Platter's

by
Diners Club
INTERNATIONAL®

2020
SOUTH AFRICAN

WINE
GUIDE

40TH **ANNIVERSARY
EDITION**

Available on the
App Store

GET IT ON
Google play

John Platter SA Wine Guide (Pty) Ltd
www.wineonaplatter.com

PUBLISHER

Jean-Pierre Rossouw

EDITOR

Philip van Zyl

ASSOCIATE EDITORS

Cathy van Zyl & Tim James

TASTERS

Winnie Bowman, Greg de Bruyn, Joanne Gibson, Tim James, Angela Lloyd, Cathy Marston, Fiona McDonald, Gregory Mutambe, Christine Rudman, Dave Swingler, Cathy van Zyl & Meryl Weaver. Previous editions: David Biggs, David Clarke, Hennie Coetzee, Christian Eedes, Higgo Jacobs, Ingrid Motteux, Khuselo Mputa, Jörg Pfützner, James Pietersen & Samarie Smith

COPYWRITERS

Greg de Bruyn, Joanne Gibson, Tim James, Angela Lloyd, Cathy Marston, Fiona McDonald, Christine Rudman, Wendy Toerien, Cathy van Zyl & Meryl Weaver

COORDINATORS

Ina de Villiers (information); Marinda Visagie & Christina Harvett (wine & tasting)

DATABASE & QR CODES

Sean de Kock, Ben van Rensburg (Modern Web Presence)

TYPESETTING & MAPS

Gawie du Toit

ADVERTISING, SALES & ADMINISTRATION

Christine Bishop ▪ T +27 (0)28-316-3049 ▪ office@wineonaplatter.com

© John Platter SA Wine Guide (Pty) Ltd 2020
PO Box 537, Hermanus 7200
T +27 (0)28-316-3049 ▪ office@wineonaplatter.com

Wineonaplatter.com
Facebook.com/wineonaplatter
Twitter.com/wineonaplatter ▪ @wineonaplatter

ISBN 978-0-9870046-9-7

Printed and bound in the Republic of South Africa by ABC Press, Cape Town

Contents

A Warm Welcome from Diners Club

It is with great pleasure that I welcome you, on behalf of Diners Club, to this 40th anniversary edition of Platter's by Diners Club South African Wine Guide.

We are proud to support the wonderful world of South African wine through Platter's, our Diners Club Winemaker of the Year and Young Winemaker of the Year awards, and also our Winelist Awards.

Platter's is the keystone in celebrating South African wine excellence, as this unique guide assesses thousands of wines a year — a monumental project of vital importance — and the wines that are judged best-of-best in these pages have really had to prove themselves.

It's not only about the top achievers, of course, and the pages of this guide are packed with indispensable knowledge for all winelovers, including background facts and figures, and information on touring our beautiful winelands. We also encourage you to download the companion app for iPhone or Android.

Thank you for being a part of, or indeed, supporting the South African wine industry, one which is world-renowned for its fine wine, welcoming people and superb spaces. For more on how Diners Club can enhance your wine, food and travel experiences, please visit www.dinersclub.co.za

Here's to a sparkling 2020!

Esh Naidoo
Managing Director, Diners Club South Africa

Some Trends in South African Wine

And the South African wine revolution rolls on...

A secondary market developing?

The increased quality (and number) of top-end SA wines in recent years has been accompanied by a stretching upwards of prices. Now, also responding to widely perceived high quality, conscious attempts are being made to build on the idea of South African wine as an investment, an 'asset class'. Two investment funds (one local and one based in London) focusing on SA wine have been established, but probably of more importance in building a secondary market has been auction activity.

A handful of SA wines have recently done well at the annual Christie's Autumn Wine auction in Hong Kong, and two local auctions of prestigious wines (mostly South African, with some 20th-century classics as well as more recent ones) have already taken place under the auspices of a leading auction house. Also significant to this drive to 'premiumise' South African wine, the venerable Nederburg Auction has rebranded itself the Cape Fine & Rare Wine Auction, offering a similar sort of selection.

The results are as yet ambiguous. Whether this trend will prove durable is still being tested; it might take a few years to be confident that there is a viable secondary market for modern South African wine, but there are, arguably, positive signs. If it happens, it is unlikely to be entirely welcomed by those who already find that prices at the top end are spiralling out of their reach.

From bulk to premium

It's useful, though, to put the elite in perspective. In terms of prestige, it is overwhelming; in quantitative terms it is minuscule. The other end of South African wine vastly predominates. In a usually over-supplied market, it seeks international and local customers for huge volumes of cheap wine off mostly high-yielding, hot and irrigated vineyards farmed industrially (with adequate irrigation hopefully becoming a widespread possibility again). Of the five price categories the authorities use in reporting on local retail sales of wine, the highest (2018 figures) accounts for some 19 million litres selling for over R108 per litre. The two lowest categories, for wines up to R48 per bottle, account for nearly three times as much. The nation is overwhelmingly drinking cheap — and sweet or sweetish — wine, especially rosé. (Though, talking of rosé and blanc de noir, South Africa seems each year to offer more of the deliciously fresh and dry kind increasingly fashionable around the world.)

One of the most exciting trends in South African wine for two decades now, however, has been the withdrawal of a growing number of vineyards from the bulk-wine scene. They are now being used for grander, not to mention more profitable, bottlings. Many of the country's most famous modern wines are off vines that are now meticulously and lovingly tended, but whose produce once disappeared into vast blending vats. And it's not only ambitious young new-wave winemakers searching the winelands and coming to pick out the best — more and more grape farmers are now making selections off their vineyards (especially carefully farmed ones) and producing their own wines. While some of the producer cellars (the 'co-ops') as well as the big merchants are also singling out special parcels for special treatment in the winery.

As a sort of by-product of this process, it's being increasingly revealed that fine table wine can come from hitherto unfashionable addresses — from Klein Karoo to Breedekloof to Prieska (that last being a Ward in the Northern Cape, if you've not heard of it before!). The time of exploration and (re)discovery is far from over.

Maximalist work in the vineyards

Understandably, in this process single vineyards (whether or not officially certified as such) are of ever-greater importance. At the top end — especially that 'asset class' end — the question of precise origin, of 'terroir', is frequently central. And, when it comes to specific vineyards, older ones have increasing cachet: thanks to the excellent work of the Old Vine Project, more premium bottles of the project's members now carry the Certified Heritage Vineyard seal, including the planting date of the vineyard from which the grapes came (the vines must be more than 35 years old).

And while plantings for table wines are still dominated by the same handful of names (chenin blanc, cabernet sauvignon, shiraz, sauvignon blanc, pinotage, chardonnay and merlot) a host of newer varieties is being planted – in tiny quantities as yet – and starting to appear on wine labels. One motive for planting newcomer grapes such as vermentino, agiorgitiko, assyrtiko and nero d'Avola is to respond to global warming's threats of greater heat and lower rainfall. The search is on for the varieties best suited to such conditions in SA.

Increased plantings of certain already established grapes like grenache are similarly motivated: they need less water, cope better in heat. This concern is, of course, part of the search for sustainability and the responsible use of resources (including human ones) – something the wider wine world is increasingly interested in, obliging all producers to respond. Many do so passionately and with conviction, some turning to organic practices where possible.

All careful, quality-oriented viticulture is expensive, mostly because it is labour-intensive rather than chemicals-intensive. If there is a tendency in mass-wine production towards mechanisation in the vineyards, there is a counter-tendency at the highest level: towards ever more concentration on vineyard work, acknowledging the best vines as the source of the best wine. Hence the respect for some – not all – of those older, lower-yielding vineyards, which have often proved their suitability for the soil and meso-climate in which they grow.

Minimalist work in the cellar

If many of the most ambitious wine producers are spending more time, effort and money in the vineyard, even more of them are (more cheaply, the sceptic might add) boasting of 'hands-off' winemaking. It's a trend that now goes beyond the 'new wave' winemakers and influences increasingly many classic producers. This is part of a return to a more 'natural' way of making wine. The aim is fewer interventions in the form of inoculated yeasts, added acidity to correct imbalances in the grapes, use of permitted additives such as hormones, etc. One trend noticeable to visitors to wine cellars is the move away from smaller oak maturation vessels (generally 225 litres), especially those made with new oak. Larger barrels – 300, 500 and 600 litres – are increasingly used for many types of red and white wine, and variants of the phrase 'only older barrels used' crop up more and more in this guide. As does reference to 'large *foudres*' – those mostly oval casks containing

thousands of litres of maturing wine are making a major comeback. Of course, the larger the vessel, and the older it is, the less the flavour influence of the oak, which continues to play a part in the slow, tiny transmission of oxygen into the wine.

Maturation is not just about oak, of course: concrete (and also polyethylene) egg-shaped tanks are now to be seen in many cellars, and large clay pots, often called amphoras, are far from rare and getting less so all the time. There are now producers going all the way with traditional, Georgian-inspired winemaking: they use clay pots, called kvevri, which are permanently buried up to their necks in earth. Two wineries are working with imported kvevri at the time of writing – such is the spirit of innovation in the SA wine scene that perhaps more have already followed.

These advances (to the past!) in terms of wine maturation are generally part of attempts to maintain the freshness and purity of fruit that is now more and more desired, and the wines matured in this way also tend to have been picked rather earlier, with resultant lower alcohol levels. But many serious wines - cabernet-based ones, for example - continue to use the 225-litre 'Bordeaux barrel', though even here, the proportion of new oak is decreasing, and there is a palpable lightening of many such wines, which are valuing freshness more.

This general trend in red wines is particularly well illustrated in the number of lighter pinotages becoming available. The grape has always produced many excellent blancs de noir as well as big, powerful, heavily oaked reds, but the charm and interest of lighter-styled versions is now apparent, and they are becoming less rare.

Winemakers

One of the socially most satisfactory components of the SA wine revolution has been the total normalisation of women making wine and managing vineyards. If the racial profile of winemakers and viticulturists has been slower to change (but note the effects of the Cape Winemakers Guild protégé programme), shifting the gender profile has moved apace. One consequence of this has been the trend among young producers for husband-and-wife teams, often with one taking primary responsibility in the cellar, the other in charge of the vineyards. Another kind of collaboration has been a crucial element of the achievements of the past few decades: eager young winemakers working together, being mutually supportive, with competition between them suppressed. In many cases this is being expressed in a new kind of small-scale co-op, with a number of winemakers sharing facilities as well as offering mutual advice and practical help.

Packaging

And what of packaging the wine once it is made? South Africans seem to be a conservative crowd on the whole, certainly at the premium end preferring glass bottles and cork closures (and not, as in Australia, wholeheartedly accepting screwcaps except for aromatic white wines — though locally there are also many top reds with screwcaps now). Wine-in-a-can is making some headway in the US, for example, but not (yet?) here. But there is a little innovation happening, with a handful of producers now offering wine 'on tap' from kegs or in larger-format glass 'growlers' (concepts familiar to beer-drinkers). Not exactly a trend yet, as it seems to be becoming in the US, but probably a space worth watching.

Editor's Note

This year we're publishing the 40th annual edition of our wine guide, and on behalf of the team I'd like to acknowledge and warmly thank everyone involved in its success over the years, especially the countless winelovers who have bought (and filled dad's Christmas stocking with), consulted, collected and recommended the book to their friends and followers.

Also to the exceptional tasting and production team members, many of whom have been involved with our venture for a decade or more.

We'd also like to salute the guide's founders, the inimitable John and Erica Platter, who created and ran, with great passion and flair, an annual winelands round-up that's become an institution on the SA wine scene and respected internationally.

Thank you, too, to eminent British winewriter Hugh Johnson, for inspiring the Platters to create their own wine guide with his still best-selling Pocket Wine Book, first published in 1977.

This 40th edition of Platter's has been fully revised, as ever, with a refreshed overview of industry trends and directions; updated tasting notes for the wines, brandies, husk spirits and sherry-style wines listed in the A–Z directory; news bulletins about the wineries and winemakers (and distilleries and distillers) featured in the A-Z, along with general information about the cellars, vineyards and amenities available to visitors.

As adjuncts to the latter, the wineland maps have been fully updated, along with the quick-lookup tables which furnish key visitor information about the wineries of a particular area.

For the benefit of those setting out on day trips or longer self-drive excursions, we've continued the partnership forged last edition with the team at What3Words, whose innovative technology makes navigation faster, easier and more accurate. W3W uses a unique 3-word address to precisely locate any person or object on the planet. Look for the 🔲 icon among the contact details of the producer listing in the A-Z, and simply type (or speak) them into the W3W app on your phone.

Icons to look out for

Amid heightened appreciation and demand for wines showcasing venerable vines, we're also continuing to use this icon �│ to highlight wines whose bottles bear the Certified Heritage Vineyard seal ('sticker'), to show they've been verified by the Old Vine Project as originating in vineyards that are officially 'old', i.e. 35 years or more. It's thought SA has the most surviving old vines of any wine-growing country, a total of some 3,500 ha, and much good work is being done to revive and extend the lives of these senior vitizens.

Growing old gracefully is the goal of wine maturation, and the 'cellar' icon 🍷 introduced last year, and continuing as a feature of the A-Z listings, is intended to draw readers' attention to wines that we believe will repay extended cellaring: at least 8-10 years for reds and fortifieds, and 4-6 years for whites. Rising interest locally and worldwide in collecting SA wine, and optimally cellaring it, will hopefully be served by this focus on ageability.

Parker & Platter's

We've had a gratifying response to the introduction last edition of scoring for wines according to the 100-point system, alongside our familiar 0-5 star rating scale. Alias 'the Parker system', the 100-point metric is the global standard, and our belief is that international readers will better understand and contextualise our judging team's pronouncements when presented with both sets of ratings.

As noted last time, there are no plans to phase out the star ratings, which have been integral to the guide since its inception. Worth mentioning is that we introduced judging on the 100-point scale internally only in 2015, and thus 100-point equivalents for vintages tasted prior to that date are not displayed in the A-Z listings.

(For visual clarity's sake, the 100-point scores are not included in the section named This Year's Ratings Summarised, where all the current edition's tasting results appear in a rapid lookup format.)

Expanding our pinnacle awards

We've also been delighted with the response to last year's expansion of our pinnacle accolades, which saw awards presented to not one but three stellar producers, namely the top performer of the year in terms of the number of 5-star wines in the particular edition; the newcomer of the year, which is the producer debuting with the highest scores;

and my Editor's Award for the individual or team whose performance on and off the track sets a benchmark for the industry.

Positive feedback has additionally prompted us to continue publishing an extended list of Wines of the Year, featuring the wines which achieved not only the maximum 5 stars, but also the highest score in their category.

We're satisfied that winelovers and the industry alike understand that these innovations underline what's recognised around the world as the much-increased depth in SA winegrowing in recent years, and in no way diminish the cachet of our 'traditional' summit wines and wineries. See page 10 for more about our rating methodology and the awards that flow from it.

With all the recent developments, it's worth mentioning that there has been no change in our long-standing goal of tasting, rating and describing as many as possible SA-made wines available during the currency of the book, both locally and overseas. To note, however, participation in the guide has always been voluntary, and a limited number of producers, for a variety of reasons, elect to be either omitted entirely or featured without wines. Of the latter, in this edition we've included a brief description in the A-Z directory for those who specifically requested it, while, for space-saving reasons, simply mentioning the remainder.

Our over-delivering team

At this point it's my pleasure to highlight the outstanding contribution of our professional and enthusiastic tasters, all over-deliverers of note. Their initials appear below the wines they tasted, as follows: Winnie Bowman (WB), Greg de Bruyn (GdB), Joanne Gibson (JG), Tim James (TJ), Angela Lloyd (AL), Cathy Marston (CM), Fiona McDonald (FM), Gregory Mutambe (GM), Christine Rudman (CR), Dave Swingler (DS), Cathy van Zyl (CvZ) and Meryl Weaver (MW). For more about these stalwarts, see page 20.

Special thanks to associate editors Cathy van Zyl (also copywriter) and Tim James (also copywriter and proofreader); copywriters Greg de Bruyn, Joanne Gibson, Angela Lloyd, Cathy Marston,

Fiona McDonald, Christine Rudman, Wendy Toerien and Meryl Weaver; information coordinator Ina de Villiers; wine coordinator Marinda Visagie, and Wines of the Year tasting coordinator Christina Harvett, both assisted by Kirschni Adams, Monique Africa, Lehandri Bothma, Thabile Cele, Anique Ceronio, Amanda Ferreira, Olga Griggs, Shannon Jacobs, Robyn-Leigh Rhode, Kurtley Snow, Theola Snow, Andrew Sutherland, Ilonka van Greunen and Marius Wantenaar; Cape Wine Masters Kristina Beuthner and Duimpie Bayly for second opinions; map and typesetting guru Gawie du Toit; Christine Bishop for book sales, administration, advertising coordination and database updates; Lara Philp and Johan Rademan of Vineyard Connection for the use of their excellent facilities; Lauren de Kock for fact-checking; Mark Whyte and XtraSmile Couriers; Christelle Reade-Jahn and the Brandy Foundation; Ben van Rensburg (Modern Web Presence) for the QR code; and the ever-helpful SAWIS and VinPro. Particular thanks to Sean de Kock for 24×7 help with the database, intranet and website.

I'm deeply grateful for the support and help of my family, commercial pilot-in-training son Luke, and Herculean wife Cathy, respected Master of Wine and Platter's taster/copywriter, whose further, behind-the-scenes contribution as associate editor is enormous; and Cessna the Staffie, pure joy and affection.

Sincere thanks to SA's wineries, without whose support the book could not be produced.

And, as always, an invitation to join us on the web, Facebook and Twitter (see page 2 for details), and to look for our apps in the on-line stores.

Finally, our ratings are the considered opinion of wine experts who understand the responsibility of adducing a star rating to a product as changeable as wine. However, because of the subjective element associated with wine assessment, we strongly recommend you view our rankings as adjuncts to the tasting notes rather than as oracular pronouncements. And we continue to urge you, in the words of a local winery's marketing slogan, to 'trust your taste'.

Philip van Zyl

Our Method & The Accolades We Award

Platter's is one of the few wine guides in the world that aims to taste and rate every wine from every South African vintage — and it's been doing so since 1980. In this endeavour, Platter's uses two judging methods: label-sighted assessment as well as blind tasting (with no label showing).

As Platter's is primarily a wine guide and not a wine competition, our expert tasters initially assess the wines sighted to have access to vital contextual details such as site, climate and style. Since Platter's not only rates wines, but also provides rich editorial content, this information enables our team to understand (and editorialise) the intent of the producer and the wine's back-story.

Annually Platter's assesses a potential 9,000 wines. Those rated 93-points or more by the sighted judges are all entered into a second round of blind tasting. Here, a single taster assesses the wines within a category (for example, Syrah/Shiraz) without sight of the label to verify the sighted tasting score. If the category has a large number of wines rated 93-points or more, it will be divided into flights, each flight tasted by a single taster. Should the verification taster disagree with the sighted taster about a wine's score, the change in score is approved by a Roving Chair, an expert taster who is not a member of the Platter's tasting team.

The wines regarded as superlative in both a South African and international context are awarded the guide's highest rating, namely Five Stars, which equates to 95-100 points.

Other important wines in our pinnacle listings are the Wines of the Year, the highest-scoring Five Star wines within each tasting category, as well as those wines which rated 94 points. The latter just missed the Five Star selection but are extremely fine and collectable in their own right. They are listed under the heading Highly Recommended.

Implicit in both the Five Star and Highly Recommended wines is the potential to improve with further bottle-maturation: 8-10 years, perhaps more, in the case of reds and fortified wines, and around 4-6 years for the whites. (Proper storage is, of course, vital for sound maturation.) However, during the sighted tasting cycle, our team identify a number of bottlings, over and above the Five Stars and Highly Recommended, which show particular potential for cellaring. A small selection of these age-worthy wines are listed under the heading Buy Now, Drink Later, and flagged in the A-Z directory with this 'cellar' icon: 🍷

Also included in this section of the guide is a selection of the wines which tasters feel are particularly worthy of note — interesting, attractive, unusual, unique, representative of an important trend, etc. Look out for these Hidden Gems in the A-Z directory; they are highlighted with this 'jewel' icon: 💎

Then, there are the Top Performing Winery, Newcomer Winery and the Editor's Award for the year.

The Editor's Award Winery of the Year recognises a team (or teams) who, based on performance in the current edition, track record and winegrowing approach, are ambassadors par excellence for South African wine.

The Newcomer Winery of the Year is awarded to the producer whose wine portfolio has been assessed by Platter's for the first time and achieved the highest ratings at the Five Star tasting, or the highest scores (should the wines not have reached the Five Star round).

The Top Performing Winery of the Year is awarded to the winery that achieves the most Five Star results after the final tasting round. In the case of an overall Five Star tie, this award goes to the winery that then has the most Wines of the Year, and so on, until the year's Top Performer is identified.

Further details about all releases listed in the Wines of the Year section will be found under the names of the relevant producers in the A-Z directory.

Wineries of the Year

Top Performing Winery of the Year 2020

MULLINEUX

It's becoming a habit, and an unparalleled achievement: Once again, like last year and in 2014 and 2016, triumph for Andrea and Chris Mullineux's winery (with Leeu Passant in Franschhoek, part of a joint venture with partners). They receive five 5-star ratings, including Shiraz of the Year for their Granite Syrah and Straw Wine of the Year for their renowned version – its ninth 5-star award. Another multiple winner, Sadie Family Wines, has in fact the same number of 5-star wines (and a White Blend of the Year), but with generally slightly lower scores. A remarkable

double achievement for Swartland, though, whose reputation as one of SA's currently most exciting wine regions both wineries have crucially helped to build. The Mullineux pair are based on their farm Roundstone, near Riebeek-Kasteel, where Andrea crafts the Signature wines as well as the Single Terroir and Kloof Street ranges – not to mention wines for the auction of the Cape Winemakers Guild, of which she's a member. Chris takes primary responsibility for work in the vineyards on the own farm and on those from which they buy in grapes – all in Swartland.

Newcomer Winery of the Year 2020

PIETER FERREIRA CAP CLASSIQUE

As one of SA wine's elder statesmen and its undisputed 'bubbly king', Pieter Ferreira is no newcomer – in fact, a pleasant coincidence is that he is cellarmaster at Graham Beck, where last year's winning newcomer, Erika Obermeyer, had been a winemaker. But this project of his and his wife Ann's is indeed a new venture – and a marvellously successful one: the first release, a superb, long-matured Blanc de Blancs 2012 is our Méthode Cap Classique of the Year, with the highest score the Guide has ever awarded a sparkling wine.

Pieter makes the wines (a Brut and a Rosé are next to be released) for Ann, the venture's owner, under contract at Graham Beck, from widely sourced grapes. Any award for Pieter will be widely welcomed, given the affectionate esteem in which he is held for more than his skills – for his unfailing generosity in sharing his knowledge with colleagues whom a lesser man might have deemed mere competitors. For Pieter, improving the breed has always been central. 'Bubbly is Pieter's life and passion', says Ann Ferreira.

Editor's Award Winery of the Year 2020

BOEKENHOUTSKLOOF WINERY

This Franschhoek-based producer (that's where the beautiful home-farm is) was our Winery of the Year for 2012. The new Boekenhoutskloof-owned brands that have been added to the list since then add further testimony to how the overall range spans a number of quality and price levels – notably producing good and even numerous 5-star wines in large enough quantities to be extremely significant, something still comparatively rare in South Africa. High-scoring Chocolate Block at well over 100,000 cases is particularly eloquent here. The scale of the magnificent new barrel cellar in Franschhoek also

speaks about a combination of quantity and quality. A large team is responsible for all this, but unquestionably the vision and leadership of Marc Kent (here from the winery's founding in 1994) is key to the success of Boekenhoutskloof's aim to make wines of integrity and value at all levels of ambition: from The Wolftrap, Porcupine Ridge and Vinologist (making its debut in this edition), to Porseleinberg, the infant Cap Maritime, and the fine wines bearing the home-farm's name. This scope, this commitment, this success are things that this guide takes pleasure in honouring by this award.

Wines of the Year

These are the highest-scoring 5-star wines within each tasting category. Please refer to the A–Z section for the points for each wine.

Cabernet Franc
☐ Anthonij Rupert 2013
☐ De Trafford 2015
☐ Raats 2017

Cabernet Sauvignon
☐ Rust en Vrede Single Vineyard 2016

Cinsaut
☐ Bosman Twyfeling 2017
☐ Savage Follow the Line 2018

Grenache Noir
☐ Sadie Soldaat 2018

Merlot
☐ Shannon Mount Bullet 2016

Pinotage
☐ Flagstone Time Manner Place 2017

Pinot Noir
☐ Storm Ignis 2017

Shiraz/Syrah
☐ Mullineux Granite Syrah 2017

Red Blends, Cape Bordeaux
☐ Van Biljon Cinq 2015

Red Blends, with Pinotage
☐ Beyerskloof Faith 2015

Red Blends, Shiraz/Syrah-based
☐ Erika Obermeyer Erica O Syrah-Grenache Noir-Cinsault 2018
☐ Rust en Vrede 1694 2016
☐ Saronsberg Full Circle 2017

Red Blends, Other
☐ Rust en Vrede Estate 2016

Chardonnay
☐ Leeu Passant Stellenbosch 2017
☐ Restless River Ava Marie 2017

Chenin Blanc
☐ Rall Ava 2018

Grenache Blanc
☐ The Foundry 2018

Sauvignon Blanc
☐ Trizanne Signature Sondagskloof Blanc Fumé 2018

Semillon
☐ Anthonij Rupert Laing Groendruif 2016
☐ Rickety Bridge The Pilgrimage 2017

Viognier
☐ Ridgeback 2018

White Blends, Cape Bordeaux
☐ Delaire Graff White Reserve 2017

White Blends, Other
☐ Sadie Palladius 2017

Méthode Cap Classique
☐ Pieter Ferreira Blanc de Blancs 2012

Natural Sweet
☐ Klein Constantia Vin de Constance 2015
☐ Laibach 2019

Noble Late Harvest
☐ Buitenverwachting 1769 2017
☐ Tokara 2017

Vin de Paille
☐ Mullineux Straw Wine 2018

Port-style
☐ Boplaas Cape Vintage Reserve 2017
☐ Upland Cape Tawny 2014

Brandy
☐ KWV Centenary

Five Stars

These are the wines achieving the guide's highest distinction, a 5-star rating, or 95 and above points. Please refer to the A–Z section for the points for each wine.

Cabernet Franc
- [ ] Anthonij Rupert 2013
- [ ] De Trafford 2015
- [ ] Raats 2017

Cabernet Sauvignon:
- [ ] Erika Obermeyer Erica O 2017
- [ ] Kanonkop 2015
- [ ] Kleine Zalze Vineyard Selection 2017
- [ ] Miles Mossop CWG Auction Reserve Maximilian 2014
- [ ] Rust en Vrede Single Vineyard 2016
- [ ] Wade Bales Regional Series Stellenbosch 2017

Cinsaut
- [ ] Bosman Twyfeling 2017
- [ ] Savage Follow The Line 2018

Grenache Noir
- [ ] Sadie Soldaat 2018

Merlot
- [ ] Shannon Mount Bullet 2016
- [ ] Thelema Reserve 2016

Pinotage
- [ ] Beeslaar 2017
- [ ] Beyerskloof Diesel 2017
- [ ] Diemersdal Reserve 2018
- [ ] Flagstone Time Manner Place 2017
- [ ] Kanonkop Black Label 2017

Pinot Noir
- [ ] Crystallum Mabalel 2018
- [ ] Storm Ignis 2018
- [ ] Storm Ignis 2017

Shiraz/Syrah
- [ ] Blackwater Cultellus Syrah 2017
- [ ] Boekenhoutskloof CWG Auction Reserve Syrah 2017
- [ ] Boekenhoutskloof Syrah 2017
- [ ] Cederberg Shiraz 2017
- [ ] De Grendel Elim Shiraz 2017
- [ ] Dorrance Cuvée Ameena Syrah 2017
- [ ] Gabriëlskloof Syrah on Shale 2017
- [ ] Leeuwenkuil Heritage Syrah 2017
- [ ] Mullineux Granite Syrah 2017
- [ ] Mullineux Iron Syrah 2017
- [ ] Mullineux Schist Syrah Roundstone 2017
- [ ] Patatsfontein Sons of Sugarland Syrah 2018
- [ ] Rall Ava Syrah 2018

- [ ] Reyneke Biodynamic Reserve Red 2017
- [ ] Rust en Vrede Single Vineyard Syrah 2016
- [ ] Savage Red 2017
- [ ] Super Single Vineyards Mount Sutherland Syrah 2016
- [ ] Van Loggerenberg Graft 2018

Red Blends, Cape Bordeaux
- [ ] De Trafford CWG Auction Reserve Perspective 2017
- [ ] Glenelly Lady May 2014
- [ ] Hidden Valley Hidden Gems 2016
- [ ] Kanonkop Paul Sauer 2016
- [ ] Tokara Director's Reserve 2015
- [ ] Van Biljon Cinq 2015
- [ ] Vergelegen GVB 2014

Red Blends, with Pinotage
- [ ] Beyerskloof Faith 2015
- [ ] Kaapzicht Vision 2017

Red Blends, Shiraz/Syrah-based
- [ ] Erika Obermeyer Erica O Syrah-Grenache Noir-Cinsault 2018
- [ ] Rust en Vrede 1694 Classification 2016
- [ ] Saronsberg Full Circle 2017

Red Blends, Other
- [ ] De Trafford Elevation 393 2013
- [ ] Glenelly Red 2014
- [ ] Rust en Vrede Estate 2016

Chardonnay
- [ ] Capensis Silene 2017
- [ ] Hamilton Russell 2018
- [ ] Jordan CWG Auction Reserve 2018
- [ ] Leeu Passant CWG Auction Reserve Radicales Libres 2014
- [ ] Leeu Passant Stellenbosch 2017
- [ ] Oak Valley Groenlandberg 2018
- [ ] Restless River Ava Marie 2017
- [ ] Rhebokskloof Sandstone Grove 2017
- [ ] Richard Kershaw Clonal Selection Elgin 2018
- [ ] Richard Kershaw GPS Series Lower Duivenhoks River 2018
- [ ] Warwick The White Lady 2018

Chenin Blanc
- [ ] AA Badenhorst Kelder Steen 2018
- [ ] AA Badenhorst Dassiekop Steen 2018
- [ ] Alheit Magnetic North 2018

Five Stars, Chenin Blanc *(continued)*

- ☐ ArtiSons The Mothership 2018
- ☐ Axle 2018
- ☐ Beaumont Hope Marguerite 2018
- ☐ Botanica Mary Delany 2018
- ☐ David & Nadia 2018
- ☐ David & Nadia Hoë-Steen 2018
- ☐ David & Nadia Plat'bos 2018
- ☐ David & Nadia Skaliekop 2018
- ☐ Gabriëlskloof Elodie 2018
- ☐ Kleine Zalze Family Reserve 2018
- ☐ Kruger Naked Wines Old Vines 2018
- ☐ Longridge Ou Steen Enkel Wingerd 2017
- ☐ Metzer & Holfeld Montane 2018
- ☐ Mount Abora Koggelbos 2017
- ☐ Raats Eden High Density Single Vineyard 2018
- ☐ Rall Ava 2018
- ☐ Sadie Mev Kirsten 2018
- ☐ Sadie Skurfberg 2018
- ☐ Spier 21 Gables 2018
- ☐ Stellenrust 54 Barrel Fermented 2018
- ☐ Stellenrust Old Bushvine 2018
- ☐ Thistle & Weed Duwweltjie 2018
- ☐ Van Loggerenberg Kameradarie 2018

Grenache Blanc

- ☐ KWV The Mentors 2017
- ☐ The Foundry 2018

Sauvignon Blanc

- ☐ Neil Ellis Amica 2018
- ☐ Tokara Reserve 2018
- ☐ Trizanne Signature Sondagskloof Blanc Fumé 2018

Semillon

- ☐ Anthonij Rupert Cape of Good Hope Laing Groendruif 2016
- ☐ Rickety Bridge The Pilgrimage 2017

Viognier

- ☐ Ridgeback 2018

White Blends, Cape Bordeaux

- ☐ Cape Point Isliedh 2018
- ☐ Delaire Graff White Reserve 2017
- ☐ Groot Constantia Gouverneurs Reserve 2017

White Blends, Other

- ☐ B Vintners Harlem to Hope 2018
- ☐ Leeuwenkuil Reserve White 2017
- ☐ Mullineux Old Vines 2018
- ☐ Rall White 2018
- ☐ Sadie Palladius 2017
- ☐ Sadie 'T Voetpad 2018
- ☐ Thorne & Daughters Rocking Horse 2018

Méthode Cap Classique

- ☐ Bon Courage Jacques Bruére Cuvée Brut Rosé 2011
- ☐ Le Lude Agrafe 2013
- ☐ Le Lude Vintage Magnum 2013
- ☐ Pieter Ferreira Blanc de Blancs 2012
- ☐ Saltare Blanc de Noirs Cuvée Camille NV

Natural Sweet

- ☐ Klein Constantia Vin de Constance 2015
- ☐ Laibach 2019

Noble Late Harvest

- ☐ Buitenverwachting 1769 2017
- ☐ Tokara 2017

Vin de Paille

- ☐ Fairview La Beryl Blanc 2018
- ☐ Mullineux Straw Wine 2018

Port-style

- ☐ Boplaas Cape Vintage Reserve 2017
- ☐ De Krans Cape Vintage Reserve 2017
- ☐ KWV Cape Tawny NV
- ☐ Upland Cape Tawny 2014

Brandy

- ☐ KWV 10 Year Old Vintage
- ☐ KWV 12 Year Old Barrel Select
- ☐ KWV 15 Year Old Alambic
- ☐ KWV 20 Year Old
- ☐ KWV Nexus
- ☐ KWV Centenary
- ☐ Van Ryn 12 Year Distillers Reserve
- ☐ Van Ryn 15 Year Fine Cask Reserve
- ☐ Van Ryn 20 Year Collectors Reserve

Husk Spirit

- ☐ Dalla Cia 10 Year Old Celebration Cabernet Sauvignon-Merlot

Highly Recommended

These are wines of exceptional merit, scoring 94 points.

Cabernet Franc
- [ ] Edgebaston David Finlayson Camino Africana 2016
- [ ] Eikendal Infused by Earth 2017
- [ ] Gabriëlskloof 2017
- [ ] Hogan Mirror for the Sun 2018
- [ ] Holden Manz Reserve 2016
- [ ] Nelson Lisha Nelson Signature 2017
- [ ] Warwick 2018

Cabernet Sauvignon
- [ ] Boekenhoutskloof Franschhoek 2017
- [ ] Boekenhoutskloof Stellenbosch 2017
- [ ] Delaire Graff Reserve 2017
- [ ] Diemersdal MM Louw 2017
- [ ] Domaine Coutelier Reserve 2013
- [ ] Edgebaston David Finlayson 'GS' 2016
- [ ] Eikendal 2017
- [ ] Ernie Els Proprietor's 2016
- [ ] Ernie Els 2017
- [ ] Excelsior Evanthuis 2015
- [ ] Neil Ellis Jonkershoek Valley 2016
- [ ] Nico van der Merwe 2017
- [ ] Rainbow's End 2017
- [ ] Restless River Main Road & Dignity 2016
- [ ] Rickety Bridge The Bridge 2016
- [ ] Stark-Condé 2017
- [ ] Stark-Condé Three Pines 2017
- [ ] Stellenbosch Reserve 2017
- [ ] Strydom Rex 2016
- [ ] The Butcher Shop & Grill Pick's Pick Gold Label 2017
- [ ] Thelema 2016
- [ ] Tokara Reserve 2016
- [ ] Vergelegen Reserve 2014
- [ ] Vergelegen V 2013
- [ ] Warwick The Blue Lady 2016
- [ ] Zorgvliet 2017

Grenache Noir
- [ ] Anysbos 2017
- [ ] ArtiSons The Phantom 2017
- [ ] Momento 2017
- [ ] Piekenierskloof Carel van Zyl 2018
- [ ] Strandveld 2018

Merlot
- [ ] De Trafford 2015
- [ ] Oldenburg 2016
- [ ] Shannon The Shannon Black 2015

Petit Verdot
- [ ] Thelema Sutherland Reserve 2016

Pinotage
- [ ] Alvi's Drift Verreaux Reserve 2017
- [ ] Ashbourne 2017
- [ ] Beyerskloof CWG Auction Reserve Traildust 2017
- [ ] Neil Ellis Bottelary Hills 2017

Pinot Noir
- [ ] Bouchard Finlayson Tête de Cuvée Galpin Peak 2017
- [ ] Cap Maritime 2018
- [ ] Catherine Marshall Pinot Noir on Clay Soils 2018
- [ ] Creation Emma 2018
- [ ] Creation The Art of Pinot Noir 2018
- [ ] Crystallum Bona Fide 2018
- [ ] Crystallum Cuvée Cinéma 2018
- [ ] La Vierge Apogée 2015
- [ ] Newton Johnson Family Vineyards 2018
- [ ] Newton Johnson Windansea 2018
- [ ] Oak Valley Groenlandberg 2018
- [ ] Paul Cluver CWG Auction Reserve 2017
- [ ] Paul Cluver Seven Flags 2017
- [ ] Radford Dale Freedom 2018
- [ ] Richard Kershaw Clonal Selection Elgin 2018
- [ ] Shannon RocknRolla 2018
- [ ] Storm Ridge 2018
- [ ] Storm Ridge 2017
- [ ] Storm Vrede 2018
- [ ] Storm Vrede 2017

Shiraz/Syrah
- [ ] ArtiSons Blueberry Hill Shiraz 2017
- [ ] Boschkloof Epilogue Shiraz 2017
- [ ] Bruce Jack Clean Slate Shiraz 2015
- [ ] De Grendel Shiraz 2017
- [ ] De Trafford Blueprint Syrah 2017
- [ ] Dewaldt Heyns Shiraz 2016
- [ ] Eagles' Nest Shiraz 2016
- [ ] Erika Obermeyer Erica O Syrah 2018
- [ ] Erika Obermeyer Erica O Syrah 2017
- [ ] Gabriëlskloof Syrah on Sandstone 2017
- [ ] Hartenberg Gravel Hill Shiraz 2015
- [ ] JC Wickens Swerver Shiraz 2018
- [ ] La Bri Syrah 570 2016
- [ ] Luddite Shiraz 2015
- [ ] Mullineux Syrah 2017
- [ ] Olifantsberg Syrah 2017
- [ ] Porseleinberg 2017

Highly recommended, Shiraz/Syrah *(continued)*

- ☐ Radford Dale Syrah 2017
- ☐ Remhoogte Reserve Syrah 2017
- ☐ Rhebokskloof Black Marble Hill Syrah 2016
- ☐ Richard Kershaw Groenland Deconstructed Bokkeveld Shale SH9C Syrah 2017
- ☐ Savage The Girl Next Door Syrah 2018
- ☐ Stark-Condé Three Pines Syrah 2017
- ☐ Trizanne Signature Reserve Syrah 2018

Tinta Barocca

- ☐ Sadie Treinspoor 2018

Red Blends, Cape Bordeaux

- ☐ Constantia Glen Five 2015
- ☐ De Toren Fusion V 2017
- ☐ Delaire Graff Botmaskop 2017
- ☐ DeMorgenzon Maestro 2017
- ☐ Diemersdal Private Collection 2017
- ☐ Groenland Steenkamp 2015
- ☐ Groot Constantia Gouverneurs Reserve 2016
- ☐ Hillcrest Hornfels 2015
- ☐ Keet First Verse 2015
- ☐ Marianne Francois Pienaar Desirade 2015
- ☐ Miles Mossop Max 2016
- ☐ Mvemve Raats MR de Compostella 2017
- ☐ Nitida Calligraphy 2017
- ☐ Oldenburg Rhodium 2016
- ☐ Ridgeback His Master's Choice Signature C 2017
- ☐ Schultz Boneyards 2016
- ☐ Simonsig Tiara 2011
- ☐ Spier Creative Block Five 2016
- ☐ Stark-Condé Oude Nektar 2016
- ☐ Strydom CWG Auction Reserve Paradigm 2016
- ☐ Thelema Rabelais 2015
- ☐ Vilafonté Series M 2016
- ☐ Warwick Trilogy 2016

Red Blends, with Pinotage

- ☐ Alvi's Drift Albertus Viljoen Bismarck 2017
- ☐ Beaumont Vitruvian 2016
- ☐ Bosman Erfenis 2016

Red Blends, Shiraz/Syrah-based

- ☐ ArtiSons JJ Handmade Eight Pillars 2016
- ☐ Eikendal Charisma 2018
- ☐ Lingen 2017
- ☐ Rall 2017
- ☐ Sadie Columella 2017
- ☐ Sijnn 2016

Red Blends, Other

- ☐ Boschkloof Conclusion 2016
- ☐ Dalla Cia Wine & Spirit Company Teano 2017
- ☐ Hogan Divergent 2018
- ☐ JC Wickens Swerwer 2018
- ☐ Mont du Toit 2014
- ☐ Mont du Toit Le Sommet 2017
- ☐ Nico van der Merwe Mas Nicolas 2017
- ☐ Plaisir de Merle Grand Plaisir 2014

Chardonnay

- ☐ Anthonij Rupert Cape of Good Hope Serruria 2017
- ☐ Boschendal Elgin 2017
- ☐ Botanica Mary Delany 2018
- ☐ Cap Maritime 2018
- ☐ Creation The Art of Chardonnay 2018
- ☐ Delaire Graff Terraced Block Reserve 2017
- ☐ Eikendal 2018
- ☐ Eikendal Infused by Earth 2017
- ☐ Glen Carlou Quartz Stone 2018
- ☐ Glenelly Reserve 2018
- ☐ Jordan Nine Yards 2018
- ☐ Kleine Zalze Vineyard Selection 2018
- ☐ Lanzerac Mrs English 2018
- ☐ Môreson FYM 2017
- ☐ Môreson Mercator 2017
- ☐ MVH Signature 2017
- ☐ Neil Ellis Whitehall 2018
- ☐ Newton Johnson Family Vineyards 2018
- ☐ Paserene 2017
- ☐ Richard Kershaw Deconstructed Lake District Cartref CY96 2018
- ☐ Richard Kershaw Deconstructed Groenland Bokkeveld Shale CY548 2018
- ☐ Uva Mira 2017

Chenin Blanc

- ☐ AA Badenhorst The Golden Slopes 2018
- ☐ Alheit Huilkrans 2018
- ☐ Alheit Nautical Dawn 2018
- ☐ Beaumont CWG Auction Reserve Leo's Whole Bunch 2017
- ☐ Bellingham The Bernard Series Old Vine 2018
- ☐ Brookdale 2018
- ☐ Cederberg Five Generations 2017
- ☐ City on a Hill 2018
- ☐ De Trafford CWG Auction Reserve 2017
- ☐ DeMorgenzon Reserve 2018
- ☐ Edgebaston David Finlayson Camino Africana 2018
- ☐ Huis van Chevallerie Nuwedam Old Vine 2018
- ☐ Joostenberg No. 19 Kaalgat Steen 2018
- ☐ KWV The Mentors 2017
- ☐ Lourens Skuinskap Steen 2018
- ☐ Malanot Asiel 2017

Highly recommended, Chenin Blanc *(continued)*

- ☐ Metzer & Holfeld Maritime 2018
- ☐ Mullineux Granite 2018
- ☐ Mullineux Quartz Leliefontein 2018
- ☐ Olifantsberg Lark 2018
- ☐ Raats Old Vine 2018
- ☐ Savage Never Been Asked To Dance 2018
- ☐ Van Loggerenberg Trust Your Gut 2018
- ☐ Waterford Stellenbosch 2018

Grenache Blanc

- ☐ Olifantsberg 2018

Sauvignon Blanc

- ☐ Bartho Eksteen CWG Auction Reserve Vloekskoot 2018
- ☐ DeMorgenzon Special Cuvée 2017
- ☐ Diemersdal 8 Rows 2019
- ☐ Erika Obermeyer Erica O 2018
- ☐ Oak Valley Fountain of Youth 2019
- ☐ Seven Springs Fumé 2015
- ☐ Skaap 47 2018
- ☐ Zevenwacht Z-Collection 360° 2018

Semillon

- ☐ Alheit La Colline 2018
- ☐ Boekenhoutskloof 2017
- ☐ Shannon Triangle Block 2018
- ☐ Steenberg 2018

Semillon Gris

- ☐ Mullineux CWG Auction Reserve The Gris 2018
- ☐ Thorne & Daughters Tin Soldier 2018

Verdelho

- ☐ Stellenbosch Vineyards 2018

Viognier

- ☐ Eagles' Nest 2018

White Blends, Cape Bordeaux

- ☐ Constantia Glen Two 2018
- ☐ Newton Johnson Resonance 2018
- ☐ Spier Frans K. Smit 2017
- ☐ Tokara Director's Reserve 2017
- ☐ Warwick Professor Black 2016

White Blends, Other

- ☐ AA Badenhorst Kalmoesfontein 2017
- ☐ Anysbos Disdit 2018
- ☐ DeMorgenzon Maestro White 2017
- ☐ Lourensford Chrysalis 2016
- ☐ Miles Mossop CWG Auction Reserve Saskia-Jo 2017
- ☐ Miles Mossop Saskia 2017
- ☐ Momento Chenin Blanc-Verdelho 2018
- ☐ Olifantsberg Blanc 2018
- ☐ Opstal Carl Everson Cape White Blend 2018
- ☐ Sadie Skerpioen 2018
- ☐ Savage White 2018
- ☐ Stark-Condé The Field Blend 2018

Méthode Cap Classique

- ☐ Altydgedacht Blanc de Blancs 2015
- ☐ Anthonij Rupert L'Ormarins Blanc de Blancs 2013
- ☐ Anthonij Rupert L'Ormarins Brut Rosé 2015
- ☐ Charles Fox Prestige Cuvée Cipher 2013
- ☐ Charles Fox Vintage Brut 2015
- ☐ Graham Beck Blanc de Blancs Brut 2015
- ☐ Graham Beck Cuvée Clive 2014
- ☐ Le Lude Rosé NV
- ☐ Le Lude Vintage Cuvée 2013
- ☐ Silverthorn The Green Man 2016
- ☐ Simonsig Cuvée Royale 2014
- ☐ Tokara Limited Release 2012
- ☐ Woolworths Signature Vintage Reserve Brut 2013

Dessert Wine, Fortified

- ☐ Bon Courage White Muscadel 2019
- ☐ Bruce Jack Vloermoer Amontillado 2000
- ☐ Villiera Dakwijn 2017

Natural Sweet

- ☐ Groot Constantia Grand Constance 2016

Noble Late Harvest

- ☐ Boekenhoutskloof 2016
- ☐ Nederburg Private Bin Eminence 2018

Vin de Paille

- ☐ Donkiesbaai Hooiwijn 2018
- ☐ Stellar Winery Heaven on Earth Muscat d'Alexandrie NV

Hidden Gems

This is a selection of wines we think are particularly good value for money or exceptionally interesting. Please look for the 'jewel' icon ⊕ in the A-Z directory for other wines receiving this distinction.

Cabernet Sauvignon
- ☐ Clairvaux 2017
- ☐ Riebeek Valley Wine Co 2018

Cinsaut
- ☐ Osbloed Rooiperd 2018

Grenache Noir
- ☐ The Horsemen The Pale Rider 2018

Merlot
- ☐ Havana Hills 2016
- ☐ Jordan Chameleon No Sulphur Added 2018
- ☐ Slanghoek Private Collection 2018

Pinot noir
- ☐ La Vierge Seduction 2018
- ☐ Paul Cluver Village 2018

Pinotage
- ☐ Eagle's Cliff-New Cape 2018
- ☐ KWV Classic 2018
- ☐ Signal Gun 2017
- ☐ Wellington Wines Duke of Wellington White Pinotage 2019
- ☐ Zevenwacht 7even 2017

Shiraz/Syrah
- ☐ Die Mas van Kakamas 2019
- ☐ Olivedale 2017
- ☐ Vinologist Swartland Syrah 2018

Tinta Barocca
- ☐ Swartland Winery Winemakers Collection 2018

Red Blends
- ☐ Aan de Doorns Route 43 Deep Red 2018
- ☐ Du Toitskloof Zola Cape Cuvée 2018
- ☐ Radford Dale Winery of Good Hope Oceanside Cabernet Sauvignon-Merlot 2018
- ☐ Thelema Mountain Red 2016

Rosé
- ☐ Allesverloren Tinta 2019
- ☐ Gabriëlskloof Rosebud 2019
- ☐ Sumaridge Tara 2019
- ☐ Waverley Hills Organic Grenache 2019

Albariño
- ☐ Springfield 2019

Bukettraube
- ☐ Darling Cellars Gustus 2018

Chardonnay
- ☐ Blue Owl 2018
- ☐ Canto Unwooded 2018
- ☐ Linton Park White Rhino 2018

Chenin Blanc
- ☐ AA Badenhorst Secateurs 2018
- ☐ Anthonij Rupert Protea 2019
- ☐ Groot Phesantekraal 2019
- ☐ Kleine Zalze Cellar Selection Bush Vines 2019
- ☐ Leeuwenkuil 2019
- ☐ Overhex Balance Winemaker's Selection 2019
- ☐ Simonsig Cultivar Selection 2019

Colombard
- ☐ Bon Courage André's Fame 2019
- ☐ The Blacksmith Barebones 2018

Fernão Pires
- ☐ Strange Kompanij Strange Bru 2018

Pinot Gris/Grigio
- ☐ Leipzig 2019
- ☐ Van Loveren Perlé du Jean Pinot Grigio 2018

Riesling
- ☐ Nederburg Winemaker's Reserve 2018

Sauvignon Blanc
- ☐ Bonnievale River Collection 2019
- ☐ Ernst Gouws & Co 2018
- ☐ Klein Roosboom Reserve 2019
- ☐ Stellenbosch Hills Polkadraai 2019
- ☐ Stellar The River's End 2018

Verdelho
- ☐ Org de Rac 2018

White Blends
- ☐ Doran Arya 2018
- ☐ Groote Post The Old Man's Blend 2019
- ☐ Saxenburg Guinea Fowl 2019
- ☐ Theuniskraal Semillon-Chardonnay 2018

Méthode Cap Classique
- ☐ Koelenhof Pinotage Rosé 2018

Dessert, Unfortified
- ☐ Van Loveren Blanc de Noir Red Muscadel 2019

Dessert, Fortified
- ☐ De Wet Hanepoot 2019

Buy Now, Drink Later

This is a selection of wines we think will reward cellaring for a good few years. Please look for the 'cellar' icon (🏠) in the A-Z directory for other wines receiving this distinction.

Cabernet Franc
- [ ] Raka 2017
- [ ] Spookfontein 2017
- [ ] Uva Mira The Dance 2016

Cabernet Sauvignon
- [ ] Aristea 2016
- [ ] Bartinney 2016
- [ ] The Fledge & Co O-Velaphi? 2017
- [ ] Wellington La Cave 2017

Cinsaut
- [ ] Neil Ellis Groenekloof 2016

Malbec
- [ ] Diemersfontein 2017
- [ ] La Couronne 2016

Merlot
- [ ] Groot Constantia 2017
- [ ] Vergelegen The Mistake 2015
- [ ] Villiera 2017

Mourvèdre
- [ ] Waterkloof Circumstance 2017

Nero d'Avola
- [ ] Bosman 2017

Petit Verdot
- [ ] Zorgvliet 2017

Pinotage
- [ ] Beyerskloof Reserve 2017
- [ ] Delheim Vera Cruz 2016
- [ ] Spioenkop 2018
- [ ] Vondelind Bowwood 2016
- [ ] Windmeul The Legend 2017

Pinot Noir
- [ ] Bruce Jack There Are Still Mysteries 2016
- [ ] Stonebird 2017
- [ ] Tesselaarsdal 2018

Shiraz/Syrah
- [ ] Esona Shiraz 2017
- [ ] Maison Shiraz 2016
- [ ] Oldenburg Stone Axe Syrah 2017
- [ ] Schultz Pepper Street Solid Syrah 2017
- [ ] Zandvliet Small Berry Pick Shiraz 2017

Tinta Barocca
- [ ] Calitzdorp Cellar Barrel Selection 2018

Red blends
- [ ] Aaldering Cabernet Sauvignon- Merlot 2016
- [ ] Alto MPHS 2015
- [ ] Belfield Magnifica 2017
- [ ] Franschhoek Cellar The Last Elephant 2017
- [ ] Idiom Cabernet Sauvignon-Merlot-Cabernet Franc-Petit Verdot 2015
- [ ] Lomond Belladonna SMV 2017

Chardonnay
- [ ] Journey's End Destination 2018
- [ ] Mont Rochelle Miko 2017
- [ ] Natasha Williams Lelie van Saron 2017

Chenin Blanc
- [ ] Botha Amyah 2018
- [ ] Creation Cool Climate 2018
- [ ] Grand Provence Amphora 2017
- [ ] Kaapzicht The 1947
- [ ] Mulderbosch Block S2 2018

Sauvignon Blanc
- [ ] The Giant Periwinkle Blanc Fumé 2018

Semillon
- [ ] Nitida 2018

Viognier
- [ ] Painted Wolf Penny 2018

White Blends
- [ ] Brunia 2018
- [ ] Darling Cellars Lady Ann Darling 2018
- [ ] Hazendal Semillon-Sauvignon Blanc 2017
- [ ] Morgenster Reserve 2018

Méthode Cap Classique
- [ ] Chantelle Blanc de Blancs Brut Reserve 2014
- [ ] KWV Laborie Blanc de Blancs 2014

Dessert Wine, Unfortified
- [ ] L'illa Noble Late Harvest 2017
- [ ] Piekenierskloof Samson Straw Wine 2018

Dessert Wine, Fortified
- [ ] De Krans Muscat de Frontignan 2019
- [ ] Weltevrede Ouma se Wyn 2018

Port-style
- [ ] Peter Bayly Cape Vintage 2014

Tasters for this Edition

Winifred Bowman

Introduced to wine at a young age, through a thimbleful of sweet muscadel with Sunday lunch, Winnie's immersion in the fruit of the vine deepened during her student days at Stellenbosch University and later through frequent travels to international winegrowing areas, and widened to include brandy and husk spirit. A qualified physiotherapist and biomedical scientist, and holder of a PhD in Education, she is a Cape Wine Master, and regular judge at several local and international wine and spirit competitions. Winnie also loves books, opera and experimenting with cocktails with her son.

Greg de Bruyn

Greg is an architect by day, and a wine devotee after hours. A casual interest in wine tasting at a social club snowballed, leading him to qualify as a wine judge in 1996 and a Cape Wine Master in 2000. He was runner-up in Wine magazine's inaugural New Wine Writer competition, after which he contributed regularly to that and other wine publications. In 1999, Greg settled in the Cape, first to establish a new wine estate in Hermanus, and later as a specialist consultant in winery construction. He has judged for Veritas, Diners Club Winemaker of the Year, Nederburg Auction and several magazine panels, lectured at Diploma level for the Cape Wine Academy and has been a taster for this guide since 2010.

Joanne Gibson

Joanne has been writing about wine for over two decades. She received her Level 4 Diploma from the Wine & Spirit Education Trust in 2003 while working for Harpers Wine & Spirit magazine in London. After returning to South Africa in 2004, she worked as deputy editor at Good Taste and then Wine magazine before going freelance in 2009. Winner of both the Du Toitskloof Wine and Franschhoek Literary Festival Wine Writer of the Year awards, she is a sought-after writer and copy editor whose passion is digging up nuggets of SA wine history.

Tim James

Tim, a Cape Wine Master, is an established and multiple award-winning winewriter, contributing freelance to local and international publications and websites, most frequently nowadays to Winemag.co.za but also a regular column to the London-based World of Fine Wine magazine. He is also SA consultant to the World Atlas of Wine. Tim's book, Wines of the New South Africa: Tradition and Revolution, was published in 2013. He has been a taster (and associate editor) for this guide for many years.

Angela Lloyd

Wine has been an important part of Angela's life for the past 50 years, since she arrived in South Africa. It began as an amateur interest stimulated by her husband, Mark, and the Wine Tasters' Guild of which he was a member. She's been a professional wine-writer and -judge since 1983, receiving innumerable commissions both locally and abroad. Travel to the world's winelands has extended her love for wine of all styles. After 34 years on Platter's tasting team, her enthusiasm for this undertaking is undiminished.

Cathy Marston

Cathy hails from Yorkshire, UK, and after completing her degree in English at Cambridge University, she joined Adnams Wine Merchants, passing all the Wine & Spirit Education Trust (WSET) exams, culminating in the Level 4 Diploma. She came to South Africa in 2001, and opened and ran The Nose Restaurant & Wine Bar, selling it after seven successful years. Cathy now concentrates on wine education. She was the first WSET Approved Programme Provider in Africa, and was named WSET Educator of the Year 2015. She also writes for various local and international publications, and judges at competitions. She is currently a Stage 2 Master of Wine (MW) student.

Fiona McDonald

Travel is said to broaden the mind, and Fiona, former editor of Wine magazine for eight years, has had her wine mind broadened by having been a long-serving jury president of several international wine competitions: International Wine Challenge, International Wine & Spirit Competition, Concours Mondial de Bruxelles and, now, Decanter World Wine Awards' regional panel chair for South Africa. Initially trained as a news journalist, she got into wine by happy accident, helping to organise The Mercury Wine Week in between reportage and newsroom management as the night news editor on that Durban broadsheet. Currently freelancing, Fiona edits Cheers magazine, and contributes to a range of publications and websites.

Gregory Mutambe

Encouraged to follow his father into accounting, Gregory instead found himself on a journey into wine and food, first as a winemaking assistant at Mukuyu, one of the handful of wineries in his home country, Zimbabwe, and later as a Cape Wine Academy student in Gauteng. Currently he heads the sommelier team at Cape Town's 12 Apostles Hotel & Spa, oversees an awarded winelist, and judges for several local competitions. Holder of the Wine Judging Academy and UCT Wine Business Management qualifications, Gregory is enrolled in the Court of Master Sommelier and University of South Africa BComm programmes, his aim being to become a wine economist. He is also founding chair of BLACC, an organisation reaching out to black Africans interested in furthering their wine knowledge.

Christine Rudman

Christine's love affair with wine started when she joined the then Stellenbosch Farmers' Winery after a Johannesburg FMCG marketing career. Enrolling in the Cape Wine Academy, she achieved her Cape Wine Master qualification in 1986; left SFW to run the CWA for seven years; and has since been occupied with consultancy work, wine-judging, -lecturing and -writing. She has been a taster for this guide since the 2003 edition. Christine has a wine column in Die Burger newspaper, writes freelance for other publications, and has published two editions of A Guide to the Winelands of the Cape. Technical director of Michelangelo International Wine Awards, she travels widely, serves on various local and international juries, and looks forward to working with wine for years to come.

Dave Swingler

A taster for this guide for over two decades, Dave has consulted to restaurants, game lodges and convention centres, taught wine courses and contributed to radio, print and other media. He is co-author of One Hundred Wines — An Insider's Guide to South African Wine, and drinks contributor to Posh Nosh. A long-standing member of the International Wine & Food Society and the South African consultant for its Annual Vintage Chart, Dave is currently cellarmaster of the Cape Town branch. A psychiatrist by day, he's intrigued by language in general, and the lexicon of wine in particular; he's collaborating on a book examining communication in wine.

Cathy van Zyl

Cathy started her wine journey on a bicycle: she asked her husband to ride SA's famed Cape Town Cycle Tour with her; he accepted if she attended a wine course with him. She has since notched up more than 21 tours - and passed the prestigious Master of Wine examination in 2005. Previously chair of the Institute of Masters of Wine's education committee, she is now a member of its Council. Cathy judges locally and internationally, occasionally contributes to wine journals and websites around the world, but spends most of her wine-time as associate editor of this guide. In 2019, she was named Institute of Cape Wine Masters' Personality of the Year for her passionate promotion of SA wine.

Meryl Weaver

The Cape winelands lured Meryl away from her legal career and, more than 20 years later, she remains firmly under their spell. She has conducted wine presentations abroad on SA wine on behalf of Wines of South Africa, lectures for the Cape Wine Academy, tastes and writes about wine, and judges for various wine competitions and magazines. Meryl qualified as a Cape Wine Master and has graduated with distinction from the Wine Judging Academy. She ensures, however, that the vinous learning curve continues by visiting wine-producing countries, combining some of her other passions, food and travel

How to use this Guide

Note: The example text used here is illustrative and not complete or up to date. See A–Z for full details.

Producer's name

Our track-record-based rating system
See next page for an explanation

Listings of wines available during the
currency of the book

Wine name, vintage, colour & style

Location: nearest major centre to winery,
vineyard, head office

Map & grid reference: see Maps section for
winery's position

WO: Wine of Origin geographical unit, region,
district or ward; wines described/rated bear the
first-mentioned WO certification unless noted

Unless noted, red wines wooded;
whites unoaked

Symbols
See next page for a complete list

Other attractions or activities available
on the property

Bartinney Private Cellar

Perched high on the slopes of the Helshoogte Pass
owned by Michael and Rose Jordaan who are incr
plantings interspersed with native fynbos on steep

★★★★ **Cabernet Sauvignon** Elegant & unders
fruit tempered by savoury Marmite hints, olive tape
lengthy finish. 12-18 months French oak, 50% new

★★★★☆ **Elevage** Poised & polished **10** oozes c
Stellenbosch fruit shows minty notes on nose givin
balanced grippy tannins. Shades of dark chocolate

★★★★☆ **Chardonnay** Classically styled **13** cor
citrus on nose before palate glides delicately into p
ity & lengthy finish.

★★★★☆ **Sauvignon Blanc** Peaches & cream **1**
green figs & quinces below. Good depth & length b

Location/map: Stellenbosch ▪ WO: Banghoek/Steller
10–4 ▪ Closed all pub hols ▪ Cellar tours by appt ▪ Bar
Stellenbosch) ▪ Owner(s) Rose & Michael Jordaan ▪ \
Ryno Maree (Oct 2010) ▪ 27ha/±17ha (cab, chard, s
BWI champion ▪ Postnet Suite 231 Private Bag X506
bartinney.co.za ▪ S 33° 55' 34.66" E 018° 55' 56.79"

Barton Vineyards

Barton is a 200-ha working farm in the hills overlc
offering a range of activities, farm produce and lux
stylish wines is still boutique in scale, critical accla
having to expand the cellar facilities to vinify othe

★★★★★ **Winemakers Reserve** Maiden **11** m
elegance & balance than barrel sample. Understat
nuance. So tailored & sleek, belies its youthful inte

★★★★ **Shiraz-Cabernet Sauvignon** Youthful
with garrigue scrub, pepper & a touch of cab's clea

Rouge 🆕 ⊘ ★★★★ 4-way blend **12**, shiraz d
ture, & merlot & malbec plump out fruit-filled inte
Blanc 13 ★★★★ **Sauvignon Blanc 13** ★★★☆

Location: Bot River ▪ Map: Elgin, Walker Bay & Bot
ing, sales & cellar tours Mon–Fri 9–5 Sat 10–4 ▪ C
olive oil, marinated olives & proteas ▪ Barton Villa
winemaker(s)/viticulturist(s) PJ Geyer (Oct 2010) ▪
raz, chenin, sauv, sem) ▪ 120t/20,000cs own label
River 7185 ▪ info@bartonvineyards.co.za ▪ www.b
2" ▪ F +27 (0)28-284-9776 ▪ **T +27 (0)28-284-**

Symbols
See next page for a complete list

rtinney Private Cellars, a boutique wine estate
heir bio-diversity credentials with new
raced slopes.

Brief introduction/news update

1 (★★★★★) improves on **10** with refined black
vanilla & spice. Delightfully gritty texture & clean

All wines dry unless noted

distinction. Cab-led Bordeaux blend from
to plushy black fruit with herbal hints & nicely
thy finish.

Abbreviations
See next page for a list of abbreviations

form of **12** showing oatmeal, cream & yellow
n pineapples & tropical fruit, balancing oak/acid-

Taster/s initials

★★) preview moves on to flinty minerality with
s concentrated appeal of **13**. — CM

Tastings, sales & cellar tour times (closed
Saturdays & Sundays but open public holidays
unless noted)

■ Est 2006 ■ 1stB 2008 ■ Tasting & sales Mon-Fri
Wine Bar Mon-Sat 11.30-9 (cnr Church & Bird Str,
ker(s) Ronell Wiid (consultant) ■ Viticulturist(s)
18t/4,000cs own label 70% red 30% white ■
nbosch 7599 ■ info@bartinney.co.za ■ www.
(0)21-885-2852 ■ **T +27 (0)21-885-1013**

Names of owner, winemaker, viticulturist &
consultant/s; year/month of appointment in
brackets

Production, in tons and/or 6-bottle cases (cs)
and red:white ratio

Postal & email address, website
(see www.wineonaplatter.com for social media
details)

T = Telephone number

he Bot River Valley, rich in biodiversity and
ommodation. Though the own portfolio of
sulting in French-trained winemaker PJ Geyer
cers' wines on contract.

d Bordeaux blend, now bottled, shows more
ed core of inky red fruit & violets with cedary
ill age with distinction.

onious **11** blend has a sappy texture, infused
ceousness. Supple structure enhanced by oak.
es though equal part cab adds pliable struc-
so tasted: **Shiraz Rosé 13 ★★★ Chenin**
: ⊘ **13 ★★★★** — MW

WO: Walker Bay ■ Est 2001 ■ 1stB 2003 ■ Tast-
aster Sun, Dec 25 & Jan 1 ■ Lavender products,
er(s) Peter J Neill ■ Cellarmaster(s)/
/30ha (cab, malbec, merlot, mourv, pinot, shi-
ed 50% white 10% rosé ■ IPW ■ PO Box 100 Bot
neyards.co.za ■ S 34° 15' 43.8" E 019° 10' 29-

Date established

Total hectares/hectares under vine (not necessarily in production); main varieties planted

GPS coordinates, based on Datum WGS 84

How To Use This Guide

Our Track-Record-Based Rating System

General rating   ★★★★ **Caldera**
For 4-star or better wines, we give the 'track-record rating' over two or more vintages in the margin. Wines rated 4½ stars or more are set in red type

Vintage-specific rating   **06 (★★★☆)**
Any differences from the general rating are noted in brackets beside the particular vintage

★★★★★	95–100 / 18–20 pts	Superlative. A South African classic
★★★★☆	90–94 / 17–17.5 pts	Outstanding
★★★★	86–89 / 16–16.5 pts	Excellent
★★★☆	83–85 / 15.5 pts	Very good/promising
★★★	80–82 / 15 pts	Good, for early drinking
★★☆	77–79 / 14.5 pts	Average, with some appeal
★★	73–76 / 14 pts	Pleasant enough
★☆	70–72 / 13 pts	Plain and simple
★	65–69 / 12 pts	Unexciting
☆	60–64 / 11 pts	Very ordinary
No star	50–59 / 10 pts	Somewhat less than ordinary

Symbols

Winery symbols

- ⓆOpen for tasting (no fee unless noted)
- 🍽Restaurant/refreshments
- 🏠Accommodation
- 📷Other tourist attractions/amenities on the property
- 🧺Bring your own (BYO) picnic
- 🧒Child friendly
- ♿Wheelchair friendly
- (NEW)New winery
- /// What3Words address*

*See Editor's Note

Wine symbols

- (88) Rating on 100-point scale (see above)
- ⊘ Good value
- (NEW) New wine
- Ⓧ Wine still selling, not retasted
- 🌱 Organic
- ◎ Biodynamic
- 🏵 Hidden gem
- ❀ From vines officially 35 years or older*
- 🐝 Worth cellaring 8-10 years (reds, fortifieds), 4-6 years (whites)*

Abbreviations

% alc	Percentage alcohol by volume		NLH	Noble Late Harvest
1stB	First bottled vintage		NV	Non-vintage. Year of harvest not stated on label
BEE	Black Economic Empowerment			
BYO	Bring your own (wine, picnic)		RS	Residual sugar
Cs	Cases		SAA	Selected to fly with SAA
CWG	Cape Winemakers Guild		SLH	Special Late Harvest
CWM	Cape Wine Master		Veritas	SA National Bottled Wine Show
Est	Date established		WIETA	Wine & Agricultural Ethical Trade Association
g/l	Grams per litre			
IPW	Integrated Production of Wine		WO	Wine of Origin
IWC	International Wine Challenge			
IWSC	International Wine & Spirit Competition		cabernet/cab	cabernet sauvignon
			pinot	pinot noir
LBV	Late Bottled Vintage		chenin	chenin blanc
Malo	Malolactic fermentation		sauvignon/sauv	sauvignon blanc
MCC	Méthode cap classique		touriga	touriga nacional
MW	Master of Wine		tinta	tinta barocca

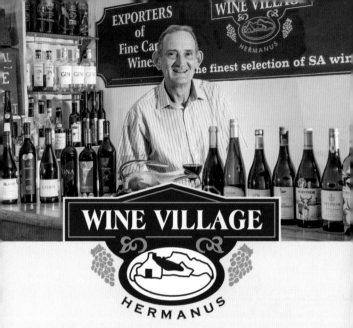

WINE VILLAGE

HERMANUS

Offering the largest selection of premium South African Wines

Available for shipping world wide - door to door

VOTED ONE OF *South Africa's Best* **WINE SHOPS**

SINCE 1998

OPEN 7 DAYS A WEEK

Mon-Fri: **09:00 - 18:00**
Sat: **09:00 - 17:00**
Sun: **10:00 - 15:00**

The most unique South African wine experience

TEL: +27 (0) 28 316 3988

Hemel-en-Aarde Village, Hermanus, South Africa

wine@hermanus.co.za | www.winevillage.co.za

GPS Coordinates: S34°24'40.7" E019°12'1.9"

Quality, Design and Innovation

Liebherr built-in Wine Coolers, provide a compact storage solution, unique to Liebherr. Yourwine collections can be magnificently presented with soft lighting, and at the perfect temperatures.

www.liebherr.com

A–Z of South African Producers

AA Badenhorst Family Wines Ⓨ ⌂ ⊚

Adi Badenhorst left a prestigious winemaking job at Rustenburg to become a pioneer of the revolutionary Swartland winemaking scene. In 2007 he and his cousin Hein bought a run-down farm on the Paardeberg, with an old cellar much in need of renovation, and inaugurated a remarkable transformation there. Not least, the vineyards have been painstakingly rehabilitated – helping the ever-dynamic Adi to shift his focus towards single-vineyard expressions of older vines. The Secateurs range of affordable but characterful wines has also been a major success, as has the reinvention of a traditional local aperitif – the Kaapse Dief Caperitif. When Jasper Wickens moved on in 2018 to concentrate on his own range, Hanneke Botha arrived to work with Adi, in hands-off fashion, on the innovative, fresh and subtly worked wines.

AA Badenhorst range

★★★★☆ **Ramnasgras Cinsault** ⓐ Perfumed red fruit on bunch-fermented **18** ⑨③, but handsome rather than pretty. There's a silky, subtle savouriness & an elegant light leanness rather than the obvious fruitiness of many cinsauts, & some delicious grippy tannins. 12% alcohol. **17** untasted.

★★★★☆ **Ringmuur Cinsault** ⓃⒺⓌ The more obviously charming & richer of the cinsaut pair, with notably pure strawberry fruit, but also very well structured. **18** ⑨③, like its partner, perfectly dry, & matured in older oak - but this one fully destemmed. 12.5% alcohol. Both also in magnum, as are Pinot & Red.

★★★★ **Bokveld Pinot Noir** ⓃⒺⓌ Fresh raspberry, herbal & coffee notes (though only older oak) on **18** ⑧⑨ from Ceres Plateau. Bright, with subtle tannins but driven more by fresh acidity. 12.5% alcohol.

★★★★☆ **Sk'windjiesvlei Tinta Barocca** ⓃⒺⓌ ⓐ Deep-coloured **18** ⑨③, intriguing spicy, plummy, dried herb & pot-pourri aromas. Pure fruit, dense & compact, Swartland's smooth but form-giving tannins. Restrained, effortless character, nothing overt - but everything delicious. Some richness, but dry finish. 13.5% alcohol. These reds great in youth but will reward keeping.

★★★★☆ **Red** ⓐ Light perfume, with red & darker fruit & ferrous savouriness on bright, vital **17** ⑨③. Shiraz (59%), cinsaut, grenache, tinta. Foot-trodden whole bunches for light extraction. Lengthy period on skins accentuates elegant, notably dry tannins. Complex & satisfying. 13.5% alcohol. **16** untasted.

★★★★★ **Dassiekop Steen** ⓐ All 5 chenin vineyards picked at similar ripeness levels; this the highest alcohol (14.5%) & richest fruit character. **18** ⑨⑥'s generous apricot & peach tones beautifully balanced by vibrant but not assertive acidity, liquorice lift. Like all the chenins, fermented in large 60 year old vats, aged in varying sizes of older oak (here 500L, 14 months) for breadth & depth, not flavour. **17** untasted.

★★★★★ **Kelder Steen** ⓃⒺⓌ Possibly the 'prettiest' of the chenins, & the only one also available in magnum. **18** ⑨⑤ intense white peach & nectarine flavours, gentle acidity & 11 months in 500L chestnut barrels delivering a smooth fantail finish.

★★★★☆ **Klip Kop Steen** ⓃⒺⓌ From low-vigour vines in shallow granite soils, **18** ⑨③ understated & assured. Nuanced quince rather than stonefruit, wet terracotta earthiness & persistent sweet-fruited finish. 11 months in large chestnut foudre aids integration, not aromatic/flavour development.

★★★★☆ **Piet Bok se Bos Steen** ⓃⒺⓌ ⓐ Named for farmer who planted these vines in 1968. Like Golden Slopes, **18** ⑨③ only faintly fruity, with greater emphasis on texture & weight. Supple, with pleasing viscosity, 4.4 g/l sugar (it's the sweetest of the whites) shot through by tangy acidity & distinct salty taste.

★★★★☆ **The Golden Slopes Chenin Blanc** ⓐ Earthy & savoury expression from vineyard on yellow granite soils. **18** ⑨④ scrub & khaki bush nuances, finely honed acid balance & lengthy saline conclusion. Almost extreme non-interventionist winemaking: lengthy natural ferment, 14 months on gross lees before bottling unfined/filtered. **17** untasted.

★★★★ **Sout van die Aarde Palomino** Bone-dry & light (12% alcohol) but **18** ⑧⑦ doesn't lack flavour or appeal; fresh herbs, salt & positive funk. Bunch pressed, fermented off its skins. No **17**.

★★★★☆ **Kalmoesfontein White** ⓐ Adds name of the home farm to the label. One of SA's best-known 'all-sorts' white blends in international markets. **17** ⑨④ usual chenin, roussanne & grenache blanc with 5 others, characterful & rich yet with satisfying dryness, commanding presence. Magnums too. WO Coastal. Last tasted was **15** ★★★★★ ⑨⑤.

Not tasted: **Raaigras Grenache**, **Méthode Ancestrale**.

Secateurs range

★★★★ **Red** Mostly cinsaut (82%) with shiraz & grenache, **18** ★★★☆ ⑧③ dry & extremely quaffable but shade less pure-fruited than last-tasted **15** ⑧⑦.

★★★★ **Riviera** 🆕 ⊘ Skin-macerated chenin & semillon, **18** ⑧⑥ distinctly phenolic with considerable tannic grip & emphatic dryness. Not to everyone's taste but perfect for solo sipping or a meal.

Chenin Blanc ⊘ 🏆 ★★★★ Popular brand at home & abroad, spirited **18** ⑧④ a juicy stonefruit & tropical mouthful, more than delivers at its price point. ±25% fermented in older casks & large foudres.

Rosé ⊘ ★★★★ Dry **19** ⑧③ pink from cinsaut, bubblegum whiffs, slight meaty element from mourvèdre, pleasing savoury farewell. — TJ, CvZ

Location: Malmesbury ▪ Map: Swartland ▪ Map grid reference: C8 ▪ WO: Swartland/Coastal/Ceres Plateau ▪ Est 2007 ▪ 1stB 2006 ▪ Tasting, sales & tours by appt Mon-Fri 8-3.30 ▪ Closed all pub hols & weekends ▪ Conferences ▪ Function venue for 130 people ▪ Conservation area ▪ Guest cottages ▪ Owner(s) Adi & Hein Badenhorst ▪ Winemaker(s) Adi Badenhorst (2006), with Hanneke Botha (2018) ▪ Viticulturist(s) Pierre Rossouw (Jan 1975) ▪ 100ha/43ha (cinsaut, grenache, shiraz, chard, chenin, rouss) ▪ 40,000cs own label 60% red 40% white ▪ PO Box 1177 Malmesbury 7299 ▪ adi@iafrica.com ▪ www.aabadenhorst.com ▪ S 33° 32' 38.01" E 018° 49' 7.42" ▪ ⁄ᵢᵢᵢ uprooting.feed.pollsters ▪ **T +27 (0)82-373-5038/+27 (0)22-125-0116 (office)**

Aaldering Vineyards & Wines   ⓥ ⌂ ♿

Entrepreneurial Dutch couple Marianne and Fons Aaldering founded their Devon Valley estate in 2004. Today their 'young, professional, dynamic and international team' includes youngest daughter Jacqueline, who looks after financial and hospitality matters, and French-trained winemaker PJ Geyer whose 'precision in vinicultural practices is ensuring top-quality grapes'. They recently purchased three additional hectares from a neighbour, where they will plant 'exciting varieties to further enhance our Bordeaux blend'.

★★★★ **Lady M** Unwooded pinotage, **18** ⑧⑦ ably puts the focus on approachability without sacrificing intensity or varietal integrity. Like last-tasted **16** ⑧⑥, fine fruit purity, satisfying weight & persistence.

★★★★ **Shiraz** Follows house's plush styling in **16** ⑧⑦: plum cake richness, cardamon & clove accents, round & ripe tannins neatly balanced by seam fresh acidity.

★★★★ **Cabernet Sauvignon-Merlot** 🐝 Classic cassis, cedar & green walnut notes, fair grip & choc/liquorice finish on 60/40 blend. **16** ⑧⑨ refreshing glassful now, structure & substance to improve 5± years.

★★★★ **Chardonnay** Rich pear tartin & orange marmalade, generous butterscotch overlay, buttery viscosity from 40% barrel-fermented portion (40% new). **18** ⑧⑦ intense & long, welcome acidity on finish.

★★★★ **Sauvignon Blanc** Elegant expression of ripe grapes. Appealing & unusual white peach, pear & hay, fresh acidity & persistent mineral conclusion. **19** ⑧⑧ should please even more with year/2 ageing.

★★★★ **Noble Late Harvest Sauvignon Blanc** 🆕 🐝 Unoaked but aged 18 months in bottle before release. Luxurious **16** ⑧⑧ apricot purée, pear & fynbos honey, sweet intensity matched with crisp acidity for light-feeling, cloy-free drinking pleasure.

Pinotage Rosé ★★★★ Shows more aroma & flavour restraint than most pink wines from this variety. **19** ⑧③ bone-dryness & underplayed berry tones countering any heaviness from 13.9% alcohol. — JG, CvZ

Location/map/WO: Stellenbosch ▪ Map grid reference: D4 ▪ Est 2004 ▪ 1stB 2007 ▪ Tasting & sales Mon-Thu 10-5 Fri 10-4 Sat (Oct-Apr) 10-3 ▪ Closed all pub hols ▪ Cellar tours by appt ▪ 3 luxury lodges (TGCSA 5 star) ▪ Owner(s) Marianne & Fons Aaldering ▪ Winemaker(s)/viticulturist(s) PJ Geyer (Sep 2017) ▪ 20ha/19.7ha (cab, merlot, ptage, shiraz, chard, sauv) ▪ ±120t/±18,300cs own label 50% red 50% white ▪ IPW ▪ PO Box 1068 Stellenbosch 7599 ▪ estate@aaldering.co.za ▪ www.aaldering.co.za ▪ S 33° 55' 9.81" E 018° 49' 8.14" ▪ ⁄ᵢᵢᵢ gliders.steamed.trek ▪ **T +27 (0)21-865-2495**

Aan de Doorns Cellar   ⓥ ♿

Grower-owned Aan de Doorns is mainly a supplier to, and shareholder in, export powerhouse FirstCape. But 25,000 cases of appealing, affordable wines are made for the house labels, available for tasting at the visitor venue near Worcester. After reduced volumes the previous harvest, 2019 produced a record crop of 33,000 tons. More cheer for longtime cellar chief Johan Morkel and his team came in the form of a new filtration unit and red-wine fermentation tanks for season 2020.

Vintage range

★★★★ **Muscat d'Alexandrie** ⓥ Fortified dessert **15** ⑧⑦, ex tank, heady grape & floral perfume harbinger of delights to come: glacé fruit & honeycomb flavours yet uncloying, refined. 375 ml. No **14**.

★★★★ **Red Muscadel** Raisin rich & full sweet without being cloying, **16** ⑧⑧ fortified muscat is mouthfilling, finishes long. A celebration of fruit & sunshine. 375 ml.

Cabernet Sauvignon ⓥ ★★☆ Oak's influence gives savoury tones to **17** ⑦⑧'s plummy fruit, has enough tannin structure for ageing or rich food. **Pinotage** ⓥ ★★★ New-oak treatment well handled, in harmony with **17** ⑧①'s fruit, a touch of salty liquorice for interest. Smooth textured, can age. **Shiraz** ⓥ ★★☆ Savoury spiced from wooding, **18** ⑦⑧ has enough dark-fruited fleshy ripeness to drink easily & well. **Doornroodt** ⓥ ★★★ Lightly oaked ruby cab & merlot blend, **17** ⑦⑧'s red berries have mocha tones, smooth & round. **Chenin Blanc** ★★★ Shows how appealing everyday chenin can be, **19** ⑦⑨ light, crisply dry & fruity. **Sauvignon Blanc** ★★ With apple freshness, elegantly dry **19** ⑦④ has ideal summer drinkability. **Sweet William Vonkelwyn** ⓥ ★★ Pink bubbly from colombard & pinotage, **NV** ⑦④ fruit gum scented, sweet & convivial, a party goer. **Cape Ruby** ⓥ ★★★★ Fruitcake richness in old-oaked **17** ⑧④ 'port', savoury spicy seam offsetting the sweetness. Long, smooth finish.

Route 43 range

· ·

Deep Red ⓥ ⑦ ★★★ Bargain priced, as all these. Shiraz & pinotage partnership in unwooded **18** ⑦⑨, dark toned & juicy, glossy berries give easy drinking.

· ·

Fruity White ⓥ ★★★ Abundant fruitiness in semi-sweet **19** ⑦⑧ from colombard, friendly 11% alcohol part of the easy drinkability. **Crisp White** ⓥ ★★★ Apt name for **19** ⑦⑧'s sauvignon & colombard blend, zesty-fresh & light (12% alcohol). Also in 3L, as for red. — CR

Location/map/WO: Worcester ▪ Map grid reference: B4 ▪ Est 1954 ▪ Tasting & sales Mon–Fri 8–5 Sat 9-1 ▪ Olive/olive oil & wine pairing by appt ▪ Closed all pub hols ▪ Tours during harvest by appt ▪ Owner(s) 27 shareholders ▪ Cellarmaster(s) Johan Morkel (Nov 1993) ▪ Winemaker(s) Gert van Deventer (Sep 1997) & Chris Geldenhuys (Sep 2016) ▪ Viticulturist(s) Pierre Snyman ▪ 1,600ha (cab, ptage, chard, chenin, cbard) ▪ 32,700t/25,000cs own label ▪ PO Box 235 Worcester 6849 ▪ info@aandedoorns.co.za ▪ www.aandedoorns. co.za ▪ S 33° 41' 47.0" E 019° 29' 26.2" ▪ ⓦ lookout.sprouts.expensively ▪ T +27 (0)23-347-2301

Aan't Vette Wine Estate   ⓥ ⑪ ⌂ ⓝⓔⓦ

This tiny estate beside the Vette River comprises a 1.2-ha block of shiraz, planted in 2008 and farmed as naturally as possible. Wines are made in a state-of-the-art facility housed in a 150-year-old barn, part of De Doornkraal Vinotel & Country Kitchen in Riversdale town. Owner (and vineyardist) is engineer and educator Pieter Steyn (founder of Cranefield College), whose forebear designed Cape Town's Castle of Good Hope.

Louis Meurant Shiraz ★★★☆ Bone-dry & bright **15** ⑧④ has a maraschino cherry & Christmas cake appeal, substantial structure assisted by year in 20% new oak. **Divine Blush** ★★★★ Pepper & scrub whiffs, spicy hints on attractive **18** ⑧③ blanc de noir from shiraz. Nicely vinous, with plenty of sweet strawberry fruit padding its supermodel derrière. — GdB, CvZ

Location: Riversdale ▪ Map: Klein Karoo & Garden Route ▪ Map grid reference: C6 ▪ WO: Western Cape ▪ Est 2009 ▪ 1stB 2012 ▪ Tasting & cellar tours by appt only ▪ Sales online ▪ Closed all pub hols ▪ Meals/refreshments (arranged by the hotel) by appt only ▪ Conference venue (max 20 pax) ▪ Aan't Vette Country Kitchen ▪ De Doornkraal Vinotel (4-star hotel) ▪ Owner(s) Pieter Steyn ▪ Winemaker(s) Piet Geldenhuys (consultant) ▪ Viticulturist(s) Pieter Steyn & Theo Geldenhuys (consultant) ▪ 1.2ha (shiraz) ▪ ±10-12t ▪ own label 90% red 10% blanc de noir ▪ kelder@dedoornkraal.com ▪ www.dedoornkraal.com ▪ S 34° 5' 20.92" E 021° 15' 42.32" ▪ ⓦ brilliance.watery.triathlete ▪ T +27 (0)28-713-1091

☐ **Abalone** *see* Whalehaven Wines
☐ **Abraham Perold Heritage Collection** *see* KWV Wines

Absolute Style Wines ⓦ ⓝ

Anne Serebolo Mogadingoane, with years of management experience behind her, founded this brand. The aim with her boldly labelled range is, she says, 'to create wines that please all the senses and over-deliver'. A specific focus is on persuading beer and spirits drinkers of the delights of wine, and Anne is confident that there are many who are 'eager to convert to wine, seeing it as a classy and socially acceptable alternative'.

Merlot ★★★ Xmas cake, herbs & vanilla scents on **15** ⑧② from Stellenbosch. Sweet fruit & satisfying grip from ripe, rounded tannins. **Cabernet Sauvignon-Petit Verdot-Malbec** ★★ Blackberry- & cassis-toned **14** ⑦④'s forthright acidity & high-toned element tempered by gentle tannins, sweet fruit on finish. **Chardonnay** ★★★ Unoaked **17** ⑦⑧ is ready now; appealing ripe orange & tangerine aromas dusted with Indian spices, brief lemon farewell. **Sweet Rosé** ★★ Modestly fruity, grapey aromas on sweet **NV** ⑦② party starter. This & white sibling uncertified. **Natural Sweet White** ★ Sweet apricot & vanilla flavours on **NV** ⑥⑨, for uncomplicated quaffing. — TJ, CvZ

Location: Cape Town ▪ Map: Cape Peninsula ▪ Map grid reference: B1 ▪ WO: Paarl/Stellenbosch ▪ Est/1stB 2017 ▪ Tasting by appt only ▪ Fee R50/5 wines, waived on purchase of 2/more btls ▪ Sales Mon-Fri 9-5 ▪ Closed Easter Fri/Sun, Dec 25/26 & Jan 1 ▪ Owner(s) Absolute Style Wines (Pty) Ltd (1 shareholder) ▪ Cellarmaster(s) various ▪ 5,000cs own label 60% red 20% white 20% rosé ▪ 1st floor JCC House, 27 Owl Str, corner Empire Rd, Milpark Johannesburg 2001 ▪ info@absolutestylewines.co.za, sales@absolutestylewines.co.za, anne@absolutestylewines.co.za ▪ www.absolutestylewines.co.za ▪ S 33° 55' 11.1" E 018° 22' 57.8" ▪ ᴀᴡ lifestyles. salivary.heptathlon ▪ T +27 (0)11-976-5827, +27 (0)82-853-9003

Accolade Wines South Africa

Part of Accolade Wines, one of the big five international wine businesses, whose portfolio includes some of the best-known New World wine labels. Accolade Wines South Africa's winemaking operation, based in Somerset West, is responsible for the global megabrand Kumala, Fish Hoek range of single varietals, and highly regarded Flagstone pinnacle wines, all listed separately.

Location: Somerset West ▪ Winemaker(s) Gerhard Swart (group winemaker), Juan Slabbert & Chandré Petersen ▪ 2.6m cs own label ▪ PO Box 769 Stellenbosch 7599 ▪ info@flagstonewines.com ▪ www.accoladewines.com ▪ T +27 (0)21-852-5052

☐ **Adama** *see* Bosman Family Vineyards

Aden's Star

These are the vintage-dated wines made by consultants for Jason Neal, CEO of Johannesburg drinks company Nicholson Smith. The NV labels, Pandora's Box and Bella Vino, are listed under Nicholson Smith.

The Golden Fleece ★★★ A rejig has merlot leading the Bordeaux blend in **17** ⑧②. Cocoa palate, with medium density & grip. Also-tasted **16** ⑧② more leathery & dry. Discontinued: **Sauvignon Blanc**. — FM

Location: Johannesburg ▪ WO: Western Cape ▪ Est 1997 ▪ 1stB 2012 ▪ Closed to public ▪ Owner(s) Jason Neal ▪ Winemaker(s) James McKenzie (reds) & John Seccombe (whites) ▪ Viticulturist(s) James McKenzie (2012) ▪ 4,000cs own label 50% red 50% white ▪ PO Box 1659 Jukskei Park 2153 ▪ jason@nicholsonsmith.co.za ▪ www.nicholsonsmith.co.za ▪ T +27 (0)11-496-2947

AD Wines ⓦ

The three vineyards from which attorney Adrian Dommisse draws grapes are all unirrigated bushvines – 'terrifying' in drought years. Would there be a 2018 harvest at all? There was, and of astonishing quality, he says, though production levels were tiny for the ex-Darling wine he settled on – made as always in minimalistic, hands-off fashion.

★★★★ **Skylark Cinsault** Very much in the lighter style of this fashionable variety (11.5% alcohol). Oodles of floral-fruity-fragrant charm on **18** ⑧⑦. Fresh & pretty, with the lightest of grips; gently persistent & beguiling. — TJ

Location: Cape Town ▪ WO: Darling ▪ Est 2013 ▪ 1stB 2014 ▪ Tasting by appt only ▪ Owner(s) Dommisse Holdings Pty Ltd, shareholder Adrian Dommisse ▪ Winemaker(s) Adrian Dommisse ▪ 2t/150cs own label 100% red ▪ PO Box 13225 Mowbray 7705 ▪ adriandommisse@gmail.com ▪ www.adwines.co.za ▪ T +27 (0)71-674-4316

☐ **Africa Five** *see* Stellenview Premium Wines
☐ **African Pride Wines** *See Editor's Note*
☐ **African Roots** *see* Seven Sisters Vineyards
☐ **Agaat** *see* Truter Family Wines
☐ **Ahrens Family** *see* The Ahrens Family

Akkerdal Wine Estate ⓠ ⌂

Family winegrowing roots may date back to 1714, but Pieter Hanekom believes in 'farming for the future' by applying biodynamic principles (without seeking certification) at his estate in Franschhoek. 'Healthy soil carried me through four years of serious drought,' he says, adding that his three main objectives are a healthy environment, economic profitability and socio-economic equity. Newly repackaged, the range has expanded to include three new red wines, untasted by us.

Limited Releases

★★★★ **Malbec** ⓠ **15** ⑧⑦ intense sour cherry & spice appeal, skilfully reins in fruit generosity to finish with elegance & focus. Attractive dinner companion, with sufficient heft to partner hearty food.

★★★★ **Kallie's Dream** ⓠ Rhône-style **15** ★★★★★ ⑨① engages on many levels, not least the unusual co-ferment of all components: shiraz (48%), mourvèdre, grenache, carignan & viognier. Fruit rich, yet plenty of tannic oomph & freshening acidity; lingering pure-fruited farewell. Worth waiting since **10** ⑧⑦.

★★★★ **Wild Boar** ⓠ **15** ⑧⑦ first since **09** ⑧⑦, 'wild' in its daredevil mix of petit verdot, cab franc, petite sirah & roobernet (20% each) with shiraz & tannat (10% apiece). Dry & firm, myriad red berry fruits to contemplate, dissect or simply enjoy.

Not tasted: **TDT**, **SG Rose**.

Akkerdal range

Occasional release: **Sauvignon Blanc**. Discontinued: **Shiraz**. — HC

Location/map/WO: Franschhoek ▪ Map grid reference: C4 ▪ Est 2000 ▪ 1stB 2001 ▪ Tasting & sales Mon-Fri 10-4 by appt only ▪ Closed all pub hols ▪ Self-catering chalet ▪ Owner(s)/cellarmaster(s)/winemaker(s) Pieter Hanekom ▪ Viticulturist(s) Pieter Hanekom, advised by Eben Archer ▪ 18ha (barbera, cab f, carignan, durif, grenache, malbec, merlot, mourv, p verdot, roobernet, shiraz, tannat, tempranillo, chard, nouvelle, sauv, sem, viog) ▪ 6,000cs own label 95% red 4% white 1% rosé ▪ IPW, WIETA ▪ PO Box 36 La Motte 7691 ▪ wine@akkerdal.co.za ▪ www.akkerdal.co.za ▪ S 33° 52' 50.9" E 019° 3' 3.8" ▪ 🌐 surges.telegraphs.campsites ▪ **T +27 (0)21-876-3481/+27 (0)82-442-1746**

Akkerdraai ⓠ ⓞ

Post retirement from international enterprise Media24, Salie de Swardt has taken his love of wine to the next level by producing it (with consultants) from his small cabernet vineyard on Annandale Road in the Helderberg. A portion of vintage '01 was blended with brought-in merlot and the result was so well received, the exercise was repeated for the '13 and now the '17, a treat for fans of Salie's well-priced bottlings.

★★★★ **Cabernet Sauvignon-Merlot** ⊘ Occasionally released Bordeaux blend, ripe & generously fruited in **17** ★★★★ ⑧⑤. Similar oaking (year, ±10 new) though fresher than sibling, & shade off **13** ⑧⑦.

Cabernet Sauvignon ⊘ ★★★★ Cassis compote with a touch of salty liquorice on **15** ⑧③. Densely packed, structure just contains ripeness & warmth. A winter comforter, for hearty fare. — MW

Location/map/WO: Stellenbosch ▪ Map grid reference: E8 ▪ Est 1956 ▪ 1stB 2007 ▪ Tasting by appt only ▪ Fee R25, waived on purchase ▪ Closed Easter Fri-Mon, Dec 25 & Jan 1 ▪ Walks/hikes ▪ Owner(s)/cellarmaster(s) Salie de Swardt ▪ Winemaker(s) Ronell Wiid (consultant), with Salie de Swardt (Jan 2013) ▪ Viticulturist(s) Ronell Wiid (consultant) ▪ 1.5ha (cab) ▪ 12t 100% red ▪ PO Box 22 Lynedoch 7603 ▪ saliedes@mweb.co.za ▪ S 33° 59' 53.52" E 018° 49' 50.94" ▪ 🌐 crossing.bossy.name ▪ **T +27 (0)21-881-3861/+27 (0)83-264-1463**

Alexanderfontein

This screwcapped range of easy-drinking wines (designed to enhance 'enjoyment of the simpler aspect of life') comes from the substantial Ormonde Private Cellar in Darling, where Razvan Macici, ex-Nederburg, is now winemaker, with Theo Basson, co-owner of the family business, in the vineyards.

Cabernet Sauvignon ⊘ ★★★ Now bottled, red-berried **15** ⑧ is easily approachable, with pleasingly firm grip & supportive oak (15% new). Coastal WO unless noted. **Merlot** ⑧ ★★★ **16** ⑦ offers ripely fruity aromas, but the palate is rather light & ungenerous. **Shiraz** ⊘ ★★★ Retasted **15** ⑦ has pleasing aromas. Soft texture, firm acid, modest tannins & sweetish, lightly fruity finish. **Chardonnay** ⑧ ★★★ Shyly fruity aromas on unoaked **17** ⑦, with a creamy texture, firm acidity & sweet-sour finish. **Chenin Blanc** ⊘ ★★★ Tasted ex-tank last year, unassertive but pleasant **18** ⑧ from Cape South Coast grapes; sweet fruit but dry. Modest 12.7% alcohol. **Sauvignon Blanc** ⊘ ★★★ A preview last time, freshly crisp & dry **18** ⑧ keeps its balance of passionfruit & green-tinged flavours. — TJ

Alheit Vineyards

Some good and bad news this year from owners and internationally celebrated husband-and-wife team, Chris and Suzaan Alheit, based in Hemel-en-Aarde Ridge and producing white wine exclusively under this family label from old, heritage-variety vineyards across the Western Cape. The much-loved Radio Lazarus chenin is no more, three years of drought plus hungry animals having finally killed one of the two Bottelary vineyards, the other yielding only 8 crates of grapes last year. The good news, however, is that the Alheits now own a farm on Swartland's prime Paardeberg, with 18 ha of old-vine chenin to hopefully spark new opportunities for their exciting, terroir-driven range. Their high-elevation riesling in Ceres has produced a first crop, and a parcel of air-dried muscat d'Alexandrie from 1890s vines is incubating in the cellar on Hemelrand farm. Chris and Suzaan have decided to discontinue their 'little brother range', Flotsam & Jetsam (but see separate entry for a delectable swansong), to concentrate solely on their quest for simplicity, identity and clarity - all three characteristics exemplified by the wines listed below.

★★★★☆ **Cartology** ⓐ ⓦ The original Alheit wine, from far-flung vineyards (WO W Cape). Just 10% semillon with chenin in **18** ⑨ but enough to add some wax & honey notes to soft yellow apple fruit & lemon zest freshness. Touch of oatmeal & nuts from old oak & 10 months on lees, a little weight mid-palate from small concrete 'egg'-fermented portion.

★★★★☆ **Fire By Night** ⓐ ⓦ Bushvines in Swartland, **18** ⑨ ridiculously low yields giving rich, concentrated stonefruit with fynbos honey & unusual saline note. Contrasting thread of lipsmacking acidity runs throughout to satisfying finish. Old, dry-farmed vineyards, bunch pressing & old neutral oak, as all the chenins.

★★★★☆ **Huilkrans** ⓐ ⓦ Richer than its Citrusdal Mountain sibling, **18** ⑨ chenin shows peaches & pineapples with caramelised marshmallow, woolly core firmly teased into line by lime marmalade acidity. Persistent & evolving through to lengthy tail. Vines planted 1974, 1986, 1989.

★★★★☆ **Magnetic North** ⓐ ⓦ Thrilling **18** ★★★★★ ⑨ from old (1981, 1984) ungrafted bushvine chenin from Citrusdal Mountain. Quiet starter, but builds on palate adding layers of tart apples, soft spice, lime zest & wet stones. Touch of creaminess balances out really zippy acidity. Just going to get better & better, as with uncompromisingly dry **17** ⑨.

★★★★☆ **Nautical Dawn** ⓐ ⓦ From False Bay side of Stellenbosch, granite soil, 1978 block produces ripest of the chenins, **18** ⑨ peaches, apricots & almonds plus gravelly texture & piquant aniseed twist. Endless finish, as racy acidity keeps it fresh & appetising throughout.

★★★★★ **La Colline Vineyard** ⓐ ⓦ Franschhoek semillon on southern slope, oldest vines in the range (84 years) goes into youngest oak (but none new - 3 year old foudres & 6 year old barrels), as **18** ★★★★★ ⑨'s concentrated, dense fruit more than handles it, as in **17** ⑨. Lemon peel, wild herb, resin & marzipan notes; clean, honeyed finish.

★★★★☆ **Hemelrand Vine Garden** ⓐ Around 30% each of roussanne, chenin, chardonnay with verdelho & muscat de Frontignan from mixed vineyard in Hemel-en-Aarde Ridge, 360 m elevation & windblown. **18** ⑨ 40% fermented in concrete 'egg', adding roundness & silky texture to peachy, Lemon Cream fruit, with racy acidity & fragrant finish.

Discontinued: **Radio Lazarus**. — CM

Location: Hermanus ▪ WO: Citrusdal Mountain/Stellenbosch/Swartland/Franschhoek/Western Cape/ Hemel-en-Aarde Ridge ▪ Est 2010 ▪ 1stB 2011 ▪ Closed to public ▪ Owner(s) Chris & Suzaan Alheit ▪ Cellarmaster(s) Chris Alheit ▪ Winemaker(s) Chris & Suzaan Alheit, with Franco Lourens (Jan 2016) ▪ 90t/4,200cs own label 100% white ▪ PO Box 711 Hermanus 7200 ▪ chris@alheitvineyards.co.za ▪ www. alheitvineyards.co.za ▪ T +27 (0)83-274-6860

Alkmaar Boutique Vineyard

Juan Möller, co-owner with Charmaine Olivier of this Wellington boutique winery, is benefitting from the wealth of knowledge of local vineyards and the wines they're capable of producing in the form of new consultant Charles Stassen. Renewed energy here sees release plans for three additional wines - 2 red blends and a chardonnay bubbly - later this year.

★★★★ **Provost Pinotage** ⓥ Full & rich, spicy dark berry & plum flavours. **17** ⑧⑧ good palate weight, supple structure & lingering savoury finish. 25% new oak ageing.

★★★★ **Dominus Merlot-Cabernet Sauvignon-Petit Verdot** ⓥ Bordeaux blend is now merlot-led, 18 months oaked **17** ⑧⑦ picks up the pace from cab-dominant **13** ★★★☆ ⑧⑤ with herb-tinged bright blackberry fruit, good balance & savoury farewell. **14 - 16** untasted.

★★★★ **Alumni Shiraz-Mourvèdre** No viognier in **17** ⑧⑨, delicious & full-bodied 67/33 Rhône blend with cured meat, leather & spice on firm tannin frame - ideal partner for grilled steak.

Chardonnay-Pinot Noir ⓥ ★★★★ Just-dry, palest pink rosé, **18** ⑧⑤ vibrant & fruity with raspberries-&-cream flavours, gentle zip of lemon on finish. **Viognier** ⓥ ★★★★ Summery fresh peach & spice appeal on unoaked **18** ⑧④, balanced & rounded. **Chardonnay-Viognier** ⓥ ★★★★ Zesty **18** ⑧⑤ in lightly aromatic style, lively & fresh for al fresco lunches & patio parties. **Méthode Cap Classique Brut** ⓥ ★★★ Deep gold-hued **11** ⑧⓪ dry sparkler from undisclosed variety/ies, evolved bruised apple, toast flavours & creamy mousse on broad palate, best enjoyed soon. — WB

Location/map/WO: Wellington ▪ Map grid reference: C4 ▪ Est 2001 ▪ 1stB 2005 ▪ Tasting & cellar tours Tue-Sat/pub hols 11-4 by appt; prefer groups of 6 and more ▪ Walks (part of Wellington Wine Walk) ▪ Owner(s) Juan Möller & Charmaine Olivier ▪ Winemaker(s) Juan Möller & Charles Stassen (consultant) ▪ 9.9ha (cab, merlot, mourv, p verdot, ptage, shiraz, chard, viog) ▪ 50t/900cs own label 83% red 17% white + 12,000L bulk ▪ PO Box 1273 Blouvlei Rd Wellington 7654 ▪ alkmaarwines@mweb.co.za ▪ www.alkmaarwines.co.za ▪ S 33° 39' 37.98" E 019° 1' 55.14" ▪ 🗺 bells.fires.flushes ▪ **T +27 (0)21-873-0191**

Allée Bleue Wines

Accessibly placed at a three-way junction of Franschhoek, Stellenbosch and Simonsberg-Paarl winelands routes, its entrance 'avenue of blue' featuring imposing bluegums, this German-owned property ticks several boxes: conference and wedding venues, bistro, historic manor accommodation (ca 1690), picnics and specialist fresh produce production. All underpinned by a tiered range of wines, widely sourced and recently book-ended by the premium Black Series and easy-drinking Blue Owl (see separate listing). Recent tweaks include relocation of the bistro (away from the busy entrance) and tasting room (now with vineyard views).

Black Series

★★★★ **Old Vine Pinotage** ⓐ 🌟 Strict 3-barrel selection for **17** ★★★★☆ ⑨① from 56 year old ungrafted Piekenierskloof bushvines. A refined freshness & purity that shows a sense of place, just masked in youth by chalky oak tannins (French, 70% new). Good ageing potential & elegant step up on **16** ⑧⑧.

★★★★ **Single Vineyard Syrah** Was 'The Lemon Grove'. Dark & rich **15** ⑧⑨, from home single-vineyard, has more time & newer oak than Platinum sibling. Generous dark chocolate & plush texture, dry tannins just keeping ripeness in check.

Platinum range

★★★★☆ **Pinotage** Combo home & Piekenierskloof grapes impart wild herb, berry & dark chocolate flavours to **17** ⑨⓪. Dry, fine-grained tannin structure from more time in oak & less plush fruit than **16** ⑨④. Quite compact & closed. Needs time to meld.

★★★★☆ **L'Amour Toujours** ⓐ Like **14** ★★★★★ ⑨⑤, the 2 cabs dominate the Bordeaux blend with merlot & drop petit verdot. Banhoek mountain vineyard fruit more tightly coiled & introverted in structured **15** ★★★★ ⑧⑨. 60% new French oak (18 months) adds chalky dryness to brisk & austere herbaceous tone.

★★★★ **Isabeau** ⓥ Chardonnay-led **15** ★★★★★ ⑨⓪ blend with semillon & viognier. Rich, aromatic flavours interwoven with zesty acidic thread. All-older oak adds a subtle nutty nuance. Graceful step up on **14** ⑧⑥. Dual Walker Bay-Coastal WO.

Premium range

★★★★ Cabernet Sauvignon-Merlot ② Minty blackcurrant fruit & plenty of firm tannin on well-structured **14** ⑧⑦, with drop petit verdot, judiciously oaked. Back to form after **13** ★★★ ⑧①, also from Banhoek grapes. Magnums available.

★★★★ Chenin Blanc ⊘ More restrained **18** ★★★☆ ⑧⑤, also has a splash of viognier. Tank & barrel fermented (15% new oak, 6 months). Sweet-fruited succulence, though touch less vibrancy than **17** ⑧⑧. WO Walker Bay-Franschhoek.

★★★★ Sauvignon Blanc ⊘ Stonefruit flavours on **19** ⑧⑥ with creamy lees substrate. Same Walker Bay source, with soupçon semillon, shade less backbone than **17** ⑧⑦ but ready to enjoy. **18** untasted.

★★★★ Méthode Cap Classique Brut ② Delicious **14** ⑧⑨ sparkling, perfectly dry, with lemony bubbles & biscuit nuance from 36 months on lees. Equal pinot noir & chardonnay, latter oaked.

Shiraz ★★★☆ Balanced & sappy **16** ⑧⑤ has a red-fruited profile with a dash of white pepper. Oak (55% new, mostly French) in sync. More finesse than previous. **Méthode Cap Classique Brut Rosé** ② ★★★☆ A little pinker & a bit more pinot noir (58%) than sibling, rest pinotage, 18 months on lees. Ex-Franschhoek **14** ⑧⑤ perfect summer bubbly. **Cape Ruby** ★★★ From pinotage, improved **18** ⑧② 'port' shows deep, scented mulberry fruit. Pleasingly drier style though more tannic grip than befits a Ruby. A winter warmer & foil for peppery sauces.

Starlette range

....

Blanc ⑦ ★★★ Similar tangy gooseberry tone on **19** ⑧②, sauvignon plus chenin & splash semillon. Lees contact adds plumpness to this cheery unoaked blend.

....

Pinotage ★★★ Home fruit & a brush of oak staves impart a dry tone & finish to piquant **18** ⑧② quaffer, tad less flavoursome than previous. **Rouge** ★★★ Still cab-led, but now equal parts merlot & shiraz. Some high-toned berry fruit on **18** ⑧⓪, a touch more rustic in style, but a good braai mate. WO W Cape. **Shiraz Rosé** ★★★ Crisp & spicy **19** ⑧① from shiraz & drop of semillon. Less fruit spark than previous, still a light, bright & balanced summer pink. — MW

Location/map: Franschhoek ▪ Map grid reference: C6 ▪ WO: Franschhoek/Walker Bay/Banghoek/Coastal/ Piekenierskloof/Piekenierskloof-Franschhoek/Walker Bay-Franschhoek/Walker Bay-Coastal ▪ Est 1690 ▪ 1stB 2001 ▪ Tasting & sales Mon-Fri 9-5 Sat 10-5 Sun/pub hols 10-4 ▪ Tasting fee R50/4 wines ▪ Cellar tours by appt ▪ Bistro Allée Bleue ▪ Picnics (booking required) ▪ Jungle gym ▪ Tour groups by appt ▪ Conferences ▪ Weddings ▪ Allée Bleue accommodation - Kendall Cottage, Manor House & Mill House ▪ Owner(s) DAUPHIN Entwicklungs-und Beteiligungs GMH (Germany) ▪ Winemaker(s) Van Zyl du Toit (Jul 2009), with Georgina Wilkenson (Jan 2019) ▪ Viticulturist(s) Douw Willemse (Sep 2008) ▪ 210ha/31ha (cab, merlot, ptage, pinot, shiraz, chard, chenin, sauv, sem, viog) ▪ 450t/30,000cs 45% red 50% white 5% MCC ▪ IPW ▪ PO Box 100 Groot Drakenstein 7680 ▪ info@alleebleue.com ▪ www.alleebleue.co.za ▪ S 33° 51' 29.0" E 018° 59' 12.9" ▪ 𝕨 havens.livelihoods.unbuckle ▪ T +27 (0)21-874-1021

Allesverloren ② ⑪ ◎ ⑧ ⑤

Last edition we flagged the then-new Chenin Blanc and the Tinta Rosé as 'hidden gems', worth seeking out for character, interest and value, and we're doing so again, having tasted the mostly red-wine portfolio vinified by ex Koelenhof winemaker Wilhelm de Vries, working with co-owner and cellarmaster Danie Malan since 2016. The focus on these slopes of Swartland's Kasteelberg remains on shiraz and Portuguese grapes, with varietals, blends and fortified all made in Allesverloren's much-loved friendly and accessible style.

★★★★ Shiraz ⊘ Tasty **17** ⑧⑦ gears up fresh forest-floor berry flavours & more elegant frame, retaining silky, savoury allure of **16** ★★★★ ⑧⑤. 18 months French oak, restrained 5% new. 14.5% alcohol the norm for reds here.

★★★★ Tinta Barocca ⊘ White pepper & dark spice mark **17** ⑧⑥, with refined tannin grip & sweet-fruited tail. Like previous, a savoury partner for venison. Year in barrel, 10% new.

★★★★ Touriga Nacional ② Cassis & crushed herb notes, deep but polished tannin grip, white pepper & dark spice persistence. **16** ⑧⑧ handsome, complex & savoury.

★★★★ Três Vermelhos Perfumed **17** ⑧⑥, unfortified blend of three port grapes - tinta, souzão & touriga. Ripe red berry & dark choc, full body, commanding but not harsh tannins, savoury farewell. No **16**.

★★★★ **Red Muscadel** Previewed **19** ★★★☆ ⑧⑤ a sweet seduction, fresh & delicious but lacks tangy acid & alcohol to slim down hefty sugar (240 g/l), as in svelte **18** ⑧⑨. Juice fortified after 24 hours on skins.

★★★★ **Fine Old Vintage** ⊘ Enduring label, accessible 'port' from traditional varieties. **12** ⑧⑨'s fruit-&-nut profile a step up on jammy **11** ⑧⑦. Fine tannins manage 101 g/l sugar, keep 21% alcohol in check. 5 years in old wood.

···

Tinta Rosé ⊘ ⑨ ★★★☆ Very few SA rosés from Portuguese grapes (here tinta & touriga, with others). **19** ⑧⑤ exuberant fruit, sweet spice & exotic tobacco note; bone-dry, with food-friendly racy acidity. **Chenin Blanc** ⊘ ⑨ ★★★☆ Deep & forthcoming ripe nectarine, pear & pineapple in plump **19** ⑧④. Unoaked yet has interest, complexity & structure.

···

Cabernet Sauvignon ★★★☆ Blackcurrant & minty notes in true-to-variety **17** ⑧⑤ matched by firm tannins, fresh acidity. Well balanced & delicious, now & for good few years. 18 months oak, 10% new. **1704 Red** ⊘ ★★★☆ Lightly wooded mix tinta & shiraz, **17** ⑧④ reined-in dark fruit & spice notes, silky tannins, some leather & plum on pleasing finish. — DS

Location: Riebeek West ▪ Map/WO: Swartland ▪ Map grid reference: D6 ▪ Est 1704 ▪ Tasting & sales Mon-Fri 9-5 Sat 9-2 ▪ Tasting R35/5 wines or R50/10 wines ▪ Closed Good Fri, Dec 25 & Jan 1 ▪ Cellar tours by appt ▪ Pleasant Pheasant Restaurant T +27 (0)22-461-2170 Tue 10.30-3 Wed-Sat 9-3 & 6-10 Sun 9-4 ▪ Facilities for children ▪ Conferences/functions T +27 (0)22-461-2253 ▪ Owner(s) Malan Boerdery Trust ▪ Cellarmaster(s) Danie Malan (Nov 1987) ▪ Winemaker(s) Wilhelm de Vries (Jan 2016) ▪ 227ha/187ha (cab, shiraz & various port varieties) ▪ 100,000cs own label 90% red 10% white ▪ PO Box 23 Riebeek West 7306 ▪ info@allesver-loren.co.za ▪ www.allesverloren.co.za ▪ S 33° 21' 32.5" E 018° 52' 24.1" ▪ ⒲ newness.attracts.reflects ▪ **T +27 (0)22-461-2589**

Almenkerk Wine Estate   ⑨ ⑪ ⊝ ◎

Last year saw cellarmaster Joris van Almenkerk mark the Belgian/Dutch family's first decade of winemaking at the showpiece Elgin property, with apples initially making way for vines from 2002. Natural, minimalist and authentic wines are the goal, and the emphasis is on focus and precision. With chardonnay and syrah established calling cards, it's no surprise that malbec and cabernet franc vines are being grafted over. A greener approach is already being applied, and more organic solutions trialled 'to see what works'. The cellar – with quick-access fireman's pole from Joris' first-floor office – might be bespoke and functional but it's also aesthetically pleasing, with its art and tasting venue appreciated by an increasing number of visitors.

★★★★★ **Merlot** ⑨ Understated & perfectly poised **15** ⑨③. Leafy, tomato, graphite & savoury elements vie with rich fruitcake & spice. Like other red, fermented with native yeasts. Rounded & plush, but reined in by 18 months French oak.

★★★★★ **Syrah** ⊘ ⑧ Bright, lively **15** ⑨② shows lovely integration of ripe black fruit & spicy oak (all old, 18 months). Seamless & beautifully knit, it is supple, textured & refined. Portion carbonic fermented. Also in 1.5, 3 & 5L.

★★★★☆ **Chardonnay** ⑧ Oatmeal & cashew creaminess in broad, rich & sophisticated **17** ⑨③, bright tangerine fruit ensuring balance. Oaking (third new, 10 months) is restrained, complexity from natural ferment, 4% in 'egg', malo on 25%, on lees 10 months without stirring. Also in 1.5L.

★★★★ **Sauvignon Blanc** Ripe pineapple & elderflower notes with light lemon-zest zip, good acid tang & defined finish. Single-vineyard **18** ⑧⑨ more tropical than **17** ★★★★★ ⑨① but given extended lees contact & stirring too. Both improve on next-to-last-tasted **13** ★★★★ ⑧④. — FM

Location/map/WO: Elgin ▪ Map grid reference: B2 ▪ Est 2004 ▪ 1stB 2009 ▪ Tasting, sales & cellar tours Tue-Sat 10-4 ▪ Open pub hols except on Sun & Mon ▪ Meals/picnics by prior booking (min 20 pax), or BYO picnic ▪ Walks/hikes ▪ Conservation area ▪ Heliport ▪ Boule court ▪ Owner(s) Van Almenkerk family ▪ Cellarmaster(s) Joris van Almenkerk ▪ Winemaker(s) Joris van Almenkerk, with Danver van Wyk (Feb 2009) ▪ Viticulturist(s) Michael Keown (Jan 2014) ▪ 104.2ha/15ha (cabs s/f, malbec, merlot, mourv, p verdot, shiraz, chard, sauv, viog) ▪ 100t/5,000cs own label 65% red 30% white 5% rosé ▪ Brands for clients: Pot Luck Club ▪ CVC member, WWF-SA Conservation Champion ▪ PO Box 1129 Grabouw 7160 ▪ info@almenkerk.co.za ▪ www.almenkerk.co.za ▪ S 34° 12' 55" E 019° 01' 57" ▪ ⒲ bookmark.prefigures.unvarying ▪ **T +27 (0)21-848-9844**

☐ **Almost Zero** *see* Van Loveren Family Vineyards

Alphabetical

David Cope, wine distributor and owner of Cape Town wine bar Publik, works with growers and winemakers to produce (in a Stellenbosch cellar) this range of wines which emphasises both drinkability and character – 'with roussanne and cabernet franc still the driving varieties we love', says David. Europe now accounts for almost two thirds of sales ('which is useful'). A few barrels of more edgy wines, including a 'cloudy white field blend', are destined mostly for mailing list sales under the Full Moon label.

Vin Ordinaire ★★★★ Attractively aromatic **17** ⑧ dominated by cab franc, with 'others thrown in for added character'. Easygoing pleasure but a firm, dry grip indicates some seriousness. **Vin Rosé** ⓥ **★★★** Light coppery pink **17** ⑧ from Darling mourvèdre & cinsaut, matured in old oak. Plenty of fruit; rounded, fresh & bone-dry. **Vin Blanc ★★★** Floral, lightly spicy **18** ⑧ mostly from Swartland roussanne with oak-matured chardonnay ex Stellenbosch. Soft texture, crisp acid; pleasant but a touch insipid. Discontinued: **Dirty Julie Dry White**. — TJ

Location: Stellenbosch ▪ WO: Western Cape ▪ Est 2010 ▪ 1stB 2008 ▪ Closed to public ▪ Owner(s) David Cope ▪ 8,500cs own label 45% red 45% white 10% rosé ▪ drink@alphabetical.co.za ▪ www.alphabetical.co.za

---

☐ **Altitude Collection** *see* Mile High Vineyards

Alto Wine Estate

On the steep northern slopes of the Helderberg, red-wine-only Alto is the top Stellenbosch winery in the portfolio of Libertas Vineyards & Estates, part of the Distell group. The estate has a long and distinguished winemaking history, the famous Alto Rouge first produced and exported to Europe in the 1920s. Bertho van der Westhuizen is one of only five winemakers since inception, his predecessors lending their first-name initials to the MPHS tribute blend. Visitors are invited to enjoy the hiking and mountain bike trails, with vistas over False Bay to Table Mountain, and a biltong-and-wine pairing with the iconic Rouge and its siblings.

★★★★ Cabernet Sauvignon Confident **16** ⑧⑨'s cassis & cedar tones more engaging than subtly meaty previous but as lithe & vibrant. Oaking (18 months, 65% new 300L barrels, smidgen American) well judged for 5+ years cellaring. Also in 1.5, 3 & 5L.

★★★★☆ Shiraz Well-crafted for medium-term ageing, **17** ⑨⓪ loses the old-Cape savouriness of the last vintage, shows exceptional balance between intense dark fruit, enlivening acidity & structuring tannins, makes up for varietal typicity with drive & energy.

★★★★ Alto Signature ⓝⒺ 4-way Bordeaux blend with cab leading cab franc & merlot, splash petit verdot. **16** ⑧⑧, like the '17s tasted here, blazes new trail for producer with brighter fruit, less astringency. Impressive fruit core encased in firm but ripe tannins augurs well for 3-5 years cellaring.

★★★★ MPHS ⓐ Much to appreciate in appropriately priced & packaged Bordeaux flagship, honouring the 4 previous winemakers. **15 ★★★★☆** ⑨⓪ from 2 cabs, like **12** ⑧⑨, well-toned tannin frame & vivacious acidity perfect foil for precise blackcurrant & black plum fruit, clean leather & charcuterie complexity. Will reward decade+ ageing. No **13**, **14**. Magnums too, like next.

★★★★ Alto Rouge ⓥ A Cape institution, made for more than half a century, intended for earlier drinking than siblings but - almost - as serious. The 2 cabs (53%) lead shiraz (28%), drops merlot & petit verdot in savoury **17** ⑧⑧ which improves on vanilla-toned **16 ★★★☆** ⑧⑤.

Not tasted: **Fine Old Vintage**. — CvZ

Location/map/WO: Stellenbosch ▪ Map grid reference: E8 ▪ Est 1693 ▪ 1stB 1921 ▪ Tasting & sales Mon-Fri 9-5 Sat/Sun 10-4 ▪ Fee R50/wine tasting ▪ Closed Good Fri & Dec 25 ▪ Biltong & wine pairing R160pp, advance booking required ▪ Hiking trail ▪ MTB track ▪ Owner(s) Libertas Vineyards & Estates, a Distell Group company ▪ Cellarmaster(s) Bertho van der Westhuizen (May 2015) ▪ Viticulturist(s) Bertho van der Westhuizen & Danie van Zyl ▪ 191ha/83ha (cabs s/f, merlot, shiraz) ▪ 800t/100,000cs own label 100% red ▪ PO Box 104 Stellenbosch 7599 ▪ info@alto.co.za ▪ www.alto.co.za ▪ S 34° 0' 10.4" E 018° 50' 49.4" ▪ ⓦ hoses.bookmakers.sweetly ▪ **T +27 (0)21-881-3884**

Altydgedacht ⓥ ⓟⓟ ⓐ

Plenty of changes at this historic Durbanville property owned by the Parkers, now with another local family, the Van der Merwes, founders of professional property services group VDMV. Long-term winemaker Etienne

Louw remains at the helm, and under his guidance the range is being focused on the farm's strengths with the aim of improving overall quality. A replanting programme in support of this goal is ongoing, though the cellar, completed in 1702 and one of the oldest in SA, remains untouched.

★★★★ **Pinotage** Bright-fruited **17** (86) swathed in smoky, charry oak (15 months, French & American) adding to firm but ripe tannins. Plenty of spices at finish of well-managed wine.

★★★★ **Gewürztraminer** Fabulous example of bone-dry style, **19** (89) tank sample is discreet & refined, with dialled-back tropical fruit notes, pleasantly citrussy flavours & bouncy acidity. Great food partner.

★★★★ **Sauvignon Blanc** Very delicious Durbanville cracker **19** (89) mingles green, clean fruit with flowers, some tropical notes, mouthwatering salinity & freshness. Well-integrated acid & lovely length.

★★★★☆ **Méthode Cap Classique Blanc de Blancs** Aromas of Lemon Cream & ginger biscuits on **16** (92) from chardonnay, leesy notes enlivened with crisp, zippy acidity & a lengthy finish. Very attractive bubbly, as fresh, zesty & moreish as retasted **15** (94), with more substance.

Barbera (Ⓥ) ★★★★ Still one of only handful of SA varietal bottlings of this north Italian variety. Individual, slightly wild **15** (84), savoury-spicy & meaty touches, food-inviting tart edge. **Bush Vine Chenin Blanc** (NEW) (🌱) ★★★★☆ From single parcel of 46 year old bushvines, caramel & toffee notes (barrel fermented in French oak, 15% new) on **18** (85) give way to cooked apples & ripe pineapples. Promising, needs time to come together. Cape Town WO, like Sauvignon. Discontinued: **Tintoretto**, **Pinotage Blanc de Noir**, **The Ollo**, **Muskarade**. — CM

Location: Durbanville ▪ Map: Durbanville, Philadelphia & Darling ▪ Map grid reference: C7 ▪ WO: Durbanville/ Cape Town ▪ Est 1698 ▪ Tasting & sales Tue-Sat 10—4 Sun 11-3 ▪ Tasting R60/5 wines R80/6 wines ▪ Cheese platters ▪ Closed Easter weekend, Dec 25/26 & Jan 1 ▪ Facilities for children ▪ Owner(s) Parker family and Van der Merwe family from VDMV Property Group ▪ Winemaker(s) Etienne Louw ▪ PO Box 213 Durbanville 7551 ▪ info@altydgedacht.co.za ▪ www.altydgedacht.co.za ▪ S 33° 50' 50.2" E 018° 37' 29" ▪ unforgettable. quiche.magnitudes ▪ **T** +27 (0)21-976-1295

Alvi's Drift Private Cellar

It's been a period of building (brand and bricks-and-mortar) as the Van der Merwe family (2nd-generation Bertie and his sons, general practitioner Alvi and lawyer Johan) combine skills with their top wine team to expand the multifaceted agribusiness on 6,000-ha property, Alfalfa, in the Worcester area. A new barrel cellar and capacity-doubling bottle store/logistics warehouse caters for growing demand for their Reserve and Albertus Viljoen ultra-premium labels (the latter adding a chardonnay), and the new Martial duo, untasted by us, echoing the African raptor theme aptly aimed at southern African game lodges. When not in the cellar, Alvi tends to farm folk in a small consulting room, part of recent homestead renovations.

Ultra Premium range

★★★★☆ **Albertus Viljoen Bismarck** (🏅) One of 2 big, bold Cape Blends, this shiraz led, 39% in **17** (94), with pinotage, cab & 4 others; showing fine interplay of ripe plum fruit & deft oaking. Complex, sleek & svelte, though presently dense tannins invite a few years cellaring.

★★★★☆ **Albertus Viljoen Chardonnay** (NEW) In lavish house-style: crème brûlée with butterscotch breadth, limy fruit in background, **18** (90) modest 13.5% alcohol but few grams sugar fill the finish. Wild yeast & French-oak fermented, half new, 10 months aged.

★★★★☆ **Albertus Viljoen Chenin Blanc** (🏅) Generous, oak-fermented (portion wild), slightly oxidative styling for this prestige label. Old gold **18** (93) folds very ripe melon fruit with creamy baked custard from 30% new wood, fairly demure 13.6% alcohol. Unrestrained but excellent, will please many.

Reserve range

★★★★☆ **Verreaux Pinotage** (🏅) High-end bottling named for majestic Black Eagle. Rich, upholstered, velvety **17** (94), svelte as previous vintages but more intensely flavoured, with brilliant balance. Juice bled off for concentration; all-new oak, 50% American, 22 months (as most reds here).

★★★★☆ **Drift Fusion** (✓) Sumptuous Cape Blend, **17** (90) abundant primary fruit & excellent vinosity. Cab with pinotage, shiraz, dashes durif, grenache & petit verdot. Superior integration of structural elements produces a smooth & sensual wine - for contemplation if you can resist glugging it! WO W Cape, as CVC.

★★★★☆ **Chardonnay** ⊘ Peach & nectarine fruit ripeness characterises **18** ★★★★ ⑧⑨), but not quite as tailored as citrus-lifted **17** ⑨⓪. Wood (French, 11 months, just 10% new) well woven into a textured structure, attractive salinity in the final flourish.

★★★★☆ **CVC** ⊘ Opulent yet measured chenin (67%) with viognier & chardonnay; sympathetic partial oaking creates creamy showcase for ripe peach, apricot & guava fruit in **18** ⑨⓪. Bunch pressed, part wild ferment, 70% barrelled, 30% new, year.

★★★★☆ **Muscat de Frontignan White** ② Exceptional fortified dessert, 18 months matured in small oak. Like last-tasted, copper-hued **10** ★★★★★ ⑨⑦, old gold **14** ⑨③ an endless, unctuous mouthful, with bright marmalade acidity energising decadent sweetness (348 g/l sugar). No **11**, **13**; **12** untasted. 375 ml.

221 range

★★★★ **Special Cuvée** ② Intriguing, harmonious union of 7 SA, Bordeaux & Rhône red/white varieties. **17** ⑧⑦ ample red-berry fruit & supportive tannin, seamlessly melded by year 30% new oak.

★★★★ **Chenin Blanc** ⊘ House-style ripe-fruited **19** ⑧⑥, generously oaked & lees rich, but steel/cement tank component & effective natural acidity (no malo) keep it fresh & lively. Pre-bottling sample still settling but looking good.

Alvi's Drift Signature range

Not tasted: **Cabernet Sauvignon**, **Merlot**, **Pinotage**, **Shiraz**, **Pinotage Rosé**, **Chardonnay**, **Chenin Blanc**, **Sauvignon Blanc**, **Viognier**, **Chardonnay-Pinot Noir**.

Sparkling range

★★★★ **Thornlands Méthode Cap Classique** ⊘ Dry bubbly from 69% chardonnay & pinot noir has fine, persistent bead, with lime & roast walnut on luxuriant finish. **NV** ⑧⑥ elegant, refined, enjoy now. ±48 months on lees. WO W Cape, as next.

Pinot Noir-Chardonnay Brut Rosé ⑭⑭ ★★★ Pretty package geared for romance; rose pink **NV** ⑧① dry bubbly with bright cherry & pomegranate fruit, zippy fizz. — DS

Location/map: Worcester ▪ Map grid reference: B5 ▪ WO: Worcester/Western Cape ▪ Est 1928 ▪ 1stB 2004 ▪ Tasting, sales & tours by appt ▪ Closed all pub hols ▪ Farm produce ▪ Owner(s) Bertie, Alvi & Johan van der Merwe ▪ Cellarmaster(s) Riaan Marais ▪ Winemaker(s) Alvi van der Merwe ▪ Viticulturist(s) Jan du Toit ▪ 6,000ha/420ha (22 varieties, mostly ptage, shiraz, chard, chenin) ▪ ±7,500t/280,000cs own label ▪ IPW ▪ PO Box 126 Worcester 6849 ▪ info@alvisdrift.co.za ▪ www.alvisdrift.co.za ▪ S 33° 46' 25.8" E 019° 31' 53.7" ▪ ⫶⫶⫶ grits.exulting.turnings ▪ **T +27 (0)23-340-4121**

☐ **Amatra** *see* Catherine Marshall Wines
☐ **Ama Ulibo** *see* Goedverwacht Wine Estate

Ambeloui Wine Cellar

Cypriot for 'small vineyard', Ambeloui led winegrowing in Cape Town's Hout Bay in the mid-1990s, Nick Christodoulou planting chardonnay and pinot noir, soon joined by a home and cellar devoted to MCC bubbly production. Each vintage is named after a family member or, latterly, a team member, the expanding clan reuniting on the first weekend of November during the annual open-day sale of the limited production. Son Alexis is now cellarmaster, his father still assisting, while daughter Miranda handles admin.

★★★★☆ **Méthode Cap Classique Brut Rosé Rosanna** Voluptuous **NV** ⑨② sparkler from pinot noir & chardonnay (as sibling), bursting with red berry fruit, nuanced with shortbread & nutmeg. Perky acidity, gentle mousse & lingering finish combine in sophisticated harmony.

★★★★☆ **Méthode Cap Classique Brut** Latest disgorgement of **16** ★★★★ ⑧⑥ (named 'Luvuyo'), now with 3 years on lees, shows convincing apple-cinnamon flavours but misses fullness & brioche of new disgorgement of **15** ⑨⓪ ('Ashley'), which spent 4 years on lees. Wholesome, well-rounded & charming, with baked apple fruit & zingy finish, borne on delicate mousse. Improves on previous, shows benefits of extended lees contact.— GdB

Location: Hout Bay ▪ WO: Western Cape ▪ Est 1994 ▪ 1stB 1998 ▪ Open for sales on 1st weekend of Nov annually ▪ Annual harvest festival (mid-March) ▪ Owner(s) Nick & Ann Christodoulou ▪ Cellarmaster(s) Alexis Christodoulou ▪ Winemaker(s) Nick Christodoulou (1994), with Alexis Christodoulou (2009) ▪ Viticulturist(s) Alexis Christodoulou (2009) ▪ 1ha/0.5ha (pinot noir/meunier, chard) ▪ 15t/3,000cs own label 100% MCC ▪ PO

Box 26800 Hout Bay 7872 ▪ wine@ambeloui.co.za ▪ www.ambeloui.co.za ▪ T +27 (0)21-790-7386/+27 (0)82-460-8399

☐ **Anchor Drift** see Viljoensdrift Fine Wines & Cruises

Andreas Wines

Former head of UK's Yorkshire Television, David Croft, and his group of wine-loving friends are full of confidence in the future of their specialist shiraz venture on one of Wellington's quintessential 18th-century Cape Dutch farms. Sustained investment since purchase in 2015, initially in luxury accommodation, continued with a recent overhaul of the small vineyard and cellar under Shaun Meyeridricks (ex top-notch Boekenhoutskloof) and the securing of additional local listings and international distribution contracts.

★★★★ **Shiraz** Handsome **17** ⑱ packed with ripe dark & red berries, violets & black pepper, silky tannins polished 18 months in old oak, ends with savoury persistence. Attractive now but can cellar. **16** skipped, **15** untasted.— GM

Location/map/WO: Wellington ▪ Map grid reference: C3 ▪ Est 2003 ▪ 1stB 2004 ▪ Tasting & sales by appt Mon-Fri 9–5 ▪ Closed all pub hols ▪ Cellar tours by appt ▪ Luxury accommodation ▪ Owner(s) Andreas Wine Trading Incorporated (England) ▪ Cellarmaster(s)/winemaker(s) Shaun Meyeridricks (Dec 2017) ▪ 6ha/4.5ha (mourv, shiraz) ▪ 43t/4,688cs own label 100% red ▪ PO Box 892 Wellington 7654 ▪ info@andreas.co.za ▪ www.andreas.co.za ▪ S 33° 37' 54.87" E 019° 2' 33.55" ▪ 🖅 absolves.repudiates.skiffs ▪ T +27 (0)21-873-2286

Andy Mitchell Wines

Continuing water shortages severely limited the crop during the past year at the small Mitchell family farm, Heuningkloof, in Greyton. However, vines are tenacious, and winemaker Olivia Mitchell Legavre undeterred, and so construction of a new boutique cellar on the hill remains on track, and the first home-grown shiraz and chardonnay are maturing nicely in the existing garage-cellar. We hope to taste them next time.

Elgin Pinot Noir ⓥ ★★★★ Good core of earthy-smoky red fruit, fresh acidity, firm tannins, **16** ⑱ shows Elgin's cooler provenance but is still tightly buttoned, needs some time to show full potential.
Décolletage ⓥ ★★★★ Merlot brings some plummy generosity & flesh to promising **13** ⑭ Bordeaux red. Cab, cab franc important structural players, need time to temper youthful astringency. Elgin & Stanford grapes, older French oak. Not tasted: **Crooked Path Pinot Noir**, **Heuningkloof Shiraz Rosé**, **Swartland Chenin Blanc**, **Méthode Cap Classique**. Discontinued: **Crooked Path Shiraz**, **Syrah-Grenache-Mourvèdre**. — MW

Location: Greyton ▪ Map: Southern Cape ▪ Map grid reference: A1 ▪ WO: Elgin/Elgin-Walker Bay ▪ Est/1stB 2003 ▪ Tasting, sales & cellar tours by appt ▪ Closed Easter Fri/Sun & Dec 25 ▪ Owner(s) Vikki Mitchell ▪ Winemaker(s) Olivia Mitchell Legavre (Jan 2008), with Stefan Legavre (2016) ▪ 1st own label 42% red 21% white 13% rosé 24% MCC + 200cs for clients ▪ PO Box 543 Paarden Eiland 7420 ▪ olivia@andymitchellwines.com ▪ www.andymitchellwines.com ▪ T +27 (0)28-254-9045/+27 (0)84-588-1309

☐ **Angels Tears** see Grande Provence Heritage Wine Estate

Annandale Wines

Long before it became trendy, 'traditional and unhurried' was the winegrowing credo of owner, winemaker and viticulturist Hempies du Toit at his charmingly rustic estate on Annandale Road in the Helderberg. Believing that vintages should be released only when ready, Hempies matures his varietal/blended cabs, merlot and shiraz for up to 8 years before bottling, hence the venerable but still-lively wines listed here.

★★★★ **Cabernet Sauvignon** ⓥ Rounded yet fresh, remarkably youthful **12** ★★★★ ⑧, concentrated & fruit driven, overtly spicy from 5 years in oak, a high-toned element too. Follows more elegant **06** ⑧.
★★★★ **Shiraz** ⓥ Improving on **04** ⑧, **05** ★★★★★ ⑨ shows vintage quality. Dark creamy plums, savoury cured meat, fragrant fynbos & fine exotic spice. Oak vanilla rounds the seamless mouthful.
★★★★ **Cavalier** ⓥ Three-way blend (shiraz, cab, merlot), 7 years barrelled; **07** ⑧ rich & spicy, bold black cherry & plum, flick of pepper & cranberry on finish. **05**, **06** not made.

CVP ② ★★★★ Fireside warming 'port', shiraz mellowed 8 years in old brandy vats. **06** ⑭ rich dark chocolate & smoky plum pudding, fiery spirit bite. Not tasted: **Merlot**. Occasional release: **Cabernet Franc**. Discontinued: **Nostalgia**. — GdB

Location/map/WO: Stellenbosch ▪ Map grid reference: E8 ▪ Est/1stB 1996 ▪ Tasting & sales Mon-Sat 9—5 ▪ Closed Easter Fri-Mon, Ascension day & Dec 25 ▪ Farm produce ▪ BYO picnic ▪ Owner(s) Hempies du Toit ▪ Winemaker(s)/viticulturist(s) Hempies du Toit (1996) ▪ 72ha/45ha (cabs s/f, merlot, shiraz) ▪ 250t/10,000cs own label 100% red ▪ PO Box 12681 Stellenbosch 7613 ▪ info@annandale.co.za ▪ www.annandale.co.za ▪ S 33° 59' 49.2" E 018° 49' 50.9" ▪ 🖰 dreaming.divide.puzzles ▪ **T +27 (0)21-881-3560**

Annex Kloof Wines

When owner/winemaker Hugo Basson isn't in his Paardeberg cellar handcrafting these wines, you'll find him somewhere in the extensive vineyards first planted by patriarch Matthys in 1906. Harvesting some 8,000 tons annually, most of it sold, he farms alongside brothers Thys and Tobie, with 'tons of sons' (seven) to follow in their footsteps, growing plums, citrus, pomegranates and wheat as well as grapes.

Annex Kloof range

★★★★ **Malbec** ② Enticing blueberries, apricots & orange peel on **16** ⑱⑨'s nose & palate, slick use of oak for support & flavour. Approachable & fruity but not frivolous, commendable dry finish.

★★★★☆ **Tulu** ② Another thoroughly enjoyable vintage, **16** ⑨③ easy to drink (& incredibly good value) but serious, deserves contemplation. Syrah (86%), grenache, mourvèdre, giving pure black fruit accented by white pepper, hint oak spice from 18 months 1st/2nd-fill barrels (as Malbec).

Xenna range

Chenin Blanc ✓ ★★★★ Unwooded **19** ⑧⑤ has real character & a body well-padded with yellow apple, pear & guava fruit, along with hints of chamomile & ginger. Nice price, too. Not tasted: **Shiraz**. — JG

Location: Malmesbury ▪ Map/WO: Swartland ▪ Map grid reference: C7 ▪ Est/1stB 2006 ▪ Tasting & cellar tours by appt only; sales daily 8-1.30 ▪ Closed Easter Fri-Mon, Ascension day, Pentecost, Dec 16/25/26 & Jan 1 ▪ Walks/hikes ▪ Conservation area ▪ Accommodation ▪ Owner(s) Hugo Basson ▪ Winemaker(s) Hugo Basson (Jan 2006) ▪ 600ha (cab, grenache, malbec, merlot, mourv, p verdot, ptage, shiraz, tinta barocca, chard, chenin, cbard, irsai oliver, sauv) ▪ 150t own label 95% red 5% white ▪ PO Box 772 Malmesbury 7299 ▪ info@annexkloofwines.co.za ▪ www.annexkloofwines.co.za ▪ S 33° 30' 39.1" E 018° 48' 22.5" ▪ 🖰 codified. surprises.olives ▪ **T +27 (0)22-487-3870**

AntHill Wines

It's 20 years since wine industry supplier and winecrafter Mark Howell and construction project manager Hylton Schwenk bottled the first wine – a Pinotage – under their boutique label (Mark at the time noting he'd found research suggesting that some of the best vineyards overlie old termite mounds or zones of past termite activity). Varying fruit sources and creative names for each new batch have been hallmarks over the years, as has a predilection for cabernet, pinot noir and sauvignon blanc. Tiny quantities mean the wines often sell out before we can taste them. See under Entre Nous for parcels made by Mark 'with others'.

Location: Somerset West ▪ Est 1999 ▪ 1stB 2000 ▪ Tasting by appt ▪ Owner(s) Mark Howell & Hylton Schwenk ▪ Winemaker(s) Mark Howell (Feb 2000) ▪ 1,200cs own label 60% red 40% white ▪ 19 Immelman Rd Somerset West 7130 ▪ www@telkomsa.net ▪ S 34° 4' 30.8" E 018° 52' 37.6" ▪ 🖰 starting.dispose.fades ▪ **T +27 (0)82-895-9008**

Anthology Wines

Johannesburg banking business analyst and boutique vintner Christian Naudé strives to create 'a collection of wines of exceptional quality, to be savoured and appreciated'. Stellenbosch's De Goede Sukses estate, home of Marklew Family Wines, is where he sources single-vineyard fruit and handcrafts his wines.

★★★★☆ **Cabernet Franc** ② Heavyweight **16** ⑨⓪'s big 15.4% alcohol, bold plum & blackberry body held in check by sizeable tannins. Shade less refinement this vintage than **15** ⑨③, more power, but could mellow into something very special given 3-5 years in the cellar.

★★★★☆ **Chardonnay** ⓥ Half barrel-fermented/aged 12 months, 50% new French, rest in (neutral) Flexcube. Self-assured **17** ㉛ less fruity than **16** ㉛, which had a citrus enlivenment, but similar well-judged oak, savoury dryness & salinity, satisfying richness.

Not tasted: **Cabernet Sauvignon**. — CvZ

Location: Stellenbosch ▪ WO: Simonsberg–Stellenbosch ▪ Est/1stB 2014 ▪ Closed to public ▪ Sales online ▪ Owner(s) Christian Naudé ▪ Winemaker(s) Christian Naudé (Feb 2014) ▪ 55ha/±40ha (cabs s/f, merlot, ptage, shiraz, chard, sauv) ▪ 2,250cs own label 66% red 34% white ▪ De Goede Sukses, R44 Muldersvlei Stellenbosch 7600 ▪ info@anthologywines.co.za ▪ www.anthologywines.co.za ▪ **T +27 (0)83-238-5887**

Anthonij Rupert Wyne   ⓥ ⓜ ⓘ ⓖ

International businessman Johann Rupert's model wine-enterprise, named for his late brother, has 18th-century Franschhoek estate L'Ormarins as its mountain-silhouetted home. The venture encompasses an internationally awarded sextet of brands, and visitor attractions such as the 100+ year retrospective Franschhoek Motor Museum, linked to two tasting venues by bespoke trams. Grapes are sourced from the venture's prime vineyards in Darling, Swartland, Elandskloof and the home farm, as well as other significant sites including old-vine parcels around the winelands. Vinified in custom, dedicated facilities such as the Cape of Good Hope Cellar, equipped with on-trend, amphora-shaped Italian concrete tanks. The team's commitment to incremental improvements in both the vineyards and cellar is reaping rewards in the bottle.

Anthonij Rupert range

★★★★☆ **Cabernet Sauvignon** Modern, ripe but deftly extracted, **14** ㉛'s dense fruit is still tightly wrapped in fine tannins, finish is pleasingly dry. Naturally fermented Franschhoek grapes, like **12** ㉝. 18-24 months oaking (as all these), 90% new, gives structure for 10+ years cellaring. **13** untasted.

★★★★☆ **Cabernet Franc** ⓐ Exceptional **13** ★★★★★ ㉟ truer to variety than ripe & brooding **12** ㉚, has franc's lovely leafiness combined with plush fruit & impressively crafted tannic frame, all-new French barrique ageing effortlessly absorbed. Will reward decade-plus in the cellar. WO Franschhoek. Wholeberry fermented & unfiltered, as all these except Optima.

★★★★★ **Merlot** ⓐ From selected sites & soil types, **14** ㉝ is admirably restrained & linear (whereas Cape of Good Hope sibling is rich & broad), still taut even after 5 years in bottle, with structure for further 5. 80% new wood. Limited 800 cases. WO Coastal.

★★★★☆ **Syrah** ⓐ First impression is of well-judged oak (85% new), giving both a precise tannin structure & a vanilla/cinnamon veneer to the sweet red fruit of **14** ㉝. Less arresting aromatically than **13** ㉝, but as sculpted & toned. Ex Franschhoek vines. Also in 1.5 & 3L, as Cabernet & Cabernet Franc.

★★★★ **Anthonij Rupert** ⓐ Still dark & intensely fruity after 6 years in bottle, with sweet vanilla from 100% new oak well integrated & adding to its charm, **13** ★★★★★ ㉚ cab, cab franc & merlot blend (42/32/26) steps up on elegant but less well-knit **11** ㉟. **12** untasted. WO Coastal.

★★★★ **Optima** ⓐ Something of SA institution, this sibling to Anthonij is cab franc-led, with merlot & cab (40/35/25). **15** ★★★★★ ㉛ attractively compact, smooth & well-formed, delicious now but can age good few years. Improves on **14** ㊱. Also in magnum.

Cape of Good Hope range

★★★★ **Parel Vallei Merlot** ⓐ Fruit from small suburban vineyard in the Helderberg, minuscule 269 cases. Vanilla-toned **14** ㊲ as rich as **13** ㊲ but also enlivened by tangy acidity, shaped by stemmy tannins. New barrique fermented, then 24 months in same vessels.

★★★★ **Sneeuwkrans Pinot Noir** From ±700-m elevation Elandskloof vineyard, picked in 2 stages. **16** ㊱ same high-toned cherry fruit, vibrant acid & gentle silky grip as previous, but greater sense of place & gravitas. Old oak. In magnum too.

★★★★ **Basson Pinotage** ⓐ ⓢ Lighter styling & less concentration in **16** ★★★★★ ㉚ than **15** ㊱, & all the better for it. Icing sugar & strawberry candyfloss nuances, bone-dry finish, older oak supporting sweetly ripe but delicate fruit. From dryland bushvines in Swartland.

★★★★☆ **Riebeeksrivier Southern Slopes** Intention of 'Slopes' pair to show aspect/soil influence; this higher clay content in Malmesbury shale. Shiraz-led **15** ㉛ the more generous. Pure fruited, with supple tannin, spice/savoury tones from mourvèdre (28%), durif & grenache. Both WO Swartland & 12-14 months older oak.

★★★★☆ **Riebeeksrivier Western Slopes** (Ⓐ) Shiraz (83%) with splashes durif, grenache & carignan. Shale/schist soils give enticing floral lift, tauter structure in **15** (93). Plenty in reserve for the cellar.

★★★★☆ **Serruria Chardonnay** (Ⓐ) Handsome **17** (94) from 2 Elandskloof vineyards, poised & precise, with rapier-like acidity (no malo), oystershell minerality. Quiet lemon-lime tones smartly accented by vanilla from partial (80%) barrel ferment/ageing, 40% new.

★★★★☆ **Riebeeksrivier Chenin Blanc** (Ⓥ) (Ⓐ) Appealingly unfruity expression of chenin, with scrub, fynbos & earth in **18** (90), as well as the animated acidity, uncompromising dryness & length of previous. Only 25% barrel fermented, mostly older oak, 7 months on lees. Worth cellaring. WO Swartland.

★★★★☆ **Van Lill & Visser Chenin Blanc** (Ⓧ) (Ⓦ) Citrusdal Mountain bushvines, 54 years old, **17** (93) extremely complex, unfruity wet earth, nut, cream nuances; leesy smoothness yet bold seam of acidity. Stately & reserved, with sense of weight (small portion oak) & profundity. Will age decade+.

★★★★ **Altima Sauvignon Blanc** Cleverly crafted **18** ★★★★★ (90) gets its wide range of aromas & flavours from 3 different pickings of the Elandskloof vineyard & various yeast strains, its breadth & weight from six months on the lees, touch of sugar. Shade more impressive than **17** (88).

★★★★☆ **Laing Groendruif Semillon** (Ⓥ) (Ⓐ) (Ⓦ) Citrusdal Mountain dryland bushvines from old-vine hero, Henk Laing. Despite lower than usual acidity given the warmer conditions, **16** ★★★★★ (95) exquisitely dry with exceptional balance & concentration, delightful quince nuance. Judiciously, only 29% portion (old) oaked, **15** (94) was 54%.

★★★★☆ **Riebeeksrivier Caroline** White Swartland blend led by chenin (46%) with marsanne, viognier & roussanne. Lively **16** ★★★★ (89) has **15** (90)'s marzipan, nougat & quinine tones, not-so-subtle vanilla oak.

Jean Roi range

★★★★ **Rosé** Chic Provence-inspired **18** (89) from cinsaut with shiraz, dash grenache. Lovely pale hue, berry & sage bouquet, sleek & dry conclusion for charcuterie or solo sipping. Also in 1.5 & 3L. WO Coastal.

L'Ormarins range

★★★★ **Méthode Cap Classique Brut Classique Rosé** (Ⓥ) Sunset-hued chardonnay & pinot noir (58/42) **NV** (87) bubbly, minimum 24 months on lees. Raspberry & strawberry attraction, creamy mousse & fruit-filled finish.

★★★★☆ **Méthode Cap Classique Brut Rosé** (Ⓐ) Revisited **15** (94) sparkler delicate & more enticing, subtle brioche & lemon curd, enlivening berry acidity, endless mineral persistence. 76/24 pinot noir & chardonnay pressed together, a rare technique worldwide; 24 months on lees.

★★★★☆ **Méthode Cap Classique Blanc de Blancs** (Ⓐ) Chardonnay sparkling's New World fruitiness offset by vibrant seam of acidity, racing tiny bubbles & fresh lemon-toned finish. **13** (94), retasted, still tightly wound, needs ±5 years to reveal full charms. 20% barrel fermented, 4 years on lees in bottle.

★★★★ **Méthode Cap Classique Brut** (Ⓥ) Vivacious **NV** (87) celebratory bubbles with honey hints, apple & lemon freshness from chardonnay (66%), vinosity from pinot. Minimum 24 months on lees.

★★★★☆ **Sagnac** First brandy in SA produced in Armagnac alambic still. From Robertson colombard & ugni blanc, 10 year old (92) is golden hued, with subtle, soft, dried apricot, peach & pear aromas. Full bodied & round, finishes silky smooth. Handsome 500 ml packaging.

Late Bottled Vintage ★★★☆ Fruitier & slightly sweeter 'port' than the classics from the Douro, but **15** (84) does have balancing fire & firm tannins. Fine winter's night companion. From touriga, 2 years older oak.

Terra del Capo range

★★★★ **Sangiovese** (Ⓥ) Sour cherry flavour, fresh tannin & acid bite, Italianate dryness, **16** (86) is variety-true & ready for food or solo enjoyment. Raises the bar on **15** ★★★★ (85). Grapes ex Darling.

Pinot Grigio (Ⓥ) ★★★☆ Rare-in-SA varietal bottling, **19** (83) fennel & aniseed notes, rounder & sleeker than most, courtesy older-vine fruit & well-managed acidity.

Protea range

Cabernet Sauvignon (Ⓥ) (Ⓣ) ★★★☆ Impressive balance of black fruit, tannin & acid in **17** (85), pleasant vanilla overlay from combo older barrels & oak staves. Punches above its price, like many in this range. **Dry Rosé** (Ⓥ) (Ⓣ) ★★★☆ Attractive aperitif or lunch accompaniment, mostly mourvèdre, as before. **19** (83) bone-dry & vibrant, leafy nuance to fresh berry aroma & flavour. Coastal WO, as next. **Chenin Blanc** ⊘ ⓥ ★★★★ Laudable complexity for this price - white peach, nut & acacia flower - lovely acid balance, **19** ⑧ good weight & dimension from 2 months on lees.

. . . .

Merlot ★★★ Plum pudding & mulberry entry, juicy centre & smooth tannins, **18** ⑧ ticks all the crowd-pleasing boxes. These in distinctive, eye-catching bottles, each a different design, with twist-off cork. **Shiraz** ⊘ ★★★★ Savoury oak & subtle pepper top note, **18** ⑧ packed with red berries & plums, supple tannins for easy drinking. **Chardonnay** ★★★ Tad shy mid-2019, but lightly oaked **19** ⑧ does show appealing lemon-peach fruit & clean dry finish. **Pinot Grigio** ⊘ ★★★★ Characterful **19** ⑧, pear drop & pink musk confectionery aromas & flavours, lightish 12.5% alcohol for al fresco quaffing. Franschhoek WO. **Sauvignon Blanc** ★★★ Water-white **19** ⑧ has Granny Smith apple in the aroma & flavour, appealing freshness, undaunting 13.5% alcohol. Slips down easily. — CvZ, WB

Location/map: Franschhoek ▪ Map grid reference: C5 ▪ WO: Western Cape/Coastal/Swartland/Franschhoek/ Elandskloof/Citrusdal Mountain ▪ Est 1714 ▪ 1stB 1982 ▪ Two tasting rooms: Anthonij Rupert & Terra del Capo, both by appt only ▪ Fee R30-R85 per flight of 3-4 wines ▪ Closed Good Fri & Dec 25 ▪ Antipasti Bar serving local artisanal produce ▪ Cheese, olive oil & honey ▪ Franschhoek Motor Museum by appt only T +27 (0)21-874-9002; admittance R80pp, seniors R60pp & children (3-12 yrs) R50pp ▪ Two specially built trams travel between the motor museum & tasting rooms ▪ Owner(s) Johann Rupert ▪ Winemaker(s) Dawie Botha (Jan 2005), Zanie Viljoen (Jan 2007), Vernon van der Hoven (2012) & Mark van Buuren (2013) ▪ 4 farms: total ±1,100ha/±210ha (cabs s/f, carignan, cinsaut, grenache, marsanne, merlot, mourv, pinot, sangio, shiraz, chard, chenin, pinot grigio, rouss) ▪ ISO 14001:2009 ▪ PO Box 435 Franschhoek 7690 ▪ tasting@ rupertwines.com ▪ www.rupertwines.com ▪ S 33° 53' 16.77" E 019° 0' 17.70" (Anthonij Rupert/Cape of Good Hope/L'Ormarins), S 33° 52' 47.36" E 019° 0' 10.91" (Terra Del Capo/Protea) ▪ 🎬 wildebeest.tapping.filmy ▪ **T +27 (0)21-874-9004/+27 (0)21-874-9041 (tasting)**

Anura Vineyards

Since the first bottling in 2001, the frog-themed Simonsberg-Paarl venture owned by Tymen Bouma and family has become ever more diverse, with an array of attractions added to the cellardoor including the Wagon Trail microbrewery, Forest Hill cheesery, Trading Post deli and attractive events space, The Cooperage. The focus remains on wine, however. Thus the new bottling unit, installed to aid production of a new ready-to-drink gin & tonic, among others, has also enabled a sparkling wine named Joy, debuting at press time.

Reserve range

★★★★ **Cabernet Sauvignon** Bold, powerful **16** ⑧ has spicy Xmas pudding framed by integrated but dry oak (2 years 60% new, combo French & American 70/30). Touch stern, so it needs time. WO W Cape. **15** untasted.

★★★★ **Malbec** ⊘ Juicy plum & blueberry galore, **17** ★★★★★ ⑨ adds baking spice from 50/50 oaking (half each American & French, old & new, for 18 months). Soft textured & plush, with yielding finish. Improves on the **16** ⑧.

★★★★ **Merlot** Previewed **16** ⑧ improves on **15** ★★★★ ⑧ in subtle oaking, 20% of which Greek, rest French, 2 years. Structured palate of liquorice & plum, cradled by sympathetic tannin.

★★★★ **Petit Verdot** ⑧ Still-rare solo bottling, black pastille succulence & focused tautness. Dry, with light spice nuance, **13** ⑧ was oaked 28 months, half new. No **12, 11** untasted.

★★★★ **Pinotage** Generous & boldly fruited **17** ⑧ is light bodied & spicy from all-American oak maturation, 80% new. Soft, with olive finish.

★★★★ **Syrah** Welcome return to form in standout **15** ⑧ vintage after last-made **12** ★★★ ⑧. Succulent lavender-tinged blue & black fruit. Well-meshed dry tannin & 16 months in 30% new oak.

★★★★ **Syrah-Mourvèdre-Grenache** ⑧ Smoky overlay to vibrant, spicy **15** ⑧, first tasted since **09** ⑧. Shiraz still leads but mourvèdre upped notably to 35%, grenache to 15%. Broad, textured plum-rich palate framed by oak, third new. Alcohol 15%.

★★★★ **Chardonnay** ⑧ Vanilla, citrus & pineapple in bold, naturally fermented **17** ⑧. Acid is lively & fresh but all-new French oak speaks loudest, in broad, reverberating tones. **16** ★★★★ ⑧ less intense.

★★★★ **Sauvignon Blanc Unfiltered** **19** ⑧, like **16** ⑧, from Darling. Pea & flint typicity balanced by bright acidity & taut focus. Seamless, long palate. No **16 - 18**.

★★★★ **Méthode Cap Classique Brut** ⓦ Crisp, dry & vivid **13** ⑧⑦ sparkling with lemon sherbet zip, portion oaked, aiding light biscuit note. **12** untasted. **11** ★★★★★ ⑨⑤ was exceptional.

Chenin Blanc ⓦ ★★★★ Stonefruit tang to **16** ⑧③ is framed by nutty oak notes. Soft & spicy. **Viognier** ⓦ ★★★☆ Nectarine & spice typicity on **16** ⑧③, creamy breadth from 4 months on lees & 10% oaked portion. Nice body & length.

Signature Series

★★★★ **Cabernet Sauvignon** ⓦ Deep, ripe cassis abundance contrasting with dry spice & prominent all-new oak backing (2 years, French). **14** ⑧⑥ needs time for elements to marry harmoniously.

★★★★ **Merlot** ⓝⓔⓦ Inky, intense & deeply alluring **15** ⑧⑨ shows impact of superb vintage. Powerful but trim, restraint evident. Harmonious, with well-knit tannin frame from 18 months oak, 80% new.

★★★★ **Nebbiolo** ⓦ Gymnastic litheness apparent on red fruit- & cinnamon-toned **14** ⑧⑦, dry & lean, with leashed power. Polished 2 years in barrel, 20% new, same in bottle.

★★★★ **Syrah** ⓦ Subtle dried herb & oregano appeal to deep red- & black-fruited **15** ⑧⑥, quite muscular & spicy from combo French/American oak, 20 months, long dry aftertaste.

★★★★ **Cape Cuvée** ⓦ Many-layered **15** ⑧⑦ pinotage (40%), cab & syrah blend; generous, persistent fruitcake, cocoa & plum flavour, structure from 70% new oak. 15% alcohol part of a forthright personality.

Carignan ⓦ ★★★ Herb & fynbos overlie vibrant red cherry fruit on **14** ⑧⓪. Serious intent evident in 2 years French wooding, 20% new, further 2 years bottle conditioning. **Grenache** ⓦ ★★★★ Appealing fynbos & herb mingle with gentle black fruit, **14** ⑧⑤ supple, light bodied & fresh despite year in older oak & 2 in bottle. **Pinotage** ⓦ ★★★★ Upfront cherry & plum vivacity on **15** ⑧③. Bright, succulent & spicy, it's backed by dry, fine tannin from new oak, 50% American, 20 months. Not tasted: **Sangiovese**.

Anura range

Grenache Noir ⓦ ★★★ Spicy tealeaf tannic dryness on **14** ⑦⑦, muted red fruit dominated by oak, despite use of older barrels only. **Merlot** ★★★☆ Plush, soft welcome on unfussy **17** ⑧⑤, mulberry ease & cigarbox frame from all-French oak, 20% new, 18 months. **Pinotage** ⓦ ★★★★ Sweet vanilla edge to ultra-ripe blueberry appeal of **16** ⑧③ courtesy 40% American oak. Slightly bitter tail. **Tempranillo** ★★★ Salami & smoky meat notes on light, smooth **16** ⑧②. Aged 2 years in old French oak. High 15.3% alcohol. **Legato** ★★★★ Inky depth to **17** ⑧⑤ merlot (60%) & cab blend. Liquorice & blue fruit with squeeze of spicy dry tannin after 14 months in combo French/American oak, 20% new. Alcohol a bold 15.2%. **Pinotage-Shiraz** ★★★★ Improves on previous with bright blueberry & baking spice appeal. Wood takes over mid-palate of **17** ⑧④, showing year in 50/50 French & American oak, 20% new. **Arpeggio** ⓦ ★★★ Light-bodied & easy blend of shiraz, mourvèdre & dab viognier, **16** ⑧① appealing spicy overlay from judicious 20% new French oak. **Rosé** ⓦ ★★★ Raspberry & cherry brightness to dry **18** ⑧⓪ from pinot noir. Succulent & effortless, it's a poolside pink. **Chardonnay** ⓦ ★★★ A tropical tack taken in **18** ⑧②, with pineapple more than typical citrus. Medium body, lively acidity & spice from oak staves. **Pinot Gris** ⓦ ★★★ Dusty lemon tang on uncomplicated **18** ⑧①. Light, fresh & perfect for summertime. **Sauvignon Blanc** ★★★ Tropical ease to grapefruit zing on **19** ⑧②, light, juicy & fresh. Some Darling grapes. — FM

Location/map: Paarl ▪ Map grid reference: C7 ▪ WO: Simonsberg-Paarl/Western Cape/Coastal/Darling ▪ Est 1990 ▪ 1stB 2001 ▪ Tasting, sales & cellar tours daily 9–5 ▪ Closed Good Fri, Dec 25 & Jan 1 ▪ Fee R60/cheese & wine, R35/wine only ▪ Trading Post Deli ▪ Farm produce & Forest Hill cheese ▪ Tour groups ▪ The Cooperage events venue (40-300 guests seated & up to 850 cocktail style) ▪ Wagon Trail Brewery & Restaurant open Tue-Sun 9-4; with craft beer tasting at R36/flight (4x100ml) ▪ Owner(s) Bouma family ▪ Cellarmaster(s) Tymen Bouma (1990) ▪ Winemaker(s) Stander Maass (2017) & Lance Bouma (Jan 2007) ▪ Viticulturist(s) Tymen Bouma & Stephen Elliot (Jan 2007) ▪ 240ha/120ha (cab, carignan, grenache, malbec, merlot, mourv, nebbiolo, p verdot, ptage, pinot, sangio, shiraz, tempranillo, chard, chenin, nouvelle, pinot gris, sauv, verdelho) ▪ 750t/60,000cs own label 80% red 17% white 2% rosé 1% fortified ▪ PO Box 244 Klapmuts 7625 ▪ info@anura.co.za, wine@anura.co.za ▪ www.anura.co.za ▪ S 33° 48' 41.4" E 018° 53' 19.8" ▪ 🖵 spinning. heiress.duplicity ▪ **T +27 (0)21-875-5360**

Anwilka ⓦ

It's 15 years since the birth of the Anwilka blend, the '05, praised by powerful US critic Robert Parker (after tasting more than 200 'rather astonishing' Bordeaux of the same vintage) as 'the finest red wine I have ever had from SA'. The near-derelict home-farm in the Helderberg was extensively redeveloped from 1997 and a cellar built in 2004 expressly to produce a premium red blend with a dedicated, on-site team, whose members have been exemplary in maintaining the lofty standard, also for the more recent 'Little Brother'. Both wines remain within the orbit of Klein Constantia, sharing owners, outlets and tasting locale.

★★★★★ **Anwilka** ⊛ Standout syrah & cab blend with petit verdot, **16** ⑨③ shows style & refinement, power & weight. Supple & velvety, with layered black fruit & charming herbal aromas, spicy oak (50% new French) still prominent, needs time to knit. Also in magnum.

★★★★ **Petit Frère** ⊘ Change in formula sees 59% cab take lead from syrah in **17** ⑧⑨, splashes petit verdot & malbec, oak up to 50%. Spicy black fruit, silky tannins speak of ripeness & unforced vinification.— GdB

Location/WO: Stellenbosch ▪ Est 1997 ▪ 1stB 2005 ▪ Tasting & sales at Klein Constantia ▪ Owner(s) Zdenek Bakala, Charles Harman, Bruno Prats & Hubert de Boüard ▪ MD Hans Aström ▪ Winemaker(s) Jean du Plessis (Aug 2008) ▪ Viticulturist(s) Piet Neethling, with Johan Wiese (consultant, both 1997) ▪ 48ha/±39ha (cab, malbec, p verdot, shiraz) ▪ 200t/±28,000cs own label 100% red ▪ PO Box 5298 Helderberg 7135 ▪ info@kleinconstantia.com ▪ www.kleinconstantia.com ▪ **T +27 (0)21-794-5188**

Anysbos   ⬧

On the Bot River farm they acquired a decade back, Johan and Sue Heyns turned fields of wheat, canola and barley into vineyards and olive groves. They imported a 30-year-old press from France, fixed it, and built a cellar in time for Marelise Niemann to vinify, in hands-off fashion, all the 2019 harvest (and some of her own Momento wines). A milk tank is used for cooling the barrel cellar, and the old goat shed has been transformed into a dry cellar.

★★★★★ **Grenache Noir** ⊛ The flavours on **17** ⑨④ resonate delicately but persistently with that of the local shrub, anysbos ('anise/liquorice bush'). Some cured meat savouriness too. Lovely purity of fruit, intensity & freshness. Naturally fermented & matured in old oak for 20 months. A beautiful terroir expression.

★★★★★ **Disdit** ⊛ Was 'White Blend'. Complex array of baked apple, clove & almond on chenin-led **18** ⑨④, with roussanne & grenache blanc (26/14). Wild ferment/10 months in older oak, further 7 in bottle. Fresh, understated yet persistent, wonderful length. Already tempting, will age gracefully for years.— MW

Location/WO: Bot River ▪ Map: Walker Bay & Bot River ▪ Map grid reference: C3 ▪ Est 2010 ▪ 1stB 2018 ▪ Tasting, sales & cellar tours by appt ▪ Owner(s) Anysbos Olywe BK ▪ Winemaker(s) Marelise Niemann (2016) ▪ Viticulturist(s) Quintus le Roux (2012) ▪ 320ha/15ha (cinsaut, grenache n/b, shiraz, chenin, marsanne, rouss) ▪ PO Box 550 Bot River 1785 ▪ info@anysbos.co.za ▪ **S** 34° 15' 23.96" **E** 019° 15' 37.84" ▪ **T +27 (0)82-601-1067**

☐ **Aphaea** see Val du Charron
☐ **Apogée** see La Vierge Private Cellar
☐ **Arboretum** see Botanica Wines

Arcangeli Vineyards   ⬧ ⑪ ⌂

Bucolic Bot River is the location of this boutique winery, but it has a much wider - multinational - perspective thanks to the people involved and wines made. Owners, construction businessman Sandro Arcangeli and his family, bring an Italian influence, and nebbiolo vines, source of the Romulus wine. It and the Verdelho, named 'Feiteiras' for the previous Portuguese owners, as well as the Semillon, a favourite of SA winemaker Krige Visser, were being released as we went to press after bottle-maturation at the cellar. Work in the vineyards continues on a sustainable route, with straw mulch used to cut chemical weed control.

★★★★ **Romulus Nebbiolo** ⓥ Winemaker Krige Visser's understanding of tannins evident in **17** ⑧⑦, if lower-key than traditional in this Italian variety. Poise, freshness & flavoursome earthy/cherry tones well set off by unintimidating grip, bone-dry finish. Rawsonville fruit.

★★★★ **Syrah-Mourvèdre** ⓥ Syrah's (72%) dark fruit the backdrop to spice, scrub, meaty complexity, firm tannic grasp in **16** ⑧⑦. Tight, brooding, mid-2017 but promising, will reward cellaring.

★★★★★ **Semillon** ⓥ Texture, structure & ageability rather than fruit main focus of individual **17** ⑨④. Intriguing almost rustic earthy, hay character, resistant grip juxtaposed with creamy weight, which age should resolve. Spontaneous ferment, portion on skins/some stalks.

★★★★☆ **Feiteiras Verdelho** ⓩ Riveting acidity, baked apple & even whiff of caramel are echoes of variety's alter ego as Madeira but no hint of maderisation in **17** ⑨①. Bigger than **16** ⑨⓪ (14% alcohol vs 12.5%), similar lean, firm frame, appetising saline length. Portion skin-fermented; 100% older oaked.

Merlot-Petit Verdot-Cabernet Sauvignon ⓩ ★★★★ Cigarbox, cassis & plum, **16** ⑧④ led by merlot (42%) but exhibits little of that variety's fruit generosity, needs few years to develop. — AL

Location: Bot River ▪ Map: Walker Bay & Bot River ▪ Map grid reference: C3 ▪ WO: Bot River/Western Cape ▪ Est/1stB 2015 ▪ Tasting & sales by appt ▪ Restaurant ▪ Luxury guest cottages ▪ Owner(s) Roodeheuvel Boerdery cc (Directors Allesandro & Fabio Arcangeli) ▪ Winemaker(s) Krige Visser ▪ 16.2ha/4.2ha (cab, merlot, mourv, p verdot, shiraz, verdelho) ▪ 3,500cs own label 70% red 30% white ▪ PO Box 234 Bot River 7185 ▪ info@arcangeliwines.com ▪ www.arcangeliwines.com ▪ S 34° 14' 3.6" E 019° 12' 33.3" ▪ thesis.freely. reassuring ▪ **T +27 (0)82-412-7795**

☐ **Arco Laarman** *see* Laarman Wines

Arendsig Handcrafted Wines

Arendsig owner and cellarmaster Lourens van der Westhuizen focuses exclusively on 'top quality single-vineyard wines' in a boutique cellar on the Robertson family farm.

Location/map: Robertson ▪ Map grid reference: C4 ▪ Est/1stB 2004 ▪ Tasting & cellar tours by appt ▪ Tour groups ▪ Pre-booked picnic baskets ▪ Wedding/function venue ▪ Accommodation available ▪ Owner(s) Lourens van der Westhuizen ▪ Cellarmaster(s)/viticulturist(s) Lourens van der Westhuizen (2004) ▪ 95ha/12ha (cab, grenache, mourv, ptage, shiraz, chard, chenin, sauv, viog) ▪ 100t/5,000cs own label 50% red 50% white ▪ PO Box 147 Robertson 6705 ▪ info@arendsig.co.za ▪ www.arendsig.co.za ▪ S 33° 55' 37.9" E 020° 0' 47.6" ▪ hence.uninterrupted.enlarging ▪ **T +27 (0)84-200-2163/+27 (0)23-616-2835**

Arendskloof-New Cape Wines ⓩ

These are the prestige wines of Christiaan Groenewald, twice Diners Club Winemaker of the Year and owner/winemaker at separately listed Eagle's Cliff Wines-New Cape Wines. Intended to complement good food, Arendskloof wines are 'made in a way to try and keep nature in the wines'.

Voetspore range

★★★★ **Merlot** ⓩ Lightly spiced red berries in **15** ⑧⑦, full of flavour & character, complexity. Silky & rounded, harmonious tannins & dried herb finish. WO W Cape, as all unless noted.

★★★★☆ **Petit Sirah** ⓩ Delicate but ripe bramble & hedgerow fruit, violet perfume & hints of fynbos on svelte **16** ⑨⓪, deep flavours & long savoury finish. 50% new oak, year, well meshed with firm but fine structure. No track record, but all set for a fine future.

★★★★ **Pinotage** ⓩ **17** ⑧⑧ similar pleasing attributes as **15** ★★★★★ ⑨⓪, a delicious coolness about it, pristine plum & spice flavours, but tannins more prominent, best kept for later. No **16**.

★★★★ **Tannat** ⓩ One of fewer than 10 varietal bottlings in our guide, **16** ⑧⑥ expectedly big & bold, ageworthy, but welcome & appealing berry succulence too, exotic spice & dark-fruit pastille finish.

★★★★ **Shiraz-Tannat** ⓩ Sweet fruited, with depth & length, **16** ⑧⑦ reveals a juicy spice-infused black cherry & plum character, tempered by supple tannins. Fine partner for hearty meat stews.

★★★★ **Tannat-Syrah** ⓩ Unusual & ambitious blend. **12** ★★★★★ ⑨② trumps last-tasted **09**. Spicy black plum & prune, firm but noble tannin (as expected from tannat).

★★★★ **Chardonnay** Fresh, fruity & lighter styled, **18** ★★★ ⑧② less complex than previous, 6 months in barrel vs 12 for also-tasted **17** ⑧⑥, which offers baked apple, vanilla biscuit & lime zest flavours. Harmonious, with delicate yet intense texture & length.

★★★★ **Witkruisarend** ⓩ From sauvignon, chardonnay & roussanne, **14** ⑧⑥ creamy, rounded, with yellow peach & nougat attractions; sufficient lemon lift to enliven vanilla finish from 40% oaked portion.

Cabernet Sauvignon ⓩ ★★★★ Judicious oak backing (30% new) for fresh black & red fruit in **17** ⑧④, medium body, balanced & smooth enough for current drinking. **Pinot Noir** ⓩ ★★★★ Misses the mark of **15** ★★★★ ⑧⑦, mashed sweet strawberries & spice, **16** ⑧④ gentle, soft, but not the length & depth of previous. **Shiraz** ⓩ ★★★★ Exuding black cherry & black pepper, **13** ⑧⑤ is commendably dry but still tight, with lively acidity. **Pinot Noir Rosé** ★★★ Salmon pink **18** ⑧② offers crushed strawberries, dry, light

& easy, with spicy grip to finish. Breede River Valley WO, as Chardonnay & Pinot Grigio. **Chenin Blanc** Ⓥ ★★★ Gentle tropical fruit on **16** ⑧① with hint of oak; easygoing, bonus of moderate 12% alcohol. **Pinot Grigio** ★★★★ Fresh & fruity **18** ⑧④, with floral & stonefruit flavours, mouthwatering, firm tangy finish. Like **16** ⑧④, lighter/lesser & complex **15** ★★★★ ⑧⑦. No **17**. **Sauvignon Blanc** Ⓥ ★★★★ Fragrant white flowers, apple & capsicum flavours on **16** ⑧④. Light & gentle for easy sipping. **Brut Rosé MCC** Ⓥ ★★★★ Classic & engaging pink sparkling, **12** ⑧④ dry, fresh & crisp, lemon sherbet notes from chardonnay, delicate red berry flavours from pinot noir. Year/2 cellaring should add complexity. — WB

☐ **Are We Having Fun Yet?** *see* Wine Village-Hermanus

Aristea Wines

This multi-national Constantia-based venture, named for an indigenous bloom, combines the expertise of consultant winemaker Matthew Krone (12th-generation offspring of Tulbagh's bubbly-pioneering family) and two overseas luminaries: British Bordeaux vineyard owner Martin Krajewski, and Bordeaux oenologist Florent Dumeau, consultant for several global giants and local ventures. Long-term contracts with Stellenbosch, Elgin and Hemel-en-Aarde growers ensure premium parcels (including a Pinot Noir '18, untasted by us), and a second, post-vinification selection reducing annual releases to maximum 6,000 bottles of each wine - 'cherry picking' - Matthew calls it, with 90% exported to five continents.

★★★★ **Cabernet Sauvignon** ⓐ Refined **16** ⑧⑨, classic cassis flavours & tobacco spicing from oak, 33% new, fine linear tannins & wonderful poise. 18 months in French barrel add sweet vanilla top note, supportive structure for good few years cellaring. Decant if drinking now.

★★★★☆ **Chardonnay** ⓐ Shows assured handling of complex vinification, inter alia some bunch-pressing & partial natural ferment. **17** ⑨⓪ marries Old and New Worlds in restraint, purity & vibrancy of citrus fruit. Beautifully dry & steely, subtle nutty nuance from deft barrelling, 40% new.

★★★★☆ **Sauvignon Blanc-Semillon** Given the owners, a fine Bordeaux white to be expected. **17** ⑨① mostly sauvignon (75%) & it shows in intense grass, green fig & passionfruit, wet pebble minerality. Smoky, suave & expressive, crushed herb lift, lemony semillon end. Elgin fruit, bunch pressed & naturally fermented/aged in combo new/2nd-fill oak. Drink now or keep.

★★★★☆ **Méthode Cap Classique Rosé** Elegant, almost ethereal packaging for all the wines particularly resonates with this sophisticated blush sparkler, both 'a crowd pleaser' (as winemaker says) & something special to contemplate in quietude. **16** ⑨⓪ chardonnay & pinot noir, uniting their red-berried richness & acid verve. Satisfying dry finish.

★★★★ **Méthode Cap Classique Blanc** Pale gold **15** ⑧⑧ dry sparkling from chardonnay & pinot noir. Rich & mouthfilling apple flavour thanks to 36 months on lees, balanced by lively effervescence & fleur de sel savouriness. WO W Cape.— WB, CvZ, AL

Location: Constantia ▪ WO: Stellenbosch/Elgin/Western Cape ▪ Est 2014 ▪ 1stB 2015 ▪ Closed to public ▪ Owner(s) Martin Krajewski, Florent Dumeau & Matthew Krone ▪ Cellarmaster(s)/winemaker(s) Matthew Krone (2014) ▪ 1,000cs per wine ▪ 13 Sillery Estate, Constantia 7806 ▪ matthew@matthewkronewines.co.za ▪ www.aristeawines.com

Arra Vineyards

Developed under the radar in the late 1990s, mostly with red wines in mind, this farm on the Paarl slopes of Klapmuts Hill has a welcoming cellardoor where the wines, some released only after extended bottle maturation, are offered for tasting and sale. At press time, a new winemaker/viticulturist was being appointed.

Arra Vineyards range

★★★★ **Cape Blend** ⊘ Representing excellent value, **13** ⑧⑦ pinotage with 27% merlot, 18% each petit verdot & mourvèdre is smooth, well-knit after 2 years in barrel, further 3 in bottle. Still fresh, full of tangy fruit, a step up on **12** ★★★★ ⑧⑤.

Cabernet Sauvignon ★★★★ After 2 years in French oak, **16** ⑧⑤ has toffee on nose, berry cordial note evolving into cassis on palate, earthy finish. **Pinotage** ⊘ ★★★★ Sweet, ripe plum & blueberry fruit on juicy **17** ⑧⑤, with lavender & mint adding to appeal, fresher & softer than previous. **Shiraz** ★★★★ With year in oak, **16** ⑧④ has subtly spiced toasted hazelnut edge to wild strawberry fruit, hints of pepper

& leather. **Shiraz-Cabernet Sauvignon** ⊘ ★★★ Shiraz-led **15** ⑧ with 33% cab shows leather & cured meat evolution but there's ample black/blueberry fruit for 2 or 3 more years of everyday enjoyment. **Blanc de Noir** ⊘ ★★★★ Pearl pink **19** ⑧, ex pinotage with 20% shiraz, is dry & refreshing at 12.5% alcohol, with piquant red fruit, Seville orange nuance. **Viognier** ⊘ ★★★★ Fragrant, unoaked **18** ⑧ has citrus blossoms on nose, hint of ginger on finish, juicy peach & tangerine in between. Real bargain. **Natural Sweet Red Blend** ★★ Caramelised berries in **17** ⑦ from equal cab & merlot, year in French oak, pleasantly sweet 31 g/l sugar. **Natural Sweet Viognier** ⊘ ★★★ Apricot & pineapple on nose, ripe papaya on palate, **14** ⑦ finishes clean with just over 34 g/l sugar. **Cape Vintage** ⑨ ★★★★ 'Port' from ruby cab, decade in French oak, **08** ⑧ soft, yielding, with flavours of boozy berries & chocolate orange. 500 ml. Coastal WO. Not tasted: **Merlot**, **Cabernet Sauvignon-Petit Verdot-Merlot**, **Shiraz-Mourvèdre**. Discontinued: **Mourvèdre**, **Chenin Blanc**.
Discontinued: **Reserve range**, **Barrel Select range**. — JG

Location/map: Paarl ▪ Map grid reference: C8 ▪ WO: Paarl/Coastal ▪ Est 1998 ▪ 1stB 2001 ▪ Tasting & sales Wed-Sun 10-4.30 ▪ Owner(s) Arra Vineyards (Pty) Ltd ▪ 72ha/28ha (cab, merlot, ptage, ruby cab, shiraz, viog) ▪ 20,000cs ▪ PO Box 298 Klapmuts 7625 ▪ sales@arrawines.com ▪ www.arrawines.com ▪ S 33° 49' 25.9" E 018° 51' 47.7" ▪ ⬜ integrate.recycle.splashing ▪ **T +27 (0)21-875-5363**

☐ **Art Collection** *see* Rascallion Wines
☐ **Artisanal Boutique Winery** *see* ArtiSons

ArtiSons   ⑨

The artisans and scions are winemaker Tertius Boshoff and viticulturist Kobie van der Westhuizen, whose work at substantial Stellenbosch winery Stellenrust dovetails with this personal venture, formerly known as Artisanal Boutique Winery. Inspired by 'renegade' Swartland vintners rediscovering traditional, sustainable winemaking methods and unlocking the potential of old vines, the duo's aim 'is not gimmicky wines, but truly a search across boundaries to create excellence'. Their latest wines refer: The Mothership Chenin, from vines circa 1964, earning our highest star rating on debut; and Blueberry Hill Shiraz, from 'crooked vine survivors in arid clay soils'. Both are from Bottelary, home to the ArtiSons' cellar.

ArtiSons range

★★★★☆ **JJ Handmade Eight Pillars** 🐝 8 pillars, 8 grapes; the Bordeaux trio plus pinotage represent the foundation of SA wine, the 4 Rhône grapes its 'sexy future'. Intricately woven **16** ⑨④ is opulent, floral & peppery, the palate full of dark berries, cured meat & spice from 2 years in oak, harmonious & persistent. 30+ year old vines in Stellenbosch, Swartland & Piekenierskloof.

SeriesRARE range

★★★★☆ **Villain Vines Carignan** 🐝 Carignan, 'slipped in' to Voor Paardeberg shiraz vineyard, now 45 years old, gives wonderfully rich & dense blueberry fruit, supple tannin structure & sumptuous palate with bramble & savoury nuances in **17** ⑨③. 32% wholebunch, older oak 16 months.

★★★★☆ **The Phantom Grenache** 🐝 1974 bushvine vineyard on 'spooky' (mist-wreathed in winter) Piekenierskloof slope is the source of **17** ⑨④, packed with mouthfilling red & black cherry & spice, earth & dried herbs, gentle vanilla & savouriness from older oak (16 months), velvety lingering finish.

★★★★☆ **After Eight Shiraz** 🐝 Bottelary Hills vines fringed by eucalyptus trees, wine maximising expression of site's overt mint chocolate character. **16** ⑨③ seductive fragrance shows that, also blackberry, violet & pepper. Forthcoming, sleek & satisfying. Spice ex half new French oak, 18 months.

★★★★☆ **Blueberry Hill Shiraz** 🆕 🐝 Fruit from 'murderous clay soil' portion of Bottelary Hills block vinified separately for its intense blueberry character. **17** ⑨③ also has mineral hints, layered complexity & generous tannins, smoothed 16 months in oak. Crisp & cool-feeling, with good focus.

★★★★★ **The Mothership Chenin Blanc** 🆕 🐝 Bottelary vines planted in 1964 make for a stellar debut in **18** ⑨⑤, full, textured (6-12 hours skin contact) & waxy, with layers of flavour unfolding to the long finish of wet stone minerality & lingering lemon blossom. Natural ferment in foudre & concrete 'egg', ageing only in concrete. Only 200 cases.

★★★★☆ **The Apprentice White Cinsault** ⓐ From Bottelary cinsaut block with mutated vines giving 'white' & light pink bunches. Only 150 cases of **18** ㉓; complex, broad & rich aromas & flavours of ripe apricot & beeswax, creamy marzipan from wild ferment & 9 months lees ageing in older oak.— WB

Location/map: Stellenbosch ▪ Map grid reference: C3 ▪ WO: Stellenbosch/Coastal ▪ Est/1stB 2013 ▪ Tasting, sales & cellar tours by appt only ▪ Closed all pub hols ▪ Owner(s) Tertius Boshoff & Kobie van der Westhuizen ▪ Cellarmaster(s) Tertius Boshoff (Jan 2005) ▪ Winemaker(s) Tertius Boshoff (Jan 2005) & Herman du Preez (Jan 2016) ▪ Viticulturist(s) Kobie van der Westhuizen (Jan 2000) ▪ 20ha/4ha (cabs s/f, carignan, cinsaut, grenache, merlot, ptage, shiraz, chenin) ▪ 10t/600cs own label 70% red 30% white ▪ PO Box 26 Koelenhof 7605 ▪ artisanswinery@gmail.com ▪ S 33° 51' 44.41" E 018° 46' 34.11" ▪ ⓦ corkscrews.installs.confetti ▪ **T +27 (0)82-455-6431**

☐ **Art Series** *see* Seven Springs Vineyards

Arumdale Cool Climate Wines ⓠ

Mark Simpson's Huguenot ancestors were from a renowned wine region, the Loire, so it's appropriate that he's invested in wine as both a brand owner – of these more serious Arumdale bottlings and the separately listed meal mates, Robin Hood Legendary Wine Series – and a merchant, via his outlet in Grabouw town.

★★★★ **St Andrew's Blend** ⓠ Cab (60%), merlot & shiraz **14** ㊇ improves on last-tasted **12** ★★★★ ㊃ in texture, depth & concentration of black fruit, supple, silky integrated tannin. Long rich finish.

Pink Shiraz ⓠ ★★★ Pomegranate pink hue to bright, tangy dry **15** ㊁ rosé. Fun, light bodied & easy.

Special LYC Sauvignon Blanc ⓠ ★★★ Maintains form with nectarine, white pepper & rich lees breadth, **15** ㊁ pleasant acid tang & dry finish. — FM

Location/map/WO: Elgin ▪ Map grid reference: B1 ▪ Est 1962 ▪ 1stB 2003 ▪ Tasting & sales Mon-Fri 10-4; pub hols by appt only ▪ No tasting fee if purchasing ▪ Closed Easter Fri-Mon, Dec 25/26 & Jan 1 ▪ Owner(s) Mark Simpson ▪ Cellarmaster(s)/winemaker(s) Christo Versfeld (Villiersdorp Cellar) ▪ (cab, merlot, shiraz, sauv) ▪ PO Box 2 Elgin 7180 ▪ royalwine@arumdale.co.za ▪ www.arumdale.co.za ▪ S 34° 9' 14.51" E 019° 1' 48.22" ▪ ⓦ trap.approach.hiking ▪ **T +27 (0)21-859-3430**

Asara Wine Estate & Hotel ⓠ ⓜ ⓐ ⓞ ⓐ

This historic Stellenbosch property, completely transformed this century, has a five-star hotel, with various dining options and arguably the largest selection of craft gin in the southern hemisphere, but 'making magnificent wine is at the heart of what Asara is all about'. To this end, seasoned vintners Abé Beukes and Achim Doër support Janette van Lill in the cellar while working with viticulturist Allan Cockcroft to drive forward a vineyard plan involving new plantings and removal of alien vegetation.

Speciality Collection

★★★★ **Bell Tower Estate Wine** ⓠ Consistently good Bordeaux-style flagship, fleshy 5-way blend in **15** ㊇, cab & cab franc (32/23) leading the cassis & foliage aromas, black fruit flavours, savoury spice & minerality. Also in magnum, as next. No **14**.

★★★★ **Avalon** ⓠ One of few SA Amarone-style wines, **13** ㊆ red & dark fruit, violet & cinnamon notes, sweetness from alcohol & some American oak artfully masked by solid tannins, freshened by acidity. Vine-dried pinotage & shiraz, lengthy 3 years in oak, 30% new.

★★★★ **Méthode Cap Classique** ⊘ Taut, tangy green-apple vibrancy to **16** ㊈ all-chardonnay bubbly, which improves on **15** ★★★★ ㊄. Bright & lively, with fantail of creamy lees notes from 18 months before disgorgement & 9 months after.

★★★★ **Carillon** ⓠ Noble Late Harvest from chenin, old oak aged. Deep gold **14** ㊇ attractive stone-fruit & rooibos aromas, bracing acidity to balance the apricot richness, uncloying marmalade conclusion.

The Red Cab ⓠ ★★★ 'Noir de noir' partner for White Cab, **17** ㊁'s mulberry & cassis tones mingle with attractive spices & herbs. Judicious 10% new-oak support, soft tannins, accessible medium body. **Passione Pinotage** ⓠ ★★★★ Full bodied & savoury, brambleberry, molasses & cinnamon complexity, **16** ㊄'s fruitiness neatly channelled by firm tannin grip, aided by year barrels & staves. **The White Cab** ★★★ Unusual white from cabernet. Gentle tang of raspberry with light body & soft acidity on **19** ㊁ summertime sipper. **Vine Dried Sauvignon Blanc** ⓥ ★★★★ Intricate vinification for **16** ⑧④ vin de paille from sauvignon, concentrated & packed with personality. Desiccated fruit flavours, vanilla tinge from oak.

Vineyard Collection

★★★★ **Pinotage** ⓥ Plum & mulberry fragrance, vanilla touches on voluptuous **17** ⑧⑥. Plush dark fruit given form by lovely broad tannins. Will reward few years patience.

Cabernet Sauvignon ★★★★ Easy appeal to fruitcake notes of light-bodied **17** ⑧⑤. Supple & easy drinking, with gentle spice from 18 months in French oak, 10% new. **Merlot** ★★★★ Dark-fruit compote charm to **17** ⑧⑤. Supple, light & easy to drink. Restrainedly oaked - just 10% new French, 14 months. No **16**. **Shiraz** ⓥ ★★★☆ Vibrant dark berries pave way for black pepper & salami notes, **15** ⑧③ supple tannin structure & savoury-smoky persistence. Also in magnum. **Cape Fusion** ⓥ ★★★★ Generously scented **16** ⑧④ trio shiraz, pinotage & malbec has red & black fruit, buchu & spice complexity. Downy tannins for immediate pleasure, sufficient padding for few years. Also in 375 ml & 1.5L. **Pinotage Rosé** ★★★☆ Quaffable blush pink **19** ⑦⑨ is softly tangy, with plum, raspberry & cherry notes. **Chardonnay Lightly Wooded** ⓥ ★★★ Carefully oaked (just 10% new) to preserve citrus, white peach & almond flavours on **17** ⑧① yet add appealing nuttiness to stonefruit finish. **Chenin Blanc** ★★★★ Attractive **18** ⑧④ shows quince & melon alongside lees breadth & nutty oatmeal from 50% barrelled portion (5% new, 8 months). **Sauvignon Blanc** ★★★ Tropical styling on juicy **18** ⑧②. Light bodied, crisp & zesty. — FM

Location/map/WO: Stellenbosch ▪ Map grid reference: D6 ▪ Est/1stB 2001 ▪ Tasting Mon-Sat 10-6 Sun 10-4 ▪ Fee R60/3 wines, R85/5 wines ▪ Sales 10-6 (summer)/10-4 (winter) ▪ Closed Dec 25 ▪ Tasting centre ▪ Cellar tours by appt Mon-Fri at 11 & 3 ▪ Tour groups ▪ 5-star TGCSA hotel ▪ Raphael's ▪ Mise en Place restaurant ▪ Sansibar bistro & gin lounge ▪ Deli ▪ Gift shop ▪ Function & banqueting facilities ▪ Conferences ▪ Weddings ▪ Vineyard walks ▪ Bikes & Wines tasting tours ▪ Cookery school ▪ Winemaker(s) Janette van Lill (Oct 2016), with consultants Abé Beukes & Achim Doër ▪ Viticulturist(s) Alan Cockcroft (2013) ▪ 180ha/102ha (cabs s/f, malbec, merlot, p verdot, ptage, shiraz, chard, chenin, sauv) ▪ 1,000t/125,000cs own label 70% red 30% white ▪ IPW, WIETA ▪ PO Box 882 Stellenbosch 7599 ▪ winery-info@asara.co.za ▪ www.asara.co.za ▪ S 33° 56' 35.00" E 018° 48' 31.00" ▪ 🔾 also.behaving.keener ▪ **T +27 (0)21-888-8000**

Ashbourne

This quality-focused venture allows the Hamilton Russell Vineyards team to expand their horizons outside Hemel-en-Aarde Valley in search of special parcels of fruit (mostly in Swartland) to partner their own carefully tended vineyards back home. (These have been joined by four blocks of pinotage, such is owner Anthony Hamilton Russell's belief in the variety.) The result is a small range of exciting wines using trending winemaking techniques and equipment such as wholebunch- and wild-yeast ferments, and amphoras. Which is great news for the children of the Hemel-en-Aarde Valley Pre-school, who benefit from a percentage of every bottle of Blanc and Rosé sold.

★★★★☆ **Pinotage** 🐝 Elegant **17** ⑨④ effortlessly asserts flavours of perfumed bright red & black fruit (50% wholeberry), balanced with ripe, integrated tannins, touch of leather & exotic spicy finish. 40% new French oak enhances & enrobes stellar fruit, assuring a great future. Also in magnum.

★★★★ **Pinotage-Cinsault** 🐝 Touch less serious than **18** ⑧⑦, cheery **19** ★★★☆ ⑧⑤ bounces forth with oodles of bright, red berried fruit, soft tannins & zippy finish. No oak (none needed) & 100% wholebunch a recipe for happy summer drinking.

★★★★ **Sandstone** Welcome return for blend of sauvignon, chardonnay, semillon (66/17/17), **18** ⑧⑨ good example of modern Cape winemaking. Preserved lemon, wild herb & slightly earthy note backed by old oak & delicious texture from ferment in amphora & clay 'egg'. Hemel-en-Aarde Valley WO, as Pinotage.

. . . .

Blanc 🐦 ★★★☆ Name change, was 'Sauvignon Blanc-Chardonnay', but same grapes (84/16) make for superior everyday sipping, **19** ⑧③ offering peas & greenpepper with candied pear drops & richer leesy finish. Walker Bay WO.

. . . .

Rosé ★★★ Crisp & savoury, bone-dry **19** ⑧② , from cinsaut, with attractive earthy finish. Tad less acid than previous. — CM

Location: Hermanus ▪ WO: Swartland/Hemel-en-Aarde Valley/Walker Bay ▪ Est 1996 ▪ 1stB 2001 ▪ Tasting & sales at Hamilton Russell Vineyards ▪ Owner(s) Anthony Hamilton Russell ▪ Winemaker(s) Emul Ross (2014)

WINE.

ANOTHER
REASON
PEOPLE
DETOUR
TO THE
GORGEOUS
GEORGE.

DON'T

BE A STRANGER

gorgeous
George.
CAPE TOWN

 A MEMBER OF
DESIGN HOTELS

STAY AND PLAY

+27 (0)878 98 6000, 118 St George's Mall, Cape Town, 8001
gorgeousgeorge.co.za

Door-to-Door Wine Delivery

to Europe, UK and Switzerland

Taste and order directly at the CAPREO partner wineries. **Free delivery for 18 bottles or more.**

- Over 50 top wineries
- More than 500 selected premium wines
- Fast & secure shipping
- Affordable prices

www.capreo.com

▪ Viticulturist(s) Johan Montgomery (2005) ▪ 64ha/24.35ha (ptage, sauv, sem) ▪ 23t/12,000cs own label 50% red 50% white ▪ PO Box 158 Hermanus 7200 ▪ info@ashbournewines.com ▪ www.ashbournewines.com ▪ **T +27 (0)28-312-3595**

☐ **Asiel** *see* Malanot Wines

Aslina Wines

Award-winning Ntsiki Biyela, formerly with Stellekaya, continues building a global market for her quartet of wines under the Aslina label (in homage to the grandmother who raised her in a small KwaZulu-Natal village, prior to her studies in oenology/viticulture at Stellenbosch University). The Somerset West-based vintner is on-trend with her 'least interference' philosophy, believing that her role is merely to provide 'a light hand of guidance to bring out the innate beauty of nature's offerings'.

★★★★ **Umsasane** Cab leads cab franc & petit verdot in both vintages of Bordeaux blend reviewed here. Step up **17** ⑧⑥ cassis & tobacco attractions, oak well integrated & shaping the long finish. **16** ★★★ ⑧⓪ soft, succulent, black-fruited mouthful which will appeal widely. ±16 months in French barriques.

Cabernet Sauvignon ★★☆ Typical cassis & fruitcake on nose of **16** ⑦⑦. Light herbal nuance on slender palate. **Chardonnay** ★★ Creamy oatmeal & nutty notes somewhat at odds with succulent citrus fruit on **18** ⑦⑤. Alcohol 12%. WO W Cape. **Sauvignon Blanc** ★★★ Appealing floral edge to tangy lemon zest vibrancy of **18** ⑧①, bright & succulent. 12% Durbanville semillon in the mix. — WB, FM, CvZ

Location: Somerset West ▪ WO: Western Cape/Stellenbosch ▪ 1stB 2013 ▪ Closed to public ▪ Owner(s)/winemaker(s) Ntsiki Biyela ▪ 2,000cs own label 50% red 50% white ▪ ntsiki@aslinawines.com ▪ www.aslinawines.co.za

☐ **Astraeus** *see* Waterkloof
☐ **Ataraxia Wines** *see* Editor's Note
☐ **Athena** *see* Thor Vintners
☐ **Atlantic Slopes** *see* Hillcrest Estate
☐ **Atlantikas** *see* Scions of Sinai
☐ **Aubergine Restaurant** *see* Migliarina Wines

Audacia Wines

Trevor Strydom, co-owner of this Stellenbosch red-wine venture, has been deeply involved in developing refined (i.e. de-flavoured and fully dissolvable) wine tannin from indigenous, antioxidant-rich honeybush and rooibos material as a substitute for sulphur in preserving wine and boosting mouthfeel, and all bottlings reviewed this edition make use of this technology. They can be sampled by appointment or at the popular Root44 weekend market on the estate.

No Sulphur Added range

★★★★ **Code Breaker** Ⓥ Characterful & unusual merlot, **13** ⑧⑦ has rooibos & honeybush as natural preservative yet more mint & lavender notes than expected fynbos. Succulent mulberry fruit, fresh finish. **Cabernet Sauvignon** ★★★ Reinvented **18** ⑧② loses signature rooibos character, focuses on blackcurrant fruit. Meaty, substantial, with velvety tannins. Tasted pre-bottling, as next. **Cabernet Franc** ⓃⒺⓌ ★★★ **18** ⑧① has convincing leafiness & graphite, also some angular tannins mid-2019, which may settle over time. **Merlot** ★★ **18** ⑦⑥ sheds its rooibos mantle, but still showing green & sappy. **Shiraz** ★★★ Medicinal nuance to previewed **18** ⑧②, with robust tannins, solid black fruit. Big-boned, intense, needs time to settle. **Premium Red Blend** Ⓥ ★★ NV ⑦④ from merlot & shiraz, forest berries dominated by tealeaf & buchu. Sweet hint & nutmeg spice make for interesting drink. Discontinued: **Natural Red Blend**. Discontinued: **Audacia range, Lower Kilojoules range**. — GdB

Location/map/WO: Stellenbosch ▪ Map grid reference: E8 ▪ Est 1930 ▪ Tasting by appt; closed pub hols ▪ On-consumption & sales at Audacia-Root44 Market Sat/Sun 11-4 ▪ Root44 Market (wine, food, arts, crafts, jewellery, kiddies area & live music from 1pm) ▪ Owner(s) Strydom & Harris families ▪ Cellarmaster(s)/winemaker(s)/viticulturist(s) Michael van Niekerk (Aug 2009) ▪ 32ha/20ha (cabs s/f, malbec, merlot, p verdot, roobernet, shiraz) ▪ 120t/18,000cs own label 100% red ▪ IPW ▪ PO Box 12679 Die Boord 7613 ▪ info@audacia.co.za ▪ www.audacia.co.za ▪ S 33° 59' 45.7" E 018° 50' 2.9" ▪ 🌐 fury.decks.qualified ▪ **T +27 (0)21-881-3052**

☐ **Aufwaerts Co-operative** *See Editor's Note*
☐ **Aureate** *see Noble Wines & Spirits*

Aurelia Wines

A double celebration for Lukas Wentzel: 20 years of his day job at the helm of Groote Post in Darling, and 10 as owner and bubbly-maker of this own boutique brand, honouring the strong women in his life — his mother and wife. Both milestones, and continuing success at satisfying SA consumers' 'hunger for crafted bubblies' deserve raising a glass this edition.

Brut Rosé ⊘ ★★★★ Pinot noir portion again upped, to 47%, rest chardonnay, for **18** (83). Fruity-style bubbly with attractive savoury edge to strawberry flavours & crisp, lipsmacking finish. **Brut** (⊗) ★★★★ Fresh, fruity, frothy crowd-pleasing **16** (84) MCC from chardonnay & pinot noir (70/30). Short lees time (14 months) adds some yeasty intensity to bouncy citrus & apple fruit. — CM

Location/WO: Darling ▪ Est 2010 ▪ 1stB 2008 ▪ Closed to public ▪ Owner(s)/cellarmaster(s)/winemaker(s) Lukas Wentzel ▪ 3t/600cs own label ▪ WIETA ▪ PO Box 102 Darling 7345 ▪ lukas@grootepost.co.za ▪ **T +27 (0)22-492-2825/+27 (0)82-306-7373**

Autumn Harvest Crackling

These long-established, lightly sparkling, lower-alcohol wines are made by Distell, and also sold in 1L & 1.5L. **Crisp Perlé Rosé** ★★ Pink **NV** (75) has gentle fizz, lingering sweetness & wintergreen bubblegum notes. **Crisp Perlé White** ★★ Lemon-apple sherbet & few grams sugar, **NV** (72)'s bubbles barely noticeable. ±12% alcohol for these. **Crisp Perlé Red** ⊘ ★★★ Dusty dark berries, gentle tannic tug & subtle sweetness make slightly pétillant **NV** (77) a party starter. Pot-pourri of varieties, as all. — CvZ

Avondale   (⊗) (⅋⅋) (◎) (⅋) (⅋)

The Grieve family owners of this Paarl farm are committed to sustainable winegrowing based on organic and biodynamic as well as scientific principles. They're among the first to import clay qvevri from Georgia, the former Soviet republic that winemaker Corné Marais visited in 2017. No wines tasted this edition.

Location/map: Paarl ▪ Map grid reference: F6 ▪ Est 1996 ▪ 1stB 1999 ▪ Tasting & sales Mon-Sun 10-4 ▪ Fee R70pp ▪ Closed Dec 25 & Jan 1 ▪ Cellar tours by appt only ▪ FABER restaurant ▪ Eco Wine Safari Wed-Sun at 10am (booking essential): R300pp incl MCC on arrival, tour & tasting in vyds, cellar tour ▪ Child friendly ▪ Owner(s) Grieve family/The Avondale Trust ▪ Winemaker(s) Corné Marais (Oct 2008), with Ivan September (Jan 2012) ▪ Viticulturist(s) Johnathan Grieve (Jul 1999) ▪ 300ha/70ha (cabs s/f, grenache, merlot, mourv, shiraz, chard, chenin, rouss, sem, viog) ▪ 500t/50,000cs own label 50% red 38% white 2% rosé 10% MCC ▪ EU Organic & USDA NOP organic ▪ PO Box 602 Paarl South 7624 ▪ wine@avondalewine.co.za ▪ www.avondalewine.co.za ▪ S 33° 45' 52.9" E 019° 0' 4.7" ▪ ⟨ɯ⟩ nitrate.loaded.salt ▪ **T +27 (0)21-863-1976**

Avontuur Estate   (⊗) (⅋⅋) (◎) (⅋)

Quality is the main focus at Avontuur, on the Helderberg between Stellenbosch and Somerset West, as 2nd-generation owners, Michael and Philip Taberer, continue the work of late father Tony, who started the brand in the 1980s. Vines are being carefully tended by both winemaking and vineyard teams, and 'improved micro-techniques' and regular input from viticulture consultant Paul Wallace are resulting in better fruit for winemaker/brandy master Jan van Rooyen to work with. 'Time spent refining and repositioning the range will lead to improvements and rationalisation over time,' the brothers anticipate. Tourist-friendly offerings include an awarded restaurant, specialised wine-and-food pairings and self-guided farm walks.

Premiere range

★★★★ **Dominion Royale Shiraz Reserve** (⊗) Dark-berried **14** (87) has complex flavours including cured meats. Less herbaceous than **12** (87), good balance & presence aided by maturation in seasoned casks only. No **13**.

★★★★ **Baccarat** (⊗) Tomato & bramble notes mingle with toasty vanilla oak & cigarbox on **12** (86) cab franc-led Bordeaux blend. Supple tannins & structure, medium body with grip for food. No **11**.

★★★★ **Luna de Miel Chardonnay Reserve** (⊗) Gorgeous **17** (87) extends uptick of last-tasted **15** ★★★☆ (84), crunchy apple freshens the butterscotch tones & dash viognier. New wood well contained.

★★★★ **Sarabande Sauvignon Blanc Reserve** More about structure than fruit, **17** ⑧⑥ has a gingery, spicy tang from partial older-oaking that will complement food. No **16**. **15** ⑧⑦ had 15% oaked chardonnay.
Legal Eagle Cabernet Franc Reserve (NEW) ★★★☆ Continues tradition of naming Premiere wines after champion racehorses bred on the estate. Sappy, herbal tones to red berry fruit supported by stern tannins; 14.5% alcohol evident on finish of **15** ⑧③. **Minelli Pinot Noir Reserve** ★★★☆ Extracted, spicy structure masks red berry fruit of **14** ⑧③, decent 'dry red' but misses variety's delicacy & finesse. Discontinued: **Natural Sweet Viognier**.

Estate range
★★★★ **Cabernet Sauvignon** Focused, elegant **16** ⑧⑦ shows bright cassis fruit, less herbaceous in style than **14** ⑧⑥. Balanced, integrated, long savoury finish. **15** not made.

....

Pinot Noir-Chardonnay ⑦ ★★★ Salmon-pink rosé not tasted in a while. A 56/44 blend, **19** ⑧② now unwooded, bone-dry, balanced & easy to like. Fabulous cranberry twist in the conclusion.

....

Pinotage ★★★ Plummy, smoky **17** ⑧② has dense, somewhat hard tannins, not as fleshy as previous.
Cabernet Sauvignon-Merlot ★★★★ A friendly fireside red, **17** ⑧⑤ has fresh berries mixed with savoury, meaty extras. **Sauvignon Blanc** ★★★ Unwooded, brisk & crisp **19** ⑧① offers tropical fruit amongst the grassy green notes. **Brut Cap Classique** ⑦ ★★★ Onion skin hue on **NV** ⑧① (**10**) traditional-method sparkling from chardonnay & pinot noir. Faint apple & black olive flavours with coarse bubbles, light. Discontinued: **Cabernet Franc**.

Brandy range
★★★★☆ **Private Collection 10 Year Old Potstill** Robustly impressive brandy ⑨⓪ from chenin. Less blatant fruitiness than many but deeply flavourful; silky, rich & rather gorgeously ingratiating.— DS, TJ

Location/WO: Stellenbosch ▪ Map: Helderberg ▪ Map grid reference: C2 ▪ Est 1850 ▪ 1stB 1984 ▪ Tasting & sales Mon-Fri 8.30–5 Sat/Sun 9–4 ▪ Fee R50/5 wines ▪ Closed Good Fri, Dec 25 & Jan 1 ▪ Cellar tours by appt ▪ Tour groups ▪ Avontuur Estate Restaurant ▪ Function venue ▪ Thoroughbred stud ▪ Self-guided farm walks ▪ Seasonal events ▪ Owner(s) Taberer family ▪ Winemaker(s) / brandy master(s) Jan van Rooyen (Jan 2011) ▪ Viticulturist(s) Pippa Mickleburgh (Sep 1999) & Paul Wallace (consultant) ▪ 110ha/40ha (cabs s/f, merlot, p verdot, ptage, pinot, shiraz, chard, sauv, viog) ▪ 300t ▪ 60% red 40% white ▪ PO Box 1128 Somerset West 7129 ▪ info@avontuurestate.co.za ▪ www.avontuurestate.co.za ▪ S 34° 1' 33.2" E 018° 49' 23.8" ▪ ⓦ pens. stronger.aground ▪ **T +27 (0)21-855-3450**

Axe Hill ⓠ
Deo volente — God willing! — shrugs Mike Neebe, pondering the prospects for rain after five years of drought in Klein Karoo. Since taking ownership in the late 2000s of what was then a 'port'-only venture, Mike joined those championing the area's equal suitability for unfortified/table wines from port varieties. With less than 2 ha under vines, drought has serious sustainability implications, and while space was always constrained at his boutique-sized cellar in Calitzdorp, this was not the solution he envisaged. But he remains as determined as the hardy vines, which amazingly continue to deliver a crop, albeit a significantly reduced one.

Axe Hill range
★★★★ **Distinta** ⊘ Calitzdorp Blend **16** ⑧⑧ now from 49% each tinta & souzão, drop touriga. Hallmark dry fruit tannins envelop dark berry & cocoa flavours but, like Machado, blossom with decanting. More balance & structure than **15** ★★★★ ⑧④.
★★★★ **Machado** All-Portuguese blend in **16** ⑧⑦, without shiraz as in richer, more polished **15** ★★★★★ ⑨⓪. Touriga-led, with tintas roriz & barocca, souzão. Dry, almondy veneer to wild berry flavours. More accessible than Distinta.
★★★★ **Ambientem 18** ⑧⑥ chenin fresher than **17** ★★★ ⑧②. Natural ferment/ageing in old oak, exudes dried peach, baked apple & almond. Creamy lees nuance & tangy farewell. Some Swartberg grapes.
★★★★ **Cape Late Bottled Vintage** Barrel-aged (8 years) 'port' from touriga, souzão & tinta exudes decadent choc/toffee appeal. **11** ⑧⑨ rich, warming & supple, as befits LBV style. 375 ml.
★★★★☆ **Cape Vintage** ⑦ 'Port' from touriga (60%) with souzão & tinta, as was equally delicious **12** ⑨② , plenty of ripe flavour in **13** ★★★★ ⑧⑦, lightly & elegantly rich, with pleasing near-dry finish, but lacks the tannic depth & intensity for Vintage style.

Cape Ruby ★★★★ Liquid dark choc & berry, warming appeal on **NV** ⑧④. More balance & brightness than previous, though colour advanced for a Ruby. 375 ml. Not tasted: **Cape White**. Occasional release: **Shiraz**, **Touriga Nacional**.

Lenie's Hof range

Red ⓥ ★★★ Older-oaked touriga & tempranillo, **16** ⑧② supple & succulent, delivers mouthfilling spiced plums & liquorice at moderate 13.5% alcohol. Affable fireside quaffer, also hearty-food mate. **Tant Lenie** ★★★★ **18** ⑧④ from old-oak-matured viognier, refined floral & dried peach tone on a gently creamy base. More sprightly & balanced than last. Discontinued: **Cardinal**. — MW

Location: Calitzdorp ▪ Map: Klein Karoo & Garden Route ▪ Map grid reference: B5 ▪ WO: Calitzdorp/Klein Karoo ▪ Est 1993 ▪ 1stB 1997 ▪ Tasting, sales & cellar tours Mon-Sat by appt ▪ Owner(s) Axe Hill Winery (Pty) Ltd ▪ Cellarmaster(s)/winemaker(s) Mike Neebe (Oct 2007) ▪ Viticulturist(s) Mike Neebe ▪ ±60ha/1.8ha (grenache, souzão, tinta barocca, tinta roriz, touriga nacional, viog) ▪ ±5t/±1,000cs own label 70% red 30% white ▪ Wesoewer Rd Calitzdorp 6660 ▪ info@axehill.co.za ▪ www.axehill.co.za ▪ S 33° 30' 54.6" E 021° 41' 23.0" ▪ 🖺 succeeds.guided.crewmen ▪ **T +27 (0)11-447-3900/+27 (0)83-676-3000**

Axle Wines ⑥

Young vintner Alexander Milner, who collaborates with brother Marcus (winemaker for Paarl boutique winery Druk My Niet) on boutique wines on the family's 300-year-old Natte Valleij property in Stellenbosch, is developing his own brand with wife Sumari (a guiding light behind their farm-chic circular Silo Cottages). First up is a 2018 chenin from 1985 Darling bushvines, reflecting new-wave treatment of SA's old vines with hand picking, basket pressing, natural ferments in seasoned barrels and extended lees time. The UK and Canada have already placed their orders.

★★★★★ **Chenin Blanc** ⓐ Quince preserve & ripe honeyed notes on naturally fermented **18** ⑨⑤. Poised, elegant & refined, with understated but intense concentration. Lovely vibrant balance of fruit, acid, lees & oak (9 months 4th-fill French barriques). Alcohol 12%.— WB, FM

Location: Stellenbosch ▪ WO: Darling ▪ Est 2018 ▪ 1stB 2019 ▪ Closed to public ▪ Owner(s)/winemaker(s) Alexander Milner ▪ 3t/200cs ▪ PO Box 4 Klapmuts 7625 ▪ wine@nattevalleij.co.za ▪ **T +27 (0)84-643-3600**

Ayama Wines ⓥ🍽🏠🏡📷🅐

Attilio and Michela Dalpiaz and their offshore partners have been 'proudly South African, truly Italian' in their approach to revitalising Voor Paardeberg hillside farm Slent, after leaving their northern Italian home over a decade ago. Embracing the best of both worlds, their wines include SA's first commercially bottled Italian variety vermentino, joining local specialities such as chenin and pinotage. A farm deli sells typical old country delicacies such as their own olive oil, fresh porcini mushrooms and artichokes. Environmental and social awareness imbues wine names celebrating local wildlife, from baboons to a resident rare Cape leopard, and community projects, particularly the Perdjieskool crèche and afterschool for farm employees.

Baboon Selection

Baboon's Back Petite Sirah ⓥ ★★★★ Ruby-hued **17** ⑧③ offers lively bramble & hedgerow fruit, subtle spice from older oak, crushed green herbs & hint of smoke. **Baboon's Cheek Viognier** ⓥ ★★★ Voluptuous melange of peaches & cream, apricot kernel & spice. **17** ⑧① delicious solo, works well with food too.

Leopard Spot range

Red ⓥ ★★★ Unwooded Cape Blend pinotage (52%), shiraz, grenache, dark berries & spice on still-fresh, mouthfilling **15** ⑧②. — WB

Location/map: Paarl ▪ Map grid reference: B2 ▪ WO: Voor Paardeberg ▪ Est 2005 ▪ 1stB 2006 ▪ Tasting & sales Mon-Sun 10-4.30 ▪ Meals/refreshments by appt; or BYO picnic ▪ Deli with fresh farm produce, olive oil, wines & much more ▪ Walks/hikes ▪ Child friendly ▪ Conservation area ▪ Ayama Rock guest house ▪ Owner(s) Slent Farms (Pty) Ltd (5 partners) ▪ Cellarmaster(s)/winemaker(s) Michela Sfiligoi (2005) ▪ Viticulturist(s) Attilio Dalpiaz (2005) ▪ 210ha/65ha (cab, carignan, grenache n/b, merlot, petite sirah, ptage, shiraz, chenin, sauv, vermentino, viog) ▪ 300t/40,000cs own label 40% red 58% white 2% rosé ▪ WIETA ▪ Suite 106 Private Bag X3041 Paarl 7620 ▪ info@slentfarms.com ▪ www.ayama.co.za ▪ S 33° 37' 22.5" E 018° 49' 19" ▪ 🖺 downloads.marigolds.swam ▪ **T +27 (0)21-869-8313**

☐ **Azania** *see* Jacques Germanier
☐ **Baboon Selection** *see* Ayama Wines

Babylon's Peak Private Cellar

A granite outcrop high on Swartland's Paardeberg, known locally as Babylonstoren, provided inspiration for 4th-generation farmer Stephan Basson when he returned to this land in 2003 and decided use the grapes from venerable vines for an own label. Increased demand has prompted him enlarge the barrel store, among other cellar extensions, and add more vines - pinotage, chenin and Rhône varieties still being the focus.

★★★★ **Pinotage** ⓥ Deliciously intense **17** ⑧⑦'s pure black pastille & plum fruit merges nicely with firm tannic grip, helps extend the finish. Attractive mocha nuance from year older barrels.

★★★★ **SMG** ⊘ Violet & white pepper perfume to succulent **17** ⑧⑧. Appealing dryness & silky grip to 51% syrah, with mourvèdre hiked to 42% from **16** ★★★★☆ ⑨⓪'s 30%, dab grenache for seasoning.

★★★★ **Viognier-Roussanne** ⓥ Older-barrel-fermented, lees-aged **17** ⑧⑨, persistent & pervasive spiced grapefruit character, white flower & peach complexity. Gram sugar smooths, doesn't unbalance food-friendly 73/37 blend.

Shiraz-Carignan ⓥ ★★★★ Thrilling tannin lift on attractive **17** ⑧④ duo shiraz (60%) & dryland carignan. Year older oak allows pristine red & black berry fruit to shine, adds subtle spice. **Chenin Blanc** ⊘ ★★★★ Pear drop & melon typicity to **19** ⑧⑤. Lively & fresh, dry leesy tail. Like previous, from old unirrigated bushvines. Discontinued: **Cabernet Sauvignon-Malbec**. — FM

Location: Malmesbury ▪ Map/WO: Swartland ▪ Map grid reference: C8 ▪ Est/1stB 2003 ▪ Tasting & sales by appt only ▪ Conservation area ▪ Dams for fishing ▪ Self-catering cottage ▪ Owner(s) Stephan Basson ▪ Cellarmaster(s)/winemaker(s)/viticulturist(s) Stephan Basson (Jan 2003) ▪ 580ha/230ha (carignan, grenache, mourv, ptage, shiraz, chenin, rouss, viog) ▪ 30,000cs own label 65% red 35% white + 500,000L bulk ▪ PO Box 161 Malmesbury 7299 ▪ info@babylonspeak.co.za ▪ www.babylonspeak.co.za ▪ S 33° 33' 15.74" E 018° 48' 30.40" ▪ ⌨ cardholder.unblock.materials ▪ **T +27 (0)21-300-1052**

Babylonstoren

The farm on the Paarl-side slopes of the Simonsberg was granted in 1692, and its original buildings date back to the mid-18th century. But its modern incarnation under the ownership of Karen Roos has been transformative — an old cowshed becoming today's Babel restaurant, for example. At the estate's heart is a splendid garden of edible and medicinal plants, apart from the vineyards and olive trees. Cellarmaster Charl Coetzee has overseen extensions to the winery, with a subterranean tunnel now linking it to the barrel cellar.

★★★★ **Shiraz** Ripe, full-fruited aromas & flavours, with tobacco-oaky notes & firm dry tannins from plenty of new wood (70%). But **17** ⑧⑧ in balance. Some sugar sweetness, but shows less than on last.

★★★★☆ **Nebukadnesar** An imposing & rather showy red, about half cab & 4 other Bordeaux grapes. All-new oak heavily dominates aroma & flavour on seriously structured **17** ⑨⓪, but sweet fruit lurks & could emerge with time, along with integration of firm dry tannins. 14.3% alcohol. Also magnums.

★★★★ **Chardonnay** In established style, **18** ⑧⑦ has forward, lemon-lime aromas & flavours mingling with toasty oak notes (50% new barrels). Ripe & full-bodied (14.2% alcohol), ready for drinking by those who enjoy assertive wood.

★★★★ **Viognier** Quietly restrained apricot notes on well-balanced **18** ⑧⑦, more elegant than many despite the big 14.5% alcohol. A touch of sweetness, but some compensating grip. Light oaking supportive, while **17** ★★★★ ⑧⑤ had a more savoury wood element.

★★★★☆ **Sprankel** Subtly citrusy, apple & brioche notes on **14** ⑨① MCC sparkling from chardonnay, 4 years on lees before disgorgement. Dry, fresh, restrained & elegant but with good flavour depth.

Babel ★★★★ Sweet ripe plummy fruit aromas on **18** ⑧⑤ from 39% shiraz plus 6 others. Less oaky than Nebukadnesar (30% new) but less fruit density, so a more exposed structure, including acidity. A touch sweet, like fleshier **17** ★★★★ ⑧⑥. WO W Cape, like Nebukadnesar. **Mourvèdre Rosé** ★★★★ Pale copper-tinged pink **19** ⑧③ with quiet fruity-floral notes; softly textured, with good acid grip giving lingering dry finish. **Chenin Blanc** ★★★★ Pleasantly straightforward **19** ⑧④, with fruity, green-tinged character. A balanced, fresh, dry & unassuming pleasure. Not tasted: **Candide**. — TJ

Location: Paarl ▪ Map: Franschhoek ▪ Map grid reference: B8 ▪ WO: Simonsberg-Paarl/Western Cape ▪ Est 1692 ▪ 1stB 2011 ▪ Wine tasting & sales daily 10–5 (winter)/10–6 (summer) ▪ Hosted cellar tours daily 11–3 ▪ Tour groups by appt ▪ Farm shop & online shop ▪ Guided garden tours at 10 daily ▪ Special collection tours at 11.30 daily ▪ Babylonstoren Farm Hotel ▪ Bakery dinners: Italian inspired evenings Mon & Fri, Carnivore evenings Wed from 7 ▪ Babel Restaurant: breakfast Mon–Sun 8–9.30, lunch Wed–Sun from 12, dinner Mon–Sun from 7; The Greenhouse Restaurant Mon–Sun 10–4 ▪ Garden Spa 8–5 ▪ Healing Garden Tue 9.30 ▪ Olive oil press ▪ Mampoer distillery ▪ Cellarmaster(s) Charl Coetzee ▪ Winemaker(s) Klaas Stoffberg, with Marina Laubser ▪ Viticulturist(s) Ian de Villiers ▪ Babylonstoren Farm, Franschhoek ▪ cellar@babylonstoren.com ▪ www.babylonstoren.com ▪ S 33° 49' 26.73" E 018° 55' 39.08" ▪ ⟨≡⟩ squeamish.cyclist.engrossed ▪ T +27 (0)21-863-3852

Backsberg Estate Cellars ⓛ ⓜ ⓒ ⓑ ⓖ

'If you find our wines easy to drink, then we are achieving what we want' is the philosophy at this 104-year-old venture in Paarl. But, according to patriarch Michael Back and son and co-owner Simon, their approach has to exist under an overall umbrella of care - for the land, the product and the people who work for the Back family. This expressed in not only social responsibility programmes and environmentally sound practices followed in the vineyards, now under the watchful eye of new appointee Morné Olivier, but also concerted efforts in broader arenas, crowned with recognition from and certification by leading organisations such as WWF-SA (as a Conservation Champion) and The Carbon Protocol of SA (for carbon neutrality).

Flagship - Backsberg Family Reserve range

★★★★☆ **Red Blend** Red & black fruit, liquorice & chocolate complexity, hint iron minerality in top-tier Bordeaux blend. Very present but balanced tannins finer than rest of red line-up. **17** ⑨① cab & merlot (36/35) lead malbec & petit verdot; **16** ⑨③ was harmonious cab, merlot, malbec trio.

★★★★☆ **White Blend** ⓐ Touch floral viognier (3%), replacing **17** ⑨④'s sauvignon, is well-judged in **18** ⑨③, characterful blend with roussanne & chardonnay (55/42). Lemons & nuts, savoury oak spice from brief 4 months in all-new oak, lingering creamy persistence.

Black Label range

★★★★ **Pumphouse Shiraz** Plenty of bouquet appeal, red plums, berries, lily notes, tannins still unyielding, though, **17** ★★★★ ⑧⑤ needs year/2 to resolve, unlike **16** ⑧⑨, lithe & accessible on release.

★★★★☆ **Klein Babylons Toren** ⓥ ⓐ Enduring Cape Bordeaux label, less cab than Flagship sibling in **17** ⑨①, with partners merlot, malbec & petit verdot. Similar to **16** ⑨③, less opulent than previous, firm tannic hold, good burst of acidity.

★★★★☆ **Sonop Chardonnay** ⓥ High-end version, shows serious intent in all-new barrel ferment. **17** ★★★★ ⑧⑥ still unsettled mid-2018, smoky whiffs, sweet oaky notes somewhat at odds with bone-dry finish. **16** ⑨①'s substantial & convincing citrus fruit handled similar woody overlay better in youth.

★★★★ **John Martin Reserve Sauvignon Blanc** Fermented (not aged) in new barriques, **19** ⑧⑦'s expressive smoky, grassy blackcurrant fruit backed by well-gauged acidity, nice silky mouthfeel. 100% wooded vs 50% for suave **18** ⑧⑨, also with dash roussanne.

★★★★ **Hillside Viognier** Oak-fermented **19** ★★★★ ⑧④ spent 4 months in barrel versus just 2 in **18** ⑧⑦. Still unsettled mid-2019, sweet fruit & vanilla oak need bit more time to knit.

Méthode Cap Classique Brut ⓥ ★★★★ Vibrant **17** ⑧⑤ dry sparkler from chardonnay (53%) & pinot noir ready for any occasion. Easygoing bubbles, lively apple flavour (green, red & candied), touch brioche from ±12 months on lees.

Premium range

★★★★ **Cabernet Sauvignon** ⓥ Robust tannins of **18** ⑧⑥ somewhat cushioned by generous strawberry & damson fruit, lifted by bright acidity, 'sweetened' by vanilla oak, but, like **17** ⑧⑥'s, would benefit from year/2 to fully settle, meld.

Merlot ⓥ ★★★★☆ Chocolate-coated plum & mulberry fruit on **17** ⑧③ sufficiently intense, juicy, to cushion firmer than usual tannins. **Pinotage** ⓥ ★★★★ Piquant **18** ⑧③, attractive & unusual rosepetal & Turkish delight whiffs, cranberry flavour, firm tannin handshake. WO Coastal, as next 3. **Dry Red** ⓥ ★★★ Wallet-pleasing **NV** ⑧② from wider-sourced grapes, various varieties smoothed by few grams sugar, slides down easily. Also in 1.5L. **Pinotage Rosé** ⓥ ★★★ Zesty & dry **19** ⑧②, palest pink, with mulberry & herb appeal, restrained 12.5% alcohol for lingering lunches. **Rosé** ⓥ ★★★ A happy pink, lightish (12.5% alcohol) & off-dry. **19** ⑦ from Paarl & Wellington, mostly pinotage with French & Italian partners. **Chardonnay** ★★★☆ Previewed **19** ⑧ echoes previous bottlings in its partial, brief oak exposure (20% new), adding nutty veneer to lemon & peach nuances, decent acidity & length. **Chenin Blanc** ⊘ ★★★ **19** ⑧ usual effortlessly drinkable self, with peaches & papaya, touch sugar & 12.5% alcohol. WO Coastal, like next. **Sauvignon Blanc** ★★★ Everyday enjoyment delivered by lightish, fruity & vivacious **19** ⑧. **Special Late Harvest** ★★★★ Fairly intense tropical tones & gentle sweetness in **19** ⑧ viognier, gewürztraminer duo.

Kosher range
Not tasted: **Merlot, Pinotage, Chardonnay, Méthode Cap Classique Brut, Kiddush Sacramental Wine**.

Fortified range
★★★★ **Pinneau** ⓥ Pineau des Charentes-style dessert, gewürztraminer & roussanne juice fortified with 10-year-old house brandy. **17** ⑧ elegant marzipan, lemon & vanilla fusion with staying power. First since **10** ★★★★ ⑧ oak-matured chenin.

Cape Vintage Reserve ⓥ ★★★☆ Obvious fortification (own 10-year brandy) on nose & palate of full-bore **17** ⑧ 'port' from barbera & zinfandel. Long & firm, tannin for keeping few years, not over-sweet.

Brandy range
★★★★ **Sydney Back First Distillation** Darkly pungent bouquet on this deep-amber 27+ year old ⑧, distilled in 1991, & a fine intensity & rich sweetness. Slightly oxidative - with even a sherry-like echo. Undoubtedly rather fascinating, but less fresh than the younger versions. 60 bottles released per year.

★★★★☆ **Sydney Back 15 Year** Floral notes starting to emerge, with a greater complexity of fruit & wood-derived character than on 10 year old. Subtler & more elegantly refined & integrated, less sweet & fiery. Some mature satisfaction here. Potstill ⑨ from chenin, as are all these.

★★★★ **Sydney Back 10 Year** Heady, fruity aromas with notes of dark honey & tobacco on 10 year old brandy ⑧. Supple & silky, with a well-controlled fieriness & a rich caramel sweetness.— CvZ, TJ

Location: Paarl ▪ Map: Franschhoek ▪ Map grid reference: B8 ▪ WO: Paarl/Coastal ▪ Est 1916 ▪ 1stB 1970 ▪ Tasting & sales Mon-Fri 9—5 Sat/Sun 10—4 ▪ Fee R50/premium tasting, R60/exclusive tasting ▪ Open 365 days a year ▪ Cellar tours by appt ▪ Self-guided tours of the cellar, brandy cellar, winery & historic corridors ▪ Wine pairings: chocolate & wine; cheese & wine ▪ Backsberg Restaurant ▪ Facilities for children ▪ Tour groups ▪ Conferences ▪ Weddings & functions ▪ Pre-ordered picnics ▪ Environmental talks (by appt only) ▪ Sunday picnic concerts (in summer) ▪ Sydney Back potstill brandy ▪ Owner(s) Michael & Simon Back ▪ Winemaker(s) Alicia Rechner (Jun 2012) ▪ Viticulturist(s) Morné Olivier (Dec 2018) ▪ 70ha (cab, merlot, ptage, shiraz, chard, sauv) ▪ 900t/160,000cs own label 65% red 30% white 5% rosé ▪ Other export brands: Tread Lightly ▪ WWF-SA Conservation Champion ▪ PO Box 537 Suider-Paarl 7624 ▪ info@backsberg.co.za ▪ www.backsberg.co.za ▪ S 33° 49' 42.9" E 018° 54' 56.9" ▪ ⒨ leaven.juror.merrily ▪ **T +27 (0)21-875-5141**

☐ **Badenhorst Family Wines** see AA Badenhorst Family Wines

Bader & Walters Family Wines
Walter Bader was literally born into the industry — at Koopmanskloof, where his namesake father made wine before moving to Riebeek Cellars (now Riebeek Valley Wine Co). In 1998, Walter jnr founded Viva Africa Wines, under whose banner this portfolio debuted last edition. The offering has since been expanded with a trio of upper-tier varietal wines from Stellenbosch and a Bordeaux blend in the Bader & Walters range.

Full Circle-Water of Life range ⓝⓔⓦ
Cabernet Sauvignon ★★★☆ Good varietal character in **16** ⑧, cassis fruit aroma/flavour, refreshing acidity & lively tannins. Well-knit, with some bottle-age character suggesting it's time to drink. **Pinotage** ★★★☆ Perhaps more Xmas cake fruit & spice than pinotage's mulberry typicity in **16** ⑧, but flavoursome & easy to like. Still brooding, so no rush to drink. **Shiraz** ★★★☆ Appealing red fruit spiced with black pepper, juicy core & smooth, supple structure on **16** ⑧.

Bader & Walters range
Cabernet Sauvignon ⓥ ★★★ Fresh & fruity **16** ⑧ doesn't shout 'cab' but has enough flavour & mouthfeel for uncomplicated early enjoyment. WO W Cape, as Pinotage & Shiraz Rosé. **Merlot** ⓝⓔⓦ ★★★

Lightly oaked (as all these reds) **18** (82), intensely sweet aromas of plum & chocolate yet palate is dry, has good tannic grip for food partnering. **Pinotage** (ℚ) ★★★ Appealing varietal aromas of plums, mulberries & banana; zesty acidity, juicy tannins a hidden strength; **16** (82) ticks all year-round drinking boxes. **Shiraz** ★★★ Ready to drink **18** (81), subtle vanilla & coffee from year in barrel, slippery-smooth tannins. **Merlot-Cabernet Sauvignon** (NEW) (✓) ★★★★ Chocolate & plum appeal on **18** (83), hint of tar but mostly packed with dark fruit, few grams sugar up drinkability, like all the reds. **Shiraz Rosé** (ℚ) ★★ Undaunting 13% alcohol, smoothing few grams sugar in the tail, **17** (74) deep-pink poolside sipper. **Sauvignon Blanc** ★★★ Cool green-grass notes, figs & gooseberries in bouquet & on palate, well-judged acid refreshment in **19** (82). — CvZ

Location: Riebeek-Kasteel ▪ WO: Stellenbosch/Western Cape ▪ Est 1998 ▪ 1stB 2017 ▪ Closed to public ▪ Online sales ▪ Owner(s) Viva Africa Wines (member Walter Bader) ▪ Cellarmaster(s) Walter Bader ▪ Winemaker(s) Johan Joubert (consultant) & Dirk Tredoux (consultant) ▪ Viticulturist(s) Johan Joubert (consultant) ▪ 100,000 L own label 60% red 25% white 15% rosé + 10,000cs for clients ▪ PO Box 548 Moorreesburg 7310 ▪ walter@bwine.co.za ▪ www.bwines.co.za ▪ **T +27 (0)65-971-1788**

Badsberg Wine Cellar

The trophy case at this established grower-owned Breedekloof winery is groaning under the weight of the silverware won at the Young Wine Show last year. While it's the sweet fortifieds and botrytis dessert wines that most attract some 2,000 attendees to its annual Soetes & Soup winter festival, the unfortified dry wines saw the team rewarded with the Pietman Hugo Trophy for winery with the best results overall.

★★★★ **Pinotage Generaal Smuts** (ℚ) Seriously conceived & modern, **16** (87) vibrant ruby colour follows through with red fruit profile, firm tannin structure & length. Elegant, shows fine complexity.

★★★★ **Chardonnay Sur Lie** (ℚ) Big mouthful aimed at fans of oaky style - 8 months mix French/Hungarian wood. **17** ★★★★ (83) citrus lightness lifts it gently. **15** (87) better balanced. No **16**.

★★★★★ **Badslese** (ℚ) Unwooded Natural Sweet dessert from chenin & muscat d'Alexandrie; only in best years (no **10**, **11**). With muscat portion upped to 30%, **12** ★★★★★ (92) is pure indulgence: melting quince, melon & grape flavours, as scintillating & precise as **09**, our 2012 White Wine of the Year.

★★★★☆ **Noble Late Harvest** (ℚ) Brulee apricot on beautifully poised **17** (90) botrytis dessert. Acid deftly balances rich sweetness (196 g/l sugar); lovely concentration, body & length with clean dry finish. Low alcohol. 375 ml.

★★★★ **Red Muscadel** (ℚ) Seductive florality of copper-hued **17** (87) fortified balances smooth sweetness, perfumed muscat typicity, spice & puréed plum flavour with defined, dry-seeming finish.

Merlot (✓) ★★★ Soft, fruity & juicy **18** (82), uncomplicated quaffer with coffee-toned tail. Also in 3L pack. **Pinotage** ★★★☆ Plush, gentle **18** (83) offers subtle spice & black fruit. Structure from 6 months in French oak. Medium body & length. **Belladonna** (✓) ★★★★ Bonfire edge to fleshy, black-fruited **17** (83) blend of equal parts cab, merlot, shiraz & petit verdot & 2 others. Light-bodied everyday appeal. **Perlé Moscato** (✓) ★★★ Tangy succulence to sweet, raspberry-toned, low-alcohol **19** (77) muscat rosé. **Barrel Fermented Chenin Blanc** (ℚ) ★★★★ Youthful **16** (84) rich & rounded, generous apricot, baked apple & clove aromas & flavours from 5 months oak ageing. **Chenin Blanc** ★★★ **19** (78) offers guava & tropical simplicity in a light body. Ideal for summer. **Sauvignon Blanc** ★★★ Grapefruit piquancy to unfussy zesty **19** (77) quaffer. Also in 3L cask. **Vin Doux** ★★★ Nice balance of grapey sweetness & acid zing on **18** (81) floral, sweet muscat sparkler. Low alcohol. **Hanepoot Jerepigo** ★★★ Jasmine & barley sugar sweetness (202 g/l RS) on **18** (82) fortified precedes a spirity mid-palate. Muscat permeates the aftertaste. **Red Jerepigo** ★★★☆ From pinotage, **18** (85) continues form of previous in bright, super-sweet cherry flavour. Balanced fortification & long finish. **Cape Vintage** (ℚ) ★★★★ Sweet, soft & dusty - more like 'fortified red wine' than 'port', needs more zip & grip. **13** (83) from undisclosed varieties. — FM

Location: Rawsonville ▪ Map/WO: Breedekloof ▪ Map grid reference: B5 ▪ Est 1951 ▪ 1stB 1958 ▪ Tasting & sales Mon-Fri 9—5 Sat 10—1 ▪ Fee R20pp ▪ Closed all pub hols ▪ Cellar tours by appt ▪ Facilities for children ▪ Farm produce ▪ Conferences (40 pax) ▪ Conservation area ▪ Soetes & Soup (Jul) ▪ Owner(s) 26 members ▪ Cellarmaster(s) Willie Burger (1998) ▪ Winemaker(s) Henri Swiegers (2002), with Stian Victor (2017) & Jaco Booysen (Jan 2007) ▪ Viticulturist(s) Shazell van den Berg (2017) ▪ ±1,500ha/±1,300ha (ptage, shiraz, chenin, cbard) ▪ ±30,000t ▪ 20% red 65% white 10% rosé 5% fortified ▪ ISO 22000:2009, IPW, WIETA ▪ PO

Box 72 Rawsonville 6845 ▪ info@badsberg.co.za ▪ www.badsberg.co.za ▪ S 33° 39' 40.1" E 019° 16' 9.2" ▪ 🔲
overlaying.layout.nettle ▪ T +27 (0)23-344-3021

☐ **Bag-in-Box Collection** *see* Jacques Germanier
☐ **Bainskloof** *see* Bergsig Estate
☐ **Balance** *see* Overhex Wines International
☐ **Bald Ibis** *see* Mile High Vineyards

Baleia Wines

There is surely mutual delight with the Joubert family's appointment of seasoned Stellenbosch winemaker Gunter Schultz (most recently of Tamboerskloof) as cellarmaster/GM of Baleia Wines. Their boutique venture draws from maturing limestone-rooted vines close to the southern Cape coast, a double delight for the surfing fanatic. He joins a vigorous young team: 3rd-generation Jan-Hendrik jnr also oversees olive groves, a merino sheep and angus cattle stud; sister Lizeth runs the Riversdale winery's La Bella eatery/deli and tasting room, the latter featuring a beautiful suspended sculpture of a whale, referencing the winery name.

Director's Reserve range

★★★★ **Sebastian** Singular, accomplished **17** (88) tempranillo, syrah, pinot noir blend has body, substance & refinement, showing intense black fruit laced with floral perfume. 12 months in barriques, 40% new. **16** untasted.

Baleia Wines range

★★★★ **Erhard Pinot Noir** ⊘ Prominent raspberries & violets on very appealing **16** (89). Impressive varietal focus, body & substance, with lingering perfumed finish, velvety tannins. No **15**.

★★★★ **Syrah** Unorthodox quince & rhubarb fruit, supple & juicy **17** (86) reflects cool Riversdale origin. Light body, with appealing peppery spice, hints of fynbos. Year in French oak barrels. **16** untasted.

★★★★ **Tempranillo** Characterful New World interpretation of Rioja's great variety, **17** (86) is elegantly lean & spicy, with savoury backbone. Plush texture from 12 months in mostly older barrels. **16** untasted.

★★★★ **Inge Chardonnay** Oak-dominated **15** (86) has body & substance, with caramel-infused lemon fruit. Should settle & integrate. 70% fermented in barrel, 30% open amphora. Riper, more extroverted than **14** ★★★★ (85).

★★★★ **Tempranillo Port** (NEW) Rich, plummy **15** (87) has fine spirit grip, tobacco & anise spiciness. Full-sweet (112 g/l), with restrained 19% alcohol, generous body & fruit. Winter nectar in 375 ml.

Deborah Rosé (NEW) ★★★★ Appealingly fruity-floral **19** (83), mostly syrah, is bone-dry, fresh & light, with mineral twist at finish. **Sauvignon Blanc** ★★★★ Pungent gooseberry/sweaty notes on ripe & cheerful **19** (85), with khaki bush, well-harnessed acidity, decent heft. — GdB

Location: Riversdale ▪ Map: Klein Karoo & Garden Route ▪ Map grid reference: C6 ▪ WO: Cape South Coast ▪ Est 2010 ▪ 1stB 2011 ▪ Tasting, sales & cellar tours Mon-Fri 9-5 Sat/pub hols 10-3 ▪ Olive oil ▪ Facilities for children ▪ Deli for refreshments/meals; or BYO picnic ▪ Pet-friendly area ▪ Videira Country House, luxury self-catering accommodation ▪ Hiking, biking & bird watching ▪ Owner(s) Fanie & Jan-Hendrik Joubert ▪ Winemaker(s) Gunter Schultz ▪ 1,000ha/9.5ha (pinot, shiraz, tempranillo, chard, sauv) ▪ 80t/600cs own label 60% red 40% white ▪ PO Box 268 Riversdale 6670 ▪ admin@baleiawines.com ▪ www.baleiawines.com ▪ S 34° 6' 36.89" E 021° 15' 18.48" ▪ 🔲 ponytailed.accent.request ▪ T +27 (0)28-713-1214

☐ **Bales Choice** *see* Wade Bales Wine Co
☐ **Balthazar** *see* Roodezandt Wines
☐ **Bamboes Bay** *see* Fryer's Cove Vineyards
☐ **Bandana** *see* Klein Roosboom
☐ **Baratok Wines** *See* Editor's Note
☐ **Barber's Wood** *see* Celestina

Barista

Bertus Fourie earned a place in SA wine's hall of fame by creating overtly mocha-toned pinotage (via selected grapes, specific yeasts, special oak treatment) while at Diemersfontein and KWV in the 2000s, spawning an entire 'coffee' genre. A whiz in the kitchen, too, 'Starbucks' has made this Vinimark wine from inception, and seen production volumes treble since debut in this guide a decade ago.

Pinotage ⓥ ★★★★☆ **19** unready at press time. **18** ⑧③ signature mocha aroma along with toffee & cherry liqueur, juicy plum & mulberry flavours. Freshness, moderate alcohol ensure food compatibility. — JG

Location/WO: Robertson ▪ Est/1stB 2009 ▪ Closed to public ▪ Owner(s) Vinimark ▪ Winemaker(s) Bertus Fourie ▪ 750t/100,000cs own label ▪ PO Box 6223 Paarl 7620 ▪ info@vinimark.co.za ▪ www.baristawine.co.za ▪ **T +27 (0)21-883-8043**

Barnardt Boyes Wines

From offices on Dorp Street in the heart of Stellenbosch, Barnardt Boyes distributes a number of wine brands to markets in more than 20 countries. The venture is part of a diverse group which has two university friends, John Boyes and Neels Barnardt, with extensive experience in agriculture and the wine industry respectively, at its centre. See separate listing for Carrol Boyes Collection.

Dorp Street range

Cabernet Sauvignon ⓥ ★★★ Appealing **16** ⑧① quite serious dark-fruit aromas, yet flavours are easygoing, fruity, with smoky twirl. Range celebrates 'historic, oak-hugged' Stellenbosch avenue. **Rosé** ⓝⓔⓦ ★★ Pretty pink pétillant **NV** ⑦⑤ light in alcohol (7.5%) & sweet, infused with tiny party-starting bubbles. **Sauvignon Blanc** ⓥ ★★ Naturally fermented **17** ⑦⑥ no mistaking the variety: grassy & zippy, brush of oak gives some palate weight for food pairing. — CvZ

Location/WO: Stellenbosch ▪ Est 2012 ▪ 1stB 2009 ▪ Closed to public ▪ Owner(s) N Barnardt & J Boyes ▪ 50,000cs own label 50% red 50% white ▪ Other export brands: Carrol Boyes Collection ▪ neels@barnardt-boyes.com, marketing@barnardtboyes.com ▪ www.barnardtboyes.com ▪ **T +27 (0)82-457-3316**

☐ **Baron Diego** see Govert Wines
☐ **Barony** see Rosendal Wines
☐ **Barrel Selection 008** see Imbuko Wines

Barrydale Winery & Distillery ⓠ ⓡ ◎

The team led by Jandre Human have recently diversified into craft beer brewing (and they highly recommend that you pair their Barry Ale and Lady Lager with the home-made pizza from the on-site restaurant on the outskirts of Barrydale town), but their mainstays are wine and Cape brandy. The latter is widely acclaimed and stylishly presented, and prominently features the 19th-century liquor tradesman Joseph Barry, who innovatively deployed a fleet of riverboats to transport goods along the Breede River.

Southern Cape Vineyards range

Shiraz ⓥ ★★★ Brims with berries & cherries, **16** ⑧⓪ soft & juicy for easy drinking (easy on the wallet, too). **Ruby Cabernet-Merlot** ⓥ ★★ Plummy merlot (20%) apparent on **17** ⑦④'s nose, not so much on the palate, which is rather stern, with sour cherry character. **Chardonnay** ⓥ ★★★ Unoaked **18** ⑧② is very smooth, subtle ginger & turmeric adding spice to zesty tangerine & citrus. **Chenin Blanc** ⓥ ★★★ White peach, guava & tangy tangerine on **18** ⑧⓪ with modest alcohol for uncomplicated summer refreshment. **Sauvignon Blanc** ⓥ ★★★ Easy-drinking **18** ⑧① shows textbook greenpepper on nose, lime on palate, zesty & balanced at 12.5% alcohol.

Cape Brandy range

★★★★★ **Joseph Barry XO** Modern packaging for complex & serious 10 year old potstill ⑨③ full & rounded with lingering vanilla on the finish, opulent dark fruit notes of prunes with some dried apricot & toasted nut. Attention to detail: bottling date included.

★★★★ **Ladismith Klein Karoo 8 Year Old** Gorgeous glistening gold potstill ⑧⑨ is delicate, harmonious & silky smooth, with dried apricot, caramelised nut & vanilla chocolate appeal. As all, only 150 cases of this new batch from colombard & chenin (replacing ugni blanc) released.

★★★★ **Joseph Barry VSOP** More power than VS in darker-hued 5 year old potstill ⑧⑧ Rich macerated plums, prunes, hints of toffee apple & dried herbs delight on rounded & smooth palate. 40% alcohol perfectly in sync, as throughout the range.

★★★★ **Joseph Barry VS** Matured 3 years, this new ⑧⑥ bottling improves on previous. Fruity & fresh, with soft dried-peach, pear drop & nut flavours on lively palate. Produced in traditional Woudberg copper stills, as all these finely crafted brandies.— JG, WB

Location: Barrydale ▪ Map: Klein Karoo & Garden Route ▪ Map grid reference: C7 ▪ WO: Klein Karoo ▪ Est 1941 ▪ 1stB 1976 ▪ Tasting & sales Tue-Fri 9–5 Sat 9–4 Sun 9-3 ▪ Fee R25 for groups of 5+ ▪ Closed Easter Fri-Mon, Dec 25/26 & Jan 1 ▪ Restaurant ▪ Craft beer brewery ▪ Owner(s) Southern Cape Vineyards (SCV) ▪ Winemaker(s) Jandre Human ▪ ±110ha (cab, merlot, shiraz, chard, cbard, sauv) ▪ 28% red 72% white ▪ PO Box 56 Ladismith 6655 ▪ info@josephbarry.co.za ▪ www.josephbarry.co.za ▪ S 33° 54' 35.83" E 020° 42' 45.20" ▪ ⟨w⟩ unlock.playground.subscriptions ▪ **T +27 (0)28-572-1012**

Barry Gould Family Wines ⓆⓎⓂⓄⒶ

'Natural' has been the approach of architect Barry Gould and family since they began growing wine on a small scale 17 years ago, and 'unhurried, to say the least' the tempo of releases from their Elgin base - '09 being the current offering (which Barry feels 'could last longer', so no rush to broach). Visitor facilities, as might be expected, are rooted in farm life, and include a country house, walking trails and fresh produce.

A Simple Red ★★★ On its 10th birthday, **09** ⑧⓪ drinks easily & well. Fragrant, subtle, with plums & savoury herbs, vanilla note from old-barrique ageing of cab & merlot (50/50), wild yeast fermented. — WB

Location/map/WO: Elgin ▪ Map grid reference: D2 ▪ Est 2003 ▪ 1stB 2004 ▪ Tasting & sales by appt ▪ Closed Good Fri, Dec 25 & Jan 1 ▪ Meals/functions by arrangement (up to 20 pax) ▪ Wildekrans Country House (B&B) + self-catering cottage ▪ Child-friendly ▪ Gifts ▪ Farm produce ▪ Conference venue (20 pax) ▪ 4-day fully guided slack-packing trail ▪ Owner(s) Barry Gould & Alison Green ▪ Cellarmaster(s) Barry Gould (2003) ▪ Winemaker(s) Barry Gould (2003), with family (2004) ▪ Viticulturist(s) Grapes bought in ▪ 50cs own label 100% red ▪ PO Box 7 Elgin 7180 ▪ barry@barrygould.co.za ▪ S 34° 12' 12.7" E 019° 8' 53.6" ▪ ⟨w⟩ reduce. explicated.conclude ▪ **T +27 (0)21-848-9788/+27 (0)82-901-4896**

Bartho Eksteen ⓆⓎⓄ

The Eksteens say they've been growing wine since 1702, when German ancestor Heinrich Oostwald Eckstein arrived at the Cape, but most recently (and most successfully) at their Hemel-en-Aarde farm, Attaquaskloof. Here award-winning Bartho Eksteen has a two-tier business model: crafting exceptional wines (assisted by son Pieter Willem) in boutique quantities, and running an academy for young winemakers and distillers (see Wijnskool, listed separately). 'Titles, trophies and other awards now make room for the ultimate reward: to see my son budding as a winemaker,' he says. Eksteen junior reports that the range will be expanding to include pinot noir, the red grape for which the area is famous. 'When in Rome, do as the Romans do!'

CWG Auction Reserves

★★★★ **Professore** Ⓐ **16** ⑧⑧ thought to be a first: Cape Blend of 3 SA crosses (pinotage, roobernet, white grape nouvelle) honouring their creators, profs Perold & Orffer. **17** ★★★★☆ ⑨⓪ benefits from more pinotage (81%), 21 months in 100% new French oak adding hints of clove & star anise to black plum & cherry fruit. WO W Cape, as Groepsdruk & Ouskool.

★★★★☆ **Vloekskoot** Ⓐ Wooded sauvignon impresses in **18** ⑨④ with fynbos aromatics, green apple & lime (fruit & zest), elegant balance between dense mouthfeel & bright acidity, less than 12.5% alcohol. Wild ferment/10 months in old 500L oak.

Flagship range

★★★★☆ **Groepsdruk** Ⓠ The best barrel (new French) of **16** ⑨① Ouskool has 13% each mourvèdre & grenache plus dash viognier to spice up syrah's intense black & red cherry/berry fruit. Floral, herbal & meaty notes, fresh acidity balancing 14.5% alcohol.

★★★★☆ **Houtskool** Ⓐ Even more structure & orange/lime verve in **18** ⑨③ than gorgeously concentrated **17** ★★★★★ ⑨⑤, now equal sauvignon & semillon wild-fermented/10 months in older oak for lemon curd creaminess. Richer than CWG white, with slightly higher alcohol (13%) but no less elegant.

Signature range

★★★★ **Ouskool** Ⓐ Rhône-style red with violet, smoke & pepper aromas, ripe dark fruit, **17** ⑧⑦ syrah with 22% mourvèdre, splashes grenache, viognier, well-knit after 21 months in new oak but also high in alcohol (15.6%). In magnum too, as Houtskool, Blom & Dom.

★★★★☆ **Blom** Exceptional Provence-style dry rosé, ferment with untoasted French oak chips adds creaminess to peach, raspberry, strawberry & red apple fruit of **19** ⑨②, 48% grenache with syrah, mourvèdre, viognier. For luxurious seafood. Coastal WO.

★★★★ **Meester** New bottling of **17** ⑧⑧ features same varieties (sauvignon, 7% semillon) but has no oak. Smooth, with toned-down acidity after year in bottle, offers fresh lime, gooseberry, granadilla.

★★★★☆ **Dom** ⓐ Aged 20 months on lees, elegant **16** ⑨③ méthode cap classique sparkler has almond cream richness, steely-clean finish, red apple, pear & stonefruit flavours from 52% pinot noir, 44% chardonnay, splash meunier. Previous releases were non-vintage.

★★★★☆ **Soetmuis** After 3-year break, their sweet treat returns in **19** ⑨⓪ as Noble Late Harvest from Upper Hemel-en-Aarde sauvignon (one of few made with that variety). Fresh & peachy, the lively acidity amply balancing 114 g/l sugar for a lovely uncloying glassful. Bunch pressed & tank fermented. Last **15** ⑨⓪ Natural Sweet ex Paarl old-vine chenin. 375 ml.

★★★★ **Bedjie Toe** ⓃⒺⓌ Delightful husk spirit ⑧⑨ is water white, fragrant, with plums, dark berries & wild herbs, palate smooth & creamy. Name recommends this as nightcap, but that's probably only the endgame! From sangiovese, cab & mourvèdre. 200 & 500 ml.— JG, WB

Location: Hermanus ▪ Map: Walker Bay & Bot River ▪ Map grid reference: A3 ▪ WO: Upper Hemel-en-Aarde Valley/Western Cape/Coastal ▪ Est/1stB 2015 ▪ Tasting & sales Mon-Sat 10-4 ▪ Closed Good Fri, Dec 16/25 & Jan 1 ▪ Cellar tours by appt ▪ Kitchen open for lunch Thu-Sat ▪ Conferences ▪ Functions & events ▪ MTB ▪ Historic building ▪ Husk spirit ▪ Owner(s) Eksteen family ▪ Winemaker(s) Bartho Eksteen (Jan 2015) & Pieter Willem Eksteen (Jan 2015) ▪ Viticulturist(s) various ▪ 5ha total ▪ 4,540cs own label 34% red 37% white 19% rosé 10% MCC ▪ PO Box 1999 Hermanus 7200 ▪ bartho@hermanus.co.za, sune@hermanus.co.za ▪ www.barthoeksteen.co.za ▪ S 34° 23' 57.31" E 019° 13' 1.17" ▪ ⓦ founds.siding.evicted ▪ **T +27 (0)82-920-7108 (Bartho), +27 (0)72-323-5060 (Suné)**

Bartinney Private Cellar   Ⓨ ⑪ ⓐ ⓞ ⓑ

Architect Rose Jordaan, owner of this scenic property in Stellenbosch's Banhoek Valley with venture capitalist and banker husband Michael, is an eco-warrior. She has banished alien invasive species, replanted indigenous vegetation, ensured carbon neutrality and biodiversity conservation champion status, not to mention re-purposing old oak staves on mountain bike and running trails which snake throughout the farm. Uprooted vine stumps have been turned into decor for the increasingly popular tasting room (drawing visitors with its unique meringue, fynbos and gin tastings), while felled trees were recycled into roofing trusses in the newest guest cottage, one of four on the estate. Loving the seasonal wine (and gin) 'challenge' is the only female winner of the sought-after Diners Club Winemaker of the Year title to date, Ronell Wiid.

Reserve range

★★★★☆ **Skyfall Cabernet Sauvignon** ⓨ Bolder than Bartinney sibling yet **14** ⑨③ elegant, refined, perhaps even tad demure on finish. Seductive Xmas pudding, cherry & tobacco on structured, firm & complex palate, fruit well-framed by oak, 18 months, 80% new French. Needs time.

★★★★☆ **Hourglass Chardonnay** ⓨ Special fruit selection from favoured high vineyard. Firm & svelte, **17** ⑨③ has yet to show its true colours, the vibrant lime flavours & creamy French oak (half new, 11 months) still at the tango-dancing stage, marriage & blissful harmony inevitable but a way off.

Bartinney range

★★★★★ **Cabernet Sauvignon** ⓐ Elegant **16** ★★★★★ ⑨② less overt than **15** ⑨⑤. Focused & refined, with cocoa earthiness to firm-bodied palate. Good concentration & harmony of cassis fruit & oak (50% new, 18 months). Deserves to be cellared.

★★★★☆ **Elevage** ⓨ Cab & petit verdot share near-equal billing in spicy, dry mouthful with merlot. **12** ⑨② blackcurrant notes temper firm grip from 50% new French oak, 12- 18 months. Certain to age well for years. Stellenbosch WO.

★★★★★ **Chardonnay** ⓐ Taut **18** ⑨② shows interplay of bright citrus with creamy breadth from barrel ferment & 11 months in oak, 33% new - like stellar **15** ★★★★★ ⑨⑤. Supple, rich & elegant, long finish. Allow time to show true colours.

★★★★ **Sauvignon Blanc** Elderflower nuance vies with zesty but rounded lemon & grapefruit typicity on **19** ⑧⑥. Refreshingly vibrant with lees breadth. Like **18** ★★★★ ⑧⑤, tasted pre-bottling.— FM

Find South Africa's best wineries with what3words

Every winery in Platter's Wine Guide is listed with its 3 word address. This refers to the precise location of the winery entrance. Enter the 3 word address into the free what3words app to make sure you arrive at the right place, relaxed and ready to enjoy South Africa's finest wines.

///dream.stardom.chart

Stellenbosch, Western Cape

Port2Port

Port2Port is South Africa's **largest fine wine marketplace**, featuring an ever growing catalogue of over 2000 products from 12 countries and arguably the **largest selection of 5 star Platter's wines available anywhere.** Rated South Africa's **best wine selection** two years running by Wine Searcher, we aim to offer you the world's finest wines sold directly from the producer at cellar door prices. **Because in the end, every bottle is SOMEONE'S story.**

Browse our wines and their stories on **port2port.wine**

BIG 5 SAFARI & SPA

Real Africa. Real Close To Cape Town.
Over 10 000-hectares of Big 5 conservancy.

AQUILA
PRIVATE GAME RESERVE
SAFARI & SPA

4-STAR ACCOMMODATION | SPA
GAME DRIVE | HORSEBACK & QUAD BIKE SAFARI

At the award-winning Aquila Private Game Reserve and Spa, guests will get the opportunity to experience a Big 5 safari, together with outstanding service; it just does not get any better than this. With game drives, quad bike and horseback safaris situated just 2 hours' drive from Cape Town, it's the closest you will get to real Africa, in the lap of luxury.

The world-class spa at Aquila adds to the already exceptional facilities and services on offer. It is a masterpiece of luxury, defined by its serenity and creative use of natural elements.

THE
LILIZELA
TOURISM AWARDS

FACILITIES & ACTIVITIES
4-STAR ESTABLISHMENT | PREMIER, FAMILY & LUXURY COTTAGES | LODGE ROOMS | DAY TRIP SAFARI | HORSEBACK SAFARI | QUAD BIKE SAFARI | STAR SAFARI | OVERNIGHT SAFARI | FLY-IN SAFARI | INDOOR & OUTDOOR RESTAURANTS | OUTDOOR POOL | WET BAR | CONFERENCE CENTRE | SPA | CURIO SHOP | CHILDREN'S FACILITIES & JUNIOR RANGER PROGRAMME

www.aquilasafari.com   AquilaSafari   AquilaSafaris

+27 (0)21 430 7260 or RES@AQUILASAFARI.COM

Location/map: Stellenbosch ▪ Map grid reference: H5 ▪ WO: Banghoek/Stellenbosch ▪ Est 2006 ▪ 1stB 2008 ▪ Tasting & sales Mon-Thu 12–5 Fri 12–8 Sat 10–3 ▪ Various tasting & pairing experiences offered; cheese & charcuterie platters ▪ Closed Dec 25/26 & Jan 1 ▪ Cellar tours by appt ▪ Bartinney Wine & Champagne Bar Mon–Sat 11.30–9 (T +27 (0)76-348-5374, 5 Bird Str Stellenbosch) ▪ MTB trails ▪ Annual trail run events ▪ Monthly live music events ▪ Vineyard guest cottages ▪ Craft beer & gin ▪ Owner(s) Rose & Michael Jordaan ▪ Winemaker(s) Ronell Wiid (consultant) ▪ Viticulturist(s) Logan Jooste (Jun 2017) ▪ 27ha/±17ha (cab, chard, sauv) ▪ 100t/4,000cs own label 70% red 30% white ▪ WWF-SA Conservation Champion ▪ Postnet Suite 231 Private Bag X5061 Stellenbosch 7599 ▪ info@bartinney.co.za, tastingshed@bartinney.co.za ▪ www.bartinney. co.za ▪ S 33° 55' 34.66" E 018° 55' 56.79" ▪ ⌖ logs.twisting.unscrew ▪ **T +27 (0)21-885-1013**

Barton Vineyards

Only one new vintage to taste this edition, as the team at the Neill family winery have been focused on selling existing stocks. Bottling will resume this year, however, under the careful watch of consultant winemaker Kobie Viljoen, who also makes his Villion wines here. The elegant Barton label features SA's national bird, the vulnerable blue crane, which has a breeding ground on the tracts of fynbos that make up most of this extensive hillside property near Bot River, and benefits, via conservation efforts, from a portion of sales.

★★★★ **Merlot** ⓥ Typical fruitcake, chocolate aromas & dry herbal twist on **15** ⑧⑧. Light-fruited sweetness (but dry enough finish). Oaking supportive (30% new). Tannins assertive, but a pleasing whole.

★★★★ **Winemakers Reserve** Splendid, complex & bold **15** ⑧⑦. Pencil shavings & crushed herbs pave way to lively mulberry & blackcurrant flavours, firm tannin grip from 22 months in oak, 20 new. Merlot-led Bordeaux blend, with cab & dab malbec. WO Walker Bay, as Rosé.

Rouge ⓥ ★★★ Pleasant & balanced, lightish-flavoured 6-way blend of Bordeaux & Rhône varieties. **15** ⑧① not dumbed down, but seriously styled for drinking over next few years. **Pinot Noir Rosé** ⓥ ★★★ Customary notes of raspberry with earthy hint on dry, salmon pink **18** ⑧②. Soft texture, but a good acid bite for freshness. **Chenin Blanc** ⓥ ★★★★ Forward, fruity & friendly aromas & flavours (mostly tending to the tropical side of things) on **17** ⑧④. It's juicy & impeccably balanced, with some real substance to it. Drinkable as ever. Not tasted: **Shiraz-Cabernet Sauvignon**, **Sauvignon Blanc**. — GM

Location: Bot River ▪ Map: Walker Bay & Bot River ▪ Map grid reference: B2 ▪ WO: Bot River/Walker Bay ▪ Est 2001 ▪ 1stB 2003 ▪ Tasting, sales & cellar tours Mon–Fri 9–5 Sat 10–4 ▪ Closed Easter Fri/Mon, Dec 25/26 & Jan 1 ▪ Lavender products, olive oil ▪ Barton Villas ▪ Owner(s) Annie & Suzy Neill ▪ Cellarmaster(s)/winemaker(s) Kobie Viljoen (Jan 2018, consultant) ▪ Viticulturist(s) consultants ▪ 200ha/30ha (cab, malbec, merlot, mourv, pinot, shiraz, chenin, sauv, sem) ▪ 120t/20,000cs own label 40% red 50% white 10% rosé ▪ IPW ▪ PO Box 100 Bot River 7185 ▪ info@bartonvineyards.co.za ▪ www.bartonvineyards.co.za ▪ S 34° 15' 43.8" E 019° 10' 29.2" ▪ ⌖ bracing.pick.ogled ▪ **T +27 (0)28-284-9283**

Bayede!

Bayede! is the traditional greeting reserved for the Zulu king. The bead-adorned wines and superb new spirit, sourced from top producers, are integral to what's believed to be one of Africa's first royal-signature 'by appointment' brands. It's focused on enterprise development, job creation and promotion of various industry sectors. Recent successes include five gold or double-gold medals at the Michelangelo awards.

7 Icon Wines

★★★★ **Pinotage Reserve** Rich **16** ⑧⑦ from Stellenbosch has black berries on the nose, super-plump fruit yet a fresh crispness, too, for balance, slightly warm vanilla-toned finish (14.8% alcohol).

Not tasted: **Cabernet Sauvignon**, **Merlot**, **Shiraz**, **Chardonnay**, **Sauvignon Blanc**.

King Shaka-Zulu range

Pinotage ★★★ Unoaked, uncomplicated **17** ⑦⑨ shows berry fruit & hints of spice. **Chenin Blanc** ★★★ Light-styled **19** ⑦⑧ misses playfulness of previous, has leaner body & briefer finish.

King & Queen range

King Goodwill Shiraz ⓥ ⓦ ★★★★ Improves on last with juicy mulberry, cured meat & leather flavours, good texture & dusty savoury notes on long finish in **17** ⑧③. Robertson WO, as next.

King Goodwill Jubilee ★★★ Cab, merlot, petit verdot in sweet, dark-fruited **18** (81). Juicy & uncompli-cated for everyday drinking. Not tasted: **Queen Nandi Méthode Cap Classique Brut Rosé**.

Prince range

Sauvignon Blanc (T) ★★★ Overflowing with tropical fruit, **19** (80) is bright & zingy, sweet pineapple tang to finish. Serve well-chilled.

Cabernet Sauvignon ★★★ Rounded & cheerful **18** (80), sweet black berries & cherries with oak spice farewell. Few grains of sugar aid drinkability. **Merlot** ★★★ Smooth & easy **18** (79) from Robertson charms with lively red fruit flavours & candied cherry aftertaste. **Pinotage** (⊘) ★★★ Everyday drinking pleasure in **18** (80), mocha & milk chocolate-dipped plums, dusty tannin grip on conclusion.

Princess range

Chardonnay-Pinot Noir (⅁) ★★★ Dry rosé with delicate pink hue, the colour & red berries courtesy **18** (81)'s 6% pinot noir component, the citrus finish from chardonnay. Robertson grapes.

Cape Brandy range (NEW)

★★★★☆ **XO Royal Cape Brandy** Handsome packaging for opulent 10 year old (93) from chenin, colombard & cinsaut, distilled in Elgin. Inviting amber glints lead to rich dried peach & pear aromas, smooth, full & rounded palate with dark chocolate, roasted nut & subtle spice. A triumph. — WB

Location/map: Paarl ▪ Map grid reference: E6 ▪ WO: Western Cape/Robertson/Stellenbosch ▪ Est 2009 ▪ Tasting & sales in showroom/office at 5 Stasie Str, Southern Paarl Mon-Fri or by appt ▪ Fee R30 ▪ Private VIP tastings at Villa Beanto Winelands Estate by appt only ▪ Closed pub hols ▪ Tour groups by appt ▪ 60% red 30% white 10% rosé ▪ PO Box 7362 Northern Paarl 7623 ▪ anto@bayede.co.za ▪ www.bayede.co.za ▪ S 33° 45' 54.77" E 018° 57' 41.03" ▪ ⌖ internal.avocado.reserved ▪ **T +27 (0)21-863-3406/+27 (0)83-650-3585**

☐ **Bayten** see Buitenverwachting
☐ **BC Wines** see Brandvlei Cellar
☐ **Beachhouse** see Douglas Green

Beau Constantia   (Q) (¶) (⊚)

'Big changes' at one of historic Constantia's younger vineyards, established by Pierre and Cecily du Preez in 2003 after buying this fire-ravaged Constantia Nek property and realising the viticultural potential of its precipitous slopes with their first wines (made off-site) in 2010. Assistant winemaker Megan van der Merwe steps up as winemaker-viticulturist, overseeing the renewing of low-yielding sauvignon, adding bushvine semillon (to up quantities of 'Pierre') and, 'most excitingly', planting pinot noir. Unchanged is the glass-fronted tasting centre and eatery with spectacular views (and artisan gins and vodkas adding allure).

★★★★★ **Stella** (⊛) Delectable **17** (92) from syrah shows meaty, malty core laced with pepper, scrub & maraschino cherry. Hands-off vinification (as all) produces unforced elegance & depth, silky texture & lingering finish. 18 months in small barrels, 33% new.

★★★★ **Lucca** Merlot & cab franc (61/39) is a harmonious blend of taut minerality & plush black fruit, with subtle liquorice notes. **16** (88) sleek, well-toned body cosseted in velvety tannins.

★★★★ **Aidan** (⊛) Muscular, opulently fruity **16** (89) is 29% shiraz with petit verdot, cab, malbec & merlot. Silky texture, plush berry fruit & well-judged oak, finishing with elegant length. 18 months in French barriques, 60% new.

★★★★ **Cecily** Varietally expressive **18** ★★★★★ (90) viognier shows deft handling of ripeness, acidity & wood, seldom achieved locally. Convincing white peach fruit with waxy-oily texture, tingling tartness & barely perceptible oak (though 100% barrel-fermented, like **17** (89)).

★★★★★ **Pierre** Barrel-fermented sauvignon & semillon, **18** ★★★★ (88) juicy apple fruit laced with nuts & salt, plumped out with lees, silky texture. Stylish but not quite as vibrant as **17** (90). — GdB

Location/WO: Constantia ▪ Map: Cape Peninsula ▪ Map grid reference: B3 ▪ Est 2003 ▪ 1stB 2010 ▪ Tasting & sales Tue-Sun 11-6 ▪ Fee R55, waved according to purchase ▪ Closed Good Fri, Dec 25/26 & Jan 1 ▪ Amphitheatre for concerts & outdoor events ▪ Chef's Warehouse ▪ Beau Constantia spirits (gin & vodka) available in tasting room ▪ Owner(s) Apostax (Pty) Ltd ▪ Winemaker(s)/viticulturist(s) Megan van der Merwe (2019) ▪ 22ha/±11ha (cabs s/f, malbec, merlot, p verdot, shiraz, sauv, sem, viog) ▪ 40t/4,000cs own label 80% red 20% white ▪ 1043

Constantia Main Rd, Constantia 7806 ▪ winesales@beauconstantia.com ▪ www.beauconstantia.com ▪ S 34° 0' 48.57" E 018° 24' 21.67" ▪ praises.wheeze.uninvolved ▪ **T +27 (0)21-794-8632**

Beaumont Family Wines

Historic Bot River farm Compagnes Drift, ca 1750, was purchased in 1974 by Jayne Beaumont and her larger-than-life late husband Raoul, who completely transformed it through 'hard work, a spirit for adventure and a proper dose of crazy'. It's now home to three generations (Jayne has seven grandchildren living on-site or nearby), with oldest son Sebastian in charge of both cellar (boasting a new press) and vineyards, where 'we are in the process of focusing on fewer grape varieties'. Meanwhile, Sebastian's wife Nici's Zest Catering partnership has been brought 'closer to the action' (next to the tasting room) to offer visitors 'a little more of a food experience', making this friendly family farm more welcoming than ever. See also listing 'Jayne's'.

★★★★☆ **Mourvèdre** From SA pioneers with this variety, powerful yet fresh **16** (91) combines savoury spice of **14** ★★★★ (88) with polished black berry fruit of **15** (90). Silky, seamless after 2 years in oak, 20% new.

★★★★ **Pinotage** Enticing rooibos tea aroma on previewed **17** (89). Middleweight but promises to be richer, smoother than **16** (86), with vibrant plum fruit easily handling slightly more (25%) new oak.

★★★★☆ **Dangerfield Syrah** Naturally fermented, 30% wholebunch in open vats, **17** (92) grips with a velvet glove, peppery freshness lifting dark fruit, 14 months in 20% new oak enhancing savoury spice impression. Also in 1.5 & 3L.

★★★★☆ **Ariane** Bordeaux blend named for founders Jayne & Raoul Beaumont's daughter. Brother Sebastian's self-declared 'best-yet' vintage is elegantly styled, has a 'cool' cabernet linearity, the antithesis of plush. **16** (90) demands & deserves time in your cellar to meld. 20 months oak, 22% new.

★★★★☆ **Vitruvian** Eclectic flagship blend, made only in best vintages, 45% mourvèdre in **16** (94), co-fermented with cab franc, pinotage & syrah. Svelte, seamless, with lovely red-fruit purity, whiffs of smoke & spice hinting at greater complexity with time. Also in 1.5, 3 & 5L, as Hope Marguerite.

★★★★ **Constable House** Pre-bottling, **17** (86) charms with pepper-spiced red fruit, mostly syrah with 35% cab, smooth after 15 months in older oak, step up on **16** ★★★☆ (83). Also in magnum for special occasions on a budget.

★★★★☆ **CWG Auction Reserve Leo's Whole Bunch Chenin Blanc** The first bottled since **11** ★★★☆ (84), remarkable **17** (94)'s clusters fermented, left 8 days on skins then pressed to barrel (100% new) for 16 months. Floral nose, savoury finish, layers of texture & peach, spice & mineral complexity in between, yet less than 12% alcohol.

★★★★★ **Hope Marguerite** A Cape benchmark chenin - **18** (95) is the 8th vintage to get our maximum 5 stars. From 40+ year old vines, unfailingly elegant & delicious. Shows taut balance between creamy, nutty richness & racy acidity, layered with tropical fruit. Naturally barrel-fermented & aged 11 months in mostly old 400L French oak.

★★★★ **Chenin Blanc** 'Baby' of cellar's chenins, **19** (87) including some Overberg fruit, unoaked & full of zest, peach & apple flavours, yet nicely rounded after 6 months on lees in tank.

★★★★☆ **The Kin Semillon** (NEW) From 22 year old vines, naturally fermented & aged 11 months in older French oak, **18** (92) has a mineral oystershell core with hay & lanolin aromas, white peach & lime flavours, spicy finish. Textured & concentrated yet alcohol is below 11.5%.

★★★★☆ **New Baby** Elegant white partner to Vitruvian, **18** (93) blends near-equal chenin & sauvignon (35/33) with semillon, chardonnay, colombard. Bright, zesty citrus flavours tempered by cream & mellow spice from 11 months in oak, 20% new. Also in 1.5 & 3L.

★★★★☆ **Cape Vintage Foot Stomped** 'Port' from equal tinta & pinotage, **17** (91) ex tank mid-2019 still very youthful & primary with black berry fruit, but Xmas spices & incense aromas hint at rich complexity to come. Not overly sweet (72.5 g/l sugar). 17.5% alcohol. 375 ml, as next.

★★★★☆ **Cape White** (NEW) White 'port' is drier than you might expect from citrus cheesecake & caramelised nut aromas (only 30 g/l sugar), skin-fermented chenin fortified by Portuguese intern Alvaro Roseira in **13** (90) is viscous, richly nutty yet fresh, lively. For tapas with a twist.

Not tasted: **Goutte d'Or**. In abeyance: **R&B**, **Chenin Blanc Demi-Sec**. Discontinued: **Starboard Dessert Wine**. — JG

Location: Bot River ▪ Map: Walker Bay & Bot River ▪ Map grid reference: C2 ▪ WO: Bot River/Cape South Coast ▪ Est 1750 ▪ 1stB 1994 ▪ Tasting & sales Mon-Fri 9.30–4.30 Sat 10–3 ▪ Tasting fee R6opp ▪ Closed Dec 25/26 & Jan 1 ▪ Platters & pre-booked picnic baskets ▪ Farm produce ▪ Walking/hiking trails ▪ Conservation area ▪ 250 year old watermill ▪ 2 historic self-catering guest cottages ▪ Owner(s) Beaumont family ▪ Winemaker(s) Sebastian Beaumont (Jun 2003) ▪ Viticulturist(s) Sebastian Beaumont (Jun 1999) ▪ 500ha/31ha (mourv, ptage, shiraz, chenin) ▪ 150t/22,000cs own label 40% red 60% white ▪ IPW ▪ PO Box 3 Bot River 7185 ▪ info@beaumont.co.za ▪ www.beaumont.co.za ▪ S 34° 13' 27.2" E 019° 12' 24.9" ▪ ⬚ advanced.textiles. telegrams ▪ T +27 (0)28-284-9194

Beeslaar Wines

Abrie Beeslaar has an unrivalled reputation in SA for superb, traditionally styled pinotage. He's the winemaker at Kanonkop, where he makes four of them, including a rosé, along with wines from other varieties. He likes to quote fellow winemaker Jan 'Boland' Coetzee about pinotage being 'not for sissies', and it's pinotage that he chose for the wine under his own label – this one coming from a single Stellenbosch vineyard with shale soils.

★★★★★ **Pinotage** ⬚ Generous aromas & flavours just hint at 50% new oak in **17** ⑼⑸, with chocolate & spicy tobacco. But the fruit is deep & dark & dense - like figured velvet. It's richly succulent, with a vital, supple tannin structure. Long-lingering, fairly dry finish. Gorgeous now & for a decade-plus. 1.5L too.— TJ

Location/WO: Stellenbosch ▪ Est 2011 ▪ 1stB 2012 ▪ Closed to public ▪ Owner(s) Abrie & Jeanne Beeslaar ▪ Cellarmaster(s)/winemaker(s) Abrie Beeslaar (Jul 2011) ▪ Viticulturist(s) Abrie Beeslaar ▪ 8t/750cs own label 100% red ▪ PO Box 93 Elsenburg 7607 ▪ info@beeslaar.co.za ▪ www.beeslaar.co.za ▪ T +27 (0)83-663-3256/+27 (0)84-255-8686

Bein Wine Cellar ⓠ

With previous careers as veterinarians, it should come as no surprise that Luca and Ingrid Bein's range of handcrafted merlots are now mostly vegan-friendly, particularly since it fits so well with their philosophy of doing all aspects of grape-growing and wine-making as naturally as possible. Their focus is on consistency, so Luca reports 'not much has changed this year', adding that concentrating on truly reflecting the individual terroirs of their farm in Stellenbosch's Polkadraai Hills is an approach which suits both them and their wines.

★★★★☆ **Merlot** ⬚ Touch more new oak (40%) than previous but **17** ⑼⓪ has more than enough dark plum & cherry fruit to cope, balancing vanilla with raspberry cream on finish. More elegant than 14.5% alcohol suggests, with plenty of time to go. Vegan-friendly, as all except Forte, & also in magnum.

★★★★ **Merlot Forte** Unusual Amarone-style **16** ⑻⑹ made from semi-dried fruit, 2 years in oak. Layers of dark chocolate, raisins & coffee, 16% alcohol & balanced 11.5 g/l sugar make for a drier alternative to port as a partner for cheese. No **15**. 375 ml.

★★★★★ **Merlot Reserve** ⓠ Only bottled in best vintages, from vines identified by aerial imaging as part of 'precision viticulture'. **16** ⑼② more intense & tannic than siblings but well structured & managed, deserves cellaring 6-8 years. All-new oak 22 months.

Little Merlot ★★★★ Becoming less 'little' by the year. **18** ⑻④ serious depth of dark-berried fruit enrobed in rich, smooth tannins & charry oak. From more vigorous vines, including tweak of petit verdot from neighbours. **Pink Merlot** ★★★★ More of a 'light red', but **19** ⑻④ has true rosé freshness & appeal, helped by usual dash muscat d'Alexandrie. Lively acidity & crisp, dry finish, perfect partner for a snoek braai. — CM

Location/map/WO: Stellenbosch ▪ Map grid reference: B6 ▪ Est/1stB 2002 ▪ Tasting, sales & cellar tours Mon-Sat by appt only ▪ Owner(s)/cellarmaster(s)/winemaker(s) Luca & Ingrid Bein ▪ Viticulturist(s) Luca Bein ▪ 3ha/2ha (merlot) ▪ 16t/2,400cs own label 80% red 20% rosé ▪ IPW ▪ PO Box 3408 Matieland 7602 ▪ lib@beinwine.com ▪ www.beinwine.com ▪ S 33° 57' 40.10" E 018° 44' 13.30 ▪ ⬚ obsession.plumbed.southward ▪ T +27 (0)21-881-3025

Belfield Wines ⓠ ⌂

Last year was one of great change at this boutique vineyard with guest cottages in Elgin, when vintage 2019 was managed without owner/vintner Mike Kreft, who had passed away in April 2018. But after help from local vintners the Almenkerks and travelling winemaker Gavin Patterson (familiar with the wines, previously

★★★★ **Hand Picked Viognier** Lively, modern, New World-style 18 ★★★★★ ⑨⓪ shows great intensity of fruit (fresh peach & ripe cantaloupe) & attractive ginger spice from 40% oak-fermented portion, third new. More interesting, satisfying than 17 ⑧⑨.

Homestead Series

★★★★ **Pinotage** ⓧ Fragrant 17 ⑧⑥ adds black fruit (plum, cherry) to spicy oak & meaty palate in very drinkable sip for superior mid-week suppers. Stellenbosch WO, as next.

★★★★ **Chardonnay** ⓧ Most enjoyable 18 ⑧⑥ balances ripe citrus fruit with gentle, creamy spiced oak. Toffee apple & almond notes, then crisp finish which lingers longer than 16 ★★★★ ⑧④. 17 untasted.

★★★★ **The Old Orchards Chenin Blanc** Was 'Chenin Blanc'. Fresh & zesty 18 ★★★★ ⑧⑤ balances soft older oak with plenty of zippy peaches, apples & pineapples. Spicy cream finish for enjoyable wine, shade less serious than 17 ⑧⑨ & exceptional debut 16 ★★★★★ ⑨③. All from Paarl, as Shiraz.

Shiraz ⓧ ★★★☆ Shy fruit 17 ⑧③ hiding behind rather forthright oak, needs time to settle but already showing pleasing peppery, cured meat notes with soft tannins & acidity. **Sauvignon Blanc** ⓧ ★★★☆ Cool ferment creates lashings of tropical fruit on exuberant 19 ⑧⑤. Grassy notes mid-palate & clean lemon sherbet finish should all harmonise with time. Cape Town WO. — CM

Location/map: Franschhoek ▪ Map grid reference: C2 ▪ WO: Coastal/Paarl/Stellenbosch/Cape Town/ Voor Paardeberg ▪ Est 1693 ▪ 1stB 1947 ▪ Tasting & sales at Bellingham cellardoor, located at Franschhoek Cellar: Mon-Thu 10-6 Fri/Sat 10-9 Sun 10-5 ▪ Closed Easter Fri/Sun, Dec 25/26 & Jan 1 ▪ Al fresco-style food & kiddies play area daily ▪ Farm produce ▪ Events venue (seat 300 pax) ▪ Owner(s) DGB (Pty) Ltd ▪ Winemaker(s) Richard Duckitt (Nov 2017), with Arlene Mains (Jan 2019) ▪ Viticulturist(s) Heinie Nel (Jul 2018) ▪ 4,000t/560,000cs own label 50% red 49% white 1% rosé ▪ ISO 9001:2000, HACCP, IPW, WIETA ▪ PO Box 52 Franschhoek 7690 ▪ bellingham@dgb.co.za ▪ www.bellinghamwines.com ▪ S 33° 54' 16.4" E 019° 6' 40.7" ▪ 🖭 receives.scoured.dumping ▪ **T +27 (0)21-876-2086**

Bellpost   ⓠ

West Coast family farms Bellevue and Buitepos each contribute to the name of the Thiart father-and-sons winery, where owner Lollies and siblings Nico (viticulturist) and Koos (winemaker) have been producing tiny parcels of wine for 15 years now. More recent is Thi Art Restaurant in nearby Vredendal, where tasting/ sales are also available. At the farm, a replanting programme, on hold due to drought, is now in progress.

C'est La Vie ⓥ ★★★ Lightly oaked white blend loses nouvelle component in 15 ⑧② but none of its charm. Lively orchard fruit & a citrus finish, delicious creaminess from lees ageing. Chardonnay & viognier.

Merlot ★★★ Rich & robust 16 ⑧⓪ has fruitcake flavours, warm spice & charry oak, will be a good partner for grilled meat. 20-50% new oak, year, for the reds. **Ruby Cabernet** ★★★ Wild cherry & berry flavours on 15 ⑧① easy & moreish, with a savoury grip to finish. **Shiraz** ★★★ Bigger (15% alcohol) & more powerful, 16 ⑧① packed with dark bramble fruit & savoury flavours, assertive tannins, yet still balanced & as food friendly as previous. **Chardonnay** ★★★☆ Bunch-pressed & unoaked 17 ⑦⑧ has bruised apple flavours & a leaner body than last, would benefit from more zip. — WB

Location: Vredendal ▪ Map: Olifants River ▪ Map grid reference: B3 ▪ WO: Western Cape ▪ Est/1stB 2005 ▪ Tasting, sales & cellar tours by appt; tasting & sales also at Thi Art Restaurant, Vredendal ▪ Owner(s) Lollies Thiart ▪ Winemaker(s) Koos Thiart (Jan 2005) ▪ Viticulturist(s) Nico Thiart (Jan 2005) ▪ 5ha/2ha (merlot, ruby cab, shiraz, chard, viog) ▪ 12t/1,800cs own label 80% red 20% white ▪ PO Box 39 Vredendal 8160 ▪ bellpost@ starmail.co.za ▪ www.bellpost.co.za ▪ S 31° 36' 24.1" E 018° 25' 0.6" ▪ 🖭 swaps.gibbering.handset ▪ **T +27 (0)27-213-2562/+27 (0)82-619-2428 (cellar); +27 (0)76-792-0806 (Thi Art restaurant)**

Bemind Wyne deur Ilse Schutte   ⓠ ⓦ ⓞ

In her must-visit cellar and visitor venue on the main street of tucked-away McGregor, Ilse Schutte makes small parcels of wine 'from the heart' (hence her brand name, which translates as Beloved Wines). She's excited about, and part of a mini-wave in her use of chenin blanc for the bubbly (replacing the classic chardonnay/pinot noir combo). Hinting at further innovation, she says to 'watch this space for a Bordeaux blend'.

Cinsault ★★★ Characterful 19 ⑧① preview is from 45 year old Breedekloof bushvines, half in old oak. Light, with wild-berry tartness & a tannic twist. **Shiraz** ★★★☆ 17 ⑧⑤ improves on bold 16 ★★★ ⑧②, with spicy dry tannins & finish tempering ripeness. Dark berry & chocolate nuances, supple, with underlying structure. **Sauvignon Blanc** ★★★ Ripe & rounded passionfruit nuance on **18** ⑧②. Refreshing, balanced, ready to celebrate summer. WO Robertson. **Méthode Cap Classique Brut** ★★★ **NV** ⑧① sparkler shows chenin's lemon, green apple flavours & tangy acidity. Invigoratingly tart, clean, bone-dry finish. In abeyance: **Langstraat**. — MW

Location: McGregor ▪ Map: Robertson ▪ Map grid reference: D6 ▪ WO: McGregor/Breedekloof/Robertson ▪ Est 2015 ▪ Garagiste winery: Tasting, sales & cellar tours Wed-Fri 10-5 Sat 10-2 ▪ Fee R30/3 wines, waived on purchase ▪ Closed Easter Fri-Sun, Pentecost, Dec 25/26 & Jan 1 ▪ Food & wine pairing on request ▪ Deli products ▪ Owner(s) Ilse Schutte ▪ Cellarmaster(s)/winemaker(s) Ilse Schutte (Jan 2015) ▪ 10-15t/±850cs own label 50% red 30% white 20% MCC ▪ IPW ▪ PO Box 446 McGregor 6708 ▪ ilse@bemindwyne.co.za ▪ www. bemindwyne.co.za ▪ S 33° 56' 49" E 019° 49' 44" ▪ ⓘ motors.coupler.stations ▪ **T +27 (0)83-380-1648**

Benguela Cove Lagoon Wine Estate ⓠ ⑪ ⓞ ⑧ ⓖ

Owned by entrepreneur Penny Streeter OBE, this wine, olive and lifestyle estate in cool-climate Walker Bay intends to become a leading wine tourism destination, with an impressive array of attractions for visitors and their families, including ones that take advantage of the location on Bot River Lagoon. The offerings from the two eateries are designed to celebrate and complement the estate-grown wine range by awarded Johann Fourie, which sees several additions this edition. Also cool-climate, though further-flung, are the vineyards in the UK, at Mannings Heath Wine & Golf Estate and Leonardslee Lakes & Gardens, which will provide the grapes for Penny's first English sparkling wine. And, in a few years, the first pinotage planted in English soil by Johann in 2018 will be ready for its first crush.

Icon range

★★★★★ **Catalina Semillon** ⓑ Sleek successor to stellar **17** ⑨⑤, **18** ★★★★☆ ⑨③ as restrained & complex, with hay & lanolin accents, smoke & oystershell minerality. Thrillingly dry & ageworthy too, despite having shade less acid & oak support (75% oaked portion, none new vs 80%, 20% new).

Vinography range

★★★★☆ **Petit Verdot** ⓝⒺⓦ ⓑ Just 645 bottles from 0.95-ha parcel, cooler ferment, some whole berries. **17** ⑨③ expressive & unforced, with tangy plum & cassis, present but unintimidating tannins. Should reward long cellaring.

★★★★☆ **Chardonnay** ⓑ Single-vineyard, barrel-fermented **18** ⑨③'s dense lemon & lime fruit shaped by deft old-oaking, lifted by precise seam of acidity, hint minerality. Long & fruit-filled, worth laying down 3+ years.

★★★★☆ **Sauvignon Blanc** ⓑ Pinpoint acidity, well-judged oak, emphatic dryness: there's exquisite control in **18** ⑨③, from 1-ha vineyard, portion vinified with non-Saccharomyces yeast. Only French oak; **17** ⑨③ had smidgen acacia wood, similarly reminiscent of iconic fumé blancs from California with smoke, tinned pea & white asparagus notes.

Estate range

★★★★ **Malbec** ⓝⒺⓦ Epitome of 'dark & brooding': **17** ⑧⑨ powerful aromas & flavours of plum & leather, stern tannic grip, astonishing persistence, brawny 14.6% alcohol & weighty bottle! Yet there's some composure, too, & plenty of potential. One to watch.

★★★★ **Pinot Noir** Aromatically & texturally correct **18** ⑧⑥, fruit-filled & with more gravitas than **17** ⑧⑥. 10% wholebunch, 90% wholeberry ferment, well-judged 30% new oak.

★★★★ **Syrah** ⓑ Intense, sweet black fruit on **17** ⑧⑥, modern but well executed, 30% new oak in good support. Tight tannins augur well for cellaring. Magnums available, as next.

★★★★ **Collage** ⓑ Serious Bordeaux blend, **17** ⑧⑦ unabashedly ripe-fruited with vanilla overlay, yet carefully managed tannins make it toned, athletic. Cab & malbec (35/23), with near-equal merlot, petit verdot & cab franc. Like previous, needs few years to mellow.

★★★★ **Chardonnay 18** ★★★★ ⑧⑤ more expressive than Vinography sibling, like **17** ⑧⑨, also less precise, its fruit dimmed in youth by 50% new oak & creamy lees. Once knit, however, the attractively lean frame & acid seam promise more sophistication.

★★★★ **Sauvignon Blanc** 'Little sister' to Vinography version, **18** ⑧⑧ nonetheless has considerable finesse & charm. Bone-dry, with 40% oaked portion for body & length; more serious than previous.

★★★★ **Joie de Vivre Brut** ⓥ Sparkler from chardonnay (57%) & pinot, with 2 years on lees, **14** ⑧⑥ full spectrum of apple aromas & flavours, some red berries, too, especially in the finish.

★★★★☆ **Noble Late Harvest** ⓥ Botrytis dessert from sauvignon blanc. **15** ⑨① vivacious & beautifully balanced by vibrant acidity. Opulent smooth texture with delicious piquancy & length.

Cabernet Sauvignon ★★★☆ Reflects maritime influence in its astringent grape tannins, piquant fruit. **17** ⑧⑤'s 40% new French oak ups the appeal for immediate enjoyment or few years ageing. Discontinued: **Semillon-Sauvignon Blanc**.

Lighthouse range
....

Moody Lagoon Red Blend (NEW) ⓦ ★★★★ Very good everyday glassful. Aromatic **17** ⑧③'s 25% new oak shows in vanilla aroma & flavour; well-formed tannin/acid structure is accessible now & will keep a few years. From two cabs, shiraz, petit verdot & merlot.
....

Syrah (NEW) ★★★ Little varietal character on youthful **17** ⑦⑨ but plenty of fruit & friendly tannins for carefree imbibing. **Rosé** ★★★ From shiraz & sauvignon blanc (22%), **19** ⑦⑨ intense berry & bubblegum aromas, fresh & light for uncomplicated sipping. **Sauvignon Blanc** ★★★ Pleasantly dry, with well-integrated acidity, whiffs of blackcurrant & dust in **19** ⑧②. **Cuvée 58 Méthode Cap Classique** (NEW) ★★★★ **NV** ⑧④ sparkling with exuberant mousse, forthcoming apple aroma & palate, breezy finish with sippability boosted by few grams sugar. From sauvignon blanc, pinot noir & chardonnay. In magnum too. — CvZ

Location: Hermanus ▪ Map: Walker Bay & Bot River ▪ Map grid reference: B2 ▪ WO: Walker Bay ▪ Est 2004 ▪ 1stB 2007 ▪ Trading hours: Mon-Sun 10-8 (summer)/10-6 (winter) ▪ Tasting fee R80pp ▪ Chocolate/cheese/oyster & wine pairing R120-R185 ▪ Millionaires tasting R40pp ▪ Cheese & charcuterie platter R320 ▪ Moody Lagoon Restaurant (fine dining); Blackbeards Diner; Tea Room; Deli ▪ Shops ▪ Facilities for children ▪ Tour groups ▪ Pirate Adventure Golf course ▪ Vineyard safaris, winery tours and pontoon cruise on the lagoon ▪ Conferencing & wedding facilities ▪ Owner(s) Benguela Cove Investments (Pty) Ltd (Penny Streeter OBE) ▪ Winemaker(s) Johann Fourie (Sep 2016), with Michelle Waldeck (Feb 2017) ▪ Viticulturist(s) Jaco Mouton ▪ 206ha/66ha (cabs s/f, malbec, merlot, p verdot, pinot, shiraz, chard, sauv, sem) ▪ 400t/30,000cs own label 50% red 50% white ▪ PO Box 327 Bellville 7535 ▪ info@benguelacove.co.za ▪ www.benguelacove.co.za ▪ S 34° 20' 45.0" E 019° 8' 15.7" ▪ cove.minerals.dismantles ▪ **T +27 (0)21-944-1041 (head office)/+27 (0)83-645-6198 (wine sales)/+27 (0)87-357-0637 (restaurant reservations)**

☐ **Berg en Dal** see Wine-of-the-Month Club

Bergheim ⓥ

Paarl general practitioner Edwin Jordaan vinifies small batches with minimum intervention in rented cellar space on Paarl Mountain. His current release, a '19 Chenin Blanc, was produced from local grapes with nearby Mooi Bly Winery as partner. 'Jorrie' intends to devote more time to his after-hours passion from this year, and has 'an exciting thing or two in the pipeline - if I'm still above ground :)'.

Location/map: Paarl ▪ Map grid reference: E6 ▪ Est/1stB 2000 ▪ Tasting by appt ▪ Owner(s) Edwin Jordaan ▪ Cellarmaster(s)/winemaker(s) Edwin Jordaan (Jan 2000) ▪ 4-6t/1,000cs own label 66% red 34% white ▪ PO Box 6020 Paarl 7622 ▪ drjordaan@gmail.com ▪ S 33° 45' 20.2" E 018° 57' 42.5" ▪ ⌨ hillside.grin.grand ▪ **T +27 (0)82-923-3115, +27 (0)21-863-1529**

☐ **Bergkelder** see Libertas Vineyards & Estates
☐ **Bergkelder Selection** see Fleur du Cap

Bergsig Estate ⓥ ⓦ ⓐ ⓑ ⓒ

The 6th-generation Lategans are honouring their past, both familial (with newly branded Reserve wines; see their website and tasting room memorabilia for more on the good ship Patmos, legendary Tant Anna and pilot Oom Prop) and vinous (by resurrecting their Riesling, last bottled in 2013). But the future is firmly in focus with chardonnay, chenin and cab plantings, and upgrades to bottling and cooling facilities.

Lategan range

★★★★ **Cabernet Sauvignon Reserve** ⓥ Solid black fruit core on **13** ★★★★ ⑧⑤ tinged with mint, coconut & sweet aromas. Gentle tannins, good structure but shade off **12** ⑧⑨. WO W Cape.

★★★★ **Oom Prop Cabernet Sauvignon Reserve** (NEW) A silk-textured & succulent debut for **15** ⑧⑨. Serious oaking (60% new, 28 months) includes 30% American barrels that impart an opulent sweet tobacco, polished leather tone to the ripe fruit. Paler hue, but the palate is still fresh, balanced & inviting, will hold for a good few years.

★★★★ **Tant Anna Chardonnay** ⓥ Year in new French oak leaves an imprint, but big-bodied **17** ⑧⑥ is generously laced with citrus, smoothly textured & lengthy on finish, & should settle with time.

★★★★ **Patmos Chenin Blanc Reserve** (NEW) Named for 18th-century sailing vessel that brought Lategan forefather to Cape. Appealing dried peach flavours a touch muted by oak (50% new) on **17** ⑧⑥, needs some time to meld. Fuller bodied, richer than Bergsig sibling.

Bergsig Estate range

★★★★ **Icarus Red** ⓥ Ripe, substantial **14** ⑧⑧ barrel selection of cab & touriga, individual & appealing, with Xmas pudding dark fruits, spiciness from new oak. No **13**. **12** ★★★★★ ⑨④ was exceptional.

★★★★☆ **Icarus White** ⓥ Oak (older) still dominant in stylish **16** ⑨③ chardonnay, chenin, riesling blend, but fruit beginning to assert itself mid-2017. Appealing mix of orange marmalade & yellow stone-fruit, spiced with vanilla & cloves. Body & freshness to match; should settle & improve.

★★★★ **Gewürztraminer Edel Laatoes** ⓥ Beguiling rosewater scents on restrained, well-judged **17** ⑧⑨ botrytis dessert, with delicate spices, tangy dried apricots filling the (unoaked) palate. 375 ml.

★★★★ **Cape LBV** ⓥ Patience rewarded in **12** ⑧⑨, first since **03** ★★★☆ ⑧④. Touriga aged in older French & American barrels for 5 years, delivers opulent caramel, mocha flavours, with a savoury, polished leather nuance. In true LBV style, the tannins are supple but structured. Ready to enjoy.

★★★★ **Cape Vintage** ⓥ Succulent, smooth & spicy 'port' from tinta. **04** ⑧⑦ generously flavoured but not sweet, sufficient fire to warm a winter night.

Cabernet Sauvignon ⓥ ★★★ Savoury tones to **14** ⑦⑧'s cherry & plum fruit, thinnish body. Also in magnum. **Pinotage** ★★★ Plummy notes & a touch of mocha on **17** ⑧②. Well balanced & fresher, for satisfying enjoyment. **Touriga Nacional** ★★★☆ Dark, brooding fruit on **15** ⑧④. Unfortified version of a traditional port grape showing characteristic dry, chalky tannins. Still quite closed, needs time to show fully. **The Family Friend** ⓥ ★★★ Shiraz-led unwooded Cape Blend **17** ⑧② makes for pleasant anytime drinking. Fruit driven, fresh & lightish, with ripe plum flavour. **Rose Gold Rosé** ★★★ Semi-dry, though fresh & balanced **19** ⑦⑦ from shiraz. Strawberry & rosepetal nuances make for appealing al fresco/sunset sipping. **Chardonnay** ⓥ ★★★☆ Dominant oak spices mask **17** ⑧③'s marmalade-tinged fruit; fresh, clean palate with decent body, clean finish. **Chenin Blanc** ★★★ **19** ⑦⑦ is dry & brisk, with some piquant green apple flavours, though less fruit than previous. Unoaked & less alcohol than Patmos sibling. **Gewürztraminer** ⓥ ★★★☆ Typically fragrant **18** ⑧③ has a touch of sweetness, lots of Turkish delight & personality, soft acidity. **Weisser Riesling** ⓥ ★★★☆ First release **19** ⑧⑤ from new vineyard. True to cultivar, with aromatic limy flavours, clean, steely acidity & some sweetness, though technically dry. Some leesy breadth too, adds to the appeal. **Sauvignon Blanc** ★★★ Gentlest hint of tropical fruit & a sprinkling of nutmeg on **19** ⑧①. Clean & light summer quaffer, also in 1.5L. **Cape Ruby** ⓥ ★★★★ Unoaked **NV** ⑧④ 'port' from tinta, delicious, approachable as this style should be. Discontinued: **Weisser Riesling Late Harvest**. — MW

Location: Wolseley ▪ Map: Breedekloof ▪ Map grid reference: A3 ▪ WO: Breedekloof/Western Cape ▪ Est 1843 ▪ 1stB 1977 ▪ Tasting & sales Mon-Fri 8—5 Sat/pub hols 9—4 ▪ Various food-&-wine pairing, winetasting options ▪ Closed Good Fri, Dec 25 & Jan 1 ▪ Cellar tours by appt ▪ Bergsig Bistro ▪ Facilities for children ▪ Farm produce ▪ Conferences ▪ Self-guided birdwatching route ▪ MTB ▪ Conservation area, visits by appt ▪ Lategan family history & historical artefacts on display ▪ Soetes & Soup (Jul) ▪ Owner(s) Lategan family ▪ Cellarmaster(s) De Wet Lategan (Jan 1989) ▪ Winemaker(s) Chris du Toit (Jul 2003) ▪ Viticulturist(s) Louis & Plum Lategan (1991) ▪ 253ha (cab, ptage, shiraz, touriga, chard, chenin, sauv) ▪ 3,200t/100,000cs own label 35% red 60% white 4% rosé 1% other ▪ 140,000cs for clients ▪ Other export brands: White River, Bulldozer Pinotage ▪ Brands for clients: Woolworths ▪ BRC, IPW, WIETA ▪ PO Box 15 Breërivier 6858 ▪ wine@bergsig.co.za ▪ www.bergsig.co.za ▪ S 33° 31' 7.78" E 019° 11' 37.14" ▪ ⌨ lighting.elastic.punch ▪ **T +27 (0)23-355-1603**

☐ **Bernard Series** *see* Bellingham
☐ **Berrio Wines** *see* The Berrio Wines

Bester Family Wines

Zakkie Bester's historic roots in Swartland (family going back to the 1700s) are only part of his eminent qualification for this private enterprise. As longtime cellarmaster/CEO of Riebeek Cellars (now Riebeek Valley Wine Co), then marketer of the winery's bulk wine in his 'retirement', his area knowledge and ability to source grapes are extraordinary. Just two wines so far, available online and at select outlets (see below).

Barbera ⓥ ★★★☆ Fruit-driven **16** ⑧⑧④ richly layered, sweet spicy & dried herb notes, a red berry succulence giving delicious drinkability enhanced by approachable tannins, suggestion of sweetness. **Chenin Blanc** ⓥ ★★★☆ From 30 year old bushvines, no oak but long lees contact, giving **17** ⑧④ palate fullness, length. Honeysuckle scents, apple & pear fruitiness, zesty-fresh. Ticks many boxes, lots to like here. — CR

Location: Riebeek-Kasteel ▪ WO: Swartland ▪ Est/1stB 2016 ▪ Closed to public ▪ Wines available for tasting & sales at Enjoy Liquors, Riebeek-Kasteel, and Toast Restaurant on Delsma Farm near Hermon ▪ Owner(s) Zakkie Bester ▪ Winemaker(s) Zakkie Bester (2016) ▪ 1,400cs own label 50% red 50% white ▪ PO Box 292 Riebeek-Kasteel 7307 ▪ zakkie@ijbester.co.za ▪ www.besterwines.com ▪ **T +27 (0)82-805-5586**

☐ **Bethani** *see* Cathedral Peak Wine Estate

Beyerskloof

Nearing four decades of winemaking, industry legend and pinotage champion Beyers Truter continues to expand the eponymous brand, based since 1988 on a Koelenhof farm serendipitously owned by Beyers family forebears a century before. He and business partners have acquired another 50 ha of vineyards, bringing chenin and sauvignon to the primarily red portfolio. A new premium pinotage is poised for release, joining an illustrious listing headlined by five-star-rated Diesel and Faith, and unusual blend Traildust, formerly available only at the tasting room, now in the trade too. FAITH also stands for the Beyers Truter Foetal Alcohol-Syndrome & Interrelated Treatment Help Fund, reflecting a deep-seated commitment to community well-being shared by the next generation, winemaker son Anri and farm bistro manager daughter Corné.

★★★★☆ **CWG Auction Reserve Traildust Pinotage** ⓐ A selection from the best barrels for the CWG annual auction, **17** ㊉④ full-throttle ripe plum & mulberry, new oak (18 months) weaving spice, chocolate & vanilla along with the fruit. Opulent & intense, polished tannins & long satisfying finish. Like previous, a wine for the long haul.

★★★★★ **Diesel Pinotage** ⓐ Only 25 barrels from 300, selected to immortalise co-founder & cellarmaster Beyers Truter's beloved dog. Never disappoints. **17** ㊉⑥ luscious, harmonious & textbook pinotage, has fruit, balance & structure from 18 months in new French oak to improve 10+ years.

★★★★ **Pinotage Reserve** ⓥ ⓐ Ripe, Ribena-like **16** ㊉⑨ followed by more complex & nuanced **17** ★★★★★ ㉠⓪. No lack of plummy fruit intensity or richness, however, or lifted fresh acidity, supple tannin frame. Only 10% new oak , enough to add delicious dark chocolate & provide scaffold for 5+ years ageing.

★★★★☆ **Winemakers Reserve Pinotage** ⓐ Tiny parcel (546 cases) of earlier-approachable Diesel. **17** ㊉③ same flavour profile: classic varietal expression, rich yet elegant, powerful yet fine tannins, exceptional length. 10% aged in older oak, 18 months.

★★★★☆ **Field Blend** ⓐ Bordeaux blend is remarkable in many ways: co-grown, -fermented, -matured, with unblemished quality record over 2 decades. Cab (80%) & merlot in textured **15** ㊉⓪, mellow, with dark berry & bramble fruit; spicy, savoury & peppery notes from 10% new French oak, 24 months.

★★★★★ **Faith** ⓐ Stellar Cape Blend from standout vintage, **15** ㊉⑥ is pinotage (34%), equal cab & merlot. Balances power & restraint, displays elegance & finesse with flavours of ripe red & black fruit, supportive structure & dash of spice from 100% new oak, 21 months.

★★★★ **Synergy Cape Blend** ⓥ Pinotage, cab, merlot (30/30/26) & 3 others combine in harmony for a succulent mouthful of ripe black cherries & plums, velvet smoothness & a wild herb finish in **17** ㊇⑧. Only 5% new oak for 13 months.

★★★★ **Traildust** Generously perfumed **17** ㊇⑨ sees pinotage united with parents cinsaut & pinot noir (33/47/30). Abundant dark berries, leather & earthy spice after year in 3rd-fill oak.

★★★★ **Lagare Cape Vintage** ⍟ Versatility of pinotage has no bounds at Beyerskloof: here it teams with shiraz (47%) & pinotage brandy for a delicious 'port', foot-crushed in traditional manner. **17** ⑧⑧ plum pudding, spice & mellow fire, a true winter warmer. 500 ml.

. . . .

Pinotage ⊘ ⍟ ★★★★ Admittedly not 'hidden', with production topping 190,000 cases, but indisputably a gem, always ticks the boxes. Smooth, fruity & plummy, touch of oak (20%) smooths any edges. Widely sourced **18** ⑧③ also in 250 ml & magnum. **Cabernet Sauvignon-Merlot** ⍟ ★★★ A real crowd pleaser. Fragrant & fruity **17** ⑧② , smooth & fresh 60/40 blend with fruitcake spice & drizzle of vanilla from 20% oaked portion. WO W Cape. **Chenin Blanc-Pinotage** ⍟ ★★★★ Tropical fruit mingles with bright red berries in a charming 'white Cape Blend' from Swartland vines. **18** ⑧③ hits the summer quaffing spot with vivacity & freshness.

. . . .

Pinotage Dry Rosé ★★★ Pair of vintages tasted. **18** ⑧⓪ has rosepetal & red cherry fruit, creamy texture from 3 months lees ageing, very refreshing. **19** ⑧⓪ in same vein with fresh grapefruit finish. Grapes from Breedekloof. — WB

Location/map: Stellenbosch ▪ Map grid reference: E3 ▪ WO: Stellenbosch/Western Cape/Coastal ▪ Est 1988 ▪ 1stB 1989 ▪ Tasting & sales Mon-Fri 9—4 Sat 9.30—4 Sun 10-3.30 ▪ Closed Easter Fri-Mon, Dec 25/26 & Jan 1 ▪ Cellar tours by appt ▪ Red Leaf Restaurant ▪ Conferences (30 pax) ▪ Owner(s) Beyers Truter, Jan Morgan & Barnie van Straten ▪ Cellarmaster(s) Beyers Truter (Jan 1988) ▪ Winemaker(s) Anri Truter (Jan 2004), with Buddy Hendricks (Jan 2010) & Elsa du Plessis (Aug 2017) ▪ Viticulturist(s) Johan Pienaar (2000, consultant) ▪ 193ha/125ha (cab, cinsaut, merlot, ptage, pinot, shiraz, chenin, sauv) ▪ 950t/350,000cs own label 96% red 2% white 2% rosé + 10,000cs for clients ▪ Brands for clients: Pick's Pick, Woolworths ▪ IPW, WIETA ▪ PO Box 107 Koelenhof 7605 ▪ reception@beyerskloof.co.za ▪ www.beyerskloof.co.za ▪ S 33° 53' 28.0" E 018° 49' 23.6" ▪ ⟲ planting.purses.living ▪ **T +27 (0)21-865-2135**

Bezalel Wine & Brandy Estate ⓠ ⑪ ⌂ ◉ ⑧

Four generations of Bezuidenhouts have turned what was once just a smallholding with rotational crops in the fertile floodplains of the Northern Cape's Gariep (Orange) River into a popular destination on the Kokerboom Food & Wine Route. In addition to wines, oak-matured fortifieds, potstill brandies and infusions, they offer 'authentic Green Kalahari hospitality' at their Garden Café and Country House accommodation.

Bezalel Estate range

★★★★ **Fortified Cape Tawny** ⍟ From 4 port grapes including rare cornifesto, 66 months older oak, **NV** ⑧⑦ luscious sweetness yet acidity to balance richness of brandied orange, caramelised nut & spice.

The Royal Oryx Pinot Noir ★★ Sporting new name (was 'Pinot Noir') & striking label, **18** ⑦④ has earthy cherry & berry jam flavours, is just-dry & full bodied (14.5% alcohol). 10 months older French oak. **Desert Rose Sauvignon Blanc** ★★★ Now named for rosette-shaped succulent - new 'succulent' semi-sweet styling, too, adding plumpness to **18** ⑦⑧ . Floral & peachy aromas, ripe tropical fruit flavours. Not tasted: **Sangiovese**, **Shiraz**, **Merlot Blanc de Noir**, **Suikerbekkie Sweet Rosé**, **Colombard**, **Zandland Viognier**. Discontinued: **Gewürztraminer Jerepigo**.

Brandy range

★★★★ **VSOP Cape Brandy** ⍟ Potstill brandy ⑧⑦ , smooth & rich, gentle dried fruit, nut & creamy marzipan flavours. Mostly colombard (with sauvignon, tinta, cab & shiraz), 5 years in Cape Tawny barrels. Not tasted: **XO Cape Brandy**. — JG, WB

Location: Upington ▪ Map: Northern Cape, Free State & North West ▪ Map grid reference: B8 ▪ WO: Northern Cape ▪ Est 1949 (farm)/1997 (cellar) ▪ 1stB 1998 ▪ Tasting, sales & cellar tours Mon-Fri 8.30—5.30 Sat 8.30—3 ▪ Fee R50-R100pp ▪ Large groups by appt ▪ Closed Easter Fri/Mon & Dec 25 ▪ Garden Café: breakfast, lunch & platters ▪ Venue for conferences & weddings ▪ Accommodation ▪ Craft beer ▪ Owner(s) Bezuidenhout family ▪ Winemaker(s) Martiens Bezuidenhout (2015) ▪ Viticulturist(s) Inus Bezuidenhout (1989) ▪ 60ha/44ha (cab, cornifesto, merlot, pinot, sangio, shiraz, touriga, cbard, gewürz, sauv, viog) ▪ ±1,000cs own label 40% red 60% white ▪ IPW ▪ PO Dyasonsklip 8805 ▪ marketing@bezalel.co.za ▪ www.bezalel.co.za ▪ S 28° 36' 28.69" E 021° 6' 19.01" ▪ ⟲ earthen.subpart.plugs ▪ **T +27 (0)54-491-1325/+27 (0)83-257-4736**

Bezuidenhout Family Wines

These Rhône-inspired boutique bottlings by Paarl Cape Wine Master Francois Bezuidenhout are intended as 'story wines', recalling his 17th-century ancestor Wijnand Leenders, from Bezuidenhout in the Netherlands, head gardener for the Dutch East India Company and one of the Cape's first vinegrowers and winemakers.

Leenders range

★★★★ Baviaan Ⓧ Harmonious chenin (72%), viognier, roussanne & grenache blanc, **18** ⑧⑦ suave creaminess from partial oaking combines attractively with vivacious pineapple & fig flavours.

Sielverkoper Ⓧ ★★★★ Lightly oaked shiraz (71%) seasoned with mourvèdre, carignan, grenache, **17** ⑧⑤ carefully extracted for good, unheavy concentration, firm but approachable tannins. **Armosyn** Ⓧ ★★★★ Dry rosé, palest pearly pink **18** ⑧③ smooth, clean guava flavour & mineral undertone, mouthfilling despite slender 12.5% alcohol, lifted leafy farewell. From Robertson mourvèdre. — JG, CvZ

Location/map: Paarl ▪ Map grid reference: E6 ▪ WO: Breedekloof/Robertson/Western Cape ▪ Est/1stB 2018 ▪ Tasting & sales by appt only ▪ Owner(s) Francois Bezuidenhout ▪ Winemaker(s) Francois Bezuidenhout (Apr 2018) ▪ 1,000cs own label 60% red 40% white ▪ Taillerfer Str Paarl 7646 ▪ francois@bezfamily.com ▪ www.bezfamily.com ▪ S 33° 45' 55.2" E 018° 57' 27.6" ▪ **T +27 (0)21-863-0872**

- ☐ **Big Bill** *see* KWV Wines
- ☐ **Big Easy** *see* Ernie Els Wines
- ☐ **Big Flower** *see* Botanica Wines

Biodynamix

The Frater brothers have several projects on the go in Paarl, Biodynamix being a joint venture between winemaker Dan and viticulturist Gerard, with grapes from the latter's Paarl Mountain farm Houmoed. Though not certified biodynamic, there's much emphasis in the farming on naturalness, and in the cellar at family seat De Zoete Inval, the wines are pampered with classical music. See under Frater Family Wines for the wines of third sibling John Robert.

★★★★ Max 1 Ⓧ Shiraz (70%) with merlot & dash cab, naturally co-fermented & older oaked, **15** ⑧⑦ has earthy scrub nuances in its hedgerow fruit, grainy tannins which should soften over time. — CR, CvZ

Location/WO: Paarl ▪ Est/1stB 2015 ▪ Closed to public ▪ Owner(s) Joint venture members: Dan & Gerard Frater ▪ Cellarmaster(s)/winemaker(s) Dan Frater (2015) ▪ Viticulturist(s) Gerard Frater (2001) ▪ 12ha/2ha (cab, merlot, shiraz) ▪ 12t/500cs own label 100% red ▪ PO Box 591 Paarl 7646 ▪ biodynamix.sales@gmail.com ▪ www.biodynamix.co.za ▪ **T +27 (0)82-328-1807**

- ☐ **Birkenhead Estate & Brewery** *see* Walker Bay Estate

Bitou Vineyards

Owner and property developer Ronald Leacy envisions a 'working winery' on the Bitou River bank beside the N2 highway, easily accessible by holidaymakers and sun-seekers who flock to nearby Plettenberg Bay. The vineyard, already in production, was recently extended, and good progress is being made with the infrastructure. Manager Derek Harvey expects the tasting venue to open soon, with a restaurant to follow.

Location: Plettenberg Bay ▪ Map: Klein Karoo & Garden Route ▪ Map grid reference: C1 ▪ Est 2009 ▪ Tasting by appt ▪ Owner(s) Ronald Leacy - Leacy Property (Pty) Ltd ▪ Winemaker(s) Anton Smal (Feb 2015, consultant) ▪ 15ha/13.5ha (malbec, pinot, chard, sauv, sem) ▪ 56t/5,000cs ▪ info@bitouvineyards.co.za ▪ www.bitouvineyards.co.za ▪ S 34° 0' 59" E 023° 23' 22" ▪ dentist.charades.gnat ▪ **T +27 (0)82-922-0809**

Bizoe Wines

Winemaking is unashamedly a love affair for Rikus Neethling, vineyardist-vintner for his Somerset West-based boutique range, made from selected blocks across the winelands. A hands-on, personal approach to his craft is reflected in the choice of name for the brand (from the French word for kiss) and individualistic wines, expressing his love of family - mother Henriëtta, father Tiny, wife Estalét and twins Retief and André, who communicate in a private patois dubbed Idioglossia.

Bizoe Wines range

★★★★ **Idioglossia Malbec** Aspirationally priced & impressively packaged **17** ⑧⑥. Deeply perfumed black fruit set on firm frame, spicy note from 18 months old oak. Improves on **16** ★★★★ ⑧⑤, also ex Swartland.

★★★★★ **Estalét Syrah** Blockbuster in weighty bottle; grapes from beloved Wolseley vines supplemented by Swartland in rounded, ripe & plush **16** ⑨②. Mulberry fruit mingles with silky tannins & American oak vanilla in dense, complex expression with lengthy finish.

★★★★ **Idioglossia Chardonnay** Vineyard source switches from Franschhoek to Elgin in wild-fermented **18** ⑧⑨. Quite a mouthful, 50% new oak asserting itself in caramel undertone to ripe orange, freshened by limy tang. 70% in oak, rest amphora, 9 months.

★★★★★ **Henriëtta** Tightly wound, oak-brushed Franschhoek semillon (70%) & Elgin sauvignon, naturally fermented. **18** ⑨① maintains house's precision & focus in textured, chalky mouthfeel tempered by vivid lemon twist. Subtle & refined, with long aftertaste, will reward few years in cellar.

Occasional release: **Tiny Noble Late Harvest**.

RNW range

Not tasted: **Cabernet Sauvignon**, **Sauvignon Blanc**. — DS

Location: Somerset West ▪ WO: Western Cape/Elgin ▪ Est/1stB 2008 ▪ Closed to public ▪ Owner(s)/cellarmaster(s)/winemaker(s)/viticulturist(s) Rikus Neethling ▪ 2,000cs ▪ Unit 189 Croydon Vineyard Estate Somerset West 7130 ▪ info@bizoe.co.za ▪ www.bizoe.co.za ▪ **T +27 (0)21-843-3307**

Blaauwklippen Vineyards ⓆⓅ◎ⒶⓈ

Winds of change are blowing fresh ideas and new life into all areas of this historic estate. The manor house has been tastefully renovated, and joined by a dramatic function venue, the Glass Cathedral. Winemaker Narina Cloete has pared down the wide range, focusing on elegant expressions of mostly classic red varieties. The signature zinfandel does still feature, in various formats, keeping its many fans happy, especially the numerous visitors to this multifaceted destination farm at the gateway to Stellenbosch.

Blaauwklippen range

★★★★ **Cabernet Sauvignon** ⓃⒺⓌ Confident **17** ⑧⑧ debuts with plenty of ripe blackcurrants, touch of lavender & savoury notes in fruit-forward but still refined style. Rounded mid-palate (courtesy 11% merlot) & fine-grained tannins softly supported by older oak.

★★★★★ **Malbec** ⓃⒺⓌ ⓥ Modern & eminently likeable **18** ⑨⓪ bursts forth with lashings of sweet ripe black plum & cherry fruit edged with signature perfume & florals. Soft ripe tannins & subtle oak (none new) nicely balanced by boisterous, attractive fruit.

★★★★ **Shiraz** ⓃⒺⓌ Shows all the hallmarks of excellent vintage, **17** ⑧⑥ balancing red plums with delightful savoury nuance & warm spices. 10% new French oak adds kiss of vanilla at the finish.

★★★★ **Zinfandel** Fresher, more modern **18** ⑧⑥ steps up on **17** ★★★ ⑧⓪, red cherries (& just a suggestion of raisin) with bold but well-managed oak, 27% new. Individual wine, now with much wider appeal.

★★★★ **Estate Blend** Ⓠ Promising barrel sample of **17** ⑧⑥ 5-way Bordeaux red, mainly cabernet with merlot. Wonderful colour, then classic notes of blackcurrant pastille, tobacco, cassis, tar with attractive freshness & excellent weight.

Winning Blend ★★★☆ 36th Blaauwklippen Blending Competition winner. Previewed **18** ⑧③ focuses on zinfandel, with merlot, petit verdot & shiraz in attendance. Cheery black fruit, soft structure & lively vanilla sweetness in tail. Magnums only. Some Wellington grapes, as next. **Zinfandel Blanc de Noir** ★★★ Tailormade for summer, **19** ⑧② light & refreshing, with stalky fruit & bone-dry finish. **Sauvignon Blanc** Ⓠ ★★★★ From mostly cool-climate grapes, **18** ⑧⑤ zippy & lively, citrus plus tweaks of peachy tropical fruit. Soft, pleasant acidity & length. WO W Cape.

Specialities

★★★★ **Zinfandel Noble Late Harvest** Ⓠ Very sweet & raisined **13** ★★★ ⑧① botrytis dessert, older oak fermented/aged. Subtle spice & tobacco notes, not the precision or freshness of **12** ⑧⑦. 375 ml.

★★★★☆ **10 Year Potstill Brandy** Inviting light amber-gold gleams on exceptional 10 year old ⑨②, 100% potstill from chenin & colombard. Subtle texture & length, lovely intensity with luxurious chocolate, vanilla & spice flavours, tropical & floral perfumes. Packaging to match the sophistication.

Diva Zinfandel Méthode Cap Classique ★★★★ Unique bubbles from zinfandel. **17** ⑧③ good yeasty notes (20 months on lees) with red apples, cranberries & peach fruit for balance. Attractive savoury snap to slightly short finish but overall improvement on previous. **Before & After Aperitif** ★★★☆ Another singularity, fortified Noble Late Harvest malbec & shiraz (81/19), strikingly presented. **NV** ⑧③ broods with dark berries, plum cake & Xmas spice. Chewy tannins counteract significant 230 g/l sugar, making for well-balanced cheese partner or fireside sipper. Not tasted: **Ons Sprankel**. — CM, WB

Location/map: Stellenbosch ▪ Map grid reference: E7 ▪ WO: Stellenbosch/Coastal/Worcester/Western Cape ▪ Est 1682 ▪ 1stB 1974 ▪ Tasting & sales Mon-Sat 10–6 (summer)/10-5 (winter) Sun/pub hols 10–5 ▪ Wine tasting; chocolate & wine pairing; macaron & wine pairing; canapé & wine pairing ▪ Closed Dec 25 & Jan 1 ▪ Wine blending on request ▪ Cellar tours daily, booking advised ▪ Family market every Sun 10-3 ▪ Bistro ▪ Facilities for children ▪ Gift shop ▪ Weddings/functions ▪ Walks/hikes & MTB ▪ Gin & brandy (tastings only) ▪ Owner(s) Blaauwklippen Agricultural Estates (Pty) Ltd ▪ Winemaker(s) Narina Cloete (Jun 2016) ▪ Viticulturist(s) Jaco van der Westhuizen (Jun 2019) ▪ 160ha ▪ 500t/60,000cs wine & 650cs (x4-btl) brandy ▪ IPW ▪ PO Box 54 Stellenbosch 7599 ▪ info@blaauwklippen.com ▪ www.blaauwklippen.com ▪ S 33° 58' 23.3" E 018° 50' 51.0" ▪ 🎞 pillow.bank.pictures ▪ **T +27 (0)21-880-0133**

Black Block Wines

Architects Derick Henstra and Peter Fehrsen have worked together for nearly 20 years, and share an even longer interest in wine. Making wine started as a hobby, then became much more. They chose pinot noir as an intriguing, elegant, evocative and versatile variety. Fruit off high-lying Tulbagh and Durbanville vines is vinified with the aid of James McKenzie.

★★★★ **Pinot Noir** ⓠ Forthright, fragrant, sweetly ripe fruit on **17** ⑧⑥. Dark cherry flavours with savouriness on slightly rustic palate; plenty of acid & light tannic grip. Last was chunkier **14** ★★★★ ⑧④.— TJ

Location: Cape Town ▪ WO: Coastal ▪ Est/1stB 2012 ▪ Closed to public ▪ Owner(s) Derick Henstra & Peter Fehrsen ▪ Winemaker(s) Derick Henstra & Peter Fehrsen, advised by James McKenzie ▪ 100% red ▪ jacqui@ blackblockwines.co.za ▪ www.blackblockwines.co.za ▪ **T +27 (0)21-421-6803**

☐ **Black Box** *see* Wineways Marketing

Black Elephant Vintners ⓠ

'Black Elephant Vintners was born of synchronicity, fortuitous friendships and a love for wine,' say the three owners of this venture, ex-stockbroker Kevin Swart (his surname meaning 'black' in Afrikaans), his business partner Raymond Ndlovu ('elephant' in the Nguni languages) and 'vintner' Jacques Wentzel. Combining business acumen with winemaking expertise has paid dividends, their commercially successful sauvignon financing increasingly 'offroad' vinous specialisation (petite sirah rather than syrah, for example). 'We are the misfits of the wine industry, the rebels of the vine,' they aver, their unconventional approach extending to music-and-wine pairings available on-site in Franschhoek or other centres by appointment.

Black Elephant range

★★★★☆ **Amazing Grace** Only wine from own grapes, elegant **15** ⑨① seductive blackcurrant & sandalwood perfume, vanilla from 2 years in 50% new French oak. Palate is velvety, with rich dark cherry & berry fruit, a big step up on **14** ★★★★ ⑧④, previously listed under 'La Petite Vigne'. Also in magnum.

★★★★ **Three Men in a Tub with a Rubberduck Pinotage** From 2 old bushvine vineyards in Wellington & Franschhoek, **15** ⑧⑨ wild fermented then basket pressed into older French oak for 2 years has exotic frankincense aroma & intense dark fruit, rich & velvety yet fresh.

★★★★ **Rosé Rebel** 🆕 ⓥ Bursting with piquant red berries & citrus, Provence-style **19** ⑧⑥, in striking 'camouflage' packaging, is dry, with spicy finish, refreshing at 12% alcohol. From pinotage. WO W Cape.

★★★★ **Two Dogs, a Peacock & a Horse Sauvignon Blanc** ⓥ From 4 Franschhoek vineyards, **19** ⑧⑨ has intense gooseberry, granadilla, guava & zesty lime flavours, very lively yet also creamy from 3 months on lees (bâtonnage twice weekly). **18** untasted.

★★★★ **The Dark Side of the Vine Semillon** (🐝) From vineyard planted in 1905, given 24 hours skin contact before natural ferment/year on lees in old French oak, **16** ★★★★★ ⑨③ has fynbos & straw perfume, layers of stonefruit & citrus peel, walnut & nutmeg. As intensely rich as **15** ⑧⑦ but fresher.

★★★★☆ **Chardonnay Blanc de Blancs MCC** (NEW) (🐝) After 6 years on secondary fermentation lees, elegant **NV** ⑨③ sparkler from single vineyard is rich, complex yet crisply balanced, dry, with creamy mousse, hints of ginger biscuit & lemon curd as well as fresh citrus & green apple flavours.

★★★★ **Chardonnay-Pinot Noir Brut MCC** Disgorged after 16 months, sparkling **NV** ⑧⑨ has very fine mousse, slight sourdough aroma, forthright lemon, apple & white peach flavours. 75/25 ratio.

★★★★ **The Honey Thief Natural Sweet** From vine-dried sauvignon, inoculated with a Sauternes yeast, aged year in 50/50 old French oak & tank, **NV** ⑨① dessert even more unctuously decadent than last, at 238 g/l sugar, yet true to grape variety with tangy tropical tones, vibrant acidity. 375 ml.

Nicholas Red ★★★★ Syrah-led Rhône blend, seamless after 2 years older French oak, **16** ⑧⑤ soft, juicy red fruit, hints of fennel & dried herbs, modest 12.5% alcohol. Not tasted: **Timothy White**. Discontinued: **Amistad Pinotage, Amistad Syrah, The Fox & The Flamingo Full Bodied Rosé**.

The Back Roads range

★★★★ **Bakenshoek Grenache Noir** Medium-bodied **15** ⑧⑦ has fresh herb & sweet spice aromas, plenty of red fruit from natural vinification (30% wholebunch), short post-ferment maceration & older oak, like next.

★★★★ **Matoppie Petite Sirah** Unashamedly big, bold, ink-black **17** ★★★★★ ⑨② heady perfume of violets & black pepper, ripe dark fruit & bittersweet chocolate that persist on palate, the rich intensity of flavour & texture cut through by a sharp burst of acidity. Worth cellaring a few years, like last-made **15** ⑧⑨.

★★★★ **Bo Lamotte Viognier** Blossoms & spice on the nose, honey-drizzled peach & apricot fruit, some aniseed & ginger on the finish, also vanilla from 16 months in French oak. **17** ⑧⑥ more complex than last-tasted **15** ★★★★ ⑧④.

Occasional release: **Die Middagkrans Malbec**. — JG

Location/map: Franschhoek ▪ Map grid reference: C1 ▪ WO: Franschhoek/Western Cape ▪ Est 2013 ▪ 1stB 2012 ▪ Tasting, sales & cellar tours by appt ▪ Owner(s) Kevin Swart, Raymond Ndlovu & Jacques Wentzel ▪ Winemaker(s) Jacques Wentzel (Jan 2013) ▪ 140t/18,000cs own label 30% red 70% white ▪ IPW ▪ PO Box 686 Franschhoek 7690 ▪ sales@bevintners.co.za, jacques@bevintners.co.za, kevin@bevintners.co.za ▪ www. bevintners.co.za ▪ S 33° 54' 9.00 E 019° 7' 14.00" , S 33° 54' 20.47" E 019° 6' 52.75" (Ryan's Kitchen) ▪ 🅐🅕 wildly.mulling.firming ▪ **T +27 (0)21-876-2903**

☐ **Black Forest** see Louis
☐ **Black Granite** see Darling Cellars
☐ **Black Label** see Backsberg Estate Cellars

Black Oystercatcher Wines   🍷🍴🏠📷🚫♿

By the end of last century, the Humans were well established on their farm on the windy Agulhas plain, near the southern tip of Africa, so Dirk Human knew well 'the unique geology and cool climate' which would shape his wines. For in 1998, a pioneer of the Elim ward, he and his family planted vines. His terroir explorations have included making sauvignon blancs in the same way off three soil types - the wines (not tasted by us) were released last year. Black Oystercatcher is now a major destination in the area for everyone from brides to cyclists to diners. For beer drinkers too, with a resident craft beer producer.

★★★★ **Triton** Piquant red sees its shiraz component upped to 90% in **15** ⑧⑥, with splash cab. Spiced cherry, plum & mulberry aromas, hint of sumac in the flavours. Usual subtle French oak support.

★★★★ **Sauvignon Blanc** A cool-climate classic with lime, gooseberry & dried figs, clean-cut acidity & a mineral core, citrus/tropical notes lingering on finish in **18** ⑧⑦. Improves on **17** ★★★★ ⑧⑤.

★★★★☆ **White Pearl** (⊘) Standout Bordeaux-style white led by oak-matured semillon (68%) & well supported by fresh & fruity sauvignon. **17** ⑨① thrilling concentration & complexity of kiwi, lime, winter melon & buchu on rich, creamy palate, fresh acidity effortlessly maintains balance.

Cabernet Sauvignon-Merlot ★★★★ Ripe-fruited bouquet with herbal nuance on **16** ⑧④, polished tannins & mint chocolate finish. Similar blend (58/42) & commendably modest alcohol (12.5%) as previous.

Rosé ★★★★ From cab & merlot, with low 10% alcohol & bright coppery colour, youthful **19** ⑭ showcases maraschino cherry & aromatic spice leading to a note of salinity on dry, crisp palate. Cape Agulhas WO.

Méthode Cap Classique Brut Rosé ★★★ Onion-skin-hued, merlot-based **16** ⑫ frother with delicious whiffs of red fruit & dried roses, fresh smooth bubbles, pomegranate persistence. Ex farm only. — GM

Location: Elim ▪ Map: Southern Cape ▪ Map grid reference: B3 ▪ WO: Elim/Cape Agulhas ▪ Est 1998 ▪ 1stB 2003 ▪ Tasting & sales Tue-Sun 9-4 ▪ Sauvignon blanc vertical tasting by appt ▪ Closed Good Fri, Dec 24/25 & Jan 1 ▪ Restaurant, function & wedding venue: kitchen open Tue-Sun 11-2.30, booking essential (venue@ blackoystercatcher.co.za) ▪ Facilities for children ▪ Tour groups ▪ Conferences ▪ Conservation area ▪ Cycling route ▪ Annual Sauvignon Blanc & Oyster Festival (Dec); peak season programme and other activities throughout the year ▪ Accommodation (stay@blackoystercatcher.co.za) ▪ Fraser's Folly craft beer R40/tasting ▪ Owner(s)/cellarmaster(s)/viticulturist(s) Dirk Human ▪ Winemaker(s) Dirk Human, with Willem Pietersen ▪ 1,550ha/18.5ha (cab, merlot, shiraz, sauv, sem) ▪ ±110t/±15,000cs own label 20% red 60% white 20% rosé ▪ IPW, WIETA ▪ PO Box 199 Bredasdorp 7280 ▪ wine@blackoystercatcher.co.za, orders@blackoystercatcher.co.za ▪ www.blackoyster-catcher.co.za ▪ S 34° 37' 58.0" E 019° 49' 39.9" ▪ 🗺 posse.clergy.lifesavers ▪ **T +27 (0)28-482-1618**

☐ **Black Pack** *see* Painted Wolf Wines

Black Pearl Vineyards ⑨ 🏠 📷 ♿

Disney is a big market for this boutique winery on Paarl Mountain which shares its name with the legendary Pirates of the Caribbean ship. Here Mary-Lou Nash, American-born, self-taught vintner and Cape Wine Master, has broken the curse of the 'killer' drought that ruled out a 2017 harvest from her dryland vines, again managing to source 'outstanding' grapes for her new releases, while her 81-year-old father, Lance, a former medical doctor, happily manages 'the least commercial tasting room in SA' - his kitchen!

★★★★★ Oro ⊘ Offering astonishing value, plush **18** ⑨2 cab-shiraz (50/50) seduces with ripe dark fruit, dark chocolate, hints of liquorice & smoke after year in oak, 15% American. More concentrated than **16** ⑨3, with slightly higher alcohol, too (15%). No **17**.

★★★★ Chenin Blanc ⊘ Unwooded but lees-rich **19** ⑧9 from Swartland over-delivers on flavour (pineapple, peach & guava), creamy texture, vibrant acidity, fresh finish & moderate 12.5% alcohol.

Not tasted: **The Mischief Maker**. Occasional release: **Cabernet Sauvignon**, **Mourvèdre**, **Grenache-Mourvèdre**. — JG

Location/map: Paarl ▪ Map grid reference: D5 ▪ WO: Paarl/Swartland ▪ Est 1998 ▪ 1stB 2001 ▪ Tasting, sales & tours just about anytime but phone ahead ▪ Closed Dec 25 ▪ Walks ▪ Lapa & camping facilities ▪ Self-catering cottage ▪ Conservation area ▪ Owner(s) Lance & Mary-Lou Nash ▪ Winemaker(s)/viticulturist(s) Mary-Lou Nash CWM ▪ 240ha/7.2ha (cab, shiraz) ▪ ±5,000cs own label 90% red 10% white ▪ IPW ▪ PO Box Suider-Paarl 7624 ▪ info@blackpearlwines.com ▪ www.blackpearlwines.com ▪ S 33° 44' 10.5" E 018° 53' 40.8" ▪ 🗺 craziness.distinct.forgotten ▪ **T +27 (0)83-297-9796/+27 (0)83-395-6999**

☐ **Blacksmith** *see* The Blacksmith
☐ **Black Swan** *see* Hout Bay Vineyards
☐ **Black Tie** *see* Wineways Marketing

Blackwater Wine ⑨

Francois Haasbroek once said he seeks to 'tell the story' of 'small blocks planted with the right vines on great sites, whether by accident or design', but whose grapes disappear into bulk blends. He still ranges widely for those grapes, working closely with the growers where possible. Then he vinifies them, with minimal intervention, into a deliciously thoughtful collection, aiming to be true to the wines' origins. The Blackwater wines' light but serious and characterful elegance (without forgetting deliciousness) is rarely paralleled in SA. The base of Francois' operations is now fully at De Meye in Stellenbosch, where he is resident winemaker.

★★★★★ Omerta Carignan ⊘ Locally rare varietal bottling, 20% wholebunch, matured in neutral old oak. Forwardly aromatic **17** ⑨0, the fruit purity, fresh energy & good balance the main attractions on a wine with fairly simple flavours. Appealingly dry finish has echoes of sweet fruit. No **16**.

★★★★☆ **Zeitgeist Cinsaut** Even lighter in colour than Omerta, **18** ⑨² ex Darling has lovely bright perfume & a softly silky palate with delicious & lingering fruit. Light, integrated tannins & lowish 12% alcohol, yet no shred of non-vinous insipidity. Concrete 'egg'; 60% wholebunch - **17** ★★★★ ⑧⑨ a little less.

★★★★☆ **Daniel Grenache** ⊘ 🐝 Fragrant aromas & flavours richer & most complex of the reds, the acidity fully integrated, the tannic structure a little more assertive (but well padded). In short, **18** ⑨³ a fine wine with a good future. Properly & elegantly dry, like all these reds. From Bot River grapes.

★★★★ **Cuvee Terra Lux Pinot Noir** ⊘ Mature strawberry aromas & a pleasant funkiness on **16** ⑧⑥ ex Elgin. More savoury than fruity-charming, but with some depth of dark fruit, like robust **15** ★★★★ ⑧④.

★★★★☆ **Cultellus Syrah** 🐝 Quintessential syrah floral-herbal perfume on **17** ★★★★★ ⑨⑤. Mere 12.5% alcohol risky for Swartland fruit, but it works. Refined richness plus lively vibrancy; tannic structure & flesh recall a swimmer's lean, sleek musculature. Like **16** ⑨④, 40+% wholebunch; no new oak.

★★★★ **Noir** ⓠ Ripest, biggest feel of reds but no loss of balance, bright flavours from wholebunch portion on **15** ⑧⑨, syrah (89%), splashes co-fermented carignan, cinsaut. Supple, well-integrated tannins & lingering savouriness for current & future enjoyment.

★★★★☆ **Picquet Chenin Blanc** From mature Piketberg vineyard, **18** ⑨²'s lovely aromas are more complex than Underdog's, featuring dry fynbos, apricot. Rich & lipsmacking, the palate broadened & integrated by 10 months in old oak. Finishes with a nice phenolic bite.

★★★★ **The Underdog Chenin Blanc** ⊘ Now bottled, generous unoaked **18** ⑧⑨ is overtly fruity by Blackwater standards, offering pure quince & pear notes. These ripe charms well controlled by firm acidity, however. Also some breadth from lees ageing.

★★★★ **Pleasure Garden Palomino** From Robertson vines planted in 1927. Exciting acidity with soft texture the real attraction on neutral yet subtly aromatic & fairly flavoursome **18** ⑧⑧. 12% alcohol gives enough vinosity.

★★★★☆ **Riesling** ⊘ Fascinating, brave version of classic grape, if mostly geeky appeal. **18** ⑨⓪'s full aromas speak more of technique (8 days on skins) than variety. Exciting acidity (variety & Elgin speaking), with fruit to carry it, despite low 10.5% alcohol. Bone-dry. Great with food, like austere **17** ★★★★ ⑧④.

★★★★ **Highroller Sauvignon Blanc** ⊘ Notably characterful **19** ⑧⑧'s aromas have floral & blackcurrant notes as well as passionfruit. Expected bright acid, modest 12.5% alcohol. Ex Darling & Robertson. **17** untasted, **18** not made.

★★★★☆ **Blanc** ⓠ Mainly chenin, barrel fermented, with clairette & palomino both skin-fermented, then oak-aged 10 months. **17** ⑨⓪ pale orange, more vinous than fruity with savoury acid backbone, rumble of tannin; very tasty; good food partner. Occasional release, last was **14** ★★★★ ⑧⑧.

Discontinued: **Prodigium Pinot Noir**. — TJ

Location/map: Stellenbosch ▪ Map grid reference: E1 ▪ WO: Swartland/Western Cape/Elgin/Robertson/Darling/Bot River ▪ Est/1stB 2010 ▪ Tasting by appt only ▪ Owner(s) Blackwater Wines & Vines ▪ Cellarmaster(s)/winemaker(s)/viticulturist(s) Francois Haasbroek (Feb 2010) ▪ (carignan, cinsaut, pinot, shiraz, chenin, palomino, sauv) ▪ 30t/5,000cs own label 70% red 30% white ▪ Rose Str, Paarl 7646 ▪ info@blackwaterwine.com ▪ www.blackwaterwine.com ▪ S 33° 49' 0.7" E 018° 49' 48.8" ▪ 🗺 movable.wisp.simulator ▪ **T +27 (0)82-329-8849**

Blake Family Wines

Swartland is a major grape-hunting ground for husband-and-wife team Andries and Marinda Blake. After working in the area for many of his more than 25 years as winemaker, Andries has a nose for finding the best blocks, mainly dryland bushvines, for their boutique label. Blending is where Andries believes a winemaker can show flair and skill. Hence the two 'gems' in the range, which also reflect the unique taste of the region. A single-vineyard version of the malbec was due at press time.

Blake's Family Wines range

★★★★ **Amethyst** Bushvine pinotage (60%) with shiraz, cab in **17** ⑧⑥. Homogeneous, savoury mix; full bodied, flesh still needs to fully emerge from tannin grip, French oak (80% new).

★★★★ **Tourmaline** Chenin-led, chardonnay, viognier blend, as usual, in previewed **18** ⑧⑦. Forthcoming, flavoursome; new oak still prominent but plentiful tangy lime fruit & nutty richness should give much pleasure once settled & integrated.

Malbec ★★★★ Fresh & tangy, **18** ⑧③ ex Franschhoek has sweet, juicy fruit & rounded tannins. Oaking, all-new French, adds toasty extras. **Chenin Blanc** ⓠ ★★★★ Full of sun-filled juicy flavours enhanced by 30% oaking, all new, **17** ⑧⑤ is characterful & satisfying. WO W Cape. — AL

Location: Malmesbury ▪ WO: Swartland/Western Cape ▪ Est 2013 ▪ 1stB 2011 ▪ Closed to public ▪ Sales via website, selected wine shops & cellar door facility ▪ Owner(s) Andries & Marinda Blake ▪ Cellarmaster(s)/wine-maker(s) Andries Blake ▪ 5t/2,000cs own label 40% red 60% white ▪ Other export brand: Blake's Boys ▪ PO Box 1121 Malmesbury 7299 ▪ info@blakefamilywines.com ▪ www.blakefamilywines.com ▪ **T +27 (0)82-922-6162**

☐ **Blake's Boys** *see* Blake Family Wines
☐ **Bloemcool** *see* Fairview

Bloemendal Wine Estate   ⓠ ⑪ ⓐ ⓑ

Andri Hanekom might be cellarmaster at this extensive corporate-owned Durbanville estate, established in 1702 to provide fresh produce for Dutch East India Company ships, but he's unafraid of mud on his boots since he doubles as the property's viticulturist (see their Facebook page for video evidence of his pruning skills!). Rock-steady winemaker Christie 'Boetman' Langeveldt has worked in the cellar since 2006, fine-tuning the ranges and particularly the two calling cards, Semillon and Suider Terras Sauvignon, from a 35+ year-old-year vineyard. Visitors flock in to enjoy weekly trail runs, market and on-site family restaurant.

Estate range

★★★★ **Tierberg Single Vineyard Syrah** ⓠ Riper dark spice on **14** ⑧⑨ than previous, richer, more immediately approachable but also sufficient structure to warrant ageing. Older French oak.

★★★★ **Single Vineyard Chardonnay** Initial citrus freshness of **15** ★★★★ ⑧④ quickly makes way for creamy vanilla oak. Rich & broad, but a little less poised than **14** ⑧⑨.

★★★★☆ **Suider Terras Sauvignon Blanc** Balances blackcurrant & tropicality with signature cool-climate flint & white pepper of windswept vineyard. **16** ⑨② taut & zesty but platform of oak (all-new, 11 months) adds structure & length.

★★★★☆ **Semillon** ⓠ Promises to be up with best of this variety. **14** ⑨④ smart oaking (seasoned 500L French) enhances naturally silky texture & citrus peel, lemongrass concentration, though there is still a sense of tightness, linearity. All suggest lengthy lifespan.

★★★★☆ **Kanonberg** ⓠ Excellent follow up to **14** ★★★★★ ⑨⑤, **15** ⑨③ sauvignon/semillon 70/30 partnership enhanced by careful oaking (50% barrel fermented, 100% oaked as blend). Dense silk texture energised by bracing acidity & 12.5% alcohol for a balanced whole, with great future.

Méthode Cap Classique ⓠ ★★★ For those who like some real pizazz in their sauvignon/semillon, **15** ⑧① displays pairing's typical fruit plus a little leesy extra dimension & refreshing bubble. Not tasted: **Semillon Noble Late Harvest**.

Waterlily range

★★★★ **Shiraz** ⓠ Most serious of range, still youthfully accessible. **15** ⑧⑦ shows medium-bodied elegance in its dark berries & spice, suppleness, well-rounded dryness. Older oak, 17 months; 40% unwooded. **Cabernet Sauvignon** ★★★☆ Hedgerow herbaceous nuance to black-fruited **15** ⑧④, swarthy presence of oak (20% new, 18 months) bulks it up from lightness of previous. **Malbec** ⓠ ★★★★ In pure, fruit-forward mode as range dictates. **16** ⑧⑤ ripe & vibrantly fresh dark berry flavours; nip of tannin lends form without disturbing early-drinking satisfaction. Older oak. **Merlot** ⓠ ★★★ Sweet-fruited **16** ⑧⓿ has juicy flesh, balanced freshness & hint toasty oak to counteract sweetish conclusion. **Pinotage** ★★★☆ Approachable & easy **16** ⑧③ offers ripe red berry fruits with inky edge. Oaking as for Cab. **Shiraz Rosé** ★★★★ Bright, light & fresh **18** ⑧④, ample plum & blueberry charm. Midweight, with good length of flavour. **Sauvignon Blanc** ★★★☆ Improves on previous in its limy zip. **18** ⑧⑤ vivid acidity balanced by grapefruit charm, lean but supple. — FM

Location/WO: Durbanville ▪ Map: Durbanville, Philadelphia & Darling ▪ Map grid reference: C7 ▪ Est 1702 ▪ 1stB 1987 ▪ Tasting & sales Mon-Sat 10-5 Sun/pub hols 11-3; larger groups by appt ▪ Tasting fee R50pp ▪ Closed Dec 25/26 & Jan 1 ▪ Bon Amis @ Bloemendal ▪ MTB ▪ Owner(s) Spirito Trade 82 (Pty) Ltd ▪ Cellarmaster(s)/viticulturist(s) Andri Hanekom (2017) ▪ Winemaker(s) Boetman Langevelt (2006) ▪ (cab, malbec, merlot, ptage, shiraz, chard, sauv, sem) ▪ 100t ▪ PO Box 466 Durbanville 7551 ▪ info@bloemendalwines.co.za ▪ www.bloemendalwines.co.za ▪ S 33° 50' 22.1" E 018° 36' 1.4" ▪ ◫ patterned.upward.perspective ▪ **T +27 (0)21-975-9591**

☐ **Blouvlei** see Mont du Toit Kelder

Blue Crane Vineyards

A breeding pair of SA's endangered national bird inspired the name of this Tulbagh property, bought by Johannesburg-based mining businessman and racehorse owner Fred Crabbia in 2009. Husband-and-wife duo Chris and Zia Fox handle the vines and wines respectively, along with the olive groves.

★★★★ Pinotage ⓠ Subtle soft plum fruit of **15** ★★★★ ⑧⑤ shaded by spicy oak (40% new, some American, as for Shiraz) mid-2018. Needs time to meld. **14** ⑧⑦ better balanced in youth.

. . . .

Pinot Noir Rosé ⓝⓔⓦ ⓥ ★★★★ Light-bodied, succulent yet zippy **18** ⑧④ oozes red berry appeal. Good fruit/acid balance. Ideal summertime sipper.

. . . .

Cabernet Sauvignon ⓠ ★★★ Perfectly correct & particularly pleasant **11** ⑧②, with dash shiraz, offers black fruit, polish & cedar spice. **Shiraz** ⓠ ★★★★ Rich, spicy **14** ⑧④ is fresh, bright & supple, with good fruit/oak balance (touch less American wood than Pinotage). **Sauvignon Blanc** ⓠ ★★★★ Produced intermittently. Signature grapefruit & lemon-pith tang on **17** ⑧④. Good body & length with lasting fruit on leesy tail. **Viognier** ⓥ ★★★★ Peach typicity & lees breadth on bold **17** ⑧④. Succulent & fresh, with oak (40% new) well integrated. Touch of heat from 15% alcohol. **First Flight** ⓥ ★★★ Easy stonefruit & lemon appeal to **18** ⑧② sauvignon, chenin & viognier blend. Less rich, ripe than previous. In abeyance: **SMV, Full Flight, Chenin Blanc**. — FM

Location/WO: Tulbagh ▪ Est 2001 ▪ 1stB 2004 ▪ Closed to public ▪ Sales via website ▪ Owner(s) Fred & Manuela Crabbia ▪ Cellarmaster(s)/winemaker(s) Zia Fox ▪ Viticulturist(s) Chris Fox ▪ 138ha/9ha (cab, mourv, ptage, pinot, shiraz, chard, chenin, sauv, viog) ▪ 4,000cs own label 75% red 25% white ▪ PO Box 306 Tulbagh 6820 ▪ info@bluecrane.co.za, wines@bluecrane.co.za ▪ www.bluecrane.co.za ▪ **T +27 (0)60-980-0384/+27 (0)82-495-8512**

☐ **Blue Moose** see The Grape Grinder

Blue Owl Wines   ⓠ

Rich wildlife on the old Franschhoek property Riversmeet, in particular a barn-lodging owl and its endearing offspring, inspired this label. The farm is now part of Allée Bleue and its fruit is vinified there.

Chardonnay ⓥ ⓥ ★★★★ Feisty, unoaked **18** ⑧⑤ packs a delicious limy melon punch from old vines, lees contact (4 months) adds a creamy nuance. Fresh & quaffable solo or with a meal.

. . . .

Merlot ⓠ ★★★★ Structured & juicy **17** ⑧⑤, ample sour cherry & blackcurrant flavour but shade less finesse than in last-tasted **15** ★★★★ ⑧⑦. — MW

Location: Franschhoek ▪ WO: Coastal ▪ 1stB 2015 ▪ Tasting at Allée Bleue Wines ▪ Winemaker(s) Van Zyl du Toit, with Georgina Wilkenson (Jan 2019) ▪ PO Box 100 Groot Drakenstein 7680 ▪ info@alleebleue.com ▪ www.alleebleue.com ▪ **T +27(0) 21-874-1021**

Boekenhoutskloof Winery   ⓠ ⓑ

There is much industry discussion about the perceived need for South Africa to ascend to the next level by producing wines that are not only superlative but also produced with sufficient consistency, depth and scale to draw large numbers of winelovers, collectors and investors worldwide into a long-term relationship. That's why Boekenhoutskloof is so relevant and exciting, and the deserved recipient of this edition's Editor's Award Winery of the Year. In 25 years, the 'Cape beech ravine' farm and winery at the southern corner of Franschhoek Valley has developed remarkably - recently and noticeably with a massive and spectacular semi-underground maturation cellar, connected by tunnel to the winery. Even more impressive is the expansion of the Boekenhoutskloof brand, which includes high-scoring Chocolate Block at well over 100,000 cases, and also owns Wolftrap, Porcupine Ridge and Vinologist (listed elsewhere), and properties in Stellenbosch, Hemel-en-Aarde (see Cap Maritime entry) and Swartland – where Porseleinberg has its own highly reputed label but now also grows much of the fruit for the famous Boekenhoutskloof Syrah. Credit for all this goes not least to prime force Marc Kent, Boekenhoutskloof's original winemaker. Although he remains very much hands-on, his place in the cellar is largely filled by Gottfried Mocke, now well settled in.

★★★★☆ **Franschhoek Cabernet Sauvignon** ⓐ Complex & intense black berry fruit, cigarbox & cool fresh herb fragrance from splash cab franc (9%) on 30% barrel-fermented **17** ⑨④. Very firm, with a fine-grain tannin structure buffed in 80% new French barriques (18 months, as next 3). Needs time to show true charm, decant in youth.

★★★★☆ **Stellenbosch Cabernet Sauvignon** ⓐ Finesse & style on **17** ⑨④, shows weighty richness & delicately perfumed fruit, power with balance & harmony. Dab cab franc (4%) brings herbal lift to the savoury long finish. 60% new small-oak. Not for the impatient. From four parcels in Helderberg & Faure.

★★★★☆ **CWG Auction Reserve Syrah** ⓐ Floral notes edge through spicy hedgerow fruit, polished leather, white pepper & cured meat in **17** ★★★★★ ⑨⑤. Fine tannin structure, intense & concentrated, made for the long haul. As with **16** ⑨③, 50/50 Swartland (Porseleinberg) & biodynamically farmed Stellenbosch fruit, 50% wholebunch fermented, only older-oaked.

★★★★★ **Syrah** ⓐ Inky purple **17** ⑨⑤ balances power & restraint, suppleness & concentration, with pristine blue-black fruit, polished leather & fine integrated oak flavours (ex 2,500L older Austrian foudres) in a sumptuous mouthful. Swartland fruit, spontaneously fermented, 35-40% wholebunch. Like **16** ★★★★★ ⑨③, will reward the patient.

★★★★☆ **The Chocolate Block** ⓐ Enviable quality plus sizeable production - 107,500 cases in **18** ⑨③. Sumptuous, with dark berry depth, long savoury finish. Syrah (69%), grenache, cinsaut, a little cab & viognier, all from Swartland. In 1.5L, 3L & 6L too. **17** ★★★★★ ⑨⑤ also plush & generous.

★★★★☆ **Semillon** ⓐ ⓦ Old vines (planted 1902, 1936 & 1942) with dash muscat d'Alexandrie (1902) for **17** ⑨④. Expressive & generous, with refined lemon, lime, stonefruit & beeswax aromas & flavours. Regal & textured, sublime. Natural ferment, 80% in new oak, rest concrete 'eggs'.

★★★★☆ **Noble Late Harvest** ⓐ Botrytised semillon dessert wine, **16** ⑨④ intense, unctuous but understated, has layer upon layer of marmalade, candied citrus peel, ginger, wax & honey flavours, superb acid balance. A triumph. 100% new oak for 30 months. 375 ml. Will age decade-plus.— WB

Location/map: Franschhoek ▪ Map grid reference: D1 ▪ WO: Franschhoek/Swartland/Coastal/Stellenbosch ▪ Est 1994 ▪ 1stB 1996 ▪ Tasting by appt only ▪ Closed all pub hols ▪ Owner(s) Boekenhoutskloof Winery (Pty) Ltd ▪ Cellarmaster(s) Marc Kent (1994) ▪ Winemaker(s) Gottfried Mocke, Johan Nesenberend, Heinrich Hugo & Eben Meiring ▪ Viticulturist(s) Takkies Cloete ▪ Boekenhoutskloof: 71ha/9ha (cabs s/f, merlot, sem); Porseleinberg: 135ha/90ha (cinsaut, grenache, shiraz); Goldmine: 65ha/40ha (cinsaut, grenache, shiraz, chenin) ▪ 60% red 39% white 1% rosé ▪ BRC, HACCP, IPW ▪ PO Box 433 Franschhoek 7690 ▪ info@boekenhoutskloof.co.za ▪ www.boekenhoutskloof.co.za ▪ S 33° 56' 33.0" E 019° 6' 28.0" ▪ Ⓜ franchiser. dipper.reduce ▪ **T** +27 (0)21-876-3320

☐ **Boer & Brit** *See Editor's Note*

Boland Cellar ⓠ ⓟ ⓒ

Paarl-based Boland Cellar's 53 grower-owners control 1,516 ha of vineyards across a wide area, a significant resource for the wine portfolio. Hence the Five Climates range, or even the winery's name, Boland. There's new strategic vision, to focus particularly on four varieties, chenin (of course, with already five wines/blends in place), shiraz (four existing wines/blends), chardonnay and merlot. The homework has been done, and the track record shows an understanding of terroir, wine styles and ranges, and the awards to back it up.

Reserve No. 1 range

★★★★ **Cabernet Sauvignon** ⓥ Previewed **17** ⑧⑧ intense cassis, oak (20 months, 20% new) in support for spicing & tannin. Very impressive fruit profile, on both concentration & silky succulence.

★★★★ **Shiraz** ⓥ True to style, **17** ⑧⑧ barrel sample shows plush dark fruit & cigarbox, firm ageing foundation yet currently accessible, no hard edges. 10% new oak, breaks from mainly new of **16** ⑧⑧.

★★★★ **Chardonnay** ⓠ Oak caramel spices dominate pre-bottled **16** ⑧⑥ from partial barrel ferment, year ageing. Appealing orange marmalade fruit, full bodied & textured. Rung above **15** ★★★☆ ⑧⑤.

★★★★ **Chenin Blanc** ⓧ Partial barrel ferment for previewed **17** ⑧⑧, total 14 months oak, long lees contact. Has intense stonefruit, good palate weight; fruit is the hero, savoury spicing subtle.

★★★★ **Chenin Blanc Unwooded** ⓧ Nice contrast to oaked sibling. **19** ⑧⑦ ex tank already expressive, melon & green fig, underlying thatch. Tightly focused freshness keeps everything lively, on track.

Merlot ⓧ ★★★★ Sweet caramel, toffee & minty notes on **12** ⑧⑤. Concentrated plummy fruit, firm body but rather abrupt finish. **Pinotage** ⓧ ★★★★ Fresh & flavourful **12** ⑧⑤ avoids variety's negatives, offering elegant, bright fruit & well-shaped tannins. Bit short on finish. WO Paarl, as previous two.

One Formation range

★★★★ **Pinotage-Shiraz-Grenache** ⓧ Equal main partners with 10% grenache, **18** ⑧⑧ pre-bottling packed with luscious dark fruit, vanilla spiced from 16 months oaking (as rest), for most of blend. Tannins evident but ripe, smooth. No **17**.

★★★★ **Shiraz-Grenache-Viognier** ⓧ Shiraz at 80% dictates in **17** ⑧⑧ preview, smoky, liquorice-toned, black plums & silky texture. Fruit is king here despite oaking for most of wine, gives flavour, supple tannin.

★★★★ **Chenin Blanc-Sauvignon Blanc-Grenache Blanc** ⓧ Tank sample **19** ⑧⑨'s style set by chenin (70%), others add nuances. Lightly oaked, initial quince & stonefruit, becoming more limy & mineral on the palate. Elegant, complex, involving. WO W Cape.

Five Climates Single Varietal range

Chardonnay ⓧ ★★★ Grapefruit & tangerine in unoaked **19** ⑧①, zesty fresh drinkability, & palate weight from 3 months on lees. **Chenin Blanc** ⓧ ★★★★ Good-value range, with varietal purity, as all Boland chenins; bruised apple & thatch in **19** ⑧④, tart apple freshness to waken the taste buds. **Sauvignon Blanc** ⓧ ★★★ Litchi, with some leafy notes, **19** ⑧⓪ shows good sauvignon typicity, even to the zesty minerality at the end.

Talent & Terroir range

Chenin Blanc ⓧ ★★★★ Tasted ex tank, citrus & winter melon, **19** ⑧④ vibrates with freshness, shows another style to Five Climates, still variety-true & delicious. WO Paarl. Not tasted: **Shiraz**. Occasional release: **Sauvignon Blanc**. — CR

Location/map: Paarl ▪ Map grid reference: E4 ▪ WO: Coastal/Paarl/Western Cape ▪ Est/1stB 1941 ▪ Tasting & sales Mon-Fri 9—5 Sat/pub hols 10-3 ▪ Closed Easter weekend, Dec 25/26 & Jan 1 ▪ Meals/refreshments - booking essential ▪ Owner(s) 53 producing shareholders ▪ Winemaker(s) Handré Barkhuizen (2009) & Bernard Smuts (2001), with Monique de Villiers (2015) & Rosco Lewis (2016) ▪ Viticulturist(s) Spekkies van Breda (2016) ▪ 1,516ha (cab, merlot, ptage, shiraz, chard, chenin, nouvelle, sauv, viog) ▪ 12,500t/205,000cs own label 48% red 50% white 2% rosé + 129,000cs for clients ▪ Other export brands: Lindenhof, Lionsway, Montestell ▪ WIETA ▪ PO Box 7007 Noorder-Paarl 7623 ▪ info@bolandkelder.co.za ▪ www.bolandkelder.co.za, www.bolandcellar.co.za ▪ S 33° 48' 47.21" E 018° 48' 31.70" (farm), S 33° 41' 19.6" E 018° 57' 20.1" (deli) ▪ [f] though.contributed.quotable ▪ **T +27 (0)21-872-1766**

☐ **Boland Kelder** see Boland Cellar

Bon Courage Estate   ⓧ ⓧ ⓧ ⓧ ⓧ

Bruwer-family-owned property in Robertson, with the members very much hands-on. Patriarch Willie planted chenin and muscats in the 1920s; his son André established the classic varieties and is now in charge of viticulture, a not insignificant task with 150 ha of vines to oversee. The three rivers on the property, which include the Breede, have all contributed to soil diversity, aiding varietal compatibility. Scion Jacques is the cellar chief, and will be joined by fourth-generation Ilse when she returns from gaining winemaking experience overseas, an example set by her father.

Inkará range

★★★★ **Cabernet Sauvignon** ⓧ More muscular than BC range version; long skin contact, 18-24 months new oak, spicy **16** ⑨⓪ is deep & dark, cocoa-rich chocolate, black plums. Tannins evident, foundation for ageing but not harsh. Serve with rich dishes, but best lies ahead.

★★★★ **Merlot** ⓧ Lovely fruit on **16** ⑧⑧, plums & berries, 18 months oaking a dark chocolate overlay plus a firm backbone for cellaring. Already accessible, enjoyable, but designed for a rewarding future.

★★★★ **Shiraz** All-new oak, 18–24 months, combo French/American, which together with dense, opulent fruit creates a delicious mocha, dark chocolate effect. Silky smooth, harmonious, **16** ★★★★☆ ⑨① is seductive, not for long ageing but who would want to? Improves on **15** ⑧⑨.

Pinot Noir ★★★☆ More restraint in **16** ⑧⑤ than **15** ⑧④, closer to variety's character: raspberry, some earthy notes, elegant, smooth textured. Mainly older French barrels, 24 months, provide svelte tannins.

Jacques Bruére Méthode Cap Classique sparkling range

★★★★☆ **Cuvée Brut Rosé** ⊘ 🐝 New disgorgement, as all. Palest pink, **11** ★★★★★ ⑨⑤ 80% pinot noir, rest chardonnay, all 3 bubblies long lees contact (60 months). Red fruit quite overt, chardonnay freshness as palate back-up, impression of vitality & surprising youth. Stylish, elegant, refined, like **10** ⑨①.

★★★★☆ **Blanc de Blancs** 🐝 **11** ⑨③ one of oldest MCCs available, as rest of range, & benefits in every way. Chardonnay, bone-dry, elegant & refined, showing lemon preserve, richly textured creamy palate. Impressive now, will still keep a few years. Also in 3L.

★★★★☆ **Brut Reserve** 60/40 pinot noir, chardonnay, small portion barrel-fermented, on lees 8 months (as rest), then bottle fermented. **11** ⑨② deepened richness, toasted brioche, baked apple & lemon preserve, flavour-loaded finish. Powerful, a statement wine. Enjoy now at peak.

Bon Courage range

★★★★ **Cabernet Sauvignon** ⊘ Wholeberry ferment, new French oak, warranted by **16** ⑧⑧'s cassis concentration. Seductive spicing, nutmeg & cloves, lots on offer, including supple tannins. Earlier drinking than Inkará sibling.

★★★★ **Le Terroir Chardonnay** ⑧ Same winemaking as Prestige Cuvée, **16** ⑧⑦ takes it to another level. Forthcoming citrus preserve perfume & flavours, laced with brightening acidity, vanilla notes an underpin. Intense, vibrant.

★★★★ **Gewürztraminer Special Late Harvest** Aromatic **19** ⑧⑨ preview is rosepetal & Turkish delight scented, full-sweet, flavours of pineapple & white peach, zesty acidity. Modest 12% alcohol but you wouldn't know, there's so much flavour richness.

★★★★☆ **Noble Late Harvest** ⊘ 🐝 Unoaked & just 9% alcohol but **18** ⑨③ riesling botrytis dessert packs quite a punch, honey & apricots, some pineapple, with wonderful sugar/fruit intensity. Piercing acidity adds tension, enlivens the fruit, finishing long & mouthfilling. No **17**. 375 ml.

★★★★☆ **White Muscadel** 🐝 Fortified muscat de Frontignan, sibling to the Red but at another level; sultana & stonefruit perfume/flavours in **19** ⑨④ preview, citrus zest on the palate. Concentrated, full-sweet, full-bodied, with revitalising acidity. Complex & involving.

. . . .

André's Fame Colombard 🍷 ★★★ And the fame is deserved: litchi/guava throughout **19** ⑧②, mouthwatering freshness & friendly 10.5% alcohol. Unerringly hits the spot. **Gewürztraminer Dry** ⊘ 🍷 ★★★★ Something special, unbottled **19** ⑧④ shows all the aromatic charm of the variety, rosewater & papaya, then changes on the palate, exotic Asian spice & tightly focused freshness. Lovely. **The Gooseberry Bush Sauvignon Blanc** 🍷 ★★★ Offers that & more, especially in the flavours, **19** ⑧② also has sage & capsicum, but the main attraction is the freshness, vibrant & alive.

. . . .

The Mulberry Bush Merlot ★★★ Apt name for lightly oaked **19** ⑧①, designed for early enjoyment, juicy & fresh. **Pinotage** ★★★ Partial barrel ferment, French/American, then 12 months maturating; **16** ⑧①'s opulent fruit easily handles that, a savoury seam, good grip at the end. **The Pepper Tree Shiraz** ★★★★ Wholeberry ferment, so the fruit focus is a given, partial barrel, then 15 months French. Boldly ripe **17** ⑧⑤ is curvaceous, has smoky, spicy tones, but also offers scrub, remains true to the variety. **Estate Red Blend** ⊘ ★★★★ Consistent style, well matched, cab-led with 40% shiraz. Cassis core with spicy, smoky top notes in **18** ⑧④ preview aided by smooth ripe tannins, the 12 months in barrel just right. **Lady of the House** 🆕 ★★★ Welcome addition, in honour of all the ladies of the house, dry rosé, in contrast to Like Father. Delicate pink from pinotage but nothing else shy, **19** ⑦⑧ is berries & candyfloss, zesty-fresh. **Chardonnay Prestige Cuvée** ★★★★ Oak's presence seen in **18** ⑧④'s vanilla top note, an appealing partner to the citrus. Full flavoured & long, a great food wine. **Chardonnay Unwooded** ★★★ Citrus freshness in **19** ⑧① tank sample, grapefruit, touch of lime, with nice rounded mouthfeel from 6 months on lees. **Estate Blend White** ★★★ Colombard dominates (70%) but **19** ⑧①'s unoaked chardonnay adds peach & citrus notes to the litchi, creating a fruit array, perked up by zesty acidity. **Blush Vin Doux** ★★★☆ From red muscadel, no surprise when you taste this latest pink sweet **NV** ⑦ carbonated bubbly. Very aromatic, grapes & raisins, the fizz turning it into party mode. **Red Muscadel ★★★★** Tasted ex tank, fortified **19** ⑧ from muscat d'Frontignan is bright pink, has raisin & dried fruit styling, wonderfully expressive. Full-sweet, with fruit-packed flavours, rich & uncloying. **Cape Vintage ★★★** Pre-bottled **18** ⑧ from equal touriga, tinta & souzão, classic port varieties. Spent 12 months in old barrels: opulent fruitcake richness with liquorice tones, smooth & mouthfilling.

Like Father Like Son range
Merlot-Cabernet Sauvignon ⊘ **★★★** Merlot 60% in **19** ⑦ unoaked blend, nothing pretentious, just fruity, smooth-textured enjoyment. **Pinotage Rosé ★★** Pale pink, strawberry-scented & -flavoured **19** ⑦ easy to like, semi-sweet & tangy-fresh. WO W Cape. **Chenin Blanc ★★★** Budget priced & made for sharing with friends, as all these. Apple & green plum in expressive **19** ⑦ preview, dry & fruity-fresh, lively. — CR

Location/map: Robertson ▪ Map grid reference: B5 ▪ WO: Robertson/Western Cape ▪ Est 1927 ▪ 1stB 1983 ▪ Tasting & sales Mon-Fri 8–5 Sat 9–3 ▪ Fee R30pp/5 wines; booking essential for groups of 10+ ▪ Closed Good Fri, Dec 25 & Jan 1 ▪ Café Maude T +27 (0)23-626-6806 ▪ Facilities for children ▪ Olive oil ▪ Owner(s) André & Jacques Bruwer ▪ Winemaker(s) Jacques Bruwer, with Phillip Viljoen (Jan 2015) ▪ Viticulturist(s) André Bruwer ▪ 150ha (cab, pinot, shiraz, chard) ▪ 40% red 50% white 10% rosé ▪ Export brand: Three Rivers ▪ PO Box 589 Robertson 6705 ▪ wine@boncourage.co.za ▪ www.boncourage.co.za ▪ S 33° 50' 43.8" E 019° 57' 38.0" ▪ 🔟 lushly.widgets.forgave ▪ **T +27 (0)23-626-4178**

☐ **Bonfire Hill** *see* Bruce Jack Wines
☐ **Bonne Esperance** *see* KWV Wines

Bonnievale Wines
The merger end-2018 of Bonnievale Wines and fellow Breede River Valley wine company Wandsbeck has CEO John Barnardt and team (now including experienced CWG protégé winemaker Heinrich Kulsen) over-seeing four modern cellars sourcing grapes from over 100 growers. They're 'only bottling the best', says brand representative Nina Steenkamp, following renewed focus on fruit quality, restructuring for greater efficiency, and rebranding (a fresh logo, more tiers to assist consumers in their choice within an expanded portfolio). New vines and varieties are coming on-stream, so 'expect to see some interesting, niche additions'.

Barrel Select range
★★★★ Shiraz ② A real fireside comforter, **15** ⑧ liquidised dark fruit & dried prunes in a generous spice-sprinkled body; balanced, with cappuccino on the finish.
Cabernet Sauvignon ② **★★★★** Ripe blackcurrant in a supple structure, **15** ⑧ medium body, dry, chocolate & vanilla notes adding depth to tasty mouthful.

River Collection
....
Cinsault Rosé ⊘ ⊕ **★★★** Palest salmon colour, dry **19** ⑧ charms with earthy spice, pulped berries & a lemon twist. Perfect for grilled fish. **Chardonnay** ⊘ ⊕ **★★★★** A sunshine wine, fleshy & bright, with apple & orchard flavours. Unoaked **19** ⑧ is delightful, finishes whistle-clean. **Chenin Blanc** ⊘ ⊕ **★★★★** Abundant tropical & citrus flavour on **19** ⑧, crisp, delicious & very pocket friendly. Stock up for summer. **Sauvignon Blanc** ⊕ **★★★** Water-white **19** ⑧ as drinkable as last plus touch more complexity in the spread of green plum, cut grass & fresh citrus flavours.
....
Merlot ② **★★★** No-worries **17** ⑧ will welcome you home, offer Christmas cake & plum pudding with mulled wine spices. **Pinotage ★★★** Easy & accessible, just-dry **18** ⑧, delightful rich berry compote flavours & espresso wafts from American oak staving. A real crowd pleaser. **Shiraz** ② **★★** Dark sweet fruit mixed with toffee, **17** ⑦ is juicy if tad less generous than last. **Cabernet Sauvignon-Merlot** ② **★★★** Sweet black fruit, spicecake & mocha touch make **17** ⑦ slip down easily. In abeyance: **Natural Sweet Shiraz**.

Nature range
Night ★★ Just-dry **NV** ⑦ red with dark berry flavours & brisk goodbye. **Dusk ★★** Light floral wafts on gently fizzy, sweet, low-alcohol **NV** ⑦ rosé. **Dawn ★★** Ripe tropical fruit in easy, sweet, quaffable **NV** ⑦ white. **Mist ★★** Easy if fleeting dry, low-alcohol **NV** ⑦ white. Discontinued: **Sushi**.

Wine Tastings & Pairings
Perdeberg boasts with
a variety of wines that's
made from quality Dry
land grapes.

Restaurant & Picnics
Honest and proudly
South African cuisine
that appeals to the whole
family.

*Treat the family to an authentic winelands experience
and visit Perdeberg! Savour and taste the quality of
award-winning dryland influenced wines, followed
by a delicious breakfast, lunch or gourmet braai picnic
prepared by the restuurant.*

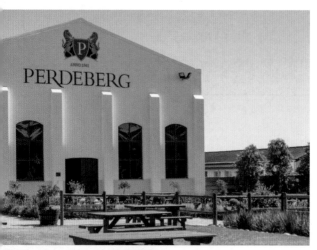

The Vale range
Cinsault Rosé Brut (NEW) ★★ Palest pink **NV** (73) fizz with earthy flavours, sweetish & light (±11% alcohol). **Sauvignon Blanc Brut** ★★★ Vigorous mousse on crisp & lean **NV** (77) bubbly, to get the party started. — WB

Location/WO: Bonnievale ▪ Map: Robertson ▪ Map grid reference: D3 ▪ Est 1950 ▪ 1stB 1977 ▪ Tasting & sales Mon-Fri 9–5 Sat 10–1 ▪ Closed Easter Fri-Mon, Dec 25/26 & Jan 1 ▪ Cheese straws ▪ Facilities for children ▪ Tour groups ▪ Conferences (12 pax) ▪ Christmas Market ▪ Owner(s) 110 members ▪ Winemaker(s) Marthinus Rademeyer (Dec 2009), Edwin Mathambo (Dec 2012), Jean Slabber (Jun 2017) & Heinrich Kulsen (2018) ▪ Viticulturist(s) Sakkie Bosman (Nov 2006) ▪ 1,697ha (cab, merlot, ptage, shiraz, chard, chenin, cbard, sauv) ▪ ISO 22 000, IPW, WIETA ▪ PO Box 206 Bonnievale 6730 ▪ info@bonnievalewines.co.za ▪ www.bonnievale-wines.co.za ▪ S 33° 57′ 27″ E 020° 06′ 06″ ▪ ⌖ article.traumas.responded ▪ **T +27 (0)23-616-2795**

Bonview Wines

From their Somerset West base, negociants Carel and Teuns Keuzenkamp target overseas markets with 'quality wines that are affordable and attuned to the tastes of everyday wine consumers', produced in association with various long-term-contracted Cape cellars. Nothing tasted for some time now.

Location: Somerset West ▪ Est 2011 ▪ 1stB 2012 ▪ Closed to public ▪ Owner(s) Carel & Teuns Keuzenkamp ▪ 7,000cs own label 95% red 5% white ▪ PO Box 1977 Somerset West 7129 ▪ bonview@telkomsa.net ▪ **T +27 (0)21-887-5812**

Boplaas Family Vineyards   (♀) (◎) (♟)

Another busy year for the Nel family and their venture in Calitzdorp, recognised internationally for 'port' and other dessert styles, 'estate' brandy and latterly also for unfortified wines featuring Portuguese varieties. Especially eventful for winemaker Margaux and husband Leon Coetzee (also wine-partners in The Fledge & Co, listed separately) who welcomed the 7th generation into the world, son William Robert, helpfully born after harvest. Sister Rozanne and brother Daniel remain fully involved in marketing and distilling respectively, all guided by their father and cellarmaster Carel. Though still committed to building a little piece of Portugal from Klein Karoo grapes, they also range further afield, sourcing from cool-climate pockets in the Southern Cape, including Outeniqua and Swartberg, and from Stellenbosch.

Heritage Reserve range
★★★★☆ **White Muscadel** (Ⓩ) Limited bottling in exceptional years to honour Nel family association with fortified muscat de Frontignan since mid-1800s. **14** (93) oozes marmalade, honey, candied ginger. Mouthfilling, complex & rich, with clean fresh finish. Will reward ageing. WO W Cape.

Family Reserve range
★★★★ **Cabernet Sauvignon** (Ⓩ) Dense & concentrated **15** (87) mixes intriguing raspberry & cherry notes with dark chocolate & mint, vanilla & cream from year new/2nd-fill oak. Ex Stellenbosch, as next 2.
★★★★ **Touriga Francesa** (Ⓩ) Scarce grape (4 ha in SA!), **12** (87) enchants with black fruit pastille flavours, hint of dark chocolate, rounded mouthfeel & fragrant mint finish.
★★★★☆ **Touriga Nacional** (Ⓩ) 'King of Portuguese grapes' sourced from 3 old blocks. **14** (90) has plum, blackberry & savoury meat flavours wrapped in supple tannins, leading to a lengthy farewell. Great for rich grilled meat dishes. 14 months French oak.
★★★★☆ **Ring of Rocks** (✓) Delicious blend of Portuguese grapes (tintas barocca & franca, souzão), tweaked with some ripe shiraz, adds up to most enjoyable **16** (90), with black fruit, chocolate, orange peel & fresh herbs. Very juicy & moreish, enjoy now or keep longer. WO W Cape, like Gamka Branca.
★★★★☆ **Gamka** (⛤) Released only when quality warrants it, **17** (93) already showing style & elegance with tarry red & black fruit spiced up with cloves, tobacco. Fine tannic structure for ageing, helped by fresh acidity. From tintas franca & barocca plus touriga & Stellenbosch shiraz. 16 months new French oak. No **16**.
★★★★ **Bobbejaanberg Sauvignon Blanc Reserve** (Ⓩ) Plenty of sappy green fruit on **18** (89) - figs, peppers, limes - held together with lively acidity, leading to flinty finish. Outeniqua vines. Most enjoyable, though shade less intense than stellar **17** ★★★★★ (93).

★★★★☆ **Gamka Branca** ⊘ Very accomplished **17** ⑨③ mixes old-vine chenin with chardonnay, grenache blanc, viognier & verdelho into seamless mouthful of peach, pith & peel, with cream & spice. Delicious texture from old oak & lees, endless finish.

Boplaas range

★★★★ **Ouma Cloete Straw Wine** Heady aromas of raisins, honey, apricots & mangoes on **16** ★★★★ ⑧⑤ unoaked dessert wine from foot-trodden viognier & muscat de Frontignan. Palate somewhat quieter, with creamy toffee-apple finish. Shade less intense than **15** ⑧⑦.

★★★★☆ **The 1932 Block Hanepoot** Exceptional fortified from small, very low-yielding single block planted along the Gamka River in 1932. **15** ⑨② wonderful freshness balancing the intense, opulent fruit & floral flavours. Concentrated, with a lemon zest finish. 500 ml.

★★★★ **Red Muscadel** ⊘ Intense & aromatic **17** ⑧⑦ shows layers of flavour - jasmine, apricot, raisin & honey - in luscious mouthful with well-integrated alcohol & excellent length.

★★★★☆ **Cape Vintage Reserve** ⊛ Stellar complexity in **17** ★★★★★ ⑨⑥ 'port'. Lusciously & concentrated, multiple layers of flavour - raisins, walnut cake, chocolate, cloves - borne on ripe velvet tannins & supportive acidity. Impeccable pedigree for long ageing, keep if you can. Mostly touriga nacional, splashes tinta barocca, touriga franca, souzão, like **16** ⑨④. 18.3% alcohol. Year Portuguese 'pipes', like Cape Vintage.

★★★★☆ **Cape Tawny** ⊘ ⊛ Savoury & complex **NV** ⑨③ 'port', from mostly tinta barocca with touriga nacional & souzão, spent 10-12 years in 500L barrel adding in layers of flavour - burnt sugar, chicory, coffee, roasted nuts. Wonderful umami saltiness to incredibly long finish. 18.7% alcohol. WO W Cape, as Vintage Reserve.

★★★★☆ **Cape Vintage** ⊘ ⊛ Appetising freshness on sturdy **17** ⑨③ 'port' from mainly touriga nacional with tinta barocca & souzão. Floral notes lift dense black cherry fruit, leather & spice while firm, already-meshed tannins & well-managed alcohol carry to a conclusion that's happiness-inducing now & for many years. 18% alcohol, as next.

★★★★ **Cape Ruby** ⊘ Uncomplicated & delicious **NV** ⑧⑥ 'port' should be consumed immediately & with gusto! Red & black fruit, well-balanced alcohol & sugar, winter warming at its best.

★★★★☆ **Cape Tawny Vintners Reserve Bin 1880** ⊘ Concentrated 'port' with many flavour layers, raisined fruit, wonderful oak/alcohol integration & unflagging finish. **NV** ⑨④ from tinta (85%) & touriga, aged minimum 10 years. 375 ml. WO W Cape.

Cabernet Sauvignon ⊘ ⊕ ★★★☆ Excellent drinking from **17** ⑧⑤, packed with black cherries, chocolate, vanilla - cake in a glass! Really juicy & most enjoyable. 10 months old oak.

Merlot ★★★ Good varietal character on **18** ⑧② , rounded & ripe with cooked black plums & touch of prunes. Stalky note freshens at finish. WO W Cape. **Pinotage** ⊘ ★★★ Moreish red fruit on just-dry **17** ⑧① makes for easy-drinking fun. 9 months older French oak add touch of coffee/toffee at finish. **Tinta Barocca** ⊘ ★★★☆ Spice bomb **17** ⑧④ , clove, star anise, cinnamon plus orange peel & dark-berried fruit add up to interesting glassful, with plenty of juicy drinkability & more intensity than before. **Touriga Nacional** ⊘ ★★★☆ Characterful **17** ⑧④ shows good typicity - dense black fruit with orange peel twists - chunky but smooth tannins & bright finish. **Stoepsit Sauvignon Blanc** ⊘ ★★★☆ Crisp & fresh **19** ⑧③ packed full of citrus (lemon, lime, grapefruit) with pleasing touch of sherbet, nicely handled acidity & clean finish. **Eerste Water Sauvignon Blanc** ⊘ ★★★☆ Floral, fresh & fruity **18** ⑧⑤ mixes tropical fruit & citrus with crunchy acidity & touch of cream. Grapes from Calitzdorp area's Groenfontein Valley. **Cape Portuguese White Blend** ⊘ ★★★★ Unusual but effective blend of verdelho, chardonnay, sauvignon (50/27/23), **19** ⑧⑤ appetising flavours of lemons & almond biscuits, honeyed finish. **Pinot Noir Brut Sparkling** ⊘ ★★★ Dry, playful & frothy, **18** ⑧② cranberry & cherry fruit whizzed up with lively acidity for the perfect Sunday brunch fizz. **Hanepoot** ★★★ Delightful floral & grapey notes on **18** ⑧① fortified muscat. Ample sweetness (230 g/l sugar) balanced by firm alcohol & freshening minty finish. **White Muscadel** ⊘ ★★★★ A festival of candied fruit & citrus rind, sweet yet bouncy, spirity & delightful. **17** ⑧④ a fortified to brighten your everyday. **Cape Vintage The Chocolate** ★★★★ Floral & perfumed **17** ⑧⑤ port-style does, indeed, have dark chocolate core, hints of leather & unusual marzipan. From tinta barocca & touriga nacional (70/30), year oaked. 375 ml. WO W Cape. In abeyance: **Cape Tawny Reserve**.

Brandy range

★★★★☆ **Potstill Reserve 15 Years** Repackaged 100% potstill ⑨② from colombard is stylish, with lively amber colour, soft aromas of dried peach, roast hazelnut, marmalade & herbs. Elegant, harmonious & a perfect after-dinner companion. Old Limousin cask & Portuguese port barrels, as all.

★★★★☆ **Potstill Reserve 8 Years** A favourite at the cellar, 8 year old potstill ⑨⓪ shows fresh, soft peach, pear & stonefruit aromas, milk chocolate & a sprinkling of spice to round the already smooth citrus-tinged & creamy vanilla finish.

★★★★ **Carel Nel Reserve 5 Years** ⊘ 5 year old blended brandy ⑧⑦, bright fruited with a floral finish, 43% alcohol well balanced within the whole. For your favourite cocktail.

Occasional release: **Potstill Reserve 20 Years**, **Potstill Reserve 12 Years**. — CM, WB

Location: Calitzdorp ▪ Map: Klein Karoo & Garden Route ▪ Map grid reference: B5 C4 ▪ WO: Calitzdorp/ Western Cape/Stellenbosch ▪ Est 1880 ▪ 1stB 1982 ▪ Tasting & sales Mon-Fri 9-5 Sat 9-4 Sun 10-3 ▪ Fee R40pp ▪ Closed Good Fri & Dec 25 ▪ Cellar tours by appt ▪ Facilities for children ▪ Gifts ▪ Farm produce ▪ Walks/ hikes ▪ Conservation area ▪ Ring of Rocks ▪ Spirits tasting incl brandy, gin & whiskey ▪ Owner(s) Carel Nel ▪ Cellarmaster(s) Carel Nel (1982) ▪ Winemaker(s) Margaux Nel (Dec 2006) ▪ Viticulturist(s) Danie Strydom ▪ 2,300ha/70ha (cab, ptage, shiraz, tinta, touriga, chard, cbard, sauv) ▪ 55% red 45% white ▪ IPW ▪ PO Box 156 Calitzdorp 6660 ▪ info@boplaas.co.za ▪ www.boplaas.co.za ▪ S 33° 32' 8.0" E 021° 41' 1.9" (Boplaas), S 34° 4' 45.40" E 022° 8' 25.22" (Boplaas on Garden Route) ▪ 🎬 traditional.external.theatrics, declined.kingpins. lotion ▪ **T +27 (0)44-213-3326**

Boschendal Wines   ⑨ 🍴 🏠 📷 👤 ♿

'Heritage' is understandably a key word at the extensive and historic Boschendal estate in Franschhoek. The name of the 1685 range indicates why – this was the year the land grant of the original Bossendal ('Wooded Valley') was made to the Huguenot Jean le Long. There's the splendid Heritage Rose Garden among the great array of visitor attractions, and now the grandly packaged Heritage range of wines (the wine business is owned by the DGB group). Two new winemakers joined the team in 2019, following the move of Lizelle Gerber: Danielle Jacobs is now in charge of the sparkling wines, with Michael Langenhoven responsible for whites, both working with cellarmaster Jacques Viljoen and DGB's group winemaker, Stephan Joubert.

Heritage Collection

★★★★★ **Grande Syrah** (NEW) (⚶) Packaged to impress, **15** ⑨③'s modern styling commendably handled, the blue & black fruit intensity contained within a gentle oak structure & deliciously spiced with black pepper. Good dry persistence, freshening grip & acid bite. Decant now, cellar decade plus.

★★★★★ **Black Angus** (NEW) (⚶) Stellenbosch fruit structured to reward lengthy ageing, with firm but not overdone tannin framing generous savoury red & black fruit, pot-pourri & orange adding exotic aromatic notes to **16** ⑨③ shiraz (59%) blend with cab, merlot & malbec.

Special Cuvée range

★★★★☆ **Nicolas** (NEW) ⊘ A variation on the Rhône/Garonne theme, **16** ⑨⓪ syrah plus all 5 Bordeaux reds. Leafier & slightly meatier than Black Angus, tannins more obvious here but well-padded by fruit, 16 months in 20% new oak giving an attractive savouriness & compaction to the sweetly ripe fruit.

Elgin Series

★★★★ **Pinot Noir** Oak-fermented/aged **17** ⑧⑨ has vivid cherry & raspberry appeal, variety's enlivening acidity, savoury & supple tannin perfect counterweights to mid-palate richness. Nudges next quality level, merits further maturation, like last-tasted **15** ⑧⑦.

★★★★ **Chardonnay** (⚶) Unlike last-reviewed **15** ⑧⑦, oak is deftly handled in **17** ★★★★☆ ⑨④, the woodsmoke character near-perfectly synced with pristine lemon & lime fruit. Better knit, too, than previous though tightly coiled, with a seam of flinty minerality that will reward cellaring.

★★★★☆ **Sauvignon Blanc** True to cool-climate origin, & needing time to unfurl & develop greater complexity, **18** ⑨① has wonderful nervous acidity carrying lightish body (12.5% alcohol) with subtly grassy & dusty khaki bush fruit. **16** ★★★★ ⑧④ more tropical toned but with some minerality. **17** not tasted.

1685 range

★★★★ Cabernet Sauvignon ⊘ Variety's affinity with Stellenbosch evident in **16** ⑧⑥, easy to drink & value priced with cut-above flavour (cassis & liquorice) & varietal definition, including freshening tannins. Like **15** ★★★ ⑧①, lengthy fruit-filled finish.

★★★★ Chardonnay-Pinot Noir ⊘ Though it has same make-up as **17** ★★★★ ⑧④, popular rosé gets more serious in **18** ⑧⑥. Drier, with more palate weight from the barrel-fermented component & tannin nibble ex 39% pinot noir. WO W Cape, as next.

★★★★ Chardonnay Intenser flavours & aromas earn a rating upgrade for **18** ⑧⑥, but the approachable personality & tasty citrus profile remain. Judicious oak (only 70% aged, 10 months, 12% new) enriches & rounds, as in **17** ★★★★ ⑧③.

Merlot ⑧ ★★★ Offers fruitcake & tobacco notes, & definite herbal twist. **16** ⑧② firmly structured & hint of sweetness. **Shiraz** ★★★★ Black fruit & a pinch of black pepper in **17** ⑧⑤, richness offset by fresh acidity. Similar gentle tannin structure as before, 30% new oak in support. **S&M** ⑧ ★★★ Usual 70/30 shiraz/mourvèdre blend in **16** ⑧②. Firmer structure than Shiraz, bolder & a little rustic. A few enriching grams of sugar, like most in range - here a bit more evident. **Chenin Blanc** ⑧ ★★★★ Dried peach, melon, thatch on **17** ⑧③. The sweet element (5 g/l sugar) more obvious here than on other whites, but with nice acid lift, for unpretentious, undemanding pleasure. **Sauvignon Blanc Grande Cuvée** ★★★★ Dash semillon broadens the palate, smooths the acidity of **18** ⑧⑤ for effortless summer drinking. Blackcurrant, passionfruit & ruby grapefruit tones reflect cooler Coastal provenance.

Reserve Collection

★★★★ Méthode Cap Classique Brut ⊘ Chardonnay leads pinot noir (44%) in latest **NV** ⑧⑦ sparkle, where drinkability is upped by a well-rounded & creamy texture. Less brioche than previous, more exuberant red, yellow & green fruit aromas & flavours, giving a lightly rich feel which will appeal widely.

★★★★☆ Méthode Cap Classique Grande Cuvée Brut ⑧ Palest gold **14** ⑨③ sparkler from equal pinot noir & chardonnay disgorged after 48 months on lees. Beguiling lemon, cheesecake & biscuit characters shot through with arresting acidity, braced by a mineral backbone. Lovely now, structured to improve. Elgin grapes, like **13** ★★★★ ⑧⑦.

★★★★☆ Méthode Cap Classique Jean Le Long ⑧ Refined **08** ⑨③ sparkling from chardonnay, lengthy 9 years on lees, further 2 on cork, is thrillingly fresh & nervy, lemon-honey nuance, endless smooth finish. Vast improvement on **07** ★★★★ ⑧④. WO Coastal.

Méthode Cap Classique Brut Rosé ⊘ ★★★★ Palest partridge eye hue to **NV** ⑧⑤ bubbly from pinot noir (& a little pinotage, chardonnay), red apple & cream notes, lovely weight & flavour depth from the red grapes. WO W Cape, as all these sparklers unless noted. **Méthode Cap Classique Demi Sec** ⊘ ★★★★ **NV** ⑧④ bubbles from chardonnay & pinot noir are elegantly off-dry, with lemon cream, gentle macadamia nut aromas & flavours to pair with charcuterie or salty cheeses. — CvZ

Location/map: Franschhoek ▪ Map grid reference: D6 ▪ WO: Coastal/Western Cape/Elgin/Stellenbosch ▪ Est 1685 ▪ 1stB 1975 ▪ Tasting & sales daily 10-6 (Oct-Mar) & 10-5 (Apr-Sep) ▪ Chocolate & wine pairing ▪ Brandy tasting ▪ Signature experiences, presented from a private room, include a Historic tasting of 5 wines representing the history of Boschendal; Connoisseur tasting of 5 limited release wines ▪ Closed Good Fri & Dec 25 ▪ Cellar tours daily 10.30, 12, 1.30 & 3 R60pp ▪ Vineyard tours 11.30 R150pp ▪ Cheese platters on request R125ea ▪ The Werf Restaurant ▪ Farmshop & deli ▪ Weddings & functions ▪ Facilities for children ▪ Tour groups ▪ Gifts ▪ The Werf Cottages & Orchards Cottages (23 luxury cottages) ▪ Owner(s) DGB (Pty) Ltd ▪ Group winemaker Stephan Joubert ▪ Cellarmaster(s) Jacques Viljoen (Aug 2018) ▪ Winemaker(s) Jacques Viljoen (reds & rosé, 2018), Michael Langenhoven (whites, Sep 2019) & Danielle Jacobs (MCC, Aug 2018) ▪ Viticulturist(s) Heinie Nel (Jul 2018) ▪ 2,240ha/200ha (shiraz, sauv) ▪ 3,100t/500,000cs own label 32% red 43% white 14% rosé 11% sparkling ▪ WIETA, WWF-SA Conservation Champion ▪ Private Bag X03 Groot Drakenstein 7680 ▪ cellardoor@boschendal.co.za ▪ www.boschendalwines.com ▪ S 33° 52' 27.5" E 018° 58' 34.4" ▪ ⬛ nooks. electronic.sweetening ▪ **T +27 (0)21-870-4200**

☐ **Boschenheuwel** *see* Wine-of-the-Month Club

Boschheim

Stellenbosch boutique vintners Andy Roediger and Mark Philp have acquired a forklift and bottling line 'to ease the physical side of work', and this has prompted a move to bigger premises. Since '08, only red wine has been produced under the Boschheim and Muse labels, but recently they've been experimenting with chenin and the result looks good.

Muse range

Cabernet Sauvignon ★★★ Xmas cake, graphite & cocoa nuances, **17** ⑧⓪ somewhat lean with green walnut finish. **Shiraz** ★★★ Easy everyday red, **17** ⑧① plums & spice, fresher & suppler than Boschheim sibling yet enough tannin grip for food. **Chenin Blanc** (NEW) ★★★ High-toned stonefruit aromas, **18** ⑧① rich honey entry, apricot & peach flavours, lees ageing & 9 months in untoasted oak add breadth & dimension. In abeyance: **Calliope**.

Boschheim range

Cabernet Sauvignon ★★★ Variety's firm tannins evident in **17** ⑧⓪, reining in the Xmas cake & chocolate flavours, pleasingly dry though fleeting. **Mourvèdre** ★★★ Very young **18** ⑦⑧, spicy black cherries & plums still in tight grip of tannin, allow more time to soften. WO Paarl. **Shiraz** ★★★ Savoury & food-styled **17** ⑦⑨, meaty/biltong spice aromas over ripe plum, standout oak tannin & tangy acidity. In abeyance: **Ella Marie**.
— FM, CvZ

Location/map: Stellenbosch ▪ Map grid reference: E5 ▪ WO: Stellenbosch/Paarl ▪ 1stB 2003 ▪ Tasting & sales by appt ▪ Owner(s) Andy Roediger ▪ Winemaker(s) Andy Roediger & Mark Philp ▪ 1,800cs own label 100% red ▪ PO Box 3202 Matieland 7602 ▪ andy@roedigeragencies.co.za ▪ S 33° 55' 54.9" E 018° 50' 10.5" ▪ [m] goes. cheat.sliders ▪ **T +27 (0)21-887-0010**

Boschkloof Wines

Jacques Borman — owner of this family farm and winery in Stellenbosch's Polkadraai Hills — has long had a particular interest in shiraz, a focus inherited by young Reenen Borman as winemaker. 'Still in pursuit to make world-class syrah,' says the latter. The 'pursuit' includes shifting to larger-format oak and using more cement vessels for ageing. Generally, the approach is hands-off, to reveal the essence of the estate's mostly decomposed granite and koffieklip soils. With the non-estate Kottabos range, Reenen can indulge more freely in more new-wave winemaking (as with his own label, Patatsfontein, separately listed), and also enjoy 'playing with and exploring' other vineyards in the area — the wines' labels mention not only the winemaker but also those of the grape-growers.

Boschkloof Wines range

★★★★ **Cabernet Sauvignon** Ripe berry fruit, hints of vanilla (but just 10% new oak) & herbs on forthright **16** ⑧⑦ - **15** not tasted. Full bodied & quite powerful, with 14.6% alcohol, but balanced, with firm dry tannins.

★★★★☆ **Epilogue** ⑥ Single-vineyard syrah, **17** ⑨④ as always more expressive & deep than the varietally named version. Herbal-floral element to the complexity of aroma & flavour. Velvety, with unassertive but influential structure - a gentle sort of power. 20% oak. Altogether convincing.

★★★★☆ **Syrah** More approachable young than Epilogue, lightly perfumed **17** ⑨⓪ had 20% whole bunches in fermentation. Firm, balanced, unobtrusive structure beneath the sweet fruit (there's also a definite savoury element), with admirably restrained oak (15% new) in support.

★★★★ **Cabernet Sauvignon-Merlot** ⊘ Dry tannins, savoury balance & good long finish mark **17** ⑧⑥ as a considerable alternative to the slightly pricier monovarietal wines - though not all will enjoy the greater touch of herbaceousness & less obvious fruit.

★★★★☆ **Conclusion** ⑥ Impressive **16** ⑨④ has more cab than previous - 65%, with cab franc, merlot & a little syrah. Cedar & tobacco aromas promise savoury more than simply fruity, though sweetish, ripe flavours are there. More harmonious than the varietal wines, with well integrated tannins & 40% new oak. 14.1% alcohol.

★★★★ **Chardonnay** Classic profile of oatmeal & citrus on **18** ⑧⑦. 70% fermented & matured in older oak on lees, giving breadth & richness, remainder in tank to add freshness of fruit. Decent balance. WO W Cape, as next.

★★★★ **Sauvignon Blanc** Unmistakeable aromas & flavours of guava & passionfruit on **19** ⑧⑦. Hardly subtle, but enjoyably fruity & fresh, nicely textured, with good long finish. Last tasted was **17** ★★★★ ⑧④.

Merlot ★★★★ Forward aromas on **17** ⑧⑤ repeated on palate: plenty of fruit but savoury element too, with tobacco & choc mingled in. Juicy, but with dry tannic grip. 14.5% alcohol shows in a warm finish.

Kottabos range

★★★★☆ **Grenache-Syrah** ⑧ Seductively perfumed **18** ⑨③ from 68% wholebunch grenache, destemmed syrah; naturally fermented, aged in older oak. Moderate 13% alcohol, light-feeling & fresh, with subtle, supple tannins. Goes deeper than the delicious charm it offers even in youth.

★★★★ **Chenin Blanc** ⑧ Naturally fermented & matured in old oak, **18** ★★★★★ ⑨③ is unshowy but subtly tasty & even more substantial than **17** ⑧⑦, with a satisfying grip. There's flint as well as fruit - the finish fantailing beautifully with dried apricot & melon.— TJ

Location/map: Stellenbosch ▪ Map grid reference: C6 ▪ WO: Stellenbosch/Western Cape ▪ Est/1stB 1996 ▪ Tasting, sales & cellar tours Mon-Fri 9-5 Sat 10-3 ▪ Fee R30 ▪ Closed Easter Fri-Sun, Dec 25 & Jan 1 ▪ Cheese & charcuterie platters ▪ BYO picnic ▪ Owner(s)/cellarmaster(s) Jacques Borman ▪ Winemaker(s) Reenen Borman (Jun 2010) ▪ Viticulturist(s) Jacques Borman, with Reenen Borman ▪ 30ha/19ha (cabs s/f, merlot, shiraz, chard) ▪ ±100-150t/6-8,000cs own label 90% red 10% white ▪ PO Box 1340 Stellenbosch 7599 ▪ boschkloof@adept.co.za, info@boschkloofwines.com ▪ www.boschkloofwines.com ▪ S 33° 57' 37.0" E 018° 46' 11.8" ▪ 🗺 mission.rates.rating ▪ **T +27 (0)21-881-3293 (office)/+27 (0)21-881-3268 (cellar)**

Boschrivier Wines - NJT de Villiers   Ⓠ Ⓨ 😀 🏠 ◎ ♿

A pioneer in the Stanford area, Theo de Villiers followed in his great-grandfather's footsteps and established vines on inherited farmland in 1998. His firstborn Shiraz since has gained siblings, and the visitor facilities on his property have grown and diversified, but Theo's day job as paediatrician in Worcester continues and his passion for wine, lived out on weekends, is as strong as ever.

Cabernet Sauvignon ★★★ Dark plums, well oak-spiced, there's vibrancy in **17** ⑧① 's fruit, giving a juicy texture, nice drinkability. **Shiraz** ★★★★ Brambleberries with a smoky overlay from 16 months in barrel, 40% new, **17** ⑧④ ticks all the boxes: savoury, spicy, no rough edges, tannins amenable. Drinks easily & well. **Rosé** ★★ Equal cab & shiraz, **19** ⑦⑤ is strawberry scented, softly rounded, ends dry. **Sauvignon Blanc** ⊘ ★★★★ Passionfruit throughout **18** ⑧④, acidity the vitaliser, brightening the flavours, extending the length. Elegant, for solo enjoyment or food. WO Coastal. — CR

Location: Stanford ▪ Map: Walker Bay & Bot River ▪ Map grid reference: C8 ▪ WO: Overberg/Coastal ▪ Est 1998 ▪ 1stB 2002 ▪ Tasting & sales Mon-Fri 8-5 Sat 9-5 Sun (Sep 1-Apr 30 only) 10-3 ▪ Closed Dec 25 ▪ Restaurant ▪ BYO picnic ▪ Gift shop ▪ Farm produce ▪ Conferences/functions (60 pax) ▪ Walking/hiking & 4x4 trails ▪ 3 self-catering farmhouses ▪ Owner(s)/viticulturist(s) Theodore de Villiers ▪ Winemaker(s) Mike Dobrovic ▪ 14ha (cab, shiraz) ▪ 7t/ha ±3,300cs own label 68.5% red 21% white 10.5% rosé ▪ Remhoogte, Caledon 7230 ▪ drnjtdevilliers@ mweb.co.za ▪ www.boschrivierwines.co.za ▪ S 34° 23' 19.4" E 019° 37' 51.0" ▪ 🗺 tandem.deems.unescorted ▪ **T +27 (0)23-347-3313/2 ext 3; +27 (0)76-736-0351; +27 (0)28-008-5031 (tasting)**

Bosjes   Ⓠ Ⓨ 🏠 ◎ Ⓐ Ⓝⓔⓦ

Israel's ancient Capernaum church ruins inspired the Breedekloof's Stofberg family to develop their 18th-century mountainside farm as a food, wine and wedding destination rich in biblical symbolism. Internationally awarded designs by top SA talent (anchored by a breathtaking curvilinear-roofed chapel, with eatery, guest house and garden landscapes) are paired with family-friendly hospitality. The small parcels of wines are selected and blended by veteran Woolworths wineman and Cape Wine Master Allan Mullins. Supporting all members of the local community, from food- and wine-growers to staff, is part of the Stofbergs' vision.

★★★★ **Shiraz Reserve** Single 600m-altitude vineyard, **16** ⑧⑥ spent 20 months in French & American barrels, portion new. Plums & prunes, vanilla, spice & pepper dusted, intensifying on palate. There's fruit density yet succulence. Tannins supple, the whole effect opulent.

Chardonnay Reserve ★★★★ Barrel fermented/aged 12 months, combo new/2nd-fill French. **18** ⑧④ has honey biscuit & citrus preserve scents, some stonefruit, becoming fresher, more lemony in the flavours. Sleek, polished, lovely assurance here. **Chenin Blanc** ★★★ Tangerine & orange perfume & flavours, **19** ⑦⑦ has fruity-fresh drinkability, for early enjoyment. **Sauvignon Blanc** ★★★ Grapefruit & green apple, **19** (78) slender (12.5% alcohol) & bone-dry but has ample flavour, crisp, flinty finish. — CR, CvZ

Location: Worcester ▪ Map/WO: Breedekloof ▪ Map grid reference: B3 ▪ Est 2017 ▪ 1stB 2018 ▪ Tasting & sales Wed-Sun 12-3 ▪ Closed Mon/Tues & Dec 25 ▪ Bosjes Kombuis Wed-Sun 12-3 & Tea Garden 10-4 ▪ Custom designed playground; special menu for children ▪ Garden & farm tours: groups to book in advance ▪ Olive oil ▪ Weddings & events ▪ Small conference/meeting venue (12 pax) ▪ Hiking trails in enclosed Bergkamp with various antelope; rare & endangered flowers ▪ Chapel - an architectural masterpiece ▪ 5-bedroomed boutique guesthouse ▪ Owner(s) Stofberg Family Trust ▪ Cellarmaster(s) Allan Mullins CWM (Feb/Mar 2018, consultant) ▪ 10ha newly planted vines ▪ WIETA ▪ PO Box 13 Botha 6857 ▪ carlen@bosjes.co.za ▪ www.bosjes. co.za ▪ S 33° 33' 20.16" E 019° 15' 52.37" ▪ ⌖ leftover.windproof.intimates ▪ **T +27 (0)23-004-0496**

Bosman Family Vineyards (Ⓠ) (🍴) (📷)

'Since 1707, when the first Bosman arrived in SA as a "sieketrooster" (sick comforter), we've believed in respecting the land and the people that farm the land,' says 8th-generation Petrus Bosman, whose family's dedication to growing terroir wines matches their commitment to sustainability and ethical initiatives (going back to 2008 and the formation of the Adama Worker Trust, which set a benchmark for transformation; the following year saw the venture certified with Fairtrade). In charge of their (renovated) 260-year-old cellar in Wellington since 2007, winemaker Corlea Fourie has unrivalled access to grapes from their Bosman Adama nursery, the largest in Africa, with vineholdings in Wellington and Hermon as well as Hemel-en-Aarde, where tastings and picnics are offered.

Adama range
★★★★ **Red** (Ⓐ) Cinnamon-spiced whole greater than sum of parts (8 cultivars, various oak treatments over 9 months) in shiraz-led **17** (87), fresh & food friendly, with choc-cherry appeal. WO W Cape, as next.
★★★★ **White** (Ⓐ) Only slightly less elegant, nuanced than **16** ★★★★☆ (91), chenin-led **17** (89) with 6 other varieties deftly oaked for smooth vanilla tones to complement cardamom-spiced citrus fruit.

Creative Space range
★★★★★ **Twyfeling Cinsaut** (✓) (🐝) Silky-smooth, with fine tannins, **17** (95) once again from Bovlei bushvines, year French oak (third new) imparting vanilla & clove nuances to vivid redcurrant & cherry fruit, underlying earthiness adding complexity. As stylish as **16** ★★★★★ (94) & debut **15** (96).
★★★★★ **Optenhorst Chenin Blanc** (🐝) (💧) Naturally fermented, aged 9 months in oak, 9% new as for **16** (93), elegant **17** (93) from Bovlei vines planted in 1952 (SA's 3rd-oldest chenin) has tangy citrus fruit with pleasantly pithy edge, ginger & baking spice, lingering mineral finish, measured 13.2% alcohol. Excellent now & for many years.
★★★★☆ **Fides Grenache Blanc** 'Amber wine' fermented naturally on skins 3 weeks then basket pressed (20% into Russian oak barrels for 9 months), **18** (90) has fresh cling peach as well as orange marmalade fruit & spice framed by finely textured tannins. Interesting potential.
Dolce Primitivo (Ⓐ) ★★★★ Sweet, textured **17** (84) dessert from zinfandel, sun-dried then bunch fermented in older oak for stewed fruit, choc-caramel richness. More charming than previous. 500 ml.

Nero range
★★★★ **Nero d'Avola** (🐝) Fresh acidity & a pinch of pepper & savoury herbs lift bold black berry & plum fruit in elegant, ageworthy **17** (89), aged year in oak (20% new, 40% American). Striking packaging for this, the guide's sole varietal bottling.

Signature range
★★★★ **Cabernet Sauvignon** From 3 Wellington sites, **15** ★★★★☆ (90) seamlessly integrated after 18 months in French oak (third new), further 3 years in bottle. Built to last but accessible now thanks to rich blackcurrant flavours, ripe tannins, smoother than in **14** (89).
★★★★ **Pinotage** (🐝) Violets & vanilla on nose of **16** (89) but palate is all ripe, juicy, dark fruit, concentrated yet fresh with edgy tannins, toasty oak from 18 months in oak (60% new, 40% American).
★★★★★ **Erfenis** (Ⓐ) Conceived as an 'ode to the vintage', blend of best barrels in **16** (94) comprises pinotage with 13% each cab, shiraz, nero d'avola & 10% each cinsaut, mourvèdre, grenache. Fresh, despite cordial-like concentration & full body, with long finish.

Upper Hemel-en-Aarde range

★★★★ Pinot Noir ⊘ **17** ⑧⑦ improves on **16 ★★★★** ⑧④ with violet perfume, wild berry flavours, hint of forest-floor earthiness, pleasant metallic tang, fine tannins & fresh acidity. Also-tasted **18 ★★★★☆** ⑨⓪ charms with a cool-climate fragrance of wild strawberries & cherries, hints of spice & earth, all carrying through to palate, quite concentrated with silky tannins. These only 15-20% wooded, 9-10 months 2nd-fill Burgundy barrels.

★★★★ Chardonnay Recent improvement continues in elegant **18** ⑧⑨, lightly wooded, just 15% of wine barrel fermented then 6 months on lees for creamy texture, subtle spicing to fresh pear & citrus fruit.

★★★★☆ Sauvignon Blanc ⊘ Maritime terroir on show in flinty undertone & finish to vibrant **18** ⑨② , bursting with zesty lime, tangy pineapple & passionfruit, a pleasant viscosity balancing the bright acidity.

★★★★ Loose Cannon Méthode Cap Classique Chardonnay with 25% pinot noir & 0.5% meunier, zero-dosage **15** ⑧⑥ fizzes with lemon & peach flavours, extra-dry yet creamy after 18 months on 2nd fermentation lees in bottle.

Generation 8 range

★★★★ Chenin Blanc ⊘ Unoaked, but luscious-bodied from extended lees contact, **19** ⑧⑧ showing white & cling peaches, sweet & savoury spices, very appealing at 12.5% alcohol.

Rosé ⊚ **★★★★** Al fresco feasting calls for rose gold **18** ⑧④, from 47 cultivars ex the Bosmans' Hermanus vine garden, packed with peach, melon & strawberry fruit, refreshing at just 11.5% alcohol.

Cabernet Sauvignon ★★★★ Fruit-driven **18** ⑧④ packed with juicy cassis, only 20% wooded (oak staves, 9 months, as all these reds) for easy drinking. **Merlot ★★★★** Medium-bodied **18** ⑧③ is smooth & approachable, tangy red cherry/berry fruit & a hint of tobacco. **Shiraz ★★★★** Fresh & food-friendly **18** ⑧⑤ has plenty of crunchy red fruit along with black pepper, spice & a hint of leather. — JG

Location: Wellington/Hermanus ▪ Map: Wellington ▪ Map grid reference: C3 ▪ WO: Wellington/Upper Hemel-en-Aarde Valley/Western Cape ▪ Map: Walker Bay & Bot River ▪ Map grid reference: B3 ▪ Est 1699 ▪ 1stB 2004 ▪ Wellington: Tasting & cellar tours by appt T +27 (0)63-052-5352/taste@bosmanwines.com ▪ Tasting fee R80pp ▪ Sales Mon-Thu 9-5 Fri 9-4.30 Sat by appt ▪ Closed Sun, Easter Fri-Mon & Dec 25 ▪ Owner(s) Bosman Adama (Pty) Ltd ▪ Cellarmaster(s) Corlea Fourie (Nov 2006) ▪ Winemaker(s) Natasha Williams (Mar 2018) ▪ Viticulturist(s) Johan Viljoen (Mar 2014) ▪ 300ha (47 varieties r/w) ▪ 5,000t/20,000cs own label 70% red 25% white 5% rosé ▪ Brands for clients: Sainsbury Supermarkets, The Cooperative ▪ BBBEE certificate (level 4), Fairtrade accredited ▪ PO Box 9 Wellington 7654 ▪ taste@bosmanwines.com ▪ www.bosmanwines.com, www.bosmanhermanus.com ▪ S 33° 37' 34.7" E019° 01' 28.9" (Wellington) ▪ ⚐ ordering.fell.pump ▪ S 34° 21' 53.28" E 019° 13' 46.15" (Hermanus) ▪ ⚐ choicest.treaty.communicate ▪ T +27 (0)21-873-3170

Botanica Wines   ⓆⓎⓐⓞ

Flowers and wine come together at Protea Heights farm in Stellenbosch's Devon Valley, where Botanica owner and winemaker Ginny Povall, a former New York corporate consultant, has 10 hectares of blooms and 5 of vineyards. Her Bordeaux red varieties are farmed organically (and certified as such from 2019), the celebrated chenin comes from a dryland vineyard high in the mountains near Clanwilliam. Ginny celebrates all things floral in her wine labels, in particular her flagships, which are named after (and feature the work of) Mary Delany, an artist who crafted breathtaking botanical collages out of thousands of pieces of cut paper in the late 1700s. 'I am fortunate to have licensed a few,' Ginny says.

Mary Delany Collection

★★★★☆ Pinot Noir ⊘ ⓐ Delicate yet by no means lightweight **18** ⑨③ has tangy red cherry, raspberry & cranberry fruit, with enticing floral perfume & spicy, lingering finish. Combo Stellenbosch & Hemel-en-Aarde Ridge fruit, matured 9 months in French oak 20% new.

★★★★★ Chardonnay ⓝⓔⓦ ⓐ Beautiful balance between tingling freshness & creamy texture in barrel-fermented **18** ⑨④ from Hemel-en-Aarde Ridge, showing lime blossom & white peach on nose, fresh grapefruit & lemon zest on palate, delicate cinnamon on lingering finish.

★★★★★ Chenin Blanc ⓐ Richly deserving of icon status, **18** ⑨⑤ is the 8th vintage since debut **09** to get our maximum 5 stars. Still sourced from venerable high-altitude Citrusdal Mountain vines, bunch-pressed (as Chardonnay), 100% older-barrel-fermented/aged on lees 8 months for rich, rounded, honeyed texture as backdrop to pure, focused citrus fruit with dry, pithy finish.

★★★★☆ **Semillon** ⓐ Adds Hemel-en-Aarde to previous Elgin source, **18** ⑨③ as beautifully poised, elegant as last. Thatch & lemongrass aromas, lime & green apple fruit, lively acidity restrained by smooth viscosity after 6 months on lees in old barrels.

Not tasted: **Three Barrels Pinot Noir**, **Fire Lily Straw Wine**. Discontinued: **Chenin Blanc Untitled No. 1**.

Arboretum range

★★★★ **Arboretum** ⓐ Rich, plush **17** ★★★★★ ⑨③ a barrel selection of cab, cab franc, merlot (53/23/21) & splash petit verdot, seamless after 11 months in mostly older oak to show off ripe dark fruit, more complex than **16** ⑧⑨ with leafy & floral aromatics.

Big Flower range

★★★★ **Cabernet Sauvignon** Despite 15% alcohol, dense cassis & dark chocolate richness, **17** ⑧⑦ is fresh thanks to balancing acidity, tannic grip. Old oak matured, like next two.

★★★★ **Cabernet Franc 17** ⑧⑨ has fresh & dried herbal notes without being herbaceous, dark mint chocolate layered with black cherry fruit, full-bodied but soft & approachable.

★★★★ **Merlot** Like predecessor, **17** ⑧⑥ voluptuously full of ripe black plum & cherry fruit, richly concentrated with violet aroma & lingering finish, alcohol above 14.5% but in balance.

Rosé ★★★★ Pale pink **19** ⑧④ is very pretty, very dry, crisp & refreshing, with cranberry & ruby grapefruit flavours. Not tasted: **Petit Verdot**.

Flower Girl range ⓃⒺⓌ

Cabernet Franc Pétillant Naturel ★★★☆ Hazy red **18** ⑧③ méthode ancestrale (single ferment) sparkling has sourdough & sour cherry aromas, red fruit & a tingle on the palate, just 11% alcohol. — JG

Location/map: Stellenbosch ▪ Map grid reference: D4 ▪ WO: Stellenbosch/Western Cape/Citrusdal Mountain/Hemel-en-Aarde Ridge ▪ Est/1stB 2008 ▪ Tasting by appt only ▪ Wine sales Mon-Fri 8-5 ▪ Farm produce ▪ Conferences ▪ Walks/hikes ▪ MTB trail ▪ Refreshments offered at Sugarbird Manor guest house ▪ Owner(s) Virginia C Povall ▪ Winemaker(s) Virginia Povall (Jan 2008) ▪ Viticulturist(s) Francois Viljoen ▪ 21.6ha/5ha (cabs s/f, merlot, p verdot, pinot) ▪ PO Box 12523 Die Boord 7613 ▪ ginny@botanicawines.com ▪ www.botanicawines.com ▪ S 33° 54' 18.5" E 018° 49' 25.4" ▪ ⧉ tabloid.simply.mountain ▪ **T +27 (0)76-340-8296/+27 (0)79-478-1515**

Botha Wine Cellar   ⓛ ⓒ ⓞ ⓐ ⓖ

It's been a year of upgrades and firsts for this grower-owned Breedekloof winery, not only in terms of its bulk production (new-generation bag presses and increased storage capacity) but also the introduction of the Amyah ultra-premium wines, showcasing special and older parcels, available for tasting at the remodelled child- and wheelchair-friendly tasting room, along with the established and ever-popular bottlings.

Amyah range ⓃⒺⓌ

★★★★ **Chenin Blanc** ⓐ Hebrew word for 'creative insight'. Riper style than chenin siblings, portion wild ferment, 10 months oaking, some new, & **18** ⑧⑧ wears that proudly. Buttered toast & stonefruit, finishing long. 29 year old dryland bushvines. Just 207 cases.

Chardonnay ★★★☆ Barrel fermented/aged, 25% new, **18** ⑧⑤ is preserved citrus & butterscotch, richly textured, full flavoured. Crisp acidity adds lift, vibrancy.

Reserve range

Merlot ★★★★ Dark berries & chocolate, some nutmeg, **17** ⑧③'s tannins firm, give structure & backbone, ageability, no barrier to current enjoyment. New oak 18 months, 25% American. **Shiraz** ★★★★ Same oak regime as Merlot, longer in barrel, adds vanilla, sweet spice to the plush fruit. **16** ⑧④'s serious side is underlying dried herbs, a supple yet definite tannin foundation. **Bush Vine Barrel Fermented Chenin Blanc** ⓛ ★★★★ From ±30 year old dryland vines. 11 months oaking, portion natural ferment, giving **17** ⑧④ toast & stonefruit flavours, acidity refreshed. Occasional release: **Cabernet Sauvignon**. Discontinued: **Barrel Fermented Chardonnay**.

Dassie's Reserve range
Dassie's Rood ⊘ ★★★ Half cinsaut, with equal cab, ruby cab, unwooded **17** ⑦⑧ is designed for early, easy enjoyment & delivers perfectly. Also in 3L cask, as next. **Dassie's Blanc** ★★ From chenin, pre-bottled dry **19** ⑦⑤ has crunchy, fresh green apple flavours, light-textured quaffability (12% alcohol). Not tasted: **Dassie's Rosé**.

Botha range
Cabernet Sauvignon ★★★ Good typicity, cassis & lead pencils, with light oaking more for flavour than structure, **17** ⑧① is smooth & round, for early drinking. **Merlot** ⓧ ★★★ Red berries & vanilla, juicy & streamlined **17** ⑦⑧ drinks well. **Pinotage** ★★★ Lightly oaked, fruit is king in **17** ⑦⑨, curvaceous & juicy. **Shiraz** ★★★ Full-ripe (15.5% alcohol) **17** ⑦⑧ offers dark-fruited succulence, oaking a savoury seam, firm finish. **Chenin Blanc** ★★★ Tiny portion oaked, adding a subtle biscuit note to **19** ⑦⑦ tank sample's apple styling. Light toned (12% alcohol) & crisply dry. **Sauvignon Blanc** ⊘ ★★★ Remaining true to style, crisply dry **19** ⑧① preview shows green fig, some minerality in the flavours. **Red Jerepigo** ⓧ ★★★ Fortified shiraz, **16** ⑦⑧ preview salty liquorice scented, wild berries, a minty note, but palate has power-packed fruit, almost jammy sweetness. **Late Bottled Vintage** ⓧ ★★★ Typical raisins, nuts, spice & dried plum on **10** ⑧① port-style offering from shiraz. Smooth & silky, with noticeable oak. Not tasted: **Chardonnay Brut**. Occasional release: **Hanepoot Jerepigo**. — CR

Location: Worcester ▪ Map/WO: Breedekloof ▪ Map grid reference: B3 ▪ Est 1949 ▪ 1stB 1974 ▪ Tasting & sales Mon-Fri 9—5 Sat 10—1 ▪ Closed Easter Fri-Sun, Dec 25/26 & Jan 1 ▪ Cellar tours by appt ▪ Play area for children ▪ Conferences ▪ BYO picnic ▪ Conservation area ▪ Breedekloof Soetes & Soup festival ▪ Owner(s) Botha Wynkelder (Edms) Bpk ▪ Production manager Johan Linde (Nov 1996) ▪ Cellarmaster(s) Gerrit van Zyl (Nov 2007) ▪ Winemaker(s) Michiel Visser (Nov 1999) & Annamarie van Niekerk (Dec 2008), with Stefan Joubert (Nov 2016) ▪ Viticulturist(s) Jan-Carel Coetzee (Nov 2010) ▪ 1,969ha (cab, merlot, ptage, shiraz, chard, chenin, cbard, sauv) ▪ 40,875t/15,000cs own label 61% red 25% white 14% fortified ▪ ISO 22000:2009 ▪ IPW, WIETA ▪ PO Box 30 PK Botha 6857 ▪ admin@bothakelder.co.za ▪ www.bothakelder.co.za ▪ S 33° 34' 1.5" E 019° 15' 27.5" ▪ ✉ saved.ultrahigh.gentler ▪ **T +27 (0)23-355-1740**

☐ **Bottega Family Wines** *see* Idiom Collection

Bouchard Finlayson   ⓧ ⑪ 🍷 📷 ♿

A year of contrasts and high drama for this acclaimed, family-owned winery in Hemel-en-Aarde. Scant months after witnessing heavy snow at the Kaaimansgat/Crocodile's Lair vineyard in far-flung Elandskloof, the team had to contend with a potentially devastating wildfire which tore through their local valley at the start of vintage, threatening buildings and vines. Thanks to the agile fire service, alert staff and helpful neighbours, they not only managed to escape serious damage, but succeeded in bringing top-quality fruit into the cellar, winemaker Chris Albrecht declaring himself delighted with the resulting wines. Most of their range is now suitable for vegans, a growing trend which cellarmaster and co-founder Peter Finlayson has observed as he travels the world, sharing his deep knowledge of this cool-climate area.

★★★★★ **Galpin Peak Pinot Noir** ⊘ 🐝 Multiple waves of red-berried fruit on attractive **17** ⑨③ edged by dried herbs & supported by lovely toasty oaking (29% new). Well-balanced now but worth keeping (1.5L & 3L bottle formats will help with that).

★★★★★ **Tête de Cuvée Galpin Peak Pinot Noir** 🐝 Selected barrels make up stellar **17** ⑨④, first since **13** ⑨④ & well worth the wait. Cascade of elegant red & black fruit enveloped by warm spices, velvety tannins & cleverly handled oak, 50% new. Grows in intensity & interest through to positive, lengthy finish.

★★★★★ **Hannibal** Highly original blend, **17** ⑨① flows confidently from the red fruit & chewy tannins of sangiovese & nebbiolo to the smoky notes & velvety breadth of shiraz & pinot noir. Charry oak (22% new) adds spice to delicious meaty mouthful. Magnums available. Walker Bay WO.

★★★★★ **Kaaimansgat Crocodile's Lair Chardonnay** Layers of flavour on **18** ⑨② add to beautifully balanced mouthful of citrus & white blossom, with attractive hints of cucumber & pepper. Slight increase in new oak (to 25%) adds cream & spice at excellent finish. Overberg WO.

★★★★★ **Missionvale Chardonnay** 🐝 Majestic **17** ⑨③ a feast for the taste buds, mingling ripe tropical fruit with sappy acidity, elegant oaking (30% new) with citrussy 10% unwooded portion making a real difference. Styled for long term, but difficult to resist drinking right now.

★★★★ **Sans Barrique Chardonnay** A leading example of the unwooded style, **18** ⑧⑥ presents wonderfully knit flavours of lemons & ginger biscuits with lively salinity & creamy finish. From own & Elandskloof fruit.

★★★★ **Sauvignon Blanc** Bursting with citrus joie de vivre, **19** ⑧⑦ mixes plenty of fresh grapefruit flavours with tropical fruits (guavas & granadillas) & herbal notes courtesy 13% semillon (unoaked). Zippy acidity & long finish.

Blanc de Mer ★★★☆ Firm favourite for seafood, **18** ⑧⑤ delivers plenty of perfumed fruit, with zesty limes & wet stones balancing out richer mid-palate. Unwooded, mostly riesling with viognier & 3 more. Cape South Coast WO. Not tasted: **Sauvignon Blanc Reserve**. Discontinued: **Walker Bay Pinot Noir**. — CM

Location: Hermanus ▪ Map: Walker Bay & Bot River ▪ Map grid reference: B4 ▪ WO: Hemel-en-Aarde Valley/ Cape South Coast/Overberg/Walker Bay ▪ Est 1989 ▪ 1stB 1991 ▪ Tasting, sales & cellar tours Mon-Fri 9—5 Sat 10—1 ▪ Fee R30pp/3 wines, R60pp/6 wines ▪ Closed all pub hols ▪ Deli platter ▪ Gift shop ▪ BYO picnic ▪ Conservation area ▪ Nature walks by appt (guided & self-guided) ▪ Owner(s) The Tollman Family Trust ▪ Cellarmaster(s) Peter Finlayson (1989) ▪ Winemaker(s) Chris Albrecht (Nov 2010), with Nelis Uys (Jun 2017) ▪ Viticulturist(s) Mortimer Lee (Dec 2009) ▪ 125ha/22ha (barbera, nebbiolo, pinot, sangio, chard, riesling, sauv) ▪ 280t/35,000cs own label 30% red 70% white ▪ IPW, WWF-SA Conservation Champion ▪ PO Box 303 Hermanus 7200 ▪ info@bouchardfinlayson.co.za ▪ www.bouchardfinlayson.co.za ▪ S 34° 22' 54.0" E 019° 14' 30.9" ▪ ⌘ freeway.nostalgia.laughing ▪ **T +27 (0)28-312-3515**

☐ **Boutinot** *see* Wildeberg Wines
☐ **Brahms** *see* Domaine Brahms Wineries

Bramon Wines

It's the 20th anniversary of this Plettenberg Bay pioneer, founded by Peter and Caroline Thorpe and named for son Bram and his sister Manon, in the cool, mountainous Crags area just 3 km from the sea (and adjacent to an elephant sanctuary!). Their then sole offering, a rare MCC sparkling from sauvignon, was crafted by Pieter Ferreira of Graham Beck; since 2010 it's been made by consultant Anton Smal, himself a local trailblazer, who has helped develop and expand the portfolio to include still and pink wines. Facilities for guests have increased, too, and now feature an upgraded tasting room, picnic area, restaurant and accommodation.

Bramon Méthode Cap Classique range

★★★★ **Blanc de Blancs** Delicious **17** ⑧⑨ bubbles from chardonnay, pretty perfumed note to crisp apple fruit. 10% barrelled reserve wine adds pleasing palate weight & firmness at finish, as do 12 months on lees.

★★★★ **Sauvignon Blanc** New release of **15** ⑧⑦ sparkler has shorter lees time (24 months) but longer on cork, leaving pronounced greenpepper & grassy notes intermingled with creamy fruit. Definitely a dramatic & unusual sparkler, shade less harmonious than last but still impresses.

The Crags range

★★★★ **Rosé** Bone-dry **18** ⑧⑥ from pinot noir & 12% chardonnay shows earthy notes with strawberries & herbs. Fresh & light (10.7% alcohol), good partner for a salade Niçoise.

★★★★☆ **Reserve** ⑭ⓔⓦ ⊘ From sauvignon, excellent debut **18** ⑨⓪ packed with pungent nettles, greenpeppers, dandelion juice. Touch of sugar (3.4 g/l) balances steely acidity & rounds out mid-palate, 6 months on lees leave lingering savoury effect.

★★★★ **Sauvignon Blanc** Full of grassy gooseberry fruit, creamy edge thanks to 6 months lees contact, **18** ⑧⑧ satisfying albeit slightly less concentrated than step-up **17** ★★★★☆ ⑨⓪.

Nectar ⑭ⓔⓦ ★★★★ Off-dry version of sauvignon, **18** ⑧④ offers easy, enjoyable sipping. Perfumed fruit, juicy acidity, great partner for seafood curries. Discontinued: **Anton's Selection**. — CM

Location/WO: Plettenberg Bay ▪ Map: Klein Karoo & Garden Route ▪ Map grid reference: C1 ▪ Est 2000 ▪ 1stB 2004 ▪ Tasting & sales daily 11-5 ▪ Fee R10/tasting glass, waived on wine purchase ▪ Closed Dec 25 ▪ Cellar tours by appt ▪ Restaurant ▪ Picnic baskets to be pre-booked ▪ Facilities for children ▪ Southern Crags Conservancy ▪ Waterfall Cottage (4 pax, self-catering) ▪ Owner(s) Private company ▪ Cellarmaster(s)/winemaker(s) Anton Smal (Feb 2010) ▪ Viticulturist(s) Private consultant ▪ 10ha/6ha (chard, sauv) ▪ 50t/6,400cs own label 100% white ▪ PO Box 1606 Plettenberg Bay 6602 ▪ accounts@bramonwines.com ▪ www.bramon-wines.co.za ▪ S 33° 57' 20.30" E 023° 28' 45.02" ▪ ⌘ bushes.roundup.predominant ▪ **T +27 (0)73-833-8183**

Brampton

This well-established DGB label has a home in the Brampton Wine Studio on Stellenbosch's trendy Church Street, and now there's also the Brampton Mobile Wine Bar, a converted food truck which enables the team to share their easy-drinking wines (not available for review by us) with crowds at festivals and events.

Location/map: Stellenbosch ▪ Map grid reference: F5 ▪ Est/1stB 1996 ▪ Opening hours Mon-Sun 10-9 pub hols 11-9, with wine tasting from 11-4 ▪ Fee R25/3 wines R50/6 wines ▪ Closed Good Fri & Dec 25 ▪ Light lunches/dinner 12-8pm; refreshments all day ▪ Craft beer ▪ Owner(s) DGB (Pty) Ltd ▪ Winemaker(s) Boschendal Cellar ▪ Viticulturist(s) Heinie Nel (Jul 2018) ▪ 500t/80,000cs own label 40% red 55% white 5% rosé ▪ WIETA ▪ 11 Church St, Stellenbosch 7600 ▪ brampton@dgb.co.za ▪ www.brampton.co.za ▪ S 33° 56' 17.42" E 018° 51' 38.08" ▪ trainer.blocks.coach ▪ T +27 (0)21-883-9097

Brandvlei Cellar

The grower-owned winery in the shadow of Jonaskop peak started out 65 years ago on premises beside Brandvlei Dam and moved to the current location between Worcester and Villiersdorp two decades later when the dam was enlarged. 'Quality wines that everyone can enjoy and afford' is the aim, and the small fraction of output that appears under the BC Wines label certainly hits that target.

BC Wines range

Cabernet Sauvignon ⊘ ★★★ 18 ⑦ has green leafy notes, primary fruit, grippy tannins. **Pinotage** ⊘ ★★★ Typical bramble & mulberry fruit profile on 18 ㉒, well-judged tannins & body. Perfect braai companion. **Shiraz** ⊘ ★★★ Sweetly fruity, unoaked 18 ㉒ offers user-friendly value. Nice spice & pepper twist at finish. **Ruby Cabernet-Merlot** ⊘ ★★★ Ripe & succulent red fruit elevates 18 ㉛ above previous. Gentle tannins, lightish body. Pleasant everyday red. **Chardonnay** ⊘ ★★★ Previewed unoaked 19 ㉘ is light bodied & still unsettled, showing youth. Convincing citrus fruit standing by. **Chenin Blanc** ⊘ ★★★ Cheerful, refreshing 19 ㉘ offers uncomplicated early-drinking pleasure, with ripe pear, guava & pineapple notes. **Sauvignon Blanc** ⊘ ★★★ 19 ㉘ is light-bodied, with khaki bush, appealing gooseberry notes. **Bacchanté** ⊘ ★★★ Pleasantly fruity, off-dry 19 ㉙ blend of chenin, colombard, viognier. **Sauvignon Blanc Brut** ⊘ ★★★ Tangy, just-dry **NV** ㉘ carbonated sparkling is pleasantly fruity, refreshing. Discontinued: **Hanepoot Jerepigo.** — GdB

Location/map/WO: Worcester ▪ Map grid reference: B5 ▪ Est 1955 ▪ Tasting & sales Mon-Fri 8–4.30 ▪ Closed all pub hols ▪ Cellar tours by appt only ▪ Conferences/weddings ▪ Owner(s) 18 members ▪ Cellarmaster(s) Jean le Roux (Aug 1995) ▪ Winemaker(s) Willie Biggs (Sep 2009) & Daneel Jacobs (Sep 2007) ▪ Viticulturist(s) Danie Conradie (Sep 2004) ▪ 1,630ha (cab, ptage, chard, chenin, cbard, sauv) ▪ 28,500t 20% red 80% white ▪ PO Box 595 Worcester 6849 ▪ sales@bcwines.co.za ▪ www.bcwines.co.za ▪ S 33° 48' 19.5" E 019° 28' 8.1" ▪ pleasant.comical.quad ▪ T +27 (0)23-340-4215

☐ **Bredell's** see JP Bredell Wines

Breëland Winery

Blessed with immense unspoilt beauty, Lizelle Marais' farm in Slanghoek Valley is a nature-, sport- and wine-lover's paradise, offering game viewing, bird watching, fishing, mountain biking, hiking and more, plus tastings of the Breëland label, part of a much bigger production from 100 hectares of vines.

Cabernet Sauvignon ⓐ ★★★ Profusion of super-ripe fruit on 15 ㉒, blackcurrants & mulberries with a nutty twist. **Pinotage** ★★★ Previewed 18 ㉘ riper, fuller than previous, with solid fruit, chewy tannins. Vinified in seasoned foudres. **Chenin Blanc Royal** ⓐ ★★★★ Fruit is the hero of barrel-fermented 14 ㉓. White peaches, lemons & flowers, appealing viscosity & crisp finish. WO W Cape. **Sauvignon Blanc** ★★★ Wet pebble dustiness on 19 ㉛ tank sample, attractively lean granadilla fruit & steely acidity. Discontinued: **Pinotage Rosé.** — GdB

Location: Rawsonville ▪ Map: Breedekloof ▪ Map grid reference: A5 ▪ WO: Slanghoek/Western Cape ▪ Est 1825 ▪ 1stB 2010 ▪ Tasting, sales & cellar tours Mon-Sat by appt ▪ Closed Ash Wed, Easter Fri-Mon, Ascension day, Dec 25 & Jan 1 ▪ Pre-booked lunches (5 days prior notice) ▪ BYO picnic ▪ Walks/hikes ▪ MTB & 4x4 trails ▪ Conservation area ▪ Wedding/function venue ▪ Self-catering guest accommodation (mountain hut/farm house) ▪ Owner(s) Lizelle Marais ▪ Cellarmaster(s)/winemaker(s) Wickus Erasmus (Dec 2008) ▪ Viticulturist(s) Wickus Erasmus ▪ 1,500ha/100ha (cab, cinsaut, nebbiolo, ptage, shiraz, tannat, chenin, cbard, hanepoot, pinot gris, sauv, sem) ▪ 3,200t/500cs own label 20% red 80% white + 500cs for clients ▪ Brands for clients: Kaap Agri, Wine Village-Hermanus, Wine Boutique l'Aghulhas ▪ PO Box 26 Rawsonville 6845 ▪ lizelle@boegoekloof.co.za ▪ www.buchukloof.co.za, www.maraiswines.co.za ▪ S 33° 39' 2.87" E 019° 13' 40.08" ▪ ⓜ undergrad.rookies.snared ▪ **T +27 (0)23-344-3129/+27 (0)78-575-2365**

Brenaissance Wine & Stud Estate

Just over a decade ago, entrepreneurial couple Tom and Hayley Breytenbach brought about a renaissance on formerly anonymous Devon Valley grape-growing property High Mead, transforming it into a winery, multi-amenity visitor venue and Boran cattle stud. Recent vintages, vinified by specialists, untasted by us.

Location/map/WO: Stellenbosch ▪ Map grid reference: D4 ▪ 1stB 2009 ▪ Tasting & sales Mon-Sun 11-5 (Oct-Apr)/Wed-Sun 11-5 (Mar-Sep) ▪ Pizza & wine pairing ▪ Brenaissance restaurant ▪ Child friendly ▪ Conferences/functions ▪ Wedding venue & chapel ▪ Accommodation ▪ Boran cattle stud ▪ Owner(s) Tom & Hayley Breytenbach ▪ Winemaker(s) various ▪ 58.23ha/31.65ha (cabs s/f, malbec, merlot, p verdot, shiraz, chard) ▪ 5,058cs own label 70% red 30% white ▪ Devon Valley Rd, Devon Valley, Stellenbosch 7600 ▪ info@brenaissance.co.za ▪ www.brenaissance.co.za ▪ S 33° 55' 4.31" E 018° 49' 7.82" ▪ ⓜ file.cages.soda ▪ **T +27 (0)21-200-2537**

☐ **Brendel Collection** *see* Le Manoir de Brendel

Brew Cru

Two locals are joined by an American in this wine (and craft beer) venture focused on producing boutique parcels from the Cape South Coast, with its 'extreme conditions, hardened landscapes and constant gusts of Atlantic sea wind': Bertus Fourie, wide-ranging consultant winemaker, Johann Fourie, Benguela Cove's cellar chief, and Jesse Balsimo, wine importer/brand developer and CEO of Minnesota's Truvino. Exploration of the area's 'back roads' for 'unique vineyard pockets to produce authentic, site-specific wines that reflect their wild origins' has resulted in the bottlings reviewed here, with a cabernet franc and chenin to follow.

★★★★ **Pinot Noir** ⊘ Rose- & strawberry-perfumed **18** ⑧⑨ entwines variety's high acidity with pure fruit flavours, slightly dusty tannins. Poised, with welcome earthiness on the finish. Some whole berries/bunches in the ferment.

★★★★ **Chardonnay** Cool maritime origins (Hemel-en-Aarde Ridge) reflected in **18** ⑧⑨'s subtle orchard fruits, fine saline mineral seam; oak tad prominent mid-2019, needs year/2 to meld. Bunch press, ferment in barrel, 40% new, portion with indigenous yeast.— WB, CvZ

WO: Walker Bay/Hemel-en-Aarde Ridge ▪ Est/1stB 2017 ▪ Tasting by appt only ▪ Owner(s) Bertus Fourie, Jesse Balsimo, Johann Fourie ▪ Cellarmaster(s) Johann Fourie & Bertus Fourie (both 2016) ▪ 2ha (pinot, chard) ▪ 10t/1,300cs own label 50% red 50% white ▪ IPW, WIETA ▪ johannlfourie@gmail.com ▪ www.brewcru.com ▪ **T +27 (0)84-559-1715**

☐ **Bridge Wines** *see* The Bridge of Hope Wines
☐ **Brink Family Vineyards** *see* Pulpit Rock Winery
☐ **Britz Brothers** *see* Under Oaks
☐ **Brocha** *see* Iona Vineyards
☐ **Broken Stone** *see* Slaley

Brookdale Estate

The first three vintages from this Paarl mountainside property have produced an old bushvine chenin. UK owner Tim Rudd has many exciting plans, including the introduction of a new range, Mason Road, not ready in time for our deadline. The first crop of a 16-variety white field-blend will be harvested this year, along with individual varietal wines. A 20-cultivar red field-blend is about to be planted, and the cellar necessary to vinify all this is planned for next year. Kiara Scott, a former CWG Protégé, takes over as winemaker, having produced the '19s with consultant Duncan Savage.

★★★★☆ **Chenin Blanc** ⓐ Begs to be noticed. Authoritative, powerful, but no heaviness in its ripe, oxidatively toned fruit. Confident acid backbone, grip, provide structure more akin to red wine. **18** ⑨④ step up on **17** ★★★★ ⑧⑤; better balanced (20% new oak vs 50%), will also grow with ageing.— AL

Location/WO: Paarl ▪ Est 2016 ▪ Closed to public ▪ Owner(s) Rudd Farms Limited (Tim Rudd) ▪ GM Schalk Pienaar (Apr 2016), with Anne Hawley ▪ Winemaker(s) Kiara Scott (Jan 2019), advised by Duncan Savage (Oct 2016, consultant) ▪ Viticulturist(s) Jaco Engelbrecht (Oct 2018, consultant), with Adam Dirkse (Oct 2016) ▪ 57ha/16ha under vine ▪ 50% red 50% white ▪ Hawequa Forest Rd, Klein Drakenstein, Paarl 7646 ▪ enquire@brookdale-estate.com ▪ www.brookdale-estate.com ▪ T +27 (0)76-400-0229

Brothers Wines

After years of tasting the wines of the world, and studying winemaking at Stellenbosch, Cape Town corporate executive Greg Castle realised his dream of an own boutique brand in 2005, naming it for sons Dylan and Alex. The wines, from top Constantia, Swartland and Stellenbosch vineyards, are available in specialist wine shops and select eateries, as well as overseas. We look forward to reviewing new vintages next edition.

Location: Cape Town ▪ Est/1stB 2005 ▪ Closed to public ▪ Owner(s) Greg Castle ▪ Cellarmaster(s)/winemaker(s) Greg Castle (2005) ▪ 10t/1,666cs own label 55% red 45% white ▪ PO Box 21681 Kloof Str Cape Town 8008 ▪ info@brotherswines.co.za ▪ www.brotherswines.com ▪ T +27 (0)82-600-2555

Bruce Jack Wines

Reflecting on his website about collecting climate data on Appelsdrift farm near Napier in the 1990s, Bruce Jack noted that the songbirds were self-conscious and 'sorrow and hardship were entwined into the bluegum branches'. But, crucially, 'the land was welcoming'. And so the remote, hilly and viticulturally extreme Overberg farm, alias The Drift, became home to the driving force behind the Flagstone success story and, until recently, group winemaker at Accolade Wines SA. He's established vineyards, olive groves, organic vegetable gardens, compost beds and much more. But there have been fires, drought and marauding animals, and plenty of physical exertion. Celebration, too, of vinifying in the recent on-site winery. And giving back, with a music school established at the Protea Primary in Napier village, a dream realised.

Bruce Jack Heritage Collection (NEW)

★★★★☆ **Clean Slate Shiraz** Seductive **15** (94) from tiny (0.45 ha) single-vineyard on shattered slate & granite. Restrained yet intense herb-brushed blue & black fruit. Light, spicy, concentrated & long, it had just 8 months in old oak. Years of life ahead.

★★★★☆ **Boer Maak 'n Plan Chenin Blanc** Vivid citrus & cream on **18** (90) from Rawsonville grapes, shows crystalline purity yet is broad & rich. Dry, with elegant restraint & long finish. Complex winemaking includes ferment in seasoned oak (portion with wild yeast) & extended (8 months) ageing on thick lees.

★★★★☆ **Vloermoer** Splendid debut in handsome packaging, **00** (94) fino sherry under flor then 13 years in solera, amontillado style. Orange gold, powerful dried fruit aromas, nuts & honey, a wonderfully savoury overlay, yet dry, elegant, classically styled. Pure class. From Stellenbosch chardonnay. 500 ml.

Bruce Jack Estate Collection

★★★★☆ **Gift Horse Single Vineyard Barbera** Tangy brightness to **17** (93) bottling of locally rare grape, on par with last-tasted **15** (92). Layered, textured & alluring. Long spontaneous ferment (25% wholebunch) & old-oak ageing for 18 months with a portion new, 18%.

★★★★☆ **There Are Still Mysteries Single Vineyard Pinot Noir** Lithe & light, **16** (91) has a wonderful interplay of sour cherry & spice, creamy mid-palate & long finish. Leashed power, perfectly poised & harmonious. Oak, just 10% new, for 18 months. Great prospects, also in the available magnums.

★★★★☆ **Over The Moon Red Blend** Creative, complex **18** (90) medley cinsaut, shiraz, touriga franca with dabs mourvèdre, pinotage & tinta barocca, none oaked. Lovely grip & vivacity from carbonic maceration, good intensity & length. Winemaker recommends light chilling. WO W Cape.

★★★★☆ **Moveable Feast Red Blend** Vibrant & creative union of partly co-fermented malbec, shiraz, tannat, touriga & pinot noir, latter back in action in **15** (93) after **14** (92)'s barbera. Unfettered by new oak, shows tight-packed black fruit, fynbos & pot-pourri. Suave & absolutely captivating.

★★★★ **Year of the Rooster Rosé** All pinotage in **18** ★★★★ (85), unlike cinsaut & touriga mix of **17** (88). Intended as suave, extra-dry wine James Bond might sip with his Scottish salmon, in fact is softly sweet this vintage, with red berry vivacity, juicy & fun. WO Coastal.

Penelope Méthode Cap Classique Rosé ★★★☆ Sparkler from malbec dedicated to Bruce Jack's wife, creator of the range's unique & inspired packaging. **16** (84) bright, tangy apple crunch & sourdough breadth from 24 months in bottle. Primary ferment in old barrels adds weight.

Bruce Jack Extreme Vineyards Collection

★★★★ Bonfire Hill White ⊘ Chenin upped to 82% in **18** (86), with roussanne & grenache blanc. Bright, honeyed richness with stonefruit tang to temper it. Oak (10% new) for 8 months frames blend. Lingering creamy finish. Improves on **17 ★★★★** (85). WO W Cape, as next.

Bonfire Hill Red ⊘ **★★★☆** Blends shiraz, 32% each cinsaut & pinotage in supple yet intense blueberry package. **18** (85) approachable & light yet concentrated, with earthy twist in the finish.

Mary Le Bow range

★★★★ Mary le Bow (②) Cherry, violet & cassis perfume elevate **14 ★★★★★** (93) blend of shiraz, cab & merlot. Velvety palate with chalky tannin & spice from mostly American oak, 15% new. Shows restraint of **09**, rather than power of **11 ★★★★** (84). Robertson WO.— FM, CR

Location: Napier ▪ Map: Southern Cape ▪ Map grid reference: B7 ▪ WO: Overberg/Western Cape/Coastal/Breedekloof/Robertson/Stellenbosch ▪ 1stB 2005 ▪ Tasting by appt only ▪ Wine sales via website ▪ Owner(s)/winemaker(s) Bruce Jack ▪ Viticulturist(s) Andre Purdy ▪ Ecocert (not vyds), WIETA ▪ PO Box 55 Napier 7270 ▪ orders@thedrift.co.za ▪ www.brucejack.com ▪ S 34° 23' 50.94" E 019° 42' 37.01" ▪ **T +27 (0)86-150-2025**

Brunia Wines (②) (◎)

On their Cold Mountain estate near Stanford, the Sander family grow 17ha of vines as well as figs and vegetables, but most of the extensive property is pristine fynbos, including the silver-hued species Brunia laevis. A sustainable approach is pursued, and conversion to organic underway. Only a portion of the grapes is bottled under the family label. Son Wade Sander, assistant winemaker at Leeu Passant in Franschhoek, sees Brunia as 'an outlet for me to experiment with small-batch production and better understand our vineyards'.

★★★★ Syrah Was 'Shiraz'. **18** (88) first tasted since **12 ★★★★★** (93). Plenty of pure sweet-fruit charm & fragrant lilies, red fruit well-focused by gentle, cool-climate structure. Should gain in interest over next few years. Natural ferment, as Semillon, 30% wholebunch.

★★★★ White (NEW) (愛) Harmonious, cool-climate sauvignon (75%), semillon blend. **18** (88) forges silky richness with bracing, lively tension. Barrel ferment/lees ageing enhance structure without disturbing overall elegance. Plenty of room to grow.

Semillon ★★★☆ First since **13** (85), **18** (84) youthfully closed, brisk natural acid leading current light earthy, waxy undertones. Has balance, structure to benefit from laying down. Lees ageing in older oak. Unfined/filtered, as White. Occasional release: **Pinot Noir**, **Sauvignon Blanc**. In abeyance: **Chardonnay**. — AL

Location: Stanford ▪ Map: Southern Cape ▪ Map grid reference: B2 ▪ WO: Sunday's Glen ▪ Est 2005 ▪ 1stB 2009 ▪ Tasting & sales by appt only ▪ Tasting R50pp ▪ Closed all pub hols ▪ Self-guided hiking trails ▪ Mountain biking ▪ Conservation area ▪ Owner(s) Sander family ▪ Winemaker(s) Wade Sander ▪ Viticulturist(s) Conrad Schutte (consultant) ▪ 417ha/17ha (pinot, shiraz, chard, sauv, sem) ▪ 75t own label 26% red 10% white, balance sold ▪ Sandies Glen Rd, Sondagskloof, Stanford 7210 ▪ info@bruniawines.co.za ▪ www.bruniawines.co.za ▪ S 34° 28' 9.25" E 019° 39' 42.60" ▪ [⚷] gridded.hauntings.cubicles ▪ **T +27 (0)28-341-0432**

☐ **Brutus Family Reserve** see Seven Sisters Vineyards
☐ **Buchu Trail** see Oude Compagnies Post Private Cellar
☐ **Buckleberry** see Louis

Buffalo Creek Wines (②)

Father-and-son growers Leroy and Mark Tolmay aim to produce affordably priced and easily drinkable wines, profits from which are distributed among the staff on their McGregor farm. Current releases, which can also be bought at Grape De-vine in McGregor village, are Merlot '16, Pinot Noir Dry Rosé and Chardonnay '18, Sunset Red NV and Sauvignon Blanc '19.

Location: McGregor ▪ Map: Robertson ▪ Map grid reference: D6 ▪ Est/1stB 2005 ▪ Tasting, sales & cellar tours Mon-Fri 9-6 Sat 9-12.30 Sun by appt only ▪ Closed Easter Sun, Dec 25 & Jan 1 ▪ Sales also available from Grape De-Vine in McGregor ▪ Owner(s) Leroy & Mark Tolmay ▪ Cellarmaster(s)/winemaker(s) Mark Tolmay

(Jun 2005) ▪ 1,328ha/30ha (p verdot, ptage, pinot, merlot, chard, chenin, cbard, sauv) ▪ ±350-380t/500-600cs own label 65% red 25% white 10% rosé ▪ PO Box 124 McGregor 6708 ▪ info@buffalocreek.co.za ▪ S 34° 0' 2.97" E 019° 53' 11.94" ▪ ⓦ outwitting.pebble.stretchy ▪ **T +27 (0)23-004-1329/1334**

Buitenverwachting   ⓠ ⓨ ⓐ ⓑ

German-owned by the Meuller family since the 1980s, with Christine Mueller's son (and co-proprietor) Lars Maack handling the day-to-day running and development, this prime Constantia estate boasts a significant history. It formed part of Simon van der Stel's original Constantia holding, with vines planted here since the 1700s. There has been management continuity, Hermann Kirschbaum, cellarmaster since 1993, took the role of estate manager to make place for Brad Paton in 2005. There is a pool of knowledge and experience which reflects in the wines, and a not insignificant 84-ha vineyard responsibility. There are core wines but the range evolves, expands, as in the Limited Release offerings, this edition with a new wine.

Buitenverwachting range

★★★★ Merlot ⓠ Fynbos & graphite temper fruitcake notes of **13** ⑧⑨. Enticing ripeness & succulence cradled by oak (20-24 months). Lovely body, concentration & length.

★★★★☆ Christine ⓠ Harmonious **13** ⑨③ adds to lustre of flagship Bordeaux blend, near-equal cab & cab franc with dabs malbec & petit verdot. Merlot (19%) added this vintage, showing deep, smooth, sexy dark fruitcake & tobacco appeal. Seamless & polished from 23 months in 90% new oak.

★★★★ Meifort ⓥ Cab franc-led 4-part Bordeaux blend, older barrels; oak shows as coriander-spiced cured beef, graphite notes in the succulent berries. **16** ⑧⑨'s tannins amenable, could still age.

★★★★☆ Chardonnay ⓐ Barrel ferment/ageing 11 months French, third new, shows in **18** ⑨③ as toasted brioche, a wild honey nuance in the citrus. Loads of flavour but great harmony between the savoury notes & fruit. Powerful, polished & assured - & truly delicious.

★★★★☆ Hussey's Vlei Sauvignon Blanc ⓐ Site selection; passionfruit & lime in **18** ⑨③, sleek & intense, a lesson on how much flavour can be packed into a svelte body. Shot through with racy acidity, mouthwateringly fresh & vibrant, a mineral note at the end.

★★★★ Sauvignon Blanc Personifies freshness, **19** ⑧⑥ ex tank has gooseberries, attractive leafy nuance, a mineral core. Zesty, the touch of sugar plumps out the body, finishes sweet/sour. More complex than **18** ★★★☆ ⑧③.

★★★★☆ 1769 ⓐ Skin ferment, then older barrels 10 months, exceptional **17** ★★★★★ ⑨⑤ Noble Late Harvest from muscat de Frontignan has the floral aromas you'd expect, sweetness (243 g/l) lifted by tangy acidity. Flavours of barley sugar, caramelised pineapple - such heady richness! Fine follow-up to **16** ⑨④. 500 ml.

....

Blanc de Noir ⓥ ⓟ **★★★★** Bright pink hue to **19** ⑧④, merlot/cab & 4 others, so expect some layering. Strawberries & red cherries with mineral/saline freshness, ending dry. Delicious, great food wine.

....

Buiten Blanc ★★★★ Deservedly popular, mainly sauvignon with 4 others, some aromatic, giving **19** ⑧③ preview floral highlights, adding to the fresh fruit interest. WO W Cape. Not tasted: **Cabernet Sauvignon**, **Méthode Cap Classique Brut**.

Limited Release range

★★★★☆ Cabernet Franc ⓐ Crammed with berries, easily handling the ±2 years in barrel, **14** ⑨② is muscular, layered & complex, densely packed, with still many years ahead. Shows a powerful version of the variety, & does it very well. The 15% alcohol not obvious.

★★★★ The Phoenix ⓝⓔⓦ ⓐ Barrel selection petit verdot, **15** ⑧⑦ a voluptuous 16% alcohol, loads of dark fruit, 30 months new French oak shows as liquorice, charcuterie. Big, bold & designed to impress.

★★★★ G That rarity, barrel-matured & bone-dry gewürztraminer, but **18** ⑧⑧ works: Turkish delight perfume, streamlined & pure, oak a subtle savoury thread. Has refinement & style, improves on **17** ★★★☆ ⑧③, also from Durbanville grapes.

★★★★☆ Maximus ⓐ Aptly named, big-personality sauvignon **17** ⑨⓪ spent 18 months in barriques, 35% new, a nice contrast to Hussey's Vlei, not only in style but in ripeness. Baked apple & honey biscuit, richly savoury & round, yet crisp acidity adds lift & drinkability.

★★★★ **3rd Time Lucky** Last was **14** ⑧⑨. Barrel-fermented/aged viognier, **18** ⑧⑧ boasts peach & apricot perfume, flavours, tangy acidity keeping it lively. Oak spice a subtle addition but fruit the main attraction. WO W Cape.

In abeyance: **Malbec, Pinot Noir Block 8, Rough Diamond**. — CR

Location: Constantia ▪ Map: Cape Peninsula ▪ Map grid reference: B3 ▪ WO: Constantia/Western Cape ▪ Est 1796 ▪ 1stB 1985 ▪ Tasting & sales Mon-Fri 9-5 Sat 10-5 ▪ Closed all pub hols ▪ Cellar tours by appt ▪ Selection of platters available in tasting room ▪ Buitenverwachting Restaurant ▪ Deli & coffee shop ▪ Conferences ▪ Owner(s) Sieglinde (Christine) Mueller & Lars Maack ▪ Estate manager Hermann Kirschbaum (Jan 1993) ▪ Cellarmaster(s) Brad Paton (Dec 2004) ▪ Winemaker(s) Brad Paton (Dec 2004), with Stephan Steyn ▪ Viticulturist(s) Peter Reynolds (Jan 2001) ▪ 84ha under vine (Bordeaux varietals, chard, sauv) ▪ 25% red 75% white ▪ PO Box 281 Constantia 7848 ▪ info@buitenverwachting.com ▪ www.buitenverwachting.com ▪ S 34° 2' 30.4" E 018° 25' 1.5" ▪ 🖂 riddles.merely.washcloths ▪ **T +27 (0)21-794-5190/1**

☐ **Bulldozer** see Bergsig Estate
☐ **Burger Family Vineyards** see Rietvallei Wine Estate

Burgershof

One of the area's original farms, Burgershof is in the Klaasvoogds ward of Robertson. Latterly the Reynecke family have focused on modern, in-demand varietal and blended wines but their heritage and biggest strength is fortified muscat. The quality's in the soil — viticulturally and according to local lore: the blood of early colonist Clas Vogt, horribly killed by an elephant, said to give the grape its special beauty in these parts.

★★★★ **Red Muscadel** ⓥ Premium-priced & -packaged **16** ⑧⑦ is complex, light footed & balanced. Gorgeous flavour array of peach through tealeaf to ginger. 375 ml intended as a gift for someone special. **Merlot** ★★★ Always pleases the crowd with its plummy tone, juicy flavours & downy texture. **17** ⑦⑨ does it again. **Pinotage** ⓥ ★★★ With dark berries, tapenade & meaty complexity, dry finish despite sweet fruit core, **16** ⑦⑧ ticks all the boxes. **Cabernet Sauvignon-Shiraz** ⓥ ★★ Uncomplex but pleasant **16** ⑦⑷ braai companion, near-equal blend has intense fruit backing its big, burly tannins. Not tasted: **Chardonnay, Sauvignon Blanc**. — WB

Location/WO: Robertson ▪ Est 1864 ▪ 1stB 2000 ▪ Closed to public ▪ Sales at La Verne Wine Boutique & Ashton Wine Boutique ▪ Owner(s) Hennie Reynecke ▪ Cellarmaster(s)/winemaker(s)/viticulturist(s) Hennie Reynecke (Jan 1979) ▪ 70ha (cab, merlot, muscadel r/w, ptage, ruby cab, shiraz, chard, chenin, cbard, sauv) ▪ IPW, WIETA ▪ PO Box 72 Klaasvoogds River 6707 ▪ burgershof@barvallei.co.za ▪ www.burgershof.com ▪ **T +27 (0)23-626-5433**

Bushmanspad Estate   ⓥ 🍴 🎁 🏠 📷

Undoubtedly a good fit for Netherlander Menno Schaafsma's vineyard, cellar and cottages on the Langeberg slopes near Bonnievale is viticulturist/winemaker Aldert Nieuwoudt. Well-settled since his first (2018) vintage here, after three with Rianie Strydom (Strydom Vintners) at prime Helderberg property Haskell, married to Roniel (now Bushmanspad marketer), father of two littlies, lover of farm life, Aldert is in his element.

★★★★ **The Menno** Flagship produced every third year, **18** ⑧⑧ worth the wait: dense, fruity & stylish malbec/shiraz-led 6-way blend. Sweetly ripe mulberries with savoury-spicy tobacco notes, silky tannins. **Cabernet Sauvignon** ★★★ Shows **17** ⑧⑤ vintage's ripeness, with bold black fruit, robust body, full tannins. Rather brisk acidity suggests red-meat matching. **Cabernet Franc** ⓥ ★★★ Toffee & plummy fruit a bit off-target for variety, but medium-bodied **15** ⑧⑵ is pleasant sipping with no rough edges. **Malbec** ★★★ Sweetly ripe black fruit with savoury notes on big, brawny **17** ⑧⑤. Hefty tannins tempered by 15 months in barrel. **Shiraz** ⓥ ★★★★ Lush, ripe & perfumed black fruit on **16** ⑧⑤ with tarry, savoury notes & suede tannins. **Cabernet Sauvignon-Merlot** ★★★ **17** ⑧⑵ revisited after time in bottle, shows slight softening of tannins, same plush red & black berry fruit. **Red Gold Blend** ★★★ 4-way Bordeaux blend with dashes shiraz & mourvèdre, retasted **17** ⑧⑤ has settled and rounded out. Plush ripe berries, soft tannins. **Pink Gold Rosé** ★★★ From malbec, **19** ⑧⑵ viscous texture, pithy red berry fruit, restrained acidity. Pleasant everyday tipple. **Sauvignon Blanc** ★★★ Restrained **19** ⑧⑵ pleasing gooseberry fruit, edgy acidity, light body. Not tasted: **Grand Reserve Merlot**. — GdB

Location: Bonnievale ▪ Map/WO: Robertson ▪ Map grid reference: C1 ▪ Est 2000 ▪ 1stB 2006 ▪ Tasting & sales Mon-Fri 8.30–5 ▪ Fee R40/5 wines ▪ Cheese platters by appt ▪ BYO picnic ▪ Walks/hikes ▪ Self-catering cottages ▪ Owner(s) Menno Schaafsma ▪ Cellarmaster(s)/winemaker(s)/viticulturist(s) Aldert Nieuwoudt (Jan 2018) ▪ 52ha (cabs s/f, malbec, merlot, mourv, shiraz, sauv) ▪ 400t own label 80% red 15% white 5% rosé ▪ PO Box 227 Bonnievale 6730 ▪ info@bushmanspad.co.za ▪ www.bushmanspad.co.za ▪ S 33° 53′ 55.0″ E 020° 11′ 46.7″ ▪ swooped.oilfield.pollsters ▪ **T +27 (0)23-616-2961**

☐ **Butcher Shop & Grill** *see* The Butcher Shop & Grill

B Vintners Vine Exploration Co

Star winemaker Bruwer Raats' out-of-the-box enterprise, with cousin Gavin Bruwer Slabbert (both of Raats Family Wines), seeks to uncover the backstory, history and potential of less illustrious varieties, alternative vinification techniques and paths less travelled. They source grapes with an untrammelled agenda and a desire to explore terroir possibilities around and beyond home-base Stellenbosch, merging the past with the present to offer an insight into the future. The range expands and contracts according to their discoveries.

★★★★☆ **De Alexandria** Rare-in-SA dry muscat d'Alexandrie from Helderberg vines, beguiling **18** ⑨② bold rosewater perfume, savoury-spicy notes & creamy tannic texture from 5 days skin contact, warmer ferment. Fine structure & elegant, fragrant finish.

★★★★★ **Harlem to Hope** Named for early Dutch settlers who brought these varieties to the Cape, stellar blend of chenin, semillon, muscats blanc & d'Alexandrie, older oaked, maintains lofty standard in **18** ⑨⑤. Robust yet silky, with delicate perfume, spices & perfectly rounded fruit. 13% alcohol.

Not tasted: **Black Bream Pinot Noir, Liberté Pinotage, Fire Heath Chardonnay**. — GdB

Location/map/WO: Stellenbosch ▪ Map grid reference: B6 ▪ Est/1stB 2014 ▪ Tasting Mon-Fri 9-5 by appt ▪ Fee R500 (2-10 pax) ▪ Closed all pub hols ▪ Owner(s)/cellarmaster(s) Bruwer Raats & Gavin Bruwer Slabbert ▪ own label 50% red 50% white ▪ PO Box 2068 Dennesig 7601 ▪ office@raats.co.za ▪ www.raatswines.co.za ▪ S 33° 58′ 16.6″ E 018° 44′ 55.3″ ▪ warps.picnic.apparent ▪ **T +27 (0)21-881-3078**

☐ **Cabrière** *see* Haute Cabrière

Cadequin Vineyard

Nothing for tasting from the minuscule parcel of pinotage and chenin on Robbie and Tarina Terheijden's property in High Riding Country Estate on the Hottentots Holland mountain slopes. 'Cadequin' was conceived by Robbie as a name for a future daughter but, after two sons, christened their wine venture instead. Nomada Wines' Riaan Oosthuizen is the consultant winemaker.

Location: Sir Lowry's Pass ▪ Map: Helderberg ▪ Map grid reference: H8 ▪ Est 2008 ▪ 1stB 2014 ▪ Tasting & sales by appt Mon-Fri 9-4 Sat/Sun 9-1 ▪ R50/tasting ▪ Closed Ash Wednesday, Easter Fri-Mon, Ascension day, Dec 25 & Jan 1 ▪ Playground ▪ Olives ▪ Airbnb Cadequin Vineyard Cottage (self-catering) ▪ Owner(s) Robbie & Tarina Terheijden ▪ Winemaker(s) Riaan Oosthuizen (Jan 2013, Nomada Wines) ▪ Viticulturist(s) Jaco Mouton (Jan 2010, consultant) ▪ 1ha (ptage, chenin) ▪ 1,6t ▪ 13 High Riding Estate, 54 Old Sir Lowry's Pass Rd, Somerset West 7130 ▪ moon@vodamail.co.za ▪ S 34° 7′ 20.89″ E 018° 55′ 30.26″ ▪ seminal.snacks. habituated ▪ **T +27 (0)71-673-5552**

☐ **Café Culture** *see* KWV Wines

Calais Wine Estate

Calais is a farm founded in 1692 by Huguenot Jean Manje, who named it after his home town. The current owners are represented by estate manager Melt van der Spuy, who oversees a portfolio of vines, wines and guest accommodation with attractive views over Paarl's bucolic Dal Josaphat area.

Klein Valley range

St Mikhail Cabernet Sauvignon ⓥ ★★★ Country-style **11** ⑺⑻ with earthy & savoury notes to plum pudding flavours, 2nd-fill oak contributing to the tannic dryness. **Applause** ⓥ ★★★ Cab/shiraz blend has clean oak & blackberry wafts, juicy berry sweetness anchored by firm tannins. **11** ⑻① could age few years. **Bel Canto** ⓥ ★★★☆ Mature **11** ⑻⑤ cab, shiraz, merlot is a hearty winter stew red, with earth, spice from older oak & red fruit, robust tannins. **St Katerina Barrel Fermented Viognier** ⓥ ★★★ Attractive, peachy **13** ⑧⑦ has some richness & texture, sufficient acidity to refresh the creamy finish.

Calais range

Chardonnay ⓥ ★★ Unoaked **13** ⑦④ straightforward easy-drinker with ripe pineapple flavour. Wellington WO, as next. **Sauvignon Blanc** ⓥ ★★ Lightly tropical **13** ⑦④ for uncomplicated quaffing. — JG

Location/map: Paarl ▪ Map grid reference: G4 ▪ WO: Paarl/Wellington ▪ Est/1stB 2000 ▪ Tasting by appt ▪ Sales daily 8-4 ▪ Guest accommodation ▪ Owner(s) Calais Wine Estate shareholders ▪ Farm manager Melt van der Spuy (Dec 2015) ▪ 23ha (cab, merlot, p verdot, ptage, ruby cab, shiraz, chard, chenin, sauv) ▪ 150t/3,000cs own label 70% red 30% white ▪ PO Box 9006 Klein Drakenstein 7628 ▪ info@calais.co.za ▪ www.calais.co.za ▪ S 33° 42' 32.1" E 019° 1' 24.6" ▪ ⓦ expect.entire.fizzy ▪ **T +27 (0)21-868-3888**

Calitzdorp Cellar

Young viti-vini man Danie van der Westhuizen has infused fresh energy and excitement into his coterie of Calitzdorp owner-growers, while still playing to the strengths of their ruggedly beautiful vineyard sites and heritage Klein Karoo styles. The former embraces on-trend exploration of unfortified wines from traditional Portuguese varieties, the latter includes production of rather fine fortified dessert wines and 'port'.

★★★★ **Tinta Barocca Barrel Selection** ⑩④ ⓥ ⓐ Best-in-cellar **18** ⑧⑦ offers variety-true lemon, orange zest & pot-pourri aromas, impresses even more on palate where there's dense but unforced dark fruit, lovely dryness & shapely tannins.

★★★★ **Tinto** Improved **NV** ⑧⑥ a vibrant, modern red full of varietal pot-pourri & orange zest appeal, piquant fruity finish, good support (not flavour) from 10% new oak. From tinta (58%) & touriga.

★★★★ **Hanepoot** Now vintage dated, fortified **17** ⑧⑥ deftly crafted for balanced sipping, the litchi & ginger aromas & flavours, honeyed sweetness all lifted by tangy lemon acidity, seamless spirit.

★★★★ **Red Muscadel** ⓥ Beautiful garnet hue, vivid sultana flavours with lavender nuance, fine balance of sweetness, alcohol & acidity for uncloying finish, **17** ⑧⑥ fortified well worth seeking out.

★★★★☆ **White Muscadel** ⓥ Gorgeous pear & white peach aromas touched with honey & fynbos, all repeated on palate with freshness & purity, delicate persistence. Even more than sibling fortifieds, **17** ⑨⓪ will reward cellaring.

★★★★ **Golden Jerepigo** Toothsome **NV** ⑧⑧ fortified benefits from moderate crop yield, giving more intensity, complexity, than before. Usual aromatic combo hanepoot & white muscadel delivers delightful, not over-sweet jasmine, rosepetal, honeysuckle & apricot flavour, perfect with sticky malva pudding.

- - - - - - - - - -

Pinotage Blanc de Noir ⓥ ⓣ ★★★ Charming **19** ⑧② delicious glassful of berries & cherries, bright acidity & pleasing body with bonus moderate 13% alcohol, smoothing touch sugar.

- - - - - - - - - -

Shiraz ⓥ ★★★ Vibrant red berries & plums, crisp acidity, **16** ⑧⓪ year in oak, 12% new. **Sauvignon Blanc** ★★★ From cool-climate Outeniqua grapes, **19** ⑧② improves on last with ample & typical grass & passionfruit tones, fuller body (13.5% alcohol) & lipsmacking dryness. Interesting dusty top note. **Cape Ruby** ⓥ ★★★★ Latest **NV** ⑧③ 'port' rings the changes: touriga & shiraz with 16% alcohol vs tinta & touriga, 18%. Has an easy, balanced charm, oozes plums & baking spices, unexpected but pleasing grip at the end. **Cape Vintage** ⓥ ★★★★ Softer-styled **17** ⑧④ 'port', equal partnership tinta & touriga, plush dark fruit with barely noticeable tannins, modest-for-style 18% alcohol for effortless fireside sipping. Not tasted: **Chardonnay, Chenin Blanc, Limited Edition Chenin Blanc-Muscat d'Alexandrie Delight**. Occasional release: **Hanepoot Muskadel Reserve**. In abeyance: **Touriga Nacional**. — CvZ

Location: Calitzdorp ▪ Map: Klein Karoo & Garden Route ▪ Map grid reference: B5 ▪ WO: Calitzdorp/Klein Karoo ▪ Est 1928 ▪ 1stB 1976 ▪ Tasting & sales Mon-Fri 9-5 Sat 9-1 ▪ Closed Good Fri & Dec 25 ▪ Cellar tours by appt ▪ Tour groups ▪ BYO picnic ▪ Conferences ▪ Owner(s) 40 members ▪ Cellarmaster(s)/viticulturist(s) Danie van der Westhuizen (Dec 2017) ▪ Winemaker(s) Danie van der Westhuizen (Dec 2017), with Abraham Pretorius ▪ 300ha (13 varieties, r/w) ▪ 5,000t/7,000cs own label ▪ IPW ▪ PO Box 193 Calitzdorp 6660 ▪ info@ calitzdorpwine.co.za ▪ www.calitzdorpwine.co.za ▪ S 33° 32' 18.9" E 021° 41' 10.6" ▪ ⓦ faltering.pianists. highlights ▪ **T +27 (0)44-213-3301**

Camberley Wines

Ⓥ Ⓥ Ⓐ Ⓐ

'The mission is simple: serve delicious wines that keep you coming back,' say John and Gaël Nel, who have been welcoming visitors to their scenic Banhoek Valley spot for over two decades. They now offer accommodation in three self-catering cottages and their son Mark and his wife Nicole run on-site Café Pavè, a refuelling stop with a bicycle showroom, especially popular among those pedalling on Helshoogte Pass.

Camberley range

★★★★ **Shiraz** Velvet **16** ⑧⑥ has ripe fruit with sweet spice from 14 months in 30% French oak, white pepper & rooibos nuances, in balance at house's generous 15% alcohol.

Illusion Ⓥ ★★★★ Pinotage's bramble & mulberry fruit, well-polished tannins from 14 months in barrel, 25% new. **NV** ⑧③ has clean leather & savoury undertones, perfect with venison. **Philosopher's Stone** ★★★☆ Bordeaux red, **16** ⑧⑤ fuller with more gravitas than previous **NV** ⑧②. Intriguing olive oil whiff adds to peppery impression. 40% each cab & cab franc, rest merlot, 14 months old oak. **Sparkling Shiraz** Ⓥ ★★★★ Luscious mulberry & cherry notes & few grams sugar on **15** ⑧④ fizz brightened by fine bubbles & acidity for clean, enjoyable & unusual drink. Not tasted: **Cabernet Franc**, **Cabernet Sauvignon-Merlot**, **Elixir Fortified Red**. Occasional release: **The 5th Element**, **Elm Tree Merlot**, **Charisma**. Discontinued: **Cabernet Sauvignon Reserve**, **Celebration**.

Prohibition range

Not tasted: **Red**, **White**. — JG

Location/map/WO: Stellenbosch ▪ Map grid reference: H4 ▪ Est 1990 ▪ 1stB 1996 ▪ Tasting & sales Mon-Sat & pub hols 9–5 Sun 9-3 ▪ Tasting fee depending on wine of choice ▪ Closed Dec 25 & Jan 1 ▪ Cellar tours by appt ▪ Café Pavè open for breakfast & light lunch Fri-Sun from 8; during high season it will be open daily - closed Jun & Jul ▪ Cycle showroom ▪ 2 self-catering guest cottages ▪ Owner(s) John & Gaël Nel ▪ Winemaker(s) John Nel ▪ Viticulturist(s) Bennie Booysen ▪ 7ha (cabs s/f, merlot, p verdot, ptage, shiraz, touriga) ▪ ±35t/6,400cs own label 100% red ▪ PO Box 6120 Uniedal 7612 ▪ john@camberley.co.za ▪ www.camberley.co.za ▪ S 33° 55' 8.9" E 018° 55' 58.3" ▪ ⓐ adopting.possible.exactly ▪ **T +27 (0)21-885-1176**

☐ **Camino Africana** *see* Edgebaston

Canto Wines

Ⓥ Ⓥ Ⓐ Ⓐ

Yoga, bubbly and macaroons - what's not to love? This boutique Durbanville winery is finding their Yoga Saturdays are proving even more successful when celebrity surfer and model, Roxy Louw, is teaching, but their wines remain the focus, with increased interest from fans locally and overseas. So much so, a new sauvignon blanc vineyard is being planted to meet the demand.

Canto Wines range

★★★★ **Merlot** Ⓥ Plenty of oak influence (18 months in barrel) only lively **16** ⑧⑥, adding smoke, tar, leather & chocolate to bright red-cherry fruit. Soft tannins & balancing acidity add to overall appeal.

★★★★ **Pinotage** Ⓥ Firmly styled **16** ⑧⑥ mixes ripe black plummy fruit with hints of coffee, smoke & tar. Tannins & zippy acidity suggest further development - certainly benefits from decanting now.

★★★★ **Chardonnay** Improving on **17** ⑧⑦ debut, **18** ⑧⑨ handles 100% new French oak with elegance & grace, edging pineapple & mango fruit with spice, biscuit & honey. Zesty acidity keeps it interesting throughout, promising improvement over few years.

Unwooded Chardonnay Ⓥ ★★★★ Fresh & lively **18** ⑧⑤, well balanced between stonefruit, touch of herbs & attractive banana bread finish, helped by 3 months lees contact.

Sauvignon Blanc ★★★☆ Subtle & elegant **18** ⑧④ balances passionfruit & white pear with Durbanville's signature dusty/grassy notes, lees ageing adds richness mid-palate.

Méthode Cap Classique range

★★★★ **Pinot Noir** Elegant, restrained rosé sparkler from Stellenbosch fruit, **17** ⑧⑨ fresher than **13** ⑧⑧, shimmers with zesty raspberry & savoury/salty tang. Well-judged lees time of 12 months. No **14** - **16**.

★★★★ **Brut** Ⓥ Fine mousse on **15** ⑧⑦ sparkler from chardonnay, lime sherbet perfume, candy apple flavour, zinging acidity keeps it focused, dry. Drink now as aperitif, can age.

Shiraz ★★★☆ Extended bottle-ageing on lees of 2 years for **15** ⑧⑤ rosé sparkling gives attractive liquorice note to spicy red-fruit core. Good acidity, though finish tails off a tad. Stellenbosch WO. **Pinot Noir-Chardonnay** ★★★☆ 18 months on lees show in richness & mid-palate weight of creamy yellow fruit. **16** ⑧④ sparkling a 55/45 blend, with bouncy bubbles & crisp finish. WO W Cape. — CM

Location: Durbanville ▪ Map: Durbanville, Philadelphia & Darling ▪ Map grid reference: C7 ▪ WO: Durbanville/ Stellenbosch/Western Cape ▪ Est/1stB 2015 ▪ Tasting & sales Tue-Fri 9-5 Sat 9-3 ▪ Wine/MCC tasting R55pp; macaroon & MCC pairing R95pp ▪ Closed Good Fri, Dec 25 & Jan 1 ▪ Deli products available from tasting room ▪ Picnics ▪ Play area for children ▪ Functions & weddings ▪ Yoga class by Roxy Louw (first Saturday of every month) ▪ MTB trail ▪ Owner(s) Marinus Neethling ▪ Winemaker(s) Anneke Potgieter (Sep 2015, consultant) ▪ 22ha/18ha (merlot, chard) ▪ 8-10t/3,500cs own label 40% red 30% white 30% MCC ▪ info@cantowines. co.za ▪ www.cantowines.co.za ▪ S 33° 48' 19.56" E 018° 37' 27.41" ▪ ⓜ antihero.many.upon ▪ **T +27 (0)21-492-2821**

Capaia Wine Estate ⓠ ⑪ ⓐ ⑧

With no expense spared, Capaia was established more than two decades ago on an old wheat farm in the Philadelphia ward north of Cape Town, just 10 km from the cool Atlantic. Ingrid von Essen, one of the original owners, has been partnered since 2015 by Stephan von Neipperg, longtime consultant here and also owner of eminent properties in Bordeaux. There are 60 hectares of mainly Bordeaux varieties (but increased plantings of shiraz), a splendid cellar and an array of hospitality options, from a deli and fine-dining to outdoor activities, all established while respecting biodiversity.

★★★★ **ONE** More restraint than power in **14** ⑧⑨, cab (78%) with shiraz, merlot & cab franc, with fine dry tannins & wood tempering fruit-sweetness. Structured, fresh & more elegant than also-tasted **15** ⑧⑦, with cab at only 29%, near-equal cab franc, shiraz & petit verdot. Dense, powerful & ripe; youthful elements will integrate & reward cellaring. Both 60% new oak, 18 months. Also in 1.5, 3, 5, 9 & 18L, as next.
Cabernet Sauvignon-Merlot ★★★★ Splashes of petit verdot, cab franc & shiraz add spice to the flavoursome, balanced blend. **17** ⑧⑤ supple oak support, juicy & approachable, with respectable dry finish.
Rosé ★★★ Delicate **19** ⑧① has cab franc's perfumed berry nuance & pale sunset blush. Crisp, modest 12.5% alcohol, lighter than previous from merlot & sauvignon blanc. Also in magnum. **Sauvignon Blanc** ★★★★ Cooler-climate **19** ⑧④ tank sample bursts with tangy gooseberry & passionfruit, succulent, creamy undertone courtesy careful yeast selection. Occasional release: **Shiraz**. Discontinued: **Mariella's**. — MW

Location/WO: Philadelphia ▪ Map: Durbanville, Philadelphia & Darling ▪ Map grid reference: C5 ▪ Est 1997 ▪ 1stB 2003 ▪ Tasting, sales & cellar tours Mon-Fri 8-5; Sat/Sun tasting & sales at Mariella's ▪ Tour groups ▪ Mariella's Restaurant T +27 (0)21-972-1103/+27 (0)72-770-9695, mariellas@capaia.co.za ▪ Deli Olivia ▪ Facilities for children ▪ Picnic baskets in summer ▪ MTB & trail running routes ▪ Owner(s) Ingrid von Essen & Stephan von Neipperg ▪ Cellarmaster(s) Bernabé Strydom (Oct 2006), assisted by Stephan von Neipperg ▪ Winemaker(s) Stephan Potgieter (Jan 2019) ▪ Viticulturist(s) Derrick Steyn (Aug 2016) ▪ 140ha/60ha (cabs s/f, merlot, p verdot, shiraz, sauv) ▪ 260t/26,000cs own label 85% red 15% white ▪ IPW ▪ PO Box 25 Philadelphia 7304 ▪ info@capaia.co.za ▪ www.capaia.co.za, www.capaia.com ▪ E 018° 34' 7.82" S 33° 42' 47.60" ▪ ⓜ unbuckle.revisit.intelligent ▪ **T +27 (0)21-972-1081 (winery); +27 (0)21-972-1103 (restaurant)**

☐ **Cape Bay** *see* FirstCape Vineyards
☐ **Cape Beach Collection** *see* Fortes Family Wines

Cape Chamonix Wine Farm ⓠ ⑪ ⓐ ⓞ

On cool mountain slopes overlooking Franschhoek, Chamonix has a history going back to the late 17th century and the French Huguenots, but its modern renaissance is due to German businessman Chris Hellinger, who renamed it and led the future direction. Vineyards are largely unirrigated, thanks to the area's high rainfall, and clay-rich soils allow red as well as white varietal success. Chamonix is more than a winefarm - its attractions include four different accommodation offerings, all with stunning views, plus a conservation area and small private game park. In addition, there is home-bottled water from an underground spring. Recent personnel changes include the appointment of Neil Bruwer as winemaker and viticulturist.

Reserve range

★★★★☆ **Cabernet Franc** ② Consistently among SA's best, variety-true **16** ⑨③ shows vivid cassis, whiffs of graphite, crushed herbs, body silky & succulent, tannins harmonious. Has fruit purity & presence, wonderful style, a cab franc template.

★★★★☆ **Pinot Noir** ② Best older vineyards, 60% new French oak, **17** ⑨④ has classic varietal elegance yet packed with fruit & interest; sour cherry intensity, savoury spice, backing freshness. Tannins masterly, firm without edges, show tensile strength.

★★★★☆ **Greywacke Pinotage** Ripasso technique used (wine reintroduced to unpressed dried-grape skins for 2nd ferment) to get fruit concentration. Intense red berries, glacé cherries in **17** ⑨③ preview, lovely succulence, polish. Oaking 18 months in evidence as spice, supple tannins. In magnum too.

★★★★☆ **Troika** Best vineyards/barrels for pre-bottled **17** ⑨③, mainly cab franc with cab, 2 other Bordeaux varieties. Glossy berries, spice array, lead pencils & cigarbox; hidden strength, built for cellaring but tannins amenable. Lovely poise, assurance.

★★★★☆ **Chardonnay** ② Older vineyards, barrel selection, **17** ⑨④ lavished with care, wild ferment, 70% new oak. Toasted brioche, lemon preserve, a suggestion of richness but nothing overt, it's all seamless, shows good breeding. Minerality on the finish, just more to admire.

★★★★☆ **White** Classic white Bordeaux blend, sauvignon & semillon (60/31), barrel fermented/14 months, 10% unoaked. Pre-bottling, **18** ⑨⓪ offers preserved lemon & buttered toast, some papaya, becoming more tropical on the palate. Complex & involving.

Not tasted: **Marco Polo**.

Cape Chamonix range

★★★★☆ **Feldspar Pinot Noir** ② Younger vineyards, less new oak than sibling, **17** ⑨② tasted ex barrel designed for earlier drinking but no lesser for that. Bright red berries, succulent, 16 months in barrel a harmonious addition for appealing spice array, supple tannins. Delicious.

★★★★☆ **Chardonnay** Younger vineyards than Reserve, but still gets plenty cellar care: ferment/14 months French oak, 40% new. Macadamia nut richness to **18** ⑨② 's marmalade fruit, flavour packed, lovely palate weight from long lees contact. Handsome. Tasted pre-bottling, as next.

★★★★ **Chardonnay Unoaked** Citrus tones, pithy grapefruit & lemon, **19** ★★★★ ⑧⑤ good example of unadorned chardonnay, has focus & fruit purity, crisp & fresh, though shade less complex than **18** ⑧⑧.

★★★★ **Sauvignon Blanc** Consistent sleek style, invigorating freshness on which is built **19** ⑧⑧ 's perfume & flavours: lime & green peas, gooseberries, intensifying on the palate. No oak, unlike last.

Rouge ② ★★★☆ Merlot & cab with malbec, dash petit verdot in **16** ⑧③ work-in-progress. Dark fruited, 18 months seasoned barrels, initial impression of being smoky, tarry, but perked up by palate's juicy freshness. Charming colourful label. Not tasted: **MCC Blanc de Blancs**. — CR

Location/map/WO: Franschhoek ▪ Map grid reference: C1 ▪ Est 1991 ▪ 1stB 1992 ▪ Tasting & sales Mon-Sun 8.30–5 ▪ Fee R60 (non reserve)/R100 (reserve tasting) ▪ Closed Dec 25 & Jan 1 ▪ Cellar tours by appt ▪ Restaurant T +27 (0)21-876-8426 ▪ Conservation area ▪ Marco Polo Lodge, Waterfall Lodge, Forest Suites & fully equipped self-catering cottages ▪ Grappa, Sweden bitters ▪ Winemaker(s)/viticulturist(s) Neil Bruwer (Jun 2019) ▪ 255ha/40ha (cabs s/f, malbec, merlot, p verdot, ptage, pinot, chard, chenin, sauv, sem) ▪ 180-220t/30,000cs own label 60% red 40% white ▪ IPW ▪ PO Box 28 Franschhoek 7690 ▪ marketing@ chamonix.co.za, winemaker@chamonix.co.za ▪ www.chamonix.co.za ▪ S 33° 53' 60.0" E 019° 7' 34.0" ▪ ⊞ matchbox.blameless.breathes ▪ **T +27 (0)21-876-8400**

Cape Classics ②

André Shearer has built his Somerset West-based wine company into the largest supplier — currently 25% — of SA bottled wines (including own brands Indaba, Jam Jar and Braai) to the US. After 25th anniversary celebrations in 2017, came a 2018 flooded with US market honours for wine quality, staff well-being and commercial success (Wine Enthusiast Importer of the Year, inter alia). In 2019 winemaker Bruwer Raats (of Raats Family Wines, this guide's 2018 Winery of the Year) was joined by Cape Winemakers Guild protégé Clayton Christians. Market research supported the release of Jam Jar in 187-ml '4-packs', and social care underlies the Indaba Foundation's long-term support for teacher training and early childhood education.

Cape Classics range

Braai ⊘ ★★★★ Delicious homage to the barbecue, beloved by most South Africans (& not just them). Cab does the cooking alone in **18** ⑧⑤; usual abundance of black fruit, broad tannins in bonhomous support.

Indaba range

★★★★ **Chenin Blanc** ⊘ Dusty **18** ⑧⑥ has texture from touch oak & 5 months on lees, bone-dry & delightful, with enough gravitas to warrant attention.

Merlot ⊘ ★★★ Previewed **18** ⑧② brims with cherry & plum touched with oak from stave contact. Affable, but tad more serious than price suggests. **Mosaic** ⊘ ★★★★ Bountiful mulberry & blueberry fruit on solid tannic backbone, toothsome **18** ⑧④ a blend of mainly cab with merlot & cab franc. Also 3L casks in some markets, as for next 2. **Chardonnay** ⊘ ★★★★ Laudably poised & shapely given the price & quantity, **18** ⑧⑤ melange of citrus fruit & butterscotch, though now no new oak. **Sauvignon Blanc** ⊘ ★★★ Incisive **18** ⑧② is ample & fresh, with tasty grapefruit & lime. Punches above its price.

Jam Jar range

Sweet White ⊘ ★★★ Perfumed muscat from Paarl. Low-alcohol **18** ⑧① isn't overly complex, but balanced. Huge fun. **Sweet Shiraz** ⊘ ★★★ Pudding in a glass! **18** ⑦⑨ is easy & likeable - if sweet red wine is your thing. — DS

Location: Somerset West ▪ Map: Helderberg ▪ Map grid reference: F4 ▪ WO: Western Cape ▪ Est 1991 ▪ 1stB 1996 ▪ Tasting by appt only ▪ Owner(s) André Shearer ▪ Winemaker(s) Bruwer Raats (Indaba & Cape Classics ranges, May 2010), Clayton Christians (Indaba & Cape Classics ranges, Jan 2019) ▪ 270,000cs ▪ PO Box 1695 Somerset West 7129 ▪ info@capeclassics.com ▪ www.capeclassics.com, www.indabawines.com, www. jamjarwines.com, www.braaiwines.com ▪ S 34° 4' 5.9" E 018° 53' 38.2" ▪ ⊞ city.leotard.trek ▪ **T +27 (0)21-847-2400**

☐ **Cape Cult** see Darling Cellars
☐ **Cape Discovery** see Stellenview Premium Wines

Cape Dreams　　　　　　　　　　　　　　　　　　　　　⑫

Eleven years ago, Bunty Khan started her company with the vision of furthering local enfranchisement and development through the creation of an internationally recognised wine brand. 'We now have an established footprint in over 20 countries,' she is justly proud to say, attributing her success to 'continuously striving to offer consumers an enhanced palate experience'.

Cape Dreams range

Cabernet Sauvignon ⑫ ★★★ Blackcurrant & cherry fruit on **17** ⑧②, a little cedar spice & graphite, too, from older oak/tanks with staves (as most of these reds). **Merlot** ⑫ ★★★ Midweight **17** ⑧⓪ has dark chocolate notes offsetting tangy berry & cherry flavours, less green than previous. **Pinotage** ★★★ Mocha tone from oak doesn't detract from attractive red plum & berry fruit in smooth, medium-bodied **18** ⑧②. **Shiraz** ★★★★ Ripe dark fruit, pepper & spice aplenty in **18** ⑧⑤, full bodied but well integrated for easy drinking. **Cabernet Sauvignon-Merlot** ⑫ ★★★ Subtly oaked for mocha dimension, **16** ⑧② also contains splash petit verdot for extra fruit concentration (black cherries, blueberries). **Selected Red** ⑫ ★★★ Super braai wine, **17** ⑦⑦ fruity unwooded blend of cab/shiraz (25% each), pinotage & others. **Pinotage Rosé** ★★★ Semi-dry **19** ⑧② good partner for Asian-spiced food, with ripe strawberry & sweet melon flavours, smooth & fruity. **Chardonnay** ★★★★ Unwooded **19** ⑧③ packed with ripe cling peach & citrus, tangy & textured from time on lees. **Chenin Blanc** ★★★ Zesty pineapple & juicy white peach flavours, **19** ⑧③ soft texture from month on lees balanced by fresh acidity. **Colombar** ⑫ ★★★ Honey-drizzled melons & pears on semi-sweet **18** ⑧⓪, uncloying thanks to balancing acidity. **Sauvignon Blanc** ★★★ Abundantly fruity, with guava, fig, melon & granadilla flavours, well-balanced acid ensuring easy summer drinking in **19** ⑧②. **Natural Sweet Red** ⑫ ★★★ Made for serving chilled with mature cheeses, not-too-sweet **17** ⑦⑧ blends 50% shiraz/cab, pinotage/merlot & others. **Natural Sweet Blanc** ⑫ ★★★ Caramelised pineapple aroma on **17** ⑦⑧ muscadel suggests more sweetness than actual 44 g/l sugar; lovely grapey flavour & bonus modest 11% alcohol.

Reserve range

Not tasted: **Cabernet Sauvignon**, **Pinotage**, **Shiraz**. — JG

Location/map/WO: Robertson ▪ Map grid reference: A6 ▪ Tasting & cellar tours by appt ▪ Owner(s) Bunty Khan ▪ Cellarmaster(s) André van Dyk ▪ Winemaker(s) Andre Schriven ▪ (cab, merlot, ptage, shiraz, chard, chenin, cbard, sauv) ▪ 60% red 40% white ▪ BEE, HACCP, IPW, ISO 9001, WIETA ▪ sales@capedreamswine. co.za ▪ www.capedreamswine.co.za ▪ S 33° 46' 35.3" E 019° 45' 42.9" ▪ ⟨⟩ highrise.hideaways.flickered ▪ **T +27 (0)83-792-7638/+27 (0)83-780-9428**

☐ **Cape Elements** *see* Nico van der Merwe Wines

Cape Elevation Vineyards

Mark Dendy Young works closely with others in crafting his range of wines from high-lying, cool Elgin sites. Firstly, with various viticulturists and farmers as he enjoys the flexibility of sourcing fruit 'from "pockets" of exceptional quality'. Secondly, with deeply experienced Elgin specialist winemaker, Catherine Marshall. 'New World meets Burgundy' sums up his stylistic aspirations.

★★★★ **Trig Beacon Pinot Noir** ⊘ Spicy more than fruity aromas on **18** ⑧⑧, but dark & red berry flavours emerge on palate, though the savoury note continues. Well balanced, with slightly lean elegance. Shows better than last-tasted **16** ★★★☆ ⑧④ preview.

★★★★☆ **Compass** (NEW) Two vintages of tasty, smart merlot-cab franc blend. **16** ★★★★ ⑧⑨ has spicy fruitcake notes, generous & fairly rich, well structured, with firmly balanced tannins. **17** ⑨① much the same, though a touch riper & fruitier, & with good dry finish.

Not tasted: **Contour Path Sauvignon Blanc**. — TJ

Location: Stellenbosch ▪ WO: Elgin ▪ Est/1stB 2015 ▪ Closed to public ▪ Owner(s) Mark Dendy Young ▪ Winemaker(s) Cathy Marshall & Mark Dendy Young (both 2015) ▪ Viticulturist(s) various Elgin growers ▪ Lavinia Cellar, Polkadraai Rd, Stellenbosch 7600 ▪ mark@elevationvineyards.co.za ▪ www.elevationvineyards. co.za ▪ **T +27 (0)72-665-5338**

☐ **Cape Fern** *see* Truter Family Wines
☐ **Cape Five** *see* Stellenview Premium Wines
☐ **Cape Fynbos** *see* The Grape Grinder
☐ **Cape Haven** *see* Pulpit Rock Winery

Capelands Estate ⓠ ⑪ ⌂

The cabernet for these sophisticated boutique wines comes from a rarity in SA: a walled vineyard. Three hectares in extent, on decomposed granite and dry-farmed, it's the vinous heart of Capelands, the Somerset West estate of Italian-born Johann Innerhofer and Laura Mauri (who creates the striking front-label art). Sharing a lovely view over False Bay with on-premises guest house and restaurant, the 18-year-old vines are tended, and their fruit vinified off-site, by consultants.

★★★★ **Redstone** (🍇) Beautiful expression of cabernet in **16** ⑨② blackcurrant, dark plum, pencil shavings & raspberry fruit in perfect harmony with silky texture & vanilla from 30 months new/older barrels. Balanced & ageworthy. Slightly firmer **14** ★★★★ ⑧⑦ also available at cellardoor. Both WO Stellenbosch. No **15**.

★★★★☆ **CR1 Redstone Reserve** (🍇) Big flavour & freshness on **16** ⑨③ cab & malbec blend (80/20) from tiny vineyard: cassis, blueberry, dried herb & hedgerow fruit all neatly held in supple tannin structure & supported by 36 months French oak. Also in larger bottle formats.

★★★★ **Whitestone Chenin Blanc** Complex, unoaked **19** ⑧⑧ has vibrant tropical & orchard fruit, waxy & creamy popcorn notes. Good balance, long lemon-zest finish. Last tasted was equally moreish **15** ★★★☆ ⑧④. WO W Cape.

Not tasted: **Whitestone Chardonnay**. Occasional release: **Klein Redstone**. — WB

Location: Somerset West ▪ Map: Helderberg ▪ Map grid reference: F7 ▪ WO: Stellenbosch/Western Cape ▪ Est 2004 ▪ 1stB 2010 ▪ Tasting available at Capelands Restaurant during operating times only - see website for trading hours ▪ Guest house ▪ Owner(s) Capelands Resort Estate (Pty) Ltd ▪ Winemaker(s) Louis Nel, with Rocco de Villiers (both consultants) ▪ Viticulturist(s) Francois Hanekom (Feb 2009, consultant) ▪ 12.5ha/3ha (cab) ▪ 6t/2,500cs own label 100% red ▪ 3 Old Sir Lowry's Pass Rd, Somerset West 7130 ▪ restaurant@capelands.com ▪ www.capelands.com ▪ S 34° 6' 29.57" E 018° 53' 4.42" ▪ ⟨⟩ swear.postage.decency ▪ **T +27 (0)21-858-1477**

HOME OF THE

AWARD WINNERS

At Checkers, our wine masters are always on the lookout for the best of the best. That's why we are the first to bring you more acclaimed wines than any other supermarket – at cellar prices.

··wine route··

ninety9cents 52975T

Checkers
better and better

UNLOCK THE A

BECOME

Club
TIONAL®

RT OF DINING

MEMBER

2264 to unlock our global village
d Entertainment experiences.

club.co.za

☐ **The Capeman** *see* Darling Cellars
☐ **Capeman** *see* Darling Cellars

Cape Moby Winery

The whale on the label speaks to these wines' origins on Walker Bay, where southern rights come to calve each spring, and specifically Springfontein Estate, where co-owner/winemaker Tariro Masayiti bottles a small range, available on the farm and exported to Europe. The latest vintages not available for tasting.

Location: Stanford ▪ Est/1stB 2007 ▪ Tasting & sales at Springfontein Wine Estate ▪ Owner(s) Springfontein Wine Estate ▪ Cellarmaster(s)/winemaker(s) Tariro Masayiti (Dec 2012) ▪ Viticulturist(s) Hildegard Witbooi (Oct 2013) ▪ 5,000cs own label 80% red 20% white ▪ PO Box 71 Stanford 7210 ▪ admin@capemoby.co.za ▪ www.capemoby.co.za ▪ **T +27 (0)28-341-0651**

Capenheimer

SA's first pétillant wine, inspired by Italian Lambrusco. Launched by Monis in 1962, now produced by Distell.

Capenheimer ★★ Blend of white varieties, light (11% alcohol) **NV** (74) semi-sweet perlé celebrates fresh-fruitiness. Also in 1.5L. — CR

Capensis

This joint venture between Antony Beck, America-based director of Graham Beck, and Barbara Banke, owner of Jackson Family Wines in California, is intended to express wines 'from the Cape', and it's devoted to one variety, chardonnay, in the belief that 'the truly great vineyard sites around the world are revealed by only a few noble grape varieties'. Currently fruit is sourced from several far-flung farms, including their own Fijnbosch property atop Banhoek Valley - at 640 m altitude, among the highest in Stellenbosch. Here, replanting of the 12 hectares is now complete. Also concluded is the fast-track construction of the Jackson-owned cellar near Paarl, spacious enough to provide a custom-crush facility for boutique wineries, with ex-DGB Mario Damon as resident winemaker.

★★★★☆ **Chardonnay** Follows exceptional form & sleek styling of previous, with pure seam of citrus, saline acidity & taut structure. **16** (93) more new oak (60% vs 30%) & richness but still sublimely fresh. Stellenbosch, Robertson & Overberg vines.

★★★★★ **Silene Chardonnay** (NEW) Less overt lemon & orange fruitiness than sibling, & less new oak (50%) give **17** (96) a more refined, even stately, bearing, the vibrancy of the vintage showing in the current of limy acid supplying energy throughout. Thrilling now, will improve 5+ years. Own Banhoek grapes plus small portion brought in from Helderberg. — CvZ

Location: Stellenbosch ▪ WO: Stellenbosch/Western Cape ▪ 1stB 2013 ▪ Closed to public ▪ Owner(s) Barbara Banke (owner of Jackson Beck, Jackson Family Wines US) & Antony Beck (director of Graham Beck Wines SA) ▪ Winemaker(s) Graham Weerts ▪ Farm manager Cedrick Delport ▪ 1,500cs own label 100% white ▪ info@capensiswines.com ▪ www.capensiswines.com ▪ **T +1 884-889-7365**

☐ **Cape of Good Hope** *see* Anthonij Rupert Wyne

Cape Point Vineyards

Sybrand van der Spuy's fine estate is the only winefarm on the Cape Peninsula's southern tip, the vineyards with their back to the mountain and with bracing exposure to the coolness of sea winds. The location makes it meaningful to specialise in white varieties, most notably – and famously – sauvignon blanc (almost invariably blended with semillon in the cellar). Its Wine of Origin area has been Cape Town for a few years now, with marketing advantages happily taken advantage of – even more so in the sister project, Cape Town Wine Co, as well as the entry-level Splattered Toad pairing (see separate entries). Riandri Visser is now into the second half of her first decade in the cellar.

★★★★☆ **Cape Town Chardonnay** Bright, appealingly fresh **18** ★★★★ (88) from own & Durbanville grapes, natural ferment, 6 months in oak (30% new). Typical citrus & stonefruit with tropical notes too. Good texture, but less intense than **17** (93). Modest 12.3% alcohol.

★★★★☆ **Noordhoek Sauvignon Blanc** ⊘ Wholebunch press, natural ferment as for Reserve, but no oaking on **18** ⑨2 except for 5% semillon addition, which adds breadth & a savoury twist. Blackcurrant & subtle tropicality, but the greener elements develop on the palate; citric acidity.

★★★★☆ **Sauvignon Blanc Reserve** ⓐ A few drops of semillon (ex amphora) as usual on old-oaked **18** ⑨3. Ripe but with a lovely freshness, the typical varietal notes transmuted into fine complexity, with a stony, liquorice lift. Finely cutting acidity, lingering bone-dry finish.

★★★★☆ **Cape Town Sauvignon Blanc** ⊘ Own & Durbanville grapes (as next), with 5% semillon, unwooded. Typical passionfruit on **19** ★★★★ ⑧8, with interesting blackcurrant notes developing as the wine opens up. Good length, & a pleasing element of richness, but a touch less impressive than **18** ⑨1.

★★★★ **Marks & Spencer Sauvignon Blanc** Silky & ripely rounded **19** ⑧7, with a dash of semillon, made for UK retailer. Restrained but lively acidity, some complexity of flavour emerging.

★★★★★ **Isliedh** ⓐ White blend, deserving of SA icon status: with 9 maximum 5-star ratings since **03** debut. **18** ⑨5 picked from one block over 5 days. Barrel-fermented sauvignon (40% new oak) with 25% semillon in clay pot. Core of sweet ripe fruit; very bright, with a stony freshness. Oak scarcely noticeable except in breadth & silkiness. Long-lingering. Will greatly benefit from good few years in bottle.

Occasional release: **Semillon**, **Noble Late Harvest**. Discontinued: **Cabernet Sauvignon**. — TJ

Location: Noordhoek ▪ Map: Cape Peninsula ▪ Map grid reference: B4 ▪ WO: Cape Town ▪ Est 1996 ▪ 1stB 2000 ▪ Tasting & sales Mon-Sun 11-6 ▪ Fee R50-R125 ▪ Cheese platters available during tasting hours ▪ Restaurant, picnics, breakfast ▪ Weddings & events ▪ Weekly Thu evening food markets ▪ Child friendly ▪ Conservation area ▪ Owner(s) Sybrand van der Spuy ▪ Winemaker(s) Riandri Visser (Jul 2014), with Adriaan Jacobs (Jun 2017) ▪ Viticulturist(s) Steffan Lochner (May 2016) ▪ 22ha (sauv, sem) ▪ 25,000cs own label 100% white; Stonehaven ±150,000cs ▪ Brands for clients: Marks & Spencer, Woolworths ▪ IPW, Farming for the Future ▪ PO Box 100 Noordhoek 7979 ▪ info@cape-point.com ▪ www.capepointvineyards.co.za ▪ S 34° 5' 45.30" E 018° 23' 10.34" ▪ ⌖ marooned.glancing.aeronautic ▪ **T +27 (0)21-789-0900**

Cape Rock Wines   ⓠ ⌂

The focus is on Rhône varieties in this boutique venture high up the Cape's Atlantic (West) coast. Willie Brand, helped by landscape architect son Gavin, makes an impressive range of wines, with a low-intervention approach ('in the simplest possible way') — mostly off their own 11 hectares of vines. Adding to the array of varieties at their disposal, grenache blanc came into production last year, and the unusual southern Rhône variety counoise has been planted 'for inclusion in our lighter red blends', says Willie.

★★★★ **Amnesty** ⓠ Juicy **17** ⑧9, equal syrah, grenache & mourvèdre, improves on **16** ★★★☆ ⑧5 with vivacious mulberry, cranberry & redcurrant fruit, delicate spice from year old oak. WO W Cape.

★★★★☆ **Red** ⓠ A hedonistic but serious blend of mostly syrah (86%), drops mourvèdre & viognier, naturally co-fermented before year older French barrels. **17** ⑨4 spice, plum & pomegranate tones, more complex than last-tasted **14** ★★★★ ⑧8.

★★★★☆ **White** ⓠ Mostly viognier, trio grenache blanc, rousanne & marsanne in support. **17** ⑨4 enticing bouquet cinnamon spice & white flowers herald full-bodied palate, attractive saline note. Satisfyingly dry (just 1.2 g/l sugar), beautifully textured from 6 months on fine lees in older barrels.

Cabernet Sauvignon ⓠ ★★★★ Succulent & expressive **17** ⑧5 showcases variety's blackberry & cassis fruit, gets chocolate nuance from year older oak (as for all the reds). Much improved from previous. **Capa Roca** ⓠ ★★★★ Happy, drinkable assemblage touriga & souzão with cab, shiraz & 3 other bit players. **15** ⑧4 juicy, creamy texture & balanced freshness, full body. In abeyance: **Carignan**, **Rosé**. — HC

Location: Vredendal ▪ Map: Olifants River ▪ Map grid reference: B4 ▪ WO: Olifants River/Western Cape ▪ Est 2001 ▪ 1stB 2002 ▪ Tasting, sales & cellar tours by appt ▪ Closed Good Fri, Dec 25 & Jan 1 ▪ BYO picnic ▪ Owner(s) Willie Brand ▪ Cellarmaster(s) Willie Brand (Jan 2001) ▪ Winemaker(s) Willie Brand (Jan 2001) & Gavin Brand ▪ 13ha/11ha (cab, carignan, grenache, mourv, shiraz, chenin, cbard, marsanne, rouss, viog) ▪ 40t/2,100cs own label 60% red 40% white ▪ PO Box 261 Vredendal 8160 ▪ caperockwines@gmail.com ▪ www.caperockwines.co.za ▪ S 31° 43' 3.12" E 018° 31' 26.37" ▪ ⌖ thigh.authenticity.freshness ▪ **T +27 (0)27-213-2567**

☐ **Cape Soleil** see Jacques Germanier
☐ **Cape to Cairo** see Rogge Cloof

Cape Town Wine Co ♀ ♍

This venture by Sybrand van der Spuy, owner of Cape Point Vineyards and a descendant of an early Dutch settler at the Cape, sources grapes only from vineyards in Cape Town WO - the District proclaimed just a few years back. A new wine-tasting room and restaurant was scheduled to be opened in November 2019 alongside the cellar on Chapman's Peak Drive in Noordhoek, just salt-spray distance from the sea.

★★★★ **Sauvignon Blanc** ⊘ Two vintages tasted, both aromatic, fresh & balanced, nothing too overt. **19** ⑧⑥ has lively stonefruit & tropical notes, with a green twist. Developing **18** ⑧⑧ includes a more complex earthy, blackcurrant element in the lipsmacking tartness.

Cabernet Sauvignon ★★★ Herbal & berry aromas & flavours on light-feeling & rather lean **18** ⑧①. Modestly firm structure, shortish dry finish. **Merlot** (NEW) ⊘ ★★★★ Spontaneously fermented, like all these reds. **18** ⑧④ offers ripe, fruity charm with a bright herbal twist. Easygoing, with a gentle tannic tug - the best balanced of these reds. **Shiraz** (NEW) ⊘ ★★★★ Lightly fruity, with smoke & spice overtones on **18** ⑧③. Some richness of fruit, despite fairly modest 12.8% alcohol, but also a bright acidity showing. Approachable now, like all these. **Cabernet Sauvignon-Merlot** (NEW) ★★★ Forward, herbaceous-tinged aromas on lightly fruited **18** ⑧① (which includes a little shiraz). Structure from rather sharp acidity as well as the undemanding tannins. Durbanville grapes, as most. **Rosé** (NEW) ⊘ ★★★★ With shiraz & merlot giving understated berry aromas & flavours, **18** ⑧③ is fresh & lively, charmingly balanced & dry. **Chardonnay** (NEW) ★★★ Fruit-driven **18** ⑧②, more tropical than the usual citrus; easy-drinking, with a good acid grip but not much intensity of fruit. 50% in old oak for breadth. **Méthode Cap Classique** ⚜ ★★★★ Salmon pink **15** ⑧⑤ dry sparkling is 100% pinot noir, frothily exuberant, with tangy red-berry fruit & cinnamon oatmeal biscuit spice/leesiness. — TJ

Location/WO: Cape Town ▪ Map: Cape Peninsula ▪ Map grid reference: A4 ▪ Est/1stB 2017 ▪ Tasting & cellar tours Mon-Sun 11-4.30 ▪ Restaurant ▪ Owner(s) Sybrand van der Spuy ▪ Winemaker(s) Riandri Visser (Jul 2014), with Adriaan Jacobs (Jun 2017) ▪ Viticulturist(s) Steffan Lochner (May 2016) ▪ own label 70% red 29% white 1% rosé ▪ PO Box 100 Noordhoek 7979 ▪ marketing@capetownwine.com ▪ www.capetownwinecom-pany.com ▪ S 34° 5' 41.36" E 018° 22' 17.48" ▪ 🌐 refereeing.reaching.semicolon ▪ **T +27 (0)21-789-0900**

Cape Venture Wine Co ♀

This eye-catchingly packaged boutique brand, inspired by Lubanzi the wandering dog, which accompanied American co-owners Charles Brain and Walker Brown on a long-ago Wild Coast hike, wants to do good while putting delicious wine in bottle (and 375-ml can). Success, mostly in the US, has allowed the friends to grow their 'give-back' to local charity Pebbles Project to 50%. Working only with farms that are Integrity & Sustainability certified, to using TreeFree labels, they're also minimising their impact on the planet.

Lubanzi range

★★★★ **Rhône Red Blend** Near-equal shiraz, grenache with splashes mourvèdre, cinsaut & carignan, **17** ⑧⑦ more serious than last-tasted **15** ★★★★ ⑧③. Enticing mixed berry & pot-pourri, beautifully dry, satisfying savoury conclusion. Minimal handling, only 50% oaked, none new.

Chenin Blanc ★★★★ From Swartland, **18** ⑧⑤ white peach, floral & waxy notes with bright acidity extending the finish, 3-6 months on lees adding breadth & weight. Also in 375 ml cans, as Red. — CvZ

WO: Coastal/Swartland ▪ Est 2016 ▪ 1stB 2017 ▪ Closed to public ▪ Owner(s) Charles Brain, Cathi & David Brain, Walker Brown ▪ Winemaker(s) Trizanne Barnard & Bruce Jack (Sep 2017, both consultants) ▪ 7,000cs own label 50% red 50% white ▪ Fair for Life ▪ 1342 Florida Ave NW Washington DC 20009 ▪ hello@capeven-turewine.com ▪ www.lubanziwines.com ▪ **T +1 202-573-7292**

☐ **Cape View** *see* Kaapzicht Wine Estate
☐ **Cape West** *see* Namaqua Wines

Cape Wine Company ♀

After a brief listing as 'Erasmus Family Wines', Paarl-based vintner Erlank Erasmus has reverted the name of his Fairtrade-accredited business to 'Cape Wine Company'. Swartland continues to supply most of the fruit for his predominantly Rhône-style wines. These are due to be joined by pair of organic bottlings under the Nieuwe Haarlem label. Exports remain Erlank's primary focus, though a national sales and marketing manager has been appointed to further establish the brand locally.

Erasmus Family range

★★★★ Cabernet Sauvignon ⓧ Cherry-choc entry on **12** ⑧⑦ opens up to dark-berried fruit, earth & tar. Plenty of intensity mid-palate, with sweet ripe fruit, chewy tannins & crisp minty finish.

★★★★ Grenache Noir 17 ⑧⑨ echoes all positives evident in **15** ⑧⑦: bright & precise wild strawberry & spice flavours on lively, medium body, well sustained with tasty, savoury length. **16** sold out untasted.

★★★★☆ Shiraz Rich, bold & ripe but not jammy thanks to rumbling grape tannins, freshness. Individual sweet dark plum, nutmeg spice concentration lingers long, warmingly. **17 ★★★★** ⑧⑨ sampled ex tank, not quite in same league as **16** ⑨③.

★★★★☆ Family Reserve ⓧ Like **15 ★★★★★** ⑨⑤, **16** ⑨⓪ a 4-way blend (mostly carignan with mourvèdre, grenache & shiraz) delivers spice bomb notes - nutmeg, cloves, allspice - mixed with ripe red plums. Elegant & restrained, lengthy complex finish. 14 months French oak, 30% new. Untasted **14** ⑨① also still available.

Chenin Blanc ⓧ **★★★** Nicely balanced **17** ⑧⓪ gains creamy spice from 50% oak (10% new) to brighten up honeyed pineapple & soft appley fruit.

The Merchant range ⓃⒺⓌ

Cabernet Sauvignon-Merlot ★★★☆ Sweet-fruited 60/40 blend ex Darling. **17** ⑧③ lightish to medium body with easy ripe strawberry flavours, bound by firm yet unharsh grip. Gram/2 sugar provide ready drinking. Fairtrade certified.

Juno range

Grenache Noir ⓃⒺⓌ **★★★** Previewed **17** ⑧② full bodied but light of touch & fresh, with smooth, spicy red fruit, ripely rounded conclusion. **Pinotage** ⊘ **★★★★** Quiet dark plum, fresh earth flavours, gentle flesh & tannins make **17** ⑧⑤ both satisfying & approachable. Small oaked portion a further enhancement. **Shiraz ★★★** Luscious **17** ⑧⓪, warmingly rich in sweet red fruit, extra spice from older-oaked portion. Good-to-go winter warmer. **Shiraz-Mourvèdre-Viognier ★★★** Spice with gamey & floral notes on shiraz-based (85%) **17** ⑧① , plenty sun-filled flavours, gentle grip eased by gram/2 sugar. — AL

Location/map: Paarl ▪ Map grid reference: E6 ▪ WO: Swartland/Darling/Western Cape ▪ Est/1stB 2010 ▪ Tasting & sales Wed-Thu 11-4 Fri/Sat 11-5 Sun/pub hols 11-2.30 ▪ Closed Good Fri, Dec 25 & Jan 1 ▪ Owner(s)/ winemaker(s) Erlank Erasmus ▪ 1,500cs own label 80% red 20% white ▪ BEE, Fairtrade, WIETA ▪ Taillerfer Str Paarl 7646 ▪ erlank@capewinecompany.co.za ▪ S 33° 45' 55.2" E 018° 57' 27.6" ▪ ⓦ deserved.eminent.edit ▪ **T +27 (0)21-863-0872**

☐ **Erasmus Family Wines** *see* Cape Wine Company

Cap Maritime

There are as yet no vines on the Upper Hemel-en-Aarde farm that Boekenhoutskloof Winery has acquired for what will be an independent label (like Porseleinberg in Swartland). But viticulturist Rosa Kruger is designing and planting chardonnay and pinot noir vineyards for the wines that will be focused on in the maritime climate that the name invokes. Until they come on-stream, Boekenhoutskloof winemaker Gottfried Mocke will take grapes off leased land in the same ward (as a once-off, the 2018 Chardonnay comes from elsewhere) and vinify them in the Franschhoek cellar – a new cellar for this venture is also being planned.

★★★★★ Pinot Noir ⓐ Precise & delicate **18** ⑨④ has perfumed, earthy strawberry fruit in harmony with a gentle but durable tannin structure, which, combined with elegance & poise, augur a long future. 50% wholebunch ferment, then 16 months in half 600L Austrian barrel, half French barrique.

★★★★☆ Chardonnay ⓐ Spontaneously fermented, like sibling, 70% in new oak, rest concrete 'eggs' (vs Pinot's 100% concrete vats). All-wholebunch **18** ⑨④ is elegant, with pristine orchard & stonefruit, hint of apple blossom, creamy vanilla. Dry, with, a grapefruit pith finish. Hemel-en-Aarde Ridge WO.— WB

Location: Hermanus ▪ WO: Upper Hemel-en-Aarde Valley/Hemel-en-Aarde Ridge ▪ Est/1stB 2017 ▪ Closed to public ▪ Owner(s) Boekenhoutskloof Winery (Pty) Ltd ▪ Cellarmaster(s) Gottfried Mocke ▪ Winemaker(s) Gottfried Mocke & Eben Meiring (Jan 2017) ▪ Viticulturist(s) Rosa Kruger ▪ 36ha ▪ 700cs own label 30% red 70% white ▪ BRC, BSCI, IPW, WIETA ▪ PO Box 433 Franschhoek 7690 ▪ info@capmaritime.co.za ▪ www.capmaritime.co.za ▪ **T +27 (0)21-842-2371**

☐ **Cappupino Ccinotage** *see* Boland Cellar

☐ **Caresse Marine** *see* Wildekrans Wine Estate

Carinus Family Vineyards

There are two Carinuses, only distantly related, involved here - Danie and Hugo, wine-loving scions of their farming families. Hugo has a Stellenbosch farm, with a hilltop shed in which Lukas van Loggerenberg makes the wines with a magic touch and minimal facilities (for his own label see Van Loggerenberg Wines); he also has a large estate in the Swartland, source of the chenins. Danie's Polkadraai Hills farm (also genuinely free-range chickens and half-Wagyu beef) provides the syrah. He's also been planting some interesting new varieties, partly in response to the drought. So, while Carinus volumes have increased greatly, perhaps we can also hope for some additions to the range.

★★★★ **Syrah** ⊘ Each vintage, this Polkadraai Hills syrah gains deeper flavour, tauter structure, more seriousness. **18** ★★★★☆ ⑩ has the fruit-forward charm of **17** ⑧⑨ & is approachable, but touch less so, promising greater rewards after a few years in bottle. Wholebunch, wild ferment, old oak, 12.9% alcohol.

★★★★☆ **Chenin Blanc** ⊘ Scarcely less impressive than Rooidraai, off the same farm, so a fine bargain. **18** ⑨① less ripe than previous, but has full fruit aroma & flavour, with savoury overtones, the texture broadened by 10 months in old oak. Well balanced & fresh, good dry finish.

★★★★☆ **Rooidraai Chenin Blanc** ⊛ Off dryland bushvines on the red-soiled Swartland farm whose name it uses. Old-oaked **18** ⑨③ a touch more complex than its partner, bringing savouriness to the pure fruit, with a fine acid thread to the texture - surprisingly rich, given the modest 12.8% alcohol.— TJ

Location: Stellenbosch ▪ WO: Swartland/Polkadraai Hills ▪ Est 2016 (cellar) ▪ 1stB 2011 ▪ Closed to public ▪ Owner(s) Hugo Carinus & Danie Carinus ▪ Winemaker(s) Lukas van Loggerenberg (Dec 2015) ▪ Viticulturist(s) Danie & Hugo Carinus ▪ 10t/810cs own label ▪ Fransmanskraal Farm, Devon Valley, Stellenbosch 7600 ▪ danie@carinusvineyards.co.za, hugo@carinusvineyards.co.za ▪ www.carinusvineyards.co.za ▪ **T +27 (0)72-249-3599**

☐ **Carpe Diem** *see* Diemersfontein Wines

Carrol Boyes Collection

Internationally hailed SA designer Carrol Boyes sadly passed away last year, but the wine brand which she founded with her brother, farmer and financier John Boyes, continues to celebrate her creative and entrepreneurial flair. The limited-edition wines feature Carrol's bold and striking designs in the packaging. See Barnardt Boyes Wines for contact details.

Carrol Boyes Collection

★★★★ **Méthode Cap Classique Gold** Beautifully presented sparkler from chardonnay & pinot noir has much to offer: energetic bubble, brioche & candy apple complexity, just enough richness to balance pleasing dryness. **13** ⑧⑥ for early enjoyment. Stellenbosch WO, rest W Cape unless noted.

Shiraz ⑧ ★★★ Natural fermentation & serious new-oaking for **15** ⑦⑦, but 'green walnut' tannins have the upper hand mid-2018, demand a hearty meal. Not tasted: **Cape Blend**, **Méthode Cap Classique Brut Rosé**. Discontinued: **Méthode Cap Classique Silver**.

Private Collection

Shiraz ★★★☆ Smooth & supple **17** ⑧⑤'s satisfying varietal red fruit & black pepper accented by green walnut notes, sweetened by noticeable vanilla oak. Stellenbosch WO.

Sketchbook range

Merlot ⑧ ★★★ Dusty plum nuance, **16** ⑦⑨ lightly flavoured & easy for summer entertaining. **Fine Red Blend** ⑧ ★★★ Bordeaux-style **16** ⑧⓪, juicy & fresh, firm tannins supporting plump black fruit. From Stellenbosch, mostly cab, with merlot & equal cab franc & petit verdot. **Chardonnay** ⑧ ★★★ Barrel fermented **17** ⑧②, ample palate appeal, salad of citrus flavours (lemon, lime, tangerine) melding with vanilla, genuine dryness making it a versatile table companion. **Chenin Blanc** ⑧ ★★★ Charming **17** ⑧③ gains creamy texture from three months on lees in tank (previous in barrel), white peach & flowers, soft mouthfeel. Not tasted: **Cabernet Sauvignon**, **Rosé**.

Discontinued: **Iconic Collection**. — CvZ

Casa Mori

Bruno Eugene Mori and son Bruno Julian share the sweet life with visitors to their Tuscan-style casa on a Devon Valley hillside, offering stay-overs along with home-grown artichokes, barrel-aged vinegars and Italianate wines. Emphasis is on sangiovese, in MCC bubbly and rosé in the making, and blended with cabernet in the next release of 'Bruno'. A varietal cab is in the works; '19 Shiraz (untasted by us) is the last.

Roberto ⊕ ★★★★☆ Mostly sangiovese, NV ⑧⑤ transports you to Italy: intense cherries on which to hang the savoury older-oak influence, yet the expected varietal dry finish. Wonderful food match.

Bianca ★★★ Was 'Viognier'. Italian-themed labels & wine styling, **17** ⑧② viognier with 20% pinot grigio, unoaked. Stonefruit & melon scented but the wine is bone-dry, zesty, designed for Mediterranean food. Occasional release: **Bruno**. — CR, CvZ

Location/map/WO: Stellenbosch ▪ Map grid reference: D3 ▪ Est 1995 ▪ 1stB 2009 ▪ Tasting, sales & tours by appt ▪ Olive oil ▪ Conferences/functions ▪ Artichoke feast ▪ B&B facilities (5 rooms) ▪ Owner(s) Eugene Mori ▪ Winemaker(s)/viticulturist(s) Bruno Julian Mori (1997, consultant), with Eugene Mori ▪ 4.4ha/2.3ha (cab, malbec, sangio, viog) ▪ 1st/1,000cs own label 97% red 1% white 2% rosé ▪ PO Box 71 Koelenhof 7605 ▪ casamoricucina@gmail.com ▪ www.casamori.co.za ▪ S 33° 53' 15.28" E 018° 48' 27.64" ▪ Ⓦ visual.thankful.goods ▪ **T +27 (0)21-948-8348/+27 (0)83-620-0016 (Eugene)**

☐ **Casa Simelia** see Simelia Wines
☐ **Cathedral Cellar** see KWV Wines

Cathedral Peak Wine Estate

Mauritz Koster and Justin Vermaak's winery is not just the only one in the central Drakensberg, but also, they say, the largest in KwaZulu-Natal. Flip Smith, in charge of the high-lying vineyards (1,100 m above sea level) and the cellar, deals with challenges that might shock his Western Cape counterparts: heavy summer rainfall and extreme weather conditions, destructive moles and ants, even peckish giraffes. But awards have started arriving. Also welcome are tasters, brides and grooms, conference-goers, and those in search of lunch. Latest releases of Merlot, Barrel Pinotage, Pinotage and Cellar Door (red blend), all under Bethani range, untasted.

Location: Winterton ▪ Map: KwaZulu-Natal ▪ Map grid reference: B2 ▪ Est 2007 ▪ 1stB 2012 ▪ Tasting & sales Mon-Fri 9.30-4 Sat/Sun 9.30-4 to be pre-booked ▪ Tasting R10pp/wine ▪ Closed Dec 25/26 & Jan 1; or when booked for weddings ▪ Light meals 9.30-3 daily ▪ Conference facility ▪ Wedding venue & chapel ▪ Christmas market ▪ Owner(s) Mauritz Koster & Justin Vermaak ▪ Cellarmaster(s) Flip Smith (Jan 2015), with Carel Smith (Jan 2015) ▪ Viticulturist(s) Flip Smith (Jan 2015) ▪ 11ha (cab, merlot, ptage, pinot, sauv) ▪ 25t/±4,200cs own label 77% red 8% white 5% rosé 5% MCC 5% jerepigo ▪ PO Box 345 Winterton KwaZulu-Natal 3340 ▪ weddings@cathpeakwines.com ▪ www.cathpeakwines.com ▪ S 28° 50' 24.88" E 029° 27' 10.29" ▪ Ⓦ unabridged.surer.combed ▪ **T +27 (0)63-075-1123**

Catherine Marshall Wines ⊕

Cathy Marshall has long focused on Elgin grapes, the cool climate there suiting the elegant, pure, fresh and vibrant style of wines for which she's built an enviable reputation over the years. But she's shifted her physical winemaking operation a few times, and she and her fellow-owners have now taken over the old Amani winery in Stellenbosch — 'a fully functional cellar with all the bells and whistles to make operations streamlined, better controlled and safe', she says with relief. Cathy's special focus on pinot noir will no doubt continue, but the chenin and riesling sections of the portfolio are being expanded, 'which means new vineyards will be used in Elgin'.

Fine Art Collection

★★★★☆ **Pinot Noir Finite Elements** ⊛ Harmonious **18** ⑨③ off shale & clay. As other pinots, 60% destemmed, but 90% new oak here, adding depth & tannic structure which well balanced with fruit, fine acidity & 13% alcohol. Supple & silky pleasure from dusky perfume to long finish. Still young.

★★★★☆ **Peter's Vision** The most robust wine in the range, **17** ⑨② from 60% merlot, cab franc. Forward aromas dark fruit, cedar, tobacco, spicy dry leaf. Sweet fruit on substantial palate (14.5% alcohol), which should meld harmoniously with a few years in bottle. 20% new oak.

★★★★☆ **Chenin Blanc Fermented in Clay** Takes in grapes from Stellenbosch as well as Elgin; fermented in clay pots, then some wine to older barrels for a year. **18** ⑨ stony-fruity character; the whole understated & subtle, fresh, lively & dry, the clay reinforcing the precision & texture.

Catherine Marshall range

★★★★☆ **Pinot Noir on Clay Soils** ⊘ ⊛ A touch fuller, more complete & complex than Sandstone version, with purer fruit profile & floral perfume. **18** ⑨ similar light touch, though 10% new oak, & perhaps more structured & weighty. Also deserves time.

★★★★ **Pinot Noir on Sandstone Soils** ⊘ Mixes perfumed fruit & a savoury touch of earthy vegetation. **18** ★★★★★ ⑨ a moderate tannic grip, but acidity even more important to the impact & to the freshness & lightness of feeling. No new oak - **17** ⑧ had 5%. Give a few years in bottle.

★★★★☆ **Riesling** Lightly peachy aromas promise an easy charm, which **19** ★★★★ ⑧ delivers with grippy freshness & sweet-edged tartness. Almost too restrained. 11.5% alcohol a bit down on last-tasted **17** ⑨.

★★★★☆ **Sauvignon Blanc** ⊘ Pure passionfruit on **18** ⑨, & a hint of cool-climate blackcurrant. Fresh, dry & balanced, softly textured (probably the minuscule oaked portion helps here), with a sense of precision & lightness of feel.

Discontinued: **Myriad**.

Amatra range

★★★★ **The Oreads Red** ⓩ Merlot from French clone, named for caves above Marshall's seaside home. Graceful **17** ⑧, supple & fresh; lovely now & for good few years. 12 months older oak.

★★★★ **Jono's Wave Chenin Blanc** Year in older oak for Elgin/Stellenbosch grapes in **18** ⑧, underlining an earthy element to the forthcoming dried peach fruitiness. Decent structure, quite rich in effect.— TJ

Location/map: Stellenbosch ▪ Map grid reference: B6 ▪ WO: Elgin/Western Cape ▪ 1stB 1997 ▪ Tasting, sales & cellar tours by appt only ▪ Closed Easter Fri-Sun, Dec 25 & Jan 1 ▪ Owner(s) / directors Catherine Marshall, Greg Mitchell, Alphan Njeru ▪ Cellarmaster(s) Catherine Marshall (Oct 1996) ▪ Winemaker(s) Jonathan Oxenham (2017) ▪ Viticulturist(s) various ▪ 50t ▪ own label 60% red 40% white ▪ IPW ▪ PO Box 13404 Mowbray 7705 ▪ cathy@cmwines.co.za ▪ www.cmwines.co.za ▪ S 33° 57' 54.3" E 018° 43' 59.5" ▪ ⎎ mistook. silver.approaching ▪ **T +27 (0)83-258-1307**

Cavalli Wine & Stud Farm ⓠ ⑾ ◎ ⑤

One of the dazzling jewels in the Helderberg's crown, this family-owned, equine-themed wine and lifestyle estate puts cabernet sauvignon and chenin blanc front and centre: in its winemaking strategy going forward, at the lake-fronted tasting and function venue, and on the wine list in the fine-dining restaurant. Here sommelier Farai Magwada maintains impeccable standards, doubtless the reason for being selected as coach for the Zimbabwe team participating in the World Blind Wine Tasting Championships in France.

Flagship Collection

★★★★ **Warlord** Handsome Bordeaux red with firm fine tannins & vibrant acidity giving form, ageability to perfectly ripe fruit. Like **16** ★★★★ ⑧, **17** ⑧ mostly cab with malbec & petit verdot, year new oak (40%) deftly handled to add savoury spice & finish. Also in magnum.

★★★★ **Cremello** Characterful barrel-fermented/aged white blend, typically chenin, chardonnay, verdelho; drop viognier adds extra perfume, opulence to **17** ⑧. Similar sophistication as 3-way **16** ⑧, same welcome seam of acidity extending lemon, lime & coconut finish.

Premium Collection

Colt Cabernet Sauvignon ★★★☆ Vibrant **17** ⑧ picks up the pace on previous with pure & plush cassis fruit, well-constructed spicy tannin frame, satisfying dry conclusion. **Filly Chenin Blanc** ★★★★ Step-up **19** ⑧ richer, more complex than last, shows flair in balancing intense peach & vanilla tones, creamy texture from 9 months on lees in barrel, vivacious acidity, bone-dry exit.

Estate Collection

Capriole Méthode Cap Classique ★★★★ Lively & engaging **17** ⑧ sparkler with brilliant lemon tones, racy acidity. From chardonnay, base-wine year on lees in tank before 2nd ferment & 18 months in bottle. Enchanting label, too. Not tasted: **The Foal Chardonnay**, **The Foal Verdelho**.

Passions range
Not tasted: **Black Beauty**, **Pink Pony**, **White Knight**. — CvZ

Location/WO: Stellenbosch ▪ Map: Helderberg ▪ Map grid reference: C1 ▪ Est/1stB 2008 ▪ Wine tasting & sales Wed-Sun 10-6 ▪ Closed Dec 26 & Jan 1 ▪ Cavalli Restaurant Wed-Sun lunch & dinner ▪ Sport & music memorabilia ▪ Art gallery ▪ Fashion boutique ▪ Conferences ▪ Banqueting facility (350 seater) ▪ Conservation area ▪ Equestrian centre: stable tours & out-rides by appt ▪ Owner(s) Smith family ▪ Winemaker(s) Craig Barnard (Nov 2014), with Kerrylea Alborough (Sep 2017) ▪ Viticulturist(s) Craig Barnard (Nov 2014) ▪ 110ha/29ha (cab, malbec, p verdot, shiraz, chard, chenin, verdelho, viog) ▪ 100t/6,500cs own label 45% red 40% white 15% rosé ▪ IPW, WIETA ▪ PO Box 102 Somerset West 7129 ▪ wines@cavalliestate.com ▪ www.cavalliestate.com ▪ S 34°0' 35.91" E 018° 48' 47.06" ▪ ⌖ keyboards.barometers.activates ▪ **T +27 (0)21-855-3218**

Cecilia Wines Ⓦ

Single-vineyard, old-vine pinotage remains the focus of boutique vintner and trained concert pianist Cerina van Niekerk, who says recent dry seasons have resulted in tiny yields, necessitating the acquisition of a small custom-made barrel. Now well-settled in Citrusdal, with husband Jaco the cellarmaster at Piekenierskloof Wine Company, she has also started a choir at Citrusdal Primary. 'The resources are few but the enthusiasm is great' – words that apply as much to her wine project as her vocal ensemble.

★★★★ **Pinotage** Ⓢ Old Citrusdal Mountain bushvines, natural ferment, seasoned oak, **17** ⑧⑨ remains true to style, deep & dark-toned, complex: campfire smoke, salty liquorice, plum/prune flavours. Smooth, supple body.— CR

Location: Citrusdal ▪ Map: Olifants River ▪ Map grid reference: D7 ▪ WO: Citrusdal Mountain ▪ Est 2010 ▪ 1stB 2013 ▪ Tasting & sales Mon-Sat 10-5 at Hebron, Piekenierskloof Pass, N7 ▪ Owner(s) Cerina van Niekerk ▪ Cellarmaster(s)/winemaker(s) Cerina van Niekerk (2010) ▪ 2t/100cs own label 100% red ▪ cerina@ ceciliawines.co.za ▪ www.ceciliawines.co.za ▪ S 32°37' 4.15" E 018° 57' 20.98" ▪ ⌖ firestorm.jolts.meaty ▪ **T +27 (0)82-334-9422**

Cederberg Private Cellar ⓌⒸⒽⒸ

In the Cederberg mountains and among SA's most elevated, the extreme, Nieuwoudt-family-owned vineyards and cellar in 2019 saw yet another year of frost damage and crop loss. As a result two unique folding frost fans have been installed, adding much-needed protection. In addition, the focus of their 12-year replanting project is now on ensuring the warmest sites for the red varieties as well as changes to row direction to maximise sun exposure while reducing wind impact. Last year the farm and UK supermarket Waitrose's Foundation established a permanent clinic on-site. A first for the area, the facility will take care, socially and medically, of the everyday needs of all members of staff.

Five Generations range
★★★★☆ **Cabernet Sauvignon** Ⓢ Ripe & opulent **17** ⑨③ flagship shines with confident flavours of black cherries, cassis, coffee & tobacco. 100% new French oak for 18 months tames the supple & integrated tannins while excellent freshening acidity lengthens the finish. Very complete wine.

★★★★☆ **Chenin Blanc** Ⓢ Prominent aromas of peaches, spanspek & dried ginger on delicious **17** ⑨④ enlivened with 5% viognier & rounded off by barrel fermentation (third new) with natural yeast. Rich & lavish, like **16** ★★★★★ ⑨⑤, but beautifully balanced by limy acidity leading to lengthy conclusion.

David Nieuwoudt Ghost Corner range
★★★★☆ **Pinot Noir** ⊘ Mixes raspberries & cranberries with wet leaves & charry oak (French, 20% new). **18** ⑨⓪ lightens up a little on palate, further couple of years should see it perfectly knit. From Elim fruit, as all this range.

★★★★☆ **Wild Ferment Sauvignon Blanc** Ⓢ All about layers of texture & flavour after natural ferment in mostly old oak (12% new). 50% wholebunch adds freshness & spice to creamy lemon meringue fruit, with acidity offset by just-dry sugar. **18** ⑨③ complex & exciting wine now & for good few years.

★★★★☆ **Sauvignon Blanc** Ⓢ Plenty of energy & interest on **18** ⑨③ using only free-run juice. Nettley notes with sappy green fruit (limes, figs) overlaid with tropical kiwis & guavas, all laced with vibrant acidity & attractive smoky/flintiness.

★★★★☆ **Semillon** Ⓢ Stand-out **17** ⑨④ is all you'd expect from cooler-climate semillon, mixing pungent grassy, stalky green-edged fruit with lovely oaking (only 30%, third new) bringing just a touch of smoke & cream. Waxy interest starting to show on lengthy citrus finish.

★★★★☆ **The Bowline** ■ Reduced oak (only 37%) on expertly done **17** ⑨④ allows sauvignon & semillon (61/39) to shine, with fresh citrus, some tropical hints of melon & mango. Classic pairing produces silky & assured combination of cream, spice & hint of soft cheese on interesting & ageworthy wine.

Cederberg Private Cellar range

★★★★☆ **Cabernet Sauvignon** Classic & elegant **17** ⑨② reins back the alcohol (now 14%) while keeping all the flavour & freshness. Melange of black-berried fruit with vanilla, leather & smoke, notch up on **16** ⑨①. French oak, 60% new.

★★★★☆ **CWG Auction Reserve Teen die Hoog Shiraz** ⓐ Deep, dark, brooding **17** ⑨③ gains extra concentration from 15% juice bleed-off prior to ferment. Huge amount of fruit (cherries, blackcurrants, plums) handles 100% new oak with aplomb. Don't drink it now - so much more to come.

★★★★★ **Shiraz** ⊘ ⓐ So much to love about **17** ⑨⑤. Classic New World shiraz flavours of black fruit, smoked meats, coriander & cloves with smoky oak (60% new, 5% American). Supple & silky tannins & fresh acidity keep interest going right through to lengthy finish. Returns to stellar form of **15** ⑨⑧ after out-there **16** ★★★★★ ⑨③.

★★★★ **Merlot-Shiraz** ⊘ Better than the average quaffer. **17** ⑧⑥ bouncy black fruit with touch of leather & spice. Juicy texture, touch of chocolate, fresh herbal finish. Only old oak, 57/43 blend.

★★★★ **Chenin Blanc** ⊘ Most agreeable melange of ripe yellow & green fruits on delightful unwooded **19** ⑧⑨. 4 months on lees add body & savoury edge, lipsmacking acidity zips through to finish.

★★★★ **Sauvignon Blanc** A fruit bowl of flavour, **19** ⑧⑨ with tropicality (bananas, guavas, litchis) vying with nettles, grapefruit & crunchy green pears. Well-managed acid & excellent length.

★★★★☆ **Blanc de Blancs Brut** ⓐ Savoury-style **14** ⑨③ MCC sparkler from chardonnay mixes yellow citrus & crisp green apples with salty, creamy brioche notes from 52 months on lees. Refreshing bubbles & attractive orange peel & fennel finish.

Sustainable Rosé ⊘ ★★★☆ Appealing just-dry pink from shiraz, **19** ⑧③ pretty strawberry milkshake flavours with herbal freshness & crisp acidity. **Buketraube** ★★★★ One of only 2 varietal bottlings in the guide. Tinned grapefruit with flowers & perfume on **19** ⑧③, off-dry favourite partner for spicy foods or solo summer sipping. — CM

Location: Citrusdal ▪ Map: Olifants River ▪ Map grid reference: D7 ▪ WO: Cederberg/Elim ▪ Est 1973 ▪ 1stB 1977 ▪ Tasting Mon-Sat 9-12 & 1.30-4.30; pub hols 9-11.30 & 4-5.30 ▪ Fee R40 ▪ Closed Good Fri & Dec 25 ▪ Sales Mon-Sat 8-12.30 & 1.30-5; Sun/pub hols 9-12 & 4-6 ▪ BYO picnic ▪ Sanddrif Holiday Resort self-catering cottages; camping ▪ Walks/hikes ▪ MTB ▪ Conservation area ▪ Rock climbing ▪ Sport climbing ▪ Observatory ▪ Craft beer brewery ▪ Owner(s) Nieuwoudt family ▪ Cellarmaster(s) David Nieuwoudt (Jan 1997) ▪ Winemaker(s) Alex Nel (whites, Aug 2011) & Tammy Turck-Nel (reds, Aug 2011) ▪ Viticulturist(s) Oubaas Laubscher (Oct 2015) ▪ 5,500ha/74ha (cab, shiraz, buketraube, chenin, sauv) ▪ 900t/90,000cs own label 40% red 60% white ▪ WWF-SA Conservation Champion ▪ PO Box 84 Clanwilliam 8135 ▪ info@ cederbergwine.com ▪ www.cederbergwine.com ▪ S 32° 30' 12.8" E 019° 15' 27.7" ▪ ⬚ withdrawn.reptile. plods ▪ **T +27 (0)27-482-2827**

Celestina

Fine-wine merchant Caroline Kilian and her husband Ray grow just under two hectares of semillon and sauvignon on their Baardskeerdersbos vineyard near cool and breezy Elim. The grapes are vinified by Dirk Human of Black Oystercatcher into the 'Little Celestial One'. The 2018 and 2019 crops were sold off but the plan is to bottle some of the 2020 vintage. The '17 is still available from Caroline's shop in central Cape Town.

★★★★☆ **Sauvignon Blanc-Semillon** Ⓢ Older-oak-fermented/aged white Bordeaux blend, equal partners sauvignon, semillon in **17** ⑨②. Intense greenpepper & grass notes, vibrant cool-climate acidity, mineral conclusion with Granny Smith apple & citrus nuances. Advances fine form of **16** ⑨①. — HC

Location: Baardskeerdersbos ▪ WO: Cape Agulhas ▪ Est 2004 ▪ 1stB 2009 ▪ Closed to public ▪ Owner(s) Caroline Kilian ▪ Winemaker(s) Dirk Human (Black Oystercatcher) ▪ Viticulturist(s) Caroline & Ray Kilian ▪ 3.4ha/1.85ha (sauv, sem) ▪ 6t/600cs own label 100% white ▪ c/o Caroline's Fine Wine Cellar, Shop 44

Matador Centre, 62 Strand Str, Cape Town 8001 ▪ carowine2@mweb.co.za ▪ www.carolineswine.com ▪ T +27 (0)21-419-8984

Cellar Cask

SA's first bag-in-box, launched 1979 and styled to meet then-rising demand for full-sweet wines with lower alcohol levels, today available in 750ml glass, 3L and 5L packs. The 1L duo debuting this year from brand owner Distell offers an undaunting path for Cellar Cask fans to transition to dry-drinking.

Smooth Dry Red (NEW) ★★★ Unpretentious **NV** (77), fruity, affable & light. **Crisp Dry White** (NEW) ★★ Uncomplicated, mildly fruity, lightweight **NV** (72). **Select Johannisberger Red** ★★ Plum-jam fruit on sweet **NV** (75) shiraz, merlot, ruby cab blend to serve lightly chilled. **Select Johannisberger Rosé** ★★ Full-sweet pink **NV** (73) from various red & white varieties. **Select Johannisberger White** ★★ Sweet, lightly fruity **NV** (73), mostly chenin & colombard, with matching modest 11.25% alcohol. — GdB

☐ **Cellar Door** see Namaqua Wines
☐ **Chabivin Champagne & MCC House** See Editor's Note
☐ **Chameleon** see Jordan Wine Estate
☐ **Chamonix** see Cape Chamonix Wine Farm

Chantelle   (Ⓠ) (NEW)

When British sculpture gallery owners Robert and Michele Bowman bought the Victorian manor house on the original 19-ha Franschhoek wine property La Ferme Chantelle, they unwittingly acquired a long-dormant yet functional 19th-century cellar and parcel of chardonnay. Beguiled by bubbly from neighbour vines, they enlisted Audacia's Michael van Niekerk to vinify their own MCC. The two vintages listed here are the commercial releases to date, some exported to the UK.

★★★★ **Méthode Cap Classique Blanc de Blancs Brut Reserve** (❀) Lean, mineral **14** (86) bubbly, pleasing brioche top note from 48 months on lees, bracing lemon freshness & subtle breadth from 10% wooded component. Impressive now, even better in a few years. Also-tasted **08** ★★★★ (85) gained honeyed charm from 36 months sur lie plus several years in bottle. Good length & freshness despite few more grams sugar.— GdB, CvZ

Location/map: Franschhoek ▪ Map grid reference: C2 ▪ WO: Franschhoek/Western Cape ▪ Est 2005 ▪ 1stB 2008 ▪ Tasting, sales & cellar tours by appt only ▪ Owner(s) Chantelle Collection Ltd (shareholders Robert & Michele Bowman) ▪ Winemaker(s)/viticulturist(s) Michael van Niekerk (May 2017, consultant) ▪ 0.5ha (chard) ▪ 6t/700cs own label 100% white ▪ PO Box 53001 Kenilworth 7745 ▪ rjeb@plot20.com ▪ www.chantelle-winery.co.za ▪ S 33° 54' 11.07" E 019° 6' 35.15" ▪ (☰) brave.stationing.capture ▪ T +27 (0)73-145-0046

☐ **Chapel** see Robertson Winery
☐ **Chapel Cellar** see Zanddrift Vineyards - Chapel Cellar

Charla Haasbroek Wines

Charla Bosman (née Haasbroek) is the winemaker at Sijnn, so knows well the remarkable quality and characters produced by the extreme, stony soils of the farm near the mouth of the Breede River. For her own label she explores them a little further, making small quantities of monovarietal wines in artisanal fashion. A Trincadeira '18 and Cabernet Sauvignon '17 were due to be released at press time.

★★★★☆ **Colourblind** (❀) Beguiling **16** (90) an unusual example of cab in its lean, light, elegant freshness (more reminiscent of a Loire cab franc than a SA cab perhaps). Yet full of flavour, with something wild, even rustic, & a stony undercurrent. Already all in vital balance, promising complexity.

★★★★☆ **Chenin Blanc** (NEW) (❀) **18** (93) spontaneously fermented & 9 months on lees in older oak barrels. Mid-gold colouring & ripe apple character speak of more oxidative handling, with flint & spicy (nutmeg, perhaps) grace notes. Quietly delicious, with fine, succulent acidic thread & rich texture.— TJ

Location/WO: Malgas ▪ Est/1stB 2016 ▪ Closed to public ▪ Winemaker(s) Charla Haasbroek (Sijnn) ▪ Lemoentuin Farm, 342 Malgas ▪ charlahaasbroek@gmail.com ▪ T +27 (0)82-782-5875

☐ **Charles Borro** see Govert Wines

Charles Fox Cap Classique Wines ⓠ ⓐ

Johannesburg businessman Charles Fox and wife Zelda decided to pursue their passion for champagne by making their own, 'proudly South African' equivalent, méthode cap classique. After an inter-regional search for the terroir best suited to the traditional champagne varieties, they decided on Elgin and purchased an old fruit farm, Furneaux. Since building a cellar, with underground storage for 200,000 bottles fifteen years ago, they haven't looked back. Reims-based consultant Nicolas Follet has made all their wines, with Kevin Watt keeping the vines in prime form. About one-third of production is now exported to six countries.

★★★★☆ **Reserve Rosé** ⓡ Copper-hued **NV** ⑨⓪ bubbly from pinot noir, 15% chardonnay & 9% meunier has intense red berry & pomegranate fruit & fine bead. Richly biscuity from minimum 2 years on lees, yet taut, dry & refreshing.

★★★★☆ **Vintage Brut Rosé** ⓐ Disgorged only after 4.5 years on lees, **13** ⑨③ sparkler with more pinot noir than previous (64%) has red berry fruit abundance plus some yeasty complexity & a savoury oystershell minerality. Very rich, with a creamy mousse. Portion oaked, as all.

★★★★☆ **Prestige Cuvée Cipher** ⓐ Flagship only in outstanding years, **13** ⑨④ is 50/50 pinot noir & chardonnay, 30% wooded, disgorged after 4.5 years on lees, for apple pie impression (buttery pastry, cinnamon-spiced fruit & vanilla cream), soft & rich, with well-integrated acidity.

★★★★☆ **Reserve Brut** Equal pinot noir & meunier with 30% chardonnay, 40% wooded, latest **NV** ⑨⓪ improves on last with biscuity richness, persistent bubble, depth of flavour: fresh apple, pear & zesty citrus.

★★★★☆ **Vintage Brut** ⓐ Meunier to the fore in vibrant **15** ⑨④, with 33% pinot, 21% chardonnay, 3.5 years on lees for buttery brioche richness, persistent fine effervescence, white peach, pear & Golden Delicious apple flavours. Pinch of herbs & spices, too. **14** sold out untasted.

Not tasted: **Prestige Cuvée Blanc de Blancs**. — JG

Location/map/WO: Elgin ▪ Map grid reference: C3 ▪ Est 2007 ▪ 1stB 2010 ▪ Tasting, sales & cellar tours Mon-Sun 10-4 ▪ Fee applicable ▪ Closed Dec 25 & Jan 1 ▪ Play area for children ▪ Owner(s) Charles & Zelda Fox ▪ Cellarmaster(s) Charles Fox (2010) ▪ Winemaker(s) Nicolas Follet (2010, consultant) ▪ Viticulturist(s) Kevin Watt (2008, consultant) ▪ 33.4ha/9ha (pinot noir/meunier, chard) ▪ 5,000cs own label 100% MCC ▪ PO Box 105 Elgin 7180 ▪ charlesfoxmcc@gmail.com ▪ www.charlesfox.co.za ▪ S 34° 14' 14.38" E 019° 04' 41.99" ▪ ⟲ when.dives.commending ▪ **T +27 (0)21-300-1065/+27 (0)82-569-2965/+27 (0)82-471-3444**

Chateau Libertas

Iconic large-volume SA red, produced since 1932 and still the epitome of value and drinkability. By Distell.

Chateau Libertas ⊘ ★★★ Affable **18** ⑦⑧, generously fruited & mocha tinged, with hints of spice & leather. Silky, friendly & tasty as ever. 5-way Bordeaux/Rhône mix, cab led. — GM

Chateau Naudé Wine Creation

After retiring as L'Avenir cellarmaster in 2005, pinotage specialist Francois Naudé started consulting to top producers, becoming convinced that, by blending their best barrels, he could produce the 'ultimate pinotage' each vintage, a wine with power, complexity and elegance. The result was Le Vin de François, of which 11 vintages were sold at an exclusive annual auction event, with son Francois and daughter Melissa joining the family business. Francois snr has now officially retired from formal employment and will dedicate more time to the venture, inter alia 'going around the world and sharing the magic'. The Naudés have decided to forego the auction 'because the wine should be available to a wider range of consumers'.

★★★★☆ **Le Vin de François** ⓐ Historically a blend of pinotages from several Cape producers advised by François Naudé; **17** ⑨⓪ narrows the focus to Stellenbosch & Tulbagh, maintains the lofty standard. Beautifully judged ripeness, with bone-dry finish to vibrant mulberry & strawberry fruit, spice dusting & tannins for many years improvement. No **16**. — WB, CvZ

Location: Stellenbosch ▪ WO: Stellenbosch-Tulbagh ▪ Est 2006 ▪ 1stB 2007 ▪ Closed to public ▪ Owner(s) Francois Naudé snr, Francois Naudé jnr & Melissa Naudé ▪ Cellarmaster(s) Francois Naudé (Jul 2007) ▪ 400cs own label 100% red ▪ 11 Weidenhof Str, Stellenbosch 7600 ▪ naude@levindefrancois.co.za ▪ www.levindefrancois.com ▪ **T +27 (0)21-883-8469**

Chennells Wines ⓠ

Vivimus Vivamus ('While we live, let us truly live') is the credo of Jeremy and Colleen Chennells, landowners and boutique vintners in prime Helderberg, who have been cultivating their vines since 2005 with personal care and total family involvement. They also strive to farm responsibly and holistically.

The Journey ⓟ ★★★☆ Named for family's life voyage. Equal cab/shiraz, French & Hungarian oak 20 months, **17** ⑧④ an explosion of flavour, cassis & mulberries, expertly spiced, smoothly curvaceous.

Cabernet Sauvignon ⓠ ★★★☆ Bold & robust **10** ⑧④ aims for seriousness in riper vintage, achieves good concentration of savoury dark berry fruit; supportive tannins & acid but 15% alcohol obvious in youth. **Saudade** ⓝⓔⓦ ★★★ Cabernet given same oak regime as The Journey, here expressed as lead pencils, **17** ⑧①'s fruit subservient, but enough flesh to offset the tannins. A savoury style. **A Handful of Summers** ⓠ ★★★☆ Oak-enriched **13** ⑧④ viognier shows ripe apricot compote features; fresher flavours, dry rather grippy conclusion. **Viognier** ⓠ ★★★☆ **14** ⑧④ is something different. Fermented in barrel, savoury oatmeal & peach flavours, variety's usual aromas tamed. Lovely! Not tasted: **Shiraz.** — CR

Location/WO: Stellenbosch ▪ Map: Helderberg ▪ Map grid reference: C2 ▪ Est 2004 ▪ 1stB 2008 ▪ Tasting, sales & cellar tours Mon-Sun 9-5 by appt ▪ Closed all pub hols ▪ Owner(s) Jeremy & Colleen Chennells ▪ Cellarmaster(s)/winemaker(s) Jeremy Chennells & Chris Keet (Jul 2009, consultant) ▪ Viticulturist(s) Francois Hanekom & Colleen Chennells ▪ 5ha/3.2ha (cab, shiraz, viog) ▪ 26t/330cs own label 85% red 15% white ▪ Cordoba Winery Rd Helderberg Somerset West 7130 ▪ chennell@iafrica.com ▪ www.chennellswines.com ▪ S 34°1' 45.99" E 018° 50' 9.05" ▪ ⌨ pretend.crooned.cranked ▪ **T +27 (0)21-855-3905**

- ☐ **Chip Off The Old Block** *see* Ormonde Private Cellar
- ☐ **Chocoholic** *see* Darling Cellars
- ☐ **Chouette!** *see* New Beginnings Wines
- ☐ **Chris Keet** *see* Keet Wines
- ☐ **Christina Van Loveren** *see* Van Loveren Family Vineyards
- ☐ **Christine-Marié** *see* Niel Joubert Estate
- ☐ **Christoffel Hazenwinkel** *see* Hazendal Wine Estate
- ☐ **Chrysalis** *see* Lourensford Wine Estate
- ☐ **Cilliers Cellars** *see* Stellendrift - SHZ Cilliers/Kuün Wyne

Cilmor Winery ⓠ

This 10,000-ton Worcester winery, vinifying six to eight million litres of Fairtrade-certified bulk wine annually from surrounding vineyards, is the legacy of early 20th-century vegetable and poultry farmer Cecil Morgan. The Cilmor Trust's urban development of his Kuils River farms underpins the winegrowing endeavours, including an extensive range of bottled wines available for on-site tasting.

Premium Collection

Cabernet Sauvignon ⓠ ★★★ Cured beef, some underlying plummy fruit, **18** ⑧① is succulent, has nice elegance & drinkability. Doesn't speak in a loud voice but is very likeable. Gently extracted, briefly oaked (staves), as all the reds. **Pinotage** ⓠ ★★★ Vanilla & blueberries, **18** ⑦⑨ aims to be friendly, appealing. Enough grip to handle food, the ideal braai wine, as back label puts it. **Shiraz** ⓠ ★★★ Fynbos & scrub notes in **18** ⑦⑧, some floral nuances & black pepper, red berries; sleek, the tannins in support. Early-picked style, has appealing drinkability. **Chardonnay** ⓠ ★★★ Oak's toastiness well partnered by **18** ⑦⑨'s orange & tangerine styling. Good mouthfeel, tangy & fresh, if not very complex. **Chenin Blanc** ⓠ ★★☆ Cool-fruit styling for **18** ⑦⑧, crunchy pear & touch of lemon, which deepens in the flavours. Also-tasted **15** ★★★☆ ⑧③ quince & melon preserve, a strong seam of citrus, lovely pine nut richness though unwooded, it's the bottle age. No **17**, **16**. **Sauvignon Blanc** ⓠ ★★★ Gooseberry & lime, some green asparagus but it's **18** ⑧②'s nervous tension that impresses, vibrates with freshness. Also-reviewed **15** ★★★☆ ⑧④ proves variety can age, thanks to good acid backbone. Melon & salted limes, an attractive pungency, long finish. At its best now. No **17**, **16**. Occasional release: **Merlot**, **Merlot Rosé**.

Popular range

Occasional release: **Berry Juicy Red**, **Candy Floss Rosé**, **Fruity Bouquet White**. — CR, CvZ

Location/map/WO: Worcester ▪ Map grid reference: B4 ▪ Est 1997 ▪ 1stB 2015 ▪ Tasting & sales Mon-Fri 9-4.30 Sat/Sun by appt ▪ Fee R50 ▪ Closed all pub hols ▪ Owner(s) Cilmor Trust ▪ Cellarmaster(s)/winemaker(s) Quintin van der Westhuizen (Dec 2012) ▪ Viticulturist(s) Rudi du Toit (July 2008) ▪ ±2,000ha/452.21ha (cab, merlot, ptage, roobernet, ruby cab, shiraz, chard, chenin, cbard, hanepoot, nouvelle, pinot gris, sauv, viog) ▪ 8,500t/±3,100cs own label 28% red 44% white 28% rosé ▪ Fairtrade, IPW, WIETA ▪ PO Box 5628 Worcester West 6862 ▪ info@cilmorwines.com ▪ www.cilmorwines.com ▪ S 33° 44' 30.02" E 019° 28' 49.02" ▪ 🅦 trim.thesis.lamps ▪ **T +27 (0)23-340-4141**

☐ **Circle of Life** *see* Waterkloof
☐ **Circumstance** *see* Waterkloof

Cirrus Wines

A Cape/Napa collaboration between Jean Engelbrecht of Rust en Vrede and Silver Oak Cellars' Duncan family, this single-label brand is made by Danielle le Roux at Guardian Peak. A Napa version has been mooted.
★★★★☆ **Cirrus Syrah** ⒶAccomplished **16** (93) continues impressive form of **15** (94), also with splash viognier. Understated, nuanced rather than forceful, showing subtle spicing, fragrant fruit. 16 months in French oak, 30% new.— GdB

Location/WO: Stellenbosch ▪ Est 2002 ▪ 1stB 2003 ▪ Tasting & sales at Guardian Peak Wines ▪ Owner(s) Jean Engelbrecht & Duncan family (Napa, CA) ▪ Winemaker(s) Danielle le Roux (Dec 2019) ▪ ±7.5t/1,200cs own label 100% red ▪ IPW ▪ PO Box 473 Stellenbosch 7599 ▪ info@cirruswines.com ▪ www.cirruswines.com ▪ **T +27 (0)21-881-3881**

City on a Hill Wine Company

André Bruyns assists David and Nadia Sadie in their Paardeberg cellar but his own brand is growing, with wines made in a similarly subtle, hands-off way from Swartland fruit. This edition sees his first red wine, a syrah off shale soils in the Kasteelberg area. His focus remains to improve and better understand all the vineyards he works with. The name and label richly evoke for André biblical and hillside vineyard themes.
★★★★☆ **Red** ⓃⒺⓌ Ⓐ Syrah, Swartland's signature red grape, on Kasteelberg shale. **18** (93) hands-off vinification, including wholebunch fermentation, ageing in seasoned wood, yields ample redcurrant fruit & appeal with lifted elegance; it's subtle, no fruit bomb this.
★★★★★ **Chenin Blanc** Super **18** ★★★★★ (94), from shy-yielding dryland vines, a harmony of complex textures & flavours. Gossamer-like yet assured, with a whisper of scrub in the elegant conclusion that lingers, though perhaps not as long as exceptional **17** (96).
★★★★ **Muscat d'Alexandrie** Intense grapiness introduces **18** (89), a paradox that's opulent on nose but quite linear on palate, partly thanks to 10 months in old casks; lipsmackingly dry, with low (11.5%) alcohol.
★★★★★ **White** Ⓐ Stellar expression of old-vine chenin on Perdeberg granite. **18** (93) has dashes viognier & muscat d'Alexandrie but isn't overtly fruity: a spicy, dusty-earth profile, elegant, dry stony finish plumped up with 10 months old oak.— DS

Location: Malmesbury ▪ Map/WO: Swartland ▪ Map grid reference: C8 ▪ Est/1stB 2015 ▪ Tasting by appt ▪ Owner(s) André Bruyns ▪ Winemaker(s) André Bruyns (2015) ▪ 1,000cs own label 20% red 80% white ▪ andre@cityonahillwine.co.za ▪ www.cityonahillwine.co.za ▪ S 33° 32' 41.41" E 018° 49' 36.14" ▪ 🅦 illogical.funds.virulently

---

☐ **CL** *see* Oldenburg Vineyards

Clairvaux Cellar

Situated on Robertson town's doorstep, Clairvaux's De Wet family owners absolutely nailed the first principle of real estate. Their winemaker/manager, Jaco van der Merwe, gets his side of things right, too. Bulk wine is the focus, but the small parcels under this label are eminently drinkable and affordably priced.
★★★★ **Straw Wine** ⓃⒺⓌ Hanepoot sun-dried on racks 2 weeks for fragrant, unctuous & intense **19** (87). Delicious flavours (grapes, barley sugar) & exotic spice in harmony with cleansing acidity. 375 ml.
★★★★ **Red Muscadel** Luminous amber **18** (88) fortified has sweet berry & boiled sweet flavours, integrated spirit giving a lovely fresh lift throughout. Solo in winter, over ice (cream) when it's hot. No 17.

Cabernet Sauvignon 🍷 ★★★ Vibrant ruby with red fruit flavours to match, cranberry, red plum & hints of lead pencil. Gentle tannins make **17** ⑧⓪ a pleasure to drink. **Shiraz** 🍷 ★★★ Friendly & generous **18** ⑧② makes you smile: ripe dark berries, savoury spice & gentle tug to make it food friendly.

Sauvignon Blanc ★★ A leaner & greener profile in **19** ⑦③, with acid nip, misses the tropical flavours & fruit padding of previous. **Good Night Irene** ★★★ Fortified hanepoot charms with sweet grapey & spicy flavours & firm, crisp spirit grip. **19** ⑧② for nightcaps & anytime prior. **Madonna's Kisses** ★★★ White muscadel fortified, **19** ⑧⓪ has aromatic sweet flavours, is easy to drink but deserves bit more time to cohere. **Cape Vintage** ⊘ ★★★ 'Port' from shiraz. 2nd bottling of **16** ⑧⓪, year longer in old oak, tad more complex, sweet fruit tempered by better-balanced spirit (17%). — WB

Location/map/WO: Robertson ▪ Map grid reference: B6 ▪ Est/1stB 2000 ▪ Tasting & sales Mon-Fri 8-5 ▪ Closed all pub hols ▪ Cellar tours by appt ▪ BYO picnic ▪ Sales (at cellar price) also from La Verne Wine Boutique T +27 (0)23-626-4314 Mon-Fri 9-5.30 Sat 9-3 ▪ Owner(s) Wouter J de Wet snr & jnr ▪ Winemaker(s) / manager Jaco van der Merwe (Oct 2011) ▪ 200ha (cab, merlot, ptage, shiraz, chard, chenin, cbard, hanepoot, muscadel, sauv) ▪ 4,000t/3.2m L bulk ▪ PO Box 179 Robertson 6705 ▪ info@clairvauxcellar.co.za ▪ www.clairvauxcellar.co.za ▪ S 33° 48' 13.8" E 019° 52' 21.1" ▪ 🖾 lively.unknowns.natures ▪ **T +27 (0)23-626-3842**

☐ **Clarington** *see* Normandie Est. 1693

Clayton Wines

Roger Clayton is a Scot who was 'captured by the spirit' of the Swartland revival. Based in Riebeek-Kasteel and sourcing many of his grapes from the area, he also expresses that spirit in his non-interventionist approach. For family reasons he and wife Natasha took a few years' break from winemaking, but are back now in full force — including working on 'an exciting small vineyard project in Constantia'.

Jolly Roger range

★★★★ **Piruju Portuguese Blend** Ⓧ Dark & red fruit freshly assembled & dusted with spice. Old-oaked, naturally fermented **15** ⑧⑦ 4-way blend is a dry, juicy, savoury-sweet delight. WO W Cape.

★★★★ **Chardonnay** Citrus & stonefruit on **16** ⑧⑥, with cool-climate freshness. Silky texture, balanced, lightish (13% alcohol) palate; fine seam of acidity. 10 months 2nd-fill oak. Ex Elgin, like last **14** ★★★☆ ⑧⑤.

Pinotage ⑭ᴇⱳ ★★★ Light berry aromas, but **14** ⑧② more savoury than fruity. Easygoing, just a touch lean from 2 years in old oak. Ready to drink. **Viognier** ⑭ᴇⱳ ★★★★ Balanced **15** ⑧⑤ retains varietal apricot charm, but probably best to drink soon. Lovely soft texture together with some grip. Fermented & 18 months in old oak. Not tasted: **Grenache**, **SMG**, **SMV**, **Syrah-Grenache**. — TJ

Location: Riebeek-Kasteel ▪ WO: Swartland/Elgin/Western Cape ▪ Est/1stB 2013 ▪ Closed to public ▪ Wines available from Wine Kollective, Riebeek-Kasteel & Vino Pronto, Cape Town ▪ Owner(s) Roger & Natasha Clayton ▪ Winemaker(s) Roger Clayton (Jan 2013) ▪ 3t/400cs own label 50% red 50% white ▪ PO Box 534 Constantia 7848 ▪ roger@unwined.co.za ▪ www.unwined.co.za ▪ **T +27 (0)76-826-8500**

☐ **Clearsprings** *see* Trizanne Signature Wines

Cloof Wine Estate   🍷 📷 🅐 ♿

Foreign owned the past two decades, the Cloof home-farm near Darling has 135 ha under vine (including venerable bushvines planted in 1966, 1976 and 1987) and a very large tract of highly endangered veld which, as a WWF-SA Conservation Champion, the estate actively protects (and allows public access to, by appointment, via game and eco drives). Environmental concern extends into the social dimension, as reflected in the new broad-based empowerment partnership with Elizabeth Petersen, whose Libby's Pride Wines were previously listed separately in this guide. Elizabeth describes herself as 'a black SA woman who prides myself on creating wines that reflect my own flamboyant and extrovert personality', and says she's proud to be collaborating with Cloof 'and putting my name to this wine for everyone to enjoy!'

Iconic range

★★★★☆ **Crucible Shiraz** Ⓧ Standard bearer, made in tiny quantities in exceptional years. Full-bodied yet refined **14** ⑨③ has concentrated fruit with white pepper & baking spice. Stablemate may be Very Sexy but this is for a long-term relationship. WO Darling. Last tasted was **06** ★★★★.

The Winemakers Selection

Merlot ⓥ ★★★★ Ripe plums on nose of **12** ⑧⑤, sweet prunes, milk chocolate & fruitcake sweetness on palate balanced by mouthwatering prickle of acidity. **Cloof Pinotage** ★★★★ Charming **17** ⑧⑤ offers spicy blue & black fruit compote with supportive oak, third new. Soft textured & lighter than **15** ★★★★ ⑧⑥. No **16**. **Cloof Lynchpin** ⓥ ★★★★ Cabernet franc leads merlot (30%) in **14** ⑧③, ample juicy blue fruit shaded by oak (60% new) & 15% alcohol; somewhat ponderous compared with **13** ★★★★ ⑧⑦. **CvD Méthode Cap Classique Blanc de Blancs** ⓥ ★★★★ Chardonnay bubbly has typical apple & brioche notes with zippy lime freshness in **14** ⑧①. WO W Cape, rest of these Darling origin. Not tasted: **Cloof Syrah**. Discontinued: **Limited Release Cabernet Sauvignon**.

The Signature range

★★★★ **The Very Sexy Shiraz** Easy **17** ★★★★ ⑧⑤ is lighter than **16** ⑧⑥ but still fruit-forward, with spicy plum & brush of herbs. Medium body & length.

The Dark Side ★★★ Ripe, fruity & friendly **NV** ⑧⓪ loses shiraz component, now entirely cab in easy-drinking style thanks to 50% unwooded portion. WO W Cape, rest WO Darling. **Inkspot** ★★★ Pinotage leads 5-way blend in **17** ⑧①. Juicy, soft & approachable, with vivid red fruit. Supple & fresh from half unoaked portion. Discontinued: **Cloof Cab Cult Cabernet Sauvignon**.

The Duckitt Collection

Cabernet Sauvignon ⓥ ★★★★ Light bodied, approachable **17** ⑧④ has trademark cassis notes. 50/50 split of tank & barrel maturation makes for a fresh & pleasant wine. WO W Cape. **Merlot** ★★★ Leafy tomato typicity on bright, gentle **18** ⑧②. Soft tannin squeeze on tail from 50/50 tank & barrel fractions. **Pinotage** ★★★ Light-bodied & juicy **17** ⑦⑦ offers floral blueberry approachability & ease. **Shiraz** ⓥ ★★★★ Deep black fruit & earthiness to **14** ⑧③. Gains freshness from tank portion blended with the oaked element, gentle tannin grip. **Cabernet Sauvignon-Merlot-Cabernet Franc** ★★★ Spicy cassis on **17** ⑧⓪ red Bordeaux blend. Somewhat slight but soft, dry grip on tail from 50% barrelled portion. **Chardonnay** ⓥ ★★★ Packs a bold nectarine wallop! Uncomplicated & unoaked, **18** ⑧⓪ is fresh & easy. **Sauvignon Blanc** ★★★ Tropical styling on pear- & guava-toned **18** ⑦⑦. Light on signature acidity.

The Bush Vines range

Merlot ⊘ ★★★★ **18** ⑧④ has black cherry, tealeaf & spicy cedar. Medium concentration & depth, with gentle grip of tannin from 25% oak portion. **Pinotage-Shiraz** ⓥ ★★★ Meaty prune notes on 85/15 blend. **16** ⑧⓪'s gentle concentration makes for easy drinking. **Rosé** ⓥ ★★★ Coral hue to **18** ⑦⑧, gently juicy poolside pink with cherry & strawberry appeal. WO Darling. **Chenin Blanc** ⓥ ★★★ A veritable fruit bowl with melon & granadilla zip, **18** ⑦⑨ appealing casual quaffer. Discontinued: **Pinotage Rosé**, **Sauvignon Blanc**.

Libby's Pride range

Cabernet Sauvignon ⊘ ★★★★ Bright cherry appeal to juicy **17** ⑧④. Light, fresh & easy blend of 50/50 tank & (seasoned) oak portions. **Shiraz** ⊘ ★★★ Pleasantly spiciness to supple **16** ⑧②. Honest, with black fruit appeal. Year in French oak adds structure. **Chardonnay** ★★★ Improves on last in honeyed ripeness, softly tangy acid to balance. **18** ⑧⓪, again, unwooded but with lees contact adding texture. — FM

Location: Darling ▪ Map: Durbanville, Philadelphia & Darling ▪ Map grid reference: B3 ▪ WO: Western Cape/Darling ▪ Est/1stB 1998 ▪ Tasting & sales Tue-Sat 10-4 ▪ Cellar tours by appt ▪ Conservation area ▪ Game & eco drives by appt ▪ Child friendly ▪ Owner(s) Cloof Wine Estate (Pty) Ltd ▪ Winemaker(s) Hennie Huskisson (Sep 2017) ▪ Viticulturist(s) Peter Duckitt (May 2004) ▪ 1,300ha/135ha (cabs s/f, merlot, ptage, shiraz, chard, chenin, viog) ▪ 600t/100,000cs own label 88% red 12% white ▪ WWF-SA Conservation Champion ▪ PO Box 269 Darling 7345 ▪ info@cloof.co.za ▪ www.cloof.co.za ▪ S 33° 28' 58.1" E 018° 31' 23.4" ▪ ⌖ overly.realtime. violets ▪ **T +27 (0)22-492-2839**

Clos Malverne

ⓧ ⓧ ⓧ ⓧ ⓧ

Family-owned and -run boutique winery in Stellenbosch's Devon Valley, inspired by a French 'clos' (walled vineyard), focused on marketing itself as a destination, a multifaceted experience. Co-owner Seymour Pritchard directs operations, wife Sophia helps to run and develop the export market, a significant part of sales, while daughter Belinda looks after the hospitality side. There's accommodation, a function centre, restaurant (growing its own organic produce) and spa; wine-and-food pairings, including, unusually, ice-cream matching, as well as craft beer and brandy, plus a range of wines at different price levels.

Clos Malverne range

★★★★ **Merlot** Red berries, macerated cherries & smoky spice, **17** ⑧⑧ is quite individual, & attractively so. Lithe, supple tannins, already drinking well. **16** not made.

★★★★ **Le Café Pinotage** Popular 'coffee' style, **18** ⑧⑧ all-new oak, French & 10% American for the sweet spice/cappuccino flavours. Sleek, smooth textured, finishes satisfyingly dry. Has some style. No **17**.

★★★★ **Pinotage Reserve** ⓐ 16 ⑧⑧ only pinotage (**14** ⑧⑥ dash cab), 20% American oak, rest French. Wonderfully perfumed; dark berries & chocolate, finishing savoury & firm. Good now, but long future. No **15**.

★★★★★ **Auret** ⓐ Flagship Cape Blend, pinotage partnered with cab (60%), dab merlot, so expect structure & longevity in **16** ⑨③. But mirrored by berry intensity adding mid-palate succulence for a streamlined effect. Delicious. **15** sold out untasted.

★★★★★ **Spirit of Malverne Limited Release** ⓩ Previewed & provisionally rated **15** ★★★★ ⑧⑦ Cape Blend is highly aromatic - scented violets over hedgerow & bramble fruit - shows lovely freshness if not (yet) the complexity of **13** ⑨③, alcohol & tannins need more time to integrate. No **14**.

★★★★ **Sauvignon Blanc 18** ⑧⑥ offers a different spectrum of flavours to sibling Devonet, winter melon, hint of Provençal herbs. Elegant (13% alcohol) & satisfyingly dry. Step up on **17** ★★★★ ⑧④.

★★★★ **Ellie Méthode Cap Classique Shiraz Rosé** Piquant wild berries in perfume & flavour, **16** ⑧⑧ bubbly displays subtle biscuit shading from 36 months on the lees. Crisply dry, very tasty. **14**, **15** not made.

. . . .

Cabernet Sauvignon-Shiraz ⓥ ★★★ Opulent styling for richly fruited **16** ⑧① well spiced, designed for enjoyment. Nice defining grip on the finish.

. . . .

Cabernet Sauvignon-Merlot ⓩ ★★★★ In this 60/40 blend, cab plays a bigger role than you'd expect; vivid cassis leading to **15** ⑧④'s well-structured body, firm but accessible tannins. **Chardonnay** ★★★★ Light oaking, French/American barrels, provide **18** ⑧③'s toasty flavours, partnering the citrus. Savoury finish makes it food compatible. **Sauvignon Blanc Brut Reserve** ★★★ Variety & styling promises freshness & **NV** ⑧⓪ sparkler delivers; summer fruits, crisply dry. Occasional release: **Auret Limited Release**.

Devonet range

Merlot-Pinotage ★★★ Earliest drinking of the reds, plumply ripe **18** ⑧① is smoothly round, fruit & oak harmonious. **Rosé** ★★★ Pale pink & delicately perfumed, flavoured, **18** ⑦⑧ is crisply dry. WO W Cape, as next. **Sauvignon Blanc** ★★★ Green apple with a leafy top note, **18** ⑧① offers what's expected, refreshment for everyday enjoyment. — CR

Location/map: Stellenbosch ▪ Map grid reference: D4 ▪ WO: Stellenbosch/Western Cape ▪ Est/1stB 1986 ▪ Tasting & sales Mon-Fri 10-4.30 Sat/Sun 10-1 pub hols 12-5 ▪ Fee R30/4 wines or R50/6 wines ▪ Closed Dec 25 & Jan 1 ▪ Cellar tours Mon-Fri (booking essential) ▪ The Restaurant @ Clos Malverne ▪ Tour groups ▪ Weddings/functions ▪ Wellness Day Spa ▪ Accommodation: 9 x 4-star rooms & 1 self-catering unit ▪ Owner(s) Seymour & Sophia Pritchard ▪ Cellarmaster(s) IP Smit (Jul 1997) ▪ Winemaker(s) IP Smit (Nov 1997) ▪ Viticulturist(s) IP Smit (Jul 2015) ▪ 7ha (merlot, ptage, shiraz, sauv) ▪ ±200t/80,000cs own label 60% red 40% white ▪ PO Box 187 Stellenbosch 7599 ▪ info@closmalverne.co.za ▪ www.closmalverne.co.za ▪ S 33° 54' 38.0" E 018° 48' 49.2" ▪ ⊞ clipped.call.bikes ▪ **T +27 (0)21-865-2022**

Clouds Wine Estate   ⓩ ⑪ ⓐ ⓞ

There's now a 'small but immaculate cellar' on the estate, says Paul Burema, owner with Jolanda van Haperen of this property on Stellenbosch's Helshoogte Pass. In 2020 it welcomed its maiden harvest, with the eminent Donovan Rall as winemaker alongside Paul (Rall also vinifies for Vuurberg and under his own name). An old block of sauvignon blanc last year made way for shiraz vines. Unchanged is the generally elegant styling of the wines, and the striking orange-dominated branding — no doubt alluding to the owners' Dutch origin.

★★★★★ **Pinot Noir** ⓥ Pure, aromatic dark cherry fruit on **18** ⑨② with a touch of savoury undergrowth. Lovely balance, with subtle but effective tannin & acid, in early, satisfying harmony with the fruit. Some Hemel-en-Aarde grapes added to estate harvest.

★★★★☆ **Shiraz** Spicy, smoky red fruit on wholebunch, natural-ferment **17** ⑨1. Smooth, savoury palate, the tannins leaner & more assertive than previously, but there's good fruit to balance. Satisfyingly dry finish. Only old barrels for maturation. From Swartland grapes.

★★★★☆ **Red Blend** The biggest, ripest & boldest of the wines here (14.5% alcohol), yet **17** ⑨2 with some leanness & restraint - 20 months in older oak playing a taming role. From estate-grown cab (67%), merlot (27%) & petit verdot giving typical fruitcake & tobacco character. Only older oak.

★★★★ **Pink Sauvignon Blanc-Syrah** 2% syrah tints **18** ⑧6 a delicate onionskin & gives definite twist to the aromatics - though typical sauvignon notes dominate. Fresh, charming, dry & refined. One of the most sophisticated local rosés.

★★★★ **Chardonnay 18** ⑧9 has breadth & depth to its light-fruited, citrusy & stony-fresh palate. Matured in oak (some new), concrete & clay pots, the latter two accentuating the dry, unassertive delicacy.

★★★★★ **Chenin Blanc** ⊛ From ripe old-vine Wellington fruit, matured in concrete 'egg' & amphora. Deeply rather than simply enjoyable **18** ⑨3; satisfying fruit with a stony dimension to the richly textured, fresh palate. The finesse characteristic of the estate.

★★★★☆ **Sauvignon Blanc** Passionfruit & citrus on **18** ★★★★ ⑧9 subtle rather than overt, the palate soft, dry, balanced & fresh. A touch less compelling than more intense **17** ⑨2.

★★★★ **Méthode Cap Classique** Sparkler is pure chardonnay in **17** ⑧9, but retains the citrusy, apple-crisp & bone-dry elegance of previous with pinot noir. Little profundity, but the finesse entirely satisfying. WO Stellenbosch. No **16**.— TJ

Location/map: Stellenbosch ▪ Map grid reference: H5 ▪ WO: Western Cape/Stellenbosch/Swartland/Wellington ▪ Est/1stB 1993 ▪ Tasting & sales by appt ▪ Breakfast, lunch & dinner - booking essential ▪ Hotel & villas ▪ Conferences ▪ Owner(s) Paul Burema & Jolanda van Haperen ▪ Cellarmaster(s) Donovan Rall (Jan 2014, Vuurberg) ▪ Winemaker(s) Donovan Rall (Jan 2014, Vuurberg), with Paul Burema (Jan 2012) ▪ 4.5ha/2.7ha (cab, carignan, grenache, merlot, p verdot, pinot, chard) ▪ 24t/2,500cs own label 50% red 50% white ▪ PO Box 540 Stellenbosch 7599 ▪ info@cloudsestate.co.za ▪ www.cloudsestate.co.za ▪ S 33° 55' 23.9" E 018° 55' 29.7" ▪ ⓜ tracks.keys.swells ▪ **T +27 (0)21-885-1819**

Cloverfield Wines ⓠ ⓖ

Pioneers in traditionally sheep- and ostrich-rearing Robertson Valley, the Marais family made their first wines in 1945. In 1978, third-generation Pietie Marais married Irish-born Liz, an event which brought three sons as well as hope, love and luck to the farm. No wonder their slogan is 'Wines of Good Fortune'.

Location/map: Robertson ▪ Map grid reference: B5 ▪ Est 1945 ▪ Tasting & sales by appt ▪ Owner(s) Henry, Cobus & Pieter Marais ▪ Cellarmaster(s)/winemaker(s) Cobus Marais (2002) ▪ Viticulturist(s) Pieter Marais ▪ ±120ha total ▪ (merlot, shiraz, chard, chenin, sauv) ▪ 40% red 60% white ▪ PO Box 429 Robertson 6705 ▪ info@cloverfield.co.za ▪ www.cloverfield.co.za ▪ S 33° 49' 57.3" E 019° 55' 34.1" ▪ ⓜ cuter.wagging. defrosting ▪ **T +27 (0)23-626-4118**

☐ **Cocoa Hill** *see* Dornier Wines
☐ **Coetzee Family** *see* Matzikama Organic Cellar
☐ **Cold Mountain** *see* Brunia Wines

Collatio Wines ⓠ

Wessel du Toit, associate professor at Stellenbosch's Viticulture & Oenology school, has been involved with wine education and research for almost two decades, so it's unsurprising his own boutique range sets out to teach as well as delight. With wine geeks, tasting clubs and educators in mind, and collatio ('bringing together and comparing') as the organising principle, Wessel seasonally sources from high-end vineyards to produce pairs of barrels, adjusting a single element of the vinification for one of them to demonstrate 'the effect that one simple intervention can have on a wine'.

★★★★ **Cabernet Sauvignon 7 Dae** ⓠ Fermented on skins just 7 days, same oak regime as partner. **16** ⑧8 almost blackcurrant jam intensity, but there's lively & very appealing natural grip on the palate.

★★★★☆ Shiraz Bloei (NEW) ✓ Illustrates effect of removing juice pre-ferment (alias saignée, bleeding, bloei). 30% drawn off in deep & plush **16** ⑨⓪, dark-toned fruit, spice, scrub nuances, & then the palate: full bodied, intense flavours, tannins dense yet ripe. Lovely.

★★★★ Shiraz Geen Bloei (NEW) No juice bled off this show-and-tell **16** ⑧⑧. Dark toned & well spiced from 16 months seasoned barrels, some scrub, prosciutto. Silky palate, polished, just touch less concentrated than sibling, tannins less dense too.

★★★★ Shiraz Nuwe Hout ② Like sibling, 18 months in barrel, but this **15** ⑧⑧ in new, lightly toasted. Spice & char complement red fruits, tannins gruffer & less supple, yet structure more pleasing.

★★★★ Chenin Blanc Een Gisting ② Shows influence of malolactic fermentation on same wine. **17** ⑧⑦ white peach & nuts, smooth & succulent enlivened by bright lemon/lime acidity courtesy no malo.

Cabernet Sauvignon 35 Dae ② ★★★★ This **16** ⑧④ fermented, macerated 35 days on skins. Similar fruit profile but a savoury gloss, grippier tannin & sterner personality. Stellenbosch WO as Cab sibling.

Shiraz Ou Hout ② ★★★★ Spent 18 months in 4 year old oak; **15** ⑧④ initially dark-toned & meaty, yet has lipsmacking acidity, bright & fresh, with restrained grip. **Chenin Blanc Twee Gisting** ② ★★★★ This **17** ⑧⑤ completed malo, secondary fermentation which converts the 'harsh' malic acid into 'soft' lactic acid. Similarly smooth & long, with an almost aloe lift on the finish, attractive peachiness. Coastal WO, as Chenin sibling. Just ±45 cases made, as all. — CR

Location: Stellenbosch ▪ Map: Helderberg ▪ Map grid reference: A3 ▪ WO: Paarl/Coastal/Stellenbosch ▪ Est 2015 ▪ 1stB 2016 ▪ Tasting by appt only ▪ Closed all pub hols ▪ Owner(s) Wessel du Toit ▪ Cellarmaster(s)/winemaker(s) Wessel du Toit (Jan 2015) ▪ 2t/180cs own label 50% red 50% white ▪ PO Box 986 Stellenbosch 7599 ▪ wessel@collatiowines.co.za ▪ www.collatiowines.co.za ▪ S 34° 2' 23.3" E 018° 45' 5.5" ▪ ◪ lakefront.bowstring.marry ▪ **T +27 (0)82-563-4418**

☐ **Collection** see Roos Family Vineyards

Colmant Cap Classique & Champagne ⓺ ⓒ

Sparkling wines – méthode cap classique, handcrafted on-site from home-grown and bought-in grapes, as well as imported champagne from select houses – are the focus of Belgium émigrés Jean-Philippe and Isabelle Colmant's wine venture on their tiny estate in Franschhoek. In an ongoing quest for excellence, they've added Paul Gerber to the winemaking team, which already includes bubbly heavyweight Pieter Ferreira as consultant (see Pieter Ferreira Cap Classique). Given Paul's reputation as both a méthode champenoise expert (he is busy with a Masters degree) and exponent, JP is 'thrilled and excited for the road ahead'.

★★★★ Brut Rosé Festive bubbly with energetic mousse, happy pink hue & forthcoming berry & lemon flavours & aromas. Latest **NV** ⑧⑨ boosts chardonnay to near-equal status with pinot noir. Extra body from 30 months on lees & - unlike previous - both reserve wine & oaked portions.

★★★★☆ Absolu Zero Dosage ⓐ Long lees-ageing (7 years), 15/15 oaked & reserve-wine portions are fundamental to uncompromising vision behind this seemingly weightless & immensely persistent **NV** ⑨③ sparkler from chardonnay, now with some Elgin fruit. Breathtakingly dry, with mineral & kelp nuances, well-toned lemon sherbet body. Begs further ageing.

★★★★☆ Blanc de Blancs Name changes (from 'Brut Chardonnay') but same variety is the solo star in exceptional **NV** ⑨① dry sparkler. Perhaps shade less delicate & with slight caramel on finish from upped oaked fraction (48% vs 34% last bottling; roughly same time on lees & reserve-wine component). Remains an assured & beautifully crafted wine.

★★★★☆ Brut Reserve ⓐ Most New World in style of these admirable sparkles, near-equal pinot noir & chardonnay **NV** ⑨③ has small oaked portion, some reserve wine & 30 months on lees for weight & length. Balances the richness with thrilling acid-fruit balance, lemon & apple piquancy.

★★★★ Sec Reserve Vivacious & fruit-filled **NV** ⑧⑨ is off-dry but so well made, the sugar (23 g/l) is indiscernible, adding only richness & weight to a lovely sparkler aged 24 months on lees, with small oaked component. All these bubblies from Franschhoek, Elgin & Robertson vines.— CvZ

Location/map: Franschhoek ▪ Map grid reference: C1 ▪ WO: Western Cape ▪ Est 2005 ▪ 1stB 2006 ▪ Tasting & sales Mon-Fri 11-1; or by appt ▪ Fee R25 per ½ glass MCC ▪ Cellar tours on request ▪ Owner(s) Jean-Philippe Colmant ▪ Cellarmaster(s) Jean-Philippe Colmant & Paul Gerber (Mar 2019) ▪ Wine consultant Pieter Ferreira

▪ 5ha/3ha (pinot, chard) ▪ 8,800cs own label 100% MCC ▪ PO Box 602 Franschhoek 7690 ▪ info@colmant. co.za ▪ www.colmant.co.za ▪ S 33° 55' 22.4" E 019° 7' 37.3" ▪ enhances.sumptuous.herds ▪ **T** +27 (0)21- **876-4348/+27 (0)83-778-8874**

Commando

Venerable label, first produced during World War I, its military moniker a sign of the times, this now Distell-owned blended brandy adheres to the strict laws ensuring quality production and contains a minimum of 30% potstill, matured in oak barrels minimum three years.

Commando ★★★ A good & versatile mixer (82), vibrant fresh peach & prune flavours, hint of caramel, spirited bite on the finish (43% alcohol). — WB

Compagniesdrift ⓥ

It's a decade since Compagniesdrift opened its doors to Stellenbosch wine producers, offering storage, bottling and labelling services – the list of clients is now impressive; and 5 years since the first of their own wines, made in the Meerlust cellar just down the road. As a black empowerment venture 'creating opportunities for growth and improving lives', it's now fully owned by the Meerlust Workers' Trust.

Cabernet Sauvignon-Merlot ★★★ Moreish **18** (82), has fresh, ripe aromas & flavour, supported by modest oaking & a bit of tannin grip. Ready for tasty drinking. **Chardonnay-Pinot Noir** ★★★ Just a drop of pinot to give a faint blush to **18** (81) dry rosé. Pleasing flavours, balance & texture for unpretentious drinking. **Chardonnay Unwooded** ★★★ Forward fruity aromas on **18** (79), but the acidity a touch out of balance with the modest flavour. — TJ

Location/WO: Stellenbosch ▪ Est 2010 ▪ 1stB 2015 ▪ Tasting by appt only ▪ Sales Mon-Thu 8-4.30 Fri 8-3.30 ▪ Closed all pub hols ▪ Owner(s) Meerlust Workers' Trust ▪ Winemaker(s) Altus Treurnicht (Nov 2018) ▪ 10% red 90% white ▪ PO Box 7121 Stellenbosch 7599 ▪ info@compagniesdrift.com ▪ www.compagniesdrift.com ▪ **T** +27 (0)21-843-3902/913/916

Conceito Vinhos ⓥ

Rita Marques, based on her family estate in Portugal's Douro Valley, has a well-established affection for South Africa and its wines. She's visited regularly since 2011, and made small parcels of own-label wine, including the Syrah listed here, which was made at Boekenhoutskloof. We look forward to more.

★★★★ **Conceito Syrah** ⓥ From Swartland, older oaked, **16** (87) preview was full but not robust, tannins a bit chalky. Youthful then, should be integrating now.— GdB, CR

WO: Swartland ▪ Est/1stB 2005 ▪ Tastings only in Douro, Portugal, by prior arrangement ▪ Owner(s) Conceito Vinhos Lda ▪ Winemaker(s) / CEO Rita Marques ▪ conceito@conceito.com.pt ▪ www.conceito.com.pt ▪ N 41° 02' 23" W 7° 18' 05" ▪ padding.deems.incisive ▪ **T** +351 279 778 059

☐ **Condé** see Stark-Condé Wines

Conradie Penhill Artisanal Wines ⓥ ⌂ ◎ ⓐ

The Conradie family have long been established in Nuy, on the lower reaches of the Langeberg, but it was only in 2004 that CP Conradie reopened the small cellar on the farm to start producing an own range from grapes kept back from the local co-op. A decade or so later, collaboration with Gareth and Kate Penny led to the double name and the introduction of wines off the Penhill estate, as well as the expansion of the winemaking facilities. CP continues to be in charge of vineyards and cellar.

Barrel Selection Reserve range

★★★★ **Pinotage** Smoky oak as yet dominates the plummy fruit on **18** (86) - the American component reinforcing the sweet ripeness, with the emphatic acidity countering it. Juicy, with well managed tannins. 14% alcohol, like Cab. **17** untasted.

Cabernet Sauvignon ★★★★ Appealing berry aromas & flavours on **17** (85), with complementary tobacco notes; the firm tannins well balanced though the acid stands out a little, as does the oaking (12 months, 50% each American/French, 40% new; as for Pinotage). WO W Cape, as next 3.

Conradie Family Vineyards range

★★★★ **Friederich Conradÿ Méthode Cap Classique Brut** Sparkling from chardonnay & 20% pinot noir, **17** ⑧⑦ is first made since **09** ★★★★ ⑧④. Attractive apple-tart aromas, the pinot showing in a hint of berry on the dry but fairly ripe & rich palate. 30 months on lees.

Pinotage-Cabernet Sauvignon ⓥ ★★★ Juicy **18** ⑦⑧ mix pinotage with 40% cab, some oak spice in tail. Few grams sugar for early drinkability. **Sweet Rosaline Perlé Rosé** ★★☆ More pale red than pink in hue, **NV** ⑦⑦ offers the charm of softly textured fruity sweetness, low 9.5% alcohol. Sauvignon blanc plus grapey muscadel & cab. **Chenin Blanc** ⑩⑨ ★★★ Understated, pleasant aromas & flavours on rounded, well-textured **19** ⑧① . House's big acid, counterposed to the just-dry sugar level, giving a sweet-sour finish. **Sauvignon Blanc** ★★★★ Riper, more interesting aromas & flavours on **19** ⑧③ than Penhill version, adding citrus to the tropical-green mix. Plenty of flavour, with a sharp acid-drop sourness on the finish. All Nuy fruit this time. Not tasted: **Red Muscadel Limited Release**.

Penhill range

Shiraz ⑩⑨ ★★★☆ Spicy fruit gleams through the shimmer of oak (half each American & French) on **16** ⑧⑤. Concentrated, sweet ripe fruit, nicely balanced smooth tannins; the acid emphatic as usual here. Big 14.5% alcohol. **Premium Sauvignon Blanc** ★★★ Forward aromas successfully mixing grassy & tropical elements on **19** ⑧② pre-bottling sample. More austerely, tartly green on the palate, with a high acid level more than a match for the 5 g/l of sugar. Not tasted: **Saw Edge Peak**. — TJ

Location/map: Worcester ▪ Map grid reference: C3 ▪ WO: Nuy/Western Cape ▪ Est/1stB 2004 ▪ Tasting, sales & cellar tours Mon-Fri 9–4.30 Sat 9-3; after-hours by appt ▪ Closed Easter Fri/Mon, Ascension day, Dec 25 & Jan 1/2 ▪ Nuy Valley Guest House ▪ Facilities for children ▪ Tour groups ▪ Conferences ▪ Walks/hikes ▪ MTB & 4x4 trails ▪ Conservation area ▪ Annual Nuy Valley Feast (May) ▪ Owner(s) CP Conradie & Gareth Penny ▪ Cellarmaster(s) CP Conradie (Jan 2004) ▪ Winemaker(s) CP Conradie (Jan 2004), with Ronwan Griffiths (Sep 2009) ▪ Viticulturist(s) CP Conradie ▪ 4,500ha/83ha (cab, ptage, red muscadel, shiraz, chard, chenin, cbard, pinot gris, sauv) ▪ 1,840t total 80t/17,000cs own label 84% red 12% white 4% rosé ▪ PO Box 5298 Worcester 6851 ▪ wine@conradiepenhill.com ▪ www.conradiepenhill.com ▪ S 33° 39' 28.0" E 019° 37' 59.6" ▪ ⊠ redevelop.aerosol.wealthiest ▪ **T +27 (0)23-342-7025**

☐ **Conservation Coast** *see* Whalehaven Wines

Constantia Glen   ⓠ ⑪

Blessed with mostly north-east facing vineyards exposed to afternoon sun for full ripeness, this Waibel-family-owned boutique estate on Constantia Nek Pass is thus able to focus on Bordeaux-style blends. Vineyards are all dryland and receive meticulous attention, such as annually replacing vines showing leafroll symptoms and thereby move the average age higher than the current 20 years. More semillon for Constantia Glen Two is being planted on the estate's steepest slopes, needing individually staked vines for stability. Always with an eye on quality, plans include the phasing out of herbicides over the next three years, and annual acquisition of more clay amphoras, due to their success in the production of the Two blend.

★★★★☆ **Constantia Glen Five** ⓐ 5-part Bordeaux-style blend, cab franc led, mainly new oak, French barriques 18 months. Wonderfully complex, black cherries, dried herbs, graphite. Despite vintage ripeness, **15** ⑨④ is designed to age: tightly packed tannins with a core of strength.

★★★★☆ **Constantia Glen Three** ⓐ Blend more than half merlot, with cab franc & cab, giving **16** ⑨③ a red berry character, plushly ripe & round. Violets in the perfume, cocoa spicing, but the main attraction is the fruit, woven around ripe tannins, a hidden power for ageing.

★★★★☆ **Sauvignon Blanc** ⓐ Dryland vineyards, different elevations, staggered harvesting & 5 months on lees all add to bone-dry **19** ⑨③'s admirable complexity & style. Cool-climate minerality, saline acidity, but also winter melon & papaya. Zesty yet satisfyingly round.

★★★★☆ **Constantia Glen Two** ⓐ Vineyard/cellar care, like different provenance barrels, clay amphoras, partial wholebunch, 7 months on lees. **18** ⑨④ sauvignon, 32% semillon, multi-layered, pithy grapefruit & greengage share space with minerality, finishing long & saline. A triumph.— CR

Location/WO: Constantia ▪ Map: Cape Peninsula ▪ Map grid reference: B3 ▪ Est 2000 ▪ 1stB 2005 ▪ Tasting & sales: in season Mon-Sun 11-8; out of season Sun-Fri 11-5 & Sat 11-8 ▪ Tasting fees from R80, waived according to purchase ▪ Closed Dec 25 & Jan 1 ▪ Various platters; gourmet flammkuchen; wine & chocolate pairing;

salads; desserts; soups during winter months ▪ Owner(s) Tumado Investments (Pty) Ltd ▪ Winemaker(s) Justin van Wyk (Dec 2011) ▪ Viticulturist(s) Justin van Wyk (Dec 2011), with Etienne Southey (Sep 2012, farm manager) ▪ 60ha/28.5ha (cabs s/f, malbec, merlot, p verdot, sauv, sem) ▪ 200t/25,000cs own label 65% red 35% white ▪ PO Box 780 Constantia 7848 ▪ wine@constantiaglen.com ▪ www.constantiaglen.com ▪ S 34° 0' 54.51" E 018° 24' 53.64" ▪ ⓶ tags.replace.retires ▪ **T +27 (0)21-795-6100**

Constantia Mist

Owned by property developer John Schooling, this boutique farm is named after 'the ethereal mist that rolls in on a windless morning and flows silently through the sprawling vineyards'. These are certified organic and managed by nearby organic estate Silvermist, which also makes the wine.

★★★★ **Sauvignon Blanc** ⓥ Fresh & zesty, with plenty of lime, grapefruit & passionfruit flavours, **18** ⑧⑧ also has wild herb & chalky mineral notes, ample layers for savouring slowly.— JG

Location/WO: Constantia ▪ Est 2004 ▪ 1stB 2009 ▪ 4-star guest house (self-catering) ▪ Owner(s) Eagles Nest Property Investments (Pty) Ltd ▪ Cellarmaster(s) John Schooling (2009) ▪ Winemaker(s)/viticulturist(s) Gregory Louw (Silvermist Organic Wine Estate) ▪ 6.6ha/2.8ha (sauv) ▪ 5.4t/ha 250cs own label 100% white ▪ Postnet Suite 96 Private Bag X16 Constantia 7848 ▪ johns@stagafrican.com ▪ www.constantiamist.co.za ▪ **T +27 (0)21-794-0904**

Constantia Nectar

This recreation of acclaimed 18th/19th-century Constantia sweet wine is from Huis-in-Bos, a portion of the historic Nova Constantia estate owned since 1950 by Peter Rawbone-Viljoen (brother of Oak Valley's Anthony). Long nurtured in barrel and bottle before release in its black ceramic flagon, vintage '10 is the second, the next being '16 and annually thereafter, amid flourishing interest (this guide's 2019 write-up wooed a Chinese importer!) Pending a bespoke tasting room, the Nectar is 'on show' in Digital Forest Studio, where sons Andrew and Jeremy work with top SA recording talent.

★★★★☆ **Natural Sweet** White muscat de Frontignan, aged 2 years in old oak, presented in show-stopping 375 ml bottle. Glistening amber **10** ⑨① dessert wine offers peach, nectarine, apricot & fynbos honey notes, complex flavours & astutely judged 115 g/l sugar lifted by brisk acidity.— DS

Location/WO: Constantia ▪ Est 2007 ▪ 1stB 2011 ▪ Tasting by appt ▪ Owner(s) Peter Rawbone-Viljoen Trust ▪ Winemaker(s) Teddy Hall (Jan 2009, consultant) ▪ Viticulturist(s) Kevin Watt (Aug 2006, consultant) ▪ 4.5ha/2.5ha (muscat de F) ▪ 9t/1,600cs own label 100% natural sweet ▪ Huis-in-Bos, Klein Constantia Rd, Constantia 7806 ▪ info@constantianectar.co.za ▪ www.constantianectar.co.za ▪ **T +27 (0)21-794-3382**

Constantia Royale

This family-owned winery in Constantia Valley is small but growing. A new sauvignon-semillon blend, Don's Reserve, after Don Rowand, husband of owner Lynn Rowand, has joined the Sauvignon Blanc. And the venture has opened a new tasting room in a highly unusual if not unique setting - a tunnel, ingeniously renovated to allow the farm tractor easy access to both the home estate, Nova Zonnestraal, and its sibling, Zonnestraal, on the other side of the M3 expressway.

★★★★ **Sauvignon Blanc** Sauvignon fleshed out by 17% silky semillon, with tiny oaked portion adding spice in **19** ⑧⑥. Pure if undramatic herbaceous, citrus flavours currently curtailed by edgy acid finish. Short ageing should see usual elegant balance restored.

★★★★ **Don's Reserve** ⑭ⓝⒺⓦ Structured, linear sauvignon-based blend. **19** ⑧⑨ full of energy, bone-dry yet not harsh, 12% semillon polishes the edges, introduces elegant & persistent cool-climate lemongrass flavours. 44% old oak. Good potential.— AL

Location/WO: Constantia ▪ Map: Cape Peninsula ▪ Map grid reference: B3 ▪ Est 1997 ▪ 1stB 2015 ▪ Tasting by appt only ▪ Closed all pub hols ▪ Owner(s) Lynn Marais Rowand ▪ Cellarmaster(s) Danna de Jongh (Jan 2018, consultant) ▪ Winemaker(s) Roger Burton (Oct 2013, consultant) ▪ Viticulturist(s) Joseph van Wyk Contractors (Nov 2013) ▪ 16ha/7.5ha (sauv, sem) ▪ 35t/3,750cs own label 100% white ▪ Suite 193 Private Bag X16 Constantia 7848 ▪ wine@constantiaroyale.co.za ▪ www.constantiaroyale.co.za ▪ S 34° 0' 18.00" E 018° 26' 60.00" ▪ ⓶ postgraduate.radiology.trombone ▪ **T +27 (0)21-794-4841**

Constantia Uitsig

Part of Simon van der Stel's vast Constantia estate in the late 1600s, this property has become a popular destination in recent years thanks to its restaurant, heritage market, bike park and, of course, wines, now made by Danna de Jongh. '2019 was my first solo harvest and the second in our newly built, state-of-the-art winery,' reports the Geisenheim University graduate. Looking ahead, she's excited about 2016 chardonnay plantings coming into production, as this will make it possible to produce the Reserve, Unwooded and MCC every year instead of alternating. They've released a second red wine, a syrah under the Red Horizon label, the flagship Bordeaux blend reverting to its original name, Constantia Red.

★★★★☆ **Constantia Red** ⓐ Was 'Red Horizon', cab-led **15** ⑨③ Bordeaux blend with 33% merlot, 15% cab franc is smooth, savoury, rich yet restrained. Fuller-bodied than **14** ★★★★ ⑧⑨, with layers of black cherry & plum fruit, hints of tobacco & spice from 20 months in 70% new oak.

★★★★ **Chardonnay Reserve** After 9 months on lees in French oak (10% new), **18** ⑧⑨ is a svelte, creamy mouthful, hints of butterscotch & toasted hazelnut complementing fresh citrus & melon fruit, lemon peel edge. This currently alternates with unwooded version (see intro), thus no **17**.

★★★★☆ **Sauvignon Blanc** ⊘ Vibrant **18** ⑨① packed with zesty citrus, tangerine & lime, freshly acidic but nicely rounded. Slight struck match note upfront & an almost saline mineral impression on the finish.

★★★★☆ **Semillon** Lanolin-smooth after 8 months in older 600L French oak, no malo or bâtonnage, **17** ⑨② fresher than **16** ★★★★ ⑧⑨, with thatch on the nose as well as bright, fresh tangerine & lime, which carry through to the palate. Lovely balance.

★★★★ **Natura Vista** Bordeaux white **17** ★★★★☆ ⑨⓪ combines (older) barrel-fermented semillon with 30% unoaked sauvignon to add lime & Granny Smith apple freshness to rich honeyed texture. Seamless after 8 months in older oak, also more complex than **16** ⑧⑧, with pinch of white pepper on finish.

★★★★ **Méthode Cap Classique** Brut sparkling from chardonnay, **16** ⑧⑨ balanced & elegant, with zippy green apple freshness rounded off by almond & lemon cream notes/texture (36 months on lees, 10% oaked portion).

★★★★ **Red Muscat d'Alexandrie** Though fresher, less sweet than floral, peach & grape-must jam aromas suggest, latest fortified **NV** ⑧⑦ blend (3 vintages) would benefit from cheese as savoury foil to 96.5 g/l sugar. 375 ml.

Not tasted: **Red Horizon**. Occasional release: **Chardonnay Unwooded**. — JG

Location/WO: Constantia ▪ Map: Cape Peninsula ▪ Map grid reference: B3 ▪ Est 1980 ▪ 1stB 1988 ▪ Tastings at the Heritage Market Tue–Sun 10–6; sales Tue–Sun 10–6 ▪ Closed Good Fri, Dec 25/26 & Jan 1 ▪ Fee R60pp/4 wines; full-range tasting by appt ▪ Artisanal cheese & charcuterie platters R225 ▪ Hanepoot grapes sold annually ▪ Block House Kitchen ▪ Chris Nixon Cycling Academy ▪ Heritage Market: Aegir Beer, Alexander Avery Fine Chocolates, Constantia Uitsig Wine Shop, Kristen's Kick-Ass Ice Cream, Nest Deli, Sushi Box ▪ Aegir Project Brewery open Mon–Sun 12–8 at the Heritage Market; production & tap room in Noordhoek ▪ Owner(s) Constantia Uitsig Holdings (Pty) Ltd ▪ Winemaker(s)/viticulturist(s) Danna de Jongh (Aug 2018) ▪ 60ha/20ha (cabs s/f, shiraz, chard, muscat d'F, sauv, sem) ▪ 100t/20,000cs own label 10% red 90% white ▪ PO Box 32 Constantia 7848 ▪ info@uitsig.co.za ▪ www.uitsig.co.za ▪ S 34° 2' 51.9" E 018° 25' 27.5" ▪ ⓦ tiles. entering.snoot ▪ **T** +27 (0)21-794-6500

☐ **Constitution Road** *see* Robertson Winery
☐ **Contours Collection** *see* Swartland Winery
☐ **Cooperative** *see* Bosman Family Vineyards

Copeland Spirits

James Copeland, electronic musician, DJ and latterly innovative small-scale distiller, focuses on rum and gin at his 'laboratory' on Cape Town's Peninsula, but he's also produced a pisco which has 'garnered quite a reputation already in the craft mixology scene' despite a delayed launch due to licensing issues, now resolved. Aromatic grape varieties from winemaker brother Matthew at Vondeling in Voor Paardeberg were cold-fermented on their skins, half then single-distilled 'for character and body', the rest double-distilled 'for finesse and aroma'. Watch for it at pop-up bars at events and locations around Cape Town and Johannesburg.

★★★★ **Pisco** ⓦ Delightfully smooth & fragrant brandy ⑧⑨, notes of passionfruit, melon, wax & almonds. Juice & skins of same grapes as Vondeling Babiana (chenin, chardonnay, viognier, grenache blanc), 50/50 single/double distilled, rested year in tank (not oak) for fruit purity. 43% alcohol.— WB

Location: Cape Town ▪ Est/1stB 2018 ▪ Closed to public ▪ Owner(s) James Copeland ▪ Cellarmaster/distiller James Copeland (Jan 2018) ▪ Postnet Suite 416 Private Bag X4 Sun Valley Cape Town 7985 ▪ james@copelandrum.com ▪ www.copelandrum.com ▪ **T +27 (0)76-481-9302**

- ☐ **Copper Collection** *see* Oneiric Wines
- ☐ **Coral Reef** *see* Wineways Marketing
- ☐ **Costa del Swart** *see* The Wine Thief
- ☐ **Coutelier** *see* Domaine Coutelier
- ☐ **Covenant** *see* Croydon Vineyard Residential Estate
- ☐ **Cranefields Wine** *See Editor's Note*

Craven Wines ⓦ

The husband-and-wife Cravens (Australian Mick and local Jeanine) focus on early picking of single-vineyard, single-variety Stellenbosch sites, freshness being a central aim for their wines, last tasted some years ago and noted for their light, interesting and delightful drinkability. Bunch- and skin-ferment on white grapes aids in giving the textural and savoury characters they seek.

Location: Stellenbosch ▪ Est 2013 ▪ 1stB 2014 ▪ Tasting & sales by appt only ▪ Owner(s) Jeanine & Mick Craven ▪ Winemaker(s) Jeanine & Mick Craven (Jan 2013) ▪ 38t own label 60% red 40% white ▪ PO Box 972 Somerset Mall 7137 ▪ www.cravenwines.com ▪ **T +27 (0)72-701-2723**

Creation Wines ⓦ ⑪ ⓐ ⓑ

Wine, food, art, nature and technology merge at this Hemel-en-Aarde farm 'created' from virgin land by Swiss-born vini-viti man Jean-Claude (JC) Martin and wife Carolyn (of the respected SA winegrowing Finlayson family). They collaborate with geologists and soil scientists in ongoing expansion of their eclectic varietal mix. Joining the area's first chenin (debuting last edition) is this year's three newcomers: interesting blends of grenache, viognier and roussanne and a Reserve Syrah. Consultation with tech gurus and international universities informs sophisticated trade and direct-to-consumer marketing and social media activities, while innovations to their ever-changing wine-and-food pairings (sometimes tied in with top art exhibits) attract the trendy and discerning (and multiple global wine tourism accolades).

Premium range

★★★★☆ **Sumac Grenache** ⓐ Sumptuous & rich, with fragrant rose, piquant lemon pip, black plum, African spice & black olive tapenade aromas & flavours. **17** ⑨③'s supple frame & savoury tone make a perfect food partner. 14 months in older barrels underpin the elegant moreishness.

★★★★ **Merlot** Silky chocolate-dipped black cherry, poached plum & ample spicy vanilla oak seduce the senses in **17** ⑧⑨. Full, rounded, with a dusty tannin conclusion.

★★★★☆ **Reserve Merlot** ⓦ Liqueur-like texture on **16** ⑨④ palate, with velvet tannins, good balance & smoky grip from 25% new oak. Will age well & deepen the complex flavour array, including spice cake, cherry, violet, dark chocolate & roasted hazelnut.

★★★★☆ **Emma Pinot Noir** ⓐ Only 3 barrels selected for opulent & expressive yet focused **18** ⑨④. Great complexity of ripe black cherry, plum & subtle spice, fabulous tannin structure & integrated 10 months oaking, 40% new. Good balance & poise. Wild fermented, 30% wholebunch.

★★★★☆ **Pinot Noir** ⊘ The 'junior' pinot is fragrant, playful & balanced in **18** ⑨②, offers bright raspberry, red plum, herbs & sprinkling of savoury spice from 10 months in 25% new oak. A well-structured & worthy wine, with delicious crunchy farewell.

★★★★☆ **Reserve Pinot Noir** ⊘ ⓐ Vineyard-selected **18** ⑨③ has wonderful brightness & lift, appealing pomegranate & brambleberry fruit mingling with earthy & peppery spice. Harmonious, with smooth tannin structure from 12 months in 35% new barrels.

★★★★☆ The Art of Pinot Noir ⓐ A further selection - in the cellar - & savoury, assertive tannin structure from 60% new oak for 12 months produce this fine pinnacle wine. **18** ⑨④ polished earthy red & black fruit, shows great concentration. Brooding & opulent yet has purity & precision, & structure to last.

★★★★☆ Reserve Syrah ⓝⓔⓦ Naturally fermented **17** ⑨③ is bold & powerful, has well-expressed varietal character - deep black fruit, hedgerow berries, undergrowth, cured meat, spice & a waft of white pepper. Mouthfilling, with savoury long finish. 30% wholebunch, 25% new oak for 18 months.

★★★★ Merlot-Cabernet Sauvignon-Petit Verdot Bordeaux blends a rarity in Hemel-en-Aarde. **17** ⑧⑨ packs a punch with dark blueberry & plum fruit, dense & firmly structured, vanilla-tinged tannin frame (14 months in 25% new oak). Like previous, needs time to unfurl.

★★★★ Syrah-Grenache ⓐ Heady, colourful & exciting as a spice market, **17** ★★★★☆ ⑨① impresses with exotic scents, sweet violets, brambles & hedgerow fruit in harmony with a firm yet supple tannin structure. Interesting to see how it develops. **16** ⑧⑨ more subdued.

★★★★ Grenache Noir-Viognier ⓝⓔⓦ Alluring soft pink rosé a satisfying mouthful of crunchy ripe red berries & lively earthy spice, subtle floral lift to dry finish. Try **19** ⑧⑧ with a summer seafood salad. Cape South Coast WO.

★★★★☆ Chardonnay Most approachable of the chardonnay siblings. Expressive & vibrant **18** ⑨⓪ shows lemon meringue pie, zesty citrus & tantalising vanilla oak from barrel-ferment/10 months in 30% new wood.

★★★★☆ Reserve Chardonnay ⓐ From a single parcel, **18** ⑨③ delights with baked apple, warm cinnamon, lemon, grapefruit zest, wet stone minerality & vanilla oak flavours (25% new barrels) on broad & sumptuous palate. Made to last.

★★★★☆ The Art of Chardonnay ⓐ Specific site within a single vineyard for this standout bottling. Reserved & regal **18** ⑨④ shows great complexity, delivers layer upon layer of flavour & structure - vanilla & almond biscuit, mango lassi & lemon verbena just some of the nuances. Still tight-wound after barrel ferment in 60% new oak with fortnightly bâtonnage.

★★★★☆ Cool Climate Chenin Blanc ⓐ As name implies, **18** ⑨② a svelte expression of the variety, with crunchy, crisp green apple, sprinkling of spice & poached quince mingling with creaminess from ferment/7 months in old oak, with regular lees stirring.

★★★★ Sauvignon Blanc 6 clones used for **19** ⑧⑦, resulting in array of gooseberry, nettle, pineapple & citrus flavours. Palate is juicy, with a salty lemon tang to finish. More generous than last-tasted **17** ★★★★ ⑧⑤. Cape South Coast WO, as next 2.

★★★★☆ Viognier ⊘ Unfettered by oak, **19** ⑨⓪ brims with stonefruit brightness & peach blossom fragrance on a slatey mineral backbone. Beautifully balanced, curves in all in the right places. Complex, rounded, made for subtly spicy fare. **18** untasted.

★★★★☆ Roussanne-Viognier ⓝⓔⓦ Characterful & bright-fruited **18** ⑨⓪, forthcoming stonefruit, baked pear, crushed almond & floral charm. Palate is voluptuous, has gentle patina of vanilla from mostly older oak, 7 months, & a stony minerality to balance it. 80/20 blend.

★★★★ Sauvignon Blanc-Semillon Immediate herbaceous notes of blackcurrant, gooseberry, beeswax & almond nuttiness, stony mineral finish. **18** ⑧⑨ is a 80/20 blend, 50% of sauvignon & all semillon barrel fermented.— WB

Location: Hermanus ▪ Map: Walker Bay & Bot River ▪ Map grid reference: C4 ▪ WO: Walker Bay/Cape South Coast ▪ Est 2002 ▪ 1stB 2006 ▪ Tasting, sales & cellar tours daily 10-5 ▪ Closed Dec 25 & Jan 1 ▪ The Story of Creation pairing; small plate pairing; brunch pairing; wine & chocolate pairing; tea pairing; charcuterie & cheese pairing; kiddies pairing; beverages & snack menu ▪ Owner(s) Jean-Claude & Carolyn Martin, Jonathan Drake ▪ Cellarmaster(s) Jean-Claude Martin (Jan 2006) ▪ Winemaker(s) Jean-Claude Martin (Jan 2006), with Gerhard Smith (Dec 2017) ▪ Viticulturist(s) Jean-Claude Martin & Peter Davison (consultant), advised by Johan Pienaar (all 2002) ▪ 50ha (cab, grenache, merlot, p verdot, pinot, shiraz, chard, chenin, rouss, sauv, sem, viog) ▪ 350t/50,000cs own label 65% red 35% white ▪ EnviroWines, IPW ▪ PO Box 1772 Hermanus 7200 ▪ info@creationwines.com ▪ www.creationwines.com ▪ S 34° 19' 51.90" E 019° 19' 35.53" ▪ ⓐⓘ rectifying.awaiting.aware ▪ **T +27 (0)28-212-1107**

☐ **Creative Block** *see* Spier

☐ **Credo** *see* Stellenbosch Vineyards
☐ **Cronier Wines** *See Editor's Note*

Croydon Vineyard Residential Estate ⓠ ⓐ ⓑ ⓒ

It's all about lifestyle at Croydon, one of the first residential estates to spring up in the Helderberg area in the early 2000s. Cape vernacular elements extend to the on-site vineyards, olives groves and cellar, where winemaker (and fellow resident) Rikus Neethling of Bizoe Wines vinifies the estate's and brought-in fruit, even getting to experiment with egg-shaped vessels for some wines.

Covenant range

★★★★ **Cabernet Sauvignon** Has a dab (5%) of malbec but **18** ⑧⑥ remains rounded, with ripe fruitcake & spice appeal. Firm, earthy cocoa frame nods to older oak used in maturation, 18 months.

★★★★ **Shiraz** Gentle violet perfume & black fruit on light **18** ★★★☆ ⑧③, which also shows firm grip of dry oak, shy spicy notes too. **17** ⑧⑥ more generous.

★★★★ **Chenin Blanc** Improving on **17** ★★★☆ ⑧④ in its richness & length, **18** ⑧⑧ shows quince & honeyed pear vivacity balancing the slippery, creamy texture from 9-month ferment & ageing in concrete 'egg'.

★★★★ **Méthode Cap Classique Brut** Improved **17** ⑧⑧ bubbly has fresh green-apple tang, chalky texture & baked sourdough. Bright & lively, with crisp acidity, breadth from 24 months on lees to balance. Franschhoek fruit, like **16** ★★★ ⑧⓪.

Merlot ★★★☆ Dry spicy oak vies with blue & black berry fruit on ripe, easy **18** ⑧⑤. Pleasantly soft but with tannin squeeze from 18 months in older French barrels. **Pinotage** ⓠ ★★★★ Deep, inky blue & black fruit on compact **17** ⑧③. Sturdy yet succulent, with bright spice lift. Improves on previous. **Sauvignon Blanc** ★★★☆ Pungent grass & white pepper aromas on vivid **18** ⑧⑤, which ups the quality on previous. Lemon zip courtesy of in-balance 7 g/l acidity. Light & refreshing.

Title Deed range

Cape Blend ★★★ Shiraz (35%) leads 5-way blend with pinotage in **18** ⑧②. Spicy, succulent, with soft fruitcake appeal & light body. **Rosé** ★★★★ Pleasing step up for dry pink, which is all-pinotage in **19** ⑧④ (previous had cab franc). Light, bright strawberry tones & juicy charm. **Chenin Blanc** ⓠ ★★★ Nectarine & pithy citrus mingle with lees breadth on light, juicy **18** ⑧⓪. Ideal summer sipper.

Croydon range

Not tasted: **Portion 20**. — FM

Location: Stellenbosch ▪ Map: Helderberg ▪ Map grid reference: A3 ▪ WO: Stellenbosch/Western Cape ▪ Est/1stB 2004 ▪ Tasting & sales Mon-Fri 8-5 ▪ Closed all pub hols ▪ Cellar tours by appt ▪ Facilities for children ▪ Tour groups ▪ Conferences ▪ Events ▪ Weddings ▪ Owner(s) Croydon Vineyard Estate ▪ Winemaker(s) Rikus Neethling (consultant), with Jannie Alexander ▪ Vineyard manager Ben van Zyl ▪ 8ha (cabs s/f, malbec, merlot, ptage, shiraz, chenin) ▪ 65t/4,000cs own label 95% red 5% white ▪ Unit 1 Croydon Vineyard Estate Somerset West 7130 ▪ finance@croydon-estate.co.za ▪ www.croydon-vineyards.com ▪ S 34° 2' 23.3" E 018° 45' 5.5" ▪ 🖵 lakefront.bowstring.marry ▪ T +27 (0)21-843-3610

☐ **Crunch** *see* Elgin Ridge

Crystallum

Brothers Peter-Allan and Andrew Finlayson are third-generation wine producers in a family known for its pioneering spirit. Like their father Peter (of Bouchard Finlayson), they focus on chardonnay and pinot noir, from sites across Hemel-en-Aarde and cool areas in the Overberg. A recent purchase of an 8-ha property beyond Hemel-en-Aarde Ridge was made to secure grape supply. Peter-Allan recalls '18 as 'pretty challenging': 'the vines really struggled to maintain their canopies leading up to harvest. In the cellar, I don't think I've ever agonised so much about barrel selections.' His vinification is at Gabriëlskloof, where he is winemaker. The birth of his and wife Nicolene's son, Theodore, has curtailed travel, but a trip to Japan, 'where Crystallum is doing very well,' last year was timed to coincide with the Rugby World Cup, 'of course!'

★★★★☆ **Bona Fide Pinot Noir** ⓐ Deep scents & great breadth of flavour reflect lowest, warmest Hemel-en-Aarde Valley origin. **18** ⑨④ has gentle richness, deliciousness & poised freshness, the profile of overall elegance. 60% bunch pressed, 20% new French barriques.

★★★★☆ **Cuvée Cinéma Pinot Noir** From Hemel-en-Aarde Ridge, **18** ⑭ pinot at its alluring, scented best; exotic note in its dark cherry & spice. Great depth of flavour, silky texture supported by complementary structure, freshness. Equal parts bunch & wholeberry pressed, 25% new oak.

★★★★☆ **Mabalel Pinot Noir** Transparent, pure, with tension from high-altitude Elandskloof origin. **18** ★★★★★ ⑮ slow to unfold from initial intense freshness; succulent black & red cherry supported by gentle yet effective tannins. Both elegance & substance. 10% wholebunch, vs just 5% for **17** ⑫, 20% new oak.

★★★★☆ **Peter Max Pinot Noir** Bright-fruited, fresh & firmly built, **18** ⑭ has grape tannins a little edgy, the fruit, with hint of mint, very primary. Deserving time to iron out awkward youth, it will offer much easygoing pleasure. 50% wholebunch. Ex 5 vineyards, 1 in Elandskloof.

★★★★☆ **Clay Shales Chardonnay** Broader, richer of the chards, **18** ⑬ no less refined in its limy, hazelnut complexity, subtle oaking. Cool, easy flow to suppleness; long finish. Already approachable, cellaring should give rewards. Hemel-en-Aarde Ridge vineyard. Bunch-pressed, fermented/10 months foudre.

★★★★☆ **The Agnes Chardonnay** Purity, freshness define **18** ⑫. Lighter, less intense than **17** ⑭ but perfectly showcases zesty citrus, oatmeal features. Needs a while for full textural richness to evolve; probably not as long-lived as **17** ⑭. Wholebunch, natural ferment/ageing 225 & 500L oak, 10% new.

Not tasted: **Whole Bunch Pinot Noir.** — AL

Location: Bot River ■ WO: Western Cape/Hemel-en-Aarde Ridge/Overberg/Hemel-en-Aarde Valley ■ Est 2006 ■ 1stB 2007 ■ Closed to public ■ Owner(s) Crystallum Coastal Vineyards (Pty) Ltd ■ Winemaker(s) Peter-Allan Finlayson (2006) ■ 60t/7,000cs own label 60% red 40% white ■ PO Box 857 Hermanus 7200 ■ info@crystallumwines.com ■ www.crystallumwines.com

---

☐ **Culemborg** *see* DGB (Pty) Ltd
☐ **Culinaria Collection** *see* Leopard's Leap Family Vineyards
☐ **Cutters Cove** *see* Robert Stanford Estate

Dâbar

Jannie Gutter's Vierfontein estate near Napier is just 30 minutes from the ocean, referenced by the anchor on the front-label. The rare endemic Agulhas Long-Billed Lark alongside is resident on the farm, also home to a cornucopia of flowers and fruit, with just 25 hectares under vine. Lourens van der Westhuizen (Arendsig) now vinifies the Chardonnay and Shiraz in Robertson, while Rianie Strydom (Strydom Family) continues to craft the MCC and Sauvignon Blanc in Stellenbosch; all the wines reflect their maritime origin.

★★★★ **Shiraz** Cool-climate clarity runs through **18** ⑧⑦, from heady white spice, floral & cinnamon fragrance, through silky flesh to finely honed, fresh tannins. Perhaps not the most complex, but so drinkable, delicious. Year older oak. No **17**, **16** sold out untasted.

Pinot Noir ★★★★ Enjoys aromatic breadth, concentration of forest floor, dark cherry flavours in its supple feel; **16** ⑧⑤ notable astringency needs time to round, reveal extent of sweet-fruited conclusion. French oak, 25% new. **Chardonnay** ★★★★ Pickled lime, butter & spice in expressive aromatic medley on **18** ⑧⑤. Medium body, ripe flavours lifted, extended by balanced natural freshness, gram/two residual sugar. Spontaneous ferment/ageing in oak, none new. **Sauvignon Blanc** ★★★★ Refreshing, cool feel on zesty **18** ⑧③, with pure, unshowy passionfruit flavours, fruity dry conclusion. **Cuvée Brut** ★★★ Easygoing méthode cap classique bubbly, **14** ⑧⓪ brief citrus, toasty notes, energetic fine mousse. From chardonnay & 40% pinot noir, old-oak fermented/aged, 4 years on lees. — AL

Location/WO: Napier ■ 1stB 2010 ■ Closed to public ■ Owner(s) Jannie Gutter ■ Winemaker(s) Rianie Strydom (Strydom Family Wine) & Lourens van der Westhuizen (Arendsig Handcrafted Wines) ■ Viticulturist(s) Conrad Schutte (consultant) ■ 25ha (pinot, shiraz, chard, sauv) ■ 50% red 50% white ■ rani@atwine.co.za ■ **T +27 (0)84-506-8024**

☐ **Da Capo Vineyards** *see* Idiom Collection

Dagbreek

Last edition we noted that 3rd-generation Peet Smith's boutique winery on the Breede River near Rawsonville was quietly gaining a following with a portfolio of local rarities, mostly black grapes from

Portugal and Italy, and latterly French variety carmenère. New vintages of these exciting wines unfortunately hadn't been released at press time. The delicious sweet muscadel listed here is still available, however.

Family Editions

★★★★ **Red Muscadel** ⊘ Fruitcake, orange peel & savoury spice on enticing **16** ⑧⑧ fortified dessert. Unctuous raisin & sultana richness, sweetness ably balanced by lively acidity.— HC

Location: Rawsonville ▪ Map/WO: Breedekloof ▪ Map grid reference: C5 ▪ Est/1stB 2009 ▪ Tasting, sales & cellar tours Mon-Sat by appt ▪ Closed all pub hols ▪ BYO picnic ▪ Walking/hiking trails ▪ Owner(s) Peet Smith ▪ Cellarmaster(s)/winemaker(s) Peet Smith (2009) ▪ Viticulturist(s) Leon Dippenaar (2009, consultant) ▪ 108ha/48ha under vine ▪ 7t/1,000cs own label 70% red 30% white ▪ WIETA ▪ PO Box 237 Rawsonville 6845 ▪ dagbreek@compnet.co.za ▪ www.dagbreek.co.za ▪ S 33° 39' 56.20" E 019° 18' 26.99" ▪ ◍ undaunted. lambing.twig ▪ **T +27 (0)82-820-2256**

DA Hanekom Familie Wyne ⊘

Andri Hanekom finds time outside his job as cellarmaster and viticulturist at Durbanville's Bloemendal Estate to winkle out special parcels of grapes his and wife Yvette's own label, which will soon include a malbec named Langrug. Vinification and tasting are at Bloemendal, and the wines are available in the Cape Town and Johannesburg trade.

★★★★ **Putfontein** Ample red fruit on **16** ⑧⑥ Bottelary pinotage vies with smoky sheen & light spice tinge. Tannins are a touch muscular & chunky after 22 months in older French oak. Retasted, as Witteberg.

★★★★ **Klipmuur** (ⓃⒺⓦ) Durbanville sauvignon shows vibrancy & lemon verbena appeal in **18** ⑧⑥. Zesty freshness & broad, structured palate from ferment/11 months in older French small-oak. Poised & long.

Witteberg ★★★★ Lively acidity on **17** ⑧⑤ chenin from Paarl. Creamy cashew oak shades the subtle spicy pear & peach fruit. Structured & bold from 10 months in older French barrique. — FM

Location: Durbanville ▪ Map: Durbanville, Philadelphia & Darling ▪ Map grid reference: C7 ▪ WO: Paarl/Stellenbosch/Durbanville ▪ Est/1stB 2016 ▪ Tasting by appt only ▪ Closed all pub hols ▪ Owner(s) Andri & Yvette Hanekom ▪ Cellarmaster(s) Andri Hanekom (Jan 2016) ▪ 4t/580cs own label 50% red 50% white ▪ WIETA ▪ andri@dahfamiliewyne.com ▪ www.dahfamiliewyne.com ▪ S 33° 50' 22.1" E 018° 36' 1.4" ▪ **T +27 (0)66-189-3371**

Dainty Bess ⊘

Jane Ferreira-Eedes' MCC sparkling is 100% pinot noir, some from a tiny parcel in Wellington planted by her father in the 1990s. The wine's popularity has required searching for grapes further afield, in Robertson and the far reaches of the Overberg which, she says, will combine the qualities of fruit grown in both warm and cool climates. The '16, with 36 months on the lees, wasn't ready for tasting.

★★★★ **Pinot Noir Méthode Cap Classique** ⊘ Delectable dry sparkler, dainty in name, appearance & taste: ballerina pink **15** ⑧⑧, gentle strawberry, cherry & spice, soft creamy mousse from 34 months on lees. Elgin & Wellington fruit.— WB

Location: Cape Town ▪ WO: Western Cape ▪ Est/1stB 2016 ▪ Tasting by appt only ▪ Owner(s) Jane Ferreira-Eedes ▪ Winemaker(s) Corné Marais (consultant) ▪ 850kg from Klein Optenhorst in Wellington, with 2t additional fruit from Shannon Vineyards in Elgin ▪ 100% MCC ▪ 44 Liesbeek Rd, Rosebank, Cape Town 7700 ▪ daintybesswine@gmail.com ▪ www.daintybess.co.za ▪ **T +27 (0)83-324-6855**

Dalla Cia Wine & Spirit Company ⊘ 🍴 ♿

Things are ticking over nicely at this Italianate family-owned winecrafting and distilling business based in Stellenbosch's trendy Bosman's Crossing. The spirit range is complete, after some bureaucratic delays over the release of their luxury potstill brandy, and company owner George Dalla Cia has become a member of the SA Brandy Foundation, adding a milestone to a journey begun by his distiller grandfather Vittorio back in Friuli in the 1920s. Their ever-popular Pane E Vino Food & Wine Bar continues to operate as an unofficial canteen for the wine industry, while the tasting area there offers a new range of custom chocolates 'corrected' with the fine house grappa.

Dalla Cia Wine range

★★★★ **Classico Cabernet Sauvignon** ⓖ Rich & ripe **16** ★★★★☆ ⑨⓪ loses splash petit verdot of **15** ⑧⑦, now 100% cab showing advertised classic flavours of blackcurrant, cedar & pleasing spice notes of cinnamon & aniseed. Well-integrated, chewy tannins (helped by 70% new oak) & light, elegant finish.

★★★★ **Pinot Noir** Spicy **17** ★★★☆ ⑧⑤ reflects 100% new French oak, which slightly dominates the red fruit mid-2019. Wet leaves & fresh herbs, plus good length at finish suggest can age, though less well-knit in youth than last-tasted **15** ⑧⑦.

★★★★☆ **Giorgio** ⓖ Cabernet with merlot & petit verdot, Bordeaux blend **15** ⑨③ is weighty & serious. Velvety black-fruit aromas/flavours of cherry, currant, perfume & polish wrapped in silky tannins. Handles hefty alcohol (15%) & 80% new oak with ease, only going to improve over next decade. No **14**.

★★★★☆ **Teano** 🍇 French & Italian grapes meet in **17** ⑨④ blend. Flavour components - strawberries, warm spice, blackcurrant, fresh herbs, savoury notes - assimilate 100% new oak effortlessly. Flavours multiply & evolve through to lengthy finish. Last tasted was **14** ⑨②. Also in magnum. WO W Cape.

★★★★ **Chardonnay** Delicately balanced **18** ⑧⑨ mainly unwooded - just 12% oak adds creamy & ginger biscuit notes to fresh peach fruit. Satisfying richness mid-palate from 6 months on lees. **17** untasted.

★★★★ **Sauvignon Blanc** Fresh & zesty **19** ⑧⑦ steps up on **18** ★★★☆ ⑧③ with tropical-fruit cocktail balancing greener nuances. Newly bottled, already harmonious & acidity integrated. Will please widely.

Dalla Cia Husk Spirit range

★★★★★ **10 Year Old Celebration Cabernet Sauvignon-Merlot** ⓖ Limited release marks distillery's 10th anniversary. Rich, with a velvet texture, delightfully mellow. Long-lasting sipper ⑨⑤ to be savoured. 500 ml, stylishly packaged.

★★★★ **Cabernet Sauvignon-Merlot Premium Selection** ⓖ Slight straw tinge to this more refined, less aggressive Premium (lightly barrelled) version ⑧⑦ of the standard husk spirit from these varieties. Supple, gently unctuous palate, lingering finish.

★★★★ **Pinot Noir-Chardonnay** ⓖ Fresh aromas of fruit & nuts; some delicacy, focus & refinement evident on a delightfully textured, smooth & balanced spirit ⑧⑦.

★★★★ **Single Cultivar Organic Merlot** ⓖ ⊘ High-toned note gives magnificent lift to red berry & floral aromas; sweet spice & some citrus buoy spirity finish (43% alcohol) of this monovarietal bottling ⑧⑦. Smooth & elegant.

Cabernet Sauvignon-Merlot ⓖ ★★★☆ Robust aromas & flavours, husk-y, quiet berry hint. This unmatured bottling ⑧④ smooth enough, but with some rusticity. Not tasted: **Limited Edition Pinot Noir**.

Brandy range

★★★★ **H&G Fine & Rare Potstill Brandy** ⓖ Evocatively packaged potstill ⑧⑥ aged 9 years. Rich & rounded, with waxy plum & orchard fruit flavours, roasted nuts all in harmony with supportive oak. Smooth & long. From semillon & shiraz.— CM, WB

Location/map: Stellenbosch ▪ Map grid reference: E5 ▪ WO: Stellenbosch/Western Cape ▪ Est 2004 ▪ Tasting, sales & traditional Italian meals at Pane E Vino Food & Wine Bar, Mon-Fri 10-6 Sat 10-5 ▪ Grappa Distillery by appt Mon-Fri 10-4 ▪ Owner(s) George Dalla Cia ▪ Winemaker(s) Giorgio Dalla Cia ▪ 18,000cs ▪ 7A Lower Dorp Str Bosman's Crossing Stellenbosch 7600 ▪ info@dallacia.com ▪ www.dallacia.com ▪ S 33° 56' 25.8" E018° 50' 50.1" ▪ 🗺 agents.tigers.tripped ▪ **T +27 (0)21-888-4120**

Damarakloof ⓠ ⌂ ◎

'Investing in people' has been the focus at this boutique Paarl family farm, once a racetrack, deemed too gravelly for cultivation, with a rolling programme of education for staff in all areas, from vineyards to hospitality. They've seen the success already, manager Jürgen Sutherland says, with an exponential increase in sales of the wines, made since 2006 by consultant Carla Pauw.

Racetrack range

★★★★ **Chenin Blanc** ⊘ From 60 year old bushvines. **15** ★★★ ⑧① shaded by toffee & vanilla, but step-up **16** ⑧⑨ has subtle & supportive oak smoothly complementing the vibrant citrus & stonefruit, acidity energising the body to utterly delicious effect.

Not tasted: **Regale**. — CM

Location/map/WO: Paarl ▪ Map grid reference: A7 ▪ Est/1stB 2006 ▪ Tasting, sales & function venue by appt ▪ Guest accommodation ▪ Museum ▪ Collectable shop ▪ Land Rover & Jaguar experience ▪ Craft beer ▪ Owner(s) Agnes de Vos ▪ Winemaker(s) Carla Pauw (Jan 2006) ▪ Farm manager Jürgen Sutherland ▪ 19ha (cabs s/f, merlot, chenin) ▪ 10t/1,300cs own label 50% red 50% white ▪ PO Box 38 Elsenburg 7607 ▪ jurgen. damarakloof@gmail.com ▪ www.damarakloof.co.za ▪ S 33° 48' 41.79" E 018° 47' 21.19" ▪ 🖬 beckoning. tectonic.retinal ▪ **T +27 (0)21-884-4304**

Damascene

David Curl, Canadian businessman and former owner of Bordeaux chateau Gaby, latterly based on Elgin farm Habibi (also home of separately listed Moya Meaker), partners with ex-Boekenhoutskloof winemaker Jean Smit on this 'epiphanic' project. The goal is to show the diversity of SA terroir in wines with 'vibrancy, purity, elegance and sense of place', made as naturally as possible. They seek out mostly high-altitude sites and mature vines (including an almost 80-year-old semillon parcel) around Stellenbosch, Franschhoek, Cederberg and Swartland, with new plantings planned for the latter. Cellar space is rented pending completion later this year of a 120-ton cellar on the home farm.

★★★★ **Stellenbosch Cabernet Franc** From elevated low-yield Bottelary site on granite, **18** ⑧⑨'s compact blue/black fruit & lifted herbal aroma true to variety. Elegant & dry, well-composed but very present tannins extending the finish.

★★★★☆ **Stellenbosch Syrah** Two granitic blocks, in Polkadraai Hills & Bottelary, in **18** ⑨⓪. Fine example of modern-Cape styling: expressive & pure red-berry & pepper notes, freshness & moderate 13.4% alcohol. Complex vinification involves variety of vessels & techniques including wholebunch & carbonic.

Franschhoek Semillon ★★★★☆ Oxidative winemaking evident in bruised apple aromas & flavours, & 'sweet' impression on (old) oak-spice-infused **18** ⑧④. Venerable (1942) vineyard on alluvials, 15% of vines with 'gris' mutation, bunch pressed. Not as harmonious in youth as red siblings, but allow time - intended to age decade minimum. — TJ, CvZ

Location: Elgin ▪ WO: Stellenbosch/Franschhoek ▪ Est 2017 ▪ 1stB 2018 ▪ Tasting & cellar tours 9-5 by appt only ▪ Sales 8-5 ▪ Owner(s) David Curl ▪ Cellarmaster(s)/viticulturist(s) Jean Smit (Oct 2017) ▪ 80t/1,200cs own label 90% red 10% white ▪ Habibi Farm PO Box 84 Elgin 7180 ▪ jean@damascenevineyards.com ▪ www.damascenevineyards.com ▪ **T +27 (0)82-334-8100**

☐ **Daniel Collection** *see* Black Elephant Vintners
☐ **Daredevils' Drums** *see* Springfontein Wine Estate

D'Aria Winery

This Durbanville winery's emblem is a flute-playing sprite, and its mission 'to awaken and celebrate the senses' through wine and food. Hence the tempting snacks and light meals offered on-site with tastings of the music-themed, pleasurable-drinking wines (and spirits, including a top-notch potstill brandy) crafted by the creative father-and-son team, Johan and Rudi von Waltsleben. The former is the longtime viticulturist here on the cooler Tygerberg Hills. Son, composer and musician Rudi is the winemaker, who this year no doubt will be working on the 'score' for a new Rhône blend from the first harvest of carignan and grenache.

Reserve range

★★★★ **The Soprano Shiraz 17** ⑧⑨ is bolder, riper than **16** ★★★★★ ⑨① & shade less complex, also needs time to integrate 100% new oak's sweet clove influence that mutes the warm fruit. More concentrated than SV sibling though.

★★★★☆ **The Songbird Sauvignon Blanc** ⊘ Portion fermented in concrete 'egg' & lees contact add plush creaminess to characteristic Durbanville dust. Riper flavour spectrum complements grapefruit nuance, makes **18** ⑨② touch more charming than **17** ⑨①, both beautifully balanced.

Artisan range

★★★★ **Cape Minstrel Pinotage** More serious intent than **15** ★★★★ ⑧④ in **16** ⑧⑥. Splashes cab & shiraz & 85% new oak give firm, dry tannic base to wild, dark berry & cherry flavours. Named for Cape Town's annual carnival.

★★★★☆ **The Following Sauvignon Blanc** ⓖ Mostly fermented & aged in concrete 'eggs', 20% in new oak. **16** ㉒ flavours develop in intensity: flint, greengage, herb & starfruit; freshening grapefruit thread with oak a creamy platform. Persistent, confident & entertaining.

Premium Cape range
★★★★ **SV Shiraz** ⓥ Continues ripe & rich style in **17** ㉘⑦, includes a splash of viognier. Cream textured, but juicy & fresh, with hint of spicy clove from 20% new oak.

★★★★ **Cabernet Sauvignon-Merlot** ⓥ More seriously structured than **16** ★★★★ ㉘⑤, **18** ㉘⑦ is a 82/18 blend. A core of cassis, touch of mint & new oak (40%) well assimilated. Balanced & tempting, but future rewards in store. **17** untasted.

★★★★ **Lullaby Noble Late Harvest** ⓖ From botrytised semillon, unctuous **15** ㉘⑦ dessert has honey-drizzled papaya, caramelised pineapple & toffee apple complexity (40% oaked). Excellent with cheese.

Merlot ★★★ More coherent than previous, & tad more dark fruit flavours & freshness on **17** ㉘①. Same firm structure, food friendliness & need for some time to unfurl. **Blush** ⓥ ★★★ From merlot & sauvignon blanc, bright **19** ㉘① rosé exudes fresh summery appeal. A few grams of sugar zested into perfect pitch by tangy acidity. **Sauvignon Blanc** ⓥ ★★★★ Lightest of the non-fizzy sauvignon quartet, gracefully balanced **18** ㉘⑤ is fresh, with appealing kiwi & starfruit flavours.

Music range
Shiraz-Cabernet Sauvignon-Merlot ⓥ ★★★★ Dapper **18** ㉘④ is flavoursome & balanced. Lighter bodied & light on the pocket, lithe & amiable. WO W Cape, as next. **Sauvignon Blanc** ★★★ Lightish & crisp **19** ㉘⓪ has a lilting tropical tone for carefree sipping.

Sparkling range
Rock Song Sparkling Shiraz ⓖ ★★★ More in the heavy metal spectrum, **17** ⑦⑦ dry fizz has a dark brooding colour, ripe berry compote flavours & savoury finish with slight tannic kick. **Love Song Sparkling Pinot Noir** ⓖ ★★★ Antithesis of Rock Song, **18** ㉘⓪ delicate sunset-pink bubbly with floral & savoury flavours, crisp balance. Very quaffable. **Pop Song Sparkling Sauvignon Blanc** ⓖ ★★★ Though dry, **18** ⑦⑨ sparkler has distinct & pleasant fruit sweetness, refreshing sherbetty citrus tang. Pure summer fun.

Brandy range
★★★★ **The Piccolo 9 Year Old Potstill** Last release was at 5 years, current 9 year old ㉘⑨ announces its longer barrelling with amber hue & more serious mien. Rich & full on palate, gentle roasted nut & dark chocolate flavours underpinning aromas of dried peach & pear. From colombard. 500 ml.— MW, WB

Location: Durbanville ▪ Map: Durbanville, Philadelphia & Darling ▪ Map grid reference: C7 ▪ WO: Durbanville/ Western Cape ▪ Est/1stB 2007 ▪ Tasting & sales Mon-Sat 10-6 Sun 11-5 ▪ Fee R20 ▪ Closed Dec 24/25 & Jan 1 ▪ Cheese platters, gourmet burgers, oysters, kiddies cookie tasting ▪ Kiddies play area ▪ Venue @ D'Aria T +27 (0)21-975-0421: conferences/events/weddings ▪ Trail running & MTB ▪ 3-star guest cottages ▪ Craft gin ▪ Owner(s) Barinor Holdings ▪ Brandy master Rudi von Waltsleben (2008) ▪ Winemaker(s) Rudi von Waltsleben (Nov 2007), with Lutske Doubell (2017) ▪ Viticulturist(s) Johan von Waltsleben (1998) ▪ 80ha/63ha (cab, merlot, shiraz, sauv) ▪ M13 Tyger Valley Rd Durbanville 7550 ▪ info@daria.co.za ▪ www. dariawinery.co.za ▪ S 33° 50' 28.6" E 018° 36' 36.2" ▪ Ⓦ steady.dices.seperators ▪ **T +27 (0)21-801-6772**

Darling Cellars   ⓖ ⑪ ⓐ ⓐ ⓑ
An industry dynamo, this extensive West Coast venture constantly fine-tunes its vineyards, upgrades its cellar facilities and enhances its wine offerings. In the past 12 months, there have been new plantings of chardonnay, pinotage and roobernet; in the cellar there's a new lees filter and MCC sparkling disgorgement line; and in the tasting room, light meals are now served. On the wine front, the popular Chocoholic Pinotage is now also available in a 3L bag-in-box, the Premium range has been discontinued and the Gustus offerings expanded to include, among others, a rare single-variety bukettraube.

Darling Heritage Collection
★★★★ **Sir Charles Darling** ⓐ Smooth & sleek flagship from cab & merlot (60/40). **17** ㉘⑨'s new oaking includes 20% American to bring forward the drinkability window (still with 3-5 years potential). Ripe & generous, yet finishes pleasingly dry.

★★★★ **The Old Grain Silo Darling** (🐝) Modern (wholeberry) styling for Cape Blend **17** (88), in contrast to savoury **16** (86), shows vivacious red fruit from shiraz (55%), subtle banana & lively acidity from pinotage. Barrel selection, as Sir Charles.

★★★★☆ **Lady Ann Darling** (🐝) Barrel-fermented Bordeaux white leads with sauvignon (60%) in **18** ★★★★ (89), shows more grass & zingy green fruit, less semillon smoke & straw as result. 100% new oak, too, more dominant than in finer **17** (90).

★★★★ **Lime Kilns Darling** Extroverted blend mostly chenin, aromatically complex & rich yet commendably dry & refreshing. **18** (89) adroitly oaked, 16% viognier for perfume, thimbleful chardonnay.

Ultra Premium range

★★★★☆ **Old Bush Vine Cinsaut** (🍇) From 30+ year old vines, well-constructed **17** (90) strawberry & raspberry tones, present but very fine tannin lattice, delicate-seeming despite 14.3% alcohol.

★★★★☆ **Old Bush Vine Chenin Blanc** (🐝) (🍇) Unshowy **18** (93)'s quiet white peach & apricot notes, toasted almond nuance, mandarin finish make for sophisticated glassful. Pinpoint acidity, well-calibrated oak (combo new & older) in support.

Gustus range

★★★★ **Skattie** (🍇) Afrikaans for 'darling'. Deliciously uncloying **16** (87) Natural Sweet dessert from pinotage, with variety's mulberry charm & fresh-fruit fragrance (no raisins). Delightful 375 ml packaging. WO Darling, rest of these W Cape unless noted.

....

Pinot Noir (NEW) (✓) (🍷) ★★★ Could be your 'everyday' pinot. Lovely strawberries & raspberries, faint hint of tobacco, gentlest of tannic tugs - **17** (82) is the real deal, & the price tag will broaden your smile.
Bukettraube (NEW) (🍷) ★★★★ Something different & satisfying, **18** (83) floral, musky & grapey bouquet, well-stocked with fruit flavours & easy to sip, good dry finish. Only 70 ha of this German variety left worldwide, according to back-label. Worth seeking out to keep Darling Cellars' ±5 ha in the ground.

....

Cabernet Sauvignon (NEW) ★★★ Grapes for **17** (83) picked very ripe but handled well, so few grams sugar, 14.5% alcohol & 70% oak are in balance, the whole not porty. **Pinotage** ★★★ Doesn't trumpet the variety, but **17** (82) is tasty, bright & fresh, big 14.8% alcohol well hidden & affability upped by vanilla from 40% American oak. **Shiraz** ★★★☆ Wholeberry fermented, **17** (83) very fruity with floral accents, gains structure & char from substantial oaking, 70% new, 20% American. **Chenin Blanc** (NEW) ★★★ Bone-dry **18** (82) from Darling vines, attractive stonefruit & apple, tingling acidity, some depth & length from 6 months on lees. **Sauvignon Blanc** (🍇) ★★★ Uncomplicated **17** (80), round, smooth & nicely dry for seafood.
Noble Late Harvest (🍇) ★★★★ From chenin, **16** (83) has enough tangy acidity to enliven caramel & dried apricot sweetness, good form from 30% oak-aged portion. Enjoy well-chilled, soon.

Reserve range

....

Old Blocks Pinotage (✓) (🍷) ★★★☆ Best of this bunch, **17** (84) has pinotage's vivaciousness, generous mulberry & raspberry fruit, attractive vanilla oak sheen. Also-tasted **16** (84) as bright & bouncy, with telltale banana top note.

....

Terra Hutton Cabernet Sauvignon ★★★ Affordable everyday-drinking range. Lightly oaked **17** (81), plummy fruit dusted with savoury oak spice. **Eveningstar Cinsault** (NEW) ★★★ For charcuterie & salty tapas, **18** (79) attractively light-textured (13% alcohol), smoothly dry with strawberry fruit & a little tannin to aid food pairing. **Six Tonner Merlot** ★★★ Rounded & plummy **17** (80), ripe & sweet fruit, vanilla from American oak ups accessibility, moreishness. **Chocoholic Pinotage** (🍇) ★★★ Slightly decadent off-dry sipper, **17** (82) packed with promised choc-mocha, mulberry & red fruit, slightly sweeter yet more vivacious than previous. Also in 1.5 & 3L. **Black Granite Shiraz** (✓) ★★★★ Appealing glassful & true to variety, **17** (83) black pepper & lilies, lively red fruit, stemmy grape tannin & well-rounded oak support. Also in 1.5L. **The Capeman SMG** (🍇) ★★★ Honest, unforced **17** (79) is mostly shiraz, with dashes mourvèdre & grenache; nice red berry fruit, fynbos nuance, just a hint of oak. **Pyjama Bush Rosé** ★★ Palest pink **19** (75), wintergreen, bubble gum & strawberry candyfloss allure, softly dry finish. From sauvignon & splash grenache. **Quercus Gold Chardonnay** ★★ Improved **18** (76), dusty oak spice nuance to blue orange flavours, salty-tangy finish. **Arum Fields Chenin Blanc** ★★★ Floral & peach flavours & aromas on **19** (79), underplayed but satisfying, 13% alcohol in balance, pleasing roundness from few grams sugar. **Bush Vine**

Sauvignon Blanc ★★★ Unashamedly 'grass-&-dust' style sauvignon, **19** ⑦⑧ zesty but doesn't linger. Discontinued: **Cinful Cinsault**.

Cellarmaster Signature Selection

No. 6 ⓋⒶ ★★★★ Mostly shiraz (61%) with six others in **15** ⑧⑤, attractive freshness & vivacious red & black fruit, integrated tannin so it's accessible on release. **No. 8** ⓋⒶ ★★★★ Rhône blend of mostly shiraz & 3 others, red fruit nicely shaped by tannin, peppery, savoury & some raisin nuances, sturdy 14.9% alcohol. **15** ⑧⑤ ready to drink now.

Darling Cellars range

Cabernet Sauvignon-Merlot ★★ Line-up of budget quaffers, all WO W Cape. Lightly oak-staved **18** ⑦⑥ slips down easily courtesy plump berries & supple tannin. **Merlot Rosé** ★★ Sunset pink **19** ⑦⑤ is the calorie counter's friend, being low in sugar & alcohol. **Chenin Blanc-Sauvignon Blanc** ⊘ ★★★ Relaxed **19** ⑦⑦ also in 500 ml. Nice & dry, with friendly 12.8% alcohol; minority partner sauvignon asserts itself in grass & dust nuances.

Sweet Darling range

Sweet Rosé ★★ Different varieties, but latest NV ⑦② bottling remains demure, with fleeting semi-sweet flavours. **Sweet White** ★★ Equal muscat & chenin deliver light, sweet but well-balanced, decently vinous **NV** ⑦⑤. **Sweet Red** ⊘ ★★★ Well-controlled sweetness on latest **NV** ⑦⑧, good grip & berry flavour from cab, merlot & cinsaut.

Méthode Cap Classique range

★★★★ **Blanc de Blancs Brut** ⓋⒶ Well-priced dry chardonnay bubbly. **17** ⑧⑥ creamy & rich, shot through with lemon acidity, persistent dry finish.

. . . .

Brut Rosé ⊘ 🍷 ★★★ From grenache noir, rare in SA, even scarcer as bottle-fermented sparkling. **17** ⑧② reminiscent of Italy's red Lambrusco in its red berry & smoke aromas, black fruit-pastille flavours, food-pairing grip. 16 months on lees. **Old Bush Vines Brut** 🆕 🍷 ★★★★ Industry focus on venerable vines evident in this sparkler from chardonnay. **16** ⑧⑤'s 36 months on lees give fine-textured mousse, Granny Smith & candy apple flavours, spun sugar nuance - all nudging next quality level.

. . . .

Demi-Sec ⊘ ★★★★ Continues cellar's theme of innovative/creative bubblies - among relatively few MCCs from chenin. **17** ⑧③ low in alcohol, too, with well-handled sweetness. Honey biscuit & lemon, tad shy & brief but nicely vinous & refreshing.

Wildflower range

Muskadel ⓋⒶ ★★★ Fortified dessert with rooibos & honey tones, fresh (not raisined) fruit. **NV** ⑧② uncomplex but pleasing fire & tug of tannin. **Cape Ruby** ⓋⒶ ★★★ Fruity **NV** ⑦⑧ from Portuguese varieties with decent warmth & grip for firesides or with ice & lime zest, as winemakers suggest. — CvZ

Location: Darling ▪ Map: Durbanville, Philadelphia & Darling ▪ Map grid reference: B2 ▪ WO: Darling/Western Cape ▪ Est 1948 ▪ 1stB 1981 ▪ Tasting & sales Mon-Fri 9—5 Sat 10—2 ▪ Closed Good Fri, Dec 25 & Jan 1 ▪ Cellar tours by appt ▪ Light meals & cheese platters ▪ Facilities for children ▪ Bottling services offered ▪ Owner(s) 20 shareholders ▪ Winemaker(s) Pieter-Niel Rossouw (Sep 2014), with Carel Hugo (Jun 2009), Anthony Meduna (Oct 2011) & Maggie Immelman (Jun 2014) ▪ 1,000ha (barbera, cab, carignan, cinsaut, durif, grenache, malbec, merlot, mourv, ptage, shiraz, bukettraube, chard, chenin, riesling, sauv, sem) ▪ 6,500—7,500t/450,000cs own label 60% red 30% white 10% rosé ▪ Other export brands: Black Granite, Cape Cult, Capeman, Chocoholic ▪ PO Box 114 Darling 7345 ▪ info@darlingcellars.co.za ▪ www.darlingcellars.co.za ▪ S 33° 26' 25.7" E 018° 31' 25.1" ▪ 🗺 climber.overruling.knotting ▪ **T +27 (0)22-492-2276/+27 (0)74-683-4454**

Daschbosch   Ⓥ 📷 &

A large wine business by any definition, and recently extended further by the merger with Goudini Wines, Daschbosch's 65 shareholders control 3,000 ha of vineyards in Breedekloof. Cellarmaster Nicolaas Rust and team annually vinify around 70,000 tons, from which some 200,000 cases are selected for the various wines in the portfolio. The site-specific Daschbosch ranges showcase various pockets of excellence as well as old vines, including hanepoot planted in 1900. Goudini and Meander are the lifestyle labels, and Palesa the Fairtrade offering, reflecting the commitment to ethical trade.

Daschbosch Experimental range (NEW)

★★★★★ **Avon** (ⓐ) (ⓦ) Clairette blanche planted 1977 on Breedekloof's Olifantsberg slopes, minuscule 0.9-1.5 t/ha yield. Wholebunch, old-barrel-fermented/matured 9 months (6 on coarse lees) for sleek **18** ㉝'s cantaloupe & nectarine perfume, but tighter flavour focus, lemon, slate & saline acidity. Remarkable.

★★★★☆ **Skin Contact** Chenin & muscat d'Alexandrie (70/30), big crop yield but standout **18** ㉝ left on skins for 6 months after ferment. Green/gold, great aromatics, stonefruit & hanepoot grapes, sultanas, then a complete switch to a mineral, savoury (yet no oak) & saline-fresh palate.

Daschbosch Heritage range

★★★★ **Cape Blend** (ⓩ) Two-thirds pinotage with petit verdot, cab & petite sirah, an unusual blend & it works. Liquorice & black plums, scrub, **16** ㊆ layered & involving, sweetly oak-spiced, succulent texture.

★★★★ **Steen** Oaked version of 4 varietal chenins across the ranges, lovely ginger biscuit & melon tones, **18** ㊆'s palate weight from lees contact, richly round, full flavoured. Has ageing potential.

★★★★★ **Hanepoot** (ⓩ) (ⓦ) Outstanding fortified from ancient muscat d'Alexandrie bushvines. Like **15** ㊌, **16** ★★★★★ ㊔ shows sultanas & dried stonefruit in a highly concentrated form, full-sweet & luscious, hedonistic texture, mouthcoating richness. Will age beautifully. 9 months small oak. 375 ml.

Daschbosch Popular Premium range

Cabernet Sauvignon ★★★ Broad shouldered & packed with flavour, **18** ㊶'s cassis easily handles the tannins, ends savoury & dry. **Merlot** (ⓩ) ★★★ Oak use positions **17** ㊶ barrel sample up the scale from Palesa sibling. Meaty, peppery, with cushion of vibrant cassis, tannins a presence but fine grained. **Sauvignon Blanc** ★★★★ Ticks all the boxes, sauvignon typicity in perfume & flavours, freshness, finishes long. **19** ㊳'s mineral palate tones ideal for seafood. WO W Cape.

Meander range

Moscato (ⓥ) ★★★ Consistent styling, latest **NV** just 5.5% alcohol, carbonated perlé from muscat d'Alexandrie; delicious, like drinking sweet hanepoot grapes. Serve well chilled.

Pinotage (✓) ★★★ Savoury spice & mocha-toned dark berries, **18** ㊶ ends dry & firm, ideal match for casseroles, meat dishes. **Shiraz** (ⓩ) ★★ Some light oaking & **17** ㊅'s red fruit gains savoury notes, but essentially still a smooth early-drinker. **Chenin Blanc** ★★ Touch of sugar in slender **19** ㊅, fits the apple styling, goes down easily. **Moscato Pink** ★★★ Pale pink version of Moscato, same grapes & low alcohol level, somehow not as zinging fresh, but **NV** ㊇ will still liven up any party.

Goudini Lifestyle range

Merlot (ⓩ) ★★★ Juicy, bouncy, fruit-forward **17** ㊈, ex tank is gluggable & pocket friendly. **Shiraz** ★★★ Dark-toned fruit, spice & some liquorice, there's typicity, ripeness & juicy appeal in **18** ㊶, the tannins supple. **Unwooded Chardonnay** (ⓩ) ★★★ Vibrant apple & floral flavours with lifted acidity on affable **18** ㊂. **Chenin Blanc** ★★ Freshly sliced apples & pears, **19** ㊍ is crisply dry, has good drinkability. **Sauvignon Blanc** (ⓩ) ★★ Dry, lean **18** ㊂ preview has a stern acid backbone. Serve well-chilled. **Brut** ★★★ Lemon drop freshness in **NV** ㊈ carbonated bubbly from sauvignon, elegantly dry, in aperitif style.

Palesa Fairtrade range

Merlot (ⓩ) ★★ Blackcurrants sprinkled with spice, **17** ㊄ is satisfyingly smooth, made for early enjoyment. **Pinotage** ★★★ Expressive variety-true fruit, juicy & smooth, **18** ㊵'s tannins harmonious, grip at the end giving definition. **Chenin Blanc** (ⓩ) ★★★ Different styling to the other chenins, mineral & fynbos, **18** ㊶ has precision & focus. Also in 3L cask. **Sauvignon Blanc** (ⓩ) ★★ Consistent style, lime with a touch of fynbos in **18** ㊄, light & fresh. — CR

Location: Rawsonville ▪ Map: Breedekloof ▪ Map grid reference: C6 ▪ WO: Breedekloof/Western Cape ▪ Est/1stB 2007 ▪ Tasting & sales at Goudini premises: Mon-Thu 8–5 Fri 8-4 Sat/pub hols 10–2 ▪ Closed Good Fri, Dec 25/26 & Jan 1 ▪ Fully licensed ▪ Conferences ▪ Owner(s) 65 shareholders ▪ Cellarmaster(s) Nicolaas Rust (Oct 2008) ▪ Senior winemaker(s) WS Visagie (Nov 2010), Schalk van der Merwe (Dec 2007) & Christo Smit (Jan 2001); with winemaker(s) Pieter van Wyk (Jun 2016), Nicolaas du Toit (2017), Lamees Isaacs (2017) & Yolandi Barnard (2018) ▪ Viticulturist(s) Nicholas Bruyns (Jul 2013) ▪ 3,000ha (cab, cinsaut, merlot, ptage, shiraz, chard, chenin, cbard, sauv) ▪ 70,000t/200,000cs own label 50% red 50% white + 50,000cs for

clients ▪ ISO 22000:2008, Fairtrade, IPW, WIETA ▪ PO Box 174 Rawsonville 6845 ▪ pro@uniwines.co.za ▪ www.
uniwines.co.za ▪ S 33° 41' 37.8" E 019° 19' 9.5" ▪ 〽 alpine.dismount.prelude ▪ **T +27 (0)23-349-1110**

☐ **Dassie's Reserve** *see* Botha Wine Cellar

David & Nadia

One of the handful of highly successful husband-and-wife partnerships in modern SA wine: David Sadie
is based in the historic cellar on Paardebosch farm (which they lease), on the slopes of the Paardeberg,
while Nadia, viticulturist and soil scientist, takes prime responsibility for the Swartland vineyards they draw
grapes from. Chenin blanc and grenache noir are their focus, and a third single-vineyard chenin adds further
depth to their portfolio of elegant and delicate but substantial wines, made in hands-off fashion. Last year
also saw the harvesting of two new single-vineyard grenaches. There are developments, too, in the cellar
itself, with new cement tanks and the first experiments with clay pots. Bill & Co, the bistro-deli-winebar in
Malmesbury, a venture between David & his brother Johann, remains the primary tasting venue.

Single Vineyard range

★★★★★ **Hoë-Steen Chenin Blanc**⭐ ⓦ Off 50 year old bushvines with roots in clay & unusually
tall shoots, hence 'High Chenin', most powerful of this trio. Customary pear & wet wool aromas, intense
bruised apple flavours in **18** ⑨⑤; same harmonious length & extraordinary presence as singular **17** ⑨⑥.

★★★★★ **Plat'bos Chenin Blanc**ⓝⓔⓦ ⓦ Astounding addition to the registered single-vineyard
chenins, from 1981 bushvines among trellised neighbours, thus 'Flat Bush'. **18** ⑨⑥ vibrates with nervous
energy, tightly wound, lean & elegant yet substantial, riveting echoes of flavour. Such focus. Same hands-
off winemaking as peers.

★★★★★ **Skaliekop Chenin Blanc**⭐ From shale ('skalie') site planted 1985; as range siblings, bunch
pressing, minimal intervention, older 300L oak. Individual, wild 'dissident' profile in steely, mineral **18** ⑨⑤,
with khaki bush & scrub features. A tense, ferrous character & exquisite saline conclusion, as in **17** ⑨⑤.

David & Nadia range

★★★★☆ **Grenache** Flavourful without being heavy is the refrain throughout the ranges, **18** ⑨⓪, like **17**
⑨⓪, is also fruit-filled without being fruity. Strawberry profile with a hint of Swartland earthiness; 60%
bunch pressed, 4 weeks on skins, year older oak. Seamless, & charming in its lightness.

★★★★☆ **Elpidios**⭐ Pace-setting Rhône-style red blend from schist & granite sites, half wholebunch
in savoury & earthy **17** ⑨③, mostly grenache (31%) & shiraz (30%) with carignan, cinsaut & pinotage,
shows linear purity, Swartland's lacy tannins, & steely presence. **16** ⑨③ was carignan-led.

★★★★★ **Chenin Blanc**⭐ ⓦ A leader of the minimal intervention/oxidative pack, yet with huge
charm & a growing following. From old (1968) Paardeberg vines, trademark ethereal white peach & pear
tones on limpid **18** ⑨⑤, hallmark dryness & profundity.

★★★★☆ **Aristargos**⭐ Authoritative white off mostly dryland bushvine blocks, some 50+ years.
Persistent **18** ⑨③ shows earth & umami tones with evocative power. Chenin with viognier, clairette, semillon, roussanne & marsanne. Old oak, native yeasts, no additives, low sulphur; no fining/filtration, as for all.

Topography range

★★★★☆ **Pinotage** Herb & scrub, strawberry & ash, a singular interpretation from dryland Paardeberg
vineyard shifting the pinotage paradigm. **18** ⑨⓪ replete with fine fruit, entices with lighter styling. As
usual, there's no shortage of endearing - or enduring - style. 20% wholebunch, year in large seasoned vats.

★★★★☆ **Semillon** ⓦ From 50 year old dryland bushvines in granite soils. Individual **18** ⑨⓪ gets 7
days skin contact in oxidative 'orange wine' genre. Lean & earthy, with hint of khaki bush, it shows precision
& freshness, echoing persistence. 12.5% alcohol, **17** ⑨① was just 11%. Year in large (2,500L) foudre.— DS

Location: Malmesbury ▪ Map/WO: Swartland ▪ Map grid reference: C8 ▪ Est/1stB 2010 ▪ Tasting by appt;
also available at Bill & Co in Malmesbury ▪ Accommodation on Paardebosch farm, contact Liesl Kruger T
+27 (0)83-280-8060 ▪ Owner(s)/winemaker(s)/viticulturist(s) David & Nadia Sadie ▪ (carignan, cinsaut,
grenache, ptage, shiraz, chenin, clairette, marsanne, rouss, sem, viog) ▪ 90t/10,800cs own label 40% red
60% white ▪ Swartland Independent Producers (2011) ▪ info@davidnadia.com ▪ www.davidnadia.com ▪ S
33° 32' 41.41" E 018° 49' 36.14" ▪ 〽 illogical.funds.virulently ▪ **T +27 (0)72-375-4336**

☐ **David Finlayson** *see* Edgebaston

David Frost Wines

South African champion golfer David Frost's wine business is being revamped, with exciting plans to produce high-quality wines and market them in America. The new portfolio will also be available locally, with
tastings by arrangement and at Bottelary Wine Centre on the outskirts of Stellenbosch once it is launched.

Location/map: Stellenbosch ▪ Map grid reference: D3 ▪ Est 1994 ▪ Tasting by appt, or at The Bottelary Hills
Wine Centre ▪ Owner(s) David Frost ▪ 30,000cs 40% red 60% white ▪ info@frostwines.com, david@
frostwine.com ▪ www.frostwine.com ▪ S 33° 52' 39.18" E 018° 48' 49.88" ▪ ⌖ special.gadgets.evenly ▪
T +27 (0)84-657-4854

☐ **David Nieuwoudt** *see* Cederberg Private Cellar
☐ **Dawn Patrol** *see* Trizanne Signature Wines

De Breede Organic Vineyards

Boutique-scale Hartebeesterivier estate just outside Worcester, its organic vines and 200-year-old cellar are
the source of these personality-packed wines, overseen and made by owner Debbie Alcock-Bousfield as a
complement to her internationally awarded Gourmet Africa condiment range.

★★★★ Syrah ⓥ ⓢ Appealing freshness on bright-fruited **11** ⑧⑦ - a bit lighter, suppler, less extracted
than the others, but still powerful & just as characterful.

Cabernet Sauvignon ⓥ ⓢ **★★** Stewed, porty notes on über-ripe **12** ⑦④ mask both varietal character
& origin; misses structure & refinement of previous. For early drinking. **1st XI Merlot** ⓥ ⓢ **★★★★**
Violets & crème de cassis abundance on **10** ⑧③. Like Cab, touch jammy but more structure-giving tannins
& finesse; good juicy acidity, too. **Little Red Rooster** ⓥ ⓢ **★★** Porty black fruit with green undertones
on **13** ⑦① Bordeaux blend led by merlot. Drink soon. **The Rooster** ⓥ ⓢ **★★★** Like sibling, **12** ⑦⑦ has
concentrated, sweet & ripe dark fruit in rustic, porty frame. More structure here, but still very evolved for its
age. **The Rooster Reserve** ⓥ ⓢ **★★★** Savoury notes to ripe black fruit on smoky **10** ⑦⑦ Bordeaux red.
Firm tannin profile gives drying effect to otherwise well-expressed, mature fruit flavours. — HJ

Location: Worcester ▪ Map/WO: Breedekloof ▪ Map grid reference: D4 ▪ Est 2006 ▪ 1stB 2009 ▪ Tasting by
appt ▪ Owner(s)/viticulturist(s) Debbie Alcock-Bousfield ▪ Winemaker(s) Debbie Alcock-Bousfield & Isaac
Mabeta (2009) ▪ 26ha/2.5ha (cabs s/f, malbec, merlot, p verdot) ▪ ±20t/2,000cs own label 99% red 1% rosé
▪ Certified organic by BCS ▪ PO Box 511 Worcester 6849 ▪ info@burchells.co.za ▪ www.gourmet-africa.com ▪ S
33° 37' 10.69" E 019° 22' 44.79" ▪ ⌖ speeded.decorate.backboard ▪ **T +27 (0)23-342-5388**

Definitum Wines

This small negociant brand was born when 'friends came together to share their passion and love for wine'.
Helderberg owners Fritz van der Merwe and De Wet Schreiber have ambitions to make definitive versions of
the blends or varieties (sometimes relatively unusual ones) in their range, hence the brand name.

Petit Verdot Reserve ★★★★ Plenty of dark, ripe berry fruit on **17** ⑧④, with big 15.6% alcohol adding
warmth & underlining the few grams of sugar. A little tannic grip, no obvious oak. Last made was drier
15 ★★★★ ⑧⑦. **Arbalest** ⓥ **★★★★** Cab-led 5-way Bordeaux blend, **16** ⑧④'s succulent red fruit underpinned by fine, gripping tannins; long & luscious. Not tasted: **Benevolence**. — TJ

Location: Strand ▪ WO: Stellenbosch ▪ Est/1stB 2009 ▪ Closed to public ▪ Owner(s) Fritz van der Merwe &
De Wet Schreiber ▪ 1,625cs own label 100% red ▪ PO Box 917 Strand 7139 ▪ info@definitum.co.za ▪ www.
definitum.co.za

De Grendel Wines

A large agribusiness (800 ha) in the form of a scenically beautiful farm which hugs the Tygerberg Hills, has
views of Cape Town's Table Mountain and its bay, and forms part of the Durbanville Wine Route. Comprising
a cattle and sheep stud, horses, game, blueberries and wine, it belongs to the Graaff family, with 4th baronet Sir De Villiers Graaff, schooled in agriculture, the current custodian, following the vision set by his father
and ably assisted by cellarmaster Charles Hopkins. Conservation forms an important part of the strategy,
with indigenous gardens and a restaurant using home-grown produce, as well as a meticulous record of all

the fynbos and wild flowers on the estate. Other family-owned properties contribute to the wine range, like cool-climate Ceres Plateau and Firgrove in Stellenbosch, and other areas sourced when needed.

★★★★☆ **Merlot** For the textbook. Vivid fruit in **17** (88), cassis & raspberries, beautifully spiced, some chocolate. A succulent, polished body, tannins a hidden strength. Outclasses **16** ★★★★ (84). Cape Town WO.

★★★★★ **Op Die Berg Pinot Noir** ⊘ Ⓐ From their Ceres Plateau property, 3 months cold maceration for colour & flavour, 13 months in barrel, **17** (91) has power & concentration. Raspberries, cherries & violets, gentle scrub note, everything beautifully in balance, savoury at the end.

★★★★☆ **Elim Shiraz** Ⓐ Only in numbered magnums, just 224 cases. **17** ★★★★★ (95) quite Rhône-like, morello cherries, black pepper, dried scrub, with a firm backbone for ageing (it's in the correct bottle), but accessible with food if you can't wait. Has power & presence. **16** (94) was first release.

★★★★☆ **Shiraz** Ⓐ Brought-in grapes, **17** (94) expertly crafted to seduce with its luscious texture, glossy fruit. Nice stylistic contrast to the Elim version: mocha chocolate, spice array & grip from French & American barrels. Doesn't put a foot wrong. WO Coastal, as next 2.

★★★★ **Rubáiyát** 4-part Bordeaux blend, cab-led, 80% new barriques 18 months, & **17** ★★★★☆ (90) preview doesn't disappoint. Deep sensuous cassis, nuances of dry scrub, dusty spice, cocoa-rich chocolate. Compact, built to age but already gives pleasure. Improves on **16** (88).

★★★★☆ **Sir David Graaff First Baronet** Ⓐ Honours the late founder. **16** (93) barrel sample from cab, petit verdot & shiraz, seriously treated as befits its status: 20 months French barrels, 80% new. Deep, intense cassis, black cherries, spice threaded through giving flavour & more to admire. For the long haul but tannins are accessible.

★★★★☆ **Op Die Berg Chardonnay** Ⓐ Respecting Ceres Plateau's cool climate, only 60% of **18** (93) oaked, half new, fermented at different temperatures. Arresting fruit concentration, the essence of citrus, oak's presence a savoury richness & length. Lithe, with signature freshness.

★★★★★ **Koetshuis Sauvignon Blanc** Carefully chosen brought-in fruit gives **19** (91) preview wet slate, oystershell intensity, the 30% oaking a gentle biscuit seam, not detracting from the core character. Classic, sophisticated & focused. WO W Cape.

★★★★ **Sauvignon Blanc** Unwooded, 100 days on lees for **19** (87)'s palate weight, flavour richness, despite the cool-climate scents: gooseberries, grapefruit, touch of fynbos. Improves on **18** ★★★★ (85).

★★★★ **Viognier** 30% ferment/ageing in French oak for palate weight. Fully expressive floral & peach aromas for **19** (87), intensifying in the flavours. Fresh & dry, variety true, character without excess. No **18**.

★★★★☆ **Winifred** Creative, admirable blend, equal viognier & semillon, 25% chardonnay, barrel fermented/aged in French & Romanian oak. **18** (92) crafted to showcase the varieties, peach/kernel aromas, a smoky charcuterie element. Good palate weight, ends crisply dry & long.

★★★★ **Méthode Cap Classique Brut** Chardonnay (64%) & pinot noir, **16** (88) bubbly has 32 months on lees, is citrus toned, lemon & grapefruit, red fruit showing in the flavours. Has elegance, finesse, bone-dry finish. Cape Town WO.

Amandelboord Pinotage ★★★☆ Pre-bottled **18** (84)'s French & American oaking nicely vanilla-spices the glossy dark fruit, tannins supple, but there's muscle tone for cellaring. More harmonious than last, not as ripe. Durbanville WO, as Sauvignon Blanc, Viognier & Winifred. **Rosé** ★★★ Equal cab & pinotage in elegant, bone-dry, pale pink **19** (81), a celebration of fruity-fresh red berries. WO Coastal. Not tasted: **Sauvignon Blanc Noble Late Harvest**. — CR

Location: Durbanville ▪ Map: Durbanville, Philadelphia & Darling ▪ Map grid reference: C8 ▪ WO: Coastal/Durbanville/Ceres Plateau/Cape Town/Elim/Western Cape ▪ Est 1720 ▪ 1stB 2004 ▪ Tasting & sales Mon-Sat 9–5 Sun 10–4 ▪ Snack selection available in tasting room ▪ Closed Dec 25 ▪ Cellar tours by appt ▪ Conferences ▪ De Grendel Restaurant ▪ Three Spades Cider ▪ Owner(s) De Villiers Graaff ▪ Cellarmaster(s) Charles Hopkins (Oct 2005) ▪ Viticulturist(s) Kudzai Mwerenga (2009) ▪ 800ha/75ha (cab f, merlot, p verdot, ptage, pinot noir/gris, shiraz, chard, sauv, sem, viog) ▪ 700t/50,000cs own label 35% red 50% white 15% rosé ▪ Plattekloof Rd Panorama 7500 ▪ info@degrendel.co.za ▪ www.degrendel.co.za ▪ S 33° 51' 2.5" E 018° 34' 18.4" ▪ 🔳 walked.approximates.doings ▪ **T +27 (0)21-558-6280**

☐ **Dekker's Valley** *see* Mellasat Vineyards

De Kleine Wijn Koöp

Already established as 'a place to express creativity and play outside the conventions of the store shelf', this winery specialising in 'piepklein' (tiny) volumes of 'niche wines with cool packaging' has been taken over by Paarl-based winemaker Wynand Grobler and wife Anya. They're expanding the portfolio with 'wines from some of the most exciting vineyards in the country'. Two of these appear in the First XI range, conceived with cricket legends Faf du Plessis, AB de Villiers, Mike Hussey and Stephen Fleming.

Klipkers range (NEW)

★★★★ **Rosé** Rose gold **19** (86) from Franschhoek is syrah with 16% mourvèdre, thimbleful grenache, smooth & dry, with red berry fruit, spice, friendly 12% alcohol. Wholebunch basket-pressed, naturally fermented, 15% in old oak, as next.

★★★★☆ **White Blend** ⊘ Voor Paarderberg grenache blanc with 17% verdelho, 9% grenache gris, old-oak-brushed **19** (90) packed with tangy apricot & granadilla fruit, some savoury spice too, quite dense yet fresh on the finish, balanced & delicious. Exceptional value.

Hoendertande range

★★★★ **Grenache Noir** From Piekenierskloof, **18** ★★★★★ (90) has bright, crunchy, tangy red fruit, also some intriguing masala spice. Fresher & more complex than last-tasted **16** (87) with smooth, lithe tannins after year in old 500L barrels.

The First XI range (NEW)

★★★★ **The Centurion** Floral perfume & cinnamon spice on **16** (89) cinsaut, aged year in stainless steel for lively, luminous expression of red berry fruit, soft & fresh but not at all lightweight. WO W Cape, as next.

★★★★ **The Belter** Shiraz opens the batting in **16** (89) with support from 10% mourvèdre, 4% grenache, scoring a deft 4 with red fruit, white pepper & spice, good teamwork after 16 months in old oak.

★★★★ **The Partnership** Cab the senior partner in **17** (88) with 15% cinsaut, 3% cab franc, latter duo providing crunchy red fruit, leafy freshness to black fruit concentration. 14 months older oak.

De Kleine Wijn Koöp range

★★★★ **Kreatuur Synachin** ② From syrah (57%), grenache (27%) & cinsaut, as name suggests. Perfumed **17** (88)'s raspberry & cranberry succulence supported by a fine tannic backbone. Well crafted but doesn't take itself too seriously. Coastal WO.

Ou Treffer Cinsaut ② ★★★★ Juicy **17** (84), abundant red berry fruit, mildly gripping tannins for early drinking; rides the wave of light, fresh SA cinsauts. Not tasted: **Heimwee Cabernet Sauvignon, Debutant, Road to Santiago.** Discontinued: **Knapse Kêrel Cabernet Franc.** — JG

Location: Paarl ▪ WO: Stellenbosch/Western Cape/Coastal/Franschhoek/Voor Paarderberg/Piekenierskloof ▪ Est/1stB 2011 ▪ Closed to public ▪ Sales via website ▪ 5,000cs own label ▪ sales@infinitywines.co.za ▪ www.dekleinewijnkoop.co.za

☐ **De Knolle Fonteyn** see Rogge Cloof

De Krans Wines   ⓦ ⑪ ⊚ ⓐ ⓖ

This substantial family winery near the Klein Karoo town of Calitzdorp has suffered from the persistent drought. MD and part-owner Boets Nel restrainedly calls 2019 'again a trying year', with an even smaller harvest than last. But, he adds, quality was fine 'because of very good water management and an excellent balance between growth and crop' – which implies kudos for brother Stroebel, caring for the vineyards for over 20 years now. Though De Krans is most famous for its port-style wines – and increasingly for its table wines from Portuguese grapes – Boets says they're putting more focus on their good-value Classic range wines. But there are also other gustatory attractions for visitors, including beer, a bistro and a deli.

Terroir range

★★★★ **Tinta Roriz** ⊘ Enticing as ever, **17** (86) leads with spicy, ripe red plum aromas to a sweet-fruited, robust palate with dry, strong tannins. Older oaked, so the fruit, while not intense, is fresh & clean.

★★★★ **Touriga Nacional** ② Another unfortified port grape bottling. Previewed **17** (87) has blackberry, cocoa & nutmeg notes - & more tannic-acid structure than **16** ★★★★ (84). Depth of flavour supported by modest oaking, like all these.

★★★★☆ **Tritonia Red** 🍇 Touriga (70%) blended with 3 tintas as usual on **17** 91 - vinified separately, then the best barrels blended. Red berry fragrance, then delightful sweet fruit on a firm, balanced structure - rather more elegant than the other reds. Needs & deserves time to soften. 13.7% alcohol.

★★★★☆ **Tritonia White** Golden blend malvasia rei (palomino) & verdelho **17** 87. Pear drop, baked apple & floral notes. Modest fruit, restrained oaking, weight from time on lees, crunchy tannic bite. 13.1% alcohol.

★★★★☆ **Zero Dosage Méthode Cap Classique** Spicy, attractive **15** 87 bubbly from 60% chardonnay with, uniquely, chenin & tinta. Delicately flavourful, with good yeasty development; well balanced, fresh & bone-dry. WO Klein Karoo, like **14** ★★★★ 85.

A Twist of Fate ★★★ Light-coloured **17** 82 blend tintas barroca & amarela with boiled sweet aromas. Easygoing & tasty; sharpish acid coping with some sweetness.

Classic range

Basket Press Cabernet Sauvignon ⊘ ★★★★ Ripe berry fruit but with herbal element, too, on easy **18** 83. Soft texture abetted by nearly off-dry level of sweetness. Smooth dry tannins. WO Klein Karoo, as Chenin. **Pinotage Rosé** ★★★ Charming berry fragrance on **19** 79 & plenty of flavour; softened by a few grams of sugar - offset by rather tart acidity. WO W Cape. **Wild Ferment Unwooded Chardonnay** ★★★☆ Pleasant, lightly flavourful, balanced & easygoing **18** 77. **Free-Run Unwooded Chenin Blanc** ★★★ Forward tropical fruit aromas on **19** 80 with a pleasing earthy touch & a zingy green nip; well textured & balanced. **Premium Moscato Perlé White** ★★★ More obviously muscatty grapey notes than on the Red. Lightly, sweetly tasty **18** 74. Both lowish 8.5% alcohol & WO W Cape. **Premium Moscato Perlé Red** ★★ Muscat with pinotage for colour; sweetish & insipid **18** 72.

Fortified range

★★★★☆ **Muscat de Frontignan** 🍇 Very sweet, softly smooth but not too unctuous fortified grape juice - **19** 90 at 15.5% alcohol. Delicious & remarkably light-feeling despite the sumptuous packed-in flavour - which is much more than typical muscat grapiness. Will last for ages. No **18**. WO Klein Karoo.

★★★★☆ **Cape Tawny Limited Release** Elegantly rich fortified, blended from wines 5-15 years in old oak to give the characteristic colour. Complexly flavourful **NV** 91 expertly crafted to be, as always, remarkably light-feeling & fresh, despite 100 g/l sugar & 18% alcohol. Mostly tinta barocca, with tinta amarela, touriga. WO W Cape.

★★★★ **Cape Vintage** ⊘ As usual, barrel sample tasted. **18** 88 blends 5 port varieties, led by touriga, in very old oak. Spicy & rich, dark-fruited & with firm but already smooth tannins & a firm acid keeping the finish quite dry. Less structured & intense than Reserve, more so than Ruby. Will keep, but good now.

★★★★★ **Cape Vintage Reserve** 🍇 'Port' with established record of quality & ageability, from touriga with tintas barocca & roriz. **17** 95 inevitably powerful in youth, with serious structure of chalky tannins, great depth of flavour, & subtle spirit fire. Impressive now, but a decade will bring harmony & complexity.

★★★★ **The Original Espresso** Always deliciously decadent, smoothly rich & enticingly balanced **NV** 86 fortified dessert from 5 port varieties. Dominant notes of coffee & choc - but plenty of fruit. 375 ml.

Premium Cape Ruby ⊘ ★★★★ Sweetly rich, gently tannic **NV** 84 fortified - the lightest, simplest of the 'ports'. Pre-bottling, a slightly intrusive, slightly grapefruity acidity, but offering great pleasure. **Original Cape Pink** ★★ Rosé-coloured, fortified **NV** 75 from port varieties; soft, smooth, candyflossy charm. — TJ

Location: Calitzdorp ▪ Map: Klein Karoo & Garden Route ▪ Map grid reference: B5 ▪ WO: Calitzdorp/Klein Karoo/Western Cape ▪ Est 1964 ▪ 1stB 1977 ▪ Wine tasting, sales & deli Mon-Sun 9-5 ▪ Tasting fee R40pp ▪ Bistro (indoor/outdoor seating) Mon-Sun 10-4.30 ▪ Biscotti & wine tasting daily (booking advised) ▪ Closed Good Fri & Dec 25 ▪ Pick your own: apricots last week Nov-1st week Dec; peaches 16-28 Dec; hanepoot grapes 2nd week Feb-1st week Mar ▪ Children's playground ▪ Walking trail ▪ Hand-crafted beer ▪ Owner(s) De Krans Wines (MD Boets Nel & directors Stroebel Nel, René Oosthuizen & Louis van der Riet) ▪ Winemaker(s) Louis van der Riet (Aug 2012) ▪ Viticulturist(s) Stroebel Nel (Jan 1988) ▪ 78ha/45ha (cab, tinta barocca/roriz, touriga nacional, chard, chenin & muscats) ▪ 600t/40–50,000cs own label 50% red 10% white 3% rosé 37% fortifieds ▪ IPW ▪ PO Box 28 Calitzdorp 6660 ▪ dekrans@mweb.co.za ▪ www.dekrans. co.za ▪ S 33° 32' 6.3" E 021° 41' 9.0" ▪ 🗺 keyholes.strolling.precise ▪ **T +27 (0)44-213-3314/64**

Delaire Graff Estate

There's no denying the glittering pull of this splendidly sited property on the highpoint of the Helshoogte Pass outside Stellenbosch town, with magnificent views. It was founded in the early 1980s by the originator of this guide, John Platter, but has changed dramatically since then, especially with the arrival in 2003 of London-based diamantaire Laurence Graff as its fifth owner. Art everywhere, both inside and out; and two restaurants, for example, with Kevin Grobler arriving in 2019 as head chef of the eponymous one; not to mention the diamond centre that one might expect, given the proprietor; and luxury accommodation that has been recently expanded. And to crown it all (in our opinion), Morné Vrey's fine range of wines, prestigious and hardly cheap – even the third tier is branded as Luxury.

Icon range

★★★★☆ **Cabernet Sauvignon Reserve** (🐾) Single-vineyard **17** (94) first since **15** ★★★★★ (95) mingles dark fruit & savoury. Classic cedar & cassis aromas & youthfully obvious oak vanilla (80% new barrels). Firm tannic structure supports deep fruit; sweet touch on finish, partly from 14.6% alcohol.

★★★★★ **Laurence Graff Reserve** (𝒥) Big, powerful cab (14.9% alcohol), but the quality of dark-bright fruit, suppleness of ripe & forceful tannins, well absorbed 80% new oak, & overall excellent balance mean that **15** (93)'s rippling musculature has some grace & is not flashily showy.

★★★★☆ **Merlot** Forthcoming fruitcake & tobacco aromas open up **17** (90); sweet, succulent fruit with no great intensity, & fresh herbal twist on lingering finish. Balanced, with rounded but firm tannins. 80% new oak will integrate. 14.6% alcohol. Should keep good few years. Ex estate's oldest single-vineyard.

★★★★☆ **Banghoek Reserve** (NEW) Powerful, sleek blend of cab franc & cab with petit verdot & malbec. Plenty of lurking fruit on **16** (92) but 60% new oak more obvious on aromas & flavours & the dry tannic structure. Some sweetness marks the finish, partly from 14.7% alcohol. Needs good few years to settle.

★★★★☆ **Terraced Block Reserve** (🐾) Hazelnut & oatmeal integrated with subtle citrus on single-vineyard **17** (94), the most interesting of the chardonnays. Bright acidity the basis of its firm structure, but intense fruit ensures generosity, & it should gain in harmony & complexity over at least 5 years.

★★★★★ **White Reserve** (🐾) Sauvignon (59%) leads wholebunch semillon in elegantly gorgeous **17** (96) - reserved but subtly intense; dry & with a fine acid seam, but also a delicious kernel of sucrosity. Unobtrusively oaked, 8% new. **16** ★★★★★ (93) was led by semillon. WO W Cape, as next two.

★★★★ **Sunrise Brut Méthode Cap Classique** Latest **NV** (88) bubbly 64% chenin with chardonnay & cab franc. Delightful ripe appley aromas & flavours; lightly sumptuous, with firm acid grip.

★★★★ **Sunburst Noble Late Harvest** (𝒥) Honeyed, marmalade aromas on **15** (87) dessert from oaked sauvignon. More charming than complex or intense; rich sweetness exposed by modest acid.

★★★★☆ **Cape Vintage** (🐾) **17** (93) as usual blends tinta (73%) with touriga, & as usual is delectable in youth, though deserving 5-10+ years bottle ageing to fully harmonise tannic structure, alcohol & extracted flavour, & bring further complexity. Amongst the elite of local 'ports'. Stellenbosch WO, as next.

Premium range

★★★★☆ **Botmaskop** (🐾) 65% cab in 5-way Bordeaux-style blend. **17** (94) as always big, forward & rather showy, with lots of dark fruit & savoury character. 45% new oak. Succulent & enjoyable in youth, but structure & depth to go a good few years, especially in magnum.

★★★★★ **Chardonnay Banghoek Reserve 18** (90) has restrained limy, nutty nose - less fruity than Summercourt, more straightforward than Terraced Block. Soft & silky, with a good seam of lemony acidity. The 40% new oak integrated.

★★★★ **Chenin Blanc Swartland Reserve** Oak gleams through modest peach & thatch notes on **18** (89) (25% new barrels). Dry & fresh; the lingering sweet fruit with a savoury tang.

★★★★★ **Coastal Cuvée Sauvignon Blanc** More perfumed nuances of aroma on this **19** (92), from widely sourced WO Coastal vineyards, than other version. Ripe, pleasingly balanced, fresh & lively, with a certain serious weight & breadth, helped by a little semillon & oaked fraction.

Luxury range

★★★★ **Summercourt Chardonnay** Attractive, forthcoming floral, citrus & stonefruit notes on **18** (86), for earlier drinking than the other chardonnays here; soft texture, charm, & just enough structure.

★★★★ Sauvignon Blanc Plenty of mostly tropical fruit aroma & flavour on **19** ⑧⑨. Splash semillon & some lees ageing give some weight, but not detracting from the fresh, light-feeling balance. WO W Cape.

★★★★ Banghoek Chardonnay Eau de Vie ⓐ Supple potstill husk spirit digestif ⑧⑥, with aromatic 'husky' nuttiness & sweet fruit reminiscences on quite fiery palate. 500 ml.

Shiraz ★★★★ Generously ripe & spicy notes on pretty straightforward **18** ⑧⑤, light grip comes more from acid than tannin. Stellenbosch WO unless noted. **Cabernet Franc Rosé ★★★★** Pale onion skin hue on **19** ⑧⑤. Lightly fruity but with a savoury edge, making an elegantly restrained, dry, fresh & lively whole. — TJ

Location/map: Stellenbosch ▪ Map grid reference: H5 ▪ WO: Banghoek/Stellenbosch/Western Cape/Coastal/Swartland ▪ Est 1983 ▪ 1stB 1984 ▪ Tasting & sales Mon-Sat 10-5 Sun 10-4 ▪ Fee R75/3 wines, R100/4 wines, R350/5 Icon range wines ▪ Cellar tours by appt (no tours during harvest) ▪ Gifts ▪ Farm produce ▪ Walks/hikes ▪ Art collection ▪ Delaire Graff & Indochine Restaurants ▪ 5-star Lodges & Spa ▪ Owner(s) Laurence Graff ▪ Winemaker(s) Morné Vrey (Jul 2009) ▪ Viticulturist(s) Kallie Fernhout (Jun 2010) ▪ 42ha/20ha (cabs s/f, malbec, merlot, p verdot, chard, sauv) ▪ 480t/30,000cs own label 36% red 48% white 16% rosé ▪ WIETA ▪ PO Box 3058 Stellenbosch 7602 ▪ info@delaire.co.za ▪ www.delaire.co.za ▪ S 33° 55' 17.70" E 018° 55' 22.08" ▪ ⓦ warmers.rise.easy ▪ **T** +27 (0)21-885-8160

Delheim Wines ⓐ ⑪ ⓒ ⓖ

A new winemaking team takes the helm at this much-loved and -admired family winery. Roelof Lotriet is the new man in charge, assisted by Nelson Buthelezi and Nongcebo Langa. Noni completed an internship at the farm, during which she wrote her university thesis on smoke taint, a topic for further investigation which saw her visit California before taking up her new role at Delheim. The trio will work with the eco-minded Sperling family to maintain their leadership in sustainable winegrowing, which has seen the farm recognised as a WWF-SA Conservation Champion. Meanwhile, visitors from around the world continue to flock to the farm high on Stellenbosch's Simonsberg Mountain, with its charming winetasting options, relaxed restaurant and year-round events.

★★★★☆ Grand Reserve ⓐ The flagship, always cab, **15** ⑨③ with dashes merlot & cab franc, latter prominent in smoky perfume & warm herbaceous aromas, giving way to rich black-berried fruit, tobacco & classic cedar twist. Positive tannins, lively acidity. 30% new oak. Keep, if possible.

★★★★☆ Vera Cruz Pinotage ⓐ From registered single-vineyard, **16** ⑨② darkly broods, oozing concentration, complexity & style. Medley of dark plums, red cherries, roasted nuts, all rounded up with beautiful ripe tannins & pliable texture. A sin to drink it now, especially from also-available magnum & other larger formats. Simonsberg-Stellenbosch WO, as VC Shiraz.

★★★★ Shiraz After **16 ★★★★** ⑧⑤, back to form in **17** ⑧⑥, glorious concoction of bright red berries, pepper, perfume & cloves. 50% new oak adds charry edge to finish, & refreshing gritty texture overall.

★★★★☆ Vera Cruz Shiraz ⓐ Premium label showing classic northern Rhône violets, cloves & pepper on elegant **15** ⑨③. Picked over 4 occasions to give layers of smoked meat, sweet spice, fresh ripe plum & cherry. Silky tannins & texture, firm positive finish. From a single site, like **14** ⑨⓪.

★★★★☆ Chardonnay Sur Lie Wonderfully poised **17** ⑨⓪ keeps ripe apricot fruit in harmony with creamy vanilla (9 months lees contact), warm honey & ginger spice (barrel ferment, 30% new). Held together seamlessly with crisp acidity through to fresh finish.

★★★★ Chenin Blanc Wild Ferment Fermented in old French oak, **18** ⑧⑦ shows crunchy apple fruit with honey, fennel & oatmeal layers. Crab apple zestiness keeps it lively & fresh throughout.

★★★★ Blanc de Blancs Brut ⓐ MCC sparkling from chardonnay, **15** ⑧⑦ spent 2 years on lees gaining attractive brioche notes & good, persistent bubbles. Soft yellow apple, pleasing salty finish. Cellardoor only.

★★★★☆ Edelspatz Noble Late Harvest ⓐ Glorious melange of ripe tropical fruit (pineapple, mango, peach), unwooded **18** ⑨③ from riesling beguiles with added botrytis notes of honey, marmalade & molasses. Elegant & balanced, excellent depth & lively acidity. Simonsberg-Stellenbosch WO. 375 ml.

Shiraz-Cabernet Sauvignon ⓟ **★★★☆** Leads with shiraz flavours - red fruit, peppered salami - before weighing in with the roundness of cab, combining beautifully for delicious drinking pleasure in **17** ⑧⑤. 40% oaked, only 15% new. Coastal WO.

Merlot ★★★☆ Bags of character on **16** (84), combines black & red fruit with attractive tar/tobacco & spice. 10% new oak gently adds to soft tannins & texture. Simonsberg-Stellenbosch WO, as next. **Pinotage** ★★★★ Plenty of typicity & cheerful comfort from **17** (85) - a black velvet, cherry, chocolate cake of a wine with fascinating tweak of savoury leather at the finish. **Pinotage Rosé** ★★★ Pretty & perfumed, fresh & fruity - what more could you want in a pink wine? **19** (81) on the cusp of dryness but 4% muscat adds appealing fruity sweet note on nose. WO Coastal. **Gewürztraminer** ★★★★ Dialled-back flavours on **18** (83) but still plenty of typicity (litchis, peaches), few grams sugar & enjoyably fresh acidity will pair perfectly with a Cape Malay curry. **Sauvignon Blanc** ★★★★ Crisp & lively tropical fruit (guava, granadilla) on **19** (83) crowd pleaser, with well-integrated acid & nutty finish. **Spatzendreck** ★★★★ Cheeky **17** (85) Natural Sweet mixes muscat, chenin & riesling in honeyed mouthful of apricots & vanilla ice cream. Oak fermented, none new, needs tad more acidity to match **16** ★★★★ (86). 500 ml. — CM

Location/map: Stellenbosch ▪ Map grid reference: F2 ▪ WO: Stellenbosch/Simonsberg–Stellenbosch/Coastal ▪ Est 1971 ▪ 1stB 1961 ▪ Tasting & sales Mon-Sun 9-5 ▪ Wine & fynbos cupcake pairing daily ▪ Closed Easter Fri/Sun, Dec 25 & Jan 1 ▪ Cellar tours daily at 10.30 & 2.30 ▪ Delheim Restaurant ▪ Delheim picnics ▪ Tour groups ▪ Gifts ▪ MTB trails ▪ Conferences ▪ Events: harvest festival, jazz & cheese fondue in winter, mushroom forages - see website for schedule ▪ Conservation area ▪ Owner(s) Sperling Trust ▪ Winemaker(s) Roelof Lotriet (Dec 2018) ▪ 375ha/130ha (cab, merlot, ptage, shiraz, chard, chenin, gewürz, riesling, sauv) ▪ 980t/120,000cs own label 50% red 30% white 20% rosé ▪ Brands for clients: Woolworths ▪ Level 8 BBEE, IPW, WIETA, WWF-SA Conservation Champion ▪ PO Box 210 Stellenbosch 7599 ▪ info@delheim.com ▪ www.delheim.com ▪ S 33° 52' 10.1" E 018° 53' 9.8" ▪ ⬚ pointed.developer.palace ▪ **T +27 (0)21-888-4600**

☐ **De Liefde** see Mountain Ridge Wines

De Meye Wines (♀) (🍴) (📷) (♿)

This family-owned estate, one of the most northerly in Stellenbosch, has been home to five generations of Myburghs, with Philip Myburgh currently farming it. Consultant winemaker Francois Haasbroek, long noted for his light touch and concern for freshness, has released the first of the wines he's vinified since his arrival in late 2018, and a few more that were bottled under his careful eye. The Table restaurant has new owners in Leigh Williamson and Brendan Thorncroft, 'who share a passion for food, fresh ingredients, seasonal produce and simple but delicious cooking' served in 'De Meye's amazing setting'.

★★★★ **Cabernet Sauvignon** Unexceptional, unshowy example of the variety, **17** (89) has youthful intensity of aroma & flavour, with a pleasant herbal twist to the typicality. Firm muscularity & a touch of ripe sweetness. Only older oak. 14.4% alcohol. No **16**.

★★★★ **Trutina** (♀) Flagship red mostly merlot in **13** (87), with cab franc, shiraz, cab. Earth, sweet tobacco, dark fruit & cocoa complexity; supple & restrained. Balance renders 14.8% alcohol unobtrusive.

Shiraz (♀) ★★★★ Splashes merlot & cab franc in **15** (85), better than last but needing time. Appealing smoky bacon & black pepper nuances in tight dry tannin framework. **Rosé** ★★★ Drops 'Shiraz' from name, as **19** (82) from Swartland grenache & cinsaut. Gently aromatic & fruity; juicy, well balanced & dry. **Chardonnay Unwooded** ★★★ Expected stonefruit & citrus on **19** (81), with a little earthiness. Dry, with modest 12% alcohol. Not tasted: **Merlot, Chenin Blanc**. — TJ

Location/map: Stellenbosch ▪ Map grid reference: E1 ▪ WO: Stellenbosch/Swartland ▪ Est/1stB 1998 ▪ Tasting & sales Wed-Sun & pub hols 11-5 ▪ Fee R40/5 wines ▪ Cellar tours Mon-Fri by appt ▪ 'The Table at De Meye' open for lunch Thu-Sun, booking essential T +27 (0)72-696-0530, www.thetablerestaurant.co.za ▪ De Meye wedding & function venue (up to 120 pax) ▪ The Garden Cottage venue (workshops/private functions up to 10 pax) ▪ Lavender ▪ Owner(s) Jan Myburgh Family Trust ▪ Winemaker(s) Francois Haasbroek (Oct 2018, consultant) ▪ Viticulturist(s) Philip Myburgh (farmer) ▪ 100ha/30ha (cabs s/f, merlot, shiraz, chard, chenin) ▪ 280t/15,000cs own label 65% red 25% white 10% rosé ▪ IPW ▪ PO Box 20 Elsenburg 7607 ▪ info@demeye.co.za ▪ www.demeye.co.za ▪ S 33° 49' 0.7" E 018° 49' 48.8" ▪ ⬚ movable.wisp.simulator ▪ **T +27 (0)21-884-4131**

DeMorgenzon (♀) (📷)

Carl van der Merwe, cellarmaster and chief executive at Wendy and Hylton Appelbaum's splendid and ambitious (and much loved) estate in Stellenboschkloof, stresses the need to continually reassess the approach to viticulture and winemaking, especially as the Cape has become drier and warmer. In the vineyards, he says 'a major focal point is increasing soil quality and minimising the use of water. In the winery, managing tannins on reds, which tend to increase in hotter and drier conditions, has become a particular focus. For our white wines, reducing vine stress and ensuring a harvest with optimal natural acid levels...' Meanwhile, no doubt the classical music played in both vineyard and cellar ('all day, and every day') also continues its positive influence on vines and wines.

Reserve range

★★★★☆ **Syrah** ⓐ Rich, authoritative & restrained **17** ⑨③ shows a dense ripe core of fruit & similar yielding grape tannins as **15** ⑨③. Unobtrusively oaked (18% new), in varying sized vessels. Still so youthful, will reward lengthy cellaring. No **16**.

★★★★☆ **Chardonnay** ⓐ Riper fruit profile though retains elegant balance in drier **18** ⑨③ vintage. Assimilates more new oak (30% new), giving an unctuous, silky texture. Quite rich & complex, already tempting, but will continue to improve.

★★★★☆ **Chenin Blanc** ⓐ ⓦ Staggered picking helped temper the drier vintage, though **18** ⑨④ a tad riper & with less verve than stellar **17** ★★★★★ ⑨⑤, but similar rich, oaked styling, reflecting the stylistic synergy between New World opulence & Old World intensity & elegance.

★★★★★ **The Divas Chenin Blanc** ⓩ ⓦ From section of oldest vineyard, made when Reserve Chenin can do without. Previously a **13** listed as 'Special Cuvée'. **17** ⑨⑦ as fine as the Chenin, but more stony & savoury (a hint of liquorice), the concentrated ripe fruit balanced by a thrilling acidity.

★★★★ **Méthode Cap Classique Chenin Blanc** ⓩ ⓦ Warm apple tart aromas with some toasted brioche too on latest, partly oaked **NV** ⑧⑦ sparkling. Lots of apple-peach flavour, fresh & dry.

★★★★☆ **Vinedried Chenin Blanc** ⓩ Complex aromas & flavours on **11** ⑨③ include typical notes of decadent grape maturity from desiccated grapes – also marmalade, marzipan, dried fruit. Would need more piercing acid to be really thrilling, but delicious & soft textured; clean finish. Only older oak. 375 ml.

Maestro range

★★★★☆ **Red** ⓐ A masterly Bordeaux blend, merlot & cab taking charge in **17** ⑨④ with cab franc, petit verdot & malbec. Distinct herbal nuance to the dark berry core, though tannins are more structured than austere. 20% new oak for 18 months in sync with complex, compact fruit. Distinguished & ageworthy.

★★★★ **Blue** Syrah-led in **17** ★★★★★ ⑨⓪ with grenache noir & splashes of mourvèdre & petite sirah. Brooding, smoky dark fruit, firm but pliable tannins, muscular & subdued. All elements in place to improve with time. More harmonious than **15** ⑧⑨. No **16**.

★★★★☆ **White** ⓐ Roussanne-led blend has more chenin & grenache blanc in **17** ⑨④ than previous, with chardonnay & viognier in equal measure. The delicately pervasive, aromatic fruit is the star, the oaked portion (20% new) seamlessly assimilated. Fresh, understated, with effortless grace.

CWG Auction Reserve range

★★★★☆ **Gravitas** ⓐ Grenache noir in the lead, with syrah & minor portions durif & mourvèdre in **17** ⑨③ Rhône-style blend. Naturally fermented & matured in old oak with musky, scented red fruit in an opulent tannin framework. Accomplished & youthful, already succulent & sensual, with rich rewards in store.

Special Release range

★★★★☆ **Special Cuvée Sauvignon Blanc** ⓐ Clean, perfumed delicacy & intensity on **17** ⑨④. A splash (3.6%) of semillon, natural fermentation & older-oak maturation in seamless, supple & waxy support. Piquantly balanced, elegant & flavourful.

DMZ range

★★★★ **Grenache Noir** Smoky, musky ripe fruit in a firm tannin grip in **17** ★★★★ ⑧⑤. Like more balanced **16** ⑧⑦, matured in old oak. A little gawky, but nothing that time or a dinner date wouldn't resolve.

★★★★ **Syrah** A supple structure, fresh acidity & generous sprinkling of spicy white pepper ensure **17** ⑧⑧'s appealing drinkability, though no impediment to future development.

★★★★ **Chardonnay** Warmer, more subdued lanolin & gentle baked pear flavours on **18** ⑧⑦. Both tank & light oaking influenced, not as bright & fresh as **17** ⑧⑨, but still satisfying.

★★★★ **Chenin Blanc** ⓩ Mildly exuberant aromas, full flavours on **18** ⑧⑥; light oaking adds breadth & texture. Undemanding but very satisfying. In awe of its senior siblings – but what chenin wouldn't be?

★★★★ **Sauvignon Blanc** Dusty nettle & grapefruit flavours on **18** ★★★★☆ ⑧⑤. Balanced & unaggressively dry, though more pensive than **17** ⑧⑦ & best with food.

Garden Vineyards range

Rosé ★★★☆ Shiraz-led 7-way varietal blend for **18** ⑧③'s dry, savoury-styled rosé. Similar dark, musky tone & bone-dry delivery to previous. Great with charcuterie. — MW

Location/map/WO: Stellenbosch ▪ Map grid reference: C5 ▪ Est 2003 ▪ 1stB 2005 ▪ Tasting & sales daily 10-5 ▪ Fee R30-R125 ▪ Closed Dec 25 & Jan 1 ▪ Cellar tours on request ▪ Conservation area ▪ Owner(s) Wendy & Hylton Appelbaum ▪ Cellarmaster(s) / chief executive Carl van der Merwe (Jul 2010), with junior winemaker Dirk van Zyl (Jun 2017) ▪ Viticulturist(s) Danie de Waal (Dec 2014) ▪ 91ha/55ha (cabs s/f, durif, grenache n/b, malbec, merlot, mourv, p verdot, pinot, shiraz, chard, chenin, rouss, sauv, sem, viog) ▪ 500t/40,000cs own label 40% red 50% white 10% rosé ▪ IPW ▪ PO Box 1388 Stellenbosch 7599 ▪ info@demorgenzon. com ▪ www.demorgenzon.com ▪ S 33° 56' 22.99" E 018° 45' 0.17" ▪ 🌐 dreaming.lobster.faces ▪ **T +27 (0)21-881-3030**

☐ **Den** *see* Painted Wolf Wines
☐ **Denneboom** *see* Oude Denneboom
☐ **De Oude Opstal** *see* Stellendrift - SHZ Cilliers/Kuün Wyne

Desert Rose Wines

Rose-like gypsum crystal formations found in their area of the West Coast, and a favourite Sting song, gave Vredendal nurseryman Alan van Niekerk and Namaqua Wines grower Herman Nel the name for their boutique wine collaboration. Minuscule production precluded a commercial release of the 2019 vintage, but the wines and vintages listed below are still available. The tasting venue remains closed for now.

Cabernet Sauvignon ⓥ ★★★ Food-inviting **09** ⑦⑧ has walnut piquancy, sour cherry flavours, & cool vintage's pleasant grip. Also-available **18** untasted. **Alex's Rose** ⓥ ★★★ Equal shiraz, merlot, cab, offers charred oaky aromas with rhubarb-laced fruit in **12** ⑧⓪. Hint of cassis, then waves of chalky tannin. — GdB

Location: Vredendal ▪ WO: Western Cape ▪ Closed to public ▪ Owner(s) Alan van Niekerk & Herman Nel ▪ Winemaker(s) Herman Nel ▪ desertrose@nashuaisp.co.za ▪ **T +27 (0)82-809-2040/+27 (0)82-800-2270**

☐ **Destiny** *see* Mont Destin Wines-Destiny Shiraz

De Toren Private Cellar ⓥ

The new team in charge of this internationally hailed boutique red-wine specialist winery on Stellenbosch's Polkadraai Hills have big plans, with renovations and upgrades for the manor house and tasting room as well as the cellar. But attention to detail in the vineyards and meticulous crafting of Bordeaux-styled wines in their gravity-flow facility remain unchanged under the watchful eye of cellarmaster Charles Williams and MD Albie Koch. Their journey to organic certification is almost complete, as they seek to farm in a more natural fashion and preserve the farm for future generations.

★★★★ **Délicate** More serious than **NV** ⑧⑦ would imply, black cherries, violets & tarry notes combine with upfront 14% alcohol in malbec, cab franc & cab blend. Older oak adds spice, softness. Intended for light chilling.

★★★★☆ **Fusion V** 🏅 Maintains quality & style in 5-way Bordeaux blend (half cab), **17** ⑨④ showing spice, tobacco, elegant blackcurrant core. Dense, dark tannins brood in the background promising plenty of satisfaction over next decade. Year oak, 50% new, 10% American. Magnums (& larger formats) highly recommended.

★★★★☆ **Z** 🏅 Also 5-way Bordeaux blend, but merlot-led (47%). **17** ⑨③ has plenty of character, black plums & cherries with hints of dust & dark chocolate. Big & bold, needing time for fruit & oak (30% new, tiny amount of American on the malbec) to settle. Halves, magnums & larger formats.— CM

Location/map/WO: Stellenbosch ▪ Map grid reference: B6 ▪ Est 1994 ▪ 1stB 1999 ▪ Tasting & cellar tours by appt only ▪ Sales Mon-Fri 9-4 (closed on pub hols) ▪ Tasting & tours are approximately 1½ hr ▪ Owner(s) De Toren Holding AG ▪ Cellarmaster(s) Charles Williams (Dec 2008) ▪ Winemaker(s) Martin Fourie (Dec 2015) ▪ Viticulturist(s) Avril Malan (Dec 2018) ▪ 25ha/±21ha (cabs s/f, malbec, merlot, p verdot) ▪ 150t/10,000cs own label 100% red ▪ PO Box 48 Vlottenburg 7604 ▪ info@de-toren.com ▪ www.de-toren.com ▪ S 33° 57′ 34.5″ E 018° 45′ 7.5″ ▪ ⌨ pleads.sportier.plunger ▪ T +27 (0)21-881-3119 / +27 (0)81-079-2297

De Trafford Wines

Freed up by winemaker Charla Haasbroek, now in full control at De Trafford's Breede River sister winery Sijnn, assistant winemaker Fred Fismer helping both there and here at De Trafford's Stellenbosch Mountain home farm, and inspired by recent trips to regions both mainstream (Rhône, Loire, Bordeaux, Piedmont, Douro) and fringe (Banyuls, Priorat, Etna, Georgia, Croatia), David Trafford, nearing his third decade as one of SA's most respected and admired non-interventionist boutique winegrowers, says he 'can play again'. Projects include 'creative, small-lot winemaking' in his original makeshift cellar: a skin-contact and Reserve chenin, wholebunch cinsaut, wholeberry cab franc in amphoras. 'Oh, and a little chardonnay and chenin.' Just as well Saturday tasting times have been extended. Maintenance continues to ensure top quality, with vine renewal keeping the blocks virus-free and allowing for conversion to more drought-resistant rootstock.

★★★★☆ **Cabernet Sauvignon** ⓐ Sophisticated & stylish **16** ⑼₃, exceptionally pure & expressive fruit aromas & flavours of blueberry, cassis, graphite & slatey minerality, structure & length from 22 months barrel ageing, 35% new. Minuscule yield, just 1.2 kg of fruit per vine; combo own (Mont Fleur) & neighbour (Keermont) grapes, as next 2. Wild-yeast fermented, as all. Also in 1.5L & 3L.

★★★★★ **Cabernet Franc** ⓥ ⓐ Superb expression of the variety from an exceptional vintage. **15** ★★★★★ ⑼₅ is seamless with dark berries wrapped in a fresh ribbon of green herbs. A keeper, & even more alluring than **14** ⑼₄. 19 months in French oak, 35% new, as next. Bottled by hand unfiltered, like all.

★★★★☆ **Merlot** ⓐ Great freshness in **15** ⑼₄, red & black fruit shining through. Curvaceous, balanced & well crafted, with Xmas spice & creamy oak complexity.

★★★★☆ **Petit Verdot** ⓐ New to the guide (**12** & **13** untasted), off Keermont vines. Intricate & concentrated notes of blackberry, pepper & cedar from 30 months in 30% new French barrels. Weighty richness & breadth in **14** ⑼₂, with good structure & poise, the fruit well-knit with the supple tannins.

★★★★☆ **Blueprint Syrah** ⓐ Thrilling complexity of bramble, plum, mulberry, liquorice & cured meat, sprinkling of white pepper on the nose & palate. Wafts of lavender & violet complete a well-balanced & generous wine. **17** ⑼₄ from mostly Keermont blocks, including alluvial Sweetwater, producing lighter but aromatic grapes. Older oak, 20 months.

★★★★☆ **Syrah 393** ⓐ Ink-tinged purple hue on svelte, home-grown **17** ⑼₃ matches dark plum & mulberry intensity, complex nuances of leather, black pepper & savoury herbs. Fine-grained tannin & serious wooding (40% new for 12 months, older small-oak for 7 more) indicate a fine future. Also in magnum.

★★★★☆ **CWG Auction Reserve Perspective** ⓐ **17** ★★★★★ ⑼₅ blend of near-equal cab franc, merlot & cab, all from Mont Fleur. Elegant, shows concentrated focus. Fine & supple tannins underpin ripe flavours of black cherry, tobacco & dried herbs. House's generous alcohol (14.9%) & 100% new oak invisible in the master-crafted whole. Last-tasted **15** ⑼₄ also exceptional. Some magnums too.

★★★★☆ **The Drawing Board** ⓥ Standout once-off Bordeaux blend, best barrels of almost-equal cab franc, merlot & cab from own high-lying sites. **16** ⑼₄ opulent yet vibrates with energy, the fine tannin structure in harmony with the pure fruit. Year new oak, further 9 months 2nd-fill casks as blend.

★★★★☆ **Elevation 393** ⓐ Beautifully aged vintage blend from single home-farm parcel at 393 m altitude. **13** ★★★★★ ⑼₆ rich, full bodied & sumptuous, still bursting with energy; enjoy now or cellar 10+ years. Mostly cab & syrah (50/30) with merlot, 24 months in mostly new French oak (blending done after 9 months). **12** ⑼₂ was syrah & 3 Bordeaux grapes.

★★★★☆ **Chenin Blanc** ⓐ Ageworthy, barrel-fermented **18** ⑼₃ has many layers of texture & depth, including cream-laced orchard fruit & roasted nuts, all in harmony with refreshing green apple acidity. From Keermont & 2 Helderberg blocks, aged 10 months in mixed barrels. Also in 1.5L & 3L.

★★★★☆ **CWG Auction Reserve Chenin Blanc** ⓝᴇᴡ ⓐ Single 225L barrel of exquisite, balanced & harmonious wine from 11 year old Keermont block, needed a year to ferment. **17** ⑼₄ rich caramel popcorn, baked apple & spice cake, with delicate apple blossom farewell. Older wood, total 21 months.

Not tasted: **Straw Wine**. — WB

Location/map/WO: Stellenbosch ▪ Map grid reference: G8 ▪ Est/1stB 1992 ▪ Tasting, sales & tours Mon-Fri by appt only; Sat 10-3 ▪ Private tasting (current releases) R200pp to the CWG Trust weekdays / Sat R150pp, waived on purchase; Vintage tasting (6 wines from library selection) R450pp; The Sijnn Experience R200pp; Vineyard Walk R200pp – all to be booked in advance ▪ Closed all pub hols ▪ Owner(s) David & Rita Trafford ▪ Winemaker(s) David Trafford & Hendry Hess, with Fred Fismer ▪ Viticulturist(s) Schalk du Toit (consultant) ▪ 200ha/5ha (cabs s/f, merlot, shiraz) ▪ 71t/7,000cs own label 70% red 30% white ▪ PO Box 495 Stellenbosch 7599 ▪ info@detrafford.co.za ▪ www.detrafford.co.za ▪ S 34° 0' 45.1" E 018° 53' 57.8" ▪ unworldly.crackle. sweeping ▪ T +27 (0)21-880-1611

Deux Frères Wines

The French name means 'two brothers', here Stellenbosch boutique winery owners Retief du Toit and Stephan as winemaker. A very personal project, the Gallic influence continuing in the grape varieties they planted in 2008, and the name of the home farm, Le Present, on the foothills of Simonsberg Mountain. The range includes, perhaps uniquely, a limited-release mourvèdre in hand-numbered magnums.

★★★★ Mourvèdre Older barrels, 30 months, for deep & dense **14** (86), dark-fruited plums/prunes, scrub & maraschino cherries. Palate also serious, foundation of compact tannins for definition, ageing.

★★★★ Fraternité Shiraz, 25% mourvèdre, **15** (87) dark toned, plush & ripe, generously spiced, prosciutto savouriness. Curvaceous, yet tannins a dry, firm presence. 2 years French/American oak, 30% new.

Liberté ★★★★ Now 100% cabernet, previewed **15** (83) mostly Hungarian barrels, 26 months, 70% new. Dusty spice & white pepper overlay to dark plummy fruit. Nice grip for food, cellaring, already accessible. **Blanc de Noir** ★★★ From grenache, coral pink & bone-dry **17** (78), perky red berries; light enough (12% alcohol) for everyday imbibing. WO Durbanville. **Chenin Blanc** ★★★★ Barrel fermented/aged year, all new. Quince & tropical notes in **17** (85), lovely ginger biscuit spicing; elegant, zesty & vibrant. The nervous tension of a racehorse. — CR

Location/map: Stellenbosch ▪ Map grid reference: E3 ▪ WO: Stellenbosch/Durbanville ▪ Est 2008 ▪ 1stB 2012 ▪ Tasting, sales & cellar tours Tue-Fri 11-4 Sat 10-2; tasting by appt 1 May to 31 Aug ▪ Closed Sun/Mon, Easter Fri-Mon, Dec 25 & Jan 1 ▪ Wine & food pairing available on request ▪ Tasting platters & picnics to be pre-booked ▪ Owner(s) Stephan & Retief du Toit ▪ Cellarmaster(s)/viticulturist(s) Stephan du Toit (Jan 2008) ▪ 2.1ha (cab, malbec, mourv, p verdot, shiraz) ▪ 1,700cs own label 80% red 20% rosé ▪ PO Box 209 Koelenhof 7605 ▪ stephan@dfwines.co.za ▪ www.dfwines.co.za ▪ S 33° 52' 51.16" E 18° 50' 44.93" ▪ molars.goat.offer ▪ T +27 (0)21-889-9865/+27 (0)82-371-4770

De Villiers Wines

Villiers de Villiers, based on his family's farm in Paarl, produces wine under contract to buyers in various international markets, latterly Taiwan, Singapore, Macao and Hong Kong, and for his own, eponymous label. See under Wineways for tasting notes and ratings.

Location/map: Paarl ▪ Map grid reference: E6 ▪ Est/1stB 1688 ▪ Tasting & sales by appt ▪ Owner(s) De Villiers Family Trust ▪ Cellarmaster(s)/winemaker(s)/viticulturist(s) Villiers de Villiers (1980) ▪ 50,000cs own label 80% red 20% white ▪ PO Box 659 Suider-Paarl 7624 ▪ info@devillierswines.com ▪ www.devillierswines.com ▪ S 33° 45' 43.3" E 018° 57' 40.8" ▪ table.pancake.purple ▪ T +27 (0)21-863-2175

☐ **Devonet** see Clos Malverne

Devonvale Golf & Wine Estate

The house wines of Devonvale, a luxury residential estate, hotel and championship golf course north of Stellenbosch, to date have included shiraz grapes grown on the property. Now, however, the vines are to be uprooted and small parcels of 'only the best' fruit selected for vinification at Stellenbosch University's Welgevallen Cellar, says longtime general manager Ryno Bernardo. As before, the wines will be sold mostly through the restaurant, function and event facilities on the estate.

Friends Forever range

Shiraz ★★★ Gluggable crowd-pleaser **17** (81), vibrant dark fruit flavours, undertones of mocha & chocolate, savoury farewell. **Sauvignon Blanc** ★★★ Zesty & fresh, but **18** (79)'s fruit is subdued, its body less substantial than previous. — WB

Location/map/WO: Stellenbosch ▪ Map grid reference: D3 ▪ Est 1997 ▪ 1stB 2004 ▪ Tasting by appt ▪ Fee R45pp ▪ Sales Mon-Sat 11-6 ▪ Chez Shiraz restaurant ▪ Tour groups ▪ Golf ▪ Pro shop ▪ Conferences ▪ Devonvale Golf Lodge ▪ Owner(s) Devonmust (Pty) Ltd ▪ Winemaker(s) Riaan Wassüng (Stellenbosch University Welgevallen Cellar) ▪ Viticulturist(s) Southern Turf Management (2015) ▪ 117ha/1.2ha (shiraz) ▪ 5t/±300cs own label 50% red 50% white ▪ PO Box 77 Koelenhof 7605 ▪ info@devonvale.co.za ▪ www. devonvale.co.za ▪ S 33° 52' 59.6" E 018° 48' 15.0" ▪ ⌨ smile.paving.drones ▪ T +27 (0)21-865-2080

DeWaal Wines   ⓠ ⓟ ⓞ

De Waals have farmed Uiterwyk estate for six generations (Stellenboschkloof neighbours Jordan and DeMorgenzon once part of the family landholding). Current owner Pieter manages the business, while brothers Chris and Daniël share vineyard and cellar duties (Chris making the whites, Daniël the reds). The production ratio might be even, but it's reds, particularly pinotages, that take pride of place. Increasingly limited Top of the Hill is a textbook expression of this heritage variety (the hilltop vines, ca 1950, the oldest in SA), as is CT de Waal (honouring the first person to vinify the grape experimentally in 1941).

DeWaal range

Pinotage ★★★ Lightly oaked **16** ⑧⓪ leaner in style, crunchy, piquant fruit, dusty tannins & very dry farewell. Not tasted: **Cabernet Sauvignon, Merlot, CT de Waal Pinotage, Top Of The Hill Pinotage, Signal Rock.**

Young Vines range

Chenin Blanc ★★★ Water-white **19** ⑧⓪ packed with tropical fruit & twist of lemon, a tasty & fun everyday drink. Sampled pre-bottling, as next. **Sauvignon Blanc ★★★** Zesty pineapple & fresh-cut grass flavours on **19** ⑧②, mouthwatering lime finish. Not tasted: **Merlot, Shiraz.** — WB

Location/map/WO: Stellenbosch ▪ Map grid reference: C5 ▪ Est 1682 ▪ 1stB 1972 ▪ Tasting & sales Mon-Sat & pub hols 10—4.30 ▪ Tasting R50/standard & R100/premium ▪ Closed Sun, Easter weekend, Dec 25/26 & Jan 1 ▪ Cheese platters in season (pre-bookings only) ▪ Top of the Hill walks in season (monthly on a Sat from Oct-Apr) ▪ Owner(s) Pieter de Waal ▪ Winemaker(s)/viticulturist(s) Chris de Waal & Daniël de Waal (whites/reds, consultants) ▪ 800t ▪ 50% red 50% white ▪ IPW ▪ PO Box 15 Vlottenburg 7604 ▪ admin@dewaal.co.za ▪ www.dewaal.co.za ▪ S 33° 56' 29.3" E 018° 45' 59.9" ▪ ⌨ sampling.think.waxes ▪ T +27 (0)21-881-3711

Dewaldt Heyns Family Wines   ⓠ

These wines are made by Dewaldt Heyns (and may be sampled) at the winery with which he is more famously associated — Saronsberg in Tulbagh. But the grapes are mostly off the old family farm in the Swartland, and the name of the range is offered as a tribute to the hard work of his father among the vines.

Weathered Hands range

★★★★ Pinotage ⓧ From old bushvines; very fine, silky **14** ⑧⑧ harmoniously melds ripe plum fruit with vanilla oak, 22 months), gears up on less structured, sweet-tasting **13 ★★★★** ⑧⑤.

★★★★☆ Shiraz ⓐ Deep, dark & brooding **16** ⑨④'s spicy bramble fruit toned by earthy elements, wonderfully fine tannins. Serious wine, delicious in youth, will reward patience. Confirms uptick in **15** ⑨③. Small berries off dryland vines on red Hutton soils, 10% wholebunch ferment, half new French barrels.

★★★★☆ Chenin Blanc ⓐ From ±40 year old bushvines on weathered granite, **18** ⑨③ is sumptuous but refined, limpid, vinous rather than fruity; like rich **17** ⑨③, its structure quickened by minerality. Bunch pressed to limit phenolics, no malo for elegance. French & Hungarian oak, 30% new.— DS

Location: Tulbagh/Swartland ▪ WO: Swartland ▪ Est/1stB 2006 ▪ Tasting by appt at Saronsberg Cellar ▪ Owner(s) Dewaldt Heyns Family Wines ▪ Cellarmaster(s)/winemaker(s)/viticulturist(s) Dewaldt Heyns ▪ (ptage, shiraz, chenin) ▪ 5t/1,100cs own label 60% red 40% white ▪ dewaldt@dewaldtheyns.com ▪ www.dewaldtheyns.com ▪ T +27 (0)82-441-4117

De Wet Cellar   ⓠ ⓟ ⓐ ⓞ ⓑ

Founded in 1946, this grower-owned winery near Worcester now processes 19,000 tons of fruit from the De Wet, Overhex and Nuy areas, mostly for export juggernaut FirstCape. However, its limited-edition own-label wines - offering quality, character and value - can be sampled alongside cheese and meat platters in the tasting lounge, also the check-in point for a 21-km MTB trail across four neighbouring farms.

★★★★ **Chardonnay** ⊘ 18 (88) half oaked, French/American, some new, shows as a buttered toast layer in the fruit, richer, fuller than slender **17** (88). A big personality.

★★★★ **Chenin Blanc Wood Matured** (Ⓥ) From single block, **17** (86) 8 months in barrel, good chenin fruit typicity, intriguing ginger savoury underpin. Individual, tasty. Up a notch on **16** ★★★★ (85).

★★★★ **Cravate** (⚬) Chardonnay, some pinot noir, **16** (88) méthode cap classique bubbly 2 years on lees. Lovely citrus aromas & flavours, bone-dry but not austere, loads of flavour, ends tangy fresh. No **13**, **14**, **15**.

★★★★ **Red Muscadel** (Ⓥ) Fortified muscat an area talent, & **17** (89) confirms it: raisins & dried stone-fruit scents, but the taste is the real pleasure, richly sweet, like drinking raisins. Well priced.

★★★★ **White Muscadel** ⊘ (⚬) Sultanas & beeswax, some citrus peel, fortified **17** (88) wonderfully layered & packed with favour. Richly sweet, so best served chilled. In its prime, long life ahead.

. . . .

Special Late Harvest (🍷) ★★★ Made by vinifying full-ripe & raisined white grapes (unspecified varieties), & **19** (80) shows it works. Sultana perfume, richly aromatic & yet not overly sweet flavours, there's balancing acidity. Delicious. **Hanepoot** ⊘ (🍷) ★★★ Never fails to impress with its grape essence character, **19** (81) is pure muscat in perfume & flavour. Fortified, richly sweet but has a tangy vibrancy that appeals. Serve well-chilled.

. . . .

Cabernet Sauvignon ★★★ French/American barrels, half new, give sleekly appealing **17** (81) its vanilla & nutmeg spicing, the tannins well integrated with the fruit. **Shiraz** (Ⓥ) ★★★ Older barrels allow **17** (80) fruit expression, cherries & hedgerow berries, nicely spiced, enough tannin grip for ageing few years. **Merlot-Cabernet Sauvignon** ⊘ ★★★ Cocoa notes from French/American oak, **18** (80) is plush & dark fruited, the gentle grip promising some ageing potential. **Cape Blend** (Ⓥ) ★★★ Petit verdot-led, with pinotage & shiraz, **16** (81) is dark toned, fruit the main player. With oak adding some spicing, definition, designed for early enjoyment. **Petillant Rosé** ⊘ ★★★ From pinotage, latest **NV** (77) perlé's touch of sweetness & moderate fizz makes this a party pleaser. **Chenin Blanc** ⊘ ★★★ Freshness personified, crunchy apples & pears, trim-figured but no lack of flavour. **19** (82) wakens the taste buds. **Petillant Fronté** ★★ Semi-sweet perlé from white muscadel, **NV** (74) offers sultana scents & flavours, perked up by the gentle fizz. Friendly 8% alcohol. **Sauvignon Blanc** ⊘ ★★★★ Showing passionfruit & fynbos, **19** (84) is sleekly elegant, with admirable purity & focus. **Cape Ruby** (Ⓥ) ★★★★ For drinking rather than cellaring, **NV** (84)'port'a fruitcake delight, enough spicing to add to attraction, smooth & satisfyingly round. — CR

Location/map/WO: Worcester ▪ Map grid reference: B3 ▪ Est 1946 ▪ 1stB 1964 ▪ Tasting & sales Mon-Fri 9-5 Sat 9-2 ▪ Closed all pub hols ▪ Cellar tours by appt ▪ Cheese platters ▪ BYO picnic ▪ Wedding/function venue for hire ▪ MTB trail ▪ Six Dogs gin available on premises ▪ Owner(s) 25 members ▪ Manager Tertius Jonck ▪ Winemaker(s) Tertius Jonck (Sep 2007) & Phillip Vercuiel (Dec 2007) ▪ Viticulturist(s) Hennie Visser (Jul 2008, VinPro) ▪ 1,000ha (cab, shiraz, chard, chenin, sauv) ▪ 19,000t/30,000cs own label 29% red 36% white 5% rosé 30% fortified + 10m L bulk ▪ ISO 22000, SGS, WIETA ▪ PO Box 16 De Wet 6853 ▪ admin@dewetcellar. co.za ▪ www.dewetcellar.co.za ▪ S 33° 36' 24.2" E 019° 30' 36.5" ▪ 🌐 ecology.network.moderate ▪ **T +27 (0)23-341-2710**

☐ **De Wit Family** *see* Signal Gun Wines

DGB (Pty) Ltd

Well-established producer with a strong portfolio of premium wine brands including Bellingham, Boschendal, Brampton, Douglas Green, Franschhoek Cellar, Old Road Wine Company, Tall Horse, The Beachhouse, The Bernard Series and The Saints, and international labels such as Culemborg, Millstream and Oude Kaap, some listed separately.

Location: Wellington ▪ Est 1942 ▪ Closed to public ▪ Owner(s) DGB Brait SE ▪ Winemaker(s)/viticulturist(s) see under Bellingham, Boschendal, Franschhoek Cellar & Old Road Wine Company ▪ Private Bag X03 Groot Drakenstein 7680 ▪ info@dgb.co.za ▪ www.dgb.co.za ▪ **T +27 (0)21-001-3150**

☐ **Diamond Collection** *see* Lutzville Vineyards
☐ **Die Bergkelder** *see* Libertas Vineyards & Estates

Die Kat se Snor

Afrikaans for 'the cat's whiskers', this is the own-label project of Gerhard Smith, whose day job is wine-making at Creation Wines. Here one of his focuses is small-batch, handcrafted pinot noir, hardly surprising given his Hemel-en-Aarde Ridge base, and eight years at Gladstone Vineyard in Wairarapa, New Zealand.

★★★★ Cinsault ⊘ Delicate, bright-fruited **19** ★★★★☆ ⑨⓪ departs from **17** ⑧⑨ with less oak (5 months) to let the fruit shine. Pristine raspberries, earthy spice, suggestion of wood & lengthy farewell in a perfect marriage. Slightly chill for best enjoyment. No **18**.

★★★★ Pinot Noir From Overberg block 'Kerksaal' (some bunch-pressed), **16** ⑧⑨ abounds with ripe strawberry, raspberry & cherry fruit wrapped in supple tannins, subtle earthy, grapefruit pithiness on the finish. Old oak aged & unfined/filtered, as all.

★★★★☆ Sauvignon Blanc (NEW) ⊘ Bunch pressed & naturally fermented (as all) in large-format barrel, **18** ⑨① more about texture & layers of flavour than aroma. Understated gooseberry, Key lime pie & crushed seashell notes, delicious kelp/umami savouriness in farewell. 11 months in oak, as Pinot. WO Hemel-en-Aarde Ridge.

Not tasted: **Chardonnay**. — WB

Location: Hermanus ▪ WO: Stellenbosch/Overberg/Hemel-en-Aarde Ridge ▪ Est/1stB 2014 ▪ Closed to public ▪ Owner(s) Gerhard Smith ▪ Winemaker(s)/viticulturist(s) Gerhard Smith (Jan 2014) ▪ Own label 70% red 30% white ▪ katsesnorwines@gmail.com ▪ **T +27 (0)76-254-0294**

☐ **Die Laan** *see* Stellenbosch University Welgevallen Cellar

Die Mas van Kakamas

Vlok and Welna Hanekom, then teachers, sallied forth more than 4 decades ago with one hectare of vines and two donkeys. Today Die Mas estate on the Orange River near Kakamas covers over 100 times that area, and the fruit is channelled into table grapes, raisins, wine and spirit. Pride in, and recognition of their location in the Kalahari echoes in the names of the sweet wines and brandies. A cornucopia awaits visitors.

Die Mas range

Merlot ⑦ ★★★ Fruitcake & coffee flavours combine with vanilla & spice in delightful **19** ⑧① easy sipper. **Shiraz** ⑦ ★★★ Beguiling violet perfume on **19** ⑧① along with sweet plums, palate is juicy with a savoury grip that invites creative food pairing. **Sauvignon Blanc** ⊘ ⑦ ★★★ Sunshine-in-a-glass styling, **19** ⑧④ nearly overflows with ripe tropical flavour, the full body (14% alcohol) mirrors lush fruit. A dusty/lemony finish reins it all in.

Cabernet Sauvignon ★★★ Smooth & easy to drink, **19** ⑦⑨ pleasing & true cassis flavours, fruity finish. Previewed, as all except Sauvignon. **Pinotage** ★★★ Wild berry & herb aromas on amiable **19** ⑧⓪, slips down very easily. Oak staved, as all except Sauvignon, 50% American for Pinotage & Merlot. **Chardonnay** ★★★ Bruised apple nuance & touch of cream, light-footed (12.5% alcohol) **19** ⑦⑧ has some texture on palate but doesn't linger.

Rooi Kalahari range

★★★★ Rooi Muskadel Gorgeous sunset hues, followed by dark plum & raisin flavour intensity, viscous mouthfeel on previewed **19** ⑧⑧ fortified. Balance comes via delicious freshness & fiery finish. 500 ml.

In abeyance: **Cape Vintage**.

Goue Kalahari range

★★★★ Hanepoot Fabulous amber-tinted fortified, **19** ⑧⑨ attracts immediately with dried peach & sultana, gaining intensity on unctuous palate. Finishes long & poised. 500 ml, as next.

★★★★☆ Wit Muskadel Extraordinary variety & concentration of flavours & aromas - dried peach, apricot kernel, barley sugar, marmalade, toasted almond. Full & sweet, but balanced spirit ensures whistle-clean, moreish conclusion. **19** ⑨⓪ tasted ex tank, as Hanepoot. Excellent value, as all the fortifieds.

Brandy range

★★★★ Die Kalahari Truffel First impression is of heightened complexity on current 5 year old ⑧⑨ from colombard & chenin (50/50) vs previous all-chenin bottling. Both 100% potstill. Array of soft flavours, dried peach, pear drop, roasted nuts & spice; full, round & poised, chocolate nuance on finish. 500 ml.

Vêr In Die Ou Kalahari ⊘ ★★★★ Robust blended brandy ⑧⑤, adds 50% colombard to previous chenin-only version. 30% potstill component. Vibrant, ripe stonefruit & nut flavours to blend with your favourite mixer for a hint of the Kalahari. — WB

Location: Kakamas ▪ Map: Northern Cape, Free State & North West ▪ Map grid reference: B8 ▪ WO: Northern Cape ▪ Est/1stB 2005 ▪ Tasting, sales & cellar tours Mon–Fri 8-5 Sat/pub hols 9-2 ▪ Closed Dec 25 ▪ Meals/ refreshments by appt; or BYO picnic ▪ Facilities for children ▪ Tour groups ▪ Gift shop ▪ Farm produce ▪ Conferences ▪ Walks/hikes ▪ MTB trail ▪ Conservation area ▪ Camping facilities, 3 self-catering chalets & large lapa/bush pub ▪ Owner(s) Die Mas Boerdery (Pty) Ltd ▪ Cellarmaster(s)/winemaker(s) André Landman (Apr 2016) ▪ 1,400ha/35ha (cab, merlot, muscadel r/w, p verdot, pinot, ptage, sangio, shiraz, souzão, tinta, touriga, chard, chenin, cbard, sauv, viog) ▪ 700t/4,000cs own label 30% red 20% white 50% brandy ▪ PO Box 193 Kakamas 8870 ▪ wine@diemas.co.za ▪ www.diemas.co.za ▪ S 28° 45' 48.59" E 020° 38' 26.45" ▪ 🖾 culturing.potting.room ▪ **T +27 (0)54-431-0245/+27 (0)71-015-7131**

Diemersdal Estate   ⑨ ⑪

In the Louw family since 1885, winemaking here dating back to 1702, this focused Durbanville farm is a sauvignon blanc producer par excellence, bottling no fewer than 11 different styles, including an unusual rosé and frozen-must wine (and a pair listed separately under Sauvignon Wines). For consumers, there's no lack of choice or interest, though, as evidenced by the recent introduction by custodian Tienie and 6th-generation winemaker son Thys (the MM flagship label references all firstborns christened Matthys Michael) of Austrian variety grüner veltliner to the range, produced from vineyards that are all unirrigated, a rarity in Durbanville. While no slouches with reds, the Louws continue exploiting the area's eminence in sauvignon, extending plantings, recruiting Janeke Beck to help with increased production, and promising another 'innovation' as we went to print.

MM Louw range

★★★★★ Cabernet Sauvignon ⊛ Fine **17** ⑨④ is firmly structured with 100% new oak for 22 months (as next) underpinning the ripe, dense blackcurrant fruit, hints of cigarbox wood & plum pudding. Shows the pedigree & elegance of this quality-driven estate.

★★★★★ Pinotage ⊛ Savoury & powerful **17** ⑨③ shows a tight mineral bouquet with graphite, salty liquorice, plum & blueberry pie, plenty of depth & broad mouthfeel. Accomplished wine with great fruit purity. WO Cape Town, as all these.

★★★★★ Sauvignon Blanc ⊛ Flagship white & one of total 11 wines featuring sauvignon. **18** ⑨③ from the oldest vineyard block & 100% oaked in 50% new barrels, 10 months. Full & intense, with unflagging stonefruit & lemon meringue pie flavours, great palate weight.

Reserve range

★★★★★ Pinotage ⊛ Dark & brooding aromas, hints of tar & roses on **18** ★★★★★ ⑨⑤, plump yet suave & finely balanced, with a fresh vanilla finish. Excellent expression of the variety, like **17** ⑨④, well-judged 40% new oak, 15 months, reining in the brashness this vintage. Be patient, this is a keeper.

★★★★★ Private Collection ⊛ Pure fruit, hint of perfume, concentrated focus in **17** ⑨④, seamless cab-led (62%) 5-way Bordeaux blend. Tannins are fine & starting to integrate for special drinking pleasure. 25% new oak for 16 months.

★★★★★ Wild Horseshoe Sauvignon Blanc ⊛ Skin-fermented (96 hours) **18** ⑨③ features a richly textured palate with grapefruit pith, quince & honey-nut biscuits, long lemon curd finish. Natural ferment, no filtration, extended lees contact & matured in older barrels for 11 months. Cape Town WO.

★★★★★ 8 Rows Sauvignon Blanc ⊛ Row selection from old block, dry farmed (as all estate's vines), unoaked. **19** ⑨④ impressive balance of richness, texture & pristine fruit flavours, notes of spring flowers & wet stone flintiness, waxy mouthfeel & enduring citrus pith finish.

★★★★☆ **Sauvignon Blanc** ⊛ Complex, concentrated & vibrant, bristling with tropical fruit flavours, slatey minerality, saline edge - all in harmony, for an exceptional expression of the variety. Unwooded **19** ⑨③ is one to keep or decant in youth.

★★★★☆ **Noble Late Harvest Sauvignon Blanc** Opulent concentration, with honey, fresh apricot, preserved melon, candied peel & dried mango all wrapped in lively, balancing sauvignon acidity. Luscious, unctuous & long, **18** ⑨② botrytis dessert will delight the fans. 9 months oaked. 375 ml. **17** untasted.

Diemersdal Estate range

★★★★ **Pinotage** Generously perfumed, supple & succulent **18** ㊏ is abundantly fruity with black plum, sweet spice & dried herbs. Tannins smoothed by year in 30% new oak for rounded & satisfying mouthful.

★★★★ **Chardonnay Unwooded** ⊘ Springtime freshness & vibrancy in **19** ㊏, Golden Delicious apple, sprinkling of spice with a lemon twist, appealing saline finale. Cape Town WO, as next 2.

★★★★☆ **Grüner Veltliner** ⊘ Still the sole SA bottling of Austrian variety. **18** ★★★★ ㊙ misses some of the complexity & substance of **17** ⑨③, grass, greengage & lemon pith notes in a lean, tight body, with vigorous acidity & graphite farewell.

★★★★ **Sauvignon Blanc** ⊘ Dependable & excellent value. Does not disappoint in crisp, fresh & zesty **19** ㊆, with citrus, tropical & apple flavours. Excellent partner for fresh seafood.

★★★★☆ **Winter Ferment Sauvignon Blanc** ⊘ ⊛ Intricate vinification: grape must kept frozen pre-ferment (in tank) till onset of winter, ±4 months, to increase flavour intensity. **19** ⑨③ delivers in spades, with full-throttle gooseberry & fig in excellent balance with grapefruit brûlée conclusion.

Sauvignon Rosé ⊘ ⊕ ★★★★ Radiant pink **19** ㊂④ has a cranberry crunch & lemon-rind zestiness in a svelte body (13.4% alcohol). Perfect for summer patio parties. Sauvignon blanc (93%) & cab combo. Cape Town WO.

Malbec ★★★★ Hedgerow fruit & earthy pepper mingle with fragrant pot-pourri & creamy coconut on friendly **18** ㊄, aged 16 months oak, some American, 40% new. **Merlot** ★★★★ Robust but juicy & cheerful, with red plum, cherry & savoury spicing from 20% new oak, year. **18** ㊝ dry & food-friendly. **Shiraz** ★★★★ All Durbanville fruit for **18** ㊄ (last had some Swartland). Generous, with lovely depth, texture & weight, perfect for a grilled steak to match the smoky meat & berry compote flavours.

Matys range

Cabernet Sauvignon-Merlot ⊕ ★★★ Easy-sipping 80/20 blend, **18** ㊆⑧ smooth & rounded, with luscious berry fruit, brush of vanilla oak.

Sauvignon Blanc ★★★★ Uncomplicated **19** ㊝ slips down easily, cheery ripe stonefruit brightness, zippy lemon end. WO W Cape for these. — WB

Location: Durbanville ▪ Map: Durbanville, Philadelphia & Darling ▪ Map grid reference: D7 ▪ WO: Durbanville/ Cape Town/Western Cape ▪ Est 1698 ▪ 1stB 1976 ▪ Tasting & sales Mon-Sat/pub hols 9–5 Sun 10–3 ▪ Closed Good Fri, Dec 25 & Jan 1 ▪ Cellar tours by appt ▪ Diemersdal Farm Eatery ▪ Owner(s) Tienie Louw ▪ Winemaker(s) Thys Louw & Mari Branders, with Juandre Bruwer & Janeke Beck ▪ Viticulturist(s) Div van Niekerk (1980) ▪ (cab, grenache, malbec, merlot, p verdot, ptage, shiraz, chard, grüner veltliner, sauv) ▪ 50% red 50% white ▪ BRC, HACCIP ▪ PO Box 27 Durbanville 7551 ▪ info@diemersdal.co.za ▪ www.diemersdal.co.za ▪ S 33° 48′ 6.3″ E 018° 38′ 25.1″ ▪ ⓜ reductive.poppy.loincloths ▪ **T +27 (0)21-976-3361**

Diemersfontein Wines   ⓠ ⓨ ⌂ ⊚

Despite drought conditions continuing through 2018, proactive owners of this Wellington winefarm, David and Susan Sonnenberg and their team went ahead with planting 2.5 hectares of the signature pinotage. Thankfully the decision was vindicated by last year's good rain (auguring well for harvest 2020) and, with more cabernet planned, hopefully repeated this winter. 'Fresh, fruit-driven' newcomer The Prodigy adds a fourth style of pinotage, showcasing the variety's versatility. With brand-new Cape Vintage 'port' and straw wine (boasting the refreshed livery), plus wines from empowerment venture Thokozani (listed separately), plus renamed restaurant Aan Tafel (under new management), it's clearly time for another visit.

Carpe Diem Reserve range

★★★★ **Malbec** ⊛ With Wellington & Robertson fruit, **17** ★★★★★ ⑨⓪ has less force, more elegance that Bot River-sourced **16** ⑧⑧. Refined berry compote with satisfying savoury notes, earthy underlay & velvet tannins. Should age with distinction.

★★★★☆ **Pinotage** Respected flagship pinotage, **17** ⑨① maintains high standard, with plush tannins, sumptuously ripe fruit easily taming 70% new French oak. Focused & intense, with subtle aromatic layers, lingering finish.

★★★★ **Chenin Blanc** Generously proportioned, wholesome **18** ⑧⑦ offers spiced stonefruit on leesy mantle, with tangy acid on finish. 35% barrel-fermented portion adds delicate oak aroma. **17** untasted.

★★★★ **Viognier** Peachy, viscous **18** ⑧⑦, prominent oak spice from 30% wood-fermented component. Weighty & richly ripe, shows good varietal character. May settle to match elegant **16** ⑧⑨. **17** untasted.

Diemersfontein range

★★★★ **Cabernet Sauvignon** Appealing racy freshness on **17** ⑧⑥ complements herbaceous, leafy cassis fruit profile. Medium bodied, smooth textured & refined. Well-judged year in older oak barrels. Step up from **16** ★★★★☆ ⑧⑤. Robertson & Tulbagh grapes.

★★★★ **Shiraz** Four-square, muscular **18** ⑧⑥ has smoky-savoury aromas, plum pudding fruit, pervasive tannin grip. 14% mourvèdre.

★★★★ **Summer's Lease** Rhône-inspired **17** ⑧⑧, syrah-mourvèdre blend with 1% viognier, plush & juicy, with wild herb & pepper appeal. Elegant, with sleek tannins & focused finish, improves on **16** ⑧⑥.

★★★★☆ **Sweet Sue** ⒩⒠⒲ ⊛ Vine-dried viognier dessert wine, **17** ⑨⓪ is sweetly concentrated, with nutty overtones, piercing acidity & opulent apricot fruit, all in graceful harmony. 10 months in older barrels add spiciness. 375 ml. Worth cellaring.

Merlot ★★★★ Sound, focused **18** ⑧⑤ has ripe plum & cherry fruit, solid tannin structure & subtle oak handling. Widely sourced. **Pinotage** ★★★ Large, loyal fan base for this original 'java' pinotage, though coffee-nutty aromas from heavily toasted oak staves very prominent on **18** ⑧②, masking bright, high-toned berry fruit. **The Prodigy** ⒩⒠⒲ ⊘ ★★★☆ Third pinotage in the portfolio, 'everyday enjoyment' the goal. With splash shiraz, **18** ⑧⑤ shows house's toffee/coffee aromas, plus sweet mint & chocolate notes. Pleasant but rather confected. WO W Cape, as next 2. **Harlequin** ★★★ Rather sullen fruit on **17** ⑧① is spiced up with hints of coffee & dark chocolate. Chalky tannins linger on finish on shiraz & pinotage (65/35) blend. **Rosé** ★★★ Light, fresh, floral-scented **19** ⑧① from grenache, mourvèdre & cinsaut is bone-dry, designed for poolside enjoyment. **Chenin Blanc** ★★★ Early preview of **19** ⑦⑨ still taut & austere, with muted peach notes. Provisional rating. **Sauvignon Blanc** ★★★ Tank sample **19** ⑧② already well-knit, showing gooseberry fruit with lime-mineral salty twist at finish. Robertson & Piekenierskloof vines. **Cape Vintage** ⒩⒠⒲ ★★★★ Fortified version of estate's signature grape, **17** ⑧⑤ still dominated by spirit, with pinotage's red berries peeking through mid-2019. 500 ml.

Brandy range

★★★★☆ **10 Year Old Potstill** Attractive modern packaging for this elegant, seamless & serious brandy ⑨②. Fruitcake, chocolate & roasted nut aromas, sprinkling of cinnamon on long & fresh finish. From chenin & crouchen. 1,380 500-ml bottles. — GdB, WB

Location/map: Wellington ▪ Map grid reference: B4 ▪ WO: Wellington/Western Cape ▪ Est 2000 ▪ 1stB 2001 ▪ Tasting & sales daily 10–5 ▪ Closed Dec 25 ▪ Cellar tours by appt ▪ Wine & biltong/artisanal sweets pairings ▪ Snack platters ▪ Aan Tafel restaurant open Tue-Sun for breakfast, lunch & supper ▪ Tour groups ▪ Conferences ▪ Weddings ▪ Amphitheatre, contact them for upcoming events ▪ Walks/hikes ▪ 3-star Diemersfontein Country House ▪ Owner(s) David & Susan Sonnenberg ▪ Winemaker(s) Francois Roode (Sep 2003), with Lauren Hulsman (Nov 2011) ▪ Viticulturist(s) Charl van der Merwe (Jun 2019) ▪ 180ha/45ha (cabs s/f, grenache, malbec, mourv, p verdot, ptage, roobernet, shiraz, chenin, viog) ▪ 600t/80,000cs own label 86% red 11% white 3% rosé ▪ HACCP, IPW, WIETA ▪ PO Box 41 Wellington 7654 ▪ tastingroom@diemersfontein. co.za ▪ www.diemersfontein.co.za ▪ S 33° 39' 41.1" E 019° 0' 31.1" ▪ 🎧 tracks.runner.rooting ▪ **T +27 (0)21-864-5050**

☐ **Die Tweede Droom** see Groot Parys Estate

Dieu Donné Vineyards

This mountainside winery is a popular stop on the Franschhoek Wine Tram route courtesy of its sweeping valley views, fine food and awarded wines. The latter are now handled by Gregory Siebrits, after the first winemaker change since 1996. He's working alongside viticulturist Hennie du Toit, a stalwart with more than 30 harvests here.

Location/map: Franschhoek ▪ Map grid reference: C1 ▪ Est 1984 ▪ 1stB 1986 ▪ Tasting & sales Mon-Fri 9–5 Sat/Sun 10.30–5 ▪ Fee R50 ▪ Closed Dec 25 & Jan 1 ▪ Cellar tours Mon-Fri by appt ▪ Cheese platters ▪ Roca Restaurant ▪ Owner(s) Robert Maingard ▪ Cellarmaster(s)/winemaker(s) Gregory Siebrits (Sep 2018) ▪ Viticulturist(s) Hennie du Toit (Apr 1988) ▪ 40ha (cab, merlot, shiraz, chard, sauv) ▪ ±280t/33,000cs own label 60% red 32% white 3% rosé 5% MCC ▪ PO Box 94 Franschhoek 7690 ▪ info@dieudonnevineyards.com ▪ www.dieudonnevineyards.com ▪ S 33° 53' 46.9" E 019° 7' 45.0" ▪ ⌂ vying.printers.dauntingly ▪ **T +27 (0)21-876-2493**

☐ **Die Waghuis** *see* Org de Rac
☐ **Dig This!** *see* Stellar Winery
☐ **Discovery Series** *see* FirstCape Vineyards

Distell Group Limited

Helmed by CEO Richard Rushton, Distell Group Limited is Africa's largest producer of wines, spirits, ciders and other ready-to-drink (RTD) beverages, and the SA leader with annual turnover of more than R21-billion and customers in more than 100 countries. From its Stellenbosch HQ, Distell produces some of SA's most successful and enduring marques. The premium- and fine-wine portfolio is now in the remit of a new company, Libertas Vineyards & Estates (LVE), and includes the following brands: Allesverloren, Alto, Durbanville Hills, Flat Roof Manor, Fleur du Cap, Inception, Nederburg, Plaisir de Merle, Pongrácz and Zonnebloem. Other Distell wine labels are Autumn Harvest Crackling, Capenheimer, Cellar Cask, Chateau Libertas, Drostdy-Hof, 4th Street, Graça, Monis (also producing sherry-style wines), Oom Tas, Overmeer, Paarl Perlé, Sedgwick's, Ship, Tassenberg, The House of JC le Roux and Two Oceans. The group's brandy labels include Commando, Flight of the Fish Eagle, Klipdrift, Mellow-Wood, Olof Bergh Solera, Richelieu, Van Ryn and Viceroy. See LVE listing for details about The Vinoteque and Bergkelder Wine Bank, and separate entries for most of the above brands.

Location: Stellenbosch ▪ Est 2000 ▪ Closed to public ▪ Winemakers/viticulturists: see individual brand entries ▪ PO Box 184 Stellenbosch 7599 ▪ info@distell.co.za ▪ www.distell.co.za ▪ **T +27 (0)21-809-7000**

☐ **DMZ** *see* DeMorgenzon

Domaine Brahms Wineries

Gesie van Deventer, live-wire co-owner and inaugural winemaker/viticulturist, recently had to take a small step back from the boutique family venture in Paarl due to manifold non-wine commitments, gratefully handing the cellar key to son Jacques. But energy levels remain high, and the restaurant has gained a dedicated area for group winetasting and special occasions; charmingly named antique shop Toeka has started catering for functions and birthday parties; and Domaine Brahms is now listed as a tractor museum.

★★★★ **Chenin Blanc** ⟨✓⟩ Nicely mature & drinking well, **15** ⑧⑦ borderline hedonistic, with creamy texture, inviting baked apple & pear flavours, spices (cinnamon & clove) & vanilla, long citrus curd finish. **Cabernet Sauvignon** ⑫ ★★★★ Creamy-rich tannin platform for pleasant & improved **14** ⑧⑭, alluring balance with just a touch of forest floor. Very youthful, will improve. **Pinotage** ⑫ ★★★ Dry, bold, even austere tannin underpin for **13** ⑧①, with raspberry fruitcake & resinous finish, touch of oak (none new). Challenging, needs time. **Shiraz** ★★★★ Juicy, spicy black fruit is appealing but coated by too-enthusiastic layer of mocha chocolate, thus **17** ⑧⑤ misses the mark of last-made **10** ★★★★ ⑧⑦. Coastal WO, like wooded Chenin. **Quartet** ⑫ ★★★★ Merlot-dominated Bordeaux blend, **12** ⑧③ bright fruited, soft & enticing. **Sonato** ⟨✓⟩ ★★★★ After skipping 6 vintages, returns with improved **18** ⑧⑤ cab/shiraz (60/40) blend. Good balance & fresh, smooth spicy farewell. Attractive upbeat, playful mien. **Unwooded Chenin Blanc** ★★★ In contrast with oaked sibling, **18** is lean, demure, the citrus flavours unlingering. — WB

Location/map: Paarl ▪ Map grid reference: C3 ▪ WO: Paarl/Coastal ▪ Est 1998 ▪ 1stB 1999 ▪ Tasting & tours (vyd/cellar/wine) by appt ▪ Fee R5/wine ▪ Chapel & wedding/function venue ▪ Toeka store for antiques, vintage tractors & cars, light lunches & traditional fare ▪ Gift shop ▪ Owner(s) Johan & Gesie van Deventer ▪ Winemaker(s)/viticulturist(s) Jacques Lategan ▪ 12ha (cab, merlot, ptage, shiraz, chenin) ▪ 50,000L 90% red 10% white ▪ PO Box 2136 Windmeul 7630 ▪ brahms@iafrica.com, toeka@mweb.co.za ▪ www. domainebrahms.co.za ▪ S 33° 40' 27.28" E 18° 53' 29.24" ▪ ⊞ flannels.rarity.steamboats ▪ T +27 (0)21-869-8555/+27 (0)76-914-5714 (Toeka)

Domaine Coutelier   ⓠ ⓐ ⓞ

The 'Home of Cutler' in Stellenbosch's Devon Valley is where Briton Quint Cutler and French wife Floriane, formerly in aviation and humanitarian aid, farm 3.5 hectares of red varieties (including some rare carmenère), buying in grapes for their white wine. Their portion of 17th-century farmland is on a ridge, offering winelovers, wedding guests and overnighters '270° views'.

Reserve range

★★★★☆ **Cabernet Sauvignon** ⓝⓔⓦ ⓐ Sophisticated & classically styled **13** ⑨④ is still wonderfully fresh. 100% French oak matured for 2 years, well assimilated. Layered & complex, with a rich core of cassis & cedar. Ready to savour, but will reward with drinking pleasure for many years.

★★★★ **Merlot** ⓥ Excellent varietal expression on **12** ⑧⑧: depth, silky tannins, ripe blackcurrant & plum fruit, earthy/meaty forest floor aromas. Elegantly poised, youthful & ambitious.

Coutelier range

★★★★ **Cabernet Sauvignon** ⓥ Primary blackcurrant & plum on big, muscular **14** ⑧⑧ showing youthful exuberance, backed by robust tannins & tarry/spicy notes. Improving label, one to watch.

★★★★ **Merlot** ⓥ Deep, brooding **14** ⑧⑨ has focused black fruit core, impressive weight & length. 18 months in 60% new French oak lend subtle spicy note, silky tannin texture. Improves on **13** ★★★★ ⑧⑤.

★★★★ **Chardonnay** ⓥ Generous, barrel-fermented **14**, leesy, with solid oak, edgy acid & nutty-lemon flavours; **15** ⑧⑧ similar but richer, riper, more nuanced wood. Durbanville vines.

Not tasted: **Méthode Cap Classique**.

Festin range

Red Blend ⓥ ★★★★ Merlot & cab show prominent mulberry fruit with meaty substance, **14** ⑧⑤ appealingly plump & rounded, ripe tannins & savoury notes. — MW

Location/map: Stellenbosch ▪ Map grid reference: D4 ▪ WO: Stellenbosch/Coastal ▪ Est/1stB 2012 ▪ Tasting, sales & cellar tours by appt ▪ Closed all pub hols ▪ Weddings/functions ▪ Two self-catering cottages ▪ Owner(s)/winemaker(s) Quint Cutler ▪ 4ha/3.5ha (cab, carmenère, merlot) ▪ ±21t/2,300cs own label 70% red 10% white 10% rosé 10% MCC ▪ 45 Blumberg Dr, Devon Vale, Stellenbosch 7600 ▪ quint.cutler@ domainecoutelier.com ▪ www.domainecoutelier.com ▪ S 33° 54' 2.80" E 018° 47' 58.46" ▪ ⊞ drainage.region. october ▪ T +27 (0)21-300-0649/+27 (0)79-498-0772

Domaine des Dieux   ⓠ ⓨ ⓐ

An emphasis at the 'Home of the Gods' on bottle-fermented bubbly grows, with the over-grafting of sauvignon vines to chardonnay under the eagle eye of esteemed new viticultural consultant Kevin Watt. Offering visitors enviable views of vines and landmark mountain peak Babylonstoren with minimal structural impediments (wines are made off-site by specialists), the vineyard further plays to the strengths of its aptly named location in Hemel-en-Aarde ('Heaven-and-Earth') with a selection of classic French and Italian varieties and a renewed commitment to farming sustainably.

★★★★ **Josephine Pinot Noir** ⊘ Exemplifies house-style extended bottle ageing at cellar. **15** ★★★★★ ⑨⓪ russet glints, mushroom aromas & layers of red berry fruits woven into gentle texture. No **14**. Still-available **13** ⑧⑥ more expressive & substantial than last. Only older oak. Also in 1.5 & 3L.

★★★★ **Sangiovese** ⓝⓔⓦ Joins just 19 varietal bottlings in the guide. Limited-release **15** ⑧⑥ lovely liquorice aroma, integrated & smooth, drinks well right now. 18 months seasoned barriques.

★★★★ **Rose of Sharon Méthode Cap Classique Brut Rosé** Classic just-pink bubbly ex near-equal pinot noir & chardonnay, **11** ★★★★★ ⑨⓪ sparkler subtle crushed berries on brioche, mature, textured finish & fine racy acidity. Remarkable 84 months on lees. Walker Bay WO, like **10** ⑧⑧.

★★★★ **Claudia Méthode Cap Classique Brut** 81% chardonnay with pinot noir, **13** ⑧ sparkling retains freshness in context of house style, long 57 months on lees gives breadth, gravitas. Now unoaked. Cape South Coast WO. **12** not tasted. Also in magnum, as above.

Syrah-Mourvèdre Ⓐ ★★★☆ Pungently savoury **13** ⑧ has distinct Rhône-like scrub aroma, with fruit-drop cherry on quite robust tannins. Pulling in several directions, but may knit in time. **Chardonnay** ★★★★ Modern **15** ⑧ reflects prior releases, with oak (28% new, 9 months) showcasing the fruit. **14** untasted. **Sauvignon Blanc** ★★★★ Tasted out of vintage sequence, **13** ⑧⑤'s edges have mellowed but classic flint, gunsmoke intensified, high acidity demands food. **16** ⑧ was unknit last edition, needing time. Not tasted: **Petit Rose**. — DS

Location: Hermanus ▪ Map: Walker Bay & Bot River ▪ Map grid reference: C4 ▪ WO: Hemel-en-Aarde Ridge/Walker Bay/Cape South Coast ▪ Est 2002 ▪ 1stB 2006 ▪ Tasting & sales at the vineyards: summer Mon-Sat 11-5 Sun 11-4; winter Mon-Sun 11-4 ▪ Closed Easter Fri/Sun, Dec 25/26 & Jan 1 ▪ Cheese & meat platters; refreshments ▪ Child-friendly ▪ Owner(s) Domaine des Dieux (Pty) Ltd ▪ Winemaker(s) consultants ▪ Vineyard manager(s) Shane Mullis & Leonore Kroukamp ▪ Viticulturist(s) Kevin Watt (consultant) ▪ 28ha/20ha under vine (pinot, mourv, shiraz & other Bordeaux and Italian red varieties, chard, sauv) ▪ 15,000cs own label 30% red 25% white 45% MCC ▪ PO Box 2082 Hermanus 7200 ▪ info@domainedesdieux.co.za ▪ www.domainedesdieux.co.za ▪ S 34° 19' 35.81" E 019° 19' 50.71" ▪ 🅦 remixing.fishers.privy ▪ **T +27 (0)28-313-2126/+27 (0)74-943-5797**

☐ **Dombeya** see Haskell Vineyards

Domein Doornkraal

With almost all their wines sold to locals and passing trade at their roadside farm stall near De Rust, co-owner and viticulturist Celia le Roux and her winemaker father, Swepie, produce styles suitable for the hot sunny days as well as chilly nights of the Klein Karoo. New vintages were bottled too late for us to taste, so there's no muscat bubbly or shocking pink ostrich feather accessory to tickle our fancy this year.

Domein Doornkraal range

★★★★ **Kaptein** Ⓐ Deep brown NV ⑧ fortified from red muscadel thrills with toasty, coffee, caramel, raisin notes. Xmas spices & roasted nuts round off delicious mouthful to warm the cockles in winter. **Tickled Pink** Ⓐ ★★★ Light, fun rosé fizz, NV ⑦ from muscadel is fresh & floral, with pretty strawberry fruit. **Kuierwyn** Ⓐ ★★★ Low-alcohol NV ⑦ Natural Sweet white is softly fruity for easy drinking, with hints of talc & perfume. Variety/ies undisclosed, as most here. **Majoor** Ⓐ ★★★★ Plenty of lemon on NV ⑧ fortified muscat d'Alexandrie - dried, glacé & spiced. Nice balance between sweetness & acid, good length. **Jerepigo** Ⓐ ★★★ Clean grapey aromas on NV ⑧ fortified, with raisins & coffee adding depth & interest. Warming alcohol suggests enjoying with food. **Luitenant** Ⓐ ★★★★ Oxidative toffee, coffee, nutty aromas & flavours on NV ⑧ red jerepiko. Try with baked camembert cheese. **Pinta** Ⓐ ★★★ Raisins & coffee on NV ⑧ 'port' followed by lashings of blackberry jam & hint toffee. Tad more acid would improve. Not tasted: **Pinotage Rosé, Tanige Port**.

Swepie Selection

Kannaland Wit Chenin Blanc Ⓐ ★★ Style change on **17** ⑦, now drier, grapefruit & lemon replacing tropical fruit, still with easy 12.5% alcohol. Not tasted: **Kannaland Rooi Merlot**. Discontinued: **Kannaland Wit Sauvignon Blanc**. — CM

Location: De Rust ▪ Map: Klein Karoo & Garden Route ▪ Map grid reference: B3 ▪ WO: Western Cape ▪ Est 1880 ▪ 1stB 1973 ▪ Tasting & sales at Doornkraal Padstal Mon-Fri & pub hols 8-5 Sat 8-3 Sun 10-2 ▪ Closed Dec 25 & Sun (mid term) ▪ Light refreshments ▪ Farm & regional produce ▪ Gifts ▪ Function venue on farm ▪ Self-catering farm cottage & lodge ▪ Owner(s) Swepie le Roux & family ▪ Cellarmaster(s) Swepie le Roux (Apr 2011) ▪ Winemaker(s) Swepie le Roux ▪ Viticulturist(s) Celia le Roux ▪ 2,000ha/10ha (cab, merlot, muscadel, ptage, tinta b, chenin) ▪ 110t/4,500cs own label 15% red 15% white 70% fortified ▪ PO Box 14 De Rust 6650 ▪ wyn@doornkraal.co.za ▪ www.doornkraal.co.za ▪ S 33° 32' 43.5" E 022° 26' 42.6" ▪ 🅦 saucepan.chuckle.fixed ▪ **T +27 (0)82-763-5296 (farm stall)**

☐ **Donatus** see Dornier Wines

Donkiesbaai

With sibling brand Stellenbosch Reserve, vigneron Jean Engelbrecht (also owner of top-ranked Rust en Vrede) pays tribute to his home town. Here he recalls happy family holidays on the West Coast at resort village Donkin Bay, whose colloquial moniker, Donkey Bay, gives its name to these Afrikaans-accented prestige wines, produced in tiny volumes from grapes grown mostly in Piekenierskloof and, latterly, Ceres. Vinification, tasting and sales are at another Engelbrecht property, Guardian Peak, in the Helderberg.

★★★★ **Pinot Noir** Ceres Plateau fruit, as previous, for **18** ⑧⑥, raspberry flavours, silky tannins, generous body & finish. Still introverted mid-2019, would benefit from few years in cellar. These saw only older oak, 9-12 months unless noted.

★★★★☆ **Rooiwijn** Fragrant cinsaut-grenache blend with dash of syrah, **18** ⑨② is lightish but oozes style & character, expresses ripeness with poise & restraint, along with the finer nuances of the varieties.

★★★★☆ **Steen** Spicy, richly aromatic **18** ⑨② chenin, alluring layers of shortbread & baked apple, lees fatness & finely judged acidity. Mix of barrel, amphora & concrete 'egg' ageing adds complexity & texture.

★★★★☆ **Hooiwijn** (Ⓡ) Intense honeyed apricots on outstanding **18** ⑨④ chenin straw wine, with massive 216 g/l sugar tamed by vibrant acidity. Viscous & textured ambrosia, the perfect foil for crème brûlée. Grapes from old vines, 6 months in 300L oak. 375 ml.

Occasional release: **Grenache Noir**. — GdB

Location: Stellenbosch ▪ WO: Piekenierskloof/Ceres Plateau ▪ Est 2010 ▪ 1stB 2011 ▪ Tasting & sales at Guardian Peak Wines (see entry) ▪ Owner(s) Jean Engelbrecht ▪ Winemaker(s) Danielle le Roux (Dec 2019) ▪ ±38t/6,000cs own label 30% red 70% white ▪ IPW ▪ PO Box 473 Stellenbosch 7599 ▪ info@donkiesbaai. com ▪ www.donkiesbaai.com ▪ **T +27 (0)21-881-3881**

☐ **Don King** *see* Govert Wines
☐ **Don Morris** *see* Govert Wines

Doolhof Wine Estate

High above Wellington, between Bain's Kloof Pass and Groenberg Mountain, this estate was named 'Labyrinth' by early settlers who found only one way in and out. Today visitors can explore parts of the 380 ha of vineyard, forest and fynbos on a walk along a 10-km stretch of river, home to abundant wildlife. Wine/vine man Gielie Beukes aims to express the many microclimates in his wines, untasted this edition.

Location/map: Wellington ▪ Map grid reference: D3 ▪ Est 1712 ▪ 1stB 2003 ▪ Tasting & sales Mon-Sat 10–5 Sun 10-4 ▪ Fee R50/5 wines, R150/Limietberg exclusive range ▪ Closed Good Fri, Dec 25/26 & Jan 1 ▪ Cellar tours by appt ▪ Light lunches Mon-Sat 11-4 Sun 11-3; picnics by appt ▪ Walks/hikes ▪ MTB trails ▪ 5-star Grand Dédale Country House; AfriCamps luxury accommodation (www.africamps.com) ▪ Craft gin ▪ Owner(s) Dennis Kerrison ▪ Winemaker(s) Gielie Beukes (Aug 2014) ▪ Viticulturist(s) Gielie Beukes (Aug 2014), with Jasper Burden (Feb 2019) ▪ 380ha/38ha (cabs s/f, malbec, merlot, p verdot, ptage, shiraz, chard, sauv) ▪ 250t/25,000cs own label 70% red 28% white 2% blanc de noir ▪ IPW, WIETA ▪ PO Box 157 Wellington 7654 ▪ wine@doolhof.com ▪ www.doolhof.com ▪ S 33° 37' 35.6" E 019° 4' 58.7" ▪ Ⓕ restates.reclassify.sharpens ▪ **T +27 (0)21-873-6911**

Doran Vineyards

André Badenhorst, viticultural revitaliser of top Constantia farms, is relishing the unlocking of Voor Paardeberg's winegrowing potential. A decade into rejuvenating Far Horizons farm with old Irish buddy Edwin Doran, he feels vindicated by the resilience during the 2018/19 growing season's drought of varieties deemed most suited to the terrain (chenin, roussanne, grenache noir/blanc, shiraz). 'New whites, especially and surprisingly, blossomed,' making Edwin's son Tom's marketing of wines in the UK that much easier. The team (awaiting a new winemaker following the post-harvest departure of Martin Lamprecht to go solo) are equally excited by local growers' ideas to 'promote our area's unique character'.

Doran Vineyards range

★★★★ **Shiraz** (Ⓥ) Lively core of fruit with tobacco & violet extras, fine-grained tannins buffed in old barrels, 12 months, touches of spice & savoury on **16** ⑧⑧. Remarkably well-priced, as all these wines.

★★★★☆ **Chenin Blanc** ⊘ From Swartland, like previous, old-barrel-fermented **16** ⑨⑴ is round & creamy yet a fresh spine of acidity keeps it balanced, accentuates the subtle array of pear, quince, almond & citrus notes. Mineral tang & a saline nuance linger on complex finish.

★★★★☆ **L'Alliance** ⓖ Delicious blend of chenin, grenache blanc & roussanne, co-fermented/year older oak. **17** ⑨⑴ sleek & effortless yet serious, almond, honey & pear flavours, persistent mineral finish.

Arya ⓦ ★★★ Same components as L'Alliance but unwooded & vinified separately. **18** ⑧② has striking freshness which highlights abundant tropical fruit & spice, creates lovely light feel for summer quaffing fun.

Pinotage ⊘ ★★★★ Vibrant ruby hue mirrored in appealing ripe red-fruit flavours on improved **18** ⑧④, spicy & smooth tannins will go well with a braai. WO Paarl, as next. **The Romy D** ⊘ ★★★★ Harmonious Bordeaux blend, cab & 30% merlot in **18** ⑧⑤, ample berry fruit seamed with dark chocolate & cigarbox from older French oak, tannins well-balanced & savoury. Step up on previous. Not tasted: **Incipio, Rosie D.**

Horse Mountain range
Not tasted: **Michele, White Blend.** Discontinued: **Pinotage, Shiraz, Chenin Blanc-Viognier.** — GM
Location/map: Paarl ▪ Map grid reference: C1 ▪ WO: Voor Paardeberg/Paarl/Swartland ▪ Est 2010 ▪ 1stB 2012 ▪ Tasting Mon-Fri by appt Sat/Sun & pub hols 10-4 ▪ Closed Good Fri, Dec 25/26 & Jan 1 ▪ Owner(s) Edwin Doran & André Badenhorst ▪ Viticulturist(s) Basson Potgieter ▪ 170ha/55ha (cabs s/f, merlot, ptage, shiraz, chenin, grenache blanc/noir, rouss) ▪ 450t/30,000cs own label ▪ PO Box 2143 Windmeul 7630 ▪ andrebad@ iafrica.com ▪ www.doranvineyards.co.za ▪ S 33° 34' 56.12" E018° 51' 59.15" ▪ 🄼 smock.debating.lavishes ▪ **T +27 (0)82-772-0016**

☐ **Doring Bay** see Fryer's Cove Vineyards

Dormershire Estate ⓠ

This 8-hectare boutique estate in Stellenbosch, with its magnificent view of Table Mountain, is owned by Paul and Sunette Frost. The focus is on red wines from cabernet and shiraz, these often undergoing lengthy barrel maturation. Longtime advisor Kowie du Toit has taken over from Sunette as winemaker.

Cabernet Sauvignon ⓖ ★★★★ As expected, juicier & earlier accessible than the Reserve, a savoury note makes **07** ⑧④ a good food match. **Reserve Cabernet Sauvignon** ⓖ ★★★☆ Selection of best barrels, 18 months oak. Despite big alcohol, **07** ⑧④ shows balance & restraint. **Shiraz** ⓖ ★★★ First tasted since **07** ⑧⑴, well-priced & ready-now **15** ⑧⓪ reflects estate's Old World styling: red plums lightly dusted with wood spices, lithe & dry tannins. **Stoep Shiraz** ⓖ ★★★ Wood here a toasty backdrop, **07** ⑧⑴ earthy & savoury blackberry fruit, pepper seasoning. **Shiraz-Cabernet Sauvignon** ⓖ ★★★ Equal partnership delivers red & black fruit, faint floral & tapenade nuances in **15** ⑧⓪. Cab's firm (not hard) tannins evident, thus age or pair with food. **Fudge Hammer Rosé** ⓖ ★★ Smoked meat, soft red & black berries - no fudge character except noticeable sweetness on **17** ⑦⑥, best served well-chilled. From shiraz, with pleasing light 11% alcohol. **Sweet Red** ⓖ ★★★★ Jerepiko-style fireside snuggler from shiraz, **NV** ⑧④ with intriguing savoury overlay. Not tasted: **Sauvignon Blanc.** — CvZ

Location: Kuils River ▪ Map/WO: Stellenbosch ▪ Map grid reference: A5 ▪ Est 1996 ▪ 1stB 2001 ▪ Tasting & sales Mon-Fri 8-2 ▪ Owner(s) SPF Family Trust ▪ Winemaker(s) Kowie du Toit ▪ Viticulturist(s) Johan Pienaar (consultant) ▪ 8ha/5ha (cab, shiraz, sauv) ▪ ±50t/8,000cs own label 85% red 10% white 5% rosé ▪ PO Box 491 Bellville 7535 ▪ wine@dormershire.co.za ▪ www.dormershire.co.za ▪ S 33° 56' 27.0" E 018° 42' 54.7" ▪ 🄼 clumsy.goad.annuals ▪ **T +27 (0)21-801-4677/+27 (0)21-801-4991**

Dornier Wines ⓠ ⓨ ⌂ ⓞ ⓹

Much has changed over the past two years at this extensive and scenic family-owned farm at the foot of Stellenbosch Mountain. The pairing of winemaker Philip van Staden and viticulturist Arjen Rijpstra is starting to show results in the wines, which GM Francois Theunissen feels are more complex and balanced than ever. Others clearly agree, as recognition and awards increasingly are falling their way. Buoyed by this success, a further 9 hectares are being developed for new plantings.

Founders range

★★★★☆ **CMD** ⓩ Smoky, savoury dark-berried allure on **14** ⑨④ flagship blend. Still malbec-led, but now with petit verdot & cab in the (75/20/5) mix. Handsome, velvet textured, suave rather than powerful, with 60% new oak in harmony. No **13**.

Donatus range

★★★★ **Red** ⓐ Cab-led 4-way Bordeaux blend **16** ★★★★ ⑨⓪ still integrating mid-2019. Big flavours - black fruit, raisin hint - & big structure with high, ripe tannins bolstered by smoky, toasty oak (33% new). Could drink now but much more lies in store. Improves on **12** ⑧⑨. No **13**, **15**; **14** untasted.

★★★★☆ **White** Smart 'Cape Blend' chenin & semillon (80/20), **17** ⑨① elegant mouthful of bright stonefruit with seam of citrus acidity livening upfront creamy oak (25% new). Better balanced than **16** ★★★★ ⑧⑦), excellent wine for serious seafood.

Dornier range

★★★★☆ **Equanimity Cabernet Sauvignon** ⊘ ⓐ Bold flavours of blackcurrants & cassis on muscular **17** ⑨⓪ handle 14.5% alcohol well, wrapping it in concentrated, fine-grained tannins & plush fruit. 15% new French oak adds toasty vanilla finish.

★★★★ **Siren Syrah** ⓩ Similar fynbos notes to previous, riper in warmer **16** ⑧⑨ vintage but well managed, balanced, with ample spicy, smoky fruit in modern, approachable style. Respectable dry finish.

★★★★ **Cabernet Sauvignon-Merlot** ⓩ Different ratio (59/41) in **16** ⑧⑦. Touch reticent, not as rich as the Cab but similar dark-fruit profile & bright acidity. Will evolve gracefully over 3-4 years.

★★★★ **Bush Vine Chenin Blanc** From Swartland fruit, **18** ★★★★ ⑧⑤ delivers creamy mouthful of soft yellow apples, oatmeal & dried apricots. 50% oaked, liquorice & honey finish, shade less concentrated than **17** ⑧⑧.

★★★★ **Semillon** Delicious example. **18** ★★★★★ ⑨⓪ balances creamy citrus notes of lemon & lime with fresh woody herbs, vanilla & nutmeg from clever oaking, 20% new. Excellent palate weight, intensity carries through to satisfying finish. Step up on **17** ⑧⑨.

★★★★☆ **Froschkönig Natural Sweet** ⓩ Preserved quince & pineapple on **16** ⑨③ 'Frog Prince', first since **13** ⑨②, also from vine-dried chenin. Decadently sweet & tangy; delightful intensity for 11.5% alcohol; a liquid dessert! 375 ml.

Malbec ★★★☆ Style change for **16** ⑧⑤ to more opulent, full bodied, with rich dark fruit, coffee hints & attractive floral note of lavender & violet. **Merlot** ★★★☆ Plenty of ripe fruit (plums, cherries) on **17** ⑧⑤ balancing warm 14.5% alcohol & leathery tannins. Needs a little time to settle, should follow footsteps of **16** ★★★★ ⑧⑨. **Petit Verdot** ★★★★ Shy black-fruited **16** ⑧⑤ needs time & air to show off charms. Well-managed oak (15% new) adds pleasing vanilla tweak to finish. Improves on previous. **Pinotage** ★★★☆ Nicely balanced **16** ⑧③ offers measured mouthful of berry fruits with softish tannins & quiet oak. Well-knit wine, perfect for a braai. **Tempranillo** ⓩ ★★★ Rare varietal bottling, offering smoke & spice with clean ripe black fruit. Like previous, **13** ⑧②'s tannins are chewy, with dry grip; best cellared or decanted. Not tasted: **Moordenaarskloof**.

Cocoa Hill range

.....
Red ⓟ ★★★☆ Good-value **17** ⑧⑤ blend of classic grapes in one juicy, fruity, moreish mouthful. Pliable tannins, lively acidity, plenty of drinking pleasure.
.....
Merlot Rosé ★★★ Ideal summer salad partner **18** ⑧② bone-dry, with pretty red cherry palate plus fresh herbal hints. WO Stellenbosch, rest WO W Cape. **Chenin Blanc** ★★★ Reliable unoaked easy-drinker. **18** ⑧② uses 6 months on lees to good effect, adding touch of richness to simple, crisp, fresh fruit. **Sauvignon Blanc** ★★★ **18** ⑧⓪ sure to find fans for dry, easy-drinking style, with tropical notes & zesty tail. — CM

Location/map: Stellenbosch ▪ Map grid reference: F7 ▪ WO: Stellenbosch/Western Cape/Swartland ▪ Est 1995 ▪ 1stB 2002 ▪ Tasting & sales daily 9-5 ▪ Cellar tours by appt ▪ Dornier Bodega Restaurant: (Oct-Apr) Mon-Sun lunch 11.30-3.30; (May-Sep) Wed-Sun lunch 11.30-3.30 ▪ Art ▪ Conference & function venues ▪ Conservation area ▪ Homestead with 6 bedrooms & large entertainment areas ▪ Owner(s) Dornier family ▪ Winemaker(s) Philip van Staden (Oct 2015) ▪ Viticulturist(s) Arjen Rijpstra (Nov 2017) ▪ 180ha/48ha (cabs s/f, malbec, merlot, p verdot, ptage, shiraz, tempranillo, chenin, sauv, sem) ▪ 380t 78% red 16% white 6% rosé ▪ PO Box

7518 Stellenbosch 7599 ▪ info@dornier.co.za ▪ www.dornier.co.za ▪ S 33° 59' 31.00" E 018° 52' 19.00" ▪ 🗺 crib.shadows.mulled ▪ **T +27 (0)21-880-0557**

☐ **Dorp Street** see Barnardt Boyes Wines

Dorrance Wines   Ⓟ Ⓨ

Christophe Durand became something of a victim of his own success in making wine. He'd moved to Cape Town from France in 1995, supplying wine barrels to the local industry. But he got completely drawn into Cape wine, to the extent of soon vinifying his own syrah — in those early years under the brand name Vins d'Orrance. A chardonnay followed, named for his and his South African wife's daughter, then a chenin and more recently an entry-level trio. Rented space became insufficient, and he established his own cellar in a heritage building in the heart of Cape Town, bringing widely sourced grapes through the city streets to make his elegant wines in non-interventionist fashion.

★★★★★ **Syrah Cuvée Ameena** ⊘ 🐝 Svelte, silk-textured **17** ⑨⑤. Older oak allows Elgin fruit purity to shine: alluring perfumed red berries infused with white pepper. Fine boned, discreet, but firm tannins streamline all elements into a thing of beauty.

★★★★☆ **Chardonnay Cuvée Anaïs** Silken elegance on **18** ⑨① now from Robertson fruit, plumped with riper than **17** ⑨③ pear flavours & delicate limy thread. Bunch pressed & naturally fermented (as all these); old oak unless noted. Balanced for earlier enjoyment & some ageing.

★★★★☆ **Chenin Blanc Cuvée Kama** Warmer, riper impression on **18** ⑨⓪, with baked apple & almond flavours, from (natural) fermentation in concrete 'egg' (no wood). Similar elegant texture to **17** ⑨③ but less complexity & depth. Already tempts, but potential to develop. WO Swartland.

Rouge ★★★ Thatchy berry jam tone to **18** ⑧② from unoaked cinsaut, a twist of tannin to dry the finish. Less concentrated & more rustic than previous. Light antipasto partner. **Rosé** ★★★ Dry & savoury styling in **19** ⑧②, hint of cranberry making it more piquant than previous, twist of tannin & acidity on the tail. **Blanc** ★★★ From chenin bushvines, **19** ⑧② supple & rounded, with gentle ripe apple tone. Less aromatics than previous from viognier, similar dry farewell. — MW

Location: Cape Town ▪ Map: Cape Peninsula ▪ Map grid reference: B1 ▪ WO: Swartland/Western Cape ▪ Est/1stB 2000 ▪ Tasting, sales & cellar tours Mon-Fri 11-6 or by appt ▪ Wine shop ▪ Bouchon bistro & wine bar Mon-Fri from 4-11, www.bouchon.co.za ▪ Owner(s) Christophe & Sabrina Durand ▪ Cellarmaster(s)/winemaker(s) Christophe Durand ▪ 11ha ▪ 30t/4,666cs own label ▪ Fairtrade ▪ 95 Hout Str Cape Town 8001 ▪ christophe@dorrancewines.com ▪ www.dorrancewines.com ▪ S 33° 55' 12.93" E 018° 25' 5.99" ▪ 🗺 mimosas.oiliness.unprovable ▪ **T +27 (0)21-422-0695/+27 (0)83-409-7071**

☐ **Double Door** see La Bri Estate

Douglas Green

Named after the original owner of the Stukvat Bottlestore in Paarl, this popular DGB-owned brand believes their mantra of 'good wine at a good price, that people enjoy' continues to create wines which hit the spot with drinkers around the world almost 80 years later. New vintages not available for tasting.

Location: Wellington ▪ Est 1942 ▪ Closed to public ▪ Owner(s) DGB (Pty) Ltd ▪ Blending manager Dico du Toit (2012) ▪ Oenologist Jaco Potgieter (2000) ▪ Viticulturist(s) Heinie Nel (Jul 2018) ▪ 50% red 49% white 1% rosé ▪ ISO 9001:2000, Fairtrade, HACCP, IPW, WIETA ▪ PO Box 246 Wellington 7654 ▪ douglasgreen@dgb.co.za ▪ www.douglasgreenwines.com ▪ **T +27 (0)21-864-5300**

☐ **Douglas Wine Cellar** see Landzicht Wine Cellar
☐ **Down to Earth** see Villiera Wines

Dragonridge   Ⓟ Ⓨ 🏠 ◎ Ⓐ

Only a small handful of Cape producers make wines that would be recognised internationally as 'natural' — off organic vines, made with no additives apart from a genuine minimum of sulphur. Dragonridge is one of them — formal organic certification for grapes, olives and lemons off the Paardeberg estate co-owned by Johan and Diana Simons came in 2019. Johan makes a large range of usually small bottlings, wines that are as a rule fresh, pure and dry, occasionally eccentric or quirky. Eco-tourism and weddings are also offered.

★★★★ **The Strawberry** ⓃⒺⓌ Charmingly aromatic **18** ⑧⑥ pinotage. Yes, strawberries, but also savoury, earthy touch on the gently but effectively structured, well-balanced palate. Good dry finish; 13% alcohol.

★★★★ **Aquila** Sangiovese with 33% cab in **17** ⑧⑥, leads with cherry & tomato leaf aromas to the customary fresh, light-feeling & balanced palate: good acid, just 12% alcohol, nice tannic grip, lingering.

★★★★ **Supernova** Yellow-gold méthode ancestrale sparkler from pinotage/chenin. **18** ⑧⑥ has forth-coming fruitiness as well as yeasty element. Succulent & fresh; bone-dry, unlike many in the category.

Cabernet Sauvignon Ⓥ ★★★ Ripe, sweet & alcoholic (15.4%) **15** ⑧① , but oak (none new) is support-ive of black berry fruits. Natural vinification, as all these. **Mourvèdre** Ⓥ ★★★ Very ripe in this context, **15** ⑧① with rustic dark-fruit notes - the aromas rather beguiling, but not enough substance to balance burning 14.5% alcohol, despite a sweet fruit core. **Pinotage** ★★ Savoury, soft-taninned but greenly acidic **17** ⑦⑥ ends with varietal bitterness. **Sangiovese** Ⓥ ★★★ Cherry typicity to **15** ⑦⑧ but more austere, grippy than previous. Acidity is high at 7.7 g/l. **Shiraz** Ⓥ ★★★★ Idiosyncratic **15** ⑧④ is juicy & ripe with a spicy, meaty edge; pliable & light bodied. Fermented with viognier skins. **Dark Star** ★★★★ **18** ⑧③ is first made since **11** ★★★ ⑧① - weighty, aromatic & flavourful blend pinotage, cab, mourvèdre. Appealing, sweetly pure–fruited character (but dry). Only older oak. **Cosmos** ★★★ Pale onion skin **18** ⑦⑨ from pinotage is bone-dry, grippy & light (11.5% alcohol); insubstantial but pleasant enough. One of first certified 'Alternative Rosé' wines in the guide. **Orion** ★★★ From chardonnay, **18** ⑧② offers citrus & stonefruit, but savoury thanks to 2 days skin contact before a year in old oak. Lightish 12.5% alcohol, serious acidity, silky texture. **Aldebaran** ⓃⒺⓌ ★★★★ A full-on 'orange wine', **17** ⑧⑤ from chenin left on skins for 2 months, in oak a year. Plenty of savoury, unfruity aroma & flavour, keeping the big acidity in check. Dry & austere - a good food wine. **Viognier** ⓃⒺⓌ ★★★ Lightly aromatic **18** ⑧② stresses earthier more than fruity side, partly thanks to 2 days on skins. Older oak gives breadth. Modest 12.5% alcohol; textured & dry. **Orion's Belt** ⓃⒺⓌ ★★★ **18** ⑦⑨ méthode ancestrale sparkler from early-picked chardonnay. Golden colour points to oxidative bruised apple notes. Firm acid grip. Bone-dry. **Rigel** Ⓥ ★★★ Faint marzipan, apricot & honeycomb notes on wooded **15** ⑧① straw wine from chenin. Oxidative & rich, broad textured, with high acid countering huge sugar level. Clean dry finish. Not tasted: **Jack's Red, Galaxy**. Occasional release: **Cygnus, Capella**. — TJ

Location: Malmesbury ▪ Map/WO: Swartland ▪ Map grid reference: C8 ▪ Est 2004 ▪ 1stB 2006 ▪ Tasting, sales & cellar tours by appt ▪ Fee R80, R40 off on purchase of 3 btls ▪ Closed Good Fri, Dec 25/26 & Jan 1 ▪ Country meals by arrangement for groups of 10+ ▪ Facilities for children ▪ Farm produce ▪ Weddings/functions ▪ Conferences ▪ Walks/hikes ▪ Simson-Simons Contract Nature Reserve ▪ Guest houses: 6-bedroom, 2 x 4-bedroom & 2 x 2-bedroom cottages ▪ De Perdestal Restaurant open for Sunday lunch (bookings only) ▪ Owner(s) Fynbos Estate (3 partners) ▪ Cellarmaster(s) Johan Simons (Jan 2004) ▪ Winemaker(s) Johan Simons (Jan 2004), Andy Kershaw (2015, consultant) ▪ Viticulturist(s) Johan Simons (Jun 1997) ▪ 320ha/13ha (cab, mourv, ptage, sangio, shiraz, chard, chenin, viog) ▪ 35t/1,400cs own label 40% red 45% white 5% rosé 10% méthode ancestrale ▪ Swartland Independent Producers ▪ Ecocert organic ▪ P O Box 526 Malmesbury 7299 ▪ info@fynbosestate.co.za, info@dragonridge.co.za ▪ www.dragonridge.co.za, www.fynbosestate.co.za ▪ S 33° 33' 28.9" E 018° 47' 5.6" ▪ ✉ newsprint.bitumen.zipping ▪ **T +27 (0)22-487-1153**

Driehoek Wines

ⓐ ⓒ ⓑ

It's just over ten years since the Du Toit family planted their 5 hectares high in the Cederberg Conservancy, and the vines are now more mature and delivering their best fruit ever, according to owner Charl du Toit. Neighbour David Nieuwoudt at Cederberg Private Cellar is responsible for vinification, keeping it simple and sustainable throughout. Next venture for the Du Toits moves underground - truffle farming, starting soon.

★★★★☆ **Mieke Pinot Noir** ⊘ ⓐ Bursting with bright, perfumed red fruit, **18** ⑨③ radiates charm & character. Smoky red cherries & tangy cranberry mix with attractive spices of nutmeg & cloves (100% oaked, 20% new). Finished off with brisk acidity & light, silky tannins.

★★★★☆ **Shiraz** Attractive fruit flavours (black cherries, blackcurrants) tweaked with classic black pepper & cloves, **17** ⑨② promises lots of pleasure to come. Tarry tannins need time to merge with fresh acidity but plenty to look forward to. 70% new oak.

★★★★☆ **Ludic Sauvignon Blanc** ⊘ Previewed **19** ⑨⓪ looks set to shine, with flinty grassy notes offset by ripe citrus, guavas & gooseberries. Bracing acidity will settle & integrate with time.— CM

Location: Citrusdal ▪ Map: Olifants River ▪ Map grid reference: D6 ▪ WO: Cederberg ▪ Est/1stB 2009 ▪ Sales Mon-Sat ▪ Closed Good Fri & Dec 25 ▪ Facilities for children ▪ Gift shop ▪ Walking/hiking & MTB trails ▪ Horse riding ▪ Bird watching ▪ Fishing ▪ Bushman paintings ▪ Conservation area ▪ Self-catering cottages & camping ▪ Beauty treatments ▪ Owner(s) Du Toit family ▪ Cellarmaster(s)/winemaker(s) David Nieuwoudt (Jan 2008, Cederberg) ▪ Viticulturist(s) Dawie Burger (Jun 2006), advised by David Nieuwoudt ▪ 375ha/5ha (pinot, shiraz, sauv) ▪ 3,500cs own label 40% red 60% white ▪ PO Box 89 Clanwilliam 8135 ▪ driehoekcederberg@gmail.com ▪ www.cederberg-accommodation.co.za ▪ S 32° 26' 34.40" E 019° 11' 24.32" ▪ ⌨ gleeful.rudder.rehash ▪ T +27 (0)27-482-2828

☐ **Drie Papen Fontein** see Fairview
☐ **Drift** see Bruce Jack Wines
☐ **Dromer Wines** See Editor's Note

Drostdy-Hof Wines

Launched in 1973, Drostdy-Hof is another Distell label with roots in SA history: the name recalls De Oude Drostdy, Tulbagh's magistracy, a national monument and for a time the brand's cellardoor. Early accessibility has remained the focus, with low-alcohol and naturally sweet wines keeping the styling current. The labels below are the domestically available bottlings in a much larger portfolio.

Core range
Claret Select ★★ Reliable for any casual meal or occasion, **NV** ⑦⑥ has a medium body, soft tannins, ripe red-berry flavours. Blend of cab & 3 others; available in various bottle/pack sizes, as all ranges.

Light range
Extra Light Rosé ★★ Copper-hued **NV** ⑦④ crisp, dry, with cranberry & strawberry flavours, 9% alcohol (as next). Serve chilled but don't add ice to either of these. Undisclosed variety/ies, as Red. **Extra Light White** ★★ Fragrant **NV** ⑦③ dry & smooth on the palate, with lemon-lime freshness. From chenin.

Natural Sweet range
Red ★★ Cherry-red **NV** ⑦③ soft & sweet, with ripe berry & plum fruit. Just 8% alcohol, like all of these, & best served chilled. **Rosé** ★★ Cheerily pink **NV** ⑦⑤ has musk sweet & candyfloss aromas, ripe strawberry flavours, fruity & fresh. Chenin & colombard, cab & cinsaut for colour. **White** ★★ Clean finish to sweet **NV** ⑦④, with very ripe grape & litchi flavours from muscat, partnering chenin & colombard. — JG

Druk My Niet Wine Estate   ⓆⓅ☺◎

After the devastating wildfire in 2017, the Kirchner and Stein families' manor house and boutique winery in Paarl was sympathetically renovated. Now it's been upgraded to include solar power, which dovetails with the ethos of farming and making wine as naturally as possible. Seasoned Marcus Milner is the man in the cellar, which dates back to 1692.

Icon Collection
★★★★ **Invictus** Sinewy but bold **14** ⑧⑨ merlot-driven blend displays hedgerow & cocoa notes. Cab & cab franc minor players. Taut & spicy, with 45% new oak evident in tannic squeeze. Needs time.

★★★★ **T3** Dry spice & cherry notes on **14** ★★★★ ⑧④, unusual blend tempranillo, tinta amarela & tannat, from 18 months in 40% new oak. Bright if a little lean, unlike bold **13** ⑧⑧.

★★★★ **C68 Chenin Blanc** Balanced **18** ⑧⑥, with fresh stonefruit vigour & creamy nuance from 50/50 tank & barrel blend. All-new oak doesn't dominate, adds length.

Mirus ★★★✩ From a shiraz single-vineyard, **16** ⑧⑤ is powerful, with herb-brushed black cherry & muscular oak, 60% new. Good concentration & length. Also in 1.5 & 3L, as Invictus & T3. Not tasted: **C68 Puella**.

Estate Collection
★★★★ **Cabernet Franc** Structured **14** ★★★★ ⑧⑤ shows typical pencil shavings & earthy nuance on textured, long palate. Good integration of oak, 40% new, whereas **13** ⑧⑥ was just 25% new.

Cabernet Sauvignon ★★★✩ Chalky texture & grip to inky blue- & black-fruited **15** ⑧③. Succulent & fresh but oak (40% new) is drying on palate. **Malbec** ★★★★ Plush, soft-textured **14** ⑧③ has lavender edge to light-bodied, blue-fruited appeal. **T3 Rosé** ⑯④ ★★★✩ Juicy strawberry & floral appeal to **19** ⑧⑤ from tempranillo, tannat & tinta amarela. Good body with leashed power & dryness. — FM

Location/map: Paarl ▪ Map grid reference: G4 ▪ WO: Paarl/Western Cape ▪ Est 2003 ▪ 1stB 2009 ▪ Tasting, sales & cellar tours by appt ▪ Tasting fees: R150pp/estate range, R400pp/full range ▪ Closed all pub hols ▪ Meals/ refreshments on request ▪ BYO picnic ▪ Tour groups ▪ Walks/hikes ▪ Conservation area ▪ Owner(s) Georg & Dorothee Kirchner, Jens-Peter Stein ▪ Winemaker(s) Marcus Milner (Aug 2018) ▪ 24.5ha/9ha (cabs s/f, malbec, merlot, shiraz, tannat, tempranillo, tinta amarela, viog) ▪ 110t cellar, 60t/3,500cs own label 80% red 20% white ▪ IPW ▪ PO Box 7383 Paarl 7620 ▪ georg.kirchner@dmnwines.co.za ▪ www.dmnwines.co.za ▪ S 33° 41' 23.26" E 019° 1' 40.23" ▪ ⌖ cleanings.boathouse.frog ▪ **T +27 (0)82-758-4106**

☐ **Duckitt** see Cloof Wine Estate

☐ **Duke of Wellington** see Wellington Wines

Dunstone Winery

(♀) (♍) (⌂) (◎) (⍟) (♿)

Owned by former British Royal Navy doctor Lee Wallis and his wife, Abbi, this farm at the foot of Wellington's Bainskloof Pass boasts luxury accommodation, bistro and boutique winery. Family, friends and guests are invited to get involved in the hands-on harvest, with recent plantings including more shiraz and grenache.

Reserve range (NEW)

★★★★ **Shiraz** (🌱) Densely fruity **17** (87) shows porty notes, hefty 15% alcohol. Ultra-ripe, weighty & thickly tannic, built for the long road.

Dunstone range

★★★★ **Grenache Noir** (NEW) From bushvines, **18** (87) shows promise. Fragrant & fruity, mid-weight, with 10% mourvèdre, has charming higher tones from partial bunch-fermentation.

★★★★ **Merlot** (✓) Honest, convincing **17** (87) delivers generous black fruit, silky tannin, good weight & finish. 14 months in older oak barrels. Solid value.

★★★★ **Shiraz** Better form than **16** ★★★★ (84), **17** (86) has bright & perky berry fruit, appealing fynbos scent, meaty core, showing promise of vintage. 25% new oak still prominent, should settle.

Shiraz Rosé (🍷) ★★★★ Appealing pale rose-pink **19** (84) is bright & fresh, charmingly juicy, with floral notes on ripe berries. Drink right now. Coastal WO.

Viognier ★★★★ **18** (85) has overt oaky flavour, with typical peach fruit notes, texture & elegance. Some Durbanville grapes. — GdB

Location/map: Wellington ▪ Map grid reference: C3 ▪ WO: Wellington/Coastal ▪ Est/1stB 2006 ▪ Tasting, sales & cellar tours Wed-Sun 8-4, Mon-Tue by appt ▪ Fee R30pp, waived on purchase ▪ Closed Dec 25 ▪ The Stone Kitchen ▪ Facilities for children ▪ Conferences ▪ Dunstone Country House luxury B&B guest house, self-catering cottage & self-catering house ▪ Owner(s) Abbi & Lee Wallis ▪ Winemaker(s) Danie de Bruyn (2018) ▪ Viticulturist(s) Johan Viljoen (Icon Vines & Wines) ▪ 6ha (grenache, merlot, mourv, shiraz, viog) ▪ 30t/3,300cs own label 65% red 25% white 10% rosé ▪ PO Box 901 Wellington 7654 ▪ wine@dunstone.co.za ▪ www. dunstone.co.za ▪ S 33° 38' 5.3" E 019° 3' 36.8" ▪ ⌖ evading.prevail.weirdness ▪ **T +27 (0)21-873-6770**

☐ **Du Plevaux** see Imbuko Wines

Du Preez Estate

(♀) (♿)

It's over a century since Hendrik Lodewyk du Preez put down roots - his own and vine ones - in Breedekloof, and over two decades since the family first released own-label wines. Hennie du Preez represents the third generation to have built up the substantial estate, with son Jean in charge of the 350 hectares of vines.

Hendrik Lodewyk range

★★★★ **Petit Verdot** (🌱) Inky **12** (87) brooding dark berries, mouthfilling liqueur-like viscosity. Smooth & complex, with freshness & savoury, gentle grip. No **11**. Goudini WO.

Cabernet Sauvignon (♀) ★★★★ Vibrant cassis, dried herbs on **15** (84), focused & light footed, showing good depth of flavour & length. WO W Cape. **Méthode Cap Classique** (♀) ★★★★ Lively & focused dry sparkling with creamy mousse, crunchy apple & citrus flavours, very appealing freshness & zest. **NV** (85) from chardonnay (85%) & pinot noir. Well priced too.

Du Preez Private Cellar range

★★★★☆ **Hanepoot** ⓥ Lemon-gold colour on **15** ⑨③ fortified entices, seduction continues on palate with voluptuous grapey barley sugar & bitter marmalade. Unctuous & super-sweet yet balanced by fiery alcohol for wonderfully clean, bright conclusion. Different league to last **11** ★★★★ ⑧④.

....

Sauvignon Blanc ⓥ ⓦ ★★★ Tropical fruit, citrus & a grassy note all there on **19** ⑧②. Neatly balanced, fresh & flavourful, with a good dry bite to it. WO W Cape, like Polla's.

....

Cabernet Sauvignon ⓥ ★★★ Dusty dark fruit with gripping tannins in **15** ⑦⑧. **Merlot** ⓥ ★★★ Plum & spice aromas, **17** ⑧① easy palate, partial oaking aids the friendly & well-rounded personality. **Shiraz** ★★★ **16** ⑧⓪ has obvious acidity coping with the sweetly soft, tasty ripeness. 14.5% alcohol. **Polla's Red** ⓥ ★★★ Undemanding crowd favourite, **16** ⑧① perky red fruit, chocolate overlay, soft smooth tannin. Pinotage & 3 others, mostly unoaked; also in magnum. — TJ

Location: Rawsonville ▪ Map: Breedekloof ▪ Map grid reference: B6 ▪ WO: Breedekloof/Western Cape/ Goudini ▪ Est 1916 ▪ 1stB 1998 ▪ Tasting & sales Mon-Fri 8–5 Sat 10–1 ▪ Closed all pub hols ▪ Cellar tours by appt, 1-day prior notice required ▪ Tour groups (max 40 pax), 1-day prior notice required ▪ Owner(s) Du Preez family ▪ Winemaker(s) Francois Joubert (Jan 2016) ▪ Viticulturist(s) Jean du Preez ▪ 350ha (cab, merlot, p verdot, ptage, shiraz, chard, chenin, cbard, nouvelle, sauv) ▪ 6,000t ▪ IPW ▪ PO Box 12 Route 101 Rawsonville 6845 ▪ info@dupreezestate.co.za ▪ www.dupreezestate.co.za ▪ S 33° 41′ 37.1″ E 019° 16′ 59.6″ ▪ ⓯ thankful. slouches.conflate ▪ T +27 (0)23-349-1995

Durbanville Hills

Last year saw this popular brand (a collaboration between local growers, a staff trust and Distell) celebrate its 21st birthday, a milestone marked with the official launch of their Collector's Reserve premium range, which links Cape Town landmarks to featured wines. Cellarmaster Martin Moore has been there from the start, and instrumental in establishing Durbanville as a region noted for top-quality cool-climate wines, uncovering different pockets of fruit each year to create not just the brand's signature Sauvignon Blanc (a staple on so many restaurant wine lists) but also more individual, handcrafted wines and labels. The brand home, high on the hills overlooking Table Bay, has also changed over the years. It now offers the newly rebranded The Tangram restaurant as well as innovative pairings and always-amazing views.

Collectors Reserve range

★★★★☆ **Cabernet Sauvignon** ⓥ Forthright & well-crafted **17** ⑨⓪, classic cabernet flavours of blackcurrant, lavender & mint, the oaking (100% French barrels, 50% new, as all reds below) adds tobacco, toffee & spice. Rich, ripe & rounded.

★★★★ **Merlot** Black Forest gateau in a glass, **17** ⑧⑨ lavishly combines black cherries, dark chocolate, cocoa powder & hint of herbs. Firm tannins & zippy acidity provide welcome backbone to ripeness.

★★★★ **Pinotage** Now fuller bodied (14.7% alcohol), plus 5% American oak added to French. Creates rich & satisfying **17** ⑧⑦ packed with savoury biltong spice, dark black plum fruit & long finish.

★★★★ **Shiraz** ⓥ ⓐ Real 'iron fist in a velvet glove' stuff. **17** ★★★★★ ⑨⓪ handles its oak (all French, 50% new) & alcohol (15%) with style, overlaying both with dense, dark blackcurrants & whiffs of violets & lavender. Plenty of spice (cloves, cumin, pepper) & excellent length. Improves on simpler **16** ⑧⑥.

★★★★ **Chardonnay** In modern New World style showing exuberant peachy fruit combined with fresh nuts & vanilla from 60% French oak, half new. **18** ⑧⑥'s unoaked portion plus lively acidity lift & freshen.

★★★★ **Chenin Blanc** Fresh peaches & pineapples of **18** ⑧⑥ slightly swamped mid-2019 by prominent oak (90% barrel-fermented, 50% new, French & 10% American). Good length & lingering aftertaste suggest time will resolve nicely.

★★★★ **Sauvignon Blanc** Pronounced grassy, greenpepper aromas on **18** ⑧⑥ relax into tropical mouthful & pleasing breadth on palate thanks to 10 months on lees. Zesty & fresh, very likeable wine.

Durbanville Hills range

★★★★ **Cabernet Sauvignon** ⓥ Exciting **18** ⑧⑥, pre-bottling shows depth of classic flavours - blackcurrant, blueberry, attractive tarry note from staves; soft juicy tannins, great acid. Cut above your everyday red.

★★★★☆ **Tangram** ⓐ Cabernet-led 5-way Bordeaux blend **16** ⑨ needs time to show off charms. Dense, dark-berried fruit with tobacco & floral top notes wrapped in charry, smoky oak (100% new French barrels, 24 months). Ripe, firm tannins & zesty acidity all suggest a keeper.

★★★★☆ **Tangram Sauvignon Blanc-Semillon** ⓐ Elegant white Bordeaux blend **18** ⑨ ups the semillon to 24%, adding appealing herbal notes to soft yellow & green sauvignon fruit. Lovely oak (100% barrel ferment, 33% new) seamlessly integrated with lipsmacking acidity & lengthy finish.

★★★★ **Méthode Cap Classique Blanc de Blancs** ⓥ Poised **16** ⑧ sparkler from chardonnay mixes elegant apple fruit with delicious touch of cream & saltiness courtesy 3 years on lees. 10% oaked component for richness & breadth, clean, fresh finish delights.

★★★★ **Cape Honey Bee Noble Late Harvest** ⓝ Botrytis dessert from sauvignon, unoaked, balances lashings of honey-sweet fruit (dried apples, apricots) with zesty marmalade, molasses & quince. **18** ⑧ pairs perfectly with malva pudding, low alcohol (9.6%) a bonus. 375 ml.

Merlot ⓥ ★★★★ Red cherry-berry mix **18** ⑧ adds fresh herbal notes & savoury bite from oak staves, mainly French plus 5% American, as for reds below. **Pinotage** ★★★ Engaging coffee notes on previewed **18** ⑧, well balanced by fresh black fruit & soft, supportive tannins. **Shiraz** ⓥ ★★★★ Ripe red & black fruit on **18** ⑧, plenty of pepper & smoked meat at the finish. **Merlot Rosé** ⓥ ★★★ Roundly dry, irrepressibly fruity **19** ⑧, crowd-pleasing pink for happy summer drinking. **Chardonnay** ⓥ ★★★☆ Peachy stonefruit **18** ⑧ with gentle acidity & creamy touch from 10% French oak staves & 6 months on lees. **Chenin Blanc** ★★★ Zesty **19** ⑧ pops with ripe fruit (pineapples & gooseberries) in uncomplicated sipper to enjoy al fresco. Very light touch of oak. **Sauvignon Blanc** ⓥ ★★★★ Ever-reliable restaurant stalwart **19** ⑧ retains good varietal character & regional typicity in mouthful of dusty green pea fruit mingled with granadilla & grapefruit. **Sparkling Rosé** ⓝ ★★★ Delightful pink fizzy party-sipper from cabernet & shiraz. Carbonated **NV** ⑧ has fresh red- & black-fruit aroma, gently dry, with clean finish. **Sparkling Sauvignon Blanc** ★★★ Perky & fresh **NV** ⑧ carbonated fizzer shows green guavas & crisp apples in almost-dry mouthful.

Discontinued: **Rhinofields range**. — CM

Location/WO: Durbanville ▪ Map: Durbanville, Philadelphia & Darling ▪ Map grid reference: C7 ▪ Est 1998 ▪ 1stB 1999 ▪ Tasting & sales Mon 12-6 Tue-Thu 10-6 Fri 10-7 Sat 10-4 Sun 11-4 (bar & kitchen close 1hr earlier) ▪ Fee R70/5 wines incl crystal glass ▪ Closed Dec 25 & Jan 1/2 ▪ Chocolate/biltong/cheese & wine pairings ▪ Tasting room menu available daily ▪ Cellar tours by appt ▪ The Tangram restaurant: breakfast 8.30-11 & lunch 12-3 Tue-Sun; dinner 6-10 Tue-Sat ▪ Facilities for children ▪ Conferences ▪ Weddings/functions ▪ Owner(s) Distell, 9 farmers & staff trust ▪ Cellarmaster(s) Martin Moore (Nov 1998) ▪ Winemaker(s) Wilhelm Coetzee (reds, Sep 2008) & Kobus Gerber (whites, Jul 2015) ▪ Viticulturist(s) Henk van Graan (consultant) ▪ 770ha ▪ 6,000t/300,000cs own label 40% red 58% white 2% rosé ▪ ISO 9000-1, ISO 14000-1, BRC, HACCP, IPW, WIETA ▪ PO Box 3276 Durbanville 7551 ▪ info@durbanvillehills.co.za ▪ www.durbanvillehills.co.za ▪ S 33° 49' 29.9" E 018° 33' 56.7" ▪ ⓜ narrowing.uppermost.incidentally ▪ **T** +27 (0)21-558-1300

Du'SwaRoo ⓥ ⓒ

The bug that turned founder-owner Tony Bailey from a hobbyist into a full-fledged vigneron lives on in his successor, judging from the many projects launched by Kallie Calitz since he took the helm of the boutique farm and cellar in Calitzdorp recently (a new irrigation dam among the developments). Tony, who named the venture after significant places in his life (Durban, South West Africa/Namibia and Klein Karoo), is still involved as co-winemaker, while Kallie's wife Pat looks after the branded farm and deli produce.

Khamsin ⓥ ★★★ Fruitcake & vanilla-rich **NV** ⑧ shiraz is well spiced from 30 months in older oak, ends nicely dry. For those who like big, flavourful reds. **Shiraz** ★★★ Savoury seam in **17** ⑧'s dark fruit, thanks to 24 months barrique (as other 2017 reds), smooth & round texture. **Bailey** ⓥ ★★★ Mulberry & plum, spicy from 2 years in barrel. Smooth-textured **NV** ⑦ uncertified tinta, best enjoyed young. **Tinta Barocca** ⓝ ★★★ Spiced fruitcake styling, yet **17** ⑧ has sleek lines, juicy, with appealing freshness. **Touriga Nacional** ⓥ ★★★ Despite 2 years oaking, **17** ⑧ designed for early drinking: plumply ripe dark berries, elegant (12.5% alcohol) & refreshing. **Ubique** ⓥ ★★★ Uncertified **NV** ⑦ touriga, mulberry & plum, sleek, with livening acidity for early drinking. **Sirocco Bin 4** ⓥ ★★★ Touriga 50%, tinta 30% with shiraz; **NV** ⑧ almost plum pudding ripeness, vanilla spiced, smooth & round, just enough grip for cellaring. **Sirocco Bin 5** ⓥ ★★★ Trim (13% alcohol) & tasty 'Calitzdorp Blend' touriga, tinta & shiraz. **NV** ⑧ (uncertified) dark plums & prunes, vanilla overlay from 36 months oaking. **Shiraz Rosé** ⊘ ★★★ Strawberries with a shot of freshness, dry **19** ⑦⑧'s friendly alcohol (12%) aids drinkability. **Chardonnay** ★★★ Unwooded **19** ⑦⑧ offers gentle peach notes, shows some citrus on the finish. **Chenin Blanc** ★★★ Light-textured & flavourful **19** ⑦⑧ shows melon & quince, crisply dry. **Cape Vintage** ⓠ ★★★☆ Vibrant nutty spice & raisin notes on **11** ⑧⑤ port-style fortified, which retains 66/34 mix of touriga & tinta. Fiery core with good spirit integration. **Cape Vintage Reserve** ⓠ ★★★☆ Touriga with tinta in **14** ⑧③ port-syle fortified, 3 years in barrel giving smoky, savoury tones to the dark plum/prune fruit. Also-tasted **12** ★★★ ⑧① , 60 months oaked, a coffee ground, liquorice character, treacly flavours. Not tasted: **Petit Verdot**, **Sharki**, **JMC Pinotage**, **Tannat**, **Tessa**, **Mistral**. — CR

Location/WO: Calitzdorp • Map: Klein Karoo & Garden Route • Map grid reference: B5 • Est/1stB 2008 • Tasting, sales & cellar tours Mon-Sat 10-4 • Closed Good Fri & Dec 25 • Farm produce & deli products • Owner(s)/cellarmaster(s) Kallie Calitz • Winemaker(s) Kallie Calitz & Tony Bailey • Viticulturist(s) Tony Bailey (2008) • 0.6ha (shiraz, tinta, touriga); 1.5ha/20t hanepoot also grown but delivered to Calitzdorp Cellar • 200cs own label 80% red 10% white 10% port • PO Box 279 Calitzdorp 6660 • sales@duswaroo.co.za • www.duswaroo.co.za • S 33° 30' 57.9" E 021° 41' 38.3" • ⌨ devout.vies.restorer • **T +27 (0)44-213-3137/+27 (0)44-213-3055/+27 (0)82-826-2419**

Du Toitskloof Winery. ⓠ ⑪ ⓒ ⓖ

A true success story: established in 1962 by six farmers to supply bulk wine to the industry's big producers, this winery has grown to become the largest accredited Fairtrade producer in the world. So far over 2,000 people have directly benefited from this certification, which has made possible children's daycare centres, clinic and mobile clinic, primary school with bus service, bursaries for high school students and tertiary education, adult literacy projects, health and safety education, computer centre and much more. Picturesquely situated near Rawsonville, Du Toitskloof has 13 owners with 22 farms comprising over 900 hectares, and produces wines in several ranges, encompassing multiple varieties and styles, most at very affordable prices.

Quest range

★★★★ **Heroes Journey 2** ⓐ Just shiraz in **16** ⑧⑥ , change from last-made **12** ⑧⑥ combo with mourvèdre. Frequent punch-downs for colour & concentration, all-new oak 24 months supports classic varietal character, brambleberries, scrub & pepper. Has ageing muscle tone.

★★★★☆ **Heroes Journey 1** ⊘ ⓐ 3-part Bordeaux blend, with cab in charge, deeply rich & ripe, **17** ⑨② is opulent, packed with cassis & tobacco, full bodied, curvy. New oak, 24 months, adds a serious note & firm tannins for a future. No **13 - 16**.

Heroes Journey Méthode Cap Classique ★★★ Blanc de blancs dry sparkling from chardonnay, **NV** ⑧④ 18 months on lees which picked up some creamy palate weight to go with the citrus character. Elegant, crisply dry.

Land's End range

Sauvignon Blanc ⑦ ★★★★ Vivid fruit, thanks to the cool-climate Agulhas origin, piquant gooseberries & kiwi, but **18** ⑧⑤ has other layers, fynbos & flint. Taut & wonderfully fresh. WO Cape South Coast for these.

Syrah ★★★★ Black cherries in ripe **17** ⑧④ , combo barrel & stainless steel gives fruit its due without losing the spice. Lovely streamlined body.

Selected Vineyard range

Dimension Red ⑦ ★★★★ Shiraz-led, but big contributions from pinotage, merlot & cab, so expect something interesting. **17** ⑧④ plums & prunes, mocha chocolate, spice array from oaking, mix French cooperages, an earthy note. Plush texture, nice grip to finish.

Cabernet Sauvignon ⓠ ★★★ Shows blackcurrants, especially expressive in the flavours, but **16** ⑦⑧ also has a savoury side, well spiced from 10 months oaking. **Merlot** ⓠ ★★★ Mulberries shot through with herbaceous notes, slight touch of mint, **17** ⑦⑧ has merlot typicity & drinks so easily. **Pinotage** ★★★ Good fruit expression, blueberries & black plums, **17** ⑧①'s savoury tannins harmonious, the whole effect smooth, juicy access. **Shiraz** ★★ Dusty spice top note, the oak influence quite strong flavour-wise in **16**

⑦⑥, not harsh, just very savoury. Best paired with rich meat dishes. **Pinotage Rosé** ★★☆ Bright pink & packed with red berries, **19** ⑦⑧ is dry & fruity-fresh. Not tasted: **Nebbiolo**.

Heritage range

Pinotage-Merlot-Ruby Cabernet ⊘ ★★★ Berries & plums, touch of oak but **18** ⑦⑨ made for early enjoyment, juicy & smooth. Also in 3L, as all except Chardonnay. **Cabernet Sauvignon-Shiraz** ⊘ ★★★ Good partnership gives **18** ⑧⓪ its plush berry fruit profile, touch of oak adds spice notes. Sleek, with appealing drinkability. **Chardonnay** ★★★ Half fermented/matured 4 months in barrel, rest stainless. Expressive citrus, tangerine, hint of lemon, light vanilla biscuit dusting, but **18** ⑧① essentially fruit driven. **Chenin Blanc** ⊘ ★★★ Well-priced range. Offering an array of fresh summer fruits, **19** ⑧① finishes crisply dry. Good example of the variety. **Sauvignon Blanc** ★★★ Forthcoming litchi & gooseberry scents, **19** ⑧① has crunchy green apple freshness. Trim-figured, with matching alcohol (12.5%), as most whites here.

Tunnel range

Robust Red ⊘ ★★★ Entire range modestly priced, designed for satisfying uncomplicated drinking. Pinotage with ruby cab, **NV** ⑦⑦ touch of oak, glossy berries, juicy & smooth. **Fragrant Rosé** ★★ Was 'Sweet Rosé'. Muscat & chenin combo, with some sauvignon & pinotage, **NV** ⑦④ is delicate pink, slim (8% alcohol, as is red) & sweet, acidity giving a tangy finish. **Crisp White** ⊘ ★★★ Name is spot on, mainly sauvignon with chenin, **NV** ⑦⑦ has apple & pear exuberant freshness. **Sweet White** ★★ More 'semi' than sweet, **NV** ⑦④ from muscat, dab chenin, has floral aromas, grapey/fruit salad flavours. **Sweet Red** ★★ Near-equal pinotage & chenin, dash ruby cab, full-sweet **NV** ⑦④ is designed to give uncomplicated drinking pleasure.

Fairtrade range

Zola Cape Cuvée ⓥ ★★★ Light oaking gives **18** ⑧① a savoury nuance, but essentially a ripe, luscious, berry-rich experience. Cab & pinotage (60/40).

Zola Pinotage Rosé ★★★ Pale pink, & different flavour profile to the other rosés. **19** ⑦⑨ red berries & musk sweets, yet dry & fresh, palate's fruit delicate. **Dimension Chardonnay** ★★★ Style change, some oak for **19** ⑧② half barrel-fermented/matured 4 months, comes through as a biscuit seam in the lemon/lime flavours. Ends crisply fresh.

Sparkling Wine range

Vin Doux ★★ Carbonated bubbly from pinotage, ruby coloured & berry-rich, **NV** ⑦④ offers low alcohol (8%) & measured sweetness, a tasty, lively party-goer. **Brut** ★★★ Carbonated bubbly from sauvignon, **NV** ⑦⑧ is like tasting foamy lemon sherbet; elegant & dry, zesty finish.

Fortified range

★★★★ **Red Muscadel** ⓐ A delight, full-sweet dried fruit & raisin powerhouse, **18** ⑧⑧ improves on **15** ★★★☆ ⑧④; hard to resist, mouthcoatingly rich flavours, & a very long future (cellar says 50 years!, as for Jerepigo). **16** untasted, no **17**. 500 ml.

Hanepoot Jerepigo ⓥ ★★★★ Ambrosial honeyed seduction of balanced **14** ⑧④ fortified from muscat d'Alexandrie. Richly sweet but with a clean finish. **Cape Ruby** ⓥ ★★★ Tinta with souzão, **13** ⑧① 'port' fits the Ruby style: fruit is the hero, rich & mellow, oak adding flavour, no firmness. 500 ml. — CR

Location: Rawsonville ▪ Map: Breedekloof ▪ Map grid reference: B6 ▪ WO: Western Cape/Cape South Coast ▪ Est 1962 ▪ Tasting & sales Mon-Fri 8–5 Sat/Sun/pub hols 9-4 ▪ Closed Dec 25 & Jan 1 ▪ Cellar tours by appt ▪ Ou Meul Bakery ▪ Owner(s) 13 members (22 farms) ▪ Cellarmaster(s) Shawn Thomson (Oct 1999) ▪ Winemaker(s) Tiaan Loubser (Nov 2016) & Willie Stofberg (Feb 2011), with Derrick Cupido (Jan 1993) ▪ Viticulturist(s) Leon Dippenaar (Jan 2005, consultant) ▪ 900ha (cab, merlot, ptage, shiraz, chard, chenin, cbard, sauv) ▪ 16,500t/±800,000cs own label 40% red 60% white ▪ Fairtrade ▪ PO Box 55 Rawsonville 6845 ▪ info@dutoitskloof.co.za ▪ www.dutoitskloof.co.za ▪ S 33° 42' 9.2" E 019° 16' 8.9" ▪ ⓦ passer.crewmen. reaming ▪ **T +27 (0)23-349-1601**

DuVon Wine Estate   ⓥ ⌂ ◎

On the Little Italy property in Robertson's Goree ward, Armand du Toit and his uncle, Alex von Klopmann, use some of 'the best grapes from the most suitable terroir that the farm has to offer' for their small-batch estate wines, made in a restored 1940s cellar. Armand's philosophy is one of minimum interference: 'I believe in soil, location, climate and one human factor, management, but with a nature-driven mindset'. **Memoire Cabernet Sauvignon** ★★★ Bright & juicy, cherry- & plum-toned **17** ⑦⑧ offers uncomplicated approachability. **Shiraz** ★★★ Succulent & ripe **17** ⑧② some berry jam notes but good freshness & crunch on palate. Touch of dried herb adds interest. **Old Vine Chenin Blanc** ★★★ Very youthful **19** ⑦⑧ still shows some ferment character. Pineapple & tropical fruit appeal, tangy summertime sipping. **Sauvignon Blanc** ★★★ Light, easy **19** ⑦⑧ has lemon zest typicity. — WB, FM

Location/map/WO: Robertson ▪ Map grid reference: B7 ▪ Est/1stB 2003 ▪ Tasting, sales & cellar tours by appt ▪ Conferences ▪ Weddings ▪ Guest house ▪ Owner(s) Armand du Toit & Alex von Klopmann ▪ Cellarmaster(s)/winemaker(s)/viticulturist(s) Armand du Toit ▪ 29.5ha/27ha (cab, ruby cab, shiraz, chenin, cbard, sauv) ▪ 400t/1,200cs own label 40% red 60% white ▪ PO Box 348 Robertson 6705 ▪ info@duvon.co.za ▪ www.duvon.co.za ▪ S 33° 48' 46.8" E 019° 47' 4.1" ▪ ⌨ nifty.report.hilltops ▪ **T +27 (0)72-514-4204**

☐ **D'Vine** see Swartland Winery
☐ **Dwyka Hills** see Eagle's Cliff Wines-New Cape Wines
☐ **Dyasonsklip** see Bezalel Wine & Brandy Estate

Eagle's Cliff Wines-New Cape Wines Ⓠ ⑪ ⓐ ⓑ ⓖ

A pair of rare Black Eagles, which made their nest in the cliffs overlooking the vineyards near Worcester, served as inspiration for the name and packaging for these good-value wines produced by two-time Diners Club Winemaker of the Year, Christiaan Groenewald. Said vineyards encircle the cellar and veranda-edged visitor venue, where conference facilities have just joined the wide range of amenities on offer. Christiaan's prestige label, Arendskloof/Voetspore, is listed separately.

Eagle's Cliff range

Pinotage ⊘ ⑬ ★★★★ Succulently ripe, with sweet plum & espresso richness, **18** ⑧③ is smooth & satisfying, a joy to drink. Touch of oak adds length & spice. Great bargain, too. **Shiraz-Pinotage** ⊘ ⑬ ★★★ Delightful, pocket-friendly **18** ⑧② fresh berries, smoked beef, dried herbs in a lipsmacking, oak-brushed body, sappy & rounded.

Cabernet Sauvignon-Merlot ⊘ ★★★ 90/10 blend in **17** ⑦⑧ easy if fleeting spice cake & coffee flavours. **Shiraz Rosé** ⊘ ★★★ Jasmine & lavender perfume on bright pink, dry & spicy **18** ⑦⑧ **Chenin Blanc** ⊘ ★★★ Light & easy tropical fun, serve **18** ⑦⑦ well-chilled. **Sauvignon Blanc** ⊘ ★★★ Steely greenpepper & crunchy green apple flavours combine on attractively juicy **19** ⑦⑦

Dwyka Hills range

Shiraz ⊘ ★★★ Fresh, fruity, with saline olive nuances, **18** ⑧② is tasty but lacks depth of previous. 20% oaked 6 months.

Hoeks Rivier range

Cabernet Sauvignon ★★ Gentle cassis & sour cherry flavours in unwooded **18** ⑦④ — WB

Location/map: Worcester ▪ Map grid reference: A6 ▪ WO: Breede River Valley ▪ Est 2000 ▪ Tasting & sales Mon-Thu 10-3 Fri 10-2 ▪ Closed all pub hols ▪ Cheese & meat platters daily ▪ Bistro (reservation only) ▪ Facilities for children ▪ Tour groups ▪ Wedding & conference venue ▪ Owner(s)/winemaker(s) Christiaan Groenewald ▪ 600ha/80ha ▪ 40% red 60% white ▪ PO Box 898 Worcester 6849 ▪ christiaan@ncw.co.za ▪ www.eaglescliff.co.za ▪ S 33° 50' 25.4" E 019° 25' 7.4" ▪ ⌨ marbles.convinces.tiled ▪ **T +27 (0)23-340-4112**

Eagles' Nest Ⓠ ⑪ ⓖ

'Showing off our curves,' the Eagles' Nest team posted on Facebook, alongside a photograph of their steep vineyard terraces high on the slopes of Constantiaberg overlooking False Bay. The Mylrea family owners switched focus completely after a fire in 2000 devastated the pine plantations on the estate. Today, the vertiginous north-, east- and west-facing slopes boast highly regarded shiraz and viognier, among others. Approaching his third harvest at the lauded winery, Duran Cornhill gets to tap into the wisdom of seasoned winemaking consultant Martin Meinert, on board since 2001. With proceeds from sales of Little Eagle wines (untasted by us) going to Western Cape Raptor Research, a highlight of the year was the successful hatching of a chick by the last breeding pair of Verreaux's eagles in adjacent Table Mountain National Park.

★★★★☆ **Merlot** Sleek, refined yet powerful **15** ㉒ offers concentrated red fruit, spice & cocoa flavour in abundance. Fruit is balanced by deep, rich & rewarding frame from 18 months in oak. Dab cab franc (8%).

★★★★☆ **Shiraz** ⓐ Spicy succulence to trademark black & blue berry fruit on **16** ㉔. Unmistakable power is reined in on the layered, nuanced yet supple palate. Oak, 35% new, is well knit after 18 months. Smart, sophisticated & long.

★★★★ **Sauvignon Blanc 18** ㊙ improves on **17** ★★★★ ㊺ with tropical ripeness poised against taut, tangy acidity. Softly zesty concentration & length from 6 months on lees. Coastal WO.

★★★★☆ **Viognier** ⓐ Interplay of rich stonefruit, cream & wood spice on **18** ㉔. Acidity balances ripeness while oak (just 15% new) supports bright nectarine flavour. Subtle yet confident & focused, long, leesy finish. — FM

Location: Constantia ▪ Map: Cape Peninsula ▪ Map grid reference: B3 ▪ WO: Constantia/Coastal ▪ Est 2001 ▪ 1stB 2005 ▪ Tasting & sales daily 10-4.30 ▪ Fee R75pp, waived on purchase of R500+ ▪ Closed Good Fri, Dec 25/26 & Jan 1 ▪ Cheese & charcuterie platters ▪ Owner(s) Mylrea family ▪ Winemaker(s) Duran Cornhill (Aug 2017), with Martin Meinert (2001, consultant) ▪ Viticulturist(s) Kobus Jordaan (2008) ▪ 38ha/12ha (merlot, shiraz, viog) ▪ 100t/15,000cs own label 85% red 15% white ▪ PO Box 535 Constantia 7848 ▪ info@ eaglesnestwines.com ▪ www.eaglesnestwines.com ▪ S 34° 0' 54.2" E 018° 24' 54.3" ▪ ⓕ graduate.shiniest. grownup ▪ **T +27 (0)21-794-4095**

☐ **Earth's Essence** *see* KWV Wines
☐ **Ecology** *see* PaardenKloof
☐ **Edenhof** *see* Schalkenbosch Wines

Edgebaston ⓟ

Owner and cellarmaster David Finlayson, one of several talented 2nd-generation winegrowers emanating from the Finlayson family (father Walter and uncle Peter helped develop top properties Hartenberg, Blaauwklippen, Glen Carlou and Bouchard Finlayson), has successfully carved out his own place in Stellenbosch's Simonsberg foothills. Acquiring land in 2004, reviving its original name (serendipitously the same as his mother's English birthplace), rooting vines in deep clay topsoil with shale subsoils ('unusual here') and building a cellar, he has cemented Edgebaston's reputation for consistently fine wines across the price spectrum. An established member of the Cape Winemakers Guild, he also collaborates with his winemaker, Pieter van der Merwe, on the Van der Merwe & Finlayson brand, listed separately.

David Finlayson range

★★★★☆ **'GS' Cabernet Sauvignon** ⓐ Tribute to George Spies & his legendary 1960s cabs, **16** ㉔ flagship shows intent with uncompromising focus on purity of fruit. Dense & plush, with finely formed blackcurrant core, delicately spiced by 18 months in all-new oak.

★★★★☆ **Camino Africana Cabernet Franc** ⓐ Splendidly lean, focused **16** ㉔ has finely textured & complex layers, showing iodine-tinged earthiness, taut blackcurrant, savoury tomato concentrate. Chiselled, densely smooth tannins from 2 years in French oak, 30% new.

★★★★ **Camino Africana Pinot Noir** Silky smooth, aromatic & savoury **18** ㉘ has heft & presence, somewhat muted berry fruit & floral scent. From small experimental block of 667 clone on Stellenbosch Mountain. First since **15** ★★★★★ ㉛.

★★★★☆ **Camino Africana Chenin Blanc** ⓐ Extraordinarily graceful **18** ㉔, from 72 & 55 year old vineyards, shows seamless savoury & mineral layers elevated by a sherry nuance, creamy lees texture. Minimum-intervention winemaking, older French barrels, no malo. Shades stellar **17** ㉝.

Edgebaston range

★★★★☆ **Cabernet Sauvignon** ⓐ Epitomises New World cab with pastille-like blackcurrant fruit leavened with herbaceous, leafy, forest floor earthiness. **17** ㉚ fine, ripe tannin structure & 14 months French oak, 30% new, in support. Improves on **16** ★★★★ ㉘, shows fine ageing potential.

★★★★ **Pinot Noir** ② Strawberry & raspberry tones are precise & vibrant yet delicate, **17** ㉗'s wooding (all older, 18 months) cleverly cossets the fruit, creates creamy platform for it to shine. WO W Cape.

★★★★ **The Pepper Pot** ⊘ Pepper (& scrub) do feature in appealing syrah-led 6-way blend, along with convincing berry fruit, silky tannin texture. **17** ⑧⑥ improves on **16** ★★★★ ⑧④. Coastal WO, as next.

★★★★ **Chardonnay** ⊘ Elegantly restrained oaking (30% new, 10 months) lends roundness & body to finely crafted **18** ★★★★★ ⑨⓪, raising bar on **17** ⑧⑧. Textural, sensual, with perfumed citrus fruit, precise acidity, lingering finish. Outstanding quality at the price.

The Berry Box Red ★★★☆ Loads of upfront plum & cherry fruit in perky, approachable **18** ⑧③ merlot with 10% cab. **17** ⑧⑤, also tasted, similar, with touch more weight. **Sauvignon Blanc** ★★★☆ With 10% semillon, wild-fermented **19** ⑧⑤ offers sweet gooseberry fruit with hints of gunsmoke & nettle, rounded by 10 months in barrel. **The Berry Box White** ★★★☆ Cheerful sipper from sauvignon, semillon & viognier, lightly oaked **19** ⑧④ has pinch of sugar, ripe pear fruit, plenty of charm. In abeyance: **Syrah**. — GdB

Location/map: Stellenbosch • Map grid reference: E3 • WO: Stellenbosch/Coastal/Western Cape • Est/1stB 2004 • Tasting by appt only • Owner(s) David Finlayson • Cellarmaster(s) David Finlayson (Jan 2004) • Winemaker(s) Pieter van der Merwe (Jan 2016) • 30ha/24ha (cab, shiraz, chard, sauv) • 300t/60,000cs own label 60% red 40% white • PO Box 2033 Dennesig 7601 • david@edgebaston.co.za • www.edgebaston.co.za • S 33° 53' 33.82" E 018° 51' 17.61" • ⌖ bolt.audible.massive • **T +27 (0)21-889-9572/+27 (0)83-263-4353**

☐ **Edward Snell & Co** *see* Wellington VO
☐ **Eendevanger** *see* illimis Wines

Eenzaamheid

The name of this 17th-century Paarl farm may mean 'Loneliness', but with 21st-century owners Christo and Karina Briers-Louw managing some 400 ha of dryland vineyard and a conference venue; winemaker son Janno handling around 3,000 tons of grapes; viticulturist André Coetzee overseeing new plantings including various clones of chenin (joining vines 35 years old in 2020 and sparking membership of the Old Vine Project); and this boutique own-brand winning friends in China, 'Lonesome' no longer covers it!

★★★★ **Cinsaut** Ⓥ Introduced by gorgeous spice, red berry fragrance, **17** ★★★★★ ⑨⓪ pure, concentrated flavours lifted by usual freshness, tangy dryness. Lightish body for lunchtime drinking. Unwooded, where **16** ⑧⑦ was older-oaked.

★★★★ **Pinotage** Ⓥ Pinotage in bright-fruited, juicy mode; **16** ⑧⑨ also has neat tannin trim. Nicely balanced for current enjoyment & keeping few years. Deftly French oaked, 5% new.

★★★★★ **Shiraz** Ⓥ Satisfyingly rich, with sweet black berries & spice, not over-ripe or heavy. **16** ⑨② will benefit from several more years. Oaking supportive, as always: 10% new French.

★★★★ **Cuvée** Ⓥ Like **15** ⑧⑥, satisfying pocket pleaser. **16** ★★★☆ ⑧⑤, shiraz-led sextet, delivers generosity of dark berry flavours, savouriness in its gently rounded form.

★★★★☆ **Chenin Blanc** From dryland vines, 33 years old, giving depth & intensity, with a minerality from deep shale soils. **17** ⑨⓪ bunch pressing, oak-fermentation & -maturation on lees give breadth & more freshness than **16** ★★★★ ⑧⑧.

Vin Blanc Ⓥ ★★★ Juicy melange chenin with semillon, viognier, clairette. Unoaked **17** ⑧② plentiful ripe melon, apricot flavours lifted by bright acid, dry finish. — MW

Location/map/WO: Paarl • Map grid reference: B5 • Est 1693 • 1stB 2010 • Tasting by appt only • Conferences • Owner(s) Christo & Karina Briers-Louw • Winemaker(s) Janno Briers-Louw (Apr 2008) • Viticulturist(s) André Coetzee (Sep 2003) • 1,185ha/400ha (cinsaut, ptage, shiraz, chenin) • 3,000t/6,000cs own label 70% red 30% white • Fairtrade, WIETA • PO Box 22 Klapmuts 7625 • wine@eenzaamheid1.co.za • www.eenzaamheidwines.co.za • S 33° 44' 52.67" E 018° 50' 12.06" • ⌖ blank.officers.captivates • **T +27 (0)82-493-9930**

Eerste Hoop Wine Cellar

Viticulturist and winemaker at this Belgian-owned, boutique-sized winery near Villiersdorp since December 2017, self-taught (with winemaker mentorship) Diané Wentzel is streamlining production. Prompted by increasing demand for the mostly exported wines, she's also overseeing the planting of a further 4 hectares of chardonnay, with more Rhône red varieties to follow.

Lemahieu range
★★★★ **Lady Brigitte Red Blend** ✓ Shiraz, grenache & mourvèdre seamlessly interwoven in **16** (87), spicy & savoury flavours in supple, dry tannin framework, with ripeness well contained & crafted. Not tasted: **Lodewijkx White Blend**.

Eerste Hoop range
★★★★ **Cabernet Sauvignon** Opulent dark berry compote & liquorice flavours, **16** ★★★☆ (83) supple & juicy, sweeter & less structured than previous **NV** (86) bottling. For fans of riper, easy-drinking reds.
Pinot Noir ★★★☆ Affable **17** (84) better balanced than previous, ample red berry & earth flavours, brush of oak char. Freshness tempers alcohol for satisfying drinking. **Shiraz** ★★★ Sweet impression from ripeness in expansive & amiably styled **16** (81). Though burly (15% alcohol), lacks concentration & structure of previous.
Blushing Bride ✓ ★★★ Rosé from pinot noir, **19** (81) much fresher & more poised than previous, clean, light-tripping berry flavours (12% alcohol). Delightful sundowner. **Chardonnay** ★★★ Similar heavily wooded style to previous, **18** (82) will appeal to fans of riper fruit & generous sweet oak spice.
Chenin Blanc (NEW) ★★★ Ripe, sweet-fruited **18** (82). Some toasty oak (better knit than on Chardonnay), body plumped by some sugar, tad soft on acidity, an afterglow needs chilling & food. **Viognier** ★★★☆ Dried yellow peach & floral tones on **18** (84). Oak & alcohol well contained in fruit ripeness & fresh acidity. Flavoursome & succulent solo or with spicy food.

Witklip range
Shiraz ✓ ★★★ Aiming to please & ready to pour, like its range siblings. **17** (81) supple, spicy, balanced & friendly. **Shiraz Rosé** ★★★ Has splash pinot noir in **19** (79), touch more savoury than Eerste Hoop sibling, piquantly fresh & dry. **Chardonnay** ★★★ Baked pear & lemon tones on **19** (81), quite viscous & round for lowish 12.5% alcohol, plump & pleasing, drinks easily. — MW

Location/map: Villiersdorp ▪ Map grid reference: A2 ▪ WO: Western Cape ▪ 1stB 2009 ▪ Tasting, sales & cellar tours by appt only ▪ Owner(s) Lodewijk Lemahieu (Belgium) ▪ Winemaker(s)/viticulturist(s) Diané Wentzel (Dec 2017) ▪ 24.5ha/11ha (cab, grenache, mourv, pinot, shiraz, chard, chenin, viog) ▪ 85t/14,000cs 55% red 42% white 3% rosé ▪ Brands for clients: Oggendau, Skoon Vallei, Stilfontein ▪ PO Box 89 Elgin 7180 ▪ admin@eerstehoop.co.za ▪ www.eerstehoop.co.za ▪ S 34° 5' 23.7" E 019° 11' 50.7" ▪ 🍷 biker.reconciles. playdate ▪ **T +27 (0)28-841-4190/+27 (0)82-754-4408**

☐ **Eikehof Wines** See Editor's Note

Eikendal Vineyards 🍷 🍴 🏠 📷 👤 ♿

A landmark on the R44 between Somerset West and Stellenbosch, thanks to its distinctive barrel-vaulted cellar and towering fountain, this welcoming Swiss-owned estate is popular for its restaurant and lodge but above all for wines made by the team led by Nico Grobler. 'In ten years of growing my roots into the soil of Eikendal, it has been my goal to infuse the wines with the beautiful character of this piece of land,' he says. 'Every year we get a little step closer.' A big step closer was last year's launch of the Infused by Earth flagships, a red and white, the latter cementing Eikendal's reputation as a 'house of chardonnay', both wines expressing Nico's belief in 'small details creating big complexities'.

Infused by Earth range
★★★★☆ **Cabernet Franc** (🏆) **17** (94) less plush, more pure than last-made **15** (94), with black fruit, black pepper, fresh mint, herbal (not herbaceous) & forest floor hints, elegant after year in untoasted 500L French oak, 10% new. Naturally fermented, like all the wines, & under 12.5% alcohol.
★★★★☆ **Chardonnay** (🏆) Fresh, pristine, elegant **17** (94), from high-lying, wind-exposed bushvines on decomposed granite, understated, with floral perfume & fresh citrus fruit. Wholebunch, wild ferment, no malo/bâtonnage, 16 months in one 300L barrel, one granite amphora.

Eikendal Vineyards range
★★★★☆ **Cabernet Sauvignon** (🏆) Both low-vigour rocky soils & drought conditions (producing less sugar) showcased in reined-in **17** (94). Fine tannins, red & black fruit, herbs & earthy mushrooms on stylish palate, tightly knit after year in 300L Burgundy oak, 25% new. 13.5% alcohol.

★★★★☆ **Merlot** ⊘ **17** ⑨ equally poised but less taut than Cab, year in 500L Burgundy barrels but none new for enticing bouquet of violets & rosemary, plummy fruit purity, tangy freshness, powdery tannins.

★★★★☆ **Classique** ⊛ Sophisticated Bordeaux blend, smooth, with sinewy tannins, black fruit, hints of clove & coriander. Mostly cab in **17** ⑨, 29% merlot, 12% cab franc, dash petit verdot, vinified separately but for first time blended before going into barrel (300L French, year) 'when wine is at its purest'.

★★★★☆ **Charisma** ⊘ ⊛ Shiraz-led, perfumed **18** ⑨ charismatic indeed with 17% petit verdot amplifying violet, black fruit & chai spice intensity, harmonious after year old wood, then 5% 2019 sangiovese added for freshness. Has good weight at moderate 13.5% alcohol.

★★★★☆ **Chardonnay** ⊛ From diverse blocks, clones, farms & areas, **18** ⑨ is 'purest ever' believes cellarmaster. Also very complex (wine & vinification), from fresh citrus & flinty minerality to subtle hazelnut kiss from year in French oak (15% new) on the lees of up to 4 previous vintages.

★★★★☆ **Mon Désir Chardonnay** ⊛ Oystershell minerality & delicate wood spice (14 months in oak, 25% new, 50% toasted) add intrigue to **18** ⑨ from Elgin, single block, CY277 clone more usually associated with sparkling wine, here expressing citrus (blossom, fruit, peel, freshness).

★★★★☆ **Janina Unwooded Chardonnay** ⊘ Own & Elgin grapes, 13 blocks, 5 clones, up to 30 stainless steel tanks & cement/polyethylene 'eggs' - unoaked but by no means simple, **18** ⑨ has fresh citrus fruit & zest, mineral core; also-tasted **19** ⑨ even more purity, flintiness, persistence.

★★★★ **Sauvignon Blanc** ⊘ Fruitier than **17** ⑧ & chardonnay siblings, with fresh melon, peach & guava flavours, **18** ★★★★★ ⑨ from Elgin has 6.1 g/l sugar (ex the wild ferment) to balance acidity & enhance texture, already creamy from skin-fermented portion & lees ageing in combo tank/old barrel.

Not tasted: **Pinotage**. — JG

Location: Stellenbosch ▪ Map: Helderberg ▪ Map grid reference: C1 ▪ WO: Stellenbosch/Elgin/Western Cape ▪ Est 1981 ▪ 1stB 1984 ▪ Tasting & sales Mon-Sat 9.30-5 (Sep-May)/10-4 (Jun-Aug) Sun 10-5 ▪ Fee R60/5 wines; pizza & wine pairing R100 (winter); cheesecake pairing R100; kiddies cookie tasting R60 ▪ Closed Good Fri, Dec 25/26 & Jan 1 ▪ Cucina di Giovanni @ Eikendal Tue-Sat lunch & dinner Sun lunch only ▪ Facilities for children ▪ Tour groups ▪ Tractor rides (weekends) ▪ Walks/hikes ▪ Cheetah Outreach (seasonal) ▪ Eikendal Lodge ▪ Owner(s) Substantia AG ▪ Cellarmaster(s) Nico Grobler (2007) ▪ Winemaker(s) Christo Hanse (2012) ▪ Farm manager Willem van Kerwel (2012) ▪ 78ha/±41ha (cabs s/f, cinsaut, grenache, malbec, merlot, mourv, p verdot, chard) ▪ 250t/40,000cs own label 50% red 50% white ▪ IPW ▪ PO Box 2261 Stellenbosch 7601 ▪ marketing@eikendal.co.za ▪ www.eikendal.com ▪ S 34° 0' 46.7" E 018° 49' 24.5" ▪ ☷ tripling.photons. installed ▪ **T +27 (0)21-855-1422, +27 (0)21-855-5033 (Restaurant)**

☐ **Elandsberg** *see* Viljoensdrift Fine Wines & Cruises

Elemental Bob

Non-interventionist boutique vintner Craig Sheard's personality-packed wines are from mostly old vineyard parcels that inspire him. He had to 'skip the 2019 vintage', he says, but is 'rebooting for the 2020 crush'. His many fans will be relieved and looking forward to new vintages of such vivacious and piquantly named gems as Graveyard Tinta Baroccoa and Farmer Red Beard Palomino. The bottlings listed below were still available from Craig's Somerset West base at press time.

My Cosmic Hand range

★★★★☆ **Somersault Cinsault** ⊘ From 25 year old vines, **17** ⑨ energetic & savoury, reminiscent of France's Arbois in its light-seeming concentration & complexity without being 'worked'. Smidgen shiraz, fermented/aged 11 months older oak.

★★★★★ **White** ⊘ Viognier, chenin, verdelho & semillon in **15** ⑨, complex lemon zest, peach & apricot aromas with distinctive white pepper spicing. Fresh & juicy, but savoury & saline, not fruit-sweet. Pithy grip from some whole bunches, skin contact & old oak. WO W Cape.— CvZ

Location: Somerset West ▪ WO: Stellenbosch/Western Cape ▪ Est/1stB 2004 ▪ Closed to public ▪ Owner(s)/ winemaker(s) Craig Sheard ▪ 1,200cs own label 40% red 60% white ▪ elementalbob@gmail.com ▪ www. elementalbob.co.za ▪ **T +27 (0)82-265-1071**

☐ **Elgin Heights** *See Editor's Note*
☐ **Elgin Highlands** *see* Iona Vineyards

Elgin Ridge ⓔ ⓐ ⓞ

Britons Brian and Marion Smith looked far and wide for a winefarm on which to pursue their vinous dream, and settled on a neglected property in Elgin. The dozen years since then have seen it grow as one of very few biodynamic farms in SA — a holistic project in which cattle, sheep, ducks and a percheron stallion named Maddox play their roles. Progress continues, as the vines mature: winemaker Kosie van der Merwe speaks of the significant increase in organic matter in the soil, of producing sufficient compost to sustain the vines, while beneficial microbes are encouraged to reduce the need for copper sprays.

★★★★ **282 Pinot Noir** ⓞ Tasted out of vintage order, **15** ⑧⑥ still a touch raw; fairly lean & light (13% alcohol), lacking overt charm, but with some persistent cherry flavours.

★★★★☆ **282 Chardonnay** ⓞ On the understated, elegant side of the variety's expressiveness, **18** ⑨① does have richness of texture & ripe stonefruit notes, along with fine, natural limy acidity. Modest, supportive oaking (20% new). Should benefit from good few years in bottle. Like Pinot Noir, also some magnums.

★★★★ **282 Sauvignon Blanc** ⓞ **17** ⑧⑦, with 14.5% alcohol, in full-bodied style of **16** ★★★★ ⑧④, but fresh acidity & fine texture satisfy. More citrus than tropical; plenty of flavour, nothing too obvious.

★★★★☆ **Chaos White** ⓞ ⓫ Restrained but subtly suggestive blend of sauvignon - 68% in **18** ⑨③ - & semillon. Lively, fresh, more earthy spice than simple fruitiness. Taut, lightly tannic grip hints at element of skin contact in complex winemaking. Speaks quietly, but has something interesting to say. 500 ml.

Not tasted: **Marion's Vineyards**. — TJ

Location/map/WO: Elgin ▪ Map grid reference: B3 ▪ Est 2007 ▪ 1stB 2009 ▪ Tasting, sales & tours Mon-Sat & pub hols 10-4 Sun 10-2 ▪ Farm produce ▪ BYO picnic ▪ Owner(s) Brian & Marion Smith ▪ Winemaker(s) Kosie van der Merwe ▪ Viticulturist(s) Kevin Watt (Apr 2007, consultant), with Taurai Mutumbwa ▪ 20.2ha/6.5ha (cab f, pinot, chard, sauv, sem) ▪ 45t/4,000cs own label 20% red 80% white ▪ Organic & biodynamic certification ▪ PO Box 143 Elgin 7180 ▪ info@elginridge.com ▪ www.elginridge.com ▪ S 34° 12' 10.68" E 019° 0' 14.34" ▪ ⓜ encounters.soloists.unflagging ▪ **T +27 (0)21-846-8060**

Elgin Vintners ⓔ ⓯ ⓐ ⓞ

The appointment of Marinda Kruger-Claassen (with postgraduate degrees in oenology, viticulture and agriscience) as business manager/winemaker at Elgin Vintners at the end of 2018 marks the 'next step up' for what originally involved six growers on multiple properties in this high-lying quality apple- and grape-growing area, outsourcing vinification to various winemakers. The venture now comprises two farms, Ridgelands and Drumearn, the former lending its name to a range debuting this edition and home to the expanded 'Painters Cottage' tasting room and elegant Victorian manor guest house.

Ridgelands range ⓝⓔⓦ

★★★★ **Pinot Noir** Alluring ripe cherry & raspberry aromas of **18** ⑧⑨ lead to spicy & savoury palate. Tangy acidity & fine-grained tannins support a deep core of seductive, perfumed berries which persist to the long finish. Touch more new oak (15%) than EV sibling.

★★★★ **Syrah** Elegant **16** ⑧⑧, subtle spice introduces vibrant plum & cherry aromas, savoury flavours, leather & white pepper notes. Nimble tannins & spice-tinged berry conclusion. Natural wholebunch ferment, shade longer in oak (20 months) than EV version.

Elgin Vintners range

★★★★ **Pinot Noir** ⓥ Modern & elegant **17** ⑧⑧, ripe cherries & perfumed rosepetals, plenty of sweet & savoury spice on a meaty core. Fresh & tangy with pillow-like tannins. Well-judged 10% new oak, year.

★★★★ **Syrah** Layers of spiced cherry, mulberry & white pepper of **16** ⑧⑥ are interlaced with clove & biltong. Rounded tannins with a savoury finish from 18 months in oak, 20% new, as Merlot.

★★★★ **Chardonnay** Lovely cool-climate freshness, minerality & moderation (13% alcohol) in **18** ⑧⑧. Pears & pineapple interwoven with rooibos & vanilla spice from ferment in 20% new barriques. Complexing kumquat citrus & mineral undertones. No **17**.

★★★★ **The Century** ⓥ Well-knit & pleasing blend in **17** ⑧⑧ is 65% sauvignon, rest semillon, giving tropical & lemon notes. Unoaked as usual. Balanced, fresh & bone-dry, with some weight & length.

Merlot ★★★★ Delicious **16** (85), dark chocolate & hazelnut whiffs leading to redcurrant & dried herb flavours, satin-smooth tannins, medium body with lingering berry aftertaste. **Sauvignon Blanc** ★★★★ Freshly gathered gooseberry & kiwi well partnered with greener notes of nettle, greengage, & on finish, lime, in light & zesty **18** (85). Not tasted: **Merlot Rosé**. Discontinued: **Viognier**. — GM

Location/map/WO: Elgin ▪ Map grid reference: B2 ▪ Est 2003 ▪ 1stB 2004 ▪ Tasting & sales Mon-Sun 10-4 ▪ Cheese platters, food & wine pairings, pizza's ▪ Function facility ▪ MTB route ▪ Fynbos walks ▪ Birding ▪ Vineyard tours ▪ 4-star guest house ▪ Winemaker(s) & business manager Marinda Kruger-Claassen ▪ ±50ha (merlot, pinot, shiraz, chard, sauv, sem) ▪ 500t/18,500cs own label ▪ IPW ▪ PO Box 121 Elgin 7180 ▪ info@elginvintners.co.za ▪ www.elginvintners.co.za ▪ S 34°10'52.18" E 019° 0'42.54" ▪ ⌨ snarl.crosses.conferred ▪ **T +27 (0)21-848-9587**

☐ **Embrace** see Stellenrust
☐ **Emineo** see Rogge Cloof

Enfin Wines   ⓠ

'It's all about passion, creativity, love and individuality with a complete hands-on approach,' says garagiste and attorney Susan van Aswegen whose home base is Huguenot Street in Franschhoek. She sources her grapes widely, focusing on syrah aged in different oak types, her decisions 'unfettered by corporate decrees and mass market considerations'.

★★★★ **Grenache Noir** (NEW) Packs a flavour punch of red fruit, from plum & cherry to pomegranate & blood orange, **17** (89) hints of smoke & spice after 8 months in 2nd-fill French oak. WO Durbanville.

★★★★ **The American Syrah** Like sibling, named for oak used, 60% new for sweet vanilla notes in **17** (88) but Elim's cool-climate white pepper & dark fruit shine through, fresh & tangy, with fine tannins.

★★★★ **The Romanian Syrah** Wood used more deftly in **17** (86) than **16** ★★★★ (85), now only 60% new for mildly earthy, nutty, spicy nuances to plush dark fruit. Also ex variety of Elim parcels.

★★★★ **Casablanca Fumé Blanc** If **17** ★★★☆ (84) lacked intensity, **18** (87) makes up for it. Succulent tropical fruit, some citrus, herbal lift, hint of gunflint, creamy texture from 7 months French oak. Undisclosed variety/ies, presumably sauvignon, as last. WO Walker Bay.

Strawberry Lane Pinot Noir ★★★★ Silky **17** (85), sour cherries & earthy strawberry notes on fruit from various Elim farms, 8 months in 60% new French oak. Naturally fermented & unfiltered, as all possibly except Casablanca, whose vinification is 'winemaker's secret'. Not tasted: **Sebastian Unfiltered Cinsaut**, **Alice Unfiltered Malbec**, **Ouma Rachel Syrah**. — JG

Location/map: Franschhoek ▪ Map grid reference: C1 ▪ WO: Elim/Walker Bay/Durbanville ▪ Est/1stB 2014 ▪ Tasting by appt ▪ Owner(s)/winemaker(s) Susan van Aswegen ▪ 6t 90% red 10% white ▪ 4 Huguenot Str Franschhoek 7690 ▪ info@enfinwines.co.za ▪ S 33° 54' 49.85" E 019° 7' 18.68" ▪ ⌨ sighing.freshening.geeky ▪ **T +27 (0)83-310-1679**

☐ **Enon** see Zandvliet Wine Estate

Entre Nous   ⓠ 🍴

Have you heard the one about the three lawyers, the quantity surveyor and the wine barrel expert? The five friends have been vinifying bought-in, mostly Stellenbosch grapes for their garagiste brand for 20 years now. All is quiet this edition on the new wines for review front, but we'll hope for a follow-up bottling or two next time.

Viognier ⓠ ★★★ Shows less of variety's peachy appeal & more of robust barrel ageing (18 months, 20% new), warm alcohol, tangy farewell. **16** (79) for fans of big, bold wines. Not tasted: **Cabernet Sauvignon**, **Chardonnay**, **Starboard**. — MW

Location/map: Stellenbosch ▪ Map grid reference: H5 ▪ WO: Western Cape ▪ Est/1stB 2000 ▪ Tasting, sales & cellar tours by appt ▪ BYO picnic ▪ Owner(s) Geoff Brooker, Mark Howell, Steve Kirk-Cohen, Andre Smalberger & Terry Winstanley ▪ Cellarmaster(s)/winemaker(s) Steve Kirk-Cohen, Andre Smalberger & Terry Winstanley (2000), Mark Howell & Geoff Brooker (2005) ▪ ±1,176cs own label 85% red 15% white ▪ PO Box 210, The Foundry, 95 Prestwich Str, Cape Town 8001 ▪ terry@winstanleyinc.com ▪ S 33° 55' 25.96" E 018° 57' 03.12" ▪ ⌨ assist.moment.hillside ▪ **T +27 (0)82-574-5173**

Epicurean Wines

The launch of the next Epicurean red (untasted this edition) will see the handsome blend joined by a chardonnay, the first white wine under this luxurious label. This will no doubt please the shade of Epicurus, the ancient Greek philosopher, who saw pleasure as the measure of what is good. The wines are made at Rupert & Rothschild, with the eminent owners having their say at blending time.

Est 2001 ▪ 1stB 2003 ▪ Closed to public ▪ Owner(s) Epicurean Wine (Pty) Ltd ▪ Cellarmaster(s) Mutle Mogase, Mbhazima Shilowa, Moss Ngoasheng ▪ Winemaker(s) Yvonne Lester (consultant) ▪ 1,000cs own label 100% red ▪ WIETA ▪ 55 Curson Str, Hyde Park 2196 ▪ info@epicureanwine.co.za ▪ www.epicureanwine.co.za ▪ **T +27 (0)11-568-3100**

Equitania

Formerly a luxurious private homestead, Equitania latterly has been the Institute of Mine Seismology's Helderberg HQ, with its own registered single-vineyards of cabernets franc and sauvignon. A '15 varietal release of the latter sold out untasted by us, and the '17 wasn't ready for review. However, we did taste the '17 blend, and the rating is a testament to several years' intense effort by the owners and viti/vini consultants Francois Hanekom and Ronell Wiid to improve viticultural practices and produce a wine of excellence.

★★★★ **Cabernet Sauvignon-Cabernet Franc** Admirable debut for near-equal blend **17** ⑧⑨, intense cassis, forest floor & ink tones soak up 50% new oak, cushion varieties' refined but present tannins. Fruit-sweet finish enlivened by cab franc's (49%) leafy lift. Decant now, cellar ±5 years.— GdB, CvZ

Location/WO: Stellenbosch ▪ Map: Helderberg ▪ Map grid reference: C3 ▪ Est 2000 ▪ 1stB 2008 ▪ Tasting & sales by appt; see website for details ▪ Closed all pub hols ▪ BYO picnic ▪ Walking/hiking trails ▪ Owner(s) Institute of Mine Seismology ▪ Winemaker(s) Ronell Wiid (consultant) ▪ Viticulturist(s) Francois Hanekom (consultant) ▪ 4.65ha/1.38ha (cabs s/f) ▪ 10.54t/12,000cs own label 100% red ▪ Postnet Suite #854 Private Bag X15 Somerset West 7130 ▪ kobus@equitania.co.za ▪ www.equitania.co.za ▪ S 34° 2' 26.15" E 018° 49' 5.51" ▪ 📍 encounter.piano.plotting ▪ **T +27 (0)21-809-2070**

☐ **Erasmus Wines** *see* Cape Wine Company
☐ **Erica** *see* Raka
☐ **Erica O** *see* Erika Obermeyer Wines

Erika Obermeyer Wines ⓛ

This is the boutique-wine portfolio of Erika Obermeyer, last edition's well-deserved and internationally fêted Newcomer of the Year. Erika is a former white-wine maker at Graham Beck, where she vinified 5-star-rated Pheasants' Run Sauvignon Blanc, amongst others, and gained an in-depth understanding of the importance of terroir, something she applies to her own range with great success. She seeks out special vineyards, mostly around Stellenbosch, to create small-batch wines which have a sense of place and showcase the diversity of South Africa — wines also with 'length, balance and concentration'. Now based at Stellenbosch Agri-Park, her agenda includes new facilities for wine production, tasting and sales

Erica O range

★★★★★ **Cabernet Sauvignon** ⓐ Awakens the senses, **17** ㊙ is deeply rich; intense blackcurrants, perfectly judged oak (24 months, 85% new) giving cigarbox spicing, crushed pepper, then as it opens up in the glass, Provençal herbs. Palate surprise is silky tannins, hinting at the latent power. No **16**.

★★★★★ **Syrah** ⓝⓔⓦ Ocean-influenced Firgrove vines (as Cab), elegant **18** � shows syrah's restraint, finesse & precision. Deeply complex, dark-toned fruit with interwoven cocoa, salty liquorice & scrub. Streamlined & polished. Tiny production. Also-tasted **17** �, same vineyards & standout styling, crafting.

★★★★★ **Syrah-Grenache Noir-Cinsault** ⓐ Syrah 68% but others make specific contributions. Layered **18** �95 has piquant wild berries, cherries with fynbos & smoky, savoury spice colouring. Elegant yet textured, there's lithe strength promising a future, but already gives pleasure. WO Coastal. Also 1.5L & 3L, as Cab & '18 Syrah. No **17**.

★★★★☆ **Sauvignon Blanc** ⓐ Dryland 21 year old Groenekloof vines, stainless steel/barrel fermented & matured; **18** � a different expression to Meticulous. Deeper, more layered, less fruit-forward, a leafy note, the oak richness vying with minerality. Good acid backbone, ends saline, ensuring ageing potential.

Premium range

★★★★ Meticulous Sauvignon Blanc From cool-climate Groenekloof, as Erika O sibling, **18** ⑧⑧ has a passionfruit core, but there's lots more going on, green peas & sage, backed by zesty, lime-toned freshness.

Flabbergast Cinsault ★★★★ Mature Agter Paarl dryland bushvines. Half older barrels, rest concrete 'eggs' for standout fruit, juicy & fresh. Not simple, **18** ⑧⑤ also has tobacco, gentle fynbos notes. — CR

Location/map: Stellenbosch ▪ Map grid reference: C7 ▪ WO: Stellenbosch/Groenekloof/Coastal/Paarl ▪ Est 2016 ▪ 1stB 2015 ▪ Tasting by appt only ▪ Owner(s)/winemaker(s) Erika Obermeyer ▪ 30t/4,000cs own label 65% red 35% white ▪ IPW ▪ Stellenbosch Agri-Park, R310 Baden Powell Dr, Stellenbosch 7600 ▪ info@erikaobermeyerwines.co.za ▪ www.erikaobermeyerwines.co.za ▪ S 33° 59' 28.62 E 018° 45' 56.74" ▪ 🅰🅰 paperback. capacitors.deliverable ▪ **T +27 (0)82-940-3499**

Ernie Els Wines

Development to fully realise the potential of this stylish property's renowned Helderberg red-wine terroir began in 1999 with sustained focus on vineyards, resulting in internationally acclaimed wines over the years. Then came closure post 2018 harvest to downsize the cellar, hardly the norm but with the intent to vinify micro batches of grapes from individual vineyard pockets (among them, 11 site-suited cabernet clones). Now, ready to play to a packed gallery, comes the cellardoor experience re-imagined, comprising the redesigned tasting area (and vinotèque) and a 120-seat, fine-dining 'restaurant with a view'. Wine remains the hero, the menu supporting cellarmaster Louis Strydom's stellar offerings, such as the Proprietor's Blend, a star-studded wine promising slow, steady maturation, not unlike co-owner Ernie Els, golf's 'Big Easy', with his effortless swing and course composure.

Ernie Els range

★★★★☆ Cabernet Sauvignon 🅰 Lovely rich fruit depth in **17** ㉔ with dark spice & cedar overlay, fine-grained tannins & restrained oaking, just 10% new. A dab of petit verdot adds complexity & gravitas. Delicious now but without doubt a keeper.

★★★★☆ Proprietor's Cabernet Sauvignon 🅰 Lavish **16** ㉔ has more pronounced oak than cab sibling (60% new). Deep aromas of cassis, followed by a graphite mineral accent to the raspberry, violet & oak spice on the firm, full-bodied palate. A drop of petit verdot too, & like sibling, ageworthy.

★★★★ Merlot Multi-layered **17** ⑧⑦ shows a profusion of red & dark berry notes enveloping cocoa, spice & dried herbs. 5% splash cabernet franc; mostly used oak.

★★★★ Proprietor's Syrah 🅰 Engaging **15** ★★★★★ ㉒, with dash of viognier, entices with perfumed aromas & gentle play of dark fruit & pepper spice. A luminosity carries through to the palate; medium body, well-judged oak & stately tannin. Outperforms **14** ⑧⑨.

★★★★☆ Ernie Els Signature 🅰 Graceful, beautifully modulated flagship, **14** ㉓ a 5-way Bordeaux blend with cab & merlot (60/25) adding a spark of freshness to the big (15%) alcohol via cool herbaceous notes & succulent red fruit. Serious 85% new French oak sets up long, fruitful future, also in 1.5, 3 & 5L.

★★★★★ CWG Auction Reserve 🅰 Mainly cab with shiraz & dash cinsaut, matured in 60% new oak for 20 months, 10% American. Attractive ripe mulberry & plum fruit in harmony with allspice & black tapenade notes. **16** ㉓'s satin-smooth tannins are complemented by a vanilla & white pepper farewell.

★★★★☆ Proprietor's Blend 🅰 Magnificent 5-way Bordeaux blend with 20% shiraz. **16** ★★★★★ ㉖ improves on **15** ㉓ with mulberry, blackcurrant in harmony with dark spice, savoury conclusion, fine tannin support. Somewhat formidable in youth, with hefty alcohol, 25% new oak. Give it plenty of time.

Sauvignon Blanc ★★★★ With a dab of (unoaked) chardonnay, **19** ⑧③ has vibrant kiwi & greengage mixing with fig, gooseberry & lime. Zesty & light summer white from Stellenbosch & Darling grapes.

Big Easy range

★★★★ Red 🅰 Satisfying shiraz-led 6-way combo, **17** ⑧⑦ steps up on already handsome **16** ★★★ ⑧① with expressive violet bouquet, polished tannins, savoury tail seasoned with older oak. Also in 1.5, 3 & 5L.

Cabernet Sauvignon 🅰 **★★★★** Inviting blackcurrant & black cherry notes of **18** ⑧④ get tobacco from old oak & floral nuance ex 15% cinsaut. Well-integrated & juicy tannins make for effortless drinkability.

Rosé ⓐ ★★★ Bone-dry, food-styled **18** ⑧②, lively pomegranates & strawberries, lightish 11.6% alcohol. Shiraz with splash viognier. **Chenin Blanc** ⓐ ★★★☆ Ripe quince, pineapple & mango appeal on generous **18** ⑧③, bright acidity & juicy tropical tail for fruity enjoyment. WO W Cape, as all these. — GM

Location/map: Stellenbosch ▪ Map grid reference: E8 ▪ WO: Stellenbosch/Western Cape ▪ Est 1999 ▪ 1stB 2000 ▪ Tasting, sales & cellar tours Mon-Sun 9-5 ▪ Restaurant Mon-Fri 11-3 Sat/Sun 11-3.30 ▪ Closed Easter Fri/Sun, Dec 25 & Jan 1 ▪ Tour groups ▪ Gift shop ▪ MTB trail ▪ Ernie Els' Trophy Room ▪ Vinoteque ▪ Owner(s) Ernie Els & Baron Hans von Staff-Reitzenstein ▪ Cellarmaster(s)/winemaker(s) Louis Strydom (Dec 1999) ▪ Viticulturist(s) Leander Koekemoer (2015) ▪ 72ha/45ha (cab, merlot, shiraz) ▪ 350t/80,000cs own label 80% red 20% white + 1,500cs for clients ▪ PO Box 7595 Stellenbosch 7599 ▪ info@ernieelswines.com ▪ www.ernieelswines.com ▪ S 34° 0' 2.8" E 018° 50' 53.5" ▪ ⓦ rinsing.resources.inhabits ▪ **T +27 (0)21-881-3588**

Ernst Gouws & Co Wines   ⓐ ⓐ ⓐ

The circular front-label reflects 'our infinite passion for wine, family and tradition and the ties that bind', says this talented clan. Having set up a well-known estate in Stellenbosch's Koelenhof area in the early 1990s, Ernst and Gwenda Gouws went on to create their own wine business a decade later, latterly joined by daughter Ezanne (she and her brother Ernst jnr are qualified winemakers). Making the circle bigger is the third generation (currently toddlers) - and a new rosé.

★★★★ **Merlot** ⓥ Muscular **17** ⑧⑦ improves on **15** ⑧⑥, same super-ripe red berry fruit & robust tannins but more poised, aromatic & savoury. No **16**.

★★★★ **Chardonnay** Mineral **18** ⑧⑦ is tank fermented, older-barrel aged 7 months, bringing fresh lime fruit into foreground. Measured, balanced richness, lingering finish. No **17**.

★★★★ **Nineteenfiftytwo** ⓐ Seriously conceived semillon (75%) & sauvignon blend, all-new barrel fermented, **16** ⑧⑨ showing wild nettle & wool aromas, restrained oak, abundant body & texture.

Sauvignon Blanc ⓥ ★★★★ Now bottled, **18** ⑧⑤ earns higher rating with vibrant cut-grass aromas & flavours adding to the racy green character, with balancing & satisfying gooseberry flesh.

Pinot Noir ⓥ ★★★★ Vivacious **17** ⑧④ raises the bar, replaces previous tarry tones with bright cherry & berry fruit, lovely texture. WO W Cape. **Pinotage** ★★★★ Textbook **17** ⑧③, generous ripe plum & bramble fruit, hints of banana & clove, robust tannins but no rough edges. **Shiraz** ⓐ ★★★★ Livelier & more defined, **16** ⑧⑤ also touch more streamlined, less ripe than **15** ⑧⑤ with its stewed fruit. In magnum, too. **Cabernet Franc Rosé** ⓝⓔⓦ ★★★ Low-key onion-skin hue contrasts pleasingly with burst of raspberry fruit, brisk upbeat finish on **19** ⑧②. **Chenin Blanc** ★★★★ Typical Stellenbosch fresh-&-fruity profile, **19** ⑧④'s crunchy apple lends crispness to tropical body, light but tasty. — DS

Location/map: Stellenbosch ▪ Map grid reference: D1 ▪ WO: Stellenbosch/Western Cape ▪ Est/1stB 2003 ▪ Tasting & sales at Koelenhof Winery Mon-Thu 9-5 Fri 9-4 Sat 10-2 ▪ Closed Easter Fri/Sun, Ascension day, Dec 25/26 & Jan 1 ▪ Facilities for children ▪ Owner(s) Gouws family ▪ Cellarmaster(s) Ernst Gouws snr ▪ 40,000cs own label 40% red 60% white ▪ IPW ▪ PO Box 7450 Stellenbosch 7599 ▪ ernst@ernstgouws.co.za ▪ www.ernstgouws.co.za ▪ S 33° 50' 3.4" E 018° 47' 52.7" ▪ ⓦ climate.helpers.spades ▪ **T +27 (0)21-865-2895**

Esau Wines   ⓐ

Chemical engineer Wim Hugo makes tiny batches of wine in the high-beamed original Schoongezicht cellar on Paarl's main street alongside another wine-bug-bitten local, general practitioner Edwin 'Jorrie' Jordaan (see under Bergheim). The duo clearly have huge fun, giving their bottlings offbeat names like 'Holy Cow' and 'Rampokker', and seeking out rarer varieties to vinify (such as mourvèdre, labelled, in house style, 'Moerwetter'). Unfortunately their new vintages were bottled too late for inclusion in this edition.

Location/map: Paarl ▪ Map grid reference: E6 ▪ Est/1stB 2010 ▪ Private tastings on request ▪ Owner(s) Wim Hugo ▪ Cellarmaster(s) Wim Hugo (2009) ▪ Winemaker(s) Wim Hugo & Jorrie Jordaan (both 2009) ▪ 3t/2,500L 100% red ▪ PO Box 3175 Paarl 7620 ▪ wim.hugo@gmail.com ▪ www.esau-wines.com ▪ S 33° 45' 20.2" E 018° 57' 42.5" ▪ ⓦ reveal.majory.towns ▪ **T +27 (0)61-453-3123**

Escapades Winery

What started as a small, fun 'escapade' among three friends 14 years ago, today is wholly-owned by Sweden-based Greek national Takis Soldatos. The range, under winemaking wing of Kiwi-born, SA-stationed Chris Kelly, focuses on the two wines tasted for this edition and a small Reserve range, yet to be bottled at press time. Bottelary Hills, Helderberg basin and Franschhoek supply fruit for the goal of terroir-driven styles. Previously all exported, Escapades wines are slowly being introduced on the local market.

★★★★ **Cabernet Sauvignon-Shiraz-Malbec** ⊘ Like **16** ★★★★ (84), **17** (86) compatible & balanced trio, each lending extra note of interest. Juicy, tangy, with fine, softish tannins - all moreish qualities for now & few years.

★★★★ **Sauvignon Blanc** ⊘ Purity of tangerine, honey tones, clean lines on **19** (86) fleshed out with portion barrel/concrete 'egg' fermented. Lengthy tangy tail, as on **17** ★★★★ (85). **18** sold out untasted.

In abeyance: **Pinotage**, **Pinotage Rosé**, **Semillon Grande Reserve**, **Semillon-Sauvignon Blanc**. Discontinued: **Semillon**. — AL

Location/map: Stellenbosch ▪ Map grid reference: B4 ▪ WO: Coastal ▪ Est/1stB 2006 ▪ Tasting by appt ▪ Owner(s) Takis Soldatos ▪ Winemaker(s) Chris Kelly (Oct 2010, consultant) ▪ (cab, malbec, shiraz, sauv, sem) ▪ 100t/10,000cs own label 60% red 40% white ▪ PO Box 99 Somerset Mall 7129 ▪ info@escapadewinery. com ▪ www.escapadewinery.com ▪ S 33° 54' 47.7" E 018° 44' 7.7" ▪ ⌨ carpenters.zing.sentence ▪ **T +27 (0)82-569-3371**

☐ **Eskdale** *see* Frater Family Wines

Esona Boutique Wine

Robertson's Esona ('The Very One') specialises in varietal wines from registered single-vineyards, produced in an on-site cellar where Bongezwa Mxokozeli, having fallen in love with wine while doing Agriculture practicals at nearby Zandvliet, has joined Charmaine Arendse as assistant winemaker. Owners Rowan and Caryl Beattie retain stocks of multiple vintages, enabling winelovers to experience the differences between the harvests in one of several tastings on offer at the visitor venue, along with delifoods and valley vistas.

Single Vineyard range

★★★★ **Shiraz** ⓐ Ripe mulberry, thatch & smoke on satisfying & succulent **17** (88). Smooth & structured palate with good fruit concentration, savoury tangy finish. 11 months barrique ageing.

★★★★ **Chardonnay** Generous gooseberry, poached quince & cinnamon intro to **17** (87), textured & layered, with lemon curd richness & bright citrus to balance. Fine expression, from certified single-vineyard (as all). 9 months oaking.

★★★★ **Chenin Blanc** ⓐ Intense orchard & tropical fruit, vanilla & roasted nut aromas leap from the glass in **18** ★★★★★ (91). Complex, rounded, with firm oak to ensure poise, layers of flavour & a rich lemon finish. Ageworthy improvement on **17** (89).

Frankly My Dear Pinot Noir Blanc de Noir ⓥ ★★★ Crushed strawberry appeal to nose & palate on nicely dry **17** (81). **Sauvignon Blanc** ★★★★ Offers stone & tropical fruit & an underpinning of bright citrus acidity, good interplay between ripe & zingy flavours in **17** (85). Not tasted: **Pinot Noir**, **Méthode Cap Classique**. — WB

Location/map/WO: Robertson ▪ Map grid reference: C4 ▪ Est 2002 ▪ 1stB 2010 ▪ Tasting & sales Mon-Fri 9-5 Sat/pub hols 10-4 ▪ Closed Dec 25 & Jan 1 ▪ Std tasting; Taste-the-Difference tasting (2 vintages/3 cultivars); fruit preserve/chocolate/music & wine/art pairing ±55 min, essential to book ▪ Taste-of-Africa ▪ Caryl's Deli ▪ Owner(s) Rowan & Caryl Beattie ▪ Winemaker(s) Charmaine Arendse (Jan 2017) & Bongezwa Mxokozeli (Feb 2019), mentored by Lourens van der Westhuizen (Jan 2010) ▪ 17ha/9.83ha (barbera, grenache, mourv, pinot, sangio, shiraz, chard, chenin, cbard, sauv) ▪ ±250t/6,000cs own label 34% red 66% white ▪ PO Box 2619 Clareinch 7400 ▪ info@esona.co.za ▪ www.esona.co.za ▪ S 33° 54' 16.14" E 020° 0' 38.66" ▪ ⌨ kayaks. glee.databank ▪ **T +27 (0)76-343-5833**

☐ **Essay** *see* MAN Family Wines
☐ **Essence du Cap** *see* Fleur du Cap

Excelsior Estate ⓆⓇⒶⒸⒶ

Combining breeding of thoroughbred racehorses and growing of fine wine, both benefiting from Robertson soil's ancient limestone deposits, Freddie and son Peter de Wet (scions of generations of De Wets farming here) name their prestige wines after their track champions. Red vines in particular flourish, malbec among new plantings, to blend with cabernet in the continuation of Johan Stemmet's full-blooded New World winemaking style, while cherishing old vines (again cabernet) dating back to the 1980s.

Excelsior Reserve range

★★★★ **Evanthuis Cabernet Sauvignon** ⊘ ⓐ Exceptional **15** ★★★★☆ ⑨④ leads trio of wines named for champion horses. Oldest vines in calcareous soil, concentrated cassis richness yet streamlined, beautifully balanced, substantial step up on fruitcake-toned **13** ⑧⑧. No **14**. 50% new barrels 20 months.

★★★★ **Gondolier Merlot** Durban July winner in usual fine fettle, **18** ⑧⑥ abundant blackberry fruit & some earthiness on bales of velvet tannin, deft oaking (just 10% new, year) completes a delicious performance. No **16**, **17**. Minuscule production, as all.

★★★★ **San Louis Shiraz** Ripe tannins control **18** ⑧⑦'s plentiful red & black berries, choc-mocha sheen from year in American oak, 20% new, adds to finessed shiraz with good few years to go. No **16**, **17**.

Discontinued: **Agricola Sauvignon Blanc**.

Excelsior Classic range

Cabernet Sauvignon ⊘ ★★★☆ Rich & ripe **18** ⑧⑤ offers sweet cassis & top note of coffee from 40% oaked component (French & American, 9 months). Splash petit verdot, as Paddock. **Merlot** ⊘ ★★★☆ What merlot fans want: a juicy wine with velvet tannin, touch of chocolate & violet fragrance. **18** ⑧③ part oaked, 6 months. **Paddock Shiraz** ⊘ ★★★☆ Generous perfume on **18** ⑧⑤, oak spice lifting succulent fruit draws you in for a second sip. **Chardonnay** ★★★ Fresh, tangy **19** ⑧② boosts drinkability by merging citrus & pear fruit, dash sugar & clever winemaking (only 25% of wine wooded). **Sauvignon Blanc** ★★★ Brisk & quite intense **19** ⑧②, loads of gooseberry & lime, long mineral flourish at the end. **Viognier** ★★★ Sunny **19** ⑦⑧ has exuberant ripe fruit from nose to sweetish tail, big 14.5% alcohol, but firm acid keeps a tight rein. Not tasted: **Caitlyn Rosé**.

Purebred range

Shiraz-Merlot ⊘ ★★★ Unoaked **17** ⑧② a good meaty mouthful, juicy & friendly, equally amicable price. **Sauvignon Blanc** ★★★ Easy **19** ⑦⑧, perky & fresh, lovely texture thanks to gram sugar. — DS

Location/map/WO: Robertson ▪ Map grid reference: C4 ▪ Est 1859 ▪ 1stB 1990 ▪ Tasting & sales Mon-Fri 10-4 Sat 10-3 ▪ Deli serving light lunches ▪ Picnics available on request ▪ Facilities for children ▪ Conferences ▪ 4-star Excelsior Manor Guest House ▪ Owner(s) Freddie & Peter de Wet ▪ Cellarmaster(s) Johan Stemmet (Aug 2003) ▪ Winemaker(s) Johan Stemmet (Aug 2003), with Kelly Gova (2005) ▪ Viticulturist(s) Freddie de Wet (1970) ▪ 320ha/220ha (cab, merlot, p verdot, shiraz, chard, sauv) ▪ 2,200t/320,000cs own label 75% red 25% white ▪ Other export brand: Stablemate ▪ BRC ▪ PO Box 17 Ashton 6715 ▪ info@excelsior.co.za ▪ www. excelsior.co.za ▪ S 33° 51' 15.1" E 020° 0' 25.6" ▪ ⬚ welder.honed.machin ▪ **T +27 (0)23-615-1980**

Excelsior Vlakteplaas ⓠ

Excelsior winery is based in the old cellar on Vlakteplaas estate near De Rust in Klein Karoo, where Danie Schoeman's family have grown grapes since the 1930s. The two fortified muscats sold under the label His Master's Choice are part of a much larger output, Danie being primarily a bulk wine producer.

His Master's Choice range

Red Muscadel ⓧ ★★★☆ Rich dried peach & honey on **15** ⑧④ fortified sweet charmer. Nicely balanced acidity gives a clean, lingering finish. **White Muscadel** ⓧ ★★★ Dusty peach & fig fruit notes on a rustic spirit base, **15** ⑧⓪ slightly cloying but tasty & warming nonetheless. — DB

Location: De Rust ▪ Map: Klein Karoo & Garden Route ▪ Map grid reference: B3 ▪ WO: Klein Karoo ▪ Est 1934 ▪ 1stB 1998 ▪ Tasting & sales by appt only ▪ Closed Easter Fri-Mon, Ascension day, Dec 16/25/26 & Jan 1 ▪ Owner(s)/winemaker(s) Danie Schoeman ▪ 31ha (merlot, ptage, ruby cab, chenin, muscadel r/w) ▪ 490t/2,000cs own label 50% red 50% white ▪ PO Box 112 De Rust 6650 ▪ jjschoeman@telkomsa.net ▪ S 33° 29' 16.74" E 022° 35' 25.50" ▪ ⬚ solar.resettling.prompting ▪ **T +27 (0)82-821-3556**

Fable Mountain Vineyards

The aspect, elevation, range of soils, as well as diurnal temperature differences bring a special quality to the wines of this US-owned boutique winery situated high on the slopes of Tulbagh's Witzenberg mountains. Tremayne Smith produced his first wines here in 2017, aiming to showcase these terroir characteristics. He employs gentler extraction methods, cooler temperatures, no post-ferment maceration, with less new and more larger-format oak. All techniques learned at Mullineux winery and in the Rhône. Syrah is the main variety here, with only small pockets of grenache and mourvèdre, as reflected in the ranges. An agent has been appointed in Ireland to distribute the wines, which include a new white in the Raptor Post line-up.

Fable Mountain Vineyards range

★★★★☆ **Syrah** Style change & riper vintage evident in **17** ★★★★ ⑧⑦: warm core of dark fruit, plush texture from softer handling; also longer oaking (24 months vs 20) & combo barrels & foudres. Less focus than in standout-vintage **15** ⑨③ but balanced & generous. No **16**.

★★★★☆ **Night Sky** Just a splash more grenache than syrah & mourvèdre (33/31) in **17** ★★★★ ⑧⑨, fresher than Syrah sibling but less fruit intensity & structure than last-made **15** ⑨③. Understatedly opulent, with all components well integrated. 18 months old 500L oak.

★★★★☆ **Jackal Bird** Ⓥ Standout white blend shows delicate vitality & purity, youthful harmony in the intricate weave of its chenin, grenache, roussanne, chardonnay & viognier make-up. **14** ⑨③ satin texture, concluding pithy grip add dimension. Natural ferment in oak (15% new), concrete 'eggs'. WO W Cape.

Belle Flower ★★★☆ Gentle savouriness & some red-berried piquancy on **18** ⑧④ dry rosé from mourvèdre, aged in old 500L oak. Though delicate, persistent fruit is the star.

Small Batch Series

★★★★ **Grenache** Ⓥ Variety's scented, sweet tobacco profile on **17** ⑧⑦. Ripe & concentrated, warm-hearted despite measured 13.7% alcohol. Silky, approachable tannins, but potential to improve.

★★★★ **Syrah SYB7** Ⓥ Clonal trio of identically made syrahs to be replaced by single varietal bottling from next vintage. Still-available **17** ⑧⑥, ex lowest-lying block, ripe & more savoury, quite dense & muscular. Youthful, needs time to develop & show full potential.

Mourvèdre Ⓥ ★★★★ Rather closed & unknit mid-2018. Dark fruit, quite fresh, not revealing enough earnest intent in youth. Feels warmer than 12.9% alcohol. **17** ⑧③ may blossom with time. Discontinued: **Syrah SYB8**, **Syrah SYB9**.

The Raptor Post range

Red ★★★ Same varieties as last, mostly syrah, mourvèdre & grenache, again supple & pleasingly dry, nice savoury tone in **17** ⑧⓪. These show same attention to detail, hands-off approach as senior wines. **Rosé** ★★★ Sunset in the glass, **18** ⑧⓪ a light aperitif with spicy, savoury tone & dry finish. Syrah & third mourvèdre. **White** ⑨ᴱᵂ ★★★ Crunchy green apple, perfumed starfruit flavours, **18** ⑧② clean-cut acidity & pleasing dry almondy conclusion. Chenin, splashes colombard & viognier, older oaked. WO W Cape. — MW

Location: Tulbagh • WO: Tulbagh/Western Cape/Coastal • Est 1989 • 1stB 2009 • Tasting at Mulderbosch Vineyards • Conservation area • Owner(s) Private partnership based in the US • Winemaker(s) Tremayne Smith (Aug 2016) • Farm manager Werner Wessels (2013) • 179ha/28ha (grenache, mourv, shiraz) • PO Box 12817 Die Boord 7613 • tremayne@fablewines.com • www.fablewines.com • **T +27 (0)21-881-8140**

☐ **Fabulous!** *see* Wineways Marketing

☐ **Fairhills** *see* Origin Wine

☐ **Fair Karoo** *see* Rogge Cloof

☐ **Fairtrade Original** *see* Piekenierskloof Wine Company

Fairvalley Wines

Ⓥ

Established in 1998 to benefit winefarm employees in Paarl, this affordable range with Fairtrade accreditation now exceeds 20,000 cases. Most are exported, chiefly to the US, Japan and Europe, but locally can be tasted by appointment.

Pinotage Ⓥ ★★★ Vibrant **17** ⑧② inky hue, matching deep raspberry & mulberry notes, juicy acidity & friendly grip. Fairtrade certified. **Chenin Blanc** ★★★ **19** ⑧⓪ pineapple- & lemon-toned summer sipper with satisfying vinosity, refreshing acidity. Coastal WO. **Sauvignon Blanc** ★★★ Subtle & delicate **18** ⑧② from Darling grapes, faint grassy aroma, pleasant wet stone flavour. In abeyance: **Cabernet Sauvignon**, **Chardonnay, Chardonnay Reserve**. — CvZ

Location: Paarl ▪ WO: Coastal/Darling/Western Cape ▪ Est 1997 ▪ 1stB 1998 ▪ Tasting by appt only ▪ Fee R25 ▪ Closed Good Fri, Dec 25 & Jan 1 ▪ Sales at Fairview ▪ Owner(s) Fairvalley Farmworkers Association ▪ Cellarmaster(s)/winemaker(s) Awie Adolf (2018) ▪ 20,000cs own label 50% red 50% white ▪ Fairtrade ▪ PO Box 6219 Paarl 7620 ▪ wine@fairvalley.co.za ▪ www.fairvalley.co.za ▪ **T +27 (0)21-863-2450**

Fairview ⑭⑭◎⑤

Acquired by Charles Back snr in 1937 and inherited by his son Cyril in 1955, this family-owned estate is now in the hands of 3rd-generation Charles (also owner of separately listed Spice Route), whose energy and drive are obvious to anybody who's visited his multifaceted venture on Paarl Mountain, with its eponymous vista over fields and vines to distant Table Mountain. It always bustles with visitors from around the world, who taste (wine and cheese), dine (at the on-site restaurant), shop (for deli fare), take selfies (with the resident goats) and more. The wines are exceptional, too. Made by Anthony de Jager, who started here almost a quarter-century ago, and more recent colleague Annette van Zyl, they cover an extensive range of sites, styles and price points with impressive skill, finesse and creativity. See also Goats do Roam entry.

Regional Revival range

★★★★★ **Caldera** ⊘ Stylish **17** ⑨2 Rhône blend grenache, shiraz & mourvèdre, densely packed fruit, silky tannin structure, subtle spice. Well-judged oaking (17 months, seasoned barrels) lends shape without intruding. Paarl WO, as Brut.

★★★★☆ **Extraño** ⊘ Inspired by Spain's famous Rioja blends, **16** ⑨1 'stranger' from tempranillo with grenache & carignan is commendably true to style in a New World way. Fine aromatic fruit with savoury undertones, supple body & pliable tannins.

★★★★☆ **Homtini** ⊘⑧ Named for the settlement of Gouna on Homtini Pass near Knysna, wine-maker Anthony de Jager's Italian ancestors' home, hence sangiovese majority in this blend. **17** ⑨3, with merlot, shiraz & cab, excels in every way. Dense, complex black fruit with heady spice & savoury notes, all beautifully integrated. Darling WO, as next.

★★★★☆ **Drie Papen Fontein** ⑧ Terroir-expressive Bordeaux-style blend of tank-fermented sauvi-gnon & barrel-fermented (third new) semillon, **17** ⑨2 showing enticingly complex nuances of seagrass, oystershell, fennel & lime. From dry-farmed vineyards.

★★★★ **Charles Back Brut** Was 'MCC Brut', remains a unique méthode champenoise dry sparkling from near-equal viognier & grenache blanc. **16** ⑧6 spent 7 months on fermentation lees, 36 in bottle. Green apple & quince fruit with piercing acidity, lively mousse.

Discontinued: **Nurok**.

Limited Releases

★★★★☆ **Stok by Paaltjie Grenache** ⑧ Referring to 'staked vine' (echalas) trellising system on Paarl home-farm, **16** ⑨2 has style & panache. Remarkably full body is packed with red berry fruit, laced with floral scents & savoury aromatics, herbal fynbos & smoky oak spices from 15 months in older wood.

★★★★ **Primo Pinotage** Intense, super-ripe **17** ⑧7 shows muscle & heft, with dense black fruit, savoury notes, velvet tannins. Name refers to Fairview-farm premium vineyard block's in-house name. 20 months in 60% new oak.

★★★★☆ **Cyril Back** ⑧ Aristocratic flagship shiraz selected from various sites, with 9% cab component, **15** ⑨3 is sumptuously ripe & full but shows fine scrub & tobacco spices. Seriously conceived, built for the long road. 29 months in 80% new barrels. No **14**.

★★★★☆ **Eenzaamheid Shiraz** ⑧ From shale site in Agter Paarl, **16** ⑨3 is terroir-revealing & intense, shows power as well as finesse. Subtle herbaceous threads in dense black cherry fruit, aromatic tobacco & subdued barrel spicing (some new). Cellarworthy, but accessible now.

★★★★☆ **Jakkalsfontein Shiraz** ⑧ Big, brawny & taut, **16** ⑨0 has savoury-tarry core, uncompromis-ing tannins, sweet plum fruit profile, hints of tobacco & liquorice. Structure promises rewarding cellaring. Swartland WO, like next.

★★★★☆ **The Beacon Shiraz** ⓖ Full-bodied **15** ⑨③ sees 10% less new oak than Eenzaamheid, allowing ripe, concentrated dark fruit to shine against complex aromatic backdrop (florals, fynbos, herbs, smoke, leather & intense pepper). Tannins firm but fine.

★★★★☆ **Beryl Back** (NEW) Intricately vinified blend of chenin, viognier, grenache blanc & roussanne, **17** ⑨⓪ flagship white combines skin-contact ferment, barrel & tank components. Elegant, supple & layered, with lingering fruit, precise balance. Paarl WO.

Not tasted: **Pegleg Carignan**.

Sweet Wines range

★★★★☆ **La Beryl Blanc** ⊘ ⊛ Perennially impressive nectar honouring family matriarch, **18** ★★★★★ ⑨⑤ straw wine retains **17** ⑨④ formula of 73% unoaked chenin with muscat de Frontignan, slow natural fermentation. Decadently honeyed, fragrant & rich, with dried apricot highlights. Paarl WO.

Sweet Red ★★★★ Fortified port-style wine, **17** ⑧⑤ is 86% petite sirah with tempranillo. Full-sweet (144 g/l) with plummy fruit, good spirit grip. Discontinued: **La Beryl Rouge**.

Fairview range

★★★★ **Stellenbosch Cabernet Sauvignon** ⊛ Precise varietal profile in **17** ⑧⑦, with earthy, leafy highlights to blackcurrant fruit, nervously poised acidity. Ripe but hefty tannins should settle with cellaring.

★★★★ **Barbera** Commendable take on northern Italian variety, with typical acidity, generous berry fruit. **17** ⑧⑥ follows form, bright & ripe, begging food partnering. Paarl WO, as next.

★★★★ **Bushvine Cinsault** ⊘ Excellent example of variety's metamorphosis, **18** ⑧⑦ from estate's own vines has depth & substance but retains signature floral scents, juicy berry fruit, supple structure.

★★★★ **Piekenierskloof Grenache** ⓖ Ex high-lying bushvines planted 1973, silky **16** ⑧⑥ delicate in terms of both fruit & spice. Fresh acidity, therefore a versatile food wine.

★★★★ **Stellenbosch Merlot** ⊘ An improvement on **15** ★★★★ ⑧③, mellow & smooth **17** ⑧⑥ has ripe plummy fruit, plenty of heft & body. Year in oak barrels lends spice & roundness. **16** untasted.

★★★★ **Mourvèdre** ⊘ Sweetly spicy scrub note on **17** ⑧⑥, with meaty, plummy fruit, tobacco aromatics, grippy tannins. Characterful, worthy rendering of variety.

★★★★☆ **Petite Sirah** ⊘ ⊛ Alias durif, showing intensity & power before elegance, **16** ⑨⓪ struts its muscular stuff. Massive tannins, fruit concentration & extract typical of variety, not for the faint-hearted, begging time in bottle to soften. Paarl WO, as next.

★★★★ **Pinotage** ⓖ Familiar face in a sea of foreigners, **17** ⑧⑥ has welcoming rush of wild-berry fruit on firm tannins. Expressive & well gauged, with appealing floral notes.

★★★★ **Shiraz** ⊘ From mostly own Paarl Mountain vines, **17** ⑧⑧ shows Rhône-like character, with supple body, scrub & pepper spicing, silky tannins, cherry & plum fruit profile. Step up on **16** ⑧⑥.

★★★★ **Tannat** ⊘ Rustic French variety has typical full body, heavy tannins, savoury stewed fruit in **16** ⑧⑦. Something different & interesting for the anorak. From Paarl vines.

★★★★ **Chardonnay** Subtle oak adds nutty appeal to plump, well-rounded **18** ⑧⑦, with spicy mixed fruit, creamy lees texture, crisply accented acid. Mix of Darling & Paarl fruit.

★★★★ **Darling Riesling** ⊘ From dryland vines, off-dry **19** ⑧⑥ has light, elegant body, sweet apple & citrus fruit, pretty floral scents. Try with spicy Asian food.

★★★★ **Darling Sauvignon Blanc** Wild khaki bush aromas, hints of flint on gravelly **19** ★★★★☆ ⑧⑤, with granadilla fruit, mineral twist on finish. Trellised dryland vines. **18** ⑧⑥ marginally fuller.

★★★★ **Verdelho** ⊘ Out-of-the-ordinary take on Madeira variety, **18** ⑧⑥ is resolutely mineral, with salty-lime accents, tropical fruit highlights. All free-run juice, 3 months on lees in tank.

★★★★ **Viognier** Fragrantly peachy **18** ⑧⑦ is a step up on **16** ★★★★ ⑧④, offering varietal fruit & viscosity, lees richness. 60% barrel-fermented portion adds spice & roundness without intruding. Paarl WO. **17** untasted.

Rose Quartz (NEW) ★★★☆ Crisply dry, refreshing **19** ⑧⑤ rosé from grenache, carignan & cinsaut with floral notes on strawberry fruit. 10% barrel fermented. Also in magnum. **Chenin Blanc** (NEW) ★★★★ Loads of youthful charm, **19** ⑧⑤ offers tropical & stonefruit with brisk, refreshing acidity. Discontinued: **Paarl Chenin Blanc**, **Darling Chenin Blanc**, **Roussanne**.

La Capra range

Chenin Blanc ⟨▽⟩ ★★★★ Cheerful fresh & fruity style **18** ⑧⑤ has loads of tropical fruit appeal, weight from 8 months on lees. Paarl Mountain grapes.

Merlot ★★★☆ Plush, juicy red fruit abounds on **17** ⑧④, youthful, exuberant everyday sipper from Stellenbosch & Paarl. **Pinotage** ★★★ Dark, musty savouriness on **17** ⑧①, hints of mulberry & bramble fruit, firm tannin structure; year older oak. **Sangiovese** ★★★☆ Attractive plummy fruit with dried tomato, **18** ⑧④ has juicy Tuscan-style appeal. Perfect pairing for pasta or pizza. **Pinot Grigio** ★★★☆ Pleasant spicy/scented notes, plum & greengage fruit, lees creaminess. Light & refreshing **19** ⑧④ from Darling dry-land vines. **Sauvignon Blanc** ★★★★ Overt passionfruit on sprightly **19** ⑧③, bright yet restrained acidity, hints of kiwi & lime. WO W Cape. — GdB

Location/map: Paarl ▪ Map grid reference: D6 ▪ WO: Coastal/Paarl/Darling/Stellenbosch/Swartland/Piekenierskloof/Western Cape ▪ Est 1693 ▪ 1stB 1974 ▪ Tasting & sales Mon-Sun 9–5, last tasting 30min before closing ▪ Standard/master tasting (applicable fees apply) ▪ Closed Dec 25 & Jan 1 ▪ The Goatshed Restaurant ▪ Deli: artisanal cheeses & fresh farm breads ▪ Owner(s) Charles Back ▪ Winemaker(s) Anthony de Jager (Dec 1996), with Annette van Zyl (2014) ▪ 500ha/300ha (cab, carignan, grenache, merlot, mourv, petite sirah, ptage, shiraz, tannat, tempranillo, chenin, sauv, viog) ▪ 2,100t/260cs own label 80% red 15% white 5% rosé ▪ ISO 9001:2001, BRC, Fairtrade, HACCP, IPW, WIETA ▪ PO Box 583 Suider-Paarl 7624 ▪ info@fairview.co.za ▪ www.fairview.co.za ▪ S 33° 46' 19.16" E 018° 55' 25.26" ▪ 🖷 breezes.sting.result ▪ **T +27 (0)21-863-2450**

False Bay Vineyards ⟨♀⟩

This label was created to give winelovers the opportunity to enjoy 'real' wine – naturally fermented and made with minimal additions – at an affordable price. Nadia Langenegger of Briton Paul Boutinot's Waterkloof winery is the maker, working with fruit from older, under-appreciated coastal vines. A red joins the Revenant line-up, styled on mid-20th century Cape classics, with cabernet supplemented by cinsaut.

Revenant range
★★★★ **Red** ⑯ Blend is cabernet-led, giving pliant structure to 20% cinsaut's perfumed appeal. **17** ⑧⑥ crossover classic/modern style, with sappy dark fruit & clean dry farewell.

White ★★★☆ Mostly sauvignon with chenin, fermented in mix of old oak, concrete 'egg' & tank. Perfumed nuance to delightfully fresh **18** ⑧⑤, succulent, balanced & engaging.

False Bay range
Bushvine Pinotage ★★★ Similar savoury liquorice flavours in **18** ⑧①, now from Stellenbosch dryland vines. Dusty tannin structure, rustic food-pairing style. **Old School Syrah** ★★★ Similar smoky bacon & dark fruit on **18** ⑧② to previous. Less (old) oak, structure & riper (14.5% alcohol) than Peacock sibling. Stellenbosch & Swartland grapes. **Whole Bunch Cinsault-Mourvèdre** ⟨✓⟩ ★★★☆ Savoury nuance to piquant red berry flavours on **19** ⑧③ rosé. Lightish (12.5% alcohol), but pleasing feistiness & flavour. Includes Swartland old-vine fruit. **Crystalline Chardonnay** ⟨✓⟩ ★★★☆ Crisp, clean pear & citrus flavours on unoaked **19** ⑧③, with a plush, leesy backdrop. Enjoy solo or at the table. Stellenbosch & Wellington vines. **Slow Chenin Blanc** ⟨✓⟩ ★★★★ Softer, rounder baked apple flavours echoing the drier growing season on **18** ★★★ ⑧①. Same older Swartland & Wellington vineyards, slow, natural ferment & sur lie treatment for richer & livelier **19** ⑧③, also tasted. Fresh pear flavours, quite plush though lower in alcohol. Both show appealing drinkability. **Windswept Sauvignon Blanc** ★★★ Aptly named **19** ⑧⓪ shows pervasive cool zest. Fresh & tarter than previous, great with seafood.

Peacock Wild Ferment range
Cabernet Sauvignon ★★★ Palate attractions more tightly wrapped in dry herbaceous tannins in **18** ⑧② than previous, needing some time & a meal to relax. Natural yeast, slow ferment & unfined, as all these. **Merlot** ⟨✓⟩ ★★★★ Red berry fruit is more piquant & herbal than before, with dry chalky tannins in food-styled **18** ⑧③. **Syrah** ⟨✓⟩ ★★★★ Distinct fynbos scrub & white pepper tone to fresh but structured **18** ⑧⑤ from Schapenberg fruit, better balanced than previous. Punch-downs by foot & aged for 20 months in old oak. **Chenin Blanc** ★★★☆ Baked apple pie with rich brioche & almond nuance. From old Helderberg bushvines, **19** ⑧④ partly wooded vs unoaked False Bay version. **Sauvignon Blanc** ★★★☆ Green apple,

gooseberry freshness & more leesy breadth than Windswept sibling. **19** (84) less ripe than previous, showing its cooler provenance. Discontinued: **Chardonnay**. — MW

Location: Somerset West ▪ WO: Stellenbosch/Coastal ▪ Est/1stB 2000 ▪ Tasting at Waterkloof ▪ Owner(s) Paul Boutinot ▪ Cellarmaster(s) Nadia Langenegger (Jan 2013) ▪ 160,000cs own label 30% red 65% white 5% rosé ▪ IPW, WIETA ▪ PO Box 2093 Somerset West 7129 ▪ info@waterkloofwines.co.za ▪ www.falsebayvineyards.co.za ▪ **T +27 (0)21-858-1292**

- ☐ **Family Tree** *see* Stamboom
- ☐ **Fantail** *see* Morgenhof Wine Estate
- ☐ **Farm Animals** *see* Osbloed Wines
- ☐ **Farm House Organic** *see* Spier
- ☐ **Fat Barrel** *see* Imbuko Wines

Fat Bastard

Robertson Winery partners with Franco-British venture Thierry & Guy to produce these 'full-bodied wines to be enjoyed with bellyfuls of laughs'. Vigneron Thierry Boudinaud and brand creator Guy Anderson made an experimental chardonnay in the late 1990s and pronounced it a 'fat bastard', launching a happy-hippo-logoed international success story.

Cabernet Sauvignon ★★★☆ Rich cassis & black cherry flavours, hint of earthiness in full-bodied **17** (84), aged 14 months in older French barrels. Robertson WO, as all. **Merlot** ★★★☆ Soft, rich, approachable **18** (84) packed with ripe plum fruit & dark chocolate; svelte, with alcohol under 13%. **Pinotage** (✓) ★★★ **17** (80) shows juicier black & blue berry fruit than previous, less overt mocha from shorter stay (14 months) in combo old/new French/American oak. **Shiraz** ★★★☆ Less jammy than last, **17** (83) well padded with red berry fruit, spiced with black pepper, cinnamon & vanilla. **Rosé** ★★★ Previewed **19** (81) from cinsaut is fresh & dry but very fruity, with oodles of red berries, spice on finish, modest 11.3% alcohol. **Chardonnay** ★★★☆ 10% wooded component adds to richness of **18** (85), bold but balanced, with ripe tropical fruit, vanilla cream flavour/texture. **Chenin Blanc** (NEW) ★★★ Half-wooded **19** (82) tad less harmonious when sampled from tank than also-tasted **18** ★★★☆ (83). The latter 10% oak-matured for appealing vanilla-laced oatmeal richness to complement ripe tropical & citrus fruit. **Sauvignon Blanc** ★★★ Textbook tropical-style sauvignon, **19** (82) has guava & melon in abundance, also zesty grapefruit & lime, lovely freshness. **The Golden Reserve** ★★★ Chocolate & ultra-ripe plum flavours to the fore in lightly oaked, soft, sweetish **18** (81), mostly cab with smidgen merlot. — JG

Felicité

A sea of sickly sweet rosés encouraged the Newton Johnson family in the late 1990s to introduce a 'classy' version, described in this guide as 'unashamedly dry rosé for grown-ups'. Now a standalone, expanded label, with Stettyn Family Vineyards as winegrowing partner, Felicité still aims for drinkability with panache.

Pinot Noir (✓) ★★★ From 3 areas, different picking dates. Wallet-pleasing **18** (81) for earlier drinking but far from simple: berry array, older barrels for an earthy, tobacco note, juicy, the tannins supple. WO Cape South Coast, next 2 W Cape. **Rosé** (✓) ★★★ Luminous coral hue, **18** (81) celebrates shiraz's red berry & strawberry fruitiness. Slender & dry, enough character to match food, share with friends. With 5% sauvignon. **Chardonnay** ★★★ Unwooded **19** (81) offers tasty fruit focus, tangerine & white peach, zesty-fresh for solo enjoyment or food. — CR

- ☐ **Fera Puer** *see* Mellasat Vineyards

Fernskloof Wines

Aided by Prince Albert Valley's relative isolation and warm climate, Diederik le Grange and family make certified-organic wine in small batches. They focus on red wine and, with a constantly evolving portfolio, invite winelovers to come to the tasting locale and see what's available. Other enticements for visiting include stay-overs, running trails and a property steeped in character and history.

Location: Prince Albert ▪ Map: Klein Karoo & Garden Route ▪ Map grid reference: A3 ▪ Est 2009 ▪ 1stB 2010 ▪ Tasting, sales & cellar tours Mon-Fri 9-5 Sat 10-5 Sun by appt 10-2 ▪ Closed Good Fri, Ascension day & Dec 25 ▪ Facilities for children ▪ BYO picnic ▪ Walks/hikes ▪ Mountain running trails (7, 10 & 16km) ▪ Conservation area ▪ Angeliersbosch guest house (up to 8 guests), no pets allowed ▪ Owner(s) Le Grange family ▪ Cellarmaster(s)/winemaker(s) Diederik le Grange (2010) ▪ Viticulturist(s) Diederik le Grange (2009) ▪ 1,026ha/7ha (cab, merlot, ptage, shiraz) ▪ 40t/1,900cs own label 42% red 29% white 29% rosé ▪ Lacon Organic ▪ PO Box 41 Prince Albert 6930 ▪ info@fernskloof.co.za ▪ www.fernskloof.co.za ▪ S 33° 16' 23.77" E 022° 10' 55.60" ▪ ⓜ arch.vitally.celebration ▪ T +27 (0)23-541-1702

☐ **Festin** see Domaine Coutelier
☐ **56Hundred** see Nederburg Wines

Fijndraai Estate ⓟ ⓐ ⓒ

On land in Stellenbosch's Lynedoch area, once part of the Meerlust and Welmoed landholdings, Laurel van Coller replanted vines after buying the property as a horse stud in the 2000s. Respected viticulturist Eben Archer advised Mediterranean varieties, soon snapped up by other labels which subsequently went on to win awards. With Ken Forrester assisting, she and brand co-owner Veronique Kritzinger now have almost a decade of own-wine under their belts.

Van Coller Family Reserve range
Shiraz-Grenache-Mourvèdre ★★★★ Supple **15** ⑧⑤ offers ample Xmas cake appeal, as shiraz & grenache blend changes to include mourvèdre (21.5%). Ripe yet succulent, with nicely knit oak. WO W Cape.
Viognier-Chenin Blanc-Roussanne ★★★ Unfussy citrus & peach notes on **19** ⑧② equal viognier & chenin blend with 2% wooded roussanne. Light & easy, but tad less characterful than previous. — FM
Location: Stellenbosch ▪ WO: Stellenbosch/Western Cape ▪ Est 2007 ▪ 1stB 2011 ▪ Tasting at Ken Forrester Wines ▪ Olive oil ▪ Walks/hikes ▪ MTB trail ▪ Self-catering accommodation ▪ Stud farm ▪ Owner(s) Laurel van Coller & Veronique Kritzinger ▪ Winemaker(s) Ken Forrester (Jan 2010, consultant) ▪ Viticulturist(s) Pieter Rossouw (Feb 2011, consultant) ▪ 93ha/11.11ha (durif, grenache, sangio, shiraz, pinot grigio, rouss, viog) ▪ 178t/1,094cs own label 77% red 23% white ▪ WIETA ▪ PO Box 24 Lynedoch Stellenbosch 7603 ▪ info@fijndraai.com ▪ www.fijndraai.com ▪ T +27 (0)83-459-5546

☐ **Fine Art Collection** see Catherine Marshall Wines
☐ **Firefly** see Stellar Winery

FirstCape Vineyards

Powerhouse export-only brand FirstCape was formed in 2002 as a joint venture between five Breede River Valley cellars and British marketer Brand Phoenix. Currently all bottling is in the UK. The wines featured below are a subset of a larger portfolio, which includes light (5.5% alcohol) wines and sparkling. Newer markets in the Netherlands, China and Canada keep growing the footprint.

FirstCape range
★★★★ Malbec Handsome packaging & wax seal, clearly the flagship. Opaque colour & dense fruit, plums, brambleberries, fynbos, smoothly succulent. **18** ⑧⑦ fine example of the variety. Unoaked, as all.
Not tasted: **Pinotage, Shiraz, Chenin Blanc**. Discontinued: **Cabernet Sauvignon**.

Five Cellars range
Cabernet Sauvignon ★★★ Expressive cassis throughout **18** ⑧②, fruit the hero here, juicy & smooth. Good example of an unwooded cab. **Merlot ★★★** Offering blackcurrant scents & flavours, streamlined **18** ⑦⑧ is designed for early drinking. **Pinotage ★★★** Fruit forward, plums & dark berries, nice succulence in **18** ⑧① for immediate enjoyment. **Chenin Blanc** ⓝⓔⓦ **★★★** Easy-drinking, citrus-toned **18** ⑦⑧ has a touch of melon in the flavours, ends freshly dry. Discontinued: **Shiraz**.

Cape Bay range
Cabernet Sauvignon-Shiraz ⓝⓔⓦ **★★★** Attractive, colourful label. Cab with 30% shiraz, some savoury nuances despite no oak; dark plums in **18** ⑧②'s sleek body, with easy accessibility.

Special Cuvée range ⓝⓔⓦ
Cabernet Sauvignon ★★★ Lightest of the red ranges (13% alcohol), **18** ⑦⑧ is dark berried, sleek & streamlined. For current drinking. **Shiraz ★★★** Range of brightly coloured labels. No oak but there's a spic-

iness in **18** ⑧①'s dark fruit; has smooth, elegant drinkability. **Chardonnay** ★★★ Gentle citrus & stonefruit flavours, softly rounded texture in **19** ⑦⑦. **Sauvignon Blanc** ★★★ Pithy grapefruit perfume & flavours, an orange blossom nuance, **19** ⑧② has lovely palate weight & freshness.

Limited Release range
Pinotage ★★★ Plums & mulberries in **18** ⑦⑧, fresh & juicy enough for everyday drinking. **Shiraz** ★★★ Expressive dark fruit, hint of spice, scrub in **18** ⑧②, despite being unwooded. Juicy & smooth, has appetite appeal. **Chenin Blanc** ★★★ Citrus & melon, good mouthfeel, **18** ⑦⑧ ends fruity-fresh. — CR

Location: Paarl ▪ WO: Western Cape ▪ Est 2002 ▪ Closed to public ▪ Owner(s) Aan de Doorns, Badsberg, De Wet & Stettyn wineries ▪ Winemaker(s) Christiaan Visser ▪ ISO 22000, WIETA ▪ PO Box 62 Simondium 7670 ▪ christiaan@firstcape.com ▪ www.firstcape.com ▪ T +27 (0)21-874-8340

☐ **First Sighting** *see* Strandveld Wines

Fish Hoek Wines Ⓠ
The middle child of Accolade Wines South Africa, and sibling to unfussy Kumala and sophisticated Flagstone (both listed separately), Fish Hoek is a 'lifestyle' label featuring only single grape varieties 'to allow the purity of taste to speak for itself'. It's also the only Fairtrade brand in global parent Accolade Wines' portfolio.

. . . .

Cinsaut Rosé ⊘ ⑨ ★★★★ Tasty pink from trendy variety, **18** ⑧④ watermelon, cranberry & lemon thyme flavours, tangy, dry & sushi friendly. **Chenin Blanc** ⊘ ⑨ ★★★ Super-fresh **19** ⑧① captures white pear & guava features of the grape with lively, dry delight.

. . . .

Merlot ⑧ ★★★ Easygoing **18** ⑧② has a sweet mixed berry feel, sprinkles pepper & cocoa from American & French oak. Good for pasta night. **Pinotage** ⊘ ★★★ Forthcoming **18** ⑦⑧'s plummy fruit spiced with clove, oak staving adds structure. **Shiraz** ⊘ ★★★ Fireside companion **18** ⑧② offers mulberries, black figs & plums; fresh acidity & brush of oak balance the ripe fruit. **Sauvignon Blanc** ★★★ Quaffable & fun, **19** ⑦⑨'s limy acidity keeps tropical exuberance in check. Discontinued: **Malbec.** — DS

Location: Somerset West ▪ WO: Western Cape ▪ Tasting & sales at Flagstone Winery ▪ Owner(s) Accolade Wines South Africa ▪ Winemaker(s) Gerhard Swart (head, Sep 2007) & Chandré Petersen (2018) ▪ 50% red 50% white ▪ Fairtrade ▪ PO Box 769 Stellenbosch 7599 ▪ info@flagstonewines.com ▪ www.fishhoekwines.com ▪ T +27 (0)21-852-5052

☐ **Five Cellars** *see* FirstCape Vineyards
☐ **Five Climates** *see* Boland Cellar
☐ **Five Generations** *see* Cederberg Private Cellar
☐ **Five's Reserve** *see* Van Loveren Family Vineyards
☐ **Flagship** *see* Stellenbosch Vineyards

Flagstone Winery Ⓠ ⑪ ♿
Flagstone does the high-end SA flag-flying for global wine giant Accolade, its characterful, applauded wines reflecting founder Bruce Jack's skill and creativity (in wine-making and -naming). One of the country's first 'wineries without a vineyard', the venture swapped its Cape Town V&A Waterfront site for a Sir Herbert Baker-designed disused dynamite factory in Somerset West, driven by growth and practicality rather than aesthetics. It's always been about the vineyards, far and wide, from which Gerhard Swart (Bruce's colleague, later successor as winemaker-in-chief) continues to source distinctive parcels. The team is delighted to be extending the easy-drinking Poetry range with a pinotage and chenin, two varieties with a strong local association. See Fish Hoek and Kumala entries for the other brands in Accolade SA's portfolio.

Super Premium range
★★★★★ **Time Manner Place Pinotage** ⓐ Heaps of sex appeal ex Breedekloof single-vineyard, tiny parcel of **17** ⑨⑦ on par with stellar **14** ⑨⑤; plush fruit with cool minty edge & authoritative oak (all new, French, American & Hungarian; **16** ★★★★★ ⑨③ only 50% new). Roast nut character, mineral freshness & compact tannins to unfurl pleasurably over next decade. No **15**.

★★★★☆ **Velvet Red Blend** ⓐ Luxury packaging (& price) for sumptuous wine from 67% shiraz with mourvèdre & cinsaut. **17** ⑨③ billows mulberry fruit laced with vanilla (mainly American oak, 50% new) in pliable tannic frame, sweet feel (not heat) from alcohol on the finish. No **15**, **16**.

Flagstone range

★★★★☆ **Music Room Cabernet Sauvignon** ⓐ Classic in style, **17** ⑨① melds fruit from both cool & warmer climes into harmonious melange of rich cassis, cooler cranberry & nuances of wild mint & fynbos. Clever oaking (68% American, 30% new, 18 months) & attention to detail create a tour de force with good prospects.

★★★★☆ **Writer's Block Pinotage** ⓐ Breedekloof single-vineyard delivers, as always; **17** ⑨⓪ both sophisticated & modern, berry compote fruit with a touch of spicy American oak, the richness & concentration also seen in **16** ⑨③ under tight control, firm tannin in place to aid longevity.

★★★★☆ **Dark Horse Shiraz 16** ⑨⓪ cements rating upturn noted in **15** ⑨⓪; beautifully composed to deliver a full-bodied, ripe-berried style, with leavening whiffs of white pepper spice. Very smooth, American oak dominance fully assimilated. Sumptuously moreish.

★★★★ **Treaty Tree Reserve Red** ⓥ Alluring cabernet-led Bordeaux-style **17** ⑧⑨, ripe, scented dark fruit, powerful tannin & toasty duo American & French oak creating a smart, focused wine that lingers.

★★★★ **Dragon Tree Cape Blend** ⓥ Multi-region **17** ⑧⑧ dominated by pinotage & shiraz, cab adding vibrancy. Bold fruited, tannins equally forthright in youth, but velvet texture hints at pleasure that awaits the patient.

★★★★ **Two Roads Chardonnay** A loud celebration of lime fruit in **18** ★★★★ ⑧⑤, amplified by 60% all-new oak & 14.5% alcohol. Rich & spiced, not as delineated, deft as **17** ⑧⑥. WO Coastal.

★★★★☆ **Tributary Chenin Blanc** ⓥ Replete with tropical charm, **18** ⑨⓪ from sunny Wellington & Paarl delivers ample peach & apricot flavour, a limy edge adds freshness to the palate while astringent acidity ensures balance. Now only French oak (35%, rest tank), portion wholebunch. Less showy than **17** ⑨⓪.

★★★★☆ **Free Run Sauvignon Blanc** ⓥ Captures essence of cool-climate Elgin, Walker Bay & Agulhas. Bright, steely grass & greenpepper fruit, tense acidity & suggestions of oystershell minerality in both aroma & texture. **18** ⑨⓪ aided by 6% (unoaked) semillon & reductive winemaking. Mouthwatering.

★★★★ **Word of Mouth Viognier** ⓥ Bunch-pressed **18** ★★★★★ ⑨⓪ proffers peach, apricot & spice; stonefruit leads on palate too, but more restrained, better defined than party-goer **17** ⑧⑧. Judicious oaking (30% wooded, 40% new French, 6 months) adds structure to mineral-toned finish.

★★★★☆ **Treaty Tree Reserve White** ⓥ Captivating sauvignon & semillon (65/35) blend. **18** ⑨⓪ shows cool Elim source, vibrating with cut-grass aromas, grapefruit flavours & tense acidity, flinty minerality spotlit by finessed oaking (30% wooded, 75% new, all French). Food wine par excellence, like **17** ⑨①.

★★★★☆ **Ice Vine Dried Sauvignon Blanc** ⓝⓔⓦ ⓥ ⓐ Stunning **16** ⑨③ nectar from vineyard-desiccated Simonsberg grapes, intended to be poured over ice. Old-gold sheen, tangerine vies with fig, mango & honey in a fruit cornucopia braced by almost startling acidity. 375 ml (notably svelte wax-sealed bottle).

....

Longitude ⓥ ⓣ ★★★ Crowd-pleaser **18** ⑧② packed with red berries, spiced with smoked meats, seamed with tealeaf. Shiraz-led sextet shows nimble tannins, restrained oak. Well priced & versatile. **Noon Gun** ⓣ ★★★ Fresh appetiser, **18** ⑧② unoaked chenin with sauvignon & viognier, unbridled fruity flavour for al fresco fun.

....

Fiona Pinot Noir ⓠ ★★★★ French, American & Hungarian oak temper the Elgin fruit of **16** ⑧⑤, adds spice to strawberry, cherry & blackcurrant flavours. Delicate & delicious everyday pinot. **Truth Tree Pinotage** ⓠ ★★★★ Again with dash pinot noir, **17** ⑧④ as interesting & delicious as previous, red berries brushed with mocha, sweet spicy oak to savour in the finish. **Last Word Cape Late Bottled Vintage** ★★★★ Port-style **14** ⑧⑤ from Swartland touriga with splash shiraz for the meal's end. 100% American oak adds spice to the plummy dark chocolate flavours, finishes sweet. 375 ml.

Poetry range

Cabernet Sauvignon ★★★ Somewhat austere **18** ⑦⑧, with chunky fruit & wood tannins freshened by a minty thread. **Merlot** ⓥ ★★★ Mulberry-toned **18** ⑧⓪, with splashes other black grapes, spiced by French & American oak to gluggable & moreish effect. **Cinsaut Rosé** ⓠ ★★★ From in-vogue grape, in fashionable drier, lighter style, crimson **18** ⑧② pretty & tasty, sweet-fruited red berries & limes, brisk finish.

Chardonnay ★★ A go-to budget chardonnay, brushed with oak. **19** ⑦ not too big, not too simple, hits the sweet spot especially when paired with chicken over coals. **Sauvignon Blanc** ★★★ Melon & granadilla perked up by zesty acid in tangy **18** ⑦. — DS

Location: Somerset West ▪ Map: Helderberg ▪ Map grid reference: B6 ▪ WO: Western Cape/Coastal/ Breedekloof/Stellenbosch/Swartland/Cape South Coast/Elim/Elgin ▪ Est 1998 ▪ 1stB 1999 ▪ Tasting & sales Tue-Fri 10-4 Sat/pub hols 10-3 ▪ Fee R10-R50pp ▪ Cheese, biltong & wine platters - please book ahead for bigger groups ▪ Closed Good Fri, Dec 25/26 & Jan 1 ▪ Cellar tours by appt ▪ Owner(s) Accolade Wines South Africa ▪ Winemaker(s) Gerhard Swart (head, Sep 2007), with Mia Boonzaier (Jan 2008) & Willene Bester (Jun 2014) ▪ 60% red 40% white ▪ WR Quinan Blvd, Paardevlei, Somerset West 7130 ▪ info@flagstonewines. com ▪ www.flagstonewines.com ▪ S 34° 5' 26.38" E 018° 48' 30.04" ▪ ⌖ smiled.common.balance ▪ **T +27 (0)21-852-5052**

- ☐ **Flash Series** see The Blacksmith
- ☐ **Flatrock** see Rhebokskloof Wine Estate
- ☐ **Flat Roof Manor** see Libertas Vineyards & Estates
- ☐ **Fledge & Co** see The Fledge & Co
- ☐ **Fleet** see Steenberg Vineyards
- ☐ **Fleur de Vie** see Fleur du Cap

Fleur du Cap

One of SA's venerable corporate-owned brands, dating back to the 1960s as a Distillers/Bergkelder product, Fleur du Cap is among several labels now managed by Distell's new standalone premium and fine-wine company Libertas Vineyards & Estates. As such it will come under what LV&E MD Kay Nash describes as the 'critical review of the large portfolio of eight brands and 40 sub-sub-brands operating in 88 markets globally across 22 varieties'. Winemaker Pieter Badenhorst is in charge of producing Fleur du Cap's five tiered ranges, including the flagship, honouring Julius Laszlo, pioneer of small-barrel ageing in SA. Seasoned Distell viticulturist Henk van Graan now oversees grape sourcing from prime locations around the winelands.

Flagship range

★★★★☆ **Laszlo** ⓥ Sumptuous & velvety, **15** ㊙ aligns classic & New World styles into structured sophistication. Prestige blend now cab-led (33%) with other 4 Bordeaux reds. Less new oak (40%, previously 100%) perfectly synchronised with the dark fruit ex Stellenbosch & Paarl.

Series Privée Unfiltered

★★★★☆ **Cabernet Sauvignon** ⊘ ⓐ Classic Stellenbosch cab, built to last decade minimum. Plush cigarbox & cedar notes over deep-piled blackcurrant & mulberry fruit, which fluently engages with firm tannins & oak spice (40% new barrels, 18 months, some American) in **16** ㊒.

★★★★☆ **Merlot** ⊘ ⓐ Poised **16** ㊑ from Stellenbosch builds a rich core of fruit on a base of firm tannin & soft but insistent acidity, auguring well for a long future. Remarkably expressive & complex - hazelnuts, violets, berries, cherries, herbs & cinnamon among the nuances, supported by sympathetic oaking (40% new, 20% American, 18 months).

★★★★☆ **Pinotage** ⊘ A notch above **16** ★★★★ ㊙, **17** ㊐ rich & complex with firm but ripe tannin structure. Bramble & plum fruit to the fore, mocha overlay from oak (30% new, some American, 20 months). WO Paarl.

★★★★☆ **Chardonnay** ⊘ ⓐ Rounded citrus, ripe peach & vanilla notes in **18** ㊙. Soft, silky cream-iness from 40% new oak embraces orange marmalade & apple, whereas the wood character from 80% new barrels on **17** ★★★★ ㊈ stood apart in youth.

★★★★ **Chenin Blanc** ⓥ Generous **17** ㊈ shows warmer Paarl provenance in ample dried yellow peach & lime. Oak quite dominant (40% new), less balanced & vibrant than **16** ★★★★★ ㊙, which included Stellenbosch grapes.

★★★★ **Sauvignon Blanc** ⓥ Darling fruit gives characteristic dusty tone to more vegetal & stonefruit flavours, **17** ㊇ not as ripe as **16** ㊇ but shows some warmth despite modest 13% alcohol. Not as scintillating as **15** ★★★★★ ㊙.

Bergkelder Selection
Not tasted: **Noble Late Harvest**.

Essence du Cap range
★★★★ Cabernet Sauvignon ⊘ Only ±20% oaked (as all these reds), so fruit is the star in **17** ⑧⑧ - blackberries, blackcurrants & plums. More intensity & complexity than **16 ★★★★** ⑧⑤, with mineral underpinning. Whiffs of cigarbox & crushed herbs, crunchy tannins provide a 3-5 year future.

★★★★ Merlot ⊘ More focused than **16 ★★★★** ⑧④, **17** ⑧⑥ delivers black cherry, plum & cocoa notes, accented by dried herbs & spice, firm backbone of tannin through to dark chocolate farewell.

Pinotage ★★★ Interesting combo of brambles, chicory & spice, savoury finish, accessible tannins provide drinking pleasure in **17** ⑧②. **Shiraz ★★★** Dark forest fruits mingle with meaty & aromatic notes of nutmeg, clove & white pepper on **17** ⑦⑨. **Chardonnay** ⊘ **★★★★** Citrus-toned **18** ⑧④ showcases apple & peach in a light, zesty body. Lightly oaked for great summer sipping. **Chenin Blanc ★★★** Melon, apple & quince in crisp **19** ⑧⓪. Chill & enjoy poolside. **Sauvignon Blanc ★★★** Good spread of riper tropical notes & greener ones (crushed herbs & nettles) in **19** ⑧①. Fresh & light, litchi & granadilla on finish.

Fleur de Vie range
Natural Light Chenin Blanc ★★ Light-hearted **18** ⑦④, off-dry & fruity, with low 9.5% alcohol. Not tasted: **Natural Light Rosé**. — GM

Location: Stellenbosch ▪ WO: Western Cape/Paarl/Stellenbosch/Coastal/Darling ▪ Est 1968 ▪ 1stB 1969 ▪ Owner(s) Libertas Vineyards & Estates, a Distell Group company ▪ Winemaker(s) Pieter Badenhorst (Dec 2006) ▪ Viticulturist(s) Henk van Graan ▪ ±17,000t/±290,000cs own label 47% red 53% white ▪ ISO 14001, ISO 9001, BRC, HACCP, IFS ▪ info@fleurducap.co.za ▪ www.fleurducap.co.za ▪ **T +27 (0)21-809-8025**

Flight of the Fish Eagle

Deservedly popular brandy, distinctive in its dark green, squared-off bottle - featuring, of course, in full flight the graceful raptor whose distinctive call many feel to be the essence of the African wild. Brand owner Distell's own call here is really to the young imbiber, hence the fresh untraditionality of brandy and image.

★★★★ Natural Potstill Brandy ⊘ Potstill ⑧⑦, light in colour & simple fresh fruitiness. At 38% alcohol, its pretty delicacy & smoothness is beyond its price point. Delicious on a rock or two, but mixers not needed. Also in 200 ml. — TJ

☐ **Flippenice** *see* Tulbagh Winery

Flotsam & Jetsam

Sad news for lovers of this 'second-label' project from star winemakers Chris and Suzaan Alheit: Flight Of The Jackass is the last wine to be produced. 'It was fun while it lasted' says Chris, but they have decided to focus on Alheit Vineyards, the main venture (listed separately), with the aim of taking those wines as high as possible. Fans of the 'kick back and enjoy' Flotsam line-up will be disappointed, but hopefully these special parcels of fruit from old Stellenbosch bushvines will find their way into future Alheit wines.

★★★★ Cinsault Flight Of The Jackass ⑨ A very worthy swansong for this label. **18** ⑧⑨ radiates drinkability with incredibly perfumed red fruit (100% wholebunch) matched to truffles, sherbet & hint of fresh rosemary. Some firmness of structure & modest 11.4% alcohol make for very satisfying drink.

Discontinued: **Cinsault Stalwart**, **Chenin Blanc Heirloom**. — CM

Location: Hermanus ▪ WO: Stellenbosch ▪ Est/1stB 2015 ▪ Closed to public ▪ Owner(s) Chris & Suzaan Alheit ▪ Winemaker(s) Chris & Suzaan Alheit (both Jan 2015), with Franco Lourens (Jan 2016) ▪ Viticulturist(s) Chris Alheit ▪ 12t 100% red ▪ PO Box 711 Hermanus 7200 ▪ www.flotsamandjetsam.co.za ▪ **T +27 (0)28-312-2083**

☐ **Flower Girl** *see* Botanica Wines
☐ **Flutterby** *see* Boland Cellar

Flying Cloud

This boutique venture is the personal passion of advocate Donald Ackerman, who sources grapes and makes wine, no more than two barrels' worth of each of the current pair of labels, always to his very high standard. His main law practice is in Cape Town but he has relocated to George on the Garden Route, where he has a satellite office, and commutes. In gestation at press time were a Pinot Noir and Fumé Blanc, sourced from the same vineyard owner in the local area.

★★★★ Sea Serpent Syrah joined by 10% grenache this vintage, just 2 barrels, 18 months oaking. **17** ⑧⑨ is sleek & savoury, peppery, the dark fruit providing enough flesh & succulence to enjoy now, but has ageing structure.

★★★★☆ Witch of the Wave ⓦ Blend switch in **17** ⑨③, semillon & sauvignon 60/40 (vice versa for **16** ⑨④), now 2 barrels. Still orange blossom & tangerine, but there's a beeswax underpin, some melon. Lovely elegance & mineral freshness.— CR

Location: George ▪ Map: Klein Karoo & Garden Route ▪ Map grid reference: C3 ▪ WO: Cape South Coast ▪ Est 2013 ▪ 1stB 2014 ▪ Tasting & sales at Ur-bin Wine Cellar (see below for address) ▪ Owner(s)/winemaker(s) Donald Ackerman ▪ 280cs own label 50% red 50% white ▪ Dynarc House, cnr Courtenay & Meade Strs, George 6529 ▪ flyingcloudwines@icloud.com ▪ S 33° 57' 24.8" E 022° 27' 43.7" ▪ 🖂 nipped.lowest.during ▪ **T +27 (0)82-610-2422/+27 (0)44-868-0086**

☐ **Foodbarn Restaurant** *see* Migliarina Wines

Foothills Vineyards

The Klein Welmoed property on Raithby Road in the Helderberg foothills was in bad shape when Glenn Hesse and Tim Featherby bought it just over a decade ago, but with input from high-calibre consultants and much TLC their boutique wine venture (and luxe guest house) is becoming more impressive by the vintage.

Monogram Collection

★★★★ Shiraz ⓦ Perhaps 'Syrah' a more apropos name, given the Old World savouriness of wild herbs, dried meat & liquorice seaming the hedgerow fruit of mouthfilling but balanced **16** ⑧⑧.

★★★★ Semillon Refined lemon & lime aromas, with brightness & slatey minerality. **18** ★★★★★ ⑨⓪ layered & complex, orchard fruit, beeswax, honey & vanilla nuances on well-structured & harmonious palate. Barrel-fermented/14 months, 20% new oak. Trumps **17** ⑧⑨.

★★★★ Méthode Cap Classique ⓦ Delicate floral & baked apple fragrances reverberate in the full, creamy mousse of **16** ⑧⑧ dry sparkling from chardonnay (65%) & pinot noir, the sleekness aided by barrel ferment/15 months on lees.

★★★★☆ Straw Wine ⓦ Air-dried & barrel-fermented viognier, **15** ⑨⓪ seduces with vibrant gold appearance, peach, honey, marmalade & toasted hazelnut richness, good viscosity & long lemon rind finish. Older oak, 2 years. 375 ml.

Foothills range

Pinot Noir ⊘ **★★★★** Silky, easy to drink **18** ⑧④, vibrant strawberries mingle with earthy wood-spice for a good dry finish. **Syrah ★★★★** Generous blackberry fruit & fynbos on velvet palate, lifted peach perfume from co-fermented 5% viognier. **17** ⑧⑤ well supported by older-oak ageing, 14 months. **Dry Rosé ★★★☆** Palest pink **18** ⑧⑤ is delicate & moreish, offers berry & tropical flavours & a dry conclusion. Semillon, viognier & blush from shiraz. **Chardonnay ★★★** Uncomplicated & shy **18** ⑧② ripe apple & vanilla from barrique ferment, some florality in an easy-drinking package. **Sauvignon Blanc ★★★★** 2 clones vinified separately for complementary tropical salad & green herb flavour profile in **19** ⑧⑤, touch unoaked semillon adds breadth & depth on full yet fresh palate. **Viognier** ⓦ **★★★** Appealing peaches-&-cream styling for **17** ⑧②, complete with aromatic spice & roasted nut topping; voluptuous & rounded. **The Partners ★★★☆** Successful & delicious liaison among sauvignon, semillon & viognier, **17** ⑧⑤ bountiful ripe stonefruit & tropical flavours, & though unoaked, concludes with food-friendly spiciness. — WB

Location/WO: Stellenbosch ▪ Map: Helderberg ▪ Map grid reference: B1 ▪ Est 2008 ▪ 1stB 2012 ▪ Tasting & sales by appt ▪ Fee R50pp ▪ Meals/refreshments by appt ▪ Olive oil ▪ Conferences ▪ 4-star luxury guesthouse (B&B), info@kleinwelmoed.co.za ▪ Owner(s) Glenn Hesse & Tim Featherby ▪ Winemaker(s) Bernard le Roux ▪ Viticulturist(s) Bennie Booysen ▪ 39ha/19ha (pinot, shiraz, chard, sauv, sem, viog) ▪ 8,000cs own label 25% red 70% white 5% rosé ▪ IPW ▪ PO Box 647 Somerset Mall 7137 ▪ info@foothillsvineyards.co.za ▪ www.klein-welmoed.co.za ▪ S 34° 0' 58.86" E 018° 47' 43.08" ▪ 🖂 armbands.busy.horizon ▪ **T +27 (0)21-842-0045**

☐ **Foot of Africa** *see* Kleine Zalze Wines

☐ **Force Majeure** *see Mother Rock Wines*
☐ **Forresters** *see Ken Forrester Wines*

Fortes Family Wines

Neil Fortes, with over 40 years of experience in the wine trade (notably with his Wine Guru company), returned to SA in 2005 and bought land in Napier Valley – a 'special terroir'. The initial plantings of sauvignon have produced small parcels of grapes vinified by Neil together with Conrad Vlok of Strandveld.

Fortes range
★★★★ Sauvignon Blanc Smoky, almost charry notes from older oak mixing with tropical & greener notes on retasted **17** ⑧⑥, giving some complexity (though perhaps dividing sauvignon lovers). A few grams of sugar add a seductive sweet touch & softened texture.

Cape Beach Collection 🆕
Camps Bay Sauvignon Blanc ★★★☆ Modest but ripe aromas & flavours on **18** ⑧⑤, a sweet fruitiness balanced by fresh acidity - the oak influence (7 months, 300L older French) not obvious. Knocks on next level. — TJ

Location/WO: Napier ▪ Map: Southern Cape ▪ Map grid reference: B2 ▪ Est 2005 ▪ 1stB 2016 ▪ Tasting, sales & cellar tours by appt only ▪ Closed all pub hols ▪ BYO picnic ▪ Owner(s) The Trojan Trust ▪ Cellarmaster(s)/ winemaker(s) Neil Fortes & Conrad Vlok (Jun 2006, consultants) ▪ Viticulturist(s) Neil Fortes (Jun 2006, consultant) ▪ 3.5ha/2ha (sauv) ▪ 5t/600cs own label 100% white ▪ PO Box 208 Napier 7270 ▪ info@ wineguru.ca ▪ www.forteswines.com ▪ S34° 27' 50.0" E 019° 53' 56.0 ▪ **T +27 (0)71-223-9927/+1 289 771 1744 (Canada)**

☐ **Fortress Hill** *see Fort Simon Wine Estate*

Fort Simon Wine Estate

Originally called Houmoed, this Bottelary Hills farm was purchased by Dr Simon Uys and his wife Anna in 1967. Now run by their sons and daughter-in-law, the cellar stands out thanks to its distinctive architecture, 'inspired by the German outpost architecture of Namibia'. The original cellar, built in 1908, is now a wedding chapel, with receptions held in the medieval-style tasting venue, Fort Anna.

Platinum Collection
★★★★ Viognier Noble Late Harvest ⓥ Unencumbered by oak, **17** ⑧⑥ has muscat-like grapey fruit; unctuously rich & intensely sweet (258 g/l sugar) but well focused & appealing. 375 ml.

Discontinued: **Viognier.**

Fort Simon range
★★★★ Cabernet Sauvignon Enticing blackcurrant, savoury liquorice & earthy notes on **15** ⑧⑧, much improved on last **13 ★★★** ⑧①. Lithe, midweight, shows poise & balance. 2 years French oak, 20% new.

★★★★ Shiraz ⓥ Sweetly ripe fruit to the fore on **15 ★★★★** ⑧⑤, with perhaps more oak spicing than **14** ⑧⑥ from 18 months in barrel, 20% new. Accessible medium body.

★★★★ Barrel Select Merlot-Malbec ⊘ Stylish **16** ⑧⑧ has heft & concentration, inky black fruit, earthy liquorice & soft, pliable tannins. 2 years French oak, 20% new, nicely integrated. 60/40 blend more serious & satisfying than **15 ★★★** ⑧①.

Merlot ⓥ **★★★☆** Dark, tarry core with sombre black berries & salty liquorice notes. **16** ⑧⑤ pleasant in an austere sort of way. **Pinotage** ⓥ **★★★☆** Oaky mocha style, **16** ⑧③ has juicy plum fruit, chewy tannins, hints of iodine & iron. **Chardonnay ★★★☆** Oak spices mask fruit on **18** ⑧④, with hints of creamy lemon peeking through. Appealing leesy texture. **Sauvignon Blanc** ⓥ **★★★** Tastily ripe tropical fruit on **18** ⑧②, with reined-in acidity. Mild mannered if unlingering. Not tasted: **Chenin Blanc.**

Fortress Hill range
Merlot ⊘ **★★★☆** Primary berry fruit tinged with menthol on **17** ⑧③, decent heft, ripe tannins, fullish acidity. Pleasant everyday quaffing. **Shiraz ★★★** Meaty, savoury **17** ⑧② has hints of scrub & wild herbs, black cherry fruit, rather rigid tannin structure. **Merlot-Cabernet Sauvignon ★★★☆** Well-rounded, wholesome **17** ⑧④ offers solid black-fruit profile, smooth tannins & generous body. **Sauvignon Blanc** ⓥ **★★★** Easygoing, nicely poised **18** ⑧⓪, pungent nettle notes over crisp passionfruit.

Michelle d'Or range

Merlot ✓ ★★★★ Appealing sweet black fruit, chocolate nuance from year in oak barrels, 15% new, on **17** ⑧③, improves on previous. WO W Cape, as all these. **Shiraz** ★★★ Meaty, smoky notes on **17** ⑧②, bolstered by ripe black fruit. Dash petit verdot adds punch to likeable everyday tipple. **Merlot-Cabernet Sauvignon** ✓ ★★★★ Nicely rounded **17** ⑧④ is uncomplicated everyday drinking pleasure, with cheerful berry fruit & a hint of caramel. **Sauvignon Blanc** ② ★★★☆ Unpretentious **18** ⑦⑧ shows typical grassy gooseberry flavours with edgy acid finish. — GdB

Location/map: Stellenbosch ▪ Map grid reference: C4 ▪ WO: Stellenbosch/Western Cape ▪ Est 1997 ▪ 1stB 1998 ▪ Tasting & sales Mon-Fri 9.30—5 Sat 10—2 ▪ Tasting R75/5 wines ▪ Closed all pub hols & long weekends ▪ Cellar tours by appt ▪ Venue for after-hours functions/weddings & conferences (120-140 guests) ▪ Wedding chapel ▪ Owner(s) Renier, Petrus & Michéle Uys ▪ Winemaker(s) Dirk Tredoux (Oct 2016) ▪ Viticulturist(s) Renier Uys ▪ 80ha (cabs s/f, malbec, merlot, p verdot, ptage, shiraz, chard, chenin, sauv, viog) ▪ 800t/80,000cs own label 70% red 30% white ▪ PO Box 43 Sanlamhof 7532 ▪ michele@fortsimon.com ▪ www.fortsimon.com ▪ S 33° 55' 9.5" E 018° 45' 19.4" ▪ 🔲 candy.evidence.patting ▪ **T +27 (0)21-906-0304**

☐ **Foundation Stone** *see* Rickety Bridge Winery
☐ **Foundry** *see* The Foundry
☐ **Four Cousins** *see* Van Loveren Family Vineyards

4G Wine Estate

Conceived a decade ago by luminaries including late Bordeaux oenologist-educator Denis Dubourdieu and local legend Giorgio Dalla Cia, this Stellenbosch cross-cultural venture is chasing 'first growth' status. Tian Scholtz works with French consultant Valérie Lavigne on reds from quality sites around the Western Cape for global distribution under directorship of Philipp Axt. Current releases not tasted.

Location: Stellenbosch ▪ Est 2009 ▪ 1stB 2010 ▪ Closed to public ▪ Owner(s) Private shareholders ▪ Winemaker(s) Valérie Lavigne & Tian G. Scholtz ▪ 20t own label 100% red ▪ Other export brands: G., The Echo of G. ▪ info@4g-wines.com ▪ www.4g-wines.com

Four Paws Wines   ⓠ

Any cat lovers irritated by the obsession with wine-farm dogs and their antics would have cheered (nonchalantly, of course) the launch 15 years ago of this boutique wine brand by feline fanatics Rob Meihuizen, Anne Jakubiec and winemaker Gerda Willers. Inaugural Bordeaux blend Pablo, in life a Brown Point Siamese, has seen his mostly Piekenierskloof-sourced family flourish, and soon it will be joined by a white blend from vines planted five seasons ago on the Franschhoek home farm, where pre-booked tastings are offered.

★★★★ **Pinotage** ② Brambleberry notes on full-bodied **11** ⑧⑦, showing vanilla tone from year 30% new oak. Drinks easily & well but underlying seriousness invites cellaring ±5 years.

★★★★ **Picatso** ② Generous floral, tropical & grapey notes contrast nicely with delicate oak (2nd fill) on **15** ⑧⑥ viognier & muscat d'Alexandrie dessert. Crackling acidity adds to enjoyment, vibrancy. 375 ml.

Grenache ② ★★★★ Elegant glassful, **14** ⑧④ with fine-grained tannins, intense red- & dark-fruit bouquet spiced with cherry tobacco & nutmeg. **Sauvignon Blanc** ★★★★ Stellenbosch grapes in attractive **17** ⑧⑤, trenchant nettle & khaki bush aromas, ripe gooseberry fruit, decent heft & focused finish. **Champurrs Méthode Cap Classique** (NEW) ★★★★ From Franschhoek chardonnay, **17** ⑧⑤ dry sparkler has steely acidity, lively bubbles & pleasant yeasty brioche from 18 months on lees. Not tasted: **Shiraz**, **Pablo**, **Vincent van Dogh**, **Rosé**, **Chardonnay**, **Calico**. — GdB

Location/map: Franschhoek ▪ Map grid reference: C3 ▪ WO: Piekenierskloof/Stellenbosch/Franschhoek/Western Cape ▪ Est 2005 ▪ 1stB 2006 ▪ Tasting by appt, R45 Franschhoek ▪ Closed weekends & pub hols ▪ Owner(s) Rob Meihuizen, Gerda Willers & Anne Jakubiec ▪ Winemaker(s) Gerda Willers (2005) ▪ Viticulturist(s) Gerda Willers ▪ 2ha (shiraz, chenin, grenache b, rouss) ▪ 20t/3,000cs own label 70% red 30% white ▪ PO Box 69 Simondium 7670 ▪ anne@southerntrade.co.za ▪ www.fourpawswines.com ▪ S 33° 53' 28.0" E 019° 5' 0.5" ▪ 🔲 rejoices.engrave.whisker ▪ **T +27 (0)83-447-1376 (Anne)**

4th Street

An unchallenging flavour profile, low alcohol and 'accessible, inclusive and unintimidating' positioning have helped propel this Distell label to the position of fastest-growing SA wine brand in the world, and one of the international Top 20 rapid risers overall.

Natural Sweet range
Red ★★ Easy, not over-sweet **NV** (72), for spicy fare. Serve well-chilled, as all. **Rosé ★** Uncomplicated, sweet-fruited **NV** (69). Latest bottling a touch cloying, needs an acid lift. Also in 1.5, 3 & 5L packs, as all. **White ★★** Floral & ripe fruit flavours on effortless **NV** (72), with friendly ±7.5% alcohol, like all. — WB

Fram Wines   ①

'Fine wines of exploration' is the rubric on the labels of this range of essentially new-wave, minimal intervention, sometimes experimental wines from the experienced Thinus Krüger. Fittingly, inspiringly, the name Fram (meaning 'Forward') is that of the ship used in polar expeditions by great Norwegian explorers around the turn of the last century. The wines come from widely sourced vineyards, with a focus on dry slopes in the Citrusdal Mountain ward – the Chenin Blanc from there took up to 9 months to ferment (naturally, of course) in its old oak barrels.

★★★★ Cinsault (ⓥ) Youthful, fresh, unwooded **17** (89) with perfumed charm, but more than simply fruity. There's vinosity (13% alcohol) & some flavour intensity supported by acidity & subtle tannins.

★★★★ Pinotage (ⓥ) New-waveish styling on **16 ★★★★☆** (92), stressing freshness, yet also rich & weighty (14.3% alcohol), with sweet, spicy fruit & a firm but unobtrusive tannic underpinning. 18 months in oak doesn't obscure the pure flavours. Less austere in youth than **15** (87).

★★★★ Chardonnay Unoaked **18** (86) from Robertson has welcoming ripe stonefruit & citrus aromas leading to a rounded, textured palate with a seam of limy tartness. More curvaceous than **17 ★★★★** (85).

★★★★☆ Chenin Blanc 18 ★★★★ (88) is notably ripe in character, almost decadently so, with bruised apple notes hinting at oxidative processes, the variety not obvious. A good grip of succulent acid & a touch of tannin. From Citrusdal Mountain, unlike more delicate **16** (94) ex Piekenierskloof & Swartland. No **17**.

★★★★ Dry White From a mixed vineyard with majority palomino. Characterful & individual **NV** (89), more savoury than obviously fruity, but full of flavour, with a firm fresh structure. Old oak, like all these.

Shiraz ★★★★ Lightly perfumed **18** (85) includes dollops of grenache & mourvèdre. Flavourful & fresh, with a bright acidity & light, smooth tannins. Not quite the charm of **17 ★★★★** (89). WO Swartland. **Grenache Gris ★★★** From unique Voor Paardeberg vineyard of the variety. 10 days on the light-red skins gives amber colour, aromatic floral & spicy notes, & a savoury tannic grip to **18** (82). Fresh & bright, more fruit-rich than previous, yet airy. — TJ

Location: Riebeek West ▪ WO: Citrusdal Mountain/Robertson/Swartland/Voor Paardeberg ▪ Est/1stB 2012 ▪ Tasting by appt only ▪ Owner(s) Thinus Krüger ▪ Cellarmaster(s)/winemaker(s) Thinus Krüger (Dec 2012) ▪ Viticulturist(s) Henk Laing ▪ 30t/2,500cs own label 45% red 55% white ▪ PO Box 2272 Dennesig Stellenbosch 7601 ▪ thinus@framwines.co.za ▪ www.framwines.co.za ▪ **T +27 (0)72-545-4959**

Francois La Garde   ①

Piet Matthée runs a specialist Stellenbosch mobile bottling and labelling company, and occasionally finds some time in the moonlight to make his small range of MCC bubblies, fulfilling 'a lifelong dream' of one of his ancestors – whose name was adopted for his project. But nothing new this year.

Location/map: Stellenbosch ▪ Map grid reference: E5 ▪ Est 2004 ▪ Tasting by appt ▪ Owner(s) PL Matthée ▪ Cellarmaster(s)/winemaker(s) Piet Matthée (Jan 2009) ▪ 15t/2,000cs own label 100% MCC ▪ PO Box 12366 Die Boord 7613 ▪ admin@technofill.co.za ▪ www.francois-lagarde.co.za, www.technofill.co.za ▪ S 33° 55' 25.45" E 018° 51' 6.25" ▪ ⊞ patio.beamed.rainy ▪ **T +27 (0)21-887-3674**

☐ **Francois le Vaillant** see Lutzville Vineyards

Franki's Vineyards

On a 700-ha farm near Malmesbury in Swartland, home to a large guest lodge and 22 ha of goblet-trained vines, Erica Joubert continues to produce tiny volumes of handcrafted wines, with a special focus on barrel-fermented viognier. 'There are no plans to increase production. These boutique wines are my passion.'

★★★★ **Grenache** ⓥ Shy cranberry scent on **16** ⑧⑨ gives way to intense, fresh palate showing fine structure & red-berry fruit, improving on **15** ★★★☆ ⑧④. Year old French oak.

★★★★ **Viognier Barrel Fermented** ⓥ Slowly fermented in seasoned wood, **18** ⑧⑥ peaches-&-cream flavours with a spicy farewell. Minuscule production, as all these.

Joubert Red Blend ⓥ ★★★☆ Characterful, well-balanced & enjoyable **15** ⑧④ blend mourvèdre (50%) with shiraz & grenache. Has rustic charm & flavour power, but modest 13% alcohol. **Mourvèdre Rosé** ⓥ ★★★ Pleasant, dry **18** ⑧② enticing summer fruits led by strawberry & just a touch of spice. — HC

Location: Malmesbury ▪ Map/WO: Swartland ▪ Map grid reference: A6 ▪ Est 2004 ▪ 1stB 2007 ▪ Tasting, sales & cellar tours Mon-Fri 8-5 by appt ▪ Closed all pub hols ▪ BYO picnic ▪ Franki's Guest Lodge ▪ Owner(s) Franco Afrique Technologies (Pty) Ltd ▪ Winemaker(s) Erica Joubert (Jan 2004) ▪ 700ha/22ha (grenache, mourv, viog) ▪ ±160t/400cs own label 50% red 50% white/rosé ▪ PO Box 972 Malmesbury 7299 ▪ erica. joubert@cropspec.co.za ▪ www.frankisvineyards.co.za ▪ S 33° 20' 59.5" E 018° 32' 12.4" ▪ ⟲ repress.mono. reprising ▪ **T +27 (0)82-888-3702**

Franschhoek Cellar

This edition we taste only the flagship blend of this long-established DGB brand; we'll catch up next time with the MCC sparking line-up and its sibling range, Village Walk, which is 'proudly Franschhoek' in referencing various landmarks in and around the town in the wines' names. The brand-home on main road is a landmark in its own right, abuzz with visitors enjoying the many wine and food options available for all ages.

★★★★☆ **The Last Elephant** ⓐ No-holds-barred show-stopper **17** ⑨⓪ has guts & power aplenty. Merlot-led 4-way Bordeaux blend with 35% new oak showing prominently mid-2019, has depth of black fruit, ripe tannins & succulent spice to integrate & bloom over the next decade.— CM

Location/map: Franschhoek ▪ Map grid reference: C2 ▪ WO: Coastal ▪ Est 1945 ▪ Tasting & sales Mon-Sat 10–6 Sun 10–5 ▪ Wine pairing: 6 wines with 6 cheeses, or with assorted chocolates ▪ Closed Easter Fri/Sun, Dec 25/26 & Jan 1 ▪ Al fresco dining daily ▪ Play area for children ▪ Farm produce ▪ Weddings ▪ Conferences ▪ Events venue (seat 300 pax) ▪ Rose & Protea cottages ▪ Owner(s) DGB (Pty) Ltd ▪ Winemaker(s) Ryan Puttick (Nov 2017) ▪ Viticulturist(s) Heinie Nel (Jul 2018) ▪ 300ha (cab, merlot, shiraz, chard, chenin, sauv, sem) ▪ 30,000t 49% red 50% white 1% rosé ▪ ISO 9001:2001, IPW ▪ PO Box 52 Franschhoek 7690 ▪ fhcellardoor@ dgb.co.za ▪ www.thefranschhoekcellar.co.za, www.franschhoek-cellar.co.za ▪ S 33° 54' 16.4" E 019° 6' 40.7" ▪ ⟲ ironed.canyon.trifle ▪ **T +27 (0)21-876-2086**

☐ **Frans K Smit** *see* Spier

Frater Family Wines

'For five generation we have been tilling these soils,' says John-Robert Frater, whose Scottish ancestors settled on historic Paarl farm De Zoete Inval in 1878. 'In contrast to commercial cellars, I have to make do with what I have. 'n Boer maak 'n plan! You won't find us in the supermarkets because our wines are unique and made in limited amounts, each one named in honour of a family member or close friend.'

Oupa Bull Pinotage Reserve ★★★ Full-ripe & voluptuous, with dark fruit, mocha & liquorice tones, **17** ⑧② offers smooth accessibility, enough structure for definition, ageing. **David Arthur Shiraz Reserve** ★★★ Plum/prune opulence on **17** ⑧⓪, well oak-spiced; smooth textured for everyday drinking, enough grip at the end for some cellaring. **Connor Cabernet Sauvignon-Petit Verdot-Malbec** ★★★★ Cab rules, vivid cassis, mixed-provenance oak staves contribute lead pencil sub-structure, firm tannins. Enjoy **15** ⑧④ now but will benefit from cellaring. Less complex than **14** ★★★★ ⑧⑥, & higher alcohol (15%). **Adrian SMG** ⓥ ★★★★ Shiraz-led with equal 14% portions mourvèdre & grenache, **14** ⑧④ swirls of spice, scrub & fresh herbs, ripe cassis fruit notes. Friendly, with latent power. **Elizabeth Viognier-Chardonnay** ⓥ ★★★ Barrel-fermented viognier (80%) leads **16** ⑧①, unoaked chardonnay gives freshness & lift. Big-boned & attractively dry with apricot & dried peach flavours. Discontinued: **Eulalia Chardonnay Unoaked**. — CR

Location/WO: Paarl ▪ Est 1878 ▪ 1stB 1976 ▪ Closed to public ▪ Owner(s) DZI Agricultural Investments cc (John Robert & Eulalia Frater) ▪ Cellarmaster(s)/winemaker(s) John Robert Frater (1999) ▪ Viticulturist(s) Robert Frater ▪ 80ha/20ha (cab, grenache, malbec, mourv, p verdot, shiraz, chard) ▪ 200t/16,000cs own label 50% red 50% white ▪ Other export brands: Eskdale, Safari ▪ PO Box 591 Suider-Paarl 7624 ▪ info@fraterfamily-wines.co.za, sales@fraterfamilywines.co.za ▪ www.fraterfamilywines.co.za ▪ T +27 (0)21-863-1535/+27 (0)82-731-3898

Freedom Hill Wines

$(\stackrel{\circ}{\downarrow})$ $(\textcircled{6})$ $(\stackrel{\circ}{\triangle})$ $(\stackrel{\circ}{\&})$

Civil engineer Francois Klomp has been the driver behind this boutique venture since inception and first bottling 20 years ago. He planted the vines on a part of the original Paarl farm, La Paris, on a Wemmershoek Mountain slope, and since added a cellar and visitor locale hosting tastings, weddings and functions.

Freedom Hill range

★★★★ **Merlot** $(\stackrel{\circ}{\downarrow})$ Second bottling of **14** ⑧⑥ as good as first. Blackcurrant & plum fruit in noble structure; has bedded down & developed well, smooth & ready to enjoy. Stellenbosch WO.

Cape Blend $(\stackrel{\circ}{\downarrow})$ ★★★ Compatible union of pinotage & cab, **15** ⑧② mild-mannered with bramble fruit, light oak spices & chunky tannin underpinning. **Chardonnay** $(\stackrel{\circ}{\downarrow})$ ★★★★ Ripe citrus fruit & beeswax, with muted oak & medium body. **15** ⑧⑤ thoroughly pleasant, well focused & convincing. WO W Cape.

Freedom Walk 1335/88 range

Pinotage $(\stackrel{\circ}{\downarrow})$ ★★★ Earthy expression of the variety, with forest floor & musk nuances to plum fruit on **15** ⑧②. French oak support is well judged. **Cape Blend** $(\stackrel{\circ}{\downarrow})$ ★★★ From pinotage & cab, understated **15** ⑧② has black berry & currant fruit, light oak spicing & earthy tannin foundation. Discontinued: **Shiraz**. — DS

Location: Paarl ▪ Map: Franschhoek ▪ Map grid reference: B5 ▪ WO: Paarl/Stellenbosch/Western Cape ▪ Est 1997 ▪ 1stB 2000 ▪ Tasting & sales Mon-Fri 9.30-5 ▪ Fee R45pp ▪ Closed all pub hols ▪ Child friendly ▪ Wedding & function venue ▪ Owner(s) Francois Klomp ▪ 82ha/19ha (cab, ptage, shiraz) ▪ ±70t/12,000cs own label 100% red ▪ PO Box 6126 Paarl 7620 ▪ info@freedomhill.co.za ▪ www.freedomhillwines.com ▪ S 33° 49' 48.33" E 019° 0' 35.90" ▪ ⌑ bottles.obediently.intermodal ▪ T +27 (0)21-867-0085

☐ **Freedom Walk** *see* Freedom Hill Wines
☐ **Free to Be** *see* Remhoogte Wine Estate
☐ **Friends Forever** *see* Devonvale Golf & Wine Estate
☐ **Friesland** *see* Kaapzicht Wine Estate

Friesland Wines

$(\stackrel{\circ}{\downarrow})$ $(\stackrel{\circ}{\P\P})$ $(\stackrel{\circ}{NEW})$

New Bottelary Hills-based wine brand Friesland is driven by Stellenbosch international trade law graduate and former KWV and Distell executive De Bruyn Steenkamp. Grapes from his uncle Piet Steenkamp's Groenland estate and his father Kosie's adjoining Friesland property (bought and replanted in 1999) are vinified by sister Marié (in Friesland's 1930s cellar) and marketed by De Bruyn and wife Marilise. Traditional winemaking methods, regional distinctiveness and personal customer interaction are mantras, the latter enhanced by a casual 'tasting deck' to woo visitors with Table Mountain/Table Bay vistas.

Merlot-Cabernet Sauvignon ★★★★ Has all the perfume & fleshy appeal one expects from a merlot-led blend (60%), **17** ⑧⑤ still has a serious side, 12 months in barrel. Ends with a firm grip, but tannins are ripe, wine is accessible, with a future. **Sauvignon Blanc** ★★★ Good typicity, some leafy notes, **19** ⑧②'s main character is piquant fruit, passionfruit, gooseberries, fresh & lively. — CR, CvZ

Location/map/WO: Stellenbosch ▪ Map grid reference: B3 ▪ Est 2018 ▪ 1stB 2017 ▪ Tasting for groups Mon-Sat by appt ▪ Meals by prior arrangement only ▪ Owner(s) Kosie Steenkamp (property); De Bruyn Steenkamp (trademark) ▪ Winemaker(s) Marié Steenkamp (Jul 2019) ▪ Viticulturist(s) Piet Steenkamp (Jan 2001, Groenland) ▪ 36.5ha/33.2ha (cab, merlot, shiraz, chenin, sauv) ▪ 365t/5,000cs own label 60% red 40% white ▪ IPW, WIETA ▪ Friesland Farm, Fischers Rd, Bottelary, Stellenbosch 7600 ▪ debruyn@frieslandwines.com ▪ www.frieslandwines.com ▪ S 33° 54' 29.29" E 018° 44' 29.74" ▪ ⌑ bodysuit.codified.basements ▪ T +27 (0)21-863-0349

Fryer's Cove Vineyards

$(\stackrel{\circ}{\downarrow})$ $(\stackrel{\circ}{\P\P})$ $(\textcircled{6})$ $(\stackrel{\circ}{\triangle})$ $(\stackrel{\circ}{\&})$

It's just over 20 years since this West Coast boutique winery established its Bamboes Bay vineyards, just a stone's throw from the icy Atlantic. It was a pioneering move for Jan 'Ponk' van Zyl and his wine-making brother-in-law Wynand Hamman, since joined as owners by the Laubscher family, one that required many hurdles to be overcome. Crops have been lost due to birds and rot, vines to virus. Despite the difficulties, Wynand is emphatic that they'd undertake it all again: 'We have a passion for what we do'. Reactions then were that they were crazy to plant vines so close to the sea, until people tasted the sauvignon blanc, which became a local benchmark. Today there is respect for what has been achieved, with many wanting to experience the area, and their unique cellar and visitor facilities on the Doring Bay waterfront, first-hand.

Bamboes Bay range

★★★★ **Pinot Noir** Positive varietal cherries & undergrowth on medium-bodied **17** (87). Supple, with balanced acidity, tannin frame. Enough concentration, structure, to assimilate 100% new oak, given time. **15** ★★★☆ (85) was readier on release. No **16**.

★★★★ **Sauvignon Blanc** (②) Vivacious, balanced & tangy **17** ★★★★☆ (91), pungent green herb & passionfruit, gooseberry flavours, creamy undertone & clean citrus farewell. Unoaked, like Doring Bay, but more substance & verve than it & (wooded) Hollebaks. Step up on **16** (89).

Not tasted: **Hollebaksstrandfontein**. Occasional release: **Noble Late Harvest**.

Doring Bay range

★★★★ **Sauvignon Blanc** (✓) Flinty, tropical, dusty appeal on **19** (86). Bright acidity tempered by weight from short time on lees, gram or 2 sugar. Combines quality with quaffability. More weight, succulence than **17** ★★★☆ (85). **18** untasted. Koekenaap grapes, as next.

· ·

Dry Pinot Noir Rosé (NEW) (🍷) ★★★★ Sprightly **19** (85) captures pinot's fruity charm with finesse & balanced freshness. Stylish addition at table or on the summer patio.

· ·

Not tasted: **Shiraz**, **The Jetty Sauvignon Blanc**. — AL

Location: Doring Bay ▪ Map: Olifants River ▪ Map grid reference: A4 ▪ WO: Coastal/Bamboes Bay ▪ Est 1999 ▪ 1stB 2002 ▪ Tasting, sales & cellar tours Mon-Fri 9-5 Sat/Sun 10-5 ▪ Tasting fee, donations for public school ▪ Closed Christian hols ▪ Child friendly ▪ The Jetty restaurant open 10-4, bookings on weekends & pub hols ▪ West Coast walking trail ▪ Craft beer ▪ Owner(s) Jan Ponk Trust, JH Laubscher Family Trust & Wynand Hamman ▪ Cellarmaster(s) Wynand Hamman (Apr 1999) ▪ Winemaker(s) Derick Koegelenberg (Apr 2017) ▪ Viticulturist(s) Jan van Zyl (Apr 1999) ▪ 6ha (pinot, sauv) ▪ 70t/5,000cs own label 20% red 80% white ▪ PO Box 93 Vredendal 8160 ▪ admin@fryerscove.co.za ▪ www.fryerscove.co.za ▪ S 31° 45' 53.1" E 018° 13' 55.8" ▪ 🗺 welded.legendary.complying ▪ **T +27 (0)27-215-1092 (office & tasting)**

☐ **Full Moon** see Alphabetical

☐ **Future Eternal** see L'Avenir Vineyards

Gabriëlskloof   (🍷)(🍴)(📷)(🛏)(♿)

Gabriëlskloof, Bernhard Heyns and partners' Bot River estate, completed its 13th harvest in 2019, the fifth under cellarmaster and Bernhard's son-in-law, Peter-Allan Finlayson, who is enjoying the ongoing new challenges and developments presented. He's delighted with sauvignon blanc in the new amphoras, which provide great texture while maintaining aromatic intensity. Era Cabernet Sauvignon (named after Bernhard's late mother) will inaugurate a new Limited Edition range, the idea being so see how the grape performs solo and ages. The more-favoured cabernet franc will soon be planted in a new 2-ha block. Harvest 2019 saw yields down anything up to 50% but on the up-side, 'leading to wonderfully concentrated wines'.

Landscape Series

★★★★☆ **Cabernet Franc** (🍇) Variety proving its compatibility with Bot River. **17** (94) shows vintage rather than stylistic difference from hedonistic **16** (93). Tighter, with spice, tobacco precision matched by freshness, lively fine tannins. Will grow & prosper.

★★★★☆ **Syrah on Sandstone** (🍇) More energetic, forward of these Syrahs. **17** (94) brims with cool-climate spice, red-fruit concentration, vitality. But there are also silky waves underneath & fine structure allowing current deliciousness to develop. Oak-enhanced, 30% new, as for sibling.

★★★★☆ **Syrah on Shale** (🍇) Quieter of the Landscape pair, **17** ★★★★★ (95) of no less quality. Sense of seamlessness in its deep, dark-fruited weight & breadth, polished grape tannins. There's power without heaviness & savoury length, all boding well for the future. Notch up on **16** (93).

★★★★☆ **Elodie** ⓐ ⓦ Chenin redolent of Swartland old vines. **18** ★★★★★ ⑨⑤ generous aromatic breadth, mouthfilling ripe flavours - baked pear, whiff of honey; added nuance via natural ferment, larger seasoned oak. Tense, mineral core carries deep flavours to great length. **17** ⑨③ included Durbanville fruit.

★★★★☆ **Magdalena** ⓐ Semillon-led **18** ⑨② variety's rich texture braced by just 15% Elgin sauvignon. Still sombre, closed in youth but has concentration, excellent structure, grip to blossom with time, which semillon needs. Larger French oak, all older, adds dimension.

Special Collection

★★★★☆ **Broken Stem Late Harvest** ⓧ Name refers to breaking bunch stems & leaving grapes to desiccate on vine. Naturally made & aged in old oak, **16** ⑨④ semillon is 375 ml of silky opulence, its intense raisin & lemon tang, acid backbone tempering richness of both 14.5% alcohol & 123 g/l RS.

★★★★ **Noble Late Harvest** ⓧ Unoaked **13** ⑧⑦ dessert from semillon with aromatic viognier (partly ex Elgin). Sweetly delicate, fresh & really charming - no great complexity or depth but poised & delightful.

Madame Lucy ★★★★ Méthode cap classique sparkling from chardonnay (54%) with pinot noir. Pleasant red fruit on refreshing **17** ⑧③; briskly dry. Cape South Coast WO.

Estate range

★★★★ **Syrah** ⊘ Flavoursome **17** ⑧⑨ combines youthful pleasure with firm structure. Spice, dark soft berries & hint of truffle, ending on satisfying savoury note. Balanced freshness lifts 14.7% alcohol.

★★★★ **The Blend** ⊘ Cabernet-based **17** ⑧⑥ has dashes cab franc, petit verdot & malbec adding further satisfaction. Fruit richness allows for approachability, refreshing fine tannins ensure potential.

★★★★ **Chenin Blanc** From Swartland, Durbanville & Franschhoek, **19** ⑧⑦ has comfortable styling; added flavour interest from honeyed hint to red apple tones & rounded grip. Spontaneous ferment, portion in older oak. **18** untasted.

★★★★ **Sauvignon Blanc** ⊘ Subtle, quite serious but eminently drinkable **19** ⑧⑧, more about texture (light grainy notes) & weight rather than overt fruit, though there's ripe flavour aplenty with impressive length. Very well-balanced, harmonised for such a young wine.

Rosebud ⓦ ★★★ Charming **19** ⑧② rosé from co-fermented shiraz (51%) & viognier peach & spice fragrance, juicy fresh flavours & food-friendly dryness. Equally attractive aperitif.

Discontinued: **Reserve range**. — AL

Location: Bot River ▪ Map: Walker Bay & Bot River ▪ Map grid reference: C3 ▪ WO: Bot River/Cape South Coast/Western Cape/Swartland ▪ Est 2002 ▪ 1stB 2007 ▪ Tasting & sales Mon-Fri 9–5 Sat 11-3 ▪ Fee R60/6 wines (Estate/Reserve) or R150/6 wines (Landscape/Broken Stem), waived on purchase ▪ Closed Dec 24/25 ▪ Cellar tours by appt ▪ Restaurant ▪ Deli ▪ Child friendly; dogs welcome ▪ Weddings (very limited availability) ▪ Annual market: see website for details ▪ Owner(s) Bernhard Heyns & shareholders Johan Heyns, Wally Clarke, Peter-Allan Finlayson & Nicolene Finlayson ▪ Cellarmaster(s)/winemaker(s) Peter-Allan Finlayson (Jul 2014) ▪ Viticulturist(s) / farm manager Adriaan Davids (2003) ▪ 66ha (cabs s/f, malbec, merlot, mourv, p verdot, pinot, shiraz, chenin, sauv, sem, viog) ▪ IPW, WIETA, WWF-SA Conservation Champion ▪ PO Box 499 Kleinmond 7195 ▪ info@gabrielskloof.co.za ▪ www.gabrielskloof.co.za ▪ S 34° 14' 19.89" E 019° 14' 58.68" ▪ ⫻ paradoxical.roused.reactors ▪ **T** +27 (0)28-284-9865

☐ **Game Reserve** see Rooiberg Winery
☐ **Garajeest** see The Garajeest

Garden Route Wines   ⓧ ⓑ

These vineyards in the Waboomskraal Valley on the Garden Route are a sort of cool-climate outpost (and a less drought-ridden one) of De Krans Wines in Calitzdorp. The grapes, grown at about 600 m above sea level, leave the Outeniqua mountains for the hour's drive to the cellar there for vinification.

★★★★ **Pinot Noir** ⓧ As usual, fresh red-cherry, raspberry aromas & flavours on previewed **17** ⑧⑧ tell of cool origins, as does firm acidity - but fully ripe. Light, silky & properly dry. Only old oak.

Sauvignon Blanc ⊘ ★★★★ Only tasted pre-bottling for some years. Billowing, fruity aromas & ripe flavours, but a fresh acidity makes for an elegant lightness of feel in **19** ⑧⑤. Discontinued: **Shiraz**. — TJ

Location: Calitzdorp-Waboomskraal ▪ Map: Klein Karoo & Garden Route ▪ Map grid reference: C3 B5 ▪ WO: Outeniqua ▪ Est/1stB 2008 ▪ Tasting & sales at De Krans, Calitzdorp (see entry) ▪ Wines also available at Outeniqua Wine Emporium, Waboomskraal on N12 between George & Oudtshoorn ▪ Owner(s) Boets Nel ▪ Cellarmaster(s) Louis van der Riet (2012) ▪ Viticulturist(s) Boets Nel (2008) ▪ 9ha (pinot, sauv) ▪ 80t/±3,000cs own label 50% red 50% white ▪ PO Box 28 Calitzdorp 6660 ▪ dekrans@mweb.co.za ▪ S 33° 50' 57.60" E 022° 21' 20.00" (Waboomskraal) S 33° 32' 6.3" E 021° 41' 9.0" (Calitzdorp) ▪ 🌐 wincing.biweekly. doormats.keyholes.strolling.precise ▪ **T +27 (0)44-213-3314**

☐ **Garden Vineyards** *see* DeMorgenzon
☐ **Gecko Ridge** *see* Thor Vintners
☐ **Generation 8** *see* Bosman Family Vineyards

Genevieve Méthode Cap Classique   ⓥ ⓒ

Brand owner Melissa Nelsen (whose middle name is Genevieve) is extending her palette of champagne-style bubblies, highlighting chardonnay to date, with one made from shiraz. Grapes first harvested in 2019 on recently acquired Klein Botrivier farm will be bottle-fermented for release in a few years' time.

★★★★ **Blanc de Blancs Brut** Extra-dry **15** ⑧⑥ sparkler from chardonnay. Rich honey & stonefruit amplified by creamy texture from 4 years on lees. Perhaps just a touch less fresh, lively than last-tasted **12** ⑧⑦, but generous & engaging.

Not tasted: **Blanc de Blancs Zero Dosage**. — MW

Location: Bot River ▪ Map: Walker Bay & Bot River ▪ Map grid reference: C2 ▪ WO: Overberg ▪ Est 2009 ▪ 1stB 2008 ▪ Tasting by appt ▪ Function venue ▪ Owner(s) Melissa Nelsen ▪ Viticulturist(s) Leon Engelke (2008) ▪ 16t/1,650cs own label 100% MCC ▪ PO Box 122 Elgin 7180 ▪ melissa@genevievemcc.co.za ▪ www.genevieve-mcc.co.za ▪ S 34° 16' 35.95" E 019° 11' 9.19" ▪ 🌐 victors.inductions.member ▪ **T +27 (0)83-302-6562**

Gentleman Spirits   ⓥ

With Swiss partner Urs Gmuer, master distiller Rolf Zeitvogel oversees the crafting of a very fine and handsomely packaged portfolio of husk spirits (and other distillates and liqueurs) for various wine estates. 'The business keeps on growing,' says Florian Leykauf, sales and marketing manager, spurring a move to larger premjses in Somerset West, where tastings are available by arrangement.

Husk Spirit range

★★★★ **Marc de Shiraz** ⓥ Violet & lavender scents, black berries & exotic spice. A smooth, elegant spirit ⑧⑦, with lovely depth & leafy freshness. 43% alcohol, as all these. 500 ml unless noted.

★★★★ **Marc de Zinfandel** ⓥ Balanced, well-integrated spirit ⑧⑦. Wild flowers, dried herbs & warm spice introduce the silky palate & delicate fire. Clean, bright, with subtle nut, mocha & red berry perfume.

★★★★☆ **Zinfandel Distiller's Reserve** ⓥ New distillation ⑨④ every bit as delightful as last, smooth & silky with a long Asian spice finish from 4 years older brandy barrels. Wild berries, cherries, preserved ginger & smoke: satisfying complexity on nose, ample flavours, too. Limited edition of 600 bottles, 750 ml.

In abeyance: **Marc de Merlot, Marc de Zinfandel Noble Late Harvest**. — WB

Location: Somerset West ▪ Map: Helderberg ▪ Map grid reference: E7 ▪ Est/1stB 2012 ▪ Tasting strictly by appt ▪ Owner(s) Urs Gmuer, Rolf Zeitvogel ▪ Master distiller/MD Rolf Zeitvogel ▪ Distillery manager Pierre du Toit ▪ 2,000cs ▪ info@triplethree.co.za ▪ www.triplethree.co.za ▪ S 34° 7' 12.98" E 018° 52' 37.63" ▪ 🌐 chucks.firmly. stick ▪ **T +27 (0)72-218-0123**

☐ **Gentleman's Reserve Boutique Wines** *See Editor's Note*
☐ **Ghost Corner** *see* Cederberg Private Cellar
☐ **Ghost Tree** *see* SylvanVale Vineyards
☐ **Giant Periwinkle** *see* The Giant Periwinkle
☐ **Gilga Wines** *See Editor's Note*
☐ **Glass Collection** *see* Glenelly Estate

Glen Carlou

Not too long after the change of ownership (Hess Family Wine Estates sold to the Pactolus Consortium in late 2016) and the change of cellarmaster (Johnnie Calitz joined from down-the-road Anura earlier that year), the well-established, widely awarded Simonsberg-Paarl winery is getting a new look, with renovations of the visitor centre aiming to improving guest experiences at the popular restaurant, art gallery and tasting facilities. International distribution is growing, with many recent listings on airlines and cruise liners, in particular. Investment in vineyard replanting sees around 5 hectares redeveloped each year. Venturing outside their appellation, The Collection of limited availability, site-specific wines continues to garner praise from critics and the winery's many fans at home and overseas.

Glen Carlou Wines

★★★★ **Cabernet Sauvignon** Freshly cooked blackcurrants & cherries, **18** ⑧⑨ keeps it clean-finishing with grippy tannins & lively acidity, making for ripe wine with delightfully elegant restraint.

★★★★☆ **Gravel Quarry Cabernet Sauvignon** ⓐ Single-vineyard wine made only in standout years. **17** ⑨③ has had the best of everything, with pungent mint, leather & vanilla aromas giving way to dense blackcurrant & cassis. 100% new oak prominent but should settle with time, helped by ripe, silky tannins. No **16**.

★★★★ **Merlot** ⓥ Middleweight, soft **17** ★★★★ ⑧④ followed by big, bold & boisterous **18** ⑧⑥ mixes ripe black plums & cherries with fresh choc-mint centre. 20% new oak adds vanilla at rather warm finish.

★★★★ **Syrah** Inky-black core of ripe dark fruit with strong peppery highlights on **17** ⑧⑧. Bold & confident, delightful oaking (15% American) making presence felt with smoked meats & cloves. Rung above **15** ★★★★ ⑧⑤. **16** untasted.

★★★★ **Grand Classique** ⓥⓐ Like **15** ⑧⑨, a 5-way Bordeaux blend, **16** ★★★★★ ⑨② shows excellent drinkability, mixes elegant black fruit with well-managed oak, tannins & acidity into harmonious mouthful. Plenty of pleasure now & for good few years. Equal cab, malbec, cab franc, ±12% each merlot & petit verdot. Paarl WO, as Cabernet Sauvignon & The Welder.

★★★★ **Chardonnay** Textbook **18** ⑧⑧ shows all the breadth & balance you could wish for. Plentiful ginger crunch & Lemon Cream biscuit notes run through, vibrant citrus acidity leading to a crisp finish. 15 different sites, French barrique ferment, 30% new.

★★★★★ **Quartz Stone Chardonnay** ⓐ Single-vineyard **18** ⑨④ opulent & lavish, as always, yet nicely restrains ripe fruit flavours (oranges, tangerines & mangoes) with excellent balancing new French oak. Small 'egg'-fermented component (10%) gives creamy texture before fragrant notes of marmalade & spice at finish.

★★★★ **The Welder** ⓩ After-dinner treat returns to Natural Sweet in **16** ⑧⑦ after Noble Late Harvest **15** ★★★★☆ ⑧③. All chenin, all sweetness & ethereal beauty, with apricot & nectarine tang. Unoaked. 375 ml.

Unwooded Chardonnay ⓦ ★★★★ Happiness abounds on lively **19** ⑧⑤ 'egg'-fermented wine delivering snappily fresh yellow fruit, bouncy acidity & attractive salinity.

Pinot Noir ⓥ ★★★★ Ripe strawberries & raspberries on **18** ⑧⑤, from fruit harvested after rosé portion. Attractive oak (30% new) adds hints of spice & tar on pleasant everyday sipper. **Pinot Noir Rosé** ⓩ ★★★ Dry subtlety to succulent, strawberry-toned summertime pink. **18** ⑧⑩ charmingly light & tangily juicy. **Sauvignon Blanc** ★★★☆ Pleasing tinned grapefruit aromas on solid **19** ⑧③, good acidity & balanced length from thrice-picked Durbanville vines. Discontinued: **Petit Verdot-Tannat**.

The Glen Carlou Collection

★★★★ **Cabernet Franc** Not discontinued as we thought, plushy & elegant **18** ⑧⑧ manages to carry off hefty 100% new French oak with dense black cherry & plum fruit, stylish tannins & freshening acidity. Needs time to settle & mesh. Stellenbosch fruit, as next.

★★★★ **Merlot** ⓝⓔⓦ Choc-mint notes on ripe **18** ⑧⑨, with plums & plum jam edged by coffee & fragrant vanilla from barrel ferment in 100% new French oak. Clean, zesty finish, nicely balanced.

★★★★ **Petite Sirah** ⓝⓔⓦ Glorious deep purple colour, **17** ⑧⑧ initially shows plenty of charry, smoky oak (100% new) before ripe cooked blackberry fruit takes over, adding hints of coffee & piquant spice. Needs time to settle - interesting times ahead.

★★★★ **Chenin Blanc** Wild fermented from 50 year old Swartland bushvines, **19** ⑧⑨ concentrated cocktail of peaches, apples, ginger & honey. Restrained oak (2nd-fill ferment) adds creamy spice with balancing acidity throughout.

★★★★☆ **Sauvignon Blanc** Signature West Coast dustiness on excellent single-vineyard **19** ⑨⓪, bright grapefruit & kiwi notes given breadth by 3 months on lees, 'egg'-fermented to give layered texture. From untrellised parcel in Groenekloof. Major improvement on last-tasted **17** ★★★★ ⑧③.

★★★★ **Verdelho** (NEW) Exciting version of Portuguese grape, **18** ⑧⑨ mixes lemon sherbet, lime marmalade with salt & spice, all tied up with zippy acidity. Older oak treatment adds to ginger tail. Must try with grilled sardines. Paarl WO.

Not tasted: **Malbec, Mourvèdre, Syrah, Red Blend, Chardonnay, Semillon-Sauvignon Blanc**.

The Haven Collection

★★★★ **Shiraz** ⊘ From younger vines, as all here, **17** ★★★☆ ⑧③ bunch fermented, giving ripe juicy black fruit with faint peppery notes & warm finish. Misses balance of **16** ⑧⑥. Coastal WO, as all these.

Cabernet Sauvignon ★★★ Simple black-fruit **18** ⑧① with warm vanilla, chocolate & jam notes rounding out mid-palate. Mostly for export, as rest. **Chardonnay** ★★★ Orange citrus gives way to toffee & marmalade notes on **19** ⑧②, portion aged in old barrels adds bit of breadth mid-palate. — CM

Location/map: Paarl ▪ Map grid reference: D7 ▪ WO: Simonsberg-Paarl/Paarl/Coastal/Stellenbosch/Swartland/Groenekloof/Cape Town ▪ Est 1985 ▪ 1stB 1988 ▪ Tasting & sales Mon–Fri 9–5 Sat/Sun 10–4 ▪ Fee R50–R150 ▪ Closed Good Fri, Dec 25 & Jan 1 ▪ Cellar tours by appt ▪ Restaurant ▪ Facilities for children ▪ Tour groups ▪ Gifts ▪ Weddings ▪ Conferences ▪ Conservation area ▪ Gallery @ Glen Carlou ▪ Owner(s) Pactolus Consortium (chair Wayne Pitout) ▪ Cellarmaster(s)/winemaker(s) Johnnie Calitz (Oct 2016) ▪ Viticulturist(s) Marius Cloete (2000) ▪ 130ha/68ha (cabs s/f, malbec, mourv, p verdot, pinot, shiraz, chard) ▪ ±700t/100,000cs own label ▪ PO Box 23 Klapmuts 7625 ▪ welcome@glencarlou.co.za ▪ www.glencarlou. co.za ▪ S 33° 48' 44.85" E 018° 54' 12.88" ▪ ⌨ consoled.restorer.swirl ▪ **T +27 (0)21-875-5528**

Glenelly Estate   ⓘ ⑪ ⓘ ⓑ

Bordeaux eminence May-Eliane de Lencquesaing's belief in Cape (Stellenbosch) terroir continues to be vindicated with this edition's two maximum ratings. The formidable Madame bought the prime viticultural Simonsberg Mountain land (then under fruit) in 2003 at the age of 78, bringing with her 250 years of family history in wine (including 30 rejuvenating top growth Château Pichon Longueville, which she sold in 2007 to focus on Glenelly). Viticulturist Heinrich Louw oversaw major vineyard plantings, with Luke O'Cuinneagain ensconced in the state-of-the-art cellar from vintage 2008. Two of May's grandchildren, Nicolas Bureau and Arthur de Lencquesaing, are now involved in her 'adventurous' investment which, after recent refurbishment, includes a bistro, beautifully located tasting room and museum for her personal glass collection.

Lady May range

★★★★★ **Lady May** ⓐ Lavish **14** ★★★★★ ⑨⑤, like **13** ⑨④, cab-based with merlot, cab franc, petit verdot to create complex, cellarworthy flagship. Bold yet lively, cassis & mulberry combine well with graphite, cedar & spices on firm but refined tannins. Natural ferment, as all; new French oak 24 months. Also magnums, as Red.

Estate Reserve range

★★★★★ **Red** ⊘ ⓐ Cab-led (40%) 5-way fusion of Bordeaux varieties with shiraz. **14** ★★★★★ ⑨⑤ reprises ripeness & power (14.5% alcohol) of **13** ⑨④, yet great detailing & precision; generous blueberry, dark plum & blackcurrant, with toasty spice (30% new oak) & savouriness on smooth, polished finish.

★★★★☆ **Chardonnay** ⓐ **18** ⑨④ perhaps best to date. Great intensity, a citrus oil note woven around creamy peach, pear, even apricot fruit. Year in 20% new oak adds subtle almond & vanilla to the finish; fine acidity gives tension to balance the opulence. Will benefit from good few years in bottle.

Glass Collection

★★★★ **Cabernet Sauvignon** ⊘ Vibrant **17** ⑧⑧ showcases mint & blackcurrant, cigarbox from year in oak, judicious ±15% new (as next two). Approachable tannin suggests early drinking but no lack of flavour or seriousness.

★★★★ **Cabernet Franc** Less herbal than previous, **17** (88) has bright fruit notes layered with violets, crushed herbs & tealeaves. Crunchy, medium-bodied, with lingering savoury/spicy farewell.

★★★★ **Merlot** ⊘ Blueberry, cherry & plum fruit notes of **17** (86) laced with cinnamon & dark chocolate from well-integrated wood. Soft & elegant, a lingering berry farewell.

★★★★ **Syrah** ⊘ Delicious varietal expression in **17** (88) given free rein by non-new oaking: mouthwatering savoury mix of white pepper, cinnamon, olive tapenade, plum & salami. Smooth, soft tannins.

★★★★ **Unoaked Chardonnay** Untrammelled by wood, **19** (88) has fruit notes in abundance, including pear, citrus & papaya. Fresh acidity ensures clean citrus-toned finish.— GM

Location/map: Stellenbosch ▪ Map grid reference: F4 ▪ WO: Simonsberg–Stellenbosch ▪ Est/1stB 2003 ▪ Tasting Tue & Wed 10-6 Thu-Sat 10-7 Sun 10-3 ▪ Closed Easter Fri/Sun, Dec 25 & Jan 1 ▪ Cellar tours by appt ▪ Glass museum ▪ Restaurant: lunch Tue-Sun 12-3; dinner Thu-Sat 6.30-8.30 (last order) ▪ Owner(s) May-Eliane de Lencquesaing ▪ Cellarmaster(s) Luke O'Cuinneagain (Jan 2008) ▪ Winemaker(s) Luke O'Cuinneagain (Jan 2008), with Jerome Likwa (Jan 2008) ▪ Viticulturist(s) Heinrich Louw (2003) ▪ 123ha/57ha (cabs s/f, merlot, p verdot, shiraz, chard) ▪ 500t/55,334cs own label 90% red 10% white ▪ PO Box 1079 Stellenbosch 7599 ▪ wine@glenelly.co.za ▪ www.glenellyestate.com ▪ S 33° 55' 6.1" E 018° 52' 45.1" ▪ quiz.ticked.hails ▪ **T +27 (0)21-809-6440**

Glen Heatlie Wines (Ⓟ)

Joan Heatlie has resumed production for her label. But for now at least she's given up a fulltime career as winemaker and is concentrating on qualifying as an accountant. She vinified grenache blanc in 2019 (not available for tasting), and continues to look out for grapes from old vineyards.

Location: Worcester ▪ Est 2006 ▪ Tasting by appt only ▪ Owner(s)/winemaker(s) Joan Heatlie ▪ joan@glenheatlie.co.za ▪ **T +27 (0)82-364-4702**

☐ **Glenrosa Vineyards** see Stettyn Family Vineyards

Glenview Wines

Vintner and surfer Robin Marks continues to do steady online business, locally and abroad, by sourcing wines from coastal vineyards for his own label ('Glen' is a popular beach near Robin's Camps Bay home). His selling point remains quality wines for everyday drinking at affordable prices. None tasted this year.

Location: Cape Town ▪ Est/1stB 1998 ▪ Closed to public ▪ Owner(s) Robin Marks ▪ Winemaker(s) Danie Steytler jnr (consultant) ▪ 14,000cs own label 50% red 50% white ▪ PO Box 32234 Camps Bay 8040 ▪ bayexport@kingsley.co.za ▪ www.glenviewwine.com ▪ **T +27 (0)21-438-1080**

GlenWood

Continuity is a big part of the focus here, in this breathtakingly beautiful Franschhoek Valley setting: 'DP' Burger has been winemaker and viticulturist for 29 years, and the property's Grand Duc chardonnay vineyard is 34 years old. Chardonnay is a core part of the focus, and unusually, has made a Franschhoek reputation. Family-owned since 1984, Alastair Wood, who had worked in the consultancy business, spearheaded conservation, such as the setting aside of 10 ha for the regeneration of Cape fynbos. In addition, he is a supporter of local community projects, including Bhabhathane, to transform the education of 5,500 learners.

Grand Duc range

★★★★☆ **Syrah** (🐝) In contrast to its sibling, **16** (93) all-new French barrels, 24 months, spice here a stronger showing but still in harmony with the fruit, richly textured, layered. Tannins are supple, streamlined, a svelte wine with presence & polish.

★★★★☆ **Chardonnay** (Ⓩ) From low-yielding (3 t/ha) vineyard. Always impressive, & curvaceous **16** (93) continues the enviable track record with beguiling buttered toast & lime preserve flavours. Naturally fermented, then 2 years in new French oak.

★★★★☆ **Semillon-Sauvignon Blanc** (Ⓩ) Light, yet profoundly focused & penetrating **17** (93) from 73% semillon & sauvignon, wild-yeast fermented & aged 12 months 50% new French oak. Flavours of thatch, butterscotch, lime & citrus in a delicious yet serious body.

★★★★☆ **Noblesse** ② Previously NV ⑨, now vintage dated. Enchanting **14** ⑨ from naturally fermented botrytised semillon cosseted in oak, 50% new, 3 years. Pure, balanced, with candied apricot & orange peel. Not as sweet as many (just 92 g/l sugar) & light-footed (13% alcohol). 375 ml.

Vigneron's Selection

★★★★ **Shiraz** Piquant blackberries, sweet-spiced from 18 months French barriques, **17** ⑧ is mainly about fruit, intense & pervading. Succulent, smooth drinkability, earlier than Grand Duc, no hardship.

★★★★☆ **Chardonnay** Bunch press, wild yeast ferment but contrasting style to its sibling, **17** ⑨ barrel aged 12 months, 60% new. Buttered toast, generously spread with lemon/lime preserve; full flavoured, rich, bold & proud of it.

GlenWood range

★★★★ **Merlot** Sprinkle of herbs & mint in **18** ⑧ as a top note, but in a good way. There's ripeness, plush fruit & amenable tannins to ensure a pleasurable experience.

★★★★ **Unwooded Chardonnay** No oak but plenty of care nevertheless: bunch pressed, 5 months on lees, **18** ⑧ offers tropical fruit, zesty-fresh & vibrant. Lovely concentration here.

★★★★ **Sauvignon Blanc-Semillon** ⊘ Unwooded sibling of Grand Duc. **18** ★★★★★ ⑨ almost equal blend, perfect partnership of crunchy-fresh fruit, svelte body, yet palate weight from semillon's 7 months on lees. Arresting purity & focus. Step up on **17** ⑧. — CR

Location/map/WO: Franschhoek ▪ Map grid reference: C2 ▪ Est/1stB 2002 ▪ Tasting & sales Mon-Sun 10-5 ▪ Closed Easter Fri/Sun, Dec 25 & Jan 1 ▪ Tasting R100 ▪ Fine Wine & Food Experience: wine & canapé pairing ▪ Cellar tours daily at 2.35; cellar tour with owner/winemaker available by prior arrangement, min 2 persons ▪ Restaurant ▪ Owner(s) Alastair G Wood ▪ Cellarmaster(s)/viticulturist(s) DP Burger (Apr 1991) ▪ Winemaker(s) Natasha Pretorius (Dec 2018, assistant) ▪ 49ha/30ha (merlot, shiraz, chard, sauv, sem) ▪ 150t/16,000cs own label 50% red 50% white ▪ IPW, WIETA ▪ PO Box 204 Franschhoek 7690 ▪ info@ glenwoodvineyards.co.za ▪ www.glenwoodvineyards.co.za ▪ S 33° 54' 56.7" E 019° 4' 57.0" ▪ ⌂ visited. increment.tapas ▪ **T +27 (0)21-876-2044**

☐ **Glorious** *see* Stellenbosch Family Wines

Goats do Roam Wine Company   ⊚

Fairview's whimsical take on Rhône (and, later, Italian) blends, with a generous dose of satire, ruffled a few French feathers when it was launched in 1998. Today the Goats do Roam brand is distributed widely around the world to appreciative chuckles. The wines themselves are good value, expressive and approachable.

Goats do Roam Red ⊘ ★★★★ Appealingly ripe & cheerful blend (syrah & 5 others), **18** ⑧ follows reliable form with bright berry fruit to the fore. WO W Cape unless noted. **The Goatfather** ⊘ ★★★☆ Sangiovese, the Italian connection here, down to 40%, but blend (with merlot & cab) remains generous & fruit driven in **17** ⑧. Darling WO. **Goats do Roam Rosé** ⊘ ★★★★ Sprightly & characterful **19** ⑧ has leesy texture & weight, appealing red berry fruit. From grenache, shiraz, mourvèdre. **Goats do Roam White** ★★★☆ Authentic Rhône character in **19** ⑧ blend of roussanne, viognier, grenache blanc & marsanne. Good fruit weight, subtle mineral touches. Discontinued: **Goat Roti**. — GdB

Goede Hoop Estate   ⊚ ⑪ ⊚

In the age of instant gratification, 3rd-generation owner Pieter Bestbier and his family want to differentiate themselves by emphasising all that's traditional and unhurried about Goede Hoop, their Bottelary Hills farm, and its wines. 'Our reds are vinified in the same open fermentation 'kuipe' as they were back in 1935, when the stables on the estate were first converted into a cellar,' says Pieter's marketer son Johan. 'That direct link to the past is becoming increasingly rare.' The wines will continue to be styled for the long term, and aged on-site so winelovers can experience the beneficial effect of time, 'an element that makes wine so unique'.

Estate range

★★★★ **Red** ⊘ Was 'Estate Wine'. Age hasn't dimmed the flavours of **12** ⑧ pinotage-led Cape Blend with shiraz, merlot & cab, all individually oak matured, as was blend (12 months in foudre), plus 5 years in bottle. Polished leather & spicy plum, smooth & inviting now & life for a few more years.

PJ Bestbier Méthode Cap Classique Brut ⓥ ★★★ Crisp, dry orange & stonefruit appeal to uncomplicated **12** ⑧⓪ dry sparkler from chardonnay & pinot noir, showing well-judged ripeness. WO W Cape. Not tasted: **White**.

Goede Hoop range

Cabernet Sauvignon ⓥ ★★★★ Velvety smooth & rich Christmas cake fruit on **11** ⑧④, up a level on previous. Taut, spicy & framed by 10% new oak. Refined & persistent. **Merlot** ★★★★ Alluring cocoa & berry on **15** ⑧④, raises bar on previous. Dapper & juicy, with some dry tannic grip. Matured in old oak & bottle (18 & 12 months), but deserves further ageing to show full potential. **Pinotage** ⓥ ★★★★ Ripe prune & berry brightness of **13** ⑧③ checked by grip of tannin from year in older oak. **Shiraz** ★★★★ Emerges from slumber in older oak & lengthy 50 months in bottle savoury, spicy & smooth. **12** ⑧④ more a balanced 'dry red' than 'varietal shiraz' but certainly better than last vintage. **Chardonnay** ⓥ ★★★ Citrus notes on **14** ⑦⑨ are fleshed out by creamy vanilla. Gentle & soft. **Sauvignon Blanc** ★★★ Riper & richer than previous, **19** ⑧① tangy dried yellow peach flavour & creamy texture. Friendly quaffer & light meal mate.

Domaine range

Not tasted: **Merlot, Chenin Blanc**. — MW

Location/map: Stellenbosch ▪ Map grid reference: C3 ▪ WO: Bottelary/Western Cape ▪ Est 1928 ▪ 1stB 1974 ▪ Tasting, sales & cellar tours Mon-Fri 9–4 Sat 10–1 ▪ Closed Easter Fri-Sun, Dec 24/25/26/31 & Jan 1 ▪ Pieter's private cellar: monthly 4-course gourmet meal with wine R480pp (subject to change), booking essential (12 seats only) ▪ MTB trail ▪ Owner(s) Pieter Bestbier ▪ Winemaker(s) Nico Vermeulen (Jan 2019, consultant) ▪ 122ha/71ha (cab, cinsaut, malbec, merlot, ptage, chard, chenin, sauv) ▪ ±600t/10,000cs own label 80% red 20% white & ±200,000L bulk ▪ PO Box 25 Kuils River 7579 ▪ info@goedehoop.co.za ▪ www.goedehoop.co.za ▪ S 33° 54' 32.0" E 018° 45' 14.0" ▪ ⌹ neon.raced.compiled ▪ **T +27 (0)81-283-1618**

☐ **Goederust** see Rooiberg Winery

Goedverwacht Wine Estate ⓥ 🍷 📷

The original Goedverwacht cellar dates from the 1950s, but it's been extensively modernised and enlarged under the ownership of Gabriël du Toit, who in the 1960s turned from civil engineering to realise his dream of growing wine, and latterly under his son Jan and grandson Gawie. The estate now comprises eight Bonnievale farms, and includes a locale on the Breede River bank where visitors can picnic and take in the beautiful valley views. SA's national bird, the Blue Crane, features on the labels, 90% of which are exported.

Maxim range

★★★★ **Cabernet Sauvignon** ⓥ From a single parcel on weathered shale, **15** ⑧⑥ elegant & sleek, modern; for earlier enjoyment courtesy less new oak than previous (40% vs 100%).

Chardonnay ⓥ ★★★★ Previewed **17** ⑧③ has creamy texture from 10 months in mostly older oak but refreshes with lemon-lime flavours, plenty of acidity.

Great Expectations range

Crane Red Merlot ★★★ Time on oak staves (like all these reds) enhances mocha appeal of **18** ⑧⓪, soft & plummy, fresher than last. **Shiraz** ★★★★ Very pleasant **17** ⑧④ with medium body, black fruit, fine tannins, enticing whiffs of violet & white pepper. **Triangle** ⓥ ★★★ Easy-drinking **16** ⑧② has plums, berries & dark chocolate from new oak. Blend of cab with 28% cab franc, 14% merlot. **Shiraz Rosé** ⊘ ★★★ Fresh & fruity **19** ⑧⓪ has strawberries-&-cream, watermelon preserve & maraschino cherry notes, friendly 11.5% alcohol. **Chardonnay** ★★★ Lightly oaked for hint vanilla, creamy texture, **19** ⑧② fresh citrus & pineapple flavours, nice depth, savoury finish. **Crane White Colombar** ★★★ Fresh & just-dry **19** ⑧② is packed with fruit - mostly guava & pear - easy to drink at modest 12% alcohol. **Sauvignon Blanc** ★★★★ Crisply refreshing yet nicely rounded from 2 months on lees, **19** ⑧③ bursts with peach & passionfruit flavours. **Sparkling Rosé Demi-Sec** ★★ Crowd-pleasing fizz **19** ⑦⑥ is carbonated shiraz, candyfloss aroma, tastes like sweet strawberries with black pepper. 11% alcohol. — JG

Location: Bonnievale ▪ Map/WO: Robertson ▪ Map grid reference: C4 ▪ Est 1960s ▪ 1stB 1994 ▪ Tasting, sales & cellar tours Mon-Fri 8.30-4.30 Sat 10-1 ▪ Closed Easter Fri/Sun, Dec 25/26 & Jan 1 ▪ BYO picnic ▪ Tour groups ▪ Conservation area ▪ Owner(s) Jan du Toit & Sons (Pty) Ltd ▪ Winemaker(s) Christiaan van Tonder (Sep 2016) ▪ Viticulturist(s) Jan du Toit, advised by Francois Viljoen ▪ 220ha/150ha (cabs s/f, merlot, p verdot, shiraz, chard, chenin, cbard, sauv) ▪ 3,000t/2.1m L 30% red 65% white 5% rosé ▪ Other export brands: Ama Ulibo, Soek die Geluk ▪ BEE, IPW, WIETA, GlobalGAP ▪ PO Box 128 Bonnievale 6730 ▪ info@goedverwacht.co.za ▪ www. goedverwacht.co.za ▪ S 33° 55' 11.3" E 020° 0' 19.1" ▪ ⅶ cosponsors.specify.violinist ▪ T +27 (0)23-616-3430

☐ **Gôiya** *see* Namaqua Wines
☐ **Golden Kaan** *see* KWV Wines
☐ **Golden Seahorse** *see* Govert Wines
☐ **Goose Wines** *see* The Goose Wines
☐ **Goudini Wines** *see* Daschbosch
☐ **Goue Kalahari** *see* Die Mas van Kakamas
☐ **Gouverneurs** *see* Groot Constantia Estate

Govert Wines

The now Somerset West-based Keuzenkamp family source wines for export from around the Cape winelands for clients and their own labels Baron Diego, Charles Borro, Don King/Morris, Golden Seahorse, Govert Family Wines, Loyal Brothers, Pegalle, Rocco Bay and Ruby Ridge.

Location: Somerset West ▪ Est 2002 ▪ 1stB 2007 ▪ Closed to public ▪ Owner(s) Teuns Keuzenkamp ▪ 180,000cs own label 80% red 5% white 15% rosé ▪ PO Box 1977 Somerset West 7129 ▪ info@govertwines.com ▪ www. govertwines.com ▪ T +27 (0)21-887-5812

☐ **GPS Series** *see* Richard Kershaw Wines

Graça

In Portuguese-inspired packaging since launch in 1983, these hugely successful Distell-owned wines are unabashed crowd pleasers, intended for 'people who live by the three Fs - fun, food and friends'.

Graça ★★ Latest **NV** ⑦⑥ appealing apple sherbet tones, gently sweet farewell. Just ±11% alcohol & with light pétillance, as next. **Rosé** ★★ Packed with strawberry sweetness - aroma, flavour & finish - for easy **NV** ⑦④ enjoyment. — CvZ

Graceland Vineyards ⓠ

Situated in Stellenbosch's 'golden triangle', this boutique family venture has grown steadily in reputation, particularly abroad, with exports to 10 different countries now accounting for 75% of production. Winemaker/viticulturist Susan McNaughton and husband Paul continue to focus on reds from Bordeaux varieties and shiraz, all elegantly packaged with beautiful label art.

★★★★ **Cabernet Sauvignon** Polished **18** ⑧⑨ has velvet tannins, cassis & dark chocolate richness, hints of cedar & tobacco. Drinks well now & for good few years. **17** untasted. These reds naturally fermented, 15-18 months oaked, 20% new French, unfined/filtered unless noted.

★★★★ **Merlot** ⓠ Appealing blueberry fruit, plums & herbs on entry, tight-grained tannins & a sappy farewell; **16** ⑧⑦ is food friendly & buffed after sojourn in 30% new French oak.

★★★★ **Strawberry Fields** Evocative name for 70/30 shiraz & cab blend, indeed shows strawberry redolence (some attractive vanilla-edged jamminess, too) in luscious **17** ⑧⑧, first since **14** ⑧⑧.

Shiraz ★★★★ Epitomises house's fullness & generosity but also shows poise & harmony, **17** ⑧⑤ ripe mulberry fruit, black pepper & baking spice in harmony with 14.7% alcohol & oak. Not tasted: **Colour Field**, **Three Graces**. In abeyance: **Rosé**. — JG

Location/map/WO: Stellenbosch ▪ Map grid reference: E7 ▪ Est/1stB 1998 ▪ Tasting & sales Mon-Fri by appt ▪ Fee R50 ▪ Closed all pub hols ▪ Owner(s) Paul & Susan McNaughton ▪ Cellarmaster(s)/winemaker(s)/ viticulturist(s) Susan McNaughton (2001) ▪ 18ha/10ha (cab, merlot, shiraz) ▪ 55t/8,333cs own label 100% red ▪ Suite 144 Private Bag X4 Die Boord 7613 ▪ graceland@iafrica.com ▪ www.gracelandvineyards.com ▪ S 33° 59' 37.5" E 018° 50' 3.1" ▪ ⅶ nurture.legs.dating ▪ T +27 (0)21-881-3121

Graham Beck ⓠ ⑪ ⓑ

It's 30 years since cellarmaster Pieter Ferreira arrived to inaugurate the first bottlings at Graham Beck — a record that would be hard to match for dedication and achievement in SA (see also his new own-label under his name). Sparkling wine has always been important for the house (and for Pieter, respected as the foremost local bubbly exponent), but it now fulfils the vision of its founder, the late mining magnate Graham Beck, in concentrating entirely on méthode cap classique wines. Substantial investments in the Robertson cellar (and a major vine replanting programme) enable the team, they say, 'to be more precise and meticulous when it comes to quality selection and fractional recovery' in assembling their final blends.

Icon Collection

★★★★☆ **Cuvée Clive** (Ⓐ) The **14** (94) flagship prestige cuvée is the pinnacle of quality, made from 100% chardonnay. Beautifully fine dry mousse & broad, mouthfilling toasty palate from 5 years on the lees (no oaking of base wine), with nutty hints & a lively freshness. Ageworthy. No **13**.

Vintage Collection

★★★★☆ **Pinot Noir Rosé** (Ⓐ) Was 'Brut Rosé'. **14** (93) has presence & verve, great depth of flavour with crushed wild raspberry & cherry fruit, creamy bubbles tinged with savouriness on dry finish from 5 years on the lees. Usual splash (4%) chardonnay, pressed with the pinot, uncommon technique in SA.

★★★★☆ **Blanc de Blancs Brut** (Ⓐ) Tasting pair of vintages - **14** (93) & **15** (94) - highlights great consistency, & stellar quality, the later release showing a little more freshness. 50% of the cuvée aged in 7% new pièce champenoise (205L barrels), 7 months, resulting in gorgeous brioche, roasted nuts, baked apple richness mingling with silky fine mousse. Sparklers with style, finesse & balance. WO Robertson.

★★★★☆ **Brut Zero** (Ⓩ) Unlike all-chardonnay **11** (93), **12** (91) mostly pinot noir (77%), 60 months on lees, no dosage (added sugar) for bone-dry palate, almost austere finish. Taut, mineral & linear, with red berry tang, notably food friendly.

Non-Vintage Collection

★★★★ **Brut Rosé** Light salmon **NV** (88), delicate & complex, pink grapefruit & cherry combining with richer pastry notes, abundant lively bubbles deliver a zingy finish. Pinot noir & chardonnay (58/42).

★★★★ **Brut** Ever-delightful fizz, 57% pinot noir with chardonnay in latest **NV** (87), festive union of fresh orchard & stonefruit, baked biscuits & smooth bubbles. Good texture & mouthfeel from 15-18 months on the lees. Also in 375 ml & magnum.

★★★★ **Bliss Demi Sec** Semi-sweet, but vigorous bubbles give terrific poise, **NV** (88) has ripe strawberry & cream flavours sprinkled with caramelised nuts. From pinot noir & chardonnay (61/39).— WB

Location/map: Robertson ▪ Map grid reference: B6 ▪ WO: Western Cape/Robertson ▪ Est 1983 ▪ 1stB 1991 ▪ Tasting & sales Mon–Fri 9–5 Sat/Sun 10–4 ▪ Cellar tours by appt only ▪ Closed on selected public holidays ▪ Tasting options: Classic R50; Vintage Méthode Cap Classique R75; Deluxe Méthode Cap Classique tasting 'A Glass Act' R125; Proprietors Collection R150/3 wines or R50/wine ▪ Cheese & charcuterie platters on request ▪ Owner(s) Graham Beck Enterprises ▪ Cellarmaster(s) Pieter Ferreira (Aug 1990) ▪ Winemaker(s) Pierre de Klerk (Oct 2010) ▪ Viticulturist(s) Pieter Fouché ▪ Robertson 140ha ▪ 2,450t/140,000cs MCC ▪ ISO 14001, IPW, SABS 1841, WIETA, WWF-SA Conservation Champion ▪ PO Box 724 Robertson 6705 ▪ market@grahambeck.com ▪ www.grahambeck.com ▪ S 33° 48' 14.95" E 019° 48' 1.41" ▪ ⓦ upfront.renaming.inkjet ▪ **T +27 (0)23-626-1214/+27 (0)21-874-1258 (marketing)**

☐ **Grand Domaine** see Le Grand Domaine
☐ **Grand Duc** see GlenWood

Grande Provence Heritage Wine Estate

Owned by a Belgian/Dutch consortium, Grande Provence is located on the immediate outskirts of Franschhoek and is one of the first stops on the popular Wine Tram route. Visitors are instantly aware of the seamlessly sympathetic merging of art, culture and history here. Sculptures dot the beautifully landscaped tasting area, there is a restaurant and art gallery to enjoy but the focus is squarely on the wines, produced from the 22 ha of vineyards and brought-in fruit. Thys Smit oversees production of the main label as well as the Angels Tears range, which has had an enthusiastic following for decades now.

Grande Provence range

★★★★ **Cabernet Sauvignon** Serious & complex **16** (89) improves on **15** ★★★★ (84) with concentration & depth. Backbone of integrated oak (40% new, 2 years) is not too firm, doesn't overwhelm blueberry/ plum fruit vivacity.

★★★★ Shiraz Cheery bright succulence of **17** ⑧⑦ shows medium-bodied appeal & ease. Affable, lithe & supple palate of spicy plum backed by gentle oak, just 30% new. No **16**.

★★★★ Chardonnay Fresh vibrancy counters rich butterscotch, honeyed peach & citrus of **18** ⑧⑨. Generous & broad, but well structured from 40% new French oak, 11 months. Lighter, more restrained than previous.

★★★★☆ Amphora ⑧ **17** ⑨② keeps up textured appeal of **16** ⑨①, from 30+ year chenin & 7.5% muscat d'Alexandrie naturally fermented/matured in clay amphoras. Apple, spice & honey richness riffs off full mouthfeel & light freshness. Refined & enduring.

★★★★☆ White ⑧ Restrained yet complex blend chenin, viognier & chardonnay in **16** ⑨⓪. Vivacious orchard fruit, spice & subtle biscuit from half oaked portion, all older wood. Taut & reined-in. Needs time.

★★★★ Méthode Cap Classique Vintage Reserve Brut ⑧ Tangy lime zip of 50/50 chardonnay & pinot noir on long-gestated **11** ⑧⑥ sparkling. 60 months on lees impart rich biscuit notes yet ample lemon zest vivacity too. No **10**.

Chenin Blanc ★★★ Unfussy pear & quince appeal to gentle, unwooded **18** ⑧②. Acidity balances fruit well. Light & easy. Franschhoek & Stellenbosch grapes. **Sauvignon Blanc ★★★★** Nuanced **18** ⑧⑤ sees Franschhoek fruit used (**17** ⑧⑤ Durbanville & Stellenbosch, **16** ★★★★ ⑧⑦ only Durbanville). Broader palate than previous, with tropical fruit notes & lively acidity. **Méthode Cap Classique Rosé Brut** ⑧ ★★★★ Frothy berry brightness to pink **NV** ⑧④ dry sparkler. Equal chardonnay & pinot noir with 2% pinotage. 15 months on lees in bottle. Not tasted: **Red**, **Méthode Cap Classique Brut**. Discontinued: **Zinfandel**, **Rosé**.

Angels Tears range

Le Chocolat Pinotage ★★★ Promised cocoa edge to vibrant raspberry fruit on **18** ⑧①, lightish body, supple & bright. Small (15%) oak-staved portion adds smoky sheen. WO W Cape, as Rosé. **Merlot-Cabernet Sauvignon ★★★** Near-equal blend gets splash petit verdot in **18** ⑧①, has dark-fruited appeal in easy, approachable style, portion (10%) oak staved for body. **Rosé ★★★** Different varieties (50/50 merlot & cab) but **19** ⑧① retains its juicy plum & cherry dryness & appeal. **Sauvignon Blanc ★★★** Tangy grapefruit simplicity on **19** ⑧⓪, bright & refreshing. Not tasted: **Moscato**. — FM

Location/map: Franschhoek ▪ Map grid reference: C2 ▪ WO: Franschhoek/Western Cape/Coastal/
Stellenbosch ▪ Est 1694 ▪ 1stB 2004 ▪ Tasting & sales Mon-Sun 10–6 (winter) & 10-7 (summer) ▪ Fee R65-
R150/4 wines, R170/food & wine pairing ▪ Group tastings under oak tree in summer and during winter in
cathedral extension of art gallery (seat up to 80 pax) ▪ Cellar & gallery tours Mon-Fri 11 & 3 Sat/Sun by appt
▪ Wine blending sessions by appt ▪ Kiddies grape juice tastings ▪ Picnics ▪ The Restaurant at Grande Provence
▪ The Bistro at Grande Provence ▪ Tour groups ▪ Gift shop ▪ Conferences & weddings ▪ Art gallery ▪ Harvest
festival ▪ The Owner's Cottage & La Provençale Villa in the Vineyard at Grande Provence ▪ On Franschhoek
Wine Tram route, express wine tram tasting option for R65/5 wines ▪ Owner(s) Dutch & Belgium consortium
▪ Winemaker(s) Thys Smit (Jun 2015) ▪ 32ha/22ha (cab, merlot, chard, sauv) ▪ Grande Provence: 80t/7,000cs
own label 50% red 50% white; Angels Tears: 200t/60,000cs own label 30% red 60% white 10% rosé ▪ PO
Box 102 Franschhoek 7690 ▪ reservations@grandeprovence.co.za ▪ www.grandeprovence.co.za ▪ S 33° 53'
57.6'' E 19° 06' 10.5'' ▪ ▥ bowhead.surfaced.mothership ▪ **T +27 (0)21-876-8600**

☐ **Grand Vin de Stellenbosch** see Le Grand Domaine

Grangehurst ⑧ ⌂

There's no guessing where Jeremy Walker's interests lie: nine of his wines are cabernet or blends thereof, pinotage a close second, with six. Owner and cellarmaster of this boutique winery on the lower Helderberg slopes, he's meticulous and won't be hurried - the wines are generally long barrel-aged and released only when he deems them ready. A far cry from the beginnings in 1992 in a converted squash court, the modern cellar is joined by a new 'pavilion' tasting room with lovely vistas. Jeremy's other passion is surfing (False Bay a 15-minute drive away), which is why he blends fellow enthusiasts' wines for the Surfing Vintners charity red, and has a joint venture, Wavescape Wines, with wave-rider and -reporter Steve Pike (see listings).

★★★★☆ Cabernet Sauvignon Reserve ⑧ Everything a mature cab should be: smooth, velvety, beautifully evolved with gentle spice & ripe black fruit. **08** ⑨① textured, refined, bright & fresh, it's at its peak. Includes splash merlot. No **07**. 28 months in wood, rest 22-26 unless noted.

★★★★☆ **The Reward** ⓠ Profits go to cellar team, hence name. 100% cabernet is broad, refined, mature & smooth, brambly hedgerow generosity framed by older French oak, 18 months. **11** ⑨④ statuesque but sexy, drinks beautifully now. In magnum too.

★★★★ **350 Pinotage Reserve** ⓠ Picked 350 years to the day from first harvest at the Cape - 2 Feb 1659, **09** ⑧⑨ pure hedgerow fruit & spice verve with supportive oak from 35 months ageing. Pliable, textured & harmoniously long.

★★★★☆ **Pinotage** ⓠ Shy red fruit & raspberry succulence on a plush palate. **08** ⑨① elegant, with structured body & good length. Splashes cab & merlot in the mix, as is dab (13%) American oak.

★★★★ **Pinotage Reserve** ⓝⓔⓦ Demonstrates cellar's pinotage expertise; **15** ⑧⑧ 30 months older barriques, tannin structure muscular but still accessible, everything else in place, plush fruit, a spice array, great length. 13% cab.

★★★★ **Cabernet Sauvignon-Merlot** ⓠ Cab leads in **08** ⑧⑧ but merlot adds leafy tomato nuance to the reined-in, black fruit compote-packed palate. Svelte & glossy, with cocoa richness lurking. Like **07** ★★★★★ ⑨①, delightfully youthful.

★★★★ **Grangehurst** ⓐ Cab dominates but merlot, petit verdot contribute, giving **09** ★★★★★ ⑨② complexity, perfume & flavour, upping the quality on **08** ⑧⑨. Lead pencils, mulberries, lovely spice array, some scrub. 32 months oaking confirms longevity. Involving, admirable. Also in magnum.

★★★★☆ **Reserve Blend** ⓝⓔⓦ ⓐ Superb cab-dominated red. **15** ⑨⓪ glossy fruit, succulence easily handling oaking 30 months French. Savoury nuances, hints campfire smoke, underbrush (dry & green). Same varieties as 'Grangehurst', cab, petit verdot, merlot, slightly different proportions, here 59/31/10.

★★★★ **Nikela** ⓠ Pliable, plush & rounded **08** ⑧⑨ from near-equal cab & pinotage, dabs shiraz, merlot & mourvèdre. Ripe, & lighter bodied than **07** ★★★★★ ⑨② yet rewarding & smooth.

★★★★ **The Point** ⓠ Confident **14** ⑧⑦ Cape Blend of cab, pinotage & shiraz, basket pressed. Silky smooth, effortless refinement of cassis, spice, plum & reined-in cedar from 18 months French oak.

. . . .

Daylea Red ⓦ ★★★★ Near-equal cab & shiraz, with mourvèdre, **09** ⑧⑤ half wholeberry, 20 months 2nd/3rd fill barrels, & showing the benefit of age. Smoky dark-toned fruit, silky palate, in perfect condition.

. . . .

Cape Rosé Blend ★★★★ Previewed last edition, **17** ⑧④ bright pink & berry-rich, dry, sleek (12.5% alcohol) & fruity-fresh. 5-way blend, mainly cab, pinotage, shiraz, splash chenin. — CR

Location/WO: Stellenbosch ▪ Map: Helderberg ▪ Map grid reference: C1 ▪ Est/1stB 1992 ▪ Tasting & sales Mon-Sat 10–4 Sun/pub hols plse phone to enquire ▪ Tasting R80pp, refundable with purchase ▪ Closed Easter Fri-Mon, Dec 25/26 & Jan 1 ▪ Self-catering guest cottages ▪ Owner(s) Grangehurst Winery (Pty) Ltd ▪ Cellarmaster(s) Jeremy Walker (Jan 1992) ▪ Winemaker(s) Jeremy Walker (Jan 1992), with Gladys Brown (Jan 2002) ▪ ±13ha/6ha own (cab) + 8ha bought in grapes (merlot, p verdot, ptage, shiraz) ▪ 8ot/8,000cs own label 90% red 10% rosé + 2,000cs for clients ▪ Brands for clients: Woolworths ▪ PO Box 206 Stellenbosch 7599 ▪ winery@grangehurst.co.za ▪ www.grangehurst.co.za ▪ S 34° 01' 02.9" E 018° 49' 50.5" ▪ 🖻 centenary.pottery.smudge ▪ **T +27 (0)21-855-3625**

☐ **Granger Bay** *see* Sauvignon Wines
☐ **Grinder** *see* The Grape Grinder
☐ **Great Expectations** *see* Goedverwacht Wine Estate
☐ **Great Five** *see* Stellenview Premium Wines
☐ **Great South African Wine Company** *see* The Great South African Wine Company
☐ **Griffin** *see* Stettyn Family Vineyards
☐ **Grimont** *see* De Krans Wines
☐ **Groblershoop** *see* Orange River Cellars

Groenland ⓠ ⓖ

Stellenbosch's Bottelary Hills, renowned for its reds, is the source of the handsomely packaged, stellar 'Steenkamp' blend, made and named by Piet Steenkamp in celebration of owner, vintner and father Kosie's 45th vintage on family farm Groenland. Both the range flagship and the fleet are available from their cellardoor and redesigned website, with label refreshes planned for most of the wines.

Premium range

★★★★ **Cabernet Sauvignon** ✓ ⊛ Scrub & appealing barnyard notes to rich cassis in polished **17** ★★★★☆ (90) which raises the game on leather-nuanced **16** (87). Complex, with fine tannins for balance, finishes beautifully dry. 75% new French oak, year, for this range.

★★★★ **Merlot** Red fruit compote with mulled-wine spice & vanilla, **17** (88)'s meaty nuance is tempered by oak, the palate weight & depth finely judged, long flavoursome finish. ⊠**Shiraz** Kaleidoscope of exotic spice, cured meat, hedgerow fruit & white pepper, extroverted **17** (89) a wine with personality & balance, appealing savoury farewell. Some American oak, as last.

★★★★☆ **Steenkamp** ⊛ Handsome, sophisticated generational tribute sees equal merlot & cab lavished year all-new oak in **15** (94). Generous blackcurrant flavours framed & restrained by pencil shavings character from oak, fruit in harmony with wood vanilla. Elegant & complex, like **14** (90), but longer finish.

★★★★ **Antoinette Marié** Berry fruit in the foreground of **17** (89), third each merlot, cab & shiraz. Abundant dark flavours coat pliable tannins in elegant support. Hint of sweet coconut balanced by firm texture on **16** (89).

Classic range

Shiraz ⓧ ★★★ Similar to sibling but older oak only. **17** (82) more accessible, too, juicy & food friendly. Also in 1.5, 3 & 5L, as next. **Antoinette Marié** ✓ ★★★★ Shiraz-led (55%) red blend with merlot & splash cab, **17** (85) dark fruited, spicy & succulent, satisfies without the gravitas of its upmarket namesake. **Sauvignon Blanc** ✓ ★★★ Fun-to-drink **18** (81) has herb & greenpepper notes, lemon zip to finish. Not tasted: **Cabernet Sauvignon**.

Landskap range

....

Shiraz-Merlot ✓ ⊛ ★★★ Windmill label motif celebrates the land, family owned almost 90 years. Equal blend **18** (82) an easygoing berry fruit melange with enough grip to take seriously.

Chenin Blanc ★★★ Dew-fresh **19** (79) billows tropical fruit untethered by oak. — DS

Location/map: Stellenbosch ▪ Map grid reference: B3 ▪ WO: Bottelary ▪ Est 1932 ▪ 1stB 1997 ▪ Tasting & sales Mon-Fri 10—4 Sat 10—1 ▪ Fee R30pp ▪ Closed Easter Fri/Sun, Dec 25 & Jan 1 ▪ Cellar tours by appt ▪ Owner(s) Kosie Steenkamp ▪ Winemaker(s) Kosie Steenkamp (Feb 1975), with Piet Steenkamp (Jan 2001) ▪ Viticulturist(s) Piet Steenkamp (Jan 2001) ▪ 192ha/154ha (cab, merlot, ptage, shiraz, chard, chenin, sauv) ▪ 1,500t/±13,000cs own label 75% red 25% white ▪ BEE level 3, IPW, PO Box 4 Kuils River 7579 ▪ steenkamp@groenland.co.za ▪ www.groenland.co.za ▪ S 33° 53' 48.9" E 018° 44' 5.3" ▪ ⬛ standouts.curtails. immaculately ▪ T +27 (0)21-903-8203

☐ **Groenlandberg** *see* Oak Valley Estate

Groot Constantia Estate   ⓧ ⓧ ⊚ ⓧ ⓧ

This year marks a personal milestone for Boela Gerber as he celebrates his 20th vintage as winemaker at this iconic Constantia property, the oldest wine-producing farm in SA. More than the numerous awards the estate has won at home and overseas, he feels his greatest achievement is the fact that during his tenure virus infection has been all but eradicated through a comprehensive replanting programme. For Boela, the effect on the wines has been seismic, and now that his vines are healthy, he is 'branching out and having fun' as he describes it, planting small parcels of different varieties (grenache, viognier, tannat) which he will use to add additional layers of complexity to the wines. All of which is highly appreciated by the many thousands of visitors who flock to the estate each year to enjoy the wine, food and history on offer.

Gouverneurs Reserve range

★★★★☆ **Red** ⊛ Powerful yet refined **16** (94) cab-dominated Bordeaux blend is heady mix of dark-berried fruit (blackcurrants, plums, prunes) well matched with upfront vanilla & toasty oak (73% new French, 14 months). Big tannins, tobacco & leathery notes suggest great ageing potential.

★★★★★ **White** ⊛ Stellar Bordeaux blanc, semillon & sauvignon (75/25) in **17** (95), back on form with medley of flavours alternating ripe peaches & litchis with waxy, herbal notes, nuanced with subtle, spicy oak (100% French, 50% new). Great acidity, long finish, will improve even further. **16** ★★★★★ (92) tad less intense than **15** (95).

Groot Constantia range

★★★★☆ **Cabernet Sauvignon** (Ⓢ) Textbook cool-climate cab in classic, restrained style. **17** (92) balances blackcurrants, cassis with cedar & vanilla (34% new French oak). Tannins are firm but ripe, adding to lengthy finish with freshening herbal notes.

★★★★☆ **Merlot** (Ⓢ) Beautifully elegant **17** (92), straight out of the Right Bank with layers of black plums & cherries joined with dark chocolate & cloves, underpinned by ripe, smooth tannins. All French oak, 35% new.

★★★★ **Pinotage** Steely red fruit (cherry & plum) stands firmly alongside plenty of oak influence (43% new French) adding tobacco & smoke on **17** (87). Ripe tannins give silky texture but wood needs time to resolve.

★★★★☆ **Shiraz** Meaty mouthful packed with peppery smoked charcuterie flavours overlaid with ripe, perfumed black fruit. **17** (92) spicy notes from French oak (25% new) add to dark chocolate core.

★★★★ **Constantia Rood** Solid & reliable drinking pleasure, **17** (87) unites pinotage & 6 others into happy, harmonious whole. 18% new oak adds lovely vanilla note at finish.

★★★★ **Lady of Abundance** (NEW) Aims to reflect vintage character & winemaker creativity, **17** (89) showing plenty of pepper & perfume highlighting elegant red-berried fruit. Near-equal pinotage, shiraz, merlot, smidgen grenache. Mostly older oak, lighter on its feet than the other blends.

★★★★☆ **Chardonnay** (Ⓢ) Exuberant fruit & toasty oak meet & marry in unashamedly New World **18** (93). A broad palate of baked yellow fruit (peach, quince) with cinnamon & toffee from barrel ferment, picks up salty note from lees while zesty acidity carries through to satisfying finish.

★★★★☆ **Sauvignon Blanc** Refined **18** (90), crisp tropical fruit (granadillas, pineapples) with racy acidity rounded out mid-palate by 4 months on lees & 7% semillon adding some richness. Quieter than oak-brushed **17** (94) but no less likeable.

★★★★ **Méthode Cap Classique Brut Rosé** Elegant summer bubbles, now from mostly pinotage with pinot noir & chardonnay. **17** (89) lees time also increased to 18 months, adding delicious savoury/umami notes to crisp cranberry fruit. **16** untasted

★★★★☆ **Grand Constance** (Ⓢ) Dazzling Natural Sweet **16** (94) delivers profusion of perfumed fruit (litchis, grapes, grainy pears) plus exotic spice notes from older oak. Week on skins adds texture & aromatics whilst rich honey-sweetness persists through to endless finish. From red & white muscat de Frontignan. 375 ml.

★★★★ **Cape Ruby** Delicious **17** (86) touriga 'port' improves in concentration & intensity on **16** ★★★☆ (83), with raisins, coffee & delightful violet notes surrounding well-managed alcohol & soft tannins.

Rosé (Ⓡ) ★★★☆ Estate's pink changes from blanc de noir to bone-dry rosé in **18** (84), component varieties make the complete 'Bordeaux blend': cab, merlot, semillon & sauvignon! Delightful floral notes mingle with strawberry & cherry, leading to lipsmacking finish.

Cape Brandy range

★★★★☆ **VSOP** Like previous 6 year old, current 8 year old (90) is 100% potstill from equal sauvignon & pinotage in stylish & modern packaging. Bright pear & soft peach aromas, satin smooth, with great depth of flavour, lingering spicy-sweet plum finish. 375 ml.— CM, WB

Location/WO: Constantia ▪ Map: Cape Peninsula ▪ Map grid reference: B3 ▪ Est 1685 ▪ 1stB 1688 ▪ Tasting & sales daily 9–6 ▪ Visitors Route tasting & tour R115 ▪ Closed Good Fri & Dec 25 ▪ Cellar tours 10-4 on the hour, every hour ▪ Simon's at Groot Constantia Restaurant; Jonkershuis Constantia Restaurant ▪ Facilities for children ▪ Tour groups ▪ Gifts ▪ Conferences ▪ Walks/hikes ▪ Conservation area ▪ Iziko Museum, manor house, historic buildings ▪ Owner(s) Groot Constantia Trust NPC RF ▪ Winemaker(s) Boela Gerber (Jan 2001), with Louise van der Westhuizen ▪ Vineyard manager Floricius Beukes ▪ Viticulturist(s) Andrew Teubes (2009) ▪ 170ha/±90ha (cab, merlot, ptage, pinot, shiraz, chard, muscat, sauv, sem) ▪ 650t/450,000cs ▪ WWF-SA Conservation Champion ▪ Private Bag X1 Constantia 7848 ▪ enquiries@grootconstantia.co.za ▪ www.grootconstantia.co.za ▪ S 34° 1' 37.44" E 018° 25' 27.39" ▪ ///anatomic.doctoral.marigolds ▪ **T +27 (0)21-794-5128**

☐ **Grootdrink** *see* Orange River Cellars
☐ **Groot Eiland** *see* Daschbosch

Groote Post Vineyards Ⓠ ⑪ ⓐ ⓑ ⓒ

It's celebration time at Groote Post, as winemaker Lukas Wentzel completes his 20th year at this family-owned farm in the Darling Hills. But there's no laurel-resting, and already plans are in train for new blocks of pinot noir and chardonnay plus new varieties as yet unrevealed. The launch of the 'Salt' pinnacle range marked a new direction into premium blends, and has been very well-received by customers near and far. On the estate, a rolling programme of events, markets, game drives, bird-watching walks and the ever-popular Hilda's Kitchen restaurant keep visitors coming all year round.

Flagship range

★★★★☆ **Salt of the Earth** Ⓠ Accomplished blend of shiraz & cinsaut (60/40), **15** ㉑ mixes sweet black cherry/berry fruit with delightful perfume, leather & game. Good grip from tannins, helped by 60% new French oak, excellent concentration & balance. Very promising debut.

★★★★ **Seasalter** ⓥ Notch up on last-tasted **15** ㊼, quietly confident **18** ★★★★★ ㉚ from sauvignon & 10% semillon has beautifully integrated green-apple fruit & oak (only 60% of wine wooded, French, 20% new), scintillating acidity & excellent length. Plenty of complexity & excitement to come.

Kapokberg range

★★★★ **Pinot Noir** Ⓠ Fresh & fragrant **15** ㊻, from elevated single block, classic pinot notes of red berries, tealeaves & herbal whiffs. Skilfully oaked (20% new) for long term, would benefit from keeping.

★★★★☆ **Chardonnay** Complex & individual **18** ㉚ ups new-oak component to 70% from 40%, adding toffee, coffee, spices & cream to sturdy apple & stonefruit flavours. Carefully balanced, should develop further.

Discontinued: **Sauvignon Blanc**.

Varietal range

★★★★ **Merlot** Powerful but contained **17** ㊽ handles hefty 14.5% alcohol nicely, wrapping it in layer of ripe blackberries with delicious choc-vanilla notes. Improves on **16** ★★★★☆ ㊺.

★★★★ **Shiraz** ⓥ Cleverly constructed **17** ★★★★★ ㉚ uses 10% American oak (& 25% new oak overall) to good effect, adding cloves, vanilla & charry notes to sweetly ripe red fruit. Classic black pepper finish & great tannins, continuing improvement from **16** ㊾.

★★★★ **Unwooded Chardonnay** Ⓠ Lipsmacking lime marmalade vies with crunchy green apple on **18** ★★★★☆ ㊺. Crisp, lively acidity, touch of warmth at finish, just a shade less thrilling than **17** ㊻.

★★★★ **Riesling** Ⓠ Brilliantly balanced **18** ㊼ treads delicate line between edgy acidity & drop softening sugar (8.7 g/l), both wonderful backdrop to blossoms, litchis & limes. Good potential, & great with food.

★★★★☆ **Sauvignon Blanc** ⓥ Stellar **19** ㉑, multiple concentrated layers of vivid flavour - green beans & peas then peaches, guavas & gooseberries. Has tiny dash residual sugar & all the better for it, adds breadth & interest to mid-palate & lengthy finish.

Pinot Noir Rosé Limited Release ★★★ An explosion of raspberries & strawberries shouts summer sunshine in all directions. **19** ㊷ nicely dry, better intensity than previous. **Chenin Blanc** ★★★ Simple yet attractive **19** ㊶ delivers fresh tropical fruit salad, backed up with zesty, fresh acidity & clean finish. WO W Cape. **Riesling Barrique** Ⓠ ★★★ Unusual **17** ㊷, 35% aged in new 500L acacia wood adding soft texture & smoky toast to slight flavours of lime & lily. Discontinued: **Semillon**.

The Old Man's Blend range

The Old Man's Blend White ⑰ ★★★☆ Happy drinking in **19** ㊸, now only sauvignon & chenin (60/40) but still packed with perky pears, pineapples & peachy fruit. Unwooded. These WO Coastal.

The Old Man's Blend Red Ⓠ ★★★★ Eminently gluggable, always-enjoyable merlot-led 4-way blend, **17** ㊸ delivers juicy black fruit, pepper & spice in spades. The large bottle formats (1.5 & 3L) highly recommended.

Méthode Cap Classique range

Brut Rosé Ⓠ ★★★☆ Pleasing improvement on latest **NV** ㊳ sparkler, delicious red fruit now happily joined by tweak of tealeaf, aniseed & salt. Chardonnay & pinot noir (70/30%), 9 months on lees. — CM

Location: Darling ▪ Map: Durbanville, Philadelphia & Darling ▪ Map grid reference: A3 ▪ WO: Darling/
Coastal/Western Cape ▪ 1stB 1999 ▪ Tasting, sales & cellar tours Mon-Fri 9–4 Sat/Sun & pub hols 10–4 ▪
Fee R25 for groups of 10+ ▪ Closed Good Fri, Dec 25/26 & Jan 1 ▪ Hilda's Kitchen open for lunch Wed-Sun,
booking essential ▪ Facilities for children ▪ Conferences ▪ Walks/hikes ▪ Game drives to be pre-booked; fee
on request ▪ Conservation area & bird hide ▪ Groote Post country market last Sunday of the month Aug-Apr
only ▪ Owner(s) Peter & Nicholas Pentz ▪ Winemaker(s) Lukas Wentzel (Nov 2000) ▪ Viticulturist(s) Jannie
de Clerk (1999), advised by Johan Pienaar ▪ 3,000ha/100ha (cabs s/f, merlot, pinot, shiraz, chard, chenin,
riesling, sauv, sem) ▪ 580t/64,000cs own label ▪ PO Box 103 Darling 7345 ▪ wine@grootepost.com ▪ www.
grootepost.com ▪ S 33° 29' 0.5" E 018° 24' 35.0" ▪ ⟨m⟩ heron.blanketed.saddles ▪ **T +27 (0)22-492-2825**

Groot Parys Estate

Ahead of the trend towards non-interventionist winemaking, Paarl-based Dutch couple Eric Verhaak and
Mariëtte Ras focused on chenin blanc and pinotage, using wild-yeast and skin ferments, and alternative
vessels long before it became fashionable. (By mentoring the Thamae family, with vines southeast of
Maseru, they also helped pioneer winegrowing in Lesotho. The first pinotage, under their Sani Wines label,
was released mid-2019.) The historic Groot Parys estate, which Eric and Mariëtte bought in 2002, is now part
of a larger (retirement) lifestyle project, and though development continues apace, the vines and wines (not
ready for tasting this edition) continue to be nurtured and made as naturally as possible.

Location/map: Paarl ▪ Map grid reference: E5 ▪ Est 1699 ▪ 1stB 1709 ▪ Tasting & sales by appt ▪ Owner(s) Eric
Verhaak & Mariëtte Ras ▪ Viticulturist(s) Donovan Boois ▪ 81ha/22ha (ptage, ruby cab, chard, chenin, cbard) ▪
100t 90% white 10% rosé ▪ PO Box 82 Huguenot 7645 ▪ grootparys@wam.co.za ▪ www.grootparys.co.za ▪ S
33° 44' 48.0" E 018° 58' 41.6" ▪ ⟨m⟩ pressing.official.airbag ▪ **T +27 (0)76-567-8082**

Groot Phesantekraal

Founded in 1698, and in the Brink family since 1897, this successful Durbanville livestock and grain farm
now has 50 ha of vines planted by current owners André and Ronelle Brink. Their boutique wines, made by
Etienne Louw of Altydgedacht, can be paired with hearty fare in the restaurant, a converted ca 1767 stable.

Flagship range

★★★★ **Anna De Koning** ⟨Ⓢ⟩ Best-years pinnacle wine shows fine complexity, baked apple & crème
brûlée on rich texture, creamy oak supports bold fruit, adds hints of spice to lifted finish. **17** ⟨89⟩ from
chenin, barrel-fermented, 10% new French, rung up from last **14** ★★★☆ ⟨83⟩.

Groot Phesantekraal range

★★★★ **Cabernet Sauvignon** ⟨✓⟩ Cedar, cassis, blueberry & vanilla with bright leafiness in **17** ⟨89⟩.
Smooth & harmonious, reined-in tannins with a cool edge. 14 months oaked, 25% new. No **16**.

★★★★ **Berliet** Named for 1927 car owned by André Brink's late father. **17** ⟨88⟩ pinotage is sweet-fruited
& spicy, luscious flavours & silk texture in harmony with oak (13 months, 30% new). Balanced & moreish.

★★★★ **Sauvignon Blanc** ⟨✓⟩ Lovely cool-climate expression of the variety. **19** ⟨86⟩ attractively lean,
with slatey minerality & flavours of gooseberry, greengage & grass, a salty tang to finish.

★★★★ **Méthode Cap Classique Blanc de Blancs** ⟨✓⟩ Chardonnay sparkler **16** ⟨88⟩ spent 15 months
on the lees, resulting in delicious layers of cream, apple cake, buttered toast & cinnamon. Elegant &
refined, a lemon twist on long, dry farewell. Durbanville WO, as Berliet.

. . . .
Chenin Blanc ⟨✓⟩ ⟨🍇⟩ ★★★☆ Unadorned by oak, **19** ⟨85⟩ is a joy to drink. Vibrant tropical fruit flavours
with good palate weight & balance, refreshing finish. Cheerful pricing, too.
. . . .

Phizante Kraal range
Not tasted: **Shiraz.** — WB

Location: Durbanville ▪ Map: Durbanville, Philadelphia & Darling ▪ Map grid reference: D7 ▪ WO: Cape Town/
Durbanville ▪ 1stB 2005 ▪ Tasting & sales Tue-Fri 8-4 Sat 9-2.30 ▪ Fee R50 ▪ Restaurant Tue-Fri b'fast 8-11 lunch
12-3 Sat brunch 9-2.30 ▪ Closed Easter weekend, Dec 25 to early Jan ▪ Owner(s) André & Ronelle Brink ▪
Winemaker(s) Etienne Louw (Jan 2017, Altydgedacht) ▪ Viticulturist(s) André Brink ▪ 50ha (cab, ptage, chenin,
sauv) ▪ 5,100cs own label ▪ PO Box 8 Durbanville 7551 ▪ wines@phesantekraal.co.za ▪ www.grootphesantekraal.
co.za ▪ S 33° 47' 46.73" E 018° 40' 12.96" ▪ ⟨m⟩ calmest.sneezed.obtains ▪ **T +27 (0)21-825-0060**

Group CDV

The initials stand for Cape Dutch Vignerons, a Netherlands-owned business supplying SA wines especially to European supermarkets, packaged locally or at their facilities in France. 'If we can't supply it... it is simply not there!' is the proud claim - bulk wines, buyers own brands, bag-in-box, etc, as well as their own portfolio, with labels such as Klein Centennial, Klein Kasteelberg, Nuwe Wynplaas and the budget range listed here.

Vry Burgher range

Cabernet Sauvignon ★★★ Unfussy everyday drinking. **18** ⑦⑧ displays red cherry & berry fruit, ripe but leanish in effect, with a spicy tail. Previewed, as next. **Dry Red** ⊘ **★★★** Slightly sweet edge to blue- & black-fruited **18** ⑦⑦. Unwooded, light, bright & approachable. — WB, FM

Location: Somerset West ▪ WO: Western Cape ▪ Est/1stB 2006 ▪ Closed to public ▪ Owner(s) Groupe LFE South Africa ▪ Cellarmaster(s) Nicky Versfeld (consultant) ▪ 1.2m cs own label 60% red 35% white 5% rosé ▪ Fairtrade ▪ PO Box 88 Somerset Mall 7137 ▪ rob@groupcdv.co.za ▪ www.groupcdv.co.za ▪ **T +27 (0)21-850-0160**

Grundheim Wines   ⓠ ⓞ ⓑ

Lingering drought has prompted the Grundling family, stalwarts of Klein Karoo grape/winegrowing and distilling, to focus less on the former and more on the latter (though small parcels of older vintages are still available from the cellardoor). Aside from the brandies listed below, they have a burgeoning range of craft gins, and are excited about a rum set to debut around press time.

Brandy range

Boegoe ★★★ Boegoe-infused brandy ⑦⑧ with 35% matured potstill component. Chartreuse colour; minty, wild herbal character. Palate less obviously attractive - but this is intended medicinally, after all (though refreshing with the right mixer). **Gemmer** ⊘ **★★★★** Natural ginger infusion works beautifully with the brandy ⑧③, giving it a rich, sweet charm - there's a herbal element too. Remarkably sippable. 5-year matured potstill component, 35%. **Kuipers** ⊘ **★★★** Blended brandy ⑧⓪, with 5-year-matured 45% potstill component. Deliciously idiosyncratic, with pungent pine & herbs to complement the prune & dried apricot. **Potstill 12 Year Old ★★★★** Charmterfully individual ⑧⑤, with herbal, gingery & sherry-like interest, complexity from the oak maturation. Clean & lively, not lacking smooth refinement, with a nicely dry finish. 40% alcohol vs the others at 43%. These all from chenin. — TJ

Location/WO: Oudtshoorn ▪ Map: Klein Karoo & Garden Route ▪ Map grid reference: B4 ▪ Est/1stB 1995 ▪ Tasting & sales Mon-Fri 9-5 Sat 9-1 ▪ Fee R40pp ▪ Closed Easter Fri/Sun, Dec 25 & Jan 1 ▪ Craft gin distillery ▪ Owner(s) Danie Grundling ▪ Winemaker(s) Dys Grundling (1997) ▪ 25ha (muscadel r/w, ruby cab, tinta, touriga, cbard, hanepoot) ▪ 360t/10,000L own label ▪ PO Box 400 Oudtshoorn 6620 ▪ grundheim@absamail. co.za ▪ www.grundheim.co.za ▪ S 33° 37' 40.1" E 022° 3' 54.6" ▪ ⱳ circulating.copier.reabsorbed ▪ **T +27 (0)44-272-6927/+27 (0)71-657-4851**

Guardian Peak Wines   ⓠ ⓟ ⓞ ⓑ

The more pocket-friendly lifestyle range in the impressive Jean Engelbrecht (Rust en Vrede) stable, targeting restaurant winelists and retail outlets. The cellar and vines on the northern slopes of the Helderberg are annexed to a grill restaurant and venue hosting tastings for the wider range of Engelbrecht wines, all with vistas of Stellenbosch's fabled 'golden triangle' of stellar-quality vineyards.

★★★★ Cabernet Sauvignon ⊘ Refined & appealing entry-level (in the Jean Engelbrecht stable), **18** ⑧⑥ has well-defined fruit, earthy notes & fine tannin backbone. Medium bodied & ready for drinking.

★★★★ Shiraz ⊘ Generous, overtly fruity **18** ⑧⑥ shows blackberries & damson, hints of floral scent, poised tannins. Unpretentious but soundly crafted, the quintessential steakhouse companion.

★★★★ Summit ⓠ Delicious, juicy syrah, mourvèdre, grenache **16** ⑧⑨ gushes red berry aromas, dense spicy compote gets a gentle tannin caress threaded with herbal scrub.

Merlot ★★★★ Sweet black berry fruit with meaty/savoury undertones, gentle tannins, **18** ⑧③ offers sound, honest drinking pleasure. **Sauvignon Blanc ★★★** Pungent khaki bush whiffs on **19** ⑦⑨, prominent acidity best with food. Discontinued: **Lapa Cabernet Sauvignon.** — GdB, CvZ

Location/map: Stellenbosch ▪ Map grid reference: E8 ▪ WO: Western Cape ▪ Est 1997 ▪ 1stB 1998 ▪ Tasting & sales Mon-Sun 9—5 ▪ Various tasting options - fee waived on purchase ▪ Closed Easter Fri/Sun, Dec 25 &

Jan 1 ▪ Guardian Peak Grill ▪ Merchandise available ▪ Owner(s) Jean Engelbrecht ▪ Winemaker(s) Danielle le Roux (Dec 2019), with Ignus Ferreira (Dec 2019), with ±400t/62,000cs own label 90% red 10% white ▪ IPW ▪ PO Box 473 Stellenbosch 7599 ▪ info@guardianpeak.com ▪ www.guardianpeak.com ▪ S 34° 0' 40.19" E 018° 50' 31.99" ▪ ⌨ converses.birdies.complications ▪ T +27 (0)21-881-3899

Guillaumé   ⓟ ⓜ ⓝⒺⓌ

Tongue in cheek, Johan Giliomee equates himself with Huguenot forebear Francois Guillaumé, tasked with starting an 18th-century Cape Colony silk business before becoming a sheep farmer (no wine-land grants apparently available at the time!). Likewise Johan, whose advertising career finally guided him 'home' to the Cape winelands where, farmless but inspired by iconic Bordeaux garagistes (Le Pin, Valandraud), he handcrafts minuscule parcels in his garage in a quest to turn out SA versions of the Left and Right Bank.

★★★★ **Cabernet Sauvignon** Seasoned with drops merlot, cab franc & petit verdot, **17** ⑧⑦ reflects strength of vintage. Stylish aromas of soft black berries, cedary new oak (51%) & sleek build, silky rich flesh framed by well-integrated, fine tannins. Properly dry finish.

Le Phenix ★★★★ Merlot-cab blend with drops cab franc & petit verdot, **17** ⑧⑤ subtle dark fruits spiced with new oak (18%). Worth cellaring 3-5 years, with good structure, balanced grip restraining fresh, concentrated flavours. More finesse than **16** ⑧③, mostly cab (75%) with merlot, cab franc & smidgen petit verdot. Opulent & sweetish from high alcohol (14.9%), contrasting firm tannins, grainy acid. Not for keeping. **Rosé** ★★★ Unusual cab, pinot noir, pinotage combo on peach-hued **18** ⑧② appearance matched by stonefruit flavours, ripe, juicy. Suggestion of sweetness though uncloying. WO W Cape. — AL, CvZ

Location: Cape Town ▪ WO: Stellenbosch/Western Cape ▪ Est 2016 ▪ 1stB 2015 ▪ Tasting by appt only ▪ Owner(s)/winemaker(s) Johan Giliomee ▪ 1t/67cs own label 90% red 10% rosé ▪ giliomee1@icloud.com ▪ **T +27 (0)82-902-4917**

- ☐ **Guinea Fowl** *see* Saxenburg Wine Farm
- ☐ **Guru** *see* Hoopenburg Wines
- ☐ **Gustus** *see* Darling Cellars
- ☐ **Habata** *see* Le Grand Chasseur Estate
- ☐ **Hagelsberg** *see* Middelvlei Estate

Hamilton Russell Vineyards   ⓟ ⓞ

This edition marks 45 years since the founding of this renowned Hemel-en-Aarde Valley estate, and an important milestone not just for the Hamilton Russell family, but also the local history of their longtime focus varieties, Burgundy's greatest grapes, pinot noir and chardonnay. Owner Anthony Hamilton Russell is hoping for a slightly larger vintage this year, after the loss of more than 10% of the pinot noir due to a wildfire which tore through the valley just before the 2019 harvest. His American pinot noir venture has proved to be very exciting, and efforts going forward will be focused on the famous Zena Crown vineyards in Oregon's Willamette Valley, which Anthony feels best reflect the HRV style of refinement, structure and minerality. All being well, winemaker Emul Ross will release the first small parcel of wines this year.

★★★★☆ **Pinot Noir** ⓐ Picture-perfect pinot, **18** ⑨③ ticks all the boxes, combines layers of red berry fruit, exotic spices, warm earth & fresh leaves. Beautifully integrated oak (35% new) highlights velvety, supportive tannins while 10% wholebunch adds sappy twist at finish. These also in magnum.

★★★★☆ **Chardonnay** ⓐ Complex & deep, **18** ★★★★★ ⑨⑤ over-delivers with lovely honeysuckle, stonefruit & citrus notes perfectly paired with immaculate oaking (21% new, 5% of wine unwooded). Pithy texture & creamy mouthfeel satisfy through to last mouthful. A little more new wood on **17** ⑨③. — CM

Location: Hermanus ▪ Map: Walker Bay & Bot River ▪ Map grid reference: B4 ▪ WO: Hemel-en-Aarde Valley ▪ Est 1975 ▪ 1stB 1981 ▪ Tasting & sales Mon-Fri 9–5 Sat 10–2 ▪ Closed Easter Fri/Mon, Dec 25/26 & Jan 1 ▪ Tours by appt ▪ Fynbos reserve & 2 wetlands ▪ Owner(s) Anthony Hamilton Russell ▪ Winemaker(s) Emul Ross (2014) ▪ Viticulturist(s) Johan Montgomery (2005) ▪ 170ha/52ha (pinot, chard) ▪ 12,900cs own label 50% red 50% white ▪ WWF-SA Conservation Champion ▪ PO Box 158 Hermanus 7200 ▪ info@hamiltonrussellvineyards.com ▪ www.hamiltonrussellvineyards.com ▪ S 34° 23' 23.0" E 019° 14' 30.6" ▪ ⌨ uncork.weathermen. exception ▪ **T +27 (0)28-312-3595**

Hannay Wines

The Hannay winery in Elgin has 'settled into a smooth-running facility' as a custom crush centre — providing working space for some leading winemakers of the area (and beyond). It is, of course, where winemaking consultants Richard Kershaw and Dudley Wilson craft the cool-climate, site-specific wines of Hannay brand owner Malcolm Dicey.

★★★★ **Cabernet Franc** ⓥ Dark fruit & dry leaf on **16** ⑧⑨. Oak supportive (10% new), but lightish palate a touch tannic & powerful for the flavour intensity. 14.7% alcohol adds sweet note to the dry finish.

Not tasted: **Chardonnay**, **Sauvignon Blanc**. — TJ

Location/map/WO: Elgin ▪ Map grid reference: B2 ▪ Est/1stB 2011 ▪ Tasting, sales & cellar tours by appt ▪ Fee R100 for groups of 10+ ▪ BYO picnic ▪ Light/buffet lunches by appt only ▪ Owner(s) Malcolm J Dicey ▪ Winemaker(s) Richard Kershaw (2012, consultant) & Dudley Wilson (2016, consultant) ▪ Viticulturist(s) Kevin Watt (2012, consultant) ▪ 72ha/11.3ha under vine ▪ 220t majority custom crush ▪ 50% red 50% white ▪ IPW, SIZA, WIETA ▪ PO Box 36 Elgin 7180 ▪ winemaker@hannaywines.co.za, elzaan@valleygreen.co.za ▪ www.hannay.co.za ▪ S 34° 12' 12.07" E 19° 02' 35.10" ▪ Ⓦ rebranded.bareness.goal ▪ **T +27 (0)21-848-9770/+27 (0)71-676-9588**

☐ **Harold's Cape Knight** *see* M'hudi Wines

Hartenberg Estate

The Mackenzie family, owners since 1987 of this friendly Bottelary Hills estate, and Carl Schultz, winemaker and latterly cellarmaster for nearly 30 years, have quietly carved a place in the industry's upper echelon. Championing SA shiraz, they offer varietal and blended versions across the quality and price spectrum, premium bottlings earning consistent local and international praise. A Bordeaux-style red, chardonnay and riesling (a Carl soft spot) are also standouts. Special wines honour special people in the farm's history (late patriarch Ken aka The Stork, his wife The Megan, and matriarch of the prolific Finlayson dynasty of wine-growers once resident here, The Eleanor). A strong focus on sustainability includes exploring indigenous cover crops, conserving a 65-ha wetland and recycling 100% of their wastewater.

Ultra Premium range

★★★★☆ **Gravel Hill Shiraz** ⓐ Estate's delicious & multifaceted flagship from parcel of poor, gravelly soil. **15** ⑨④ has compact core of dark plum, mulberry & olive tapenade, poised tannin structure, great refinement & savouriness; 19 months oak, 90% new. Built to last at least a decade. Magnums too.

Super Premium range

★★★★★ **The Stork** ⓐ Shiraz off deep, clay-rich loam soil. **16** ⑨③ is superb, savoury, with layers of aromatic blackcurrant & plum laced with spice & white pepper. Effortlessly assimilates all-new wood, giving substantial but malleable structure, tannins very smooth. Hard to resist now, but good for many years.

★★★★★ **The Mackenzie** ⓐ Blend always cab-driven, with merlot, petit verdot & malbec (72/19/7/2). **16** ⑨③ a bold dark-fruit expression includes blackcurrant, plum & cherry with graphite mineral notes, faint herb nuance on the lingering finish. Also in magnum.

★★★★ **The Megan** Rhône is the template, shiraz, mourvèdre & grenache the materials (85/12/3). Smooth & refined, with fruitcake richness & shake of spice & pepper. **16** ⑧⑧ has carefully judged oak, 92% new for 18 months, ensuring balance, charm & a savoury note at the end.

★★★★★ **The Eleanor** ⓐ From best-performing chardonnay parcel of Burgundy CY95 clone. Steely **17** ⑨③ citrus-infused, with yellow peach & quince notes playing off the stony mineral element & adding complexity. Bright acidity keeps palate balanced, as does moderate 13.5% alcohol. Fine length & finish.

CWG Auction Reserves

★★★★★ **Shiraz** ⓐ A lavish, easy-to-love marriage of The Stork & Gravel Hill parcels. **16** ⑨③ has ample dark & red berries fused with oak spice & lavender aromas, leading to violets & pepper. Full body, tense & bright, featuring a core of fine-grained tannins. Follows exceptional, harmonious **15** ★★★★★ ⑨⑤.

Premium range

★★★★☆ **Cabernet Sauvignon** ⓐ Classic varietal expression on **17** ⑨⓪. Vibrant dark-fruit whiffs interwoven with cedarwood spice & tobacco, dense tannins from 19 months in oak, 50% new. Delicious now if you decant but cellaring will reward. Magnums available, as for Merlot & Shiraz.

★★★★☆ **Merlot** Rhubarb & dark chocolate whiffs envelop deep-piled raspberry, cherry & plum fruit in **17** (92). Harmonious tannins buffed 20 months in oak, 40% new, give balance & spice undertones. More complex, satisfying than **16** ★★★☆ (85).

★★★★ **Shiraz** A racy style, buoyed by a refined structure, presenting perfumed cherry & mulberry with hints of bay, white pepper & salami. **17** (88) ends on a lingering savoury note. Tempting now, but no rush.

★★★★ **Chardonnay** Well-judged oak (14% new) ensures unhindered expression of bright fruit in **18** (88) - bags of peaches, pears & apple with lemon meringue topping. Alluring vanilla in the persistent length.

★★★★ **Riesling** Bone-dry **18** (86) features the usual touch of botrytis, giving honey & orange marma-lade notes which later reveal fragrant lime, granadilla & litchi. 6 months on lees, as previous.

Cabernet Sauvignon-Shiraz ⑦ ★★★★ Near-equal blend in **17** (85), offering profusion of dark berries, spice & savoury notes, soft, smooth tannins to enjoy by the braai. Magnums, too, for extra conviviality.

Doorkeeper Shiraz ★★★☆ From younger vines, for earlier drinking. Vivacious red & dark fruit in **17** (83). Elegant, with smooth tannins, light oaking (older barrels for 12 months), spicy finish. **Sauvignon Blanc** ★★★☆ Interesting combo of ripe tropical fruit, dried herbs & grassy notes as a result of **18** (84)'s grapes picked at different ripeness levels. Crisp acidity & pleasing light feel. Occasional release: **Occasional Chardonnay, Occasional Riesling.** — GM

Location/map/WO: Stellenbosch ▪ Map grid reference: C4 ▪ Est/1stB 1978 ▪ Tasting & sales Mon-Fri 9-5 Sat 9-4 Sun 10-4 ▪ Closed Good Fri, Dec 25 & Jan 1 ▪ Tasting fee refunded with purchase ▪ Cellar tours by appt ▪ Picnics & lunches 12-3 Tue-Sun (summer); lazy lunches Wed-Sun (winter) ▪ Light snacks, charcuterie & cheese platters served throughout the day ▪ Facilities for children ▪ Walks/hikes ▪ Bird watching ▪ Bottelary Renosterveld Conservancy ▪ Owner(s) Hartenberg Holdings ▪ Cellarmaster(s) Carl Schultz (Nov 1993) ▪ Winemaker(s) Patrick Ngamane (Jan 2001), with Oscar Robyn (Nov 2003) ▪ Viticulturist(s) Wilhelm Joubert (May 2006) ▪ 187ha/85ha (cab, merlot, shiraz, chard, riesling, sauv) ▪ 550t/60,000c own label 80% red 20% white ▪ IPW ▪ PO Box 12756 Die Boord 7613 ▪ info@hartenbergestate.com ▪ www.hartenbergestate.com ▪ S 33°53' 52.5" E 018°47' 30.4" ▪ 🖳 uptake.website.showdown ▪ **T +27 (0)21-865-2541**

☐ **Hartswater** *see* Orange River Cellars

Haskell Vineyards   ⑨ ⑪ ⓐ ⓐ ⓑ

There have been a few changes over the past year at this 25-ha Helderberg mountainside property, owned since 2002 by American-born international real estate magnate Preston Haskell IV. Rianie Strydom, winemaker since 2005, officially handed over to Rudolph Steenkamp, who also looks after the 14 ha of vines. These are now being converted to organic, official certification expected three years hence. A move to trim the single-site shiraz range will see the best blocks channelled into Pillars, ultimately the one remaining label. 'It's hard to sell three premium shirazes,' Rudolph explains. The Dombeya sibling will also benefit from some of that fruit. Of his first solo vintage, Rudolph says: '2019 in my book is a white-wine year, with some amazing flavours in sauvignon blanc and chardonnay.'

Haskell range

★★★★☆ **Aeon Syrah** ⑨ This now one of a pair of syrahs from different sites to showcase differences. Expressive red berries in **14** (92), svelte & streamlined till the end, when the firm dry finish reminds you the wine is built to last.

★★★★☆ **Pillars Syrah** ⑨ Range flagship, **14** (92) similar oaking to Aeon but open fermenters, long skin contact, natural yeast. Most textbook of the 3 shirazes, wild dark berries, scrub, cloves & pepper. Sleek & compact, enough fine-grained tannins for ageing.

★★★★☆ **Haskell IV** Cabernet-based Bordeaux blend, merlot adding flesh to still youthfully firm **14** (91). There's power in its ripe flavours, zesty acid, also attractive spicing from drops cab franc, petit verdot & new oak. Should benefit from further few years.

★★★★☆ **Haskell II** ⑨ Syrah & cab an underrated combination in SA, 60/40 in **14** (90) illustrates its merit both in accessibility & ageworthiness. Syrah's suave dark-fruited richness leads, companion cab providing necessary tannin restraint. Partners in pleasure now & for future.

★★★★☆ **Anvil Chardonnay** From 30 year old vineyard, **18** ⑨ is composed, with nutty interest backed by creamy lees, firm acid. Lacks some complexity, length of **17** ★★★★★ ⑨ but should offer characterful drinking once sweet vanilla note from oak (35% new) harmonises.

Discontinued: **Hades Syrah**.

Dombeya range

★★★★ **Fenix Cabernet Sauvignon** Ⓥ Strength of vintage evident in **15** ⑧; rich blackberry, cedar-spiced layers, firm yet unforbidding build. Freshness, & juicy ripe tannins enhance current accessibility, promote future promise. 18 months French oak, 20% new.

★★★★ **Merlot** Firm structure, deep, rich flavours reflect strength of vintage **17** ⑧. More serious, ageworthy than **16** ⑧, which ready sooner, though has balance for current enjoyment. 30% new oak.

★★★★ **Boulder Road Shiraz** Ⓥ Silky & fresh, **15** ⑧'s comfortable grip, pure peppery & dark berry flavours provide ready satisfaction. Ripe yet unheavy & dry make this a versatile food partner.

★★★★ **Chardonnay** Quieter than previous, **18** ⑧ more nutty, tropical restraint than pronounced limy zest. Interest lies in texture: creamy lees freshened by clean acid, allowing for current & future pleasure.

Sauvignon Blanc ★★★★ Ex-tank **19** ⑧ offers usual herby, tropical tones. Keen acid tempered by lees ageing, small oaked portion. — AL

Location/map/WO: Stellenbosch ▪ Map grid reference: F8 ▪ Est 2002 ▪ 1stB 2008 ▪ Tasting & sales Tue-Fri 9–5 Sat/Sun & pub hols 10-5 ▪ Tasting fee applies ▪ Closed Mon, Easter Fri/Mon, Dec 25 & Jan 1 ▪ Cellar tours on special request only ▪ Facilities for children ▪ Long Table Restaurant Tue-Sun 11.30-6 ▪ Picnics (Oct-Mar), booking essential ▪ Self-catering accommodation in The Residence and Cottage ▪ Owner(s) Preston Haskell ▪ Winemaker(s)/viticulturist(s) Rudolph Steenkamp (Oct 2018) ▪ 25ha/14ha (cabs s/f, merlot, shiraz, chard) ▪ ±80t/3,600cs own label 80% red 20% white ▪ PO Box 12766 Die Boord 7613 ▪ info@haskellvineyards.com ▪ www.haskellvineyards.com ▪ S 34° 0' 13.9" E 018° 51' 38.4" ▪ ⦿ lampshades.toughening.wheat ▪ **T +27 (0)21-881-3895**

Haute Cabrière   Ⓟ Ⓜ Ⓖ

Established in the early 1980s by Achim and Hildegard von Arnim, Haute Cabrière has 2nd-generation Takuan building on the family legacy of Burgundy-inspired chardonnay and pinot noir specialisation. The Haute Cabrière range (including Achim's trailblazing blush) introduces a dry rosé. Taking quality up a notch is the new small-batch Haute Collection, featuring trendy amphora vinification. The Pierre Jourdan label, reflecting traditional Champagne winemaking, adds a rare sweetish bottle-fermented bubbly. They're all grist to the mill of the wine-and-food pairing menu (one of SA's first) in the refurbished restaurant, recessed into Middagkrans Mountain overlooking Franschhoek, offering views quite as mouthwatering.

The Haute Collection Ⓝⓔⓦ

★★★★☆ **Pinot Noir** Ⓥ Floral-tinged raspberries, earthy spices & strawberry compote feature on elegantly proportioned **17** ⑨. Svelte & fragrant, shows considerable style. 15% wholebunch ferment, 11 months in 40% new French oak. Ex registered single-vineyard & Franschhoek WO, as all these.

★★★★☆ **Chardonnay** Ⓐ Very impressive **17** ⑨ debut from 1983 vines, showing exceptional depth, weight & texture. Restrained oaking, together with clay amphora component, add subtle spiciness & nuance. Promises bright future.

★★★★☆ **Amphora Chardonnay** Brilliant **17** ⑨, unwooded but matured, as name suggests, in 450L terracotta vessel. Noble varietal expression, with fine fruit purity, sleek texture, concentrated citrus on finish. Minuscule 28-case production.

Haute Cabrière range

★★★★ **Pinot Noir Réserve** Ⓥ Floral aromas with herbaceous & earthy highlights in smoothly subtle **16** ⑧, showing ripe raspberry & rose hip fruit. 11 months in Burgundian oak, 33% new. Step up from **15** ⑧. WO Franschhoek. Also in magnum.

★★★★ **Chardonnay-Pinot Noir** Ⓥ Very pale **19** ⑧ dry rosé is 78% chardonnay, offering satisfyingly full & generous body, bright peachy fruit, velvet texture, nice salty twist on finish. A pioneer of this trendy style. In magnum too.

Unwooded Pinot Noir ⊘ 🏵 ★★★★ Remarkably well-priced **19** (83) a big improvement on last, with floral-scented accents on cheerful red berry fruit. Serve slightly chilled.

Pinot Noir Rosé (NEW) ★★★★ Light & dry, upbeat **19** (84) has strawberry fruit & hints of varietal floral perfume. Perfect summer sipper. Discontinued: **Chardonnay Reserve**.

Pierre Jourdan range

★★★★ **Belle Rose** ⊘ Competent **NV** (87) dry rosé MCC sparkler, mostly pinot noir with a dash of chardonnay, has a creamy mousse, grippy acidity & a red berry undercurrent.

★★★★★ **Blanc de Blancs** Silky smooth, rich & elegant **NV** (90) MCC sparkling spent a remarkable 9 years on lees. Chardonnay, 40% barrel matured, shows fine citrus & shortbread notes on gentle but persistent mousse, focused lingering finish.

★★★★ **Brut** ⊘ Dependable, appealing & pocket-pleasing **NV** (86) MCC, brisk bubbles & refreshing green-apple fruit tang. Chardonnay with 11% pinot noir from Robertson & Franschhoek.

★★★★ **Ratafia** Named for Champagne's traditional fortified unfermented grape juice, chardonnay-based aperitif/dessert is now vintage-dated (**18** (86)) & a delightfully fruity winter warmer. 375 ml.

Tranquille ⊘ ★★★★ Pretty onion-skin-hued **NV** (85) dry rosé from pinot noir & chardonnay has scented lime & strawberry fruit, creamy texture. 1.5L also available, as Belle Rose & Brut. **Belle Nectar** (NEW) ★★★★ Semi-sweet (37 g/l sugar) **NV** (84) rosé MCC is frothy & approachable. From Robertson chardonnay & splash pinot noir, year on lees. — GdB

Location/map: Franschhoek ▪ Map grid reference: C1 ▪ WO: Western Cape/Franschhoek ▪ Est 1982 ▪ 1stB 1984 ▪ Tasting & sales Mon-Sat & pub hols 8-8 Sun 8-4 ▪ Cellar tours Mon-Sat at 11; private tasting/tour to be pre-booked ▪ Haute Cabrière Restaurant ▪ Owner(s) Clos Cabrière (Pty) Ltd ▪ Cellarmaster(s) Takuan von Arnim (2005), with Tim Hoek (Dec 2014) ▪ Viticulturist(s) Tim Hoek (Dec 2014) ▪ 30ha (pinot, chard) ▪ 40% red 60% white ▪ PO Box 245 Franschhoek 7690 ▪ info@cabriere.co.za ▪ www.cabriere.co.za, www.pierrejourdan.co.za ▪ S 33° 54' 51.8" E 019° 8' 8.2" ▪ 🅦 contingent.chairlifts.bushy ▪ **T +27 (0)21-876-8500**

Haut Espoir   🍷 📷 ♿

Environmental awareness is at the heart of all aspects of this family-owned farm in the Franschhoek Conservancy (where catch-and-releasing protected puff adders makes an interesting addition to the daily routine!) Biodynamic principles and practices are followed, and viticulturist and co-owner Rob Armstrong firmly believes they have a positive effect on his vines and Marozanne Bieldt's wines. The popular fynbos walks and wetland trail pass through stunning mountain scenery.

★★★★ **Cabernet Sauvignon** Fruity aromas of **12** ★★★★ (85) followed by dense blackberries with stalky edge from 80% wholebunch ferment, 43 months in old oak leave drier tannins than last **10** (86).

★★★★ **Shiraz** ⓥ Plenty of dried fruit, leather, earthy notes & touch portiness, **12** (86) carries off hefty 15.4% alcohol with style. Lovely tannin integration & really delicious red fruit/vanilla combo at finish. Steps up on **11** ★★★★ (85) but is ready, needs broaching soon.

★★★★ **Gentle Giant** ⓥ Mainly merlot with petit verdot & cab, **14** (89) delivers complex mix of ripe blackcurrant, dried herbs, liquorice & toffee. 2 years old oak give supple tannins & coffee hints before ripe red-fruit finish. No **13**.

★★★★ **Chardonnay** On an upward curve of quality, **18** ★★★★★ (90) shines with ample bright citrus melded with beautifully reined-in older oak, creating overall fresher, more appealing style than **17** (86). Lively acidity with nutty crisp finish.

★★★★ **Semillon** Step up for **18** (87), showing attractive balance of creamy yellow fruit, warm spice & fresh garden herbs. 15 months in old oak add richness, balancing out lively acidity. Good improvement in freshness & appeal from **17** ★★★★ (85).

Shiraz Rosé ⓥ ★★★ Rich & quite serious, gaining weight from barrel ageing & warm alcohol, balancing acid brings it all together. Enjoy **17** (81) with charcuterie or terrines. **Cloudfall** ⓥ ★★★★ 5-way blend led by sauvignon & semillon. **16** (84) brush of oak lets luscious stonefruit prevail, with balancing citrus edge, greengage freshness & creamy mouthfeel. Discontinued: **Cabernet Franc**, **White Port**. — CM

Location/map/WO: Franschhoek ▪ Map grid reference: D1 ▪ Est 1999 ▪ 1stB 2004 ▪ Tasting & sales Mon-Fri 11-4 Sat/Sun by appt ▪ Closed all pub hols ▪ Cellar tours by appt ▪ Fynbos walks by appt ▪ Wetland trail ▪

Conservation area ▪ Craft beer & gin ▪ Owner(s) Armstrong family ▪ Winemaker(s) Marozanne Bieldt, with Bradley Ewerts (Jan 2018) ▪ Viticulturist(s) Rob Armstrong ▪ ±23ha/12ha (cab, merlot, p verdot, shiraz) ▪ 50t/7,000cs own label 60% red 40% white ▪ PO Box 681 Franschhoek 7690 ▪ wine@hautespoir.com ▪ www. hautespoir.com ▪ S 33° 56′ 23.6″ E 019° 6′ 20.9″ ▪ ▥ feed.honed.strolling ▪ T +27 (0)21-876-4000

Havana Hills ⓠ

These eminently drinkable wines bear testimony to not only a state-of-the-art cellar but also a successful farming conversion from wheat to wine in the late 1990s. The home farm, in the Philadelphia ward north of Cape Town, has ancient shale soils, many south-facing slopes, and is cooled by the Atlantic some 8 km distant. Owner Xinxing Pang's investments are bearing fine fruit, and new canopy management techniques are being applied to ensure that they continue to do so. A Natural Sweet and MCC sparkling are on the way.

Kobus range

★★★★☆ **Red** More cab (53%), with merlot (38%) & cab franc in **16** ⑨¹, showing both modern & classic styling. Balanced, savoury & svelte, with oaking (80% new French) in sync. Already tempts, but credentials to age. WO W Cape.

Occasional release: **Chardonnay**.

Havana Hills range

★★★★ **Cabernet Sauvignon** ⊘ Same savoury, dark-fruited profile, though all-older oak & riper vintage render **16** ⑧⑦ more balanced & flavoursome than **15** ⑧⑥. Approachable, but will develop nicely.

★★★★ **Shiraz Reserve** ⒩ⒺⓌ All-new oak (French & American) lavished on **16** ⑧⑥, giving sweet coconut & white pepper impression. Dry chalky tannins need time to meld & allow fruit to shine.

Merlot ⓦ ★★★★ Unoaked, fresh-faced **16** ⑧⑤ continues in juicy, supple style. Showcases merlot's red berry appeal, clean dry farewell.

Sangiovese ★★★ Similar friendly styling for both vintages tasted this edition, though unoaked **15** ⑧¹ shows more earthy tobacco flavours than slightly fresher, brighter **16** ⑧², which had 12 months old wood. Equally pleasant solo or as antipasto partner. **Shiraz** ★★★★ Style change from richly fruited (& new wood) in **15** ★★★★ ⑧⑨ to unknit & old-oaked **16** ⑧³. Chunky ripe fruit jostles with dry chalky tannins. A barbecue would resolve. Occasional release: **Pinot Noir**, **Cabernet Sauvignon-Barbera**, **Chardonnay-Pinot Noir**, **Sauvignon Blanc Sparkling**. In abeyance: **Sauvignon Blanc**.

Lime Road range

Cabernet Sauvignon-Merlot-Cabernet Franc ⊘ ⓦ ★★★★ Unoaked **16** ⑧⑤ Bordeaux blend brims with juicy berries. Bright & balanced, ready to entertain at a pocket-friendly price. Also in 3L bag-in-box.

Occasional release: **Shiraz-Mourvèdre-Viognier**, **Cabernet Sauvignon Rosé**. In abeyance: **Shiraz**, **Sauvignon Blanc**. — MW

Location: Philadelphia ▪ Map: Durbanville, Philadelphia & Darling ▪ Map grid reference: C5 ▪ WO: Philadelphia/Western Cape ▪ Est 1999 ▪ 1stB 2000 ▪ Tasting, sales & cellar tours by appt only ▪ Owner(s) Xinxing Pang ▪ Winemaker(s) Joseph Gertse (Jan 2000) ▪ Farm manager Rudi Benn (Jan 2001) ▪ 260ha/60ha (barbera, cabs s/f, merlot, mourv, sangio, shiraz, sauv) ▪ 70,000cs own label 70% red 30% white ▪ IPW ▪ PO Box 451 Melkbosstrand 7437 ▪ sales@havanahills.co.za ▪ www.havanahills.co.za ▪ S 33° 43′ 17.2″ E 018° 33′ 31.6″ ▪ ▥ reanimate.seethed.projecting ▪ T +27 (0)21-972-1110

Hawksmoor at Matjieskuil ⓠ ⑪ ⌂ ⓞ

Wine is almost overlooked when visiting this historic and beautiful southern Paarl country retreat and guest house. Popular for intimate weddings and conferences, the boutique venture also boasts 24 ha of vines, mostly Rhône varieties, and sought after by buyers. Its small own-label production is marketed very personally, with groups enjoying the ambience of the place and its engaging wine stories.

Signature range

★★★★ **Algernon Stitch** ⓩ Mourvèdre & shiraz share equal billing in **14** ⑧⑥, spicy black fruit is succulent yet the whole is leaner than **12** ⑧⑧, with dry tannin from 2 years in old oak, further 2 in bottle. No **13**.

★★★★ **Saint Alfege's** ② Gentle, juicy mouthful of plum & smoke on **14** ⑧ shiraz & mourvèdre, which improves on **12** ★★★★ ⑧. Supple & restrained. Older French oak seamless & integrated. No **13**.
Cabernet Franc ② ★★★ Earth-, coffee- & cocoa-tinged blackcurrant fruit on chunky **15** ⑧. Bold & powerful, cries out for food. **Mourvèdre** ② ★★★★ Fruit carries the day on unoaked **15** ⑧. Spice, herbs, berries with a graphite nuance, balanced & deep. Svelte & dark-toned **14** ⑧ also still available.

Limited Releases

Magdalen ② ★★★★ Light berry notes of **17** ⑧ rosé belie the mid-palate presence of gentle grip. Dry, succulent, with hint of flint. Not tasted: **Buurman**, **Shiraz**, **Triginta**. Discontinued: **Cape Blend**, **French Blend With A Cape Twist**.

Classic range

Pinotage Lightly Oaked ② ★★★ Subtle old oak frames sour cherry & brambly black fruit compote on succulent **14** ⑧. **Serliana** ② ★★★★ Vivid apricot & nectarine on **17** ⑧ chenin. Light & zippy, with easy charm. From 35 year old bushvines, unoaked. Not tasted: **Vanburgh Pinotage Unoaked**. — FM

Location/map/WO: Paarl ▪ Map grid reference: A7 ▪ Est 1692 ▪ 1stB 2005 ▪ Tasting by appt 10-4 daily ▪ Fee dependent on number of people/wines tasted ▪ Sales by appt daily ▪ Specialise in group tastings (8-20 pax), with option of lunch in the Cape Dutch manor house - prior arrangement essential ▪ Closed Easter Fri-Sun, Dec 25/31 & Jan 1 ▪ Luxury guest house ▪ Wedding & function venue ▪ Owner(s) Brameld Haigh ▪ Winemaker(s) various ▪ Viticulturist(s) Paul Wallace (2004) ▪ Farm manager Jan Lategan ▪ ±23ha (cab f, mourv, ptage, shiraz, chenin) ▪ ±130t/1,000cs own label 65% red 25% white 10% rosé ▪ PO Box 9 Elsenburg 7607 ▪ wines@hawksmoor.co.za ▪ www.hawksmoor.co.za ▪ S 33° 48' 47.4" E 018° 46' 14.1" ▪ ✉ beckoning. tectonic.retinal ▪ **T +27 (0)21-884-4587**

Hazendal Wine Estate ② ⑪ ⑥ ⑧ ⑥

Originally granted to German free burgher Christoffel Hazenwinkel in 1699, this Bottelary Hills estate has been transformed into a multifaceted 'heritage destination with a contemporary twist' by Russian businessman, investor and philanthropist Mark Voloshin and daughters Simone and Ina. From the Wonderdal edu-play centre for children to the 'floating' wedding pavilion, art gallery and fine-dining restaurant, it's a seamless blend of old and new, SA craftsmanship and Russian traditions (notably the special tea ceremony). At its heart, a modern cellar. Not forgetting the craft vodka distillery, beer garden, deli, MTB park . . .

Hazendal range

★★★★ **Chardonnay** ⑭ Voluptuous, with barrel ferment/9 months in oak (some Hungarian barrels) showing a little more here than on siblings, though the buttery richness is ably offset by acidity from 30% unwooded component. **17** ⑧ lemon custard & blue orange scents in keeping with the ripe profile.

★★★★ **Chenin Blanc** Elegant & white peach, honeysuckle & almond aromas, **17** ⑧ has smidgen sugar to glide over the palate, well-judged oak (as for Chardonnay) provides support. Moderate 13.5% alcohol, like most in the ranges.

★★★★ **Semillon-Sauvignon Blanc** ⑭ ⑧ Well-executed 'fumé' styling on refined & poised **17** ⑧ Bordeaux white (same oaking as Chardonnay). Semillon (67%) asserts more on palate, in weight & lanolin texture, sauvignon adds attractive tinned pea & white asparagus aromas. Delicious now & for several years.

Christoffel Hazenwinkel range

The Red Blend ★★★★ Cape Blend as creative & witty as the front-labels for this range, depicting estate's founder posing in 17th-century opulent finery - with a hare's face! Shiraz, pinotage & its parent pinot noir, **17** ⑧ happy & perfumed, zesty & fruit-filled, 50% oaked portion well knit. **The Blanc de Noir** ★★★★ Deep pink **18** ⑧ has rose & strawberry aromas, soft berry flavours. Nicely dry, with satisfying vinosity & perky acidity. From shiraz. **The White Blend** ★★★★ Unoaked, but several months on lees lend weight & smooth texture to **18** ⑧, from chenin & 3 others. Mostly green fruit & foliage in the flavours & aromas. Good everyday white, doesn't need food.

Scarlet Sails range ⑭

★★★★ **Méthode Cap Classique** Dry sparkler from pinot noir (54%) & chardonnay reflects house's adventurous packaging. Richness the keynote on **15** ⑧, 48 months on lees give toasted brioche, toffee apple, apple pie characters & creamy texture. Energetic bubbles refresh for now, but best enjoyed soon. WO Coastal.— GdB, CvZ

Location/map: Stellenbosch ▪ Map grid reference: B3 ▪ WO: Stellenbosch/Coastal ▪ Est 1699 ▪ 1stB 1996 ▪
Wine tasting Tue-Sun 9-5 ▪ Cellar tours by appt ▪ Craft vodka distillery ▪ Avant-Garde Restaurant ▪ Babushka
deli & picnics ▪ Pivnushka beer garden ▪ Wonderdal children's edutainment centre ▪ Conferences, weddings
& functions ▪ Marvol art gallery ▪ Family MTB park ▪ Golf course (opening 2020) ▪ Owner(s) Mark Voloshin ▪
Cellarmaster(s)/winemaker(s) Clarise Sciocatti-Langeveldt (Jul 2016) ▪ Viticulturist(s) Clarise Sciocatti-
Langeveldt (Jun 2016) ▪ 145ha/12ha (cab, carignan, carménère, ptage, pinot, shiraz, albariño, chard, chenin,
marsanne, rouss, sauv, sem) ▪ 100t/26,000cs own label 50% red 50% white ▪ Bottelary Rd Stellenbosch
7600 ▪ bookings@hazendal.co.za ▪ www.hazendal.co.za ▪ S 33° 54' 2.7" E 018° 43' 9.1" ▪ ⬚ coyote.shortness.
drifts ▪ T +27 (0)21-903-5034

☐ **HB Vineyards** see Hout Bay Vineyards
☐ **Headbutt** see Rooiberg Winery
☐ **Heart of Africa** see The Grape Grinder
☐ **Heaven on Earth** see Stellar Winery
☐ **Hendrik Lodewyk** see Du Preez Estate
☐ **Hercules Paragon** see Simonsvlei International
☐ **Heritage Heroes** see Nederburg Wines

Hermit on the Hill Wines   ⓟ

Pieter de Waal and wife Lohra's boutique collection of paradigm-shifting wines is now, in Pieter's words,
'totally legit'. Not that there was anything untoward, of course; just that the duo's management style was
more T-shirt than suit and tie. But now, after 20 years, they've committed to a permanent brand-home in
Cape Town 'with a very attractive by-appointment tasting area' from where they're driving the venture. Pieter
will continue as stakeholder in Mount Abora Vineyards, and no doubt the trip to the half-hectare of vines,
small house and cellar in Globoka, Slovenia, bought a few years ago, will remain an annual fixture.

★★★★ **Stellenbosch Syrah** ⓠ **15** ★★★★ ⑧④ opens in glass to sweet black cherry fruit, meaty notes,
medium body & freshening acidity. Last-tasted **13** ⑧⑧ also needed time to unfold. 18 months in older oak.

★★★★ **Skermunkel Semillon** ⓠ Aptly named 'Rascal' in **16** ⑧⑦ flouts convention with oxidative,
sherry-like bouquet, bruised apple & barley sugar palate. Rich, smooth, saline, intriguing.

The Red Knight ⓠ ★★★ Laudably dry, light (12% alcohol) & succulent **16** ⑧② Lightly chill & enjoy this
summer. Mourvèdre (35%), grenache, shiraz & cinsaut from Swartland. **The White Knight** ⓠ ★★★★
Smoky & light-footed (just 12.5% alcohol) **17** ⑧⑤, attractive floral & lemongrass tones, earthy natural
winemaking nuance & pleasant tannic tug. From semillon, older oaked. Not tasted: **Knights in Tights
Mourvèdre Luminoir, The Second Crusade Chenin Blanc, Grenache Blanc, The Round Table
Roussanne, The Starry Knight**. — CvZ

Location: Cape Town ▪ Map: Durbanville, Philadelphia & Darling ▪ Map grid reference: C8 ▪ WO:
Stellenbosch/Swartland ▪ Est/1stB 2000 ▪ Tasting & sales by appt ▪ Owner(s)/cellarmaster(s) Pieter de Waal
▪ Winemaker(s) Pieter & Lohra de Waal ▪ mourv, shiraz, chenin, grenache b, rouss, sem ▪ 10t/1,000cs own
label 40% red 60% white ▪ PO Box 995 Bellville 7535 ▪ pieter@dw.co.za ▪ www.hermitonthehill.co.za ▪ S 33°
54' 14.48" E 018° 36' 18.21" ▪ ⬚ goodness.dose.dairies ▪ T +27 (0)83-357-3864

Herold Wines   ⓟ ⑪ ⌂ �◎ ⓐ ⓖ

Cool conditions in Nico and Maureen Fourie's farm at the foot of Cradock Peak in Outeniqua Ward prompted
the first planting of pinot noir two decades ago – the vineyard almost surrounded by a nature reserve
that unhelpfully harbours baboons, bush pigs and fruit-eating birds. Pinot remains the focus of the now
wide-ranging plantings and of Nico's wines, all marked by the freshness the climate encourages.

★★★★ **Pinot Noir** ⊘ Confident berry aromas & classic undergrowth accent on **16** ⑧⑦ Fresh, brightly
sweet-fruited & ready to drink, though well structured & with time to go. Older oak; 12.9% alcohol.

★★★★ **John Segon** ⊘ Fresh, lively **16** ⑧⑦ merlot, shiraz & pinotage, none of them stands out; nor
does 14% alcohol. No great intensity but far from trivial, with good structure of acid & tannin. Old oak.

★★★★ **Sauvignon Blanc** ⊘ Deliciously lively green-apple freshness on **18** ⑧⑨, enticing blackcurrant
fragrance. But softly textured & some weight from 8 months on lees. Attractive, balanced & satisfying.

Pinot Noir 'Screwcap' ② ★★★☆ Bright red fruit & wild herbal element on aromatic **15** ⑧₃. Lively & fresh, rather simple & unlingering, but a wholly delightful drink. **Riesling** ★★★☆ **18** ⑧₃ back from very sweet style of **17** ★★★ ⑧₀, the prominent acidity more than balancing the off-dry peachy charm. Might well bloom in a few years. Not tasted: **Private Collection Pinot Noir Reserve**, **Syrah**, **Red Men**, **Schaam Schaap**, **Laatlammetjie Natural Sweet**. Occasional release: **Pinot Noir Reserve**. — TJ

Location: George ▪ Map: Klein Karoo & Garden Route ▪ Map grid reference: C3 ▪ WO: Outeniqua ▪ Est 1999 ▪ 1stB 2003 ▪ Tasting, sales & cellar tours Mon-Sat 10-4 ▪ Fee R20, waived on purchase ▪ Closed Easter Sun & Dec 25 ▪ Light refreshments/cheese platters during opening hours ▪ Picnic baskets/farm lunches with 2 days prior notice ▪ Facilities for children ▪ Tour groups ▪ Gifts ▪ Farm produce ▪ Conferences ▪ Walks/hikes ▪ MTB ▪ Conservation area ▪ Self-catering cottages ▪ Owner(s) Nico & Maureen Fourie ▪ Winemaker(s)/viticulturist(s) Nico Fourie (Jul 2011) ▪ 324ha/8ha (cab, merlot, pinot, shiraz, chard, riesling, sauv, sem) ▪ 45t/5,400cs own label 55% red 25% white 20% rosé ▪ PO Box 10 Herold 6615 ▪ info@heroldwines.co.za ▪ www.heroldwines.co.za ▪ S 33° 51' 49.4" E 022° 28' 9.9" ▪ ⌨ alleviates.taller.notions ▪ **T +27 (0)72-833-8223/+27 (0)83-653-5770**

Hidden Valley Wines

② ⑪ ⌂ ◎ ⑤

Winemaker Annalie van Dyk, who describes this modern cellar among vineyards in a fold of Helderberg Mountain as a 'gem', is producing some jewels of her own. New to the collection are two MCC bubblies, joining an exceptional Bordeaux red and unusual blend featuring locally rare tannat (a varietal bottling is mooted). 'Hard work in the vineyard to improve the quality of our sauvignon blanc' generated an experimental parcel of barrel-fermented Blanc Fumé, available end-2019 to visitors and Wine Society members. Overall, investment by owner Riaan Stassen has resulted in a 'wine, dine and art experience' to dazzle.

★★★★☆ **Hidden Gems** ⊘ ⊛ Rich & dense, dark fruit & bitter chocolate on more impressive cab-led **16** ★★★★★ ⑨₅, with 34% petit verdot, 10% merlot. Similar deft oaking to **15** ⑨₂ (18 months in French barrels, 20% new) & slight herbal nuance. All quite compact but streamlined, augurs well for the future.

★★★★ **Hidden Secret** Spicy dark fruit & cocoa flavours on **16** ⑧₉. Shows more warmth & has more shiraz (80%) in the mix (with tannat & cab) than structured **15** ★★★★★ ⑨₃. Dry, chalky tannin framework & same oak regime as Hidden Gems.

★★★★ **Méthode Cap Classique Brut Rosé** ⑧ Identical blend & time on lees as Brut. **17** ⑧₆ sparkler more of a savoury, cranberry tone, befitting the style, rosy hue from pinot noir skin contact. Similar freshness, with a more piquant twist on the tail. Cellardoor only, as sibling.

★★★★ **Méthode Cap Classique Brut** ⑧ Dry oystershell, lemon & green apple nuances on **17** ⑧₆ bubbly from equal portions chardonnay & pinot noir. Refreshing acidity, with some creamy breadth from 2 years lees contact.

Hidden Treasure ★★★ Similar merlot-led mix in both unoaked dry rosés tasted this edition. **18** ★★★ ⑦₉ more delicate, almost dilute. Fresher **19** ⑧₁ has more fruity verve & character, from a touch more cab. Both light & genial. **Sauvignon Blanc** ★★★★ Less verve, complexity & flavour in **18** ★★★ ⑧₀. Softer, muted dried vegetation impression, also more alcohol (13.9%) than **19** ⑧₃, also tasted, which has fresher, brighter stonefruit flavours. Both less impressive than more complex **17** ★★★★ ⑧₉. **Sauvignon Blanc-Viognier** ★★★ A touch more viognier (38%) in **19** ⑧₂ & a brush of oak. Similar gentle peachy tone & just enough freshness for balance. Clean, delicately aromatic quaffer. — MW

Location/map/WO: Stellenbosch ▪ Map grid reference: E8 ▪ Est/1stB 1995 ▪ Tasting & sales: summer Mon-Sun 9-6 (sundowners Fri 5-8); winter Mon-Sun 9-5 ▪ Fee R65pp ▪ Open pub hols, but closed Dec 25 & Jan 1 ▪ Cellar tours by appt ▪ Overture Restaurant ▪ The Deck at Hidden Valley ▪ Cheese/winter/chocolate platters ▪ Picnics, to be pre-booked ▪ Table olives & olive oil ▪ Tour groups by appt ▪ Boardroom & conference facilities ▪ Functions ▪ Sculpture studio ▪ Bush Lodge luxury accommodation ▪ Walks/hikes ▪ Conservation area ▪ Owner(s) Riaan Stassen ▪ Winemaker(s) Annalie van Dyk (Nov 2014) ▪ Viticulturist(s) Daniël Roux (Nov 2013) ▪ 40ha/21ha (cab, merlot, p verdot, shiraz, tannat, sauv, viog) & 3ha olives ▪ 150t/24,000cs own label 70% red 30% white ▪ WWF-SA Conservation Champion ▪ PO Box 12334 Die Boord 7613 ▪ winetasting@hiddenvalleywines.co.za ▪ www.hiddenvalleywines.co.za ▪ S 34° 1' 14.80" E 018° 51' 9.78" ▪ ⌨ sparkly.captivated.redeems ▪ **T +27 (0)21-880-2646**

Highberry Wines

The two partners in the production of these wines from wind-cooled Schapenberg in the Helderberg are grower Andre Parker and long-time SA wine entrepreneur Jabulani Ntshangase, latterly New York resident. (Third partner and winemaker Werner Engelbrecht has since moved on.) New vintages weren't ready for tasting, but the '17 Sauvignon featured here will still be available during the currency of the guide.

★★★★ Sauvignon Blanc Ⓢ Vibrant gooseberry, apple & lime fruit on **17** ⑧⑦, acidity a freshening counterpoint to richness from barrelled component, 10% semillon (oaked) & 8 months on lees.

Not tasted: **Cabernet Sauvignon.** — GM

Location: Sir Lowry's Pass ▪ Map: Helderberg ▪ Map grid reference: F6 ▪ WO: Stellenbosch ▪ 1stB 2014 ▪ Tasting by appt only ▪ Function venue ▪ Owner(s) Andre Parker & Jabulani Ntshangase ▪ Viticulturist(s) Edward Etson (Jul 2003) ▪ 65ha/49ha (cabs s/f, malbec, merlot, p verdot, shiraz, chard, sauv, sem) ▪ 350t/3,000cs own label 50% red 50% white ▪ accounts@highberry.co.za ▪ www.highberry.co.za ▪ S 34° 6' 3.29" E 018° 54' 8.92" ▪ ✉ exhaled.tenacious.noodles ▪ **T +27 (0)21-852-3754**

☐ **High Constantia Wine Cellar** *See Editor's Note*

Highgate Wine Estate

Rudi and Cindy Kassier helped pioneer winegrowing in KwaZulu-Natal when they test-planted some 25 varieties in 2005, bottling their first wines in 2010. Climatic and other challenges induced a brief hiatus before vintage 2016 heralded Highgate's next-generation releases. Thornton Pillay, ensconced in a custom-designed, red-brick cellar, is one of the youngsters (including daughter Cathryn Kassier) applying Stellenbosch work and study experience to highlighting Highgate's many charms as an integral part of the Piggly Wiggly lifestyle destination near Lion's River and the larger Midlands Meander tourism route.

Black Edition Cabernet Sauvignon Ⓢ ★★★ Dark plummy fruit in **17** ⑦⑦, gentle savoury tone from 15 months oak, sleek & perky-fresh. Displays more ripeness than you'd expect from 12% alcohol. Acidity bit high, stands out. **Cabernet Sauvignon** Ⓢ ★★★ Blackcurrant & liquorice, hint of fennel, **17** ⑦⑧ is streamlined, elegant, with house-style freshness aiding drinkability. Not tasted: **Merlot**, **Pinotage**, **Tomcat Pinotage**, **Syrah**, **Rosé**, **Chardonnay.** — CR

Location: Lions River ▪ Map/WO: KwaZulu-Natal ▪ Map grid reference: B2 ▪ Est/1stB 2010 ▪ Tasting, sales & cellar tours Wed-Sun 10-3; cellar tours available by appt Mon/Tue ▪ Closed Dec 25 ▪ Menu Restaurant open for lunch & dinner, www.menuathighgate.com ▪ Wine etiquette courses ▪ Events & weddings ▪ Country shops catering for all ages adjacent to cellar (Piggly Wiggly) ▪ Owner(s) Rudi & Cindy Kassier ▪ Winemaker(s) Thornton Pillay ▪ 57ha/4ha (cab, merlot, ptage, shiraz, chard) ▪ 12t/1,250cs own label 75% red 25% white ▪ PO Box 1025 Howick 3290 ▪ wine@highgatewineestate.co.za ▪ www.highgatewineestate.co.za ▪ S 29° 27' 29.92" E 030° 8' 8.66" ▪ ✉ consistency.looses.vigilantly ▪ **T +27 (0)82-345-5706/+27 (0)82-895-1667/+27 (0)33-234-2002**

Highlands Road Estate

Consistency is a key consideration at Michael White's boutique estate in Elgin. Thus the range remains focused on white wines (a Bordeaux blend and varietals), along with a small number of reds from grapes which flourish in the lower temperatures of this late-ripening area. Viticulturist Paul Wallace continues to keep abreast of the latest vineyard management techniques, while winemaker Vanessa Simkiss celebrates another vintage of crafting pure and elegant wines in the small but well-equipped cellar.

★★★★ Pinot Noir Ⓢ Well-balanced **15** ⑧⑨ starting to show pleasing development (game, earth, leather) to fresh strawberries & sweet spice. Nicely handled oak (25% new) supports good structure & tannins through to just-dry finish. Rung above **14** ★★★★ ⑧⑤.

★★★★ Syrah Ⓢ Stately **15** ★★★★ ⑨① oozes Old World charm, generous tobacco, leather notes supporting stewed black plums & cherries, spice accents from 30% new oak & nice textural finish. Set to improve over next 5 years. Confident step up on **14** ⑧⑨.

★★★★☆ Chardonnay Previewed **18** ⑨② already very polished & pure, showing steely peach fruit, wet stones plus creamy oatmeal notes from sensitively done oak (barrel fermented, 35% new). Meshing well, expect more pleasure to come.

★★★★★ **Sauvignon Blanc White Reserve** ⓐ Multi-layered, complex **17** ★★★★★ ⑨③ reverberates with vibrant orange citrus & guava, flint & smoke courtesy of barrel ferment, 50% new. Excellent balance of different components, already well-knit but long finish & zesty acidity indicate plenty more pleasure in store. Fine successor to stellar **15** ⑨⑦. No **16**.

★★★★☆ **Sauvignon Blanc** ⊘ Gamut of flavour in **17** ⑨② from mandarins & tangy green herbs to peas, peppers & poached guava on finish. Creamy mid-palate from 12 months lees contact, excellent food wine with classic goats' cheese match. No **16**.

★★★★ **Semillon** Pre-bottling, **18** ⑧⑨ combines classic flavours of lemons, herbs, orange blossom & wax with forthright vanilla oak & sharp acidity, all needing a little more time to settle.

★★★★☆ **Sine Cera** ⓐ Delightful Bordeaux white blend, 50/50 semillon & sauvignon, **17** ⑨③ dials back the oaked fraction very slightly, to 15%, half new, adding spice edges to fresh woody herbal notes & zesty citrus. Excellent balance & enough intensity to enjoy now or keep a while.

★★★★☆ **Noble Late Harvest** ⊘ Barrel-aged dessert from sauvignon **17** ⑨② with honey, lemons, pineapples plus lime marmalade botrytis notes. Racy acidity more than balances out fairly modest 126 g/l sugar, tad more length needed to match **15** ⑨④. No **16**.

Occasional release: **Pinot Noir Rosé**, **Pinot Noir Late Harvest**. — CM

Location/map/WO: Elgin ▪ Map grid reference: C3 ▪ Est 2005 ▪ 1stB 2007 ▪ Tasting, sales & cellar tours Mon-Sun 10—4 ▪ Cheese & charcuterie platters ▪ Facilities for children ▪ Boule court ▪ Owner(s) Michael White ▪ Winemaker(s) Vanessa Simkiss ▪ Viticulturist(s) Paul Wallace ▪ 28ha/10ha (pinot, shiraz, chard, sauv, sem) ▪ 70t/4,500cs own label 35% red 65% white ▪ PO Box 94 Elgin 7180 ▪ info@highlandsroadestate.co.za ▪ www.highlandsroadestate.co.za ▪ S 34° 14' 4.4" E 019° 4' 14.3" ▪ [m] deemed.kitchen.tigers ▪ **T +27 (0)71-271-0161/+27 (0)78-332-5782**

☐ **High Road** *see* The High Road

Hildenbrand Wine & Olive Estate ⓐ ⓟ ⓐ ⓑ

Reni Hildenbrand is the live wire behind this characterful Wellington boutique estate, where wine is handcrafted, extra virgin olive oil produced, feet put up (by guests of the country house) and time somehow found to rescue animals and name wines after them, like Justi & Semi, the shiraz-malbec blend.

Location/map: Wellington ▪ Map grid reference: B4 ▪ Est 1991 ▪ 1stB 1999 ▪ Tasting & sales Mon-Fri 10-4 Sat/Sun 9-12 by appt ▪ Wine tasting R50pp; olive & oil tasting R15pp ▪ Closed Easter Sat/Sun, Dec 24/25 & Jan 1 ▪ Food & wine evenings/lunch by appt ▪ Klein Rhebokskloof Country & Guest House ▪ Owner(s)/cellarmaster(s)/winemaker(s) Reni Hildenbrand ▪ ±4,500cs ▪ PO Box 270 Wellington 7654 ▪ info@wine-estate-hildenbrand.co.za ▪ www.wine-estate-hildenbrand.co.za ▪ S 33° 39' 33.3" E 019° 1' 46.3" ▪ [m] limit.tickles.fevered ▪ **T +27 (0)82-656-6007**

Hill & Dale Wines

This brand had its origins in 2003 as a subsidiary to Stellenzicht. With the sale of Stellenzicht, the Schreiber family owners decided to retain Hill & Dale — and its winemaker Guy Webber — and re-base it at their Neethlingshof estate, also in Stellenbosch. Guy promised 'exciting changes' last year, and they've taken the form of two new Prosecco-styled bubblies. 'People are going nuts for them!' reports their ebullient creator. Since the premise was always to deliver 'estate-quality wines at supermarket prices' while celebrating the Stellenbosch provenance, it's little wonder corks are popping.

Dry Rosé Merlot ⊘ ⓥ ★★★☆ Takes a step up in strawberry vivacity & succulence in **19** ⑧⑤. Broad-textured palate with long tail from time on lees. Summer sipper with attitude & a bargain price.

Merlot ⓐ ★★★ Leafy cassis varietal character, **17** ⑧⓪ with tarry edge & prominent tannins. **Pinotage** ⓐ ★★★ Sweetly ripe berry compote on **17** ⑧②, slight steely edge & chalky tannins. **Cabernet Sauvignon-Shiraz** ⓐ ★★★ Pleasantly quaffable **17** ⑧② has blackcurrant & cherry fruitiness, medium body, chewy tannins on finish. **Chardonnay** ⊘ ★★★☆ Seamless ease to poised unwooded **19** ⑧⑤. Abundant juicy citrus, quince & zesty freshness. Light, with a creamy lees breadth. **Sauvignon Blanc** ⊘ ★★★☆ Vibrant **19** ⑧③ improves on previous with pea & flint typicity. Bright, fresh, with touch of white pepper. Good body & length. **Sparkling Brut Rosé** ⓝⓔⓦ ⊘ ★★★☆ Perky pink fizz, full of raspberry &

candyfloss fun. **NV** ⑧③ light & zesty, with good balance of sweetness & acidity. Variety/ies undeclared, as next. **Sparkling Brut** (NEW) ✓ ★★★★ Crisp yet friendly **NV** ⑧⑤ sparkler, inspired by Prosecco (as sibling). Ample apple & pear appeal, lively acid & impressive palate length. Both bubblies carbonated. — FM

Location/WO: Stellenbosch ▪ Est 2003 ▪ 1stB 2001 ▪ Closed to public ▪ Online wine shop ▪ Owner(s) Schreiber family ▪ Winemaker(s) Guy Webber (Oct 1998) ▪ 112,000cs own label 30% red 35% white 35% rosé ▪ IPW, WIETA ▪ PO Box 104 Stellenbosch 7599 ▪ info@hillanddale.co.za ▪ www.hillanddale.co.za ▪ **T +27 (0)21-883-8988**

Hillcrest Estate ⚲ 🍴 📷

This Durbanville hilltop farm's ancient soils were quarried before the owners, in the construction business, decided early this century to plant vines (and later olives) and convert a storeroom into a small cellar. Much development later, Arno Smith is in charge of vineyard and cellar, and the focus continues to be on boutique quantities of the Bordeaux varieties — both black and white grapes — expressed with restraint and elegance, though also with some ripe richness. The Hillcrest Restaurant, under new owner Mike Crafford, is now also open for dinner on the weekends. Also newly available is a tasting pairing wine and chocolate.

Atlantic Slopes range

★★★★ **Quarry Merlot** Successfully combines a rich opulence of flavour & texture with a degree of elegant refinement. **16** ★★★★★ ⑨⓪ firm but smoothly silky tannin structure, well-considered oak support (50% new), appropriate 13.4% alcohol. Like **15** ⑧⑨, with enlivening acidity. Durbanville WO.

★★★★☆ **Hornfels Bordeaux-Style Blend** (🍇) Already approachable, **15** ⑨④ from 5 Bordeaux red grapes (30% petit verdot in the lead). Classic aromas of brightly dark fruit, with tobacco spice. The fruit is persistent, but there's a savoury, dry dimension; the tannins are firm but smooth. Plenty of time to go.

★★★★☆ **Atlantic Slopes Sauvignon Blanc** ✓ (🍇) With 14% semillon, **18** ⑨③ has multidimensional aromas & flavours, both riper & grassy-citrus - more so than Estate version, & more impressive than last **16** ★★★★ ⑧⑨ (pure sauvignon). Fine racy structure. 20% of blend lightly oaked.

Saartjie Single Vineyard Selections

★★★★ **Cabernet Franc** Leafy, herbal notes on pleasantly aromatic **18** ⑧⑥, a green element despite ripeness indicated by big but balanced 14.5% alcohol. Decent structure. These varietal reds judiciously oaked, 30% new.

★★★★ **Malbec** Full dark fruit character on **18** ⑧⑧, juicy & tasty despite its obvious raw youth - decant now, rather wait a few years, though the tannins are easygoing but useful. 13.8% alcohol, as next.

★★★★ **Petit Verdot** The most firmly structured of the 3 varietal reds, **18** ⑧⑦ with a slightly rough tannic bite to its rich dark fruit. Overall quite savoury & serious-minded.

★★★★ **Semillon** Pre-bottling, **19** ⑧⑦ looks promising - first tasted since **16** ★★★☆ ⑧④. Forward tropical, lemon & earthy notes, ripe & rich, with a succulent acidity controlling any excess.

Hillcrest Estate range

★★★★ **Sauvignon Blanc** ✓ Forward, enticing tropical fruit character on aromatic **18** ★★★★★ ⑨⓪, with grassy & stony mineral notes emerging on the beautifully structured, grippy but unaggressive palate. 12.8% alcohol & great value. Up a notch on last-tasted **16** ⑧⑨.

Red Shale Blend (🍇) ★★★ Bordeaux quartet, merlot uppermost in **17** ⑧① juicy, with plump tannins. Comfortable braai wine. **Robbenzicht** ★★★★ Cab & merlot **17** ⑧④, mostly aged in older oak. Pleasant fruitcake aromas & flavours, sweetly easygoing & juicy. **Cabernet Sauvignon Rosé** ✓ ★★★ Copperpink **18** ⑧② dry & savoury, with a little sweet fruit, smooth texture & slightly sour, green acidity. — TJ

Location: Durbanville ▪ Map: Durbanville, Philadelphia & Darling ▪ Map grid reference: C7 ▪ WO: Cape Town/Durbanville ▪ Est/1stB 2002 ▪ Tasting & sales daily 10-5 ▪ Fee R30/estate range, R75/full range ▪ Chocolate & wine pairing ▪ Olive platter ▪ Closed Dec 25/26 & Jan 1 ▪ Cellar tours by appt ▪ Hillcrest Restaurant T +27 (0)21-975-2346 open Tue-Sun for b'fast & lunch; dinner Fri & Sat (kitchen close at 9) ▪ Outdoor beer garden ▪ Wedding/function venue ▪ Farm produce ▪ MTB ▪ Conservation area ▪ Craft beer brewery: Tasting & sales Tue-Sun 11-4; tasting fee R60pp ▪ Owner(s) PD Inglis, R Haw, G du Toit & E Menegablo ▪ Winemaker(s) Arno Smith (Jan 2014) ▪ Viticulturist(s) Arno Smith ▪ 25ha (cabs s/f, malbec, merlot, p verdot, sauv) ▪ 60t/±6,000cs own label 45% red 55% white ▪ Private Bag X3 Durbanville 7551 ▪ info@hillcrestfarm.co.za ▪ www.hillcrestfarm.co.za ▪ S 33° 49' 38.2" E 018° 35' 25.9" ▪ (w) flog.worthier.transistor ▪ **T +27 (0)21-970-5800**

☐ **Hillock Wines** *See Editor's Note*
☐ **Hill of Enon** *see* Zandvliet Wine Estate
☐ **Hills** *see* The Hills
☐ **Hilton Vineyards** *see* Richard Hilton Vineyards

Hirst Wines

Yorkshireman, rugby enthusiast and entrepreneur Luke Hirst's Vino Pronto wine shop in Cape Town is well-known for its hard-to-find, young-gun and fine-wine selection. But there's another good reason to pop in: Luke's own-label bottling, currently from Swartland, a satisfying high-quality wine at a friendly price.

The Front Row range
★★★★ **Chenin Blanc** ② Lightish, gentle & charming **14** ⑧⑦ surprisingly intense flavour for just 12% alcohol. Oxidative winemaking shows in bruised apple finish.
Not tasted: **Shiraz**.

Hirst Wines range
Not tasted: **Riverhorse**. — HC

Location: Cape Town ▪ WO: Swartland ▪ Est/1stB 2013 ▪ See website for sales hours ▪ Owner(s) Luke Hirst ▪ Own label 50% red 50% white ▪ PO Box 12066 Hout Bay 7872 ▪ lukeh@vinopronto.co.za ▪ www.vinopronto.co.za ▪ **T +27 (0)82-751-8169**

☐ **His Master's Choice** *see* Excelsior Vlakteplaas, Ridgeback
☐ **Hoeks Rivier** *see* Eagle's Cliff Wines-New Cape Wines

Hofstraat Kelder ② ⑪ ◎
Located at Myrtledene near Malmesbury, this garagiste cellar is named for the street where friends Wim Smit and Jerry Finley's wine journey began — a journey that took Wim to Piedmont in Italy last year. 'My love for nebbiolo has grown and I'm now paying particular attention to this noble cultivar.'

Renosterbos range
Cabernet Sauvignon ★★★ First since **14**, muscular **17** ⑧② packed with dark-toned fruit, spice & chocolate seasoning; smoothly accessible. **Nebbiolo** ★★★ One of few single bottlings, **17** ⑧⓪'s cherry/berries anchored by firm tannins, ageable. WO Breedekloof. **Pinotage** ★★★ Dark fruit & liquorice in full, ripe, rustic **18** ⑧⓪, tannins still youthfully firm. **Shiraz** ★★★★ Wild yeast ferment, as rest. Spice-dusted plush hedgerow fruit in **17** ⑧③, underpinned by firm tannins for ageing, though already drinkable. **Tinta Barocca** ★★★ Spiced pruney fruit in full ripe **17** ⑧②, tannins providing welcome grip. As rest, 11 months barrel ageing. **Myrtledene** ⑭ ★★★★ Shiraz, cab & pinotage blend, black plums, spice array, almost meaty tones, smoothly curvaceous. **17** ⑧④ bold but tasty. Not tasted: **Barbera**, **Merlot**, **Chenin Blanc**, **Die Solder**, **Cape Vintage**.

Oesland range
Cabernet Sauvignon ★★★ Ripe, dark-fruited **17** ⑦⑧ shows its oaking on the finish, savoury & dry. — CR
Location: Malmesbury ▪ Map: Swartland ▪ Map grid reference: C7 ▪ WO: Swartland/Breedekloof ▪ Est 2002 ▪ 1stB 2003 ▪ Tasting, sales & tours by appt ▪ Scheduled tasting evenings every first Thu of the month ▪ Dine at the cellar on Fri evenings ▪ Functions (up to 80 pax) ▪ Owner(s) Wim & Karin Smit, Jerry Finley ▪ Cellarmaster(s)/winemaker(s) Wim Smit & Jerry Finley ▪ 4t/505cs own label 100% red ▪ PO Box 1172 Malmesbury 7299 ▪ renosterbos@cornergate.com ▪ S 33° 26' 56.1" E 018° 44' 1.8" ▪ 🌐 activity.awaiting.pans ▪ **T +27 (0)83-270-2352**

Hogan Wines
A busy two years for Stellenbosch-based Jocelyn Hogan Wilson have seen much exciting growth, not least the addition of a chardonnay and cabernet franc to her boutique label. The names are inspired by The Chemical Brothers and Red Hot Chili Peppers, whose music also animates Jocelyn when she's running and thinking. The cabernet franc, modelled on Loire versions, reflects her enjoyment of working with fruit from a particular Helderberg farm. The results have encouraged her to craft a more Bordeaux-like wine from a

nearby site. Exports have also grown, with good success in the US, and Japan where she visited for the first time. 'I was humbled by the culture and how thrilled they are about spreading news of our wines'.

★★★★☆ **Mirror for the Sun Cabernet Franc** (NEW) (⚤) From lower Helderberg slope, **18** (94) has spicy, leafy intensity but no greenness in its sweet fruit. Great verve & freshness though still tightly wound, taut grip accented by bone-dry finish. Highest alcohol in range, 14%, but house-style clarity, lightness not compromised. Natural ferment, older oak, as all.

★★★★☆ **Divergent** (⚤) Delicious & individual blend, **18** (94) near-equal cab, partly bunch-fermented cinsaut (both Stellenbosch) & carignan (Wellington). Great purity of wild-berry fruit & fragrance of scented shrubs; juicy yet firm build, freshness adding to light feel but no shortage of beneficial staying power.

★★★★☆ **The Galvanised Chardonnay** (NEW) From 1 Elandskloof & 2 Stellenbosch sites. **18** (90) has cool-climate feel with understated, yet great, depth of lime flavour, creamy lees, acid tension & sustained dry conclusion. Balance & structure assure a good future. Oaked 11 months, as next.

★★★★☆ **Chenin Blanc** (⚤) Shows transparency & elegance, goal of its gentle, minimal treatment. **18** (93) poised, sense of lightness in its depth of floral, red apple & spice flavours. Natural freshness & savoury dry finish complete a most attractive wine from Swartland bushvines.— AL

Location: Stellenbosch ▪ WO: Cape Coast/Coastal/Stellenbosch/Swartland ▪ Est 2013 ▪ 1stB 2014 ▪ Closed to public ▪ Owner(s) Jocelyn Hogan Wilson ▪ Winemaker(s) Jocelyn Hogan Wilson (Nov 2013) ▪ 16t/1,700cs own label 40% red 60% white ▪ PO Box 2226 Dennesig 7601 ▪ jocelyn@mweb.co.za ▪ www.hoganwines.co.za ▪ **T +27 (0)21-885-1275**

Holden Manz Wine Estate

Situated in the southernmost corner of Franschhoek Valley, with spectacular mountain views, is this restored family farm owned by Gerard Holden and Migo Manz. Boasting luxury accommodation, spa, restaurant and impressive contemporary African art collection (on show in the guest house and Franschhoek village), it is eco-conscious, with increasingly more solar panels supplying its needs, and natural vinification applied in the cellar. Bordeaux University-trained winemaker Thierry Haberer uses own fruit as well as sourcing selected terroir sites for his small-batch wines (three new ones this edition), using to good effect the knowledge gained by working with French consultant Michel Rolland prior to joining Holden Manz in 2014.

Reserve range

★★★★☆ **Cabernet Franc** (⚤) Glossy fruit core but **16** (94) has lots going on, graphite notes, hint of Provençal herbs. Good firm foundation for cellaring but tannins are ripe, supple, in harmony with the fruit. There's polish here, assurance: a class act.

★★★★ **Merlot** (⚤) Showcasing prime fruit, plums & blackcurrants, **16** ★★★★☆ (91) a classic varietal rendition, improves on **15** (89): sleek, supple, lovely succulence. 22 months new oak a compatible partner, giving structure, a future, not detracting from the glossiness.

★★★★☆ **Syrah** (⚤) Big/bold track record, **16** (90) still has complexity: black plums & espresso, cocoa-rich chocolate, even scrub, the dry firm tannins providing an anchor, some restraint. A dense wine, not for immediate enjoyment, but with a long future.

★★★★☆ **Chardonnay** (NEW) (⚤) More oak than its sibling, 11 months, 80% new, but masterly balance in **17** (93); lemon/lime preserve, shot through with roasted walnuts, a well-matched partnership. Overall effect is powerful, intense, vital. New World with flair. WO W Cape.

Avant Garde range

★★★★ **Big G** (⚤) Cab leads, with cab franc, merlot, **15** (88)'s fruit density allows serious oaking, 20 months in barriques, 40% new. Fleshy, a savoury thread, backbone for ageing, yet great drinkability.

★★★★ **Visionaire** (∅) Packed with forest fruits, more elegant than stablemates, **14** (89) 22 months in barriques has cab in ascendancy (37%) with merlot, shiraz, splashes cab franc & malbec.

★★★★ **Chardonnay** Oak shows in **18** (88)'s character, 8 months French, half new, becomes butterscotch, which, with caramelised citrus, presents as a bold, rich wine. Finishes long & full-flavoured. WO W Cape.

Good Sport Cape Vintage ★★★★☆ From syrah, **14** (85) fitting the 'vintage port' barrel age/sugar/alcohol requirements. Richly flavoured, brandied fruitcake, sweetly spiced, nutmeg & cinnamon, smooth & round.

Modern range

★★★★ **Vernissage** ⓥ Juicy red fruit to the fore in lightly oaked **15** ⑧⑥, blending spicy shiraz with ±30% merlot & cab, dash cab franc. At 14% alcohol, more approachable & refreshing than **14** ★★★★ ⑧③.

Rosé ⓣ ★★★★ Eclectic blend, mainly grenache & shiraz, with 3 others, **18** ⑧④ takes you straight to Provence. Bone-dry, slender, with red berries & minerality, a touch of earthiness. For solo enjoyment or food match. WO W Cape.

Contemporary range

★★★★ **Cabernet Sauvignon** ⓐ Dense & dark, cassis, black cherries & cocoa, 22 months in barrels adds lovely savoury spice to **17** ★★★★★ ⑨①, yet another layer. Good tannin foundation for cellaring but plush fruit makes current access pleasurable. More polish & presence than **16** ⑧⑦.

★★★★ **Syrah** ⓝⒺⓦ ⓐ Deep & dark-toned, muscular **17** ⑧⑧ is power-packed with flavour, black plums & liquorice, spice-laden (oaked 21 months). Enough tannin grip for ageing & food, but hard to resist now.

★★★★ **Proprietors' Blend** ⓝⒺⓦ Syrah, merlot & cab, dash cab franc, 18 months French barrels for vivid fruit, cassis & raspberries, lovely smooth lines. Delicious **15** ⑧⑧ ageable, but why postpone the pleasure?

★★★★ **Chenin Blanc** ⓐ Vineyard selection, minimal handling. **18** ⑧⑨ variety-true, quince & minerality, some thatch, & unexpected palate richness. Bone-dry but has texture, curves. Small portion oaked. WO W Cape.— CR

Location/map: Franschhoek ▪ Map grid reference: D1 ▪ WO: Franschhoek/Western Cape ▪ Est 2010 ▪ 1stB 2005 ▪ Tasting & sales daily 10-5 ▪ Fee R30 ▪ Cellar tours by appt ▪ Franschhoek Kitchen ▪ Spa ▪ Picnic area ▪ Holden Manz Country House ▪ Owner(s) Gerard Holden & Migo Manz ▪ Winemaker(s) Thierry Haberer (Dec 2014), with Annamarie Fourie (Apr 2015) ▪ Viticulturist(s) Lourens Bester (Nov 2018) & Marko Roux (Oct 2016, consultant) ▪ 20ha/16ha (cabs s/f, merlot, shiraz) ▪ 110t/13,332cs own label 85% red 3.85% white 6.65% rosé 4.5% port ▪ IPW ▪ PO Box 620 Franschhoek 7690 ▪ info@holdenmanz.com ▪ www.holdenmanz.com ▪ S 33° 56' 6.3" E 019° 7' 8.3" ▪ ⓜ yodel.parody.prefaces ▪ **T +27 (0)21-876-2738**

Holder Vineyard & Wines ⓠ ⓝⒺⓦ

The experienced Reg Holder, formerly winemaker at Delheim and before that at Neil Ellis, is focusing on pinotage in his new label, working with old vineyards on the slopes of the Helderberg and Simonsberg in his native Stellenbosch (with consultant viticulturist Etienne Terblanche). The aim is to craft pinotage in a more elegant and fresh style than has been the tradition, while recognising the challenges and opportunities of work in the vineyards.

★★★★ **Dorper Pinotage** The charming label well suited to **17** ⑧⑦, whose perfumed notes of candyfloss & musk are part of a more complex whole. In a modern, light & bright style but with sufficient vinosity at 13% alcohol, soft texture, plenty of flavour & a good dry grip. Only older oak.

★★★★ **Elmie Rosé** In Provence style, from the pale onion-skin hue to the light, dry & delicate palate - though **18** ⑧⑦ from pinotage certainly not lacking flavour. A little oak influence.— TJ, CvZ

Location/WO: Stellenbosch ▪ Est/1stB 2017 ▪ Tasting only by prior arrangement ▪ Closed all pub hols ▪ Owner(s) Holder Vineyard & Wines (Pty) Ltd ▪ Winemaker(s) Reg Holder (2018) ▪ Viticulturist(s) Etienne Terblanche (2018, consultant) ▪ 9t ▪ reg@holderwines.co.za ▪ **T +27 (0)83-678-9598**

☐ **Home of Erasmus** see Cape Wine Company
☐ **Homestead Series** see Bellingham

Hoopenburg Wines ⓠ ⓔ ⓖ ⓞ

Every year something new from Gregor Schmitz's Stellenbosch farm. This edition it's a pinot noir, following last year's Bordeaux red. That both boast the premium Integer label underlines a steady upward quality trajectory, new plantings coming on-stream, boosting production and allowing for more stringent selection for the various ranges. The 2017 red-wine releases, winemaker Anton Bothma's first vintage here, are evidence of a sure touch, tweaks including the addition of cab franc to the Integer cab-based blend.

Integer range

★★★★ **Cabernet Sauvignon** ⊘ Much improved **15** ⑧⑨ shows resolute earthy-mineral & liquorice backbone, convincing blackcurrant fruit. Brooding & muscular, promising rewards with cellaring. Step up from **14** ★★★ ⑧①.

★★★★ **Pinot Noir** (NEW) ⊘ Impressive debut for top-tier **17** ⑧⑦, with solid body, robust tannins & scented floral bouquet. Year in 2nd-fill barrels fleshes out, doesn't intrude. 14.8% alcohol.

★★★★ **Cabernet Sauvignon-Cabernet Franc-Petit Verdot-Merlot** ⊘ Merlot-driven **16** ⑧⑨ succeeded by cab-led **17** ⑧⑨, with succulently ripe black fruit core, velvet tannins. Plenty of muscle, yet supple & approachable now. 2 years in 2nd-fill French oak. Great value, as throughout the ranges.

★★★★☆ **Syrah-Mourvèdre-Carignan** ⊘ Previewed **17** ⑨⓪ follows form, shows enticing layers of ripe red & black cherry fruit, plums & charming tobacco-tinged spice. 71% syrah with near-equal mourvèdre & carignan, all in subtle harmony after 18 months in 2nd-fill barrels. Coastal WO.

★★★★☆ **Chardonnay** ⊘ Pre-bottling, **18** ★★★★ ⑧⑨ still muted & unsettled, but showing glimpses of potential. Year in older oak lends body but subtly so. Honest, forthright citrus fruit emerging. Possibly shaded by fine **17** ⑨②. Rating provisional.

★★★★ **Méthode Cap Classique Brut** ⊘ Very likeable **NV** ⑧⑧ sparkler from chardonnay is resolutely dry, with yeasty brioche, ginger-spiced apple tart, lively mousse. Previous releases were vintage-dated.

Hoopenburg Bush Vine range

★★★★ **Cabernet Sauvignon** ⊘ Convincing varietal shape & noble blackcurrant fruit raise **17** ⑧⑥ above edgy, high-toned **16** ★★★ ⑧①. Muscular, broad shouldered, with fine tannins.

★★★★ **Pinot Noir** ⊘ Herbaceous aromatics with floral & farmyard notes on appealing **17** ⑧⑥. Light bodied but lithe, with silky tannins & minerality on finish.

....

Chardonnay ⊘ ⑦ ★★★★ Attractive unwooded **18** ⑧④ shows vibrant citrus fruit, crisp acidity, lingering finish. Bonus of house's friendly pricing.

....

Merlot ★★★☆ Riper, fresher, more focused than previous. **17** ⑧④ nicely rounded plummy fruit, gentle tannins. **Pinotage** ★★★ Sweetly aromatic blackberry fruit dominates **17** ⑧②, with ripe, grippy tannins, powdery texture. **Shiraz** ★★★ Previewed **17** ⑧② offers sour cherry fruit, lightish body & mouthcoating tannin. Needs time to knit. **Rosé** ★★★ From cabernet, **18** ⑧② has pretty pale salmon hue, charming leesy texture, rosewater scent. Bone-dry this vintage. **Chenin Blanc** ★★★ Fruit-driven, cheerful, light-bodied **19** ⑧① is unoaked, fresh & youthful. Greengage & pineapple notes, crisp acidity. **Sauvignon Blanc** ★★★☆ Pungent nettle aromas, glacé fruit notes on lean **18** ⑦⑨, with modest 12.6% alcohol.

Guru range

Merlot ★★★☆ Medium-bodied **18** ⑦⑧ has sweet red berry fruit, caramel & dusty oak notes. **Merlot-Cabernet Sauvignon** ★★★ Bordeaux blend switches to merlot-led in **17** ⑧⓪, unpretentious, with plummy fruit, light tannins, nutty finish. **Sauvignon Blanc** ★★ Somewhat flabby in **18** ⑦⑥, with green-tinged fruit. — GdB

Location/map: Stellenbosch ▪ Map grid reference: E1 ▪ WO: Stellenbosch/Western Cape/Coastal ▪ Est/1stB 1992 ▪ Tasting, sales & cellar tours Mon-Fri 8.30-4 ▪ Fee R30/6-8 wines ▪ Closed all pub hols ▪ BYO picnic ▪ Conferences ▪ Guest house T +27 (0)21-884-4534 ▪ Owner(s) Gregor Schmitz ▪ GM Anton Beukes (Aug 2009) ▪ Winemaker(s) Anton Bothma (Jan 2017) ▪ Viticulturist(s) Gert Snyders ▪ 70ha/30ha (cab, merlot, ptage, pinot, shiraz, chard, chenin) ▪ 180t/40,000cs own label 80% red 18% white 2% MCC ▪ PO Box 1233 Stellenbosch 7599 ▪ info@hoopenburg.com ▪ www.hoopenburgwines.co.za ▪ S 33° 49′ 33.4″ E 018° 49′ 9.3″ ▪ ⟨w⟩ narrations.monuments.reconnect ▪ **T +27 (0)21-884-4221**

☐ **Horsemen** *see* The Horsemen
☐ **Horse Mountain** *see* Doran Vineyards
☐ **Houdamond** *see* Bellevue Estate Stellenbosch
☐ **House of GM & Ahrens** *see* The House of GM&AHRENS
☐ **House of JC le Roux** *see* The House of JC le Roux
☐ **House of Krone** *see* Krone

House of Mandela

Businesswoman Makaziwe Mandela, daughter of late SA statesman and Nobel laureate Nelson Mandela, owns this brand with her daughter Tukwini. The wines commemorate 'the life and spirit of a great African soul', and are made in conjunction with Durbanville's D'Aria, where tastings are available by appointment.

King Vusani range

★★★★ **Cabernet Sauvignon** New bottling of **17** ⑧⑦ is in rich & riper style than previous, & with more new oak (40%) than Thembu sibling. Good fruit depth & some freshness in a pliable but chalky tannin framework. Already harmonious & approachable, with ageing potential.

Shiraz ★★★★ Plusher-styled **17** ⑧⑤ has more oak, sugar & body than Thembu version. Opulence, befitting nobility, but too generous a sweet & spicy clove tone. Less structured than **16** ★★★★ ⑧⑥, ready now. Not tasted: **Chardonnay**.

Phumla range

Pinotage ★★★★ More new oak (20%), & barrels not staves, in **18** ⑧④ create a firm, dry tannin framework for dark berry & cherry flavours. Better than previous, this one is for the table. **Chenin Blanc** ⓠ ★★★ Mandarin vibrancy to wild-fermented **16** ⑧①, creamy breadth from half the wine ageing 8 months in oak.

Thembu Tribute range

Cabernet Sauvignon ★★★ Similar appealing ripe raspberry flavours, but **17** ⑧① more structured than previous, from Elgin & Stellenbosch fruit. Poised, with respectable dry farewell. **Shiraz** ★★★ A touch fresher & brighter in **17** ⑦⑨, with a dash of white pepper spicing the fynbos & smoky plum flavours. Pair with a hearty meal or barbecue. **Sauvignon Blanc** ★★★ Clean, crisp lemongrass & gentle tropical flavours on **19** ⑧⓪ from Lutzville grapes. Fresh, flavoursome & balanced step up on previous, ready to enjoy. — MW

Location: Durbanville ▪ Map: Durbanville, Philadelphia & Darling ▪ Map grid reference: C7 ▪ WO: Western Cape ▪ Est 2009 ▪ Tasting by appt ▪ Owner(s) Makaziwe & Tukwini Mandela ▪ Winemaker(s)/viticulturist(s) Rudi von Waltsleben (D'Aria Winery) ▪ 50% red 50% white ▪ capewinematch@gmail.com ▪ www.house-of-mandela.com ▪ S 33° 50' 28.6" E 018° 36' 36.2" ▪ 🗺 steady.dices.seperators ▪ **T +27 (0)82-686-6854**

Hout Bay Vineyards

On their small mountainside Hout Bay property, Peter and Catharine Roeloffze established a vineyard (including the locally rare grape, meunier), as well as a cellar and house, carving out the slopes to do so. They also bring in some grapes to complement their tiny harvest, from as far afield as Wellington. It's as intensely hands-on as you'd expect from a pair who've taught themselves about winegrowing from scratch.

Hout Bay Vineyards range

★★★★ **Shiraz** Spicy & ripe aromas with classic floral-herbal character on **16** ⑧⑥. Sweet fruit, the oaking not obvious; finish warmed by 14.2% alcohol. Fairly easygoing but with effective tannin-acid backbone.

★★★★ **Petrus** Shiraz (41%) leads **15** ⑧⑧, plus 4 Rhône varieties. Clear wood influence (60% new, oak & 15% acacia) but plenty of fruit flavour. Smooth, fairly rich but with firm acidity. Grapes ex Wellington. Also in 1.5 & 3L.

★★★★ **Klasiek by Catherine** Chardonnay-led **16** ⑧⑦ méthode cap classique sparkler with 20% pinot noir & a drop of meunier. Mid-gold, spiced apple & hint of brioche lead to richly flavourful, silky & genuinely bone-dry palate.

Merlot ★★★☆ Bright fruitcake aromas with oak-mocha & herbal notes on **17** ⑧⑤, the herbaceousness more obvious on the palate. Approachably but usefully structured with ripe tannin. 15% alcohol. **Blush** ★★★ Previewed lightly aromatic, flavourful & individual **19** ⑧⓪ rosé from 60% chardonnay, plus pinot noir & meunier. Lightish 12% alcohol, dry, soft texture. **Sauvignon Blanc** ★★★★ Intense aroma & flavour on pre-bottling **19** ⑧④, with tropical & grassy elements, plus a little earthiness. Gentle texture shot through with bright acidity; nicely balanced & dry.

Black Swan range

★★★★ **Cape Vintage** ⓠ Tasty modern-style 'port', **13** ⑧⑨ lovely pepperiness on deep core of dark fruit & molasses, dry pliable tannins, 19% alcohol nicely knit. Equal parts 5 traditional varieties. WO W Cape.— TJ

Location: Hout Bay ▪ Map: Cape Peninsula ▪ Map grid reference: A3 ▪ WO: Hout Bay/Western Cape ▪ Est 2001
▪ 1stB 2004 ▪ Tasting, sales & cellar tours by appt ▪ Fee R50pp (min R300) ▪ Facilities for children ▪ Owner(s)
Peter & Catharine Roeloffze ▪ Cellarmaster(s)/winemaker(s)/viticulturist(s) Peter & Catharine Roeloffze
(both Jan 2004) ▪ 3.5ha/1.1ha (merlot, meunier, pinot noir, shiraz, chard, sauv, viog) ▪ 24t/2,800cs own
label 40% red 20% white 20% rosé 20% MCC ▪ Other brand: HB Vineyards ▪ PO Box 26659 Hout Bay 7872
▪ cathy@4mb.co.za ▪ www.houtbayvineyards.co.za ▪ S 34° 1' 31.0" E 018° 22' 31.0" ▪ ⟨ℳ⟩ hatches.invariably.
shrugged ▪ **T +27 (0)83-790-3303**

Houw Hoek Vineyards   (ⱴ) (ᵞᵞ) (◎) (⅄)

Much larger in size and scope than the norm, Clive Heward's farm stall on Elgin's Houw Hoek pass has an
extensive collection of local wines on its shelves, lately including this house label, vinified off-site by a
consultant from home-grown chardonnay and some brought-in shiraz.

★★★★ **Chardonnay** (ⱴ) Expressive fruit, intense citrus dusted with sweet spice, **15** (87) still in prime of
health. Racy acidity is an appealing underpin, the whole effect lively, vibrant, packed with flavour.

Shiraz (ⱴ) ★★★ Opaque colour, deep & dense, smoky liquorice tones, some prosciutto, **15** (82) generous
flavours, dark fruit & streamlined body. — GdB, CR

Location/map/WO: Elgin ▪ Map grid reference: D3 ▪ Est 2004 ▪ 1stB 2012 ▪ Tasting & sales Mon-Sat 9.30-5 ▪
Closed Dec 25 ▪ Farm stall ▪ Coffee shop Mon-Sun 7.30-5.30 b'fast & lunch ▪ Gift shop ▪ Facilities for children
▪ Tour groups ▪ Walking/hiking trails ▪ Craft beer ▪ Owner(s) Clive Heward ▪ Cellarmaster(s)/winemaker(s)
Kevin Grant (Jan 2013, consultant) ▪ Viticulturist(s) Braam Gericke (consultant) ▪ 10ha/2ha (chard) ▪ 8t/800cs
own label ▪ houwhoekfarmstall@gmail.com ▪ www.houwhoekfarmstall.co.za ▪ S 34° 12' 24.62" E 019° 8'
55.19" ▪ ⟨ℳ⟩ incident.survive.clans ▪ **T +27 (0)28-284-9015 (farm stall)**

Hughes Family Wines   (ⱴ)

Output from Billy Hughes' organically farmed Swartland vines, mostly Mediterranean varieties, was already
affected by drought, but much of the vinified remainder was destroyed end-2018 in a fire at the facility
bottling and storing his wines. 'With a lot of positivity from friends and customers', plus support from
winemaker Lieze Norval and new co-owner, daughter Kiki, the Argentina-born, SA-naturalised marine
engineer 'managed to recover and continues to grow' their Nativo brand. A creatively constructed cellar and
tasting room is 'now fully functional, ready to receive visitors'.

Nativo range

★★★★☆ **Red Blend** (☉) Creative, individual & delicious blend of shiraz, grenache, mourvèdre, tempranillo & pinotage, latter upped from 6% to 27% in **17** (90). Still very youthful, with rich dark fruit & earthy
touch, firm tannin grip. Some wholebunch; 50% of wine old-oaked, rest tank & 'egg'. No **16**.

★★★★☆ **White Blend** (ⱴ) (☉) Singular **15** (92) melange chenin, grenache blanc & roussanne led by
70% viognier in new-wave Swartland style: minimal intervention & just a whisper of old oak allow fruit to
shine. Viognier component pleasingly restrained; balanced, poised & bone-dry.— WB

Location: Malmesbury ▪ Map/WO: Swartland ▪ Map grid reference: C6 ▪ Est 2000 ▪ 1stB 2004 ▪ Tasting
by appt ▪ Owner(s) Billy & Kiki Hughes ▪ Cellarmaster(s) Billy Hughes ▪ Winemaker(s) Lieze Norval ▪
Viticulturist(s) Kevin Watt (Jul 2005, consultant) ▪ 52ha/27ha (grenache n/b, mourv, ptage, tempranillo,
shiraz, chenin, rouss, viog) ▪ 180t total 25t/3,600cs own label 50% red 50% white ▪ Organic ▪ 6 Riverstone
Rd, Tierboskloof, Hout Bay 7806 ▪ billy@nativo.co.za ▪ www.nativo.co.za ▪ S 33° 20' 37.71" E 018° 43' 45.09" ▪
⟨ℳ⟩ erase.stylings.guesses ▪ **T +27 (0)83-270-2457**

☐ **Huguenot Wine Farmers** See Editor's Note

Huis van Chevallerie   (ⱴ) (◎)

Christa von La Chevallerie worked tirelessly on family farm Nuwedam on Swartland's Paardeberg Mountain
to rehabilitate the old bushvine vineyards, till the grapes they ripened were of such quality they attracted
the attention of some of the great names in modern SA wine. Two of those, husband and wife Chris and
Suzaan Alheit (Alheit Vineyards), bought the property last year. Christa will continue with her own label of
sparkling and still wines, including the chenin named for the farm and the first to be released bearing the
Certified Heritage Vineyard seal of the Old Vine Project.

★★★★☆ **Nuwedam Old Vine Chenin Blanc** (🏵) (🍷) Seductive white peach & earth, well-judged oxidative styling (natural old-oak ferment), trenchant dryness in **18** (94). Thrilling acidity & salinity deepen & extend the unfruity flavours, heighten the sense of being able to reach out & touch the gnarled vines.

★★★★ **Filia Chenin Blanc Kaap Klassiek** (🏵) (🍷) MCC bubbly from old-vine chenin. Oxidative bruised apple aromas on intriguing **15** (87). Persistent varietal flavours but no typical development from 18 months on lees. Zero dosage, bone-dry. **14** (87) also available. Also in 1.5L.

★★★★ **Springhaas Vin Blanc** (NEW) Swartland chenin (55%) leads Voor Paardeberg verdelho in upbeat, bone-dry, bunch-fermented (in old oak) **18** (88). Fruit-filled, with good acid verve from both grapes.

★★★★☆ **Filia Chenin Blanc Kaap Klassiek Reserve** (NEW) (🏵) (🍷) Same base wine as Filia, this 30 months on lees in bottle. Vibrant zero-dosage **15** (93) sparkler's apple nuances (green, yellow & candied), apple pie richness pierced by brilliant acidity & bone-dryness. A triumph for chenin. Also in magnum.

★★★★ **Circa Rosecco** Lightly sparkling pinotage with 18% colombard, styled on Italy's Prosecco. **NV** (88) palest pink hue, myriad tiny bubbles, savoury & umami tones for food partnering or solo.

Not tasted: **The Hummingbird Colibri**. — CvZ

Location: Riebeek-Kasteel ▪ Map: Swartland ▪ Map grid reference: D6 ▪ WO: Swartland/Western Cape ▪ Est 1956 ▪ 1stB 2011 ▪ Tasting by appt only ▪ Pub hols by prior arrangement ▪ Tours & tastings in the Swartland available by appt ▪ Owner(s)/winemaker(s) Christa von La Chevallerie ▪ Viticulturist(s) Christa von La Chevallerie & several consultants ▪ (vyds: ptage, chenin; bought in: verdelho, viura) ▪ 90% MCC 10% still wines ▪ 32 Main Str, Riebeek-Kasteel 7307 ▪ info@huisvanchevallerie.com ▪ S 33° 23′ 0.77″ E 018° 53′ 46.13″ ▪ (📍) mismatched.tungsten.flammable ▪ **T +27 (0)72-237-1166**

Hunneyball Wines   (💡) (🏠) (📷)

Swedish transplants and boutique vignerons Jim Hunneyball and wife Marie source grapes from Stellenbosch, where local winemakers encourage and mentor. The couple also have a guest house in Stellenbosch town, and offer guided wine tours to selected cellars in the area. No wines to taste this edition.

Location/map: Stellenbosch ▪ Map grid reference: F5 ▪ Est 2012 ▪ 1stB 2011 ▪ Tasting by appt ▪ Guided wine/regional tours ▪ Hunneyball House, 32 Herold Str, Stellenbosch ▪ Winemaker(s) Jim & Marie Hunneyball ▪ 5t ▪ 100% red ▪ PO Box 795 Stellenbosch 7599 ▪ jim@africaninvite.com, marie@hunneyballhouse.com ▪ www.africaninvite.com ▪ www.hunneyballhouse.com ▪ S 33° 56′ 13.99″ E 018° 51′ 7.58″ ▪ (📍) craft.shades.belonged ▪ **T +27 (0)71-674-9379**

☐ **Hunterspeak** see Niel Joubert Estate
☐ **Hunting Family** see Slaley
☐ **IBN Negociants** see O'Connell's
☐ **Idelia** see Swartland Winery
☐ **Ideology** see Spier

Idiom Collection   (💡) (🍴) (📷)

The addition of four stellar reds to the 900 range of this Helderberg cellar, vineyards and visitor centre, developed by the Italian Bottega family, follows last year's expansion of the Idiom Collection. Clearly a good return on viticultural investment, including imported Italian expertise on pruning techniques, especially instructive given the Italian varieties in the mix. Sign, too, of the belief in the potential of the site on the mountainside above Sir Lowry's Pass village (grapes also used for separately listed sibling Whalehaven).

900 Series

★★★★☆ **Cabernet Sauvignon** (NEW) (🏵) Impressive **15** (93) shows quintessential varietal form, lithe yet powerful structure, nervous herbaceous notes & beguiling forest floor, liquorice & cassis. Sweetly ripe, with silky tannins, refined & precise.

★★★★ **Cabernet Franc** Opulent & dense black fruit on **15** (86) is atypical for variety, but very appealing. Thick tannins need time to unfurl. Last tasted was red-fruited **06** ★★★.

★★★★☆ **Merlot** (NEW) Blockbuster **15** (90) has generously ripe black fruit, plump body, silky texture, thumping 15.2% alcohol. Big & overtly New World style expresses weight & density in place of elegance.

★★★★☆ **Pinotage** (NEW) Strong varietal identity, with strident wild berry fruit, mineral nuances, massive body & concentration in **15** (90). 24 months in mostly new oak not intrusive.

★★★★☆ **Syrah** (NEW) Massive & muscular **14** (91) has extract to burn, with brooding black fruit, dense tannins laced with whiffs of fragrant scrub. Hefty 14.6% alcohol. 2 years in mostly new French oak.

Occasional release: **Barbera**, **Mourvèdre**, **Nebbiolo**, **Sangiovese**.

Idiom Collection

★★★★ **Malbec** (✓) Though big, ripe & full bodied, **15** (86) better modulated than **14** ★★★ (82), with fresh mulberry & cherry fruit, strong oak spice, riper tannins.

★★★★ **Sangiovese** Laudable effort with classic Tuscan grape, **16** (89) has New World influence but retains typical acidity, sleekness & bright red fruit. Full oak presence (40% new barrique) should integrate.

★★★★ **Zinfandel** Spicy stewed fruit profile with overt minty-herbal notes, **16** ★★★☆ (83) atypically light & sinewy, with chewy tannins. **15** (88) had lovely intensity of fruit, polished finish.

★★★★☆ **Cabernet Sauvignon-Merlot-Cabernet Franc-Petit Verdot** (✓) Convincing Bordeaux blend, **15** (91) is earthy & rigidly structured, with fine-tuned currant fruit, leafy herbaceousness & dominant tannins. Very satisfying, with potential to cellar several years.

★★★★ **Cape Blend** Solid **15** (88), from pinotage, merlot, cab & shiraz, offers black cherry, damson & currants plus leather & sweet spices. Intense & concentrated, with formidable tannin cloak, needs time.

★★★★ **Shiraz-Mourvèdre-Viognier** Very appealing Rhône blend, **15** (88) exudes ripeness & radiant health. Mix of French & American oak adds background spice. Step up from **14** ★★★☆ (84).

★★★★ **Semillon** Wet wool, oak spice, ginger & sherry nuance in characterful **17** (86) preview, with textured mouthfeel & piquant acid. Barrel ferment/8-12 months. Improves on more mineral **16** ★★★☆ (85).

★★★★ **Viognier** Up to 12 months in French oak & acacia barriques, 20% new, mean **17** (88) has prominent wood character but also appealing peach fruit, varietal fatness, tangy acidity on finish.

Grenache-Tempranillo (✓) ★★★★ Strident minty-medicinal tones detract somewhat on **15** (83) Spanish pairing. Fresh & juicy, with reined-in tannins. Alcohol a bold 15.5%. Not tasted: **Nebbiolo**. Occasional release: **Barbera**.

Heritage Series

Rosso di Stellenbosch (✓) ★★★★ Rhubarb & tomato paste notes on cheerful, juicy **16** (84). Sangiovese with 3% barbera. **Bianco di Stellenbosch** ★★★★ Hints of anise on **18** (83) pinot grigio, offering wholesome body & fruit, appealing texture. — GdB

Location: Sir Lowry's Pass ▪ Map: Helderberg ▪ Map grid reference: H7 ▪ WO: Stellenbosch ▪ Est 1999/1stB 2003/4 ▪ Tasting & sales Tue-Sun 10-5 and Restaurant Tue-Sun 11-5 (see website for extended hours in summer) ▪ Wine tasting & canapés; food & wine experience; deli & restaurant ▪ Fynbos perfumery & imported Vinotria Italian wine library ▪ Italian festival (Feb/Mar) ▪ Owner(s) Bottega family ▪ Winemaker(s) Reino Thiart ▪ 35ha (barbera, cabs s/f, merlot, mourv, nebbiolo, p verdot, ptage, sangio, shiraz, zin, sauv, sem, viog) ▪ 85% red 15% white ▪ PO Box 3802 Somerset West 7129 ▪ wine@idiom.co.za ▪ www.idiom.co.za, www.bottegafamilywine.co.za ▪ S 34° 6' 17.25" E 018° 56' 26.11" ▪ [W] coolest.operate.reclassify ▪ **T +27 (0)21-858-1088 (tasting/restaurant)/+27 (0)21-852-3590 (distribution/sales)**

Idun

Albert Rousset, born in Mauritius into a French-Danish 'family of dreamers', and introduced at an early age to 'the poetry of wine', after a successful career in apparel was pushed towards setting out on his dream journey — making wine — by a midlife crisis. Now he and wife Joanne are based on an Elgin farm named Idun, after the Norse goddess of eternal youth, and making up for lost time with a slew of new releases. There's more due this year and next: Syrah, MCC sparkling and two red blends in the Poetic range.

Poetic range (NEW)

★★★★ **Crepuscule** Classic styling for **18** (88) pinot noir, elegance, red berries, faintest hint of forest floor in the flavours, the oak (50% new) in support, not intruding. Has finesse, refinement.

★★★★ **Renaissance** 300L barrels, 45% new oak & more maturation than Reverie gives **18** (87) chardonnay lovely balance, depth of flavour. Citrus & stonefruit, an oat biscuit seam, long finish. Unshowy, just quality & style. Elgin WO, as all this range.

Jouvence ★★★ Differently packaged to other range. Chardonnay unadorned, no oak, wild yeast ferment (as rest), **18** ⑧① is softly fruity, mainly citrus, with good palate weight despite its 12.5% alcohol sleekness.

Reverie range

★★★★ **Sauvignon Blanc** Intense passionfruit throughout; **18** ⑧⑥'s other layers include some leafy notes & appealing saline acidity. Tightly focused, pure. Up a notch on **17** ★★★ ⑧②.

Merlot ★★★ Older oak, but a strong presence in **17** ⑧①; black pepper & cloves, a firm foundation for ageing, the fruit subservient. Nice dark chocolate notes. **Syrah** ★★★★ Smoky, spicy, dark-fruited **17** ⑧④ is unmistakably syrah, muscular & savoury, nice grip; cries out for charcuterie & hearty food, venison, to show its suitability. **Chardonnay** ★★★★ Boldly New World, though mainly older barrels for **17** ⑧③, showing on the nose as roasted almonds in the fruit, becoming quite savoury & prominent in the flavours. — CR

Location: Elgin ▪ WO: Cape South Coast/Elgin ▪ 1stB 2017 ▪ Closed to public ▪ Owner/s) Albert & Joanne Rousset ▪ Winemaker(s) Albert Rousset, Kobie Viljoen (consultant) ▪ info@idun.co.za ▪ www.idun.co.za

---

illimis Wines

A decade of hands-on involvement in vineyards and cellars locally and in California and Italy helped shape Somerset West boutique-brand owner and winemaker Lucinda Heyns' vision for illimis. 'Wine should be a window to the place its vines are rooted,' she believes, and her vinification decisions are made accordingly, notably minimal intervention and neutral oak for fermentation and ageing. Respect for the environment and society is also key, hence support for Horizon House, a residential and sheltered-employment centre specialising in the holistic care of people with a primary intellectual disability.

★★★★ **Cinsault** Bone-dry, supple & vibrant **18** ⑧⑨ follows pleasing light-textured style of previous. Even lower alcohol, just 11.4%, yet no lack of seriousness. 50/50 carbonic maceration/bunch ferment.

★★★★☆ **Chenin Blanc** A lovely expression of variety not readily associated with Elgin. **18** ⑨⓪ slightly riper than previous (14% alcohol) but equally composed & balanced. Brilliant acid structure, smooth persistence from neutral-oak ferment, 6 month on lees.

★★★★ **Riesling** Locally uncommon grape, this rarer still in being barrel fermented (as for Chenin), which gives **18** ⑧⑦ more texture, breadth & weight than the norm. Engaging appley lift in the finish, balances the few grams of sugar.— CvZ

Location: Somerset West ▪ WO: Darling/Elgin ▪ Est/1stB 2015 ▪ Tasting by appt ▪ Owner(s)/winemaker(s) Lucinda Heyns ▪ 940cs ▪ lucinda@illimiswines.com ▪ www.illimiswines.com ▪ **T +27 (0)84-370-4282**

☐ **Imagine** *see* Southern Sky Wines

Imbuko Wines

From Uitkyk, their deceptively tranquil home-farm in Wellington, the Van Zyl family owners continue to build a hugely successful business with numerous export brands, all Fairtrade-certified, some organic, but founder-cellarmaster Theunis van Zyl reports on surging local popularity, too, thanks to 'keeping our tasting room offerings fresh and interesting, and engaging with all our followers as diversely as possible'.

Du Plevaux Private Collection

Jean Prieur Pinotage ★★★ Dark fruit & mocha but also slight aloe vera edge to **16** ⑧②, year in 2nd/3rd-fill French barrels, like next. Oak staves for all other reds unless noted. **Daniël Johannes Shiraz** ★★★★ Smooth **16** ⑧⑤ less sweet than choc-vanilla nose suggests, packed with red fruit, spice & pepper especially on the finish. WO W Cape, rest of these Wellington origin. **Madeleine Menanteau Sauvignon Blanc** ★★★ Previewed last time, **18** ⑧① now more expressive of tropical fig & guava, with lime peel & asparagus on finish. **Elizabeth Albertha Chenin Blanc-Viognier** ★★★★ Pre-bottling last edition, **18** ⑧③ still has high-toned floral aromatics from 7% viognier, creamy texture, ripe peach & apricot flavours.

Van Zijl Family Vintners range

★★★★ **Reserve Blue Ink** Was 100% cab previously, adds 30% merlot, 5% each cab franc & petit verdot in notch-up **16** ⑧⑧. Fresh acidity enlivens rich dark fruit, seamless after year French oak. Big, bold yet alcohol below 13.5%.

Cabernet Sauvignon ★★★ Fruit-driven **17** ⑧② well-stocked with ripe black berries & hints of vanilla. Few grams sugar for easy-drinking appeal, as with reds in all ranges. **Coffee Pinotage** ★★★ Plenty of ripe plum & blueberry fruit in **18** ⑧ to complement advertised roast bean (coffee & cocoa) tones. **Pinotage** ⓧ ★★★ Gluggable bright berries, cocoa & pleasantly grippy tannins in **16** ⑦. **Shiraz-Mourvèdre** ★★★ As previous, just a splash of mourvèdre, but the **17** ⑧ blend is smoother than last, for easier everyday drinking. Tangy red fruit, hints of pepper & spice. **Bushvine Chenin Blanc** ⊘ ★★★★ After lean **18** ★★★ ⑦, **19** ⑧ has more fruity substance, cling peach & citrus flavours. Refreshing, with reined-in alcohol (±12%). **Sauvignon Blanc** ★★★ Crisp, dry, zesty **19** ⑦ has herbaceous aromas & lime/green apple fruit. **Chardonnay-Viognier** ⓧ ★★★ Creamy baked apple, vibrant fresh stonefruit & sprinkle of spice (though unwooded), **18** ⑧ delightful, softly dry summer white.

Imbuko range

Cabernet Sauvignon ⊘ ★★★ Black berries & plums in **18** ⑦, along with oak-derived clove & vanilla notes. **Merlot** ⊘ ★★★ Sawdust & Xmas spice on nose of soft, juicy, plummy **18** ⑦. **Chenin Blanc** ⊘ ★★★ Unwooded **19** ⑦ offers tropical fruit salad flavours for fresh, lively, casual quaffing. **Sauvignon Blanc** ★★ Brisk **19** ⑦ has cut-grass & lemongrass aromas, zesty lime on the palate. **Iswithi Pinotage** ⊘ ★★★ As name hints, **17** ⑦ is sweet (23 g/l sugar), with cherry cola flavours, but finishes clean & fresh. Unoaked. **Discontinued: Chardonnay.**

Shortwood range

Premium Shiraz ⊘ ★★★ Ample cherry (fruit, pip, liqueur) & a medium body in **16** ⑦, generous grind of black pepper, too. **Premium Cabernet Sauvignon-Merlot** ⊘ ★★★ Smooth, easy-drinking **17** ⑦, 60/40 blend with Ribena-like intensity of black berry & plum fruit, lick of vanilla oak. **Red** ★★ Latest **NV** ⑦ burger/braai wine is soft, succulent, with red berry flavours. Undisclosed varieties, as next. **Rosé** ⒩⒠⒲ ★★ Semi-dry **19** ⑦ has strawberry, tangerine & ruby grapefruit flavours, sub-12% alcohol, for serving chilled with a picnic. **Chenin Blanc** ⊘ ★★★ Likeable, easy-to-drink **19** ⑦ returns to the guide (& changes name, was 'White') with greengage & melon fruit, fresh & dry, pithy finish. **Premium Sauvignon Blanc** ★★★ Crisp, clean, dry refreshment, with lemon/lime verve in **19** ⑦. — JG

Location/map: Wellington ▪ Map grid reference: B4 ▪ WO: Western Cape/Wellington ▪ Est/1stB 2004 ▪ Tasting Mon-Fri 9-5 Sat/pub hols 9-2 ▪ Fee R50/5 wines, waived on purchase ▪ Sales 8-5 ▪ Closed Easter weekend, Dec 25 & Jan 1 ▪ Cellar tours by appt only ▪ Food & wine pairing - booking advised ▪ Farm produce ▪ Child friendly ▪ Owner(s) Imbuko Wines (Pty) Ltd ▪ Cellarmaster(s) Theunis van Zyl (2004) ▪ Viticulturist(s) Jan-Louw du Plessis ▪ 60ha (cab, cinsaut, merlot, ptage, shiraz, chenin, sauv, viog) ▪ 570,000cs own label 60% red 40% white ▪ Other export brands: Barrel Selection 008, Fat Barrel, King Shaka, Kleine Kaap, Makulu, Rebourne Fairtrade & Releaf Organic ▪ Fairtrade, IPW, ISO, Organic ▪ PO Box 810 Wellington 7654 ▪ info@ imbuko.co.za ▪ www.imbuko.co.za ▪ S 33° 40' 30.84" E 019° 01' 18.87" ▪ ⌨ bonanza.conceding.clinch ▪ **T +27 (0)21-873-7350**

☐ **Imoya** see KWV Brandies
☐ **Imprint** see Wellington Wines
☐ **Inception** see Libertas Vineyards & Estates
☐ **Indaba** see Cape Classics
☐ **Indwe** see Trizanne Signature Wines

Inevitable Wines ⒩⒠⒲

Neville 'Nev' Lotz ('"Inevitable" is part play on my name, part statement to what's in the bottle') is an AAA School of Advertising alum with Cape Wine Academy courses guiding him to brand management, wine consulting and sommelier services. Encouraged by a wine producer friend, he made a '19 Chardonnay and Shiraz in a custom crush cellar. Confident that 'handmade, small-batch, niche wines' will sell in a 'flooded market', he hopes to double production and release two more bottlings this year.

Location: Stellenbosch ▪ Est/1stB 2019 ▪ Closed to public ▪ Owner(s) Neville Lotz ▪ ±2t/291cs own label 51% red 49% white & 280cs for clients ▪ IPW ▪ inevitablewine@gmail.com ▪ **T +27 (0)61-311-5369**

☐ **Infiniti** see Stellenbosch Vineyards
☐ **Infused by Earth** see Eikendal Vineyards
☐ **Ingenuity** see Nederburg Wines
☐ **Inkará** see Bon Courage Estate

☐ **Integer** *see* Hoopenburg Wines
☐ **Intellego Wines** *See Editor's Note*

Iona Vineyards

'Boys and their toys,' quips GM (and Cape Wine Master) Brad Gold, but he can't resist sharing high-resolution images taken by his camera drone of the unique cloud which blankets Iona, even on the hottest summer days. Remote and isolated, the estate in the Elgin highlands benefits from moist Atlantic air borne by the southeast wind, rising and cooling over the Kogelberg mountains to form misty clouds that then blanket the farm before dissipating into Elgin Valley. Andrew Gunn is the custodian of this special piece of land; wife Rozy's lower-lying Brocha is farmed increasingly organically; a third parcel to the north is home to interesting varieties such as nebbiolo. The portfolio has been refined to best express unique vineyard sites.

Elgin Highlands range

★★★★☆ **Chardonnay** Ⓥ Rich, intense aromas & flavours on **17** ⑨③ yet not without characteristic elegance, thanks to the convincing balance between fruit & structure - notably the fine acidity off cool Iona vineyards. Oak support vital for complexity, but invisible.

★★★★☆ **Sauvignon Blanc** Twist of grapefruit pith & flinty typicity mark lively **18** ★★★★ ⑧⑦. Customary dab (4%) semillon (now oaked, after natural ferment) adds subtle nuance to fresh, zesty & succulent palate. **17** ⑨⓪ more exuberant.

★★★★☆ **Wild Ferment Sauvignon Blanc** Was 'Barrel Fermented', still is vinified (with ambient yeast) in oak, none new this time, 11 months on lees, giving body & texture to **18** ⑨⓪. Well structured, with delightful freshness & citric acidity that leads to bone-dry finish. Vivid granadilla & grapefruit tang.

Not tasted: **Pinot Noir**.

Single Vineyard range ⓃⒺⓌ

★★★★☆ **Fynbos Chardonnay** ⒷⒾⓄ Refined **17** ⑨③ from 3 clones on clay-underlain decomposed sandstone. Rich yet balanced citrus & butterscotch from wild ferment in quarter new French oak & extended (12 months) lees contact. Tauter & more focused than sibling, with layered palate.

★★★★ **Kloof Chardonnay** Confident **17** ⑧⑨ from dryland vines on soils having large silica quartz deposits. Elegant, with citrus tang & creamy breadth ex wild ferment in 25% new oak. Lees stirring during 12-month maturation adds breadth & length.

One Man Band range

★★★★☆ **Red** Bold, spicy cherry & plum vivacity to wild-fermented **14** ⑨⓪, 5-way Bordeaux/Rhône blend from Iona & Brocha farms, led by shiraz (60%). Lower 13.5% alcohol than **13** ⑨① but dry oak notes still prominent (12-16 months, 25% new).

★★★★☆ **White** Equal billing for sauvignon & semillon in **17** ⑨⓪. Crisp grapefruit & nettle, poised fruit & acid with good minerality. Sinewy & refreshing, natural ferment in seasoned oak adding complexity.

Brocha range

★★★★☆ **Solace** Was 'Solace Syrah', still from that variety, on Brocha property, grapes farmed with organic/biodynamic ethos. Naturally fermented **16** ⑨①, like **15** ⑨③, understated dark fruit with big squeeze of tannin & dried herb from 16 months in oak. Complex, nuanced & long, with good density.

Husk Spirit range

Corretto Ⓥ ★★★ From cab & merlot; light amber hue, playful label, fragrant black-fruit perfume; alcohol quite prominent - perhaps better to 'correct' your shot ⑧① with an espresso. — FM, WB

Location/map/WO: Elgin ▪ Map grid reference: C4 ▪ Est 1997 ▪ 1stB 2001 ▪ Tasting, sales & tours Mon-Fri 8–5 Sat by appt ▪ Closed all pub hols ▪ Walks/hikes ▪ MTB ▪ Conservation area ▪ Owner(s) Andrew & Rozanne Gunn, Workers Trust ▪ Winemaker(s) Werner Muller (May 2011), with Thapelo Hlasa (Jun 1997) & Bobby Wallace (May 2017) ▪ Vineyard manager(s) Joseph Sebulana & Bobby Wallace (May 2017) ▪ Viticulturist(s) Jaco Engelbrecht (consultant) ▪ 100ha/40ha (cab, merlot, mourv, p verdot, pinot, shiraz, chard, sauv) ▪ 250t/24,000cs own label 25% red 75% white ▪ PO Box 527 Grabouw 7160 ▪ orders@iona.co.za ▪ www.iona. co.za ▪ S 34° 16' 42.2" E 019° 4' 58.2" ▪ ⓌⒾⒻ refills.hikers.androids ▪ **T +27 (0)28-284-9678**

☐ **Italian Collection** *see* Morgenster Estate

☐ **Iwayini** *see* Maiden Wine Cellars

Izak van der Vyver Wines

With praiseworthy consistency and craftsmanship, Elgin general practitioner and after-hours vigneron Izak van der Vyver sources a tiny parcel of sauvignon from mountain vines behind the home of his friend Paul Cluver and vinifies it in the Paul Cluver Wines production facility, cellarmaster Andries Burger facilitating.

★★★★ **Limited Release Sauvignon Blanc** ⊘ Gorgeous **18** (88), round & full courtesy long lees ageing, fragrant green herb flavours delivered elegantly, finishes unaggressively fresh.— DS

Location/WO: Elgin ▪ 1stB 2002 ▪ Closed to public ▪ Owner(s) Izak van der Vyver ▪ Cellarmaster(s) Andries Burger (Paul Cluver Wines) ▪ Winemaker(s) Izak van der Vyver (Jan 2002) ▪ 1.4t/±166cs own label ▪ PO Box 42 Grabouw 7160 ▪ drs@telkomsa.net ▪ **T +27 (0)21-859-2508**

J9 Wine   ⓠ ⓟ

'The J9 challenge is for everyone to go out and live their 9 lives and do the 9 things they have always wanted to do,' says Janine Petersen, who founded this young wine venture after gaining experience in wine-making, -marketing and -distribution alongside several 'big names', who continue to support her. She's delighted now to be part of the buy-local initiative Proudly South African and have her wines available through its e-store, RSAMade.co.za.

Merlot ★★★★ Earthy, leafy notes on **17** (84) with honest, focused currant fruit. Improved ripeness & varietal expression. **Cabernet Sauvignon-Merlot** ★★★ Cab takes over as senior partner in this two-way blend, **16** (80) lighter-seeming than last (though ±15% alcohol), with juicy blackcurrant fruit, prominent oak & tannin. Not tasted: **Chenin Blanc**, **Sauvignon Blanc**. — GdB

Location/map/WO: Stellenbosch ▪ Map grid reference: E1 ▪ Est 2016 ▪ 1stB 2017 ▪ Tasting Mon-Fri 9-5 Sat 9-2 ▪ Fee R45pp ▪ Closed Easter Sat/Sun, Dec 25 & Jan 1 ▪ Food pairing, chocolate & biltong pairing ▪ Owner(s) Janine Petersen ▪ info@j9wine.com ▪ www.j9wine.com ▪ S 33° 49' 33.4" E 018° 49' 9.3" ▪ ⅷ narrations. monuments.reconnect ▪ **T +27 (0)21-884-4221/+27 (0)62-797-4974**

☐ **Jack Parow Brandy** *see* Parow Brandy

Jacobsdal   ⓠ

This Stellenbosch family farm sees 3rd-generation Cornelis Dumas and son Hannes vinifying a few eminently drinkable wines off substantial vineyards. Fermentation is in traditional open concrete tanks, using wild yeasts. Bottling and marketing have long been done by Distell, and the vintages below are still selling through their network, but Dumas père et fils will be managing the logistics themselves in the future.

★★★★ **Cabernet Sauvignon** ⓠ Unshowy, quietly classic. Blackcurrant & cigarbox on well & restrainedly structured **15** (87). Naturally & traditionally made. Will mature yet.

Pinotage ⓠ ★★★ Unusually light-coloured **14** (81) has charming red-fruited perfume over darker notes. Lightness of fruit is rather elegant, but substantial dry tannins a little unbalanced. — TJ

Location/map/WO: Stellenbosch ▪ Map grid reference: B6 ▪ Est 1916 ▪ 1stB 1974 ▪ Tasting on the farm by appt only ▪ Owner(s) Dumas Ondernemings (Pty) Ltd ▪ Cellarmaster(s) Cornelis Dumas ▪ Winemaker(s)/viticulturist(s) Cornelis Dumas, with Hannes Dumas ▪ 73ha (cab, merlot, ptage, chenin, sauv) ▪ 300t/10,000cs own label 100% red ▪ PO Box 11 Kuils River 7579 ▪ info@jacobsdal.co.za ▪ www.jacobsdal.co.za ▪ S 33° 58' 4.9" E 018° 43' 34.6" ▪ ⅷ coupler.triumphing.palatial ▪ **T +27 (0)21-881-3336**

☐ **Jacoline Haasbroek Wines** *see* My Wyn
☐ **Jacques Bruére** *see* Bon Courage Estate

Jacques Germanier   ⓠ ⓟ ⌂ ◎

A pioneer (as 'African Terroir') of sustainable winefarming in SA, Swiss-owned Jacques Germanier aims to 'delight people with our wines' while caring for the environment and community. The wines reviewed here are part of a much larger portfolio, offered for tasting at the brand home, Sonop Farm near Paarl, along with conference and function facilities, accommodation and book-ahead lunches with lovely valley vistas.

Organic range
Cabernet Sauvignon-Merlot (NEW) ⚐ ★★★ Red & black berry infused **18** ⑧⓪ has dusty top notes, round & smooth tannins that slip down easily. Voor Paardeberg grapes, as next. **Chardonnay-Sauvignon Blanc** (NEW) ⚐ ★★★☆ Refreshing **19** ⑧③, bone-dry, with modest 12% alcohol & vibrant acidity. Sauvignon (37%) grassiness is the main impression though there's an interesting saline/savoury nuance too. — CvZ

Location/map: Paarl ▪ Map grid reference: C1 ▪ WO: Western Cape ▪ Est/1stB 1991 ▪ Tasting & cellar tours by appt ▪ Lunch available for larger groups on request - to book ahead ▪ Conferences ▪ Functions ▪ Conservation area ▪ Guest house ▪ Owner(s) Sophie Germanier ▪ Winemaker(s) Jaco Marais (Nov 2012) ▪ Viticulturist(s) Hanno Roux (2018) ▪ 75ha organic vineyards (cab, merlot, ptage, shiraz, chard, sauv, viog) ▪ Brands for clients: Azania, Bag in Box Collection, Cape Soleil, Landela, Milton Grove, Out of Africa, Sonop (Organic), The Big 5, Tribal, Winds of Change (Organic) ▪ IPW, Organic, WIETA ▪ PO Box 2029 Windmeul Paarl 7630 ▪ admin@germanier.co.za ▪ www.germanier.co.za ▪ S 33° 37' 1.8" E 018° 50' 38.4" ▪ 🖵 ultimate.dimension. consults ▪ **T +27 (0)21-869-8103**

Jacques Smit Wines ⓠ ⓐ

Wellington-based vintner Jacques Smit is also a long-standing vine nurseryman, and a lover of 'port', so it's appropriate that both his currently available Cape Vintages are made from a grape variety that's rare and has a particular viticultural significance - the red-fleshed roobernet, a 1950s crossing of cabernet and alicante bouschet by the eminent prof Chris Orffer. Personally, Jacques rates the LBV over the Vintage, saying the latter is best served with ice.

Limited Releases
Cabernet Sauvignon ⓠ ★★★★ Juicy & appealing **07** ⑧④ easygoing mealtime companion. **Vine Valley** ⓠ ★★★★ Boldly fruited **06** ⑧④ blend cab (67%) & shiraz nicely integrated, pleasing firm handshake. **Cape Late Bottled Vintage Roobernet** ⓠ ★★★★ 'Port' from uncommon red variety, **08** ⑧④ forthcoming, almost pruney fruitcake intensity, cinnamon & nutmeg dusting from different size barrels. Full-sweet & curvy, scarcely showing its age. Retasted, as next. **Cape Vintage Roobernet** ⓠ ★★★ Unoaked, dark-fruited **11** ⑦⑦ shows some maturity year later. Smoky, treacly flavours, not as layered as LBV. Not tasted: **Shiraz**. — CR

Location/map/WO: Wellington ▪ Map grid reference: B3 ▪ Est/1stB 2003 ▪ Tasting, sales & tours by appt ▪ Closed Easter Fri/Sun/Mon, Ascension day, Dec 25/26 & Jan 1 ▪ Facilities for children ▪ Owner(s) Jacques & Marina Smit ▪ Cellarmaster(s)/winemaker(s)/viticulturist(s) Jacques Smit ▪ 60ha/32ha (cab, roobernet, shiraz, Cape riesling, chenin) ▪ 300t total 100% red ▪ Welvanpas PO Box 137 Wellington 7654 ▪ info@ vines2wine.com ▪ www.vines2wine.com ▪ S 33° 39' 2.2" E 019° 1' 9.0" ▪ 🖵 teachers.submits.lipstick ▪ **T +27 (0)21-873-1265**

☐ **Jailbreak** *see* Mountain Ridge Wines
☐ **Jakkalskloof** *see* Wine-of-the-Month Club
☐ **Jakkalsvlei Private Cellar** *See Editor's Note*

Jakob's Vineyards ⓠ

'A labour of love,' says André de Lange, but he and wife Yvonne still have 'a lot of fun'. 2019 saw the 13th harvest off their tiny Hemel-en-Aarde vineyard. The wine, vinified by Peter-Allan Finlayson at Gabriëlskloof, offers (mostly via their online shop) the rare advantage of being released only when drinking well.

★★★★ **Cabernet Sauvignon** A little fynbos, a little tobacco mingle with dark berries on **14** ⑧⑨, attractive & ready now - but no hurry. Ripe flavours, with a sweet opulence from 14.5% alcohol supported by gentle but informing tannins & well-integrated oak. No **13**. — TJ

Location: Hermanus ▪ Map: Walker Bay & Bot River ▪ Map grid reference: C4 ▪ WO: Hemel-en-Aarde Ridge ▪ Est 2002 ▪ 1stB 2006 ▪ Tasting by appt ▪ Wine & olive products available via online shop ▪ Owner(s) André & Yvonne de Lange ▪ Farm manager Peter Davison ▪ Winemaker(s) Peter-Allan Finlayson (2010, consultant) ▪ Viticulturist(s) Johan Pienaar (Jun 2003, consultant) ▪ 5ha/1ha (cab) ▪ 5t/±500cs own label 100% red ▪ PO Box 15885 Vlaeberg 8018 ▪ wine@jakobsvineyards.co.za ▪ www.jakobsvineyards.co.za ▪ S 34° 19' 43.48" E 019° 19' 46.41" ▪ 🖵 tones.unplugging.accruing ▪ **T +27 (0)82-371-5686**

☐ **Jam Jar** *see* Cape Classics

Jan Harmsgat (♀) (🍴) (🏠) (📷)

The unusual name of this large Robertson farm on the Langeberg foothills seems to be a corruption of the original (1723) 'Jan Harmansz Schat', meaning the 'treasure' of its founding owner. Wine (made by Lourens van der Westhuizen of Arendsig) is a small part of agricultural production here, and there are also luxury accommodation, functions facilities and a restaurant.

JHG Wine Collection

★★★★ **Pinot Noir** (NEW) (✓) Totally beguiling **19** (87) has a charming, aromatic fruitiness supported by light, unobtrusive oaking, subtle tannins & a bright freshness. All making for happy early drinkability.

★★★★ **Chenin Blanc** Juicy, flavourful & rich (but not excessively, even quite light-feeling) **19** (86). As usual, unobtrusively supportive oaking adds breadth, succulent acidity adds freshness & sippability. No **18**.

★★★★ **Sauvignon Blanc** (✓) Uneffusive but generously friendly **19** (86) offers ripe tropical aroma & flavour. Zesty but not aggressively so, with pleasing grip to the juiciness. **18** untasted.

Cabernet Sauvignon ★★★★ Pleasing savoury succulence on full-fruited, sweet-noted **17** (85). Softly ripe texture, sufficient grip, & easy balance make for ready drinkability. Wild-yeast fermented, as all except Pinot & Sauvignon. **Pinotage** ★★★★ Bright, clean fruit aromas on **17** (85), with some tantalising perfume. Lighter-feeling than many from this variety, with a modest drily tannic structure. Only older oak as on all these reds. **Shiraz** ★★★★ Spice & ripe plumminess on easygoing **17** (83), a notable sweet element to the fruit, with a compensating acidity. **Chardonnay** ★★★★ Lightly oaked, nutty **17** (85) has forward ripe fruitiness & smoothly rich texture. Marked, like many in range, by a certain sweetness (3.6 g/l sugar). **16** ★★★★ (86) was in better balance & more intense. — TJ

Location: Bonnievale ▪ Map/WO: Robertson ▪ Map grid reference: C2 ▪ Est 1723 ▪ Tasting & sales Mon-Sun 8-5 ▪ Fee R40 ▪ Open all year round ▪ 5-star Country Guest Lodge & Restaurant ▪ Gift shop ▪ Farm produce ▪ Conferences ▪ Walks/hikes ▪ MTB trail ▪ Heritage property ▪ Vineyard tours; farm & nature 4x4 tour ▪ Owner(s) XH Mkhwanazi/AH Kleinhans-Curd ▪ Winemaker(s) Lourens van der Westhuizen (Jan 2011, consultant) ▪ Viticulturist(s) Kowie Smit (Dec 2012, consultant) ▪ 625.05ha/16.35ha (cab, ptage, pinot, shiraz, chard, sauv, viog) ▪ 260t/3,300cs own label 65% red 35% white ▪ IPW, GlobalGAP, Siza, WIETA ▪ PO Box 161 Swellendam 6740 ▪ wine@janharmsgat.com ▪ www.janharmsgat.com ▪ S 33° 56' 48" E 020° 12' 58" ▪ 🎦 validates.understudy.ungraded ▪ **T +27 (0)23-616-3407**

JAN Wines (♀)

The own brand of South Africa's first Michelin-starred chef, Jan Hendrik van der Westhuizen, named for his restaurant JAN, based in Nice, France. The wines are a selection from organic winery Org de Rac's top Waghuis range and bear superbly elegant labels - both rich and restrained, not entirely unlike the wines.

★★★★☆ **Special Cuvée Red** (✓) Shiraz the largest component of **17** (90) with grenache, mourvèdre & verdelho. Aromatic, ripe & juicy yet not over-exuberant. The sweet fruit balanced & supported by bright acidity & firm dry tannins. Well-integrated, supportive oaking.

★★★★☆ **Special Cuvée White** (✓) Retasted **17** (91) has 51% verdelho with roussanne & chenin. Quietly impressive, though unshowy & subtle, with a fine balance. Floral & stonefruit notes, softly textured with a firm acidity, the new-oak element well integrated.— TJ

WO: Swartland ▪ Tasting for groups & sales at Org de Rac (see entry) ▪ Wines also available online ▪ Owner(s) Jan Hendrik van der Westhuizen ▪ Cellarmaster(s) Frank Meaker (Org de Rac) ▪ Winemaker(s) Jurgen Siebritz (Org de Rac) ▪ Viticulturist(s) Heini Grobler (Org de Rac) ▪ pro@orgderac.co.za ▪ www.janhendrik.com ▪ **T +27 (0)22-913-2397**

☐ **Jardin** *see* Jordan Wine Estate
☐ **Jason's Creek** *see* Jason's Hill Private Cellar

Jason's Hill Private Cellar (♀) (📷) (👤) (♿)

It's almost 20 years since Ivy du Toit, then just 21, converted a garage on her family's farm, Jasonsfontein, in Slanghoek Valley, into a mini-cellar and produced the first wine, a Shiraz '01, after six generations of grape growing, going on to gain Diners Club Young Winemaker and Woman Winemaker of the Year titles. The winery is named after an old shepherd, and latterly Ivy's partner in the enterprise has been her husband, Alister Oates, who takes care of the vineyards.

Reserve range

★★★★ **Izak** ⓧ All 5 Bordeaux red varieties, but unusually **15** ⑧⑦ equal petit verdot & cab franc-led. Graphite, scrub, earthiness with the fruit, 18 months oak (80% new) showing serious intent. Needs time.

★★★★ **Beatrix** From chenin, honouring area's 19th-century pioneering woman farmer. Half Hungarian barrels, rest amphoras, **19** ⑧⑨ distinctive ginger biscuit nuance, with thatch, grapefruit & minerality. Not showy, has focus & precision. No **17**, **18**.

Jason's Hill range

★★★★ **Cabernet Sauvignon** ⊘ Classic cassis styling, savoury top note from 14 months oaking, 60% new. **16** ⑧⑦ enough tannin structure for some ageing but balanced, harmonious.

Merlot ⓧ ★★★ Vanilla & bright red berries, **16** ⑦⑧'s perfume draws you in, but firm dry tannins need more time, will reward bottle ageing. Or match with rich dishes. **Shiraz** ⓧ ★★★ Nice combo vivid fruit & oak seasoning in **15** ⑧①, vanilla & sweet spice, tannins end dry, no barrier to enjoyment.

Jason's Creek range

Classic Red ⊘ ⓦ ★★★☆ Creative blend of pinotage, malbec & tannat, punches above its price. **16** ⑧④ glossy red berries, 10 months oak a savoury seam but tannins ripe, palate succulent. — CR

Location: Rawsonville • Map/WO: Breedekloof • Map grid reference: A5 • Est/1stB 2001 • Tasting & sales Mon-Fri 8—5 Sat 10-3 • Shop • Facilities for children • Weddings/functions • 6.5km hiking trail • Owner(s) Du Toit family • Cellarmaster(s) Ivy du Toit (Jan 2001) • Viticulturist(s) Alister Oates (Jan 2004) • 100ha • 45% red 55% white • PO Box 14 Rawsonville 6845 • info@jasonshill.co.za • www.jasonshill.co.za • S 33° 39' 52.3" E 019° 13' 40.6" • ⬚ chilled.armbands.wiper • **T +27 (0)23-344-3256**

Jasper Raats Single Vineyard Wines ⓠ

Longridge cellarmaster Jasper Raats' small but impressive own-label is built on his belief that the fruit of a single vineyard, planted with a single variety, grown according to organic and biodynamic principles and vinified naturally, produces the purest expression of terroir. The new sangiovese is an elaboration of the theme, and a local rarity, in that the single parcel is trellised with one of the Italian pergola systems. The wine salutes the fortitude and resourcefulness of 19th-century Italian weavers who found their new home in the eastern Cape wholly unsuited to silkworm farming. Like many of his peers, Jasper is using clay amphoras 'to reduce the role of oak' in the cellar.

★★★★☆ **Die Plek Cinsault** ⓧ From 40+ year old Helderberg vines, naturally fermented (as all these wines), older oak 13 months. **16** ⑨② wonderfully poised & delicate, with considerable presence - at just 12.3% alcohol - courtesy regal tannin frame, acid backbone. Less fragrant than **15** ⑨① but just as fine.

★★★★ **The Silk Weaver Sangiovese** ⓝⓔⓦ Ready-now **17** ⑧⑧ has variety's dried cherry aromas & flavours, bright acidity. Juicy yet not plush, with savoury tannin grip. From lower Helderberg slopes, as next.

★★★★☆ **Driefontein Organic Syrah** ⊘ ⓐ One of the sterner expressions of the variety, showing densely packed blue fruit, tight-wound tannin, structure to reward the patient. **16** ⑨③ less fruity & heady than **15** ⑨③ (15% alcohol), more mineral.

★★★★ **Driefontein Organic Sauvignon Blanc** ⓧ ⊘ Bunch-pressed, old barrel fermented/10 months, which tempers acidity, adds signature creamy texture. **16** ⑧⑦ back on track after **15** ★★★★☆ ⑧④, with Loire-like yellow fruit tones. Also in 1.5L.

Not tasted: **Cuvée Rika Pinot Noir**. — CvZ

Location/WO: Stellenbosch • Map: Helderberg • Map grid reference: C1 • Est 2010 • 1stB 2011 • Tasting & sales Mon-Sat 11-6 • Closed Good Fri & Dec 25 • Owner(s) Vigneron Consulting Ltd • Winemaker(s)/viticulturist(s) Jasper Raats (2010) • 5.5ha (cinsaut, pinot, sangio, shiraz, sauv) • 17t/2,300cs own label 60% red 40% white • info@jasperraats.co.za • www.jasperraats.co.za • S 34° 0' 55.2" E 018° 49' 60.0" • ⬚ flows.habitats. recliners • **T +27 (0)76-752-5270**

☐ **Jasper Wickens** *see* JC Wickens Wines

Jayne's

Although Jayne Beaumont sold Beaumont Family Wines to son Sebastian in 2015, she continues to live (and make wine) on the farm. 'This is where I belong – in the Botriviera of the Overberg!' She and late husband Raoul always dreamt of growing pinot noir and chardonnay on the hillside here: 'He sadly reneged on his side of the bargain in 2008 but I decided to make the wine anyway as a tribute to him.'

★★★★ **Pinot Noir** Still plenty of red fruit, hint smoky bacon in silky **12** ⑧⑦ (WO Overberg) while smooth **14** ⑧⑥ shows spice & leather, **15** ⑧⑥ is darker, more brooding, with cherries rather than the cranberries of very delicate, pretty **16** ⑧⑧. All 50/50 wholebunch/berry, naturally fermented, year older oak. **13** untasted.

★★★★☆ **Electrique Chardonnay** Own grapes from 21 year old vineyard gently crushed, wild fermented/matured year in 3rd-fill barrels. **18** ⑨⓪, with just 11% alcohol, fresh & flinty yet creamy, with delicate lemon-lime fruit & zest, while equally elegant **17** ⑨⓪ & **16** ⑨⓪ prove merits of cellaring, acquiring biscuit & toasted hazelnut nuances, depth, complexity.— JG

Location: Bot River ▪ WO: Bot River/Overberg ▪ Est/1stB 2011 ▪ Tasting & sales at Beaumont Family Wines ▪ Owner(s)/winemaker(s) Jayne Beaumont ▪ PO Box 3 Bot River 7185 ▪ jayne@beaumont.co.za ▪ www.beaumont.co.za ▪ **T +27 (0)82-928-2300/+27 (0)28-284-9194**

☐ **JC le Roux** see The House of JC le Roux

JC Wickens Wines

A busy and celebratory time it's been for Jasper and Franziska Wickens (the former the winemaker, no longer also working at AA Badenhorst, the latter the viticulturist): 2019 saw the first harvest brought into the century-old cellar they've renovated on Franziska's family farm on Swartland's Paardeberg. Plus planting a tinta barocca vineyard and bottling two new wines for their growing range, including one from 'the first and only 100% semillon gris (red-skinned) vineyard in South Africa'. Not to mention, adds Jasper, 'the arrival of a future winemaker (4th generation), a baby boy for Franziska and me!'

Swerwer range

★★★★☆ **Shiraz** ⓐ Enticingly perfumed aromas lead to elegantly structured palate: harmonious & subtly intense with smooth but vibrant tannins; fresh, 13% alcohol on **18** ⑨④. A touch deeper-fruited than Red Blend. Like that wine, part wholebunch; like all, 12 months old oak, unfined. No **17**.

★★★★☆ **Touriga Nacional** ⓝⓔⓦ Intriguing, succulent charm on maiden **18** ⑨⓪. A perfumed, lingering sweet fruitiness with good balancing acidity & big but rounded tannins; rather less precise than the other reds. Light-feeling; just 12.5% alcohol. Part wholebunch, adding to brightness.

★★★★☆ **Swartland Red Blend** ⓐ Cinsaut announces its dominance (53%) on **18** ⑨④ with aromatic fruity charm & sweet fruit (but a savoury dimension too); with grenache (35%), & tinta barocca to reinforce the serious tannic structure complementing a fresh lightness of touch. Needs time - decant in youth.

★★★★☆ **Chenin Blanc** ⓐ Ripeness of bunch-pressed **18** ⑨③ gives a core of sweet dried peach fruit, but there are also earthy, stony, dry grass elements & a touch of fine austerity, pointed by a vein of fresh acidity. All leading to a satisfying, dry & lingering finish.

★★★★☆ **Rooi-Groen Semillon** ⓝⓔⓦ Mid red-gold hue on **18** ⑨① points to skin contact (6 days) with red version of semillon, as does the savoury lift. Rich texture - almost oily, full of flavour. Like chenin, natural ferment in old oak & matured there 10 months.— TJ

Location: Malmesbury ▪ Map/WO: Swartland ▪ Map grid reference: C8 ▪ Est 2012 ▪ Tasting strictly by appt only ▪ Owner(s)/winemaker(s) Jasper Wickens ▪ Viticulturist(s) Franziska Wickens ▪ 2,000cs ▪ jcwickens@gmail.com ▪ S 33° 33' 44" E 018° 49' 9" ▪ **T +27 (0)72-461-4249**

☐ **JD Initial Series** see Jean Daneel Wines

Jean Daneel Wines

After an illustrious career helping kick-start modern winemaking at such stellar properties as Buitenverwachting and Morgenhof, Jean Daneel is enjoying his 'second' incarnation as a pioneering wine-grower in ancient Overberg soils. While son Jean-Pierre has been handling recent vintages in their Napier village cellar, Jean is still very much involved, 'especially with Jean-Pierre spending much of the time in the US'. The line-up below, reflecting the family's long association with top-quality chenin and red blends, remains unchanged, the Daneels choosing to hold back on new vintage releases 'until later this year'. A stop at their JD Bistro for meals (and winetasting) is a must for lovers of country chic.

Signature Series

★★★★☆ **Red** ⓥ Its succulent fruit sequestered by fairly austere tannins mid-2018, **15** ★★★★ ⑧⑧ Bordeaux/shiraz blend needs a meal accompaniment or, preferably, cellaring to harmonise the serious vinification: ferment in 500L barrel, then 2 years smaller oak, half new. First rated since **11** ⑨⓪.

★★★★☆ **Chenin Blanc** ⓥ Old bushvines supply the apple, pear & stewed quince fruit, & the fresh acidity, 20% new oak the rich oatmeal texture, peanut brittle & almond features. All harmoniously melded in **16** ⑨⓪ with enough verve for food pairing.

Not tasted: **Méthode Cap Classique**.

Directors Signature Series

★★★★☆ **Red** ⓥ Clean black berry fruit in a fine structure, remarkably measured considering all-new wood, 28 months, & 15% alcohol. Cab, cab franc & merlot, **15** ★★★★★ ⑨④ a pleasure now but will amply reward patience. First tasted since **05**.

Not tasted: **Chenin Blanc**, **Sauvignon Blanc**.

JD Initial Series

Red ⓥ ★★★☆ Svelte, with iodine & white pepper, berry fruit ably supported by 2 years old oak. **14** ⑧⑤ is 94% shiraz, dash merlot. Napier grapes but WO Overberg. — DS

Location: Napier ▪ Map: Southern Cape ▪ Map grid reference: B2 ▪ WO: Western Cape/Overberg ▪ Est/1stB 1997 ▪ Tasting, sales & cellar tours by appt ▪ Closed Dec 25 & Jan 1 ▪ JD Bistro ▪ Owner(s) Jean & Renée Daneel ▪ Winemaker(s) Jean-Pierre Daneel ▪ 70t 40% red 60% white ▪ PO Box 200 Napier 7270 ▪ info@ jdwines.co.za ▪ www.jdwinesandbistro.co.za ▪ S 34° 28' 37.82" E 019° 54' 17.09" ▪ 🔲 bowling.exiled.stapling ▪ **T +27 (0)28-423-3724**

☐ **Jean Roi** *see* Anthonij Rupert Wyne
☐ **Jemma** *see* Painted Wolf Wines
☐ **JHG Wine Collection** *see* Jan Harmsgat

JH Meyer Signature Wines ⓥ

A non-interventionist young-gun winemaker who revels in time spent with growers advancing sustainable and organic farming methods, Johan 'Stompie' Meyer fell in love with pinot noir and chardonnay while in Santa Barbara, California. He sources the grapes for this boutique range from special vineyards in cool climates. He also partners a UK importer on au naturel Mother Rock Wines, and is one of the winemakers at Mount Abora Vineyards (see separate entries). None of his solo-venture wines were ready for tasting.

Location: Hermon ▪ Est/1stB 2011 ▪ Private tastings on request ▪ Owner(s) Johan Meyer ▪ Cellarmaster(s)/ winemaker(s)/viticulturist(s) Johan Meyer (2011) ▪ 25t ▪ Own label 80% red 20% white ▪ 1 Main Rd, Hermon 7308 ▪ jhmeyerwines1984@gmail.com ▪ www.jhmeyerwines.co.za ▪ **T +27 (0)79-280-0237**

☐ **Jikken Bareru Experimental Barrels** *see* The Fledge & Co
☐ **Joachim Scholtz** *see* Rogge Cloof

Johan Joubert Wines

Stellenbosch boutique winemaker Johan Joubert, member of the prestigious Cape Winemakers Guild and currently independent after an acclaimed residence at top-ranked Kleine Zalze, focuses on 'playing a role in the SA wine industry by helping cellars making specialised wines'. Johan's latest vintages unfortunately weren't ready for tasting. Previous focused on his favourite varieties, chenin and cabernet, in granite soils.

Location: Stellenbosch ▪ Est 2016 ▪ 1stB 2015 ▪ Closed to public ▪ Owner(s) Johan Joubert ▪ Cellarmaster(s)/ winemaker(s)/viticulturist(s) Johan Joubert (Aug 2016) ▪ 8t total/600cs own label 70% red 30% white + 15,111cs for clients ▪ WIETA ▪ 18 Santa Rosa Str, Die Boord, Stellenbosch 7600 ▪ info@johanjoubertwines.com ▪ www.johanjoubertwines.com ▪ **T +27 (0)21-887-4425**

☐ **John B** *see* Rietvallei Wine Estate

☐ **Jolly Roger** *see* Clayton Wines

Joostenberg Wines ⓘ 🍴 🏠 📷 ⓐ

'Good food, good wine and good friends' is the perfect mantra for the Myburgh-owned and -run venture in Paarl. Long famed for their family-friendly bistro at the Klein Joostenberg venue, winemaker Tyrrel and wife Anette have now opened The Kraal restaurant in converted old buildings at the winery nearby, offering leisurely lunches seated amongst the olive trees (booking essential). Wine-wise, Tyrrel continues to push boundaries with experimental batches and old/new techniques, making wines from the organically farmed vineyards, some of which fall into the realm of the burgeoning Old Vine Project. Separately, Tyrrel and co-owner and brother Philip also make wine under the Myburgh Bros tribute label.

Estate range

★★★★ **Philip Albert Cabernet Sauvignon** 🍇 Attractive **17** ⑧⑦ shows good intensity of ripe black fruit (commendably non-jammy despite hefty 14.5% alcohol) along with supportive tannins & vanilla twist at finish. Small amount of merlot adds roundness.

★★★★☆ **Bakermat** 🍇 🍇 Syrah (43%) leads cab in **16** ⑨② with mourvèdre, touriga - clever, successful blend, the spicy berry fruit with an edge of wildness. Balanced, succulent acid, firm but unag-gressive tannins, some fruit-rich power to carry it to maturity, but already appealing. Properly dry.

★★★★ **Die Agteros Chenin Blanc** 🍇 ✦ Bruised apple notes on **18** ★★★★ ⑧⑤ add rusticity whilst old oak gives ample cinnamon & clove spice though shade less intensity than **17** ⑧⑦. Mostly wholebunch, 10 months on lees.

★★★★ **Fairhead** 🍇 Versatile & food-friendly blend of roussanne, chenin & viognier, **18** ⑧⑨ achieves delicate stonefruit perfume with soft toffee & spicy cream, all edged with lively acidity. Mainly concrete 'egg' & some older oak.

★★★★☆ **Chenin Blanc Noble Late Harvest** 🍇 🍇 Rich & robust **18** ⑨③ ups the sugar (now 140 g/l) but alcohol is dialled down from previous, making for balanced & elegant botrytis dessert. Apricots, marmalade, pineapples all take turns in the spotlight before lengthy honeyed finish rounds out satisfying mouthful. 375 ml.

Not tasted: **Klippe Kou Syrah**.

Family Wines range

The Family Blend ⓘ 🍇 ★★★★ Mostly shiraz in blend. **17** ⑧③ quite light coloured; mildly fruity & easygoing, with a respectable grip. Modestly oaked. **Chenin Blanc** ★★★ Eminently quaffable **18** ⑧② given breadth from 5 months on lees. Crunchy apples, crisp, fresh acidity, delicious everyday enjoyment. Unoaked.

Small Batch Collection

★★★★☆ **No. 19 Kaalgat Steen** 🆕 🍇 🍇 Single barrel of skin-fermented chenin **18** ⑨④ justifies all the hype around 'orange' wines. Layers of flavours - pineapples, cream, spiced apples - with distinctive salty/savoury tang lead to a lipsmacking finish. Bone-dry, 11% alcohol.

Occasional release: **No. 11 Mourvèdre**, **No. 7 Lightweight Syrah**, **No. 10 Touriga Nacional**, **Early Bird Chenin Blanc**. — CM

Location/map/WO: Paarl ▪ Map grid reference: A7 ▪ Est/1stB 1999 ▪ Tasting & cellar tours by appt at Joostenberg Wines ▪ The Kraal restaurant open for Sunday lunches and first Friday suppers - booking essential ▪ Sales daily 10—5 at the Joostenberg Deli & Bistro on Klein Joostenberg Farm ▪ Closed Dec 25 & Jan 1 ▪ Joostenberg Bistro ▪ Facilities for children ▪ Tour groups ▪ Gifts ▪ Farm produce ▪ Conferences ▪ Ludwig's rose nursery & Van den Berg garden centre ▪ Guest accommodation (3 double rooms), contact anette@joostenberg.co.za ▪ Owner(s) Philip & Tyrrel Myburgh ▪ Cellarmaster(s)/viticulturist(s) Tyrrel Myburgh (1999) ▪ Winemaker(s) Tyrrel Myburgh (1999), with Elmerie Joubert (2017) ▪ 29.53ha (cab, merlot, mourv, shiraz, touriga nacional, alvarinho, chenin, rouss, viog) ▪ 120t/6,000cs own label 35% red 50% white 15% NLH ▪ PO Box 82 Elsenburg 7607 ▪ winery@joostenberg.co.za ▪ www.joostenberg.co.za ▪ S 33° 48' 47.21" E 018° 48' 31.70 (Joostenberg Wines/The Kraal), S 33° 49' 34.8" E 018° 47' 45.5" (Joostenberg Deli & Bistro) ▪ 🗺 expensively.premixed.distract, chieftain.peaceful.wheat ▪ **T +27 (0)21-200-9903 (Joostenberg Wines/ The Kraal); +27 (0)21-884-4141 (Joostenberg Deli & Bistro)**

Jordan Wine Estate

Husband-and-wife team Gary and Kathy Jordan have steered the fortunes of their internationally acclaimed Stellenboschkloof family estate since 1993, consistently improving on its reputation through precision winemaking and careful curation of the terroir-matched classic varieties planted by Gary's parents, Ted and Sheelagh after they bought the farm in 1982. With the upgrade of the tasting venue complete, and renovation of their recently acquired boutique country estate in the UK well underway, they're now ticking another item off their bucket list: the planting of assyrtiko, paying homage to Kathy's Greek heritage, to be trained in traditional Santorini manner with ground-hugging baskets to minimise wind damage. Winemaker Sjaak Nelson has already installed the correct amphoras in the Jordan underground cellar in anticipation.

CWG Auction Reserve range

★★★★☆ Sophia ⓐ Only the best Cobblers Hill's French barrels plus 'reserve' cab used for this impressive Bordeaux blend, total 2 years in barrique. **16** ⑨③ follows the styling to a T: dense, sweet cassis fruit & tightly packed tannins, beautiful dry mineral persistence, elegant seam of acidity for the long haul.

★★★★☆ Chardonnay ⓐ Fruit selection from Nine Yards terroir. Less new oak in **18 ★★★★★** ⑨⑤ - 41% versus 80% in **17** ⑨③, 100% in **16** ⑨② - puts purity, minerality & chalkiness of vineyard soil centre stage. Light textured, with vibrant lime, lemon & kumquat flavours seamed by bright acidity. Intended for cellaring 6-10 years.

Reserve range

★★★★☆ Cobblers Hill ⓐ Always a fine & noble Bordeaux red. Eschews **15** ⑨①'s drop cab franc in **16** ⑨② for 2-way blend, cab (72%) & merlot. Cool elegance & fine, taut tannin structure, whisper of coconut from 29% American oak. Fruitier than red siblings, & still youthful, good for 10+ years. Also in magnum.

★★★★☆ Sophia ⓐ Refined Bordeaux blend, smooth & accessible but built for long ageing. Epitomised by **15** ⑨③, which has a berried nose & palate imbued with vanilla from 2 years in oak; seamless & taut, with an assured future. Mostly cab (60%) & merlot selected from Cobblers Hill barrels, like CWG sibling, but including some American casks.

★★★★☆ Nine Yards Chardonnay ⓐ From eponymous stellar vineyard, **18** ⑨④ lavished with 70% new oak but not at the expense of its fruit, which is captivatingly pure & fresh. Meticulous & detailed winemaking as ever, including portion natural ferment. Superb now & worth cellaring many years (the also-available magnums in particular).

★★★★ Méthode Cap Classique Blanc de Blancs ⓩ Jordans limbering up ahead of launching English sparkling from their new Sussex estate? **15** ⑧⑦ from chardonnay, extra-dry, creamy & smooth from 2 years on lees, persistent freshness for solo sipping or celebratory meals.

★★★★☆ Mellifera Natural Sweet Minuscule quantity of Natural Sweet from riesling, named for Cape honey bee. Understated **18** less than half the sugar (53.4 g/l) of **16** ⑨② yet as sophisticated, delicate & graceful. Occasional label - no **17** ⑨② produced. 375 ml.

Jordan Estate range

★★★★☆ The Long Fuse Cabernet Sauvignon Per the name, this is a slow burn, the wine team mooting 11+ years as maturation window for **16** ⑨⓪. Classically styled, as previous, with dense fruit & tight tannins, nervy acidity. 18 months in barrique, portion new, give cigarbox & cedar spice. Also in 1.5L.

★★★★ Black Magic Merlot Partial wholeberry ferment & soft extraction give well-structured **16** ⑧⑥ its plush black fruit, gentle spice ex older oak, slight leafiness also contributes to attractive glassful. Drier & more vivacious than Chameleon sibling.

★★★★☆ The Prospector Syrah Distinguished **17** ⑨② continues quality improvement noted on **16** ⑨⓪. Lovely fynbos & black pepper spicing to the fruit, appealing fantail finish. Less tightly wound in youth than other reds from this producer yet able to age good few years.

★★★★☆ Barrel Fermented Chardonnay Unashamedly New World in style, with robust oaking - 93% of **18** ⑨① saw wood, 27% new, with occasional barrel rolling - & malo, also for the tank-fermented portion. But brilliantly executed, with pure fruit & enlivening acidity ensuring balance, drinkability. Magnums available.

★★★★ Unoaked Chardonnay Relies on varietal fruit & lees ageing for flavour, structure & quality. **18** ⑧⑧ has satin mouthfeel, lemon-lime vivacity. Also-tasted **19** ⑧⑧ preview reticent mid-2019 but exceedingly persistent.

★★★★☆ Inspector Péringuey Chenin Blanc ⊘ ⑧ Fermented & aged 7 months in older barrels, **18** ⑨③ effortlessly balances weight & power with finesse & freshness, retains variety's inherent enlivening acidity via 30% unoaked portion.

★★★★ The Real McCoy Riesling Cleverly juxtaposes acidity & few grams of sugar, delivers generous lime & ginger flavours in a pleasingly light body (12.6% alcohol) in **19** ⑧⑨ tank sample. WO W Cape.

★★★★☆ The Outlier Sauvignon Blanc ⊘ ⑧ Not your average SA sauvignon. (Partly) barrel fermented, for starters, & aged with occasional lees stirring for gravitas, texture & length. But **18** ⑨③ also very tightly wound, giving it a future & making for a thrilling drink in youth.

★★★★ The Cold Fact Sauvignon Blanc Tasted ex tank, **19** ⑧⑦ fruitier than barrel-fermented sibling & for earlier drinking. Blackcurrant & passionfruit nuances, well-judged weight.

Chameleon range

....

No Added Sulphur Merlot ⊘ ⑨ **★★★★** Ready-now **18** ⑧③'s rich plummy fruit lifted by bright acidity, slight ferrous minerality. Nice dry finish, too, with whisper of vanilla from American oak. **Cabernet Sauvignon-Merlot** ⊘ ⑨ **★★★★** Most serious of these reds, with greater varietal distinctivevess & poise, well composed oak structure. **16** ⑧④ liquorice & cigarbox details, cassis fruit tightly packed but delicious now & for a few years.

....

Syrah ⑩④ **★★★** Lightly textured mouthfeel, faint herbs & touch oak spice (15% American), **17** ⑧② appealing & more softly spoken than Prospector sibling. WO W Cape, for export only. **No Added Sulphur Cabernet Franc-Cabernet Sauvignon ★★★** No merlot component in 78/22 combo **18** ⑧① Attractive fennel nuance, softer than expected (& than previous) courtesy vanilla overlay from 67% American oak. **Rosé** ⊘ **★★★★** Syrah & merlot (51/49) the stars in **19** ⑧③ berry & cream glassful. Bone-dry, with 13.5% alcohol to match the fairly grown-up styling. **Chenin Blanc** ⑧ **★★★★** Characterful weekday drinking delivered by tropical- & whiteflower-toned **17**, with exuberant green & yellow apple palate. Previewed **18** ⑧③ similar nuances but more intense. **Sauvignon Blanc-Chardonnay ★★★** Two vintages tasted. Breezy **19** ⑧② tank sample boasts sauvignon's grassy tones & chardonnay's lemon nuances, whereas **18** ⑧① more lemon/lime toned, slightly nutty & less lively. Whimsical illustrations of Cape Dwarf Chameleon by Linda Kathryn Wright for this range. — CvZ

Location/map: Stellenbosch ▪ Map grid reference: C5 ▪ WO: Stellenbosch/Western Cape ▪ Est 1982 ▪ 1stB 1993 ▪ Tasting & sales daily 9.30–4.30 ▪ Tasting fee R90pp ▪ Cellar tours by appt Mon-Fri 11 & 1.30 ▪ Pre-booking required for: tasting & cellar tour R180pp; speciality tasting from R250pp; exclusive vineyard & cellar wine safari from R600pp ▪ Jordan Restaurant ▪ Jordan Bakery ▪ Conferences (30 pax) ▪ Mountain biking ▪ Conservation area ▪ Jordan Luxury Suites ▪ Owner(s) Jordan family ▪ Cellarmaster(s) Gary & Kathy Jordan (1993) ▪ Winemaker(s) Sjaak Nelson (Jan 2002), with Wade Roger-Lund (2014) ▪ Viticulturist(s) Gary Jordan (1983), with Hilton Phipson (2014) ▪ 160ha/105ha (cab, merlot, shiraz, chard, chenin, riesling, sauv) ▪ 750t/80,000cs own label 45% red 54% white 1% rosé ▪ Other export brand: Jardin ▪ Brands for clients: Pick's Pick, Woolworths ▪ PO Box 12592 Die Boord Stellenbosch 7613 ▪ info@jordanwines.com ▪ www.jordanwines.com ▪ S 33° 56' 33.7" E 018° 44' 41.3" ▪ ✉ birdcalls.thereby.shivered ▪ **T +27 (0)21-881-3441**

☐ **Joseph Barry** *see* Barrydale Winery & Distillery

Joubert-Tradauw Wingerde & Kelder   ⑨ ⑪ ⌂ ◎ ⑧ ♿

It was while working in California's Napa Valley that the 3rd-generation owner of this Klein Karoo farm, Meyer Joubert, resolved to pursue his childhood dream of handcrafting premium wine from the family vineyards, and seeing the R62 (which he duly trademarked as a wine brand) turn into a popular tourist trail similar to America's Route 66. Many called him crazy but his vision is now very much a reality, and his boutique cellar (and the deli-bistro run by wife and award-winning cookbook author, Beate) worth visiting.

★★★★ R62 ⑧ Cedar spice complements wild black berry/forest fruit flavours in medium-bodied **14** ⑧⑦, tangy, with fresh acidity, savoury spices on finish. 100% cab (**13 ★★★★** ⑧④ a blend), 30% new oak.

★★★★☆ **Reserve Cabernet Franc** Having shown promise ex barrel last year, **16** ⑨ now over-delivers on complexity, flavour, with secondary smoked meat & leather notes adding to allure of ripe dark fruit, also pepper, liquorice & mocha from 2 years in 50% new French oak. Substantially improves on **15** ★★★☆ ⑧.

★★★★ **Syrah** ⑧ Still fresh & lively, **16** ⑧ previewed last year after 2 years in older French oak now has earthy nuances & savoury spice but eucalyptus has mellowed into dark mint chocolate. Traditional vinification, no filtration, as all.

★★★★ **Chardonnay Barrel Fermented** More savoury, nutty, spicy than tasted from barrel (French, year, 50% new), **16** ⑧ still rich & creamy, with zesty citrus providing ample freshness, balance.

Discontinued: **Redfin Pinot Noir**. — JG

Location: Barrydale • Map: Klein Karoo & Garden Route • Map grid reference: C7 • WO: Tradouw • Est/1stB 1999 • Tasting, sales & cellar tours Mon-Fri 9–5 Sat 10–2 • Closed Easter Fri/Sun & Dec 25 • R62 Deli Mon-Fri 9-3 Sat 10-1 breakfasts, lunches & Klein Karoo tapas • Walks/hikes • MTB • Conservation area • Lentelus B&B (www.lentelus.co.za) • Owner(s) Lentelus Family Trust • Cellarmaster(s)/winemaker(s)/viticulturist(s) Meyer Joubert (1999) • 1,100ha/20ha (cab, merlot, shiraz, chard) • 8,000cs own label 70% red 30% white • PO Box 15 Barrydale 6750 • info@joubert-tradauw.co.za • www.joubert-tradauw.com • S 33° 55' 26.4" E 020° 35' 40.6" • ⟨≡⟩ fine.cowbirds.installs • **T +27 (0)28-125-0086/+27 (0)82-815-3737/+27 (0)71-656-1230**

Journey's End Vineyards ⓠ ⑪ ⊕ ◎

The Gabb family have owned this scenic Sir Lowry's Pass property overlooking False Bay since 1995. Rollo, son of Roger, a founder of Western Wines and popular Kumala brand, has been at the helm since 2007 and overseen many refinements, the latest of which is a stratification of the wine portfolio. The Tales line-up tells a story, the V range is varietally driven, and the Precision series incorporates the trio of top-tier offerings.

Precision range

★★★★☆ **Cape Doctor Cabernet Sauvignon 14** ⑨ continues where **12** ⑨ left off. (No **13** made.) Rich, spicy, deep dark fruit with layered palate, firm oak support (75% new, 18 months) & lingering finish. Shows refinement & restraint.

★★★★ **The Griffin Syrah** Was 'Griffin Shiraz'. Dried lavender & plum succulence on **16** ⑧. Firm backbone of French & American oak tussles with plush, ripe fruit character from carbonic maceration.

★★★★ **Destination Chardonnay** ⑥ Influence of 10 months in 50% new French oak on **18** ⑧ is marked mid-2019, with creamy vanilla shading tangy orange & lemon cream flavour. Structured, spicy & broad, with long finish. Should settle, allow time. Also in magnum. Fairtrade certified, as all ranges.

V-Series

★★★★ **Cabernet Sauvignon** ⑥ Exotic perfumed edge to rounded, approachable **16** ⑧. Medium bodied & gentle, oak (35% new, 20 months) well knit after a further 18 months marrying in bottle.

★★★★ **Shiraz** ⑥ Ripe blueberry plum & spice vivacity to juicy, rounded **15** ⑧. Fresh, soft & supple, it was aged in French & American oak (80/20) for 18 months, just third new.

★★★★ **Chardonnay 18** ★★★★☆ ⑧ continues trend towards lightness while retaining fresh elderflower & citrus tang. Like **17** ⑧, creamy & broad from third new oak, nine months.

Merlot ★★★★ Supple, easy red- & black-fruited **16** ⑧ less generous than previous. Layered palate, with pleasant spice & succulence but a brusque tannin edge.

Tales Series

Pastor's Blend ★★★☆ Reduced to three-way Bordeaux blend with cab in the majority in **17** ⑧. Dry, spicy vibrancy with light herb sheen on black fruit. Good structure. **The Huntsman Shiraz-Mourvèdre-Viognier** ★★★★ Black olive & spice highlights on big, dark-fruited **17** ⑧. Savoury & refreshing, with good platform of well-knit older French & American oak. **Haystack Chardonnay** ★★★ Light, bright & soft **18** ⑧ with ample marmalade, peach appeal. Creamy breadth from lees contact, honeyed nuance on tail. WO W Cape, as next. **Weather Station Sauvignon Blanc** ★★★ Grapefruit tang on rounded yet fresh **18** ⑧. Easy & light, with signature vivacity of grape. Few months on lees add interest. — FM

Location: Sir Lowry's Pass • Map: Helderberg • Map grid reference: G7 • WO: Stellenbosch/Western Cape • Est 1995 • 1stB 2001 • Tasting & sales by appt Mon-Fri 10-5 • Fee R50pp • Closed Easter Fri-Mon, Dec 25 & Jan 1 • Cheese platters & snacks by appt; or BYO picnic • Walks/hikes • Horse riding • MTB • Conservation area •

Owner(s) Gabb family ▪ Cellarmaster(s) Leon Esterhuizen (Jun 2006) ▪ Winemaker(s) Leon Esterhuizen (Jun 2006) & Mike Dawson (Jun 2015) ▪ Viticulturist(s) Lodewyk Retief (Jun 2011) ▪ 50ha/30ha (cabs s/f, malbec, merlot, mourv, p verdot, shiraz, chard, sauv, sem, viog) ▪ 300t/30,000c own label 60% red 40% white ▪ Fairtrade, HACCP, IPW, WIETA ▪ PO Box 3040 Somerset West 7129 ▪ info@journeysend.co.za ▪ www.journeysend.co.za ▪ S 34° 6' 35.11" E 018° 54' 54.06" ▪ ⌨ payouts.unbolted.overlays ▪ T +27 (0)21-858-1929

JP Bredell Wines ⓠ

With Anton Bredell at the helm, the JP Bredell brand in the 1990s became synonymous with quality red wines and, perhaps more so, port-style wines standing shoulder to shoulder with those grown in the Douro. With the sale of the Helderberg farm and cellar, the venture is based in the Langeberg-Garcia ward near Riversdale. Well-matured limited releases of the table wines and famed fortifieds are available for tasting/sale by appointment, along with a 'tribute' Cape Vintage Reserve (untasted by us) produced in 2017 with winemaker son Bernhard (see Scions of Sinai) from the last port vines in the Helderberg.

Bredell's range

★★★★ **Shiraz** ⓠ Featured in our 2007 edition, **03** ⑧⑦ was noted as improvement on previous **01**, with oak cosseting berry fruit, attractive spice on finish.

★★★★ **De Rigueur** ⓠ Cab-led Bordeaux blend, **08** ⑧⑦ bramble & cedar aromas, ripe (but just 13% alcohol), earthy & fruity palate absorbs 14 months oak. Smooth, rich texture, good dry finish.

★★★★★ **Cape Vintage Reserve** ⓠ Long-admired benchmark Cape 'port', splendid blend tinta, touriga, souzão, showing refined power, tremendous length. 60 cases of **00** held back to monitor development, now available. **03** (without 'Reserve' in name) 400 cases of never-before-available 375 ml on offer. **07** ⑨⑦ is the current, more plentiful release.

★★★★ **Late Bottled Vintage** ⓠ 'Port' now released for 1st time in 375 ml, **99** rich, silky, fragranced; also available is a further parcel of seductive, plushly ripe **04** ⑧⑦ in 375 ml. Tinta, souzão, touriga nacional & franca; 3-4 years older barrels.

Merlot ⓠ ★★★☆ Intended as Auction Reserve when Anton Bredell was CWG member, & never released, this parcel of **99** ⑧⑤ shows lovely tertiary earth, leather & undergrowth whiffs, silken sweet-fruited palate. Delicious, enjoy soon. — CM, CvZ

Location: Riversdale ▪ Map: Klein Karoo & Garden Route ▪ Map grid reference: C5 ▪ WO: Stellenbosch ▪ 1stB 1991 ▪ Tasting & sales by appt only ▪ Owner(s) Helderzicht Trust ▪ Winemaker(s)/viticulturist(s) Anton Bredell (1988) ▪ 2ha (port cultivars & some other experimentals) ▪ 500cs own label 20% red 80% port ▪ PO Box 275 Riversdal 6670 ▪ antonbredellwines@gmail.com ▪ www.bredellwines.co.za ▪ S 33° 55' 13.58" E 021° 30' 52.13" ▪ ⌨ tabloid.enchants.headlock ▪ T +27 (0)82-550-0684

Julien Schaal ⓠ

Former sommelier Julien Schaal and winemaker wife Sophie shuttle from their Alsace home, where they produce grand cru riesling, to the Cape where the main focus recently has been on chardonnay. Now, rejoining the vintage 2018 releases of their acclaimed trio from Upper Hemel-en-Aarde and Elgin (where they vinify in the Paul Cluver cellar), is the Syrah, this time 'from two superb sites, in Bot River and on the lagoon side, emphasising the style of cool-climate syrah we love'. Also noteworthy is that, as of vintage 2018, the Schaals have committed to screwcap closures for all their wines.

★★★★ **Syrah** Returns to the guide in fine fettle, **18** ⑧⑧ from pair of Bot River vineyards has Rhône spiciness with fynbos notes. Elegantly weighted, showing velvet tannins & sprightly black cherry fruit.

★★★★☆ **Confluence Chardonnay** Elegantly wrought **18** ⑨③ from Upper Hemel-en-Aarde fruit (as **17** ⑨④) expresses variety's charm & complexity, with richness, texture & finely poised acidity. Imperceptible oak from partial barrel fermentation (25% new), 14 months ageing.

★★★★☆ **Evidence Chardonnay** Accomplished & gracious **18** ⑨③ from single farm in cool-climate Elgin speaks of restraint, in both handling & maturation (14 months in oak, 25% new), with notes of lime & lemon, crisp but balanced acidity & creamy lees-mineral structure.

★★★★☆ **Mountain Vineyards Chardonnay** From Elgin & Upper Hemel-en-Aarde vines, **18** ⑨⓪ has voluptuous marmalade fruit, racy acidity ensuring balance. Fine body & texture promise improvement with few years cellaring. Wild yeasts for all; portion fermented in tank for the whites. — GdB

Location: Elgin ▪ WO: Walker Bay/Cape South Coast/Elgin/Upper Hemel-en-Aarde Valley ▪ Est 2004 ▪ 1stB 2005 ▪ Tasting by appt only ▪ Owner(s) Julien Schaal ▪ Winemaker(s) Sophie & Julien Schaal ▪ 28t/4,000cs own label 20% red 80% white ▪ c/o PO Box 48 Grabouw 7160 ▪ julien@vins-schaal.com ▪ www.julien-schaal.com ▪ T +33 (0)6-10-89-72-14

☐ **Juno** *see* Cape Wine Company
☐ **Kaap Agri** *see* Breëland Winery

Kaapse Familie Wingerde ⚲

The Cape families alluded to in the name of this joint venture have a combined 30 generations' winegrowing expertise: the De Waals in Paarl's Voor Paardeberg ward, marketing as Oude Denneboom, the Loubsers near Philadelphia (Kuyperskraal) and the Le Rouxs in Paarl (Vendôme). See separate entries, and under Vendôme for tasting details. New vintages under this collective label not ready for review this edition.

Paarl Families range

Ingrid's Blush Pinotage Rosé ⚲ ★★★ Much to like about strawberries-&-cream **16** ⑧①, dry, but teensy sprinkle sugar perks up the palate, makes it very tippleable, as does sensible 12.6% alcohol. Not tasted: **Cabernet Sauvignon**, **Sauvignon Blanc**. — CvZ

Location: Paarl ▪ WO: Coastal ▪ Est 1688 ▪ 1stB 2014 ▪ Tasting & sales at Vendôme ▪ Owner(s) Loubser, Le Roux & De Waal families ▪ Winemaker(s) Jannie le Roux & Altus le Roux (consultant) ▪ Viticulturist(s) Viljee Loubser ▪ WIETA ▪ Arboretum Ave, Paarl 7620 ▪ info@kaapsefamiliewingerde.com ▪ www.kaapsefamiliewingerde.com ▪ T +27 (0)21-863-3905

Kaapzicht Wine Estate ⚲ 🏠 📷

The Steytler family have farmed this large Bottelary hillside property since 1946, and are proud that their 1947 chenin vineyard is one which has certified Old Vine status. Danie Steytler jnr, now in his second decade as winemaker, has played a key role in celebrating both family and viticultural heritage through an emphasis on pinotage, chenin and latterly cinsaut. Another focus is on preserving their venerable bushvines through improved soil health and biodiversity. For the first time, a cover crop of turnips was planted between the rows. This not only prevented soil loss during the wet winter season, but also provided organic matter and nutrients for the soil — and ingredients for hearty soups!

Steytler range

★★★★☆ **Pinotage** 🍇 Selection of vintage's best pinotage, **17** ⑨⓪ true to form, elegant, refined & serious, with all-new oak. Powerful & structured but restrained. Layered juicy palate with fruit & tannin in harmony. Needs time. No **16**.

★★★★☆ **Pentagon** 🍇 Statuesque Bordeaux blend showing elegance & leashed power in **17** ⑨①. Succulent, but with squeeze of tannin from all-new oak, rich fruitcake & spice showing well. Majority cab (60%), equal 15% merlot & cab franc, splashes petit verdot & malbec. Stellenbosch WO, as next. No **16**.

★★★★★ **Vision** 🍇 Sophisticated & stellar Cape Blend sees cab lead pinotage & merlot (35/10) in **17** ⑨⑤. Powerful, with cocoa & dark-fruit richness, yet sleek & supple. Vinified & aged separately 28 months before blending. Lovely concentration, poise & persistence. **15** ★★★★★ ⑨③ was first since **12** ⑨⑤. No **16**.

★★★★☆ **The 1947 Chenin Blanc** 🍇 ⚘ Single-vineyard, SA's 2nd-oldest chenin, produces signature rich apricot & nutty flavour on **18** ⑨②, gentle freshness & refinement with a delightful pithy finish. From low-key winemaking; oak kept to 30% new for 1 year. Worth keeping.

Kaapzicht range

★★★★ **Cabernet Sauvignon** Effortlessly combines fruitcake lightness with inky depth & leashed power. **16** ⑧⑧ layered palate with beautifully knit oak, 50% new. Smooth, silky texture & long finish.

★★★★☆ **Cabernet Franc** ⊘ Not discontinued as we thought, **17** ⑨② has signature cocoa, ink & graphite mingling with riper, succulent hedgerow fruits, seductive perfumed edge. Mellow, with leashed power. Oak as for Cab.

★★★★☆ **Skuinsberg Cinsaut** From estate's steepest slope, **18** ★★★★ ⑧⑧ offers trademark cheery, bright red-berry succulence. Light bodied, pliable & dry, saw only older oak. **17** ⑨④ & **15** ★★★★★ ⑨⑦ more generously structured. **16** not made.

★★★★ **Merlot 17** ★★★☆ ⑧⑤ is ripe & appealing but softer, more approachable than last-made **15** ⑧⑨. Coffee tinge to rounded black fruits. Subtle frame of oak, just 30% new.

★★★★ **Pinotage** Plump, pillowy & plush, **17** ★★★★ ⑧⑤ generous in its raspberry & blueberry succulence. Light to medium-bodied, it's less concentrated than inky, dark **16** ⑧⑨.

★★★★ **Kliprug Chenin Blanc** (❀) Rich apricot & honeyed melon flavour on **18** ⑧⑧ single-vineyard offering. Lovely harmony of fruit & wood (old barrels for just 80% of wine). Broad, creamy & structured.

Shiraz ★★★☆ Fynbos & herb edge to attractive blue-fruited **17** ⑧⑤ which follows **15** ★★★★ ⑧⑥. No **16** made. Supple, with good restraint & judicious oak (30% new). Palate is rich & long. **Kaleidoscope Red** ⊘ ★★★ Smoky cherry, plum & liquorice on **18** ⑧② easy-drinking blend. Fun & friendly, made for sharing. **Bin 3** ⊘ ★★★★ Undisclosed red blend again over-delivers in approachability, bags of flavour, soft-textured yet structured body. **16** ⑧⑤ medium concentration & density but long rewarding finish. **Estate Red** ⊘ ★★★☆ Subtle smokiness to yielding yet structured **16** ⑧④ blend, nice squeeze of tannin to the medium body. Gentle, rounded finish. **Pinotage Rosé** ⊘ ★★★ Cheery pink **19** ⑧① offers ample succulence & refreshment, dry cherry & berry flavour. Unfussy & vibrant, with easy charm & alcohol (12.2%). **Chenin Blanc** ⊘ ★★★ Everyday quaffer, **19** ⑧① light & bright, has guava & pear vivacity & zip. No oak in the appealing mix. **Sauvignon Blanc** ★★★ Taut & tangy **19** ⑧⓪, typical grapefruit & zesty vibrancy. Succulent & light. Not tasted: **Pinot Noir**. Discontinued: **Kaleidoscope White, Hanepoot Jerepigo**.

Brandy & Husk Spirit range

★★★★ **15 Year Potstill** (🥃) As the brandy ⑧⑦ matured, it kept harmony & texture, gained in flavour complexity (the almond note particularly attractive), but perhaps lost some brightness, freshness.

Grape Husk Spirit (🥃) ★★★☆ Fresh & persistent spirit ⑧④ from aromatic varieties gewürztraminer & riesling, giving a gentle fragrant quality, the nuttiness touched with grape & raisin notes. 375 ml. — FM, TJ

Location/map: Stellenbosch ▪ Map grid reference: B4 ▪ WO: Bottelary/Stellenbosch ▪ Est 1946 ▪ 1stB 1984 ▪ Tasting & sales Mon-Fri 9–4 Sat/pub hols 10–1 ▪ Closed Good Fri, Dec 24/25/26 & Jan 1 ▪ Conference/ function/wedding & braai venues ▪ MTB trail ▪ Conservation area ▪ Self-catering cottage ▪ Potstill brandy & grappa ▪ Owner(s) Steytdal Farm (Pty) Ltd/Steytler Family Trusts ▪ Cellarmaster(s) Danie Steytler jnr (Jan 2009) ▪ Assistant winemaker Kayleigh Hattingh (Nov 2018) ▪ Viticulturist(s) George Steytler (Jan 1984) & Callie Hefer (Apr 2019) ▪ 190ha/162ha (cabs s/f, cinsaut, malbec, merlot, p verdot, ptage, shiraz, chard, chenin, hanepoot, rouss, sauv, sem, verdelho) ▪ 1,100t/60,000cs own label 70% red 30% white + 20,000cs for clients ▪ Other export brands: Cape View, Friesland, Vet Rooi Olifant ▪ PO Box 35 Koelenhof 7605 ▪ carin@ kaapzicht.co.za ▪ www.kaapzicht.co.za ▪ S 33° 54' 47.7" E 018° 44' 7.7" ▪ ⟨ꟷ⟩ hideout.binders.relation ▪ **T +27 (0)21-906-1620/1**

☐ **Kadette** see Kanonkop Estate
☐ **Kakamas** see Orange River Cellars
☐ **Kalkveld** see Zandvliet Wine Estate

Kanonkop Estate (🥃)(🍴)(🖐)(📷)(♿)

Near-universally regarded as one of SA's 'first-growths', this dynamic and progressive 4th-generation family estate on Stellenbosch's Simonsberg has three cornerstones for quality: only the best fruit (whether estate-grown or brought-in), inspired winemaking (cellarmaster Abrie Beeslaar three times International Winemaker of the Year at the International Wine & Spirit Competition) and ongoing investment in both vineyard and cellar. Recently owners and brothers Paul and Johann Krige acquired a state-of-the-art optical sorter and automatic punch-down machines for their new open fermenters. But technological advancement is always tempered with respect for tradition. Hence the sustained focus on pinotage, the venerable bushvines, the manual punch-down regimes for many of the old cement 'kuipe'. Not forgetting the time-honoured snoek barbecue, available to groups by arrangement, along with other visitor attractions.

Kanonkop Estate range

★★★★☆ **Cabernet Sauvignon** (🍇) A Cape classic & consistent top performer in this guide, 5 stars (one of only 2) in the inaugural edition, **15** ★★★★★ ⑨⑤ makes it 12 maximum ratings total. Refined & sensual rather than austere & cerebral, with forthcoming textbook cassis aromas/flavours, cedar seasoning, polished tannins from 2 years in 50% new oak. Like **14** ⑨④ & previous, has both immediate appeal & minimum 10 years cellaring potential. This range also in formats up to 18L except next.

★★★★★ **Black Label** (symbol) Single-vineyard wine, an always-stellar expression of old-vines pinotage. **17** (96) concentrated & expressive, with lively, piquant core, extravagant vanilla & cedar oak tones. Possibly a little too flamboyant now, but the provenance, the compact fruit, the stern structure from all-new oak/grape tannin interplay - needed for decades-long cellaring - are all there.

★★★★☆ **Pinotage** (symbol) Variety's signature racy acidity & well-judged 80% new oak are key to the exceptional balance & freshness of **17** (93). Always a serious rendering of SA's home-grown grape; rich, dark toned & concentrated but unforced. Superb now & for decade-plus.

★★★★★ **Paul Sauer** (symbol) Stately & ageworthy Bordeaux blend. Mostly cab, as ever, in **16** (96) with merlot, cab franc (62/25/13); classic bouquet of cassis, lead pencil & hedgerow fruit with extra flesh from slightly more merlot than usual. Hallmark oystershell minerality, fine powdery tannins. Like Cab sibling, proud record of, now, 12 maximum ratings.

Kadette range

★★★★ **Cabernet Sauvignon** (NEW) 'Little brother' **18** (89) is for early enjoyment (as all these), with less concentration & more approachable tannins than sibling, yet no lack of typicity in its cassis & cedar tones, or firm grip. Only ex cellardoor & Woolworths outlets.

★★★★ **Pinotage** (✓) Previewed **18** (89) already shows variety's vital acidity & mulberry scents, house's sleek tannins. Also in larger bottle formats, like Cape Blend. All Kadettes Stellenbosch origin unless noted.

★★★★ **Cape Blend** (✓) Vast fan club for this well-priced combo pinotage & 3 Bordeaux varieties, plenty to go round too: 250,000 cases. Previewed & tentatively rated **18** (88) tad unknit, usual friendly tannins more sombre & masking deep red & black fruit, but pleasing spice & leaf top notes.

★★★★ **Pinotage Dry Rosé** (✓) Hugely satisfying **19** (86) has burst of tangy acidity, good weight (14.3% alcohol), long dry finish. Pale Provençal hue, strawberries-&-cream aromas a bonus. Like **18** ★★★☆ (84), combo Stellenbosch & Malmesbury grapes.— CvZ

Location/map: Stellenbosch ▪ Map grid reference: F2 ▪ WO: Simonsberg–Stellenbosch/Stellenbosch/Coastal ▪ Est 1910 ▪ 1stB 1973 ▪ Tasting & sales Mon-Fri 9-5 Sat 9-2 pub hols 10-4 ▪ Fee R70 ▪ Closed Good Fri, Dec 25 & Jan 1 ▪ Cheese platters in summer; traditional snoek barbecues by appt (min 15 people); or BYO picnic ▪ Conservation area ▪ Art gallery ▪ Owner(s) Johann & Paul Krige ▪ Cellarmaster(s) Abrie Beeslaar (Jan 2002) ▪ Winemaker(s) Alet de Wet (Dec 2014) ▪ Viticulturist(s) Ryno Maree (May 2016) & Annelie Viljoen (2017) ▪ 120ha/100ha (cabs s/f, merlot, ptage) ▪ 3,000t/500,000cs own label 98% red 2% rosé ▪ WIETA ▪ PO Box 19 Elsenburg 7607 ▪ wine@kanonkop.co.za ▪ www.kanonkop.co.za ▪ S 33° 51' 18.4" E 018° 51' 36.1" ▪ boggles.could.piglet ▪ **T +27 (0)21-884-4656**

Kanu Wines

Passers-by on the R304 near Stellenbosch cannot have missed the changes happening at Kanu. Investment by the corporate owner, ABC GROUP & Caratex, has seen significant redevelopment, from the entrance through the vineyards to the cellar complex on the hillside. Among many new amenities are a restaurant, curio shop and even mini-golf course to keep children entertained while parents enjoy tastings. Long-time winemaker Johan Grimbeek is invigorated by the new facilities and energy (though, as a keen cook, just a tad disappointed that a planned herb garden made way for putting greens!).

Ultra Premium range

Pinotage (symbol) ★★★☆ Vibrant seam of tangy brambles runs through elegant **17** (83), accentuating its fruitiness. Easy, soft tannin grip for current drinking, fynbos & berry farewell.

Premium range

★★★★ **Shiraz** (✓) Reflects **17** (89) vintage in density & interest. Layered plum, spice, pepper & graphite. Nice body, definition & mouthfeel from 16 months older oak. Step up on **14** ★★★ (81); **15** & **16** untasted.

★★★★ **Keystone** Bordeaux blend tweaked in **17** ★★★☆ (85), cab, petit verdot & cab franc. Fruitcake & cedar appeal, firm backbone & pleasant dry finish from 21 months older oak. Last-tasted **15** (87) had merlot & malbec.

★★★★ **Nu Era** (✓) (symbol) Seductive **17** (86) shiraz & mourvèdre blend delivers blackcurrant pliability with gentle tannic grip & spice vibrancy. Nuanced, succulent & with few grams sugar, will age well. WO W Cape.

★★★★ KCB Chenin Blanc Poised & precise **17** ⑧⑧ with trademark creamy vanilla breadth from 11 months oaking (20% new) & ripe honeyed orange & apricot flavour. Vivid zesty lime tang offsets the 9 g/l sugar beautifully. Harmonious & long. Coastal WO, as unwooded sibling.

Merlot ★★★☆ Improves on previous in concentration, depth of black berry flavour. **18** ⑧⑤ plush texture & dry spicy grip from American oak staves, approachable but structured. **Chenin Blanc ★★★** Light, succulent nectarine vivacity on **18** ⑧② Bright & approachable, with touch sugar balanced by acid freshness for satisfying summer sipping. **Sauvignon Blanc ★★★** Goes up a notch in **19** ⑧⓪ Flint & lemon zest typicity with bright acid freshness. **Angelina Méthode Cap Classique** ⑨ᴇᴡ **★★★★** Pink sparkler from pinot noir with coconut marshmallow appeal. **NV** ⑧④ medium body, balanced & dry with green apple tang after 12 months on lees. **Giselle Méthode Cap Classique ★★★☆** Sourdough & bright citrus marmalade attractions on **NV** ⑧⑤ bubbly from chardonnay & pinot noir. Refreshing, dry, with good body & length from year on lees. **Sauvignon Blanc Noble Late Harvest** ⑨ᴇᴡ **★★★★** Brûléed pineapple & mango sweetness on **15** ⑧④ wooded botrytis dessert. Tangy acid offsets the richness & sugar effectively. Lees breadth on clean, dry-seeming finish. 375 ml. Not tasted: **Viognier**.

Black Label range

Rifle Range Red ⊘ ⑨ **★★★★** Merlot & cab franc with brooding, swarthy depth, cocoa & black cherry verve in **NV** ⑧⑤ Good squeeze of dry tannin & focused finish. Improves on previous. Coastal WO.

Rifle Range White ⑨ **★★** Brief delight from tropical sauvignon, chenin **NV** ⑦① blend. WO W Cape.
Natural Sweet Shiraz ⑨ **★★** Maraschino cherry & cinnamon spicing on Glühwein-like **14** ⑦① Sweet & uncomplicated. — FM

Location/map: Stellenbosch ▪ Map grid reference: E3 ▪ WO: Stellenbosch/Coastal/Western Cape ▪ Est/1stB 1998 ▪ Tasting & sales Mon-Fri 10–4.30 Sat-Sun 10-3 ▪ Fee R60pp ▪ DuVin restaurant ▪ Curio shop ▪ Putt-putt course ▪ Owner(s) ABC GROUP & Caratex (Pty) Ltd ▪ Cellarmaster(s)/winemaker(s) Johan Grimbeek (Jan 2002) ▪ 48ha/20ha (cab, merlot, chard, sauv) ▪ 200t/60,000cs own label 50% red 45% white 5% rosé ▪ WIETA ▪ PO Box 548 Stellenbosch 7599 ▪ info@kanu.co.za ▪ www.kanu.co.za ▪ S 33° 53' 23.35" E 018° 49' 8.44" ▪ ⓦ scooter.mimic.tins ▪ **T +27 (0)21-865-2488**

☐ **Kap Hase** *see* Migliarina Wines
☐ **Kapokberg** *see* Groote Post Vineyards
☐ **Kap Vino Estate** *see* Kunjani Wines

Kara-Tara ⑨ ⑨ᴇᴡ

Young Cape Winemakers Guild protégé and Stellenbosch University oenology graduate Rüdger van Wyk, winemaker at Jonkershoek's Stark-Condé, has vinified his first wine under an own label here with backing from owner-vintner José Conde. That it's a pinot noir is not surprising given Rüdger's postgrad harvest in Burgundy. Kara-Tara is a river near his southern Cape hometown of George.

★★★★ Pinot Noir ⊘ From Elgin & Overberg fruit, **17** ⑧⑨ more New Zealand in style than Burgundy, with pure bright fruit to the fore on a supple acid/tannin base, new oak scaled back to just 10%, persistent dry finish. Doesn't set out to charm or impress, but does so anyway, packaging inclusive.— FM, CvZ

Location: Stellenbosch ▪ WO: Cape South Coast ▪ Est/1stB 2017 ▪ Tasting at Stark-Condé Wines ▪ Owner(s) Kara-Tara (Pty) Ltd ▪ Cellarmaster(s)/winemaker(s) Rüdger van Wyk (2017) ▪ 3,000cs own label ▪ PO Box 389 Stellenbosch 7500 ▪ info@stark-conde.co.za ▪ **T +27 (0)21-861-7700**

☐ **Karate Water** *see* Parow Brandy
☐ **Karoobossie** *see* Teubes Family Wines

Karusa Premium Wines & Craft Brewery ⑨ ⑨⑨ ⓞ ⓑ

Visitors exploring the Klein Karoo will find a smorgasbord of attractions at Karusa near Oudtshoorn: small-parcel wines, from still to bubbly to fortified, a microbrewery, tapas restaurant and deli and, at road's end in the Swartberg mountain foothills, the famous Cango Caves.

Location: Oudtshoorn ▪ Map: Klein Karoo & Garden Route ▪ Map grid reference: B3 ▪ Est/1stB 2004 ▪ Tasting & sales Mon-Fri 9.30–4 Sat 10–2.30 ▪ Closed Sun, Good Fri & Dec 25 ▪ Karoo Tapas Restaurant &

Deli ▪ Conferences (30-40 pax) ▪ Microbrewery ▪ Owner(s) Karusa Partnership ▪ Cellarmaster(s) Jacques Conradie (2004) ▪ 8ha (grenache, mourv, muscadel r, ptage, shiraz, touriga nacional, chard, sauv, viog) ▪ 50-70t/5,000cs own label 30% red 50% white 5% rosé 15% other ▪ PO Box 1061 Oudtshoorn 6620 ▪ info@ karusa.co.za ▪ www.karusa.co.za ▪ S 33° 28' 36.0" E 022° 14' 33.2" ▪ ⓜ zoologists.concepts.prequel ▪ **T +27 (0)44-272-8717**

☐ **Kasteelberg** *see* Riebeek Valley Wine Co

Katbakkies Wine ⓠ

Stellenbosch wine producer and distiller Andries van der Walt vinifies small parcels for his Katbakkies and other labels. In his own words: 'If it can ferment, I will ferment and distil it and make something elegant out of it.'

★★★★ **Cabernet Sauvignon** ⓠ Classically styled **11** ⑧⑦, built around its crunchy ripe fruit & form-giving grape tannins; well proportioned for current enjoyment & further few years.

Syrah ⓠ ★★★★ Last sampled was suave, spicy & unshowily fruity **08** ⑧④. — AL

Location/map/WO: Stellenbosch ▪ Map grid reference: D5 ▪ Est/1stB 1999 ▪ Tasting & sales Mon-Sat by appt ▪ Closed all pub hols ▪ Owner(s) Andries van der Walt ▪ Cellarmaster(s)/winemaker(s) Andries van der Walt (1999) ▪ 29ha/4ha (cab, merlot, shiraz) ▪ 100cs own label 50% red 50% white ▪ PO Box 305 Stellenbosch 7599 ▪ info@katbakkies.co.za ▪ www.katbakkies.co.za ▪ S 33° 55' 37.4" E 018° 49' 14.6" ▪ ⓜ pink.primed.oval ▪ **T +27 (0)82-882-9022**

☐ **Kattekwaaad** *see* Maiden Wine Cellars

Kay & Monty Vineyards ⓠ ⓟ ⌂ ◎

The sauvignon blanc, pair of MCC bubblies and red blend from John Legh's polo and wine estate (also a scenic wedding and lunching spot) are named SAV, Champu and Big Red respectively (untasted by us for some time). They come from a tiny parcel of vines, among the first to be planted in the Plettenberg Bay area. Recently viticulturist Lloyd Kasimbi added ±3 ha for consultant winemaker Anton Smal to work with. Kay and Monty? They're the Legh grandparents, who loved their glass of chilled 'champu' at sundown.

Location: Plettenberg Bay ▪ Map: Klein Karoo & Garden Route ▪ Map grid reference: C1 ▪ Est 2009 ▪ 1stB 2012 ▪ Tasting & restaurant Tue-Sun 11-4 ▪ Restaurant ▪ Weddings & events (200 seater venue) ▪ Guest house ▪ Owner(s) John Legh ▪ Cellarmaster(s)/winemaker(s) Anton Smal (2012, consultant) ▪ Viticulturist(s) Lloyd Kasimbi ▪ 163ha/7.09ha (carignan, grenache, mourv, pinot, shiraz, chard, sauv) ▪ PO Box 295 The Crags 6602 ▪ hello@kayandmonty.com ▪ www.kayandmonty.com ▪ S 33° 55'49.55" E 023° 26' 03.48" ▪ ⓜ kebab.variant. turnings ▪ **T +27 (0)79-965-9779**

☐ **KC** *see* Klein Constantia Estate

Keermont Vineyards ⓠ ⌂

It's not only the drier winegrowing areas of the Western Cape that were impacted by the recent drought. In relatively wet Stellenbosch, mountain sites that drain exceptionally well, like those on this estate owned by the Wraith family since 2003, also suffered. It was the final straw for the Homestead block of old-vine cabernet, uprooted a few months before the new hectare of syrah was planted at the top of the Steepside block. This after a delay prompted by, yes, the drought. There's been increased activity in the tasting area, now open on Saturday morning. The venue also hosts exclusive dinners of the recently launched Companion Club, and welcomes participants in the Upper Blaauwklippen Valley Hop, a one-day wine-tasting and food-pairing event staged with neighbours De Trafford and Tamboerskloof/Kleinood. In the cellar, 15-vintage 'veteran' Alex Starey continues his gentle, natural vinifications using traditional methods only.

Single Vineyard Series

★★★★ **Pondok Rug Cabernet Franc** ⓠ **15** ★★★★★ ⑨① a pleasing mix of austerity & fruit-rich flavour depth, firm tannins in control. Powerful, but 14.5% alcohol is in balance, & the totality even quite elegant, thanks to balance & dry finish. Impresses more than **14** ⑧⑨. Also in magnum, as all these.

★★★★☆ **Steepside Syrah** ⓠ Impressive **15** ⑨③ denser in colour than Topside, notably riper & darker-fruited. The palate broader & softer, with intense flavours & supple tannins; everything in balance, including 14.8% alcohol. All reds no added yeast, fining or filtration; mostly older oak.

★★★★☆ **Topside Syrah** ⓠ In **15** ⑨② this has the lighter colour & brighter, redder spicy fruit of the pair of single-vineyard syrahs, as in **14** ★★★★★ ⑨⑤ - though also with darker aspects. Well structured & elegant; sweet fruit lurks in the depths, before a good dry finish.

★★★★☆ **Riverside Chenin Blanc** ⓠ Subtly oaked **17** ⑨④ offers early complexity, with dried peach & earthy undertone. Fine integration of acid with fruit for lively & compelling full, sweet flavour (but bone-dry). No **16**.

Annual Release range

★★★★ **Cabernet Sauvignon** ⓐ Classically styled **16** ★★★★★ ⑨⓪ handles hot, dry vintage superbly, shows textbook cassis & cedar profile, tight tannin & commendably restrained ripeness so there's ample fruit yet no sweetness, alcohol a full degree lower at 14% than big but balanced **15** ⑧⑧. From single block; splashes cab franc & malbec for complexity.

★★★★☆ **Merlot** Delicious & accessible in youth, **17** ⑨⓪ has sweet plum fruit & a light texture, plus a fine tannin-acid structure for cellaring. Support & complexity from (older) oak & smidgens cab, malbec.

★★★★ **Syrah** ⓐ Step-up **15** ★★★★★ ⑨③'s intense sweet red fruit lifted by fresh acidity & slightly saline edge, given form by fine-grained tannins. Elegant, like **14** ⑧⑦, with better balance & freshness. From 3 sites; portion mourvèdre adds 'another aspect to the tannin structure'. Magnums available.

★★★★☆ **Estate Reserve** ⓐ Refined flagship blend, 5 Bordeaux varieties with dash syrah. **14** ⑨⓪ ripe, as previous, but it shows more this vintage in subtle prune nuance to the dense fruit. Spent 2 years in oak, further 3 in bottle yet tannins still (attractively) firm, will reward good few years ageing.

★★★★☆ **Terrasse** ⓠ Old-oaked **16** ⑨② another successful blend of chenin with viognier (some peachy perfume), sauvignon (green-tinged freshness), chardonnay (lemon notes). Has weight, intensity & seductive charm without overt fruitiness, succulent acid verve. **15** ★★★★ ⑧⑦ fell a fraction short.

★★★★ **Fleurfontein** ⓠ Pre-bottling, **17** ★★★★★ ⑨⓪ dessert wine from vine-dried sauvignon is velvet-soft with a range of aromas & flavours, marmalade to raisins. Low 11% alcohol, high 268 g/l sugar, yet good acidity provides touch more liveliness than last-tasted **15** ⑧⑦. 375 ml.— CvZ

Location/map/WO: Stellenbosch ▪ Map grid reference: G8 ▪ Est 2003 ▪ 1stB 2007 ▪ Tasting & sales Fri & Sat 10.30-1.30 or by appt ▪ Tasting fees apply ▪ Cellar tours by appt ▪ Luxury self-catering accommodation ▪ Owner(s) Wraith family ▪ Winemaker(s)/viticulturist(s) Alex Starey (Jan 2005) ▪ 156ha/29ha (cab, merlot, shiraz, chenin) ▪ ±90t/10,000cs own label 65% red 33% white 2% dessert ▪ IPW ▪ PO Box 21739 Kloof Str Cape Town 8008 ▪ info@keermont.co.za ▪ www.keermont.co.za ▪ S 34° 0' 27.0" E 018° 53' 39.0" ▪ 🅦 mellow. creased.drum ▪ **T +27 (0)21-880-0397**

Keet Wines ⓠ

Christopher Keet owns neither cellar nor vines, but the boutique-scale production of his 'proudly South African' red gives great satisfaction to a loyal and serious fan-base. The Bordeaux blend from Stellenbosch grapes is made at the Van Biljon cellar, proportions differing in response to each vintage. The vinification gets fine-tuned, but the wines are remarkably consistent in their elegant style and quality. This was clearly demonstrated in a recent vertical tasting of the bottlings since debut '09. Ageworthy, maturing slowly and beautifully, all achieve Chris's aim to craft wines that are 'refined, focused, elegant and timeless'.

★★★★☆ **First Verse** ⓐ Reflects the sheathed power of a classic vintage in **15** ⑨④. Cab & cab franc lead in 5-way assembly from 4 pockets around Stellenbosch. Tight, toned & muscular restrains core of dark fruit & cocoa. Complexity & intensity in sync with alcohol.— MW

Location/WO: Stellenbosch ▪ Est 2008 ▪ 1stB 2009 ▪ Tasting by appt ▪ Owner(s) Christopher Keet ▪ Cellarmaster(s)/winemaker(s)/viticulturist(s) Christopher Keet (Oct 2008) ▪ 1st/2,000cs own label 100% red ▪ PO Box 5508 Helderberg 7135 ▪ chris@keetwines.co.za ▪ www.keetwines.co.za ▪ **T +27 (0)82-853-1707**

☐ **Keimoes** see Orange River Cellars
☐ **Keizer's Creek** see Roodezandt Wines
☐ **Keldermeester Versameling** see Lanzerac Wine Estate

Ken Forrester Wines ⓘ ⑪ ⑤

The ingenious weather prediction system still hangs outside the Scholtzenhof home-farm which Ken Forrester and family bought 25 years ago, but the tasting room is almost unrecognisable courtesy of the revamp facilitated by the 2016 buy-in by international wine specialist AdVini. The team are also adapting to the adjacent new cellar and storage space, also completed last year. Ken spent much of the year celebrating the quarter-century anniversary with customary bonhomie by sharing vintage wines – many from his private cellar – with guests throughout South Africa. The proceeds went to Spark, a winelands education cause Ken Forrester Wines is happy to support. Capping the celebrations was a place in the annual Chenin Blanc Top 10 for The FMC, breaking years of drought for this iconic wine at the prestigious competition.

Icon range

★★★★☆ **The Gypsy** No mourvèdre, so **15** ⑨⓪ is 2-way blend of grenache & syrah (65/35) showing subtle hedgerow fruit vibrancy. Layered, lithe & supple, with supportive oak, year, all old. Light & spicy but well proportioned, long & generous.

★★★★★ **The FMC** ⓐ ⓦ A pioneer of the SA chenin renaissance. Refined **18** ⑨③ is rich, with signature ripeness, sun-dried pineapple & honeyed notes balanced by refreshing acidity. Creamy macadamia nuance from year in oak, sur lie. Low-yielding old bushvines (1974). **17** untasted. Stellenbosch WO, as next.

★★★★ **FMC Première Sélection Moelleux** Only possible in special - riper - years, **17** ★★★★★ ⑨① offers gentle barley sugar sweetness (33 g/L sugar) but acid tang to balance. Expressive & rich, with broad, textured palate that finishes clean. Natural ferment, 14 months in oak. Last was **10**.

Not tasted: **'T' Noble Late Harvest**.

Cellar Exclusives range

★★★★★ **Three Halves** ⓩ Vibrantly spicy, dry mourvèdre, shiraz & grenache is swarthy & brooding; **15** ⑨③ structured & firm after 18 months in older French oak, yet also generous & rich. Layered & complex with long, rewarding finish. Better balanced than **13** ★★★★ ⑧⑨, which had 15% alcohol. No **14**.

★★★★★ **Roussanne** ⓩ Richly textured, **16** ⑨① has trademark stonefruit & tarte tatin spice. Restrained but fresh, fruit supported by subtle frame of oak from large older barrels. Elegant & subtle, the unusual (for SA) Rhône grape is well expressed. Stellenbosch WO, like next.

★★★★ **Sparklehorse** ⓦ Crisp green-apple vigour to **16** ⑧⑥ all-chenin MCC sparkling. Chalky, with good grip, intensity & lees notes from 18 months in bottle. Balanced & dry. Improves on **15** ★★★★ ⑧⑤.

Reserve range

★★★★☆ **Renegade** Typically pepper- & spice-seasoned Rhône blend, **16** ★★★★ ⑧⑨ preview is dry, focused & well integrated. Squeeze of oak tannin balances generous, pliable blue & black fruits. Less muscular than last **14** ⑨⓪.

★★★★☆ **Old Vine Chenin Blanc** ⊘ Poised **18** ⑨⓪ marries barrel- & tank-fermented parts seamlessly. Rich, complex, with honeyed apricot matched by lees & cleansing acid. Long, nuanced finish with lingering flavour memory. Stellenbosch WO, as next.

Merlot Pat's Garden ★★★★ Generous Black Forest cake appeal to plush, expressive **16** ⑧⑤. Good texture & body, with oak cradle from year in barrel. **Sauvignon Blanc** ★★★★ Tangy & crisp lemon & fig notes on **18** ⑧⑤. As last, a blend of 3 regions. Succulent & light bodied with tropical edge.

Petit range

Cabernet Sauvignon ★★★ Juicy, bright & unfussy cassis verve on light-bodied, easy **18** ⑧②. **Pinotage** ⊘ ★★★★ Raspberry & cranberry shine bright on uncomplicated **18** ⑧④. Juicy, approachable & quaffable. Stellenbosch WO. **Rosé** ⊘ ★★★★ Improves on previous in vivacious strawberry & plum tang from grenache & viognier mix. **19** ⑧③ light bodied, crisp & easy. Ideal for summer. **Chardonnay** ★★★ Offers signature citrus flavour with bright, light body & abundant appeal. **19** ⑧② unoaked & all too easy to drink with its fresh acid tang. **Chenin Blanc** ⓩ ★★★ Melon, guava & pear on **18** ⑧①. Fresh & tasty as usual, dry & bright. **Sauvignon Blanc** ★★★ Grapefruit zest & fig leaf typicity on **19** ⑧② poolside quaffer. Fresh, lively & vivacious, with zippy acidity. **Natural Sweet** ★★★ Honeysuckle & peach appeal to mostly chenin **18** ⑧①. Delicious succulence, light & approachable, balanced acidity on clean finish. — FM

Location: Stellenbosch ▪ Map: Helderberg ▪ Map grid reference: C2 B2 ▪ WO: Western Cape/Stellenbosch ▪ Est/1stB 1994 ▪ Tasting & sales on home farm, cnr R44 & Winery Rd: Mon-Fri 9-5 Sat 9.30-3.30 ▪ Tasting options: Petit R60/5 wines; Chenin 101 & Connoisseur R100/5 wines or R150/7 wines; Best of Both Worlds R100/4 wines; Rhône Connoisseur R150/5 wines - tasting fee deductable with purchases over R400pp ▪ Closed Good Fri, Dec 25 & Jan 1 ▪ Sundays & after hours tasting available at 96 Winery Rd Restaurant ▪ Owner(s) Forrester Vineyards Pty Ltd ▪ Cellarmaster(s)/winemaker(s) Ken Forrester (1994) ▪ Viticulturist(s) Pieter Rossouw (Oct 2009) ▪ (grenache, merlot, mourv, shiraz, chenin) ▪ 1,325t/190,000cs own label 45% red 55% white ▪ Other export brand: Workhorse (Marks & Spencer) ▪ Brands for clients: Woolworths ▪ ISO 9001:2000, HACCP, SEDEX, WIETA ▪ PO Box 1253 Stellenbosch 7599 ▪ info@kenforresterwines.com ▪ www. kenforresterwines.com ▪ S 34° 1' 31.06" E 018° 49' 05.92" (home farm) ▪ S 34° 1' 38.30" E 018° 48' 31.99" (96 Winery Rd Restaurant) ▪ ⌖ airships.plums.braves, recoil.shockwaves.megabits ▪ **T +27 (0)21-855-2374**

☐ **Kershaw** *see* Richard Kershaw Wines
☐ **Kevin Arnold** *see* Waterford Estate
☐ **Kevin King** *see* South Hill Vineyards
☐ **KFK Reserve** *see* Stellenview Premium Wines

Kingna Distillery   ⓠ ⓒ

At Norbert Engel's boutique farm near Montagu, brandy master Ruan Hunlun has been crafting colombard grapes into premium brandies since 2007, using a 2,000L still and French/American oak barrels. He's released a pair to date, and though we'd hoped to sample a new bottling this edition, Ruan confirms 'at present we have only the 5 and 8 Year Old'. Given the up-trend in quality with advancing age, patience will be rewarded. Tasting is available at the distillery, along with wedding, function and conference facilities.

★★★★ **Potstill Brandy 8 Year Old** ⓠ Sunshine-in-a-bottle fruitiness in this gorgeous bottling ⑧⑦, aromas of violets & orange blossoms leading to smooth, enveloping candied fruit flavours, entwined with gentle cinnamon spice & chocolate.

Potstill Brandy 5 Year Old ⓠ ★★★ Smooth textured, light & elegant brandy ⑧①, with fresh apricot, fynbos, clove & floral perfume, rather obvious but not unbalanced oak. — WB, TJ

Location: Montagu ▪ Map: Klein Karoo & Garden Route ▪ Map grid reference: C8 ▪ Est 2007 ▪ 1stB 2012 ▪ Tasting, sales & distillery tours Mon-Fri 10-5 Sat/Sun by appt ▪ Closed Easter Sat/Sun, Dec 25/26 & Jan 1 ▪ Tour groups ▪ Conferences ▪ Weddings/functions ▪ Owner(s) Norbert Engel ▪ Brandy master Ruan Hunlun (Jan 2005, consultant) ▪ 1,000ha/8ha (chenin, cbard) ▪ 140t/9,000L ▪ PO Box 395 Montagu 6720 ▪ ruan@ kingna.co.za ▪ www.kingna.co.za ▪ S 33° 49' 45.87" E 20° 15' 39.10" ▪ ⌖ singled.bliss.chores ▪ **T +27 (0)71-637-3958**

☐ **King & Queen** *see* Bayede!
☐ **King Shaka** *see* Imbuko Wines
☐ **King Shaka-Zulu** *see* Bayede!

Kings Kloof Vineyards   ⓠ

The Newton-King family bought the upper portion of an historic Somerset West farm in 1936, which the Newton-King women managed for many years. High on Helderberg Mountain, Kings Kloof has 12 ha of vineyards, used to supply Spier with grapes for its ranges. It basically remained under the consumer radar until the Spier team, led by Frans Smit, started vinifying small parcels of its fruit for an own-label range.

Family Reserve range

★★★★ **Merlot** ⓥ Vivid fruit, cassis in pre-bottling **17** ⑧⑨, with bluegum/mint notes part of the pleasure. Masterly oaking, 24 months in older barrel, tannins integrated, the whole effect luscious.

★★★★ **Syrah 17** ⑧⑦ preview ticks all the boxes, hedgerow fruit, pepper & spice, some woodsmoke, with palate succulence adding to the enjoyment. Tannins supple but there's muscle tone for ageing.

★★★★ **Sauvignon Blanc** ⓥ Classic cool-fruit style for **19** ⑧⑨, vivid litchi & passionfruit, becoming more mineral on the palate, finishes saline. Admirable focus, tension. No **17, 18**.

★★★★ **Semillon** ⓠ Emphatic dusty stone minerality, wet wool note on lean, racy **17** ⑧⑦. Unoaked, leesy, with shapely elegance, lingering finish.— CR

Location: Somerset West ▪ Map: Helderberg ▪ Map grid reference: E4 ▪ WO: Stellenbosch ▪ Est 1939 ▪ 1stB 1986 ▪ Tasting by appt ▪ Owner(s) Newton-King family ▪ Cellarmaster(s) Frans Smit (1995, Spier) ▪

Winemaker(s) Frans Smit & Spier winemaking team ▪ Viticulturist(s) Bennie Liebenberg (Spier) ▪ 73ha/12ha (merlot, shiraz, sauv, sem) ▪ 120t/600cs own label 30% red 70% white ▪ WIETA ▪ PO Box 2 Somerset West 7129 ▪ richardnk@kingskloof.co.za ▪ www.kingskloof.co.za ▪ S 34° 3' 12.68" E 018°51'49.34" ▪ ⓜ served. evening.hush ▪ **T** +27 (0)21-851-9080

Kirabo Private Cellar   Ⓠ ⑪ ◎ ⑧

Pieter le Roux, winegrower on Watervalkloof estate in Breedekloof, sells off most of his output. But he and wife Karen since 2003 have produced small parcels of red under the label Kirabo ('Gift from God'), available to private clients and visitors enjoying the many facilities and activities on the property. The 7th-generation Le Roux, son Ronald, now does the handcrafting, after seasons in Stellenbosch and California.

Merlot ★★★ Broad-shouldered & generous (14.9% alcohol), with warm plum cake & clove aromas in **16** ⑧⓪. Older oak, as all. **Petit Verdot ★★★** Cherry cola & spice in **17** ⑧①, very ripe but 14.8% alcohol well-absorbed by the fruit, tannins rounded & limber. **Shiraz ★★☆** Blueberry aromas & flavours, smooth texture, **17** ⑦⑨ fruity & easy to enjoy. Not tasted: **Cupcake, No. 4our.** — WB, CvZ

Location: Rawsonville ▪ Map/WO: Breedekloof ▪ Map grid reference: C6 ▪ Est 2002 ▪ 1stB 2003 ▪ Tasting, sales & cellar/vineyard tours Mon-Fri 8.30-5 Sat/Sun 10-2 ▪ Closed all pub hols ▪ Meals by appt only; platters ▪ Facilities for children ▪ Tour groups ▪ Farm produce ▪ Walking/hiking trails ▪ Weddings/functions ▪ Conservation area ▪ Owner(s) Pieter & Karen le Roux ▪ Cellarmaster(s) Pieter le Roux (2002) ▪ Winemaker(s) Ronald le Roux (2019) ▪ Viticulturist(s) Pieter le Roux ▪ 21t/3,000cs own label 100% red ▪ IPW ▪ PO Box 96 Rawsonville 6845 ▪ info@kirabocellar.co.za ▪ www.kiraboprivatecellar.com ▪ S 33° 42' 36.68" E 019° 21' 27.55" ▪ ⓜ transitive.part.reprinted ▪ **T** +27 (0)71-681-9019/+27 (0)83-228-5191

☐ **Kitchen Sink** see The Kitchen Sink
☐ **Klaasenbosch** see Wine-of-the-Month Club

Klawer Wine Cellars   Ⓠ ⊖ ⑧ ⑤

This primarily bulk-wine producer, with two cellars (at Klawer and Trawal) drawing from over 2,000 hectares of vines on the West Coast, is always eager to innovate. Witness the Vino Sacci duo in 375-ml resealable pouches, tailor-made for hikers and campers, alongside the Villa Esposto premium parcels. For visitors, there are all manner of wine-pairing options, with something sweet and even infused with indigenous rooibos.

Villa Esposto range

★★★★ Chenin Blanc ⊛ Now settled in bottle, **18** ⑧⑨ reveals creamy stonefruit & citrus flavours in harmony with the nutty oak (6 months older French).

★★★★☆ Straw Wine ⊘ ⊛ ⊛ Attractive packaging for sun-kissed **17** ⑨③ stunner from muscat d'Alexandrie, vines 51 years old, hand harvested & bunches straw-dried. Unctuous & intense, dried peach & apricot flavours that linger forever on spicy finish. 375 ml.

Pinotage ★★★★ Tangy plum & mulberry fruits mingle with gentle spice on robust yet smooth & rounded **17** ⑧⑤, good food companion. **Pinotage Rosé ★★★** Delicate pink **19** ⑧⓪, fresh spice-tinged berries, lingering tangy-dry finish. Tad more complex than last.

Klawer range

★★★★ Hanepoot ⊘ Variety's litchi & rosepetal signatures in abundance, **17** ⑧⑨ fortified dessert supported by an alluring, long-lingering sweetness. Delicious ice cold. First since **14** ⑧⑨.

★★★★ African Ruby Rooibos A step up for **NV** ⑧⑥ fortified red muscadel infused with rooibos. Fresh, aromatic, with perfect balance of fruit & warming alcohol. Both different & delightful.

★★★★ White Muscadel ⊘ Perennial favourite, fortified **17** ⑧⑥ offers petals, spice & boiled sweet intensity & flavour. Rounded, mouthfilling, enduring dried herb farewell.

. . . .

Chenin Blanc ⊘ ⊕ **★★★** Riot of tropical flavour on unoaked **19** ⑧① pocket friendly & perfect for everyday enjoyment.

. . . .

Cabernet Sauvignon ⊘ **★★★** Smoky cherry notes on **18** ⑦⑨, with firm, astringent goodbye. Misses mark of previous. **Merlot ★★** Black fruit & savoury meat flavours on **18** ⑦⑥ everyday sipper. **Pinotage** ⊘ **★★★** Fresh, fruity & friendly **18** ⑧⓪ delights with berry & cherry flavours. Slips down easily, finishing dry. **Shiraz** ★★ Uncomplicated **18** (74) shows hedgerow fruit, dry tannin & brisk exit. **Shiraz-Malbec** (Ⓩ) ★★★ Unusual blend is plump & succulent, ample blackberry goodness sure to be an instant hit. **17** (80) good braai red. **Chardonnay** (Ⓩ) ★★★ Friendly & easy, delicious citrus entry & marzipan finish. **18** (78) fruit driven & fresh. **Sauvignon Blanc** ★★★ Grapefruit, tropical & green plum flavours, zippy finish, **19** (77) more substantial & enjoyable than previous. **Michelle Vin Doux Sparkling** (⊘) ★★★ Fruity & floral fun in soft, sweet pink **NV** (78) sparkler from muscat, with low 8.5% alcohol. **Red Muscadel** (Ⓩ) ★★★★ Seductive sweet fortified, **17** (84) with beautiful light pink hue. Pairs perfectly with vanilla ice cream to delight & impress dinner party guests. **Cape Vintage** (⊘) ★★★ Less complex then previous, **16** (82) 'port' offers grippy plums, berries & still-dominant charry oak flavours, needing more time to cohere.

Vino Sacci range

Merlot ★★ Fruity red **18** (71) in modern, spill-resistant, go-anywhere 375-ml pouch, as sibling. **Chenin Blanc** ★★ Light & easy tropical flavours, **19** (70) good for picnics & boating trips.

Discontinued: **Travino range**. — WB

Location: Klawer ▪ Map/WO: Olifants River ▪ Map grid reference: B4 ▪ Est 1956 ▪ Tasting & sales Mon-Fri 8–5 Sat 9–1 ▪ Facilities for children ▪ BYO picnic ▪ 4 wine pairing options from R40–R45 pp/pairing ▪ Owner(s) 87 members ▪ Manager Andries Blake ▪ Cellarmaster(s) Pieter van Aarde (Nov 2011) ▪ Winemaker(s) Roelof van Schalkwyk, Tiaan van Zyl, Neill Gellatly & Christo Beukes ▪ Viticulturist(s) Johannes Mellet ▪ 2,095ha (cab, merlot, ptage, ruby cab, shiraz, chard, chenin, cbard, hanepoot, muscadel, sauv, viog) ▪ 34,000t/50,000cs own label 40% red 40% white 5% rosé 15% other ▪ ISO 22000:2009, Organic, DLG, IPW ▪ PO Box 8 Klawer 8145 ▪ info@klawerwyn.co.za ▪ www.klawerwine.co.za ▪ S 31° 47' 34.9" E 018° 37' 36.1" ▪ Ⓕ primly.netball.handsomest ▪ **T +27 (0)27-216-1530**

☐ **Klein Centennial** *see* Group CDV

Klein Constantia Estate   (Ⓩ) (Ⓧ) ⓞ (Ⓖ)

A jewel in the crown of SA's wine empire, this historic property was part of the farm that produced the legendary Constantia wines that enthralled European royalty in the 18th century. The legacy lives on in their celebrated Vin de Constance dessert muscat. Restored and revitalised by the Jooste family in the 1980s, the estate's current owners (including internationally reputed vignerons Bruno Prats and Hubert de Boüard) took the baton and initiated Project Sauvignon, cataloguing and analysing every row of each precious block to express its unique character. The results are there to be experienced. The winery, designed by architect Gawie Fagan and recently extended, is a deservedly popular wine-tourism destination, with offerings like winetasting, cellar and vineyard tours by arrangement, and jacaranda-shaded The Bistro @ Klein Constantia.

Estate Wines

★★★★☆ **Estate Red Blend** (⚶) Lone red in Estate line-up, aristocratic **16** (91) Bordeaux-shiraz blend shows cedar spices woven into dense black fruit, brawny body with robust tannins. 12 months in small French oak, 40% new. Worth cellaring. Magnums also available.

★★★★ **Chardonnay** (Ⓩ) Svelte barrel-fermented **16** (89) gushes with sweetly ripe orange marmalade & glacé fruit, laced with restrained oak spices. Nascent complexity, already showing fine balance & poise.

★★★★ **Riesling** (Ⓩ) Serious & convincing effort sees expressive dry **16** (89) bear out promise of previous years. Persistent terpene with steely mineral notes, evolved fruit & lees richness. Build for 3-5 years.

★★★★★ **Clara Sauvignon Blanc** (⚶) Was 'Block 361/372'. Occasional release of high-end barrel selection, blended from single-block vinifications, **17** ★★★★★ (93) is elegant, seamless & fragrant, showing complex aromas, silky texture. 9 months in oak & acacia, 25% new. Improves on last-tasted **15** (89).

★★★★☆ **Glen Dirk Sauvignon Blanc** Characterful block selection, **18** (92) has heady aromatic herbaceousness with almost floral fragrance, hints of anise & bergamot. Barrel maturation doesn't intrude in the least: 9 months 500L oak & acacia.

★★★★★ **Metis Sauvignon Blanc** (Ⓩ) In collaboration with Pascal Jolivet, **17** (93) from high-lying estate vines expresses Sancerre character: intense aromatics, oyster juice & flint. Sublime weight, focus & balance. Also-available magnum especially worth laying down.

★★★★☆ **Perdeblokke Sauvignon Blanc** Ⓢ Signature best-years-only blend of selected high-lying blocks, **18** (93) follows impressive form of **17** (92). 9 months in older oak & acacia rounds out delightfully intricate tapestry of herbs, spices & mineral-underpinned kiwifruit.

★★★★ **Sauvignon Blanc** Poised & refined mainstay, **18** (88) follows form with sweet ripe fruit, crisply precise acidity & satisfying heft. Unoaked, 7 months on lees. 1.5L also available, as Perdeblokke.

★★★★ **Brut Méthode Cap Classique** Lean & racy chardonnay sparkling, **15** (87) richer brioche notes, more roundness than **14** ★★★☆ (85). As previously, base wine unoaked, 33 months on lees.

★★★★☆ **Brut Méthode Cap Classique Reserve** Ⓡ Exceptionally fine chardonnay sparkling, **11** (94) has panache in abundance, 60 months on lees yet youthful & vibrant. Rich brioche, crisp acid & spicy apple flavour from optimally harvested fruit & 100% barrel fermentation in older oak.

★★★★★ **Vin de Constance** Ⓢ Iconic reprise of legendary 18th-century Constantia sweet wine, eagerly awaited **15** (95) is spectacular. Muscat de Frontignan, harvested through the season as ripe berries (for acidity) & raisins (for sugar concentration), delivers fragrant aromatic spices, honeyed floral highlights & piercing freshness, all in perfect balance & harmony after 42 months in 500L barrels. 500 ml & magnum.

Not tasted: **Sauvignon Blanc Block 382**. Occasional release: **Sauvignon Blanc Block 371**, **Sauvignon Blanc Block 381**. Discontinued: **Organic Sauvignon Blanc**.

KC range

Cabernet Sauvignon-Merlot ★★★☆ Likeable middleweight, **17** (83) has perky blackcurrant & mulberry fruit, sleek tannin structure. Year in older barrels. WO W Cape for these. **Rosé** Ⓡ ★★★☆ Previewed **18** (83) bone-dry pink from cab franc offers earthy notes with appealing floral scents. Crisp acidity, silky texture. **Sauvignon Blanc** Ⓡ ★★★☆ Substantial fruit weight & body, **18** (84) shows good poise & focus, Constantia & Stellenbosch vines deliver more than a quaffer. Discontinued: **Pinot Noir**. — GdB

Location: Constantia ▪ Map: Cape Peninsula ▪ Map grid reference: B3 ▪ WO: Constantia/Western Cape ▪ Est 1823 ▪ 1stB 1824 ▪ Tasting & sales Mon-Sat 10–5 Sun & pub hols 10-4 ▪ Closed Good Fri & Dec 25 ▪ Tasting from R100 ▪ The Bistro @ Klein Constantia Tue-Sun 12-4 ▪ Gift shop ▪ Cellar tour & vineyard tours (bookings in advance) ▪ Collection of original Constantia bottles on display ▪ Owner(s) Zdenek Bakala, Charles Harman, Bruno Prats & Hubert de Boüard ▪ MD Hans Aström ▪ Winemaker(s) Matthew Day (2009) ▪ Viticulturist(s) Craig Harris (Oct 2013) ▪ 146ha/64ha (cab, malbec, p verdot, shiraz, chard, muscat de F, riesling, sauv, sem) ▪ 500t/80,000cs own label 30% red 70% white ▪ WWF-SA Conservation Champion ▪ PO Box 375 Constantia 7848 ▪ info@kleinconstantia.com ▪ www.kleinconstantia.com ▪ S 34° 2' 19.0" E 018° 24' 46.5" ▪ flattest.recyclers.herewith ▪ **T +27 (0)21-794-5188**

☐ **Klein DasBosch** *See Editor's Note*
☐ **Kleine Draken** *see* Zandwijk
☐ **Kleine Kaap** *see* Imbuko Wines
☐ **Kleine Rust** *see* Stellenrust

Kleine Schuur Estate

Due to the lingering drought, the tiny dryland vineyard in Durbanville co-owned by Danie Louw and Liezel Falck didn't bear enough fruit in 2018 to produce a commercial bottling. No-one, therefore, will begrudge fans who stock up on the current release ('17). Fortunately 2019 did deliver a viable crop - albeit small - and Danie was thrilled to slip on his winemaker's boots, ready his Flexcubes and get to work.

Shiraz ✓ ★★★☆ As in **16** (84), scrubby **17** (84)'s plump fruit is balanced by bright acidity, deft touch of oak, commendable dryness. Appealing, tasty, punches above its weight. — CvZ

Location/WO: Durbanville ▪ Est 2005 ▪ Closed to public ▪ Owner(s) Danie Louw & Liezel Falck ▪ Winemaker(s) Danie Louw ▪ 0.9ha/0.25ha (shiraz) ▪ 2.1t/241cs own label 100% red ▪ PO Box 2603 Durbanville 7551 ▪ info@kleineschuur.co.za ▪ **T +27 (0)83-231-4346**

Kleine Zalze Wines

Entrepreneurial Stellenbosch attorney Kobus Basson, supported by an always-talented team, transformed what was in the 1990s a neglected corporate-owned cellar and vineyard into a model winelands lifestyle development. Incorporating the De Zalze luxury residential and golf estate, this enterprise's heart remains the modern cellar under stewardship of experienced Alastair Rimmer and winemaker RJ Botha, shepherding grapes from rejuvenated home and quality-driven partner vineyards into bottle. The extensive range, expertly tiered, provides quality across the board. And Kleine Zalze's constancy, while earning consumer loyalty (in-demand in over 20 countries), does not preclude the introduction of exciting new wines.

Family Reserve range

★★★★☆ **Cabernet Sauvignon** ⓐ Violet & mint in the bouquet of knockout **16** ⑨③, followed by blackcurrant & dark chocolate on the deep palate. Well structured, voluminous & powerful, with vibrancy & intensity. 75% new French oak, 20 months, for the long haul. Stellenbosch fruit for these unless noted.

★★★★☆ **Shiraz** ⓐ Aromas of dark berries, clove & warm spice lead to succulent palate full of mulberries & dried herbs, long & rewarding. The richly layered texture shows French oak ageing (70% new, 22 months). **16** ⑨③ needs time, perhaps 6+ years to reveal full charm.

★★★★☆ **Chenin Blanc** ⓐ White flagship from 3 different sites, textbook **18** ★★★★★ ⑨⑤ has vibrant orchard fruit, nuts, fresh citrus & creamy vanilla from barrel ferment/8 months in older wood, like **17** ⑨④. Rich & curvy yet vivacious. Drinks well now, but has a long journey ahead.

★★★★☆ **Sauvignon Blanc** ⓐ Impressive balance of richness, texture, bright fruit flavours & wet stone minerality in **18** ⑨③. Tight & harmonious, with excellent focus & purity. Stellenbosch, Durbanville & Darling grapes, 7 months on lees. Cellar for future pleasure.

Not tasted: **Pinotage**.

Vineyard Selection

★★★★★ **Cabernet Sauvignon** ⓥ ⓐ Deliciously rich dark-berry fruit flavours are supported by black plum, dark chocolate & floral hints, robust tannin frame in **17** ⑨⑤. Shows great elegance & precision, benefits from less new oak than older sibling (40%, 18 months). Exceptional value, too, like **16** ★★★★★ ⑨④ & equally stellar **15** ⑨⑤. Stellenbosch WO, as Shiraz.

★★★★ **Grenache** ⓝⓔⓦ Unadorned by oak, **17** ⑧⑥ from Darling grapes shows great intensity of flavour & freshness along with red & black fruit, earthy spice & a savoury undertone.

★★★★ **Shiraz** ⓧ Voluptuous, with sweet-savoury finish of black pepper & tapenade, **16** ⑧⑦ inherently a food partner. Ripe & full-flavoured, mulberry, exotic spice & cured meat undertones.

★★★★ **Shiraz-Mourvèdre-Viognier** Lovely complexity & savouriness in shiraz-dominated (92%) **17** ⑧⑥, chocolate, fresh earth & florals, the juicy fruit sprinkled with spice from 14 months in older wood.

★★★★☆ **Chardonnay** ⓥ ⓐ Bright **18** ⑨④ brims with apple blossom, vanilla, dew-fresh orchard fruit & crème brûlée flavours. Intense, vibrant palate, creamy richness from 60% new oak (8 months) balanced by freshening acidity. Will age well. Stellenbosch & Robertson fruit.

★★★★☆ **Chenin Blanc** ⓥ ⓐ Pure drinking pleasure from various sites in Stellenbosch. **18** ⑨③'s tropical fruit given texture, shape & delicious vanilla coating by older-oak ferment/ageing, as Reserve sibling, but only 6 months. Stylish, excellent value to boot.

★★★★☆ **Sauvignon Blanc** ⓥ Complex & characterful **18** ⑨⓪ from Stellenbosch & Durbanville, only free-run juice, long (10 months) lees-aged in stainless steel. Layered & persistent flavours of blackcurrant, gooseberry & slatey minerality, citrus emerging on the finish. Lovely restrained 12.5% alcohol.

Discontinued: **Pinot Noir**.

Cellar Selection

....

Cinsault Rosé ⓥ Ⓣ ★★★ Pulpy strawberries in harmony with earthy spice in **19** ⑧①, light, balanced & dry - will put a big smile on your face. From Stellenbosch & Paarl vines, as Chenin. **Chardonnay Unwooded** ⓥ Ⓣ ★★★★ Pocket-friendly **19** ⑧⑤ is a mouthful of vibrant orchard fruit given a creamy texture from 4-month lie-in on lees, finishes with pleasantly drying citrus twist. **Chenin Blanc Bush Vines** ⓥ Ⓣ ★★★★ Never fails to delight. Sun-ripe tropical flavours on a wave of fresh citrus, **19** ⑧⑤ satisfying, bright & moreish, reined-in 13.3% alcohol.

....

Merlot ★★★ Everyday quaffer with inviting plum compote aroma, spice & smooth mouthfeel in **18** ⑧①. Coastal WO, as next. **Cabernet Sauvignon-Merlot** ⓧ ★★★ Wholeberry-fermented **17** ⑧① showcases pristine fruit, freshness & rounded texture. **Sauvignon Blanc** ⓥ ★★★★ Wet stone, greenpepper & zingy gooseberry on well-balanced, lively **19** ⑧④, good varietal expression from widely sourced fruit, Lutzville to Sunday's Glen. A must for summer. Not tasted: **Cabernet Sauvignon**, **Pinotage**. Discontinued: **Cinsault**.

Méthode Cap Classique Sparkling range

★★★★ **Brut Rosé** ⓥ Elegant & stylish 60/40 pinot noir/chardonnay bubbly. NV ⑧'s red berries get a citrus underpin from the white grape; all come together nicely in an acid-brightened palate.

★★★★ **Brut** ⓥ Impressively consistent styling for these sparklers. Expected elegance & finesse in latest NV ⑧; zesty, fresh berry & citrus flavours courtesy 60/40 chardonnay & pinot noir.

★★★★ **Vintage Brut** Creamy, yeasty **13** ⑧ sparkler from Robertson & Stellenbosch chardonnay & pinot noir (60/40), floral, green apple & earthy strawberry aromas & flavours, fine mouthfeel with persistent gentle bubbles. No **12**.

Zalze range

Vineyard Reserve Cabernet Sauvignon ⓥ ★★★ Fairtrade-certified **17** ⑧, sweet blackcurrants & blackberries, hints of cedar, lively tannins on sleek body. Coastal WO. For export, as all this & next range. **Shiraz-Grenache-Viognier** ★★★★ Wholeberry shiraz & grenache components, & ageing 14 months in older barrels give **17** ⑧ rich mulberry & hedgerow fruit, a dried herb nuance. Floral lift from dash viognier. **Shiraz-Mourvèdre-Viognier** ★★★ Fragrant, juicy & friendly barbecue red, **18** ⑧ with bright, bouncy red fruit in harmony with savoury accents. **Vineyard Reserve Bush Vine Chenin Blanc** ★★★★ Apple cake, spice & freshening citrus in **18** ⑧, aged 6 months in only old barrels to preserve fruit character. Delicious. **Bush Vine Chenin Blanc** ★★★ The boisterous younger sibling oozes pristine tropical fruit flavours, textured mouthfeel from 4-month lees ageing & long lemon zest finish in unoaked **19** ⑧. **Sauvignon Blanc** (NEW) ★★★★ Packed with fragrant & vigorous fruit salad flavours, lipsmacking saline finish, **18** ⑧ showcases mostly cool areas. Discontinued: **Pinotage**.

Foot of Africa range

Cabernet Sauvignon Reserve (NEW) ★★★★ Expensive graphite tones to blackcurrant & dried herb flavours in **17** ⑧. Well balanced, smooth & savoury from year older barrels. Coastal WO. **Shiraz Reserve** ★★★ Dark fruit mingles with robust though balanced oak & mocha in **17** ⑧. **Chenin Blanc Reserve** ★★★ Unfettered by oak, **19** ⑧ showcases freshly sliced apple & tang of lemon on long aftertaste. — WB

Location/map: Stellenbosch ▪ Map grid reference: E7 ▪ WO: Western Cape/Coastal/Stellenbosch ▪ Est 1695 ▪ 1stB 1997 ▪ Tasting & sales Mon-Sat 9–6 Sun 11–6 ▪ Fee R25/5 wines or R15/3 wines ▪ Closed Good Fri, Dec 25 & Jan 1 ▪ Terroir Restaurant ▪ De Zalze Golf Course ▪ Owner(s) Kobus Basson ▪ Cellarmaster(s) Alastair Rimmer (Sep 2014) ▪ Winemaker(s) RJ Botha (Dec 2012) ▪ Viticulturist(s) Henning Retief (May 2006) ▪ 130ha/80ha under vine ▪ 2,300t/400,000cs own label 40% red 50% white 10% rosé ▪ PO Box 12837 Die Boord 7613 ▪ quality@kleinezalze.co.za ▪ www.kleinezalze.co.za ▪ S 33° 58' 14.1" E 018° 50' 8.9" ▪ ⓦ cave. rally.lifelong ▪ **T +27 (0)21-880-0717**

Klein Gustrouw Estate

After businessman Jannie Mouton bought Klein Gustrouw Estate in Stellenbosch's Jonkershoek Valley just over a decade ago, he introduced several varieties, including rare alicante bouschet. However, only the better-known French grapes have made it into the bottlings we've tasted, latterly produced on contract by the eminent Warren Ellis of Neil Ellis Wines.

★★★★ **Reserve** ⓐ Black orchard & hedge fruit on polished **15** ⑧'s well-formed tannin frame, has vintage plushness & varietal depth (blend cab, cab franc & merlot); smooth vanilla overlay from 18 months French oak. Deftly constructed.

Not tasted: **Sauvignon Blanc**. — CR, CvZ

Location/WO: Stellenbosch ▪ Est 1817 ▪ 1stB 1993 ▪ Private tastings by special arrangement only ▪ Owner(s) Klein Gustrouw (Pty) Ltd ▪ Winemaker(s) Warren Ellis (2006) ▪ Viticulturist(s) Danie Malherbe (consultant) ▪ ±23ha/±14ha under vine ▪ 70% red 30% white ▪ PO Box 6168 Uniedal 7612 ▪ info@kleingustrouw.co.za ▪ **T +27 (0)21-882-8152/+27 (0)72-584-5314**

Kleinhoekkloof   ⓥ

Former international steel man Theunis de Jongh fell in love with a farm in the higher folds of the Langeberg mountains near Ashton, where altitude and aspect help him produce small parcels from French varieties, recently including cabernet franc and malbec. Wines untasted this year.

Location: Ashton ▪ Map: Robertson ▪ Map grid reference: B4 ▪ Est 2004 ▪ 1stB 2006 ▪ Phone ahead for opening hours ▪ Owner(s) Raudan Trust ▪ Cellarmaster(s)/winemaker(s)/viticulturist(s) Theunis de Jongh (2011) ▪ 114ha/11.8ha (cab f, merlot, malbec, p verdot, pinot, shiraz, sauv, viog) ▪ 110t/5,000cs own label 68% red 25% white 7% rosé ▪ Other export brand: Mountain Eye ▪ PO Box 244 Ashton 6715 ▪ theunis@khk.co.za ▪ www.kleinhoekkloof.co.za ▪ S 33° 46′ 51.87″ E 020° 03′ 17.30″ ▪ 🗺 rhinos.attributions.cultivates ▪ **T +27 (0)82-332-5474**

☐ **Klein Kasteelberg** *see* Group CDV
☐ **Kleinood** *see* Tamboerskloof Wine – Kleinood Farm
☐ **Klein Optenhorst** *see* Dainty Bess
☐ **Klein Parys Vineyards** *See Editor's Note*

Klein Roosboom   (♀) (🍴) (◎) (🖐) (♿)

Durbanville's 'Little Rose Bush' has grown a little bigger, says cellarmaster Karin de Villiers. Two new 5,000-litre fermentation tanks have upped production, and a restaurant named after her late husband, owner and viticulturist Jéan, has opened. Sons Johan and Nicol (now tending vines) are part of the close-knit venture.

Reserve range

Sauvignon Blanc ⊛ ★★★★ Selected 23 year old single block. **19** ㉘ more mineral than its sibling, wet pebbles & slate, with pithy grapefruit flavours. Great for seafood, & has some ageing potential.

Klein Roosboom range

Johan Cabernet Sauvignon (♀) ★★ Aptly recognises a 'strong & robust' son. Prosciutto & white pepper, the oak's influence prominent in **17** ㉖'s character, firm foundation for cellaring, the berry fruit muted, not yet holding its own. **Nicol Merlot** (♀) ★★★ Red berries at core of **17** ㉘, some chocolate, savoury spice, tannin still youthful, firm & dry, needing a year/2 to soften. **Janét Shiraz** (♀) ★★★ Oaking 12 months, some new barrels, as all the varietal reds, giving toasty, sweet spice tones to **17** ㉛'s dark fruit, the body smooth & round, ready to enjoy. **My Way** (♀) ★★★ Merlot/cab & 75% new oak, 16 months for **15** ㉗. Dark-toned in fruit, hint salinity, firm finish; a bit dry & grainy. **Marianna Rosé** ★★★ Bright pink **19** ㉛ has distinctive styling, piquant red berries but also mineral notes in the flavours, ends dry. Good food match. **Dear Diary Chardonnay** ★★★ Unwooded but **19** ㉛ none the worse for that. Citrus & Bosc pear, zesty fresh. **Jéan Sauvignon Blanc** ★★★★ Durbanville's green pea & just-picked gooseberry intensity in **19** ㉓, touch of fynbos, then palate minerality. Ends fresh & dry. **Marné Brut Méthode Cap Classique** ★★★ Pinot noir with 49% chardonnay, 20 months on lees, no oak in **NV** ㉛ sparkling, unlike last. Lively citrus, red berry seamed; tasty aperitif, celebration bubbly. WO W Cape.

Bandana range

Occasional release: **Blanc**. — CR

Location: Durbanville ▪ Map: Durbanville, Philadelphia & Darling ▪ Map grid reference: C7 ▪ WO: Durbanville/Western Cape ▪ Est 1984 ▪ 1stB 2007 ▪ Tasting, sales & cellar tours Tue–Sun 10-4.30 ▪ Fee R50pp, waived on purchase (6 wines) ▪ Wine tasting in a 'cave' ▪ Closed Good Fri, Dec 25/26 & Jan 1 ▪ Jéan restaurant ▪ Facilities for children ▪ Tour groups ▪ Owner(s) Jéan de Villiers Trust ▪ Cellarmaster(s) Karin de Villiers (2007) ▪ Winemaker(s) Piti Coetzee (2019) ▪ Viticulturist(s) Nicol de Villiers (2017) ▪ 260ha/150ha (cab, merlot, shiraz, chard, sauv) ▪ 8,500cs own label 30% red 70% white ▪ Postnet Suite #3 Private Bag X19 Durbanville 7551 ▪ info@kleinroosboom.co.za ▪ www.kleinroosboom.co.za ▪ S 33° 49′ 6.24″ E 018° 34′ 25.86″ ▪ 🗺 unmatched. blabbed.alleviates ▪ **T +27 (0)60-877-2678**

☐ **Klein Simonsvlei** *see* Niel Joubert Estate
☐ **Klein Tulbagh** *see* Tulbagh Winery
☐ **Klein Valley** *see* Calais Wine Estate
☐ **Klein Welmoed Wine & Olive Estate** *see* Foothills Vineyards

Klipdrift

At exactly 8.02pm in 1938, so the story goes, the first drops of Klipdrift were distilled on his Robertson farm by JP Marais. It grew into an iconic South African brand (the distillery in Robertson town) – frequently in its coupling with cola (now available ready-mixed). Remarkably good value, the original Export version, with its label showing a clockface at 8.02, has been joined over the years by more ambitious bottlings. By Distell.

★★★★☆ **Gold** A qualitative leap ⑨⓪ from the siblings, its refinement including a 38% alcohol level vs their 43%. Darker from greater ageing - all potstill components, 3-21 years old. Nutty, spicy elements speak of the oak, with the fruit (including citrus & apricot) subordinated to complexity of the whole.

Export ⊘ ★★★★ Blended brandy ⑧③, with standard 30% potstill component. Destined for mixing (famously with cola), the fiery apricot flavours offer little complexity, but it's balanced & smooth & lingering enough for small neat sips. **Premium** ⊘ ★★★☆ The 30% potstill component aged for 5 years, so this ⑧④ richer, more intense & interesting than Export, with tobacco, nutty notes from oak. Available in larger & smaller formats, 1L to 50 ml, as all these. — TJ

☐ **Kloof Street** *see* Mullineux

Kloovenburg Wine & Olives   ⓟ ⑪ ⓐ ⓕ

This substantial Swartland estate just outside Riebeek-Kasteel has attained WWF Conservation Champion status. Other good news is that wine and olive tasting is now free (private, paid 'experiences' can be booked on the website). Winemaker Jolandie Fouché has settled into the second half of her first decade here, working alongside owner/cellarmaster Pieter du Toit in lightening the wines and bringing in exciting new varieties, while respecting Kloovenburg's vinous traditions. The other tradition – a range of olive products – is in the creative hands of Pieter's wife, Annalene.

★★★★ **Grenache Noir** Lightly perfumed **18** ⑧⑧, with floral & cherry notes, is pure & fresh - the charm of the Carignan but more depth & interest. Balanced, the older oak well integrated, a pleasing tannic grip.

★★★★ **Riebeekberg Syrah** ⊘ Supple, ethereal lightness to inky black palate of naturally fermented **17** ★★★★★ ⑨⓪. Plush yet dense & nuanced, with spicy pliability, long satisfying aftertaste. Third bunch-pressed, no new oak. Step up on debut **16** ⑧⑨.

★★★★ **Shiraz** Light-feeling **17** ⑧⑧ despite 14.8% alcohol & firm structure. Spicy & clean-finishing, if not intense. 20% new oak well integrated. Portion bunch-pressed, as Carignan, Grenache. Also in magnum.

★★★★ **Eight Feet Red** 55% shiraz on **17** ⑧⑨, with grenache, carignan & mourvèdre. A little fuller, richer & more complete than the monovarietals. Mostly older oak; portions wholebunch; native yeasts.

★★★★ **Barrel Fermented Chardonnay** ⊘ A nutty, toasty oak touch on **18** ⑧⑥'s aroma (20% new barrels) but integrated into the light citrus flavours on softly rounded palate. Half natural ferment. More depth than Unwooded version.

★★★★ **Eight Feet White 18** ⑧⑨ chenin & grenache blanc with roussanne & verdelho; charachterful & pleasing, though the flavours not intense. Some richness of texture, with older oak giving breadth.

Carignan ★★★☆ **18** ⑧⑤ is bright & refreshing, balanced & lively, simple & easy-drinking, the pure fruit untrammeled by obvious oak, with just 12.5% alcohol. **Merlot** ★★★★ Good varietal typicity on **17** ⑧⑤, with fruitcake notes & a herbal twist. Flavourful & decently structured; 20% new oak in support, as in **16** ★★★★ ⑧⑥. **Unwooded Chardonnay** ★★★ Forthcoming pear drop character on pleasantly balanced, easygoing **19** ⑧②. Soft texture, just enough backbone. **Sauvignon Blanc** ⊘ ★★★ Zesty grapefruit tang on lively **18** ⑧②, unfussy & refreshing. **Shiraz Blanc de Noir Brut Sparkling** ⊘ ★★★★ Strawberry & cherry vivacity on coral pink **NV** ⑧③ carbonated fizz. Tangily tasty, dry & easy to enjoy. Not tasted: **Cape Vintage Shiraz**. — TJ

Location: Riebeek-Kasteel ▪ Map/WO: Swartland ▪ Map grid reference: D6 ▪ Est 1704 ▪ 1stB 1998 ▪ Tasting & sales Mon-Fri 9–4.30 Sat 9–2 ▪ Closed Good Fri, Dec 25/26 & Jan 1 ▪ Wine & olive pairing/tasting options: to be booked online by selecting 'book an experience' ▪ Gift shop ▪ Farm produce/olive products ▪ 'Build your own picnic' from a wide selection of products ▪ Conservation area ▪ Owner(s) Pieter du Toit ▪ Cellarmaster(s) Pieter du Toit (Jan 1998) ▪ Winemaker(s) Jolandie Fouché (Dec 2014) ▪ 300ha/130ha (carignan, grenache n/b, merlot, mourv, shiraz, chard, chenin, rouss, sauv, verdelho) ▪ 200t/12,000cs own label 55% red 40% white 4% rosé 1% sparkling ▪ WWF-SA Conservation Champion ▪ PO Box 2 Riebeek-Kasteel 7307 ▪ info@kloovenburg.com ▪ www.kloovenburg.com ▪ S 33° 23' 36.3" E 018° 53' 27.5" ▪ ⒜ barbers.spirals.robes ▪ **T +27 (0)22-448-1635**

Knorhoek Wines

Knorhoek farm on Stellenbosch's high Simonsberg slopes, its facilities and wine brand have been sold to private investors, and at press time the first of a new portfolio of wines — Cabernet Sauvignon and Chenin Blanc — were being readied for release. Meanwhile the Namysto range by neighbour Quoin Rock will be available for tasting and sale. Popular estate amenities continue to welcome wedding couples, conferees, outdoor enthusiasts, stay-over seekers and diners.

Location/map: Stellenbosch ▪ Map grid reference: F3 ▪ Est 1827 ▪ 1stB 1997 ▪ Tasting & sales Wed-Sun 10–5 ▪ Closed Jan 1 ▪ Towerbosch Restaurant Wed-Sun 11-4 (Sat/Sun booking essential T +27 (0)21-865-2958) ▪ Facilities for children ▪ Tour groups ▪ Weddings/conferences ▪ Hiking trail ▪ 3-star guesthouse & self-catering cottages ▪ Owner(s) Private investors ▪ Cellarmaster(s) Chris Keet (consultant) ▪ Viticulturist(s) Nico Walters (Jan 2019) ▪ ±60ha ▪ PO Box 23 Elsenburg 7607 ▪ cellar@knorhoek.co.za, towerbosch@knorhoek.co.za ▪ www.knorhoek.co.za ▪ S 33° 52' 44.8" E 018° 52' 19.1" ▪ loosens.having.animated ▪ **T +27 (0)21-865-2114**

☐ **Kobus** *see* Havana Hills
☐ **Koelenbosch** *see* Koelenhof Winery

Koelenhof Winery

The 'nice and settled' winemaking team at this forward-looking grower-owned winery, providing a range of industry services while vinifying for its own labels from select Stellenbosch pockets, last year enjoyed a 'very productive second harvest together'. To emphasise the quality side of their production, on top of consistency and affordability, the team released a new pinnacle chenin under the label Stellenbosch 1679, and will follow it up with a red blend. More reasons to visit the 'relaxed, cheerful' tasting venue.

Stellenbosch 1679 range (NEW)

★★★★ **Bush Vine Chenin Blanc** Concentrated **17** ⑧⑥ from Stellenbosch bushvines stands up well to barrel-ferment in 80% new French oak. Peaches, yellow apples & cream handle 14.5% alcohol, carrying intensity through to lengthy finish.

Koelenbosch range

Shiraz ⓥ ★★★ Nice step up for characterful **17** ⑧② balancing smoked meats with ripe black fruit & pleasing vanilla finish (French & American oak, 50% new). **Nineteenfortyone** ⓥ ★★★★ Very appealing blend of cab, shiraz, merlot & pinotage, **17** ⑧⑤ is brimful of ripe black fruit, with soft tannins & positive finish. Good intensity more than handles 12 months in oak, 50% new. **Pinotage Rosé Méthode Cap Classique** ⓥ ⓥ ★★★★ Style change on **18** ⑧③ sparkling from savoury, more oxidative last release. Now only 12 months on lees, much fresher but still with yeasty depth & perky strawberry fruit. Good-value weekend morning fizz.

Merlot ★★★ Cherry-choc flavours on **17** ⑧⓪ matched with charry, smoky oak (50% new, half American), needing time to settle. **Pinotage** ★★★ Cheerful **17** ⑧⓪ seems perfect partner for a sociable braai - soft, juicy, smoky & a slightly sweetish finish. **Sangiovese** ★★★ All-new French oak shows strongly on **17** ⑦⑨ giving smoked meat, savoury quality to shy fruit. **Dry Pinotage Rosé** ⓥ ★★★ Leap forward in quality, **19** ⑧⓪ full of fresh red berries with pleasing crisp acidity. **Chenin Blanc** ★★★ Candyfloss confection on **19** ⑦⑨ nevertheless appeals with lemon sherbet, pear drops & dry finish. Big improvement. **Sauvignon Blanc** ★★★ Tropical notes of **19** ⑦⑧ combined with fresh acidity will please many this summer. **Chardonnay Méthode Cap Classique** ⓥ ★★★ Now only 12 months lees time for **18** ⑧① & far livelier than previous. Fresh & fruity fizz, with green apples & peachy tang. Discontinued: **Koelenhof 1941 Limited Release**, **Chenin Blanc Wooded**.

Koelenhof range

Pinotage ★★★ Plenty of typicity on **18** ⑧⓪ mixing black fruits with stony minerality. Handles 100% new French oak well, charry note just creeping through at the end. **Koelenberg** ★★★ Merlot-led blend **18** ⑦⑧ dominated by 100% new oak, black cherry fruit struggles against meaty, smoky notes. **Koelnektar** ★★ Now 100% gewürztraminer, **19** ⑦⑤ less intense than last but still has some character. 30 g/l sugar to go with desserts. **Koelenhoffer** ★★ Easy-drinking **19** ⑦⑥ will definitely have fans with this soft, fruity off-dry sauvignon. **Pinotage Rosé Vin Sec** ★★ Semi-sweet pink sparkling lacks freshness in **18** ⑦③ with caramel & toffee in place of fruit flavours. **Sauvignon Blanc Vin Sec ★★** Semi-sweet bubbles to make a party go with a swing. **18** ⑭ shade more neutral than before. **Pinorto ★★★** Vintage-style 'port' from pinotage, **18** ㉒ perfect partner for winter evenings & chocolate desserts. Higher alcohol than previous (19.5% vs 15.5%). — CM

Location/map/WO: Stellenbosch ▪ Map grid reference: D1 ▪ Est 1941 ▪ 1stB 1970's ▪ Tasting & sales Mon-Thu 9–5 Fri 9–4 Sat/pub hols 10–2 ▪ Guided cellar tours daily ▪ Closed Easter Fri/Sun, Ascension day & Dec 25 ▪ Facilities for children ▪ Picnics to be pre-booked; fresh roosterkoek available daily ▪ Conference/function venue ▪ Distillique training courses available at Koelenhof ▪ Owner(s) 67 shareholders ▪ GM Andrew de Vries (2006) ▪ Winemaker(s) Nicholas Husselman (Oct 2017), with Handré Visagie & Estian Matthee (both Jan 2018) ▪ 16,500t/30,000cs own label 45% red 45% white 8% rosé 2% fortified + 2,000cs for clients & 100,000L bulk ▪ Other export brand: Simonsbosch ▪ IPW ▪ PO Box 1 Koelenhof 7605 ▪ koelwyn@mweb.co.za ▪ www.koelenhof.co.za ▪ S 33° 50' 5.2" E 018° 47' 52.7" ▪ ⟨⟩ toolkit.sounds.junction ▪ **T** +27 (0)21-865-2020/1

Koelfontein

This cool-climate mountainside property in Ceres, farming mostly fruit and nuts, started making own wine off their small vineyard in 2002. A devastating fire a few years back and the drought have brought setbacks, especially in terms of yield, but the mood is optimistic. Dewaldt Heyns makes the wines at Saronsberg.

★★★★ Shiraz Ripe, juicy, sweet-fruited & flavourful **15** ⑧⑨ given balance, even a touch of elegance, by luscious acidity, fine tannins. 90% new oak just hinted at. Approachable, but should keep.

Chardonnay ★★★☆ Full-bodied **17** ⑧⑤ less ripe, oaky & bold than previous, though no real model of restraint - 14.4% alcohol, 3.7 g/l sugar giving a sweet touch to the pleasant character. — TJ

Location/WO: Ceres ▪ Map: Tulbagh ▪ Map grid reference: H5 ▪ Est 1832 ▪ 1stB 2002 ▪ Tasting & sales Mon-Fri 11-4 Sat 11-2 ▪ Closed all pub hols ▪ Farm produce ▪ Hikes ▪ Conservation area ▪ Die Kloof self-catering historic house (sleeps 6) ▪ Owner(s) Handri Conradie ▪ Winemaker(s) Dewaldt Heyns (2004) ▪ Viticulturist(s) Hennie van Noordwyk ▪ 950ha/±6ha (shiraz, chard) ▪ ±24t/2,400cs own label 50% red 50% white ▪ WWF-SA Conservation Champion ▪ PO Box 4 Prince Alfred's Hamlet 6840 ▪ wine@koelfontein.co.za ▪ www.koel-fontein.co.za ▪ S 33° 15' 54.70" E 019° 19' 29.28" ▪ ⟨⟩ narrator.repaint.ducts ▪ **T** +27 (0)23-313-3304/+27 (0)71-413-3869

Koni Wines

After a successful career in human resources management, Soweto-born, Cape Town-based Koni Maliehe decided to pursue her passion for wine while adding value to the economy through job creation. The result is this range of 'premium-quality wines at a reasonable price' that she aims to export to Africa and Asia, 'targeting smaller countries where wine is not widely known and therefore being positively received'. Next step is a formal distribution service in Johannesburg 'to reach our market in the north more quickly'.

Cabernet Sauvignon (NEW) **★★★** For current drinking, **16** ⑧① has meaty & savoury tones, unshowy but pleasing. **Shiraz ★★★★** Good heft in middleweight **17** ⑧④, with prominent oak from 20% new barrels, gentle tannins, appealingly high-toned fruit. **Sauvignon Blanc ★★** Lean, light (12.5% alcohol) **18** ⑦⑤ has unusual 'green twig' nuance, sappy fruit. Discontinued: **Cabernet Sauvignon-Merlot**. — GdB

Location: Cape Town ▪ Map/WO: Stellenbosch ▪ Map grid reference: E1 ▪ Est 2015 ▪ 1stB 2014 ▪ Tasting & cellar tours Mon-Fri 11-3 Sat/pub hols on request ▪ Fee R50pp ▪ Sales Mon-Fri 8-5 ▪ Owner(s) Koni Maliehe ▪ maliehe@live.com ▪ www.konempire.com ▪ S 33° 49' 33.4" E 018° 49' 9.3" ▪ ⟨⟩ narrations.monuments.reconnect ▪ **T** +27 (0)74-112-6769

Konkelberg

Targeting 'a younger wine-drinking public', this Longridge-owned label with approachable and wallet-friendly wines is making inroads into China and Europe. The brand takes its name from a rumoured 'connivance corner' in the crook of the Stellenbosch and Helderberg mountains, where early settlers rendez-voused secretly with local traders in defiance of a Dutch East India Company ban.

Rouge ⟨⟩ **★★★★** Ideal summer red, **18** ⑧⑤ light textured, vibrant & fruit-filled, dry, just enough tannin grip for food or drinking solo. Mostly shiraz with dash cabernet franc, from Helderberg.

Sauvignon Blanc ⊘ ★★★☆ Now bottled, **18** ⑧⑤ has settled & relaxed, acidity now zesty rather than sharp, tropical tones instead of green. Also-reviewed **19** ⑧③ tank sample is racier, with cool blackcurrant flavours & grassy tail. — CvZ

Location: Stellenbosch ▪ Map: Helderberg ▪ Map grid reference: C1 ▪ WO: Western Cape ▪ Est 2011 ▪ 1stB 2012 ▪ Tasting & sales Mon-Sat 10-6 ▪ Closed Good Fri & Dec 25 ▪ Owner(s) Longridge Wynlandgoed ▪ Winemaker(s) Hendrien de Munck (2014) ▪ Viticulturist(s) Huey Janse van Rensburg ▪ 20ha/18ha (cab, cinsaut, ptage, sangio, shiraz, sauv) ▪ 180t/25,000cs own label 60% red 40% white plus 1,000cs for clients ▪ Suite 116 Private Bag X4 Die Boord 7613 ▪ info@konkelberg.co.za ▪ www.konkelberg.co.za ▪ S 34° 0' 55.2" E 018° 49' 60.0" ▪ ⌨ promptness.anatomy.quotes ▪ T +27 (0)21-855-2005

☐ **Kookfontein** *See Editor's Note*

Koopmanskloof Vineyards ◎

A large venture by Stellenbosch standards, with 456 ha on six farms on the Bottelary Hills, one an empowerment project, staff-owned and -managed. Broadly sustainability accredited, including Fairtrade, with a history going back to the 18th century, it was given new life by hiker and conservationist, the late Stevie Smit, who established a 98-ha private nature reserve with walking trails.

Reserve range 🆕

Cabernet Sauvignon ★★★☆ Handsome black & gold label. Only new French barrels for **17** ⑧④, still youthfully firm & dry but enough plush fruit to balance. Even better in a year or two.

Koopmanskloof range

Cabernet Sauvignon ⊘ ★★★ Mulberries & dark plums, savoury oak-influenced spicing, **18** ⑧② has friendly tannins, just enough grip for food pairing. Fairtrade certified, as all below. **Merlot** ⊘ ★★★ Packed with berries, some smoky tones from French/American oak, **18** ⑦⑧ is smooth-drinking, accessible. **Mocha Pinotage** ⊘ ★★★ Mocha, chocolate-toned from toasted staves, **18** ⑦⑧ tank sample lives up to its name. Good grip at the end, but juicy fruit has palate appeal. **Pinotage** ⊘ ★★★ More fruit expression than Mocha sibling, pre-bottling **18** ⑧① also has savoury spice notes, appealing succulence for early enjoyment. **Shiraz** ⊘ ★★★ Brambleberries, a toasty top note from staves, 30% American, **18** ⑦⑧ is quite savoury, a hearty food partner. **Pinotage Rosé** ⊘ ★★★ Musk sweets & red berries, **19** ⑧⓪ is highly perfumed, the flavours fruity-fresh, dry yet mouthfilling. **Chardonnay** ⊘ ★★★☆ Unwooded version, with winter melon freshness, **19** ⑦⑧ offers zesty drinkability. **Chenin Blanc** ⊘ ★★★ Crunchy green apple on **19** ⑦⑧, good varietal purity, crisply dry. **Sauvignon Blanc** ⊘ ★★★ Good typicity in **19** ⑧① capsicum & lime, refreshingly dry. — CR

Location/WO: Stellenbosch ▪ Est 1801 ▪ 1stB 1970 ▪ Closed to public ▪ Private Nature Reserve ▪ Owner(s) Managed by Koopmanskloof Wingerde (Pty) Ltd ▪ MD Rydal Jeftha ▪ Winemaker(s) Stephan Smit ▪ Viticulturist(s) Japie de Villiers ▪ 456ha (cab, carignan, merlot, ptage, roobernet, ruby cab, shiraz, chard, chenin, sauv, sem) ▪ ±3,700t/±2.5m L 50% red 50% white ▪ Other brand: The Fair Trade ▪ Fairtrade, IPW, WIETA ▪ PO Box 19 Koelenhof 7605 ▪ info@koopmanskloof.co.za ▪ www.koopmanskloof.co.za ▪ T +27 (0)21-842-0810

☐ **Kottabos** *see Boschkloof Wines*

Kranskop Wines ♀ ♍

Néwald Marais celebrates a decade as owner of this boutique winery on its eponymous rocky outcrop, proudly emphasising the distinctiveness of Robertson's Klaasvoogds ward. The former Nederburg cellarmaster is relishing being a traditional, hands-on grower for a family concern, recently WIETA accredited, currently redesigning its open-air tasting area for an all-weather welcome, cheese platters already on offer.

Petite Sirah-Viognier Rosé Sec ⑦ ★★★ Candyfloss pink **19** ⑧② unusual varietal pairing (50/50) co-vinified. Sampled ex tank, forthcoming peach blossom & floral aromas, quite delicate yet juicy & vibrant, good dry finish. **Chenin Blanc** ⑦ ★★★★ Fully ripe tropical fruit, hint of oak & crisp, zesty character give **18** ⑧③ drinkability, complexity & texture. 31 year old vines, 30% oaked.

Pinot Noir ⊘ ★★★ Fleshier, less food-styled than previous, **17** ⑧⓪ has ripe strawberry & spice, good balance & peppery grip to finish. **Shiraz** ★★★ Savoury & meaty flavours mingle with generous black fruit & ripe tannin for a delicious mouthful in moreish **16** ⑧⓪, 25% new oak, 12 months, in good support. **Tannat** ★★★☆ Still-rare varietal bottling. Inky ruby **17** ⑧③ brims with dark plum & mulberry fruit, shows balance & length. Good meaty meal option & will reward a little patience. **Chardonnay** ★★★ Now bottled, **18** ⑧② harmonious melange of Golden Delicious apple & creamy vanilla from combo 50/50 barrelled & unoaked portions. **Sauvignon Blanc** ★★★ Melon, pineapple & granadilla abound on previewed **19** ⑧①, piquant & lively lemon twist conclusion. **Viognier** ★★★ Overt peach & apricot fragrance & flavours on gentle oak-vanilla base in **18** ⑧⓪. Typical, but could linger longer. Not tasted: **Cabernet Sauvignon**, **Merlot**, **Viognier Noble Late Harvest**. — WB

Location/map: Robertson ▪ Map grid reference: B4 ▪ WO: Klaasvoogds ▪ Est 2001 ▪ 1stB 2003 ▪ Tasting, sales & tours Mon-Fri 10-4.30 Sat/pub hols 10-2 ▪ Closed Easter Sun & Dec 25 ▪ Cheese platters ▪ Owner(s)/viticulturist(s) Néwald Marais ▪ Cellarmaster(s)/winemaker(s) Néwald Marais (2008) ▪ 43ha/30ha (cab, merlot, pinot, shiraz, tannat, chard, sauv, viog) ▪ 240t/3,000cs own label 75% red 25% white ▪ IPW, WIETA ▪ PO Box 49 Klaasvoogds 6707 ▪ newald@kranskopwines.co.za ▪ www.kranskopwines.co.za ▪ S 33° 47' 53.1" E 019° 59' 56.6" ▪ ⌖ purest.touted.mapmaking ▪ **T +27 (0)23-626-3200**

Krone   ⓠ ⓞ

Dating back to 1710, Twee Jonge Gezellen in Tulbagh is home to this collection of méthode champenoise bubblies. Since being bought by giant wine business Vinimark in 2012, the cellar has been upgraded yet retains 'a feel as timeless as the 300-year-old estate itself'. Only vintage-dated MCCs are produced 'to celebrate a unique moment in time and place', and the range has now expanded to include two new blancs de blancs: terroir-driven Kaaimansgat and clay-fermented Amphora, the latter exclusively available at the estate, also worth visiting for its WHATIFTHEWORLD art gallery.

★★★★ **Rosé Vintage Cuvée Brut** ⊘ Salmon pink **18** ⑧⑦ sparkling from 92% pinot, rest chardonnay, has vibrant cranberry & juicy pomegranate notes, fresh but creamy bubbles, with hints of toasted hazelnuts after 9-12 months on lees.

★★★★ **Night Nectar Rosé Demi-Sec** ⊘ Strawberries & cream in a bottle, **18** ⑧⑨ has sweet raspberries, too, plus ample acidity to balance 43 g/l sugar, fine, rich, velvety mousse. Like sibling pink fizz, 92% pinot noir & 11% alcohol.

★★★★☆ **Amphora Blanc De Blancs** (NEW) (ⓐ) **17** ⑨③ sparkling, cool-climate Elandskloof chardonnay fermented in clay vessels, bottled unfiltered with zero dosage & matured 21 months on lees, already richly textured with layers of lemon cream, ginger shortbread & toasted nuts, beautifully balanced by brisk acid.

★★★★ **Borealis Vintage Cuvée Brut** ⊘ Splash pinot blanc joins 67% chardonnay, 27% pinot noir in dry, fresh, saline/steely sparkler, **18** ⑧⑦ with citrus, orange peel & ginger notes opening up in glass, promising more complexity with time.

★★★★☆ **Kaaimansgat Blanc De Blancs** (NEW) (ⓐ) Showcases famed vineyard, 700 m altitude in cool Elandskloof, & made to age, **16** ⑨③ in youth is very pure, focused, flinty, with lime & apple notes, but nascent creamy oatmeal (32 months on lees) & oystershell minerality hint at future complexity.

★★★★☆ **RD 2006** (ⓐ) Prestige sparkling, recently disgorged after remarkable 13 years on lees, **06** ⑨③ dry & vibrant yet immensely rich in texture & flavour: dried apples, apricots, toasted nuts, honey, rooibos, nutmeg & buttery pastry. Mostly chardonnay with 26% pinot, 23% pinot blanc. Limited release (450 cases), as Kaaimansgat (520) & Amphora (318). Previous was seductive **02** ⑨③. Tulbagh WO.

★★★★ **Night Nectar Demi-Sec** Semi-sweet version of Borealis (43 g/l sugar), **18** ⑧⑧ luxurious, creamy, lemon tart rather than fresh citrus notes, indulgent yet refined. Gossamer mousse & bright acidity.

Chardonnay-Pinot Noir ★★★ Non-sparkling **18** ⑧② rosé has faintest blush from 11% pinot, very dry, with lemon & ruby grapefruit tang, refreshing at modest 11.5% alcohol. — JG

Location/map: Tulbagh ▪ Map grid reference: F4 ▪ WO: Western Cape/Elandskloof/Tulbagh ▪ Est 1710 ▪ 1stB 1937 ▪ Tasting & sales Mon-Sat 10–4 ▪ Tasting fee R50pp ▪ Closed all pub hols ▪ Cellar tours Mon-Sat at 11 ▪ Annual festival: Christmas in Winter (Jun) ▪ Art gallery ▪ Owner(s) TJG Estate (Pty) Ltd ▪ Winemaker(s) Stephan de Beer (2008), with Tanya Fourie (Jan 2018) ▪ Viticulturist(s) Rosa Kruger ▪ PO Box 16 Tulbagh 6820

▪ info@tjg.co.za, info@kronemcc.com ▪ www.tweejongegezellen.co.za ▪ S 33° 14' 18.1" E 019° 6' 51.8" ▪ sightseers.headgear.brilliance ▪ T +27 (0)23-230-0680

Kronendal Boutique Winery

This small rural Durbanville winery (sprouted from an indigenous plant-growing venture), where Pieter and Magdaleen Kroon nurture a handcrafted red blend of naturally cultivated Rhône varieties, has gone international, with the first batch of Kronendal-branded wine exported to Germany. Hosting visitors by appointment, and seasonal communal 'long table' lunches, reflect their personal touch.

★★★★ **Mirari** ⓥ Latin for 'to wonder at'. As one does this naturally fermented blend of shiraz, mourvèdre & viognier. Plush **15** ★★★★☆ ⑨⓪, ripe berry fruit supported by generous oak (50% new), more hedonistic than spicy **14** ⑧⑨.— DS

Location: Durbanville ▪ Map: Durbanville, Philadelphia & Darling ▪ Map grid reference: C7 ▪ WO: Cape Town ▪ Est 2003 ▪ 1stB 2006 ▪ Tasting, sales & cellar tours by appt ▪ Seasonal 'langtafel' lunches ▪ Owner(s) Pieter & Magdaleen Kroon ▪ Winemaker(s) Magdaleen Kroon ▪ 2ha/0.6ha (mourv, shiraz, viog) ▪ 4t/520cs own label 100% red ▪ PO Box 4433 Durbanville 7551 ▪ info@kronendalwine.co.za ▪ www.kronendalwine.co.za ▪ S 33° 48' 30.78" E 018° 36' 50.82" ▪ deliverer.breadth.milkshakes ▪ T +27 (0)82-499-0198

☐ **Kruger Family** see Stellenview Premium Wines

Kruger Family Wines

Travelling is very much part of tenant winemaker Johan Kruger's life, not only to his international markets (Belgium, wife Sophie's home country, joined the list in 2019) but also to far corners of the winelands, from Upper Hemel-en-Aarde to Piekenierskloof, where he enjoys good working relationships with his vineyard partners. Johan's focus has turned to saving older vineyards, and he currently works with eight. The 43-year-old Wellington chenin blanc block was thanks to UK customer-funded Naked Wines, which also helped rescue an old tinta barocca vineyard ('So far my wine of 2019'). MCC sparkling rosé from Upper Hemel-en-Aarde and grenache rosé from Piekenierskloof are upcoming new members of his Family range.

Kruger Family Wines range

★★★★ **Old Vines Cinsault** ⓥ **18** ★★★★☆ ⑨⓪, like **17** ⑧⑦, from Piekenierskloof vines planted 1976. Natural ferment (as all KFW wines), older oak; 30% wholebunch ensures house-style freshness to silky, concentrated fruit - perfumed & spicy. Balanced tannin trim for current & future drinking.

★★★★☆ **Pearly Gates Pinot Noir** ⊘ Ruby translucence introduces **18** ⑨②, a wine of both clarity & complexity. Portion wholebunch enhances scented dark fruit, undergrowth layers; these lengthily sustained by natural acidity, fine grip. Oak, 5% new, 10 months. A charmer. Ex Upper Hemel-en-Aarde, like **17** ★★★★ ⑧④.

★★★★☆ **Klipkop Chardonnay** Sunny-hued **18** ⑨⓪; old Piekenierskloof, high-lying vines, tiny 1.5 t/ha yield imparts extraordinary concentration. Cool lemon & lime features enriched with touch vanilla (25% new oak) gain precision from savoury acid backbone. Will reward few years' ageing.

★★★★☆ **Walker Bay Chardonnay** ⓐ Delicacy & precision hallmarks of sophisticated **18** ⑨③. Natural ferment, mainly older oak (10% new) augment gentle citrus, saline notes. Sense of lively tension, cool ripeness rather than overt fruit; complementary dry, long tail.

Old Vines Grenache ⓝⒺⓦ ⓥ ★★★★ From 47 year old Piekenierskloof vines. Initial funky notes hide spice-edged red fruits on **18** ⑧④; brighter, juicy flavours clipped by dense tannin. Maybe will benefit from decanting, time. Older oak, 10 months. **Sans Chêne Chardonnay** ★★★★ Lots nutty citrus flavour, creamy substance with hint of grip in **18** ⑧⑤. Unoaked, natural ferment in mix stainless steel, concrete 'egg' enhances personality. Piekenierskloof WO.

Naked Wines range

★★★★ **Elements** Quality of **15** ⑧⑨ shines in cab-led quintet, especially cedary-oak enhanced pure, dark berry fragrance. Silkily rich, full bodied but nicely reined in, freshened by vibrant tannins, dry finish. Step up on **14** ★★★★ ⑧④.

★★★★ **Chardonnay 18** ★★★★☆ ⑧⑤ fresher but tad less distinctive than **17** ⑧⑥; similar natural ferment/oak ageing (25% new). Tasty tangy citrus, oak spice/vanilla flavours, some creamy lees. Bone-dry.

★★★★★ **Old Vines Chenin Blanc** (NEW) (🌿) (🏅) From 43 year old Wellington vines. Older oak, concrete 'egg' (50/50) vinification give full rein in striking **18** (95) to dense texture, delicious red apple concentration, complexity. Freshness, medium body add to focus, persistence. To enjoy at best, don't over-chill.

Merlot ★★★ still youthfully shy, tight, **17** (82)'s sternish tannins should harmonise with underlying ripe plummy flavours & juiciness with year/2 ageing. Stellenbosch WO, like next. **Pinotage** ★★★★ Juicy **18** (83) with plenty ripe mulberry, plum fruit & light spicing from older wood. More youthful grip than previous, which short ageing should resolve. **Matteo Reserve** ★★★★ Cab-shiraz **18** (84), dark berries & spice attractions in harmony with ripe flesh, rounded tannins. Satisfying, approachable. Minty, spicy exuberance on shiraz-led **17** (83), also tasted, flavoursome, savoury, equal parts merlot, cab add respectively juiciness, fresh tannic edge. **16** (83) included pinotage. **Unoaked Chardonnay** (NEW) ★★★★ Bright, zesty citrus notes underpinned by creamy texture. **18** (84) refreshingly dry, medium bodied. Franschhoek WO. **Angels Selection** ★★★★ Flavoursome ripe apple/pear notes in **18** (85) chenin-led blend; older-vine colombard & chardonnay add freshness, palate weight. Not tasted: **Maxime Reserve**. — AL

Location: Somerset West ▪ WO: Coastal/Piekenierskloof/Stellenbosch/Walker Bay/Franschhoek/Wellington/ Upper Hemel-en-Aarde Valley ▪ Est/1stB 2015 ▪ Tasting by appt only ▪ Owner(s) Johan & Sofie Kruger ▪ Cellarmaster(s)/winemaker(s) Johan Kruger (Sep 2015) ▪ 80t/25,000cs own label 50% red 50% white + 40,000cs for clients ▪ Brands for clients: Naked Wines (UK) ▪ WIETA ▪ johan@krugerfamilywines.co.za ▪ www.krugerfamilywines.co.za ▪ **T +27 (0)83-411-0757**

Kruishof Wines (NEW)

Swedish corporate executive Bengt Kvarnbäck retired to 355-ha Wellington farm Kruishof in 2008. He restored the 1812 manor house and replaced under-performing vines with pomegranates and a prime hectare with shiraz. As a surprise for wife Cecilia's 50th, Bengt had a shiraz specialist vinify vintage 2013. Subsequent vintages were mainly exported (Sweden, Germany). The intention is to up local sales under the redesigned YMER label, depicting the geometric tortoise (the organically farmed property is part of the Renosterveld Conservancy, this critically endangered reptile's home range).

★★★★ **YMER Shiraz** (✓) Scrub, sweet red berries & hint liquorice with cinnamon & clove spice, vibrant acidity, hefty structure characteristics of all vintages reviewed. **14** ★★★★ (85) the ripest, with slightly malty notes, big 15.5% alcohol; **15** ★★★★ (85), cooler year, more vibrant. **16** (86) vital & engaging, cracked black pepper attraction, commendable dry finish, less new oak (20%) than others, too. — GdB, CvZ

Location/WO: Wellington ▪ Est 2010 ▪ 1stB 2013 ▪ Closed to public ▪ Owner(s) Letuche Farming (Pty) Ltd (Bengt Kvarnbäck, Sweden) ▪ Winemaker(s) Ossie Sauermann (2013) & Marozanne Bieldt (2015, both consultants) ▪ Viticulturist(s) Ossie Sauermann (2012, consultant) ▪ 355ha/1.02ha (shiraz) ▪ 8t/1,000cs own label 100% white ▪ GlobalGAP, IPW, WIETA ▪ PO Box 2165 Windmeul 7630 ▪ kruishofwines@gmail.com ▪ www.kruishofwines.com ▪ **T +27 (0)83-633-2835**

Kumala (🏆)

Accolade Wines SA's export powerhouse Kumala is the top-selling SA wine brand in the world by volume. Building on more than 20 years' success, and vinifying grapes from diverse areas, head winemaker Gerhard Swart and his team aim for 'a versatile range of everyday wines, full of life'. The wines below are only ones available locally, the numerous export labels are untasted.

Reserve range

Pinotage (NEW) ★★ Plump plum fruit well-supported by wood tannin for comfortable early drinking; **18** (76) for firesides & barbecues. **Shiraz** (🌿) ★★★ A handsome rustic, **17** (80) dark plummy fruit & florals layered with fragrant mocha. Perky tannin & lively acidity balance few grams sugar & 14.5% alcohol. **Chenin Blanc** ★★★ Bold pear & melon fruit lightly buffed by French oak in **18** (77). Built for quaffing: just chill & enjoy. **Sauvignon Blanc** ★★ Breedekloof fruit (including splash semillon) has a vanilla glow from light oaking (some American) in brisk **18** (75). Discontinued: **Malbec, Chardonnay**.

Zenith range

Shiraz-Cabernet Sauvignon-Pinotage ★★ Shiraz (72%) leads friendly blend, pinotage replaces merlot of previous. Juicy **18** (75) has twist of pepper; simple but enjoyable. Also in magnum. WO W Cape. — DS

Location: Somerset West ▪ WO: Swartland/Breedekloof/Western Cape ▪ Tasting & sales at Flagstone Winery ▪ Owner(s) Accolade Wines South Africa ▪ Winemaker(s) Gerhard Swart (head, Sep 2007) & Juan Slabbert (Jan 2018) ▪ 50% red 50% white ▪ PO Box 769 Stellenbosch 7599 ▪ info@flagstonewines.com ▪ www.kumala.co.za ▪ **T +27 (0)21-852-5052**

Kumusha Wines

Shona for 'home/origin/roots', Kumusha marks Zimbabwe-born Cape Town sommelier Tinashe Nyamudoka's debut as wine producer. From arrival here in 2008, 'having never tasted wine', to work as a waiter, through Cape Wine Academy food and wine courses, and wine-steward award wins, to acclaimed The Test Kitchen beverage manager and head sommelier, Tinashe now sources wines from 'trusted winemakers' for blending at a facility in the city. 'The wine and food culture is rapidly changing among black millennials and Kumusha aims to join the conversation.'

★★★★ **Merlot** Supple & lithe **17** (87), plummy with liquorice & chocolate accents, fresh, balanced & easygoing glassful with enough grip for food, structure for few years improvement.

★★★★ **Red Blend** On-trend traditional pairing of cabernet & cinsaut (55/45), **18** (86) treads lightly (12.9% alcohol) but is packed with sweet red fruit, pleasantly stemmy tannin & bright acidity give balanced form, extend the palate appeal. WO Slanghoek, like White Blend.

★★★★☆ **Sauvignon Blanc** Ripe & complex varietal fruit flavours & aromas (gooseberry, passionfruit, tinned pea) in stylish **18** (90). Vigorous acidity provides excellent balance to enjoy solo or with food, seamless fantail finish.

★★★★☆ **White Blend** (🍇) Old-oak-matured **17** (93) sees majority chenin (48%) contributing richness & silky texture, semillon & roussanne adding vibrancy, viognier subtle perfume. Understated gravitas, considerable presence at moderate 13.2% alcohol.

Shiraz ★★★ Bright-fruited **17** (82), appealing scrub & leather nuances, obvious farmyard notes. For current drinking. — GdB, CvZ

Location: Cape Town ▪ WO: Cape Agulhas/Slanghoek ▪ 1stB 2016 ▪ Closed to public ▪ Owner(s)/cellarmaster(s) Tinashe Nyamudoka ▪ Winemaker(s) Hannes Meyer (Lomond) & Attie Louw (Opstal) ▪ Unit 3B, Tygerberg Park, Railway Str, Parow Industrial 7499 ▪ tnyamudoka@yahoo.com ▪ **T +27 (0)83-432-5400**

Kunjani Wines

'Kunjani means "Hi, how are you?" and that is exactly how friendships start,' say Paul Barth and Pia Watermeyer, the German/South African husband-and-wife owners of this boutique winery in the Bottelary Hills overlooking Devon Valley. Their industrial-chic tasting lounge and restaurant are now open every day, and their improved wines — made by Carmen Stevens — have undergone a sophisticated packaging transformation, their labels featuring a fist-bump logo with the words 'two cultures, one passion'.

Cabernet Sauvignon (NEW) ★★★★ **17** (83) has earthy aromas leading to sweet, ripe blackcurrant & blueberry fruit, choc-nut notes, nicely rounded. **Merlot** (NEW) ★★★ Ripe plum fruit, hint milk choc/vanilla oak sweetness, **17** (80) also some tobacco & aniseed which linger on finish. **Shiraz** ★★★ Step up on previous, **17** (82) brims with ripe black fruit, hints of cocoa, cola & smoke after year in 2nd/3rd-fill oak. **Stolen Chicken Rosé** ★★★ Fresher, drier than previous, with guava & cranberry flavours, **18** (80) ex shiraz & splash merlot is quite full-bodied yet elegant. **Chenin Blanc** ★★★ Made oxidatively, 3 months on lees, **18** (80) has cling peach & Golden Delicious apple flavours, moderate 12% alcohol for easy drinking. Coastal WO. **Sauvignon Blanc** ★★★★ Tropical **18** (83) from Paarl has ripe fig, kiwi & granadilla fruit, viscous texture (3 months on lees) cut through by bracing acidity. Discontinued: **Red Blend**. — JG

Location/map: Stellenbosch ▪ Map grid reference: D3 ▪ WO: Devon Valley/Coastal/Paarl ▪ Est 2017 ▪ 1stB 2011 ▪ Tasting & sales Mon-Sun 9-5 ▪ Fee R60pp ▪ Restaurant open daily for breakfast & lunch ▪ 4 self-catering villas ▪ Conference/function venue ▪ Farm produce ▪ Walks/hikes ▪ Owner(s) Kap Vino Estate (Paul Barth & Pia Watermeyer) ▪ Farm 90, 20 Blumberg Dr, Devonvale, Stellenbosch 7600 ▪ info@kunjaniwines.co.za ▪ www.kunjaniwines.co.za ▪ S 33° 53' 40.98" E 018° 48' 21.46" ▪ **T +27 (0)87-630-0409**

Kuypers Kraal ⓠ

Sibling to dairy products brand Fair Cape, Kuyperskraal originates in the Philadelphia area, where the Loubser family has been farming for 150 years. The current generation, five brothers, is part of collaborative marketing venture Kaapse Familie Wingerde, with Oude Denneboom and Vendôme, the latter also the tasting venue for the wines below.

Pinotage ⓠ ★★★ Vanilla caramel-laced mulberry fruit will take fans of old-school pinotage back to the halcyon days. Previewed **16** ⑧⑴ wholesome if somewhat chunky. **Sauvignon Blanc** ⊘ ★★★★ Vivacious tropical fruit & grass, delicious lemon tang on persistent farewell in **19** ⑧⑷ from Durbanville vines. — WB

Location: Philadelphia ▪ WO: Coastal/Durbanville ▪ Est 1991 ▪ 1stB 2014 ▪ Tasting & sales at Vendôme ▪ Owner(s) Loubser brothers ▪ Cellarmaster(s) Altus le Roux (consultant) ▪ Viticulturist(s) Viljee Loubser ▪ 1,500ha/100ha (cab, ptage, sauv) ▪ 1,000t/400cs own label 30% red 70% white ▪ WIETA ▪ Malanshoogte Rd Durbanville 7550 ▪ viljee@faircape.com ▪ www.faircape.com, www.kaapsefamiliewingerde.com ▪ **T +27 (0)86-169-6455**

KWV ⓠ ⓘ ⓒ ⓖ

Founded in 1918, KWV has evolved into a producer of over 100 products represented in more than 100 markets globally. The company's century-long reputation for quality is reflected in its long-standing global status for fine wines, fortifieds and brandies (see separate listings). Visitors to HQ in Paarl are greeted by venerable production facilities transformed into modern and memorable tourist spaces: the House of Fire, originally the distilling cellar for KWV's brandies, and the imposing, vaulted Cathedral Cellar, built in 1930 and now lovingly refurbished.

Location: Paarl ▪ KWV Wine Emporium: Kohler Str, T +27 (0)21-807-3007/8 F +27 (0)21-807-3119, wineemporium@kwv.co.za, www.kwvwineemporium.co.za ▪ Tasting & sales Mon-Sat 9—4.30 Sun 10-3 ▪ Several food & wine pairings available ▪ Cellar tours: Eng Mon-Sat 10, 10.30 & 2.15; Ger 10.15; Sun Eng 11 ▪ Tour groups by appt ▪ Closed Good Fri, Dec 25 & Jan 1 ▪ KWV House of Fire: Kohler Str, contact details same as for KWV Wine Emporium, or houseoffire@kwv.co.za ▪ House of Fire tour & brandy tasting: Eng Mon-Fri 11.30 & 2.30 reservations essential (max 14 persons per tour), regret no under 18s allowed ▪ KWV Sensorium: 57 Main Rd, T +27 (0)21-807-3094, sensorium@kwv.co.za, www.kwvsensorium.co.za ▪ Tasting & art museum Mon-Fri 9-4.30 ▪ Art & wine pairing ▪ Owner(s) Warshay Investment (Pty) Ltd ta KWV ▪ Chief winemaker Wim Truter ▪ Winemaker(s) Izele van Blerk, Louwritz Louw, Carla Cutting, Kobus van der Merwe & Sacha Muller ▪ Viticulturist(s) Marco Ventrella, Anneke du Plessis & Oursula Lenee ▪ PO Box 528 Suider-Paarl 7624 ▪ customer@kwv.co.za ▪ www.kwv.co.za ▪ S 33° 45' 46.87" E 018° 57' 59.92" (Emporium/House of Fire), S 33° 45' 43.26" E 018° 57' 44.06" (Sensorium) ▪ **T +27 (0)21-807-3911 (office)**

KWV Brandies

Since 1918, KWV has been crafting world-class spirits - potstill brandy in particular - garnering an international reputation and many prestigious awards including World-Class Distillery at the World Spirits Award 2019. The portfolio is crafted by master distiller Pieter de Bod and a team who are also responsible for Imoya VSOP Cognac, a collaboration with Cognac house Maison Charpentier. The House of Fire at KWV Wine Emporium in Paarl (see KWV 'corporate' listing) provides a multifaceted showcase for these fine brandies.

★★★★★ **Centenary** ⑯⑷ Just 100 hugely expensive bottles of this magnificent brandy ⑨⑼ to celebrate 100 years of KWV. SA's oldest, with portion distilled in 1926 & average maturation period 37 years. Combines ethereal, elegant delicacy with subtle intensity. Delectable rancio/sherry note within its complexity, but so fresh! Mellow & deeply satisfying, reverberating endlessly.

★★★★★ **Nexus** Superb packaging featuring individually crafted bottle & wooden case sets the scene for this 30 year old ⑨⑸: fine floral notes, wafts of soft spice, dried pears & apple follow on to intense fruit on the palate. Elegant, regal & oh so smooth, with a dry lingering citrus bite. Astounding quality.

★★★★★ **20 Year Old** Exquisite aromas - sandalwood, apricot, scented flowers, hints spice & oxidative maturity. Rich & full, yet ultra-refined & delicate. This ⑨⑹ touch less forceful than 15YO, but more grace. Beautifully balanced, with supreme oak support. Long, mellow, mature notes carry to sweetish finish.

★★★★ **Imoya Fine Potstill** Modern, beautifully presented brandy ⑧⑧. Fresh fruity aromas & flavours; elegant, rich balance, subtle texture with nutty, spicy oak in support, lifted with a fresh spirity finish. 100% potstill of up to 20 years.

★★★★★ **15 Year Old Alambic** Attractive honey, soft spice & dried fruit with floral backing & some fine oak on this brandy ⑨⑦. Smooth, fine texture & good balance; great complexity from a range of citrus & rich fruitcake flavours. Mellow & mature, with everlasting finish.

★★★★★ **12 Year Old Barrel Select** ⊘ A triumph ⑨⑤. Rich, robust with caramelised nuts, sun-dried peaches, pear drop on the nose. The palate is that & more. Layers of cashew nut flavours melt in the mouth, honey, dark chocolate & fine sprinkling of spice.

★★★★★ **10 Year Old Vintage** ⊘ Exquisite 100% potstill ⑨⑤. Jewel bright & delicate, with citrus aromas, dried apple, spice & dark chocolate on the palate. Rounded & full bodied, long mellow finish.

★★★★ **5 Year Old Superior** ⊘ Notes of sweet caramel, fruit, nuts & vanilla. Excellent balance, clean & lightly fiery on sweet-tinged finish. Blended brandy ⑧⑨; could compete with pure potstills on their turf!

3 Year Old Finest Blend ⊘ ★★★★ This ⑧④ less aggressive than many young blended brandies - sippable neat. Fruity nose with caramel, dark molasses, tealeaves. Sufficiently complex, balanced. — WB

KWV Sherry-Style Wines

KWV's awarded fortified range consists of a Red Muscadel, Ruby and Tawny 'ports' (see KWV Wines), plus these three sherry-style wines. The trio is made from chenin blanc and colombard, and aged in small barrels for the first year. They are then transferred to a solera for a further 3–6 years' maturation.

★★★★ **Cape Full Cream** ⓧ Golden brown **NV** ⑧⑦ shows the candied fruit profile, velvety sweetness & gentle spirity lift that proclaims KWV's expertise with fortified wine.

★★★★ **Cape Medium Cream** ⓧ Amber **NV** ⑧⑦ trademark stewed fruit & caramelised apples, the flavours rich & sweet yet uncloying. Finish is savoury, brightened by alcohol.

★★★★ **Cape Pale Dry** ⓧ **NV** ⑧⑦ shows typical flor character of tealeaf & pear, almond, hints of dried fruit simmering under. Bone-dry, good freshness & spirit lift. — CR

KWV Wines

Now in its second century of production, KWV is a globally recognised, award-winning wine and spirits company, and the highest-ranking SA wine brand in a Drinks International magazine Top 50 Most Admired Wine Brands in the World listing. The ranges featured below are created under the leadership of chief winemaker Wim Truter, with 'drinkability first' as mantra and the goal of 'elegant, balanced and fresh wines of high quality'. Tastings and sales of the wines and separately listed brandies and sherry-style wines are at KWV's well-appointed Wine Emporium in Paarl (see KWV 'corporate' entry).

Abraham Perold Heritage Collection

★★★★☆ **Tributum** ⓰ Best barrels selected to honour father of pinotage. Very fine Cape Blend is mostly shiraz & pinotage, with malbec, cab & splash petite sirah in **14** ⑨②. Lush dark fruit, savoury spice & a structure (70% new French & American, 18 months) which should carry the wine 10+ years. Coastal WO.

The Mentors range

★★★★☆ **Cabernet Sauvignon Darling** ⓧ Elegant expression of Darling's cool maritime climate: **14** ⑨② generous but reined-in blackberry fruit, hint of mint, firm but ripe tannins. 18 months, 70% new oak, as most reds this range. This & all below WO W Cape unless noted.

★★★★ **Cabernet Sauvignon Stellenbosch** ⓧ Deep & dark but not extracted, with fresh acidity & vibrant fruit, oak-driven finish. **14** ⑧⑦ needs year/2 to show at best.

★★★★☆ **Petit Verdot** ⓧ Variety-true **16** ⑨① rich & concentrated, notes of blueberry, lavender, dark chocolate & toasty oak. Polished, firm tannins provide backbone & balance, & bode well for the future.

★★★★☆ **Pinotage** ⓧ Switching from Stellenbosch to Darling origin, **16** ⑨⓪'s fruit is dark & plummy, the body full & rounded, hints of vanilla & coconut from French & American barrels. Will reward ageing.

★★★★ **Shiraz** ⓧ Like last-tasted **09**, **14** ★★★★☆ ⑨⓪ ripe & expressive but not unrestrained. Violet & cassis notes, well-judged oak (some American), long spicy finish. Coastal WO, as next 2.

★★★★ **Orchestra** ② Best barrels selection for this cab-led, 5-way Bordeaux blend. **16** ⑧⑧ a symphony of black & red berry fruit, vivacious & succulent yet structured by cocoa-tinged oak & fresh finish.

★★★★☆ **Canvas** ② Shiraz (39%) with grenache, tempranillo, petite sirah, cinsaut & tannat colours the **16** ⑨④ canvas in bright aromas & flavours. Lipsmacking & complex, with a savoury freshness. A masterclass in blending. 50% new oak.

★★★★☆ **Chenin Blanc** ⊘ ⓐ Complex & rich barrel-fermented **17** ⑨④ from 3 parcels in Paarl, different yeasts & long lees contact. Rounded & expressive, with mellow orchard fruit, buttery texture & freshening drizzle of lime. Drinks well now, but no rush. **16** not made.

★★★★☆ **Grenache Blanc** ⊘ ⓐ Complex vinification - barrel-fermented (with wild yeast) & tank-vinified (65%) portions, both lees-aged in old oak. **17** ★★★★★ ⑨⑤ rewards the effort with unfolding layers of flavour, stonefruit, wax & stony minerality, textured & long with lingering freshness. Very modern, sleek, like last-made **15** ⑨③.

★★★★ **Sauvignon Blanc Darling** Packs a punch in **17** ⑧⑨ with bold gooseberry & melon flavours, palate weight boosted by 60 days on lees, stirred weekly. Finish is fresh, sustained, with lime zest nuance.

★★★★ **Sauvignon Blanc Elim** ② Attractively austere **14** ⑨③ from ocean-cooled vines, mineral expression with salty hints; interesting contrast to sibling's tropical generosity. Well-judged acidity, herbal length with just enough grip from 2 months on lees. Will reward few years cellaring.

★★★★ **Semillon** ② Quintessential semillon notes of hay, smoke plus variety's signature acid tension in impressive **15** ⑧⑦ from Darling. Partial barrel ferment adds subtle creaminess.

★★★★ **Sauvignon Blanc-Semillon** ② Accomplished barrelled version with 2 months on lees for extra texture & weight. **15** ⑧⑦'s toastiness gives way to forthcoming capsicum & passionfruit. Delicious now, should improve year/2. Coastal WO.

Cathedral Cellar range

★★★★ **Shiraz** ② Previewed **16** ⑧⑧ is spicy, with robust black hedgerow fruit, meaty undertone, long finish & savouriness from 40% new oak, 6% American. Delightful wine - very lively & youthful.

★★★★☆ **Triptych** ② Well-structured vintage blend, mostly cab & shiraz in **16** ⑨⓪, plus merlot & pinotage. Full bodied, amply layered with berry, spice & cured meat. Tasted pre-bottling, rating provisional, but everything set for usual pleasurable drinking.

★★★★ **Chardonnay** Lovely interplay of unoaked (4%) & wooded components, different yeast strains in **18** ⑧⑦. Rich & rounded, baked apple cake & spice notes ending with a fresh lemon flourish. Extended lees contact adds complexity.

Cabernet Sauvignon ★★★☆ Rich & smooth **17** ⑧④ brims with red berry & bramble character, lovely vanilla note from 35% new oak, 14-16 months, to enhance the juicy palate. **Sauvignon Blanc** ★★★☆ Tropical & greenpepper flavours abound on **18** ⑧④, yet generosity & ripeness reined back by well-judged lees contact & lime zest twist.

Roodeberg range

★★★★ **Dr Charles Niehaus** ② Roodeberg an iconic name in SA wine, this wine honours its father. 'Dr Charles' also early proponent of shiraz, hence variety's lead in **16** ★★★★☆ ⑨⓪ characterful blend with cab, merlot, malbec. Sweet, intense black cherry flavours, deepening earthy herb notes, savoury finish. Dab American oak, as in **15** ⑧⑦. Coastal WO.

★★★★☆ **Roodeberg 1949** ⒩ⓔⓦ ⓐ Marks 70 years of Roodeberg with expressive, well-structured & creative blend cab, tempranillo, carignan & carmenère. Mouthfilling dark plum, mulberry, savoury meat flavours coupled with 18 months oaking, 50% new, will easily carry **17** ⑨⓪ through to the 80th anniversary celebrations. Stellenbosch WO.

....

Red ⓥ ★★★ Enduring label, synonymous with KWV & always a gem. **18** ⑧② true to form: easy, friendly, spicy fruit & supple tannins to enjoy without ceremony. Mostly cab & shiraz.

....

Rosé ★★★ Ever-charming & vibrant dry pink, **19** ⑧⓪ from cab, shiraz, mourvèdre, has gentle strawberry flavours & hint of spice.

Laborie range

★★★★☆ **Signature Shiraz** (NEW) ⊘ (🏭) A barrel selection, showing fine intensity & concentration of thatchy hedgerow fruit & wild berries. Inky ruby hue matched with solid tannin backbone, long creamy farewell. 18 months in barrel, 35% new, mostly French, prepare **16** (90) for the long haul.

★★★★ **Méthode Cap Classique Brut Rosé** ⊘ Dry sparkling from pinot noir, chardonnay, touch pinotage, **NV** (89) is seriously conceived but so vibrantly berried, its bubbles so creamy, fresh & upbeat, it will jump-start even the dullest party.

★★★★☆ **Méthode Cap Classique Blanc de Blancs** ⊘ (🏭) Chardonnay sparkler with 36 months on lees, giving rich brioche, cinnamon-baked apple & lemon curd flavours. **14** (91) intense, full, with gentle, fine lingering mousse. Finishes long with a roasted nut, savoury note. First tasted since **11** (90).

★★★★ **Méthode Cap Classique Brut** ⊘ Beautifully packaged (& well priced), like sibling sparklings, **NV** (88) chardonnay, pinot noir & meunier spent 24 months on lees for a wonderfully balanced, silky mouthfeel. Finessed fruit, with toasty richness & fine bubbles.

Shiraz (🍇) ★★★ Brings a smile to your face with generous, juicy spiced berries. **18** (82) poised, with buffed tannins. **Chardonnay** (🍇) ★★★ Partly oaked & lees aged for some complexity, but **19** (80) is all about gluggability, with delicious creamy baked apple flavour, complete with pinch of cinnamon.

Cabernet Sauvignon ★★★ 18 (78) is medium bodied, with spiced dark fruit & a plum skin tang to finish. **Merlot** ★★☆ Perky 18 (79), nice & smooth with blueberry notes, hint of espresso. **Merlot-Cabernet Sauvignon** ★★★ Showing spice-dusted tangy red berries, **18** (77) tastes a bit sweet so the firm tannin grip comes as a surprise. **Rosé** ★★★ Previewed **19** (79) is dry but soft, bright fruited, with nice bite to finish. Mostly mourvèdre & 5 other black grapes. **Chenin Blanc** (NEW) ★★★ Water-white **19** (79) has tropical fruit flavours & barely perceptible brush of oak, zippy citrus farewell. **Sauvignon Blanc** ★★★ Floral & delicate **19** (79), greenpepper & herb wafts, lemon zest aftertaste. **Pineau de Laborie** ★★★☆ Sweet fortified pinotage dessert wine, unoaked **NV** (84) is plummy & spicy, with a warming finish. 500 ml.

Classic Collection

★★★★★ **Cape Tawny** ⊘ (🏭) Always-impressive **NV** (95) 'port' from tinta, cinsaut, souzão, touriga & shiraz. Roast nuts, caramel, dried fruit, toffee, hints of coffee & dark chocolate in a gorgeous amber body, spirit & fruit in harmony after 8-10 years in older wood. Even more notable than previous bottling.

Petit Verdot (🍇) ★★★ Variety not usually associated with carefree quaffing, but **18** (81) ticks that box (& the food-partnering one) with generous black fruit, appealing depth of accessible flavour. **Pinotage** (🍇) ★★★ Pure joy to drink, lightly oaked **18** (81)'s dark-berry flavours are ripe, juicy & underpinned by an appetising warm spiciness. **Chardonnay** (🍇) ★★★ Subtly satisfying **19** (82), gentle butterscotch overlay to the bright fruit, fragrant baked apple flavour, creamy & smooth. Well weighted & balanced. **Moscato** (🍇) ★★★ Perfumed honeysuckle & jasmine on charming sweet muscat d'Alexandrie, **19** (82) delightful with Asian fare or chilled on its own.

Cabernet Sauvignon ★★☆ Partly oaked, **18** (79) has soft-textured black berries, is very easy to enjoy. **Merlot** ★★☆ Fruitcake & plums, gentle tannin grip on easy, light-bodied **18** (78). **Shiraz** ★★★ Generous & welcoming ripe plum, chocolate & savoury flavours in **18** (80), easy & friendly, a great pasta partner. **Rosé** ★★ Was 'Shiraz Rosé' but no longer only from that grape. Bright pink in hue but the rest of **19** (74) less outspoken, the body slender, the fruit favours demure. Serve chilled. **Chenin Blanc** ★★☆ Zippy & punchy, with crunchy Granny Smith apple flavours, **19** (79) will cheer up your everyday. **Grenache Blanc** (✗) ★★★☆ Standout among the whites here: oak-brushed **18** (84) pleasingly intense & flavourful, excellent value for money. **Sauvignon Blanc** ★★★ Has an attractive cool tone in **19** (77), with green herbs & balanced acidity. **Sparkling Cuvée Brut** ★★★ Refreshing & vibrant green-toned sparkler, **NV** (79) for picnic popping. **Sparkling Demi-Sec** ★★ Semi-sweet & frothy, **NV** (76) is creamy & gentle with subtle balance. **Red Muscadel** ★★★☆ Dried fruit, spice, toffee & raisin flavours leap from the glass of winter-warming fortified **NV** (85). Rich & flavoursome, with a good long fiery finish. **Cape Ruby** ★★★☆ Sweet mouthful of red plums, mulberry & warm spice on **NV** (85) 'port', all tempered by vibrant spirit. Good example of the style from tinta, shiraz & pinotage.

Café Culture range
Pinotage ★★☆ Perfect for lovers of the 'java' style: warm plum fruit in a dark coffee embrace. **19** ⑦⑧ funkily packaged, too.

Earth's Essence No Sulphur Added range
Shiraz ★★ Ex-tank **19** ⑦④ shows lively raspberry fruit in a lean sour-cherry grip. **Chenin Blanc** ⓧ ★★ Previewed **18** ⑦③ very demure, some bruised apple flavour, lick of lemon.

Contemporary range
Cabernet Sauvignon-Merlot (NEW) ★★☆ All older-oak ageing for **18** ⑦⑧, berries & cherries in light & friendly style. **Chenin Blanc-Chardonnay** (NEW) ★★☆ Fleeting crunchy green apple flavour & citrus bite on **19** ⑦⑦ preview.

Golden Kaan range
Cabernet Sauvignon ★★ Part oaked, as red siblings, just-dry **18** ⑦⑥ offers dusty sweet/sour berry flavours. **Merlot** ★★☆ Juicy, fleshy **18** ⑦⑨ charms with easy just-dry fruit flavours. **Shiraz** ★★☆ Liquorice & gentle spice on **18** ⑦⑨'s ripe, sweet/savoury red fruit. **Sauvignon Blanc** ★★☆ A riot of tropical fruit in **19** ⑦⑨, intense flavours, but the grippy farewell doesn't linger.

Big Bill range
Not tasted: **Red**, **White**.

Bonne Esperance range
Not tasted: **Red**, **White**.

Pearly Bay range
Not tasted: **Celebrations Rosé**, **Celebrations**. — WB

Kyburg Wine Estate ⓠ ⌂
It's been more than two decades since Fred and Rosmarie Ruest bought their boutique farm in Stellenbosch's Devon Valley. Each year they return to Switzerland to present a tasting near the medieval castle Kyburg in Winterthur, where they both grew up. Consultant Jacques Fourie vinifies just 20% of the grape crop, the rest is snapped up by other labels. Fred prefers to sample grapes from his quad bike, not the shiny red 1953 delivery pickup which daughter Tanya blogs about. It's travelled from Kruger to KwaZulu-Natal, but the new markets in Brazil, Canada and China may be a stretch.

★★★★ **Cabernet Sauvignon** Better than **11** ★★★★ ⑧③, **12** ⑧⑧ drinks well after 16 months in oak (20% new) & 5 years in bottle. Understated yet plush, velvety & ripe with subtle mint brush to cassis palate. Good for years yet, as next 3.

★★★★ **Merlot** Another step up for this label. Rich, cocoa-toned **12** ⑧⑨, lovely succulence, fruit, texture & breadth. Structured & long. Improves on **11** ★★★★ ⑧⑤. Same oak & bottle-age regime as Cab.

★★★★ **Shiraz** Red fruit succulence vies with dry spice on **12** ⑧⑧ & raises the bar on **11** ★★★★ ⑧⑤. Firm tannin supports tertiary fruit well, for a sleek, supple effect. Maturation as above.

★★★★ **33 Latitude Select** Same **12** ⑧⑧ blend as namesake but handled differently: 28 months in new oak, 4 years in bottle. Fruitcake, plum richness with inky depth. Soft & supple, with oak better integrated than **10** ★★★☆ ⑧⑤. **11** untasted.

33 Latitude ★★★☆ Shows influence of hot year in jammy notes on cab (60%) mix with merlot & shiraz. **12** ⑧④ textured but a tad light & short, unlike impressive **11** ★★★★ ⑧⑥. Not tasted: **Chenin Blanc**. — FM

Location/map: Stellenbosch ▪ Map grid reference: D4 ▪ WO: Devon Valley ▪ Est 1998 ▪ 1stB 2006 ▪ Tasting by appt ▪ Self-catering guest house (exclusive use, rental min 2 weeks) ▪ Owner(s) Fred & Rosmarie Ruest ▪ Winemaker(s) Jacques Fourie (Jan 2006, consultant) ▪ Viticulturist(s) Frans Snyman (Jul 2006, consultant) ▪ 28ha/16ha (cab, merlot, shiraz) ▪ 160t/3,000cs own label 90% red 10% white ▪ PO Box 12799 Die Board 7613 ▪ info@kyburgwine.com ▪ www.kyburgwine.com ▪ S 33° 54' 59.3" E 018° 49' 28.4" ▪ impulses.huddled. hush ▪ **T +27 (0)21-865-2876/+27 (0)82-651-5688**

Laarman Wines ⓠ
Winemaker Arco Laarman, solo the past few years after an early career at acclaimed cellars Glen Carlou and Kaapzicht, says his Paarl-based venture is 'expanding nicely' and now has followers in the US, Japan and

South Korea. His love for classic Bordeaux and Burgundy varieties (debut Focal Point Chardonnay making him a contender for 2018 Diners Club Winemaker of the Year) dovetails with an emphasis on SA heritage grapes, hence an old-vine Chenin Blanc slated to join the Cinsault in the course of this year.

Focal Point range

★★★★☆ **Cinsault** Perfume, cherry & white pepper on flavoursome, svelte & succulent **18** ⑨⑴ from Paarl bushvines. Natural ferment & old oak allow fruit to shine. Like previous, an elegant example of the variety.

★★★★ **Chardonnay** Lovely concentration, focus & length on **18** ★★★★☆ ⑨⓪ from cool Vermaaklikheid vineyard. Part natural fermentation & maturation in a range of barrels (now 39% new). Bursts with juicy vitality, raises the bar on **17** ⑧⑧.— MW

Location: Paarl ▪ WO: Paarl/Cape South Coast ▪ Est 2016 ▪ 1stB 2017 ▪ Tasting by appt only ▪ Owner(s)/winemaker(s) Arco Laarman ▪ 5,000cs own label 40% red 60% white ▪ 84 Wilderbosch Str, Paryskloof Estate, Paarl 7646 ▪ arco@laarmanwines.com ▪ www.laarmanwines.com ▪ T +27 (0)83-546-1146

☐ **Labeye** see Radford Dale
☐ **La Bonne Vigne** see Wonderfontein
☐ **Laborie** see KWV Wines

La Bri Estate   ⑨ ⑪ ◎

'A small, quiet, beautiful place' was how owner Robin Hamilton described La Bri, one of the first farms granted to Huguenot settlers in Franschhoek 300 years ago. It's become a popular stop for the local Wine Tram, reports GM and cellarmaster Irene de Fleuriot, in her tenth vintage here. (Her right hand, Glen Isaacs, ahead of her by a year.) Ever energetic and enthusiastic, Irene bottled the first varietal petit verdot under the Double Door label, and notes that the young chardonnay and cabernet vines have borne their first crop.

Limited Release range

★★★★☆ **Cabernet Sauvignon** ⊛ Seductive understated appeal of nose & palate on **16** ⑨③, barrel selection off 25 year old single parcel. Subtle entry becomes a fantail of gently voluptuous black fruit & cedar (2 years new oak), velvet texture harmonised by structure in a refined, noble wine with a long future.

★★★★☆ **Syrah 570** ⊛ Was 'Syrah 1045'. Lavender sheen to plush **16** ⑨④ vineyard selection. Supple cherry & plum fruit on broad, rich & savoury palate showing good concentration & density. Deft lightness & refinement doesn't allow all-new oak (2 years) to dominate. Just 570 bottles made. No **14, 15**.

★★★★☆ **Chardonnay** ⑨ 2nd, riper picking of 26 year old block & cask selection result in refined & elegant **17** ⑨③, showing cashew, orange & spice subtlety. Integrated & complex, many layers of flavour on rich palate, creaminess ex all-new French oak.

★★★★☆ **Viognier** ⊘ ⊛ Lime edge to ripe nectarine fruit imparts appealing verve on creamy **18** ⑨③. Big jump from last-made **13** ★★★☆ ⑧④. Impressively rich & broad from 12 months in older oak. Bunch pressed, barrel fermented with no acid adjustment. Balanced. Lingering dry peach tail.

★★★★☆ **Sauvage La Bri Blanc de Blancs** ⊛ Marine breeze, oystershell & grapefruit on **13** ⑨③ dry, crisp all-chardonnay méthode cap classique sparkler. Primary ferment in old oak & zero dosage, with 60 months on lees (vs 48 for previous). Thrillingly taut yet expressive, rich & creamy. Vibrant yet refined.

Estate range

★★★★ **Merlot** ⊘ Complex, considered & nuanced **17** ★★★★☆ ⑨① improves on **16** ⑧⑦. Oak (30% new) frames richly textured mulberry & red fruit. Medium bodied but with ample freshness & length, seamless integration. Also in magnum.

★★★★ **Syrah** ⊘ More than in **16** ⑧⑧, co-ferment of **17** ★★★★☆ ⑨① shiraz & 2% viognier is seamless, lithe, perfumed & peppery, aiming for Côte Rôtie. Velvet textured, refined & long, it had 2 years in oak (43% new) & year in bottle.

★★★★ **Affinity** ⑨ Cab leads in **15** ⑧⑦ appealing 4-way Bordeaux blend. Complex, cohesive, soft-textured & rich mouthful that tapers off on cocoa note. Poised, with deft oaking, mainly old French.

★★★★ **Chardonnay** ⊘ Latest ups quality on **17** ⑧⑧ with wholebunch pressing & barrel fermentation. **18** ★★★★☆ ⑨⓪ beautiful interplay of kumquat tang & vibrancy, with creamy, refined oak (54% new, 12 months). Statuesque but with a bright, elegant vivacity too.

Double Door range

★★★★☆ **Petit Verdot** (NEW) ⊘ Confident debut in **15** (92). Exotic perfume to intense black fruit & squeeze of dry tannin from 2 years in 60% new French oak. Firm but supple structure, with layers of inky flavour. Minuscule 30 cases from old Franschhoek block; next will be '17 in larger volume.

★★★★ **Semillon** (ℤ) Beeswax & honey notes of **17** (86) layered with spice & citrus. Light & juicy but with creamy breadth. Half oaked, all-new French oak aids both richness & definition/focus; long aftertaste. Neighbours' grapes, as next.

★★★★ **White** Components trimmed to 50/50 roussanne & semillon but **18** (87) remains poised, confident, broad & textured. Spicy stonefruit vies with creamy vanilla from year in older oak. **17** (87) had splashes chardonnay, viognier.

Merlot Rosé ⊘ ★★★☆ Light & bright **19** (85) charms with easy strawberry appeal. Unfussy yet juicy, dry & defined. — FM

Location/map/WO: Franschhoek ▪ Map grid reference: C1 ▪ Est 1694 ▪ Tasting, sales & cellar tours Mon-Fri 9.30-5 Sat/Sun & pub hols 10-4 ▪ Fee varies ▪ Closed Good Fri, Dec 25 & Jan 1 ▪ Chocolate & wine pairing; biltong & wine experience; Turkish delight & wine pairing ▪ Cheese platters; bespoke picnics ▪ Bicycle friendly ▪ Weddings & functions ▪ Part of Franschhoek Tram route ▪ Owner(s) Robin Hamilton ▪ Winemaker(s) Irene de Fleuriot (Oct 2010), with Glen Isaacs (Jun 2009) ▪ Viticulturist(s) Gerard Olivier (Oct 2010) ▪ ±20ha/±15ha (cabs s/f, merlot, p verdot, shiraz, chard, viog) ▪ 100t/10,000cs own label 80% red 20% white ▪ WIETA ▪ PO Box 180 Franschhoek 7690 ▪ info@labri.co.za ▪ www.labri.co.za ▪ S 33° 55' 18.3" E 019° 7' 1.5" ▪ 🗺 resource.tweaked.implicit ▪ **T +27 (0)21-876-2593**

☐ **La Capra** *see* Fairview
☐ **La Cave** *see* Wellington Wines

La Chataigne   (ℤ) (🏠) (♿)

When the Parkfelt family moved from Gothenburg in Sweden to this Franschhoek property in 1972, it was already a working wine farm. Sections were subsequently sold off, and the lovely riverside spread Julie and Richard now own and run features guest cottages and a vineyard boasting some older vines, including semillon from 1942. The wines, by consultant Gerda Willers and neighbour Martin Smith (Paserene), feature unusual packaging, names and descriptions handwritten directly onto the bottles.

Kastanje (ℤ) ★★★ From chenin bushvines, giving expressive citrus- & apple-toned fruit to **17** (82). Light textured, crisply dry, tasty. **Sauvignon Blanc** (ℤ) ★★★ Nice sauvignon styling, leafy, capsicum, with lime-fresh flavours & finish. **17** (81) just the thing to perk up your taste buds. **18** also available but untasted by us. Not tasted: **Marron**, **Rosé**, **Semillon**. — CR

Location/map/WO: Franschhoek ▪ Map grid reference: C4 ▪ Est 1972 ▪ 1stB 2003 ▪ Tasting & sales Mon-Fri 10-4 Sat/Sun & pub hols by appt ▪ 5 guest cottages ▪ Owner(s) Parkfelt family ▪ Winemaker(s) Gerda Willers (2003, consultant) & Martin Smith ▪ 17ha/10ha (merlot, ptage, sauv, sem) ▪ 120t/1,500cs own label 25% red 65% white 10% rosé ▪ PO Box 301 Franschhoek 7690 ▪ info@lachat.co.za ▪ www.lachat.co.za ▪ S 33° 52' 59.77" E 019° 3' 11.29" ▪ 🗺 admire.rosters.grappling ▪ **T +27 (0)21-876-3220**

La Couronne Wines   (ℤ) (🍴) (🏠) (📷)

This Franschhoek boutique winery and lifestyle estate has undergone extensive redevelopment recently, including the replanting of vineyards, and the team is delighted that their 'passion and hard work are now shining through' in the form of, among others, 'fantastic awards' at wine competitions. Also gratifying is the growing number of visitors disembarking here from the popular Wine Tram, drawn by family-friendly dining and wine-pairing options, including pre-booked 'secret garden' picnics and traditional braais. Ongoing rejuvenation sees the wine portfolio streamlined and the range names changed.

Premium Collection

★★★★ **Malbec** (🐝) Bolder oaking on **16** (89) (French & American, 80% new, 33 months) amplifies spicy profile, succulence & structure. Handsome, full bodied & flavoursome, with good ageing potential.

★★★★☆ **Pinotage Limited Edition** (ℤ) With gravitas to match the weighty bottle, **15** (91) is full, firm & dry, with plum, smoke & piquant meatiness in an elegant structure. Far more refined than many of the genre. 21 months seasoned oak, some American. Stellenbosch WO.

★★★★ **Shiraz** Now bottled, 16 (88) still dominated by sweet oak (100% new, 24 months). Sappy spiced fruit & white pepper should emerge with cellaring. Bold, modern style, needing time.

★★★★ **Barrel Fermented Chardonnay** Big, curvaceous & beautiful, 17 (89), ratchets up oak regime (30% new, 11 months). Fruit intensity & limy acidity to carry it; needs time to meld.

★★★★ **Barrel Fermented Viognier** 17 (88) aroma's promise of peachy richness restrained by more overt oaking (as for Chardonnay) than 16 (87). Acidity trims the figure & alcohol. All in sync in a few years.

★★★★★ **Muscadel** Preview of old-oak-matured, fortified elixir from Nuy Valley grapes. 17 ★★★★☆ (93) billows barley sugar, dried fig & orange blossoms. Uncloyingly sweet (despite 251 g/l sugar) & with zesty citrus farewell. A decadent delight, like previous **NV** (98). 375 ml.

Signature Collection

Le Petite Malbec ★★★ Lower-key version of Premium sibling. All older oak allows savoury dark fruit to shine. 16 (81) balanced & approachable. **Portside Red** (②) ★★★ Malbec-led quintet of Bordeaux varieties delivers winter fireside enjoyment. 15 (78) firmer than previous, allow year to soften. **Merlot Rosé** ★★★ Similar delicate, sleek but tangy rosepetal/candyfloss flavours in 19 (82), drier farewell. **Chenin Blanc** ★★★ More flavoursome 19 (79) shows crunchy bright fruit in a balanced & lighter style. WO W Cape. Discontinued: **Merlot, Upper Deck Red, Sauvignon Blanc**. — MW

Location/map: Franschhoek ▪ Map grid reference: C1 ▪ WO: Franschhoek/Stellenbosch/Nuy/Western Cape ▪ Tasting & sales Mon-Sun 10-5; closed some Sundays during winter ▪ Chocolate & wine tasting ▪ Closed Christian religious hols ▪ Wine tram ▪ Traditional braai & picnics to be booked in advance ▪ Tour groups ▪ Weddings & functions ▪ Le Chais Villa (6 en-suite rooms) ▪ Winemaker(s) Henk Swart (May 2015) ▪ 21ha (cabs s/f, malbec, merlot, p verdot, ptage, shiraz, chard, sauv, viog) ▪ 160t/±25,000cs own label 70% red 30% white ▪ info@lacouronnewines.co.za ▪ www.lacouronnewines.co.za ▪ S 33° 55' 8.9" E 019° 6' 40.9" ▪ ⬛ ballads.currency.thumbnail ▪ **T** +27 (0)21-876-3939/+27 (0)82-861-9669

☐ **Ladismith Winery & Distillery** *see* Barrydale Winery & Distillery
☐ **Ladybird** *see* Laibach Vineyards
☐ **Lady May** *see* Glenelly Estate
☐ **Lady Somerset** *see* Somerset Wines
☐ **La Famille** *see* Mischa Estate

Laibach Vineyards

(Ⓠ) (⌂)

Natural balance and minimal intervention are the guiding principles at this German-family-owned winery outside Stellenbosch. Organic certification since 2012 means nature is encouraged to take its course, as with the ladybird population to control vineyard mealy bug (and supply naming inspiration for their best-selling range, which receives a pink extension this edition). Long-standing winemaker Francois van Zyl increasingly uses natural and on-trend winemaking techniques, like carbonic maceration and wild-yeast ferment. One of the stars in the line up is Claypot Merlot, originally referencing the clay-rich soils in the vineyard and now also the Italian amphoras in which it ferments and ages.

Reserve range

★★★★☆ **Widow's Block Cabernet Sauvignon** (②) Rich, dark & brooding 14 (93) has more new oak (75%) than previous, masking the tight, concentrated fruit; very firm cedary tannins. Appeals less on release than 12 (93). Has pedigree to age harmoniously, though, just needs time. No 13.

★★★★☆ **Claypot Merlot** (♡) (≋) Long skin contact, Italian clay pots & 60% new barrels, 16 (93) rewards with vibrant colour, intense cassis, a spice array. Tannin still firm, but ripe, doing justice to the fruit, promising good ageing potential. Impressive.

★★★★ **Pinotage RR** (②) (♡) Wild ferment, mainly new oak, 16 (88) different to its Classic sibling. Loads of savoury spice/salty liquorice, glossy blueberry fruit; tannin structure more evident, firm but ripe, geared for cellaring. Also in 1.5, 3 & 5L.

★★★★☆ **Friedrich Laibach** (②) Honours founder. Merlot, with cab, dash cab franc, 16 (90) new oak 14 months, vintage's 18 best barrels: shows spicy meat extract, almost toasty, but red fruit equal to it. Sleek texture & appealing freshness, ready but built for the long haul. No 15.

★★★★ **Chenin Blanc Sur Lie** ⊘ ⊗ ⊛ Diverse methods, 75% carbonic maceration, 21 days skin contact, wild ferment, half each French oak & concrete 'eggs' to create **18** ★★★★☆ (93). Lime peel & quince, savoury underpin, ends saline, but it's mainly about precision & style. Improves on **17** (88). Stellenbosch WO.

Ladybird range

★★★★ **Red** ⊘ ⊗ ⊛ 5-part Bordeaux blend, half merlot, so **17** (87)'s cassis concentration is a given. Wonderfully spiced, a step up on **16** ★★★★ (83) but tannins still firm, need a year or two to meld.

★★★★☆ **White** ⊘ ⊗ ⊛ Naturally made, combo older barrels, concrete 'eggs' & stainless steel, chardonnay plus 15% chenin. Citrus, with most of the players - grapefruit, lemon, tangerine - while **18** (93)'s almond seam adds richness, complexity, length. Individual, sophisticated.

Rosé (NEW) ⊗ ★★★ Chenin (60%) & sauvignon, 5% pinotage giving **19** (81) delicate pink hue. Light & crisply dry, worthy addition to range. WO W Cape, as White. **Chenin Blanc** (⊘) ★★★ Melon & apple in **18** (81), fresh & lively, shows good typicity, fruity all the way through. Discontinued: **Méthode Cap Classique**.

Classic range

★★★★ **Merlot** (⊘) Less oaking than Claypot, same great vines: **17** (87) expressive fruit, cassis & plums, spice overlay. Suave tannins, polished & succulent for pleasure now but can age. Stellenbosch WO, as next.

★★★★☆ **Natural Sweet** ⊛ 'Modern-day German/Mosel-style winemaking' applied to **19** ★★★★★ (95) Bottelary bushvine chenin: low 7% alcohol & piercing acidity. Liquidised apricots & pineapple; nervy intensity adds vibrancy to the sweetness, the effect mouthwateringly tangy. **18** (93) also thrilling. 375 ml.

Pinotage ★★★☆ Blueberries, vanilla-spiced thanks to 12 months French barrels, third new. Hard not to like **17** (83) for its juicy & fresh-fruity drinkability. Not tasted: **Cabernet Sauvignon**. — CR

Location/map: Stellenbosch ▪ Map grid reference: F1 ▪ WO: Simonsberg–Stellenbosch/Western Cape/ Stellenbosch ▪ Est 1994 ▪ 1stB 1997 ▪ Tasting & sales Mon-Fri 10–5 Sat (Nov-Apr)/pub hols 10–1 ▪ Fee R40/4 wines ▪ Closed Easter Fri/Sun, Dec 25/26 & Jan 1 ▪ Cellar tours by appt ▪ Laibach Vineyards Lodge ▪ Owner(s) Petra Laibach-Kühner & Rudhier Kühner ▪ Cellarmaster(s)/winemaker(s) Francois van Zyl (Jan 2000) ▪ Viticulturist(s) / MD Michael Malherbe (Jun 1994) ▪ 50ha/37ha (cabs s/f, malbec, merlot, p verdot, ptage, chard, chenin) ▪ 380t/48,000cs own label 70% red 30% white + 20,000cs for Woolworths ▪ Organic ▪ PO Box 7109 Stellenbosch 7599 ▪ info@laibachwines.com ▪ www.laibachwines.com ▪ S 33° 50' 43.3" E 018° 51' 44.2" ▪ (AW) records.pool.premises ▪ **T +27 (0)21-884-4511/+27 (0)82-413-4346**

☐ **Lakehurst** *see* Wine-of-the-Month Club

Lammershoek Winery   (⊘)

This Paardeberg, Swartland estate was proclaimed in 1718 and vines were planted soon after – though the cellar (now extended and modernised) dates to the mid-1800s. It hadn't been used for 50 years when a new owner started keeping grapes back from the cooperative at the turn of this century. The farm was acquired in 2013 by a German consortium, with football legend Franz Beckenbauer as the main investor. Major upgrades in vineyards, cellar and visitor facilities followed. Tweaking of the ranges has continued, with now a substantial expansion of the Mysteries range. The name of the fine-value Innocent range recalls the origin of the farm's name, 'lamb's corner', as a place where ewes and lambs sought shelter from black eagles.

The Mysteries range

★★★★ **Die Onderstok** (NEW) ⊛ Sleek & light-hearted old-vine carignan, **17** (86) artfully vinified to showcase vivid cranberry & raspberry fruit, pillow-like tannins. Savoury/biltong & baking spice notes from 9 months in old oak barrels & foudres.

★★★★ **Die Duiker** (⊘) Impressive grenache from two dryland blocks. **16** (88) fruit-filled & complex, cherry tobacco & violet nuances, fine dry tannins & grip from partly destemmed component.

★★★★ **Die Ou Man** (⊘) ⊛ Among oldest tinta in SA, planted 1969, 1973. **16** (89) perfumed & spiced with prune, cherry & leather, ripe tannin structure. Entirely destemmed, unlike Duiker, yet similar good dryness. Same 12-month older vat/barrel ferment/ageing. Improves on chunky **15** ★★★☆ (85).

★★★★ **Ounooi** (NEW) ⊛ From chardonnay bushvines planted in 1981, understood to be oldest in SA. Impressive array of aromas: citrus blossom, pie crust, vanilla, spice & starfruit, all echo on persistent mineral palate. **18** (88) elegant & focused, with subtle oak, 30% new French barrels for 9 months.

★★★★ **Die Oranje** (Ⓦ) As name ('The Orange') suggests, **17** ⑧⑥ chenin fermented on skins 7 weeks, basket pressed to old barrels, 12 months. Stonefruit, caramel & spice, rich & full but plenty of acidity to freshen, fine grape tannin ending on saline note. Better realised than **15** ★★★★ ⑧⑤. No **16**.

★★★★ **Die Harde Blaar** (Ⓦ) Hárslevelü, widely planted in Hungary, clearly at home here in Swartland too. Creamy, light- to medium-bodied white, hints of cashews & minerals in the fresh flavours of lemon peel, quince & pineapple on **17** ⑧⑦. Older 500L barrels. Wild yeast fermented, as next.

★★★★☆ **White Blend** (NEW) (Ⓐ) (Ⓦ) Melange of majority chenin (60%) with viognier & chardonnay. Complexly vinified **17** ⑨③ has skin contact, basket press & naturally fermented portions coming together to reveal fresh figs, pears & lemon meringue notes, rich & creamy palate balanced with vibrant acidity, noticeable grape tannins.

★★★★☆ **Die Swart Strooi** Unusual & delicious dessert from syrah, grapes desiccated 4 weeks on the vine. **16** ⑨⓪ bold notes of dark plum, mulberry & paprika. Sweet (50 g/l sugar), with fine tannins for poise. Unwooded, unlike **15** ⑨⓪, noted as equally good with fruit salad, choc tart & ripe cheese. 500 ml.

Die Varkhok (NEW) (Ⓦ) ★★★★ Naturally fermented chenin, **18** ⑧④ fresh & alluring pear, baked apple & persimmon notes well lifted by bright acidity. From 50 year old dryland vines, oak as for Ounooi.

The Reserve range

★★★★ **Syrah** (Ⓩ) Embodiment of house style: old dryland vines, partial bunch ferment, aged in big seasoned oak. Piercing pepper & pimento spice lead out **16** ⑧⑧'s sweet berry fruit, viscosity in the finish.

★★★★☆ **Terravinum Chenin Blanc** (Ⓥ) (Ⓦ) Low-yield (2 t/ha), 51 year old vines deliver great depth in **17** ⑨⓪, wet pebble, chamomile & honeysuckle aromas & flavours on a steely backbone of fresh apple & quince. Ambient yeasts, foudre & old barrel matured, 7 months on lees.

Discontinued: **Terravinum Red Blend**, **Terravinum White**.

The Innocent range

★★★★ **White Blend** (Ⓥ) Mainly chenin plus viognier & sauvignon in **18** ⑧⑦, only 40% in older wood to not overwhelm vibrant quince & pear aromas & flavours. Zesty & light, with a perfumed apricot finish. Same varieties as exceptional **17** ★★★★☆ ⑨⓪. Debut **15** ★★★★ ⑧⑤'s quintet included hárslevelü. All with ample appeal & vivacity. **16** untasted.

Pinotage ★★★★ Beaujolais-styled **18** ⑧③ is light, fresh & crunchy, cherries & plums leading to a spicy finish. Wholebunch/berry ferment & 9 months in concrete. **Syrah** (Ⓩ) ★★★★ Intricate vinification/ageing for 3 bushvine parcels. Youthful & vibrant **17** ⑧③, juicy, with violet & nutmeg spicing, perfect for lamb or venison. **Red Blend** (Ⓩ) ★★★★ Rainbow blend of 6 red varieties & dash chenin, year old oak. **15** ⑧④ white pepper whiffs, red berry fruits & fennel intrigue. **SMG** (Ⓩ) ★★★★ Handsome **17** ⑧④, 50% syrah, equal grenache, mourvèdre fermented separately & aged in mix concrete, old foudres & used barrels. Packed with dark fruit, accented by cloves & black pepper. Coastal WO. **Rosé** ★★★★ Striking freshness from shiraz (54%), matured in stainless steel, matched by deep cherry fruit & spice of equal grenache & mourvèdre which had a touch of oak. **19** ⑧③ bright acidity & moderate 12.5% alcohol. — GM

Location: Malmesbury ▪ Map: Swartland ▪ Map grid reference: C8 ▪ WO: Swartland/Coastal ▪ Est 1999 ▪ 1stB 2000 ▪ Tasting, sales & cellar tours by appt ▪ Owner(s) Lammershoek Farms & Winery (Pty) Ltd ▪ Winemaker(s) Schalk Opperman (Jan 2015) ▪ Viticulturist(s) Marius Kotze (2018) ▪ 60ha (carignan, grenache, merlot, mourv, ptage, shiraz, tinta barocca, chard, chenin, hárslevelü, marsanne, sauv, viog) ▪ PO Box 597 Malmesbury 7299 ▪ info@lammershoek.co.za ▪ www.lammershoek.co.za ▪ S 33° 31' 30.2" E 018° 48' 21.1" ▪ ⟨AW⟩ escapes.boasted.handset ▪ **T +27 (0)22-482-2835**

La Motte

(Ⓨ) (Ⓨ) (Ⓐ) (Ⓐ) (Ⓐ)

The Rupert-Koegelenberg family have entered the second half-century of ownership of this historic Franschhoek estate, one of SA's richest in terms of visitor attractions, something recognised and multiply recognised by the Great Wine Capitals of the World Global Network. History, art, culture and sustainability are key tenets here, hence the heritage and fynbos walks, magnificent gallery of works by renowned artist JH Pierneef, acclaimed restaurant and farm shop selling some of the lavender products of the employee empowerment venture — all supplementing the lustre of the wine ranges. Cellarmaster Edmund Terblanche has been here 20 years, and still is stimulated each vintage by the difference in site-specific vineyards, as well as the contribution that cool-climate Cape South Coast vines make to many of the wines.

The Pierneef Collection

★★★★☆ **Syrah-Viognier** ⓐ **17** ⑨③ maintains tone set by previous. Structured, elegant, Rhône-styled with peppery plum fruit & vibrancy from 5% viognier. Lovely concentration & depth. Some fruit from cool Elim & Walker Bay used again. 1,000 magnums bottled.

★★★★ **Sauvignon Blanc** ⊘ **18** ★★★★☆ ⑨⓪ steps up on **17** ⑧⑥ in its crisp, taut & nervy verve. Typically flinty, but with lovely acid succulence to balance. Features (unoaked) 12% semillon & fruit from cool-climate Elim & Napier.

La Motte Collection

★★★★ **Syrah** ⊘ ⓐ Showing influence of stellar vintage, **17** ★★★★☆ ⑨② raises the bar on **16** ⑧⑥ in rich, rounded concentration. Darkly seductive, it's harmonious, plush & long. Oak (30% new) well integrated. Dab durif for colour. Available in 1.5 to 18L. Franschhoek WO for this range.

★★★★ **Chardonnay 18** ⑧⑧ improves on **17** ★★★☆ ⑧④. Vibrant citrus freshness plays off light-bodied cashew & lees breadth. Seamless oak (25% new) frames fruit impeccably. Long finish.

★★★★ **Méthode Cap Classique Brut** Zingy citrus zip to **16** ⑧⑧ zero-dosage sparkler from chardonnay (65%) & pinot noir. Taut but long, with broad creamy texture from 36 months on lees. Complexity added by small oaked portion (15%).

Classic Collection

★★★★ **Cabernet Sauvignon** ⊘ Vintage influence ups **17** ★★★★☆ ⑨⓪ status from **16** ⑧⑧. Silky, refined & supple, ripe black fruit superbly balanced by well-knit oak (25% new). Cinsaut (5%) adds succulence. Blend of Stellenbosch, Bot River & Franschhoek grapes on granite, shale & sandy soils respectively.

★★★★ **Millennium** ⊘ Herb edge to red & black fruit generosity on **17** ⑧⑨. As ever, merlot-led 4-way Bordeaux blend that is lithe, approachable & structured from year in old oak. Long finish. Magnums too.

★★★★☆ **Straw Wine** Sweet dried pineapple tang to **NV** ⑨① dessert from Franschhoek air-desiccated, barrel-fermented viognier. Less sweet (163 g/l) than previous. Precise & defined, with long, rich brûlée tail which ends clean & seemingly dry. 375 ml.

Sauvignon Blanc ★★★★ Pear drop & tropical fruit to tangy & zesty **19** ⑧④, using grapes from many areas. Light & juicy, it has 8% semillon too. — FM

Location/map: Franschhoek ▪ Map grid reference: C3 ▪ WO: Western Cape/Franschhoek/Cape South Coast ▪ Est 1969 ▪ 1stB 1984 ▪ Tasting & sales Mon-Sat 9–5 ▪ Fee R60pp ▪ Booking essential for: group tastings 8-16 R70pp; themed tastings R250pp; food & wine pairing Fri 10 R250pp by appt only ▪ Closed Good Fri & Dec 25 ▪ Pierneef à La Motte Restaurant ▪ Facilities for children ▪ Tour groups (max 16), booking essential ▪ Farm shop: seasonal flowers, bread, confectionery, gifts ▪ Booking essential for: hiking trail Mon-Sat 9-2 R60pp (duration 1.5-2.5hrs, not recommended for children under 10); guided hike Mon 9 R120pp; historic walk Wed 10-11 R60pp; sculpture walk Thu 10-11 R60pp ▪ 35ha conservation area ▪ Museum Tue-Sun 9-5: Rupert family, history of La Motte, Cape Dutch architecture, life/art of JH Pierneef & other SA artists ▪ Monthly classical music concerts ▪ Owner(s) Hanneli Rupert-Koegelenberg ▪ CEO Hein Koegelenberg ▪ Cellarmaster(s) Edmund Terblanche (Dec 2000) ▪ Viticulturist(s) Pietie le Roux (May 1986) ▪ 170ha/75ha (merlot, pinot, shiraz, chard, sauv, sem) ▪ 2,000t/240,000cs own label 38.2% red 61.5% white 0.3% sparkling + 38,000cs for clients ▪ Brands for clients: Woolworths ▪ ISO 14001:2004, EnviroWines, Farming for the Future, HACCP, IPW, WIETA, WWF-SA Conservation Champion ▪ PO Box 685 Franschhoek 7690 ▪ info@la-motte.co.za ▪ www.la-motte. com ▪ S 33° 52' 52.20" E 019° 4' 25.76" ▪ 🔲 industrious.entrance.prolongs ▪ **T +27 (0)21-876-8000**

Landau du Val ⓠ

Basil and Jane Landau take their custodianship of La Brie, one of Franschhoek's oldest properties (ca 1689) seriously, nurturing vines that are not quite as aged but, in the case of the 4 hectares of semillon planted in 1905, comfortably old enough to qualify for membership of the Old Vine Project. Veteran Pietie le Roux is the vineyard consultant, while Donovan Ackermann, new winemaker at nearby Rickety Bridge, makes the wine, available at top local wine shop La Cotte Inn.

★★★★ **Semillon Private Selection** ⓐ Waxy, honeyed notes on **17** ⑧⑨ from low-yield, venerable 115 year old vines. Graceful, understated, smooth & rich; natural ferment in combo old oak & cement tanks, with variety's lingering freshness & moderate 12.8% alcohol. Will charm for many years. No **16**.— MW

Location/map/WO: Franschhoek ▪ Map grid reference: D2 ▪ Tasting by appt only ▪ Sales at La Cotte Inn, Franschhoek ▪ Owner(s) Basil & Jane Landau ▪ Winemaker(s) Donovan Ackermann (Rickety Bridge Winery) ▪ Viticulturist(s) Pietie le Roux (consultant) ▪ 15ha under vine ▪ La Brie, Robertsvlei Rd, Franschhoek 7690 ▪ landau@mweb.co.za ▪ S 33° 55' 34.3" E 019° 6' 34.1" ▪ 🗺 feast.cloves.lodges ▪ T +27 (0)83-261-1573

- ☐ **Landela** see Jacques Germanier
- ☐ **Land of Hope** see Radford Dale
- ☐ **Landscape Series** see Gabriëlskloof
- ☐ **Land's End** see Du Toitskloof Winery
- ☐ **Landskap** see Groenland

Landskroon Wines

It's 45 years since the De Villiers family bottled the first wine under the label Landskroon, after Landskrona, home of the original Swedish farm owner, and 145 years since they took possession of their property on Paarl Mountain. Knowledge of the terroir, acquired over five generations, helps ensure consistency under the current custodianship of brothers Paul and Hugo. Reds are their forte, the Cabernet and Merlot enduring best sellers. Pinotage is the focus of their current older-vine replacement programme, designed to provide continuity. Value for money, another pillar of the brand, springs from ever consumer-conscious pricing.

Paul de Villiers range

★★★★ **Cabernet Sauvignon** Abundant oak (French & American, 63% new) jostles with fruit mid-2019, but given time **17** ⑧⑧ should settle & reveal more piquant black berries among the layers of mocha.

★★★★ **Merlot** Expression of floral, berry fruit of **17** ⑧⑦ masked by luscious oak vanilla (100% French, 50% new, 16 months). **16** ⑧⑨'s bramble fruits were supported rather than smothered, the finish refined.

★★★★ **Shiraz** Plump berries overlaid with mocha, **17** ⑧⑥'s interplay of ripe fruit, full body & 18 months in 87% new American oak makes it almost a meal in itself - dessert included!

★★★★ **Reserve** ⊘ Graceful flagship blend of cabs sauvignon (52%) & franc plus merlot, **17** ★★★★★ ⑨① gains appealing graphite & cedar aromas from partly new French oak. Cassis & sappy red berry fruit still tightly wound, will develop in elegant frame. Altogether more refined than **16** ⑧⑨.

Chenin Blanc Barrel Fermented ★★★★ Expansive vanilla overlay to cling peach & pear fruit of **18** ⑧⑤, 10 months in barrel, some new, give attractive oak-sweet finish. A big wine despite its modest 13% alcohol.

Landskroon range

★★★★☆ **Cape Vintage** ⊘ Awarded 'port' from tintas barocca & amarela, souzão & touriga, super **15** ⑨① 34 months in old oak, like **13** ⑨⓪, but gears up with exceptional balance between exuberant fruitiness & finely integrated spirit. For green leather armchairs, dried fruit & nuts over the next five years. No **14**.

Cabernet Franc-Merlot ⓟ ★★★ A standout 'housewine', accessible, immensely likeable. **17** ⑧② teams unwooded cab franc with French-oak-seasoned merlot & splash shiraz for flavourful quaffing. **Chenin Blanc Dry** ⊘ ⓟ ★★★ Crisp & refreshing; fruit salad flavours of **19** ⑧② enlivened by tangy tail.

Cabernet Sauvignon ⊘ ★★★★ Hints of cassis & cedar herald athletic **17** ⑧⑤, accessible, pliable, for early enjoyment. French oak (5% new) well assimilated. **Cinsaut** ⓧ ★★★ More concentrated styling continues in **16** ⑦⑦, with similar perky tealeaf tweak to strawberry fruit. **Merlot** ⊘ ★★★★ Vibrant everyday sipper, **17** ⑧④ offers generous mulberry flavours & choc-coffee note from mix French & American barrels. **Pinotage** ★★★ Lipsmacking **17** ⑧② a robust mix of plum fruit & oak vanilla from American & French casks; for matching with food. **Shiraz** ⊘ ★★★★ Sweet redcurrant fruit wrapped in supple tannins, **17** ⑧⑤ glides down easily; enough charry grip from used mixed-origin barrels for food. **Cinsaut-Shiraz** ⊘ ★★★ Savoury, tasty & affordable anytime red. **17** ⑧⓪ a 64/36 combo fermented on French oak staves. **Paul Hugo Red** ★★★ Blend cab franc, shiraz & merlot, **18** ⑦⑨ is filled with fruit but firmed by tannins from oak staves (French & American). **Blanc de Noir Pinotage Off-Dry** ⊘ ★★★ Understated **19** ⑧① has vinous appeal; acidity lifts gently sweet cranberry flavours. **Chardonnay** ★★★ Super-fresh racy summer fruits on previewed **19** ⑧②; also-tasted **18** ⑧② mellower, with some nutty complexity. Both unoaked. **Chenin Blanc Off-Dry** ⓧ Hint of sweetness amplifies freshly sliced summer fruit profile of gluggable **18** ⑧②. **Sauvignon Blanc** ★★★ Zesty acidity & friendly 12% alcohol, **19** ⑧② perfect for al fresco lunches. WO W

Cape. **Paul Hugo White** ⊘ ★★★ 80% chenin buoyed by sauvignon in easy yet flavoursome **19** ⑧⓪. Stock up for summer. — DS

Location/map: Paarl ▪ Map grid reference: D6 ▪ WO: Paarl/Western Cape ▪ Est 1874 ▪ 1stB 1974 ▪ Tasting & sales Mon-Fri 8.30–5 Sat (Sep-Apr) 9.30-1 ▪ Closed Sun, Easter weekend, Dec 25 & Jan 1 ▪ Fee R35/5 wines, waived on purchase of 6 btls ▪ Heritage food & wine pairing R95 ▪ 5 Paul's food & wine pairing R135 ▪ Cellar tours by appt Mon-Fri 9-4 ▪ BYO picnic ▪ Pre-packed picnics available - booking essential ▪ Play area for children ▪ Permanent display of Stone Age artefacts ▪ Self-catering cottage ▪ Owner(s) Paul & Hugo de Villiers Family Trusts ▪ Cellarmaster(s) Paul de Villiers (Jan 1980) ▪ Winemaker(s) Michiel du Toit (Nov 2014), with Dani Brown (Jul 2018) ▪ Viticulturist(s) Hugo de Villiers (1995) ▪ 330ha/190ha (cab, cinsaut, merlot, ptage, shiraz, souzão, tinta amarela/barocca, touriga nacional, chenin, chard, sauv, viog) ▪ 80% red (incl port) 20% white ▪ IPW, WIETA ▪ PO Box 519 Suider-Paarl 7624 ▪ huguette@landskroonwines.com ▪ www.landskroonwines.com ▪ S 33° 45' 38.34" E 018° 54' 58.38" ▪ ⫐ wagging.gooseberry.discussions ▪ **T +27 (0)21-863-1039**

Landzicht Wine Cellar ⓠ ⓐ

There's now an all-woman team at the helm of this dynamic Northern Cape winery (owned by extensive agribusiness GWK and previously listed in the guide as 'Douglas Wine Cellar'), Sanmari Snyman having been promoted to cellarmaster and Elsaré van der Merwe stepping into her assistant winemaker boots. Their range of friendly, everyday drinkers continues to find favour, particularly with visitors to the town of Douglas, where the wine portfolio can be sampled at the tasting venue along with the house brandy and gin.

Winemakers Reserve range
Sauvignon Blanc ⓠ ★★★ Very pleasant mouthful of grapefruit & gooseberry, **18** ⑧① slightly confected but no harm done, all set for summer sunshine. WO W Cape. Not tasted: **Cabernet Sauvignon Reserve**, **Merlot Reserve**, **Petit Verdot**.

Landzicht range

Colombar ⒩⒠⒲ ⊘ ⓣ ★★★ Semi-sweet **19** ⑧⓪ has attractive pink grapefruit & crunchy apple flavours, nicely balanced sugar & acidity. A zesty partner for full-flavoured curries.

Cabernet Sauvignon ★★ Lots of oak flavours slightly overwhelm **19** ⑦⑥, though time may help subdued black cherry fruit to emerge. **Merlot** ★★ Clean, fresh-fruited **19** ⑦⑥ struggles somewhat with stalky tannins & warmth (15% alcohol) at finish. **Chenin Blanc** ★★★ Friendly & fruity **19** ⑦⑧, plenty of pineapples & mangoes on light, off-dry easy-drinker. **Rosenblümchen** ★★★ Ripe strawberries & raspberries in confected Natural Sweet rosé, **NV** ⑦⑦ from red & white muscadel with chenin & shiraz. **Blümchen** ★★★ Stonefruit, flowers & pleasant aniseed finish on **NV** ⑦⑦ Natural Sweet white from chenin & duo of muscats. **Hanepoot** ⓠ ★★★ Bright **17** ⑦⑧ fortified shows litchi, peach & rosepetal notes with still-fiery alcohol - needs time to settle. **Red Muscadel** ⓠ ★★★ Now vintage dated, **17** ⑧⓪ fortified steps up on previous with touch more acidity balancing flowery flavours with luscious oxidative notes (toffee, nuts). **White Muscadel** ★★★ Lovely perfume & flowers, though **19** ⑧⓪'s hefty sugar (272 g/l) slightly cloys. Soupçon more acidity needed to match previous. **Red Jerepigo** ⓠ ★★★ From touriga & souzão, fortified **17** ⑦⑧ mixes raisins & black cherry jam with warm alcohol. Needs to go with a good winter pud! **Cape Ruby** ⓠ ★★★ Deep, intense colour of **15** ⑦⑧ 'port' matched by deep, intense flavours of liquorice, aniseed & spice, hints of mint & herbs. Touriga & souzão. **Brandy** ⓠ ★★★ Potstill brandy ⑧① from chenin & colombard aged 3–5 years in oak. Less fruity than nutty & leathery, with a caramel hint. Fiery 43% alcohol, best for blending; a bitter tinge & a pleasing dryness if one samples it solo. 350 & 750 ml. Not tasted: **Nagmaalwyn**, **Oak Matured Full Cream**. — CM, TJ

Location: Douglas ▪ Map: Northern Cape, Free State & North West ▪ Map grid reference: C5 ▪ WO: Northern Cape/Western Cape ▪ Est 1968 ▪ 1stB 1977 ▪ Tasting & sales Mon-Fri 8-1 & 2-5 ▪ Closed all pub hols ▪ Cellar tours by appt ▪ Function/lapa venue (up to 60 pax) ▪ Owner(s) GWK Ltd ▪ Cellarmaster(s) Sanmari Snyman ▪ Winemaker(s) Sanmari Snyman, with Elsaré van der Merwe (Jun 2019) ▪ Douglas + Landzicht GWK: 350ha (cab, ruby cab, shiraz, chard, chenin, cbard, muscadels r/w) ▪ 40,000cs own label 20% red 40% white 5% rosé 35% fortified ▪ PO Box 47 Douglas 8730 ▪ wynkelder@gwk.co.za ▪ www.gwk.co.za, www.landzicht.co.za ▪ S 29° 3' 57.0" E 023° 46' 7.8" ▪ ⫐ hardy.streams.inhibitor ▪ **T +27 (0)53-298-8314/5**

☐ **Landzicht Wyn** see Landzicht Wine Cellar
☐ **Langeberg Wineries** see Wonderfontein
☐ **Langtafel** see Mooiplaas Wine Estate & Private Nature Reserve

Langverwacht Wynkelder

In addition to bulk wines, grower-owned Langverwacht in Bonnievale produces its own limited-release label. 'They're fruity wines that everyone enjoys,' says winemaker Theunis Botha, reporting on new chardonnay plantings and the installation of a new transformer, generator and cooling unit in response to cellar expansion and larger crops in recent years.

★★★★ **4 Barrel Shiraz** ⊘ Differently packaged to rest of range, **17** ⑧⑥ special bottling of four best-performing barrels after 14 months, 30% new French. Peppery notes, piquant hedgerow berries & blackcurrants, admirable fruit intensity more than handles the tannins.

Chardonnay ⊘ ⊕ ★★★ Selected block (as most of these), unwooded, but the fruit richness & few years bottle-age make up for it. **17** ⑧② tropical tones, & despite its dryness, a deep wild honey layer that has lovely palate appeal.

Cabernet Sauvignon ★★★ Wallet-pleasing **17** ⑧⓪, appealing blackcurrant note, whiff cedar, smoky spice from French barrique ageing; juicy palate with satisfying structure, gentle tannic tug. **Ruby Cabernet** ⊘ ★★★ Lightly oaked, just enough to add savoury notes without detracting from **18** ⑦⑧'s juicy fruit flavours. **Chenin Blanc** ★★★ Like freshly sliced green apple & pear, **19** ⑦⑧ vibrates with freshness. **Colombard** ⊘ ★★★ Bright-fruited **19** ⑧⓪ is packed with litchi & guava, zinging fresh, appealing drinkability. **Sauvignon Blanc** ★★★ Dewdrop freshness, **19** ⑦⑦ pithy grapefruit, touch of lime, nice mineral finish. A cool-climate character. Discontinued: **Shiraz**. — CR, CvZ

Location: Bonnievale ▪ Map/WO: Robertson ▪ Map grid reference: D4 ▪ Est 1954 ▪ Tasting, sales & tours Mon-Fri 8-5 ▪ Closed all pub hols ▪ Owner(s) 25 members ▪ Cellarmaster(s) Johan Gerber (Dec 1986) ▪ Winemaker(s) Theunis Botha (Dec 2005) ▪ Viticulturist(s) Hennie Visser (Jul 2008) ▪ 640ha (cab, ruby cab, shiraz, chenin, chard, cbard, sauv) ▪ 14,500t/4,500cs own label 50% red 50% white ▪ IPW, WIETA ▪ PO Box 87 Bonnievale 6730 ▪ info@langverwachtwines.co.za ▪ www.langverwachtwines.co.za ▪ S 33° 57' 32.8" E 020° 1' 35.3" ▪ ▨ prevail.rehearsed.fervently ▪ **T +27 (0)23-616-2815**

Lanzerac Wine Estate

It's almost unfair how many advantages this country hotel and wine estate just outside Stellenbosch has: historic and beautifully restored buildings with diverse hospitality offerings, mountain views and vineyards, and a wine range with heritage. Recovery from a fire in 2017 is complete (a benefit was exposure of an earlier history in the buildings). Cellarmaster Wynand Lategan also acknowledges historical figures and key local players in his innovative ranges. Bearing the name of the first commercially launched pinotage (the '59, released 1961) has prompted the collection of all available older Lanzerac pinotages, now cellared here.

Heritage range

★★★★☆ **Pionier Pinotage** ⊛ Honours SA's first commercial pinotage released 1961. High-altitude (400 m) single-vineyard, ±20 years old; wild ferment, 21 months older barriques. Vivid, glossy fruit & creamy ripeness, **17** ⑨③ delicious now but a tannin backbone for cellaring.

★★★★ **Le Général** ⊛ Salutes French general Charles Lanrezac, hence fittingly, 4-part cab-led Bordeaux blend. **16** ⑧⑨ enough fruit intensity to balance tannins, & enough polish for current appreciation but best lies ahead.

★★★★ **Mrs English** ⊛ Single-vineyard chardonnay, natural ferment/ageing 11 months in half-new barrels, **18** ⑨④ has presence & personality. Nutty savouriness vies with orange preserve, acid balance keeps it fresh, lively, finishing very long. Impressive crafting.

Premium range

★★★★ **Cabernet Sauvignon** Cassis & savoury spice, hint of mint, **17** ⑧⑦ ticks all the cab boxes yet is streamlined, in juicy mode for earlier enjoyment. Finishes with enough firmness to satisfy food requirements.

★★★★ **Merlot** Berry-rich, an intriguing thatch top note, 17 ⑧⑧ is as fleshy & succulent as its predecessors. 12 months French oaking, 60% new, but tannins a hidden strength.

★★★★ **Pinotage** Always gets it right, liquorice richness, plush dark fruit, spice-laden from 15 months older barrels, 17 ⑧⑧ is a silky-smooth seduction. For earlier drinking than Pionier, no hardship. Stellenbosch WO, as Sauvignon Blanc.

★★★★ **Syrah** Pepper, some campfire smoke, even cloves, but 17 ⑧⑧'s dark fruit matches these savoury tones, gives smooth-textured drinkability. Only half wine oaked to manage tannins, texture.

★★★★ **Cabernet Sauvignon-Merlot-Petit Verdot** ⊘ Prosciutto & scrub top notes for pre-bottling 16 ⑧⑧'s dark plum character, savouriness a feature here. There's depth & interest, tannins finely judged to provide definition, ageability.

★★★★ **Chardonnay** Nice contrast to Mrs English; 18 ⑧⑧ portion unoaked, no new barrels, fruit profile more expressive, lime & tangerine. Bone-dry, with tangy freshness, almost sweet-sour; very appealing.

★★★★ **Sauvignon Blanc** ⊘ Ex tank, 19 ⑧⑨ reflects its mountain slope site; pithy grapefruit, some leafy notes, tightly focused & zesty, vibrant. Wakens the taste buds, & a great seafood accompaniment.

Pinotage Rosé ★★★ Nicely captures pinotage's berries to accompany light-textured 19 ⑧① 's refreshing drinkability. Dry yet fruity. **Chenin Blanc** ★★★ Lightly oaked, with melon & apple tones, 18 ⑧② is curvy, with fruity freshness adding to the appeal. **Blanc de Blancs Brut** ★★★★ Handsomely packaged **NV** ⑧⑤ MCC bubbly from chardonnay. Pronounced citrus preserve & brioche flavours, bone-dry but seems richer, has good palate weight from 16 months on lees.

Keldermeester Versameling

★★★★ **Dok** ⊘ Honours doyen of SA rugby 'Doc' Danie Craven. Single-vineyard malbec, tiny crop (3 t/ha), wild ferment. Inky colour, 16 ★★★★☆ ⑨③ packed with fruit, has variety's distinctive herbaceous seam. Older oak to support the plush texture. Improves on 15 ⑧⑦.

★★★★ **Prof** Blend pinot noir & cinsaut, honours prof Abraham Perold, who created pinotage from them. 17 ⑧⑧ light texture yet beguiling depth of flavour. Just 6 months oaking, so the tannins don't affect the refinement. WO W Cape.

★★★★ **Bergpad** Pinot blanc, rare in SA. 18 ⑧⑦ aged in older oak but fruit takes centre stage, starfruit & winter melon, litchi, with racy acidity that fits the character, keeps things tight, pristine.

Bergstroom ⊘ ★★★★ Sauvignon with a third semillon from Elgin, 17 ⑧④ combines green melon & citrus, has oatmeal tones from 9 months in seasoned barrels. Taut, crisp finish. — CR

Location/map: Stellenbosch ▪ Map grid reference: G5 ▪ WO: Jonkershoek Valley/Stellenbosch/Western Cape ▪ Est 1692 ▪ 1stB 1957 ▪ Tasting & sales daily 9–5 ▪ Cellar tours on request ▪ Open all pub hols ▪ Deli platters; wine & chocolate tasting ▪ 5-star Lanzerac Hotel, Spa & Restaurants ▪ Conferences ▪ Weddings/functions ▪ Owner(s) Lanzerac Estate Investments ▪ Cellarmaster(s) Wynand Lategan (Jan 2005) ▪ Viticulturist(s) Danie Malherbe (2008) ▪ 163ha/45ha (cab, malbec, merlot, ptage, shiraz, chard, chenin, pinot blanc, sauv) ▪ 500t/24-26,000cs own label 55% red 30% white 15% rosé ▪ PO Box 6233 Uniedal 7612 ▪ wine@lanzerac.co.za, winetasting@lanzerac.co.za ▪ www.lanzeracwines.co.za ▪ S 33° 56' 14.7" E 018° 53' 35.5" ▪ ⊞ slices.slowly.nuance ▪ **T** +27 (0)21-886-5641

La Petite Ferme Winery ⓠ ⑪ ⌂ ◎

Meeting expectations has long been the way at aptly named 'The Small Farm' on Franschhoek Pass. A reputation for warm hospitality, dreamy valley views, delicious food and luxury lodgings, paired with lovingly made wines, was built by former owners, the Dendy Young family. It's being upheld by the recent team under GM Riaan Kruger, with wine/vine man Wikus Pretorius, supported by long-time farm manager Frans Malies, making good on last edition's promise of new white and red blends.

★★★★☆ **Cabernet Sauvignon** Excellent 17 ⑨⓪ has firm ripe tannins on guard in youth, but heady violets & cassis, leading to dense ripe black berry & plump fruit will offer much pleasure in years to come - as for 16 ⑨① , tuck this one away. Now only Franschhoek vines, 15 months in 30% new wood.

★★★★ **Merlot** More restrained than 16 ⑧⑥ , which was Xmas pudding in a bottle, 17 ⑧⑥ mulberry fruit & cherry deftly spiced with cinnamon & vanilla from oak (25% new), now all local grapes.

★★★★ **Shiraz** ⊘ Pimento & white pepper spirals, elegant 16 ⑧⑥ more Old World than New, with reined-in red berry fruit & hints of charcuterie lingering on savoury finish.

★★★★ The Verdict If the jury was out previously, it will undoubtedly find for **17 ★★★★★** ⑨, attention-grabbing Cape Blend from the 2 cabs & 21% pinotage. Violet & cherry perfumes lead to a super palate of lively cassis fruit & pliable tannins, full of energy & flavour. 30% new oak, 15 months, supportive & well judged. **16** ⑧⑧ more austere.

★★★★★ Variation ⑩ Rhône red promised last edition arrives in style, shiraz co-fermented with 1% viognier, plus 12% grenache, in a welcomely refined & delicate expression of the style. **17** ⑨ vibrantly spicy, the fruit accessible in youth, acid/tannin structure finely balanced. 20% new wood.

★★★★ Barrel Fermented Chardonnay Orange blossom aroma & lingering marmalade finish attract, & though bold, **18** ⑧⑥ is beautifully textured, balanced. Bunch pressed, all oaked, third new, 8 months. Some Elim grapes.

★★★★ Winemaker's Edition Wikus ⑩ Bordeaux-style white blend of gravelly Elim semillon (61%, oaked 6 months) with tropical Franschhoek sauvignon fermented in tank; **18** ⑧⑨ bracing but with enough beguiling fruit focus to enjoy as aperitif or seafood partner.

Rosé ★★★ From merlot, briskly fresh & racy **18** ⑦⑨ pink is bone-dry & perfect for sipping on the patio. **Sauvignon Blanc ★★★★** Super-fresh **18** ⑧④ is a fine, grassy pick-me-up, with hints of green apple in the zesty mix. **Viognier ★★★★** Unoaked **18** ⑧⑤ bursts with variety's apricot & peach, but shows some restraint in crisp dry finish, which reins in viscosity & breadth. Not tasted: **Baboon Rock Unwooded Chardonnay Wild Yeast Fermented**. — DS

Location/map: Franschhoek ▪ Map grid reference: C1 ▪ WO: Franschhoek/Western Cape ▪ Est 1972 ▪ 1stB 1996 ▪ Tasting daily at 10.30 by appt ▪ Fee R100pp ▪ Sales daily 8.30-5 ▪ Restaurant ▪ Guest suites ▪ Tour groups ▪ Gift shop ▪ Owner(s) The Nest Estate South Africa (Pty) Ltd, t/a La Petite Ferme ▪ GM Riaan Kruger ▪ Winemaker(s) Wikus Pretorius (Oct 2015) ▪ Viticulturist(s) Wikus Pretorius (Oct 2015) ▪ Farm manager Frans Malies ▪ 16ha/14ha (cabs s/f, merlot, shiraz, chard, sauv, viog) ▪ 60-70t/10,000cs own label 40% red 50% white 10% rosé ▪ PO Box 683 Franschhoek 7690 ▪ info@lapetiteferme.co.za ▪ www.lapetiteferme.co.za ▪ S 33° 55' 6.43" E 019° 8' 10.32" ▪ 🖅 posturing.foil.softly ▪ **T +27 (0)21-876-3016**

La Petite Provence Wine Company ⑨

The 2017 vintage release marks the first time the fruit from La Petite Provence residential estate in Franschhoek was vinified by Simonsvlei, previously being made by a wine-making neighbour. Just 3.5 ha of cabernet sauvignon and merlot are planted, so that's what residents, their friends and family get to enjoy.

Cabernet Sauvignon ★★★★ Light & supple **17** ⑧⑤, cassis, cigarbox & spicy dark notes. Easy approachability from 10 months on French oak staves in tank. Previewed last time, now bottled, as next. **Merlot ★★★★** Cocoa, dark berry & dried herb on nuanced, gentle **17** ⑧⑤. Pleasant ease from judicious maturation (as for Cab). **Mélange ★★★★** Cab leads merlot in **17** ⑧⑤ blend, ripe blue & black fruit with spice on light frame. Same oak regime as others. — FM

Location/WO: Franschhoek ▪ Est 2001 ▪ 1stB 2005 ▪ Tasting & sales Wed/Sat by appt ▪ Owner(s) La Petite Provence Wine Trust ▪ Winemaker(s) Helena Senekal (2017, Simonsvlei) ▪ 3.5ha (cab, merlot) ▪ 30t/900cs own label 100% red ▪ 2 Cabernet Dr, La Petite Provence, Franschhoek 7690 ▪ info@lapetiteprovence.co.za ▪ www.lapetiteprovence.co.za ▪ **T +27 (0)21-876-4178/+27 (0)21-876-4554**

☐ **La Petite Vigne** *see* Black Elephant Vintners
☐ **Lategan** *see* Bergsig Estate

Lateganskop Winery ⑨

The Lategan family have been tending vines in the Wolseley area for more than 100 years. Oupa Willie, who reached a remarkable 102, built a cellar in 1969, founding a legacy that continues today in mostly bulk-wine production. The recent granting of an on-consumption liquor licence creates new and exciting possibilities for the parcels that find their way into bottle, currently a minuscule 600 cases.

The Zahir range

★★★★ Red ⑨ Previewed **13** ⑧⑦ cab, pinotage, cinsaut aged extraordinary 4 years in old oak, adding nuance & complexity. Lighter in style but packs a savoury berry punch, improves on **12 ★★★** ⑧④.

★★★★ **White** Ex 24 year old bushvines, **17** ⑧⑧ chenin steps up on **16** ★★★★ ⑧④ with luscious tropical fruit, melt-in-the-mouth crème brûlée texture & flavour. Balanced acidity completes a delicious wine, 13 months old-oak aged.

Lateganskop range

Livia's Laughter Méthode Cap Classique ⑫ ★★★★ Delightful dry bubbles from chardonnay & pinot noir, **13** ⑧⑤ baked apple, ginger & biscuit notes, full & smooth, long-lingering lemon curd aftertaste. WO W Cape, as Sauvignon. **Muscat d'Alexandrie '102'** ⑫ ★★★★ Attractively packaged solera-aged **NV** ⑧⑤ fortified dessert honours centenarian patriarch. **13** sweet grape & boiled sweet flavours, good viscosity, whistle-clean conclusion. 500 ml.

Twins range

Sauvignon Blanc ★★★ Departure from fresh & fruity easy-drinking styling, **19** ⑦⑨ bigger (14% alcohol) & richer but lifted by vibrant acidity. — WB, CvZ

Location: Wolseley ▪ Map: Breedekloof ▪ Map grid reference: A2 ▪ WO: Breedekloof/Western Cape ▪ Est 1969 ▪ 1stB 2004 ▪ Tasting & sales Mon-Fri 8–12 & 1–5 ▪ Closed Easter Fri-Mon, Dec 25/26 & Jan 1 ▪ Cellar tours by appt ▪ Owner(s) 5 members ▪ Cellarmaster(s) Heinrich Lategan (Oct 2008) ▪ Winemaker(s) Heinrich Lategan, with Kéan Oosthuizen (May 2011) ▪ 238ha (cab, ptage, chard, chenin, sauv, sem) ▪ 2,900t/600cs own label 30% red 70% white & ±2m L bulk ▪ PO Box 44 Breërivier 6858 ▪ lateganskop@breede.co.za ▪ www.lateganskop.co.za ▪ S 33° 30' 57.27" E 019° 11' 13.65" ▪ ⓜ prim.quarries.conflating ▪ **T +27 (0)23-355-1719**

La Terre La Mer

Undaunted by the 1,000 km separating them from the Cape winelands, a group of East London friends and winelovers started this boutique venture in 2008 'to have fun while aiming to make a serious wine'. The cellar overlooks the Indian Ocean (La Mer) while grapes are sourced from Swartland (La Terre).

Shiraz ⑫ ★★★ Plums & red berries in older-oaked **14** ⑧① retasted, shows some liquorice notes, softly fruity appeal, satisfying palate weight. — CR

Location: East London ▪ Map: Eastern Cape ▪ Map grid reference: B2 ▪ WO: Swartland ▪ Est/1stB 2008 ▪ Tasting & cellar tours by appt ▪ Owner(s)/winemaker(s) Mark Wiehahn, Jon Liesching, Nicholas Cooke & Nelanie Kaiser ▪ 2.5t shiraz ▪ 30 Plymouth Dr, Nahoon Mouth, East London 5241 ▪ mw-assoc@mweb.co.za ▪ S 32° 59' 09.5" E 027° 56' 28.9" ▪ ⓜ instead.tribune.shields ▪ **T +27 (0)83-701-3148**

☐ **Lautus** *see* Woolworths

L'Avenir Vineyards

The motto for this fine-wine estate on the Simonsberg foothills of Stellenbosch, is 'Proudly SA with a touch of French flair'. That covers a number of aspects. Firstly, L'Avenir means 'The Future' in French and it's owned by France-based AdVini, which has encouraged winemaker Dirk Coetzee to interact with his French counterparts, adding to his skills base. And there's the focus on chenin and pinotage, the proudly local part. There are meticulously cared-for single vineyards of both, plus other range options, including a beautifully packaged rosé from pinotage. A new feature on the property is a multifaceted hands-on garden, created by the employees and in their honour, which links the cellar, cellardoor venue and the Country Lodge.

Single Block range

★★★★★ **Pinotage** ⑳ Top of the pinotages, 100% new oak but careful handling ensures **17** ⑨② 's fruit is up to it. Multi-layered & involving: dark berries, espresso notes, well spiced; generously constructed, the body compact, enough muscle tone for long cellaring. Registered single-vineyard, as Chenin.

★★★★★ **Chenin Blanc** ⑳ Fruit from 45+ year old vines. In contrast to other chenin, **18** ⑨③ fully oaked: stonefruit, grapefruit, gentle almond thread, then tightening on the palate, more savoury, peach kernel, graphite nuance. Long life ahead. Admirable.

Glenrosé ⑰ ★★★★ Lovely packaging, glass stopper, bevelled punt gives jewel-like effect to flint bottle. Pale copper hue, **18** ⑧④ from pinotage, portion older barrels. Shows berries but also minerality, slight biscuit nuance. Grown-up rosé.

Provenance range

★★★★ **Pinotage** Tasted as preview, **17** (89) not as ripe as **16** (88). 85% older barrels 15 months, wonderfully perfumed, violets, blueberries & plums, some cinnamon, the tannins supple, harmonious. Has poise & presence.

★★★★ **Chenin Blanc** Stylistic change from **17** (88)'s 85% oaked, down to **18** (89)'s 40%, half whole-bunch ferment. Showcases the fruit, lime & winter melon, brightened by zesty acidity, giving vigour & length. Lovely.

Stellenbosch Classic ★★★★ Bordeaux blend, cab 65% with merlot, cab franc, small portion unoaked, rest older barrels, **17** (84) proudly displays cassis & dusty cedar. Smooth, enough grip for ageing yet accessible. Discontinued: **Cabernet Sauvignon**, **Merlot**.

Future Eternal range

★★★★ **Méthode Cap Classique Brut** Blend change to 6-part chardonnay-led, rest red. Orange gold hue, 34 months on lees, powerful toasted brioche, mix stonefruit & red berries. **16** (88) bubbly more developed style. **15** sold out untasted.

Méthode Cap Classique Brut Rosé (✷) ★★★★ Red fruit dominates **16** (84), made up of 6 varieties, including 31% chardonnay. Spent 14 months on the lees; vibrant berries, a strawberry note, sleekly built.

L'Horizon range (NEW)

. . . .

Sauvignon Blanc (✿) ★★★★ Good debut. Passionfruit & kiwi in bone-dry **19** (84), zinging freshness highlights a mineral seam, extends the flavours, wakens the taste buds.

. . . .

Pinotage ★★★ Unoaked **18** (82) designed for earlier drinking than other 2 pinotages, & nicely done too. Dark berries, touch of liquorice, gentle grip from skin contact. Streamlined, smooth texture. **Rosé** ★★★★ Appealing pale pink, with the expected pinotage berry fruitiness, but dry **19** (83) unexpectedly has minerality, ends almost saline. Lovely food wine, noteworthy debut. — CR

Location/map/WO: Stellenbosch ▪ Map grid reference: E3 ▪ Est/1stB 1992 ▪ Tasting & sales: Mon-Sat 10-7 (Oct-Apr)/10-5 (May-Sep) Sun/pub hols 10-4 ▪ Fee based on tasting option selected ▪ Closed Good Fri, Dec 25 & Jan 1 ▪ Cellar tours by appt ▪ Light meals ▪ Child friendly ▪ Function venue ▪ Luxury 4-star Country Lodge ▪ Owner(s) AdVini ▪ Winemaker(s) Dirk Coetzee (Aug 2009), with Mattheus Thabo (Jan 2007) & Francois Conradie (Jan 2014) ▪ Viticulturist(s) Leigh Diedericks, with Johan Pienaar ▪ 64.9ha/34.05ha (cabs s/f, merlot, ptage, chenin, sauv) ▪ 300t/41,000cs own label 44% red 38% white 18% rosé ▪ IPW, WIETA ▪ PO Box 7267 Stellenbosch 7599 ▪ info@lavenir.co.za ▪ www.lavenirestate.co.za ▪ S 33° 53' 7.78" E 018° 50' 37.12" ▪ (⬚) padding.march.steps ▪ **T +27 (0)21-889-5001**

La Vierge Private Cellar   (✷) (🍴) (♿)

Developed in the late 1990s on virgin land (hence the name) in what is now Hemel-en-Aarde Ridge, La Vierge winery is situated on Babylon Farm, the vineyards rooted in shale soils, the cellar and visitor facilities atop a steep slope, giving panoramic views. Going into this season, the team in charge since 2017 (winemaker Christo Kotze, viticulturist Juan Louw and GM Tania Theron-Joubert) were 'very pleased' to welcome leading vine guru Kevin Watt. A fresh perspective and new vineyard practices promise to 'take our young vineyards to the next level', while experimentation continues in the cellar to 'keep pushing the boundaries on our wine quality'. Various new projects will come to fruition over the next two years, 'assisting with brand building and cementing our capabilities as a fine-wine producer'.

Icon range

★★★★★ **Apogée Pinot Noir** (🍷) Opulent, multi-layered **15** (94), naturally fermented & styled for the long haul: new oak 18 months, then 6 months older. Fine typicity of sour cherry & raspberry interwoven with spice & black tea. Fine-textured tannins & a savoury edge, balanced mouthwatering acidity.

★★★★★ **Apogée Chardonnay** (🍷) Power & oatmeal richness but also a beguiling charisma rooted in pristine fruit (pears, stonefruit) & bright acidity. Honey & vanilla from new oak, year, give way to citrus on vivacious finish of **17** ★★★★★ (93). Like debut **15** (97), set to bloom over 3-5 years. No **16**.

Ultra Premium range
★★★★☆ **Royal Nymphomane** Poised & polished Bordeaux red, majority cab & merlot (56/27), 2 others, some fruit from Hemel-en-Aarde Valley. Cassis & mulberry whiffs of **15** (91) adorned with graphite & cedar from 2 years new oak. Svelte tannins complemented by a dried herb finish.

Flagship range
★★★★ **La Vierge Noir** ⊘ The 'noir' is 'pinot', from highest block on farm. Elegant **16** (87) lovely red berry aromas, earthy & savoury notes reflecting a subtle oak treatment, 20% new for 9 months.

Premium range
★★★★ **The Affair** ⊘ From pinot noir, fine & focused in **18** (87), with cherry, redcurrant & raspberry fruit meshing well with savoury spice & meat nuances, ending on piquant cherry note.

★★★★ **Satyricon** Seductive **18** (87) from sangiovese aged in older oak, good varietal cherry, strawberry & almond notes, leather & floral elements adding depth on long, earth/mineral conclusion. **17** not made.

★★★★ **Anthelia** Shiraz in usual unshowy style, **17** (88) has firm tannins (that will soften with time), leather & herbal notes to persistent dark cherry, plum & mulberry fruit, spice from barrique sojourn.

★★★★ **Nymphomane** Artfully crafted Bordeaux quartet, mostly cab & merlot (49/35), **17** (87) is dark toned, savoury & food styled, like **16** (88), the lingering forest fruits having cigarbox, spice & dried herb nuances. Walker Bay WO.

★★★★ **Jezebelle** ⊘ 🍇 The 2nd chardonnay, but no understudy to the Apogée bottling in **18** ★★★★★ (93), which outshines **17** (88) in its dialled-back oaking (20% new puncheons, 8 months) ceding centre stage to enticing pear, peach & kumquat fruit. No lack of creamy richness, but ably balanced by fresh acidity.

★★★★ **Original Sin** Unoaked white Bordeaux blend, sauvignon (85%) & semillon, **18** (86) has lime, kiwi & fig fruit nuances, bracing acidity & lingering citrus finish.

. . . .

Seduction ⊘ ★★★★ Two vintages of unoaked pinot noir tasted, both light, fresh, spicily red-fruited & brimming with joie de vivre. Wild-fermented **17** (84) is juicy, **18** (84) crunchy, both delicious & well priced.

The Last Temptation ★★★★ Aromatic **17** (84) riesling shows some Old World appeal: grapefruit, floral & terpene wafts, dry, with lipsmacking acidity to savour with seafood. — GM

Location: Hermanus ▪ Map: Walker Bay & Bot River ▪ Map grid reference: B4 ▪ WO: Hemel-en-Aarde Ridge/Walker Bay/Cape South Coast ▪ Est 1997 ▪ 1stB 2006 ▪ Tasting & sales Mon-Sun 10–5 ▪ Closed Good Fri & Dec 25 ▪ La Vierge Restaurant & Champagne Verandah ▪ Tour groups by appt ▪ Owner(s) La Vierge Wines (Pty) Ltd & Viking Pony Properties 355 (Pty) Ltd ▪ Winemaker(s) Christo Kotze (Jul 2017) ▪ Viticulturist(s) Juan Louw (Jul 2017), Kevin Watt (consultant) ▪ 44ha (cab f, p verdot, pinot, sangio, shiraz, chard, riesling, sauv, sem) ▪ 200t 60% red 40% white ▪ PO Box 1580 Hermanus 7200 ▪ info@lavierge.co.za ▪ www.lavierge.co.za ▪ S 34° 22' 22.3" E 019° 14' 29.4" ▪ 🔲 referees.newness.timeliness ▪ **T +27 (0)28-313-0130**

☐ **Lavine & Mackenzie** *see* The Wine Thief

Lazanou Organic Vineyards (♀) (🍴) (🏠) (📷)
When Josef Lazarus and Candice Stephanou bought this tiny Wellington property in 2002, there was just one block of chenin. The vineyards have grown — all are certified organic — and there are now also olives and livestock, biodiversity zones and visitor attractions. The wines, made by a consultant, not tasted this time.

Location/map: Wellington ▪ Map grid reference: B2 ▪ Est 2002 ▪ 1stB 2006 ▪ Tasting & sales by appt ▪ Open days with wine & food pairing - booking required ▪ Tour groups ▪ Farm produce ▪ Cow Shed Cottage ▪ Owner(s) Josef Lazarus & Candice Stephanou ▪ Winemaker(s) Rolanie Lotz (Jan 2011, consultant) ▪ Viticulturist(s) Johan Wiese (Jan 2006, consultant) ▪ 8.48ha/5.54ha (mourv, shiraz, chard, chenin, viog) ▪ 50t/6,000cs own label 50% red 50% white ▪ Certified organic by Ecocert ▪ PO Box 834 Wellington 7654 ▪ wine@lazanou.co.za ▪ www.lazanou.co.za ▪ S 33° 35' 59.58" E 018° 59' 36.12" ▪ 🔲 countdown.sandbags. tabulated ▪ **T +27 (0)83-265-6341**

☐ **Leaf Plucker** *see* Sauvignon Wines

Le Belle Rebelle

'The Beautiful Rebel' arose from former Stofberg Family Vineyards to avoid confusion with another Stofberg cellar in Breedekloof. Winemaker Mariëtte Stofberg-Coetzee's ambitions and adventurousness seem to be kindled by the change. She promises 'different and risky' wines (and labels) for the Rebelle range — including a 'chenin blanc battle between Swartland and Breedekloof', indicating, as does the new sauvignon blanc from Darling, that grapes from other regions will be coming into her rebellious winery. Plenty of vinous excitement, then, but other liquors also among the attractions, with beer, gin and rum tastings on offer.

Mariëtte range

★★★★ **Syrah** Inky black allure on **15** ⑧⑧, leather, mulberry, black plum & savoury meat spice. Firm & concentrated, dusty tannins (30 months barrique) to the firm cocoa finish. Needs time.

★★★★ **Chardonnay** (NEW) Crisp Golden Delicious apple, sprinkling of cinnamon & clove spice on barrel-fermented **18** ⑧⑦. Elegant, with toasty oak flavours reined in by a citrus core & lemon zest farewell.

★★★★ **Chenin Blanc** 18 ★★★★★ ⑨⓪ steps up from **17** ⑧⑨ with rich tropical & stonefruit flavours in perfect harmony with sweet vanilla oak. Understated & layered nuttiness from barrel-fermentation. Lovely spine of citrus throughout.

★★★★☆ **Pinot Blanc** (🍸) A joy to drink (& pair food with) this rare varietal bottling. **18** ⑨③ oozes apricot, melon, wet hay, orchard fruit flavours, mingled on sustained finish with toasted almond, touch of caramel & exotic spice from older oak. Only the white grapes picked from 33 year mixed blanc/gris vines.

★★★★ **Méthode Cap Classique Chardonnay** Rich & rounded, **14** ⑧⑦ sparkling delights with baked apple, buttery biscuit & a lemon tang. Smooth, creamy bubbles on mouthfilling, long conclusion.

Cabernet Sauvignon ★★★★ Abundant ripe black berry, cherry & cassis fruit smoothed 2 years in barrel, vanilla & chocolate hints on finish of **16** ⑧⑤.

Special range

★★★★☆ **Israel Chardonnay** (🍸) Delicate ripe apple, white blossom & orchard fruit aromas on barrel-fermented **17** ⑨⓪, made by a treasured member of staff. Just-dry but harmonious, with crème brûlée flavours, lengthy & elegant.

Rebelle range (NEW)

★★★★ **Butcher Bird Sauvignon Blanc** (✓) Pear drop & tropical fruit with saline edge on **19** ⑧⑧ from high Durbanville slope. Vibrant & fresh, with clean lemon squeeze & crushed stone minerality to finish.

Mía range

Shiraz ★★★★☆ Younger, somewhat trimmer (14.5% alcohol vs 15%) sibling of Mariëtte is bouncy & fresh, **17** ⑧③ red & black fruit, immaculately judged oak & savoury meaty finish. **Pinot Noir Rosé** (🍸) ★★★ Vibrant blush on **17** ⑧① mirrored in riot of red-berry fruit, lemony acidity on dry exit is food friendly. **Chenin Blanc** ★★★ Carefree, for everyday enjoyment, **18** ⑦⑨ apple & pear fruit with spicy edge (though unoaked). In the same vein as also-tasted **19** ⑦⑨, just a bit less fresh. — WB

Location: Rawsonville ▪ Map: Breedekloof ▪ Map grid reference: C5 ▪ WO: Breedekloof/Durbanville ▪ Est 2011 ▪ 1stB 2012 ▪ Tasting, sales & restaurant Mon-Thu 11-9 Fri/Sat 11-10 Sun 11-3 ▪ Tasting R25/3 Mia wines, R45/4 Mariëtte wines or R65 for all 7; gin experience R55/2 gins & 2 tonics with dressings; craft beer tasting R50/4 Feather beers, R60/4 Rock beers; Pirate rum tasting R55/2 rums paired with appletizer & coke ▪ Cellar tours by appt ▪ Closed Dec 25 & Jan 1 ▪ Ou Stokery Restaurant, admin@oustokery.co.za ▪ Play area for children ▪ Craft gin/brandy distillery ▪ Craft beer brewery ▪ Owner(s) PJD Stofberg, M Stofberg-Coetzee & GJN Coetzee ▪ Cellarmaster(s)/winemaker(s) Mariëtte Stofberg-Coetzee (Nov 2011) ▪ Viticulturist(s) Pieter Jacobus Daniël Stofberg (Jan 1981), Andries de Wet (Jun 2002, consultant) & Gideon Jacobus Nicolaas Coetzee (Nov 2011) ▪ ±102ha ▪ 42.5t 19% red 25% white 12% MCC 9% rosé 35% brandy ▪ PO Box 298 Rawsonville 6845 ▪ info@lebellerebelle.com ▪ www.lebellerebelle.com ▪ S 33° 40' 17.24" E 019° 18' 37.27" ▪ patterns.trumpeters. dragging ▪ **T +27 (0)82-867-6958 (cellar); +27 (0)82-511-0500 (restaurant)**

Le Bonheur Wine Estate (🍷)

After buying historic Stellenbosch estate Le Bonheur in 2016, rejuvenating vines and renovating the cellar, international wine specialist AdVini has tasked winemaker William Wilkinson with identifying single-vineyard gems for limited release from 2020. Included is a barrel-fermented sauvignon from 40-something vines

(Le Bonheur's Blanc Fumé was a star during the tenure of 1970s/80s prime mover, soil scientist and early 'terroirist' Michael Woodhead). A standout petit verdot and cabernet franc may also feature. William's first Prima and Cabernet Sauvignon were released last year.

★★★★ **Cabernet Sauvignon** Young, muscular **18** (88) has bramble fruit & scrub, with wood in good support (30% new, 15 months), promises much - sampled pre-bottling, as all new releases this edition. **17**, **16** untasted.

★★★★ **The Manor Meander Merlot** (NEW) ⊘ Evidence of quality makeover in progress, **18** (89) thrilling fruit marshalled by soft ripe tannins, long succulent finish. Mostly from block planted 1984 beside manor house, possibly oldest merlot in Stellenbosch.

★★★★ **Prima** Merlot-led Bordeaux blend with cab, cab franc & splash petit verdot. Vibrant **18** (86) a rung up on previous, juicy fruit shoehorned into tense tannic frame. More potential than **16** ★★★☆ (84). **17** untasted.

★★★★ **The Weather Blocks Sauvignon Blanc** (NEW) Concentrated gunflint profile of **19** (88), from combo old (1977) & high altitude parcels of 'weerstasie' (weather station) clone, fleshed out by part barrel ferment, 5 months in oak, 10% new.

Cinsault (♀) ★★★☆ Piquant red fruit - cranberry, pomegranate - give sweet-sour twist to light & deft **17** (84) from Swartland, one third briefly aged in barrel. **Chardonnay** ★★★☆ Generous lime fruit of **19** (85) served with crème caramel richness of oak (half new, 5 months), balanced by fresh acidity. **Sauvignon Blanc** ★★★☆ Quintessential Stellenbosch sauvignon from mature block at 500 m, **19** (83)'s ample tropical fruit checked by zesty acid for deliciously dry finish. — DS

Location/map: Stellenbosch ▪ Map grid reference: F1 ▪ WO: Simonsberg–Stellenbosch/Swartland ▪ Est 1790s ▪ 1stB 1972 ▪ Tasting by appt only ▪ Owner(s) AdVini South Africa ▪ Winemaker(s) William Wilkinson (May 2017) ▪ 163ha/75ha (cab, merlot, chard, sauv) ▪ 600t/60,000cs own label 40% red 60% white ▪ cellar@ lebonheur.co.za ▪ www.lebonheur.co.za ▪ S 33° 50' 1.0" E 018° 52' 21.4" ▪ [☒] droplet.necks.loaders ▪ **T +27 (0)21-889-5001/+27 (0)21-875-5478**

▢ **Leenders** see Bezuidenhout Family Wines
▢ **Leeumasker** see Maske Wines

Leeu Passant ♀

The Cape's extended drought, relieved only in 2019, negatively impacted many vineyards. But celebrated winegrowing couple Chris and Andrea Mullineux, partnered with Indian businessman Analjit Singh and Peter Dart in this Franschhoek-based venture, are pleased that rehabilitation of the old vineyards they nurture with the assistance of consultant Rosa Kruger has resulted in increased drought resistance and more balanced fruit. This small but acclaimed range celebrates history and honours terroir. It features, among others, vines producing for nearly 12 decades and, in the Dry Red, a union of cabernet and cinsaut modelled on what Chris and Andrea believe were the first red blends made in the Cape. While completely different in focus to the wines the Mullineuxs craft in Swartland (see Mullineux listing), these parcels are just as thoughtfully conceived and impeccably executed.

Leeu Passant range
★★★★★ **Dry Red Wine** (🏅) (🏆) Intended as 'deconstruction/reconstruction' of venerable Cape wines of the past', hence cab & cinsaut (56/26), with cab franc supplying leafy top note in **17** (93). Intense berry & plum aromas & flavours, fine tannin/acid structure for decade-plus ageing. Dryland vineyards, some up to 119 years old. Natural ferment, as all. Magnums too, as next. WO W Cape.

★★★★★ **Stellenbosch Chardonnay** (🏅) Pure & fine **17** (97) has subtle citrus complexity, discreet white peach fleshiness, hint perfumed oak. Incredibly well crafted, totally unforced, all elements moulded into cohesive whole, hallmark savoury conclusion. For ageing many years. Barrel fermented, wholebunch, year in 225/500L oak, 30% new, unfiltered.

CWG Auction Reserve range (NEW)
★★★★★ **Radicales Libres** (🏅) Inspired by a Rioja winemaker, hence the Spanish name & 'extended barrel-age' styling. Riveting **14** (96) from Barrydale chardonnay, matured in neutral oak in evaporative

environment for 5 years, during which time 'everything' concentrated & turned savoury, resulting in a saltiness persisting through to thrillingly dry finish. — CvZ

Location/map: Franschhoek ▪ Map grid reference: C2 ▪ WO: Klein Karoo/Stellenbosch/Western Cape ▪ Est 2013 ▪ 1stB 2015 ▪ Tasting & sales Mon-Sun 10-5 at the Wine Studio, Leeu Estates, Franschhoek (booking recommended) ▪ Fee R110-R300 depending on tasting ▪ Closed Good Fri, Dec 25 & Jan 1 ▪ Owner(s) Chris & Andrea Mullineux, Analjit Singh, Peter Dart ▪ Cellarmaster(s) Andrea Mullineux ▪ Winemaker(s) Andrea Mullineux, with Wade Sander (Dec 2015) ▪ Viticulturist(s) Chris Mullineux & Rosa Kruger (consultant) ▪ 25t/1,684cs own label 55% red 45% white ▪ WIETA ▪ info@mlfwines.com ▪ www.mlfwines.com ▪ S 33° 54' 33.43" E 019° 6' 14.85" ▪ 📟 prospects.versions.cigar ▪ **T +27 (0)21-492-2455 (office)/+27 (0)21-492-2224 (Wine Studio)**

Leeurivier Wyn & Olyf   ⓟ

Extremely rocky soils, once quarried, in relatively new viticultural land in the hills between Bot River and Hermanus are now home to olive orchards and a small vineyard. Here Overberger Ewald Groenewald, formerly in the truck and transport business, vinifies a handful of reds in a stone cellar for co-owners and long-time friends Jakobus du Plessis and Leo Pistorius.

Leo Wyn range

Mourvèdre ⓠ ★★★ Almost porty in its ripeness, deep & dense, black fruited, oak not much in evidence. **13** ㉘ big & bold, for those who like swashbuckling wines. **Pinot Noir** ⓠ ★★ Full-ripe style, shows in perfume despite Walker Bay origin. **13** ㉒ toasted oak, savoury spice threaded through, tannins still firm, ending dry. Less fresh than expected, could have offset the wooding. **Petit Verdot** ⓠ ★★★★ Dark plum fruit, mocha overlay, intense & somewhat extracted **13** ★★★ ㉜'s tannins needing year/2 more to knit. More vibrant & herbaceous **14** ㉞ has savoury, umami notes but also firm tannins & needs few years. **Sangiovese** ⓠ ★★★ Dusty nose, cherries as an underpin, the ripeness (15.5% alcohol) shows in opulence, curvaceous body. **13** ㉚ has enough juiciness to counterbalance the dry tannins. Big but tasty. **Shiraz** ⓠ ★★★ Two vintages, different origins & styles. **13** ㉜ ex Walker Bay the riper, black plus/prunes, gentle savoury notes, body smooth & round. **12** ㉛ from Klein Karoo showing more complexity, hedgerow fruit, brambleberries, touch of scrub & liquorice. Streamlined, sleek, nice grip on the end. — CR, CvZ

Location: Bot River ▪ Map: Walker Bay & Bot River ▪ Map grid reference: C3 ▪ WO: Walker Bay/Klein Karoo ▪ Est 2005 ▪ 1stB 2008 ▪ Tasting & sales by appt ▪ Closed Easter Fri-Mon, Ascension day & Dec 25 ▪ Owner(s) Leeurivier Wyn & Olyf (Pty) Ltd ▪ Winemaker(s) Ewald Groenewald ▪ 70ha/4ha (malbec, mourv, p verdot, pinot, sangio) ▪ PO Box 345 Kleinmond 7195 ▪ ewald@leeurivier.co.za ▪ S 34° 16' 39.99" E 019° 13' 36.22" ▪ 📟 response.ally.work ▪ **T +27 (0)82-883-3329**

Leeuwenkuil Family Vineyards

Leeuwenkuil, Willie and Emma Dreyer's expansive Swartland farm, boasts 1,250 ha under vine, with many varieties planted. They provide cellarmaster Pieter Carstens with an infinite palette of flavours and textures for his favourite style, blends. His first ('17) Reserve White, from chenin with an eclectic array of other varieties, attracted international and local acclaim, vindicating the goal for both this wine and the Reserve Red sibling to produce quality in significant volume - the latter not something the recent drought vintages have offered, however. 'Quantities were already low in 2018,' Carstens recalls, 'we hoped for a similar-size crop in 2019, but vines cared more about their survival than fruit, and yields were down another 16%.' On the upside, he considers 2019 superior in quality and longevity.

Heritage series

★★★★★ **Syrah** ⊘ ⓐ A blue-blood Swartland syrah. **17** ㊲ captivating spice, berries both fragrant & flavoursome, precise rather than showy. Even tighter than previously made **15** ㊲ but silky concentration bides time behind fine, fresh grip. So elegant, so stylish.

★★★★ **Chenin Blanc** ⓐ **18** ㊙, first since **14** ㊼, echoes latter's subtle fruit, rich texture, both well-sustained. Still youthful, yet to absorb 90% new oak; has concentration for that & to grow with age.

Reserve range

★★★★ **Red** ⊘ Previewed last edition, **17** ㊘ rich in fruit, suggestion of red earth sometimes found in Swartland syrah (60%, with 3 other Rhône varieties). Medium body, gentle tannins & balanced freshness all help approachability. Harmonised in older oak.

★★★★★ **White** ⊘ ⓐ More than lives up to tank sample tasted previously, **17** ㉟ a consummate blend, headed by chenin with 20% seven others - notably grenache blanc, marsanne, verdelho. All create complexity, individuality & freshness without assistance of oak. Modern, delicious.

Occasional release: **Rosé**.

Leeuwenkuil range

★★★★ **Shiraz** More youthfully approachable than Heritage, **17** ㉘ lacks nothing in quality. Captivates with floral, red fruit & spice fragrance, silkily flowing texture & savoury flavours. Freshness, gentle yet lively tannins encourage current enjoyment, worth saving for few years too. **16** ★★★★ ㉟ for early drinking.

. . . .

Chenin Blanc ⊘ ⓟ ★★★★ Generous, sunny Swartland chenin; **19** ㉞ preview brims with ripe apple, tropical tones, refreshing fruity acids. Immensely likeable, plenty of character.

. . . .

Occasional release: **Cinsaut Rosé**.

Varietal range

Occasional release: **Cinsault**, **Grenache Noir**, **Grenache Blanc**, **Marsanne**. — AL

Location: Stellenbosch ▪ WO: Swartland ▪ Est 2008 ▪ 1stB 2011 ▪ Closed to public ▪ Owner(s) Willie & Emma Dreyer ▪ Cellarmaster(s) Pieter Carstens (Aug 2008) ▪ Winemaker(s) Riaan van der Spuy (Dec 2016), Corrien Basson (Jan 2012), Bernard Allison (Jan 2012), Jean Aubrey (Aug 2017) & Madré van der Walt (Sep 2013), with Jehan de Jongh (Aug 2008) ▪ Viticulturist(s) Koos van der Merwe (Dec 2008) & Claude Uren (Jan 2012) ▪ 4,550ha ▪ 36,500t/27m L 70% red 30% white ▪ Fairtrade, WIETA ▪ PO Box 249 Koelenhof 7605 ▪ kobus@leeuwenkuilfv.co.za ▪ www.leeuwenkuilfv.co.za ▪ **T +27 (0)21-865-2455**

☐ **Legends** *see* Slanghoek Winery
☐ **Legends of the Labyrinth** *see* Doolhof Wine Estate

Le Grand Chasseur Estate ⓠ ⓖ

Owned by successful Eastern Cape fresh produce enterprise Habata, Le Grand Chasseur is planted with wine- as well as table-grape vines. The former are about 220 ha in extent and yield around 4,500 tons a season, vinified since 2011 by Carel Botha. Tastings have moved from Robertson town back to the farm beside the Breede River, where the namesake 'great hunter', the African Fish Eagle, makes its home.

Habata Reserve Selection

Pinotage ⓖ ★★★★ Oak-spice-dusted maraschino cherry flavours, reined-in 13.5% alcohol attractive & welcome but **17** ㉞'s firm tannins (abetted by new oak) need time to resolve. **Shiraz** ★★★★ Remains big & bold, at 15% alcohol, but **17** ㉝ dials back the new oak (from 100% to zero), loses the gram sugar. Tannins are firm but offset by fresh plum fruit. **Chardonnay** ⓖ ★★★ Intense joiner's workshop fragrance (year 2nd-fill oak) suffuses ripe tangerine fruit, **16** ㉜ drier than Habata sibling but richer, fuller, the wood notes returning on finish.

Habata range

Cabernet Sauvignon-Merlot ⓖ ★★★ Unoaked, juicy **18** ㉚, with cab at 70%, is light-footed (12.6% alcohol) & supple for early/easy sipping. **Chardonnay Unwooded** ⓖ ★★★ Lemon & peach tones accented by subtle salinity, **18** ㉜ has smidgen sugar to smooth & extend the finish. **Sauvignon Blanc Tropical** ⓖ ★★★ Trust the label: granadilla, papaya & mango all present on **18** ㉛, bone-dry & lightish for lingering lunches. **Muscat de Frontignan** ⓖ ★★★★ Appealing **17** ㉟ fortified, lemon, white peach, dried apricot & pear complexity; silky 204 g/l sweetness perhaps needs dash more acidity. 500 ml. — CvZ

Location/map/WO: Robertson ▪ Map grid reference: B7 ▪ Est 1881 ▪ 1stB 1999 ▪ Tasting by appt ▪ Closed all pub hols ▪ Owner(s) Hannes Joubert (Habata Boerdery) ▪ Cellarmaster(s)/winemaker(s) Carel Botha (Jan 2011) ▪ Viticulturist(s) Jan Rabie (Sep 2015) ▪ ±1,300ha/220ha (cab, merlot, ptage, ruby cab, shiraz, chard, chenin, cbard, muscadel w, nouvelle, sauv) ▪ ±4,500t ▪ IPW ▪ PO Box 439 Robertson 6705 ▪ cellar@lgc.co.za, sales@lgc.co.za ▪ www.habata.co.za ▪ S 33° 51' 47.7" E 019° 43' 10.6" ▪ ⊞ meltingly.zoologists.resistors ▪ **T +27 (0)23-626-1048**

Le Grand Domaine ⓠ

Owned by Origin Wine founder Bernard Fontannaz, this property on the crest of Stellenbosch's Devon Valley is planted with red Bordeaux varieties, now grown in a 'softer' way, with 'a reduction in the use of chemicals and other interventions'. It also provides a 'gorgeous setting with breathtakingly colourful sunset views' for pop-up restaurants where chefs pair their specialities with wines that now include a Provence-style rosé.

The Pledge range

★★★★ **Sauvignon Blanc** ⊘ Vivacious **18** ★★★★★ ⑨⓪ from 10 different areas, Lutzville to Stanford. Steps up from **17** ⑧⑦ with intensity & complexity, hint of smoke on succulent citrus & tropical fruit. Lovely pithy grapefruit note on the finish. 2% oaked for 3 months.

Grand Vin de Stellenbosch range

★★★★ **Sauvignon Blanc** All-Stellenbosch fruit for **18** ⑧⑧, expressive greengage, lemon zest & hint of greenpepper. Bouncy & fresh, with a long finish. Same wooding as Pledge.

- - -

Shiraz (NEW) ⑦ ★★★ Unfettered by oak, **18** ⑧② is juicy & meaty, with hints of spice for braais & steak-house suppers. **Chenin Blanc** (NEW) ⊘ ⑦ ★★★★ Light-hearted & -bodied **18** ⑧③, balanced & generous, full of sunshine fruit to serve al fresco this summer. **Chardonnay-Viognier** ⑦ ★★★ Now unoaked, & showing a more fun side in **18** ⑧①. Exuberant orchard fruit & blossomy perfumes leap from the glass in a delicious taste experience.

- - -

Cabernet Sauvignon-Merlot ★★★★ **17** ⑧⑤ 80/20 Bordeaux blend shade more complex than previous, full of dark fruit flavours, cassis, some old leather-bound book aromas. Harmonious & fresh. 20% new wood, 18-24 months. Not tasted: **Shiraz-Mourvèdre**. — WB

Location/map: Stellenbosch ▪ Map grid reference: D4 ▪ WO: Stellenbosch/Western Cape ▪ Est/1stB 2014 ▪ Tasting strictly by appt ▪ Owner(s) Bernard Fontannaz ▪ Viticulturist(s) Deon Joubert ▪ 40% red 50% white 10% rosé ▪ PO Box 7177 Stellenbosch 7599 ▪ info@granddomaine.co.za ▪ www.granddomaine.co.za ▪ S 33° 54' 0.61" E 018° 48' 23.49" ▪ T +27 (0)71-398-3011

☐ **Leipoldt 1880** *see* Wineways Marketing

Leipzig Winery ⑨ ⑪ ⌂ ⑥ ⑧

Locally born Lida Smit and husband Francois revived their 19th-century Worcester farm's Leipzig label, ending decades as a grape supplier to Nuy Winery. Two consulting winemakers vinify home and brought-in grapes in a new boutique cellar (the historic old one now a wedding chapel), and daughter Alida Bester and husband Vian manage the venture, growing exports to Europe and adding more visitor facilities.

★★★★★ **Grand Master** ⑨ Superior Bordeaux red, gently crafted in medium-bodied, elegant style; demure cassis & mulberry, subtle spice, very supple tannins & gentle 13% alcohol. Merlot-led, 5-way **17** ⑨⓪ delicious in youth. 9 months in old oak.

★★★★ **Master Blend** ⑨ Cape Blend of mostly pinotage plus merlot, 3 others. Grippy **17** ⑧⑧ in mould of **15** ⑧⑥, plum fruit constrained by brusque tannins mid-2018, needs year/2 to relax. **16** not tasted.

★★★★ **Heimat** Was 'Shiraz-Mourvèdre-Viognier', **17** ⑧⑥ still from those varieties. Steps up on **16** ★★★☆ ⑧⑤ with abundance of deep plum & hedgerow fruit, gentle creamy tannins & long, spicy, lifted farewell. Delightful drinking now & for few years.

★★★★ **White Leipzig** White flagship from chardonnay, chenin & viognier. **18** ⑧⑨ opulent mouthful of apple & melon, pineapple, peach melba & subtle oak spice from older barrels, 9 months. Concentrated yet well rounded, refined. 13.7% alcohol.

- - -

Pinot Gris ⑦ ★★★ Palest pink **19** ⑧⓪ packed with fresh melon, pear & spice, zippy acid for balance, good intensity. Something really tasty & different for everyday. WO Stellenbosch. **Sauvignon Blanc** ⑦ ★★★★ Good energy in **19** ⑧④ from Elim, Stellenbosch & Worcester vines, pleasing spread of flavours from tropical fruit & lemon zest to nettle & wet stone. Also in 1.5L.

- - -

Cabernet Sauvignon ★★★★ Vibrant ruby **17** ⑧⑤, black berries, leather, tealeaves on palate, finishing dry. All old oak for 12 months. Stellenbosch WO, as next. **Shiraz** ★★★ Just shy of previous, **18** ⑧② less intense & leaner, with mulberry, wild berry, smoke & savoury nuances. Needs time or food. **Chenin Blanc** ★★★★ Cape Town WO bushvine grapes for gently oaked **18** ⑧④, rounded & showing good acid balance. Baked apple & buttered popcorn flavours make it very moreish. Not tasted: **Pinotage**, **Viognier**. In abeyance: **Chardonnay**. — WB

Location/map: Worcester ▪ Map grid reference: C3 ▪ WO: Western Cape/Stellenbosch/Cape Town ▪ Est/1stB 2013 ▪ Tasting, sales & cellar tours Tue-Fri 10-4 Sat 10-2; or by appt ▪ Closed Ash Wednesday, Easter Mon, Dec 25 & Jan 1 ▪ Cheese & charcuterie platters by appt ▪ Facilities for children ▪ Tour groups ▪ Conferences ▪ Weddings/functions ▪ Walks/hikes ▪ MTB trail ▪ Guided tours by appt: historic buildings & art ▪ Leipzig Country House ▪ Owner(s) Francois & Lida Smit ▪ Winery manager Vian Bester ▪ Winemaker(s) Jacques Fourie & Wynand Pienaar (May 2018, consultants) ▪ 10ha/4.5ha (sauv) ▪ 28,505t own label 75% red 25% white ▪ PO Box 5104 Worcester 6849 ▪ winery@leipzigcountryhouse.co.za ▪ www.leipzigcountryhouse.co.za ▪ S33° 38' 29.90" E 019° 38' 9.44" ▪ winery.inundate.utensil ▪ **T +27 (0)23-347-8422**

☐ **Lelie van Saron** *see* Natasha Williams Signature Wines

Le Lude Méthode Cap Classique ⓥ ⑾ ⌂

Le Lude estate in Franschhoek, owned by Nic and Ferda Barrow, specialises in méthode cap classique. The expanding range includes SA's first agrafe sparkling, a production method which involves a second fermentation under cork rather than crown cap, before disgorgement by hand and further ageing under a new cork. At Orangerie restaurant on the premises, chef Nicolene Barrow crafts classic dishes to pair with the elegant sparklers.

★★★★☆ **Rosé** ⓐ Blends pinot noir with chardonnay (35%) & meunier (5%). **NV** ⑨④ subtle, complex red fruit & biscuit flavours partnered by stream of pinprick bubbles. Still youthful, emphatically dry; can beneficially develop further. 30 months on lees.

★★★★★ **Agrafe** ⓐ Cellarworthy **13** ⑨⑥ bottle-fermented/aged under cork as opposed to more usual crown cap, gives more harmonious, evolved wine. Classic lees, citrus, ginger spice medley for fans of 'drier brut' (just 3.8 g/l sugar) with pleasing tension, mineral seam. Chardonnay with 36% pinot noir. Like Cuvée, Magnum & Brut '13, includes some Stellenbosch fruit.

★★★★ **Brut** Classic pairing of chardonnay & pinot noir (60/40) & the 30 months on lees reflect house's traditional approach to MCC. **NV** ⑧⑧ has precise if understated lees, ginger spice whiffs with balanced fresh acidity, creamy mousse. Fruit for this & Rosé ex Robertson, Bonnievale, Franschhoek.

★★★★ **Brut** ⑩④ More developed, expressive than others with leesy richness & light saline note. Heaviness avoided thanks to delicacy of mousse, acid/residual sugar balance creating crisp yet soft conclusion. **13** ⑧⑦ includes reserve wine held in oak vats. Aged 66 months on lees, as all wines noted.

★★★★☆ **Vintage Cuvée** ⓐ Best parcels for assured **13** ⑨④, same blend, very similar analysis to Agrafe. Most fruity of the line-up, with unabashed apple/lemon notes, & vivid freshness as expected with crown-cap ageing. Great energy & acid tension; creamy undercurrent ready to emerge with time.

★★★★★ **Vintage Magnum** ⓐ Selection of best parcels in **13** ⑨⑥, chardonnay with 36% pinot noir. Crisp acidity well to fore, just a hint of fresh limes, more mineral & oystershell tone. Nascent creaminess from extended lees contact will develop with ageing (longer than Cuvée). — AL, CvZ

Location/map: Franschhoek ▪ Map grid reference: C1 ▪ WO: Western Cape ▪ Est 2009 ▪ 1stB 2012 ▪ Tasting, sales & cellar tours Mon-Sun & pub hols 10-6 ▪ Orangerie restaurant ▪ Lily Pond guest villa ▪ Owner(s) Nic & Ferda Barrow ▪ Winemaker(s) Emma Bruwer ▪ Viticulturist(s) Etienne Terblanche (consultant) ▪ 6.2ha/3.4ha (pinot noir/meunier, chard) ▪ 210t/120,000 btls plus magnums own label 100% MCC ▪ PO Box 578 Franschhoek 7690 ▪ info@lelude.co.za ▪ www.lelude.co.za ▪ S 33° 54' 49.24" E 019° 7' 32.78" ▪ index. depended.wholeness ▪ **T +27 (0)21-100-3464/3465**

☐ **Lemahieu** *see* Eerste Hoop Wine Cellar

Le Manoir de Brendel ⓥ ⌂ ⊚ ⓐ

Consultants are employed by Christian and Maren Brendel, German proprietors of this exclusive Franschhoek guest house and winelands function venue, to vinify house wines from the small vineyard.

Brendel Collection

Cabernet Sauvignon ⓥ ★★★ Mature **07** ⑧① rhubarb & prune notes, firm tannin structure for food pairing. **Merlot** ⓥ ★★★ Tobacco, dried tomato & fruit-sweet edge to **06** ⑦⑧, was nearing drink-by date when last reviewed. **Pinotage** ⓥ ★★★ Sweet fruit, spicy aromas & typical acetone whiffs on ready **08** ⑦⑧; handles 15% alcohol with aplomb. **Shiraz** ⓥ ★★★ Engaging sweet-sour tang on meaty **06** ⑦⑧;

soft textured, slips down easily. **Chardonnay** ㉒ ★★ Ripe yellow citrus & light nutty aromas on **16** (74), creamily soft, with hint of spice in tail. WO W Cape, as Sauvignon-Viognier. **Sauvignon Blanc** ㉒ ★★☆ Quiet tropical ripeness on **15** (78) offset by invigorating freshness. **Sauvignon Blanc-Viognier** ㉒ ★☆ Bone-dry **16** (71), very soft, short on verve & fruit.

Le Manoir de Brendel Collection

Shiraz ㉒ ★★★ Stewed fruit & bottle-age nutty character, drink **05** (81) soon. — AL

Location/map: Franschhoek ▪ Map grid reference: C3 ▪ WO: Franschhoek/Western Cape ▪ Est/1stB 2003 ▪ Tasting daily 12-4 ▪ Fee R40pp, waived on purchase ▪ Sales daily 7.30-4 ▪ Open daily, closed when booked for weddings/conferences ▪ Facilities for children ▪ Gift shop ▪ Conferences: day package (60 pax)/overnight package incl 10 rooms & 2 private cottages ▪ Walks ▪ Weddings (up to 60 pax) with chapel ▪ 5-star guest house (10 suites) ▪ Owner(s) Christian & Maren Brendel ▪ Winemaker(s) Cerina van Niekerk & Gerda Willers ▪ Viticulturist(s) Paul Wallace (consultant) ▪ 30ha/±23ha (cab, merlot, ptage, shiraz, chard, chenin, sauv, sem) ▪ ±150t ▪ PO Box 117 La Motte Franschhoek 7691 ▪ lmb@brendel.co.za ▪ www.le-manoir-de-brendel.com ▪ S 33° 52' 52.8" E 019° 3' 42.2" ▪ suburbs.dominantly.fruitfully ▪ **T +27 (0)21-876-4525**

Lemberg Wine Estate

Beloved bulldogs Spencer and Lady are in doggie heaven but Nelson, Louis, Rose and Ella still welcome visitors at this boutique Tulbagh estate, formerly owned by pioneering woman winemaker Janey Muller. The Hungarian grape she introduced to the SA repertoire, hárslevelü, remains a 'labour of love' for current owners Henk du Bruyn and Suzette Jansen van Rensburg, alongside their premium reds. They have picked up their 'consistent pace of patience and passion' by diversifying into handcrafted gin.

Yellow Label range

★★★★☆ **Spencer** From pinotage, **17** (92) lower alcohol (14.5%) & far less new oak (only 5% versus 60% for **14** (92)) to showcase ripe dark cherry, plum & berry fruit, silky-smooth, with subtle spice & dark chocolate, fresh finish. Also in magnum, as Nelson. **15** & **16** untasted.

★★★★ **Nelson** Syrah sold out untasted in **15** & **16**. **17** (87) big, bold at 15% alcohol, ripe cherry concentration & savoury hints of dried herbs, fennel, smoked meat from 15 months older oak.

★★★★ **Louis** Syrah plus 28% grenache, 22% mourvèdre, **17** (89) nudges higher rating with tangy red fruit, smoke & pepper nuances, subtle oak spice (French with soupçons American & Hungarian).

★★★★ **Hárslevelü** Hungarian white grape, naturally fermented, oxidatively handled, **18** ★★★★☆ (91) a step up on last-made **15** (89), worth seeking out for silky texture, spiced marmalade as well as fresh citrus fruit/zest flavours. Rich yet very refreshing, elegant, alcohol below 13%.

★★★★☆ **Lady** ✓ Also naturally fermented, oxidatively handled, here hárslevelü plays 2nd fiddle to 53% viognier plus 11% each sauvignon/semillon in fragrant, full-bodied **18** (90) bursting with succulent white peach, creamy guava & mouthwatering grapefruit. No **16**, **17**.

Pinot Noir ✓ ★★★☆ Lightly oaked **18** (83) has deep ruby hue, powdery tannins, berry flavours, earthy as well as savoury olive notes.

White Label range

Pinotage ㉒ ★★★ Characterful early-drinking **14** (81) mixes berries with slight leathery note, sweet-sour palate. Older oak, wholeberry ferment. WO W Cape. **Cape Blend** ★★★ Lightly oaked **18** (82) is 40% syrah with pinotage, equal grenache & pinot noir for lively red fruit, ready to drink at friendly 13% alcohol. **Blanc de Noir** ✓ ★★★☆ Pale coral **19** (84) is dry, with crisp red-apple & -berry freshness, subtle white pepper on finish. Syrah with 22% grenache. **Rosie's Blanc de Noir** (NEW) ★★★ Rose gold **19** (82), made from pinot noir, fresh & dry with piquant cranberry & ruby grapefruit, refreshing at 12% alcohol. **Sauvignon Blanc** ✓ ★★★☆ Crisp, bone-dry **19** (83) has peach & passionfruit aromas, zesty lemon-lime flavours, clean & slightly flinty finish. Occasional release: **Syrah**. — JG

Location/map: Tulbagh ▪ Map grid reference: F5 ▪ WO: Tulbagh/Western Cape ▪ Est 1978 ▪ Tasting, sales & cellar tours Mon-Fri 9-5 Sat 10-3.30 Sun 10-3 ▪ Fee R50 ▪ Closed Dec 25 ▪ Meals, cheese platters & picnics by appt - book prior to visit ▪ BYO picnic ▪ Table olives & olive oil ▪ Function venue (40-60 pax) ▪ Self-catering guest cottage (sleeps 4) ▪ Owner(s)/winemaker(s) Henk du Bruyn ▪ Viticulturist(s) Lemberg team ▪ 21ha/9ha (grenache, ptage, pinot, shiraz, hárslevelü, sauv, viog) ▪ 70t/10,000cs own label 53% red 36%

white 11% blanc de noir ▪ IPW ▪ PO Box 221 Tulbagh 6820 ▪ suzette@lemberg.co.za ▪ www.lemberg.co.za ▪ S 33° 18' 8.27" E 019° 6' 23.06" ▪ 🅜 footfalls.venue.ponytail ▪ **T +27 (0)21-300-1130**

☐ **Lenie's Hof** *see* Axe Hill
☐ **Leopard Frog Vineyards** *See Editor's Note*

Leopard's Leap Family Vineyards   Ⓨ Ⓨ Ⓒ Ⓐ

Wine is one of life's great pleasures, and for Hein and Hanneli Rupert-Koegelenberg of Leopard's Leap, it would be less enjoyable without food. Hence their increasingly exported label's emphasis on culinary harmony, and the brand-home being situated in Franschhoek, for many the food capital of South Africa. Responsibility takes the form of supporting the Cape Leopard Trust, lightening the carbon footprint with rooftop photovoltaic panels, and introducing a range of de-alcoholised wines.

Culinaria Collection

★★★★ **Pinot Noir** ⊘ From Elgin, as before, **17** ⑧⑦ shows abundant typical red berry fruit. Light, pliable & juicy, with deeper, darker concentrated finish. Oak, 30% new, well integrated.

★★★★ **Grand Vin** ⊘ ⓐ **17** ★★★★★ ⑨⓪ improves on **16** ⑧⑧ in cohesion of rich fruitcake & spicy cedar flavours. Oak, 40% new French, dialled down in better vintage. Appealingly dry yet rich & textured. As before, cab-led 4-way Bordeaux red from Darling & Stellenbosch fruit.

★★★★ **Muscat de Frontignan** Bold jasmine & sun-dried pineapple flavours on **18** ⑧⑧ rosé. Bright & refined, lovely acid freshness balances 80 g/l sugar, finishes crisp. More restrained than **17** ★★★ ⑧⓪.

★★★★ **Chenin Blanc** Ⓨ Happy trifecta of dryland, Paardeberg bushvines & partial barrel ferment make **17** ⑧⑦ complex & rich. Lovely interplay of ripe fruit, polished oak & vivid acid from 30% tank portion.

Pinot Noir-Chardonnay Ⓨ ★★★★ Subtle floral brush to gentle cranberry & nectarine flavours on **18** ⑧⑷ dry rosé. Juicy, light & vivid, good body & length. **Brut Méthode Cap Classique** ★★★★ Granny Smith apple & oyster aromas on dry **NV** ⑧⑤ bubbly from chardonnay, pinot noir & meunier. Tinge of red fruit & biscuit on defined finish. 24 months on lees.

Special Editions

Pinotage ⊘ ★★★★ Bold raspberry & cranberry with sheen of coffee & smoke on **17** ⑧⑷, from dryland Swartland bushvines. Light bodied & slight.

Family Collection

★★★★ **Cabernet Sauvignon** Ⓨ Dark-berried **16** ⑧⑥ improves on **15** ★★★★ ⑧⑷ with concentration & depth. Refined, velvety & plush without being overripe. Only older oak used for 15 months maturation.

Classic range

Cabernet Sauvignon Ⓨ ★★★ Lighter-styled **17** ⑧② is approachable & appealing in its floral, red-berry simplicity. Perdeberg & Swartland fruit, combo barrel & oak staves. **Merlot** Ⓨ ★★★ Cocoa edge to blue/black fruit on light-bodied **17** ⑧②, touch grippy & tannic from combo oak barrels (20%) & staves. **Shiraz** ⊘ ★★★★ Mocha-toned juiciness & ease on pliable **17** ⑧⑤. Light fynbos & toast from oak stave maturation in tank. **Cabernet Sauvignon-Merlot** Ⓨ ★★★ Light-bodied, fynbos-brushed berry compote is eminently sippable in **17** ⑧②. Near-equal billing for cab & merlot, ex Swartland & Stellenbosch. **Chardonnay-Pinot Noir** ⊘ ★★★★ Coral-hued **19** ⑧⑷ dry rosé improves on previous in crisp, vivacious pomegranate flavour; juicy & bright, ideal for summer. **Unwooded Chardonnay** ★★★ Soft lemon sherbet & pear drop appeal to light-bodied, rounded yet crisp **19** ⑧①. **Chenin Blanc** ⊘ ★★★ Pineapple & lemon zest on tropical-styled **19** ⑧②. Young, vibrant & succulent, with bright acidity. Fruit from Agter Paarl. **Sauvignon Blanc** ★★★ Improves on previous: **19** ⑧① taut, tangy citrus influence of cooler Elgin & Walker Bay grapes & longer lees contact. **Sparkling Chardonnay-Pinot Noir** ★★★ Pomegranate & blueberry on zippy **NV** ⑧② pink sparkler. Vivid berries balanced by acidity & lingering creamy lees notes.

Natura range 🅝

De-Alcoholised Classic Red ★★ **NV** ⑦② blend of cinsaut & cabernet offers berry cordial flavour & sweet/sour tang. Less than 0.5% alcohol, as next. **De-Alcoholised Classic White** ★★ Oddly sweet-yet-sour **NV** ⑦② blend of chenin & muscat is light in every way. — FM

Location/map: Franschhoek ▪ Map grid reference: C3 ▪ WO: Western Cape ▪ Est 2000 ▪ Tasting & sales Tue-Sat 9-5 Sun 11-5 ▪ Standard tasting R40/6 wines; Culinaria tasting R55/6 wines; Group tasting R65, booking essential

▪ Rotisserie lunches Wed–Sun 11.30–3.30 ▪ South African Table Wed–Sat from 12–1 ▪ Family Table Sun 12–3.30, booking essential ▪ Cooking demonstrations & classes on request ▪ Shop: lifestyle gifts, wine accessories, tableware, linen ware, kitchen utensils & equipment, food literature ▪ Child friendly ▪ Owner(s) Hanneli Rupert-Koegelenberg & Hein Koegelenberg ▪ Winemaker(s) Renier van Deventer (Nov 2014) ▪ 600,000cs own label 60% red 39% white 1% rosé ▪ PO Box 1 La Motte 7691 ▪ info@leopardsleap.co.za ▪ www.leopardsleap.co.za ▪ S 33° 53' 08.7" E 019° 04' 49.1" ▪ ⓦ unstrapped.global.zone ▪ T +27 (0)21-876-8002

☐ **Leopard Spot** see Ayama Wines
☐ **Leo Wyn** see Leeurivier Wyn & Olyf
☐ **Le Piquet** see Org de Rac

Le Pommier Wines

Like many other properties at the top of Stellenbosch's Helshoogte, this was originally an apple farm, hence the name. Today it has country-style accommodation, a restaurant and other family-friendly amenities. The boutique wines are made at Zorgvliet in the valley below, from mostly own vines, soon to include more cab franc and malbec, the latter thankfully spared the attentions of Jonathan, the late grape-snacking bull.

★★★★ **Cabernet Franc** Returns to guide in fine form after lengthy break. **18** ⑧⑦ rich & essency thanks to ripe berry fruit but ample freshness via lively acidity, firm tannins & minerality on lingering farewell. 30% new oak adds spice & tobacco nuances.

★★★★ **Red Blend** ⊘ Delightful fresh herbs, tealeaves & floral notes are layered with generous dark cherry, mulberry & blueberry fruits. **18** ⑧⑧ is elegant, has fine malleable tannins to match. Cab franc (68%) & merlot. No **17**.

★★★★ **Sauvignon Blanc** Tropical fruit aroma on **19** ★★★★ ⑧④ leads to nettle & mineral flavours, riper fig & gooseberry on the aftertaste. Clean-cut acidity supplies energy & freshness. Shade less intense, complex than **18** ⑧⑧ & previous.

Jonathan's Malbec ★★★☆ Alluring red fruit aromas backed by violets & spices, tannins silky smooth after 12 months in old barriques, **18** ⑧⑤ concludes with plum pudding persistence. **Rosé** ★★★ Sauvignon blanc with 2% cab franc for colour & red berry notes, **19** ⑧⓪ bright acidity, light & fresh, extended grapefruit & buchu finish. Discontinued: **Cabernet Sauvignon Reserve**, **Olivia**. — GM

Location/map: Stellenbosch ▪ Map grid reference: H4 ▪ WO: Banghoek ▪ Est/1stB 2003 ▪ Wine tasting Mon–Sun 11–5 ▪ Facilities for children ▪ Picnics ▪ Le Pommier Restaurant ▪ Country lodge & self-catering units ▪ Conferences & weddings ▪ Owner(s) Johan & Melanie van Schalkwyk ▪ Winemaker(s) Bernard le Roux (Zorgvliet) ▪ Viticulturist(s) Hannes Jansen van Vuuren ▪ 16ha/4.8ha (cab f, malbec, sauv) ▪ 5,000cs own label 45% red 55% white ▪ PO Box 1595 Stellenbosch 7599 ▪ gm@lepommier.co.za ▪ www.lepommier.co.za ▪ S 33° 55' 8.58" E 018° 55' 43.14" ▪ ⓦ mashing.port.rise ▪ T +27 (0)21-885-1269

Le Riche Wines

The younger generation Le Riches run this extremely well-reputed small family business and winery in the foothills of the Helderberg, not too far (well, still within the Stellenbosch WO) from where Etienne le Riche founded it nearly a quarter-century back. Son Christo commands the cellar, which substantially replicates the old Jonkershoek premises, complete with open fermenters, and pursues a specialisation in cabernet sauvignon. Grapes are sourced mostly elsewhere in Stellenbosch, the home vineyard being small. (Fittingly Christo is also a leading player in the ambitious Stellenbosch Cabernet Collective organisation.) Keeping it in the family, sister Yvonne, a Cape Wine Master, is now joined by their cousin, Francois le Riche, in marketing and general management. South Africa remains the main market, the balance widely exported.

★★★★☆ **Cabernet Sauvignon** Both vintages share the same fruit source & similar winemaking. Tad more new oak on riper, contemplative **16** ★★★★ ⑧⑦. **17** ⑨⓪ is more expressive, fresher, with bright fruit, clean cedary tannins & potential to age, though less intensity than **15** ⑨②.

★★★★☆ **Cabernet Sauvignon Reserve** ⓐ From Firgrove, Raithby & Jonkershoek fruit, **16** ⑨③ cuts a handsome figure, suave richness with velvet tannin integration. As for Cab, 24 months in oak, but 85% new here, tempers unctuous dark fruit. Shade less elegant, structured than **15** ★★★★★ ⑨⑤. Also in 1.5L.

★★★★ **Richesse** A similar 6-way, cab-led blend in **17** ⑧⑦ continues to charm with fresh spectrum of berry fruit in supple, streamlined framework. Older-oak matured, balanced, with a good few years ahead.

★★★★ **Chardonnay** Alluring citrus & toasted nut flavours from bunch pressing & equal parts tank/oak ferment (latter natural). Suppressed malo enhances zesty character, anchors confident Polkadraai fruit. **17** ★★★★★ ⑨⓪ tangy & vivacious step up on **16** ★★★★ ⑧⑤ & **15** ⑧⑦. — MW

Location/WO: Stellenbosch ▪ Map: Helderberg ▪ Map grid reference: B1 ▪ Est 1996 ▪ 1stB 1997 ▪ Tasting, sales & cellar tours Mon-Fri 8.30-4.30 Sat by appt ▪ Closed all pub hols ▪ Hanepoot grapes (Feb & Mar) ▪ Owner(s) Le Riche Wines (Pty) Ltd ▪ Cellarmaster(s) Christo le Riche ▪ Winemaker(s) Christo le Riche (Jan 2010), with Mark Daniels (Sep 2000) ▪ 70t/9,000cs own label 90% red 10% white ▪ PO Box 5274 Helderberg 7135 ▪ wine@leriche.co.za ▪ www.leriche.co.za ▪ S 34° 0'52.87" E 018° 48' 9.06" ▪ 🗺 cleverest.promenades.thirst ▪ **T +27 (0)21-842-3472**

☐ **Les Coteaux** see Mont du Toit Kelder

Le Sueur Wines

The home of Louis van der Riet's project has moved from De Krans (where he is winemaker) to Jakkalsvlei on the Garden Route – the wines are available there for tasting. While the aim remains to strengthen perceptions of Klein Karoo dry table wines, the drought which has affected the area so badly has meant having to look beyond its boundaries for the latest releases. A fascinating concept in wine sales means that the Wild Card wines are also being sold 'on tap' (like draught beer) in many Garden Route restaurants.

Le Sueur range
★★★★☆ **Paradoks** The usual 50/50 blend of pinotage's paradoxically lighter parents, but now cinsaut & pinot noir ex Elgin & Swartland. **18** ⑨② perfumed interplay of red & darker fruit on aromas; fresh & light-feeling, but firm & full at just 12.5% alcohol. First tasted since **16** ★★★★★ ⑨⑤ & **15** ★★★★ ⑧⑧.

★★★★ **Kluisenaar** Naturally fermented chenin blanc from Klein Karoo. **18** ★★★★★ ⑨② has a richness of texture & core of sweet peachy fruit, & a light, fresh grip - making for a well-balanced, rather elegant whole with a lingering finish. More intense than **17** ⑧⑨. Old oak, as Paradoks.

Wild Card range
★★★★ **Sauvignon Blanc** Unusually undemonstrative for the variety, but **18** ★★★☆ ⑧③ ex Klein Karoo is fresh & pleasing enough in its quiet way, though less expressive than **17** ⑧⑥.

Queen of Hearts Merlot ⊘ ★★★☆ Ripe fruitcake on **18** ⑧⑤ with a spearmint note. Balanced, smoothly easygoing but with a good grip; few grams of sugar add fullness not sweetness. Old oak. WO W Cape. — TJ

Location: Herbertsdale ▪ Map: Klein Karoo & Garden Route ▪ Map grid reference: C5 ▪ WO: Klein Karoo/Western Cape/Elgin-Swartland ▪ Est 1987 ▪ 1stB 2014 ▪ Tasting & sales at Jakkalsvlei, booking essential ▪ Wild Card tasting & sales at Oak Barrel Wine Shop ▪ Owner(s)/winemaker(s) Louis van der Riet ▪ 23t/1,500cs own label 40% red 60% white ▪ PO Box 28 Calitzdorp 6660 ▪ louis@lesueurwines.co.za ▪ www.lesueurwines.co.za ▪ S 33° 59' 15.31" E 021° 43' 9.33" ▪ 🗺 outcomes.smiles.married ▪ **T +27 (0)79-602-2161**

☐ **L'Horizon** see L'Avenir Vineyards
☐ **L'Huguenot** see Val de Vie & Polo Club Wines

Libby's Pride Wines

With star sign Leo, which she associates with strength and pride, Elizabeth 'Libby' Peterson is an entrepreneurial vintner focused on developing her good-value Libby's Pride label through a new BEE partnership with Cloof Wine Estate, under whose heading her wines are now listed in our guide.

Location: Darling ▪ Tasting & sales by appt ▪ Owner(s) Elizabeth Petersen ▪ Winemaker(s) Hennie Huskisson (2019, Cloof Wine Estate) ▪ Viticulturist(s) Peter Duckitt (2019, Cloof Wine Estate) ▪ info@libbyspridewines.com ▪ www.libbyspridewines.com ▪ **T +27 (0)82-745-5550**

☐ **Liberator** see The Liberator

Libertas Vineyards & Estates (NEW)

Launched in 2019, Libertas Vineyards & Estates is Distell's premium- and fine-wine company whose purpose is to support and drive the upselling and premiumisation of SA wine on the global stage. Headed by Kay Nash, the company will, among others, renew focus on Distell's top-tier wine brands, many of them revered names in SA wine culture. The company manages The Vinoteque (www.vinoteque.co.za), the online shopping experience for premium and well-matured wines, as well as wine brands Allesverloren, Alto, Durbanville Hills, Flat Roof Manor, Fleur du Cap, Inception, Nederburg, Plaisir de Merle, Pongrácz and Zonnebloem. The heritage assets of Chateau Libertas, Zonnebloem, Oude Libertas and the Libertas Tabernacle, the irreplaceable wine library with iconic SA wines, form part of the company's focus.

Location: Stellenbosch ▪ Est 2019 ▪ Closed to public ▪ Owner(s) Distell Group Limited ▪ Winemaker(s)/viticul-turist(s) see under Allesverloren, Alto, Durbanville Hills, Fleur du Cap, Nederburg, Plaisir de Merle, Pongrácz & Zonnebloem ▪ Cnr Adam Tas & Oude Libertas Rds Stellenbosch 7600 ▪ info@libertasvineyards.co.za ▪ www.libertasvineyards.co.za ▪ T +27 (0)21-809-8200

☐ **Liberty** *see* Piekenierskloof Wine Company

Lieben Wines ⓠ

A 'big year', was 2019 for widely consulted Walker Bay-based winemaker Alwyn Liebenberg (advisory roles have taken him to emerging Chinese regions Ningxia and Yunnan). Origami-themed Lieben's expansion included not only a trio of new wines (including a Roussanne, inspiring future exploration of rare-in-SA varieties), but also five gins distilled on an organic Overberg farm, all exported to Europe and China.

★★★★☆ **Cabernet Franc** (NEW) Confident styling on fynbos- & cocoa-brushed **17** ⑨② from Franschhoek. Good concentration of black fruit & grip from 16 months in oak, 30% new. Partial wild ferment adds complexity & length.

★★★★ **Chardonnay** Has trademark citrus but is broad & creamy from 50% barrel ferment & 16 months in seasoned oak. **17** ⑧⑥ grapes from McGregor, not Stellenbosch like last-tasted **14** ★★★★ ⑧⑤.

★★★★ **Chenin Blanc** (NEW) From 38 year old untrellised single-vineyard, **18** ⑧⑥ is savoury, with fresh acidity & stonefruit appeal. 9 months in old oak add breadth before a persistent finish.

★★★★ **Roussanne** (NEW) Gentle body & concentration, with lifted nectarine & apple on **18** ⑧⑦. Like other whites, 50/50 barrel & tank ferment with some skin contact. Also 9 months in older oak.

Pinot Noir ★★★★ Light & tangy **18** ⑧⑤ follows last-tasted **13** ⑧④ in easy cherry & berry succulence. Walker Bay grapes allowed to ferment naturally before inoculation halfway through. — WB, FM

Location: Hermanus ▪ WO: Walker Bay/Franschhoek/McGregor ▪ Est 2005 ▪ 1stB 2008 ▪ Visits by appt ▪ Gin ▪ Owner(s) Alwyn Liebenberg ▪ Cellarmaster(s)/winemaker(s) Alwyn Liebenberg (Jun 2005) ▪ 54 Siffie Crescent, Vermont 7201 ▪ alwyn@lieben.wine ▪ www.lieben.wine ▪ T +27 (0)82-610-2279

Lievland Vineyards ⓠ ♿

'A sleeping beauty of a property' was how José Conde described Lievland, on the slopes of the Simonsberg between Stellenbosch and Paarl, when the MAN Family Wines venture bought it as its new home. 'It just needs some loving care and a confidence boost.' And a resplendent rooster – Piet – which confidently struts the Cape Dutch werf and loaned his image rights to the limited-release Hanekraai blend! With renovations to the tasting room and cellar (once birthplace to a much-loved and -lauded shiraz and SA's first Natural Sweet) complete, and new vineyards planted, the awakening has begun.

★★★★ **Cabernet Sauvignon** (NEW) Gentle, softly rounded & silky **17** ⑧⑨ offers trademark Xmas cake flavour with cedar spice. Dabs cinsaut (8%) & syrah, 13 months in oak, just 5% new. Paarl & Stellenbosch grapes.

★★★★ **Old Vine Chenin Blanc** (NEW) Lovely honeyed pineapple on **18** ⑧⑨ balanced by zingy stonefruit vibrancy of 50% tank-fermented portion. Harmonious, rich, structured & long. From 2 old bushvine blocks.

★★★★☆ **Oogappel Chenin Blanc** (NEW) Peach cobbler spice appeal to rounded **18** ⑨⓪ off high Simonsberg vineyard (Stellenbosch WO). Multidimensional, with pear & quince fruit in harmony with acid. Added complexity from seasoned-barrel ferment & 10 months on lees.

★★★★ **Hanekraai Sauvignon Blanc-Semillon** (NEW) Confident, textured **18** ⑧⑦ 65/35 blend from 2 oldest blocks on Lievland (1983 & 1991). Typical grapefruit tang with creamy breadth from long lees contact & semillon portion skin- & barrel-fermented.

Bushvine Pinotage (NEW) ★★★★ Brambly blue fruit & muted spice on **17** ⑧⑤. Lithe & sinewy succulence, with just 15% new oak for 13-month maturation. Splash old-vine cinsaut. **Liefkoos Rosé** (NEW) ★★★★ Light perfume to dry pomegranate crunch of **18** 84, 50/50 syrah & mourvèdre from estate vines with Provence styling & hue. Chalky grip & vivid acidity. — FM

Location/map: Stellenbosch ▪ Map grid reference: F1 ▪ WO: Paarl/Simonsberg–Stellenbosch/Coastal/Stellenbosch ▪ Tasting & sales Mon-Sun 10-4 ▪ Closed Good Fri, Dec 25 & Jan 1 ▪ Owner(s) MAN Vintners (Pty) Ltd ▪ Cellarmaster(s) Tyrrel Myburgh ▪ Winemaker(s) Riaan Möller ▪ 3,500cs own label ▪ PO Box 37 Klapmuts 7625 ▪ info@lievland.co.za ▪ www.lievland.co.za ▪ S 33° 50' 29.5" E 018° 52' 34.8" ▪ kindest.quieter.hedge ▪ **T +27 (0)21-875-3079**

☐ **Lighthouse Series** see Benguela Cove Lagoon Wine Estate
☐ **Like Father Like Son** see Bon Courage Estate

L'illa

The Catalan name (pronounced leeya) means 'island', alluding to the farm in Eilandia, Robertson, where the family of Nadia Cilliers has been for 6 generations. It produces the grapes for a Noble Late Harvest, made by Nadia and husband Gordon Newton Johnson in the Newton Johnson cellar in Hemel-en-Aarde.

★★★★☆ **Noble Late Harvest** Botrytis dessert from 1976 chenin, wild ferment in oak, barrel aged year, but fruit is king in **17** 92. Apricot & Seville marmalade, barley sugar & almond savouriness; full sweet but gets the balance right, brightening acidity gives a delicious tangy effect. No **16**. 375 ml. — CR

Location: Hermanus ▪ WO: Eilandia ▪ Est/1stB 2006 ▪ Tasting & sales at Newton Johnson Vineyards ▪ Owner(s)/winemaker(s) Gordon & Nadia Newton Johnson ▪ Viticulturist(s) AA Cilliers (Jan 1973) ▪ (chenin) ▪ 220cs own label 100% white ▪ PO Box 225 Hermanus 7200 ▪ gordon@newtonjohnson.com, nadia@newtonjohnson.com ▪ www.newtonjohnson.com ▪ **T +27 (0)28-312-3862**

☐ **Lime Road** see Havana Hills
☐ **Limestone Rocks** see Springfontein Wine Estate
☐ **Limietberg Site Exclusive** see Doolhof Wine Estate
☐ **Lindenhof** see Boland Cellar

Lingen

Newly crowned Diners Club Young Winemaker of the Year and former Cape Winemakers Guild protégé Rüdger van Wyk vinifies fruit from the Krige family's tiny vineyard at the neighbouring Stark-Condé cellar in Stellenbosch's Jonkershoek Valley. In conversion to organic, the vineyard also has some mourvèdre and grenache which will form part of the blend from the 2018 vintage.

★★★★★ **Lingen** Understated & refined, **17** 94 shiraz (66%), petit verdot & petite sirah blend thrills with its silky mouthful of spicy blue & black fruits, superb structure & composure. Deep inky, earthy notes. Complex winemaking with 22 months in French, Hungarian & American oak, 30% new. — FM

Location: Stellenbosch ▪ WO: Jonkershoek Valley ▪ Est 2003 ▪ 1stB 2008 ▪ Tasting & sales at Stark-Condé Wines ▪ Owner(s) JD Krige Family Trust ▪ Cellarmaster(s) José Conde (2003) ▪ Winemaker(s) Rüdger van Wyk (2017) ▪ Viticulturist(s) Andrew Klinck ▪ 7ha/2ha (grenache, mourv, p verdot, shiraz) ▪ 14t/508cs own label 100% red ▪ PO Box 389 Stellenbosch 7599 ▪ info@stark-conde.co.za ▪ www.stark-conde.co.za ▪ **T +27 (0)21-861-7700**

Linton Park Wines

The Wellington home-farm traces its roots back to the 17th century, when it was named for the winding Slange Rivier ('Snake River') which still flows down Groenberg Mountain. Today the team are part of London-based multinational Camellia, crafting premium estate wines as well as the everyday Rhino ranges.

Linton Park Estate range

★★★★ **Malbec** From single block, **17** 89 shows plenty of promise. Big structure & flavours (black plums, vanilla, lavender & violets), smoky oak spices & fresh acidity. Should improve.

★★★★ **Merlot** Sweetly fruited **16** 87 is plump & appetising, offering soft pudding spices, plum-cake, prunes, chocolate & smoke. Ripe but firm tannins (helped by year French oak), good acid & length.

★★★★ **Pinotage** Lots going on in **16** 87, from black cherries, sweet spices, leather & smoke, with over-arching coffee/mocha highlights. Nicely balanced palate, with good tannins & structure.

★★★★ **Shiraz** ⊘ Appealing black-fruit entry on **16** ⑧⑧ given perfumed lift with liquorice & violets, fresh mint tweak & 40% American oak make their presence felt at soft, spicy finish.

★★★★ **De Slange Rivier** ⊘ Bordeaux red changes to 3-way blend (equal cab & cab franc plus 20% merlot) in **17** ⑧⑦ (**15** ⑧⑦) cab & merlot). Firm tannins, attractive aniseed notes & roasty, toasty oak (50% new) vie with red- & black-berried fruit. No **16**. WO W Cape.

★★★★ **Wild Ferment Chardonnay** ⓺ Rich & creamy **17** ⑧⑥ spreads lavish oak-derived flavours - butter, toast & spice - over tinned mango & melon. Interesting notes of nuts, muesli & smoke developing, suggesting more to come.

Cabernet Sauvignon ★★★★ Solid example, **17** ⑧④ mixes blackcurrants, cherries, plums & tobacco with chewy tannins & a warm finish. WO W Cape, as next. **Café Cabernet** ★★★ Popular 'coffee' style **18** ⑧① sure to find fans, with ripe black fruit & easy-drinking sprinkle of sugar at the finish. **Café Malbec** ⓺ ★★★ All present & correct, with black fruit, coffee & chocolate showing quite powerfully on **17** ⑧②. **Chardonnay** ★★★ Toffee apple notes on **17** ⑧③, pleasant enough but lacks fruity freshness of previous. Year in oak, 50% new. **Unwooded Chardonnay** ⓺ ★★★ Plenty of tinned & cooked fruit on **17** ⑧⓪, weighty on palate, needs drop more acid to balance. **Sauvignon Blanc** ★★★ Shy **18** ⑦⑦ has subtle pineapple fruit, 3 months lees time add some richness. **Méthode Cap Classique Rosé** ⓺ ★★★ Equal pinot noir & chardonnay **NV** ⑧② dry fizz spent 36 months on lees acquiring its pretty onion-skin hue, full body & bubbles showing plenty of salty tang. **Méthode Cap Classique Brut** ⓺ ★★★ Fizzer from 50/50 pinot noir & chardonnay, **NV** ⑧② had 36 months on lees giving rich flavours of nuts, toffee, salty yeast.

Red Rhino range

Cabernet Sauvignon ⓺ ★★★ Plenty of herbs & spices on easy-drinking **17** ⑧⓪. Unwooded, as all reds in this range. **Merlot** ⊘ ★★★ Drier than previous, **17** ⑧⓪ soft black fruit & herbal notes add to charm & early-drinking appeal. **Pinotage** ⓺ ★★ Overwhelming spice notes a detraction in just-dry **17** ⑦③. **Shiraz** ⓺ ★★★ Uncomplicated drinking fun, **17** ⑧① melange of red & black fruit, touches of tar & fresh herbs. WO W Cape, as all except Pinotage.

White Rhino range

. . . .

Chardonnay ⓦ ★★★ Cheerful, characterful **18** ⑧① gives burst of ripe tropical fruit (litchi, melon) for happy summer sipping. Unoaked & WO W Cape, as all these.

Chenin Blanc ★★ Neutral fruit on **18** ⑦⑥, light bodied, perfect for a summer spritzer. **Sauvignon Blanc** ★★★ Zesty **18** ⑧⓪ improves on previous with all flavours present & correct (limes, lemons) & fresh sherbet finish.

Discontinued: **Reserve range**, **The Rhino range**. — CM

Location/map: Wellington ▪ Map grid reference: C2 ▪ WO: Wellington/Western Cape ▪ Est 1995 ▪ 1stB 1998 ▪ Tasting & sales Mon–Fri 9-4.30 Sat/pub hols 10-3 ▪ Cellar tours by appt ▪ Uncorked Restaurant Tue–Sat 11-3 ▪ Owner(s) Camellia PLC UK ▪ Winemaker(s) JG Auret (2007) ▪ Viticulturist(s) Rudolf Jansen van Vuuren (2012) ▪ 294ha/75ha (cabs s/f, malbec, merlot, ptage, shiraz, chard, sauv) ▪ 550t/80,000cs own label 60% red 40% white ▪ IPW, WIETA ▪ PO Box 1234 Wellington 7654 ▪ tasting@lintonparkwines.co.za ▪ www.lintonparkwines.co.za ▪ S 33° 36' 40.1" E 019° 2' 15.0" ▪ ⌖ types.mountainous.powers ▪ **T +27 (0)21-873-1625**

☐ **Lion Creek** *see* Napier Vineyards
☐ **Lionel Smit Collaboration Series** *see* Scions of Sinai
☐ **Lion's Drift** *see* Silkbush Mountain Vineyards
☐ **Lion's Pride** *see* Stellenrust
☐ **Lions River Vineyards** *see* Highgate Wine Estate
☐ **Lionsway** *see* Boland Cellar
☐ **Lisha Nelson Signature Wines** *see* Nelson Family Vineyards
☐ **Lismore Estate Vineyards** *See* Editor's Note

Litigo Wines

After-hours vintner Eben van Wyk focuses on small-scale, minimum-intervention wines, but vintage 2018, the third consecutive dry season, saw 'small' reduced to a minuscule ±1,000 bottles, sold on allocation and to a few retailers. With a second varietal wine in mind, chardonnay has joined pinot noir on the Overberg farm near Shaw's Mountain which Eben owns with Crystallum's Peter-Allan Finlayson, who is also the co-winecrafter. In the meantime, Eben's day job as trademark lawyer helps fund 'this amazing venture'.

★★★★☆ **Pinot Noir** Very ripe, yet **18** ★★★★ (88) also quite austere, with toned-down mint & black cherry features. Just a little flesh, should emerge with short ageing, but not the generosity, enticement of **17** (92). Spontaneous ferment; ±25% wholebunch; 15% new oak, 11 months.— AL

Location: Hermanus ▪ WO: Overberg ▪ Est 2011 ▪ 1stB 2012 ▪ Closed to public ▪ Owner(s) Eben van Wyk ▪ Winemaker(s) Eben van Wyk & Peter-Allan Finlayson (both 2011) ▪ 2t/200cs own label 100% red ▪ Postnet Suite 134 Private Bag X1005 Claremont 7735 ▪ info@litigowines.com ▪ www.litigowines.com ▪ **T +27 (0)82-803-4503**

☐ **Little Rock** *see* Mont Rochelle Hotel & Vineyard
☐ **Live-A-Little** *see* Stellar Winery
☐ **Lobola** *see* Taillard Family Wines

Lodestone Wines & Olives   (♀) (¶¶) (◎)

Owners Ingrid and Jon Tonkin have rung the changes at their boutique winery in Plettenberg Bay, putting globe-trotting Jaco van der Watt in charge of the cellar, and Jon 'as his assistant'. Jaco's task in the cool maritime climate is to craft wines of greater complexity and body while retaining natural elegance and crispness.

★★★★ **Pinot Noir** ⊘ Bright cherry & raspberry fruit, understated but good presence at just 12% alcohol courtesy cool maritime origin. On **18** (86), like debut **17** ★★★☆ (84), fresh acidity is tempered by tealeaf tannins, well-judged older oak.

Miss Lottie Rosé ★★★☆ Was 'Stoepsit'. Deep pink **19** (84) from pinot noir, happy & flavoursome glassful of berries & cream, technically dry but a few grams sugar nicely balance the tangy acidity. Tasted pre-bottling, as next 3. **Chardonnay** ★★★ Faint lemon tones commendably undimmed by oak (only 3 months on staves), **19** (81) light (12% alcohol) & brief. **Strandloper Sauvignon Blanc** ★★★☆ Green gooseberry & grassy notes, a mineral seam, **19** (83) good weight & vinosity courtesy 14% alcohol (high for Plettenberg Bay) & touch sugar. **Sauvignon Blanc-Semillon** ★★★☆ 26% semillon adds subtle & appealing hay & waxy tone to **19** (83). Good poise & length. **Stonechat Méthode Cap Classique Brut Rosé** (⅌) ★★★★ Characterful sunset pink dry sparkler with cured meat & strawberry notes from pinot noir (70%), Granny Smith apple acidity from chardonnay. **16** (85) 15 months on lees, so no bread/brioche whiffs yet, but impressively fine bubbles, creamy mousse. Not tasted: **The Jimdog**. — CvZ

Location/WO: Plettenberg Bay ▪ Map: Klein Karoo & Garden Route ▪ Map grid reference: C1 ▪ Est 2012 ▪ 1stB 2014 ▪ Tasting & sales Tue-Sun 11-4 in high season, with reduced opening times in quieter seasons (see Facebook for details) ▪ Fee R10/tasting per wine, R20/tasting for MCC & pinot noir ▪ Closed Good Fri, mid-May to mid-Jun, Dec 25 & Jan 1 ▪ Light seasonal meals; cheese & charcuterie platters ▪ Farm produce ▪ MTB trail ▪ Owner(s) Tonkin family ▪ Winemaker(s) Jaco van der Watt ▪ 4.3ha (pinot, chard, sauv, sem) ▪ 28t/3,000cs own label 15% red 35% white 15% rosé 35% MCC ▪ PO Box 2747 Plettenberg Bay 6600 ▪ info@lodestonewines.com ▪ www.lodestonewines.co.za ▪ S 33° 56' 27.70" E 023° 26' 4.20" ▪ 🚗 insulated. invitingly.complexism ▪ **T +27 (0)44-534-8015/+27 (0)82-600-7835**

Loki Wines   (NEW)

Durbanite Nick le Roux, latterly Cape winelands based, a specialist wine consultant, with certification from the Court of Master Sommeliers, in 2016 started sourcing fruit from 'cherry-picked' vineyards in Elgin and Stellenbosch to make his own small-batch wines. He avoids additives and machinery 'at all costs', and personally bottles each wine and signs the label. Hopefully we'll get a taste next edition.

Location: Somerset West ▪ Est 2016 ▪ 1stB 2017 ▪ Closed to public ▪ Owner(s)/winemaker(s) Nick le Roux ▪ ±333cs own label 70% red 30% white ▪ nick@therelouxcollective.com

Lomond   (♀) (¶¶) (◎)

Ex-Simonsig winemaker Hannes Meyer celebrated a double maiden in 2019: his first harvest at this pioneer estate in the cool-climate Cape Agulhas appellation, in its brand-new 600-ton cellar. There's a focus on sauvignon here, with a further 10 ha planted in the past year, but 18 different soil types make it possible to produce a wide range of wines including a number of distinctive single-vineyard bottlings, each named for a floral species from this biodiversity hotspot, part of the Walker Bay Fynbos Conservancy.

Icon range

★★★★ **Snowbush** Ⓡ Unoaked sauvignon, nouvelle balanced by oaked semillon, viognier, in **13** (86). Good weight, zestily clean conclusion - if a bit light on fruit intensity compared to **12** ★★★★☆.

Single Vineyard range

★★★★ **Pincushion Sauvignon Blanc** Ⓡ Alcohol toned down in vibrant **17** (89) to offer greater elegance. Floral aromas & salad of green tropical fruit, including lime, honeydew melon & greengage.

★★★★ **Sugarbush Sauvignon Blanc** Ⓡ After blowsy **16** ★★★☆ (83), **17** (87) returns to form with fresh fig, guava & gooseberry fruit, stony minerality, clean finish.

Phantom Pinot Noir ★★★☆ Pot-pourri aroma leads to forest berry flavours, **18** (85) more intense than light appearance suggests, with subtle spice & earthiness, silky texture & pleasing 12.5% alcohol. No **17**. Not tasted: **Cat's Tail Syrah**, **Conebush Syrah**.

Ultra Premium range

★★★★☆ **Belladonna SMV** Ⓑ Named for shrubland lily, **17** (90) shiraz with 20% mourvèdre, splash viognier is fynbos-scented, an intriguing hint of fynbos honey carrying through to palate. Fresh & elegant, with ripe red fruit, & spice from 14 months in 25% new oak.

Not tasted: **Candelabra Cabernet Sauvignon**.

Estate range

★★★★ **Syrah** Smooth, after 14 months in mostly older oak, balanced, though over 14.5% alcohol, complex **16** (88) has plenty of red & black fruit, also some vegetal rhubarb & tomato, smoky bacon & pepper.

★★★★ **Sauvignon Blanc** ✓ Fynbos & nettle aromas on **19** (88), same pleasing racy-yet-rounded character as **17** (87) from 6 weeks on lees & ripeness of the lime & white peach fruit. **18** not tasted.

★★★★ **SSV** ✓ 15% semillon & splash viognier, both fermented/aged 4 months in 3rd-fill oak, add weight, texture to fresh, zingy sauvignon in balanced **17** (87), redolent of peach & passionfruit.

★★★★☆ **Noble Late Harvest** Ⓡ From botrytised viognier, 9 months in barrel, liquid gold **17** (94) syrupy sweet yet uncloying thanks to racy acidity, tangy apricot & pineapple fruit, ginger preserve-like bite & clean finish. Just 7.4% alcohol. Only 900 bottles of 500 ml.

Merlot ★★★☆ Red plums, cherry cola & pinch of cinnamon on juicy, medium-bodied **17** (85), portion aged 14 months in French oak. **Merlot Rosé** ★★★ Coral pink **19** (82) has rosepetal perfume but is dry, smooth, with spanspek melon as well as red berry flavours. — JG

Location: Gansbaai ▪ Map: Southern Cape ▪ Map grid reference: C8 ▪ WO: Cape Agulhas ▪ Est 1999 ▪ 1stB 2005 ▪ Tasting & sales Mon-Sun 10-4 ▪ Food platters ▪ Craft beer ▪ Part of Walker Bay Conservancy ▪ Winemaker(s) Hannes Meyer (Jun 2018) ▪ 1,100ha/120ha (merlot, mourv, shiraz, nouvelle, sauv, sem) ▪ 850t 60% red 40% white ▪ PO Box 1269 Gansbaai 7200 ▪ info@lomond.co.za ▪ www.lomond.co.za ▪ S 34° 34' 12" E 019° 26' 24.00" ▪ whittle.shrubbery.joyriding ▪ **T +27 (0)28-388-0095/+27 (0)82-908-0099**

☐ **Longmarket** *see* Woolworths
☐ **Long Mountain** *see* Thor Vintners

Longridge Wine Estate

Owned by two families, Dutch Van der Laans and South African Raats, this winery on the slopes of the Helderberg might have to invest in a larger trophy cabinet to accommodate the recent spate of hardware from local and international critics and judges, including a trio of gold medals ex the Grand International Organic Wine Awards. Committed to a vine-to-bottle 'natural first' approach, Longridge has now launched the first wines labelled as made from organically grown grapes. Assisting viticulturist, winemaker and MD Jasper Raats with his 'green' responsibilities in the vineyard is newcomer Huey Janse van Rensburg.

Ultra Premium range

★★★★☆ **Misterie** (NEW) Ⓑ Intended to raise the bar for SA merlot (& priced accordingly), **15** (93) very polished & modern but not overwhelmingly so, plenty of latent structure from 2 years oak (old & new) for lengthy cellaring. Dash cab franc adds spearmint top note, touch extra grip. Helderberg grapes, as all these.

★★★★☆ **Ekliptika** ⓐ Flagship & Bordeaux blend, name & front-label intended to convey alignment of house's winemaking approach with biodynamic principles. **16** ⑨③ compact dark fruit, oystershell minerality, well-controlled grape & oak tannins for decade-plus ageing or decanting now. Cab, cab franc with merlot, like shade more impressive **15** ★★★★★ ⑨⑤.

★★★★☆ **Clos du Ciel** ⓧ ⓐ Suave barrel-fermented chardonnay from organic, low-cropped single-vineyard. Hallmark white peach, honey & almond nuances overlay refined citrus. Present oak nudge (30% new) in **16** ⑨④, but remains a poised & respectworthy glassful. Also in magnum.

★★★★☆ **Ou Steen Enkel Wingerd Chenin Blanc** ⓥ ⓐ ⓦ Small, low-yield, 38 year old block shows beautiful balance, vivacious acidity underpinning 14.4 g/l sugar. **17** ★★★★★ ⑨⑤ less oxidative than **16** ⑨②, less boldly oaked; the barrel ferment/year on lees adds support, not flavour or sweetness.

Premium range

★★★★ **Cabernet Sauvignon** Cedar-toned **16** ⑧⑦ raises the bar on similarly styled **15** ★★★☆ ⑧⑤ with impressively dry structuring tannins, lively seam of acidity, plush cassis fruit.

★★★★ **Merlot** Younger sibling of Misterie is very good in its own right, for earlier drinking. **17** ⑧⑦ sweet plum dusted with savoury & vanilla oak spice, smooth but with sufficient grip for food.

★★★★ **Pinotage** Trendily light-styled, unlike the other reds here. Variety's natural verve an appealing contrast with sweet-fruited flavours (strawberry & mulberry) on **18** ⑧⑨. Satisfying dry finish & smart oaking for easygoing summer drinking with a touch of style.

★★★★ **Organic Chardonnay** ⓥ Complex handling in the cellar: portions fermented in barrel, 'egg' & amphora; year in barrel. **17** ⑧⑨ lemon & lime with barley sugar hint, lovely weight, chalky minerality.

★★★★ **Organic Chenin Blanc** ⓥ Delicate grass, blackcurrant & white peach, understated oak barrel influence, **17** ⑧⑨ is all about the palate: tightly wound, tense acidity, salty lift - intriguing & exciting.

★★★★ **Edelgoud** ⓥ Ginger & honey, fynbos & umami, oak-matured **16** ⑧⑧ Noble Late Harvest from riesling is a more savoury, less sweet & weighty botrytis dessert style, underscored by light 11.4% alcohol.

The Emily ★★★☆ Rosé from mostly chardonnay & a little oaked Elgin pinot noir. **18** ⑧④ lavender & berries, tangy lemon acidity, just-dry impression. Dedicated to 'brave women fighting for what is right, all over the world'.

Méthode Cap Classique range

★★★★ **Brut Rosé NV** ⑧⑦ Sunset-hued sparkler, attractive interweave of toast on nose & palate from 40 months on lees, gentle berries from 40% pinot noir, verve & floral notes ex chardonnay.

★★★★☆ **Brut Vintage Reserve** ⓐ In best years only. **14** ⑨③ zero-dosage bubbly from chardonnay has quiet presence, exceptional depth & richness from 60 months on lees & pinpoint acid balance. Bone-dry house styling, as for last-made chardonnay/pinot noir **09** ⑨③.

★★★★ **Chardonnay-Pinot Noir Brut** Minority pinot noir (20%) makes its presence felt in energetic **NV** ⑧⑥ fizz with candy apple whiffs, satisfying weight. Just 40 months on lees, already showing honey & bruised apple development.— CvZ

Location: Stellenbosch ▪ Map: Helderberg ▪ Map grid reference: C1 ▪ WO: Stellenbosch/Western Cape ▪ Est 1841 ▪ 1stB 1992 ▪ Tasting & sales Mon-Sat 11-6; booking essential for groups of 8+ ▪ Closed Good Fri & Dec 25 ▪ Cellar tours by appt ▪ Longridge Restaurant T +27 (0)21-855-4082, restaurant@longridge.co.za ▪ Tour groups ▪ Gift shop ▪ Owner(s) Van der Laan & Raats families ▪ Cellarmaster(s) Jasper Raats ▪ Winemaker(s) Jasper Raats & Hendrien de Munck ▪ Viticulturist(s) Jasper Raats & Huey Janse van Rensburg ▪ 38ha (cab, merlot, pinot, chard, chenin) ▪ 215t/30,000cs own label 45% red 50% white 5% MCC ▪ Suite 116 Private Bag X4 Die Boord 7613 ▪ info@longridge.co.za ▪ www.longridge.co.za ▪ S 34° 0' 55.2" E 018° 49' 60.0" ▪ 🖵 flows. habitats.recliners ▪ **T +27 (0)21-855-2005**

☐ **Lookout** see Leopard's Leap Family Vineyards
☐ **Lord Somerset** see Somerset Wines

Lord's Wines

ⓧ ⓜ ⓞ ⓐ

Now family owned, Lord's boutique winery was established 15 years ago by a group of cricket fanatics among indigenous fynbos high in the mountains behind McGregor town. Beside the thatched cellar is a new function venue with spectacular views of the vines and valley below, making it much in demand as a dramatic wedding setting and for other celebrations, all perfectly accompanied by their MCC sparklers.

Limited Releases

★★★★ **Three Barrel Shiraz** ⊛ Ample spice (clove, star anise, cinnamon) interleave ripe red & black cherries & plums in characterful **16** ⑧⑨, warm breadth tweaked up with hints of cough drops & eucalyptus before lengthy finish. 100% French oak, 50% new. First since **12** ⑧⑧.

Lord's Wines range

★★★★ **Chardonnay** Barrel-fermented **18** ⑧⑥ is rich & fat, with caramelised grapefruit, toffee & candied limes. Citrus acidity races through & adds freshness & length. **17** untasted.

★★★★ **Méthode Cap Classique Brut** Change in style for tight & nervy **NV** ⑧⑦ sparkler: moves to zero dosage, adding austere acidity to creamy apple pie fruit. Appealing savoury notes, now from 28 months on lees, should develop further on cork. Pinot noir & chardonnay (70/30).

Pinot Noir The Legend ⊘ ★★★ Ripe raspberries & cherries mingle with attractive spices from 100% French oak. A little more fruit intensity at the finish would improve **18** ⑧⓪. **Shiraz** ★★★ Crunchy black fruit with smoked meats & cinnamon sticks combine in youthful **16** ⑧②. Time needed to knit & resolve. **Pinot Noir Rosé** ★★★☆ Explosion of berry fruit (rasp/cran/straw) on dry **19** ⑧③, crisp acidity & sherbet finish. Improved intensity from previous. **Sauvignon Blanc** ★★★ Multi-stage picking in **19** ⑧⓪ mixes the 'g's - gooseberry, grass, granadilla & guava - in delicious fruit bomb, with better acid than previous. **Méthode Cap Classique Brut Rosé** ★★★☆ From pinot noir, **NV** ⑧③ sparkling returns to form, gains savoury intensity from 18 months on lees, balanced on palate by soft red plums & apples, clean fresh finish. — CM

Location/WO: McGregor ▪ Map: Robertson ▪ Map grid reference: D7 ▪ Est 2005 ▪ 1stB 2006 ▪ Tasting, sales & cellar tours Mon-Fri 9-4 Sat 10-4 Sun/pub hols 10-2 ▪ Light meals ▪ Function & wedding venue ▪ Child friendly ▪ Owner(s) Jacie Oosthuizen ▪ GM Louwrens Rademeyer (Mar 2018) ▪ Cellarmaster(s) Jacie Oosthuizen (2006) ▪ Winemaker(s) Jacie Oosthuizen (2006), with Samuel Lekay (2006) ▪ Viticulturist(s) Jacie Oosthuizen (Jan 2003) ▪ 33ha/13ha (pinot, shiraz, chard, sauv) ▪ 90t/13,200cs own label 50% red 45% white 5% rosé ▪ PO Box 165 McGregor 6708 ▪ lordswinery@breede.co.za, sales@lordswinery.com ▪ www.lordswinery.com ▪ S 33° 59' 20.98" E 019° 44' 28.39" ▪ ⌕ swerved.jointly.nettle ▪ **T +27 (0)23-625-1265**

☐ **L'Ormarins** *see* Anthonij Rupert Wyne

Lothian Vineyards   ⓠ ⌂ ⊙

The Wilson family's farm on the banks of Elgin's Palmiet River has seen the completion of the warehouse which will in time also house the estate winery. Meanwhile the wines are being made in the local Valley Green cellar by Dudley Wilson and the eminent Richard Kershaw (also vinifier of his own eponymous range). The Lothian vines, cared for by the equally eminent Kevin Watt, are also seeing a little change, with a new small vineyard of grüner veltliner, a variety grown most notably in Austria and still rare in the Cape.

Vineyard Selections

★★★★ **Pinot Noir** ⊘ Ripe dark berry aromas & flavour on **18** ⑧⑧, more savoury & deep-feeling than previous - this underlined by 25% new oak. Firm, fresh acidity but fairly rich.

★★★★ **Chardonnay** Typical oatmeal & citrus notes on **18** ⑧⑧. Ripely flavoured, firm & fleshy, balanced by a notably lemony acidity & unobtrusive oaking - 25% new. Still youthful, should develop a few years. Also in magnum.

★★★★☆ **Noble Late Harvest** Marmalade & honeyed character on **18** ★★★★ ⑧⑥ from viognier. Softly textured & charming, but less nervy & the acidity less elegantly integrated than **17** ⑨⓪. No oaking. 375 ml.

Isobel Mourvèdre Rosé ⊘ ★★★★ As usual, more substance & character than many rosés on copper-pink **18** ⑧③. Dry & fresh. **Riesling** ★★★★ As previous, peachy earthiness & an early note of petrol on the intense aromas of **18** ⑧⑤. More forceful than delicate, with grippy cool-climate acidity, succulently dry. **Méthode Cap Classique Brut Rosé** ⒩ ★★★ **15** ⑧② sparkler from pinot noir, as aroma & flavour attest. In fact, in colour & character more like a very light, savoury red with bubbles than MCC. Pleasant enough & dry. — TJ

Location/map/WO: Elgin ▪ Map grid reference: A2 ▪ Est 2004 ▪ 1stB 2010 ▪ Tasting by appt only ▪ Honey ▪ Conferences ▪ Weddings/functions ▪ Conservation area ▪ Luxury guest house (8 double en-suite rooms) ▪

Open for Elgin Open Gardens (Nov) ▪ Owner(s) Wilson family ▪ Winemaker(s) Richard Kershaw & Dudley Wilson (Jan 2016) ▪ Viticulturist(s) Kevin Watt (Mar 2009) ▪ 46ha/13ha (mourv, pinot, chard, grüner, riesling, sauv, viog) ▪ 60t 25% red 75% white ▪ IPW ▪ 68 Reservoir Rd, Somerset West 7130 ▪ info@lothianvineyards. com ▪ www.lothianvineyards.com ▪ S 34° 11' 31.49" E 018° 58' 57.78" ▪ ⌁ rearranges.shaker.scrabbled ▪ **T +27 (0)21-859-9901/+27 (0)82-565-7869**

Louis

Winemaker and consultant Louis Nel's experience runs wide and deep, and boutique producers in his home base of Stellenbosch as well as areas beyond benefit from his know-how. These are two of his own-label ranges, the Buckleberry and Louis portfolios being out of stock at press time.

Black Forest range

Shiraz-Mourvèdre Ⓥ ★★★★ A real crowd pleaser. With shiraz at 85%, **16** ⑧④ Xmas cake & baking spice, wonderfully dry yet with a plushness that begs another sip.

Titanic range

Cabernet Sauvignon Ⓥ ★★★ Modestly oaked **16** ⑦⑧, blackcurrant fruit on a bed of bone-dry tannins & sharp, lingering freshness. — HC

Location: Stellenbosch ▪ WO: Western Cape ▪ Est/1stB 2007 ▪ Closed to public ▪ Owner(s) Louis Nel ▪ Cellarmaster(s)/winemaker(s) Louis Nel (Jan 2007) ▪ 15t/3,000cs own label 50% red 50% white ▪ 9 Forest Str Stellenbosch 7600 ▪ louis@louiswines.com ▪ www.louiswines.com ▪ **T +27 (0)82-775-8726**

Louis 57 Wines   Ⓥ 🍴 📷

Route 57 is the combined tasting HQ, shop and restaurant of this brand, in Mossel Bay on the Garden Route – not far from the golf course where Louis Oosthuizen made his record-breaking low score of 57. The golfing connection will explain some of the names of the wines, which are made by Jacques and Reenen Borman at Boschkloof in Stellenbosch.

★★★★ **Jasoma Conclusion** Ⓥ Cab with cab franc, merlot, petit verdot. **16** ⑧⑥ classic berry & cigar-box aromas. Dry tannic firmness, big acidity & plenty of sweet fruit balance 15% alcohol. No **15**. **Merlot** ★★★ Plenty of herbal-tinged fruitcake character on **17** ⑧②, with oak, dry tannin & acid influence giving a touch of harshness to the good fruit. **Pinotage** Ⓥ ★★★★ Expressive red fruit, maraschino cherries & plums, **15** ⑧④ has variety's typical succulence for immediate enjoyment, the tannin backbone ensures ageing ability. WO W Cape, like Jasoma. **Open Champion Syrah** Ⓥ ★★★★ Dark, spiced plummy ripeness on **16** ⑧⑤. Big 14.5% alcohol, but balanced by plenty of flavour. Easygoing but form-giving tannins. **Shiraz** Ⓥ ★★★★ Sappy hedgerow fruit, some peppery notes, ends savoury & dry. **15** ⑧④ ideal casserole companion now & for few years. **Fifty Seven Red Blend** ★★★★ Berry fruit aromas & flavours on bright, well-balanced **17** ⑧⑤ cab-merlot blend. More ambitious than previous (cab-shiraz), with notable tannic structure, but fruit to balance. 12.9% alcohol. **Nelmari Rosé** (NEW) ★★★ Lightly aromatic, tasty **19** ⑧② with earthy note adding interest. Full flavours, well built, juicy & dry. Shiraz-grenache, like perlé version. **Sweet Swing Rosé** (NEW) ★★★ Bubbles added to aromatic & vaguely fruity-earthy **19** ⑦⑨. The unfussy, sweet-toothed crowd will down it with gusto. **Double Eagle Chardonnay** (NEW) ★★★★ Lightly oaked **19** ⑧⑤ is fresh & light-feeling, yet with some richness & plenty of fruit flavour, as well as stony, herbal elements. Unlingering, but enjoyable. WO W Cape, like next. **Sauvignon Blanc** Ⓥ ★★★★ Quintessential sauvignon ex Somerset West & Wellington fruit. Nice intensity, gooseberries & capsicum, **17** ⑧④ becomes more mineral in the flavours. — TJ

Location: Mossel Bay ▪ Map: Klein Karoo & Garden Route ▪ Map grid reference: C4 ▪ WO: Stellenbosch/ Western Cape ▪ Est/1stB 2009 ▪ Tasting & sales Mon-Sat 10-9.30 at 12 Marsh Str Mossel Bay ▪ Closed Dec 25 ▪ Sales also via online shop ▪ Route 57 Restaurant ▪ Gift shop ▪ Craft beer & gin ▪ Owner(s) Louis 57 Group (Pty) Ltd ▪ Winemaker(s) Jacques & Reenen Borman (Boschkloof) ▪ bertu@louis57.co.za ▪ www. louis57wines.com ▪ S 34° 10' 59.46" E 022° 9' 10.78" ▪ ⌁ worker.quieter.message ▪ **T +27 (0)82-893-6848**

☐ **Louisa** *see* Pulpit Rock Winery

Louisvale Wines

Focused on chardonnay since inception more than 3 decades ago, this Devon Valley estate continues to place the Burgundy variety front and centre of the handful of still wines and MCC sparklers made from home-grown fruit. The Stone Road wines, in striking minimalist packaging, are sourced from far-flung and neighbour vineyards, some of which form part of the panorama from the attractive, modern visitor centre.

Louisvale range

★★★★☆ **Five Barrels Cabernet Sauvignon** ⊛ Stringent selection for this assured, ageworthy flagship. **17** ⑨⓪ more composed & less powerful than last, with 14% alcohol & 80% new wood (scaled back from 15% & 100%). Polished, with sweet cassis fruit ably reined-in by commendable dryness. No **16**.

★★★★ **Dominique** ⊘ ⊛ Confident cab-led (70%), 3-way Bordeaux blend with trademark well-judged tannins, pleasingly dry conclusion in **17** ⑧⑥. As before, merlot's plummy exuberance well contained. Worth cellaring.

★★★★ **Chardonnay** Ferment/12 months in 50% new oak result in intense toast & vanilla notes in **18** ⑧⑥, very attractive but not yet in balance with the lemon-lime fruit, should harmonise with ageing.

Chavant ★★★ Their lighter-oaked (20% new barrels) chardonnay. **18** ⑧② slightly sweet impression, needs more of previous' invigorating acidity to counter ripe citrus fruit & few grams sugar. **Chardonnay Unwooded** ★★★ Easygoing **19** ⑧②, gentle lemon & lemongrass tones, not-overdone hint of sweetness in the farewell. WO W Cape. **Méthode Cap Classique Rosé Brut** ★★★★ Well-balanced & energetic **NV** ⑧④ dry sparkler's pinot noir takes care of the colour & berry aromas, chardonnay does the zest. Also in magnum. **Méthode Cap Classique Brut** ★★★★ From chardonnay, **NV** ⑧③'s racing bubbles, toffee & candy apple aromas, Granny Smith apple acidity will get any new union off to a fine start at the on-site wedding venue.

Stone Road range

Cabernet Sauvignon ★★★ Cab's distinctive tannins & bright acidity to the fore in lightly oaked **16** ⑦⑨, though cherry & raspberry tones less typical of the variety. **Merlot** ★★★ Subtle vanilla from 10% oaked portion, fresh plum fruit on nicely dry, supple **17** ⑧⓪. **Shiraz** ★★★ Doesn't shout 'shiraz', but **18** ⑧⓪ is ripe & smooth, glides down easily. **Cinsault Rosé** ⑰ ★★ Subtle strawberries-&-cream character, **18** ⑦⑥ light & dry. **Sauvignon Blanc** ★★★ Most forthcoming of these wines, **19** ⑧② cool green notes mingle with riper passionfruit & papaya, deft few grams sugar up the drinkability. — CvZ

Location/map: Stellenbosch ▪ Map grid reference: D4 ▪ WO: Stellenbosch/Western Cape ▪ Est/1stB 1989 ▪ Tasting & sales Mon-Sat 10-4 ▪ Fee R40 ▪ Closed on selected pub hols ▪ Wedding/function venue (150 pax) ▪ Owner(s) Louisvale Wines (Pty) Ltd ▪ Directors Altmann Allers, Hendrik Kluever, Johann Kirsten & Zane Meyer ▪ Winemaker(s)/viticulturist(s) Simon Smith (Jul 1997) ▪ 34ha/23ha (cab, merlot, chard) ▪ 220t/16,000cs own label 50% red 50% white ▪ PO Box 542 Stellenbosch 7599 ▪ winery@louisvale.com ▪ www.louisvale.com ▪ S 33° 54' 32.3" E 018° 48' 24.3" ▪ ⊞ snapper.guardian.earliest ▪ **T +27 (0)21-865-2422**

Lourens Family Wines

Last year was a massive one for Franco Lourens and wife Lindi, as they welcomed daughter Lua to the family, timing her arrival perfectly - right after the end of harvest. With the current range already containing wines named after Lindi and Franco's father Howard John, 'expect another special wine to join the portfolio very soon!' Which will work well for the many 'Franco-philes', as volumes of his boutique handmade wines were much reduced in 2018, the Blouklip Steen '18 skipped entirely as it didn't meet his very high standards. Thankfully 2019 looks promising, says the winemaker who also helps craft the stellar Alheit Vineyards wines.

★★★★☆ **Howard John** Pronounced aromatics on perfumed & peppery **18** ⑨② southern French blend (mainly grenache & cinsaut with syrah & carignan, all dryland bushvines) courtesy 80% wholebunch component. Strawberry jam spiced up with generous clove & cinnamon, pleasing tannic squeeze just at finish. Only old oak, as all these.

★★★★☆ **Skuinskap Steen** ⊛ From a 43 year old chenin vineyard in Piekenierskloof, **18** ⑨④ delivers fascinating melange of fruit (pineapples, apples) honey/oatmeal texture & unusual liquorice tweak. Zesty acidity keeps interest up right through to satisfying finish. A keeper. Natural ferment (as all) in barriques.

★★★★★ **Lindi Carien** ⊛ Stylish **18** ★★★★★ ⑨③ from mainly chenin & verdelho (SA's oldest) with grenache blanc & roussanne, bunch fermented in old oak to produce fruit-driven wine (melons, apricots) with crunchy muesli texture & fresh, lively acidity. Slightly richer style than more linear **17** ⑨⑤.

Not tasted: **Blouklip Steen**. — CM

Location: Hermanus ▪ WO: Western Cape/Piekenierskloof ▪ Est/1stB 2016 ▪ Closed to public ▪ Owner(s) Franco Lourens ▪ Winemaker(s) Franco Lourens (Jan 2016) ▪ ±14t/±1,600cs own label 35% red 65% white ▪ Private Bag X15 Suite 189 Hermanus 7200 ▪ info@lourensfamilywines.co.za ▪ www.lourensfamilywines.co.za ▪ **T +27 (0)84-919-4206**

Lourensford Wine Estate   ⓠ ⑪ ◎ ⑤

This vast, multifaceted property sprawls over 4,000 hectares of Hottentots Holland and Helderberg mountain slopes and valleys in Somerset West — and just 100 are under vine. Belonging to businessman Christo Wiese, the showpiece estate boasts a market, restaurant, brewery and even a coffee roastery. Winemaker Hannes Nel has helped refocus and realign the portfolio over the past two years, with ranges culled and new ones introduced (new wines, too, the debut Bordeaux blend this edition recognises the philanthropic daughter of early 20th-century Lourensford owner JW Jagger). In the vineyards, blocks have been uprooted, and the emphasis placed on plantings suited to terroir and climate. A new 4x4 safari vehicle is ideal for taking trade guests around the more remote areas of the farm to demonstrate ongoing conservation, alien invasive vegetation clearance and green energy projects.

Chrysalis range

★★★★☆ **Red** Flagship Bordeaux blend of cab, merlot & cabernet franc, **16** ⑨② alluring, structured & complex, with seamless interplay of fruit & oak (73% new, 19 months). Powerful yet restrained, it will reward patience.

★★★★☆ **White** ⑧ Intricately vinified blend, sauvignon (73%) leads with chardonnay & viognier in savoury, sophisticated **16** ⑨④. Nuanced fruit - fig & asparagus vying with creamy spice. Complex, poised; silky texture but vivid freshness too. Dimension from part natural ferment & 8 months on lees in barrel.

Limited Releases

★★★★☆ **Merlot** Bold yet plush **17** ⑨① offers cocoa powder depth with spice & ripe plum fruit countered by squeeze of tannin from 19 months in 65% new French oak. Balanced, harmonious & structured, with fine concentration & depth.

★★★★☆ **Shiraz-Mourvèdre-Viognier 17** ⑨⓪ improves on **16** ★★★★ ⑧⑧ in its deceptively light, pliable ease. Core of ripe, concentrated dark fruit with bright freshness to balance. Dry spicy tannin grip courtesy of 16 months in 39% new oak barrels.

★★★★☆ **Chardonnay** Statuesque & voluptuous **18** ⑨⓪ goes up a level on **17** ★★★★ ⑧⑨. Winemaking is complex, with parts natural, barrel & tank ferment. Fresh & lively but balanced by creamy breadth, textured & persistent. Registered single-vineyard.

★★★★ **Viognier** Peach cobbler appeal to barrel-fermented **18** ★★★★☆ ⑨② (percentage Hungarian oak). Taut & lively yet generously creamy. Structured & vital, good line of acidity balancing ripe flavour. Surpasses **17** ⑧⑨.

★★★★☆ **Noble Late Harvest** ⑧ Lively sun-dried pineapple & apricot opulence on botrytised **14** ⑨① semillon, lightly wooded. Vivid acid checks ripe honeyed sweetness. Long but clean & focused, with precise, pure tail. Light 10.5% alcohol. 375 ml.

★★★★☆ **Kurkbos Chardonnay Cape Vintage** (NEW) ⑧ Intriguing & unusual **15** ⑨③ white 'port' from best site. Nutty almond skin with saline edge to bright acidity. Sweetness (84.9 g/l RS) is balanced & it finishes clean. 34 months on lees in barrel. Named for ancient cork oak forest near the single-vineyard.

The Dome range

★★★★ **Pinot Noir** ⊘ **18** ★★★★☆ ⑨① raises the bar on **17** ⑧⑧ in its restraint while retaining lithe, sinewy yet succulent cherry/berry vibrancy. Subtle nutty oak support, 11 months, 12% new. WO W Cape.

★★★★☆ **Ethel** (NEW) Two-part harmony of cab (87%) & merlot in **16** ⑨⓪. Hedgerow fruit, graphite depth & subtle violet nuance on long finish. Substantial but restrained. 19 months in oak, 27% new.

★★★★ **Chardonnay** ⊘ Oatmeal & nuts are livened by bright tangerine vigour on cohesive **18** ★★★★☆ ⑨①, ups the palate appeal on **17** ⑧⑨. Complex winemaking, with wild, barrel & tank ferments & lees ageing. Lovely integration, breadth & texture. Poised mouthful.

Méthode Cap Classiques

★★★★ **Brut Rosé** Salmon pink hue to 60/40 pinot noir/chardonnay dry sparkling in **16** ⑧⑧. Crisp, tangy with broad, leesy, red fruit flavour. Also-tasted **15** ⑧⑨ more zesty & toasty, with grapefruit & sourdough, likewise from 27 months on lees.

★★★★ **Brut 13** ★★★★★ ⑨⓪ dry sparkler, like **12** ⑧⑧, is mostly chardonnay. Marine tang with marmalade & brioche appeal. Lovely lime zest finale. Long 59 months on lees & hand riddled before November 2018 disgorgement.

Not tasted: **Brut Zero Cuvée 89**. — FM

Location: Somerset West ▪ Map: Helderberg ▪ Map grid reference: F4 ▪ WO: Stellenbosch/Western Cape ▪ Est 1999 ▪ 1stB 2003 ▪ Tasting, sales & cellar tours daily 9-5 ▪ Fee R45-R60 ▪ Closed Good Fri & Dec 25 ▪ Millhouse Kitchen ▪ Tour groups ▪ Market ▪ Coffee Roastery ▪ Function hall ▪ Conservation area ▪ Craft beer: sales at market ▪ Owner(s) Christo Wiese ▪ Winemaker(s) Hannes Nel (Nov 2002), with Timothy Witbooi (May 2005) ▪ Viticulturist(s) Piet Uys ▪ 4,000ha/100ha (cab, merlot, pinot, shiraz, chard, sauv, viog) ▪ 1,200t/240,000cs own label 40% red 58% white 2% rosé ▪ BRC, CVC, HACCP, WIETA, WWF-SA Conservation Champion ▪ PO Box 16 Somerset West 7129 ▪ info@lourensford.co.za ▪ www.lourensford.co.za ▪ S 34° 4' 3.7" E 018° 53' 44.2" ▪ spirit.dairy.anchors ▪ **T +27 (0)21-847-2333**

Lovane Boutique Wine Estate & Guest House ⑨ ⌂ ◎

Strategically located at the entrance to Stellenboschkloof, the old wagon road between Cape Town and Stellenbosch, is Theresa and Hennie Visser's 2.5-ha boutique vineyard and luxury guest house. It's a popular conference venue, and a great stepping off point for wine-routing weekenders and holidaymakers.

Cabernet Sauvignon ★★★★ Vivid cassis in **16** ⑧④, 24 months French oaking (as all reds) appearing in the flavours, giving spice, touch of dark chocolate. Tannins supple. **Shiraz** ⑨ ★★★ Typical ripe plum spice of **16** ⑧② shaded by dominant oak (all-new French, 2 years) as well as big 15.7% alcohol. Hot & tad dry, grippy. **Isikhati** ★★★★ Bordeaux blend, cab in charge (79%), with cab franc & petit verdot. **16** ⑧⑤'s oak expressive here, smoky spice, beef extract on plummy fruit, & yet succulent, streamlined texture, already drinking well. **Pinotage-Petit Verdot** ⑨⑤ ★★★ Cape Blend, pinotage at 67%, **17** ⑧①'s oaking shows as vanilla-tinged dark berries, some cocoa notes. Texture is plush, ready to drink. **Theresa Blanc de Noir** ★★★ Pale pink **19** ⑦⑦ from cab has effusive berry/candyfloss scents, touch of sugar making it more appealing. **Sauvignon Blanc** ★★★ Lemon drop freshness in dry **19** ⑦⑨, nuance of lemongrass, crisply clean finish. **Méthode Cap Classique** ⑨ ★★★ Apple & lime tang on coral pink **NV** ⑧⓪ fizz, sherbet zip vies with creamy yeast note on chardonnay/pinot noir blend. Not tasted: **Cape Vintage**. Occasional release: **Cabernet Franc**, **Petit Verdot**, **Chenin Blanc**. — CR

Location/map/WO: Stellenbosch ▪ Map grid reference: D6 ▪ Tasting, sales & cellar tours Mon-Sun 10-5 ▪ Tasting fee R35, waived on purchase ▪ Conferences ▪ 4-star guest house (16 rooms) ▪ Owner(s) Hennie & Theresa Visser ▪ Winemaker(s)/viticulturist(s) Hennie Visser ▪ 3.6ha/2.5ha (cabs s/f, p verdot) ▪ PO Box 91 Vlottenburg 7604 ▪ info@lovane.co.za ▪ www.lovane.co.za ▪ S 33° 57' 09.74" E 018° 48' 02.38" ▪ bachelor.drip.fairly ▪ **T +27 (0)21-881-3827**

☐ **Love Boat** *see* The Love Boat Wines

Lowerland ⑨

The Coetzee's family farm on the banks of the Orange River in the Northern Cape runs mostly to grain, nuts and livestock. But there are 9 hectares of organic vines - much of whose crops disappear into co-op tanks. But the work of young Bertie Coetzee, and his growing confidence that excellence is (surprisingly to many) possible from the semi-arid Prieska ward, has led to some grapes being cool-trucked far south, where they are vinified – in hands-off, natural fashion – by a few of the Cape's great winemaking talents into increasingly hailed wines. Exports are growing, along with listings in restaurants of note.

Lowerland range

★★★★ **Tolbos Tannat** ⓥ Half wholebunch fruit on **18** ⑧⑧ adds bright freshness to a riper, sweeter element. Tannin unusually subtle for tannat; good berry character, silky texture. Still very youthful. No **17**.

★★★★ **Vaalkameel Colombard** ⓥ Beguiling **18** ★★★★★ ⑨② a rare example of ambitious colombard. Ripe apple notes dominate aromas & full, rounded but elegant palate, the few grams of sugar kept invisible by succulent acid & a touch of phenolic grip. At 12.9% alcohol, delicious & impressive, as was drier **17** ⑧⑧.

★★★★ **Witgat Viognier** Lightly aromatic, floral & understatedly peachy, old-oaked **18** ⑧⑧ is dry & fresh, even bracing, with moderate intensity. Million miles from the blowsy, overdone model of the grape.

★★★★ **Méthode Cap Classique** ⚲ **16** ⑧⑧ bubbly from colombard, in wood before year+ on lees, adding delicious spice to apple-Danish flavours & savoury finish. Zero dosage for dry, appetising freshness. Occasional release: **Herd Sire Reserve**.

#WOPrieska range

Die Verlore Bokooi ★★★☆ Latest **NV** ⑧⑤ as charming as its label: balanced, fresh, dry & light-feeling (12.7% alcohol), with red cherry freshness & ready drinkability. Mostly syrah & merlot, plus cab, petit verdot. — TJ

Location/WO: Prieska ▪ Map: Northern Cape, Free State & North West ▪ Map grid reference: C6 ▪ Est 2000 ▪ 1stB 2006 ▪ Tasting & cellar tours by appt ▪ Owner(s) Lowerland (Pty) Ltd ▪ Winemaker(s) JD Pretorius & Lukas van Loggerenberg ▪ Viticulturist(s) Terblanche Viticulture & Bertie Coetzee (May 2013) ▪ 12,000ha/9ha (cab, merlot, p verdot, shiraz, tannat, chard, cbard, viog) ▪ 90t/1,300cs own label 60% red 40% white ▪ Organic vyd (Ecocert), GlobalGap, Siza ▪ PO Box 292 Lowerland Prieska 8940 ▪ bertie@lowerland.co.za, alette@lowerland.co.za ▪ www.lowerland.co.za ▪ S 29° 29' 15.28" E 023° 0' 28.41" ▪ ⌗ seat.monument. reissuing ▪ **T +27 (0)83-349-9559/+27 (0)82-854-9109**

☐ **Loyal Brothers** see Govert Wines

Lozärn Wines

The Smuts brothers in 2019 inaugurated a new cellar, where Salómé Buys-Vermeulen vinifies a small portfolio headlined by red blend Kay's Legacy, honouring late relative Granny Kay who tended a flock of ducks. The birds, in stylised and creative form, adorn the striking front-labels. Besides a Sauvignon and Chardonnay, a single-varietal red and rosé from rare-in-SA carmenère should tempt visitors to the Bonnievale venue for pre-booked casual tastings among the barrels.

★★★★ **Kay's Legacy** Cab franc-led blend with merlot, cab & dab carmenère (3%). Bold entry of spicy black cherry balanced by supportive tannin from 9 months older oak. Impressive depth & length on **17** ⑧⑨.

★★★★ **Chardonnay** ⑭ Confident debut for **18** ⑧⑨, with creamy cashew oak notes (just 80% wooded, 10% new) & lively citrus freshness. Ideally poised & seamless, good breadth & depth.

Carmenère Rosé ★★★☆ Majority Philadelphia grapes with 3 hours skin contact for **19** ⑧④ pink charmer. Raspberry cordial vibrancy but lovely zip of acid & dryness to balance. Not tasted: **Carmenère, Sauvignon Blanc**. Discontinued: **Shiraz**. — WB, FM

Location: Bonnievale ▪ Map: Robertson ▪ Map grid reference: D3 ▪ WO: Robertson/Western Cape ▪ Est/1stB 2017 ▪ Tasting, sales & cellar tours by appt ▪ Owner(s) Smuts Brothers Agri (Pty) Ltd (Directors Grant & Juan Ivan Smuts) ▪ Winemaker(s) Salómé Buys-Vermeulen (Jun 2017) ▪ 18ha under vine (1.9ha carmenère) ▪ 30t/1,400cs own label 70% red 20% white 10% rosé ▪ PO Box 6 Robertson 6707 ▪ winemaker@lozarn.co.za ▪ www.lozarn.co.za ▪ S 33° 58' 1.49" E 020° 8' 12.01" ▪ ⌗ contravene.movie.blend ▪ **T +27 (0)82-576-8093**

☐ **Lubanzi** see Cape Venture Wine Co
☐ **Luca & Ingrid Bein** see Bein Wine Cellar

Luddite Wines

Luddite, on the slopes of the Houw Hoek mountains overlooking Bot River village, is a family concern, with Niels Verburg making the wine with daughter and cellar assistant Alice, and wife Penny tending the vines. Niels going solo after working for prestigious wineries was prompted by his passion for shiraz and wish to make it his way, with minimal intervention. Chenin was added to that mission, and these two varieties form the core of the Verburgs' project. But, typically, not in a conventional way - one has only to look at the positioning of the Saboteur wines and their award-winning packaging to appreciate that.

★★★★☆ **Shiraz** ⑯ Only 2.3 t/ha yield, 4 weeks on skins, 24 months mainly French barrels, 30% new, & **15** ⑨④ is a powerhouse of perfume & flavour: black cherries, scrub, white pepper notes, salty liquorice. Richly textured, handsome, as **14** ★★★★★ ⑨⑤, but muscles more toned. Various bottle formats.

★★★★☆ **Saboteur Red** ⓥ Blend change, shiraz-led with cab, mourvèdre, less oaking than Shiraz (year), **16** ⑨② for earlier drinking. No less impressive for that: vivid dark fruit & tobacco, juicy texture & a backbone for ageing. Cape South Coast WO, as White.

★★★★☆ **Chenin Blanc** ⓐ Lowest alcohol ever, 11.5% because of dry weather/earlier picking, but nothing else trim. Wild ferment on skins, 12 months on lees in older barrels, taut, savoury, sleek **18** ⑨③ has ginger biscuit, crushed walnut scents, the fruit peach & melon. Winemaker Niels calls it 'cerebral'. Spot on.

★★★★☆ **Saboteur White** ⓐ Crown cap closure, tag-like neck label lauding saboteurs, as Red. Chenin (71%) with sauvignon & viognier, treated differently for fruit expression. **18** ⑨③ prominent lime aromas, pear & peach in the flavours, 9 months lees contact giving palate weight, savoury notes.— CR

Location: Bot River ▪ Map: Walker Bay & Bot River ▪ Map grid reference: D2 ▪ WO: Bot River/Cape South Coast ▪ Est/1stB 2000 ▪ Tasting & sales Mon-Fri 9-3 Sat/Sun by appt ▪ Cellar tours by appt ▪ Closed Dec 25 & Jan 1 ▪ Farm produce ▪ Walks/hikes ▪ Conservation area ▪ Owner(s) Niels Verburg & Hillie Meyer ▪ Cellarmaster(s) Niels Verburg (2000) ▪ Winemaker(s) Niels Verburg (2000), with cellar assistant Alice Verburg (Jan 2018) ▪ Viticulturist(s) Penny Verburg (2000) ▪ 17ha/8.5ha (cab, grenache, mourv, shiraz, chenin) ▪ 60t ▪ Own label 70% red 30% white + 1,000cs for clients ▪ PO Box 656 Bot River 7185 ▪ info@luddite.co.za, niels@luddite.co.za ▪ www.luddite.co.za ▪ S 34° 12' 50.5" E 019° 12' 24.1" ▪ 🄰 piecing.opener.embalmer ▪ **T +27 (0)28-284-9308/+27 (0)83-444-3537**

LuKa Wine Estate　　　　　　　　　　　　　　　　ⓥ

Older sibling in the family of Plettenberg Bay boutique wine producers (and one also drawing on the experience of veteran winemaking consultant Anton Smal), LuKa more recently became the idyllic Garden Route home of Mark and Anneke Barnard and their two youngsters. An established vineyard producing awarded sauvignon has been expanded with a parcel of pinot noir and chardonnay for a future bubbly.

Rosé ⓥ ★★★ Raspberry & strawberry mingle with spice & dried herbs. Rich & mouthfilling (though only ±12.5% alcohol) with spiced berry finish on **18** ⑧②. **Sauvignon Blanc** ⓥ ★★★★ Lime, greengage & kiwi fruit merge well with grass & nettle notes, all speaking of grapes' cool-climate provenance. **18** ⑧④ has fresh acidity, ends with a melon persistence. — GM

Location/WO: Plettenberg Bay ▪ Map: Klein Karoo & Garden Route ▪ Map grid reference: C1 ▪ Est 2008 ▪ 1stB 2011 ▪ Tasting Mon-Sat 11-3.30 ▪ Owner(s) Mark & Anneke Barnard ▪ Cellarmaster(s)/winemaker(s) Anton Smal (Bramon Wines) ▪ Viticulturist(s) Mark Barnard ▪ ±7ha/2.5ha (pinot, chard, sauv) ▪ 8t/1,122cs own label 100% white ▪ PO Box 92 Knysna 6570 ▪ info@lukawines.co.za ▪ www.lukawines.co.za ▪ S 34° 2' 28.14" E 023° 15' 57.56" ▪ 🄰 mediating.buffets.landings ▪ **T +27 (0)83-767-6218/+27 (0)82-498-7112**

Lutzville Vineyards　　　　　　　　　　　　ⓥ ⑪ ⓞ ⓖ

Crushing 48,000 tons off 2,100 hectares to produce 400,000 cases of own-label wines, this West Coast winery is one of SA's largest. Its portfolio comprises mostly varietal and low-alcohol sweet wines for early consumption, but there are more ambitious ranges, from select sites in Lutzville Valley: Francois le Vaillant is named for a French explorer and naturalist, and features a new port-style wine; Diamond Collection references the gem- (and shipwreck-) strewn Diamond Coast north of the cellar's home-base, Lutzville.

Francois le Vaillant range

★★★★ **Cabernet Sauvignon** ⓥ Strikes a fine balance between intense cassis fruit & enlivening tannins, **15** ⑧⑦ easily soaks up 100% new oak.

★★★★ **Pinotage** ⓥ Supple black fruit on **16** ⑧⑥, sweetly ripe & dense, with smooth tannins, noticeable acidity. New oak adds char hint but also structure for year/2 cellaring. No **15**.

★★★★☆ **Noble Late Harvest** ⓥ Worthy addition to botrytis dessert category. From chenin, hedonistic **12** ⑨② distinctive dried apricot & citrus peel flavour, lovely freshening acidity.

Cape Vintage ⓝⒺⓦ ★★★★ Unlike most Vintage 'port', released young for lengthy cellaring, **16** ⑧③ ready to be poured. No concluding tannic grip or structure, more cherry liqueur-like, bitter choc finish. From ruby cab, in 500 ml.

Diamond Collection

★★★★ **Cabernet Sauvignon** ⓥ Undaunting tannin structure the attraction in **15** ⑧⑦, with voluptuous fruit. Only 10-20% oak for these reds vs 100% for Le Vaillant. **14** untasted.

★★★★ **Ebenaezer** ⓥ Flagship mostly cab & shiraz, ruby cab for extra fruitiness. **15** ⑧⑦ initially oaky, opens to black berry & clove; reined-in tannin & salty finish. Distinct tapenade savoury nuance, like Shiraz.

★★★★ **Oaked Chenin Blanc** ⓥ Full, rich & fruity **15** ★★★★ ⑧④, judiciously wooded to preserve fine mineral notes. Succeeds **13** ⑧⑦ from cooler Koekenaap & warmer Lutzville blocks. No **14**.

★★★★☆ **White Muscadel** ⓥ Delicate, yet no pushover, **16** ⑨⓪ fortified muscat de Frontignan intoxicating bouquet of jasmine, litchi, pear & white peach. Silky, seductive, with just enough fortification to blush the cheek, let fruit shine.

Shiraz ⓥ ★★★★ Savoury & sweet vanilla overtones on **15** ⑧④'s sweet cherry fruit. Decent dryness, overt acidity; lacks varietal character but is appealing. **Sauvignon Blanc** ⓥ ★★★★ Round & soft **17** ⑧④ tank sample, restrained cool green aromas; fruit-sweet entry with 14% alcohol padding out crisp acidity, adding body, texture.

Lutzville range

Cabernet Sauvignon ⓥ ★★ Similar terse tannins as last vintage but less cushioning juiciness in **17** ⑦②. **Merlot** ★★ Bright acidity for lift, **18** ⑦⑥ engaging candyfloss tones, stewed fruit finish. **Pinotage** ★★☆ Upbeat **18** ⑦⑧ packed with variety's strawberry, mulberry fruit, vibrant acidity. Like other reds & Chenin, few grams sugar for easy drinkability. **Shiraz** ★★☆ Crisp red fruit with black pepper & faint lily notes. **18** ⑦⑦ lightly oak-staved, combo French/American, as all these reds. **Shiraz Rosé** ★★ Mere whisper of berry aroma & flavour on **19** ⑦④, driest of all these at 2.5 g/l sugar. **Chardonnay** ★★☆ Faint lemony charm, unwooded **19** ⑦⑦ grassy finish, noticeable acidity. **Chenin Blanc** ★★ Tropical & floral appeal, **19** ⑦②'s few grams sugar not quite balancing piercing acidity. **Sauvignon Blanc** ★ Strident acidity, **19** ⑥④ barely vinous but aromas are true to variety. **Sparkling Rosé** ★★☆ New to the guide, **NV** ⑦⑦ from undisclosed variety/ies, pleasing combo of heady berries, low 8% alcohol & pleasant sweetness for parties. **Natural Sweet Red** ⓥ ★★☆ Berry-packed **NV** ⑦⑦ sipper from chenin & pinotage, refreshing & light, with low ±8.5% alcohol, as all the Natural Sweets. **Natural Sweet Rosé** ⓥ ★★ Loses the hanepoot & its grapey, musky attraction, so latest **NV** ⑦③ from chenin & pinotage tad vapid by comparison. **Natural Sweet White** ⓥ ★★☆ Attractive **NV** ⑦⑧ from chenin commendably intense tropical aromas & flavours. — CvZ

Location: Lutzville ▪ Map: Olifants River ▪ Map grid reference: B3 ▪ WO: Lutzville Valley ▪ Est 1961 ▪ 1stB 1980 ▪ Tasting & sales Mon-Fri 9-5 Sat 10-2 ▪ Closed Sun, Easter Sat, Dec 25 & Jan 1 ▪ Cellar tours by appt only ▪ Coffee shop & restaurant Mon-Fri 9-5 Sat 10-2 (kitchen closes 1hr earlier) ▪ Function/conference venue ▪ Owner(s) Lutzville Wingerde Beperk ▪ Cellarmaster(s) Brenda Thiart (Nov 2011) ▪ Winemaker(s) Christo Basson (Feb 2019), Andries Eygelaar (Jan 2014) & Christoff de Wet (Jan 2018) ▪ Viticulturist(s) Gideon Engelbrecht (Sep 2009) & Hugo Lamprecht (Sep 2009) ▪ 2,100ha (cab, merlot, ptage, pinot, ruby cab, shiraz, chard, chenin, cbard, nouvelle, sauv, sem, viog) ▪ ±48,000t/400,000cs own label 15% red 85% white ▪ BRC, Fairtrade, IPW, WIETA ▪ PO Box 50 Lutzville 8165 ▪ catherine@lutzvillevineyards.com ▪ www.lutzvillevineyards.com ▪ S 31° 33' 35.9" E 018° 21' 0.2" ▪ ⓦ supreme.laced.tributary ▪ **T +27 (0)27-217-1516**

Lyngrove   ⓠ ⓐ ⓞ

Lyngrove 5-star country house and conference centre in the Helderberg overlooks close to 80 ha of vines, part of a palette from which the cellar/vineyard team of Danie van Tonder and André van den Berg produce four defined tiers - Platinum: best barrels for structure and ageing; Reserve: full, complex, bold oak; Lyngrove Collection: fruit forward, easy drinking; Lyngrove: méthode cap classique and other sparkling.

Platinum range

★★★★ **Pinotage** Consistent style, ripe & voluptuous, well vanilla-spiced by 15 months combo French & American oak. Good fruit, plums, prunes, gives **17** ⑧⑧ smooth accessibility, yet with ageing ability.

★★★★ **Shiraz** ⓥ Handsome big brother to Collection version in packaging & style. Loads of spice, 16 months in barrel, 40% new (as next), **16** ⑧⑧'s dark fruit an equal partner. Also scrub, violets, a curvy body.

★★★★ **Latitude** ⓐ Cape Blend, pinotage with high percentages cab & shiraz; **17** ⑧⑨ multi-layered, richly fruited & spiced. Longest in barrel of the reds, 18 months, 45% new, deservedly so. More amenable than **16** ⑧⑧, still a long future.

Not tasted: **Old Bush Vine Chenin Blanc**.

Reserve range

Shiraz-Pinotage ⑦ ★★★★ Shiraz dictates at 76%, smoky, vanilla-spiced from French/American oak, 14 months. **17** ⑧⑤ brambleberries & prosciutto, pinotage makes its mark with juicy texture, ease of access.

Cabernet Sauvignon ★★★ Cassis at core but oak has given **17** ⑧⓪ quite a few savoury notes, beef extract, tobacco & cloves. Tannins well managed, balanced, accessible. **Chardonnay** ★★★★ Only 30% of wine oaked, **18** ⑧③ is about the fruit, citrus & white peach, but there's a delicious sweet/sour intensity in the flavours, adding to the attraction.

Lyngrove Collection

Chenin Blanc ⑦ ★★★ Scents of crunchy Granny Smith apples, hint of winter melon, & then minerality, seamed throughout, making **19** ⑧① a good food partner.

Merlot ★★★★ Tiny portion oaked for spice, but **18** ⑧④ essentially unwooded. Luscious cassis, some violets & dark chocolate, the lightly savoury palate adding interest. **Pinotage** ★★★ Glossy blueberries & spice from light oaking (as next) gives **18** ⑧⓪ plush texture, appealing drinkability. Ends savoury. **Shiraz** ★★★ Nice effect & good typicity, wild fruit, scrub, a toasty top note, **17** ⑧② offers flavourful, smooth enjoyment. **Sauvignon Blanc** ★★★ Slender (12% alcohol), yet **19** ⑧① has all the fruity freshness you need in sauvignon, passionfruit & green figs, crisply dry.

Lyngrove range

Sparkling Brut ⊘ ★★★ Carbonated bubbly from chenin, **NV** ⑦⑧ apple & pear freshness, frothy mousse, crisply dry. Not tasted: **Pinot Noir Brut.** — CR

Location/WO: Stellenbosch ▪ Map: Helderberg ▪ Map grid reference: B1 ▪ Est/1stB 2000 ▪ Tasting & sales by appt only ▪ Guest house ▪ Conferences (12 pax) ▪ Winemaker(s) Danie van Tonder (2015) ▪ Viticulturist(s) André van den Berg ▪ 76ha (cab, merlot, p verdot, ptage, shiraz, chard, chenin, sauv) ▪ 100,000cs own label 70% red 20% white 10% rosé ▪ WIETA ▪ PO Box 7275 Stellenbosch 7599 ▪ wine@lyngrove.co.za ▪ www. lyngrove.co.za ▪ S 34° 1′ 8.7″ E 018° 48′ 10.2″ ▪ ⬛ pomegranates.botch.faxed ▪ **T +27 (0)21-880-1221**

Lynx Wines ⓠ ⓐ

The indigenous caracal, which shares distinctive tufted ears with the lynx, names these boutique wines from mostly Franschhoek mountain vineyards. Owners since 2018, Germans Manuel and Brigitte Konen are placing a personal stamp on their passion project, expanded to offer guest accommodation from this summer. Newcomer Pierre Louw supports stalwart Helgard van Schalkwyk in a 'fresher look and feel', the flagship red blend renamed The Spirit of Lynx and new Hemel-en-Aarde-origin wines showing their cool climate.

Ultra Premium range

★★★★☆ **The Spirit of Lynx** ⊛ Name change adds 'Spirit of' to flagship red blend that's ever changing; **17** ⑨③ cab driven, with 33% cab franc, drops merlot & petit verdot. Bold & brawny like **16** ⑨②, a gush of super-ripe cassis fruit borne on sturdy tannins, but layered, needs time to unfurl. 2 years all-new oak.

Reserve range ⓝⓔⓦ

★★★★ **The Cabernet Sauvignon** Redolent of blackcurrant, **17** ⑧⑨ large-framed & generous, pliable tannins will unveil juicy fruit in 1-2 years.

★★★★☆ **The Cabernet Franc** Best balanced of these showy wines. **17** ⑨⓪ ripe & juicy but a sappy seam freshens, 70% new-oak tannin is well judged, crisp acidity brightens the finish. 2 top barrels (225L) selected at 1 year, aged further 6 months for the reds in this limited-release line-up.

★★★★☆ **The Pinot Noir** ⊘ ⊛ Upper Hemel-en-Aarde Valley grapes sensitively handled to retain ethereal perfumes, red berry fruits, supple texture & lovely balance of benevolent **17** ⑨⓪ vintage. Just 10% new oak, just right. A must for any pinotphile's collection.

★★★★ **The Shiraz** New French oak for this fruit bomb. **17** ⑧⑨ full, ripe, with pastille succulence in a massive frame (14.5% alcohol).

★★★★ **The Chardonnay** 100% barrel-aged (third new, 10 months) expression of Upper Hemel-en-Aarde Valley fruit. Focused vein of citrus penetrates the leesy oatmeal richness of **18** ⑧⑨, delivers echoing layers of flavour.

★★★★ **The Viognier** All-new-barrel selection **18** ⑧⑦ packs sweet-fruit characters into oak-buttressed structure with 14.5% alcohol, full-ripe harvesting creates near-overwhelming cornucopia of flavours.

Lynx range

★★★★ **SMG** Shiraz with splashes mourvèdre & grenache in **18** ⑧⑧. Charming spice, berry fruit, hints of tobacco & caramel from year oak (now just 15% new) complete plush package. **17** ⑧⑥ had drop viognier.

★★★★ **Viognier** Typical white peach & apricot pip aromas, with vanilla & cinnamon spicing. Full-bodied **18** ⑧⑥ has pleasing rounded shape, creamy texture, lengthy finish. 58% barrel fermented.

Cabernet Sauvignon ★★★☆ Steely varietal edginess of **17** ★★★★ ⑧⑦ persists in leafy **18** ⑧⑤, leaner than its stablemates. Solid tannin backbone, well-defined shape & structure. **Grenache** ★★★☆ Jammy fruit, silky texture & glacé cherry flavour on **18** ⑧③, 20% new wood, year, some American. 15% alcohol evident. **Pinot Noir** ★★★★ Hot, baked-earth character to **18** ⑧③, ready now but perhaps too indulged with new oak (50%) for drinking without food. **Shiraz** ★★★★ Toasty mocha flavours from year in 60% new oak, 20% American, jostle with plum & wood spice in medium-bodied **18** ⑧⑤. **The Tinto** ★★★ Was 'Vino Tinto', still a bits-&-bobs red, mostly cab, with earthy, gamey nature in **18** ⑧⓪ & pleasantly sweet fruit. Year older mixed-source oak. **Blanc de Noir** ★★★ Pretty salmon-hued **19** ⑦⑨ from merlot, rosepetal scent & juicy berry fruit, few grams sugar smooth the tail. **Chardonnay** (NEW) ★★★★ Unoaked **18** ⑧⑤ light on its feet, true to its Upper Hemel-en-Aarde Valley provenance. Tangy lime profile, refreshingly steely send-off. Not tasted: **Cabernet Franc, Xanache.** Discontinued: **Tardio, Vino Blanco.** — DS

Location/map: Franschhoek ▪ Map grid reference: C4 ▪ WO: Franschhoek/Upper Hemel-en-Aarde Valley ▪ Est/1stB 2002 ▪ Tasting, sales & cellar tours Mon-Thu 10—5 Fri/Sat 10-3 Sun/pub hols by appt ▪ Fee R50 (tasting & tour) ▪ Guest house ▪ Owner(s) Brigitte & Manuel Konen ▪ Winemaker(s) Helgard van Schalkwyk (Nov 2010) & Pierre Louw (Apr 2018) ▪ Viticulturist(s) Quinton Daniels ▪ 26ha/11ha (cabs s/f, grenache, merlot, mourv, p verdot, pinot, shiraz, viog) ▪ 130t/8,000cs own label 46% red 13% white 41% rosé ▪ IPW ▪ PO Box 566 Franschhoek 7690 ▪ winemaker@lynxwines.co.za ▪ www.lynxwines.co.za ▪ S 33° 51' 46.1" E 019° 2' 14.6" ▪ ✉ jive.diction.degenerate ▪ **T +27 (0)21-867-0406**

☐ **Maankloof** *see* Mountain River Wines

Maanschijn

Paul Hoogwerf and Doug Mylrea make their fresh, minimal-intervention wines in a renovated barn between Hermanus and Stanford, beneath a peak called Maanschynkop, which gives the brand its 'moonshine' name. But the grapes are brought in from elsewhere: This year sees a new trendy méthode ancestrale bubbly made from Stellenbosch muscat join two wines from Voor Paardeberg, the latter crafted to fit the official 'Alternative white' category.

★★★★☆ **Kolonel Mostert en die Twee Souties** ⓥ Cinsaut, shiraz & grenache, partly destemmed, on **17** ⑨② ; more convincing now than as an infant sample. Gorgeous pure fruit fragrance, supple, easy tannins & fresh acid. Not intense, but more vinous than many lightish wines (13% alcohol).

★★★★☆ **Easy, Tiger** Apricot-gold hue on **18** ⑨⓪ grenache gris. Offers bruised apple, spice & savoury notes - primary fruit not the point here, but the flavour is full & enticing. Citrus zest marks the fresh acidity. Light-feeling & bone-dry. This & next among a handful of wines certified 'Alternative white'.

★★★★ **Spin Cycle** Cloudy gold **18** ⑧⑦ verdelho. Stony, dried herb & oxidative notes lead to ripe appley richness; good bite of lemony acid, a tannic touch from skin contact. 13.6% alcohol adds a little warmth.

Brunch Club (NEW) ★★★☆ Crown-capped **19** ⑧⑤ méthode ancestrale sparkling from Stellenbosch muscat blanc shows typical grapey character with ginger-beer earthiness. Bone-dry & delightfully fresh, though the flavours rather fugitive. In abeyance: **Goldmember.** — TJ

Location: Hermanus ▪ WO: Voor Paardeberg/Stellenbosch ▪ Est 2016 ▪ Closed to public ▪ Winemaker(s) Douglas Mylrea & Paul Hoogwerf ▪ info@maanschijn.co.za ▪ www.maanschijn.co.za

Maastricht Estate   ⓥ ⑪

Palpably pleased to join the Durbanville Wine Valley visitors' route in 2019, major grape growers 'Wheaty' Louw and son Thys of early 18th-century Maastricht farm (part of the Durbanville Hills venture nearby) showcase their own-label wines with tasty platters in an historic barn, newly converted in a garden setting.

★★★★ **Sauvignon Blanc** Awakens the senses with a spectrum of greengage, apple, gooseberry & capsicum aromas & flavours around a core of smooth, mouthwatering acid. **19** ⑧⑧ full, intense & persistent, with a nettle & wet pebble piquancy.

Cabernet Sauvignon ★★★★ More concentrated **17** ⑧⑤, red & blue berries join cigar smoke & coffee on smooth palate with tannins & well-integrated 50% new oak. **Merlot** ★★★★ Uncomplicated **18** ⑧③ shows lively dark-berry fruit & a coffee/mocha undertone, finishes with a toasty oak grip (40% new barriques, 16 months). **Pinot Noir** ★★★★ Fresh fruit (cherry, strawberry) made more complex by forest floor nuance, **17** ⑧③ toastiness from 40% new oak but in harmony with fruit & lingering savoury note. **Pinotage** ★★★★ Dark plums & cherries on fruity & amiable **18** ⑧⑤. Balanced & smooth, chocolate from 25% new oak on finish. For everyday enjoyment. **Pinotage Rosé** (NEW) ★★★ Prettily pink **19** ⑧① chock-full of ripe red berry fruit & spice, zingy, with citrus also in the flavour mix. **Chardonnay** (NEW) ★★★★ Ripe baked apple, cinnamon spice & sprinkling of vanilla from 50% new oak, **18** ⑧④ creamy & rounded, though tad short for higher rating. Discontinued: **Shiraz**. — WB

Location: Durbanville • Map: Durbanville, Philadelphia & Darling • Map grid reference: C7 • WO: Cape Town • Est 1702 • 1stB 2009 • Tasting & sales Tue-Fri 10-5 Sat & pub hols 10-3 • Closed Sun/Mon, Good Fri, Dec 25/26 & Jan 1 • Small platters • Owner(s) Johannes Beyers Louw • Cellarmaster(s) Thys Louw jnr (Jan 2009) • Viticulturist(s) Johannes Beyers Louw (1986) & Thys Louw jnr • 90ha (cab, ptage, pinot, shiraz, sauv) • ±1,000t/3,000cs own label 40% red 60% white • info@maastricht.co.za • www.maastricht.co.za • S 33° 50' 22.86" E 018° 35' 26.79" • ⑩ whisker.eared.moisten • **T +27 (0)21-976-1995**

☐ **Maestro** see DeMorgenzon

Magna Carta Wines

From rural KwaZulu-Natal origins to investment banking, 30-something Mphumeleli 'Mphumi' Ndlangisa now makes wine in Cape Town suburb Woodstock. He lauds mentors (Hermit on the Hill's Pieter de Waal and Lammershoek's Schalk Opperman, among others); industry NPO VinPro's bursary for a postgrad wine-business course; and owners, liquor industry brand manager (and fiancée) Nomfundo Makhanya and cosmetic surgeon Keith Cronwright. Since debut '14, his diverse, organic range (not tasted) is largely exported. Grapes are sourced for production that's truly 'hands-on', from foot crushing to label design.

Location: Cape Town • Map: Cape Peninsula • Map grid reference: B1 • Est/1stB 2014 • Tasting, sales & cellar tours Mon-Fri 12-7 Sat/Sun 12-5 • Owner(s) Nomfundo Makhanya & Keith Cronwright • Winemaker(s) Mphumeleli Ndlangisa • 156 Victoria Rd, Woodstock 7925 • mphumi@magnacartawines.com • www.magnacartawines.com • S 33° 55' 46.24" E 018° 26' 55.53" • ⑩ portable.winch.hooking • **T +27 (0)21-671-6024/+27 (0)61-738-0812**

Maiden Wine Cellars

Helderberg negociant Danie Hattingh's export business was founded 25 years ago with America and Europe as focuses, gradually expanding to Asia. His starter label, Private Reserve, was later joined by Iwayini and now he's added Kattekwaaad, the Afrikaans word for mischief playfully misspelt.

Location: Gordon's Bay • Est 1995 • 1stB 1999 • Tasting/tours by appt; also tailor-made wine tours (max 6 people) • Owner(s) Danie Hattingh • 12,000cs own label 100% red • Other export labels: Iwayini, Kattekwaaad • PO Box 185 Gordon's Bay 7151 • mwines@mweb.co.za • www.maidenwines.co.za • **T +27 (0)82-554-9395**

Maison

Kim Smith and Chris Weylandt (a surname synonymous with casual-contemporary homeware in South Africa) invite you to visit their boutique Franschhoek estate, where one of chef Liam Tomlin's popular Chefs Warehouse restaurants specialises in pairing 'global tapas' with the characterful wines made by Antwan Bondesio. As this guide went to press, the self-described 'plaasboer' was happy to report that production of his Reserve Chenin has resumed and his 2016 malbec plantings have borne fruit.

★★★★ **Shiraz** Fermented with a handful of viognier raisins, aged 15 months in French oak, third new, **16** ★★★★★ ⑨① better balanced than **15** ⑧⑧, with alcohol in check at 14%, ripe forest fruit, intense black pepper, hints of black olive & masala spices.

★★★★ **Blanc de Noir** Pale coral **19** ⑧⑥ from shiraz is dry, very creamy after 3 months on lees in older oak, gently filtered for delicate red cherry, ruby grapefruit & pink peppercorn flavours, more complex than **18** ★★★★ ⑧⑤.

★★★★☆ **Chardonnay** Elegant **18** ⑨① comprises 21 barrels, 7 new, fermented using 3 different yeasts (including wild), aged 9 months sur lie with bâtonnage for concentrated pineapple & citrus fruit, creamy texture balanced by tangy freshness.

★★★★ **Single Vineyard Chenin Blanc** ⑨ Unwooded yet richly textured from 4 months on lees, imparting very pleasant yeasty undertone to fresh citrus fruit in **18** ⑧⑦. From registered single block.

★★★★ **Viognier** Fragrant **18** ⑧⑧ has exotic floral & spice notes leading to white peach & Golden Delicious apple flavours, fresh acidity cutting through oily texture after 6 months in older barrels.

★★★★ **Méthode Cap Classique** Zero dosage chardonnay sparkler with 5 years on lees before disgorgement. Vibrant citrus, with buttery biscuit richness, more to celebrate in **12** ⑧⑧ than bone-dry **11** ★★★ ⑧②.

★★★★ **Straw Wine** Chenin sun-dried on straw, fermented/aged year in French oak, 20% new. **17** ⑧⑨ has honey & dried apricot concentration, 150 g/l sugar yet no cloy thanks to nervy acidity. 500 ml.

Not tasted: **Single Vineyard Chenin Blanc Reserve**. — JG

Location/map/WO: Franschhoek ▪ Map grid reference: C3 ▪ Est 2005 ▪ 1stB 2008 ▪ Tasting & sales Mon-Sun 10-5 ▪ Chefs Warehouse @ Maison ▪ Owner(s) Chris Weylandt & Kim Smith ▪ Winemaker(s)/viticulturist(s) Antwan Bondesio ▪ 11ha/4.5ha (malbec, shiraz, chard, chenin, viog) ▪ 50% red 50% white ▪ PO Box 587 Franschhoek 7690 ▪ cw.maisonestate.co.za, cw.maison@gmail.com ▪ www.maisonestate.co.za ▪ S 33° 53′ 09.7″ E 019° 4′ 39.80″ ▪ ⓜ unanimously.unforgettable.goods ▪ **T +27 (0)21-876-2116**

Maison de Teijger ⓥ

Whether there's any room for vehicles in Durbanville anaesthetist and small-scale winemaker Charl van Teijlingen's garage, which doubles as a 'cellar' during harvest, is unknown. Wife Danél provides assistance making and marketing the wines through friends, wineclubs and tasting groups.

Chardonnay range
Chardonnay Wooded ★★★ Shy citrus & creamy lees on understated **18** ⑧②, 8-month oaking, all old, not apparent. Shade less nuanced than last. **Chardonnay Unwooded** ⓥ ★★★ Shows trademark orange blossom & spice, nice lees richness & breadth; **17** ⑧② tangy & vibrant.

Malbec range
Malbec Reserve ⓥ ★★★ Exotic **15** ⑧① with rum-&-raisin spicing, mandarin & plum notes; salty, zesty & mouthfilling. Love it or hate it - it definitely makes a statement! Also in magnum.

Petit Verdot range
Petit Verdot ⓥ ★★★☆ Plummy, vanilla-dusted **15** ⑧④ takes step up with fresher acid-tannin structure; despite ripeness, remarkably unheavy & sippable. Also in magnum.

Sauvignon Blanc range
Sauvignon Blanc Unwooded ⓥ ★★★ Cool-climate (Durbanville) fruit makes **18** ⑧⓪ leaner, zestier than previous. Bright, tangy & succulent. Occasional release: **Sauvignon Blanc Wooded**.

Bush Vine range
Cabernet Sauvignon ★★★ Confected, jammy **17** ⑦⑧ from Agter Paarl grapes, with prominent oak, 22 months in barrique, despite none new. **Cinsaut** ★★★ Juicy, bright **17** ⑦⑧ from Bottelary fruit, straightforward, with dry vanilla spice courtesy 15 months in 30% American oak, none new. **Cinsaut Reserve** ⑭ⓔⓐ ★★★ Light, soft **17** ⑧⓪ displays variety's blueberry notes. Gentle & easy, 15 months oaking not obvious. Same grape source as sibling. **Merlot** ★★★ Tealeaf & Xmas cake notes on **17** ⑦⑧ from Stellenbosch grapes. Uncomplicated, lacks structure despite 22 months in old oak. **Pinotage** ★★ Raspberry simplicity on **17** ⑦⑥ off very old low-yielding Durbanville bushvines. **Chenin Blanc** ⑭ⓔⓐ ⓥ ★★★ Light pineapple & melon vibrancy, **19** ⑧② unchallenging, with ample tang from acid (6.8 g/l). Old Paarl vines; unwooded.

Méthode Cap Classique range
Pinot Noir-Chardonnay ⓥ ★★★☆ Overt apple & toast on **15** ⑧④ zero-dosage sparkler (pinot 52%), nice dry lime twist & lees notes from 38 months on lees. Not tasted: **Chardonnay, Pinot Noir**. — FM

Location: Durbanville ▪ Map: Durbanville, Philadelphia & Darling ▪ Map grid reference: D7 ▪ WO: Durbanville/Bottelary/Paarl ▪ Est/1stB 2004 ▪ Tasting Sat by appt only ▪ Owner(s) Charl van Teijlingen ▪ Cellarmaster(s) Charl van Teijlingen (2004) ▪Winemaker(s) Charl van Teijlingen, with Danél van Teijlingen (both 2004) & Matthew van Teijlingen (2016) ▪ 5-9t/±300cs own label 80% red 20% white ▪ PO Box 2703 Durbanville 7551 ▪ cteijlingen@gmail.com ▪ S 33° 49' 02.20" E 018° 39' 01.56" ▪ handover.stoically.piercingly ▪ **T +27 (0)21-975-0806/+27 (0)83-456-9410**

☐ **Major's Hill Estate** *See Editor's Note*
☐ **Makulu** *see Imbuko Wines*

Malanot Wines

'People think I'm crazy,' says Marius Malan, who cobbled together a brand name from his surname and the Afrikaans word for pleasure – 'genot'. He admits he too sometimes thinks he's nuts to winkle out special parcels of grapes for increasingly natural vinification. Which might explain why he called a labour-of-love, skin-contact, natural-ferment chenin blanc Asiel (asylum)! This seasoned vintner has made wines and consulted far and wide, and qualified as a Cape Wine Master, one of few winemakers to do so.

Asiel range (NEW)
★★★★☆ **Chenin Blanc** 🌿 Seamless **17** ⑨④ shows nectarine, baked apple & cream with thrilling crystalline acid to balance. Portion fermented with stalks & skins. Year in oak, all old. Textured, with long, rewarding fresh finish. Also in 1.5L.

★★★★ **Semillon** Succulent, crisp & zesty **18** ⑧⑦ from Elgin fruit. Flint & apple blossom vivacity. 2-day skin contact & all-natural ferment before year in mainly old oak add mouthfeel & breadth. Minuscule quantity produced & worth keeping, as Chenin.

Family Reserve range
★★★★ **Triton Syrah** Restrained & characterful **18** ⑧⑨ follows form of **16** ⑧⑧. Spicy purple fruit with lithe pliability & lean muscle. Well-knit oak (25% new) limited to 1 year. WO Paarl. **17** untasted.

★★★★☆ **Chardonnay** 🌿 Bunch fermented/aged in barrel, natural yeasts. Restrained elegance in **16** ⑨② from Elgin & Franschhoek, nothing showy, citrus & toasted almonds seamlessly meshed. Lovely poise.

Malanot range
Sauvignon Blanc 🌿 ★★★★ Pineapple & gooseberry typicity on tangy **18** ⑧④, balanced & long. Perfect poolsider. In abeyance: **Vino Café Pinotage, Cherry Blossom, Rosé, Bush Pig Chenin Blanc, Flower Pot.** — FM

Location/map: Stellenbosch ▪ Map grid reference: E3 ▪ WO: Stellenbosch/Paarl/Elgin/Western Cape ▪ Est/1stB 2006 ▪ Tasting & sales by appt ▪ Cellar tours by appt & during harvest only ▪ Owner(s) Malanot Wine Projects cc ▪ Cellarmaster(s)/winemaker(s)/viticulturist(s) Marius Malan (Jan 2006) ▪ 500t/40,000cs own label 80% red 20% white + 2,000cs for clients ▪ PO Box 592 Strand 7139 ▪ marius@malanot.com ▪ www.malanotwines.co.za ▪ S 33° 52' 57.71" E 018° 50' 49.39" ▪ shears.yards.seat ▪ **T +27 (0)72-124-7462**

☐ **Malkopbaai** *see Teubes Family Wines*
☐ **Mandela** *see House of Mandela*

MAN Family Wines

The team behind MAN Family Wines have swapped the tractor shed where they started their 300-case 'weekend project' in 2001 for an elegantly renovated Cape-Dutch-gabled home at the Lievland estate between Stellenbosch and Paarl. A welcoming tasting lounge has opened there, converting yet more fans to their well-priced, ultra-drinkable range. Now producing 280,000 cases and exporting to more than 30 countries globally, the trio of winemaking husbands – José Conde of Stark-Condé, Philip and Tyrell Myburgh of Joostenberg – still answer to the wives who lent their initials to this brand: Marie, Anette and Nicky.

MAN Family Wines range
★★★★ **Skaapveld Shiraz** ✓ Firm frame of **17** ⑧⑥ supports peppery black fruit. Like **16** ⑧⑥, layered & medium bodied with year in older American oak. Dabs mourvèdre & grenache.

Ou Kalant Cabernet Sauvignon ⊗ ★★★☆ Ripe softness & buxom appeal on plummy **17** ⑧⑤. Light fynbos & spice nuance from oak (30% wooded, 5% new American, rest older). Dryland Agter Paarl vines unless noted. **Jan Fiskaal Merlot** ⊘ ★★★★ Gentle interplay of berry fruit & deeper spicy vanilla oak on **17** ⑧④. Medium bodied, pleasant, easy & approachable. **Bosstok Pinotage** ⊘ ★★★☆ Better than previous, but **17** ⑧④ retains coffee sheen on raspberry fruit. Light tannic note from year in quarter American oak, 20% new. **Padstal Chardonnay** ★★★☆ Citrus & butterscotch from combo tank- & barrel-fermented/ aged portions intermingle on lively **18** ⑧④. Offers good length of flavour. **Free-Run Steen Chenin Blanc** ★★★☆ Quince & melon vim to **19** ⑧③. Unoaked, it's fresh yet leesy with good length. **Warrelwind Sauvignon Blanc** ★★★ Dusty nettle & lemon zest to **19** ⑧② from widely sourced fruit. 15% portion semillon added. Light & bright but touch less intense than last. **Méthode Cap Classique Brut** ⊗ ★★★☆ Oystershell & lemon tang counter richer cream, biscuit & sourdough notes on **NV** ⑧⑤ dry sparkler from chenin. Quite complex, structured & rich from 13 months on lees & dab oaked wine added with dosage.

Essay range

Syrah-Mourvèdre-Grenache-Cinsault ⊘ ★★★☆ Inky depth to light, supple & spicy **17** ⑧④ blend. Gentle leather note & tannin from older oak. **Chenin Blanc-Viognier-Roussanne** ★★★★ Unwooded **19** ⑧⑤ offers quince, apple & leesy creaminess, lovely weight & breadth with fresh acid to balance. Finishes clean & dry, poised. Roussanne from Stellenbosch. — FM

Location: Stellenbosch/Paarl ▪ WO: Coastal/Western Cape ▪ Est 2001 ▪ Tasting & sales at Lievland Vineyards ▪ Owner(s) MAN Vintners (Pty) Ltd ▪ Cellarmaster(s) Tyrrel Myburgh (2001) ▪ Winemaker(s) Riaan Möller (Dec 2016) ▪ 280,000cs own label 60% red 40% white ▪ PO Box 37 Klapmuts 7625 ▪ info@manwines.com ▪ www. manwines.com ▪ **T +27 (0)21-875-3026**

Manley Private Cellar   ⓠ ⑪ ⑩ ⓪

Though part of a broader tourism and lifestyle venture, involving accommodation, meals, function venues and outdoor attractions, wine is no afterthought at Tulbagh's Manley Private Cellar. It's been a feature here since founder David Manley Jordan planted vines in the late 1990s, and later converted the dairy and stables into a boutique cellar. The man now in charge of said facility is Joshua van Blommestein, previously assistant at nearby top-ranked Saronsberg. Mostly exported, the wines currently selling were not available for review.

Location/map: Tulbagh ▪ Map grid reference: F5 ▪ Est/1stB 2002 ▪ Tasting Mon-Fri by appt, Sat/Sun 10-3 ▪ Fee R30, waived on purchase ▪ Belgium chocolate & wine tasting ▪ Cellar tours by appt ▪ Closed Good Fri, Dec 25 & Jan 1 ▪ Luxury B&B ▪ Restaurant Wed-Fri 12—9 Sat/Sun 9-9 ▪ Wedding & conference facilities ▪ Chapel ▪ Owner(s) Manley Wine Lodge (Pty) Ltd ▪ Winemaker(s)/viticulturist(s) Joshua van Blommestein (Sep 2019) ▪ 38ha/8ha (cab, merlot, ptage, shiraz) ▪ PO Box 318 Tulbagh 6820 ▪ bookings@manleywinelodge.co.za ▪ www.manleywinelodge.co.za ▪ S 33° 16' 15.8" E 019° 8' 43.8" ▪ ⟨⟩ modifying.escapees.glistened ▪ **T +27 (0)23-230-0582**

☐ **Manor House** see Nederburg Wines
☐ **Marais Family** see Wonderfontein

Maree Family Wines   (NEW)

Upcoming young winemaker Jacques Maree (helping re-establish Quoin Rock on Simonsberg Mountain) joins his father and namesake on a mission to celebrate nature's role in winemaking, by showcasing vintage variations in red wines from the Helderberg. Vinified from bought-in grapes in rented cellar space, the debut '16 blend recalls the relationship between Pieter, a tame Brahman bull on the family's Namibia cattle farm, and mischievous young Jacques jnr, alias 'Jakkals', Afrikaans for jackal.

Pieter & The Jackal ★★★☆ Bold, with firm tannins, **16** ⑧③'s red/black fruit compote from shiraz, cab, dab cab franc has cloves & black pepper, scrub notes & light vanilla dusting. Charming label. — CR, CvZ

Location: Somerset West ▪ WO: Stellenbosch ▪ Est/1stB 2016 ▪ Closed to public ▪ Owner(s) Maree Family Wines (Pty) Ltd (shareholders Jacques Maree snr & jnr) ▪ Winemaker(s) Jacques Maree (2016) ▪ Own label 100% red ▪ 94 Lourensford Rd, Somerset West 7130 ▪ jacques@mareefamilywines.com ▪ www.mareefamily-wines.com ▪ **T +27 (0)82-925-9493**

Marianne Wine Estate

French and SA cultures blend seamlessly at this Simonsberg wine and luxury guest farm. It's owned by Bordeaux's Dauriac family, with French-born GM Soline Lippe de Thoisy and Bordeaux-trained consultant oenologist Thierry Haberer backing locals Jos van Wyk (winemaker) and Ernest Manuel (viticulturist). The debut viognier is one of only two in the guide using acacia wood for maturation, and the '15 Desirade, launched ahead of the 2019 Rugby World Cup, bears the name of the captain of the 1995 winning Springboks, 'a huge honour for the farm'.

Marianne range

★★★★☆ **Cabernet Sauvignon** ⓐ Excellent varietal character & complexity: aromas of blackberry, mulberry, graphite & notes of dried herb & liquorice. **17** ⑨③ rich yet & elegant, with supple tannin frame & oak in support (40% French, 16-18 months). Deserves time to unfurl. No **16**. Coastal WO.

★★★★ **Merlot 15** ⑧⑧ steps up from **14** ★★★★ ⑧④ with more focus & lush berry fruit flavours, enhanced by hints of plum pudding & dark chocolate from older oak, 16-18 months. Balanced, house's big alcohol (14.9%) well hidden.

★★★★ **Shiraz** Improving on **14** ★★★★ ⑧④, **15** ⑧⑨ billows wild berries, spice & fragrant fynbos, flavours well arranged on firm tannin bed (30% new) & in harmony with 14.9% alcohol. Well structured for ageing.

★★★★ **Floreal** ⓐ Harmonious, balanced flagship. Current release **10** ★★★★☆ ⑨③, revisited, has aged well, with lavender perfume, mulled wine & savoury flavours. Rounded & perfectly mature for present enjoyment though enough freshness for few more years. Cab, merlot, shiraz, as last-tasted **13** ⑧⑦.

★★★★ **Sauvignon Blanc** Effusive tropical, greenpepper & waxy aromas in **18** ⑧⑨, plus floral notes & richness from 50% barrel-aged (French & Acacia) component. 11% semillon adds further complexity & mouthfeel. Some fruit from Somerset West.

★★★★☆ **Viognier** ⓝⓔⓦ Exceptional **18** ⑨① reined-in expression of the variety, with subtle peach, apricot kernel & spice bouquet. Intense on palate with creamy vanilla & floral echo on finish. Good food companion. 100% wooded, third new French oak, rest acacia, 10 months.

Cape Blend ★★★★ Juicy but sweetish & warming **15** ⑧⑤ is for early enjoyment with grilled meat. From shiraz, pinotage & merlot. **Rosé** ★★★★ Improved **18** ⑧⑤, candyfloss pink hue, floral & perfumed aromas with good structure & flavour. From 4 Rhône black grapes vs some white varieties for previous. Not tasted: **Pinotage**.

Private Collection

★★★★ **Francois Pienaar Desirade** ⓐ Adds Springbok rugby captain's name. Stylish **15** ★★★★☆ ⑨④ is 50/30 merlot & cab with splashes shiraz & pinotage, showing fine concentration of dark berry fruit & chocolate, supple tannin structure & enduring finish. More finesse than **14** ⑧⑨.

Natana range

Not tasted: **Syrah**, **Cuvée Rouge**.

Selena range

Not tasted: **Syrah**, **Cuvée Rouge**. — WB

Location/map: Stellenbosch ▪ Map grid reference: G1 ▪ WO: Simonsberg-Paarl/Coastal/Western Cape ▪ Est/1stB 2004 ▪ Tasting, sales & cellar tours Mon–Sun & pub hols 10-7 (summer)/10-6 (winter) ▪ Fee R70/5 wines; R115/wine & biltong pairing ▪ Cellar tour, barrel tasting & vertical tasting of flagship wines ▪ Meat & cheese platters ▪ Picnics ▪ The Floreal Brasserie, www.floreal.co.za ▪ Panoramic tasting deck ▪ Gift shop ▪ 4-star accommodation ▪ Owner(s) Dauriac family ▪ Winemaker(s) Jos van Wyk, with Thierry Haberer (consultant) ▪ Viticulturist(s) Ernest Manuel (Sep 2017) ▪ 36ha/±26ha (cabs s/f, cinsaut, grenache, merlot, mourv, ptage, shiraz, sauv, viog) ▪ 100t/16,000cs own label 90% red 5% white 5% rosé ▪ PO Box 7300 Stellenbosch 7599 ▪ info@mariannewinefarm.co.za, hospitality@mariannewinefarm.co.za ▪ www.marian-newines.com ▪ S 33° 49' 57.6" E 018° 53' 37.4" ▪ ⌖ busting.waffle.retracing ▪ **T +27 (0)21-875-5040**

☐ **Mariëtte** see Le Belle Rebelle
☐ **Marimba** see Southern Sky Wines

Marklew Family Wines

Long a supplier of prime grapes in sought-after Simonsberg-Stellenbosch, the Marklew family of the farm De Goede Sukses renovated a 180-year-old cellar in the early 2000s to begin producing for an own label. Bill Marklew tends to the vines, while his sister Haidee keeps the wheels of the business running. Neil Strydom makes the boutique wines.

★★★★ **Cabernet Sauvignon** ⓥ Ripe mulberry & blackcurrant aromas dusted with cedar, **17** ⑧⑦ persistent, with deep blueberry palate, dense tannin structure. No **16**.

★★★★ **Cape Flora Pinotage** ⓥ Perfumed **17** ⑧⑧ same generous fruit as last. Primary berry & violet notes, ripe juicy core & supple tannins for now or keeping a few years. **16** untasted. Coastal WO.

★★★★ **Shiraz Reserve** ⓥ Widely sourced **17** ⑧⑦, plum & Xmas cake spicing, youthful & firm with taut tannin grip, heady 15% alcohol, yet enough savoury appeal for food pairing.

★★★★ **Family Reserve** ⓥ Bordeaux red with cab (52%), dashes merlot, cab franc. Laudable **16** ⑧⑧ authentic forest fruit, oak spice & minerality. Poised & full, dark berry persistence. Worth keeping.

★★★★ **Chardonnay** ⓥ Svelte **16** ⑧⑧'s alluring nectarine & pear interwoven with almond & vanilla ex 13 months French oak. Creamy & mouthfilling but fresh, too, with judicious 13% alcohol, enlivening acidity.

Sauvignon Blanc ★★★ Seriously zesty acid tang on **19** ⑧⓪, gentle elderflower & tropical fruit notes as well. **Méthode Cap Classique Brut Reserve** ⓜⓒⓒ ★★★★ Citrus marmalade & apple on all-chardonnay **NV** ⑧⑤ sparkling. Light, bright & zesty, creamy tail from 14 months on lees. Not tasted: **Merlot**. — FM

Location/map: Stellenbosch ▪ Map grid reference: F1 ▪ WO: Simonsberg–Stellenbosch/Coastal/Western Cape ▪ Est 1970 ▪ 1stB 2003 ▪ Tasting, sales & tours by appt ▪ Tour groups (max 20) ▪ Private/business functions for small groups ▪ Walks ▪ Mountain biking ▪ Conservation area ▪ Owner(s) Marklew family (Edward Dudley, Edward William, Lyn & Haidee) ▪ Winemaker(s) Neil Strydom (Oct 2015) ▪ Viticulturist(s) Billy Marklew (Jun 2001), with Neil Strydom (Oct 2015) ▪ 58ha/45ha (cabs s/f, merlot, ptage, shiraz, chard, sauv) ▪ ±300t/5,000cs own label 65% red 30% white 5% MCC ▪ IPW ▪ PO Box 17 Elsenburg 7607 ▪ wine@marklew.co.za ▪ www.marklew.co.za ▪ S 33° 50' 35.7" E 018° 51' 50.3" ▪ 🖵 item.puzzles.charge ▪ **T +27 (0)21-884-4412**

☐ **Martindale** *see* Wine-of-the-Month Club
☐ **Marvelous** *see* Yardstick Wines
☐ **Mary Delany** *see* Botanica Wines
☐ **Mary Le Bow** *see* Bruce Jack Wines

Maske Wines ⓥ

For 20 years now, Wellington vintners Erich and Janine Maske have contracted with various winemakers and viticulturists to produce a boutique portfolio for export. The past year has been 'very quiet on the wine front but challenging on others', yet they're hearted by their '15 Cabernet which 'has been doing a little self-improvement in the bottle and is now ready for release'.

Maske range
Cabernet Sauvignon ★★★★ Shy cedar & tobacco notes, clean savoury & earthy whiffs, fruitier on palate with dry tannins reining in the exuberance & lending structure. Drink **15** ⑧④ now & over 3+ years. Discontinued: **Merlot, Tattoo, Chenin Blanc**.
Discontinued: **Leeumasker range**. — CvZ

Location/map/WO: Wellington ▪ Map grid reference: C4 ▪ Est/1stB 2000 ▪ Tasting & sales by appt only ▪ Closed Ash Wed, Easter Fri/Sun & Dec 25 ▪ Owner(s) Erich & Janine Maske ▪ Winemaker(s)/viticulturist(s) outsourced ▪ 7ha/5ha (cab, merlot, shiraz, chenin) ▪ 80% red 20% white ▪ Klein Waterval PO Box 206 Wellington 7654 ▪ laureat@iafrica.com ▪ www.maskewines.co.za ▪ S 33° 40' 4.2" E 019° 2' 37.3" ▪ 🖵 clutches.pocket.triathlete ▪ **T +27 (0)21-873-3407**

☐ **Mason Road** *see* Brookdale Estate
☐ **Maties** *see* Stellenbosch University Welgevallen Cellar
☐ **Matys** *see* Diemersdal Estate

Matzikama Organic Cellar

When not nurturing over 200 hectares of vines and making wine for ground-breaking West Coast winery Stellar (putting SA on the world stage with organic Fairtrade and no-added-sulphur wines), Klaas Coetzee produces this boutique brand, named 'Place of Water'. Also certified organic, the small parcels of wine, including a rare varietal bottling of petite sirah (durif), are from the maritime Koekenaap ward.

Coetzee Family Wines range

Blomveld se Vlei Petite Sirah ⊘ ★★★★ A celebration of vibrant, bright red-berry fruit, prune & herb nuances in tarry finish. **17** ⑧⑤ still tight but promising, needs year/two for 50% new French oak to settle. Discontinued: **Blomveld se Vlei Chenin Blanc**. — DS

Location: Vredendal ▪ WO: Olifants River ▪ Est/1stB 2001 ▪ Closed to public ▪ Owner(s)/winemaker(s)/ viticulturist(s) Klaas Coetzee ▪ 12ha/2.5ha (cab, shiraz, tannat) ▪ 24t 100% red ▪ PO Box 387 Vredendal 8160 ▪ klaas@matzikamawyn.co.za ▪ www.matzikamawyn.co.za ▪ **T +27 (0)82-801-3737**

☐ **Maxim** *see* Goedverwacht Wine Estate

McGregor Wines ⓠ ⓑ

Barely out of celebratory mode for the 70th anniversary of the founding of this industrious producer-owned winery near McGregor village, the team is getting ready to pop corks marking seven decades since the crush of the first grapes here, on 21 February 1950. The vision for the next three score and ten is to produce innovative wines that excite and inspire the growers, the community and of course lovers of wine.

Winemaker's Reserve range

★★★★ **Cabernet Sauvignon** Fresh blackcurrant, cranberry & graphite note from 16 months in oak, appealing crunchy finish, yet leaner fruit & more exposed tannins mean **17** ★★★★ ⑧⑤ misses the mark of last-made **15** ⑧⑦.

McGregor range

Chardonnay ⓦ ★★★ Unwooded & very easy to like, **19** ⑦⑨ offers ripe apple & floral notes, lemon on the finish. **Colombard** ⓦ ★★★ Jam-packed with variety's guava on palate, joined by fragrant orchard fruit in the bouquet, piquant spice on the finish. **19** ⑧⓪ balanced & delightful.

Pinotage ★★★ Dark plums & dusty fynbos, also hint of mocha though **18** ⑦⑨ is unoaked. **Shiraz** ★★ Juicy **18** ⑦⑥ is friendlier than last, with more fruit & softer spicy grip. **Chenin Blanc** ★★ Lean & lemony **19** ⑦③ is water-white & unoaked, has a fleeting crisp farewell. **Sauvignon Blanc** ★★ Light, barely-there capsicum & pineapple wafts in **19** ⑦③. **Red Muscadel** ⓠ ★★★ Brick-red jerepiko is grapey, fragrant, with caramel aftertaste. **16** ⑦⑨ appeals but could use more zip. WO W Cape, as next. **White Muscadel** ⓠ ★★★ Dried peach & boiled sweet notes on **16** ⑧① fortified dessert. Very sweet despite spirity bite. Not tasted: **Cabernet Sauvignon-Merlot, The Delicious Monster**. Discontinued: **Cape Ruby**. — WB

Location: McGregor ▪ Map: Robertson ▪ Map grid reference: D6 ▪ WO: McGregor/Western Cape ▪ Est 1948 ▪ 1stB 1978 ▪ Tasting & sales Mon-Fri 8—5 Sat 9-1 ▪ Closed Good Fri, Dec 25/26 & Jan 1 ▪ Owner(s) 27 members ▪ Winemaker(s) Elmo du Plessis (Jan 2009) ▪ 14,000t 22% red 78% white ▪ IPW, WIETA ▪ PO Box 519 McGregor 6708 ▪ info@mcgregorwinery.co.za ▪ www.mcgregorwinery.co.za ▪ S 33° 56' 5.4" E 019° 50' 56.3" ▪ 🖾 limousines.promptness.phenomenal ▪ **T +27 (0)23-625-1741/1109**

☐ **Meander** *see* Daschbosch

Meerendal Wine Estate ⓠ ⓜ ⓐ ⓞ ⓢ ⓑ

Among many recent upgrades at this historic, family-owned Durbanville estate, established in 1702, is a new vinoteque for its old wines, an important consideration for a producer that celebrated half a century of pinotage last year. Yet winemaker Liza Goodwin continues to innovate with wines such as the Ripasso-style Pinotage Vine and a Natural Sweet sauvignon blanc with vine-dried and botrytised elements. And if the wines (now all Wine of Origin Cape Town) aren't enough to entice visitors, there are various activities, a market, distillery, gallery, boutique hotel and three restaurants, new iL Tesoro offering farm-to-table fare.

Prestige range

★★★★☆ **Heritage Block Pinotage** ⊛ From bushvines planted in 1955, Durbanville's oldest block, previewed **17** ⑨③ has floral aromatics, bright blueberry & plum fruit, vanilla & cocoa from 20 months in new French oak. Tannin structure & brisk acid suggest good keepability.

★★★★☆ **Intensio** Fascinating collaboration with Italian vintner Stefano Contini, Amarone-style **18** ⑨⓪ from vine-dried pinotage is very full & ripe, as expected, barely dry on taste, yet shows lovely freshness & little wood influence after only 4 months in 4th-fill barrels. Tasted pre-bottling.

★★★★☆ **The Pinotage Vine** (NEW) Another compelling, boundary-pushing, Italianate expression of pinotage. After triple fermentation (alcoholic, malolactic & Ripasso-style on skins of 2018 grapes from Heritage Block), **16** ⑨① is very fresh, dry, with attractive dark fruit, moderate 13.5% alcohol, no overt wood notes after 14 months in 2nd/3rd-fill oak.

★★★★ **Sauvignon Blanc Natural Sweet** (NEW) Vine-dried grapes with 20% botrytised component, **18** ⑧⑨ unoaked dessert wine has dried apple & yoghurt-coated almond flavours, intensely sweet at 160 g/l sugar but fresh thanks to vivacious acidity. 375 ml.

Not tasted: **Heritage Reserve**, **Méthode Cap Classique Brut**. Occasional release: **Merlot Prestige**, **Merlot Reserve**, **Bin159 Shiraz**, **Liza**.

Standard range

★★★★ **Merlot** With pinch of fresh herbs, plenty of red fruit (plums, cherries), **16** ⑧⑧ is smooth after year in mostly older barrels, less choc-mocha & masala oak spice than last.

★★★★ **Sauvignon Blanc** ⊘ Wonderful complexity in **19** ★★★★☆ ⑨⓪, granadilla & grapefruit plus hints of lemongrass & gunflint. Benefits from 3 months on lees (with regular stirring), gains even more character, substance, depth & length than **18** ⑧⑥.

Pinot Noir ★★★☆ Prior to bottling, **19** ⑧④ shows densely packed fruit cradled by mostly older oak, earthy wild strawberries in the flavour profile. **Pinotage** ★★★☆ Fresh-earth nuance to red & black berry fruit in easy-drinking **16** ⑧④, 13 months in older oak lend subtle spice & soft tannins. **Shiraz** ★★★★ While **16** & **17** await release, **18** ⑧③ preview shows dark fruit & dark chocolate, liquorice from 7 months in 50% new oak. **Pinotage Blanc de Noir** ★★★☆ Copper-hued **19** ⑧④, ex tank packed with red berries, creamy texture cut through by fresh acidity for drier effect than previous. **Chardonnay Unwooded** ★★★☆ Smoothed by 2 months on lees, **19** ⑧⑤ shows lemon & lime freshness, pleasingly restrained 12.5% alcohol. Ex tank seems just a fraction less complex than **18** ★★★★ ⑧⑥. Occasional release: **Cabernet Sauvignon**. Discontinued: **Méthode Cap Classique**. — JG

Location: Durbanville ▪ Map: Durbanville, Philadelphia & Darling ▪ Map grid reference: C7 ▪ WO: Cape Town ▪ Est 1702 ▪ 1stB 1969 ▪ Tasting & sales Mon-Sat 10-6 Sun 11-6 ▪ Closed Good Fri, Dec 25 & Jan 1 ▪ Cellar tours by appt ▪ Crown Restaurant & Wine Bar at Meerendal T +27 (0)21-975-0383, Mon-Sun 7am-10pm ▪ Carlucci's Deli T +27 (0)21-612-0015, Sun/Mon 7-5 Tue-Sat 7am-8.30pm ▪ iL Tesoro at Meerendal T +27 (0)21-612-0015, Wed-Sat 6pm-10pm Sun 12-4 ▪ Facilities for children ▪ Tour groups ▪ Weddings/functions ▪ Walking/running/MTB trails ▪ Renosterveld conservation area ▪ Meerendal Wine Academy ▪ The Meerendal Boutique Hotel ▪ Owner(s) Coertze family ▪ Cellarmaster(s)/winemaker(s) Líza Goodwin (Sep 2006) ▪ Viticulturist(s) Altus van Lill (Jun 2018) ▪ 227ha/54ha (cab, merlot, ptage, pinot, shiraz, chard, sauv) ▪ 500t/50,000cs own label 75% red 20% white 5% rosé ▪ IPW ▪ Private Bag X1702 Durbanville 7551 ▪ info@meerendal.co.za ▪ www.meerendal.co.za ▪ S 33° 47' 55.8" E 018° 37' 26.2" ▪ ⓕ fiery.kettles.funnier ▪ **T +27 (0)21-975-1655**

Meerhof Wines ⓘ 🍴 📷

There's obvious new energy here: the range has already expanded by 9 wines, so the new teams in cellar and vineyards are clearly fully productive. The Jansen van Rensburgs were maize and game farmers on the Highveld for 40 years before relocating to buy these high-lying vineyards and cellar near Riebeek-Kasteel in Swartland. Koos and son Eric direct operations across two farms, this and Rheeboksfontein, and while expansion is the main focus, speciality wines are also appearing, like blends and a straw wine. Building of expanded facilities at the restaurant are now complete, with visitors very welcome.

Premium range (NEW)

★★★★ **Shiraz-Grenache** Shiraz in control, 30% grenache, **18** ⑧⑧ is smoky, dark toned, meaty, some dried herbs. 12 months new oak's firm grip in the finish, otherwise there's succulence, ample curves.

★★★★☆ White Blend ⊘ Chenin dominates **18** ⑨⓪, with chardonnay, grenache blanc, dab roussanne; new oak & half each French/American (as all these). Showy: roasted almonds, stonefruit, some caramelised orange zest, & then a palate surprise, is mineral & savoury. Worthy debut.

Grenache Rosé ⊛ **★★★☆** A rarity, barrel-fermented rosé, 8 months new oak. Cranberries & toast in delicately hued **18** ⑧④, slender (12% alcohol) but ample fruit for ambitious food pairing. Has personality.

Speciality Wines ⑭

★★★★ Arbeidsgenot Grenache Noir Vanilla- & mixed spice-perfumed from mainly new oak; piquant cranberries, wild fruit & scrub, **18** ⑧⑧ is complex, involving. Streamlined, enough basic structure for ageing.

★★★★ Arbeidsgenot Shiraz New oak, heaps of flavour, seductively rich, blackberries & spice, black pepper, multi-layered **18** ⑧⑧'s texture the bonus, smooth & supple, curvy, long finish.

★★★★☆ Mooistrooi ⊛ Vin de paille from muscat d'Alexandrie air-dried on straw-lined racks ±2 weeks, **18** ⑨③'s name ('Lovely Straw') is spot on. Caramelised citrus & pineapple, molten apricots, barley sugar from 5 months new oak. Full-sweet but no barrier to enjoyment, needs the right occasion. 500 ml.

Meerhof range

Red Blend ⑭ ⊛ **★★★☆** Shiraz's dark fruit dominates **18** ⑧④, cab's cassis adds a berry-rich layer. Careful use of staves contributes spice, no edginess, this succulent blend is about pleasure. Splash grenache.

Cabernet Sauvignon ⑭ **★★★☆** New barrels 12 months for **18** ⑧④, showing as lead pencils, firm dry finish. Plums & blackcurrants sheath the tannins, aid current enjoyment but wine designed for cellaring. **Pinotage** ⑭ **★★★☆** Blueberries & smoky spice, **18** ⑧⑤ has lovely juiciness, fresh & fruity, the tannins amenable, a stable foundation providing structure & a future. All-new barrels, well managed. **Shiraz ★★★☆** Lots going on in **18** ⑧③, scrub & black pepper, dark wild berries, a lovely campfire smokiness that will pair well with meat dishes. Combo barrels & oak staves 12 months. **Grenache Rosé** ⊘ **★★★☆** Pale pink but the rest is far from wan, wild red berries, notes of dry scrub in **18** ⑧④, the voice of grenache speaks clearly. Dry, with a mineral finish. Lovely. Fairtrade, as most. **Chardonnay** ⊘ **★★☆** Lightly oaked **18** ⑦⑧ is citrus-styled, fruity-fresh, delicate biscuit shading adds interest. **Chenin Blanc** ⊘ ⊛ **★★★☆** Stonefruit, granadilla & a mineral top note, **18** ⑧③ has lots to offer. No oaking, a flinty savouriness at the end. Great food wine. **Sauvignon Blanc** ⊘ **★★★☆** Variety-true **18** ⑦⑧ has appealing drinkability, melon & citrus flavours, fresh & dry. **White Blend** ⊘ **★★★☆** Creative & appealing Swartland blend of roussanne, viognier, grenache blanc. **18** ⑧④'s light oaking only evident in the flavours, white-fleshed nectarines, some lemon zest. Discontinued: **Petrolhead Red Blend**, **Saffronne Rosé**, **Joseph & Herman Fraternity Chenin Blanc**, **Petrolhead White Blend**. — CR

Location: Riebeek-Kasteel ▪ Map/WO: Swartland ▪ Map grid reference: D6 ▪ 1stB 2017 ▪ Tasting, sales & cellar tours Mon-Fri 9-5 Sat/Sun 9-3 ▪ Fee R35pp ▪ Closed Dec 25 ▪ Restaurant Wed-Fri 9-5 Sat/Sun 9-3 ▪ Farm produce ▪ Conferences ▪ Walking/hiking trails ▪ Conservation area ▪ Owner(s) Koos & Hestia Jansen van Rensburg ▪ Cellarmaster(s)/winemaker(s) Jaco Brand (Oct 2017) ▪ Viticulturist(s) Johan Kellerman (Oct 2017) ▪ 230ha/130ha (cab, merlot, pinot noir/gris, shiraz, chard, chenin, grenache b, rouss, sauv, verdelho, viog) ▪ 1,000t/65,000L own label 40% red 40% white 20% rosé ▪ Fairtrade ▪ PO Box 148 Riebeek-Kasteel 7307 ▪ admin@meerhofwines.co.za ▪ www.meerhofwines.co.za ▪ S 33° 24' 19.8" E 018° 52' 15.0" ▪ ✉ emancipate. diplomacy.determining ▪ **T +27 (0)22-125-0422/3**

☐ **Meerkat Wines** *see* Welbedacht Wine Estate

Meerlust Estate ⑨ ⓐ

This is one of great old estates of the Cape. Occupying the lovely Cape Dutch manor house is Hannes Myburgh, whose family have owned the property since 1757, when Johannes Myburgh bought it and started developing the land and charming complex of buildings. There will now be a rare change in the cellar, with Chris Williams moving on to devote more time to his own winemaking project (see The Foundry), after some 15 years as cellarmaster, mingling classical vinous virtues of restraint and longevity with riper opulence and earlier charm. He leaves Meerlust in excellent shape. His replacement was being considered at press time, but continuity will be provided by Altus Treurnicht, back in the cellar after three years' absence. And by Roelie Joubert, who has been caring for the vines for nearly two decades now.

★★★★☆ **Cabernet Sauvignon** Usual classic notes of dark berry fruit & cigarbox on **16** (91), with plenty of fruit depth & a hint of herbal quality - perhaps a little more relaxed than some vintages. A slightly sombre, serious wine, balanced & well structured. 55% new oak needs a few years to absorb.

★★★★☆ **Merlot** Both sombre & lively notes of spicy tobacco along with dark fruit on **16** (92) - with dollops of cab franc & petit verdot adding as usual to complexity. Serious, richly flavoured, with sweet, bright fruit. Many years to go.

★★★★☆ **Pinot Noir** **18** (91) fresher-fruited aromas & lighter in feel & structure than usual, with more fruity charm, in what is often one of the Cape's more tannic, burly pinots. But perhaps less intensity, though it handles 50% new oak effortlessly. Lovely dry finish.

★★★★☆ **Rubicon** Fine cab-based flagship - 49% in **16** (93) (a bit less cab each year it seems) - with merlot, cab franc & petit verdot. Elegant, fresh & refined, yet with a touch of velvet opulence. Just under 14% alcohol, firm structure, all in balance, though 55% cedary new oak needs time to harmonise.

★★★★☆ **Chardonnay** Nutty, toasty notes dominate **18** (91) in youth (45% new barrels), but there's plenty of sweet fruit & a serious acidity in the balance on the palate, which is rich, lemony & nicely dry (**17** ★★★★ (87) had a heavier, sweeter character). More forceful than 12.9% alcohol would suggest.

Occasional release: **Red**. — TJ

Location/map/WO: Stellenbosch ▪ Map grid reference: C8 ▪ Est 1693 ▪ 1stB 1975 ▪ Tasting & sales Mon-Fri 9–5 Sat 10–2 ▪ Fee R30 ▪ Closed all pub hols ▪ Cellar tours by appt ▪ Quarters self-contained cottage ▪ Owner(s) Hannes Myburgh ▪ Winemaker(s) Altus Treurnicht (Nov 2018) ▪ Viticulturist(s) Roelie Joubert (2001) ▪ 400ha/110ha (cabs s/f, merlot, p verdot, pinot, chard) ▪ 500t/60,000cs own label 90% red 10% white ▪ PO Box 7121 Stellenbosch 7599 ▪ info@meerlust.co.za ▪ www.meerlust.co.za ▪ S 34° 1' 1.7" E 018° 45' 24.7" ▪ gold.hits.chilled ▪ **T +27 (0)21-843-3587**

Meinert Wines

Cape Wine Master Brendan Butler wears multiple hats as general manager, winemaker and viticulturist at this winery in Stellenbosch's Devon Valley. But so did Martin Meinert for 20 years before he sold his eponymous label to a trio of Johannesburg partners. Martin still provides some gentle guidance as a consultant but Brendan has made a seamless transition, which included extending the winery to up capacity. Not one to meddle with the brand's entrenched solid positioning in the local industry, he has ensured that merlot remains the core. But he also hints at range extensions in the next year, with exciting projects in the pipeline.

Meinert Wines range

★★★★ **Cabernet Sauvignon** Gentle fruitcake & cigarbox on **16** (88) with dab (6%) merlot that follows form of elegant **15** (87). Delicate brush of herbs & structured oak frame, 40% new, 18 months.

★★★★ **Merlot** Despite low rainfall, **16** ★★★★☆ (90) a good vintage here, improves on **15** (86). Silky smooth, succulent, with elegance. Refined harmony of tealeaf, cocoa, blue fruit & oak, 30% new. Natural ferment, as next 2.

★★★★ **Printer's Ink Pinotage** Cheery red fruit on **17** (88) livened by portion carbonic ferment, & 5% of '18 wine instead of usual dab merlot. Good concentration & length, serious structure from year in old oak. Improves on **15** ★★★☆ (83). WO Stellenbosch. **16** untasted.

★★★★☆ **Synchronicity** Improving on **15** (90) but remaining a 5-way blend, **16** (92) has equal cab & cab franc with dabs merlot, pinotage & petit verdot. Nuanced, with Black Forest cake richness balanced by tannin grip from oak, 80% new. Seductive & long. Also in magnum.

★★★★ **The German Job Riesling** Zippy taut signature wax & green apple on dry, flinty **16** (88) from Elgin. Lipsmackingly fresh & vibrant, with great fruit/acid tension. Will last well.

★★★★ **La Barry Sauvignon Blanc** Trademark succulence & vivacity in **18** (86) from Elgin. Elderflower & waxy/leafy lime notes with structured mid-palate & lingering, defined finish. Unwooded this vintage. Modest 12.5% alcohol. Ideal with summer sunshine. No **17**.

★★★★☆ **Semillon Straw Wine** Richly sweet apple & honey with subtle wax nuance on **15** ★★★★ (86). Balanced acidity ensures clean, dry finish, as with memorable **14** (93). Mostly in 375 ml.

La Barry Red ② ★★★★ Bold, bright & cheerful blend of merlot, cabs franc & sauvignon. Light-bodied, easy charmer which would partner a braai or pasta equally well. Now **NV** ⑧③. WO Coastal. **Sauvignon Blanc** ★★★★ Blends Elgin fruit & 12.4% Stellenbosch semillon to good effect, **18** ⑧⑤ tangy yet rounded & vibrant. Both oak & lees contact add flesh & breadth.

Limited Editions

★★★★ **The Italian Job White Merlot** Exotic tea & berry fruit on white, bright **18** ⑧⑥. Lovely succulence & lightness, with gentle cream overtone from occasional bâtonnage over 9 months in old oak. Dabs chenin & semillon. Coastal WO.

The Graduate Syrah ★★★★ Soft, supple & creamy **17** ⑧⑤ from Upper Hemel-en-Aarde grapes is medium bodied & easy, with floral violet nuance at the end. **Semillon** ② ★★★★ Only 10% oaked but 5 months on the lees, giving **15** ⑧④ fruit focus & good palate weight, brightening freshness calls for a second glass. Occasional release: **Pinot Noir**. Discontinued: **Chardonnay**. — FM

Location/map: Stellenbosch ▪ Map grid reference: D4 ▪ WO: Devon Valley/Coastal/Elgin/Stellenbosch/Upper Hemel-en-Aarde Valley/Western Cape ▪ Est 1987 ▪ 1stB 1997 ▪ Tasting Mon-Sat strictly by appt only ▪ Closed all pub hols ▪ Owner(s) Hesticap (Pty) Ltd ▪ Cellarmaster(s) /winemaker / GM Brendan Butler CWM (Aug 2017); Martin Meinert (1997, consultant) ▪ Viticulturist(s) Brendan Butler CWM (Aug 2017) & Henk Marconi (Jan 1991) ▪ 19ha (cabs s/f, merlot, p verdot, ptage, shiraz, sem) ▪ 90t/10,000cs own label 67% red 33% white ▪ PO Box 375 Stellenbosch 7599 ▪ info@meinertwines.com ▪ www.meinertwines.com ▪ S 33° 54' 1.8" E 018° 48' 50.2" ▪ 🖼 evidence.thus.improve ▪ **T +27 (0)21-865-2363**

Mellasat Vineyards   ② ⑪ ⑨ ⑥

Since reinventing 17th-century Dekkersvlei farm against Paarl's Klein Drakenstein crags in the late 1990s, winegrower Stephen Richardson concedes his unusual, gone-global White Pinotage remains a big drawcard. Yet he's pretty pleased with the reception of niche Mediterranean varieties viognier and tempranillo, and with the progress of natural-winemaking trials for new label, Fera Puer ('Wild Child'), all tastily paired with wife Janet's kitchen creations (see below for details).

Premium Exclusives

★★★★ **'M' Cabernet Sauvignon** ② **13** ⑧⑦ more malleable than **12** ★★★★ ⑧④ but equally robust. Menthol & cedar accents on dark-fruit bouquet & palate.

★★★★ **Tempranillo** One of fewer than a dozen in the guide. Spice & violet accents on **17** ⑧⑧'s core of cherry & blackberry fruit, laced with savoury acidity, supported by smooth tannins. Oak (40% new, some American) gives vanilla on persistent finish.

★★★★ **Viognier** Like previous, **18** ⑧⑥ carefully wooded to retain varietal character (quince, yellow peach, fresh hay) while adding layers of complexity (saffron, vanilla). Soft acidity on stonefruit finish. 11 months in mix Romanian, French & Hungarian barrels.

Mellasat range

★★★★ **'Sigma' White Pinotage** Unusual blanc de noir with bright gold hue. Alluring whiffs of banana & pear pave way for sweet spice & almond, creaminess from Romanian oaking. Fresh acidity accentuates the dried herb & nut notes which persistent to the end in previewed **18** ⑧⑥.

Chardonnay ★★★★ Usual light brush of (old French) wood gives rich citrus & melon fruit flavours free rein, some roasted pine nuts & subtle oak notes a pleasing backdrop in **17** ⑧⑤, orange peel on exit. In abeyance: **Tuin Wyn**.

Dekker's Valley range

Shiraz ★★★★ Ripe notes of redcurrant, cherry & plum are backed by moderately astringent tannins & smooth acidity. **16** ⑧④ has leather & spice showing towards the finish. **Revelation** ★★★★ Shiraz (63%) & cab in **17** ⑧④, dark fruit (blue berry & mulberry) interleaving white pepper, clove & tobacco, firm tannins with good fruit support, nice spicy tinge ex seasoned oak. **Shiraz Rosé** ★★★ Extra-dry & zesty **18** ⑧① oozes cherries & raspberries, cinnamon spice & watermelon on finish. Enjoy this summer. **Seraphic** ★★★ Chenin-based blend with chardonnay & viognier, **18** ⑧② offers plenty of quaffing fun with tropical fruit on palate, peachy aftertaste. — GM

Location/map/WO: Paarl ▪ Map grid reference: G5 ▪ Est 1996 ▪ 1stB 1999 ▪ Tasting & sales Mon-Sat 9.30-5.30 Sun/pub hols 10-4 ▪ Closed Good Fri, Dec 25 & Jan 1 ▪ Cellar tours by appt ▪ Cellarmaster's reserve tasting

• Light lunches for groups/tours or private dinner functions by appt; picnics in summer; cheese platters; pop-up seasonal restaurant & other food-based events • Tour groups • Paarl Harvest Celebration • Owner(s) Stephen Richardson • Cellarmaster(s) Stephen Richardson (Jan 1999) • Winemaker(s) Gizelle Coetzee (2016) • Viticulturist(s) Poena Malherbe (Sep 1996) • 13ha/8ha (cab, ptage, shiraz, tempranillo, chard, chenin, viog) • 50t/3,500cs own label 40% red 50% white 10% rosé • IPW • PO Box 7169 Paarl 7623 • tastingroom@mellasat. com • www.mellasat.com • S 33° 44' 30.0" E 019° 2' 31.0" • ⬚ presses.pits.supply • **T +27 (0)21-862-4525**

☐ **Mellow-Wood** *see* Distell Group Limited

☐ **Mensa** *see* Overhex Wines International

☐ **Mentors** *see* KWV Wines

☐ **Mercia Collection** *see* Mooiplaas Wine Estate & Private Nature Reserve

---

Merwida Winery   ⓠ ⓕ

The Merwida cellar vinifies grapes from several Breedekloof properties owned by the Van der Merwe family, here for over 170 years. Cousins Schalk and Pierre farm with eco and social responsibility in mind, hence their certification by WIETA for ethical practice and elite status as WWF-SA Conservation Champions for saving 800 ha of untouched wetland. They also support the preservation of the area's vinous heritage via the Breedekloof Makers initiative, under which banner the Reserve Chenin Blanc is produced and marketed.

Family Vintners range

★★★★ Reserve Chenin Blanc ⓠ Smooth & creamy from part oaking (57%, mostly older), **17** ⑧⑦ very well-made/judged, plays to variety's strengths with opulence from baked apple, lemon brûlée flavours in perfect harmony with inherent freshness that lingers.

Merwida Winery range

★★★★ Barbera ⊘ Lovely expression of this Italian variety: spicy plum with a dry savoury twist. **16** ⑧⑦ dapper & bright, infused with vanilla oak (40% new French). Good food-pairing length & freshness.

★★★★ Sauvignon Blanc ⊘ Whole spectrum of tropical fruit in **19 ★★★★** ⑧⑤ on mouthfilling, creamy yet fresh base, from 3 months on lees. Engaging & flavoursome, albeit shade off **18** ⑧⑦.

Cabernet Sauvignon ★★★ Unashamedly ripe & gutsy, but **17** ⑧⓪'s warm maraschino cherry appeal reined in by firm, dusty tannin structure. A bit at odds, a barbecue may resolve. **Pinotage** ⓠ **★★★** Tutti-frutti **15** ⑧② is soft & supple, an easy sip. Breedekloof WO. **Pinotage Rosé** ⓠ **★★★** Pretty-in-pink **18** ⑧①, amiable dry al fresco partner with alluring red berries, citrus & spice. **Chardonnay ★★★** Part American oak on **19** ⑧② adds a spiced nuance to ripe pear, lees stirring (as for Sauvignon) a rich succulence & food matching potential. **Chenin Blanc ★★★** Amiable **19** ⑧① is unwooded, ripe & rounded with dried fruit flavour. Tad less sprightly & fresh than previous, but very quaffable. **Cuvée Brut** ⓠ **★★** Frothy & fruity **NV** ⑦⑤ fizzer from sauvignon, dry & zesty, a party starter. **White Muscadel** ⓠ **★★★★** Jerepiko **18** ⑧③ ex tank delivers the expected sunshine-in-a-bottle richness, adding boiled sweet, honeysuckle, raisin & spice to the seduction. Discontinued: **Pinot Grigio**. — MW

Location: Rawsonville • Map: Breedekloof • Map grid reference: C6 • WO: Western Cape/Breedekloof • Est 1963 • 1stB 1975 • Tasting & sales Mon-Fri 9-12.30 & 1.30-5 Sat 9-1 • Closed Easter Fri-Mon, Dec 25-Jan 1 • Owner(s) Schalk & Pierre van der Merwe • Cellarmaster(s)/viticulturist(s) Magnus Kriel • Winemaker(s) Magnus Kriel (Dec 2000), with Sarel van Staden (Aug 1982) & Lieza van der Merwe (Jan 2015) • 800ha (cab, merlot, shiraz, chard, chenin, sauv, sem, viog) • 17,500t/10,000cs own label 40% red 60% white • ISO 22000, Fairtrade, IPW, WIETA, WWF-SA Conservation Champion • PO Box 4 Rawsonville 6845 • wines@ merwida.com • www.merwida.com • S 33° 41' 24.9" E 019° 20' 31.1" • ⬚ pizzerias.applicants.reconsidered • **T +27 (0)23-349-1144**

☐ **Metafisika** *see* Osbloed Wines

Metzer & Holfeld Family Wines   ⓠ

The thread running through boutique winemaker and co-owner Wade Metzer's wines in this portfolio (see also his separately listed The Kitchen Sink bottlings) is the desire to achieve something uniquely South African, hence focusing on heritage grapes chenin blanc and cinsaut. It continues with his new cabernet, where drops of shiraz and cinsaut add 'local flavour' as well as early drinkability. Viewing the Helderberg, where he's based, as 'the heart of the SA cabernet scene' ensured the variety would become part of the range; the '17 is the result of a four-year project. With seven wines made in 2018, he's not looking to further expand the range, 'but I'm always stumbling on unique old-vine parcels, so don't take my word for it!'

★★★★☆ **Cabernet Sauvignon** (NEW) From 20 year old Helderberg vineyard, **17** (90) showcases elegance, quality of vintage. Pure ripe fruit, silky texture are framed by finely tuned, gentle yet effective tannins. Subtly French oak polished, 30% new. Includes splashes shiraz, cinsaut. Natural ferment, unfined/filtered.

★★★★ **Cinsault** (⚡) In the vanguard of rediscovery of SA cinsaut, **17** (89) from Helderberg vines planted 1992 has strawberry fruit & rosewater perfume; full flavoured yet light of foot, despite 14.4% alcohol.

★★★★☆ **Shiraz** (⚡) White pepper introduction to savoury, spicy **17** (92), like **16** (92), less burly than previous; plum/blackberry fruit in rich yet elegant package. Single Helderberg block on 3 soil types, minimalist winemaking with 30% bunch ferment, year French barrels, now 10% new.

★★★★ **3 Miles to Milk Bay** (⚡) Untamed scrub, red berry & savoury notes jostle in **17** (87) shiraz combo with cinsaut, mourvèdre, cab & splash viognier. 20% whole bunch ferment, 14 months old cask.

★★★★☆ **Maritime Chenin Blanc** (🍃) (🌸) Single bushvine block within seabreeze of coast, planted 1981. **18** (94) sings with freshness, agility; natural ferment adds nuance to pear, red apple aromas. Weight without loss of purity via older oak, 9 months lees ageing, no stirring. Lovely now, plenty in store.

★★★★★ **Montane Chenin Blanc** (🍃) (🌸) 'Montane' subtitle reflects Helderberg foothills origin of 50+ year old single-site bushvines. **18** (95) broader, more stately than Maritime sibling, though lower alcohol (13%). Ripely scented, mouthfilling richness with a dry, lengthy conclusion. For now & many years.

PetNat (NEW) ★★★★ Different take on the lightly sparkling méthode ancestrale style; **18** (85) old-vine chenin, natural ferment in used French oak to 9 g/l residual sugar, completed dry in bottle. Concentrated, with ripe pear flavours in its rich, creamy texture & gentle, harmonious pinprick mousse. Perhaps not for the purist, who'd expect a slightly sweeter wine, enjoyable nonetheless. — AL

Location: Somerset West ▪ WO: Stellenbosch ▪ Est/1stB 2006 ▪ Tasting by appt ▪ Owner(s) Wade Metzer & Barry Holfeld ▪ Winemaker(s) Wade Metzer ▪ 30t/4,500cs 60% red 40% white ▪ info@mhfwines.co.za ▪ www.mhfwines.com ▪ **T +27 (0)72-279-7645**

M'hudi Wines

Originally from upcountry, the Rangaka family bought a Stellenbosch vegetable, fruit and wine farm in the early 2000s with scant farming experience and limited wine knowledge. That they've grown from a boutique 3,000 to very substantial 160,000 cases a year, after 'hard lessons and rude awakenings', is testament to what they've called 'a relentless pursuit of one's aspirations'. As matriarch Malmsey Rangaka likes to say: life's more exciting if you take risks. Giving back, they donate a portion of revenue from Harold's wine sales to Cape Town hygiene and health advocacy non-profit Health Promoters.

M'hudi Boutique Family Wines range

★★★★ **Cabernet Sauvignon** (✓) Drinking well, **15** ★★★★ (85)'s tertiary notes of forest floor & leather mingle with still-lively cassis fruit, melded tannins giving satisfactory form & grip. First tasted since **11** (87).

★★★★ **Pinotage** (✓) Not as typically pinotage on nose as Harold's sibling, but **15** ★★★★ (83) more concentrated & persistent on palate, with variety's lifted acidity, pleasant astringency. Last-tasted **11** (87) was plusher.

★★★★ **Foro's Legacy** Pleasing black pepper & mixed berries on **15** (86), 6-way blend mostly shiraz & cab. Generous & flavoursome, juicy fruit cradled by gently sweet oak. Drink soon while at best.

★★★★☆ **Barrel Fermented Chenin Blanc** Myriad aromas & flavours including white & yellow stonefruit, well-judged wood part of an attractive, detailed whole. **17** (90) smooth, with mouthcoating vinosity (14% alcohol), long full-fruited finish. Very drinkable yet no lack of gravitas, could age few more years.

Discontinued: **Shiraz**.

Harold's Cape Knight range (NEW)

Cabernet Sauvignon ★★★ Forthright ripe, almost jammy blackberry character on **18** (83), enlivened by touch grape tannin. Light bodied for everyday, as all this range. **Pinotage** ★★★ Laudably intense sweet strawberry attraction, pleasant stemmy grip & light texture on **18** (81). **Medley** ★★☆ Shiraz, cinsaut & both cabs in **17** (78), toasty top note, made extra-drinkable by hint of sweetness. **Chenin Blanc ★★★** Pears & peaches, subtle earthiness, **19** (79) well-balanced & refreshing summer white. WO W Cape, as all these. Discontinued: **Say Lovey Sparkling range**. — CvZ

Location: Stellenbosch ▪ WO: Coastal/Western Cape ▪ Est 2005 ▪ Closed to public ▪ Owner(s) Rangaka family ▪ Winemaker(s) Albertus Louw (consultant) ▪ 160,000cs own label 90% red 10% white ▪ WIETA ▪ PO Box 30 Koelenhof 7605 ▪ malmsey@mhudi.com ▪ www.mhudi.com ▪ **T +27 (0)61-476-9365**

Michaella Wines

Businessman Adrian Dix has great ambitions for his young label, bent on establishing a venture that his children, Michael and Ella (source of the brand name), can develop. His concern for quality is testified by his engaging young but already eminent Lukas van Loggerenberg to oversee the minimal-intervention winemaking. And testified too by the reluctant decision to not bottle the 2018 vintage, which the drought had rendered insufficiently good for the Michaella label.

★★★★★ Shiraz ⓥ Lighter in colour, extraction & body than most Stellenbosch examples, yet no lack of intensity or personality. **17** (93) scrub, pepper nuances to pure & succulent fruit, real grip & structure, serious intent. Bunch ferment, old oak ageing, minuscule quantities for both.

★★★★★ Chenin Blanc ⓥ Unfurls in glass to gorgeous fennel, earth & thatch perfumes, impresses with clever juxtaposition of silky ripeness & mineral salinity. **17** (94) elegant & engaging, with persistent, tapering conclusion. Native yeasts, no additions, like sibling. Stellenbosch & Paarl fruit.— TJ, CvZ

Location: Stellenbosch ▪ WO: Stellenbosch/Stellenbosch-Paarl ▪ Est/1stB 2016 ▪ Closed to public ▪ Owner(s) Adrian Dix ▪ Cellarmaster(s)/winemaker(s) Lukas van Loggerenberg (Jan 2016, consultant) ▪ 2t/140cs own label 70% red 30% white ▪ adrian@dixaluminium.co.za ▪ www.michaella.co.za ▪ **T +27 (0)21-712-2978/+27 (0)83-230-1634**

☐ **Michelle d'Or** see Fort Simon Wine Estate

Micu Narunsky Wines ⓥ

Micu Narunsky, jazz pianist, boutique winemaker and Brazilian music and culture fan, is now a barista too, his mobile coffee station a familiar sight around home-base Somerset West. Bordeaux University-trained Micu's predilection for SA's heritage varieties and Portuguese cultivars continues in the new 'port', which he calls a 'homage to the old style of off-dry tinta wines prevalent in the 1960s and 70s in the Swartland'.

★★★★ Iemanjá First since **12** (86), **16** (86) is all-touriga (no tinta, souzão). Impeccably ripe mulberry & blueberry mingle with Xmas pudding & cherry tobacco, impressively downy tannins & spicy finish.

★★★★ La Complicité A rarity, wooded colombard. Fascinating aroma/flavour profile of dried fig & pear, thyme, green tea & buchu. Creamy & rich, with flor/sherry note on finish. **17** (86) spent 2 years in one older barrique. Characterful, involving, if shade less successful than **16** ★★★★★ (90), which improved on previously made **13** ★★★★ (85) colombard blend.

Olodum ⓥ ★★★★ 50 year old Swartland tinta, intense **11** (83) handles 4.5 years in oak nicely, adding leathery tannins & medicinal notes to slightly raisined black fruit. **Tinta** (NEW) ★★★★ 'Reverse-engineered' port from old-vine Swartland tinta barocca: high-alcohol wine (16.8%) oak-matured 30 months, then sweetened to 18.8 g/l. Earthy & spicy notes, the sugar masked by soft tannins. **13** (83) ready to enjoy. — GM

Location: Somerset West ▪ WO: Stellenbosch/Swartland ▪ Est 2005 ▪ 1stB 2006 ▪ Tasting by appt ▪ Owner(s)/cellarmaster(s)/viticulturist(s) Micu Narunsky ▪ Winemaker(s) Micu Narunsky, advised by Francois Naudé ▪ 4.8t/450cs own label 85% red 15% white ▪ 3 De Hoop Cres Somerset West 7130 ▪ micunarunsky@gmail.com ▪ www.micunarunsky.com ▪ **T +27 (0)73-600-3031**

Middelvlei Estate ⓥ ⓥ ⌂ ◎ ⓥ ⓥ

But a quick jog from the centre of Stellenbosch, the Momberg family estate offers attractions for everyone, locals as well as those from further afield. The boerebraai (outdoor BBQ, with marshmallows for children), Burgers & Beats (with live music) and wine blending experience are but a sampler. To mark the 100th anniversary last year, winemaker Tinnie Momberg made two yet-unreleased wines for the Estate range: wooded chardonnay and oak-aged pinotage, the latter a variety that has proved its ageability here.

Estate range

★★★★ **Cabernet Sauvignon** ⊘ Smart cabernet from excellent vintage, **17** ★★★★☆ ⑨⓪ stylish scents of perfectly ripe blackberry polished with cedary tones of carefully judged new oak (30%). Well fleshed, fresh & confidently but not intimidatingly structured, augurs well for ageing, steps up on **16** ⑧⑥.

★★★★ **Shiraz** Comfortable & flavoursome **18** ⑧⑦ is fruit focused, with ripe, soft dark berries & spice contained by gentle yet effective tannins. Oak, some American, none new, subtly adds to approachability.

★★★★ **Momberg** Finely fused Cape Blend, **17** ⑧⑨ shiraz (45%) with pinotage & cab. First two provide waves of rich fruit, which cab's neat tannin confidently contains. Roundly dry, but maintains good thread of freshness; promises more savouriness with age. French/American oak, 50% new, 15 months.

· ·

Pinotage-Merlot ⑨ ★★★ Partnership with natural affinity on Middelvlei. **17** ⑧② (85/15) invitingly bright plum pudding, mulberry juiciness, freshness & lively tannins. All harmonised for ready enjoyment.

Free-Run Pinotage ★★★★ Pinotage is house's calling card. **18** ⑧⑤ modern, lighter style; fresh, with ripe juicy plum, mulberry flavours & finest of well-meshed tannins; all vindicate the 'pure run' moniker. Good drinking now, interesting to see how it ages. Not tasted: **Chardonnay Unoaked**.

Rooster range

Merlot ★★☆ Ripe, but with balanced freshness in **18** ⑦⑨ to focus rather shy dark choc, plummy sweetness. Rounded tannin for ready enjoyment. WO W Cape, as all these. **Shiraz** ★★ Just a pinch of spice, red fruit on smooth, sweetish **18** ⑦⑥ crowd pleaser. **Chardonnay** ⑨ ★★★ Easy yet satisfying, **17** ⑧① has lightly oak-spiced citrus lifted by bright, balanced acidity. Firm yet rounded, dry & clean fruity memory. — AL

Location/map: Stellenbosch ▪ Map grid reference: E4 ▪ WO: Stellenbosch/Western Cape ▪ Est 1941 ▪ 1stB 1973 ▪ Tasting & sales daily 10–4.30 ▪ Fee R25pp ▪ Closed Good Fri, Dec 25 & Jan 1 ▪ Cellar tours by appt ▪ Traditional lunchtime braai 7 days a week; evenings by prior arrangement for groups of 35 pax ▪ The Wine Barn function venue (150 pax) ▪ Facilities for children ▪ Conferences ▪ Walking/hiking & MTB trails ▪ Cottage (2 pax) ▪ Owner(s) Momberg family ▪ Cellarmaster(s)/winemaker(s)/viticulturist(s) Tinnie Momberg (Feb 1992) ▪ 160ha/110ha (cab, merlot, ptage, shiraz, chard, sauv) ▪ 650t/60,000cs own label 95% red 5% white ▪ Other export brands: Hagelsberg, Red Falcon ▪ IPW, WIETA ▪ PO Box 66 Stellenbosch 7599 ▪ info@middelvlei. co.za ▪ www.middelvlei.co.za ▪ S 33° 55' 41.2" E 018° 49' 55.9" ▪ 🌐 charmingly.butter.resolved ▪ **T +27 (0)21-883-2565**

Midgard

This worthy private venture, now in its eighth year, supports the Elkana Hostel at the Alta du Toit Aftercare Centre in Cape Town, where adults with special care needs from all Western Cape communities live and work. Quality grapes are bought in from the Durbanville area, and Nomada Wines' Riaan Oosthuizen donates his skill and knowledge to vinify the wine. All profits from sales are donated to the hostel.

Sauvignon Blanc ⑨ ★★★★ Remarkably well priced, **18** ⑧⑤ showcases Durbanville terroir, sleek (12.5% alcohol), fynbos & zesty lime. A delight. — CR

Location/WO: Durbanville ▪ Est/1stB 2012 ▪ Closed to public ▪ Winemaker(s) Riaan Oosthuizen (Nomada Wines) ▪ 2-3t/±300cs own label 100% white ▪ PO Box 2703 Durbanville 7551 ▪ cteijlingen@gmail.com ▪ **T +27 (0)83-456-9410**

Migliarina Wines ⑨

As an internationally experienced sommelier and winemaker, Carsten Migliarina brings rare insight and creativity to bear on wines that tick the box for top eateries and discerning foodies alike. Widely sourcing premium parcels of exciting, often lesser-known varieties, he has been tweaking techniques for clarifying the wines, allowing for 'natural' settling. This results in a longer wait for tasting- and market-ready wines, hence no new vintages from this Somerset West perfectionist. Happily, the boutique bottlings below were still available at press time, and wines-in-waiting include a first-time white blend, ready for next edition.

Migliarina range

★★★★☆ **Grenache** ⑨ Usual ruby luminescent eye-appeal; **17** ⑨① from Wellington slightly fuller than **16** ⑨④ (which also had some Stellenbosch fruit), more crushed raspberry substance than spice, herbs. Still refreshingly dry, with appetising savoury conclusion.

★★★★ **Syrah** (Ⓥ) Ex Stellenbosch has perfectly pitched fresh ripe fruit, supple core currently held by imposing grape tannin (2 months on skins). **15** (89) deserves benefit of time. 14 months older oak.

★★★★ **Syrah-Cabernet Sauvignon** (Ⓥ) Blends spicy syrah with 25% dark-berried cab. **15** (88) velvet mouthfeel balanced by natural freshness, tannin, harmonised in older oak. Can age.

★★★★ **Chardonnay** (Ⓥ) Elgin's vibrancy, steeliness, hallmarks of **15** (88), as is house's understatement, including oak - just 10% new. Bright citrus, creamy breadth satisfy now, even more after few years.

★★★★ **Chardonnay Single Vineyard** (Ⓥ) Has trademark Elgin intensity, taut acid but also richness from oak (35% new); **16** (88) needs time to integrate with more familiar pickled-lime zest, lingering tail.

★★★★ **Chenin Blanc** (Ⓥ) Light-of-foot but depth, intensity of flavour in **17** (89). Lees ageing adds creamy dimension, balances bone-dry conclusion. Spicy lift from 50% natural ferment, older oak.

Creative range

★★★★☆ **Parquet** (Ⓥ) Shiraz & splashes interest from carignan, grenache, **16** (94) delivers Migliarina's usual unshowy precision. Cool feel in its flavoursome, gently spiced red fruit; lithe, supple, light tannin squeeze allow for early enjoyment. Year older oak. Stellenbosch, Swartland, Wellington fruit.

★★★★ **Grey Matters Pinot Gris** (Ⓥ) These once-offs allow for 'exploration, creativity & fun'. Punning name a mind-changing wine, **17** (89) substantial, for food rather than aperitif; deep smoky peach flavours, 50% old oak enriched. Emphatically dry. Bottelary WO.— AL

Location: Somerset West ▪ WO: Stellenbosch/Elgin/Coastal/Wellington/Bottelary ▪ Est 2001 ▪ 1stB 2002 ▪ Tasting by appt only ▪ Owner(s)/winemaker(s) Carsten Migliarina ▪ 4,000cs own label 40% red 60% white + 900cs for clients ▪ Brands for clients: Aubergine Restaurant, Foodbarn Restaurant, Kap Hase ▪ PO Box 673 Stellenbosch 7599 ▪ carsten@migliarina.co.za ▪ www.migliarina.co.za ▪ **T +27 (0)72-233-4138**

☐ **Miko** *see* Mont Rochelle Hotel & Vineyard

Mile High Vineyards   Ⓘ 🍴 🏠 📷

If drought in the Western Cape has produced headaches for winegrowers, imagine having to contend with the reverse - 900 mm of rain, along with hail - during harvest. That's the reality of John and Trish Critchley at their Mile High Vineyards (previously listed as 'The Bald Ibis'), at altitude 1,680 m near Fouriesburg in eastern Free State province. Their approach is artisanal, from manual harvesting, basket pressing into used oak, small steel and concrete vats, using gravity as much as possible, to hand bottling into recycled bottles. They are the only growers in the area, so selecting which varieties to plant is a matter of trial and error. Bordeaux grapes have been ruled out; pinot noir, pinotage and shiraz is much more suited to the terroir, and tempranillo, hopefully, will produce its first crop this year.

Estate Altitude Collection

Pinot Noir (NEW) ★★★★ Own organically grown grapes, 1,680 m high in Free State, as all. Plenty of interest in **18** (85), dark fruit with hint undergrowth intensified by bright, natural freshness. Supple feel, gentle forming tannins & subtle oak, all older, further enhancements. Should give pleasure for several more years.

Pinotage ★★★ Easy-drinking but not simple, **18** (82) plentiful juicy fruity acids, raspberry & pomegranate flavours, concluding with nip of tannin. Also-tasted **17** (82) fresh, fruity & smoothly rounded for immediate enjoyment. Could take light chilling. **Shiraz** ★★★ Two vintages tasted. Shy earthy, spicy whiffs on **18** (78); full-bodied, balanced structure but light on fruit. **17** ★★ (74) high-toned spice notes, lean & short.

Discontinued: **The Bald Ibis range**. — AL

Location: Fouriesburg ▪ WO: Free State ▪ Est 2008/2009 ▪ 1stB 2013 ▪ Tasting & sales Mon-Sat 10-4 ▪ Tasting fee ▪ Closed Easter Sun, Dec 25/26 & Jan 1 ▪ Cellar tours by appt ▪ The Rose Hip lunch venue 11-3 ▪ Farm produce ▪ Walking/hiking trails ▪ The Rose House: 2 garden suites & 1 garden cottage (B&B); 2 barn cottages (self-catering) ▪ Owner(s)/cellarmaster(s)/winemaker(s) John & Trish Critchley ▪ Viticulturist(s) Johan Wiese (Aug 2008) ▪ ±460ha/1.5ha (ptage, pinot, shiraz) ▪ 6-8t/800cs own label 100% red ▪ PO Box 149 Fouriesburg 9725 ▪ critch@netactive.co.za ▪ www.therosehouse.co.za ▪ S 28° 37' 34.76" E 028° 15' 32.51" ▪ 🌐 jumbled.excerpts.shawl ▪ **T +27 (0)82-319-0722**

Miles Mossop Wines

The 2018 and 2019 vintages were ones 'of great experimentation and discovery' for Miles Mossop, he having left his job as (much-lauded) winemaker at Tokara estate to concentrate fully on his own, equally praised brand. He's been 'playing around' with new vineyard sites in Stellenbosch — the prime source of his grapes. But he's also been seeking farther afield, as witnessed by the Swartland wines in his new Chapters range - which documents 'a new journey in viticulture and winemaking'. Chapters, which falls in price between The Introduction and Family wines, looks set to be experimental, with wines possibly once-offs, possibly repeated. At press time, Miles was vinifying at Tokara, but seeking a permanent new home for his wines.

The Family range

★★★★☆ **Max** (🐝) There's a touch of ripe sweetness on **16** (94) blend of 44% cab, 33% merlot, 23% petit verdot, though 14.5% alcohol doesn't detract from fine balance. Well & smoothly structured, excellently oaked (29% new). A sense of luxury. Can only gain in harmony & complexity over a long future. Larger bottle formats too.

★★★★☆ **Saskia** (🐝) **17** (94) chenin-based blend as usual, with viognier, verdelho & clairette. Gently perfumed, light-feeling, dry & elegant - the floral, peachy fruit only subtly intense, the oaking supportive (14% new adding a hazelnut touch), the fresh acidity part of the harmony. WO Coastal.

★★★★☆ **Kika** (🍯) Poised & elegant chenin Noble Late Harvest, barrel fermented. **17** (94) voluptuous & unctuous, oozing honey, crème brûlée & sweet vanilla. An enduring fresh citrus finish follows a velvet rush of tropical fruit. 375 ml.

CWG Auction Reserves (NEW)

★★★★★ **Maximilian Cabernet Sauvignon** (🐝) Classic aromas of cassis & cedary cigarbox on **14** (95). More intense & muscular, a greater sense of glories to come than in the Max blend (this 100% cab) - it's still very young. A sweetness of intense, ripe fruit (14.5% alcohol), silkily textured & balanced. 50% new oak well absorbed.

★★★★☆ **Saskia-Jo** (🐝) All-Swartland **17** (94) from chenin (78%) & clairette - the latter underlining a taut mineral freshness that's a great thing here, giving a thrilling light & lively feel. Pure, stony fruit, with a kernel of sweet peachiness to the long, lithe finish. Only older oak.

The Chapters range (NEW)

★★★★ **Chapter One Swartland Cinsault 18** (89) aromatic & light (12% alcohol), but offering vinous depth beyond variety's pretty charm. Gently structured by acid & smooth tannin, restrained & dry, with generous pure flavours. Older oak.

★★★★ **Chapter Two Swartland Chenin Blanc** Subtle dried stonefruit & earthy element on aromas of **18** (88), leading via a balanced, not-too-fruity palate, to a long, peachy finish. Ripe, but rather urbanely elegant, like most Mossop wines. Only older oak on both these chenins; 13.5% alcohol.

★★★★ **Chapter Three Stellenbosch Chenin Blanc** A green glint in this **18** (88) announces a slightly tighter, stonier elegance than on other version, with a green flavour twist too, despite the ripeness (14% alcohol).

The Introduction range

★★★★ **Red** Welcoming fruitcake & cedar aromas on **17** (86) - now merlot-led (46%) with cab down to 35%, plus cab franc, petit verdot. Smoothly approachable but present tannins, ripe 14% alcohol. No hurry.

★★★★ **Chenin Blanc** Lightly fruity, spicy notes on **18** (86) from Swartland & Stellenbosch grapes, plus subtle green edge. Bright & fresh, the easiest of the 3 chenins; a final touch of rich sweetness.— TJ

Location: Stellenbosch ▪ WO: Stellenbosch/Swartland/Coastal ▪ Est/1stB 2004 ▪ Closed to public ▪ Owner(s)/winemaker(s)/viticulturist(s) Miles Mossop ▪ 80t/5,000cs own label 61% red 36% white 3% NLH ▪ PO Box 7339 Stellenbosch 7599 ▪ miles@milesmossopwines.com ▪ www.milesmossopwines.com ▪ **T +27 (0)82-413-4335**

☐ **Milkwood** *see* The Grape Grinder
☐ **Mill** *see* Windmeul Cellar
☐ **Millstone** *see* Stettyn Family Vineyards
☐ **Millstream** *see* DGB (Pty) Ltd
☐ **Milton Grove** *see* Jacques Germanier

Mimosa Wines

Mimosa owners Bernhard Hess and Richard Weilers have 'finally,' they say, opened an 'official wine cellar and tasting venue,' as well as a new restaurant, BluVines (see the Touring Wine Country section), on Montagu town's main road. The vines are tended, and the wines off them are made, by Lourens van der Westhuizen of Arendsig in Robertson. Elegant packaging is a feature, mostly with black labels touched with gold.

Reserve range

★★★★☆ **Chenin Blanc** Peach & quince notes on the forward, generous aromas of **18 ★★★★ ⑧⑧**, with a little oak spice (10 months, none new). Less intense than **17 ⑨⓪**, & few extra grams of sugar work with the lemony acid to give a slightly sweet-sour finish.

★★★★ **Méthode Cap Classique Blanc de Blancs Brut** A brioche note on the aroma & a touch of Marmite on the palate signal the 60 months on lees of **13 ⑧⑥**, but there's a danger of losing freshness. Satisfyingly dry, crisp finish. Robertson WO, as next.

★★★★ **Natural Sweet** Had 'Weisser Riesling' in the name for last-tasted **16 ⑧⑦**, but **18 ★★★☆ ⑧③** from gewürztraminer. Forward aromas more raisin than varietal, with light fruit, some grapefruity acidity & a bitter edge on palate. 500 ml.

★★★★ **Alambic 8 Year Old Potstill** Last tasted as 5 Year Old. This 8YO ⑧⑥ has nutty oak on the bouquet, with a characteristic dried pear note (peach more common). Rich caramel sweetness to the smooth, bright palate.

Natus MMX ⑨ ★★★★☆ Bordeaux blend, led by cab in **15 ⑧⑤** with 3 others. In big, ripe house style but with notable herbaceous element & perhaps more tannin-acid structure than fruit. **14 ★★★★ ⑧⑦** something-of a standout. Not tasted: **Pinotage**. In abeyance: **Méthode Cap Classique Special Cuvée**.

Mimosa range

★★★★ **Cabernet Sauvignon** Classic aromatic notes of cassis & cedar on **17 ⑧⑦**. As usual, restrained fruit, with dry tannins nicely in balance. Approachable now, but should go a good few years.

★★★★ **Shiraz** Bright & pleasing **17 ⑧⑥**, with a tobacco twist to the fruit, is generous, sweet-fruited & approachable now thanks to its balance (but no hurry). 14.2% alcohol unobtrusive.

★★★★ **Mysterium** (NEW) Ripe plumminess & oak spice on **18 ⑧⑦** from half shiraz with mourvèdre & grenache. Softly rich, bright-fruited, with cushiony tannins; delicious in youth. 15.2% alcohol unobtrusive.

★★★★ **Chardonnay** Citric & ripe apple character on **18 ★★★★ ⑧⑤** & a firm pickled lime acidity, but 3.6 grams of sugar leave it a little too sweet for seriousness - more so than **17 ⑧⑥**. Robertson WO.

Not tasted: **Sauvignon Blanc**. — TJ

Location: Montagu ▪ Map: Klein Karoo & Garden Route ▪ Map grid reference: B8 ▪ WO: Western Cape/Robertson ▪ Est 2004 ▪ 1stB 2003 ▪ Tasting, sales & restaurant Fri-Tue 9-5 ▪ Tour groups ▪ BluVines Restaurant ▪ Owner(s) Bernhard Hess & Richard Weilers ▪ Cellarmaster(s)/winemaker(s)/viticulturist(s) Lourens van der Westhuizen (consultant) ▪ 5ha/3ha (cab, shiraz, chard, sauv) ▪ 20t/2,480cs own label 70% red 30% white ▪ PO Box 323 Montagu 6720 ▪ bernhard@mimosa.co.za ▪ www.mimosawines.co.za ▪ S 33° 47' 29.33" E 020° 6' 39.81" ▪ 🚗 yardage.skimmers.stencils ▪ **T +27 (0)23-614-1512**

☐ **Miner** *see* Taillard Family Wines

Minimalist Wines

The hands-off young winecrafter here is Sam Lambson, Stellenbosch University trained, with harvests at prestige cellars DeMorgenzon, Van Loggerenberg and Alheit Vineyards. His approach, very much on trend, is 'focusing on what matters and allowing vineyards to talk without influencing them more than necessary'. Wines not available for review.

Location: Stellenbosch ▪ Est/1stB 2018 ▪ Closed to public ▪ Owner(s)/winemaker(s) Sam Lambson ▪ 140cs own label 100% red ▪ sam@minimalistwines.com ▪ www.minimalistwines.com ▪ **T +27 (0)71-898-8969**

Miravel

Maarten and Janine van Beuningen sold their vineyard in 2014 but still live on the Helderberg property and continue with the Miravel brand, named for children Mark, Michael, Melanie and David. The former

Zimbabwe fruit and livestock farmers offer pre-booked meals/platters, as well as tastings of their boutique wines, produced by contracted winemakers from grapes grown by the new owner and neighbours.

....

Nigma ⊕ ★★★★ Sauvignon oaked 11 months, riper in style than unwooded version. **17** ⑧⑤ shows brioche & greengage, lipsmacking freshness. Just 760 bottles. **Sauvignon Blanc** ⊕ ★★★★ Noteworthy as always, varietal-true **18** ⑧⑤ crackles with freshness: mineral & leafy, crisp limy finish.

Cabernet Sauvignon ★★★ Ripeness shows in **15** ⑧⓪, deep black plums, opulent cassis, big & bold (15.5% alcohol), smoothly round. **Ella Family Reserve Cabernet Sauvignon** ★★★★ Mainly new oak for **16** ⑧⑤ as befits its flagship status. Richly fruited, layers of interest, spice & dried herbs, still long life ahead. Borders next level. **Merlot** ★★★★ Savoury shading from 24 months French barriques (as all these) nicely offsets **16** ⑧④'s intense cassis. Full, round & tasty. **Petit Verdot** ⊘ ★★★★ Full-ripe style, as all the reds, but **15** ⑧④ has enough fruit/oak balance to be both interesting & delicious. Hint of scrub adds to the appeal. **Pinotage** ⊘ ★★★★ Dark toned, plum compote, **15** ⑧③ backed by 2 years in wood for appealing savoury flavours, ageing potential. **1952 Family Blend** ⊘ ★★★★ Cab-dominant Bordeaux-style red, **15** ⑧③ shows cocoa & plush dark fruit, a firm tannin foundation for further ageing. — CR

Location/WO: Stellenbosch ▪ Map: Helderberg ▪ Map grid reference: A3 ▪ Est 2002 ▪ 1stB 2005 ▪ Tasting & sales Mon-Sat & pub hols by appt ▪ Closed Ash Wed, Easter Fri-Mon, Ascension day, Pentecost, Dec 25/26 & Jan 1 ▪ Meals & cheese platters by prior arrangement ▪ Owner(s) Maarten & Janine van Beuningen ▪ Winemaker(s) Gerda Willers (whites, 2007) & André Liebenberg (reds, 2012) ▪ 750cs own label 55% red 45% white ▪ PO Box 5144 Helderberg 7135 ▪ maarten@miravel.co.za ▪ www.miravel.co.za ▪ S 34° 1' 58.7" E 018° 46' 46.9" ▪ ▥ riverbeds.self.sectional ▪ **T +27 (0)21-842-3154/+27 (0)72-212-4668**

Mischa Estate   ⊘ ⑪ ⊚

Owned by brothers Andrew and Gary Barns, alias The Vine Guys, this 3rd-generation Wellington estate with its boutique winery is also home to a thriving vine nursery and regenerative farming business with a 'pure focus' on soil health. 'We believe in growing the best grapes and then not messing with them until they get into the bottle.'

Estate Reserve range

★★★★☆ **Petite Sirah** ⑰ Fine future in store for pre-bottled **18** ⑨① with its lifted floral violet & fynbos perfume, ripe yet fresh & tangy bramble fruit, hints of black pepper & mocha, serious tannin/acid structure.

★★★★ **Merlot-Cabernet Sauvignon** ⑧ 10% cab adds to black-fruit intensity in **18** ⑧⑨, full bodied & rich yet tangy, balanced, with fresh acidity, subtle cinnamon spice from 20% new oak. Good prospects.

Estate Limited Edition range

★★★★ **Cabernet Franc** ⑰ Previewed **18** ⑧⑨ promises to be rich & full bodied, with bold black cherry, blackberry & mocha flavours well-knit after 18 months in oak, drying tannins should soften with time.

★★★★☆ **Grenache** ⊘ Sheer drinking pleasure offered by **17** ⑨③, with its ripe, juicy, red berry fruit, also some ruby grapefruit along with cinnamon spice & pepper ex 15 months oak, 20% new. Medium bodied & fresh, soft chalky tannins. Wellington WO.

★★★★ **Malbec** ⑰ ⑧ Robust, full-bodied **18** ⑧⑦ has black cherry & mulberry fruit, hints of tobacco & leather, bitter chocolate on finish (15 months in 30% new oak).

★★★★ **Créer** ⑧ Mostly mourvèdre with 16.5% each grenache, petite sirah, **18** ⑧⑧ has hints of black pepper, smoke & leather, plenty of juicy black & red fruit, smooth texture from 15 months in barrel.

Estate range

★★★★ **Cabernet Sauvignon** ⑧ Newly bottled after 15 months in 30% new oak (some Hungarian/ American, as all these reds), voluptuous **18** ⑧⑦ shows ripe black fruit, dark chocolate, plush but effective tannins for long ageing.

★★★★ **Merlot** ⊘ Fresh, aromatic **16** ⑧⑧, with black wine gums & aniseed over ripe plum & black berry intensity. 2 years in oak, 20% new.

★★★★ **Roussanne** ⊘ Fresh **18** ⑧⑦ steps up on viscous **17** ★★★★ ⑧⑤ thanks to lower alcohol (under 12.5%), intriguing sweet melon & Toff-o-Luxe richness despite being very dry, with underlying minerality.

Shiraz ⊘ ★★★★ Ripe dark fruit & velvety mouthfeel, **15** ⑧⑤ succulent, white spice & vanilla from 3 years oak, 25% new, alcohol high (15%) but not hot.

Mischa range

★★★★ **Sauvignon Blanc** (NEW) At under 12.5% alcohol, vibrantly dry **19** (86) offers both refreshment & tropical fruit intensity, from figs & granadilla to zesty grapefruit. WO W Cape, like next.

La Famille range

Cabernet Sauvignon (⊘) ★★★★ Packed with ripe black cherries & berries, **16** (85) nicely balanced, smooth tannins making it youthfully approachable. **Merlot** ★★★★ 15 months in oak, 20% new, have given **18** (85) some mocha sweetness as well as tangy berry & plum flavours. Smoother, richer than previous.

The Vine Guys range

Occasional release: **Sauvignon Blanc**. — JG

Location/map: Wellington ▪ Map grid reference: B2 ▪ WO: Groenberg/Western Cape/Wellington ▪ Est/1stB 1999 ▪ Tasting, sales & tours (vine nursery in winter & cellar in summer) by appt ▪ Fee R125pp, waived if purchase equals/exceed it ▪ Open pub hols by appt ▪ Snacks & meals by appt ▪ Walks ▪ MTB ▪ Owner(s) Andrew & Gary Barns ▪ Cellarmaster(s)/winemaker(s) Andrew Barns (Jan 1999) ▪ Viticulturist(s) Ruiter Smit (Jun 1960) & Eben Archer ▪ 40ha (cabs s/f, malbec, merlot, mourv, p verdot, petite sirah, shiraz, rouss, sauv, viog) ▪ 97t/4,000cs own label 75% red 25% white ▪ Oakdene Rd, Wellington 7654 ▪ sales@mischaestate.com ▪ www.mischaestate. com ▪ S 33° 36′ 13.1″ E 019° 0′ 46.8″ ▪ ⟨☷⟩ asteroids.brandishes.newsstands ▪ **T +27 (0)21-864-1016/19/20**

Miss Molly

These characterful wines are listed separately from their Môreson siblings to 'move the Miss Molly brand out of the entry-level wine stigma' while raising quality standards, explains Clayton Reabow, head of the wine team in Franschhoek. Their naughty but loveable Weimaraner inspired the label's name and charming logo.

★★★★ **The Huntress Pinot Noir** (⊘) From single, very low-crop block, **16** (87) ripe redcurrant & strawberry fruit, hints exotic spice & forest floor, balanced & moreish. Can age.

★★★★ **Kitchen Thief Sauvignon Blanc** (⊘) Orange blossom aroma on **16** (86), crisp & zesty lem-on-lime fruit, 13% semillon fermented in older oak/concrete 'eggs' providing rounded mouthfeel.

★★★★ **Manor Born Chardonnay-Semillon** (⊘) Elegant **16** (88) gets vanilla biscuit nuance to tangy citrus fruit from 40% new oak; complex, lengthy flavours with waxy overlay. Very attractive 78/22 blend.

★★★★ **Petit Rosé** (⊘) Pretty & playful **NV** (86) MCC pink sparkler. Fresh red-fruit flavours, creamy mousse, long dry lemon curd finish from year on lees (as next). Chardonnay & 27% pinot noir. Well priced.

★★★★ **Bubbly** (⊘) Refreshing, smooth & mouthfilling MCC bubbles from chardonnay & splash chenin achieve winemaker's goal of showcasing fruit (tropical & orchard in latest **NV** (86)) rather than yeasty character. WO W Cape, rest Franschhoek.

Not tasted: **In My Bed Red Blend**. — WB

Misty Mountains Estate   (⊘) (🍴) (🏠) (📷)

The mountains are the pleasant Klein River hills near Stanford, where the estate has evolved from a natural spring to a vineyard to a winery (gin, beer and cider on offer as well), with numerous cellar and visitor attractions, including guest cottages, for those travelling the R43 from Hermanus.

★★★★ **Sauvignon Blanc-Semillon** (NEW) Aromatic sauvignon (74%) dominant in pre-bottling **19** (87), semillon adding notes of lemon & wax. Fresh, lively & grippy, needs time. Some richness & flavour depth.

Rosé ★★★ Prettily pink **19** (79) from mourvèdre tasted ex tank; dry & a little more savoury than expected, with light fruitiness. **Sauvignon Blanc** ★★★★ Good varietal typicity on tank sample **19** (84), the full fla-vour complemented by bright lemon-tart acidity, with some weight & texture. Not tasted: **Shiraz, Family Reserve Sauvignon Blanc, Méthode Cap Classique**. — TJ

Location: Stanford ▪ Map: Walker Bay & Bot River ▪ Map grid reference: B5 ▪ WO: Walker Bay ▪ Est 2004 ▪ 1stB 2008 ▪ Tasting & sales Mon-Sun 9-5 ▪ Closed Good Fri, Dec 25 & Jan 1 ▪ Cellar tours by appt ▪ Conferences (±60 pax) ▪ Self-catering cottages ▪ Restaurant & farm stall ▪ Craft beer, gin & cider ▪ Owner(s) Misty Mountains Estates (director A van Vuuren) ▪ Winemaker(s) Neil Patterson ▪ Vineyard manager(s) Robert Davis ▪ 46ha/16ha (mourv, shiraz, sauv, sem) ▪ PO Box 26 Stanford 7201 ▪ info@mistymountains.co.za ▪ www.mistymountains. co.za ▪ S 34° 25′ 04″ E 019° 25′ 35″ ▪ ⟨☷⟩ encoded.crosswords.retry ▪ **T +27 (0)82-973-5943**

Mitre's Edge

A 'special anniversary' happened at this estate on the Stellenbosch edge of Paarl in 2019 — 50 years since the farm was bought by Lola Nicholls' father. The Mitre 2016 blend is therefore being offered as a celebratory 'Limited Release'. And, we note, it's 20 years since Lola and mechanical engineer husband Bernard took over and established the wine business, with Lola now crafting a full range of wines, focusing on the red Bordeaux varieties. Daughter Jenny is joining the team 'to focus on special events, including small weddings'.

Flagship range

★★★★ **Cabernet Sauvignon** Classic aromas of cassis & cedary tobacco on **16** ⑧⑦. Less powerful than previous, but shows varietal structure - more tannic as well as a littler sweeter than the others.

★★★★☆ **Cabernet Franc** As usual, **17** ⑨①. the most elegantly balanced of these big reds. Inviting aromas of dark fruit with spicy dry leaf & tobacco. Subtly rich flavours, beautifully managed tannic structure. Fine, restrained balance makes for early approachability, but still very young. No **16**.

★★★★ **Malbec** Almost light-feeling **17** ⑧⑨ offers usual loganberry charm, the flavours held in check by effective yet unobtrusive structure. Good dry finish adds to sense of restraint. Very drinkable.

★★★★ **Merlot** Well behaved, even rather demure **17** ⑧⑦ has fruitcake character with herbal & milk choc hints. Attractive & quite easygoing; good balance with a sufficient but modest grip. **16** not made.

★★★★☆ **Sholto** ⑧ **15** ⑨③ half cab, with other 4 Bordeaux red varieties. Intense, dense ripe flavours, firmly structured, savoury element; properly dry conclusion in established house style. A serious, substantial wine worth keeping a good few years. 5-10% new oak, as on all these.

★★★★ **The Mitre** Moves to top range with **16** ⑧⑦. Previous had 73% cab franc, this one 40%, with 40% petit verdot, 20% merlot. Sweet, ripe flavours offer plenty of charm, with firm tannins giving a sterner note. No **15**.

Occasional release: **Petit Verdot**.

Mitre's Edge range

Shiraz ⑧ ★★★★ Spicy, smoky aromas on big, flavourful **15** ⑧⑤ with pleasing savoury edge; surprisingly well balanced given 15.3% alcohol. Also-tasted **16** ⑧③ less big & ripe, with redder fruit & herbal notes. Not tasted: **Chenin Blanc, Viognier**. Occasional release: **Cabernet Sauvignon, Rosé**.

ME range

nvME Classic Red ⑧ ★★★★ Bordeaux/shiraz blend **14** ⑧⑤'s attractions bound up in dry tannins mid-2016, might since have softened & opened. — TJ

Location/map: Paarl ▪ Map grid reference: C8 ▪ WO: Simonsberg-Paarl ▪ Est 1999 ▪ 1stB 2004 ▪ Tasting & sales by appt Mon-Fri 9-5 Sat/Sun 9-4 ▪ Cellar tours by appt ▪ Olive oil ▪ Guest house B&B ▪ Owner(s) Bernard & Lola Nicholls ▪ Winemaker(s) Lola Nicholls (2004), with Bernard Nicholls ▪ Viticulturist(s) Danie Kritzinger (consultant) ▪ Vineyard manager Bertus de Clerk ▪ 58ha/18ha (cabs s/f, malbec, merlot, p verdot, shiraz, chenin, viog) ▪ 34t/4,500cs own label 88% red 12% white ▪ IPW, WIETA ▪ PO Box 12290 Die Boord 7613 ▪ info@mitres-edge.co.za ▪ www.mitres-edge.co.za ▪ S 33° 49' 47.3" E 018° 52' 34.4" ▪ ⟨⟩ embedded.shifting. apron ▪ **T** +27 (0)21-875-5960

☐ **MM Louw** *see* Diemersdal Estate

MolenVliet Oosthuizen Family Vineyards Ⓠ ⓐ ⓞ

These Stellenbosch wines, vinified by a contract winemaker, emanate from Banhoek Valley vines owned, together with exclusive wedding, conference and accommodation facilities, by former Springbok rugby prop Ockie Oosthuizen and wife Susan.

Private Collection

Cabernet Sauvignon ⑧ ★★★★ Variety's firm tannins, prominent acidity, modest oaking (10% new) give form to **14** ⑧④'s sweet berry fruitiness. Should reward few years cellaring. **Merlot** ⑧ ★★★ Appealing confectionery sugar & black plum aromas, **14** ⑧⓪ drinks easily & well courtesy very soft tannins. **Duet** ⑧ ★★★ Marries 60% cab, merlot in milk chocolate- & berry-infused mouthful, **13** ⑧① good food partner now & for the next year/2. Stellenbosch WO, as Quartet. **Proprietors Blend** ⑧ ★★★★ **13** ⑧⑤ cab franc, cab & merlot combo with very ripe rum-&-raisin profile lifted by cab franc's leafiness. Briefer, with sweeter impression than Selection. 10% new oak is well-judged. First tasted since **05** ★★★★ ⑧⑦. **Proprietors**

Selection Ⓩ ★★★★ Equal cab/merlot blend in **14** ⑧④. Rich & plummy, with nutmeg note, vibrant fantail conclusion. Judicious 10% new oak. **Quartet** Ⓩ ★★★★ Cab, merlot with splashes petit verdot, cab franc in **13** ⑧③ successful, if somewhat stern, nod to Bordeaux. **Sauvignon Blanc** Ⓩ ★★★ Subdued acacia aroma, **17** ⑧② smooth & easy, variety's brisk acidity smoothed by few grams sugar. — GM, CvZ

Location/map: Stellenbosch ▪ Map grid reference: H4 ▪ WO: Simonsberg–Stellenbosch/Stellenbosch ▪ Est/1stB 2005 ▪ Tasting only available to in-house guests ▪ Wedding/conference venue ▪ 5-star luxury accommodation ▪ Owner(s) Ockie & Susan Oosthuizen ▪ Winemaker(s) Barry van Niekerk ▪ 14ha/8ha (cab, merlot, shiraz) ▪ 13t/±2,500cs own label 100% red ▪ PO Box 6288 Uniedal 7612 ▪ info@molenvliet.co.za ▪ www.molenvliet.co.za ▪ S 33° 54' 52.9" E 018° 56' 30.6" ▪ 🄼 kitchen.dream.truth ▪ **T +27 (0)21-885-1597**

Momento Wines

Shortages and a growing population's pressure on water resources mean 'dryland bushvines are the way forward'. Hence boutique vintner Marelise Niemann's focus on unirrigated vineyards and drought-tolerant Mediterranean varieties, particularly grenache, which she 'fell utterly and ridiculously in love with' after working with ancient vines in Spain while at Bot River's Beaumont Wines, before going solo in 2014. Having rented space at Gabriëlskloof, she's found a permanent new home at neighbouring Anysbos (whose separately listed wines she also vinifies). Her old/unusual parcels are made naturally, to reflect their source.

★★★★★ **Grenache Noir** Ⓐ Feisty yet focused & elegant, trademark Niemann power without force in beautiful **17** ⑨④, perfumed rose, white pepper & buchu kept in line by lively acidity & tannic grip from extended skin contact. Ex Swartland & Voor Paardeberg, 30% wholebunch, 16 months in barrique. Follows lighter **16** ★★★★ ⑧⑦ sourced from Paardeberg & Bot River.

★★★★ **Tinta Barocca** Delicate expression of 4+ decade old vines. **18** ⑧⑦'s bright acidity lights up wild berries, lively dry tannins add polished leather undertone. Bot River, Stellenbosch & Swartland provenance, as **17** ★★★★ ⑧⑤.

★★★★ **Grenache Gris** Unshowy, fine & satisfying **18** ⑧⑦ ex young Voor Paardeberg vines, like **17** ★★★★ ⑧⑤; subtle flavour yet feisty texture, skin contact adds pithy nuance, 10 months old oak (like next) buffs edges. Promising.

★★★★★ **Chenin Blanc-Verdelho** Ⓐ Chenin from Swartland decomposed granite gives breadth, Bot River shale & clay contributes austere structure, both components given vivacity by 33% Voor Paardeberg verdelho. **18** ⑨④ lime, baked apple & nut flavours in a nuanced wine, more extrovert than **17** ⑨⓪, as persistent & engaging with potential for some ageing.— DS

Location: Bot River ▪ WO: Western Cape/Voor Paardeberg ▪ 1stB 2012 ▪ Private tastings on request ▪ Owner(s)/winemaker(s) Marelise Niemann ▪ 2,500cs own label 50% red 50% white ▪ marelise@momentowines.co.za ▪ www.momentowines.co.za ▪ **T +27 (0)82-968-8588**

Monis Wines

Tuscan brothers Giuseppe and Roberto Moni's turn of the 20th century cheese, olive oil, pasta and wine trading company today is a fortifieds-only business based in Paarl. Cellarmaster Michael Bucholz and his team source locally and from Breede River, Calitzdorp and Stellenbosch for their muscadel, port- and sherry-style wines. The fortifying brandy spirit is from parent Distell's own distilleries.

Monis Wines range

★★★★★ **Wood Matured Muscadel** Ⓩ 500 ml of irresistible dried orange zest, spice, muscat complexity. Fortified **04** ⑨②'s rich, silky sweetness balanced by 5 years older oak, tangy acid. Breede River fruit.

★★★★ **Tawny Port** Ⓩ Gorgeous **96** ⑧⑦ complex bouquet of spice, burnt caramel, nuts & dried fruit; slippery tail. Paarlberg tinta & cinsaut.

Vintage Port Ⓩ ★★★★ Touriga's fragrance enhances ex-Calitzdorp **06** ⑧④, with warming spirity tail.

Monis Sherry-Style Wines range

★★★★ **Full Cream** ⊘ Richest, sweetest of this fortified range, & yet **NV** ⑧⑧ tastes drier than it is. Red amber, concentrated dried fruit & nuts with savoury depths, a tealeaf note. Complex, involving & delicious.

Medium Cream ★★★★ Orange gold & sweet, but **NV** ⑧④ has plenty to offer: classic flor & nutty nose, candied fruit flavours, with an alcohol lift that makes it a perfect aperitif. **Pale Dry** ★★★★ From chenin, matured under flor 3 years, then further 3 in solera (average barrel age 64 years!), like all these. Orange gold, touch sugar but **NV** (84) tastes dry. Rock salt & tealeaf, underlying preserved citrus zest, ends savoury. Serve chilled, as aperitif. — CR

Location: Paarl ▪ WO: Western Cape/Breede River Valley/Paarl/Calitzdorp ▪ Est 1906 ▪ Closed to public ▪ Owner(s) Distell ▪ Cellarmaster(s) Michael Bucholz (Jul 2017) ▪ 52,000cs 100% fortified ▪ PO Box 266 Paarl 7620 ▪ mbucholz@distell.co.za ▪ www.moniswines.co.za ▪ **T +27 (0)21-860-1601**

☐ **Monogram Collection** *see* Foothills Vineyards

Montagu Wine Cellar

Changes to the management team at this grower-owned cellar on the outskirts of the Montagu town mean promotions up the ladder for Hermias Vollgraaff and Chris de Villiers, who become production manager and winemaker respectively. Their new single-vineyard range (as yet untasted by us) is their passion project, and last year saw investment in winery equipment to help them fulfil the potential of these special wines.

Location: Montagu ▪ Map: Klein Karoo & Garden Route ▪ Map grid reference: B8 ▪ Est 1941 ▪ 1stB 1975 ▪ Tasting & sales Mon-Fri 8–5 ▪ Closed all pub hols ▪ Farm produce ▪ Owner(s) 54 members ▪ Production manager Hermias Vollgraaff (Aug 2013) ▪ Winemaker(s) Chris de Villiers (Aug 2017) ▪ 620ha (11 varieties r/w) ▪ 16,000t/11,000cs own label 12% red 82% white 6% muscadel ▪ IPW, WIETA ▪ PO Box 29 Montagu 6720 ▪ sales@montaguwines.co.za ▪ www.montaguwines.co.za ▪ S 33° 46' 37.3" E 020° 7' 58.4" ▪ ⊞ suborbital. typewriter.untying ▪ **T +27 (0)23-614-1125**

Mont Blois Wynlandgoed

This large Robertson estate, which Ernst Bruwer is the 6th generation of his family to own, is expanding its range of own-label wines – most of the crop is sold to big merchants and some prestigious private labels. It is Nina-Mari Bruwer who has revived the winemaking tradition here, and has a corner of the 1884 cellar in which to do so, keeping everything 'simple, old-school'. For the first time, red wines join the list, as does a sauvignon blanc made by Raymond Kirby, on the estate for 35 years. By-appointment tastings are now held in the stylishly converted silo on the farm.

★★★★☆ **Tarentaalsdraai Pinotage** ⊕ Lightly perfumed red & black fruit aromas on not-too-assertive **16** (90), with notes of spicy tobacco & chocolate. Soft texture, ripe & fairly easygoing dry tannins. The big 15% alcohol unobtrusive except helping in some sweetness on the finish. Only older oak.

★★★★☆ **Bacchus Red Blend** ⊕ Named for a beloved dog, **16** (92) blends 80% cab with petit verdot. Gorgeously fruity aromas with more savoury herbal & tobacco notes. Palate also combines charm & seriousness. Balanced, with forming but unforceful tannins; approachable now but with room to grow.

★★★★ **Hoog & Laag Chardonnay** Off clay soil, as usual **18** (86) is richer, broader & more deeply coloured than Kweekkamp, with nutty, lightly toasty notes to the fruit (both with only older oak maturation). Definite sugar sweetness (6.3 g/l), but complementing good acid.

★★★★☆ **Kweekkamp Chardonnay** From a single-vineyard on limestone, **18** ★★★★ (89) as previously the subtler, more focused of the chardonnays. With 12.5% alcohol, lighter & more obviously green-limy than **17** (92), appealingly fresh & grippy, with some finesse but less depth & intensity than previous.

★★★★☆ **Groot Steen Chenin Blanc** Ripely forward, fruity charm balanced by a firm acidity marks **18** (90), off 33 year old single-vineyard. The peachy sweetness marks it from more austere chenins but freshness & elegant structure redeem it, & deliciousness is the decider.

★★★★☆ **Pomphuis Muscadel** ⊘ Single-vineyard **16** (92) harks back to 1988 White Muscadel in 1993 guide. Panoply of aromas & flavours, redolent of grapes, flowers, marmalade, mint humbug. Very sweet & viscous, but nicely balanced for seductiveness. Year in old oak. 500 ml. Should develop for ages.

★★★★☆ **Harpie Muscadel** ⊘ Second single-vineyard fortified, matured in oak. **16** (92) packed with multitudinous flavours, from raisin to marmalade & beyond. Silky texture, good, balanced acid keeping from cloy, the 16% alcohol not fiery. More refined than many examples.

Kirby Sauvignon Blanc ⊕ ★★★★ Made by long-serving Raymond Kirby, **18** (85) offers appealing passionfruit aromas & flavours, with balanced grippy lemony acid. A touch short of weight & intensity, but the restraint is pleasing. The only inoculated wine here. Not tasted: **Grenache Blanc**. — TJ

Location/map/WO: Robertson ▪ Map grid reference: A5 ▪ Est 1869/1884 (farm/cellar) ▪ Tasting, sales & cellar tours by appt only ▪ Closed Easter Fri-Mon & Dec 25 ▪ Conservation area ▪ MTB trail ▪ Owner(s) Ernst Bruwer ▪ Cellarmaster(s) Raymond Kirby (Jun 1984) ▪ Winemaker(s) Nina-Mari Bruwer (Apr 2008) ▪ Viticulturist(s) Andries Colyn (Mar 1999) & Dean Kriel (Jul 2013) ▪ 301ha (cab, merlot, p verdot, ptage, pinot, shiraz, cbard, chard, chenin, muscadel w) ▪ Own label 20% red 80% white ▪ IPW, WIETA ▪ PO Box 181 Robertson 6705 ▪ info@montblois.co.za ▪ www.montblois.co.za ▪ S 33° 46' 4.00" E 019° 55' 35.06" ▪ ⌖ admirably.attended. ranked ▪ T +27 (0)23-626-4052/+27 (0)82-561-4139

Mont Destin Wines-Destiny Shiraz

The Stellenbosch farm with its view of Table Mountain (their 'mountain of destiny') has been sold and Samantha Bürgin has moved to Franschhoek, but she continues to celebrate the legacy of her late husband, Erny, through the wine they created together – Destiny Shiraz. Only 500 bottles are produced, each hand-labelled and -numbered, signed and sealed with gold wax using the Bürgin family heirloom ring.

★★★★☆ **Destiny Shiraz** Polished tannins create a plush backdrop for mulberry, cassis & plum flavours in **13** ⑨③, notes of cedar & white pepper in lingering aftertaste. Still not at peak, whereas also-tasted **12** ⑨③ is ready now, with lively & persistent dried cherry, liquorice, cinnamon & smoked pepper flavours, refined tannic grip. A spirited & precise wine. Both vintages 18 months French oak, 50% new.

In abeyance: **Passioné, 11 Barrels.** — GM

Location: Franschhoek ▪ WO: Simonsberg-Paarl ▪ Est/1stB 1998 ▪ Closed to public; sales by email/phone ▪ Owner(s) Samantha Bürgin ▪ Winemaker(s) Samantha Bürgin (May 1996) ▪ Own label 100% red ▪ PO Box 1237 Stellenbosch 7599 ▪ info@montdestin.co.za ▪ www.destinyshiraz.co.za ▪ T +27 (0)83-288-4985

Mont du Toit Kelder

Title to this Wellington property overlooked by Hawequa Mountain has rested in Du Toit family hands since first granted in 1691. Current custodian is Johannesburg senior advocate Stephan du Toit, who has maintained the property's red-wine consistency with the long-term assistance of renowned German vintner Bernd Philippi (of Koehler-Ruprecht), a believer in balancing a fine line of acidity with fruit purity and tannin structure. Though there are new varietal wines in the portfolio, blends remain the strength here.

Mont du Toit range

★★★★ **Cabernet Sauvignon** (NEW) (🐝) Confident debut of **16** ⑧⑨. Young but promising, with cassis & spice generosity & fine dry tannin backbone. 18 months in bottle matches time in 20% new oak.

★★★★ **Merlot** (NEW) Succulent ripe mulberry, cocoa & tomato typicity in total harmony with spice & oak, which adds stature & length to **16** ⑧⑨.

★★★★☆ **Le Sommet** (🐝) Suitably exceptional, as cab franc (44%) takes lead on best-years 'Pinnacle' blend with 32% cab & equal parts shiraz & petit verdot. **17** ⑨④ lithe, supple, layered, with concentrated blackcurrant & graphite appeal. Effortlessly sophisticated & enduring.

★★★★☆ **Mont du Toit** (🐝) Alluring **14** ⑨④ improves on **12** ⑨① in complexity, sleek dark-fruited depth. Cab franc upped to 25% but cab leads merlot & shiraz (15% each) & dab tinta barocca. Harmonious & refined. **13** went untasted by us.

★★★★ **La Colline** (🍷) From dryland vines in Paarl, **16** ⑧⑧ chenin has intense tropical flavours, ranging from guava to tangy pineapple, creamy vanilla softness & spice after 9 months in barrel.

Not tasted: **Hawequas**.

Les Coteaux range

★★★★ **Cabernet Franc** (🐝) **16** ⑧⑦ picks up where **14** ⑧⑦ left off: graphite, cocoa vibrancy with gentle squeeze of dry tannin. Lithe & sexy, needs some time. No **15**.

★★★★ **Sélection** (✓) Cab franc takes the lead in **15** ⑧⑨ 8-way blend. Deep, complex & suave, with pencil shavings, plum pudding, liquorice & spice cradled by oak. Harmonious, supple & long.

Cabernet Sauvignon ★★★☆ Cherry tobacco & cigarbox vie for attention on **16** ⑧⑤. Rounded & plush, it's slighter than statuesque sibling but as appealing. **Merlot** ★★★☆ Light spice & floral element on **17** ⑧⑤. Tangy, succulent acidity set against spicy oak & ripe blue, black fruit. **Shiraz** (🍷) ★★★★ Very ripe, dense dark fruit in **15** ⑧⑤ with nuances of black pepper, cocoa & smoke, smooth, with powdery tannins.

Blouvlei range

Selection ★★★ Trimmed to 5-way blend with equal parts merlot & cab leading in **17** ⑧②. Light-bodied, juicy & gentle pastille appeal. No **16**. In abeyance: **Sauvignon Blanc.** — FM

Location/map: Wellington ▪ Map grid reference: C4 ▪ WO: Wellington/Paarl ▪ Est 1996 ▪ 1stB 1998 ▪ Tasting, sales & cellar tours by appt only ▪ Closed all pub hols ▪ Hiking trails ▪ Owner(s) Stephan du Toit ▪ Cellarmaster(s) Bernd Philippi (1997) ▪ Winemaker(s) Chris Roux (2012), with Abraham Cloete (Jan 2005) ▪ ±40ha/±28ha (alicante bouschet, cabs s/f, merlot, mourv, p verdot, shiraz, tinta barocca) ▪ ±16st/±1,200cs own label 100% red ▪ IPW ▪ PO Box 704 Wellington 7654 ▪ kelder@montdutoit.co.za, marketing@montdutoit.co.za ▪ www.montdutoit.co.za ▪ S 33° 39' 27.72" E 019° 1' 45.81" ▪ 🖮 rummage.super.talker ▪ **T +27 (0)21-873-7745**

Montegray Vineyards ⓥ ⑪ ⓒ

It started with a singular vineyard, a stone's throw away from Bartinney farm in Stellenbosch's Banhoek Valley. Energetic architect, mountain biker, trail runner, conservationist, wife and mom to three daughters Rose Jordaan saw the opportunity for a special wine, vinified by consultant Ronell Wiid. And that led to other distinctive parcels, and pouring the resultant wines at the Montegray wine bar in Stellenbosch, in a building restored by Rose which is also her venture capitalist husband Michael's office.

★★★★ Petit Verdot ⓥ Muscular but refined **15** ⑧⑥ shows chunky blue & black fruit abundance. Succulent & bright, with light tannic grip from just 8 months in older French oak, none new.

★★★★ Syrah Black pepper vibrancy to **16** ⑧⑨ from Banhoek single block. Succulent black fruit framed by dry, fine, integrated tannin & 15 months old oak. Structured & long, with distinct smoky finish.

★★★★ Chenin Blanc ⓝⓔⓦ Effortlessly poised **17** ⑧⑨, with ripe honeyed stonefruit, creamy oak cradle (50/50 tank & barrel, none new) & vivacious acid counterpoint. Lovely long aftertaste.

★★★★ Grenache Blanc-Roussanne ⓥ Rich stonefruit appeal in 50/50 **16** ⑧⑥ blend. Honeyed nectarine countered by supportive, well-knit oak (all old). Lively acid keeps whole fresh & focused.— FM

Location/map/WO: Stellenbosch ▪ Map grid reference: F5 ▪ Est 2014 ▪ 1stB 2015 ▪ Tasting & sales Mon-Sat 11-9 at Montegray & Independents Wine Bar T +27 (0)63-677-7928, 6 Bird Str Stellenbosch ▪ Closed Dec 25/26 & Jan 1 ▪ Wine, craft beer, gin & sharing plates ▪ Owner(s) Rose & Michael Jordaan ▪ Winemaker(s) Ronell Wiid (consultant) ▪ Viticulturist(s) Logan Jooste (Jun 2017) ▪ 3.5ha ▪ Postnet Suite 231 Private Bag X5061 Stellenbosch 7599 ▪ info@bartinney.co.za, enquiries@montegrayvineyards.co.za ▪ www.montegray-vineyards.co.za ▪ S 33° 56' 18.85" E 018° 51' 36.89" ▪ **T +27 (0)21-885-1013**

☐ **Montestell** *see* Boland Cellar
☐ **Montino** *see* Riebeek Valley Wine Co
☐ **Montpellier** *See Editor's Note*

Mont Rochelle Hotel & Vineyard ⓥ ⑪ ⓰ ⓒ

Part of UK entrepreneur Sir Richard Branson's Virgin Limited Edition portfolio since 2014, its exclusive country hotel and restaurant redeveloped as an international drawcard, Mont Rochelle winery's recent focus has been on replanting vineyards. Matching varieties, clones and rootstocks to sites on some 13 hectares for terroir-specific wines reaches the final phase this year. The mission now, says winemaker/viticulturist Dustin Osborne, is to keep vines virus-free, and cover crops with varying flowering times to attract beneficial insects timeously are being tested. So too larger barrels 'for more elegant, less oak-extracted wines'.

Miko range

★★★★☆ Chardonnay ⓐ Barrel fermented/12 months in all-new oak, **17** ⑨② packs a fruit & spice punch, with quince & baked cinnamon apple flavours. Long, persistent & intense, with a slatey minerality. Built to last.

Not tasted: **Syrah**.

Mont Rochelle range

★★★★ Cabernet Sauvignon ⓐ Altogether more serious & long-lived than **15** ★★★★ ⑧③, **16** ⑧⑨'s cassis, lead pencil, leather & cigarbox (from 18 months in 35% new oak) are tightly wound around firm but supple tannins. Extra complexity from dab petit verdot.

★★★★ Syrah ⓐ Expressive black plums, cherries, mulberries, cured meat & scrub - a delightful fantail on the palate of **16** (88). Full body, with firm backbone supplemented by 13% cab & supported by 35% new oak, 20 months.

Chardonnay ★★★☆ Contrast with Miko sibling, **19** (84) preview only partly barrel fermented & aged just 6 months in old wood. Result is vivacious tropical fruit flavours with lemon zest twist on the finish.

Sauvignon Blanc ★★★★ Clean & lively passionfruit-, nettle- & capsicum-toned **18** (84) has 15% oaked semillon adding mouthfeel & texture.

Little Rock range

Rouge ⓥ **★★★★** Adds syrah to previous release's Bordeaux-only grapes in **16** (83), fruity & delicious fireside drinker. **Blanc** ⓥ **★★★** Semillon-driven **16** (82) with chardonnay, sauvignon & viognier, unoaked. Light & zesty picnic fare. — WB

Location/map/WO: Franschhoek ▪ Map grid reference: C2 ▪ Est 1994 ▪ 1stB 1996 ▪ Tasting & sales 10–7 daily ▪ Fee available on request ▪ Wine tasting closed Dec 25 ▪ Cellar tours Mon, Wed, Fri at 11 (pre-booking required) ▪ Winemaker tutored tastings by appt only ▪ Miko Restaurant & The Country Kitchen ▪ Mont Rochelle Hotel & Vineyard ▪ Picnics ▪ Owner(s) Virgin Limited Edition ▪ Cellarmaster(s)/winemaker(s)/viti-culturist(s) Dustin Osborne ▪ 33ha/14.32ha (cabs s/f, shiraz, chard, nouvelle, sauv, sem) ▪ 90-120t/12,000cs own label 60% red 40% white ▪ PO Box 448 Franschhoek 7690 ▪ wine@montrochelle.virgin.com ▪ www.montrochelle.virgin.com ▪ S 33° 54' 52.1" E 019° 6' 21.9" ▪ ⬛ rusting.nudged.crept ▪ **T +27 (0)21-876-2770**

Mooi Bly Winery ⓥ 🍴 🏠 📷

Erik Schouteden nurtures the vines and wines at this boutique property owned by his Belgian in-laws, the Wouters. The small selection of classic-variety wines is supplemented by uncommon solo bottlings of malbec and tannat. Accommodation is offered in self-catering cottages overlooking Paarl's Dal Josafat area.

Cultivar range

★★★★ Malbec Perfumed **14** (87), spicy, succulent & packed with black fruit. Supple & soft, with a long earthy conclusion. Oak, all French, 50% new for 24 months, further 3 years in bottle.

Tannat ★★★★ Rare varietal bottling of signature high-tannin grape. **14** (83) has blue & black berry flavour with notable dry tannic grip. Structured & evolved from 2 years oaking (50% new) & 3 years in bottle. Last tasted was lovely **10 ★★★★** (86). **Chenin Blanc ★★★★** Dried pineapple & honeyed richness to **19** (83) preview. Orchard fruit is balanced by fresh acidity though lees is prominent. Not tasted: **Cabernet Sauvignon, Shiraz, Chardonnay**. — WB, FM

Location/map/WO: Paarl ▪ Map grid reference: F4 ▪ Est/1stB 2005 ▪ Tasting, sales & cellar tours by appt ▪ Fee R75pp ▪ Closed Dec 25 & Jan 1 ▪ BYO picnic ▪ Walks ▪ 6 self-catering cottages ▪ Owner(s) Wouters family ▪ Cellarmaster(s)/winemaker(s) Erik Schouteden (Jan 2005) ▪ Viticulturist(s) Erik Schouteden (Feb 2001) ▪ 32ha/18ha (cab, malbec, shiraz, tannat, chard, chenin) ▪ 70t/6,000cs own label 50% red 50% white ▪ PO Box 801 Huguenot 7645 ▪ wine@mooibly.com ▪ www.mooibly.com ▪ S 33° 41' 7.0" E 019° 1' 21.9" ▪ ⬛ anyone.cleared.sneaker ▪ **T +27 (0)21-868-2808**

Mooiplaas Wine Estate & Private Nature Reserve ⓥ 🍽 🏠 📷 ⓐ

It's a quarter-century since the Roos family started to bottle under their label on the Bottelary Hills estate, where wine, hospitality and conservation are interwoven. Preservation centres on a 70-ha private nature reserve, which shelters endangered fynbos, benefits outdoor enthusiasts and provides a habitat for predators of vineyard pests. Hospitality comes in many forms, from pre-booked dining in the manor, a national monument, to learning to horse-ride. And wine? It's made by cellarmaster Louis Roos, his viticulturist brother Tielman and their teams, for the local market and export to almost 30 countries. The younger generation is very much involved in various capacities. Equally important are the loyal staff, for whom a church and community centre have been established. See also Roos Family Vineyards listing.

Mercia Collection

★★★★☆ Tabakland Cabernet Sauvignon Reserve ⓐ Fruit concentration on barrel-selected **17** (90) a tad masked by sweet-oak character from the 70% new portion, though the 18-month sojourn in cask does beneficially temper the herbaceous tannins. Streamlined & sophisticated, will give greater rewards with ageing. Ex 27 year old vines. No **16**.

★★★★ **Watershed Pinot Noir** ⒩ⒺⓌ Graceful debut for **18** ⑧⑧. Soft, earthy berry nuances, silk textured, bright & deftly oaked. Plenty of varietal charm, ready for the table.

★★★★ **Rosalind** Elegant **17** ⑧⑨ cab franc blend with cab, merlot & petit verdot. Sappy & structured, oak maturation (50% new, 18 months) in sync with rich fruit. Ageworthy, though less than last-made **15** ⑧⑨.

★★★★ **Houmoed Bushvine Chenin Blanc** Ⓖ Mixed-oak ferment/maturation enhances fruit from 48 year old dryland single-vineyard. **18** ⑧⑧ richer than Bushvine sibling, apple pie in a glass. No **16**, **17**.

★★★★ **Laatlam Noble Late Harvest** Light & uncloyingly sweet (172 g/l sugar) **14** ⑧⑨, caramelised sugar flavours from botrytised sauvignon aged 48 months in old oak. Delicious dessert in a glass. 375 ml.

Duel Méthode Cap Classique ★★★★ Latest **NV** ⑧⑤ now chardonnay-led (73/27) with pinot noir, shows more piquant, bruised apple nuances. Similar brioche & 36 months lees ageing to previous, though less rich. Discontinued: **Watershed Syrah**.

Roos Family range

★★★★ **Cabernet Sauvignon** Ⓖ From Tabakland block, **17** ⑧⑨ less ripe & bold than **15** ⑧⑥, more classic, more tannin restraint & freshness. Older oak highlights fruit well. Will evolve elegantly. No **16**.

★★★★ **Merlot-Cabernet Franc** ⒩ⒺⓌ Flamboyant debut for 66/34 duo in standout **15** ⑧⑨ vintage. Lovely concentration & structure, perfume & plush charm. Already tempting but ageworthy.

Pinotage ★★★★ Spiced red fruit shines through older oak, underscored by chalky tannins. **17** ⑧④ youthful & better balanced than previous, with development potential. **Chenin Blanc Bush Vine** Ⓖ ★★★★ Unoaked **19** ⑧⑤ from older vines (35 years average) including Houmoed vineyard, shows depth & smooth texture. Yeasty, almond nuances (50% natural fermentation) need time to integrate. **Sauvignon Blanc** ★★★ Clean herbaceous flavours, balanced with some creamy breadth courtesy 9 months lees ageing. **18** ⑧② less spark & flavour than last.

Langtafel range

Vino Baruzzo Novella ★★ Nouveau-style cab, **18** ⑦⑥ follows style of & improves on previous. Ripe but drier finish. Chill, quaff & enjoy the low 9.96% alcohol. **Red** ★★★ Mostly cab & shiraz with pinotage, **18** ⑦⑧ unwooded, fruit-forward & ready to entertain. WO W Cape, as next 2. **Rosé** ★★★ **19** ⑦⑦ a dry, gentle strawberry/cherry-toned aperitif from pinotage. **White** ★★★ Chenin & colombard duo. **18** ⑦⑧ light, fresh & fragrant, for a summer langtafel lunch. — MW

Location/map: Stellenbosch ▪ Map grid reference: B4 ▪ WO: Stellenbosch/Western Cape ▪ Est 1806 ▪ 1stB 1995 ▪ Tasting & sales: summer Mon-Fri 9-4.30 Sat 10-4 Sun 10.30-3.30; winter Mon-Fri 9-4.30 Sat 10-4 ▪ Tasting options: R50/4 Langtafel wines, R85/5 Mooiplaas Estate wines ▪ Closed Good Fri, Dec 25 & Jan 1 ▪ Gourmet picnic hampers & cheese platters, booking essential ▪ Private dinners/luncheons or tutored tastings in the manor house (a national monument), by appt ▪ Accommodation ▪ Walks/hikes ▪ MTB ▪ Horse riding, riding lessons & trail rides ▪ Child friendly ▪ 70ha private nature reserve ▪ Owner(s) Louis & Tielman Roos ▪ Winemaker(s) Louis Roos (1983) & Bertus Basson (2017) ▪ Viticulturist(s) Tielman Roos (1981) ▪ 240ha/90ha (cabs s/f, merlot, p verdot, ptage, pinot, shiraz, chard, chenin, sauv, viog) ▪ 650t/50,000cs own label 56% red 40% white 4% rosé ▪ IPW, WIETA ▪ PO Box 104 Koelenhof 7605 ▪ info@mooiplaas.co.za ▪ www.mooip-laas.co.za ▪ S 33° 55' 16.3" E 018° 44' 21.4" ▪ ⓘⓝⓕ reunion.capping.museums ▪ **T +27 (0)21-200-7493**

☐ **Mooiuitsig Wine Cellars** *See Editor's Note*
☐ **Moonlight Organics** *see Stellar Winery*

Môrelig Vineyards ⓛ

The home-vinified grapes off the unirrigated bushvines on Andrew Wightman's Swartland farm on the rather famous Paardeberg, Môrelig ('Morning Light'), are now marketed under the name Wightman & Sons — some grapes are still sold off to other prestigious producers. At present the son most relevant for the winemaking is Brandon, who works alongside Andrew — they're the 'A' and 'B' of the new white blend. The approach is resolutely 'natural', in line with the precepts of the Swartland Independent Producers organisation.

Wightman & Sons range

★★★★☆ **The Hedge** ⊘ Bursting with vitality, brightly aromatic **18** ⑨① is both full-fruited & dry-spicy. It's succulent & savoury, with a good dry tannic grip. From syrah with 15% each carignan & cinsaut. Only older oak, to preserve the purity of fruit.

★★★★ **Chenin Blanc** As in 17 ★★★★ ⑧⑤, old-oaked, mid-gold **18** ⑧⑥ has spicy, bruised apple notes, suggesting oxidative winemaking. Silky, but pleasing acidic grip & dry finish. Many, not all, will revel in it.

★★★★ **A&B's Blend** (NEW) **18** ⑧⑦ from chenin with 30% clairette adding vibrant freshness & some complexity compared with the straight chenin, also matured in older oak; generous texture & bone-dry.

Not tasted: **Syrah**. — TJ

Location: Malmesbury ▪ Map/WO: Swartland ▪ Map grid reference: C8 ▪ Est/1stB 2015 ▪ Tasting by appt only ▪ Owner(s) Andrew Wightman ▪ Winemaker(s) Andrew & Brandon Wightman ▪ 42ha/24ha (carignan, ptage, shiraz, tinta barocca, chenin, clairette) ▪ 90-100t/1,000cs own label 30% red 65% white 5% rosé ▪ PO Box 1133 Malmesbury 7299 ▪ moreligvineyards@paarlonline.co.za ▪ www.moreligvineyards.co.za ▪ S 33° 31' 12.73" E 018° 48' 49.40" ▪ ⊞ swirly.database.timepieces ▪ **T +27 (0)82-658-1101**

Môreson   ⓠ ⓒ

'Morning Sun' in Franschhoek Valley was acquired in the early 1980s by Richard Friedman, one of the forces behind the rise of the area as an international food and wine destination. Under current co-owner and daughter Nikki, the estate continues to draw visitors with attractions such as Happy Valley Distillery and the Gin Palace function venue. Winemaking is focused on pinotage, chardonnay and sparkling wine (see also Miss Molly listing). Clayton Reabow, with Diners Club Winemaker and Young Winemaker of the Year awards to his name, and viticulturist Zach Moolman employ modern vineyard practices, and farm as organically as possible to produce increasingly impressive wines from own and mostly Valley-sourced grapes.

★★★★☆ **Magia** (🐝) Only in exceptional years, 100% cabernet, now from single Franschhoek parcel (**15** ⑨②) & previous had some Stellenbosch fruit). **17** ⑨③ fragrant & concentrated, with lashings of fynbos-scented cassis, graphite & silky tannins after 20 months in 87% new oak. Full bodied but refined & elegant. No **16**.

★★★★☆ **Cabernet Franc** (🐝) From a single block, **17** ⑨③ combines elegance with underlying power: spice & fine herb notes mingle with rich redcurrant, blueberry & raspberry fruit on a supple bed of tannin, all in harmony after 18 months in 44% new barrels, 1st 6 without being sulphured.

★★★★☆ **MKM** (🐝) Vineyard & cellar selection of Stellenbosch pinotage. Ferment in clay amphoras, some wholebunch, then 100% new oak for 16 months. **16** ⑨③ is rich, rounded & regal, with pristine black plums, a cocoa dusting, supple tannins & highly polished texture.

★★★★☆ **The Widow Maker Pinotage** (🐝) Dryland vines in Stellenbosch planted 1994, 25% fermented wholebunch. **17** ⑨③ brooding but vibrant dark plums, spice & well-judged oak (40% new, 15 months). Balanced, with long, 'cool' mineral finish. Also-tasted **16** ⑨③ wonderfully rich & taut, full of black berries on nose & piquant saline note on palate. Pinpoint focus, texture & tension. Slightly more new wood this vintage (50%).

★★★★☆ **FYM** (🐝) From usual minuscule, 26 year old registered single-vineyard & rare CY18 chardonnay clone. **17** ⑨④ pure & pointed aromas of ripe, slightly honeyed stonefruit leading to palate of fresh citrus, toasted nuts & orange blossom. A serious wine, barrel-fermented/11 months in 80% new oak, for luxury dishes such as fruits de mer. No **16**.

★★★★☆ **Mercator Chardonnay** (🐝) Marzipan & brioche aromas enhance the fresh tropical flavours, while beautiful concentration & perfectly judged oak structure (45% new, 10 months) give **17** ⑨④ a long future. Finishes on a wet stone mineral note.

★★★★ **Dr Reason Why** (✓) Bunch pressed & fermented in concrete 'eggs' & clay amphoras to preserve the freshness & flavour, **18** ★★★★★ ⑨⑩ chardonnay has no oak but is no shrinking violet, shows concentrated apple, citrus & elderflower perfume & flavour, long zesty farewell. Steps up on **17** ⑧⑧.

★★★★ **Pink Brut Rosé Méthode Cap Classique** Pinot noir & chardonnay (69/31) NV ⑧⑧ sparkling has fruity strawberry flavours & earthy spice combined with toasty richness & fine bubbles. Mouthfilling yet finessed, for special celebrations. Striking packaging, as sibling.

★★★★ **Solitaire Blanc de Blancs Méthode Cap Classique** Vivacious & refreshing chardonnay sparkler, NV ⑧⑨ shines with floral, pear & citrus fruit character, full body & persistent tiny bubbles. Unoaked, 24 months lees aged, as Pink.

★★★★☆ **The Fudge** Dessert wine from vine-desiccated, naturally fermented chardonnay. Terrific concentration in **15** ⑨③, honey, caramelised nuts & marmalade with a rapier acid backbone. Super-sweet but finishes whistle-clean. Extraordinarily balanced, more so than **14** (90), with similarly intense toffee apple, marmalade & vanilla cake flavours. 12 & 24 months respectively in 100% new oak. 375 ml.— WB

Location/map: Franschhoek ▪ Map grid reference: C3 ▪ WO: Franschhoek/Stellenbosch ▪ Est 1983 ▪ 1stB 1994 ▪ Tasting, sales & cellar tours daily 9.30–5 ▪ Fee R60 ▪ Closed Dec 25 ▪ Happy Valley Distillery: tasting by appt only ▪ Owner(s) One Happy Valley (Pty) Ltd ▪ Winemaker(s) Clayton Reabow (May 2007), Gerald Ludwinski (consultant) ▪ Viticulturist(s) Zach Moolman ▪ 35ha/±18ha (chard) ▪ ±120t 10% red 20% white 70% MCC ▪ EuroGAP, IPW ▪ 1 Happy Valley Rd, Franschhoek 7690 ▪ sales@moreson.co.za ▪ www.moreson.co.za ▪ S 33° 53' 11.9" E 019° 3' 30.6" ▪ ⌨ inductions.vacancy.photographs ▪ **T +27 (0)21-876-8525**

Morgenhof Wine Estate

Owner Anne Cointreau (of the famous French champagne and cognac family) led the rejuvenation of this Simonsberg foothills property in the 1990s as an early international investor during newly democratic SA's return to the world stage. She created a showpiece wine tourism destination, converting 17th-century Cape Dutch buildings into a variety of venues, constructing a cutting-edge underground cellar in the French château vernacular and replanting vineyards, drawing top cellar talent. Incumbent winemaker and self-described traditionalist Andries de Klerk continues the classic styling, and his goal of producing terroir wine includes farming entirely without irrigation, something uncommon in Stellenbosch.

Morgenhof Estate range

★★★★ Cabernet Sauvignon ✓ ⊛ Multifaceted **14** (86), alluring, graphite-tinged deep black fruit, powerful yet silky with integrated oak (20% new, 24 months). Delicious now & for good few years. Improves on **13** ★★★★ (84).

★★★★☆ Malbec Vintage Select (Ⓩ) Varietal characteristics well expressed on **14** (92). Older oak showcases dark, ripe & spicy fruit-laden profile. Modern, compact style, with smooth dry tannins. Already tempting but plenty of potential.

★★★★ The Morgenhof Estate (Ⓩ) All five red Bordeaux varieties, led by cab & merlot (41/39) in slow-evolving **12** ★★★ (80). Very dry & firm still, fruit held in tight tannin embrace. May benefit from further cellaring but currently best paired with robust food. Last tasted was **06** (87).

★★★★ Brut Reserve (Ⓩ) Full, persistent mousse carries red pear flavours of bone-dry **10** (86) chardonnay, pinot noir MCC sparkling. Couple of years on lees imparts freshness & complexity to lean, focused style.

Cabernet Franc (Ⓩ) ★★★★ Variety's piquant walnut tone on **13** (84), taut & youthful with hint of perfume emerging. Not austere, but would certainly benefit from few years cellaring. **Merlot** ★★★★ Initial mint chocolate note on **13** (85) leads to hazelnut & plum on palate. Firm yet rounded tannins, well-judged oak (as for Cab), interesting dried rosepetal-earthy echo on finish. **Pinotage** (Ⓩ) ★★★★ Dark mulberry fruit & nice savoury tone, **13** (84) drier than Fantail, similar cedary tannins, supple balance, oak well integrated. **Chardonnay** ★★★★ Array of ripe pear, kumquat, marmalade & stonefruit on **16** (84), subtle oak (none new, 12 months) adds to appeal of balanced, smooth palate. **Chenin Blanc** (Ⓩ) ★★★★ Solo or meal partner (for next few years), **17** (85) marries richer baked apple & quince flavours with fresh crunchy acidity. Medium body, brush of old oak & less overt ripe fruit than on **16** (83). **Sauvignon Blanc** ★★★ Tropical fruit abundance on vibrant **18** (80), hints of lemon peel & fig on crisp palate. Pack for picnic this summer. Not tasted: **Merlot-Cabernet Franc, Cape LBV.**

Fantail range

Pinotage (Ⓩ) ★★★ Bright, bouncy **14** (82), spiced berry fruit framed by clean, dry tannin structure. Offers sappy drinkability with a meal. **Pinotage Rosé** ✓ ★★★ Attractive sherbet, watermelon & pomegranate aromas, **17** (80) dry & light, smooth texture for easy sunset sipping. Stellenbosch WO. — GM

Location/map: Stellenbosch ▪ Map grid reference: F3 ▪ WO: Simonsberg–Stellenbosch/Stellenbosch ▪ Est 1692 ▪ 1stB 1984 ▪ Tasting & sales Mon–Fri 9–5.30 (Nov–Apr) & 9–4.30 (May–Oct); Sat/Sun 10–5 (Nov–Apr) & 10–3 (May–Oct) ▪ Fee R40pp ▪ Closed Good Fri, Dec 25 & Jan 1 ▪ Cellar tours/viewing of underground barrel cellar on request ▪ Cheese platters ▪ Morgenhof Restaurant ▪ Facilities for children ▪ Conferences ▪ Weddings/functions ▪ Helipad ▪ Conservation area ▪ Morgenhof Manor House ▪ Owner(s) Anne Cointreau ▪ Winemaker(s) Andries de Klerk (Jan 2012) ▪ Viticulturist(s) Rohan Breytenbach (Dec 2017) ▪ 212ha/78ha (cabs s/f, malbec, merlot, chenin, chard) ▪ 410t/70,000cs own label 60% red 38% white 2% rosé ▪ IPW ▪ PO.

Box 365 Stellenbosch 7599 ▪ info@morgenhof.com ▪ www.morgenhof.com ▪ S 33° 53' 38.5" E 018° 51' 39.2"
▪ *fb* chatting.reminder.letter ▪ **T +27 (0)21-001-9416**

Morgenster Estate

This renowned estate, as famous for its olive oil as for its wine, lies on the slopes of Somerset West's fabled Schapenberg. The name means 'Morning Star', imaged on the gable of the 1786 Cape Dutch manor house, a design borrowed for the logo on the labels. The inspired force behind the restoration and development of the property was an Italian industrialist, the late Giulio Bertrand, whose transformation of Morgenster included persuading Pierre Lurton of the famous Château Cheval Blanc to become his wine consultant. The red-wine focus remains on, especially, Bordeaux Right Bank specialist varieties merlot and cabernet franc. A later addition to the range was a series of wines made from Italian varieties, most given operatic names. Inherited by Giulio's daughters, along with his vision, Morgenster remains in good hands.

Morgenster Estate range

★★★★☆ **Lourens River Valley** Ⓠ Merlot & cab franc (38/34) take lead in **15** Ⓨ91Ⓨ, with cab & petit verdot. Perfumed, plush berries, violets, spice array, hint of herbs, bolstered by firm but ripe tannins. 20% new oak, 18 months. Less extracted than **14** ★★★★ Ⓨ87Ⓨ. Also in magnum.

★★★★☆ **White Reserve** Ⓐ Oaked sauvignon with semillon (46%), resulting in an oatmeal overlay to **18** Ⓨ92Ⓨ's wonderfully complex perfumes & flavours. Orange blossom, white peach, with pine nut richness on the palate. Keeps rewarding with other layers, finishes long. No **17**.

Cuvée Alessandra Ⓠ ★★★ Prosecco-style bubbly from cab franc: in oak 12 months, 21 months on lees in bottle. Pale gold, energetic mousse, **16** Ⓨ82Ⓨ mixture pear & grapes; elegant, bone-dry. Not tasted: **Reserve**.

Italian Collection

★★★★ **Nabucco** Ⓠ 15 Ⓨ88Ⓨ lovely fruit expression, plums, dark berries, better able to handle the tannins than when previewed. Some melding, but still firm; varietal character, as in Italy, nebbiolo is long-lived, needs time. But can be enjoyed now.

★★★★ **Tosca** Ⓠ 15 Ⓨ86Ⓨ 80% sangiovese with both cabs; glossy cherries, rich & ripe, year later better tannins, still dry but compact rather than forceful. For food, ageing.

★★★★☆ **Vermentino** ⊘ Was 'Vespri'. Sicilian clone exclusive to 2 farms & different to most white varieties in SA. Touch of muscat, yet also mineral & mustard leaf, complex & intriguing. **19** Ⓨ92Ⓨ's flavours are ruby grapefruit in partnership with muscat grapiness. Wow! WO W Cape.

Dry Rosé ★★★★ Previously 'Caruso'. Delicate pink **19** Ⓨ84Ⓨ reflects sangiovese in its cherry styling; elegantly structured (12.5% alcohol) & bone-dry. Would work as an aperitif or with food.

Single Varietal range

★★★★ **Cabernet Franc** ⊘ Ⓐ Dark fruit & savoury tones, cassis, dried herbs, graphite, many layers of interest. **18** Ⓨ89Ⓨ shows ageing structure/strength while still giving current access, a fine balance & gets it right. No **17**.

★★★★ **Sauvignon Blanc** ⊘ 15% semillon for weight & flavour, expressive **19** Ⓨ89Ⓨ gooseberries & litchi, a lime top note. Palate less green than **18** Ⓨ88Ⓨ, more tropical, acidity giving lift, shine to the fruit.

Cabernet Sauvignon ★★★★ Not the longest cellaring promise in the line up, **16** Ⓨ83Ⓨ has other attractions: cassis typicity with lovely spice, savoury notes, a juicy appeal. Just enough grip for food, some ageing.

Merlot ★★★★ Impressive concentration, glacé cherries, dark chocolate, loads of spice, **16** Ⓨ84Ⓨ is seductive even on the palate, streamlined, polished. Earlier drinking than some other range reds. **Sangiovese** ★★★★ Lightly oaked, **19** Ⓨ84Ⓨ's aromatics include cherries & raspberries, some subtle vanilla. There's lovely freshness in the flavours, primary fruit tones, juicy & accessible. — CR

Location: Somerset West ▪ Map: Helderberg ▪ Map grid reference: F5 ▪ WO: Stellenbosch/Western Cape ▪ Est 1993 ▪ 1stB 1998 ▪ Tasting & sales Mon-Sun 10-5 ▪ Tasting fee R50-R95 wine/R55 olive oil & olive products ▪ Closed Good Fri & Dec 25 ▪ Restaurant 95@morgenster ▪ Owner(s) Bertrand family ▪ Cellarmaster(s) Henry Kotzé (Oct 2009), with consultant Pierre Lurton (Nov 1997) ▪ 200ha/30ha (cabs s/f, merlot, nebbiolo, p verdot, sangio, sauv, sem, vermentino) ▪ 70% red 25% white 5% rosé ▪ IPW, SIZA ▪ PO Box 1616 Somerset West 7129 ▪ info@morgenster.co.za ▪ www.morgenster.co.za ▪ S 34° 5' 2.9" E 018° 53' 7.8" ▪ *fb* shelters. braked.sock ▪ **T +27 (0)21-852-1738**

☐ **Morkel** *see* Bellevue Estate Stellenbosch
☐ **Mortons** *see* Wine-of-the-Month Club

Mostertsdrift Noble Wines   ⓥ ⑪ ⓞ ⓑ

For several years, siblings and owners André Mostert and Anna-Mareè Uys sold off most of the grapes from their family estate but last year made and bottled a small parcel of sauvignon blanc, which is available from their cellardoor just outside Stellenbosch. Passionate about hockey, Anna-Mareè is delighted with the newest addition to the farm amenities: an AstroTurf mini pitch.

Location/map: Stellenbosch ▪ Map grid reference: E4 ▪ Est/1stB 2001 ▪ Tasting, sales & cellar tours by appt ▪ Meals for groups by prior arrangement ▪ Facilities for children ▪ Conference venue ▪ AstroTurf mini pitch ▪ Owner(s) André Mostert & Anna-Mareè Uys (Mostert) ▪ Cellarmaster(s)/winemaker(s) Anna-Mareè Uys (Jan 2001) ▪ 13ha/±8ha (cab, merlot, pinot, chard, hanepoot) ▪ ±80-100t/3,986cs own label 70% red 10% white 20% rosé ▪ PO Box 2061 Dennesig Stellenbosch 7601 ▪ winemaker@mostertsdrift.co.za ▪ www.mostertsdrift.co.za ▪ S 33° 53' 31.7" E 018° 50' 17.6" ▪ ⟨m⟩ steered.tone.painting ▪ **T +27 (0)73-194-9221**

Mother Rock Wines

This eclectic, cerebral and idiosyncratically delicious range is a joint venture between 'au natural' winemaker Johan Meyer (see also JH Meyer Signature Wines) and UK importer Ben Henshaw, crafted using practices like early picking, skin contact for whites and old-oak maturation. The new vintages unfortunately were still works in progress at print time.

Location: Hermon ▪ Est/1stB 2014 ▪ Closed to public ▪ Owner(s) Johan Meyer & Ben Henshaw ▪ Winemaker(s) Johan Meyer ▪ 75t/12,500cs own label ▪ 1 Main Rd, Hermon 7308 ▪ motherrockwines@gmail.com ▪ www.motherrockwines.com ▪ **T +27 (0)79-280-0237**

Mount Abora Vineyards   ⓥ

Partners in this boutique venture, Pieter de Waal and Krige Visser, since the first vintage in 2011 have focused on vineyard sites in Swartland. In 2018 they decided to look further afield and, with Krige latterly responsible for winemaking at Arcangeli Vineyards in Bot River, it's to this area they turned. Both men are fans of Loire Valley wines, cabernet franc in particular, and this locally fashionable grape was duly sourced and vinified in usual hands-off, low-alcohol style - much appreciated in their major export markets, the US and Japan.

★★★★ **Saffraan** ⓥ A pioneer of modern, fresh & light cinsauts. Unoaked **17** ⑧⑨ a charmer; gorgeous breadth of ripe raspberry perfume; good substance, fruit intensity & length at a light but convincing 11.2% alcohol. **16** ★★★★ ⑧④ shade less satisfying.

★★★★★ **The Abyssinian** ⊘ Another successful tweak of this 4-way Rhône blend in **16** ⑨⓪: mourvèdre & cinsaut (57/27) lead syrah, drop grenache. Freshness, vibrancy, light tannic structure remain constants, give starring role to pure savoury concentration. 12% alcohol. Natural ferment/year in older oak.

★★★★★ **Koggelbos** ⓐ A stellar, individual & delicious chenin from 37 year old Malmesbury vines. Emphatically dry **17** ⑨⑤ continues in oxidative style, delivering intense flavour & earthy minerality rather than simple fruit. Extra textural dimension from portion fermented, matured in concrete 'egg'; balance in old oak, all natural ferment. No **16**.— AL

Location: Bot River/Cape Town ▪ WO: Swartland ▪ Est/1stB 2011 ▪ Tasting & sales by appt at MojoVino Wine Warehouse, Parow East Industrial ▪ Owner(s) Vinotage CC ▪ Cellarmaster(s) Pieter & Lohra de Waal ▪ Winemaker(s) Johan Meyer & Krige Visser ▪ 2,000cs own label 50% red 50% white ▪ PO Box 995 Bellville 7535 ▪ wine@abora.co.za ▪ www.abora.co.za ▪ **T +27 (0)82-413-6719 (Krige)/+27 (0)83-357-3864 (Pieter)**

☐ **Mountain Eye** *see* Kleinhoekkloof

Mountain Ridge Wines   ⓥ ⓞ ⓑ

This winery is centred (with its cellar) in Wolseley in Breedekloof, where there's also the visitor locale, though the grower-owners are very widely spread. They've been celebrating their 70th birthday last year — though the birthname was Romansrivier Kelder (first bottling under that name was in 1976 — a dry cinsaut); it changed to this more evocative one only in 2011.

Mountain Ridge range

Cabernet Sauvignon ⓥ ★★★☆ Velvety tannin underpinning for attractive cassis, eucalyptus & subtle vanilla on **14** ⑧④, which improves on previous. **Merlot** ★★★ Fruitcake & tobacco notes on **17** ⑦⑦, with a herbaceousness amplified on the firmly tannic palate. **Shiraz** ★★★★ Smoked meat, spice, raspberry & herbal notes on mouthfillingly flavourful **17** ⑧⑤. Dry tannic backbone, a little sweetness & warmth from 14.5% alcohol. 10% new oak, as on last-made **14** ★★★★ ⑧⑦. **Sauvignon Blanc** ⓥ ★★ Unchallenging **18** ⑦④, forthcoming grassy & tropical notes, light & bright. Breedekloof WO.

Romansrivier range

Cabernet Sauvignon Reserve ⓥ ★★★☆ Big & juicy **14** ⑧④, bold tannins offset by pleasant herbal note, nicely rounded off by a sweet farewell. **Shiraz Reserve** ⓥ ★★★☆ Perfumed with generous charry oak, juicy **14** ⑧④ has fine floral palate & still-firm tannin - will reward a bit of patience.

Jailbreak range

Pinotage ⓝⓔⓦ ★★★ Aromatic charm on easygoing **17** ⑧②, with a sweet juiciness as well as a good succulent grip. Eminently drinkable. **Shiraz** ★★★ Pleasant smokiness on **17** ⑧②. There's a balanced firmness & good oaking to support the sweet fruity charm. The 14.5% alcohol doesn't intrude. **Chenin Blanc** ★★★☆ Packed with tropical, boiled sweet aromas & flavours, **18** ⑦⑧ has soft texture & some obvious sugar sweetness. **Viognier** ⓝⓔⓦ ★★★ Billowing peach perfume on **18** ⑦⑧, but more restraint on the fleshy, juicily fruity palate.

De Liefde range

Aanstap Rooies Dry Red ★★ Ripe berries on sweetly mouthfilling, easygoing **NV** ⑦④ from cab & merlot. **The Long & Wine'ing Road Dry White** ★★★ Exuberant & outgoing **NV** ⑦⑧ from chenin: tasty, fruity, not too sweet. Good company after travelling that road. **Smooch Vonkelwyn** ★★ Light & frothy **NV** ⑦③ pink sparkler offers simple, brief & innocuous fun. — TJ

Location: Wolseley • Map: Breedekloof • Map grid reference: A2 • WO: Western Cape/Breedekloof • Est 1949 • 1stB 1976 • Tasting & sales Mon-Thu 8–5 Fri 8-4 Sat 9-1 • Closed all pub hols • Cellar tours by appt only • Ramkiekie farmer's market • Wedding & function venue (140-160 pax) • Owner(s) 17 members • Cellarmaster(s) / CEO Justin Corrans (May 2017) • Winemaker(s) Karel Hugo (Jul 2019) • 400ha (cab, grenache, merlot, ptage, shiraz, chenin, sauv) • 8,000t/10,000cs own label 37% red 48% white 15% rosé • IPW, WIETA • PO Box 108 Wolseley 6830 • sales@mountainridge.co.za • www.mountainridge.co.za • S 33° 28' 26.04" E 019° 12' 10.44" • ⓦ wealthier.restrictions.wafting • **T +27 (0)74-185-3780/+27 (0)74-125-8096**

Mountain River Wines

Founded in the early 1990s when newly democratic SA's wine exports took off, and run from one of historic Paarl Main Street's elegantly restored homes, De Villiers Brits' negociant business has carved a place for both bulk and bottled wines in markets around the world.

Zaràfa range

Pinotage ★★ Pliable tannins provide support for **18** ⑦⑥'s warm plum pudding features. Unwooded, as all these. **Shiraz** ⊘ ★★★ Loud purple label mirrors exuberant mulberry fruit & sweet spice on ripe, slightly baked **18** ⑦⑧. **Chardonnay** ⊘ ★★★ Somewhat neutral **18** ⑦⑦ has waxy edge to lime fruit. **Sauvignon Blanc** ⊘ ★★★ Less steely than previous but still fresh, tasty **19** ⑦⑦ offers tropical fruit flavours. Not tasted: **Cabernet Sauvignon**, **Rosé**.

Mountain River range

Pinotage ⓥ ★★★☆ Tropical/plum tones of **16** ⑧④ lavished with new French oak, sweet fruited, with firm tannins for good food partnering. Not tasted: **Chardonnay**.

Maankloof range

Not tasted: **Cabernet Sauvignon**, **Pinotage**, **Shiraz**, **Sauvignon Blanc**. Occasional release: **Chenin Blanc**.

Ukuzala range

Occasional release: **Dry Red**, **Dry White**. — DS

Location: Paarl • WO: Western Cape • Est 1993 • 1stB 1998 • Closed to public • Owner(s) De Villiers Brits • Cellarmaster(s) De Villiers Brits, with consultants • 1.2ha (shiraz) • 80,000cs own label 60% red 40% white

▪ ▪ 146 Main Rd, Paarl 7646 ▪ dev@mountainriverwines.co.za, mattie@mountainriverwines.co.za ▪ www.mountainriverwines.co.za ▪ **T** +27 (0)21-872-3256

☐ **Mountain Shadows** *see* Wineways Marketing

Mount Babylon Vineyards

Johan and Yolanda Holzhausen's Hemel-en-Aarde Ridge vines, with local landmark Babylonstoren Peak in their sight, produce fruit for specialist boutique méthode cap classique production, currently a classic pinot/chardonnay and New World-style sparkling shiraz, made with neighbour JC Martin of Creation Wines.

Location: Hermanus ▪ Map: Walker Bay & Bot River ▪ Map grid reference: C4 ▪ Est 2002 ▪ 1stB 2007 ▪ By invitation only ▪ Exclusive events venue ▪ Owner(s) Johan Holtzhausen ▪ Winemaker(s) Jean-Claude Martin (2008, consultant), Johan & Yolanda Holtzhausen ▪ Viticulturist(s) Johan Pienaar (2002, consultant) ▪ 6sha/16ha (pinot, shiraz, sauv, sem, viog) ▪ ±38t/±400cs own label 90% red 10% white ▪ PO Box 7370 Stellenbosch 7599 ▪ info@mountbabylon.co.za ▪ www.mountbabylon.co.za ▪ S 34° 19' 44.0" E 019° 19' 34.3" ▪ *f* unplug.poem.matured ▪ **T** +27 (0)84-511-8180

Mount Pleasant Vineyards

Former London banker, now active music patron in Darling, Alfred Legner also tends a tiny walled shiraz block in this West Coast town. The grapes are vinified in Malmesbury by Wim Smit of Hofstraat Kelder.

Darling Pascale's Shiraz ⓥ ★★★★ Elegant **13** (84) sports a vibrant label & clearly shows cool origin in white pepper, bitter cherry & savoury, earthy notes. Tightly wound still, decant or cellar year/2. — HJ

Location/WO: Darling ▪ Est 2009 ▪ 1stB 2011 ▪ Closed to public ▪ Owner(s) Legner family ▪ Winemaker(s) Wim Smit (Dec 2010, Hofstraat) ▪ Viticulturist(s) Alfred Legner (Jun 2006) ▪ 0.2ha/0.1ha (shiraz) ▪ 2t/ha 66cs own label 100% red ▪ 11 High Str, Darling 7345 ▪ info@darlingmusic.org ▪ **T** +27 (0)72-015-1653

☐ **Mount Sutherland Continental** *see* Super Single Vineyards
☐ **Mount Vernon Estate** *See Editor's Note*

Moya Meaker

Canadian businessman and wine enthusiast David Curl and SA-born wife Genevieve, former owners of Bordeaux's Château Gaby, bought Elgin apple farm Habibi in 2010 and almost immediately planted 3 ha of pinot noir on a ridge of clay-rich Bokkeveld shale. In 2017 they were joined by Jean Smit, former senior winemaker at Boekenhoutskloof, who vinified the 2018 vintage featured below off-site. A 120-ton cellar on the estate is due for completion midyear. Moya Meaker, Genevieve's mother and Miss SA 1959, 'radiated life, elegance and freedom of spirit' and the namesake wine 'seeks to celebrate those qualities'.

★★★★ **Pinot Noir** Attractive floral, earth & raspberry/cherry tones, lithe tannins giving form & few years ageing, variety's signature bright acidity, **18** (88) delicious step up on last-made **14** ★★★ (81). Complex vinification, including 5 separate ferments, 30% new oak, various toastings.— DS, CvZ

Location/WO: Elgin ▪ Est 2010 ▪ 1stB 2012 ▪ Tasting by appt only ▪ Owner(s) David Curl ▪ Winemaker(s) Jean Smit (Oct 2017) ▪ Viticulturist(s) Jean Smit (Oct 2017) ▪ Farm manager Danie du Plessis ▪ 3.12ha (pinot) ▪ 20t own label 100% red ▪ Habibi Farm, Valley Rd, Elgin 7180 ▪ jean@moyameaker.com ▪ www.moyameaker.com ▪ **T** +27 (0)82-334-8100

Moya's Vineyards

With fewer than 10 ha under vine, and miserly yields, this sustainably farmed hillside property in Upper Hemel-en-Aarde Valley adds just 6,000 bottles to each year's inventory with assistance of independent winemaker Hannes Storm (based a few farm gates along), and Johan Montgomery, viticulturist at Hamilton Russell Vineyards (some kilometres back). The Sauvignon, released later than most, is particularly worth seeking out for its mellow bottle-age nuance, gentler acidity and attractive price.

★★★★☆ **Pinot Noir** ⊘ Ripe but tending to savoury in style, **18** (91) shows some earthy, sombre notes but also the lively acidity, barely noticeable tannins of **17** (93). Perhaps touch less characterful but delicious & well-constructed. From low-crop official single-vineyard.

★★★★☆ **Sauvignon Blanc** ⊘ Aromatically complex - tinned peas, white asparagus & stonefruit among the aromas - a subtle granadilla note that extends to palate, **18** ⑨⓪ is dry & fresh, has supple acidity & balance.— CvZ

Location: Hermanus ▪ Map: Walker Bay & Bot River ▪ Map grid reference: B4 ▪ WO: Upper Hemel-en-Aarde Valley ▪ Est 2008 ▪ 1stB 2013 ▪ Tasting Sat/Sun by appt ▪ Closed Good Fri, Dec 25/26 & Jan 1 ▪ Part of the greater Hemel-en-Aarde MTB trails ▪ Owner(s) Hemel & Aarde Country Retreat (Pty) Ltd ▪ Winemaker(s) Hannes Storm (Jan 2013, consultant) ▪ Viticulturist(s) Johan Montgomery (Jul 2008, consultant) ▪ 46ha/8.93ha (pinot, sauv) ▪ 28t/3,000cs own label 50% red 50% white ▪ IPW (vineyards) ▪ PO Box 6367 Uniedal 7612 ▪ collin@bishopcf.co.za ▪ S 34° 21' 51.48" E 019° 15' 32.63" ▪ ⌨ quizzed.channels.graduate ▪ **T** +27 (0)82-551-0088

Mulderbosch Vineyards

In the Stellenboschkloof basin outside Stellenbosch, Mulderbosch uses own fruit and sources from selected vineyards elsewhere in the winelands. A particular focus is chenin, with four variants in the range, three from single pockets, vividly reflecting the influence of terroir. Ownership has changed to a US private part-nership, but the team is confident the right decisions are being made and welcomes the resulting additional capital to further develop, grow and improve the brand. That includes new agency appointments in America and Europe. Adam Mason remains at the winemaking helm, and his personal wine project, Yardstick (see listing), not only has management support but Mulderbosch is there as a partner.

1000 Miles range
★★★★☆ **Sauvignon Blanc** ⓈĲ From 3 Stellenbosch sites, **17** ⑨⓪ vivacious & zesty, with rich stonefruit & tinge of lime. Enriched by 10 months lees ageing in old oak, though less intensity & flinty verve than scintillating **15** ★★★★★ ⑨⑤, from wider range of vineyard sources. No **16**.

Single Vineyards range
★★★★ **Chenin Blanc Block A** One of trio of identically vinified chenins from registered single-vine-yards. **18** ⑧⑨ ex sandy Polkadraai soils, melon & bruised apple, oak's almond overlay, yet trim (12.5% alcohol), ending fresh. Bunch pressed, fermented/10 months in older 1,500L foudres.

★★★★☆ **Chenin Blanc Block S2** Ⓢ Koelenhof shale-based block shows the most citrus, lemon & tangerine, palate enriched by a nutty, savoury effect. Zesty & flavour packed, **18** ⑨② appears the most full bodied (though alcohol is same for all 3 wines).

★★★★☆ **Chenin Blanc Block W** Ⓢ Firgrove parcel on decomposed granite, **18** ⑨③ has bruised apple & citrus perfume, the citrus intensifying on palate, lemon & lime, a slight mineral edge, saline acidity. Tightly focused, has purity & freshness.

Mulderbosch Vineyards range
★★★★☆ **Cabernet Franc** ⓈĲ Exciting prospects for **16** ⑨④ from special block 9B on Stellenboschkloof home-farm. Plush layers of scented fruit, lithe structure, velvety tannins & fresh, sappy farewell. Already tempting but time will bring handsome rewards.

★★★★☆ **Faithful Hound** Ⓢ Classic 5-part Bordeaux blend, with merlot, cab, cab franc leading the pack, now mostly from own vines. Plums & smoky spice, lead pencils, **17** ⑨⓪ ticks all the boxes, even some beef extract. Body is smooth, streamlined, luscious, in perfect drinking mode after 18 months French oak.

★★★★ **Chardonnay** Partial oaking (third) allows **18** ⑧⑧'s citrus & stonefruit to shine, adds complexity, a gentle toastiness & palate roundness. Elegant yet full-flavoured.

★★★★ **Chenin Blanc Steen op Hout** ⊘ Alcohol lowish 12.5% but **18** ⑧⑧ appears fuller, richer due to part oaking in barrels/foudres. Apples & stonefruit, enlivening acidity, savoury biscuit seam throughout.

★★★★ **Sauvignon Blanc** Appealing tropical ripeness in **18** ⑧⑥, 24% oaking a palate weight contribu-tion, round & full. Zesty freshness as an underpin, adds length. **17** ★★★★ ⑧③ very tangy, for food.

Cabernet Sauvignon Rosé ★★★★ Vineyard-sourced style, elegantly (12.5% alcohol) dry, pink **19** ⑧⑤ showcases cab's berries, touch of fynbos. Zesty & vibrant. Also in 1.5L & (Scandinavia only) 3L bag-in-box. WO Coastal. **Méthode Cap Classique Brut** ★★★★ Toasted brioche, red berries, underlying citrus, **15** ⑧④ bubbly is bone-dry, elegant yet packed with flavour. Pinot noir led, with chardonnay, meunier, part barrel fermented/matured 12 months, 3 years on lees. Discontinued: **Chardonnay Barrel Fermented**. — CR

Location/map: Stellenbosch ▪ Map grid reference: C5 ▪ WO: Stellenbosch/Coastal ▪ Est 1989 ▪ 1stB 1991 ▪ Tasting & sales Tue–Sun & pub hols 10–6 ▪ Fee R60–R75 ▪ Closed Easter Fri/Mon, July (annual winter break), Dec 25 & Jan 1 ▪ Pizzas & cheese boards, gourmet burgers, cappuccinos, artisanal beer, juice ▪ Olive oil ▪ Bocce ball courts (Italian boule) ▪ Conservation area ▪ Devil's Peak and The Italian Job craft beer on tasting destination menu ▪ Owner(s) Private partnership based in the USA ▪ Winemaker(s) Adam Mason (Dec 2011), with Mick Craven (Jan 2013) ▪ Viticulturist(s) Adam Mason (Jun 2013) ▪ 80ha/45.2ha (cabs s/f, merlot, p verdot, shiraz, chard, chenin, sauv, viog) ▪ IPW, WIETA ▪ PO Box 12817 Die Boord Stellenbosch 7613 ▪ info@mulderbosch.co.za ▪ www. mulderbosch.co.za ▪ S 33° 56' 56.00" E 018° 45' 57.00" ▪ 🖂 stadium.bridge.hunches ▪ T +27 (0)21-881-8140

Mullineux

If this was a multimedia guide, the words you're reading would be accompanied with thunderous applause for the team this edition achieving an unparalleled fourth coveted pinnacle award in this guide. They've been Winery of the Year in both 2014 and 2016, then Top Performing Winery of the Year last year, and now (cue fireworks) they clinch a second consecutive Top Performing Winery accolade, with five maximum ratings, including Shiraz of the Year and Vin de Paille of the Year. All the more extraordinary for the modesty of the team led by Andrea and Chris Mullineux, wife-and-husband founders and co-owners (with Indian businessman Analjit Singh) of this non-interventionist venture based on Swartland farm Roundstone. Their aim is to reflect the diverse soils of the area using shiraz and chenin blanc as the lens in the varietal bottlings, and as cornerstone of the blends. While acknowledging that old vines play an important role, an eye on the changing climate has seen Chris and consultant Rosa Kruger initiate a planting programme. Look forward to – depending on performance – macabeu/viura, verdelho, assyrtiko and/or vermentino, among others, entering in the cellar, where Andrea and assistant Wade Sander weave their magic. For the team's near-equally stellar Franschhoek-based project, see under Leeu Passant.

Single Terroir range

★★★★☆ **Granite Syrah** 🐝 Same winemaking for 3 syrahs puts terroir in the spotlight: wholebunch natural ferment, older 500L barrels/large foudres, unfined/filtered. **17** ★★★★★ ⑨⑧ from Paardeberg dryland vines, trademark lily perfume & sleek succulence, oystershell minerality, similar tightly wound tannin frame as **16** ⑨③. Magnums too, as for most.

★★★★★ **Iron Syrah** 🐝 Lily, tobacco & black pepper nuances, ferrous character from dryland Malmesbury hills vineyard with deep, iron-rich koffieklip (ferricrete) soil. **17** ⑨⑦ less compact & athletic than siblings but has excellent muscle tone, will be stellar for next decade or more.

★★★★★ **Schist Syrah Roundstone** 🐝 From vineyard on Kasteelberg home-farm. Soil deeper, denser, little water-holding capacity, vines & bunches smaller. Fynbos scent, some smokiness, **17** ⑨⑥ shows seamless elegance with a fine tannin structure, exceptional purity & vivacity. Long life ahead.

★★★★☆ **Granite Chenin Blanc** 🐝 🍃 Amongst oldest vineyards on Paardeberg, deep soils allow dryland farming with minimal stress. Perfectly poised **18** ⑨④ is chenin pared back, showcases the unfruity loveliness of variety: persistent saline acidity, crystalline minerality, only then a quince nuance, including slight (positive) bitter lift.

★★★★★ **Quartz Chenin Blanc Leliefontein** 🐝 Rare concentration of quartz in this single Kasteelberg block, stones reflect sunlight into the canopy, aiding ripeness without sugar increase. Fine **18** ⑨④ reined-in fruit, linear, with terse seam of minerality. Same vinification as chenin sibling to emphasise site: wholebunch, natural ferment, older 225L/500L barrels, unfined/filtered.

Occasional release: **Schist Chenin Blanc**.

CWG Auction Reserve range

★★★★☆ **The Gris Semillon Old Vines** 🐝 🍃 From semillon on granite soil, 1960 Paardeberg dryland parcel, red-skinned bunches isolated from rest & bunch-pressed straight to barrel. Though still breathtakingly dry, **18** ⑨④ intentionally richer than previous, says Andrea Mullineux, to enhance the sensuality of the pear & beeswax flavours as wine ages over next 10 years or more.

Signature range

★★★★☆ **Syrah** 🐝 Blend of 3 soil types featured in terroir range, half the barrel time (12 months). **17** ⑨④ quintessential shiraz scrub & hedgerow fruit, white pepper & charcuterie notes, limber tannins. Graceful wine now & minimum 5 years.

★★★★★ **Old Vines White** ⓐ ⓨ Senior vines, some veterans of 80 seasons, in 4 main Swartland soils. **18** ⑨⑥ chenin-led with 4 others, harmonious melody of stonefruit, minerals & flowers, same brightening saline acidity as previous. A wine with soul & character, & only one beside Rouge with portion new oak, 20%, deftly handled.

★★★★★ **Straw Wine** ⓐ Unbeaten 5-star track record, 9 of 10 vintages. Fruit from 3 vineyards air-dried al fresco for week, then old-barrel fermented 10 months. Bewitching **18** ⑨⑦ chenin's myriad sweet, fruity & savoury layers interleaved with vibrant tangerine & lime acidity, subtle nutty oak. Tad less sugar (303 g/l) perfectly balanced with 9.8 g/l acid, will carry the wine a great many years. 375 ml.

Occasional release: **Essence Straw Wine, Olerasay Straw Wine**.

Kloof Street range

★★★★ **Swartland Rouge** Earlier-drinking option, varieties chosen for area history. **18** ⑧⑨ step change, with 45% tinta just leading syrah, splashes grenache, cinsaut, carignan. Light textured & fruity as ever, enough in reserve for few years.

★★★★ **Old Vine Chenin Blanc** 'Intro to the Swartland, rather than entry-level wine.' From 2 granite sites on Paardeberg, just 10% oaked in new-livery **19** ⑧⑦ Lively & bright, mulled pear & terracotta earthiness, long mineral finish. **18** untasted.— CvZ

Location: Riebeek-Kasteel ▪ Map: Franschhoek ▪ Map grid reference: C2 ▪ WO: Swartland ▪ Map: Swartland ▪ Map grid reference: D6 ▪ Est 2007 ▪ 1stB 2008 ▪ Tasting & sales Mon-Sun 10-5 at the Wine Studio, Leeu Estates, Franschhoek (booking recommended); Roundstone Farm, Riebeek-Kasteel by appt only ▪ Owner(s) Mullineux & Leeu Family Wines (Pty) Ltd ▪ Cellarmaster(s) Chris & Andrea Mullineux (May 2007) ▪ Winemaker(s) Andrea Mullineux (May 2007), with Wade Sander (2016) ▪ Viticulturist(s) Chris Mullineux (May 2007), with Rosa Kruger ▪ 38ha (carignan, cinsaut, mourv, shiraz, chenin, clairette, sem, viog) ▪ 160t/16,000cs own label 58% red 40% white 2% dessert ▪ PO Box 369 Riebeek-Kasteel 7307 ▪ info@ mlfwines.com ▪ www.mlfwines.com ▪ S 33° 54' 33.43" E 019° 6' 14.85" (Franschhoek) ▪ 📍 lotions.concretely. pitting ▪ S 33° 22' 34.13" E 018°50' 23.74" (Riebeek-Kasteel) ▪ 📍 menu.evaluations.twinkle ▪ **T +27 (0)21-492-2455 (office)/+27 (0)21-492-2224 (Wine Studio)**

Muratie Wine Estate ⓨ 🍴 ◎

Family, tradition, hospitality and wine are interlinked themes at Muratie, steeped in early Cape history, with gnarled roots firmly entrenched in the higher reaches of Stellenbosch's Simonsberg. Behind the proud relics of the past - old oaks, cobwebbed tasting room and historically themed wine labels - there is a dynamic team dealing with contemporary challenges. Winemaker Hattingh de Villiers has had to adapt his cellar techniques to deal with the drought-reduced crop, while owner Rijk Melck tackles the business sustainability issue, championing a more realistic price for undervalued SA wines abroad, to ensure a fair and dignified salary for staff back home. Besides the array of wine-related hospitality already offered here, locals were treated to tasting rare vinous gems dating back to 1993 at the first Retro Rouge festival.

Premium range

★★★★ **Martin Melck Cabernet Sauvignon** ⓐ Authoritative & restrained, **15** ★★★★★ ⑨③ ticks all the varietal boxes & takes a confident step up on **14** ⑧⑧. Seriously structured, classically styled, with a dense core of dark fruit streamlined by firm dry tannins. Infanticide now, so much more to enjoy in 6-10 years. Like previous, only 10% new oak.

★★★★☆ **Martin Melck Cabernet Sauvignon Family Reserve** ⓨ Premium grapes & all-new oak (previously 60%) for this label. **15** ⑨④ concentrated, intense, yet more elegant & fresh than **14** ⑨②, with touch of mint. Complex & layered, already enticing, but will handsomely reward ageing. Simonsberg-Stellenbosch WO, as Ronnie, Ansela, Isabella Reserve, Lady Alice & Ben Prins.

★★★★ **Alberta Annemarie Merlot** Ripe red cherry & berry flavours, well crafted, good fruit balancing firm, lithe tannins, eschewing new oak the right decision in **16** ⑧⑨. Augurs well for development.

★★★★ **George Paul Canitz Pinot Noir** ⓨ Smoky, perfumed red fruit, lithe dry tannins, all enveloped in creamy oak & alcohol embrace. **16** ⑧⑥ engaging dinner partner, with structure for 3-5 years, though shade off **15** ⑧⑦.

★★★★★ **Ronnie Melck Shiraz** Smoky, brooding & riper-style **16** ★★★★ ⑧⑧, similar smooth tannins & dark fruit, with a warm liquorice tone, but shade less structure & gravitas than **15** ⑨②.

★★★★☆ **Ansela van de Caab** ⓐ Continues as cab-led Bordeaux blend in **16** ⑨③ & similar 24 months in 60% new oak. Ample riper, dark-berry fruit in a supple, dry tannin structure. Balanced, layered & inviting, though shade off the complexity & intensity of stellar **15** ★★★★★ ⑨⑤.

★★★★ **Melck's Blended Red** ⓿ Shiraz-led, with cab, merlot & cab franc in **15** ⑧⑨. Mostly savoury, clean dark choc & berry core in elegant, structured tannin framework. Already balanced, with potential. Improves on **14** ★★★★ ⑧③. WO W Cape, like Melck's Sauvignon & Amber Forever.

★★★★ **Isabella Chardonnay** Natural ferment, ageing in 40% new oak add spice & breadth to **18** ⑧⑦. Succulent, more rounded & richer than **17** ★★★☆ ⑧⑤.

★★★★ **Isabella Chardonnay Reserve** ⓠ Barrel selection from **17** ⑧⑧ vintage. All-new oak tempers acidity, adds silky texture but also masks the more delicate lemon/starfruit profile. Finer than sibling but rung below more complex **14. 16** & **15** not made.

★★★★ **Laurens Campher Blended White** Like **17** ⑧⑦, a chenin-led quartet. Quite rich & plumper in **18** ⑧⑥, with warmer aromatic dried-fruit impression. Creamy, gentle twist of acidity on the finish.

★★★★ **Lady Alice Méthode Cap Classique Rosé** ⓠ Brut sparkler from pinot noir honours ex owner & perennial celebrant Lady Alice Sarah Stanford. **15** ★★★★ ⑧⑤ engaging, light-hearted & tangy, but reduced lees time (20 months) less impressive than **14** ★★★★☆ ⑨① & **13** ⑧⑧.

Johanna Pinot Noir Rosé ★★★ Adds variety to name in delightfully fresh **19** ⑧①, & continues to charm with scented berry/cherry flavours. Dry, light & tangy al fresco wine. **Melck's Sauvignon Blanc** ★★★ Combo tropical & crunchy green-apple notes on **19** ⑧①. Feisty malic nuance, better with food than solo.

Fortified Wines

★★★★☆ **Amber Forever** ⓠ Perfumed raisin flavours on oak-matured fortified hanepoot, creamy, warming centre with thread of citrus freshness. **16** ★★★★ ⑧⑦ more delicate than heady **15** ⑨②. 375 ml.

★★★★ **Ben Prins Cape Vintage** ⓠ Modern, delicious 'port' from traditional varieties. **15** ★★★★★ ⑨② concentrated black fruit, firm, dry & peppery tannins, sweetness well contained, finishes with a fiery twist. An infant, deserves decade ageing. Also-tasted **16** ⑧⑦ riper & rounder, appealing but will peak much earlier.

Discontinued: **Cape Ruby**. — MW

Location/map: Stellenbosch ▪ Map grid reference: F3 ▪ WO: Stellenbosch/Simonsberg–Stellenbosch/Western Cape ▪ Est 1685 ▪ 1stB ca 1920 ▪ Tasting & sales daily 10-5 ▪ Tasting fees: R60/classic, R95/premium, R80/chocolate pairing, R300/heritage tasting - by appt only ▪ Closed Good Fri, Dec 25 & Jan 1 ▪ Farm Kitchen Mon-Sun 9-3.30 ▪ R30/cellar tours ▪ Group bookings by appt only ▪ Cheese platters ▪ Function venue ▪ MOK art gallery/exhibit ▪ Harvest festival ▪ Live music ▪ MTB ▪ Trail running ▪ Owner(s) Melck Family Trust ▪ Winemaker(s) Hattingh de Villiers (Jul 2014) ▪ Viticulturist(s) Conrad Schutte ▪ 110ha/40ha (cabs s/f, grenache, merlot, mourv, p verdot, pinot, shiraz, chard, chenin, hanepoot, port, verdelho) ▪ 300t/320,000cs own label 70% red 20% white 1% rosé 19% other ▪ IPW ▪ PO Box 133 Koelenhof 7605 ▪ info@muratie.co.za ▪ www.muratie.co.za ▪ S 33° 52' 14.8" E 018° 52' 35.1" ▪ ⓦ include.trailer.drove ▪ **T +27 (0)21-865-2330/2336**

☐ **Muse** *see* Boschheim
☐ **Music by D'Aria** *see* D'Aria Winery

Mvemve Raats   ⓠ

Friends and collaborators Mzokhona Mvemve and Bruwer Raats (also of Raats Family Wines) since debuting with the '04 vintage have focused on a single wine, a red blend named De Compostella, signifying 'a collection or compilation of stars'. The wine has indeed achieved stellar success, with international recognition and acclaim. A major reason, no doubt, is the emphasis on quality above style, and an unwavering approach: source the very best pockets of each of the 5 Bordeaux varieties from top sites around Stellenbosch, vinify separately, taste and rate 'blind', then compose the blend according to the results.

★★★★☆ **MR de Compostella** ⓐ Iconic cab-driven, 5-way Bordeaux blend shows consummate craftsmanship. **17** ⑨④ an uncompromising, visceral expression of earthy currants, with thumping tannins & muscular body, yet refined, pure & focused.— GdB

Location/map/WO: Stellenbosch ▪ Map grid reference: B6 ▪ Est/1stB 2004 ▪ Tasting & sales Mon-Fri 9-5 by appt only ▪ Closed all pub hols ▪ Owner(s) Bruwer Raats & Mzokhona Mvemve ▪ Cellarmaster(s)/viticulturist(s) Bruwer Raats & Mzokhona Mvemve (both Jan 2004) ▪ Winemaker(s) Bruwer Raats & Mzokhona Mvemve (both Jan 2004), with Gavin Bruwer Slabbert (Feb 2010) ▪ (cabs s/f, malbec, merlot, p verdot) ▪ 10t/900cs own label 100% red ▪ PO Box 2068 Dennesig Stellenbosch 7601 ▪ office@raats.co.za ▪ www. raatswines.co.za ▪ S 33° 58' 16.6" E 018° 44' 55.3" ▪ *tinged.guzzle.newness* ▪ **T +27 (0)21-881-3078**

MVH Signature Wines

Boutique production for this eponymous Burgundy-focused label is non-negotiable for Matthew van Heerden, thoughtful vigneron and former Diners Club Young Winemaker of the Year. His fruit is sourced in cool-climate areas which, he's delighted to report, rode out the drought really well. Having experimented with careful water management, Matthew praises 'exceptional soils' for leading to balanced growth, with small bunches and berries providing 'exceptional concentration'. He believes hands-on viticulture, and achieving greater efficiency in farming more naturally are the way forward.

★★★★☆ **Pinot Noir** ⊘ Seductive **18** ⑨⓪ again carefully sorted & pressed, cool-climate Elgin fruit, naturally fermented. Bright & pure, with supportive oak (third new, 12 months) adding to refined, broad, spicy, long finish. No **17**. Also in magnum, as next.

★★★★☆ **Chardonnay** ⓐ Refined **17** ⑨④ picks up where **16** ⑨④ left off, grapes from Helderberg & Elgin fermented naturally. Oatmeal, marmalade richness cradled by sympathetic oak (50% new, 10 months), rewarding & long.— FM

Location: Stellenbosch ▪ WO: Elgin/Western Cape ▪ Est/1stB 2013 ▪ Tasting by appt only ▪ Owner(s) Matthew van Heerden ▪ Winemaker(s)/viticulturist(s) Matthew van Heerden (Jan 2013) ▪ 5t/400cs own label 50% red 50% white ▪ IPW ▪ PO Box 2134 Dennesig Stellenbosch 7601 ▪ mvhwines@gmail.com ▪ **T +27 (0)82-771-7969/+27 (0)82-520-9338**

☐ **My Best Friend** *see* Zandvliet Wine Estate

Myburgh Bros

Myburgh siblings Tyrrel and Philip honour their great-grandfather Johannes and his brother with this well-made range of varietal wines, listed separately from their main Joostenberg venture. They aim to make wines which are pure and honest, sticking to traditional winemaking practices. The result is fresh, clean wines, farmed organically where possible and shepherded into the bottle with the minimum of fuss.

★★★★ **Cinsault** ⊘ Fruity **18** ⑧⑥ hits the summer drinking mark with soft red berries, hint of dried herbs & juicy texture courtesy of 1/3 wholebunch ferment, restrained 12.5% alcohol. Serve lightly chilled.

★★★★ **Viognier** ⓥ Lovely varietal typicity on **18** ★★★★☆ ⑧④, showing bright stonefruit backed up by nice touch of soft oak. Tails off somewhat at finish, shade less balanced than delightful **17** ⑧⑧.— CM

Location/map/WO: Paarl ▪ Map grid reference: A7 ▪ Est/1stB 2017 ▪ Tasting, sales & cellar tours by appt ▪ Owner(s) Tyrrel & Philip Myburgh ▪ Cellarmaster(s)/viticulturist(s) Tyrrel Myburgh (2017) ▪ Winemaker(s) Tyrrel Myburgh (2017), with Elmerie Joubert (2017) ▪ ±8,000cs own label 50% red 50% white ▪ Control Union (Organic), IPW ▪ PO Box 82 Elsenburg 7607 ▪ tyrrel@joostenberg.co.za, winery@joostenberg.co.za ▪ S 33° 48' 47.21" E 018° 48' 31.70 ▪ *centipedes.bridesmaids.dinners* ▪ **T +27 (0)21-200-9903**

☐ **My Cosmic Hand** *see* Elemental Bob

My Wyn

Jacoline Haasbroek's pride in 'My Wine', her almost two-decade-old artisan venture housed in a tiny Franschhoek mountain cellar, vinifying brought-in grapes, knew no bounds last year when Cabernet Franc Challenge judges awarded her varietal bottling ('16) a gold medal, and the blended version, Rouge '15, a top three place in its category. Jacoline has fans around the world who rave about her convivial personalised tastings and by-arrangement delicacies. Book now (and take your own picnic if preferred).

Les Grandes Horizontales range

★★★★ **Rouge** Au naturel female figure in front-label artwork of many of these wines intended to communicate 'unadorned & authentic' nature of the content; this range, the subject reclines in classic pose (hence name). **15** ⑧⑥ creatively pairs 5 Bordeaux & Rhône grapes in savoury-meaty blend with dark fruit & admirable accessibility despite 26 months oaking & tannin grip.

Not tasted: **Blanc**.

My Wyn range

★★★★ **Cabernet Franc** Richly fruited **16** (88), blackcurrant pastilles, had 17 months in 2nd-fill barrels, easily assimilated, curvaceous body, ripe tannins, the serious side showing as firmness at the end.

★★★★ **Méthode Cap Classique Blanc de Blancs Extra Brut** Oaked, 48 months on lees, **14** (88) bubbly from chardonnay is amber-gold, has lemon sherbet & toasted brioche perfume, flavours. Classically styled, with fine bead & elegant finish. Drink soon to catch at best.

★★★★ **Méthode Cap Classique Extra Brut** Medium gold, oaked & 37 months on lees, **14** (86) sparkling from chardonnay & 38% pinot noir, has bruised apple scents & flavours, toasted brioche, vigorous mousse. Sleek, ends dry. Lots of personality here, best enjoyed in next year/2.

Petit Verdot ★★★☆ Some scrub notes in **15** (83), deep & dark-toned, liquorice, some beef extract, with firm dry tannins needing more time. In barrique 24 months, 3 weeks skin maceration, promise well for the future. Variety true. **Shiraz-Viognier** ★★★☆ Just a dab of viognier; **16** (85) is dark fruited, ripe & robust, 20 months 2nd-fill barrels, so spice is plentiful yet tannins supple. Smooth textured, eminently drinkable. **Méthode Cap Classique Brut Rosé** ★★★☆ Pale pink bubbly from pinot noir (88%) & chardonnay, oaked & 14 months on the lees, **17** (83) has red berry appeal lifted by racy acidity; zesty, fresh & dry. Elegant 11.5% alcohol. **My Robyn Cape Vintage** ★★★☆ From shiraz, 3 weeks skin maceration, 31 months in barrel, port-style **16** (84) moderately sweet jammy fruit, nice tar, anise & candy/sherbet notes, finishing grip. **My Amber** ★★★ White 'port' from viognier, **NV** (80) yellow-gold colour, scents of wild honey, preserved melon & ginger spice from older oak ageing, sweetness kept in check by edgy spirit. Uncertified. 375 ml to be served well-chilled. Not tasted: **Viognier**, **Sauvignier**. Discontinued: **Semillon**. — GdB, CR

Location/map/WO: Franschhoek ▪ Map grid reference: B1 ▪ Est/1stB 2001 ▪ Tasting, sales & cellar tours by appt, or as indicated on the gate ▪ Open pub hols by appt ▪ Tasting R75pp ▪ Cheese platters by prior arrangement, or BYO picnic ▪ Wine clubs, team building groups welcome for intimate food & wine pairing - various options available, to be pre-booked ▪ Owner(s) Jacoline Haasbroek ▪ Winemaker(s) Jacoline Haasbroek (2001) ▪ 1,250cs own label 50% red 20% port 30% MCC ▪ PO Box 112 Franschhoek 7690 ▪ tastewine@telkomsa.net ▪ www.mywynfranschhoek.co.za ▪ S 33° 53' 29.3" E 019° 8' 3.6" ▪ 🖵 witticism.mouthparts. placebos ▪ **T +27 (0)21-876-2518/+27 (0)83-302-5556**

☐ **Naked Wines** *see* Richard Kershaw Wines

Namaqua Wines

There's a wine to suit almost every palate (and pocket) at Namaqua, one of SA's biggest and most successful producers, with 200 owner-growers, ±5,000ha under vine and 9.3 million cases leaving the cellar each year. From the evocative old-vine Doornkraal Chenin Blanc, to the sleek Spencer Bay Reserve reds from selected vineyards, to the easy-drinking whites, reds, rosés, bubblies, fortified and sweet wines in the Namaqua, Gôiya and hugely popular bag-in-box ranges, 'quality' is the watchword for production chief Len Knoetze and his team of five winemakers and viticulturist Dirk de Bruyn. Why not drive up the scenic West Coast and taste for yourself at Die Keldery, the modern visitor centre and restaurant just outside Vredendal town?

Doornkraal range

★★★★☆ **Chenin Blanc** ⊘ From low-yield Lutzville vines trained with the echalas (staked vine) system, handled minimally in the cellar. Unoaked **18** (90) slightly denser, broader than **17** (90); similar white peach & floral notes, positive earthy touch, refreshing acidity & length.

Spencer Bay Winemakers Reserve range

★★★★ **Pinotage** ⊘ Most attractive wine in the line-up. **13** (86) modern, with house's vivacious acidity, lingering dry finish; lovely interplay between structuring tannins & succulent mulberry, plum fruit.

★★★★ **The Blend** 🍷 Cab-led, 5-way Bordeaux red. **14** (86) repeats pleasing **11** (86) formula: dark fruit, mint accent, oak adding complexity & structure, hint sweetness.

Pinot Noir ⊘ 🍸 ★★★★ First since **13** (83), **17** (85) subtle cherry aromas & flavours with light smoky overlay, invigorating freshness. Worth seeking out.

Cabernet Sauvignon ★★★★ Youthful **14** ⑧⑤ as polished & generous as previous, with plush cassis fruit & hint meatiness. Loses the vanilla sweetness for a more satisfying conclusion. Nudges next level. From selected top-performing blocks, 70% new oak, mostly American, 12-18 months, as all these. **Merlot** (NEW) ★★★★ Sweet plums, hint Christmas spices, **17** ⑧③ engages from the first sip; finishes well, too, with enlivening acidity & pleasantly firm tannin. **Shiraz** ⊘ ★★★★ Still-youthful **12** ⑧③, with bright acidity, firm tannins as counterpoint to vanilla overlay.

Cellar Door range
Occasional release: **Merlot**, **Pinotage**, **Pinotage-Malbec**, **Sauvignon Blanc**.

Cape West Limited Releases
Cabernet Sauvignon-Malbec-Pinotage ⊘ ★★★ Smooth & easy **17** ⑧② with attractive spiciness, charry finish. Good everyday drinking, as all these (but note big 14.5% alcohol here). **Cabernet Sauvignon-Pinotage** ⊘ ★★★ Bright acidity for food pairing, firm tannins but no rough edges on fruity **17** ⑧②. **Shiraz-Pinotage** ⊘ ★★★ Attractively spicy, smoky & savoury 67/33 blend, **17** ⑧② soaks up 70% new wood (50/50 French/American, as for all), so it's less oak-sweet than siblings. Not tasted: **Chardonnay**, **Sauvignon Blanc**.

Namaqua range
....

Shiraz ⊘ ⊛ ★★★ Spicy aromas, bright fruit & bouncy acidity: **17** ⑦⑨ has everything needed for pleasurable casual drinking.
....

Cabernet Sauvignon ⊘ ★★★ Well-priced, candyfloss-toned **16** ⑦⑦ has just enough tannin for everyday sipping. Few grams sugar, high portion American oak aid drinkability, aromatic appeal, as all these reds. **Merlot** ⊘ ★★★ Sweetness well balanced by brisk acidity, **17** ⑦⑦ slight leafiness & hint of clove. **Pinotage** ★★ Little varietal character, but **18** ⑦④'s fruit is sweet & slips down easily. **Chenin Blanc** ★★ **19** ⑦② nicely dry, pineapple-toned easy sipper. **Sauvignon Blanc** ★★ Modest in aroma & flavour departments, yet **19** ⑦② has zip & is quaffable. **Guinevere Méthode Cap Classique** ⊘ ★★★★ **10** ⑧⑤ celebratory sparkling from 60% pinot noir with chardonnay has rather unorthodox orange hue, impresses with fine bead, creamy mousse, savoury/umami finish from 5 years on lees. **Noble Late Harvest** ⊘ ★★★ Unusual but pleasant **14** ⑧② botrytis dessert from pinotage, unoaked, with delightful savouriness, giving strawberries in balsamic vinegar effect. Would work well with soft cheeses or fresh fruit desserts. 375 ml. **Red Muscadel** ⊘ ★★★★ Partly oaked **17** ⑧⑤ fortified, with exotic allure of tangerine, tealeaf & cardamom. Persistent, sweet but uncloying flavours. **White Muscadel** ⊘ ★★★★ Well-integrated alcohol, tangy acidity, intense citrus & honeysuckle aromas & flavours: **17** ⑧③ part-oaked fortified dessert ticks all the boxes. **Hanepoot Jerepigo** ★★★ Charming rainy day companion, **17** ⑦⑨ fortified big-hearted & grapey, rounded by touch old oak. **Cape Vintage** ⊘ ★★ From shiraz, **17** ⑦④ more jerepiko than 'port' in style, with lower alcohol (17%) & more sugar (130 g/l) than purists would expect.

Gôiya range
Not tasted: **Sauvignon Blanc-Chardonnay**.

3L Box range
....

Cabernet Sauvignon ⊘ ⊛ ★★★ Take-me-camping **NV** ⑦⑧ more vibrant & drier than the bottled version.
....

Merlot ★★ Less feisty than Cab, with same mostly American oak giving **NV** ⑦③ an appealing vanilla-toned drinkability. **Sauvignon Blanc** ★★ Grassy **19** ⑦⑥ has bracing acidity that needs food. — CvZ

Location: Vredendal ▪ Map/WO: Olifants River ▪ Map grid reference: B4 ▪ Est/1stB 1947 ▪ Tasting & sales Mon-Sat 8–5 ▪ Closed Easter Fri-Mon, Ascension day & Dec 25/26 ▪ Cellar tours Mon-Fri 10 & 3, book ahead ▪ Die Keldery Restaurant T +27 (0)27-213-3699/8 Mon-Fri 8-5 Sat 9-5 & dinner Thu 7-10 ▪ Facilities for children ▪ Conferences ▪ Owner(s) 200 members ▪ Production manager Len Knoetze ▪ Winemaker(s) Driaan van der Merwe, Rudi de Wet, Koos Thiart, Johan Weideman & Reinier van Greunen ▪ Viticulturist(s) Dirk de Bruyn ▪ 4,990ha ▪ 113,692t/9.3m cs 20% red 80% white ▪ PO Box 75 Vredendal 8160 ▪ info@namaquawines.com ▪ www.namaquawines.com ▪ S 31° 42' 34.9" E 018° 30' 15.6" ▪ ⌖ scattered.overactive.centenary ▪ **T +27 (0)27-213-1080**

Napier Vineyards

Owned by German wine powerhouse Reh Kendermann since 2017, this winery is scenically sited on the slopes of the Groenberg in Wellington. It has 89 ha of predominantly black grapes, and the cellar capacity was recently increased to handle the entire crop of 750 tons. Recognition has been received from the Business Social Compliance Initiative (BSCI) for social compliance in the global supply chain and, excitingly, the wine-brand that funds social upliftment for employees, '14 Homes', was successfully launched in Europe.

Napier range

★★★★ Cabernet Sauvignon Single-vineyard **15** ★★★★ ⑧④'s sense of ripeness & fruit-sweetness amplified by few grams sugar & burly 15% alcohol, partly balanced by tailored tannins & little nip acidity. Shade off better-modulated **14** ⑧⑨.

★★★★ Red Medallion ⑧ Cabernet (45%) leads cab franc, just, in 5-way Bordeaux flagship, **15** ⑧⑧ has freshness & grip, handles 15% alcohol better than noticeably warm **14** ⑧⑦ & the varietal Cab. Effect is one of luxury, with 100% new oak well handled.

★★★★ Cape Blend ⑭ ⊘ ⑧ Pinotage & equal cab franc & shiraz in **18** ⑧⑥. All-older oak well-supports the medley of red & black fruit, helps give lighter feel, earlier approachability than other reds, as do more moderate 13.5% alcohol & properly dry finish. WO Coastal.

★★★★ St Catherine Chardonnay Continues tendency towards elegance & understatement in **18** ⑧⑧ from single-vineyard. Subtle lemon & tangerine gently brushed with 10% new oak, lengthy dry end.

★★★★ St Helen Chenin Blanc ⑭ ⊘ Third single-vineyard wine in line-up, **18** ⑧⑥ mostly unwooded but the 16% new-barrelled portion makes its presence felt. Poise achieved through ample yellow fruit & vibrant acidity. Impressively dry & long.

Petite Marie Rosé ★★★ Exchanges grenache for cab franc, retains well-hidden gram sugar, which gives extra appeal in uncomplicated **19** ⑦⑨, with demure berry aromas & flavours. **Little Lara Chenin Blanc** ⑭ ★★★ Unoaked sibling picked early & thus light in alcohol (12%), with delicate peach & floral tones. **19** ⑧② bone-dry, undemanding but balanced, flavoursome.

Lion Creek range

Cabernet Sauvignon ★★★ As always, berry toned & smooth, with friendly tannins & light oaking. **17** ⑧② makes for good everyday sipping. **Cabernet Sauvignon-Shiraz** ★★★ Unlike previous, no smidgen sugar in **17** ⑧⓪, sparingly wooded to showcase fruit, 49% shiraz providing charcuterie platter aromas & flavours. **Chenin Blanc-Sauvignon Blanc** ★★★ Lightly does it - in fruity perfume, alcohol (12%) & daub sweetness - brisk acidity adds to the airy feel in **18** ⑧② blend with 10% colombard. WO W Cape.

Brandy range

★★★★ Sir George Potstill Brandy ⑨ From 100% chenin, vibrant gold hues on this sophisticated brandy ⑧⑦, matured 5 years. Well structured, smooth & elegant; appropriately packaged.— CvZ, WB

Location/map: Wellington ▪ Map grid reference: C3 ▪ WO: Wellington/Coastal/Western Cape ▪ Est 1989/1stB 1999 ▪ Tasting & sales Mon-Thu 8-5 Fri 8–3 ▪ Fee R30/R60/R100 ▪ Cellar tours by appt ▪ Closed all pub hols ▪ Owner(s) Reh Kendermann GmbH Weinkellerei ▪ Cellarmaster(s) Leon Bester (Apr 2000) ▪ Winemaker(s) Leon Bester (Apr 2000), with Hanlie Schönborn (Sep 2012) ▪ Viticulturist(s) JP van der Merwe (Aug 2017) ▪ 135ha/89ha (cabs s/f, malbec, merlot, p verdot, shiraz, chard, chenin) ▪ 750t/30,000cs own label 78% red 20% white 2% rosé ▪ BSCI, WIETA ▪ PO Box 638 Wellington 7654 ▪ info@napierwinery.co.za ▪ www.napier-vineyards.co.za ▪ S 33° 38' 37.0" E 019° 2' 24.8" ▪ 🖥 shopper.internet.phones ▪ **T +27 (0)21-873-7829**

☐ **Natana** see Marianne Wine Estate

Natasha Williams Signature Wines

Following her Stellenbosch University oenology degree with an internship at acclaimed Jordan and a stint in California, Natasha Williams joined the Bosman Family Vineyards team in 2014. The up-and-coming young winemaker's own label pays tribute to her tiny Tulbagh hometown of Lelie van Saron, and features fruit from the Bosmans' De Bos vine garden and vineyards in cool-climate Upper Hemel-en-Aarde. The Chardonnay is from a single block and the Syrah a clonal selection, produced with minimal intervention.

Lelie van Saron range

★★★★☆ **Syrah** Seductive **18** ⑨⓪ has marvellous profusion of flavours & aromas, from cassis & black cherries through violets & rosepetals to herbs & pepper, encased in a fine tannin lattice. Outstanding complexity & structure at moderate 13.4% alcohol. Only older oak, as sibling.

★★★★☆ **Chardonnay** ⑧ Deftly balances lime & orange fruit with oak character ex ferment/16 months in 225/300L barrels. **17** ⑨① beautifully dry, with a stony minerality, shows real elegance & restraint (just 13% alcohol). Bunch pressed & wild fermented. Also in magnum.— JG, CvZ

Location: Wellington ▪ WO: Upper Hemel-en-Aarde Valley ▪ 1stB 2017 ▪ Tasting & cellar tours by appt ▪ Closed all pub hols ▪ Owner(s)/winemaker(s) Natasha Williams ▪ 2-3t/360cs own label 50% red 50% white ▪ IPW ▪ natasha25w10@gmail.com ▪ **T +27 (0)73-034-4846**

☐ **Nativo** see Hughes Family Wines

Natte Valleij Wines

The Milner family's 300-year-old Stellenbosch cellar, fairly unchanged over the centuries, is the source of a critically acclaimed 'four pack' of site-specific varietal cinsaut bottlings, untasted by us. Now also a stellar chenin by winemaker and cycling enthusiast Alex Milner, listed separately under Axle Wines.

Location/map: Stellenbosch ▪ Map grid reference: F1 ▪ Est 1715 ▪ Tasting, sales & cellar tours Mon-Sat by appt ▪ Closed all pub hols ▪ Wedding venue ▪ Art gallery & art classes ▪ Natte Valleij self-catering cottages ▪ Owner(s)/winemaker(s) Milner family ▪ 28ha total ▪ 40t/5,000cs own label 90% red 10% white ▪ PO Box 4 Klapmuts 7625 ▪ wine@nattevalleij.co.za ▪ www.nattevalleij.co.za ▪ S 33° 50' 3.6" E 018° 52' 43.2" ▪ ⌖ sofa.cardinal.same ▪ **T +27 (0)21-875-5171**

☐ **Natura** see Leopard's Leap Family Vineyards
☐ **Natural Star** see Stellar Winery
☐ **Nature** see Bonnievale Wines
☐ **Naudé Old Vines** see Naudé Wines

Naudé Wines

Long before 'old' became an industry focus - and latterly a certification - Ian Naudé, now located in Stellenbosch, was seeking out old vines for grapes for his wines. 'It's about respect,' he says, going on to explain that vines that have been in the soil for 30 to 50 years have an authenticity and character that no younger vines can offer. He doesn't always seek to express single vineyards, but also does blending across a number of sites, characterising these wines as 'multi-terroir', to bring out the best in a variety. His wines have presence and authenticity, speaking of a man who cares deeply about what he produces. And, as the Naudé White so ably demonstrates, ageing ability is a given.

Naudé Old Vines range

★★★★☆ **Cinsaut** ⑨ ⓦ Single Darling vineyard, **15** ⑨③ follows maiden **14** ⑨④ in red fruit intensity, yet also earthy, scrubby, with textured savouriness. Elegant, with nothing missing, has sleek musculature. As winemaker says: 'Young at heart with an old soul.'

★★★★☆ **Grenache** ⑨ Naturally fermented **14** ⑨④ is light, understated, almost austere - but undeniably complex, with red cherry, pot-pourri & a pinch of pepper. Silky, with a fresh, bright finish. Swartland vines; only older oak.

★★★★☆ **Chenin Blanc** ⑧ ⓦ Blend of 3 old-vine terroirs in Durbanville, Stellenbosch & Swartland. **16** ⑨③ wild ferment, 12 months in barrel, 10% new, nut/fruit concentration, tangerine & preserved quince. And then the palate surprise, minerality, a finish that's saline & very long.

★★★★☆ **Semillon** ⑨ ⓦ Wild ferment, 10 months oak, 25% new, **16** ⑨③ melon & ginger preserve richness but not overt, in a restrained, quietly assured way, deep rather than flashy. Lovely brightening acidity, almost saline, keeps it in perfect health. No **15**.

★★★★☆ **Naudé White** ⑨ ⓦ Small parcels of older vintages on current release. Masterly **09** ⑨② blend semillon, sauvignon (both barrel fermented) & chenin (43/41/16). Refined & integrated, with beguiling flavour twists & turns - grass, lemon, almond. Agreeably moderate ±13% alcohol.— CR

Location: Stellenbosch ▪ WO: Western Cape/Swartland ▪ Est 2017 ▪ 1stB 2000 ▪ Closed to public ▪ Owner(s)/winemaker(s) Ian Naudé ▪ 50% red 50% white ▪ PO Box 982 Stellenbosch 7599 ▪ naudewines@gmail.com, iannaude7@gmail.com ▪ www.naudewines.co.za ▪ **T** +27 **(0)83-630-3794**

☐ **Nectar** *see* The House of JC le Roux

Nederburg Wines

Now under the aegis of Distell group company Libertas Vineyards & Estates, Nederburg is one of SA's best-known and most-loved brands, and since commencement of quality-wine production under Johann Graue from 1937, a major player locally and ultimately worldwide. The stately gabled manor near Paarl, completed in 1800, is a national monument and icon, and latterly a part of an extensive hospitality offering, experienced by thousands of visitors from around the globe. The wine range is similarly wide ranging, covering everything from easy-drinkers to fine thoroughbreds deserving of this guide's Winery of the Year accolade in 2011 and 2017. The famous Wine Auction, held on the estate since 1975, has been re-imagined as the Cape Fine & Rare Wine Auction and moved off-site, though the spacious auction venue continues to host numerous events, including non-wine ones. Last year, Lizelle Gerber was announced as the new cellarmaster, overseeing production of upwards of 2 million cases of wine annually.

Two Centuries range

★★★★☆ **Cabernet Sauvignon** ⓠ Dense & dark **15** ⑭ continues effortlessly in similar spectacular vein as **14** ★★★★★ ⑲, our 2018 Red Wine of the Year, with extra elegance & restraint. 22 months new French oak add layers of spice - cinnamon & nutmeg - along with smoky overtones to ripe black-berried fruit. Solid tannins & fresh acid build to long finish. Paarl grapes.

★★★★☆ **Sauvignon Blanc** ⓠ Everything is green & cream on nose of exceptional **17** ⑭ - limes, peppers, pine needles, vanilla, touch of wax. 9 months barrel ferment/ageing add lick of spice & salt as well as weight & texture on palate, & a bright, lengthy finish. Classic example, like **16** ⑬.

Ingenuity range

★★★★☆ **Red Italian Blend** ⓠ Shy nose takes time to shine on **15** ⑬ blend, mostly sangiovese with barbera & 10% nebbiolo. Palate more forthcoming with cherries, tar, tobacco, plenty of big ripe tannins & lively acidity. Definitely needs keeping but good times ahead. New oak, some American, 30 months.

★★★★☆ **Red Spanish Blend** ⓠ Plenty of black & red fruit on enjoyable **15** ★★★★ ⑧⑦, edged with coffee & sweet leather. Mainly tempranillo with graciano, both picking up lots of spice from mix of French, American & Hungarian oak. Follows style of **14** ⑭.

★★★★☆ **White Blend** ⓠ Sauvignon-led 8-way blend **17** ⑨① is intriguing melange of peachstones, apples, guavas & flowers. Oak touch on chardonnay component adds almonds, cream & spice while slightly bitter note at finish adds to conviction that this is a great food wine.

Manor House range

★★★★ **Cabernet Sauvignon** Announces itself with authority, unashamedly New World, smooth & muscular with solid black fruit, gentle oak spices. **17** ⑧⑨ would benefit from more varietal tension & subtlety. Coastal WO, as next.

★★★★ **Shiraz** ⓐ Focuses on ripe fruit, supple & textural, with subtle notes of scrub & tar, yet **17** ⑧⑨'s opulence is restrained, the body well-judged & the tannins fine.

★★★★☆ **Sauvignon Blanc** Darling vines provide a complex fruit salad in **19** ⑨①, granadilla & gooseberry to the fore, appealing wet-pebble dustiness. Forceful & lingering, with fine acid balance. Back to form after lesser **18** ★★★★ ⑧⑨.

Heritage Heroes range

★★★★☆ **The Brew Master** ⓥ Honouring German brewer Johann Graue who acquired the estate in 1937. Previewed **17** ⑨② cab-led 5-way Bordeaux blend is succulent yet aristocratic, with plush fruit, velvet tannins & finely etched structure aided by 2 years in mixed oak barrels. Coastal WO.

★★★★☆ **The Motorcycle Marvel** ⓥ Salutes legendary winemaker Günter Brözel, who made his vineyard rounds on his 1954 BSA. 5-way Rhône-style blend led by carignan, grenache & shiraz, **17** ⑨① is lithe, supple & juicy. Very impressive though shade off high-flying **16** ⑬.

★★★★ **The Anchorman** ⊘ Intricate winemaking for **18** ★★★★★ ⑨ chenin, tribute to estate founder Philippus Wolvaart, includes carbonic maceration, amphoras, barrels & tanks. Results are impressive: sumptuous fruit, texture, complexity & length, improving on **17** ㉘.

★★★★ **The Beautiful Lady** Distinctly 'feminine' **19** ㉙ gewürztraminer, pre-bottling is svelte & shapely, delightful rosewater & litchi filled out by 13 g/l sugar. Poised & balanced, with noble deportment.

★★★★★ **The Young Airhawk** ⊘ Elegantly poised **18** ⑨ sauvignon, partly barrel fermented, has plenty of mild-mannered varietal character, focused fruit tinged with dust, creamy lees richness. Brightly aromatic lime cordial finish, understated & stylish.

Private Bin range

★★★★☆ **Eminence** ⊛ Lauded & awarded dessert wine. Last tasted was **13** ⑨, a Natural Sweet from muscat blanc; unoaked **18** ⑨ from same variety but now with botrytis component, thus certified as Noble Late Harvest. Beguiles with seductively spicy pineapple, complex aromatics, subtle & nuanced despite massive sweetness.

Occasional release: **Edelkeur**.

Winemaster's Reserve range

★★★★ **Merlot** ⊘ Cheerfully fruity **18** ★★★★ ㉘ is soundly structured but a shade off **17** ㉘, showing hints of green leaf, less lingering finish.

★★★★ **Shiraz** ⊘ Supple & sleek, with generous black cherry fruit, hints of smoked bacon, tobacco & pepper. **17** ㉘ returns to form after lesser **16** ★★★★ ㉝. Oak staves, as all these reds.

★★★★ **Edelrood** ⊘ Expressive 60/40 cab-merlot blend, **17** ★★★★ ㉝ offers generous blackberry compote with vanilla & caramel. Appealing but not quite up to **16** ㉙.

★★★★ **Special Late Harvest** ⊘ Well-judged **18** ㉘ is full-sweet (120 g/l) with balancing acid. Delectable mix of melon preserve, glacé rind, honey melon flavours from healthy, fully ripe chenin, gewürztraminer & super-rare Romanian grape grasa de Cotnari (which also features in the NLH).

★★★★☆ **Noble Late Harvest** ⊘ Unctuous botrytised chenin & muscat de Frontignan with splashes of others, **18** ㉙ has full, expressey grapey fruit with mulled honey, apricot notes. Pure & focused from cold ferment in tank with no subsequent oaking. Follows fine **17** ㉙. 375 ml.

. . . .

Carignan-Grenache Rosé ㉟ ★★★★ Appealing honeyed strawberry fruit, gentle acid kiss on dry **19** ㉘ near-equal blend with floral aftertaste. Paarl WO. **Riesling** ⊘ ㉟ ★★★★ Convincing varietal grapefruit profile, laced with faint terpene & sherbet, piercing acidity on moreish **18** ㉝.

. . . .

Cabernet Sauvignon ⊘ ★★★★ Medium-bodied **17** ㉛ has slightly green leafy-stalky notes, with blackcurrant fruit peeking through. Hefty tannins need time. Also in 1.5L & 250ml. **Pinotage** ⊘ ★★★★ Fruit-driven **18** ㉘ with mulberry & bramble, fullish body & big tannins, typical high-toned aromas. **Albariño** ⓧ ★★★ Interesting debut for this trendy Spanish grape, **18** ㉜ pretty floral notes with hints of tinned peach & pear. **Chardonnay** ⊘ ★★★★ Pleasant citrus fruitiness on **18** ㉘, with reined-in oak spices from brief wooding. **Pinot Grigio** ★★★ Fruity profile on **19** ㉝ emphasised few grams sugar, dash colombard. Light & crisp, with pear, guava & melon taste. **Sauvignon Blanc** ⊘ ★★★★ Typical dusty gravel with bright grassy notes, well-judged acidity on substantial **19** ㉝, showing ripe fig & gooseberry fruit. Discontinued: **Malbec**.

56Hundred range

Cabernet Sauvignon ★★★ Toffee-toned, off-dry **18** ㉞ has thickish tannins, leafy blackcurrant fruit. **Merlot** ⊘ ★★★ Undemanding, fruit-driven **18** ㉙ for everyday enjoyment. Hints of oak spice, soft tannins, crunchy ripe berries. **Pinot Noir** ⓧ ★★★ Lively, light, easy-drinking **17** ㉙ mixes spice, biltong & berries. Chill in summer. **Chenin Blanc** ★★★ Cheerfully ripe fruit, firm acid offset by few grams sugar on **19** ㉞. Modest 12% alcohol. **Pinot Grigio** ★★ **19** ㉖ is uncomplicated, fresh & crisp, borderline austere. **Sauvignon Blanc** ⊘ ★★★ Characterful **19** ㉙ is crisp & fresh, nicely weighted, with honest gooseberry fruit, perky finish. Not tasted: **Pinotage**, **Shiraz**, **Cabernet Sauvignon-Shiraz**.

1791 range

Merlot ★★★ Cherry-drop fruit, light tannins on mediumweight, uncomplicated **18** ㉞. **Rosé** ★★★ Off-dry **19** ㉗ is a pleasantly fruity, undemanding sipper from 4 black grapes. Not tasted: **Cabernet Sauvignon**, **Pinotage**, **Shiraz**, **Chardonnay**, **Sauvignon Blanc**.

Nederburg range

Duet ✓ ★★★ Rather insubstantial shiraz-pinotage blend, just-dry **18** ⑦ offers candied berry fruit.
Baronne ✓ ★★★★ Big-volume steakhouse standard, **18** ⑧ cab-shiraz blend has plush plum & cherry fruit, soft approachable tannins. **Lyric** ✓ ★★★ Reliable everyday quaffer, just-dry **19** ⑦ from sauvignon & chenin, dash chardonnay. **Stein** ✓ ★★★ Pleasant semi-sweet chenin, **19** ⑦ fresh & fruity, as always.
Première Cuvée Brut Ⓠ ★★★ Fresh, fruity & frothy **NV** ⑧ sparkling from chenin & sauvignon, great for Sunday brunch. — GdB

Location/map: Paarl ▪ Map grid reference: F5 ▪ WO: Western Cape/Coastal/Paarl/Darling ▪ Est 1791 ▪ 1stB ca 1940 ▪ Tasting & sales May-Sep: Mon-Fri 9-5 Sat/Sun 10-4; Oct-Apr: Mon-Fri 9-6 Sat/Sun 10-4 ▪ Various tasting fees, waived on purchase of R300+ ▪ Closed Good Fri, Dec 25 & Jan 1 ▪ Cellar tours Mon-Fri 10.30 & 3 Sat 11 Sun 11 (Oct-Apr) ▪ Large groups/foreign language tours by appt only ▪ Visitors' centre: wine tasting, cheese & wine pairing ▪ Historic manor house (national monument) featuring the Red Table restaurant, open Tue-Sun T +27 (0)21-877-5155 ▪ Tour groups ▪ Gifts ▪ Conferences ▪ Museum ▪ Conservation area ▪ Owner(s) Libertas Vineyards & Estates, a Distell Group company ▪ Cellarmaster(s) Lizelle Gerber (Aug 2019) ▪ Winemaker(s) Samuel Viljoen (reds, Oct 2014) & Elmarie Botes (whites, Dec 2017) ▪ Viticulturist(s) Henk van Graan ▪ 1,680ha (cab, carignan, grenache, malbec, merlot, p verdot, ptage, shiraz, tannat, tempranillo, chard, chenin, riesling, sauv, sem) ▪ 13,000t/2m cs own label ▪ ISO 0001:2008, ISO 14001:2004, HACCP, IPW, BRC, SGS organic ▪ Private Bag X3006 Paarl 7620 ▪ info@nederburg.com ▪ www.nederburg.co.za ▪ S 33° 43' 15.4" E 019° 0' 9.4" ▪ 🗐 steeped.fighters.playful ▪ **T +27 (0)21-862-3104**

Neethlingshof Estate

Bought in the 1980s by one of SA's first major foreign wine investors, German financier Hans-Joachim Schreiber, Neethlingshof remains under Schreiber family custodianship. It combines a colourful Cape Dutch heritage (starting in 1692 and including a widow as owner and winemaker in the early 1800s) with what is deemed one of Stellenbosch's finest terroirs, sustainably farmed as an elite WWF-SA Conservation Champion. Hence the new ultra-premium 'Ode to Nature' label, for vintage standouts released only in exceptional years and sold only on the estate. The debut Riesling is in 3,290 individually numbered bottles.

Short Story Collection

★★★★★ **Owl Post** ⓐ Single-block pinotage recognises wild owls' role in reducing pesticide use on estate. Dark ripe cherry, berry & plum fruit in balance with plush & rich structure of **18** ⑨, silky dry finish. 15 months mainly Hungarian oak, 70% new.

★★★★★ **Caracal** ⓐ Bordeaux blend of 50% cab, merlot, malbec & cab franc a tribute to 'enigmatic presence' of wild cat linked to local renosterveld restoration. **17** ⑨ well fruited yet sleek & muscular, with focused ripe tannins & not-overdone 14% alcohol. 70% new oak, mostly French. 1.5 & 3L available.

★★★★☆ **Jackals Dance** ✓ Superb single-vineyard sauvignon spotlit in this prestige range. Meagre 4 t/ha crop of **19** ⑨ carefully handled to preserve flinty green (grass/nettle) aromas; contrasting ripe fruit (fig & gooseberry) fills out balanced, dry palate. Lovely tension in sync with 13.4% alcohol.

★★★★★ **Six Flowers** ✓ Unusual 6-way blend in homage to Maria Marais & her five children; sauvignon leads **19** ⑨, adding steely backbone for creamy chardonnay & chenin, opulent viognier & aromatic riesling & gewürztraminer. All-new oak fills already ample frame & adds to exotic decadence. **18** untasted.

★★★★★ **Maria Magdalena Noble Late Harvest** Ⓠ Unoaked botrytis dessert from riesling. **17** ⑨ billows honeyed apricot, then tangy melon & Golden Delicious apple kick in, & wonderful sugar-acid balance focuses the rich crème brûlée texture. A low-alcohol (10%) beauty with great prospects. 375 ml.

Ode To Nature range 🆕

★★★★ **Weisser Riesling** From registered single-vineyard planted 1986, **18** ⑧ intense floral & riverstone aromas introduce leesy spice & greengage flavour, dry, food-friendly finish.

Neethlingshof range

★★★★ **Chenin Blanc** ✓ Pear drop aroma, tropical fruit flavour & zesty, dry finish lift creamy oatmeal texture of **19** ⑧, which saw weekly lees stirring but no wood contact.

★★★★ **Gewürztraminer** ✓ Redolent of litchi, rosewater & Turkish delight, fresh & tangy with lime & ginger nuance on finish. **19** ⑧ has gram broadening sugar, ideal partner for spicy food.

Cabernet Sauvignon ★★★★ Pliable, sweet tannins tether the cool brambly fruit of **16** ⑧⑤ but the delicious, moreish juiciness wins out! 18 months oak, 90/10 French & American, 30% new, as for most of these reds. 3 & 5L too for the inevitable parties. **Malbec** ★★★★ Something to perk up your taste buds: earthy mineral tones offset by a bright pomegranate tang; velvety tannins & whiff American oak vanilla up the appeal. **18** ⑧④ also in 3, 5 & 9L, as next. **Merlot** ★★★★ Mulberry & smoked bacon features on **17** ⑧③, elegant but still generous thanks to padding of ripe fruit. **Pinotage** ★★★★ Quintessential pinotage plum & banana made more piquant, tasty, by cinnamon spice from French & American oak, 40% new. **18** ⑧④ full yet gentle enough for solo sipping. **Shiraz** ★★★★ Suave **16** ⑧④ has red berry & smoked meat profile with sweet mocha overlay & chewy tannins, brawny texture holds 14.3% alcohol. 15% American oak. Also in 3L & 5L. **Cabernet Sauvignon-Merlot** ⓥ ★★★★ Ample black berry fruit of **16** ⑧⑤ amplified by American oak (10%), generous but not as measured, balanced as previous, which better absorbed the wooding. **Chardonnay Unwooded** ★★★☆ Young & vibrant, punchy **19** ⑧④'s citrus & pear profile a good bet on winelists. **Sauvignon Blanc** ★★★ Light & refreshing, has Stellenbosch's signature riper fruit flavours, granadilla & grapefruit in **19** ⑧①. — DS

Location/map/WO: Stellenbosch ▪ Map grid reference: D5 ▪ Est 1692 ▪ 1stB 1880 ▪ Tasting & sales Mon-Fri 9–5 Sat/Sun 10-4 ▪ Tasting fees: R55/5 Estate wines; R85/5 Short Story Collection wines; R70/5 Selection wines ▪ Closed Good Fri & Dec 25 ▪ Cellar tours by appt R40pp ▪ 'Flash Food & Slow Wine' pairing: summer/R130pp, winter R120pp - booking recommended for 6+ ▪ 'Truffle & Wine' pairing R70pp ▪ Kiddies pairing R60pp ▪ Pizzas & platters available in winegarden ▪ Jungle gym ▪ Tour groups ▪ Conferences ▪ Conservation area ▪ Wednesday night live music (summer & winter) ▪ The Restaurant at Neethlingshof & Palm Terrace open Mon/Tue/Thu 9-5 Wed/Sat 9-9 Sun 12-4 ▪ Owner(s) Schreiber family ▪ Cellarmaster(s) De Wet Viljoen (Jun 2003) ▪ Winemaker(s) Jacobus van Zyl ▪ Viticulturist(s) Hannes van Zyl ▪ 273ha/95ha (cabs s/f, malbec, merlot, p verdot, ptage, shiraz, chard, chenin, gewürz, riesling, sauv, viog) ▪ 500t/70,000cs own label 55% red 45% white ▪ WIETA, WWF-SA Conservation Champion ▪ PO Box 104 Stellenbosch 7599 ▪ info@neethlingshof.co.za ▪ www.neethlingshof.co.za ▪ S 33° 56' 28.2" E 018° 48' 6.7" ▪ ⊞ unwind.trailers.trail ▪ **T +27 (0)21-883-8988**

Neil Ellis Wines

There's something both comforting and admirable when the new generation driving this successful Stellenbosch-based wine business is proud to invoke tradition. Today, they say, 'the experience and knowl-edge of the past are applied to modern techniques and technologies for a new generation of winemaking'. Neil Ellis was, in the 1980s, the Cape's first real negociant winemaker, seeking widely for interesting vine-yards and bottling the wines under his name. He has stepped back somewhat in recent years and lets his children do much of the work (Charl heads the financial team, Margot is brand manager, and Warren rules the cellar). Warren's impact on the house tradition of rather grand, substantial wines has largely been one of 'ongoing refinement of style', but there are many signs of his incorporating new-wave techniques and styles.

Terrain Specific range

★★★★☆ **Jonkershoek Valley Cabernet Sauvignon** Ⓐ SA classic from prime Stellenbosch terroir, built to last 10+ years. **16** ⑨④ packed with pure blackcurrant, graphite, polished leather & fresh herbs on a frame of supple, ripe tannin & new French oak, 18 months.

★★★★☆ **Groenekloof Cinsaut** Ⓐ Vibrant in colour & personality, **16** ⑨⓪ has redcurrant, plum & dried Mediterranean herbs in aroma & flavour. Well structured & balanced, finishes with a twist of pepper. Sympathetically aged 16 months in older 500L oak, as next 2.

★★★★☆ **Piekenierskloof Grenache** Ⓐ Grenache noir a still-small but growing category, with much to offer the adventurous palate in alluring **16** ⑨②. Cherries, perfumed violet & earthy spice, juicy fruit deftly masking 14.9% alcohol, smooth texture. Delicious now, will reward patience.

★★★★☆ **Bottelary Hills Pinotage** Ⓐ Modern take on the variety, with fruit-forward plum, mulberry, hints of creamy chocolate supported by well-judged, fine-grain tannin. **17** ⑨④ is sumptuous yet elegant & memorable.

★★★★ **Rodanos** ⓥ Rhône blend shiraz (70%), cinsaut & grenache in **14** ★★★★★ ⑨⓪ more complex & deep than **13** ⑧⑦. Dark berry compote & lashings of warm spice, satisfying bone-dry savoury finish. 25% new oak, 16 months.

★★★★☆ **Whitehall Chardonnay** ⊛ Elgin fruit bunch-pressed on champagne cycle (as next) for gentle extraction & fruit purity. **18** ⑨④ displays fragrant baked apple sprinkled with cinnamon, creamy vanilla oak from 300L barrels, 9 months, & fresh, lemon blossom farewell.

★★★★☆ **Amica** ⊛ From Jonkershoek sauvignon, **18** ★★★★★ ⑨⑤ is serene & elegant yet has a richness & intensity above **17** ⑨④'s. Pristine blackcurrant fruit, zingy notes of gooseberry & citrus, gentle smoke from 9 months in seasoned 500L oak. Lovely wet stone minerality as it lingers. Ample concentration for cellaring several years.

★★★★☆ **Op Sy Moer** ⊛ Afrikaans name tells you to expect cloudiness & sediment in very attractive, minimally handled **18** ⑨③, certified as 'Alternative white'. Concentrated, textured, with apple freshness & candied lemon-rind lift, dusty tannic grip. 45/28/27 grenache, palomino & chenin from Piekenierskloof, bunch pressed & naturally fermented in old oak. No sulphur added.

★★★★☆ **Semillon Noble Late Harvest** ⑨ Lovely light-footed **16** ⑨⓪ botrytis dessert from bunch-pressed, barrel-fermented Elgin fruit. Delicate floral & roasted nut flavours & aromas, fine structure & 'cool' balancing acidity. First since **11**, untasted by us. 375 ml.

Regional range

★★★★ **Stellenbosch Cabernet Sauvignon** Generous **17** ⑧⑧, fascinating aromas & flavours of spiced black cherry, cassis, old leather-bound books & garden herbs. Splashes cab franc & petit verdot add backbone to lush fruit. Cellar for later enjoyment. Also-tasted **16** ⑧⑥ softer & silkier, drinks well now, cassis & olive tapenade in the flavours. Also has dash petit verdot balancing the plushness.

★★★★ **Groenekloof Syrah** ⊛ Textured & sumptuous **17** ⑧⑨ has dash cinsaut (12%), delivers flavour in spades: mulberry, scrub, hedgerow fruit, cured meat & sprinkling of pepper on a firm structure with vanilla from 16 months in 500L barrels.

★★★★ **Cabernet Sauvignon-Merlot** Luscious **17** ⑧⑥ has dark berry, pencil shaving & herb (dried & fresh) appeal. Satisfying as always, with light grip on the finish. 47/38 blend with soupçon cab franc.

★★★★ **Groenekloof Sauvignon Blanc** ⊘ Always a standout, expressive & flavour packed, achieves complexity without wood. **19** ⑨① has all the expected greenpeppers & gooseberries, plus minerality & persistent lemon-lime finish. No rush to uncork: the creators mooch this as 6-10 year wine.

Aenigma ⑨ ★★★★ Always easy-to-enjoy red from enigmatic variety/ies. **16** ⑧⑤ for al fresco dining, just enough tannin bite to balance the rich fruit flavours. — WB

Location/map: Stellenbosch ▪ Map grid reference: G5 ▪ WO: Stellenbosch/Groenekloof/Jonkershoek Valley/Piekenierskloof/Elgin/Western Cape/Bottelary ▪ Est 1986 ▪ 1stB 1984 ▪ Tasting & sales Mon-Fri 9.30-4.30 Sat/pub hols 10—5 ▪ Fee R40 regional range/R60 terrain specific range/R100 exclusive range ▪ Closed Good Fri, Dec 25/26 & Jan 1 ▪ Antipasto platters ▪ Pesto & wine pairing ▪ Tour groups ▪ Owner(s) Neil Ellis Wines (Pty) Ltd ▪ Winemaker(s) Warren Ellis (2006) & Christiaan van der Merwe (2016) ▪ Viticulturist(s) Warren Ellis (2006) ▪ 50,000cs own label 50% red 50% white ▪ Brands for clients: Woolworths ▪ PO Box 917 Stellenbosch 7599 ▪ info@neilellis.com ▪ www.neilellis.com ▪ S 33° 55' 34.92" E 018° 53' 32.46" ▪ 🌐 blows.imposes.briskly ▪ **T +27 (0)21-887-0649**

Nelson Family Vineyards   ⑨ 🏠 ⓐ ⓑ ⓒ

The early history of this estate between Paarl and Wellington includes the substantial presence of a remarkable, much-storied freed slave, Angela of Bengal (who died in 1720). Much more recently it was acquired, and greatly developed by lawyer Alan Nelson. Now most of his family are involved 'in one way or another' in the venture, which includes wedding and function venues, and accommodation. Daughter Lisha Nelson makes the wines, with cabernet franc having proved to be particularly suited to the terroir.

Lisha Nelson Signature Wines

★★★★☆ **Cabernet Franc** ⊛ Concentrated core of dark fruit in a tightly woven structure in **17** ⑨④, first tasted since **14** ⑨③. Serious oak regime (80% new, 18 months) effortlessly assimilated into rich & plush profile, with a light minty nuance that adds a graceful lift. Sophisticated crafting of this classic cultivar.

Not tasted: **Dad`s Blend**.

Nelson Estate range

★★★★ **Shiraz** Bold style on **14** ⑧⑥ has ample fruit restrained by a supple tannin structure. New oak adds a spicy note (80% new, 18 months), with enough fruit to match.

★★★★ **Cabernet Sauvignon-Merlot** ⓨ Scented & opulent dark-berry compote restrained by very dry chalky tannins in **14** ⑧⑧, cellaring will bring more poise, already better than **12** ★★★ ⑧①. **13** untasted.
Noble Late Harvest ⓨ ★★★★ Faint apricot botrytis notes with ginger accents on **15** ⑧④ dessert from semillon. Charming delicacy from 12.5% alcohol, exact sugar-acid balance. Caramel nuance on conclusion from 80% new oak.

Family Vineyards range

Rosé ★★☆ Vermilion hue from equal portions petit verdot & cab franc in **19** ⑦⑧. Aromatic & dry, for friendly sunset sipping. **Chardonnay** ★★★ Like previous, plenty of toasty oak (80% new) holding sway over demure fruit in **18** ⑧①. Rich butterscotch & creamy texture will however charm fans of this style.
Sauvignon Blanc ★★★ Gooseberry pungency & a pithy nuance on crisp **19** ⑧②. Light & summery, ready to enjoy. WO W Cape.

Nelson's Creek range

Shiraz ⓨ ★★★ Now bottled, **17** ⑧① interesting spread of dark smoked meat & sweet-spicy florals, supple but quite robust. A barbecue & country cooking partner. **Chenin Blanc** ★★☆ Subtle apple & pear flavours on balanced & friendly **19** ⑦⑨. **Rosé** ★★ Cabernet franc in candyfloss, light & floral mode. **19** ⑦③ is for the sweeter-toothed rosé fans. — MW

Location/map: Paarl ▪ Map grid reference: D3 ▪ WO: Paarl/Western Cape ▪ Tasting, sales & cellar tours by appt only ▪ Closed all pub hols ▪ Facilities for children ▪ Tour groups ▪ Conferences ▪ Weddings ▪ Walks/hikes ▪ MTB trails ▪ Guest accommodation ▪ Owner(s) Alan Nelson ▪ Cellarmaster(s) Lisha Nelson (Nov 2007) ▪ Winemaker(s) Lisha Nelson (Nov 2007), with Solly Hendriks (Apr 2011) ▪ Viticulturist(s) Petrus de Villiers ▪ 142ha/41ha (cabs s/f, merlot, p verdot, ptage, shiraz, chard, chenin, sauv, sem) ▪ 210t/9,340cs own label 30% red 60% white 10% rosé ▪ IPW ▪ PO Box 2009 Windmeul 7630 ▪ lisha@nelsonscreek.co.za ▪ www.nelson-screek.co.za ▪ S 33° 39' 31.2" E 018° 56' 17.3" ▪ 🎧 named.unchanged.bridesmaid ▪ **T +27 (0)21-869-8453**

☐ **Nelson's Creek** *see* Nelson Family Vineyards
☐ **Nest Egg** *see* The Fledge & Co

New Beginnings Wines ⓨ

Owned by vineyard staff, and guided by Cape Town wine marketers FMS Food & Beverages, the brand focuses on exports – with Japan a particularly important supporter since its inception. Some tweaks in the range continue, but the idea remains for a wider new beginning, they say: 'See it as a spiritual journey to rise to this challenge every single day.'

Renaissance Collection

★★★★ **Pinotage** (NEW) Dark aromas on **16** ⑧⑥, tinged with oak vanilla (20% new barrels). Full & rich, more intense than Skipper's version; sweet-savoury fruit checked by firm dry tannin & balanced acidity.
Méthode Cap Classique Blanc de Blancs Brut (NEW) ★★★☆ Clean, fresh aromas of fresh apple & biscuit on **17** ⑧⑤ sparkling from chardonnay. Focused, balanced & sufficiently flavourful; satisfyingly dry. Coastal WO. Not tasted: **Méthode Cap Classique Demi-Sec**.

Skipper's Collection

Pinotage (NEW) ★★★★ Inviting dark fruity aromas on unoaked **17** ⑧③, & juicy palate doesn't disappoint. Just the right amount of tannic grip for early drinking without triviality! **Chenin Blanc** (NEW) ★★★ Thoroughly pleasing **18** ⑧② is fresh & juicy, balanced & dry - even if not long-lingering. Discontinued: **Classic Dry Red, Classic Dry White**.

Family Collection

Merlot ⓨ ★★★★ Vivacious **15** ⑧⑤, intense plum perfume, pure black fruit & balanced grip (no new oak), light-seeming despite 14.5% alcohol. Companionable sipper solo or at mealtimes. **Chardonnay** ⓨ ★★ Slightly earthy **17** ⑦③, with faint fennel & apple notes. Though lightly wooded, oak still tad obvious mid-2018, perhaps just needs time to settle. Not tasted: **Cabernet Sauvignon, Shiraz, Pinotage Rosé**. Discontinued: **Pinotage, Chenin Blanc**.

Chouette! Collection

Not tasted: **Gewürztraminer**. — TJ

Location: Cape Town ▪ Map: Cape Peninsula ▪ Map grid reference: B1 ▪ WO: Stellenbosch/Coastal/Paarl ▪ Est 1996 ▪ 1stB 1999 ▪ Tasting by appt only ▪ Owner(s) Klein Begin Farming Association ▪ Brand manager FMS Food & Beverages SA cc ▪ 13ha/10ha (cab, merlot, ptage, shiraz, chard, chenin) ▪ 20,000cs own label 80% red 20% white ▪ Unit 106 Rapallo, 292 Beach Rd, Sea Point, Cape Town 8005 ▪ info@fms-wine-marketing.co.za ▪ www.fms-wine-marketing.co.za ▪ S 33° 55' 11.1" E 018° 22' 57.8" ▪ lifestyles.salivary.heptathlon ▪ **T +27 (0)21-426-5037**

☐ **New Cape Wines** *see* Eagle's Cliff Wines-New Cape Wines

Newstead Lund Family Vineyards

Among the number of boutique winegrowers near oceanside resort town Plettenberg Bay on the tourist Garden Route, Doug and Sue Lund are making their mark with a pair of MCC bubblies produced by prolific local consultant Anton Smal. This leaves not much of their chardonnay and pinot for still wines, hence the 'occasional release' notices below. With a sauvignon blanc, craft beer and gin, these bubbles make up a range of appealing libations to accompany the vineyard amenities available here.

★★★★☆ **Méthode Cap Classique Rosé** From pinot noir & chardonnay, **16** ⑨⓪ continues **15** ㊲'s improved form. Finely structured & piquant but not lean. Cranberry, citrus impression, shows freshness & refinement. 24 months on lees. Tangier than sibling - a sparkler for the table.

★★★★ **Méthode Cap Classique Brut** From chardonnay, **15** ★★★★★ ⑨⓪ bubbly ups the pleasure. Incisively clean & dry, like **14** ⑧⑧, but with 36 months on lees shows appealing toasted hazelnut & a hint of saltiness. Lovely freshness & length. Appealing to the last drop.

Sauvignon Blanc ★★★ Green herb, starfruit flavours in crisp & clean **18** ⑧②. A lunchtime/light meal partner. Occasional release: **Pinot Noir, Chardonnay.** — MW

Location/WO: Plettenberg Bay ▪ Map: Klein Karoo & Garden Route ▪ Map grid reference: C1 ▪ Est 2008 ▪ 1stB 2012 ▪ Tasting & sales Tue-Sat 10-4 ▪ Closed Dec 25 ▪ Vineyard lunches, weddings & celebrations - booking required ▪ Tour groups ▪ Gift shop ▪ Farm produce ▪ Walks ▪ MTB/guided cycle tours ▪ Accommodation ▪ Craft beer & gin ▪ Owner(s) Doug & Sue Lund ▪ Cellarmaster(s)/winemaker(s) Anton Smal (Jan 2011, consultant) ▪ Viticulturist(s) Doug Lund & Gift Lwazi ▪ 11ha/6.5ha (pinot, chard, sauv) ▪ 24t/4,500cs own label white & MCC ▪ PO Box 295 The Crags 6602 ▪ info@newsteadwines.com ▪ www.newsteadwines.com ▪ S 33° 57' 7.24" E 023° 28' 18.66" ▪ tins.goals.centenary ▪ **T +27 (0)76-300-9740 (office)**

Newton Johnson Vineyards

A family business in Upper Hemel-en-Aarde Valley started by Dave and Felicity Johnson (née Newton) in the mid-1990s, now run by their sons, Bevan as marketer and Gordon as winemaker, with his wife Nadia. This is a pinot noir mecca. There are four in the range: top growths Seadragon and Windandsea, multi-parcel Family Vineyards and younger-vineyard Walker Bay, from different aspects and soils, including challenging rocky slopes, and each quite individual. The sensitive winemaking has minimal intervention as its focus (spontaneous ferment, older oak, no fining, filtration) in the gravity-fed cellar, so the wines are allowed full site expression. There are other varieties and styles in the line-up, all expertly crafted with the same core integrity, which comes from the family philosophy: be honest and true, respect the terroir.

Family Vineyards range

★★★★☆ **CWG Auction Reserve The Awakening Mourvèdre** (NEW) Bushvines grown in granite & claystone soils give **18** ㉝ its densely rich fruit, but also has graphite, scrub & salty liquorice, all resting on a bed of firm but ripe tannin. Handsome, has gravitas, but an infant, the best still lies ahead.

★★★★☆ **Pinot Noir** ⊘ From all soils of farm's sites, range's archetype. Vivid fruit, **18** ㉞'s perfume of oak-spiced cranberries & cherries, violet top note, gets richer, denser in the flavours, thanks to clay-rich vineyards. Chewy tannins from higher-lying gravel, promising longevity, as in **17** ★★★★★ ㉟.

★★★★☆ **Seadragon Pinot Noir** Farm's oldest pinot noir block & richest-fruit wine. Multi-layered **18** ㉝ offers intense cherries, raspberries, but also violets, with an underlying earthy, savoury element. Spent 20 days on skins, 15 months small barrels. Epitomises the variety, sinewy elegance & power.

★★★★☆ **Windandsea Pinot Noir** Single 2.5 ha, high-lying vineyard, with wind exposure (hence name), resulting in thicker skins, denser structure. Morello cherries, brambleberries, oak-fragrant **18** ㉞ seamed with minerality, house-style earthiness. Sleekly muscular but tannins ripe, long life ahead.

★★★★☆ **Granum** ⓐ Cellar as adept with Rhône varieties as Burgundy grapes. Shiraz with 23% mourvèdre, on iron-rich granite (as name suggests), **16** ⑨③ shows fynbos, dark wild berries & distinctively earthy slate notes. Well-managed supple tannins for access, longevity.

★★★★☆ **Chardonnay** ⓐ Different aspects of 3 granite vineyards, hence **18** ⑨④'s layers. Bunch pressed & wild fermented in barrel (as all): stonefruit & citrus, complex scents & flavours open up in the glass, roasted nut & oatmeal, lime & tangerine. Layered & involving.

★★★★☆ **CWG Auction Reserve Sandford Chardonnay** ⓝⓔⓦ ⓐ More oak than other chardonnays, 15 months, an almond seam in the peach & citrus flavours, but **18** ⑨③ also has minerality, everything working in harmony, nothing showy, overt. Textured palate yet elegant, balancing acidity the underpin. Immensely stylish wine.

Newton Johnson range

★★★★ **Walker Bay Pinot Noir** ⓥ Own younger, lower-elevation vineyards, variety-true **17** ⑧⑨ meticulously made. Red cherries, raspberries, with Burgundy oak's earthy, truffle nuances. Streamlined, tannins supple.

★★★★ **Full Stop Rock** ⓩ Syrah with grenache, dab mourvèdre, **17** ⑧⑨ a symphony of fruits & flavours. Mulberries sweetly spiced, palate succulent, luscious fruit holding sway, tannins polished.

★★★★☆ **Albariño** Iberian grape, first in SA. Combo stainless steel, older oak & concrete 'egg', allowing **18** ⑨①'s fragrant character to surface. Apple blossom & quince, white peach, not showy, just subtle complexity. Ends with beeswax texture, lightly savoury, tangy fresh.

★★★★☆ **Southend Chardonnay** Cool-climate mountain vineyards owned by neighbours, barrel fermented/matured in oak & stainless steel, **18** ⑨③ preview has the sleek lines & nervous energy of a racehorse. Green-tinged lime intensity with mineral tones in the flavours & finish, acidity almost saline. Wonderful precision & focus.

★★★★ **Sauvignon Blanc** ⓥ Character from different Cape South Coast vineyard elevations & soils, plus 14% oaked semillon. Mineral core, lemon & ruby grapefruit top notes, with palate heft, round & full, **19** ★★★★★ ⑨① ends vibrantly lemon-fresh. Incredible purity & focus, up a notch from **18** ⑧⑨.

★★★★★ **Resonance** ⓐ Own cool-climate-influenced, mountain-vineyard sauvignon & 40% oaked semillon from neighbour. **18** ⑨④ a compelling perfume/flavour interplay: mineral seamed, with whiffs of fynbos, lemongrass, green fig. Textured palate despite elegance, brightening saline acidity lengthening the flavours.— CR

Location: Hermanus ▪ Map: Walker Bay & Bot River ▪ Map grid reference: B4 ▪ WO: Upper Hemel-en-Aarde Valley/Cape South Coast ▪ Est 1996 ▪ 1stB 1997 ▪ Tasting & sales Mon-Fri 9-4 Sat 10-2 ▪ Closed all pub hols ▪ 'Restaurant @ Newton Johnson' lunch 12-3 Wed-Sun (Apr-Nov)/Tue-Sun (Dec-Mar) ▪ Owner(s) Newton Johnson family ▪ Winemaker(s) Gordon Newton Johnson (Jan 2001) & Nadia Newton Johnson (Aug 2006) ▪ Viticulturist(s) Dean Leppan (Sep 2010) ▪ 140ha/18ha (grenache, mourv, pinot, shiraz, albariño, chard, sauv) ▪ 240t/20,000cs own label 50% red 50% white ▪ PO Box 225 Hermanus 7200 ▪ wine@newtonjohnson. com ▪ www.newtonjohnson.com ▪ S 34° 22' 9.7" E 019° 15' 33.3" ▪ 🖵 royalties.conception.tripods ▪ **T +27 (0)28-312-3862**

Nicholson Smith

It started less than a decade ago with Jason Neal, CEO of Nicholson Smith Agencies in Johannesburg representing the wines of Wellington-based James McKenzie. Now the duo are united in selling (Jason) and making (James) this ever-expanding range of approachable, well priced, non-vintage wines. See under Aden's Star for the vintage-dated portfolio.

Pandora's Box range

Bell Pepper Cabernet Sauvignon ⓥ ★★☆ Unfussy **NV** ⑦⑨ red, sweet-fruited & juicy with some cassis notes. **The Black Bird Merlot** ⓥ ★★☆ Plum & spice ease on **NV** ⑦⑧ red. Light & supple. **The Professor's Pinotage** ★★ Light & dry **NV** ⑦⑥, with brief blueberry flavour. **The Persian Connection Shiraz** ⓥ ★★☆ Overtly commercial, **NV** ⑦⑧ has juicy plum ripeness. **Lock 1855 Merlot-Cabernet Sauvignon** ⓥ ★★☆ 55/45 **NV** ⑦⑦ blend is simplicity personified, light & effortless. **The Italian Job** ★★ Jammy raspberry aroma to skinny **NV** ⑦⑥ dry red. **La Dolce Vita Moscato** ★★ Shy grapey florality & tang on light, just-dry **NV** ⑦④ from muscat blanc. **The Godfather Pinot Gris** ⓝⓔⓦ ★★ Apple & lemon flavours on **NV** (74), with light 12% alcohol. **The Gooseberry Sauvignon Blanc** ★★ Gentle tang to, yes, gooseberry-toned, unchallenging **NV** (75). **The Honeysuckle Sweet Red** ★★ Sweetness dominates light, dilute low-alcohol **NV** (74) red.

Bella Vino range
Sultry Red ★★ Smoky cherry & boiled sweets on **NV** (74) Bordeaux/sangiovese blend. **Perky Pink** ★★ Gentle pink hue to sweet **NV** (72), with confected strawberry & candyfloss aroma & low 8.5% alcohol. **Sublime White** ★★ Uncomplicated, light & juicy **NV** (73). **Seductively Sweet White** ★★ Lemon zest nuance to light, low-alcohol **NV** (75). **Sassy Sweet Red** ★★ Confected boiled sweets on **NV** (74), sweet & light at 12% alcohol. — FM

Location: Johannesburg ▪ WO: Western Cape ▪ Est 1997 ▪ 1stB 2012 ▪ Closed to public ▪ Owner(s) Jason Neal ▪ Winemaker(s)/viticulturist(s) James McKenzie (2012) ▪ 265,000cs own label 70% red 20% white 10% other ▪ PO Box 1659 Jukskei Park 2153 ▪ jason@nicholsonsmith.co.za ▪ www.nicholsonsmith.co.za ▪ **T +27 (0)11-496-2947**

Nick & Forti's Wines

'Nick' is Nick van Huyssteen, owner of Saronsberg in Tulbagh (where the wines are made), 'Forti' is restaurateur Fortunato Mazzone - and this is their joint venture. The range is available at the winery and at Forti's restaurants and stores as well as selected outlets and eateries.

★★★★☆ **Epicentre** From all 5 Bordeaux varieties. Even more so than **15** ★★★★ (85), **17** (87) delivers a lot of flavour - mostly cassis - for your money. Supple tannin structure, the 14.4% alcohol not too obvious. Tulbagh WO. **16** untasted.

Shiraz ⓥ ★★★☆ Irresistible **17** (85) absolutely packed with spicy plum fruit, deftly balanced by fresh acidity & moderate tannin grip. Oak (25% new, 20 months) is well judged.

Artspace Chenin Blanc ★★★★☆ Was 'White', still is chenin but now 5% fermented in old oak, **19** (84) peach & tropical fruit in a zesty, versatile food partner. — DS

Location: Tulbagh/Pretoria ▪ WO: Western Cape/Tulbagh ▪ Est/1stB 2004 ▪ Tasting at Saronsberg Cellar ▪ Owner(s) Fortunato Mazzone & Saronsberg ▪ Winemaker(s) Dewaldt Heyns (2004) ▪ 4,000cs own label 85% red 15% white ▪ Box 25032 Monument Park Pretoria 0105 ▪ ritrovo@mweb.co.za ▪ www.saronsberg.com ▪ **T +27 (0)12-460-4367**

Nicky Versfeld Wines

After studying cellar technology at Elsenburg Agricultural College, Nicky Versfeld over many years has been involved with wineries of varying sizes and types, locally and in Bordeaux and Sancerre, as winemaker and latterly also consultant. Given those French connections, it's unsurprising that his personal boutique project has focused on sauvignon blanc and semillon, and that his wines have been unfailingly classic in style.

★★★★☆ **Sauvignon Blanc** ⓥ Previewed **19** (92) ex same area as previous but fruit profile is more savoury/spicy (capsicum, dust & white pepper vs white asparagus & tinned pea). Usual deep, satisfying flavour, signature pinpoint acidity & breadth from 6 months on lees, just a shade shorter than last.— CvZ

Location: Somerset West ▪ WO: Darling ▪ Est 2016 ▪ 1stB 2015 ▪ Closed to public ▪ Winemaker(s) Nicky Versfeld ▪ 1,000cs own label 100% white ▪ Building No 8, Fairways Office Park, 5 Niblick Way, Somerset West 7130 ▪ ncversfeld@gmail.com ▪ **T +27 (0)21-850-0160/1, +27 (0)83-675-8436**

Nico van der Merwe Wines

It's a few decades since Nico van der Merwe started making his own wine while still the eminent winemaker at Saxenburg; much less since he started concentrating fully on his boutique venture on Stellenbosch's Polkadraai Hills, where he and wife Petra are now based. Here he can be fussy: wines not on par are sold off in bulk, as in 2016. His most celebrated wines involve shiraz, the grape he says he is most 'relaxed' with — not 'confident', he modestly points out, as that would imply arrogance. A degree of confidence would be justified, we'd suggest, by the local and international recognition received.

Flagship range

★★★★☆ **Mas Nicolas Cape** ⓐ A gentle giant, usual cab-shiraz duo (54/46). Beguiling dark tarry layers on a fine structure, **17** ⑭ plum, coriander, meat & mocha also in the unfolding flavour profile. Great depth, complexity. 50% new wood, 15 months. 14.5% alcohol. 100 magnums too. No **16**, as all below.

Nicolas van der Merwe range

★★★★☆ **Cabernet Sauvignon** ⑩ ⓐ Nico van der Merwe's 'ego project in exceptional **17** ⑭ vintage'. A barrel-selected blockbuster, intense cassis fruit lavished 15 months all-new oak, beautifully constructed tannins support a body that vibrates with energy. A triumph. Minuscule 600-bottle production sold ex cellardoor only.

★★★★☆ **Syrah** ⓐ Was big & muscular like Cabernet, recently more polished & buffed. **17** ⑬, like **15** ★★★★★ ⑮, sumptuous yet stylish, replete with berry & spice yet refined, beautifully balanced. Vinified for long ageing though lovely to drink now. Also in magnum.

★★★★ **Merlot-Cabernet Sauvignon-Cabernet Franc** Was 'Red', still merlot-dominant (52%) Bordeaux blend. Crunchy fruits & pliable tannins, just 10% new oak in deliciously accessible **17** ㊇. 'Trimmer but sexier than **15** ㊆' per winemaker.

★★★★ **Geelbos Steen** ⑩ Geelbos ('Yellowbush'), a local plant with medicinal value, headlines winery's striking first chenin/steen, ex high-elevation vines, partly oaked, 3 months on lees. **18** ㊈ rich in oatmeal & stewed quince comfort.

★★★★☆ **White** ⓠ Unwooded Stellenbosch sauvignon (68%) & new-oak-fermented Somerset West semillon intertwine in saline **17** ㊑, with an intense, tingling oystershell minerality. Yard ahead of mostly Robertson-sourced **15** ★★★★ ㊇.

★★★★ **Méthode Cap Classique Brut** ⓠ Latest **NV** ㊅ sparkler from chardonnay, 2 years on lees (previous 5 years). Well measured & elegant, refreshing rather than rich & weighty. WO W Cape.

Five to Nine Sauvignon Blanc ★★★★ Harvested between 5 & 9 am. Racy style of **18** ㊃ shows a gunsmoke steeliness cushioned by few grams sugar & time on lees.

Robert Alexander range

★★★★ **Shiraz** ⓥ Spicy **17** ㊅ offers many layers of flavour - ripe black fruit, dried herbs, cured meat, along with a tarry richness; firm but accessible. Year seasoned oak. Super value.

Merlot ★★★★ Violet perfume & meat spice lift gentle berry fruit, rounded in older wood, **17** ㊃ a pleasure to drink.

Cape Elements range

Shiraz-Grenache ★★★★ Mostly Stellenbosch shiraz, splash Wellington grenache, omitting usual cinsaut component yielded 'more exciting' blend in **17** ㊄. Juicy, older-oak brushed, good anytime drinking. — DS

Location/map: Stellenbosch ▪ Map grid reference: B6 ▪ WO: Stellenbosch/Western Cape ▪ Est/1stB 1999 ▪ Tasting & sales Wed 12-5 Fri 10-5 Sat 10-2, otherwise by appt ▪ Owner(s) Nico & Petra van der Merwe ▪ Cellarmaster(s)/winemaker(s) Nico van der Merwe ▪ 50t/4,000cs own label 80% red 20% white ▪ PO Box 12200 Stellenbosch 7613 ▪ nvdmwines@vodamail.co.za ▪ www.nvdmwines.com ▪ S 33° 57' 48.2" E 018° 43' 51.8" ▪ 🖃 fishmonger.monthly.trudges ▪ **T +27 (0)21-881-3063**

Nico Vermeulen Wines ⓠ

As a wine consultant and bulk trader for the past three decades, Paarl-based Nico Vermeulen is well placed to source vinous gems for his family brand. The wines, made in rented space, offer good value for money and sport refreshingly clear, simple labels, depicting the grape berry/ies used.

★★★★ **The Right Red** ⓠ From shiraz, **14** ★★★★ ㊃ spicy, piquant red fruit, brisk acidity & tannins that are supple but need a meal or time to settle. Misses elegance of **13** ㊅. Coastal WO.

★★★★ **The Right White** ⓠ Two vintages, different expressions of sauvignon character & terroir. **18** ㊅ mostly ex Langeberg-Garcia, cool purity of green fruit, smooth, almost delicate. **17** ㊆ Darling & Lambert's Bay, signature dusty minerality & freshness, some depth & gravelly substance.

★★★★ **The Right Two Whites** ⓠ Complementary blend sauvignon (75%) & semillon in **17** ㊆. Delicately scented cool green fruit, elegant & fine with partial oaking (50% new) seamlessly integrated. Well-crafted step above **15** ★★★★ ㊃. No **16**.

The Right Two Reds ⓥ ★★★☆ Dark-fruited equal cab & merlot blend. **14** ⑧⑤ quite juicy, with sprinkling of cocoa & fresh, balanced acidity, sound but supple tannins. Well constructed, but touch off sophisticated **13** ★★★★ ⑧⑦. **Life From Old Wood** ⓥ ★★★☆ Chenin from old Paardeberg & Malmesbury bushvines. Straw-gold **17** ⑧⑤ subtle preserved quince & baked apple underscored by toasty hazelnut & clove from part oaking (2nd-fill barrels). Understated flavours but zestily fresh, good food pairer. **Wit Muskadel** ⓥ ★★★☆ Jerepiko-style white muscat de Frontignan, aged in older oak. Brassy-gold **16** ⑧④ grapey, barley sugar flavours, clean & light-tripping, 16.5% spirit well-integrated. Robertson WO. — MW

Location: Paarl • WO: Western Cape/Coastal/Robertson • Est/1stB 2003 • Tasting by appt only • Owner(s)/viticulturist(s) Nico Vermeulen • Winemaker(s) Nico Vermeulen, with Judy & Izelle Vermeulen • 3,000cs own label & 240,000L bulk export • 3 Pieter Hugo Str, Courtrai, Suider-Paarl 7646 • nicovermeulen@webmail.co.za • **T** +27 (0)21-863-2048/+27 (0)82-553-2024

Niel Joubert Estate ⓠ

Much to celebrate on this Paarl estate, in the Joubert family for over a century: notably the birth of the 5th generation, a son born to Mari Joubert. The self-styled 'down-to-earth, honest wines' of the family label make use of a third of the crop, the remainder is sold off. Note the strikingly packaged new Reserve range.

Reserve range (NEW)

★★★★ **Chenin Blanc** On debut, **17** ⑧⑧ shows aromatic spiced apple & citrus, with some gentle toasty oak enhancement. Lighter (12.5% alcohol) than unwooded Estate sibling. Fresh, with a silky elegance.

★★★★ **Grenache Blanc** Subtle floral tone to baked quince on maiden **17** ⑧⑨. New oak adds plush spice, interwoven with a freshening limy thread. Svelte, lingering & tempting, but will continue to charm.

Proprietor range

★★★★ **Malbec** ⓥ Welcome entry to this small but growing category. **14** ⑧⑦ interesting dried apricot & meat aromas; cranberries, red cherries & dried herbs on firm tannic base. Could develop well.

Christine-Marié range

★★★★ **Cabernet Sauvignon** ⓥ Full expression of warm-climate fruit & 100% new oak, **14** ⑧⑥ unashamedly New World in style, with matching alcohol (15.7%). No **10**, **12**, **13**.

★★★★ **Shiraz** ⓥ More freshness, balance than other red, all-new oak in harmony with persistent spice & perfumed fruit. **12** ⑧⑧ inviting now & over next few years. WO W Cape for these except next, WO Paarl.

★★★★ **Méthode Cap Classique** ⓥ **14** ★★★ ⑧② chardonnay bubbly follows **09** ⑧⑦ though lacks its freshness, creamy texture, despite 36 months on lees. Quite ripe, with apple cider nuance. **12**, **13** untasted.

Chardonnay ⓥ ★★★★ Extra toasted dimension to clean pear & lime flavours from wood regime (100% of wine oaked, 10% new). **17** ⑧⑤ tad less poised than partly wooded **15** ★★★★ ⑧⑦. **16** untasted. **First Kiss Fortified Chenin Blanc** ⓥ ★★★☆ Creamy honey & ginger flavours on oak-matured (9 months) **12** ⑧④, warming, delightful nightcap & alternative to 'port'. Discontinued: **Merlot**.

Niel Joubert Estate range

Cabernet Sauvignon ★★★ Unpretentious & friendly **17** ⑧⓪ exudes sweet raspberry flavours. Mostly unoaked, this is pure berry enjoyment, fresh & accessible. **Merlot** ★★★ Friendlier & more overt fruit in **17** ⑧② than previous. Supple structure with a brush of old oak & a clean minty farewell. **Pinotage** ⓥ ★★★ Unoaked **16** ⑧① leaner than last though ample earthy-spicy berry flavours, good freshness, finishes with dry, piquant twist which works well with tomato-based dishes & BBQ meat. WO W Cape, like Herr Leicht. **Shiraz** ★★★★ Riper & rounder in **16** ⑧④ than previous, with smoky bacon & clove impression. Mostly older oak in sync with ample fruit. Ready. **Blanc de Noir** ★★ Forthright & tangy **19** ⑦⑤ from pinotage, in a dry, light (12% alcohol) style, perfect for sunset canapés. **Chardonnay** ⓥ ★★★★ Gentle poached pear, zested through with lime, brightens **18** ⑧④. A low 12% alcohol adds to the easy-drinking pleasure. Unoaked this vintage. **Chenin Blanc** ⓥ ★★★ Crunchy Golden Delicious apple on unoaked **19** ⑧⓪. Fresher & fruitier than previous for attractive easy drinking. **Sauvignon Blanc** ★★★ Similar stonefruit & dried grassy tone on **19** ⑦⑦, with a tangy farewell twist. **Herr Leicht** ⓥ ★★★ Unoaked **17** ⑦⑨ blend changes to nouvelle, sauvignon, chenin. Crunchy green apples & herbs, trips lightly. — MW

Location/map: Paarl • Map grid reference: C8 • WO: Paarl/Western Cape • Est 1898 • 1stB 1996 • Tasting & sales Mon-Fri 9-4 by appt • Closed all pub hols • Owner(s) Joubert family • Cellarmaster(s) Ernst Leicht

(Oct 2000) ▪ Winemaker(s) Ernst Leicht, with Niel Joubert jnr (May 2011) ▪ Viticulturist(s) Daan Joubert ▪ 1,000ha/300ha (cab, cinsaut, grenache n/b, malbec, merlot, ptage, shiraz, tempranillo, touriga nacional, chard, chenin, grüner veltliner, sauv) ▪ 1,953t/±160,000cs own label 49% red 50% white 1% rosé ▪ Other export brand: Hunterspeak ▪ GlobalGAP, IPW ▪ PO Box 17 Klapmuts 7625 ▪ wine@nieljoubert.co.za ▪ www.nieljoubert.co.za ▪ S 33° 49' 54.7" E 018° 54' 3.2" ▪ ☞ alchemy.dazzled.seated ▪ **T +27 (0)21-875-5936**

☐ **Niels Verburg** *see* Luddite Wines

Niemandsrivier

Featuring an elegant front-label drawing of The Treasury, the ancient Jordanian city of Petra's most elaborate temple, the '17 reviewed here is the last shiraz vintage produced by consultants for Lawrence Hyslop. Businessman and new proprietor of the boutique Niemandsrivier farm in Elgin, Johan Vosloo, retained the services of viticulturist Rob Semple and winemaker Niels Verburg after acquiring both land and brand in 2018, providing continuity.

Petra Shiraz ★★★★ Not as brooding as previous but still - attractively - restrained, **17** ⑧⑤ peppery nuances, well-masked 15.3% alcohol, bright seam of acidity adds structure & potential for few years ageing. — CvZ

Location/WO: Elgin ▪ Est 2006 ▪ 1stB 2009 ▪ Closed to public ▪ Owner(s) Johan Vosloo ▪ Cellarmaster(s)/winemaker(s) Niels Verburg (Jan 2015, consultant) ▪ Viticulturist(s) Rob Semple (Jun 2006, consultant) ▪ 17.4ha/3.2ha (shiraz) ▪ 35t/200cs own label 100% red ▪ WIETA (farm) ▪ Niemandsrivier Farm PO Box 157 Elgin 7180 ▪ niemandsrivier@mweb.co.za ▪ **T +27 (0)83-440-5581**

Nietgegund

Jan Dreyer, boutique vintner in Stellenbosch's Blaauwklippen Valley, taps into the vast experience of advisers Ronell Wiid (cellar) and Francois Hanekom (vineyard) to maintain high standards for his wines, thus ensuring that 'the friend you enjoy them with remains your friend!'

★★★★ **Pro Amico** ⊘ Merlot anchors this accomplished blend, partners elegantly with cab franc (94/6) in standout **15** ⑧⑧ vintage. Pristine black fruit with a cool leafiness, balanced & sustained. **13** ★★★★ ⑧④ was merlot & shiraz. No **14**. — WB

Location/WO: Stellenbosch ▪ Est 2004 ▪ 1stB 2008 ▪ Closed to public ▪ Owner(s) Nietgegund Boerdery (Edms) Bpk ▪ Winemaker(s) Ronell Wiid (Jan 2013, consultant) ▪ Viticulturist(s) Francois Hanekom (Sep 2006, consultant) ▪ 3.4ha/1ha (cabs s/f, merlot) ▪ 4t/100cs own label 100% red ▪ IPW ▪ PO Box 12684 Die Boord 7613 ▪ jan@nietgegund.com ▪ www.proamico.co.za ▪ **T +27 (0)21-880-0738**

Nieuwedrift Vineyards   ⑨ ⑪ ⌂ ◎ ⑧

A love of wine prompted Johan Mostert to build a boutique cellar on his 7th-generation Piketberg farm in 2002. He says the tasting room doubles as a gallery for his wife Karin's paintings, while the restaurant helps with wine sales. 'And accommodation in our cottage makes a visit even nicer.'

★★★★ **Méthode Cap Classique** ⊘ Joyful, delicious & well-priced sparkler from chardonnay. **18** ⑧⑥ ripe but bone-dry palate, green apple zing balanced by creaminess of light oak & 11 months on lees.

. . . .

Shiraz ⑦ ★★★★ Seriously conceived (2 years cask, third new) but actually fun to drink. **17** ⑧⑤ packed with red berry fruit, roast coffee/mocha & spice features, 15% alcohol neatly tucked away.

. . . .

Blanc de Noir ★★☆ Salmon pink hue on bone-dry **19** ⑦⑧ from shiraz, fruity, easy & honest.

Chardonnay ⑭ ★★★ Lemon & lime twist of fresh **18** ⑧⓪ plumped up by oak treatment, which stands apart mid-2019. **Chenin Blanc** ★★★ Unassuming **19** ⑧② is textured, fresh & dry, abundant guava, melon & gooseberry on offer. — DS

Location: Piketberg ▪ Map/WO: Swartland ▪ Map grid reference: C2 ▪ Est/1stB 2002 ▪ Tasting, sales & cellar tours Mon-Sat 9–6 ▪ Closed Easter Fri/Sun, Dec 25/26 & Jan 1 ▪ Nieuwedrift Wine Estate Restaurant: lunch Mon-Sun 11-3; dinner Fri/Sat 6-9 ▪ Facilities for children ▪ Tour groups ▪ Conferences ▪ Nieuwedrift Cottage ▪ Owner(s)/viticulturist(s) Johan Mostert ▪ Cellarmaster(s) Johan Mostert (Jan 2002) ▪ 151ha/15ha (shiraz, chard, chenin) ▪ 200t total 14t/1,560cs own label 14% red 38% white 25% rosé 23% MCC ▪ PO Box 492 Piketberg 7320 ▪ nieuwedrift@patat.co.za ▪ S 32° 58' 28.1" E 018° 45' 10.6" ▪ ☞ chatty.porcupines.surnames ▪ **T +27 (0)22-913-1966/+27 (0)82-824-8104**

☐ **Nieuwe Haarlem** *see* Cape Wine Company

☐ **1900** *see* Spioenkop Wines

Nitida Cellars

With responsibility for both vines and wines on these cool slopes on the outskirts of Durbanville suburbia, Danie Keulder has a lot on his plate but revels in the challenge. Five years on from his first vintage, he's clearly at home on the property, a rundown former sheep farm bought 30 years ago and developed by engineer Bernhard Veller and his family. Sauvignon blanc and semillon remain the calling cards, and in addition to wine, people visit for the mountain biking, restaurant dining, conferencing and eventing. There may soon even be a boutique hotel to stay over in.

★★★★☆ **Cabernet Sauvignon** ✓ ⊛ Seductive **17** ⑨③ raises the bar on **16** ⑨② in complexity, elegance, but retains approachability, Xmas cake flavour profile. Structure & poise from usual 33% new oak for 12 months. Dry, fine tannins support cool-climate fruit well.

★★★★ **Merlot** ✓ Accomplished **17** ⑧⑨ shows Italianate dry tannin grip but beautifully countered by succulent ripe plum & black berry flavour. Acidity & oak (20% new) balance fruit & add length.

★★★★☆ **Pinot Noir** ✓ Trademark strawberry & cherry notes on **17** ★★★★ ⑧⑧. Lighter, less complex than **16** ⑨①. Succulent, with oak, none new, apparent in supportive frame rather than flavour.

★★★★ **Shiraz** ⊛ Continues form of previous in effortlessly combining dark fruit concentration, spice & pepper with supportive seasoned oak. Deceptively soft-textured **17** ⑧⑨ has ample length & richness.

★★★★☆ **Calligraphy** ✓ Merlot (32%) leads equal parts cabs sauvignon & franc on **17** ⑨④ with dabs malbec, petit verdot. Alluring fruitcake, graphite & cocoa on textured, layered palate. Complex & refined, sleek, long finish. 14 months 43% new French oak. No **16**.

★★★★ **Riesling** Lime marmalade tang shows typicity to best effect on **18** ⑧⑨. Residual sugar (10 g/l) lower than **17** ⑧⑦ but in total harmony with vibrant acidity. Lovely intensity & succulence.

★★★★☆ **Wild Child** From sauvignon, **18** ⑨② improves on **17** ★★★★ ⑧⑧ & expresses farm's cool-climate sites well. Granadilla tropicality vies with flint typicity. Portion naturally fermented in old oak blended with tank component that had 4 months on lees, adding texture, complexity.

★★★★☆ **Golden Orb** ⊛ High-lying, south-facing single-site sauvignon picked multiple times. Singular **18** ⑨① shows intense, tautly concentrated grapefruit, lemon & flint. Focused, with zingy typicity, it will age well.

★★★★ **Sauvignon Blanc** ✓ Gooseberry & citrus jostle with tropical stonefruit on succulent, approachable **18** ⑧⑦. Melange of picking dates produces rounded, ripe & refreshing mouthful.

★★★★ **Semillon** ⊛ Made to age, 70% portion of **18** ⑧⑧ was fermented in new French oak with lees stirring for texture, breadth. Ripe nectarine fruit & contrasting wet pebble note, the long-lasting flavours are taut & vibrant.

★★★★ **The Tinkery** ⚲ Experimental label. **17** ★★★☆ ⑧⑤ barrel-fermented viognier. Signature nectarine & peach, simultaneously tangy & spicy creamy palate. **16** ⑧⑦ lower-alcohol, higher-sugar riesling.

★★★★☆ **Coronata Integration** ✓ ⊛ Complex **17** ⑨② Bordeaux white balances taut citrus vibrancy with creamy breadth courtesy of barrel-fermented semillon & tank-fermented sauvignon, like **16** ⑨②, blended 50/50 & oaked, third new, for 8 months. Focused & precise.

★★★★☆ **The Grande Matriarch Méthode Cap Classique** ⑩⑭ Winery's first 100% pinot noir bubbly, **15** ⑨⓪ pale coral hue with marmalade, apple skin & light almond nuance. Rich biscuity flavour from 39 months on lees, gaining concentration & intensity.

★★★★ **The Matriarch Méthode Cap Classique** Improves on previous in richness & concentration. **17** ⑧⑧, 50/50 chardonnay & pinot noir bubbly on lees for 13 months, has tarte tatin & cinnamon vibrancy & long, rewarding tail.

Occasional release: **Modjadji Semillon Noble Late Harvest**. Discontinued: **Chardonnay**. — FM

Location/WO: Durbanville ▪ Map: Durbanville, Philadelphia & Darling ▪ Map grid reference: C7 ▪ Est/1stB 1995 ▪ Tasting & sales Mon-Fri 9–5 Sat 11–4 Sun 11-3 ▪ Fee R40/R60 4 wines range ▪ Closed Good Fri, Dec 25/26 & Jan 1 ▪ Cassia Restaurant T +27 (0)21-976-0640; conference & function venue at Cassia (200 pax) ▪ Tables at Nitida T +27 (0)21-975-9357, www.tablesatnitida.co.za ▪ Facilities for children ▪ MTB, part of Hillcrest/Majik forest trail (www.tygerbergmtb.co.za) ▪ Conservation area ▪ Owner(s) Bernhard Veller ▪ Winemaker(s)/

viticulturist(s) Daniel Keulder (Jan 2015) ▪ 35ha/16ha (cabs s/f, p verdot, riesling, sauv, sem) ▪ 220t/18,000cs own label 30% red 70% white + 3,000cs for clients ▪ Brands for clients: Woolworths, Checkers ▪ PO Box 1423 Durbanville 7551 ▪ info@nitida.co.za ▪ www.nitida.co.za ▪ S 33° 50' 3.8" E 018° 35' 37.0" ▪ predictable. march.telephoto ▪ **T +27 (0)21-976-1467**

Noble Hill Wine Estate

There's pride and pleasure in growing and working with your own farm's grapes, and they're conscious of it at this family estate on the granitic northern (Paarl-side) slopes of the mighty Simonsberg - a noble hill indeed. Co-owner and winemaker Kristofer Tillery takes the satisfaction further by aiming to be in harmony with the environment and to vinify with as little intervention as possible. New in the cellar are locally produced 10,000L concrete fermenters, and a Reserve White blend maturing in barrel.

★★★★ **Cabernet Sauvignon** Sleek & muscular **15** (89), embraces dark fruit core with fine-grained tannins. Naturally fermented in tank & 15% new-oak maturation, as for Estate Reserve. A rewarding future & structured step up on **14** (86).

★★★★ **Merlot** Some wild red-berry pungency in concentrated **15** ★★★★ (84), quite edgy & unknit in youth, tannins on the austere side, time should resolve though less ripe fruit & balance than **14** (86).

★★★★ **Syrah** Splashes mourvèdre & viognier in ripe & succulent **16** (86), smoky bacon flavours, smooth tannins & warm-hearted 14% alcohol. Drink before more structured, elegant **15** (89).

★★★★ **Estate Reserve** Spectrum of succulent dark fruit from cab-led **16** (89) Bordeaux blend, with merlot, cab franc & petit verdot. Fine, dry tannins streamline ripeness. More balanced than tighter **15** (86), but still ageworthy. Also 200 magnums.

★★★★ **Viognier** Like **17** ★★★★ (85), **18** (87) showcases viognier's aromatic charm; even more elegance & intensity at a measured 12.5% alcohol. Oak-fermented & -matured, 10% new; creamy breadth from 9 months on lees.

★★★★ **Blanc de Blancs** Baked apple & soft brioche tone to **16** ★★★★ (85) méthode cap classique sparkling from chardonnay. Same 24 months lees ageing & ultra-dry style, but less vibrant & flavoursome than **15** (88).

Not tasted: **Mourvèdre Rosé**, **Sauvignon Blanc**. — MW

Location: Paarl ▪ Map: Franschhoek ▪ Map grid reference: B7 ▪ WO: Simonsberg-Paarl ▪ Est/1stB 2001 ▪ Tasting & sales daily 10—5 ▪ Fee R50, waived on purchase ▪ Cellar tours by appt only ▪ Food & wine pairing option ▪ cosecha Restaurant ▪ Picnic baskets ▪ Facilities for children ▪ Farm-produced extra virgin olive oil ▪ Conservation area ▪ Hitachino Nest Japanese craft beer available at winery ▪ Owner(s) Noble Hill Trust ▪ Winemaker(s) Kristopher Tillery ▪ Viticulturist(s) Kristopher Tillery, Rodney Zimba & Johan Viljoen (consultant) ▪ 62ha/40ha (cabs s/f, merlot, mourv, p verdot, shiraz, chard, chenin, grenache blanc, marsanne, sauv, viog) ▪ PO Box 111 Simondium 7670 ▪ info@noblehill.com ▪ www.noblehill.com ▪ S 33° 49' 38.0" E 018° 56' 12.1" ▪ circulates.reaping.picket ▪ **T +27 (0)21-874-3844**

☐ **Noble Nomad** see Rosendal Wines

Noble Savage

Produced at Bartinney Private Cellar by consultant Ronell Wiid for owners Michael and Rose Jordaan, this 'feisty, fun range of serious wines with real character' can be found at the Bartinney Wine & Champagne Bar in central Stellenbosch.

★★★★ **Cabernet Sauvignon-Merlot** Subtle violet scents tempt on fruitcake-rich **14** (86), 80/20 blend of Banhoek grapes which improves on **13** ★★★ (81). Concentrated & broad, with fine tannin.

★★★★ **Chenin Blanc** Lemon verbena-brushed stonefruit appeal on light, zesty **18** ★★★★ (85). Rounded, with pleasant breadth from extended lees contact. Touch less substance than **17** (86).

Rosé ★★★★ Strawberry appeal with light herb dusting on bright, succulent **19** (84) pink charmer. Broader lees note & dry tail make it ideal for summer. Tasted pre-bottling, as next. **Sauvignon Blanc** ★★★★ Taut, tangy & vibrant, with pithy grapefruit flavour on **19** (85). Lees contact adds breadth. — FM

Location/map: Stellenbosch ▪ Map grid reference: F5 ▪ WO: Western Cape/Stellenbosch ▪ Est 2006 ▪ 1stB 2008 ▪ Sales Mon-Sat 11.30-9 at Bartinney Wine & Champagne Bar T +27 (0)76-348-5374, 5 Bird

Str, Stellenbosch ▪ Closed Dec 25/26 & Jan 1 ▪ Owner(s) Rose & Michael Jordaan ▪ Winemaker(s) Ronell Wiid (2012, consultant) ▪ 13,000cs own label 50% red 50% white ▪ Postnet Suite 231 Private Bag X5061 Stellenbosch 7599 ▪ info@bartinney.co.za ▪ www.noblesavage.co.za, www.bartinney.co.za ▪ S 33° 56' 18.36" E 018° 51' 36.81" ▪ [🗺] scuba.pictures.sunshine ▪ T +27 (0)21-885-1013

Noble Wines & Spirits

Owned by Indian-born, Cape Town-based businessman Goutham Reddy, this diversified venture sources Stellenbosch wines for bottling at third-party facilities, and produces brandy (inter alia) at its distillery in Somerset West. On the wine side, consultant Johan du Preez oversees the Noble and premium Aureate labels, hopes to introduce an ultra-premium wine this year, and is working on MCC bubbles. Expansion of exports (currently to Africa) is planned for south and east Asia and Europe. We hope to taste next time.

Location: Somerset West ▪ Est 2015 ▪ 1stB 2017 ▪ Closed to public ▪ Sales Mon-Fri 9-4 ▪ Distillery ▪ Owner(s) Goutham Reddy ▪ 20,000cs own label 60% red 30% white 10% rosé ▪ info@noblespirits.co.za ▪ T +27 (0)21-845-4853

☐ **No House Wine** *see* Stellar Winery

Nomada Wines

Based in Durbanville, but using cellar space outside Stellenbosch on the R44, Riaan Oosthuizen does contract winemaking for clients there, as well as producing Nomada, an own-label wine venture using Durbanville fruit. Wife and project partner Gina handles the marketing and packaging.

★★★★ **Sauvignon Blanc** ⊘ Reductively made, 8 months on lees, fraction oaked, **18** ⑧⑨ grown-up sauvignon. Gooseberries, leafy nuances, mineral seam, racy acidity adding vibrancy. **17** untasted.

Not tasted: **Cabernet Franc**, **Georgina**, **Rustica Sauvignon Blanc**, **Rustica**. — CR

Location: Durbanville/Stellenbosch ▪ Map: Helderberg ▪ Map grid reference: D2 ▪ WO: Durbanville ▪ Est/1stB 2007 ▪ Tasting by appt only ▪ Owner(s) Riaan & Gina Oosthuizen ▪ Winemaker(s)/viticulturist(s) Riaan Oosthuizen (2007) ▪ 66ha/7ha (cabs s/f, merlot, chenin, sauv) ▪ 55t total 10t/2,000cs own label 40% red 60% white + 6,000cs for clients ▪ Brands for clients: Cadequin, Skaap (Netherlands) ▪ PO Box 5145 Tygervalley 7536 ▪ nomadawines@gmail.com ▪ S 34° 1' 18.4" E 018° 50' 54.6" ▪ [🗺] scruff.unbridled.eclipse ▪ T +27 (0)83-280-7690

☐ **Nordic Wines** See Editor's Note

Normandie Est. 1693

Mature vines on 17th-century Franschhoek farm Normandie contribute to a mostly exported portfolio of high-end wines (untasted this edition) produced by Johan Viljoen for SA-born international designer Mark Eisen and wife Karen. Given the owners, packaging is a particular emphasis, the high-gloss, ink-coated bottle design for the Clarington range being several years in development and patented internationally.

Location: Franschhoek ▪ Est 2008 ▪ 1stB 2009 ▪ Closed to public ▪ Owner(s) Mark & Karen Eisen ▪ Cellarmaster(s)/winemaker(s) Johan Viljoen (Feb 2008) ▪ Viticulturist(s) Johan Viljoen & Bennie Booysen (both Feb 2008) ▪ 47ha/17ha (cab, merlot, p verdot) ▪ ±130t/12,000cs own label 50% red 30% white 20% rosé ▪ WIETA ▪ PO Box 398 Pniel 7681 ▪ info@normandie1693.com ▪ www.normandie1693.com, www.claringtonwines.com ▪ T +27 (0)21-874-1039

☐ **Nova Zonnestraal** *see* Constantia Royale
☐ **Ntsiki Biyela Wines** *see* Aslina Wines

Nuiba Wines

A happy childhood on her family's Nuiba cattle ranch near Gobabis in Namibia inspired the naming of Suzanne Coetzee's boutique brand, and the 'post' theme, referring to a cattle staging/drinking station. She makes her wines at Clos Malverne (where she was cellar chief for several years), and now offers by-appointment tastings of them at newly opened offices in Stellenbosch town centre. Involvement with recent successful theatre productions is prompting greater Nuiba facilitation of cultural events.

★★★★★ **Third Post** ⓖ Half pinotage, with cab & grenache, **16** ⑨③ is a perfumed delight, an array of vivid fruit, cinnamon- & nutmeg-spiced from 18 months in old oak. Sleek musculature, succulent, yet enough grip for a future. Doesn't put a foot wrong. Piekenierskloof grapes.

★★★★ **First Post** Semillon, sauvignon (60/40), partially aged in older barrels but **18** ⑧⑦ still honours the fruit. Prominent granadilla, underpinned by a savoury seam, strengthening on the palate. No **17**.

Second Post ⓖ ★★★★☆ Plush red fruit, **16** ⑧④'s oaking in support, adds savoury notes, doesn't detract from the fruit-driven shiraz styling. Just enough grip at the end for definition. Simonsberg-Paarl WO. Not tasted: **Fourth Post**. — CR

Location: Stellenbosch ▪ WO: Stellenbosch/Simonsberg-Paarl/Piekenierskloof ▪ Est/1stB 2016 ▪ Closed to public; private tastings by arrangement only ▪ Owner(s) Suzanne Coetzee ▪ Winemaker(s) Suzanne Coetzee (Jan 2016) ▪ 350cs own label 70% red 15% white 15% rosé ▪ 25 Herold Str, Stellenbosch 7600 ▪ suzanne@nuibawines.co.za ▪ www.nuibawines.co.za ▪ **T +27 (0)21-883-3617**

☐ **Nuwehoop** see Daschbosch
☐ **Nuwe Wynplaas** see Group CDV

Nuy Wine Cellar ⓛ ⓜ ⓞ ⓖ

This large grower-owned cellar in Worcester's Nuy Valley vinifies both bulk and boutique-scale wines. The latter category, which goes much wider than the famous long-lived muscadels, amounts to only 5% of production. But its success has warranted the appointment of two new managers to extend the well-priced ranges into the Western Cape and Gauteng, and enhance the hospitality experience of visitors to the Nuy on the Hill wine centre and restaurant. A new Exclusive Wine Club will offer special deals to its members.

Legacy range

★★★★ **Argilla** ⓖ Named for area's soils, **15** ⑧⑥ New World-styled blend mostly pinotage & cab, with shiraz & merlot. Spicy dark fruit, warm hearted but a touch brooding, needs more time. No **14**.

★★★★☆ **Calcareo** ⊘ Deliciously fresh & tangy dried peach & lime flavours on **18** ⑨⓪ chenin, off limestone soils. All-French new oak, 8 months, doesn't obscure fruit, though shade off sumptuous **17** ⑨①.

★★★★☆ **Barbieri Idro** ⓖ Stellar debut for **13** ⑨③ fortified muscat de Frontignan. 3 years in old oak has honed it into a finely polished cross between tawny 'port' & muscadel, the raisin character interleaved with citrus rind & dried apricot, tempered by tangy acidity.

Celine Méthode Cap Classique ★★★★ Brioche & similar smoky nuance to latest **NV** ⑧⑤ brut sparkling from chardonnay & pinot noir. Some shortbread & honeyed flavours, fresh but quite open-textured & less finessed than previous. Robertson grapes.

Mastery range

★★★★ **Cabernet Sauvignon** Preview of **17** ★★★★ ⑧⑤ shows tighter fruit profile, firmer acidity & pungent wood tone from more new oak (60%) than **16** ⑧⑥. Some American barrels, as for all these reds.

★★★★ **Pinotage** ⊘ Scented red fruit pastille flavours, touch of mocha & supple balance allow **17** ⑧⑦ full rein for satisfying drinkability. Like **16** ★★★★ ⑧⑤, mostly French oak, but better structure & freshness.

★★★★ **Shiraz** ⊘ Touch more new oak & less American in the **17** ⑧⑥ mix than Inspiration sibling, underpins dense spicy fruit. Balanced & succulent, ready to enjoy.

Chardonnay ⓖ ★★★★☆ Open-textured & appealing **17** ⑧⑤, gentle poached pear & subtle brush of sweet toasty oak. Silky, balanced, with gentle freshness. A serial crowd pleaser. Not tasted: **Sauvignon Blanc**.

Inspiration range

★★★★☆ **Red Muscadel** Richer, more aromatic & sweeter than sibling fortified muscat. Spirit stands a little proud in **18** ⑨⓪, shade less delicately balanced than **17** ⑨①. Ample heart-warming charm & raisiny flavours. Still a fine example of this unoaked style.

★★★★ **White Muscadel** Ever-popular winter warmer shows similar alluring barley sugar, jasmine & dried peach flavours on **18** ⑧⑨, but fresher & more delicately balanced than **16** ⑧⑥. Uncloying sweetness courtesy integrated 'dry' spirit. **17** sold out untasted.

Cabernet Sauvignon ⊘ ★★★★☆ Amiable sweet berry fruit on **17** ⑧③, supported by pliable dry tannins. Like Shiraz & Pinotage, half each French & American oak add spicy appeal. **Koffiepit Pinotage** ★★★ Your morning cuppa in **19** ⑧② pre-bottling sample. All-new oak, cleverly toasted to impart sweet & popular mocha/coffee flavours. Friendly, easy drinking. **Shiraz** ★★★ Riper than Mastery version, **17** ⑧⓪ less balanced than previous. Chunky & hearty barbecue style. **Rouge de Nuy** ⓥ ★★★ Cab & equal shiraz & pinotage, latter's ripe mulberry tones dominant, some sweet new-oak too. **NV** ⑧② supple & juicy, accessible. **Chenin Blanc** ⓥ ★★★ Similar ripe Golden Delicious apple flavours & appealing smooth texture on **19** ⑧①, with an extra limy twist to freshen. **Colombar Semi-Sweet** ★★ Crunchy green fruit & floral profile on **19** ⑦⑥'s semi-sweet delivery. Easygoing summer tipple. **Sauvignon Blanc** ⓥ ★★★ A tad brisker in **19** ⑧①, with a piquant, sherbetty freshness to tropical flavours. Bright al fresco quaffer. **Chant de Nuit** ★★★ Crisp, dry & light **NV** ⑦⑧ quaffer from mostly chenin & colombard, splash rare, aromatic Ferdinand de Lesseps gives a distinct experience, like drinking unsweetened pineapple juice. Refreshing at 12% alcohol. **Muscat Sparkling Wine** ⓥ ★★★ Scented grapey sweetness surprisingly uncloying on **19** ⑦⑨ light rosé sparkling. Solo or with a mild Thai curry. **Sauvignon Blanc Sparkling Wine** ⓥ ★★★ Fresh, apple- & sherbet-flavoured sparkler. **19** ⑦⑦ dry & quaffable, touch of sweetness lifted by ample fizz.

Brandy range
★★★★ **Copper Potstilled** ⓧ The 10% component aged 20 years makes all the difference in this brandy ⑧⑦ (the rest 3-year & 5-year). It adds smoothness, complexity, depth, & tempers the fire. A little sweet; very sippable.— MW, TJ

Location/map: Worcester ▪ Map grid reference: C4 ▪ WO: Nuy/Western Cape ▪ Est 1963 ▪ Tasting & sales Mon–Fri 9–5 Sat/Sun 9–4 ▪ Closed Good Fri & Dec 25 ▪ Bistro & deli ▪ MTB ▪ Brandy & gin also available for tasting/sale at Nuy on the Hill wine centre ▪ Owner(s) 19 members ▪ Cellarmaster(s) Christo Pienaar (Sep 2003) ▪ Winemaker(s) Paul Burger (Nov 2016, senior) ▪ Viticulturist(s) Pierre Snyman (VinPro) ▪ 770ha (cab, merlot, muscadel, ptage, shiraz, chard, chenin, cbard, nouvelle, sauv) ▪ 18,200t/20,000cs own label ▪ PO Box 5225 Worcester 6849 ▪ wines@nuywinery.co.za ▪ www.nuywinery.co.za ▪ S 33° 41' 8.77" E 019° 35' 17.96" ▪ 🅦 chive.bitter.transitive ▪ T +27 (0)23-347-0272

Oak Valley Estate   ⓥ 🏠 ◎ ⓰

Established by the pioneering Sir Antonie Viljoen in 1898, now owned by son Anthony and run by grandson and CEO Christopher Rawbone-Viljoen, this estate in the heart of Elgin Valley is renowned for its apples and pears, free-range wagyu beef and acorn-fed pork, greenhouse cut-flowers, MTB trails, charming 1902 cottage and, of course, cool-climate wines being made by Jacques du Plessis (ex Constantia Uitsig) in a cellar that was upgraded and expanded last year. A successful agribusiness with a long history of environmental management, Oak Valley is a founder member of the Groenlandberg Conservancy and the Green Mountain Eco Route, formed to promote ecotourism in the region.

Groenlandberg range
★★★★★ **Pinot Noir** ⓥ 🐝 Following in footsteps of aromatic **17** ⑨③, beguiling **18** ⑨④ has floral perfume & intense, succulent red fruit augmented by tobacco & spice; small portion wholebunch fermented, 10 months in mostly 3rd-fill French oak for silky texture.
★★★★★ **Chardonnay** 🐝 These from high-lying (±430 m), south-facing blocks on Groenlandberg. Barrel-fermented **18** ⑨⑥ has wonderful cool-climate citrus fruit intensity, oatmeal creaminess from 9 months in French oak (38% new). Stylish & elegant.

Elgin range
★★★★ **Sounds of Silence Pinot Noir** ⓥ Ruby-bright **18** ⑧⑦ lightly oaked, packed with ripe red cherry & raspberry fruit, rosepetal perfume & caramelised note adding to sweet impression despite only 1.3 g/l sugar.
★★★★★ **Beneath The Clouds Chardonnay** ⓥ 🐝 Restrainedly wooded **18** ⑨③ (only 10% new, 8 months French) is remarkably fresh, focused, flinty, with lemon peel nuances adding to intense, lingering citrus impression.
★★★★★ **Stone & Steel Riesling** ⓥ Acid (7 g/l) & sugar (3.8 g/l) perfectly balanced in dry, bracingly fresh yet fruity & pleasingly viscous **19** ⑨② showing green apple, white peach, lime & lemon peel against a pebbly mineral backdrop.
★★★★★ **Fountain of Youth Sauvignon Blanc** ⓥ 🐝 Oystershell minerality & good palate weight from 2 months on lees add depth & interest to **19** ⑨④, with zesty lime, lemon & ruby grapefruit as well as some more tropical passionfruit & white peach notes.— JG

Location/map/WO: Elgin ▪ Map grid reference: B1 ▪ Est 1898 ▪ 1stB 2003 ▪ Tasting & sales Mon-Fri 9—5 Sat/Sun 10-4 ▪ Closed Easter Mon, Dec 25/26 & Jan 1 ▪ The Pool Room tasting facility ▪ Self-catering 1-bedroom cottage ▪ MTB trails ▪ Conservation area ▪ Owner(s) AG Rawbone-Viljoen Trust ▪ Winemaker(s) Jacques du Plessis (Oct 2018) ▪ Viticulturist(s) Jacques du Plessis (Oct 2018), assisted by Kevin Watt ▪ 32ha (pinot, chard, riesling, sauv) ▪ ±250t/±35,000cs own label 20% red 80% white ▪ GlobalGAP, IPW, WIETA, WWF-SA Conservation Champion ▪ PO Box 30 Elgin 7180 ▪ wines@oak-valley.co.za ▪ www.oakvalley.co.za ▪ S 34° 9' 24.4" E 019° 2' 55.5" ▪ ⬛ inspectors.soon.sunscreen ▪ **T +27 (0)21-859-4110**

☐ **Obscura** *see* Spice Route Winery

O'Connell's

Paarl-based negociant Lukas O'Connell owns and markets multiple wine brands locally and in international markets, including this eponymous label which, he says, 'is for people who know what they enjoy'. To achieve the consistency his customers expect, he selects specific wine parcels irrespective of terroir and region, and blends them to deliver 'a guaranteed taste sensation, year after year'. Low sulphur and tannin are part of the package. A sibling brand is Rara Sunt Cara.

Location: Paarl ▪ Est 1995 ▪ 1stB 2016 ▪ Closed to public ▪ Owner(s) Lukas O'Connell ▪ 14,000cs own label 76% red 24% white + 22,500cs for clients ▪ PO Box 7206 Noorder-Paarl Paarl 7623 ▪ lukasoconnell34@gmail.com ▪ www.ibnn.co.za ▪ **T +27 (0)82-499-4995**

☐ **Ode To Nature** *see* Neethlingshof Estate
☐ **Oesland** *see* Hofstraat Kelder
☐ **Oggendau** *see* Eerste Hoop Wine Cellar
☐ **Oh!** *see* Oneiric Wines
☐ **Old Brown** *see* Sedgwick's Old Brown

Oldenburg Vineyards

Based in Switzerland, Adrian Vanderspuy spent happy childhood holidays in this mountain amphitheatre high up in Stellenbosch's Banhoek when the land belonged to his grandmother. But he and wife Vanessa had more ambitious plans when they purchased it in 2003 - and they must be close to achieving them after implementing several important strategic changes over the past year: new winemaker, new cellar and new brand positioning (from the debut CL 'concept range' targeting the millennial market to the top-tier Rondekop label). 'We have created the platform from which we will continue to work towards our ultimate goal: to make exceptional wines from this extraordinary terroir,' says MD Judi Dyer.

Rondekop range

★★★★☆ **Per Se Cabernet Sauvignon** Stellar debut **15** ⑨③ a hard act to follow, but lithe **16** ⑨② comes close with intense blackcurrant fruit, forest floor earthiness, hints of baking spice from 20 months in new oak. Also available in magnum, as all reds except Grenache & CL Red.

★★★★ **Stone Axe Syrah** Ⓐ Sweet ripe red fruit & peppery finish on **17** ★★★★☆ ⑨②, youthfully tight after 20 months in 50% new oak but balance between structure/concentration & perfumed elegance promises even brighter future than **16** ⑧⑨.

★★★★☆ **Rhodium** Ⓐ Gracefully lean rather than powerful, with 20 months in new oak imparting cinnamon spice to brambleberry fruit, **16** ⑨④ Bordeaux blend sees 10% each malbec & petit verdot added to usual duo of merlot (60%) & cab franc (20%).

Oldenburg range

★★★★☆ **Cabernet Sauvignon** Ⓐ After the concentration of **15** ⑨③, **16** ⑨① is a little more restrained yet shows hallmark cassis with hints of thyme, also cedar from 20 months in 40% new oak. Classically styled with firm, fine tannins.

★★★★☆ **Cabernet Franc Barrel Select** Ⓐ Deliciously savoury fennel, black olive & herbal edge to cherry & mulberry fruit of lively **16** ⑨①. Powdery tannins enhance hints of cinnamon & toasted nut from 25% new oak, well integrated.

★★★★☆ **Merlot** ⊛ Richly concentrated **15** ★★★★★ ⑨⑤ followed by sleek, succulent **16** ⑨④, with floral perfume & hint of dark chocolate adding to appeal of black berry & plum fruit. Slightly more new oak (40% vs 35%).

★★★★ **Syrah 16** ⑧⑨ sees a return to understated elegance, a pinch of pepper & allspice (40% new oak) enlivening juicy red cherry & plum fruit, with supple tannins.

★★★★ **Chardonnay** ⊘ Now 100% naturally fermented in barrel (35% new), **18** ★★★★★ ⑨⓪ a deft step up on **17** ⑧⑨ with subtle hints of toasted hazelnut & butterscotch adding depth of flavour to creamy texture, cut through by citrus freshness which lingers.

★★★★ **Chenin Blanc** Wild fermented (as all whites) then aged 9 months in mostly older 300L barrels, **18** ⑧⑨ has almond cream richness balanced by crisp acidity, showcasing tangy apple & passionfruit notes.

★★★★ **Viognier** 100% fermented/aged in Hungarian oak, 33% new, **18** ⑧⑧ has cling peach & crème brûlée aromas carrying through to palate, linear acidity & flinty finish bringing lovely balance.

Grenache Noir ⊗ ★★★★ Identically made **17** ⑧⑤ darker in colour & flavour profile than **16** ⑧③. More of everything, in fact, including vibrant freshness & succulence that lifts it above more rounded, lighter-bodied & smoother predecessor. Both have charm, but different personalities.

CL range (NEW)
★★★★ **Red Blend** ⊘ Fun back-label 'formula' proves Oldenburg 'cooler' than CL (Stellenbosch vehicle registration). Smooth blend syrah with 13% merlot in juicy **17** ⑧⑥, packed with ripe berry & plum fruit, cocoa powdery tannins.

★★★★ **White Blend** Chardonnay with 37% chenin in **18** ⑧⑥, 15% fermented in 'egg', rest in older oak, 9 months lees contact imparting soft texture & yoghurt-coated nut flavour to citrus & pineapple fruit.— JG

Location/map/WO: Stellenbosch ▪ Map grid reference: H5 ▪ Est 1960s ▪ 1stB 2007 ▪ Tasting & sales Mon-Fri 10-4.30 Sat & pub hols 10-4 ▪ Reservations highly recommended ▪ Closed Good Fri, Dec 25/26 & Jan 1 ▪ Luxury accommodation in The Homestead (exclusive use, sleeps up to 12 in 6 bedrooms) ▪ Owner(s) Adrian & Vanessa Vanderspuy ▪ MD Judi Dyer (Apr 2017) ▪ Winemaker(s) Nic van Aarde (Nov 2018) ▪ Viticulturist(s) Zelda Shaik (Jun 2018), with Etienne Terblanche (consultant) ▪ 50ha/30ha (cabs s/f, merlot, shiraz, chard, chenin) ▪ 136t/7,400cs own label 57% red 43% white ▪ PO Box 2246 Dennesig 7601 ▪ tastingroom@oldenburgvineyards.com ▪ www.oldenburgvineyards.com ▪ S 33° 55' 7.61" E 018° 56' 8.75" ▪ 🎦 chickens.splits.teaspoons ▪ **T +27 (0)21-885-1618 (winery), +27 (0)87-057-4515 (homestead reservations)**

☐ **Old Harbour** see Whalehaven Wines
☐ **Old Man's Blend** see Groote Post Vineyards

Old Road Wine Company
🖳 🍴 📷

Franschhoek Valley's heritage of venerable vines and fascinating backstories is the inspiration for this boutique DGB-owned brand. Winemaker Ryan Puttick and his team have done much work sourcing special small pockets, often from aged vineyards, and their care and attention continues in the cellar, where they work with amphoras, whole bunches and natural ferments, among others, to bring out the best of each parcel. The wines, with their unusual names and striking labels, can be enjoyed at the brand-home and popular restaurant on Franschhoek's main road.

Single Vineyards range (NEW)
★★★★ **Grand-Mère Semillon** ⊛ From registered Franschhoek single-vineyard (as Elite duo), **17** ⑧⑨ dynamic debut with plenty of semillon character (lemons, wax & honey) balanced by firm oaking (wholebunch barrel-fermented, 25% new French). Old vines, as name implies.

The Elite range (NEW)
★★★★ **12 Mile Syrah** Well-made **17** ⑧⑦ offers typical flavours of black pepper & black fruit, with pliable, leathery tannins. Handles 14% alcohol with elegance aided by nicely judged oak (25% new). Franschhoek WO.

★★★★ **Anemos Chenin Blanc** ⊛ Lively **17** ⑧⑦ shimmers with sherbety lemons, pineapples & herbs underpinned by subtle oak, all larger format, only 20% new. Starts better than it finishes but smartly done.

The French Corner range (NEW)
★★★★ **White Blend** Spent year on lees in older oak gaining creamy richness to citrus palate, **18** ⑧⑥ plenty of ginger & cinnamon spice, too, suggesting Asian food matches. Mainly verdelho, tweaks of viognier & grenache blanc.

....

Red Blend ⑦ ★★★★ Unusual mourvèdre-led Rhône red, including splash viognier, **18** ⑧⑤ perfumed raspberries & strawberries with soft, juicy tannins & plenty of peppery bite. Very enjoyable drinking indeed.

....

The Quirky Ones range (NEW)
Pardonnez-Moi Cinsaut ★★★ Juicy, red gummy bear notes on **19** ⑧②, just-dry, very soft tannins, fresh acidity - everything cries 'chill me & enjoy all summer long!' WO W Cape. **The Butcher & Cleaver Cape Blend** ★★★★ Mainly shiraz but 30% pinotage rounds out **15** ⑧⑤ with warm black fruit, touch of tar & smoky oak (old barrels). Good midweek drinking. **Spotted Hound Red Blend** ★★★★ Fermented on oak staves then into old barrels, **18** ⑧⑤ grenache-led Rhône blend is melange of ripe red fruit & pleasing herbal whiffs, aniseed finish. **Juliette Sauvignon Blanc** ★★★ Grassy notes with peppers & peas, **18** ⑧① adds tropical fruit on palate with steely-green finish. WO Elgin. — CM

Location/map: Franschhoek ▪ Map grid reference: C2 ▪ WO: Coastal/Franschhoek/Elgin/Western Cape ▪ 1stB 2015 ▪ Tasting Tue-Sat 11-10 Sun 11-9 ▪ Sales Tue-Sat 11-5 ▪ Closed Easter Sun & Dec 25 ▪ Restaurant open for lunch & dinner ▪ Tour groups ▪ Gift shop ▪ Farm produce ▪ Owner(s) DGB (Pty) Ltd ▪ Winemaker(s) Ryan Puttick (Sep 2017) ▪ Viticulturist(s) Heinie Nel (Jul 2018) ▪ 7ha/14ha (shiraz, chenin, sem) ▪ 40% red 60% white ▪ info@orwc.co.za ▪ www.oldroadwinecompany.com ▪ S 33° 54' 16.4" E 019° 6' 40.7" ▪ ⓦ rebuffing.enticingly.capita ▪ **T +27 (0)21-271-0379**

Old Vines Cellars

The two generations of women behind this Cape Town boutique brand are taking a small step back from their business this year to refocus. Cape Wine Master Irina von Holdt and daughter Fran Botha have been long-time advocates for chenin blanc - 'we still dream, live and drink it!' - and it will surely feature prominently when they re-launch, both in the premium selections and their charming, everyday Springvalley range. Meanwhile, attention is also on the next generation of the family - Fran's two young sons. Will they be the next winemaker or viticulturist? 'Probably more likely to be filmmakers!' chuckles Irina.

Location: Cape Town ▪ Est/1stB 1995 ▪ Closed to public ▪ Owner(s) Irina von Holdt ▪ Winemaker(s) Irina von Holdt & Rocco de Villiers ▪ 12,000cs own label 20% red 80% white ▪ 50 Liesbeek Rd, Rosebank 7700 ▪ info@oldvines.co.za ▪ www.oldvines.co.za ▪ **T +27 (0)21-685-6428**

☐ **Old Vine Series** see Sadie Family Wines

Olifantsberg Family Vineyards
⑨

When international critics start beating a path to the door, it's obvious that a winery is doing something right. The focus on Paul and Corine Leeuwerik's property is boldly Rhône, with grapes — some echalas trained — planted in shale and schist, suited to the high-elevation, windblown location. Dynamic winemaker Elizma Visser has vinified only a handful of vintages on these slopes of the Brandwacht mountains in Breedekloof, but all the omens are positive. She intends to continue experimenting with skin exposure, natural ferments and alternative vessel usage. Sustainability of the vineyard remains paramount and specialist assistance is called in at pruning to train staff and pursue ever-improving quality.

★★★★ **Grenache Noir** ⊘ **18** ★★★★★ ⑨① improves on **17** ⑧⑥ in subtlety & complexity. Bright fruited, refreshing but with nuanced, layered palate. Natural ferment & time in older oak add depth & grip. Could take light chilling.

★★★★ **Pinotage** ⊘ Lighter, modern-styled **18** ★★★★★ ⑨⓪ better than **17** ⑧⑦. Similar bright juiciness but with darker, deeper tones referencing variety's pinot noir heritage. Wholeberry open ferment results in good concentration & length. 10 months in French oak, all old.

★★★★ **Syrah** ⊘ ⓐ Understated but powerful **17** ★★★★★ ⑨④ steps up on **16** ⑧⑨. Echalas vines, portion wholebunch & open ferment lead to complex, herb-tinged spicy mouthful of black fruit reminiscent of the Rhône. Structured, textured, broad & long from combo barrels, casks & foudres, 5% new.

★★★★☆ **Silhouette** ⓐ Near-equal grenache noir, shiraz, carignan & mourvèdre in refined **16** ⑨③ blend. Bold yet restrained, with spice, lavender & dark berries cradled by oak, 5% new, 10 months in 225L - 2,000L French. Complex & rewarding. Lovely in every respect.

★★★★ **Chenin Blanc** ⓥ Poised yet refreshing **18** ★★★★★ ⑨⓪ from 37 year old bushvine fruit improves on lighter **17** ⑧⑨. Sun-dried pineapple richness balanced by lively acidity & brush of oak (9 months, 225L - 2,000L). Freshness from tank-fermented portion. **16** untasted.

★★★★ **Lark Chenin Blanc** ⓥ ⓐ Leashed power on improved **18** ★★★★★ ⑨④. Creamy vanilla & stonefruit succulence from natural & inoculated ferment in French & Hungarian oak. Textured, rich, balanced, structured & dry yet simultaneously fresh & svelte. Just 10% new oak used, less than **17** ⑧⑨.

★★★★☆ **Grenache Blanc** ⓥ ⓐ Vibrant **18** ⑨④ ups the quality on **17** ⑨②. Ripe stonefruit with lemon tang & savoury notes. As with others, complex winemaking: natural ferment, 5% skin & portion in 600L 'egg'. Result is weighty yet lively, layered wine contained in subtle oak frame with lees breadth.

★★★★☆ **Blanc** ⓥ ⓐ Marries roussanne (56%), grenache blanc & dab chenin in stellar **18** ⑨④ blend. Spicy, creamy, light, with chalky grip. Self-contained & confident. Bunch press, natural ferment in old oak & 10 months on lees in combo French/Hungarian barrels (10% new) & plastic 'egg'.

Not tasted: **Blanc de Noir**. — FM

Location: Worcester ▪ Map/WO: Breedekloof ▪ Map grid reference: C4 ▪ Est 2003 ▪ 1stB 2005 ▪ Tasting & sales Mon-Sat by appt ▪ Owner(s) Paul J Leeuwerik ▪ Winemaker(s)/viticulturist(s) Elizma Visser (Jun 2015) ▪ 95ha/17ha (carignan, grenache n/b, mourv, ptage, shiraz, chard, chenin, rouss) ▪ 100t/±13,000cs own label 60% red 40% white ▪ PO Box 942 Worcester 6849 ▪ winemaker@olifantsberg.com ▪ www.olifantsberg.com ▪ S 33° 35' 42.76" E 019° 21' 42.39" ▪ 🖃 oscillates.tribune.cuddled ▪ **T +27 (0)71-301-9440**

Olivedale Private Vineyards Ⓠ

There's never a dull moment for viticulturist Carl van Wyk and consultants Abé Beukes and Jolene le Roux at these Belgian-owned, 20-hectare Southern Cape vineyards and cellar (producing the only WO Swellendam wines in the guide). Not with 18 varieties rooted in soils ranging from stony clay to – mere metres distant – free-draining Breede riversand. Most recently, the focus has been on a skin-fermented white blend from four of those cultivars, debuting this edition, and, to follow, an alternative red from seldom-seen rooibernet.

Olivedale range

★★★★ **Chardonnay** Lemon- & almond-toned **18** ⑧⑥ less ripe, more refined than **17** ★★★ ⑧②. Deftly oaked (just 30% new), enough bright acidity to lift few grams sugar.

★★★★ **Wild Olive Semillon** Ⓠ Natural ferment, 40 days on skins, 6 months ageing, all in older oak. **17** ⑧⑥ full & rich, in contrast to semillon's usual racier profile; challenges convention.

★★★★ **Wild Melody** (ⁿᵉʷ) Certified as skin-fermented white, **18** ⑧⑥ viognier with roussanne, semillon & verdelho (27/22/14); 30% oaked, mainly French. Nutty & earthy, with faint peach & floral notes, long & bone-dry, balanced finish.

★★★★ **Red Muscadel** Ⓠ New-wave fortified muscat de Frontignan with higher alcohol, reined-in sweetness, greater focus on fresh rather than dried fruit character, **17** ⑧⑥ still satisfyingly grapey, with uplifting bitter hint. Year in oak, some new. 500 ml.

Shiraz (ⁿᵉʷ) ⓥ ★★★★ Sweet vanilla notes give way to scrub, black pepper & charcuterie on older-oaked **17** ⑧⑤. Well-formed tannins, bright acidity & dry finish complete a package worth seeking out.

Syrah Ⓠ ★★★☆ Oak-forward **17** ⑧⑤ is opaque, with faint pepper, black/red berry scents & core of dark fruit. Very young, needs few more years to knit. **Tempranillo** Ⓠ ★★★★ Barrel sample **17** ⑧③ atypically dark hued, like previous, with similar pleasing dry tannic grip & bracing acidity. Perfect osso bucco companion. **Shiraz-Mourvèdre-Grenache** Ⓠ ★★★ Well-crafted, part-oaked **NV** ⑧① with fruit intensity, vibrant colour from shiraz. Supple, smooth, tannins amenable for satisfying easy sipping. Not tasted: **Rosé**.

Queen of Africa range

★★★★☆ **Edel Laat Oes** Ⓠ Distinctively & charmingly packaged in 375-ml bottle, **15** ⑨④. Darling semillon is a classically styled Noble Late Harvest dessert. Gold colour, liquidised stonefruit & pineapple richness, brief oaking giving almond shading. Vibrant, the acidity freshening the sweetness. Gorgeous.— CvZ

Location: Swellendam ▪ Map: Southern Cape ▪ Map grid reference: D1 ▪ WO: Swellendam/Western Cape ▪ 1stB 2016 ▪ Tasting by appt only ▪ Closed all pub hols ▪ Owner(s) 8 shareholders ▪ Cellarmaster(s) Abé Beukes (2014) ▪ Winemaker(s) Jolene le Roux (Jan 2016) ▪ Viticulturist(s) Carl van Wyk ▪ 20ha (carignan, grenache, malbec, mourv, p verdot, red muscadel, roobernet, shiraz, tannat, tempranillo, touriga, chard, riesling, rouss, sauv, sem, verdelho, viog) ▪ 85t own labels 70% red 30% white ▪ Buffeljagsrivier Olivedale Swellendam 6740 ▪ jolene@olivedalewines.com ▪ www.olivedalewines.com ▪ S 34° 05' 08.2" E 020° 30' 00.8" ▪ ⬚ acquisition.entrusts.quips ▪ T +27 (0)28-007-0087

Olof Bergh Solera

A rarity in the local brandy arena, Distell's Olof Bergh is matured in a dedicated cellar at Goudini in the Breede River Valley using a solera, where different batches are racked down tiers of barrels for a final product with a greater percentage of cask-aged distillate than the usual blended brandy.

Olof Bergh Solera ⊘ ★★★ Straightforward, balanced blended brandy ⑧⑴ for cocktails & mixing (43% alcohol). Fruity & fresh, with caramel & nut notes. — WB

Olsen Private Vineyards

The debut sparkling from this boutique Paarl farm on the Klein Drakenstein mountain foothills is named for the third civilian in space, American Greg Olsen, who bought the property in 2002 and now co-owns it with daughters Kimberly and Krista. Local front man Armand Botha tends both the vines and the cellar, and crushes just a few tons of the six varieties planted for the strikingly packaged own-label wines.

★★★★ **Shiraz** ⊘ 🐝 Ticks the boxes in **16** ⑧⑧ & improves on last-tasted **12** ★★★★ ⑧⑷ with plentiful plum & mulberry fruit to balance the savoury & floral nuances, & sweet spice from oak. Authoritative tannins & flavour depth invite cellaring.

Merlot ★★★★ Pleasing fireside sipper, **16** ⑧⑸ redcurrant & rhubarb notes followed by cocoa & dried herbs. Firm tannins & oaking (90% new, French & American, 24 months, as red siblings) add some gravitas. **Pinotage** ★★★★ Generous, ripe bramble fruit handles oak-derived mocha & vanilla spice well on **16** ⑧⑷. Interesting meaty nuance, full body & dark spice finish. **Chardonnay** ★★★★ Copious fruit on **17** ⑧⑸ laced with chamomile, vanilla & oatmeal from serious woodsing (year new barriques). Creamy & fresh palate, good stonefruit persistence. **Gregory Hammond Méthode Cap Classique** ⓃⒺⓌ ★★★ Joyful brut celebrator from chardonnay, **17** ⑧⑵ pops with citrus & crunchy apple fruit flavours, Lemon Cream biscuit overtone from 9 months on lees. Not tasted: **Cabernet Sauvignon**, **Cape Blend**, **Chenin Blanc**. — GM

Location/map/WO: Paarl ▪ Map grid reference: G5 ▪ Est/1stB 2002 ▪ Tasting by appt only ▪ Fee R50pp depending on sales ▪ Farm-style jams & olive oil ▪ Owner(s) Greg Olsen & daughters ▪ Cellarmaster(s)/viticulturist(s) Armand Botha (2000) ▪ Winemaker(s) Armand Botha (2007) & Loftie Ellis (consultant) ▪ 15ha ▪ 1,500cs own label 80% red 20% white ▪ PO Box 9052 Huguenot 7645 ▪ admin@olsenprivatevineyards.co.za ▪ www.olsenprivatevineyards.co.za ▪ S 33° 44' 4.7" E 019° 3' 5.0" ▪ ⬚ parables.backdrops.pulsations ▪ T +27 (0)21-862-3653/+27 (0)83-400-1909

☐ **Ondine** see Ormonde Private Cellar
☐ **One Formation** see Boland Cellar

100 Reserve

Produced in the reputed Oude Molen distillery, 100 Reserve's name suggests that all components are aged in oak, going a step above what's legally required in the blended brandy category.

Premium Brandy ⊘ ★★★★ Blended brandy ⑧⑷, the wine spirit component aged 100 days, potstill 3 years. Simple, with sherry-like nuttiness & dried peach. Best as a mixer, but not too harsh to go solo. — TJ

Oneiric Wines

Blessed with a magnificent setting in Elgin, the farm of prime mover Shan Pascall and her family is mostly undeveloped and provides a habitat for numerous species, as well as a scenic backdrop for various visitor amenities, including picnics, walks and hikes. The wines are made by recent appointee, Mark Wallace, whose father and veteran viticultural consultant Paul has looked after Oneiric's 8 hectares since inception. Much of the branding of the portfolio (untasted by us) is related to copper, referencing Shan's father's mining career.

Location/map: Elgin ▪ Map grid reference: C4 ▪ Est 2007 ▪ 1stB 2009 ▪ Tasting & sales Wed-Sun 10-4; otherwise by appt ▪ Long cellar table lunches - booking essential ▪ Gift shop ▪ Walks/hikes ▪ Picnics to be ordered 3 days prior ▪ Conservation area ▪ Owner(s) Pascall family ▪ Winemaker(s) Mark Wallace ▪ Viticulturist(s) Paul Wallace (Aug 2007, consultant) ▪ 64ha/8ha (cab, merlot, shiraz, chard, sauv) ▪ ±180t/10,000cs own label 65% red 35% white ▪ 76 Highlands Rd, Elgin 7180 ▪ shan@oneiric.co.za ▪ www.oneiric.co.za ▪ S 34° 14' 31.0" E 019° 03' 05.8" ▪ valuable.phenomenally.poking ▪ **T +27 (0)71-481-9560**

☐ **One Man Band** *see* Iona Vineyards

Onoma Private Cellar

The late Com Yiannakis bought Stellenbosch farm Felicia in 1999, nurturing some 17 ha of vineyards (including 30-year-old chardonnay) to become a sought-after grape supplier to prestigious local producers. His passing in 2015, the year of their first commercial bottling, a cabernet vinified by consultant winemaker, Matthew van Heerden, makes the 2020 release 'bittersweet'. Son Blaise speaks of honouring his father's legacy and heritage by adhering to a terroir-driven classic style, reflected in the name Onoma (Greek for 'of repute') and the image of an amphora on the front-labels, limited to 2,000 cases per vintage.

Cabernet Sauvignon ★★★☆ Seriously conceived **15** (85), wholeberry ferment & 2 years new oak, vintage's bounty shows in heady cherry liqueur, hedgerow fruit & typical fruitcake tones, all reined-in by tannins, pliable enough for solo sipping or with food. Also in magnum. **Chardonnay** ★★★ Gentle citrus & light floral aroma, fruit-filled lemon & lime palate, tangy finish on **16** (82), for current drinking. — FM, CvZ

Location/WO: Stellenbosch ▪ Est 2016 ▪ 1stB 2015 ▪ Entire villa available on Airbnb ▪ Owner(s) Full Imput 146 (Pty) Ltd (shareholder Com Yiannakis Family Trust) ▪ Winemaker(s) Matthew van Heerden (consultant) ▪ 31ha/17.5ha (cab, merlot, shiraz, chard) ▪ 140t/1,350cs own label 60% red 40% white ▪ WIETA ▪ blaise@onomawines.com ▪ www.onomawines.com ▪ **T +27 (0)82-468-3788**

Oom Tas

Distell big-volume white depicts winefarmer 'Uncle Tas' beaming from retro label. In 1, 2 & 5L bottles.
Oom Tas ★ Amber **NV** (64), light (11.5% alcohol), faintly grapey, dry & tangy. Undisclosed grapes. — CvZ

☐ **Openers** *see* Stellenview Premium Wines

Opstal Estate

Attie Louw, 7th-generation custodian of this noteworthy estate, together with brother Zak as production manager, is at the forefront of the Breedekloof Makers grouping, young guns showing the world the true potential of their valley by challenging convention, exploring new concepts, handcrafting special batches and nurturing old vines. The area as a whole, and this farm in particular, are worth watching as future stars of the industry. The Louws' visitor-friendly property in mountain-fringed Slanghoek offers a restaurant, 5 guest cottages and a wedding venue, all presented with down-to-earth family hospitality.

Heritage range

★★★★☆ **Carl Everson Cape Blend** Poised, elegant & supple **17** (92), complex layers of fruit laced with sweet floral scents, white pepper & fynbos, all wrapped in suede tannins. Creative, stylish near-equal blend pinotage, cab & carignan, splash cinsaut, 20 months in older oak barrels.

★★★★☆ **Carl Everson Chenin Blanc** (🍇) (🍂) Sophisticated & accomplished single-vineyard flagship, **18** (93) follows impressive form. Muscular, expressive yet nuanced & complex, showing multi-layered stonefruit, creamy lees richness from 10 months in old large barrels, natural-yeast ferment.

★★★★☆ **The Barber Semillon** Outstanding example of variety, **18** (92) is plush yet lithe & refined, with charming lemon notes, spicy scrub highlights. Named for winemaker's grandfather & namesake, post-WW2 barbershop proprietor, before taking over estate's reins. Ex riverine vines planted 1998.

★★★★☆ **Carl Everson Cape White Blend** (🍇) Opulent & seductive roussanne-led blend with chenin, semillon, viognier & colombard, **18** (94) maintains the standard set by debut **17** (94). Complex natural-yeast vinification, multi-vessel oaking lend focus & detail, weight & texture.

The Barber Cinsault (NEW) ★★★ Beaujolais-like **18** (82) is floral scented & sweetly juicy, but lacks substance of siblings. 30% wholebunch, old oak.

Opstal Estate range

★★★★ **Cabernet Sauvignon-Cinsault** ⊘ Near-equal blend is supple, light bodied & enticingly juicy, with signature floral scent, peppery spice of cinsaut highlighting bright cassis fruit. **18** ⑧⑦ step up from **17** ★★★★ ⑧⑤.

★★★★ **Chenin Blanc** ⊘ Characterful, partly wooded (oak foudres) **18** ⑧⑥ is silk textured, bursts with tropical fruit appeal. Wild-yeast ferment, deftly handled lees lend richness. Improves on **17** ★★★★ ⑧⑤.

★★★★ **Hanepoot** Heavenly fortified fireside warmer from 32 year old vines, **18** ⑧⑨ offers intense, concentrated muscat fruit with melon preserve, ginger & lemon zest. Well-judged alcohol & sugar (15.6%, 174 g/l). No **17**.

Syrah-Viognier Blush ⊘ ★★★★ Appealing dry rosé, varieties (60/40) co-harvested & -vinified, **19** ⑧④ bright floral & berry scents with hint of flint. **Sauvignon Blanc Sparkling Sec** ⊘ ★★★ Uncomplicated off-dry carbonated bubbly, **19** ⑧⓪ has varietal granadilla fruit, refreshing crispness.

Sixpence range

Cabernet Sauvignon-Merlot ⊘ ★★★ Undemanding, fruit-driven braai companion, **18** ⑧⓪ delivers at the price, offers ripe tannins, red berries. **Sauvignon Blanc-Semillon** ★★★ Nicely balanced, vibrant & crisp **19** ⑧② offers great-value everyday drinking. Appealing melon & kiwi profile. — GdB

Location: Rawsonville ▪ Map: Breedekloof ▪ Map grid reference: A5 ▪ WO: Slanghoek ▪ Est 1847 ▪ 1stB 1978 ▪ Tasting, sales & cellar tours Mon–Fri 9–5 Sat 11–3 Sun by appt ▪ Closed Easter Fri-Mon, Dec 25/26 & Jan 1 ▪ Cheese platters ▪ Restaurant Wed-Sun 9–5 ▪ Facilities for children ▪ Tour groups ▪ Gift shop ▪ Farm produce ▪ Conferences ▪ Weddings ▪ Conservation area ▪ MTB trail ▪ Opstal Stay (5 exclusive self-catering units) ▪ Owner(s) Stanley Louw ▪ Winemaker(s) Attie Louw (Sep 2010) ▪ Viticulturist(s) Gerhard Theron (Jan 2002) & Zak Louw (Jan 2016) ▪ 419ha/101ha (cab, cinsaut, ptage, shiraz, chard, chenin, muscat d'A, sauv, sem, viog) ▪ 1,600t/25,000cs own label 30% red 55% white 10% rosé 5% dessert ▪ IPW, WIETA ▪ PO Box 27 Rawsonville 6845 ▪ wine@opstal.co.za ▪ www.opstal.co.za ▪ S 33° 38' 19.8" E 019° 13' 40.8" ▪ 🖾 bloomed.summons. finished ▪ **T +27 (0)23-344-3001**

Orange River Cellars   ⓠ ⓖ

The figures attached to this dynamic winery's five production cellars, spread out along the Northern Cape's Orange River, are impressive: between them, Kakamas, Keimoes, Upington, Grootdrink and Groblershoop annually receive around 117,000 tons of grapes produced by their 750 owner-growers across 3,700 hectares. Another impressive figure is the 26 million litres packaged under their own label. In the semiarid to arid climate, fine harvest conditions are never a given; all the more laudable, then, is the quality achieved across the board. The 2019 season, as it happens, was excellent, frost-free, with a bumper crop showing unusually aromatic whites and deep-coloured reds. This follows from 2018, where the cellars achieved outstanding results, including Best Producer with 10 or Fewer Entries at Veritas, and Best Producer at the Young Wine Show, with the new Cellar Master whites taking champion or runner-up trophies. Delighting the team even more is that business is booming, with sales showing healthy growth.

Reserve range

★★★★ **Lyra Shiraz** ⊘ From 100% shiraz (last had splash petit verdot), **15** ⑧⑧ shows some evolution, greater depth than **14** ★★★★ ⑧⑤ in its dark berry, spice & meaty character. The flavours are rich, savoury & bound by rounded tannins. These & a balanced freshness make for tasty drinking now, further few years. Oak matured, French/American 48% new.

★★★★ **Lyra Quasar** 🆕 ⊘ Unusual take on colombard, **18** ⑧⑥ tank-fermented, aged 10 months on lees. Intriguing aromatic interweave of guava, subtle orange citrus, green mangoes. Gains weight from lees without loss of purity, saline persistence. Seafood a great partner for it.

★★★★★ **Straw Wine** ⊘ Brilliant red-gold **18** ★★★★ ⑧⑨ from air-dried chenin, unwooded. Raisiny rich, with honeyed apricot flavours; just enough acidity to keep more luscious sweetness under control. Not quite as riveting as oaked **17** ⑨④. 375 ml.

Lyra Irsai Olivér Demi-Sec Sparkling 🆕 ⓦ ★★★ Low-alcohol **19** ⑧⓪ carbonated bubbly from Hungarian variety irsai olivér. Spicy muscat flavours partnered by gentle mousse, sweetness.

Lyra Vega ★★★★ Blends shiraz with 20% petit verdot in **17** ⑧③. Big & forthright, sweet vanilla tones of new oak (61%, mix French/American) in lead. Softish, supple texture, some spice & glow from 15% alcohol. Needs careful monitoring if keeping.

Cellar Master range (NEW)

Omstaan Colombard ★★★ Similar vinification as sibling, started in tank, completed in seasoned 300L American oak. **18** ⑧⓪ light on fruit, also lowish 11.4% alcohol. Both leave wood, bracing acid more exposed.

Omstaan Sauvignon Blanc ★★★★ Cool passionfruit, tropical tones on **18** ⑧⑤ advanced by hint oak fragrance. Medium bodied, lively, with intensity & lingering flavours. Bone-dry. Interesting few years potential.

Orange River Cellars range

★★★★ Hanepoot Was 'Soet Hanepoot'. Fortified **17** ★★★ ⑧② quieter than distinctive **16** ⑧⑦. Shy nutty, grapey character, down-toned spirity verve; both rather overshadowed by luscious sweetness.

★★★★ Red Muscadel ⊘ Flame-licked hue inviting introduction to lush **17** ⑧⑨. Generous, delicious mix raisins, dried citrus peel, spice enriched with warming fortification. Sweetly persistent.

★★★★☆ White Muscadel ⊘ Fortified (unoaked) muscat de Frontignan. In footsteps of stellar **16** ★★★★★ ⑨⑤, **17** ⑨④ so elegant, such fresh, cool spiced citrus peel flavours beautifully merged with warming, not overly fiery spirit. Great balance between typical grapey sweetness & clean finish.

★★★★ White Jerepigo Roast nuts & honey aromas on **18** ⑧⑥ fortified chenin. Rich fruity sweetness contrasted by clean lingering tail. Improves on smooth, fruitily sweet **16** ★★★★ ⑧③. **17** sold out untasted.

Sparkling Doux ⊘ ⑦ **★★★** From chenin & morio muscat, **18** ⑧⓪ enjoys fruitily sweet floral, litchi flavours, invigorating fizz, crisp finish. Light 9% alcohol. Has appeal beyond those with sweet tooth.

Cabernet Sauvignon ★★☆ Dark berries with some cedary oak spice on **17** ⑦⑦. Despite a little sweetness, tannins remain gruff, drying. **Pinotage** ⊘ **★★★** Plenty zesty, red-berry appeal in **18** ⑧②. Full bodied but unheavy, balanced by nip of lively tannin. Tiny portion oaked, 40% new. **Ruby Cabernet ★★★** Modest berry fruit on lightly oaked **18** ⑦⑧. Smooth, few grams sugar aid easy drinking. **Shiraz ★★★** Light oaking on **17** ⑦⑨ adds spice to ripe red berry fruit. Flavours plumped out, smoothed by gram/2 sugar. **Chardonnay** ⊘ **★★★** Quiet lemon, spice touches on **17** ⑧⓪; drop chenin, 8 months older oak add extra interest, satisfaction. **Chenin Blanc** ⊘ **★★★** Gentle tropical tones on very brisk, dry **19** ⑦⑦. **Colombard** ⊘ **★★★** Mouthful of freshly picked, juicy guavas lifted by gentle sweetness. **19** ⑧① light, zesty & refreshing. **Sauvignon Blanc ★★** Brief green grassy notes on **19** ⑦⑥. Dry, with assertive acid. **Sparkling Rosé ★★☆** Cherry pink fizz from chenin, morio muscat & pinotage. **18** ⑦⑧ low alcohol, sweet, with creamy mousse. **Sparkling Brut** ⊘ **★★★** Gently fruity, truly dry bubbly from chenin. **19** ⑧① lightish & refreshing. **Rosé Natural Sweet ★★** Morio muscat, chenin & pinotage in vivid pink **18** ⑦④. Luscious & overly cloying. **Nouveau Natural Sweet ★★** Was 'Nouveau Blanc'. Now from colombard. **19** ⑦③ gentle fruit lifted by sprightly acid. Refreshing summer sipping at just 9% alcohol. **Red Jerepigo ★★★** Ruby cab & shiraz in very fruity, richly sweet **18** ⑧② fortified. Warmingly smooth & a little cloying. **Cape Ruby** ⊘ **★★★** Simple ripe plums on sweet **17** ⑦⑦ 'port' from ruby cab, tannat, shiraz. Smoothly warming, if light on flavour. — AL

Location: Upington ▪ Map: Northern Cape, Free State & North West ▪ Map grid reference: B8 ▪ WO: Northern Cape ▪ Est 1965 ▪ 1stB 1968 ▪ Tasting & sales at Upington visitor centre Mon-Fri 10–6 Sat 10-3 & at Kakamas, Keimoes & Grootdrink cellars Mon-Fri 8–5 Sat 8.30–12; closed Sun, Good Fri, Dec 25 & Jan 1 ▪ Also at Upington visitor centre: virtual cellar tours, tasting & sales of Kalahari craft beer & Die Mas van Kakamas brandy ▪ Owner(s) ±750 shareholders ▪ CEO Charl du Plessis ▪ Cellarmaster(s) Gert Visser ▪ Cellar managers George Kruger (Kakamas), Johan Dippenaar (Keimoes), Johan Esterhuizen (Upington), Ferdi Laubscher (Grootdrink), with winemakers (in same cellar order) Marko Pentz, Stefan Steenkamp; Rianco van Rooyen; Jopie Faul, Jodie Johannes, Philani Gumede; Mynhardt van der Merwe ▪ Viticulturist(s) Henning Burger (viticultural services manager), with Francois Ozrovech ▪ 3,700ha (ptage, ruby cab, shiraz, chard, chenin, cbard, muscat varieties) ▪ 117,000t/26m L own label 10% red 50% white 25% rosé 15% other + 30m L for clients/bulk ▪ PO Box 544 Upington 8800 ▪ info@orangeriverwines.com ▪ www.orangeriverwines.com ▪ S 28° 26' 26.30" E 021° 16' 27.66" ▪ [IW] palace.mimed.heeding ▪ **T +27 (0)54-337-8800**

☐ **Oranjerivier Wynkelders** *see* Orange River Cellars
☐ **Oranjezicht** *see* Rogge Cloof

Org de Rac

Two decades back, this large estate at the foot of the Piketberg was a neglected grain farm. Now – quite apart from lavender, rosemary and olives – over 50 hectares of sustainably farmed, organic vineyards are thriving, and Org de Rac is offered as the 'green heartbeat of the Swartland'. Somewhat unusually for the serious producers of the area, a wide range of varieties are grown and successfully vinified – not just those associated with the Mediterranean. The wines are now also confirmed as vegan-friendly.

Die Waghuis range

★★★★☆ **Rooi** ⊘ ⊙ **17** ⑨ blends shiraz with grenache, mourvèdre & verdelho for an aromatic, ripe & juicy yet quite restrained whole. The sweet fruit balanced & supported by bright acidity & firm dry tannins. Oak unobtrusive & supportive of the fruit.

★★★★ **Blanc** ⊘ ⊙ Verdelho-based **17** ★★★★☆ ⑨, with roussanne & chenin, retasted & now showing a fine balance & understated, subtle impressiveness. Floral & stonefruit notes, softly textured with a firm acidity, the 40% new oak now integrating well. Previewed **16** ⑧⑦ had less verdelho in blend.

Reserve range

★★★★☆ **Cabernet Sauvignon** ⑫ ⊙ Charming as **15** ⑨, impressive, too, **16** ⑨ admirable concentration, serious oak backbone (year, new French & American), lavish cassis fruit. Drinks well now, will reward cellaring few years.

★★★★ **Shiraz** ⑫ ⊙ White pepper & vanilla welcome, appealing powdery tannin & satisfying dry finish. **16** ⑧⑥ nicely spiced, sculpted by year 90% new French/American oak.

★★★★ **Chardonnay** ⊙ Pleasantly but modestly flavoured **18** ⑧⑥, introduced by nutty, toasty, limy aromas. Silky texture, oak integrated on palate, with bright but balanced acid & lingering citric finish.

Merlot ⑫ ★★★★ Plum, bramble fruit & blueberry, soupçon mint for freshness, with limber tannins, **15** ⑧④ for now or few years.

Org de Rac

★★★★ **Roussanne** ⊘ ⊙ Gently aromatic, waxy, pithy **18** ★★★★ ⑧④ is easygoing, well balanced & fresh; no great fruit intensity but satisfying. Good value for a fashionable, still quite rare variety. Small wood influence, as with **17** ⑧⑧.

★★★★ **Sauvignon Blanc** ⊘ ⊙ Succulent, fresh **18** ⑧⑥ from Constantia grapes, nicely mixing ripely tropical & grassy notes but unmistakeably cooler climate. A few months on lees & a small portion barrel fermented, both adding breadth.

★★★★ **La Verne Méthode Cap Classique** ⊘ ⊙ Notes of ripe apple & biscuit on **16** ★★★☆ ⑧③ sparkling from chardonnay; fresh & nicely dry, but rather short & lacking in depth of fruit. **14** ⑧⑦ was the last one made.

. . . .

Verdelho ⊘ ⊚ ⊙ ★★★★ Gingery spice, a touch of earthiness & some tropicality on well-textured, lightly gripping **18** ⑧⑤ from not-so-common Portuguese variety. Easy-drinking but not trivial.

. . . .

Cabernet Sauvignon ⊘ ⊙ ★★★☆ Classic blackcurrant & cigarbox aromas on **17** ⑧④. Less opulent & intensely fruited than **16** ★★★★ ⑧⑦, even a little lean, with forthright dry tannins, though with sweet note on the finish. **Merlot** ⊘ ⊙ ★★★★ Pleasing fruitcake character on ripely flavourful, dry **17** ⑧⑤. Serious but balanced tannic structure. 14.6% alcohol not too obvious. As usual here, mostly French oak, some American. **Shiraz** ⊘ ⊙ ★★★★ Warm, generous & spicy **17** ⑧⑤ offers fairly juicy palate, supported by grippy tannin & acid. Finishes a little sweeter than **16** ★★★★ ⑧⑦. **Shiraz-Cabernet Sauvignon-Merlot** ⑫ ⊙ ★★★★ Spicy berries entice on near-equal partnership, **17** ⑧④ preview gets grip & structure from grape tannin & 80% oak-staved portion. Well-priced everyday red. **Chardonnay** ⑫ ⊙ ★★★★ Light 20% new-oak touch supports expressive fruit salad tones, lifted by brisk citrus acidity. **18** ⑧③ step up on new-oaked previous. **The Old Pumphouse Cape Ruby Port** ⑫ ⊙ ★★★ NV ⑧① from cab & shiraz pleasingly sweet, cooked plum fruit & raisins, sufficient tannic grip & lively acidity.

Le Piquet range

Cabernet Sauvignon-Merlot ⑫ ⊙ ★★★ Savoury notes & juicy fruit, all balanced by pleasantly firm tannins. Previewed **15** ⑧⓪ perfect fireside companion. **Blanc** ⑫ ⊙ ★★★☆ Laid-back poolside sipper, **17** ⑧③ fruity, fresh & uncomplicated trio chenin, roussanne & verdelho.

Husk Spirit range

★★★★ **Le Genio** Water-white **17** (87) from merlot, fine balance & complexity, delicious length & spicy spirit bite; strawberries & cream on the nose, smooth & husk-y on palate.— TJ, WB

Location: Piketberg ▪ Map: Swartland ▪ Map grid reference: C2 ▪ WO: Swartland/Constantia ▪ Est 2001 ▪ 1stB 2005 ▪ Tasting, sales & tours Mon-Fri 9–5 Sat/pub hols 9.30–2 ▪ Closed Good Fri, Dec 25 & Jan 1 ▪ Meals/refreshments/cheese platters by prior arrangement ▪ Facilities for children ▪ Tour groups ▪ Farm produce ▪ Weddings/functions (100 pax) ▪ Conferences ▪ Conservation area ▪ Owner(s) Nico Bacon ▪ Cellarmaster/GM Frank Meaker (Jul 2013) ▪ Winemaker(s) Jurgen Siebritz (Sep 2014) ▪ Viticulturist(s) Heini Grobler (Jan 2019) ▪ 220ha/54ha (cab, grenache, merlot, mourv, shiraz, chard, chenin, rouss, verdelho) ▪ 650t/62,500cs own label 85% red 10% white 5% rosé ▪ BSCI, Control Union (Organic), IPW, WIETA ▪ PO Box 268 Piketberg 7320 ▪ wine@orgderac.co.za ▪ www.orgderac.co.za ▪ S 32° 57' 44.3" E 018° 44' 57.4" ▪ bathhouses.teardrop.hybrid ▪ **T +27 (0)22-913-2397/3924**

Origin Wine

In fewer than two decades, Bernard Fontannaz's Origin Wine has grown into one of SA most extensive wineries, producing some 7 million cases a year, including a significant portion certified as Fairtrade and marketed under the Fairhills label. Recently they discontinued a number of brands 'not delivering exceptional value to the consumer', and a current area of focus at their Stellenbosch facilities is 'to deliver a world-class service to customers and third-party contractors alike'.

Location/map: Stellenbosch ▪ Map grid reference: D3 ▪ Est/1stB 2002 ▪ Tasting strictly by appt ▪ Owner(s) Bernard Fontannaz ▪ COO Jac Lourens (2018) ▪ Production director Grant Michaels (2004) ▪ Sales director Liezl Retief (2004) ▪ Wine sourcing manager Johan Gerber (2016) ▪ Cellarmaster(s) Chris Smit (2019) ▪ Winemaker(s) Seugnét Rossouw (2007), with Helienne van Zyl ▪ 7m cs ▪ 50% red 40% white 10% rosé ▪ BRC, DLG, Fairtrade, HACCP, IFS, WIETA ▪ PO Box 7177 Stellenbosch 7599 ▪ info@originwine.co.za ▪ www.originwine.co.za ▪ S 33° 52' 39.07" E 018° 48' 35.50" ▪ travel.explains.instant ▪ **T +27 (0)21-865-8100**

Ormonde Private Cellar

This large family estate in Darling moved into its third decade of own-label wine production (a good proportion of the grapes off 300 hectares of vines goes elsewhere) by appointing as winemaker Razvan Macici, the Romanian expatriate who headed up Nederburg winemaking with great distinction for many years. So co-owner and viticulturist Theo Basson can return full-time to the vineyards. There's a welcome return of wines to the flagship Heritage Collection, including an impressive new dessert wine. Ormonde's easy-drinking range, Alexanderfontein, is listed separately.

Ormonde Heritage Collection

★★★★☆ **Vernon Basson** First since **08** (91), **13** (91) from cab & 30% cab franc maturing nicely; tannins still youthful & all-new oak shows on tobacco-fruitcake aromas & palate, with herbal element. Touch sweet on finish. Flavourful & rich but not over-bold at 14.2% alcohol. Still many years to go.

★★★★☆ **Theodore Eksteen** All-new oak dominates the aromas of **13** (92), with the lighter perfumed charm of grenache (35%) & the weightier ripe richness of shiraz. Firm structure beneath the sweet, fairly intense fruit. Has benefited from time in bottle, but will do so further. First made since **08** ★★★☆ (84).

★★★★☆ **Noble Late Harvest** (NEW) Charming delicacy as well as delicious but subtle fullness of fruit on **15** (93) botrytis dessert from chenin. Lovely balance: light (just over 11% alcohol) but not lacking in presence. Only older oak barrels used. 184 g/l sugar leaves no cloy at all on lingering finish. 375 ml.

Ormonde Barrel Selected range

★★★★ **Cabernet Sauvignon** Berry aromas & flavours mingle with tobacco-oak layer on **15** (87). Succulent acid balanced by sweet element & firm but integrated tannin. Juicy & drinkable, but will keep.

★★★★ **Shiraz** Plush, ripe **15** (86) has tobacco, spice & more expressive fruit, with chocolate note on the palate, than the Old Block version. Softly textured, lingering & not too challenging.

★★★★ **Chardonnay** Forward citrus aromas on **15** (86) preview lead to tangy palate with pleasing texture, lemon acidity & plenty of flavour supported by good oak (25% new), considerable finish.

★★★★ Wholebunch Press Sauvignon Blanc Adds essential winemaking description to the varietal name in **19** ⑧⑧ - all free-run juice, no skin contact. Vibrant, well balanced & softly rounded, a touch less fruity than Old Block version. Tasted pre-bottling & very young. No **18**.

Merlot (NEW) **★★★☆** Oaky tobacco notes & dark berries on **15** ⑧⑤. Ripe flavours but also a minty, herbal element. Burly 14.7% alcohol. Dry, grippy tannins, slightly edgy acidity. **Pinot Noir** ⓥ **★★★★** Needs time; **15** ⑧③ unusually dark with intense black berry flavours (versus red fruit of Ondine version). Soft tannins & some earthy mushroom notes.

Ondine Specialities

★★★★ Cabernet Franc ⊘ Attractive as ever, **15** ⑧⑥ has customary perfumed, vanilla-edged aromas & ripe berry notes. Doesn't advertise its 14.4% alcohol, but acid a little overt. Pleasingly grippy.

★★★★ Chardonnay ⓥ Tasted ex tank few years back, **15** ⑧⑥ had liquorice note with oats, nuts, citrus. Rich texture but restrained in effect. Supportively oaked (25% new), as **14 ★★★★** ⑧⑤.

★★★★ Sauvignon Blanc Previewed last year, bottled **17** ⑧⑧ now less overtly fruity, but still with clear passionfruit & a succulent grassy greenness; refreshing acidity part of a pleasing example of the style.

Grenache ★★★★ Fragrant red fruitiness on **16** ⑧⑤. Light & fresh (just 11.9% alcohol), easy but far from trivial; well balanced, with a welcome dry conclusion. **Malbec ★★★☆ 18** ⑧⑤ tank sample - first tasted since **15** ⑧③. Full, fruity aromas & flavours (not intense or lingering) contrast rather nicely with the good dry grip. Unobtrusive oaking, for easy approachability. **Pinot Noir** ⓥ **★★★★** Opening up slowly, **15** ⑧③ light & lithe with earthy strawberries & warm spice, slight rusty metal tang on finish. **Chenin Blanc** ⓥ **★★★☆** Purer fruit on **17** ⑧⑤ than Old Block version though some similar aromas & flavours. Riper, richer, though. Sweet fruit but good dry finish. Discontinued: **Merlot**.

Single-Vineyard Chip Off The Old Block range

★★★★ Sauvignon Blanc ⊘ Ex tank, **19** ⑧⑧ riper in effect than last-tasted **17** ⑧⑥, with stonefruit, ripe apple & some tropical notes. Softly textured, packed with flavour, with good balancing acidity.

Cabernet Sauvignon ⓥ **★★★★ 14** ⑧⑤ pleasing ripe fruit flavours with a herbal element. Sappy tannins, bright acidity, supportive oaking (15% new, 9 months). **Merlot** ⓥ **★★★★ 14** ⑧④ appeals with dark plum & blackberry nose, fruitcake richness, hints of milk chocolate & vanilla. **Shiraz** ⓥ **★★★** Ripe, spicy aromas on fleshy, flavourful **15** ⑧②, with easygoing tannins & very bright acidity giving sweet-sour finish. **Chenin Blanc** ⓥ **★★★★** Peach & melon on **17** ⑧⑤, with a more savoury element of straw & earth too. Nothing too overt. Fresh, balanced. — TJ

Location/WO: Darling ▪ Map: Durbanville, Philadelphia & Darling ▪ Map grid reference: A1 ▪ 1stB 1999 ▪ Tasting & sales Mon-Fri 9—4 Sat/pub hols 9—3 ▪ Closed Good Fri, Dec 25/26 & Jan 1 ▪ Chocolate & Wine and Nougat & Wine pairings by appt @ R60pp ▪ Facilities for children ▪ Walks ▪ Owner(s) Basson family ▪ Winemaker(s) Razvan Macici (Aug 2017, consultant) ▪ Viticulturist(s) Theo Basson ▪ ±300ha (cabs s/f, merlot, mourv, p verdot, pinot, shiraz, chard, chenin, sauv, sem) ▪ 1,000t/70,000cs own label 40% red 60% white ▪ PO Box 201 Darling 7345 ▪ info@ormonde.co.za ▪ www.ormonde.co.za ▪ S 33° 22' 20.2" E 018° 21' 23.6" ▪ ⓦ refereed.resembled.handlebars ▪ **T +27 (0)22-492-3540**

☐ **Orpheus & The Raven** *see* The Vinoneers

Osbloed Wines ⓥ

Celebrating a decade of bottling wine as naturally and adventurously as possible in the garage of his sub-urban Somerset West home, ex-pastor Bertus van Niekerk never runs out of wine ideas or biblical names to give his wines. There are four additions this edition, two featuring grape varieties very rare in SA. His children seem set to follow in his footsteps, qualified winemaker son Hendrik has just done a harvest in California, and daughter Renée is enrolled to study oenology at Stellenbosch University.

Metafisika range

★★★★ Ongelowige Thomas (NEW) Creative, admirable crouchen-led blend with semillon, co-fermented, unfiltered, **16** ⑧⑦ melon & thatch perfume, some preserved lemon, but flavours pure citrus, lemon & lime, with racy acidity giving lift, taut focus. Coastal WO.

Rooiperd ⓦ **★★★☆** Pale crimson wooded cinsaut, **18** ⑧④ follows previous in its cranberry & scrub tones, elegance (12% alcohol). Juicy & flavour packed. Delicious.

Swartperd ★★★★ Inky colour alone makes 'Black Horse' name apt, but **18** ⑧④ cab goes further, rich & densely fruited, plums & mulberries, smoky spice throughout, tannins end firm. A wine to age or match with the right food. **Baäl** (NEW) ★★★ Villard noir (& Blanc sibling hybrid variety) very rare in SA; this & Astarte sole varietal bottlings in guide. Ruby, with crimson edge, intense raspberries on entry but somewhat dissipated by light-textured body (11.5% alcohol). **18** ⑧⓪ nice enough, for early drinking. **Wonderbare Raadsman** ★★★★ Pinotage & its parents, cinsaut & pinot noir (66/22) in **18** ⑧⑤. Co-fermented, older oaked, as Kultus. Piquant red berries, cherries & spice, ripe & smooth, fuller bodied than expected. Single 225L barrel. **Kultus** ★★★★ Inspired by Ch Musar & the Lebanon. Cab with cinsaut, dash shiraz, **18** ⑧⑤ ripe, deep layers of cassis & plums, fleshy & round, enough oak spice for seasoning without tannins being intrusive, ends with nice grip. Single barrique. Previous was NV. **Vaalperd** ★★★★ Barrel wild ferment, as all unless noted, unfiltered chenin, **18** ⑧③'s quince & melon seamed with gentle biscuit, crisp acidity giving length, brightness to the flavours. **Astarte** (NEW) ★★★ Villard blanc, French hybrid variety, as Noir. **18** ⑧① quince & stonefruit, an orange blossom highlight. Low 11% alcohol, but good acidity adds freshness to the gentle flavours. **Buiteperd** ★★★★ 'Outsider' experimental label, last was early-picked crouchen, now extended skin-contact Elgin viognier. Orange gold, sherry-like aromas, **18** ⑧③ has gone beyond fruit, palate still reflecting peach but more kernel than flesh. Ends savoury, Marmite-like tone. Not tasted: **Offerlam**.

Farm Animals range

★★★★ **Blommetjie Fumé Blanc** (NEW) Channels California in fermenting sauvignon in wood, **19** ⑧⑨'s capsicum & grassy tones shine through in perfume & flavours, an intense limy finish wakening the taste buds. Lovely purity. Inoculated ferment, on lees 3 months, unfiltered.

Osbloed ★★★ Blend of red varieties after single barrels filled, 7 here from the range, unfiltered. **18** ⑧① quite savoury, with toasted oak scents, white pepper & spice, ends smoky, but enough fruity succulence for early enjoyment. — CR

Location: Somerset West ▪ Map: Helderberg ▪ Map grid reference: E6 ▪ WO: Stellenbosch/Coastal/Elgin ▪ Est 2009 ▪ 1stB 2010 ▪ Open daily, please call ahead ▪ Tasting fee R50 ▪ Owner(s) Bertus van Niekerk ▪ Cellarmaster(s) Bertus van Niekerk (Jan 2010) ▪ Winemaker(s) Bertus van Niekerk (Jan 2010), with Hendrik van Niekerk (2011) ▪ 18 barrels, some for friends ▪ 60% red 40% white ▪ 33 Eagle Cres Somerset West 7130 ▪ bertus@osbloed.com ▪ www.osbloed.com ▪ S 34° 5' 26.22" E 018° 51' 55.87" ▪ 🖤 invented.preoccupied. deliver ▪ T +27 (0)83-400-2999

Oude Compagnies Post Private Cellar   ⓠ ⌂ ⌾

The Swanepoel family's boutique winery in Tulbagh is being re-energised by Elsenburg-trained, California-seasoned winemaker and son Dirk, who took over the helm from father Jerry in 2018. Dirk has introduced several new wines including a rare white pinotage and an unusual light-styled fortified made with a Greek friend. The visitor venue promised last edition is now open, and other options are available, such as winemaker-presented mountain-top tastings and samplings from barrel. More guest accommodation has been added, and events such as weddings and birthdays are catered for.

Swanepoel range

★★★★ **Syrah Rosé** Palest salmon pink **19** ⑧⑥ blooms in the glass with fragrant berry & spice aromas. Palate is super-fresh, shows good texture & fresh grip for food partnering. Huge improvement on **18** ★★ ⑦④. Previewed, as next.

★★★★ **White Pinotage** (NEW) One of handful on the shelves. **19** ⑧⑥ soft berry fruit & fynbos aromas, good overall balance, creaminess from extended lees ageing, fresh acid balance & mineral tannins softened 6 months in older oak.

Pinotage (NEW) ★★★★ Succulent & dark-fruited **18** ⑧⑤, vibrant & smooth with good depth & blueberry crumble flavours on a clean, crisp palate. Older oak aged, 12 months.

Compagnies Wijn range

★★★★ **SMG** (NEW) Perfumed lavender entices in previewed **18** ⑧⑥, with generous bramble, wild heather & roasted nuts unfolding on supple palate, firm savoury finish. Good balance & well-judged oaking (all older) on near-equal syrah, mourvèdre, grenache.

Cabernet Sauvignon ★★★ An abundance of dark berry & plum flavours with quite a stern tannin structure in **17** ⑧②. Needs time for lovely fruit to unfurl. **Mourvèdre** ★★★ Mulberry, black cherry, liquorice

& olive paste mingle with still-meshing tannins. Pre-bottling, **18** ⑧ has potential, could age interestingly.
Vassileon GPS ⑭ ★★★ Ruby 'port' **18** ⑧ from grenache & pinotage, splash shiraz. Spicy, & though sweet, has low sugar & alcohol for this style, therefore is light-textured & refreshing. 375 ml. Not tasted: **Grenache**, **Pinotage**, **Shiraz**. Occasional release: **The Buchu Trail**. — WB

Location/map/WO: Tulbagh ▪ Map grid reference: F4 ▪ Est 1995 ▪ 1stB 2003 ▪ Tasting & sales Mon-Sat 11-4 ▪ Walking trail ▪ Hiking trail 1-2 days (sleepover on Obiqua mountain in own tent) ▪ Guest accommodation ▪ Weddings & events ▪ Owner(s) Jerry Swanepoel Family Trust ▪ Cellarmaster(s)/winemaker(s) Dirk Swanepoel ▪ Viticulturist(s) Dirk Swanepoel, with Marius Roberts (consultant) ▪ 235ha/10ha (cab, grenache, mourv, ptage, shiraz) ▪ 50t own label 90% red 10% rosé ▪ Other export brands: Buchu Trail, Swanepoel Wines ▪ PO Box 11 Tulbagh 6820 ▪ swanepoel@compagnies.co.za ▪ www.oudecompagnies.com ▪ S 33° 14' 56.9" E 019° 6' 49.1" ▪ **T +27 (0)76-013-8613/+27 (0)82-829-8404**

Oude Denneboom

The De Waal family have farmed in the Voor Paardeberg area for more than 140 years. Concern for the environment led them, among others, to establish a private game reserve on their estate, and it informs their practice of assigning the name of an endangered raptor to their shiraz in exceptional years. The wines are produced off-site by consultants, and marketed in collaboration with two other family ventures, Vendôme and Kuyperskraal, under the banner of Kaapse Familie Wingerde.

★★★★ **Black Harrier Shiraz** ⑫ Ripe, fruity, **16** ⑧ spicy berries, clove, fynbos & hedgerow fruit on nose & palate; well balanced, smooth; the lovely fresh grip begs to be paired with grilled meat. No **15**.

Chenin Blanc ⑦ ★★★ Rewarding & fun everyday white, lively tropical fruit with intriguing soft spiciness (though unoaked), nice tang on exit in **19** ⑧. — WB

Location/map/WO: Paarl ▪ Map grid reference: C2 ▪ 1stB 2003 ▪ Tasting by appt at the estate; also at Vendôme ▪ 4-star self-catering cottages ▪ Private game reserve ▪ Owner(s) De Waal family ▪ GM Willem de Waal ▪ Winemaker(s) Altus le Roux (consultant) ▪ Viticulturist(s) Willem de Waal ▪ 199ha/±62ha (cab, mourv, ptage, shiraz, chenin, nouvelle, viog) ▪ 600t/1,000cs own label 60% red 40% white ▪ WIETA ▪ PO Box 2087 Windmeul 7630 ▪ info@oudedenneboom.co.za ▪ www.oudedenneboom.co.za, www.kaapsefamiliewingerde.com ▪ S 33° 37' 47.28" E 018° 51' 55.08" ▪ ⓔ granules.hawking.remainder ▪ **T +27 (0)21-869-8072/+27 (0)83-357-9756**

☐ **Oude Kaap** see DGB (Pty) Ltd
☐ **Oudekloof Winery** See Editor's Note

Oude Molen Distillery

This famous distillery was founded over a century back in Stellenbosch but is now based in Elgin, where visitors can now enjoy an interactive distillery tour. Oude Molen's founding distiller, French-born René Santhagens, played a crucial role in the history of Cape spirits, encouraging superior brandy-making based on double distillation in copper potstills. The French connection has been reinforced by Oude Molen using the traditional Cognac labels VS, VSOP and XO to distinguish quality for their potstill brandies.

Cape Brandy range
★★★★★ **XO** ⑭ Longer ageing (minimum 10 years) of the XO ⑨③ adds lighter, airier fruit (peach, pear) & floral, nutty notes to the bouquet, & silkier slippery smoothness to the palate. Not without richness, but also elegance. Like all these, from a mix of chenin, colombard, cinsaut.

★★★★ **VSOP** Minimum 5 years ageing. The VSOP ⑧⑨ more elegant, smooth, integrated & complex than VS. Nutty, subtly peach-fruity, with chocolate & orange-peel. Lingering power.

★★★★ **VS** All potstill ⑧⑥, minimum 3 years aged in a solera system. Forceful, but dry, refined & smooth enough, & not too fiery for solo sipping. Sweet apricot notes & wood overtones.— TJ

Location/map: Elgin ▪ Map grid reference: B1 ▪ Tastings Mon-Fri 11-4 (booking advisable) ▪ Fee R85pp ▪ Sales Mon-Fri 11-5 ▪ Closed all pub hols ▪ Interactive tasting experience ▪ Tour groups ▪ MD Andre Simonis ▪ Brandy master(s) Kobus Gelderblom (Jun 2013, consultant), with Andy Neil & Lara Patrick ▪ PO Box 494 Grabouw

7160 ▪ info@oudemolen.co.za ▪ www.oudemolen.co.za ▪ S 34° 8' 27.77" E 019° 1' 15.64" ▪ ⬛ fines.moisture. passport ▪ **T +27 (0)21-859-2517**

☐ **Out of Africa** *see* Jacques Germanier
☐ **Ovation** *see* Thokozani Wines

Overgaauw Wine Estate

Fourth-generation winemaker David van Velden sees no need to change what his forebears established on this charming Victorian-era Stellenboschkloof farm, its tin roofs and lacy veranda trim a rarity in the winelands. The family's low-key mien belies a trailblazing heritage: planting classic Portuguese varieties for port wine; introducing small oak barrels for red-wine maturation; helping pioneer single-variety merlots; co-founding the Stellenbosch Wine Route and Cape Winemakers Guild, among others. David is simply consolidating – scrapping the Shepherd's Cottage label – and focusing on heritage: SA's only sylvaner, marching towards its 50th vintage; the new sauvignon celebrating the farm's founder; and the return of the former CWG Auction-only DC Classic red blend.

★★★★ **Merlot** Youthful **17** ⑧⑥ has a distinctly piquant, minty nuance to red-fruited core. Less integrated & even more tightly coiled than **16** ⑧⑧, needing time to resolve.

★★★★☆ **DC Classic** Stellar return to the guide of this Bordeaux blend, previously for CWG auctions, now a 3-bottle wooden box set. Bright merlot (85%) & cab franc duo in **15** ⑨⓪. Minty nuance to perfumed red fruit & fine dry tannins, from strict fruit selection & all-new French oak (24 months). Still tightly woven, will unfurl gracefully over a few years.

★★★★☆ **Tria Corda** Similar cab, merlot, cab franc blend partners & oak (60% new) to **14** ⑨①, but more complexity in fine **15** ⑨②. Smoky cassis, cedar & polished leather all hint at future delights.

★★★★ **Sylvaner** Unique varietal bottling in SA. Previewed **19** ⑧⑦ lanolin, almond & starfruit flavours, gently insistent, with some viscosity. Mature vines also impart a flor-like character, dry freshness & minerality. Unoaked, like last-made **16** ★★★★ ⑧③.

★★★★☆ **Cape Vintage** ⓿ Classic, superbly dry, vibrantly spicy & rich **98** ★★★★★ ⑨⑤ 'port' calls on touriga nacional & equal tintas barocca & roriz, touriga franca, souzão & cornifesto for complexity. Bold & nutty, it's structured from 30 months in 1,300L vats. Good for further half-decade. Last tasted was **96** ⑨⓪.

Abraham Sauvignon Blanc (NEW) ★★★★ Tribute to estate's founder. 5% new-oak fraction adds a touch of toasty magic to clean, lingering starfruit flavours in **18** ⑧⑤. Not tasted: **Touriga Nacional**. Discontinued: **Shepherd's Cottage Cabernet Sauvignon-Merlot, Shepherd's Cottage Sauvignon Blanc**. — MW

Location/map/WO: Stellenbosch ▪ Map grid reference: D5 ▪ Est 1905 ▪ 1stB 1970 ▪ Tasting by appt only on weekdays ▪ Closed Easter Fri-Mon, Dec 25/26 & Jan 1 ▪ Venue facilities available ▪ Owner(s) Braam & David van Velden ▪ Winemaker(s) David van Velden (Jan 2003) ▪ Viticulturist(s) David van Velden ▪ 100ha/60ha (cabs s/f, merlot, ptage, touriga, sauv, sylvaner) ▪ 60% red 40% white ▪ HACCP, IPW ▪ PO Box 3 Vlottenburg 7604 ▪ info@overgaauw.co.za, venue@overgaauw.co.za ▪ www.overgaauw.co.za ▪ S 33° 56' 52.1" E 018° 47' 33.4" ▪ ⬛ passport.groomed.suitcase ▪ **T +27 (0)21-881-3815**

Overhex Wines International

This large Worcester-based winery continues to develop its brand-building digital marketing technology. Some of their wines (still as friendly to the pocket as to the palate) have creative, digitally interactive labels. The Mensa range was the first in SA supported by an augmented reality app, now further improved, to bring the story to life, while the Balance wines are linked to an online game relating to the range's alignment with the conservation of desert elephants. Aloof from high-tech (for now) are the top-tier wines, joined by the medalled Survivor Pinotage Reserve and Wild Yeast Syrah.

Survivor range
★★★★ **Cabernet Sauvignon** Dark & spicy fruit constrained by more new oak (now 20%, French & Hungarian) on **18** ⑧⑦ barrel sample. Gives a drier, leaner impression than **17** ⑧⑨. Like the pinotages, matured 15 months. This range WO Swartland unless noted.

★★★★ **Pinotage** More appealing dark & spicy plum tone to **18** ⑧⑧ preview. Same oak regime (20%, 15 months) but more balanced than **17** ⑧⑥, with clean dry farewell & potential for development.

★★★★ **Pinotage Reserve** (NEW) Ripe & brooding in its intensity, with dark plum & liquorice flavours. 20% new oak maturation adds further spice to **17** (86). Robust & almost overblown, will have its fans.

★★★★ **Wild Yeast Syrah** (NEW) Pre-bottling, **18** (86) billows white pepper & fragrant scrub. Partly bunch pressed, naturally fermented & older-oak matured 12 months. Bold & ripe, almost chewy, but finishes drier. Ample flavour & drinkability. WO W Cape.

★★★★ **Chenin Blanc** Similar tangy dried peach flavours on **19** (89) pre-bottling sample. And, like previous, well-crafted oak (70% new French, fermented & matured) adds a rich, toasted nut nuance.

★★★★ **Sauvignon Blanc** Fresher profile on **19** (87), sampled ex tank, than drier & smoother **18** (86). Also partly oak fermented/matured, with similar grapefruit/nectarine flavours & food-styled feisty acidity.

Not tasted: Wild Yeast Chardonnay. Discontinued: **Méthode Cap Classique Brut**.

Survivor Offspring range

Not tasted: **Cape Red Blend**, **Cape White Blend**.

Balance Winemaker's Selection

Chardonnay ⊘ 🏵 ★★★★ Supple & creamy **19** (83) has a hint of butterscotch from a brush of oak, balanced by twist of lime. Lithe & light - 12.5% alcohol (or less for the other whites). **Chenin Blanc** ⊘ 🏵 ★★★★ Golden Delicious apple in a glass. Tangy & light **19** (83) exudes flavour, with lees-infused smooth texture. A summer delight. **Pinot Grigio** ⊘ 🏵 ★★★ Not discontinued as we thought, cool-as-a-cucumber **19** (81) is a fine example of the variety, with appealing hint of florality. A dew-fresh al fresco quaffer.

Cabernet Sauvignon (ℤ) ★★★ Distinct cocoa flavour with touch tannin to structure juicy dark fruit, nice freshness too. **17** (81) good barbecue/campfire partner. **Merlot** ★★★ Piquant red fruit & minty nuance to ex-barrel **18** (80). Some tannic grip, too, from oak ageing (staves, as for all these reds), nothing a nice lamb chop wouldn't resolve. **Pinot Noir** ⊘ ★★★ A tad less harmonious & friendly in **18** (80). Still a good core of fruit, just needing time for the charry oak nuance to integrate. **Shiraz** ★★★ Preview of **18** (81) has pliable dry tannins with a ripe, salty liquorice tone. **Sauvignon Blanc** ⊘ ★★★★ Graceful **19** (83) shows clean starfruit flavours & subtle waxy undertone. Touch more sugar than Mensa version, & fresh, balanced step up on previous. Discontinued: **Pinotage**.

Mensa range

Chenin Blanc-Pinot Grigio 🏵 ★★★★ Mostly chenin with 20% pinot grigio giving a bright floral lift to **19** (84). Like previous, creamy but fresh, engaging & different.

Cabernet Sauvignon ★★★ Drier, more savoury tone to **18** (82). Still balanced, with enough fruit for pleasurable armchair enjoyment. **Shiraz-Malbec** ★★★ 70/30 blend with brush of oak. **18** (81) pre-bottling more savoury, drier styled, still balanced & enough sappy fruit to enjoy. Feels lighter than 14.5 % alcohol. **Chardonnay-Pinot Noir** ★★★ Laid-back quaffing with a book on the deck. Preview of **19** (81) (80/20 mix) rosé shows stonefruit & cranberry flavours in dry, juicy & fresh style. **Sauvignon Blanc** ★★★ Driest of the sauvignons, **19** (82) has good stonefruit & citrus backing, with similar creamy lees undertone. More breadth than both siblings. Succulent step up on previous.

Balance Classic range

Cabernet Sauvignon-Merlot ★★☆ Piquantly fresh & cheery **18** (79) with gentle berry flavours. A relaxed sipper, unoaked. **Semi-Sweet Rosé** ★★☆ Pinotage & shiraz in this **19** (79) strawberry-toned tipple. Light (12%), fragrant & friendly, could also work with a light curry. **Muscat** ★★☆ All raisined charm, with jasmine & citrus blossom too. **19** (79) muscat d'Alexandrie in semi-sweet style but fresh & delicate. **Sauvignon Blanc** ★★☆ Bright **19** (79) has tangy & crunchy green apple, herb flavours. Some sugar to balance. Light & summery. Not tasted: **Pinotage-Shiraz**, **Shiraz-Merlot**, **Chenin Blanc-Colombar**.

Balance Sparklings

Sweet Temptation Sparkling (ℤ) ★★ Sweet strawberry pink fizz from pinotage, **NV** (74) friendly fun for the sweeter toothed, at a low 8% alcohol. **Boldly Brut Sparkling** (ℤ) ★★★ From sauvignon, dry styled, but plenty sweet green herb/starfruit flavour & fizz to ensure **NV** (78) will have many fans.

Discontinued: **Limited Edition range**, **Magaliesburg range**. — MW

Location/map: Worcester ▪ Map grid reference: B3 ▪ WO: Western Cape/Swartland ▪ Est/1stB 2006 ▪ Tasting & sales Mon-Thu 8—5 Fri 8-4 Sat/Sun 9-4 ▪ Tasting fees: Balance R10/2 wines, R20/4 wines; Survivor R15/2 wines, R30/4 wines; Mensa R10/3 wines ▪ Closed Easter Fri-Tue & Dec 23-Jan 3 ▪ Cellar tours by appt ▪ Overhex Winery & Bistro Mon-Sun 9.30-3.30 ▪ Facilities for children ▪ Tour groups ▪ Conferences ▪ Weddings & functions ▪ Owner(s) G van der Wath ▪ MD Gert van Wyk ▪ Winemaker(s) Willie Malan (2002) & Ben Snyman (Dec 2010), with Dirk Rust (Jan 2012) & Heinrich Carstens (Jan 2014) ▪ Viticulturist(s) Hennie Visser & Hanno van Schalkwyk ▪ 12,500t 35% red 62% white 3% rosé ▪ ISO 22000, Fairtrade, IPW, WIETA ▪ PO Box 139 Worcester 6849 ▪ marketing@overhex.com ▪ www.overhex.com ▪ S 33° 39' 28.6" E 019° 30' 55.8" ▪ ⓦ patrol.cross.surfed ▪ T +27 (0)23-347-5012

Overmeer Cellars

Enduring (since 1986) no-frills range by Distell, with modest alcohol levels. In 3L & 5L packs.
Red ✓ ★★★ Pinotage, ruby cab & cinsaut work well together to give NV (77) its red berry character, smooth easy drinkability. **Grand Cru** ★★ Mainly chenin & colombard, latest NV (74) is dry & fruity-fresh. **Stein** ✓ ★★★ Chenin & colombard partnership gives NV (77) apple & pear flavours, nicely rounded body from semi-sweet styling, fresh finish. **Late Harvest** ★★ Like with Stein, blend of chenin & colombard, this NV (74) sweeter, has fruit salad flavours, softly round. **Sweet Rosé** ★★ Sweetest of the range, bright-coloured & berry-fruited NV (74) goes down easily. — CR

☐ **Over the Mountain** *see* Seven Springs Vineyards

PaardenKloof

Three rivers form the boundaries of the PaardenKloof home-farm, which is very extensive at 1,430 hectares yet has fewer than 25 ha planted with vines, the remainder is given over to nature to run its course. The wines from this cool coastal parcel are produced by top consultants and available at nearby Ecology Lifestyle Farm on the R43 between Hermanus and Bot River, with amenities to entertain the whole family.

PaardenKloof Private Collection
★★★★★ **Die Fynboshuis Cabernet Sauvignon** Ⓥ Sumptuous & concentrated red berry fruit, exotic dried flower aromas & flavours on **10** (92), with outstanding structure & dimension.
Springtide Sauvignon Blanc Ⓥ ★★★★ Vivid & tangy grapefruit, fynbos & granadilla, **17** (84) broad on palate with long flinty tail.

Peter Clarke Collection
★★★★ **The Kiss Pinot Noir** Ⓥ Eight months in 20% new French oak & further 50 months in bottle result in seamless integration of bright acidity, spicy cherry fruit & deeper oak notes on **13** (87).
★★★★ **The Long Road Shiraz** Ⓥ Aromatic plum, fynbos & white pepper aromas on **10** (87). Perfectly judged oak provides framework for lush, bright fruit, rounded mouthfeel & restraint.
★★★★ **Bend In The Road Sauvignon Blanc** Ⓥ Cool-climate expression, **14** (88) with lime & grapefruit; bright & focused flavours, refreshing orchard & fynbos notes with piquant conclusion.
Gaiety Sauvignon Blanc Ⓥ ★★★ Gunsmoke whiffs, attractive gravelly minerality, **10** (81) lightly flavoured so acidity is apparent.

Ecology range
★★★★ **Cabernet Sauvignon** Ⓥ Fynbos nuances to structured, gentle succulence on **14** (86); shows good intensity; long, fruity, tobacco-tinged finish.
Shiraz Ⓥ ★★★★ Blueberry ease & plushness on **14** (85), juicy black fruit framed by soft squeeze of tannin from 25% new oak. Not tasted: **Sauvignon Blanc**. — FM

Location/WO: Bot River ▪ Map: Walker Bay & Bot River ▪ Map grid reference: C3 C2 ▪ Est 2003 ▪ 1stB 2007 ▪ PaardenKloof & Ecology wines: tasting & sales at Ecology Lifestyle Farm Mon-Sun 9-5; PaardenKloof estate visits by appt ▪ Ecology Restaurant Mon-Sun 8.30-5 ▪ Farmyard animals & jungle gym ▪ Wedding venue ▪ Day conference venue ▪ Tour groups ▪ Protea & fynbos nursery ▪ Decor service ▪ Farmstall ▪ Craft beer ▪ Winemaker(s) Kobie Viljoen, Niels Verburg & Adam Mason ▪ Viticulturist(s) Kevin Watt (Dec 2006) ▪ 23.6ha (cab, pinot, shiraz, sauv) ▪ IPW, WIETA ▪ PO Box 381 Bot River 7185 ▪ info@paardenkloof.co.za, info@ecologylifestyle.co.za ▪ www.paardenkloof.co.za, www.ecologylifestyle.co.za ▪ S 34° 17' 44.1" E 019° 14' 5.4" (PaardenKloof), S 34° 15' 39.98" E 019° 11' 04.96" (Ecology Lifestyle Farm) ▪ ⓦ stockpile.baking.actuality, participate.pebbled.zoologists ▪ T +27 (0)28-284-9824 (PaardenKloof)/+27 (0)28-284-9809 (Ecology Lifestyle Farm)

☐ **Paarl Families** *see* Kaapse Familie Wingerde

Paarl Perlé

This Distillers Corporation brand became a hit fifty years ago when lightly fizzy wines were all the rage, and it retains its sweetly sparkling character under Distillers' successor, Distell.

Paarl Perlé ★★ Unchanging style, **NV** ⑦⑤ blend of chenin & muscat d'Alexandrie; has grapey aromas, gentle sweetness. Also in 1L, 2L. — CR

Packwood Wines   ⓠ ⑪ ⌂ ◉

There's much to keep visitors to this Garden Route country estate and boutique winery owned by UK émigrés Peter and Vicky Gent occupied and content, from 4-star luxury accommodation to mountain bike trails. Of course there's wine, too, reflective of the maritime climate. Vicky tends the source small vineyard herself but recently enlisted winemaking support in the person of Sollie Sauerman, previously at Glen Carlou.

★★★★ Sauvignon Blanc Reflects cool origins in restrained 11% alcohol, piquant acidity, lipsmacking dryness. **18 ★★★☆** ⑧④ green apple in aroma, flavour & pithiness, shade less intensity than **17** ⑧⑥. **Blanc de Noir ★★★☆** Partridge eye hue of **18** ⑧④ from pinot noir. Satisfying weight & vinosity at modest alcohol, understated toastiness from 8 months in older oak. **Chardonnay ★★★☆** Barrel-fermented/aged **18** ⑧③ packs plenty of flavour into a slender body. Lemons, interesting apricot kernel note, lively acidity & creamy finish from regular bâtonnage. **Gent Méthode Cap Classique Brut ★★★** Chardonnay (80%) with pinot noir in **NV** ⑧② celebratory sparkler, lovely & dry, lightish, with overt toasty aromas & flavours, subtler lemon & berry nuances. Not tasted: **Pinot Noir**. Discontinued: **Pinot Noir Rosé**. — CvZ

Location/WO: Plettenberg Bay ▪ Map: Klein Karoo & Garden Route ▪ Map grid reference: C1 ▪ Est 2006 ▪ 1stB 2009 ▪ Tasting & sales Mon-Fri 11-3 Sat/Sun 10-3 pub hols by prior arrangement ▪ Cheese & wine lunch - book ahead ▪ Small tour groups by appt ▪ Farm produce ▪ Hikes ▪ MTB trail ▪ 4-star country house & self-catering cottages ▪ Owner(s) Peter & Vicky Gent ▪ Winemaker(s) Vicky Gent (2009) & Sollie Sauerman (2019) ▪ Viticulturist(s) Vicky Gent (Jan 2006) ▪ 380ha/3.5ha (pinot, chard, sauv) ▪ 5t/10,000cs own label 30% red 70% white ▪ PO Box 622 Knysna 6570 ▪ vicky@packwood.co.za ▪ www.packwood.co.za ▪ S 34° 0' 18.77" E 023° 13' 43.33" ▪ 🖳 signposts.visiting.zing ▪ T +27 (0)82-253-9621

☐ **Paddagang** *see* Tulbagh Winery
☐ **Painted Dog** *see* Painted Wolf Wines

Painted Wolf Wines   ⓠ ⑪

Named best producer overall at the 2019 Trophy Wine Show, the 'pack' led by Jeremy and Emma Borg was also recognised by Forbes magazine as one of four outstanding SA producers doing things in a different and dynamic way – in short, helping conserve the endangered Painted Wolf (African Wild Dog) while producing 'wines with character that offer fair value across the board'. More good news, for their wine fans and conservation partners alike, is that they're now also sourcing grapes from Breedekloof, Wellington and Walker Bay 'to offset the possibility of yet another dry period and to position ourselves for future growth'.

Pictus range

★★★★☆ VII ⓝⓔⓦ Limited-edition blend, 'Lycaon pictus' scientific name for wild dog, **17** ⑨① combines Swartland grenache & 34% shiraz with 15% old-vine carignan ex Wellington. Wild ferment & judicious oaking for red fruit concentration with pepper & spice.

Discontinued: **IV, V, VI**.

Black Pack range

★★★★☆ Mourvèdre ⓝⓔⓦ ⊘ ⍟ Usually blended in Pictus, tiny yields bottled varietally with 5% syrah in **17** ⑨③, 11 months in combo French/American oak, 30% new, adding to cocoa-enrobed dark berry appeal, concentrated yet silky & remarkably fresh. Organically grown Swartland grapes.

★★★★☆ **Walker Bay Pinot Noir** (NEW) ⊘ Grapes ex Stanford, 20% wholebunch, 11 months in old oak. **18** (90) has tangy red fruit galore, cherries & cranberries layered with earthy & herbal nuances, spicy finish enhanced by fresh acidity.

★★★★ **Walker Bay Syrah** (NEW) 9 months in barrel (20% new, mostly French) underpin **18** (87)'s violet perfume, plum & cherry fruit; quite tannic, acidic, in youth less harmonious than Swartland sibling.

★★★★ **Chenin Blanc** Happily not discontinued as we thought. Wild/barrel-fermented **18** (86), aged 9 months in 40% new French oak, has rich & creamy texture, subtle citrus fruit, still tight.

In abeyance: **Paarl Pinotage**.

Pack range

★★★★☆ **Guillermo Swartland Pinotage** Honours longtime grower Billy 'Guillermo' Hughes, though **17** (91) sourced from others due to drought-reduced crop; also-tasted **18** (90) does have some BH fruit. Both wines wild fermented, aged in 30% new French and American oak, vibrant & juicy with subtle spice, soft tannins.

★★★★ **Swartland Syrah** Silky **17** ★★★★★ (92) leaner, more elegant than **15** (87), 14 months in oak (20% new) adding hints of baking spice to scents/flavours of fynbos, white pepper & tangy red fruit. Seamless & seductive. Off organically farmed vines. No **16**.

★★★★ **Lycaon Old Vine Chenin Blanc** (NEW) (⊛) Intense concentration of apricot & citrus fruit on **18** (89), from 45 year old vines in Wellington, 50% barrel-fermented/aged 9 months for creamy texture & savoury spice.

★★★★ **Old Vine Chenin Blanc** (⊘) Wild/barrel-fermented **17** ★★★★★ (90) from two 30+ year old blocks in Paarl, creamy, complex with luscious melange melon, guava & stonefruit, touch vanilla from 15% new oak, zesty/pithy grapefruit finish, fresh acidity & pleasing 12.5% alcohol. Step up on **15** (87). No **16**.

★★★★ **Paarl Roussanne** (⊛) Wild-fermented in light-toast 500L barrels, 50% new, **18** ★★★★★ (93) impresses with broad, beeswaxy mouthfeel, savoury spice as well as chamomile & vanilla complementing white peach & pear fruit. More mouthfilling & delicious than last-made **15** (87). Paarl WO.

★★★★ **Penny Viognier** (⊛) Tribute to 'beautiful & poised' late wife of Swartland grower Billy Hughes, **18** (88) now ex Breedekloof mountain vines, mineral finesse balancing spiced peaches & cream (5 months in new French oak). No **15 - 17**.

Not tasted: **Lycaon Grenache**.

Peloton range

★★★★ **Blanc** Looks to 'capture the spirit of southern France... where wine, cycling & conservation meet'. Chenin-led **18** (87) with 20% grenache blanc, 10% viognier (9 months in oak) well-padded with stonefruit, cream & spice. No **17**.

Not tasted: **Rouge**.

The Den Comfort Wines

Cabernet Sauvignon ★★★ 'Social wines to be enjoyed with friends & family.' Middleweight **18** (80) preview has black fruit buffed with oak staves in tank, as all these reds. Coastal WO. **Pinotage** ★★★ Chocolate on the nose, **18** (82) juicy mulberries & plums on well-formed palate, ideal partner for Mexican fajitas, says winemaker (a trained chef). WO W Cape. **Shiraz** ★★★ Bright berries vie with obvious wood in **18** (82), smooth & quite savoury. **Pinotage Rosé** ★★★ Less acerbic than previous, dry, fresh & food-friendly **19** (80) has sweet-sour cranberry & fresh ruby grapefruit flavours. **Chenin Blanc** ★★★☆ Ex Swartland, 2 batches naturally fermented, riper portion with staves, pre-bottling **19** (85) has cling peach & guava flavours, creamy depth & spicy finish. **Sauvignon Blanc** ★★★☆ Tropical **19** (84) blends cooler Darling & warmer Swartland fruit, smooth & refreshing, with fig, granadilla & gooseberry flavours.

Cape 'Hunting' Blends

Not tasted: **Madach**. — JG

Location/map: Paarl ▪ Map grid reference: E5 ▪ WO: Swartland/Coastal/Paarl/Walker Bay/Breedekloof/ Wellington/Western Cape ▪ Est/1stB 2007 ▪ Tasting, wine by the glass & sales Tue-Sat (seasonal hrs) ▪ Fee various; 5% of sales donated to conservation & social upliftment ▪ Closed Sun/Mon, Easter Fri-Mon, Dec 25 & Jan 1 ▪ SIT Café ▪ Owner(s) Jeremy & Emma Borg, & 16 'pack members' ▪ Cellarmaster(s) Madre van der Walt ▪ Winemaker(s) Jeremy Borg ▪ 20ha (grenache, mourv, ptage, shiraz, viog) ▪ 30t/20,000cs own label 75% red 20% white 5% rosé ▪ Other export brands: Painted Dog, Jemma ▪ 125 Main Rd, Paarl 7646 ▪ wines@paintedwolfwines.com ▪ www.paintedwolfwines.com ▪ S 33° 45' 9.34" E 018° 57' 44.06" ▪ ☒ fish. graphic.chapters ▪ **T +27 (0)21-863-2492**

☐ **Palesa Fairtrade** *see* Daschbosch
☐ **Pandora's Box** *see* Nicholson Smith
☐ **Papillon** *see* Van Loveren Family Vineyards

Parow Brandy

Afrikaans rapper Jack Parow is a keen brandy drinker, like his 'fan demographic'. 'Brandy should be a fun and edgy drink' the thinking goes, so the packaging is wild and funny and brilliant, and the contents, developed by brandy master Kobus Gelderblom at Oude Molen, impressive for the category.

Parow Brandy ⓧ ★★★★ 30% potstill brandy ⑧④ from colombard & chenin, smooth, flavourful & unfiery enough to sip solo - helped by dryness rare for this type. Mostly destined for mixing, however. — TJ

Location: Cape Town ▪ Closed to public ▪ Owner(s) Natures Own Beverages (Pty) Ltd ▪ Brandy master Kobus Gelderblom (Oude Molen Distillery) ▪ PO Box 369 Bonnievale 6730 ▪ info@parowbrandy.co.za ▪ www. parowbrandy.co.za ▪ **T +27 (0)23-616-2010**

Paserene   ⓧ ⑪

Martin Smith's venture began while he still made wine at Vilafonté in Stellenbosch. He has since gained a business partner in Ndabe Mareda, relocated to Franschhoek, where he recently opened a stylish visitor lounge, and devotes his time to building his boutique wine portfolio, with another range, Shiner, to follow. The winery name comes from Passeriformes, the order of 'travelling and free' birds that includes martins and the swallows featured on his labels — aptly so, given his previous extended working residence in California.

★★★★☆ **Union** ⓧ Expressive & voluptuous Rhône-style blend from Tulbagh fruit, **16** ⑨③ red berry, violet & lavender, Xmas spice perfume from 22 months older oak, savoury truffle finish. Syrah (44%), carignan (34%) & mourvèdre.

★★★★☆ **Marathon** ⓧ Impressive three-way partnership cab (53%), petit verdot & splash rare-in-SA carmenère; **16** ⑨④ blackcurrant, mulberry & cedar tones; like petit verdot-dominated **15** ⑨③, tight-knit tannins for the long haul but with sufficient fruit, freshness to broach young.

★★★★☆ **Chardonnay** ⓐ Wild yeast fermented/aged 18 months, 40% new, **17** ⑨④ from Elgin shows a cool-climate citrus profile, given breadth & richness by nutty biscuit savouriness. Not a shy bone in its body, lovely personality & style. — CR

Location/map: Franschhoek ▪ Map grid reference: C4 ▪ WO: Tulbagh/Elgin/Western Cape ▪ Est/1stB 2013 ▪ Tasting Mon-Sun 10-5 ▪ Cheese platters ▪ Owner(s) Martin Smith & Ndabe Mareda ▪ Cellarmaster(s)/ winemaker(s) Martin Smith (Jan 2013) ▪ Viticulturist(s) Martin Smith ▪ 60t/1,400cs own label 60% red 40% white ▪ Farm 1665, on R45 Franschhoek 7690 ▪ info@paserene.co.za ▪ www.paserene.co.za ▪ S 33° 52' 43.8" E 019° 3' 34.1" ▪ ☒ endorsed.lifesavers.dunk ▪ **T +27 (0)21-876-2714**

☐ **Passions** *see* Cavalli Wine & Stud Farm

Patatsfontein

This remarkable wine venture (formerly under the name Ron Burgundy) showcases the talents — and the commitment to terroir expression and hands-off winemaking — of Reenen Borman of Boschkloof. But here, in partnership with friends Fritz Schoon and Henk Kotze, he also moves beyond Stellenbosch for grapes. Notably to often under-appreciated Montagu — and even less appreciated colombard. He's still waiting for the right vintage, he says, to make his first single-vineyard wine from that grape. Meanwhile, in Boschkloof's cellar, cement tanks play an ever-growing role in making these wines, with the brilliant 2018 Syrah being matured entirely in them.

★★★★★ **Sons of Sugarland Syrah** ⓐ No oaking on outstanding, best-yet **18** ★★★★★ ⑨⑦ - just cement vessels for 11 months. From a single Polkadraai Hills vineyard. Pure & precise, almost ethereal, yet with a fine sensual richness of fruit & dry spice, & firm structure. Even more impressive than **17** ⑨④.

★★★★☆ **Patatsfontein Steen** ⊛ From a chenin single-vineyard in Montagu, the grapes wholebunch & naturally fermented, like all these. **18** ⑨③'s fragrance leads to a supple, silky palate with a bright acidic line & lingering apricot finish. In youth, gains in harmony with decanting, but best in a good few years.

★★★★☆ **Patatsblanc 18** ★★★★ ⑧⑧ has 52% colombard, the chenin component up on **17** ⑨②. Fresh, attractive fairly shy aromas; modest, easygoing palate with a stony element. More austere than previous, & less lingering, but still a good advertisement for an underrated, usually simply fruity variety.— TJ

Location: Stellenbosch ▪ WO: Montagu/Stellenbosch ▪ 1stB 2014 ▪ Closed to public ▪ Owner(s) Fritz Schoon, Reenen Borman & Henk Kotze ▪ Winemaker(s) Reenen Borman ▪ 1,500cs own label ▪ reenen@boschkloofwines.com

Paul Cluver Estate Wines ⑨ ⑪ ◎ ⑤

This substantial estate pioneered commercial winefarming in Elgin in the late 1980s. As in the valley as a whole, applegrowing remains important, but the Paul Cluver wines continue to gather prestige, with the family of the founder, neurosurgeon Dr Paul Cluver, fully involved. The focus is on white wines in this cooler climate, with pinot noir the only red. All of them tend to the classic in style and are widely regarded as benchmarks. Social and environmental sustainability have always been of central concern – the latter reflected in WWF-SA Conservation Champion status. The restaurant on the estate has been refurbished (its name, Salt, reflects the personal collection of one of the owners of 147 salts from around the world), and the mountain bike route has been revamped.

CWG Auction Reserve range
★★★★☆ **Pinot Noir** ⊛ Sourced from highest-lying vineyards, **17** ⑨④ reflects this in delightful purity of red-berry fruit, mingled with spicy & savoury hints. Refined tannins (after 9 months polishing in 20% new oak), smooth acidity & mineral notes bode well for cellaring.

Estate range
★★★★ **Pinot Noir** More new (27%) & longer oak than Seven Flags, but fruit notes of sour cherry & cranberry are undimmed, in fact expressed quite flamboyantly, & mesh well with spice & savoury undertones from the wood. Fine tannins & fresh acidity in harmonious balance in **18** ⑧⑧.

★★★★☆ **Seven Flags Pinot Noir** ⊛ Best barrels for the flagship. Splendid **17** ⑨④, vibrant cherry fruit paves way for spice & savoury nuances from 11 months in 300L barrels, 14% new. Bright natural acidity combined with soft & fine tannins interwoven with deep minerality.

★★★★☆ **Chardonnay** ⊛ Subtler oaking (9 months, 20% new) than Seven Flags & only 15% malo give lively citrus, peach & honey tones centre stage in wild-fermented **18** ⑨③. Seamless & fresh, ends with a delicious baked apple persistence.

★★★★☆ **Seven Flags Chardonnay** ⊛ Naturally fermented/9 months in 40% new oak & 30% malo create a lavish wine with a rich fruit core of peach, melon & fig fruit. Rich, creamy palate balanced by clean-cut acidity, flint & oak spice emerge on the finish of poised **18** ⑨③.

★★★★☆ **Riesling** ⊘ ⊛ Excellent varietal expression. Aromatic & floral **18** ⑨③ has citrus blossom, perfumed apple & lime with sweet spice undertone from quarter old-oaked component. Semi-dry style, the sugar effortlessly matched by zippy acidity (19.5, 7.9 g/l).

★★★★☆ **Sauvignon Blanc** ⊘ Quintessential cool-climate styling. **19** ⑨② lime, greengage, fig & gooseberry abundance, touches nettle & crunchy apple on palate, lovely texture from a dash of semillon & touch of oak.

Village Pinot Noir ⊘ ⑪ ★★★★ Light-hearted & delicious **18** ⑧④, generous cherry & redcurrant fruit fused with spice & salami undertones, much subtler oak character (combo 300L/500L barrel & vat, just 11% new) than pinot siblings. Appetising price, too.

Not tasted: **Riesling Noble Late Harvest**. Discontinued: **Dry Encounter Riesling**. — GM

Location/map/WO: Elgin ▪ Map grid reference: C2 ▪ Est 1896 ▪ 1stB 1997 ▪ Tasting centre: tasting & sales Tue-Fri 9-4 Sat/Sun 10-4 ▪ Fee R50-70pp; groups by appt only ▪ Closed Mondays, Easter Fri/Mon, Dec 25/26 & Jan 1; tasting centre closed Sundays for period of 12 weeks in winter ▪ SALT restaurant T +27 (0)21-844-0012, saltatpaulcluver@gmail.com: Tue-Sun 8.30-4, booking essential ▪ Conservation area (part of Kogelberg Biosphere UNESCO heritage site) ▪ MTB track & bike park open to public, fee payable ▪ Owner(s) Cluver family ▪ Cellarmaster(s) Andries Burger (Nov 1996) ▪ Winemaker(s) Anné van Heerden (Dec 2016) ▪ Viticulturist(s) Rudi

Zandberg (Dec 2013) ▪ 8oha (pinot, chard, riesling, sauv) ▪ 20% red 80% white ▪ Brands for clients: Woolworths, ScruCap ▪ WWF-SA Conservation Champion ▪ PO Box 48 Grabouw 7160 ▪ info@cluver.com ▪ www.cluver.com ▪ S 34° 10' 7.25" E 019° 5' 9.35" ▪ *uphill.crested.strop* ▪ **T +27 (0)21-844-0605**

☐ **Paul de Villiers** *see* Landskroon Wines
☐ **Paulina's Reserve** *see* Rickety Bridge Winery
☐ **Paul René** *see* Wonderfontein

Paul Roos Farming

Most of the grapes off Tjuks and Johan Roos' Helderberg farm go elsewhere. But Gus Dale and Ricardo Adams make a few wines in traditional manner - their names ('Philanthropist' and 'School Principal') alluding to the educational benevolence behind this brand, named for a famous rugby player and educationist relative. A crèche for the children of farm personnel is long established, but a grander new one has been opened. Meanwhile the wines are being more widely exported.

★★★★☆ **Die Filantroop** Bright, clean aromas on **17** ⑨ blend of 72% shiraz with cab & pinotage (no merlot this year). 13.5% alcohol & touch richer & riper than previous, but properly dry & still a feeling of restraint. Wholeberry, natural ferment. Well & firmly structured; should benefit from keeping.

★★★★☆ **Susan** ② This **16** ⑨ a once-off tribute to Susan Roos, with Filantroop's varieties but cab now in the lead (64%). Tobacco aromas & more obvious sweet fruit is the result - perhaps more immediately charming too, but still a very serious structure.

★★★★☆ **Die Skoolhoof** ② Chenin with 18% chardonnay adding a lemony note in **17** ㊲, but maintaining the distinctive earthy tinge to the good fruit. Lively & fresh, with fine (natural) acidity, but also weight & texture; sweet-fruited elegance & dry, lingering finish. Native yeasts for all these.— TJ

Location/WO: Stellenbosch ▪ Map: Helderberg ▪ Map grid reference: C1 ▪ Est 2008 ▪ 1stB 2014 ▪ Tasting, sales & cellar tours by appt ▪ Owner(s) Tjuks & Johan Roos, Paul Roos Farming Trust ▪ Cellarmaster(s) Augustus Dale (Jun 2012) ▪ Winemaker(s) Ricardo Adams (1998) ▪ Viticulturist(s) Piet Adams (1974), with Jan Julius ▪ 24ha/18ha (cab, merlot, ptage, shiraz, chard, chenin) ▪ 7t/±800cs own label 40% red 60% white ▪ IPW, GlobalGAP, WIETA ▪ PO Box 397 Stellenbosch 7599 ▪ info@paulroosswine.com ▪ www.paulroosswine.com ▪ S 34° 0' 57.5" E 018° 49' 2.6" ▪ *keyboards.barometers.activates* ▪ **T +27 (0)21-855-3628**

Paulus Wine Co

When the experienced winemaker of premier-league Sadie Family Wines sets out to make his own Swartland wine, it's worth paying close attention. Paul Jordaan and his partner Pauline Roux (a French-born vigneronne) have set out to follow their 'shared dreams of making a fine wine the way they wanted to'. The future is unclear at this stage, they say, but they're aiming to make just one wine ('evolving with time through our journey'), a naturally made chenin blanc based on a 'partnership with nature'.

★★★★☆ **Bosberaad** ㊛ Chenin off mature Paardeberg bushvines, the granitic soils giving brightly aromatic, flint-inflected fruit. **18** ㊲ depth & intensity of flavour, good mouthfeel, some breadth from 10 months on lees in old oak, decent acidic grip. Altogether well balanced.— TJ, CvZ

Location: Malmesbury ▪ WO: Swartland ▪ Est 2017 ▪ 1stB 2018 ▪ Closed to public ▪ Owner(s)/winemaker(s) Paul Jordaan ▪ 2t/200cs own label 100% white ▪ Aprilskloof, Paardeberg, Malmesbury 7299 ▪ hello@pauluswineco.com ▪ **T +27 (0)63-708-3506**

Paul Wallace Wines

This hands-on family business started in 2003, when the Wallaces bought their 25-hectare Elgin farm. Paul, a respected consulting viticulturist, the following year began converting the apple orchards to vineyards, and set about producing his own wines with the help of some local winemaker friends. Partner and wife Nicky takes care of the tasting room, marketing and guest cottages. Their two sons, both winemaking graduates, currently work elsewhere but are set to take over the reins in future.

★★★★ **Black Dog Malbec** Small portion concrete 'egg', rest French barrique, **17** ㊛ plush dark fruit, palate-pleasing freshness in its succulence. Tannins supple, harmonious, not for long keeping, no hardship.

★★★★ **Brave Heart Pinot Noir** Red fruit to the fore, **17** ㊅'s oaking careful (10 months) to respect the variety's lighter structure. Juicy, some savoury spicing, no barriers to current enjoyment. Has vivacity.

★★★★ **Crackerjack** ⨀ Merlot-led Bordeaux blend, **16** ⑧⑧ typical fruitcake flavour lifted by fresh acid & subtly spicy, well-knit oak (22% new). Some non-estate fruit.

★★★★☆ **Reflection Chardonnay** ⓐ Citrus at core, lemon & lime, oak's oatmeal enriching **18** ⑨③'s fruit. Nicely done, got the balance right, remaining taut & focused without sacrificing character & flavour.

★★★★☆ **The Nix Noble Late Harvest** ⓐ Back on track after **16** ★★★★ ⑧⑦. Botrytised sauvignon, older barrels 6 months but **17** ⑨③'s fruit the hero, tangerine & preserved lemon, vividly perfumed. Richness to come unexpected, intense & mouthfilling sweetness, acid giving a tangy offset. 375 ml.

Little Flirt Sauvignon Blanc ★★★☆ Cool-climate passionfruit & grapefruit tones, the latter deepening in the flavours. Zesty freshness, **18** ⑧⑤ wakens the taste buds. — CR

Location/map/WO: Elgin ▪ Map grid reference: C3 ▪ Est 2004 (vineyard)/2013 (brand) ▪ 1stB 2004 ▪ Tasting facility open Saturdays, other days by appt or when open sign is displayed ▪ Tasting fee R60, waived on purchase ▪ Chocolate & wine pairing ▪ Self-catering accommodation ▪ Owner(s) Paul & Nicky Wallace ▪ Winemaker(s) Paul Wallace, advised by various other winemakers ▪ Viticulturist(s) Paul Wallace ▪ 25ha/12.5ha (cab f, malbec, pinot, chard, sauv) ▪ 120t/7,000cs own label 60% red 40% white ▪ IPW ▪ PO Box 141 Elgin 7180 ▪ nicky@paulwallace-wines.co.za ▪ www.paulwallacewines.co.za ▪ S 34° 12' 58.67" E 019° 03' 32.18 ▪ ⒨ marigolds.ordinate.blondie ▪ **T +27 (0)21-848-9744/+27 (0)83-255-1884/+27 (0)82-572-1406**

☐ **Peacock Wild Ferment** see False Bay Vineyards
☐ **Pearce Predhomme** see Radford Dale

Pearl Mountain   ⓠ ⑾ ⓘ

Cooler east-facing vines on the northern slope of Paarl Mountain — famous for its smooth, gleaming plutons resembling pearls — are the mainstay of the Retief family's two ranges. Viticulturist Graham is steadily adopting an organic approach, which son and GM David (one of three 5th-generation Retiefs now involved) is convinced is improving quality. New wine styles have been explored and the results will be bottled 'soon'. Good news, no doubt, for the F&B team at the on-site Blacksmith's Kitchen and wedding/functions venue.

Pearl Mountain range

★★★★ **Three Oaks Cabernet Sauvignon** ⓐ Black-fruit core has hints of nuts & herb leafiness in heavyweight **17** ⑧⑥, soundly crafted but chewy tannins, muted aromas beg cellaring to settle & unfold. Last-made **14** ★★★★ ⑧④ also needed time. Magnums available, as next 2.

★★★★ **Above The Mist Merlot** ⓐ Dense & concentrated **17** ⑧⑦, with massive extraction yet good focus & expression of cocoa-seamed plum fruit. Thick tannins suggest benefit from cellaring. No **15**, **16**.

★★★★ **Wagon Trail Shiraz** Four-square **17** ⑧⑥ shows baked black fruit, meaty liquorice on robust tannin structure. Like red siblings, deserves further maturation to realise its potential.

Avis Chardonnay ★★★☆ Toasty oak spiciness with appealing citrus fruit backing up. Natural yeast ferment/9 months in barrel on lees lend weight to **18** ⑧④. **Witkaree Chenin Blanc** ★★★ Reined-in oak on **18** ⑧② in sync with early-harvested fruit, tangy acidity. Pleasing lightness though finish could linger longer.

Stubborn Man range

Rosé ★★★ Pleasant summer sipping in **19** ⑧⓪, light & cheerful pink from cab, merlot & shiraz.
Chardonnay Unwooded ⨀ ★★★ Still showing fermentation notes mid-2018, **18** ⑦⑧ has understated pear drop fruit. **Chenin Blanc** ⨀ ★★★ Fruity, unfussy **18** ⑧⓪ made for easy everyday drinking, with generous tropical notes, light body. **Sauvignon Blanc** ⨀ ★★★ Dominant khaki bush aromatic edge to **18** ⑧②, with primary granadilla fruit. Unsubtle but striking. Durbanville grapes. In abeyance: **Merlot**. — GdB

Location/map: Paarl ▪ Map grid reference: E4 ▪ WO: Paarl/Western Cape ▪ Est 1747 ▪ 1stB 2004 ▪ Tasting & sales Tue-Sun 11.30-4 ▪ Closed Mon, Dec 25 & Jan 1 ▪ Blacksmith's Kitchen Tue-Sat 12-10 Sun 11.30-4 ▪ The Venue @ Pearl Mountain for weddings & functions ▪ Owner(s) Pearl Mountain Wines (Pty) Ltd ▪ Winemaker(s) Lisha Nelson (2016, Nelson Family Vineyards) ▪ Viticulturist(s) David & Graham Retief ▪ 14ha (cab, grenache, merlot, shiraz, chard, chenin, sauv) ▪ 120t/7,000cs own label 50% red 50% white ▪ PO Box 709 Northern Paarl 7623 ▪ info@pearlmountain.co.za ▪ www.pearlmountain.co.za ▪ S 33° 41' 44.4" E 018° 57' 11.1" ▪ ⒨ younger.vitamins.whispers ▪ **T 021-872-9507/+27 (0)21-870-1550 restaurant & tasting**

☐ **Pearly Bay** see KWV Wines
☐ **Pecan Stream** see Waterford Estate

☐ **Pegalle** *see* Govert Wines
☐ **Pella** *see* Super Single Vineyards
☐ **Peloton** *see* Painted Wolf Wines
☐ **Penhill** *see* Conradie Penhill Artisanal Wines

Perdeberg Wines

Funky zebra-striped capsules on this progressive venture's bottles – a nod to the 'wild horses' which once roamed here – would have been unthinkable 20 years ago. But there has been a quiet revolution since, in which this former co-operative cellar has become a quality-focused, visitor-friendly winery which makes the most of its trove of thousands of hectares of vines, mainly unirrigated, and many advanced in age, in Paarl's Voor Paardeberg area. Amenity-wise there is much on offer, including fun tasting options, craft beer, conference and meeting venues, and a new restaurant.

Perdeberg Speciality range

★★★★☆ **Red Blend** ⓐ Elegant Cape Blend of pinotage, shiraz, malbec, grenache noir, **14** ⑨⑨ youthful ruby colour; brooding black fruit, game, gunsmoke & violets saturate the palate for a full-bodied, smooth generous offering with definition & freshness.

★★★★ **Endura Chenin Blanc** Expressive tropical fruit on subsequent bottling of **17** ⑧⑨. Like previous, ripe peach balanced by lime tang & signature marmalade notes. Serious winemaking in combo tank, amphora & oak (none new) which lends structure. Registered Swartland single-vineyard.

The Dryland Collection

★★★★ **Conqueror Cabernet Sauvignon** ⓐ Inky cassis on **15** ⑧⑥ in leaner, less opulent style than **13** ⑧⑨. Taut, reined-in & tensile from 18 months French oak, just 10% new. WO Paarl for these unless noted.

★★★★ **Tenacious Shiraz** ⓥ Smoky coffee nuance to **15** ⑧⑦. Medium body, soft & gentle in its mouthfeel, fruit & length. Oak (80/20 French/American) is restrained.

★★★★ **Joseph's Legacy** ⓐ Almost equal shiraz & cab lead 6-way blend, **15** ⑧⑦ black fruit compote & spice lift, supple & pliable texture with good length. 20% American oak. Coastal WO.

★★★★☆ **Courageous Barrel Fermented Chenin Blanc** ⓥ Cream overlay to ripe apricot & citrus on **18** ⑨⑨. Lovely succulence but good structure from supportive cradle of oak, 10 months, 10% new French. Poised, refreshing & rewardingly long.

★★★★ **Rossouw's Heritage** Grenache blanc & viognier follow chenin blanc (59%) in new batch of **17** ⑧⑧. Granadilla, peach & pear tropicality with lively acidity & tang. Oaked for 10 months in 10% new French barrels. WO W Cape.

★★★★★ **Longevity Natural Sweet Chenin Blanc** ⓐ Ambrosial sweetness of **17** ★★★★★ ⑨⓪ suffused with sun-ripe pineapple, mango & apricot flavours so typical of the grape. Acid freshness prevents cloy on defined tail. Light yet structured from 7 months French oak, only 10% new, like **16** ⑨⑤. 375 ml.

Resolve Pinotage ★★★★ Spicy red-fruit vivacity of **17** ⑧⑥ is shaded by creamy vanilla notes from portion (20%) American oak ageing. Supple & juicy. **Pioneer Pinot Noir-Chardonnay** ⓐ ★★★☆ Hint of blush on **18** ⑧⑧, light, tangy & pleasant dry summer rosé. Coastal WO.

The Vineyard Collection

★★★★ **Grenache Blanc** ⓥ Nectarine & pear life to **19** ⑧⑥, well balanced by fresh line of acid. Third oaked (all-new French), adds structure & length, slots into the mix seamlessly. WO W Cape. **18** untasted.

★★★★ **Méthode Cap Classique Pinot Noir Rosé** ⓐ Frothy dry sparkler, red-berry tang to **15** ★★★ ⑧⓪, good body & length. **13** ⑧⑦ savoury, more serious. No **14**.

★★★★ **Méthode Cap Classique Chenin Brut** ⓐ New disgorgement of **12** ⑧⑥ dry bubbly presents crunchy apple fruit over shortbread & brioche, fine, lingering creamy mousse.

Chenin Blanc ⓥ ⓣ ★★★★ Easy drinker **19** ⑧④ is light, with vibrant granadilla zip & tang. Unfussy & gluggable, good fruit & acid balance.

Cinsault ★★★☆ Bright, lively & piquant **18** ⑧⑤ is perky, with cranberry succulence. Tannin grip from older-oaked portion (30%) adds a deeper, darker nuance. Good length. Paarl WO, like Shiraz & Chenin Brut.

Malbec ★★★☆ Plum & blueberry lightness on **18** ⑧⑤, soft textured, with gentle squeeze of tannin from year in oak, 15% new. **Pinotage** ★★★ Heady raspberry perfume on **18** ⑧⑵ is echoed by rounded yet juicy mouthful. Like last, light & easy despite year in oak, 20% American. **Shiraz** ⊘ ★★★★ **18** ⑧⑷ improves on last in density & body. Herb-brushed blue & black fruit appeal, which lingers. Structured from year in 80/20 French/American oak, 10% new. **Cinsault Rosé** ⑵ ★★★ Vivid raspberry & strawberry on **18** ⑺⑼ fresh, light, dry summer sipper. **Sauvignon Blanc** ★★★ Zippy pea shoot & asparagus verve to effortless, tangy **19** ⑧⑵. Perfect poolside companion. WO W Cape.

Perdeberg Classic range
Cabernet Sauvignon ⑵ ★★★★ Ever-reliable, well-priced cab. Blue & black berry fruit appeal on part-oaked **17** ⑧⑶, medium bodied & easy to drink. **Merlot** ⊘ ★★★★ Fruitcake friendliness to **18** ⑧⑷, portion (40%) oaked for 6 months, all new, adding structure & length. Affable braai buddy. Paarl WO, as Sparkling Rosé **Pinotage** ⊘ ★★★ Easy cherry & berry appeal to bright & juicy **18** ⑧⓪. Combo of 80/20 French & American oak used on 40% portion for 6 months. **Shiraz** ⊘ ★★★★ Blueberry & plum fruit is overlaid with a smoky note in **18** ⑧⑶. Medium body & length. Same oak regime as pinotage. **Chenin Blanc** ★★★ Lives up to uncomplicated everyday drinker tag. **19** ⑺⑼ light & juicy with pear & melon attraction. **Sauvignon Blanc** ★★★ White pepper & flint typicity on bright, light & succulent **19** ⑺⑻. **Sparkling Rosé** ★★ Gently sweet low-alcohol (9.5%) fizz from pinotage & hanepoot. **19** ⑺⑹ strawberry & candyfloss palate appeal & lightness.

Perdeberg Soft Smooth range
Rosé ⊘ ★★☆ Subtle Turkish delight on **19** ⑺⑺ semi-sweet, berry-toned pink charmer. Gentle & easy. WO W Cape, as all these. **White** ★★ Blend change on **19** ⑺⑷ semi-sweet: chenin (78%) leads nouvelle & viognier. Guava- & capsicum-toned, light, juicy mouthful. **Red** ★★ Unchallenging **17** ⑺⑷ shiraz-led blend with cinsaut, cab s & cab franc is berry packed & semi-sweet. — FM

Location/map: Paarl ▪ Map grid reference: B2 ▪ WO: Coastal/Paarl/Western Cape/Swartland ▪ Est 1941 ▪ 1stB 1942 ▪ Tasting & sales Mon-Fri 8-5 Sat/Sun 9-5 ▪ Closed Good Fri & Dec 25 ▪ Cellar tours Mon-Fri by appt ▪ Light meals, book for groups of 10+ ▪ Child friendly ▪ Eat @ Perdeberg restaurant open Wed-Sun 9-5 ▪ Function venue (up to 200 pax) ▪ Weddings ▪ Conferences ▪ Tutored tastings ▪ Wine pairings ▪ Wine blending/bottle your own wine, to be pre-booked ▪ Craft beer brewery ▪ Owner(s) 27 shareholders ▪ Cellarmaster(s) Albertus Louw (Oct 2008) ▪ Winemaker(s) Andri le Roux (Jun 2019), Natalie Kühne (Dec 2015), Lodewyk Botha (Oct 2017) & Arthur Basson (Dec 2017) ▪ Viticulturist(s) Tharien Hansen (Aug 2018) ▪ 6,000ha/2,564ha (cab, cinsaut, merlot, ptage, shiraz, chard, chenin, sauv) ▪ 18,000t/300,000cs own label 60% red 40% white ▪ Fairtrade, HACCP, IPW, WIETA ▪ PO Box 214 Paarl 7620 ▪ info@perdeberg.co.za ▪ www.perdeberg.co.za ▪ S 33° 39' 30.00" E 018° 49' 37.00" ▪ 🖳 intentional.popup.crewmen ▪ **T** +27 (0)21-869-8244

Peter Bayly Wines ⑨
The drought has been tough on Calitzdorp-based Peter and Yvonne Bayly's boutique wine business, affecting their plans for future growth. Following good winter rains, however, hopes are high that this year they can finally plant the albariño and verdelho they've been wanting to add to their stable of interesting port-style and Portuguese varietal wines.

★★★★☆ III Delicious (unfortified) trio of Portuguese grapes, touriga taking the lead, with souzão & tinta, older oaked 18 months. Three vintages tasted: **16** ⑨⓪ broods with dark plum fruit, attractive spice, needs & deserves time. Similar vein to **15** ⑨⓪; lighter **14** ★★★★ ⑧⑼ shows red berries & cocoa hints. All significantly better than **13** ★★★ ⑧⓪.

★★★★ **Cape Vintage** Classically styled, touriga-led 'port', **14** ⑧⑻ attractive fresh red cherries & raisins, grippy tannins & as yet unresolved alcohol point to a bright future. **12** ⑧⑻, also tasted, already showing the rewards patience will bring. 18 months old 500L oak, 19% alcohol. 375 ml, some **12** ⑧⑻ in 750 ml too. Bright, concentrated **10** ⑧⑹ still selling at cellardoor. No **11**, **13**.

Chenin Blanc (NEW) ★★★ From Jonkershoek Valley vines, unwooded, **18** ⑧⓪ soft & gentle peachy fruit, simple & attractive, with slight grip at finish. **Cape Late Bottled Vintage** ⑵ ★★★ Ripe plum & malty berry compote, **08** ⑺⑻ chiefly souzão (58%) & tinta, dash touriga. Soft & accessible, as per the LBV style. **Cape White** ⑵ ★★★★ Satisfying **NV** ⑧⑷ white 'port' from chenin. Full of golden raisins, candied peel, with touches apricot & honey. Recommended served on ice with tonic, mint & lemon. Occasional release: **Tinta Barocca**, **Cape Pink**. — CM

Location: Calitzdorp ▪ Map: Klein Karoo & Garden Route ▪ Map grid reference: B5 ▪ WO
Est 2002 ▪ 1stB 2004 ▪ Tasting, sales & tours by appt ▪ Owner(s) Peter Bayly Wines (Pty
viticulturist(s) Peter Bayly ▪ 6.6ha/1.2ha (tinta, touriga, souzão) ▪ ±8t/±1,320cs own
Calitzdorp 6660 ▪ info@baylys.co.za ▪ www.peterbayly.co.za ▪ S 33° 27' 16.70" E 021°
tortoise.satellite ▪ **T +27 (0)44-213-3702/+27 (0)83-457-5037**

☐ **Peter Clarke Collection** see PaardenKloof

Peter Falke Wines ⓛ ⓜ

German entrepreneur Franz-Peter Falke bought Groenvlei, with its stately Cape Dutch homestead, in 1995
– fulfilling his dream to own a farm. The vineyards on the lower slopes of the Helderberg have grown to 9
hectares, and fruit is also brought in as necessary, to be vinified by Werner Schrenk and consultant Louis Nel
in the plush, big but balanced style that characterises the estate.

Signature range

★★★★ **Syrah** Opulent, ripe, weighty & sweet-fruited **16** ⑧⑥ shows chocolatey oak, with easygoing,
rounded tannins in a balanced whole - the 14.8% alcohol not too obtrusive.

★★★★ **Exclusive Blend** Cabernet with 12% merlot in **15** ⑧⑧. Cigarbox & ripe, dark berry aromas, spicy
oak evident here & on juicy, full-fruited & attractive palate, structured with big but cushiony tannins.

★★★★ **Muscat d'Alexandrie** As ever, NV ⑧⑧ fortified offers more complexity than just obvious floral,
grapey charm. Silky texture; intense flavour & fine balance ensure the sweetness doesn't cloy. 500 ml.

PF range

★★★★ **Cabernet Sauvignon** Classic fruit & cigarbox aromas on ripe, flavourful **16** ⑧⑥ with easy
grip making for early approachability. 14.8% alcohol part of the plush, ripe house style. Perhaps more
harmonious than **15** ★★★★ ⑧③.

★★★★ **Méthode Cap Classique** Tasted out of vintage sequence, **13** ⑧⑦ sparkling from chardonnay
shows brioche development, along with ripe apple character. Rich but with good acid balance; ingratiating, flavourful charm.

Pinot Noir ★★★★ Lightly perfumed **17** ⑧⑤ with red berry fruit complemented by earthy, savoury
element. Velvet-textured & juicy, with unassertive grip. Not long, but most enjoyable. **Ruby Blend**
★★★★ Ripe, dark fruit on juicy & fruity **16** ⑧③ - thoroughly approachable in its youth, without too much
structure dominating the smooth softness or flavours. **Blanc de Noir** ★★★★ Partridge-eye hue & plenty
of charming fruit, with an earthy edge on dry-enough **18** ⑧③ from cab. Light-feeling & fresh, even elegant.
Chardonnay ★★★ Quiet citrus notes on **17** ⑦⑦. Off-dry, with awkward acidity. **Sauvignon Blanc**
★★★★ Typical passionfruit & guava on zesty but richly textured **18** ⑧③. — TJ

Location/map/WO: Stellenbosch ▪ Map grid reference: E8 ▪ 1stB 2003 ▪ Tasting & sales Tue-Sun 11-7 ▪ Fee
R65 ▪ Closed Good Fri, Dec 25 & Jan 1 ▪ Cheese platters, charcuterie & salads ▪ Owner(s) Franz-Peter Falke ▪
GM Werner Schrenk ▪ Winemaker(s) Werner Schrenk (2007) & Louis Nel (2013, consultant) ▪ Viticulturist(s)
Werner Schrenk (2007) ▪ 24ha/9ha under vine ▪ PO Box 12605 Stellenbosch 7613 ▪ marketing@peterfalkew-
ines.co.za ▪ www.peterfalkewines.com ▪ S 34° 0' 2.1" E 018° 50' 19.3" ▪ ▦ factorial.overheated.enticed ▪
T +27 (0)21-881-3677

☐ **Petit** see Ken Forrester Wines
☐ **Philip Jonker** see Weltevrede Estate
☐ **Phizante Kraal** see Groot Phesantekraal
☐ **Phoenix** see Stellenbosch Family Wines
☐ **Phumla** see House of Mandela
☐ **Picardi ReBEL** See Editor's Note
☐ **Pickled Fish Collection** see Asara Wine Estate & Hotel
☐ **Pick's Pick** see The Butcher Shop & Grill
☐ **Pictus** see Painted Wolf Wines
☐ **Piekeniers** see Tierhoek

...ierskloof Wine Company

...ty shareholders at this Citrusdal winery, Oubaas and Potgieter van Zyl, are delighted about increased ...mily involvement thanks to Potgieter's daughter, Bridget, having joined as business developer. In the upland Piekenierskloof, where their forebears pioneered vinegrowing, they continue to expand and refine their premium offering from six Old Vine Project-certified vineyards. 'Stylistically the emphasis is increasingly on respect for terroir and toning down the use of overt oak, especially on grenache noir and cinsault,' they say, excited to have introduced some amphoras and foudres for fermentation.

Old Vine range

★★★★☆ **Heidedal Cinsault** (NEW) ⊛ ⊛ Very easy to drink thanks to plush tannins, purity of red cherry & pomegranate fruit, but worth pausing to savour **18** (93) for its fynbos & thyme nuances, earth & subtle wood spice from year in 500L French barrels, 20% new. Also in magnum, as next 2.

★★★★☆ **Carel van Zyl Grenache Noir** (NEW) ⊛ ⊛ Remarkable red fruit concentration in lean, lithe & lively **18** (94), year in 500L French barrels (30% new) adding to subtle clove, cardamom, cured meat complexity, fine tannins & refreshing acidity showing good potential for development.

★★★★ **Bergendal Chenin Blanc** ⊛ A step up in **18** ★★★★☆ (90) on last-tasted **16** (87), with less oak (only 20% new, no American) adding creamy texture, subtle vanilla & spice to ripe pear & white peach flavours, highlighted by vibrant acidity.

★★★★ **Samson Straw Wine** ⊛ ⊛ Stylish 375 ml packaging for muscat de Frontignan dessert, **18** (88) fermented/aged year in older oak for dried peach & candied orange peel flavours, fresh acidity balancing 191 g/l sugar.

Reserve range

★★★★ **Heirloom Red** Was 'Red'. Grenache & shiraz with mourvèdre, 14 months mostly older oak, **16** (89) smooth, fruitcake nose leading to ripe red fruit with vanilla & rooibos hints, chalky tannins.

★★★★ **Heirloom White** ⊘ Chenin with 20% each grenache, chardonnay, 9% verdelho, fermented & matured 4 months 50% new oak (20% American, rest French). **17** ★★★★☆ (90) richer than **16** (87) with leavening acidity, lovely stonefruit purity, subtle oak spice.

Piekenierskloof range

★★★★ **Cinsault 18** (87) more interesting than **16** ★★★★ (84), with cured meat & herb aromas, crunchy red fruit & stemmy freshness on palate rounded out by year in older oak. No **17**.

★★★★ **Grenache Noir** Previewed last time, after year in 30% new French oak, **17** (89) still fresh & delicious, nudges higher rating with delicate perfume, lithe tannins, lively acidity & purity of red fruit.

★★★★ **Shiraz** (NEW) Plenty of smoky spice on nose of **18** (86), black pepper & ripe dark cherry/berry fruit persisting on the palate, soft & smooth after 14 months in large oak vats.

★★★★ **Grenache Blanc** ⊘ Racked to older 500L barrels for 14 months, previewed **18** (86) promises more than **17** ★★★ (82), with creamy texture, peach & kiwi, savoury yet fresh cucumber & fennel finish.

Grenache Rosé ★★★ Fragrant, dry **19** (82) has tangy red berry, luscious watermelon & creamy guava fruit, finishes with a burst of ruby grapefruit. **Chenin Blanc** ★★★★ Loses oaked component to showcase peach & melon freshness, **18** (83) fruity, with slightly earthy finish.

Stonedance range

Cabernet Sauvignon ★★★ Previewed last year, medium-bodied **17** (81) still has meaty edge to juicy black fruit, also dark chocolate after year in French/American oak. Fairtrade certified & WO Swartland, like all these. **Shiraz** ★★★ Ex-tank **18** (82) promises easy drinking pleasure with black pepper & spice-kissed plum fruit, 80% wooded (year in older oak). **Chenin Blanc** ★★★ Previewed **19** (82) has vibrant peach & nectarine flavours, pithy citrus finish, great summertime refreshment at 12.5% alcohol. **Sauvignon Blanc** ★★★ With reined-in 13% alcohol, **19** (82) tank sample slips down easily, has zesty lime & green apple flavours.

Six Hats Fairtrade range

Cabernet Sauvignon ⊘ ★★★ Blend Piekenierskloof/Swartland fruit & Fairtrade certified, like all these, **17** (81) medium bodied with dark berry fruit, subtle oak spice (80% on staves, as next). **Pinotage** ⊘ ★★★☆ Juicy **18** (83) packed with fresh blueberry & strawberry fruit, sweet vanilla/milk chocolate finish. **Shiraz** ⊘ ★★★☆ Black pepper & spice lift very ripe, slightly jammy red fruit in **17** (83), aged 9 months in older French & American barrels. **Rosé** ⊘ ★★★ Chenin, with 5% pinotage for deep coral hue, **19** (80) is dry & very fruity, offers peach, tangerine, pineapple & strawberry flavours. **Chardonnay** ⊘ ★★★ Unwooded **19** ⑧ has creamy texture, Cream Cracker finish, refreshing citrus in between. **Chenin Blanc** ⊘ ★★★★ Less than 12% alcohol for poolside quaffing, **19** ⑧ over-delivers on tropical flavour, weight, length, refreshment. **Sauvignon Blanc** ⊘ ★★★★ Easygoing **19** ⑧ is crisp & dry, quite steely, with tropical hints of granadilla & gooseberry. **Viognier** 🆕 ⊘ ★★★ Savoury edge to apricot & nectarine fruit in **19** ⑧, fragrant, with sweetish finish, calls for moderately spicy food. — JG

Location: Citrusdal ▪ Map: Olifants River ▪ Map grid reference: D7 ▪ WO: Piekenierskloof/Western Cape/Swartland ▪ Est/1stB 2007 ▪ Tasting room at Hebron, Piekenierskloof Pass, N7 ▪ Wine pairing ▪ Winery tours by appt only ▪ Carmién gin ▪ Owner(s) Majority shareholding Oubaas & Potgieter van Zyl ▪ Cellarmaster(s) Jaco van Niekerk (Dec 2017) ▪ Winemaker(s) Jaco van Niekerk (Dec 2017), with Andries de Klerk ▪ Viticulturist(s) Hanno van Schalkwyk (Nov 2017) ▪ 550ha (cab, cinsaut, grenache n/b, merlot, mourv, ptage, ruby cab, shiraz, tannat, chard, chenin, hanepoot, pinot grigio, sauv, viog) ▪ 5,000t/30,000cs own label 45% red 50% white 5% rosé ▪ Brands for clients: Fairtrade Original, Liberty ▪ Fairtrade, HACCP, IPW, WIETA ▪ PO Box 41 Citrusdal 7340 ▪ info@pkwc. co.za ▪ www.piekenierskloofwines.co.za ▪ S 32° 37' 05.17" E 018° 57' 21.66" ▪ **T +27 (0)22-921-2233**

☐ **Pierneef Collection** see La Motte
☐ **Pierre Jourdan** see Haute Cabrière
☐ **Pieter Cruythoff** see Riebeek Valley Wine Co

Pieter Ferreira Cap Classique 🆕

Pieter Ferreira's status as the Cape's leading exponent of traditional-method sparkling wine means that he is far from being a 'newcomer', but this own-label brand is new — and in fact so brilliantly successful in its first appearance in this guide that it is our Newcomer Winery of the Year. The project arose from Pieter's need for a 'retirement plan' for when he leaves Graham Beck, where he is cellarmaster (though that retirement now looks likely to be substantially delayed). That professional connection means the project is officially owned by wife Ann Ferreira (arguably the Cape's second-most knowledgeable bubbly expert), and the wines are made by Pieter under contract at Graham Beck.

★★★★★ **Blanc de Blancs** 🍾 A new SA classic from the 'Bubbly King'. **12** ⑨⑦ taut, & so vibrant & youthful it's hard to credit 72 months sur lie on crown cap, & a further 12 sur point on cork. But it's this - & attention to detail - that creates the super-fine mousse, creamy texture, subtle brioche & persistent finish. Chardonnay's lemon & lime, a mineral seam, bone-dry finish. Robertson & Darling vines.— WB, CvZ

Location: Franschhoek ▪ WO: Western Cape ▪ Est/1stB 2012 ▪ Closed to public ▪ Owner(s) Pieter Ferreira Wines (Pty) Ltd - Ann Ferreira ▪ Cellarmaster(s) Pieter Ferreira (Graham Beck) ▪ 300cs own label 100% cap classique ▪ PO Box 102 La Motte 7691 ▪ ann@pieterferreiramcc.co.za ▪ www.pieterferreiramcc.co.za ▪ **T +27 (0)82-909-1116**

☐ **Pillar & Post** see Stellenrust
☐ **PK Morkel** see Bellevue Estate Stellenbosch

Plaisir de Merle 🍷 🍽 🏠 📷 🎦 ♿

As of 2019, Plaisir de Merle is among the long-established and respected fine-wine brands run by Distell's new standalone company, Libertas Vineyards & Estates. Plaisir, based on a prime Simonsberg-Paarl mountainside property with a showpiece cellar melding Cape Dutch heritage with modern winemaking, been run along classic Bordeaux lines since the first vintage in 1993, most notably reflected in a predominantly red portfolio of traditional Médoc varieties, and the behind-the-scenes continuity brought by cellarmaster Niel Bester, approaching his 30th vintage here. His 20th was celebrated with the making of the Signature Blend '12, debuting with five stars in last year's edition, our Cape Bordeaux Blend of the Year.

★★★★ **Cabernet Sauvignon** 🍷 Stylish **16** ★★★★★ ⑨⓪ has real Old World charm, with earthy forest floor leafiness, strands of liquorice & iodine, all spicing up ripe, opulent black fruit. Well-judged weight & balance, velvet tannin cloak. Outshines **15** ⑧⑦, with better balance, heft.

★★★★ **Cabernet Franc** 🍷 Fine varietal definition on **17** ★★★★★ ⑨⓪, with nervous leafiness, minerally pencil shavings & sumptuously ripe blackcurrant fruit. Bold & muscular yet focused, with grippy tannin, lingering finish. Improves on already fine **15** ⑧⑨. No **16**.

★★★★ **Merlot** Taut, well-defined black cherry fruit dominates finely shaped **17** (89), laced with cassis, underscored by honest earthiness. 14.5% cab adds muscle without loss of refinement.

★★★★ **Shiraz** (✷) Concentrated black cherry fruit on blockbuster **16** (88), with appealing tobacco spices & smoked meat aromas. Plump & generous, with plush tannin texture.

★★★★☆ **Charles Marais** (✷) Statuesque offering debuts with **13** (93) 4-way Cape Bordeaux blend headed by cab (30%). Layers of blackcurrant fruit, intense forest floor scents, plush velvet tannins, & earthy liquorice, all delivered with poise & grace. Very impressive. Paarl WO.

★★★★★ **Signature Blend** (✷) 'Anniversary edition', marking winemaker's 20th vintage here. Superb 5-way Bordeaux red, cab & petit verdot (33/25) leading. **12** (96) shows impeccable form & substance. Rich & earthy, with herbaceous notes to blackcurrant fruit core, elegantly rounded body & lengthy finish. Hefty oak regime (90% new French) in perfect harmony.

★★★★ **Petit Plaisir** (✓) Earthy, mineral notes on shiraz-led **17** (86) with cab & cab franc, bolstered by solid, ripe black-fruit core. 17 months in French & American oak barrels. Improves on **16** ★★★★ (85).

★★★★☆ **Grand Plaisir** (🐝) Segues from Bordeaux to Bordeaux/Rhône blend, retains its stature & aristocratic bearing in **14** (94). 58% cab supported by petit verdot & shiraz deliver intense blackcurrant/ cassis fruit, sumptuously ripe tannins, intriguing earthy, mineral highlights, lingering farewell. No **12**, **13**.

★★★★ **Chardonnay** Oak prevails over fruit in **18** (86), with spicy caramel to the fore mid-2019. Elegantly structured, with ripe citrus, lees texture & richness. Should knit with cellaring.

★★★★ **Grand Brut Méthode Cap Classique** (✷) Near equal pinot noir & chardonnay sparkling, **16** (86) is lean & focused, showing green apple fruit & primary acid on generous, foamy mousse. WO W Cape.

Malbec ★★★★ Leafy spearmint notes dominate **17** (83), with bay & anise threads. Big, chewy tannins flesh out robust body. Not tasted: **Petit Verdot**. — GdB

Location: Paarl ▪ Map: Franschhoek ▪ Map grid reference: C6 ▪ WO: Simonsberg-Paarl/Paarl/Western Cape ▪ Est/1stB 1993 ▪ Tasting, sales & cellar tours Mon-Sun 10-6 (Sep-Apr) & 10-5 (May-Aug) pub hols 10-4; last tastings winter/pub hols half an hour before closing ▪ Closed Good Fri, Dec 25 & Jan 1 ▪ Tasting fee R60 ▪ Cheese platters available during trading hours R140 or R180 ▪ Children welcome ▪ Gifts ▪ Manor House (sleeps 8) can be booked for functions, conferences & weddings ▪ Owner(s) Libertas Vineyards & Estates, a Distell Group company ▪ Farm manager(s) Paul Laas, with Heinright Prins ▪ Cellarmaster(s) Niel Bester (1993) ▪ Viticulturist(s) Drikus Heyns & Morne Steyn ▪ 974ha/400ha (cabs s/f, malbec, merlot, p verdot, pinot, shiraz, chard, sauv) ▪ 800t/80,000cs own label 80% red 20% white ▪ ISO 9001:2008, ISO 14001:2004, BRC, SGS, WIETA, WWF-SA Conservation Champion ▪ PO Box 121 Simondium 7670 ▪ info@plaisirdemerle. co.za ▪ www.plaisirdemerle.co.za ▪ S 33° 51′ 0.0″ E 018° 56′ 36.2″ ▪ ⌨ patrons.flooring.satchel ▪ **T +27 (0)21-874-1071**

Plettenvale Wines   (℗)

They're working to get the vineyard back to optimum health at Gloria Strack van Schyndel's boutique wine operation at Plettenberg Bay, after years of drought. Part of the farm had also been destroyed by drought-fuelled wildfires in 2017. But the undaunted Gloria reports that the young viognier vines are growing vigorously – enough so to contribute to the 2019 Rosé.

Dry Rosé ★★★ Berry fruit, soft texture & bright acidity on light (11% alcohol), dryish **NV** (79) from pinot, chardonnay & a drop syrah. **Brut Rosé Méthode Cap Classique** ★★★ Pink onion-skin **NV** (80) sparkling from pinot noir & chardonnay, with some floral, musky, sweet berry aromas & flavours. Light-feeling, dry & fresh. Not tasted: **Ruby Rush Our Blend**, **Chardonnay**. — TJ

Location/WO: Plettenberg Bay ▪ Map: Klein Karoo & Garden Route ▪ Map grid reference: C1 ▪ Est 2008 ▪ 1stB 2011 ▪ Tasting & sales every Sat 10-1, all other times by appt ▪ Short tour of cellar available with tasting ▪ Owner(s)/winemaker(s) Gloria Strack van Schyndel ▪ Viticulturist(s) Paul Wallace (Nov 2007, consultant) ▪ 5.3ha/2.5ha (pinot, shiraz, chard, viog) ▪ PO Box 2103 Plettenberg Bay 6600 ▪ info@plettenvalewines.co.za ▪ www.plettenvalewines.co.za ▪ S 34° 04′ 53.9″ E 023° 19′ 41.4″ ▪ ⌨ endures.bronze.wing ▪ **T +27 (0)44-533-9146/+27 (0)82-322-0765**

☐ **Poetic** see Idun
☐ **Poetry** see Flagstone Winery

☐ **Poker Hill** *see* Somerbosch Wines
☐ **Polkadraai** *see* Stellenbosch Hills Wines
☐ **Polo Club** *see* Val de Vie & Polo Club Wines
☐ **Pomüla** *see* Imbuko Wines

Pongrácz

Change is afoot at this specialist méthode cap classique sparkling house, bearing the name of Hungarian nobleman and refugee Desiderius Pongrácz, who settled in Stellenbosch in 1958 and became a famed viti-cultural adviser. The brand has a new owner, Libertas Vineyards & Estates, part of Distell, and a successor to long-term cellarmaster Elunda Basson was unconfirmed at press time. The popularity and critical success of the bubblies are undiminished, top honours at the 2019 MCC Challenge being one of several recent awards.

★★★★ **Brut Rosé** ⊘ Appealing **NV** (87) bubbles from pinot noir & chardonnay (60/40), crisp, fresh & lively. Stewed cranberries, wet leaves & light, savoury lees (24 months), 10.5 g/l sugar balances mid-palate beautifully. Also in halves & magnums.

★★★★☆ **Blanc de Blancs** Less time on lees (36 months) for latest **NV** (91) sparkling from chardonnay proves a winner. Crunchy apple fruit, lemon cake & salty oyster juice character, small portion barrel fermented for added complexity. Whole is delightfully poised, persistent & elegant.

★★★★ **Brut** ⊘ Well-made & delightful **NV** (87) sparkler now chardonnay-led with 40% pinot noir. Lemon Cream biscuits & apple Danish pastry, savoury smoothness from 24 months lees contact. Significant achievement to make this quality in such quantity. Also in 375 ml, 1.5L & 3L.

★★★★☆ **Desiderius** ⊗ Fine, pedigreed flagship bubbly, **11** (92) 55% chardonnay plus pinot noir. Wonderfully refined, with lengthy fresh focus, smoky toasted hazelnut & brioche tones from 77 months on lees – less than marginally more impressive **09** ★★★★★ (95) (90 months). No **10**.

★★★★ **Noble Nectar Demi-Sec** ⊘ Fruit-driven semi-sweet **NV** (86) from chardonnay & pinot noir had 24 months on lees, adding gentle umami-note to creamy orange, apple pie & honey. Sugar (40 g/l) ably offset by fine, brisk acidity. Improves on previous.— CM

Location: Stellenbosch ▪ WO: Western Cape ▪ Owner(s) Libertas Vineyards & Estates, a Distell Group company ▪ 27ha own vyds ▪ 20% red 80% white ▪ ISO 9200 ▪ PO Box 184 Stellenbosch 7599 ▪ www.pongracz.co.za

Porcupine Ridge

The first wine bearing this label, with a pen and ink drawing of the indigenous Crested Porcupine by acclaimed wildlife artist Zakkie Eloff, was a Sauvignon Blanc '97. Since then, the range has grown substantially (and the volumes enormously), gaining an identity apart from that of the label's owner, Boekenhoutskloof. Also grown has been its reputation for palate and pocket friendliness.

Syrah ⊘ ⊗ ★★★☆ Simply delicious **18** (85) from Swartland, savoury & spicy, with dark brooding fruit & signature lavender hint. Rounded & moreish.

Cabernet Sauvignon ⊘ ★★★☆ Full of dark berry fruit, easy & smooth for everyday, splash cab franc adds appealing leafiness in **18** (84). 80% older-oaked for 9 months, as red siblings. **Merlot** ⊘ ★★★☆ Fruity **18** (83) is silky, with fruitcake & mulled wine flavours, gentle grip to finish. Slips down easily, as all. **Rosé** ★★★ Light & soft yet vibrant, bone-dry, with crunchy cranberries & sour cherry tang. **19** (80) from mostly cinsaut, dash syrah. **Chardonnay** ⊘ ★★★☆ Delightful fresh-baked cinnamon apple pie aromas & flavours in **18** (84), complexity & palate appeal aided by gentle oak & lees ageing. **Chenin Blanc** ⊘ ★★★☆ Bursts with tropical fruit & exotic spice, **18** (85) lovely intensity, lipsmacking finish. Also-tasted **19** (85) similar flavour profile & attention to detail, just tad fresher. Swartland fruit, admirable complexity achieved without oak. **Sauvignon Blanc** ★★★ Riot of fruit salad flavour in **19** (81), juicy & zippy, lovely lemon twist in the tail. WO W Cape, rest Coastal unless noted. — WB

Porseleinberg

Taking its name from the stony hills in the Swartland, not far from Riebeek-Kasteel, this farm's 90 ha of vineyards are planted with red Rhône varieties, the majority of grapes from which go to the Franschhoek cellar of the owner, Boekenhoutskloof, for use in its ranges. A small portion from the oldest vines is used to vinify the single wine produced here, a syrah of international acclaim. Callie Louw is both winemaker and viticulturist, with an unerring talent for getting the best from the grapes. The cellar is modest, and the wine made in a natural, minimal-interference way, according to Swartland Independent Producers' guidelines.

★★★★☆ **Porseleinberg** ⓐ Syrah from a special site, wholebunch fermented/12 months large old oak & concrete 'egg'. **17** ㉚ unshowy, this is about intrinsic class & style. Plush fruit, deeply perfumed; like **16** ★★★★★ ㉟, musculature for long ageing yet lithe, with succulence, polish.— CR

Location: Riebeek-Kasteel ▪ WO: Swartland ▪ Est 2009 ▪ 1stB 2010 ▪ Closed to public ▪ Owner(s) Boekenhoutskloof Winery (Pty) Ltd ▪ Winemaker(s)/viticulturist(s) Callie Louw (Jun 2009) ▪ 130ha/90ha (cinsaut, grenache, shiraz) ▪ 50t/1,000cs own label 100% red ▪ PO Box 433 Franschhoek 7690 ▪ callie@ porseleinberg.com ▪ www.porseleinberg.com ▪ **T +27 (0)79-884-2309**

☐ **Postcard Series** *see* Stark-Condé Wines

Post House Vineyards

Once planted with tobacco (as well as bushvines), this family property in the Helderberg foothills between Stellenbosch and Somerset West is unabashed red-wine country, and owner/winemaker Nick Gebers is delighted to have added grenache to his varietal mix. Taking its philatelic theme and brand name from its home in an old post office in the missionary village of Raithby, Post House is all about unhurried, traditional winemaking with as little interference as possible.

★★★★ **Bulls Eye Cabernet Sauvignon** Ripe cassis tinged with violet on **17** ㉘. Refined & rounded from natural ferment (as for all bar Blueish White) & 24 months in third new French oak. Layered, integrated palate with long rewarding finish.

★★★★ **Black Mail Merlot** Gentle yet firm tannic grip on **17** ㉘ is matched by ripe fruit, herb & cigar-box abundance. Lithe & pliable, it is fresh & dry. Alcohol is 15% but absorbed within the whole.

★★★★ **Merry Widow Shiraz** Spicy plum, dried herb & apparent sweetness on **17** ㉚ belies its low sugar (1.6 g/l) but is balanced by chalky tannin. As with **16** ★★★★☆ ㉟, oak is 20% new, French & American (4:1), needs time to knit.

★★★★ **Missing Virgin** Generously ripe & plump blue/black fruit & spice on interesting **17** ㉘ Cape Blend led by pinotage (67%) with petit verdot in support. Oak, 20% new for 2 years, frames lush palate. Alcohol 15%, in house's bold style.

★★★★ **Penny Black** Signature herbs on eclectic blend shiraz, 3 Bordeaux grapes & dab chenin blanc. Notable firm tannin grip & dryness on **17** ㉘, spicy but a touch brusque, whereas **16** ★★★★★ ㉙ was plush, with layers of flavour.

Blueish Black ★★★☆ Inky black appeal to **17** ㉔ shiraz-led blend with pinotage, merlot & cab, 25% in barrel, rest in tank with oak staves. Soft, light bodied & easy. WO W Cape, as next. **Golden Monkey** ★★★★ Shiraz upped to 77% in **18** ㉟ Rhône blend with mourvèdre & grenache. Soft, supple spicy cherry appeal is framed by dry tannin from oak staves, 13 months. **Stamp Of Chenin** ★★★☆ Creamy caramel & vanilla on **18** ㉔ tells of oak ferment & maturation (10 months, 10% new). Leesy stonefruit lightness muted by wood. **17** ★★★★ ㉚ bolder & vibrant. **Blueish White** ★★★☆ Subtle pear, melon & apricot fruit on **18** ㉟ unoaked sauvignon & chenin blend. Succulent, light & easy. Improves on previous in verve & tang. Not tasted: **Treskilling Yellow**. — FM

Location: Stellenbosch ▪ Map: Helderberg ▪ Map grid reference: C1 ▪ WO: Stellenbosch/Western Cape ▪ Est/1stB 1997 ▪ Tasting, sales & cellar tours Mon-Fri 9-5 Sat by appt ▪ Fee R50 ▪ Closed all pub hols ▪ BYO picnic ▪ Guest house ▪ Function/wedding venue (up to 150 pax) ▪ Owner(s) Nicholas Gebers ▪ Cellarmaster(s) Nick Gebers ▪ Winemaker(s) Nick Gebers, with Madri Dreyer ▪ 70ha/39ha (cab, merlot, p verdot, ptage, shiraz, chenin, sauv) ▪ 200t/16,000cs own label 65% red 35% white ▪ PO Box 5635 Helderberg 7135 ▪ nick@posthousewines.co.za ▪ www.posthousewines.co.za ▪ S 34° 1' 8.1" E 018° 48' 41.6" ▪ Ⓦ softest. materialistic.quickening ▪ **T +27 (0)21-842-2409**

☐ **Pot Luck Club** *see* Almenkerk Wine Estate
☐ **Pride of Kings** *see* Stellenview Premium Wines
☐ **Prince** *see* Bayede!
☐ **Princess** *see* Bayede!

☐ **Printer's Devil** *see* Rickety Bridge Winery
☐ **Private Collection** *see* Saxenburg Wine Farm
☐ **Prohibition** *see* Camberley Wines
☐ **Protea** *see* Anthonij Rupert Wyne
☐ **Provenance** *see* Saronsberg Cellar

Pulpit Rock Winery

The Brink family's extensive farm just outside Riebeek West in the Swartland is named for a craggy outcrop on the Kasteelberg. The hiking trail to the top is a steep climb rewarded by 'breathtaking views' – and, after the descent, by what's on offer over weekends at the new Wine & Snack Bar, including the generally easy-drinking and modestly priced bottlings in their own wine ranges.

Pulpit Rock range

★★★★ **Petit Verdot** Ⓡ Naturally fermented **16** (89), typical inky depth & spicy black fruit, muscular but with some subtlety, tannic grip for food from 16 months French/American wood.

Louisa range

★★★★ **Cape Blend** Ⓡ Pinotage with shiraz & petit verdot, individually vinified & best barrels blended. **15** (87) dense & packed with flavour, spicy fruit given form by nicely dry tannin. **14** untasted.

★★★★ **Méthode Cap Classique** Ⓡ Creamy dry sparkling from chardonnay. **17** (89) vivacious mousse, apple & lemon favours, persistent tail. Delicious in youth, perhaps to gain complexity over next year/2.

Brink Family Vineyards range

★★★★ **Barrel Fermented Chardonnay** Ⓡ Subtle honeysuckle, citrus & oatmeal on **17** (87), sumptuous courtesy oak ferment/ageing & regular bâtonnage but with focused seam of enlivening acidity.

Cabernet Sauvignon Ⓡ ★★★ Big, bold **16** (82)'s dry tannins underpin ripe blackberry & cassis fruit. At 15% alcohol, balance is shade off previous. **Merlot** Ⓡ ★★★☆ Velvet tannin & violet appeal in **16** (84), herbal note, chocolate complexity from year French oak, satisfying length & dryness. **Pinotage** ✓ ★★★☆ Rich, sweet-fruited & juicy, **17** (83) has some balanced firmness of structure, & contains its big 15% alcohol quite well. **Shiraz** ★★★ Easygoing **17** (80) has plentiful ripe berry flavours; generously built with the 14.5% alcohol warming the finish. **Chardonnay** ★★★ Peardrop & honeysuckle notes on attractive, richly textured, unwooded **19** (80). **Chenin Blanc** ✓ ★★★☆ Pleasingly & freshly aromatic **19** (84) has a gentle acidic bite as part of its good balance. **18** ★★★★ (88) was something of a standout. **Sauvignon Blanc** ★★★ Forthright ripe guava & passionfruit notes on **19** (82). Soft & light, tasty. Like **18** ★★★★ (89), from Darling vines.

Swartland Stories

Shiraz-Pinotage-Grenache ★★☆ Ripe, fruity, juicy **17** (79) has a savoury tang to its flavourfulness; only just dry, with a thick texture. **Pinotage Rosé** ✓ ★★☆ Dusty ripe strawberry aroma & full flavour on **18** (78), fruity but fairly dry. **Chenin Blanc-Viognier** ★★★ Generous peach, apricot & pear notes on ingratiatingly likeable, softly textured & sweet-fruited **19** (82). — TJ

Location: Riebeek West ▪ Map: Swartland ▪ Map grid reference: D6 ▪ WO: Swartland/Coastal ▪ Est 2003 ▪ 1stB 2004 ▪ Tasting & sales Mon-Fri 9–5 Sat 10–2 ▪ Closed Easter Fri-Sun, Dec 25/26 & Jan 1 ▪ Cellar tours by appt ▪ Wine & Snack Bar open Sat & Sun 9-4 ▪ BYO picnic ▪ Pulpit Rock hiking trail (±2km) ▪ Annual olive festival (May) ▪ Self-catering accommodation ▪ Owner(s) Brink family ▪ Winemaker(s) Dewald Huisamen (Dec 2016) ▪ 600ha/475ha (cab, grenache, merlot, mourv, p verdot, ptage, shiraz, chard, chenin) ▪ 650t/30,000cs own label 70% red 29% white 1% rosé + 3m L bulk ▪ Other export brand: Cape Haven ▪ PO Box 1 Riebeek West 7306 ▪ info@pulpitrock.co.za ▪ www.pulpitrock.co.za ▪ S 33° 20' 47.4" E 018° 51' 14.1" ▪ buds.exploration.jitters ▪ **T +27 (0)22-461-2025**

☐ **Purebred** *see* Excelsior Estate

Quando Vineyards & Winery

Two Bruwer brothers are the current generation driving the Robertson Valley family farm: Fanus responsible for the winemaking and marketing, Martin tending the vineyards. Their first own-label wine was a '01

Sauvignon and, though the range has grown, only a limited number of Quando wines are made each vintage, the rest of the grapes going elsewhere.

Pinot Noir ⊘ ★★★★ Attractive perfumed aromas give way to a feistier persona, with firm tannins supporting sappy, fresh berry fruit. Best barrels, from higher-lying vines on Karoo shale. **16** ⑧④ deserves year/2 to fully evolve. **Mourvèdre Rosé** ★★☆ Savoury-style aperitif. **19** ⑦⑨ dry, cranberry toned, with a twist of tannin. Shade off previous. **Sauvignon Blanc** ★★★★ Bright tropical & citrus flavours on **19** ⑧⑤, from single parcel in deep alluvial soil. Staggered picking & blending ensure balance & freshness. **Chenin Blanc-Viognier** ⊘ ★★★★ Richness from old-vine chenin, co-fermented with viognier (29%), makes for creamy, aromatic, unoaked **17** ⑧⑤. Fruit-packed & accessible. Not tasted: **Mourvèdre**, **Natural Sweet Sauvignon Blanc**. — MW

Location: Bonnievale ▪ Map/WO: Robertson ▪ Map grid reference: D4 ▪ Est/1stB 2001 ▪ Tasting & sales by appt ▪ Closed all pub hols ▪ Owner(s) FM Bruwer cc ▪ Cellarmaster(s)/winemaker(s) Fanus Bruwer (Jan 1991) ▪ Viticulturist(s) Martin Bruwer (Jan 1991) ▪ 190ha/80ha (mourv, chenin, sauv) ▪ 6,000cs own label 10% red 90% white ▪ PO Box 82 Bonnievale 6730 ▪ info@quando.co.za ▪ www.quando.co.za ▪ S 33° 56' 9.6" E 020° 1' 28.8" ▪ 🗺 articles.searchers.ducking ▪ **T +27 (0)82-926-0805**

☐ **Quartet** see Wine-of-the-Month Club
☐ **Queen of Africa** see Olivedale Private Vineyards
☐ **Quest** see Du Toitskloof Winery

Quoin Rock Wines

This family-owned estate high on Stellenbosch's Simonsberg Mountain recently underwent extensive redevelopment to be a showpiece of luxury and refinement, with elegant architecture, eye-catching interior design and a molecular gastronomy experience at Gate Restaurant. The new-generation wines are impressive, too, and have been very well received, and the team advised by the estimable Chris Keet is doing much detailed work to maintain the flow of awards.

Quoin Rock range

★★★★☆ **Shiraz** ⊘ Wild fruit, morello cherries, peppery savouriness, **15** ⑨② shows masterly oaking (20 months French, just over half new, like Red Blend) which gives a scrub-toned dry finish, yet the texture is supple, polished. High alcohol, as all the reds, but masked by the fruit. Simonsberg-Stellenbosch WO.

★★★★ **Red Blend** ⊘ Cab (66%), with cab franc & merlot, liquorice-nuanced **15** ⑧⑨ projects opulence in its creamy dark fruit, spice array, until you get to the palate, where it's all business. Firm, dry tannins guarantee a rewarding long life, no barrier to current enjoyment.

★★★★☆ **Chardonnay** ⚜ Barrel-fermented **18** ⑨③ is precise & polished. Slightly richer & broader, despite trim 12.6% alcohol, courtesy 15% concrete 'egg' matured portion, but effective counterweight of lime & grapefruit; smoky attraction from oak, which will integrate with time. WO W Cape, as next.

★★★★ **White Blend** ⊘ Sauvignon with 15% semillon, nearly half the wine oaked, **17** ⑧⑧'s profile is tinned pea & fynbos, bolstered by a cedar-spiced seam that takes the edge off the green notes.

★★★★ **Méthode Cap Classique** ⊘ Elgin pinot noir & chardonnay, 52 months on lees, trim-figured & bone-dry **13** ⑧⑧ sparkling has toasted brioche & citrus richness in its perfume & flavours, then comes the unexpected racy acidity adding vigour & vitality, & a saline-mineral note to the finish.

★★★★ **Husk Spirit Sauvignon Blanc** ⑭ Beautifully clean & fresh spirit ⑧⑨, with lightly perfumed aromas & flavours. On the more delicate side, balanced, integrated alcohol giving a soft fieriness. 500 ml. Not tasted: **Vine Dried Sauvignon Blanc**.

Tribute range

★★★★ **Namysto Shiraz-Cabernet Sauvignon** ⊘ Also a dab of merlot, cab franc in **15** ⑧⑧, but shiraz dictates the styling: dark fruit, smoke, savoury spicing including black pepper. Oaked 20 months, 30% new, tannins a hidden strength, the body curvaceous, silky. Simonsberg-Stellenbosch WO.

★★★★ **Namysto Rosé** ⑭ From cabernet, **19** ⑧⑧ sophisticated & attractively food styled, lipsmacking dryness (1.4 g/l) & grip, with savoury acid support, palate presence from oak & concrete 'egg' components.

Namysto Sauvignon Blanc-Semillon ⊘ ★★★☆ Just 5% semillon in **17** ⑧④, that portion oaked. Very distinctive, a nervy intensity that's more Old World than New, wild grasses & tinned pea, the semillon's role

more evident on the palate texture, smooth & lightly savoury. WO W Cape. Not tasted: **Namysto Sweet**.
— CvZ, TJ

Location/map: Stellenbosch ▪ Map grid reference: F3 ▪ WO: Stellenbosch/Western Cape/Simonsberg–
Stellenbosch/Elgin ▪ Est 1998 ▪ 1stB 2001 ▪ Tasting & sales Tue-Sat 10-4 ▪ Closed Jan 1 ▪ Meals/refreshments ▪
Function venue ▪ Gâte Restaurant ▪ Accommodation ▪ Owner(s) Quoin Rock Wines (Pty) Ltd ▪ Cellarmaster(s)
Chris Keet (consultant) ▪ Viticulturist(s) Nico Walters ▪ PO Box 23 Elsenburg 7607 ▪ info@quoinrock.co.za ▪ www.
quoinrock.com ▪ S 33° 52' 42.5" E 018° 52' 2.3" ▪ 🏠 avid.refuse.readily ▪ **T +27 (0)21-888-4740**

☐ **Route 43** see Aan de Doorns Cellar

Raats Family Wines

This guide's Winery of the Year in 2018, Raats Family Wines specialises in cabernet franc and chenin blanc
with enviable success. Founded in 2000, with a philosophy of vineyard perfection and a striving for
excellence, the Stellenbosch venture can count itself among the biggest drivers of cab franc's awakening and
champions of chenin's revival in SA. The high-density vine project initiated by owner/viticulturist Bruwer
Raats and winemaker and cousin Gavin Bruwer sees small vineyard sites planted with up to 8,000 vines
per hectare, producing tiny yields of truly unique fruit. They are founder-members of marketing collective
Premium Independent Wineries of South Africa (PIWOSA), and Bruwer Raats was inducted into the prestigious Cape Winemakers Guild in 2016. The multifaceted operation, incorporating B-Vintners and Mvemve
Raats (see separate entries), is based on their property on Polkadraai Hills.

★★★★★ **Cabernet Franc** 🏵 Complex, showing sense of place, masterly restraint, **17** ⑨⑤ is expressive
yet lean & refined. Earthy, leafy, with iodine & mulberry infusions, olive tapenade, finely integrated oak.
Standout example in the SA industry. 18 months in 300L French oak, as all the reds. This 25% new.

★★★★☆ **Dolomite Cabernet Franc** ⊘ Pocket-friendly yet exceptionally good & precise varietal
expression, **17** ⑨⓪ has modest weight, finely judged ripeness & vibrancy, earthy charm & leafy herbal
highlights. Shade off spectacular **16** ★★★★★ ⑨⑤ but still punches above its weight. Older oak, like Jasper.

★★★★☆ **Eden High Density Single Vineyard Cabernet Franc** Uncompromising, pricey & rare
(50 cases) rendition from 0.2 ha vineyard planted to 8,000 vines/ha, rather muted in **17** ⑨⓪ but deserves
respect. Peppery spices from 20% wholebunch ferment & 50% new oak, resolutely earthy, elegant &
supple, but a notch down from **16** ⑨④.

★★★★☆ **Jasper Red Blend** Boldly expressive **17** ⑨② follows illustrious line, with sublime cab franc
leading 5-way Bordeaux blend. Haunting mineral notes, nervously poised leaf & earth undertones
combine with impressive balance & silky texture.

★★★★★ **Eden High Density Single Vineyard Chenin Blanc** 🏵 Star of an impressive line-up, **18**
⑨⑤ is a masterclass in poise & balance: heft with grace, fruit with minerals, spice with perfume. Sweetly
subtle stonefruit lightly brushed with oak (just 10% new), rounded by 11 months on lees. Shades also-
great **16** ★★★★★ ⑨④. No **17**.

★★★★☆ **Old Vine Chenin Blanc** 🏵 Elegant, stately **18** ⑨④ follows illustrious record with heady
aromatics woven into generous, refined tropical fruit. 50% older-barrel-fermented fraction rounds out rich
& plush texture, adding body & mouthfeel. Outstanding.

★★★★☆ **Original Chenin Blanc** ⊘ 🏵 The wine that started it all: unpretentious, unembellished,
unoaked but irresistibly delicious, **18** ⑨③ is true to esteemed pedigree, with precisely defined stonefruit,
cheerful demeanour & spicy highlights.— GdB

Location/map/WO: Stellenbosch ▪ Map grid reference: B6 ▪ Est/1stB 2000 ▪ Tasting & sales Mon-Fri 9-5 by
appt only ▪ Fee R500 per group (2-10 pax) ▪ Closed all pub hols ▪ Owner(s) Bruwer Raats ▪ Cellarmaster(s)
Bruwer Raats (Jan 2000) ▪ Winemaker(s) Gavin Bruwer Slabbert (Feb 2010) ▪ Viticulturist(s) Bruwer Raats
(Jan 2000) & Gavin Bruwer Slabbert (Feb 2010) ▪ 30ha (cab f, chenin) ▪ 150t/20,000cs own label 40% red
60% white ▪ PO Box 2068 Dennesig Stellenbosch 7601 ▪ office@raats.co.za ▪ www.raatswines.co.za ▪ S 33°
58' 16.6" E 018° 44' 55.3" ▪ 🏠 shredded.balance.undefended ▪ **T +27 (0)21-881-3078**

☐ **Racetrack** see Damarakloof

Radford Dale ℗

Harvest 2019 marked this high-end Helderberg winery's official rebranding (from The Winery of Good Hope) in response to the consistent acclaim and widespread recognition of their flagship range, Radford Dale, namechecking UK-born Alex Dale and Australian Ben Radford, who form a United Nations of co-owners with French cellarmaster Edouard Labeye, SA winemaker Jacques de Klerk (see also under Reverie) and others driving a progressive, inclusive and sustainable venture. A new Pinotage twins with the Vinum Chenin (in its 20th vintage), both 'resonating with customers globally as SA heritage varieties'. Gathering pace is a decade-long move away from Bordeaux-style wines towards lighter reds (more gamay plantings, wholeberry carbonic pinotage) and fresher whites (partial early-pick chenins) with lower alcohols, achieved by terroir-driven viticulture requiring minimal cellar intervention.

Radford Dale range

★★★★ **The Antidote Gamay Noir** Bunch/berry carbonic ferment, like Thirst Gamay, but in 7,000L oak vessel then to barrel for year (sibling is unoaked), giving savoury meat spicing to raspberry fruit of **18** ⑧⑨. Energetic, with bone-dry finish.

★★★★ **Thirst Gamay Noir** Vibrant red cherry notes on light, fresh **19** ⑧⑥, fruity Beaujolais nou-veau-style red, best served chilled. Just 10.8% alcohol for lunch - & beyond.

★★★★☆ **AD Pinot Noir** ⓐ The most fragrant, perhaps most delicate of the house's pinots. Elgin fruit destemmed & wholeberry fermented; **17** ⑨④ no lightweight given its black cherry intensity & serious structure, with grippy tannins. Bone-dry, naturally low 10.5% alcohol.

★★★★☆ **Freedom Pinot Noir** ⊘ ⓐ Best of the top 3 Elgin pinots, all destemmed & wholeberry fermented to capture pure fruit, 10 months in oak, this 10% new, rest old wood. Riveting perfume, tangy black berry fruit, fresh acidity & fine-grained tannins lift **18** ⑨④. Also in magnum, as next 3.

★★★★☆ **Frankenstein Pinotage** Handled much like Gamay (wholebunch/berry ferment & semi-car-bonic maceration in 7,000L vat before 10 months finishing in 600L barrels). **17** ⑨① reflects clay soils with textured power - but no monster, at 11% alcohol actually rather elegant, perfumed & refreshing.

★★★★☆ **Nudity Syrah** ⓐ 'Natural wine' (no additives, not even sulphur) from organic Voor Paardeberg vines, picked early for low 10.5% alcohol & bone-dry finish. Nothing pared down about intensely aromatic **17** ⑨③ though; vibrant pepper tones, wild berries, hints of fynbos & smoked meat, a chalky minerality. Old oak.

★★★★☆ **Syrah** ⓐ Singular Stellenbosch rendition, more muscular, less fragrant than Nudity. **17** ⑨④ inch up on **15** ⑨③; scrub & fynbos profile heralds savoury intensity - hints of iodine - with lovely balance in a long conclusion. 30% wholebunch, some post-ferment maceration. 20% new oak, 18 months. No **16**.

★★★★☆ **Gravity** ⓐ Gravitational pressing extracts components of syrah, merlot & cabernet gently; 2 years in seasoned oak & 6 in bottle mould a **11** ⑨③ sensation ready for pleasure. Lively red & black berries on a firm base balances fruitiness & savoury depths to give complexity, as in **10** ⑨②. Also 1.5 & 3L.

★★★★★ **Black Rock** ⓐ **17** ★★★★☆ ⑨③ shows fine form after **16** skipped. Gorgeous fynbos perfume, brambly berries & spice from 41% cinsaut, 39% syrah & carignan, co-fermented/aged in oak, 16 months, 15% new. Naturally fermented Swartland fruit. **15** ⑨⑤ was syrah with splashes grenache & mourvèdre.

★★★★☆ **Chardonnay** Winemaker as chaperone rather than surgeon allows natural processes to yield multi-layered, complex **18** ⑨②. Like more nuanced **17** ⑨④, fresh peachy fruit nests in firm but pliable support, moderate 12.5% alcohol. There's added allure of vanilla-spiced creaminess from 10 months in French oak, 15% new.

★★★★ **Chenin Blanc** ⑯④ From Stanford vines, sappy, steely fruit of **18** ⑧⑨ lets mineral, saline features centre stage. Wild-yeast, old-oak ferment, 10 months on lees. 11.5% alcohol.

★★★★☆ **The Renaissance of Chenin Blanc** More sumptuous vinosity than above newcomer, sensual **18** ⑨① from dryland Helderberg bushvines, partial bunch-press, wild-yeast ferment, 10% new oak, bone-dry, modest 12.5% alcohol. Honeysuckle aromas & velvety structure support fresh citrus & waxy lanolin.

★★★★ **Vinum Chenin Blanc** Bunch press, 20% skin contact, wild ferment (part in cask) & long lees contact build **18** ⑧⑦'s savoury/umami backbone. Ripe melon centre freshened by acidity, steely finish.

Vinum Pinotage (NEW) ★★★☆ Lighter house style; wholeberry semi-carbonic maceration & ferment in very large old oak. **18** (85) preserves plum fruit, pliable tannins & fresh piquant finish. Not tasted: **Thirst Cinsault**, **Thirst Clairette Blanche**, **Vine Dried Chenin Blanc**.

Labeye range

★★★★☆ **Pinot Noir** (Ⓥ) Like Freedom sibling, destemmed Elgin grapes are not crushed to allow semi-carbonic maceration. Reflecting the persona of the cellarmaster, **17** (93) brawniest of the pinots with earthy wild strawberry & morello cherry fruit, enticing fynbos perfume & savoury truffle hints.

Pearce Predhomme range

★★★★☆ **Cinsault-Syrah** Duo for export customer. Pot-pourri on nose of 'whole-cluster, wild-ferment' **18** (90) fabulously expressive of red berry fruit from 73/27 blend. Stellar **17** (91) was 65/35 & lighter **16** ★★★★ (89) 'Syrah-Cinsault' a 55/45 mix. Lovely 12.5% alcohol throughout.

★★★★☆ **Chenin Blanc** From 5 parcels in collaboration with 'like-minded' Canadian sommeliers, elegant old-vine, wild-ferment **18** (90) more vinous than fruity, but balanced. Like **17** (91), peachy fruit cut by very bright acidity, super for food accompaniment. Now only seasoned oak. Trademark moderate alcohol.

Land of Hope range

★★★★ **Reserve Cabernet Sauvignon** Plush yet poised, ripe yet restrained **17** (89) has tobacco & leather notes complementing red berry fruit. Elegant finish lifts rating. 25% new French barrels, 20 months

★★★★ **Chardonnay** To deciduous & stonefruit ex Stellenbosch & Robertson, partial oaking adds vanilla spice, 8 months on lees a creamy mouthfeel. **18** (86) fuller at 13.5% alcohol than **16** (86). **17** untasted.

★★★★ **Reserve Chenin Blanc** (Ⓥ) Part bunch-pressed, natural-yeast fermented in barrel. **17** (88) fuller, tighter, more palate traction than range siblings, cling peach & yellow apple features with subtle oak spice.

Syrah ★★★★ Farmyard aromas spiral around streamlined fruit in **17** (84), from destemmed & crushed grapes. More nuanced than previous. Year old oak. Not tasted: **Reserve Pinot Noir**.

Winery of Good Hope range

★★★★ **Reserve Pinot Noir** (⊘) Fresh & bright, with tangy red berry fruit. Great-value **18** (87) Stellenbosch & Stanford grapes naturally fermented wholeberry in steel before brief 4 months in older oak.

. . . .

Oceanside Cabernet Sauvignon-Merlot (🍇) ★★★★ 86/14 blend offers blackcurrant & mulberry fruit in soft-textured mouthful, framed by brief old-oaking. **18** (85) fairly serious but charming & generous, too.

. . . .

Full Berry Fermentation Pinotage ★★★★ Was 'Whole Berry', still undergoes wholeberry ferment & semi-carbonic maceration. Unoaked **19** (85) is pure fruited, tense but not astringent, bone-dry. WO Coastal, as Oceanside. **Mountainside Syrah** (Ⓥ) ★★★★ Previewed **17** (83) shows relative restraint; white pepper woven into somewhat stern texture. Year seasoned casks. **Granite Ridge Reserve** (Ⓥ) ★★★★ Syrah combo with cab & merlot rests 18 months in seasoned oak. **16** (84) peppery nuance & firm tannin, for food. WO W Cape, like next. **Unoaked Chardonnay** ★★★★ Made for early & easy drinking, **19** (85) brims with citrus fruit, fresh acidity & even some stony minerality. Not tasted: **Bush Vine Chenin Blanc**. — DS

Location: Stellenbosch ▪ Map: Helderberg ▪ Map grid reference: C1 ▪ WO: Stellenbosch/Western Cape/ Elgin/Coastal/Swartland/Walker Bay/Voor Paardeberg ▪ Est/1stB 1998 ▪ Tasting by appt at cellar door; sales Mon-Fri 9-5 ▪ Closed all pub hols ▪ Owner(s) Alex Dale, Andy Openshaw, Yalumba, Edouard Labeye, Cliff Roberson, Ben Radford, Heather Whitman, Kathleen Krone & Jacques de Klerk ▪ Cellarmaster(s) Edouard Labeye (1998) ▪ Winemaker(s) Jacques de Klerk (Oct 2009), with Gerhard Joubert (Jun 2016) ▪ Viticulturist(s) Edouard Labeye, Jacques de Klerk & Gerhard Joubert ▪ ±100ha (cab, carignan, cinsaut, gamay, grenache, mourv, ptage, pinot, shiraz, chard, chenin, clairette, verdelho) ▪ 700t/40,000cs own label 60% red 40% white ▪ Level 2 BEE, IPW, WIETA ▪ Postnet Suite 124 Private Bag X15 Somerset West 7129 ▪ thirsty@ radforddale.com ▪ www.radforddale.com ▪ S 34° 0' 57.5" E 018° 49' 2.6" ▪ 🄰 dancing.lessened.carbonates ▪ **T** +27 (0)21-855-5528

Rainbow's End Wine Estate   (Ⓥ) (📷)

The pot at the end of this rainbow contains some very fine, mostly red wines from grapes grown on Banhoek mountain slopes rising 540 m above sea level. Engineer Jacques Malan and wife Ingrid settled here in 1978. Encouraged by surrounding Banhoek Valley success stories (and firstborn son Anton's wine studies and St Emilion work stint), they started planting vines in 2000. Second son Francois subsequently joined the family endeavour, helping handcraft wines in a repurposed home cellar and outbuildings.

Reserve range

★★★★☆ **Family Reserve** ⓐ Flagship Bordeaux red sheds malbec & cab in **16** ⑨③ for near-equal merlot, cab franc & petit verdot. Complex & bold, plethora of dark berry notes, violets & spice. Lovely tannin grip, full body, lead pencil whiff on exit from 2 years oak, 60% new (vs 30-45% for Estate reds).

Estate range

★★★★☆ **Cabernet Sauvignon** ⓐ Youthfully tight, **17** ⑨④ highlights a range of forest fruit notes upfront, a deep mineral core & cedary oak following through to the finish, which is firm & precise.

★★★★ **Cabernet Franc 17** ⑧⑨ with dark- & red-fruit notes backed by violets, tealeaves & spice. Polished tannins, savoury farewell. Delightful now, but enough structure & substance for many years.

★★★★☆ **Cabernet Franc Limited Release** ⓐ More depth & precision than sibling. Dab more oak too (45% new), setting stage for long ageing. **17** ⑨③ is lavish & alluring, sage, menthol notes on ripe blackberry, plum & blackcurrant fruit. Waft of tobacco emerges on the finish. 600 cases.

★★★★☆ **Merlot** Dark chocolate, plum & spiced cherry. Youthful but tannins are harmonious in handsome **18** ⑨⓪. Also in magnum, as all above except Cabernet.

★★★★ **Shiraz** Blackcurrant, red plum & dried raspberry fruit laced with black pepper, backed by savoury touch & nimble tannin. Lemony sumac detail on lengthy finish. **17** ★★★★☆ ⑨⓪ notch above **16** ⑧⑨.

Mystical Corner ⓥ ★★★★ 3-way Bordeaux red with dab of shiraz is sleek & elegant. Mulberry, mint & dark chocolate of **18** ⑧⑤ go all the way to the finish. Old oak.

Rosé ★★★ Summertime sipper from 6 red varieties. Light & zesty **18** ⑧① has red berry & spice notes, dry fruity finish. **Chenin Blanc** ★★★☆ Fresh tropical fruit nuances, light, with vibrant acidity. **18** ⑧③ has wafts of almond from a touch of older oak. Stellenbosch WO. — GM

Location/map: Stellenbosch ▪ Map grid reference: H6 ▪ WO: Banghoek/Stellenbosch ▪ Est 1978 ▪ 1stB 2002 ▪ Tasting, sales & tours by appt ▪ Fees: R50 tasting/R80 tour, waived on purchase of R250+ ▪ Closed all pub hols ▪ Sales also via website, delivery free of charge ▪ Conservation area ▪ Owner(s) Malan family ▪ Cellarmaster(s) Anton Malan (Nov 2000) ▪ Winemaker(s) Anton Malan (Nov 2000) & Francois Malan (Jan 2005) ▪ Viticulturist(s) Francois Malan (Jan 2005) ▪ 42ha/19ha (cabs s/f, malbec, merlot, p verdot, shiraz) ▪ 120t/8,200cs own label 90% red 10% rosé ▪ IPW, WIETA ▪ PO Box 2253 Dennesig 7601 ▪ info@rainbowsend.co.za ▪ www.rainbowsend.co.za ▪ S 33° 56′ 25.8″ E 018° 56′ 42.6″ ▪ ⓦ tracking.either.dinosaur ▪ **T +27 (0)21-885-1719/+27 (0)83-411-0170/+27 (0)82-404-1085**

☐ **Raised By Wolves** *see* Yardstick Wines

Raka   ⓥ ⓐ ⓐ ⓐ ⓐ

Two tough years of drought saw yields decline - but that's part of farming, maintains Piet Dreyer, patriarch of this family venture. The former squid fisherman could never have foreseen, when he bought the home-farm at the foot of Akkedisberg in 1982, that 20 years later he'd build a cellar and two decades beyond that, have 60-plus hectares under vine, with one son (Josef) making wine and another (Pieter) in the vineyards, and a daughter (Jorika) handling sales. (And the eldest son, Gerhard, succeeding him in the fishing business.) With an expanded outdoor area, their venue is a popular destination for visitors to relax and enjoy the views of the mountains and Klein River Valley near Stanford.

Raka range

★★★★☆ **Cabernet Sauvignon** ⓩ Svelte, spicy & amply fruited, **16** ⑨⓪ everything a cab should be. Smart, nuanced, focused, with backbone of oak (25% new French) beautifully supporting core of ripe, supple black fruit. Long & rewarding.

★★★★ **Cabernet Franc** ⓐ Lithe **17** ⑧⑧ shows graphite, liquorice & floral nuances on refined, textured palate with notable chalky tannin grip. Like **16** ⑧⑨, light bodied & long.

★★★★☆ **Barrel Select Merlot** ⓥ Stellar **17** ⑨⓪ vintage surpasses **16** ★★★★ ⑧⑨ with savoury appeal of dark fruit richness, cocoa & spice. Good firm grip from year in oak, 25% new, but well knit. Concentrated & long. Selection of best 30 barrels.

★★★★ **Petit Verdot** Ripe cherry brightness of 17 ⑧⑦ step up on 16 ★★★★ ⑧⑤. Trademark dry tannin grip from house-standard 12–14 months in 25% new oak. Good density & body.

★★★★☆ **Biography Shiraz** ⊘ Elegant 17 ⑨⓪ maintains standard set by previous with dried herb-tinged blue & black fruit succulence. Compact yet nimble, with fine dry tannin from 25% new oak. Layered, refined yet rich & long.

★★★★☆ **Five Maidens** ⓰ Knockout 11 ⑨⓪ 5-way cab-led Bordeaux-style commemorates 10 years of the Dreyer family in wine. Elegant intensity, without excess weight. Great vibrancy & persistence.

★★★★☆ **Quinary** ⊘ ⓰ Cab upped to 53% in 17 ⑨① vintage of dependable 5-way Bordeaux red. Typical cedar-edged fruitcake generosity with integrated oak grip & structure. Pliable & plush, it drinks well now but will reward patience. Also in 1.5L to 15L.

★★★★ **Figurehead Cape Blend** Rich fruitcake appeal to 17 ⑧⑨, with 15% pinotage adding succulence to cab-led blend. Subtle dry grip from oaking, 25% new, good concentration & density. 16 untasted.

Malbec ★★★★ Bright cherry & spice appeal to light & succulent 17 ⑧⑤. Bold oak (25% new) on medium tail. **Pinotage** ★★★★ Approachable, soft & plush, red-fruited 17 ⑧⑤ maintains standard of previous. Vanilla spice note from portion American oak. **Sangiovese** ★★★★☆ Spicy dry tannin so typical of Italian grape, 16 ⑧④ is light, supple & cherry toned. Perfect accompaniment to pasta. **Spliced** ⊘ ★★★☆ Brooding plum & spice appeal on cab-led 17 ⑧⑤, a 5-way Bordeaux/shiraz blend which improves on previous. Soft, succulent & approachable, with earthy depth. WO Cape South Coast. **Rosé** ⊘ ★★★ Simply appealing 19 ⑧② blends malbec, shiraz, cab, mourvèdre & petit verdot. Unfussy dry berry fun for poolside quaffing. **Sauvignon Blanc** ⊘ ★★★☆ Tropical pineapple & granadilla vibrancy to 19 ⑧⑤. Extra nuance from four blocks on different slopes, skin & lees contact.

Erica range ⓝⓔⓦ

★★★★☆ **Cabernet Sauvignon** ⓰ Rounded, spicy & pliable 16 ⑨⓪. Fruit bold enough to counter 3 years all-new oak. Juicy & fresh, with a long, piquant finish, nicely integrated tannin. Alcohol 15%.

★★★★ **Shiraz** Graphite & ink depth to 16 ⑧⑨. Plush, gentle & silk-textured palate which balances fruit & oak, also 36 months, new French. Smoky nuance to firm exit.— FM

Location: Stanford ▪ Map: Walker Bay & Bot River ▪ Map grid reference: C8 ▪ WO: Klein River/Cape South Coast ▪ Est/1stB 2002 ▪ Tasting & sales Mon-Fri 9-5 Sat 10-2.30 ▪ Tasting fee: R30/6 wines on daily tasting list, or R110/ whole range ▪ Closed Sun, Good Fri & Dec 25 ▪ Cellar tours & large groups by appt ▪ BYO picnic ▪ Kiddies play area ▪ Conservation area ▪ Owner(s) Piet Dreyer ▪ Winemaker(s) Josef Dreyer (Jan 2007) ▪ Viticulturist(s) Pieter Dreyer (Jan 2007) ▪ 760ha/62ha (5 Bdx, mourv, ptage, sangio, shiraz, sauv, viog) ▪ 35oꞇ/30,000cs own label 75% red 17% white 8% rosé ▪ IPW ▪ PO Box 124 Caledon 7230 ▪ info@rakawine.co.za ▪ www.rakawine.co.za ▪ S 34° 23' 56.1" E 019° 37' 26.7" ▪ ✉ captain.charmer.finders ▪ **T +27 (0)28-341-0676**

Rall Wines ⓠ

Donovan Rall's focus on the Swartland (though not exclusive) has meant having to cope with the exigencies of the drought in that dryland area. He's been using larger-format barrels, for example, 'to keep the wines fresher'. Other tweaks include bottling the reds earlier (and ageing them in bottle longer before release) to preserve the fruit. Outside the cellar, he's also managing some vineyards himself, to have more control over quality. This year sees the 10th release of his justly renowned Red – the equally prestigious White having passed that mark last year. He's still looking for a permanent home in the Swartland, and meanwhile makes his Swartland Independent Producers wines there in rented space. The others are vinified in Stellenbosch, where he also makes wine for Clouds and Vuurberg.

★★★★☆ **Cinsault** Brightly aromatic 18 ⑨⓪ from Swartland & Darling grapes is notably light-feeling, thanks to low 12% alcohol, yet has some richness of red fruit alongside savoury element. Firm dry tannins. 50% wholebunch fermented; matured in mix of concrete & old oak.

★★★★★ **Ava Syrah** ⓰ Fresh, complex aromas with herbal-floral notes on poised, refined, superbly balanced 18 ⑨⑥ - the 13.5% alcohol & acidity just right, the tannins big but powdery-smooth, the flavours deep. Like Red, bunch ferment; year in old oak. Just 1,200 bottles - all deserving time to develop further.

★★★★☆ **Red** ⓰ The syrah down to 58% on 17 ⑨④, with carignan, grenache, cinsaut - winningly perfumed, but that's just the teaser. Concentrated, dense flavours but not at all heavy, the palate with large but well-upholstered tannin structure. Already complex, but needing a good few years to fully resolve.

★★★★★ **Ava Chenin Blanc** (🏵) The expected pure, mineral-fruity aromas & flavours on individual, outstanding **18** (97), intense without being too overt. Almost slippery silkiness, but a gripping brilliant acidity. Saline note on the long, fantailing finish. 13% alcohol.

★★★★ **Cinsault Blanc** A rarity, from old Wellington vines. **18** (86) had 5 days on skins before 8 months in clay pots. Tight & very light (11.5% alcohol). Fairly neutral, but a hint of sweet fruit on lingering finish.

★★★★☆ **Grenache Blanc** (🏵) Floral, stony, spicy aromas on **18** (93), leading to understatedly intense palate showing more of the lingering sweet fruit. Maturation in concrete 'eggs' & clay accentuates dry, fresh precision. Fascinatingly distinctive wine off Piekenierskloof vines. Opens up in the glass & would benefit from decanting in youth.

★★★★★ **White** (🏵) Complex opening to **18** (97) (fruit, flowers, spice...) & no less profoundly interesting palate, supple & silky, lively & intense. The core of sweet fruit moves to a long finish on a firm, balanced structure. 13.5% alcohol. Wholebunch ferment; old oak-aged. Exactly the same blend as **17** (95), chenin & verdelho (71/24) & a little viognier, mostly ex Swartland, some Helderberg.— TJ

Location: Malmesbury ▪ Map: Swartland ▪ Map grid reference: C7 ▪ WO: Swartland/Coastal/Wellington/Piekenierskloof ▪ Est/1stB 2008 ▪ Tasting, sales & cellar tours by appt ▪ Owner(s)/winemaker(s)/viticulturist(s) Donovan Rall ▪ 30t/1,500cs own label 50% red 50% white ▪ info@rallwines.co.za ▪ www.rallwines.co.za ▪ S 33° 30' 39.1" E 018° 48' 22.5" ▪ **T +27 (0)72-182-7571**

Rannoch Farm

The lake and the scenery in general of Rory and Ricky Antrobus' Helderberg farm reminded them of the Scottish highlands, hence the name they chose. There's a tiny vineyard of cabernet, tended by Rory, whose wine is vinified at Avondale in Paarl.

★★★★ **Cabernet Sauvignon** (🥂) Lovely, pure expression of blackcurrant fruit, subtle tobacco & cedar, **15** (89)'s seamless integration of new French oak, 18 months, aided by 3 years bottle ageing at cellar.— JG

Location/WO: Stellenbosch ▪ Est 1999 ▪ 1stB 2003 ▪ Closed to public ▪ Owner(s) Rory & Ricky Antrobus ▪ Winemaker(s) Corné Marais, with Ivan September (both Jan 2010, Avondale) ▪ Viticulturist(s) Rory Antrobus (Mar 1999) ▪ 8ha/1ha (cab) ▪ 6t/500cs own label 100% white ▪ PO Box 5667 Helderberg 7135 ▪ rory@gmint.co.za ▪ **T +27 (0)82-570-3106**

☐ **Raptor Post** *see* Fable Mountain Vineyards
☐ **Rara Sunt Cara** *see* O'Connell's
☐ **Rare Sightings** *see* The Fledge & Co

Rascallion Wines   (Ⓟ)

The Kretzmar family of Broad Valley wine and olive farm in the Overberg collaborate with marketing maven Ross Sleet on this newer Stellenbosch-based negociant business. Homed on Distillery Road in Bosman's Crossing, their creatively conceived Collections (Word and Vinyl) now include an Art portfolio of blends from grapes widely sourced. Focus the past year has been on building distribution in SA and abroad (including Kenya and European countries) with plans to 'expand aggressively in North America'.

Word Collection

★★★★ **Bombinate** Time has been kind to **16** (89), older sibling of Pandiculation, savoury & powerful, with intense spicy fruit, smooth texture & satisfying long finish. 100% oaked for 18 months.

★★★★ **Pandiculation** (✓) Another year in bottle has allowed serious **15** (88) shiraz & grenache (85/15) to harmonise. Tannins are smooth & knit with the lively black, earthy fruit for a rounded mouthfeel. Shiraz component oaked 18 months. Retasted, as all except Rouge.

★★★★ **Aquiver** Same varieties as Susurrous, mostly unoaked, **16** (87) now shows ripe peach & floral tones, roasted nuts on the finish, balanced & well meshed.

★★★★ **Susurrous** Barrel-fermented chenin (70%) & grenache blanc with 10% tank-vinified sauvignon for freshness. **16** (89) flavours have melded, giving a rich, creamy apple soufflé & buttery vanilla character.

Art Collection (NEW)

★★★★ **Impress Rouge** (✓) From Swartland shiraz, cab & pinotage, **18** (88) is bright-fruited, with hint of espresso from 6 months oaking, good structure & balance of tannin & summer pudding fruit.

Vinyl Collection
45 RPM ★★★ Unoaked **16** ⑧⓪ grenache, cinsaut, mourvèdre & tannat now ~~~
red fruit that's easy to drink. From Piekenierskloof & Swartland vines, as next. ~~~
17 ⑧①, white orchard fruit & spice, aromatic flavours smoothly rounded. Equal ~~~
grenache blanc, viognier & verdelho. — WB

Location/map: Stellenbosch ▪ Map grid reference: E5 ▪ WO: Western Cape/Swartla~~~ ~~~ 2015
▪ Tasting & sales Mon-Sun 10-6 (Nov-Apr) & Mon-Sat 10-5 (May-Oct) ▪ Owner(s) R~~~eet, A Kretzmar
Family Trust ▪ Winemaker(s) consultants ▪ 12,000cs own label 55% red 45% white ▪ PO Box 15176 Vlaeberg
Cape Town 8018 ▪ ross@rascallionwines.co.za ▪ www.rascallionwines.co.za ▪ S 33° 56' 27.6" E 018° 50' 47.3"
▪ T +27 (0)78-886-2246

- ☐ **Ready Steady** see Southern Sky Wines
- ☐ **Rebelle** see Le Belle Rebelle
- ☐ **Rebourne Fairtrade** see Imbuko Wines

Rebus

A momentous time for André and Rhona Liebenberg. After 25 years at Romond Vineyards on the Helderberg,
they've sold the farm 'to embark on new adventures'. The Rebus brand name continues, and André will
continue his 'love affair with cab franc'. Now that he is released from the demands of farming, he says, he
can concentrate even more on making his range of wines, sourcing grapes from the same terroir.

★★★★ Extempore Pinotage (NEW) Delightfully drinkable **18** ⑧⑦ in new-wave, lighter & modestly (older)
oaked style: aromatic, flavourful & fresh, with easygoing but form-giving tannic grip & properly dry finish.

★★★★ Fanfaronne (ⓥ) Blend 59% cab franc with cab. **15** ⑧⑦ ripe, rich & powerful (warming 15%
alcohol), hints at oak influence - 30 months, 5% new. Firm & well-rounded, nicely succulent. Last-tasted
09 ★★★★★ ⑨② included merlot.

★★★★ Cape Cuvée (ⓥ) Pinotage, merlot & the 2 cabs on charming **16** ⑧⑦. 15% alcohol, dry firmness
ex 30 months oak, yet easier, lighter-feeling than most of these reds. Last tasted was **11 ★★★★** ⑧④.

Cabernet Franc (ⓥ) **★★★★** Ripe, dark-fruited & tobacco aromas & well-structured palate with a herbal
twist on **15** ⑧⑤ (first tasted since **10** ⑧④). 15% alcohol adds warmth & a sweet note to the dry finish.
Pinotage (ⓥ) **★★★★** Fruity but serious, balanced & juicy, with delicious grip to finish. **09** ⑧④ tasted few
years back. **Ad Libitum Merlot Rosé** (NEW) **★★★★** Lightest in colour of the 3 rosés & the least assertive.
18 ⑧③ same soft texture, the modest flavours well balanced, the finish dry & lightly gripping. **Ad Libitum
Pinotage Rosé** (NEW) **★★★★** Deeper pink colour on this version, also deeper berry notes. Good, fresh grip
with tannic touch. **18** ⑧④, like other rosés, dry 4 months in older oak. **Impromptu Rosé Traditionelle**
★★★★ Was 'Merlot Rosé'. **18** ⑧⑤ from pinotage (56%) & merlot offers appealing fruity aromas, flavours too,
on creamy palate. Balanced, bone-dry, for rather elegant sipping. Discontinued: **Merlot**. — TJ

Location/WO: Stellenbosch ▪ Est 1994 ▪ 1stB 2003 ▪ Closed to public ▪ Owner(s) André & Rhona Liebenberg ▪
Winemaker(s) André Liebenberg ▪ Viticulturist(s) Francois Hanekom (May 2007) ▪ PO Box 5634 Helderberg
7135 ▪ info@rebuswine.co.za ▪ www.rebuswine.co.za ▪ T +27 (0)82-445-8838

- ☐ **Red Chair** see Rooiberg Winery
- ☐ **Red Falcon** see Middelvlei Estate
- ☐ **Red Rhino** see Linton Park Wines
- ☐ **Releaf Organic** see Imbuko Wines

Remhoogte Wine Estate   ⓠ ⓜ ⓗ ⓞ ⓖ

When it comes to the vineyard and boutique cellar, the Boustred family of Remhoogte believe less is more
– except for rainfall! A good quantity of which fell in winter, causing patriarch Murray and sons Chris (winemaker) and Rob (sales and marketing) to be upbeat about the prospects for the new harvest. 'It's the first
time in years the dam filled up and overflowed.' The visitor venue at this special spot, where wagons once
braked while descending the sloping trail to Stellenbosch town (hence the farm name), has the ubiquitous
winelands views of vineyards (inlcuding of new cab franc, pinotage and chenin) but much rarer ones, too, of
wildebeest, springbok and zebra in the game camp below.

★★★★★ **...bernet Sauvignon** ⊛ **17** ★★★★★ ⑨⓪ notch up on **16** ⑧⑦ in its concentration & depth. ...plush black fruit with dry, fine tannins & acid to balance. Powerful but refined. Wild-yeast ferment ...open 500L French barrels, like next.

★★★★★ **Syrah** ⊛ Impressive, broad-shouldered **17** ⑨④ maintains standard of previous. Bold black-fruited palate which stays fresh & light. 50% wholebunch component & 80% new French oak, 24 months, add to overall elegance, undisturbed by 14% alcohol.

★★★★★ **Sir Thomas Cullinan** ⊛ Merlot leads 30% cabernet in **16** ⑨①. Row & berry selection make for a plush, textured palate with earthy fruitcake & spice notes. Succulent, yet well framed with oak (60% new), it is long, elegant & refined. 13.5% alcohol lower than previous.

★★★★★ **Honeybunch Chenin Blanc** Bold, golden **18** ⑨② had 12 hours skin contact & 20% new oak. Ripe, honeyed tropical tones mingle effortlessly with integrated vanilla oak. Rich, statuesque & structured. 32 year old vines, native-yeast ferment & 11 months on lees add breadth while acid keeps it fresh.

Premium range

★★★★ **Aspect Merlot** ② Shows fruitcake, choc, with a herbal twist & oaky overlay. **15** ⑧⑥ lots of flavour, with big, dry tannic structure exacerbated by 2 years in barrel (30% new). Burly 14.8% alcohol.

★★★★ **Vantage Pinotage** ⊛ Lithe, spicy, cherry-toned **17** ★★★★☆ ⑨③ is darkly alluring & improves on **16** ⑧⑦. Supple, nuanced palate with oak (30% new) cradling rich, juicy fruit. Third wholebunch & portion open ferment make for a complex mouthful. Fine dry tannin finish.

★★★★ **Chronicle Cape Blend** Estate's 4 red grapes combine well in flavourful **16** ⑧⑧ blend. Spicy cassis & cherry overlay 30% new oak frame. Less plush than other reds but succulence holds its own appeal.

★★★★ **First Light Chenin Blanc** ② Always a small oaked component (from Honeybunch) in fresh, fruit-driven style. Tasted very young, **18** ⑧⑥ exuberantly flavourful, with serious core of crisp acidity, usual marmalade sweet-sour element. Like all, unfined & unfiltered.

Free to Be range

★★★★☆ **Carbonic Syrah** Exuberant wholebunch, spontaneous fermented syrah/petite sirah blend. **18** ⑨① lively red berries, gentle squeeze of grape tannin & overarching florality. Alluring in its subtle concentration & intensity, & a step up on last-tasted **16** ★★★★ ⑧④. Stellenbosch WO.

Weisser Riesling NEW ★★★★ Shy apple & lime zest aroma on **19** ⑧⑤. Spontaneously fermented in tank, it's light bodied, tangy & fresh, with good length. Occasional release: **Orange Chenin Blanc**. — FM

Location/map: Stellenbosch ▪ Map grid reference: F3 ▪ WO: Simonsberg–Stellenbosch/Stellenbosch ▪ Est 1812 ▪ 1stB 1995 ▪ Tasting & sales Mon-Fri 9—5 Sat 10-4 ▪ Closed Easter Fri-Sun, Dec 25/26 & Jan 1 ▪ Cellar tours by appt ▪ Cheese platters, flat breads, craft beer ▪ Functions ▪ Walks/hikes ▪ Game ▪ Guest cottage ▪ Wild Beast Craft Brewery ▪ Owner(s) Murray Boustred Trust ▪ Cellarmaster(s) Chris Boustred (Jan 2011) ▪ Winemaker(s)/viticulturist(s) Chris Boustred (Jan 2007) ▪ 55ha/25ha (cabs s/f, merlot, ptage, shiraz, chenin) ▪ 130t/10,000cs own label 80% red 20% white ▪ IPW ▪ PO Box 2032 Dennesig 7601 ▪ info@remhoogte.co.za ▪ www.remhoogte.co.za ▪ S 33° 53' 4.2" E 018° 51' 4.6" ▪ ✉ nobody.tweaked.whom ▪ **T +27 (0)21-889-5005**

☐ **Re'Mogo** see Walking Woods Wines
☐ **Renaissance Collection** see New Beginnings Wines
☐ **Renosterbos** see Hofstraat Kelder

Restless River ⚲

Craig and Anne Wessels, owners of this boutique winery, have a clear philosophy: 'Our vineyards are fundamental to our future. A smart cellar will never be a substitute for terroir.' They expand: 'We need old, virus-free vines growing in healthy soils, on the right site.' A legacy they want to leave for the next generation. Further plantings include 3 hectares of cabernet sauvignon, with chardonnay and pinot noir following this year and next. The first, minuscule bottling of pinot came and went; the Wessels promise a more viable quantity to review next year. The Upper Hemel-en-Aarde Valley proved its cool-climate credentials when vintage 2019 produced a record: the last cabernet was harvested on 7th May and pressed on 19th July.

★★★★☆ **Main Road & Dignity Cabernet Sauvignon** ⊛ Named for two blocks on the farm. Unmistakably cool-climate, as perfumed intensity of fresh black fruits, compact build, bracing, steely but ripely firm grape tannins on **16** (94) reveal. Flavoursome & richly textured flesh brings whole into balance. Natural ferment in open oak vats; 21 months on lees in barriques, 25% new. Deserves years in bottle.

★★★★★★ **Ava Marie Chardonnay** (🏵) Five pickings from single-vineyard, natural ferment in oak, aged in mix of barrel, amphora, stainless steel. **17** (97) has thrilling tension, purity & complexity in spice-edged, ripe lime flavours. Texture is as important; density, fine grip, ensure a long lifespan.— AL

Location: Hermanus ▪ Map: Walker Bay & Bot River ▪ Map grid reference: B4 ▪ WO: Upper Hemel-en-Aarde Valley ▪ Est 1999 ▪ 1stB 2005 ▪ Tasting & sales by appt ▪ Closed all pub hols ▪ Owner(s) Craig & Anne Wessels ▪ Winemaker(s) Craig Wessels (Jan 2005) ▪ Viticulturist(s) Kevin Watt (2012) ▪ 20ha/7ha (cab, pinot, chard) ▪ 25t/3,000cs own label 50% red 50% white ▪ PO Box 1739 Hermanus 7200 ▪ anne@restlessriver.com ▪ www.restlessriver.com ▪ S 34° 21' 26.11" E 19° 16' 32.80" ▪ ⌖ parental.earmark.inform ▪ **T +27 (0)28-313-2881/+27 (0)82-650-3544**

☐ **Retief Reserve** *see* Van Loveren Family Vineyards
☐ **Retief Wines** *see* Pearl Mountain
☐ **Retro Series** *see* Elemental Bob
☐ **Revenant** *see* False Bay Vineyards

Reverie   (♀)

Jacques de Klerk, winemaker/viticulturist for Radford Dale, embraces the challenges — including drought conditions in recent years — of dryland farming when it produces the level of quality for which his old-vine chenin has become renowned since the 2012 debut. He's delighted to now have found a worthy match in the form of a pinotage from Voor Paardeberg. With French wife Amelie, he is exploring European markets, encouraged by 'exciting developments' in UK distribution based on growing 'but still manageable' volumes, also feeding the local, mostly on-consumption trade.

★★★★☆ **Pinotage** (NEW) Voor Paardeberg grapes picked early for freshness, natural acidity & trim 12% alcohol; wholebunch carbonic maceration then basket press to older cask preserves delicate red berry fruit in a refreshing wine that dances on the palate. Lithe tannin/acid frame adds gravitas to **18** (90).

★★★★☆ **Chenin Blanc** (🏵) Finessed from tiny berries off 40+ year old Swartland dryland bushvines, 4-day skin contact, natural ferment in old oak. **18** (93) is in the groove, with limpid oystershell minerality, salinity & exceptional elegance at sub-12% alcohol.— DS

Location: Stellenbosch ▪ WO: Swartland/Voor Paardeberg ▪ Est 2011 ▪ 1stB 2012 ▪ Tasting & sales by appt ▪ Closed all pub hols ▪ Owner(s) Jacques de Klerk ▪ Cellarmaster(s)/viticulturist(s) Jacques de Klerk (Nov 2011) ▪ Winemaker(s) Jacques de Klerk (Nov 2011), with Amelie de Klerk (Nov 2011) ▪ 300cs own label 50% red 50% white ▪ 15 Seaview Rd Somerset West 7130 ▪ reveriechenin@gmail.com ▪ **T +27 (0)82-783-7647**

Reyneke Wines   (♀) (📷)

Johan Reyneke is particularly proud of the fact that the original family-owned farm, Uitzicht, outside Stellenbosch, since inception of their wine brand 22 year ago has grown to 60 ha of biodynamically farmed vineyards. Biodynamic certification is a rare distinction, there still being only two officially (Demeter) certified farms in SA. Johan has an Environmental Philosophy postgraduate degree, and has been a passionate proponent of nature-centric farming from the outset. He has also spread the gospel to the neighbours, and another 16.3 ha of certified-biodynamic land is now also farmed by the Reyneke team. The latter includes viticulture guru Rosa Kruger, assisting with the planting of additional sauvignon, semillon and chenin vines this year. The packaging of the Cornerstone blend has also been revamped. It is named as a tribute to the loyal staff whose efforts underscore the success of the business, and who benefit directly from its sales.

Biodynamic Reserve range

★★★★☆ **Cabernet Sauvignon** (♀) (◉) Classic cassis & cedar, pencil shavings, lithe tannins, lovely core of sweet fruit, **15** ★★★★★ (95) more streamlined & polished than **14** (90), the result of stringent selection in the cellar, 24 months in new oak after natural fermentation (as all here except Cornerstone & Sauvignon-Semillon) in concrete tanks.

★★★★☆ **Red** (◉) (Ⓐ) A triumph for biodynamic & organic viticulture, from single syrah vineyard. 35% bunch-pressed **17** ★★★★★ (95) intense, elegant & fresh, with characteristic white pepper & scrub.

More concentration & longer (old) oak maturation than Biodynamic sibling, & even finer than 16 (94). Distinguished development ahead.

★★★★★ **Natural Chenin Blanc** (⊘) (◉) (☀) A single clay amphora made, with no fining, filtration or added sulphur in 17 (90). Lovely fruit purity though more demure in style than more expressive, oaked 16 (94). Quietly elegant & contemplative, with modest 12.5% alcohol. Needs some time to unfurl.

★★★★★ **White** (⊘) (◉) Elegant expression of sauvignon in 17 (93), mostly new oak vs older wood for Biodynamic sibling. This a much more outgoing personality, with white peach, florals & lime, developing more yeasty almond nuances on palate. Both vibrant & quite textural courtesy lees contact.

Biodynamic range

★★★★★ **Syrah** (⊘) Youthful & bright 17 (92) has a tightly coiled structure & lovely white pepper impression. Like previous, part wholebunch, foot trodden. Tannins still resolutely firm, embracing a core of dark fruit that will enchant with proper ageing. Step up on 16 ★★★★ (89), lower alcohol & less oak (14 months vs 20, none new) than reserve Red.

★★★★ **Cornerstone** (⊘) Riper & plusher 16 (88) blend also has 30% new oak, but is now cab franc-led with cab & merlot. Some perfumed elegance, perhaps less depth, but as pleasing.

★★★★ **Chenin Blanc** (☀) Similar appealing beeswax & aromatic dried peach flavours on 18 (89), from two old, biodynamically farmed vineyards. Natural ferment & lees maturation in older oak add a gentle opulence. More graceful intensity & freshness than 17 (86).

★★★★ **Sauvignon Blanc** (⊘) Fermented in old oak & tank, 18 (86) retains fresh, flinty profile despite the dry vintage conditions. Subtle stonefruit & lime, with gentle leesy undertone.

Organic range

Cabernet Sauvignon-Merlot (⊘) ★★★ A riper, fruitier 60/40 blend in 18 (82). Less bright, though more friendly & supple than previous. Still enough substance & ready to entertain. These all WO W Cape. **Shiraz-Cabernet Sauvignon** (⊘) ★★★ 85% shiraz in 18 (82), a third from home fruit, similar smoky, savoury tone, some ripe spicy fruit & pliable tannins. A friendly solo glassful or meal partner. **Chenin Blanc** (⊘) ★★★★ Broader, creamy profile on 19 (83) from a special vineyard in semi-arid region. Shortbread & baked apple flavours (though unoaked), more understated than previous, but balanced. **Sauvignon Blanc-Semillon** (⊘) ★★★ More subdued in 19 (81) than before, with lanolin & oatmeal flavours. Supple, waxy texture with a lemon twist on unoaked, 54% sauvignon quaffer. — MW

Location/map: Stellenbosch ▪ Map grid reference: B6 ▪ WO: Stellenbosch/Western Cape ▪ Est 1863 ▪ 1stB 1998 ▪ Tasting by appt only ▪ Fee R50/R150pp ▪ VIP tasting & vineyard walk with viticulturist and/or winemaker at R250pp (max 20), booking essential ▪ Sales Mon-Thu 9-5 Fri 9-3.30 ▪ Paintings by Mila Posthumus on display ▪ Owner(s) Reyneke Wines (Pty) Ltd ▪ Cellarmaster(s) Rudiger Gretschel ▪ Winemaker(s) Rudiger Gretschel, with Nuschka de Vos (Dec 2015) ▪ Viticulturist(s) Johan Reyneke, guided by Rosa Kruger ▪ 80ha/60ha (cabs s/f, merlot, ptage, shiraz, chenin, sauv) ▪ 70,000cs own label 70% red 30% white + 5,000cs for clients ▪ CERES (organic), Demeter (biodynamic), IPW ▪ PO Box 61 Vlottenburg 7604 ▪ lizanne@reynekewines.co.za ▪ www.reynekewines.co.za ▪ S 33° 57' 13.00 E 018° 44' 26.50 ▪ ⟨ⁱⁱⁱ⟩ railings.gingers. strategists ▪ T +27 (0)21-881-3451(main)/3517

Rhebokskloof Wine Estate   (Ⓟ)(Ⓨ�)(◎)(Ⓐ)(♿)

This historic Paarl Mountain estate, converted in recent years into a multi-purpose function, business and leisure venue, has at the same time made the most of the viticultural potential of its decomposed granite slopes. Well-established cellar duo Rolanie Lotz and Karin Louw are relishing working with quality fruit off young vines in full production (nursed by experienced consulting viticulturist André Rousseau). The portfolio has been trimmed and tiered, packaging refreshed and innovative 187-ml pouches introduced for active outdoors enjoyment. Executive chef Kim Cox presides over a renovated restaurant, while Martin Gebers as new GM oversees the whole.

Reserve range

★★★★★ **Black Marble Hill Syrah** (🏵) From single block on decomposed granite. Multifaceted 16 (94) follows exceptional 15 ★★★★★ (95), reveals dark plum, black olive tapenade, violets & black pepper. Firm tannins & full body, with meaty & savoury finish from new French oak, 24 months. Will continue to improve over a decade.

★★★★☆ **The Rhebok** (🐾) Singular & creative blend shiraz & pinotage (50/37), splash durif. Plum & raspberry purée are the focus, clove, meat & violet alluring embellishments. **15** ⑨⓪ full, with poised tannins & serious oaking (all-new French, 2 years), balance & fine fruit concentration. All suggest long ageing.

★★★★☆ **Sandstone Grove Chardonnay** (🐾) Lavish use of oak, 33% new French, year, so **17** ★★★★★ ⑨⑥ richer & more complex than Rhebokskloof sibling. Flamboyant, like **16** ⑨①, with deep, creamy core of honeyed peach & ripe kumquat yet ably freshened with minerals & clean acidity.

Rhebokskloof range

★★★★ **Pinotage** (⊘)(🐾) Fine-grained & dignified **17** ★★★★★ ⑨① lifts the bar on **16** ⑧⑨, shows weight & presence with finesse. Should cellar well & reveal full potential of the lovely black cherry, plum & brambleberry fruit, subtle mocha, meat & juniper accents. Oak as for Shiraz.

★★★★ **Shiraz** Has splashes viognier & durif, & 30% new French oak adding cedarwood, spice & pepper to dark plum & mulberry. Fine & accessible tannins cradle spicy, persistent core of fruit. **17** ⑧⑧ also in hiking-friendly 187 ml pouch.

★★★★ **Mourvèdre-Durif-Shiraz** With a dab of carignan in **17** ⑧⑥, all in great harmony. Rich yet elegant & vivacious, with refined tannins supporting mulberry & black cherry fruit, violets & sumac spice adding to the luxurious profile. Tad less new oak (25%) but same duration (16 months) as red siblings.

★★★★ **Chardonnay** Handsome **18** ⑧⑧ has cornucopia fruit flavours - orange marmalade, quince, yellow stonefruit - vanilla & toasted almond from 20% new oak emerging on elegant palate. Lengthy citrus farewell.

Chenin Blanc ★★★☆ Youthful & vibrant **19** ⑧④, floral overtones to pineapple, pear & nectarine flavours, inspired 13% splash grenache blanc provides great support on palate.

Flatrock range

Red ★★★ Was 'The Flatrock'. 7-way combo headlined by equal shiraz & durif. Satisfying & quite refined, red & dark berries with whiffs of spice, **17** ⑧⓪ excellent partner for lamb on spit. **White** ★★★ Previously 'Flatrock White'. Chenin (35%) with equal chardonnay & viognier, **19** ⑧② offers bright, breezy quaffing fun this summer. Expect tropical fruit & flowers in a light & zesty body.

Sparkling Wines

★★★★ **Méthode Cap Classique** (⊘) Returns after extended break as elegant & fine **NV** ⑧⑦ blanc de blancs. Chardonnay's lemon sorbet tone deepens into brioche & apple cake from 2 years on lees, delicate mousse makes it even more delightful, especially with shellfish.— GM

Location/map/WO: Paarl ▪ Map grid reference: D3 ▪ 1stB 1975 ▪ Tasting & sales Mon-Sun 9-5, open 365 days/year ▪ Fee R30/5 wines, waived on purchase ▪ Rhebokskloof Restaurant open daily for b'fast & lunch ▪ Facilities for children ▪ Tour groups ▪ Weddings, functions & conferences ▪ MTB & hiking trails ▪ Owner(s) Siebrits & Albie Laker, ASLA Group ▪ Winemaker(s) Rolanie Lotz (Jan 2007), with Karin Louw (2007) ▪ Viticulturist(s) André Rousseau (2017) ▪ 180ha/38ha (cab, carignan, durif, grenache n/b, mourv, p verdot, ptage, shiraz, chard, chenin, viog) ▪ 300t/30,000cs own label 75% red 25% white + 3,000cs for buyers own brands ▪ CVC member ▪ PO Box 2637 Paarl 7620 ▪ info@rhebokskloof.co.za ▪ www.rhebokskloof.co.za ▪ S 33° 41' 6.1" E 018° 55' 56.6" ▪ (🗺) labyrinths.overhauls.starfish ▪ **T +27 (0)21-869-8386**

☐ **Rhinofields** see Durbanville Hills
☐ **Rhino Run** see Van Loveren Family Vineyards

Richard Hilton Vineyards

The past year has shown encouraging signs for Richard Hilton and his Stellenbosch boutique venture. Exports are expanding - a first shipment to China included the whole range, and sales to Sweden were boosted with a listing by Forsea Ferries, operating in Scandinavia. Richard's desire for a cool-climate syrah will be realised this year with a '18 from Elgin. Meanwhile, plans are on hold for 'orange' (skin-fermented) wine The Ancient, after current stocks sell out, as Richard acknowledges it's 'quirky and niche'.

Richard Hilton range

★★★★ **Ironstone** Full of energy in its compact, steely yet unharsh build, **17** ★★★★★ ⑨① syrah's structure provides great support for full flavours - raw meat, spice & concluding savoury flourish - harmonised but undimmed by 18 months French oak, all older. Further rewards in store, as **15** ⑧⑧. No **16**.

★★★★☆ **The Dalmatian** 🌿 Broader, rounder, richer than Ironstone, though **17** ⑨③ syrah doesn't lack grip or freshness. Scented with dark spice, berries & unobtrusive new oak (20%), all woven in its silky layers, concluding with delicious length. No **16**. Stellenbosch WO, as Ironstone.

★★★★ **Rose Quartz** Elgin's cool-climate profile evident on understated yet distinctive **18** ⑧⑧ viognier. Carefully handled, with gentle freshness, the subtle flavours will still benefit from full integration with oak, all older for ferment & lees ageing.

★★★★☆ **The Ancient** ⑳ A remarkable viognier, **17** ⑨③ fermented & aged on skins in 500L barrel, further ageing in oak, all old. Rich in orange hue, dried apricot, peach scents & sweet-fruited silky waves; the freshening tannins, mineral thread bring all to life & allow for lengthy flavour intensity.

★★★★☆ **The Emperor Probus** This viognier a little more outspoken than Rose Quartz, both in fruit & build, while maintaining elegance, balance. Apricot, spice, honeysuckle fragrance on **18** ⑨② heightened by richness, light finishing grip. Oak enhanced, 20% new. Remember for Asian dishes.

Husk Spirit range

★★★★ **Eau de Vie de Marc de Viognier** ⑳ Very smooth & satisfying spirit ⑧⑦, with a lanolin texture. Delicate flavours of stonefruit & spice, warming grip on the finish. Harmonious & moreish. Ex Elgin; unusually, made from wine as well as husks.— AL, WB

Location: Stellenbosch ▪ WO: Elgin/Stellenbosch ▪ Est 2003 ▪ Closed to public ▪ Owner(s) Richard Hilton ▪ Cellarmaster(s)/winemaker(s) Richard Hilton (2003) & Riaan Wassüng (2005) ▪ Viticulturist(s) Francois Hanekom ▪ (shiraz, viog) ▪ 20t/2,700cs own label 55% red 45% white ▪ info@hiltonvineyards.co.za ▪ www.hiltonvineyards.co.za ▪ **T +27 (0)83-650-5661**

Richard Kershaw Wines ⑨

The remarkable success of the label of British-born Master of Wine Richard Kershaw is attested by the growth of the portfolio in well under a decade (the seventh release of the chardonnay which started it all is reviewed below) and the expansion of exports to 20 countries. The focus remains cool-climate Elgin, where Richard is based, including not just the flagship varietal wines but also the remarkable Deconstructed ranges of chardonnay and syrah, small-volume expressions of clonal and site differences, to delight geeks (and other sensualists). The terroir dimension is taken further by explorations of further-flung regions, with a new pinot noir from Hemel-en-Aarde now joining the Grape Positioning System range. And the availability of a small number of magnum and double-magnum bottlings offers, say the team, 'a unique insight into large-format maturation potential'.

Kershaw Clonal Selection

★★★★☆ **Elgin Pinot Noir** 🌿 Fragrant, bright berries & cherry on **18** ⑨④ with usual hint of forest floor. Silky richness & sweet fruit balanced by light dry tannins & firm acidity. Altogether poised & refined, with a subtle intensity. Savoury in effect, but with some sweetness on the finish.

★★★★☆ **Elgin Syrah** 🌿 Customary pure, clean fruit & light perfume on **17** ⑨③. Intense, dense fruit on richly textured palate, with ripely smooth tannins. Very youthful still, showing some oak (41% new, 17 months). Magnums too, as Pinot & Chardonnay. All wines 13.5-13.9% alcohol.

★★★★★ **Elgin Chardonnay** 🌿 Subtle, complex, ripe aromas on **18** ⑨⑥. A rich intensity, yet refined & finely balanced, with silky acidity giving a lively vibrancy & lemony grip. Long, widening finish seems to reverberate for ever. 40% new oak average. Like **17** ★★★★★ ⑨④, delicately powerful. Malo discouraged on all the chardonnays.

Kershaw Deconstructed range

★★★★☆ **Groenland Bokkeveld Shale SH9C Syrah** 🌿 Dark, savoury, even earthy notes on this **17** ⑨④ version of SH9C clone. Big, dense, sweet fruit, bright & balanced & with fine tannin, but heaviest of the syrahs & showing most toasty oak (50% new for all). Magnums & a few 3L bottles for these syrahs.

★★★★☆ **Lake District Cartref SH22 Syrah** 🌿 Perfumed, fresh & lighter-feeling **17** ⑨③, with supple, smooth tannic structure & bright acidity. The most youthfully approachable of the syrahs, despite a little gruff oakiness on the good dry finish.

★★★★☆ **Lake District Cartref SH9C Syrah** 🌿 Impressive **17** ⑨③ linked by a certain robustness & darkness to other SH9C, though a touch more showy & bright, less weighty & sweet-fruited. Plenty of fine acid/tannin structure.

★★★★☆ **Groenland Bokkeveld Shale CY548 Chardonnay** (&) This **18** (94) had a little more new oak (59%) than others, & it shows in youth on the broad, limy-green aroma. Citrus prominent on palate too, the intense flavour & lovely creaminess complemented by a serious acidic bite.

★★★★☆ **Lake District Bokkeveld Shale CY95 Chardonnay** (&) Full-fruited, ripely intense **18** (93), the citrus deepened by an earthy-stony note. Cutting finesse & notably bright acidity makes for a forceful attack in youth, but there is promise of substantial complexity & elegance to come.

★★★★☆ **Lake District Cartref CY96 Chardonnay** (&) Citrus notes on lithely graceful **18** (94), with floral & vanilla hints & a stony force. Recalls previous in its elegance, but particularly harmonious this vintage, with a lifted lightness, creamy texture & long-lingering finish. These small-quantity chardonnays all in magnum too.

Kershaw GPS Series

★★★★☆ **Hemel-en-Aarde Pinot Noir** (NEW) (&) From Hemel-en-Aarde Ridge, **18** (93) with ripe strawberry aromas has more obvious charm in youth than its stablemate, more richness (though balanced by firm acidity & less tannin) but less intensity. A subtle savoury element, though, on the good finish.

★★★★☆ **Klein River Syrah** (&) Clear, spicy red fruit with herbal hints on **17** (93). Bright, fresh acidity & gently grippy tannins, the oak (38% new) supportive. Should harmonise into a robust elegance with a few years in bottle, & develop longer.

★★★★☆ **Lower Duivenhoks River Chardonnay** (&) Immediately expressive, beguiling **18** ★★★★★ (95) already showing spicy-floral citrus complexity. Notably refined & fresh, with the same softness of texture & finely penetrating acidity as **17** (94). 44% new oak; 13% alcohol a little lower than others.

Smuggler's Boot range

★★★★ **Chardonnay** (NEW) Unlike all other wines, **17** (88) only part natural ferment. Rounded rich & flavourful, more stonefruit than citrus, but a fresh lemony acidity cuts the creamy texture. Readier for drinking than the senior ranges. WO W Cape.

Not tasted: **GSM Blend**, **SBS Blend**. — TJ

Location/map: Elgin ▪ Map grid reference: B2 ▪ WO: Elgin/Klein River/Western Cape/Hemel-en-Aarde Ridge/Lower Duivenhoks River ▪ Est/1stB 2012 ▪ Tasting by appt ▪ Owner(s) Richard Kershaw ▪ Winemaker(s) Richard Kershaw (2012) & Dudley Wilson (2016) ▪ ±8,000cs own label 50% red 50% white ▪ PO Box 77 Grabouw 7160 ▪ info@richardkershawwines.co.za ▪ www.richardkershawwines.co.za ▪ S 34° 12' 12.07" E 19° 02' 35.10" ▪ (m) rebranded.bareness.goal ▪ **T +27 (0)21-200-2589**

☐ **Richard's** *see* Richard Kershaw Wines

Richelieu

This famous Distell-owned brand pays tribute to the origins of brandy though its French name and distinctive French-inspired flavour profile. A sibling of the SA-produced brandies, multi-award-winning Richelieu XO Cognac Fine Champagne, is no longer marketed.

★★★★ **10 Year Vintage Brandy** One of only 2 in this category in SA: minimum 30% potstill & brandy spirit matured 10 years. This (89) is elegant, rich & smooth, with floral, fig, caramel & toasty hazelnut complexity. Also in 50 ml.

Richelieu International ⊘ ★★★ Blended brandy (82), upbeat peach caramel flavours, rich & robust (43% alcohol) for mixing. Also in 1L, 375 ml, 200 ml, 50 ml. — WB

Rickety Bridge Winery   (luminosity) (fork) (house) (camera) (person) (wheelchair)

This British-owned Franschhoek winery invokes the past with some of the names used. The Paulina's Reserve range honours original owner Paulina de Villiers, as does the restaurant. But the rickety bridge itself is long-since restored as part of a substantial renewal programme over the years, which included converting the historic cellar into a barrel facility when the new winery was built. Other ranges have their own stories: Foundation Stone has drawings of a winery (spot the dog!); Printer's Devil refers to those dreaded printing mishaps. There are significant changes to the vinicultural team to report: cellarmaster Donovan Ackermann and winemaker Mari Kotze arrived in time for vintage 2019; Rayno White nurtures the vines.

Icon range

★★★★☆ **The Bridge** ⓐ Mere 1 t/ha yield, so **16** ⑨④ cabernet got the full treatment: 2 months skin contact, 24 months all-new French barriques. Glossy fruit, almost creamy richness (& 15% alcohol!), backed by ageworthy tannins, savoury & dry. Deep muscle tone, long future ahead.

★★★★★ **The Pilgrimage** ⓐ ⓦ Was 'Road to Santiago'. From 1905 vines, wholebunch, wild ferment, mainly older barrels/foudres, cement tanks. **17** ⑨⑤ the essence of semillon: beeswax & melon, pine nuts; elegant yet textured palate, ends dry & long, savoury. Almost ageless - cellar it to discover.

Not tasted: **The Crossover**, **The Sleeper**.

Paulina's Reserve range

★★★★ **Cabernet Sauvignon** ⓐ **17** ⑧⑧ pullback from **15** ⑧⑧'s oaking, mainly older barriques, only 15 months from 24, but no worse off. Cassis richness & power, firm tannins for ageing but well crafted. **16** sold out untasted.

★★★★ **Chenin Blanc** Wild ferment in older barrels & stainless steel lets elegant **18** ⑧⑧'s fruit shine, quince & citrus zest, then savoury biscuit at the end. Nice flavour juxtaposition: grown-up chenin. WO W Cape.

★★★★ **Semillon** ⓐ Wild ferment, older barrels & vats, **17** ⑧⑨ wonderfully expressive, melon & green apple, shot though with almonds. Offers more than its elegance suggests: has intrinsic health, long future.

Foundation Stone range

★★★★ **White** Mainly chenin, grenache blanc with 3 others, wild ferment, 80% older barrels, dry **17** ⑧⑧ rewards with stonefruit, barley sugar, lovely ginger biscuit savouriness. Has depth of flavour & interest.

. . . .

Rosé ⓥ ★★★☆ Mainly shiraz, grenache, 2 others, so expect something different in **19** ⑧⑤, strawberries, scrub, intriguing dusty note, yet lovely elegance & lively freshness. Also in 1.5L. WO W Cape, as White.

. . . .

Not tasted: **Red**.

Rickety Bridge range

★★★★ **Merlot** Vivid berries & dusty cedar, **17** ⑧⑧ more approachable, balanced than austere **16** ★★★☆ ⑧④. Still serious, backbone firm, will provide for the future, but there's enough succulence to offset.

★★★★ **Shiraz** ⓐ Long skin contact, 15 months oak, 30% new, but **17** ⑧⑦'s tannin extraction polished, matches the fruit. Classic shiraz, dark & spicy, grip for cellaring. WO W Cape, as Sauvignon. No **16**.

★★★★ **Chardonnay** ⓐ 30% new, rest older barrel & concrete 'egg', **18** ⑧⑧ toasted brioche greeting, flavours, lemon & lime seasoning. Svelte (12.5% alcohol) more oak presence than last. Great food pairing.

★★★★ **Noble Late Harvest 18** ⑧⑨ muscat blanc botrytised dessert (last tasted was chenin, **17** unreviewed); pale copper hue, expected grapiness, 12 months older barrels for a savoury effect, contrast to the sweetness. Individual. 375 ml. Stellenbosch WO.

Pinotage ★★★ Fruit takes more of a back seat in **18** ⑧⓪, oak's contribution spicy, peppery tones, yet still smoothly accessible. **Sauvignon Blanc** ★★★ Cool fruit notes in **19** ⑧① litchi, meadow grasses, racy acidity keeping it zesty-fresh. **Méthode Cap Classique Blanc de Blancs** ⓥ ★★★ Sparkling from chardonnay, now **NV** ⑧②, 18 months on lees, small portion oaked. Appealing citrus & toasted brioche, but its most distinguishing feature is a steely bite of acid that invigorates. Lovely aperitif. Not tasted: **Chenin Blanc**, **Méthode Cap Classique Brut Rosé**, **Méthode Cap Classique Blanc de Blancs**.

Printer's Devil range

Rosé ★★★ From grenache, 6 months on lees, copper-hued **18** ⑧② has cranberry & earthy notes, true to variety; dry, sleek & food friendly. WO Darling. Not tasted: **Red**, **White**. — CR

Location/map: Franschhoek ▪ Map grid reference: C2 ▪ WO: Franschhoek/Western Cape/Darling/Stellenbosch ▪ Est 1990 ▪ Tasting, sales & cellar tours Mon-Sun 10—5 (May-Aug)/10-6 (Sep-Apr) ▪ Closed Dec 25 & Jan 1 ▪ Fee R50/5 wines ▪ Panna cotta & wine pairing ▪ Wine blending ▪ Paulina's at Rickety Bridge ▪ Facilities for children ▪ Gift shop ▪ Conferences ▪ Weddings ▪ Rickety Bridge Manor House ▪ Owner(s) Duncan Spence ▪ Cellarmaster(s) Donovan Ackermann (Dec 2018) ▪ Winemaker(s) Mari Kotze (Nov 2018) ▪ Viticulturist(s) Rayno White ▪ 50ha/25ha (cab, grenache n/b, merlot, mourv, shiraz, chard, chenin, marsanne, rouss, sauv, sem) ▪ 500t/60,000cs own label 60% red 30% white 10% rosé ▪ PO Box 455 Franschhoek 7690 ▪ info@ricketybridge.com ▪ www.ricketybridge.com ▪ S 33° 53' 58.5" E 019° 5' 27.6" ▪ ⬛ craved.informal. steeper ▪ **T** +27 (0)21-876-2129

Ridgeback 🔍 🍴 🏠 📷 👤 ♿

The inspiration for this Agter Paarl farm's name and labels is Rhodesian Ridgebacks, dogs whose breeding can be traced to the semi-domesticated, ridged hunting dogs of southern Africa, and which were brought here by the estate's Zimbabwean founders. Subsequent generations welcome visitors to the property. With mountainside vineyards and a variety of aspects, there was much to attract Toit Wessels here 20 years ago. Now winemaker, viticulturist and GM, he has guided range development over the years. There are two new wines (neither tasted here): Lucky Lady Rosé, only available at cellardoor, and Mischief bubbly. Expanding on the many visitor attractions already available, Ridgeback has become the starting point of Hero Adventures' mountain bike trail around Paarl Mountain.

His Master's Choice range

★★★★★ **Signature C** 🐾 Cab franc-led (70%), with equal cab, merlot, petit verdot; 18 months in oak, 80% new. **17** ★★★★★ (94) made for a future: cocoa-rich chocolate, graphite, the glossy fruit partnering the tannins, but deep muscle tone proclaims its serious intent. **16** (95) was similarly worth cellaring.

★★★★☆ **Signature S** 🐾 Shiraz with mourvèdre & grenache, no viognier as in previous, but great compatibility in **17** (93). Dark toned, compact, with concentration & musculature, deeply seamed layers of interest. Mainly new oak, 16 months, accessible but the best lies ahead.

Ridgeback range

★★★★ **Cabernet Sauvignon** 🐾 Third new barrels in **16** (89) brings oak spice to the fore, partnering the molten dark plums, subtle element of fynbos. Nice expression of cab, plush, compact, balanced.

★★★★☆ **Cabernet Franc** 🐾 Lovely typicity in **16** (93), a sprinkle of herbs over red berries, even graphite shading, a complex, involving wine. There's enough succulence for immediate enjoyment but its true worth lies in the future, the dry finish attests to that.

★★★★ **Merlot** 🐾 Expressive fruit & dark chocolate in **16** (88), strikes the right oaking balance, enough for a future but no barrier to current enjoyment. Supple, streamlined, well made.

★★★★ **Shiraz** 🐾 Savoury without austerity, **16** (88) is built to age but the dark fruit is an equal partner, giving flesh to the tannins. More Old World style than New in its tobacco & black pepper tones.

★★★★ **Journey** 🐾 Bordeaux blend, equal merlot/cab, & cab franc, petit verdot. Glossy fruit, cassis & plums throughout, cedar spiced, **16** (88) very likeable but firm ageworthy tannins demand respect.

★★★★☆ **Chenin Blanc** ✅ 🐾 Mainly wholeberry ferment, 8 months mixed-provenance older barrels for 80% of wine, as for Viognier. **18** (93) upholds standard set by **17** (93). Orange blossom & preserved melon, honey biscuit savouriness & a brisk, zesty lemon finish. Lots to offer.

★★★★☆ **Viognier** ✅ 🐾 Standout version of the variety. Proudly displays its aromatic charms, yet **18** ★★★★★ (95) has refinement, finesse in the flavours & structure. Peach pip, almond biscotti, a savoury core that's almost elemental. Good enough solo or for a creative food match, like **17** (94).

★★★★ **Natural Sweet Viognier** 🐾 Continues in piquantly fresh style. **15** (87) lively, light (10.5% alcohol) & racy dessert wine that exudes pineapple & lime.

....

Viognier Méthode Cap Classique 🍾 ★★★★ Unique in the guide, champagne-method sparkling from viognier, small portion oaked, 36 months bottle aged, **15** (84) wears the varietal floral/peach pip character with pride, while retaining svelte freshness. Aperitif with difference, personality.

....

African Ember ★★★ Was 'SGMV', **16** (82) same blend, shiraz-led with grenache, dabs mourvèdre, viognier. Dark fruit & liquorice, some mocha flavours, smooth & tasty. **Sauvignon Blanc** ★★★ Care taken to preserve **19** (81)'s freshness, minerality at core, gentle fruit notes adding interest. Sleek & dry. — CR

Location/map/WO: Paarl ▪ Map grid reference: D3 ▪ Est 1997 ▪ 1stB 2001 ▪ Tasting & sales Mon-Sat 10-5 (summer)/10-4 (winter) Sun 10-4 ▪ Fee R30pp/6 wines, R50pp/6 premium wines ▪ Closed Good Fri, Dec 25 & Jan 1 ▪ Cellar tours by appt ▪ The Deck Restaurant Tue-Sun 9.30-3.30 ▪ 4-star/5-room Ridgeback Guest House ▪ Hiking & MTB trails ▪ Children's play area ▪ Owner(s) Kilimanjaro Investments ▪ Cellarmaster(s)/winemaker(s) Toit Wessels (Jan 2007) ▪ Viticulturist(s) Toit Wessels (Mar 2000) ▪ 65ha/35ha (cabs s/f, grenache, merlot, mourv, p verdot, shiraz, sauv, viog) ▪ 300t/30,000cs own label 60% red 35% white 5% sweet ▪ WIETA ▪ PO Box 2076 Windmeul Paarl 7630 ▪ tasting@ridgeback.co.za ▪ www.ridgebackwines.co.za ▪ S 33° 40' 24.9" E 018° 54' 53.5" ▪ 🗺 suddenly.zippy.unabridged ▪ **T +27 (0)21-869-8068**

☐ **Ridgelands** *see* Elgin Vintners
☐ **Riebeek Cellars** *see* Riebeek Valley Wine Co

Riebeek Valley Wine Co

December 2018 marked the beginning of a new era for Riebeek Cellars, the self-described 'authentically Swartland' venture in Riebeek-Kasteel founded during the co-operative boom of the 1940s. Unveiling a new company name, Riebeek Valley Wine Co, the team indicated they'd re-focused on sustainability through collaboration, and noted significant investments in the vineyard and production facilities, including a new boutique wine cellar. These made possible the provision of a range of wine-industry services, as well as a step up in the quality of the company's own wine, especially the Riebeek Cellars Collection, whose packaging had been upgraded accordingly.

Kasteelberg range

★★★★ **Pinotage** Allure ramped up on **17** ★★★★★ ⑨⓪: bright, rounded blue & red fruit appeal & succulence. Balanced, with good concentration & depth. Textured & long despite high alcohol (15.5%). **16** ⑧⑨, subtler & more restrained but equally spicy & fruit forward.

★★★★ **Shiraz** Seductive dried herb sprinkle to spicy, richly fruited **17** ⑧⑧. Soft & succulent, with voluptuous depths but light bodied & supple.

★★★★ **Chenin Blanc** Toned ripeness on **18** ★★★★★ ⑨① improves on **17** ⑧⑧. Equilibrium of honeyed apricot & creamy vanilla breadth from time in oak is appealing. Structured, fresh & rewardingly long. Full bodied but poised.

Riebeek Cellars Collection

Cabernet Sauvignon ⊘ ⑨ ★★★★ Ticks all the boxes again: **18** ⑧⑤ ripe fruit, balance & structure with ample drinking pleasure. Only older oak used for maturation, like all these reds.

Merlot ⊘ ★★★★ Tealeaf & mulberry appeal on medium-bodied **18** ⑧⑤, poised but has light squeeze of tannin. Fresh, lively to end. **Pinotage** ⊘ ★★★★ Plum & berry vivacity on **18** ⑧③. Light & soft, good restraint in ripeness & oak which supports the fruit. Juicy charmer. **Shiraz** ⊘ ★★★★ Inky blue & black fruit depth on subtly smoky **18** ⑧③ which improves on previous. Nice dry twist of tannin in sync with leaner fruit profile. **Pinotage Rosé** ⊘ ★★★ Cherry & berry ease on dry **19** ⑧②. Good body from time on lees. Bright & refreshing, ample summer enjoyment guaranteed. **Chardonnay** ⊘ ★★★★ Goes up a notch in unoaked **19** ⑧⑤. Trademark citrus & nectarine succulence with lively balancing acidity. Good length & texture. **Chenin Blanc** ⊘ ★★★★ A step up, **19** ⑧③ quince & apricot verve balanced by creamy breadth from time on lees. Structured yet refreshing, persistent. **Sauvignon Blanc** ★★★ Fig & grapefruit typicity to **19** ⑧②. Lively & fresh, with unfussy appeal, ideal for summer. **Pieter Cruythoff Brut** ★★★ Subtle blush-pink hue to dry Charmat-method bubbly. Zippy, with marmalade, green apple tang & lime zest. Uncomplicated & fun **NV** ⑧② from chardonnay & pinot noir. **Cape Ruby** ⊘ ★★★★ Sweet plum spice, raisins & nuts on **NV** ⑧④ 'port'. Balanced & appealing, fiery spirit heart to chase away winter chill. Mostly touriga, splash shiraz. Discontinued: **Shiraz-Cinsaut**. — FM

Location: Riebeek-Kasteel ▪ Map/WO: Swartland ▪ Map grid reference: D6 ▪ Est 1941 ▪ Tasting & sales Mon-Fri 9-5 Sat 9-4 Sun 10.30-4 (wine boutique) ▪ Closed Good Fri, Dec 25 & Jan 1 ▪ Cellar tours by appt ▪ Owner(s) 30 shareholders ▪ CEO Werner Engelbrecht ▪ Production manager Alecia Boshoff ▪ Winemaker(s) Alecia Boshoff (Dec 2004), Jacques Theron (Dec 2017) & Thembile Ntloko (Nov 2016) ▪ Viticulturist(s) Claude Uren (Aug 2018) ▪ 950ha (cab, cinsaut, grenache n/b, merlot, mourv, ptage, shiraz, touriga nacional, chenin, sauv, viog) ▪ 40% red 50% white 10% rosé ▪ ±100,000cs for clients ▪ PO Box 13 Riebeek-Kasteel 7307 ▪ info@riebeekwineco.co.za ▪ www.riebeekvalleywineco.com, www.riebeekcellarscollection.com ▪ S 33° 22' 58.0" E 018° 54' 54.5" ▪ ⌖ spades.tradition.partaking ▪ **T +27 (0)22-448-1213**

Rietvallei Wine Estate ⑨ ⑾ ⊚ ⑤

One of the oldest wine estates in Robertson, that of the Burger family, with owner/winemaker Kobus the 6th generation here. It boasts red muscadel vines planted by a 2nd-generation Burger in 1908, the oldest in SA, and the bottle label proudly carries that as part of its design. The up-market range offers many other delights, including creative blends and a highly rated cabernet franc. The Burger Family Vineyards, John B and Stonedale brands untasted.

Heritage Collection

★★★★ **JMB Cabernet Franc** ⓥ Plush & streamlined **14** ⑧⑦; blackcurrants, hint of graphite, chopped herbs, good freshness supplying a lift. All-new French oak 24 months. Tasted last edition out of vintage sequence. Like **15** ⑧⑦, built for the future, but also current enjoyment

★★★★ **JMB Chardonnay** ⓥ New-oak-fermented **18** ★★★★★ ⑨⑩ preview is citrus themed, elegance & purity with admirable intensity. Oak well-judged, in progress but promises well. Improves on **17** ⑧⑦

★★★★ **Estéanna Chardonnay-Sauvignon Blanc-Chenin Blanc-Viognier-Nouvelle** ⓥ Portion barrel fermented/aged, rest tank; though chardonnay dominates at 40%, **17** ⑧⑦ different profile to a varietal chard: green fig & melon, creamy palate with balancing freshness & length.

★★★★☆ **1908 Red Muscadel** ⓥ Muscat de Frontignan bushvines planted 1908, fortified style passed down the Burger generations. Deeper colour than Classic sibling, grapiness in the dried fruit, also barley sugar, fynbos honey. No oak, would have spoilt **15** ⑨④: sweet but beautifully proportioned. No **14**. 375 ml.

Estéanna Sauvignon Blanc ⓥ ★★★★ Tasted from second-fill barrel & provisionally rated, **18** ⑧③ combination citrus & leafy tobacco, racy saline acidity. Wine could still change, but what's there already admirable. Not tasted: **Dark Cin, Estéanna Cabernet Sauvignon-Cabernet Franc-Petit Verdot.**

Classic Collection

Cabernet Sauvignon ⓥ ★★★☆ Fruitcake richness to **16** ⑧④, loads of flavour, generously spiced by 14 months in barrel, half new, tannins approachable. Attractive, well put together. **Red Muscadel** ⓥ ★★★★ Pale red colour but rest of fortified **17** ⑧④ is a power trip: intense dried fruit richness, tantalising floral nuances, round & syrupy, mouthcoating. Not tasted: **Shiraz, Classic Chardonnay, Natural Chardonnay, Chenin Blanc, Sauvignon Blanc.** Discontinued: **Shiraz-Petit Verdot-Viognier.** — CR

Location/map/WO: Robertson ▪ Map grid reference: B4 ▪ Est 1864 ▪ 1stB 1975 ▪ Tasting & sales Mon-Fri 8–5 Sat 10–2 ▪ Tasting fee standard ▪ Closed Easter Fri/Sat, Dec 25 & Jan 1 ▪ Cheese platters, book ahead for groups of 6+ ▪ Function/wedding venue ▪ Owner(s) Kobus Burger ▪ Cellarmaster(s)/winemaker(s) Kobus Burger (2003) ▪ 215ha/100ha (cab, red muscadel, shiraz, chard, sauv) ▪ 2,000t/150,000cs own label 40% red 50% white 5% rosé 5% fortified + 800,000L bulk ▪ PO Box 386 Robertson 6705 ▪ info@rietvallei.co.za ▪ www.rietvallei.co.za ▪ S 33° 49' 25.7" E 019° 58' 39.4" ▪ ▣ mountains.confederate.attended ▪ **T +27 (0)23-626-3596**

☐ **Rijk's** *See Editor's Note*
☐ **Rita Marques** *see Conceito Vinhos*

Rivendell Boutique Wine Farm ⓠ ⑪ ⓒ ⓐ

Austrian émigrés Heimo and Maria Thalhammer specialise in sauvignon and shiraz, their Bot River vines, planted just over a decade ago, now under the experienced eye of nearby Elgin-based adviser Paul Wallace. He's overseeing more organic viticulture, in sync with traditionalist consulting winemaker Kobie Viljoen (Villion). Family-friendly and function facilities are anchored by The Singing Cook eatery.

Reserve range

★★★★ **Shiraz** ⓥ Modern, suave **15** ⑧⑨, opulent smoky fruit elevated by maritime influence, so 15% alcohol is less intrusive. Bigger, more interesting personality than Rivendell sibling, deserves a dinner date.

★★★★ **Sauvignon Blanc** ⓥ Part-fermented in 100% new wood, lending distinct sweet toasty nuance to passionfruit & pungent green herbs. **17** ⑧⑧ dry, tangy & fresh, with plenty of palate appeal.

Rivendell range

★★★★ **Sauvignon Blanc** ⓥ Cool-grown herb & greengage flavours on **16** ⑧⑥, though less acid zing this vintage. 6 months on lees add breadth, but shade less verve & intensity than in **15** ★★★★★ ⑨③.

Shiraz ⓥ ★★★★ Liquid berry jam character in **14** ⑧⑤ but fresh, juicy & bright, uncloying. Smoky twist from well-integrated oak, supple tannins; a food-friendly wine also in magnum. **Shiraz Rosé** ⓥ ★★★☆ Nixes sauvignon & viognier for 100% shiraz, **17** ⑦⑨ gains savoury overtone to red fruit; dry & crisply balanced, creaminess from part oaking. — MW

Location/WO: Bot River ▪ Map: Walker Bay & Bot River ▪ Map grid reference: B2 ▪ Est 2008 ▪ 1stB 2011 ▪ Tasting & sales daily 9-5 ▪ Light meals & platters ▪ The Singing Cook **T +27 (0)72-462-4271** (Antonio)/+27

(0)82-896-5106 (Louise) open for lunch & pre-booked dinners; cater for functions of various sizes ▪ Pre-booked picnics in summer ▪ Child friendly ▪ Tour groups ▪ Venue for weddings & corporate functions (in & outdoor; 80 pax inside) with fully equipped kitchen ▪ Large secured parking area ▪ Owner(s) Whales & Castle Investments (Pty) Ltd (shareholders Heimo & Maria Thalhammer) ▪ Winemaker(s) Kobie Viljoen (Mar 2010, Villion Family Wines) ▪ Viticulturist(s) Paul Wallace (Jan 2019) ▪ ±8.3ha/±4.8ha (shiraz, sauv) ▪ 30t/3,000cs own label 33% red 67% white ▪ PO Box 570 Onrusrivier 7201 ▪ office@rivendell-estate.co.za ▪ www.riven-dell-estate.co.za ▪ S 34° 18' 5.22" E 019° 8' 32.23" ▪ ⌨ rebates.ended.lampshades ▪ **T +27 (0)28-284-9185**

☐ **River Collection** *see* Bonnievale Wines
☐ **River Grandeur** *see* Viljoensdrift Fine Wines & Cruises
☐ **The River's End** *see* Stellar Winery
☐ **RNW** *see* Bizoe Wines
☐ **Robert Alexander** *see* Nico van der Merwe Wines

Robertson Winery

This enterprising winery on Robertson's main road was established in 1941 but bottled its own-label wines for the first time only in 1987, the winemaking philosophy (then and now) being 'minimal handling and gentle pressing in order to capture the natural flavours of the fruit'. Today the winemaking team led by Francois Weich and Thys Loubser under veteran cellarmaster Bowen Botha produces more than 100 products, exported to over 60 countries, while Briaan Stipp's team of viticulturists oversees 7.5 million vines grown on over 40 farms, many of which have been supplying RW with grapes for decades. 'This collaboration between nature, staff, farmers, winemakers and the grape already implies a product to be shared and enjoyed together,' says marketing coordinator Annalize Cooper.

Constitution Road range

★★★★☆ **Shiraz** Ⓥ Inky, opulent **15** ⑨① flagship from two blocks on Wolfkloof estate, concentrated fruit pastille aroma, ripe almost jammy black berry & plum flavours; full body & fruit richness lifted by black pepper & allspice; dark chocolate nuance ex 36 months new French barrels.

★★★★ **Chardonnay** Only 10% new French oak in **17** ⑧⑨, 18 months on lees for creamy texture & subtle spice to accompany fresh citrus & pineapple, nicely balanced, almost as elegant as **16** ★★★★★ ⑨⓪.

Winery range

Cabernet Sauvignon ★★★ Confected nuance to ripe dark fruit in **18** ⑧① , soft & approachable, with subtle oak spice from staves, as most of these reds. **Merlot** ★★★ Milk chocolate note adds to plummy, easy-drinking appeal of **18** ⑧⓪. **Pinot Noir** Ⓥ ★★★ Choc-dipped strawberries & red cherries in fruity, lightly wooded **17** ⑦⑧, made for early drinking. **Pinotage** ★★★ Light oaking adds hint of smoke to caramelised berry, plum compote notes in **18** ⑦⑧. **Ruby Cabernet** ★★★ Packed with ripe dark cherries, **18** ⑦⑦ soft & approachable, less than 13% alcohol. **Shiraz** ★★★★ Appealing choc-vanilla oak notes on **18** ⑧⑤, along with black fruit, black pepper, hints of smoke & mushroom. **Cabernet Sauvignon-Shiraz** Ⓥ ★★★ Carefree quaffing in **17** ⑧①, 49% shiraz bringing subtle pepper & sweet American oak spice to ripe black-fruit melange. **Lightly Sparkling Rosé** Ⓥ ★★ Frothy strawberries-&-cream on zingy **18** ⑦④, semi-dry, with mild 10.5% alcohol. From pinot noir. **Chardonnay** ★★★☆ Partly wooded **18** ⑧④ has smooth mouthfeel, hint of vanilla, lots of citrus & stonefruit. **Chenin Blanc** ★★★ Flowers in bouquet of **19** ⑧⓪, generous ripe tropical fruit on the palate, fresh acidity. **Lightly Sparkling Sauvignon Blanc** ★★★ Crisp & fresh, with delicate froth, **18** ⑦⑦ just-dry perlé wine is like Appletiser with 11.5% alcohol. **Sauvignon Blanc** ★★★ At 12.5% alcohol, with zesty lime & green apple tones, **19** ⑦⑨ is summery & refreshing. **Beaukett** Ⓥ ★★★ Aromatic **18** ⑧⓪, semi-sweet equal blend colombard & muscadel with ripe apple & melon notes balanced by fresh acidity. **Gewürztraminer Special Late Harvest** Ⓥ ★★★ Honeyed both in taste & texture, **18** ⑧①'s sweet litchi flavour doesn't cloy thanks to lively acidity & apricot tang. **Red Muscadel** Ⓥ ★★★ Ginger & barley sugar nuances to sweet muscat richness of **15** ⑧②. Rich & rewarding yet uncloying thanks to well-judged fortification. **White Muscadel** Ⓥ ★★★ Clean, sweet muscat seduction on well-balanced & -defined **12** ⑧①. **Cape Ruby** Ⓥ ★★★★ Aged 18 months in old oak, **14** ⑧③ delicious berry compote of a wine, with vanilla & Xmas spice. Not tasted: **Viognier**.

Chapel range

Red ★★★ Range named for chapel used as wine cellar since 1941. Unoaked **18** ⑦⑦ cab-merlot soft & juicy, with forest fruit flavours, under 13% alcohol for enjoying around the braai. Also in 500ml, 1.5L. **Extra**

Light ★☆ Low-kilojoule **NV** (72) is crisp & dry, just 9.5% alcohol for chilled summer sipping. **White** (②) **★★** Peachy **18** (76) chenin & colombard, refreshingly dry & nicely rounded. **Sweet White ★★** Was 'Semi-Sweet', but latest **NV** (72) has 3 times the sugar to tempt the sweet toothed. Finishes clean & fresh, though; low 7.5% alcohol a bonus. Also in 500ml, 1.5L, as next 2. **Sweet Rosé ★★** Cheerful cherry-pink **NV** (72) has perky red apple & berry flavours, almost 62 g/l sugar balanced by brisk acid. **Sweet Red ★★** Wine gum fruit intensity, sweet red fruit balanced by acidity, alcohol just under 8% on newest **NV** (73).

Light Cultivar range

Extra Light Merlot ★★ Juicy plums & berries in low-alcohol (9.6%) **18** (74). **Pinotage Rosé ★★** Rose gold **19** (75) is smooth, dry, with rosepetal aroma, guava on palate, friendly 9% alcohol. **Chenin Blanc ★★** Dry but fruity **18** (73) slips down easily, with tropical fruit flavours, while also-tasted **19** (75) tank sample promises to be even more crisp & refreshing at less than 9% alcohol. **Extra Light Sauvignon Blanc ★☆** Offers dry refreshment to those who enjoy leaner, greener style of sauvignon. **19** (72) just 9.5% alcohol.

Natural Sweet range

Red ★☆ Seductive **NV** (72) tastes like berry cordial & red wine gums at under 8% alcohol. **Rosé ★★** Latest pink **NV** (72) a succulent mouthful of ripe red berry & spanspek flavours. **White ★★** Fragrant, peachy **NV** (73) with fresh, clean finish.

Sparkling Wines

Sweet Red ★☆ Slightly higher ±8% alcohol in this year's **NV** (74) carbonated red, with berry jam flavours. **Brut Rosé** (104) **★★★** Charming pink **NV** (77) bubbly has floral aroma, creamy mouthfeel, forest fruit flavours, alcohol below 10.5%. **Sweet Rosé ★★☆** Strawberries, redcurrants & cranberries galore in sweet pink **NV** (77) fizz with ±7.5% alcohol. **Brut ★★★** Much to celebrate in crisp & dry **NV** (78) fizz, fresh green apple & lime notes, alcohol below 10.5%. **Sweet White ★★** Sweet, frothy **NV** (76) pops with peach, pear & apple, not cloying thanks to high acidity for a fresh finish. Alcohol 7.5%.

One-Litre Combibloc range

Cabernet Sauvignon ★★★ Soft & accessible **18** (81) has subtle oak-stave spicing to ripe dark fruit. **Merlot ★★★** An attractive easy-drinker, as previous, **18** (80) with chocolate note to plummy fruit. **Smooth Dry Red ★★** Smooth & dry indeed, **NV** (74) has ripe black fruit & modest 12.5% alcohol. Good match with pizza. **Chardonnay ★★★★** Ample citrus & stonefruit in **18** (84), smooth, hint of vanilla from partial oaking. **Sauvignon Blanc ★★★** Zesty & fresh, **19** (79) has lime & green apple fruit, gentle 12.5% alcohol for light meals on the patio. **Crisp Dry White ★★** Serve chilled, but don't add ice to latest **NV** (72), it's light bodied enough - & pleasantly lemon-fresh. **Crisp Extra Light ★★** Low-kilojoule **NV** (70) is crisp as advertised, & bone-dry, with pleasing 9.5% alcohol. **Selected Stein ★★** Semi-sweet **NV** (71) is very fruity, packing apricots, tangerines & a hint of marmalade into a trim body. **Fruity Late Harvest ★★** Ripe fruit salad flavours in gently sweet **NV** (72) with pleasant balancing tang, just over 10% alcohol. **Natural Sweet Rosé ★★** Ripe red berry & cantaloupe flavours in juicy pink **NV** (72). **Natural Sweet White ★★** Latest **NV** (73) not over-sweet, ends fresh & clean with a peachy note in the aftertaste. **Smooth Sweet Red ★☆** Concentrated, almost essency berry flavours in **NV** (72), all the more appealing given the 8% alcohol.

Two-Litre Certified Cultivar Slimline range

Cabernet Sauvignon ★★★ Touch of confection on **18** (81) but plenty else to like. Ripe dark fruit, soft texture, hint of spice from oak staves. **Merlot ★★★** Plummy fruit drizzled with milk chocolate in appealing, easy-to-like **18** (80). **Pinotage ★★☆** Cooked berries & plums & a whiff of campfire smokiness in **18** (78). **Ruby Cabernet ★★☆** Packs a generous amount of cherry fruit into a neat body (13% alcohol), **18** (77) soft textured & ready to enjoy. **Shiraz ★★★★** Appealing combo of black fruit, vanilla oak & savoury/peppery notes on **18** (85). **Chardonnay ★★★★** Smooth vanilla-toned citrus & stonefruit in **18** (84), sparingly wooded as previous. **Chenin Blanc ★★★** Copious ripe tropical fruits & florals on **19** (80), upbeat & fresh finish. **Sauvignon Blanc ★★★** As last, **19** (79) offers lime & green apple zing, balanced 12.5% alcohol for poolsides & barbecues.

Three-Litre Cultivar Slimline range

Cabernet Sauvignon ★★★ No rough or hard edges, just approachable ripe dark fruit in **18** (81), deftly spiced with oak staves. **Merlot ★★★** Appealing, as always, & ready to drink, **18** (80) adds a chocolatey nuance to the plummy flavour. **Pinotage ★★★** Smoke-tinged plums & berries, **18** (78) darker-toned than previous but as fresh & accessible. **Shiraz ★★★☆** Pizza & pasta partner **18** (85) mixes savoury, pepper &

fruit flavours, serves with oak vanilla for an appealing glassful. **Chardonnay** ★★★☆ Applies successful template of gently oaking the citrus & stonefruit to create a smooth mouthfeel & hint of vanilla in **18** ⑧④. **Chenin Blanc** ★★★ Ripe tropical fruit & some floral fragrance in generous **19** ⑧⓪, nice fresh lift on the finish. **Extra Light Sauvignon Blanc** ★★ Always a racy, green-tinged version, **19** ⑦② no exception, plenty of zing for fans of this bare-bones (9.5% alcohol) style. **Sauvignon Blanc** ★★★ Zesty, rather than bracing like its Light sibling, also green-toned with limes & apples & restrained 12.5% alcohol in **19** ⑦⑨. **Natural Sweet White** ★★ Peachy, aromatic **NV** ⑦③, not too sweet, good acid clean-out.

Three-Litre Blended Slimline range
Smooth Dry Red ★★ As label says, smooth, dry, with easy black fruit & temperate alcohol in newest **NV** ⑦④ slimline pack. **Crisp Dry White** ★★ Keep in fridge door, so **NV** ⑦② will be well-chilled to show its light lemony flavour at its best. **Refreshing Extra Light** ★★ Slimmer's friend **NV** ⑦⓪, with low 9.5% alcohol in a crisp, bone-dry glassful, to be served chilled but undiluted. **Johannisberger Semi-Sweet White** ★★ Pear, litchi & banana fruit in gently sweet **NV** ⑦①, soft & smooth, with just over 10% alcohol. **Natural Sweet Red** ★★ As previous, a cordial-like berry intensity on the latest **NV** ⑦②, well-managed sweetness & alcohol (8%). **Natural Sweet Rosé** ★★ Latest **NV** ⑦② pink is sweet & sappy, with ripe red berries & tropical fruit flavours. **Johannisberger Semi-Sweet Red** ★★ Berry plum & pomegranate flavours in semi-sweet **NV** ⑦②, a match for hot curry.

Five-Litre Blended Slimline range
Chapel Red ★★ Medium-bodied **NV** ⑦⑥ has ripe, juicy black fruit, drinks easily solo or with casual meals.

Brandy range
★★★★ **William Robertson 7 Year Potstill** Ⓟ Smooth & refined, with more ripe fruit complexity (built around apricot) than the two blended versions - this 100% potstill ⑧⑥ - though recognisably family in stressing the less obviously fruity components. Lower 38% alcohol gives more elegance.

William Robertson 5 Year Ⓟ ★★★ Prunes, dried peach & nuts, & hint of mustiness on this blended brandy ⑦⑧, designed for mixing, but neither very heavy nor very fiery. Like other 5 year version, has 40% potstill component. **5 Year** Ⓟ ★★★ Rather fresher aromas of prunes & dried peach on this version ⑧① of 5 year matured blended brandy, though also a trifle idiosyncratic. Fairly smooth & not too fiery, dry conclusion. These brandies all from colombard & distilled at Oude Molen. — JG, TJ

Location/map/WO: Robertson ▪ Map grid reference: B5 ▪ Est 1941 ▪ 1stB 1987 ▪ Tasting & sales Mon-Fri 9-5.30 Sat/pub hols 9-3 Sun 9-1 ▪ Closed Good Fri, Dec 25/26 & Jan 1 ▪ Cellar tours by appt ▪ Conferences ▪ Cellarmaster(s) Bowen Botha (Jan 1982) ▪ Winemaker(s) Francois Weich (Sep 1997) & Thys Loubser (Jan 2012) ▪ Viticulturist(s) Briaan Stipp (May 2005) ▪ 2,400ha under vine ▪ 42,000t ▪ BRC, FSSC 22000, WIETA ▪ PO Box 566 Robertson 6705 ▪ info@robertsonwinery.co.za, sales@robertsonwinery.co.za, customercare@robertsonwinery.co.za ▪ www.robertsonwinery.co.za ▪ S 33° 48' 36.8" E 019° 52' 51.4" ▪ ⓜ jelly.conga.solve ▪ **T +27 (0)23-626-3059/+27 (0)23-626-8817 (sales)**

Robert Stanford Estate Ⓟ Ⓜ Ⓐ Ⓞ Ⓐ
Winemaking here dates back to the late 1800s when owned by the Robert Stanford after whom the nearby Walker Bay hamlet was named. Vines re-introduced over a century later produce wines, made by Villiersdorp Cellar's Christo Versfeld, that are among an array of attractions to please all ages and interests.

Sir Robert Stanford range
★★★★ **The Hansom** Ⓟ Complex fruit notes, cigarbox & thyme, restrained 12.5% alcohol in **15** ⑧⑦. Cab (60%) & equal merlot, cab franc give firm structure, should reward few years cellaring.

★★★★ **Chenin Blanc** Ⓟ Unoaked **17** ⑧⑦ preview, lovely spicy lift to white peach & floral notes; fresh & persistent, gently gripping.

★★★★ **Sauvignon Blanc** Ⓟ Ex-tank **17** ⑧⑦'s maritime influence shows in cool/green tone, lively but not bracing acidity & passionfruit pithiness. Satisfying anytime companion.

Pinot Noir Ⓟ ★★★ Packed with youthful red fruit, **17** ⑦⑧ finishes on delicate spicy note. Tasty now & for a few years. **Méthode Cap Classique Brut** Ⓟ ★★★ Fresh, dry **12** ⑧② sparkling, appealing golden hue, tiny energising bubbles, some apple pie richness & lively quince farewell. From chardonnay, pinot noir & meunier. Not tasted: **Shiraz**, **Rosé**.

Cutters Cove range
Pinot Noir ⓥ ★★★ Touch sweetness on **15** ⑦⑧ palate but mostly succulent strawberry & red cherry fruit, neatly shaped by powdery tannins. Not tasted: **Chenin Blanc**. — GM

Location: Stanford ▪ Map: Walker Bay & Bot River ▪ Map grid reference: B6 ▪ WO: Walker Bay ▪ Est 1855 ▪ 1stB 2008 ▪ Tasting & sales Thu-Mon 9-4 ▪ Closed Good Fri, Dec 25 & Jan 1 ▪ The Zesty Lemon Restaurant Thu-Mon 9-4 ▪ Facilities for children ▪ Gift shop ▪ Farm produce ▪ Conservation area ▪ Tractor tours/vineyard walks by appt ▪ Amphitheatre ▪ Accommodation ▪ Owner(s) Robert Stanford Vineyards (Pty) Ltd ▪ Winemaker(s) Christo Versfeld (Villiersdorp Cellar) ▪ Viticulturist(s) Jan Malan (Jan 2003) ▪ 176ha/60ha (pinot, shiraz, chenin, sauv) ▪ 320t/2,500cs own label 40% red 30% white 15% rosé 15% MCC ▪ wines@robertstanford-estate.co.za ▪ www.robertstanfordestate.co.za ▪ S 34° 25' 49.41" E 019° 27' 49.98" ▪ ⓦ tending.yielding.flowerpots ▪ **T +27 (0)82-304-4849**

Robin Hood Legendary Wine Series
Elgin-based brand owner Mark Simpson describes himself light-heartedly as a 'Huguenot-blooded orchard-ist', and in similar playful fashion, his Robin Hood wine quartet pairs a figure from Sherwood Forest legend with a course in a four-part meal, rosé Maid Marian the starter to port-style Friar Tuck the cheese. Available from Mark's Elgin wine shop; his more serious Arumdale wines are listed separately.

Robin Hood ⓥ ★★★★ Cab & merlot has trademark sweet note but it's offset by toned fruitcake & spicy berry flavours. **NV** ⑧③ improves on previous in body & length. **Maid Marian** ⓥ ★★★ Deep pink hues of **NV** ⑦⑨ off-dry rosé lead to juicy raspberry palate, pleasantly uncomplicated & easy. From shiraz & merlot. **Little John** ⓥ ★★★ Stonefruit & flint on bright **NV** ⑦⑦ from sauvignon, sweetish edge to pithy grapefruit zest, light & touch short. **Friar Tuck** ⓥ ★★ Semi-sweet merlot & shiraz, **NV** ⑦③ offers leathery plum fruit & gentle spice simplicity. — FM

☐ **Rocco Bay** see Govert Wines

Rogge Cloof ⓨ ⓟ ⓐ ⓞ ⓑ
Winegrowing is rare in high-altitude Sutherland-Karoo, perhaps unsurprisingly when one reads of the history of this farm since 1756 and its various owners 'enduring lions, droughts, snow and freezing winds'. But at press time planting of chardonnay and pinot noir were set to begin on the estate, understood to be the highest in SA. No on-site cellar yet, but there are facilities for tasting the off-site vinified brands listed below, a restaurant 'with sweeping views', accommodation and many other amenities.

Location: Sutherland ▪ Est 1756 ▪ 1stB 2006 ▪ Tasting, sales & cellar tours by appt ▪ Meals & picnics available ▪ Facilities for children ▪ Tour groups ▪ Gift shop ▪ Farm produce ▪ Walks/hikes ▪ Conservation area ▪ 4x4 trail ▪ MTB trail ▪ Museum ▪ Guest house ▪ Stargazing ▪ Nature reserve ▪ 95% red 4% white 1% fortified ▪ Other brands: Cape to Cairo, De Knolle Fonteyn, Emineo, Fair Karoo, Joachim Scholtz, Oranjezicht, Salpeterkop, Sneeukop ▪ Off the R354, Roggeveld Karoo, Sutherland 6920 ▪ info@roggecloof.com ▪ www.roggecloof.com ▪ S 32° 31' 24.79" E 20° 38' 13.00" ▪ ⓦ modules.stipulate.fortify ▪ **T +27 (0)23-004-1161**

☐ **Romansrivier** see Mountain Ridge Wines
☐ **Romond Vineyards** see Rebus
☐ **Ron Burgundy Wines** see Patatsfontein
☐ **Rondekop** see Oldenburg Vineyards
☐ **Roodeberg** see KWV Wines

Roodezandt Wines ⓨ ⓑ ⓖ
It's a remarkable 40 years since Christie Steytler first walked through the doors of this winery. Today, as cel-larmaster, he oversees a flourishing grower-owned venture, in process of constructing a major new facility equipped with combi-tanks of varying sizes and a combined storage capacity of 4.6 million litres. Increased demand for Roodezandt's wine is also reflected in the vineyard, where 'new plantings are showing a positive trend'. The focus is on bulk wine, but the team also bottles a small volume under its proprietary label, and invites winelovers to taste and buy at the visitor centre in Robertson town.

Roodezandt range

Chenin Blanc ⊘ ⊛ ★★★ Brimful of bright tropical & orchard fruit, **19** ⑧⑴ is exceptionally drinkable & well priced, a go-to white for summer.

Cabernet Sauvignon ★★★ Dark-fruited **18** ⑧⓪ is juicy, has a chocolate-tinged finish, smooth tannins for early enjoyment. **Syrah** ⑫ ★★☆ Spice & forthcoming dark fruit on easygoing **17** ⑺⑼. **Sauvignon Blanc** ★★★ Greengage, capsicum & zesty citrus flavours in light, taut **19** ⑧⓪, mouthwatering & dry. Try with goats cheese crostini. **Late Harvest** ⑫ ★★★ Balanced, juicy sweetness & lively lemon fruit made **NV** ⑧② a good solo sip & equally amenable partner for spicy fare. **Red Muscadel** ★★★★ Candyfloss, rosepetal & intense raisin flavours on **18** ⑧⑤ fortified, the sugar very well balanced by fiery alcohol.

Keizer's Creek range

The Red ⊘ ★★☆ From pinotage, cab & merlot, **NV** ⑺⑺ is unoaked & offers uncomplicated drinking with succulent berry & chocolate flavours.

Balthazar range

Not tasted: **Chardonnay Brut Méthode Cap Classique**. — WB

Location/map/WO: Robertson ▪ Map grid reference: B5 ▪ Est 1953 ▪ Tasting & sales Mon-Fri 9-5 ▪ Cellar tours by appt Mon-Fri 8-12 & 2-5 ▪ Closed all pub hols ▪ Sales (at cellar price) also from La Verne Wine Boutique Mon-Fri 9-5.30 Sat 9-5 ▪ Facilities for children ▪ Owner(s) 45 members ▪ Cellarmaster(s) Christie Steytler (May 1980) ▪ Winemaker(s) Jean du Plessis (2012), with Tiaan Blom (Oct 2005) ▪ Viticulturist(s) Jaco Lategan (Dec 2006) ▪ 1,700ha (cab, malbec, merlot, ptage, ruby cab, shiraz, tannat, chard, chenin, cbard, muscadel w, sauv) ▪ 34,000t/26.5m L bulk ▪ BSCI, HACCP, IPW, WIETA ▪ PO Box 164 Robertson 6705 ▪ info@roodezandt.co.za ▪ www. roodezandt.co.za ▪ S 33° 48' 33.2" E 019° 52' 47.3" ▪ ⒥⒥ gallons.immunity.sugar ▪ **T +27 (0)23-626-1160**

Rooiberg Winery ⑫ ⑪ ⓐ ⓐ ⓑ

Established in 1964, this private company with 25 shareholders strives to over-deliver on quality, not only in its own signature Rooiberg wines but also its many export labels and brands produced for clients. The modern tasting venue, Bodega de Vinho restaurant and exuberant red land-art make it a distinctive landmark at the western end of the Robertson Valley. Cultivating some 20 farms around the Breede, Vink and Noree rivers, Rooiberg has become a leader in green production and nature conservation, exemplified by The Game Reserve range, a portion of whose sales contribute to the Wilderness Foundation.

Reserve range

★★★★ **Cabernet Sauvignon** ⊘ Tasted pre-bottling, dark-fruited **18** ⑧⑧ has mocha, caramel & a hint of sawdust on the nose from a year in 50% new oak, some American (as next two reds).

★★★★☆ **Pinotage** ⊘ Previewed **18** ★★★★ ⑧⑨ has vibrant plum, mulberry, banana & dark chocolate flavours, big & bold but not quite as balanced as **17** ⑨⓪ with alcohol over 14.5%.

★★★★ **Shiraz** ⊘ Tank sample **18** ⑧⑧ rich & concentrated, with black pepper & smoked meat bringing savoury spice to ripe dark fruit & sweet vanilla wood notes, alcohol a high 15%.

★★★★ **Cape Blend** ⑫ Pinotage, shiraz, cab blend, **15** ⑧⑥ over-delivers & improves on **13** ★★★☆ ⑧④. Fruit driven (older oak) with softening tannins. No **14**.

★★★★ **Chardonnay** ⊘ 10 months on fine lees in combo French/American oak, 50% new, provides **18** ⑧⑥ with soft vanilla cream texture & baking spice, doesn't diminish lemon & grapefruit freshness. No **17**.

Premium range

★★★★ **Cabernet Sauvignon** ⑫ Juicy dark plum & berry fruit in **15** ⑧⑺, with chocolate richness, soft tannins after older oaking, 2 years in bottle. Sub-14% alcohol.

★★★★ **Shiraz** ⑫ Excellent food wine (think juicy steaks & meaty pastas), **14** ⑧⑥ ripe dark plums on spicy black pepper base; tangy cranberry finish lingers forever.

★★★★ **Chenin Blanc** ⑫ Intense white peach & subtle almond nuance from older barrels on smooth, balanced **16** ⑧⑺, has enough substance to pair with creamy pasta dishes.

Merlot ⑫ ★★★ Mocha & savoury notes on **15** ⑧⑴, plum & cranberry flavours with nicely managed tannin, juicy finish. **Pinotage** ⑫ ★★★★ Slightly high-toned red berry, plum & mulberry notes with savoury undertone, fruit-sweet exit. **14** ⑧④ ready & could age a bit.

The Game Reserve range

★★★★ Sauvignon Blanc ⊘ Conservation-minded range, African Fish Eagle on label of **18** ⑧⑥, with lime & lemongrass nose, green apple as well as grapefruit & granadilla flavours. Punchier than **16** ★★★☆ ⑧④. Coastal WO. **17** untasted.

Cabernet Sauvignon ⊘ ★★★★ Ripe dark fruit on nose of **16** ⑧⑤, palate less generous than last-tasted **14** ★★★★ ⑧⑦, though smooth after year in oak, 20% new, as for all these reds. **Merlot** ⑧ ★★★ Violet-scented **15** ⑧② packed with ripe plum & chocolate, buffed tannins. **Pinotage** ⊘ ★★★★ Red, blue & black fruit galore in **16** ⑧④, spice too, soft & juicy but nicely structured, better balanced than last. WO W Cape for these unless noted. **Shiraz** ⊘ ★★★★ Ripe, tangy, black berry & cherry succulence, **16** ⑧③ rich & full bodied at over 14.5% alcohol. **Chardonnay** ⊘ ★★★★ Lightly oaked **18** ⑧⑤ is full bodied & creamy after 11 months on lees. Very fresh, with lime & grapefruit flavours. WO Robertson. **Chenin Blanc** ⊘ ★★★★ Aromatic **18** ⑧⑤ packed with tropical melon & juicy orange, not only fresh & fruity but also smooth, well rounded. Coastal WO.

Rooiberg range

★★★★☆ Red Muscadel Serious fortified returns in **18** ★★★★ ⑧⑨ with slightly less sugar (226 g/l) & also slightly less complexity than **16** ⑨⓪. Still delicious, with sun-dried raisin & maraschino cherry flavours.

Cabernet Sauvignon ⊘ ★★★ Older barrels/tanks with staves for most of these reds. Medium-bodied **18** ⑧① has cinnamon & mocha notes, dark berry fruit. **Merlot** ⊘ ★★★ No green notes on **18** ⑧⓪, only ripe plum & dark chocolate, soft tannins, nice for a braai. **Pinotage** ⊘ ★★★ Mocha tone to midweight **18** ⑧②, complementing ripe red plum & berry fruit. **Shiraz** ⊘ ★★★★ Ripe dark fruit, pepper & spice abound in **18** ⑧④, big boned but well integrated for easy drinking. **Cabernet Sauvignon-Merlot (Roodewyn)** ⊘ ★★★ Aged on staves, **18** ⑧① is mostly cab with 30% merlot, 10% petit verdot adding to generous ripe fruit & extraction. **Mountain Red** ⊘ ★★★ Ideal barbecue buddy, unwooded, shiraz-led **18** ⑦⑨ with 20% each cab & pinotage has plenty of juicy, tangy, red berry fruit. **Pinotage Rosé** ⊘ ★★★ Smooth **19** ⑧② semi-dry but fresh, with ripe white peach & strawberry fruit, good foil for Asian spice. **Chardonnay** ⊘ ★★★ **19** ⑧④ tangy & fresh, with plenty of citrus fruit, unwooded but nicely textured from time on lees. **Chenin Blanc** ⊘ ★★★ Fresh & zesty **19** ⑧② has soft texture (month on lees) cushioning tropical pineapple & white peach flavours. **Cape White Colombar** ⊘ ★★★ Zippy acid keeps **19** ⑧⓪ from being cloying at 19 g/l sugar. Pear & honeyed melon notes, under 12% alcohol. **Sauvignon Blanc** ⊘ ★★★ Easy-drinking, flavourful **19** ⑧② a tropical fruit salad of guava, fig & granadilla, refreshed with burst of acidity. **Flamingo Sparkling** ★★★ Pink **NV** ⑦⑨ froths with all the sweetness of cotton candy & ripe red berries. Low 9.5% alcohol. **Brut Sparkling** ★★★ Clean, almost firm finish on this **NV** ⑦⑨ bubbly, frothy & fresh with lime & green apple notes. **Red Natural Sweet** ★★ Best served chilled, low-alcohol **18** ⑦⑥ blend shiraz with 20% each cab, pinotage has sweet cherry cola appeal. **Rosé Natural Sweet** ★★★ Watermelon, pomegranate & maraschino cherry flavours in light **19** ⑦⑧ from red muscadel, pinch of spice too. **Blanc Natural Sweet** ★★★ Honey-drizzled fruit salad flavours in **19** ⑦⑨ white muscadel, a sweet treat at just over 10% alcohol. Discontinued: **Cape Vintage**.

Red Chair range

Pinotage ★★★ Aimed at 'beginner' red-wine drinkers, **18** ⑧⓪ has subtle choc/mocha rather than overt coffee notes. **Sauvignon Blanc** ⊘ ★★★ Fresh & fruity **19** ⑧① made in a tropical style, with smooth mouthfeel after month on lees. — JG

Location/map: Robertson ▪ Map grid reference: A7 ▪ WO: Robertson/Western Cape ▪ Est 1964 ▪ 1stB 1974 ▪ Tasting & sales Mon-Fri 9–5.30 Sat 9–4 ▪ Fee R20pp for tour groups ▪ Closed Good Fri, Dec 25 & Jan 1 ▪ Bodega de Vinho restaurant & bakery Mon-Fri 8–5 Sat 9–4 ▪ Facilities for children ▪ Tour groups ▪ Gift shop ▪ Rooiberg Conservancy ▪ Owner(s) 25 shareholders ▪ Cellarmaster(s) André van Dyk (Oct 2002) ▪ Winemaker(s) André Scriven (Jan 2008), with Gerhard Augustyn (2019) ▪ Viticulturist(s) Hennie Visser (2007, VinPro consultant) ▪ 743ha (cab, merlot, ptage, ruby cab, shiraz, chard, chenin, cbard, sauv) ▪ 12,000t/130,000cs own label 35% red 65% white ▪ Other export brands: Zebra Collection ▪ Brands for clients: Cape Dreams, Goederust (Protea Hotels), Headbutt, Woolworths, Zikomo ▪ ISO 9001:2008, HACCP (SANS 10330:2007), IPW, LACON Organic, WIETA ▪ PO Box 358 Robertson 6705 ▪ info@rooiberg.co.za ▪ www.rooiberg.co.za ▪ S 33° 46' 35.3" E 019° 45' 42.9" ▪ 🖅 undigested.domains.dripping ▪ **T +27 (0)23-626-1663**

☐ **Rooibos Ridge** see Fairview

☐ **Rooi Kalahari** *see* Die Mas van Kakamas

Roos Family Vineyards Ⓠ

The Collection was conceived and developed by the younger Roos generation for a modern, youthful market, but has developed a much wider fan base, offering quality wines at a fair price. These export wines are also used locally and offered for tasting, on request, at the Mooiplaas estate in Stellenbosch.

The Collection

The Coco ★★★ Soft berry, mocha on **18** ⑧ from merlot, touch less engaging than previous but still amiable. Same toasted oak-stave treatment as for Bean. WO W Cape, as all. **The Bean ★★★** From pinotage, **18** ⑦ with tangy plums & rustic edge to the roasted coffee bean impression that detracts from balance of last vintage. **The Strawberry ★★★** Crisp, piquant & dry summer pick-me-up. **19** ⑦ rosé from pinotage has lively, fresh... yes, strawberry tone, moderate 12.5% alcohol. **The Lemongrass ★★★** Lighter (12%) & leaner than last, **18** ⑦ clean & crisp summer sauvignon. **The Peach ★★★** Chenin & viognier (76/24) blend **18** ⑧, now without semillon, less creamy than previous. Still suitably crisp, aromatic & easy to drink. **The Mulberry ★★** Plump namesake berries & spice on **18** ⑦, from shiraz. Usual teaspoon sugar, but tastes drier & better than last. Undemanding winter quaffer. — MW

☐ **Rooster** *see* Middelvlei Estate
☐ **Rose House** *see* Mile High Vineyards

Rosendal Wines ⓆⓀ⌂ⓄⓀ

The link between wine and wellness is no stretch here, with the owners of Rosendal luxury spa retreat, guest house and restaurant in the Robertson winelands harnessing the talents of Therese de Beer to vinify selected parcels and bottle special wines from top producers under various labels for clients and regular customers. The bottlings are available online, via Private Home Tastings (see website) and at selected eateries.

Reserve range

★★★★☆ Hilltop Cabernet Sauvignon ⓐ Classic cassis, lead pencil, dried herbs on beautifully balanced **17** ⑨ from Stellenboschkloof fruit. Full yet with admirable restraint, layered fruit & spice, a slatey grip to finish. 20% new French oak, 22 months. First since robuster **14 ★★★★** ⑧.

★★★★ Hilltop Shiraz Attractive lifted aromas of violet, cinnamon & berry, paired with savoury flavours on palate & balanced with supple tannin structure & oak (all older, 14 months) in **17** ⑧. **15**, **16** not made.

★★★★ Reserve Mistral ⓝ Rhône-style **15** ⑧ is smooth & creamy, the dark, earthy fruit in harmony with supple tannins & wood (older, 2 years). Naturally fermented blend shiraz, grenache, mourvèdre.

★★★★☆ Classic Cuvée Bordeaux blend gets splash shiraz in rich, robust **16** ⑨. Good depth, with multi-layered fruit plus spice & vanilla from older barrels, 18 months. Fresh, lingering finish. Massive improvement on last **11 ★★★** ⑧.

★★★★ Cape Ruby All about the fruit, as it should be for this style of 'port'. **NV** ⑧ vibrant, fresh cherry & berry fruit, hint of spice to finish. Mostly touriga, tinta, souzão ex Calitzdorp, ±5 years in old oak.

Occasional release: **Hilltop Merlot**, **Hilltop Pinot Noir**, **Cape Francolin**, **Red Rock**, **Vexator**, **Black Eagle**, **Black Spice**, **Serenity Chardonnay**.

Rosendal range

★★★★ Merlot Dark brooding aromas of plum, chocolate & black cherry, **17** ⑧ fleshy & round with silky tannins for earlier drinking. Older oak, 16 months.

★★★★ Sauvignon Blanc Lively lime, greenpepper & tropical abundance in **18** ⑧ from Darling. Broad, with an assertive acid backbone & food-friendly saline, wet pebble nuance on finish. More flavour & intensity than last **15 ★★★★** ⑧.

Occasional release: **Syrah**, **Pinotage Rosé**, **Chenin Blanc**, **HVIT**.

Barony range

★★★★ Skadi Grenache ⓝ Stellenbosch fruit delivers earthy flavours & red berries in **17** ⑧. Sumptuous, with mouthfilling red plums & spice from year older-oak maturation, fresh lifted finish.

Occasional release: **August Cabernet Sauvignon**, **Bønne Pinotage**, **Candelabra**, **Heidi Shiraz**, **Sophie**, **Røsslyng Chardonnay**, **Cecile Sauvignon Blanc**.

Noble Nomad range

He Stole My Horse Shiraz-Cabernet Sauvignon ⓥ ★★★☆ All about dark berries & spice, **16** ⑧③ generous & juicy, a savoury coriander note in aftertaste of 60/40 blend. Discontinued: **He Was My Lover Pinotage Rosé**, **He Slept Beneath The Stars Sauvignon Blanc**. — WB

Location/map: Robertson ▪ Map grid reference: B4 ▪ WO: Western Cape/Calitzdorp ▪ 1stB 2003 ▪ Tasting & sales Mon-Sat 10-5 Sun 10-2 ▪ R130 tasting fee only charged for groups of 6+ ▪ Wine & Lindt chocolate tastings ▪ Restaurant & guest house ▪ Spa & wellness centre ▪ Conferences ▪ Owner(s) Du Toit Britz, Mike Harvey & Geir Tellefsen ▪ Cellarmaster(s)/winemaker(s) Therese de Beer (Jan 2012) ▪ 18ha ▪ 80% red 15% white 5% rosé ▪ PO Box 3 Suite 128 Roggebaai 8012 ▪ wine@rosendalwinery.com ▪ www.rosendalwines.com ▪ S 33° 48' 7.8" E 019° 59' 19.0" ▪ ⓦ unloaded.flatter.bulk ▪ **T +27 (0)21-424-4498 (sales)/+27 (0)23-626-1570 (farm)**

Rossouw, Gouws & Clarke

This boutique venture has a new supplier, Scholtz Rossouw (hence the brand name change from 'Wightman, Gouws & Clarke'), who grows the grapes on Swartland's Paardeberg in a 1968 vineyard. The owners, David and Jeannette Clarke of Ex Animo wine distributors, and winemaker, Jurgen Gouws of Intellego Wines, are unchanged, as is the focus on a new-wave pinotage, labelled Dry Red, which invariably sells out before we can taste it. A sizeable portion of the production goes to David's native Australia.

Location: Cape Town ▪ Closed to public ▪ Owner(s) Ex Animo Wine Co ▪ Winemaker(s) Jurgen Gouws ▪ Viticulturist(s) Scholtz Rossouw ▪ 2t ▪ PO Box 386 Newlands Cape Town 7725 ▪ david@exanimo.co.za ▪ **T +27 (0)81-011-8505**

☐ **Rough Diamond** see Van der Merwe & Finlayson

Rousseau Wines
ⓥ

André Rousseau is very much at home in, and thoroughly in tune with the Constantia Valley after nearly two decades here, having helped replant Constantia Uitsig's vineyards as viticulturist and then becoming its winemaker too, before going solo in 2015. His trio of wines, names paying tribute to special women from the Rousseau family, are made in the Steenberg cellar with grapes from regular sources in Constantia, Elgin, Darling and Stellenbosch. A shiraz and bubbly may be next; all available directly from André.

★★★★☆ **Babette** ⓥ ⓐ Elegant & complex Bordeaux blend is cab franc-driven (60%) with cab, merlot ex Stellenbosch, Darling & Constantia. **16** ⑨① cassis, mulberry & tealeaf flavours are wrapped around a firm vanilla-scented core from 15 months in 60% new oak.

★★★★ **Grace Sauvignon Blanc** ⓥ Same deft 'tripartite' construction as **18** ★★★☆ ⑧⑤, but fresher, more vivid flavours in previewed **19** ⑧⑦: cool, leafy blackcurrant top layer, followed by vibrant tropical fruit on creamy base from 10% barrel-fermented semillon (7 months). WO Constantia

★★★★ **Sacharia Wooded Sauvignon Blanc** Full-bodied & harmonious **18** ⑧⑥ is from Elgin whole-bunch fruit, 100% oak-fermented & -matured 10 months, giving creamy, leesy palate yet with tropical fruit flavours shining through, long & satisfying finish.— WB

Location: Constantia ▪ Map: Cape Peninsula ▪ Map grid reference: B4 ▪ WO: Coastal/Constantia/Elgin ▪ Est/1stB 2015 ▪ Tasting by appt ▪ Sales to the public via email/phone orders ▪ Owner(s) André Rousseau ▪ Winemaker(s) André Rousseau (2015) ▪ ±2,000cs own label 30% red 70% white ▪ c/o Steenberg Wine Estate PO Box 224 Steenberg 7947 ▪ andre@rousseauwines.co.za ▪ S 34° 4' 17.0" E 018° 25' 31.1" ▪ ⓦ nominations.moonlit.lily ▪ **T +27 (0)21-713-2211/+27 (0)83-460-4037**

☐ **Ruby Ridge** see Govert Wines

Rudera Wines
ⓥ

Psychologist turned vintner Riana Hall allowed herself a nostalgic moment beside her hearth in the winter of 2019, contemplating the upcoming 20th harvest of Rudera and 'living the dream dreamt of in front of a fireplace many winters ago'. Sourcing Stellenbosch grapes, and working in a characterful old Jonkershoek cellar, she candidly says she's 'sometimes thriving, other times only surviving, but still going strong - and looking forward to the next 20!' Her highly rated reds and chenins have conquered China and Canada, and are now wooing the UK and US.

★★★★ **Cabernet Sauvignon** Previewed after 2 years in barrel (now only 15% new), **17** ⑧⑥ riper than Platinum, supple framework contains brooding dark fruit with a compote character. **15** & **16** not tasted.

★★★★☆ **Platinum Cabernet Sauvignon** ⓥ Simonsberg grapes, both berry & barrel selected, which shows in bright flavours & lovely dry cedary tannins. Layered, fresh & elegant, 80% new oak in sync. Though quality's a tiny fraction off **11** ⑨③, **14** ⑨② richly deserves cellaring. No **12**, **13** untasted.

★★★★ **Syrah** In forthright house style, pre-bottling **17** ⑧⑥ features plump berry, dark prune, sweet tobacco & ripe 14.5% alcohol. Naturally fermented, as all tasted this edition, 2 years in cask. Enjoy soon, while in balance. **15**, **16** untasted.

★★★★ **De Tradisie Chenin Blanc** ⓥ From old Piekenierskloof vines, **15** ⑧⑥ subtly nuanced, mid-2017 still waiting for obvious oak to settle & allow pear & lime flavours to shine through.

★★★★☆ **Noble Late Harvest** Old gold **17** ★★★★ ⑧⑨, oak-matured dessert from chenin, welcoming honeyed botrytis aromas, luscious ripe peach sweetness leavened by tangy apricot, very well balanced. Year 15% new French barrels. Last tasted was **10** ⑨② which included splashes chardonnay, viognier & sauvignon. 375 ml.

Occasional release: **Platinum Chenin Blanc**, **Robusto Chenin Blanc**. — DS

Location/map: Stellenbosch ▪ Map grid reference: G6 ▪ WO: Stellenbosch/Piekenierskloof ▪ Est 1999 ▪ 1stB 2000 ▪ Tasting & cellar tours by appt only ▪ Fee R120pp/5 wines, waived on purchase ▪ Owner(s) Riana Hall ▪ Winemaker(s) Riana Hall (2017) ▪ 15ha/10ha (cab, shiraz, chenin) ▪ ±160t/20,000cs own label & BOB 70% red 30% white ▪ IPW ▪ PO Box 589 Stellenbosch 7599 ▪ riana@rudera.co.za ▪ www.rudera.co.za ▪ S 33° 56' 26.5' E 018° 54' 14.3" ▪ ⌑ freed.starters.rotation ▪ **T +27 (0)21-882-8214**

☐ **Rudi Schultz Wines** see Schultz Family Wines

☐ **Runner Duck** see Vergenoegd Löw The Wine Estate

☐ **Running Duck** see Stellar Winery

Rupert & Rothschild Vignerons   ⓥ ⑪ ⓞ ♿

The internationally acclaimed wines from this joint venture between the Rupert family and Baron Benjamin de Rothschild were not available for review, but the current releases are '16 Baron Edmond (Bordeaux red), '17 Classique (red blend) and '18 Baroness Nadine (wooded chardonnay).

Location: Paarl ▪ Map: Franschhoek ▪ Map grid reference: B7 ▪ Est 1997 ▪ 1stB 1998 ▪ Tasting & wine sales Tue-Fri 10-4.30 Sat/Sun 10-4 ▪ Restaurant hours Tue-Sun 12-3 ▪ Seasonal menu and wine-&-food pairing menu ▪ Closed Christian religious holidays, Dec 26 & Jan 1 ▪ Owner(s) Rupert family & Baron Benjamin de Rothschild ▪ Head winemaker Yvonne Lester (Sep 2001), with winemaker André Roux (Oct 2013) ▪ ISO 14001, HACCP, IPW ▪ PO Box 412 Franschhoek Valley 7690 ▪ info@rupert-rothschildvignerons.com ▪ www.rupert-rothschildvignerons.com ▪ S 33° 50' 14.5" E 018° 56' 51.1" ▪ ⌑ outsides.flood.thermos ▪ **T +27 (0)21-874-1648**

☐ **Rupert Wines** see Anthonij Rupert Wyne

Rustenberg Wines   ⓥ ⓞ ♿

Celebrated and historic Stellenbosch family estate Rustenberg, with its old buildings, beautiful gardens and vineyards high on Simonsberg Mountain, was founded in 1682. In modern terms, 1945 is important as the year industrialist Peter Barlow bought and reunited the Rustenberg and Schoongezicht properties, split in 1810. Also significant is 1892, since when wine has been bottled every year. Sadly, wildfires in 2016 meant some wines weren't even made let alone bottled, including the acclaimed cabernet, Peter Barlow. Some blocks rebounded, others had to be replanted. Murray Barlow, cellarmaster and son of owner Simon Barlow, says the issue of climate change is being tackled with suitable rootstocks, clones and planting density rather than new varieties. 'We're sticking with the farm's belt and braces, chardonnay and cabernet, for which there are many suitable sites.' The popularity of the new trio, including a chenin blanc from bought-in fruit, should ensure they become permanent members of the range.

Flagship range

★★★★☆ **Buzzard Kloof Syrah 17** ⑨② captures benefits of specific cooler site in its medium-bodied freshness, also highlights variety's vibrant white spice. For now there's a sense of youthful tightness, evident oak vanilla (40% new, some American) but all appropriate for required ageing. No **16**.

★★★★☆ **John X Merriman** ⓐ Cab-led Bordeaux quintet, **16** ⑨③ harmonious & already showing complexity in its dark berry, oak spice weave. Opulent, richly flavoured yet unshowy due to balanced freshness, bracing tannins. Nice potential. Also 375 ml & 1.5L. Simonsberg-Stellenbosch WO, as Buzzard Kloof & Five Soldiers.

★★★★☆ **Stellenbosch Chardonnay** ⓐ Youthful **18** ⑨① still displaying primary lemon-lime, nutty & creamy-lees tones. Rich texture, flavours & oak (25% new, 300L) complementary partners, controlled, freshened by firm acid. All confidently structured to benefit from ageing.

Site Specific range

★★★★☆ **Five Soldiers** ⓐ Latest **17** ⑨③ reflects increased flinty tension, agile lightness of foot enhanced by bright citrus zest. None at expense of characteristic creamy lees, oatmeal & nutty savoury concentration. Oak (70% new 300L) complementary. Lovely potential. No **16**.

Not tasted: **Peter Barlow**.

Regional range

★★★★☆ **Stellenbosch Cabernet Sauvignon** ⊘ ⓐ Lovely example of Stellenbosch cab, **17** ⑨③ has all classic trimmings: generous dark berry fragrance, subtle oak spice (20% new), sweet flesh, freshness & appropriate dense tannin grip. None of such power as to spoil current enjoyment; ageing will also reward.

★★★★ **Stellenbosch Grenache 17** ★★★★ ⑧⑤ a little sombre, less extroverted than **16** ⑧⑦. Quiet spice, soft but also full bodied & gripped by dense, lively tannins. A few years may offer greater rewards.

★★★★ **Stellenbosch Malbec** (NEW) ⊘ Deep-hued **17** ⑧⑥ is youthfully approachable & easy to enjoy with its deep, rich fruit supported by fine, tangy tannins. Savoury & soundly dry.

★★★★ **Stellenbosch Merlot** ⊘ Restrained plummy, herbal notes on **18** ⑧⑥. Still youthful, with plenty freshness, dry tannin grip dominating sweet flesh. Needs year/2; possibly ready sooner than **16** ⑧⑥. **17** untasted.

★★★★ **Stellenbosch Shiraz** ⊘ ⓐ Serious & seriously delicious, **17** ⑧⑨ also approachable thanks to balanced tannins, supple texture. Deep spice, dark berry concentration backed by well-judged oak (20% new). Simonsberg-Stellenbosch WO, as Roussanne & Wild Ferment Sauvignon.

★★★★ **RM Nicholson** ⊘ **17** ⑧⑦ follows previous 50% shiraz with merlot & cab mix but more firmly structured. Plenty bold dark berries, spice lifted by sweet oak hints. Big, but eased by freshening acid core.

★★★★ **Stellenbosch Chenin Blanc** (NEW) ⊘ From mature Bottelary bushvines, **18** ⑧⑦ exudes ripe red apple, pear appeal in plump, lees-enriched body; dry & lingering. Balanced freshness for current enjoyment & few years' ageing. Also-tasted **19** ⑧⑥ similar flavour profile & lees richness, buoyed by juicy fruity acids for crisp & clean finish. Both unwooded.

★★★★ **Stellenbosch Roussanne** A wine of character. Unoaked **19** ⑧⑥ shows floral, spiced fruit aromatics, concentrated yet unshowy flavours, firm structure with plenty of verve to balance full body. **16 - 18** untasted.

★★★★ **Wild Ferment Sauvignon Blanc** (NEW) **18** ⑧⑥ reflects coolness of high-lying vineyards in its gooseberry purity. Wild ferment, oak spice add extra, subtle dimension. Rich flavours lengthened by firm acid backbone. French oak, 12% new, 6 months on lees.

★★★★☆ **Straw Wine** ⊘ Honeyed hedonism, **18** ⑨② chenin with 18% viognier. Honey again with apricot in its precise, silky concentration; very sweet but nothing cloying or heavy thanks to thrilling acid, low 10% alcohol. Unwooded; **17** ⑨② older-oak aged. 375 ml.

★★★★ **Red Muscadel** ⑧ There's no denying the soft, sweet grapey & floral delights of this fresh, airy **15** ⑧⑦ fortified (16% alcohol) from Calitzdorp grapes. Lightly oaked & not quite trivial. 375 ml.

Stellenbosch Petit Verdot Rosé ★★★ Generous red fruit aromas, rich flavours on smooth, just-dry **18** ⑧①. **Unwooded Chardonnay** ★★★★ Nicely structured **19** ⑧⑤, good citrus flavours & freshness, balanced lees richness, clean & dry. Bit more restrained than **17** ★★★★ ⑧⑥ but a versatile aperitif & food parter. **18** untasted. Not tasted: **Stellenbosch Sauvignon Blanc**. — AL

Location/map: Stellenbosch ▪ Map grid reference: F4 ▪ WO: Stellenbosch/Simonsberg—Stellenbosch/ Western Cape ▪ Est 1682 ▪ 1stB 1892 ▪ Tasting & sales Mon-Fri 9—4.30 Sat 10—4 Sun 10-3 ▪ Closed Good Fri, Dec 25 & Jan 1 ▪ Gardens ▪ Filming ▪ Owner(s) Simon Barlow ▪ Cellarmaster(s) Murray Barlow (Nov 2011) ▪ Winemaker(s) Randolph Christians (Nov 1995), with Craig Christians (Jun 2012) ▪ Viticulturist(s) Simon

Barlow (Aug 1987), with Tessa Moffat (Nov 2013) & Nick van Zyl (Nov 2015) ▪ 880ha/±110ha (cabs s/f, grenache n/b, malbec, merlot, p verdot, shiraz, chard, rouss, sauv) ▪ ±1,200t/120,000cs own label 51% red 47% white 2% other ▪ IPW ▪ PO Box 33 Stellenbosch 7599 ▪ wine@rustenberg.co.za ▪ www.rustenberg.co.za ▪ S 33° 53' 44.8" E 018° 53' 33.6" ▪ 🌐 tickles.usages.medium ▪ **T +27 (0)21-809-1200**

Rust en Vrede Wine Estate ⓠ ⓜ ⓐ

This historic Stellenbosch property, first granted in 1694, was rescued from decay and restored by Springbok rugby legend Jannie Engelbrecht in the early 1970s and has been listed in this guide since its inception (described in the 1980 first edition as 'a promising newcomer'). The graceful Cape Dutch buildings preside over pristine vineyards, cellars, tasting facilities and a celebrated fine-dining restaurant, offering a memorable tourism experience. Latterly under the custodianship of son Jean, the brand has established itself among the Cape's wine aristocracy, producing only high-end reds based on their signature cabernet and syrah plantings. Winemaker and Cape Winemakers Guild member Coenie Snyman has held the reins since 2006, honing, fine tuning and extending the range.

Estate Vineyards range

★★★★☆ **Cabernet Sauvignon** ⓐ Perfectly pitched **17** ⑨② shows classic R&V cab styling: deep, intense blackcurrant fruit tinged with rose scent, velvet texture & understated earthiness. Pedigree suggests excellent ageing potential. Usual 50% new oak, 22 months, 300L barrels, as next.

★★★★★ **Single Vineyard Cabernet Sauvignon** ⓐ Quintessential Cape cab has it all: ethereally fragrant & robustly assertive, enlivened by trace of nervous acidity. **16** ⑨⑥ already stunning, but made for future decades. Worthy successor to formidable **15** ★★★★★ ⑨④.

★★★★ **Merlot** ⓐ Shy, muted **17** ⑧⑧ is already showing promise of vintage but needs time in bottle. Plush, ripe & finely crafted, a study in graceful balance.

★★★★★ **Single Vineyard Syrah** ⓐ Aristocratic **16** ⑨⑥ maintains heady standards, with more detail & nuance than sibling. Restrained power & body, with exquisitely etched structure, silky texture & lingering finish. Fine herbaceous profile complemented by 16 months oaking, 50% new, 500L barrels.

★★★★ **Syrah** ⓐ Intense black fruit with plush, velvet tannins, **17** ⑧⑦ ripe New World styling, placing power ahead of subtlety without losing cellar's hallmark sophistication. 16 months in oak, 20% new.

★★★★★ **1694 Classification** ⓐ Premium-priced flagship of an impressive fleet, syrah & cab since debut a decade back, **16** ⑨⑤ 61/39 blend is succulently ripe & big-boned yet shows sublime balance & texture. Substantial yet stylish, like **15** ★★★★★ ⑨④. Wooding as for the cabs, combo 300L & 500L barrels.

★★★★★ **Estate** ⓐ Standout Cape red for over 30 years, the lustre undimmed in **16** ⑨⑦ cab-shiraz blend (52/39, splash merlot), 40% new oak, 22 months. Demands attention, with gravitas & impossibly dense fruit, yet has poise, nobility. Cellarworthy, as **15** ⑨⑤ & previous. Bottle formats up to 27L.— GdB

Location/map/WO: Stellenbosch ▪ Map grid reference: E8 ▪ Est 1694 ▪ 1stB 1979 ▪ Tasting & sales Mon-Sat 9–5 Sun seasonal, call to enquire ▪ Various tasting options - fee waived on purchase ▪ Closed Easter Fri/Sun, Dec 25 & Jan 1 ▪ Rust en Vrede Restaurant (fine dining, evenings only) ▪ Rust en Vrede Winemaker's Lunch ▪ Merchandise available ▪ Owner(s) Jean Engelbrecht ▪ Winemaker(s) Coenie Snyman (Dec 2006), with Malie McGregor (Jan 2018) ▪ Viticulturist(s) Dirkie Mouton (Jun 2010) ▪ 50ha/34ha (cab, merlot, shiraz) ▪ ±250t/40,000cs own label 100% red ▪ IPW, WWF-SA Conservation Champion ▪ PO Box 473 Stellenbosch 7599 ▪ info@rustenvrede.com ▪ www.rustenvrede.com ▪ S 33° 59' 54.0" E 018° 51' 22.5" ▪ 🌐 snaps.proposes.years ▪ **T +27 (0)21-881-3881**

☐ **Ruyter's Bin** *see* Stellenrust
☐ **Ryk Neethling** *see* Val de Vie & Polo Club Wines
☐ **Saam Mountain Vineyards** *see* Perdeberg Wines
☐ **Saartjie Single Vineyard Selections** *see* Hillcrest Estate
☐ **Sabi Sabi** *see* Stellenrust

Sadie Family Wines ⓠ

Ten years ago Eben Sadie launched his Ouwingerdreeks (Old Vine Series), another landmark in his illustrious career (and in the Cape wine revolution), honouring old, dryland single vineyards. It is testament to the time, energy and capital spent on them by the farmers and Eben that they have survived the recent drought years: '2019 was even more extreme than 2018; winter rains could not fill the subsoil reservoirs', he says. Quantity was severely affected, quality and distinction were not. The same is true of the blended Signature pair, reflecting the wider Swartland with increasing complexity and freshness: 'A variety of terroirs achieves the most stable representation of our region'. Work in the cellar, where Paul Jordaan is centrally responsible, is directed, with minimal intervention, to expressing what the vineyards deliver. And the first vineyard planted on the small Paardeberg home-farm, Rotsvas, gave its first meaningful harvest last year. That vineyard is of mixed red-wine grapes; a second, of numerous white varieties, was planted in 2019.

Signature Series

★★★★☆ **Columella** ⓐ Shiraz with mourvèdre, grenache, carignan, cinsaut & tinta blended as representative of Swartland. **17** ⑨④ among finest yet, exhibits great freshness, tension & secure core of tightly knit, ripe tannins. Incipient wild herb & sweet fruit complexities are temptations worth the long wait this benchmark deserves. Year in barrel, just 5% new, further 12 months in foudre. Unfined/filtered, as all. Also in 1.5 & 3L, as next.

★★★★★ **Palladius** ⓐ Consummate white blend & one of this guide's highest-rated wines, **17** ⑨⑧ being the 9th with the maximum 5 stars. Reflects Swartland rather than any of 11 varieties, including chenin. Has great energy, tension & sense of coolness in its intricate flavours & layers of texture. Striking & distinguished. Fermented/aged year on lees in clay amphora & concrete 'egg', further year older foudre.

Old Vine Series

★★★★☆ **Pofadder** ⓦ Named for shape of Riebeek Mountain origin of old cinsaut vines; this the most challenging wine here, Eben Sadie says. More so in **18** ⑨① drought. Gently perfumed, light & fresh but not without gravitas in its wild berry, scrub fruit. Youthfully austere, grippy but may be ready earlier than usual.

★★★★★ **Soldaat** ⓐ ⓦ Benefit of altitude, great climate on these Piekenierskloof grenache dryland vineyards clearly evident in **18** ⑨⑥. Intensity, depth of wild strawberry, earthy tones; plenty of flesh attached to fresh, resilient tannins. Less ethereal than some previous, but acidity gives sense of cool energy.

★★★★☆ **Treinspoor** ⓐ ⓦ Member of range which has blossomed most since first vintage. 'Tinta das baroccas', the local name, from 1974 unirrigated bushvines growing by old railway line ('treinspoor'). **18** ⑨④ textbook floral, spice, orange zest fragrance, concentration, length, & above all, refined tannins. Confident & full of personality.

★★★★★ **Skurfberg** ⓐ ⓦ Chenin off three old-vine dryland parcels in Olifants River, crop decimated by drought to around 30%. **18** ⑨⑥ triumphs over adversity. Harmonious, spare but not insubstantial build; shy earthy, peachy notes leading to mineral, firmly dry conclusion. Speaks of place rather than variety.

★★★★☆ **Mev. Kirsten** ⓐ ⓦ SA's oldest chenin, Stellenbosch block mostly planted 100+ years ago. Undergoes initial carbonic maceration to protect oxidation-prone juice. **18** ★★★★★ ⑨⑤ stately & opulent but also has thrilling acidity lighting up gorgeous red apple, peachy fruit. Precision, as in **17** ⑨④. Possibly longest-lived of these whites.

★★★★☆ **Kokerboom** ⓦ Olifants River vineyard nearing 90 years old bearing both white & red semillon. **18** ⑨① yielded under 30% of norm, harvested very early to save vineyard reserves, results in more typical cool-climate lemongrass character. Not overly lean; promises to fill out after few years.

★★★★★ **'T Voetpad** ⓐ ⓦ Isolated ungrafted Swartland vines, co-fermented field blend chenin, semillon blanc/gris, palomino & muscat d'Alexandrie. **18** ⑨⑤ tiny quantity yet star quality, easily tops breathtaking **17** ★★★★★ ⑨③. Kaleidoscope of flavour: white peach, orange citrus, spice, across textured palate. Full of energy, great potential.

★★★★☆ **Skerpioen** ⓐ ⓦ Interplanted & co-vinified chenin & palomino ex 60 year old vines near Swartland's cool Atlantic coast. **18** ⑨④ delicate citrus blossom & honey scents; flavours more emphatic yet still pure, earthy, saline; chalky texture from limestone soil; finish lifted, lengthened by fresh acidity.— AL

Location: Malmesbury ▪ Map: Swartland ▪ Map grid reference: C8 ▪ WO: Swartland/Olifants River/ Stellenbosch/Piekenierskloof ▪ Est 1999 ▪ 1stB 2000 ▪ Only scheduled tastings - bookings essential, contact office@thesadiefamily.com ▪ Owner(s) The Sadie Family (Pty) Ltd ▪ Winemaker(s) Eben Sadie (1999), Paul Jordaan (2017) ▪ Viticulturist(s) Morné Steyn (2019) ▪ 25ha (cinsaut, grenache n/b, mourv, shiraz, tinta barocca, chenin, clairette, palomino, rouss, sem, verdelho, viog) ▪ 90t/10,000cs own label 50% red 50%

white ▪ PO Box 1019 Malmesbury 7299 ▪ office@thesadiefamily.com ▪ www.thesadiefamily.com ▪ S 33° 31' 31.0" E 018° 48' 18.1" ▪ ⌖ broomstick.gargled.tomorrow ▪ **T +27 (0)76-151-7131**

☐ **Safari** *see* Frater Family Wines

Safriel House
The portfolio under the Safriel House label is described by SA-born and -bred, Florida-based brand owners, clinician Yair Safriel and wife Lynne, as the culmination of their ambassadorship for SA wine in the US and international markets. It currently comprises a '16 Chardonnay, '17 Rosé, '15 Select Vineyards White Blend, '17 Cabernet and '17 Select Vineyards Reserve Cabernet, made by local winemakers from Stellenbosch, Paarl, Franschhoek and Elgin grapes. Tastings by appointment in Florida and New York City, purchases on-line.

Tasting only in Florida & New York City by app ▪ Closed all pub hols ▪ Owner(s) Pharmascan LLC ▪ 900cs own label 55% red 45% white ▪ info@safrielhouse.com ▪ www.safrielhouse.com ▪ **T +27 (0)11-083-8886 / +1(612)235-6369**

☐ **Sainsbury** *see* Bosman Family Vineyards
☐ **Saints** *see* DGB (Pty) Ltd
☐ **Salpeterkop** *see* Rogge Cloof

Saltare
Winemaker Carla Pauw, co-owner with husband Christoff of boutique brand Saltare ('Dance') – their central-Stellenbosch cellar and tasting room just a hop and a skip across the Eerste River from each other - last year celebrated two 'long-awaited' arrivals. Their maiden Blanc de Noirs sparkling was released in September, commemorating the first birthday of daughter Camille after whom it's named. (Our present to Camille: a five-star rating!). Distribution of their other star-studded MCCs and still wines is going 'from strength to strength, thanks to the amazing team at [Cape Town's] Publik, doing something very special for SA's boutique producers' who share a philosophy of sustainable farming and minimal cellar intervention.

★★★★★ **Syrah** Opulent black fruit to the fore on standout **15** ⑨①, mingling delightfully with aromatic tobacco & spices. Broad shouldered & muscular, yet silky smooth, textural & sleek. Malmesbury (Swartland) fruit has splash of carignan. Improves on **14** ★★★★ ⑧⑨.

★★★★ **Specialis** ⑳ Occasional release. **15** ★★★☆ ⑧⑤ Bordeaux red from Paarl vines lighter than **12** ★★★★☆ ⑨③ & **08** ⑧⑦, salty & iodine hints on supple blackcurrant fruit. Cab & merlot, dash cab franc.

★★★★ **Old Vines Chenin Blanc 16** ★★★★☆ ⑨⓪ is big, ripe & honeyed. Appealing sherry- yeastiness underscores yellow stonefruit, with lees fatness, impressive finish. 9 months in older French barrels add weight without intruding. From Paardeberg vines, like **15** ⑧⑧.

★★★★ **Méthode Cap Classique Brut Rosé** Plush & savoury, pinot noir **NV** ⑧⑧ sparkler expresses ripe berry fruit with structured shortbread & brioche yeastiness. Resolutely dry, with commendable body, vigorous mousse. WO Stellenbosch. Also in magnum, as all below except Brut Nature.

★★★★★ **Méthode Cap Classique Blanc de Noirs Cuvée Camille** 🆕 🐝 Delightfully bright & fruity **NV** ⑨⑤ sparkling from Helderberg pinot noir has faintest blush, infinite charm. Once-off release to celebrate Christoff & Carla's daughter's first birthday, spent 42 months on lees. Rich, textural & refined.

★★★★☆ **Méthode Cap Classique Brut Blanc de Blancs** Rich & opulent, with yeasty undertone, latest **NV** ⑨② maintains impressive standard. Robertson chardonnay yields lime-mineral profile, with lemon highlights & firm acid backbone. 15% oak-matured component lends heft.

★★★★☆ **Méthode Cap Classique Brut Nature** Bone-dry, zero-dosage **NV** ⑨① from 59% Helderberg pinot noir with Robertson chardonnay has 20% reserve component. Appealingly yeasty, with toasty brioche & baked apple notes, vigorous mousse & lingering piquant finish.

★★★★☆ **Méthode Cap Classique Brut Reserve** 🐝 **NV** ⑨③ from Robertson chardonnay & Helderberg pinot noir follows form. 20% reserve, 20% in older oak, minimal dosage, all result in sumptuous, precise & elegant bubbly. Creamy brioche, apple-tinged shortbread, tingling acidity.

Not tasted: **Single Vineyard Chenin Blanc**. — GdB

Location/map: Stellenbosch ▪ Map grid reference: F5 ▪ WO: Stellenbosch/Swartland/Western Cape/ Robertson/Paarl ▪ 1stB 2005 ▪ Tasting & cellar tour by appt ▪ Olive oil ▪ Owner(s) Christoff & Carla Pauw ▪

Cellarmaster(s)/winemaker(s) Carla Pauw (2005) ▪ 19t/2,200cs own label 15% red 15% white 70% MCC ▪ 30 Die Laan Stellenbosch 7600 ▪ info@saltare.co.za ▪ www.saltare.co.za ▪ S 33° 56' 18.4" E 018° 52' 05.7" ▪ 🅰 briefer.kebabs.fills ▪ **T** +27 (0)21-883-9568

☐ **Sandveld** *see* Tierhoek

☐ **Sani Wines** *see* Groot Parys Estate

☐ **Sanniesrust** *see* Van der Merwe & Finlayson

Sarah's Creek

Stockwell, the Malherbe estate in Robertson Valley, has been in the family since 1888. Here, grapes for export brand Sarah's Creek (untasted by us) are grown on the scenic slopes of the Langeberg mountains, and vinified by Marga Malherbe, daughter-in-law of current custodian Dirk. A different family member, whose fascination with a farm stream made her habitually late for school, is recalled in the branding.

Location: Robertson ▪ Closed to public ▪ Owner(s) Dirk C Malherbe ▪ Winemaker(s) Marga Malherbe ▪ 25ha (cab, ptage, ruby cab, shiraz, chenin) ▪ PO Box 6531 Welgemoed 7538 ▪ marga@scwines.co.za ▪ www.sarahscreek.co.za ▪ **T** +27 (0)21-300-1731/+27 (0)84-941-2526

Saronsberg Cellar   ⊙ ☺ ⌂ ◎

Saronsberg, along with Rijk's, provided early proof this century of the potential for quality in the Tulbagh area, beyond the few white wines it had been known for. In fact, it is now red wines for which the estate is most renowned – although, ironically, the first release under the Saronsberg label was a Sauvignon Blanc '04! The reds are substantial, rich and powerful, yet winemaker Dewaldt Heyns (here from the start) endows them with a degree of finesse that eludes many similarly-styled warm-country wines. The two farms making up the estate, one on the slopes of the mountain that gives Saronsberg its name, one stretching down the valley, give Dewaldt varied terroirs to work with. Fruit orchards and olives groves are planted on the more fertile soils.

Saronsberg range

★★★★ **Grenache** Light on its feet, with elegant thread to earthy, game meat profile. **17** ⑧⑦'s measured palate has seasoned oak neatly sewn in. Mere 1,600 bottles for discovery at cellardoor only, as next.

★★★★ **Mourvèdre** House's full-throttle styling evident in lipsmacking **17** ⑧⑨, ripe mulberry fruit, plush tannins, 20-month oaking & 14.5% alcohol, all need year or so to marry.

★★★★☆ **Shiraz** ⓐ As rich in local & international awards as in ripe, near-sweet power, expressed with signature refinement in **17** ⑨③. Usual whiffs of white pepper, lovely supple tannin, plenty of French oak (70% new, 20 months) & 14.6% alcohol continue the big, bold & rewarding styling.

★★★★★ **Full Circle** ⓐ Depth, complexity & power combine in scintillating **17** ⑨⑤; mostly shiraz with splashes grenache, mourvèdre & dash separately vinified viognier - the last adds perfume & lingering finish. As **16** ⑨⑤, the Saronsberg way - weighty but still agile, commanding but balanced, muscular but not chunky, the all-new oak unobtrusive.

★★★★ **Brut Méthode Cap Classique** ⓺ Notes of biscuit & sweet citrus on **16** ⑧⑧ dry bubbly from chardonnay, plumped by 2 years on lees. Balanced & flavourful, pleasing steeliness behind the fruit.

★★★★ **Six Point Three Straw Wine** ⓺ Gorgeous **11** ⑧⑦ dessert from air-dried viognier, nurtured 4 years in oak. Old gold & oozing tropical fruit, it's very sweet & luscious but doesn't cloy. 375 ml.

Sauvignon Blanc ★★★★ Grapes ex estate's oldest vineyard (1998) produce fresh, juicy **19** ⑧⑤, exuberant tropical aromas jostle with greener grassy notes. **Viognier** ★★★★ Decorous rather than blockbusterish thanks to winemaking (wholebunch, 30% wild yeasts, 30% new barrels, no malo) which keeps **18** ⑧⑤'s apricot ebullience in check, seals in freshness.

Provenance range
....

Shiraz ⑦ ★★★★ Scrumptious **17** ⑧⑤ loaded with spiced plum fruit, well balanced by fresh acidity & modest tannic grip. Utterly moreish. WO W Cape. **Seismic** ⑦ ★★★★ Cellar's sole Bordeaux red from all 5 varieties, **16** ⑧⑤ delivers spades of cassis fruit in an accessible tannic structure, big 14.5% alcohol not too obvious. Delicious.
....

Shiraz-Mourvèdre Rosé ★★★ Fun-filled **19** ⑧② with overt red-fruit notes finishes bone-dry. This, next, WO Coastal. **Earth in Motion** ★★★ Dominant sauvignon perks up voluptuous chenin in tasty **19** ⑧②, full of summery charm. — DS

Location/map: Tulbagh ▪ Map grid reference: F4 ▪ WO: Tulbagh/Coastal/Western Cape ▪ Est 2002 ▪ 1stB 2004 ▪ Tasting & sales Mon-Fri 8.30-5 Sat 10-2 Sun 10-1 ▪ Fee R80pp ▪ Closed Good Fri, Ascension day & Dec 25 ▪ Cellar tours by appt ▪ Olive oil ▪ BYO picnic ▪ Artworks & sculptures on display ▪ Christmas in Winter Tulbagh festival (Jun) ▪ Self-catering guest cottages ▪ Wedding venue ▪ Owner(s) Saronsberg Cellar (Pty) Ltd ▪ Cellarmaster(s) Dewaldt Heyns (2003) ▪ Winemaker(s) Dewaldt Heyns (2003), with Joshua van Blommestein & Maryna Huyshamen ▪ Viticulturist(s) Dewaldt Heyns & Marchand du Plessis ▪ 550ha/50ha (shiraz) ▪ 500t own label 70% red 30% white ▪ WIETA ▪ PO Box 361 Tulbagh 6820 ▪ info@saronsberg.com ▪ www.saronsberg.com ▪ S 33° 14' 48.2" E 019° 7' 2.0" ▪ 🗺 fishers.assets.cosmos ▪ **T +27 (0)23-230-0707**

Saurwein Wines Ⓨ

Jessica Saurwein (her surname seems desperately ironical, given the delights of her totally un-sour wines) has trebled her range. The weight is still on pinot noir, with a second joining the debut release, alongside a riesling. These are, she says, 'my favourite cultivars and probably the most challenging wines to get right in terms of the growing and making. I love a challenge!' Until she can establish her own set-up, she makes her wines in rented space in Stellenbosch.

★★★★ **Nom Pinot Noir** ⊘ This ex Elandskloof grapes, like Om spontaneous ferment, seasoned oak, 'head-to-toe' vinification (using both press & free-run fractions). **18** ★★★★☆ ⑨① brims with vivacious fruit in fine structure, less austere than **17** ⑧⑨. Intensity augurs well for 3+ years in cellar.

★★★★☆ **Om Pinot Noir** 🆕 ⊘ 🍂 From pinot noir's heartland - Hemel-en-Aarde - a sibling with resonant name: 'Om' a symbol of universal creation, peace. **18** ⑨③ is riveting, its bright cherry fruit layered with silky tannins in a powerful yet refined & elegant whole. Natural winemaking as for Nom.

★★★★☆ **Chi Riesling** 🆕 Celebrates the 'life force', which **18** ⑨⓪ has in abundance: steely, stony & vibrant, it crackles with freshness, the few grams residual sugar buffed by a thrilling acidity. Grapes from cool Elgin vines. Agreeable 12% alcohol. Lovely, versatile aperitif & food partner.— DS

Location: Stellenbosch ▪ WO: Elandskloof/Elgin/Hemel-en-Aarde Ridge ▪ 1stB 2015 ▪ Tasting by appt ▪ Sales online only ▪ Owner(s)/winemaker(s) Jessica Saurwein ▪ 7t/1,000cs own label 60% red 40% white ▪ c/o Cape Crush, Winery Rd Stellenbosch 7599 ▪ saurweinwines@gmail.com ▪ www.saurwein.co.za ▪ **T +27 (0)76-228-3116**

Sauvignon Wines

Durbanville's Diemersdal is the celebrated sauvignon blanc specialist behind this pair of labels, Leaf Plucker aimed exclusively at overseas winelovers. See also separate listing for the estate.

Granger Bay range
Cabernet Sauvignon-Merlot ⊘ ★★★ Succulent **18** ⑧② charms with fragrant dark berry & spice cake aromas & flavours, underpinned by sweet vanilla oak. **Sauvignon Blanc** ⊘ ★★★ Bright tropical fruit on **19** ⑧⓪, touch leaner than previous but still crisp, limy, will complement creamy pasta.

Leaf Plucker range
Sauvignon Blanc ★★★★ Fragrant leafy fig, green plum & grass flavours, creamy, leesy mouthfeel with savoury touch to finish **19** ⑧⑤. Export only. Both ranges WO W Cape. — WB

Savage Wines Ⓨ

'Life on the Salt Riviera just gets better and better,' enthuses Duncan Savage, joking about the rather humdrum commercial setting of the Savage cellar in the Cape Town inner-city suburb of Salt River. Having his own premises also makes quality control easier and better for Duncan, both viticulturist and winemaker at this boutique family venture. Focus is now on leasing the vineyards they work with to ensure continuity of supply in the long term. In the cellar, that focus turns to showcasing the sites. Despite the drought, Duncan declares he's 'super happy' with the '18s, all individuals, sensitively interpreted. The straw wine was an experiment, 'for fun, but it turned out so lekker, we're releasing it'. We doubt many will say 'Not tonight, Josephine'!

★★★★☆ **Follow The Line** (🐝) Cinsaut ex Darling goes solo in **18** ★★★★★ (95) (**17** (94)) had 7% syrah). Both purity & complexity in its delicious ripe fruit, spice & fresh earth medley. Light-footed, vibrant but not insubstantial & with a firmness suggesting ageing will reap rewards. 50% wholebunch ferment, large oak vats.

★★★★☆ **Red** (🐝) **17** ★★★★★ (95) all syrah (**16** (93) & previous syrah-led blends). Ripe, concentrated; many layers in its spice, soft berry & savoury notes; all balanced, focused by lively ripe tannins, overall freshness. Already appetising, but future rewards. Wholebunch ferment, large-oak matured, none new. Coastal WO.

★★★★☆ **The Girl Next Door** (🐝) Striking cool-climate syrah ex Cape Peninsula. **18** (94) vivid youthful hue, heady spice & red fruit scents with energy & freshness. Concentration of flavour rather than high alcohol give sense of body. Bone-dry, still bit edgy but will round with even short ageing. 13% alcohol.

★★★★☆ **Are We There Yet?** (🐝) Equal syrah & touriga ex Malgas. **18** (93) possibly most distinctive yet, with perfumed floral, soft dark fruit tones. Fresh ripe flavours paced by equally ripe, lively grape tannins make for youthful enjoyment; but should benefit from few years cellaring. Spontaneous ferment, 50% wholebunch.

★★★★☆ **Thief In The Night** Grenache, syrah, cinsaut combo but **18** (91) has a bit more gutsy structure than previous, not at expense of freshness, energy; full appetising flavour spectrum - red/dark fruits, zesty spice, savouriness - & comfortable richness. 20% wholebunch; oak matured, 10% new.

★★★★★ **Never Been Asked To Dance** (🐝) Openness, generosity in oaked **18** ★★★★☆ (94) chenin's ripe peach, honey aromas but also a sense of composure. Dense, fleshy texture supports juicy layers of flavour, seamlessly carried with great persistence by natural acid. Maiden was **17** (95). Spontaneous ferment. Paarl WO.

★★★★★ **White** (🐝) No one variety outshines others in **18** ★★★★☆ (94), sauvignon, semillon, chenin blend, as **17** (95). Sense of ripe calmness, textural flow, balanced by focusing savoury acid. More contemplative than arresting. Natural ferment, older oak 10 months. WO W Cape.

★★★★☆ **Not Tonight Josephine** (NEW) Air-dried chenin from Piekenierskloof. **18** (91) satiny, with intense, luscious peach flavours rounded by older-oak ferment/ageing. Good balance between sugar (300 g/l) & acid ensures clean, uncloying finish. Just 11% alcohol. 375 ml. — AL

Location: Cape Town ▪ Map: Cape Peninsula ▪ Map grid reference: C2 ▪ WO: Piekenierskloof/Coastal/Darling/Paarl/Malgas/Cape Town/Western Cape ▪ Est 2006 ▪ 1stB 2011 ▪ Tasting by appt only ▪ Owner(s) Duncan Savage ▪ Winemaker(s) Duncan Savage (Jan 2006) ▪ 60t/7,000cs own label 75% red 25% white ▪ 6 Spencer Rd, Salt River, Cape Town 7925 ▪ info@savagewines.com ▪ www.savagewines.com ▪ S 33° 55' 45.10" E 018° 27' 54.30" ▪ 🖳 evaporation.beacons.morals ▪ **T +27 (0)21-447-3022**

Saxenburg Wine Farm (💡) (🍴) (🏠) (📷)

Careful attention to vineyards continues at Saxenburg, with new plantings of shiraz last year and cabernet planned for this year as part of a vine renewal plan. Viticulturist Donovan Diedericks rose to the challenge of the drought (hopefully now somewhat relieved), making full use of modern moisture probe technology and satellite imagery to assess water requirements for stress-free, balanced vines. The rest was up to the cellar team, which at press time was due to change, Edwin Grace having moved on in 2019. The values and traditions of the Bührer family, who've owned and run this multifaceted wine and hospitality business in Stellenbosch's Polkadraai Hills since 1989, are continued by the second generation, Fiona and Vincent, who are now focused on growing Saxenburg's national and international distribution footprint.

Saxenburg Limited Release

★★★★☆ **Shiraz Select** Flagship from meticulous, 3-vineyard grape selection. **13** (92) New World styling, sleek & supple, sumptuous richness enhanced by 21 months new French & American (50/50) oak. Lovely fresh thread retains balance. Already tempting, but an ageworthy beauty. **10** - **12** not made.

Private Collection

★★★★ **Cabernet Sauvignon** (💡) Less new oak (30%, year) for **15** ★★★★★ (92) than **13** (89), aiding lovely cassis fruit purity, freshness & lithe tannin support. Already balanced, but deserves 3-5 years ageing, with further rewards in time. Seamless, elegant step up. No **14**.

★★★★☆ **Shiraz** ⓥ Ripe & spicy berries from 2 weeks skin contact (no sulphur), mostly older oak (some American) well integrated. **16** ★★★★ (88) succulently poised, more modern-style than **15** (93), vintage warmth contained, though, despite 14.5% alcohol.

★★★★☆ **Chardonnay** ⓥ Rich toast & lime flavours on **17** ★★★★ (88), all-oak ferment/ageing adds a creamy nuance (new barrels upped to 15%, previously 10%). Elegant & approachable, with potential to age, but shade off fresher, brighter **15** (90). **16** untasted.

★★★★ **Sauvignon Blanc 19** (87) preview reflects Stellenbosch's crisp, grassy, white peach varietal character. A range of yeasts & 3 months on the lees give freshness & body.

Pinotage ★★★ Savoury & earthy tone to **17** (81), with warm berry jam sweetness. Similar supple tannins, but lacks freshness & balance of last-tasted **15** ★★★★ (87). **Méthode Cap Classique** ★★★★ Latest **NV** (85) brut sparkling from chardonnay & pinot noir (80/20) even plumper, richer than previous. Old-oak maturation of base wine & lees ageing (48 months) amplify both fruit sweetness & lack of fresh balance. Not tasted: **Merlot**.

Guinea Fowl range

. . . .

White ⓥ ★★★★ From chenin, **19** (84) tank sample shows clean lines & crunchy apple flavours. Brush of oak & lengthy lees contact add attractive substance & highlights variety's charm.

. . . .

Red ⓥ ★★★★ Smoky red fruit & cedar on old-oak-matured **16** (84) Bordeaux blend, takes juicy step up with lithe tannins & lovely freshness. Perfect table mate over next few years. — MW

Location: Kuils River ▪ Map/WO: Stellenbosch ▪ Map grid reference: A5 ▪ Est 1693 ▪ 1stB 1990 ▪ Tasting & sales Mon-Sun 10-6 ▪ Wine tasting fee R45/R75 ▪ Chocolate & wine pairing R75/3 wines ▪ Safari tasting R350pp (incl all wines, glass of MCC, cheese platter with biltong & nuts) - to book in advance, minimum 4 guests ▪ Closed Good Fri, Dec 25 & Jan 1 ▪ Cheese platters ▪ Cattle Baron Grill Room restaurant T +27 (0)21-906-5232, www.cattlebaron.co.za ▪ Gifts ▪ Game park ▪ Guest cottages ▪ Owner(s) Adrian & Birgit Bührer ▪ Viticulturist(s) Donovan Diedericks (Apr 2008) ▪ 195ha/85ha (cabs s/f, malbec, merlot, ptage, shiraz, chard, chenin, sauv) ▪ 650t/100,000cs own label 80% red 20% white ▪ PO Box 171 Kuils River 7580 ▪ info@saxenburg.co.za ▪ www.saxenburg.co.za ▪ S 33° 56' 47.9" E 018° 43' 9.4" ▪ 🌐 visits.lively.waistband ▪ **T +27 (0)21-903-6113**

☐ **Say Lovey** *see* M'hudi Wines
☐ **Scarlet Sails** *see* Hazendal Wine Estate
☐ **Schaap** *see* Skaap Wines
☐ **Schalk Burger & Sons** *see* Welbedacht Wine Estate

Schalkenbosch Wines   ⓥ ⌂ ◎

This enormous estate in Tulbagh dates back to the latter 18th century, with the manor house completed in 1792. There's a wide range of farming operations besides the vineyards – but a substantial proportion of the property is conserved for wildlife and indigenous vegetation. Taking advantage of this attraction, there are extensive walking, hiking and biking trails, as well as luxury cottages and function venues.

Schalkenbosch range

Grenache Noir ⓥ ★★★★ Light but ripe fruit mingles with savoury, oak-supported notes on **15** (84). Juicy berry flavours, & sour-sweet element on finish warmed by 15% alcohol. **Pinotage** ★★★★ Pleasant, easygoing fruitiness on **18** (83) - first made since **12**. Smooth ripe tannins & the just-off-dry sweetness showing on the warm finish. **Cumulus** ⓥ ★★★★ Quintet of Bordeaux black grapes in ripe & burly **15** (84). Solid, sweet fruit copes well with muscular structure. Finishes with sweetish, warming glow from 15.1% alcohol. **Stratus** ⓥ ★★★★ Bold shiraz-led blend with grenache, mourvèdre & a little viognier. **12** (84) sweet-fruited succulence accompanying rather austere structure to substantial finish. Not tasted: **Malbec**. Discontinued: **Méthode Cap Classique**.

Edenhof range

Shiraz ★★★ Ripely warm aromas with a vanilla oak shimmer (though no new barrels used) on **17** (82). Heavily extracted, with juicy fruit, the acidity standing a little apart. **Rosé** ⓥ ★★☆ Pleasant, zippy & fruity-savoury character on friendly dry **17** (78) from mostly shiraz. **Sauvignon Blanc** ★★★ Forthright guava character to full-flavoured, zesty & succulent **19** (80). Not tasted: **Cabernet Sauvignon**, **Chenin**

Blanc. Occasional release: **Pinotage, Cabernet Sauvignon-Merlot, Nighthawk 409, Chardonnay, Viognier**. — TJ

Location/map/WO: Tulbagh ▪ Map grid reference: G5 ▪ Est 1792 ▪ 1stB 2002 ▪ Tasting, sales & tours by appt ▪ Closed all pub hols ▪ Tour groups ▪ Weddings/functions ▪ Walking/hiking & MTB trails ▪ Conservation area ▪ Self-catering cottages ▪ Owner(s) Platinum Mile Investments ▪ Winemaker(s) Suzanne Hartman & Josef Krammer (consultants) ▪ Viticulturist(s) Johan Wiese & Andrew Teubes ▪ 1,800ha/30ha (cab, shiraz) ▪ 140t/20,000cs own label 80% red 18% white 2% rosé ▪ WWF-SA Conservation Champion ▪ PO Box 95 Tulbagh 6820 ▪ info@schalkenbosch.co.za ▪ www.schalkenbosch.co.za ▪ S 33° 18' 49.7" E 019° 11' 59.9" ▪ ✉ unlocks.kiosk.ornately ▪ **T +27 (0)23-230-0654/1488**

Schenkfontein Kelders Ⓨ

Sibling to separately co-listed Winkelshoek and Weskus, and historically a supplier of bulk wine to one of the majors, Schenkfontein entered the packaged-wine arena six years ago with a trio of wines from own and partners' grapes in the Piketberg-Citrusdal area. Owner Hennie Hanekom and winemaker/viticulturist Hendrik Hanekom since extended the range, and now they have a range of spirits in the pipeline.

Merlot Ⓨ ★★ Plum & high-toned icing sugar tones, racy acidity on **17** ⑦⑷ early-drinker. **Pinotage** Ⓨ ★★★ Appealing mulberry aromas & flavours, enough grip for food, good dry finish. **17** ⑧⓪ would rate higher but for prominent acid. WO W Cape. **Shiraz** ★★★ For current drinking, **18** ⑧② 's red fruit accented by light fynbos & black pepper, pleasant tealeaf finish. **Chardonnay** ★★★ From Swartland grapes, just-bottled **19** ⑦⑧ faint lemon sherbet & flowers, tangy unoaked refreshment. **Chenin Blanc** ★★★ Step-up **19** ⑧② 's fresh & fruity styling very pretty, floral, spice & khaki bush complexity. WO Swartland. Not tasted: **Rosé**. In abeyance: **Cabernet Sauvignon**. Discontinued: **Colombar, Sauvignon Blanc**. — CvZ

Location: Piketberg ▪ Map: Olifants River ▪ Map grid reference: C7 ▪ WO: Coastal/Swartland/Western Cape ▪ Est 2000 ▪ 1stB 2014 ▪ Tasting & cellar tours available montly by appt - contact Alicia Hanekom +27 (0)74-584-1234 ▪ Owner(s) Hennie Hanekom ▪ Cellarmaster(s)/winemaker(s)/viticulturist(s) Hendrik Hanekom (Nov 2010) ▪ 500ha/60ha (muscadel r/w, ptage, shiraz, chenin, cbard, grenache b, hanepoot) ▪ 800t/150,000L own label 30% red 70% white ▪ PO Box 2 Eendekuil 7335 ▪ hendrik@winkelshoek.co.za ▪ www.winkelshoek.co.za ▪ S 32° 42' 18.85" E 018° 47' 43.09" ▪ **T +27 (0)22-942-1484**

Schultz Family Wines Ⓨ

One of three winemaking brothers (Hartenberg's Carl, Baleia's Gunter), Rudi called dibs on the family name for this own venture, started in 2002 shortly after joining Thelema, where he's still making 5-star wines. Rudi continues an emphasis on reds (cab and syrah) with the debut blend. It forms part of his attractively labelled 'fun but serious' wines, recently featuring names of some of southern Africa's top surf breaks (another shared Schultz brother passion). His only white, a chenin, is now from two rehabilitated blocks.

★★★★☆ **Dungeons Cabernet Sauvignon** 🐝 Adds big-wave spot off Hout Bay to name. Exemplary **16** ⑨② has glossy fruit, supple tannins, long finish - latent power for decade ageing. Polished, assured. Usual winemaking care, hand sorting, wild ferment, 18 months in barrique, 30% new.

★★★★★ **Pepper Street Solid Syrah** ⊘ 🐝 The road down to Supertubes in Jeffreys Bay. Fabulous fruit concentration, notes of violets, Provençal herbs. Savoury **17** ⑨① has solid tannic core for ageing but it's admirably dry & food friendly, so no barrier to early enjoyment. 10% new oak.

★★★★★ **Boneyards** 🆕 🐝 Celebrated surf spot names Bordeaux flagship. 66% cab merges with malbec & petit verdot into a dense compendium of flavours & sensations: pungent perfume, lilting black fruits, lacy tannins; **16** ⑨④ accessible but compact, needs few years to show. Half new oak, 18 months.

★★★★ **Skeleton Bay Chenin Blanc** ⊘ Now references world's longest left-handed surfing wave, **18** ★★★★★ ⑨⓪ ex two parcels (Somerset West & Paarl), average age 50 years. Bunch pressed, barrel fermented/aged for smoky savouriness to partner the honeysuckle & pear. **17** ⑧⑨ from 30 year old vines, similarly sophisticated.

Occasional release: **Reserve Syrah**. — DS

Location: Stellenbosch ▪ WO: Stellenbosch/Western Cape ▪ Est 2002 ▪ Tasting by appt ▪ Closed all pub hols ▪ Owner(s) Rudi Schultz ▪ Cellarmaster(s)/winemaker(s) Rudi Schultz (Jan 2002) ▪ Viticulturist(s) Dirkie Morkel ▪ 12t/1,000cs own label 100% red ▪ 8 Fraser Rd, Somerset West 7130 ▪ rudi@thelema.co.za ▪ **T +27 (0)82-928-1841**

Scions of Sinai

The 'scions' in the brand name are 7th-generation winemaker Bernhard Bredell and some precious old dryland bushvines, formerly part of his family's holdings in the Helderberg, centred around a hill colloquially known as Sinai. Now based on Klein Helderberg farm in a renovated cellar used by an earlier Bredell generation, Bernhard also works with vines in Voor Paardeberg and Klein Karoo (see JP Bredell Wines listing). Related brands in Bernhard's purview include Lionel Smit Collaboration Series and Atlantikas Wines.

Location: Stellenbosch ▪ Est 2016 ▪ 1stB 2017 ▪ Closed to public ▪ Owner(s) Bernhard Bredell ▪ Winemaker(s)/viticulturist(s) Bernhard Bredell (Jun 2016) ▪ 18t/1,200cs own label 70% red 15% white 15% orange ▪ info@scionsofsinai.com ▪ www.scionsofsinai.com ▪ T +27 (0)82-772-8657

Scrucap Wines

Consultant Kent Scheermeyer and a sextet of elite SA producers are behind this refreshingly modern selection of wines, designed to dovetail with the philosophy of LUX* Resorts & Hotels in the Indian Ocean, China and the Middle East to offer a lighter, brighter alternative to traditional five-star holidays.

★★★★ **Cabernet Sauvignon** Plush dark berry fruit on **16** (88) is balanced with earth, leather & tobacco notes, restrained by slightly more/longer new oak, 35%, 20 months. By Radford Dale, as Chenin.

★★★★ **Chardonnay** ⊘ Very subtle oak, just 4 months in mixed barrels, none new. **19** (86) packed with peach, melon & citrus fruit, a honey thread focuses the elements, gives length. By Paul Cluver, as next 3.

★★★★ **Gewürztraminer** (Ⓥ) Oh-so-lovely **17** (86), litchi, pineapple & pot-pourri perfumes are pure hedonism yet the palate is swept dry & made moreish by freshening grapefruit acidity. 375 ml.

★★★★ **Riesling** ⊘ Perfumed litchi, pear & granadilla accentuate lime cordial & floral notes. Well-made **18** (89) is poised, the residual sugar of 19.8 g/l effortlessly balanced by bracing acidity.

★★★★ **Sauvignon Blanc** ⊘ Gooseberry & lime fruit on fresh **19** (88). Dusty floral aromas, steely mineral notes emerge on palate to offset richness & rounded texture from 5 months on lees & splash semillon, clean citrus farewell.

★★★★ **Sauvignon Blanc** (18A) Multiple vineyard blocks provide complexity & persistent acidity in attractive **19** (87), preview shows classic cool-climate flavours of greenpepper, grass & lime. By Steenberg, as next 2.

★★★★ **Popcap Méthode Cap Classique Rosé** ⊘ Subtle & savoury **NV** (89) pink sparkler from pinot noir. Appealing saline quality to the bubbles, along with fruit notes of cranberry & apple, & a fresh yeasty element from 12 months on lees.

★★★★ **Popcap Méthode Cap Classique Brut** Robertson chardonnay is the source of this crisp & mouthwatering **NV** (89) sparkler. Bursts with appley freshness, hints of pear & almond, & oven-fresh brioche nuance from 12 months on lees.

. . . .

Pinot Noir ⊘ (Ⓥ) ★★★☆ Paul Cluver's satisfying 'everyday' pinot is from younger vines. **17** (84) has appealing cherry fruit & spice, ripe tannin & lively farewell. Also in 375 ml.

. . . .

Merlot (Ⓥ) ★★★☆ Bright fruit with savoury spice from older French barrels, **14** (83) rounded tannins for easy, satisfying enjoyment. By Jordan. **Shiraz** ★★★☆ Juicy & elegant **17** (83) shows good energy & typicity. Blackberries & plums, hint of clove, all wrapped up tightly mid-2019. Should unwind in the near term. By Lammershoek, as next. **Rosé** (Ⓥ) ★★★ Delicious take on Provence dry rosé: mostly syrah tweaked in old oak to make it savoury, food friendly. **18** (81) herby & sweet spicy nuance to vibrant cherries. **Chenin Blanc** ★★★☆ Brims with peach & pear, tropical fruit unfettered by oak, but taut, bone-dry finish brings balance. **18** (85) uncomplicated yet deep-flavoured. — Various tasters

WO: Various ▪ Est 2011 ▪ Closed to public ▪ Cellarmaster(s) Andries Burger (Paul Cluver), JD Pretorius/Elunda Basson (Steenberg), Edouard Labeye (Radford Dale), Sjaak Nelson (Jordan), Schalk Opperman (Lammershoek) ▪ 20,000cs own label 40% red 40% white 10% rosé 10% MCC ▪ ksconsult@icloud.com ▪ www.theluxcollective.com ▪ T +27 (0)83-484-8781

☐ **Seaward** see Spier
☐ **Secateurs** see AA Badenhorst Family Wines

Sedgwick's Old Brown

Fortified cockle warmer since 1916; today produced by Distell in bottle sizes from 200ml to 2L.

The Original Old Brown ⊘ ★★★ Jerepiko & dry 'sherry' **NV** ⑧⑴ blend, unchanging style otherwise fans would rebel. Amber hue, sherry & raisin/dried fruit richness, molasses tone, eminently drinkable. — CR

☐ **Selection Vivante** *see* The House of JC le Roux
☐ **Selena** *see* Marianne Wine Estate
☐ **Semara** *see* Wine-of-the-Month Club
☐ **Sentinel** *see* Wine-of-the-Month Club
☐ **Series Privée Unfiltered** *see* Fleur du Cap
☐ **SeriesRARE** *see* ArtiSons
☐ **Seriously Cool** *see* Waterkloof

Ses'Fikile

Founded by former teacher and Cape Town-based entrepreneurial vintner Nondumiso Pikashe, Ses'fikile means 'We have arrived. . . in style', a phrase that sparkles with a sense of adventure. The choice of wine, too, ranges wider than the norm and includes an unusual chenin-roussanne blend, chosen by Nondumiso because the varieties 'beautifully synchronise together'. Exports are currently to Sweden only, but other EU countries are also in her sights, as is the local market.

Cabernet Sauvignon-Merlot ★★ Straightforward fresh, fruity **18** ⑦⑥. Ripe, juicy red berry flavours, gentle grip smoothed by gram/two sugar. **Shiraz-Cinsault** ⊘ ★★ Near-equal blend, **16** ⑦⑥ has earthy, leathery styling, the fruit more evident on palate than nose. Smooth, light, easy drinking. **Chenin Blanc-Roussanne** ★★★ Fresh, light & crisply dry **18** ⑧⑽; chenin's red apple with extra floral, tropical interest from roussanne. — AL

Location: Cape Town ▪ WO: Western Cape ▪ Est 2008 ▪ Tasting by arrangement in Gugulethu ▪ Owner(s) Ses'Fikile Wine Services ▪ Winemaker(s) Madré van der Walt (Leeuwenkuil Family Vineyards) ▪ 50,000cs own label 70% red 30% white ▪ sesfikile@gmail.com, ndumi@sesfikile.co.za ▪ www.sesfikile.co.za ▪ **T +27 (0)83-431-0254**

☐ **7even** *see* Zevenwacht
☐ **7 Icon Wines** *see* Bayede!

Seven Sisters Vineyards   ⊘ ⑴⑪ ◎

The eponymous Brutus siblings (and brother John, who recently made it on to a label too!) grew up in the West Coast village of Paternoster. Sister Vivian (Kleynhans) led the formation of their African Roots company more than a decade back, and now they have a wine-base further south, on their farm in Stellenbosch.

Brutus Family Reserve range

Shiraz ⊘ ★★★★ Starts with aromatic notes of smoked meat, spice & plums. **15** ⑧④ lightly oaked, with smooth tannic structure supporting the pleasantly juicy sweet fruit. **John Brutus** ⊘ ★★★★ Tobacco notes with ripe fruit on aromas of **14** ⑧④ from petit verdot, cab, cab franc & merlot. Flavoursome, generous & rounded. Approachable young, to give substantial but easy satisfaction. **Chardonnay** ⊘ ★★★★ Notes of toasty oak on aromas & flavours, but there's good ripe citrus & stonefruit in support. **16** ⑧④ fairly well balanced, intense & structured.

Seven Sisters range

Not tasted: **Cabernet Sauvignon, Shiraz, Chardonnay, Moscato, Sauvignon Blanc**. — TJ

Location/map/WO: Stellenbosch ▪ Map grid reference: C7 ▪ Call gate for entry +27 (0)60-696-9814 ▪ Wine & food pairings 9-4 daily ▪ Weddings/conferences/special functions ▪ Owner(s) African Roots Wine ▪ Winemaker(s) Vivian Kleynhans ▪ PO Box 4560 Tygervalley 7536 ▪ vivian@africanrootswines.com ▪ www.sevensisters.co.za ▪ S 33° 59' 23.41" E 018° 46' 34.35" ▪ 🗺 adornment.modern.escalating ▪ **T +27 (0)71-049-4109/+27 (0)60-696-9814**

Seven Springs Vineyards   ⊘ ⑴

Development has continued apace at Britons Tim and Vaughan Pearson's winery in the Shaw's Mountain foothills just beyond Hemel-en-Aarde Ridge. The new tasting venue was inaugurated as planned, farmstall-restaurant The Onion Shed opened next door (Seven Springs wines to be available once a licence is obtained) and Augustus Dale took over in the cellar. Enthusing about returning to this part of the winelands after 10 years, he notes that '2019 vintage was an absolute delight; the cooler temperatures resulting in extremely good-quality grape juice'. His longer-term goals are to improve quality further and make vineyard and cellar practices more sustainable.

Seven Springs range

★★★★ **Pinot Noir** ⊘ Greater vine age sees increased concentration each vintage. **15** ⑧⑧ has usual freshness, light feel complemented by charming black cherry & spice flavours. These focused by older oak, gentle tannins. Enjoy over next 2-3 years.

★★★★ **Syrah** Expressive, ripe black berries & spice in delicious, still-youthful **15** ⑧⑧. Supple, rich yet unheavy, framed by fine, fresh tannins; older oak an unobtrusive harmonising factor.

★★★★☆ **Sauvignon Blanc** ⊘ **17** ⑨② lovely follow up to glorious **16** ⑨④, if in slightly gentler, less intense style. Retains cool-climate blackcurrant, tropical fragrance, freshness, balancing leesy weight & endless fruity length.

Chardonnay ★★★★ Usual orange, lemon highlights on **17** ⑧④. Older oak provides shoulder & spice to gentle creamy lees but these somewhat overshadowed by bracing acidity. **Unoaked Chardonnay** ★★★☆ Satisfying combination of fruit purity with textural interest. **16** ⑧⑤ intense lime & lemon flavours broadened by nutty lees; zestily dry, lingering. Not tasted: **Syrah Rosé**.

Art Series

★★★★ **Syrah** ② Tasted out of vintage sequence, **12** ⑧⑨ opens in glass to Xmas spice & tapenade, chewy tannins yet backed by juicy fruit, promising a good future. Limited release in magnum, only ex farm.

★★★★☆ **Sauvignon Blanc Fumé** ⑭ⓔⓦ ⊛ Tantalises with heady, cool-climate blackcurrant fragrance, rich flavours shot through with mineral energy. Few years' ageing of **15** ⑨④ have polished youthful edges but freshness, precision remain. Memorably long. 6 months on lees in old French oak.

Occasional release: **Pinot Noir**. — AL

Location: Hermanus ▪ Map: Walker Bay & Bot River ▪ Map grid reference: C5 ▪ WO: Overberg ▪ Est 2007 ▪ 1stB 2010 ▪ Tasting & sales Mon-Fri 11-4 ▪ The Onion Shed farmstall & restaurant ▪ Owner(s) Tim & Vaughan Pearson ▪ Winemaker(s) Augustus Dale (Nov 2018), with Renico Botes (Nov 2017, snr cellar assistant) ▪ Vineyard manager(s) Peter Davison (Jul 2007) ▪ 12ha/±8ha (pinot, shiraz, chard, sauv) ▪ ±67t/10,000cs own label 55% red 40% white 5% rosé ▪ Other export brand: Over the Mountain ▪ Private Bag X15 Suite 162 Hermanus 7200 ▪ tim@7springs.co.za ▪ www.7springs.co.za ▪ S 34° 19' 36.76" E 019° 22' 38.65" ▪ Ⓦ purchased.taillights.vowing ▪ **T +27 (0)28-316-4994 (office)/+27 (0)76-600-3228 (winemaker)**

☐ **1791** *see* Nederburg Wines

Shannon Vineyards

⑨ ⓖ

The lovely Elgin farm of brothers James and Stuart Downes had been known to some lucky recipients of grapes for many years as the source of excellent fruit – thanks to the cool terroir and James' meticulous viti-culture. But, as we noted in Shannon's first entry in this guide a decade back, it took seven years of research and experimentation before they felt happy to release three wines (to great acclaim) under their own name. Those wines were made by Gordon and Nadia Newton Johnson at their family winery in Hemel-en-Aarde, as are all those, ten years on, in the expanded range. And the acclaim is, if anything, even louder. A new chardonnay vineyard and a replanted pinot noir one are likely to be represented in the line-up soon.

★★★★★ **Mount Bullet Merlot** ⊛ Dark but radiant, full-fruited & spicy aromas on big (14.5% alcohol) **16** ⑨⑥ from French & Italian clones. Very serious wine, sumptuous, with great depth of flavour, but also an element of refined austerity. Still far off its best, as was **15** ★★★★★ ⑨④ at this early stage.

★★★★★ **The Shannon Black** ⊛ Big, showy & exciting, & not exactly subtle. Merlot from a single Italian clone. Dense & sweetly deep **15** ★★★★★ ⑨④ easily bears weight of 50% new oak, with dry but balanced tannins; altogether beautifully structured. Something joyful & triumphant here. Just 48 cases. **13** ⑨⑤ was debut vintage. No **14**.

★★★★☆ **RocknRolla** ⓐ Pinot noir from the farm's oldest parcel, a registered single-vineyard. Wholly impressive, assertive **18** ⑨④ rather dominated in youth by oak (50% new barrels, 12 months), but there's intense, pure, sweet berry fruit flavour lurking, needing at least a few years in bottle. No **17**.

★★★★☆ **Rockview Ridge Pinot Noir** ⓥ Plenty of raspberry & cherry on **18** ⑨②, with savoury hints of forest floor. Sweet, sensual fruitiness controlled & balanced by firm acidity & informing but subtle tannins. Mostly wild yeast. Year in oak, 30% new.

★★★★☆ **Sanctuary Peak Sauvignon Blanc** ⓥ Tropical fruit & touches of blackcurrant & stoniness on fresh, flavourful **18** ⑨②. 6% fermented naturally & briefly matured in oak to add some breadth & support the richness of texture.

★★★★☆ **Triangle Block Semillon** ⓐ Oak maturation (30% new) on lees adds dimension & complexity to fine **18** ⑨④. Poised & well balanced, with grippy, lemony acid firmness. Natural ferment, as next. Takes time to open in youth - preferably decant, or leave a few years for flavour to blossom.

★★★★★ **Capall Bán** ⓐ Blends best barrels of semillon (70%) & sauvignon. Initially latter's aromas dominate **16** ★★★★★ ⑨③ - later semillon's lanolin & lemon emerge, with blackcurrant. Soft texture cut by penetrating (but balanced) acid. Not an easy wine in youth, but most impressive. Good oaking, like **15** ⑨⑤.

Occasional release: **Macushla Pinot Noir Noble Late Harvest**. — TJ

Location/map/WO: Elgin • Map grid reference: A2 • Est 2000 • 1stB 2003 • Tasting by appt Mon-Fri 10-3 • Owner(s) Stuart & James Downes • Winemaker(s) Gordon & Nadia Newton Johnson • Viticulturist(s) Kevin Watt (consultant) • 75ha/11.5ha (merlot, pinot, sauv, sem) • 100t/10,000cs own label 66% red 34% white • GlobalGAP, IPW, Tesco's Natures Choice • PO Box 20 Elgin 7180 • james@shannonwines.com • www.shannonwines.com • S 34° 11' 3.9" E 018° 59' 3.6" • ✉ beckons.lemon.decibel • **T +27 (0)21-859-2491**

☐ **Shepherd's Cottage** *see* Overgaauw Wine Estate
☐ **Shiner** *see* Paserene

Ship

Originally 'Ship Sherry', this Distell-owned piece of South African wine patrimony was launched in 1929.
Ship Fortified Wine ★★ Stalwart jerepiko in distinctive tall, flat bottle with eponymous 17th-century merchantman De Goede Hoop on retro label. **NV** ⑦④ powerfully raisiny, sweet, full-bodied. — CR

☐ **Shoprite Checkers** *See* Editor's Note
☐ **Short Story** *see* Neethlingshof Estate
☐ **Short Street** *see* Riebeek Valley Wine Co
☐ **Shortwood** *see* Imbuko Wines
☐ **SHZ Cilliers/Kuün Wyne** *see* Stellendrift - SHZ Cilliers/Kuün Wyne
☐ **Signal Cannon** *see* Vondeling

Signal Gun Wines   ⓛ ⓜ ⓞ

The Signal Gun wine brand, owned by the De Wit family, is so named because of a 300-year-old signal cannon on the Durbanville home farm, which is still fired at 13h00 on the first Saturday of each month. The high-lying Hooggelegen property is particularly suited to sauvignon blanc, an area speciality and solo player in two of the wines. Another part of the business is craft beer, produced on-site by Hoogeberg Brewing Co.

De Wit Family Reserves
★★★★ **Sea Smoke Sauvignon Blanc** Misty/foggy single block, Durbanville's highest (455 m), which **18** ⑧⑧ reflects in capsicum & passionfruit intensity. Slender (12.7% alcohol), but packs a flavour punch, finishes long & tangy.

Gun Smoke Merlot ⓥ ★★★★ Expressive perfume, cassis, violets, tobacco, **16** ⑧⑤ spent 12 months in barrel, 45% new. Tannins supple, palate smooth, polished, finishes long. WO W Cape. **B Loved Méthode Cap Classique** ★★★☆ Blanc de blancs brut bubbly from chardonnay, no pinot noir as previous. Attractive toasted brioche in **14** ⑧④, giving richness & depth to the preserved citrus. Heaps of flavour, character.

Signal Gun range
★★★★ **Shiraz** Powerful & ripe (15% alcohol), black plums & brambleberries, **17** ⑧⑧'s variety-true gamy notes, lovely long spicy finish. Curvaceous, yet 18 months oaking suggests serious intent for cellaring.

★★★★ **Sauvignon Blanc** ⊘ Combines gooseberries & fynbos, some minerality at the end. **19** ⑧⑦ wonderfully complex & involving, goes up a level from **18** ★★★★ ⑧④.

....

Pinotage ⊗ ★★★☆ Luscious blueberries & dark plums, **17** ⑧④'s fruit concentration & smooth texture are major parts of its appeal. Doesn't put a foot wrong, tannins ripe, integrated.

....

Chardonnay ★★★☆ Toastiness in the flavours from oaking but suits **18** ⑧④'s profile, citrus peel with a savoury edge. Has character, confidently New World. Occasional release: **Chenin Blanc**.

Tin Hill range

Cape Blend ⊗ ★★★ Only half of **17** ⑧① oaked, pinotage/merlot duo designed for easy drinking, with character. Red & dark berries, sweet spice, smooth & juicy. — CR

Location: Durbanville ▪ Map: Durbanville, Philadelphia & Darling ▪ Map grid reference: C7 ▪ WO: Durbanville/Western Cape ▪ Est/1stB 2006 ▪ Tasting & sales Tue-Sat 10-5 Sun 11-5 ▪ Fee depends on tasting R50-R70 ▪ Wine & food pairing ▪ Closed Good Fri, Dec 25 & Jan 1 ▪ Ke-Monate Restaurant ▪ Conferences ▪ Game drives ▪ Craft beer brewery ▪ Owner(s) WRM de Wit ▪ Cellarmaster(s) Riaan Oosthuizen (2011), MJ de Wit (Jan 2006) ▪ Winemaker(s) Liani de Wet (2019), MJ de Wit (Jan 2006) ▪ Viticulturist(s) Walter Smith ▪ 210ha/95ha (cab, merlot, ptage, shiraz, chard, sauv) ▪ 19t/3,000cs own label 50% red 50% white ▪ PO Box 364 Durbanville 7551 ▪ wine@signalgun.com ▪ www.signalgun.com ▪ S 33° 49' 13.26" E 018° 36' 40.32" ▪ 𝍐 seasoned. scholars.hallways ▪ **T +27 (0)21-976-7343**

Signal Hill Wines

Signal Hill moved to Cape Town's city centre in 2001, becoming one of SA's first urban boutique wineries, and remained there till 2018, when water restrictions made on-site production impossible. 'No water to clean, no wine,' laments owner and French-born vigneron Jean-Vincent Ridon, who now vinifies in rented Stellenbosch space. His grape source is another 'JV' innovation/creation: a tiny syrah block on lower Table Mountain, encircled by residences, inspired by Paris' famed Clos Montmartre. Making wine is just one of his passions. He also judges locally and abroad, and manages the Sommeliers Academy in Cape Town as part of his mission to uplift wine service standards.

★★★★☆ **Clos d'Oranje** Organically grown syrah, tasted mere hours after bottling & provisionally rated, **18** ★★★★ ⑧⑧ sweet red & black fruit, maraschino cherry top note & saline lilt, needing more time to settle, meld. Older oak, like last **13** ⑨⓪, 15 months.— CvZ

Location/WO: Cape Town ▪ 1stB 1997 ▪ Closed to public; only the city vineyard can be visited by appt ▪ Clos d' Oranje vineyard: tasting & visit by appt in season; masterclass for organic farming ▪ Owner(s) Signal Hill Wines cc ▪ Cellarmaster(s) Jean-Vincent Ridon ▪ 1ha ▪ PO Box 12481 Cape Town 8010 ▪ info@winery.co.za ▪ www.winery.co.za ▪ **T +27 (0)21-422-5206**

☐ **Signatures of Doolhof** *see* Doolhof Wine Estate

Sijnn

David Trafford, trained architect, acclaimed boutique vintner and co-owner acknowledges the role played by 'gut feel' in the development of this internationally acclaimed pioneer winery and vineyard in stony, uncompromising terroir at Malgas near the Breede River mouth. The project's success has much to do with a commitment to farming sustainably – 'the French call it "la lutte raisonnée", the reasoned struggle' – but also experience gained in founding and running top-ranked De Trafford winery in Stellenbosch since the early 1990s. Appropriately, sketches and photographs by David of Sijnn's cellar and bushvines (barbera, vermentino, petit manseng in the mix) adorn the new label for the White and Red blends. Sijnn (rhymes with 'Seine') is also collaborating with 'similar-minded individuals to cement this location [the local area bounded by Bredasdorp, Arniston and Agulhas, aka 'Agulhas triangle'] as an exotic winemaking destination producing some of the most exciting wines in the Western Cape'.

★★★★☆ **Syrah** ⊗ Uniquely charactered, stony-spicy-earthy **15** ⑨⓪ replete with fruit depth & intensity. Far from showy, but with subtle power, fine & supple tannins; long dry finish echoing sweet fruit. Only old oak. Also in magnum.

★★★★☆ **Touriga Nacional** Fine local example of the great Portuguese grape better known for port-styles. **17** ★★★★ ⑧⑧, first since **14** ⑨②, complex ripe fruit marshalled by serious tannins. Delicious, but needs plenty of time to show at best. All these spontaneous ferment, unfined & unfiltered.

★★★★ **Low Profile** A lighter-oaked, less intense version of Sijnn Red, though **17** ⑧⑨ no pushover with its firm structure. More mourvèdre than sibling, similarly distinctive. Juicy fruit, vibrant freshness, dry stony finish. Magnums too.

★★★★☆ **Sijnn Red** ⊛ Distinctive shiraz-driven flagship with touriga, mourvèdre, trincadeira & splash cab. **16** ⑨④ elegantly powerful, its rich dark spice, chocolate & sweet fruit offset by lively acidity, firm tannins. 20% new oak 22 months. **14** yet unreleased. Also in 1.5 & 3L, as White.

★★★★☆ **Free Reign 2nd Edition** ⊛ Shiraz & touriga, 22 months in oak (25% new), then bottle-aged several years at cellar. 2nd **NV** ⑨③ release (59/41 blend) similar character to debut, extended maturation adding complexity & sinewy structure giving austere note to full, sweet fruit; lingering dry finish.

★★★★ **Saignée** Juice drained off pre-ferment of mourvèdre, touriga & shiraz for a lighter-styled but well-structured red. **17** ⑧⑧ full & richly flavoured: meaty, spicy, earthy, sweet fruit. Firm & balanced.

★★★★☆ **Sijnn White** ⊛ Individual & rather gorgeous, limpid gold **18** ⑨③, from 70% chenin, has viognier & roussanne adding floral aromas & apricot notes. More savoury than fruity, richly full of flavour, with texture & a fine natural acidity. Unobtrusive 15% new oak supports 14% alcohol.— DS

Location/WO: Malgas ▪ Map: Southern Cape ▪ Map grid reference: D1 ▪ 2003 ▪ 1stB 2007 ▪ Tasting, sales & cellar tours at Sijnn Sat 10-3, or by appt ▪ Vintners platters ▪ Wines are also sold at De Trafford ▪ Owner(s) David & Rita Trafford, Simon Farr, Quentin Hurt ▪ Winemaker(s) David Trafford & Charla Haasbroek (Dec 2014), with Fred Fismer ▪ Viticulturist(s) Schalk du Toit (2002, consultant) ▪ 125ha/25ha (cab, grenache, mourv, shiraz, tempranillo, touriga nacional, trincadeira, chenin, rouss, viog) ▪ 60t/5,400cs own label 52% red 48% white ▪ 1.5ha olives ▪ PO Box 495 Stellenbosch 7599 ▪ info@sijnn.co.za ▪ www.sijnn.co.za ▪ S 34° 19' 0.27" E 020° 36' 41.37" ▪ 🖾 picturesque.consist.tenacious ▪ **T +27 (0)21-880-1398**

Silkbush Mountain Vineyards   ⌂

Guarded by Breedekloof's Sybasberg (Silkbush Mountain), amidst wild fynbos, the high-elevation vines here supply quality grapes to some of SA's majors as well as Silkbush's own labels, vinified by Chris du Toit of nearby Bergsig. Overseeing California-owned Silkbush is Anton Roos, who developed most of the 80-plus hectares and also looks after the on-site accommodation, Kingsbury Cottage.

Pinotage ⓥ ★★★★ High-toned **17** ⑧④, with generous mulberry & plum fruit, plush texture, good body & finish. **Shiraz** ⓥ ★★★★ Herbal aromas & ripe red fruit to the fore on **16** ⑧④. Elegant, with nice tannin grip. **Altitude** ★★★★ Revised Cape Blend in **18** ⑧⑤ has shiraz (32%), pinotage, petit verdot & malbec, offering substance & shape. Spiced black fruit has hints of scrub & tobacco. Year in older oak barrels. **Hillside Red** ★★★ Fruity, approachable unwooded pinotage-shiraz blend, **17** ⑧① offers ripe primary berries, smooth texture. **Rosé** ★★★ Vibrant **19** ⑧② from shiraz is pure strawberries-&-cream, with marsh-mallow texture & highlights. Ideal poolside sipper. **Summer White** ★★★ Switches from blend to varietal chenin in **19** ⑦⑧, light & fruity, tart tangy finish. **Sauvignon Blanc** ★★★ Prominent acid, flinty gunsmoke whiff with green fig & guava. **19** ⑧① crisp & refreshing, alcohol a reined-in 12.5%. **Viognier** ★★★★ Prominent peach profile on substantial, well-rounded **18** ⑧③, with crisp acidity, sweet spiciness. — GdB

Location: Wolseley ▪ WO: Breedekloof ▪ Est 2000 ▪ 1stB 2007 ▪ Closed to public ▪ Kingsbury Cottage (self-catering), www.silkbush.com/guest-house ▪ Owner(s) Silkbush Holdings LP ▪ Winemaker(s) Chris du Toit (2015, Bergsig Estate) ▪ Viticulturist(s) Anton Roos (2000) ▪ 143ha/87ha (cabs s/f, malbec, merlot, mourv, p verdot, ptage, shiraz, sauv, sem, viog) ▪ 1,200t/10,000cs own label 100% red ▪ Other export brand: Lion's Drift ▪ PO Box 91 Breërivier 6858 ▪ anton@silkbush.co.za ▪ www.silkbush.com ▪ **T +27 (0)83-629-1735**

Silvermist Organic Wine Estate   ⓥ ⑪ ⌂ ⊚

On Constantia Nek, with views over False Bay, Silvermist boutique wine estate is the only one on the Cape Peninsula that's certified organic. In addition to two restaurants (fine-dining La Colombe and casual Green Vine), luxury accommodation and various activities, it also now offers a Wine Garden Experience, with tasting hosted from the Silvermist Wine Truck. 'It's worth the visit,' assures GM Tessa Melck-Louw.

★★★★ **Cabernet Sauvignon** ⓥ ⓐ None reviewed since **10** ㉘, so it's a pleasure to taste pair of vintages: **15** ㉙, ripe & rich yet fresh, with tangy black fruit, cedar nuances; **16** ㉘ Cape Peninsula WO, shows dense blackcurrant, overt liquorice, needs more time for French oak to integrate.

★★★★ **Sauvignon Blanc** ⓥ A sauvignon for savouring (& cellaring few years), **18** ㉘ has pungent wild herb & tingling mineral notes adding interest to zesty granadilla, lime & grapefruit.

★★★★ **Sauvignon Blanc Reserve** ⓝⓔⓦ ⓥ Youthful **18** ㉙ has all the tropical fruit intensity of its sibling, just a little more compelling. Good palate weight & some white pepper on the finish. Could age. Not tasted: **Rocket Dog Red**. — JG

Location: Constantia ▪ Map: Cape Peninsula ▪ Map grid reference: B3 ▪ WO: Constantia/Cape Peninsula ▪ Est 1984 ▪ 1stB 2010 ▪ Wine tasting & sales: see website for opening times ▪ The Green Vine, www. greenvineeatery.com: Mon-Sun 8-5 for breakfast, lunch & all-day foods ▪ Events: events@silvermistestate. co.za ▪ Silvermist Boutique Hotel: hotel@silvermistestate.co.za ▪ Walks & hikes ▪ Conservation area ▪ La Colombe Restaurant: www.lacolombe.co.za / reservations@lacolombe.co.za ▪ Owner(s) Constantia Ridge Estates (Pty) Ltd ▪ Cellarmaster(s)/winemaker(s)/viticulturist(s) Gregory Brink Louw (Jan 2005) ▪ 22ha/6ha (cab, shiraz, sauv) ▪ 5.2t/580cs own label 30% red 70% white ▪ CERES organic ▪ PO Box 608 Constantia 7848 ▪ silvermistvineyards@gmail.com ▪ www.silvermistestate.co.za ▪ S 34° 0' 51.93" E 018° 24' 5.13" ▪ ⌨ refilling. diffidence.interests ▪ T +27 (0)21-794-7601

☐ **Silver Myn** *see* Zorgvliet Wines

Silverthorn Wines ⓟ

March 18th 2019 saw the fulfilment of a lifelong dream for John and Karen Loubser, as they 'started building a specialised méthode cap classique cellar and tasting facility on our Silverthorn farm' in Robertson. While the infrastructure is new, viticulturist/winemaker John's vines are mature, helping his goal of terroir-influenced bubblies: the chardonnay is 28 years old, shiraz for Genie a slightly younger 21. Pinot noir is sourced from Darling. A new release this year will be MCC from a 35-year-old block of colombard, the base wine to be naturally fermented in acacia barrels ('We can then join the Old Vine Project!'). The Loubsers promise visitors incredible views of the Breede River and Riviersonderend Mountains.

Méthode Cap Classique range

★★★★ **The Genie** Eye-catching pearly pink **NV** ㉙ rosé sparkling from shiraz. Enticing ensemble of biscuity notes, florals & red fruit wrapped in creamy mousse. 16 months lees- & further 8 months bottle-ageing add complexity, weight.

★★★★★ **CWG Auction Reserve Big Dog V** ⓐ Sophisticated & satisfying **14** ㉝ sparkler. Restrained apple, nut & hay complexity, enlivened by bright acidity. Depth thanks to 50 months on lees; dry & lengthy finish. Chardonnay up to 70%, old oak fermented/matured; plus unoaked pinot noir (as for Jewel).

★★★★★ **Jewel Box** ⓐ Elegant, refined bubbly, **15** ㉝ initial lemon pith zestiness yields to baked apple, red fruit richness partnered by brightening bubble. Can age with benefit. Chardonnay & pinot noir (70/30), 40 months on lees, 6 months on cork. WO W Cape, as Big Dog.

★★★★★ **The Green Man** ⓐ Suggestion of toasty, nutty evolution alongside fresh lemony zest on **16** ㉞ from 100% chardonnay. Satisfying creamy weight from 29 months on lees & really fine, energetic bubble deliver MCC of elegance, intensity & length. 10% older oak fermented.— AL

Location/map: Robertson ▪ Map grid reference: C4 ▪ WO: Robertson/Western Cape ▪ Est 1998 ▪ 1stB 2004 ▪ Tasting & cellar tours by appt Mon-Fri 12-3 Sat & select pub hols 10-2 ▪ Closed Good Fri, mid-June to mid-July for annual vacation, Dec 25/26 & Jan 1 ▪ Owner(s) Silverthorn Wines (Pty) Ltd ▪ Cellarmaster(s)/ winemaker(s)/viticulturist(s) John Loubser (1998) ▪ 10.5ha/4ha (cab, shiraz, chard, cbard) ▪ 60t/6,000cs own label 60% white 40% rosé ▪ IPW ▪ PO Box 381 Robertson 6705 ▪ john@silverthornwines.co.za, karen@ silverthornwines.co.za ▪ www.silverthornwines.co.za ▪ S 33° 55' 48.77" E 020° 1' 53.39" ▪ ⌨ passionately. shaves.expanding ▪ T +27 (0)21-788-1706

☐ **Silwervis** *see* Terracura Wines

Simelia Wines

Founded in 2012 by newly-married couple, German-born Simon Obholzer and Celia Hoogenhout, daughter of Wellington winegrower and nurseryman Ben Hoogenhout, Simelia (derived from their names) is clearly a passion project. Traditionally vinified wines by consultant Louis Nel come from vines on the Hoogenhouts' 19th-century Groenberg Mountain farm Woestkloof. New plantings are joining established ones, including venerable single blocks (among them a syrah of rare age), prompting affiliation with the Old Vine Project.

Reserve range (NEW)

★★★★☆ **Fluvius Merlot** Dark fruited, plum pudding notes, Xmas spice & mulled wine nuances on **16** ⓖ. Intense flavours, good balance & a supple tannin structure. Lovely dark chocolate notes from 30% new French oak, 36 months, on the satisfying finish. Also in magnum.

★★★★☆ **Senectus Syrah** ⓐ Opulent blackberry, mulberry, spiced meat, fynbos & dried herbs mingle with fragrant violet & white pepper in **16** ⓗ. Firmly structured, with tannins & oak (as Merlot) supporting the classic balance. Dry & very moreish, made to age.

Simelia range

Not tasted: **Merlot**, **Syrah**.

Casa Simelia range

★★★★ **Syrah** ⓩ A savoury, smoky bouquet welcomes & follows through to **17** ⓗ's perfectly dry palate, showing pristine fruit sweetness & balanced ripe tannins, well-absorbed wood (20% new).

★★★★ **Merlot-Cabernet Sauvignon** ⓩ Cab's 30% contribution shows in intense - not unpleasant - grip, buffered by luscious mulberry, cassis & plum. Pampering in 20% new oak, 15 months, aids fine texture & length in **17** ⓗ. — WB

Location/WO: Wellington ▪ Est Woestkloof farm 1837/Simelia wine label 2012 ▪ 1stB 2013 ▪ Access by invitation only ▪ Casa Simelia luxury self-catering country house ▪ Owner(s) Simon A Obholzer & Celia Hoogenhout-Obholzer ▪ Winemaker(s) Louis Nel (Nov 2012) & Simon A Obholzer ▪ 42ha/4.5ha (cab, merlot, shiraz) ▪ 8t/ha total ▪ ±3,500cs/ha plus ±500 magnum btls/ha 100% red ▪ PO Box 15587 Vlaeberg Cape Town 8018 ▪ info@simelia.co.za ▪ www.simelia.co.za ▪ **T +27 (0)21-300-5025**

☐ **Simonsbosch** *see* Koelenhof Winery

Simonsig Wine Estate (⚲) (🍴) (📷) (♿) (👓)

Just shy of 40 vintages at this significant Stellenbosch family estate, cellarmaster Johan Malan has passed the reins to Debbie Thompson, practically a clan member herself after 20 vintages here. Johan's son Michael focuses on reds, Charl Schoeman on whites and bubblies. Johan, now 'global ambassador for the family and its wines', goes forth with a history of innovation and industry leadership, from his father Frans pioneering SA bottle-fermented bubbly to co-founding the first wine route, to his own versatility and skill guiding an internationally reputed portfolio into the 21st century. For another example of which, see The Grapesmith.

The Garland range

★★★★☆ **Cabernet Sauvignon** ⓐ Awarded label design features arresting image of Stellenbosch's Simonsberg Mountain, source of this single-site flagship, 100% cabernet. **11** ⓗ seductive violet perfume, opulent fruit & harmonious structure of fine tannins, polished 23 months in 100% new French oak. Elegant & impressive finish. Will reward cellaring a decade or longer.

Malan Family Selection

★★★★☆ **Redhill Pinotage** ⓐ Lifted aromas of peach tea & red orchard fruit in **17** ⓗ. Palate is toasty from 15 months in 89% new oak, some American, with plump black plums & piquant tannin finish. Harmonious, shows good depth. From single bushvine parcel named for soil colour.

★★★★☆ **Merindol Syrah** ⓐ Ex single parcel on deep weathered granite. **16** ⓗ vibrant & satisfying, juicy black-fruit concentration, firm backbone of tannin & oak (100% new French, 18 months) to last 10+ years. Powerful but balanced for versatile food matching. Recalls Malan family's original French home.

★★★★☆ **Tiara** Bordeaux-style blend is rounded & expressive in **16** ⓖ, with generous plum & mulberry flavours, fine structure for a long life. Also-tasted **15** ⓙ is luscious with ripe tannins, blackcurrant fruit &

long finish. Wonderful food wine with a great future. Similar blends: cab (±70%) with merlot, petit verdot & cab franc; ±51% new French oak, 17 months.

★★★★ **Frans Malan Cape Blend** ⓥ Pinotage (70%), cab & merlot named for Malan patriarch, estate founder. Plush dark fruit coils around supple tannin spine, **16** ⑧⑨ glossy, & built to age but approachable in youth, too.

★★★★ **Chenin Avec Chêne** ⓥ Literally, 'With Oak', & in **17** ★★★★☆ ⑨⓪ the wood is all older, 12 months. Voluptuous Golden Delicious apple, nectarine, cinnamon-spiced quince & roasted nuts complexity. Similar refreshing conclusion to elegant **16** ⑧⑧, with more concentration in the flavours.

Cultivar Selection

★★★★ **Sunbird Sauvignon Blanc** ⓥ Pre-bottling, **19** ⑧⑦ steps up from **18** ★★★☆ ⑧⑤ with more concentrated tropical & stonefruit flavours, fuller body & lovely texture, fresh citrus zest finish. Dual Stellenbosch & Walker Bay WO.

Chenin Blanc ⓥ ⓣ ★★★★ Now in its 6th decade, still a delightfully drinkable, shareable, affordable wine. **19** ⑧④ easy & bright, unfettered by oak, abounds with tropical fruit flavours.

Labyrinth Cabernet Sauvignon ★★★ Ripe berry fruit sprinkled with mulled-wine spices charms in **17** ⑧④, dab of merlot adds complexity. Mostly older oak. **Pinotage** ★★★ Juicy, fruity & fun, **17** ⑧④ no edges, gentle tannins & a lifted cranberry squeeze to say goodbye. **Mr Borio's Shiraz** ★★★★ Generous dark berries, earthy spice, cured meat & whiff of dried herbs in charming **17** ⑧⑤. Nicely judged 10 months in variety of vessels, none new. **Cabernet Sauvignon-Shiraz** ★★★ Blackberry, mulberry, graphite & savoury meat flavours on **18** ⑧① , succulent 66/34 blend & a super pizza partner. **The GSM** ⓥ ★★★ Large portion of **17** ⑧①'s fruit picked early, given carbonic fermentation, delivering deliciously drinkable red-berry flavours. Grenache noir (24%), shiraz (30%) & mourvèdre. **Chardonnay** ★★★★ Full-bodied, barrel-fermented **18** ⑧⑤ delicious melange of stonefruit, caramel popcorn, melon & creamy vanilla. Good balance, spiced apple finish. **Gewürztraminer** ★★★ Aromatic semi-sweet from Durbanville grapes billows Turkish delight & rosepetals in **19** ⑧⑤, dab morio muscat adding to the heady perfume. Concludes with a litchi tang, for savoury fare or solo. Discontinued: **Roussanne**.

Export Market range

Cabernet Sauvignon-Merlot ★★★ Medium-bodied & easy **18** ⑦⑨ has lively berry fruit flavours, smooth tannins & dry finish. **Chenin Blanc-Pinotage Rosé** 🆕 ★★★ Fashionably pale-hued **19** ⑧⓪ is dry, vibrant & zesty, light bodied, with plentiful red berries & citrus for a summer party. WO W Cape, as next. **Sauvignon Blanc-Semillon** ★★★★ Just 2% semillon, but enough to give delicious waxy lemon twist on the farewell of **19** ⑧④, the sauvignon majority packs a gooseberry & greenpepper punch in fragrant & cheerful blend.

Méthode Cap Classique range

★★★★ **Kaapse Vonkel Brut Rosé** Candyfloss-scented **18** ⑧⑧ sparkling ex pinot noir & pinotage (76/24), dry & vivacious, creamy-savoury berry fruit in fine, melting mousse. Elegant & ready to celebrate.

★★★★ **Kaapse Vonkel Satin Nectar Rosé** 🆕 Demi-sec pink bubbly tastes fruity rather than sweet &, in fact, **17** ⑧⑦ has delicate pastry note which would partner well with canapés. Mouthfilling & fine, pleasing strawberry & raspberry intensity in aroma & flavour. Pinot noir, pinotage & meunier. WO W Cape, as Vonkel Brut & Nectar sibling.

★★★★☆ **Cuvée Royale** 🍂 Prestige blanc de blancs MCC from chardonnay, longest on lees of range (4-5 years). Elegant **14** ⑨④ shows meticulous attention to detail, admirable delicate harmony between stonefruit, apple blossom, vanilla biscuit & smooth persistent creamy mousse. No **13**.

★★★★ **Kaapse Vonkel Brut** First MCC in SA in 1971, still a pleasure to drink & instantly recognisable. Chardonnay (barrel fermented, 55%), pinot noir & drop meunier shows floral & fresh fruit aromas in **18** ⑧⑨ alongside nutty, toasty notes, dry finish.

★★★★ **Kaapse Vonkel Satin Nectar** Name changes (from 'Demi-Sec') but **17** ⑧⑧ still a sweeter (39 g/l sugar) sparkler yet with tiny tickling bubbles avoiding cloy. Alluring candied apple & roasted almond (though unoaked) tones, rounded & full. Same varieties as Vonkel Brut, fraction more pinot & meunier.

Dessert Wines & Digestifs

★★★★ **Vin de Liza** ⓠ Light-footed & perfectly balanced **17** ⑧⑥ Noble Late Harvest from wooded sauvignon & semillon, soft dried-apricot & roasted hazelnut flavours, tangerine zest finish. 375 ml.

★★★★ **Cape Vintage Reserve** ⓠ From shiraz, port-style **14** ⑧⑧ shows brambleberry & fruitcake richness, 25 months older oak giving welcome tannic grip, adding to drinkability & appeal. No **10 - 13**.

★★★★ **Gees Van Die Wingerd Husk Spirit Gewürztraminer** ⓠ Fragrant & aromatic **15** ⑧⑦, smooth & refreshing after dinner tipple or a shot in your espresso. Harmonious, with warm, clean farewell. Occasional release: **Straw Wine.** — WB

Location/map: Stellenbosch ▪ Map grid reference: E2 ▪ WO: Stellenbosch/Western Cape/Stellenbosch-Walker Bay ▪ Est 1953 ▪ 1stB 1968 ▪ Tasting & sales Mon-Fri 8.30–5 Sat/pub hols 8.30–4 Sun 11-3 ▪ Closed Good Fri, Dec 25 & Jan 1 ▪ Cellar tours by appt ▪ Cuvée restaurant: Mon-Sat breakfast 8.30-11 lunch 12-4; Fri 4-7 bubbles & tapas; Sun breakfast 8.30-11 family feast lunch 12-3 ▪ Fireplace ▪ Facilities for children ▪ Tour groups ▪ Conferences ▪ First Fizzday every first Thursday of the month: Oct-Apr ▪ Owner(s) Malan Family Trusts ▪ Cellarmaster(s) Debbie Thompson (Nov 1999) ▪ Winemaker(s) Michael Malan (reds, Oct 2017) & Charl Schoeman (whites & MCC, Dec 2012) ▪ Viticulturist(s) Francois Malan (Jan 1981) & Tommie Corbett (Nov 2008), with Etienne Terblanche (VinPro) ▪ 210ha (cab, merlot, ptage, pinot, shiraz, chard, chenin, sauv) ▪ 2,700t/340,000cs own label 20% red 48% white 32% MCC ▪ HACCP, IPW, SANAS, WIETA ▪ PO Box 6 Koelenhof 7605 ▪ wine@simonsig.co.za ▪ www.simonsig.co.za ▪ S 33° 52' 12.1" E 018° 49' 31.7" ▪ ⌨ gazette.stylist.wants ▪ **T +27 (0)21-888-4900 (general), +27 (0)21-888-4915 (tasting), +27 (0)21-888-4932/+27 (0)76-207-8930 (Cuvée)**

Simonsvlei International   ⓠ ⑪ ⑩ ⑧ ⑤

Founded by growers in the 1940s, Simonsvlei today has 65 shareholders and 33 active producers. The annual crush – 60% of which is white – is vinified into mostly wallet-friendly ranges destined for local and international markets, as well as brands for local clients like Woolworths. The large visitor-friendly 'campus' is located just off the N1 motorway near Paarl and comprises wine-making, -tasting and -sales facilities, conference and function venue, restaurant and an area to keep the youngsters amused.

Hercules Paragon range

★★★★ **SMCV** ⓠ Abundant red fruit, gentle spice from mostly older oak & fresh acidity, **16** ⑧⑥ successful quartet shiraz, mourvèdre, cinsaut & viognier, perennial cellardoor favourite.

New Generation range

Ja-Mocha Pinotage ★★★ Chocolate, more than mocha, nuance to variety's attractive strawberry & mulberry fruit, tingling acidity in **18** ⑦⑨. **Toffee Chunk Syrah** ★★★ Step-up **17** ⑦⑨ delivers promised caramel coating to vivacious red fruit & dry tail for satisfying sipping.

Premier range

Shiraz Rosé ⊘ ⑨ ★★★ A standout in this range, **19** ⑧⓪ dry but fruit-filled, flavoursome berry finish very easy to drink. **Chardonnay** ⊘ ⑨ ★★★ Well-balanced & nicely vinous, **18** ⑧⓪ subtle straw & nut highlights, lemon & cream finish.

Cabernet Sauvignon ★★ Food-styled **18** ⑦⑥ dry red with herbaceous tannins. **Pinotage** ★★☆ Ready-to-drink **18** ⑦⑨ packs plenty of variety's mulberry & strawberry fruit, refreshing acidity. Has few grams smoothing sugar, as all these reds. **Shiraz** ★★★ Light-seeming, even at 14.5% alcohol, **18** ⑦⑦'s piquant red fruit slips down easily. **Zenzela Pinotage Rosé** ★★ Pretty pink **19** ⑦⑷ has boiled sweet/lollipop aromas, pleasant suggestion of sweetness (though technically dry). **Chenin Blanc** ★★ Bright & friendly **19** ⑦⑥ has sauvignon-like grassy aromas & flavours. **Humbro Red Jerepiko** ★★★ Grapey **NV** ⑦⑨ fortified dessert is a cellar stalwart, well-judged spirit for solo in winter, over ice in summer.

Lifestyle range

Simonsrood ⊘ ⑨ ★★★ As usual, **NV** ⑦⑨ exactly as per label: 'smooth red for easy drinking'. Treads lightly with just 12.5% alcohol, perfect picnic red.

Cabernet Sauvignon ★★ Wallet-friendly range in attractive packaging. Choc-coffee tones, slightly astringent tannins, **18** ⑦⑥ best with a meal. **Merlot** ★★ Brooding plum fruit, firm grape tannins smoothed by spoonful sugar in **19** ⑦⑥, as all reds in line-up. **Pinotage** ⊘ ★★★ Most accessible of these reds. **18** ⑦⑨ soft & rounded, with mulberry flavours, unripe strawberry tang. **Shiraz** ⊘ ★★★ Shade less variety-true than previous, cranberry-toned **18** ⑦⑨ makes up with pleasing freshness & weight. **Chenin Blanc** ★★ Brisk & brief **19** ⑦⑤, with faint grass & lemon tones. **Sauvignon Blanc** ⑧ ★★ Water-white & subtly grassy, **18** ⑦② balanced but shade less substance, flavour than usual.

Simonsvlei range

Dry Red ★★ Uncomplicated but fruity **NV** ⑦⑤, slightly higher (13%) alcohol than Lifestyle offering, drier & bit more satisfying. 5L pack, as all these. **Dry White** ★★ **NV** ⑦③ expressive grass, melon & peach notes, energetic acidity & dash sugar for extra sip appeal. **Natural Sweet Rosé** ★★ Raspberry & strawberry tones, lively acidity neatly counters sweetness on low-alcohol (7.6%) **NV** ⑦④.

Villa Cape Kosher range

Merlot ★★★ Bold but well-concealed 14.7% alcohol, **18** ⑧⓪ plum & interesting salted caramel note, silky conclusion. **Pinotage** ★★★ Firm grape tannins add extra dimension to **18** ⑦⑨'s sweet mulberry fruit. **17** ⑦⑧, also tasted, candyfloss toned & slightly less persistent. Both decently dry supper mates. **Shiraz** ⑯④ ★★★ Least generous fruit in the range, but **18** ⑦⑦ does have an engaging spicy character. **Chardonnay** ⑧ ★★ Unwooded, creamy **18** ⑦③, tropical fruit flavours & nice mouthfeel for solo sipping. **Chenin Blanc** ⑧ ★★★ Fresh **18** ⑦⑧'s white peach & dried pear flavours highlighted by bouncy acidity. Not tasted: **Cabernet Sauvignon**, **Shiraz Rosé**. — CvZ

Location/map: Paarl ▪ Map grid reference: D7 ▪ WO: Western Cape ▪ Est/1stB 1945 ▪ Tasting & sales Mon-Fri 8–5 Sat/pub hols 8.30–4.30 Sun 11–3; last tasting 30 minutes prior to closing ▪ Fee R25pp/3 wines R40pp/6 wines ▪ Cellar tours by prior arrangement ▪ Closed Good Fri, Dec 25 & Jan 1 ▪ Kids indoor & outdoor play areas ▪ Restaurant ▪ Conference & function venue ▪ Karoo Craft Breweries (www.kcbrew.co.za) ▪ Owner(s) 65 shareholders ▪ 33 active producers ▪ Cellarmaster(s) Helena Senekal (Oct 2016) ▪ 5,200t 40% red 60% white ▪ Brands for clients: Woolworths ▪ BRC, E-Mark, Fairtrade, IPW, WIETA ▪ PO Box 584 Suider-Paarl 7624 ▪ info@simonsvlei.co.za, steven@simonsvlei.co.za ▪ www.simonsvlei.co.za ▪ S 33° 47' 23.31" E 018° 55' 48.15" ▪ ⌖ luckier.metro.start ▪ **T +27 (0)21-863-3040**

☐ **Simplicity** see Weltevrede Estate
☐ **Since 1922** see Villiersdorp Winery
☐ **Sir George** see Napier Vineyards

Sir Lambert Wines   ⑫

The Sir Lambert brand originated from a small seaside sauvignon blanc vineyard at Lamberts Bay developed by veteran viticulturist Johan Teubes with fellow vine-man John Hayes and vintner Thys Louw of Diemersdal. After a restructure, the label is now jointly owned by Johan and John, with Johan's son Sybrand and granddaughter Mariska making the wine and intending 'to build on growing demand for West Coast wines with our unique terroir and story'. Tasting/sales are at the Teubes family's venue in Lamberts Bay.

★★★★ **Sauvignon Blanc** Fresh granadilla, gooseberry & vivacious citrus flavours interwoven in complex **19** ⑧⑥. Balanced & mouthfilling, with length & saline nuance on finish.— WB

Location/WO: Lamberts Bay ▪ Map: Olifants River ▪ Map grid reference: B5 ▪ Est 2004 ▪ 1stB 2007 ▪ Tasting & sales at Teubes Family Wines ▪ Owner(s) John Hayes & Johan Teubes ▪ Cellarmaster(s) Sybrand Teubes ▪ Winemaker(s) Sybrand Teubes, with Mariska Teubes ▪ Viticulturist(s) John Hayes ▪ 10ha (shiraz, sauv) ▪ PO Box 791 Vredendal 8160 ▪ info@teubeswines.co.za ▪ www.teubeswines.co.za ▪ S 32° 5' 52.40" E 018° 18' 19.50" ▪ ⌖ feathered.yearned.paid ▪ **T +27 (0)27-213-2377**

☐ **Sir Robert Stanford Estate** see Robert Stanford Estate
☐ **Six Hats** see Piekenierskloof Wine Company
☐ **Sixpence** see Opstal Estate
☐ **1685** see Boschendal Wines
☐ **Sixty 40** see Boland Cellar

Skaap Wines   ⑪ ⌂ ◎ ⑧

Dutch banker Thierry Schaap made some important decisions when he bought his Sir Lowry's Pass property, with access to renowned Schapenberg (must be fate!): focus on quality; personalise the wines (his name, 'sheep', reflected in the charming 'woolly' labels); work with a winemaker you respect, as in Nomada's Riaan Oosthuizen. Now, reaping the benefit, all the wines except rosé are off home vines, and the ratings speak for themselves. The numbers on the shiraz and sauvignon are Thierry's age - he started his wine career at 40.

★★★★ **Shiraz 46** (醤) Seriously made, long skin contact, 18 months oaking, mixed provenance, half new. Individual **17** (88) shows scrub & pepper, red berry mix, meat extract savouriness. Complex & assured.

★★★★☆ **Sauvignon Blanc 47** (✓)(醤) Vibrant passionfruit on entry but oak-touched **18** (94) is multi-layered on track record, will reveal more over time, including minerality already hinted at. Nervy, tightly focused, in the prime of health.

Not tasted: **Rosalie Reserve Shiraz, Nathan Blend, Okuphinki, Méthode Cap Classique Brut**. — CR

Location: Sir Lowry's Pass ▪ WO: Stellenbosch ▪ Est/1stB 2011 ▪ Wine sales daily ▪ Private functions/dinner by appt ▪ Local art on display & for sale ▪ Conferences (up to 16 pax) ▪ Walks/hikes ▪ Conservation area ▪ 5-bedroom guest house, dining room with chef & 2 self-catering lodges plus villa ▪ Swimming pool ▪ Owner(s) Thierry Schaap ▪ Cellarmaster(s)/winemaker(s) Riaan Oosthuizen (Jan 2011) ▪ 17ha/4ha (shiraz, sauv) ▪ 1,700cs own label 50% red 50% white ▪ IPW ▪ PO Box 3794 Somerset West 7130 ▪ info@skaapwines. com ▪ www.skaapwines.com ▪ S 34° 06' 11.35" E 018° 55' 05.87" ▪ 🖼 truce.product.freestyle ▪ **T +27 (0)21-858-1982**

☐ **Sketchbook** *see* Carrol Boyes Collection

Skilpadvlei Wines   (♀)(🍴)(🏠)(📷)(🛏)(♿)

Wine pairings and a deli have been added to the numerous food, wine and hospitality attractions at the Polkadraai Hills farm of the Joubert family — who arrived here in 1917, long after a resident colony of water tortoises had given their name to it. Only more recently (this century, in fact) did fourth-generation Willie Joubert start diverting some of the estate's grapes into wines for an own label.

★★★★ **ML Joubert** Usual equal blend of cab & merlot on **17** (86), & usual spicy fruitcake, dark choc & cigarbox. Plenty of flavour, supported by good oaking (25% new), ripe tannins & balanced acidity. No hurry to drink.

Grenache Noir (NEW) ★★★★ Dark cherry notes on **17** (84); generous flavours & structure but also a lean, dry element, with restrained but form-giving tannins. 20% wholebunch ferment; only older oak. **Pinotage** (✓) ★★★★ Ripe & fruity aromas on **18** (84) promise the sweet, juicy flavours that indeed follow. Firm but cushiony structure doesn't detract from approachability. **Shiraz** ★★★ Spicy, dark, sweet fruit on juicy, easygoing & simply straightforward **18** (82). **Grenache Rosé** ★★★ Copper-pink **18** (82) lightly aromatic, an earthy tug to the sweet berry fruit & a fairly dry finish. **Chenin Blanc Wooded** (NEW) ★★★★ Oaking (25% new) adds a dominant savoury element to aromas & flavours of **17** (83) & broadens the palate, balanced by a tartly green acidity. **Chenin Blanc** (✓) ★★★ Deftly made, balanced, fruity & fresh **18** (82) - not varietally typical, given the tropical notes, but satisfying. **Sauvignon Blanc** ★★★ Quaffable, exuberant **19** (81) is forwardly aromatic & fruity, with a neat green acid balance & dry finish. — TJ

Location/map/WO: Stellenbosch ▪ Map grid reference: C6 ▪ Est 2004 ▪ 1stB 2001 ▪ Tasting & sales Mon-Sat 8-5 Sun 8-4 ▪ Fee R30/4 wines R40/6 wines R50/8 wines ▪ Food & wine pairings; kiddies tasting ▪ Closed Dec 25/26 & Jan 1/2 ▪ Restaurant Mon-Sat 8-late Sun 8-4 ▪ Facilities for children ▪ Gift/decor shop ▪ Deli ▪ Conferences ▪ Weddings & functions ▪ B&B guest house & self-catering cottages ▪ Owner(s) WD Joubert ▪ Cellarmaster(s) Kowie du Toit (consultant) ▪ Viticulturist(s) Johan Pienaar & Eben Archer (consultants) ▪ 78ha/55ha (cab, merlot, ptage, shiraz, chenin, sauv) ▪ 652t/12,000cs own label 80% red 20% white ▪ PO Box 17 Vlottenburg 7604 ▪ wines@skilpadvlei.co.za ▪ www.skilpadvlei.co.za ▪ S 33° 57' 31.5" E 018° 45' 52.4" ▪ 🖼 ahead.both.budding ▪ **T +27 (0)21-881-3237**

☐ **Skipper's** *see* New Beginnings Wines

Skipskop Wines   (♀)(📷)(NEW)

Home for below naturally-made boutique wines (and a future MCC bubbly) is Napier in the Overberg (nearby Skipskop is the site of several 19th-century shipwrecks). Bottlings since 2003 of petit verdot from a back-garden vineyard inspired renovation in 2012 of an old barn into a rustic red-wine cellar, soon joined by facilities for white-wine making. Latterly British geologist and vintner Jonathan de Thierry has also been vinifying and blending-in fruit from vines on his farm in a warmer climate, Klein Karoo, tended by Dirk Viljoen. Nebbiolo will join fellow Italian sangiovese there to feed growing export markets.

Petit Verdot ★★★★ 16 ⑧④ showcases variety well. Deeply coloured, dense & dark toned yet with touches of green scrub, savoury spice, woodsmoke - many layers of interest. 18 months oak, an equal partner, no edges to interfere with immediate enjoyment - but has ageing potential. Napier & Klein Karoo grapes.

Sauvignon Blanc-Semillon ★★★★ Capsicum & sage, svelte unwooded **19** ⑧④ speaks of cool growing conditions, racy acidity in support, giving vibrancy, length & ageing ability. — CR, CvZ

Location: Napier ▪ Map: Southern Cape ▪ Map grid reference: C6 ▪ WO: Napier/Western Cape ▪ Est 2012 ▪ 1stB 2014 ▪ Tasting by appt only ▪ Craft brandy still ▪ Owner(s) Tweedal Estate cc ▪ Winemaker(s) Jonathan de Thierry ▪ Viticulturist(s) Dirk Viljoen ▪ Napier 2ha (p verdot, pinot, shiraz, sauv, sem, viog) + Voorbaat (Klein Karoo) 2.5ha (p verdot, sangio, shiraz, white muscadel) ▪ 33t/1,000cs own label 80% red 20% white ▪ Meul Str, Napier 7270 ▪ skipskopwines@gmail.com ▪ S 34° 28' 26.22" E 019° 54' 5.86" ▪ 🖂 soothingly.souffles. voluntary ▪ **T** +27 (0)82-093-1791

☐ **Skoon Vallei** *see* Eerste Hoop Wine Cellar

Slaley

The third generation of the Hunting family running this Stellenbosch winery reports 'many new developments'. They welcomed experienced consultants Jacques Fourie (winemaker, working alongside incumbent Marjean Smit) and Wynand Pienaar (viticulturist). 'Massive effort in the vineyard' included nurturing 1955 pinotage vines, cellar development provided for MCC bubbly production (wines currently on the lees) and the guest house reopened its doors.

Slaley range

★★★★ Merlot ⓠ Big & bold, but **08** ⑧⑦ has aged gracefully, revealing plum compote & spice in well-integrated tannin frame. Serious oaking: 36 months in 50% new oak, as for Pinotage.

★★★★ Shiraz ⓠ Plush, plump & supple **07** ⑧⑥ is ready to drink but still bright & perky. Expressive black plum & stewed prune fruit. Similar mint nuance as tannic **06 ★★★★** ⑧④.

★★★★ Merlot-Cabernet Sauvignon ⓠ Brooding **08** ⑧⑥ beginning to emerge from dense tannin cloak, revealing ripe damson & blackcurrant fruit, aromatic liquorice & tobacco. Well up on **07 ★★★** ⑧①.

Pinotage ⓠ **★★★★** Opulent ripe dark berry fruit & big alcohol (15%) have melded into engaging, smooth **08** ⑧④ offering, ready to drink. Occasional release: **Reserve Noble Late Harvest Chardonnay**. Discontinued: **Chardonnay**.

Broken Stone range

★★★★ Pinotage ⓠ Dark prune & pot-pourri nuances, **11★★★** ⑦⑧ flagging somewhat, burly alcohol (16.2%) standing apart. Last tasted was polished & elegant **06** ⑧⑦.

Cabernet Sauvignon ⓠ **★★★** Supple **11** ⑧② showing its age in mature Xmas cake flavours, generous sprinkle of spice & some warmth (15.5%). Best to drink soon. **Chardonnay** ⓠ **★★★** Now bottled, **17** ⑦⑦ pronounced bruised apple & pear flavours, fleeting honeyed finish. Not tasted: **Shiraz**, **Cabernet Sauvignon-Shiraz-Pinotage**.

Social range

Lindsay's Whimsy Red ⓠ **★★★** Wholesome & robust **11** ⑧② pinotage, shiraz & cab, intense black fruit & plum pudding richness on solid tannins. **Lindsay's Whimsy Rosé** ⓠ **★★★** Dry **13** ⑦⑨ from pinotage, deliberately weightier in style, says team, so wine will 'stay wine as opposed to water if you add ice'! **The Whimsy Sauvignon Blanc** ⓠ **★★★** Pleasingly different fruit profile of citrus & orchard fruit, **17** ⑧⓪ light & breezy for early drinking. — WB

Location/map: Stellenbosch ▪ Map grid reference: E2 ▪ WO: Simonsberg—Stellenbosch/Western Cape ▪ Est 1955 ▪ 1stB 1997 ▪ Tasting & sales Tue-Fri 10-4 Sat/Sun 9—5 ▪ Fee R45, waived on purchase ▪ Closed Good Fri, Dec 24/25 & Jan 1 ▪ Bistro: light meals during tasting hours ▪ Venue & conference facility with AV capacity ▪ Guesthouse ▪ Owner(s) Hunting family ▪ Winemaker(s) Jacques Fourie (consultant) & Marjean Smit (Jan 2018) ▪ Viticulturist(s) Wynand Pienaar (consultant) ▪ 183ha/30ha (cab, merlot, ptage, shiraz, chard, sauv) ▪ 220t/15—20,000cs own label 90% red 9% white 1% rosé ▪ IPW ▪ PO Box 119 Koelenhof 7605 ▪ venue@slaley.

co.za, accounts@slaley.co.za ▪ www.slaley.co.za ▪ S 33° 51' 53.7'' E 018° 50' 51.1'' ▪ 🖾 paint.awesome.scoots
▪ T +27 (0)21-865-2123

Slanghoek Winery Ⓨ ⓒ ⓑ

The vineyards of the 25 growers that own this winery spread across the valley, surrounded by spectacular
berg scenery, the cellar deriving its name from the Slanghoek Mountains. Taking in their grapes and running
operations, with the aid of innovative technology and modern equipment, is a staff whose core has a depth
of experience acquired over nearly two decades. There's not only a large and diverse range of wines, but also
much to tempt visitors, like 4x4 trails, mountain biking, hiking, canoeing, fishing and seasonal area festivals.

Legends range

★★★★ **Barrel Fermented Chenin Blanc** Seriously made **17** ⑧⑧ similar styling to previous, 20 months
new French barrels, stonefruit & vanilla biscuit, richly textured, ends limy-fresh. Only 2,000 bottles.

Private Selection

★★★★ **Crème de Chenin** ⓧ Bargain-priced Natural Sweet, **16** ⑧⑦ captures the essence of sweet
chenin. Intense apricot & pear, piercing acidity cutting a swathe through 91 g/l sugar, keeping it vibrant.

★★★★ **Noble Late Harvest** ⓧ **16** ⑧⑨ retasted, extra year deepened, enriched the flavours. Crème
caramel & honey, 60% oaking giving ginger biscuit overlay, ends racy-fresh. Chenin, dash muscat.

··

Merlot ⓦ ★★★ Merlot at its likeable best: berry-rich, hint of mint, **18** ⑧② is smooth-textured, eminently
drinkable. **Chardonnay** ★★★ Portion **19** ⑧② in new French barrels, nicely combines citrus with biscuit
tones, ends limy-fresh. Similar flavours for **18** ⑧②, touch more melon development says it's ready to drink.
Sauvignon Blanc ⓦ ★★★ Sparking with life: gooseberry freshness in svelte **19** ⑧②, ending with
food-friendly minerality.

··

Cabernet Sauvignon ★★★ Longer oaking than other range reds, 18 months, no barrier to **17** ⑧①'s
accessibility. Dark berries & chocolate, lithe appeal. **Pinotage** ★★★ Offering easy drinkability, **17** ⑧① is
liquorice- & black plum-toned, sleek & juicy. Year oaked, as most of the reds. **Shiraz** ★★★ Dark-toned &
harmoniously oaked, smooth, succulent **17** ⑧② finishes on a tasty fresh note. **Camerca** ⊘ ★★★ Cab,
merlot, dab cab franc (name gives the clue!). Berry fruit supported by **17** ⑧①'s tannin backbone, giving
definition. **Chenin Blanc** ★★ Apple & pear flavours in light-textured (12% alcohol) **19** ⑦④, dry & zesty.
Discontinued: **Special Late Harvest**.

Slanghoek range

··

Hanepoot Jerepigo ⓦ ★★★★ Distinctive fortified wine-style of the area. **18** ⑧④ celebrates muscat
d'Alexandrie in its tangy rich array of sultanas & dried fruit.

··

Cuvée Brut ★★ Mainly chardonnay, touch chenin in carbonated NV ⑦⑤ bubbly. Consistent styling, lemon
sherbet, finishes crisply dry. **Vin Doux** ★★★ Muscat d'Alexandrie gives NV ⑦⑧ sweet grapiness with floral
highlights, the bubbles a lively refresher. **Red Muscadel** ★★★ Sweetest of the fortified wines, **18** ⑧① is
raisiny with mouthcoating luscious richness. Perfect winter fare. **Red Jerepigo** ★★★ Vivid scarlet-hued **18**
⑦⑧ from pinotage offers fruit gum flavours, tangy sweetness. **Cape Ruby** ⊘ ★★★ Unwooded 'port' from
touriga, **18** ⑧① is fruity & sweet with rich, smooth, tasty drinkability.

Vinay range

Vin Rouge ⊘ ★★★ Name change from 'Smooth Blended Red' but NV ⑦⑧'s styling & blend remain:
pinotage, malbec & petit verdot, dark toned & juicy, smoothly dry. **Vin Blanc** ★★ Was 'Crispy White',
remains true in flavour: sauvignon, chenin, colombard, unwooded NV ⑦⑤, low 12% alcohol. **Vin Rosé**
★★★ Previously 'Natural Sweet Rosé'. Sweetest of range, NV ⑦⑦ from red muscadel; raisins & candyfloss,
with friendly low 9.5% alcohol. **Vin Semi-Doux** ⑯④ ★★★ Muscat d'Alexandrie (70%) with chenin gives
NV ⑦⑧ loads of grapey aromas & flavours. Balanced sweetness & just 8% alcohol add to the appeal. — CR

Location: Rawsonville ▪ Map: Breedekloof ▪ Map grid reference: A5 ▪ WO: Slanghoek ▪ Est 1951 ▪ 1stB 1970 ▪
Tasting & sales Mon-Fri 9–5 Sat 10–1 ▪ Closed Easter Fri/Sun, Dec 25 & Jan 1 ▪ Cellar tours by appt ▪ Slanghoek
MTB Route, fee R20: 13km ride with optional extra, more challenging 4km ▪ Owner(s) 25 producers ▪
Cellarmaster(s) Pieter Carstens (Aug 2002) ▪ Winemaker(s) Nico Grundling (Dec 2002) & Werner du Plessis (Aug
2014), with Jacques de Goede (Dec 2001) & Elaine Conradie (Nov 2016) ▪ Viticulturist(s) Callie Coetzee (Nov

2010) ▪ 1,830ha ▪ 30,000t/80,000cs own label 25% red 55% white 10% rosé 10% fortified ▪ Other export brand: Zonneweelde ▪ ISO 22000, IPW ▪ PO Box 75 Rawsonville 6845 ▪ info@slanghoek.co.za ▪ www.slanghoek.co.za ▪ S 33° 39' 1.1" E 019° 13' 49.0" ▪ ⌷ equates.reflectors.booking ▪ T +27 (0)23-344-3026

☐ **Slent** *see* Ayama Wines
☐ **Slowine** *see* Villiersdorp Winery
☐ **Sluk Jou Woorde** *See Editor's Note*
☐ **Smiley** *see* Terracura Wines
☐ **Smuggler's Boot** *see* Richard Kershaw Wines
☐ **Sneeukop** *see* Rogge Cloof
☐ **Social** *see* Slaley
☐ **Soek Die Geluk** *see* Goedverwacht Wine Estate

SoetKaroo Wine Estate   ⓠ ⓖ

Crafting sweet ('soet') wines since 2004 from varieties that include a rare red-skinned mutation of hanepoot, garagiste winemaker Susan Perold and viticulturist husband Herman have seen the dire effect of climate change on their small vineyard in the town centre of Groot Karoo's Prins Albert. Excessive heat and insufficient dormancy means that from 2019, production will be from 'adopted children', the '18 Jerepigo being the last from their beloved parcel. Other current releases (none tasted) are '16 Cape Vintage 'port', '17 fortified Touriga Nacional, and a '19 hanepoot named Die Laatlam.

Location: Prince Albert ▪ Map: Klein Karoo & Garden Route ▪ Map grid reference: A4 ▪ Est 2000 ▪ 1stB 2004 ▪ Tasting & sales Mon-Sat 9-1; afternoons by appt ▪ Closed Dec 25 ▪ Owner(s) Herman & Susan Perold ▪ Cellarmaster(s)/winemaker(s) Susan Perold (Jan 2007) ▪ 2t ▪ 56 Church Str Prince Albert 6930 ▪ soetkaroo@gmail.com ▪ S 33° 13' 21.9" E 022° 1' 48.0" ▪ ⌷ catching.hideouts.lapping ▪ T +27 (0)23-541-1768

☐ **Soleil de Karoo** *see* Karusa Premium Wines & Craft Brewery

Solitary Wine

Jozua Joubert was winemaker at A-league Warwick when he took over family winegrowing farm Karibib in Stellenbosch's Polkadraai Hills in 2010. He's produced these own-brand single-vineyard wines in minuscule quantities since 2014. Having inherited some 52 ha of mature vines (including 32-year-old chenin, which debuts in bottle this edition), he strives for minimalist, intense wines from the farm's granitic soils.

★★★★ **Bankrot Chenin Blanc** ⓝⓔⓦ 'Bankrupt' name of farm's last workhorse, which died 1988 when chenin vineyard was planted. **19** ⑧⑦ fully oaked; citrus & fynbos vie with almond savouriness; vibrant acidity adds brightness & vigour, great length. Can age.

Morning Bell Pinot Noir ★★★★ Forest floor, chopped herbs, fresh red berries, **18** ⑧④ has cool-climate intensity. Barrel aged 16 months, finishes savoury. **Owl House Sauvignon Blanc** ★★★★ Barrel contact for half **19** ⑧⑤, gooseberry styling remains dominant, some leafy notes which follow onto the palate. Crisply dry, ends saline. — CR

Location: Stellenbosch ▪ WO: Polkadraai Hills ▪ Est/1stB 2014 ▪ Closed to public ▪ Owner(s) Jozua Joubert ▪ Cellarmaster(s)/winemaker(s) Jozua Joubert (Jun 2014) ▪ Viticulturist(s) Jozua Joubert (Oct 2010) ▪ 56ha/52ha (cab, pinot, chenin, sauv) ▪ 7t/ha 500cs own label 40% red 60% white ▪ PO Box 81 Kuils River 7579 ▪ jozua@solitarywine.co.za ▪ www.solitarywine.co.za ▪ T +27 (0)82-336-3370

Somerbosch Wines   ⓠ ⓨ ⓞ ⓐ ⓖ

Owned by the winemaking Roux family for over half a century, the multi-amenity farm Die Fonteine is exactly halfway between Somerset West and Stellenbosch, hence the name of these wines, the premium range now with a matt black label and gold print to 'better represent Somerbosch Wines'.

Somerbosch range

Cabernet Sauvignon ★★★ Supportive wooding, combo older French/American, so there is black-berried fruit galore in **18** ⑧②, nicely buffed tannins too, moderate 13.5% alcohol. **Merlot** ★★★ Lightly oaked **18** ⑧⓪ is accessible, with ripe plum & subtle mocha notes. **17** to be released later. **Pinotage** ★★★ **17** ⑦⑨ has ripe black cherries & blueberries wrapped in sweet vanilla from 100% American oak staves. **Shiraz** ★★★

Youthful **18** (81) opens up in glass to reveal red fruit & baking spice from partial ageing in 70% American barrels. Give it a little time/air to show its charms. **Shiraz-Merlot** ★★★ Equal marriage for everyday drinking, **18** (80) brings together red & black fruit, smoke & mocha courtesy 20% portion oaked in older barrels. **Rosé** ★★★ Pack a picnic for coral-hued **18** (81), watermelon, strawberry & peach flavours. Drier, fresher than previous (12.5% alcohol). **Chenin Blanc** ★★★ Pineapple on nose combines with litchi & guava on **19** (82) palate to deliver toothsome, fruit salady easy-drinker. **Sauvignon Blanc** ★★★ Fruitier than last, **19** (81) has Granny Smith apples & luscious white peaches, appealing slight chalkiness. **Sauvignon Blanc-Semillon** (2) ★★★ Pre-bottling, unoaked 50/50 blend refreshes, with lingering mineral tone on clean finish. **18** (82) quite smooth despite zestiness. **Méthode Cap Classique Brut** (2) ★★★★ Underlying chalkiness to **NV** (83) sparkling, 100% chardonnay from Elgin fruit gives sherbetty citrus & green apple profile. **Late Bottled Vintage Port** (2) ★★★ From cab, aged 2 years in old barrels, **NV** (81) decadently sweet with spiced fruitcake richness. Not tasted: **Kylix**, **Chardonnay**. — JG

Location: Stellenbosch ▪ Map: Helderberg ▪ Map grid reference: C1 ▪ WO: Stellenbosch/Western Cape ▪ Est 1950 ▪ 1stB 1995 ▪ Tasting & sales daily 9–5 ▪ Fee R50/6 wines, waived on purchase of any 3 btls; R70pp/ice cream & red wine tasting ▪ Closed Dec 24/25 ▪ Cellar tours by appt ▪ Somersbosch Bistro: breakfast & lunch daily ▪ Facilities for children ▪ Farm produce ▪ Conferences ▪ Craft beer ▪ Owner(s) Somersbosch Wines cc ▪ Cellarmaster(s)/winemaker(s)/viticulturist(s) Marius & Japie Roux (both 1995) ▪ 55ha/43ha (cab, merlot, shiraz, sauv) ▪ 350t 55% red 45% white ▪ PO Box 12181 Die Boord 7613 ▪ enquiries@somersbosch.co.za, sales@somersbosch.co.za ▪ www.somersbosch.co.za ▪ S 34° 0' 28.6" E 018° 49' 6.9" ▪ 🗺 sayings.realists.clinic ▪ T +27 (0)21-855-3615

Somerset Wines

Based in the Helderberg, Somerset Wines is a national sales, marketing and distribution company with a wide selection of SA's best-loved wine, brandy, spirit and ready-to-drink labels in its portfolio. Listed here are proprietor and industry stalwart Boetie Rietoff's own value-for-money ranges, made by Pieter-Niel Rossouw of Darling Cellars with another wine-business veteran, Jeff Wedgwood, consulting.

Lord Somerset range

Cabernet Sauvignon (2) ★★★ Well-priced **16** (78)'s forthcoming blackberry aromas, cranberry flavours & juicy food-friendly tannins will win many fans. **Shiraz** (2) ★★★ Very lightly wooded **15** (79) is unexpectedly tart given its port-like nose of prunes & caramel. **Cabernet Sauvignon-Merlot** ⊘ ★★★ Loads of black & red berries, subtle tannic grip, **18** (79) lively mouthful best enjoyed now. **Sauvignon Blanc** ★★ **19** (76) light, brief & breezy with subtle grassiness. **Soft Smooth Red** ★★ As advertised, soft & smooth rather than sweet, the sugar offset by tannin. Latest **NV** (74) bright red/black fruits, light enough for summer. Not tasted: **Chenin Blanc**.

Lady Somerset range

Merlot Rosé (NEW) ★★ Delicate strawberry aromas & tastes, **18** (72) dry & understated. **Crisp Dry White** ★★ **NV** (76) from chenin & sauvignon, tropical & indeed crisp for relaxed imbibing. **Sweet Rosé** ★★ Faintly berried & pineappley **NV** (72), gently sweet, refreshing when served well-chilled. 3 white grapes tinged by pinotage. **Sweet White** ★★ Not over-sweet **NV** (75) is light (10.9% alcohol) & grapey, fun to drink. From muscat & chenin. **Sweet Red** ⊘ ★★★ Obvious sweetness on latest plummy **NV** (77) balanced by good tannic grip. Not tasted: **Stylish Elegant Red**, **Sparkling Blush**. — CvZ

Location: Somerset West ▪ Map: Helderberg ▪ Map grid reference: E6 ▪ WO: Western Cape ▪ Est 2010 ▪ 1stB 2011 ▪ Tasting & sales Mon-Fri 9–5 Sat 9–1 ▪ Closed all pub hols ▪ Tour groups ▪ Wine shop ▪ Craft gin tasting event every 3 months - entry fees going to Rotary charity ▪ Owner(s) Boetie Rietoff ▪ Winemaker(s) Pieter-Niel Rossouw (Darling Cellars) & Jeff Wedgwood (consultant) ▪ 200,000cs 80% red 20% white ▪ PO Box 2240 Somerset West 7129 ▪ orders@swdirect.co.za ▪ www.swdirect.co.za ▪ S 34° 6' 12.27" E 018° 51' 25.83" ▪ 🗺 believer.starting.actors ▪ T +27 (0)21-851-0734/+27 (0)21-852-5473

Sonklip Wine

Producing just 200 cases annually, Stellenbosch engineer Frik Kirsten personifies the country's vibrant garagiste movement, crafting wine after hours using traditional techniques and equipment. His venture, named for a massive boulder on Botmaskop Peak, is now in its 2nd decade and still focused exclusively on reds.

★★★★ **Malbec** (NEW) One of Frik Kirsten's best, characterful **17** (86) markedly dry with savoury overtone to red & black plum fruit, better acid integration than Red Blend, good persistence. Could age few years. Bottelary grapes, as Special Red.

Red Blend ★★★☆ Returns as 5-way Bordeaux mix (previous had some Rhône varieties), mostly merlot & cab (61/22). **17** (84)'s concentrated & ripe black fruit shaped by sweet-sour acidity, dense tannins. **Special Red Blend** (②) ★★★★ Polished trio cab, malbec, petit verdot shows serious intent in **16** (85). Vibrant, involving, vanilla overlay to dark berries & slightly elevated acidity. Also in magnum. Coastal WO. — CvZ

Location/map: Stellenbosch ▪ Map grid reference: G5 ▪ WO: Stellenbosch/Coastal ▪ 1stB 2009 ▪ Tasting & cellar tours by appt ▪ Owner(s)/winemaker(s) Frik Kirsten ▪ 200cs own label 100% red ▪ PO Box 6198 Uniedal 7612 ▪ frik.kirsten@gmail.com ▪ S 33° 56' 3.55" E 018° 53' 44.95" ▪ ⌖ basin.dart.scooter ▪ **T +27 (0)83-284-3821**

☐ **Sonop** *see* Jacques Germanier

Sophie & Mr P

This range is from Iona – who take it very seriously, despite light-hearted labels on the screwcapped bottles. Mr P comes from pinot noir on an Elgin farm owned by Iona, while Sophie Te'blanche (a local nickname for sauvignon blanc) is partly from own grapes, but also draws more widely from the Cape South Coast.

Location: Elgin ▪ Est/1stB 2009 ▪ Closed to public ▪ Owner(s) Andrew Gunn ▪ Cellarmaster(s) Werner Muller (May 2011) ▪ (pinot, sauv) ▪ 150t/20,000cs own label 90% white 10% rosé ▪ PO Box 527 Grabouw 7160 ▪ orders@sophie.co.za ▪ www.sophie.co.za ▪ **T +27 (0)28-284-9678**

☐ **Southern Cape Vineyards** *see* Barrydale Winery & Distillery

Southern Right   (②) (◎) (&)

Twenty-five years have passed and co-owner Anthony Hamilton Russell still sees no need to expand the two-wine portfolio of this cool-climate wine brand. But that's not to say that there aren't other changes afoot, principally with the sauvignon, already consistently excellent, which they believe can offer even more quality and value. Following a trip to Sancerre for winemaker Emul Ross, experiments with different yeasts, ferment temperatures and a small amount of old oak appear to be paying dividends. 'It's all about adding complexity and palate depth - not fruit,' explains Anthony.

★★★★ **Pinotage** Forthright explosion of flavour on **18** (89), mixing black plums & cherries with cleverly managed charry oak (only 9% new). Excellent vanilla & spice finish, chewy tannins suggest a match made in heaven for meaty dishes.

★★★★ **Sauvignon Blanc** Lipsmacking flavours on previewed **19** (89) a cut above your average sauvignon. Beautifully focused green fruits & herbs balanced by candied lemons. Tiny amount of old oak (4%) & 5 months lees add richness & breadth.— CM

Location: Hermanus ▪ Map: Walker Bay & Bot River ▪ Map grid reference: A3 ▪ WO: Walker Bay ▪ Est 1994 ▪ 1stB 1995 ▪ Tasting & sales Mon-Fri 9-5 Sat 10-2 ▪ Cellar tours by appt ▪ Closed Easter Fri/Mon, Dec 25/26 & Jan 1 ▪ Fynbos reserve, renosterveld reserve & 3 wetlands ▪ Quad bike route ▪ Owner(s) Mark Willcox, Mikki Xayiya & Anthony Hamilton Russell ▪ Winemaker(s) Emul Ross (2014) ▪ Viticulturist(s) Johan Montgomery (2005) ▪ 447ha/±36ha (ptage, sauv) ▪ 225-280t/30-40,000cs own label 20% red 80% white ▪ PO Box 158 Hermanus 7200 ▪ info@southernright.co.za ▪ www.southernright.co.za ▪ S 34° 24' 3.2" E 019° 13' 0.4" ▪ ⌖ unduly.energetics.steamy ▪ **T +27 (0)28-312-3595**

Southern Sky Wines   (②)

From offices on Paarl's historic main street, negociant Andrew Milne markets various own-label wines, including Imagine, Marimba, Ready Steady and Tara Hill, none tasted this edition. He also provides a range of services, such as bulk-wine sourcing, and brand-development and -positioning consulting.

Location/map: Paarl ▪ Map grid reference: E6 ▪ Est/1stB 2002 ▪ Tasting & sales by appt ▪ Owner(s) Andrew Milne ▪ Winemaker(s) Andrew Milne (Jan 2003) ▪ 10,000cs own label 95% red 5% white ▪ 78 Main Str, Paarl 7646 ▪ andrew@ssw.co.za ▪ www.ssw.co.za ▪ S 33° 45' 8.78" E 018° 57' 42.55" ▪ ⌖ elaborate.client.boating ▪ **T +27 (0)21-863-4440**

South Hill Vineyards

Among the many attractions on this Elgin boutique farm owned by the King family are a restaurant, art gallery, accommodation, and conference and function venue. Absent till now has been a cellar, the past 14 vintages being vinified at other Elgin wineries. Emotions therefore must have run high when Sean Skibbe, winemaker since inception, received the first grapes last harvest in an on-site facility. A new attraction for visitors is one of very few vineyard mazes in SA, created from a portion of the cabernet block.

South Hill range

★★★★ **Cabernet Sauvignon** ⓥ Ripe, pure varietal character with a herbal twist on **16** ⑧⑥. Warming 15.1% alcohol, but saved from over-boldness by modest oaking. **15** untasted.

★★★★ **Pinot Noir** ⓥ Some enticement in **17** ★★★★☆ ⑧⑤'s earthy, undergrowth aromas but flavours diminished by very ripe fruit. Good acid lifts rich, somewhat sturdy structure. If cellaring, best monitor to catch at peak. Short on delicacy, balance of **15** ⑧⑦. No **16**.

★★★★ **Syrah** ⓥ Spicy, bright aromas on **16** ⑧⑦ lead to well-built, youthful palate. Only older oak maturation, leaving sweet fruit flavours clean & clear. Good dry finish.

★★★★ **Sauvignon Blanc** Ex tank, **19** ⑧⑦ similar attributes to previous; moderate intensity of tropical & herbaceous flavours, crisp & dry. Assertive acid should benefit from calming period post-bottling.

Rosé ⓥ ★★★★☆ Spicy, fresh & fruity-savoury character on pale pink-red **18** ⑧⑤ from undisclosed varieties. Bone-dry, for crisp, light elegance.

Kevin King range

★★★★ **BBK** Tangy & rich in flavour as good malbec can be. **16** ⑧⑧ expressive but also restrained, with zippy acid, bone-dry finish highlighting the sour cherry & loganberry succulence. Older oak.

★★★★ **Micah** ⓥ Unusual blend half shiraz with mourvèdre & barbera, **15** ⑧⑨ with ripe, fairly fruity & pure aromas & palate. Firmly structured, a serious but friendly wine. Last tasted was **13** ⑧⑨.

★★★★ **Bassey** ⓥ Sauvignon leads semillon in older-oaked **15** ⑧⑧ blend, but latter's wax & lemon dominant in youth, though lifted by grass & blackcurrant notes. Fresh, softly silky & well balanced.— AL

Location/map/WO: Elgin ▪ Map grid reference: C3 ▪ Est 2001 ▪ 1stB 2006 ▪ Tasting Mon-Sun 10-4 ▪ Cellar tours by appt ▪ The Gallery @ South Hill (original artworks) ▪ South Hill Restaurant open daily for breakfast & lunch ▪ The Guest House & Pumphouse Cottage ▪ Function venue for conferences & weddings ▪ Conservation area ▪ Owner(s) South Hill Vineyards (Pty) Ltd ▪ Winemaker(s) Sean Skibbe (Jun 2005) ▪ Viticulturist(s) Kevin Watt (Jun 2015, consultant) ▪ 57ha/28ha (cab, pinot, shiraz, chard, riesling, sauv, sem, viog) ▪ 130t/7,000cs own label 20% red 80% white ▪ PO Box 120 Elgin 7180 ▪ info@southhill.co.za ▪ www.southhill.co.za ▪ S 34° 14' 6.22" E 019° 6' 32.77" ▪ ⌨ bubbly.disbanding.unloading ▪ **T +27 (0)21-844-0888**

☐ **Spencer Bay** *see* Namaqua Wines

Spice Route Winery

Honouring the trading mariners of yore, and firmly rooted in Swartland, this Mediterranean-accented Charles Back-owned winery (sibling of Fairview) is based on Klein Amoskuil farm near Malmesbury, working with own grapes and selected neighbours'. It boasts the oldest sauvignon blanc in the Cape, and an array of Rhône and other varieties. Charles and long-term cellar chief Charl du Plessis' latest venture explores the ancient origins of winemaking, using Georgian terracotta qvevri to produce wholebunch, natural wines; look out for the new Obscura range. The Spice Route tasting room and visitor destination on Paarl Mountain, near Fairview, offers wide-ranging craft workshops, food and drinks, including a chocolatier, distillery, beer brewer, ceramic and glass studios, and lots more. Newly opened Jewell's Restaurant under star chefs Neil and Tina Jewell with Liam Tomlin has already garnered critical acclaim.

★★★★☆ **Grenache** ⓥ Strikingly pristine berry fruit, supple body on **16** ⑨③ make for pure drinking pleasure. Poised & lithe, charmingly approachable, showcasing Swartland's affinity with Mediterranean varieties. 15 months older French oak.

★★★★ **Terra de Bron Swartland Grenache** ⓥ Concentrated berry fruit dominates **16** ★★★★☆ ⑨⓪ from single block of dryland bushvines on home farm, with fine tannin structure, supple body, sweetly ripe lingering finish. Subtle spice & oak notes from 16 months in barrel. Improves on **15** ⑧⑧.

★★★★ **Mourvèdre** Real Rhône character in **16** ⑧⑨ from unirrigated/untrellised vines: scrub, earthy savouriness & hints of white pepper. Appealing morello cherry fruit profile.

★★★★ **Pinotage** ⓥ Impressively rounded & balanced, with sweet cherry fruit, **17** ⑧⑧ from single home-farm bushvine vineyard is juicy, generous, yet restrained. Vanilla notes from year American oak.

★★★★☆ **Malabar** ⓥ Brilliant syrah-driven blend with mourvèdre, petite sirah & carignan has depth, detail & elegance in **15** ⑨③. Supple & succulent, exemplifying its conducive terroir, unfurling layers of spice, cherry fruit, herbal scrub & tobacco.

★★★★☆ **Chakalaka** Characterful, creative, mourvèdre-based 6-way blend from mostly dry-farmed bushvines. Rhône-accented **16** ⑨② offers dense, spicy multifaceted fruit, broad shoulders & velvet texture. Named after feisty local spice blend. Shaded (just) by stand-out **15** ⑨④.

★★★★☆ **Chenin Blanc** ⓥ Enticing melon & peach on restrained **17** ⑨②, with fruit to the fore, subtle minerality balancing & broadening the palate. Poised & measured, master-handled to express Swartland terroir. Portion fermented & 9 months in older barrels.

★★★★ **Sauvignon Blanc** WO Darling **18** ⑧⑨ hits all the right West Coast notes: dusty pebbles, grassy gooseberry fruit, bracing acidity. Mineral salty twist & lees texture add to drinking pleasure.

★★★★ **The Amos Block Sauvignon Blanc** ⊘ ⊛ 1965 vineyard, oldest sauvignon in SA, yields exciting, crisp & textural wines from its minute 0.94 t/ha yield. **19** ★★★★☆ ⑨⓪ no exception, shows aromatic nettle, gooseberry & green fig, finely focused finish. Outdoes excellent **17** ⑧⑧. No **18**.

★★★★ **Viognier** ⓥ Luscious yellow peach introduction to **17** ⑧⑨, with sweet perfumed highlights & tingling acidity to balance the generously full, leesy body. Fermented & 10 months in old French barrels.

★★★★☆ **The Amos Block Perpetual Reserve Under Flor** ⊛ Amazing depth & complexity in fino-styled **NV** ⑨①. New blend of '14–'16 sauvignon from SA's oldest block improves on previous. Nutty, rich & layered, the perfect aperitif. Picked under-ripe, natural yeast fermented, fortified to 15% alcohol & flor inoculated. Bottled 'en rama' (unfiltered). 500 ml.

Not tasted: **Saffron Rosé**. Discontinued: **Terra de Bron Swartland Carignan**, **Terra de Bron Swartland Mourvèdre**, **Terra de Bron Darling Syrah**, **Terra de Bron Swartland Syrah**, **Terra de Bron Darling Semillon**. — GdB, CR

Location: Malmesbury/Paarl ▪ Map: Paarl ▪ Map grid reference: D6 ▪ WO: Swartland/Darling ▪ Tasting & sales Mon-Sun 9-5, last tasting 30min before closing ▪ Standard/master tasting (applicable fees apply) ▪ Closed Dec 25 & Jan 1 ▪ Jewell's Restaurant ▪ Red Hot Glass Studio ▪ DV Artisan Chocolate Roastery & Espresso Bar ▪ Barley & Biltong Emporium ▪ Brenda's Deli ▪ Richard Bosman's ▪ The Trading Company ▪ The Barn Artist Studio ▪ Wilderer's Distillery & La Grapperia Restaurant ▪ Cape Brewing Company ▪ Owner(s) Charles Back ▪ Winemaker(s) Charl du Plessis (Dec 2001), with Licia Solomons (Jan 2006) ▪ 90ha (barbera, carignan, grenache, mourv, petite sirah, sangio, shiraz, tannat, chenin, rouss, sauv, sem, viog) ▪ 60% red 40% white ▪ Fairtrade, HACCP, IPW, WIETA ▪ PO Box 583 Suider-Paarl 7624 ▪ info@spiceroute.co.za ▪ www.spiceroutewines.co.za ▪ S 33° 45' 50.5" E 018° 55' 9.7" ▪ 🗺 jarring.chills.pavers ▪ **T +27 (0)21-863-5200**

Spider Pig Wines ⓃⒺⓌ

Two Davids - Nel and Wibberley – in the hospitality and wine business have joined forces to create this 'concept brand', with eye-catching, creative and fun packaging; and marketing that will, they hope, 'take away the intimidation factor of wine-drinking'. The brand name recalls Homer Simpson's parody of the Spiderman theme song, which makes for a good start, while working with various established winemakers in the Cape to produce the wines takes the strategy much further.

★★★★ **The Black Pig** Characterful & dry **18** ⑧⑥, bright strawberry fruit from 43 year old Stellenbosch bushvine cinsaut & 50% wholebunch ferment, hint cedar & firm tannins from 25% cab. Seriously conceived - we'd keep this little piggy at home a few years.

Cinsational Cinsault ★★★☆ Perhaps not quite stunning but **18** ⑧④ is very good & satisfying, not just 'pretty' as variety can be. Light hued yet fruit-filled, with crisp acidity, pleasing stemminess (30% stalks added back), good dry persistence. Swartland & Simonsberg-Paarl fruit. **Grenache Noir** ★★★☆ Just 10% new oak for translucent, slightly leathery **18** ⑧③, with decent tannic grip, lowish 13% alcohol for solo sipping or food. **Roam Piggy Roam** ★★★ With a label-design award, **15** ⑧② shiraz & grenache (67/33) is perfumed & sweet-fruited, attractively dry though unlingering. **Bro/Zay Rosé** ★★★ Festive & fun **18** ⑧① from colombard (60%) &

cinsaut, tangy if brief, touch sugar well-hidden. **Chenin Blanc ★★★★** Understated on nose (some peach & pear brushed with oak spice), **18** (83) has plenty of presence on palate, gentle cream (possibly from 11 months on lees) & smoothing smidgen sugar, moderate 13.5% alcohol. — TJ, CvZ

Location: Cape Town ▪ WO: Western Cape/Coastal ▪ Est/1stB 2015 ▪ Closed to public ▪ Owner(s) David Nel & David Wibberley ▪ Winemaker(s) various ▪ 3,000cs own label 60% red 20% white 20% rosé ▪ david@ spiderpigwines.com ▪ www.spiderpigwines.com ▪ **T +27 (0)72-117-2147 / +27 (0)83-235-5748**

Spier

There is a discernible ethical underpin to everything that happens at this extensive, internationally known and recognised estate outside Stellenbosch, owned by the Enthoven family since 1993. Historic, with 17th-century buildings and ancient oaks, it's a tourist magnet with multiple hospitality attractions. Also a strong eco and social focus, with sourcing from local producers, and empowerment for employees to supply produce ('Growing for Good' icon on labels), among many examples. There are 11 ranges, produced from own and brought-in grapes, an impressive 650 ha's worth, with dedicated winemakers for the reds, whites and organic wines, and cellarmaster (and Cape Winemakers Guild member) Frans Smit's sure hand at the helm. New line-up this edition is Seaward, named for the proximity of the source vineyards to the ocean. Tying in with the ethical theme is the news that Spier is the world's first winery to receive Control Union's Vegan Standard certification, for the Seaward, Creative Block, 21 Gables and Frans K Smit lines.

Frans K. Smit range

★★★★★ Frans K. Smit White (🍇) Bordeaux blend with sauvignon, 20% semillon, French barrel fermented/aged 11 months, 80% new. Hard to pin **17** (94) down, so much going on, green fig & tobacco, slate, oystershell & good palate weight, brightened by limy acidity. The longer in the glass, the more it reveals.

Not tasted: **Frans K. Smit Red**.

21 Gables range

★★★★☆ Cabernet Sauvignon (🍇) Built to last, but like these reds, there's earlier access. **16** (93) spent 24 months in French barrels, 75% new, for vanilla & sweet spice seasoning to the intense blackcurrant. Palate contrasts with lead pencil savouriness, ending dry, with sleek muscle tone. Stellenbosch WO, as next.

★★★★☆ Pinotage (🍇) Bold & handsome, dense & ripe, plums & prunes, vanilla & other spices, liquorice, mocha chocolate, all found in hedonistic **17** (91). Oaked 18 months, 85% new, mixed barrels; built for the long haul but fruit gives earlier pleasure. Also in 1.5L, like Cab.

★★★★★ Chenin Blanc (🍇) Green-gold; barrel fermented/aged, 40% new, 10% unoaked portion. **18** (95) offers tropical fruit & citrus, subtle Lemon Cream biscuit savouriness. Not overt, just interwoven complexity, silky texture. Pure class from stringently sorted Durbanville grapes. Also in 1.5L.

★★★★☆ Sauvignon Blanc (🍇) From single Durbanville block, 3 months lees contact, **19** (93)'s fruit profile is passionfruit & lime, taken to another level by steely minerality. Vibrantly fresh & focused, there's admirable purity & precision here.

Creative Block range

★★★★☆ Five (🌿) (🍇) Classic Bordeaux blend, cab with 4 others, **16** (94) has lots to offer. Cassis & plums, lead pencils, fynbos tinge, well oak-spiced. Expectation would be for long ageing but there's enough flesh & succulence for current enjoyment. These reds also in magnum.

★★★★ Eight Cape Blend, pinotage & 7 others, notably cab, merlot & shiraz. Black plums & salty liquorice in **17** (89), lovely cedar notes from French & American barrels, 45% new. Supple tannins, but can age.

★★★★☆ Three (🌿) Rhône blend, shiraz with dashes mourvèdre, viognier, **16** (90) is generously proportioned, ample plush dark fruit, nicely curvaceous. Plenty seasoning from 18 months oaking, 85% new: smoky spice, black pepper, charcuterie. Firm, ripe tannins say this is no pushover.

★★★★ Two White Bordeaux blend, sauvignon with 10% semillon, stainless steel tank & older barrel ferment, previewed **19** (87) has classic styling, gooseberries & flint, crisp limy acidity adding lift & vibrancy.

Farm House Organic range

★★★★ Red (NEW) (🌿) Merlot & cab, wild yeast ferment, older barrels 24 months, **17** (88)'s results impressive. Vivid cassis, cigarbox seasoning, fynbos whiffs. Tannins chewy but promise well, intrinsics in place.

★★★★☆ **Rosé** ⊘ Two pickings, early acidity, later ripeness, **17** ㉜'s shiraz a serious rosé: wild ferment, combo 2nd fill barrels, ceramic 'eggs'. Tealeaf tone to the red berry compote, brioche-savoury & dry, some minerality. Wonderfully complex & different, for grown-ups. Stellenbosch WO for these.

★★★★★ **Chenin Blanc** ⊘ 🐝 Wild ferment on skins in barrel in the dedicated organic cellar; tiny yield of 0.1 t/ha, just 53 cases. Touch of wild honey in **17** ★★★★★ ㉝'s stonefruit & pineapple scents, almond overlay from 16 months oak, palate weight a major attraction. Follows standout **16** ㉝.

Occasional release: **Straw Wine**.

Organic range

★★★★☆ **First Stone** ⊘ Merlot/cab 68:32, similar to Farmhouse but here 85% new oak, **16** ㉜ preview's cassis in full play with spice, lead pencils & tobacco leaf, a violet top note. Tannins still firm but ripe, time will reveal its full potential. Serious, muscular, imposing. Stellenbosch WO.

....

Yellow Wood White 🆕 ▼ ⊘ ★★★★ Chenin & viognier combo, small portion oaked, **19** ㉘ an aromatic delight, floral & peach, with almost muscaty flavours, but ends dry, fruity-fresh. To charm your friends or pair with exotic dishes.

Yellow Wood Red ⊘ ★★★★ Merlot with 18% cab, **17** ㉘'s oak component (16 months French) dominant, dusty spice & mocha chocolate, fruit subservient at this youthful stage. Will integrate over time; well crafted otherwise. **Yellow Wood Rosé** ⊘ ★★★★ From shiraz, cranberry-scented & -flavoured **19** ㉘ had no oak, unlike last, this is purely about the fruit. Dry & elegant, good enough to drink solo, without food.

Ideology range

★★★★ **Chenin Blanc** ⊘ Single Darling vineyard, as next; common thread is the intensity, tight focus: winter melon & citrus, especially lime, **19** ㉘ has signature freshness, is ageable. Portion oaked. No **17**, **18**.

★★★★ **Sauvignon Blanc** Passionfruit & lime, mouthwateringly fresh & fruit-filled, lovely sweet/sour quality has you reaching for more. Sleek, taut & intense, **19** ㉙ so tightly structured it could age. No **18**. **17** ★★★★★ ㉝ ex Helderberg was exceptional.

Occasional release: **Wild Ferment Pinotage**, **Rhône Blend**, **Chardonnay-Pinot Noir**, **Merlot Rosé**.

Signature range

....

Chenin Blanc ▼ ★★★ Apple-rich summer fruit salad, satisfyingly fresh, **19** ㉒ has 'drink me' written all over it. Proves why this chenin remains so popular.

....

Cabernet Sauvignon ★★★ Variety-true **18** ㉒ offers plummy fruit, an earthy/scrub nuance from the light oaking (includes 15% American), tannins firm but approachable. **Merlot** ★★★ Plums & mocha chocolate, **18** ㉛ is very easy to like, which is the intention with this lightly oaked, spicy, smooth-textured wine. Stellenbosch WO, rest W Cape. **Pinotage** ★★★ For early drinking, no hardship, **18** ㉒ fruit is dense & smooth, the light oaking for spice, a gentle grip. **Shiraz** ★★★ Designed for earlier drinking, **18** ㉒ still delivers the expected attributes, smoky dark fruit, medium body, taste appeal. **Cabernet Sauvignon-Merlot-Shiraz** ★★★ Successful combination in **18** ㉒, providing plums & glossy berries, savoury notes for food matching, sleek & juicy palate. **Chardonnay-Pinot Noir** ★★★ Pale salmon hue from pinot noir's 30% contribution, **19** ㉒ dry rosé gets the varietal balance right, red berries on the nose, zesty freshness in the flavours. **Chardonnay** ⊘ ★★★★ Small portion barrel fermented, but oak influence is subtle, **19** ㉓ proudly displays its citrus fruit, lemon & tangerine, brightened by acidity, adding length & drinking appeal. **Sauvignon Blanc** ⊘ ★★★☆ Gooseberry & passionfruit scents & flavours, **19** ㉟ made to enjoy, its tangy acidity lengthens the experience, adds vibrancy.

Seaward range 🆕

....

Chardonnay ▼ ★★★★ Oaking 40%, **18** ㉟ spent 4 more months on lees; citrus, lemon & grapefruit, toned with a crushed almond seam. There's palate weight, some curves, & a gentle savouriness at the end. Cape Town WO.

....

Cabernet Sauvignon ★★★☆ Nice fruit/spice partnership, **17** ㉘'s 12 months in barrel (15% American) a smoky, savoury interleave to the plums. Later earthy, lead pencil notes part of the character. **Pinotage** ★★★★ Lovely typicity, blueberries, brambleberries, herbaceous hint another layer; **17** ㉟'s barrel time a savoury, almost meaty effect. Lots going on, all good, which includes the lithe body, ripe but firm tannins. **Shiraz** ★★★★ Black plums, prune richness in **17** (84), well spiced by 14 months in barrel (French/American), a black pepper note. Well-managed tannins, an ageing backbone & dry finish but enjoyable with the right food. **Sauvignon Blanc** ★★★★ Single parcel in Darling, portion barrel-fermented. **19** (85) passionfruit & citrus, good palate breadth, long lime-fresh finish. Loads of flavour, a sauvignon to enjoy more than admire.

Méthode Cap Classique range

★★★★ **Brut** ✓ Classic chardonnay & pinot noir bubbly, 10% barrel ferment (as next), 23 months on lees. Vibrant freshness **17** (86)'s major asset, lemon & lime, brioche seasoning. **16** untasted.

★★★★☆ **Brut RD** (NEW) Special sparkler, handsome packaging, on lees 102 months, disgorged in 2018. Just 1,300 bottles. Same blend & Stellenbosch WO as sibling, **09** (93) has power & richness, toasted brioche & marmalade, wild honey, brightening acidity for length & vitality.

Collaborative Series

Occasional release: **These Waves Merlot**, **Blind Astronomer Pinotage**, **Blind Astronomer Chenin Blanc**, **These Waves Viognier**, **Noble Late Harvest**.

Vintage Selection range

Occasional release: **Weisser Riesling**. — CR

Location/map: Stellenbosch ▪ Map grid reference: C7 ▪ WO: Coastal/Stellenbosch/Western Cape/Cape Town/ Darling ▪ Est 1692 ▪ 1stB 1770 ▪ Tasting & sales Mon-Sun 9-5 (seasonal times apply) ▪ Tasting from R40 ▪ Facilities for children ▪ Tour groups ▪ Farm produce ▪ Picnics ▪ Conferences ▪ Manor House & Heritage Walk ▪ Spier Artisan Studio Stellenbosch ▪ Conservation area ▪ 4-star Spier Hotel ▪ Spier Farm Café & Spier Hotel Restaurant ▪ Vadas Smokehouse & Bakery ▪ Owner(s) Enthoven family ▪ Cellarmaster(s) Frans Smit (Dec 1995) ▪ Winemaker(s) Johan Jordaan (reds, Jul 2007), Jacques Erasmus (whites, Apr 2007) & Tania Kleintjes (organic wine, Jan 2016) ▪ Wine procurement/winemaker(s) Johan de Villiers, Anton Swarts (CWM) & Lizanne Jordaan ▪ Viticulturist(s) Bennie Liebenberg (Jun 2019) ▪ 650ha (barbera, cabs s/f, malbec, merlot, mourv, p verdot, ptage, shiraz, chard, chenin, sauv, sem, viog) ▪ 3,850t own label 65% red 31% white 3% rosé 1% MCC ▪ Fairtrade, FSSC 22000, IPW, Organic, WIETA, WWF-SA Conservation Champion ▪ PO Box 99 Lynedoch 7603 ▪ info@spier.co.za ▪ www.spier.co.za ▪ S 33° 58' 24.63" E 018° 47' 2.23" ▪ 🌐 induce.breathe. mufflers ▪ T +27 (0)21-809-1100 (wine tasting)

Spioenkop Wines ⓠ

There's been a shake-up in the ranges from Koen Roose. The trimmed Spioenkop estate range continues its tradition of fine, fresh and characterful wines off unirrigated vines - the latter a rare choice in Elgin, but part of Koen's uncompromising determination to make 'pure, tight and elegant terroir wines from our unique Spioenkop hill'. The focus here is now on pinotage, chenin and riesling. The 1900 line (still with a Stellenbosch contribution) correspondingly expands, and there's a new range named, in accord with the Anglo-Boer War theme, for the Tugela River in KwaZulu-Natal, where the original Spioenkop rises. More easily affordable, these, but the philosophy of natural fermentation and no additives still applies.

1900 range

★★★★ **Pinot Noir** (NEW) ✓ From 2 vineyards; 30% wholebunch. **16** (87) cherry & berry character but more savoury than simply fruity. Bright, refined & well balanced; firm structure but gentler than Tugela.

★★★★☆ **Pinotage** ✓ ⚥ Always one of SA's freshest, purest. Black & red berry notes on **18** (93) - more luxuriously fruity than other version. Well balanced, the firm tannins & succulent acid held in check by depth of flavour; fairly modest 13.3% alcohol; 55% new oak unobtrusively supportive. WO Stellenbosch.

★★★★ **Sauvignon Blanc** Some developed green bean hints on **16** (86). Attractive, quite light fruit; silky texture; fresh, with a gripping mineral acidity that will serve food well over the next few years. No **15**.

Spioenkop range

★★★★☆ **Pinotage** ✓ ⚥ The expected bright elegance on **18** (91), darkly aromatic. More edgy & nervy than 1900 version, a touch austere on the palate despite the good fruit: the tannins forthright, the freshness a little tart in youth - best to keep this a good few years to allow it to bloom.

★★★★☆ **Johanna Brandt** (⚥) Of the pair of estate chenins, this off shale. **17** (94) offers generous fruit aromas with floral & citric notes; broader than Sarah (11 months on lees in older barrels), but with penetrating 'mineral' acidity, intense & focused flavours, firm & effectively dry finish.

★★★★☆ **Sarah Raal** ⊘ ⓐ Chenin off ferricrete soil. **18** ⑨③ pure, complex aromas & flavours, with a subtle earthy nuttiness. Crisp & refined, unshowy but intense, with fine vein of citric acidity. Lightly oaked & on lees for added breadth. Drier & less rich than notably impressive **17** ★★★★★ ⑨⑤.

★★★★★ **Riesling** ⓟ Thrilling peach complexity on **17** ⑨①, with an early aromatic note of kerosene. Bone-dry, with good balance & texture, the fresh acidity integrated with concentrated fruit to lively, moreish effect. Should develop a good few years. Natural ferment.

Discontinued: **Pinot Noir**, **Sauvignon Blanc**.

Tugela River range ⓃⒺⓌ

★★★★ **Ghandi** Forward dark aromas & flavours on **16** ⑧⑥ pinot noir, but mostly earthy-savoury in effect. Fresh, with a certain dry tannic elegance, but not much real depth of fruit or pinot charm.

★★★★ **Red Blend** From merlot, cab franc & syrah, sourced around Elgin. **16** ⑧⑥ fruitcake & spicy cigarbox notes. House restraint & slightly austere acidity designed for food, with balanced dry tannins.

★★★★ **Chardonnay** More tropical & stonefruit than citrus on attractive **17** ⑧⑦, but a limy freshness emerges to control the ripe, slightly sweet richness & creamy texture. 20% new oak well integrated.— TJ

Location/map: Elgin ▪ Map grid reference: C4 ▪ WO: Elgin/Stellenbosch ▪ Est 2008 ▪ 1stB 2010 ▪ Tasting & sales by appt only ▪ Tasting fee R100pp; waived on purchase ▪ Pre-booking required for: tasting & cellar tour R100pp; speciality tasting, exclusive vineyard walk with winemaker R150pp ▪ Closed all pub hols ▪ Owner(s) Valuline 119 (Pty) Ltd, 5 shareholders ▪ Cellarmaster(s)/winemaker(s)/viticulturist(s) Koen Roose-Vandenbroucke (2008) ▪ ±47ha/12ha (ptage, pinot, chenin, riesling, sauv) ▪ 60t/8,000cs own label 63% red 37% white ▪ PO Box 340 Grabouw 7160 ▪ info@spioenkopwines.co.za ▪ www.spioenkopwines.co.za ▪ S 34° 14' 14" E 019° 3' 50" ▪ ✉ bidders.costume.achiever ▪ **T +27 (0)72-440-2944**

Splattered Toad ⓠ

The point is, really, that the Western Leopard Toad, a legally protected but severely threatened species endemic to Cape Town, should avoid being splattered as they hop across the busy roads. Look out for them! This easy-drinking range drawing attention to the problem comes from Cape Point Vineyards. See under sibling winery Cape Town Wine Co for tasting details.

Shiraz ★★★ Bright, flavourful **18** ⑧② is easygoing but not dumbed down; fruity & rather succulently lipsmacking. WO W Cape, as next. **Sauvignon Blanc** ⊘ ★★★★ Exuberant tropical aromas & flavours - especially passionfruit - on **19** ⑧③. Zippy & zingy, without much in the way of depth, but pleasing. 15% plumping chenin. — TJ

☐ **Splendidior 150** *see* Welgevallen Wines - Splendidior 150

Spookfontein Wines ⓠ ⑪ ⓐ ⓞ

Businessman Mike Davis purchased this ca 1840 farm and 'fynbos heaven' in Upper Hemel-en-Aarde Valley as a weekend retreat for his family. Two decades later, it boasts an architect-designed cellar, restaurant, two self-catering guest cottages and range of wines made by neighbour Hannes Storm (Storm Wines). The namesake ghost, said to haunt the spring, has given way to happy diners and imbibers.

★★★★ **Cabernet Sauvignon** ⓐ Black cherry & mulberry fruit in **16** ⑧⑥ lifted by fynbos notes, smooth, with soft tannins & subtle wood spice after year in French oak (20% new). More herbs, less chocolate than **15** ★★★★ ⑧⑤.

★★★★ **Cabernet Franc** ⓐ Midweight **17** ⑧⑧ less tight than **16** ★★★★ ⑧③ after 18 months in French oak, 20% new, more intensely flavoured, fresh raspberry & redcurrant fruit, some ripe capsicum, too.

★★★★ **Pinot Noir** ⊘ ⓐ Silky **17** ⑧⑦ has none of the stalkiness of **16** ★★★★ ⑧③, floral perfume & earthiness adding complexity to delicate cranberry & strawberry fruit. 11 months French oak, 20% new.

★★★★ **Syrah** Even more spicy than **16** ⑧⑦, with clove & a pinch of cayenne pepper, **17** ★★★★★ ⑨⓪ lightly oaked (13 months in older barrels) to showcase plush dark cassis & cherry fruit.

★★★★ **Phantom** Whole greater than sum of parts (merlot, cab, cab franc) in elegant **17** ⑧⑨, seamless after 18 months in French oak, 25% new, to frame succulent dark fruit with cedar spice.

★★★★☆ **Chardonnay** Light oaking (8 months, 25% new) apparent in creamy texture of **18** ⑨⓪, in youth still dominated by bright citrus & white peach flavours, with very lively acidity, fruit purity & mineral undertones promising further elegant development.

★★★★ **Sauvignon Blanc** ⓥ Definite seaside salinity to **18** ⑧⑥ pre-bottling, crisply dry yet shapely from 3 months on lees, fruit quite restrained but should open up.

★★★★ **Full Moon** ⓥ Unwooded equal sauvignon & semillon ex Hemel-en-Aarde Ridge nudges higher rating. **18** ⑧⑨ fruity yet flinty, mouthwatering natural acidity promising long future.

Merlot ★★★☆ More herbaceous than last, **16** ⑧④ aged year in mostly older oak, tobacco & tealeaf as well as bright red-cherry fruit. **Merlot Rosé** ⓥ ★★ Tentatively rated **18** ⑦⑥ early preview promises red berry & glacé cherry fruit, dry finish. Not tasted: **Méthode Cap Classique**, **Noble Late Harvest**. — JG

Location: Hermanus ▪ Map: Walker Bay & Bot River ▪ Map grid reference: B4 ▪ WO: Upper Hemel-en-Aarde Valley/Hemel-en-Aarde Ridge ▪ Est 2000 ▪ 1stB 2004 ▪ Tasting & sales Mon-Sat 10-4.30 Sun/pub hols 10-4 ▪ Closed Dec 25/26 & Jan 1 ▪ Restaurant @ Spookfontein open for lunch ▪ Functions T +27 (0)73-067-7936 Vaughan ▪ Two self-catering guest cottages ▪ Conservation area ▪ Owner(s) Spookfontein Wines cc (Mike Davis) ▪ Winemaker(s) Hannes Storm (2014) ▪ Viticulturist(s) Andries Gotze (Jan 2000) ▪ 313ha/±12ha (cabs s/f, merlot, pinot, chard) ▪ 50t/2,000cs own label 85% red 5% white 10% rosé ▪ PO Box 12031 Mill Str, Cape Town 8010 ▪ admin@spookfontein.co.za ▪ www.spookfontein.co.za ▪ S 34° 21' 19.5" E 019° 17' 20.8" ▪ ⌨ quarterfinals.pieced.avenging ▪ **T +27 (0)28-125-0128**

Spotswood Wines ⓠ

The Spotswood family moved from Polokwane in the north to boutique farm Down The Road in Stellenbosch's Blaauwklippen Valley in 2007. Bill and son Nick, both engineers, took a (calculated) risk in planting locally rare French variety durif, but it has been a hit for them, latterly and innovatively also as a dry rosé. Vintage 2020, their 12th, will be vinified by a new winemaker – 'watch this space!'

Durif Dry Rosé ⓥ ⓣ ★★★☆ Dry & refreshingly savoury pink from unusual variety (aka petite sirah). Piquant cranberry flavours, crisp, feisty step up in **19** ⑧④ on previous.

Not tasted: **Durif, Shiraz, Chardonnay, Viognier**. — MW

Location/map/WO: Stellenbosch ▪ Map grid reference: F7 ▪ Est 2007 ▪ 1stB 2008 ▪ Tasting & sales by appt ▪ Owner(s) Spotswood family ▪ Winemaker(s) Guy Webber (Jan 2012, consultant) & Gunter Schultz (consultant) ▪ Viticulturist(s) Bill Spotswood (Sep 2007) ▪ 7.05ha/3ha (durif, shiraz, chard, viog) ▪ 28t/3,000cs own label 56% red 19% white 25% rosé ▪ Suite 200 Private Bag X4 Die Boord 7613 ▪ spotswoodwines@gmail.com ▪ www. spotswoodwines.com ▪ S 33° 59' 2.0" E 018° 51' 35.0" ▪ ⌨ carry.enlarge.bashed ▪ **T +27 (0)21-880-2893**

Springfield Estate ⓠ ⌂

Renewal is a constant at this highly successful, much-admired and dynamic family estate in Robertson, where present custodians, brother and sister Abrie and Jeanette Bruwer, believe in investing and building for future generations of Bruwers and their dedicated staff. In addition to replanting vineyards in 2019, they also invested in four automatic frost fans, installed a larger and faster bottling line, nearly doubled the capacity of their reservoir, revamped the tasting room deck, and added cellar tours to the list of attractions. And, kicking back a little, celebrated the debut of their Albariño ('18), which sold out in just five days.

★★★★☆ **Méthode Ancienne Cabernet Sauvignon** Naturally fermented **13** ★★★★ ⑧⑨ a balanced glassful with mellow tannins & alcohol (13.2%), aromas of cassis & cedar spice from new oak, 2 years, with bottle-age notes of forest floor & leather. **09** ⑨③ similarly elegant. No **10** & **12**, **11** untasted.

★★★★ **Whole Berry Cabernet Sauvignon** Lighter styled & thus on-trend, nevertheless has fine fruit intensity in **17** ⑧⑦ together with hallmark leafy tobacco overlay, refreshing seam of acidity, judicious oaking, 40% new for 12 months.

★★★★☆ **The Work of Time** ⓥ Cab franc takes the lead in quietly impressive 4-way Bordeaux blend from old vines. **13** ⑨⓪ polished, poised & persistent, with characteristic fine-grained tannins. As ever, unhurriedly made: 3-week natural ferment, 2 years in oak, 4 in bottle. **12** untasted.

★★★★ **Méthode Ancienne Chardonnay** Opulent styling continues with **17** ⑧⑥ being 100% barrel fermented (using ambient yeasts) & undergoing full malo, giving hallmark blue orange bouquet, tangerine palate, soft acidity. Less new oak this time (just 10% vs 30%), so vanilla & toast notes are dialled down.

★★★★☆ **Wild Yeast Chardonnay** ⊘ Unwooded, with body & silky texture from 60-day natural fer-ment in tank. As expected, **18** ⑨⓪ tauter than sibling, less ripe, with signature purity & subtle minerality, lime & lemon adding vigour & zesty flavour.

★★★★ **Life From Stone Sauvignon Blanc** ⊘ Among SA's best-known & most-loved sauvignons, ex fully mature vines that keep delivering (& thus quashing occasional thoughts of replanting). **19** ★★★★☆ ⑨⓪ inherits **18** ⑧⑨'s flint, feisty acid, bone-dryness; pronounced mineral seam this vintage raises the bar.

★★★★ **Special Cuvée Sauvignon Blanc** Night harvested to preserve freshness & flavour, **19** ⑧⑨ as thrilling as previous with similar assertive pea shoot tone & acidity. More aromatic & flavoursome than sibling, restrained 12.5% alcohol on both.

....

Albariño ⓥ ★★★★☆ New to the guide, with characterful label evoking Spanish heritage of variety, one of only three in these pages. **19** ⑧⑤ has expected sauvignon-like green aromas & flavours, also appealing white peach nuance & good vinosity.

....

Pinot Noir ★★★★ Vibrant **16** ⑧③ from high-density vineyard has immediate cherry & raspberry appeal, sufficient fruit to soak up 80% new oak. **Miss Lucy** ★★★★ Blend change sees pinot gris (40%) in majority, with sauvignon & semillon helping conserve the threatened Red Stumpnose fish, alias Miss Lucy. **19** ⑧③ house's most approachable white even with signature untamed acidity. — CvZ

Location/map/WO: Robertson ▪ Map grid reference: B5 ▪ Est/1stB 1995 ▪ Tasting & sales Mon-Fri 8-5 Sat 9-3 ▪ Closed Easter Fri/Sun, Dec 25 & Jan 1 ▪ Cellar tours Mon-Fri 10 & 3 by appt ▪ BYO picnic ▪ Owner(s) Bruwer family ▪ Cellarmaster(s)/viticulturist(s) Abrie Bruwer ▪ Winemaker(s) Abrie Bruwer, with Johan van Zyl ▪ 150ha (cabs s/f, merlot, p verdot, albariño, chard, pinot gris, sauv, sem) ▪ IPW ▪ PO Box 770 Robertson 6705 ▪ wine@springfieldestate.com ▪ www.springfieldestate.com ▪ S 33° 50' 12.1" E 019° 54' 54.0" ▪ ⊞ cross. layover.pancake ▪ **T +27 (0)23-626-3661**

Springfontein Wine Estate ⊙ ⑪ ⌂ ⌾

Among the vanguard of viticultural developers around the Walker Bay hamlet of Stanford since the 1990s, German former mining engineer Johst Weber, partners, family and friends celebrated a watershed 2019 vintage. It was the first bottled as Wine of Origin Springfontein Rim, newly demarcated for its limestone soils, unique in the area (remarkable agglomerations of ancient seashells are everywhere in the vineyards). After years of working naturally, Springfontein is now certified organic for both vineyards (under Hildegard Witbooi's care) and cellar (husband Tariro Masayiti's domain). Uniquely for an extensive range, their 'proudly SA' wines all have some pinotage and/or chenin. The Ulumbaza ('House of Joy') label-moniker is now also attached to their convivial tasting venue, Ulumbaza Wine Bar(n) @ Springfontein. See also Cape Moby.

Limestone Rocks range

★★★★ **Gadda da Vida** Open-barrel-fermented pinotage with 14% petit verdot, **16** ⑧⑧ shows sweetly ripe plum fruit, muscular structure. **15** ⑧⑥, also tasted, has more mocha-tinged wild berry fruit. Both a step up from **14** ★★★★☆ ⑧⑤.

★★★★ **Child in Time** Big & brawny, dark & sombre. **16** ⑧⑧ 86% petit verdot tempered with pinotage, offering leathery tannins, meaty plum-pudding fruit, inky black hue. Spice from French & American oak.

★★★★☆ **Whole Lotta Love** Pinotage-led (55%) Cape Blend really rocks in **16** ⑨② , with bold black fruit profile, supple tannins, sleek texture. Wholebunch barrel fermented, 18 months in mixed all-new oak, some American. Poised now, but meant for cellaring. Equal petit verdot, shiraz.

★★★★☆ **Dark Side of The Moon** Unlikely but successful blend of skin-contact chenin & chardonnay with pinotage vinified as white, all wild-yeast fermented. **17** ⑨① is fresher, brighter than **16** ⑨⓪, retaining charming marmalade notes, plumply rounded body. 18 months in oak don't intrude.

Single Vineyard range

★★★★☆ **Jonathan's Ridge Pinotage** Sumptuously ripe berry fruit dominates **16** ⑨⓪ from registered single-vineyard (as next), high-toned aromatic notes, firm but velvety tannins in support. Better balanced than **15** ★★★★ ⑧⑧, with bulk & power reined in.

★★★★☆ **Jil's Dune Chenin Blanc** Much-improved **17** ⑨⓪ shows restraint in oaking, with mellow stonefruit & subtle brioche to the fore. Natural yeast, gentle handling are reflected in richness & texture, body & finish. A big step up on wood-driven **16** ★★★☆ ⑧④.

Daredevils' Drums range

★★★★ **Blushes Inverse** Unusual straw-hued blanc from pinotage, barrel-fermented **18** ⑧⑥ has subtle oak spice with canned peach fruit profile. Full bodied but smooth & steely-fresh, showing no varietal provenance. Like Terroir Chenin & Ulumbaza Pink/White, first wine in the guide from new Springfontein Rim appellation.

In abeyance: **Mashes Extreme Cabernet Sauvignon**, **Bunches Broken Shiraz**, **Juices Untamed Chardonnay**, **Skins Agleam Sauvignon Blanc**.

Terroir Selection

★★★★ **Pinotage** Fruit-driven, with brambleberry & plums to the fore, **16** ⑧⑦ is dark, big & full, bolstered by 10% petit verdot. Spicy seasoning from 18 months in mixed oak barrels. Also-tasted **15** ⑧⑥ from 100% pinotage, similar profile.

★★★★ **Chenin Blanc** Very appealing **18** ⑧⑧ has 70% barrel-fermented portion, balance in concrete 'egg'. Minerality & crisp acid reflect limestone soils, with stonefruit highlights & lees texture on finish.

★★★★☆ **Ikhalezi Noble Late Harvest** ⑫ Highly unusual but fascinating **09** ⑨⓪ botrytis dessert from chenin spent a remarkable 7 years in oak acquiring deep brown colour & complex flavours. Incredibly sweet (372 g/l sugar) but with savoury/umami notes coming through on lengthy finish.

Ulumbaza range

Red of Springfontein ★★★★ Variable blend, **16** ⑧④ is pinotage-led with cab, shiraz & petit verdot, older oaked. Solid fruit core, smooth texture, dusty oak lacing. **Pink of Springfontein** ★★★★ Dark salmon pinotage-merlot rosé, **18** ⑧③ bright rose-scented berry fruit, leesy richness. Unwooded, natural-yeast ferment in 'egg', 9 months on lees. **White of Springfontein** ★★★★☆ Characterful unoaked blend of sauvignon, chardonnay, semillon & pinotage, **18** ⑧④ shows tangy Granny Smith apple fruit. — GdB

Location: Stanford ▪ Map: Walker Bay & Bot River ▪ Map grid reference: B5 ▪ WO: Walker Bay/Springfontein Rim ▪ Est 1996 ▪ 1stB 2004 ▪ Ulumbaza Wine Bar(n) @ Springfontein open daily 11-9: wine tasting & sales; bits & bites (wine pairing with small warm/cold dishes); dry-aged steaks every day & night ▪ Springfontein Eats fine dining ▪ Cellar tours ▪ Walking/hiking trail ▪ Springfontein Sleeps lodging ▪ Olive oil ▪ Fynbos vermouth ▪ Owner(s) Johst Weber, with Tariro Masayiti, Hildegard Witbooi, family & friends ▪ Cellarmaster(s) Tariro Masayiti (Dec 2012) ▪ Winemaker(s) Tariro Masayiti ▪ Viticulturist(s) Hildegard Witbooi (Oct 2013) ▪ 275ha/30ha (cab, merlot, p verdot, ptage, shiraz, chard, chenel, chenin, sauv, sem) ▪ 100t/12,500cs own label 70% red 25% white 5% rosé ▪ Certified organic by Ecocert (vyds & cellar) ▪ PO Box 71 Stanford 7210 ▪ info@springfontein.co.za ▪ www.springfontein.co.za ▪ S 34° 25' 38.5" E 019° 24' 32.7" ▪ ✍ calories.restricts. brotherly ▪ **T +27 (0)28-341-0651 Office/+27 (0)28-341-0571 Eats/+27 (0)28-341-0651 Ulumbaza Wine Bar(n)**

☐ **Springlights** see Kay & Monty Vineyards
☐ **Springvalley** see Old Vines Cellars
☐ **Stablemate** see Excelsior Estate

Stamboom

This Vlok family wine (the name means 'family tree') is made by Conrad Vlok, winemaker at Strandveld. The Elim farm is the source of the grapes, which also represent a family: pinotage and its parents, cinsaut and pinot noir. The '17 will be released only later this year, once it has acquired more maturity. Future vintages will come in slightly larger volumes, says Conrad.

★★★★☆ **Stamboom** ⑫ Pinot noir dominates blend (50%) & cherry, raspberry notes on **17** ★★★★ ⑧⑨; cinsaut shares credit for fragrance. Pinotage plumminess shows on quite easygoing palate, with modest dry tannins, & harmless bitter tinge on finish. Older oak. Touch off last-made **15** ⑨⓪. — TJ

Location/WO: Elim ▪ 1stB 2004 ▪ Closed to public ▪ Winemaker(s) Conrad Vlok ▪ info@zush.co.za ▪ www.stamboomwines.co.za ▪ **T +27 (0)82-328-3824**

Stanford Hills Winery Ⓠ ⑪ ⓐ ⓞ ⓑ

Peter and Jami Kastner's farm near charming Stanford town (not far inland from Hermanus) offers not only wine but also, amongst others, accommodation (including luxury 'glamping'), a restaurant, horse-riding and lovely valley views. A new recruit, Mark Stephens, will be 'taking care of the wines from vine to bottle', while Peter focuses on the vineyards.

Stanford Hills range

★★★★ **Jacksons Pinotage** Ⓠ Perfumed fruit charm & more detracting sticking-plaster notes on **16** ★★★☆ (83). Lightish flavours, fairly firm, supportive oak. Like **15** (86), big alcohol (14.5%) in balance.

★★★★ **Sauvignon Blanc** ⊘ Understatedly but thoroughly charming **19** (87) with typical sauvignon notes & an earthy tinge adding character. Rounded, well textured, grippy & dry, but unaggressive.

★★★★ **Méthode Cap Classique** New disgorgement of **15** (86) bubbly from chardonnay & 30% pinotage still shows red berry twist on brioche-rich aromas, & a note of pinotage bitterness. Flavourful, fresh & bone-dry.

Reserve Shiraz ★★★☆ Pleasantly rustic, characterful & tasty **16** (83) has good ripe fruit, integrated oak (15% new), dry but ripely soft tannins, & a slightly warming finish from 14.5% alcohol. **Rosé** ★★☆ Pale pink, dry & soft-textured **19** (79) from syrah with berry & earth notes; firm acid leaves it a little sweet-sour. 11.5% alcohol. Walker Bay WO, as MCC & Cape Blend. Not tasted: **Chardonnay**.

Veldfire range

Pinotage Ⓠ ★★★ Attractive wild fruitiness on dry **17** (79), with the slightly funky twist also on Jacksons version. Light fruit. **Cape Blend** ★★★ **17** (82) from shiraz with 35% pinotage shows dark fruit, tobacco & spice. Dry & savoury; pinotage's occasional bitterness on finish. Only older oak. **Rosé** Ⓠ ★★★ From pinotage in **18** (80) (last was shiraz). Light-feeling & fresh, mildly fruity & dry. — TJ

Location: Stanford ▪ Map: Walker Bay & Bot River ▪ Map grid reference: B6 ▪ WO: Stanford Foothills/Walker Bay ▪ Est 1856 ▪ 1stB 2002 ▪ Tasting, sales & restaurant Mon-Sun 8.30-5 ▪ Grappa, preserves ▪ Restaurant: breakfast & lunch, chalkboard menu changes daily ▪ Functions & events (up to 180 pax) ▪ Hiking/MTB trails ▪ Horse riding ▪ Fishing ▪ Whale watching flights from own airfield ▪ 5 self-catering cottages & main farmhouse (sleeps up to 32 pax) plus AfriCamps at Stanford Hills (up to 25 guests) ▪ Owner(s) Stanford Hills Estate (Pty) Ltd ▪ Cellarmaster(s) Peter Kastner (Apr 2005) ▪ Winemaker(s) Peter Kastner (Apr 2005), with Mark Stephens (Feb 2019) ▪ Viticulturist(s) Peter Kastner ▪ 131ha/12ha (ptage, shiraz, chard, sauv) ▪ 60t/4,000cs own label 66% red 34% white ▪ PO Box 1052 Stanford 7210 ▪ info@stanfordhills.co.za ▪ www.stanfordhills.co.za ▪ S 34° 25' 21.4" E 019° 28' 25.7" ▪ 🌐 pickling.impacts.barnacle ▪ **T +27 (0)28-341-0841**

Stark-Condé Wines Ⓠ ⑪ ⓑ

Kansas City-born graphic designer José Conde turned his hand to wine more than two decades ago, and continues to produce some of SA's most classic cabernets from this scenically spectacular property in Stellenbosch's Jonkershoek, in the family since father-in-law Hans-Peter Schröder settled here in the late 1980s. José reports that his right hand, Rüdger van Wyk, former Cape Winemakers Guild protégé and newly minted Diners Club Young Winemaker of the Year, traded in his wedding tuxedo to get back to business (the harvest providing smaller yields but excellent concentration). Conversion to organic has the vineyard team hard at work, while the new glass-enclosed tasting centre, 'floating' in the lake, offers exceptional vistas.

Three Pines range

★★★★★ **Cabernet Sauvignon** ⓐ Sleek, seductive **17** (94) reflects vintage excellence. Understated yet powerful black fruit, graphite & tobacco notes on layered, refined palate. Differs from **16** (93) in 3% petit verdot addition. Seamless velvety tannins from harmoniously integrated oak, 70% new French. Old, high-lying vines.

★★★★★ **Syrah** ⓐ Iron fist in velvet glove, **17** (94) like nuanced **16** (93), has leashed power cloaked by sexy violet-tinged black fruit & brooding inky notes. Balance of fruit & oak (22 months, 30% new) is superb. Like most of the reds, bottled unfined/filtered.

Stark-Condé range

★★★★☆ **Cabernet Sauvignon** ⓐ 17 ⑭ follows 16 ⑬ form in subtle influence of dabs petit verdot, petite sirah, malbec & cab franc. Deeply alluring fruitcake spice yet light, elegant & pliant. Natural ferment with maturation in third new oak, 20 months. WO Stellenbosch, as next 2.

★★★★☆ **Petite Sirah** Soft yet powerful 17 ⑫ differs from 16 ⑪ in that splashes petit verdot & shiraz add interest. Chalky tannin grip from 25% new oak (some American) doesn't dominate bright floral, spicy blue fruit succulence. Silky texture & long finish.

★★★★☆ **Syrah** Broad, layered 17 ⑫ as intricately constructed as 16 ⑭ with portions wholebunch, co-fermented viognier & roussanne, new (10%) & old oak. Silk textured, liquorice & pepper toned, with understated yet refined charms. Reined-in power.

★★★★☆ **Oude Nektar** ⓐ Tealeaf & hedgerow fruit mark 16 ⑭, only the third from farm's highest vineyard (500 m), wiped out by fire in 2009 & replanted. Like 15 ⑬, controlled power, elegant & svelte. Dabs petit verdot, cab franc & malbec. Fruit assimilates 70% new oak (20 months) effortlessly.

★★★★☆ **Round Mountain Sauvignon Blanc** Expressive but subtle 18 ⑨⓪, from 28 year old vines shows fynbos, thatch & lemon zest with vivid acidity & life. Composed structure & breadth courtesy of 'slightly dirty' barrel ferment & 8 months on lees, occasionally stirred. Long, dry tangy finish.

★★★★☆ **The Field Blend** ⓐ Chenin (42%) leads roussanne, verdelho & viognier in 18 ⑭ co-planted vineyard blend. Beautiful balance of ripe stonefruit, spice, creamy oak & lees. Like 17 ★★★★★ ⑨⑤, complex vinification involving barrel ferment, 'egg' & tank portions. Thrilling, taut & focused.

Not tasted: **Petit Verdot**, **Jan Lui's Chenin Blanc**.

Postcard Series

In abeyance: **Pinot Noir**, **Chenin Blanc**, **Sauvignon Blanc**. — FM

Location/map: Stellenbosch ▪ Map grid reference: G6 ▪ WO: Jonkershoek Valley/Stellenbosch ▪ Est/1stB 1998 ▪ Tasting & sales Mon-Sun 9.30–4 ▪ Fee from R60pp ▪ Closed most pub hols (please call to confirm) ▪ Postcard Café open Wed-Sun 9-4 ▪ Owner(s) Jonkershoek Cellars (Pty) Ltd ▪ Cellarmaster(s) José Conde (1998) ▪ Winemaker(s) Rüdger van Wyk (2017), with Mahalia Kotjane (2019) ▪ Viticulturist(s) Andrew Klinck ▪ 250ha/40ha (cabs s/f, p verdot, shiraz) ▪ 250t/12,000cs own label 80% red 20% white ▪ PO Box 389 Stellenbosch 7599 ▪ info@stark-conde.co.za ▪ www.stark-conde.co.za, www.postcardcafe.co.za ▪ S 33° 57' 13.83" E 018° 54' 37.59" ▪ ⓦ voices.monkeys.hangs ▪ **T +27 (0)21-861-7700**

☐ **Starlette** *see* Allée Bleue Wines

Steenberg Vineyards ⓠ ⓟ ⓗ ⓞ ⓖ

It's all change at this venerable old Constantia estate, as new cellarmaster Elunda Basson takes over the reins. She brings with her a wealth of bubbly expertise from her previous position in charge of production at The House of JC le Roux, and is looking forward to adding her stamp and taking the range to even greater heights. Other changes include a make-over for the fine-dining offering at Steenberg Hotel & Spa after 21 years of delighting customers. New Tryn Restaurant has opened its doors and looks set to take its place among the culinary hotspots of the Cape. Meanwhile the ever-popular Bistro Sixteen82 continues to offer informal dining for many, including the locals on the property's residential and golf estate.

Icon range

★★★★☆ **Magna Carta** ⓥ Perennially impressive white Bordeaux blend, sauvignon & semillon (60/40), 30% new oak in 17 ⑭. Approachable in youth, with bountiful lemongrass, spice, citrus & melon succulence, yet also coiled & profound, crisp acid platform to carry it forward.

Flagship range

★★★★☆ **Nebbiolo** ⓥ Standout red in very smart line-up. 16 ⑨⑪ raspberry & sour cherry on dry tannin bed, ably supported by older oak. Crystalline & fresh but hiding its true charm, needs year/2 to show at best.

★★★★☆ **Catharina** ⓥ Flagship blend named for estate's original owner, usually merlot-led. Hallmark power with elegance & poise in 16 ⑬, which lifts the bar on 15 ⑨⑪ with greater concentration & form, 20% syrah & 5% petit verdot augmenting merlot's black fruit, bolstering structure & length.

★★★★☆ **The Black Swan Sauvignon Blanc** Beautifully crafted **18** (93) follows refined, elegant path of **17** ★★★★★ (95), uniting crisp citrus fruit with wet pebbles, nettles & hay. 9 months lees add breadth, tertiary notes of wax & wool just beginning to add complexity, with plenty more to come. From 2 selected vineyards, no oak.

★★★★☆ **Semillon** Stellar example, **18** (94) leans towards the savoury side as discreet oak (fermented in large-format barrel, 35% new) adds wax, resin, lanolin to elegant orange blossom & tangerine fruit. Lively acidity, excellently integrated, with more excitement to come.

Fleet range

★★★★ **Stately Red** Enjoyable black-fruited blend, **17** (87) is fragranced with spice (clove & anise) from older oak, the barrelling also helping soften, smooth the tannins. 67% cab, rest shiraz. WO W Cape, as next.

Ruby Rosé ★★★☆ Bone-dry pink from mainly syrah with some cinsaut, **19** (83) crackles with crisp cranberry fruit, hint of ripe pomegranate & bouncy acidity.

Sphynx Chardonnay ★★★☆ Citrussy mouthful, with orange, grapefruit & marmalade & well-handled oak (only 60% barrelled, 40% new) adding hints of caramel & nuts to pithy finish in **19** (85) preview from Robertson fruit.

Estate range

★★★★☆ **Merlot** Delicious mix of red & black fruit, **16** ★★★★ (89) is 100% merlot with plushy tannins, notes of chocolate & coffee, & good length. Shade less structure than **15** (90), which had petit verdot adding extra depth. For earlier drinking.

★★★★ **Rattlesnake Sauvignon Blanc** Barrel- & concrete-fermented **18** (86) adds texture & vanilla/toffee flavour to flinty-green fruit. Lively acidity suggests keeping could be worthwhile.

★★★★ **Sauvignon Blanc** With classic flavours of greenpepper, grass & lime **19** (87), tank sample is set fair to shine. Different blocks provide complexity & persistent acidity for most attractive wine.

Not tasted: **Syrah**.

Sparkling Wines

★★★★ **1682 Pinot Noir Méthode Cap Classique** Subtle & savoury **NV** (89) rosé bubbly, more discreet than chardonnay sibling, with appealing salty/pithy finish after cranberries, apples & fresh yeasty notes from 12 months on lees. WO W Cape unless noted.

★★★★ **1682 Chardonnay Méthode Cap Classique** Bursting with appley freshness, **NV** (89) sparkling is crisp & lipsmacking, with hints of pears, almonds & just-baked brioche. 12 months on lees, also in magnums. Robertson grapes.

★★★★☆ **Lady R Méthode Cap Classique** Wonderful intensity on multi-layered **14** (93) sparkler from 1st ferment in old oak, 48 months on lees, further 9 months on cork. Bruised apples, crab apples, cranberries with savoury bite & elegant seam of acidity. Pinot noir & chardonnay (70/30).

Sparkling Sauvignon Blanc ★★★☆ Happy summer bubbles, **NV** (84) short-aged sparkler with grassy top-notes then some tropical fruit shining at finish. Frothy & fun. — CM

Location: Constantia ▪ Map: Cape Peninsula ▪ Map grid reference: B4 ▪ WO: Constantia/Western Cape/Robertson ▪ Est 1990 ▪ 1stB 1996 ▪ Tasting & sales Mon-Sun 10–6 ▪ Tasting from R50-R150pp subject to availability ▪ Closed Dec 25 ▪ Cellar tours Mon-Fri 11 & 3 ▪ Bistro Sixteen82; Tryn Restaurant ▪ Steenberg Hotel & Spa; conferences; access to a world-class golf course, walking trail ▪ Extensive merchandising area ▪ Annual festival: Constantia Fresh (Feb) ▪ Owner(s) Graham Beck Enterprises ▪ Cellarmaster(s) Elunda Basson (Jun 2019) ▪ 60ha (cab, malbec, merlot, nebbiolo, shiraz, sauv, sem) ▪ 1,054t ▪ own label 40% red 60% white ▪ WIETA ▪ PO Box 224 Steenberg 7947 ▪ info@steenbergfarm.com ▪ www.steenbergfarm.com ▪ S 34° 4' 17.0" E 018° 25' 31.1" ▪ nominations.moonlit.lily ▪ **T +27 (0)21-713-2211**

☐ **Steenhuis** *see* Wine-of-the-Month Club
☐ **STELL** *see* Stellenrust

Stellar Winery

A family-owned winery, bar 23% held by an empowerment trust and others, Stellar has enjoyed remarkable successes. Based near Vredendal, and taking full advantage of the conditions there, with its low rainfall and minimal vine disease, as well as cooler terroir near the Atlantic, it has grown into the world's largest maker of no-sulphur-added wines, and SA's largest producer of certified-organic Fairtrade bottlings. Demand has outstripped own supply (now accounting for only one third) but its West Coast partners are fully committed to the organic vision. Evocative wine names and labels tell the story verbally and graphically, and prices remain affordable.

The River's End range

★★★★ Chenin Blanc ⊘ ⊙ Cool-climate fruit shows in **18** ㊆, intense lime & grapefruit, easily handles the oaking, a honey biscuit interweave, the whole experience about flavour. Admirable complexity & assurance. Fairtrade certified, as all ranges.

★★★★ Sauvignon Blanc ㋿ ⊘ ⊙ Oaked & nicely done, **18** ㊅'s toasted almond effect doesn't detract from green fig & minerals, there's harmony, layered interest. Zesty saline finish perfect for food.

Pinot Noir ⊘ ⊙ **★★★★** Classic light texture, red berries & damp earth nuance; quite savoury, 12–18 months oaking, half new, **17** ㊃'s firm dry finish promising some longevity. WO Koekenaap, as all these.

The Sensory Collection

★★★★ Grande Reserve Shiraz ⊙ Barrel aged 18–24 months, half new, as next, compatible with **17** ㊆'s dark fruit; has layered interest, scrub, cocoa-rich chocolate. Whole effect richly savoury, characterful.

Grande Reserve Pinotage ⊙ **★★★★** Oak's contribution is spicing in **17** ㊃'s dark fruit, notes of cocoa, liquorice. Ripe & forceful, muscular, with enough tannin backbone for ageing. These all WO Koekenaap.

Grande Reserve Chardonnay ⊙ **★★★★** Spent 12 months on lees in barrel & it shows as buttered toast in **17** ㊃'s dried peach flavours. Statement wine, quite bold, but it works.

The Storyteller range

NSA Cabernet Sauvignon ⊙ **★★★** Meaty & dark toned, heaps of savoury spice, **18** ㊀'s fruit more expressive in the flavours, has good enlivening freshness in a sleek body. WO Koekenaap.

Running Duck range

Merlot ⊙ **★★★** Bright-fruited, slender **19** ㊆'s oak treatment contributes more spice than tannin, has easy drinkability. **Shiraz** ⊙ **★★★** Oak staves used, sleek texture (13% alcohol) but **19** ㊁ has good varietal character, white pepper & cloves, some underbrush, juicy dark fruit to aid enjoyment. **Reserve Cabernet Sauvignon-Pinotage** ⓧ ⊙ **★★★** Only 50% oaked to allow greater fruit expression in **17** ㊆. Fynbos/scrub notes, mulberry vibrancy, especially in the flavours. **Chardonnay** ⊙ **★★★** No wood, citrus notes in dry **19** ㊆, refreshing appeal. **Chenin Blanc** ⊙ **★★★** Consistent styling, **19** ㊁ has crunchy green apple freshness, is sleek (12.5% alcohol) & vibrant. **Sauvignon Blanc** ⊙ **★★★** Svelte (12% alcohol) & refreshingly dry, **19** ㊁'s pear & winter melon flavours a good varietal fit. **Reserve Sauvignon Blanc-Semillon** ⓧ ⊙ **★★★** Crunchy summer fruits, **18** ㊁'s backing limy acidity & trim lines make for ideal food accompaniment.

Stellar Organics range

Chardonnay-Pinot Noir Sparkling ⊙ **★★★** Soupçon pinot noir for **NV** ㊁ carbonated bubbly's pale pink colour, red berry top note. Chardonnay provides the rest: crisply dry citrus, & elegance at just 11.5% alcohol. **Extra Dry Sparkling** ⊙ **★★★** From chenin, zippy **19** ㊁ carbonated bubbly packed with apple & grapefruit freshness, wakens the taste buds.

Stellar Organics No-Sulphur-Added range

Cabernet Sauvignon ⊙ **★★★** Berry fruit is there, but oaking plays a prominent role in **19** ㊆, savoury & dark toned. Match with rich dishes. **Merlot** ⊙ **★★★** Prominent blackberries, a herbal note, some oak-driven savoury spice, **19** ㊇ is light & juicy. **Pinotage** ⊙ **★★★** Barrel treatment gives **19** ㊆'s dark fruit a distinctly savoury overlay, almost mocha chocolate. Tannins supple, accessible. Nice match for venison, robust casseroles. **Shiraz** ⊙ **★★★** Use of oak staves in **19** ㊈ carefully done, adding savoury spice, cocoa but no tannin barrier to the fruit's succulence. Not tasted: **Rosé**, **Limited Release Blanc de Blanc**.

Heaven on Earth range

★★★★★ Muscat d'Alexandrie ⊘ ⊙ ㊗ Classic air-drying process (on bed of straw, rooibos no longer used), this exceptional **NV** ㊈ dessert wine is about richness, concentration, yet still with a varietal grapiness, caramelised fruit. Despite the high sugar, there's astonishing elegance, finesse. 375 ml. — CR

Location: Vredendal ▪ Map: Olifants River ▪ Map grid reference: B4 ▪ WO: Western Cape/Koekenaap ▪ Est 2000 ▪ 1stB 2001 ▪ Tasting & sales Mon-Fri 8–5 ▪ Closed all pub hols ▪ Cellar tours by appt ▪ Owner(s) Rossouw family, Stellar Empowerment Trust & others ▪ Winemaker(s) Klaas Coetzee (Aug 2010) & Mauritius Naude ▪ Viticulturist(s) Klaas Coetzee ▪ ±68ha Stellar Farming, ±149ha independent organic producers (cab, merlot, ptage, pinot, ruby cab, shiraz, chenin, chard, muscat d'A, sauv) ▪ 11,900t ▪ Other export brands: Dig This!, Firefly, Live-A-Little, Moonlight Organics, Natural Star, No House Wine ▪ PO Box 308 Vredendal 8160 ▪ info@stellarorganics.co.za ▪ www.stellarorganics.co.za ▪ S 31° 42' 24.70" E 018° 33' 33.70" ▪ ⬚ legislate.contoured.arachnid ▪ T +27 (0)27-216-1310

Stellekaya Winery ⓠ

The all-red portfolio of Dave and Jane Lello's Stellenbosch winery has been increasingly concentrated on grapes off their Blaauwklippen Valley farm. The vinification, for a year or two in the hands of Rose Kruger, takes place at Bosman's Crossing, on the edge of the town, where there are also the visitor facilities. Most of the wines are released with a good few years' maturation, both in barrel and bottle, making them more accessible on release than many, as well as generally more savoury than upfront-fruity.

Limited Releases

★★★★ **Malbec** ⓥ Serious-minded single-vineyard bottling. **12** ⑧⑦'s generous mulberry & plum fruit in harmony with gripping yet ripe tannins, but will reward few years patience. Only 700 numbered bottles.

★★★★ **Orion Reserve** ⓥ Cab with merlot plus drops cab franc, malbec. Retasted, **12** ⑧⑨ showing well mid-2018. Developed character, bringing more complex, oxidative, savoury, even sombre notes to the dark fruit. Fine tannins - rather dry thanks to 44 months in oak. Great food wine for a few more years.

Stellekaya range

★★★★ **Cabernet Sauvignon** Tobacco, cedar & dark fruit on **15** ⑧⑧, with a drop of malbec, pleasingly savoury; balanced, with good structure. A sweet, juicy note, but 40 months in oak give notably dry tannins.

★★★★ **Malbec** ⓥ By house's unshowy standards, **14** ⑧⑥ quite forward juicy fruit to complement the firm tannic structure, savoury element & long oaking. Nice loganberry finish.

★★★★ **Merlot** ⓥ Lovely rich red-fruited aromas & flavours on **14** ⑧⑦ preview. Properly ripe, supple tannins, balanced & fresh, oak well judged. Shows good potential.

★★★★ **Pinot Noir** ⓥ Sour cherry fruit & some earthiness, brisk acidity, quite high toned. **13** ★★★ ⑦⑧ best enjoyed soon with a meal. Less beguiling than last **11**. WO W Cape.

★★★★ **Hercules 15** ⑧⑥ has same majority sangiovese as **14** ★★★★ ⑧⑤ with 15% cab. Bright savoury-sweet cherry, balanced, with smooth dry tannins (37 months oak a little much), & silky mouthfeel.

★★★★ **Orion** ⓥ 50% cab, with merlot, cab franc, malbec - **14** ⑧⑧ fleshier, less severe than Cab; quite elegant, good savoury balance & hints of sweet fruit. Also 44 months oak, but firm tannins not too dry.

Not tasted: **Pinotage**, **Shiraz**. Discontinued: **Cape Cross**, **Pinot Grigio**. — TJ

Location/map: Stellenbosch ▪ Map grid reference: E5 ▪ WO: Stellenbosch/Western Cape ▪ Est 1998 ▪1stB 1999 ▪ Tasting, sales & cellar tours Wed-Fri 10-5 Sat 10-2 ▪ Closed all pub hols ▪ Owner(s) Dave & Jane Lello ▪ Winemaker(s) Rose Kruger (Jan 2018) ▪ Viticulturist(s) Wynand Pienaar ▪ 23ha/15ha under vine ▪ 12,000cs own label ▪ IPW ▪ PO Box 12426 Die Boord Stellenbosch 7613 ▪ info@stellekaya.co.za ▪ www.stellekaya.co.za ▪ S 33° 56' 27.6" E 018° 50' 47.3" ▪ ⬚ circling.swan.sang ▪ T +27 (0)21-883-3873

☐ **Stellenbosch 1679** see Koelenhof Winery

Stellenbosch Family Wines ⓠ

The beautiful rising phoenix labels of the international range of this boutique Stellenbosch venture are joined by a collection aimed at the local market, named Glorious, featuring equally creative packaging by artist Michelle-Lize van Wyk, a member of one of the three families behind the brand. Vinification is at Koelenhof Winery by the amazingly youthful Carlo de Vries, just 15 years old, and his father Andrew, a seasoned winemaker and Koelenhof's general manager.

Phoenix range

Cabernet Sauvignon ⓥ ★★★ Unusual **17** ⑧⓪ has medicinal nuance to ripe black fruit, fragrant notes of violets & mint, soft tannins despite 100% new oak. **Merlot** ⓥ ★★★ Wood dominates **17** ⑦⑦ though ripe chocolate-dipped cherry fruit suggests it may harmonise with time. **Pinot Noir** ⓥ ★★★ Jammy red-fruit confection but **16** ⑦ handles the spicy barrelling well, attractive earthy notes developing. **Pinotage** ⓥ ★★★ Cherry fruit on ripe **17** ⑧, good balance & pleasant tannins. Less oak than others & the better for it. **Family Blend** ⓥ ★★ Merlot/cab show their compatibility in the plummy/berry character; gentle spice & structure from oak staves in **13** ⑦. **CMP Legacy Red** ⓥ ★★ Mostly cab with merlot & pinot noir. **13** ⑦ red berries & gentle savoury spice, slight herbaceous note but the palate is accessible, drinks easily. **Chardonnay** ⓥ ★★★★ Interesting citrus/tropical vibe on lively **17** ⑧ - orange, grapefruit, touch melon - good balance, judicious oak (50%, none new) adding clove & vanilla tweaks.

Glorious range

Cabernet Sauvignon ⓥ ★★★ Tar-tinted sweet cassis fruit still gripped by tannins, **15** ⑧ needs food or few years cellaring to soften. **Merlot** ⓥ ★★ Same charry choc overlay on cherry fruit as previous, **17** ⑦ finishes on astringent note. **Pinot Noir** ⓥ ★★ Revisited, **15** ⑦'s oak dominates slight red-fruit aromas, shows as smoky & charry on palate. **Pinotage** ⓥ ★★★ Reined-in wooding lets appealing fresh-fruit profile shine, **15** ⑧ mulberries, strawberries, fair intensity, bold but unharsh tannins. **Family Blend** ⓥ ★★★★ Restrained hedgerow fruit, zippy acidity & friendly tannic hold, **15** ⑧ merlot (51%) & cab combo slips down easily. **CMP Legacy Red** ⓥ ★★★ Mainly cab with merlot & pinot noir, **15** ⑧ mouthcoating tannins & brisk acidity for beefy stews & potjies. **Chardonnay** ⓥ ★★★★ Aperitif-style **15** ⑧ will have broad appeal with its attractive nut, citrus & lemon thyme bouquet, toast & vanilla flavours. — CM

Location/map/WO: Stellenbosch ▪ Map grid reference: D1 ▪ Est/1stB 2013 ▪ Tasting by appt ▪ Fee R30/6 wines ▪ Sales Mon-Sat 8-6 by appt ▪ Owner(s) Renata de Vries, Michelle-Lize van Wyk & Christel Truter ▪ Winemaker(s) Carlo de Vries, with Andrew de Vries (both Jan 2013, consultants) ▪ 2,900cs own label 90% red 10% white ▪ c/o PO Box 1 Koelenhof 7605 ▪ info@stellenboschfamilywines.co.za ▪ www.stellenbos-chfamilywines.co.za ▪ S 33° 50' 5.2" E 018° 47' 52.7" ▪ 🄵 toolkit.sounds.junction ▪ **T +27 (0)82-835-7107**

Stellenbosch Hills Wines ⓥ ♿

Stellenbosch Hills epitomises the modern grower-owned wine business, its Polkadraai Hills vineyards and wines managed in tiers of quality, style and price. This edition there are new wines at both ends of the spectrum: the premium Sense of Place range gets a wooded chenin, pinotage blend and, soon, MCC bubbly, and to celebrate the 10th anniversary of the cheerful Polkadraai range, with its colourful polka dot capsules, a rosé, proceeds from sales of which support a farm community school nearby.

Sense of Place range

★★★★☆ **Suikerboschrand** (NEW) (🍾) Pinotage in the lead for tightly structured **15** ⑨ Cape Blend, with shiraz, merlot, cab & petit verdot. Firm, dry, but fine fruit & oak tannins (100% new, French) augur well for a long & rewarding future for this youthful beauty.

★★★★ **Kastanjeberg** (NEW) Ripe & rich **17** ⑧ will charm fans of boldly oaked chenin. Stave ferment & new barrel maturation accentuate ample sweetness. Like liquid dried peach, but errs on the generous side.

★★★★☆ **La Serena** ⓥ Prestige limited bottling of rare muscat de Hambourg, long a signature grape of this winery, fortified with 7 year old brandy. **14** ⑨ pomegranate, nougat & nut packed into full-sweet explosion of flavour, the spirit smoothly integrated. Lightly chill for luxurious aperitif or serve with cheese.

1707 Reserve range

★★★★ **Red** Syrah-led complementary blend with merlot, cab & petit verdot in **16** ⑧. Ample ripe fruit tempered into drier, streamlined framework by 24 months wood maturation (60% new, French).

★★★★ **White** More new oak (100%, French) on chardonnay-led **18** ⑧ blend, continues bold styling of **16** ⑧ & highlights toasted nut, buttered pear flavours. More curvaceous & succulent than intense. No **17**.

Stellenbosch Hills range

★★★★ **Muscat de Hambourg** Alluring jasmine-, incense- & Turkish delight-infused fortified, **18** ⑧ lovely acidity & spiritous lift, not cloying. Decadent & heart-warming, chilled or straight. No **17**.

Cabernet Sauvignon ⊘ ★★★★ Herbaceous nuance to dark fruit on **17** ⑧, tannins firm, but not aus-tere. Some mixed French & American oak, as most of these reds. Sappy & fresh, nice dry farewell. **Merlot** ★★★ Tight, minty **17** ⑧, skin maceration & all-French oak maturation 14 months up the dry cedary tannins. Order the lamb! **Bushvine Pinotage** ★★★ Drier styling, but balanced in **17** ⑧, with lively acidity & piquant plummy fruit. **Shiraz** ★★★ Spicy, savoury impression on fresh & lively **17** ⑧. Balanced, juicy & approachable. **Chenin Blanc** ⊘ ★★★ Friendly in style & on the pocket, **19** ⑧⓪'s ripe but crisp apple flavours make for attractive easy drinking. **Sauvignon Blanc** ★★★ **19** ⑧② has clean passionfruit flavours, plumped by some creamy lees.

Polkadraai range

Sauvignon Blanc ⊘ ⑨ ★★★ Burst of summer fruit & crunchy freshness on **19** ⑧⓪. Bright & balanced, with plenty to share in super-value 3L cask. Polkadraai Hills WO, as all here.

....

Pinotage-Merlot ⊘ ★★★ Pinotage's high-toned mulberry fruit to the fore on **18** ⑦⑦. Dry, spiced tannins for robust fare. **Merlot-Shiraz** ⑧ ★★ Ripe mulberry features ushered into a toasty frame, **17** ⑦③ easy, succulent, good value. 3L cask only. **Rosé** ⒩ ⊘ ★★★ From shiraz. **19** ⑦⑧ sundowner hue & styling, with spiced cherry flavours & a dry, clean finish. **Chenin Blanc-Sauvignon Blanc** ⊘ ★★★ Cool & tangy **19** ⑦⑧ duo, perfect for relaxed & refreshing summer sipping, at a restrained 12.7% alcohol. Not tasted: **Pinot Noir Sparkling Rosé**, **Sauvignon Blanc Sparkling Brut**. — MW

Location/map: Stellenbosch ▪ Map grid reference: D6 ▪ WO: Stellenbosch/Polkadraai Hills ▪ Est 1945 ▪ 1stB 1972 ▪ Tasting & sales Mon-Fri 9-5 Sat 10-3 ▪ Fee R20; R75 wine, biltong & droëwors tasting ▪ Closed Sun & all pub hols ▪ Owner(s) 16 members ▪ Cellarmaster(s) PG Slabbert (Jan 1997) ▪ Winemaker(s) James Ochse (Sep 2016) ▪ Viticulturist(s) Johan Pienaar & Eben Archer (consultants) ▪ 715ha (cab, merlot, ptage, shiraz, chard, chenin, muscat de Hambourg, sauv) ▪ 6,000t/20,000cs own label 68% red 30% white 2% other ▪ IPW ▪ PO Box 40 Vlottenburg 7604 ▪ info@stellenbosch-hills.co.za ▪ www.stellenbosch-hills.co.za ▪ S 33° 57' 38.2" E 018° 48' 1.8" ▪ 🖃 pilots.brittle.withdrew ▪ **T +27 (0)21-881-3828**

☐ **Stellenbosch Manor** see Stellenrust

Stellenbosch Reserve   ⓠ

Rust en Vrede proprietor Jean Engelbrecht here pays tribute to his birthplace, 'a unique town and home to many of South Africa's greatest leaders, intellectuals, artists, scientists, sportsmen and winemakers'. A branding update underway at press time includes new packaging and the phasing out of heritage wine names ('Ou Hoofgebou', 'Kweekskool' et al). Seasoned Stellenbosch winemaker Danielle le Roux takes the reins in time for the 15th vintage of this accomplished prestige portfolio.

★★★★★ **Cabernet Sauvignon** ⊘ ⓐ Masterly varietal expression, bold & forceful yet showing finesse & detail, underscored by restrained oak (20% new). Dark blackcurrant core interwoven with liquorice, earthy iodine & wild herbs. **17** ★★★★★ ⑨④ worthy successor to stellar **16** ⑨⑤.

★★★★ **Merlot** Distinct menthol aromas, following to bright, spicy red berries. **17** ⑧⑥ carefully crafted & elegant, as is the whole range, offering impressive value.

★★★★☆ **Vanderstel** ⑧ Stately elegance persists in **16** ⑨⓪, though touch less impressive than high-flying **15** ★★★★★ ⑨⑦. Cab-led 4-way Bordeaux blend has poise, ripeness & complexity. **17** ⑨③, also tasted, 5-way assemblage is deeper, fuller, with brooding cassis & forest floor notes.

★★★★ **Chardonnay** Judicious oaking on **18** ⑧⑨ expresses charming citrus & honeysuckle scent. Very appealing, medium bodied & subtly accomplished, restrained & focused.

★★★★ **Chenin Blanc** ⒩ Lightly oaked, middleweight **18** ⑧⑦ shows control & finesse. Honeyed stonefruit with brisk acidity, leesy substance & lingering finish. One to watch.— GdB

Location/WO: Stellenbosch ▪ Est 2004 ▪ 1stB 2005 ▪ Tasting & sales at Guardian Peak Wines ▪ Owner(s) Jean Engelbrecht ▪ Winemaker(s) Danielle le Roux (Dec 2019) ▪ ±170t/27,000cs own label 65% red 35% white ▪ IPW ▪ PO Box 473 Stellenbosch 7599 ▪ info@stellenboschreserve.com ▪ www.stellenboschreserve.com ▪ **T +27 (0)21-881-3881**

Stellenbosch University Welgevallen Cellar   ⓠ

Yes, the university in the heart of SA's winelands, with a renowned oenology faculty, does have its own wine brand. Two, in fact. Made (and offered for tasting/sale) in a cellar dating to the birth of its home town (1680) from grapes grown on the Welgevallen experimental farm and selected private estates around Stellenbosch.

Die Laan range

★★★★ **Shiraz** ⊘ Plenty of spicy appeal to **17** ⑧⑦ middleweight, morello cherry tang to black fruit, characterful & poised. 17 months in 20% new oak well absorbed. No **16**.

★★★★ **Chenin Blanc Reserve** Accomplished barrel-fermented **18** ⑧⑨ delivers on many levels, has heft & texture, absorbs richly ripe tropical fruit & buttery fatness from 8 months in 30% new oak into a balanced whole.

....

Sauvignon Blanc ⑰ ★★★★ Exuberantly fruity, aromatic **19** ⑧④ gushes granadilla & gooseberry, injects the ripe flavour with perky acidity for a poised glassful.

Cabernet Sauvignon ★★★★ Offers overt berry fruit, **17** ⑧④ perfectly pleasant but could do with more varietal nerve & tension. Oak (17 months, 20% new) shows through. **Merlot** ⊘ ★★★★ Distinctive herbal-leafy tones in **17** ⑧⑤, underpinned by sweetly ripe blackcurrant & plum fruit. **Merlot Reserve** ⊘ ★★★★ Brawny, tannic **17** ⑧④ shows good varietal fruit & leafy herbaceousness. Rather rough at the edges, chalky finish. **Pinotage** ★★★★ Mild-mannered, with vibrant berry fruit, **17** ⑧⑤ has plenty of varietal character & appeal, medium body, fullish ripe tannins. Touch less interesting, satisfying than **15** ★★★★ ⑧⑦. No **16**. **Chenin Blanc** ★★★★ Candied rind, dried apricot & pineapple, **18** ⑧⑤ has ample fruit-driven charm, amplified by 20% barrelled component & splash sauvignon. **Cape Fortified** ⊘ ★★★ Ripe fruitcake notes on still-available **05** ⑧① 'port' from tintas barocca & roriz, in old oak 8 years. Neither too sweet nor fiery, the tannins soft & easygoing. Not tasted: **Rector's Reserve Pinotage**. Occasional release: **Chardonnay Méthode Cap Classique**. Discontinued: **Viognier**.

Maties range

Rooiplein ⊘ ★★★ Unpretentious but competent **NV** ⑧② pinotage-cab blend, showing cheerfully ripe red berries, smooth tannins. — GdB

Location/map/WO: Stellenbosch ▪ Map grid reference: F5 ▪ Est 2001 ▪ 1stB 2009 ▪ Tasting Mon-Fri 9-4 ▪ Fee R45pp ▪ Closed all pub hols & Dec 15-Jan 10 ▪ Owner(s) Stellenbosch University ▪ Cellarmaster(s)/winemaker(s) Riaan Wassüng (Jan 2004) ▪ 11ha/10ha (cab, ptage, shiraz, sauv) ▪ 4,600cs own label 68% red 32% white ▪ Faculty AgriSciences Private Bag X1 Matieland 7602 ▪ winesales@sun.ac.za, rfw@sun.ac.za ▪ http://academic.sun.ac.za/viti_oenol/ ▪ S 33° 56' 22.38" E 018° 52' 1.92" ▪ ⬜ anyone.crusher.likely ▪ **T** +27 (0)21-808-2925/+27 (0)83-622-6394

Stellenbosch Vineyards ⑨ ⑧ ⑤

This extensive and dynamic global wine business – it exports close to 80% of production – is located on Welmoed, a 17th-century farm in Stellenbosch. Since last edition, France-based international wine specialist AdVini has further increased its majority shareholding, and a 5,500 m2 warehouse was erected to replace the facility gutted by fire during the 2019 harvest. There's also refreshed packaging for the Stellenbosch Vineyards range, a new single-site chenin blanc from 50-year-old bushvines in the Limited Release range, and increasing focus on varieties, like therona and verdelho, which tolerate the drier and warmer conditions linked to climate change. See separate listing for the Welmoed range.

The Flagship range

★★★★★ **Petit Verdot** ⊘ Assured, uncompromising yet unforced **12** ⑨③, opulent plum fruit given near-perfect form by commanding tannins, vibrant acidity, emphatic dry finish & well-integrated oak (48 months, 80% new). Coastal WO.

★★★★★ **Right Bank** ⊘ Firm & linear interpretation of merlot-dominated (67%) Bordeaux blend, **15** ⑨④ with equal splashes cab, cab franc & petit verdot; judicious spicing from 2 years in 50% new oak, beautiful dry end. Ideally structured to reward 10+ years cellaring.

Not tasted: **Cabernet Franc**.

Limited Release range

★★★★★ **Cinsault** Like **17** ⑨③, cherry-toned **18** ⑨⓪ in modern, lightly oaked, medium-intensity style. Attractive gentle stalky grip, house's impressive acid-tannin balance. Only older wood, as for red sibling.

★★★★★ **Grenache** On-trend for lighter-oaked & -styled reds, with variety's signature strawberry & charcuterie notes, **18** ⑨② has similar stemmy tone on nose & palate as previous.

★★★★ **Single Vineyard Chenin Blanc** (NEW) From registered single block, **17** (87) Rubenesque but well-formed, delicious; rich bruised apple character, sweet vanilla aromas & flavours from 50% new oak, plump tail (8 g/l sugar) lifted by bright acidity.

★★★★ **Therona** Seldom-seen locally developed white grape. Old-oak-matured **18** (87) improves on **17** ★★★☆ (85). More elegance, pleasing dryness & vinosity, similar white peach & nectarine fruit profile.

★★★★☆ **Verdelho** (🍇) Less big-boned than **17** (93) (13.5% alcohol vs 14.9%), barrel-fermented **18** (94) sleek & racy, 30% new-oak gloss to mandarin & yellow apple fruit, subtly adding texture & length.

Credo range

★★★★★ **Shiraz** (✓) (🍇) Gently extracted **17** (93), even more sophistication, nuance & elegance than **15** (91) & **14** ★★★★ (87) (**16** sold out untasted). Pepper seasoning & lily fragrance to black fruit, well-judged acidity & powdery tannins add poise & freshness. Excellent value.

★★★★ **SMV** 'M' on most 'SMV' labels means mourvèdre, here it's merlot - just 16%, with shiraz & splash viognier. **17** (86) florals & light oak, just enough fruit on beautifully dry palate. Step up on **16** ★★★★ (85).

★★★★ **Chardonnay** With considerable intensity of vanilla oak & citrus flavour, & lively acidity, **18** (89) is bold but so well crafted, it retains plenty of palate appeal & refreshment, like **17** (88).

★★★★☆ **Chenin Blanc** (✓) Vivacious **17** (90) benefits from cooler vintage, steps up on full-bore **16** ★★★★ (89) while handling 50% new oak with aplomb. Effortless, & not at all fruit-sweet.

Occasional release: **Pinotage Reserve**.

Stellenbosch Vineyards range

★★★★ **Bushvine Pinotage** (✓) Consistently outperforms range siblings, flies the varietal flag (strawberry & mulberry tones, hint banana, bright acidity) with panache. **17** (86) tad bigger than usual at 14.5% alcohol.

Cabernet Sauvignon ★★★ Lightly oaked **18** (82), dusty dark plums & blackberries, slightly astringent tannins no impediment to pleasurable sipping. **Shiraz** ★★★☆ Laudably dry & fresh, **17** (84) with confected strawberry candyfloss aroma, appealing if unusual for variety. **Unwooded Chardonnay** ★★★ For early, uncomplicated enjoyment, **18** (82) faint lemon notes, sleek body & finish. **Bushvine Chenin Blanc** ★★★☆ Quite luxurious at the price, with partial wooding & few grams sugar adding richness to white peach & pineapple aromas & flavours, while feisty acid touch keeps **19** (84) poised & vibrant. **Sauvignon Blanc** ★★★ Shows usual leanness & zing from racy acidity in **19** (82), along with blackcurrant & musk nuances.

Discontinued: **Infiniti range**. — CvZ

Location/map: Stellenbosch ▪ Map grid reference: C7 ▪ WO: Stellenbosch/Coastal ▪ Est 2004 ▪ Tasting & sales Tue–Fri 9–5 Sat/Sun & pub hols 10–5 ▪ Tasting fee R50pp/standard & R80pp/premium ▪ Closed Good Fri, Dec 25 & Jan 1 ▪ Facilities for children ▪ Owner(s) 12 shareholders ▪ Winemaker(s) Abraham de Villiers (Dec 2004) & Bernard Claassen (Feb 2005), with Petri de Beer (Jan 2015) ▪ Viticulturist(s) Francois de Villiers (1998) ▪ 5,500t ▪ 55% red 35% white 10% rosé ▪ BEE, Fairtrade, IPW, WIETA ▪ PO Box 465 Stellenbosch 7599 ▪ info@stellvine.co.za ▪ www.stellenboschvineyards.co.za ▪ S 33° 59' 26.06" E 018° 46' 2.21" ▪ 🗺 wingspans. sprinkler.hotspots ▪ T +27 (0)21-881-3870

Stellendrift - SHZ Cilliers/Kuün Wyne

The names of Fanie Cilliers' wines reflect his Huguenot grape-growing and wine-making family's history from their arrival at the Cape in 1700. Some of his wines are collaborations with other cellars and winemakers, and some are produced intermittently.

Stellendrift range

Cabernet Sauvignon Reserve ★★★ Later bottling of **13** (80) more accessible than the **14** ★★★ (78) vintage we tasted last edition. Meaty, savoury, dark-fruited with herbal nuances, smooth & easy. **Kruyspad Pinotage** ★★★ Opulent & dark-toned, **15** (81)'s 30 months in older barrels shows in the savoury spice seam, firm tannin finish. Good venison & meat casserole match. **VOC Syrah** ★★★ Later bottling of **13** (80), retains its plum/prune richness, shot through with sweet & savoury spice from 30 months oaking. Dry, food-friendly finish. For those who like their syrah burly. In abeyance: **Cabernet Sauvignon, Josué Merlot, Merlot-Cabernet Sauvignon Blitz, Rosa Rosaceae Red Select, Cape Huguenot Merlot-Pinotage, Giant Sauvignon Blanc, Cape White Savour**.

Cilliers Cellars range
In abeyance.

De Oude Opstal range
In abeyance.— CR

Location/WO: Stellenbosch ▪ Est 1995 ▪ 1stB 1996 ▪ Closed to public ▪ Owner(s) Fanie Cilliers (SHZ Cilliers/Kuün Wines) ▪ Winemaker(s)/viticulturist(s) Fanie Cilliers (Nov 1995) ▪ 2,200cs own label 90% red 10% white ▪ PO Box 6340 Uniedal 7612 ▪ fcilliers@vodamail.co.za ▪ www.stellendrift.co.za ▪ T +27 (0)21-887-6561/+27 (0)82-372-5180

Stellenrust

This Stellenbosch family winery boasts 200 hectares of vines ranged across the Helderberg's 'golden triangle', Devon Valley and Bottelary Hills. Many vineyards are old, 35 years or more, and most are nourished with a compost system from their Hereford pure-bred stud's waste. Sustainability is just one element driving a 25% annual increase in sales and production, mostly of chenin and pinotage. Rewards from attention to detail are manifold. For example, the '54' Chenin achieves a fourth consecutive maximum rating in this guide; Stellenrust has been in the Top Ten every year since the inauguration of the Chenin Blanc Challenge; and trophies are regularly won at the International Wine Challenge. Cellarmaster Tertius Boshoff is also delighted that listings in retail chains Waitrose and Sainsbury's, and presentations at major restaurants, are helping build chenin into an increasingly strong category in the key UK market.

Super Premium range

★★★★ **Barrel Selection Cabernet Franc** Helderberg fruit for **16** ⑧⑦, just light dusting of spice on ripe, sweet fruit. Appropriately structured to balance, not overwhelm; French oak, 30% new, 18 months. Ready sooner than distinguished **15** ★★★★☆ ⑨③.

★★★★ **Cornerstone Pinotage** Bold **16** ⑧⑨ ex 51 year old Bottelary bushvines. Pronounced spice, black cherry fruit, oak enhanced (35% new). Ripe & creamily rich, though short on depth of **15** ★★★★☆ ⑨⓪. Needs time for stern tannins to relax.

★★★★ **Peppergrinder's Shiraz** Aromatic **16** ⑧⑨, florals, spice including some oak (French with a little American, 35% new). Silky texture backed by firm tannins. Should gain more savouriness with few years but lacks depth of **15** ★★★★☆ ⑨⓪ for longer term.

★★★★☆ **Timeless** Ⓐ Cab with merlot, cab franc. **16** ⑨③ classic cassis aromas with smart cedary oak decoration. Well fleshed, sweet fruit held by fine, determined grip & fresh acidity. Concluding savouriness should increase with time. Varieties vinified/oak-aged separately, then 6 months as a blend. Also in 1.5L.

★★★★☆ **Barrel Fermented Chardonnay** Familiar ripe pickled lime, oatmeal undertones on approachable **18** ⑨①. Lots of juicy flavours, keen acidity, lightly weighted by clean, creamy lees, subtle oak. A little ageing should achieve greater harmony. Natural ferment, French oak, 32% new.

★★★★★ **54 Barrel Fermented Chenin Blanc** Ⓐ Consistently stellar wild-fermented chenin; **18** ⑨⑥ stylish as ever, chalking up Bottelary Hills bushvines' 54th birthday with 6th maximum rating in the guide, 4th in succession. Whisper of honeyed botrytis, juicy peach flavours - delicious, complex & carried to sweet-fruited conclusion on wave of ripe acidity. Resist for few years at least, especially in magnum.

★★★★★ **Old Bushvine Chenin Blanc** ⓃⒺⓌ Ⓐ Hedonistic newcomer to this remarkable chenin collection, from 43 year old bushvines. **18** ⑨⑤ gorgeously ripe, juicy & concentrated red apple, peach flavours enriched by subtle oak, all old. Clean natural acid & freshness leave fruity rather than sweet (3.6 g/l sugar) finish.

★★★★☆ **Barrel Fermented Sauvignon Blanc** Usual concentration from 40+ year old bushvine block in **18** ⑨⓪. Bit more plush than **17** ⑨④ but no lack of incisive acid backbone to focus the blackcurrant, greengage interest. Old-oak ferment & lees ageing add balancing flesh. Still needs to fully harmonise.

★★★★☆ **Chenin d'Muscat** Ⓐ Bright citrus scents on **16** ⑨③ Natural Sweet from old-vine chenin & muscat d'Alexandrie, accessorised by gentle dusting of botrytis. Fresh-as-a-daisy fruity acids, moderate 121 g/l sugar. Just under 11% alcohol. Refreshing, moreish. Natural ferment, old French oak. 375 ml.

Old Bush Vine Cinsaut ★★★☆ From unirrigated 54 year old bushvines in Bottelary. **18** ⑧⑤ in understated, lighter style with pretty if straightforward raspberry flavours. Freshness, lively tannins suggest early drinking, even lightly chilled. Not on par with complex **17** ★★★★ ⑧⑨.

Premium range

★★★★ **Chenin Blanc** ⊘ **19** ⑧⑧ out of the blocks with verve, delightful red apple juiciness & tangy acidity. Just as irresistible as Super Premium siblings. Also from mature vines; treated with equal care, natural ferment, 16% in older oak, 5 months on lees.

★★★★ **Sauvignon Blanc** ⊘ Both intense & easy to enjoy thanks to great balance between its ripe, juicy, tropical flavours & riveting acid. **19** ⑧⑦ a wine that doesn't want to be forgotten in a hurry! Also in 375 ml, like **18** ★★★★ ⑧⑤.

. . . .

Cabernet Sauvignon ⊘ ⑦ ★★★★ Following in footsteps of previous, **18** ⑧⑤ shows clear blackberry & cassis scents, oak (20% new) & 8% cab franc add extra interest. Youthful approachability matched by sound structure for few years further enjoyment, as all this range. **Merlot** ⊘ ⑦ ★★★☆ A real crowd pleaser. **18** ⑧④ plentiful spicy, plummy flavours, sweet flesh & nip of framing tannin; all oak-harmonised, 30% new. **Pinotage** ⊘ ⑦ ★★★★ Fruit-forward **18** ⑧④ comfortably styled with gentle tannins, attractive fresh berry fruit medley. **Shiraz** ⊘ ⑦ ★★★★ Entices with its rich black berries & spice flavours, downy feel & complementary oaking. **18** ⑧⑤ has enough body, freshness to benefit from a few years' ageing too. **Simplicity** ⊘ ⑦ ★★★★ Tasty trio, mainly shiraz with cab, merlot. **18** ⑧⑤ satisfying spice, plum, blackberry mix; savoury conclusion. Ripe, full bodied yet avoids heaviness thanks to fresh acidity, gentle grip. Also 375 ml. **Chardonnay** ⊘ ⑦ ★★★★ Bright lime & lemon fruit on lipsmacking **19** ⑧④ are just tempered by some creamy lees. Plenty to enjoy, more so after short settling. Small portion older-oak fermented.

. . . .

Kleine Rust range

. . . .

Chenin Blanc-Sauvignon Blanc ⑦ ★★★ Reliable blend, **19** ⑦⑨ has 18% sauvignon blanc. Plump & juicy tropical flavours lifted by few grams sugar & zesty acid. Also in 375 ml & 1.5L, as Pinotage-Shiraz. **Semi-Sweet** ⑦ ★★★ Lively grape & citrus flavours, mouthwatering juicy acids in chenin-based **19** ⑦⑨. Offers much more than 'semi-sweet' would suggest. Coastal WO.

. . . .

Pinotage-Shiraz ⊘ ★★★ Smooth, rich-fruited blend, **18** ⑦⑧ includes splash cinsaut. Older oak rounded. Fairtrade certified range. **Pinotage Rosé** ⊘ ★★★ Peachy-pink **19** ⑦⑨, ripe strawberry & cream juiciness, extended on crisp, fruity tail. — AL

Location/map: Stellenbosch ▪ Map grid reference: E7, C3 ▪ WO: Stellenbosch/Coastal ▪ Est/1stB 1928 ▪ Tasting & sales (Hberg & Btlry) Mon-Fri 10—5 Sat 10-3 ▪ Closed Ash Wed, Easter Fri-Mon, Ascension day, Dec 25/26 & Jan 1 ▪ Cellar tours by appt ▪ Farm-style platters & pre-arranged lunches/dinners ▪ BYO picnic ▪ Tour groups ▪ Grape stomping/make your own wine ▪ Gifts ▪ Conferences ▪ Weddings/functions (300+ pax) ▪ Walking/ hiking & MTB trails ▪ Art exhibition ▪ Owner(s) Stellenrust Family Trust ▪ Cellarmaster(s) Tertius Boshoff (Jan 2004) ▪ Winemaker(s) Herman du Preez (2014) ▪ Viticulturist(s) Kobie van der Westhuizen (Jan 2000) ▪ 200ha (cabs s/f, carignan, cinsaut, grenache noir, merlot, ptage, shiraz, chard, chenin, muscat d'A, sauv) ▪ 2,000t/300,000cs own label 50% red 40% white 10% rosé + 40,000cs for clients ▪ Other export brands: Pillar & Post, STELL, Stellenbosch Manor, Steynsrust, Xaro ▪ Brands for clients: Embrace, Lion's Pride, Ruyter's Bin, Sabi Sabi Private Game Lodge ▪ Fairtrade, HACCP, WIETA ▪ PO Box 26 Koelenhof 7605 ▪ info@stellenrust. co.za ▪ www.stellenrust.co.za ▪ S 33° 59' 18.0" E 018° 50' 57.9" (Helderberg) S 33° 51' 44.41" E 018° 46' 34.11" (Bottelary) ▪ ✉ spark.sailor.pancake, newness.realist.sessions ▪ **T +27 (0)21-880-2283**

Stellenview Premium Wines   ⑫

Started in 2015, this Stellenbosch-based company has had astonishing success, with a recent two-year growth from 200,000 to 500,000 cases, vinifying mainly brought-in fruit. The driving force behind Stellenview is Reino Kruger, cellarmaster, entrepreneur and marketer. Expansion into Asia, Russia and Africa accounts for some of the growth, but the real secret is understanding consumer needs. There are multiple and ever-expanding ranges (not all listed here), many unoaked reds for immediate drinkability, and wild-life-themed labels for a sense of Africanness. A number of awards confirm that it's not just clever marketing.

Stellenview Reserve range

Cabernet Sauvignon ★★★★ Cassis & black plums in **17** ⑧④, savoury tone another layer. Smooth textured, accessible, with ageing potential. Also-tasted **16** ⑧④ seems spicier, vanilla & nutmeg, the same plush fruit. Similar styling to Kruger sibling, same oak regime. **Shiraz** ★★★★ Spice array, dark fruit an equal partner, just enough tannin firmness in **16** (84) for ageing, food. Drinking easily & well, as befits the standard bearer. Stellenbosch WO this range & next.

Kruger Family Reserve range

Cabernet Sauvignon ★★★★ Longer oaking at this range level, 16 months, 30% new, as rest, without fruit sacrifice. **17** (84)'s cassis richness coats the tannins, but there's intrinsic power for a future. Meatier notes in also-tasted **16** (84), more savoury styling though good succulence & freshness. **Shiraz** ★★★★ Good quality progression from Great Five & Cape Five ranges, as for Cab. Plum/raspberry fruit, admirable intensity, **16** (84) resting on a savoury, spicy bed of tannins, supple, accessible. **Chardonnay** ★★★★ Second bottling of **16** (83), elegant & citrus toned, lemon/lime given good palate weight by lees contact. Dry & crisply fresh, ends savoury, Lemon Cream biscuit from time in barrel. **17** (83) tasted last edition also still available. **Sauvignon Blanc** (∅) ★★★ Early picked **17** (81), just 12.5% alcohol; lemon purity & zesty-fresh, some pear & mineral notes making it even more food friendly.

Cape Five Reserve range

Cabernet Sauvignon ★★★ Fully oaked, 10% new, as rest. **17** (82) has depth of flavour, fruit concentration, classic cassis, white pepper dustiness adding interest. Palate smooth, curvaceous. **Merlot** (∅) ★★★ More oak than Great Five sibling gives **16** (81) a meaty scent, notes of cloves/allspice, but the red berries are there in the flavours. Streamlined, nice freshness. **Pinotage** (∅) ★★★ Blueberries & mulberries, well-spiced **17** (81) has variety's trademark juicy palate, fresh & fruity, but a serious note in the tannins, firm but ripe, promising a future. **Shiraz** (∅) ★★★ Dark toned, there's opulence & ripeness in **15** (81); curvaceous body, nicely smooth. Marriage of vanilla-spiced oak & plummy fruit adds to the appeal. **Cape Premier Red** ★★★ Shiraz 60% with merlot, small portion unwooded, second bottling of **15** (81). It's all about spice & rich dark fruit, round, smooth & juicy, tannins fully integrated. **Red Reserve Organic** ★★★ Six-part blend of mainly shiraz, cab & merlot, **14** (82) seriously oaked, 36 months, 20% new, but enough ripe fruit flesh to handle it. Good body & length, ends savoury. Later bottling of **13** (82), also tasted this edition, mocha chocolate tones, tannins well partnered with plush fruit.

KFK Reserve range (NEW)

Pinotage ★★★ Fully oaked, older barrels, 10% new, as next. Pronounced mocha on **17** (79), dark plum fruit more evident in the flavours. Streamlined texture, tannins accessible. **Shiraz** ★★★ Plush-fruited **16** (79) is succulent, just enough oak for spicing, dry grip. Drinks well.

Great Five Reserve range

Cabernet Sauvignon ★★★ Small portion unoaked, as rest of range, fruit is king in these. Juicy & smooth cassis & fruitcake, attractive smokiness to **17** (81), especially in the flavours. Will make many friends. **Merlot** ★★★ Plumply ripe berries, a minty nuance, **17** (80)'s body sleek & welcoming. Drinks well. **Pinotage** ★★★ **17** (81) has an appealing fruit profile, blueberries, mulberries, well spiced by vanilla, the palate juicy & smooth. **Shiraz** ★★★ **16** (78) ripe-fruited, some meaty notes, smooth & round, ends savoury. **Cape Premier Red** ★★★ Shiraz & merlot 60/40 working well together in **16** (79) for fruit-driven early enjoyment. — CR

Location/map: Stellenbosch ▪ Map grid reference: D4 ▪ WO: Coastal/Stellenbosch ▪ Est/1stB 2015 ▪ Tasting, sales & cellar tours Mon-Fri 8-5 Sat/Sun by appt ▪ Closed all pub hols ▪ Owner(s) Reino Kruger ▪ Cellarmaster(s) Reino Kruger (Apr 2015) ▪ Winemaker(s) Monique Fourie (Jan 2018), Skye Nolan (Jan 2017) ▪ 12ha (cabs s/f, merlot, p verdot) ▪ 450t/500,000cs own label 80% red 20% white ▪ Other export brands: Africa Five, Cape Discovery, Openers, Pride of Kings, Top Five, Wild Instinct ▪ PO Box 7177 Stellenbosch 7599 ▪ info@stellenviewwines.com ▪ www.stellenviewwines.com ▪ S 33° 54' 0.61" E 018° 48' 23.49" ▪ 🖥 unique. pencils.kite ▪ **T +27 (0)87-152-0997/+27 (0)76-248-4739**

Stellenzicht Wines

This 218-ha Helderberg Mountain estate, long hailed for top-quality wine, was acquired in 2017 by Baron Hans von Staff-Reitzenstein, also co-owner of nearby Ernie Els Wines, and closed to the public while major rejuvenation takes place. The vineyards are being redeveloped and natural vegetation re-established in unplanted areas. The 1980s cellar has undergone significant upgrades, and the team is now focusing on creating a new tasting venue, set to open in early 2022. The new-look wines are due next year.

Location/map: Stellenbosch ▪ Map grid reference: F8 ▪ Est 1982 ▪ 1stB 1989 ▪ Tasting room closed for renovations - please phone ahead ▪ Owner(s) Stellenzicht Wines ▪ Winemaker(s) L'Re Burger, with Matthew Andersen ▪ Viticulturist(s) Nico Nortjé ▪ 218ha/55ha (cab, cinsaut, malbec, shiraz, sauv, viog) ▪ PO Box 7595 Stellenbosch 7599 ▪ info@stellenzichtwines.com ▪ S 33° 59' 50.0" E 018° 51' 59.8" ▪ 🗺 nozzles.drilling. pegged ▪ **T +27 (0)21-880-1103**

Stettyn Family Vineyards

This is the only winery in the recently demarcated Stettyn ward near Villiersdorp, its modern cellar supplied with grapes from four adjoining farms, all part of the original 18th-century farm Stettyn, named by the Botha family owners for their ancestral home, Stettin, in Prussia. Via a BEE partnership, Paarl's Adama Wines has a stakeholding in the venture, which supplies leading export brands including FirstCape.

Stettyn Family Vineyards range
Cabernet Sauvignon ⊘ ★★★★ Lightly wooded **17** ⑧⑧ represents excellent value with its soft texture, ripe black fruit, savoury hints of olive & smoked mussel. **Shiraz** ★★★ Less jammy than last, **17** ⑧② has Glühwein spice & black pepper aroma/finish framing fresh ripe blackcurrants on the palate.

Stettyn Cellar range
Chardonnay-Pinot Noir ⊘ ★★★ Rose gold **19** ⑧② a versatile food partner with tangerine & peach flavours as well as tangy cranberry from 30% pinot noir. Worcester WO. **Sauvignon Blanc** ★★★ Smooth **19** ⑧② refreshes with zesty lime & lemon, tangy granadilla & gooseberry flavours. Discontinued: **Reserve Straw Wine, Reserve Cape Vintage**.

Stone range
Not tasted: **Red**, **White**.

Signature range
Not tasted: **The Guardian**. — JG

Location: Villiersdorp ▪ Map: Worcester ▪ Map grid reference: A6 ▪ WO: Stettyn/Worcester ▪ Est 1964 ▪ 1stB 1984 ▪ Tasting & sales Mon-Fri 9–4.30 Sat (Oct-Apr) 10-1 ▪ Closed all pub hols ▪ Cheese platters ▪ Nursery ▪ Owner(s) 4 major producers (3 family owned), Glenrosa Vineyards (BEE partnership with Adama Wines) ▪ Cellarmaster(s) Albie Treurnicht (Nov 2000) ▪ Winemaker(s) Albie Treurnicht (Nov 2000), with JM Crafford (Nov 2012) ▪ Viticulturist(s) Pierre Snyman (VinPro) ▪ 400ha (cab, merlot, ptage, shiraz, chard, chenin, sauv) ▪ 7,500t/19,000cs own label 25% red 75% white ▪ Brands for clients: FirstCape ▪ ARA, BEE, HACCP, IPW, WIETA ▪ PO Box 1520 Worcester 6849 ▪ info@stettynwines.co.za ▪ www.stettynwines.co.za ▪ S 33° 52' 14.8" E 019° 22' 2.3" ▪ 🗺 exporting.trouble.solving ▪ **T +27 (0)23-340-4220**

☐ **Steynsrust** *see* Stellenrust
☐ **Steytler** *see* Kaapzicht Wine Estate
☐ **Stilfontein** *see* Eerste Hoop Wine Cellar

Stoep

Garagiste label Stoep is owned by SA asset manager Gerrit Mars and Swiss partners, and the blended Red produced with a contract winemaker. The current vintage has had one of the longest gestations in the entire guide, having been released in 2019 - on its 10th birthday! Untasted, but dare we say 'ready to drink'?

Location: Stellenbosch ▪ Est/1stB 2001 ▪ Tasting, sales & tours by appt ▪ Owner(s) Zelpy 1023 (Pty) Ltd: 3 shareholders Gerrit Mars (SA), Sven Haefner (Swiss) & Daniel Hofer (Swiss) ▪ Cellarmaster(s)/winemaker(s) André Liebenberg (Romond) & Gerrit Mars ▪ 50% red 50% white ▪ gerritmars@mweb.co.za ▪ **T +27 (0)82-352-5583**

☐ **Stofberg Family Vineyards** *see* Le Belle Rebelle
☐ **Stone** *see* Stettyn Family Vineyards

Stonebird Wines

Gavin Patterson has flown to the UK - with his amphora - to take up a winemaking job there. His vision for Stonebird ('a mythical birdlike creature' symbolising a connection to earth and nature) has always been to vinify grapes from rocky sites, whether in SA or the UK. So, while the vintage reported on here is the last for the time being, the plan remains to find further appropriate sites, sometime – whether here or there.

★★★★☆ **Pinot Noir** ⊛ From a rocky shale vineyard in Elgin. **17** ⑨① has varietal notes of raspberry, cherry, some undergrowth, all kept pure & focused by ferment & maturation in clay pots - the modestly firm tannin is all ex grapes, not oak. Balanced, fresh acidity. Should mature well.

★★★★☆ **Chardonnay** ⊛ Aromatic touches of liquorice, marzipan & stony earth over more typical yellow & white stonefruit & citrus. **17** ⑨③ ex Stanford Foothills & Upper Hemel-en-Aarde is poised & confident, with a real sense of precision - partly thanks to amphora fermentation/maturation. Fine lemony acid.

★★★★ **Gonzo** Ⓥ Why make, in a solera, fortified pinot noir with very ripe fruit & pinot husk spirit? Well, because it can interest like this **NV** ⑧⑨. It's bright, dry in effect (67 g/l sugar; 18% alcohol). Not complex but a little strange & very moreish. 375 ml. Walker Bay WO.— TJ

Location: Elgin ▪ WO: Cape South Coast/Walker Bay ▪ Est/1stB 2016 ▪ Owner(s)/winemaker(s) Gavin Patterson ▪ 450cs own label 46% red 46% white 8% fortified ▪ c/o Farm No. 7, Viljoenshoop Rd, Elgin 7180 ▪ gavin@stonebirdwines.com ▪ www.stonebirdwines.com

☐ **Stonedale** see Rietvallei Wine Estate
☐ **Stonedance** see Piekenierskloof Wine Company
☐ **Stone Ridge Wines** See Editor's Note
☐ **Stone Road** see Louisvale Wines
☐ **Stones in the Sun** see Dunstone Winery

Stonewall Wines   Ⓥ ⑪ ⊚

De Waal Koch's farm Happy Vale, close by the busy R44 between Stellenbosch and Somerset West, is probably the best advertisement for his boutique wine range, being a picture-perfect example of a heritage Cape winefarm, complete with gabled cellar, werf and ringmuur – white-washed stone perimeter wall already nearly 50 years old when the owner-winemaker's forebears took ownership in 1873.

★★★★ **Cabernet Sauvignon** Black forest fruits, spice & cherry on succulent **17** ★★★★ ⑧⑤. Like **16** ⑧⑥, good body & frame of dry oak (60% new, 18 months) but tad less length & definition. In 375 ml too.

★★★★ **Rubér** ⊘ As before, cab franc has top billing in **17** ⑧⑧ Bordeaux blend. Hedgerow fruit & cocoa appeal balanced by spicy dry wood (40% new, 18 months). Supple & textured. Some ageing potential.

Chardonnay Ⓥ ★★★ Oak-fermented & -aged **16** ⑧① ripe & rounded, ready to drink. — FM

Location/WO: Stellenbosch ▪ Map: Helderberg ▪ Map grid reference: C2 ▪ Est 1828 ▪ 1stB 1997 ▪ Tasting & sales by appt Mon-Fri 10—5 Sat 10—1 ▪ Closed Easter Fri-Sun, Dec 25/26 & Jan 1 ▪ Refreshments by appt ▪ Helderberg Wine Festival ▪ Owner(s) De Waal Koch ▪ Cellarmaster(s) Ronell Wiid (Jan 2000, consultant) ▪ Winemaker(s) De Waal Koch (Jan 2000) ▪ Viticulturist(s) De Waal Koch (Jun 1984) ▪ 90ha/70ha (cabs s/f, merlot, ptage, shiraz, chard, pinot gris, sauv) ▪ 300t/4,000cs own label 80% red 20% white ▪ PO Box 5145 Helderberg 7135 ▪ stonewall@mweb.co.za ▪ www.stonewallwines.co.za ▪ S 34° 1' 59.0" E 018° 49' 14.6" ▪ 🖽 resting.approximates.qualifying ▪ **T +27 (0)21-855-3675/+27 (0)83-310-2407**

Stony Brook   Ⓥ ⌂ ♿

The McNaught family, long-time Franschhoek vintners, produce an eclectic collection of wines from both classic and more uncommon varieties at their Stony Brook cellar and vineyard. Though using mainly local fruit, winemaker son Craig also sources from cooler Elgin and Walker Bay, as well as further afield for some notable varietal bottlings and equally accomplished blends. The McNaughts' self-catering cottages, with a grand valley view, provide a perfect place to explore the portfolio.

★★★★☆ **Ghost Gum** ⊛ As always, 100% cab from hand-sorted grapes. **15** ⑨③ blackcurrant & cocoa richness paving way on palate for graphite, thyme & savoury notes, firm tannin grip but well rounded, structured for decade or more. Like **14** ⑨③, seriousness underscored by 30 months in new French oak.

★★★★ **Pinot Noir** Ⓥ Vibrant & alluring **16** ⑧⑦'s sour black cherry enveloped in fine-textured tannin, sympathetic oaking (18 months, older barrels) adds depth, richness, on bone-dry finish.

★★★★☆ **Syrah Reserve** Appealing precision to the spice-laced plum, black cherry & leather notes on **16** (91), nutmeg & black tea nuances linger on finish, where tannins are dense but polished. More classic than **15** ★★★★ (89), which has 15% alcohol.

★★★★☆ **Ovidius** Tempranillo from Franschhoek, **16** (93) full in body & texture, with smoky wood notes & tobacco ex 60% new French oak, 26 months, over plum & cassis. A poised tannin structure, dried herb & cherry farewell.

★★★★☆ **The Max** 4-way Bordeaux blend, mostly cab, **16** (93) showing excellent integration & silkiness, ample charm in its mulberry & prune fruit, wood spice & soft acidity. Noticeably grippy tannins & serious oak (40% new, French, 28 months) for keepability.

★★★★ **SMV** Near-identical blend to **15** (88): shiraz & mourvèdre (53/45), splash viognier; **16** (87) medium body, with dusty tannins holding ebullient black cherry and raspberry fruit in check. Ends with hints of violet & salami.

★★★★ **Heart of the Lees** Unusual winemaking technique for Elgin sauvignon: bunch pressed & settled, lees then fermented in older wood. Only 2 barrels of **16** (89), leesy richness punctuated, lifted by zesty farewell. Excellent, involving, though not quite as impactful as **15** ★★★★☆ (90).

★★★★ **Sauvignon Blanc** Alluring & complex notes of melon, lime & kiwi, along with fig & greengage. **18** (88) vibrant, smooth & clean, leaves a lasting impression of freshness. Walker Bay WO.

★★★★☆ **Ghost Gum White** Like **17** (93) & previous, **18** (93) mostly chardonnay & splash semillon. Ripe fruit (pear & white peach) & custard pie richness abetted by vanilla & chamomile, but winemaker is aiming for fresher style, leaves 10% of wine unwooded, creating zesty citrus tone on palate, concluding on interesting saffron note.

★★★★ **The 'J'** Multi-region blend led by viognier with chenin, semillon, chardonnay & sauvignon, part barrel fermented. Floral, spicy & fruity **17** (87) light-tripping yet full of flavour. WO W Cape.

★★★★☆ **Lyle** Champagne-style brut sparkler from chardonnay, **14** (91) usual tiny barrel-fermented component & solera-aged reserve wine blended in before second ferment in bottle & remarkable 50 months on lees, giving brioche overlay to gorgeous citrus-scented, mineral-tinged bubbles.

Not tasted: **Cabernet Franc**. Occasional release: **Mourvèdre**, **Camissa**, **Snow Gum**. Discontinued: **V on A**. — GM

Location/map: Franschhoek ▪ Map grid reference: D1 ▪ WO: Franschhoek/Walker Bay/Elgin/Western Cape ▪ Est 1995 ▪ 1stB 1996 ▪ Tasting by appt ▪ Fee R50 ▪ Sales Mon-Fri 10–5 Sat 10-1; enquire about pub hols ▪ Self-catering cottages ▪ Owner(s) Nigel & Joy McNaught ▪ Winemaker(s) Craig McNaught (2011), with Michael Blaauw (Jan 2008) ▪ 23ha/14ha (cab, merlot, mourv, p verdot, pinot, shiraz, tempranillo, chard, sem, viog) ▪ 120t/8,000cs own label 65% red 35% white ▪ ISO 14001:2003 ▪ PO Box 22 Franschhoek 7690 ▪ info@stonybrook.co.za ▪ www.stonybrook.co.za ▪ S 33° 56' 28.7" E 019° 7' 4.1" ▪ annual.offsets.bushes ▪ **T +27 (0)21-876-2182**

Storm Wines

Terroirist Hannes Storm, who worked at Hamilton Russell Vineyards before going solo, is the only producer to offer single-vineyard pinot noirs from each of the three Hemel-en-Aarde wards. They're made in identical hands-off fashion in an unwaveringly classic and serious style, so their distinctive personalities and characters come only from their vineyard origins. This edition celebrates two vintages from each parcel, with both '17 and '18 Ignis achieving our highest accolade - 5 stars. Ignis, Latin for 'fire', alludes to the igneous rock formation underlying the vineyard and hence the wine's metaphorical journey from fire to stone to (stellar) liquid. Hannes' young pinot and chardonnay vines are 'doing well', and he's upgraded the boutique cellar (in Upper Hemel-en-Aarde) to enable more efficient, gravity processing. He'll also launch a new chardonnay, from the 2019 vintage, from a tiny parcel in the Ridge. Dare we anticipate a full house soon?

★★★★★ **Ignis Pinot Noir** The 3 Storm pinots treated identically in the cellar (except for 3% variance in new-oak portion) to express terroir. From more light-structured decomposed granite of Upper Hemel-en-Aarde, Ignis more fruit forward than siblings & thus more approachable in youth but with such precise acid tension it could easily prove the most long-lived. **18** (96) exceptional pure-fruited charm; long-lingering **17** (97) unshowy but similar honed athletic frame. Both 30% new wood. Also in magnum, like all the wines.

★★★★☆ **Vrede Pinot Noir** Hallmark fruity-savoury persistence, brooding intensity from bouquet to finish on Hemel-en-Aarde Valley offering. Compact body, latent power from clay-rich, low-vigour

Bokkeveld soil most noticeable on **17** (94); **18** (94) showing more of the vineyard's overt acid character. Both deserve 5+ years cellaring to deliver on potential. New oak 28% & 30% respectively. Natural ferment, as all the wines; unfined/filtered as all reds.

★★★★☆ **Ridge Pinot Noir** From clay-rich, low-crop Hemel-en-Aarde Ridge soil, this typically more unsettled in youth, all elements finely judged but needing year/2 to harmonise. **18** (94)'s black cherry & plum fruit brushed with savoury oak spice (28% new); **17** (94) (27% new) has a pleasant ferrous nuance.

★★★★☆ **Vrede Chardonnay** (Ⓐ) Has house's fine acidity, deft touch new oak (22%) & subtle flavours. **18** (93) more citrus toned than previous stonefruit & oatmeal; attractive oxidative notes & saline conclusion. Barrel fermented/aged 8 months on lees.— CvZ

Location: Hermanus • Map: Walker Bay & Bot River • Map grid reference: B4 • WO: Hemel-en-Aarde Valley/ Upper Hemel-en-Aarde Valley/Hemel-en-Aarde Ridge • Est 2011 • 1stB 2012 • Tasting by appt • Closed Easter Fri/Sun, Ascension day, Dec 25/26 & Jan 1 • Owner(s) Hannes Storm • Winemaker(s)/viticulturist(s) Hannes Storm (Dec 2011) • 6.5ha (pinot, chard) • 18t/1,400cs own label 80% red 20% white • IPW • PO Box 431 Hermanus 7200 • info@stormwines.co.za • www.stormwines.co.za • S 34° 21' 16.99" E 019° 16' 59.23" • excavating.vacuuming.flocked • **T +27 (0)28-125-0073**

Strandveld Wines   Ⓠ Ⓐ Ⓐ Ⓒ

Less than two decades back, before Strandveld was established as a collaborative venture among a group of friends, it was a neglected sheep farm. New plantings continue, testifying to the dynamism at this, Africa's most southerly winery. Viticulture is not easy in the wind-bitten, often misty conditions, but winemaker Conrad Vlok gets the distinctive grapes he wants. The range has now expanded with a fine, maiden grenache, which speaks of its cool maritime origins just as the sauvignons do. But Strandveld goes wider than wine: it is part of the Nuwejaars project, protecting the precious wetlands and their endemic populations.

Strandveld range

★★★★☆ **Grenache** (NEW) (Ⓐ) **18** (94) lighter in feeling than other reds, 25% wholebunch fermentation brightening the red berry notes, adding to spicy, white pepper fragrance. Succulent freshness, old-oaking & moderate tannic grip make it approachable early, but should gain in harmony. 14.2% alcohol.

★★★★ **Anders Sparrman Pinot Noir** (Ⓩ) Raspberry, cherry on **15** (88) lead to ripe, rich, sweetly fruited palate, with firm tannins. Tight, youthful; less charm & generosity than power. Needs time. Elim WO.

★★★★☆ **Syrah** Usual splash of viognier adding subtle aromatics on **16** (92). Riper, richer, bigger than FS version, balanced by firm structure with good acidity, the 35% new oak unobtrusively supportive. 14.8% alcohol taken in its stride. WO Cape Agulhas, as FS Pinot Noir & Sauvignon Blanc.

★★★★☆ **The Navigator** Half shiraz, with grenache, mourvèdre, viognier. Spicy & lively aromas announce **16** (92) as another very ripe, bold, richly generous red (14.5% alcohol), kept in trim by firm structure, including a decent acidity, & good oaking (third new).

★★★★☆ **Pofadderbos Sauvignon Blanc** (✓) (Ⓐ) Less obviously fruity aromas on **18** (93) than FS version, a little earthy even, adding to notes of citrus & blackcurrant. Intense, intriguing flavours with stony, bracing acid support. Should develop interestingly for a few years. WO Elim, as next two.

★★★★ **Adamastor** Oaked semillon leads sauvignon in **17** ★★★★☆ (92), unlike **16** (89) & earlier, adding hints of lemon & wax to sauvignon notes of blackcurrant, as well as weight & texture. Less exuberant than straight sauvignon, a touch more severe, accentuated by the partial oaking.

Skaamgesiggie Méthode Cap Classique (Ⓩ) ★★★★ Name aptly suggests a shy blush for this rosé sparkling from pinot noir - though the fruity charm of berries & red apple is not held back. **16** (85) dry, fresh, balanced & pleasing.

First Sighting range

★★★★ **Shiraz** (✓) Attractive, fresh aromas on **17** (86), with drops of other varieties as in **16** ★★★★ (84). Ripe but light-feeling; modest oaking supports easy balanced drinkability, but it has a useful grip.

★★★★ **Sauvignon Blanc** (✓) Delightful forward aromas of citrus & passionfruit on **18** ★★★★☆ (91), with a grassy note pointed by a few drops of nouvelle - there's also 10% semillon adding weight. Luscious, powerful acidity drives the flavourful palate. More complex & impressive than **17** (89).

Pinot Noir ⚲ ★★★ Fresh, modest aromas & lightish fruit on **15** ⑧②, with grippy acid, a tannic touch & some toasty oak notes. A little severe. **Rosé** ⊘ ★★★★ Dry, light (12.1% alcohol) **19** ⑧③ from grenache & shiraz. Less trivial than previous, more charming & elegant in its balance. — TJ

Location: Elim ▪ Map: Southern Cape ▪ Map grid reference: B3 ▪ WO: Cape South Coast/Elim/Cape Agulhas ▪ Est 2002 ▪ 1stB 2003 ▪ Tasting, sales & cellar tours Mon–Thu 8–5 Fri 8-4 Sat 10–3 ▪ Closed Good Fri, Dec 25 & Jan 1 ▪ Farm produce ▪ BYO picnic ▪ Walks/hikes ▪ MTB ▪ Conservation area ▪ Two self-catering cottages ▪ Owner(s) Strandveld Vineyards & Rietfontein Trust ▪ Winemaker(s) Conrad Vlok (Dec 2004) ▪ Viticulturist(s) Tienie Wentzel (Oct 2009) ▪ 64ha (grenache, mourv, pinot, shiraz, sauv, sem, viog) ▪ 280t/33,000cs own label 45% red 55% white ▪ IPW ▪ PO Box 1020 Bredasdorp 7280 ▪ info@strandveld.co.za ▪ www.strandveld. co.za ▪ S 34° 39' 59.2" E 019° 47' 26.8" ▪ 🖭 logbook.resentful.promise ▪ **T +27 (0)28-482-1902/6**

Strange Kompanjie
⚐

An offshoot of Wildeberg (UK-based wine company Boutinot's local venture) which grew out of existing wines and labels. As the name suggests, they will do things a little differently in South Africa. Their purpose is to champion underdog varieties, the unusual or unfashionable, producing wines that are of interest and presenting them in an engaging way to the consumer; the strange names are part of this story. The idea is also to have fun and experiment, even if 'mistakes are likely.'

★★★★ **Underworld Grenache Blanc** Unwooded to show off pure ripe citrus, fresh hay aromas; **18** ★★★★ ⑧⑤ fruit & weight emphasised by gram/2 sugar. Good solo & with spicy dishes, like **17** ⑧⑥.

Underworld Blend 3 🆕 ⊘ ⑦ ★★★★ Unusual, appetising grenache, durif, carignan, mourvèdre combo. **18** ⑧④ harmonious, rounded; not so complex but offers plenty savoury satisfaction. Great value.
Strange Bru Fernão Pires 🆕 ⑦ ★★★ Only varietal representative of this Portuguese white grape in the guide. **18** ⑧② lightish, gently refreshing, brightened by herby, spicy, quiet muscat tang. Pair with a warm summer's evening.

Mantlepiece Cinsault ⚲ ★★★★ Delicious ripe red fruit (strawberry & raspberry) on light & perfumed **17** ⑧④. Softest of tannins, zippy acidity, perfect summer red. Coastal WO, as Blend 3. **Strange Bru Ruby Cabernet** 🆕 ★★★ Generous, mouthfilling mix juicy red berries & wild herb notes on unoaked **18** ⑧②. Full body but soft tannins, balanced freshness offer immediate pleasure. Swartland WO, like next.
Wandering Beeste Syrah ⚲ ★★★ Appetising & enjoyable **17** ⑧② bright black fruit, supportive tannins, slight bitter twist at finish. **Tea Leaf Chenin Blanc-Palomino-Grenache Blanc** ⚘ ★★★★ Initial juicy peach attractions on **18** ⑧③ somewhat dimmed by still-assertive oak, bitter note on tail. May better harmonise with further few months. Natural ferment, French oak, 23% new. Not tasted: **On Reflection Chenin Blanc**. Discontinued: **Filigree Blanc de Blancs**. — AL

Location/map: Franschhoek ▪ Map grid reference: D1 ▪ WO: Western Cape/Coastal/Swartland ▪ Tasting, sales & cellar tours by invitation ▪ Closed all pub hols ▪ Owner(s) Wildeberg & Kompanjie ▪ Winemaker(s) Ryno Booysen & JD Rossouw ▪ 150t ▪ own label 50% red 50% white ▪ henrietteh@boutinot.com ▪ www.wildeberg.co.za ▪ S 33° 56' 13" E 019° 08' 03" ▪ 🖭 clubs.cheering.dust ▪ **T +27 (0)82-895-4111/+27 (0)72-605-9817**

☐ **String of Pearls** see Francois La Garde

Strydom Family Wine
⚐

Rianie Strydom, now an independent consultant for a couple of wineries after just over a decade establishing a stellar reputation for Helderberg's Haskell, is one half of this Simonsberg-Stellenbosch family venture (a hop and a skip away from Morgenhof where she started her illustrious career). The other half is husband Louis, MD and cellarmaster at another premium Helderberg property, Ernie Els. Having been 'moonlighting' here for the past decade, this talented, energetic couple (both Cape Winemakers Guild members and parents to three young adults) are thrilled to have Rianie 'dedicated full-time to our project'. While Louis continues to tend their own and leased vineyards, Rianie is busy renovating a tasting room and 'possible cellar facility'.
★★★★★ **Rex Cabernet Sauvignon** ⚘ Textbook cabernet, **16** ⑨④ from Helderberg vines. Dark forest fruit nuances mingle with graphite mineral & cedar whiffs from 18 months French oak, 30% new, effortlessly absorbed. Full body & poised structure, good now but will surely improve over at least a decade.

★★★★ **Rock Star Syrah** Delicious as ever, **16** (89) has pristine plum & mulberry fruit spiced with clove & nutmeg. Savoury palate has noticeable & malleable tannins, ends on a spicy note.

★★★★☆ **CWG Auction Reserve Paradigm** (★) Like last **12** (93), **16** (94) classic Bordeaux red headed by king cab (74%), attended by merlot & splashes cab franc & petit verdot. Elegant & sophisticated, dark berry generosity, cedar & spice notes from judicious oak, 40 new. Unified & well built, to keep for 10 years.

★★★★ **Danièle Chenin Blanc** Striking freshness of **18** (88) achieved by picking Helderberg grapes early; 2nd/later harvest delivers ripe fruit (pears, citrus). Subtle florality preserved by sparing old-oak use - just 50%, rest tank & amphora. As captivating, flavourful as **17** (88).

. . . .

Retro (🍇) ★★★★ Celebrates the traditional cab & cinsaut blend, with support from a little merlot. **17** (85) is super-juicy & smooth, with blueberry fruit & spicy farewell. Includes Robertson fruit.

. . . .

The Freshman (✓) ★★★★ Full of youth & vigour, as name suggests, **19** (84) Groenekloof sauvignon has bursts of tropical fruit & bright acidity, zingy kiwi & lime on finish. Grab sushi, chill & enjoy. — GM

Location: Stellenbosch ▪ WO: Stellenbosch/Western Cape ▪ Est 2012 ▪ 1stB 2009 ▪ Tasting by appt only ▪ Owner(s) Louis & Rianie Strydom ▪ Cellarmaster(s) Rianie Strydom ▪ 8.5ha (cab, shiraz) ▪ 1,000cs own label 70% red 30% white ▪ IPW ▪ PO Box 1290 Stellenbosch 7599 ▪ rianie@strydomvineyards.com ▪ www.strydomvineyards.com ▪ **T +27 (0)21-889-8553/+27 (0)82-290-6399**

──

☐ **Strydom Vintners** see Strydom Family Wine
☐ **Stubborn Man** see Pearl Mountain

──

Sumaridge Wines   (🍷) (🍴) (🏠) (📷) (👤) (♿)

British owners Simon Turner and wife Holly Bellingham set out to make a difference at this Upper Hemel-en-Aarde Valley farm, not only to staff welfare but also to the environment. They've succeeded admirably. The first Walker Bay-area producers to get WIETA ethical accreditation, they practise sustainable farming and have set aside close to a third of the property for fynbos conservation. There is much to interest visitors, like conference and wedding facilities, a restaurant and accommodation, nature trails, mountain biking and fishing. And it's child-friendly. Winemaker Walter Pretorius is gearing up for his fourth vintage in charge, ably assisted by an experienced team, so all is well on the wine front too.

★★★★ **Merlot** (🍷) With full dark-fruited ripeness, **16** (87) is curvaceous, confident, has much to give. Well spiced, some cocoa, rich chocolate notes from 18 months in barrel, tannins firm but accessible.

★★★★☆ **Pinot Noir** (🍷) Elegant & balanced **13** (94), freshness, malleable tannins, spice & earthy notes adding to the drinking pleasure now & at least 5 years to come. Like **12** ★★★★★ (97), needs time to develop. Also in 1.5 & 3L.

★★★★ **Pinotage** (🍷) Care lavished, half wild ferment, 18 months French barriques, 30% new, **15** (88) shows ripe plum/prune ripeness, dusting of sweet spice, supple tannins. Handsome, loads of personality.

★★★★ **Syrah** (🍷) Complex savoury, white pepper & spice aromas, modest 12.6% alcohol, **13** (88) ripe yet not jammy, tannins still chewy after 2 years 25% new oak, some Hungarian.

★★★★ **Bushell** (🍷) Merlot leads, with cab franc, malbec, **15** (86)'s 15 months French/Hungarian oak giving cocoa styling, allspice/clove savoury spicing, solid bed of tannin. Deep, dark & dense in an interesting way.

★★★★ **Epitome** (🍷) Cape Blend **11** (89), shiraz & 48% pinotage, the former dominates & gives opulent spice, merging well with the bramble fruit, elegant tannins. Fine follow-up to **10** ★★★★★ (91).

★★★★☆ **Chardonnay** (🍷) Opulent **15** (92) seduces with roasted almond, oatmeal & fresh honey, crisp acidity keeps creamy palate in check, sympathetic oak (30% new) allows flinty-fresh fruit to shine.

★★★★ **Sauvignon Blanc** Cool-climate expression in bone-dry **18** (89), sage leaf & intense passionfruit, with minerality appearing in the flavours & finish. Vibrantly alive, lovely nervous tension.

★★★★ **Klip Kop** (✓) Mainly sauvignon, the 16% semillon fermented in older oak, adds oatmeal savouriness to **18** (89)'s layers. Fruit a strong focus, bright & pure, sparked by racy acidity. Minerality to finish. Walker Bay WO, like Tara & Bushell.

★★★★ **Maritimus** (🍷) Intended for site expression & ageing, natural-ferment **13** (89) is 45% sauvignon with chardonnay & semillon. Intriguing savoury seaweed nuance, zesty acidity, touch oak adds palate weight. Similar profile to **12** ★★★★★ (90). Also in 1.5 & 3L.

★★★★ **The Wayfarer** ⓥ Not discontinued as we thought, cerise-coloured berry-rich **15** ★★★★ ⑧③ MCC sparkling also has herbal top notes, presenting variety-true character. Dry, elegant, touch of oak, could do with more freshness. From pinot noir, like last-tasted **10** ⑧⑦.

Tara Rosé ⓥ ★★★★ Mainly merlot for its red berries but also malbec & cab franc, giving **19** ⑧③ more serious dimensions, slate, a touch of fynbos. Nice food wine. — CR

Location: Hermanus ▪ Map: Walker Bay & Bot River ▪ Map grid reference: B4 ▪ WO: Upper Hemel-en-Aarde Valley/Walker Bay ▪ Est 1997 ▪ 1stB 2000 ▪ Tasting & sales daily 11—5 ▪ Tasting fee applicable, waived on purchase ▪ Closed Dec 25 & Jan 1 ▪ Seasonal tasting platters and soups available plus kiddies platters ▪ Facilities for children ▪ Tour groups ▪ Conferences ▪ Weddings ▪ Luxury self-catering lodge ▪ Conservation area ▪ Extensive nature trails ▪ Mountain biking ▪ Bass & fly fishing by arrangement ▪ Owner(s) Holly & Simon Bellingham-Turner ▪ Winemaker(s) Walter Pretorius (Jul 2013), with Reginald Maphumulo (Jun 2000) ▪ Viticulturist(s) Petrus Bothma (Jul 2017) ▪ 210ha/35ha (cab f, malbec, merlot, ptage, pinot, shiraz, chard, sauv, sem) ▪ 150t/20,000cs own label 45% red 50% white 5% rosé ▪ IPW, WIETA ▪ PO Box 1413 Hermanus 7200 ▪ info@sumaridge.co.za ▪ www.sumaridge.co.za ▪ S 34° 22' 1.6" E 019° 15' 18.6" ▪ 🔲 phrased.seating. incurring ▪ **T +27 (0)28-312-1097**

Summerhill Wines   ⓠ ⑪ ⓞ

Much that's new at Charles Hunting's vineyards and cellar at the foot Simonsberg Mountain near Stellenbosch: consultant winemaker Lola Nicholls, whose own boutique winery, Mitre's Edge, is based a few farms down the road; vines, as part of a continuing replanting programme; and a farm dam, hopefully filling up nicely after the drought-relieving rains. The cellardoor remains welcoming and on trend, with Sir Thomas Brewing Co handcrafting beer and a pizzeria also on the premises.

Merlot ⓃⒺⓦ ★★★ Good intensity of berry fruit on **17** ⑧⓪, chocolate coating from French oak ageing, 5% new (as next), easygoing but warm (15.7% alcohol). **Shiraz** ⓃⒺⓦ ★★★ Lively blackberries & brambles mingle with spice on savoury & juicy **17** ⑧②. Friendly & moreish, with good tannin grip. **Chenin Blanc** ★★★ Misses a touch of the generosity of previous, **19** ⑧⓪ some tropical notes, leanish body & firm acidity. Not tasted: **Rosé**. — WB

Location/map/WO: Stellenbosch ▪ Map grid reference: E3 ▪ 1stB 2008 ▪ Tasting & sales Mon-Thu 9-4.30 Fri 9-2 ▪ Private tastings in manor house by appt; or anytime at the brewery ▪ Closed all pub hols ▪ Pizzeria ▪ Craft beer & gin ▪ Owner(s) Summerhill Wines cc, Charles R Hunting ▪ Winemaker(s) Lola Nicholls (Mitre's Edge) ▪ Viticulturist(s) Paul Wallace (consultant) ▪ 15ha/10ha (cab, grenache, malbec, merlot, pinot, shiraz, chard, chenin) ▪ 24t/2,500cs own label 40% red 60% white ▪ PO Box 12448 Die Boord 7613 ▪ charles@ summerhillwines.co.za, manager@summerhillwines.co.za ▪ www.summerhillwines.co.za ▪ S 33° 52' 57.71" E 018° 50' 49.39" ▪ 🔲 comfort.twist.veered ▪ **T +27 (0)21-889-5015**

☐ **Sumsaré Wines** See Editor's Note
☐ **Suo** see Aslina Wines

Super Single Vineyards   ⓠ

Just off the original wagon route between Cape Town and Stellenbosch, in what's now Stellenboschkloof, is family farm Canettevallei, home to Daniël de Waal. From here, he seeks out special parcels, mainly older, always intriguing for the Pella range. And, more than 300 km away in Sutherland, at 1,500 metres in elevation, he sources the Mount Sutherland wines. Since working in Italy's Antinori cellars in 1993, Daniël has been hunting for the perfect pocket of sangiovese. He's found his thrill - on Bottelary Hill, a stone's throw away.

Pella Coastal Wines

★★★★☆ **Granietbult Cabernet Sauvignon** ⓥ Svelte **14** ⑨③ announced by ripe dark berries judiciously scented with new French oak (40%). Sleek, sweet-fruited length with complementary tailored tannins for requisite ageing.

★★★★ **Oukliprant Malbec** Spicy **17** ⑧⑧ continues form of last **14** ⑧⑨. Dry oak tannin (22% new, 18 months) stands up to juicy blue & black fruit, counters bright acidity too. Small dab (10%) cab in the mix.

★★★★ **Verlatenkloof Merlot** 15 ★★★★ ⑧④ lighter & less concentrated than last-tasted **13** ⑧⑨. Hedgerow fruit, herb & spice less abundant but gentleness remains. 10% cab used again.

★★★★☆ **Thomas Se Dolland Pinotage** 16 ⑨⓪ continues where **14** ⑨⓪ ended: well-fruited but not fruity, with integrated oak (35% new, 18 months). Appealing balance & concentration on nuanced, savoury palate. No **15**.

★★★★ **Die Hang Sangiovese** ⑭ⓔⓦ Confident debut of bright cherry-toned **16** ⑧⑨, with trademark dry, Italianate tannic grip. Agile & pliable, only seasoned oak used (18 months). Bottelary fruit.

★★★★☆ **Family Reserve** ⓐ Brambly dark hedgerow fruit on **15** ⑨② cab-driven blend with merlot (15%). Structured, broad, with squeeze of fine tannin courtesy 18 months older French oak (30% new) yet succulently rewarding. Patient cellaring will further improve enjoyment. No **14**.

★★★★ **Kanniedood Chenin Blanc** Creamy oatmeal & succulent softness on **18** ⑧⑥, echoing the marzipan, honeycomb richness of also-tasted **17** ⑧⑥, both from 30+ year Stellenbosch single block. Lighter, less concentrated than **16** ★★★★☆ ⑨③ ex Swartland. Juicy & bright, just 25% new oak used.

Mount Sutherland Continental Wines

★★★★ **Nebbiolo** ⓛ Maiden crop from high-lying vineyards, just 1 t/ha. **14** ⑧⑦ much to like, if unusually approachable in its attractive floral aromas, savoury fruit & close tannin weave. Older oak.

★★★★ **Pinot Noir** ⓛ Exciting **15** ⑧⑦ bunch-fermented for fruit focus, older French oak matured. **15** ⑧⑦ still harmonising mid-2017, needed time to reveal underlying dark fruit richness.

★★★★☆ **Ouberg Syrah** ⓛ From older of the two syrah blocks, planted 6,000 vines/ha. **13** ⑨③ has cool precision, lithe feel, if yet to reveal full array of its lifted spice & dark berry concentration. Judicious oaking, 20% new, adds a little plushness but not at expense of firm, emphatically dry conclusion.

★★★★☆ **Syrah** ⓐ Stellar **16** ★★★★★ ⑨⑤ improves on **15** ⑨③ in purity & complexity. Textured, dry yet lithe, signature pepper keeping ripe dark fruit in check. Restrained oak (none new) matched by 18 months bottle ageing. Poised & elegant, with savoury finish. Sutherland-Karoo WO, as all these.

★★★★☆ **Tempranillo** ⓛ Cool purity & depth of character in splendid **15** ⑨③. Full bodied yet unheavy, silky texture, spice & tobacco features lifted by fresh, fine tannins. Memorably long. French oak enhanced, 20% new. Straddles modern/traditional styling. **14** ★★★★ ⑧⑧ bigger, more tannic.— FM

Location/map: Stellenbosch ▪ Map grid reference: C5 ▪ WO: Stellenbosch/Sutherland-Karoo ▪ Est/1stB 2004 ▪ Tasting Mon-Sat 10-5 ▪ Closed all pub hols ▪ Owner(s)/viticulturist(s) Daniël de Waal ▪ Winemaker(s) Daniël de Waal, with Kyle Zulch (also marketing/sales) ▪ 60ha Canettevallei farm ▪ (cab, malbec, nebbiolo, ptage, pinot, sangio, shiraz, tempranillo, chenin, riesling) ▪ 2,000cs own label 80% red 20% white ▪ PO Box 89 Vlottenburg 7604 ▪ marketing@ssvineyards.co.za ▪ www.supersinglevineyards.co.za ▪ S 33° 56' 29.73" E 018° 45' 15.20" ▪ ⓜ arrived.reply.master ▪ **T +27 (0)72-200-5552 (Daniël)/+27 (0)82-556-0205 (Kyle)**

Surfing Vintners

Wine-makers, -marketers and viticulturists gather for the annual Vintners Surf Classic to not only ride the waves but donate 50L of wine, blended at Grangehurst in Stellenbosch to create a 'benevolent causes' wine. Proceeds from sales go to non-profit Surf4Life, which welcomes disadvantaged folk into the surfing family.

★★★★ **Big Red** ⓛ Red & black berry fruit & gentle squeeze of dry, fine tannin, **15** ⑧⑥ has subtle density & body with long, rewarding finish. Near-equal cab, pinotage, shiraz in magnum only.— FM

Location: Stellenbosch ▪ WO: Coastal-Cape South Coast ▪ Est/1stB 2000 ▪ Closed to public ▪ Winemaker(s) various, led by Jeremy Walker, Gunter Schultz & Miles Mossop ▪ 700 magnums own label 100% red ▪ PO Box 206 Stellenbosch 7599 ▪ jeremy@grangehurst.co.za ▪ **T +27 (0)21-855-3625**

☐ **Survivor** *see* Overhex Wines International
☐ **Sutherland** *see* Thelema Mountain Vineyards
☐ **Sutherland Continental** *see* Super Single Vineyards
☐ **Swallow** *see* Natte Valleij Wines

Swallow Hill Single Vineyard Wine Estate 🅀 🍴 🏠

Di and Brian Dawes' boutique winery in Greyton looks across their modest hectarage of viognier and tempranillo vines to the Riviersonderend mountains. The organically tended vineyards suffered from three years of drought — a sad explanation for the lack of offerings this year.

Location: Greyton ▪ Map: Southern Cape ▪ Map grid reference: A1 ▪ Est 2009 ▪ 1stB 2013 ▪ Tasting, sales & cellar tours by appt only ▪ Tapas & tasting ▪ Open between Oct to May (inclusive) for lunch (2 pax/more) & dinner (4 pax/more) - booking essential ▪ Conservation area ▪ Farm stay: en suite guest room (2 pax) ▪ Owner(s) Di & Brian Dawes ▪ Cellarmaster(s) John Brian Dawes ▪ Winemaker(s) Di Dawes, with John Brian Dawes ▪ Viticulturist(s) Di & John Brian Dawes ▪ 21ha/2ha (tempranillo, viog) ▪ 2t own label 50% red 50% white ▪ IPW, SAWIS ▪ PO Box 299 Greyton 7233 ▪ wine@swallowhill.co.za ▪ www.swallowhill.co.za ▪ S 34° 6' 10.10" E 019° 36' 35.46" ▪ ⓜ searchable.fortify.outsold ▪ T +27 (0)82-423-9634

☐ **Swallows' Tale** see Trizanne Signature Wines
☐ **Swanepoel Wines** see Oude Compagnies Post Private Cellar

Swartberg Wingerde (NEW)

The eminent Rudiger Gretschel is production director for major wine company Vinimark and cellarmaster at top-league Reyneke. But, he says modestly, it's taken '18 years of working with vineyards and wine to have finally gained the necessary experience to make a wine under my own brand'. The vines for it are on the high-lying Swartberg farm owned by Jurgens Hanekom in Piekenierskloof, and farmed 'holistically'. Grapes are taken to Stellenbosch for vinification. Apart from the pinotage block, there's a vineyard of mixed white varieties, from which we also hope to see a wine soon.

★★★★☆ **Sangiro** ⓐ Perfumed pure-fruit charm on **17** ⑨③ pinotage, also herbs, fynbos. Natural ferment, older oak, 13.2% alcohol. Ripe but elegant, firm lithe tannins; tight & compact; good dry finish. Interestingly, successfully placed between modern lighter, fresher style & traditional bigness.— TJ, CvZ

Location: Stellenbosch ▪ WO: Piekenierskloof ▪ Est/1stB 2017 ▪ Closed to public ▪ Owner(s) Swartberg Wingerde (Pty) Ltd ▪ Cellarmaster(s)/winemaker(s) Rudiger Gretschel (2017) ▪ Viticulturist(s) Jurgens Hanekom ▪ 1,000ha/2.5ha (ptage, chenin, palomino, sauv) ▪ 300cs own label 80% red 20% white ▪ rudiger@swartbergwingerde.co.za

☐ **Swartland Stories** see Pulpit Rock Winery

Swartland Winery 🅀 📷 🅰 ♿

Established in 1948, this substantial winery based on the outskirts of Malmesbury has 60 producer-owners and 2,689 ha of vineyards. That includes mature unirrigated bushvines, a particular feature of one range. The wines are diverse, with classic varieties, local focus, and a number of traditional fortifieds. At multi-level price points, they're widely distributed locally and abroad. The winery's ability to vinify special batches separately allows the expression of terroir, contributing to a reputation for reflecting and promoting the area.

Idelia range

★★★★ **Cape Blend** Ex 40 year old dryland bushvines, pinotage with cab & shiraz. **17** ★★★★★ ⑨⓪ reflects best of those & winemaking care: intense berries vanilla-spiced from new oak, silky mouthfeel, tannins perfectly judged for backbone. Improves on **15** ⑧⑧, no **16**.

Bush Vine range

Chenin Blanc ⓥ ★★★★ Quintessential chenin, **18** ⑧④'s quince & melon given intensity, focus by old bushvines. Partial oaking a harmonious savoury layer; mouthfilling, finishes long.

Cabernet Sauvignon ★★★★ Spice from 12 months in barrel (as all these reds) shows as dark chocolate in **17** ⑧④, black plum fruit subservient but still attractive. Smooth-textured, balanced. **Pinotage** ★★★★ Liquorice & dark fruit, **17** ⑧④ promises richness & succulence, delivers with ease. From barrels, spice notes & supple structure. **Syrah** ★★★★ Full-ripe in flavour but **17** ⑧④ isn't chunky, has an attractive smooth-textured body, fleshy vibrancy.

Reserve range

Limited Selection Cabernet Sauvignon-Merlot ⚲ ★★★ Occasional release. Equal blend, half barrel-matured, rest staves, **17** ⑧① nicely combines piquant berries & savoury notes. Drinks smoothly. Not tasted: **Pinotage, Cabernet Sauvignon-Merlot**.

Winemakers Collection

. . . .

Merlot ⊘ 🍷 ★★★ Berry concentration & appealing plushness, **18** ⑧① has tannin grip at the end, adding a serious note. **Syrah** ⊘ 🍷 ★★★ Unmistakably syrah, **18** ⑧② offers smoky dark fruit, hints of underbrush, appealing succulence. **Tinta Barocca** ⊘ 🍷 ★★★ Unoaked, as rest of these reds, piquant hedgerow berries add lift & interest to **18** ⑧①'s smooth, streamlined body. **Sauvignon Blanc** ⊘ 🍷 ★★★ Offering purity & citrus zest, **19** ⑧⓪ delivers the tangy freshness one expects from good sauvignon. **White Jerepigo** 🍷 ★★★★ Uncommon grenache blanc for latest fortified **NV** ⑧③ (last was chenin), but the pleasure remains. Intense nectarine scent & flavour, full-sweet without cloy. Serve well-chilled & watch the faces.

. . . .

Cabernet Sauvignon ⚲ ★★★ Succulent berries & plums, **17** ⑧① is cab at its friendly, early-drinking best. **Pinotage** ⊘ ★★★ In contrast to Bush Vine version, **18** ⑧⓪ made for earlier drinking; succulent black fruit, touch of liquorice. **Dry Red** ⊘ ★★★ Bargain-priced **NV** ⑦⑨ from equal cab/merlot for smooth dark-fruited enjoyment. **Blanc de Noir** ⊘ ★★★ From pinotage, light-textured **19** ⑦⑦'s fruit gum flavours make for easy, flavourful quaffing. WO W Cape, as Bouquett. **Chardonnay** ⊘ ★★★ Unwooded, dry **19** ⑧⓪ has fresh-fruity appeal, zesty & bright, food friendly & for solo enjoyment. **Chenin Blanc** ★★★ Contrasting with its Bushvine sibling, dry **19** ⑦⑧ is unoaked, with pear & grapefruit tones. **Bouquett** ⊘ ★★★ Mainly chenin (70%) but **19** ⑦⑧ has enough muscat d'Alexandrie effect to justify the name. Grapey & semi-sweet. WO W Cape, as next 2. **Natural Sweet Sparkling Rosé** ⊘ ★★★ Appley top note to **NV** ⑦⑦ from pinotage, but the rest is about berries, sweet & lively. Friendly 10.5% alcohol. **Cuvée Brut** ★★★ Apple & pear freshness in latest sparkling **NV** ⑦⑦ from sauvignon, fruity dry finish. **Hanepoot** ★★★ Tastes like liquidised sultanas, latest **NV** ⑧① fortified is full-sweet & mouthfilling. **Red Jerepigo** ★★★ Ruby cab in latest fortified **NV** ⑧① (last was pinotage) giving it appealing red berry/cherry piquancy, mediumweight structure. **Cape Ruby** ⊘ ★★★ **NV** ⑧① has the scrub & fruitcake character touriga brings to 'port', with sleek lines & appealing sweetness. No oak. WO W Cape.

Contours Collection

Not tasted: **Merlot, Merlot-Cabernet Sauvignon, Chenin Blanc, Moscato, Sauvignon Blanc**.

D' Vine range

Not tasted: **Cabernet Sauvignon-Merlot, Rosé, Chenin Blanc-Sauvignon Blanc**. — CR

Location: Malmesbury ▪ Map: Swartland ▪ Map grid reference: C7 ▪ WO: Swartland/Western Cape ▪ Est/1stB 1948 ▪ Tasting & sales Mon-Thu 9-5 Fri 9–4 Sat 9–2 Sun closed ▪ Closed Easter Fri/Sun, Dec 25/26 & Jan 1 ▪ Facilities for children ▪ Tour groups ▪ Farm produce ▪ Owner(s) 60 producers ▪ Wine coordinator Marius Prins ▪ Viticulturist(s) Claude Uren (Nov 2010) ▪ 2,689ha (cab, malbec, merlot, ptage, shiraz, chard, chenin, sauv) ▪ 20,000t 38% red 55% white 5% rosé 2% sparkling ▪ BRC, IFS, IPW, WIETA ▪ PO Box 95 Malmesbury 7299 ▪ susan@swwines.co.za ▪ www.swartlandwinery.co.za ▪ S 33° 27' 12.7" E 018° 45' 17.7" ▪ ⚞ footfalls.purring. checking ▪ **T +27 (0)22-482-1134**

☐ **Sweet Darling** see Darling Cellars
☐ **Swepie Selection** see Domein Doornkraal
☐ **Swerwer** see JC Wickens Wines

SylvanVale Vineyards   ⚲ 🍴 🏠 📷 ⚥ ♿

Though luxurious and picturesque Devon Valley Hotel has its own vines, the house-label wines served to guests are produced by consultants elsewhere in Stellenbosch. The Ghost Tree line-up has been tweaked, and both ranges are getting informative new back labels.

Ghost Tree range

Three Colours Red ★★★ Now a cab/merlot (52/48) blend (last was pinotage). **16** ⑧② earth, berry & bitter chocolate flavours & brush of tannin afford satisfying drinkability with a barbecue. **Three Colours**

White ★★★ Smooth, unoaked chardonnay, **17** ⑦⑨ showing bottle age, honeyed citrus nuances. Shade off previous chenin. Discontinued: **Bristle White**.

SylvanVale range

Cape Blend Rosé ★★★ Light (12.5%), savoury & smooth, with a piquant twist, **17** ⑧② flavoursome sunset tipple from pinotage & 3 other reds plus splash chenin. — MW

Location/map/WO: Stellenbosch ▪ Map grid reference: D4 ▪ Est 1997 ▪ 1stB 1998 ▪ Tasting & sales daily 11-7 ▪ Open pub hols ▪ Flavours Restaurant: 120 seater; Vineyard Terrace; Cedarwood Bar & Lounge ▪ The Devon Valley Hotel: 50 rooms ▪ Facilities for children ▪ Tour groups ▪ Conferences ▪ 6 banqueting venues (max capacity 98 pax) ▪ Walking/hiking trails ▪ Gin, whisky & craft beer tastings 12-8 daily ▪ Owner(s) Alan Louis Trust ▪ Viticulturist(s) Lorna Hughes (1997, consultant) ▪ 8ha/4.3ha (cab, ptage, chenin) ▪ PO Box 68 Stellenbosch 7599 ▪ info@sylvanvale.com ▪ www.sylvanvale.com ▪ S 33° 54' 12.5" E 018° 48' 57.7" ▪ 🖵 trails. square.recover ▪ T +27 (0)21-865-2012

□ **Taaibosch** *See Editor's Note*

Taillard Family Wines   ⓥ ♿

At the time of going to print, the Taljaard family's Voor Paardeberg property Kersfontein, growing grapes for Pieter and daughter Anelise's Taillard wines, was in the process of being sold. The intention remains to continue production of the Taillard and Lobola ranges, assisted by winemaker Hugo Truter, using alternative grape sources and cellar facilities.

Taillard Premiere Collection

★★★★ **Pinotage Reserve** ⓥ Whiffs of raspberry freshen **16** ⑧⑦'s dark fruit features, as do old oak & firm tannic structure though perhaps touch more acidity would bring real balance. **15** untasted.

★★★★ **Watershed** ⓥ Toned Bordeaux blend cab (40%), equal cab franc & merlot. Like **14** ⑧⑦, **15** ★★★★½ ⑨⓪ least overt wine here. Classic cedar & graphite introduce svelte palate displaying precise balance, supple tannins, integrated oak.

★★★★ **Chenin Blanc Reserve** Big, bold **18** ⑧⑥ in peaches-&-cream style, oozes ripe quince preserve, vanilla oak from year 80% new barrels, all amplified by oxidative notes. Serious if not subtle. **17** not tasted.

Lobola range

★★★★ **Beau Rouge** Accessible, but far from cheap-&-cheerful 75/25 cab & shiraz blend. Dark-berried **16** ⑧⑥ full, rich flavour, juicy tannins in ripe house style, 14.5% alcohol warms the finish.

Discontinued: **Belle Blanc**.

Miner range

★★★★ **Cabernet Sauvignon** ⊘ Bulges with black berries in ample, ripe style. Perhaps in need of more balance, restraint, but **16** ⑧⑥ will have many fans. No new oak.

Bedrock Merlot ⓥ ★★★★ Savoury meat-spice tones of **16** ⑧⑤ somewhat leaven rather stern, tarry tannins that mask more delicate fruit in youth. **Bullion Pinotage** ⓥ ★★★★ Pleasingly less ebullient than some earlier versions, **16** ⑧⑤ is plum fruited, with measured tannins & alcohol. **Deep Level Shiraz** ⓥ ★★★★ Improved **15** ⑧③ is savoury & tasty, with leather notes, succulent flavourful palate & slightly dry tannins. **Gully Chenin Blanc** ⓥ ★★★★ Fresh & fruity **18** ⑧⑤, short sojourn in old oak adds breadth for more serious quaffing. **Prospectors Seekers Red** ★★★★ Fortified dessert with relatively high sugar & low alcohol, **NV** ⑧⑤ from traditional port varieties & pinotage. Last was cabernet. WO W Cape. — DS

Location/map: Paarl ▪ Map grid reference: C1 ▪ WO: Paarl/Western Cape ▪ Tasting, sales & tours by appt ▪ Closed all pub hols ▪ Owner(s) Pacas Winery (Pty) Ltd (Pieter Taljaard) ▪ Cellarmaster(s)/winemaker(s) Hugo Truter (2018) ▪ Viticulturist(s) Morné van Greunen (Feb 2009) ▪ ±44ha (cabs s/f, merlot, p verdot, ptage, shiraz, chenin) ▪ 1,000cs own label 80% red 20% white ▪ IPW ▪ PO Box 7274 Noorder-Paarl 7623 ▪ admin@taillardwines.com ▪ www.taillardwines.com ▪ S 33° 35' 22.5" E 018° 52' 45.0" (VP) ▪ 🖵 tofu.mobiles. interlaced ▪ T +27 (0)21-869-8384

□ **Taillefert** *see* Cape Wine Company
□ **Talent & Terroir** *see* Boland Cellar
□ **Tall Horse** *see* DGB (Pty) Ltd

Tamboerskloof Wine – Kleinood Farm

Prominent winery engineer Gerard de Villiers' boutique winery reposes on an idyllic farm named 'Small & Precious' between high-profile neighbours in Stellenbosch's Blaauwklippen Valley, handcrafting small quantities of Rhône-inspired wine from own vineyards in a technically advanced cellar. Winemaker Reynie Oosthuizen has completed his first vintage there and declares himself well satisfied with the results.

★★★★☆ Syrah ⓐ Elegantly wrought **16** ⑨③ has spicy damson & maraschino cherry fruit core cosseted in sleek tannins. Complex, layered aromas mingle with meaty, savoury notes, all in serene harmony. Splashes mourvèdre & viognier; 18 months in oak, 15% new. Also in magnums.

★★★★ Katharien Syrah Rosé Charming strawberry & raspberry characters in dry, well-textured **19** ⑧⑥, with hint of tannic grip, loads of appeal. Retasted **18** ⑧⑥ similar, showing smoothness from time in bottle.

★★★★☆ Viognier Exquisite layers of ripe peach & spicy baked apple, borne on rich leesy texture, elevate **19** ⑨① & also-tasted **18** ⑨① well above **17** ★★★★ ⑧⑥. 15% roussanne, mix of older oak, concrete 'egg' & tank.

Not tasted: **John Spicer Syrah**. — GdB

Location/map/WO: Stellenbosch ▪ Map grid reference: F7 ▪ Est 2000 ▪ 1stB 2002 ▪ Tasting, sales & cellar tours Mon-Thu by appt; Fri (except pub hols) open from 10-2; open first Sat of every month ▪ Closed all pub hols ▪ Olive oil ▪ Tree identification route ▪ Owner(s) Gerard & Libby de Villiers ▪ Winemaker(s) Reynie Oosthuizen (Oct 2018), with Julio Engelbrecht (Jan 2008) ▪ Viticulturist(s) Reynie Oosthuizen (Oct 2018) ▪ 22ha/10ha (mourv, shiraz, rouss, viog) ▪ 100t/8,500cs own label 70% red 7% white 23% rosé ▪ IPW ▪ PO Box 12584 Die Boord 7613 ▪ office@kleinood.com ▪ www.kleinood.com ▪ S 33° 59' 42.6" E 018° 52' 14.8" ▪ 🖃 stuns.lion.case ▪ T +27 (0)21-880-2527

Tanagra Winery & Distillery

On their McGregor farm, German owners Anette and Robert Rosenbach focus on single-vineyard wines and spirits made with minimal interference. The drought has shown them which vineyards cope best (cab franc, shiraz and colombard) and which ones struggle (merlot in particular). 'This year the plan is to strengthen the vines by improving soil structure (more mulching, adding gypsum to remove salts, etc).' They're also expanding their distillery to cater for 'growing customer demands'.

Tanagra range

★★★★ Cabernet Franc ⓐ Floral edge to refined, serious **16** ⑧⑧, fermented naturally, as all the wines. Ample blue & black fruit well framed by integrated oak (14 months, none new). Structured & poised.

★★★★ Shiraz ⓐ Reined-in **16** ⑧⑦, earthy spice & succulent ripeness, excellent structure & persistence of flavour. Oak same as Cab; ex registered single-vineyard, as all except Carah & Chaos.

★★★★ Heavenly Chaos ⊘ Merlot-driven (74%) Bordeaux blend with cab & cab franc, **17** ⑧⑧ sweet cherry & blackberry flavours with a cool leafiness for balance. Smooth & fresh. 14 months in older oak.

★★★★ Carah ⓐ Equal cab & shiraz blend is savoury & rich, with dry fine tannin. **16** ⑧⑧ pleasant interplay of fruit generosity & oak backbone from 14 months in older French oak.

Cabernet Sauvignon ⓐ ★★★☆ Approachable, easy **16** ⑧③. Medium body, with fruitcake & sweet spice, dry finish from 14 months in older oak. **Cabernet Franc Blanc de Noir** ★★★☆ Provençal pink **19** ⑧④, fresh & dry with appealing savoury overlay, fantail berry finish, modest 12.5% alcohol. **Colombard** ★★★☆ Lovely guava & lime freshness, natural ferment & 10 months on lees in tank add to mouthfeel & structure on **18** ⑧⑤.

Husk Spirit range

★★★★☆ Cabernet Sauvignon Eau de Vie de Lie 5 Years Reserve ⓐ Gorgeous golden colour, with enticing melange of dark berry, chocolate, liquorice & vanilla aromas. **12** ⑨② intense on the palate but satiny, light footed, with lifted spirit finish. Aged 5 years in old red-wine barrels. Well worth seeking out.

★★★★☆ Marc de Chardonnay Barrique (NEW) ⊘ From Springfield Estate (Robertson) grape pomace, matured 2 years in older chardonnay barrels. **14** ⑨⓪ billows baked apple, marmalade & light cinnamon spice aromas & flavours. Silky smooth, full bodied, with lingering farewell. 500 ml, as next.

★★★★☆ **Marc de Hanepoot** ⊘ Previous spent 3 years in old muscat barrels. **16** ⑨¹ is unmatured, beautiful glint & exotic spice perfume. Delicate yet rich & round, with raisin, barley sugar & fine fresh-herb notes on long warming finish. Elegantly packaged, as all.— WB, CvZ

Location: McGregor ▪ Map: Robertson ▪ Map grid reference: C6 ▪ WO: McGregor/Robertson ▪ Est/1stB 2003 ▪ Tasting (wine/grappa), sales & cellar/distillery tours daily by appt ▪ Fee R40pp, refunded on purchase of R200 ▪ Farm produce ▪ Luxury farm accommodation in 6 cottages (self-catering) ▪ Adjoining Vrolijkheid Nature Reserve ▪ Craft distillery ▪ Owner(s) Robert & Anette Rosenbach ▪ Distiller(s) Robert Rosenbach ▪ Cellarmaster(s)/winemaker(s)/viticulturist(s) Lourens van der Westhuizen ▪ 78ha/12.5ha (cabs s/f, merlot, ptage, shiraz, cbard) ▪ 120t/4,000cs own label 70% red 15% white 15% rosé; 600cs spirits ▪ IPW, WIETA ▪ PO Box 92 McGregor 6708 ▪ tanagra@tanagra.co.za ▪ www.tanagra.co.za ▪ S 33° 55' 29.6" E 019° 52' 15.9" ▪ ⬜ leaves.fruitfully.husky ▪ **T +27 (0)23-625-1780**

Tangled Tree

These eco-friendly wines from Robertson have entwined Karee trees on their labels, symbols of the bond between Van Loveren founders and passionate gardeners Hennie and Jean Retief. Packaged in light, robust, recyclable, low-carbon PET (plastic) bottles, they're perfect for active and outdoorsy winelovers. **Chocolate Cabernet Sauvignon** ⊘ ★★★ Apt description: **18** ⑧¹ nicely combines oak-induced dark chocolate with black plum flavours, satisfyingly rich. **Spicy Shiraz** ★★ Spice & woodsmoke from oaking, **18** ⑦⁴ is more savoury than fruity, a match made for hearty stews. Body plumped by touch of sugar, as for Cab. **Rose Petal Moscato Rosé** ⊘ ★★☆ Sweetest of range but **18** ⑦⁸ not excessive, & with just 10% alcohol, fits the aromatic variety, delivering promised rosepetal perfume. **Butterscotch Chardonnay** ⊘ ★★☆ Name is spot on, **18** ⑦⁸'s peachy fruit enriched by oak, but carefully done, it's about flavour not grip. Not tasted: **Tropical Sauvignon Blanc**. — CR

Tanzanite Wines   ⓥ

After 'declassifying' the 2018 vintage, quality not meeting the Tanzanite standard, MCC sparkling specialist Melanie van der Merwe and husband Wentzel are delighted with the 2019 harvest, describing as 'exceptional' the grapes from Robertson vines on limestone soils. Exports keep growing, to Belgium, the US and UK in particular. Locally the wines can be tasted at a new venue on Val de Vie estate outside Paarl.
★★★★ **Méthode Cap Classique Brut Rosé** Steadily improving **NV** ⑧⁹ sparkler marries pinot's depth & weight with chardonnay's elegance & freshness. Pinpoint acid balance, delicate persistence. Also in 1.5L.
★★★★☆ **Méthode Cap Classique Brut** ⊘ 🅐 Always-impressive & delicious sparkling, **NV** ⑨³ is chardonnay-led with 20% pinot noir for hint richness, depth. Expertly combines New World fruit generosity with Old World restraint, oystershell & wet pebble minerality. ±30 months on lees, as Rosé.— CvZ

Location: Worcester ▪ Map: Franschhoek ▪ Map grid reference: A7 ▪ WO: Robertson ▪ Est 2006 ▪ Tasting Mon-Fri by appt ▪ Owner(s) Wentzel & Melanie van der Merwe ▪ Cellarmaster(s) Melanie van der Merwe (Apr 2006) ▪ 2,000cs own label ▪ PO Box 5102 Worcester 6850 ▪ melanie@tanzanitewines.co.za ▪ www. tanzanitewines.co.za ▪ S 33° 48' 5.22" E 018° 58' 38.39" ▪ ⬜ glove.occupancy.jams ▪ **T +27 (0)82-555-8105**

☐ **Tara Hill** see Southern Sky Wines

Tassenberg

A South African wine institution, Tassenberg is an affable dry red that since 1936 has launched millions on a wine journey. Affectionately known as 'Tassies', it's available in 750 ml, 2L & 5L. By Distell.
Tassenberg ⊘ ★★☆ Legendary cab-cinsaut **NV** ⑦⁸ is smooth, fruit driven & quaffable. — GdB

☐ **Taste** see Truter Family Wines

Tempel Wines   ⓥ 🅟 🏠 📷

Tom Heeremans, recent Belgian owner with Tatjana Holkina of this Paarl farm (its 1784 Cape Dutch farmhouse once a Jewish place of worship) is shifting attention to Mediterranean reds, adding tempranillo and bushvine grenache noir and mourvèdre to inherited pinotage in 2019, to be farmed as naturally as possible.

So too winemaking, Neil Marais' maiden vintage below (from bought-in grapes) using traditional open cement tanks retained during cellar renovations (as were decorative murals by SA street artists).

★★★★ **Sorgvry Cinsaut** Pleasing savoury-fruity, boiled sweet fragrance on **18** ⑧⑦ from Wellington grapes. Rather four-square tannic structure, balancing acidity. On the more serious side of Cape cinsauts.

★★★★ **Oogwink Shiraz** Youthfully purple **18** ⑧⑥ offers ripe-fruited, spicy aromas, with hints of vanilla & tobacco. Rich sweet fruit, with moderate dry tannins & firm acidity. WO Elgin. Like Sorgvry, 30% wholebunch natural ferment & maturation in oak (25% new only for this wine) & concrete 'egg'. Both in larger formats too.— TJ, CvZ

Location/map: Paarl ▪ Map grid reference: E3 ▪ WO: Wellington/Elgin ▪ Est 2000 ▪ 1stB 2003 ▪ Tasting, sales & cellar tours by appt ▪ Fee R50 ▪ Wine, beer & tasting platters available ▪ Guest house/B&B (5-star) ▪ Gin ▪ Owner(s) Tom Heeremans & Tatjana Holkina ▪ Winemaker(s) Neil Marais (Jan 2018, consultant) ▪ Viticulturist(s) Marko Roux (Mar 2018, consultant) ▪ 6ha ▪ 24t own label 100% red ▪ Suite 12 Private Bag X3041 Paarl 7620 ▪ info@tempelwines.com ▪ www.tempelwines.com ▪ S 33° 40' 34.0" E 018° 58' 32.2" ▪ 📍 steroids.goodness.hatch ▪ **T +27 (0)79-833-9617**

Terracura Wines

Husband-and-wife team Ryan Mostert (winemaking) and Samantha Suddons (everything else) are among the most uncompromising devotees of non-interventionism in SA's winescape. Their boutique portfolio, with grapes from selected growers in Swartland, includes the idiosyncratic Smiley range (chenin is particularly unusual — but delicious — combining 'fresh' wine with flor-matured and 'sun wine' components) alongside the fine Terracura and Silwervis bottlings. With businessman Michael Roets as partner, the couple released their first single-vineyard Terracura, Trinity Syrah '17, late last year, after this edition went to print.

Silwervis range
★★★★☆ **Cinsault** 🐝 From single Paardeberg vineyard, **17** ⑨③ is unoaked yet avoids the 'pretty strawberry' stereotype with characteristic piquant fruit, mineral seam, gains structure & length from lively acidity & lithe tannins. Like **16** ⑨④, naturally fermented wholebunch in stainless steel, aged year each in concrete 'egg' & stainless steel.

★★★★★ **Chenin Blanc** 🐝 Terse tannic grip - yes, on a white wine - striking acidity, lengthy beeswax & almond finish, **17** ⑨② could challenge some drinkers, thrill others. Not ungenerous, though, especially if decanted (or aged, up to 10 years its creator says). Venerable (1966) Paardeberg alluvial vineyard.

Smiley range
★★★★ **Dry Red** Fourth release of wittily labelled **NV** ⑧⑧, blend of cinsaut, tinta, syrah & mourvèdre from 2016-2019 vintages, various Swartland terroirs. Fruitier than Silwervis red yet fine & dry.

★★★★☆ **Chenin Blanc** Inspired by the wines of Jura & Jerez, brilliant **NV** ⑨⓪ (5th release) marries 14 different batches from 2016-2019 vintages, including skin-contact, 'sun wine' & flor-matured components. Expect freshness, umami savouriness & latent power.

Terracura Wines range
Not tasted: **Syrah**, **White**. — CvZ

Location: Hermon ▪ Map: Tulbagh ▪ Map grid reference: A7 ▪ WO: Swartland ▪ Est 2010▪ 1stB 2011 ▪ Tasting, sales & cellar tours by appt only ▪ Closed all pub hols ▪ Owner(s) M. Roets & R.P. Mostert ▪ Winemaker(s) Ryan Mostert (Nov 2013) ▪ Viticulturist(s) various ▪ 45ha (cinsaut, mourv, shiraz, tinta barocca, chenin, sem) ▪ 40t 50% red 50% white ▪ Hermon 7308 ▪ samantha@terracura.co.za ▪ www.terracura.co.za, www.silwervis. com ▪ S 33° 26' 16.97" E 018° 58' 2.29" ▪ 📍 since.scooting.busting ▪ **T +27 (0)76-392-4301**

☐ **Terra Del Capo** see Anthonij Rupert Wyne

Tesselaarsdal Wines

Exciting news from Berene Sauls' boutique wine business was the doubling of wines in her range when she released her first chardonnay last year. Her property purchase in Tesselaarsdal in the Overberg is nearing completion, allowing her to fulfil her dream of growing grapes on her own land. Meanwhile she divides her time between her day job at Hamilton Russell Vineyards in Hemel-en-Aarde Valley (HRV winemaker Emul Ross assists Berene with production) and her rapidly expanding wine brand.

★★★★☆ **Pinot Noir** ⓐ Delicious **18** ㉒ employs 10% wholebunch ferment to good effect, the ripe red fruit vividly rendered along with interesting saline note, sappy tannic structure & attractive charry oak (25% new, ±9 months). Better balanced than previous, can keep or enjoy now.

★★★★ **Chardonnay** ⓝⓔⓦ Preview shows much promise. **19** ㊆ crunchy apples, hints of pineapples & orange blossom, creamy texture from old oak & amphora ferment, partial malo. Looking good. — CM

Location: Hermanus ▪ WO: Hemel-en-Aarde Ridge ▪ Est/1stB 2015 ▪ Tasting by appt ▪ Owner(s) Berene Sauls ▪ Winemaker(s) Emul Ross (Jan 2015, Hamilton Russell Vineyards) ▪ 645cs own label 100% red ▪ PO Box 158 Hermanus 7200 ▪ berene@tesselaarsdalwines.co.za ▪ www.tesselaarsdalwines.co.za ▪ **T +27 (0)28-312-3595/+27 (0)73-322-9499**

Teubes Family Wines ⓞ ⓜ ⓐ ⓘ ⓐ ♿

The Teubes family have been making wines for half a century, they say, and for ten years have had their own label - the maiden '10 Cabernet was made elsewhere while awaiting completion of their cellar. The home farm is near Vredendal on the Atlantic coast, its certified organic vineyards cared for by Johan Teubes, also a well-known consultant. They are increasingly focusing on their organic wines and a new unsulphured range.

Teubes Family Wines range

★★★★ **Cabernet Sauvignon** ⓥ Rich, ripe & lively **18** ㊆. Firm tannins, 40% new oak & bright acidity matched by fruit concentration. Tasty now, should improve. Quality leap since last-made **14** ★★★ ㊀.

★★★★ **Sauvignon Blanc 19** ㊅ has some riper tropical character - more so than Malkopbaai, & more generous on the palate too, with a fairly balanced acid thread & good lingering flavours. First WO Nieuwoudtville wine in the guide. Back on form after light-fruited **17** ★★★★ ㊂.

Pinotage Reserve ⓐ ⓥ ★★★★ Offers a mix of dark, ripe fruit with pronounced herbal note. **16** ㊄ effectively oaked, with good balance & texture. Hint of varietal bitterness on end. Needs a few years. **Shiraz** ⓥ ★★★ Deep plummy fruit on **16** ㊁, though a touch harsh & hot from big acid & 14.5% alcohol. **Barrel Fermented Chenin Blanc** ⓐ ★★★★ Shows oak-enhanced ripe melon, floral features. Few grams sugar lift fruit, smooth effects of 14.3% alcohol. **15** ㊃ may benefit from short-term ageing.

Karoobossie range

★★★★ **Méthode Cap Classique Brut Rosé** ⓐ Pale pink **16** ㊇ from pinot noir, pinotage, meunier. Delightful aromas of brioche, light berry. Dry & elegant, with full flavours & good freshness. WO W Cape

Malkopbaai range

Sauvignon Blanc ★★★★ From various West Coast sources, **19** ㊂ has more green & lemondrop notes than tropical. Tasty & notably zippy. Good step up on previously tasted **17** ★★ ㊆. Not tasted: **Pinotage**, **Lightly Wooded Chenin Blanc**. — TJ

Location: Vredendal ▪ Map: Olifants River ▪ Map grid reference: B4 B5 ▪ WO: Olifants River/Western Cape/ Nieuwoudtville ▪ Est 2010 ▪ 1stB 2011 ▪ Tasting & sales Mon-Fri 8-5 Sat 9.30-5; Lambert's Bay tasting venue & Kreefhuis restaurant Mon-Sat 10-5 ▪ Tasting fee ▪ Cellar tours ▪ Tour groups ▪ Facilities for children ▪ Farm produce ▪ Cheese platters & pizza ▪ Conferences/functions ▪ Walks/hikes ▪ Bergkraal 4x4 trail ▪ MTB ▪ Conservation area ▪ Guest cottages ▪ Owner(s) Johan & Ella Teubes ▪ Cellarmaster(s) Sybrand Teubes ▪ Winemaker(s) Sybrand Teubes, with Mariska Teubes ▪ Viticulturist(s) Johan Teubes ▪ (cab, ptage, shiraz, chard, sauv) ▪ 300t ▪ Organic, WIETA ▪ PO Box 791 Vredendal 8160 ▪ info@teubeswines.co.za, sybrand@teubeswines.co.za ▪ www.teubeswines.co.za ▪ S 31° 43' 19.1" E 018° 30' 14.5" (Vredendal) S 32° 5' 35.35" E 018° 18' 10.12" (Lambert's Bay) ▪ 🖪 forever.passive.weirdly ▪ **T +27 (0)27-213-2377**

That Wine Demesne ⓐ ⓐ

David and Joanna Butler, owners of this minuscule but significant domaine in rugged The Crags near Plettenberg Bay, pioneered the establishment of pinot noir clones best suited for serious red-wine making rather than champagne-method sparkling, the area speciality. They've added 2,200 vines, bringing the total vineyard size to 1.5 hectares, fruit vinified by Plettenberg's go-to winemaker, Anton Smal. David and Joanna are justly proud of their '18, a challenging vintage which nonetheless doubled in size to 3,030 bottles.

★★★★ **Pinot Noir** ⓥ At 12.5% alcohol, **18** ㊇ touch riper than **17** ★★★★ ㊄ but still classically styled & charming, with wonderful freshness, drinkability & fruit purity, supported by delicate oak. — CvZ

Location/WO: Plettenberg Bay ▪ Est 2012 ▪ 1stB 2016 ▪ That Place & Ons Hoek - both self-catering & pet-friendly cottages ▪ Owner(s) David & Joanna Butler ▪ Winemaker(s) Anton Smal (Bramon Wines) ▪ 1.5ha (pinot) ▪ 50cs own label 100% red ▪ PO Box 197 The Crags 6602 ▪ thatwine@thatplace.co.za ▪ www. thatwine.co.za ▪ **T +27 (0)82-578-1939**

The Ahrens Family

Growing wine was never on the radar of upcountry-raised Albert Ahrens, till he watched a Stellenbosch University promotional film featuring a vigneron (whom he chanced to meet years later) tending his barrels in an atmospheric cellar. Via numerous wine countries, regions and cellars, notably Lammershoek during the Swartland revolution, Albert is now based in Paarl. Here he handcrafts selected parcels as naturally as possible, believing that 'address speaks louder', meaning place of origin outweighs grape variety and winemaker as the main determinant of a wine's character and personality. See also The House of GM&Ahrens entry.

★★★★ **Black** Albert Ahrens' first wine under his own label, the name alludes to Swartland & its heralded syrah blends. 9th vintage **17** ★★★★★ ⑨⓪ lovely lily & scrub perfume, lacy tannins, vintage's enlivening acidity. Like **16** ⑧⑧, mostly syrah (±70%), grenache, carignan & cinsaut in support.

★★★★ **Paarl Rooiwijn** (NEW) The newcomer 'Red Wine' is a vivacious melange of red & black fruit, with brisk acidity, orange zest & pot-pourri notes. **17** ⑧⑧ smidgen more sugar than other reds, smooths the firm tannins. Syrah (±70%) & cinsaut. Wild ferment, long skin contact, ±12 months old French oak, as all.

★★★★ **Bottelary Seventy** Rewinds to 1970s & the cab/cinsaut blends de rigueur then (& now). **17** ⑧⑧ an aromatic, black-fruited 60/40 mix, approachable, with compact core & tannin/acid structure for good few years cellaring.

★★★★☆ **Bottelary OVC** Ⓐ Chenin from 38 year old vines & the coolest site of the OVCs, with picking dates staggered to achieve 'freshness as well as ripeness'. Nails it in **17** ⑨③, shows impressive juxtaposition of rich tropical/deciduous tones, palate weight & arresting acidity in poised & harmonious mouthful.

★★★★ **Paarl OVC** (NEW) From two chenin vineyards, elder planted in 1977, on well-drained shale. Attractive **17** ⑧⑨ broad & creamy mouthfeel with lemony acid enlivenment, yellow/white peach & nectarine in the aromas & flavours.

★★★★☆ **Swartland OVC** (NEW) Single 1984 chenin vineyard in sand over ferricrete, latter delivering disguised power, richness & great persistence. **17** ⑨① complex medley of orchard & stonefruit, khaki bush & earthy top notes, pleasant bitter pithiness on the finish.

★★★★☆ **The WhiteBlack** Ⓐ Swartland-inspired white Rhône blend from decomposed granite vineyards in Voor Paardeberg. **17** ⑨③ marries roussanne, marsanne & grenache blanc, lifts the bar with remarkable fruit intensity, purity & poise.— CvZ

Location/map: Paarl ▪ Map grid reference: G6 ▪ WO: Paarl/Stellenbosch/Swartland/Voor Paardeberg ▪ Est/1stB 2008 ▪ Tasting & sales by appt only ▪ Tastings with either lunch or dinner by appt only; private tastings for groups in Gauteng, Bloemfontein & KZN ▪ Owner(s) Albert Ahrens ▪ Cellarmaster(s)/winemaker(s)/viticulturist(s) Albert Ahrens (2008) ▪ 35t/4,000cs own label 50% red 50% white ▪ tastewine@theahrensfamily.co.za ▪ S 33° 45' 11.30" E 019° 1' 48.19" ▪ 🎦 openings.perkily.locked ▪ **T +27 (0)79-196-6887**

☐ **Theater of Wine** *see* Val du Charron
☐ **The Back Roads** *see* Black Elephant Vintners
☐ **The Bald Ibis** *see* Mile High Vineyards
☐ **The Beachhouse** *see* Douglas Green
☐ **The Bernard Series** *see* Bellingham

The Berrio Wines

Growing grapes right at the foot of Africa was never going to be easy, but after more than a score of years coping with the extreme climate of the Agulhas Plain, and despite the problems of drought, vinegrower Francis Pratt's boutique brand is going from strength to strength. Volumes, though boutique, are increasing (to 3,500 cases), while ongoing rejuvenation and empathetic winemaking (by Cederberg Private Cellar's David Nieuwoudt, who vinifies these grapes alongside his own fruit from the area) will help ensure that the wines continue to reflect their unique site - its viticultural soils amongst the oldest in the world.

★★★★☆ **Shiraz** ⓥ Many layers of flavour in **16** ⑨⓪, from cranberry, plum & cherry to tobacco, wild herbs, meat & mint. 20% new oak adds appealing smoky-charry notes to soft tannins. Delicious drinking, like sleek & suave **15** ⑨②, also still available.

★★★★☆ **Sauvignon Blanc** ⓥ Previewed **19** ⑨① builds & builds in glass, adding layers of greenpepper, crisp apple & fresh grapefruit, all with an attractive saline bite & zippy acidity. Free-run juice only.
Not tasted: **Weather Girl**. — CM

Location/WO: Elim ▪ Est 1997 ▪ 1stB 2002 ▪ Closed to public ▪ Owner(s)/viticulturist(s) Francis Pratt ▪ Cellarmaster(s) David Nieuwoudt (Cederberg) ▪ Winemaker(s) David Nieuwoudt (2013, Cederberg) ▪ 2,276ha/34ha (pinot, shiraz, sauv, sem) ▪ 40t/3,500cs own label 20% red 80% white ▪ PO Box 622 Bredasdorp 7280 ▪ wine@theberrio.co.za ▪ www.theberrio.co.za ▪ **T +27 (0)28-482-1880/+27 (0)27-482-2827**

☐ **The Big 5** *see* Jacques Germanier

The Blacksmith

Everything about Fable Mountain Vineyards winemaker Tremayne Smith's own small but growing brand and 'personal passion project' is refreshingly innovative and extroverted. Also detailed and considered, with a hands-off approach to reflect the integrity of the varieties, from parcels in three diverse areas. The wine names are drawn from both the vineyard characteristics and Tremayne's fascination with the medieval era and symbolism. He regards chenin as the 'king' of whites and cinsaut the 'prince' of reds, while 'old bones' refers to aged vineyards. The labels, designed by tattoo artist Tamar Thorn, are unique and impactful.

The Flash Series
★★★★ **The Basilisk** Rare varietal bottling of durif/petite sirah is quite the charmer, with polished plum fruit & white pepper accent, yet **18** ⑧⑥ also shows wonderful vinosity, well-judged tannin structure.

★★★★ **The King's Spirit** From old chenin in Darling, **18** ⑧⑥ unshowy but with satisfying almond & apple tones, fine balance & delicate freshness. Also good weight & depth at a very dry 1.3 g/l sugar.

★★★★ **Bloodline** Méthode ancestrale (single-ferment) sparkling from Swartland chenin. **18** ⑧⑥ fruity & refreshing with idiosyncratic - but pleasant - ginger nut character. Light feel thanks to modest alcohol & sugar (12%, 6.4 g/l). 10 months on lees.

Blacksmith range
★★★★ **These Old Bones White Field Blend** From 43 year old vineyard, officially chenin, but at least 9 other varieties interspersed. **18** ⑧⑧ pure & delicate fruit, fine energy, freshness & length. Just 12.5% alcohol. Fermented/aged in plastic 'egg'.

....

Barebones Colombard ⓥ ★★★★☆ Bursts with tangy greengage & lime, **18** ⑧⑤ creamy nuance from some old oak, lovely freshness from 50% unwooded portion to balance a few grams of sugar. Heirloom grape given a modern twist - with panache.

....

Barebones Cinsault ★★★ Only unoaked red in this portfolio, 6 months stainless steel, **18** ⑧② earthy & herbaceous tones, relatively soft acidity but like most Blacksmith wines - dare we say it? - bone-dry. Also in 1L 'growlers', like Barebones sibling & Hell Yeah. **Prince Of Bones** ★★★★ Strawberry-toned **18** ⑧③ from Swartland cinsaut has more fruit intensity than Barebones, svelte & creamy texture. Just 25% wholebunch (most others 100%), 10 months old 500L barrels. **Hell Yeah** ★★★ From pinotage, characterful **18** ⑧⓪ a sure hit with the in-crowd. Variety-true strawberry, mulberry & smoke aromas & flavours, positive funkiness & house's emphatic dry styling. — CvZ, MW

Location: Riebeek-Kasteel ▪ WO: Paarl/Swartland/Darling ▪ 1stB 2014 ▪ Closed to public ▪ Owner(s)/winemaker(s) Tremayne Smith ▪ 38t own label 60% red 40% white ▪ tremayne@theblacksmithwines.co.za

The Bridge of Hope Wines   ⓥ

The three ranges of owner Rosemary Mosia's burgeoning wine brand are designed to suit all tastes and wallets, 'bridging the gap' between everyday wines and more seriously styled ones. Her day job as a new-business advisor has proved a blessing for this side-venture, now entering its eighth successful year.

Ultra Premium range

Shiraz ★★★ Showy oak (50% new, 60/40 French/American) dominates **14** ⑧② adding smoked meats, spice & salami to fairly quiet fruit. Good braai wine, drink soon.

Premium range

Cabernet Sauvignon ⓠ ★★★ Attractive Xmas mince pie notes on ripe **16** ⑧②, dried fruit & peel spicing up jammy black fruit. For earlier drinking than last. **Café Cabernet** ⓠ ★★★★ In popular 'coffee' style, **17** ⑧③ balances ripe dark fruit & mocha notes well. Few grams sugar for easy drinkability. **Merlot** ⓠ ★★★ Plummy, almond features on **14** ⑦⑦. WO W Cape, rest Wellington. **Chardonnay** ★★★☆ Old-style but attractive **17** ⑧③ creates layers of flavour - toffee apples, cinnamon, spice - in slightly oxidative & food-friendly wine. **Sauvignon Blanc** ⓠ ★★★☆ Clean, zippy, fresh **17** ⑦⑨, light flavours of yellow & green fruit.

Classic range

Cabernet Sauvignon ⓥ ★★★ Plenty of flavour **17** ⑦⑨, but dried fruit character suggests not a keeper. Less freshness than last. Unwooded, as all these. **Merlot** ⓝⒺⓦ ⓥ ★★★ Easy-drinking **17** ⑦⑨, dark stewed fruit with hints of chocolate & herbs. **Pinotage** ⓥ ★★★ Simple yet pleasing red & black fruit on **17** ⑦⑧, though finish is tad high-toned. **Shiraz** ⓝⒺⓦ ★★ Raisins & smoked meat flavours on **17** ⑦⑥ just manage to carry off hefty 14.5% alcohol. **Unwooded Chardonnay** ⓥ ★★★ Perky **18** ⑧①, straightforward yellow & tropical fruit edged with candyfloss & just enough acidity. **Natural Sweet Red** ⓠ ★★★ Who needs dessert when it's already in the glass? **NV** ⑦⑦'s mocha-laden flavours glide down effortlessly. Mostly merlot, shiraz. **Natural Sweet Rosé** ⓠ ★★ As sweet as it is ruby in hue, **NV** ⑦⓪ will charm many. — CM

Location: Cape Town ▪ WO: Western Cape/Wellington ▪ Est 2012 ▪ 1stB 2010 ▪ Pre-booked private tasting only ▪ Owner(s) Rosemary P Mosia ▪ Winemaker(s) JG Auret (2012, Linton Park) ▪ Viticulturist(s) Rudolf Jansen van Vuuren (2012, Linton Park) ▪ 70% red 30% white ▪ 66 Loch Rd Rondebosch 7700 ▪ rmosia@yahoo.com, rmosia@thebridgeofhopewines.co.za ▪ www.thebridgeofhopewines.co.za ▪ **T +27 (0)21-686-2294/+27 (0)83-276-3759**

☐ **The Bridge Wines** *see* The Bridge of Hope Wines

The Butcher Shop & Grill

The Butcher Shop & Grill is a local restaurant industry institution with outlets in Sandton's Nelson Mandela Square and Cape Town's Mouille Point. The cut-above house labels are sourced from top producers, including Cape Winemakers Guild members, and include a fully mature red that, on track record, should be stellar now.

Limited Editions

★★★★☆ **Morgenster** ⓠ Currently available **01** ⑨② merlot-led Bordeaux red tasted for our 2005 edition & noted as 'probably destined for Cape showcase greatness'. Delicate, with already tertiary nose, but tight restrained palate suggested keeping. More ripely opulent & big than previous, though still refined. With cab & cab franc, 16 months French oak, 80% new.

★★★★☆ **Niels Verburg Red Blend** ⓠ Opulence & intensity of **15** ⑨④ mirrors **13** ⑨④: mulberries, molten black plums, sweetly spiced, supple tannins, finishing dry. Powerful, impressive, packed with flavour & interest. 77% shiraz, cab & mourvèdre, pinch cab franc. By Luddite's Niels Verburg. No **14**.

Discontinued: **The Natalie**.

Pick's Pick Gold Label range

★★★★☆ **Cabernet Sauvignon** ⓐ Dark-toned **17** ⑨④ has forthcoming cherry & tobacco whiffs, polished tannins, earthy minerality well-integrated with the fruit flavours & underlying spice & herbal notes. Has dab petit verdot. Crafted by Ernie Els.

★★★★ **Reserve Pinot Noir** ⓠ Fragrant, bright & expressive **17** ⑧⑦, Elgin grapes fermented whole-berry in steel for aroma & freshness, then 9 months in seasoned oak. Succulent, delicious. By Radford Dale. **Shiraz** ⓠ ★★★★ Medium body, with ample smoky blue fruit & cherry appeal on **15** ⑧④ by Montpellier. Succulent but firm grip of oak. **Selection Rouge** ⓠ ★★★ Cab & merlot blend by Montpellier is tad brusque, with dry spicy oak (10% new) shading red cherry fruit on **15** ⑧①. **Sauvignon Blanc** ⓠ ★★★☆ Not as exuberant or persistent as some, but fresh & pleasing **17** ⑧③, with good stonefruit & citrus flavours. By Iona Vineyards. Not tasted: **Merlot**, **Pinotage**.

Pick's Pick Platinum range
Not tasted: **Cabernet Sauvignon**.

Pick's Pick range

★★★★ **Merlot** Restrained black plum fruit, subtle dusting of oak spice & hint of leafiness, **16** ⑧⑥ judiciously extracted, fresh & harmonious, drinks well. From Jordan.

★★★★ **Shiraz** ⓥ Like still-available **15** ⑧⑦, **16** ⑧⑦ savoury toned, subtle & confident. Approachable dinner companion or solo sipper from Zevenwacht.

★★★★ **Shiraz-Cabernet Sauvignon** Savoury blend, splashes merlot & carignan joining the main players in **17** ⑧⑦ from Ernie Els. Shows leather & spice over ripe black plums & blackberries, ripe tannins polished in combo French & American oak, none new.

★★★★ **Unoaked Chardonnay** By Jordan, **18** ⑧⑧ has smooth & creamy texture from 4 months on lees, balanced by a zingy lemon freshness, lunchtime-friendly 12.5% alcohol.

★★★★ **Sauvignon Blanc** Previewed **19** ⑧⑦ best enjoyed in youth to get most from attractive blackcurrant & white peach complexity, wet pebble minerality & satisfying weight. By Jordan.

Pinotage ⓥ ★★★☆ From pinotage specialist Beyerskloof, **17** ⑧③ plummy & very smooth, perfect with the spare ribs. **Rosé** ★★★★ Jordan's **19** ⑧③ is plump & juicy, bone-dry & polished. From near-equal syrah & merlot. **Chardonnay** ⓥ ★★★★ Reined in, & with a saltiness that pairs well with food, Radford Dale's unoaked **18** ⑧⑤ delivers appealing lemon tones, easy drinkability. Discontinued: **Cabernet Sauvignon**, **Bubbly**. — Various tasters

Location: Cape Town/Sandton ▪ WO: Various ▪ Owner(s) Alan Pick ▪ Beach Rd Mouille Point (opposite lighthouse) Cape Town 8005; Shop 30 Nelson Mandela Square Sandton 2196 ▪ thebutchershop@mweb.co.za ▪ T +27 (0)11-784-8676/7

☐ **The Chapters** *see* Miles Mossop Wines
☐ **The Cinsault Collective** *see* Natte Valleij Wines
☐ **The Cirrus Wine Company** *see* Cirrus Wines
☐ **The Collection** *see* Roos Family Vineyards
☐ **The Cooperative** *see* Bosman Family Vineyards
☐ **The Crags** *see* Bramon Wines
☐ **The Cross Collection** *see* Dieu Donné Vineyards
☐ **The Den** *see* Painted Wolf Wines
☐ **The Dome** *see* Lourensford Wine Estate
☐ **The Drift** *see* Bruce Jack Wines
☐ **The Elite** *see* Old Road Wine Company

Theescombe Estate Wine   ⓥ ⑪ ⊙

This tiny boutique venture on the outskirts of Port Elizabeth has just one hectare of vines, planted with five varieties. But the Futter husband-and-wife team run their wine business with passion, hands-on, Roger in the vineyard and Sandra as winemaker and welcomer of visitors. The confidence to try new things has resulted in individual wines, like the unique aged dry muscat featured below.

★★★★ **White Muscadel Dry** Held back for further maturation, unwooded preview **13** ⑧⑨ shows **17** ★★ ⑦④'s grapey/sultana aromas, with subtle floral notes, some barley sugar. A sleek dryness, almost slatey, yet a seam of freshness. There's an elemental quality here, the variety reduced to its essence. Something very rare.

Cabernet Sauvignon ⓥ ★ Light colour & texture, **17** ⑥⑦ very savoury, no fruit showing, pepper & forest floor the predominant flavours. **Rosé** ⓥ ★ Pale copper-hued, off-dry **17** ⑥⑦ from cab shows no fruit, just light-textured (11% alcohol) freshness. **Chenin Blanc** ⓥ ★★★★ Has maturity, scents of preserved melon, baked apple, marzipan - & savoury bacon crackers (yet unoaked). Flavours the same: rich, full & tasty. **13** ⑧⑤ unusual, almost solera-style umami character but it works. Not tasted: **Pinotage**. — CR

Location: Port Elizabeth ▪ Map/WO: Eastern Cape ▪ Map grid reference: D5 ▪ Est/1stB 2010 ▪ Tasting, sales & cellar tours by appt ▪ Fee R200pp (R80/tasting, R55/tour, R65/cheese platter) ▪ Meals/platters (cheese, olives & biltong) to be pre-booked ▪ Functions ▪ Card facilities available ▪ Owner(s) Futter family ▪ Winemaker(s)

Sandra Futter (Oct 2007) ▪ Viticulturist(s) Roger Futter (Jun 2006) ▪ 1.94ha/1ha (cab, ptage, chenin, sem, white muscadel) ▪ 1–4t ▪ PO Box 28642 Sunridge Park Port Elizabeth 6008 ▪ theescombewines@hotmail. co.za ▪ www.theescombewines.wixsite.com/wine, www.theescombewines.yolasite.com ▪ S 33° 58' 44.82" E 025° 28' 27.46" ▪ 🔲 length.iceberg.vows ▪ T +27 (0)41-379-4035/+27(0)73-889-6663

☐ **The Fair Trade** *see* Koopmanskloof Vineyards
☐ **The Flagship** *see* Stellenbosch Vineyards
☐ **The Flash Series** *see* The Blacksmith

The Fledge & Co ⓥ

Boutique label The Fledge & Co, under husband-and-wife owners Leon Coetzee and Margaux Nel, continues to grow. Based in Calitzdorp, they now work with 40 vineyards and 21 varieties across the winelands, from Piketberg to Agulhas, which sees Leon on the road for much of the year. The wide range of sites provides an ongoing learning experience, especially in the increasingly challenging climatic conditions. New labels have been introduced: a site-specific pair under the O-Velaphi? moniker, an isiXhosa phrase roughly meaning 'where were you born?', and Redemption of a Rogue, marking the passing of vineyards through drought or vagaries of fashion. But the year's best newcomer is Leon and Margaux's first fledgling, William Robert.

Rare Sightings range

★★★★ **O-Velaphi? Stellenbosch Cabernet Sauvignon** (NEW) ⓐ Single, dry-farmed Bottelary site gave birth to this **17** (88) cab. Unambiguous bright cassis aromas, sweet crunchy fruit & well-tempered grape tannins. Both structure & depth of flavour indicate greater interest with time. French oak, none new.

★★★★☆ **Pinot Noir Elgin** ⊘ ⓐ Area's thumbprint of cool-climate freshness, elegance defines **17** (93). Charming red cherry fragrance, pure flavours also suggestion of complexing undergrowth. Fine, lacy tannins promise a future. Portion wholeberry. Selection of 5 best barrels, 20% new.

★★★★★ **Red Blend** ⓥ In best vintages only. **15** (93) local take on Douro red table wines; mostly touriga, tinta with splash touriga franca; rich, earthy aromas brightened with fragrant florals. Quite powerful but well controlled; good acid thread avoids any heaviness & lengthens sweet fruit.

★★★★ **O-Velaphi? Elgin Chardonnay** (NEW) Single clone, Elgin site close to Rockview Dam. **17** (87) quietly assured, with lemony zest, bright acidity tempered by creamy lees. Supportively older-oaked.
Not tasted: **Hatchi**.

Nest Egg range

★★★★ **Syrah** Tradouw syrah co-fermented with 5% viognier. **17** (87) still closed, needing time to harmonise toasty oak with varietal soft black berry & spice. Worth the wait; otherwise nicely balanced, supple & sweet-fruited, with freshness, gentle grip. French, American oak, 40% new.

★★★★☆ **Hoeksteen Stellenbosch Chenin Blanc** ⓐ Two dryland bushvine sites (Bottelary & Faure) dating from early 1980s. **18** (93) tremendous concentration, intensity yet still silky, graceful, with purity in its crunchy green apple flavours. Old 400L French oak ferment, 4 months lees-ageing added complexities.

★★★★ **Klipspringer Swartland Steen** From two old unirrigated bushvine blocks. **18** (89) expressive blossom, red apple scents; plenty of steely tension, firm grip but not overly harsh. 40% barrel ferment, old oak; lees ageing 9 months adds dimension, weight. Should age few years with interest.

★★★★ **Fumé Blanc** ⓥ Old-oak-fermented sauvignon with 5% semillon; **17** (87) more vinous than fruity, a little citrus & earthy features. Sleek, dense satin texture, lemongrass, honey flavours lifted by firm acidity. Unfined/filtered. Better suited to food than aperitif. **16** not tasted.

★★★★ **Vagabond** Adds roussanne to chenin-led, widely-sourced sextet. **17** (88) restrained floral, apricot scents, like **16** (88), showing some evolution. Comfortable plump juiciness coupled with freshness & light grip make for appealing drinking now, further few years. Fermented/aged older oak, 9 months.

Katvis Pinot Noir ★★★★ Ex Elgin & Napier (60/40), **17** (85) delivers richness of dark cherry fruit bolstered by firm structure, enlivening freshness. Few years' rounding of benefit. Well-judged oak, 8% new. **Red/ Tinto** ★★★★ Mostly touriga nacional with touriga franca, splashes souzão & shiraz from Stellenbosch, Tradouw & Klein Karoo. **16** (85) friendly & warmingly spicy; rich, chunky flavours, their ripely sweet conclusion unhindered by rounded tannins. For winter & a hearty stew.

Jikken Bareru Experimental Barrels range

★★★★☆ **Redemption of a Rogue Elgin Viognier** (NEW) Cool-climate charmer with persuasive yet delicate fragrance, flavours. **18** (91) poised, lively, subtly broadened - without loss of purity - by barrel ferment, old French, one new 500L Hungarian & lees ageing. Sadly, a swansong: vineyard since overgrafted.

Elgin Riesling ★★★★ Zesty **18** (84), light terpene & spice, bracing acidity tempered by juicy flavours, few grams sugar. Not tasted: **Nel & Coetzee Steen, Sauvignon Blanc**. — AL

Location: Calitzdorp/Riebeek West ▪ WO: Western Cape/Elgin/Stellenbosch/Swartland ▪ Est 2007 ▪ 1stB 2010 ▪ Tasting & sales by appt at Boplaas ▪ Closed all pub hols ▪ Owner(s) Margaux Nel & Leon Coetzee ▪ Winemaker(s) Margaux Nel & Leon Coetzee (both Jan 2007) ▪ Viticulturist(s) Margaux Nel (Jan 2007) & Leon Coetzee (Jan 2015) ▪ 45% red 55% white ▪ IPW ▪ wine@thefledge.co.za ▪ www.thefledge.co.za ▪ **T +27 (0)82-828-8416/+27 (0)72-385-6503**

The Foundry ⓥ

It's been a long time coming, but Chris Williams has resigned from his prestigious job as Meerlust cellarmaster and is to concentrate full-time on his own projects — notably this well established range of terroir-expressive wines. His partner in the business remains James Reid, operations director of Accolade Wines and owner of a historic Voor Paardeberg farm with an old cellar that will be upgraded to provide a suitable home for The Foundry vinifications. The winemaking aim will continue to be purity and authenticity. Looking for ever-greater depth and intricacy, Chris looks forward to harvest 2020 when new vessels will be used to improve the complexity of all five wines in the range. As ever, the emphasis remains on mature, well-sited venerable vines and viticulture to deliver the best possible grapes.

★★★★☆ **Grenache Noir 17** (91) picks up where **15** (92) left off. Light tannin grip with wholebunch portion hiked to 40% & only half of wine aged in oak, none new. Understated, with fruit succulence & quiet concentration. No **16**.

★★★★★ **Syrah** (🍇) Welcome return for **16** (93) (no **13**, **14** or **15**). Gentle, pliable & broad, has restrained blue & black fruit charm. Lovely dry, fine tannin grip after 16 months in seasoned French oak. Parts wholebunch, natural ferment & malo add depth & interest.

★★★★★ **Grenache Blanc** (🍇) Another standout in **18** (96), restrained, delicate yet vivid & exciting. Round & supple yet broad too. Dry citrus twist with creamy finish from 7 months on lees. Superb harmony of fruit, acid & (older) oak. Voor Paardeberg grapes, as **17** ★★★★★ (94) & previous.

★★★★☆ **Roussanne** (ⓥ) A leader of the pack in this small but growing category. Delicate **17** (93) is floral, stonefruit toned. 7 months older oak, few grams of sugar add palate weight. Finishes perfectly fresh.

★★★★☆ **Viognier** Effortlessly elegant & rewarding, as befits a Cape benchmark. Typical nectarine & citrus vibrancy in **18** (90), which vies with spice, creamy breadth & depth from oak fermentation, part natural. Just a shade less subtle than last **16** (92). — FM

Location/map: Paarl ▪ Map grid reference: C2 ▪ WO: Stellenbosch/Voor Paardeberg ▪ Est 2000 ▪ 1stB 2001 ▪ Tasting, sales & cellar tours by appt ▪ Closed all pub hols ▪ Owner(s) Chris Williams & James Reid ▪ Cellarmaster(s)/winemaker(s) Chris Williams (Nov 2000) ▪ Viticulturist(s) Chris Williams (Nov 2000), with growers ▪ 11ha (grenache, shiraz, rouss, viog) ▪ ±30t/4,000cs own label 40% red 60% white ▪ PO Box 12423, Die Boord 7613 ▪ thefoundry@mweb.co.za ▪ www.thefoundry.co.za ▪ S 33° 37' 47.1" E 018° 50' 08.4" ▪ [m] reliant.clouding.trimmed ▪ **T +27 (0)82-577-0491**

☐ **The French Corner** *see* Old Road Wine Company
☐ **The Front Row** *see* Hirst Wines
☐ **The Game Reserve** *see* Rooiberg Winery

The Garajeest ⓥ

The playful, unconventional spelling of her brand name signals the spirit of small-scale vintner Callan Williams. Her boldly labelled wines are named for favourite rock stars and sourced in Elgin, though she's based in Somerset West. End-2019 was destined for the launch of a new blanc de noir, as well as a new set of just 100 magnums in what is becoming a biennial tradition — the wine's varietal make-up kept secret.

★★★★ **Jim Semillon** Like still-selling **17** (86), **18** (88) is 50% older-oaked. Attractive ripe fullness of flavour, with usual bruised apple note. Silky soft, shot through with balanced, freshly succulent charm.

Bruce Cabernet Franc ⓥ ★★★☆ Big, bold & ripely rich **16** ⑧③ has soft but useful tannins, firm acidity & some warmth & sweetness on the finish. Only old oak barrels used. **'Blanc de Noir'** ⑭ ★★★★ Name of pinkly pretty **19** ⑧③ from cab franc yet to be decided at press time. Pre-bottling sample (so rating tentative) shows ripe fruitiness but savoury element, too, on balanced, freshly grippy palate. — TJ

Location: Somerset West ▪ WO: Elgin ▪ Est 2014 ▪ 1stB 2015 ▪ Tasting by appt ▪ Owner(s) Callan Williams ▪ Cellarmaster(s)/winemaker(s) Callan Williams (May 2014) ▪ (cab f, sem, blanc de noir) ▪ 12t/±1,800cs own label 70% red 30% white ▪ IPW ▪ Oudehuis Centre, 122 Main Rd, Somerset West 7130 ▪ callan@thegarajeest. co.za ▪ www.thegarajeest.co.za ▪ **T +27 (0)72-524-2921**

The Giant Periwinkle ⓥ

Every year sees something new for Giant Periwinkle and Cape Town advocate Pierre Rabie, with co-owners Robert Stelzner and Karen van Helden. The cellar, opened in 2018 in the maritime hamlet of Baardskeerdersbos, was joined by tasting facilities (by appointment) in 2019. Now there are new wines, and the team are particularly excited about the pinotage, which they consider a true reflection of its Cape Agulhas origin. Pierre summarises the realisation of a longtime dream as: 'Making cool-climate wine on a small scale, garagiste style, the way I like it!'

★★★★☆ **Sun Spider Pinotage** ⑭ ⓥ Cool-climate pinotage flaunting its pinot noir parentage. **18** ⑨① fresh, fragrant cherry & spice notes poised on delicate, lively base; finest of tannins on its dry farewell. A charmer. Just 12% alcohol.

★★★★ **Kelp Forest Syrah 18** ⑧⑨ first since **15** ⑧⑦, bigger alcohol (14%), but similar freshness, delicacy as other reds. Lovely fruit purity - soft red berries, white spice - set off by supple texture, fine grape tannins. Even better in year/2. 500L older French oak.

★★★★ **Baardbek** Cinsaut, shiraz, newly spiced with home-grown viognier, previous included malbec. **18** ⑧⑧ maintains house-style approachability & layered satisfaction in its supple, fresh feel, unshowy yet sustained spice, dark berry flavours. WO W Cape.

★★★★☆ **Blanc Fumé** ⓐ Invigorating, cool-climate sauvignon, **18** ⑨② mixes tropical tones with cutting-edge fruity acids & suggestion of salinity from these seaside vineyards. Ferment in 1,000L Flexcube with new Russian oak insert adds weight, dimension, enhances ageability.

★★★★☆ **Wind Scorpion** ⓥ Unoaked sauvignon, **18** ⑨⓪ about structure, racy agile acid, mineral vitality; fruit an undercurrent. Heady freshness, saline length reflection of most southerly, maritime Cape Agulhas vineyards & winemaker's aim of expressing typicity & place. Interesting potential.

★★★★ **The Bard** ⓥ Cool lemongrass-scented **18** ⑧⑨ mainly semillon with important herbal, delicate floral infusion from nouvelle, viognier, splash sauvignon. Old oak fermented, aged in Flexcube without wood to maintain fruit purity & persistence. Cape South Coast WO.

Coenraad de Buys ★★★★ Multi-source origin for **18** ⑧③ pinotage, shiraz, cinsaut, dab viognier blend. A little muted, bottled month prior to tasting, with youthful edginess but light touch, decent structure suggest better to come, if not in class of **17** ★★★★ ⑧⑦. **Viognier** ⑭ ★★★★ Tasted just post-bottling, **19** ⑧③ agreeably unshowy, subtly oak-spiced. Freshness lifts weighty texture, provides clean, crisp conclusion. May rate higher after time to settle, integrate. **South Cape White** ⑭ ★★★★ Unusual take on white Bordeaux. Semillon wholeberry fermented 3 weeks in amphora, blended with older-oak-fermented sauvignon. **18** ⑧⑤ interesting heavy silk/grainy texture; youthfully shy, should grow, show better cohesion with few years. Discontinued: **Old Lady On The Corner Pinot Noir, Sea Witch Pinot Noir.** — AL

Location: Baardskeerdersbos ▪ Map: Southern Cape ▪ Map grid reference: A3 ▪ WO: Cape Agulhas/ Western Cape/Cape South Coast ▪ Est 2009 ▪ 1stB 2012 ▪ Tasting by appt only T +27 (0)82-465-8350 or +27 (0)82-821-2301 ▪ Owner(s) Pierre Jacques Rabie, Robert Stelzner & Karen van Helden ▪ Winemaker(s) Pierre Jacques Rabie ▪ 2.46ha (Baardskeerdersbos: ptage, albariño, sauv, sem; Bredasdorp: pinot, sauv) ▪ PO Box 415 Bredasdorp 7280 ▪ pjrabie@giantperiwinkle.com ▪ S 34° 34' 31.25" E 019° 35' 39.74" ▪ 🎦 trophy. physicists.trancelike ▪ **T +27 (0)21-426-2653**

The Goose Wines

Retief Goosen, co-owner, and the man whose nickname provided the branding for this venture, was inducted into the World Golf Hall of Fame in 2019 - clutching a bottle of Expression, we hope. His farm,

Ganzekraal ('Goose Pen'), is high in the Outeniqua mountains near George, in the heart of the Garden Route. Its coolness ensures fine natural acidity in the wines, made in the Lourensford cellar in Somerset West.

★★★★ **Expression** Pure sweet fruit & a cool-climate herbaceous element on **14** ⑧⑦, first since **09** ⑧⑦. 60% home cab with Stellenbosch shiraz. Combines plushness with good freshness. 14.3% alcohol. 30% new oak. Also in 1.5 & 3L.

★★★★ **Sauvignon Blanc** ⊘ More citrus than tropical fruit on previewed **19** ⑧⑥, despite ripeness (14.5% alcohol). Really zippy & tangy, but integrated acidity & a good juicy core of sweet flavour.

Cabernet Sauvignon ★★★☆ Ripe, fruity aromas & juicy, flavourful palate on **17** ⑧③, but leaner than 14.5% alcohol suggests - balanced by good acidity. Mostly older oaking for breadth. **Pinot Noir** ⑧ ★★★★ Alluring earth, spice & red berry aromas, turning more savoury on palate. **14** ⑧⑤ balanced & approachable, satisfying now, with potential for good few years. **Shiraz** ★★★☆ Ripe & spicy **17** ⑧⑤, powerful in effect, with an oaky note (30% new), notable bright acids & firm dry tannins supporting the sweet fruit. 14.5% alcohol. Not tasted: **Chardonnay**. — TJ

Location: George ▪ Map: Klein Karoo & Garden Route ▪ Map grid reference: C3 ▪ WO: Upper Langkloof/ Western Cape ▪ Est 2005 ▪ Tasting by appt ▪ Meals/refreshments by appt; or BYO picnic ▪ Family friendly ▪ Owner(s) Retief Goosen & Werner Roux ▪ GM Pieter Haasbroek (Jul 2015) ▪ Winemaker(s) Rocco de Villiers (2018 vintage, consultant) ▪ Viticulturist(s) Bennie Botha (Jan 2009) ▪ 500ha/21ha (cab, shiraz, sauv) ▪ 120t/18,666cs own label 66% red 34% white ▪ HACCP ▪ PO Box 2053 George 6530/The Goose Office, 37 Mark Str, Stellenbosch 7600 ▪ michele@thegoosewines.com ▪ www.thegoosewines.com ▪ S 33° 47' 25.72" E 022° 41' 45.36" ▪ ⬚ fancy.hyper.waistline ▪ **T +27 (0)82-610-2276**

The Grape Grinder

Paarl negociants Johan du Toit and Oliver Kirsten aim to create 'excellently branded, consumer-focused, award-winning' wines through partnerships with 'the best cellars' (social and environmental responsibility an important concern). Their new Heart of Africa range, featuring striking animal labels by local artist Tertia du Toit, is untasted by us but 'already overwhelmingly popular', as is their artisan fynbos-infused gin.

The Grinder range
Pinotage ⊘ ★★★ Special yeasts & 'abundant oaking' (barrels, staves) give **18** ⑧② its overt & desired coffee/choc/mocha character but there's ripe berry & plum fruit, too. WO W Cape. **Shiraz** ⊘ ★★★ Slightly less soft & approachable than previous, **17** ⑧② with sour cherries, leathery hints, spicy kick. Half wooded. **Rosé** ★★★ From Paarl & Swartland cinsaut, **19** ⑧② dry, fruity & refreshing, ample red berry, watermelon, pomegranate & pink grapefruit flavours. **Chenin Blanc** ⊘ ★★★★ From old dryland Swartland vines, **19** ⑧③ aged 6 months on lees is smooth, with nectarine, apricot & yellow apple fruit.

Blue Moose range
Cabernet Sauvignon-Shiraz ⊘ ★★★★ Approachable **18** ⑧⑤ ex Swartland has black fruit, subtle baking spice from 10 months older oak, 4% shiraz contributes peppery hint.

Cape Fynbos range
Chenin Blanc ⊘ ★★★ Only free-run juice in **19** ⑧① , 2 months on lees add texture, leesy quality to tropical fruit. Worth buying for the pretty 3L pack alone.

Milkwood range
Shiraz-Viognier ⊘ ★★★★ **17** ⑧③ again sees 4% viognier co-fermented with shiraz for fynbos & dried herb aromas, red fruit, sweet spice from year oak. WO W Cape.

Wild Olive range
Old Vines Chenin Blanc ⊘ ★★★★ From Swartland, **19** ⑧③ concentrated stonefruit & some pithiness, smooth texture after 6 months on lees. Occasional release: **Rosé**. — JG

Location: Paarl ▪ WO: Coastal/Western Cape/Swartland ▪ Est/1stB 2010 ▪ Closed to public ▪ Owner(s) Oliver Kirsten & Johan du Toit ▪ Cellarmaster(s) Pieter Carstens (Dec 2010, consultant) ▪ Winemaker(s) Madré van der Walt (Jul 2015, consultant) ▪ Viticulturist(s) Koos van der Merwe (Dec 2010, consultant) ▪ 70,000cs own label 75% red 20% white 5% rosé ▪ ISO 2009, BRC, WIETA ▪ PO Box 606 Paarl 7624 ▪ oliver@grapegrinder. com ▪ www.grapegrinder.com ▪ **T +27 (0)21-863-3943**

The Grapesmith

These new releases were produced by the awarded Simonsig team 'using minimalist natural winemaking' with bunch pressing, unsettled juice, wild ferments and the like. The inspiration is the Rhône, Die Kluisenaar modelled on white Hermitage and its sibling on white Châteauneuf-du-Pape. Both are 'proudly WO Stellenbosch' and raised in older French oak.

★★★★☆ **Die Kluisenaar** ⓐ 'The Hermit' is a multi-layered blend of roussanne & marsanne (60/40), **16** ⑨③ with lemon blossom, tropical fruit, hay, vanilla oak & wax notes in mouthfilling yet balanced union. Beautifully packaged, as sibling.

★★★★☆ **Mediterraneo** ⓐ Roussanne, marsanne, grenache blanc, clairette blanche & splash from SA's oldest verdelho (1997) vines combine for a taste sensation in **17** ⑨③. Perfumed & lush, an array of stonefruit, crushed herb & gentle vanilla in harmony with refreshing acidity. — WB

The Great South African Wine Company

This venture is a partnership between Wendy Appelbaum and Carl van der Merwe — respectively owner and winemaker of DeMorgenzon, where the wines are made. The search continues, says Carl, 'for unique parcels of mature vineyards that exude a sense of heritage', focusing on high-lying vineyards in Stellenbosch (while the witty label also conveys tradition, alluding as it does to old medicine bottles). The winemaking, Carl adds, 'remains as natural and minimal as possible'.

★★★★ **The Great Red** ⓖ Blends 60% cab, 24% cinsaut (half fermented with stems) with cab franc & petit verdot. **17** ★★★★☆ ⑨③ heady light perfume; fresh, lively & light-feeling; gentle but firm structure. No new oak, unlike last-made **15** ⑧⑦, where it showed. This one altogether better balanced.

★★★★☆ **The Grand Blanc** Was 'The Great White'. **18** ⑨① a 42/41/17 blend of semillon, chenin, sauvignon from 3 sources, naturally fermented & matured in older oak. Lanolin & dried peach interwoven with feisty acidity, less integrated in youth than **17** ⑨③, will harmonise elegantly with time.— MW

Location/map/WO: Stellenbosch ▪ Map grid reference: C5 ▪ Est 2014 ▪ 1stB 2015 ▪ Tasting by appt only ▪ Owner(s) Wendy Appelbaum & Carl van der Merwe ▪ Cellarmaster(s)/winemaker(s) Carl van der Merwe (2014) ▪ 12-15t ▪ 1,000cs own label 50% red 50% white ▪ PO Box 1388 Stellenbosch 7599 ▪ carl@greatsawineco.com ▪ www.greatsawineco.com ▪ S 33° 56' 22.99" E 018° 45' 0.17" ▪ ⬛ totals.pictures.buddy ▪ **T +27 (0)82-600-9457**

☐ **The Griffin** *see* Stettyn Family Vineyards
☐ **The Grinder** *see* The Grape Grinder
☐ **The Haute Collection** *see* Haute Cabrière
☐ **The Haven Collection** *see* Glen Carlou

The High Road

It's full steam ahead for brand co-owners Les Sweidan and Mike Church with their Bordeaux-inspired reds, including a Reserve Cabernet in magnum soon. From home base at Stellenbosch's Bosman's Crossing, they can now ship to private clients 'almost anywhere in the world', celebrating a first parcel to Russia. Acclaimed Miles Mossop, replacing Mark Carmichael-Green as wine consultant; new website offering online ordering; Instagram account; monthly tastings/lunches with wineclub members... We did say 'full steam ahead'!

★★★★ **Cabernet Sauvignon** ⊘ Appealing black fruit-pastille flavours underscored by dry, chalky tannins. Now matured in old barrels, **17** ⑧⑦ still quite closed in youth, will benefit from further cellaring.

★★★★☆ **Classique** Now 4-part, cab-led Bordeaux blend from 3 Stellenbosch sources. **16** ⑨① dark sappy fruit interwoven with svelte dry tannins in refined balance. Especially well-crafted in difficult vintage. Already appealing, with potential.

★★★★☆ **Director's Reserve** ⓐ Cab-dominated, 5-way Bordeaux blend. All-new cedary oak (16 months) more prominent on **16** ⑨③ vintage than previous, muting core of dark, ripe fruit. Cellar time will harmonise. Still layered & complex, with silky, refined tannins. Also in 3,5 & 12L.— MW

Location/map/WO: Stellenbosch ▪ Map grid reference: E5 ▪ Est/1stB 2003 ▪ Tasting by appt only ▪ Closed all pub hols ▪ Online wine shop ▪ Boardroom facilities ▪ Owner(s) Les Sweidan & Mike Church ▪ Winemaker(s) Miles Mossop (2018, consultant) ▪ Viticulturist(s) Paul Wallace (2004, consultant) ▪ 50t/3,500cs own label 100% red

▪ 7D Lower Dorp Str/Distillery Rd, Bosman's Crossing Stellenbosch 7600 ▪ wine@thehighroad.co.za ▪ www.thehighroad.co.za ▪ S 33° 56' 27.1" E 018° 50' 49.1" ▪ ⌑ myth.heats.uptown ▪ **T +27 (0)76-044-5020**

The Hills ⓠ

Vic Hills is 'looking forward to something new in a few years', having decided to replace some older cabernet with, probably, a Rhône variety at his boutique estate in Stellenbosch's Devon Valley. Grapes grown on the property, named Chimanimani and in Vic's family for over 50 years, are mostly sold off but since 2006 small parcels have been produced for The Hills label by consultants.

Cabernet Sauvignon ★★★ Leafy notes on blackcurrant backbone, salty-savoury **16** ⑧② is lightish, rather brief, with minty finish. **Pinot Noir** ⓠ ★★★ Spicy smoked meat notes to **15** ⑦⑦, aged in old oak. Stellenbosch WO. **Dry Red** ⓠ ★★★★ From shiraz, **13** ⑧④ delivers much more than its name, sleek & juicy with intense red berries, extended oaking fully assimilated. **Shiraz** ★★★ Forward fruit tinged with toffee on heavily wooded **16** ⑦⑨. **Ensemble** ★★★ Lightish cab-shiraz with 11% cab franc, **16** ⑧② has pleasant fruit, minty notes, gentle tannins. 24 months in barrel. **Chenin Blanc** ★★★★ Cheerful, fresh & effusively fruity **18** ⑧③ shows yellow stonefruit with spicy-savoury threads, gentle acidity. — GdB

Location/map: Stellenbosch ▪ Map grid reference: D4 ▪ WO: Devon Valley/Stellenbosch ▪ Est/1stB 2006 ▪ Tasting & sales by appt ▪ Owner(s) The Victor Hills Family Trust ▪ Winemaker(s) Nicky Claasens (2016, consultant) & Danie Steytler (consultant) ▪ Viticulturist(s) Vic Hills (Jan 1998) ▪ 6ha/5ha (cab, pinot, shiraz, chenin) ▪ 40t/600cs own label 80% red 20% white ▪ PO Box 12012 Die Boord Stellenbosch 7613 ▪ vwhills@iafrica.com ▪ www.thehillswine.co.za ▪ S 33° 55' 04.1" E 018° 48' 47.1" ▪ ⌑ among.paper.darkest ▪ **T +27 (0)21-865-2939/+27 (0)82-493-6837**

The Horsemen ⓝⓔⓦ

Debuting this edition (though a few years in the making) is this small-scale joint venture between two friends and former Elsenburg students, viticulturist Jaco Engelbrecht and winemaker Tremayne Smith. Both young, talented and innovative, they have focused their skills on some lesser-known varieties from interesting, far-flung vineyards. The wines are all made naturally, using older neutral oak or plastic 'eggs', ensuring the integrity of the fruit. The striking labels were designed by tattoo artist Tamar Thorn.

★★★★ **The Black Rider** Pure & precise chenin from Philadelphia, **18** ⑧⑨ delicate fruit with hint of spice & some earthy notes, well-balanced freshness & great length. Just 12.5% alcohol. Bunch pressed, as all.

The Pale Rider ⊛ ★★★ Charming, bright & fresh **18** ⑧① ex Darling grenache. Piquant spiced cherry flavours & light texture (12.5% alcohol) make a terrific summer red, could even take light chilling.

The Red Rider ⊘ ★★★ Carignan from Darling, **18** ⑧② introverted mid-2019, low-key red & black berries with gentle spice from 10 months in old oak, well-controlled, supple tannin structure. **The White Rider** ★★★★ Same variety & vinification as Black Rider, different region (Paarl) & outcome: **18** ⑧④ personality packed, rich & ripe, plenty of dried-peach tang & vibrant acidity to maintain poise, interesting pithy end. — CvZ, MW

Location: Riebeek-Kasteel ▪ WO: Darling/Paarl/Philadelphia ▪ 1stB 2018 ▪ Closed to public ▪ Owner(s) Tremayne Smith & Jaco Engelbrecht ▪ Winemaker(s) Tremayne Smith ▪ Viticulturist(s) Jaco Engelbrecht ▪ 8.5t own label 50% red 50% white ▪ tremayne@theblacksmithwines.co.za, jaco@visualviticulture.co.za

The House of GM&AHRENS ⓠ ⓥ⑂

Independent vintner Albert Ahrens' (see The Ahrens Family) desire to make sparkling wine was lit by his first sip of one of the world's most revered bubblies, Clos le Mesnil '90, in the Krug cellar in Champagne. Today, he and Gerrit Maritz, attorney and co-owner of this Franschhoek-based brand, produce just 1,000 5-bottle cases of premium méthode cap classique sparkling, the 2015 vintage of which we'll review next time.

Location/map: Franschhoek ▪ Map grid reference: C1 ▪ Est 2007 ▪ 1stB 2008 ▪ Tasting, sales & cellar tours by appt ▪ Closed all pub hols ▪ Meals/refreshments by appt ▪ Owner(s) Albert Ahrens & Gerrit Maritz ▪ Cellarmaster(s)/viticulturist(s) Albert Ahrens (Jan 2007) ▪ 15t/1,000 x 5-btl cs own label 100% MCC ▪ info@gmahrens.com ▪ www.gmahrens.co.za ▪ S 33° 54' 14" E 019° 07' 08" ▪ ⌑ multilayer.shower.along ▪ **T +27 (0)79-196-6887 (Albert)/+27 (0)83-348-1230 (Gerrit)**

The House of JC le Roux

One of SA's most recognised brands, Distell-owned bubbly specialist JC le Roux is housed in an attractive multi-function cellar in Stellenbosch's Devon Valley, combining production facilities with educational self-guided tours, on-site restaurant and cocktail bar, and amazing views. With much to delight both local and international visitors, the venue specialises in pairing the sparklers with options including chocolate truffles and nougat, as well as a fun kiddies pairing with sweets and flavoured milk. Wine-wise, long-term cellarmaster Elunda Basson has moved on, leaving an experienced team in place, well-versed in producing the champagne-method and popular carbonated bubblies for which the brand is renowned.

Méthode Cap Classique range

La Vallée Rosé Demi-Sec ✓ 🍷 ★★★ Very attractive dessert bubbly, NV ⑧ mixes strawberries & raspberries with creamy sweetness plus freshening acidity.

Brut ✓ ★★★★ Well-priced NV ⑧ everyday sparkler shows fresh lemons & crunchy apples, creamy marshmallow notes & dryish finish. **Pinot Noir** ② ★★★ Subtle berry & savoury tones in still-available **10** ⑧, dry, crisp & crunchy, very fine mousse. **La Vallée Demi-Sec** ✓ ★★★ Charming apple pie & cream notes on NV ⑧ bubbly. Slightly sweeter than pink partner but just as nicely integrated & enjoyable. These from pinot noir & chardonnay unless noted. Not tasted: **Scintilla**. Discontinued: **Pinot Noir Rosé**.

Nectar range

Rosé Demi-Sec ★★★ Pink NV ⑦ is light, crisp & refreshingly off-dry. Fun party fizz from mainly sauvignon with pinotage, muscat & shiraz. 10% alcohol, like White. Carbonated, as all below. **White Demi-Sec** ★★ Semi-sweet NV ⑦ foam has slight honey/floral notes but less intensity than previous. Mostly sauvignon with muscadel.

Sélection Vivante

La Chanson ★★ Sweet red NV ⑦ bubbly shows sophisticated grapey flavours, attractive pepper & spice. From pinotage & others. **La Fleurette** ★★ Pretty colour & perfume on NV ⑦ floral rosé. Appealing low alcohol (7.5% as all these unless noted) & well-managed sweetness make for toothsome pairing with strawberries & cream. **Sauvignon Blanc** ★★★ Pleasantly crisp & fresh **18** ⑦, softly dry, engaging grassy notes & hints of lemon & lime. ±13% alcohol. **Le Domaine** ★★ Frothy & fun NV ⑦ full of grapes & blossoms from the muscadel component, finishes sweet but clean. Perfect Sunday morning sparkle. — CM

Location/map: Stellenbosch ▪ Map grid reference: D4 ▪ WO: Western Cape ▪ 1stB 1983 ▪ Tasting & sales Mon-Fri 10—4 Sat/pub hols 10—3 Sun 10—2; booking essential ▪ Fee R80-R120 ▪ Closed Good Fri, Dec 25 & Jan 1 ▪ Nougat Experience, Truffle Experience ▪ Self-tour available during opening hrs ▪ Cocktails & platters ▪ Gifts ▪ Restaurant open for breakfast & lunch, booking essential ▪ Conference/wedding facilities ▪ Owner(s) Distell ▪ Viticulturist(s) Bennie Liebenberg (Jan 2000) ▪ Farm manager(s) Graham Daniels (2015) ▪ 27ha own vyds ▪ 20% red 80% white ▪ ISO 9200 ▪ PO Box 184 Stellenbosch 7599 ▪ info@jcleroux.co.za ▪ www.jcleroux.co.za ▪ S 33° 54' 16.6" E 018° 48' 37.4" ▪ 🖭 running.shares.belong ▪ **T +27 (0)21-865-8200**

☐ **The House of Krone** see Krone
☐ **The House of Mandela** see House of Mandela
☐ **The Innocent** see Lammershoek Winery
☐ **The Introduction** see Miles Mossop Wines

The Kitchen Sink

Originally a second label within the Metzer & Holfeld Family Wines portfolio, The Kitchen Sink has evolved into a standalone brand, hence this separate listing. 'Distinctive vineyard parcels' across the Western Cape are vinified in Stellenbosch by minimalist Wade Metzer 'to retain as much terroir and fruit character as possible'.
★★★★ **Red Blend** ② Complex multi-region **16** ⑧ led by shiraz, naturally fermented. Seductive choc-laced dark-berry depths without tannic edges, lower 14.5% alcohol after 15% in lush **15** ⑧.
Not tasted: **White Blend**. — DS

Location: Somerset West ▪ WO: Western Cape ▪ Tasting by appt ▪ Owner(s) Wade Metzer & Barry Holfeld ▪ Winemaker(s) Wade Metzer ▪ info@kitchensinkwine.com ▪ www.kitchensinkwine.com ▪ **T +27 (0)72-279-7645**

☐ **The Legend** *see* Windmeul Cellar

Thelema Mountain Vineyards

The phoenix on Thelema's label speaks volumes about both farm and family. Gyles Webb swapped accounting for winemaking in the early 1980s, fledging from an old Helshoogte Pass fruit farm one of SA's best-loved quality-wine producers by the 1990s. Drive and success (similarly cool-climate Elgin property Sutherland was bought in 2002 to supplement Thelema's wines, flying out of the cellar) never compromised the personal touch. In the early days Gyles' redoubtable mother-in-law Edna 'Ed' McLean entertained winelovers and wife Barbara did deliveries, now son Thomas manages affairs while Gyles guides the cellar team (introducing a second Sutherland pinot noir). It was the turn of visitors and staff in 2019, treated respectively to an extended tasting area (incorporating a scenic deck, private venue and underground bottle cellar) and a tea/lunch room with scenic vineyard views.

Thelema range

★★★★☆ **Cabernet Sauvignon** ⊛ Impressive crafting & balance, confirms why Stellenbosch is renowned for cabernet. Intensely perfumed & flavoured, cassis & spice, hint of graphite supported by fine-grained tannins, toned 18 months (as all these reds unless noted) in 45% new oak. **16** ⑨④ has musculature for a long life. Also in magnum.

★★★★ **Merlot** Long-standing SA benchmark & paragon of reliability. **16** ★★★★☆ ⑨⓪ bright fruited, with choc/mocha notes & tobacco from third new oak, as smooth & elegant as **15** ⑧⑦ & even more effortlessly enjoyable. Well made, with good few years cellaring potential.

★★★★★ **Merlot Reserve** ⊛ All-new oak & selection of special vineyard parcels show in the fruit intensity, layers of spicing & sleek structure. Impressive **15** ⑨⑤ beat off contenders in Wine Cellar's 2019 SA versus Bordeaux blind taste-off, **16** ⑨⑤ as beautiful & built to last - a great future ahead.

★★★★ **Shiraz** ⊘ Different styling to Sutherland, **15** ⑧⑨ is smoky, savoury, its dark fruit well matched to supple tannins, texture silky, curvaceous. But hidden strength here, good ageing potential.

★★★★☆ **Rabelais** ⊛ In youth, **15** ⑨④ 90/10 cabernet & petit verdot duo is quietly stellar, shows striking focus of blackcurrant flavour lifted by ethereal kelp/iodine tones, exceptionally well-managed tannin structure contains the sleek fruit. 20 months French oak, 80% new, perfect platform for ageing.

★★★★ **Chardonnay** A great table accompaniment, **16** ★★★★★ ⑨⓪ improves on **15** ⑧⑦ with packed flavour, citrus & buttered toast, zesty freshness brightening the palate, extending the sensations. Bolder than Sutherland sibling but lovely balance, well-crafted oak, 15% new.

★★★★ **Ed's Reserve Chardonnay** ⊘ Ed was co-owner Gyles Webb's feisty, memorable late mother-in-law. From unusual 'muscat' clone of chardonnay, **16** ⑧⑧ barrel fermented/aged, gives aromatic zesty grapiness, it's one-of-a-kind, much like Ed.

★★★★ **Riesling** ⊘ Distinctive **16** ⑧⑧ from estate's oldest block, planted 1984. Floral notes vie with pineapple, bottle age intensifying the flavours. Racy freshness & dry, sleek body, hard to resist.

★★★★☆ **Sauvignon Blanc** ⊘ Different style to Sutherland, though both have cool growing conditions. Citrus with a mineral core to polished pre-bottling sample of **19** ⑨① tangy limy acidity giving it focus & startling length. Used to sell out on release 1 July each year when the field was less crowded; still the same consistent quality.

★★★★ **Méthode Cap Classique Brut** ⊘ Elgin-sourced sparkling, 32 months on lees, classic chardonnay/pinot noir blend, **14** ⑧⑨ ticks all boxes: lemon/lime & brioche, elegant yet great length.

★★★★ **Semillon Late Harvest 15** ⑧⑨ continues the uptick of **14** ⑧⑦, celebrates melon fruit & citrus preserve with honey overlay. Explosive flavour perked by tense acidity. This & next 11% alcohol & 375 ml.

★★★★ **Vin de Hel Late Harvest** Named for Helshoogte Pass, home of Thelema. Grapey, with notes of honey blossom, **16** ⑧⑨ muscat blanc is rich & sweet, a fresh acid lift adds length & delicious drinkability.

....

Mountain Red ⊘ ★★★★ Creative shiraz-led blend, **16** ⑧⑤ with petit verdot, merlot & splashes cab & grenache. Again punches above its price, with wild berries, salty liquorice & peppery notes, food friendly, firm & dry. WO W Cape. **Muscat** ⊘ ★★★☆ Piercing grapiness heralds fresh, dry & zesty (unfortified) **19** ⑧⑤, the gorgeous perfume beguiles & lingers forever. Versatile, merits a place at picnics, barbecues & even silver service meals. Tasted pre-bottling.

....

Not tasted: **The Mint Cabernet Sauvignon**.

Sutherland range

★★★★☆ **Reserve Grenache** ⓥ An impressive debut, **16** ⑨③ shows scrub & red berries & violets. Nails the variety by showing that intensity is possible with elegance & grace. Ripeness without excess; polished, harmonious, a long life ahead. Elgin WO, as all these.

★★★★ **Pinot Noir** ⓥ **16** ⑧⑥ brims with mulberries & raspberries framed by ripe tannins. Evolved, with an earthy character, ready to savour while firm **15** ★★★★ ⑧④ rests awhile in cellar. 9 months cask, 15% new.

★★★★☆ **Reserve Pinot Noir** ⓝⒺⓦ ⓐ Barrel selection **16** ⑨⓪ sends spirals of perfume to tempt, & black cherry entices before super texture offers fabulous grip for food (or contemplation). Slightly more new (20%) wood, but altogether more refined than sibling.

★★★★★ **Reserve Petit Verdot** ⓐ All-new French oak signals refined **16** ★★★★★ ⑨④'s serious intent, as did stellar debut **15** ⑨⑤. Almost as complex, notes of violets & wild berries beautifully threaded through with scrub & cigarbox, but massive tannic lattice still in infancy, demands the cellar.

★★★★ **Syrah** ⓥ Lilting whiffs of white pepper overlay dark berries of **15** ★★★★★ ⑨⓪, which reflects sleek vintage & shares **14** ⑧⑨'s fine-grained savoury tannin backbone, promising years of pleasure ahead. 18 months oak, 20% new.

★★★★ **Chardonnay** Lemon Cream biscuit & buttered toast, **18** ⑧⑨ wears its oaking with pride (fermented/10 months in seasoned wood), the citrus core keeping it fresh & lively. Delicious food wine.

★★★★☆ **Reserve Chardonnay** ⓥ A barrel selection, long lees contact & bottle age providing orange preserve richness & palate weight. **16** ⑨③ has latent power, belying its elegance (just 13% alcohol).

★★★★ **Riesling** Always noteworthy for varietal elegance & refinement. **18** ⑧⑧ a step up on **17** ★★★★ ⑧④, riverstone aromatics, racy acidity offset by a dab of sweetness, adding to the appeal.

★★★★☆ **Sauvignon Blanc** ⓥ Sampled ex tank, **19** ⑨⓪ thrills with vibrant nettle & lime reflecting the cool climate. Sleek, focused & pure, a true palate awakener before or with the meal. Intense **18** ⑨③ led the uptick from **17** ★★★★ ⑧⑧.

★★★★☆ **Viognier-Roussanne** ⓐ Intriguing white blend, viognier in the vanguard (80%) but far from blowsy. Aromas abound in **16** ⑨③, stonefruit given a savoury overlay by 10 months seasoned-oak ferment/ageing. Elegant, a range trademark, without sacrificing flavour intensity.

Cabernet Sauvignon ★★★☆ Nice combo cassis & oak spice, elegant **15** ⑧⑤'s tannins are supple for immediate enjoyment. Discontinued: **Grenache Rosé**, **Unwooded Chardonnay**. — DS

Location/map: Stellenbosch ▪ Map grid reference: G4 ▪ WO: Stellenbosch/Elgin/Western Cape ▪ Est 1983 ▪ 1stB 1988 ▪ Tasting & sales Mon-Fri 9–5 Sat 10–3 ▪ Fee R80/6 wines, waived on purchase ▪ Owner(s) McLean & Webb family trusts ▪ Cellarmaster(s) Gyles Webb (1983) ▪ Winemaker(s) Rudi Schultz (Dec 2000), with Duncan Clarke (Jan 2009) ▪ 257ha/90ha (cab, grenache, merlot, p verdot, pinot, shiraz, chard, muscat, riesling, rouss, sauv, viog) ▪ 1,000t/60,000cs own label 40% red 60% white ▪ PO Box 2234 Dennesig Stellenbosch 7601 ▪ info@thelema.co.za ▪ www.thelema.co.za ▪ S 33° 54' 30.0" E 018° 55' 23.4" ▪ ⓘ slap. testing.march ▪ **T** +27 (0)21-885-1924

The Liberator

'Expect the unexpected,' says Rick the Cape Crusader, aka Richard Kelley MW, UK authority on SA wine, who visits several times a year to 'liberate' experimental batches or interesting offcuts that might otherwise be blended away or sold in bulk. Each once-off bottling is an 'episode' that tells a story. 'There is no set style or quantity. No fixed price point. Rest assured that whatever the wine, it's received Rick's own seal of approval.'

★★★★ **P.S. I Love You** Delicious, fresh petite sirah from Stellenbosch's DeMorgenzon, **16** ⑧⑧ naturally fermented, year in old oak, packed with juicy plum & blueberry fruit, pinch pepper & herbs.

★★★★ **The Teeth Of The Dog** Chardonnay from Glen Carlou, name inspired by tiny Dents de Chien vineyard in Burgundy, **17** ⑧⑨ fermented/aged year in half oak, half 'egg', is creamy with zesty citrus freshness, nutty finish.

★★★★☆ **Perfectly Flawed** Cinnamon, cardamom, tangerine rind & coconut, **15** ⑨① chenin ex Fable Mountain Vineyards smells like Cape Malay koeksisters but is dry, distinctive, deliciously tangy thanks to flor yeast that developed while maturing 20 months in concrete 'egg'. Tiny parcel available locally through Wine Cellar. Swartland WO.— JG

WO: Stellenbosch/Swartland/Simonsberg-Paarl ▪ Est 2010 ▪ 1stB 2008 ▪ Closed to public ▪ Owner(s) Richard Kelley MW & Eduard Haumann ▪ 50% red 50% white ▪ richard@dreyfus-ashby.co.uk ▪ www.theliberator-wine.com ▪ T +44 (0)1476-870717

☐ **The Lion Hound** see Ridgeback

The Love Boat Wines

Winemaker friends Duncan Savage and Adi Badenhorst shared some 'interesting' Airbnbs on a marketing trip to Norway. A 'compromising' selfie in a one-bed studio, widely shared on Twitter, caused much hilarity. Never ones to miss a marketing opportunity, the duo developed a pair of joint-venture wines sold on the annual Cape Winemakers Guild auction, when Adi was still a CWG member. A one-off? 'The Love Boat has left the harbour but our GPS is on the blink!' They hope to be back on course in 2020, if the wine makes the grade.

Location: Cape Town ▪ Est 2017 ▪ 1stB 2016 ▪ Closed to public ▪ Owner(s) Adi Badenhorst & Duncan Savage ▪ ±200cs own label 60% red 40% white ▪ info@savagewines.com ▪ T +27 (0)21-447-3022

☐ **The Marais Family** see Wonderfontein
☐ **Thembu Tribute** see House of Mandela
☐ **The Mentors** see KWV Wines
☐ **The Merchant** see Cape Wine Company

Themika ⓠ ⌂ ◎

Cape Town doctors Paul and Dagmar Whitaker named their fruit and olive farm in Tulbagh after daughters Kim and Thea. There already were 40-year-old chenin vines, and a small winery was awaiting official recognition as we went to press. Nothing new to taste, but Paul says a chenin in barrel is looking promising.

Location/map: Tulbagh ▪ Map grid reference: F4 ▪ 1stB 2013 ▪ Tasting by appt only ▪ Themika guest house (farm house & 3 self-catering cottages) T +27 (0)78-472-0934 (Douglas) ▪ MTB routes ▪ Owner(s) Paul & Dagmar Whitaker ▪ Winemaker(s)/viticulturist(s) Paul Whitaker ▪ 56ha/2ha (chenin) ▪ 4.5t/220cs own label 100% white ▪ ansec166@docswhitaker.co.za ▪ www.themika.com ▪ S 33° 13' 4.14" E 019° 6' 35.44" ▪ 🏧 flowerbeds.redoubts.mossy

---

☐ **The Mysteries** see Lammershoek Winery
☐ **The Old Man's Blend** see Groote Post Vineyards
☐ **The Pierneef Collection** see La Motte
☐ **The Pledge** see Le Grand Domaine
☐ **The Quirky Ones** see Old Road Wine Company
☐ **The Raptor Post** see Fable Mountain Vineyards
☐ **The Rhino Run** see Van Loveren Family Vineyards
☐ **The Rose House** see Mile High Vineyards
☐ **The Sadie Family** see Sadie Family Wines
☐ **The Saints** see DGB (Pty) Ltd
☐ **The Search** see Trizanne Signature Wines
☐ **The Sensory Collection** see Stellar Winery
☐ **The Spice Route Winery** see Spice Route Winery
☐ **The Stellenbosch Reserve** see Stellenbosch Reserve
☐ **The Storyteller** see Stellar Winery
☐ **The Tin Mine** see Zevenwacht
☐ **The Township Winery** see Township Winery

Theuniskraal ⓠ ♿

Named for a son of one of the earliest families to settle in Tulbagh (circa 1699), Theuniskraal has been farmed by the Jordaan family since 1927. These paragons of continuity are set to produce the 73rd vintage of their consumer favourite, Cape Riesling, meanwhile adding a trio of wines in the same crowd-pleasing style.

Semillon-Chardonnay ⊘ ⊛ ★★★ Cheerful & fragrant, with sunshiny peach flavour untrammelled by oak. **18** ⑧⓪ just-dry but crisp, balanced, oh so easy to drink.

....

Cabernet Sauvignon (NEW) ★★★ Light hearted **17** ⑧① shows sweet black berry, mocha & vanilla wafts, offers smooth & effortless drinking. **Shiraz** (NEW) ★★★ Bold & spicy black fruit, smooth tannin & lingering savoury finish in **17** ⑦⑨. **Prestige** ★★★ Dark berries, dried herbs & hints of coffee on light-bodied, oak-brushed **17** ⑦⑨ cab/shiraz blend, with splash ruby cab. **Moscato Rosé** ★★ Light (10.5% alcohol) & sweet pink from muscat ottonel & shiraz charms with delicate rose perfume in **18** ⑦⑥. **Cape Riesling** ★★☆ A Cape institution since 1948; **18** ⑦⑨ shy, dry & light, with hints of orchard fruit. Alcohol a friendly 11.5%.
Sauvignon Blanc (NEW) ★★☆ Uncomplicated **18** ⑦⑧ is light & fleeting, with tropical fruit & grassy notes.
Bouquet Blanc ★★ From gewürztraminer & white muscadel, **18** ⑦⑥ is soft, with fleshy berries & spicy edge, touch sweeter than previous. — WB

Location/map/WO: Tulbagh ▪ Map grid reference: F4 ▪ Est 1705 ▪ 1stB 1947 ▪ Tasting & sales Mon-Fri 9–5 Sat 9–2 ▪ Closed Easter Sat/Sun, Dec 25 & Jan 1 ▪ Owner(s)/viticulturist(s) Jordaan family ▪ Cellarmaster(s) Andries Jordaan (1991) ▪ Winemaker(s) Andries Jordaan (1991) & Wagner Jordaan ▪ 140ha total ▪ PO Box 34 Tulbagh 6820 ▪ admin@tkraal.co.za ▪ www.theuniskraal.co.za ▪ S 33° 13' 41.3" E 019° 8' 7.1" ▪ ⊠ seesaws. consulate.autobiography ▪ **T** +**27 (0)23-230-0689**

──────────────────────────────────────

☐ **The Vale** *see* Bonnievale Wines
☐ **The Vine Guys** *see* Mischa Estate
☐ **The Vinologist** *see* Vinologist Wine Company

The Vinoneers

Some of the talents of both owners of this Durbanville wine collaboration are on display, both in the elegant labels created by graphic designer Brenden Schwartz, and the contents, crafted by winemaker Etienne Louw (also of Altydgedacht). The project aims to show their creativity and depict their love for wine as art, their next challenge being how to incorporate Etienne's chops as a rock guitarist in the bottle!

Orpheus & The Raven range

★★★★★ **No. 42 Cape Blend** A very 'Cape' blend of pinotage & its parents pinot noir & cinsaut (58/35/7), **17** ⑨⓪ is a delight with snappy red fruit (cranberries & cherries), spicy, toasty oak (35% new), smooth tannins & savoury notes of Marmite, smoke & meat. Durbanville, Walker Bay & Bottelary grapes.

★★★★ **No. 42 Old Bush Vine Chenin Blanc** Intricate & intriguing labels perfectly mirror contents of **18** ★★★★★ ⑨⓪, from 40 year old bushvines providing concentrated citrus & cooked apple flavours, perfectly married to creamy honey notes from barrel ferment (10% new). Step up on **17** ⑧⑨. Cape Town WO.

★★★★★ **The Swansong** (?) From 35 year old gewürztraminer vines uprooted after this harvest, hence name. **16** ⑨① pure litchi & rosepetal aromas, fresh & linear, just off-dry. Seductive & playful on nose, but so sophisticated on the palate: pristine & focused.— CM

Location: Durbanville ▪ WO: Durbanville/Cape Town/Western Cape ▪ Est/1stB 2016 ▪ Closed to public ▪ Owner(s) Etienne Louw & Brenden Schwartz ▪ Winemaker(s) Etienne Louw (2015) ▪ 2,000cs own label 66% red 34% white ▪ etienne@vinoneers.com ▪ www.vinoneers.com ▪ **T** +**27 (0)21-461-0245**

──────────────────────────────────────

☐ **The Winery of Good Hope** *see* Radford Dale

The Wine Thief   ⊙

Ewan Mackenzie is less of a sommelier these days than a wine negociant, collaborating with established winemakers in cellars around the Western Cape — at present mostly in Stellenbosch and the Swartland. Perhaps there's an ironical allusion to his vinous acquisitions in his brand name, though it less humorously refers to the pipette used for taking samples of wine through barrel bungholes.

The Wine Thief range

★★★★★ **Mourvèdre** (NEW) Ripe, full aromas on **17** ⑨② with savoury dark fruit & spice, presage a rich & robust, generous palate. Big but smooth tannins, 14.2% alcohol, sweet fruity & fresh acidity all well-balanced to make a deliciously exuberant whole, with a firm dry finish.

★★★★ **Colombard** (NEW) Characterful, fresh **18** (87) from Slanghoek, naturally fermented like all these; fruity-savoury with white flowers & honey. Ripe-tasting, though lightish 12% alcohol.

★★★★☆ **Marsanne** (NEW) Distinctive old-oaked **18** (90) also with 7% viognier adding to the complexity of lively fresh aromas & flavour, making for intensity as well as subtlety. Light rich, silky & satisfyingly dry.

★★★★☆ **Cape White** (NEW) **17** (93) has 50% chenin & 5 other varieties making up a pleasingly aromatic & flavourful, rather intriguing whole. Fresh grip, good texture, dry & refined, with a lingering stony-mineral finish. Maturation in old oak barrels.

Not tasted: **Petit Verdot Blanc de Noir**.

Costa del Swart range

★★★★ **Tinta Barocca** (NEW) Gorgeously perfumed aromas on **15** (89) from early-picked Swartland grapes. Light 11.5% alcohol, but enough vinosity; expressive fruit though without intensity. Restrained dry tannins.

★★★★ **Viura Vonkelwyn** (NEW) Sparkling **17** (88), 2nd ferment in bottle, made with locally rare Spanish white grape (aka macabeo) - giving, unsurprisingly, unusual aromas & flavours. Forward, even bold & a touch rustic, but with a good fresh grip, dry & most attractive. WO Voor Paardeberg.

Occasional release: **Chenin Blanc**. — TJ

Location: Cape Town ▪ WO: Stellenbosch/Swartland/Slanghoek/Voor Paardeberg ▪ Est 2015 ▪ 1stB 2013 ▪ Consultant sommelier, staff training, events & functions, private dinners & sommelier-led tours ▪ Owner(s) Ewan Mackenzie ▪ Cellarmaster(s)/winemaker(s)/viticulturist(s) Various ▪ 50-160cs own label 30% red 45% white 25% rosé ▪ Other consulting brands: Ben Wren Wines, Grub & Vine, Jason Bakery, Khayelitsha's Finest Wines ▪ ewan@winethief.co.za ▪ **T +27 (0)71-116-8129**

The Wolftrap

There never have been wolves in the Cape, but on the Boekenhoutskloof estate in Franschhoek (the owner of this brand) an old wolftrap was found — whence this reminder of 'the mysteries and legends of days gone by'. That there's great value to be found in the modern, widely sourced trio is, however, no mere tale.

★★★★ **White** ⊘ Ever-dependable, delicious & best value on the shelf. **18** (88) has viognier ahead, for intense floral aromas & rich texture, near-equal chenin & grenache blanc add vibrant apple & stonefruit, partial oaking lends spice emporium piquancy.

Red ⊘ ★★★★ Super-drinkable **18** (85), smooth, juicy black fruit, olive tapenade nuance & a floral lift. Mostly syrah with mourvèdre & viognier. **Rosé** ★★★ Dry, juicy & fresh **19** (82) from cinsaut, syrah & grenache slips down easily. WO W Cape, as all. — WB

☐ **The Woodstock Winery** See Editor's Note
☐ **The Zahir** see Lateganskop Winery
☐ **Thierry & Guy** see Fat Bastard
☐ **Thierry Haberer** see Verspieren Haberer Family Wines

Thistle & Weed ⓛ

Channelling the Mumford & Sons song, Thistle & Weeds, but also reflecting on the relationships between vines and vineyard pests, the dynamic wine partnership between winemaker Stephanie Wiid, ex Fairview, now full-time T&W, and viticulturist Etienne Terblanche, recent PhD and part of the estimable VinPro team, is going places fast. Both joyfully announced new arrivals in their respective families, as well as their site-specific wine range. The focus is on minimal intervention, expression of terroir and small-volume, high-quality wines. No visitor centre, flashy cellar or other frills.

★★★★ **Knapsekêrel** (NEW) Appealingly lean & subtle cab franc from biodynamically farmed vines, **17** (89) wholeberry fermented for brighter fruit accents. Heady notes of liquorice & bay, silky texture.

★★★★☆ **Nastergal** Unique & wonderfully quirky blend tempranillo & red-fleshed alicante bouschet, **18** (90) from Stellenbosch grapes exudes appeal. Lashings of succulent berry fruit, spiced with scrub & pepper, borne on a muscular, robust framework. Simply delicious. Also-tasted **17** (91) adds Paarl grapes, ramps up the appeal on debut **16** ★★★★☆ (84).

★★★★☆ **Brandnetel** Simple, old-school winemaking at its best: bunch pressed, wild yeast, older barrels, unfiltered; **18** ⑨ underscores promise of excellent **17** ⑨. Chenin from old experimental block (30 rootstocks!), expressing varietal nobility with shape, delicacy & focus.

★★★★★ **Duuweltjie** ⓐ Stunning chenin from 1956 Paarl bushvines, **18** ⑨ minimally worked & bottled unfined/filtered. Commanding presence, elegant poise & layered complexity, all rounded out by 11 months in older barrels.

★★★★☆ **Khakibos** ⓝⓔⓦ Exotic spicy aromas, viscous texture, & lingering mineral & glacé fruit flavours make for a unique taste experience in **18** ⑨ verdelho. Quince-like tannin structure, apple & rhubarb notes, burnished by year in very old barrels. A bright future predicted.— GdB

Location: Stellenbosch ▪ WO: Stellenbosch/Coastal/Paarl ▪ Est 2015 ▪ 1stB 2016 ▪ Tasting by appt only ▪ Wines available online ▪ Owner(s) Etienne Terblanche & Stephanie Wiid ▪ Winemaker(s) Stephanie Wiid (Sep 2015) ▪ Viticulturist(s) Etienne Terblanche (Sep 2015) ▪ 1,000cs own label 30% red 70% white ▪ PO Box 62 Koelenhof 7605 ▪ info@thistleandweed.co.za ▪ www.thistleandweed.co.za

---

Thokozani Wines   ⓆⓅⓖⓞ

David Sonnenberg of Diemersfontein Wines was the wind beneath the wings of Thokozani, but the Wellington wine venture is now flying high, 80% owned by staff and so successful, international pundits are studying its rise and rise. There are an office and facilities on Diemersfontein where visitors can 'engage with our business of transformation'. The vision is to further develop 'in a steady and responsible way, with no short cuts, to lead eventually to true capacity building and autonomy'.

Thokozani range
★★★★ **SMV** ⊘ Ample yet elegant **18** ㉠, fresh berries spiced with pepper & scrub. Supple & plush, smooth, subtle savoury notes from 10 months in oak. Shiraz & mourvèdre (77/11), splash viognier. Wellington WO.
Discontinued: **Rosé**, **CCV**.

Ovation range
Merlot Ⓠ ★★★ Juicy **17** ㉜ from Robertson & Wellington grapes offers fair intensity, berry complexity for uncomplicated, early enjoyment. **Cabernet Sauvignon-Merlot** ★★★ Sound everyday drinker **17** ㉠, flavoursome, its fruit front & centre, accessible. **Sauvignon Blanc** ★★★ Elgin & Piekenierskloof-sourced **18** ㉠ shows cool-climate pungency; fruit-forward, with pleasing shape & substance. **Spumante** Ⓠ ★★ Light-hearted off-dry sauvignon blanc from Robertson grapes. **NV** ㉕ fresh, with a slight spritz. — GdB
Location/map: Wellington ▪ Map grid reference: B4 ▪ WO: Western Cape/Wellington ▪ Est/1stB 2005 ▪ Tasting & sales daily 10-5 ▪ Closed Dec 25 ▪ Cellar tours by appt ▪ Aan Tafel restaurant ▪ Tour groups ▪ Conferences ▪ Walks/hikes ▪ 4-star Thokozani Cottages ▪ Owner(s) Diemersfontein employees & Diemersfontein Wines ▪ Winemaker(s) Francois Roode (Sep 2003), with Lauren Hulsman (Nov 2011) ▪ Viticulturist(s) Charl van der Merwe (Jun 2019) ▪ 180ha/45ha (cabs s/f, grenache, malbec, mourv, p verdot, ptage, roobernet, shiraz, chenin, viog) ▪ 15,000cs own label 60% red 40% white ▪ WIETA ▪ PO Box 41 Wellington 7654 ▪ denisestubbs@thokozani.co.za ▪ www.thokozani.co.za ▪ S 33° 39' 41.1" E 019° 0' 31.1" ▪ ⓜ gates.cakes.mere ▪ **T +27 (0)21-864-5050**

Thorne & Daughters Wines   Ⓠ

In little more than half a decade, John Seccombe has built a reputation as a leader of the school of modern (traditionally made!), fresh winemaking, achieving a sometimes ethereal elegance and characterfulness that is his own. He sources his grapes primarily in the Swartland, and makes his wine in the Gabriëlskloof cellar in the Overberg, as part of a small, harmonious 'winemaking clan'. Beyond the family link in the brand name, childhood is behind all the names of the wines, even that of the sole red in the range, Wanderer's Heart, which derives from a character in children's stories written by a friend. New to the winemaking team is Albert van Niekerk, working for both Thorne & Daughters and Peter-Allan Finlayson's Crystallum.

★★★★☆ **Wanderer's Heart** ⓐ Blends grenache with cinsaut, mourvèdre & syrah. **18** ㉝ pure-fruited & perfumed, but much more than charming, light (12.9% alcohol), fresh & vibrant: it's serious, with a fine structure to match the core of sweet fruit. Ageable too, though delicious in youth. WO W Cape.

★★★★☆ **Cat's Cradle Chenin Blanc** ⊛ ⊛ Aromatic, mid-gold **18** ⑨③ echoes with peach, quince & ripe apple. Subtle, understated intensity, with succulent freshness & a dry grip controlling the lingering finish. 9 months in old oak add breadth & texture.

★★★★☆ **Tin Soldier Semillon** ⊛ Apricot-gold hue points to red-skinned version of the grape. 7-10 days on skins adds tannic touch as well as colour. Intense aromas on **18** ⑨④: lanolin, lemon, gingery spice. Fresh acid infuses velvet texture; modest 12.6% alcohol part of ethereal finesse. Even finer than **17** ⑨②.

★★★★★ **Paper Kite Old Vine Semillon** ⊛ ⊛ Serene & gently assertive **18** ⑨③ has great depth of fruit allied with savoury complexity. Smooth, even a touch oily. At 13.4%, the highest alcohol here - ripeness achieved with sufficient acidity for excellent balance.

★★★★★ **Rocking Horse Cape White Blend** ⊛ Roussanne, semillon, chardonnay, clairette & chenin make a seamless, complex whole in lightly rich & ripe, delicate but forceful **18** ⑨⑦. Texture like rippling silk, shot through with fresh lemony acidity. Tantalising but satisfying to the long-lingering finish. WO W Cape. Natural ferment & maturation in old oak, as for all these wines.— TJ

Location: Bot River ▪ WO: Swartland/Western Cape ▪ Est 2012 ▪ 1stB 2013 ▪ Tastings by prior arrangement ▪ Owner(s) John & Tasha Seccombe ▪ Cellarmaster(s)/viticulturist(s) John Seccombe (Dec 2012) ▪ Winemaker(s) John Seccombe (Dec 2012), with Albert van Niekerk (consultant) ▪ 35t/2,000cs own label 25% red 75% white ▪ 36 Main Rd, Onrus 7201 ▪ john@thorneanddaughters.com ▪ www.thorneanddaughters.com ▪ T +27 (0)76-036-7116

Thor Vintners

Durbanville vintner Emile Gentis produces a small range of wines under his Age of the Rebel label, aptly named given they are 'premium, experimental, think-out-the-box, rebel small batches, made once or twice before moving on to a new blend, terroir, style or origin'. As a broker of grapes, bulk and bottled wine for clients, he also manages local labels Long Mountain, Gecko Ridge and Athena for their Ghanaian owners.

Age of the Rebel range ⑭ⓔ⑭

Cabernet Franc ★★★★ Richly fruited & ripe **17** ⑧③ ticks some varietal boxes in its graphite & dried herb nuances, a fuller style than the elegance the variety can give, but there's tasty drinkability here. **Cinsaut** ★★★★ Light-coloured & - textured **18** ⑧④ perhaps not delicate but shows distinct varietal character. Expressive red berries, spicing from mostly old oak, juicy & smooth. Splash grenache. WO Stellenbosch. **Merlot** ★★★ From Bot River, **13** ⑦⑦ on skins 2 months post ferment, then 26 months in barrel, to create a wine for ageing. Deep ripe cassis but tannins grippy: cellar says 'More for the collector'. **Agostinelli Syrah** ★★★ Intense raspberries & cherries, **17** ⑧① in nouveau style for easy drinkability. Oaked 10 months, grip & vanilla at the end but fruit is in charge. Durbanville grapes, including dashes cinsaut & grenache. **Semillon** ★★★ Oaked **18** ⑦⑦ shows oat biscuit savouriness throughout, fruit remains subservient but good light texture (12.5% alcohol) & freshness. **Chardonnay-Semillon-Roussanne** ★★★ Stonefruit & toasted almonds on elegant **18** ⑧②, more expressive in perfume flavours but appealing nonetheless. 14 months oaked, 70% new. Also-tasted **17** ⑧⓪, 50% new wood, stonefruit & touch of honey from bottle age. Riper style, palate more savoury than fruity. **Semillon-Roussanne** ★★★ Floral notes & ginger biscuit (oaked 12 months, 40% new), **18** ⑧①'s fruit is yellow peach but not very forthcoming, has a delicacy. Ends soft & smooth. Splashes chardonnay & viognier. — CR, CvZ

Location: Durbanville ▪ WO: Franschhoek/Stellenbosch/Bot River/Durbanville ▪ Est 2016 ▪ 1stB 2010 ▪ Closed to public ▪ Cellarmaster(s) Emile Gentis ▪ Other export ranges: Voyageur, Wind Song ▪ PO Box 46140 Durbanville 7550 ▪ emile@thorvintners.com, jeanne@thorvintners.com ▪ www.thorvintners.com

☐ **1000 Miles** *see* Mulderbosch Vineyards
☐ **Three Pines** *see* Stark-Condé Wines
☐ **Three Rivers** *see* Bon Courage Estate

Thunderchild

In 2003, Robertson farmers got together to plant vines on land owned by the community's children's home. The fruit is vinified, also pro bono, by sympathetic wineries and sold from their cellardoors and nearby fine-wine shops. Profits go to Die Herberg's 'thunderchildren', helping lighten 'dark and threatening clouds'.

★★★★ **Thunderchild** ⊘ Satisfies on many levels. Wild-yeast-fermented, modestly oaked merlot, cab franc & cab **16** ⑧⑧ packed with blackberry fruit & charcuterie spice. Even better - & better priced - than delightful **15** ★★★★ ⑧⑤. — DS

Location/WO: Robertson ▪ Est 2003 ▪ 1stB 2008 ▪ Wines available from Affie Plaas Farmstall, Ashton Wine Boutique, Ashton Winery, Bon Courage Estate, De Wetshof Estate, La Verne Wine Boutique, Platform 62, Robertson Winery, Rooiberg Winery, Tanagra Winery & Distillery ▪ Owner(s) Thunderchild Wingerd Trust ▪ Cellarmaster(s) Various Robertson winegrowers ▪ 5ha (cabs s/f, merlot) ▪ PO Box 770 Robertson 6705 ▪ info@thunderchild.co.za ▪ www.thunderchild.co.za ▪ **T +27 (0)23-626-3661**

Tierhoek   ⓠ ⓐ ⓗ ⓞ

The coolness of this high-lying farm in Piekenierskloof is apparent in the bright freshness of the wines. The remoteness and wild beauty need a visit to be appreciated. Shelley and the late Tony Sandell did just that and bought the run-down property back in 2001, restoring the derelict buildings and planting more vines, supplementing the old grenache and chenin blanc. Wines are made as naturally as possible: no pesticides or herbicides in the vineyards, spontaneous fermentation in the cellar, the aim always being that freshness and purity of fruit. The rosé joining the range epitomises this stylistic objective.

Tierhoek range

★★★★☆ **Grenache** Very pale **18** ★★★★ ⑧⑥ with delicately pretty red fruit aromas. Fresh & lively; fruit light but tannins restrained to match; marked cranberry tartness. Only old oak, like more intense **17** ⑨⓪.

★★★★ **Mourvèdre-Grenache-Syrah** ⊘ Name tweaked in response to blend - 51% mourvèdre in **18** ⑧⑦; **17** ★★★★ ⑧⑤ had grenache majority. Charming fruity, spicy notes; more structure & fruit than the Grenache this year, still restrained, fresh & balanced. 13% alcohol; natural ferment & old oak barrels.

★★★★ **Chardonnay** Classic varietal notes on **18** ⑧⑥. Dry, fairly lean, with bright acidic trim, good limy finish. Half fermented & matured in older oak, half in stainless steel to enhance fruit purity.

★★★★ **Chenin Blanc 18** ⑧⑥ shows ripe, pleasing aromas & flavours, though not intense, with a touch of sweetness to balance the bright acidity. Half matured in older oak, half in tank.

★★★★ **Chenin Blanc** Was 'Old Blocks', still for export only to UK client. Dried apricot, thatch & an earthy element on textured, well-balanced **18** ⑧⑧. Lovely fresh fruit flavours disciplined by savoury, stony acidity.

★★★★☆ **Sauvignon Blanc** ⊘ Now bottled, **18** ★★★★★ ⑨⓪, with small oaked portion, has more savoury breadth on flavourful palate than Sandveld version. Also a ripely soft texture, with balanced but grippy acid structure, as racy as **17** ⑧⑨. 14.5% alcohol.

★★★★☆ **Méthode Cap Classique** ⓥ Natural ferment, 5 months on lees in tank, before 4 years bottle-ageing. From chardonnay, **NV** ⑨① sparkling arresting fruit purity, vivid citrus perfume & flavours, mouthwatering limy acidity.

★★★★☆ **Straw Wine** Latest light-amber **NV** ⑨② from air-dried chenin, matured in solera (older oak barrels, multiple vintages). Raisin & toffee hints at oxidative ageing, but there's also a piercing fruitiness. Very sweet, but cool-climate high acidity comes into its own in the balance. 11.5% alcohol. 375 ml.

Rosé ⓃⒺⓌ ★★★★ From sauvignon (74%) & oaked grenache & viognier, tank sample of **19** ⑧⑤ is deep rose-pink & enticingly aromatic. Allies fruitiness with bright, elegant freshness, for a dry, satisfying whole. Occasional release: **Grenache Private Reserve**, **Mourvèdre**, **Chenin Blanc Reserve**.

Sandveld range

★★★★☆ **Sauvignon Blanc** ⊘ Unoaked **18** ★★★★ ⑧⑧ is, unlike **17** ⑨③, a touch less impressive than Tierhoek version. Stresses green elements rather than tropical ones, but clear, clean passionfruit notes on softly textured yet very zingily fresh palate.

Piekeniers range

★★★★ **White** ⊘ Fresh **18** ⑧⑧ shows sauvignon majority (70%) in green figgy aromas, but lemony chardonnay & apricotty viognier are revealed later to very pleasing effect. Mix of oaked & tank-aged wines. — TJ

Location: Citrusdal ▪ Map: Olifants River ▪ Map grid reference: C6 ▪ WO: Piekenierskloof ▪ Est 2001 ▪ 1stB 2003 ▪ Tasting, sales & cellar tours on the farm Mon-Sun 8.30-4.30 by appt ▪ Tasting fee applicable, waived on purchase ▪ Closed all pub hols ▪ BYO picnic ▪ Walks/hikes ▪ Conservation area ▪ Guest house (sleeps 9)

▪ Owner(s) Shelley Sandell ▪ Winemaker(s) Roger Burton (Aug 2006, consultant), with Basie Snyers (Oct 2006) ▪ Viticulturist(s) Ryno Kellerman (Aug 2006) ▪ 700ha/16ha (grenache, mourv, shiraz, chard, chenin, sauv) ▪ 70t/6,000cs own label 40% red 60% white ▪ IPW ▪ PO Box 53372 Kenilworth 7745 ▪ info@tierhoek.com ▪ www.tierhoek.com ▪ S 32° 23' 27.49" E 018° 51' 24.14" ▪ 🚩 leagues.byways.radiate ▪ T +27 (0)21-674-3041/+27 (0)82-536-7132 (owner), +27 (0)22-125-0249/0179 (farm)

☐ **Timestone Vineyards** see Trizanne Signature Wines
☐ **Tin Cups** see Wineways Marketing
☐ **Tin Hill** see Signal Gun Wines
☐ **Tin Mine** see Zevenwacht
☐ **Titanic** see Louis
☐ **Title Deed** see Croydon Vineyard Residential Estate

Tokara
🍷 🍴 📷 🛅 ♿

The views might tempt a visitor to undervalue the really important intrinsics of this fine Stellenbosch property, but can't be ignored: a stunning 360-degree panorama, including a fan of vineyards and olive groves on the undulating slopes below. For this is an olive and wine farm, owned by GT and Anne-Marie Ferreira, part of whose art collection is dotted around the buildings and gardens. As successful business-people do, they have put the right people in place. This includes Aidan Morton, longtime and deeply experienced viticulturist, looking after the extensive Elgin vineyards, too; and a more recent arrival, winemaker Stuart Botha who, apart from taking a firm grip on the valuable Tokara tradition, has experimented with concrete small fermenters with good results. The management guiding hand is that of Karl Lambour, executing day-to-day operations and future strategy.

Reserve Collection

★★★★☆ **Cabernet Sauvignon** 🌱 Top cab, so best cellar-care for **16** ⑨⑷: wild ferment combo stainless/foudres, 22 months French oak, 63% new, no fining, filtration. Deeply rich cassis, cigarbox spicing, sleekly curvaceous, enough flesh to balance the tannins. Polished & assured.

★★★★ **Syrah** 🌱 Admirable balance in **15** ★★★★★ ⑨⑵, less bold than **14** ⑧⑧, a step up, shows Rhône characteristics, pepper & scrub, hedgerow fruit. Masterly oaking, 20 months third new, giving silky tannins yet a backbone for ageing. Stylish, has poise.

★★★★☆ **Director's Reserve Red** 🌱 Classic 5-part Bordeaux-style blend, cab-led for structure & complexity. Admirable polish, cassis at **15** ★★★★★ ⑨⑸'s core but given wings by cigarbox spicing, espresso notes. Streamlined body yet hidden power. That rarity, delicious, but a great future, like **14** ⑨⑷.

★★★★☆ **Chardonnay** 🌱 Best vineyard blocks, **18** ⑨⑶ portion bunch pressed, barrel fermented, third new, 11 months on lees. Essence of citrus, oak in support as buttered toast underpin, brisk acidity keeping it youthfully vibrant, promising a future.

★★★★★ **Sauvignon Blanc** ✓ 🌱 Tightly focused, vibrates with nervous tension: nettles & lime, green papaya, the palate dry, with mouthwatering tangy acidity. **18** ⑨⑸ already drinking well but a long life ahead as it unfolds over time. Cool-climate style from Elgin.

★★★★☆ **Director's Reserve White** 🌱 Only best blocks, sauvignon leads, 31% semillon. **17** ⑨⑷ has great precision, fruit is variety-true, lime & minerality, but pared down to the essence of freshness. Oak in support, but the fruit is too intense to allow much effect.

Limited Release Collection

★★★★☆ **Pinotage** 🌱 Generously fruited, lush dark berries, **17** ⑨⑶ has depth & complexity, is seriously made. Expertly oaked, 22 months in French barrels, half new, but tannins supple, the whole effect seductive, with enough core strength for a future.

★★★★☆ **Méthode Cap Classique** 🌱 Elgin blanc de blancs sparkling, **12** ⑨⑷'s chardonnay is concentrated lemon preserve, oaked 15 months, 48 months on lees in bottle. There's richness plus acid's steely precision: toasted brioche, a honey overlay, flavours that never end. Elegance yet power.

★★★★★ **Noble Late Harvest** 🌱 **17** ⑨⑸ Elgin botrytised sauvignon has similar molten apricot & caramelised citrus scents & flavours to equally superb **16** ⑨⑸, seductively rich yet lifted by the tangy acidity. Barrel ferment, some new but not showing, the fruit is king. A triumph.

Discontinued: **Cabernet Franc**, **Grenache**.

Premium range

★★★★☆ **Cabernet Sauvignon** ⊘ ⊛ Compact, with admirable cassis fruit expression, which, together with **16** ⑨③'s other layers, involve & seduce: graphite, finest charcuterie, hint of dark chocolate. Different styling to **15** ⑨③, equally impressive, & also good cellaring potential.

★★★★ **Chardonnay** ⊛ Different handling to Reserve, **17** ⑧⑨ combo barrel/stainless steel ferment, then oaked 8 months, giving subtle savoury tone to citrus intensity. Tightly knit, has purity & focus.

★★★★ **Sauvignon Blanc** ⊘ Tropical fruit salad but in a fresh way, **18** ⑧⑧'s acid seam holds everything in place, giving vigour, vitality & incredible length. The ultimate food wine but good enough to enjoy solo.

Shiraz ★★★★ Touch mourvèdre in smoky, peppery **17** ⑧⑤, the hedgerow fruit deep & dark. Great typicity, a muscular version with a good future. WO W Cape, like Chardonnay. **Rosé** ★★★★ Blend change in **18** ⑧④ to shiraz, merlot, some cab franc; fruit-forward & elegant with all the freshness one desires from a dry rosé. Appealing saline note at the end. — CR

Location/map: Stellenbosch ▪ Map grid reference: G4 ▪ WO: Stellenbosch/Elgin/Western Cape ▪ 1stB 2001 ▪ Tasting & sales Mon-Sun 10—6 ▪ Closed Dec 25 & Jan 1 ▪ Tokara Restaurant Tue-Sun lunch 12.30-2.30 & dinner 7-9.30 ▪ Delicatessen Tue-Sun 10-4 ▪ Facilities for children ▪ Gift shop ▪ Art exhibitions ▪ Owner(s) GT & Anne-Marie Ferreira ▪ Winemaker(s) Stuart Botha (Sep 2017), with Timothy Whitfield (May 2018) ▪ Viticulturist(s) Aidan Morton (Nov 2000) ▪ 104ha (cabs s/f, grenache, malbec, merlot, mourv, p verdot, ptage, shiraz, chard, chenin, sauv, sem) ▪ 70st/100,000cs own label 40% red 59% white 1% rosé ▪ PO Box 662 Stellenbosch 7599 ▪ wine@tokara.com ▪ www.tokara.com ▪ S 33° 55' 2.9" E 018° 55' 13.7" ▪ ◫ feeds. avid.curiosity ▪ **T +27 (0)21-808-5900**

☐ **Top Five** see Stellenview Premium Wines

Topiary Wines

It's 15 years since boutique winery Topiary was established on a hillside Franschhoek fruit farm, and 6 since it was acquired by Burgundian vigneron Philippe Colin. Given Philippe's Chassagne-Montrachet connections, it is unsurprising that there is a focus (and a greatly beneficial one it has proved to be) on chardonnay, but the new blend reveals ambitions for red too. For visitors wanting 'a little luxury on a working wine farm', there are cottages with views down the lovely valley, while a restaurant was due to open as we went to press.

★★★★ **Innocence** (NEW) From cab (66%) & syrah, well-balanced **17** ⑧⑨ straddles generous sweet fruitiness & restrained elegance in very satisfactory manner. 14.3% alcohol unassertive, as is 10% new oak. Farm's best red yet.

★★★★☆ **Chardonnay** ⊛ Serious, subtle & savoury **18** ⑨③ is unshowy but has an assured presence. A little lighter-feeling & drier than previous, equally graceful & fresh, silky & balanced, with a good finish. 25% new oak is supportive & shaping, not assertive.

Rosé ⊘ ⊕ ★★★★ Made from syrah, **18** ⑧⑤ has a sophisticated onion skin hue well-suited to its fine balance; quietly aromatic & flavourful, with a lingering, bone-dry, liquorice-tinged finish. Also in magnum.

Discontinued: **Cabernet Sauvignon**, **Syrah**, **Blanc de Blancs Brut**. — TJ

Location/map/WO: Franschhoek ▪ Map grid reference: C4 ▪ Est 2005 ▪ 1stB 2006 ▪ Tasting & sales Tue-Sat 9-5 Sun/Mon by appt only ▪ Fee R30, waived on purchase ▪ Closed Easter Sun, Dec 24/25 & Jan 1 ▪ Restaurant ▪ Cellar tours on special request ▪ BYO picnic ▪ Small tour groups ▪ 1.7km fynbos hiking trail ▪ Conservation area ▪ Honeymoon suite plus 2 self-catering cottages ▪ Owner(s) Philippe Colin ▪ Cellarmaster(s)/winemaker(s) Philippe Colin (Aug 2014) ▪ Viticulturist(s) Carlo Popolillo (Jun 2019) ▪ 63ha/20ha (cab, shiraz, chard) ▪ 44t/1,500cs own label 90% red 10% white ▪ PO Box 108 La Motte 7691 ▪ sales@topiarywines.co.za ▪ www.topiaryvineyards.simplesite.com ▪ S 33° 51' 52.2" E 019° 2' 39.0" ▪ ◫ spirals.pancake.therapy ▪ **T +27 (0)21-867-0258**

☐ **Topography** see David & Nadia

Township Winery   ℗

This innovative community project encourages householders in Philippi, Nyanga and Crossroads, economically challenged areas of Cape Town, to plant backyard vines and supply grapes to a small Philippi Village cellar, where the resulting wines can also be tasted and bought. Original impetus came from low-income housing developer Kate Jambela, supported by Wellington entrepreneur and vintner Graham Knox, who made the current releases from wider-sourced fruit.

★★★★ **Philippi Merlot-Cabernet Sauvignon** ⓥ Elegant & poised **14** ⑧⑥, plum- & currant-infused mouthful laced with wood spice & crushed herbs. Helderberg merlot & Durbanville cab, ready now but with some years to go. Last **12** ⑧⑦ was 'Cab-Merlot'.

Philippi Sauvignon Blanc ⓥ ★★★★ Vivacious **15** ⑧③ from West Coast vines within 10 km of Atlantic, hence cool lemongrass & lime tone; juicy, involving, lingering greengage & fig finish. Not tasted: **The Flats Pinotage**, **The Flats Viognier**. — GM

Location: Philippi ▪ Map: Cape Peninsula ▪ Map grid reference: D3 ▪ WO: Coastal/Western Cape ▪ Est 2009 ▪ 1stB 2010 ▪ Tasting Mon-Fri 10-4 ▪ Owner(s) The Township Winery cc ▪ Cellarmaster(s) Graham Knox ▪ 800cs own label 50% red 50% white ▪ 13 Arnold Str, Observatory 7925 ▪ graham@townshipwinery.com ▪ S 34° 0' 1.02" E 018° 35' 37.71" ▪ ⌖ munched.cabin.elevate ▪ **T** +27 (0)83-625-2865

☐ **Travino** *see* Klawer Wine Cellars

☐ **Tread Lightly** *see* Backsberg Estate Cellars

☐ **Tree of Knowledge** *see* Wijnskool

☐ **Treintjiewyn** *see* Villiersdorp Winery

☐ **Tribal** *see* Jacques Germanier

Trizanne Signature Wines

Given Cape Town-based Trizanne Barnard's passion for surfing, it's no surprise she looked to vineyards near the ocean when casting her terroir net wider than beloved Elim, Darling and Swartland for her elegant boutique label. Sunday's Glen, the tiny ward in cool-climate Walker Bay, fits the stylistic profile and her lifestyle perfectly. With 21 harvests under the belt, more than half as owner-winemaker of TSW, Trizanne is a role model for women in the industry: her business model includes a healthy export element, both bottled and bulk, and it shows that with focus, passion - and an eye for a good break - you can 'have it all'.

Reserve range

★★★★☆ **Syrah** ⓐ Effortless, pure & precise expression of Elim's cool maritime climate. Fynbos & black pepper on naturally fermented **18** ⑨④, gentle fruitfulness, seamless integration of fine grape tannins with 15% new oak.

★★★★☆ **Sauvignon Blanc-Semillon** Unlike old-barrel-fermented & semillon-led **17** ⑨④, sauvignon-based (64%) **18** ⑨② gets much of its character from 30% new oak. Toasty nose & palate, faint grass, fig & asparagus tones; vivacious but needs more time to unfurl & knit.

Wine Of Origin range

★★★★☆ **Darling Barbera** Sour cherry tones, bright acidity & noticeably dry grape tannins true to the Italian variety's character. Lightish (12% alcohol) yet serious in its intent. **18** ⑨② continues fine form of previous. Wild ferment, as Syrah & Semillon.

★★★★☆ **Sondagskloof Syrah** ⓝⒺⓦ ⓐ From maritime Sunday's Glen ward near Stanford. Minimal intervention & old-oak maturation highlight **18** ⑨③'s pure black & red fruit. Neat & compact, less aromatic complexity than Reserve, but no less stylish.

★★★★★ **Sondagskloof Blanc Fumé** ⓝⒺⓦ ⓐ Sauvignon's evocative hay & wild grasses accents, & smoky whiffs from 50% barrel ferment in old wood on **18** ⑨⑥. Mineral rather than fruity, with poise & persistence, & gentle grip from the other half that was skin-fermented in new 500L oak.

★★★★ **Elim Semillon** Portion new oak (30%) plays role in elegant **18** ⑧⑨, as it does - unusually - in many of Trizanne Barnard's wines of this vintage. Toasty & nutty, very smooth & long ex 16 months on lees.

Signature range

★★★★ **Swartland Syrah** ⓥ Floral & red-fruited **17** ⑧⑧ is admirably 'unworked', with a light tannin bite & delicate brush of older oak. From 17 year old vines on schist soils. No grenache component as before.

★★★★ **Sauvignon Blanc** Widely sourced **19** ⑧⑦ has tiny oaked portion, dash semillon & few months on lees. Present but rounded acidity, charming 'cool' feel.— CvZ

Location: Cape Town ▪ WO: Elim/Sunday's Glen/Darling/Swartland/Western Cape ▪ Est 2008 ▪ 1stB 2009 ▪ Closed to public ▪ Wine sales via website ▪ Owner(s)/winemaker(s) Trizanne Barnard ▪ 25,000cs own label 45% red 65% white + 2.5m L bulk wine export ▪ Export-only brands: Clearsprings, Dawn Patrol, Indwe, Swallows' Tale, The Search, Timestone Vineyards ▪ 14 Van der Horst Ave, Kommetjie 7975 ▪ info@trizanne. co.za ▪ www.trizanne.co.za ▪ **T +27 (0)21-783-0617/+27 (0)82-383-6664**

Truter Family Wines

Wellington winemakers Hugo Truter and wife Celeste mine widely for their 'gems', launched over a decade ago and labelled Agaat ('Agate' in Afrikaans). Still favouring blends, ensuring quality (and domestic harmony!) by bottling only if they agree on style, they've recently added two ranges, including varietal wines and a debut rosé.

Agaat range
★★★★ **Christina** Still sauvignon-majority blend in **18** ⑧⑥ with chenin, nouvelle & viognier (70/20/9/1). Succulent array of subtle green herbs & fruits. Clean & smooth texture interwoven with freshening acidity. More graceful than **17** ★★★★ ⑧③, for solo or mealtime enjoyment.
John David ★★★★ Cape Blend **17** ⑧⑤, pinotage-led (32%) with shiraz, cab & petite sirah. Oak adds spicy nuance to smoky red-berried fruit. Plush & supple, already inviting.

Cape Fern range
Shiraz ⊘ ★★★☆ Mix oak-barrel & -stave maturation on more-appealing **17** ⑧⑤, imparts rich & spicy tone, with generous white pepper dusting to dark fruit. Balanced & inviting, respectable dry finish.
Sauvignon Blanc ★★★☆ Appealing starfruit & elderflower nuances to light, balanced & fresh **18** ⑧④. Pleasing persistence for its moderate 12.7% alcohol.

Taste range
Shiraz-Cabernet Sauvignon ★★★ 30% cab in good support on **17** ⑧② . Similar light tannin framework as before for spiced blackberry flavours & amiable drinkability. **Rosé** ⑭ ⊘ ★★★ Appealing cranberry/cherry flavours on light & cheery sunset quaffer. **18** ⑦⑦ hint of sweetness, but twist of lime to freshen.
Chenin Blanc ★★★ Tropical fruit salad with the cream & twist of lime. **19** ⑧⓪ is a friendly summer white.
Sauvignon Blanc ★★★ Piquant gooseberry & citrus peel flavour & freshness on **19** ⑧⓪. Even more sipping pleasure than previous at a pleasing price. — MW

Location: Wellington ▪ WO: Western Cape ▪ Est 2008 ▪ 1stB 2010 ▪ Closed to public ▪ Owner(s) Hugo & Celeste Truter ▪ Winemaker(s) Hugo Truter ▪ 3,000cs own label 50% red 50% white ▪ hugo@truterfamilywines.co.za ▪ www.truterfamilywines.co.za ▪ **T +27 (0)83-639-6288**

☐ **Tugela River** *see* Spioenkop Wines

Tulbagh Winery   ⑨ ⑩ ⑤

Based in SA's 4th-oldest town, charming mid-17th century Tulbagh, this grower-owned concern has a venerable heritage too, being founded in 1906. Bulk wine is the focus, but small parcels are bottled for clients and the house brands. One of these, Flippenice, is now family-friendly, with lime- and litchi-flavoured grape juice in 275-ml glass bottles joining the line-up. Staffing is also 'kept in the family', with cellar personnel Johan Jacobs and Wilfred Morris joining production manager Naude Bruwer as assistant winemakers.

Klein Tulbagh range
Cabernet Sauvignon ⑫ ★★★★ Lots going on in **14** ⑧④, cassis, hint of mint, interwoven with oak-driven espresso. You'd expect sterner tannins but the texture is supple, flavours fruity-fresh. From official single-vineyard & Tulbagh WO, as all these. **Pinotage** ⑫ ★★★★ Expressive **15** ⑧③ shows intense mulberries & sweet spice, more savoury on the palate. Oaking well handled, giving smooth tasty appeal plus ageability. **Shiraz** ⑫ ★★★★ **14** ⑧④ received 18 months oaking, half new, as all these reds, intensifying the meaty dark fruit, spicy flavours. In perfect drinking condition but can still age. Occasional release: **Merlot**. Discontinued: **Port**.

Tulbagh range

Cabernet Sauvignon (Ⓧ) ★★★ Mocha, meaty overlay to **17** (78)'s berry fruit, tannins sturdy enough for food matching, ageing. **Merlot** (Ⓧ) ★★★ Red berries & chocolate savouriness, **17** (78) has appealing succulent freshness, smooth & round. **Pinotage** (Ⓧ) ★★★ Blueberries & gentle toastiness, some liquorice, **17** (81) has good typicity, smooth mouth appeal, is very easy to like. **Syrah** (Ⓧ) ★★★ Black plums & sweet spice from French/American oak treatment, **17** (81) has a supple texture, appealing juicy accessibility.
Shiraz-Pinotage (Ⓧ) ★★★ Some barrel ageing in **NV** (78) but essentially designed for earlier drinking: dark fruit, savoury seamed, juicy accessibility. **Pinotage Rosé** (✓) ★★☆ Light-textured (11.5% alcohol) & fruity-fresh, **17** (77)'s red berries provide tasty drinkability. **Chardonnay** (Ⓧ) ★★★ Tangerine perfume/ flavours in **17** (78), a biscuit seam from light oaking, finishes bone-dry. **Chenin Blanc** (✓) ★★★ Sleek, dry yet satisfyingly fruity, **19** (80) a template for chenin, apple & pear, with minerality on the finish. **Sauvignon Blanc** (Ⓧ) ★★ With lemon drops, **17** (76) has tasty, tangy flavours. Light (11.5% alcohol) & dry enough for summertime quaffing. **Blanc de Blancs Méthode Cap Classique** (Ⓧ) ★★★ **NV** (81) from chardonnay, 48 months on lees, giving brioche/barley sugar tones, ends crisply dry & long. For those who like more mature-style bubblies.

Paddagang range

CCM (Ⓧ) ★★★ Cab-led with cab franc, merlot, **14** (81) is ready to drink: plush cassis with a mint chocolate nuance & softly textured body. **Paddapoot Hanepoot** (Ⓧ) ★★★ Buy it for the frog-themed label alone, but **NV** (82) fortified is worth it in its own right. Intensely grapey, with melon, ginger & barley sugar notes, sweet but moreish. **Sopkoppie Rooi Muskadel** (Ⓧ) ★★★ Fortified red muscadel, a raisin-saturated, full-sweet **NV** (81) that's too good not to share. Improves on previous. Tulbagh WO, rest of these W Cape.

Flippenice range

Cabernet Sauvignon-Merlot ★★★ 60/40 blend, 6 months stave oaking; red-fruited **NV** (77) is streamlined, has juicy appeal. WO W Cape. **Xtra Lite** ★★★ Aptly named, a skinny 9% alcohol, bone-dry **NV** (78) from fernão pires, dab muscat d'Alexandrie. Fresh yet fruity, drinks well. **Chenin Blanc-Sauvignon Blanc** ★★ Good partnership with a touch of sugar, delicate melon-flavoured **NV** (74) goes down easily. **Pinotage Doux** ★★ Dark-hued carbonated bubbly, **NV** (74) is sweet & berry-rich, the fizz turning it into party mode. Tulbagh WO, as next. **Sauvignon Blanc Brut** ★★★ Lemon drops in perky-fresh & dry **NV** (77) carbonated bubbly, an ideal aperitif. **XLite Natural Sweet Rosé** ★★ Just 9% alcohol in **NV** (75) from pinotage. Red berries & semi-sweet style make it easy to like. — CR

Location/map: Tulbagh ▪ Map grid reference: F5 ▪ WO: Coastal/Tulbagh/Western Cape ▪ Est 1906 ▪ 1stB 1910 ▪ Tasting & sales Mon-Fri 9—5 Sat & pub hols 9—1; closed Easter Fri-Sun, Dec 25/26 & Jan 1 ▪ Gifts ▪ Farm produce ▪ MTB in the area ▪ Owner(s) 86 members ▪ Production manager / senior winemaker Naude Bruwer (Jan 2010), with Johan Jacobs & Wilfred Morris ▪ Viticulturist(s) Carl Allen (Aug 2003) ▪ 740ha (cab, merlot, ptage, shiraz, chenin, chard, sauv) ▪ 9,600t own label 65% red 30% white 5% rosé & 8m L bulk + 40,000cs for clients ▪ PO Box 85 Tulbagh 6820 ▪ info@tulbaghwine.co.za ▪ www.tulbaghwine.co.za ▪ S 33° 15' 8.8" E 019° 8' 36.5" ▪ 🗺 soldiers.incursions.waistband ▪ **T** +27 (0)23-230-1001

☐ **Tunnel** *see Du Toitskloof Winery*
☐ **Twee Jonge Gezellen** *see Krone*
☐ **Twelve Apostles Winery** *See Editor's Note*
☐ **21 Gables** *see Spier*
☐ **Twins** *see Lateganskop Winery*
☐ **TwoCenturies** *see Nederburg Wines*

Two Oceans

Distell's global brand Two Oceans, introduced in the early 1990s and now in some 80 countries, is styled for easy/early enjoyment, hence some wines also being available in fast-growing bag-in-box format. The labels listed below are ones available in South Africa.

Shiraz (✓) ★★★ Soft & juicy, **18** (78) earthy wild strawberry fruit in a medium body. **Cabernet Sauvignon-Merlot** (Ⓧ) ★★★ Approachable **18** (78), light dusting of cocoa on juicy plum & berry fruit. Also in 3L, as Sauvignon. **Shiraz Rosé** (Ⓧ) ★★★ Bright cherry-pink **18** (77) is semi-dry, like strawberry cordial for grown-ups with a clean, fresh finish. **Chenin Blanc** (ⓝⒶ) ★★★ Smooth, dry **18** (79) has rounded

mouthfeel, guava & luscious white peach flavours. **Pinot Grigio** ⊘ ★★★ Less zesty than last, fruity **19**
⑱ has litchi & honeydew melon flavours, easy 12.5% alcohol. **Sauvignon Blanc** ⊘ ★★★ Passionfruit &
pineapple aromas lead to mango & papaya on palate in **19** ⑰, not as tangy & fresh as last. — JG

☐ **221** see Alvi's Drift Private Cellar
☐ **Ukuzala** see Mountain River Wines
☐ **Ulumbaza** see Springfontein Wine Estate

Under Oaks   ⓠ ⑪ ⌂

Co-owner of this Paarl Mountain boutique winefarm and luxury guest house, Theresa Britz, has taken
control of plans for a tasting room addition – since the wine-plan was hatched without her! Experienced
and long-standing consultant Bertus Fourie vinifies grapes grown on the property, first granted to freed
slave Ansela van Bengale in 1706.

Premium range

★★★★☆ **Just B** ⓠ Textured mouthful of olives, herbs & black fruit on **15** ⑨⓪ well-judged Bordeaux
blend, mostly petit verdot with cab & merlot. Savoury, structured, with depth & concentration. Fine dry
tannin, firm body & long finish.

★★★★ **Three Twenty** ⓠ Lovely freshness, with cling peach & spice on one-off **15** ⑧⑧ grenache blanc,
viognier & roussanne to mark 320 years of farming the land. Balanced, delicate, with creamy oak support.

French Flair ⓠ ★★★★ Initial grip on **15** ⑧③ mix of equal grenache noir, mourvèdre, carignan with dab
shiraz tempered by juicy freshness. Spicy & tangy.

Under Oaks range

★★★★ **Cabernet Sauvignon Reserve** Big step up for **16** ⑧⑨ in enhanced intensity, structure, refinement & length. Silky feel to dark-fruited palate, integrated oak (18 months). **15** ★★★ ⑧① simpler & lighter.

★★★★ **Merlot** ⊘ Softly ripe & supple **16** ⑧⑨ improves on **15** ★★★ ⑧⓪ with integration, poise &
understated charm. Ripe black berry fruit succulence has ample appeal.

★★★★ **Pinotage Reserve** Like **15** ★★★ ⑧⓪, **16** ⑧⑦ shows cocoa & coffee nuances but with juicy blue
& red fruit to counter. Nice accessible body, dry tannin twist on the tail.

★★★★ **Shiraz Reserve** Dried herb & pepper lift to rounded plum palate on **16** ⑧⑨, which is better than
15 ★★★★ ⑧③. Serious, structured, but agile & lithe. Good concentration & balance.

★★★★ **Gemini** Was 'Cab-Syrah', still is a blend (50/50) of those varieties in **17** ⑧⑧. Muscular (15%
alcohol), inky, dark & brooding but oak (50 new, 15 months) is well knit. Major improvement on last-tasted
10 ★★★ ⑦⑧. Also in 3L.

★★★★ **Chardonnay** ⊘ **18** ⑧⑥ trumps **17** ★★★ ⑧② in subtlety, length & presence. Lightly wooded
cream & vanilla notes mesh seamlessly with lively citrus tang.

Chenin Blanc ⊘ ★★★★ Juicy & tropical **18** ⑧⑤ offers pear & guava affability. Rounded tail & gently dry
farewell. **Sauvignon Blanc** ⊘ ★★★★ Elderflower & granadilla zip in **18** ⑧④. Light, tangy & pleasant,
soft body & dry finish. Ideal for summertime sipping.

Britz Brothers range

Not tasted: **The Secret**. — FM

Location/map: Paarl ▪ Map grid reference: E3 ▪ WO: Coastal ▪ 1stB 2003 ▪ Tasting & sales Tue-Sun 11-4 ▪ Fee
R50pp standard tasting, various seasonal pairings ▪ Cellar tours/private tastings by appt only ▪ Pizzeria
Sep-Mar: Tue-Sat 11.30-10 Sun 12-3.30; Apr-Aug: Wed-Sat 11.30-9.30 Sun 12-3.30 ▪ 4-star country house ▪
Winemaker(s) Bertus Fourie (2002, consultant) ▪ wine@underoaks.co.za ▪ www.underoaks.co.za ▪ S 33° 40'
30.0" E 018° 56' 32.2" ▪ 🗺 erosional.gongs.ropes ▪ **T +27 (0)21-869-8045**

☐ **United Nations of Wine** See Editor's Note
☐ **Unorthodox** see Zandwijk
☐ **Upington** see Orange River Cellars

Upland Organic Estate

Edmund Oettlé marches to the beat of his own drum in rustic surrounds: farming sustainably and vinifying and distilling wines and spirits, certified organic since the 1990s, way ahead of trends. The debut Cape Tawny typifies his natural, unhurried approach, and the exceptionally fine méthode ancienne sparkling - notoriously difficult to produce - showcases the winecrafting skills of this Wellington veterinarian turned vintner.

Estate range

★★★★☆ **Earth Song** ⊘ Méthode ancestrale (single-ferment) bubbly from chenin, splash pinot noir. Rain-on-parched-earth character & most satisfying dry finish in **18** ⑨⓪.

★★★★★ **Cape Tawny Port** ⓃⒺⓦ ⊘ ⊘ ⊛ Scintillating addition to the portfolio. Ex cab yet classic in style, 5 years in barrel. Shimmering russet hues set the scene for exquisitely light rendition of nutty fruitcake- & tobacco-styled **14** ⑨⑥, its sensual finish unblemished by any jagging spirit.

★★★★ **Tandem Cape Ruby** Ⓐ ⊘ From cabernet, individual, less obviously fruity than many Ruby 'ports'. 3 years in oak & 4 in bottle give **NV** ⑧⑧ beautiful integration of clean spirit (18% alcohol), firm dry-tasting finish. Leap up on sterner previous.

Cabernet Sauvignon Ⓐ ⊘ ★★★★ Restasted mid-2015, **09** ⑧④ had benefited from another year in bottle, showed suppler structure, mature dark-berry fruit. **Intuition Pinot Noir** ⊘ ⊘ ★★★★ Bold **18** ⑧⑤ veers off course of elegant **17** ★★★★ ⑧⑨ with highly concentrated, sweet-fruited package. Far from classic, but very drinkable. No sulphur added, as for Earth Song; just 240 bottles made.

Brandy range

★★★★☆ **Drakenwijn** Ⓐ ⊘ Handsome packaging for 15 year old brandy ⑨⓪ from chenin & crouchen (as next 2). Rich amber hue introduces fine floral & prune compote notes; on palate great intensity of fruit, warm spice & roasted nuts, creamy dark chocolate hints on long finish.

★★★★ **Pure Potstill Brandy** Ⓐ ⊘ 10 year old ⑧⑨ with jewel-bright amber glints, nuances of dried peach, prune & sandalwood; smooth, rich & full bodied, ginger spice aftertaste. 500 ml.

★★★★ **Undiluted Cask Strength Potstill Brandy** ⊘ Only local cask-strength brandy ⑧⑨, 10 years in French oak. Intense, perfumed peach & nut, powerful yet smooth & balanced. 62% alcohol, small sips only! 375 ml.

Witblitz Ⓐ ⊘ ★★★★ Fun retro 200-ml 'half-jack' packaging for unmatured brandy ⑧⑤ from chenin & colombard. Water-white, aromatic, subtle notes of florals, fynbos & fresh fruit. For mixing (50% alcohol).

Husk Spirit range

★★★★ **Grapé** Ⓐ ⊘ Fragrant dried herbs, wildflower notes on 15 year old ⑧⑧ from pinot noir & cabernet husks. Smooth, raisin & gentle nut notes, rounded & perfect for after a rich dinner. 375 ml. — DS, WB

Location/map/WO: Wellington ▪ Map grid reference: C4 ▪ Est 1990 ▪ 1stB 1996 ▪ Tasting, sales & tours by appt ▪ Closed Easter Fri-Mon & Dec 25 ▪ Organic olives, olive oil, dried fruit & nuts ▪ Craft workshop ▪ Distillery: brandy, grappa, witblits, limoncello, gin ▪ Owner(s) Edmund & Elsie Oettlé ▪ Cellarmaster(s) / brandy master(s) Edmund Oettlé ▪ Winemaker(s)/viticulturist(s) Edmund Oettlé ▪ 46ha/10ha (cab, pinot, chenin, cbard, crouchen) ▪ 20t/1,200cs own label 100% red & 2,000L brandy ▪ QCS organic certification ▪ PO Box 152 Wellington 7654 ▪ info@organicwine.co.za ▪ www.organicwine.co.za ▪ S 33° 40' 19.9" E 019° 2' 40.0" ▪ Ⓜ corded.rejoin.tipping ▪ **T +27 (0)82-731-4774**

☐ **Usana** see Winshaw Vineyards

Uva Mira Mountain Vineyards

Consistent quality, elegance and sophistication are pervasive threads woven into every aspect of this winery on the elevated slopes of Helderberg Mountain in Stellenbosch's 'golden triangle'. Owner and family man Toby Venter (also CEO of Porsche South Africa) had sought a wine estate, his wife a horse farm, Uva Mira took precedence and has exceeded all expectations. From the elegant neck tags of the wine bottles that pay meaningful tribute to founders and family, as well as fauna and flora on the farm, to the precision-cultivated vineyards (classified as level II on the Winkler temperature index, much cooler than IV for Stellenbosch generally) on a wide range of soil types. The resultant award-winning wines speak for themselves. The window-side wine tastings, with panoramic views and savoury platters on offer, make this a worthwhile visit.

★★★★☆ **The Mira Cabernet Sauvignon** ⓐ Similar polished & understated varietal character on **16** ⑨⑶, though in a lower key. Refined cassis flavours in sync with less new oak (50%) than previous. Streamlined, classic & ageworthy, but will peak before stellar **15** ★★★★★ ⑨⑸.

★★★★☆ **The Dance Cabernet Franc** ⓐ Perfumed red fruit with a herbal touch on **16** ⑨⑴. 'Feminine' & fresh, with more fruit to carry similar oaking than DW Shiraz. Riper, less piquant than more structured **15** ⑨⑵, with potential to age. Name inspired by courtship display of farm's resident pair of Verreaux's eagles.

★★★★ **The Mira Merlot** ② **16** ★★★☆ ⑻⑷ appears even more subdued & savoury than **15** ⑻⑹. Youthful & tightly buttoned, with food-friendly tannins still evolving. Cellar time or decanting will resolve.

★★★★☆ **DW Syrah** New oak (60% for 16 months) masks some of the fruit in **16** ⑨⓪ vintage. Demure white pepper & savoury tone with dry chalky tannins. Youthful & introverted, will reward time in the cellar & glass. Shade less intensity & polish than **15** ⑨⑷.

★★★★ **The Mira Shiraz** ⓐ Earthy red fruit on **16** ⑻⑺, quite tight, all elements in place, needing time. Less oak (now 40% new) & fruit expression at this young stage than impressive **15** ★★★★☆ ⑨⑶.

★★★★☆ **OTV** ⓐ Refined cab franc-led (65%) blend with cab, shows more freshness in **16** ⑨⑶ than the red siblings. The most new oak too (70%), & more than previous, in sync with perfumed dark fruit. Will reward cellaring, though to be broached before **15** ⑨⑷.

★★★★ **The Mira Chardonnay** ⓐ Piercing lemon & oystershell minerality on **17** ⑻⑻. Zesty acidity, bright clean style, also lowest alcohol (13.4%) & new oak of the trio. Youthful & compact table wine.

★★★★☆ **The Single Tree Chardonnay** ⓐ Name alludes to lone tree in this vineyard. **17** ⑨⑶ shows characteristic stonefruit intensity, enhanced by new oak (60%). Less acidity than Uva Mira sibling yet vivaciously fresh & vibrant. Still youthful, future rewards in store.

★★★★☆ **Uva Mira Chardonnay** ⓐ Clean, fresh-sliced pear & lime flavours on **17** ⑨⑷, from 0.2 ha, ocean-facing section of Single Tree vineyard. Similar 50% new oak, integrated into bright, more linear fruit profile than sibling. Still youthful & ageworthy, has more charm than **16** ⑨⑶.

★★★★☆ **Sing-a-Wing Sauvignon Blanc** Similar fine-dining style in **18** ⑨⑴, from highest vineyards (470 m) on the farm. Tad less intensity in this drier season, though still elegant, with bright starfruit & kiwi flavours. Graceful, with a lingering cool, limy farewell.

★★★★ **The Mira Sauvignon Blanc** More tropical nuance to green-fruit flavours in **18** ⑻⑼. Touch more sugar than Sing-a-Wing, though vineyard elevation ensures lime freshness to creamy texture.— MW

Location/map/WO: Stellenbosch ▪ Map grid reference: E8 ▪ Est 1997 ▪ 1stB 1998 ▪ Tasting & sales Mon-Sun 10-5 (tasting & platters) ▪ Fee R70/3 wines, R110/5 wines, call to confirm ▪ Closed Easter Fri/Sun, Dec 25/26 & Jan 1 ▪ Artisan cheese platters & savoury meat platters ▪ Olive oil, honey ▪ Conservation area ▪ Owner(s) Toby Venter ▪ Winemaker(s) Christiaan Coetzee (2012) ▪ Viticulturist(s) Christo Crous (2014) ▪ 127ha/33ha (cabs s/f, merlot, shiraz, chard, sauv) ▪ 200t/20,000cs 60% red 40% white ▪ Off Annandale Rd, Stellenbosch 7600 ▪ info@uvamira.co.za ▪ www.uvamira.co.za ▪ S 34° 1' 31.3" E 018° 51' 26.1" ▪ ⓦ cofounder.transact. advertisement ▪ **T +27 (0)21-880-1683**

Vaalvlei Wines ⓠ ⓐ ⓒ

Conservationists as well as winegrowers, Naas Terblanche and family on moving to their Stanford-area farm in 2005 were delighted to discover the air thick with frog calls, hence the endangered Western Leopard Toad emblem on their labels. The focus remains on shiraz and sauvignon blanc, grown on sandstone and ferricrete, touched by what Naas describes as Walker Bay's 'unique four-seasons-in-a-day weather patterns'. **Shiraz** ★★★ Firm tannins on **16** ⑻⑴, but enough floral & red-fruited flesh to enjoy solo. Satisfying length & freshness. **Sauvignon Blanc** ⓥ ★★★★ Nicely dry & lightish (13%), **18** ⑻⑶ rings the aromatic/flavour changes: plenty of riper gooseberry & peach, less of previous capsicum & grass. **Cape Vintage** ★★★★ Fiery **17** ⑻⑶ 'port' from shiraz true to house style: drier than most, pot-pourri & citrus zest, savoury finish from 18 months in old oak. 375 ml. — CvZ

Location: Stanford ▪ Map: Walker Bay & Bot River ▪ Map grid reference: B7 ▪ WO: Walker Bay ▪ Est 2005 ▪ 1stB 2008 ▪ Tasting & sales Mon-Fri 9-5 Sat 9-1 ▪ Closed Good Fri & Dec 25 ▪ 2 self-catering cottages ▪ Fly-fishing ▪ Owner(s) Terblanche family ▪ Cellarmaster(s)/viticulturist(s) Naas Terblanche (Mar 2005) ▪ Winemaker(s) Naas Terblanche (Mar 2005) & Josef Dreyer (Aug 2005, Raka), advised by Charl van Teijlingen (Mar 2008) ▪ 50ha/3ha (shiraz, sauv) ▪ 19t/650cs own label 40% red 60% white ▪ PO Box 92 Stanford 7210 ▪ info@

vaalvlei.co.za ▪ www.vaalvlei.co.za ▪ S 34° 26' 56.11" E 019° 33' 07.05" ▪ 🗺 sprayed.redecorate.elongates ▪ T +27 (0)28-341-0170/+27 (0)72-782-3431

☐ **Val de Valley Life** *see* Val de Vie & Polo Club Wines

Val de Vie & Polo Club Wines   ⓨ 🍴 ⊚ ⓰

Luxury Paarl residential estate Val de Vie is nirvana for winelovers, too, with its own wine production cellar, brand and charismatic ambassador in the person of Ryk Neethling, the internationally celebrated swimmer and latterly businessman. He lends his name to Val de Vie's pinnacle wine, joined this edition by a second red blend and varietal chenin blanc, for sampling by appointment at the L'Huguenot Venue & Vinoteque.

Val de Vie range

★★★★ **Ryk Neethling** The flagship, named for SA swimming Olympian & Val de Vie marketing director. **11** ⑧⑥, shiraz-led 5-way Rhône blend, followed by **16** ⑧⑥, just shiraz & grenache, deftly oaked (40% new, 18 months) & very sleek, with forest floor tertiary notes, sweet-fruit finish.

★★★★ **Méthode Cap Classique Cuvée de Vie** Bone-dry **17** ⑧⑥ sparkling most engaging wine in the line-up; chardonnay, with 30% pinot noir & 15% meunier giving richness, creamy texture, balanced by lovely lemony acidity.

Valley of Life ⑭🆕 ★★★★ Restrained Bordeaux blend, a limited release, as both ranges, **14** ⑧⑤ black & red berries, unobtrusive brush 20% new oak, touch sugar rounds out the finish. Cab & dashes merlot & malbec.

Perfect Host 🆕 ★★★★ Handsomely packaged chenin, in heavyweight bottle. **17** ⑧④ peach & apple notes, piquant green-apple acidity, roasted nuts from 10 months oaking, subtle breadth & generosity from 20% new wood.

Polo Club range

Merlot ★★★ Soft bouquet of plums & liquorice on **17** ⑧⓪ followed by surprisingly firm palate & tannic bite that needs food. **Chardonnay-Pinot Noir** ★★★ Dry rosé gets its pretty pink hue & enlivening berry tang from 30% pinot noir. **19** ⑧① svelte & smooth, albeit unlingering. **Sauvignon Blanc** ★★★ Blackcurrant & passionfruit flavours & aromas, **19** ⑦⑧ fresh but fleeting. — CR, CvZ

Location: Paarl ▪ Map: Franschhoek ▪ Map grid reference: A7 ▪ WO: Western Cape ▪ Est 2003 ▪ 1stB 2004 ▪ Tasting by appt ▪ Sales Mon-Thu 11-4 Fri 11-7 ▪ Closed weekends & pub hols ▪ L'Huguenot Venue & Vinoteque at Val de Vie ▪ Pizzas & cheese platters ▪ Fleet Coffee Roastery ▪ Owner(s) Val de Vie Wines (Pty) Ltd ▪ Jan van Riebeeck Drive, Paarl 7646 ▪ experience@lhuguenot.com ▪ www.valdevie.co.za ▪ S 33° 48' 15.0" E 018° 58' 4.0" ▪ 🗺 quickened.diets.nightshade ▪ T +27 (0)21-876-8847

Val du Charron   ⓨ 🍴 🏠 ⊚ ⓧ ⓰

Owned by the Entwistle family, this Wellington 'wine and leisure estate' now offers MTB and trail runs in addition to 4- and 5-star accommodation, spa, conference facility and two restaurants (also serving craft beer and gin). 'But the most exciting addition is our new winemaker, Juhan Hunlun, who is always ready for a new challenge and eager to get his hands dirty, not only in the cellar, but starting in the vineyard.'

Estate Reserve range

★★★★ **Chardonnay** Full-bodied **19** ⑧⑥ had 3 months on lees with 70% new French oak staves, adding creamy texture & subtle vanilla frame for quince, citrus & lemon peel notes.

★★★★ **Pinot Gris** More serious than most, **18** ⑧⑦ is 100% varietal (vs **17** ★★★★ ⑧⑤) which had dashes viognier & chardonnay), with nearly 14% alcohol yet retains freshness through green melon & greengage fruit, mineral undertone.

Not tasted: **Cabernet Sauvignon**, **Malbec**, **Merlot**, **Syrah**.

Theater of Wine range

★★★★ **Erasmus** Previously cab based, **16** ⑧⑥ is shiraz with 13% each pinotage, mourvèdre, grenache, some grapes ex Paarl (as Countess). Showcases ripe red fruit with pepper & spice seasoning from year on 50% new oak staves.

★★★★ **Black Countess** Velvety, after year in 50% new oak, **16** ⑧⑦ is fresher than **15** ★★★★ ⑧⑤ (& Erasmus), with blueberry & plum fruit, cinnamon spice. Shiraz with 15% cab, 13% each mourvèdre & grenache, also in 3L.

★★★★ **Four White Legs** Characterful vintage blend loses half **18** ⑧⑥'s varieties & all wooding in **19** ⑧⑥, chardonnay with 19% viognier, splash pinot gris. Intense lavender & dried apricot aromas, toned down on palate, quite weighty with just over 14% alcohol.

Aphaea range

Silk Rosé ★★☆ Cherry pink **19** ⑦⑨, musky perfume, few grams sugar balanced by red-berry tang. 7 black grapes plus chenin. WO W Cape. **Aphaea White** ★★★ Chardonnay with grenache blanc & roussanne, **19** ⑧① white peach & grapefruit notes, tad less fresh & focused than last. Not tasted: **Aphaea Red**. — JG

Location/map: Wellington ▪ Map grid reference: C3 ▪ WO: Wellington/Western Cape ▪ Est 2007 ▪ 1stB 2009 ▪ Tasting daily 10-4 ▪ Sales Mon-Fri 8-5 Sat/Sun 10-4 ▪ Cellar tours by appt ▪ The Grillroom; Pizza Vista ▪ Children play area ▪ Tour groups ▪ Conferences ▪ Spa ▪ 4 & 5 star guest house (stay@vdcwines.com) ▪ Wild Boar MTB & trail runs ▪ Craft beer & artisan gin ▪ Owner(s) Val du Charron Wines (Pty) Ltd ▪ Winemaker(s) Juhan Hunlun (Apr 2019) ▪ Viticulturist(s) Heinie Nel (Apr 2010, consultant) ▪ 43ha/21ha (cab, ptage, shiraz, chard, chenin) ▪ ±300t ▪ IPW ▪ PO Box 890 Wellington 7654 ▪ ce@vdcwines.com ▪ www.vdcwines.com ▪ S 33° 37' 28.14" E 019° 2' 55.32" ▪ ⌖ precollege.aubergine.shrivels ▪ **T +27 (0)21-873-1256**

Van Biljon Wines   ⓠ ⓖ

It's a matter of conscious pride and privilege for Anton and Julia van Biljon to produce their own wine off their own small estate in the Polkadraai Hills, just outside Stellenbosch town. And such a wine! The eminent Chris Keet consults to Anton in its making; unsurprisingly, it reflects Chris' orientation to classic, understated styling in a Cape context. Chris also nurtures the four hectares of now fully mature vineyard which carry the five ('cinq' in French) black Bordeaux grapes that go into the blend.

★★★★★ **Cinq** ⓐ Intensity of **15** ★★★★★ ⑨⑦ vintage reflected in refined & elegant manner in cab-led 47%) blend with merlot, malbec, cab franc, petit verdot. Deftly oaked, shows real finesse & balance, sappy fruit & fine dry tannins. 3 years in bottle at cellar, but deserves longer, like **14** ⑨④ & earlier. — MW

Location/map/WO: Stellenbosch ▪ Map grid reference: B6 ▪ Est 2004 ▪ 1stB 2013 ▪ Tasting, sales & cellar tours Mon-Sat by appt ▪ Closed all pub hols ▪ Self-catering Tarentaal Cottage ▪ Owner(s) Anton & Julia van Biljon ▪ Winemaker(s) Christopher Keet (Oct 2008, consultant), with Anton van Biljon (Jan 2011) ▪ Viticulturist(s) Christopher Keet (Oct 2008, consultant) ▪ 5ha/4ha (cabs s/f, malbec, merlot, p verdot) ▪ 15t/500cs own label 100% red ▪ IPW ▪ PO Box 1292 Hermanus 7200 ▪ info@vanbiljonwines.co.za ▪ www.vanbiljonwines.co.za ▪ S 33° 58' 4.98" E 018° 45' 8.39" ▪ ⌖ pleasant.stockings.consorts ▪ **T +27 (0)21-882-8445**

☐ **Van Coller Family** see Fijndraai Estate

Van der Merwe & Finlayson   ⓠ

The seemingly incongruous combination of traditional Afrikaans and quintessential Scottish surnames belies a seamless SA collaboration between Pieter van der Merwe and David Finlayson, winemaker and owner-cellarmaster respectively of Stellenbosch's Edgebaston. The Sanniesrust range, named after Pieter's Free State family farm, features varieties he particularly enjoys drinking. The Rough Diamond label of lesser-known varieties has been discontinued.

Sanniesrust range

★★★★ **Cinsaut** Light-bodied, fragrant **18** ⑧⑥ improves on **17** ★★★★ ⑧④, offers juicy cherry & redcurrant fruit on silk-textured tannins. Natural yeast ferment & older barrels (as next). 9 months oaked; 20% wholebunch.

★★★★ **Grenache** Commendable fruit weight in wholeberry-fermented **17** ⑧⑨, with primary red berry flavours to the fore. Plush & supple, cosseted in gentle tannin cloak. 20 months wooded. — GdB

Location/WO: Stellenbosch ▪ Est/1stB 2016 ▪ Tasting by appt only ▪ Closed all pub hols ▪ Owner(s) David Finlayson & Pieter van der Merwe ▪ Winemaker(s) David Finlayson & Pieter van der Merwe (both Jan 2016) ▪ 8t/390cs own label 94% red 6% white ▪ PO Box 2033 Dennesig 7601 ▪ pwavandermerwe@gmail.com, sanniesrust@gmail.com ▪ **T +27 (0)21-300-1168/+27 (0)84-512-5266**

Van Loggerenberg Wines

Apart from some lower yields, says Lukas van Loggerenberg, the Cape's drought has meant 'added work going into the vineyards and cellar to ensure the quality of our wines amidst very difficult growing and harvesting conditions'. In 2019 he was still making his wine in a simple shed atop a Devon Valley hill, where he also crafts the Carinus Family wines in exchange for the hospitality –such 'very basic' conditions being adequate for the rigorously non-interventionist approach behind these fresh, elegant (and much-ac-claimed) wines. But he spoke of 'hoping to move into a slightly bigger cellar soon, with an eye on increasing future production, though still remaining quite small'.

★★★★★ **Breton** 🥂 With 13.4% alcohol, **18** ㉛ cab franc a touch richer & more powerful than **17** ★★★★★ ㉟, but still in lighter style than most local examples, stressing its Loire rather than Bordeaux inspiration. Pure-fruited, a touch of dry leaf aromatic. Silky & harmonious, quietly insistent but elegant.

★★★★★ **Geronimo** 🥂 Gorgeous, appealing, aromatic but not trivially pretty, this always one of SA's most serious versions of fashionable cinsaut. **18** ㉛ has gentle but significant dry tannins, sweet & spicy fruit, great purity & freshness. Wholebunch ferment; only old oak. WO Stellenbosch, as Breton.

★★★★★ **Graft** 🥂 Syrah from Polkadraai Hills in **18** ★★★★★ ㉟, drops the cinsaut of **17** ㉛ & earlier. Dry spiciness, with ripe plum fruit plus brightness of wholebunch ferment. Elegant, light-feeling, almost ethereal, yet with commanding presence. Dry, firm but melting tannins. Great length. Deserves time.

★★★★★ **Break a Leg** Old-oaked blanc de noir from cinsaut, a long way from the standard trivial, off-dry rosé. **18** ★★★★ ㉘ has usual restraint & savoury finesse, spicy cranberry freshness, but a touch less intensity & vinosity than **17** ㉚. Old oak 7 months; 11.7% alcohol.

★★★★★ **Kameradarie** 🥂 Drought meant tiny volumes of **18** ★★★★★ ㉟ Paarl chenin, but subtle, unshowy complexity as in **17** ㉞. Interplay of intense fruit & stony savour with firm acidic structure. Even in youth (& it will gain with time in bottle), a marvellous fantailing finish with apricot & almond notes.

★★★★★ **Trust Your Gut** 🥂 Expressive **18** ㉞ old-oaked chenin from Polkadraai Hills & Swartland more generous, sweetly fruity & exuberant than Kameraderie. But also a savoury, flinty element to the density, & fair acid balance to 4.6 g/l sugar. Will gain from a good few years in bottle, yet lovely now.— TJ

Location: Stellenbosch ▪ WO: Paarl/Stellenbosch/Polkadraai Hills/Western Cape ▪ Est/1stB 2016 ▪ Tasting by appt only ▪ Closed all pub hols ▪ Owner(s) Lukas & Roxanne van Loggerenberg ▪ Winemaker(s) Lukas van Loggerenberg (Jan 2016) ▪ 25t/3,300cs own label 40% red 18% white 42% rosé ▪ PO Box 94 Somerset Mall 7137 ▪ lukas@vanloggerenbergwines.co.za ▪ www.vanloggerenbergwines.co.za ▪ **T** +27 (0)82-093-8091

Van Loveren Family Vineyards 🥂 🍴 📷 ♿

Robertson's Van Loveren winery has come a long way since 1937, with current co-owners Wynand and Nico Retief's parents supplying bulk wine to the industry, to the major player it is today. Key to the venture's growth has been the complementary brand, Four Cousins, with its own home in Robertson town and recognising the third generation, Wynand and Nico's sons, each with their own particular skill set, running the business: Bussell for winemaking, Neil and Hennie as viticulturists (with ±800 hectares under their control), and Phillip on the commercial side. Nothing stands still here, and there's a new unique rosé from pinot grigio honouring the late matriarch, Jean Retief, and a de-alcoholised range, among the first in SA, tapping into the latest worldwide health trend.

Christina Van Loveren Limited Releases

★★★★ **Cabernet Sauvignon** 🥂 Designed for pleasure, without stinting on quality, **16** ㉘ plush dark fruit, intriguing aromatic scrub/Provençal herb top note. Sleekly muscled for cellaring, already accessible.

★★★★★ **Pinotage** (NEW) 🥂 Handsome packaging, declares '9 barrels' & depicts Christina's bridal chest lock. Best grapes, new French barrels 18 months, & **17** ㉛ offers cocoa, spice & pepper, black fruit yet with silky tannins, curvaceous body. Enough muscle tone for a long future.

★★★★ **Shiraz** ⊘ Always beautifully constructed. **17** ★★★★★ ㉜ oaked 14 months, 30% new French, respecting the vivid fruit; layered complexity, spice, prosciutto, whiffs of scrub. Tannins supple, enjoyment assured. Even more polished than **16** ㉘.

★★★★★ **Chardonnay** ⊘ 🥂 Single vineyard. With fruit that good, new French barrels for 5 months an easy decision. Buttered toast, a citrus array, **18** ㉛'s flavours remaining long after the glass is empty. Has intensity without going over the top; stylish & delicious.

★★★★☆ **Sauvignon Blanc** ⓧ Following standout **17** ★★★★★ ⑨⑤ & with the same focus, nervy intensity, **18** ⑨③ is mineral at core, graphite, wet slate, with grassy, meadow top notes. More Old World than New.

★★★★ **Méthode Cap Classique Brut Rosé** ⓐ From pinot noir, which proudly displays its fruit in latest **NV** ⑧⑧ bubbly; strawberries throughout, fresh, elegant, admirable purity. Good varietal expression, improves on last.

★★★★ **Méthode Cap Classique Brut** ⓐ Chardonnay dictates styling in latest **NV** ⑧⑧ refined bubbly: citrus freshness, vibrancy, pinot noir (29%) giving a piquant berry tone, palate weight. All satisfyingly harmonious & impressive.

★★★★ **10 Year Old Brandy** ⓧ Small release of potstill ⑧⑦ from chenin, only ex cellardoor. Delicate bouquet of caramel & nuts, with fresher peach & apricot, plus chocolate notes, on restrained palate.

Noble Late Harvest Chenin Blanc ⓧ ★★★★ Rich but not over-sweet **13** ⑧④, unwooded, with notes of honey nougat, hazelnuts & watermelon jam. Perfect match for blue cheese. 375 ml.

Retief Reserve range

Cape White ⓝⓔⓦ ⓣ ★★★★ Chenin-based (65%, rest colombard & chardonnay) partner to the red, vineyard selections, majority oaked. Intense tropical flavours, wood influence subtle, **18** ⑧④ vibrates with health & vitality.

Cape Blend ⓐ ★★★★ Pinotage, equal cab, some shiraz. Gentle coffee notes in dark-fruited **17** ⑧④, the body smoothly curvaceous. Label shows the famous roadside red cannas at the farm, as White.

Five's Reserve range

Cabernet Sauvignon ⓐ ★★★ Unoaked, as rest, **18** ⑧① remains variety-true, blackcurrants, sprinkle of herbs, appealing plush palate. **Pinotage** ⓐ ★★★ **18** ⑧① is about the fruit & succulence, made to enjoy. Has an intriguing smoky top note. **Merlot Rosé** ⓐ ★★★ Pale pink & lightish in alcohol (12.5% as rest) but not in fruitiness; red berries abound in **19** ⑦⑨, dry food-friendly finish. **Chenin Blanc** ⓐ ★★★ Scents & flavours of freshly sliced pears, **19** ⑦⑧ is sleek & bone-dry, nice fruity finish. **5 Year Old Brandy** ⓧ ★★★ Blended brandy ⑧① from chenin with plenty of nuts & fruitiness (apple, pear, raisin). Enough sweetness to benefit from ice or a mixer, but sippable neat (in gingerly fashion!).

The Rhino Run range

Cabernet Sauvignon ★★★ Like rest of range, fruit-filled & honest, for early enjoyment. Lightly oaked (as next), just enough to spice **18** ⑧①'s blackcurrants, give a dry finish. **Pinotage** ★★★ Fruit's the hero in **18** ⑧①, smooth & round, just a hint of mocha chocolate to keep it interesting. Palate- & wallet-pleasing, as rest. **Ian Player** ⓧ ★★★ Named for the renowned international conservationist; sales contribute to rhino protection. Cab/merlot blend for **16** ⑧①, plush fruit, well spiced & savoury, enough grip for food. **Chardonnay** ★★★ Breadth of flavour in **17** ⑧①, citrus & stonefruit, given appealing biscuit seam by oak treatment. Ends zesty & fresh.

Van Loveren range

River Red ⓐ ⓣ ★★★ Perennial favourite, shiraz & pinotage work well together to give unoaked **18** ⑧⓪ fruit-rich succulent appeal. Also in 500 ml, 1.5L. **Blanc de Noir Red Muscadel** ⓐ ⓣ ★★★ Intense grape aroma plus Turkish delight, thanks to the variety, **19** ⑧① has enough sweetness to fit the styling. Something exotic & tasty. **Neil's Pick Colombar** ⓐ ⓣ ★★★ Consistently good & popular. **19** ⑧②'s litchi/guava flavours perfectly fit the touch of sugar, giving an effect of fruit intensity rather than sweetness. **Perlé du Jean Pinot Grigio** ⓝⓔⓦ ⓐ ⓣ ★★★★ An individual, 'noir de blanc', rosé from rosy-skinned white grape pinot grigio, with year in barrel adding serious element & gentle bubble adding lift; litchi & spice interplay on light (12% alcohol) & dry **18** ⑧④. Honours Jean Retief, matriarch & garden creator there, reflected by the colourful label.

Cabernet Sauvignon ⓐ ★★★ In contrast to Five's Reserve, **18** ⑧① given 10 month French oaking, nicely partnered by cassis. Just enough savoury spicing & grip for food pairing. **Merlot** ★★★ Short-duration oaking contributes sweet spicing to **18** ⑦⑧, light grip at the end, but fruit remains the star. **Blue Velvet Pinot Noir** ⓐ ★★★ Carefully made so as not to overwhelm the variety's intrinsic delicacy, **18** ⑧① is fruit expressive, oaking harmonious. Nice savoury finish. **African Java Pinotage** ⓐ ★★★ Consistent style, toasted oak to give the 'coffee' character, & **18** ⑧⓪ is right there. Touch of sugar makes it even more appealing, smooth & round. **Cabernet Sauvignon-Merlot** ⊘ ★★★ Cab (60%) in charge, prominent cassis, while **18** ⑧①'s smoothly rounded body is from both partners & judicious oaking. **A Dry Syrah Rosé** ⓃⒺⓌ ⊘ ★★★ Just-picked strawberries, but salmon-coloured **19** ⑧⓪ also has some minerality in its dry finish, for creative food matching. **Daydream Chardonnay-Pinot Noir** ⊘ ★★★ Delicate pink colour in well-matched elegant, dry **19** ⑧①; red berry perfume & flavours, with main player chardonnay's crispness & citrus tones at the end. **Chardonnay** ★★★ Nice contrast to Rhino Run, **19** ⑦⑨ handles light oaking confidently, tangerine & grapefruit the main attraction. Dry & fruity-fresh. **Chenin No 5** ⊘ ★★★ Extra-dry but no lack of fruit in **19** ⑦⑧, apple & pear freshness throughout. **Sauvignon Blanc** ⊘ ★★★ **19** ⑧① stays true to style, green figs & just-picked gooseberries, streamlined & zesty-fresh. **Blanc de Blanc** ⊘ ★★★ Colombard with 20% sauvignon, **19** ⑧⓪'s whole focus is freshness, litchi & passionfruit, more fruit expression than modest alcohol (±12%, as all whites & rosés) leads you to expect. Also in 500 ml. **Special Late Harvest Gewürztraminer** ⊘ ★★★★ Powerfully scented, glacé pineapple & rosewater, **19** ⑧④'s sweetness has a very attractive delicacy, refinement. **Red Muscadel** Ⓠ ★★★★ Liquidised raisins & stonefruit, bargain-priced **16** ⑧⑤ postprandial fortified has admirable concentration. Full-sweet, mouthcoatingly luscious, demands respect. Sip slowly & speak of wise things. **Cape Ruby** Ⓠ ★★★ Xmas cake richness, **NV** ⑧② 'port' has ultra-smooth drinkability - as a good Ruby should. From touriga. Also in 500 ml. Discontinued: **Pinot Grigio**.

Four Cousins Skinny range
Red ★★ Bargain-priced, Weigh-Less endorsed, reduced kilojoule, low ±8.5% alcohol (as rest), **NV** ⑦⑤'s dab sweetness plumps the body, merlot's berry flavours smooth & easy. **Rosé** ★★ Sweetest of range, as befits **NV** ⑦④'s red muscadel; grapey, aromatic, goes down easily. Could partner spicy dishes. **White** ★★ From semillon, **NV** ⑦⑤ reflects its green apple personality; crisp enough for food or everyday drinking.

Almost Zero range ⓃⒺⓌ
Ravishing Rosé ★★ De-alcoholised range, only 0.05%. Stylish label, as rest, red muscadel gives both the pale pink hue & **19** ⑦⑥'s appealing grapey/muscat character. **Wonderful White** ★★ Has sauvignon's gooseberry character, light textured & very fresh, in spite of **19** ⑦⑤'s semi-sweet sugar level, as for Rosé. **Radiant Red** ★★★ Red-berried merlot, **19** ⑦⑦ is juicy, the sugar more evident here than siblings, giving a fuller body. — CR, TJ

Location/map/WO: Robertson ▪ Map grid reference: B5 C4 ▪ Est 1937 ▪ 1stB 1980 ▪ Tasting & sales: Van Loveren wines (only at home-farm) Mon-Fri 8.30-5 Sat 9.30-3 Sun 11-2; Four Cousins wines (only at @Four Cousins venue, Robertson) Mon-Fri 8.30-5 Sat 9.30-4 Sun 11-3 pub hols 9.30-4 ▪ Closed Easter Fri/Sun, Dec 25 & Jan 1 ▪ Cellar tours by appt ▪ Garden tours ▪ Food & wine tasting platters ▪ Fish Eagle hiking trail ▪ MTB trails ▪ Christina's @ Van Loveren bistro open daily ▪ Amenities @Four Cousins: Food & wine pairings; craft Boet Beer tasting; whiskey pairings ▪ Tasting platters R65pp; R20/gin, R20/10yr brandy, any other 4 wines R20pp ▪ @Four Cousins restaurant open daily ▪ Owner(s) Nico, Wynand, Phillip, Hennie, Bussell & Neil Retief ▪ Cellarmaster(s) Bussell Retief ▪ Winemaker(s) Danelle Conradie (Jan 2007), Chris Crafford (Nov 2014) & Willie Conradie (Jan 2019), with Jonas Cupido & Jakob Pieterse ▪ Viticulturist(s) Neil & Hennie Retief ▪ 800ha (cab, merlot, mourv, muscadel r/w, ptage, pinot noir/gris, ruby cab, shiraz, touriga nacional, chard, chenin, cbard, gewürz, irsai olivér, morio muscat, nouvelle, sauv, sem, viog) ▪ 16,000t/1.4m cs own label 33% red 33% white 34% rosé ▪ Brands for clients: Liquor City, Ultra Liquors, Woolworths ▪ Fairtrade, HACCP, IPW, WIETA ▪ PO Box 19 Klaasvoogds 6707 ▪ info@vanloveren.co.za ▪ www.vanloveren.co.za ▪ S 33° 48' 17.36" E 019° 52' 26.62" (@Four Cousins) S 33° 52' 31.3" E 020° 0' 9.1" (home-farm) ▪ ⓌⒷ insides.hawks.riverboats, subtle.insulators.adventure ▪ **T +27 (0)23-615-1505**

Van Ryn

Distell's flagship brandy range garners much local and overseas praise for its premium potstill products. Best Brandy Worldwide and Distiller of the Year crowns at the International Wine & Spirit Competition are just some of the more recent plaudits. Also globally recognised is Van Ryn's century-old, visitor-friendly premises near Stellenbosch, offering tours (including rare on-site cooperage), exhibits and special events, and various tasting options such as Decadent Delight, pairing the 12, 15 and 20 YO brandies with bite-size confectionery.

★★★★★ **20 Year Old Potstill** A light mahogany gleam at the heart of this very fine brandy ⑨⑦. The most refined & subtle bouquet in the range & the darkest; the complex, smooth & silky palate with cigarbox & spice recalling the many years in oak, but still reverberating echoes of pure dried fruit.

★★★★★ **15 Year Old Potstill** This ⑨⑥ a touch silkier & richer than the 12 year old, but maybe less ethereal, with a delicate spicy tobacco becoming more obvious. The fruit (citrus, dried peach & prune) underplayed as in all these, part of a savoury complexity that includes chocolate & spice.

★★★★★ **12 Year Old Potstill** Always a particularly successful bottling ⑨⑦. A remarkable leap in complexity & subtlety from the 10 year old, announcing the sublimation of fruit into the refined but rich style of the house. Here the power plays especially well with delicacy. Fresh, balanced, complete.

★★★★☆ **10 Year Old Potstill** An excellent introduction, ⑨⓪, to the combination of flavourful, lightly fiery power with finesse that characterises the whole range. This just less subtle by comparison & a little sweeter & fruitier, though clean & fine. All from chenin & colombard, widely sourced.— TJ

Location/map: Stellenbosch ▪ Map grid reference: D6 ▪ Est 1905 ▪ Tasting & sales Mon-Fri 9-5 (May-Sep) 9-6 (Oct-Apr) Sat 9-4 Sun (Oct-Apr only) 11-4 ▪ Tasting options: Cape Smoke, Brandy & Chocolate, Decadent Delight ▪ Closed Good Fri, Dec 25 & Jan 1 ▪ Cellar tours Mon-Fri 10, 11.30 & 3 Sat 10, 11.30 & 1 ▪ Tour groups ▪ Gift shop ▪ Conference & boardroom facilities ▪ Exhibitions & special events ▪ Museum collection of historical brandies on display ▪ Owner(s) Distell ▪ Brandy master(s) Marlene Bester (Jul 2009) ▪ ISO 9001:1995 ▪ Van Ryn Rd Vlottenburg Stellenbosch 7604 ▪ info@vanryns.co.za ▪ www.vanryn.co.za ▪ S 33° 57' 43.26" E 018° 48' 4.87" ▪ *www* successes.harps.mint ▪ **T +27 (0)21-881-3875**

☐ **Vansha** *see* Ridgeback

Van Wyk Family Wines

Constantia Glen winemaker Justin van Wyk's eponymous label comprises parcels reflecting a particular, though not exclusive interest in old vineyards. These include chenin and cinsaut pre-dating his birth (1984), a 'reasonable abundance' of which has allowed him to secure additional grapes. Among his young-vine sources are Elgin syrah, and roussanne which he hopes to include in his white blend. Lastly, 'a leap of faith': non-vintage riesling, 'best to express the nearly 40-year-old vines and their site'.

★★★★ **Syrah** 🍇 Coming of age for distinctly Rhône-style, cool-climate, older-oaked **17** ★★★★☆ ⑨③. Succulent black cherry fruit, bright scrub & pepper spicing, supple body & silky texture, all in graceful harmony. Will age, but why wait? From Elgin vines, like **16** ⑧⑦.

★★★★ **Rebecca May** Delicately structured **18** ★★★★☆ ⑨⓪ from Darling, Slanghoek & Constantia cinsaut, syrah & grenache offers charming violet & rose scents, sweetly fragrant spices. Bunch ferment in older barriques expresses purity of fruit. Auspicious step up on **17** ⑧⑥.

★★★★ **Chenin Blanc** Now sourced from Stellenbosch, minimalistically vinified in old 600L barrels, **18** ⑧⑨ shows ripe stonefruit, lees texture. Poised & subtle, improves on **17** ★★★★ ⑧⑤ ex Darling.

★★★★☆ **Riesling** 🆕 Radical handling of fruit from 1982 Stellenbosch vineyard has pleasing, if atypical, results. Beguiling **NV** ⑨⓪ blend of 20% new-barrel-fermented 2017 & 80% concrete-'egg'-fermented 2018 is rich & creamy, with elegant mineral finish.

★★★★ **Olivia Grace** Intricately vinified eclectic chenin, chardonnay, riesling & viognier from Darling & Stellenbosch. **18** ★★★★★ ⑨② rich, layered & intensely satisfying, with floral scents, mineral undertones & lingering finish. Improves on wider-sourced **17** ⑧⑧.— GdB

Location: Constantia ▪ WO: Stellenbosch/Western Cape/Elgin ▪ Est/1stB 2016 ▪ Wines available for tasting & sale from Constantia Glen tasting room ▪ Owner(s) Van Wyk Family Wines (Pty) Ltd ▪ Winemaker(s)/viti-culturist(s) Justin van Wyk (Jan 2016) ▪ 1st/2,000cs own label 40% red 60% white ▪ PO Box 780 Constantia 7848 ▪ justin@vanwykfamilywines.co.za ▪ www.vanwykfamilywines.co.za ▪ **T +27 (0)84-582-0107**

☐ **Van Zijl Family Vintners** *see* Imbuko Wines

Van Zylshof Estate

Third-generation Andri van Zyl is the owner, viticulturist and winemaker at this small family farm in Bonnievale, celebrating its 80th anniversary this year. Andri uses only a fraction of the grapes grown on the property for the proprietary label, crafting flavoursome, easy-drinking wines. More importantly, he loves what he does, and though there are 4th and 5th generation Van Zyls, Andri has no definite succession plan.

Riverain Unwooded Chardonnay ⓥ ★★★ Angelica, pear & starfruit flavours, rounded, with brisk thread of acidity. **18** ⑧⓪ is ready for carefree quaffing. **Chenin Blanc** ★★★★ Golden Delicious apple flavours on crisp & creamy **19** ⑧③. Less feisty than before, but such an easy, refreshing summer drink. **Sauvignon Blanc** ★★★ Friendlier than previous, **19** ⑧② clean starfuit & tropical flavours, enough balancing acidity for an appealing summer staple. Not tasted: **Cabernet Sauvignon-Merlot**. — MW

Location: Bonnievale ▪ Map/WO: Robertson ▪ Map grid reference: D3 ▪ Est 1940 ▪ 1stB 1994 ▪ Tasting & sales Mon-Fri 9—5 Sat 9—1 ▪ Closed Good Fri, Ascension day, Dec 25 & Jan 1 ▪ Cellar tours by appt ▪ Owner(s) Van Zylshof Trust ▪ Cellarmaster(s)/winemaker(s)/viticulturist(s) Andri van Zyl (Mar 1993) ▪ 37ha/32ha under vine ▪ 450t/±8,000cs own label 15% red 80% white 5% rosé ▪ PO Box 64 Bonnievale 6730 ▪ vanzylshof@lando.co.za ▪ www.vanzylshof.co.za ▪ S 33° 56' 18.5" E 020° 6' 23.4" ▪ ☒ undulates.automobiles.woods ▪ T +27 (0)23-616-2401

Varkenskraal ⓥ ⌂

Continuing water deficits meant that André and Gail Cockcroft had to skip certain recent vintages, but the boutique vignerons are pleased with the '19 Chenin Blanc (not ready for review) and hoping to resume bottling the Chardonnay this harvest. Guest accommodation on their farm near De Rust in Klein Karoo is 'very popular', with great reviews regarding location, facilities and being able to relax in beautiful surroundings'.

Merlot ★★★ Nice red fruit shares space with earthy savouriness in **17** ⑧①, some meaty nuances. Palate smooth & juicy, grip at the end. **Chardonnay** ⓥ ★★★ Light oak-spice adds interest to ripe citrus flavours on tangy-dry **16** ⑦⑨. **Chenin Blanc** ⓥ ★★★ Ripe melon, apple juiciness in **17** ⑦⑨; brisk, just-dry. — CR

Location: De Rust ▪ Map: Klein Karoo & Garden Route ▪ Map grid reference: B3 ▪ WO: Klein Karoo ▪ Est 1995 ▪ 1stB 2014 ▪ Tasting by appt ▪ 2 self-catering guest houses ▪ Owner(s) André & Gail Cockcroft ▪ Cellarmaster(s) Jacques Conradie (Feb 2017, Karusa) ▪ Viticulturist(s) Herman van der Walt & VinPro (Mar 2014, consultant) ▪ 82ha/7.18ha (merlot, chard, chenin) ▪ 28t/1,700cs own label 26% red 74% white ▪ PO Box 93 De Rust 6651 ▪ andre@varkenskraal.co.za ▪ www.varkenskraal.co.za ▪ S 33° 27' 19.21" E 022° 33' 29.70" ▪ ☒ sways.quirkiness.stacked ▪ T +27 (0)44-241-2352

☐ **Veenwouden Private Cellar** See Editor's Note
☐ **Veldfire** see Stanford Hills Winery
☐ **Velo** see Wildehurst Wines

Vendôme ⓥ ⑪ ◎ ♿

Farmed by the Le Rouxs for 10 generations, Vendôme on the Berg River in Paarl was named for their ancestral home in central France. They are part of marketing venture Kaapse Familie Wingerde, with Oude Denneboom and Kuyperskraal, and host tastings for all the brands here. The Vendôme wines unreviewed.

Location/map: Paarl ▪ Map grid reference: E6 ▪ Est 1692 ▪ 1stB 1999 ▪ Tasting & sales by appt ▪ Closed all pub hols ▪ Restaurant open Tue/Thu/Fri/Sat 8—5 Wed 8-10pm Sun 8-3 ▪ Functions ▪ Owner(s)/winemaker(s)/viticulturist(s) Jannie le Roux ▪ 20ha (cab, merlot, shiraz, chard, chenin, cbard, sauv, sem) ▪ 5t/600cs own label 50% red 50% white ▪ PO Box 36 Paarl 7645 ▪ lerouxjg@icon.co.za ▪ www.vendome.co.za, www.kaapsefamiliewingerde.com ▪ S 33° 45' 27.8" E 018° 58' 42.4" ▪ ☒ panels.minus.clauses ▪ T +27 (0)21-863-3905

☐ **Vera Cruz Estate** see Delheim Wines

Vergelegen Wines ⓥ ⑪ ◎ ♿ ♿

Recently announced as one of the 50 best vineyards in the world by a global survey, Anglo American's splendid Somerset West property has it all. This sprawling 3,000 ha spread at the foot of the Hottentots Holland mountains is a biodiversity champion, with more than 2,200 ha dedicated to conservation projects, including a herd of rare Bontebok, recently augmented by 9 new calves. The meticulously restored Cape Dutch buildings, formal gardens, fine restaurants (including SA Top 10 Camphors) and exceptional wines all make for a memorable experience. The iconic semi-subterranean, gravity-driven cellar on Schapenberg Hill, overseen by veteran winemaker André van Rensburg, has a dedicated laboratory where wife and co-winemaker Maritza has been doing crucial behind-the-scenes work in one of Vergelegen's biggest accomplishments, eradicating quality-impacting leafroll virus.

Flagship range

★★★★☆ **Vergelegen V** ⊛ Towering flagship of impressive line-up, **13** ⑨④ is cab with splashes cab franc, merlot, petit verdot. Elegant, restrained & confident, with reined-in power, supple body & texture, seductive detail. Oak as for GVB. Improves on all-cab **12** ⑨⓪. Also in 1.5, 3, 5 & 9L.

★★★★☆ **Vergelegen GVB Red** ⊛ Aristocratic cab-led (81%) Bordeaux blend with cab franc & merlot, **14** ★★★★★ ⑨⑤ exudes class & refinement. Plush velvet tannins cosset rich cassis & black cherry fruit. Barely emerging after 18 months in new oak, 4 years in bottle. Tops also-stellar **13** ⑨③.

★★★★☆ **Vergelegen GVB White** Outstanding semillon-led Bordeaux blend has a lofty track record. 2 vintages tasted: **17** ⑨③ is 59% semillon, showing body & texture, sweetly aromatic fruit profile; **16** ⑨③, 80% semillon, is less expressive, with piercing salty-mineral notes. Fermented & 10 months French oak, ±30% new, larger (500L) barrels for sauvignon component.

Reserve range

★★★★☆ **Cabernet Sauvignon** ⊛ Combines New World exuberance & stately elegance, **14** ⑨④ is packed with ripe currant & berry fruit, cosseted in satin tannins polished 18 months in small French barrels, 40% new. Precise, focused & balanced, a cellar treasure for the long haul.

★★★★☆ **Merlot** ⊛ Perfect balance & structure on **14** ⑨② shows ripeness & complexity, layered fruit on silky mantle. Plush & textured, finely integrated & seamless, ready now with promise of future pleasure.

★★★★☆ **Shiraz** ⊘ Reflects the exceptional quality of the vintage. **15** ⑨③ concentrated yet finely nuanced, with plum pudding, tobacco & delicate herbs in graceful harmony. Silky & approachable in youth, but worth laying down.

★★★★☆ **DNA** ⊛ Precise & nuanced cab franc-dominant (68%) Bordeaux blend, with merlot & dash of cab. **14** ⑨② is just emerging into drinking window, with delightful mineral & earthy highlights to cassis-dominated fruit. Notch up from fine **13** ⑨⓪.

★★★★☆ **Chardonnay** ⊘ Understated, subtly complex **16** ⑨③ has finely detailed citrus, showing zest, marmalade & blossom notes. Also-tasted **17** ⑨③ follows form, less butter & oak spice emphasis. Both elegantly weighted, with lingering finish. Bunch pressed, barrel fermented, matured 9 months.

★★★★☆ **Sauvignon Blanc SV Schaapenberg** ⊛ The cool, wind-swept sea-facing tract of Schaapenberg Hill yields unmistakably pungent, flinty flavours. **18** ⑨③ single-vineyard follows form with striking minerality, sublime poise & elegance. Fermented/8-9 months in 2,500L Austrian oak ovals.

★★★★☆ **Semillon** ⊘ Refined, finely focused **17** ⑨③ upholds Cape benchmark standard. Exquisite layers of minerality, dusty lanolin & floral scents, with subtle oak highlights. Sumptuous texture & lingering, fragrant finish. Excellent potential.

★★★★☆ **Semillon Straw Wine** ⊘ Luscious but understated dessert wine from air-dried semillon, **15** ⑨② was fermented on skins & spent 15 months in older oak. Modest 96 g/l sugar, steely acid core, sumptuous raisin fruit, lingering finish. No **14**. 375 ml.

Not tasted: **MMV**.

Vineyard range ⑭

★★★★☆ **First Thought Cabernet Sauvignon** ⊛ Enigmatically named trio of single-vineyard (& once-off? - see 'The Mistake') offerings. Exceptional **15** ⑨② blending component stands proudly on its own, showing aristocratic black fruit, liquorice & forest-floor earthiness.

★★★★☆ **Last Word Cabernet Sauvignon** ⊛ Characterful & very satisfying, **15** ⑨① shows svelte shape & firm backbone, solid ripe black fruit. Ferment & 17 months in all-new oak round out body, don't intrude.

★★★★☆ **The Mistake Merlot** ⊛ Named for a misunderstanding about volumes on consultant Michel Rolland's blend 'recipe', **15** ⑨① left-over component shows generously ripe black fruit, lithe form & elegant finish. Aromatic lift from wholeberry ferment.

Premium range

★★★★ **Shiraz** Exudes ripeness & sunshine, with meaty plum fruit, silky texture. **17** ⑧⑧ charming scrub & tobacco aromas, harmonious oak spicing.

★★★★ **Cabernet Sauvignon-Merlot** Concentrated plum & prune fruit to the fore in elegantly balanced **15** (89), with dabs petit verdot & cab franc, signature earthy & leafy notes lending detail. No **13**, **14**.

★★★★ **Chardonnay** Deftly handled wood lends roundness & buttery texture to citrus-driven fruit profile on **18** (88). Highlights of honeysuckle & hazelnut, fine acidity.

★★★★ **Sauvignon Blanc** Wholesome, piquant & expressive **18** (88) has tiny 2.5% barrel-matured component. Signature nettle & flint aromas with ripe granadilla, lees richness, all elegantly integrated.— GdB

Location: Somerset West ▪ Map: Helderberg ▪ Map grid reference: F5 ▪ WO: Stellenbosch ▪ Est 1987 ▪ 1stB 1991 ▪ Tasting & sales daily 9–4.30 (gate closes at 4) ▪ Estate closed Good Fri, May 1 & Dec 25 ▪ Daily heritage & gardens tour at 9.30; cellar tours at 11 & 3 ▪ All tours R30pp (reservations advised) ▪ Tastings from R30pp ▪ Camphors Restaurant ▪ Stables Bistro & Forest Picnic (child-friendly) ▪ Gift shop ▪ Historic Cape Dutch homestead ▪ Library ▪ Exhibition corridor ▪ Ancient camphor trees (National Monuments since 1942) ▪ Conservation area ▪ 17 gardens including Camellia garden of excellence & children's adventure garden & maze ▪ Owner(s) Anglo American plc ▪ Winemaker(s) André van Rensburg (Jan 1998) ▪ 3,000ha/126ha (cab, merlot, sauv) ▪ 900t/120,000cs own label 58% red 42% white ▪ ISO 9001, ISO 14001, ISO 22000, OSHAS 18000, WIETA, WWF-SA Conservation Champion ▪ PO Box 17 Somerset West 7129 ▪ info@vergelegen.co.za ▪ www.vergelegen.co.za ▪ S 34° 4' 38.33" E 018° 53' 30.03" ▪ ⓦ bottle.locating.cobbles ▪ **T +27 (0)21-847-2100**

Vergenoegd Löw The Wine Estate   (Ⓠ) (🍴) (◎) (Ⓐ) (Ⓖ)

Significant changes are under way at this centuries-old German-owned Stellenbosch property with regard to wine production and hospitality, but their famous and unique vineyard pest control — more than 1,600 Indian runner ducks — remain faithfully on duty. In fact, conservation and sustainability are front of mind in all planning, specifically habitat and research into indigenous waterbirds. The cellar has been modernised and extended, solar power generation is being installed, and branding and labelling is undergoing an extreme makeover. Even the deli fare is being reworked, and the popular weekend market is on hold while new programmes and events are planned.

Premium range

★★★★ **Cabernet Sauvignon** Inky, earthy **14** (89) shows generous tarry iodine aromas, fragrant liquorice, tinged with port & caramel. Brawny & forceful, with bold, ripe tannins & 50% new oak to match.

★★★★ **Estate Blend** Released drink-ready, **10** ★★★★★ (90) is elegantly evolved, with supple tannins, complex berry compote fruit, precise finish. Cab-led 5-way Bordeaux blend spent 14 months in mostly French oak barrels, 80% new, 7 years in bottle. Improves on **09** (89).

★★★★ **Cape Vintage** Authentic **11** (86) 'port', previewed last time, now has bold, spicy plum fruit, well-judged 105 g/l sugar & 21% alcohol in harmony & balance. Equal touriga & tinta, naturally co-fermented.

Mid-Tier range

★★★★ **Shiraz** Meaty, savoury profile, with tobacco & liquorice highlights on **16** (86), showing some muscle behind black cherry & sweet plum fruit. Riper, more appealing than **15** ★★★ (80).

★★★★ **Little Flower Brut** Rich brioche, apple pie, piercing acidity & lively mousse on dependable **NV** (87) méthode cap classique sparkling, 63% chardonnay with pinot noir, 18 months on lees.

Merlot ★★★★ Rounded & ripe **16** (85) offers generous berry fruit laced with spiciness from year in mixed barrels, 30% new. **Terrace Bay** ★★★★ Shiraz & merlot blend with dashes malbec, cab franc, tinta, subsequent bottling of **15** (85) has generous fruit, decent heft, better definition than previous.

Runner Duck range

Red ★★★★ 5-way blend, mostly shiraz & merlot, **16** (84) has appealing black fruit with tarry notes, ripe tannins. 40% oaked. **Rosé** ★★★ Previewed **19** (81) from shiraz has restrained berry fruit, perky acidity. Modest 12% alcohol makes for great poolside quaffing. **Sauvignon Blanc** ★★★ Cheerfully fresh, light-bodied **18** (80) offers unchallenging everyday enjoyment. Different bottling to last edition; this from Robertson plus Stellenbosch vines. Discontinued: **Reserve White**.

Discontinued: **Limited Edition range**. — GdB

Location/map: Stellenbosch ▪ Map grid reference: B8 ▪ WO: Stellenbosch/Western Cape ▪ Est 1696 ▪ 1stB 1972 ▪ Open 365 days a year from 8-5 ▪ Tasting Mon-Sat 9-5 Sun 10-4 ▪ Farm Deli & picnic area ▪ Picnic baskets ▪ Wine experiences ▪ Wine club ▪ Cellar & vineyard tours by appt ▪ Facilities for children ▪ Tour groups

▪ Wine-related gifts ▪ Lawn games available ▪ Duck parades daily 10.30, 12.30 & 3.30 ▪ Waterbird habitat project ▪ Bird hides ▪ Owner(s) Livia Investment Group ▪ Winemaker(s) Marlize Jacobs (Dec 2007) ▪ Vineyard manager(s) Louis Horn (Jun 2017) ▪ 161ha/57ha (cabs s/f, malbec, merlot, p verdot, shiraz, tinta, touriga) ▪ 20,000cs own label 90% red 7% white 3% rosé ▪ IPW, WIETA, WWF-SA Conservation Champion ▪ PO Box 1 Faure 7131 ▪ info@vergenoegd.co.za ▪ www.vergenoegd.co.za ▪ S 34° 2' 2.8" E 018° 44' 20.1" ▪ ⊞ online. spoiler.themes ▪ **T +27 (0)21-843-3248**

☐ **Versailles** *See Editor's Note*

Verspieren Haberer Family Wines

This is a collaboration between two French émigrés: Bordeaux-educated consulting winemaker Thierry Haberer (clients include Franschhoek's Holden Manz) and Julien Verspieren, entrepreneurial founder of Work & Co, offering clients access to a hi-tech Cape Town-based physical and digital workspace. The current releases (unavailable for tasting) were made in Holden Manz's boutique cellar from widely sourced grapes, comprising the dry Rosalie Rosé '16, Sagra Red '17 (grenache/syrah) and Alma White '18 (chardonnay).

Location: Franschhoek ▪ Closed to public ▪ Owner(s) Julien Verspieren & Thierry Haberer ▪ Winemaker(s) Thierry Haberer ▪ thierry.haberer@me.com ▪ **T +27 (0)78-217-3300/+33 (0)6-12-48-96-13**

☐ **Vet Rooi Olifant** *see* Kaapzicht Wine Estate

Viceroy

Among SA's most enduring blended brandies, with mid-1800s ties to the Van Ryn Wine & Spirit Company. The original, which upped the ante in its category with five years' barrelling, has since been joined by a 3YO, forming a power couple that ranks among owner Distell's Top 15 brands, alongside mighty Nederburg.
5 Year ⊘ ★★★★ 5 year old blended brandy ⑧⑤ is fairly serious-minded with a lingering finish, but 43% alcohol (as next) inclines it more towards mixing than solo. Serendipitously, it has ginger among the flavours so practically made for ginger ale & ice. Also in 375 ml & 200 ml. **Makoya** ⊘ ★★★★ Younger & more recent sibling, lively blended 3 year old ⑧④ has fresh pear & dried peach, floral notes & a spirity finish. For mixing. Also in 200 ml. — WB

Vierkoppen

Britons David and Daphne Briscoe and another couple founded this boutique winery just over a decade ago, naming it for the 'four heads' involved, and the hilly terrain in Robertson's Klaasvoogds ward. Latterly vinifying as a duo, the Briscoes achieved increasingly impressive results with cab and pinotage. Sadly David passed away in early 2018, and Daphne is winding down the venture, though stocks of the Merlot listed below, and untasted '15 Weavers Nest Reserve (Bordeaux blend) and Cabernet Sauvignon are still available.
The Basket Case Merlot ⓧ ★★★★ Primary flavours - berries, violets, smoked meat - to the fore in just-bottled **15** ⑧④, accessible & moreish. — DS

Location: Robertson ▪ WO: Klaasvoogds ▪ Est 2008 ▪ 1stB 2009 ▪ Owner(s) Daphne Briscoe ▪ PO Box 950 Robertson 6705 ▪ info@vierkoppen.com ▪ www.vierkoppen.com ▪ **T +27 (0)78-413-1733**

Vilafonté   ⓛ

Named for the 'seriously old dirt' (alias vilafontes soils) of their Simonsberg-Paarl vineyards, this luxe wine collaboration between one of America's most famous winemakers, Zelma Long, viticulturist husband Phil Freese, and SA marketer Mike Ratcliffe is flying high (literally, with listings in First and Business Class on Emirates). While Zelma continues to consult internationally, and receive plaudits such as a Lifetime Award from Innovation + Quality, an annual forum focused on cutting-edge advancements in wine quality in California, SA winemaker Chris de Vries handles day-to-day operations at the Bosman's Crossing cellar in Stellenbosch, and viticulturist Edward Pietersen is planting more vines, in particular cabernet for Series C.
★★★★★ **Series C** Ⓐ Refined, ageworthy cab-led Bordeaux blend with merlot, malbec & cab franc (15/12/11), **16** ⑨③ less dense, more elegant than previous. Black-fruit intensity & length, also dark chocolate & pencil shavings from 22 months in 77% new French oak. In magnum, too, as next.

★★★★☆ **Series M** (🐝) Merlot (36%) plays 2nd fiddle to malbec in rich, velvety yet bright, fresh **16** (94), with 12% cab, 2% cab franc, aged 22 months in 21% new French oak. Cellarworthy, but youthfully accessible thanks to succulent fruit, subtle spice & soft tannins.

★★★★☆ **Seriously Old Dirt** 'Your everyday Vilafonté' is modern & fruit-forward, yet **17** (92) related to Series M in its make-up, with malbec & merlot dominant (& near equal), 26/1 cab & cab franc providing support as well as herb & tealeaf notes, light oaking showcasing mixed berry fruit. **16** untasted.— JG

Location/map: Stellenbosch ▪ Map grid reference: E5 ▪ WO: Paarl ▪ Est 1996 ▪ 1stB 2003 ▪ Tasting, sales & tours by appt only ▪ Owner(s) Mike Ratcliffe, Zelma Long & Phil Freese ▪ Winemaker(s) Zelma Long & Chris de Vries (Oct 2016) ▪ Viticulturist(s) Phil Freese & Edward Pietersen (2006) ▪ 19ha (cabs s/f, malbec, merlot) ▪ 70t/4,000cs own label 100% red ▪ Unit 7C, Lower Dorp Str, Bosman's Crossing, Stellenbosch 7600 ▪ info@ vilafonte.com ▪ www.vilafonte.com ▪ S 33° 56' 26.8" E 018° 50' 49.8" ▪ [⌖] abacus.blizzard.rather ▪ **T +27 (0)21-886-4083**

Viljoensdrift Fine Wines & Cruises   (🍷) (🍴) (📷)

Manie and Fred Viljoen are the 5th generation to grow and make wine in Robertson. The brothers restored the old cellar on the family farm, where forebears made sweet wines and brandy, and began bottling under the Viljoensdrift label in 1998, that year's entire production snapped up by Dutch buyers who arrived unannounced. Even then, the visitor facilities were among the most unusual in the winelands, and have been enduringly popular, with cruises on riverboat Uncle Ben and, latterly, a self-help deli for leisurely picnics.

River Grandeur range
Cabernet Sauvignon (🍷) ★★★ Juicy ripe plums with a cocoa dusting, **16** (81) is smooth & lifted by a berry finish. **Merlot** ★★★ Stewed plums, spiced cherries & polished tannins make **17** (82) an enjoyable mouthful. **Pinotage Single Vineyard** (🍷) ★★★★ Big & bold, in house style, yet **17** (84) balanced, too, its ripe plum fruit checked by a raspberry freshness, firm grip of oak & nice savoury finish. **Shiraz** (🍷) ★★★ Generous hedgerow fruit, cured meat & exotic spice mingle with savoury oak in **17** (80) pleasant everyday red. **Cape Blend** (🍷) ★★★★ Equal pinotage & cab in muscular **17** (84), upfront dark berry flavours & hints of violets & dried herbs. Appealing but robust, needs time to show at best. **Chardonnay** ★★★ Leesy **18** (80) offers bruised apple & poached quince flavours for uncomplicated drinking. **Crispy Sauvignon Blanc** ★★★ Attractively packaged **19** (80) improves on previous. Crisp, as intended, with tropical flavours & an assertive citrus finish.

Viljoensdrift range
Muskapino Sweet Pink Sparkling Wine ★★ Sweet, lively pink fizz with low 7.5% alcohol & billows of rosepetals & Turkish delight. **19** (76) muscadel & pinotage is easy & fun. **Cape Vintage Reserve** (🍷) ★★★★ Vivacious red fruit & plum pudding on **15** (83) 'port' from tinta. Gentle vanilla spice ex 3 years in oak, good spirity farewell. Not tasted: **Villion**.

Anchor Drift range
Dry Red (✓) ★★★ From pinotage & cinsaut, NV (77) juicy, fruity & light, with a smooth mouthfeel. **Dry White** ★★★ Just-dry NV (77) from semillon is balanced & mouthfilling, slips down easily. — WB

Location/map/WO: Robertson ▪ Map grid reference: C5 ▪ Est/1stB 1998 ▪ Tasting, sales & river cruises at riverside venue Mon-Fri 10—5 Sat 10-4 & 1st Sun/month 10-3; open 7 days/week Dec-Feb ▪ Closed Good Fri, Dec 25 & Jan 1 ▪ Self-help deli - create your own picnic basket ▪ Tour groups ▪ Conferences ▪ Owner(s) Fred & Manie Viljoen ▪ Winemaker(s) Fred Viljoen, with Zonia Lategan ▪ Viticulturist(s) Manie Viljoen ▪ 240ha/120ha (cab, merlot, ptage, shiraz, chard, sauv) ▪ 2,000t/±160,000cs own label 55% red 40% white 4% rosé 1% port + 15,000L for clients ▪ Other export brand: Elandsberg ▪ IPW, WIETA ▪ PO Box 653 Robertson 6705 ▪ rivercruises@viljoensdrift.co.za ▪ www.viljoensdrift.co.za ▪ S 33° 52' 8.4" E 019° 59' 13.6" ▪ [⌖] cucumber. toothless.logo ▪ **T +27 (0)23-615-1901 (cellar)/+27 (0)23-615-1017 (tasting/cruises)**

☐ **Villa Cape Kosher** *see* Simonsvlei International

☐ **Villa Esposto** *see* Klawer Wine Cellars

☐ **Village Walk** *see* Franschhoek Cellar

Villiera Wines ⒧ ⑪ ◎ ⒧

The Grier family winery fizzes with ideas and projects to push their winemaking envelope – entirely appropriate given their status as pioneers of méthode cap classique sparkling from 1983 under cellar chief and Cape Winemakers Guild member Jeff Grier. Natural ferments and use of amphoras and 'eggs' are but a few examples of such advances. More radically, they placed demijohns of fortified chenin on the tasting room roof and let them maderise al fresco for a delicious new 'sun wine' debuting this edition. Major emphasis remains on MCC production, however, and here 2nd-generation Xander Grier is the young cellar kingpin, colleague Nathan Valentine looking after the non-sparkling wines, both mentored by Jeff and his cousin, the viticulturist Simon Grier. Sustainability, eco and social, is central, hence solar panels and a rainwater recovery system, and homing winelands charity Pebbles on the Stellenbosch estate.

Villiera Wines range

★★★★ **Cabernet Sauvignon** ⒲ Effortless ease to **16** ⑧⑥. Supple, smooth, black fruited & spicy, with well-knit oak (25% new), including 10% dab American. Confident & structured for the long haul.

★★★★ **Stand Alone Gamay** ⒩⒠⒲ ⒲ Smoky edge to cranberry & cherry fruit on **18** ⑧⑧ off certified Heritage Vineyard. Lipsmacking succulence & defined structure. Spontaneous ferment, 30% wholebunch.

★★★★ **Merlot** ⊘ ⒲ **17** ⑧⑧ improves on **16** ★★★☆ ⑧⑤ with subtle berry fruit vibrancy from one-third wholebunch pressing. Good oak frame from just 20% new oak means nothing is overplayed. Harmonious, elegant, with long spicy finish. Worth cellaring.

★★★★☆ **Monro Merlot** Deceptively light yet concentrated **17** ⑨① continues form of **16** ⑨①. Layered with hedgerow fruit & light tannin grip from 18 months in 50% new oak, rich & refined, with lingering cocoa finish.

★★★★ **Stand Alone Pinot Noir** Light as a forest sprite, **16** ⑧⑨ spicily ethereal yet succulent, with good berry core & concentration. Hemel-en-Aarde Ridge grapes, spontaneous ferment, 30% wholebunch.

★★★★☆ **The Clan** ⒲ Superb, unusual blend of cab franc & 10% carignan. **16** ⑨④ muscular but silky, complex & nuanced. Rich & powerful yet controlled; 18 months oak, 60% new.

★★★★☆ **Barrel Fermented Chenin Blanc** Complex, as befits its intricate making (portion wholebunch, natural ferment, some malo in 50% new oak, some bâtonnage...) Rich honeyed citrus & pineapple, fruit & acid balanced on platform of well-knit oak. **18** ★★★★ ⑧⑧ less hedonistic than **17** ⑨④.

★★★★ **Bush Vine Blanc Fumé 18** ⑧⑨ sees a style tweak: portions wholebunch & oak fermented, malo avoided to retain freshness. Zippy lemon verbena appeal, bright but structured & long.

★★★★☆ **Sauvignon Blanc** ⊘ From Stellenbosch & Elgin grapes, **19** ⑨⓪ taut & vital, with zingy grapefruit freshness but also rounded tropical nuance. Skin contact & 20% portion natural ferment in old oak add complexity, body & length. Different league to **18** ★★★☆ ⑧③ & previous.

★★★★☆ **Dakwijn** ⒩⒠⒲ ⒲ Intriguing & delicious **17** ⑨④ chenin fortified dessert. Nutty oxidative nose & palate with well-gauged spirit & sweetness (94 g/l sugar) balanced by vivacious acid. Spicy, savoury, with saline nuance. Natural ferment in 'egg', aged outdoors in demijohns 8 months, then year in old oak. 500 ml.

Pinotage ⒲ ★★★★ Instant appeal of juicy raspberry & plum tones on **17** ⑧⑤. Concentration & depth belie vivacity. Lithe & persistent. Like previous, 25% new oak. **Chenin Blanc** ⊘ ★★★☆ Bright pear & lemon zest on **19** ⑧④. Lively yet rich from dabs oak, natural ferment & lees contact. Easy, clean & poised. **Jasmine** ⊘ ★★★★ Seductive pot-pourri nose on **19** ⑧⑤ tangy, semi-sweet muscat-led blend with gewürztraminer & riesling. Gently succulent, with good acidity. In abeyance: **Antithesis**, **Inspiration**.

Méthode Cap Classique range

★★★★ **Tradition Brut Rosé** ⊘ Subtle pink hue to improved pinot noir-led **NV** ⑧⑨ sparkler with equal parts chardonnay & pinotage & dab meunier. Bright lime zest entry followed by fantail of lees & nuts from 18 months sur lie. Also in magnum.

★★★★ **Brut Natural** Creamy, rounded yet vivid **15** ⑧⑧, all-chardonnay bubbly boasting zero dosage & 42 months on lees. Broad & complex, with zesty dry finish, like harmonious **14** ⑧⑨.

★★★★☆ **Monro Brut** ⒲ **13** ⑨③ follows stellar **12** ★★★★★ ⑨⑤ flagship bubbly in maritime/oyster-shell complexity. Taut, nuanced & lengthy. Chardonnay leads pinot noir (30%) & meunier. Powerful yet restrained & refined. Freshness defies 72 months on lees.

★★★★ Tradition Brut ✓ Their original **NV** (87) sparkler, ever reliable but capable of change: chardonnay (70%) leads pinot noir, but lees contact (18 months) & 6 months in bottle are standard. Lime zest tang is balanced by creamy sourdough & toast. Also in 1.5L & 375 ml.

Starlight Brut ✓ ★★★★ Citrus vibrancy to low-alcohol **NV** (85) bubbly. Chardonnay leads (50%), with pinot noir & pinotage. Lively, light & zesty with crisp finish.

Down to Earth range

Red ✓ ★★★★ Plush, spicy & soft **17** (85) blend of touriga & shiraz. Good frame from 6 months in 35% new oak. Unfussy yet rewarding. **White** ★★★ Ripe tropical tinge to **19** (82) blend of sauvignon (82%) & semillon. Tangy, succulent & fresh. — FM

Location/map: Stellenbosch ▪ Map grid reference: D1 ▪ WO: Stellenbosch/Hemel-en-Aarde Ridge/Stellenbosch-Elgin ▪ Est/1stB 1983 ▪ Tasting, sales & self-guided cellar tours Mon-Fri 9–5 Sat 9–3 ▪ Closed Good Fri, Dec 25 & Jan 1 ▪ MCC & nougat pairing; MCC & chocolate pairing; cheese platters ▪ Wildlife sanctuary ▪ Game drive safaris & birding (incl tasting & self-guided tour of cellar), phone for cost and to book ahead ▪ Owner(s) Grier family ▪ Cellarmaster(s) Jeff Grier (1983) ▪ Winemaker(s) Nathan Valentine (reds/whites) & Xander Grier (MCC/reserve wines) ▪ Viticulturist(s) Simon Grier ▪ 180ha (cab, merlot, ptage, pinot, shiraz, chard, chenin, sauv) ▪ 1,600t/110,000cs own label 25% red 30% white 45% MCC ▪ Brands for clients: Woolworths (local); Marks & Spencer (export) ▪ B-BBEE, HACCP, IPW, WIETA ▪ PO Box 66 Koelenhof 7605 ▪ wine@villiera.com ▪ www.villiera.com ▪ S 33° 50' 14.4" E 018° 47' 34.4" ▪ concoct.launchpad.layouts ▪ T +27 (0)21-865-2002/3

Villiersdorp Winery

A name change (from Villiersdorp Cellar) and new business partners (Iona's Andrew Gunn becomes the majority shareholder) means a new impetus for this grower co-owned venture in the heart of the Cape South Coast. The different wine ranges have been clearly defined and focused on their various markets, the pinnacle Since 1922 tier of terroir-driven wines now aiming to showcase the potential of specific top-quality, mostly cool-climate sites. In Villiersdorp town, investment in the cellar and cellardoor means better facilities for the winemaking team and visitors alike.

Since 1922 range

★★★★ Kiara (NEW) Flagship Bordeaux red **15** (88) has plenty to shout about. Stewed black fruit pervaded with spice (vanilla, anise, liquorice), soft rounded tannins & good length. Showy but substantial. Co-ferment of cab franc, cab & merlot, 100% new French & Hungarian barrels.

★★★★ Mosko (NEW) Moskonfyt (unctuous must jam), this cellar's speciality for many years, remembered in excellent blend of semillon, viognier, chardonnay, chenin. **18** (89) alive with bright yellow fruit (pineapples, apples) wrapped in delicate, creamy oak (none new, 10% Hungarian). Extremely good length, fresh acidic bite. One to watch.

★★★★ Last Straw (NEW) Delightful sweet treat from vine-dried chenin, fermented/6 months in old oak, 20% Hungarian. **18** (89) great depth of flavour (honey, apricots, orange peel) with creamy vanilla custard notes, well-balanced sugar/acid. Delicious partner for puddings & blue cheese. WO W Cape. 375 ml.

Villiersdorp Winery range

Pinotage (NEW) ★★★ Fruity little number (cranberries & blackberries) with coffee & chocolate from oak-stave ageing. **18** (80) tasted pre-bottling, as next 3. **Shiraz** (NEW) ★★★ Attractive floral notes on **18** (80) along with rich black fruit, smoked meats & pepper spice. Pleasant everyday drinking. **Chardonnay** (NEW) ★★★ Gentle lemon fruit on **19** (81), with creamy overtones from 4 months on oak staves. Tinned litchi finish, should all come together nicely. **Sauvignon Blanc** (NEW) ★★★★ Promising **19** (83), fresh mouthful of crisp green fruit, lively acidity & good length. Ideal for summer sipping. **Cape Ruby** ★★★ Winter-warming **NV** (80) 'port' with fiery alcohol knitting together dark chocolate, spiced raisins & stewed plums. Tinta, 10% pontac, co-fermented. WO W Cape, as Pinotage.

Slow range

Van Der Stel ✓ ⊤ ★★★ Happy summer drinker **19** (82), crisp, fresh lemon fruit plus perfumed flowers, hint of ginger & bouncy acidity. Just-dry blend of chenin & viognier. WO W Cape, as next 2.

Cabernet Sauvignon (NEW) ★★★ Fresh & juicy black fruit on **18** (79) tad unbalanced by overt oak & forthright tannins but should settle & improve. Previewed from tank, like all these. **Bossieveld** ⊘ ★★★ 60/40 cab/merlot blend **18** (81) showing nice black fruit, rounded juiciness aided by gram sugar, soft tannins. Appealing wine also in 3L pack, as Van Der Stel. **Rosé** (NEW) ⊘ ★★★ Bone-dry **19** (81), crunchy red fruit with creamy palate, good weight & soft finish. Interesting shiraz, pinot noir & merlot combo. **Chenin Blanc** (NEW) ⊘ ★★★ Very decent drop **19** (80) mixes tropical & apple fruit in crisp, clean, sappy mouthful.

Treintjiewyn range

Hanepoot Jerepiko ★★★ Well-balanced **NV** (81) fortified with appetising grapey notes, litchis & fresh blossoms. Plenty of sweetness held in check by nicely integrated alcohol. WO W Cape. — CM

Location/map: Villiersdorp ▪ Map grid reference: C1 ▪ WO: Cape South Coast/Western Cape ▪ Est 1922 ▪ 1stB 1974 ▪ Tasting & sales Mon-Fri 8—5 Sat 9-1 ▪ Fee R10 for groups of 7+ ▪ Closed Easter Fri-Mon & Dec 25/26 ▪ Cellar tours by appt ▪ Kelkiewyn Restaurant ▪ Farm produce ▪ Tractor museum open on request ▪ Owner(s) 37 shareholders ▪ GM Christo Versfeld ▪ Winemaker(s) Christo Versfeld, with Richard Schroeder ▪ Viticulturist(s) Richard Schroeder ▪ 141ha under vine ▪ IPW ▪ PO Box 151 Villiersdorp 6848 ▪ cellaradmin@villiersdorpcellar. co.za ▪ www.villiersdorpcellar.co.za ▪ S 33° 59' 11.2" E 019° 17' 48.5" ▪ 🗺 custard.crackle.stretcher ▪ **T +27 (0)28-840-0083**

Villion Family Wines

Once wide-ranging, viti-vini consultant Kobie Viljoen fledged his own brand in 2015, honouring 17th-century French forebear Francois Villion. For his eclectic range, he selects from parcels close to the ocean and high-altitude sites, mindful of vine age, limited yields, clone differences and sustainable cultivation. Grapes are wild-yeast fermented in open vessels. Working at Bot River's Barton Vineyards, a winemaking consultancy - now a residency, with Villion allocated its own space - he and wife Elnette (with young Willem shadowing dad in the vineyards) welcome all, including the Hermanus-based ChillGuru Bus.

★★★★☆ **Cabernet Sauvignon** (🍇) Copybook cabernet packed with blackberry, cassis & spice in **16** (93). 21 months French oak, 25% new 300L, deliver well-tamed tannins as well as graphite & cigarbox overlays. WO Bot River.

★★★★ **Pinot Noir** Alluring sour cherry & cranberry are laced with spice & savoury from mostly 2nd-fill wood on naturally fermented **16** (86), bright acidity with saline persistence. Steps up on **15** ★★★ (82).

★★★★ **Syrah** Unshowy but impressive **17** (88) has splashes mourvèdre & viognier. Shows real aromatic complexity (dark plum, mulberry, clove & nutmeg), with white pepper, violets & olive tapenade nuances in the flavours. Tannins are smooth after 21 months in French oak, 20 new.

★★★★ **Henning Chenin Blanc** From 37 year old Bot River vines, wild-fermented **18** (87) shows a laudably subtle oaking regime which showcases fresh quince & peach fruit notes & hay wafts, stonefruit finish lifted by vibrant acidity.

★★★★ **Blanc de l'Atlantique** Like **16** ★★★★ (84), **17** (86) a mix of Elgin viognier & chardonnay, Bot River skin-fermented chenin, with apricot, orange marmalade & a vanilla note from light oaking. Textured & fresh, ideal for seafood platters.

Chardonnay ★★★★ Fresh kumquat, pear & peach fruits on **18** (85) mingle well with cinnamon & vanilla spice from judicious partial oaking, elegant citrus finish. WO Elgin. **White Merlot Solo** (NEW) ★★★★ Crisp & svelte **15** (83) a once-off parcel of just 750 bottles. 11 months in old oak deliver restrained whiffs of pears & citrus leading to chamomile & oatmeal flavours. — GM

Location: Bot River ▪ Map: Walker Bay & Bot River ▪ Map grid reference: B2 ▪ WO: Cape South Coast/Bot River/Elgin ▪ Est 2015 ▪ 1stB 2012 ▪ Tasting Mon-Fri 10-5 Sat & pub hols 10-3 ▪ Owner(s)/winemaker(s) Kobie Viljoen ▪ 15t/3,000cs own label 48% red 52% white ▪ R43/Hermanus Rd Bot River 7185 ▪ elnette@ villionwines.com, kobie@villionwines.com ▪ www.villionwines.com ▪ S 34° 15' 43.8" E 019° 10' 29.2" ▪ **T +27 (0)28-284-9248**

☐ **Vinay** see Slanghoek Winery

Vinimark

The largest independent wine-specialist company in SA, distributing and marketing more than 50 well-known brands, including wholly owned ones, many listed in these pages.

Location: Stellenbosch ▪ Closed to public ▪ Directors Gys Naudé, Cindy Jordaan, Geoff Harvey, Eckhardt Gerber, Rudiger Gretschel & Guy Pause ▪ Exports: Geoff Harvey ▪ PO Box 441 Stellenbosch 7599 ▪ geoff@vinimark.co.za ▪ www.vinimark.co.za ▪ **T +27 (0)21-883-8043/4**

☐ **Vinography** *see* Benguela Cove Lagoon Wine Estate

Vinologist Wine Company

A new label from Boekenhoutskloof and their expert team of winemakers must be a notable event (see Porcupine Ridge and Wolftrap as proof). The Vinologist's aim is to find 'vineyards of single origin which produce grape varieties that thrive in those places'. In the cellar, the mantra is 'simple and honest winemaking'. The packaging is designed to be inviting and unpretentious, avoiding alienating the average consumer; the contents designed to be quality wines that 'speak in a simple and relatable tone'.

Swartland Syrah ⊘ ⊛ ★★★☆ Variety-true **18** ⑧⑤ has highly appealing savoury aromas & flavours of cured meat & coriander, brooding dark fruit, slatey minerality & succulent finish. **Swartland Dry Rosé** ⊛ ★★★☆ Mostly cinsaut, splash syrah in this delightful pink. **19** ⑧⑤ is all fragrant berries, fynbos & earthy herbs, to serve chilled & celebrate summer. Very attractively packaged, as all. **Cape Town Sauvignon Blanc** ⊛ ★★★☆ 'Cool' & deliciously dry **19** ⑧⑤ offers tropical fruit flavours, good balance & grip, with a citrus tang in its tail.

Stellenbosch Cabernet Sauvignon ★★★ Perfumed & fragrant blackberry, vanilla & polished leather on the nose in **18** ⑧⓪, but terse tannins need time or food. **Franschhoek Merlot** ★★★ Notes of plum, mulberry & bramble fruit on approachable **18** ⑧② part oaked (as Syrah), with supple tannin structure & cranberry finish. **Swartland Chenin Blanc** ★★★ Fleeting apple, stonefruit & gentle spice (though unoaked), **19** ⑧⓪ pleasing creaminess from extended lees ageing. — WB

Location: Franschhoek ▪ WO: Swartland/Stellenbosch/Franschhoek/Cape Town ▪ Est/1stB 2017 ▪ Closed to public ▪ Owner(s) Boekenhoutskloof Winery (Pty) Ltd ▪ Cellarmaster(s) Marc Kent ▪ Winemaker(s) Johan Nesenberend & Heinrich Hugo (both Jan 2017) ▪ 30,000cs own label 50% red 33% white 17% rosé ▪ BRC, BSCI, IPW, WIETA ▪ PO Box 433 Franschhoek 7690 ▪ vin@vinologist.co.za ▪ www.vinologist.co.za ▪ **T +27 (0)21-842-2371**

☐ **Vinoneers** *see* The Vinoneers
☐ **Vino Pronto** *see* Hirst Wines
☐ **Vino Sacci** *see* Klawer Wine Cellars

Vintales Wines International ⓆⓇ

'Every wine has a story' is the premise of this lifestyle brand, owned by Paarl-based Anneli Karsten and a large SA winery. Vintales' own narrative, begun in 2012, continues with the establishment of new export markets (Russia and Poland), helping make possible increased contributions to Living Legends, a local youth development and training project. In the next chapter, two Fairtrade wines will join the portfolio.

Crowded Café Cabernet Sauvignon Ⓠ ★★ With some chocolate & cassis, few grams sugar & light tannin, **17** ⑦③ slips down effortlessly. **Road Trip Pinotage** ★★★ Ups freshness with brisk acidity in **18** ⑦⑧, retains drinkability with mulberries-&-cream flavours, a few well-judged grams of sugar. **Last Call Shiraz** Ⓠ ★★ Smoke & char notes, fresh & fruity flavours plumped out by few grams sugar in **17** ⑦⑤. **Sunset Rosé** Ⓠ ★★ Gently sweet **18** ⑦⑥ pink, packed with cherry fruit to get the party started. **Serenade Chardonnay** Ⓠ ★★ Offers sherbet & Lemon Cream tones, but unwooded **18** ⑦③ waves goodbye all too soon. **Lazy Days Chenin Blanc** Ⓠ ★★ Demure **18** ⑦④ faint gooseberry appeal, suggestion of vinosity & sweetness. **Sea Breeze Sauvignon Blanc** Ⓠ ★★ Water-white **18** ⑦⑤, understated grass & gooseberry, feisty acidity to partner creamy food. **Espontaneo Sparkling Sweet Rosé** Ⓠ ★★ Plenty of racy bubbles in pink **NV** ⑦⑤ fizz with red-boiled-sweet character, dab sugar for drinkability. **Espontaneo Sparkling Brut** Ⓠ ★ Dry **NV** ⑥⑦ sparkler is smooth & vinous, with quickly dissipating bubbles. **Espontaneo Sparkling Moscato** ★★ Grapey bouquet, frothy mousse, lemon sherbet zing & balanced sweetness, charming **NV** ⑦⑥ ticks all the party-starting boxes. **Bloomin' Late Moscato** Ⓠ ★★ Engaging spice nuance on **18** ⑦⑥'s grapey nose & palate; to enjoy well-chilled. **Sugar & Spice Natural Sweet Red** Ⓠ ★★ Forthright red berries & spice, sweetness curbed by nudge tannin, lowish 11% alcohol on **NV** ⑦⑤ casual sipper. **Best Of Both Natural Sweet Rosé** Ⓠ ★★ Appealing sunset hue, sweet berries & cherries on **NV** (74) carefree quaffer. **Head Over Heels Natural Sweet White** (Ⓥ) ★★ Full-sweet **NV** (72) grape juice for adults. — CvZ

Location: Paarl ▪ WO: Western Cape ▪ Est 2012 ▪ 1stB 2015 ▪ Tasting & tours/excursions by appt ▪ Sales via website or by appt ▪ Meals/refreshments by prior arrangement ▪ Owner(s) 2 shareholders ▪ WIETA ▪ 13 Constantia Str Paarl 7646 ▪ story@vintaleswine.com, anneli@vintaleswine.com ▪ www.vintaleswine.com ▪ **T +27 (0)82-783-9935**

☐ **Vinum** see Radford Dale
☐ **Vinyl Collection** see Rascallion Wines
☐ **Viva Africa Wines** see Bader & Walters Family Wines
☐ **Voetspore** see Arendskloof-New Cape Wines

Vondeling

The Vondeling home-farm in Voor Paardeberg ward lies at the foot of Paarderberg Mountain, estimated to have 1,000 plant species, nearly 200 threatened or endangered. As WWF-SA Conservation Champions, the team's efforts have helped highlight this rich diversity. Sustainability drives both viticultural and wine-making practices, as well as management of the fynbos, which is again flourishing after 2019's good rains. Vondeling's green credentials are boosted by the on-site solar array, which powers over half the property, houses and two large cellars. Winemaker Matthew Copeland's plans for Rurale, SA's first certified méthode ancestrale sparkling, are to include pinotage, increase production and upgrade the packaging to place it alongside other premium sparkling wines.

Flagship Wines

★★★★☆ **Monsonia** (🐝) Shiraz-led blend with 3 other Rhône varieties. **16** (90) easy-drinking but not simple; supple, broad mouthfilling spice, meat & truffle complexity, long savoury conclusion. Freshness & balanced structure portend well for the future. Larger French oak, 33% new, 16 months.

★★★★☆ **Babiana** Regular quartet led by 30+ year chenin with viognier, roussanne & grenache blanc. **18** (92) gorgeous ripe yellow peach, honeysuckle fragrance; succulent but also good energy; rounded off with light grip. Very moreish. Natural ferment in oak, 10 months lees ageing.

★★★★☆ **Sweet Carolyn** (Ⓥ) Vine-dried white muscat de Frontignan, unoaked, wholeberry fermented on skins to enhance alluring varietal flavours. Zesty, fresh citrus ensures balance, uncloying despite decadent 203 grams sugar. Light 10.5% alcohol. **17** (92) stylish dessert though shade off **16** (94). 500 ml.

Limited Releases

★★★★☆ **Bowwood Pinotage** (🐝) Barrel selection from single block produces smart, modern-style **16** (90). Refined clove & raspberry concentration; rich texture held by well-managed tannins. Still some evidence of new/used American oak but sound building blocks to allow for more savouriness over time. **15** ★★★★ (89) wood was more centre-stage.

★★★★☆ **Philosophie** (Ⓥ) Low yields, careful barrel selection & fine **15** (94) vintage align in rich, concentrated cab-led Bordeaux blend. Seamless & polished, with fine dry tannins, 100% French oak in sync with fruit intensity. Like **14** (93), deserves ageing.

★★★★ **Rurale Méthode Ancestrale** One of local pioneers of méthode ancestrale (single-ferment) sparkling. Quality has increased since debut **13** (88). **16** ★★★★☆ (90) from chardonnay, best to date. Gorgeous baked apple, lemon zest character, pinprick creamy mousse & bright acid cutting through natural 26 g/l sugar. Lowish 11% alcohol adds to refreshment, as in **15** (89).

Discontinued: **Rurale Blanc de Noir**.

Vondeling range

★★★★ **Cabernet Sauvignon** Combination of high-lying, temperate vineyards, quality vintage evident in promising **17** (89). Inviting aromas of dark, soft berries, complementary cedary notes suggest future complexity. Well fleshed with ripe fruit, but retains balance thanks to freshness & fine dry tannins. Previewed, could rate higher once bottled.

★★★★ **Merlot** (NEW) In ripe, fruit-driven style. **17** (86) full bodied, with juicy plummy flavours, oak spice (300L Hungarian barrels); fruit currently dimmed by apparent finishing sweetness though technically dry. Should benefit from couple of years rounding.

★★★★ Baldrick Shiraz ⓦ Spice, white pepper, floral & plummy tones on **17** ⑧⑥, 100% shiraz (no mourvèdre). Supple tannins, (older) oak secondary, bright fruit is the star, finishes respectably dry. More earnest intent than **16** ★★★★ ⑧④.

★★★★ Chardonnay Consistent performer. **18** ⑧⑧ offers usual approachability with layers of interest. Yellow peach, ginger spice, oatmeal & creamy lees, showcased by tangy freshness; subtle oak a harmonising extra. Natural ferment, maturation 400L French oak, lees enriched.

Sauvignon Blanc ★★★★ Appetising tropical, granadilla fruity acids on **19** ⑧③ plumped out by 4 months on lees. Fresh yet unaggressive.

Lifestyle range

Rosé ⓦ **★★★** Brims with summer red berries, juicily fresh, tangy dry finish. **19** ⑧② easy-drinking & very moreish but not trivial. Mainly merlot, 2 other reds. **Petit Blanc Chenin Blanc** ⓦ **★★★** Concentrated ripe, red apple flavour on **19** ⑧① backed by zesty fruity acids, lightish body, gentle persistence.

Petit Rouge ⓦ **★★★★** Bright as a button, with berry & cherry flavours, supple & juicy, raring to entertain solo or with meaty meals. **18** ⑧④ 100% merlot, still pocket friendly. — AL

Location/map: Paarl ▪ Map grid reference: C1 ▪ WO: Voor Paardeberg ▪ Est 2001 ▪ 1stB 2005 ▪ Tasting & sales Mon-Fri 10-5 Sat/pub hols by appt ▪ Wedding/function/conference venue ▪ St Clement's Chapel ▪ Owner(s) Julian Johnsen & Anthony Ward ▪ Winemaker(s) Matthew Copeland (Jul 2007), with Emile van der Merwe (Dec 2011) ▪ Viticulturist(s) Magnus Joubert (Jul 2012) ▪ 100ha (cabs s/f, carignan, grenache r/w, malbec, merlot, mourv, p verdot, shiraz, chard, chenin, muscat de F, sauv, viog) ▪ 900t/100,000cs own label 40% red 40% white 20% rosé ▪ Other export brand: Signal Cannon ▪ WWF-SA Conservation Champion ▪ PO Box 57 Wellington 7654 ▪ admin@vondelingwines.co.za ▪ www.vondelingwines.co.za ▪ S 33° 35' 22.50" E 018° 52' 45.00" ▪ ✉ closest.each.cruised ▪ **T +27 (0)21-869-8595**

☐ **Age of the Rebel** *see* Thor Vintners
☐ **Voyageur** *see* Thor Vintners

Vrede en Lust Wine Farm   ⓦ ⓫ ⌂ ⊙ ⓐ ⓹

Buys family vines in Simonsberg-Paarl and Elgin are the source of the Vrede en Lust wine range, untasted by us. A cornucopia of amenities awaits visitors to the stylishly appointed and historic estate, founded in 1688 by a Flemish merchant, Jacques de Savoye.

Location: Paarl ▪ Map: Franschhoek ▪ Map grid reference: B7 ▪ Est 1688 ▪ 1stB 2002 ▪ Tasting & sales daily 10–5 ▪ Closed Good Fri & Dec 25 ▪ Tours 10–4 by appt ▪ Lust Bistro & Bakery ▪ Guest accommodation in deluxe suites & manor house ▪ Tour groups by appt ▪ Conferences, functions & weddings ▪ Play area for children ▪ Pétanque courts ▪ Run2Wine (5km fun run) ▪ Owner(s) Buys family ▪ Cellarmaster(s) Karlin Nel (Sep 2017) ▪ Winemaker(s) Karlin Nel (Sep 2017), with Duan Engelbrecht (May 2017) ▪ Viticulturist(s) Etienne Buys (Jun 1998) & Annette Davel (Oct 2017, Casey's Ridge) ▪ 275ha total ▪ Vrede en Lust: 66ha (cab, grenache, malbec, merlot, p verdot, shiraz, chard, viog); Casey's Ridge, Elgin: 88.9ha (cabs s/f, merlot, shiraz, chard, chenin, pinots g/n, riesling, sauv, sem, viog); Ricton: 127ha (cab, cinsaut, ptage, shiraz, chard) ▪ 800t/45,000cs own label ▪ WIETA ▪ PO Box 171 Groot Drakenstein 7680 ▪ info@vnl.co.za ▪ www.vnl.co.za ▪ S 33° 50' 15.9" E 018° 57' 13.4" ▪ ✉ houseplant.dedicating.reached ▪ **T +27 (0)21-874-1611**

Vredenheim Wines   ⓦ ⓫ ⌂ ⊙ ⓹

Beside wine, family-owned Vredenheim estate in Stellenbosch is recognised and frequented for its smorgasbord of visitor amenities. Matriarch and 'gracious lady' Rikie Bezuidenhout and late husband 'M'Lord' Coen moved here from a KwaZulu-Natal game farm in 1986, hence the large antelope enclosure and popular Big Cats Park. To note, however, the Jaguars for hire are of the four-wheeled sort.

Cabernet Sauvignon ⓦ **★★★★** Dark chocolate & blackcurrant mingle with dusty, firm but not harsh tannins, **16** ⑧③'s fruit well-balanced with the oak (30% new French, 22 months). **Merlot** ⓦ **★★★** Improved **15** ⑧⓪ has more presence but remains easy to drink thanks to soft, plump plums & spice sprinkle from 25% new oak. **Pinotage ★★★** Juicy & friendly **18** ⑧⓪, wild plums & berries dusted with cocoa, dry savoury notes on the finish. WO W Cape. **Shiraz** ⓦ **★★★★** Somewhat old-style but satisfying, well executed. **14** ⑧③ meat & leather, fruit plushness reined in by firm tannins, savoury finish. **Gracious**

Lady ★★★★ Loses shiraz component, but **16** ⑧⑤ cab/merlot blend continues to charm with creamy vanilla-tinged blackcurrant, plum & dried herb flavours. Rounded & smooth. **Rosé ★★★** Delicate pink blush on semi-dry **NV** ⑦⑨ from sauvignon & dab merlot, bright fruited & friendly. **Chenin Blanc** (NEW) **★★★** Shy green-apple wafts on light-bodied (±12% alcohol), bracing **19** ⑦⑦. Serve well-chilled. **Sauvignon Blanc ★★** Lean & green **18** ⑦⑤, little light on flavour, finishes rather crisp. **Vredenvonkel ★★★** Party-starting **NV** ⑦⑨ sparkler from sauvignon & merlot. Dry, with green plum, piquant strawberry flavours. In abeyance: **M'Lord Chardonnay**. — WB

Location/map: Stellenbosch ▪ Map grid reference: D6 ▪ WO: Stellenbosch/Western Cape ▪ Tasting & sales Mon-Sat 9-4.30 ▪ Closed Good Fri & Dec 25 ▪ Restaurant Barrique T +27 (0)21-881-3001 ▪ Hudson's Coffee Shop T +27 (0)21-881-3590 ▪ Conferences/functions ▪ Vredenheim Angus Stud ▪ Big Cats Park ▪ Jaguar cars for hire ▪ Curio shop ▪ Guest house ▪ Craft beer brewery & gin distillery: tasting Tue-Sun 10-5 ▪ Owner(s) Bezuidenhout family ▪ Winemaker(s) Kowie du Toit ▪ Viticulturist(s) Kalie Kirsten ▪ 80ha under vine ▪ 20,000cs own label 60% red 40% white ▪ PO Box 369 Stellenbosch 7599 ▪ wine@vredenheim.co.za ▪ www. vredenheim.co.za ▪ S 33° 57' 38.2" E 018° 48' 29.4" ▪ ☒ premiums.widgets.cover ▪ **T +27 (0)21-881-3637**

Vriesenhof Vineyards ⓘ

Harvest 2019, winegrower Jan Coetzee's 53rd vintage, was briefly but momentously interrupted by his alma mater, Stellenbosch University, to award him an Honorary Doctorate of Science in Agriculture. The 1970s Springbok rugby hero was acknowledged for his 'engaged citizenship, work ethic and generosity of spirit' through involvement in and support of wine research, better farm working conditions, and industry leadership and mentoring as founder-member of the Cape Winemakers Guild and its protégé programme. Homage was paid to his fine winecraft, first at Kanonkop, then here at his own Stellenbosch Mountain property, the portfolio reflecting his abiding passions, the new grenache rosé the explorative bent of a vintner who has been, as GM Eddie Smit attests, 'a humble servant of nature'.

★★★★ Grenache Tasted pre-bottling, as next 3. **18** ⑧⑦ shows great promise. Supple, juicy red berries & delicate spicy highlights, lithe body & smooth tannins. Piekenierskloof fruit spent 16 months in oak barrels. Magnums available, as Kallista.

★★★★ Pinot Noir ⊘ Delicately perfumed red berry fruit, silky tannins. **18** ⑧⑦ light but elegantly formed, with better balance & harmony than **16 ★★★★** ⑧⑤. 15% new oak, 18 months, well judged. No **17**.

★★★★ Kallista High-toned, brooding **16** ⑧⑨ cab franc, cab & merlot blend (40/35/25) tones down the muscle, bringing form, texture & nuance to the fore. Still unknit, but showing well.

★★★★ Chardonnay Still under hefty oak mantle, **18** ⑧⑥ offers glimpses of sweet citrus fruit, promises well. Robustly structured yet even in extreme youth, better balanced than last-tasted **16 ★★★★** ⑧④.

Pinotage ⊘ **★★★★** Signature wild berries & high aromatics announce variety in **17** ⑧⑤, showing restrained weight, supple juicy fruit. **Grenache-Shiraz-Mourvèdre** ⊘ **★★★★** Cheerfully fruity, pocket-friendly **17** ⑧④ offers mixed berry compote & velvety tannin structure. **Grenache Rosé** (NEW) ⊘ **★★★★** Rather garish pink **19** ⑧③ has tannin texture & weight, concentrated strawberry fruit, makes for refreshing summer sipping & creative food pairing. **Ongehoute Chardonnay ★★★★** Improves on previous in **18** ⑧⑤ with glacé citrus rind, white nuts & appealing mineral notes, creamy lees texture. Discontinued: **Cabernet Sauvignon**. — GdB

Location/map: Stellenbosch ▪ Map grid reference: F7 ▪ WO: Stellenbosch/Piekenierskloof ▪ Est 1980 ▪ 1stB 1981 ▪ Tasting & sales Mon-Thu 10—4 Fri 10—3.30 Sat by appt ▪ Fee R50 ▪ Closed all pub hols ▪ Cellar tours by appt ▪ Owner(s) Landgoed Vriesenhof (Pty) Ltd ▪ Cellarmaster(s) Jan Coetzee ▪ Winemaker(s) Nicky Claasens (2008), with Richard Phillips (2001) ▪ 60ha/45ha (cabs s/f, grenache, merlot, ptage, pinot, chard) ▪ 300t 90% red 10% white ▪ PO Box 155 Stellenbosch 7599 ▪ info@vriesenhof.co.za ▪ www.vriesenhof.co.za ▪ S 33° 58' 16.7" E 018° 52' 2.8" ▪ ☒ manager.ports.cactus ▪ **T +27 (0)21-880-0284**

☐ **Vry Burgher** *see* Group CDV
☐ **King Vusani** *see* House of Mandela

Vuurberg ⓘ

Netherlander Sebastiaan Klaassen was seduced by the beauty of Stellenbosch while visiting the Cape on a kite-surfing holiday in 2000, and acquired this small Banhoek estate. Winemaker Donovan Rall (who also has his own 'new wave' label and makes wine for nearby Clouds) brings in grapes from outside Stellenbosch to complement the home vineyards. The drought has had its effect and he's been incorporating more varieties that could be picked early to naturally add freshness to the wines. Reducing the flavour impact of oak on the red, in addition to adding cinsaut, has been aimed at the same end.

★★★★☆ **Reserve Red** Ⓐ Blend of **16** (93) tweaked to less home-grown cab (57%), more petit verdot (36%) & just 7% Swartland cinsaut. Still a big, ripe, assertive wine (15% alcohol), plenty of dense fruit, strong, dry tannin structure needing time to mellow. Some warm sweetness on the finish. 10% new oak.

★★★★☆ **White 18** (90) as usual blends 6 varieties (chenin in the lead) from 3 regions. Wholebunch, natural ferment & maturation in oak, 10% new. Also as usual, it's full-fruited, rich & ripe, with a velvet smoothness made livelier by a firm, balanced acidity.— TJ

Location/map: Stellenbosch ▪ Map grid reference: H4 ▪ WO: Coastal/Western Cape ▪ Tasting, sales & cellar tours by appt ▪ Closed all pub hols ▪ Owner(s) Sebastiaan Klaassen ▪ Cellarmaster(s) Donovan Rall ▪ Winemaker(s) Donovan Rall (Oct 2010) ▪ 8ha (cabs s/f, malbec, merlot, p verdot, chenin, viog) ▪ 2,000cs own label 50% red 50% white ▪ PO Box 449 Stellenbosch 7599 ▪ info@vuurberg.com ▪ www.vuurberg.com ▪ S 33° 54' 28.9" E 018° 56' 52.7" ▪ princes.projects.defender ▪ **T +27 (0)72-182-7571**

Waboomsrivier Winery

One of few Protea species to grow into trees, the waboom used to provide wood for wagon wheels. Seventy years ago it also provided a name for what is now a modern, grower-owned, northern Breedekloof winery, producing mostly bulk wines but also this 'fresh and fruity' range under its own label.

Wagenboom range

Pinotage ★★★ Mocha aroma hints at year in half new oak (50/50 French/American) for **17** (80), soft & approachable, with juicy dark berries. **Arborea** ★★★ **17** (82) pinotage, cab & shiraz has black berries, intriguing hint bitter aloe, also vanilla from half new oak, 40% American. **Shiraz-Pinotage** ★★☆ Dark berries, slightly caramelised, in juicy 50/50 **NV** (78) blend. **Chenin Blanc** ★★★ Fresh, fragrant & fruity **19** (80) offers plenty of everyday drinking appeal. **Sauvignon Blanc** ★★★ Easy summertime sipping at 12.5% alcohol, **19** (79) is crisp & dry, with refreshing green apple & lime flavours. **Hanepoot** ★★★☆ Well-handled, freshening spirit gives **13** (84) fortified extra warmth & charm, lifts its tropical pineapple & papaya flavours. **Cape Vintage** ★★★ More Ruby than Vintage 'port' in style, with fairly low alcohol, highish sugar, yet **14** (81) very drinkable, like all under this wallet-friendly label. — JG

Location: Worcester ▪ Map/WO: Breedekloof ▪ Map grid reference: A3 ▪ Est 1949 ▪ Tasting & sales Mon-Fri 8-5 ▪ Closed all pub hols ▪ Cellar tours by appt only ▪ Cellarmaster(s) Bennie Wannenburg (Sep 2005) ▪ Winemaker(s) Charl Myburgh (Oct 2016), with Lara Prins (Nov 2016) ▪ Viticulturist(s) Pierre Snyman (VinPro) ▪ ±971.10ha ▪ 17,075t ▪ ISO 22000:2005 ▪ PO Box 24 Breërivier 6858 ▪ sales@wabooms.co.za ▪ www.waboomsrivier.com ▪ S 33° 31' 43.08" E 019° 12' 35.24" ▪ catalytic.shimmy.pizzerias ▪ **T +27 (0)23-355-1730**

Wade Bales Wine Co

Wade Bales is a long-established, Constantia-based specialist wine merchant who sources fine wines from producers and sells them directly to private clients. He offers the convenience of buying wine monthly through membership of his Wade Bales Wine Club. Wade is also a negociant bottling and marketing exclusive and limited-release wines under his Regional and Winemaker Selection labels.

Wade Bales Regional Series (NEW)

★★★★★ **Stellenbosch Cabernet Sauvignon** Ⓐ Exceptional debut for this superb multi-producer blend, built for a decade or longer ageing. **17** (95) hedgerow fruit, cigarbox & spice, vibrant yet sleek & refined, layered & complex. Dry tannic grip doesn't detract from supple pliability. 60% new French oak, 18 months.

★★★★☆ **Constantia Sauvignon Blanc-Semillon** Ⓐ Grapefruit zest & grassy typicity on 8-producer blend (67/33). **18** (91) has lovely intensity, structure & texture from oaked portion (70%, all old) but fruit remains the hero. Succulent, with long waxy finish. Give it time to fully reveal myriad charms.— WB, FM

Location: Constantia ▪ Map: Cape Peninsula ▪ Map grid reference: B3 ▪ WO: Stellenbosch/Constantia ▪ Est 1992 ▪ Tasting & sales Mon-Fri 8.30-5 ▪ Closed all pub hols ▪ Owner(s) Wade Bales ▪ 10,000cs own label ▪ Private Bag X2 Constantia 7848 ▪ info@wadebales.co.za ▪ www.wadebales.co.za ▪ S 34° 2' 5.43" E018° 25' 32.98" ▪ reposed.unpaged.picnicked ▪ **T +27 (0)21-794-2151**

☐ **Wade Bales Winemaker Selection** *see* Wade Bales Wine Co
☐ **Wagenboom** *see* Waboomsrivier Winery

Walker Bay Estate

There has been a changing of the guard at this small venture near Stanford. David Smit comes from export giant FirstCape to take responsibility as viticulturist, winemaker and marketer. He's looking to differentiate the winery from Birkenhead, its perhaps better-known, craft-beer-producing sibling on the same property, partly by emphasising that it produces only 'estate'-grown wine. South Africans and, soon, winelovers in Europe and Asia will notice a new drive to promote the produce from ocean-cooled vines.

★★★★ **Pinot Noir** (NEW) ✓ Graceful debut for **18** (86) with a gentle smoky plum, earthy nuance. Deft older oaking adds breadth without obscuring the fruit. Not overly complex, but fresh, elegantly balanced & satisfying.

★★★★ **Petit Verdot** Black cherry & some smoky tones on **17** (86), pliable but structured tannins & older oak in support. Less alcohol & a touch more fruit intensity & depth than **16** ★★★☆ (84).

★★★★ **Barrel Fermented Sauvignon Blanc** Older-oak ferment & ageing add sweet spicing to greener fruit profile of pre-bottled **19** (87). Nice intensity, lower alcohol & sugar than sibling.

Merlot ★★★ Youthful **18** (82) preview shows piquant red fruit, firm structure, freshness & some development potential. **Amesteca** (Ⓡ) ★★★☆ Bordeaux-style blend; merlot's sweet red-fruit fragrance/flesh in command on **15** (83). Fresh acid, modicum grip allow good drinking now, further year/2. **Shiraz Rosé** ✓ ★★★ Bright vermilion **18** (82) has dry, spicy red fruit flavours. Balanced, quite creamy, a summer quaffer with enough substance for food pairing. **Chardonnay** (Ⓡ) ★★ Earthy, lemony impression on **17** (76). Dry, subtle oak in leaner style. **Limestone Sauvignon Blanc** ★★★☆ Pre-bottling, unoaked **19** (85) from vines on broken limestone outcrops shows similar minerality, juicy grapefruit tone & food-friendly appeal as previous. **Méthode Cap Classique** (NEW) ★★★ Subdued honey/bottle age character on **NV** (82) dry sparkling from pinot noir & chardonnay (60/40). Gentle cider tone, some creaminess & clean acidity; has fizz, needs more sizzle. Not tasted: **Cabernet Sauvignon**, **Shiraz**, **Sauvignon Blanc**. Discontinued: **Chardonnay Unoaked**. — MW

Location: Stanford ▪ Map: Walker Bay & Bot River ▪ Map grid reference: B6 ▪ WO: Walker Bay ▪ Est 1997 ▪ 1stB 2007 ▪ Tasting & sales Mon-Sun 10-5 ▪ Tasting fee applicable ▪ Closed Dec 25 ▪ Cellar tours by appt ▪ Restaurant ▪ Facilities for children ▪ Tour groups ▪ Craft beer brewery ▪ Winemaker(s)/viticulturist(s) David Smit (Nov 2018) ▪ 300ha/24ha (cab, merlot, p verdot, pinot, shiraz, chard, sauv, sem) ▪ 100t/14,000cs own label 40% red 60% white ▪ PO Box 530 Stanford 7210 ▪ walkerbayvineyards@birkenhead.co.za ▪ www.walkerbayestate.com ▪ S 34° 26' 30.5" E 019° 27' 40.5" ▪ compactly.pomegranates.unanswered ▪ **T +27 (0)28-341-0013**

Walking Woods Wines

Founded in 2004 as 'Re'Mogo' by a group of black entrepreneurs exploring business interests in wine, among other sectors, this now Pretoria-based venture is fronted by Thamsanqa Hombana, and sources wines mainly from Olifants River and latterly also Stellenbosch.

Location: Pretoria ▪ Est 2004, Trust est 2011 ▪ Sales Mon-Fri & pub hols 9-3 by appt only ▪ Online shop ▪ Owner(s) Simatule Trust ▪ Winemaker(s) Stellar Winery & Koopmanskloof Wingerde ▪ 50% red 50% white ▪ 1 Meiring Naude Rd, Brummeria, Pretoria 0184 ▪ woods.southafrica@gmail.com ▪ www.walkingwoods.co.za ▪ **T +27 (0)82-638-6774**

Warwick Wine Estate

'We intend to continue building a brand to rival the top in the world,' state the recent owners of this fine property, undergoing vineyard and wine rejuvenation from 2017 under Charles Marston and Kishore Bopardikar of San Francisco investment company Eileses Capital. The subsequent purchase of neighbour Uitkyk amalgamated a formidable team (now boosted by ex-Steenberg Cape Winemakers Guild member JD Pretorius), drawing on 700 ha of prime Simonsberg-Stellenbosch vineyard land. A terroir-driven viticultural programme focuses on classic Bordeaux varieties, starting with some 170 ha being replanted with cabernet, cab franc and merlot. It's already reflected in the portfolio, with erstwhile Cape Blend, Three Cape Ladies, now Left Bank styled, and former sauvignon, Prof Black, reinvented as a duo with semillon. Meanwhile

The White Lady from Burgundy continues her five-star run - in homage to Warwick's former co-owner and pioneering woman vintner Norma Ratcliffe, perhaps?

★★★★☆ **The Blue Lady** Ⓐ Classic Simonsberg-Stellenbosch cabernet. **16** (94) has detail, allure & gravitas. Ripe dark berry fruit lined with cedar, lead pencil & spice from 27 months French oak, 25% new, expected firm tannin grip, long-lingering spiced blackberry finish. Drinks well now, like **15** ★★★★★ (95) on release, but so much better & more complete in a decade or more.

★★★★☆ **Cabernet Franc** Ⓐ One of SA's finest, **16** (94) shows customary excellent varietal character, dark spice & dried herbs over generous dark forest fruits. On palate, mulberry & blueberry to the fore with firm tannins & savoury undertone from serious barrique ageing, 27 months, 65% new. Simonsberg-Stellenbosch WO, as Trilogy. Magnums available.

★★★★☆ **Three Cape Ladies** Ⓐ Restyled as cab-based Bordeaux trio from **15** (94), with cab franc & merlot, **16** (93) similar proportions (41/31/28) with beneficially less oak influence than the other reds, 18 months, 20% new. Rich entry, then a tight, concentrated core of fruit, in balance yet probably best decanted now, ideally cellared few years. Stellenbosch WO, like The White Lady.

★★★★☆ **Trilogy** Ⓐ Flagship from estate grapes, imposing & ageworthy Bordeaux blend with majority cab franc in **16** (94), with 34% cab & 15% merlot. Full & boldly complex, with lively black cherry, basil & toasted spice, firm tannins that will carry a decade or more. 1.5L, 5L, 9L & 12L also available.

★★★★★ **The White Lady** Ⓐ Classic expression of chardonnay, with perfectly ripe fruit (citrus & stonefruit) the focus. Full & rich but with crisp acidity, only a portion through malo to maintain freshness. Subtle oak nuances of vanilla & spice (35% new, 9 months) add to the complexity of **18** (95) but in no way overpower. Lovely citrus & mineral finish. Like **17** (95), naturally fermented in barrique.

★★★★☆ **Professor Black** Ⓐ Since **17** ★★★★★ (95), a white Bordeaux blend, **18** (94) has 65% sauvignon with semillon (both bunch-fermented in barrel) in an intriguing marriage of bright apples, figs & gooseberries with lime, pistachio nuts & slatey minerals. Full & rich, with just the right amount of oak (20% new, 9 months).

The First Lady Cabernet Sauvignon ★★★☆ Reliable, delicious & drinkable, almost gluggable, cab. **17** (84) offers a mixed basket of dark berries & red cherries, soft tannins & blackberry farewell. Expertly wooded, mostly with staves. Magnums available, as next. **The First Lady Dry Rosé** ★★★ Bone-dry & zesty **19** (81), light bodied with spice & pomegranate flavours, laudably moderate 11.5% alcohol for carefree sipping. From pinotage. **The First Lady Chardonnay** ★★★★ A chardonnay to simply chill & enjoy. Citrus-toned **19** (83) is fresh, light & crisp, almost entirely fermented in stainless steel, so there's minimal oak to complicate the fruit flavours. **The First Lady Sauvignon Blanc** ★★★★ Pleasant **19** (83) presents an array of passionfruit, white blossoms & figs. Bone-dry, with bright acidity, zingy lime finish. Discontinued: **The Black Lady**, **Méthode Cap Classique**. — GM

Location/map: Stellenbosch ▪ Map grid reference: F1 ▪ WO: Western Cape/Simonsberg–Stellenbosch/Stellenbosch ▪ Est 1964 ▪ 1stB 1983 ▪ Tasting & sales daily 9–5 ▪ Cellar tours by appt ▪ 'Big 5' vineyard safari ▪ Gourmet picnics in summer; à la carte winter menu ▪ Facilities for children ▪ Gifts ▪ Conferences ▪ Weddings ▪ Owner(s) Charles Marston & Kishore Bopardikar ▪ CEO Christiane von Arnim ▪ Winemaker(s) JD Pretorius (May 2019) & Estelle Lourens (May 2018) ▪ Viticulturist(s) Ronald Spies (Nov 2001) & Rudi Buys (May 2018) ▪ 700ha/135ha (cabs s/f, merlot, chard, chenin, sauv) ▪ 1,200t/300,000cs own label 60% red 40% white ▪ WIETA ▪ IPW ▪ PO Box 2 Elsenburg 7607 ▪ info@warwickwine.com ▪ www.warwickwine.com ▪ S 33° 50' 27" E 018° 51' 54.0" ▪ 🖳 outdone.reader.graphics ▪ **T +27 (0)21-884-4410**

Waterford Estate   Ⓠ Ⓐ Ⓖ

This handsome estate in Stellenbosch's Blaauwklippen Valley was bought by Jeremy and Leigh Ord late last century, and rejuvenated and developed with the crucial help of accomplished cellarmaster and business partner Kevin Arnold (the Italianate buildings and courtyard date from then). The farm's planting diversity is well expressed in the flagship red blend, The Jem, which is now to be released annually on the 'founding day' of the estate, 1 April. The Library Collection, of mostly experimental wines, can now be sampled, together with the Estate bottlings, in a dedicated room in the upgraded visitor facilities. Other developments include new plantings of cabernet sauvignon and shiraz, and, in the cellar, more concrete 'eggs' and large oak vats to expand the range of winemaking possibilities.

Waterford Estate range

★★★★☆ **Cabernet Sauvignon** ⊛ Elegant & complex cabernet with poise. **16** ⑨⑴ has dark black fruit & spice with fynbos nuance; generous, silky, dabs merlot, petit verdot & cab franc add to the layers. Receives house's wholeberry ferment, 18 months in barrel, 32% new. Also in 375 ml, 1.5, 3, 5 & 18L.

★★★★★ **The Jem** ⊘ Flagship from selection of estate's 11 black grapes - Italian, Spanish & French - majority planted since 1999. Cab-led **14** ⑨⑸ is tall, dark & handsome; packed with juicy berry fruit & savoury spice, 32% new oak in harmonious support. Rich, lithe & deeply alluring, a wine for the long haul.

★★★★ **Single Vineyard Chardonnay** Peach pip & lime intensity from 30+ year old vines; **17** ⑧⑨ gets 18% new oak, 10 months, giving a vanilla patina to the citrus tang; suave if not greatly complex. Also 1.5L.

⋯⋯⋯⋯⋯⋯⋯⋯⋯⋯⋯⋯⋯⋯⋯⋯⋯⋯⋯⋯⋯⋯⋯⋯⋯⋯⋯⋯⋯⋯⋯⋯⋯

Rose-Mary ⊗ ★★★ Flashes of salmon light up vibrant red-berry, low-alcohol (11%) **19** ⑧⑵ rosé. Zesty, bone-dry, has a festive air about it. Shiraz leads black-grape quintet, sampled ex tank. 1.5L also available.

⋯⋯⋯⋯⋯⋯⋯⋯⋯⋯⋯⋯⋯⋯⋯⋯⋯⋯⋯⋯⋯⋯⋯⋯⋯⋯⋯⋯⋯⋯⋯⋯⋯

Grenache Noir ★★★☆ Characterful single-vineyard **17** ⑧⑸, farmyard & gamey whiffs, fleshy cranberry fruit & tense tannins; old oak supports. Third matured in porcelain jars.

Library Collection

Not tasted: **Cabernet Sauvignon**, **Cabernet Franc**, **2BB**, **Antique Chenin**, **Chenin Blanc**, **Edition: Riesling**.

Waterford range

★★★★ **Elgin Pinot Noir** Expressive, bright fruit from 12 year old cool-climate single block. Filigree tannin of **18** ⑧⑻ frames tangy sour-cherry fruit, in balance with modest 12% alcohol, bone-dry finish.

★★★★☆ **Kevin Arnold Shiraz** Subtitled 'Katherine Leigh', impressive **15** ⑨⑵ straddles flavour spectrum from peppery spice to earthy leather; deep, dark & concentrated fruit in velvety core, dash mourvèdre adds panache. Only seasoned oak. Supple, balanced, flavourful. Also in 1.5, 3, 5 & 18L.

★★★★☆ **Stellenbosch Chenin Blanc** ⓃⒺⓌ ⊛ ⊛ From 1966 vines, vinified in mostly concrete 'eggs', **18** ⑨⑷ is a wine of limpid glints, gossamer perfumes, fine minerality. A deeply textured, rich & full taste sensation, tensioned by a line of freshest acidity. Its beauty stops you in your tracks & demands attention.

★★★★☆ **Méthode Cap Classique Brut 11** ⑨⓪ bubbly confirms recent uptick; chardonnay joined by pinot noir & meunier (**09** ⑨⑶ was chardonnay, **10** not made) remarkably long 7 years on lees, then year under cork. Rich brioche aromas & creamy texture borne on surprisingly lively fruit.

★★★★ **Heatherleigh** Solera-aged Natural Sweet dessert of muscat d'Alexandrie with chardonnay, viognier & chenin. **NV** ⑧⑻ beautifully balanced; piquant marmalade, brûlée delicacy, dryish finish. 375 ml.

Elgin Sauvignon Blanc ★★★☆ Penetrating, pure-fruited lemongrass & nettle highlight **19** ⑧⑸ tank sample, good body & length, lipsmacking tang on finish. Also in 500 ml & 1.5 L.

Pecan Stream range

Pebble Hill ⊗ ★★★☆ 'Mini Jem' - shiraz, mourvèdre, tempranillo, sangiovese & merlot made as if for flagship - punches way above its weight. **16** ⑧⑸ is juicy, has supple plum-fruit allure. **Chenin Blanc** ⊗ ★★★☆ Pre-bottling **19** ⑧⑸ loaded with refreshing tangy stonefruit, a bright & juicy oak-touched chenin.

Sauvignon Blanc ★★★ Plump passionfruit profile to satisfying tank sample **19** ⑧⑵. WO W Cape, as all these. — DS

Location/map: Stellenbosch ▪ Map grid reference: F8 ▪ WO: Stellenbosch/Western Cape/Elgin ▪ Est/1stB 1998 ▪ Tasting, sales & cellar tours Mon-Fri 9—5 Sat 10—5 ▪ Tasting fees: R90/portfolio; R95/chocolate; R125/Estate; R115/The Jem (current vintage only); R250/Library; R450/wine walk & R1,150/wine drive, pre-booking essential ▪ Closed Good Fri, Dec 25 & Jan 1 ▪ Tea/coffee/soft drinks & chocolates ▪ Olive oil ▪ Owner(s) Jeremy & Leigh Ord; Kevin Arnold (partner) ▪ Cellarmaster(s) Kevin Arnold (1998) ▪ Winemaker(s) Mark le Roux (Jul 2009) ▪ Viticulturist(s) David van Schalkwyk (Jun 2014) ▪ 120ha/60ha (barbera, cabs s/f, grenache, malbec, merlot, mourv, p verdot, sangio, shiraz, tempranillo, chard) ▪ 550t/54,000cs own label 70% red 30% white ▪ 27.3ha conserved land ▪ WWF-SA Conservation Champion ▪ PO Box 635 Stellenbosch 7599 ▪ info@waterfordestate.co.za ▪ www.waterfordestate.co.za ▪ S 33° 59' 54.6" E 018° 52' 12.7" ▪ ⌖ shots.slipping.traffic ▪ T +27 (0)21-880-5300

Waterkloof

Waterkloof's Circle of Life brand was inspired by the story of Briton Paul Boutinot's discovery and conversion of this once conventionally farmed Helderberg property, in a beautiful mountainous amphitheatre overlooking False Bay, into vibrantly alive, biodynamic vineyards. Though official certification is no longer sought, Christiaan Loots' farming practices continue steadfastly according to biodynamic principles. A range of animals, from chickens (producing manure) to Percheron horses (for ploughing) contribute to the greater sustainable whole. Winemaker Nadia Langenegger has changed her surname but not her winemaking philosophy, crafting elegant wines as gently and naturally as possible. More chenin and mourvèdre vineyards have been planted and, following a winter with rain and sufficient coldness for proper vine dormancy, Nadia at press time was optimistic about the forthcoming harvest.

Waterkloof range

★★★★☆ **Sauvignon Blanc** The flagship, **18** ⑨ from a low-yield single parcel on Schapenberg Hill delivers leafy elegance & delicate yet pervasive starfruit & greengage flavours. Shade off **17** ⑨, richer, more refined than Circumstance sibling. This & all wines from Waterkloof undergo natural, slow ferments, lees ageing & are unfined.

Circle of Life range

★★★★ **Red** ⑨ **15** ★★★★★ ⑨ trumps **14** ⑧, with savoury, white pepper from syrah in leading role, merlot & petit verdot the structured support cast. Layers of flavour, lively dry tannins, rich, creamy texture, real depth & intensity. Bordeaux varieties destemmed, others bunch pressed, as all reds.

★★★★☆ **White** Sauvignon-led blend with chenin & drop of semillon, co-fermented in old oak & concrete 'egg'. **16** ⑨ shows riverstone flintiness, stonefruit & signature waxy undertone. Svelte & fresh, well crafted in a more difficult vintage than **15** ⑨.

Seriously Cool range

Cinsault ★★★★ From old (35+ years) bushvines, **18** ⑧ is leaner than previous. Perfumed red berries, lithe & lingering, with a dry, dusty spice nuance. Fresh & light at 11.5% alcohol. **Chenin Blanc** ★★★★ Low-crop old bushvines deliver their signature cool stonefruit & apple flavours in **18** ⑧. Part oak, part concrete 'egg' ferment, with lees enhancement for sleek & succulent enjoyment.

Circumstance range

★★★★ **Cabernet Sauvignon** Brooding cassis with herbaceous nuance on riper **16** ⑧. Tad austere, with less gravitas & elegance than **15** ⑧. Should show better with time.

★★★★ **Merlot** ⑧ More appealing juicy fruit & balance than tightly coiled **15** ★★★★ ⑧. Fruit handling is gentle, as for all their grapes, giving refined tannin structure. More at ease, takes a confident step up in **16** ⑧, though structured to still age elegantly. This & cab only wines with touch of new oak.

★★★★☆ **Mourvèdre** ⑧ Earthy & savoury, with cardamom spice in a lithe, dry tannin framework. **17** ⑨ foot treading of grapes (as for Merlot) results in a more pliable structure. Similar fruit intensity, even fresher than **16** ★★★★ ⑧ & potential for handsome development.

★★★★☆ **Syrah** ⑧ Subtle earthy, white pepper impression on **17** ⑨. Balanced, but still in a youthful dry tannic frame. Restrained cool elegance, with delicious savoury length. Raises the bar on **16** ★★★★ ⑧, structured for future enjoyment.

★★★★ **Sauvignon Blanc** ⊘ Appealing dried fig & stonefruit flavours on **18** ★★★★★ ⑨, an elegant rung up on **17** ⑧. More sweet/sour tension than flagship version despite lower acidity & longer lees time. Vivacious intensity from vineyard cooled by south-easterly winds.

Cabernet Franc ⑨ ★★★★ Scented herb & floral aromas/flavours restrained by very firm chalky tannins from smaller, tougher-skinned grapes. Like previous, **16** ⑧ slow evolving, needs time. **Cape Coral Mourvèdre Rosé** ★★★ Supple & savoury, **18** ⑧ is dry with an earthy cranberry tone. A good sushi or charcuterie partner. **Chenin Blanc** ★★★★ Plumper & riper nectarine & honey flavours in **18** ⑧, still with balance, freshness & seductive silky texture. Ferment only in old oak & longer lees contact than Seriously sibling. Not tasted: **Chardonnay**, **Viognier**.

Astraeus range

★★★★ **Méthode Cap Classique Reserve Pinot Noir** Fresh cranberry & touch of savouriness on dry rosé sparkling from organically grown Elgin grapes. **NV** ⑧⑧ fruitier than sibling, with touch more sugar. Both have oak-fermented base wines, though this 11 months on lees, then 7 months in bottle.

★★★★☆ **Méthode Cap Classique Reserve Chardonnay Brut** Lemon, brioche & toasted nut impression on latest **NV** ⑨② 15% reserve from 2009 adds depth to organically grown Elgin fruit. Extra-dry but well balanced, with refined fruitiness, some minerality & freshness from 2 years on lees. The more elegant & intense of the sparklings & even better than previous.— MW

Location: Somerset West ▪ Map: Helderberg ▪ Map grid reference: F6 ▪ WO: Stellenbosch/Elgin/Western Cape ▪ Est 2004 ▪ 1stB 2005 ▪ Tasting & sales daily 10–5 ▪ Fee: standard R40/6 wines, premium R50/6 wines ▪ Closed Dec 25 & Jan 1 ▪ Healey's cheese tasting ▪ Waterkloof platters R150 with selection of cheese, olives, meat terrine, gherkins, pickles, chutney & bread ▪ Cellar tours by appt ▪ The Restaurant at Waterkloof ▪ Walking/hiking/horse riding trails ▪ Conservation area ▪ Art collection on display ▪ Tutored horse riding & biodynamic walking tours with ploughman's platter & wine tasting ▪ Healey's Cheesery & Deli open Mon-Sat 10–5 Sun 10–2 ▪ Owner(s) Paul Boutinot ▪ Cellarmaster(s)/winemaker(s) Nadia Langenegger (Jan 2013) ▪ Viticulturist(s) Christiaan Loots (Jan 2010) ▪ 149ha/61ha (cabs s/f, grenache, merlot, mourv, p verdot, shiraz, chard, chenin, sauv, sem, viog) ▪ 450t/20,000cs own label 50% red 45% white 5% rosé ▪ Ecocert organic, IPW, WIETA, WWF-SA Conservation Champion ▪ PO Box 2093 Somerset West 7129 ▪ info@waterkloofwines.co.za ▪ www.waterkloofwines.co.za ▪ S 34° 5′ 55.4″ E 018° 53′ 22.8″ ▪ ⓜ lush.wagers.slippers ▪ **T +27 (0)21-858-1292**

☐ **Waterlily** see Bloemendal Wine Estate

Waverley Hills Organic Wines & Olives ⓠ ⑪ ⓐ ⓑ ⓔ

'Defined by the earth, crafted by nature' is the slogan of the Du Toit family's farm and winery on the foothills of the Witzenberg range between Tulbagh and Ceres. The estate is certified organic and has WWF-SA Conservation Champion status, with some 20% of the land set aside. In accord with these concerns, the wine labels have fynbos as the unifying theme. The 'biggest news' for some time, says cellarmaster Johan Delport, is that one of the wines, the SMV '13, won the International Organic Trophy at the International Wine & Spirit Competition. Drought-tolerant marselan, a French cross of cab and grenache, has been planted.

Premium range

★★★★ **Grenache** ⓐ ⓒ Earthy & fragrant **17** ⑧⑨ charms with lively red fruit, herbs & spice, smooth gentle tannins from year large older barrels. 10% wholebunch.

★★★★☆ **CW Reserve Shiraz** ⓒ ⓐ Now bottled, **15** ⑨③ from a parcel of small-bunch grapes within a block has settled & grown. Pristine black fruit, dried herbs, scrub & vanilla spice. Elegant, harmonious & rich, tannins are integrated & supple after 3 years in 100% new oak. Different league to **14** ★★★★ ⑧⑨.

★★★★ **De Huijsbosch** ⓒ Cab, cab franc, merlot & splash pinotage in **17** ⑧⑧ produce sweet black fruit, cassis & scrub, entwined with dried herbs & spice from 50% new oak, 14 months.

★★★★ **Shiraz-Mourvèdre-Viognier** ⓒ Mulberry & earthy dark fruit lifted by floral notes in **15** ⑧⑧. Full on the palate, rounded & luscious, with hints of espresso & smoke after 34 months in 40% new oak.

★★★★ **Chardonnay** ⓒ **18** ⑧⑧ somewhat misses the mark of complex **17** ★★★★☆ ⑨⓪, previewed last edition. Flavours of apple & tropical fruit a tad subdued, mouthfeel boosted by splash co-fermented semillon but oak (60% new, 11 months) not yet melded. Possibly just needs more time.

....

Grenache Rosé ⓝⓔⓦ ⓣ ⓒ ★★★☆ Previewed dry **19** ⑧④ is ballerina pink, shows candyfloss & earthy spice, lovely texture with a cranberry tang to accompany a summer salad.

....

Méthode Cap Classique Brut ⓒ ★★★★ 100% chardonnay in **18** ⑧⑤ sparkling, baked apple & spiced pear flavours, savoury persistent mousse. Taut & lean, with steely citrus finish.

Estate range

....

Shiraz ⓣ ⓒ ★★★☆ Sweet black berries, plums, dark chocolate & spice mingle harmoniously with gentle tannins (all older oak) in now-bottled **17** ⑧⑤. Touch mourvèdre adds earthiness to long finish.

....

Cabernet Sauvignon-Shiraz ⊘ ★★★ **18** ⑧① has dash merlot for extra fruitiness & fruitcake spice. Juicy & friendly for everyday. **Pinot Grigio** ⊘ ★★★ Floral, fresh & fun **19** ⑦⑨ is very easy to drink. Serve well chilled. **Sauvignon Blanc-Semillon** ⑧ ⊘ ★★★★ Unoaked **18** ⑧④ brims with bright orchard & tropical fruit, poised, succulent & harmonious. Perfect for flame-roast chicken. Discontinued: **Red Jerepigo**.

No Sulphites Added range

Cabernet Sauvignon ⊘ ★★★ Lightly oaked **18** ⑧⓪ steps up, shows bright berry character, hints of chocolate & wood spice add some complexity to a tasty everyday sipper. — WB

Location/map/WO: Tulbagh ▪ Map grid reference: G6 ▪ Est 2006 ▪ 1stB 2004 ▪ Tasting, sales & cellar tours Mon-Sat 10-4 Sun 11-3 ▪ Closed Easter Mon & Dec 25 ▪ Restaurant Tue-Sat 10-4 Sun 11-3 & Wed evenings ▪ Picnic baskets by appt ▪ Facilities for children ▪ Tour groups ▪ Conferences ▪ Wedding venue & chapel ▪ Walks/hikes ▪ Conservation area ▪ Owner(s) Brenn-O-Kem (Pty) Ltd ▪ Cellarmaster(s) Johan Delport (Oct 2008) ▪ Winemaker(s) Eric Frieslaar (May 2017) ▪ Viticulturist(s) Johan Greeff (May 2012) ▪ 80ha/30ha (cab, grenache, marselan, merlot, mourv, ptage, shiraz, chard, pinot gris, sauv, sem, viog) ▪ 230t/20,000cs own label 80% red 15% white 5% MCC ▪ Cape Nature Stewardship, WIETA, WWF-SA Conservation Champion ▪ PO Box 71 Wolseley 6830 ▪ info@waverleyhills.co.za ▪ www.waverleyhills.co.za ▪ S 33° 24' 21.2" E 019° 14' 19.6" ▪ 🗺 nominally.innovating.humble ▪ **T +27 (0)23-231-0002**

Wavescape Wines

'Vibrant blends of surfing and winemaking' are the aim of freelance journalist and author Steve Pike, and fellow wave-rider Jeremy Walker, owner and cellarmaster to highly regarded Grangehurst, who produces the wines at his cellar in Stellenbosch. Sourced, of course, from Coastal vineyards.

Red Barrel ⑧ ★★★★ Balanced, ready **09** ⑧⑤, cab-shiraz & drop mourvèdre unobstructed by oak, with good fruit complexity. Mid-wave between serious & fun. Not tasted: **White Curl**. — FM

Location: Stellenbosch ▪ WO: Coastal ▪ Est 2014 ▪ 1stB 2009 ▪ Closed to public ▪ Sales by telephone or web-sites ▪ Owner(s) Grangehurst Winery (Jeremy Walker) & Wavescape (Steve Pike) ▪ Cellarmaster(s) Jeremy Walker ▪ 1,700cs own label 70% red 30% white ▪ PO Box 206 Stellenbosch 7599 ▪ jeremy@grangehurst. co.za, spike@wavescape.co.za ▪ www.wavescape.co.za, www.grangehurst.co.za ▪ **T +27 (0)21-855-3625**

☐ **Wazu Wine Merchants** *See Editor's Note*

☐ **Weathered Hands** *see Dewaldt Heyns Family Wines*

Webersburg Wines   ⑨ ⑪ 🏠 ◎ ⑤

Originally part of Groenerivier, one of the earliest land grants in the Helderberg during the 18th century, the Webersburg home-farm was acquired by businessman Fred Weber in the mid-1990s and latterly developed into a showpiece accommodation, conference and events venue. The beautiful setting and luxury facilities are joined by a range of boutique wines, headed by a pair of ageworthy reds, made by Matthew van Heerden. Five more hectares of cabernet have been planted for future vinification and release only when deemed ready to drink, in the house's unhurried style.

★★★★☆ **Cabernet Sauvignon** 🐝 Refined **15** ⑨② revels in exceptional vintage conditions. Trademark fruitcake & spice with graphite depth, effortlessly integrated oak, 70% new for 2 years, provides backbone & a long life. Layered & concentrated. Also in 1.5L to 18L.

★★★★ **Webersburg Blend** Cab (65%) takes lead over merlot & petit verdot on **17** ⑧⑥. Gentle & light bodied but with good concentration on cocoa-tinged palate. Oak spice (also 70% new for 2 years) a touch forward but good depth & breadth. **15**, **16** untasted. In magnum, too.

Rosé 🆕 ★★★☆ Vivacious cherry & strawberry debut, previewed **19** ⑧③ from cab nice flesh & body, dry pithy tail, good balance. **Sauvignon Blanc** ★★★☆ Grapefruit & white pepper appeal to **19** ⑧⑤ tank sample. Vibrantly zesty & fresh, good body & concentration. Some Elgin grapes, as last. **Méthode Cap Classique Brut Rosé** ⑧ ★★★★ Creamy lees & red fruit notes characterise **NV** ⑧③ pink bubbly. Light citrus tang but a touch sweet. 60 months on lees. WO W Cape, as next. **Méthode Cap Classique Brut** ⑧ ★★★★ Lemon sherbet zip on **NV** ⑧③ bubbly vies with biscuit & yeast fullness. Dry & crisp, with long toasty finish. Five years on lees. — FM

Location/map: Stellenbosch ▪ Map grid reference: E8 ▪ WO: Stellenbosch/Western Cape/Stellenbosch-Elgin ▪ Est 1995 ▪ 1stB 1996 ▪ Tasting, sales & cellar tours Mon-Fri 10—5 Sat/Sun 10-4 ▪ Closed for lunch on Mondays

▪ Bistro ▪ Tour groups ▪ Historic buildings: manor house 1786; cellar & jonkershuis 1796 ▪ 5-star Cape Dutch guest house ▪ Conferences ▪ Weddings/functions ▪ Owner(s) Fred Weber ▪ Winemaker(s) Matthew van Heerden (2009-2015; 2018) ▪ 20ha/5ha under vine ▪ 30t/4,000cs own label 80% red 20% white ▪ PO Box 3428 Somerset West 7129 ▪ info@webersburg.co.za ▪ www.webersburg.co.za ▪ S 34° 0' 22.1" E 018° 50' 34.5" ▪ ⌖ flatland.smokers.standouts ▪ T +27 (0)21-881-3636

Wederom Boutique Winery   ⓥ ⑾ ⌂ ⊚

The main business on this small Robertson farm is hospitality and functions. However, the 3 ha of vines are the 'exciting part' for recent owners, the Meyer and Viljoen families. The 2016 and 2017 grapes were sold off, and the '18 Giovanni Salvadori Shiraz, in established, well-loved style, is maturing at the cellar. A merlot is to join the range, thematically linked to the Italian Prisoners of War Museum on the property.

Location/map: Robertson ▪ Map grid reference: B7 ▪ Est 2002 ▪ Tasting, sales & cellar tours by appt ▪ Fee R60pp tasting/tour ▪ Meals by appt ▪ Weddings, conferences, tours ▪ Italian Prisoners of War Museum ▪ Hanepoot Huisies guest house ▪ Owner(s) Meyer & Viljoen families ▪ Cellarmaster(s)/winemaker(s)/viticulturist(s) Ferdie Viljoen ▪ 3ha (merlot, shiraz) ▪ IPW ▪ Goree Rd, Robertson 6705 ▪ info@wederom.co.za, bookings@wederom.co.za ▪ www.wederom.co.za ▪ S 33° 49' 5.5" E 019° 47' 15.8" ▪ ⌖ shelving.captaincy.imposition ▪ T +27 (0)23-626-4139

Welbedacht Wine Estate   ⓥ ⑾ ⌂ ⊚ Ⓐ Ⓑ

Originally part of the Wellington farm Driefontein, Welbedacht ('Well Thought Out') is owned by one of SA's best-known rugby families, the Burgers. Former Springbok Schalk snr's dream cellar was ready by the end of 2004, the year son Schalk jnr was named International Rugby Player of the Year, with capacity expanded to 1,200 tons in 2009 to process fruit from 18 varieties planted and cope with demand for the popular Meerkat wines. The facility is now the domain of Piet Kleinhans, ex Havana Hills winemaker. He and the team summarise their approach as 'love is in the detail'.

Schalk Burger & Sons Proprietors Reserve range

★★★★☆ **No. 6** Terroir expression the aim, only best barrels from their premium blocks for limited release (280 cases). **16** ⑨① continues '6' theme in sextet varieties: shiraz flanking 20% carignan, splashes grenache, cinsaut, pinotage, petite sirah, scrumming down well after 2 years in French oak (20% new). Floral & cured meat aromas, bright red-fruit flavours. Big, bold but balanced.

★★★★ **Myra** ⓥ Old bushvine chenin & 4 others in (unwooded) **15** ⑧⑧, more focused, less oxidative than previous. Stonefruit & citrus, nicely layered, becoming more mineral on the palate.

Mon René ⓥ ★★★★ Chardonnay MCC sparkling; current **NV** ⑧④ nicely captures variety's citrus tones, enriched by lees ageing. Though elegantly dry, has almost honeyed flavours.

Welbedacht Estate range

★★★★ **Old Bush Vine Pinotage** ⓥ From 30-season vines. In sleek **16** ⑧⑥, 5% cinsaut enhances sweet tangy red fruit, pleasant earthiness, fresh fynbos notes. No obvious oak from 20 months old barrels (some Hungarian). Improves on **15** ★★★★ ⑧④.

★★★★ **Bohemian Syrah** ⓥ With splash petite sirah, 20 months older oak, **16** ⑧⑨ has violets & five-spice adding layers to lush dark fruit. Accessible, with ample tannic staying power.

★★★★ **Cricket Pitch** ⓥ Merlot-led 4-part Bordeaux blend, **13** ⑧⑥ is beautifully scented, cedar-nuanced cassis & violets. Palate more serious, firm but ripe tannins promise a long future. **11**, **12** untasted.

★★★★ **Hat Trick** ⓥ Alcohol over 15% but in balance on **15** ⑧⑥ Cape Blend, 58% pinotage with equal grenache & merlot, showing red & dark fruit with hints of tobacco, velvet tannic grip. No **13**, **14**.

★★★★ **Patriot** ⓥ Where **12** ★★★★ ⑧④ was a showy cab-led blend with 30% new wood, **14** ⑧⑧ mostly pinotage with 25% grenache, 12.5% each malbec & cab, more deftly oaked & harmonious. No **13**.

★★★★ **Old Bush Vine Chenin Blanc** ⓥ ⓦ Plenty of oxidative richness (marmalade, almond, lemon crème brûlée) on **15** ⑧⑥, aged year in old oak, further year in tank. **13**, **14** not made.

Cabernet Sauvignon Barrique Select ⓥ ★★★★ 20 months in seasoned oak (5% Hungarian), **16** ⑧⑤ has velvet texture with ripe macerated black fruit upfront. **Merlot Barrique Select** ⓥ ★★★★ Fairly lush **16** ⑧③ has dark plum & cherry fruit, chocolate nuance after 18 months in older oak, quite chewy tannins.

Barrel Fermented Chardonnay ⓨ ★★★★ 15 ⑧③ citrus & melon fruit, lively acidity, medium body with biscuit nuances from 10-12 months on lees in older wood.

Meerkat range

Burrow Blend ⓥ ⓣ ★★★ Mostly shiraz (39%) with 8 others, **17** ⑧② bursts with juicy wild forest fruit, soft & approachable. Great BBQ red, bargain priced. Also in 187 ml. Groenberg WO, as next 2.

Chenin Blanc ⓥ ★★★ Offers uncomplicated tropical & stonefruit refreshment in **19** ⑧⓪, moderate 13.3% alcohol a plus. **Sauvignon Blanc** ⓥ ★★★ Hot summer evenings call for crisp, dry, lively **19** ⑧①, green apple, lime & granadilla flavours, just over 12% alcohol. **Sun Angel Semi-Sweet** ⓨ ★★ Unspecified blend, melon-flavoured **NV** ⑦⑤ has enough freshening acidity to offset its sweetness, tastes drier than it is. Not tasted: **Pinotage**, **Pinotage Rosé**, **Unwooded Chardonnay**. — JG

Location/map: Wellington ▪ Map grid reference: B1 ▪ WO: Wellington/Groenberg ▪ Est/1stB 2005 ▪ Tasting, sales & cellar tours Mon-Fri 9-5 Sat 10-2 Sun by appt 10-2 ▪ Fee R15 ▪ Closed Easter Fri & Mon, Dec 25 & Jan 1 ▪ No. 6 Restaurant @ Welbedacht ▪ Picnics ▪ Facilities for children ▪ Tour groups ▪ Gifts ▪ Conferences ▪ Functions ▪ Welbedacht cricket oval ▪ Bradgate manor house ▪ Owner(s) Schalk Burger Family Trust ▪ Winemaker(s) Piet Kleinhans (Jun 2019) ▪ 140ha/110ha (19 varieties r/w) ▪ 1,000t ▪ 75% red 20% white 5% rosé ▪ CVC, IPW, OVP, WIETA ▪ PO Box 51 Wellington 7654 ▪ info@welbedacht.co.za ▪ www.meerkatwines. co.za, www.schalkburgerandsons.co.za, www.welbedacht.co.za ▪ S 33° 34' 39.8" E 019° 1' 12.8" ▪ 📍 victors. will.trout ▪ **T +27 (0)21-873-1877**

Welgegund Heritage Wines

The Brimacombe family, owners of this old Wellington estate, have added a pair of wines to their portfolio. Both are vinified in the trendy 'light red' style yet not insubstantial, thanks to fruit from old vines. With three parcels older than the qualifying 35 years, the Brimacombes are proud members of the Old Vine Project but, looking to the future, have established a 1.7-ha shiraz block and are extending their grenache plantings.

★★★★☆ **Cinsault** 🆕 🍷 Stylish, understated packaging for the two new offerings; wines in similar vein. Smoky whiffs from 20% wooded component (12 months, 20% new), **17** ⑨① ex venerable-vines (45 years), single-vineyard fruit, saline edge, quiet presence.

★★★★ **Grenache Noir** 🆕 Off younger vines than Cinsault, **17** ⑧⑧ shows more fruit, less oak (only 50% wooded, none new). Bright & engaging, with satisfying grape tannin, strawberry finish.

★★★★ **Providence** ⓨ 🍷 Red fruit melange, lovely freshness & supple tannins, **15** ⑧⑥ shiraz with 30% old-vine (42 years) cinsaut, dash carignan, adroitly oaked (30% new).

★★★★ **Chenin Blanc** ⓨ 🍷 Shows serious intent at modest 12.5% alcohol, good depth & dryness, **17** ⑧⑥ subtly saline & earthy, well-handled partial oaking, 33% new. Similar attractive unfruity styling to last **15** ★★★★ ⑧⑤. 45 year old dryland vines.— CvZ

Location/map: Wellington ▪ Map grid reference: C4 ▪ WO: Wellington/Coastal ▪ Est 1777 ▪ 1stB 1997 ▪ Tasting & sales by appt ▪ Olive oil ▪ Guest accommodation ▪ Owner(s) Brimacombe family ▪ Winemaker & vineyard manager Friedrich Kühne ▪ 35ha/13ha (carignan, cinsaut, grenache, shiraz, chard, chenin) ▪ 1,550cs 80% red 20% white ▪ PO Box 683 Wellington 7654 ▪ sales@welgegund.co.za ▪ www.welgegund.co.za ▪ S 33° 39' 38.3" E 019° 2' 13.6" ▪ 📍 taker.chef.blurred ▪ **T +27 (0)21-873-2123**

☐ **Welgevallen Cellar-Stellenbosch University** *see* Stellenbosch University Welgevallen Cellar

Welgevallen Wines - Splendidior 150

Named for the farm on which Stellenbosch's prestigious Paul Roos Gymnasium was built in 1866, Welgevallen wines are donated by old boys who are now winemakers and estate owners. Sales generate funds enabling talented youngsters from economically disadvantaged families to attend the school.

★★★★ **Splendidior 150 Cabernet Sauvignon** ⓨ Magnum commemorating Paul Roos Gymnasium's 150th anniversary, barrel each from 12 past students - a who's who of Stellenbosch wine. Enough pride at stake, there's cassis & cedar, silky smooth body, a long life ahead. **13** ⑧⑦ splendid indeed. Not tasted: **Pinotage**. Discontinued: **Cabernet Sauvignon-Merlot**, **Sauvignon Blanc**. — CR

Location/map: Stellenbosch ▪ Map grid reference: F5 ▪ WO: Bottelary ▪ Est/1stB 2000 ▪ Visits Mon-Fri 10—2 ▪ Closed pub & school hols ▪ Owner(s) Paul Roos Gymnasium Old Boys Union ▪ Winemaker(s)/viticulturist(s) Wouter Pienaar, Tinnie Momberg, Danie Steytler & Coenie Snyman (consultants) ▪ 800cs own label 75% red 25% white ▪ c/o Paul Roos Gymnasium Old Boys Union Suidwal Stellenbosch 7600 ▪ oldboys@paulroos.co.za ▪ www.paulroos.co.za ▪ S 33° 56′ 31.2″ E 018° 51′ 41.1″ ▪ animated.wiggly.spark ▪ T +27 (0)21-883-8627

Wellington VO

The 5-year-aged component has been nixed, meaning the potstill portion of Edward Snell & Co's 'brandy for the regular South African guy' now 3 years old. It's still produced at Oude Molen in Elgin, and notable for being one of the few local blended brandies without legal natural flavouring agents known as bonificateurs. **Wellington VO ★★★☆** Fruity, apricot/peach straightforwardness on this mixer brandy ⑲, with a caramel note. A touch too sweet & powerfully fiery for solo sipping (43% alcohol). — TJ

Wellington Wines

A substantial and significant producer, Wellington Wines dates its origins back to 1906/7 with the establishment of Wellington Wine Cellar and Bovlei Cellar on opposite ends of Wellington town. Today it produces a wide range of wines for consumers around the world from three facilities, where new technology investment is planned to 'ensure our focus remains on quality and style improvements'. A newly renovated underground space in the original WWC cellar will soon be home to the La Cave range, while the old BC building on the Hawequa Mountain slope is the venue for tasting the larger portfolio 'in a homely atmosphere'.

La Cave range

★★★★ Cabernet Sauvignon ⓐ Lithe, fine-grained **17 ★★★★☆** ⑨⓪ combines power of **16** ⑧⑥ with restraint, refinement; cassis fruit swaddled in new oak (as all this range, reds 18 months) but wine carries it with assurance. Worth cellaring 3-5 years.

★★★★ Pinotage ⓐ Generous plump fruit laced with spice & lavished with new wood; **18** ⑧⑦ berries & plums vie with heady vanilla in riot of flavour; stern tannins keep the gates of hedonism shut in youth. Allow time to soften, settle, like **17 ★★★★☆** ⑨⓪.

★★★★ Shiraz ⓐ Under **17** ⑧⑥'s enthusiastic tannin extraction & new small-oaking lies succulent ripe cherry fruit waiting for time to bring harmony. Be patient or serve with country food.

★★★★ Cape Blend ⓐ Intuitively divergent components (pinotage leads cab, roobernet & merlot) in fact harmonise well in spicy **17** ⑧⑦, with elegant cassis fruit. Fine but still-dense tannic core needs food or a cellar.

★★★★ Chenin Blanc Broad, oaky (500L barrel, year) & oxidative, **17** ⑧⑦'s baked custard styling has immediate & considerable appeal, perhaps best enjoyed soon while still at peak.

Duke of Wellington range

Shiraz ⊘ ⓣ **★★★☆** Pick of the bunch, **18** ⑧④ even more moreish than previous. Fresh minty nuance to plump blueberries, smoked meat & dark spice, delicious succulence within balanced frame. **White Pinotage** ⓣ **★★★** Free-run juice of black grape made as a dry white wine, slightest hint of pink in **19** ⑧②. Savoury, wild scrub notes add interest to red berry fruit, unfettered by any oak.

Cabernet Sauvignon ⓠ **★★★★** Herb-toned **17** ⑧③ cements uptick of recent vintages; juicy bramble fruit with pliable tannin support, savoury tail. Decent drinking, not at all trivial. **Merlot** ⓠ **★★★** Lavender & violet aromas lift, & firm tannic structure anchors the ripe berry features of **17** ⑧②; oak in harmony. **Pinotage ★★★** Vibrant plum, banana & clove flavours on fleshy **18** ⑧②, firm tannins & 14% alcohol in balance. **Chenin Blanc ★★★** Clean, fresh & uncluttered ripe-fruit profile to crisp **19** ⑧①. **Sauvignon Blanc ★★★** Riper green fig & gooseberry flavours livened by vibrant cut-grass freshness in **19** ⑧⓪, brisk acid tempered by few grams sugar.

Imprint range

Frizzante Blush ⓠ **★★** Was 'Blushing Pino Frizzante'. Lightly sparkling Natural Sweet rosé. Carnival pink NV ⑦⓪ is hanepoot with chenin, dash pinotage. Low 9% alcohol, as next. **Frizzante Blanc** ⓠ **★★** Was

'Moscato Frizzante'. Pétillant Natural Sweet from hanepoot & chenin. **NV** ⑦ is frothy & grapey, to kick-start a party. These WO W Cape. — DS

Location/map: Wellington ▪ Map grid reference: B3 C3 ▪ WO: Wellington/Western Cape ▪ Est 1941 ▪ Tasting & sales Tue/Wed/Sat 9-5 Thu/Fri 9-6 Sun/pub hols 11-3 (only Bovlei tasting room) ▪ Fee R40/5 wines ▪ BYO picnic ▪ Gift shop ▪ Seasonal wine pairing menu ▪ Venue for private functions ▪ Owner(s) ▪ Production team: Francois van Niekerk (2014), Erik van Wyk (2015) & Daniel Slabber (2019) ▪ Viticulturist(s) Nikey van Zyl (2017) ▪ 2,400ha ▪ 27,000t 60% red 40% white ▪ BRC, Fairtrade, HACCP, IPW, WIETA ▪ PO Box 509 Wellington 7654 ▪ marketing@wellingtonwines.com ▪ www.wellingtonwines.com ▪ S 33° 38' 4.68" E 018° 59' 24.39" (Wellington), S 33° 38' 18.4" E 019° 1' 54.2" (Bovlei) ▪ ⌨ lemons.songs.then, books.steers.natural ▪ **T +27 (0)21-873-1582**

Welmoed

Well-priced, easy-drinking range named for the property whose 17th-century owner, Jacobus van der Heyden, resisted government corruption and earned the people's admiration for his 'moed' (courage). The site is now home to brand owner Stellenbosch Vineyards.

Pinotage ⊘ 🏵 ★★★ Star of this good-value range in **18** ⑧: varietal mulberries & cream, tasty fruit-laden farewell.

Cabernet Sauvignon ⊘ ★★★ Unpretentious everyday companion; **18** ⑦ sweet black fruit, malleable tannins. **Merlot** ⊘ ★★★ Gentle plum & mulberry appeal, **18** ⑦ tangy & charry mouthful. **Shiraz** ⊘ ★★★ **18** ⑦ not as savoury, dry as previous; juicy, with good bite of tannin. **Chenin Blanc** ★★★ Understated, in house style, **19** ⑦ some khaki bush & floral notes, satisfying breadth. **Sauvignon Blanc** ★★★ Attractive wet-pebble texture & intense grassiness make **19** ⑦ easy & pleasant to drink - but note sturdy 14% alcohol. Stellenbosch WO, as all. Not tasted: **Rosé, Chardonnay, Gewürztraminer, Pinot Grigio, Sparkling Brut.** — CvZ

Weltevrede Estate   ⑨ ⑪ 🏠 📷 ♿

Philip Jonker is the fourth generation on this Breede riverside estate between Robertson and Bonnievale. While his father Lourens, a former industry leader who re-energised the Weltevrede label in the 1970s, remains a 'free consultant', Philip has expanded the portfolio, adding MCC production, exploring chardonnay's versatility and testing new sites for shiraz. The farm's sizeable conservation portion, vineyard guest cottages and new-look tasting area (in progress) further occupy a family, rooted here since 1912, whose social commitment helped spearhead a remarkable new community school. Built with local contributions (money and expertise) to a trust fund, with some 40% government input, on 12 hectares donated by Weltevrede, Jakes Gerwel Technical High School opened in Bonnievale town in 2018.

Estate range

★★★★ **Bedrock Black Syrah** 🐝 Year on, **16** ⑧ shows still-compact but juicy fruit, appealing white pepper hint, better integration of 40% new oak, 18 months, similar firm but easygoing tannins as **15** ★★★★ ⑧. Robertson WO, as all this range & Entheos.

★★★★ **Place of Rocks Chardonnay** Sleek & smooth **18** ⑧'s pure lemon-lime fruit, vivacious acidity & bone-dry finish perfectly complemented by 30% new oak. Like also-lightish **16** ★★★★ ⑧, less oaky than wooded siblings. **17** untasted.

★★★★ **Poet's Prayer Chardonnay** Flagship white, for fans of oak-sweet chardonnay. Like **16** ⑧, deepish colour of **17** ★★★ ⑧ reflects its ferment/2 years in an older barrique. Vibrant melange of citrus fruit in a broad frame (15% alcohol), coconut sheen to finish. Limited release of just 42 cases.

Hardrock Cabernet Sauvignon ★★★ Tasted out of sequence, **15** ⑧ is fresh, has well-judged ripeness & controlled tannic grip. Also appealingly bone-dry vs **16** ⑧'s few grams sugar. Oak as for Syrah.

Weltevrede 1912 Collection

Cabernet Sauvignon ⑨ ★★★★ Clean berry aromas & flavours on **16** ⑧. Juicy sweet fruit, with undominating firm structure. Oak well integrated. Should develop well a good few years. **Merlot-Cabernet Sauvignon** ★★★ Revisited, 80/20 blend has settled over the year, edgy acidity mellower, sweet cassis fruit more to the fore though **15** ⑧ still slightly herbaceous on palate. **Chardonnay** ★★★★ Barrel-fermented/year aged, yet oak subtler on **17** ⑧ than previous, does not overwhelm tangerine &

ruby grapefruit flavours, or attractive frangipani note. Soft textured for easy sipping. Discontinued: **Malbec**, **Pinotage**.

Philip Jonker Brut Méthode Cap Classique Collection

Entheos ⊘ ★★★ Chardonnay (60%) leads pinot noir in light (11.5% alcohol) & bouncy **NV** ⑧② sparkler. Fruit is shy, but fresh as an ocean wave. Not tasted: **The Ring**.

Simplicity range

Chocmint Cabernet Sauvignon ⨂ ★★ A really easy drinker, this **16** ⑦⑥. Adds a pleasing touch of tobacco to the announced flavour; off-dry but balanced. **Cherrychoc Merlot** ★★ Soft & flavourful **17** ⑦⑥, revisited, still very easy, just-dry & supple. For current drinking. **Cigarbox Shiraz** ★★★ Less tobacco character than usual in **18** ⑦⑧, more lovely pure red fruit, gentle tug of tannin & smoothing smidgen sugar. **Vanilla Chardonnay** ★★★ Blue orange & oak-derived vanilla on ready-to-enjoy **17** ⑦⑦, a year later still slips down easily. **Lemon Zest Chardonnay** ★★★ As it says on the label: zesty lemon tones, brisk & perky, though unoaked **19** ⑦⑨ shade off flavoursome & much lighter previous. Not tasted: **Turkish Delight Rosé**. Discontinued: **Trop!co Sauvignon Blanc**.

Heritage range

★★★★ Ouma se Wyn ⊛ 'Granny's Wine' is fortified white muscat de Frontignan, always commendably, uncloyingly sweet. **18** ⑧⑧ similar Turkish delight scents as last-tasted **15** ⑧⑥, more orange rind, lemon pith & fresh ginger complexity. 375 ml, as next.

Oupa se Wyn ⨂ ★★★ Grandpa's favourite is fortified red muscadel. **17** ⑧① forthright grapiness, slippery-sweet & quite fiery, with a resin edge to the aftertaste. — CvZ

Location: Bonnievale ▪ Map: Robertson ▪ Map grid reference: D3 ▪ WO: Western Cape/Robertson ▪ Est 1912 ▪ 1stB 1945 ▪ Tasting & sales Mon-Fri 8—5 Sat 9—3.30 ▪ Closed Easter Fri/Sun, Dec 25/26 & Jan 1 ▪ Cellar tours & underground tasting by appt ▪ Restaurant Tue-Sat 9-3 ▪ Walks/hikes ▪ Conservation area ▪ Weddings/functions ▪ 4 self-catering guest cottages ▪ Owner(s) Lourens Jonker ▪ Cellarmaster(s) Philip Jonker (Jan 1997) ▪ Viticulturist(s) Francois Viljoen (consultant) ▪ 360ha/106ha (cab, merlot, pinot, shiraz, chard, cbard, gewürz, sauv) ▪ 1,300t/50,000cs own label 15% red 75% white 10% other ▪ Brands for clients: Woolworths ▪ PO Box 6 Bonnievale 6730 ▪ info@weltevrede.com ▪ www.weltevrede.com ▪ S 33° 56′ 30.9″ E 020° 3′ 4.4″ ▪ ⌖ dangles.shires.unicorn ▪ **T +27 (0)23-616-2141**

Welvanpas   ⨂ ⑪ ◎ ⑧

Dan Retief, owner, winemaker and viticulturist of Wellington estate Welvanpas, is the custodian of a heritage spanning more than 300 years and 10 generations. Yet even if he lacked a sturdy family tree, including Voortrekker leader Piet Retief, or the farm a long backstory, which Dan shares during the pre-booked History Package lunch and talk, both would still be admired by lovers of heartfelt, handcrafted wines, and the scores of MTB riders, trail runners and hikers using some 60 km of mountain foothill paths made available to them.

Daniel Pinotage ⨂ ★★★ Adds 3 year old son to wine's name in unwooded **16** ⑦⑧. Nice typicity: blueberries, succulence, a bit of grape tannin giving definition. **De Krakeelhoek Rood** ⨂ ★★★ **14** ⑧① merlot (71%) with shiraz, relaxed & confident & ready now, cassis sharing the limelight with smoked meat tones, supple tannins. **Revival Red** ⨂ ★★ Cab-led with merlot & shiraz, good dark-fruit expression, clean leather & forest floor in **14** ⑦④; juicy tannins for early drinking but a gentle grip at the end says it can age a bit. **Suzanne Pinotage Rosé** ⨂ ★★★ Elegant & dry, **16** ⑦⑧ packed with red berries, a vibrant patio sipper. **Chardonnay** ⨂ ★★ Savoury notes dominate **16** ⑦④'s buttered toast, whiffs of olive oil, shy stonefruit; portion American oak adds a sweet vanilla farewell. **Sauvignon Blanc** ⨂ ★★ Melon, whiffs of capsicum in **16** ⑦④ following through to the palate. Dry, light textured, slips down easily. — CR, CvZ

Location/map/WO: Wellington ▪ Map grid reference: C3 ▪ Est 1704 ▪ 1stB 1994 ▪ Tasting & sales Tue-Fri 8—5 Sat/Sun 8—3 ▪ Fee R30pp ▪ Closed Easter Fri-Mon, Dec 16-Jan 2 ▪ Die Ou Meul coffee shop Tue-Fri 8-5 Sat/Sun 8-3 ▪ Facilities for children ▪ Tour groups ▪ History Package incl lunch & talk on Piet Retief family, booking required ▪ Farm produce ▪ Walks/hikes ▪ Bains MTB trails ▪ Craft beer ▪ Owner(s)/viticulturist(s) Dan Retief ▪ Cellarmaster(s) Dan Retief (Jan 1999) ▪ Winemaker(s) Dan Retief (Jan 1990), with Neels Kruger (Jan 1999) ▪ 260ha/50ha (11 varieties r/w) ▪ 25t own label 80% red 15% white 5% rosé ▪ PO Box 75 Wellington 7654 ▪ welvanpas@gmail.com ▪ S 33° 37′ 59.9″ E 019° 4′ 12.5″ ▪ ⌖ brunt.stating.ultrahigh ▪ **T +27 (0)21-300-5708**

☐ **Weskus** see Winkelshoek Wine Cellar

Whalehaven Wines

Owned by the Italian Bottega family, this artisanal winery in Hermanus has a sibling, Idiom Collection, with a home in a different appellation, Stellenbosch, specifically the mountain slopes high above Sir Lowry's Pass village. They share a winemaker, Reino Thiart, and a fruit source (Idiom's Da Capo vineyards), though grapes for Whalehaven are also brought in from Walker Bay and elsewhere in the Coastal region, giving its wines a distinct identity. The recently revamped home base offers all sorts of wine-and-food taste treats.

Conservation Coast range

★★★★ **Pinot Noir** ⊘ Delectably fragrant **17** ★★★★☆ ⑨⓪ shows rose-scented berries & spicy aromas on firm tannin structure. Well-judged oak adds dimension without intruding. Promising step up from **16** ⑧⑦. Upper Hemel-en-Aarde fruit, as next.

★★★★☆ **Chardonnay** Solid, full-bodied **17** ⑨⓪ has boldly ripe citrus fruit over still-prominent oak spice, hints of zest & ginger. Bunch pressed, barrel fermented & matured, 30% new wood. Continues improved form of **16** ⑨⓪.

Classic range

★★★★ **Cabernet Franc** Two vintages tasted. **15** ⑧⑧ shows malty evolution, with convincing blackcurrant fruit. Generous & ripe. Coastal WO. **14** ⑧⑧ lacks varietal austerity but compensates with solid blackberry fruit, smooth texture.

★★★★ **Merlot** Darkly sombre **15** ⑧⑥, black cherry & damson fruit with cocoa highlights. Full bodied & ripe, with chewy tannins, gentle acidity.

★★★★ **Pinot Noir** ⑧ Subtle, fragrant berry & cherry fruit with faint floral scents, **16** ⑧⑥ lighter than **15** ⑧⑦ but charmingly supple & silky. Hemel-en-Aarde Ridge vines.

★★★★ **Pinotage** Nicely weighted, berry-fruited body, ripe tannins, sweet oak spices on **15** ★★★★☆ ⑧⑤, also more of the variety's high tones than on **14** ⑧⑥.

Sauvignon Blanc ★★★★ Elegant & flavoursome **18** ⑧⑤, crisp but restrained acidity, ripe kiwi fruit, fragrant finish. From Upper Hemel-en-Aarde vines, like **17** ★★★★ ⑧⑦, which improved on previous. In abeyance: **Unwooded Viognier**.

Abalone range

Pinotage-Merlot ★★★ Middleweight **15** ⑧② has juicy mixed berry fruit, prominent tannins, rather brief finish. In abeyance: **Chenin Blanc-Viognier**.

Old Harbour range

Red ★★★ Switches to merlot & cab blend in **15** ⑧⓪, with farmyard notes, decent heft & solid fruit for pleasant quaffing. Occasional release: **Pinotage Rosé**, **White**. — GdB

Location: Hermanus ▪ Map: Walker Bay & Bot River ▪ Map grid reference: A3 ▪WO: Western Cape/Coastal ▪ Est/1stB 1995 ▪ Tasting & sales Mon-Fri 9.30-5 Sat/Sun 10.30-4.30 ▪ Wine tasting R50-R100 for paired tastings with fine floral chocolates & aromatic jams ▪ Tour groups (up to 40 pax) ▪ Private tasting room can be booked for small functions/corporate events (up to 14 pax) ▪ Owner(s) Bottega family ▪Winemaker(s) Reino Thiart ▪ 120t capacity ▪ Private Bag X14 Hermanus 7200 ▪ experience@whalehaven.co.za, info@bottegafamilywine.co.za ▪ www.whalehaven.co.za, www.bottegafamilywine.co.za ▪ S 34° 24' 36.9" E 019° 11' 60.0" ▪ 🌐 lineage.disappearance.hooks ▪ **T +27 (0)28-316-1633**

☐ **White Hill** *see* Skipskop Wines
☐ **White Rhino** *see* Linton Park Wines
☐ **White River** *see* Bergsig Estate
☐ **Wightman & Sons** *see* Môrelig Vineyards
☐ **Wightman, Gouws & Clarke** *see* Rossouw, Gouws & Clarke

Wijnskool

Seasoned winemaker Bartho Eksteen (see separate listing) started this wine academy with his wife, Suné, to teach the next generation of potential winemakers - high school pupils - about different wine styles, winemaking techniques, industry-related career options and ('very importantly') responsible use of alcohol. Previously the course was only offered to boys attending Boland Agricultural High School in Paarl, but the

Eksteens now have facilities on their Hemel-en-Aarde farm, enabling them to draw girls as well as boys from the local community. Part of the hands-on educational process is to produce these two wines.

★★★★ **Tree of Knowledge Shiraz** ⊘ Reverts to varietal shiraz, takes a step up in **17** ⑧⑥ after Rhône blend **16** ★★★★ ⑧⑤. Fresh & tangy, raised in older French oak only (18 months) for lovely purity of ripe black fruit, plush tannins, hints of smoke & black pepper.

★★★★ **Tree of Knowledge Sauvignon Blanc** Shy, delicate floral perfume, then **19** ⑧⑨ blooms on palate with peach, green apple & zesty lime, leaving flinty nuance on lingering finish. No **18**.— JG

Location: Hermanus ▪ WO: Western Cape ▪ Est/1stB 2011 ▪ Tasting, sales & cellar tours at Bartho Eksteen (see entry) ▪ Owner(s) Bartho & Suné Eksteen ▪ Winemaker(s) Bartho Eksteen (Feb 2011), with Pieter Willem Eksteen (Jan 2012) & learners at Boland Agricultural High School & other schools ▪ Viticulturist(s) Gerhard Bruwer (De Bos Estate, Hermanus); Jaco Mouton (Benguela Cove, Hermanus) - bought in grapes ▪ 30t/3,680cs own label 50% red 50% white ▪ PO Box 1999 Hermanus 7200 ▪ bartho@hermanus.co.za, sune@hermanus.co.za ▪ www. barthoeksteen.co.za ▪ **T +27 (0)82-920-7108 (Bartho), +27 (0)72-323-5060 (Suné)**

☐ **Wild Card** see Le Sueur Wines

Wildeberg Wines

The home-farm, owned by UK-based wine company Boutinot, covers 144 hectares on the eastern Franschhoek mountains, and all but nine are (as the brand name implies) 'raw mountain, flora and fauna'. So far 6 ha have been planted on this virgin land, 'where soil and slope change every 10 metres; it's a challenging hillside', acknowledges winemaker JD Rossouw. Semillon, chardonnay, syrah and durif are shortly to be joined by some more exotic varieties; a first harvest is anticipated in 2022. Meanwhile Paarl chenin and Banghoek sauvignon, from contract growers, have the team smiling. See also Strange Kompanjie listing.

Terroirs range (NEW)

★★★★ **Sauvignon Blanc** Granadilla, touch of sweat & vigorous fruity acids on **18** ⑧⑦ will appeal to those who like full-on sauvignon flavour. Balanced & persistent, it should provide enjoyment for few years. Banghoek WO. Also in 1.5L, as next.

Chenin Blanc ★★★★ **18** ⑧③ shows lush fruit - pear, baked apple - with cleansing acid in easy-drinking style. Barrel ferment, 18% new, adds concluding sweet vanilla note, though technically dry.

Wildeberg range

★★★★ **White** (NEW) ⊛ Typical Franschhoek semillon; **18** ⑧⑧ more neutral on fruit, beeswaxy with suggestion citrus lift; interest lies in textural breadth yet to fully unwrap from its zippy freshness, oak spice (barrel fermented, 33% new).

Discontinued: **Chrome Yellow Semillon**. — AL

Location/map: Franschhoek ▪ Map grid reference: D1 ▪ WO: Paarl/Franschhoek/Banghoek ▪ Est/1stB 2016 ▪ Tasting, sales & cellar tours by invitation ▪ Closed all pub hols ▪ Owner(s) Wildeberg & Kompanjie ▪ Winemaker(s) JD Rossouw ▪ 60t ▪ Own label 50% red 50% white ▪ henrietteh@boutinot.com ▪ www. wildeberg.co.za ▪ S 33° 56' 13'' E 019° 08' 03'' ▪ ᴀᴠ clubs.cheering.dust ▪ **T +27 (0)82-895-4111/+27 (0)72-605-9817**

Wildehurst Wines

Joanne Hurst's small winery and home vineyard in Swartland hamlet Koringberg is the centre of great energy and creativity. Numerous small bottlings mostly come from grapes brought in from elsewhere in the appellation — Wildehurst is a member of Swartland Independent Producers, meeting their hands-off winemaking criteria. Winemaker Sheree Nothnagel loves new cultivars, new projects. Two new wines to report on this year, while newcomers in barrel include nebbiolo, tinta barocca, durif and a straw wine.

Wildehurst range

★★★★ **Cinsaut** Sour cherry tang of light, refreshing **18** ⑧⑥ a delight; fine tannic structure with rosemary & spice flavours. Minuscule production & only older oak, as all. Wild yeast ferment except MCC Cinsaut.

★★★★ **Merlot** (NEW) 30 year old Berg riverside vines yield fabulous **17** ⑧⑥; meaty aromas & understated mulberry fruit, elegant acidity underpins the finish. 3 barrels, aged 18 months.

★★★★ **Tempranillo** (NEW) Comparatively rare for the Cape. Single barrique of **17** (87) loaded with black fruit & cured meat characters in superbly toned, elegant frame, 18 months ageing quietly adds gravitas.

★★★★☆ **Red** (🏅) Power with poise & restraint in **15** (93) Rhône blend; ever-improving, up a level from **14** (90). Co-fermented syrah & viognier, plus mourvèdre, splash cinsaut deliver a lovely, generous spice-laden mouthful of redcurrant pastilles; 18 months oak integrated & supportive.

★★★★☆ **Chenin Blanc** Quintessential pure-fruited Swartland chenin, sunshine-in-a-glass styling but ripe tropical fruit of **18** (91) is finessed, textured. Like **17** (93), serious enough to contemplate, easy enough to want to quaff. From 30 year old Paardeberg bushvines; barrel fermented/matured 6 months.

★★★★ **The Wilde Le Premier Or** 'The Wilde' a witty name for winemaker's experimental space. Debut **15** ★★★ (81) a red blend (no **16**), **17** (89) nebbiolo; going up another notch, **18** ★★★★☆ (90) skin-mac-erated (& certified as such) semillon from bushvines on Paardeberg, 6 months oaked. Truly special wine, delivers sumptuous flavour in an unforced, almost serene way.

★★★★ **Viognier** From Paardeberg & Malmesbury vineyards, just 900 bottles. Elegant & light (12% alco-hol), yet **18** (89) has peach & spice intensity &, like **16** ★★★★☆ (90), hint of pineapple in farewell. No **17**.

★★★★ **Méthode Cap Classique Cinsaut** (NEW) Novel, pink-tinged, fun-but-high-quality bubbles from a trendy grape. Zero-dosage, bone-dry **17** (86) offers red berry fruit ahead of biscuit notes. 1 year on lees.

★★★★ **Méthode Cap Classique Chenin Blanc-Chardonnay** Chenin-led (69%) dry **17** (86) offers drinking pleasure & interest. Creamy citrus & apple notes; mouthwatering acidity, good complexity.

Occasional release: **Petit Wilde**, **Méthode Cap Classique**, **Méthode Cap Classique Chardonnay**.

Unlabelled range

★★★★ **Red Blend** (🔂) Franco-SA allsorts mix headed by cinsaut & featuring dash pinotage. **16** (88) spice box aroma focused by old oak, joined on palate by generous red berries & pepper. Structured yet easy.

Velo range

★★★★ **Red** (✓) Grenache (73%) leads delicious & well-priced **16** (86), with shiraz & mourvèdre in the mix (no viognier like previous). Berry profile has bottle-age breadth.

Rosé ★★★ Ex old cinsaut vines, **19** (77) lacks friendly fruit profile of previous. **Blanc** ★★★☆ Colombard & chenin duo gets oomph from barrel-fermented viognier in **18** (85). A super summer white. — DS

Location: Koringberg ▪ Map/WO: Swartland ▪ Map grid reference: B2 ▪ Est 2006 ▪ 1stB 2009 ▪ Cellar tours & tasting by appt at 1 Main Rd, Koringberg ▪ Owner(s) Joanne Hurst ▪ Winemaker(s) Sheree Nothnagel (Dec 2013) ▪ 1.1ha (carignan, cinsaut, mourv, shiraz, viog) ▪ 24t ▪ own label 45% red 45% white 10% rosé ▪ PO Box 103 Koringberg 7312 ▪ info@wildehurst.com ▪ www.wildehurst.com ▪ S 33° 01' 10.10" E 018° 40' 26.42" ▪ 🗺 eruptions.intervals.invoice ▪ **T +27 (0)60-374-9267**

Wildekrans Wine Estate   (🍷)(🍴)(🏠)(📷)(♿)

The Harlow family owners and their long-time viticulturist Braam Gericke (now winemaker too) regard a new cabernet franc and grenache blanc (untasted here) as highlights among the site- and varietal-specific, small-batch wines from their Bot River terroir. They're now enrolled with the Old Vine Project, courtesy of 1982 chenin, and have added membership of Sustainability Initiative of SA (SIZA) to their listing of organisations promoting ethical, environmental and quality-driven farming practices.

Barrel Select Reserve range

★★★★ **Pinot Noir** Delicate fruit profile on **18** ★★★★ (85) mid-2019 masked by new oak (60%). Time should resolve. Piquant freshness invites food pairing. Not as elegant as last-tasted older-oaked **14** (87).

★★★★☆ **Pinotage** Vanilla-polished, bold, modern styling on riper **16** (92) vintage, pinotage's opulent dark cherry flavours easily assimilate 70% new oak. Balanced, but touch less structure than **15** (94).

★★★★ **Shiraz** Similar herbal, minty nuance to spicy wild berry flavours on **16** (87). Same oak maturation (60% new, 22 months) as Cape Blend, lends a respectable dryer tone. Already tempting.

★★★★ **Cape Blend** Pinotage-led (71%) **16** (89), with cab, pinot noir & shiraz. Dry tannin structure contains vintage's ripeness. Less intense than **15** ★★★★★ (93) but balanced, with development prospects.

★★★★☆ **Chenin Blanc** (🏅) (🌱) Bunch-pressed **17** (93) from 38 year old vines. Tangy apple & marzipan flavours focused by bright acidity. Deftly oaked (30% new), with fruit purity & intensity for a fine future.

Estate range

★★★★ **Sauvignon Blanc** ⓥ Maritime influence reflected in crisp **19** ⑧⑨. Nettle, passionfruit, ruby grapefruit flavours in fine, tensile balance with racy acidity. Great food pairer & even better than **18** ⑧⑦.

Pinotage ★★★★ Succulent, supple & smooth but fresh, with ample plummy fruit. **17** ⑧③ all older oak, poised, friendly & eminently quaffable. Not tasted: **Shiraz, Cabernet Franc-Merlot.**

Méthode Cap Classique range

★★★★ **Brut Rosé** Palest blush on savoury-style **16** ⑧⑧ sparkling, now chardonnay-led with pinot noir, chenin, pinotage. Fresher, brighter structure than sibling; appealing creamy brioche undertone though shade off finer **15** ★★★★☆ ⑨⓪.

Chenin Blanc ⓥ ★★★★ Brush of oak adds a honeyed nuance to apple, dried pineapple & almond flavours of **15** ⑧⑤ sparkler. Plush waxy texture, with a tart almondy twist. — MW

Location/WO: Bot River ▪ Map: Walker Bay & Bot River ▪ Map grid reference: B1 ▪ Est/1stB 1993 ▪ Tasting, sales & cellar tours Mon-Fri 8.30–5 Sat 11–5 Sun 11-4 ▪ Restaurant ▪ Picnics to order ▪ Olive oil ▪ Tour groups ▪ Conferences/functions ▪ Self-catering cottages ▪ Walks/hikes ▪ MTB ▪ Birding ▪ Horseback riding ▪ Conservation area ▪ Grappa still, tour/tasting to be pre-booked; grappas & ports available for sale at the cellar ▪ Owner(s) Gary & Amanda Harlow ▪ Winemaker(s) Braam Gericke (2017), with Andre Olkers ▪ Viticulturist(s) Braam Gericke (2008) ▪ 1,015ha/71.8ha (cabs s/f, merlot, ptage, pinot, shiraz, chard, chenin, grenache b, hanepoot, riesling, sauv, sem) ▪ 350t own label 55% red 40% white 5% rosé; ±13,200cs for clients ▪ CVC, OVP, SIZA, WIETA, WWF-SA Conservation Champion ▪ PO Box 31 Botriver 7185 ▪ wines@ wildekrans.com ▪ www.wildekrans.com ▪ S 34° 14' 23.50" E 019° 11' 54.42" (home farm, Bot River) ▪ ⬛ unlocking.heartless.dealmakers ▪ **T +27 (0)28-284-9902**

Wilderer Distilleries   ⓨ ⑪ ⓞ ⓑ

Christian Wilderer is proud to claim that his late father Helmut, a German restaurateur, founded the first SA private husk spirit distillery, in the mid 1990s, and became a leading producer of fruit-based eaux de vie. Now a wide, innovative range of spirits and liqueurs is produced at the Paarl distillery (there's a second tasting and dining location, at Spice Route Destination). Despite such successes as Fynbos Gin, the oak-matured grappas remain what the team recognise as 'the foundation spirits on which the company is built'.

★★★★☆ **Grappa Muscato** ⓥ Grapey & floral notes dominate straw-hued **18** ⑨⓪ spirit from morio muscat, 6 months in oak like all these. Immensely smooth & seductive, clean & fresh - with that muscat quality guiding to a stylish finish. 500 ml, as all.

★★★★ **Grappa Pinotage** Matured in ex-pinotage casks, adding a delicate pink tint. Aroma & subtly intense red berry flavour also recall the pinotage grapeskins. A special, unusual charm to **18** ⑧⑧.

★★★★☆ **Grappa Shiraz** ⓥ More husk notes as well as a light smoky toast from the time in oak make **18** ⑨① less fruity, but more complexly aromatic & characterful than the others. Same Italian-style elegance, the pale fire of the 43% alcohol finely & tensely in balance.— TJ

Location/map: Paarl ▪ Map grid reference: D7 ▪ Est/1stB 1995 ▪ Tasting, sales & distillery tours daily 10-5 ▪ Fee R30 ▪ Closed Dec 25 & Jan 1 ▪ Restaurant open for lunch & dinner Tue-Sun ▪ Facilities for children ▪ Gift shop ▪ Gin blending experiences available during tasting room hours ▪ Owner(s) Christian Wilderer ▪ Distiller Johan Mönnig (2014) ▪ 2ha ▪ ±22,000cs (6x500ml) ▪ PO Box 150 Paarl-Simondium 7670 ▪ info@ wilderer.co.za ▪ www.wilderer.co.za ▪ S 33° 48' 1.12" E 018° 57' 5.81" ▪ ⬛ precollege.wasabi.volatiles ▪ **T +27 (0)21-863-3555**

☐ **Wildflower** *see* Darling Cellars
☐ **Wild Instinct** *see* Stellenview Premium Wines
☐ **Wild Olive** *see* The Grape Grinder

William Everson Wines   ⓨ ⓗ

William Everson's flourishing craft apple-cider venture has been front and centre the past few years, but the Grabouw garagiste has kept his hand in with production of small parcels of wine - uncertified '11 Cab, '12 Shiraz and '17 Chenin currently available from Everson's Cider Tasting facility at nearby Peregrine Farm Stall, to be joined by his latest bottlings, Durbanville Cab and Elgin Shiraz (both '19), not ready for review.

Location: Grabouw ▪ Map: Elgin ▪ Map grid reference: B2 ▪ Est/1stB 2001 ▪ Tasting, sales & tours by appt ▪ Self-catering accommodation ▪ Owner(s)/winemaker(s) William Everson ▪ 4t/800cs own label 60% red 40% white ▪ 2281 Essenhout Ave, Klipkop, Grabouw 7160 ▪ william@eversonwine.co.za, william@eversonscider.com ▪ www.eversonwine.co.za, www.eversonscider.com ▪ S 34° 9' 52.06" E 019° 2' 6.19" ▪ mini.laying.primary ▪ **T** +27 (0)82-554-6357

☐ **Willowbrook** *see* Wine-of-the-Month Club

Windfall Wine Farm

After acquiring Windfall from cricketing legend Eddie Barlow, KwaZulu-Natal businessman Robert Alexander set about rejuvenating the property, restoring dams, drilling new boreholes, replanting vineyards and establishing a boutique cellar. Today, the venture in Robertson's scenic Agterkliphoogte Valley offers a fine potstill brandy, extra virgin olive oil and stays in colourful cottages, in addition to its range of food-friendly wines.

Windfall Wine range

Chenin Blanc ⑦ ★★★ Picked early but **19** ⑧⑴'s acidity is reined in & well-matched with stonefruit & guava intensity, & the modest oaked portion, for a sleek & satisfying glassful.

Cabernet Sauvignon ★★★★ Previewed **18** ⑧③ enticing cassis notes, hint of baking spices from French oak, 18 months (like all the reds). As always, no rough edges, just great drinkability thanks to ripe tannins, plush fruit & smidgen sugar. **Shiraz** ★★★ Toasty & high-toned cherry liqueur notes on **16** ⑦⑺, slightly warming finish (14.5% alcohol vs balanced 13% last time). **Barrel 41** ★★★ Characterful **17** ⑧② layers vanilla oak on base of ripe black fruit, creatively & tastily blends 7 Rhône & Bordeaux grapes, shiraz in majority at 52%. WO W Cape. **Grenache Rosé** ★★ One of relatively few pink grenaches. Pre-bottled **19** ⑺⑸ still muted on nose but easy to drink, usual friendly alcohol (11%), piquant lemon finish. **Sauvignon Blanc** ★★★ A little new oak adds complexity & breadth to **19** ⑦⑺, showing fermentation character when previewed mid-2019 along with attractive Granny Smith & yellow apples. **Mendola** ★★★ Dry MCC sparkler from chardonnay. Retasted **15** ⑧② has gained in complexity, peach, apricot & yellow apple in the bouquet, palate is creamy but could linger longer. Not tasted: **Pinot Noir, Pinotage, Kibali.**

Brandy range

★★★★ **The Hunter** Beautifully packaged 6 year old potstill ⑧⑺ from chenin is vibrant, smooth & satisfying. Peach, pear & spice notes, with a trace of citrus on the long finish. 500 ml. — CvZ, WB

Location/map: Robertson ▪ Map grid reference: C8 ▪ WO: Robertson/Western Cape ▪ Est 1998 ▪ 1stB 2006 ▪ Tasting, sales & tours by appt ▪ Closed all pub hols ▪ 5 self-catering cottages (sleeps between 2 & 4 people) R500pp/n ▪ Owner(s) Bianca Weingartz, Sarah Alexander & Jaco de Wet ▪ Cellarmaster(s) Kobus van der Merwe (Jan 2006, consultant) & Jaco de Wet ▪ Winemaker(s) Kobus van der Merwe (Jan 2006, consultant), with Van Zyl de Wet (Jan 2009, consultant) ▪ Viticulturist(s) Jaco de Wet (Jan 2003) ▪ 300ha/63ha (cab, merlot, pinot, ruby cab, chard, chenin, sauv) ▪ 1,100t/1,250cs own label 75% red 25% white ▪ PO Box 22 Robertson 6705 ▪ info@windfallwine.co.za ▪ www.windfallwine.co.za ▪ S 33° 56' 33.37" E 019° 38' 42.98" ▪ greatness.chronicle.trainee ▪ **T** +27 (0)83-320-8473

Windmeul Cellar

The grower-owners of this Paarl venture are celebrating 75 years of bottling under their label, named for Blake's Mill, an engineering wonder of its day. This gives cellarmaster Danie Marais extra incentive to keep his promise of launching another wine in The Legend series, a barrel-selected pinotage recognising a former Windmeul director. Danie and team have added a second new wine, which we commend as a 'Hidden Gem'.

Reserve range

★★★★ **Cabernet Sauvignon** ⑦ Pot-pourri & tangerine notes on dark-fruited **16** ⑧⑥. More generous than **15** ⑧⑼, lovely balance & freshness from well-judged oak, acidity.

★★★★☆ **Pinotage** ⊘ ⑧ Exceptional fruit purity & freshness key to **17** ⑼⑴'s appeal. Tightly wound, 85% new oak & tannin grip for few years ageing, though still as quintessentially 'pinotage' as its siblings.

★★★★☆ **Shiraz** ⓐ Lily- & white pepper-toned **16** ★★★★ ⑧⑧, generous & plump black & red fruit supported by well-composed grape/oak tannin frame. Savoury, despite smidgen sugar broadening the finish. Follows impressively concentrated **15** ⑨④.

★★★★☆ **Cape Blend** ⓩ Repeats successful formula of recent years: 55% pinotage with mostly cab, smidgens merlot, petit verdot. Lead variety's inherent bright acidity key to **16** ⑨⓪'s structure but doesn't detract from impressively tight-packed fruit, muscular tannins. Will reward many years patience.

Chardonnay ⓩ ★★★★ Lightly oaked **17** ⑧⑤ takes time to reveal scented bouquet of lemon, lemongrass & lemon thyme, fruit-sweet tail in which oak provides form not flavour. **VSOP Brandy** ⓩ ★★★★ Delightfully different brandy ⑧④, light-feeling - no doubt due to the rare sauvignon blanc component giving more apple & pear notes than apricot & peach. Sweetly smooth, with no need of mixer or ice. 40.5% alcohol. Aged 5-6 years in oak.

The Legend Collection

★★★★☆ **Pinotage** ⓝⒺⓦ ⓐ Selection of best barrels, honours former Windmeul director & rugby Springbok TPD Briers. **17** ⑨⓪ similar to Reserve in its vivid perfume, variety-true acidity, supportive oaking & keepability - all done with a light touch.

★★★★ **Left Wing** ⓩ Confident **16** ★★★★★ ⑨⓪ cab (57%) blend with equal merlot, petit verdot, 5% cab franc. Classic walnut, cigarbox & lead pencil complexity, plush but not sweet cassis tones throughout, precise tannin structure for 5+ years ageing. More restrained than bold, earthy **15** ⑧⑨.

★★★★ **Chenin Blanc** ⓩ ⊛ Nicely dry **17** ⑧⑦'s nuttiness & palate breadth from year in barrel add extra dimension to ripe white peach, floral & earth aromas, rich & lengthy palate.

Windmeul range

Pinotage ⊘ ⓣ ★★★★ Unmistakable pinotage mulberry & strawberry tones, crackling acidity, brush of oak & satisfying dryness. **17** ⑧③ perfect supper companion or lightly chilled summer red. **Pinotage Rosé** ⓝⒺⓦ ⓣ ★★★ Trendy pale pink à la Provence, raspberry & mulberry aromas & flavours, **19** ⑧② tangy & piquant al fresco sipping.

Cabernet Sauvignon ⓩ ★★★ Less convincing than previous, **16** ⑦⑨ brief but not easy, with astringent tannins. **Merlot** ⊘ ★★★ Sugared plum fragrance, juicy fruit core, limber tannins, **16** ⑧② ticks the boxes for easy sippability. **Shiraz** ⊘ ★★★ Cranberry & red plum fruit seasoned with black pepper, oak spice. **17** ⑧① fleshy, with attractive stemmy farewell. **Chardonnay** ⊘ ★★★ Unwooded **18** ⑧⓪ happy mouthful of lemon & tangerine, brisk acidity & creamy lees finish. Not tasted: **Cabernet Sauvignon-Merlot**, **Chenin Blanc**, **Sauvignon Blanc**. Discontinued: **White Muscadel**, **Port**.

Discontinued: **Mill range**. — CvZ, TJ

Location/map: Paarl ▪ Map grid reference: D3 ▪ WO: Coastal ▪ Est 1944 ▪ 1stB 1945 ▪ Tasting & sales Mon-Fri 9–5 Sat 9–3 ▪ Roosterkoek & wine pairing ▪ Closed all pub hols ▪ Cellar tours by appt ▪ Parskuip Neighbourhood Marketplace Mon-Fri 8-5 Sat 9-3 ▪ Farmers' market every 1st Sat of each month (excl Jan) ▪ Function/tasting area ▪ Facilities for children ▪ Owner(s) 34 members ▪ Cellarmaster(s) Danie Marais (Oct 1999) ▪ Winemaker(s) Abraham van Heerden (Nov 2014), with Berto Dippenaar (Dec 2016) ▪ Viticulturist(s) Anton Laas (Oct 2007) ▪ 1,700ha ▪ 11,000t/20,000cs own label 54% red 44% white 1% rosé 1% fortified ▪ PO Box 2013 Paarl 7620 ▪ windmeul@iafrica.com ▪ www.windmeul.com ▪ S 33° 40' 18.1" E 018° 54' 30.6" ▪ 🌐 educational.riffraff.megawatt ▪ **T** +27 (0)21-869-8100/8043

☐ **Winds of Change** *see* Jacques Germanier

☐ **Wind Song** *see* Thor Vintners

☐ **Wine Boutique l'Aghulhas** *see* Breëland Winery

☐ **Winemaster's Reserve** *see* Nederburg Wines

Wine-of-the-Month Club

Wine-of-the-Month is SA's longest-standing and largest wine club, offering members the best-scoring wines in blind tastings by an independent panel of twelve judges. Aside from the familiar delivered-to-your-door service, WotM now also has walk-in outlets, branded as Wine Tonight?, offering both club selections and more widely curated wines, with daily and after-hours private tastings. Claremont and Kenilworth in Cape Town are the first of an envisaged national roll-out. Aside from third-party wines, the club also has its own labels, including Berg en Dal, Boschenheuwel, Jakkalskloof, Klaasenbosch, Lakehurst, Martindale, Mortons, Quartet, Semara, Sentinel, Steenhuis and Willowbrook.

Location: Cape Town ▪ Est 1986 ▪ MD Cliff Collard ▪ Private Bag X2 Glosderry 7702 ▪ cheers@wineofthemonth. co.za ▪ www.wineofthemonth.co.za ▪ **T** +27 (0)21-492-4100

☐ **Winery of Good Hope** *see* Radford Dale
☐ **Wine Thief** *see* The Wine Thief

Wine Village-Hermanus   ⓠ ⓖ

Wine Village at the entrance to Hemel-en-Aarde Valley is the realisation of retailers Paul and Cathy du Toit's dream to bring together the fine wines of South Africa under one roof. Daughter Ulla manages events and the popular annual Hermanus Wine & Food Festival. Their (untasted) house brand is Are We Having Fun Yet?

Location: Hermanus ▪ Map: Walker Bay & Bot River ▪ Map grid reference: A3 ▪ Est 1998 ▪ 1stB 2004 ▪ Open Mon-Fri 9-6 Sat 9-5 Sun 10-3 ▪ Closed Good Fri & Dec 25 ▪ Tasting of wine, craft beer, gin, brandy & olive oil ▪ Owner(s) Paul & Cathy du Toit ▪ ±2,000cs 50% red 50% white ▪ PO Box 465 Hermanus 7200 ▪ winevillage@ hermanus.co.za ▪ www.winevillage.co.za ▪ S 34° 24' 40.7" E 019° 12' 1.9" ▪ ⌨ kilos.amendment.graduating ▪ **T** +27 (0)28-316-3988

Wineways Marketing

Headquartered in Blackheath near Kuils River, substantial negociant business Wineways Marketing buys grapes across the winelands for vinification at Leeuwenkuil and Stellenbosch Vineyards, and marketing under a variety of brand names. The wines, some in bag-in-box, are available locally and in many export markets. Wineways also distributes the De Villiers Wines range. See listing for tasting details.

Black Box range

Merlot ⊘ ★★★ Soft & easy **NV** ⑦ with red berry flavours & a savoury finish. 5L pack, as all this range. **Pinotage** ★★ Plummy sweetness, with hints of dark chocolate on pleasant **NV** ⑦. **Shiraz** ★★ Uncomplicated everyday **NV** ⑦, almost dry, spicy dark-berried fun. **Merlot-Cabernet Sauvignon** ⊘ ★★★ Bouncy red & black berries in smooth, gluggable **NV** ⑦. Unwooded, as all ranges.

Black Tie range

Cabernet Sauvignon ⊘ ★★★ Light bodied, juicy, with plum & chocolate flavours, hint of sweetness on **18** ⑦. **Merlot** ★★ Rounded **19** ⑦ has cheery cherry fruit & a spicy hit. **Pinotage** ★★ Loads of fresh black fruit on juicy & friendly **19** ⑦. **Merlot-Cabernet Sauvignon** ⊘ ★★★ Silky, bursting with succulent fruit & savoury nuances in **19** ⑦. A party animal! **Sauvignon Blanc** ⊘ ★★★ Tropical fruit salad flavours on light-textured **19** ⑦. **Shiraz Natural Sweet** ★★ Sweet dark-berry appeal in **19** ⑦, attractive spice for extra interest.

Coral Reef range

Cabernet Sauvignon ⊘ ★★★ Light, juicy **18** ⑦, plums & chocolate in the flavours, suggestion of sweetness on finish. **Merlot** ★★ Smooth **19** ⑦ offers spice-laced cherries & nice dry conclusion. **Pinotage** ★★ Affable **19** ⑦, generous black fruit in a fresh & sappy body. **Merlot-Cabernet Sauvignon** ⊘ ★★★ Delightful easy-drinker, quite lush & sweet fruited, with balancing touch of savoury in **19** ⑦. **Sauvignon Blanc** ⊘ ★★★ Light, dry & crisp **19** ⑦, with melange of tropical fruits on offer. **Shiraz Natural Sweet** ★★ Dark berries & plenty of sweet appeal to **19** ⑦, also a piquancy that prevents any cloy.

De Villiers Wines range

Cabernet Sauvignon ⓧ ★★★ Raspberry toned, with variety's gripping fruit tannins in **17** ⑦, tad short, as last vintage. **Merlot** ⊘ ★★★ Sunshiny fruit with hints of Xmas spice on very fresh **19** ⑦. **Pinotage** ⊘ ★★★ Generous & rounded, **19** ⑧ nicely layered, too, with dark plum, scrub, smoke & espresso.

Leipoldt 1880 range

Merlot-Cabernet Sauvignon ⊘ ★★★ Equal blend **18** ⑦ is silky, well padded with cranberry & cassis, good grip for food. Satisfying everyday red. **Sauvignon Blanc** ⊘ ★★★ Tropical fruit salad flavours on lightly structured, dry & grassy **19** ⑦. **Fruity Dry White** ⑭ ★★ Name says it all: **NV** ⑦ is dry, friendly, with an apple crunch finish. **Shiraz Natural Sweet** ★★ Balanced sweetness, spice & dark fruit flavours in **19** ⑦⑤, lingers a while. **Smooth Red** (NEW) ★★ Sweet & juicy **NV** ⑦④, red plums & cherries, tasty & balanced sipping.

Tin Cups Screw Cap range
Merlot-Cabernet Sauvignon ★★ Soft, fruity & undemanding **19** ⑦④ slips down easily. **Sauvignon Blanc** ★★ Capsicum, greenpepper & light herbal pleasure on improved **19** ⑦⑥. **Fruity Dry White** (NEW) ★★ Gentle tropical fruit on easygoing **NV** ⑦⑤, concludes with a fresh bite. **Smooth Red** ★★ Light, easy, with dab of sweetness on berried mouthful of latest **NV** ⑦③. Discontinued: **Sweet Rosé**.

Mountain Shadows range
Not tasted: **Cabernet Sauvignon, Merlot, Pinotage, Shiraz, Sauvignon Blanc**.
Discontinued: **Fabulous! range**. — WB

Location: Kuils River ▪ WO: Western Cape ▪ Est 2000 ▪ Closed to public ▪ Owner(s) Carl Schmidt, Stephen Vermeulen & Fanie Marais ▪ Winemaker(s) Pieter Carstens & Corrien Basson (Leeuwenkuil), Bernard Claassen (Stellenbosch Vineyards) ▪ 400,000cs own label 80% red 20% white ▪ Plot 689, Zinfandel Str, Saxenburg Park 2, Blackheath 7580 ▪ info@wine-ways.co.za ▪ www.wine-ways.co.za ▪ **T +27 (0)21-905-7713/6/9**

Winkelshoek Wine Cellar ⓥ
Hennie Hanekom's Winkelshoek portfolio, made by Hendrik Hanekom, includes the Weskus range of easygoing and wallet-friendly table wines and Winkelshoek fortified sweet desserts. Available in retail and hospitality establishments on the West Coast, and sibling winery Schenkfontein near Piketberg (see listing).

Weskus range
Pinotage ⓥ ★★★ Mulberry & plum bouquet, enlivening acidity, decent grip & friendly price: unwooded **17** ⑦⑧ ticks all the everyday red boxes - but note 15% alcohol. **Rooigety** ⓥ ★★★ With moderate tannin & 12.5% alcohol, 'Red Tide' an alternative to white or rosé during the day. Unwooded **17** ⑦⑨ merlot & cab with juicy fruit & crunchy acidity. **Sweet Rosé** ⓥ ★★ Wild strawberries & spice, **17** ⑦① pink's perky acidity lifts its 52 g/l sweetness for casual, uncomplicated sipping. **Chenin Blanc** ⓥ ★★ Bone-dry, light **18** ⑦③ fleeting apricot aromas & flavours. **Sauvignon Blanc** ⓥ ★★ Restrained grassiness, fresh acidity & granadilla finish on **17** ⑦④ preview. **Natural Sweet White** ⓥ ★★ Peaches & florals on **17** ⑦④, pleasing sweetness best enjoyed well chilled.

Winkelshoek range
Hanepoot ⓥ ★★★ Fortified **17** ⑧⓪ marries grapes from white & rare red muscat d'Alexandrie for interesting spiced fruit mouthful energised by bite of 18% alcohol. **Red Muscadel** ⓥ ★★★★ Unctuous **15** ⑧④ fortified dessert has pink-tinged tawny hue, flavours of honey & raisin, gentle alcohol grip. **White Muscadel** ⓥ ★★★ Bright gold in appearance, **16** ⑦⑧ fortified dessert has high-toned talcum powder aroma, very sweet raisin flavours. **Red Jerepigo** ⓥ ★★★ Tentatively rated **17** ⑧① fortified, youthful orangey pink, unusual tomato juice nuance to more classic tealeaf, decidedly sweet yet light footed. **White Jerepigo** ⓥ ★★★★ Tank sample shows some complexity in dried sultana, apple & campfire ash characters; vibrant acidity & alcohol fire keep **17** ⑧④ lively. Not tasted: **Cape Vintage**. — CvZ

Location: Piketberg ▪ WO: Western Cape ▪ Tasting by appt at Schenkfontein Kelders ▪ Owner(s)/cellarmaster(s) Hennie Hanekom ▪ Winemaker(s) Hendrik Hanekom (2011) ▪ PO Box 395 Piketberg 7320 ▪ info@winkelshoek.co.za ▪ www.winkelshoek.co.za ▪ **T +27 (0)22-913-1092**

Winshaw Vineyards ⓥ ⓞ
As well as vineyards, there are pasture-reared chickens and cattle on the substantial Stellenbosch farm owned by the Winshaw family. Winshaw is a resonant name in the last century of Cape wine so it's appropriate that some of the wine off their vines has been going into their own-label range since 2003 - under the Usana name, which was also previously the name under which this entry was given.

Usana range
★★★★ **The Fox Cabernet Sauvignon** Oaky, tobacco aromas on **16** ⑧⑥, reflecting 25% new oak. There's sweet-fruited power, with 14.5% alcohol but also a pronounced herbal note. **15** ★★★★★ ⑨⓪ was a step up.

★★★★ **Chardonnay** (NEW) Restrained & unflashy **18** ⑧⑦, but with good fruit overlaid with spicy, nutty element from 29% new oak. Pleasant richness of texture, everything modestly balanced.

★★★★ Barrel Fermented Chenin Blanc ⓔ Enticing honeysuckle aromas before a platter of pure yellow stonefruit, honey & beeswax. Long & intense **16** ⑧⑥ helped by judicious old oak, natural ferment. Improves on **15 ★★★★** ⑧④, also from Elgin fruit.

★★★★ Pinot Gris Perfumed & charming **18** ⑧⑦, partly oaked, is ripe & rounded but with a little fresh bite. Dry & rather delicious in an unshowy way. Spontaneous ferment, as for all these.

★★★★ Sauvignon Blanc ⓥ Panoply of aromas & flavours on **18** ⑧⑦, with floral, citrus & stonefruit - less green than **17 ★★★★** ⑧④. Attractive, well integrated & balanced, much less aggressive than many.— TJ

Location/map: Stellenbosch ▪ Map grid reference: C8 ▪ WO: Stellenbosch/Elgin ▪ Est/1stB 2003 ▪ Tasting & sales by appt ▪ Farm produce ▪ Weddings & functions ▪ Owner(s) JP & Pierre Winshaw ▪ Winemaker(s) Pierre Winshaw, with Hendrien de Munck (2010, consultant) ▪ Viticulturist(s) Pierre Winshaw ▪ 300ha/45ha (cabs s/f, malbec, merlot, chard, pinot gris, sauv) ▪ 29t/4,000cs own label 40% red 60% white ▪ PO Box 68 Lynedoch 7603 ▪ jp@usana.co.za, pierre@usana.co.za ▪ www.usana.co.za ▪ S 34° 0' 14.42" E 018° 45' 36.97" ▪ ⌨ posterity.firestorm.mayonnaise ▪ **T +27 (0)83-650-9528**

Withington

Charles Withington's easygoing but serious-minded wines are sourced from Darling district, where he's based. Export successes are particularly pleasing — none more so than Voorkamer brandy, entered by his Canadian importer in the Alberta Beverage Awards, where it was 'placed on the podium alongside a French cognac at twice the price!'

Withington range

Malbec ⓔ **★★★★** Tobacco note (but only old oak), good fruit presence on **15** ⑧④, hints of varietal loganberry. Firmly structured & not without seriousness despite tasty drinkability. **Roan Ranger ★★★** From 62% cinsaut with grenache & a dash mourvèdre, **17** ⑧② lacks the expected perfumed fruity charm. Tends to the savoury; fruit there, but the structure a bit lean. Not tasted: **NBC Chardonnay**.

Brandy range

★★★★ Voorkamer 7-year potstilled colombard ⑧⑨ ex Klein Karoo is smooth & charming, with plenty of apricot fruit touched up by spice & floral notes. Aged half in old bourbon barrels, half French oak. Drier & more elegant than many local brandies.— TJ

Location/WO: Darling ▪ Map: Durbanville, Philadelphia & Darling ▪ Map grid reference: A1 ▪ Est 2001 ▪ 1stB 2003 ▪ Tasting & sales at Darling Wine Shop Mon-Sat 10-6 (10-7 in summer) Sun 11-2 ▪ Closed Mar 21, Easter Fri/Sun & Dec 25/26 ▪ Fresh West Coast mussels on order every Friday ▪ Owner(s) Withington family ▪ 2,000cs own label 85% red 10% white 5% potstill brandy ▪ PO Box 236 Darling 7345 ▪ taste@withington. co.za ▪ www.withington.co.za ▪ S 33° 22' 28" E 018° 22' 38" ▪ ⌨ nudge.excluder.lionesses ▪ **T +27 (0)22-492-3971/+27 (0)74-194-1711**

☐ **Withoek** *See Editor's Note*
☐ **Witklip** *see Eerste Hoop Wine Cellar*
☐ **Woestkloof** *see Simelia Wines*
☐ **Wolfkloof** *See Editor's Note*
☐ **Wolftrap** *see The Wolftrap*

Wolf & Woman Wines ⓝⓔⓦ

The woman is maybe Jolandie Fouché herself, crafter of these wines. She does so at Kloovenburg in Swartland, where she is winemaker, bringing in grapes from special areas and soils, working with old vineyards for her own range. The wolf? Her wild spirit, perhaps. Jolandie is 'inspired by the fierce, untamed nature of these glorious creatures'. Both wolf and woman are painted there on the splendid labels. In the bottle is wine expressing origin, rather than intervention in the cellar.

★★★★ Pinotage Joins the welcome, emerging range of new-wave pinotage: **18** ⑧⑦ fresh, light & perfumed, expressing the variety's good acidity, with tannins restrained & not astringent. Arguably just a little short on vinosity & substance. Just 12% alcohol.

★★★★☆ **Chenin Blanc** Another thoroughly satisfying old-oaked Swartland example. Aromas of dried peach, apple & thatch on **18** ⑨① lead to a balanced, harmonious palate with silky texture & good grip, then a fine dry finish with a salty note.— TJ, CvZ

Location: Malmesbury ▪ WO: Swartland ▪ Est/1stB 2018 ▪ Closed to public ▪ Owner(s) Jolandie Fouché ▪ Winemaker(s) Jolandie Fouché (Jan 2018) ▪ 3t/335cs own label 34% red 76% white ▪ 20 Loubser Str, Malmesbury 7300 ▪ jolandie@wolfandwomanwines.com ▪ www.wolfandwomanwines.com ▪ T +27 (0)83-602-5602

☐ **Wolvendrift Private Cellar** *See Editor's Note*
☐ **Women in Wine** *See Editor's Note*

Wonderfontein ⑫

Champagne-method bubbly remains the focus of this family business based in Robertson, lovingly packaged in 'treasure chest' boxes and smart 'handbags' for an unforgettable gift! Last year saw new plantings of pinot noir to increase production, and this has led to new buildings in which to store the fizz as it matures.

Paul René Méthode Cap Classique range

★★★★ **Brut Rosé** Continuing upward curve of quality from **15** ⑧⑦, **16** ★★★★★ ⑨⓪ sparkler radiates style & elegance. Savouriness from 2 years on lees combines with delicate notes of crushed strawberries & rosepetals, sassy acidity & excellent length. For superior celebrations. Pinot noir (75%) & chardonnay.

★★★★ **Brut** Richer style than its pink partner, **16** ⑧⑦ from chardonnay mixes apples, pears & yeasty brioche notes to good effect with fresh acidity & lengthy finish. 24 months on lees.

Wonderfontein range

★★★★ **Wonderfontein Red Muscadel** ⑫ Perfume & flowers on **16** ★★★★ ⑧③ give way to toffee, coffee hints with warm alcohol & just enough acid. Should improve. Last-tasted **11** ⑧⑦ also fragrant, fresh.

La Bonne Vigne Shiraz ★★★ Improved **17** ⑧⓪ shows plenty of typicity with black cherries, warm spices & attractive hint of coffee. Soft tannins & juicy finish add to all-round appeal. **La Bonne Vigne Sauvignon Blanc** ★★★ Straightforward everyday quaffing **19** ⑦⑧, gooseberries, pear drops & slight sweetness at finish. **Wonderfontein White Muscadel** ⑫ ★★★ Appealing floral notes, **16** ⑧⓪'s alcohol still fiery, needs time to integrate, tad more acid would improve. Not tasted: **La Bonne Vigne Merlot**.

The Marais Family range

Merlot ⑫ ★★ Anytime companion **15** ⑦④ has subtle nudge of tannin, light plummy fruit. — CM
Location/map/WO: Robertson ▪ Map grid reference: B6 ▪ Est ca 1884 ▪ Tasting Mon-Fri 9-4 Sat/Sun & pub hols by appt only ▪ Sales Mon-Fri 9–4.30 Sat 9–1 ▪ Tour groups ▪ Owner(s) Paul René Marais ▪ Winemaker(s) Stefan Bruwer ▪ Viticulturist(s) Gert Visser & Gerald Stemmet ▪ (merlot, muscadel r/w, pinot, shiraz, chard, sauv) ▪ PO Box 4 Robertson 6705 ▪ info@wonderfonteinestate.co.za, admin@paulrenemcc.co.za ▪ www.wonderfonteinestate.co.za, www.paulrenemcc.co.za ▪ S 33° 49' 3.5" E 019° 52' 2.1" ▪ 🌐 selling.cross.soloist ▪ T +27 (0)23-626-2212

Woolworths

Universally and affectionately known as 'Woolies', this upmarket, nationwide retail giant has been selling wine for 35 years now, and the philosophy behind its selections has never wavered. 'At Woolworths, we aim to provide the best-edited choice of wines, keeping up with innovations and trends,' explains Rebecca Constable, one of the trio recently running the wine department. She's the buyer for whites and bubblies, Rob Gower handles reds and imports, and both are supported by the vastly experienced Allan Mullins, Cape Wine Master and wine selector for 27 of those 35 years. More than 200 wines are made, blended or selected especially for the Woolworths 'house' label, and these involve boutique to big-brand producers, covering a comprehensive array of styles, varieties and price points (including box packaging). Other wine brands, such as de-alcoholised Lautus, stand side by side on the always-interesting and reasonably priced shelves.

Cabernet Sauvignon range

★★★★ **Diemersdal Reserve Collection Cabernet Sauvignon** Smooth, succulent & creamy **18** ⑧⑧, ripe dark berry fruit & spice from older oak, rich yet beautifully dry & savoury, ready to drink.

★★★★☆ **Grangehurst Cabernet Sauvignon** Ⓑ Smooth & refined **13** ⑨⓪, fruitcake richness & brush of herbs, lovely integration & depth on long, nuanced palate. Follows improved **11** ⑨②. No **12**.

★★★★ **Spier Private Collection Cabernet Sauvignon** Deep & dense, packed with cassis, **17** ⑧⑦'s 18 months oak maturation, 65% new, providing a bed of fine tannins, mixed spice aromas & flavours. Already delicious, can age.

★★★★ **Villiera Cabernet Sauvignon** ⊘ 🐝 Deep cassis, olive & spice on ripe, structured **17** ⑧⑨. Rich, rounded palate framed by judicious oak, 25% new French. Poised & rewarding, it will age well.

Diemersfontein Blackberry Cabernet Sauvignon ★★★ Light bodied & juicy, fruit-filled **18** ⑧② ticks the boxes for everyday enjoyment. **Fairview Cabernet Sauvignon** Ⓑ ★★★★ Lighter, easy-drinking **16** ⑧③ has savoury tone with expressive black fruit, suede tannins. **Kleine Zalze Cabernet Sauvignon** ⓃⒺⓌ ★★★ For earlier drinking, **17** ⑧① fleshy dark berries & plums, juicy, with succulent tannins in support. **Organic NSA Cabernet Sauvignon** ⊘ ★★☆ From Stellar Winery. Berry fruit is there but oaking plays a prominent role in **19** ⑦⑧, savoury & dark toned, perfect for rich dishes. Fairtrade certified. **Spier Woolworths Cabernet Sauvignon** ★★★★ Different styling to last, no new oak, not as boldly ripe or dark-fruited. **18** ⑧④ is smooth & succulent, with immediate taste appeal despite its youth. **Warwick Cape Lady Cabernet Sauvignon** ★★★☆ A get-together with friends wine, consistent & satisfying. Offers tasty mix of dark berries & red cherries in **17** ⑧④, soft tannins & blackberry aftertaste. **Woolworths Cabernet Sauvignon** ⊘ ★★★ Mulberries & dark plums, savoury oak-influenced spicing, **18** ⑧② has friendly tannins, just enough grip for food pairing. Fairtrade certified, by Koopmanskloof.

Merlot range

★★★★ **Jordan Reserve Collection Merlot** A stylish dinner companion, **16** ⑧⑥ has leafy top notes & piquant fruit, creamy texture from French oaking, sleek & food-friendly dry finish.

★★★★ **Shannon Merlot** Fruitcake, dark choc & some pleasing earthiness introduce **18** ⑧⑦. There's sweet fruit on the palate, but no great generosity, with the dry tannin structure almost severe.

★★★★ **Signature Series Merlot** Lovely fruit focus in **17** ⑧⑧ from Spier, plush berries, some spice & chocolate notes from oaking (70% new barrels), tannins supple, texture streamlined, succulent.

★★★★ **Vergelegen Merlot** Splashes of petit verdot & cab franc add heft in **16** ⑧⑦. Stylish & balanced, with ripe berry fruit, supple texture, supportive 16 months French oaking, 40% new.

★★★★ **Villiera Merlot** ⊘ **17** ⑧⑧ improves on **16** ★★★★ ⑧⑤ in density & concentration. Leafy tomato, cedar & spicy fruitcake generosity in soft, rounded package. Supportive cradle of oak, 25% new.

Hartenberg Merlot Reserve Collection ★★★☆ Aromas of plum, coffee & cocoa, **17** ⑧⑤ nimble tannins, spice & berry persistence, perfect winter warmer with hearty dishes. **La Motte Platinum Merlot** ★★★☆ Gentle, textured **17** ⑧④ maintains form in spicy fruitcake appeal. Layered, sleek & rewarding. **Organic NSA Merlot** ⊘ ★★☆ Prominent blackcurrants, a herbal note, some oak-derived savoury spice, **19** ⑦⑦ is light & juicy. Fairtrade certified, from Stellar Winery. **Origami NSA Merlot** ⊘ ★★★☆ No sulphur added to **18** ⑧③, in flush of youth with juicy choc-plum fruit given form & satisfying dryness by ripe grape tannins, deft touch oak (67% American). From Jordan. **Spier Merlot** ⓃⒺⓌ ⊘ ★★★★ Good typicity, red fruit, hint crushed herbs, lightly oaked **18** ⑧③ is sleek & juicy, designed for early drinking. **Woolworths House Cultivar Merlot** ⓃⒺⓌ ⊘ ★★★ From Koopmanskloof, **18** ⑦⑧ is packed with berries, has some smoky tones from French/American oak. Smooth & accessible.

Pinot Noir range

★★★★ **Catherine Marshall Pinot Noir** ⊘ Pleasing aromas on **18** ⑧⑨ from Elgin promise the flavour & refinement then delivered. Clean, fresh & pure, with light tannins & a savoury dimension. Only older oak.

★★★★ **Shannon Pinot Noir** ⊘ Mostly natural ferment, older oak on **18** ⑧⑧. Forceful fruit profile, with a savoury, mushroom element. Muscular structure, grippy tannins, but there's plenty of flavour too.

DMZ Pinot Noir ⊘ ★★★ Smoky plums & damp forest floor, earthy nuances on **18** ⑧⑤ from DeMorgenzon. Balanced, for appealing drinkability. Some substance & food pairing prospects.

Pinotage range

★★★★ **Diemersfontein Pinotage** ⊘ Previewed **18** ★★★★ ⑧⑤ shows focused, concentrated wild berries, varietally typical & fruit driven albeit shade off quality of **17** ⑧⑦.

★★★★ **Diemersfontein Pinotage Reserve** High-toned varietal fruit is prominent in ripe, well-judged **17** ⑧⑧, shows fine structure & texture. Rounded bramble fruit & aromatic notes. 16 months, 50% new oak.

★★★★ **Signature Series Pinotage** Rich & rounded **17** (89) from Beyerskloof shows typical upfront fragrant plum & hint of scrub. The palate is juicy, harmonious & complex, older oak ageing, year, adds creamy vanilla & chocolate.

Bellevue Reserve Collection Pinotage ★★★★ Fresh, juicy **16** (84), ripe raspberry & mulberry fruit, components harmonised by year in mostly older American oak. **Beyerskloof Reserve Collection Pinotage** (Ⓩ) ★★★★ Few months on French oak staves give concentrated black berry & ripe plum fruit of **17** (84) a vanilla sweetness, also evident last vintage. **Coffee Pinotage** ★★★ Overt mocha & charred oak dominate **17** (80) from Diemersfontein, masking red berry fruit. Will have its fans. **Longmarket Pinotage** ★★★ Cocoa dusting for plum & blueberry fruit in juicy **18** (82) from Rooiberg, oak-matured in older barrels & tanks with staves. **Organic NSA Pinotage** (☺) ★★★ From Stellar Winery. Fairtrade certified. Barrel treatment gives **19** (78)'s dark fruit a distinctly savoury overlay, almost mocha chocolate, tannins supple, accessible. Nice match for venison, robust casseroles. **Woolworths Pinotage** (✓) ★★★ Supple, light-bodied & friendly **18** (82) with vivid red & blue berry fruit. By Ken Forrester.

Shiraz range

★★★★ **Hartenberg Shiraz Reserve Collection** A blend of different Hartenberg parcels. **17** (86) spice & new leather laced with plum & violet, full body with firm tannins, savoury notes linger on finish.

★★★★ **Neil Ellis Groenekloof Bush Vine Shiraz** (✓) Delicious aromas & flavours of violet, blackberry, earthy spice & cured meat in **17** (87). Generous but balanced structure, with lifted minerality & floral notes courtesy dash cinsaut (12%).

★★★★ **Reserve Radford Dale Syrah** (Ⓩ) Natural ferment, only 15% new oak enhance immediate appeal of pepper- & scrub-toned **15** ★★★★★ (90); pristine red fruit, agile tannins, a sense of weightless intensity. Superb. Decant now or cellar 5+ years. **14** (87) also very fine.

★★★★ **Saronsberg Life is Fine Shiraz** Powerful, with prominent fruit sweetness elbowing out ethereal spice, but **17** (87) full of interest, structure & drinkability with food. 40% new oak.

★★★★ **Signature Shiraz** By Hartenberg. Friendly **17** (86)'s plush plum flavours complemented by dark choc aromas, finish is savoury with soft tannins, great for pairing with lamb.

. . . .

Kleine Zalze Shiraz (✓) (🍷) ★★★ Spice & vibrant red plums, mulberries, with a good sprinkling of dried herbs in **17** (85). Rounded, smooth & very food-friendly.

. . . .

Chocolate Shiraz (Ⓩ) ★★★ More coffee & vanilla than chocolate, **17** (80) from Diemersfontein will appeal to fans of the aromatised style. Generously full bodied, densely fruity. **Organic NSA Shiraz** (☺) ★★★ In Stellar Winery's **19** (79), use of oak staves carefully done, adding spice, cocoa but no tannin barrier to the fruit's succulence. Fairtrade approved. **Woolworths Shiraz** (✓) ★★★ From Darling Cellars, **18** (82) has variety-true lily & red berry fruit, friendly tannins, tarry finish, is ready to enjoy.

Niche Red Cultivars

★★★★ **Bellevue Reserve Collection Malbec** (✓) Very smooth after year in 50% new French oak, fynbos & dried herb aromas adding nuance to black plum & berry fruit on **16** (87)'s generous mid-palate.

★★★★ **Diemersfontein Malbec Reserve** Stylish **17** (87) has fine, ripe tannins, savoury-aromatic fruit, credible heft supported by 14 months in French oak barrels, 50% new. Splash roobernet.

★★★★ **Terra del Capo Reserve Collection Sangiovese** (✓) Variety-true **16** (86) has sour cherry flavour, fresh tannin & acid bite, Italianate dryness. Ready now for food or solo. By Anthonij Rupert Wyne, like more delicate **15** ★★★★ (85).

Ken Forrester Reserve Collection Grenache (✓) ★★★★ Chalky grip on bright **18** (85) balances lively raspberry fruit & spice. Succulent, vibrant, with good pliability & texture. Deep & long yet approachable.

Boplaas Tinta Barocca (Ⓩ) ★★★★ Eminently drinkable **17** (84) shows black fruit & leather, with lively acid & soft tannins.

Red Blends

★★★★★ **Jordan Cobblers Hill** Always-impressive & -delicious Bordeaux blend, mostly cab & merlot, splash cab franc, **15** (91) textbook cigarbox, hedgerow & cedar tones, firm tannins framing pure dark fruit. Better knit than **14** (91), with uncharacteristic vanilla nuance from portion American oak.

★★★★ **La Motte Platinum Cabernet Sauvignon-Merlot** (✓) Succulent black fruit appeal on **17** (87) improves on **16** ★★★★ (84). Subtle spicy oak, rich textured length. Merlot just 25%.

★★★★ **Neil Ellis Reserve Cabernet Sauvignon-Merlot** ⊘ Fresh & bright **17** (86), upfront red fruit flavours & leafy coolness from 3% cab franc. Smooth tannin structure makes for easy drinking.

★★★★ **Warwick Cape Lady Cape Blend** ⊘ Trio pinotage, shiraz & cab. Ripe plum, red & dark cherry aromas lead to dark spice & savoury flavours, nimble tannins make **17** (87) enjoyable now & for a few years.

★★★★ **Alto 1693** ⊘ Tasty, well-priced red from same stable as SA stalwart Alto Rouge. **17** (86) piquant berries, creamy vanilla from smidgen American oak, just-right tannins for solo, food pairing or cellaring few years. Similar shiraz blend as **16** ★★★★ (85), with more to offer.

★★★★ **La Motte Platinum Shiraz-Grenache** Deep, rich & concentrated palate on **17** (89) 50/50 blend. Black fruit with herb sheen adds appeal. Supple, rounded & approachable.

★★★★ **Reserve Collection Shiraz-Grenache-Mourvèdre** ⊘ Seductive rosepetal nuance to spicy, black cherry-toned **16** (86) from Ken Forrester. Structured, dry & inky, the seasoned oak is unnoticeable but supports the fruit.

★★★★ **Saronsberg SGM** Enticing **17** (86) mostly shiraz (74%), with grenache & mourvèdre; ripely rich, berried rather than spiced, structure from 25% new oak & good tannic grip. Finishes tad sweet, as **16** (89).

Delheim Reserve Collection Cabernet Sauvignon-Merlot (⨂) ★★★★ Very enjoyable everyday drinking in **16** (85), mixing plenty of blackcurrants & cassis with juicy red plums & cherries. **Diemersdal Reserve Collection Merlot-Malbec** ★★★☆ Abundant red & black berries mingle with earthy spice in **18** (83), generous savoury conclusion. 14 months older-oak ageing give dark chocolate nuance. **Grand Rouge** ⊘ ★★★☆ Cab leads 30% merlot in succulent, spicy fruitcake-toned **17** (85) blend from La Motte. Subtle & approachable, with light tannic grip. **Ovation Cabernet Sauvignon-Merlot** ★★★ Tasty, accessible, fruit-forward Bordeaux blend by Thokozani, **17** (80) sound everyday drinking. **DMZ Concerto Red** ⊘ ★★★☆ Ripe, generous, warm-hearted shiraz blend from DeMorgenzon. **17** (85) full of flavour, easygoing, with just enough grip. Last-made **14** ★★★★ (87) was more structured. **Longmarket Shiraz-Cabernet Sauvignon** ★★★ Produced by Rooiberg, mostly shiraz **18** (81) has splashes cab & petit verdot for ripe, soft, juicy black fruit & subtle spice. **Diemersfontein Cabernet Sauvignon-Shiraz** ⊘ ★★★☆ Soundly formed, fruit-driven **17** (85) is 60% cab. Appealingly savoury core, with hints of tobacco & liquorice. **Portuguese Connection** ★★★☆ Earthy red- & black-berried fruit with soft spice & tannins in **17** (83), from near-equal tinta & cab with 25% touriga. By Boplaas.

Rosé Wines

Bellingham Strawberry Rosé (⨂) ★★★ Pretty dry pink from mainly pinotage **18** (82) is fragrant & perfumed, with lovely strawberry & lemon favours. **Delaire Graff Empress Rosé** (NEW) ★★★☆ Chic onionskin hue on **19** (85) is part of the smart, restrained & refined whole. Subtle sweet fruit, lively & dry. From cab franc. **Delheim Pinotage-Shiraz Rosé** (⨂) ★★★ Cheerful & pretty **18** (81) gains from tiny touch of muscat. Technically dry, but few grams sugar add delicious confected note to jammy red fruit. **Diemersdal Rosé** ★★★ Candyfloss pink **19** (80) goes up a notch on previous with delicate rosepetal aroma, crunchy cranberry fruit & zippy dry finish. Delightful summery wine from grenache. **Light Rosé** ⊘ ★★★ Blueberry & raspberry appeal to bright, low-alcohol (9%) pink from pinot noir. **19** (82) by Villiera. **Organic Ladybird Rosé** (⊘) ★★★ From Laibach. Chenin (60%) & sauvignon, with 5% pinotage giving **19** (81) its delicate pink hue. Light, crisply dry, the predominantly white varieties emphasise freshness. **Steenberg Rosé** ⊘ ★★★★ Bone-dry **19** (83) pink from mainly syrah with 20% cinsaut, lipsmackingly fresh & zesty, with cranberry, pomegranate & herbal finish. **Tranquille Blush** ⊘ ★★★☆ From Haute Cabrière. NV (85) dry rosé from pinot noir & chardonnay with lime & strawberry fruit, creamy conclusion. **Villiera Pinot Noir Rosé** (⨂) ★★★ Fruit basket & floral whiffs, **17** (78) a light, dry & zesty easy-sipper. **Warwick Cape Lady Rosé** ★★★ Bone-dry & zesty **19** (81). Light bodied, with restrained 11.5% alcohol, spice & red berry flavours. Super sashimi/sushi partner from pinotage. **Longmarket Pinotage Rosé** (⨂) ★★★ Cherry & strawberry ease & approachability to semi-dry **17** (82) pink from Villiera. Bright, light & refreshing, just 11.3% alcohol.

Chardonnay range

★★★★ **DMZ Chardonnay** ⊘ Appealing vanilla & pear flavours on **18** (87) from DeMorgenzon. Light oak influence, more breadth than **17** ★★★★ (85), succulent & satisfying.

★★★★ **Hartenberg Reserve Collection Chardonnay** From various parcels on the Hartenberg estate. **18** (87) intense lime & chamomile notes offer great drinking pleasure. Vanilla spice & citrus in the aftertaste.

★★★★☆ **Ladybird Chardonnay** ⊘ ⊘ 🐝 By Laibach. Naturally made, combo older barrels, concrete 'eggs' & stainless steel; splash chenin. Citrus the main players, grapefruit, lemon, tangerine, while **18** ⑨③'s almond seam adds richness, length, complexity. Individual, sophisticated.

★★★★☆ **Neil Ellis Barrel Fermented Elgin Chardonnay** ⊘ Stewed quince & baked apple pie on **18** ⑨①, smooth, with vanilla crème brûlée flavours & texture, a fresh citrus bite to finish. Rounded & harmonious, with depth & length.

★★★★ **Reserve Collection Unoaked Chardonnay** Food-styled **18** ⑧⑦, restrained lemon & lime fruit, taut body & brisk acidity. Impressive & tasty example of unwooded style by chardonnay specialist Jordan.

Organic Chardonnay ⊘ ★★★ No oak used in Stellar Winery's Fairtrade-certified dry **19** ⑦⑧; gentle citrus notes, refreshing appeal. **Woolworths Chardonnay** ★★☆ Unwooded **19** ⑦⑨ from Weltevrede zesty lemon tones, brisk & perky.

Chenin Blanc range

★★★★ **Ken Forrester Reserve Collection Chenin Blanc** ⊘ Gentle oak gloss (just 5% of wine wooded) to vibrant nectarine fruit on **18** ★★★★ ⑧⑤. Ripe but restrained, with fresh balanced acidity & long honeyed finish. Less nuanced than **17** ⑧⑥.

★★★★ **Spier Private Collection Chenin Blanc** Barrel fermented/aged 12 months on lees, **18** ⑧⑥ almond-layered from oaking, its stonefruit brightened by citrus notes. Essentially a full-bodied, full-flavoured wine, offers a lot of pleasure.

Kleine Zalze Chenin Blanc ⑦ ★★★☆ Creamy & rounded, brimming with fleshy orchard & tropical fruit, zesty lemon finish in **19** ⑧⑤. Very moreish. **Reserve Collection Unwooded Chenin Blanc** ⊘ ⑦ ★★★☆ Forthcoming pear, nectarine & ripe apple in the aromas & flavours of **19** ⑧⑤ from Simonsig. Delightful & bargain priced.

DMZ Chenin Blanc ⊘ ★★★★ Feisty **19** ⑧③ not as easygoing, with tad less ripe fruit than previous. Pithy almond paste nuance invites some creamy food pairing. **Villiera Chenin Blanc** ⊘ ★★★★ Lively **19** ⑧⑤, with good nectarine succulence, breadth from extended lees contact & 35% barrel-fermented portion. **Longmarket Chenin Blanc** ★★★ Tropical fruit appeal on **18** ⑧② matched by vivacious acidity. Unoaked, succulent & crisply zesty, from Ken Forrester. **Organic Chenin Blanc** ⊘ ★★★ Consistent styling in Stellar Winery's **19** ⑧①, crunchy green apple freshness, sleek (12.5% alcohol) & vibrant. Backed by Fairtrade. Not tasted: **Woolworths Chenin Blanc**.

Sauvignon Blanc range

★★★★ **Cape Point Vineyards Cape Town Sauvignon Blanc** A splash of (unoaked) semillon adds breadth to the bright freshness of **19** ⑧⑥ - & perhaps the hint of citrus, though ripe passionfruit notes dominate. Integrated & balanced.

★★★★ **Delaire Graff White Rock** ⊘ Generously aromatic **19** ⑧⑥ packed with tropical & subtle citrus flavour. Softly silky texture, broadened by a little semillon, sauvignon's bright acidity giving stony firmness.

★★★★ **Diemersdal Sauvignon Blanc** Orchard fruit, gooseberry & citrus appeal on **19** ⑧⑦. Balanced, complex with fruity depth, signature freshness & wet stone finish. More serious sibling of 'Passionfruit'.

★★★★ **Reserve Collection Nitida Sauvignon Blanc** Light **18** ★★★☆ ⑧④ offers signature grapefruit & lemon zest appeal & succulence. Bright, easy acidity guarantees summertime refreshment, though tad less impressive, concentrated than **17** ⑧⑨.

★★★★☆ **Shannon Sauvignon Blanc** ⊘ Fresh passionfruit dominates aromas of **18** ⑨⓪, with a little peach & blackcurrant & stony element. Good texture & grip, with succulently bright but unaggressive acidity.

★★★★ **Spier Sauvignon Blanc** 🆕 ⊘ Gooseberries & passionfruit fill the glass, **19** ⑧⑧ is expressively fruity, zesty fresh, the touch of minerality at the end an ideal food match. Good sauvignon typicity.

★★★★ **Steenberg Sauvignon Blanc** Crisp, elegant **19** ⑧⑦ gains extra weight from lees contact (no semillon component this vintage). Fruit forward, zesty gooseberry & blackcurrant, good length & finish.

Durbanville Hills Sauvignon Blanc ★★★☆ Plenty of attractive typicity in **19** ⑧③. Mixes green peas, peppers & tropical passionfruit in easy-drinking, enjoyable wine. **Kleine Zalze Sauvignon Blanc** ★★★☆ Grass, tinned pea & pineapple fruit on zesty **19** ⑧③, fresh & vibrant for a summer picnic. **Organic Sauvignon Blanc** ⊘ ★★★ Slender (12% alcohol) & refreshingly dry, **19** ⑧①'s pear & winter melon flavours a good varietal fit. By Stellar Winery, Fairtrade endorsed. **Ovation Sauvignon Blanc** ★★★

Grape source changes from Robertson to cool Elgin & Piekenierskloof in **18** (80), shows pleasing intensity, substance & structure. By Thokozani. **Passionfruit Sauvignon Blanc ★★★** Green, grassy effortlessness in **19** (80), some tropical fruit nuances & bright lemon tang on the finish. By Diemersdal.

Niche White Cultivars

★★★★ Noble Late Harvest ⊘ From viognier, **18** (87) botrytis dessert offers richly sweet honeysuckle, marmalade & peach flavours but has ample acidity to freshen. Harmony of fruit, acidity & oak (9 months, none new) is impeccable. Clean & poised finish. 375 ml by Ken Forrester.

Woolworths Moscato ★★★ Trademark grapey sweetness of rare muscats morio & ottonel on charmer from Villiera is balanced by zippy acidity in **19** (82). Pleasantly tangy. Additional appeal in lowish 11.7% alcohol. **Woolworths Pinot Grigio ★★☆** One of only a few on the market, from Van Loveren. **19** (78) crisp summer fruit, some food-friendly minerality on the finish, elegantly dry. **Ken Forrester Reserve Collection Viognier** ⊘ **★★★★** Trademark peach notes on fresh, unwooded **19** (83). Lively citrus flavour & vibrant acidity. Shorter & lighter than impressive **17 ★★★★** (87).

White Blends

★★★★ Chardonnay-Pinot Noir ⊘ Very pale **19** (86) dry rosé from Haute Cabrière is 78% chardonnay, satisfyingly full & generous body with a nice salty twist on finish.

★★★★ Reserve Collection Nitida Sauvignon Blanc-Semillon ⊘ Fynbos edge to gooseberry-toned **18** (87), creamy yet tangy & taut, improves on **17 ★★★☆** (85), more sauvignon (60%) than semillon but harmony & long succulence result.

....

Chenin Blanc-Pinotage Reserve Collection (🏆) **★★★** Simonsig's palest pink **19** (81) bursts with tropical & orchard fruit flavours, fresh & lively with lipsmacking lemon tang.

....

Longmarket Sauvignon Blanc-Chenin Blanc ⊘ **★★★★** Granadilla & grapefruit vivacity on bright **19** (85) 60/40 mix. Good intensity & balance of fresh acid on summer sipper from Villiera. **Villiera Dry White ★★★** Was 'Natural White', remains a zero-additive unwooded blend by Villiera. Unfussy but creative mix of riesling & chardonnay, **19** (82) usual lime & pineapple tang, rounded body from natural ferment. **Cape Sweet White** (⊗) **★** Wellington Wines's charming **NV** (69) for the sweet tooth, but doesn't cloy.

Méthode Cap Classique Sparkling range

★★★★ Brut Rosé ⊘ Cranberry tang to improved **NV** (89) dry pink sparkler from chardonnay, pinotage, pinot noir & meunier. Rounded & creamy notes balanced by fresh, crisp acidity. Long rich finish from 18 months on lees. Also in 375 ml. By Villiera, as all these unless noted.

★★★★ NSA Pinot Noir Rosé No-sulphur-added dry sparkler by MCC pioneer Simonsig. Fresh & cheerful salmon-pink **18** (88) has fine & persistent mousse, vibrant red berry fruit, with delicate spice & savoury undertone from 10 months on the lees.

★★★★ Brut Natural 15 (88) follows **14** (89) in quality & zero dosage as well as 42 months on lees. Creamy, evolved marmalade notes balanced by vivid acid & pithy verve. Complex & poised.

★★★★☆ Signature Vintage Reserve Brut (🏅) Adds 'Signature' to name. Brioche, limestone & sea air complexity on **13** (94) bubbles. Like standout **12 ★★★★★** (95), rich yet taut & tangy. Lovely breadth of flavour from chardonnay (60%), pinot noir & dab meunier, 72 months on lees with 25% portion in (older) oak for 6. Poised & long.

Brut ⊘ **★★★★** Zippy citrus & maritime notes on **NV** (85) bubbly from chardonnay (50%), pinot noir & pinotage (replacing meunier). Toasty biscuit richness from 18 months on lees, like previous, but tad less serious, complex. **Light Brut** ⊘ **★★★☆** Crisp **NV** (85) fun bubbly, citrus-tangy & low in alcohol (9.6%), from chardonnay, pinot noir & pinotage. **Demi Sec ★★★★** Ripe apple & sourdough appeal to off-dry **NV** (83) sparkler from Villiera. Acid brightness offsets gentle sweetness & yeasty lees notes.

Sparkling Wines

Spumante Rosé ★★★ Strawberry, cranberry & piquant ruby grapefruit flavours pop in sweet pink **NV** (77) fizzer by Rooiberg. **Avivado Sec-Si** ⊘ **★★★★** Fizz from chenin (60%) & chardonnay in novel crown-capped bottle. **NV** (85) appealing crisp apricot & lime zest with light sweetness. By Villiera. **Spumante Brut ★★★** Fun times call for **NV** (79) with lively sparkle, green apple sherbet intensity, great for Buck's Fizz. By Rooiberg. **Steenberg Sparkling Sauvignon Blanc** ⊘ **★★★★** Short-aged sparkler, not officially méthode cap classique, but so happy & fun it hardly matters. **NV** (84) has grassy notes & tropical fruit in its ovely summery froth. **Spumante Doux** ★★☆ Sweet **NV** (79) bubbly by Rooiberg has less than 9% alcohol with sweet, uncloying grape, white peach & red apple flavours.

1L Box range

Dry Red ★★ Uncomplicated, friendly (13% alcohol) **NV** (75), plenty of fruity flavours but dry enough for food matching. From Simonsvlei, as all below. **Light Red** ★★ Appealing if light berry aromas & flavours to match translucent cherry hue & low 9% alcohol of **NV** (75), less plump than last so acid flick in tail more obvious. **Crisp White** ★★ Generous melon & peach fruit, lively acidity & dash sugar for extra sippability in latest **NV** (73). **Light White** ★★ Low-alcohol (9.5%) **NV** (72) is also light on aroma & flavour but has plenty of tart appley acidity. **Sweet Red** ★★ Natural Sweet **NV** (75) shows appealing berries & slight leafiness, well-judged sugar for uncloying quaffing. Just 11% alcohol, too. **Natural Sweet Rosé** ★★ Raspberry- & strawberry-toned **NV** (74) has lively acidity to neatly balance the sweetness, bonus of low alcohol.

2L Box range

Woolworths Merlot ⟨✓⟩ ★★★ Ripe plums & prunes of **19** (77) joined by touch of leafiness in the flavours, astringent nuance on finish. Enjoy with food. **Woolworths Sauvignon Blanc** ★★ Bright & breezy **19** (76) has grassy aromas & flavours, lively finish, reined-in 11% alcohol.

3L Box range

Dry Red ★★ Fruity, uncomplicated & easygoing **NV** (75) for get-togethers with friends. **Light Red** ⟨✓⟩ ★★★ Low-alcohol (9%) **NV** (77) has aromas & flavours of berries, bright acidity & whisper of tannin. **Crisp White** ★★ Few grams sugar up the drinkability of latest **NV** (73), fruit filled & zesty. **Light White** ★★ The calorie counter's friend, with its low (9.5%) alcohol, though **NV** (72) a tad neutral & brisk. **Natural Sweet Red** ★★ Soft & balanced **NV** (75) has gentle nibble of tannin, modest 11% alcohol, slips down easily. **Natural Sweet Rosé** ★★ Lively acidity balancing the sugar, low alcohol (7.6%), & raspberry & strawberry flavours make latest **NV** (74) an attractive, not over-sweet drink. **Sweet White** ★★ Enough grapey flavour, sugar & alcohol (9%) to ensure **NV** (73) is a smooth, silky & satisfying glassful.

5L Box range

Dry Red ★★ Just the right wine, & pack size, for a party! Fresh & fruity **NV** (75) slips down smoothly. **Crisp White** ★★ As advertised, **NV** (73) is white & crisp, with melon & peach appeal. **Sweet Red** ★★ Smooth Natural Sweet **NV** (75), understated but pleasant berry aromas & flavours, well-balanced sugar & satisfying vinosity (11% alcohol). **Natural Sweet Rosé** ★★ Low-alcohol **NV** (74) has bright acidity & ripe berry fruit for fresh, uncloying sipping. — Various tasters

WO: Various ▪ Buyer Rob Gower T +27 (0)21-407-7644 RobGower@woolworths.co.za ▪ Buyer Rebecca Constable T +27 (0)21-407-3162 RebeccaConstable@woolworths.co.za ▪ Selector Allan Mullins T +27 (0)21-407-7443 AllanMullins@woolworths.co.za ▪ Owner(s) Woolworths Holdings ▪ Woolworths House 93 Longmarket Str Cape Town 8000 ▪ www.woolworths.co.za ▪ T +27 (0)21-407-9111

☐ **#WOPrieska** *see* Lowerland
☐ **Word Collection** *see* Rascallion Wines
☐ **Workhorse** *see* Ken Forrester Wines
☐ **Xaro** *see* Stellenrust
☐ **Xenna** *see* Annex Kloof Wines
☐ **Y** *see* Yonder Hill

Yardstick Wines

⟨♀⟩

The driving force behind Yardstick Wines is Adam Mason, winemaker/viticulturist for Stellenbosch's Mulderbosch Vineyards, who are partners in this enterprise. Adam finds the vineyards and, using Mulderbosch facilities, makes the wines to best reflect their terroir. Named after their single vineyards, except for Old School, a stylistic inspiration, there's a story behind every site, including the lamentable uprooting of rare Montpellier-clone chenin at Driehoek, '18 being the last vintage. Though volumes are boutique, at only 1,000 cases, there has been international success: two top New York listings, a restaurant and wine bar, La Colline Semillon winning a Norwegian tender, and top professional ratings for the rosé.

Raised By Wolves range

★★★★ Bonniemile Cabernet Sauvignon Enclosed 1986 vineyard on koffieklip (ferricrete) Stellenbosch soils. **17** ★★★★★ ⑨⓪ nothing overt, just lovely restraint & balance: blackcurrant & spice, hint of dried herbs, graphite, sleek & polished. Improves on **16** ⑧⑧.

★★★★ Old School As implied, this a traditional blend of cab & cinsaut. Latter's 66% dictates, 18 months older barrels for spicing, but **17** ⑧⑥'s vivid cranberry fruit shines through. Light textured & succulent, just enough grip for food. Also in 375 ml & 1.5L, as La Colline Semillon.

★★★★☆ 777 Chardonnay ⓐ Name refers to Piekenierskloof vines' altitude. **18** ⑨③ has great fruit intensity, white peach (flesh & kernel), tangerine hint, then lime finish, but all taut, tightly focused. Only external influence is subtle oak, just 17% new.

★★★★ Driehoek Chenin Blanc Rare old Montpellier clone, vines since uprooted, **18** ⑧⑧ has restraint, finesse, elegance (12.5% alcohol). Stonefruit & kernels, 9 months French oak, as all the whites & rosé, for cinnamon & nutmeg spicing. Fresh, finishes long.

★★★★ Errigal Sauvignon Blanc ⓃⒺⓌ From Elgin, a slatey entry, delicate lemon & lemongrass nuances. Bunch-pressed **18** ⑧⑦ is oaked, shows in the flavours & finish as a toasty note. Lovely food wine.

★★★★☆ La Colline Semillon ⓐ Textbook semillon from 1930s Franschhoek block, fermented/matured in neutral oak, **18** ⑨③ waxy, subtle green plum, becoming mineral & saline on the palate. Wonderfully balanced, spice the merest hint; masterly respect of terroir.

★★★★ La Colline 'Semillon Gris' As sibling, from venerable Franschhoek vines, but copper-hued 'gris' much rarer, possibly red semillon mutation. Carbonic maceration & oaking, trim **18** ⑧⑧ hard to pin down: subtle red berries, leafy, but also mineral. Intriguing, individual.

Newlands Meunier ★★★☆ Only varietal bottling in guide of this locally rare black grape, aka pinot meunier, associated with bubbly production. Pale copper colour, rosé-like, elegant (11% alcohol) & dry **18** ⑧⑤ has gentle cranberry & raspberry notes, ends zesty-fresh. In abeyance: **Limestone Pinot Noir**, **Karibib Chardonnay**, **Bonniemile Muscat Blanc**.

Yardstick range
In abeyance: **Pinot Noir**, **Chardonnay**.
Discontinued: **Marvelous range**. — CR

Location/map: Stellenbosch ▪ Map grid reference: C5 ▪ WO: Stellenbosch/Franschhoek/Piekenierskloof/Elgin ▪ Est/1stB 2009 ▪ Tasting by appt ▪ Owner(s) Adam Mason in partnership with Mulderbosch Vineyards ▪ Winemaker(s) Adam Mason ▪ Raised By Wolves 1,000cs 25% red 75% white ▪ adam@yardstickwines.com ▪ S 33° 53' 22.8" E 018° 49' 8.3" ▪ ⒨ jacket.panels.dwelled ▪ **T +27 (0)82-924-3286**

Yonder Hill   ⓠ ⑪ ⓞ ⓑ

Seasoned winemaker/viticulturist Abé Beukes, consulting for this boutique winery on the Helderberg, has been busy introducing tannat and new cabernet vines to the classic Bordeaux red mix. Meanwhile the Naudé family owners have been hard at work upgrading the tasting room, re-landscaping the gardens and opening a deli, stocking their own Ankole craft beer, named for the breed of their resident big-horn cattle.

Premium range

★★★★ Merlot ② Seductive nose of dark berries, spicy fruitcake & vanilla oak, **14** ⑧⑥ creamy & full, supple tannins & fresh grip on the finish. Perfect for grilled meat.

★★★★ Inanda ② More complexity on cab franc-led Bordeaux blend **15** ⑧⑦ than **14** ★★★★ ⑧④. Floral aromas, a good black-fruit flavour punch balanced by silky tannins.

★★★★ Nicola The other cab is in charge of this 4-way Bordeaux sibling to Inanda, cab franc reduced to 18%, equal with merlot & petit verdot. **16** ⑧⑥ intense dark fruit flavour with hints of dried thyme & cedary French oak (66% new), spiced plum finish shaped by firm tannins.

Danilo Rosé ★★★ Enticing peach & maraschino cherry notes woven with sweet spice. **19** ⑧① fresh, dry, with appetising zestiness. Merlot & grenache, concluding on ripe berry note. Tasted ex tank, as next. **Sauvignon Blanc** ★★★ Restrained aromas of gooseberry & melon, **19** ⑧⓪ dry & crisp, elegant & very drinkable.

Y range

Merlot ★★★ Preview of **18** ⑧⓪ promises copious drinking pleasure. Cherry & plum aromas, adding dark chocolate & cinnamon on juicy, soft & svelte palate. — GM

Location/WO: Stellenbosch ▪ Map: Helderberg ▪ Map grid reference: C3 ▪ Est 1989 ▪ 1stB 1993 ▪ Tasting & sales Mon-Fri 9—4 Sat (Nov-Feb) 10-4 ▪ Closed all pub hols ▪ Cellar tours by appt only ▪ Function & conference venue: functions@yonderhill.co.za ▪ Tour groups ▪ Gift shop ▪ Deli ▪ Olives & olive oil tasting ▪ Ankole craft beer ▪ Owner(s) Naudé family ▪ Cellarmaster(s)/winemaker(s) Abé Beukes (2014) ▪ Viticulturist(s) Abé Beukes ▪ 14ha/5ha (cabs s/f, merlot, p verdot) ▪ 50t/15,000cs own label 80% red 15% white 5% rosé ▪ PO Box 914 Stellenbosch 7599 ▪ wines@yonderhill.co.za ▪ www.yonderhill.co.za ▪ S 34° 2' 22.5" E 018° 49' 40.2" ▪ 📷 superstore.rekindling.handwritten ▪ **T +27 (0)21-855-1008**

☐ **Zahir** *see* Lateganskop Winery
☐ **Zakkie Bester** *see* Bester Family Wines
☐ **Zalze** *see* Kleine Zalze Wines

Zanddrift Vineyards - Chapel Cellar

Owned by retired Singapore architect Koh Seow Chuan, Zanddrift boutique winery's mostly exported cab/shiraz blend, Chapel Cellar Myrna, named for the arch-roofed visitor locale near Paarl, is untasted this edition, and the visitor facilities closed till next year due to redevelopment.

Location: Paarl ▪ Est 1995 ▪ Closed to public ▪ Owner(s) Windsharp Trading 23, Koh Seow Chuan (Singapore) ▪ Winemaker(s)/viticulturist(s) Christo Jacobs ▪ 8.5ha (cab, shiraz) ▪ PO Box 1302 Suider-Paarl 7624 ▪ zanddrift@telkomsa.net ▪ **T +27 (0)21-863-2076/+27 (0)82-256-5006**

Zandvliet Wine Estate   ⓘ ◎ ♿

A shiraz specialist for over four decades, this historic Robertson estate was purchased in 2015 by ANB Investments (best known for its ClemenGold mandarin brand), raising concern about citrus replacing grapes. 'Rest assured, Zandvliet wines are here to stay,' says GM/winemaker Jacques Cilliers, whose vintages enjoy growing critical success. 'We've planted more shiraz, and we've also established mourvèdre, grenache and carignan for a Rhône-style blend.'

Hill of Enon range

★★★★ Small Berry Pick Shiraz ⓐ Flagship from chalky outcrop, **17** ⑧⑧ bunch-selected & -fermented, luscious, ripe, tangy black & blue fruit, sweet wood spice & dark chocolate after 20 months in equal French/American oak, 50% new. Shade less fresh/elegant than standout **16 ★★★★☆** ⑨⓪, still delicious, ageworthy.

Occasional release: **Terroir Chardonnay**.

Kalkveld range

★★★★ Shiraz Poised & refined at 13.5% alcohol, **16** ⑧⑨ leaves chalky impression (mouthfeel & taste), also brims with plums, berries & subtle oak spice from larger French oak barrels, 30% new.

Zandvliet Estate range

★★★★ Shiraz ⊘ Aged 2 years in mostly older French oak, **16** ⑧⑦ has juicy red fruit seasoned with pepper, chocolate on the finish. Approachable in youth but chalky tannins suggest some ageing potential.

★★★★ Chardonnay Naturally fermented, aged 4 months in older French barrels, **19** ⑧⑨ has tangy citrus & stonefruit flavours, satin texture, fresh & spicy finish. **18** sold out untasted.

★★★★ Sauvignon Blanc ⓧ Brief lees contact gives some weight & mineral smoothness to **18** ⑧⑥, redolent of lime & passionfruit, focused & refreshing at under 13% alcohol. **17** sold out untasted.

★★★★ VLW Cape Vintage Shiraz Estate's signature grape inspanned for 'port'; **14** ⑧⑥ more complex than **13 ★★★★** ⑧③ after 4 years in very old oak, with liquorice & smoke notes persisting beyond overt, decadent black cherry & mocha sweetness.

White Muscat Natural Sweet ★★★★ Friendly low-alcohol (±7%) **19** ⑧⑤ packed with fresh peach & grape flavours, floral on the nose & spicy on the finish.

My Best Friend range
Cape Red ★★★ Well-padded with juicy red berry fruit, unwooded **NV** ⑦⑧ perfect for pizza nights. **Semi-Sweet** Ⓠ ★★☆ Lemon-drop tangy sweetness on light **18** ⑦⑧, a good Asian food match. **Cape White** Ⓠ ★★★ Fruity, easy-drinking **18** ⑦⑦ mostly chenin, with partners sauvignon & chardonnay. — JG
Location: Ashton ▪ Map/WO: Robertson ▪ Map grid reference: C4 ▪ Est 1867 ▪ 1stB 1975 ▪ Tasting, sales & cellar tours Mon-Fri 9–5 Sat 10-4 ▪ Closed Easter Fri/Sun, Dec 25/26 & Jan 1 ▪ Tour groups ▪ Private tastings by appt ▪ Art exhibition ▪ Winemaker(s) / GM Jacques Cilliers (Dec 2011) ▪ PO Box 36 Ashton 6715 ▪ info@zandvliet.co.za ▪ www.zandvliet.co.za ▪ S 33° 50' 50.7" E 020° 2' 13.7" ▪ ⓦ stringency.spasmed.senator ▪ **T +27 (0)23-615-1146**

Zandwijk ⓠ ⑪ ⓺

Dating back to 1693, this Paarl mountainside farm is SA's only fully kosher boutique cellar, where both the sweet Kleine Draken and dry Unorthodox ranges are produced under strict supervision of the Cape Beth Din, with a mashgiach present from grape crushing through flash pasteurisation and fermentation to bottling.

Unorthodox range
Merlot-Cabernet Sauvignon Ⓠ ★★★★ Mevushal & kosher for Passover (as both ranges) blend aimed at the fine-wine market, **14** ⑧③ suitably careful oaking (French only for cab, some American for merlot) adds attractive spicing to concentrated fruit. Paarl WO. **Chenin Blanc** Ⓠ ★★★ Pineapple & baked apple pie flavours with a viscous texture, some plumpness from lees contact & alcohol, just enough acidity to balance smooth & affable **18** ⑧② . **Sauvignon Blanc** ★★★★ Fruity & forthcoming, gooseberries & green papaya, bone-dry **18** ⑧③ delivers the variety's required freshness & length; even a touch of minerality.

Kleine Draken range
Vin Doux Ⓠ ★★ Watermelon notes on **NV** ⑦③ sweet sparkler from sauvignon & riesling. Low-alcohol for all these (7–9%). Paarl WO. **Natural Sweet Red** Ⓠ ★★ Now from merlot, **NV** ⑦① is gently sweet, with very slight dark cherry & berry flavour. **Natural Sweet White** Ⓠ ★★ Delicate jasmine-scented sweetness, light, with a hint of lime sherbet. **NV** ⑦② from riesling. **Kiddush** Ⓠ ★★ Sacramental wine, **NV** ⑦④ with cherry, grapey tones from 15% red muscadel & merlot, cloying sweetness. — CR
Location/map: Paarl ▪ Map grid reference: D6 ▪ WO: Coastal/Paarl ▪ Est 1983 ▪ 1stB 1988 ▪ Tasting & sales Mon-Fri 8–4 ▪ Closed all pub hols & Jewish holy days ▪ Cellar tours by appt ▪ Pre-booked kosher picnics available ▪ Owner/s Cape Gate (Pty) Ltd ▪ Winemaker(s) Jean van Rooyen (Dec 2007) ▪ Viticulturist(s) Frank Pietersen (1984) ▪ 12.5ha/8ha under vine ▪ 55t/20,000cs own label 60% red 40% white ▪ IPW, OU certified ▪ PO Box 2674 Paarl 7620 ▪ zandwijk@capegate.co.za ▪ www.zandwijk.co.za ▪ S 33° 46' 33.3" E 018° 56' 50.4" ▪ ⓦ stole.retrial.secrets ▪ **T +27 (0)21-863-2368**

☐ **Zaràfa** see Mountain River Wines
☐ **Z-Collection** see Zevenwacht
☐ **Zebra Collection** see Rooiberg Winery
☐ **Zenith** see Kumala

Zevenwacht ⓠ ⑪ ⓐ ◎ ⓧ ⓺

Given the extensive soil-study project spanning Zevenwacht, the Johnson family's home-farm outside Stellenbosch, and their second property, Zevenrivieren in Banhoek, it's not surprising the team's mantra is 'vineyards are news'. This year sees plantings of bushvine grenache and trellised cabernet franc on high-altitude sites on Zevenrivieren, while on Zevenwacht the focus is on nurturing 39-year-old chenin and gewürztraminer. This edition features wines from winemaker Hagen Viljoen's first harvest (2019) here. He's looking forward to vinifying the first grapes from young sauvignon during the current crush.

Estate range
★★★★ **Cabernet Sauvignon** ⊘ **16** ⑧⑥ repeats polished wooding (30% new, 18 months) of **15** ⑧⑦. Savoury overlay to sweet blackberry & plum fruit, subtle earthiness, satisfying tannin-acid structure.
★★★★ **Syrah** ⊘ Well-crafted for early accessibility & 5+ years ageing, **17** ⑧⑨ animated & engaging, with lily accents, restrained dark fruit. No new oak (vs 30% in **16** ⑧⑦), not over-extracted.

★★★★ **Chenin Blanc** ⊛ Poise & richness (apricot & yellow cling peach) from dryland vines planted 1981. Well-judged oaking (15% new, 15 months) adds whiff of vanilla & some shape in **18** ⑧⑥ while preserving variety's spirited acidity, bone-dry finish.

★★★★☆ **Sauvignon Blanc** ⊘ From highest, sea-facing vines, with 8% semillon, 5% barrel-fermented portion & 5 months lees contact for extra depth & breadth, **19** ★★★★ ⑧⑨ unshowy & mineral expression. Gentle acidity, like poised **18** ⑨⓪, shade briefer.

......

Merlot ⊛ ★★★☆ As usual, unfettered by new oak, fruit-filled & understated, with hint cinnamon/clove, rounded finish. **16** ⑧⑤ nudges next level.

......

Chardonnay ★★★☆ Was 'Barrel Fermented', **18** ⑧⑤ still is vinified in wood, 20% new, yet emphasis is on freshness to complement the understated lemon fruit, emphatic dry finish.

Z-Collection

★★★★ **Reserve** Big-boned (14.7% alcohol) **15** ⑧⑧ more cab than **14** ⑧⑦ (88% vs 74%), same 40% new oak & splashes other four Bordeaux varieties. Cassis & blueberries, sweet vanilla on nose & palate, good grip for freshness & few years ageing.

★★★★☆ **360° Sauvignon Blanc** ⊛ From 19 year old vines on breeze-cooled site with view of False Bay, delivering complex green & white fruit flavours, pinpoint acidity. **18** ⑨④, like **17** ⑨③, confident, refined & enduring; gets some heft from 8 months on lees & 8% oaked semillon.

Gewürztraminer ⊛ ★★★★ One of increasingly rare single-variety bottlings in SA. Dry **17** ⑧⑤'s effusive rosepetal perfume, litchi flavour tempered - slightly - by year older oak. Occasional release: **Grenache**.

The Tin Mine Collection

★★★★ **Red** ⊗ Serious but friendly Rhône blend, **15** ⑧⑥ mostly shiraz (57%) with lovely pepperiness from grenache. Approachable, but tannins have legs for a few years. Well-priced, especially in 1.5L format.

★★★★ **White** Myriad orchid fruit aromas & flavours courtesy chenin & chardonnay, splashes viognier, semillon (replacing roussanne in **17** ★★★★ ⑧⑤), mostly older oaked. **18** ⑧⑥ best served nicely chilled to enhance the sleek citrus thread which balances the richness, extends the finish.

7even range

......

Pinotage ⊘ ⊛ ★★★★ Punches above its price in **17** ⑧③, while paying homage to its parent, cinsaut, in lovely strawberry/candyfloss aromas & flavours, lively stemmy grip.

......

Rood ★★★ Reliable easy-sipping red boasts red-berry melange, crisp acidity in **17** ⑧⓪. Mostly shiraz (88%) with grenache, year older barrels. **Rosé** ★★★ From cab franc & more serious than most lunchtime pinks, **19** ⑧⓪ delicate & nicely dry, with attractive herby finish. **Sauvignon Blanc** ★★★ Wide array of cool green & ripe tropical fruits, perky acidity, **19** ⑧⓪ ticks all the easy, flavoursome boxes. **Bouquet** ★★★ Sweet, intensely aromatic **19** ⑦⑨, slight rose gold bush, billows of Turkish delight from 85% gewürztraminer & muscat de Frontignan. Enjoy chilled. — CvZ

Location: Kuils River ▪ Map/WO: Stellenbosch ▪ Map grid reference: B5 ▪ Est 1980 ▪ 1stB 1983 ▪ Tasting & sales Mon-Fri 8.30–5 Sat/Sun 9.30–5 ▪ Fee R35 ▪ Closed Dec 25 ▪ Cellar tours by appt ▪ Restaurant ▪ Picnics in summer ▪ Facilities for children ▪ Conferences ▪ Weddings/banqueting ▪ Walking & MTB trails ▪ Conservation area ▪ Bakwena Spa ▪ 4-star Country Inn ▪ Owner(s) Harold Johnson ▪ Winemaker(s) Hagen Viljoen (Aug 2018), with Charles Lourens (Jun 2014) ▪ Viticulturist(s) Eduard van den Berg (Jan 2001) ▪ 473ha/100ha (cabs s/f, grenache, merlot, mourv, ptage, primitivo, shiraz, chard, chenin, gewürz, muscat de F, rouss, sauv, sem, viog) ▪ 657t/100,000cs own label 48% red 48% white 4% rosé ▪ IPW ▪ PO Box 387 Kuils River 7579 ▪ info@ zevenwacht.co.za ▪ www.zevenwacht.co.za ▪ S 33° 55' 46.0" E 018° 43' 38.2" ▪ ⌨ hearse.postings.fending ▪ **T +27 (0)21-900-5700**

☐ **Zidela Wines** *See Editor's Note*

☐ **Zikomo** *see Rooiberg Winery*

Zoetendal Wines

⊙ ⊛ ◎

This small Elim estate was an early entrant into the ranks of winegrowing in the southerly, wind-riven Elim ward near Africa's southern tip, as well as being committed to the Nuwejaars Wetland Special Management

Area. The Zoetendal brand has now been revitalised by new owners Jan and Christine Becker. The new wines, elegantly expressive of their cool-climate origins, are made elsewhere: the sauvignon by Trizanne Barnard (of Trizanne Signature Wines); the rosé by CP Conradie (Conradie Penhill).

★★★★ **Red Dune Rosé** (NEW) Dark onion-skin hue on subtly fruity **18** (86) from shiraz. Light raspberry character, with fresh lemony acidity. Bone-dry, 12.4% alcohol. Elegantly satisfying.

★★★★ **Sauvignon Blanc** The first tasted since **12** ★★★☆, **18** (88) shows cool origins in its fresh citrus & blackcurrant, with a subtle grassy element. Acid is tangy but not aggressive, finish crisp & bone-dry. Not tasted: **Shiraz.** — TJ, CvZ

Location/WO: Elim ▪ Map: Southern Cape ▪ Map grid reference: C7 ▪ Est 2002 ▪ 1stB 2004 ▪ Tasting & sales Mon-Sat 10-4 ▪ Closed Good Fri, Dec 25 & Jan 1 ▪ Restaurant & venue (up to 40 pax) ▪ Conservation area ▪ Craft beer ▪ Owner(s) Jan & Christine Becker ▪ 125ha/10.3ha (shiraz, sauv) ▪ 39t/4,000cs own label 15% red 85% white ▪ IPW ▪ PO Box 22 Elim 7284 ▪ tradingpost@zoetendalwinefarm.co.za ▪ www.zoetendalwine-farm.co.za ▪ S 34° 36' 2.57" E 019° 47' 27.44" ▪ 🎯 commend.absorbs.dovetailed ▪ **T +27 (0)82-789-9848**

Zonnebloem

A name held in affection and respect since the beginning of the modern commercial winemaking era – a recent heritage-vintage tasting of several producers had this brand's cabernets from the late 1960s and early 1970s still showing particularly well – Zonnebloem is the last (alphabetically speaking) of Distell's leading labels to fall under the auspices of new standalone premium wine company Libertas Vineyards & Estates. The team has been consolidated, now proudly all women (see below).

Zonnebloem range

★★★★ **Lauréat** ⊘ Similar style & serious oaking (75% new barrels, 2 years) for flagship red, from mostly cab & merlot, though **16** (89) has petit verdot & cab franc in the blend. Riper, warmer & touch less gravitas than **15** ★★★★★ (90). Still sumptuous & tempting, but will continue to develop.

★★★★ **Shiraz-Mourvèdre-Viognier** ⊘ Satisfying trio (shiraz 87%), **17** (89) has added spice & substance from new, mixed-origin oak maturation. More plush & generous than **16** (89), but equally inviting & ageable.

Cabernet Sauvignon ⊘ ★★★☆ Consistently ticks the varietal boxes, **17** (85) is firm but balanced, with cassis & herbal flavours that end respectably dry. Mixed-origin oak maturation, 12 months, as all varietal reds here. **Merlot** ★★★ Violet & red berry flavours on a fresh base in **17** (82). Some piquancy & drier tannins make this a good tablemate. **Pinotage** ★★★ Some high-toned plum & mulberry flavours tempered to a chalky finish on **17** (81). Both warming & dry, one for the barbecue. **Shiraz** ⊘ ★★★★ Quite succulent, ripe & spicy **17** (85)'s ample fruit & pliable tannins allowed full rein for satisfying drinkability. **Chardonnay** ⊘ ★★★☆ Vivacious balance of freshness & flavour on **18** (85). Pear & lime spiced with oak on a creamy base. Perennial favourite for quaffing or mealtime enjoyment. **Sauvignon Blanc** ⊘ ★★★★ Spectrum of greener to tropical flavours on crisp & tangy **19** (83). A fresh step up on previous for this balanced summer staple. **Blanc de Blanc** ⊘ ★★★ Chenin-led blend with 20% sauvignon. Crunchy green apple freshness & flavours on **19** (81). Amiable, dry everyday quaffer. WO W Cape.

Limited Editions

In abeyance: **Cabernet Sauvignon, Pinotage, Shiraz, Chenin Blanc, Sauvignon Blanc.** — MW

Location: Stellenbosch ▪ WO: Stellenbosch/Western Cape ▪ Est 1893 ▪ Owner(s) Libertas Vineyards & Estates, a Distell Group company ▪ Cellarmaster(s) Elize Coetzee (Nov 2015) ▪ Winemaker(s) Bonny van Niekerk (reds, Oct 2007) & Kelly-Marie Jacobs (whites, Jun 2019) ▪ Viticulturist(s) Isabel Habets ▪ (cab, merlot, shiraz, chard, sauv, sem) ▪ 9,500t/±109,000cs own label 60% red 40% white ▪ ISO 9002, Fairtrade ▪ PO Box 184 Stellenbosch 7599 ▪ info@zonnebloem.co.za ▪ www.zonnebloem.co.za ▪ **T +27 (0)21-809-7000**

☐ **Zonneweelde** *see* Slanghoek Winery

Zorgvliet Wines (🍷)(🍴)(🏠)(📷)(👤)(♿)

The gradual conversion to a classic Bordeaux mix of varieties continues on Stephan and Izelle van der Merwe's Banhoek Valley wine and guest farm on the southern Simonsberg slopes. Harvest 2019 saw the first crop off new cabernet and cab franc vines, followed by a winter in which more non-Bordeaux varieties were removed in preparation for replanting. Recent cellar investments have included a new sorter/destemmer, all geared to give winemaker Bernard le Roux the tools to make the most of terroir as viticulturally blessed as it is beautiful.

Grand Cuvée range

★★★★☆ **Richelle** ⓐ Multi-layered Bordeaux red, **17** ⑨③ is cab led, like **16** ⑨③, with serious structure for decade ageing. Overt spicy oak wraps around black cherry, blackcurrant & subtle graphite notes. Stately & broad, lingering aftertaste of dark fruit & cedar from 20 months in French barriques. Should develop well.

★★★★☆ **Simoné** ⓐ Classic Bordeaux white, sauvignon with substantial (43%) semillon component. **18** ⑨③ aromas are lifted by accents of dried sage & fynbos, leading to crisp citrus fruit flavours. Granny Smith & lime notes show on the lingering finish.

Zorgvliet range

★★★★☆ **Cabernet Sauvignon** ⊘ ⓐ Rich, spiced aromas of blueberry, blackberry & dark currant, firm tannin grip bolstered by 37% new oak, 18 months, chocolate mousse notes & graphite minerality in conclusion. **17** ⑨④ just as delicious as **16** ⑨③, good to last at least a decade.

★★★★ **Cabernet Franc** Raspberry & strawberry notes accented by earthy/gravel & bellpepper notes in bold & steely **17** ⑧⑦. Firm tannins, 20 months in oak, 17% new, ensure a spicy & savoury long finish.

★★★★ **Malbec** Abundant seductive red plum & blackcurrant in a graceful structure, **17** ⑧⑥ has complexity, polished texture & good density. Leafy & cocoa notes add interest, as does vanilla persistence.

★★★★ **Merlot** Forward cherry & plum aromas in **17** ⑧⑦, & some bold bay & mint chocolate. Opulent & soft textured, with a generous fruit expression on the palate. As harmonious as last.

★★★★ **Petit Verdot** ⓐ Mulberry & blackcurrant flamboyance & subtler coffee & sage in aroma. Palate shows typical tannin structure, expectedly grippy & firm, with deep, dark cherry core & finish in **17** ⑧⑧. Lay it down for a decade for maximum pleasure.

★★★★ **Cabernet Franc Rosé** Bone-dry **18** ⑧⑦ maintains high standard with alluring pomegranate & strawberry fruit notes interwoven with a striking jasmine & sherbet bouquet. Well balanced by vibrant acidity, lingering spiced-watermelon farewell.

★★★★☆ **Single Vineyard Sauvignon Blanc** ⊘ ⓐ From selected block, **18** ⑨③ had 10 hours skin contact to build complexity in already intricate array of kiwi & lemon peel, fig & fynbos aromas. Same intensity as **17** ⑨④, bright acidity & moderate alcohol help maintain balance. Exceptionally well priced.

Silver Myn range

Argentum ⓥ ★★★★ Handsome & sleek 4-way Bordeaux red, merlot led in **18** ⑧④. Affable & red-fruit toned, smooth tannins ensure early drinking with potential for few years in cellar.

Rosé ★★★ Bone-dry & refreshing **19** ⑧⓪ summer sipper. Sauvignon & semillon provide acid backbone, cabernet franc the blush, cherries & cinnamon spice. Stellenbosch WO, as all. **Sauvignon Blanc** ★★★ Tropical fruited, light & zesty **19** ⑧② reveals gooseberry & grapefruit bursts with bellpepper undertones. Enjoy with sushi. — GM

Location/map: Stellenbosch ▪ Map grid reference: H4 ▪ WO: Banghoek/Stellenbosch ▪ Est/1stB 2000 ▪ Tasting & sales Mon-Fri 9–5 Sat 10-6 Sun/pub hols 11–5 ▪ Closed Good Fri, Dec 25 & Jan 1 ▪ Tasting fee, waived on purchase ▪ Cellar tours by appt ▪ Zorgvliet picnic Sep-Apr ▪ Facilities for children ▪ Tour groups ▪ Gifts ▪ Conferences ▪ Walks/hikes ▪ Zorgvliet Country Lodge (17 rooms) ▪ Owner(s) Stephan & Izelle van der Merwe ▪ Winemaker(s) Bernard le Roux (Dec 2013), with Ruben Adams ▪ Viticulturist(s) Hannes Jansen van Vuuren ▪ 58ha/25ha (cabs s/f, merlot, p verdot, sauv, sem) ▪ 350t/35,000cs own label 32% red 64% white 4% rosé + 150t for clients ▪ PO Box 1595 Stellenbosch 7599 ▪ winecellar@zorgvliet.com ▪ www.zorgvlietwines.com ▪ S 33° 54' 41.7" E 018° 56' 32.0" ▪ 🖭 instant.spreads.averts ▪ **T +27 (0)21-885-1399**

This Year's Ratings Summarised

Here we summarise the wines featured in the A-Z section, with their ratings, sorted first by wine style, in alphabetical order, and then by producer or brand. New wines in **bolder type**. **NS** = no star; **NT** = not tasted; **NR** = tasted but not rated; **D** = discontinued. Where wineries produce more than one version of a particular style, the number of versions is indicated in brackets after the name. A number of wines were tasted as pre-bottling barrel or tank samples, and therefore ratings are provisional. Refer to the A-Z for details.

Albariño

★★★★★ Newton Johnson

★★★★ Springfield ★★★ Nederburg

Alternative white/red

★★★★★ Neil Ellis (White blends, wooded, dry); Maanschijn (Grenache gris); Môrelig (Red blends, shiraz/syrah-based)

★★★★ Olivedale (Semillon wooded); **AA Badenhorst** (White blends, wooded, dry; Skin-macerated white); Maanschijn (Verdelho); Mount Abora (Cinsaut)

★★★☆ **Dragonridge** (Chenin blanc wooded, dry) ★★★ Dragonridge (Rosé dry) ★★ Dragonridge (Pinotage) **NT** Dragonridge (3) (Red blends, with pinotage; Chenin blanc unwooded dry; White blends, wooded, dry)

Barbera

★★★★★ Bruce Jack; Trizanne

★★★★ Fairview; Merwida

★★★☆ Altydgedacht; Bester **NT** Hofstraat; Idiom (2)

Biodynamic

★★★★★ Reyneke (2) (Cabernet sauvignon; Shiraz/syrah)

★★★★★ Reyneke (2) (Chenin blanc unwooded dry; Sauvignon blanc wooded; Old Vines); Elgin Ridge (2) (Chardonnay wooded; White blends, wooded, dry)

★★★★ Elgin Ridge (2) (Pinot noir; Sauvignon blanc unwooded)

Blanc de noir

★★★★ Maison; Van Loggerenberg

★★★☆ **Aan't Vette** Arra; Buitenverwachting; Hazendal; Lemberg; Meerendal; Packwood; Peter Falke; Tanagra; **The Garajeest** ★★★ Blaauwklippen; Calitzdorp; Esona; Landskroon; **Lemberg**; Van Loveren★★★ Deux Frères; Lovane; Lynx; Nieuwedrift; Swartland ★★ Niel Joubert **NT** Aaldering; Bezalel; Doolhof; Olifantsberg; The Wine Thief **D** Altydgedacht; Signal Gun

Brandy

★★★★★ KWV Brandies (6); Van Ryn (3)

★★★★☆ Anthonij Rupert; Avontuur; Backsberg; Barrydale; **Bayede!**; Blaauwklippen; Boplaas (2); Diemersfontein; Groot Constantia; Klipdrift; Oude Molen; Upland (Organic); Van Ryn

★★★★ Backsberg (2); Barrydale (3); Bezalel; Boplaas; Copeland; D'Aria; Dalla Cia; Die Mas; Flight of the Fish Eagle; Kaapzicht; Kingna; KWV Brandies (2); Mimosa; Napier; Nuy; Oude Molen (2); Richelieu; Robertson; Upland (2) (Organic); Van Loveren; Windfall; Withington

★★★☆ 100 Reserve; Die Mas; Grundheim (2); Klipdrift (2); KWV Brandies; Parow; Upland (Organic); Viceroy (2); Windmeul ★★★ Commando; Grundheim; Kingna; Landzicht; Olof Bergh; Richelieu; Robertson; Van Loveren★★★ Grundheim; Robertson; Wellington VO **NT** Bezalel; Boplaas (2); Tokara

Bukettraube

★★★★ Cederberg; **Darling Cellars**

Cabernet franc

★★★★★ Anthonij Rupert; De Trafford; Raats

★★★★☆ Anthology; Buitenverwachting; Cape Chamonix; Edgebaston; Eikendal; Gabriëlskloof; **Hogan**; Holden Manz; Joubert-Tradauw; Kaapzicht; Keermont; **Lieben**; **Lynx**; Mitre's Edge; Môreson; Mulderbosch; Nelson; Oldenburg; Plaisir de Merle; Raats (2); Rainbow's End; Ridgeback; Uva Mira; Warwick Loggerenberg; Warwick

★★★★ Botanica; **Damascene**; Glen Carlou; Glenelly; Hannay; Hillcrest; Idiom; Le Pommier; **Mischa**; Mont du Toit (Natural/non-fortified pale); Morgenster; My Wyn; Ormonde; Rainbow's End; Raka; Rietvallei; Spookfontein; Stellenrust; Tanagra; **Thistle & Weed**; Whalehaven (2); Zorgvliet

★★★☆ **Avontuur**; Druk My Niet; Morgenhof; Rebus; The Garajeest; **Thor**; Waterkloof ★★★ **Audacia**; Bushmanspad; Hawksmoor **NT** Annandale; Camberley; Doolhof; Kleinhoekkloof; Lovane; Lynx; Nomada; Stellenbosch Vineyards; Stony Brook; Waterford; Woolworths **D** Audacia; Avontuur; De Kleine Wijn Koöp; Haut Espoir; Knorhoek; Tokara; Vergenoegd

Cabernet sauvignon

★★★★★ Erika Obermeyer; Kanonkop; Kleine Zalze; **Miles Mossop**; Reyneke (Biodynamic); Rust en Vrede; **Wade Bales**

★★★★☆ Anthonij Rupert; Bartinney (2); Black Elephant; Boekenhoutskloof (2); Bon Courage; Bosman; Capelands; Cederberg (2); Charla Haasbroek; Dalla Cia; De Trafford; Delaire Graff (2); Delheim; Diemersdal; **Domaine Coutelier**; Dornier; Durbanville Hills; Edgebaston (2); Eikendal; Ernie Els (2); Excelsior; Flagstone; Fleur du Cap; Glen Carlou; Grangehurst; Groenland; Groot Constantia; Hartenberg; Holden Manz; **Idiom**; Jordan; Journey's End (Fairtrade); Keermont; Kleine Zalze; KWV; La Bri; La Motte; La Petite Ferme; Laibach; Le Riche (2); Louisvale; Marianne; Meerlust; **Metzer**; Middelvlei; Mooiplaas; Môreson; Muratie (2); Nederburg; Neil Ellis; **Nico van der Merwe**; Nitida; Oldenburg (2); Org de Rac (Organic); PaardenKloof; Plaisir de Merle; Rainbow's End; **Raka** (2); Remhoogte; Restless River; Rickety Bridge; Rosendal; Rudera; Rust en Vrede; Rustenberg; Saxenburg; Schultz Family; Simonsig; Spier; Stark-Condé (2); Stellenbosch Reserve; Stony Brook; Strydom; Super Single Vineyards; The Butcher Shop; Thelema; Tokara (2); Uva Mira; **Vergelegen** (4); Villion; Warwick; Waterford; Webersburg; Wellington Winery; Woolworths; Yardstick; Zorgvliet

★★★★ Alto; Anura (2); **Aristea**; Avontuur; Backsberg; Belfield; **Bergsig**; **Blaauwklippen**; Boland; Bon Courage; Boplaas; Boschendal; Boschkloof; Botanica; Brenaissance; Cape Wine Company; Collatio; Croydon; De Meye; Diemersfontein; Domaine Coutelier; Durbanville Hills; Fairview; Fleur du Cap; Fort Simon; Glen Carlou; Glenelly; Goedvertwacht; Graceland; Grande Provence; Groot Phesantekraal; Guardian Peak; **Guillaumé**; Haskell; Havana Hills; Hoopenburg (2); House of Mandela; Jacobsdal; Jakob's Vineyards; Jason's Hill; Joostenberg (Organic); Joubert-Tradauw; Journey's End (Fairtrade); Kaapzicht; **Kanonkop**; Katbakkies; KWV; Kyburg; Landskroon; Lanzerac; Le Bonheur; Le Riche; Leopard's Leap; **Lievland**; Longridge; Lutzville (2); **Lynx**; Marklew; Meinert; Mellasat; Mimosa; Mischa; Mitre's Edge; **Mont du Toit** (Natural/non-fortified pale); Mont Rochelle; Mooiplaas; Morgenhof; Nederburg; Neil Ellis (2); Niel Joubert; Noble Hill; Ormonde; Overhex (Nouveau); PaardenKloof; Pearl Mountain; Perdeberg; Peter Falke; Post House; Radford Dale; Rannoch; Rickety Bridge; Ridgeback; Rooiberg (2); Rudera; Scrucap; Silvermist (2) (Organic); South

Hill; Spookfontein; Springfield (2); Stellekaya; Taillard; Teubes (Organic); **The Fledge**; The High Road; Under Oaks; Van Loveren; Vergenoegd; Villiera; Vondeling; Waterkloof; Welgevallen; Windmeul; Winshaw; Woolworths (3); Zevenwacht

★★★☆ Akkerdraai; Allesverloren; Annandale; Anthonij Rupert; Arendskloof; Arra; Asara; **Bader & Walters**; Benguela Cove; Bergsig; Bloemendal; Bonnievale; Boplaas; Bosman; Bushmanspad; Cape Classics; Cape Rock; Cavalli; Chennells; Cloof (2); Collatio; Conradie; **Darling Cellars**; De Krans; Domaine Brahms; Dormershire (2); Druk My Niet; Du Preez; Eerste Hoop; Ernie Els; Excelsior; Fat Bastard; Goede Hoop; Haut Espoir; Jacques Smit; Jan Harmsgat (Fairtrade); **Kleine Zalze**; **Koopmanskloof**; **Kunjani**; KWV; La Petite Provence; Landskroon; Le Belle Rebelle; Leipzig; Linton Park; Lovane; Lynx; **M'hudi** (2); Maastricht; MAN Family; Maske; McGregor; **Meerhof** (Fairtrade); Miravel; Mischa; MolenVliet; Mont du Toit (Natural/non-fortified pale); Morgenster; Mountain Ridge (2); Namaqua; Napier; Nederburg; Neethlingshof; Nuy (2); **Onoma**; Org de Rac (Fairtrade; Organic); Ormonde; Osbloed; Perdeberg; Porcupine Ridge; Riebeek Valley; Rietvallei; Rooiberg; Simonsig; **Spier**; Stellenbosch Hills; Stellenbosch University; Stellenrust; Stellenview (4); Stettyn; Stonewall; Swartland; Tanagra; The Bridge of Hope; The Goose; Thelema; Tulbagh Winery; Upland (Organic); Vredenheim; Warwick; Welbedacht; Wellington Winery; Weltevrede (2); Windfall; Woolworths (3); Zonnebloem ★★★ Alexandersfontein; Asara; Audacia; Bader & Walters; Barnardt Boyes; Bayede!; Blue Crane; Boschheim (2); Boschrivier; Botha; Breëland; Cape Dreams; Cape Town Wine Co; **Chennells**; Cilmor; Clairvaux; Cloof; Darling Cellars; Daschbosch; De Wet; Dragonridge; False Bay; FirstCape; Glen Carlou; Hofstraat; House of Mandela; Imbuko (Fairtrade); Ken Forrester; Kleine Zalze (Fairtrade); **Koni**; Koopmanskloof (Fairtrade); Langverwacht; Le Manoir de Brendel; Leopard's Leap; Linton Park (2); Lyngrove; Merwida; Miravel; Napier; Niel Joubert; Oude Compagnies Post; Overhex (2) (Nouveau); Painted Wolf; Piekenierskloof (2) (Fairtrade); Pulpit Rock; Robertson (4); Roodezandt; Rooiberg; Slaley; Slanghoek; Somersbosch; Spier; Stellar (Fairtrade; Organic); Stellenbosch Family Wines (2); Stellenbosch Vineyards; Stellendrift; Stellenview (2); Swartland; Tangled Tree; The Bridge of Hope; The Hills; **Theuniskraal**; Van Loveren (3); Viljoensdrift; **Vinologist**; Waverley Hills (Organic); **Woolworths** (3) ★★☆ Aan de Doorns; Aslina; Bergsig; Brandvlei;

Calais; Desert Rose; Die Mas; Du Preez; Du Toitskloof; DuVon; **FirstCape**; Flagstone; Group CDV; Highgate (2); Hofstraat; Imbuko (Fairtrade); Klawer; KWV (2); Louis; Louisvale; Maison de Teijger; Namaqua (2); Nederburg; Nicholson Smith; Orange River; Somerset Wines; Stellar (Fairtrade; Organic); The Bridge of Hope; Tulbagh Winery; **Villiersdorp**; Welmoed; Windmeul; Wineways (3); Woolworths ★★ De Breede (Organic); Eagle's Cliff; Klein Roosboom; KWV; Landzicht; Mooiplaas (Light & low-alcohol); Simonsvlei (2); Vintales; Weltevrede ★★ Lutzville ★ Theescombe **NT** Alvi's Drift; Anthology; Arendsig (2); Bayede!; Bizoe; Black Pearl; Botha; Brampton; Buitenverwachting; Camberley; Cape Dreams; Carrol Boyes; De Kleine Wijn Koöp; DeWaal; Dieu Donné; Doolhof; Douglas Green; Drostdy-Hof; Entre Nous; Esau; Fairvalley (Fairtrade); Fernskloof (Organic); Franschhoek Cellar; Groenland; **Hawksmoor**; Highberry; Hildenbrand; Hunneyball; Kaapse Familie Wingerde; Kleine Zalze; Kranskop; Laibach; Landzicht; Lomond; Louis; Manley; Meerendal; Mitre's Edge; Montagu Wine Cellar; Mooi Bly; Mountain River (2); Nederburg; New Beginnings; Olsen; Oneiric (2); Rietvallei; Rosendal; Rustenberg; **Safriel** (2); Schalkenbosch (Fairtrade); Schenkfontein; Seven Sisters; Simonsvlei (Kosher); Southern Sky (3); Springfontein; Stellendrift (3); The Butcher Shop; Thelema; Val du Charron; Vierkoppen; Walker Bay Estate; Waterford; Wineways; **Woolworths** (4); Zonnebloem **D** Arra (2); Audacia; Camberley; Cape Point; Cloof (2); Darling Cellars; FirstCape; Guardian Peak; Knorhoek (2); L'Avenir; Le Pommier; Linton Park; MAN Family; Simonsvlei; The Butcher Shop; Topiary; Vriesenhof; Woolworths

Cape Riesling
★★★ Theuniskraal **NT** Hildenbrand

Carignan
★★★★☆ ArtiSons; Blackwater

★★★★ **Lammershoek**

★★★★☆ Kloovenburg ★★★ Anura; **The Horsemen NT** Cape Rock; Fairview **D** Signal Hill; Spice Route

Carmenère
NT Dagbreek; Lozärn

Chardonnay unwooded
★★★★☆ Eikendal (2); **Haute Cabrière**; Môreson; Springfield; Stonebird

★★★★ Bouchard Finlayson; Diemersdal; Fram; Glenelly; GlenWood; Jordan (3); The Butcher Shop; Woolworths

★★★☆ Blue Owl; Bonnievale; Canto; Cape Chamonix; Cape Dreams; False Bay; Glen Carlou; Groote Post; Hill & Dale; Hoopenburg; Idun; Kleine

Zalze; **Kruger Family** (2); Lynx; Meerendal; Neethlingshof; Niel Joubert; Radford Dale; Riebeek Valley; Rooiberg; Rustenberg; Seven Springs; The Butcher Shop; Vriesenhof; **Warwick** ★★★ Barrydale; Boland; Bon Courage; Brandvlei; Cloof (2); Daschbosch; De Meye; Felicité; **Idun**; Journey's End (Fairtrade); Ken Forrester; Klein Roosboom; Kloovenburg; Landskroon (2); Le Grand Chasseur; Leopard's Leap; Linton Park; Louisvale; Maison de Teijger; **Onoma**; Piekenierskloof (Fairtrade); Pulpit Rock; Stellenbosch Vineyards; Swartland; The Bridge of Hope; Van Zylshof; Viljoensdrift; Windmeul ★★★ **Absolute Style**; Alexanderfontein; Bellpost; Compagniesdrift; De Krans; Du'SwaRoo; **FirstCape**; Klawer; Koopmanskloof (Fairtrade); Linton Park; Lutzville; McGregor; Mountain River; Pearl Mountain; Schenkfontein; Slaley; Stellar (Fairtrade; Organic); SylvanVale; Weltevrede; Woolworths (2) (Fairtrade; Organic); Zandvliet ★★ Calais; Flagstone; Simonsvlei (Kosher); Vintales **NT** Aaldering; Backsberg (Kosher); Brampton; Brunia; Buffalo Creek; Constantia Uitsig; Dieu Donné; Doolhof; Elemental Bob; Franschhoek Cellar; Hartenberg; Hildenbrand; La Petite Ferme; Middelvlei; Newstead; Oneiric; Plettenvale; Rietvallei; Somersbosch; The Goose; Welbedacht; Withington; Woolworths **D** Bellevue; False Bay; Frater; Stettyn; Thelema; Walker Bay Estate

Chardonnay wooded
★★★★★ **Capensis**; Hamilton Russell; Jordan; **Leeu Passant** (2); Oak Valley; Restless River; Rhebokskloof; Richard Kershaw (2); Warwick

★★★★☆ Almenkerk; **Alvi's Drift**; Anthology; Anthonij Rupert; **Aristea**; Bartinney (2); Benguela Cove; Boschendal; **Botanica**; Bouchard Finlayson (2); Buitenverwachting; Cap Maritime; Cape Chamonix (2); Capensis; Creation (3); Crystallum (2); De Grendel; Delaire Graff (2); Delheim; DeMorgenzon; Dorrance (Fairtrade); Edgebaston; Eikendal (3); Elgin Ridge (Biodynamic); Fleur du Cap; Glen Carlou; Glenelly; GlenWood (2); Groot Constantia; Groote Post; Hartenberg; Haskell; Haut Espoir; **Haute Cabrière**; Highlands Road; **Hogan**; **Holden Manz**; **Iona** (2); **Jayne's**; Jordan (2); Julien Schaal (3); Kleine Zalze; Kruger Family (2); La Bri (2); La Vierge (2); Laarman; Laibach (Organic); Lanzerac; Le Belle Rebelle; Le Riche; Longridge (Organic); Lourensford (2); Maison; Malanot; Meerlust; Mont Rochelle; Môreson (2); MVH Signature Wines; **Natasha Williams**; Neil Ellis; **Newton Johnson** (3); Oak Valley; Oldenburg; Paserene; Paul Cluver (2); Paul Wallace; Quoin Rock; Radford Dale; Richard Kershaw (3); Rietvallei; Rustenberg (2); Spookfontein; Stellenrust; Storm;

Sumaridge; Thelema (2); Tokara; Topiary; Uva Mira (2); Van Loveren; Vergelegen; Whalehaven; Woolworths (2) (Organic); Yardstick

★★★★ Aaldering; Alvi's Drift; Anura; Arendskloof; Avontuur; Babylonstoren; Backsberg; Baleia; **Bellevue**; Bellingham; Bergsig; Bizoe; Boland; Bon Courage; Boschendal; Boschkloof; Bosman; **Brew Cru**; Canto; Cape Point; Clayton; Clouds; Constantia Uitsig; Dalla Cia; De Wet; Delaire Graff; DeMorgenzon; Domaine Coutelier; Durbanville Hills; Elgin Vintners; Ernst Gouws; Esona; Fairview; Glen Carlou; Grande Provence; Hartenberg; Haskell; **Hazendal**; Holden Manz; Hoopenburg; Houw Hoek; **Idun**; **Iona**; Joubert-Tradauw; Journey's End (Fairtrade); Klein Constantia; Kloovenburg; KWV; La Couronne; La Motte; La Petite Ferme; **Lammershoek** (Old Vines); Lanzerac; **Le Belle Rebelle**; Lieben; Linton Park; Longridge (Organic); Lord's; Lothian; Louisvale; **Lozärn**; **Lynx**; Marklew; Migliarina (2); Mont Blois (2); Mulderbosch; Muratie (2); Napier; Olivedale; Org de Rac (Organic); Ormonde (2); Plaisir de Merle; Pulpit Rock; Radford Dale; Rhebokskloof; **Richard Kershaw**; Rickety Bridge; Robertson; Rooiberg; Saxenburg; Scrucap; **Spioenkop**; Springfield; Stellenbosch Reserve; Stellenbosch Vineyards; **Tesselaarsdal**; **The Fledge**; The Liberator; Thelema (2); Tierhoek; Tokara; Under Oaks; Uva Mira; Val du Charron; Vergelegen; Vondeling; Vriesenhof; Waterford; Waverley Hills (Organic); Weltevrede; **Winshaw**; Woolworths (2); Zandvliet

★★★☆ Backsberg; Badsberg; Benguela Cove; Bergsig; Bloemendal; Bon Courage; **Bosjes**; **Botha**; Cape Classics; Clos Malverne; Dâbar; Domaine des Dieux; Durbanville Hills; Fat Bastard; Flagstone; Fleur du Cap; Fort Simon; Freedom Hill; Goedverwacht; Jan Harmsgat (Fairtrade); Journey's End (Fairtrade); Koelfontein; Kruger Family; Le Bonheur; Linton Park; **Louis 57**; Lyngrove; **Maastricht**; MAN Family; Mellasat; Mimosa; Mont Rochelle; Morgenhof; Nederburg; Niel Joubert; Nuy; Olsen; Org de Rac (Organic); Overhex (Nouveau); Packwood; Pearl Mountain; Porcupine Ridge; Robertson (4); Rooiberg; Seven Sisters; Seven Springs; Signal Gun; Simonsig; **Spier** (2); Steenberg; Stellar (Fairtrade; Organic); Stellenbosch Family Wines (2); Stellenrust; Stellenview (2); The Bridge of Hope; Villion; Welbedacht; Weltevrede; Windmeul; Zevenwacht; Zonnebloem ★★★ Anthonij Rupert; Anura; Arendskloof; Asara; **Cape Town Wine Co**; Carrol Boyes; Dragonridge; Du Toitskloof (2) (Fairtrade); Eerste Hoop (2); Excelsior; Foothills; Glen Carlou; Goedverwacht; Kranskop; KWV (2); Langverwacht;

Le Grand Chasseur; Lodestone; Louisvale; Maison de Teijger; Merwida; Middelvlei; Nelson; **Nieuwedrift**; Orange River; Simonsvlei; Slanghoek (2); Stonewall; Van Loveren; **Villiersdorp**; Weltevrede ★★★ Cilmor; Die Mas; Goede Hoop; Meerhof (Fairtrade); Peter Falke; Tangled Tree; Tulbagh Winery; Van Loveren; Varkenskraal; Weltevrede ★★ Aslina; Darling Cellars; Le Manoir de Brendel; New Beginnings; Walker Bay Estate; Welvanpas **NT** Alvi's Drift; Arendsig; B Vintners; Bayede!; Burgershof; Calitzdorp; Capelands; Cavalli; Die Kat; Dieu Donné (2); Douglas Green; Drostdy-Hof; Entre Nous; Fairvalley (2) (Fairtrade); Four Paws; Glen Carlou (2); Groot Parys; Hannay; Havana Hills; Highgate; Hildenbrand (2); House of Mandela; JH Meyer; Lazanou (Organic); Leipzig; Mooi Bly; Mountain River; Namaqua; Oneiric; Overhex; Rietvallei (2); Rosendal (2); Rupert & Rothschild; **Safriel**; Schalkenbosch; Seven Sisters; Spotswood; Springfontein (Skin-macerated white); Stanford Hills; Two Oceans; **Verspieren**; Vredenheim; Walking Woods (Organic); Waterkloof; Welmoed; **Woolworths** (5); Yardstick (2); Zandvliet **D** Botha; Durbanville Hills; Haute Cabrière; Imbuko; Kumala; Meinert; Mulderbosch; Nitida; Riebeek Valley; Slaley

Chenin blanc off-dry/semi-sweet (w & u/w)

★★★★★ Longridge

★★★★☆ Ken Forrester

★★★★ Kanu; Slanghoek

★★★ Landzicht ★★ Bonnievale (Perlé); Fleur du Cap **NT** Beaumont; Dagbreek; Landskroon; Seven Sisters

Chenin blanc unwooded dry

★★★★★ Sadie

★★★★☆ Clouds; Dorrance (Fairtrade); Grande Provence; Namaqua; Raats; Reyneke (Biodynamic; Old Vines); Terracura (Old Vines); **Waterford**

★★★★ Beaumont; Black Pearl; Blackwater; Boland; Bosman; Capelands; Cederberg; Croydon; Glen Carlou; Huis van Chevallerie (Old Vines); Maison; Neethlingshof; **Rustenberg** (2); Tierhoek

★★★☆ Allesverloren; **Altydgedacht** (Old Vines); Annex Kloof; Anthonij Rupert; Babylon's Peak; Babylonstoren; Barton; Bester; Boland (2); Bonnievale; Boschendal; Cape Dreams; Cape Venture (Fairtrade); Carrol Boyes; Ernie Els; Ernst Gouws; **Fairview** (2); False Bay; Groot Phesantekraal; Hawksmoor; Imbuko (Fairtrade); Jordan; Kleine Zalze; **Le Grand Domaine**; Leeuwenkuil; MAN Family; Meerhof (Fairtrade; Old Vines); Mooi Bly; Mooiplaas (Old Vines); Noble Savage; Ormonde (2); Overhex (Nouveau); Perdeberg; Piekenierskloof (2) (Fairtrade); Porcupine Ridge

(2); Pulpit Rock; Reyneke (Organic); Rhebokskloof;
Riebeek Valley; Saxenburg; Scrucap; Simonsig;
The Grape Grinder (2); The Hills; Theescombe;
Under Oaks; Van Zylshof; Woolworths (2) ★★★
Alexanderfontein; Backsberg; Barrydale; Brandvlei;
Conradie; Croydon; **Darling Cellars**; Daschbosch
(Fairtrade); De Krans; De Wet; DeWaal; Dornier;
Du Toitskloof; Fairvalley (Fairtrade); False Bay; Fish
Hoek (Fairtrade); Grande Provence; Groote Post;
Hoopenburg; Joostenberg; Kaapzicht; Kanu; Ken
Forrester; Klawer; Kleine Zalze (2); Kunjani; La
Chataigne; Laibach; Landskroon; Leopard's Leap;
Lyngrove; **Maison de Teijger**; Merwida; **Napier**;
New Beginnings; Niel Joubert; Nieuwedrift;
Nuy; Oude Denneboom; Pearl Mountain; **Peter
Bayly**; Piekenierskloof (Fairtrade); Robertson (3);
Roodezandt; Rooiberg; Schenkfontein; Skilpadvlei;
Somerbosch; Spier; Stellar (Fairtrade; Organic);
Stellenbosch Hills; Summerhill; The Grape Grinder;
Truter Family; Tulbagh Winery; **Villiersdorp**;
Vinologist; Vondeling; Waboomsrivier; Welbedacht;
Wellington Winery; Woolworths (2) (Fairtrade;
Organic); Zandwijk★★★ Aan de Doorns; Badsberg;
Bayedє!; Bergsig; Bon Courage; **Bosjes**; Cilmor;
Cloof; Darling Cellars; Diemersfontein; Domaine
Brahms; Du'SwaRoo; DuVon; Eagle's Cliff;
FirstCape (2); Groenland; Imbuko (2) (Fairtrade);
Koelenhof; Koopmanskloof (Fairtrade); KWV; La
Couronne; Langverwacht; Le Belle Rebelle (2);
M'hudi; Mountain Ridge; Nederburg; Nelson;
Orange River; Perdeberg; Silkbush; Simonsvlei
(Kosher); Swartland; **Two Oceans**; Van Loveren
(2); Varkenskraal; **Vredenheim**; Welmoed;
Woolworths★★ Botha; Daschbosch (2); Domein
Doornkraal; Drostdy-Hof (Light & low-alcohol);
KWV; Linton Park; McGregor; Robertson (2) (Light
& low-alcohol); Simonsvlei (2); Slanghoek; Vintales;
Winkelshoek ★★ Klawer; Lutzville; Namaqua **NT**
Alvi's Drift; Arendsig; Ayama (2); Calitzdorp; Cavalli;
De Meye; Doolhof; Douglas Green; Dragonridge
(Alternative white/red); Drostdy-Hof; Elemental
Bob; FirstCape; Franschhoek Cellar; Goede Hoop;
Groot Parys (2) (Organic); Hildenbrand; J9;
Kyburg; Lazanou (Organic); Lovane; Malanot;
Mitre's Edge; Montagu Wine Cellar; Mountain
River; Nederburg; Olsen; Radford Dale; Rietvallei;
Rosendal; Schalkenbosch; Signal Gun; Somerset
Wines; Stettyn; Strange Kompanjie; Swartland;
The Fledge; Walking Woods (Fairtrade; Organic);
Windmeul; Wine Village-Hermanus; Woolworths (3)
(Light & low-alcohol); Zonnebloem **D** Alheit (Old
Vines); Arra; Cloof; Fairview; Knorhoek (2); Maske;
Nederburg; New Beginnings; Stettyn; Windmeul

Chenin blanc wooded, dry

★★★★★ AA Badenhorst (2); Alheit (Old Vines);
ArtiSons; **Axle**; Beaumont (Old Vines); Botanica;
David & Nadia (4) (Old Vines); DeMorgenzon
(Old Vines); Gabriëlskloof (Old Vines); Kleine Zalze;
Kruger Family (Old Vines); Metzer (Old Vines);
Mount Abora; Raats; Rall; Sadie (Old Vines); Spier;
Stellenrust (2); Thistle & Weed; Van Loggerenberg

★★★★☆ AA Badenhorst (3); Alheit (4) (Old
Vines); Alvi's Drift; Anthonij Rupert (2) (Old Vines);
Beaumont; Bellingham (Old Vines); Blackwater;
Boschkloof; Bosman (Old Vines); Brookdale; **Bruce
Jack**; Carinus Family (2); Catherine Marshall;
Cederberg; **Charla Haasbroek**; City on a Hill;
Creation; Darling Cellars (Old Vines); **De Trafford**
(2); DeMorgenzon (Old Vines); DewaldtHeyns;
Donkiesbaai; Doran; Edgebaston; Eenzaamheid;
Esona; Flagstone; Hogan; Huis van Chevallerie
(Old Vines); Illimis; JC Wickens; Jean Daneel;
Joostenberg (Organic; Skin-macerated white);
Jordan; Kaapzicht (Old Vines); Keermont; Ken
Forrester (2) (Old Vines); Kleine Zalze; KWV;
L'Avenir; Laibach (Organic; Skin-macerated white);
Lammershoek (Old Vines); Le Belle Rebelle; Le
Sueur; **Lievland**; Lourens Family; Luddite; M'hudi;
Malanot; Metzer (Old Vines); Michaella; Mont
Blois; Mulderbosch (2); Mullineux (2) (Old Vines);
Naudé (Old Vines); Nederburg; Nuy; Olifantsberg
(2); Opstal (Old Vines); Painted Wolf; Patatsfontein;
Paulus; Perdeberg; Piekenierskloof (Old Vines);
Raats; Radford Dale (2); Remhoogte; Reverie;
Ridgeback; Riebeek Valley; Saltare; Savage; Schultz
Family; Simonsig; Spice Route; Spier (Organic);
Spioenkop (2); Springfontein; Stellenbosch
Vineyards; Terracura; **The Ahrens Family** (2);
The Fledge; The Liberator; The Vinoneers; Thistle
& Weed; Thorne & Daughters (Old Vines); Van
Loggerenberg; Wildehurst; Wildekrans (Old Vines);
Wolf & Woman

★★★★ Alvi's Drift; Axe Hill; **Bergsig**; Boland;
Botha; Cape Classics; Catherine Marshall; Collatio;
Damarakloof; Daschbosch; De Wet; Delaire
Graff; Delheim; DeMorgenzon; Diemersfontein;
Domaine Brahms; Druk My Niet; Durbanville
Hills; Fleur du Cap; Fram; Gabriëlskloof; Groot
Phesantekraal; Hawksmoor; Hazendal; Hirst;
Holden Manz; Jan Harmsgat; Jason's Hill; Kaapzicht
(Old Vines); Klawer (Old Vines); **Koelenhof**;
L'Avenir; Lammershoek (Old Vines); Lateganskop;
Leeuwenkuil; Leopard's Leap; **Lieben**; **Lievland**;
Longridge (Organic); Merwida; Migliarina; **Miles
Mossop** (3); Mimosa; Mont du Toit; **Montegray**;
Mooiplaas (Old Vines); Môrelig; Mulderbosch

(2); Mullineux; **Napier; Nico van der Merwe; Niel Joubert; Old Road** (Old Vines); Oldenburg; Olifantsberg; Opstal; Overhex (Nouveau); **Painted Wolf** (2) (Old Vines); Perdeberg; **Radford Dale** (3); Remhoogte; Reyneke (Old Vines); Rickety Bridge; Robert Stanford; Rooiberg; Rudera; Slanghoek; **Solitary;** Spier; Springfontein; Stellar (Fairtrade; Organic); **Stellenbosch Hills; Stellenbosch Reserve;** Stellenbosch University; **Stellenbosch Vineyards;** Stellenrust; Strydom; Super Single Vineyards (2); Taillard; **The Ahrens Family;** The Blacksmith; The Fledge; **The Horsemen;** Tierhoek; Van Wyk; Villiera; Villion; Welbedacht (Old Vines); Welgegund (Old Vines); Wellington Winery; Windmeul (Old Vines); Winshaw; Woolworths; Yardstick; Zevenwacht

★★★★ AA Badenhorst; Allée Bleue; Anura; Asara; Badsberg; Bellevue (Old Vines); Bellingham; Blake; Botha; Breëland; Cavalli; Collatio; DA Hanekom; Deux Frères; Dornier; **Dragonridge** (Alternative white/red; Skin-macerated white); False Bay; **Fat Bastard;** Joostenberg (Old Vines; Organic); Kleine Zalze; Kranskop; **Lammershoek** (Old Vines); Landskroon; Leipzig; Lutzville; Morgenhof; Nick & Forti's; Nico Vermeulen; Osbloed; Painted Wolf; Post House; Rainbow's End; Rooiberg; **Skilpadvlei; Spider Pig;** Stellenbosch University; Stellenbosch Vineyards; Swartland; Taillard; Teubes; **The Horsemen; Val de Vie;** Villiera; Waterford; Waterkloof (2); **Wildeberg;** Woolworths (3) ★★★ Arendskloof; **Boschheim;** Cape Wine Company; Dorrance; Durbanville Hills; **Eerste Hoop; Fat Bastard;** Fleur du Cap; House of Mandela; Lanzerac; Pearl Mountain; Windfall ★★★ Botha; Kumala; **KWV;** Mountain Ridge **NT** Andy Mitchell; Avondale (Organic); Blue Crane; Craven; Dagbreek; Doolhof; Dornier; Dragonridge; Elemental Bob (2); Fort Simon; Groot Parys; Hermit on the Hill; Hildenbrand; Hofstraat; Jean Daneel; Joostenberg (Organic); Lourens Family; Lyngrove; Maison; Mother Rock (3); Mullineux (2); Remhoogte; Rickety Bridge; Rietvallei; Robert Stanford; Rudera (2); Saltare; Spier (Organic); Stark-Condé (2); Terracura; Teubes; The Kitchen Sink; The Wine Thief; Themika; Tierhoek; Waterford (2) (Old Vines); Woolworths **D** Botanica; Fairview; Flotsam & Jetsam (Old Vines); Knorhoek; Koelenhof; MAN Family; Matzikama (Fairtrade; Organic); Meerhof; Signal Hill

Cinsaut

★★★★★ Bosman; Savage

★★★★☆ AA Badenhorst (2); Blackwater; Die Kat; Eenzaamheid; Elemental Bob; Jasper Raats; Kruger Family (Old Vines); Laarman; Naudé (Old Vines); Neil Ellis; **Piekenierskloof** (Old Vines); Rall;

Sadie (Old Vines); Stellenbosch Vineyards; Terracura; Van Loggerenberg; **Welgegund**

★★★★ AD Wines; **De Kleine Wijn Koöp;** Fairview; **Flotsam & Jetsam;** Fram; Illimis; Kaapzicht; Metzer; **Miles Mossop;** Mount Abora (Alternative white/red); Myburgh Bros; Piekenierskloof; **Tempel;** Van der Merwe & Finlayson; Wildehurst

★★★☆ Bellevue; De Kleine Wijn Koöp; Erika Obermeyer; Le Bonheur; Osbloed; Perdeberg; **Spider Pig;** Stellenrust; Strange Kompanjie; The Blacksmith; **Thor;** Waterkloof ★★★ Bemind; Dorrance; **Maison de Teijger; Old Road; Opstal;** The Blacksmith ★★☆ Darling Cellars; Landskroon; Maison de Teijger **NT** Craven; Enfin; Leeuwenkuil; Radford Dale; Rickety Bridge; Rietvallei **D** Darling Cellars; Flotsam & Jetsam (Old Vines); Kleine Zalze; MAN Family; Overhex; Signal Hill; Super Single Vineyards

Cinsaut blanc
★★★★ Rall

Clairette blanche
★★★★★☆ Daschbosch

NT Craven; Radford Dale **D** Thorne & Daughters

Colombard
★★★★★☆ Lowerland

★★★★ Micu Narunsky; **Orange River; The Wine Thief**

★★★☆ Tanagra; The Blacksmith ★★★ Bon Courage; Cape Dreams; Goedverwacht; **Landzicht;** Langverwacht; McGregor; **Orange River** (2); Rooiberg; Van Loveren ★★★ Aan de Doorns ★★ Nuy **NT** Bezalel; Stellar (Fairtrade; Organic); Woolworths **D** Schenkfontein

De-alcoholised
★★★☆ Van Loveren (Sweet red) ★★ Van Loveren (Sauvignon blanc unwooded)

Fairtrade
★★★★★ Dorrance (Shiraz/syrah)

★★★★★ Journey's End (Cabernet sauvignon); **Meerhof** (2) (White blends, wooded, dry; Vin de paille/straw wine); Stellar (Vin de paille/straw wine; Organic); Dorrance (2) (Chardonnay wooded; Chenin blanc unwooded dry)

★★★★ Stellar (3) (Chenin blanc wooded, dry; Sauvignon blanc wooded; Shiraz/syrah; Organic); Bosman (2) (Red blends, shiraz/syrah-based; White blends, wooded, dry); Asara (Red blends, Cape Bordeaux); Org de Rac (Shiraz/syrah; Organic); Imbuko (Red blends, Cape Bordeaux); Journey's End (2) (Shiraz/syrah; Chardonnay wooded); Fairview (Pinotage); Journey's End (2) (Cabernet sauvignon; Shiraz/syrah); Rivendell (Sauvignon blanc unwooded); Jan Harmsgat (Sauvignon blanc unwooded); Spice Route (Mourvèdre); Cape Venture (Red blends, shiraz/syrah-based) ★★★★☆ Stellar (3) (Pinot noir; Pinotage; Chardonnay wooded; Organic); Imbuko (2) (Shiraz/syrah; White blends, unwooded, dry); Org de Rac (2) (Merlot; Cabernet sauvignon; Organic); Imbuko (Chenin blanc unwooded dry); **Meerhof** (Rosé dry); Org de Rac (White blends, unwooded, dry; Organic); **Cape Wine Company** (Red blends, Cape Bordeaux); Journey's End (2) (Merlot; Chardonnay wooded); Cape Wine Company (Pinotage); **Meerhof** (7) (Cabernet sauvignon; Pinotage; Shiraz/syrah; Red blends, shiraz/syrah-based; Rosé dry; Chenin blanc unwooded dry; White blends, wooded, dry; Old Vines); Piekenierskloof (4) (Pinotage; Shiraz/syrah; Chenin blanc unwooded dry; Sauvignon blanc unwooded); Fish Hoek (Rosé dry); Goats do Roam (Red blends, shiraz/syrah-based); Jan Harmsgat (4) (Cabernet sauvignon; Pinotage; Shiraz/syrah; Chardonnay wooded); Matzikama (Petite sirah/durif; Organic); Cape Venture (Chenin blanc unwooded dry); Journey's End (2) (Red blends, Cape Bordeaux; Red blends, shiraz/syrah-based) ★★★★ Woolworths (2) (Chenin blanc unwooded dry; Sauvignon blanc unwooded; Organic); Stellar (7) (Cabernet sauvignon; Shiraz/syrah; Chenin blanc unwooded dry; Sauvignon blanc unwooded; White blends, unwooded, dry; Sparkling, Non-MCC, rosé, dry; Sparkling, Non-MCC, white, dry; Organic); Imbuko (2) (Pinotage; Sauvignon blanc unwooded); Asara (White from red/black grapes (not Blanc de noir)); Imbuko (3) (Cabernet sauvignon; Pinotage; Red blends, shiraz/syrah-based); Du Toitskloof (2) (Red blends, with pinotage; Chardonnay wooded); Daschbosch (2) (Pinotage; Chenin blanc unwooded dry); Piekenierskloof (4) (Cabernet sauvignon; Shiraz/syrah; Chenin blanc unwooded dry; Sauvignon blanc unwooded); Kleine Zalze (Cabernet sauvignon); Koopmanskloof (4) (Cabernet sauvignon; Pinotage; Rosé dry; Sauvignon blanc unwooded); **Cape Wine Company** (3) (Grenache noir; Shiraz/syrah; Red blends, shiraz/syrah-based); Piekenierskloof (4) (Cabernet sauvignon; Rosé dry; Chardonnay unwooded; Viognier); Fairvalley (3) (Pinotage; Chenin blanc unwooded dry; Sauvignon blanc unwooded); Fish Hoek (3) (Merlot; Shiraz/syrah; Chenin blanc unwooded dry); Schalkenbosch (Shiraz/syrah); Journey's End (2) (Chardonnay unwooded; Sauvignon blanc unwooded) ★★★ Woolworths (6) (Cabernet sauvignon; Merlot; Pinotage; Shiraz/syrah; Chardonnay unwooded;

Chenin blanc unwooded dry; Organic); Stellar (7) (Merlot; Red blends, with pinotage; Chardonnay unwooded; Cabernet sauvignon; Merlot; Pinotage; Shiraz/syrah; Organic); Imbuko (Pinotage); Du Toitskloof (Rosé dry); Imbuko (8) (Cabernet sauvignon; Merlot; Chenin blanc unwooded dry; Sweet red; Shiraz/syrah; Red blends, Cape Bordeaux; Chenin blanc unwooded dry; Sauvignon blanc unwooded); Koopmanskloof (5) (Merlot; Pinotage; Shiraz/syrah; Chardonnay unwooded; Chenin blanc unwooded dry); Stellenrust (4) (Red blends, with pinotage; Rosé dry; White blends, unwooded, dry; White blends, off-dry/semi-sweet (w & u/w)); Meerhof (2) (Chardonnay wooded; Sauvignon blanc unwooded); Rivendell (Rosé dry); Fish Hoek (2) (Pinotage; Sauvignon blanc unwooded) ★★ Imbuko (Sauvignon blanc unwooded); Daschbosch (2) (Merlot; Sauvignon blanc unwooded); **Imbuko** (5) (Red blends, other; Rosé off-dry/semi-sweet; Muscadel, white, unfortified; Muscadel, white, unfortified; Non-muscat, white, fortified; Light & low-alcohol; Perlé) **NT** Stellar (14) (Viognier; Malbec; Red blends, shiraz/syrah-based; White blends, unwooded, dry; Rosé dry; Colombard; Shiraz/syrah; White blends, unwooded, dry; Red blends, shiraz/syrah-based; Rosé dry; White blends, unwooded, dry; White blends, off-dry/semi-sweet (w & u/w); Sparkling, Non-MCC, rosé, off-dry/semi-sweet; Sweet red; Organic); Township Winery (2) (Pinotage; Viognier); Fairvalley (3) (Cabernet sauvignon; Chardonnay wooded; Chardonnay wooded); Walking Woods (7) (Pinotage; Red blends, with pinotage; Rosé dry; Chardonnay wooded; Chenin blanc unwooded dry; Sparkling, Méthode cap classique, white, dry; Sparkling, Non-MCC, rosé, off-dry/semi-sweet; Organic); Schalkenbosch (Cabernet sauvignon); Havana Hills (Rosé dry) **D** Fish Hoek (Malbec); Spice Route (4) (Mourvèdre; Shiraz/syrah; Shiraz/syrah; Semillon wooded); Matzikama (Chenin blanc wooded, dry)

Fernão pires
★★★ Strange Kompanjie

Gamay noir
★★★★ Radford Dale (2); **Villiera**

Gewürztraminer
★★★★★☆ The Vinoneers

★★★★ Altydgedacht; Buitenverwachting; Nederburg; Neethlingshof; Scrucap

★★★★ Bergsig; Bon Courage; Delheim; Simonsig; Zevenwacht ★★ Koelenhof **NT** New Beginnings; Welmoed

Grenache blanc

★★★★★ KWV; The Foundry

★★★★☆ Bellingham; Bosman; Olifantsberg; Rall

★★★★ Niel Joubert; Perdeberg; Piekenierskloof

★★★☆ KWV; Strange Kompanjie NT Elemental Bob; Glen Heatlie; Hermit on the Hill; Leeuwenkuil; Mont Blois D Signal Hill

Grenache gris

★★★★☆ Maanschijn

★★★★ Momento

★★★ Fram

Grenache noir

★★★★★ Sadie

★★★★☆ Anysbos; ArtiSons; Blackwater; Creation; David & Nadia; De Kleine Wijn Koöp; Fairview; Migliarina; Mischa; Momento; Naudé; Neil Ellis; Olifantsberg; Piekenierskloof (Old Vines); Spice Route (2); Stellenbosch Vineyards; Strandveld; The Foundry; Thelema

★★★★ Black Elephant; Cape Wine Company; Dunstone; Enfin; Fable; Fairview; Franki's; Kleine Zalze; Kloovenburg; Lammershoek; Meerhof; Piekenierskloof; Rosendal; Saronsberg; Tierhoek; Van der Merwe & Finlayson; Vriesenhof; Waverley Hills (Organic); Welgegund

★★★☆ Anura; DeMorgenzon; Four Paws; Kruger Family (Old Vines); Lynx; Oldenburg; Ormonde; Rustenberg; Schalkenbosch; Skilpadvlei; Spider Pig; Waterford; Woolworths ★★★ Cape Wine Company (Fairtrade); The Horsemen ★★☆ Anura NT AA Badenhorst; Arendsig; Clayton; Donkiesbaai; Elemental Bob; Esau; Leeuwenkuil; Mother Rock; Oude Compagnies Post; Painted Wolf (Organic); Tierhoek; Zevenwacht D Signal Hill; Tokara

Grüner veltliner

★★★★ Diemersdal

Hanepoot fortified

★★★★☆ Boplaas; Daschbosch (Old Vines); Du Preez

★★★★ Aan de Doorns; Calitzdorp; Constantia Uitsig (Skin-macerated white); Die Mas; Klawer; Muratie; Opstal; Peter Falke

★★★☆ Domein Doornkraal; Du Toitskloof; Slanghoek; Waboomsrivier ★★★ Badsberg; Boplaas; Clairvaux; De Wet; Orange River; Swartland; Tulbagh Winery; Villiersdorp; Winkelshoek★★★ Landzicht NT Calitzdorp D Kaapzicht; Signal Hill

Hanepoot unfortified

★★★★☆ B Vintners

★★★★ City on a Hill

★★★ Cape Classics; KWV★★★ Overhex NT Hofstraat (Light & low-alcohol); Swartland D Bellevue

Hárslevelü

★★★★☆ Lemberg

★★★★ Lammershoek

Husk spirit/grappa-styles

★★★★★ Dalla Cia

★★★★☆ Gentleman Spirits; Tanagra (3); Wilderer (2)

★★★★ Bartho Eksteen; Dalla Cia (3) (Organic); Delaire Graff; Gentleman Spirits (2); Org de Rac (Organic); Quoin Rock; Richard Hilton; Simonsig; Upland (Organic); Wilderer

★★★☆ Dalla Cia; Kaapzicht ★★★ Iona NT Dalla Cia; Gentleman Spirits (2)

Jerepigo red

★★★★ Stonebird

★★★☆ Badsberg; Blaauwklippen; Domein Doornkraal; KWV ★★★ Domein Doornkraal; Orange River; Swartland; Winkelshoek★★★ Botha; Landzicht; Simonsvlei; Slanghoek NT Camberley; Grundheim D Catherine Marshall; Waverley Hills

Jerepigo white

★★★★ Backsberg; Calitzdorp; Haute Cabrière; Orange River

★★★☆ Lateganskop; Niel Joubert; Swartland; Winkelshoek ★★★ Sedgwick's Old Brown★★★ Namaqua ★★ Ship NT Botha D Bezalel; Brandvlei; Riebeek Valley; Signal Hill

Kosher

★★★☆ Zandwijk (2) (Red blends, Cape Bordeaux; Sauvignon blanc unwooded) ★★★ Zandwijk (Chenin blanc unwooded dry); Simonsvlei (Merlot) ★★★ Simonsvlei (4) (Pinotage; Pinotage; Shiraz/syrah; Chenin blanc unwooded dry) ★★ Zandwijk (2) (Sparkling, Non-MCC, white, off-dry/semi-sweet; Sweet red; Light & low-alcohol; Sacramental); Simonsvlei (Chardonnay unwooded) ★★ Zandwijk (2) (Natural Sweet, red; Natural Sweet, white; Light & low-alcohol) NT Backsberg (5) (Merlot; Pinotage; Chardonnay unwooded; Sparkling, Méthode cap classique, white, dry; Sweet red; Sacramental); Simonsvlei (2) (Cabernet sauvignon; Rosé dry)

Late Harvest

★★★★☆ Gabriëlskloof

★★★★ Gabriëlskloof; Thelema (2)

★★★ Roodezandt ★★ Overmeer Cellars; Vintales ★★☆ Robertson NT Drostdy-Hof (2); Highlands Road D Bergsig

Light & low-alcohol

★★★★★ Mullineux (Vin de paille/straw wine); Laibach (Natural Sweet, white)

★★★★☆ Bon Courage (Noble Late Harvest)

★★★★ **Durbanville Hills** (Noble Late Harvest); Glen Carlou (Noble Late Harvest); **Meerendal** (Natural Sweet, white)

★★★★ Woolworths (Sparkling, Méthode cap classique, white, dry); Villiera (Sparkling, Méthode cap classique, white, dry); Darling Cellars (Sparkling, Méthode cap classique, white, off-dry/semi-sweet); Zandvliet (Natural Sweet, white); **Maanschijn** (Sparkling, Méthode ancestrale) ★★★ Woolworths (Rosé dry); Daschbosch (Natural Sweet, white; Perlé); **Orange River** (Sparkling, Non-MCC, white, off-dry/semi-sweet); Namaqua (Noble Late Harvest); Orange River (Sparkling, Non-MCC, white, off-dry/semi-sweet); Blaauwklippen (Noble Late Harvest); Badsberg (Sparkling, Non-MCC, white, off-dry/semi-sweet) ★★★ Robertson (Sparkling, Non-MCC, rosé, off-dry/semi-sweet); Woolworths (Sparkling, Non-MCC, white, off-dry/semi-sweet); Lutzville (3) (Sparkling, Non-MCC, rosé, off-dry/semi-sweet; Natural Sweet, red; Natural Sweet, white); Daschbosch (Natural Sweet, rosé; Perlé); Klawer (Sparkling, Non-MCC, rosé, off-dry/semi-sweet); Rooiberg (Sparkling, Non-MCC, rosé, off-dry/semi-sweet); Woolworths (Red blends, other); Conradie (Rosé off-dry/semi-sweet; Perlé); Tulbagh Winery (White blends, unwooded, dry); Landzicht (2) (Natural Sweet, rosé; Natural Sweet, white); Orange River (Sparkling, Non-MCC, rosé, off-dry/semi-sweet); **Slanghoek** (2) (Natural Sweet, rosé; Natural Sweet, white); Badsberg (Rosé off-dry/semi-sweet; Perlé); Domein Doornkraal (Natural Sweet, white); Tangled Tree (Rosé off-dry/semi-sweet); **Van Loveren** (Sweet red) ★★ Robertson (10) (Sweet red; Merlot; Rosé dry; Chenin blanc unwooded dry; Chenin blanc unwooded dry; Natural Sweet, white; Sparkling, Non-MCC, red, off-dry/semi-sweet; Sparkling, Non-MCC, white, off-dry/semi-sweet; Natural Sweet, white; Natural Sweet, white); Woolworths (2) (Red blends, other; Natural Sweet, rosé); Lutzville (Natural Sweet, rosé); Perdeberg (Sparkling, Non-MCC, rosé, off-dry/semi-sweet); Du Toitskloof (2) (Rosé off-dry/semi-sweet; Sweet red); Simonsvlei (Natural Sweet, rosé); Rooiberg (Natural Sweet, red); Woolworths (Natural Sweet, rosé); Overhex (Sparkling, Non-MCC, rosé off-dry/semi-sweet); De Krans (White blends, off-dry/semi-sweet (w & u/w); Perlé); Tulbagh Winery (Natural Sweet, rosé); Du Toitskloof (Sparkling, Non-MCC, red, off-dry/semi-sweet);

Viljoensdrift (Sparkling, Non-MCC, rosé, off-dry/semi-sweet); Zandwijk (2) (Sparkling, Non-MCC, white, off-dry/semi-sweet; Sweet red; Kosher; Sacramental); Woolworths (Natural Sweet, rosé); Fleur du Cap (Chenin blanc off-dry/semi-sweet (w & u/w)); Van Loveren (3) (Merlot; Rosé off-dry/semi-sweet; Semillon unwooded); Mooiplaas (Cabernet sauvignon); Orange River (Natural Sweet, white); The House of JC le Roux (3) (Sparkling, Non-MCC, red, dry; Sparkling, Non-MCC, rosé, off-dry/semi-sweet; Sparkling, Non-MCC, white, off-dry/semi-sweet); De Wet (Muscadel, white, unfortified); Perlé); **Barnardt Boyes** (Rosé off-dry/semi-sweet); Perlé); **Van Loveren** (2) (Rosé off-dry/semi-sweet; Sauvignon blanc unwooded; De-alcoholised); Drostdy-Hof (5) (Rosé dry; Chenin blanc unwooded dry; Natural Sweet, red; Natural Sweet, rosé; Natural Sweet, white) ★★ Robertson (12) (White blends, unwooded, dry; White blends, off-dry/semi-sweet (w & u/w); Natural Sweet, rosé; Sauvignon blanc unwooded; Natural Sweet, red; Natural Sweet, rosé; Natural Sweet, rosé; Sweet red; Sauvignon blanc unwooded; White blends, unwooded, dry; Natural Sweet, red; Natural Sweet, rosé); Woolworths (White blends, unwooded, dry); 4th Street (2) (Natural Sweet, red; Natural Sweet, white); Woolworths (White blends, unwooded, dry); Nicholson Smith (Rosé off-dry/semi-sweet); De Krans (Sweet red; Perlé); Zandwijk (2) (Natural Sweet, red; Natural Sweet, white; Kosher); Bonnievale (Rosé off-dry/semi-sweet; Perlé); Wellington Winery (2) (Natural Sweet, rosé; Natural Sweet, white; Perlé); **Leopard's Leap** (2) (Red blends, other; White blends, unwooded, dry) ★ Woolworths (Natural Sweet, white); 4th Street (Natural Sweet, rosé); Theescombe (Cabernet sauvignon) **NT** Woolworths (10) (Merlot; Red blends, other; Natural Sweet, red; Sweet red; Natural Sweet, rosé; Chardonnay unwooded; Chenin blanc unwooded dry; Sauvignon blanc unwooded; Colombard; Natural Sweet, white); Fleur du Cap (Noble Late Harvest); Paul Cluver (Noble Late Harvest); Druk My Niet (Vin de paille/straw wine); Swartland (Hanepoot unfortified); Mullineux (Vin de paille/straw wine); Swartland (Rosé off-dry/semi-sweet); Fleur du Cap (Rosé dry); De Grendel (Noble Late Harvest); Quando (Natural Sweet, white); Hofstraat (Hanepoot unfortified); Somerset Wines (Sparkling, Non-MCC, rosé, dry) **D** Wineways (Natural Sweet, rosé); Simonsvlei (Natural Sweet, rosé); Douglas Green (2) (Natural Sweet, rosé; Natural Sweet, white); Audacia (Shiraz/syrah); Overhex (3) (Rosé off-dry/semi-sweet; White blends, off-dry/semi-sweet (w & u/w); Sweet red);

Bonnievale (White blends, off-dry/semi-sweet (w & u/w); Perlé); Durbanville Hills (Noble Late Harvest)

Malbec

★★★★☆ Anura; **Blaauwklippen**; Diemersfontein; Lanzerac; Morgenhof

★★★★ Akkerdal; Annex Kloof; Bellevue; **Benguela Cove**; Bizoe; FirstCape; Hillcrest; **Idiom**; La Couronne; Linton Park; **Mischa**; Mitre's Edge; Mooi Bly; Niel Joubert; Paul Wallace; **Rustenberg**; **Sonklip**; South Hill; Stellakaya (2); Super Single Vineyards; Woolworths (2); Zorgvliet

★★★☆ Blake; Bloemendal; Bushmanspad; Diemersdal; Dornier; Druk My Niet; Le Pommier; Neethlingshof; Ormonde; Perdeberg; Plaisir de Merle; Raka; Withington ★★★ La Couronne; Linton Park; Maison de Teijger **NT** Black Elephant; Buitenverwachting; Doolhof; Enfin; Glen Carlou; Hildenbrand; Schalkenbosch; Southern Sky; Stellar (Fairtrade; Organic); Val du Charron **D** Fish Hoek (Fairtrade); Kumala; Nederburg; Overhex; Signal Hill; Vergenoegd; Weltevrede

Marsanne

★★★★☆ The Wine Thief

NT Leeuwenkuil; Maanschijn

Merlot

★★★★★ Shannon; Thelema

★★★★☆ Almenkerk; Anthonij Rupert; Bein (2); Creation; De Trafford; Delaire Graff; Eagles' Nest; Eikendal; Fleur du Cap; Groot Constantia; Hartenberg; Hillcrest; Holden Manz; **Idiom**; Keermont; La Bri; Laibach (Organic); **Longridge**; Lourensford; Meerlust; Meinert; Oldenburg; Rainbow's End; Raka; Shannon; **Simelia**; Thelema; **Vergelegen** (2); Villiera

★★★★ Anthonij Rupert; **Anura** (2); Arendskloof; Audacia; Barton; Bein; Belfield; Bon Courage; Botanica; Buitenverwachting; Canto; Catherine Marshall; Clos Malverne; Creation; De Grendel; Domaine Coutelier (2); Dunstone; Durbanville Hills; Ernie Els; Ernst Gouws; Excelsior; Fairview; Fleur du Cap; Freedom Hill; **Glen Carlou** (2); Glenelly; GlenWood; Graceland; Groenland; Groote Post; Haskell; Jordan; Kings Kloof; **Kumasha**; Kyburg; La Petite Ferme; Laibach; Landskroon; Lanzerac; **Le Bonheur**; Linton Park; Longridge; Marianne; Meerendal; Mischa; Mitre's Edge; **Mont du Toit**; Muratie; Nitida; Overgaauw; Pearl Mountain; Plaisir de Merle; Post House; Remhoogte; Rickety Bridge; Ridgeback; Rosendal; Rust en Vrede; Rustenberg; Slaley; Steenberg; Stellakaya; Stellenbosch Reserve; Sumaridge; The Butcher Shop; Township Winery; Under Oaks; Villiera; **Vondeling**; Waterkloof;

Whalehaven; **Wildehurst**; Woolworths (5); Yonder Hill; Zorgvliet

★★★★ Anura; Asara; Backsberg; Bein; Blue Owl; Boland; Boschkloof; Bosman; Botha; **Cape Town Wine Co**; Cloof (2); Croydon; De Breede (Organic); Delheim; Diemersdal; Diemersfontein; Dornier; Durbanville Hills; Elgin Vintners; Excelsior; Fairview; False Bay; Fat Bastard; Fort Simon (3); Goede Hoop; Guardian Peak; Havana Hills; Hoopenburg; Hout Bay; Jg; Jordan; Journey's End (Fairtrade); JP Bredell; Kaapzicht; Kanu; Ken Forrester; Kloovenburg; La Petite Provence; Landskroon; Le Sueur; Lomond; Lyngrove; Maastricht; MAN Family; Marklew; Miravel; Mischa; Mont du Toit (Natural/ non-fortified pale); Morgenhof; Morgenster; **Namaqua**; Nederburg; Neethlingshof; New Beginnings; Nico van der Merwe; Noble Hill; Olsen; Org de Rac (2) (Fairtrade; Organic); **Ormonde** (2); Perdeberg; Porcupine Ridge; Pulpit Rock; Riebeek Valley; Scrucap; Signal Gun; Spookfontein; Stellenbosch University (2); Stellenrust; Super Single Vineyards; Taillard; Uva Mira; Vergenoegd; Vierkoppen; Vondeling; Welbedacht; **Woolworths** (4); Zevenwacht ★★★ **Absolute Style**; Anthonij Rupert; **Bader & Walters**; Badsberg; Bellpost; Bloemendal; Bon Courage; Bonnievale; Boplaas; Boschendal; Cape Classics; Cape Dreams; Cloof; D'Aria; Darling Cellars; Daschbosch; Die Mas; Du Preez; Fish Hoek (Fairtrade); Flagstone; Goedverwacht; Hill & Dale; Hillcrest; Idun; Kirabo; Klein Roosboom; Kleine Zalze; Koelenhof; Kruger Family; **Kunjani**; Leopard's Leap; Linton Park; Louis 57; Louisvale; MolenVliet; Nederburg; Niel Joubert; Overhex (Nouveau); Robertson (4); Rooiberg (3); Roos Family; Simonsvlei (Kosher); Slanghoek; Somerbosch; Spier; Stellenbosch Hills; Stellenview (2); **Summerhill**; Swartland; Thokozani; Val de Vie; Varkenskraal; Viljoensdrift; **Vinologist**; Vredenheim; Walker Bay Estate; Wellington Winery; Windmeul; Yonder Hill; Zonnebloem ★★★ Alexanderfontein; Bayede!; Botha; Burgershof; Carrol Boyes; Daschbosch; Du Toitskloof; FirstCape; Hoopenburg; Imbuko (Fairtrade); Jason's Hill; Koopmanskloof (Fairtrade); KWV (3); Le Manoir de Brendel; Maison de Teijger; Middelvlei; Mountain Ridge; Namaqua; Nederburg; Nicholson Smith; Stellar (2) (Fairtrade; Organic); Stellenbosch Family Wines; **The Bridge of Hope** (2); **Thor**; Tulbagh Winery; Van Loveren; Viljoensdrift; Welmoed; Wineways (2); **Woolworths** (3) (Fairtrade; Organic) ★★ Audacia; Daschbosch (Fairtrade); Klawer; Landzicht; Lutzville; Namaqua; Robertson (Light & low-alcohol); Schenkfontein; Simonsvlei; Stellenbosch Family Wines; Van Loveren

(Light & low-alcohol); Weltevrede; Wineways (2); Wonderfontein ★★ Klawer NT Alvi's Drift; Annandale; Arra; Backsberg (Kosher); Bayede!; Bemind; Buffalo Creek; Bushmanspad; Camberley; Cathedral Peak; Cilmor; De Meye; DeWaal (2); Dieu Donné; Domein Doornkraal; Doolhof; Douglas Green; Drostdy-Hof; Fernskloof (Organic); Franschhoek Cellar; Glenview; Goede Hoop; Highgate; Hofstraat; Kleinhoekkloof; Kranskop; Landzicht; Meerendal (2); Namaqua; Oneiric; Pearl Mountain; Rietvallei; Rosendal; Saxenburg; Simelia; Spier; Stellendrift (2); Swartland; The Butcher Shop; Tulbagh Winery; Val du Charron; Wineways; Wonderfontein; **Woolworths** (8) (Light & low-alcohol; Organic) **D** Audacia (3); Durbanville Hills; Knorhoek; L'Avenir; La Couronne; Linton Park; Maske; Niel Joubert; Ormonde; Rebus; Stettyn

Meunier/pinot meunier
★★★★ Yardstick

Morio Muscat unfortified
★★★ Woolworths

Mourvèdre
★★★★☆ Beaumont; Newton Johnson; Painted Wolf; The Wine Thief; Waterkloof

★★★★ Deux Frères; Fairview; Saronsberg; Spice Route

★★★★☆ Fable; Hawksmoor ★★★ Dragonridge; Oude Compagnies Post★★★ Boschheim; Leeurivier NT Arendsig; Black Pearl; Glen Carlou; Hermit on the Hill; Idiom; Joostenberg (Organic); Quando; Stony Brook; Tierhoek **D** Arra (2); MAN Family; Spice Route

Muscadel, red, fortified
★★★★★ Nuy (2); Rietvallei

★★★★ Aan de Doorns; Badsberg; Boplaas; Burgershof; Calitzdorp; Clairvaux; Dagbreek; De Wet; Die Mas; Domein Doornkraal; Du Toitskloof; Klawer; Olivedale; Orange River; Rooiberg; Rustenberg

★★★★☆ Allesverloren; Bon Courage; Excelsior Vlakteplaas; Klawer; KWV; Namaqua; Rietvallei; Roodezandt; Van Loveren; Winkelshoek; Wonderfontein ★★★ Darling Cellars; Landzicht; Robertson; Slanghoek; Tulbagh Winery; Weltevrede ★★★☆ McGregor NT Conradie; Grundheim; Montagu Wine Cellar

Muscadel, red, unfortified
NT Landzicht

Muscadel, white, fortified
★★★★☆ Alvi's Drift; Bon Courage; Boplaas; Calitzdorp; De Krans; Die Mas; La Couronne; Lutzville; Monis; Mont Blois (2); Orange River

★★★★ De Wet; Klawer; Nuy; Weltevrede

★★★★ Boplaas; Le Grand Chasseur; Merwida; Namaqua; Nico Vermeulen ★★★ Clairvaux; Excelsior Vlakteplaas; Landzicht; McGregor; Robertson; Wonderfontein ★★★☆ Winkelshoek NT Grundheim; Montagu Wine Cellar **D** Windmeul

Muscadel, white, unfortified
★★★★ Theescombe

★★★★ Thelema ★★ De Wet (Light & low-alcohol; Perlé); Nicholson Smith NT The Fledge; Yardstick

Muscat de Hambourg fortified
★★★★★ Stellenbosch Hills

★★★★ Stellenbosch Hills

Méthode ancestrale
★★★★☆ Upland (Sparkling, Méthode ancestrale)

★★★★ Dragonridge (Sparkling, Méthode ancestrale)

★★★★☆ **Maanschijn** (Sparkling, Méthode ancestrale; Light & low-alcohol); **Botanica** (Sparkling, Méthode ancestrale) ★★★ **Dragonridge** (Sparkling, Méthode ancestrale)

Natural Sweet, red
★★★★ Darling Cellars

★★★ Cape Dreams; Lutzville (Light & low-alcohol); The Bridge of Hope ★★ Arra; Cellar Cask; Drostdy-Hof (Light & low-alcohol); Rooiberg (Light & low-alcohol); Vintales; **Wineways** (4); Woolworths (3) ★★ 4th Street (Light & low-alcohol); Kanu; Robertson (2) (Light & low-alcohol); Zandwijk NT Bonnievale; Woolworths **D** Douglas Green; Wineways

Natural Sweet, rosé
★★★★☆ Groot Constantia

★★★ Daschbosch (Light & low-alcohol; Perlé); Landzicht (Light & low-alcohol); Rooiberg; Slanghoek ★★ Cellar Cask; Drostdy-Hof (Light & low-alcohol); Lutzville (Light & low-alcohol); Nelson; Orange River; Overmeer Cellars; Simonsvlei (Light & low-alcohol); Tulbagh Winery (Light & low-alcohol); Vintales; Woolworths (3) (Light & low-alcohol) ★★ **Absolute Style**; Robertson (4) (Light & low-alcohol); Somerset Wines; The Bridge of Hope; Wellington Winery ★ 4th Street NT Woolworths (2) (Light & low-alcohol) **D** Douglas Green (Light & low-alcohol); Linton Park; Simonsvlei (Light & low-alcohol); Wineways (2) (Light & low-alcohol)

Natural Sweet, white
★★★★★ Klein Constantia; Laibach

★★★★☆ Badsberg; Bartho Eksteen; Black Elephant; Constantia Nectar; Dornier; Jordan; Perdeberg; Stellenrust

★★★★ **Meerendal** (Light & low-alcohol); Ridgeback; Waterford

★★★★ Delheim; Mimosa; Zandvliet ★★★ Daschbosch★★★ Arra; Cape Dreams; Domein Doornkraal (Light & low-alcohol); Landzicht (Light & low-alcohol); Lutzville (Light & low-alcohol); Rooiberg; **Slanghoek** ★★ Cellar Cask; Drostdy-Hof (Light & low-alcohol); Nicholson Smith; Orange River (Light & low-alcohol); Robertson (3) (Light & low-alcohol); Somerset Wines; Theuniskraal; Winkelshoek; Woolworths ★★ 4th Street (Light & low-alcohol); Vintales; Wellington Winery (Light & low-alcohol; Perlé); Zandwijk ★ Absolute Style; Woolworths **NT** Herold; Quando (Light & low-alcohol); Quoin Rock (2); Woolworths **D** Avontuur; Douglas Green (Light & low-alcohol); Stony Brook; Wineways

Natural/non-fortified pale

★★★★ **Mont du Toit** (3) (Cabernet sauvignon; Cabernet franc; Red blends, other)

★★★★ Mont du Toit (2) (Cabernet sauvignon; Merlot)★★★ Koelenhof (Sauvignon blanc unwooded)

Nebbiolo

★★★★★ Steenberg

★★★★ Anura; Arcangeli; Morgenster; Super Single Vineyards

★★★ Hofstraat **NT** Dagbreek; Du Toitskloof; Idiom (2)

Nero d'Avola

★★★★ Bosman

Noble Late Harvest

★★★★★ Buitenverwachting; Tokara

★★★★★ Badsberg; Benguela Cove; Boekenhoutskloof; Bon Courage (Light & low-alcohol); Delheim; Diemersdal; GlenWood; Highlands Road; Joostenberg (Organic); L'illa; Lomond; Lourensford; Lutzville; Miles Mossop; Nederburg (2); Neethlingshof; Neil Ellis; Olivedale; **Ormonde**; Paul Wallace; Springfontein

★★★★ **Aaldering**; Asara; Bergsig; D'Aria; Delaire Graff; **Durbanville Hills** (Light & low-alcohol); Fort Simon; Glen Carlou (Light & low-alcohol); Longridge; Lothian; Mooiplaas; Rickety Bridge; Rudera; Simonsig; Slanghoek; Woolworths

★★★★ Darling Cellars; **Kanu**; Nelson; Van Loveren ★★★ Blaauwklippen (Light & low-alcohol); Namaqua **NT** Beaumont; Bizoe; Bloemendal; Cape Point; De Grendel (Light & low-alcohol); Dieu Donné; Fleur du Cap (Light & low-alcohol); Fryer's Cove; Hildenbrand; Ken Forrester; Kranskop;

Nederburg; Nitida; Paul Cluver (Light & low-alcohol); Post House; Shannon; Slaley; Spier; Spookfontein; Villiera **D** Darling Cellars; Durbanville Hills (Light & low-alcohol); Signal Hill (2); Stellenbosch Vineyards

Non-muscat, white, fortified

★★★★☆ Villiera

Nouveau

★★★★ **Overhex** (6) (Cabernet sauvignon; Pinotage; Pinotage; Shiraz/syrah; Chenin blanc wooded, dry; Sauvignon blanc wooded)

★★★★ Overhex (4) (Chardonnay wooded; Chenin blanc unwooded dry; Sauvignon blanc unwooded; White blends, unwooded, dry); Org de Rac (Sparkling, Méthode cap classique, white, dry) ★★★ Overhex (7) (Merlot; Pinot noir; Shiraz/syrah; Pinot gris/grigio; Cabernet sauvignon; Red blends, shiraz/syrah-based; Rosé dry)★★★ Overhex (4) (Red blends, Cape Bordeaux; Rosé off-dry/semi-sweet; Hanepoot unfortified; Sauvignon blanc unwooded) **NT** Groot Parys (Pinotage)

Organic

★★★★★ Longridge (Chenin blanc off-dry/semi-sweet (w & u/w); Old Vines); **Upland** (Port-style, red)

★★★★☆ Woolworths (Chardonnay wooded); Spier (3) (Rosé dry; Chenin blanc wooded, dry; Red blends, Cape Bordeaux); Org de Rac (3) (Red blends, shiraz/syrah-based; White blends, wooded, dry; Cabernet sauvignon); Longridge (Chardonnay wooded); Joostenberg (2) (Red blends, other; Noble Late Harvest); Laibach (2) (Merlot; Chenin blanc wooded, dry; Skin-macerated white); Waverley Hills (Shiraz/syrah); Reyneke (Shiraz/syrah); Laibach (Chardonnay wooded); **Joostenberg** (Chenin blanc wooded, dry; Skin-macerated white); Stellar (Vin de paille/straw wine; Fairtrade); Upland (Sparkling, Méthode ancestrale; Méthode ancestrale); JAN Wines (2) (Red blends, shiraz/syrah-based; White blends, wooded, dry); Jasper Raats (Shiraz/syrah); Lowerland (Colombard); Hughes Family (2) (Red blends, with pinotage; White blends, wooded, dry); Upland (Brandy)

★★★★ **Stellar** (3) (Chenin blanc wooded, dry; Sauvignon blanc wooded; Shiraz/syrah; Fairtrade); **Spier** (Red blends, Cape Bordeaux); Teubes (Cabernet sauvignon); Org de Rac (2) (Shiraz/syrah; Chardonnay wooded; Fairtrade); Joostenberg (2) (Cabernet sauvignon; White blends, wooded, dry); Laibach (Pinotage); Org de Rac (Sauvignon blanc wooded); Waverley Hills (4) (Grenache noir; Red blends, with pinotage; Red blends, shiraz/

syrah-based; Chardonnay wooded); Longridge (2) (Chardonnay wooded; Chenin blanc wooded, dry); Reyneke (2) (Red blends, Cape Bordeaux; Sauvignon blanc wooded); Dalla Cia (Husk spirit/grappa-styles); Laibach (Red blends, Cape Bordeaux); Org de Rac (Husk spirit/grappa-styles); Constantia Mist (Sauvignon blanc unwooded); De Breede (Shiraz/syrah); Upland (Port-style, red); Jasper Raats (Sauvignon blanc wooded); Lowerland (Tannat); **Silvermist** (4) (Cabernet sauvignon; Cabernet sauvignon; Sauvignon blanc unwooded; Sauvignon blanc unwooded); Upland (3) (Brandy; Brandy; Husk spirit/grappa-styles)

★★★★ Stellar (3) (Pinot noir; Pinotage; Chardonnay wooded; Fairtrade); **Spier** (3) (Red blends, Cape Bordeaux; Rosé dry; White blends, wooded, dry); Teubes (Pinotage); Joostenberg (Chenin blanc wooded, dry; Old Vines); Org de Rac (8) (Cabernet sauvignon; Merlot; Shiraz/syrah; Red blends, shiraz/syrah-based; Chardonnay wooded; Roussanne; Verdelho; Sparkling, Méthode cap classique, white, dry; Fairtrade; Nouveau); **Waverley Hills** (4) (Rosé dry; Sparkling, Méthode cap classique, white, dry; Shiraz/syrah; White blends, unwooded, dry); Joostenberg (Red blends, shiraz/syrah-based); Org de Rac (White blends, unwooded, dry; Fairtrade); Reyneke (Chenin blanc unwooded dry); De Breede (Merlot); Upland (2) (Cabernet sauvignon; Pinot noir); Myburgh Bros (Viognier); Upland (Brandy); Matzikama (Petite sirah/durif; Fairtrade); **Jacques Germanier** (White blends, unwooded, dry) ★★★ Woolworths (3) (Rosé dry; Chenin blanc unwooded dry; Sauvignon blanc unwooded; Fairtrade); Stellar (7) (Cabernet sauvignon; Shiraz/syrah; Chenin blanc unwooded dry; Sauvignon blanc unwooded; White blends, unwooded, dry; Sparkling, Non-MCC, rosé, dry; Sparkling, Non-MCC, white, dry; Fairtrade); Teubes (Shiraz/syrah); Org de Rac (Port-style, red); Stellenview (Red blends, shiraz/syrah-based); Waverley Hills (Red blends, other); Org de Rac (Red blends, Cape Bordeaux); **Laibach** (Rosé dry); Waverley Hills (Cabernet sauvignon); Reyneke (3) (Red blends, Cape Bordeaux; Red blends, shiraz/syrah-based; White blends, unwooded, dry); **The Horsemen** (Carignan); **Jacques Germanier** (Red blends, Cape Bordeaux) ★★★ Woolworths (5) (Cabernet sauvignon; Merlot; Pinotage; Shiraz/syrah; Chardonnay unwooded; Fairtrade); Stellar (7) (Merlot; Red blends, with pinotage; Chardonnay unwooded; Cabernet sauvignon; Merlot; Pinotage; Shiraz/syrah; Fairtrade); Waverley Hills (Pinot gris/grigio); De Breede (2) (Red blends, Cape Bordeaux; Red blends, Cape Bordeaux) ★★ De Breede

(Cabernet sauvignon) ★★ De Breede (Red blends, Cape Bordeaux) **NT** Woolworths (Merlot); Avondale (7) (Shiraz/syrah; Red blends, Cape Bordeaux; Red blends, shiraz/syrah-based; Rosé dry; Chenin blanc wooded, dry; White blends, wooded, dry; Sparkling, Méthode cap classique, white, dry); Spier (Vin de paille/straw wine); Stellar (4) (Viognier; Malbec; Red blends, shiraz/syrah-based; White blends, unwooded, dry; Fairtrade); Painted Wolf (Grenache noir); Woolworths (Sparkling, Non-MCC, white, dry); Joostenberg (Shiraz/syrah); Stellar (4) (Rosé dry; Colombard; Shiraz/syrah; White blends, unwooded, dry; Fairtrade); Spier (Chenin blanc wooded, dry); Stellar (6) (Red blends, shiraz/syrah-based; Rosé dry; White blends, unwooded, dry; White blends, off-dry/semi-sweet (w & u/w); Sparkling, Non-MCC, rosé, off-dry/semi-sweet; Sweet red; Fairtrade); Joostenberg (4) (Mourvèdre; Shiraz/syrah; Touriga nacional; Chenin blanc wooded, dry); Groot Parys (2) (Pinotage; Chenin blanc unwooded dry; Nouveau); Fernskloof (5) (Cabernet sauvignon; Merlot; Pinotage; Red blends, shiraz/syrah-based; Rosé dry); Lazanou (7) (Shiraz/syrah; Red blends, shiraz/syrah-based; Chardonnay wooded; Chenin blanc unwooded dry; Viognier; White blends, unwooded, dry); Silvermist (Red blends, other); Walking Woods (7) (Pinotage; Red blends, with pinotage; Rosé dry; Chardonnay wooded; Chenin blanc unwooded dry; Sparkling, Méthode cap classique, white, dry; Sparkling, Non-MCC, off-dry/semi-sweet; Fairtrade) **D** Woolworths (2) (Sparkling, Méthode cap classique, rosé, dry; Sparkling, Non-MCC, rosé, dry); Waverley Hills (Jerepigo red); Klein Constantia (Sauvignon blanc unwooded); Groot Parys (Vin de paille/straw wine); Matzikama (Chenin blanc wooded, dry)

Old Vines

★★★★★ DeMorgenzon (Chenin blanc wooded, dry); Anthonij Rupert (Semillon wooded); Longridge (Chenin blanc off-dry/semi-sweet (w & u/w); Organic); Rickety Bridge (Semillon wooded); Gabriëlskloof (Chenin blanc wooded, dry); **David & Nadia** (3) (Chenin blanc wooded, dry; Chenin blanc wooded, dry; Chenin blanc wooded, dry); Mullineux (White blends, wooded, dry); Alheit (Chenin blanc wooded, dry); Beaumont (Chenin blanc wooded, dry); Metzer (Chenin blanc wooded, dry); **Kruger Family** (Chenin blanc wooded, dry); Sadie (4) (Grenache noir; Chenin blanc wooded, dry; Chenin blanc unwooded dry; White blends, wooded, dry)

★★★★☆ Daschbosch (Clairette blanche); Darling Cellars (2) (Red blends, other; Chenin blanc wooded, dry); Daschbosch (Hanepoot fortified); DeMorgenzon (Chenin blanc wooded, dry); Bosman (Chenin blanc wooded, dry); Bellingham (Chenin blanc wooded, dry); Anthonij Rupert (2) (Pinotage; Chenin blanc wooded, dry); **Piekenierskloof** (3) (Cinsaut; Grenache noir; Chenin blanc wooded, dry); Ken Forrester (Chenin blanc wooded, dry); Mullineux (Chenin blanc wooded, dry); Klawer (Vin de paille/ straw wine); Reyneke (Chenin blanc unwooded dry; Biodynamic); Boekenhoutskloof (Semillon wooded); Kaapzicht (Chenin blanc wooded, dry); Mullineux (Semillon gris); Terracura (Chenin blanc unwooded dry); **Lammershoek** (White blends, wooded, dry); Bellevue (Pinotage); Naudé (4) (Cinsaut; Chenin blanc wooded, dry; Semillon wooded; White blends, wooded, dry); Lammershoek (Chenin blanc wooded, dry); **Waterford** (Chenin blanc unwooded dry); David & Nadia (Semillon wooded); Alheit (5) (Chenin blanc wooded, dry; Chenin blanc wooded, dry; Chenin blanc wooded, dry; Chenin blanc wooded, dry; Semillon wooded); Wildekrans (Chenin blanc wooded, dry); Opstal (Chenin blanc wooded, dry); **Huis van Chevallerie** (2) (Chenin blanc wooded, dry; Sparkling, Méthode cap classique, white, dry); Kruger Family (Cinsaut); Leeu Passant (Red blends, other); Metzer (Chenin blanc wooded, dry); Meerendal (Pinotage); Spice Route (2) (Sauvignon blanc unwooded; Sherry-style wines); Thorne & Daughters (2) (Chenin blanc wooded, dry; Semillon wooded); Allée Bleue (Pinotage); Sadie (4) (Cinsaut; Tinta barocca; Semillon wooded; White blends, wooded, dry); **Welgegund** (Cinsaut)

★★★★ Zevenwacht (Chenin blanc wooded, dry); Piekenierskloof (Vin de paille/straw wine); **Painted Wolf** (Chenin blanc wooded, dry); **Old Road** (Semillon wooded); Klawer (Chenin blanc wooded, dry); Mooiplaas (Chenin blanc wooded, dry); **Villiera** (Gamay noir); Ken Forrester (Sparkling, Méthode cap classique, white, dry); **Old Road** (Chenin blanc wooded, dry); Windmeul (Chenin blanc wooded, dry); **Lammershoek** (5) (Carignan; Tinta barocca; Chardonnay wooded; Chenin blanc wooded, dry; Hárslevelü); Welbedacht (Chenin blanc wooded, dry); Reyneke (Chenin blanc wooded, dry); Kaapzicht (Chenin blanc wooded, dry); Cecilia (Pinotage); Huis van Chevallerie (Chenin blanc unwooded dry); Landau du Val (Semillon wooded); Welgegund (2) (Red blends, shiraz/syrah-based; Chenin blanc wooded, dry); Wildeberg (Semillon wooded)

★★★★ Joostenberg (Chenin blanc wooded, dry; Organic); Zevenwacht (Gewürztraminer); **Lammershoek** (Chenin blanc wooded, dry); Bellevue (Chenin blanc wooded, dry); Mooiplaas (Chenin blanc unwooded dry); Meerhof (Chenin blanc unwooded dry; Fairtrade); **Altydgedacht** (Chenin blanc unwooded dry); Ashbourne (Red blends, with pinotage); **Kruger Family** (Grenache noir); Strange Kompanjie (White blends, wooded, dry) **NT** Fairview (Carignan); Waterford (Chenin blanc wooded, dry); De Kleine Wijn Koöp (Semillon wooded); Leeu Passant (Red blends, other); Rickety Bridge (White blends, unwooded, dry) **D** Alheit (Chenin blanc unwooded dry); Flotsam & Jetsam (2) (Cinsaut; Chenin blanc wooded, dry)

Palomino/malvasia rei

★★★★ AA Badenhorst; Blackwater

NT Elemental Bob

Perlé Wines

★★★★ **Van Loveren** (Pinot gris/grigio) ★★★ Daschbosch (Natural Sweet, white) ★★★ Robertson (Sauvignon blanc unwooded; Perlé); Daschbosch (2) (Natural Sweet, rosé; Sparkling, Non-MCC, white, dry; Light & low-alcohol; Perlé); Conradie (Rosé off-dry/semi-sweet; Light & low-alcohol; Perlé); Autumn Harvest Crackling (Sweet red; Perlé); Badsberg (Rosé off-dry/semi-sweet; Light & low-alcohol; Perlé); De Wet (Rosé off-dry/semi-sweet; Perlé); **Louis 57** (Rosé off-dry/semi-sweet) ★★ Robertson (Rosé off-dry/semi-sweet; Perlé); De Krans (White blends, off-dry/semi-sweet (w & u/w); Light & low-alcohol; Perlé); Bonnievale (Chenin blanc off-dry/semi-sweet (w & u/w); Perlé); Autumn Harvest Crackling (Rosé off-dry/ semi-sweet; Perlé); Capenheimer (White blends, off-dry/semi-sweet (w & u/w); Perlé); De Wet (Muscadel, white, unfortified; Light & low-alcohol; Perlé); **Barnardt Boyes** (Rosé off-dry/semi-sweet; Light & low-alcohol; Perlé); Paarl Perlé (White blends, off-dry/semi-sweet (w & u/w); Perlé); Thokozani (Sauvignon blanc unwooded) ★★ De Krans (Sweet red; Light & low-alcohol; Perlé); Bonnievale (Rosé off-dry/semi-sweet; Light & low-alcohol; Perlé); Autumn Harvest Crackling (White blends, off-dry/semi-sweet (w & u/w); Perlé); Wellington Winery (2) (Natural Sweet, rosé; Natural Sweet, white; Light & low-alcohol; Perlé) **NT** Seven Sisters (Chenin blanc off-dry/semi-sweet (w & u/w); Perlé); Blaauwklippen (Sparkling, Non-MCC, rosé, dry; Perlé); Calitzdorp (White blends, off-dry/ semi-sweet (w & u/w)) **D** Bonnievale (White blends, off-dry/semi-sweet (w & u/w))

Petit verdot

★★★★☆ Benguela Cove; De Trafford; KWV; **La Bri**; Stellenbosch Vineyards; Thelema

★★★★ Anura; **Buitenverwachting**; Du Preez; Hillcrest; Montegray; Pulpit Rock; Raka; Walker Bay Estate; Zorgvliet

★★★☆ Definitum; Dornier; Leeurivier; Maison de Teijger; Miravel; My Wyn; **Skipskop** ★★★ Kirabo; KWV **NT** Bellevue; Botanica; Du'SwaRoo (2); Kleinhoekkloof; Landzicht; Lovane; Mitre's Edge; Plaisir de Merle; Stark-Condé **D** Super Single Vineyards; Vergenoegd

Petite sirah/durif

★★★★☆ Arendskloof; Black Elephant; Fairview; Mischa; Stark-Condé

★★★★ **Glen Carlou**; The Blacksmith; The Liberator

★★★☆ Ayama; Matzikama **NT** Spotswood; The Blacksmith; Wildehurst

Pinot blanc

★★★★☆ Le Belle Rebelle

★★★★ Lanzerac

Pinot gris/grigio

★★★★ Migliarina; Val du Charron; Winshaw

★★★☆ Anthonij Rupert (2); Arendskloof; Fairview; Idiom; Nederburg; **Van Loveren** ★★★ Anura; Leipzig; Overhex ★★★ Two Oceans; Waverley Hills (Organic); Woolworths ★★ Nederburg; **Nicholson Smith NT** Craven; Welmoed **D** Merwida; Overhex; Stellekaya; Stettyn; Van Loveren

Pinot noir

★★★★★ Crystallum; Storm (2)

★★★★☆ Bosman; Botanica; Bouchard Finlayson (2); Bruce Jack; Cap Maritime; Cape Chamonix (2); Catherine Marshall (3); Cederberg; Clouds; Creation (4); Crystallum (3); De Grendel; Domaine des Dieux; Driehoek; Hamilton Russell; **Haute Cabrière**; Kruger Family; La Vierge; Lourensford; **Lynx**; Meerlust; Moya's; MVH Signature Wines; Newton Johnson (3); Oak Valley; **Painted Wolf**; Paul Cluver (2); Radford Dale (3); **Richard Kershaw** (2); **Saurwein** (2); Shannon (2); Stonebird; Storm (4); Sumaridge; Tesselaarsdal; The Fledge; Thelema; Whalehaven

★★★★ AA Badenhorst; Anthonij Rupert; Baleia; Benguela Cove; Black Block; Blackwater; Boschendal; Bosman; **Brew Cru**; Cape Elevation; Die Kat; Donkiesbaai; Edgebaston (2); Elgin Ridge (Biodynamic); **Elgin Vintners** (2); Fryer's Cove; Garden Route; Groote Post; Haute Cabrière; Herold; Highlands Road; **Hoopenburg** (2); Idun; Jan

Harmsgat; **Jayne's** (4); **Kara-Tara**; La Vierge (2); Leopard's Leap; Litigo; Lodestone; Lothian; Miss Molly; **Mooiplaas**; Moya Meaker; Muratie; Newton Johnson; Nitida; Oak Valley; PaardenKloof; Paul Cluver; Paul Wallace; Radford Dale; Seven Springs; **Spioenkop** (2); Spookfontein; Stony Brook; Strandveld; Super Single Vineyards; That Wine Demesne; The Butcher Shop; Thelema; Villiera; Villion; Vriesenhof; **Walker Bay Estate**; Waterford; Whalehaven; Woolworths (2)

★★★★ Andy Mitchell; Arendskloof; Avontuur; Bon Courage; Dâbar; Dalla Cia; Eerste Hoop; Enfin; Ernst Gouws; Flagstone; Foothills; Glen Carlou; Haute Cabrière; Herold; La Vierge (2); Lemberg; Lieben; Lomond; Lynx; Maastricht; Meerendal; **Mile High**; Namaqua; Ormonde (2); Paul Cluver; Peter Falke; Quando; Scrucap; Solitary; South Hill; Springfield; Stellar (Fairtrade; Organic); The Fledge; The Goose; Upland (Organic); Wildekrans; Woolworths

★★★ **Darling Cellars**; Felicité; Kranskop; Lord's; Nederburg; Overhex (Nouveau); Strandveld; Van Loveren ★★★ Robert Stanford (2); Robertson; Stellekaya; Stellenbosch Family Wines; The Hills ★★ Bezalel ★★ Leeurivier; Stellenbosch Family Wines **NT** Andy Mitchell; Arendsig (2); B Vintners; Botanica; Brunia; Buitenverwachting; Craven; Crystallum; Elemental Bob (2); Esona; Havana Hills; Herold (2); Iona; Jasper Raats; JH Meyer (5); Kaapzicht; Kleinhoekkloof; Meinert; Newstead; Packwood; Radford Dale; Rosendal; Seven Springs; Stark-Condé; Two Oceans; Windfall; Woolworths; Yardstick (2) **D** Bellevue; Blackwater; Bouchard Finlayson; Joubert-Tradauw; Klein Constantia; Kleine Zalze; Signal Hill; Spioenkop; The Giant Periwinkle (2)

Pinotage

★★★★★ Beeslaar; Beyerskloof; Diemersdal; Flagstone; Kanonkop

★★★★☆ Allée Bleue (2) (Old Vines); Alvi's Drift; Anthonij Rupert (Old Vines); Ashbourne; **Bellevue** (2) (Old Vines); Bellingham; Beyerskloof (3); Cape Chamonix; Chateau Naudé; David & Nadia; Delheim; Diemersdal; Diemersfontein; Flagstone; Fleur du Cap; Fram; Grangehurst; **Idiom**; Kaapzicht; Kanonkop; KWV; L'Avenir; La Couronne; Lanzerac; Lemberg; **Meerendal** (3) (Old Vines); **Mont Blois**; Môreson (3); Neethlingshof; Neil Ellis; Olifantsberg; Painted Wolf (2); Radford Dale; Remhoogte; **Reverie**; Rhebokskloof; Riebeek Valley; Simonsig; Spier; Spioenkop (2); Springfontein; Super Single Vineyards; **Swartberg**; **The Giant Periwinkle**; Tokara; **Van Loveren**; Vondeling; Wildekrans; **Windmeul** (2)

★★★★★ Aaldering; Alkmaar; Altydgedacht; Anura; Arendskloof; Asara; Babylon's Peak; Badsberg; Bayede!; Beaumont; Bellingham; Black Elephant; Bosman; Canto; Cecilia (Old Vines); Clos Malverne (2); Conradie; D'Aria; DA Hanekom; DewaldtHeyns; Diemersdal; **Dragonridge**; Durbanville Hills; Eenzaamheid; Fairview (2) (Fairtrade); Four Paws; **Grangehurst** (2); Groot Constantia; Groot Phesantekraal; **Holder**; Kanonkop; L'Avenir; Laibach (Organic); Lanzerac; Linton Park; Longridge; Lutzville; Lyngrove; Marklew; Meinert; Namaqua; **New Beginnings**; Nuy; **Overhex** (2) (Nouveau); **Rebus**; Rooiberg; Southern Right; Spice Route; Springfontein (4); Stellenbosch Vineyards; Stellenrust; Sumaridge; Taillard; The Butcher Shop; Under Oaks; Welbedacht; Wellington Winery; **Wolf & Woman**; Woolworths (2)

★★★★☆ Anura (2); Arra; Asara; Backsberg; **Bader & Walters**; Badsberg; Barista; Bellevue; Beyerskloof; Bloemendal; Blue Crane; Boland; Camberley; Cape Wine Company (Fairtrade); Cloof; Croydon; Darling Cellars (2); De Grendel; Delheim; **Diemersfontein**; Doran; Dornier; Eagle's Cliff; Ernst Gouws; Flagstone; Fort Simon; Goede Hoop; House of Mandela; Jan Harmsgat (Fairtrade); Kaapzicht; Kanu; Ken Forrester; Klawer; Kruger Family; Laibach; Lammershoek; Le Grand Chasseur; Leopard's Leap; **Lievland**; Louis 57; M'hudi; Maastricht; MAN Family; Meerendal; **Meerhof** (Fairtrade); Middelvlei; Miravel; Mooiplaas; Morgenhof; Mountain River; Nederburg; Neethlingshof; **New Beginnings**; Olsen; **Oude Compagnies Post**; Perdeberg; Piekenierskloof (Fairtrade); Pulpit Rock; **Radford Dale** (2); Raka; Rebus; Riebeek Valley; Rooiberg (2); Schalkenbosch; Signal Gun; Silkbush; Simonsig; Skilpadvlei; Slaley; **Spier**; Stanford Hills; Stellar (Organic; Fairtrade); Stellenbosch University; Stellenrust; Swartland; Taillard; Teubes (Organic); The Butcher Shop; Tulbagh Winery; Viljoensdrift; Villiera; Vriesenhof; Whalehaven; Wildekrans; Windmeul; Woolworths (3); Zevenwacht ★★★ Aan de Doorns; Allée Bleue; Avontuur; Bader & Walters; Bayede!; Bergsig; Bon Courage; Bonnievale; Boplaas; Brandvlei; Cape Dreams; **Clayton**; Darling Cellars (2); Daschbosch (2) (Fairtrade); DeWaal; Die Mas; Diemersfontein; Domaine Brahms; Du Toitskloof; Durbanville Hills; Fairvalley; Fairview; False Bay; Fat Bastard; FirstCape; Fleur du Cap; Frater; Freedom Hill; Grande Provence; Hawksmoor; Hill & Dale; Hofstraat; Hoopenburg; Imbuko (2) (Fairtrade); Jacobsdal; Klawer; Koelenhof (2); Koopmanskloof (Fairtrade); Kuypers Kraal; KWV; **L'Avenir**; Landskroon; Lemberg; Lyngrove; **M'hudi**; Merwida; Mile High (2);

Morgenhof; **Mountain Ridge**; Niel Joubert; Nuy; Orange River; Painted Wolf; Perdeberg (2); Rickety Bridge; Rooiberg (2); Saxenburg; Schenkenfontein; Slanghoek; Spier; Stellenbosch Family Wines (2); Stellenbosch Hills; Stellendrift; Stellenview (2); Swartland; The Blacksmith; The Grape Grinder; Tulbagh Winery; Van Loveren (2); **Villiersdorp**; Vredenheim; Waboomsrivier; Wellington Winery; Welmoed; Wineways; Woolworths (3); Zonnebloem ★★★ Bayede!; Botha; Breëland; Burgershof; Cilmor; Cloof; FirstCape; Fish Hoek (Fairtrade); Imbuko (Fairtrade); Koopmanskloof (Fairtrade); KWV; Le Manoir de Brendel; Lutzville; McGregor; Robertson (3); Roos Family; Simonsvlei (5) (Kosher); Slaley; Somerbosch; Stanford Hills; Stellar (Fairtrade; Organic); **Stellenview**; The Bridge of Hope; Vintales; Welvanpas; Winkelshoek; Woolworths ★★ Dragonridge (Alternative white/red); **Kumala**; Linton Park; Maison de Teijger; Mountain River; Namaqua; Nicholson Smith; Wineways (3) **NT** Aaldering; Alvi's Drift; Arendsig (2); Ayama; B Vintners; Backsberg (Kosher); Brampton; Buffalo Creek; Cadequin; Cape Dreams; Cathedral Peak (2); DeWaal; Doolhof (2); Douglas Green; Drostdy-Hof; Du'SwaRoo; Eikendal; Escapades; Fernskloof (Organic); FirstCape; Franschhoek Cellar; Groot Parys (Nouveau; Organic); Hawksmoor; Highgate (2); Kleine Zalze (2); Leipzig; Malanot; Manley; Marianne; Mimosa; Mountain River; Namaqua; Nederburg (2); Oude Compagnies Post; Painted Wolf; Rickety Bridge; Rosendal; Rossouw, Gouws & Clarke; Schalkenbosch; Spier (2); Stellekaya; Stellenbosch University; Stellenbosch Vineyards; Swartland; Teubes; Theescombe; Township Winery (Fairtrade); Two Oceans; Walking Woods (Fairtrade; Organic); Welbedacht; Welgevallen; Windfall; Wineways; Zonnebloem **D** Arra; Bellevue; Black Elephant; Dagbreek; Darling Cellars; Doran; Durbanville Hills; Kleine Zalze; Knorhoek (2); MAN Family; Mile High; New Beginnings; Overhex; Stettyn; Weltevrede

Port-style, pink
★★ De Krans **NT** Peter Bayly

Port-style, red
★★★★★ Boplaas; De Krans; JP Bredell; KWV; Overgaauw; **Upland**

★★★★☆ Beaumont; Boplaas (3); De Krans; Delaire Graff; Landskroon

★★★★ Allesverloren; Axe Hill (2); **Baleia**; Bergsig (2); Beyerskloof; Bezalel; Boplaas; De Krans (2); Groot Constantia; Hout Bay; JP Bredell; Monis; Muratie; Peter Bayly (2); Rosendal; Simonsig; Upland (Organic); Vergenoegd; Zandvliet

★★★★ Aan de Doorns; Annandale; Anthonij Rupert; Arra; Axe Hill; Backsberg; Badsberg; Bergsig; Boplaas; Calitzdorp (2); De Krans; De Wet; **Diemersfontein**; Du'SwaRoo (2); Fairview; Flagstone; Holden Manz; Jacques Smit; KWV; **Lutzville**; **Micu Narunsky**; Monis; My Wyn; Riebeek Valley; Robertson; Taillard; Vaalvlei; Viljoensdrift ★★★ Allée Bleue; Bon Courage; Botha; Clairvaux; Domein Doornkraal; Du Toitskloof; Klawer; Koelenhof; Org de Rac (Organic); **Oude Compagnies Post**; Slanghoek; Somersbosch; Stellenbosch University; Swartland; Van Loveren; Villiersdorp; Waboomsrivier ★★★ Darling Cellars; Jacques Smit; Landzicht; Orange River; Peter Bayly ★★ Namaqua; Robin Hood **NT** Alto; Boplaas; Die Mas; Domein Doornkraal; Entre Nous; Grundheim (3); Hofstraat; Kloovenburg; Lovane; Morgenhof; Winkelshoek **D** Beaumont; Dagbreek; Douglas Green; Klawer; McGregor; Muratie; Rooiberg; Stettyn; Tulbagh Winery; Vergenoegd; Windmeul

Port-style, white

★★★★☆ Beaumont; Lourensford
★★★★☆ Peter Bayly ★★★ My Wyn **NT** Axe Hill; Grundheim **D** Haut Espoir

Red blends, Cape Bordeaux

★★★★★ De Trafford; Glenelly; Hidden Valley; Kanonkop; Plaisir de Merle; Tokara; Van Biljon; Vergelegen
★★★★☆ Alto; Anthonij Rupert (2); Babylonstoren; Backsberg (2); Bartinney; Beaumont; Beyerskloof; Botanica; Buitenverwachting; Cape Chamonix; **Cape Elevation**; Capelands; Catherine Marshall; Clouds; Constantia Glen (2); Constantia Uitsig; Dalla Cia; De Grendel; De Toren (2); De Trafford; **Delaire Graff** (2); DeMorgenzon; Diemersdal; Dornier (2); Du Toitskloof; Durbanville Hills; Eikendal; Ernie Els; Fleur du Cap; Franschhoek Cellar; Glen Carlou; **Grangehurst** (2); Groenland; Groot Constantia; Hartenberg; Haskell; Havana Hills; Hillcrest; Idiom; Jean Daneel; Jordan (3); Kaapzicht; Keet; La Vierge; Laibach; Landskroon; Leipzig; Leopard's Leap; Longridge; **Lourensford** (2); Lynx; Meerlust; Miles Mossop; Mitre's Edge; **Mont Blois**; Morgenster; Mulderbosch; Muratie; Mvemve Raats; Nederburg; Neethlingshof; Nitida; Oldenburg; Ormonde; Overgaauw (2); Plaisir de Merle; Raats; Rainbow's End; Raka (2); Remhoogte; Ridgeback; Rousseau; Rustenberg; **Schultz Family**; Simonsig (2); Spier (2) (Organic); Springfield; Stark-Condé; Stellenbosch Reserve; Stellenbosch Vineyards; Stellenrust; Stony Brook; Strydom; Super Single Vineyards; Taillard; The Butcher Shop; The

High Road (2); Thelema; Under Oaks; Uva Mira; Vergelegen; Vergenoegd; Vilafonté (3); Vondeling; Warwick (2); Windmeul; Woolworths; Zorgvliet

★★★★ Aaldering; Alkmaar; Allée Bleue (2); **Alto**; Asara (Fairtrade); Aslina; Avontuur; Barton; Beau Constantia; Benguela Cove; Blaauwklippen; Boschkloof; Buitenverwachting; Cape Elevation; Cavalli; Creation; D'Aria; Darling Cellars; De Toren; Dornier; Druk My Niet; Equitania; Flagstone; Fort Simon; Gabriëlskloof; Grangehurst; Haut Espoir; Holden Manz; Hoopenburg; Imbuko (Fairtrade); Jason's Hill; JP Bredell; Klein Gustrouw; Kruger Family; KWV; La Bri; La Motte; La Vierge; Laibach (Organic); Lanzerac (2); Le Bonheur; Le Pommier; Linton Park; Louis 57; Louisvale; Marklew; Miles Mossop; Mischa; Mitre's Edge; **Mooiplaas** (2); Namaqua; Napier; Neil Ellis; Nelson; Nick & Forti's; Nico van der Merwe; Nietgegund; Noble Hill; Noble Savage; Paul Wallace; Peter Falke; Quoin Rock; Rebus; Reyneke (Organic); Ridgeback; Robert Stanford; Simelia; Skilpadvlei; Slaley; **Spier** (Organic); Spookfontein; Stellekaya (2); Stonewall; Sumaridge; Tanagra; Thunderchild; Vergelegen; **Villiersdorp**; Vriesenhof; Webersburg; Welbedacht; Woolworths; Yonder Hill (2); Zevenwacht; Zonnebloem

★★★★ Akkerdraai; Andy Mitchell; Anura; Arcangeli; Avontuur; **Bader & Walters**; **Bellascene**; Black Oystercatcher; Camberley; Capaia; Cape Chamonix; Cape Classics; **Cape Wine Company** (Fairtrade); Cloof; Clos Malverne; Definitum; Deux Frères; Domaine Brahms; Domaine Coutelier; Doran; Edgebaston (2); Fort Simon (2); Frater; **Friesland**; **Guillaumé** (2); Havana Hills; Hillcrest; Journey's End (Fairtrade); Kanu (2); Klein Constantia; L'Avenir; La Petite Provence; Le Grand Domaine; Louis 57; Lovane; Meinert; Mimosa; Miravel; MolenVliet (3); Nederburg; Neethlingshof; Nico Vermeulen; Radford Dale; Robin Hood; Saltare; Saronsberg; Saxenburg; Schalckenbosch; Seven Sisters; Sonklip (2); Spier (Organic); Stellenbosch Family Wines; **Val de Vie**; Vredenheim; Walker Bay Estate; Woolworths (3); Zandwijk (Kosher); Zorgvliet ★★★ Aden's Star (2); Aslina; Barry Gould; Bayede!; Beyerskloof; Bushmanspad; Cape Dreams; **Cape Town Wine Co**; Carrol Boyes; Cloof; Compagniesdrift; De Wet; Goedverwacht; Grande Provence; Hoopenburg; J9; **Jacques Germanier** (Organic); Jordan; Kleine Zalze; Le Grand Chasseur; Leopard's Leap; MolenVliet; Morgenhof; Opstal; Org de Rac (Organic); Reyneke (Organic); Rooiberg; Sauvignon Wines; Slanghoek; Swartland; SylvanVale; The Butcher Shop; Thokozani; Tulbagh Winery; Van Loveren (2); Villiersdorp;

Weltevrede; Whalehaven; Woolworths★★★ Bon Courage; Bonnievale; De Breede (2) (Organic); Diemersdal; Eagle's Cliff; Imbuko (Fairtrade); Klein Roosboom; **KVW** (2); La Couronne; Nicholson Smith; Overhex (Nouveau); Robertson; Simonsig; Somerset Wines; Swartland; Tulbagh Winery; Two Oceans; Wineways (4); Winkelshoek ★★ **Absolute Style**; Darling Cellars; Mountain Ridge; Robertson; Ses'Fikile; Stellenbosch Family Wines; Wineways ★★ De Breede **NT** Arra; Avondale (Organic); Bellevue; Buitenverwachting; Camberley (2); Cape Chamonix; Capelands; Conradie; Damarakloof; Dieu Donné; Doolhof (2); Doran; Epicurean; Fernskloof; Glen Carlou; Grande Provence; Hirst; Lowerland; Lynx; McGregor; Meerlust; Morgenhof; Morgenster; Nelson; Nomada; Oneiric; Rietvallei; Rogge Cloof; Rosendal (4); Rupert & Rothschild; Schalkenbosch; **Skaap**; Stellendrift (3); Stettyn; Stoep; Stony Brook; Swartland (3); Van Zylshof; Vierkoppen; Waterford; Wildekrans; Windmeul; Woolworths (4) **D** Audacia; Babylon's Peak; Douglas Green; Knorhoek; Koni; Kunjani; Overgaauw; Simonsvlei; The Butcher Shop; Welgevallen; Woolworths; Yardstick

Red blends, other

★★★★★ De Trafford; Ernie Els; Glenelly; Rust en Vrede; Waterford

★★★★☆ Arendskloof; Black Pearl; Boplaas (2); Boschkloof (2); Bouchard Finlayson; Bruce Jack; Cape Wine Company; Dalla Cia; Darling Cellars (Old Vines); De Grendel; De Krans; DeMorgenzon; Donkiesbaai; Ernie Els; Fairview (3); Hogan; JC Wickens; Joostenberg (Organic); Keermont; Ken Forrester (2); Klein Constantia; **KVW**; Le Sueur; Leeu Passant (Old Vines); Lourens Family; Maanschijn; Marianne; Mont du Toit (2); Mount Abora; Nederburg (2); Nico van der Merwe; Olifantsberg; **Painted Wolf**; Paserene; Peter Bayly (2); Plaisir de Merle; Radford Dale (2); Rosendal; Savage; Sijnn; Spice Route; Steenberg; The Fledge; The Great SA Wine Co; Thistle & Weed (2); Thorne & Daughters; Van Wyk; Villiera; Vuurberg

★★★★ Akkerdal; Allesverloren; Alto; Anwilka; Arumdale; Axe Hill (2); Baleia; Bergsig; Bushmanspad; Calitzdorp; Capaia (2); Cederberg; Clayton; **De Kleine Wijn Koöp**; De Meye; Dragonridge; Escapades; Fable; **False Bay**; Groenland; Holden Manz; Jean Daneel; **Kumusha**; Kyburg; Lanzerac; Le Riche; Lozärn; M'hudi; Mischa; Mont du Toit (Natural/non-fortified pale); Morgenster; Mullineux; My Wyn; Nederburg; Opstal; Peter Bayly; Rhebokskloof; Sijnn; **Spider Pig**; **Spioenkop**; Stamboom; Steenberg; Taillard; Tanagra; Terracura; The Ahrens Family; The Giant

Periwinkle; The Goose; Tierhoek; **Topiary**; Under Oaks; Wildehurst; Yardstick

★★★★☆ AA Badenhorst; Allesverloren; Alphabetical; Badsberg; **Benguela Cove**; Blaauwklippen; Bon Courage; Bushmanspad; Calais; Cape Rock; Chennells; Domaine Brahms; Dornier; Druk My Niet; Franki's; Goats do Roam; Grangehurst; Groote Post; Hartenberg; Idiom (2); Jacques Smit; Jordan; Kaapzicht (2); Kruger Family; Kyburg; Lowerland; **Maree Family**; Mitre's Edge; Mont Rochelle; Nederburg; Neil Ellis; **Old Road** (2); Orange River; Osbloed; Peter Falke; Rainbow's End; Raka; **Strange Kompanjie**; Strydom; The Fledge; The Grape Grinder; Under Oaks; Villiera; Vriesenhof; Wavescape; Woolworths (2) ★★★ Allée Bleue; Arra; Axe Hill; Backsberg; Barton; Brandvlei; Calais; Clos Malverne; De Krans; Du Toitskloof; Du'SwaRoo (2); Fable; **FirstCape**; Hermit on the Hill; Hill & Dale; KVW; Landskroon (2); Lynx; Mont du Toit; Napier; Osbloed; Rascallion; Robertson; Simonsig (2); Spier; Stellenbosch Family Wines; The Hills; Waverley Hills (Organic); Welvanpas; Withington ★★★ Aan de Doorns; Botha; Chateau Libertas; Group CDV; Koelenhof; Landskroon; Tassenberg; Theuniskraal; Woolworths (Light & low-alcohol); Zandvliet ★★ Audacia; Barrydale; Burgershof; Imbuko (Fairtrade); Nicholson Smith (2); Robertson (2); Simonsvlei; Stellenbosch Family Wines; Stellenbosch Hills; Welvanpas; Woolworths (4) (Light & low-alcohol)

★★ Bonnievale; **Leopard's Leap NT** 4G Wine Estate (2); Akkerdal; Black Pearl; Blue Crane; Boschheim (2); Brampton; Buffalo Creek; Camberley; Casa Mori; Desert Rose; Dieu Donné; Du'SwaRoo; Elemental Bob; Esau (3); Four Paws; Graceland (2); Havana Hills; Herold; Kay & Monty; Kirabo (2); KWV (2); La Chataigne; Leeu Passant (Old Vines); Malanot; Mont Destin; Mont du Toit; Montagu Wine Cellar; Mother Rock; Mountain River; Nederburg; Oneiric; Plettenvale; Richard Kershaw; Rietvallei (2); Schalkenbosch; Silvermist (Organic); Somersbosch; Somerset Wines; Southern Sky; Spier (2); Stettyn; Stony Brook; Swallow Hill; Under Oaks; Val du Charron; **Verspieren**; **Woolworths** (2) (Light & low-alcohol); Zanddrift **D** Annandale; Audacia; Axe Hill; Capaia; Glen Carlou; La Couronne; Windmeul; Woolworths (2); Yardstick

Red blends, shiraz/syrah-based

★★★★★ Erika Obermeyer; Rust en Vrede; Saronsberg

★★★★☆ AA Badenhorst; Akkerdal; Annex Kloof; Anthonij Rupert (2); Anwilka; Bartho Eksteen; Bellingham; Boekenhoutskloof; **Boschendal** (2); Bruce Jack; Cape Rock; Creation;

DeMorgenzon; Eikendal; Flagstone; Groote Post; Haskell; Hoopenburg; Iona; JAN Wines (Organic); Kronendal; KWV (2); **La Petite Ferme**; Lingen; Lomond; Lourensford; Luddite; Migliarina; Môrelig (Alternative white/red); Neil Ellis; Newton Johnson; Org de Rac (Organic); Ormonde; Paserene; Radford Dale; Rall; Ridgeback; Sadie; Savage; Sijnn; Spice Route; Spier; Strandveld; The Ahrens Family; The Butcher Shop; Vondeling; Waterkloof; Welbedacht; Wildehurst

★★★★ Alkmaar; Annandale; Anura; Arcangeli; Arendskloof; Babylon's Peak; Bartho Eksteen; Beau Constantia; Beaumont; Biodynamix; Black Oystercatcher; Blackwater; Boland; Bosman (Fairtrade); Cape Rock; Cape Venture (Fairtrade); **De Kleine Wijn Koöp** (2); Deux Frères; Diemersfontein; Edgebaston; Eerste Hoop; Ernie Els; Graceland; Guardian Peak; Hartenberg; Hawksmoor (2); Hidden Valley; **Holden Manz** (2); Hout Bay; Idiom; Kanu; Ken Forrester; Kleine Zalze; Kloovenburg; Leeuwenkuil; Leipzig; Lemberg; Lynx; **Meerhof**; Metzer; Migliarina; **Mimosa**; Muratie; Newton Johnson; **Oldenburg**; **Oude Compagnies Post**; Perdeberg; Piekenierskloof; Plaisir de Merle; Post House; Quoin Rock; Rascallion (2); **Rosendal**; Rustenberg; Sijnn; Simonsvlei; South Hill; Stellenbosch Hills; Stellenbosch Vineyards; Stony Brook; **The Ahrens Family**; The Butcher Shop; The Kitchen Sink; Thokozani; Val de Vie; Val du Charron; Waverley Hills (Organic); Welgegund (Old Vines); Woolworths (4); Zevenwacht; Zonnebloem

★★★★ Babylon's Peak; Bezuidenhout Family; Black Elephant; D'Aria; Darling Cellars (2); Delheim; Domaine des Dieux; Fijndraai; Frater; Goats do Roam (Fairtrade); Groenland; Joostenberg (Organic); Journey's End (Fairtrade); Kleine Zalze; Konkelberg; Kruger Family; Lammershoek (2); Louis; MAN Family; **Meerhof** (Fairtrade); Mellasat; My Wyn; Nico van der Merwe; Org de Rac (Organic); Post House; Radford Dale; Rosendal; Schalkenbosch; Stellenrust; The Grape Grinder; The Wolftrap; Thelema; Vergenoegd (2); Waterford; Woolworths ★★★ Anura; Boschendal; Cape Wine Company (Fairtrade); Desert Rose; Dormershire; Eagle's Cliff; Excelsior; Flagstone; Groenland; Imbuko (Fairtrade); Klawer; Kleine Zalze; Olivedale; Overhex (Nouveau); Reyneke (Organic); Ridgeback; Somersbosch; **Spider Pig**; Stellenview (3) (Organic); Truter Family; Windfall; Woolworths; Zevenwacht★★★ Darling Cellars; **M'hudi**; Simonsvlei; Stellenview ★★ Ses'Fikile **NT** Aaldering; Arra; Avondale (Organic); Barton; Black Pearl; Blue Crane; Brampton; Cecilia; Cilmor; Clayton (3); Dieu Donné; Doran; Drostdy-Hof (2);

Esau (2); Fernskloof (Organic); Four Paws; Havana Hills; Hildenbrand; Hunneyball; Kleinhoekkloof; Kruger Family; Lazanou (2) (Organic); Le Grand Domaine; Lodestone; Louis; **Marianne**; Mont Destin; Myburgh Bros; Oude Compagnies Post; Overhex; Rickety Bridge; Rogge Cloof; Rosendal (2); Stellar (2) (Fairtrade; Organic); Two Oceans; Windfall; Wine Village-Hermanus; Woolworths **D** Andy Mitchell; Arra; Goats do Roam; Klawer; Knorhoek (2); Lammershoek; MAN Family (2); Maske; Meerhof; Mother Rock; Nederburg; Painted Wolf; Riebeek Valley (2); Rietvallei; Simonsvlei; Summerhill

Red blends, with pinotage

★★★★★ Beyerskloof; Kaapzicht

★★★★☆ Alvi's Drift (2); ArtiSons; Bartho Eksteen; Beaumont; Bosman; Bruce Jack; Clos Malverne; David & Nadia; Hughes Family (Organic); KWV (2); La Petite Ferme; Marianne; Meinert; Nuiba; Opstal; Paul Roos (2); Perdeberg; Rhebokskloof; Springfontein; **Stellenbosch Hills**; Swartland; The Vinoneers; Windmeul

★★★★ Alvi's Drift; Anura; Arra; Asara; Beyerskloof (2); Blake; Boland; Clos Malverne; Darling Cellars; Daschbosch; Flagstone; Goede Hoop; Grangehurst (2); **Groot Constantia** (2); Herold; Idiom; Kanonkop; Lateganskop; Leipzig; Lutzville; Lyngrove; Middelvlei; **Napier**; Nuy; Post House; Pulpit Rock; Raka; **Rascallion**; Rebus; Remhoogte; Rooiberg; Simonsig; Spier; Springfontein; Sumaridge; Surfing Vintners; Val du Charron; Waverley Hills (Organic); Welbedacht (2); Wellington Winery; Wildehurst; Wildekrans; Woolworths

★★★★ Anura; Asara; Ashbourne (Old Vines); Babylonstoren; Bruce Jack; Dragonridge; Du Toitskloof; Eenzaamheid; Hazendal; **Hofstraat**; Jason's Hill; Koelenhof; Lyngrove; Marianne; **Old Road**; Osbloed; Post House; Silkbush; Springfontein; The Giant Periwinkle; Truter Family; Van Loveren; Viljoensdrift ★★★ Ayama; Bergsig; Cloof (2); Clos Malverne; Croydon; De Wet; Diemersfontein; Du Preez; Du Toitskloof (Fairtrade); Freedom Hill (2); Kaapzicht; Lemberg; **Lovane**; Middelvlei; Namaqua (3); Nuy; Rhebokskloof; Signal Gun; Silkbush; Slaley; Stanford Hills; Stellenbosch University; Van Loveren; Waboomsrivier; Welbedacht; Whalehaven★★★ Aan de Doorns; Cape Dreams; Conradie; Du Toitskloof (2); Mooiplaas; Nederburg; Overmeer Cellars; Pulpit Rock; Roodezandt; Rooiberg; Slanghoek; Stellar (Fairtrade; Organic); Stellenbosch Hills; Stellenrust (Fairtrade); Tulbagh Winery; Waboomsrivier ★★ Drostdy-Hof; Kumala **NT** Beaumont; Bellevue; Carrol Boyes; Cathedral Peak; Clos Malverne; Croydon;

Definitum; DeWaal; Doolhof (3); Dragonridge (Alternative white/red); Esau; Fernskloof; Manley; Marianne; Meerendal (2); Miss Molly; Namaqua; Olsen; Overhex (2); Painted Wolf (2); Rogge Cloof; Rupert & Rothschild; Slaley; Stellendrift (2); Two Oceans; Walking Woods **D** Altydgedacht; Douglas Green (2); Hawksmoor (2); Koelenhof; Maske; Môreson; New Beginnings; Stellekaya

Riesling

★★★★☆ Blackwater; Oak Valley; Paul Cluver; **Saurwein**; Spioenkop; **Van Wyk**

★★★★ Catherine Marshall; Fairview; Groote Post; Hartenberg; Illimis; Jordan; Klein Constantia; Meinert; **Neethlingshof**; Nitida; Scrucap; Thelema (2)

★★★☆ Bergsig; Herold; La Vierge; Lothian; Nederburg; **Remhoogte**; The Fledge ★★★ Groote Post **NT** Hartenberg; Rietvallei; Spier; Waterford; Woolworths **D** Migliarina; Paul Cluver; Super Single Vineyards

Rosé dry

★★★★☆ Bartho Eksteen; Spier

★★★★ Anthonij Rupert; **Black Elephant**; Boschendal; Bramon; Clouds; **Creation**; **De Kleine Wijn Koöp**; Haute Cabrière; **Holder**; Kanonkop; Oude Compagnies Post; **Quoin Rock**; Tamboerskloof (2); **Zoetendal**; Zorgvliet

★★★☆ AA Badenhorst; Aaldering; Alkmaar; Allesverloren; Anthonij Rupert; Babylonstoren; **Baleia**; Bein; Bezuidenhout Family; Black Oystercatcher; Bloemendal; **Blue Crane**; Bosman; Botanica; Bruce Jack; **Cape Town Wine Co**; Cederberg; Croydon; Delaire Graff; DeMorgenzon; Diemersdal; **Druk My Niet**; Dunstone; Fable; **Fairview**; False Bay; Fish Hoek (Fairtrade); Foothills; **Fryer's Cove**; Goats do Roam; Grangehurst; Groot Constantia; **Haute Cabrière** (2); Hawksmoor; Hill & Dale; Holden Manz; Jordan; Ken Forrester; Klein Constantia; **L'Avenir** (2); La Bri; Lammershoek; Leopard's Leap (2); **Lievland**; Lodestone; Longridge; Lord's; Lothian; Lozärn; Marianne; **Meerhof** (2) (Fairtrade); Morgenster; Mulderbosch; Nederburg; Noble Savage; Opstal; Perdeberg; **Rebus** (3); Rickety Bridge; South Hill; Spier (Organic); Spotswood; Springfontein; Steenberg; Strandveld; Sumaridge; The Butcher Shop; **Tierhoek**; Tokara; Topiary; **Vinologist**; **Vriesenhof**; **Waverley Hills** (Organic); **Webersburg**; **Woolworths** (3) ★★★ Allée Bleue; Alphabetical; Anura; Arendskloof; Arumdale; Ashbourne; Avontuur; Backsberg; Barton; Bayede!; Beyerskloof (2); Bonnievale; Bushmanspad; Capaia; Compagniesdrift; D'Aria;

De Grendel; De Meye; Delheim; Diemersfontein; Dornier; Dorrance; Durbanville Hills; Eerste Hoop; Ernie Els; **Ernst Gouws**; Fable; Fat Bastard; Felicité; Flagstone; Franki's; Gabriëlskloof; Glen Carlou; Goedverwacht; Grande Provence; Groote Post; **Guillaumé**; Haut Espoir; Hidden Valley; Hillcrest; Hoopenburg; Hout Bay; Kaapse Familie Wingerde; Kaapzicht; Klawer; Klein Roosboom; Kleine Zalze; Koelenhof; Koopmanskloof (Fairtrade); Kranskop; Krone; Kunjani; KWV; La Couronne; **Laibach** (Organic); Lanzerac; Le Belle Rebelle; Le Pommier; Lomond; **Louis 57**; LuKa; **Maastricht**; Mellasat; Merwida; Morgenhof; Muratie; Overhex (Nouveau); Painted Wolf; Pearl Mountain; Piekenierskloof (2) (Fairtrade); Porcupine Ridge; Rainbow's End; Raka; Rickety Bridge; Riebeek Valley; Rustenberg; Saronsberg; Scrucap; Silkbush; **Simonsig**; Simonsvlei; Somerbosch; **Spider Pig**; Spier; Stanford Hills; Stettyn; SylvanVale; The Grape Grinder; The Wolftrap; Val de Vie; **Van Loveren** (2); Vergenoegd; **Villiersdorp**; Vondeling; Walker Bay Estate; Warwick; Waterford; Waterkloof; **Windmeul**; Woolworths (6) (Light & low-alcohol; Organic); Yonder Hill; Zevenwacht; Zorgvliet ★★★ Asara; Benguela Cove; **Bon Courage**; Cloof; Clos Malverne; De Krans; Dragonridge (Alternative white/red); Du Toitskloof (2) (Fairtrade); Du'SwaRoo; Eagle's Cliff; Eerste Hoop; Hidden Valley; KWV; La Petite Ferme; Misty Mountains; Mooiplaas; Nelson; Perdeberg; Plettenvale; Pulpit Rock; Quando; Rivendell (Fairtrade); Roos Family; Schalkenbosch; Slaley; Stanford Hills; **Stellenbosch Hills** (Fairtrade); **Truter Family**; Tulbagh Winery; Two Oceans; Van Loveren; Welvanpas; Wildehurst; Woolworths ★★ Boschrivier; Darling Cellars (2); Drostdy-Hof (Light & low-alcohol); KWV; Louisvale; Lutzville; Robertson (Light & low-alcohol); Simonsvlei; Spookfontein; Windfall ★★ **Somerset Wines NT** Akkerdal; Alvi's Drift; Andy Mitchell; Avondale (Organic); Belfield; Brampton; Cape Rock; Carrol Boyes; Cavalli; Gilmor; Desert Rose; Domaine des Dieux; Doran; Drostdy-Hof; Du'SwaRoo; Elgin Vintners; Escapades; Excelsior; Fernskloof (Organic); Fleur du Cap (Light & low-alcohol); Four Paws; Franschhoek Cellar; Graceland; Havana Hills (2) (Fairtrade); Herold; Highgate; Highlands Road; Hildenbrand; Kleinhoekkloof; La Chataigne; Leeuwenkuil (2); Malanot; Mitre's Edge; Mother Rock; Mountain River; New Beginnings; Noble Hill; Nuiba; Olivedale; Oneiric; Rietvallei; Robert Stanford; Rosendal; **Safriel**; Schenkfontein; Seven Springs; Simonsvlei (Kosher); Skaap; Spice Route; Spier (2); Stellar (2) (Fairtrade; Organic); Summerhill; Swallow

Hill; The Grape Grinder; **Verspieren**; Walking Woods (Fairtrade; Organic); Welmoed; Whalehaven; **Woolworths** (2) **D** Black Elephant; Cloof; Fryer's Cove; Grande Provence; Knorhoek; Louis 57; Meerhof; Packwood; Rosendal; Signal Gun; Thelema; Thokozani; Windmeul

Rosé off-dry/semi-sweet

★★★★ Leopard's Leap

★★★ Cape Dreams; Rooiberg; Skilpadvlei; Woolworths★★★ Backsberg; Badsberg (Light & low-alcohol; Perlé); Bergsig; Conradie (Light & low-alcohol; Perlé); De Wet (Perlé); **Louis 57** (Perlé); Napier; Nederburg; Overhex (Nouveau); Perdeberg; Robin Hood; Tangled Tree (Light & low-alcohol); Val du Charron; Vredenheim ★★ Autumn Harvest Crackling (Perlé); Bader & Walters; **Barnardt Boyes** (Light & low-alcohol; Perlé); Bon Courage; Dormershire; Du Toitskloof (Light & low-alcohol); Graça; **Imbuko** (Fairtrade); Robertson (Perlé); Theuniskraal; **Van Loveren** (2) (Light & low-alcohol); Vintales ★★ Bonnievale (Light & low-alcohol; Perlé); Darling Cellars; Nicholson Smith (Light & low-alcohol); Winkelshoek ★ Theescombe **NT** Bezalel; Botha; Buffalo Creek; Cilmor; Dieu Donné; Domein Doornkraal; KWV; Rietvallei; Swartland (Light & low-alcohol); Welbedacht; Weltevrede **D** Breëland; Douglas Green; Klawer; Linton Park; Overhex

Roussanne

★★★★★ Bellingham; Ken Forrester; Painted Wolf; The Foundry

★★★★ **Lieben**; Mischa; Rustenberg

★★★★ Org de Rac **NT** Hermit on the Hill **D** Fairview; Simonsig

Ruby cabernet

★★★ Bellpost; **Strange Kompanjie** ★★★ Langverwacht; Orange River; Robertson (2)

Sacramental Wines

★★ Zandwijk (Sweet red) **NT** Backsberg (Sweet red; Kosher; Sacramental); Landzicht (Muscadel, red, unfortified)

Sangiovese

★★★★ Anthonij Rupert; **Domaine des Dieux**; Idiom; **Jasper Raats**; La Vierge; Stellakaya; **Super Single Vineyards**; Woolworths

★★★★ Casa Mori; Fairview; Morgenster; Raka ★★★ Havana Hills (2); Leeurivier★★★ Dragonridge; Koelenhof **NT** Anura; Bezalel; Idiom

Sauvignon blanc unwooded

★★★★★ Tokara

★★★★ Anthonij Rupert; Benguela Cove; Boschendal; Bosman; **Bramon**; Buitenverwachting; Cederberg; Constantia Glen; Constantia Uitsig; D'Aria; Diemersdal (3); Driehoek; Flagstone; Fryer's Cove; Glen Carlou; Groot Constantia; Groote Post; Highlands Road; Hillcrest; Kleine Zalze (2); **Kumusha**; KWV; La Motte; Meerendal; Moya's; Nederburg; Neethlingshof; Neil Ellis; Nicky Versfeld; Nitida; Oak Valley; Seven Springs; Spice Route (Old Vines); Spier; Springfield; Steenberg; Strandveld (2); The Berrio; The Giant Periwinkle; Thelema (2); Uva Mira; Van Loveren; Woolworths; Zorgvliet

★★★★ Aaldering; Allée Bleue; Almenkerk; Altydgedacht; Anura; Bartho Eksteen; Bartinney; Black Elephant; Black Oystercatcher; Blackwater; Boplaas; Boschkloof; Bouchard Finlayson; Bramon; Buitenverwachting; Cape Chamonix; Cape Point (2); Cape Town Wine Co (2); Cederberg; Clos Malverne; Clouds; Constantia Mist (Organic); Creation; Dalla Cia; De Grendel; Delaire Graff; Diemersdal; Durbanville Hills; Eagles' Nest; Elgin Ridge (Biodynamic); Erika Obermeyer; Fleur du Cap; Fryer's Cove; Gabriëlskloof; Groot Phesantekraal; Herold; Idun; Izak van der Vyver; Jan Harmsgat (Fairtrade); Jordan; Kings Kloof; Klein Constantia; KWV; La Vierge; Lanzerac; **Le Belle Rebelle**; Lomond (3); Maastricht; Meinert; **Mischa**; Morgenster; Nico Vermeulen; Nitida; Ormonde (3); PaardenKloof; Rivendell (Fairtrade); Robert Stanford; Rooiberg; Rosendal; Saxenburg; **Scrucap** (2); Signal Gun (2); **Silvermist** (2) (Organic); Simonsig; Sir Lambert; South Hill; Southern Right; Spice Route; Spioenkop; Spookfontein; Springfield; Stanford Hills; Steenberg; Stellenrust; Stony Brook; Sumaridge; Teubes; The Butcher Shop; The Goose; Tierhoek; Tokara; Trizanne; Uva Mira; Wijnskool; **Wildeberg**; Wildekrans; Winshaw; **Woolworths** (5); Zandvliet; Zevenwacht; Zoetendal

★★★★ Arendskloof; Bellingham; Blaauwklippen; Bloemendal; Blue Crane; Boplaas (2); Boschendal; Boschrivier; **Bramon**; Canto; Capaia; Conradie; Croydon; D'Aria; Dâbar; Daschbosch; De Wet; Delheim; DeMorgenzon; Die Mas; Diemersdal; Domaine des Dieux; Du Toitskloof; Durbanville Hills; Elgin Vintners; Ernie Els; Ernst Gouws; Esona; Fairview (2); False Bay; Foothills; Four Paws; Garden Route; Glen Carlou; Goedvertrouw; Grande Provence; Hartenberg; Hidden Valley; Hill & Dale; Hout Bay; Ken Forrester; Klein Constantia; Klein Roosboom (2); **Kleine Zalze** (2); Konkelberg (2); Kunjani; Kuypers Kraal; KWV; **L'Avenir**; La Motte; La Petite Ferme; Le Pommier; Le Sueur; Leipzig; Lemberg; Lodestone; Louis 57; LuKa; Lutzville; Malanot;

Merwida; Midgard; Miravel; Misty Mountains; **Mont Blois**; Nederburg; Nico van der Merwe; Noble Savage; Overhex (Nouveau); PaardenKloof; Packwood; Paul Wallace; Peter Falke; Piekenierskloof (Fairtrade); Quando; Raka; Saronsberg; Sauvignon Wines; **Spier** (2); Splattered Toad; Stellenbosch University; Strydom; Teubes; The Butcher Shop; Township Winery; Truter Family; Under Oaks; Vaalvlei; **Villiersdorp**; **Vinologist**; Vondeling; Walker Bay Estate; Warwick; Waterford; Webersburg; Whalehaven; Woolworths (3); Zandwijk (Kosher); Zonnebloem ★★★ Alexanderfontein; Anthonij Rupert; Anura; Arumdale; Asara; Aslina; Avontuur; Backsberg; Bader & Walters; Barrydale; Bayede!; Bellevue; Bemind; Benguela Cove; Bergsig; Boland; Bon Courage; Bonnievale; Breëland; Bushmanspad; Calitzdorp; Cape Classics; Cape Dreams; Cilmor; Clos Malverne; Conradie; D'Aria; Darling Cellars; DeWaal; Diemersfontein; Dornier; Du Preez; Du Toitskloof; Excelsior; Fairvalley (Fairtrade); False Bay; Fat Bastard; **FirstCape**; Fleur du Cap; Fort Simon (2); **Friesland**; Goede Hoop; Grande Provence; Groenland; Hidden Valley; House of Mandela; Imbuko (Fairtrade); Journey's End (Fairtrade); Kaapzicht; Kanu; Ken Forrester; Kloovenburg; Koopmanskloof (Fairtrade); Kranskop; La Chataigne; Landskroon; Landzicht; Le Grand Chasseur; Leopard's Leap; Linton Park; Lord's; Louisvale; Lyngrove; Maison de Teijger; MAN Family; Marklew; MolenVliet; Mooiplaas; Morgenhof; Muratie; Nederburg; Neethlingshof; Nelson; Newstead; Nuy; **Old Road**; Overhex; PaardenKloof; Pearl Mountain; Perdeberg; Piekenierskloof (Fairtrade); Porcupine Ridge; Pulpit Rock; Rickety Bridge; Ridgeback; Riebeek Valley; Roodezandt; Rooiberg (2); Sauvignon Wines; Schalkenbosch; Silkbush; Skilpadvlei; Slaley; Slanghoek; Somerbosch; Stellar (Fairtrade; Organic); Stellenbosch Hills (2); Stellenbosch Vineyards; Stellenview (Skin-macerated white); Stettyn; Swartland; Thokozani; Truter Family; Van Loveren; Van Zylshof; Vergenoegd; Viljoensdrift; Waterford; Welbedacht; Wellington Winery; Woolworths (3) (Fairtrade; Organic); Yonder Hill; Zevenwacht; Zorgvliet ★★★ Badsberg; Bezalel; **Bosjes**; Brandvlei; Cloof; Darling Cellars; Devonvale; DuVon; Eagle's Cliff; Excelsior; Fish Hoek (Fairtrade); Flagstone; Fort Simon; Guardian Peak; Hoopenburg; Imbuko (2) (Fairtrade); Klawer; Koelenhof (Natural/non-fortified pale); KWV (3); Langverwacht; Lateganskop; Le Manoir de Brendel; Linton Park; Lovane; Meerhof (Fairtrade); Mountain River; Niel Joubert; Overhex (Nouveau); Perdeberg; Robertson (5) (Perlé); Robin Hood; Roos Family;

The Bridge of Hope; **Theuniskraal**; Two Oceans; Val de Vie; Waboomsrivier; Welmoed; Wineways (3); Wonderfontein ★★ Aan de Doorns; Calais; Clairvaux; Daschbosch (2) (Fairtrade); Hoopenburg; Imbuko (Fairtrade); Koelenhof; Koni; McGregor; Mountain Ridge; Namaqua; Nicholson Smith (2); Orange River; Somerset Wines; Thokozani (Perlé); Tulbagh Winery; **Van Loveren** (De-alcoholised; Light & low-alcohol); Vintales; Vredenheim; Welvanpas; Wineways; Winkelshoek; Woolworths ★★ Namaqua; Robertson (2) (Light & low-alcohol); Simonsvlei ★ Lutzville **NT** Akkerdal; Arendsig (2); Barton; Bayede!; Bitou; Bizoe; Boland; Bouchard Finlayson; Brampton; Brunia; Buffalo Creek; Burgerhof; Camberley; Cape Elevation; Dieu Donné; Doolhof; Dormershire; Douglas Green; Drostdy-Hof; Franschhoek Cellar; Fryer's Cove; Glenview; Hannay; Havana Hills (2); J9; Kaapse Familie Wingerde; Kay & Monty; Klein Gustrouw; Klein Roosboom; Kleinhoekkloof; Louis; Lozärn; Mimosa; Mischa; Misty Mountains; Mont du Toit; Mountain River; Nederburg; Noble Hill; Nomada; Nuy; Oneiric; PaardenKloof; Rietvallei (4); Rosendal; Rustenberg; Seven Sisters; Stellendrift; Tangled Tree; The Fledge; Walker Bay Estate; Windmeul; Wineways; **Woolworths** (9) (Light & low-alcohol); Zonnebloem **D** Aden's Star; Bramon; Cloof (2); Domein Doornkraal; Douglas Green; Durbanville Hills; Excelsior; Groote Post; Klein Constantia (Organic); Knorhoek (2); La Couronne; M'hudi; Overgaauw; Rosendal; Schenkfontein; Simonsvlei (2); Spioenkop; Welgevallen; Weltevrede; Woolworths

Sauvignon blanc wooded
★★★★★ Neil Ellis; **Trizanne**

★★★★☆ Bartho Eksteen (2); Bloemendal; Buitenverwachting; Cape Point (2); Catherine Marshall; Cederberg; D'Aria; De Grendel; Delaire Graff; DeMorgenzon; **Die Kat**; Diemersdal (2); Eikendal; Erika Obermeyer; Highlands Road; Hillcrest; Iona; Jordan; Klein Constantia (4); Le Grand Domaine; Mulderbosch; Nederburg (2); Newton Johnson; Nitida; Paul Cluver; Reyneke (Biodynamic); **Seven Springs**; Shannon; Skaap; Stark-Condé; Stellenrust; The Giant Periwinkle; Tierhoek; Vergelegen; Villiera; Waterkloof (2); Zevenwacht

★★★★ Avontuur; Backsberg; Benguela Cove; Constantia Royale; **DA Hanekom**; Enfin; Escapades; Fortes; Highberry; Iona; Jasper Raats (Organic); **Le Bonheur**; Le Grand Domaine; Marianne; Miss Molly; Mulderbosch; Nomada; Org de Rac (Organic); **Osbloed**; Overhex (Nouveau); Reyneke (Organic); Rivendell; Rousseau (2); **Rustenberg**;

Spier (2); Steenberg; **Stellar** (Fairtrade; Organic); Stony Brook; The Fledge; Vergelegen; Villiera; Walker Bay Estate; **Yardstick**

★★★☆ Baleia; Edgebaston; **Fortes**; Haskell; Le Bonheur; Meinert; Miravel; Mont Rochelle; **Orange River**; **Overgaauw**; Painted Wolf; Quoin Rock; Rietvallei; Solitary ★★★ Botha ★★★ Windfall ★★ Barnardt Boyes; Kumala **NT** Alvi's Drift; Fryer's Cove; Jean Daneel; Klein Constantia (4); Louis; Maison de Teijger; Namaqua (2); Springfontein; Stark-Condé; Swartland; Woolworths (2) **D** Darling Cellars

Semillon gris
★★★★☆ **JC Wickens**; Mullineux (Old Vines); Thorne & Daughters

Semillon unwooded
★★★★☆ Benguela Cove

★★★★ Kings Kloof

★★★ Viljoensdrift ★★ Van Loveren **D** Wildeberg

Semillon wooded
★★★★★ Anthonij Rupert (Old Vines); Rickety Bridge

★★★★☆ Alheit (Old Vines); Arcangeli; **Beaumont**; Black Elephant; Bloemendal; Boekenhoutskloof (Old Vines); Botanica; Cederberg; Constantia Uitsig; David & Nadia (Old Vines); Dornier; Foothills; Naudé (Old Vines); Opstal; Sadie (Old Vines); Shannon; Steenberg; Thorne & Daughters (Old Vines); Vergelegen; Wildehurst; Yardstick

★★★★ Haut Espoir; Hermit on the Hill; Highlands Road; Hillcrest; **Idiom**; KWV; La Bri; Landau du Val (Old Vines); **Malanot**; Nitida; **Old Road** (Old Vines); Olivedale (Alternative white/red); Rickety Bridge; The Garajeest; Trizanne; **Wildeberg** (Old Vines); Yardstick

★★★☆ Brunia; **Damascene**; Meinert ★★★ **Thor NT** Cape Point; **De Kleine Wijn Koöp** (2) (Old Vines); Escapades; Hildenbrand; La Chataigne **D** Escapades; Groote Post; My Wyn; Nicky Versfeld; Signal Hill; Spice Route

Sherry-style wines
★★★★☆ **Bruce Jack**; Spice Route

★★★★ KWV Sherry-Style Wines (3); Monis

★★★☆ Monis (2) **NT** Landzicht

Shiraz/syrah
★★★★★ Blackwater; Boekenhoutskloof (2); Cederberg; De Grendel; Dorrance (Fairtrade); Gabriëlskloof; Leeuwenkuil; Mullineux (3); Patatsfontein; Rall; Reyneke (Biodynamic); Rust en Vrede; Savage; Super Single Vineyards; Van Loggerenberg

★★★★☆ Almenkerk; Alto; Annandale; Anthonij Rupert; **ArtiSons** (2); Beau Constantia; Beaumont; Bellingham; Bizoe; Bon Courage; **Boschendal**; Boschkloof (2); **Bruce Jack** Family; Cederberg; Cirrus; **City on a Hill**; Cloof; Clouds; **Collatio**; **Creation**; **Damascene**; De Grendel; De Trafford (2); Delheim; DeMorgenzon; DewaldtHeyns; Driehoek; Durbanville Hills; Eagles' Nest; Eenzaamheid; **Erika Obermeyer** (2); Ernie Els; Fairview (4); Flagstone; Gabriëlskloof; GlenWood; Groot Constantia; Groote Post; Hartenberg (3); Haskell (2); Highlands Road; Holden Manz; **Idiom**; Iona; Jasper Raats (Organic); JC Wickens; Jordan; Keermont (3); Kleine Zalze; Kloovenburg; **KWV** (2); La Bri (2); La Motte (2); Luddite; Maison; Metzer; Michaella; Mont Destin (2); Mullineux; **Natasha Williams**; Nico van der Merwe; Oldenburg; Olifantsberg; Painted Wolf; Porseleinberg; Quoin Rock; Radford Dale (2); Rainbow's End; Raka; Remhoogte (2); Reyneke (Organic); Rhebokskloof; Richard Hilton (2); Richard Kershaw (5); Robertson; Rustenberg; Saltare; Saronsberg; Savage; Saxenburg; Schultz Family; Sijnn; **Simelia**; Simonsig; Spookfontein; Stark-Condé (2); Stellenbosch Vineyards; Stony Brook; Strandveld; Super Single Vineyards; Tamboerskloof; The Berrio; The Foundry; Thelema; Tokara; **Trizanne** (2); Uva Mira; Van Loveren; Van Wyk; Vergelegen; Waterford; Waterkloof; Waverley Hills (Organic); Woolworths

★★★★ Aaldering; Allée Bleue; Allesverloren; Andreas; Anura (2); Avontuur; Babylonstoren; Baleia; Benguela Cove; **Blaauwklippen**; Bloemendal (2); Boland; Bonnievale; **Bosjes**; Brunia; Camberley; Cape Wine Company; **Collatio** (2); Conceito; D'Aria (2); Dâbar; De Breede (Organic); Delheim; DeMorgenzon; Diemersfontein; Doran; Dornier; Du Toitskloof; **Dunstone** (2); **Elgin Vintners** (2); Enfin (2); Esona; Excelsior; Fable (2); Fairview; Flying Cloud; Foothills; Gabriëlskloof; Glen Carlou; Glenelly; GlenWood; Grande Provence; Groenland; Guardian Peak; Hartenberg; Haskell; Haut Espoir; **Havana Hills**; **Holden Manz**; Hout Bay; Joubert-Tradauw; Journey's End (2) (Fairtrade); JP Bredell; Julien Schaal; Kanu; Kings Kloof; Kleine Zalze; Kloovenburg; Koelfontein; **Kruishof**; KWV; Kyburg; La Couronne; La Petite Ferme; La Vierge; Lammershoek; Landskroon; Langverwacht; Lanzerac; Le Belle Rebelle; Leeuwenkuil; Lemberg; Linton Park; Lomond; Lord's; Lyngrove; **Lynx**; Malanot; MAN Family; Marianne; Marklew; **Meerhof**; Middelvlei; Migliarina; Mimosa; Mont Rochelle; Montegray;

Muratie; Nederburg (2); Neil Ellis; Nelson; Nico van der Merwe; Niel Joubert; Nitida; Noble Hill; Nuy; **Old Road**; Oldenburg; Olsen; Orange River; Org de Rac (Fairtrade; Organic); Ormonde; Oude Denneboom; **Overhex** (Nouveau); PaardenKloof; **Painted Wolf**; Pearl Mountain; Perdeberg; Peter Falke; **Piekenierskloof**; Plaisir de Merle; Post House; **Raka**; Rhebokskloof; Rickety Bridge; Ridgeback; Riebeek Valley; Rivendell; Rooiberg (2); Rosendal; Rudera; Rust en Vrede; Rustenberg; Saxenburg; Seven Springs (2); Signal Gun; Signal Hill; Simelia; Skaap; Slaley; South Hill; Stellar (Fairtrade; Organic); Stellenbosch University; Stellenrust; Strandveld; Strydom; Sumaridge; Tanagra; **Tempel**; The Butcher Shop; The Fledge; The Giant Periwinkle; Thelema; Trizanne; Under Oaks; Uva Mira; Vergelegen; Vergenoegd; Villion; Vondeling; Welbedacht; Wellington Winery; Weltevrede; Wijnskool; Wildekrans; Windmeul; Woolworths (4); Zandvliet (3); Zevenwacht

★★★★ Aan't Vette; Allée Bleue; Anthonij Rupert; Arendskloof; Arra; Asara; Backsberg; **Bader & Walters**; Bayedé; **Bellascene**; Bellingham; Bemind; Blue Crane; Bon Courage; Boschendal; Boschrivier; Bosman; Botha; Bushmanspad; Cape Dreams; **Cape Town Wine Co**; Carrol Boyes; Cloof (2); Collatio; **Conradie**; Croydon; Darling Cellars (2); De Meye; Delaire Graff; Diemersdal; Domaine Brahms; Dragonridge; Druk My Niet; Du Toitskloof; Durbanville Hills; Ernst Gouws; Excelsior; False Bay; Fat Bastard; Foothills; Fort Simon; Fram; Glen Carlou; Goede Hoop; Goedverwacht; Graceland; Hartenberg; Havana Hills; Hermit on the Hill; Hofstraat; House of Mandela; Idun; Imbuko (Fairtrade); Jan Harmsgat (Fairtrade); Jean Daneel; Kaapzicht; Katbakkies; Kleine Schuur; Koni; **Kruishof** (2); Lammershoek; Landskroon; Le Belle Rebelle; Le Grand Chasseur; Leopard's Leap; Louis 57 (2); Lutzville; Lynx; Meerendal; Meerhof (Fairtrade); Meinert; Mellasat; Mischa; Mitre's Edge; Mont du Toit; Mount Pleasant; Mountain Ridge (2); Namaqua; Neethlingshof; Nick & Forti's; Nico Vermeulen; Niel Joubert; Niemandsrivier; Nieuwedrift; Nuiba; **Olivedale** (2); Org de Rac (Organic); PaardenKloof; Perdeberg (2); Piekenierskloof (Fairtrade); Porcupine Ridge; Radford Dale (2); Riebeek Valley; Rivendell; Robertson (3); Rooiberg (2); Saronsberg; Scrucap; Seven Sisters; Silkbush; Simonsig; **Spier**; Stanford Hills; Stellenbosch Vineyards; Stellenrust; Stellenview (2); Swartland; Taillard; The Butcher Shop; The Goose; The Hills; Tokara; Truter Family; Tulbagh Winery; **Vinologist**; Vredenheim; Waverley Hills (Organic); Wellington Winery; Woolworths;

Zonnebloem **★★★** Audacia; Bader & Walters; Barrydale; Bellevue; Bellpost; Boschheim; Brandvlei; Calitzdorp; Cape Wine Company (Fairtrade); Clairvaux; Cloof; Daschbosch; De Wet; Devonvale; Die Mas; Dormershire (2); Du Preez; Du'SwaRoo (2); DuVon; Eagle's Cliff; Eerste Hoop (2); False Bay; **FirstCape** (2); Fish Hoek (Fairtrade); Fort Simon (2); Frater; Groenland; Hoopenburg; Houw Hoek; Jason's Hill; **Jordan**; Klein Roosboom; Kleine Zalze; Koelenhof; Kranskop; Kumala; **Kumusha**; Kunjani; KWV (2); La Terre La Mer; **Le Grand Domaine**; Le Manoir de Brendel; Leeurivier; Leipzig; Linton Park; Lord's; Louisvale; Lovane; Lyngrove; Mountain Ridge; Nelson; Nuy; Ormonde; Overhex (Nouveau); Painted Wolf; Piekenierskloof (Fairtrade); Pulpit Rock; Schalkenbosch (Fairtrade); Schenkfontein; Skilpadvlei; Slanghoek; Somerbosch; Spier; Splattered Toad; Stellar (Fairtrade; Organic); Stellenbosch Hills; Stellendrift; Stellenview; Stettyn; Strange Kompanjie; **Summerhill**; Swartland; Teubes (Organic); The Bridge of Hope; The Grape Grinder; **Thor**; Tulbagh Winery; Vaalvlei; Viljoensdrift; **Villiersdorp**; Windmeul; Wonderfontein; Woolworths (2) **★★★** Aan de Doorns; Alexanderfontein; **Benguela Cove**; Boschheim; Botha; Carrol Boyes; Cilmor; Fleur du Cap; House of Mandela; Imbuko (Fairtrade); Kirabo; Koopmanskloof (Fairtrade); KWV; Le Manoir de Brendel; Lutzville; Mile High; Mountain River; Namaqua; Nicholson Smith; Orange River; Roodezandt; **Simonsvlei** (4) (Kosher); Somerset Wines; Stellar (Fairtrade; Organic); **Stellenview** (2); The Hills; **Theuniskraal**; Two Oceans; Welmoed; Weltevrede; Windfall; Woolworths **★★** Bonnievale; Daschbosch; Du Toitskloof; Klawer; KWV; McGregor; Middelvlei; Mile High; Tangled Tree; **The Bridge of Hope**; Vintales; Wineways **NT** Alvi's Drift; Annex Kloof; Arendsig; Avondale (Organic); Axe Hill; Bayedé; Belfield; Bezalel; Boland; Brampton; Capaia; Cape Dreams; Cavalli; Chennells; Cloof; Constantia Uitsig; Craven (2); Desert Rose; DeWaal; Dieu Donné; Douglas Green; Drostdy-Hof; Edgebaston; Enfin; Fernskloof; FirstCape; Four Paws; Franschhoek Cellar; Fryer's Cove; Glen Carlou; Groot Phesantekraal; Grundheim; Havana Hills; Hawksmoor (2); Herold; Highgate; Hildenbrand (2); Hirst; Jacques Smit; Joostenberg (2) (Organic); Kleinhoekkloof; Lazanou (Organic); Lemberg; Lomond (2); Manley; Marianne (2); Meerendal; Misty Mountains; Mont Rochelle; Mooi Bly; Mörelig; Mother Rock; Mountain River; Nederburg (2); New Beginnings; Oneiric (2); Oude Compagnies Post; Rickety Bridge; **Rietvallei** (2); Robert Stanford; Rogge Cloof; Rosendal (3); Schultz

Family; Seven Sisters; Simelia; **Skaap**; Slaley; Spotswood; Springfontein; Steenberg; Stellar (Fairtrade; Organic); Stellekaya; Tamboerskloof; Terracura; Val du Charron; Walker Bay Estate; Wederom; Wildekrans; Wineways; Woolworths (2); Zoetendal; Zonnebloem **D** Akkerdal; Andy Mitchell; Arra (2); Audacia (2) (Light & low-alcohol); Ayama; Black Elephant; Camberley; Creation; Darling Cellars; Doran; Durbanville Hills; Fable (2); FirstCape; Freedom Hill; Gabriëlskloof; Garden Route; Haskell; Knorhoek; Langverwacht; Linton Park; Lozärn; M'hudi; Maastricht; Mooiplaas; Simonsvlei; Spice Route (2) (Fairtrade); Topiary; Warwick

Skin-macerated white

★★★★☆ Laibach (Chenin blanc wooded, dry; Organic); **Joostenberg** (Chenin blanc wooded, dry)

★★★★ **Olivedale** (White blends, wooded, dry); **AA Badenhorst** (White blends, wooded, dry; Alternative white/red); Constantia Uitsig (Hanepoot fortified)

★★★★☆ **Dragonridge** (Chenin blanc wooded, dry)

★★★ Stellenview (Sauvignon blanc unwooded) **NT** Springfontein (Chardonnay wooded)

Sparkling, Méthode ancestrale

★★★★☆ Upland (Méthode ancestrale; Organic); Vondeling

★★★★ Dragonridge (Méthode ancestrale); The Blacksmith

★★★★ **Botanica** (Méthode ancestrale); **Maanschijn** (Light & low-alcohol; Méthode ancestrale); Metzer★★★ Dragonridge **NT** AA Badenhorst; The Blacksmith **D** Groot Parys; Vondeling

Sparkling, Méthode cap classique, red, dry

★★★★☆ Camberley **NT** Mount Babylon

Sparkling, Méthode cap classique, rosé, dry

★★★★★ Bon Courage

★★★★☆ Ambelouï; Anthonij Rupert; **Aristea**; Charles Fox (2); Domaine des Dieux; Graham Beck; Le Lude; Newstead; **Nitida**; Wonderfontein

★★★★ Anthonij Rupert; Canto; Clos Malverne; Colmant; Dainty Bess; Graham Beck; Groot Constantia; Haute Cabrière; **Hidden Valley**; Kleine Zalze; Krone; KWV; Longridge; Lourensford (2); Miss Molly; Môreson; Pongrácz; Saltare; Scrucap; Silverthorn; Simonsig; Steenberg; Tanzanite; Teubes; Van Loveren; Villiera; Waterkloof; **Wildehurst**; Wildekrans; Woolworths (2)

★★★☆ Allée Bleue; Arendskloof; Aurelia; Boschendal; Bruce Jack; Canto; Cape Town Wine Co; Grande Provence; Groote Post; **Kanu**; Koelenhof;

L'Avenir; Lodestone; Lord's; Louisvale; My Wyn; Namaqua; Strandveld; Sumaridge; Webersburg

★★★ Black Oystercatcher; Darling Cellars; Linton Park; **Lothian**; Lovane; Packwood; Perdeberg; Plettenvale **NT** Bayede!; Carrol Boyes; Dieu Donné; Elgin Ridge; Francois La Garde; Franschhoek Cellar; Lyngrove; Misty Mountains; Rickety Bridge **D** Ayama; The House of JC le Roux; Woolworths

Sparkling, Méthode cap classique, rosé, off-dry/semi-sweet

★★★★ Krone; **Simonsig**

★★★ The House of JC le Roux

Sparkling, Méthode cap classique, white, dry

★★★★★ Le Lude (2); **Pieter Ferreira**; Saltare

★★★★☆ Altydgedacht (2); Ambelouï; Anthonij Rupert; Babylonstoren; Bartho Eksteen; **Black Elephant**; Bon Courage (2); Boschendal (2); Cederberg; Charles Fox (3); Colmant (3); Graham Beck (4); Haute Cabrière; **Huis van Chevallerie** (Old Vines); Klein Constantia; **Krone** (3); KWV; La Bri; Le Lude; Longridge; Lourensford; Newstead; Pongrácz (2); Saltare (3); Silverthorn (3); Simonsig; **Spier**; Steenberg; Stony Brook; Tanzanite; Tierhoek; Tokara; Villiera; Waterford; Waterkloof; Woolworths

★★★★ Allée Bleue; Alvi's Drift; Amelouï; Anthonij Rupert; Anura; **Aristea**; Asara; Benguela Cove; Black Elephant; Boschendal; Bosman; Bramon (2); Canto; Carrol Boyes; **Chantelle**; Clouds; Conradie; Constantia Uitsig; Croydon; Darling Cellars; De Grendel; De Krans; De Wet; Delaire Graff; Delheim; DeMorgenzon; Domaine des Dieux; Durbanville Hills; Fairview; Foothills; Genevieve; Graham Beck; Grande Provence; Groot Phesantekraal; Haute Cabrière; **Hazendal**; **Hidden Valley**; Hoopenburg; Hout Bay; Ken Forrester (Old Vines); Klein Constantia; Kleine Zalze (2); Krone; KWV; L'Avenir; La Motte; Le Belle Rebelle; **Le Lude** (2); Longridge; Lord's; Lowerland; Maison; Mimosa; Miss Molly; Môreson; Morgenhof; My Wyn (2); Nico van der Merwe; Nieuwedrift; Nitida; Perdeberg; Peter Falke; Plaisir de Merle; Pongrácz; Pulpit Rock; Quoin Rock; Rhebokskloof; Saronsberg; Scrucap; Simonsig; Spier; Stanford Hills; Steenberg; **The Wine Thief**; Thelema; Val de Vie; Van Loveren; Vergenoegd; Villiera (2); Wildehurst; Wonderfontein; Woolworths

★★★☆ Aurelia; Backsberg; **Benguela Cove**; Blaauwklippen; Canto; Cavalli; **Chantelle**; **Darling Cellars**; Du Preez; Du Toitskloof; **Four Paws**; Gabriëlskloof; Kanu; Lanzerac; Lateganskop; Leopard's Leap; Louisvale; Maison de Teijger; **MAN Family**; **Marklew**; Mooiplaas; Mulderbosch; Muratie;

New Beginnings; Noble Hill; Nuy; Org de Rac (Nouveau; Organic); Ridgeback; Saxenburg; Signal Gun; Somerbosch; The House of JC le Roux; Villiera (Light & low-alcohol); Waverley Hills (Organic); Webersburg; Welbedacht; Wildekrans; Woolworths (2) (Light & low-alcohol) ★★★ Alkmaar; Avontuur; Bernind; Bloemendal; Cloof; Dâbar; Goede Hoop; Klein Roosboom; Koelenhof; Linton Park; Morgenster; Niel Joubert; **Olsen**; Rickety Bridge; Robert Stanford; The House of JC le Roux; Tulbagh Winery; **Walker Bay Estate**; Weltevrede; Windfall **NT** Andy Mitchell; Avondale (Organic); Backsberg (Kosher); Buitenverwachting; Cape Chamonix; Charles Fox; Dieu Donné; Domaine Coutelier; Esona; Francois La Garde; Franschhoek Cellar; Genevieve; Grande Provence; Hildenbrand; Huis van Chevallerie; Jean Daneel; Kay & Monty (2); Lourensford; Maison de Teijger (2); **Meerendal**; Mimosa; Mount Babylon; Rickety Bridge; Riebeek Valley; Roodezandt; Skaap; Spookfontein; Stellenbosch University; The House of GM&AHRENS; The House of JC le Roux; Vergelegen; Viljoensdrift; Walking Woods (Fairtrade; Organic); Weltevrede; Wildehurst (2) **D** Ayama (2); Carrol Boyes (2); Laibach; Meerendal; Overhex; Schalkenbosch; Signal Hill; Stellenbosch Vineyards; Strange Kompanjie; The Butcher Shop; Topiary; Warwick

Sparkling, Méthode cap classique, white, off-dry/semi-sweet

★★★★ Graham Beck; Pongrácz; Simonsig ★★★☆ Boschendal; Darling Cellars (Light & low-alcohol); **Haute Cabrière**; Woolworths ★★★ The House of JC le Roux **NT** New Beginnings

Sparkling, Non-MCC, red, dry

★★★ D'Aria ★★ The House of JC le Roux **D** M'hudi

Sparkling, Non-MCC, red, off-dry/semi-sweet

★★ Du Toitskloof (Light & low-alcohol); Robertson

Sparkling, Non-MCC, rosé, dry

★★★★ Huis van Chevallerie

★★★★ Hill & Dale; Kloovenburg ★★★ Alvi's Drift; Boplaas; D'Aria; **Durbanville Hills**; Riebeek Valley; Stellar★★★ **Robertson NT** Blaauwklippen (Perlé); Somerset Wines **D** Knorhoek; Woolworths

Sparkling, Non-MCC, rosé, off-dry/semi-sweet

★★★ Bon Courage; Domein Doornkraal; Klawer (Light & low-alcohol); Lutzville (Light & low-alcohol); Nuy; Orange River (Light & low-alcohol); Robertson (Light & low-alcohol); Rooiberg (Light & low-alcohol); Swartland; The House of JC le Roux; Vredenheim; Woolworths ★★ Aan de Doorns; **Bonnievale**; Goedverwacht; Koelenhof; Mountain

Ridge; Overhex (Light & low-alcohol); Perdeberg (Light & low-alcohol); The House of JC le Roux (Light & low-alcohol); Tulbagh Winery; Viljoensdrift (Light & low-alcohol); Vintales **NT** Rietvallei; Stellar (Fairtrade; Organic); Stellenbosch Hills; Walking Woods

Sparkling, Non-MCC, white, dry

★★★★ Colmant

★★★☆ **Hill & Dale**; Steenberg; Woolworths (2) ★★★ Clos Malverne; Durbanville Hills; Leopard's Leap; Nederburg; Orange River; Stellar★★★ Bonnievale; Brandvlei; D'Aria; Daschbosch (Perlé); Du Toitskloof; KWV; Lyngrove; Overhex; Robertson; Rooiberg; Swartland; The House of JC le Roux; Tulbagh Winery; Woolworths ★★ Merwida; Slanghoek ★ Vintales **NT** Botha; Havana Hills; Hermit on the Hill; Rietvallei; Stellenbosch Hills; Welmoed; Woolworths

Sparkling, Non-MCC, white, off-dry/semi-sweet

★★★★ Krone

★★★ Badsberg (Light & low-alcohol); Opstal; **Orange River** (2) (Light & low-alcohol)★★★ Nuy; Slanghoek; Woolworths ★★ Koelenhof; KWV; Robertson (Light & low-alcohol); The House of JC le Roux (2) (Light & low-alcohol); Vintales; Zandwijk

Special Late Harvest

★★★★ Bon Courage; Nederburg ★★★★ Backsberg; Van Loveren ★★★ De Wet; Robertson **D** Slanghoek

Sweet red

★★★★ Dormershire ★★★ Fat Bastard ★★★ Autumn Harvest Crackling (Perlé); Cape Classics; Darling Cellars; Imbuko (Fairtrade); Somerset Wines; **Van Loveren** ★★ Du Toitskloof (Light & low-alcohol); Nicholson Smith (2); Perdeberg; Robertson (Light & low-alcohol); Roos Family; Somerset Wines; Wineways; Zandwijk ★★ De Krans (Light & low-alcohol; Perlé); Robertson (2) (Light & low-alcohol) **NT** Backsberg (Kosher; Sacramental); Stellar (Fairtrade; Organic); Woolworths **D** Overhex

Sylvaner

★★★★ Overgaauw

Tannat

★★★★ Arendskloof; Fairview; Lowerland ★★★★ Kranskop; Mooi Bly **NT** Du'SwaRoo

Tempranillo/tinta roriz

★★★★☆ Stony Brook; Super Single Vineyards ★★★★ Baleia; De Krans; Mellasat; **Wildehurst** ★★★★ Olivedale ★★★ Anura; Dornier **NT** Swallow Hill **D** Van der Merwe & Finlayson

Therona
★★★★ Stellenbosch Vineyards

Tinta barocca
★★★★☆ AA Badenhorst; Sadie
★★★★ Allesverloren; **Calitzdorp**; Lammershoek
(Old Vines); Momento; **The Wine Thief**
★★★☆ Boplaas; Micu Narunsky; Woolworths ★★★
Du'SwaRoo; Hofstraat; Swartland★★★ Du'SwaRoo
NT Dagbreek; Elemental Bob; Peter Bayly

Touriga franca
★★★★ Boplaas

Touriga nacional
★★★★★ Boplaas; JC Wickens
★★★★ Allesverloren; De Krans; Micu Narunsky;
Sijnn
★★★☆ Bergsig; Boplaas ★★★ Du'SwaRoo★★★
Du'SwaRoo NT Axe Hill; Calitzdorp; Dagbreek;
Joostenberg (Organic); Overgaauw D MAN Family

Trincadeira/tinta amarela
NT Charla Haasbroek; Dagbreek

Verdelho
★★★★★ Arcangeli; Stellenbosch Vineyards;
Thistle & Weed
★★★★ Fairview; **Glen Carlou**; Maanschijn
★★★☆ Org de Rac NT Cavalli D Alphabetical

Vermentino
★★★★★ Morgenster

Villard blanc
★★★ Osbloed

Villard noir
★★★ Osbloed

Vin de paille/straw wine
★★★★★ Fairview; Mullineux
★★★★☆ DeMorgenzon; **Diemersfontein**;
Donkiesbaai; **Flagstone**; Foothills; Keermont;
Klawer (Old Vines); La Motte; Lammershoek;
Meerhof (Fairtrade); Môreson (2); Rustenberg;
Savage; Stellar (Fairtrade; Organic); Tierhoek;
Vergelegen; Vondeling
★★★★ **Clairvaux**; Maison; Meinert; Orange
River; Piekenierskloof (Old Vines); Saronsberg;
Villiersdorp
★★★☆ Asara; Boplaas; Bosman ★★★ Dragonridge
NT Botanica; De Trafford; Druk My Niet (Light &
low-alcohol); Mellasat; Mullineux (2) (Light &
low-alcohol); Radford Dale; Simonsig; Spier D
Dagbreek; Fairview; Groot Parys (Organic); Signal
Hill; Stettyn

Viognier
★★★★★ Ridgeback
★★★★☆ Beau Constantia; Bellingham; Creation;
Eagles' Nest; Flagstone; La Bri; Lourensford;
Marianne; Richard Hilton (2); Tamboerskloof (2);
The Fledge; The Foundry
★★★★ Babylonstoren; Black Elephant;
Buitenverwachting; De Grendel; Diemersfontein;
Fairview; Franki's; Idiom; La Couronne; Lowerland;
Lynx (2); Maison; Mellasat; Noble Hill; Oldenburg;
Painted Wolf; Richard Hilton; Spice Route;
Wildehurst
★★★☆ Alkmaar; Anura; Arra; Axe Hill; Backsberg;
Blue Crane; Chennells (2); **Clayton**; Dunstone; Eerste
Hoop; La Petite Ferme; Myburgh Bros (Organic);
Nitida; Osbloed; Saronsberg; Silkbush; **The Giant
Periwinkle**; Woolworths ★★★ Ayama; Calais;
Dragonridge; Foothills; Kranskop; **Piekenierskloof**
★★★ Entre Nous; Excelsior; **Mountain Ridge NT**
Alvi's Drift; Arendsig (2); Bezalel; Dieu Donné; Kanu;
Lazanou (Organic); Leipzig; Mitre's Edge; My Wyn;
Robertson; Schalkenbosch; Spier; Spotswood; Stellar
(Fairtrade; Organic); Swallow Hill; Township Winery
(Fairtrade); Waterkloof; Whalehaven (2) D Arra (2);
Elgin Vintners; Fort Simon; Lynx; Riebeek Valley;
Stellenbosch University; SylvanVale; Van der Merwe
& Finlayson; Vergenoegd

White blends, off-dry/semi-sweet (w & u/w)
★★★★ Four Paws
★★★☆ Villiera ★★★ Ken Forrester; Robertson
★★★ Brandvlei; Nederburg; Overmeer Cellars;
Stellenrust (Fairtrade); Swartland; Zevenwacht
★★ Capenheimer (Perlé); Darling Cellars; De Krans
(Light & low-alcohol; Perlé); Du Toitskloof; Graça;
Paarl Perlé (Perlé); Perdeberg; Tulbagh Winery;
Welbedacht ★★ Autumn Harvest Crackling (Perlé);
Robertson (3) (Light & low-alcohol) NT Calitzdorp
(Perlé); Drostdy-Hof (2); Grande Provence; KWV;
Stellar (Fairtrade; Organic); Swartland; Two Oceans
D Altydgedacht; Bonnievale (Light & low-alcohol;
Perlé); Overhex (Light & low-alcohol); Signal Gun

White blends, unwooded, dry
★★★★★ Leeuwenkuil
★★★★☆ **Daschbosch**; GlenWood
★★★★ Elgin Vintners; KWV; **Misty Mountains**;
Nico Vermeulen; Spookfontein; The Blacksmith;
Truter Family; Welbedacht; Woolworths (2)
★★★☆ Alkmaar; Ashbourne; Beyerskloof; Boplaas;
Bouchard Finlayson; Buitenverwachting; Foothills;
Goats do Roam; Groote Post; Hazendal; Imbuko
(Fairtrade); **Jacques Germanier** (Organic);
Kruger Family; Lodestone; MAN Family; Org de

Rac (Fairtrade; Organic); Overhex (Nouveau); Post House; Quando; Simonsig; **Skipskop**; Springfield; Springfontein; Waverley Hills (Organic); Wildehurst; Woolworths ★★★ Allée Bleue; Bon Courage; Casa Mori; Doran; Flagstone; Frater; Imbuko; Jordan (2); Landskroon; Le Grand Domaine; Mellasat; Napier; Opstal; Pulpit Rock; Rascallion; Reyneke (Organic); Rhebokskloof; Roos Family; Saronsberg; Ses'Fikile; Somersbosch; Stellar (Fairtrade; Organic); Theuniskraal; Val du Charron; Van Loveren; Villiera; Villiersdorp; Woolworths (2); Zonnebloem ★★☆ Aan de Doorns; Darling Cellars; Du Toitskloof; **KWV**; Mooiplaas; Nederburg; Niel Joubert; Nuy; Stellenbosch Hills; Stellenrust (Fairtrade); Tulbagh Winery (Light & low-alcohol); Zandvliet ★★ Overmeer Cellars; Robertson; Simonsvlei; Slanghoek; Somerset Wines; **Wineways** (2); Woolworths (3) ★★ Bonnievale; Kanu; Le Manoir de Brendel; **Leopard's Leap** (Light & low-alcohol); Robertson (5) (Light & low-alcohol); Woolworths (2) (Light & low-alcohol) ★ Oom Tas **NT** Aaldering; Alvi's Drift; Cilmor; Doran; Drostdy-Hof; Four Paws; Kleinhoekkloof; KWV (2); Lazanou (Organic); McGregor; Mountain River; My Wyn; Myburgh Bros; Namaqua; Osbloed; Overhex (2); Rickety Bridge (Old Vines); Rosendal; Stellar (3) (Fairtrade; Organic); Stellendrift; The Berrio; Wavescape; Whalehaven; **Woolworths** (5) **D** Douglas Green; Kaapzicht; Klawer; Knorhoek; Lynx; New Beginnings; Riebeek Valley; Signal Gun; Simonsvlei; Thokozani; Wineways; Woolworths

White blends, wooded, dry

★★★★★ B Vintners; Cape Point; Delaire Graff; Groot Constantia; Mullineux (Old Vines); Rall; Sadie (2) (Old Vines); Thorne & Daughters

★★★★☆ AA Badenhorst; Alheit; Allée Bleue; Alvi's Drift; Anysbos; **Aristea**; Backsberg; Beaumont; Bergsig; Bizoe; Black Oystercatcher; Blackwater; Bloemendal; Boplaas; Cape Chamonix; Cape Rock; Cederberg; Celestina; City on a Hill; Constantia Glen; Constantia Uitsig; **Creation**; David & Nadia; De Grendel; **De Kleine Wijn Koöp**; DeMorgenzon; Doran; Dornier; Durbanville Hills; Elemental Bob; Elgin Ridge (Biodynamic); Fable; **Fairview** (2); Flagstone; Flying Cloud; Gabriëlskloof; GlenWood; Grande Provence; Groote Post; Highlands Road; Hughes Family (Organic); Iona; JAN Wines (Organic); Keermont; **Kumusha**; **Lammershoek** (Old Vines); Lemberg; Lourens Family; Lourensford; Luddite; **Meerhof** (Fairtrade); **Miles Mossop** (2); Momento; Morgenster; Naudé (Old Vines); Nederburg; Neethlingshof; Neil Ellis (Alternative white/red); Newton Johnson; Nico

van der Merwe; Nitida; Olifantsberg; Opstal; Org de Rac (Organic); Paul Roos; Piekenierskloof; Sadie (Old Vines); Savage; Shannon; Sijnn; Spier; Springfontein; Stark-Condé; Steenberg; Stony Brook; Strandveld; The Ahrens Family; **The Grapesmith** (2); The Great SA Wine Co; **The Wine Thief**; Thelema; Tokara; Trizanne; Van Wyk; Vergelegen (2); Vondeling; Vuurberg; **Wade Bales**; Warwick; Waterkloof; Zorgvliet

★★★★ AA Badenhorst (Alternative white/ red; Skin-macerated white); Anthonij Rupert; Arendskloof; Ashbourne; Babylon's Peak; Beau Constantia; Bezuidenhout Family; Blake; Boland; Bosman (Fairtrade); Bruce Jack; **Brunia**; Cavalli; **Constantia Royale**; Creation; Darling Cellars (2); De Krans; Ernst Gouws; Fram; **Hazendal**; **Huis van Chevallerie**; Joostenberg (Organic); Kloovenburg; La Bri; **La Petite Ferme**; Lammershoek; Leipzig; **Lievland**; Lomond (2); Miss Molly; Montegray; **Môrelig**; Muratie; Nuiba; **Old Road**; **Oldenburg**; **Olivedale** (Skin-macerated white); **Osbloed**; Painted Wolf; Patatsfontein; Perdeberg; Quoin Rock; Rascallion (2); Rickety Bridge; Rietvallei; South Hill; Stellenbosch Hills; Stony Brook; Sumaridge (2); The Fledge; The Giant Periwinkle; The Wolftrap; Tierhoek; Under Oaks; Val du Charron; **Villiersdorp**; Villion; Zevenwacht

★★★☆ Edgebaston; False Bay; Haut Espoir; Hermit on the Hill; Lanzerac; Meerhof (Fairtrade); **Spier** (Organic); Strange Kompanjie (Old Vines); **The Giant Periwinkle**; **Van Loveren** ★★★ Alphabetical; Bellpost; Blue Crane; Eenzaamheid; **Fable**; Fijndraai; Hidden Valley; Mont Rochelle; **Thor** (3) **NT** Avondale (Organic); Babylonstoren; Black Elephant; Doolhof; Dragonridge (Alternative white/red); Eerste Hoop; Elemental Bob; Escapades; Glen Carlou; **Goede Hoop**; Hildenbrand (2); Malanot; Mother Rock; My Wyn; Nomada; Richard Kershaw; **Safriel**; Swallow Hill; Themika; Two Oceans; Villiera **D** Altydgedacht; Benguela Cove; Doran; Fairview; Lammershoek; Le Pommier; Meerhof; Nederburg; Painted Wolf (2); Taillard; Yardstick

White from red/black grapes (not Blanc de noir)

★★★★☆ ArtiSons

★★★★ Meinert; Mellasat; **Oude Compagnies Post**; Springfontein

★★★☆ Villion ★★★ Asara (Fairtrade); Wellington Winery

Zinfandel/Primitivo

★★★★ Blaauwklippen

★★★☆ Idiom **D** Grande Provence

The Industry

Overview

According to the latest available data (2018), South Africa is the 9th-largest wine-producing nation by volume, down from 8th largest in 2017. Italy, having increased its share to 18.7% of global production, remains the number one producer, followed by France, which also increased its share (to 16.8%), Spain (15.2%, also up) and the US (down slightly, to 8.2%). SA, with 950 m litres (excluding grape juice and grape juice concentrate), in 2018 contributed 3.3% to global volume, down from 4.1%.

The number of SA wine-grape growers continued to decline (2,873 compared with 3,029 in 2017), along with the hectares under vine (93,021 vs 94,545) and the overall number of wine cellars crushing grapes (542 vs 546). Total private cellars also dipped, from 472 to 468, as did co-operatives – 'producer cellars' in officialese – from 48 to 47. Producing wholesalers crushing grapes increased from 26 to 27. Micro-cellars, vinifying less than 100 tons, fell from 224 to 222 but at 47% of the total, remained a strong force in the industry.

Vineyards

After slumping to a new low of 1,198 ha in 2017 (revised figure), vineyard establishment recovered slightly to 1,506 ha. Planting for white wine far outstripped that for red (1,101 ha vs 496), with sauvignon blanc taking the long-held number one spot from chenin blanc as most-planted variety (337 ha added). More chenin (242), colombard (177) and chardonnay (143) were also planted in 2018 vs 2017.

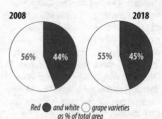

Red ● and white ○ grape varieties as % of total area

Of the red-wine varieties, cabernet (151) remained the most planted, followed again by shiraz (90) but merlot (which in 2017 grew only 26 ha) passed pinotage (40) as 3rd most-planted grape, with 72 ha. Cinsaut edged into 5th position (34).

Chenin (806) was the most-uprooted variety in 2018, followed by colombard (790), but the former still led the overall hectareage table, with 18.5% of the total 93,021 ha. Cabernet, with ±11%, remained the leading red. The percentage of very young vines (under 4 years) remained at ±6%, while the portion older than 20 again rose, from ±24% to over 27%.

Exports

Exports in 2018 of 420 m litres were down on the 448 m litres of 2017, yet accounted for just over half of SA's total wine production, up on the 49% share in 2017. In the white-wine class, chenin and 'other white' categories improved markedly on their 2017 packaged and bottled export performance; only 'other single red varieties' did so for red wines.

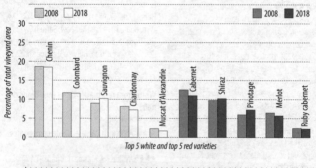

Top 5 white and top 5 red varieties

South African Wine Industry – Ten-Year Overview

	2009	2010	2011	2012	2013	2014	2015	2016	2017	2018
Number of wineries	604	573	582	582	564	559	566	568	546	542
Total vine area (excl sultana) (hectares)	101 259	101 016	100 568	100 097	99 687	99 472	98 594	95 775	94 545	93 021
Producing area 4 yrs & older (excl sultana) (hectares)	93 220	93 119	92 594	91 810	91 958	92 010	91 453	88 747	88 624	87 578
Avg yield (tons/hectare)	14.46	13.55	14.07	15.41	16.29	16.52	16.15	15.84	16.22	14.20
Grapes crushed (millions of tons)	1.35	1.26	1.30	1.41	1.50	1.52	1.48	1.41	1.44	1.24
Total production (millions of litres)	1 033.4	984.8	1 012.8	1 097.0	1 156.9	1 181.1	1 154.0	1 089.0	1 118.0	960.1
Domestic sales (millions of litres)	338.3	346.4	353.3	361.4	368.3	395.3	425.1	436.9	449.7	431.4
Consumption per capita (litres SA wine)	6.75	6.81	6.85	6.90	6.93	7.33	7.76	7.86	7.96	7.47
Export volume (millions of litres)	395.6	378.5	357.4	417.2	525.6	422.7	420.0	428.4	448.4	420.2

The big winners in 2018 on the export markets were pinks and sparkling wines. The UK, Germany, France, the Netherlands and Denmark were the top five markets for SA wine (packaged and bulk) in 2018, with the US – in 3rd place in 2017 – falling to 9th. For packaged wine only, once again, the UK, Germany, the Netherlands, Sweden and the US remained the five biggest outlets.

Local wine consumption

After 8 years of growth, SA's per-capita wine consumption dipped from 7.91L in 2017 (the highest mark since 2002) to 7.47L in 2018. As a result, wine's combined market share (natural, fortified and sparkling) fell from 18.7% to 17.9%. This remained substantially lower than beer (55%). Brandy maintained ±5% share of the market and whisky fell slightly to 5.3%.

Of natural wine sold domestically (including locally bottled imports), ±44% was in glass (largely unchanged from 2017), and of that ±61% was in the standard 750-ml bottle. Wine in bag-in-box grew to 39% of total sales, while plastic containers accounted for ±13% and Tetra packs ±4%. Foil bags – the notorious papsakke, now carefully regulated – were a minuscule 0.1%.

SA wine consumption per capita (litres)

Note

Statistical data was provided by SAWIS NPC.

Industry Organisations

Agricultural Ethical Trade Initiative See Wine & Agricultural Ethical Trade Association.

ARC Infruitec-Nietvoorbij Senior manager, research: prof Bongani Ndimba ▪ Winemaker: Craig Paulsen ▪ T +27 (0)21-809-3091 ▪ PaulsenC@arc. agric.za ▪ Marketing & communications: Derusha Crank ▪ T +27 (0)21-809-3100 ▪ infocape@arc. agric.za ▪ www.arc.agric.za

ARC Infruitec-Nietvoorbij focuses on research and development as well as technology transfer on the breeding, cultivation, protection and post-harvest technology of deciduous fruit, grape vines, alternative crops and indigenous herbal teas. Nietvoorbij, ARC's internationally acclaimed research farm, is synonymous with quality research in oenology and viticulture. Annually, 1,000 small-batch wines are made for research purposes, along with commercial wines for sale to the public.

Biodiversity & Wine Initiative (BWI) See WWF-SA Conservation Champion Programme

Biodynamic & Organic Wines of South Africa (BOWSA) Chair: Marion Smith ▪ marion@ elginridge.com ▪ T +27 (0)79-433-9400 ▪ www. bowsa.co.za

Recently formed association aiming to help consumers and media easily see which local wine producers and grape growers are officially certified as biodynamic and organic.

Cape Brandy Distillers Guild (CBDG) Patron: Dave Hughes ▪ Trustees: Kobus Gelderblom (kobus@capebrandy.org) & Charles Withington (charles@capebrandy.org) ▪ www.capebrandy.org

Communication and promotion platform for positioning Cape Brandy in terms of its provenance and integrity. In consumer terms, Cape Brandies have traditionally and widely (as well as in the legislation) been described as 'Potstill Brandies', which at present comprise only 5% of the total brandy market. Members enjoy access to skills and expertise, and benefit from collective marketing and attendance at local/international trade shows under the Cape Brandy banner.

Cape Port Producers' Association (CAPPA)
Chair: Margaux Nel ▪ **T** +27 (0)44-213-3326 ▪
F +27 (0)44-213-3750 ▪ boplaas@mweb.co.za ▪

Producer group aiming to further improve
the quality and market for Cape 'ports' and
Portuguese-variety table wines in SA.

Cape Vintner Classification (CVC) CEO Charl
Theron ▪ **T** +27(0)83-269-0577 ▪ F +27(0)86-
275-8887 ▪ info@cvc1659.co.za ▪ www.cvc1659.
co.za

Independent body committed to the accreditation, governance, representation and promotion
of distinctive site-specific wines. Through a
system of certification and classification, CVC
endorsement underscores its members' commitment to terroir-specific winemaking as well
as excellence in cellar practices, environmental
championing and cellardoor experience.

Cape Winemakers Guild (CWG) Chair: Boela
Gerber ▪ General manager: Kate Jonker ▪ **T** +27
(0)21-852-0408 ▪ F +27 (0)21-852-0409 ▪ info@
capewinemakersguild.com ▪ www.capewinemak-
ersguild.com

Independent, invitation-only association,
founded in 1982 to promote winemaking
excellence among its members. Since 1985, the
CWG has held an annual public auction of rare
and unique wines, produced by its members
exclusively for the auction. The Nedbank CWG
Development Trust, established in 1999, supports
social development in the winelands through its
oenology and viticulture protégé programmes,
Billy Hofmeyr AgriSeta bursaries and support of
Wine Training South Africa.

Chardonnay Forum of South Africa Chair:
Johann de Wet ▪ johanndewet@dewetshof.com ▪
T +27 (0)23-615-1853 ▪ F +27 (0)23-615-1915

Producers and people creating awareness and
stimulating interest in SA chardonnay among
consumers, buyers, media and producers locally
and internationally.

Chenin Blanc Association (CBA) Chair: Ken
Forrester ▪ **T** +27 (0)21-855-2374 / +27
(0)82-783-7203 ▪ F +27 (0)21-855-2373 ▪ ken@
kenforresterwines.com ▪ www.chenin.co.za ▪
Manager: Ina Smith ▪ **T** +27 (0)82-467-4331 ▪
cheninblancasso@gmail.com ▪ @CheninBlancAsso

Formed in 2000 by a few concerned winemakers in response to dramatic decreases in plantings.
The focus is to promote the variety and raise the
image of chenin blanc.

**Fairtrade Africa - Southern Africa Network
(FTA-SAN)** Regional head: Zachary Kiarie ▪ **T**+27

(0)21-447-3486 ▪ z.kiarie@fairtradeafrica.net ▪
www.fairtradeafrica.net

Fairtrade Africa (FTA) is the independent
non-profit umbrella organisation representing
all Fairtrade-certified producers in Africa. FTA is
owned by its members, who are African producer
organisations certified against international
Fairtrade standards. The Southern Africa Network
(SAN), located in Cape Town, is one of four FTA
regional networks which represent Fairtrade-
certified producers (smallholder farmers,
farm-workers and -owners) in southern Africa.
SAN provides technical support on Fairtrade
standards; facilitates trade linkages and markets
access opportunities; advocates on behalf of
and with its producers on relevant issues; and
enhances knowledge and capacity around social
and environmental issues.

Garagiste Movement of South Africa See under
Make Your Own Wine or Brandy

Institute of Cape Wine Masters National chair:
De Bruyn Steenkamp ▪ **T** +27 (0)79-598-5274
▪ National vice-chair: Harry Melck ▪ **T** +27
(0)79-789-1844 ▪ Secretary: Raymond Noppé
▪ **T** +27 (0)82-335-2020 ▪ info@icwm.co.za ▪
www.icwm.co.za

The title of Cape Wine Master, first instituted in
1983, is one of the most sought-after formal qualifications in SA wine. To date 99 candidates have
qualified, and a further 3 have been awarded the
title Honorary Cape Wine Master. The purpose of
ICWM is to harness the collective ability of CWMs
to open the world of wine and brandy to others
through knowledge, deep understanding and love
for the products.

Integrated Production of Wine (IPW)
Manager: Daniël Schietekat ▪ **T** +27 (0)21-889-
6555 ▪ F +27 (0)866-903-224 ▪ daniel@ipw.co.za
▪ www.ipw.co.za

Innovative, widely supported initiative aimed
at producing wine in an environmentally sustainable, profitable way by means of guidelines
for both farm and cellar, embracing all aspects of
grape production, winemaking and biodiversity
conservation. See also Sustainable Wine South
Africa.

**Méthode Cap Classique Producers'
Association** Chair: Pieter Ferreira ▪ bubbles-
ferreira@gmail.com ▪ Admin: Elsabé Ferreira ▪
T +27(0)21-863-1599 ▪ F +27 (0)21-863-1552 ▪
info@capclassique.co.za

Muscadel SA Chair: Henri Swiegers ▪ **T** +27 (0)23-
344-3021 ▪ henri@badsberg.co.za ▪ Vice-chair:

André Scriven ▪ T +27 (0)23-626-1664 ▪ andres@rooiberg.co.za

Old Vine Project (OVP) Marketing & communications consultant: André Morgenthal ▪ T +27 (0)82-658-3883 ▪ andre@oldvineproject.co.za ▪ www.oldvineproject.co.za

Believing that old vines produce wines with a unique character – pure and delicate yet powerful – OVP strives to preserve as many of SA's 3,505 gnarled-vine hectares as possible, while creating a culture of helping young vineyards mature into stellar seniors. The Certified Heritage Vineyards seal which, affixed to a bottle, assures winelovers these wines are from genuinely venerable vines (35+ years) and reflects authenticity, traceability and integrity. See also Editor's Note.

Pinotage Association Chair: Beyers Truter ▪ T +27 (0)21-865-1235 ▪ F +27 (0)21-865-2683 ▪ reception@beyerskloof.co.za ▪ Manager: Elsabé Ferreira ▪ T +27 (0)21-863-1599 ▪ F +27 (0)21-863-1552 ▪ admin@pinotage.co.za ▪ Marketing manager: Johan Schwardtz ▪ T +27 (0)82-660-0702 ▪ marketing@pinotage.co.za ▪ www.pinotage.co.za

Sauvignon Blanc South Africa (SBSA) Chair: RJ Botha ▪ T +27 (0)21-880-0717 ▪ RJBotha@kleinezalze.co.za ▪ Manager: Eunice Joubert ▪ T +27 (0)21-975-4440 / +27 (0)82-808-1114 ▪ admin@sauvignonblanc.com

Fosters excellence in making and marketing SA sauvignon blanc locally and internationally via members' networking, information exchange and wine competitions, including the annual FNB Sauvignon Blanc Top 10.

Shiraz South Africa Chair: Edmund Terblanche ▪ T +27 (0)82-770-2929 ▪ F +27 (0)21-876-3446 ▪ et.cellar@la-motte.co.za ▪ Secretary: Sandra Lotz ▪ T +27 (0)82-924-7254 ▪ F +27 (0)86-267-4333 ▪ info@shirazsa.co.za

Founded in 2008, and today representing more than 200 members, Shiraz SA aims to promote the image of wine produced from this noble grape, with the purpose of establishing acceptance and enjoyment of SA shiraz locally and internationally.

South African Brandy Foundation (SABF) Director: Christelle Reade-Jahn ▪ T +27 (0)64-754-6552 ▪ christelle@sabrandy.co.za ▪ www.sabrandy.co.za

A registered non-profit organisation representing more than 95% of local brandy producers, SABF facilitates long-term growth and helps preserve the integrity and heritage of the SA brandy industry.

South African Pinot Noir Association Chair: Emul Ross ▪ emul@hamiltonrussellvineyards.com ▪ T +27 (0)28-312-3595 ▪ F +27 (0)28-312-1797 ▪ Admin: Vanessa Hoek ▪ vanessa@winemachinerygroup.com

Producer group aiming to further improve the general quality of local pinot noir still-wines by sharing ideas, and ultimately finding an identity for the variety in SA.

South African Sommelier Association (SASA) Chair: Barry Scholfield ▪ Vice-chair: Spencer Fondaumiere ▪ T +27(0)21-012-5367 ▪ info@sommeliers.org.za ▪ www.sommeliers.org.za

Membership-driven, non-profit, voluntary private organisation established in 2012 to promote a culture of fine wine, food and service excellence in South Africa; formalise the profession of sommelier; and provide a forum for dialogue, exchange of ideas, knowledge and skills.

SA Wine Industry Information & Systems NPC (SAWIS) Executive manager: Yvette van der Merwe ▪ T +27 (0)21-807-5700 ▪ info@sawis.co.za

Responsible for the collection, processing and dissemination of industry information. Administers the Wine of Origin (WO) system.

Southern Africa Fairtrade Network (SAFN) See Fairtrade Africa-Southern Africa Network

Sustainable Wine South Africa (SWSA) www.swsa.co.za ▪ Contact details as for individual organisations.

Alliance between the Wine & Spirit Board (WSB), Integrated Production of Wine (IPW), WWF-SA Conservation Champion Programme (CCP) and Wines of South Africa (WOSA), driving the industry's commitment to sustainable, eco-friendly production.

Swartland Independent Producers (SIP) Chair: Thinus Krüger ▪ T +27 (0)72-545-4959 ▪ swartlandindependent@gmail.com, swartlandsocialmedia@gmail.com ▪ www.swartlandindependent.co.za

Alliance of like-minded Swartland producers seeking to make wines that are a true expression of their Swartland origin. SIP members share a number of core values, such as natural vinification and minimal intervention, and follow an evolving set of guidelines covering vineyard and cellar practices.

Wine & Agricultural Ethical Trade Association (WIETA) CEO: Linda Lipparoni ▪ T +27 (0)21-880-0580 ▪ F +27 (0)21-880-0580 ▪ linda@

wieta.org.za, info@wieta.org.za ▪ www.wieta. org.za

Multi-stakeholder, non-profit, voluntary organisation established in 2002 to promote ethical trade in wine and general agriculture. WIETA's members have adopted a code of ethical and labour standards for the wine industry. WIETA's main task is to support, enhance and promote members' ethical performance, encourage best practice and promote improved working conditions on farm and at the cellar through training, capacity-building projects and third-party ethical auditing. WIETA also issues a Fair Labour Certification seal on individual wines, which has been endorsed by the wine industry in recognition of wine supply chains' ethical commitment to good working conditions on farms and in cellars.

Wine & Spirit Board Chair: Matome Mbatha ▪ Secretary: Olivia Poonah ▪ **T +27 (0)21-889-6555** ▪ F +27 (0)21-889-5823 ▪ olivia@wsb.org.za

Administers the Wine of Origin, Estate Brandy and Integrated Production of Wine (IPW) schemes.

Wines of South Africa (WOSA) CEO: Siobhan Thompson ▪ Non-executive chair: Carina Gous ▪ info@wosa.co.za ▪ **T +27 (0)21-883-3860** ▪ F +27 (0)21-883-3861 ▪ www.wosa.co.za

Generic marketing organisation, responsible for raising the profile of SA wine in key export markets.

Wine Industry Network of Expertise & Technology (WINETECH) Executive manager: Gerard Martin ▪ **T +27 (0)21-276 0498** ▪ F +27 (0)86-611-7846 ▪ marting@winetech.co.za

Coordinates research, development, innovation and knowledge transfer in the SA wine industry, to strengthen both local and international competitiveness and profitability.

WWF-SA Biodiversity & Wine Initiative See WWF-SA Conservation Champion Programme.

WWF-SA Conservation Champion Programme manager: Shelly Fuller ▪ **T +27 (0)21-881-3086** ▪ sfuller@wwf.org.za ▪ Head of extension: Joan Isham ▪ **T +27 (0) 21-881-3086** ▪ jisham@wwf. org.za

In 2005 the Biodiversity & Wine Initiative (BWI) started as a world-leading partnership between the SA wine industry and the conservation sector to minimise further loss of threatened natural habitat in the Cape Floral Kingdom, and contribute to sustainable wine production through better environmental management practices on farm and in cellar. After 10 years of successful implementation, the needs of the membership base shifted to a more holistic approach of managing environmental risk. The BWI name fell away, and today consumers can support WWF-SA Conservation Champions by buying wines displaying the colourful sugarbird and protea logo, recognising industry leaders who have a strong commitment to biodiversity conservation and show continual improvement of production practices, energy-efficiency measures and water stewardship.

Winegrowing Areas

From modest beginnings in the Dutch East India Company's 17th-century gardens below Table Mountain, South Africa's vineyards now cover 93,021 ha and more than 100 official appellations. Changes to the Wine of Origin (WO) scheme of 1972/3 saw 'geographical units' incorporated into the WO classification alongside 'regions', 'districts' and 'wards' (the latter have the smallest footprint of the WO areas, following earlier amendments to the 'estate' legislation). Below are brief notes on the most noteworthy grape cultivation zones. Information supplied by Wines of South Africa (WOSA) and SA Wine Industry Information & Systems NPC (SAWIS), and reflects 2018 data for the WO areas. Note: Area maps are not to the same scale.

Breedekloof Large (12,604 ha) Breede River Valley district producing mainly for brandy industry and merchant trade, but also featuring some quality-focused boutiques, family estates and some grower-owned ventures with ever-greater ambitions for pinotage, chenin, chardonnay and semillon, particularly from old vines. Major varieties (ha): chenin (2,796), colombard (1,893), sauvignon (1,184), pinotage (920), chardonnay (806). See under Robertson for climate, geology etc.

Cape Coast New overarching region for Cape South Coast and Coastal regions.

Cape South Coast 'Umbrella' region (2,632 ha) for Cape Agulhas, Elgin, Lower Duivenhoks River (now upgraded from ward status), Overberg, Plettenberg Bay, Swellendam and Walker Bay districts, and Herbertsdale, Napier and Stilbaai East wards.

Cape Town Maritime district (2,717 ha) incorporating Constantia, Durbanville, Hout Bay and Philadelphia wards, and vines in Cape Town city.

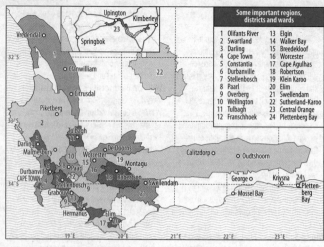

Some important regions, districts and wards			
1	Olifants River	13	Elgin
2	Swartland	14	Walker Bay
3	Darling	15	Breedekloof
4	Cape Town	16	Worcester
5	Constantia	17	Cape Agulhas
6	Durbanville	18	Robertson
7	Stellenbosch	19	Klein Karoo
8	Paarl	20	Elim
9	Overberg	21	Swellendam
10	Wellington	22	Sutherland-Karoo
11	Tulbagh	23	Central Orange
12	Franschhoek	24	Plettenberg Bay

Cederberg 101-ha standlone ward in the Cederberg Mountain range, with some of SA's remotest and highest vineyards (950–1,100 m). Best known for shiraz (18), chenin (17) and sauvignon (16). Also cab (12) and bukettraube (11).

Central Orange River This large ward (3,187 ha) along the Orange River (Gariep) is a production zone within the Northern Cape Geographical Unit. Altitude: 500–1,000 m; Mean February Temperature (MFT) 25.3℃; rain total/summer: 250/208 mm; geology: granite, dolorite, shale, alluvial. Overwhelmingly a white-grape area but red plantings are increasing. Sultana (5,655), colombard (1,739), chenin (832), villard blanc (182), muscat d'Alexandrie (105).

Constantia Premium viticultural ward (430 ha) and cradle of SA winemaking on the eastern slopes of the Cape Peninsula, cooled by south-easterly sea breezes. Recognised for whites generally, notably sauvignon, semillon and muscat. Altitude: 100–300 m; temp 20.6℃; rain: 1,056/335 mm; geology: granite (sandstone). Major varieties: sauvignon (186), cab (36), merlot (35), shiraz (29), chardonnay (28).

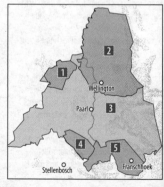

1	Philadelphia	3	Cape Town
2	Durbanville	4	Hout Bay
		5	Constantia

1	Voor Paardeberg	4	Simonsberg-Paarl
2	Wellington	5	Franschhoek
3	Paarl		

1 Polkadraai Hills
2 Bottelary
3 Devon Valley
4 Papegaaiberg
5 Stellenbosch
6 Simonsberg-Stellenbosch
7 Jonkershoek Valley
8 Banghoek

Darling District (2,754 ha) encircling the eponymous West Coast town, best known for the wines from higher-lying ward Groenekloof, long the source of top sauvignon; also a reputation for full-flavoured reds, especially shiraz; source of interesting young-gun bottlings. Groenekloof: sauvignon (476), cab (436), shiraz (366), pinotage (186), merlot (183).

Durbanville Ocean-tempered hilly ward (1,421 ha) in Cape Town district with reputation for sauvignon (519) and merlot (208). Cab (193), shiraz (159) and pinotage (105). Altitude: 150-350 m; temp 22.4°C; rain: 481/140 mm; geology: shale.

Elgin Cool upland district (739 ha) in Cape South Coast region producing many stellar aromatic whites and elegant reds. Altitude: 200-250 m; temp 19.7°C; rain: 1,011/366 mm; geology: shale (sandstone). Sauvignon (277), chardonnay (110), pinot noir (107), shiraz (61), cab (51).

Elim Maritime ward in Cape Agulhas district, its 140 ha of windswept vineyards arrayed around the old mission village of Elim near Africa's most southerly point. Sauvignon (80), shiraz (29), semillon (14), pinot noir (9), merlot (3).

Franschhoek Increasingly dynamic, and stylistically diverse, Coastal district with 1,234 ha under vine, perhaps best known for cab (181) and semillon (82), latter among SA's oldest vines. Chardonnay (194), sauvignon (185), shiraz (154), merlot (117).

Hemel-en-Aarde See Walker Bay.

Klein Karoo Scrubby semi-arid region (2,150 ha), reliant on irrigation. Recognised for 'ports' and fortifieds generally; increasingly a hunting ground for young terroirists. Calitzdorp district: muscat

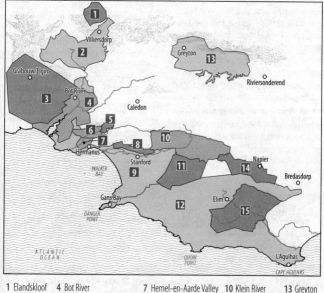

1 Elandskloof
2 Theewater
3 Elgin
4 Bot River
5 Hemel-en-Aarde Ridge
6 Upper Hemel-en-Aarde
7 Hemel-en-Aarde Valley
8 Stanford Foothills
9 Walker Bay
10 Klein River
11 Sunday's Glen
12 Cape Agulhas
13 Greyton
14 Napier
15 Elim

1 Swartland   **3** Malmesbury   **5** Riebeekberg
2 Darling   **4** Riebeeksrivier   **6** Tulbagh

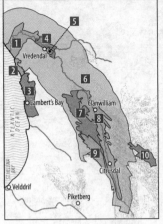

1 Lutzville Valley   **6** Olifants River
2 Bamboes Bay   **7** Citrusdal Mountain
3 Lamberts Bay   **8** Citrusdal Valley
4 Vredendal   **9** Piekenierskloof
5 Spruitdrift   **10** Cederberg

d'Alexandrie (69), colombard (65), chenin (45), touriga and cab (17). Tradouw ward: merlot (7), colombard and sauvignon (5), shiraz and ruby cab (4). Boutique-scale plantings in Langeberg-Garcia district (43), and Cango Valley (9), Tradouw Highlands (10) and Upper Langkloof (52) wards.

Lutzville Valley See Olifants River

Northern Cape Quality moves afoot in this geographical unit, particularly Sutherland-Karoo, a high-altitude (1,450 m), semi-arid district around Sutherland, SA's coldest town. The smallest SA district by far (5 ha, mostly pinot noir, shiraz, chardonnay), but big on character, quality. Also-exciting ward Prieska (neighbour of Central Orange River - see separate entry above), with 13 ha of mostly reds, including rare tannat.

Olifants River Grapes for SA's highest-rated wines increasingly originate from this north-westerly region (9,531 ha), particularly the Citrusdal Mountain district (565), cool upland ward of Piekenierskloof (451). (The

Bamboes Bay 'micro-ward' (6 ha) is now a standalone appellation, while Lutzville Valley district (3,020) near the Atlantic now part of Coastal region.) Inland, a climate conducive to organic cultivation is exploited to that end. Altitude: 20-100 m; temp 23°C; rain: 139/47 mm; geology: mainly schist and alluvial deposits. Koekenaap ward (Lutzville Valley): chenin (300), colombard (210), sauvignon (159), cab (61), pinotage (49). Piekenierskloof: pinotage (72), grenache noir (60), chenin (49), palomino (41), sauvignon (37). Citrusdal Mountain: chenin (90), pinotage (83), grenache noir (61) sauvignon (46), palomino (42).

Orange River See Central Orange River.

Paarl This district has many meso-climates, soils and aspects, and thus succeeds with a variety of styles and grapes. Altitude: 100-300 m; temp 23.2°C;

1 Montagu   **5** Malgas   **9** Langeberg-Garcia   **13** Prince Albert   **16** Swartberg
2 Stormsvlei   **6** Buffeljags   **10** Still Bay East   Valley   **17** Upper Langkloof
3 Swellendam   **7** Tradouw   **11** Herbertsdale   **14** Cango Valley   **18** Plettenberg Bay
4 Tradouw Highlands **8** Klein Karoo **12** Calitzdorp   **15** Outeniqua

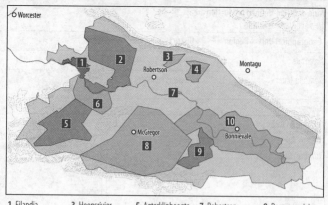

1 Eilandia 　　 3 Hoopsrivier 　　 5 Agterkliphoogte 　　 7 Robertson 　　 9 Boesmansrivier
2 Vinkrivier 　　 4 Klaasvoogds 　　 6 Le Chasseur 　　 8 McGregor 　　 10 Bonnievale

rain: 945/273 mm; geology: granite and shale. Paarl proper is recognised for shiraz and, more recently, viognier and mourvèdre grown on warmer slopes. Chenin (1,362), shiraz (841), cab (825), pinotage (586), cinsaut (356). The following are wards: Simonsberg-Paarl, on the warmer slopes of the

Simonsberg, recognised for red blends, shiraz and chardonnay. Cab (257), chardonnay (187), sauvignon (168), shiraz (163), chenin (145); Voor Paardeberg, long an uncredited source of top-quality grapes, now a star in own right. Cab (384), shiraz (294), chenin (218), merlot (182), pinotage (168); and

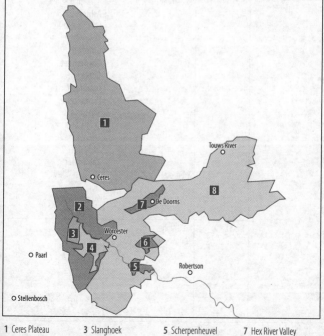

1 Ceres Plateau 　　 3 Slanghoek 　　 5 Scherpenheuvel 　　 7 Hex River Valley
2 Breedekloof 　　 4 Goudini 　　 6 Nuy 　　 8 Worcester

Wine of Origin-defined production areas
(New appellation/s in **bold**.)

Geographical Unit	Region	District	Ward
Free State	—	—	Rietrivier
KwaZulu-Natal	— —	Central Drakensberg Lions River	— —
Limpopo	—	—	—
GREATER CAPE			
Eastern Cape	—	—	St Francis Bay
Northern Cape	— — — — —	Douglas — — — Sutherland-Karoo	— Central Orange River Hartswater Prieska —
Western Cape	— — — — — —	— Ceres Plateau — — — —	Cederberg Ceres **Leipoldtville-Sandveld** **Nieuwoudtville** Prince Albert Valley Swartberg
	Breede River Valley	Breedekloof Robertson	Goudini Slanghoek Agterkliphoogte **Ashton** Boesmansrivier Bonnievale Eilandia **Goedemoet** **Goree** **Goudmyn** Hoopsrivier Klaasvoogds Le Chasseur McGregor Vinkrivier **Zandrivier**
		Worcester	Hex River Valley Nuy Scherpenheuwel Stettyn
	Klein Karoo	Calitzdorp Langeberg-Garcia — — — — — —	— — Cango Valley Montagu Outeniqua Tradouw Tradouw Highlands Upper Langkloof

Geographical Unit	Region	District	Ward
Western Cape (*continued*)	Olifants River	Citrusdal Mountain	Piekenierskloof
		Citrusdal Valley	—
		—	Spruitdrift
		—	Vredendal
	CAPE COAST		
	Cape South Coast	Cape Agulhas	Elim
		Elgin	—
		Overberg	Elandskloof
			Greyton
			Klein River
			Theewater
		Lower Duivenhoks River	—
		Plettenberg Bay	—
		Swellendam	Buffelsjags
			Malgas
			Stormsvlei
		Walker Bay	Bot River
			Hemel-en-Aarde Ridge
			Hemel-en-Aarde Valley
			Springfontein Rim
			Stanford Foothills
			Sunday's Glen
			Upper Hemel-en-Aarde Valley
		—	Herbertsdale
		—	Napier
		—	Stilbaai East
	Coastal	Cape Town	Constantia
			Durbanville
			Hout Bay
			Philadelphia
		Darling	Groenekloof
		Franschhoek	—
		Lutzville Valley	Koekenaap
		Paarl	Agter Paarl
			Simonsberg-Paarl
			Voor Paardeberg
		Stellenbosch	Banghoek
			Bottelary
			Devon Valley
			Jonkershoek Valley
			Papagaaiberg
			Polkadraai Hills
			Simonsberg-Stellenbosch
		Swartland	Malmesbury
			Paardeberg
			Paardeberg-South
			Riebeekberg
			Riebeeksrivier
			St Helena Bay

Geographical Unit	Region	District	Ward
Western Cape (*continued*)	Coastal (*continued*)	Tulbagh Wellington	— Blouvlei Bovlei Groenberg Limietberg Mid-Berg River
		—	Bamboes Bay
		—	Lamberts Bay

Source: SAWS NPC

recent Agter Paarl: chenin (502), shiraz (220), cab (216), cinsaut (213), pinotage (206).

Robertson Traditionally a white-wine district (12,910), latterly also recognised for shiraz and cab though chardonnay, sauvignon and sparkling remain standouts. Has five new wards: Ashton, Goedemoed, Goree, Goudmyn and Zandrivier. Altitude: 150–250 m; temp 23°C; rain: 280/116 mm; geology: shale and alluvial. Colombard (1,982), chardonnay (1,685), sauvignon (1,573), chenin (1,546), cab (1,296).

Stellenbosch To many, this intensively farmed district (12,339) is the wine capital of SA. Key contributors to quality are the cooler mountain slopes, varied soil types and breezes off False Bay which moderate summer temperatures. Altitude: 200–400 m; temp 21.5°C; rain: 713/229 mm; geology: granite (sandstone). Jonkershoek Valley, a ward east of Stellenbosch town, is recognised for cab and cab blends. Cab (55), chardonnay (21), pinotage (20), sauvignon and merlot (19). Simonsberg-Stellenbosch, in the south-western foothills of the Simonsberg Mountain, especially recognised for cab, cab blends and pinotage, and reds generally. Cab (299), merlot (168), sauvignon (167), chardonnay (132), shiraz (126). North-west of Stellenbosch town are four adjoining wards: Papegaaiberg - sauvignon (27), chenin (21), chardonnay (12), pinotage (11), cab (8); Devon Valley, recognised mainly for red blends - merlot (97), sauvignon (92), cab (86), shiraz (61), pinotage (46); Bottelary, noted for chenin, pinotage, shiraz and warm-blooded blends - chenin (387), cab (357), pinotage (270), shiraz (252), sauvignon (241); the most westerly ward, Polkadraai Hills - sauvignon (147), cab (140), shiraz (117), merlot (84), chenin (68); and Banghoek, the mountain amphitheatre above the village of Pniel - cab (61), shiraz (40), merlot (29), chardonnay (26), sauvignon (23). The remainder of the Stellenbosch district, as yet officially undemarcated, includes Stellenboschberg, Helderberg and Faure, recognised for red blends,

chenin and sauvignon. Cab (1,497), shiraz (1,081), sauvignon (942), merlot (791), chenin (694).

Sutherland-Karoo See Northen Cape.

Swartland Traditionally associated with hearty wines, but latterly with elegant, personality-packed chenins, Mediterranean-style reds and whites, and revived heirloom varieties, this fashionable district (10,075) north of Cape Town now has six wards, Malmesbury, Riebeekberg, Riebeeksrivier, St Helena Bay and new Paardeberg and Paardeberg South, plus a large unappellated area. Malmesbury: cab (663), shiraz (578), chenin (482), pinotage (476), sauvignon (321); Riebeekberg: chenin (208), shiraz (177), pinotage (117), cab (75), chardonnay (72); Riebeeksrivier: shiraz (16), chenin (9), cinsaut (5), grenache (5), clairette (1); St Helena Bay: sauvignon (13), chenin (7), semillon (4), shiraz and muscat d'Alexandrie (3). 'Swartland': chenin (1,614), shiraz (850), pinotage (638), cab (627), chardonnay (334). Altitude: 100–300 m; temp 23.3°C; rain: 523/154 mm; geology: mostly granite and shale.

Tulbagh Inland district (1,003) traditionally known for sparkling and lightish whites, more recently also for quality reds and serious white blends. Altitude: 160–400 m; temp 24°C; rain: 551/175 mm; geology: sandstone boulderbeds and shale. Chenin (199), shiraz (129), colombard (101), cab (89), chardonnay (78).

Walker Bay Highly regarded maritime district (1,014) south-east of Cape Town, recognised for pinot noir, pinotage, sauvignon and chardonnay. Altitude: 100–250 m; temp 20.3°C; rain: 722/322 mm; geology: shale, granite and sandstone. Sauvignon (261), shiraz and pinot noir (141), chardonnay (109), cab (73). Bot River, Hemel-en-Aarde Ridge, Hemel-en-Aarde Valley, Stanford Foothills, Sunday's Glen, Upper Hemel-en-Aarde Valley and new Springfontein Rim are wards.

Wellington District (3,874) in the Coastal region increasingly reputed for shiraz and gutsy red blends.

Chenin (814), cab (622), shiraz (564), pinotage (415), chardonnay (302).

Worcester District (6,388) producing chiefly for the brandy industry and merchant trade, but small quantities bottled under own labels are increasingly impressive. Recognised for red and white blends, chenin and fortifieds. Chenin (1,852), colombard (1,176), sauvignon (566), chardonnay (420), shiraz (396). See under Robertson for climate, geology etc.

Grape Varieties

Below are brief notes on the grape varieties mentioned in the guide, and their contribution to the national vineyard (statistics from SAWIS NPC). See under Winegrowing Areas for details of the most widely planted and best-performing varieties in the major vine cultivation zones.

Red-wine varieties

Barbera Piedmont's second grape (after nebbiolo), its natural high acidity suiting warm climates; sought after, too, for low tannins, good colour. 0.04% of total vineyard area.

Cabernet franc Like its descendant cabernet sauvignon, with which it is often partnered, a classic part of the Bordeaux blend, but in SA and elsewhere – particularly in the Loire – also used for varietal wines. (0.86%)

Cabernet sauvignon Adaptable and internationally planted black grape making some of the world's finest and longest-lasting wines. And retaining some of its inherent qualities even when over-cropped in less suitable soils and climates. Can stand alone triumphantly, but frequently blended with a wide range of other varieties: traditionally, as in Bordeaux, with cab franc, merlot and a few minor others, but also in SA sometimes partnering varieties such as shiraz and pinotage. Number of different clones, with differing characteristics. (11%)

Carignan Hugely planted in the south of France, where it is not much respected. But there, as in SA, older, low-yielding vines can produce pleasant surprises. (0.13%)

Carmenère Dark-skinned, late-ripening parent of cabernet franc; once important in Bordeaux, today most significant in Chile. Deep-hued/flavoured wines if picked fully ripe. Handful of bottlings in SA - varietals as well as blends. (0.01%)

Cinsaut (noir) 'Cinsault' in France. Another of the mass, undistinguished plantings of southern France,

which only occasionally comes up trumps. Used to be known locally as hermitage, the name reflected in its offspring (with pinot noir), pinotage. (1.84%)

Durif See *Petite sirah.*

Gamay noir Although it produces some serious long-lived wines in Beaujolais, its use for (mainly) early- and easy-drinking 'nouveau' wines there, often using carbonic maceration, is the model mostly copied in SA. (0.01%)

Grenache (noir) The international (ie French) name for the Spanish grape garnacha. Widespread in Spain and southern France, generally used in blends (as in Rioja and Châteauneuf), but occasionally solo. A favourite for rosés. When vigour restrained, capable of greatness, but this is rare. (0.42%) White/pink versions also occur.

Malbec Once a significant part of Bordeaux's blend, now most important in Cahors in western France (where it is known as cot), and as Argentina's signature variety. In SA a small but rising number of varietal and some blended examples. (0.53%)

Mataro See *Mourvèdre.*

Merlot Classic blending partner (as in Bordeaux) for cabernet, fashionable around the world, where it tends to be seen as an 'easier' version of cab – although this is perhaps because it is often made in a less ambitious manner. Merlot varietal wines increasingly common in SA too. (5.82%)

Meunier Aka meunier, a mutation of pinot noir and, like pinot noir and chardonnay, significant in France's Champagne region where it adds fruitiness

Approximate ripening dates in the Stellenbosch area for some important grape varieties

to blended sparklings. Rare in SA; also mostly for bubbly, lone varietal bottling. (0.02%)

Mourvèdre Internationally known by its French name, though originally Spanish (monastrell). In Australia and California also called mataro. Particularly successful in some serious southern French blends, and increasingly modish internationally. (0.51%)

Nebbiolo Perhaps the greatest red grape to have scarcely ventured from its home – Piedmont in this case, where it makes massive, tannic, long-lived wines. (0.02%)

Nero d'Avola Sicily's major red grape, aka calabrese, of interest to SA because of heat tolerance and ability to produce full-flavoured/coloured wines. Locally, only one single-varietal bottling.

Petite sirah/durif Originally from southern France, a cross of peloursin and syrah/shiraz. Produces tannic, densely fruited wines. (0.20%)

Petit verdot Use of this excellent variety in the Médoc limited by its late ripening. Recently appearing in some local blends, and a few varietals. (0.80%)

Pinotage A 1920s cross between pinot noir and cinsaut ('hermitage'). Made in a range of styles, from simply fruity to ambitious, well-oaked examples. (7.30%)

Pinot Meunier See Meunier.

Pinot noir Notoriously difficult grape to succeed with outside its native Burgundy, but SA, along with the rest of the New World, now produces some excellent examples. (1.26%)

Roobernet Relatively recent local crossing of cabernet sauvignon and what was thought to be pontac, in fact alicante bouschet. Mostly blended. (0.30%)

Ruby cabernet US cross between cabernet sauvignon and carignan, designed for heat tolerance. Rather rustic, used mostly in cheaper blends. (2.26%)

Sangiovese Tuscany's signature black grape, producing light or big wines, depending on how it is grown. Can be unacceptably acidic and tannic with little colour unless well managed in the vineyard. (0.08%)

Shiraz Better known as syrah outside SA and Australia (and on some local labels too). Internationally increasing in popularity, with northern Rhône and now also Australia as its major domiciles. Made here in a variety of styles – generally wooded. (10.21%)

Syrah See Shiraz.

Tannat From France's Basque region, recently Uruguay's calling card but still little more than a curiosity in SA. Known for deep colour and high tannin. (0.12%)

Tempranillo Aka tinta roriz. The soul of Spain's storied Rioja and Ribera del Duero. Low tannin, balanced acidity and plush fruit; suited to warm climates but hardly on the SA radar – yet. (0.11%)

Tinta amarela See Trincadeira.

Tinta barocca Elsewhere spelt 'barroca'. One of the important Portuguese port-making grapes, which is its primary role in SA, usually blended. Also used for some varietal unfortified wines, and namelessly in some 'dry reds'. (0.21%)

Touriga franca Formerly known as touriga francesa. Most-planted grape in Portugal's Douro Valley, used for port as well as unfortified reds. Only a few hectares in SA.

Touriga francesa See Touriga franca.

Touriga nacional Important Portuguese port-making grape, usefully grown here for similar ends, along with tinta barocca, tinta roriz (tempranillo) and souzão. (0.11%)

Trincadeira Also 'tinta amarela'; from Portugal, deep coloured with good black fruit and big tannins. (0.01%)

Zinfandel The quintessential Californian grape (of European origin, and the same as Italy's primitivo), used here in a small way for some big wines. (0.03%)

White-wine varieties

Albariño Aromatic, high-acid white grape from Spain's damp north-west (also grown in Portugal, as alvarinho), recently fashionable in New World. Mostly varietals, occasionally oaked, potentially ageworthy. Just three bottlings - varietal - in SA. (0.03%)

Bukettraube Light and acidic variety, mostly used to add zing to white blends. (0.05%)

Chardonnay In SA, as elsewhere, many new vineyards of this grape have come on-stream, with wines showing a wide range of styles, quality and price. Generally used varietally, but also in blends, and for sparkling. Wooded, lately with a lighter touch, in more ambitious wines. (7.16%)

Cape Riesling See Riesling

Chenin blanc SA has more chenin (locally also called steen) than even France's Loire Valley, the variety's home. Used here for everything from generic 'dry white' to ambitious sweet wines, to brandy.

Increasing numbers of table-wine successes in recent years, as well as inexpensive but flavoursome easy-drinkers. (18.54%)

Clairette blanche High-alcohol, low-acid, musky component of southern Rhône white blends; bottled as single variety only off superior sites. In SA, also mainly used in blends. (0.19%)

Colombar(d) One of the mainstays of brandy production in SA, colombard (usually without the 'd' in SA) is also used for numerous varietal and blended wines, ranging from dry to sweet – seldom wooded. (11.63%)

Crouchen Blanc See Riesling

Fernão pires Aromatic workhorse from Portugal; can be used for wide range of wine styles. (0.06%)

Gewürztraminer Readily identifiable from its rosepetal fragrance, best known in its Alsatian guise. In SA usually made off-dry. (0.10%)

Grenache blanc Staple of Rhône white blends, finding adherents in SA, particularly when given skin contact, oak fermentation/ageing. Needs careful handling. (0.14%) Also very rare gris plantings/ vinifications.

Grüner veltliner Austria's no. 1 white grape (by hectare and repute) venturing west (to America), east (Australasia) and south to SA, where plantings are still tiny and vinification follows dry, full, aromatic style of home country's top examples. (0.01%)

Hanepoot Traditional Afrikaans name for muscat d'Alexandrie, SA's most common muscat variety (see also muscadel below). (1.79%, some for raisins and table grapes). Also minuscule red plantings.

Hárslevelü From Tokaj, Hungary; delicate when fermented dry, fat and smoky in sweeter styles. Only 24 ha in SA (0.01%).

Marsanne Rhône grape, more widely planted than twin' roussanne. Dependable, but flabby in too-warm terroir, bland in too-cool. (0.02%)

Muscadel Name used here for both muscat de Frontignan and muscat blanc à petits grains (both red and white versions). The grape associated with the famous Constantia dessert wines of the 18th century today is used chiefly for dessert and fortified wines and for touching up blends. (1.32% red and white). Morio muscat, muscat de Hambourg and muscat Ottonel also bottled on small scale, mostly as fortifieds.

Muscat See Hanepoot and Muscadel.

Nouvelle Local crossing of semillon and neutral ugni blanc/trebbiano, produces intense grass and greenpepper characters. Typically blended. (0.45%)

Palomino Aka malvasia rei, fransdruif, white french. Once important in Spain's sherry industry and locally for distilling, palomino fino is now just 0.13% of the total vineholding. Roles in some hipster bottlings may help raise the profile.

Pinot blanc Import from north-east Italy; very few serious examples locally. (0.01%)

Pinot gris/grigio In north-east Italy prized for acidity, France's Alsace for plump richness. Tiny quantities in SA, named 'gris' or 'grigio' depending on style. (0.41%)

Riesling The name by itself now refers to the great German grape (as it does in this guide). Previously, the grape by law had to carry the prefix 'Rhine' or 'weisser', and the 'riesling' was an official SA synonym for the inferior crouchen blanc, also known as Cape riesling and mostly used anonymously in blends, occasionally varietally. Rhine riesling often off-dry here, in blends or varietally, some excellent botrytised dessert examples. (Rhine: 0.15%, crouchen: 0.24%)

Roussanne Like frequent blending partner marsanne, from the northern Rhône. Also aromatic component of Châteauneuf du Pape. Gaining a following in SA. (0.09%)

Sauvignon blanc Prestigious vine most associated with eastern Loire regions, Bordeaux and New Zealand – whose wines have helped restore fashionability to the grape. The SA version no longer a poor relation of these. Usually dry, but some sweet wines; sometimes wooded (and occasionally called fumé blanc/blanc fumé), more often not. (10.25%)

Semillon Spelt sémillon in French. Sometimes heavily wooded, sometimes sweet, more often in blends. (1.14%, including rare red-skinned version)

Sylvaner Native of Germany's Franken, more about style and texture than flavour. Just 1 ha and one varietal bottling in SA.

Verdelho From Portugal (not to be confused with Spain's verdejo). Both a grape and a (sweet) fortified style in Madeira; mostly dry in the southern hemisphere. (0.08%)

Vermentino Sardinia and Corsica's premier white grape is new in SA but holds potential to deliver aroma, flavour and verve in a warming climate. Both local versions made, appropriately, by Italians.

Viognier Increasingly fashionable variety internationally, spreading out from its home in the northern Rhône, now showing promise here. Usually wooded. (0.82%)

Competitions, Challenges & Awards

An increasing number of wine competitions, awards and challenges are run by liquor industry bodies, independent companies, publishing houses and individuals. Below are the main national events:

Absa Top 10 Pinotage Competition Run annually by the Pinotage Association and a major financial institution to help set international quality targets for growers of pinotage. Local/overseas judges. See under Industry Organisations for contact details.

Amorim Cap Classique Challenge Annual competition to appoint SA's top bottle-fermented sparkling wines. Mostly local judges. ▪ admin@capclassique.co.za ▪ www.capclassique.co.za ▪ T +27 (0)21-863-1599 ▪ F +27 (0)21-863-1552

Cabernet Franc Challenge Annual wine competition aimed at raising public awareness and rewarding quality in the production of cabernet franc varietals and blends. 'Museum' category spotlights maturation potential; Best Value category rewards value-for-money entries. Local judges. ▪ cobie@cvomarketing.co.za ▪ T +27 (0)21-981-0216 / +27 (0)83-556-3740

CAPPA Cape Port & Wine Challenge Organised by the Cape Port Producers' Association to award best in class and gold medals in each of the port categories, and select the Top 10 Portuguese-style wines. Local judges. ▪ info@boplaas.co.za ▪ www.capeportproducers.co.za ▪ T +27 (0)44-213-3326 ▪ F +27 (0)44-213-3750

Chenin Blanc Top 10 Challenge See Standard Bank Chenin Blanc Top 10 Challenge.

Diners Club Winemaker of the Year Inaugurated in 1981, this prestigious competition features a different category each year. The Young Winemaker of the Year recognises the winning entrant aged 30 years or younger. Local panel with some overseas representation.

Winemaker of the Year since inception

1981 Walter Finlayson, Blaauwklippen Zinfandel 1980
1982 Walter Finlayson, Blaauwklippen Cabernet Sauvignon 1980
1983 Günter Brözel, Nederburg Rhine Riesling 1983
1984 Manie Rossouw, Eersterivier Sauvignon Blanc 1984
1985 Günter Brözel, Nederburg Gewürztraminer 1985
1986 Sydney Back, Backsberg Chardonnay 1985
1987 Beyers Truter, Kanonkop Pinotage 1985
1988 Wilhelm Linde, Nuy White Muscadel 1985
1989 Peter Finlayson, Hamilton Russell Pinot Noir 1986
1990 André Bruwer, Bon Courage Gewürztraminer Special Late Harvest 1989
1991 Wilhelm Linde, Nuy Riesling 1991

1992 Jean Daneel, Buitenverwachting Reserve Merlot 1991
1993 Danie de Wet, De Wetshof Finesse Chardonnay 1993
1994 Gyles Webb, Thelema Cabernet Sauvignon-Merlot 1992
1995 Nicky Krone, Twee Jonge Gezellen Krone Borealis Brut 1993 **1996** Gyles Webb, Thelema Cabernet Sauvignon 1994
1997 Jeff Grier, Villiera Bush Vine Sauvignon Blanc 1997
1998 Danie Malan, Allesverloren Shiraz 1996
1999 Ronell Wiid, Hazendal Shiraz-Cabernet Sauvignon 1998
2000 Paul de Villiers, Landskroon Port 1997
2001 Teddy Hall, Kanu Chenin Blanc 2001
2002 Danie de Waal, Uiterwyk De Waal Top of the Hill 2001
2003 John Loubser, Constantia Uitsig Reserve Semillon 2002
2004 Pieter Ferreira, Graham Beck Brut Blanc de Blancs 1999
2005 Carl Schultz, Hartenberg Merlot 2004
2006 Gottfried Möcke, Chamonix Reserve Chardonnay 2005
2007 Marc Kent, Boekenhoutskloof Syrah 2005
2008 Not awarded
2009 Coenie Snyman, Rust en Vrede Cabernet Sauvignon 2007
2010 Bartho Eksteen, Hermanuspietersfontein Nr. 5 Sauvignon Blanc 2009
2011 Johan Jordaan, Spier Creative Block 5 2009
2012 Razvan Macici, Nederburg Private Bin Eminence 2007
2013 Christiaan Groenewald, Arendskloof Voetspoere Tannat-Syrah 2011
2014 Jacques Erasmus, Spier Creative Block 2 2014
2015 Johann Fourie, KWV The Mentors Pinotage 2013
2016 Pierre Wahl, Rijk's Chenin Blanc 2014
2017 Christiaan Groenewald, Eagle's Cliff Pinotage 2017
2018 Clayton Reabow, Môreson Mercator Chardonnay 2017

Young Winemaker of the Year since inception

2001 Henri Swiegers, Slanghoek Noble Late Harvest 2001
2002 Boela Gerber, Groot Constantia Merlot 2001
2003 Ivy du Toit, Jason's Hill Sauvignon Blanc 2003
2004 Johan Nesenberend, For My Friends Shiraz 2002
2005 Johan Kruger, Sterhuis Chardonnay 2004
2006 Francois Agenbag, Mountain Ridge Seven Oaks 6+1 Reserve Cabernet Sauvignon-Shiraz 2004

2007 Ruth Penfold, Steenberg Semillon 2007

2008 Ossie Sauermann, La Vigne Single Vineyard Shiraz 2007

2009 Clayton Reabow, Môreson Premium Chardonnay 2007

2010 RJ Botha, Nitida Calligraphy 2009

2011 Matthew van Heerden, Uva Mira Chardonnay 2009

2012 Anri Truter, Beyerskloof Diesel Pinotage 2010

2013 Murray Barlow, Rustenberg Stellenbosch Chardonnay 2012

2014 JD Pretorius, Steenberg Merlot 2012

2015 Philip Viljoen, Bon Courage Noble Late Harvest 2015

2016 Murray Barlow, Rustenberg RM Nicholson 2015

2017 Wade Roger-Lund, Jordan Blanc de Blancs Méthode Cap Classique 2015

2018 Rüdger van Wyk, Stark-Condé Stellenbosch Syrah 2016

▪ winemaker@dinersclub.co.za ▪ www. dinersclub.co.za ▪ T +27 (0)21- 795-5400 ▪ F +27 (0)21-794-8185

FNB Sauvignon Blanc Top 10 Annual competition hosted by Sauvignon Blanc South Africa since 2007 to promote innovation and excellence of the sauvignon blanc cultivar, and reward those making wines of true distinction. Local judges. admin@ sauvignonblanc.com ▪ www.sauvignonblanc.com ▪ T +27 (0)21-975-4440

Michelangelo International Wine & Spirits Awards Run in SA since 1997, Michelangelo is said to be the largest international drinks competition in the southern hemisphere, 2036 entries from 12 countries being received in 2019. Thirty accredited experts representing 22 countries sit on specialist wine and spirit judging panels. Entries are judged under OIV guidelines and awarded trophies as well as Platinum, Gran d'Or, Gold and Silver medals. QR codes on award stickers add value for consumers and producers. ▪ orraine@michelangeloawards.com ▪ www.michelan-geloawards.com ▪ T +27 (0)82-556-8679

Muscadel Award for Excellence Annual competition aimed at raising consumer awareness and recognising quality in the creation, packaging and promotion of SA's muscadel wines. Local judges. ▪ henri@badsberg.co.za, andres@rooiberg.co.za ▪ T +27 (0)23-344-3021 / +27 (0)23-626-1664

National Wine Challenge Fine-wine competition incorporating Top 100 SA Wines. Uses key international and local judges with a focus on MW qualifications. Blind-tasted audited results yield Double Platinum/ Top 100 status for the top-scoring 100 wines, National Champion 'Grand Cru' status for best-in-class wines, and either Double Gold or Double Silver awards for high-scoring wines. Winning wines are showcased via a free Android/iOS app and at tasting events around the world. ▪ operations@buybetterwine.com ▪ www. buybetterwine.com, www.thenationalwinechallenge. com

Novare South African Terroir Wine Awards Established 15 years ago and now run by the SA National Wine Show Association (also responsible for the SA Young Wine Show and Veritas), the Terroir Wine Awards focus on soil and climatic factors in narrowly defined cultivation areas. Only wines certified as originating from single vineyards, units registered for the production of estate wine, wards or districts (last-mentioned not divided into more than one ward) may be entered, making this one of the most exclusive wine competitions in the world. Top Wine, Top Single-Vineyard Wine, Top Wine Area, Top Wine Estate and Top Producer trophies also awarded. Five local judges ▪ entries@terroirwineawards.co.za ▪ www. terroirwineawards.co.za ▪ T +27 (0)21-863 1599 ▪ F +27 (0)21-863-1552

Old Mutual Trophy Spirits Show Inaugural event in 2019. Convened by Michael Fridjhon and sponsored by Old Mutual. Seeks to identify the best spirits available in SA and award trophies to the top gold medal winners. Local and international judges. ▪ alex@outsorceress.co.za ▪ www.trophywine-show.co.za ▪ T +27 (0)11-482-5936 ▪ F +27 (0)86-532-5177

Old Mutual Trophy Wine Show Convened by Michael Fridjhon and sponsored by Old Mutual. Seeks to identify the best wines in SA and award trophies to the top gold medal winners, as well as the top producer overall. Local and international judges. ▪ alex@outsorceress.co.za ▪ www.trophywineshow.co.za ▪ T +27 (0)11-482-5936 ▪ F +27 (0)86-532-5177

Perold Absa Cape Blend Competition Launched in 2011 and aimed at creating a signature style for Cape Blends (see SA Wine Styles section). Local judges. Contacts as for Absa Top Ten Pinotage.

Shiraz SA Wine Challenge Annual competition to identify the 12 best varietal shirazes and 3 best shiraz blends across all regions and styles. Local/international judges. ▪ info@shirazsa.co.za ▪ www.shirazsa.co.za ▪ T +27 (0)82 924 7254 ▪ F +27 (0)86-267 4333

South African Airways (SAA) Wine Awards Annual selection of wines to fly with the national carrier (drinkability in flight conditions an important consideration). Local and overseas palates. ▪ NompumeleloSambo@flysaa.com T

+27(0)11-978-9301 ▪ MotshabiPaile@flysaa.com
T +27(0)11-978-9305 ▪ MelindaUys@flysaa.com T
+27(0)11-978-6482 ▪ YolandeSchutte@flysaa.com ▪
T +27 (0)11-978-3982

SA National Bottled Wine Show See Veritas.

South African Terroir Wine Awards See Novare
South African Terroir Wine Awards.

**South African Wine Tasting Championship
(SAWTC)** In the spirit of ongoing education, and
in an attempt to encourage new converts to wine,
SAWTC offers all winelovers the chance to put their
talents to the test and be the centre of a local wine
event, with an opportunity to compete internationally.
▪ sawtc@wine.co.za ▪ www.sawtc.co.za ▪ T +27
(0)21-422-5206

South African Young Wine Show Inaugurated
1975 to gauge the quality of embryo wines, prior
to finishing and bottling, thereby also recognising
wineries which sell their products in bulk. The grand
champion receives the General Smuts Trophy. Local
judges. ▪ info@veritas.co.za ▪ www.youngwineshow.
co.za ▪ T +27 (0)21-863 1599 ▪ F +27 (0)21-863-1552

**Standard Bank Chenin Blanc Top 10
Challenge** Annual event in which varietal chenins
and chenin-dominated (85%) blends in the drier
spectrum (max 12 g/L sugar) are assessed by a panel
of five judges (one from abroad) and an associate. The
ten winners each receive R25,000, to be used to reinforce economic and social benefits in the workplace.
▪ cheninblancasso@gmail.com ▪ www.chenin.co.za ▪
T +27 (0)82-467-4331

Top 100 South African Wines See National Wine
Challenge.

Trophy Wine Show See Old Mutual Trophy Wine
Show.

Ultra Value Wine Challenge Provides an
objective, independent and professional annual
rating of SA wines selling for under R150/bottle.
These are tasted blind for quality, then an algorithm
factors in price attractiveness. Top performers are
awarded double-gold, gold or silver medals. Local
judges. ▪ accounts@buybetterwine.com ▪ www.
ultravaluewines.com, www.buybetterwine.com

Veritas SA's biggest competition for market-ready
wines, awarding double-gold, gold, silver and bronze
medals across a wide range of categories. Local palates
with some overseas input. ▪ info@veritas.co.za ▪
www.veritas.co.za ▪ T +27 (0)21-863 1599 ▪ F +27
(0)21-863-1552

Wine & Brandy Education

**Brandy Course for Hospitality
Staff** Underwritten by the Cape Wine Academy
(CWA) and subsidised by the SA Brandy Foundation,
this quarterly training programme is aimed
specifically at tasting room and other hospitality
staff. Topics covered include the history of brandy,
brandy production and conducting a brandy tasting.
Successful students receive a CWA certificate. T +27
(0)64-754-6552 ▪ christelle@sabrandy.co.za

Cape Wine Academy Recognised leader in wine
education and appreciation in SA for over 40 years,
CWA focuses on the development of skills and knowledge for all sectors of the wine and related industries,
as well as private wine enthusiasts and corporates.
Educational, training and experiential courses are
held in public venues and tertiary institutions in
various provinces, and presented by wine industry
experts, winemakers and Cape Wine Masters. ▪ info@
capewineacademy.co.za ▪ www.capewineacademy.
co.za ▪ Stellenbosch: T +27 (0)21-889-8844 ▪ F +27
(0)21-889-7391 ▪ Johannesburg: T +27 (0)11-024-
3616 ▪ F +27 (0)86-559-7329.

Sommeliers Academy Founded in 2016, with
campuses in Johannesburg, Durban, Cape Town
and, recently, Harare. Provides wine and hospitality
education for local (SASA) and international (ASI)
qualifications. Also runs exchange programs with
counterparts in France and Switzerland. Online
learning available. ▪ somm.academy@gmail.com ▪
www.sommellerie.co.za ▪ T +27 (0)21-422-5206

The School of Fine Wine For wine enthusiasts,
The School of Fine Wine offers a month-long wine
appreciation course in central Cape Town and Tokai.
Presented in four sessions, it is an informative and
enjoyable course about SA wine, with tastings of
some of the best local wines. For the hospitality
industry, there are three interactive, excursion-based
courses. Students visit winefarms to experience
winemaking, meet winemakers, tour vineyards and
taste wines, so acquiring a practical understanding
of the production of wine. Courses are presented by
qualified winemaker and teacher Lieze Norval in
association with Caroline's Fine Wine Cellar. ▪ T +27
(0)21-419-8984 ▪ carowine6@mweb.co.za

**University of Stellenbosch Garagiste
Winemaking Course** See under Make Your Own
Wine or Brandy

Wine Judging Academy Run by Michael Fridjhon
in association with the University of Cape Town's
Graduate School of Business, this intensive 3-day

tasting and wine judging course aims to increase the number of competent wine judges at work in the local industry. ▪ crossley@reciprocal.co.za

WSET in South Africa with the International Wine Education Centre Led by WSET Educator of the Year, Cathy Marston, IWEC was the first provider of the UK-based Wine & Spirit Education Trust's (WSET) courses in SA, catering for enthusiastic amateurs and wine industry professionals alike. WSET wine and spirit qualifications are recognised as the industry standard in over 70 countries. The IWEC offers all WSET wine and spirit courses, and is the only provider of the flagship qualification, WSET Level 4, in Africa and the Middle East. In-house training and ad hoc courses are also offered, and for those wanting to take their wine education to the highest level, WSET is the direct path to Master of Wine (MW) and Master Sommelier (MS). ▪ courses@thewinecentre.co.za ▪ www.thewinecentre. co.za ▪ T +27 (0)21-012-5349

Make Your Own Wine or Brandy

BuytheBarrel Sign up and buy a barrel, choose your grapes and decide which style of wine you want to make. Either pick and press the grapes — the hard part — or fast-forward to taste and blend your wine with the help of the qualified resident winemaker. Then design your label, bottle your wine (you get 300 bottles!) and sip, ship, sell or share it as you see fit. ▪ alex@icloud.com ▪ www.buythebarrel.co.za ▪ T +27 (0)84-582-6376

Hofstraat Kelder Wim Smit and Jerry Finley, owners and winemakers at Malmesbury's Hofstraat Kelder, act as mentors to aspirant winemakers by arrangement, facilitating grape sourcing through to labelling. See listing in A-Z directory.

Sign Your Name in Wine at Stellenrust Stellenrust wine farm near Stellenbosch offers groups of 20 or more the opportunity to pick grapes, crush them in 3-ton open-tank fermenters and put a personal signature on their very own wine. Packages include a full-day excursion followed by traditional braai lunch and bottles of participants' handcrafted wine (after proper barrel maturation in the boutique cellar). info@stellenrust. co.za ▪ www.stellenrust.co.za ▪ T +27 (0)21-880-2283 ▪ F +27 (0)21-880-2284

University of Stellenbosch Garagiste Winemaking Course The premium short course for people interested in producing quality small-scale wines at home or simply expanding their wine knowledge. Attendees receive a set of notes; observe the use of garagiste winemaking equipment; taste different vinifications; bottle their own wine; and receive a certificate from Stellenbosch University. A follow-on, advanced course was introduced in 2016. ▪ wdutoit@sun.ac.za ▪ T +27 (0)21-808-2022 ▪ F +27 (0)21-808-4781

A-Code Numbers & Certification Codes

Many wines appear on the market under brand names, with, at first glance, no reference to their producers or purveyors. However, consumers need not buy 'blind', and may trace a wine's provenance by checking the official 'A-number' which appears on the bottle or pack. This identity code tells you either who produced the wine, or who sourced it for resale. In the latter case, an enquiry to the merchant should elicit the source. The list keeps growing and being revised, and is too lengthy to reproduce in this guide. Via the SAWIS NPC web page **www.sawis.co.za/ sealsearch.php**, it is possible however to search the list of A-codes, as well as the certification codes issued for each wine by the Wine & Spirit Board, for details about the production area, variety and vintage.

Styles & Vintages

Recent South African Vintages

South African wines do not exhibit the major vintage variations seen in some other winegrowing areas. There are, nevertheless, perceptible differences from year to year. Dry, hot summers are the norm but a variety of factors make generalisations difficult and possibly misleading.

2019 Like 2017, bone-dry but cool, small but pristine crop showing freshness and concentration. Some pick this as an exceptional white-wine vintage. Likely longer-lived than 2018.

2018 Challenging year for reds and whites, lingering drought requiring particular focus on optimal picking times. Sound, concentrated if perhaps earlier-peaking wines.

2017 Dry but surprisingly cool, resulting in smaller but excellent crop with vivacity and fine flavour concentration on reds as well as whites.

2016 Exceptionally hot and dry, later-ripening varieties benefiting from lower temperatures. In cool climates, healthy fruit yielded some stellar wines.

2015 Near-perfect conditions produced less but perfect fruit. One of the great vintages, possibly surpassing 2009.

2014 Later, slightly smaller and unusually cool. Lighter, less powerful wines; potential for fine concentration with elegance if picked judiciously.

2013 Biggest crop to date; moderate conditions yielded good to very good reds and whites, lighter alcohol levels.

2012 Unusually dry, hot January strained unirrigated vineyards; otherwise good to very good vintage for both reds and whites; moderate alcohol levels.

2011 Yet more variable than the last, impossible to generalise. As in 2010, producer's track record should guide the buying/cellaring decision.

2010 A real test of the winegrower's savvy, and one of the toughest recent harvests to call. Be guided by producer's track record.

2009 Perhaps one of the greatest vintages. Late, gruelling, but whites and reds both stellar.

2008 Long, wet, late and challenging but also unusually cool, favouring elegance in reds and whites.

2007 Elegant, structured whites; smaller red-grape berries gave intense colour and fruit concentration.

2006 Perhaps the best white-wine vintage in a decade. Fleshy, mild-tannined reds, lower alcohols.

Older Vintages

2005 Concentrated if alcoholic reds; mostly average whites, some exceptions. **2004** Cooler dry conditions yielded elegant, often ageworthy wines with lower alcohols, softer tannins. **2003** Outstanding, especially for reds — concentrated and structured, and often slow to show their best. **2002** Challenging and patchy, but top producers show fine concentration and moderate alcohols. **2001** Some excellent reds — fruity and concentrated, best are long lived. Flavourful if alcoholic whites. **2000** Powerful, concentrated reds, befitting a hot year; the best have kept very well. Whites generally less impressive, not for long ageing. **1999** Fat, alcoholic reds with ripe fruit for earlier drinking. Generally not too much excitement among the whites. **1998** Excellent red vintage with enough fruit for extended cellaring; whites generally not for keeping. **1997** Among coolest and latest vintages on record. Supple, elegant reds; some excellent and stylish whites. **1996** Generally awkward reds, not for keeping; whites, except for top NLHs, best drunk up. **1995** For many, the vintage of the 90s. Concentrated reds, some still maturing spectacularly. **1994** Hottest, driest vintage in decades; variable quality; new-clone cabs and early ripening reds fared well. **1993** Without serious mishaps; some excellent sauvignons; above-average reds. **1992** Coolish season, favouring whites, especially sauvignon; the reds (notably pinotage) very good; **1991** Dry, warm to hot, favouring early to mid-season ripeners; some long-lasting reds. **1990** Uneven year, alternately cool and warm; average whites and reds; not for further ageing. **1980s**: even years ('82, '84, '86) usually more favourable for reds; uneven years, marginally cooler, favoured whites, but 'white' years '87 and, especially, '89 produced remarkable reds. **1970s**: again, even years generally favoured reds. Best was '74; but top wines from some other vintages are still delicious. **1960s** and earlier yielded some astonishingly long-lived wines.

South African Wine Styles

Agrafe/agraffe See Sparkling wine.

Air-dried See Straw wine.

Alternative white/red Intended to allow for greater flexibility within the official certification framework, recent category provides for dry (≤4 g/L), lower-sulphur wines with colours ranging from light gold to amber (white) and light red to purple (red). Certification is mandatory.

Amber wine See Orange wine.

Biodynamic See Winemaking Terms section.

Blanc de blancs White wine made from white grapes only; also used for champagne and cap classique. Alternative name is 'vin gris'.

Blanc de noir A pink wine (shades range from off-white through peach to pink) made from red grapes. See also Rosé.

Blanc fumé or **fumé blanc** Dry white from sauvignon, usually but not necessarily wooded (nor smoked, smoky).

Blend See Varietal wine, and Cape Blend.

Brut See Sugar or sweetness, and Sparkling wine.

Cap classique See Sparkling wine.

Cape Blend Usually denotes a (red) blend with pinotage, the 'local' grape making up a significant part of the assemblage; sometimes simply a blend showing a distinct 'Cape' character; occasionally used for chenin-based blends.

Carbonated See Sparkling wine.

Cultivar Grape variety (a contraction of 'cultivated variety').

Cuvée French term for the blend of a wine.

Demi-sec See Sugar or sweetness.

Dessert wine A sweet wine, often to accompany the dessert but sometimes pleasurably prior, as in the famous Sauternes/foie gras combo.

Dry to sweet See Sugar or sweetness.

Estate wine Term now reserved for wine originating from an officially registered 'unit for the production of estate wine' (see www.sawis.co.za/cert/about.php for current list).

Extended barrel-aged white/gris Category of vintage-dated, dry (≤4 g/L) wine from white/gris grapes, light gold to amber in colour, matured in oak for at least 2 years and showing a nutty/oxidative character.

Fortified wines Increased in alcoholic strength by the addition of spirit, by SA law to minimum 15% alcohol by volume.

Grand cru See Premier Grand Cru.

Ice wine Intensely sweet wine from ripe grapes picked and pressed while frozen. Not an official category.

Jerepiko or **jerepigo** Red or white wine produced without fermentation; grape juice is fortified with grape spirit, preventing fermentation; very sweet, with considerable unfermented grape flavours.

Kosher See Winemaking Terms section.

Late Harvest Unfortified wine from late-harvested and therefore sweeter grapes. Alcohol by volume (ABV) must exceed 10%. See also Sugar or sweetness.

Méthode ancestrale See Sparkling wine.

Méthode cap classique (MCC) See Sparkling wine.

Natural pale/non-fortified pale Class of white wines oak-matured (under a film of flor yeast, for minimum of 2 years) with discernible almond, flor yeast and wood characters.

Natural Sweet Aka Sweet Natural. Unfortified wine with residual sugar greater than 20 g/L. See also Sugar or sweetness.

Noble Late Harvest (NLH) Sweet dessert wine (still, perlé or sparkling) exhibiting a noble rot (botrytis) character, from grapes infected by the botrytis cinerea fungus. This mould, in warm, misty autumn weather, attacks the skins of ripe grapes, causing much of the juice to evaporate. As the berries wither, their sweetness and flavour become powerfully concentrated. SA law dictates that grapes for NLH must be harvested at a minimum of 28° Balling and residual sugar must exceed 50 g/L.

Nouveau Term originated in Beaujolais for fruity young and light red, usually from gamay and made by the carbonic maceration method. Bottled soon after vintage to capture the youthful, fresh flavour of fruit and yeasty fermentation.

Orange wine Unofficial name for fashionable style of white-wine making using extended skin contact (see Winemaking Terms section), as for red wine, resulting in darker hues and greater flavour/aroma intensity, sometimes with an (attractive) oxidative character and/or noticeable tannins. See also Skin-macerated white.

Organic See Winemaking Terms section.

Perlant, perlé, pétillant Lightly sparkling, usually carbonated wine.

Port Fortified dessert with excellent quality record in SA since late 1980s, partly through efforts of Cape Port Producers' Association which has adopted 'Cape' to identify the local product. Following are CAPPA-defined styles: **Cape White**: non-muscat grapes, oak-aged min 6 months, any size vessel, drier to full-sweet; **Cape Pink**:

non-muscat varieties, pink hue, barrel/tank-aged min 6 months; **Cape Ruby**: full bodied, fruity; min 50% barrel/tank-aged 6-36 months; can be vintage dated; **Cape Vintage**: fruit of one harvest; dark, full-bodied; tank/cask-aged min 1 year; must be certified, sold in glass, vintage dated; **Cape Vintage Reserve**: as for Vintage, but 'superior quality'; **Cape Late Bottled Vintage** (LBV): fruit of single year, full-bodied, slightly tawny colour, barrel/bottle aged min 3 years (of which min 2 years in oak); **Cape Tawny**: min 80% wood matured, amber-orange (tawny) colour, smooth, slightly nutty taste; **Cape Dated Tawny**: single-vintage tawny.

Premier Grand Cru Unlike in France, not a quality rating in SA — usually an austerely dry white.

Residual sugar See Sugar or sweetness.

Rosé Pink wine, made from red or a blend of red and white grapes. The red grape skins are removed before the wine takes up too much colour.

Single-vineyard wine Classification for wines from officially registered vineyards, no larger than 6ha in size and planted with a single variety.

Skin-macerated white Dry (≤4 g/L) white wine, light gold to deep orange in colour, macerated on-skin for at least 96 hours.

Sparkling wine Bubbly, or 'champagne', usually white but sometimes rosé and even red, given its effervescence by carbon dioxide — allowed to escape in the normal winemaking process. **Champagne** undergoes its second fermentation in the bottle. Under an agreement with France, SA does not use the term, which describes the sparkling wines from the Champagne area. Instead, **méthode cap classique** (MCC) is the SA term to describe sparkling wines made by the classic method, with a second ferment in bottle. **Méthode ancestrale** results from a single ferment, spontaneously initiated in tank and completed in bottle. **Charmat** undergoes its second, bubble-forming fermentation in a tank and is bottled under pressure. **Carbonated** sparklers are made by the injection of carbon dioxide bubbles (as in fizzy soft drinks). **Agrafe** (or agraffe) bubblies undergo bottle-fermentation under cork instead of the usual metal crown cap. See also Sugar or sweetness.

Special Late Harvest (SLH) SA designation for a lighter dessert-style wine. There is no legal stipulation for residual sugar content, but if the RS is below 20 g/L, the label must state 'extra dry', 'dry', 'semi-dry' or 'sweet', as the case may be. The minimum alcohol content is 11% by volume.

Stein Semi-sweet white wine, usually a blend and often confused with steen, a grape variety (chenin blanc), though most steins are at least made partly from steen grapes.

Straw wine Vin de paille in French; sweet, unfortified wine from ripe grapes that are 'naturally dried' (optionally on straw mats). Minimum ABV is 16%.

Sugar or sweetness In still wines: extra-dry or bone-dry wines have less than 2.5 g/L residual sugar, undetectable to the taster. A wine legally is dry up to 5 g/L*. Taste buds begin picking up a slight sweetness, or softness, in a wine — depending on its acidity — at about 6 g/L, when it is still off-dry. By about 8–9 g/L a definite sweetness can usually be noticed. However, an acidity of 8–9 g/L can render a sweet wine fairly crisp even with a sugar content of 20 g/L plus. Official sweetness levels in SA wine are listed in the table below.

Wine	Sugar (g/L)
Still wines	
Extra-dry	≤ 2.5
Dry*	≤ 5
Semi-dry*	> 5 ≤ 12
Semi-sweet	> 5 <30
Late Harvest	≥ 20
Special Late Harvest (SLH)	—
Natural Sweet (or Sweet Natural)	> 20
Noble Late Harvest (NLH)	> 50
Naturally dried grape wine (straw wine)	> 30
Sparkling wines	
Brut nature	<3
Extra brut	<6
Brut	<12
Extra-dry	12–17
Dry	17–32
Semi-sweet	32–50
Sweet	> 50

* Recent amendments allow for higher sugar levels for dry (9 g/L) and semi-dry (18 g/L) if the total acidity is within 2 g/L or 10 g/L respectively of the sugar level.

Sun wine Bottlings in this fortified category must be from white grapes, pale to deep gold in colour and show a maderised character (see under Winetasting Terms section). Must be certified and vintage dated.

Sweet Natural See Natural Sweet.

Varietal wine From a single variety of grape. Legislation requires the presence in the wine of 85% of the stated variety or vintage. Blends may name component parts only if those components were vinified separately, prior to blending; then they are listed with the larger contributor(s) named first. If any one of the blend partners is less than 20%, percentages for all the varieties must be given. Blends may be vinified separately in any recognised WO area; component areas may be named, as above except the threshold is 30%.

Vin de paille See Straw wine.

Vine-dried wine Often – but not necessarily – sweet, from grapes desiccated on the vine.

Vintage In SA primarily used to denote year of harvest. Not a quality classification (a 'vintage' port in Europe means one from an officially declared great port-grape year).

South African Brandy, Husk Spirit & Sherry-Style Wines

Brandy and Husk Spirit

SA brandy is divided into three main stylistic categories. Put simply and reductively, these are as follows:

- **Blended brandy** must by law contain at least 30% per LAA (litres absolute alcohol) brandy distilled in a potstill and aged for at least three years in oak barrels smaller than 340L each. The remaining component will be of wine spirit (made in a continuous still). More often than not, these brandies are intended to partner mixers or to play a role in cocktails. The alcohol by volume (ABV) must be at least 43% (in practice it usually is 43%).
- **Vintage brandy** (a small category) must have at least 30% potstill brandy, but not more than 80%, aged minimum eight years. Up to 70% wine spirit, but not less than 20%, is permitted but it too must be matured at least eight years.
- **Potstill brandy** must be 100% potstilled and matured at least three years in oak barrels. The ABV is a minimum of 38%, as for Vintage brandy. Increasingly labelled 'Cape Brandy'.

Estate brandy is brandy in any of the above categories in which all stages of production, from vineyard to maturation, took place on one property (as for 'estate' wine).

Not (yet) regulated locally, these official French (cognac) designations are increasingly used here, with minimum age adjustments for VS to comply with local legislation:

- **VS (Very Special)** - youngest component is at least 3 years old (2 for cognac).
- **VSOP (Very Superior Old Pale)** - youngest component is at least 4 years old.
- **XO (Extra Old)** - youngest component is at least 10 years old.
- **XXO (Extra Extra Old)** - youngest component is at least 20 years old.

Husk Spirit will have an ABV level of at least 43% and not be matured; **Premium Husk Spirit** must be at least 40% ABV, and be matured in oak for between three and six months.

Sherry-Style Fortified Wines

There are eight classes of sherry-style wines described in South Africa's Liquor Products Act. The colour of these wines must range – depending on the class – from pale straw to amber. Their aromas and flavours must be 'nutty' and 'woody'. Five of the eight classes must have a discernible flor yeast and/or wood character. In addition:

- In the case of **Fino**, the residual sugar shall not exceed 20 g/L, and the alcohol content must not exceed 16%. It should have an almond flavour.
- The alcohol content of an **Amontillado** must be at least 16%, and it should have a flavour of hazelnuts.
- **Oloroso** must have rich, nutty flavours, a minimum of 50 g/L residual sugar, and at least 16% alcohol by volume.
- The residual sugar content of a **Pale Dry** wine cannot exceed 30 g/L, and its alcohol content should exceed 16%.

- Similarly, the alcohol content of a **Pale Cream** must exceed 16%, but its residual sugar must range between 30 g/L and 80 g/L.
- The remaining three classes need only exhibit a discernible wood character.
- In addition, the residual sugar and alcohol content of a **Medium Cream** must be between 80 g/L and 115 g/L, and above 16% respectively.
- A **Full Cream** wine must have at least 115 g/L residual sugar, and an alcohol content above 16%.
- A muscat character and an aldehyde content of at least 80 mg/L, a residual sugar content of at least 100 g/L, and at least 16% alcohol by volume is necessary for an **Old Brown**. This may also only be sweetened with concentrated must, or with fortified wine with a residual sugar content of at least 180 g/L.

Words & Phrases

Winetasting Terms

Short of a ready description? Here are a few frequently used words, phrases and explanations that may be helpful. See also Winemaking Terms, and SA Wine Styles.

Accessible, approachable Flavours and feel of the wine are harmonious, easily recognised; it is ready to drink.

Aftertaste The lingering flavours and impressions of a wine; its persistence — the longer, the better.

Alcoholic 'Hot' or, in excess, burning character caused by imbalanced or excessive alcohol. Also simply spirituous.

Astringent Mouth-puckering sensation, associated with high tannin (and sometimes acid); also bitter, sharp.

Aroma Smells in the bouquet, or nose, especially the odours associated with the grape rather than the winemaking process.

Attack First sensations on palate/nose — pungent, aggressive, quiet etc.

Austere Usually meaning unyielding, sometimes harsh. Sometimes, more favourably, to imply a notable restraint/refinement.

Backbone The wine is well formed, firm, not flabby or insipid.

Baked 'Hot', earthy quality. Usually from scorched/shrivelled grapes which have been exposed too long to the sun, or from too warm a ferment, especially in some whites.

Balance Desirable attribute. The wine's chief constituents — alcohol, acid, tannin, fruit and wood (where used) — are in harmony.

Bead Bubbles in sparkling wine; a fine, long-lasting bead is the most desirable. See also Mousse.

Big Expansive in the mouth, weighty, full-bodied, as a result of high alcohol and/or fruit concentration.

Bite or **grip** Imparted by tannin, acid and/or alcohol, important in young wines designed for ageing. If overdone can impart undesirable bitterness, harshness or spirity 'glow'.

Bitter Sensation perceived mainly on the back of the tongue, and in the finish of the wine. Usually unpleasant, though an accepted if not immediately admired character of certain Italian wines. Sometimes more positively associated with the taste of a specific fruit or nut, such as cherry-kernel or almond.

Body Fullness on the palate.

Botrytis/ed Exhibits a noble rot/botrytis character, from grapes infected by the *botrytis cinerea* fungus.

Bottle-age Negative or positive, depending on context. Positively describes development of aromas/flavours (i.e. complexity) as wine moves from youth to maturity. Much-prized attribute in fine whites and reds. Negatively, bottle age results in a wine with stale, empty or even off odours.

Buttery Flavour and texture associated with barrel-fermented white wines, especially chardonnays; rich, creamy smoothness.

Claret Another name for a dry red Bordeaux or Bordeaux-like red.

Classic Showing characteristics of the classics of Bordeaux, Burgundy etc; usually implying balance, elegance, subtlety.

Coarse Rough, unbalanced tannins, acid, alcohol or oak.

Complexity Strong recommendation. A complex wine has several layers of flavour, usually developing with age/maturation. See Bottle-age.

Concentration See Intensity.

Confected Over-elaborately constructed, artificial, forced; sometimes overly sweet.

Corked, corky Wine is faulty; its flavours have been tainted by yeast, fungal or bacterial infections, often but not necessarily from the cork. It smells damp and mouldy in its worst stages — but sometimes it's barely detectable. In a restaurant, a corked wine should be rejected and returned immediately; producers are honour-bound to replace corked wine.

Creamy Not literally creamy, of course; more a silky, buttery feel and texture.

Crisp Refers to acidity. Positively, means fresh, clean; negatively, too tart, sharp.

Deep and **depth** Having many layers; intense; also descriptive of a serious wine.

Dense Well-padded texture, flavour packed.

Deposits (also sediment or crust) Tasteless and harmless tartrates, acid crystals or tannin in older red wines. Evidence that wine has not been harshly fined, filtered or cold-stabilised.

Dried out Bereft of fruit, harder constituents remaining; tired.

Earthy Usually positive, wine showing its origins from soil, minerals, damp leaves, mushrooms etc.

Easy Undemanding (and hopefully inexpensive).

Elegant Stylish, refined, 'classic'.

WORDS & PHRASES · 631

Esters Scents and smells usually generated by alcohols and acids in wine. A wine may be 'estery' when these characteristics are prominent.

Extract An indication of the 'substance' of a wine, expressed as sugar-free or total extract (which would include some sugars). 18 g/L would be low, light; anything much above 23 g/L in whites is significant; the corresponding threshold for reds is around 30g/L.

Fat Big, full, ample in the mouth.

Finesse/d Graceful, polished. Nothing excessive.

Finish The residual sensations – tastes and textures – after swallowing. Should be pleasant (crisp, lively) and enduring, not short, dull or flat. See also Aftertaste and Length.

Firm Compact, has good backbone.

Flabby Usually lacking backbone, especially acid.

Flat Characterless, unexciting, lacks acid. Or bubbly which has lost its fizz.

Fleshy Very positive, meaning a wine is well fleshed out with texture and grape flavours.

Flowery, floral Flower-like (i.e. smell of rose, honeysuckle, jasmine etc.). Distinct from 'fruity' (i.e. smell/taste of papaya, cantaloupe, grape! etc.).

Forward rather than shy; advancing in age too; mature.

Fresh Lively, youthful, invigorating. Closely related to the amount of acid in the wine and absence of oxidative character: a big, intensely sweet dessert without a backbone of acidity will taste flat and sickly; enough acid and the taste is fresh and uncloying.

Fruity See Flowery.

Full High in alcohol and extract.

Gamey Overripe, decadent, not universally unattractive; also meaty, 'wild'.

Gravel/ly With suggestions of mineral, earthy quality; also firm texture.

Green Usually unripe, sour; also herbaceous; sometimes simply youthful.

Grip Gripping, firm on palate, in finish. Acid, tannin, alcohol are contributors.

Heady Usually refers to the smell of a wine. High in alcohol; intense, high-toned.

Herbaceous Grassy, hay-like, heathery; can also indicate under-ripeness.

Hollow Lacking substance, flavours.

Honey or **honeyed** Sometimes literally a honey/beeswax taste or flavour; a sign of developing maturity in some varieties or more generally a sign of bottle age.

Hot Burning sensation of alcohol in finish.

Intensity No flab, plenty of driving flavour; also deep colour.

Lean Thin, mean, lacking charm of ample fruit; also, more positively, compact, sinewy.

Lees/leesy Taste-imparting dead yeast cells (with grape skins and other solid matter) remaining with wine in tank/barrel (or bottle in the case of méthode champenoise sparkling wines) after fermentation. The longer the wine is 'on its lees' (sur lie) the more richness and flavour it should absorb.

Light/lite Officially wines under 10% alcohol by volume; also light in body (and often short on taste); a health-conscious trend in both reds and whites.

Lively Bouncy, fresh flavours.

Long or **length** Enduring; wine's flavours reverberate on the palate long after swallowing.

Maderised Oxidised and flat; colour is often brownish. Over-mature. More positively, a madeira-like oxidative quality, with 'cooked'/caramelised flavours.

Meaty Sometimes suggesting a general savouriness; but also literally the aroma of meat – raw, smoked etc.

Mousse Fizz in sparkling wines; usually refers also to quality, size and effervescence of the bubbles. See also Bead.

Mouthfeel, mouthfilling Texture, feel; racy, crispness (fine with appropriate dishes) or generous, supple, smooth.

Neutral What it says, neither here nor there.

New World Generally implies accessible, bold, often extrovert (in terms of fruit and use of oak). **Old World** embraces terms like subtle, complex, less oaky, more varied and generally more vinous (than fruity). See also Classic.

Oaky Having exaggerated oak aromas/flavours (vanilla, spice, char, woodsmoke etc.). Oak balanced by fruit in young wines may lessen with age, but over-oaked young wines (where fruit is not in balance) will become over-oaked old wines.

Palate Combination of flavour, taste and texture of a wine.

Pebbly See Gravelly.

Perfumed or **scented** Strong fragrances (fruity, flowery, animal etc)

Phenolic Astringency or bitterness, usually in white wine, attributed to excessive phenolic compounds.

Plump Well fleshed in a charming, cherubic way.

Porty Heavy, over-ripe, stewed; a negative in unfortified wine.

Rich Flavourful, intense, generous. Not necessarily sweet.

Robust Strapping, full-bodied (but not aggressive).

Rough Bull-in-a-china-shop wine, or throat sand-papering quality.

Round Well balanced, without gawkiness or jagged edges.

Sharp or **tart** All about acid, usually unbalanced. But occasionally sharpish, fresh wine is right for the occasion.

Short or **quick** Insubstantial wine, leaving little impression.

Simple One-dimensional or no flavour excitement.

Stalky Unripe, bitter, stemmy.

Stewed Over-ripe, cooked, soft, soggy fruit.

Structure The wine's make up (fruit, acid, tannin, alcohol etc), also in relation to its ageing ability; if a wine is deemed to have 'the structure to age' it suggests these principal elements are in place.

Stylish Classy, distinguished; also voguish.

Supple Very desirable (not necessarily subtle), yielding, refined texture and flavours. See also Mouthfeel.

Tannic Tannins are prominent in the wine, imparting, positively, a mouth-puckering, grippy, tangy quality; negatively, a harsh, unyielding character.

Tension Racy, nervy fruit-acid play on the palate.

Terpene(s)/terpenoid Strong, floral compounds influencing the aromas of especially riesling, gewürztraminer and the muscats; with bottle-age, terpenes can develop a pungent resinous oiliness.

Texture Tactile 'feel' in the mouth: hard, acidic, coarse and alcoholic; or, smooth, velvety, 'warm'.

Toasty Often used for barrel-fermented or -aged wines showing a pleasant biscuity, charry character.

Vegetal Grassy, leafy, herby – in contrast to fruity, flowery, oaky. Overdone, a no-no.

Yeasty Warm bakery smells, often evident in barrel-fermented whites and méthode champenoise sparkling wines, where yeasts stay in contact with the wine after fermentation.

Winemaking Terms

A few brief reference explanations. See also sections on Winetasting Terms and SA Wine Styles.

Acid and **acidity** The fresh – or, in excess, sharp or tart – taste of wine. Too little acid and the wine tastes dull and flat. In SA, winemakers are permitted to adjust acidity either by adding acid – at any stage before bottling – or by lowering the acid level with a de-acidifier. See also Volatile acid and Malolactic.

Alcohol Essential component of wine, providing fullness, richness and, at higher levels, sometimes an impression of sweetness. Also a preservative, helping keep wines in good condition. Produced by yeasts fermenting the sugars in the grape. Measured by volume of the total liquid. Most unfortified table wines in SA have between 11% and 14.5% alc by vol; fortifieds range from ±15% to 21%. A variation of up to 1% between the strength stated on the label and the laboratory analysis is permitted by local law. Various techniques (such as reverse osmosis and 'spinning cone', also the addition of water) exist to address the increasingly important issue of high alcohol levels in wine, and some are legal in SA (though not for export to, e.g., Europe).

Barrels (**barrel-aged**; **barrel-fermented**) Wines are transferred to barrels to age, pick up oaky flavours etc. When must or fermenting must is put into barrels, the resulting wine is called barrel-fermented. A barrel or cask is generally a 225–500L oak container; barrique is a French word for a 225-L barrel; pipe, adapted from the Portuguese

pipa, usually indicates a vessel of 530–630L; vat and foudre are terms generally used for larger (2,000–5,000L) wooden vessels.

Bâtonnage See Lees.

Biodynamic See Organic.

Blend A wine made from two or more different grape varieties, vintages, vineyards or containers. Some of the world's finest wines are blends.

Bottles While the 750-ml (75-cl) bottle is now the most widely used size of container for wine, it is by no means the only one. Smaller bottles (375 and 500 ml) are popular with restaurants and airlines, and larger sizes are prized by collectors because of their novelty value and/or their tendency to promote slower wine ageing. The following are the larger bottle sizes (note: some no longer in production):

Capacity		Bordeaux	Champagne/Burgundy
litres	bottles		
1.5	2	Magnum	Magnum
3	4	Double magnum	Jéroboam
4.5	6	Jéroboam	Rehoboam
6	8	Impériale	Methuselah
9	12	—	Salmanazar
12	16	—	Balthazar

Capacity		Bordeaux	Champagne/Burgundy
litres	*bottles*		
15	20	—	Nebuchadnezzar

Brettanomyces or **'brett'** Naturally occurring yeast, usually associated with red wine and regarded as a spoilage factor, because its growth triggers the formation of volatile acids, phenols and other compounds which, in sufficient concentration, impart a range of unpleasant characters, from barnyard to sweat to cheese. At low concentrations, can enhance complexity and character.

Carbonic maceration or **maceration carbonique** Method of fermenting wine without first crushing the grapes. Whole clusters with stalks etc. are put into closed vat; intracellular fermentation occurs within the grape berries, which then burst.

Chaptalisation Originally French term for the addition of sugar to grape must to raise the alcohol of a wine. Selectively legal in northern Europe, where acid adjustments are not allowed as they are in SA.

Charmat Method of making sparkling wine in a sealed tank (cuvée close) under pressure. Easier, cheaper than méthode champenoise.

Chips See Oak chips.

Cold ferment 'Cold' is a relative term; applied to ferment of mainly white wines in temperature-controlled tanks, it refers to a temperature around usually 13–16°C. The benefits, especially important in a warm country, include conserving the primary fruit aromas and ensuring fermentation is carried out steadily and thoroughly.

Cold soak or **cold maceration**. Red-wine making method carried out prior to fermentation. Skins and juice are held, usually for a few days, at a sufficiently cool temperature to prevent fermentation. The theory is that this extracts more favourable colour and aromas than after fermentation.

Cold stabilisation Keeping a wine at about -4°C for a week or more to precipitate tartaric acid and 'clean up' the wine, preventing later formation of (harmless) tartrate crystals in bottle. Some winemakers believe this process damages flavour and prefer to avoid it.

Concrete Traditionally the preferred construction material for larger fermentation and storage containers, largely superseded since the 1970s by stainless steel. More recently concrete 'eggs', their shape reminiscent of the amphoras of antiquity, have found favour for reasons varying from more-uniform fermentations to improved wine structure, texture and flavour.

Disgorgement (dégorgement in French) Important stage in the production of traditionally fermented sparkling where accumulated sediment (or lees), which could cloud the finished wine, is removed from the neck of the bottle.

Dosage The sugar added to sparkling wine after the second fermentation.

Fermentation The conversion of sugar in grapes into alcohol and carbon dioxide, a function of enzymes secreted by yeasts. In modern SA winemaking, cultured yeasts are normally added to secure the process, but along with the growth of the natural winemaking movement, ferments using wild yeasts (which occur both in vineyard and cellar) are increasing. Beyond about 15% of alcohol, yeasts are overwhelmed and fermentation ceases, although it usually is stopped (for instance by cooling, filtration or the addition of alcohol) before this stage. See also Malolactic.

Filtration Removes last impurities including yeast cells. Done excessively, can thin a wine. Some traditionalists bottle without cold- or protein-stabilisation or filtration.

Fining and **protein stabilisation** Fining is ridding wine of suspended particles by adding substances that attract and draw the particles from the wine.

Flash-pasteurisation See Kosher.

Free run After grapes have been de-stalked and crushed, juice runs freely.

Garage wine Generic term for wine made in minuscule quantities, sometimes literally in a garage; a grower of such wine is sometimes called a garagiste.

Glycerol Minor product of alcoholic fermentation; from the Greek for sweet. Has an apparent sweetening effect on even dry wines and also gives a viscous, mouthfilling character.

Icewine Sweet, concentrated wine from grapes picked and pressed while frozen. Not a recognised category for SA wine production.

Kosher Wine made 'correctly', ie under rabbinical supervision, to be suitable for use by religious Jews. Vinification and any initial movement of the wine must be done by an observant Jew. Flash-pasteurisation, increasingly by means of flavour-preserving processes such as Thermoflash, renders the resulting meshuval wine (literally 'boiled' or 'cooked') fit for handling by non-Jews.

Leafroll virus Virus (or complex of viruses), widespread throughout the winegrowing world, which causes the vine to perform below its potential and thereby produce wine which is lower in colour, body and flavour than that derived from virus-free or 'cleaned-up' plants.

Lees Spent yeast cells and other matter which collect at the bottom of any container in winemaking. Yeast autolysis, or decomposition, can impart richness and flavour to a wine, sometimes referred to as leesy. Lees stirring or bâtonnage involves mixing the bed of lees in a barrel or tank through the wine, which is said to be sur lie; it is employed primarily on barrel-fermented white wines. The main effects of mixing lees and wine are to prevent off-odours developing from lack of oxygen, to limit the amount of wood tannin and oak character extracted, and to increase flavour.

Malolactic fermentation (malo) Occurs when bacteria convert malic into lactic acids. This reduces the acidity of a wine, a normal and healthy process, especially in reds – provided, of course, it occurs before bottling.

Maturation Ageing properties are closely related to tannin and/or fixed acid content of a wine. A relatively full red wine with tannin has lasting power. With age, it may develop complexity, subtlety and smooth mellowness. Lighter wines with lower tannins are drinkable sooner but probably will not reach the same level of complexity. A rising number of SA whites mature well over several years, but most are best drunk in their fruity youth, up to 18 months.

Méthode champenoise Classic method of making champagne by inducing secondary fermentation in the bottle and producing fine bubbles. Due to French restrictions on terminology, Cape sparkling wines made in this way are called méthode cap classique (MCC).

Micro-oxygenation Technique enabling introduction of precise, controlled doses of oxygen to must/ wine. Advocates claim softer tannins, more stable colours and other advantages.

Oak chips, either in older barrels or stainless steel tanks, are widely used in SA, as are oak **staves**. Still frowned on by some purists, the 'additives' approximate the flavour effects of a new barrel, far more cheaply, more easily handled.

Oak-matured See Barrels.

Organic viticulture/winemaking Increasingly popular alternative to 'conventional' or 'industrialised' winegrowing, emphasising natural and sustainable farming methods and cellar techniques. A variant is biodynamic viticulture, influenced by anthroposophy, focused on improving wine quality through harmony with nature and its rhythms.

Oxidation Change (usually for the worse) due to exposure to air, in whites often producing dark yellow or yellowish colour (called maderisation), altering, 'ageing' the taste. Controlled oxidation can be used to produce positive development in wine (see next entry).

Oxidative winemaking Intentional exposure to oxygen during vinification, imparting in a nutty/ biscuity quality to the wine. Contrast with protective winemaking, where contact with oxygen is avoided as much as possible.

Pasteurisation See Kosher.

pH A chemical notation, used in winemaking and evaluation. The pH of a wine is its effective, active acidity – not in volume but by strength or degree. The reading provides a guide to a wine's keepability. The optimum pH in a wine is somewhere between 3.1 and 3.4 – which significantly improves a wine's protection from bacterial spoilage, so permitting it to mature and develop if properly stored.

Racking Drawing or pumping wine off from one cask or tank to another, to leave behind the deposit or lees.

Reductive Wine in an unevolved, unoxidised state is said to be 'reductive'; usually with a tight, sometimes unyielding character. The absence of air (in a bottled wine) or the presence of substantial sulphur dioxide (anti-oxidant) levels, will inhibit both oxidation and reduction processes, which are linked and complementary.

Reverse osmosis A specialised filtration technique, permitted in SA for various purposes, including the removal of water from wine. See also Alcohol.

Skin contact After crushing and de-stemming, white grapes may be left for a period with the juice, remaining in contact with skins (before being moved into the press, from which the grape juice is squeezed). Some winemakers believe the colours and flavours in and under the grape skins should be maximised in this way; others believe extended (or any) contact can lead to coarseness, even bitterness.

Sulphur dioxide (SO_2) Sterilising agent and preservative, near-ubiquitous in winemaking since antiquity, now strictly controlled. In SA, max total SO_2 level for dry wines is 150–160 mg/L; for wines with 5+ g/L sugar it is 200 mg/L; and botrytis-style wines 300 mg/L. Any wine with more than 10 mg/L total SO_2 must carry the warning 'Contains sulphites' (or 'sulfites') on the label.

Sur lie See Lees.

Tannin Vital preservative in wine, derives primarily from the grape skins. Necessary for a red wine's longevity. A young wine's raw tannin can give it a harshness, but no red wine matures into a great one without tannin, which itself undergoes change, combines with other substances and mellows. Tannin leaves a mouth-puckering dryness about the gums, gives 'grip' to a wine. A wooded wine will usually also contain some wood tannin.

Tartrates Harmless crystals formed by tartaric acid precipitating in non-cold-stabilised wine. Because of lack of public acceptance, usually avoided through cold stabilisation.

Terroir Important, controversial (and in SA over-used) French term embracing soil, climate, topography and other elements which constitute the natural environment of a vineyard site and give it a unique character.

Thermovinification/Thermoflash See Kosher.

Unfiltered See Filtration.

Virus or **virused** See Leafroll.

Volatile acid (VA) The part of the acidity which can become volatile. A high reading indicates a wine is prone to spoilage. Recognised at high levels by a sharp, 'hot', vinegary smell. In SA, most wines must by law be below 1.2 g/L of VA; in practice, the majority are well below 1 g/L.

Wholebunch pressing or **cluster pressing** Some SA cellars use this age-old process of placing whole bunches directly in the press and gently squeezing. The more usual method is to de-stem and crush the berries before pressing. Wholebunch pressing is said to yield fresher, cleaner must, and wine lower in polyphenols which, in excess, tend to age wines faster and render them coarser.

Wood-fermented/matured See Barrels.

Yeasts Micro-organisms that secrete enzymes which convert or ferment sugar into alcohol. See Fermentation.

Touring Wine Country

Wine Routes, Trusts & Associations

For localised information about regional official wine routes and wineries, contact these organisations:

Agulhas Wine Triangle ▪ T +27 (0)82-658-3883 (André Morgenthal) ▪ andre@andremorgenthal.com

Breedekloof Wine & Tourism ▪ T +27 (0)23-349-1791 ▪ info@breedekloof.com ▪ www.breedekloof.com

Constantia Wine Route ▪ T +27 (0)83-679-4495 (Carryn Wiltshire) ▪ info@constantiawineroute.com ▪ www.constantiawineroute.com

Darling Wine & Food Experience ▪ +27 (0)22-492-3971 ▪ taste@darlingwine.co.za ▪ www.hellodarling.org.za

Elim Winegrowers See Agulhas Wine Triangle.

Franschhoek See Vignerons de Franschhoek.

Helderberg See Stellenbosch.

Hemel-en-Aarde Wines ▪ T +27 (0)84-581-6023 (Emul Ross) ▪ info@hemelenaardewines.com ▪ www.hemelenaardewines.com

Klein Karoo Wine Route ▪ T +27(0)44-272-7492 / +27 (0)82-214-5910 ▪ F +27 (0)86-528-4055 (Ellen Marais) ▪ info@kleinkaroowines.co.za ▪ www.kleinkaroowines.co.za

Northern Cape Wine Association See Orange River Wine Route

Olifants River Vodacom Wine Route See West Coast Wine Route

Orange River Wine Route ▪ T +27 (0)54-337-8800 (Jorine Viviers) ▪ F +27 (0)54-332-4408 ▪ info@orangeriverwines.com

Paarl Wine Tourism Office ▪ T +27 (0)21-872-4842 ▪ paarlwineroute@dlta.co.za ▪ www.paarlonline.com

Plett Winelands (Plettenberg Bay) ▪ T +27 (0)44-553-4065 ▪ info@plettwinelands.com ▪ www.plettwinelands.com

Robertson Wine Valley ▪ T +27 (0)23-626-3167 / +27 (0)83-701-5404 ▪ manager@robertsonwinevalley.com ▪ www.robertsonwinevalley.com

Santam Swartland Wine & Olive Route ▪ T +27 (0)22-487-1133 ▪ F +27 (0)22-487-2063 ▪ swartlandinfo@westc.co.za ▪ www.swartland-wineandolives.co.za

Stanford Wine Route ▪ T +27 (0)82-572-5856 / +27 (0)82-927-0979 ▪ stanfordwr@gmail.com

Stellenbosch Wine Routes ▪ T +27 (0)21-886-4310 ▪ info@wineroute.co.za ▪ www.wineroute.co.za

Tulbagh Wine Route ▪ T/F +27 (0)23-230-1348/75 ▪ info@tulbaghtourism.co.za ▪ www.tulbaghwineroute.com ▪ www.tulbaghtourism.co.za

Vignerons de Franschhoek ▪ T +27 (0)21-876-2861 ▪ F +27 (0)21-876-2768 ▪ info@franschhoek.org.za ▪ www.franschhoek.org.za

Walker Bay Wine Wander ▪ T +27 (0)28-316-3988 ▪ F +27 (0)86-509-4931 ▪ wine@hermanus.co.za

Wellington Wine Tourism Office ▪ T +27 (0)21-864-1378 ▪ wellingtoninfo@dlta.co.za ▪ www.wellington.co.za

West Coast Wine Route ▪ T +27 (0)83-446-6930 / +27 (0)27-201-3376 ▪ wine@visitnwc.com ▪ www.visitnwc.com

Worcester Wine & Olive Route ▪ T +27 (0)84-245-3922 ▪ info@worcesterwineroute.co.za ▪ www.worcesterwineroute.com

Winelands Tourism Offices

For additional accommodation options, brochures and local advice, contact the information offices and/or publicity associations of the wine areas you plan to visit.

Breedekloof Wine & Tourism ▪ T +27 (0)23-349-1791 ▪ info@breedekloof.com ▪ www.breedekloof.com

Calitzdorp Tourism ▪ T +27 (0)44-213-3775 ▪ tourism@calitzdorp.co.za ▪ www.calitzdorp.org.za

Elgin Valley Tourism ▪ T +27 (0)21-848-9838 ▪ F +27 (0)86-660-0398 ▪ info@elginvalley.co.za ▪ www.elginvalley.co.za

Franschhoek Wine Valley ▪ T +27 (0)21-876-2861 ▪ F +27 (0)21-876-2768 ▪ info@franschhoek.org.za ▪ www.franschhoek.org.za

McGregor Tourism ▪ T +27 (0)23-625-1954 ▪ info@tourismmcgregor.co.za ▪ www.tourism-mcgregor.co.za

Paarl Visitor Information Centre ▪ T +27 (0)21-872-4842 ▪ paarlinfo@dlta.co.za ▪ www.paarlonline.com

Route 62 ▪ info@route62.co.za ▪ www.route62.co.za

Stellenbosch 360 ▪ T +27 (0)21-883-3584 ▪ F +27 (0)21-882-9550 ▪ info@stellenbosch360.co.za ▪ www.stellenbosch.travel

Tulbagh Tourism ▪ T/F +27 (0)23-230-1348/75 ▪ info@tulbaghtourism.co.za ▪ www.tulbaghwineroute.com ▪ www.tulbaghtourism.co.za

Wellington Visitor Information Centre ▪ T +27 (0)21-864-1378 ▪ wellingtoninfo@dlta.co.za ▪ www.wellington.co.za

Worcester Tourism Association ▪ T +27 (0)23-342-6244 / +27 (0)76-200-8742 ▪ info@worcestertourism.com ▪ www.worcestertourism.com

---

Specialist Wine Tours

Below are some specialist wine tour guides operating in Cape Town and the winelands. These are paid entries. The guides supplied information on their services, which was then edited for consistency of style.

African Story Wine Tours Contact Bruce Storey ▪ info@africanstorytours.com ▪ www.africanstorytours.com ▪ English ▪ T +27 (0)73-755-0444 / +27 (0)79-694-7915 ▪ Tour times: about 8.30am-5.30pm daily, pick-up/drop-off in Cape Town city centre ▪ Closed Christmas & New Year ▪ Facebook/Twitter/Flickr/YouTube: African Story Tours ▪ 109 Son Vida Flats, 79 Somerset Rd, Green Point ▪ PO Box 15039, Vlaeberg 8018 ▪ Special/unique facilities & features: private and group tours also offered.

The scheduled tour leaves from Cape Town city centre and is fun but informative, visiting Paarl, Franschhoek and Stellenbosch wine regions. The day includes four wineries and a delicious gourmet lunch, plus pairings of cheese, chocolate and wine. Cellar tours are included. Private and group tours are also offered.

Bikes 'n Wines bookings@bikesnwines.com ▪ www.bikesnwines.com ▪ English, Afrikaans ▪ Facebook: Bikesnwines ▪ Instagram: @bikesnwines ▪ T +27 (0)21-823-8790 ▪ &Bikes Café, 32 Loop Street, Cape Town ▪ Special/unique facilities & features: guided bicycle tours, bicycle rentals, hiking tours and coffee shop.

Cape Town's premier bicycle touring and rental company, Bikes 'n Wines offer guided bike tours in Stellenbosch, Franschhoek, Wellington, Hermanus, Elgin, Grabouw as well as Cape Town and the Cape peninsula, with departures daily. Hiking tours are also available. The &Bikes coffee shop in the trendy heart of Cape Town is the perfect place to plan your winelands excursions.

Cape Fine Wine Tours Contact John Lawrence ▪ john@capefinewinetours.com ▪ www.capefinewinetours.com ▪ English, German, Italian ▪ T +27 (0)82-258-2951 ▪ 41 Loresta, St Andrews Rd, Rondebosch, Cape Town ▪ Special/unique facilities & features: introductions to winemakers.

Cape Fine Wine Tours' winelands excursions are private and customised, and include cellar tours, vineyard walks, barrel tastings and library tastings. Overnight tours are a speciality, and feature fine wines and fine dining.

Caroline's Fine Wine Tours Contact Lieze Norval ▪ carowine6@mweb.co.za ▪ www.carolineswine.com ▪ English, Afrikaans ▪ T +27 (0)21-419-8984 / +27 (0)82-828-5249 ▪ 62 Strand Str, Cape Town ▪ Special/unique facilities & features: winemaker-led wine tours.

Caroline's Fine Wine Tours takes novice or connoisseur winelovers through the greater Cape winelands to discover hidden gems, travelling routes based on clients' particular preferences, interests and tastes. Guide Lieze Norval is a winemaker herself, and thus the tours are extraordinarily informative, as well as enjoyable and memorable. Private tours are a focus, and special interest groups are catered for.

Explore Sideways info@exploresideways.com ▪ www.exploresideways.com ▪ English, French, German, Italian, Dutch, Spanish, Portuguese ▪ T +27 (0)79-607-1978 ▪ Facebook/Twitter: @ ExploreSideways ▪ 401A, 66 Albert Rd, Woodstock Exchange, Woodstock, Cape Town ▪ Special/unique facilities & features: insider access, exclusive experiences, expert wine guides, highly curated, flexible itineraries using industry connections and long-standing relationships.

Explore Sideways is the leader in highly curated, private gourmet food, wine and cultural day tours in the winelands involving industry experts, specialist guides and handcrafted itineraries. Each unique tour offers off-the-beaten track access and can be personalised to suit your interests and palate. Visit the Explore Sideways TripAdvisor page to see our Certificate of Excellence and 5-star reviews.

Go Cape Tours bookings@gocape.co.za ▪ www.gocape.co.za ▪ English, German, Afrikaans ▪ T +27 (0)72-630-7907 ▪ 24 Tarentaal Rd, Stellenbosch, 7600

Go Cape Tours has been crafting private wine tour itineraries across the major regions of the Cape since 2002. Be it focused programmes for wine connoisseurs, intimate days in wine country for honeymoon couples or child-friendly excursions for wine-loving families, Go Cape Tours will design day tours or multi-day packages that showcase the best of SA's amazing winelands.

Gourmet Wine Tours Contact Stephen Flesch ▪ sflesch@iafrica.com ▪ www.gourmetwinetours.co.za ▪ English, Afrikaans ▪ **T +27 (0)21-710-5454 / +27 (0)83-229-3581** ▪ F +27 (0)86-241-1685 ▪ 213 Fernbridge, Alnwick Rd, Diep River, Cape Town ▪ Special/unique facilities & features: tours are led personally by Stephen Flesch, who is passionate and knowledgeable about the Cape winelands.

Explore the scenically stunning winelands of the Western Cape — an epicurean's dream — and experience the best of South African wine and food. Private tours are offered for individuals or small groups, covering the principal wine areas and estates, combined with meals in selected leading restaurants.

Kiff Kombi Tours Contact Drew Campbell ▪ bookings@kiffkombitours.co.za ▪ www.kiffkombitours.co.za ▪ English ▪ Facebook: Kiff Kombi Tours ▪ Twitter: @kiffkombitours ▪ LinkedIn: Kiff Kombi Tours ▪ **T +27 (0)72-213-3888** ▪ 7th Floor, Buitenkloof Studios, 8 Kloof Street, Gardens, Cape Town ▪ Special/unique facilities & features: flexible and extended booking hours, unique combinations of experiences.

Splendour in the Winelands: in this unforgettable excursion, you visit five of the Cape's most high-end wineries, with tastings, cellar tour, biltong pairing, lunch and chocolate pairing included. Wine, Beer & Biltong Safari: South Africa being renowned for both beer and wine, this authentic tour stops at two wine farms and two breweries, and includes tastings, biltong-and-wine pairing and typical South African lunch braai.

La Rochelle Wine & Gourmet Tours Contact Johan Barnard ▪ info@larochelletours.com ▪ www.larochelletours.com ▪ www.franschhoektaxis.co.za ▪ www.franschhoekvineyardhopper.co.za ▪ English, Afrikaans ▪ **T +27 (0)83-301-6774 / +27 (0)82-256-1606** ▪ Twitter/Instagram: @capewinetours ▪ Franschhoek, Stellenbosch, Paarl

Established in 2000 and ranked #1 on TripAdvisor, La Rochelle Wine & Gourmet Tours strive to offer a once-in-a-lifetime experience. Specialist wine guides provide personalised scheduled/private wine tours, with collections from Franschhoek, Stellenbosch and Paarl. Tours cater for everyone, from novices who wish to learn more about wine in a relaxed manner, to connoisseurs with more specific requests. Non-guided driver services are available

for repeat visitors who prefer to follow their own itinerary. Taxi/transfer services are also available.

Luhambo Tours Contact Cedric Jones ▪ bookings@luhambotours.com ▪ www.luhambo-tours.com ▪ English, Afrikaans, German ▪ **T +27 (0)21-551-0467 / +27 (0)82-306-4141** ▪ Twitter: @CapeTownWine ▪ Facebook: @LuhamboTours ▪ 31B Platinum Junction, School Str, Milnerton 7441 ▪ Special/unique facilities & features: specialist wine guides, air-conditioned vehicles, private and customised tours.

Luhambo Tours offers high-quality wine tours in Cape Town, Stellenbosch, Franschhoek, Paarl and the greater Cape winelands. Small, personalised groups with a maximum of seven participants enable Luhambo Tours to provide guests with the ultimate winelands experience. Tours depart daily from Cape Town.

Magical Mystery Tours Contact Gerda Bücker ▪ info@magicalmysterytours.co.za ▪ www.magicalmysterytours.co.za ▪ English, Afrikaans ▪ Facebook: Magical Mystery Tours ▪ **T +27 (0)83-245-1657** ▪ Special/unique facilities and features: private and exclusive chaperone to single tourists or older couples.

Believing that the taste of wine is unique to each individual, Magical Mystery Tours offer exclusive and private excursions designed to help wine novices discover their favourite grape varieties and styles, and start developing their tasting superpowers by learning about their particular palate. Your guide, Hermanus-based Gerda Bücker, also assists more experienced winelovers visit wineries suited to their tastes and preferences while endeavouring to introduce fresh experiences from the Cape's exciting and ever-expanding repertoire.

Nine Yards Travel Contact Maria Steyn ▪ info@nineyardstravel.com ▪ www.nineyardstravel.com ▪ English ▪ **T +27 (0)21-881-3441 / +27 (0)60-998-8426** ▪ F +27 (0)21-881-3426 ▪ Facebook/Twitter/LinkedIn: Nine Yards Travel ▪ Stellenboschkloof Rd, Stellenbosch ▪ Special/unique facilities & features: with strong links to the winelands, via Jordan Wine Estate, Nine Yards Travel places an emphasis on promoting wine tourism and supporting the wine industry.

Nine Yards Travel, derived from the famous Jordan Nine Yards Chardonnay, is a destination management business founded by Gary and Kathy Jordan, also proud owners of Jordan Wine Estate. As the company name implies, Nine Yards Travel covers the full spectrum of client requests and preferences, including guided winelands excursions in partnership with select, experienced and knowledgeable local tour operators. For self-drive visitors, Nine Yards Travel joins with leading wine estates, restaurants and guest lodges to offer customised itineraries in wine-country and beyond. The extensive offering encompasses international and domestic flights, accommodation, transfers, car rental and activities – in short, the whole nine yards.

Percy Tours Hermanus Contact Percy Heywood ▪ travel@percytours.com ▪ www.percytours.com ▪ www.hermanuswinetours.com ▪ English, Afrikaans, some French ▪ **T +27 (0)72-062-8500** ▪ WhatsApp/Instagram/Facebook: Percy Tours Hermanus ▪ PO Box 488, Hermanus 7200 ▪ Special/unique facilities & features: registered and accredited with Cape Wine Academy; Cape Town and Hermanus & Overberg tourism boards; registered tour guides and PDP professional chauffeurs; insured to the highest levels (Passenger Liability and General Liability policies).

Established in 2004, Percy Tours specialise in fully tailor-made, personalised, door-to-door wine tours of Hermanus, Stellenbosch, Franschhoek and the Cape winelands in all their remarkable diversity. A fleet of spacious and luxurious minibuses (and cars) with knowledgeable chauffeur wine-tour guides collect you from your accommodation and supply many comforts on board. The guides have completed Cape Wine Academy courses, so they will discuss many wine topics - and much more - while you sip delicious wines. Flexibility is key, meaning individuals or groups of any size can be hosted. Wine-and-food pairings, and restaurant lunches at scenic wineries are increasingly popular and highly recommended, and Percy Tours can easily advise you and make the necessary reservations. Visit Percy Tours' TripAdvisor page for reviews by many delighted clients.

Plett WINE Tours Contact Monica Botha ▪ bookings@plettwinetours.com ▪ www.plettwinetours.com ▪ English, Afrikaans ▪ **T +27 (0)60-608-8473 / +27 (0)81-270-0658** ▪ Airport Rd, Plettenberg Bay 6600 ▪ PO Box 2041 Plettenberg Bay 6600 ▪ Facebook: @plettwinetours ▪ Twitter: @PlettWineTours ▪ Special/unique facilities & features: tailor-made tours; specialising in Bachelor, Bachelorette and corporate events; air-conditioned vehicles; knowledgeable guides.

Whatever your passion, or your experience of wine, Plett WINE Tours have the experience for you! Sit back and relax in one of their luxury vehicles and allow a knowledgeable team member to be your guide to the numerous joys of the winelands. Whether you're a wine connoisseur or a complete

newbie – or even if your preference is beer – your excursion will be tailor-made to ensure an unforgettable experience. Your guide will return you safely to your accommodation, so there's no drinking and driving.

Sunswept Tours Contact Glynis van Rooyen ▪ glynis@hermanus.co.za ▪ www.sunswept.co.za ▪ English, Afrikaans ▪ **T +27 (0)82-775-8843** ▪ Facebook: Sunswept Tours ▪ PO Box 1216, Hermanus 7200 ▪ Special/unique facilities & features: wine and olive oil tasting specialist, author of wine and extra virgin olive oil guides, extensive winelands contacts, registered tour guide.

Personal, exclusive tours will immerse you in the taste, feel, look, sound and smell of the Cape, with explorations of less-travelled roads leading to cellars and dining rooms of wine-makers and -lovers. Discover hidden gems and extraordinary experiences. Day excursions and longer tours are tailor-made for discerning visitors.

Taste The Cape Travel & Tours Contact Delight Aitken ▪ info@tastethecape.co.za ▪ www.tastethecape.co.za ▪ English ▪ **T +27 (0) 82-090-2278 / +27 (0)71-952-1986** ▪ Special/unique facilities & features: Taste the Cape specialises in distinctive private tours, with small exclusive groups allowing an attentive personal touch to help you experience some of the Cape's lesser-known but internationally acclaimed wines and vineyards.

Taste the Cape's owner, Delight Aitken, is well-travelled as a former executive in the corporate world, and a qualified and registered tour guide for Cape Town and the Western Cape. A wine specialist with a passion for food and golf, she has excellent contacts and relationships with winemakers, vineyards and restaurants. She will work closely with you to prepare a unique itinerary to ensure that your travels and stay in the Cape are memorable. From providing a relaxing day out in the winelands in a luxury air-conditioned vehicle, the Taste the Cape service extends to designing and booking your perfect vacation from start to finish.

Vineyard Ventures (Glen Christie) Contact Glen Christie ▪ vinven@iafrica.com ▪ www.vineyard-ventures.co.za ▪ English, Afrikaans, German; other languages on request ▪ **T +27 (0)21-434-8888 / +27 (0)82-920-2825** ▪ F +27 (0)86-579-9430 ▪ A82 Punta Del Mar, Milton Rd, Sea Point ▪ PO Box 554, Sea Point 8060

Vineyard Ventures creates private, personalised, all-inclusive tours of Cape Town and southern Africa. Glen Christie and her team are wine specialists, and with more than 30 years' experience, their contacts in the industry can't be matched. They deal with the widest range of travel requirements when arranging an itinerary or travel booking tailored to each individual client. Their special expertise is introducing clients to the captivating world of South African wines.

Wine Desk Contact Ligia de Coito ▪ info@winedesk.co.za ▪ www.winedesk.co.za ▪ English, Afrikaans, Dutch, Flemish, French, German, Portuguese (conversational only) & Spanish ▪ **T +27 (0)87-701-3492 / +27 (0)79-513-8145** ▪ PO Box 51460, Waterfront 8002 ▪ Facebook: Wine Desk ▪ Special/unique facilities & features: specialist wine guides/tours.

Wine Desk offers tours tailor-made to your personal interests and preferences, led by specialists in wine and food who are passionate and great story-tellers. Private tours are the focus, but if preferred, you are welcome to join a scheduled small group-tour operating daily (full- and half-day).

Prepare to be educated, have fun and see your expectations exceeded!

Winetour Contact Will Hamann ▪ info@winetour.co.za ▪ www.winetour.co.za ▪ English, Afrikaans ▪ Facebook: Easy Africa Tours ▪ **T +27 (0)21-886-4651 / +27 (0)76-509-2261** ▪ 12 Market Str, Stellenbosch ▪ Special/unique facilities and features: scheduled, fun, all-inclusive tours departing daily from Cape Town and Stellenbosch. Private-, group- and half day-tours available.

Creating memories for international visitors and locals since 1994, and with a base in the picturesque university town of Stellenbosch, Winetour offers all-encompassing experiences around the Cape winelands. Whether you're a novice or connoisseur, young or wise, you'll improve your wine knowledge during a fun day out with plenty of food, photo opportunities and lifelong memories. Qualified and registered guides are top-rated, always up for a good laugh and keen to share their local knowledge.

Restaurants in the Winelands and Cape Town

Below are some dining out options in Cape Town and the winelands. These are paid entries. The venues supplied information on their cuisine, menus and attractions, which was then edited for consistency of style. For more restaurants among the vines, consult the A–Z section of the guide for wineries that offer light lunches, picnics etc. Look for the (♈) symbol beside the individual entries. Unless stated to the contrary, all allow you to bring your own (BYO) wine – the corkage fee is indicated at the start of each entry. Should you wish to know about wheelchair access, please discuss with the relevant restaurant.

INDEX OF RESTAURANTS

BREEDEKLOOF

Bergsig Bistro Bergsig Estate, Route 43, Breërivier ▪ Bistro ▪ Open Mon-Fri 8am-4pm, Sat & pub hols 9am-3pm ▪ Closed Sun, Christmas Day & Good Friday ▪ Booking advised ▪ Children welcome ▪ Major credit cards accepted ▪ No BYO ▪ Owner De Wet Lategan ▪ wine@bergsig.co.za ▪ www.bergsig.co.za ▪ **T +27 (0)23-355-1603**

The Bistro on Bergsig Wine Estate is stylishly decorated and offers a friendly, relaxed dining atmosphere for up to 36 guests. In summer, request a table in the Balcony Room on the terrace and enjoy sweeping views of vineyards and the Bainskloof mountain range; in winter, especially when those peaks become snowcapped, a log fire will keep you cosy. Functions and special occasions can be catered for by prior arrangement. (See also Bergsig Estate in A-Z section.)

CAMPS BAY

Azure The Twelve Apostles Hotel & Spa, Victoria Rd, Camps Bay, Cape Town ▪ Contemporary South African cuisine with global culinary influences ▪ Open daily for breakfast 7am-10.30am, lunch 12.30pm-3.30pm & dinner 6pm-10pm ▪ Booking advised ▪ Children welcome ▪ No BYO ▪ Major credit cards accepted ▪ Owners Tollman family/Red Carnation Hotels ▪ Executive chef Christo Pretorius ▪ restaurants@12apostles.co.za ▪ www.12apostleshotel.com ▪ **T +27 (0)21-437-9000** ▪ F +27 (0)21-437-9062

Azure is the fine-dining restaurant at Cape Town's Twelve Apostles Hotel & Spa, where mesmerising ocean views vie for attention with executive chef Christo Pretorius' creations. Azure offers leisurely breakfasts including fresh oysters and sparkling wine, degustation dinners, food-&-wine-dinners, à la carte lunches and dinners, special tasting menus, a vegan offering and Sunday buffet lunches on the Atlantic-facing terrace — the perfect spot for spectacular sunsets and cocktails. (See also The Twelve Apostles Hotel & Spa in Accommodation section.)

CAPE TOWN CENTRAL

Aubergine Restaurant 39 Barnet Str, Gardens, Cape Town ▪ Classical cuisine with innovative twists & Asian influence ▪ Outdoor terrace ▪ Lunch Wed-Fri 12pm-2pm in summer, dinner Mon-Sat 6pm-10pm ▪ Closed Sun & alternate Mon ▪ Booking advised ▪ Children 5+ welcome ▪ Major credit cards accepted ▪ No BYO ▪ Owner/chef Harald Bresselschmidt ▪ info@aubergine.co.za ▪ www.aubergine.co.za ▪ **T +27 (0)21-465-0000** ▪ F +27 (0)86-671-0835

At this warmly sophisticated restaurant revolving round wine pairing, a 15,000-bottle cellar gives chef/patron Harald Bresselschmidt's keen palate and culinary skills free rein to accent flavour, aroma and texture, whether preparing seafood, prime aged meat or produce from the restaurant's own garden. Degustation menu taste teasers include duck breast with lentils and duck liver emulsion, seafood potpourri with crayfish clouds, venison loin with cocoa tortellini, and lime gastrique with fennel parfait, pineapple and coconut. (See also Auslese Function Venue under Restaurants.)

Auslese Function Venue 115 Hope Str, Gardens, Cape Town ▪ Wines paired with sophisticated menus in classic yet innovative style ▪ Booking advised ▪ Open for pre-booked functions only ▪ Closed Sun & alternate Mon ▪ Children welcome ▪ Major credit cards accepted ▪ BYO by arrangement ▪ Owner/chef Harald Bresselschmidt ▪ info@auslese.co.za ▪ www.auslese.co.za ▪ **T +27 (0)21-461-9727** (reservations/enquiries **T+27 (0)21-465-0000**) ▪ F +27 (0)86-671-0835

At this sister venue to elegant Aubergine, chef/patron Harald Bresselschmidt can tailor any occasion for you, from a private birthday party to a corporate event — or simply when you want the perfect pairing for your wine gems but don't feel like cooking. Custom designed for functions, whether cocktail events with canapés and tapas or sit-down wine-pairing dinners, Auslese also hosts regular music evenings and winemaker events. (See also Aubergine Restaurant under Restaurants.)

Sotano 121 Beach Rd, Mouille Point & 199 Bree Str, Cape Town ▪ Mediterranean, classic tapas ▪ Open daily 7am-10.30pm ▪ Booking advised ▪ Children welcome ▪ Major credit cards accepted ▪ No BYO ▪ Owner Brendon Crew ▪ Executive chef Russel Jalil ▪ info@sotano.co.za ▪ www.sotano.co.za ▪ **T +27 (0)21-433-1757** (Mouille Point) **+27 (0)21-422-0567** (Bree Str)

Mediterranean-inspired food is the star at this vibey eatery in two great City locations, overlooking the famous Mouille Point lighthouse and on trendy foodie hub on Bree Street. Sip bubbly while watching the sunset or indulge in the array of tapas such as calamari a la plancha, beef croquettes and patatas bravas. After work, visit Bree Street's exciting new pintxos bar and help yourself to these delicious small mouthfuls while sipping on a beautiful cocktail or perfectly chilled glass of wine. The rest of Sotano's menu features hearty mains such as the signature paella, and tempting lighter options such as salads and sushi. Or try the spicy Lebanese shakshouka or delicious eggs benedict at brunch. The winelist is well curated.

CONSTANTIA

Jonkershuis Constantia Groot Constantia Wine Estate, Groot Constantia Rd, Constantia, Cape Town ▪ Cape Malay/global cuisine ▪ Summer trading (Sep-Apr) Mon-Sat 9am-9pm & Sun 9am-5pm ▪ Reduced winter trading hours ▪ Breakfast daily 9am-11.30am ▪ Booking essential ▪ Children welcome ▪ Function facilities ▪ Major credit cards & Zapper accepted ▪ No BYO ▪ Owners Chris Coetzee, Tammy Botbyl & Angelina Moepana ▪ info@jonkershuisconstantia.

co.za ▪ www.jonkershuisconstantia.co.za ▪ T +27 (0)21-794-6255 ▪ F +27 (0)86-532-6961

Nestled in the historic core of the Groot Constantia Estate, with sweeping views over the oldest wine-producing vineyards in SA and across the coastline of False Bay, Jonkershuis Constantia offers fireside and al fresco dining on the front lawns, main restaurant or courtyard areas. The menu reflects sustainability and a rich Cape Malay heritage. (See also Groot Constantia Estate in A–Z section.)

ELGIN

South Hill Vineyards 113 Valley Rd, Elgin ▪ Contemporary, bistro, country-style tapas & platters ▪ Open 7 days a week for breakfast & lunch 8am-4pm ▪ Open pub hols ▪ Closed 25/26 December & 1 Jan ▪ Winetasting Mon-Sun 10am-5pm ▪ Booking advised ▪ Children welcome ▪ BYO allowed but not encouraged ▪ Corkage R50/bottle ▪ VISA & MasterCard accepted ▪ Conferences ▪ Weddings/functions ▪ Owners Kevin & Sandra King ▪ info@southhill.co.za ▪ www.southhill.co.za ▪ T +27 (0)21-844-0888

The restaurant in South Hill's gallery space serves breakfasts and lunches of country platters, tapas and a selection of daily specials, with homemade breads and deli items also available. Produce is sourced from the kitchen garden and local suppliers. A variety of artworks is on display, including paintings, small- and large-scale sculptures, photographs, ceramics and mixed-medium works, as well as conceptual work. (See also South Hill Vineyards under Accommodation and in A–Z section.)

FRANSCHHOEK

Franschhoek Cellar Restaurant Franschhoek Cellar, R45/Franschhoek Main Rd, Franschhoek ▪ Bistro cuisine ▪ Open Mon-Sat 10am-6pm & Sun 10am-5pm ▪ Open pub hols ▪ Closed Good Friday, Easter Monday & 25 Dec ▪ Booking advised ▪ Children welcome ▪ VISA & MasterCard accepted ▪ No BYO ▪ Chef Jerry Kennedy ▪ fhcellardoor@dgb.co.za ▪ www.franschhoekcellar.co.za ▪ T +27 (0)21-876-2086

The kitchen opens at 11am and serves light snacks, lunches and cakes throughout the day. Expect hearty and delicious artisanal food using home-grown ingredients and fresh produce from local markets and suppliers in Franschhoek Valley. Chef Jerry Kennedy garners inspiration from the natural goodness of farm life, and expertly combines modern and traditional techniques to produce a menu that is as exciting as it is wholesome. (See also Franschhoek Cellar – Rose & Protea Cottages under Accommodation and Franschhoek Cellar in A–Z section.)

Old Road Wine Co R45, Main Rd, Franschhoek ▪ International fusion cuisine (specialities: flatbreads and sesame-seared tuna) ▪ Open Tue-Sat 11am-9pm, Sun 11am-8pm, pub hols 11am-9pm ▪ Closed Mon, 25 & 31 December ▪ Booking advised ▪ Children welcome (but no kids' menu) ▪ VISA & MasterCard accepted ▪ No BYO ▪ Head chef Reimond van der Walt ▪ info@orwc.co.za ▪ www.oldroadwinecompany.com ▪ T +27 (0)21-271-0379

With a beautiful, historically significant location between Franschhoek's old main road and railway line, the Old Road Wine Co winery and restaurant are colourful visual tributes to the village artisans of the past. Guests enjoy sundowner wines on a deck with views of the Franschhoek mountains, followed by delicious contemporary cuisine prepared under the creative watch of chef Reimond van der Walt. (See also Old Road Wine Co in A–Z section.)

Orangerie @ Le Lude Le Lude Méthode Cap Classique, Bowling Green Ave (Lambrechts Rd), Franschhoek ▪ Contemporary cuisine ▪ Open daily for tastings & canapés 10am-6pm ▪ Tue-Sun for lunch 12pm-4pm & high tea 3pm-6pm ▪ Booking advised ▪ Major credit cards accepted ▪ Owners Nic & Ferda Barrow ▪ Chef Nicolene Barrow ▪ info@lelude.co.za ▪ www.lelude.co.za ▪ T +27 (0)21-100-3464

Orangerie @ Le Lude is a grape throw away from the iconic Huguenot Monument. The interior is spacious and light, with a French flair, while outdoors there is a gorgeous terrace with a magnificent view of the Franschhoek mountains. Fresh herbs and vegetables from the kitchen garden are transformed into dishes that reflect the seasonal abundance. Enjoy a lazy lunch or high tea, or try the carefully paired canapés with Le Lude méthode cap classique. (See also Le Lude Méthode Cap Classique in A–Z section.)

Pierneef à La Motte Restaurant R45, Main Rd, Franschhoek ▪ South African culinary heritage ▪ Open Tue-Sun 11am-5pm ▪ Closed Mon, Christian religious pub hols & a winter break ▪ Booking advised ▪ Children welcome ▪ VISA, MasterCard & AMEX accepted ▪ No BYO ▪ Head chef Eric Bulpitt ▪ Owner Hanneli Rupert-Koegelenberg ▪ pierneef@la-motte.co.za ▪ www.la-motte.com ▪ T +27 (0)21-876-8800

Inspired by La Motte's admiration of South African artist JH Pierneef (1886–1957) and his appreciation of the country's diversity, Pierneef à La Motte Restaurant celebrates SA's culinary heritage. Chef

ic Bulpitt treats guests to a sophisticated à la carte
enu within the restaurant's elegant ambience,
eautifully embraced by tranquil gardens where the
fresco summertime Garden Menu can be enjoyed.
ee also La Motte in A-Z section.)

he Restaurant at La Petite Ferme Pass Rd,
anschhoek ▪ Country contemporary cuisine ▪ Open
aily 12pm-3pm, dinners in season 6.30pm-9pm
Nov-Apr), winter 6.30pm-8.30pm (Fri & Sat) ▪
poking advised ▪ Children welcome ▪ No BYO
Major credit cards accepted ▪ Owners The Nest
state ▪ reception@lapetiteferme.co.za ▪ www.
petiteferme.co.za ▪ T +27 (0)21-876-3016

   The Restaurant at La Petite Ferme Boutique Hotel
Winery offers a culinary experience like no other.
he best and freshest ingredients are sourced locally
 Franschhoek and a combination of international
ethods are used to deliver flavours in a unique
ountry contemporary style. (See also La Petite
erme under Accommodation and La Petite Ferme
Vinery in A-Z section.)

HERMANUS

's Stro@Lavierge R320, Hemel-en-Aarde Valley,
ermanus ▪ Traditional South African steak & local
wists to popular cuisines ▪ Lunch Tue-Sun, dinner
at ▪ Open pub hols ▪ Closed Mon & sometime
 July 2020 but please check with tasting room ▪
ooking advised ▪ Children welcome ▪ Major credit
ards accepted ▪ No BYO ▪ Owner/head chef Bruce
enderson ▪ bruce@lavierge.co.za ▪ www.lavierge.
o.za ▪ T +27 (0)28-313-2007

   At the summit of an infamous cycling hill, with
superb view over Hemel-en-Aarde Valley, B's
tro@Lavierge continues where local legend B's
teakhouse left off, serving exceptional grain-fed
outh African beef, game in season and plenty of
ther traditional - and different - fare to please
ll palates (speciality dish: 350g sirloin with
oraged mushroom sauce). Acclaimed La Vierge
nd Domaine des Dieux wines complement the
xperience. Excellent venue for weddings, corporate
unctions, private parties, product launches and
nore. (See also La Vierge Private Cellar in A-Z
ection.)

Moody Lagoon Benguela Cove Lagoon Wine
state, R43 Walker Bay, Hermanus ▪ South African
uisine ▪ Open for brunch Sat-Sun 10am-11:30am;
unch Mon-Sun 12pm-3pm; dinner Thu-Sat
pm-9pm ▪ Booking advised ▪ Children welcome ▪
Major credit cards accepted ▪ Corkage fee R150 per
ottle ▪ Owner Penny Streeter OBE ▪ Head chef Annie
adenhorst ▪ dine@benguelacove.co.za ▪ www.
enguelacove.co.za ▪ T +27 (0)87-357-0637

   Moody Lagoon restaurant is set in the heart
of Benguela Cove Lagoon Wine Estate, with an
elevated setting and expansive views of the lagoon
and Atlantic Ocean. Namibian-born chef Annie
Badenhorst heads up the kitchen. She is a talented
young woman with a passion for using only the best
fresh produce. Annie and her team create simple yet
creative menu items. Guests can expect a choice of
delicious dishes, paired with sensational Benguela
Cove wines. (See also Lakeside Lodge & Spa under
Accommodation, Nom Nom under Restaurants and
Benguela Cove Lagoon Wine Estate in A-Z section.)

KUILS RIVER

Zevenwacht Restaurant Zevenwacht Wine
Estate, Langverwacht Rd, Kuils River, Cape Town ▪
Contemporary country cuisine ▪ Breakfast Mon-Fri
7am-10am, Sat/Sun & pub hols 8am-11am, lunch
12pm-3pm & dinner 6pm-10pm daily ▪ Booking
advised ▪ Children welcome ▪ Major credit cards
accepted ▪ No BYO ▪ Executive chef Henna von
Wielligh ▪ restaurant@zevenwacht.co.za ▪ www.
zevenwacht.co.za ▪ T +27 (0)21-900-5800 ▪ F +27
(0)21-903-5257

   Decorated with finesse and charm, Zevenwacht
Restaurant is located within a turn-of-the-19th
century Cape Dutch manor house with views of
a tranquil lake and park-like gardens. Open for
breakfast, lunch and dinner seven days a week, the
restaurant offers contemporary country cuisine,
perfectly prepared, as well as a range of picnic
baskets (including a braai basket) served on tree-
shaded lawns sloping down to the lake. (See also
Zevenwacht Country Inn under Accommodation and
Zevenwacht in A-Z section.)

MONTAGU

BluVines Restaurant 12 Long Str, Montagu ▪
Contemporary fusion ▪ Open Fri-Tue 9am-5pm ▪
Closed Wed & Thu (and pub hols falling on those
days) ▪ Booking advised ▪ Children welcome ▪ Major
credit cards accepted ▪ No BYO ▪ Executive chef Sean
Bassett ▪ info@bluvines.co.za ▪ www.bluvines.co.za
▪ T +27 (0)23-614-1663 / (0)23-614-1512

   For business partners Richard Weilers and Swiss
chef Bernhard Hess, BluVines is a passion project that
combines excellent food, quality wine and top-notch
coffee with social development and responsible
job creation. In a glamorously refurbished old
farmhouse, the restaurant offers a gastronomic
encounter unlike any other on Route 62. Bernhard
designed the menu such that unique dishes like
picanha and new-age sashimi happily coexist with
popular favourites like all-day breakfasts, gourmet

burgers and steaming cups of Truth coffee. (See also Mimosa Wines in A-Z section.)

PAARL

Restaurant @ Glen Carlou Simondium Rd, Klapmuts ▪ South African contemporary cuisine ▪ Open Mon-Sun 12pm-4pm incl pub hols ▪ Closed 25 Dec, 1 Jan & Good Friday ▪ Booking advised ▪ Children welcome ▪ Major credit cards accepted ▪ Corkage R60/bottle ▪ Owner Pactolus Consortium ▪ Head chef Johan Stander ▪ restaurant@glencarlou.co.za ▪ www.glencarlou.co.za ▪ **T +27 (0)21-875-5528**

Consistency, expertise and a commitment to always deliver beyond expectations is what Glen Carlou strives for - not just with every bottle of wine but also every plate of food. Guests enjoy innovative dishes while taking in the breathtaking landscape from inside the architect-designed building or the shaded terrace deck. Chef Johan Stander uses the rhythm of the seasons, panoramic views and selection of awarded wines to produce a classic menu with a contemporary twist. (See also Glen Carlou in A-Z section.)

RIEBEEK-KASTEEL

The Royal Restaurant 33 Main Str, Riebeek-Kasteel ▪ Modern South African cuisine ▪ Open daily 7.30am-9.30pm ▪ Booking advised ▪ Children welcome ▪ BYO allowed ▪ Corkage R50 (wine), R75 (sparkling) ▪ Major credit cards & EFT accepted ▪ info@royalinriebeek.com ▪ www.royalinriebeek.com ▪ **T +27 (0)22-448-1378** ▪ F +27 (0)86-545-3559

'More than anything, food should satisfy.' Set in the oldest Hotel in the Cape, The Royal Restaurant uses the latest techniques and best produce, yet remains faithful to its rich heritage and diverse influences. Enjoy lunch or dinner imbued with the flavours of the Swartland and paired with some of the best wines from the region and beyond. Stroll down memory lane with a world-famous gin & tonic from the 150-year-old bar. Life doesn't get much better. 2017 Eat Out Top 500 Award. (See also The Royal Hotel under Accommodation.)

SOMERSET WEST

Nom Nom C/o Main Rd & Coronation Ave, Somerset West ▪ South African cuisine ▪ Open Tue-Sat 10am-10pm ▪ Closed Mon & Sun ▪ Children welcome ▪ Major credit cards accepted ▪ No corkage fee ▪ Open during load shedding ▪ Owner Penny Streeter OBE ▪ Head chef Andrias Ntshangase ▪ nomnom@benguelacove.co.za ▪ www.nomnom.co.za ▪ **T +27 (0)21-851-6197**

Nom Nom has the perfect ingredients for a long lazy lunch or dinner in Somerset West: the freshest local seafood and sushi, and wonderfully tender, succulent steaks, expertly prepared and cooked to order. Plus great cocktails, beers and estate wines. All served in a relaxed vibe that will make you feel like you're on holiday. Award-winning Benguela Cove wines are available at cellardoor prices, and if you prefer to bring your own wines, there is no corkage policy, so feel free. (See also Moody Lagoon under Restaurants, Lakeside Lodge & Spa under Accommodation and Benguela Cove Lagoon Wine Estate in A-Z section.)

The Restaurant at Waterkloof Waterkloof Estate, Sir Lowry's Pass Village Rd, Somerset West ▪ Classic French cuisine with a modern twist ▪ Open daily Mon-Sat 12pm-2pm & 7pm-9pm & Sun 12pm-2pm ▪ Closed Mon & Tue in winter ▪ Closed mid-Jun to mid-July, 25 Dec & 1 Jan ▪ Booking advised ▪ Major credit cards accepted ▪ No BYO ▪ Owner Paul Boutinot ▪ Executive chef Grégory Czarnecki ▪ restaurant@waterkloofwines.co.za ▪ www.waterkloofwines.co.za ▪ **T +27 (0)21-858-1491** ▪ F +27 (0)21-858-1293

High on the slopes of the Schapenberg, Waterkloof's 'restaurant in the sky' is stylishly appointed in a 10-meter-high, all-glass promontory flowing from a slick tasting lounge and gravitational cellar. Here chef Grégory Czarnecki, 2016 Eat Out San Pellegrino Chef of the Year, gives sophisticated contemporary classics a whimsical and polished edge. Showcasing confidence and immense skill, his dishes are not only consistently beautiful to look at, they also beg to be eaten. The Restaurant at Waterkloof received the No 1 Restaurant in South Africa position in the 2018 Mercedes-Benz Eat Out Awards. (See also Waterkloof in A-Z section.)

Vergelegen Vergelegen Wine Estate, Lourensford Rd, Somerset West ▪ **Camphors at Vergelegen** (à la carte/contemporary/global) lunch Wed-Sun 12pm-3pm, dinner Fri & Sat 6.30pm-9pm; **Stables at Vergelegen** (bistro) open Mon-Sun for breakfast 9am-11.30am, lunch 11.30am-3.30pm, tea/coffee & cakes 9am-4pm; **Picnic at Vergelegen** (luxury/elegant picnic) pre-booked baskets Nov-Apr 12.15pm-1.30pm ▪ Estate closed Good Friday, 1 May & 25 Dec ▪ Bookings essential ▪ Picnic & Stables specifically child friendly ▪ Major credit cards accepted ▪ No BYO ▪ Owners Anglo American plc ▪ info@vergelegen.co.za ▪ www.vergelegen.co.za ▪ Camphors Restaurant/Picnic at Vergelegen **T +27 (0)21-847-2131** ▪ Stables **T +27 (0)21-847-2156**

Experience the world of Vergelegen first-hand – from spectacular gardens to arts and culture, historic homestead and ancient camphor trees, winetasting and cellar tours, and restaurants to suit all tastes. The Camphors at Vergelegen signature restaurant, Stables at Vergelegen bistro restaurant and the seasonal luxury Picnic at Vergelegen are only a few of many enjoyable activities at Vergelegen. (See also Vergelegen in A-Z section.)

STELLENBOSCH

Delaire Graff Restaurant Delaire Graff Estate, Helshoogte Pass, Stellenbosch ▪ Bistro-chic cuisine ▪ Open daily (times change according to the season) ▪ Booking advised ▪ Children welcome during lunch only ▪ Major credit cards accepted ▪ Corkage fee ▪ Owner Laurence Graff ▪ reservations@delaire.co.za ▪ www.delaire.co.za ▪ **T +27 (0)21-885-8160**

The dining experience here on the exquisite Delaire Graff Estate is an expression of the seasons, underpinned by the belief that the best food starts with the best ingredients. Classic bistro favourites are served with the finest South African touches, enriched by the restaurant's high-altitude location, affording unique views from the terrace of Simonsberg Mountain and its mantle of vines and olives, down into the steep-sloped Banhoek Valley. Inside, the David Collins Studio designed interiors include curving orange leather banquettes and handpicked art. (See also Indochine Restaurant under Restaurants, Delaire Graff Lodges & Spa under Accommodation and Delaire Graff Estate in A-Z section.)

Eight Spier Wine Farm, R310, Baden Powell Rd, Stellenbosch ▪ Farm-to-table South African fare ▪ Open Tue-Sun (call ahead for opening hours) ▪ Booking advised ▪ Children welcome ▪ Major credit cards accepted ▪ No BYO ▪ eight@spier.co.za ▪ www.spier.co.za ▪ **T +27 (0)21-809-1188** ▪ F +27 (0)21-881-3087

Eight is Spier's farm-to-table eating experience. Like its name, the restaurant is an expression of balance, cycles, harmony, infinity and abundance. The produce used at Eight is either grown on the farm or sourced from nearby farmers. Natural and organic ingredients are preferred and combined to create nourishing, healthy and delicious food. (See also Spier Hotel under Accommodation and Spier in A-Z section.)

Guardian Peak Winery & Grill Guardian Peak Wines, Annandale Rd (off R44), Stellenbosch ▪ Grill house ▪ Open Mon-Sun 12pm-3.30pm, Wed-Sat 6pm-10pm ▪ Closed Good Friday, Easter Sunday, Christmas Day, New Year's Day ▪ Reservations advised ▪ Children welcome ▪ Major credit cards accepted ▪ No BYO ▪ Owner Jean Engelbrecht ▪ Executive chef Willie Mostert ▪ info@guardian-peak.com ▪ www.guardianpeak.com ▪ **T +27 (0)21-881-3899**

A relaxed Stellenbosch winelands experience with vineyard and mountain vistas, appreciated from a wide veranda and adjacent deck. Generous lunches and dinners, with focus on prime-quality beef and venison, enjoyed with Guardian Peak wines, as well as other family wine brands Stellenbosch Reserve, Donkiesbaai and Cirrus. (See also Rust en Vrede Restaurant (Dinner Only)/Winemaker's Lunch under Restaurants, and Guardian Peak Wines and Rust en Vrede Estate in A-Z section.)

Indochine Restaurant Delaire Graff Estate, Helshoogte Pass, Stellenbosch ▪ Asian-influenced cuisine ▪ Open daily for lunch 12pm-2.30pm & dinner 6.30pm-9pm ▪ Booking advised ▪ Children welcome ▪ Major credit cards accepted ▪ Corkage fee ▪ Owner Laurence Graff ▪ Head chef Virgil Kahn ▪ guest.relations@delaire.co.za ▪ www.delaire.co.za ▪ **T +27 (0)21-885-8160**

Indochine is more than a restaurant: it's a fine-dining food theatre, where delicate Asian-inspired flavours come alive and exquisitely balanced dishes are synonymous with vitality, wellness and healthy living. Discover tapas turned into an art form, experience a tea ceremony, savour signature dishes like pork belly and duck. You'll find that all elements are finely crafted to create a multi-sensory dining experience, including the intimate setting, featuring a calming blue and copper colour palette and stunning aerial art installation by Lionel Smit and André Stead, with over 1,000 swallows becoming part of the panoramic views stretching to Table Mountain. (See also Delaire Graff Restaurant under Restaurants, Delaire Graff Lodges & Spa under Accommodation and Delaire Graff Estate in A-Z section.)

Jordan Restaurant Jordan Wine Estate, Stellenbosch Kloof Rd, Stellenbosch ▪ Continental cuisine ▪ Open for lunch Mon-Sun 12pm-2pm & dinner Thu, Fri & Sat 6.30pm-10pm (Oct-Apr) ▪ Closed Mon-Wed & Sat dinner (May-Sep) ▪ Open pub hols ▪ Booking advised ▪ No under 12s at dinner ▪ Major credit cards accepted ▪ BYO allowed if not on winelist (corkage R80, 1 bottle/table) ▪ Owners George & Louise Jardine ▪ Chefs George Jardine & Kyle Burn ▪ restaurant@jordanwines.com ▪ www.jordanwines.com ▪ **T +27 (0)21-881-3612**

Jordan Restaurant has been open for 11 years and continues to serve modern continental food in a relaxed outdoor setting. The menu changes weekly according to the best seasonal produce available. (See also Jordan Luxury Suites under Accommodation and Jordan Wine Estate in A-Z section.)

Lanzerac Wine Estate – Dining No.1 Lanzerac Rd, Stellenbosch ▪ Culinary classics reimagined ▪ Open daily from 7am-midnight ▪ Booking advised ▪ Children welcome ▪ Corkage R80 ▪ Major credit cards accepted ▪ Executive chef Stephen Fraser ▪ fandb@lanzerac.co.za ▪ www.lanzerac.co.za ▪ **T +27 (0)21-887-1132** ▪ F +27 (0)21-887-2310

The Manor Kitchen, the main à la carte restaurant at Lanzerac, opens daily to welcome guests with contemporary and seasonal dishes, served with the estate's own award-winning wines. Generous buffet-style breakfasts, appetising lunches and delicious dinners are served daily on the estate, with gourmet sharing dishes offered on the outdoor terrace of the Taphuis, overlooking the historic manor house. Light meals and platters are served at the Lanzerac Deli. (See also Lanzerac Wine Estate – Hotel under Accommodation and Lanzerac Wine Estate in A-Z section.)

Longtable Restaurant Haskell Vineyards, Annandale Rd, Lynedoch, Stellenbosch ▪ Continental small-plates menu ▪ Open Tue-Sun & pub hols 11:30am-6pm ▪ Fri & Sat sunset dinners till 9pm Nov–Mar ▪ Closed Mon, Christmas Day & New Years' Day ▪ Booking advised ▪ Children welcome ▪ VISA, MasterCard & Diners Club accepted ▪ No BYO ▪ Owner Haskell Vineyards ▪ Head chef Cornelle Minie ▪ longtable@haskellvineyards.co.za ▪ www.haskellvineyards.co.za ▪ **T +27 (0)21-881-3746**

The culinary team on Haskell Vineyards estate has created the relaxing and convivial Longtable venue among the vines, where you can take time to savour unpretentious yet mouthwatering food and wine. Each dish is a fitting match for the multi-award-winning Haskell and Dombeya wines. (See also The Residence at Haskell Vineyards under Accommodation and Haskell Vineyards in A-Z section.)

Peter Falke Wines - Restaurant Annandale Rd, Stellenbosch ▪ Continental cuisine (specialising in cheese platters) ▪ Open Tue-Sun 11am-7pm ▪ Closed Mon, 24/25 December, 30/31 January ▪ Booking advised ▪ Major credit cards accepted ▪ No BYO ▪ Owners Peter & Danielle Falke ▪ tasting@peterfalkewines.co.za ▪ www.peterfalkewines.co.za ▪ **T +27 (0)21-881-3677**

The winery's contemporary Wine Bar, with its elegant furnishings and soft music, is a cosy sanctuary in which to savour a glass of wine and delectable bite to eat. The French-inspired menu, from cheese to charcuterie, nachos and a selection of salads, is complemented by a selection of top wines and beautiful mountain and garden views. The Little Store has a variety of artwork on display, while the lavish lawns add to an unforgettable experience. (See also Peter Falke Wines in A-Z section.)

Rust en Vrede Restaurant (Dinner Only) Rust en Vrede Wine Estate, Annandale Rd (off R44), Stellenbosch ▪ Fine dining ▪ Tue-Sat 6.30pm till late ▪ Closed Good Friday, Christmas Day, New Year's Day ▪ Reservations essential ▪ Major credit cards accepted ▪ No BYO ▪ Owner Jean Engelbrecht ▪ Executive chef Fabio Daniel ▪ dining@rustenvrede.com ▪ www.rustenvrede.com ▪ **T +27 (0)21-881-3757**

Contemporary fine dining within Rust en Vrede Wine Estate's historic former cellar (also a national monument), where the front-and-centre kitchen, fine stemware and bespoke crockery enhance creative four- and six-course menus. A comprehensive winelist carries wide local and international selections, leaving little to be desired. (See also Guardian Peak Winery & Grill and Rust en Vrede Restaurant Winemaker's Lunch under Restaurants, and Guardian Peak Wines and Rust en Vrede Estate in A-Z section.)

Rust en Vrede Winemaker's Lunch Rust en Vrede Wine Estate, Annandale Road (off R44), Stellenbosch ▪ Set menu ▪ Mon-Sat 12pm-3pm, Sun seasonal - call to enquire ▪ Closed Good Friday, Easter Sunday, Christmas Day, New Year's Day ▪ No reservations; first come, first served ▪ Major credit cards accepted ▪ No BYO ▪ Owner Jean Engelbrecht ▪ Executive chef Rommel Rodriguez ▪ sales@rustenvrede.com ▪ www.rustenvrede.com ▪ **T +27 (0)21-881-3881**

Comprising a two-item set menu, salmon and steak, historic Stellenbosch estate Rust en Vrede's lunch experience is a no-fuss version of its celebrated fine-dining dinner. Tables set under ancient oaks suggest a laid-back approach, yet the linen is classily crisp and white, the cookery flawless and the service impeccable. Enjoy your choice of meal with a glass of red or white. (See also Guardian Peak Winery & Grill and Rust en Vrede Restaurant (Dinner Only) under Restaurants, and Guardian Peak Wines and Rust en Vrede Estate in A-Z section.)

The Restaurant at Neethlingshof Neethlingshof Wine Estate, Polkadraai Rd, Stellenbosch ▪ Contemporary bistro-style South African cuisine & light meals ▪ Open Mon, Tue & Thu 9am-5pm; Wed, Fri & Sat 9am-9pm, un 12pm-4pm ▪ Open pub hols & Christmas lunch ▪ Closed Christmas Eve & Good Friday ▪ Booking advised ▪ Children welcome ▪ Major credit cards accepted ▪ No BYO ▪ Owner Stone Pine Wines (Pty) Ltd ▪ Head chef Brendan Stein ▪ restaurant@neethlingshof.co.za ▪ www.neethlingshof.co.za ▪ T +27 (0)21-883-8966 / +27 (0)81-353-2039

The Restaurant at Neethlingshof Wine Estate is situated in the original manor house, built in 1814. The history-steeped setting, complete with ancient oaks, is mirrored in the menu, with its emphasis on long-time-favourite South African ingredients and dishes, presented bistro-style with contemporary touches. Springbok shank, ostrich fillet, grilled miso aubergine and gourmet burgers are among the choices, served (weather permitting) on the terrace with vistas of manicured gardens, vineyards and mountains. The Restaurant proudly supports StreetSmart SA. (See also Neethlingshof Estate in A-Z section.)

Warwick Wine Estate - Gourmet Picnics Warwick Wine Estate, R44 between Stellenbosch & Paarl ▪ Gourmet picnics ▪ Open Mon-Sun 9am-5pm ▪ Booking advised ▪ Children welcome ▪ Major credit cards accepted ▪ No BYO ▪ Owners Eileses Capital ▪ Executive chef Mariaan Jacobs▪ visit@warwickwine.com ▪ www.warwickwine.com ▪ T +27 (0)21-884-4410

Warwick has a well-deserved reputation for its gourmet picnics, which combine the highest-quality ingredients from locally sourced artisan suppliers. Vegetarian and vegan options are available too, and prepared with love. These delicious offerings are perfect for that special occasion or just a lazy day out in wine country. Gourmands rave about the picnics and keep coming back — you will too. For families, there are delicious children's picnics designed by parents who 'get it'. (See also Warwick Wine Estate in A-Z section.)

WORCESTER

Overhex Winery & Bistro R60 between Worcester and Robertson ▪ Bistro specialising in pizzas ▪ Open daily (including pub hols) 9.30am-3.30pm ▪ Booking advised ▪ Children welcome ▪ Major credit cards accepted ▪ No BYO ▪ Owner Gerhard van der Wath ▪ functions@overhex.com ▪ www.overhex.com ▪ T +27 (0)23-347-5012

Situated on the scenic Route 60 between Worcester and Robertson, the delectably different Overhex Winery & Bistro has become a popular meeting place for friends and families, colleagues and business associates. Stylish, with a touch of Old World charm, vivacious and trendy, with typical Breede River Valley warmth and hospitality, Overhex Winery & Bistro offers bespoke breakfasts, artisanal pizzas, designer burgers and home-style meals - all freshly prepared using hand-picked ingredients and served with panache. The award-winning wines will please the most fastidious connoisseur. (See also Overhex Wines International in A-Z section.)

Accommodation in the Winelands and Cape Town

Featured below are some guest lodges, hotels, country inns, B&Bs and self-catering cottages in the winelands, many of them on wine farms (look for the ⌂ symbol beside the individual entries in the A–Z section of this guide). These are paid entries. The venues supplied information on their facilities and attractions, which was then edited for consistency of style. Unless stated to the contrary, all speak English and Afrikaans, have parking and gardens/terraces. Rates are for standard double rooms unless otherwise specified – for example per person (pp) or breakfast included (B&B). Tourism Grading Council of South Africa (TGCSA) ratings where provided. Should you wish to know about wheelchair access, please discuss with the relevant venue.

INDEX OF ACCOMMODATION

CALITZDORP

The Retreat at Groenfontein Groenfontein Rd, district Calitzdorp (20km from Calitzdorp, off Route 62) ▪ TGCSA 3 & 4-star guest house; AA Quality Assured highly recommended ▪ Rates on request ▪ VISA & MasterCard accepted ▪ Restaurant (problem diets catered for - advise when booking) ▪ Pool ▪ Children & pets welcome ▪ Mountain biking & walking trails ▪ Birding ▪ River with rock pools ▪ Secure parking ▪ Laundry service ▪ Safe ▪ Wifi in lounge ▪ French, German, Italian & Swedish spoken ▪ Owner Marie Holstensson ▪ info@groenfontein.com ▪ www.groenfontein.com ▪ **T +27 (0)44-213-3880 / (0)44-213-3168** ▪ F +27 (0)86-271-5373

A consistent award winner, this welcoming, personally run, 3- and 4-star Victorian farmhouse offers both standard and garden rooms. You'll enjoy personal pampering, hearty breakfasts and tasty dinners. The inviting lounge and dining room overlook sweeping lawns and the majestic Swartberg. Take leisurely walks, challenging trails, explore the rock pools in the river, bird-watch or simply laze at the pool, soaking up the peace and silence.

CAMPS BAY

The Twelve Apostles Hotel & Spa Victoria Rd, Camps Bay, Cape Town ▪ TGCSA 5-star hotel ▪ 70 rooms ▪ Best available seasonal rates B&B ▪ Major credit cards accepted ▪ Azure and Café Grill restaurants with Sushi By 12A sushi bar ▪ Conferences ▪ Weddings/functions ▪ Spa ▪ Gym ▪ Hydrotherapy pools ▪ Walks/hikes ▪ Birding ▪ Wine, gin & craft beer tasting ▪ Secure parking ▪ Shuttle service ▪ Laundry service ▪ Air-conditioning ▪ TV ▪ DStv ▪ DVD player ▪ Wifi ▪ Safe ▪ French, Mandarin & Dutch spoken ▪ Owners Tollman family/Red Carnation Hotels ▪ reservations1@12apostles.co.za ▪ www.12apostleshotel.com ▪ **T +27 (0)21-437-9000** ▪ F +27 (0)21-437-9062

Award-winning Twelve Apostles Hotel & Spa is situated on Cape Town's most scenic route, flanking Table Mountain National Park and overlooking the Atlantic Ocean. Part of the family-run Red Carnation Hotel Collection, it offers 55 deluxe guest rooms and 15 luxurious suites, not to mention a holistic spa and private cinema, with Azure Restaurant serving up breathtaking views in addition to legendary local cuisine. (See also Azure under Restaurants.)

ELGIN

South Hill Vineyards 113 Valley Rd, Elgin ▪ TGCSA 4-star self-catering (Exclusive Category) ▪ Rates from R1,330 per room B&B, exclusive use of the Guest House (6 rooms, self-catering) from R6,660 per night, Pumphouse Cottage (sleeps 2) from R1,730 per night B&B ▪ Major credit cards accepted ▪ Restaurant ▪ Conferences ▪ Weddings/functions ▪ Jacuzzi (Pumphouse Cottage) ▪ Pool (Guest House) ▪ Fireplace ▪ Mountain biking ▪ Walks/hikes ▪ Birding ▪ Fishing ▪ Boule court ▪ Winetasting ▪ TV (Guest House) ▪ DStv ▪ Wifi ▪ stay@southhill.co.za ▪ www.southhill.co.za ▪ **T +27 (0)21-844-0888**

South Hill Guest House is a six-bedroom, en suite luxury villa with full guest amenities. Rooms have vineyard, orchard or garden views, with mountain ranges in the distance. The secluded, self-contained Pumphouse Cottage has a private courtyard, overlooks one of the farm dams and is surrounded by indigenous fynbos gardens and vineyards. Whether you are visiting for a wedding, weekend, holiday or just a complete chill-out in the week, South Hill has much to offer! (See also South Hill Vineyards under Restaurants and in A-Z section.)

FRANSCHHOEK

Franschhoek Cellar – Rose & Protea Cottages Franschhoek Cellar, R45, Franschhoek Main Rd, Franschhoek ▪ 2 cottages sleeping 4 pax per cottage ▪ R2,000-R2,500 per cottage ▪ VISA & MasterCard accepted ▪ Restaurant ▪ Conference facilities ▪ Weddings/functions ▪ Winetasting ▪ Secure parking ▪ Air-conditioning ▪ Fireplace ▪ Safe ▪ TV ▪ DStv ▪ Wifi ▪ accommodation@franschhoekcellar.co.za ▪ www.franschhoekcellar.co.za ▪ **T +27 (0)21-876-2086**

Ideal for winelovers wanting to be close to the action, Rose and Protea cottages are situated beside the production cellar on the premises in the heart of Franschhoek. Both cottages have been remodelled to match the contemporary-chic styling of the visitor venue, which is also on the property. The self-catering homes each sleep four adults and have been fitted with all modern conveniences to ensure you have a relaxing stay in one of South Africa's food capitals. (See also Franschhoek Cellar Restaurant under Restaurants and Franschhoek Cellar in A-Z section.)

La Petite Ferme Pass Road, Franschhoek ▪ TGCSA 4-star boutique hotel ▪ 9 rooms ▪ Rates from R3,314-R10,230 per room ▪ Breakfast included ▪ Major credit cards accepted ▪ Restaurant ▪ Vine Orientation tours ▪ Winetasting ▪ Secure parking ▪ Air-conditioning ▪ Ceiling fans ▪ Fireplace ▪ Under-floor heating ▪ Safe ▪ TV ▪ DStv ▪ Wifi ▪ Some rooms have plunge pools ▪ Owners The Nest Estate ▪ accommodation@lapetiteferme.co.za ▪ www.lapetiteferme.co.za ▪ **T +27 (0)21-876-3016**

La Petite Ferme Boutique Hotel & Winery offers the perfect combination of private, contemporary country-style accommodation, luxury amenities and heart-warming hospitality. Situated on the Oliphants Pass high on the Middagkrans Mountain slopes, the Manor House and Vineyard Suites each have all the creature comforts you'd expect plus spectacular views of Franschhoek Valley – a picture-perfect paradise in which to relax. (See also The Restaurant at La Petite Ferme under Restaurants and La Petite Ferme Winery in A-Z section.)

Leeu Estates Dassenberg Rd, Franschhoek ▪ TGCSA 5-star boutique hotel ▪ 17 rooms ▪ Rates from R9,200 per room per night ▪ Breakfast included ▪ All major credit cards accepted ▪ 1 hour from Cape Town ▪ Restaurant ▪ Spa ▪ Gym ▪ Swimming pool ▪ Walks/hikes ▪ Winetasting ▪ Shuttle service ▪ Secure parking ▪ Laundry service ▪ Fully air-conditioned ▪ Ceiling fans & fireplaces (selected rooms) ▪ Under-floor heating ▪ TV ▪ DStv ▪ Safe ▪ Wifi ▪ Owner Leeu Collection ▪ reservations@leeucollection.com ▪ www.leeucollection.com ▪ **T +27 (0)21-492-2222**

One of three properties in Leeu Collection Franschhoek, Leeu Estates is an exclusive boutique hotel and winery in scenic Franschhoek Valley, just an hour from Cape Town. The focal point of this elegant and sophisticated private hideaway is the refurbished 19th-century manor house with its six guest rooms, dining room, reading room and living room. Adjacent is Leeu Spa & Gym, plus five spacious cottages scattered among gardens, oak trees and vineyards. (See also Leeu House/Le Quartier Français in Accommodation section.)

Leeu House 12 Huguenot Str, Franschhoek ▪ TGCSA 5-star boutique hotel ▪ 12 rooms ▪ Rates from R7,800 per room per night ▪ Breakfast included ▪ All major credit cards accepted ▪ 1 hour from Cape Town ▪ Restaurant ▪ Swimming pool ▪ Winetasting ▪ Shuttle service ▪ Secure parking ▪ Laundry service ▪ Fully air-conditioned ▪ Ceiling fans (selected rooms) ▪ Under-floor heating ▪ TV ▪ DStv ▪ Safe ▪ Wifi ▪ Owner Leeu Collection ▪ reservations@leeucollection.com ▪ www.leeucollection.com ▪ **T +27 (0)21-492-2222**

Leeu House is an oasis of tranquillity and comfort in the heart of Franschhoek, one of the world's great food and wine destinations, a mere hour from Cape Town. Leeu House's special appeal is its country ambience despite being located on the village's vibrant main street, very near award-winning restaurants, art galleries and boutiques. The hotel's stylish interiors are a contemporary take on Franschhoek's Cape Dutch heritage, with its strong French influences. (See also Leeu Estates/Le Quartier Français in Accommodation section.)

Le Quartier Français Cnr Wilhelmina & Berg Str, Franschhoek ▪ TGCSA 5-star ▪ 32 rooms ▪ Rates from R8,200 per room per night ▪ All major credit cards accepted ▪ 1 hour from Cape Town ▪ Restaurant ▪ Spa ▪ Gym ▪ Swimming pool ▪ Winetasting ▪ Shuttle service ▪ Laundry service ▪ Fully air-conditioned ▪ Ceiling fans & fireplaces (selected rooms) ▪ Under-floor heating ▪ TV ▪ DStv ▪ Safe ▪ Wifi ▪ Owner Leeu Collection ▪ reservations@leeucollection.com ▪ www.leeucollection.com ▪ **T +27 (0)21-492-2222**

Tucked away in the heart of Franschhoek, just an hour from Cape Town, Le Quartier Français is an exclusive and romantic 32-room boutique hotel with two separate villas, revered culinary landmark and member of Leeu Collection. This peaceful auberge's ideal location makes it easy to wander out from its scented gardens to explore the quaint charms of the village and the wonders of the winelands beyond. (See also Leeu Estates/Leeu House in Accommodation section.)

HERMANUS

High Season Farm Cottages Hemel-en-Aarde Valley, Hermanus ▪ TGCSA 4-star self-catering ▪ Rates from R360 pp (low season) to R500 pp (high season) ▪ 8 cottages ▪ VISA, MasterCard, Diners Club & Amex accepted ▪ Weddings/functions ▪ Pool ▪ Mountain biking ▪ Walks/hikes ▪ Birding ▪ Cellar tours ▪ Winetasting ▪ Secure parking ▪ Laundry service ▪ Air-conditioning ▪ Ceiling fans ▪ Fireplace ▪ Underfloor heating ▪ Safe ▪ TV ▪ DStv ▪ Wifi ▪ info@highseasonfarm.co.za ▪ www.highseasonfarm.co.za ▪ **T +27 (0)21-200-2514**

High Season Farm is ideally located near the whale-watching hotspot of Hermanus, and within walking distance of all the top pinot noir vineyards of the Upper Hemel-en-Aarde Valley. Beautifully decorated 4-star farm cottages are ideal for groups or couples travelling to this internationally hailed and wonderfully scenic wine region.

KUILS RIVER

Zevenwacht Country Inn Zevenwacht Wine Estate, Langverwacht Rd, Kuils River ▪ TGCSA 4-star country house (Country Inn honeymoon and luxury suites only) ▪ Total 38 rooms: 1 honeymoon suite (deluxe), 12 Country Inn luxury suites, 7 x 3-bedroom cottages, 1 x 4-bedroom self-catering chalet ▪ Low season from R905 pps B&B, high season from R1,145 pps B&B ▪ Major credit cards accepted ▪ Restaurant ▪ Conferences ▪ Weddings/functions ▪ Spa ▪ Sauna ▪ Pool ▪ Tennis court ▪ Mountain biking ▪ Walks/hikes ▪

Birding ▪ Cellar tours ▪ Winetasting ▪ Secure parking ▪ Shuttle service ▪ Laundry service ▪ Air-conditioning ▪ TV ▪ DStv ▪ Wifi ▪ Safe ▪ Owners Harold & Denise Johnson ▪ reservations@zevenwacht.co.za ▪ www.zevenwacht.co.za ▪ **T +27 (0)21-900-5700** ▪ F +27 (0)21-906-1570

Meaning 'Seven Expectations', the name Zevenwacht encapsulates several delights that await visitors at this historic estate. Choose between the Country Inn, offering four-star accommodation in luxuriously appointed, air-conditioned suites; three-bedroom Vineyard Cottages; or self-catering four-bedroom chalet. (See also Zevenwacht Restaurant under Restaurants and Zevenwacht in A-Z section.)

PAARL

Under Oaks Guest House Noord Agter Paarl Rd, Paarl ▪ TGCSA 4-star country house ▪ Rates from R1,100 single/R1,350 double (low season) to R1,565/R1,970 (high season), breakfast included ▪ 7 bedrooms ▪ VISA, MasterCard & Amex accepted ▪ Pizzeria ▪ Conference facilities ▪ Pool ▪ Winetasting ▪ Secure parking ▪ Air-conditioning ▪ Safe ▪ TV ▪ DStv ▪ Wifi ▪ Coffee & tea station ▪ Iron plus ironing board ▪ Owners The Britz family ▪ accommodation@underoaks.co.za ▪ www.underoaks.co.za ▪ **T +27 (0)21-869-8535 ext 1**

Four-star graded, newly built and limited to seven spacious en suite rooms, the suites on working farm Under Oaks are stylish and luxurious, with personalised designs and decor ensuring exclusivity in a vine-fringed, tranquil setting. All suites feature a private patio and uplifting vistas of vineyards and mountains. Historic Paarl town and the Cape winelands' myriad allures are within easy reach. (See also Under Oaks in A-Z section.)

RIEBEEK-KASTEEL

The Royal Hotel 33 Main Str, Riebeek-Kasteel ▪ AA Superior Hotel ▪ 1 Grand Garden room: low season (16 May-30 Sep) R995 pp-R1,990 pp, high season (1 Oct-15 May) R1,245 pp-R2,490 B&B; 9 Standard rooms: low season from R845-R1,690 pps B&B, high season R1,245 pp-R2,190 B&B; 4 King suites: low season R1,495 pp-R2,990, high season R1,625 pp-R3,250 B&B ▪ Major credit cards & EFT accepted ▪ The Royal Restaurant ▪ Conferences ▪ Weddings/functions ▪ Pool ▪ Laundry service ▪ Air-conditioning ▪ Under-floor heating ▪ Safe ▪ TV ▪ DStv ▪ DVD player ▪ Free wifi ▪ Owner Robert Brendel ▪ info@royalinriebeek.com ▪ www.royalinriebeek.com ▪ **T +27 (0)22-448-1378** ▪ F +27 (0)86-545-3559

Located in Riebeek-Kasteel, the Royal Hotel is the Western Cape's oldest and most colonial hotel. It offers beautiful and luxurious accommodation with great valley and Kasteelberg views from the garden, swimming pool and pool deck. Listed in 2006 among the government's 50 most fabulous places to visit in South Africa, the hotel boasts a 150-year-old bar and the longest stoep south of the Limpopo. (See also The Royal Restaurant under Restaurants.)

ROBERTSON

Windfall Guest Cottages Retreat, Agterkliphoogte Valley, Robertson ▪ Self-catering guest cottages ▪ Rates from R400 pp sharing (low season), R500 pp sharing (high season) ▪ 5 cottages ▪ VISA & MasterCard accepted ▪ Pool ▪ Mountain biking ▪ Walks/hikes ▪ Fishing ▪ Children welcome ▪ Winetasting on request ▪ Air-conditioning ▪ TV ▪ DStv ▪ info@windfallwine.co.za ▪ www.windfall-wine.co.za ▪ **T +27 (0)83-320-8473**

Splashes of bright, inviting colour in a quiet Robertson valley, the individually decorated self-catering cottages on Windfall farm will lift your spirit just by looking at them! There are different units for families and couples, all with own braai area, along with refreshing pool to cool off in and variety of kids' activities on offer. It's the perfect getaway to recharge, with the bonus of handcrafted, award-winning Windfall wines and brandy to taste by arrangement. (See also Windfall Wine Farm in A-Z section.)

SEDGEFIELD

Lakeside Lodge & Spa 3 Lakeside Dr, Swartrivier, Sedgefield ▪ TGCSA 4-star boutique hotel ▪ Rates on request ▪ 9 bedroom suites ▪ VISA & MasterCard accepted ▪ Weddings/functions ▪ Spa ▪ Pool ▪ Jacuzzi ▪ Children welcome ▪ Walks/hikes ▪ Birding ▪ Fishing ▪ Winetasting ▪ Secure parking ▪ Shuttle service ▪ Laundry service ▪ Pontoon cruises ▪ Air-conditioning ▪ In-room safe ▪ DStv ▪ iPod docking station ▪ Wifi ▪ 2016 & 2018 Sanlam Top Destination and 2017 LTG Africa & Middle East awards ▪ Owner Penny Streeter OBE ▪ info@lakesidelodge.co.za ▪ www.lakesidelodge.co.za ▪ **T +27 (0)44-343-1844**

Lakeside Lodge & Spa is a 4-star boutique hotel with one of the highest ratings from the Tourism Grading Council of South Africa (TGCSA). The lodge has nine luxurious bedroom suites, all with breathtaking views of the Swartvlei Lagoon. Guests can look forward to luxury accommodation and various water sport activities on the beautiful lake. (See also Moody Lagoon and Nom Nom under

Restaurants, and Benguela Cove Lagoon Wine Estate in A-Z section.)

STELLENBOSCH

Delaire Graff Lodges & Spa Helshoogte Pass, Stellenbosch ▪ Villa, Owners, Presidential, Superior, Luxury & Deluxe lodges ▪ Rates from R8,100 pps ▪ Breakfast included ▪ VISA, MasterCard & international money transfer accepted (Amex & Diners Club cards not accepted) ▪ Delaire Graff & Indochine restaurants ▪ Functions ▪ Spa ▪ Sauna ▪ Gym ▪ Pool ▪ Jacuzzi ▪ Mountain biking ▪ Walks/hikes ▪ Cellar tours ▪ Winetasting ▪ Secure parking ▪ Shuttle service ▪ Helipad ▪ In-room tea & coffee facilities ▪ Laundry service ▪ Air-conditioning ▪ Fireplace ▪ Under-floor heating ▪ Safe ▪ TV ▪ DStv ▪ DVD player ▪ Wifi ▪ Condé Nast Traveller Gold List - Top 20 Best Hotels in the World (Feb 2018) ▪ guest.relations@delaire.co.za, lodge.reservations@delaire.co.za ▪ www.delaire. co.za ▪ **T** +27 (0)21-885-8160

A magnificent Cape winelands property flanked by majestic mountain ranges, Delaire Graff Estate is a unique destination offering exceptional experiences born of exclusive lodges & villa, a destination spa, two outstanding restaurants, state-of-the-art winery and wine lounge, and luxury boutiques. (See also Delaire Graff Restaurant and Indochine Restaurant under Restaurants and Delaire Graff Estate in A-Z section.)

Jordan Luxury Suites Jordan Wine Estate, Stellenbosch Kloof Rd, Stellenbosch ▪ Klink Award best accommodation in a wine estate ▪ 13 rooms ▪ Rates on request (breakfast included) ▪ Major credit cards accepted ▪ Restaurant ▪ Conference facilities ▪ Weddings/functions ▪ Cellar tours ▪ Winetasting ▪ Secure parking ▪ Laundry service ▪ Air-conditioning ▪ Fireplace ▪ Safe ▪ TV ▪ DStv ▪ Wifi ▪ English & Afrikaans spoken ▪ Owners Jordan family ▪ accommodation@jordanwines.com ▪ www.jordanwines. com ▪ **T** +27 (0)21-881-3048

Tucked away close to the wine cellar, restaurant and bakery, the new luxury suites on Jordan Wine Estate offer panoramic views of the vineyards and Stellenbosch mountains. Each suite has spacious interiors that are individually designed and uniquely decorated, making Jordan Luxury Suites an ideal choice for a perfect winelands getaway. (See also Jordan Restaurant under Restaurants and Jordan Wine Estate in A-Z section.)

Laibach Vineyards Lodge Laibach Vineyards, R44, Klapmuts Rd, Stellenbosch ▪ TGCSA 4-star self-catering apartments ▪ 5 apartments ▪ R800 pps, single R1,350 ▪ Major credit cards accepted ▪ Pool ▪ Walks/hikes ▪ Winetasting ▪ Secure parking ▪ Ceiling fans ▪ TV ▪ DStv ▪ Wifi ▪ Safe ▪ Owners Laibach family from Germany ▪ info@laibachwines.com ▪ www. laibachwines.com ▪ **T** +27 (0)21-884-4511 ▪ F +27 (0)86-665-2839

Laibach Vineyards invites you to its lodge in the middle of a sea of organic vines. At this 50-hectare working wine farm, just a few kilometres north of Stellenbosch, five spacious and comfortable self-catering apartments are offered, each with a private en suite bathroom, small but fully furnished kitchen, LCD satellite TV and wifi, and deck with magnificent Table Mountain views. (See also Laibach Vineyards in A-Z section.)

Lanzerac Wine Estate – Hotel No.1 Lanzerac Rd, Stellenbosch ▪ TGCSA 5-star boutique hotel ▪ 53 rooms & suites ▪ Seasonal rates on request ▪ Major credit cards accepted ▪ Main restaurant, cigar bar, pub & casual deli ▪ Conferences ▪ Weddings/ functions ▪ Day spa ▪ Sauna ▪ Gym ▪ Pool ▪ Jacuzzi ▪ Helipad ▪ Horse riding ▪ Mountain biking ▪ Walks/ hikes ▪ Birding ▪ Cellar tours ▪ Winetasting on-site ▪ Secure parking ▪ Shuttle service ▪ Laundry service ▪ Air-conditioning ▪ Under-floor heating ▪ TV ▪ DStv ▪ Wifi ▪ In-room tea & coffee facilities ▪ Safe ▪ info@ lanzerac.co.za ▪ www.lanzerac.co.za ▪ **T** +27 (0)21-887-1132 ▪ F +27 (0)21-887-2310

Steeped in history, and nestled in Stellenbosch's idyllic Jonkershoek Valley, 328-year-old Lanzerac is synonymous with Old World charm and rich Cape heritage. Staying in exquisitely styled rooms and suites, blending period grandeur with contemporary style, guests are indulged with warm and passionate service, and the best wine and cuisine – in short, the finest hospitality the Cape winelands has to offer. (See also Lanzerac Wine Estate - Dining under Restaurants and Lanzerac Wine Estate in A-Z section.)

Marianne Wine Estate & Guest Apartments Valley Rd, off R44, Klapmuts, Stellenbosch ▪ TGCSA 4-star guest house ▪ Rates from R2,700 (low season) to R3,900 (high season) including breakfast ▪ 16 bedrooms ▪ VISA, MasterCard, Diners Club & AMEX accepted ▪ The Floréal Brasserie ▪ Conference facilities ▪ Weddings/ functions ▪ Pool ▪ Boule court ▪ Children welcome ▪ Winetasting ▪ Secure parking ▪ Shuttle service ▪ Laundry service ▪ Air-conditioning ▪ Under-floor heating ▪ Safe ▪ TV ▪ DStv ▪ Wifi ▪ English & French spoken ▪ Owners Dauriac family ▪ info@mariannewinefarm.co.za ▪ www.mariannewines.com ▪ **T** +27 (0)21-875-5040

Scenic Marianne Wine Estate on the slopes of Simonsberg Mountain is fringed by pine trees and bordered by a private game reserve. The estate's Cape Dutch-inspired Manor House and The Lofts are tucked away among citrus orchards, gardens and vineyards. L'Ermitage, the most recent addition to the accommodation portfolio, is a newly renovated villa with six delightful bedrooms encircled by vines. (See also Marianne Wine Estate in A-Z section.)

Spier Hotel Spier Hotel R310, Baden Powell Rd, Stellenbosch ▪ 4-star hotel ▪ 153 rooms ▪ From R3,250 per room B&B ▪ Major credit cards accepted ▪ Eight restaurant ▪ Conferences ▪ Weddings/functions ▪ Spa ▪ Pool ▪ Mountain biking ▪ Walks/hikes ▪ Segway tours, Eagle Encounters & self-guided VoiceMap walks ▪ Birding ▪ Winetasting ▪ Secure parking ▪ Shuttle service ▪ Laundry service ▪ Air-conditioning ▪ Ceiling fans ▪ TV ▪ DStv ▪ Wifi ▪ Safe ▪ TripAdvisor Hall of Fame ▪ Dutch & French spoken ▪ Vadas Smokehouse & Bakery ▪ Spier Shop ▪ info@spier. co.za ▪ www.spier.co.za ▪ **T +27 (0)21-809-1100** ▪ F +27 (0)21-881-3087

Village-style buildings, lush green lawns and spacious rooms beside the calming Eerste River are the defining characteristics of the 4-star Spier Hotel. The rooms are clustered around six courtyards, each with its own swimming pool. The design is reminiscent of the Bo-Kaap or Mediterranean villages where pedestrians have right of way. The hotel is situated on the historic Spier wine farm in the heart of the Stellenbosch winelands, just 20 minutes from Cape Town International Airport. (See also Eight under Restaurants and Spier in A-Z section.)

The Homestead at Oldenburg Vineyards Zevenrivieren Rd, Banghoek, Stellenbosch ▪ Luxury guest villa sleeping max 12 pax ▪ Rates from R24,530-R41,030 (breakfast included) ▪ Guests staying min 3 nights treated to signature SA braai or 3-course dinner (included in rate) ▪ 6 bedrooms ▪ Major credit cards accepted ▪ Gym ▪ Pool ▪ Mobile spa (extra cost) ▪ Mountain biking (extra cost for hiring bikes) ▪ Walks/hikes ▪ Birding ▪ Winetasting ▪ Secure parking ▪ Shuttle

service available (extra cost) ▪ Laundry service ▪ Safe ▪ Air-conditioning ▪ Fireplace in common areas ▪ Under-floor heating in bathrooms ▪ TV ▪ DStv ▪ Wifi ▪ homestead@oldenburgvineyards.com ▪ www. oldenburgvineyards.com ▪ **T +27 (0)87-095-1139 / +27 (0)21-885-1618**

Spacious and elegantly proportioned, the 200-year-old Oldenburg homestead has been meticulously restored and modernised to create a seamless flow of indoor and outdoor spaces for relaxed family living and sophisticated entertaining. Sleeping up to 12 in six bedrooms, this luxury guest villa is well suited to a multi-generational family, party of friends or corporate team in need of a discreet setting for high-powered meetings. Fringed by a well-established garden, olive groves and vineyards, the two-level house has deep verandas, large swimming pool and glass-walled gym from which to appreciate the dramatic Groot Drakenstein mountains. It comes with resident manager and two housekeepers; additional staff can be arranged. (See also Oldenburg Vineyards in A-Z section.)

The Residence at Haskell Vineyards Annandale Rd, Lynedoch, Stellenbosch ▪ Luxury country house ▪ Rates from R1,500-R3,700 per night ▪ 2-bedroom house & 1-bedroom cottage ▪ Major cards, EFT & cash accepted ▪ Restaurant ▪ Conference facilities ▪ Weddings/functions ▪ Children welcome ▪ Walks/hikes ▪ Winetasting ▪ Secure parking ▪ Laundry service ▪ Safe ▪ Air-conditioning ▪ Fireplace ▪ TV ▪ DStv ▪ Wifi ▪ German spoken ▪ Owner Haskell Vineyards ▪ theresidence@haskellvineyards. co.za ▪ www.haskellvineyards.com ▪ **T +27 (0)21-881-3895**

The Residence and the Cottage are set in the foothills of Helderberg Mountain, within 9 km of De Zalze Golf Estate. Secluded and fringed by vines, both homes offer tranquillity and stunning mountain views. The historic town of Stellenbosch is just a 15-minute drive distant, and the surrounding countryside offers nature lovers outstanding hiking and walking opportunities in a beautiful part of South Africa. (See also Longtable Restaurant under Restaurants and Haskell Vineyards in A-Z section.)

Winelands Maps

The maps in this section show locales where wine is available for tasting/sale either at set times or by appointment. The larger-scale map below shows the areas covered by the maps, and the table starting on the next page lists some details for prospective visitors.

Areas covered by the maps

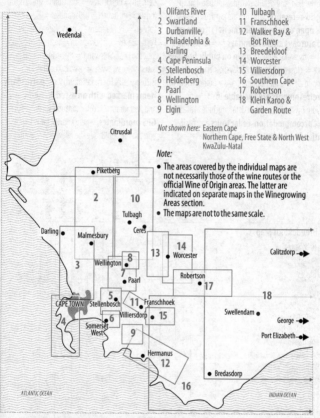

1 Olifants River
2 Swartland
3 Durbanville, Philadelphia & Darling
4 Cape Peninsula
5 Stellenbosch
6 Helderberg
7 Paarl
8 Wellington
9 Elgin
10 Tulbagh
11 Franschhoek
12 Walker Bay & Bot River
13 Breedekloof
14 Worcester
15 Villiersdorp
16 Southern Cape
17 Robertson
18 Klein Karoo & Garden Route

Not shown here: Eastern Cape
Northern Cape, Free State & North West
KwaZulu-Natal

Note:
- The areas covered by the individual maps are not necessarily those of the wine routes or the official Wine of Origin areas. The latter are indicated on separate maps in the Winegrowing Areas section.
- The maps are not to the same scale.

Some distances from Cape Town (kilometres)

Calitzdorp	370	Paarl	60	Tulbagh	125
Franschhoek	80	Plettenberg Bay	520	Upington	800
Hermanus	120	Robertson	160	Vredendal	300
Malmesbury	70	Stellenbosch	50	Worcester	110

Key for maps

——— Main access roads	R62 R60 = Road numbers
——— Roads	Towns
······· Gravel roads	

Details of Locales Shown on Maps

The tables below are intended to facilitate winery visits by providing summary information about all the winetasting venues which are open to the public, either at set times or by appointment, and appear on our winelands maps. Venues are listed by region, and details provided include a **map grid-reference**; whether the particular venue is **open only by appointment** (T); **open on Saturdays and/or Sundays** (√ = at set times; T = by appointment); **open on public holidays** (× = closed all public holidays; otherwise assume open all or some holidays); and whether **meals/refreshments are available** (BYO = bring your own picnic). Other details include availability of **accommodation**, **cellar tours** and **facilities for children**. Venues which have tasting

facilities **friendly to individuals with reduced mobility**, as audited by our disability consultants, are highlighted. **Other languages spoken** (besides English and Afrikaans) are also noted (Danish = da, Dutch/Flemish = nl, French = fr, German = de, Hebrew = he, Hungarian = hu, Indian = in, Italian = it, Japanese = ja, Latvian = lv, Mandarin = mdr, Norwegian = nn, Portuguese = pt, Romanian = ro, Russian = ru, Sesotho = st, Setswana = tn, Spanish = sp, Swedish = sv, Swiss = gsw, isiXhosa = xh, isiZulu = zu). For more information, **particularly items marked with an asterisk**, see the A–Z and Restaurants/Accommodation sections. For **GPS coordinates**, where known, for wineries open to the public, see the relevant A–Z entries.

	Grid reference	Open by appt. only	Open Saturdays	Open Sundays	Open public holidays	Meals/refreshments	Accommodation	Cellar tours	Disabled friendly	Child friendly	Languages spoken
Breedekloof Map											
Badsberg	B5		√		×			T	√	√	
Bergsig	A3		√			√		T	√	√	
Bosjes	B3		√	√		√	√			√	
Botha	B3		√			BYO		T	√	√	
Breëland	A5	T*				T/BYO*	√	T			
Dagbreek	C5	T			×	BYO		T			
Daschbosch	C6		√						√		
De Breede	D4	T									
Du Preez	B6		√		×			T*	√		
Du Toitskloof	B6		√	√		√		T	√		de
Jason's Hill	A5		√						√	√	
Kirabo	C6		√	√	×	T*		√		√	
Lateganskop	A2							T	×		
Le Belle Rebelle	C5		√	√		√*		T		√	
Merwida	C6		√						√		
Mountain Ridge	A2		√		×			T	√		
Olifantsberg	C4	T*									
Opstal	A5		√	T		√*	√	√*	√	√	
Slanghoek	A5		√					T	√		
Waboomsrivier	A3				×			T			
Cape Peninsula Map											
Absolute Style	B1	T*									fr
Beau Constantia	B3		√	√		√					
Buitenverwachting	B3		√		×	√		T	√		

	Grid reference	Open by appt. only	Open Saturdays	Open Sundays	Open public holidays	Meals/refreshments	Accommodation	Cellar tours	Disabled friendly	Child friendly	Languages spoken
Cape Point	B4		✓	✓		✓*			✓	✓	
Cape Town Wine Co	A4		✓	✓		✓		✓			
Constantia Glen	B3		✓	✓		✓*					
Constantia Royale	B3	T			X						
Constantia Uitsig	B3		✓*	✓*		✓			X		
Dorrance	B1					✓		✓			fr
Eagles' Nest	B3		✓	✓		✓*		✓			
Groot Constantia	B3		✓	✓		✓		✓	✓	✓	fr
Hout Bay	A3	T						T		✓	de
Klein Constantia	B3		✓	✓		✓*		✓*	✓		fr/sv
Magna Carta	B1		✓	✓				✓			fr/xh/zu
New Beginnings	B1	T									fr
Rousseau	B4	T									
Savage	C2	T									
Silvermist	B3		✓	✓		✓*	✓				
Steenberg	B4		✓	✓		✓	✓	✓	✓		
Township Winery	D3										
Wade Bales	B3				X						

Durbanville, Philadelphia & Darling Map

	Grid reference	Open by appt. only	Open Saturdays	Open Sundays	Open public holidays	Meals/refreshments	Accommodation	Cellar tours	Disabled friendly	Child friendly	Languages spoken
Altydgedacht	C7		✓	✓		✓*				✓	
Bloemendal	C7		✓	✓		✓			✓		
Canto	C7		✓			✓*				✓	
Capaia	C5		✓*	✓*		✓		✓		✓	de
Cloof	B3		✓					T	✓	✓	
DA Hanekom	C7	T			X						
D'Aria	C7		✓	✓		✓	✓			✓	nl
Darling Cellars	B2		✓			✓*		T	✓	✓	xh
De Grendel	C8		✓	✓		✓		T	✓		
Diemersdal	D7		✓	✓		✓					
Durbanville Hills	C7		✓	✓		✓*		T	✓	✓	
Groot Phesantekraal	D7		✓								
Groote Post	A3		✓	✓		✓*		✓	✓	✓	
Havana Hills	C5	T						T			
Hermit on the Hill	C8	T									
Hillcrest	C7		✓	✓		✓		T			
House of Mandela	C7	T									
Klein Roosboom	C7		✓	✓		✓		✓	✓	✓	
Kronendal	C7	T				✓*		T	✓		
Maastricht	C7		✓			✓*					
Maison de Teijger	D7	T*									
Meerendal	C7		✓	✓		✓	✓	T	✓	✓	xh/zu
Nitida	C7		✓	✓		✓			✓	✓	
Ormonde	A1		✓						X	✓	

	Grid reference	Open by appt. only	Open Saturdays	Open Sundays	Open public holidays	Meals/refreshments	Accommodation	Cellar tours	Disabled friendly	Child friendly	Languages spoken
Signal Gun	C7		✓	✓		✓					
Withington	A1		✓	✓					✓		
Eastern Cape Map											
La Terre La Mer	B2	T						T			
Theescombe	D5	T				T*		T			
Elgin Map											
Almenkerk	B2		✓			✓/BYO*		✓*			nl/fr
Arumdale	B1				T						
Barry Gould	D2	T				T*	✓			✓	
Belfield	B2	T					✓	T			
Charles Fox	C3		✓	✓				✓		✓	
Elgin Ridge	B3		✓	✓		BYO		✓			fr
Elgin Vintners	B2		✓	✓		✓*	✓				
Hannay	B2	T				T/BYO		T			
Highlands Road	C3		✓	✓		✓*		✓	✓	✓	
Houw Hoek	D3		✓			✓				✓	
Iona	C4		T		×			✓			
Lothian	A2	T					✓				sp
Oak Valley	B1		✓	✓			✓		✓		it/fr
Oneiric	C4		✓	✓		✓*					
Oude Molen	B1				×						
Paul Cluver	C2		✓	✓*		✓*			✓		
Paul Wallace	C3	T*	✓				✓				
Richard Kershaw	B2	T									fr
Shannon	A2	T*							✓		de/sp
South Hill	C3		✓	✓		✓*	✓	T	✓		
Spioenkop	C4	T			×			T*			fr/nl
William Everson	B2	T					T	T			
Franschhoek Map											
Akkerdal	C4	T*			×		✓				
Allée Bleue	C6		✓	✓		✓	✓	T	✓	✓	de
Anthonij Rupert	C5	T				✓			✓		
Babylonstoren	B8		✓	✓		✓*	✓	✓	✓		
Backsberg	B8		✓	✓		✓*		T*	✓	✓	
Bellingham	C2		✓	✓		✓*				✓	
Black Elephant	C1	T						T			
Boekenhoutskloof	D1	T			×				✓		xh
Boschendal	D6		✓	✓		✓	✓	✓	✓	✓	
Cape Chamonix	C1		✓	✓		✓		T			
Chantelle	C2	T						T			
Colmant	C1							✓*	✓		fr
Dieu Donné	C1		✓	✓		✓		T*			

	Grid reference	Open by appt. only	Open Saturdays	Open Sundays	Open public holidays	Meals/refreshments	Accommodation	Cellar tours	Disabled friendly	Child friendly	Languages spoken
Enfin	C1	T									
Four Paws	C3	T			x						
Franschhoek Cellar	C2		✓	✓		✓*	✓		✓	✓	
Freedom Hill	B5				x				✓	✓	
GlenWood	C2		✓	✓		✓		✓*			
Grande Provence	C2		✓	✓		✓	✓	✓*	✓	✓	
Haut Espoir	D1		T	T	x			T	✓		
Haute Cabrière	C1		✓	✓		✓		✓*	✓		fr/de
Holden Manz	D1		✓	✓		✓	✓	T	✓		de
La Bri	C1		✓	✓		✓*		✓			
La Chataigne	C4		T	T	T		✓		✓		sv
La Couronne	C1		✓	✓*		✓*	✓				
La Motte	C3		✓			✓			✓	✓	xh
La Petite Ferme	C1	T*				✓	✓				
Landau du Val	D2	T*									
Le Lude	C1		✓	✓		✓		✓			
Le Manoir de Brendel	C3		✓	✓			✓			✓	
Leeu Passant	C2		✓	✓							
Leopard's Leap	C3		✓	✓		✓				✓	
Lynx	C4		✓	T	T		✓	✓			de/sp
Maison	C3		✓	✓		✓					
Mont Rochelle	C2		✓	✓		✓	✓	✓*			
Môreson	C3		✓	✓				✓			
Mullineux	C2		✓	✓							
My Wyn	B1	T*			T	T/BYO*		T			
Noble Hill	B7		✓	✓				T	✓	✓	fr
Old Road	C2		✓			✓					
Paserene	C4		✓	✓		✓*					
Plaisir de Merle	C6		✓	✓		✓*	*	✓	✓	✓	de
Rickety Bridge	C2		✓	✓		✓	✓	✓	✓	✓	
Rupert & Rothschild	B7		✓	✓		✓*		✓			
Stony Brook	D1	T*					✓		✓		
Strange Kompanjie	D1	T*			x			T*			
Tanzanite	A7	T*									
The House of GM&AHRENS	C1	T			x	T		T			
Topiary	C4		✓	T		✓/BYO	✓	T	✓		fr
Val de Vie	A7	T*			x	✓*			✓		
Vrede en Lust	B7		✓	✓		✓	✓	T*	✓	✓	
Wildeberg	D1	T*			x			T*			
Helderberg Map											
Avontuur	C2		✓	✓		✓		T	✓		de/pt
Cadequin	H8	T*					✓			✓	nl
Cape Classics	F4	T									

	Grid reference	Open by appt. only	Open Saturdays	Open Sundays	Open public holidays	Meals/refreshments	Accommodation	Cellar tours	Disabled friendly	Child friendly	Languages spoken
Capelands	F7					✓*	✓				
Cavalli	C1		✓	✓		✓*			✓		
Chennells	C2	T*			x			T			de/sp
Collatio	A3	T			x						
Croydon	A3				x			T	✓	✓	
Eikendal	C1		✓*	✓		✓*	✓		✓	✓	de
Equitania	C3	T*			x	BYO					
Flagstone	B6		✓			✓*		T	✓		
Foothills	B1	T				T	✓				
Gentleman Spirits	E7	T									de
Grangehurst	C1		✓	T*	T		✓				
Highberry	F6	T									
Idiom	H7		✓	✓		✓*					it
Jasper Raats	C1		✓								
Journey's End	G7	T*				T/BYO*					
Ken Forrester	C2 B2		✓	✓*		✓*			✓		
Kings Kloof	E4	T									
Konkelberg	C1		✓								
Le Riche	B1		T		x			✓			de
Longridge	C1		✓			✓		T	✓		
Lourensford	F4		✓	✓		✓		✓	✓		
Lyngrove	B1	T					✓				
Miravel	A3	T			T	T					nl/fr
Morgenster	F5		✓	✓		✓					
Nomada	D2	T									
Osbloed	E6	T*									
Paul Roos	C1	T						T			fr
Post House	C1		T		x	BYO	✓	✓	✓		
Radford Dale	C1	T*			x						fr/sv
Somerbosch	C1		✓	✓		✓		T	✓	✓	
Somerset Wines	E6		✓		x						
Stonewall	C2	T*				T					
Vergelegen	F5		✓	✓		✓		✓*	✓	✓	.
Waterkloof	F6		✓	✓		✓*		T	✓		
Yonder Hill	C3		✓*		x	✓*		T	✓		

Klein Karoo & Garden Route Map

	Grid reference	Open by appt. only	Open Saturdays	Open Sundays	Open public holidays	Meals/refreshments	Accommodation	Cellar tours	Disabled friendly	Child friendly	Languages spoken
Aan't Vette	C6	T			x	✓*	✓	✓			
Axe Hill	B5	T						T			
Baleia	C6		✓			✓/BYO	✓	✓		✓	
Barrydale	C7		✓	✓		✓					
Bitou	C1	T									
Boplaas	B5 C4		✓	✓				T		✓	
Bramon	C1		✓	✓		✓	✓	T	✓	✓	

	Grid reference	Open by appt. only	Open Saturdays	Open Sundays	Open public holidays	Meals/refreshments	Accommodation	Cellar tours	Disabled friendly	Child friendly	Languages spoken
Calitzdorp	B5		✓			BYO		T	✓		
De Krans	B5		✓	✓		✓*			✓	✓	
Domein Doornkraal	B3		✓	✓*		✓*	✓				
Du'SwaRoo	B5		✓					✓			
Excelsior Vlakteplaas	B3	T									
Fernskloof	A3		✓	T*		BYO				✓	sp
Flying Cloud	C3										
Garden Route	C3 B5		✓*						✓		
Grundheim	B4		✓								
Herold	C3		✓			✓*	✓	✓	✓	✓	
Joubert-Tradauw	C7		✓			✓	✓	✓	✓	✓	
JP Bredell	C5	T						✓			
Karusa	B3		✓			✓			✓		
Kay & Monty	C1		✓	✓		✓	✓				
Kingna	C8		T	T				✓*			de
Le Sueur	C5										
Lodestone	C1		✓	✓		✓					
Louis 57	C4		✓			✓					
LuKa	C1		✓								
Mimosa	B8		✓	✓		✓*			✓		de/gsw
Montagu Wine Cellar	B8				X				✓		
Newstead	C1		✓			T*	✓				zu
Packwood	C1		✓	✓	T	✓*	✓				
Peter Bayly	B5	T						T			
Plettenvale	C1	T*						T*			
SoetKaroo	A4		✓*						✓		de
The Goose	C3	T				T/BYO				✓	
Varkenskraal	B3	T					✓				
KwaZulu-Natal Map											
Cathedral Peak	B2		✓*	✓*		✓					zu
Highgate	B2		✓	✓		✓		✓*		✓	de
Northern Cape, Free State & North West Map											
Bezalel	B8		✓			✓*	✓	✓		✓	nl
Die Mas	B8		✓			T/BYO*	✓	✓		✓	
Landzicht	C5				X			T			
Lowerland	C6	T						T			
Orange River	B8		✓					✓*	✓		
Olifants River Map											
Bellpost	B3	T*						T			
Cape Rock	B4	T				BYO		T			
Cecilia	D7		✓								
Cederberg	D7		✓	✓*		BYO	✓				
Driehoek	D6		✓				✓			✓	

	Grid reference	Open by appt. only	Open Saturdays	Open Sundays	Open public holidays	Meals/refreshments	Accommodation	Cellar tours	Disabled friendly	Child friendly	Languages spoken
Fryer's Cove	A4		✓	✓		✓*		✓	✓	✓	
Klawer	B4		✓			BYO			✓	✓	
Lutzville	B3		✓			✓		T	✓		
Namaqua	B4		✓			✓*		✓*	✗	✓	
Piekenierskloof	D7	T*						T			
Schenkfontein	C7	T*						T*			
Sir Lambert	B5										
Stellar	B4				✗			T			
Teubes	B4 B5		✓			✓*	✓	✓	✓	✓	
Tierhoek	C6	T*			✗	BYO	✓	T*			
Paarl Map											
Anura	C7		✓	✓		✓*		✓	✓		de
Arra	C8		✓	✓							
Avondale	F6		✓	✓		✓		T	✓	✓	
Ayama	B2		✓	✓		T/BYO*	✓			✓	it
Bayede!	E6		T	T	✗						
Bergheim	E6	T									
Bezuidenhout Family	E6	T									
Black Pearl	D5	T*					✓	T*	✓		
Boland	E4		✓			✓*			✗		
Calais	G4	T*					✓				
Cape Wine Company	E6		✓	✓							
Damarakloof	A7	T*					✓				
De Villiers	E6	T									
Domaine Brahms	C3	T			T	✓		T			
Doran	C1	T*	✓	✓					✓		
Druk My Niet	G4	T			✗	T/BYO		T			de
Eenzaamheid	B5	T									
Esau	E6	T									
Fairview	D6		✓	✓		✓			✓		
Glen Carlou	D7		✓	✓		✓		T	✓	✓	de
Groot Parys	E5	T									nl
Hawksmoor	A7	T*				T*	✓				fr/de/ja
Jacques Germanier	C1	T				✓*	✓	T			fr
Joostenberg	A7	T*				✓*	✓	T		✓	
KWV	E6		✓	✓		✓*		✓	✓		de
Landskroon	D6	✓*				BYO*	✓	T*		✓	
Mellasat	G5		✓	✓		T*		T	✓		
Mitre's Edge	C8	T*						✓	T		
Mooi Bly	F4	T				BYO	✓	T			nl
Myburgh Bros	A7	T						T			de
Nederburg	F5		✓	✓		✓*		✓	✓		de
Nelson	D3	T			✗		✓	T	✓	✓	

	Grid reference	Open by appt. only	Open Saturdays	Open Sundays	Open public holidays	Meals/refreshments	Accommodation	Cellar tours	Disabled friendly	Child friendly	Languages spoken
Niel Joubert	C8	T*			×						
Olsen	G5	T									
Oude Denneboom	C2	T*					√				
Painted Wolf	E5		√*			√					fr
Pearl Mountain	E4		√	√		√					
Perdeberg	B2		√	√		√*		T*		√	
Rhebokskloof	D3		√	√		√			√	√	
Ridgeback	D3		√	√		√	√	T	√	√	
Simonsvlei	D7		√	√		√		T	√	√	
Southern Sky	E6	T									
Spice Route	D6		√	√		√			√		
Taillard	C1	T			×			T	√		
Tempel	E3	T				T*	√	T			fr/lv/nl/ru
The Ahrens Family	G6	T				T*					
The Foundry	C2	T			×			T			
Under Oaks	E3		√	√		√*	√	T			
Vendôme	E6	T			×	√			√		
Vondeling	C1		T		T				√		
Wilderer	D7		√	√		√*		√		√	de
Windmuel	D3		√		×	√*		T	√	√	
Zandwijk	D6				×	T*		T	√		
Robertson Map											
Arendsig	C4	T				T*	√	T			
Bemind	D6		√			T*		√			
Bon Courage	B5		√			√			√	√	
Bonnievale	D3		√						√	√	
Buffalo Creek	D6		√	T				√*			
Bushmanspad	C1					T/BYO*	√				nl
Cape Dreams	A6	T						T			
Clairvaux	B6				×	BYO		T	√		
Cloverfield	B5	T							√		
DuVon	B7	T					√	T			
Esona	C4		√			√*					
Excelsior	C4		√			√*	√			√	
Goedverwacht	C4		√			BYO		√			
Graham Beck	B6		√	√		√*		T	√		
Jan Harmsgat	C2		√	√		√	√				
Kleinhoekkloof	B4	T*									
Kranskop	B4		√			√*		√			de
Langverwacht	D4				×			√	√		
Le Grand Chasseur	B7	T			×				√		
Lord's	D7		√	√		√		√		√	
Lozärn	D3	T						T			

	Grid reference	Open by appt. only	Open Saturdays	Open Sundays	Open public holidays	Meals/refreshments	Accommodation	Cellar tours	Disabled friendly	Child friendly	Languages spoken
McGregor	D6		✓						✓		
Mont Blois	A5	T						T			fr
Quando	D4	T			x						de
Rietvallei	B4		✓			✓*			✓		
Robertson	B5		✓	✓				T	✓		
Roodezandt	B5				x			T*	✓	✓	
Rooiberg	A7					✓			✓	✓	
Rosendal	B4		✓	✓		✓	✓		✓		nn
Silverthorn	C4	T*						T*			
Springfield	B5		✓			BYO		T*			
Tanagra	C6	T*					✓	T			de
Van Loveren	B5 C4		✓	✓		✓		T	✓		
Van Zylshof	D3		✓					T	✓		
Viljoensdrift	C5		✓	✓*		✓*					fr
Wederom	B7	T			T	T	✓	T			de
Weltevrede	D3		✓			✓*	✓	T	✓		
Windfall	C8	T			x		✓	T			
Wonderfontein	B6		T*	T	T						
Zandvliet	C4		✓						✓	✓	
Southern Cape Map											
Andy Mitchell	A1	T						T			
Black Oystercatcher	B3		✓	✓		✓*	✓		✓	✓	
Bruce Jack	B7	T									
Brunia	B2	T			x						
Fortes	B2	T			x	BYO		T			
Jean Daneel	B2	T				✓		T			de
Lomond	C8		✓	✓		✓*					
Olivedale	D1	T			x						
Sijnn	D1		✓*			✓*		✓*			
Skipskop	C6	T									
Strandveld	B3		✓			BYO	✓	✓			
Swallow Hill	A1	T				T*	✓	T			de/fr/sp
The Giant Periwinkle	A3	T*									
Zoetendal	C7		✓			✓					
Stellenbosch Map											
Aaldering	D4		✓*		x		✓	T	✓		
Akkerdraai	E8	T									de
Alto	E8		✓	✓							
Annandale	E8		✓			BYO			✓		
ArtiSons	C3	T			x			T			
Asara	D6		✓	✓		✓	✓	T*		✓	de
Audacia	E8	T*	✓	✓	x	✓*			✓	✓	
B Vintners	B6	T*			x						

	Grid reference	Open by appt. only	Open Saturdays	Open Sundays	Open public holidays	Meals/refreshments	Accommodation	Cellar tours	Disabled friendly	Child friendly	Languages spoken
Bartinney	H5		✓*			✓*	✓	T	✓		
Bein	B6	T						T			de/fr
Bellevue	C3		✓	✓		✓*				✓	
Beyerskloof	E3		✓	✓		✓		T	✓		
Blaauwklippen	E7		✓	✓		✓		✓*	✓	✓	de
Blackwater	E1	T									
Boschheim	E5	T									de
Boschkloof	C6		✓			✓/BYO		✓			
Botanica	D4	T*				✓*	✓				
Brampton	F5		✓	✓		✓*					
Brenaissance	D4		✓	✓		✓	✓			✓	
Camberley	H4		✓	✓		✓*	✓	T			
Casa Mori	D3	T						✓	T		it/fr
Catherine Marshall	B6	T						T			
Clos Malverne	D4		✓	✓		✓	✓	✓*	✓		
Clouds	H5	T				✓*	✓				
Dalla Cia	E5		✓			✓		T*	✓		it
David Frost	D3	T*									
De Meye	E1		✓	✓		✓*		T*	✓		
De Toren	B6	T*			✗			T			
De Trafford	G8	T*	✓		✗			T*			
Delaire Graff	H5		✓	✓		✓	✓	T*	✓		
Delheim	F2		✓	✓		✓		✓	✓		de
DeMorgenzon	C5		✓	✓				T			
Deux Frères	E3		✓*			T*		✓			
Devonvale	D3	T*				✓	✓		✓		de/fr
DeWaal	C5		✓			✓*					de
Domaine Coutelier	D4	T			✗			✓	T		fr
Dormershire	A5										
Dornier	F7		✓	✓		✓*	✓	T	✓		
Edgebaston	E3	T									
Entre Nous	H5	T			T	BYO		T			
Erika Obermeyer	C7	T									
Ernie Els	E8		✓	✓		✓		✓	✓		
Ernst Gouws	D1		✓						✓	✓	de
Escapades	B4	T									
Fort Simon	C4		✓		✗			T	✓		
Francois La Garde	E5	T									
Friesland	B3	T*				T*					
Glenelly	F4		✓	✓		✓		T	✓		de/fr
Goede Hoop	C3		✓			T*		✓			
Graceland	E7	T*			✗						
Groenland	B3		✓					T	✓		

	Grid reference	Open by appt. only	Open Saturdays	Open Sundays	Open public holidays	Meals/refreshments	Accommodation	Cellar tours	Disabled friendly	Child friendly	Languages spoken
Guardian Peak	E8		✓	✓		✓			✓		
Hartenberg	C4		✓	✓		✓*		T	✓	✓	de
Haskell	F8		✓	✓*		✓*	✓	T	✓	✓	
Hazendal	B3		✓	✓		✓		T	✓	✓	de/ru
Hidden Valley	E8		✓	✓		✓*	✓	T	✓		
Hoopenburg	E1				X	BYO	✓	✓			
Hunneyball	F5	T					✓				
J9	E1		✓			✓*					
Jacobsdal	B6	T*									
Jordan	C5		✓	✓		✓*	✓	T*	✓		
Kaapzicht	B4		✓				✓				de
Kanonkop	F2					T/BYO*		✓			
Kanu	E3		✓	✓		✓		✓			
Katbakkies	D5	T*			X						
Keermont	G8	T*	✓				✓	T			
Kleine Zalze	E7		✓	✓		✓	✓		✓		
Knorhoek	F3		✓			✓*	✓		✓	✓	
Koelenhof	D1		✓			✓*		✓	✓	✓	de
Koni	E1		T		T			✓			st/xh/zu
Kunjani	D3		✓	✓		✓	✓				de
Kyburg	D4	T					✓				fr/de
Laibach	F1		✓*				✓	T			
Lanzerac	G5		✓	✓		✓	✓	✓*	✓		
L'Avenir	E3		✓	✓		✓	✓	T	✓	✓	fr
Le Bonheur	F1	T									
Le Grand Domaine	D4	T									
Le Pommier	H4		✓	✓		✓	✓			✓	
Lievland	F1		✓	✓					✓		
Louisvale	D4		✓						✓		
Lovane	D6		✓	✓			✓	✓			
Malanot	E3	T						T*	✓		
Marianne	G1		✓	✓		✓	✓	✓	✓	✓	de/fr
Marklew	F1	T						T			
Meerlust	C8		✓		X		✓	T			
Meinert	D4	T*			X						de
Middelvlei	E4		✓	✓		✓*	✓	T	✓	✓	
MolenVliet	H4	T*					✓				
Montegray	F5		✓			✓*					
Mooiplaas	B4		✓	✓*		T*	✓			✓	
Morgenhof	F3		✓*	✓*		✓	✓	T	✓	✓	de
Mostertsdrift	E4	T				T*		T		✓	
Mulderbosch	C5		✓	✓		✓*			✓		fr
Muratie	F3		✓	✓		✓*		✓*			

	Grid reference	Open by appt. only	Open Saturdays	Open Sundays	Open public holidays	Meals/refreshments	Accommodation	Cellar tours	Disabled friendly	Child friendly	Languages spoken
Mvemve Raats	B6	T*			x						
Natte Valleij	F1	T*			x		✓	T*			
Neethlingshof	D5		✓	✓		✓*		T	✓	✓	de
Neil Ellis	G5		✓			✓*			✓		
Nico van der Merwe	B6		✓								fr/de
Noble Savage	F5		✓								
Oldenburg	H5		✓				*		✓		
Origin	D3	T									fr/de
Overgaauw	D5	T*							✓		
Peter Falke	E8		✓	✓		✓*					
Quoin Rock	F3		✓			✓	T				
Raats	B6	T*			x						
Rainbow's End	H6	T			x			T			
Rascallion	E5		✓	✓*							
Remhoogte	F3		✓			✓*	✓	T	✓		
Reyneke	B6	T*						T			
Roos Family	B4	T									
Rudera	G6	T						T			
Rust en Vrede	E8		✓	✓*		✓*					
Rustenberg	F4		✓	✓					✓		
Saltare	F5	T						T			
Saxenburg	A5		✓	✓		✓	✓				
Seven Sisters	C7		✓	✓		✓*					
Simonsig	E2		✓	✓		✓		T	✓	✓	
Skilpadvlei	C6		✓	✓		✓	✓	✓	✓		
Slaley	E2		✓	✓		✓					
Sonklip	G5	T						T			
Spier	C7		✓	✓		✓	✓		✓	✓	de/xh
Spotswood	F7	T									
Stark-Condé	G6		✓	✓	x*	✓			✓		ja
Stellekaya	E5		✓		x			✓*	x		zu
Stellenbosch Family Wines	D1	T									
Stellenbosch Hills	D6		✓		x				✓		
Stellenbosch University	F5				x						
Stellenbosch Vineyards	C7		✓	✓					✓	✓	xh
Stellenrust	E7, C3		✓		x*	✓/BYO*		T			xh
Stellenview	D4		T	T	x			✓*			
Stellenzicht	F8	T*									
Summerhill	E3				x	✓					
Super Single Vineyards	C5		✓		x						
SylvanVale	D4		✓	✓		✓	✓		✓	✓	de/xh
Tamboerskloof	F7	T*			x			T			de/fr
The Great SA Wine Co	C5	T									

	Grid reference	Open by appt. only	Open Saturdays	Open Sundays	Open public holidays	Meals/refreshments	Accommodation	Cellar tours	Disabled friendly	Child friendly	Languages spoken
The High Road	E5	T			x				✓		
The Hills	D4	T									
The House of JC le Roux	D4		✓	✓		✓*		✓*	✓		
Thelema	G4		✓						✓		
Tokara	G4		✓	✓		✓			✓	✓	
Uva Mira	E8		✓	✓		✓*			✓		
Van Biljon	B6	T			x		✓	T			
Van Ryn	D6		✓	✓*				✓*			
Vergenoegd	B8		✓	✓		✓*		T	✓	✓	xh
Vilafonté	E5	T						T			
Villiera	D1		✓			✓*		✓	✓		fr
Vredenheim	D6		✓			✓	✓	✓			
Vriesenhof	F7		T		x			T			
Vuurberg	H4	T			x			T			
Warwick	F1		✓	✓		✓*		T	✓	✓	
Waterford	F8		✓					✓	✓		
Webersburg	E8		✓	✓		✓		✓	✓	✓	
Welgevallen	F5				x			✓			
Winshaw	C8	T									
Yardstick	C5										
Zevenwacht	B5		✓	✓		✓	✓	T	✓	✓	xh
Zorgvliet	H4		✓	✓		T*	✓	T	✓	✓	

Swartland Map

	Grid reference	Open by appt. only	Open Saturdays	Open Sundays	Open public holidays	Meals/refreshments	Accommodation	Cellar tours	Disabled friendly	Child friendly	Languages spoken
AA Badenhorst	C8	T*			x		T	T*			
Allesverloren	D6		✓			✓*		T	✓	✓	
Annex Kloof	C7	T*			x*		✓	T	✓		
Babylon's Peak	C8	T					✓		✓		
City on a Hill	C8	T									
David & Nadia	C8	T*					*				
Dragonridge	C8	T				T*	✓	T		✓	
Franki's	A6	T*			x	BYO*	✓	T*			
Hofstraat	C7	T*				✓*		T			
Hughes Family	C6	T									sp
Huis van Chevallerie	D6	T			T						de/fr/it
JC Wickens	C8	T									
Kloovenburg	D6		✓			✓*			✓		
Lammershoek	C8	T						T			
Meerhof	D6		✓	✓		✓		✓			
Môrelig	C8	T									
Mullineux	D6	T									
Nieuwedrift	C2		✓			✓*	✓	✓		✓	
Org de Rac	C2		✓			✓*		✓	✓	✓	de
Pulpit Rock	D6		✓			✓/BYO*	✓	T	✓		

	Grid reference	Open by appt. only	Open Saturdays	Open Sundays	Open public holidays	Meals/refreshments	Accommodation	Cellar tours	Disabled friendly	Child friendly	Languages spoken
Rall	C7	T						T			
Riebeek Valley	D6		✓	✓				T	✓		
Sadie	C8	T*									
Swartland	C7		✓						✓	✓	
Wildehurst	B2	T*						T*			
Tulbagh Map											
Koelfontein	H5		✓		×		✓				
Krone	F4		✓		×			✓			pt/sp
Lemberg	F5		✓	✓		T/BYO*	✓	✓	✓		
Manley	F5	T*	✓	✓		✓*	✓	T			
Oude Compagnies Post	F4		✓				✓				
Saronsberg	F4		✓	✓		BYO	✓	T			
Schalkenbosch	G5	T			×		✓	T			de
Terracura	A7	T			×			T			
Themika	F4	T					✓				
Theuniskraal	F4		✓						✓		
Tulbagh Winery	F5		✓						✓		
Waverley Hills	G6		✓	✓		✓*		✓	✓	✓	
Villiersdorp Map											
Eerste Hoop	A2	T						T			
Villiersdorp	C1		✓			✓		T	✓		
Walker Bay & Bot River Map											
Anysbos	C3	T						T			
Arcangeli	C3	T				✓	✓				
Bartho Eksteen	A3		✓			✓*		T			fr/xh
Barton	B2		✓				✓	✓	✓		
Beaumont	C2		✓			✓*	✓		✓		
Benguela Cove	B2		✓	✓		✓*		✓	✓	✓	
Boschrivier	C8		✓	✓*		✓/BYO	✓		✓		
Bosman	B3	T*				T*					
Bouchard Finlayson	B4		✓		×	✓/BYO*		✓	✓		de/fr
Creation	C4		✓	✓		✓		✓	✓	✓	de/fr
Domaine des Dieux	C4		✓	✓		✓*				✓	
Gabriëlskloof	C3		✓			✓		T	✓	✓	
Genevieve	C2	T									
Hamilton Russell	B4		✓					T			tn/xh
Jakob's Vineyards	C4	T									
La Vierge	B4		✓	✓		✓			✓		
Leeurivier	C3	T									
Luddite	D2		T	T				T	✓		nl
Misty Mountains	B5		✓	✓		✓	✓	T			
Mount Babylon	C4	T*									

	Grid reference	Open by appt. only	Open Saturdays	Open Sundays	Open public holidays	Meals/refreshments	Accommodation	Cellar tours	Disabled friendly	Child friendly	Languages spoken
Moya's	B4	T*									
Newton Johnson	B4		✓		×	✓			✓		
PaardenKloof	C3 C2		✓	✓*		✓				✓	xh
Raka	C8		✓			BYO		T	✓	✓	
Restless River	B4	T			×						
Rivendell	B2		✓	✓		✓*				✓	
Robert Stanford	B6		✓	✓		✓*	✓			✓	
Seven Springs	C5					✓					
Southern Right	A3		✓					T	✓		
Spookfontein	B4		✓	✓		✓	✓				
Springfontein	B5		✓	✓		✓*	✓	✓			
Stanford Hills	B6		✓	✓		✓	✓		✓		
Storm	B4	T									
Sumaridge	B4		✓	✓		✓*	✓		✓	✓	
Vaalvlei	B7		✓				✓				
Villion	B2		✓								
Walker Bay Estate	B6		✓	✓		✓		T	✓	✓	
Whalehaven	A3		✓	✓							
Wildekrans	B1		✓	✓		✓	✓	✓	✓		
Wine Village–Hermanus	A3		✓	✓					✓		
Wellington Map											
Alkmaar	C4	T*		T				T*			
Andreas	C3	T*			×		✓	T			sv
Bosman	C3	T*						T			
Diemersfontein	B4		✓	✓		✓	✓	T			
Doolhof	D3		✓	✓		✓*	✓	T	✓		
Dunstone	C3		✓	✓		✓	✓	✓*	✓	✓	
Hildenbrand	B4		T*	T*		T*			✓		de
Imbuko	B4					✓*		T		✓	
Jacques Smit	B3	T						T		✓	
Lazanou	B2	T*				T*	✓				
Linton Park	C2		✓			✓		T			
Maske	C4	T									de
Mischa	B2	T		T		T		T*			
Mont du Toit	C4	T			×			T	✓		de
Napier	C3				×			T	✓		
Thokozani	B4		✓	✓		✓	✓	T			
Upland	C4	T		T				T			de
Val du Charron	C3		✓	✓		✓	✓	T	✓	✓	
Welbedacht	B1		✓	T*		✓	✓	✓	✓	✓	de
Welgegund	C4	T					✓				
Wellington Winery	B3 C3		✓	✓		BYO			✓		
Welvanpas	C3		✓	✓		✓*				✓	nl

	Grid reference	Open by appt. only	Open Saturdays	Open Sundays	Open public holidays	Meals/refreshments	Accommodation	Cellar tours	Disabled friendly	Child friendly	Languages spoken
Worcester Map											
Aan de Doorns	B4		√		×			T*	√		
Alvi's Drift	B5	T			×			T			
Brandvlei	B5				×			T	√		
Cilmor	B4		T	T	×						
Conradie	C3		√				√	√		√	
De Wet	B3		√		×	√/BYO*		T	√		
Eagle's Cliff	A6				×	√*			√	√	
Leipzig	C3		√			T*	√	√*		√	ru
Nuy	C4		√	√		√			√		
Overhex	B3		√	√		√		T	√	√	
Stettyn	A6		√*		×	√*			√		

Olifants River & West Coast

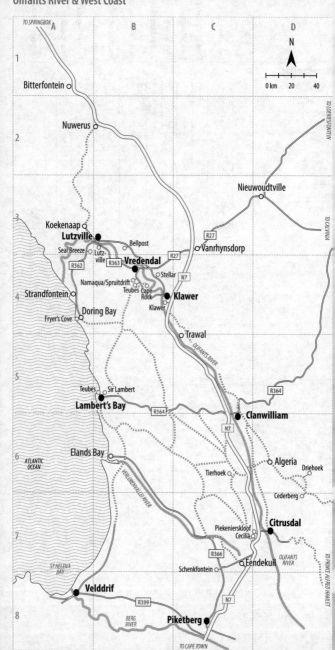

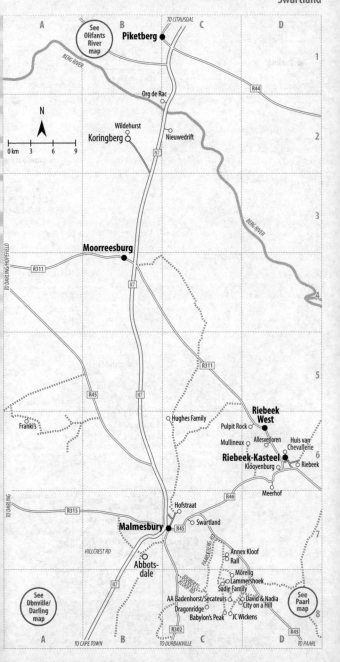

A
B
C
D

See Olifants River map

Piketberg ●

TO CITRUSDAL

1

BERG RIVER

R44

Org de Rac ○

N

2

0 km   3   6   9

Wildehurst ○
Koringberg ○
Nieuwedrift ○

N7

3

BERG RIVER

TO DARLING/HOPEFIELD

Moorreesburg ●

R311

N7

4

BERG RIVER

R311

5

R45

N7

Hughes Family ○

Riebeek West ●

Pulpit Rock ○

Franki's ○

Allesverloren ○

Mullineux ○

Huis van Chevallerie ○

Riebeek-Kasteel ●

6

Klóoyenburg ○

Riebeek ○

Meerhof ○

TO DARLING

R315

R46

Hofstraat ○

Malmesbury ●

R45

Swartland ○

7

HILLCREST RD

Annex Kloof ○

Rall ○

Abbotsdale

Môrelig ○

Lammershoek ○

Sadie Family ○

PAARDEBERG RD

AA Badenhorst/Secateurs ○

David & Nadia ○

City on a Hill ○

See Dbnville/Darling map

Dragonridge ○

Babylon's Peak ○

JC Wickens ○

See Paarl map

8

R302

R45

A
B
C
D

TO CAPE TOWN

TO DURBANVILLE

TO PAARL

Durbanville, Philadelphia & Darling

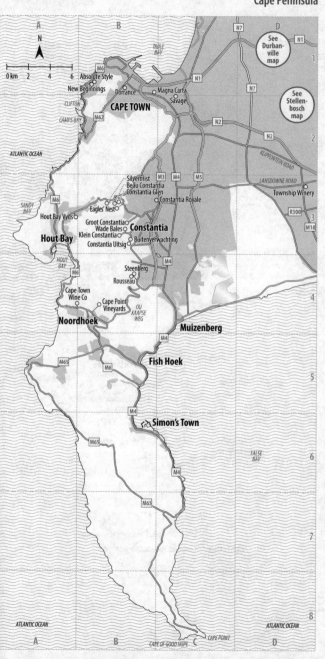

Stellenbosch

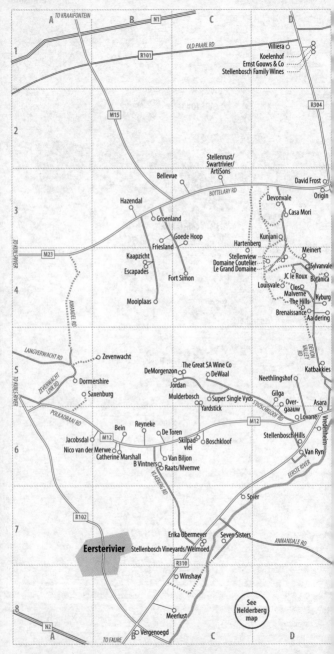

TO KRAAIFONTEIN

N1

R101

OLD PAARL RD

Villiera
Koelenhof
Ernst Gouws & Co
Stellenbosch Family Wines

R304

M15

Stellenrust/
Swartrivier/
ArtiSons

Bellevue

BOTTELARY RD

David Frost
Origin

Hazendal

Devonvale

Groenland

Casa Mori

Goede Hoop

Kunjani

Meinert

Friesland

Hartenberg

Stellenview

Sylvanvale

TO KUILSRIVIER

Kaapzicht

Domaine Coutelier
Le Grand Domaine

Botanica

M23

Escapades

JC le Roux

Louisvale

Clos
Malverne

Fort Simon

The Hills

Kyburg

Mooiplaas

Brenaissance

Aaldering

AMANDEL RD

LANGVERWACHT RD

Zevenwacht

DEVON VALLEY RD

The Great SA Wine Co

Katbakkies

DeMorgenzon

DeWaal

TO KUILS RIVIER

ZEVENWACHT LINK RD

Dormershire

Jordan

Neethlingshof

Saxenburg

Mulderbosch

Gilga

Asara

POLKADRAAI RD

Super Single Vyds

Overgaauw

Vredenheim

Yardstick

Lovane

M12

Bein

Reyneke

Stellenbosch Hills

STROCKKLOOF RD

Jacobsdal

M12

De Toren

Nico van der Merwe

Skilpad
vlei

Boschkloof

Van Ryn

Catherine Marshall

B Vintners

Van Biljon

EERSTE RIVER

Raats/Mvemve

VLAEBERG RD

R102

Spier

ANNANDALE RD

Erika Obermeyer

Seven Sisters

Eersterivier

Stellenbosch Vineyards/Welmoed

R310

Winshaw

See
Helderberg
map

N2

Meerlust

Vergenoegd

TO FAURE

TO KRAAIFONTEIN

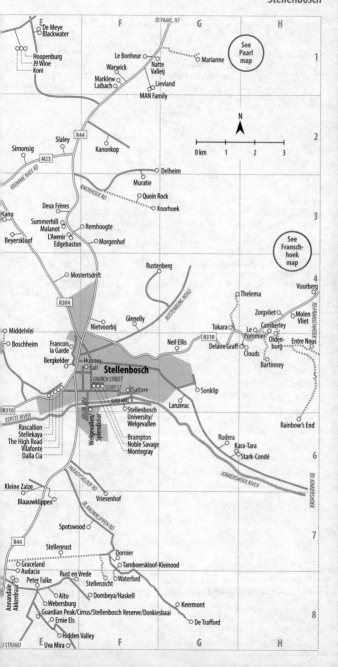

E
De Meye
Blackwater
Hoopenburg
J9 Wine
Koni

F
Le Bonheur
Warwick
Marklew
Laibach
MAN Family

TO PAARL, N1

G
Natte
Valleij
Lievland
Marianne

H
See Paarl map

Simonsig
R44
Slaley
M23
KROMME RHEE RD
KNORHOEK RD

Kanonkop

N
0 km   1   2   3

Delheim
Muratie
Deux Frères
Quoin Rock
Knorhoek

See Franschhoek map

Kanu
Summerhill
Malanot
L'Avenir
Edgebaston
Remhoogte
Morgenhof

Beyerskloof

Mostertsdrift

Rustenberg

R304

RUSTENBURG ROAD

Thelema
Vuurberg

Zorgvliet
Camberley
Molen Vliet

Middelvlei
Glenelly
Nietvoorbij
Tokara
Le Pommier
Oldenburg
Entre Nous

Boschheim
Francois la Garde
Bergkelder
Hunney-ball
Neil Ellis
Delaire Graff
Clouds
Bartinney

Stellenbosch
CHURCH STREET
DORP ST
Saltare
Sonklip

R310
EERSTE RIVER
PIET RETIEF
BIRD ST
SNID WAL

Rascallion
Stellekaya
The High Road
Vilafonté
Dalla Cia

Welgevallen
Splendidior
Stellenbosch University/ Welgevallen
Lanzerac
Rainbow's End

Brampton
Noble Savage
Montegray

Rudera
Kara-Tara
Stark-Condé

Kleine Zalze
Blaauwklippen

PARADYSKLOOF RD
Vriesenhof

JONKERSHOEK RIVER

TO JONKERSHOEK

Spotswood

R44
BLAAUWKLIPPEN RD

Stellenrust
Dornier
Tamboerskloof-Kleinood

Graceland
Audacia
Peter Falke
Rust en Vrede
Stellenzicht
Waterford
Alto
Webersburg
Dombeya/Haskell
Annandale
Akkerdraai
Guardian Peak/Cirrus/Stellenbosch Reserve/Donkiesbaai
Ernie Els
Keermont
De Trafford
Hidden Valley
Uva Mira

TO STRAND

E   **F**   **G**   **H**

Helderberg

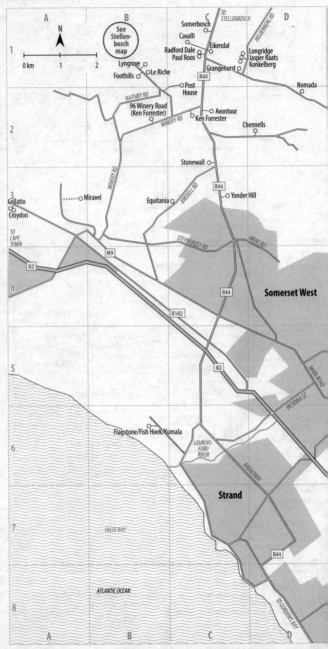

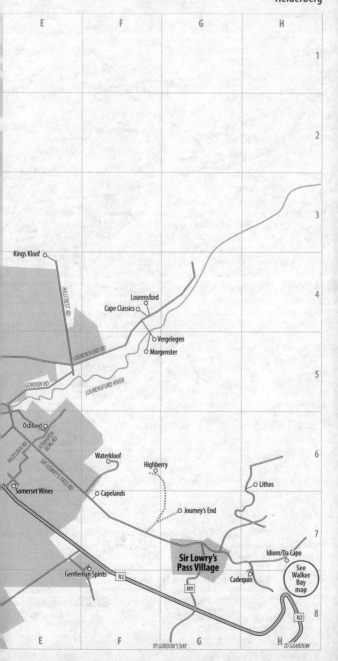

Paarl

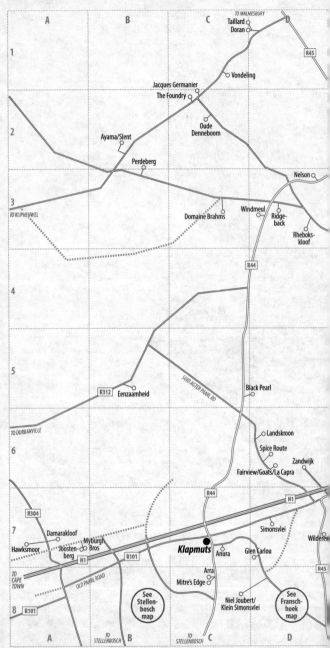

TO MALMESBURY

A · B · C · D

Taillard
Doran
R45

Vondeling

Jacques Germanier
The Foundry

Oude
Denneboom

Ayama/Slent

Perdeberg

Nelson

TO KLIPHEUWEL

Domaine Brahms

Windmeul

Ridge-
back

Rheboks-
kloof

R44

R312
Eenzaamheid

SUID AGTER PAARL RD

Black Pearl

TO DURBANVILLE

Landskroon

Spice Route

Zandwijk

Fairview/Goats/La Capra

R44

N1

R304

Damarakloof

Simonsvlei

Hawksmoor

Myburgh
Bros

Wildere

Jöosten-
berg

N1

R101

Klapmuts

Anura

Glen Carlou

R45

TO
CAPE
TOWN

OLD PAARL ROAD

Arra

R101

Mitre's Edge

See
Stellen-
bosch
map

Niel Joubert/
Klein Simonsvlei

See
Fransch-
hoek
map

A · B · C · D

TO
STELLENBOSCH

TO
STELLENBOSCH

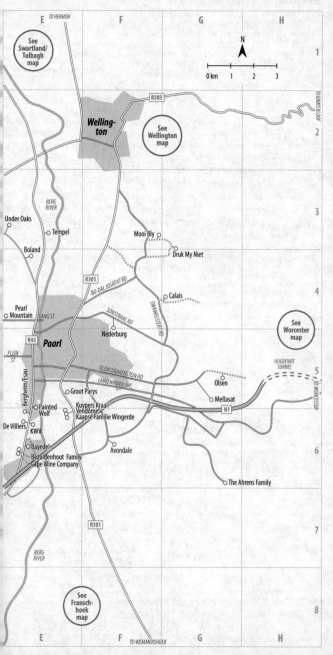

N

0 km 1 2 3

TO HERMON

See Swartland/Tulbagh map

R303

Wellington

See Wellington map

TO BAINS KLOOF

BERG RIVER

Under Oaks

Tempel

Boland

Mooi Bly

Druk My Niet

R301

BO-DAL JOSAFAT RD

SONSTRAAL RD

SWAWESTER RD

Calais

Pearl Mountain

LANG ST

R45

See Worcester map

Paarl

Nederburg

PLEIN ST

KLEIN DRAKENSTEIN RD

LANGENHOVEN AVE

HUGUENOT TUNNEL

TO WORCESTER

Olsen

Groot Parys

Bergheim/Esau

Kuypers Kraal

Vendome

Kaapse Familie Wingerde

Mellasat

N1

Painted Wolf

De Villiers

KWV

Bayede!

Bezuidenhout Family

Cape Wine Company

Avondale

The Ahrens Family

R301

BERG RIVER

See Franschhoek map

TO WEMMERSHOEK

Wellington

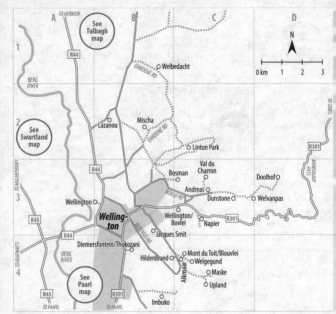

Elgin

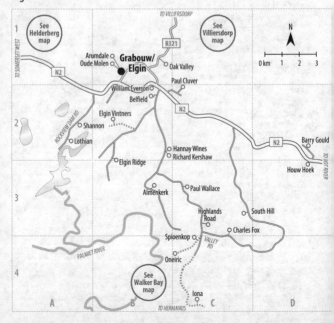

Franschhoek

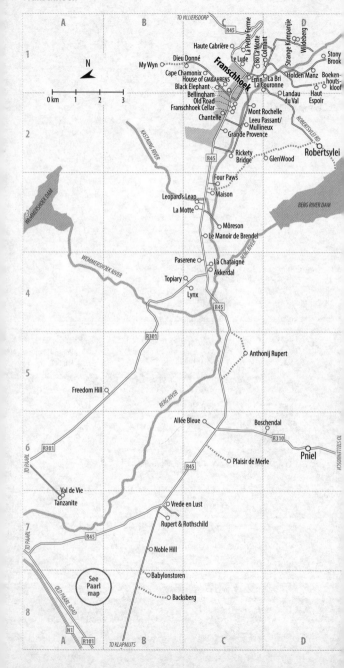

Walker Bay & Bot River

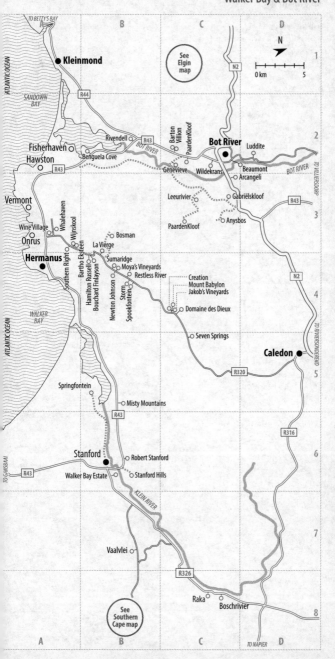

Breedekloof

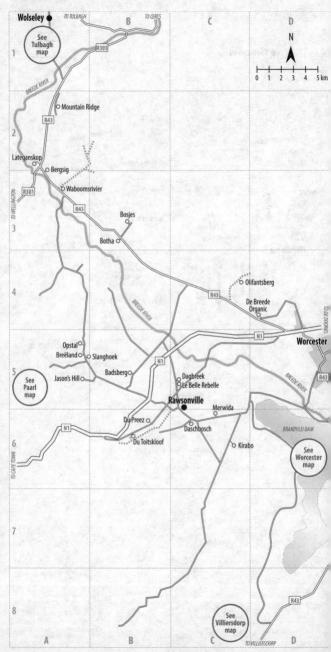

Worcester

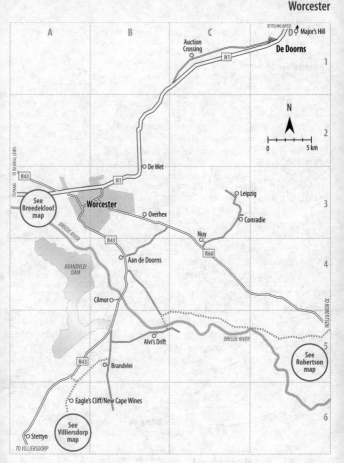

Villiersdorp

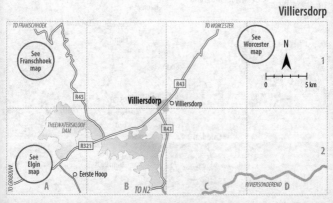

Southern Cape

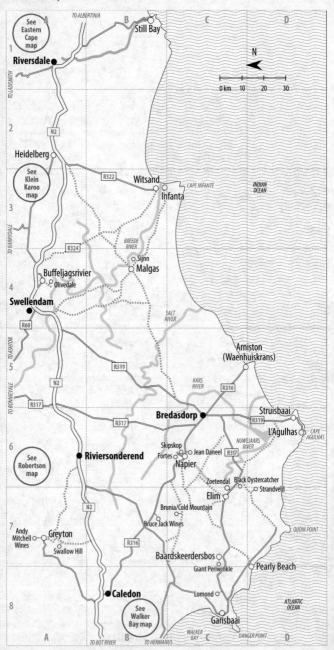

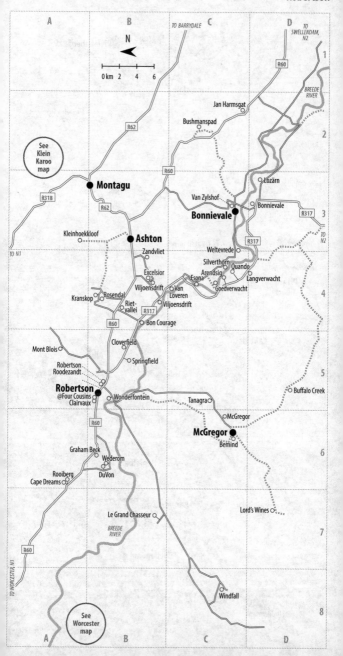

Klein Karoo & Garden Route

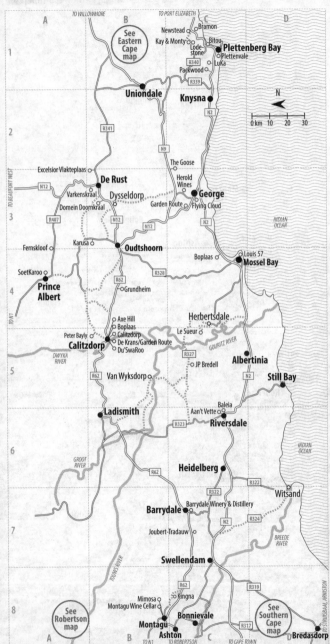

Northern Cape, Free State & North West

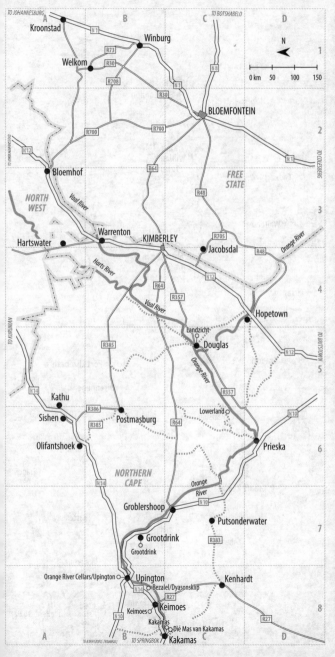

Eastern Cape

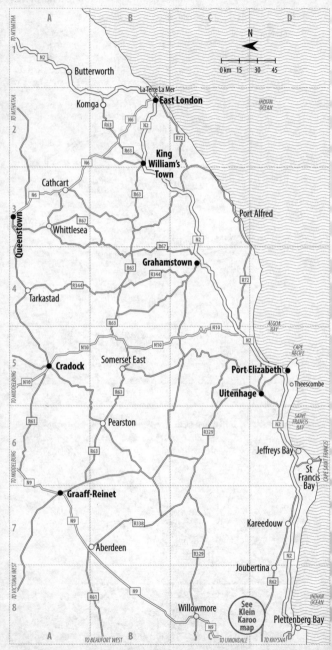

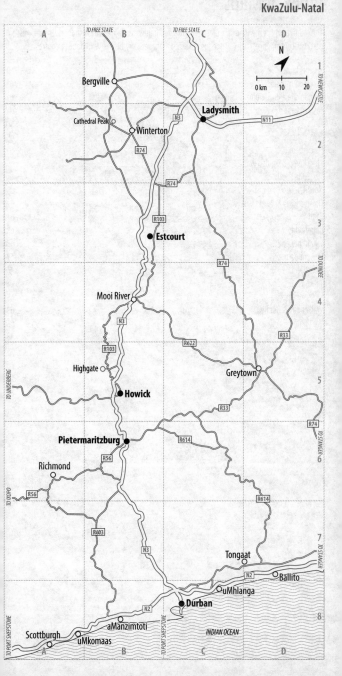

Index of Maps

The order in which the maps are placed follows geography, reading from north to south and west to east. For convenience, individual maps are listed alphabetically below, with page references.

Notes

Notes

Notes

Notes